The Oxford Paperback Thesaurus

EDITED BY
Maurice Waite

OXFORD
UNIVERSITY PRESS

Great Clarendon Street, Oxford OX2 6DP

Oxford University Press is a department of the University of Oxford.
It furthers the University's objective of excellence in research, scholarship,
and education by publishing worldwide in

Oxford New York

Auckland Bangkok Buenos Aires Cape Town Chennai
Dar es Salaam Delhi Hong Kong Istanbul Karachi Kolkata
Kuala Lumpur Madrid Melbourne Mexico City Mumbai Nairobi
São Paulo Shanghai Singapore Taipei Tokyo Toronto

and an associated company in Berlin

Published in the United States
by Oxford University Press Inc., New York

First edition 1994
Second edition 2001

British Library Cataloguing in Publication Data

Data available

Library of Congress Cataloging in Publication Data

Data available

ISBN 0-19-860371-1

10 9 8 7 6 5 4 3 2

Typeset in Swift and Arial
by Kolam Information Services, Pondicherry, India
Printed in Great Britain by
Clays Ltd, Bungay, Suffolk

Editorial staff

Editor
Maurice Waite

Project Editor
Sara Hawker

Senior Assistant Editors
Catherine Bailey
Chris Cowley

Introduction

This Second Edition of the *Oxford Paperback Thesaurus* is an abridgement of the *New Oxford Thesaurus of English*, published in 2000. Using computational techniques to analyse real language collected in the British National Corpus and the database of the Oxford Reading Programme, the editors were able to determine better than ever before how words are really used and thus to give better-matching sets of synonyms.

In making this abridgement, we have had to exclude only five per cent of entries, and principally only synonyms that were rare, specialized, archaic, restricted to less common varieties of English, or marginal to the sense of the entry word.

Arrangement of synonyms

The synonyms in each entry are grouped in numbered 'synonym sets'. Major synonym sets correspond roughly to different senses of the word in a dictionary, and many sets contain finer distinctions, which are signalled by semicolons.

The synonyms in each set that are closest in meaning to the entry word are given first, usually starting with a 'core synonym' in SMALL CAPITALS. Some synonym sets have more than one core synonym if two synonyms are very close to the entry word but neither covers the whole sense; for example, at *audience*, both *spectators* and *listeners* are given as core synonyms. Two different core synonyms may also emphasize slightly different aspects of the meaning of the entry word. For example, at *prosperous*, the first core synonym given is *thriving*, followed by a group of words closely related to that aspect of its meaning, such as *flourishing* and *successful*. Then, after a semicolon, a second core synonym, *affluent*, is given, with an allied group of synonyms such as *wealthy* and *rich*.

Guidance on the use of synonyms

Most of the synonyms are part of standard English, but some are suitable only in certain contexts. These are grouped at the end of their synonym set and given the following labels:

informal, e.g. *swig*, *dodgy*: the kind of vocabulary used in speech or informal writing.

formal, e.g. *perquisite*, *adjure*: normally only used in writing.

technical, e.g. *occlusion*, *admixture*; words used in specific fields are labelled Medicine, Nautical, etc.

poetic/literary, e.g. *forsake*, *plenteous*.

dated, e.g. *toodle-oo*, *rotter*.

historical, e.g. *serfdom*, *ballista*: still used today, but only to refer to some practice or article that is no longer part of the modern world.

humorous, e.g. *retail therapy*, *transmogrify*.

archaic, e.g. *bootless*, *in sooth*: very old-fashioned language, not used today except for effect.

rare, e.g. *funambulist*, *reprehend*.

Synonyms are also labelled if they are used exclusively or mainly in the English spoken in a particular part of the world, namely: British (abbreviated to Brit.), North American (N. Amer.), United States (US), Canadian, Australian (Austral.), New Zealand (NZ), South African (S. Afr.), or West Indian (W. Ind.).

Major features of the thesaurus

part of speech of the entry word

assign ▶ verb ❶ *a young doctor was assigned the task* ALLOCATE, allot, give, set; charge with, entrust with. ❷ *she was assigned to a new post* APPOINT, promote, delegate, commission, post, co-opt; select for, choose for, install in; *Military* detail. ❸ *we assign large sums of money to travel budgets* EARMARK, designate, set aside, reserve, appropriate, allot, allocate, apportion. ❹ *he assigned the opinion to the Prince* ASCRIBE, attribute, put down, accredit, credit, chalk up, impute; pin on, lay at the door of. ❺ *he may assign the money to a third party* TRANSFER, make over, give, pass, hand over/down, convey, consign; *Law* attorn, devise.

example of use, to help distinguish different senses

label indicating the specialist field in which the following synonym(s) are used

combined synonym group standing for *hand over* and *hand down*

bag ▶ noun ❶ *I dug around in my bag for my lipstick* HANDBAG, shoulder bag, clutch bag, evening bag, pochette; *N. Amer.* pocketbook, purse; *historical* reticule, scrip. ❷ *she began to unpack her bags* SUITCASE, case, valise, portmanteau, holdall, grip, overnighter; backpack, rucksack, knapsack, haversack, kitbag, duffel bag; satchel; (**bags**) luggage, baggage.
▶ verb ❶ *locals bagged the most fish* CATCH, land, capture, trap, snare, ensnare; kill, shoot. ❷ *he bagged seven medals* GET, secure, obtain, acquire, pick up; win, achieve, attain; commandeer, grab, appropriate, take; *informal* get one's hands on, land, net.

label indicating the region of the world in which the following synonym(s) are used (see Introduction for abbreviations)

form of the entry word for which the following synonym(s) can be substituted

label indicating the style of English in which the following synonym(s) are used

infrequent ▶ adjective RARE, uncommon, unusual, exceptional, few (and far between), like gold dust, as scarce as hens' teeth; unaccustomed, unwonted; isolated, scarce, scattered; sporadic, irregular, intermittent; *informal* once in a blue moon; *dated* seldom.
–OPPOSITES common.

core synonym—the closest synonym to the entry word

combined synonym group standing for *few* and *few and far between*

word(s) meaning the opposite of the entry word; most have entries of their own, where a wider choice can be found

lip ▶ noun ❶ *the lip of the crater* EDGE, rim, brim, border, verge, brink. ❷ (*informal*) *I'll have no more of your lip!* INSOLENCE, impertinence, impudence, cheek, rudeness, audacity, effrontery, disrespect, presumptuousness; *informal* mouth; *Brit. informal* sauce, backchat.
–RELATED TERMS labial, labio-.
■ **keep a stiff upper lip** KEEP CONTROL OF ONESELF, not show emotion, appear unaffected; *informal* keep one's cool.

label indicating the style of English in which this sense of *lip* is used

words, prefixes, or suffixes with meanings that are closely related to the entry word but are not actual synonyms

night ▶ noun night-time; (hours of) darkness, dark.
–RELATED TERMS nocturnal.
–OPPOSITES day.
■ **night and day** ALL THE TIME, around the clock, {morning, noon, and night}, {day in, day out}, ceaselessly, endlessly, incessantly, unceasingly, interminably, constantly, perpetually, continually, relentlessly; *informal* 24–7.

brackets showing that the phrase they contain is one complete synonym

Aa

aback
■ **take someone aback** SURPRISE, shock, stun, stagger, astound, astonish, startle, take by surprise; dumbfound, nonplus, stop someone in their tracks; shake (up), jolt, throw, unnerve, disconcert, unsettle, bewilder; *informal* flabbergast, knock sideways, floor; *Brit. informal* knock for six.

abandon ▶ verb ❶ *the party abandoned policies which made it unelectable* RENOUNCE, relinquish, dispense with, disclaim, disown, disavow, discard, wash one's hands of; give up, drop, jettison, do away with, axe; *informal* ditch, scrap, scrub, junk; *formal* forswear. ❷ *by that stage, she had abandoned painting* GIVE UP, stop, cease, drop, forgo, desist from, have done with, abstain from, discontinue, break off, refrain from, set aside; *informal* cut out, kick, pack in, quit; *Brit. informal* jack in; *formal* abjure. ❸ *he abandoned his wife and children* DESERT, leave, leave high and dry, turn one's back on, cast aside, break (up) with; jilt, strand, leave stranded, leave in the lurch, throw over; *informal* walk out on, run out on, dump, ditch; *poetic/literary* forsake. ❹ *the skipper gave the order to abandon ship* VACATE, leave, depart from, withdraw from, quit, evacuate. ❺ *a vast expanse of territory was abandoned to the invaders* RELINQUISH, surrender, give up, cede, yield, leave. ❻ *she abandoned herself to the sensuousness of the music* INDULGE IN, give way to, give oneself up to, yield to, lose oneself to/in.
– OPPOSITES keep, retain, continue.
▶ noun *reckless abandon* UNINHIBITEDNESS, recklessness, lack of restraint, lack of inhibition, wildness, impulsiveness, impetuosity, immoderation, wantonness.
– OPPOSITES self-control.

abandoned ▶ adjective ❶ *an abandoned child* DESERTED, forsaken, cast aside/off; jilted, stranded, rejected; *informal* dumped, ditched. ❷ *an abandoned tin mine* UNUSED, disused, neglected, idle; deserted, unoccupied, uninhabited, empty. ❸ *a wild, abandoned dance* UNINHIBITED, reckless, unrestrained, wild, unbridled, impulsive, impetuous; immoderate, wanton.

abase ▶ verb HUMBLE, humiliate, belittle, demean, lower, degrade, debase, cheapen, discredit, bring low; (**abase oneself**) grovel, kowtow, bow and scrape, toady, fawn; *informal* crawl, suck up to someone, lick someone's boots.

abasement ▶ noun HUMILIATION, belittlement, lowering, degradation, debasement.

abashed ▶ adjective EMBARRASSED, ashamed, shamefaced, remorseful, conscience-stricken, mortified, humiliated, humbled, chagrined, crestfallen, sheepish, red-faced, blushing, put out of countenance, discountenanced, with one's tail between one's legs.

abate ▶ verb ❶ *the storm had abated* SUBSIDE, die down/away/out, lessen, ease (off), let up, decrease, diminish, moderate, decline, fade, dwindle, recede, tail off, peter out, taper off, wane, ebb, weaken, come to an end; *archaic* remit. ❷ *nothing abated his crusading zeal* DECREASE, lessen, diminish, reduce, moderate, ease, soothe, dampen, calm, tone down, allay, temper.
– OPPOSITES intensify, increase.

abatement ▶ noun ❶ *the storm still rages with no sign of abatement* SUBSIDING, dying down/away/out, lessening, easing (off), let-up, decrease, moderation, decline, ebb. ❷ *noise abatement* DECREASE, reduction, lowering.

abattoir ▶ noun SLAUGHTERHOUSE; *Brit.* butchery; *archaic* shambles.

abbey ▶ noun MONASTERY, CONVENT, priory, cloister, friary, nunnery; *historical* charterhouse; *rare* coenobium.

abbreviate ▶ verb SHORTEN, reduce, cut, contract, condense, compress, abridge, truncate, pare down, prune, shrink, telescope; summarize, abstract, precis, synopsize, digest, edit.
– OPPOSITES lengthen, expand.

abbreviated ▶ adjective SHORTENED, reduced, cut, condensed, abridged, concise, compact, succinct; summary, thumbnail, synoptic; *formal* compendious.
– OPPOSITES long.

abbreviation ▶ noun SHORTENED FORM, short form, contraction, acronym, initialism, symbol, diminutive; elision.

abdicate ▶ verb ❶ *the king abdicated in 1936* RESIGN, retire, stand down, step down, bow out, renounce the throne; *archaic* demit. ❷ *Ferdinand abdicated the throne* RESIGN FROM, relinquish, renounce, give up, surrender, vacate, cede; *Law* disclaim; *formal* abjure. ❸ *the state abdicated all responsibility for their welfare* DISOWN, reject, renounce, give up, refuse, relinquish, repudiate, abandon, turn one's back on, wash one's hands of; *formal* abjure; *poetic/literary* forsake.

abdication ▶ noun ❶ *Edward VIII's abdication* RESIGNATION, retirement; relinquishment, renunciation, surrender; *formal* abjuration; *archaic* demission. ❷ *an abdication of responsibility* DISOWNING, renunciation, rejection, refusal, relinquishment, repudiation, abandonment.

abdomen ▶ noun STOMACH, belly, gut, middle, intestines; *informal* tummy, tum, insides, guts, maw, breadbasket, pot, paunch; *Austral. informal* bingy; *dated* corporation.

abdominal ▶ adjective GASTRIC, intestinal, stomach, stomachic, enteric, duodenal, visceral, coeliac, ventral.

abduct ▶ verb KIDNAP, carry off, seize, capture, run away/off with, make off with, spirit away, hold hostage, hold to ransom; *informal* snatch.

aberrant ▶ adjective DEVIANT, deviating, divergent, abnormal, atypical, anomalous, irregular, rogue; strange, odd, peculiar, uncommon, freakish; twisted, warped, perverted.
–OPPOSITES normal, typical.

aberration ▶ noun *a statistical aberration* ANOMALY, deviation, departure from the norm, divergence, abnormality, irregularity, variation, freak, rarity, oddity, peculiarity, curiosity; mistake.

abet ▶ verb ASSIST, aid, help, lend a hand, support, back, encourage; cooperate with, collaborate with, work with, collude with, be in collusion with, be hand in glove with, side with; second, endorse, sanction; promote, champion, further, expedite, connive at.
–OPPOSITES hinder.

abeyance ▶ noun SUSPENSION, a state of suspension, a state of uncertainty, remission; (**in abeyance**) pending, suspended, deferred, postponed, put off, put to one side, unresolved, up in the air; *informal* in cold storage, on ice, on the back burner, hanging fire.

abhor ▶ verb DETEST, hate, loathe, despise, execrate, regard with disgust, shrink from, recoil from, shudder at; *formal* abominate.
–OPPOSITES love, admire.

abhorrence ▶ noun HATRED, loathing, detestation, execration, revulsion, abomination, disgust, repugnance, horror, odium, aversion.

abhorrent ▶ adjective DETESTABLE, hateful, loathsome, despicable, abominable, execrable, repellent, repugnant, repulsive, revolting, disgusting, distasteful, horrible, horrid, horrifying, awful, heinous, reprehensible, obnoxious, odious, nauseating, offensive, contemptible.
–OPPOSITES admirable.

abide ▶ verb ❶ *he expected everybody to abide by the rules* COMPLY WITH, obey, observe, follow, keep to, hold to, conform to, adhere to, stick to, stand by, act in accordance with, uphold, heed, accept, go along with, acknowledge, respect, defer to. ❷ (*informal*) *I can't abide the smell of cigarettes* TOLERATE, bear, stand, put up with, endure, take, countenance; *informal* stomach; *Brit. informal* stick; *formal* brook; *archaic* suffer. ❸ *at least one memory will abide* CONTINUE, remain, survive, last, persist, stay, live on.
–OPPOSITES flout, disobey.

abiding ▶ adjective ENDURING, lasting, persisting, long-lasting, lifelong, continuing, remaining, surviving, standing, durable, everlasting, perpetual, eternal, unending, constant, permanent, unchanging, steadfast, immutable.
–OPPOSITES short-lived, ephemeral.

ability ▶ noun ❶ *the ability to read and write* CAPACITY, capability, potential, potentiality, power, faculty, aptness, facility; wherewithal, means. ❷ *the president's leadership ability* TALENT, skill, expertise, adeptness, aptitude, savoir faire, skilfulness, prowess, mastery, accomplishment; competence, proficiency; dexterity, adroitness, deftness, cleverness, flair, finesse, gift, knack, genius; qualification, resources; *informal* know-how.

abject ▶ adjective ❶ *abject poverty* WRETCHED, miserable, hopeless, pathetic, pitiful, pitiable, piteous, sorry, woeful, lamentable, degrading, appalling, atrocious, awful. ❷ *an abject sinner* CONTEMPTIBLE, base, low, vile, worthless, debased, degraded, despicable, ignominious, mean, unworthy, ignoble. ❸ *an abject apology* OBSEQUIOUS, grovelling, fawning, toadyish, servile, cringing, sycophantic, submissive, craven.

abjure ▶ verb (*formal*) RENOUNCE, relinquish, reject, forgo, disavow, abandon, deny, repudiate, give up, wash one's hands of; eschew, abstain from, refrain from; *informal* kick, pack in; *Brit. informal* jack in; *Law* disaffirm; *poetic/literary* forsake; *formal* forswear, abnegate.

ablaze ▶ adjective ❶ *several vehicles were ablaze* ON FIRE, alight, aflame, in flames, flaming, burning, blazing; *poetic/literary* afire. ❷ *every window was ablaze with light* LIT UP, alight, gleaming, glowing, aglow, illuminated, bright, shining, radiant, shimmering, sparkling, flashing, dazzling, luminous, incandescent. ❸ *his eyes were ablaze with fury* PASSIONATE, impassioned, aroused, excited, stimulated, eager, animated, intense, ardent, fervent, frenzied.

able ▶ adjective ❶ *he will soon be able to resume his duties* CAPABLE OF, competent to, equal to, up to, fit to, prepared to, qualified to; allowed to, free to, in a position to. ❷ *an able student* INTELLIGENT, clever, talented, skilful, skilled, accomplished, gifted; proficient, apt, good, adroit, adept; capable, competent, efficient, effective.
–OPPOSITES incompetent, incapable.

able-bodied ▶ adjective HEALTHY, FIT, in good health, robust, strong, sound, sturdy, vigorous, hardy, hale and hearty, athletic, muscular, strapping, burly, brawny, lusty; in good shape, in good trim, in fine fettle, fighting fit,

as fit as a fiddle, as fit as a flea; *informal* husky; *dated* stalwart.
– OPPOSITES infirm, frail, disabled.

ablutions ▶ **plural noun** (*formal*) WASHING, cleansing, bathing, showering, scrubbing; wash, bath, shower, toilet, soak, dip, douche; *rare* lavage, lavation.

abnegation ▶ **noun** (*formal*) ❶ *a serious abnegation of their responsibilities* RENUNCIATION, rejection, refusal, abandonment, abdication, surrender, relinquishment, repudiation, denial; *formal* abjuration. ❷ *people capable of abnegation and unselfishness* SELF-DENIAL, self-sacrifice, abstinence, temperance, continence, asceticism, abstemiousness, austerity.
– OPPOSITES acceptance, self-indulgence.

abnormal ▶ **adjective** UNUSUAL, uncommon, atypical, untypical, non-typical, unrepresentative, rare, isolated, irregular, anomalous, deviant, divergent, aberrant, freak, freakish; STRANGE, odd, peculiar, curious, bizarre, weird, queer; eccentric, idiosyncratic, quirky; unexpected, unfamiliar, unconventional, surprising, unorthodox, singular, exceptional, extraordinary, out of the ordinary, out of the way; unnatural, perverse, perverted, twisted, warped, unhealthy, distorted; *Brit.* out of the common; *informal* funny, freaky, kinky.
– OPPOSITES normal, typical, common.

abnormality ▶ **noun** ❶ *babies born with physical or mental abnormalities* MALFORMATION, deformity, irregularity, flaw, defect. ❷ *the abnormality of such behaviour* UNUSUALNESS, uncommonness, atypicality, irregularity, anomalousness, deviation, divergence, aberrance, aberration, freakishness; strangeness, oddness, peculiarity, unexpectedness, singularity.

abode ▶ **noun** (*formal*) HOME, house, place of residence, accommodation, seat; quarters, lodgings, rooms; address; *informal* pad, digs; *formal* dwelling, dwelling place, residence, habitation.

abolish ▶ **verb** PUT AN END TO, get rid of, scrap, end, stop, terminate, axe, eradicate, eliminate, exterminate, destroy, annihilate, stamp out, obliterate, wipe out, extinguish, quash, expunge, extirpate; annul, cancel, invalidate, nullify, void, dissolve; rescind, repeal, revoke, overturn; discontinue, remove, excise, drop, jettison; *informal* do away with, ditch, junk, scrub, dump, chop, give something the chop, knock something on the head; *formal* abrogate.
– OPPOSITES retain, create.

abolition ▶ **noun** SCRAPPING, ending, termination, eradication, elimination, extermination, destruction, annihilation, obliteration, extirpation; annulment, cancellation, invalidation, nullification, dissolution; revocation, repeal, rescindment, discontinuation, removal; *formal* abrogation.

abominable ▶ **adjective** LOATHSOME, detestable, hateful, odious, obnoxious, despicable, contemptible, damnable, diabolical; disgusting, revolting, repellent, repulsive, offensive, repugnant, abhorrent, reprehensible, atrocious, horrifying, execrable, foul, vile, wretched, base, horrible, awful, dreadful, appalling, nauseating; horrid, nasty, disagreeable, unpleasant, distasteful; *informal* terrible, shocking, God-awful; *Brit. informal* beastly; *dated* cursed, accursed.
– OPPOSITES good, admirable.

abominate ▶ **verb** (*formal*) DETEST, loathe, hate, abhor, despise, execrate, shudder at, recoil from, shrink from, be repelled by.
– OPPOSITES like, love.

abomination ▶ **noun** ❶ *in both wars, internment was an abomination* ATROCITY, disgrace, horror, obscenity, outrage, evil, crime, monstrosity, anathema, bane. ❷ *he had a Calvinist abomination of indulgence* DETESTATION, loathing, hatred, aversion, antipathy, revulsion, repugnance, abhorrence, odium, execration, disgust, horror, hostility.
– OPPOSITES liking, love.

aboriginal ▶ **adjective** *the area's aboriginal inhabitants* INDIGENOUS, native; original, earliest, first; ancient, primitive, primeval, primordial; *rare* autochthonous, autochthonic.
▶ **noun** *the social structure of the aboriginals* NATIVE, aborigine, original inhabitant; *rare* autochthon, indigene.

abort ▶ **verb** ❶ *I decided not to abort the pregnancy* TERMINATE, end. ❷ *the organism can cause pregnant ewes to abort* MISCARRY, have a miscarriage. ❸ *the crew aborted the take-off* HALT, stop, end, axe, call off, cut short, discontinue, terminate, arrest; *informal* pull the plug on. ❹ *the mission aborted* COME TO A HALT, end, terminate, fail, miscarry, go wrong, fall through, collapse, founder, come to grief.

abortion ▶ **noun** TERMINATION, miscarriage; *rare* feticide.

abortive ▶ **adjective** UNSUCCESSFUL, failed, vain, thwarted, futile, useless, worthless, ineffective, ineffectual, to no effect, inefficacious, fruitless, unproductive, unavailing, to no avail, sterile, nugatory; *archaic* bootless.
– OPPOSITES successful, fruitful.

abound ▶ **verb** ❶ *cafes and bars abound in the narrow streets* BE PLENTIFUL, be abundant, be numerous, proliferate, superabound, be thick on the ground; *informal* grow on trees, be two/ten a penny. ❷ *a stream which abounded with trout and eels* BE FULL OF, overflow with, teem with, be packed with, be crowded with, be thronged with; be alive with, be crawling with, be overrun by/with, swarm with, bristle with, be infested with, be thick with; *informal* be lousy with, be stuffed with, be jam-packed with, be chock-a-block with, be chock-full of.

abounding ▶ **adjective** ABUNDANT, plentiful,

superabundant, considerable, copious, ample, lavish, luxuriant, profuse, boundless, prolific, inexhaustible, generous; galore; *poetic/literary* plenteous.

– OPPOSITES meagre, scanty.

about ▶ **preposition** ❶ *a book about ancient Greece* REGARDING, concerning, with reference to, referring to, with regard to, with respect to, respecting, relating to, on, touching on, dealing with, relevant to, connected with, in connection with, on the subject of, in the matter of, apropos, re. ❷ *two hundred people were milling about the room* AROUND, round, throughout, over, through, on every side of.

▶ **adverb** ❶ *there were babies crawling about in the grass* AROUND, here and there, to and fro, back and forth, from place to place, hither and thither, in all directions. ❷ *I knew he was about somewhere* NEAR, nearby, around, hereabouts, not far off/away, close by, in the vicinity, in the neighbourhood. ❸ *the explosion caused about £15,000 worth of damage* APPROXIMATELY, roughly, around, round about, in the region of, circa, of the order of, something like; or so, or thereabouts, there or thereabouts, more or less, give or take a few, not far off; *Brit.* getting on for; *informal* as near as dammit; *N. Amer. informal* in the ballpark of. ❹ *there's a lot of flu about* AROUND, in circulation, in existence, current, going on, prevailing, prevalent, happening, in the air, abroad.

■ **about to** (JUST) GOING TO, ready to, all set to, preparing to, intending to, soon to; on the point of, on the verge of, on the brink of, within an ace of.

about-turn (*Brit.*) ▶ **noun** ❶ *he saluted and did an about-turn* ABOUT-FACE, volte-face, turnaround, turnabout, U-turn; *informal* U-ey, one-eighty. ❷ *the government was forced to make an about-turn* VOLTE-FACE, U-turn, reversal, retraction, backtracking, swing, swerve; change of heart, change of mind, sea change.

above ▶ **preposition** ❶ *a tiny window above the door* OVER, higher (up) than; on top of, atop, on, upon. ❷ *those above the rank of Colonel* SUPERIOR TO, senior to, over, higher (up) than, more powerful than; in charge of, commanding. ❸ *you must be above suspicion* BEYOND, not liable to, not open to, not vulnerable to, out of reach of; immune to, exempt from. ❹ *the Chinese valued pearls above gold* MORE THAN, over, before, rather than, in preference to, instead of. ❺ *an increase above the rate of inflation* GREATER THAN, more than, higher than, exceeding, in excess of, over, over and above, beyond, surpassing, upwards of.

– OPPOSITES below, under, beneath.

▶ **adverb** ❶ *in the darkness above, something moved* OVERHEAD, on/at the top, high up, on high, up above, (up) in the sky, high above one's head, aloft. ❷ *the two cases described above* EARLIER, previously, before, formerly.

▶ **adjective** *the above example* PRECEDING, previous, earlier, former, foregoing, prior, above-stated, aforementioned, aforesaid.

■ **above all** MOST IMPORTANTLY, before everything, beyond everything, first of all, most of all, chiefly, primarily, in the first place, first and foremost, mainly, principally, predominantly, especially, essentially, basically, in essence, at bottom; *informal* at the end of the day, when all is said and done.

■ **above oneself** CONCEITED, proud, arrogant, self-important, cocky, haughty, disdainful, snobbish, snobby, supercilious; *informal* stuck-up, high and mighty, snooty, uppity, big-headed, swollen-headed, too big for one's boots.

above board ▶ **adjective** *the proceedings were completely above board* LEGITIMATE, lawful, legal, licit, honest, fair, open, frank, straight, overt, candid, forthright, unconcealed, trustworthy, unequivocal; *informal* legit, kosher, pukka, by the book, fair and square, square, on the level, on the up and up, upfront.

– OPPOSITES dishonest, shady.

abrade ▶ **verb** WEAR AWAY, wear down, erode, scrape away, corrode, eat away at, gnaw away at.

abrasion ▶ **noun** ❶ *he had abrasions to his forehead* GRAZE, cut, scrape, scratch, gash, laceration, injury, contusion; sore, ulcer; *Medicine* trauma. ❷ *the metal is resistant to abrasion* EROSION, wearing away/down, corrosion.

abrasive ▶ **adjective** ❶ *abrasive kitchen cleaners* CORROSIVE, corroding, erosive; caustic, harsh, coarse. ❷ *her abrasive manner* CAUSTIC, cutting, biting, acerbic; rough, harsh, hard, tough, sharp, curt, brusque, stern, severe; wounding, nasty, cruel, callous, insensitive, unfeeling, unsympathetic, inconsiderate; *N. Amer.* acerb.

– OPPOSITES kind, gentle.

abreast ▶ **adverb** ❶ *they walked three abreast* IN A ROW, side by side, alongside, level, beside each other, shoulder to shoulder. ❷ *try to keep abreast of current affairs* UP TO DATE WITH, up with, in touch with, informed about, acquainted with, knowledgeable about, conversant with, familiar with, au courant with, au fait with.

abridge ▶ **verb** SHORTEN, cut, cut short/down, curtail, truncate, trim, crop, clip, pare down, prune; abbreviate, condense, contract, compress, reduce, decrease, shrink; summarize, sum up, abstract, precis, synopsize, give a digest of, put in a nutshell, edit; *rare* epitomize.

– OPPOSITES lengthen.

abridged ▶ **adjective** SHORTENED, cut, cut down, concise, condensed, abbreviated; summary, outline, thumbnail; bowdlerized, censored, expurgated; *informal* potted.

abridgement ▶ **noun** SUMMARY, abstract, synopsis, precis, outline, résumé, sketch, digest.

abroad ▶ **adverb** ❶ *he regularly travels abroad*

OVERSEAS, out of the country, to/in foreign parts, to/in a foreign country/land. ❷ *rumours were abroad* IN CIRCULATION, circulating, widely current, everywhere, in the air, {here, there, and everywhere}; about, around; at large.

abrogate ▶ verb (*formal*) REPEAL, revoke, rescind, repudiate, overturn, annul, cancel, invalidate, nullify, void, negate, dissolve, countermand, declare null and void, discontinue; reverse, retract, remove, withdraw, abolish, put an end to, do away with, get rid of, end, stop, quash, scrap; *Law* disaffirm.
– OPPOSITES institute, introduce.

abrogation ▶ noun (*formal*) REPEAL, revocation, repudiation, rescindment, overturning, annulment, cancellation, invalidation, nullification, negation, dissolution, discontinuation; reversal, retraction, removal, withdrawal, abolition; *formal* recission; *Law* disaffirmation.

abrupt ▶ adjective ❶ *an abrupt halt* | *an abrupt change of subject* SUDDEN, unexpected, without warning, unanticipated, unforeseen, precipitate, surprising, startling; quick, swift, rapid, hurried, hasty, immediate, instantaneous. ❷ *an abrupt manner* CURT, brusque, blunt, short, sharp, terse, brisk, crisp, gruff, rude, discourteous, uncivil, snappish, unceremonious, offhand, rough, harsh; bluff, no-nonsense, to the point; *informal* snappy. ❸ *abrupt, epigrammatic paragraphs* DISJOINTED, jerky, uneven, disconnected, inelegant. ❹ *an abrupt slope* STEEP, sheer, precipitous, bluff, sharp, sudden; perpendicular, vertical, dizzy, vertiginous.
– OPPOSITES gradual, gentle.

abscess ▶ noun ULCER, ulceration, cyst, boil, blister, sore, pustule, carbuncle, pimple, wen, whitlow, canker; inflammation, infection, eruption.

abscond ▶ verb RUN AWAY, escape, bolt, flee, make off, take flight, take off, decamp; make a break for it, take to one's heels, make a quick getaway, beat a hasty retreat, show a clean pair of heels, run for it, make a run for it; disappear, vanish, slip away, steal away, sneak away; *informal* do a moonlight flit, clear out, cut and run, skedaddle, skip, head for the hills, do a disappearing act, fly the coop, take French leave, scarper, vamoose; *Brit. informal* do a bunk, do a runner; *N. Amer. informal* take a powder.

absence ▶ noun ❶ *his absence from the office* NON-ATTENDANCE, non-appearance, absenteeism; TRUANCY, playing truant; leave, holiday, vacation, sabbatical. ❷ *the absence of any other suitable candidate* LACK, want, non-existence, unavailability, deficiency, dearth; need.
– OPPOSITES presence.

absent ▶ adjective ❶ *she was absent from work* AWAY, off, out, non-attending, truant; off duty, on holiday, on leave; gone, missing, lacking, unavailable, non-existent; *informal* AWOL. ❷ *an absent look* DISTRACTED, preoccupied, inattentive, vague, absorbed, abstracted, unheeding, oblivious, distrait, absent-minded, dreamy, far away, in a world of one's own, lost in thought, in a brown study; blank, empty, vacant; *informal* miles away.
– OPPOSITES present, attentive, alert.
▶ verb *Rose absented herself from the occasion* STAY AWAY, be absent, withdraw, retire, take one's leave, remove oneself.

absent-minded ▶ adjective FORGETFUL, distracted, preoccupied, inattentive, vague, abstracted, unheeding, oblivious, distrait, in a brown study, wool-gathering; lost in thought, pensive, thoughtful, brooding; *informal* scatterbrained, miles away, having a mind/memory like a sieve.

absolute ▶ adjective ❶ *absolute silence* | *an absolute disgrace* COMPLETE, total, utter, out-and-out, outright, entire, perfect, pure, decided; thorough, thoroughgoing, undivided, unqualified, unadulterated, unalloyed, unmodified, unreserved, downright, undiluted, consummate, unmitigated, sheer, arrant, rank, dyed-in-the wool. ❷ *the absolute truth* DEFINITE, certain, positive, unconditional, categorical, unquestionable, incontrovertible, undoubted, unequivocal, decisive, conclusive, confirmed, infallible. ❸ *absolute power* UNLIMITED, unrestricted, unrestrained, unbounded, boundless, infinite, ultimate, total, supreme, unconditional. ❹ *an absolute monarch* AUTOCRATIC, despotic, dictatorial, tyrannical, tyrannous, authoritarian, arbitrary, autonomous, sovereign, autarchic, omnipotent. ❺ *absolute moral standards* UNIVERSAL, fixed, independent, non-relative, non-variable, absolutist.
– OPPOSITES partial, qualified, limited, conditional.

absolutely ▶ adverb *you're absolutely right* COMPLETELY, totally, utterly, perfectly, entirely, wholly, fully, quite, thoroughly, unreservedly; definitely, certainly, positively, unconditionally, categorically, unquestionably, undoubtedly, without (a) doubt, without question, surely, unequivocally; exactly, precisely, decisively, conclusively, manifestly, in every way/respect, one hundred per cent, every inch, to the hilt; *informal* dead.
▶ exclamation (*informal*) *'Have I made myself clear?' 'Absolutely!'* YES, indeed, of course, definitely, certainly, quite, without (a) doubt, without question, unquestionably; affirmative, by all means.

absolution ▶ noun FORGIVENESS, pardon, exoneration, remission, dispensation, indulgence, clemency, mercy; discharge, acquittal; freedom, deliverance, release; vindication; *informal* let-off; *formal* exculpation; *archaic* shrift.

absolve ▶ verb ❶ *this fact does not absolve you from responsibility* EXONERATE, discharge, acquit,

vindicate; release, relieve, liberate, free, deliver, clear, exempt, let off; *formal* exculpate. ❷ (*Christianity*) *I absolve you from your sins* FORGIVE, pardon.
– OPPOSITES blame, condemn.

absorb ▶ **verb** ❶ *a sponge-like material which absorbs water* SOAK UP, suck up, draw up/in, take up/in, blot up, mop up, sop up. ❷ *she absorbed the information in silence* ASSIMILATE, digest, take in. ❸ *the company was absorbed into the new concern* INCORPORATE, assimilate, integrate, take in, subsume, include, co-opt, swallow up. ❹ *these roles absorb most of his time and energy* USE (UP), consume, take up, occupy. ❺ *she was totally abosrbed in her book* ENGROSS, captivate, occupy, preoccupy, engage, rivet, grip, hold, interest, intrigue, immerse, involve, enthral, spellbind, fascinate.

absorbent ▶ **adjective** POROUS, spongy, sponge-like, permeable, pervious, absorptive; *technical* spongiform; *rare* sorbefacient.

absorbing ▶ **adjective** FASCINATING, interesting, captivating, gripping, engrossing, compelling, compulsive, enthralling, riveting, spellbinding, intriguing, thrilling, exciting; *informal* unputdownable.
– OPPOSITES boring, uninteresting.

absorption ▶ **noun** ❶ *the absorption of water* SOAKING UP, sucking up; *technical* osmosis. ❷ *the company's absorption into a larger concern* INCORPORATION, assimilation, integration, inclusion. ❸ *her total absorption in the music* INVOLVEMENT, immersion, raptness, engrossment, occupation, preoccupation, engagement, captivation, fascination, enthralment.

abstain ▶ **verb** ❶ *Benjamin abstained from wine* REFRAIN, desist, hold back, forbear; give up, renounce, avoid, shun, eschew, forgo, go without, do without; refuse, decline; *informal* cut out; *formal* abjure. ❷ *most pregnant women abstain, or drink very little* BE TEETOTAL, take the pledge; *informal* be on the wagon. ❸ *262 voted against, 38 abstained* NOT VOTE, decline to vote.

abstemious ▶ **adjective** SELF-DENYING, temperate, abstinent, moderate, self-disciplined, restrained, self-restrained, sober, austere, ascetic, puritanical, spartan, self-abnegating, hair-shirt.
– OPPOSITES self-indulgent.

abstinence ▶ **noun** SELF-DENIAL, self-restraint; teetotalism, temperance, sobriety, abstemiousness, abstention.

abstract ▶ **adjective** ❶ *abstract concepts* THEORETICAL, conceptual, notional, intellectual, metaphysical, philosophical, academic; *rare* ideational. ❷ *abstract art* NON-REPRESENTATIONAL, non-pictorial.
– OPPOSITES actual, concrete.
▶ **verb** ❶ *staff abstract material for an online database* SUMMARIZE, precis, abridge, condense, compress, shorten, cut down, abbreviate, synopsize; *rare* epitomize. ❷ *a scheme to abstract more water from the river* EXTRACT, pump, draw (off), withdraw, remove, take out/away; separate, isolate.
▶ **noun** *an abstract of her speech* SUMMARY, synopsis, precis, résumé, outline, abridgement, digest, summation; *N. Amer.* wrap-up; *archaic* argument.

abstracted ▶ **adjective** ABSENT-MINDED, distracted, preoccupied, in a world of one's own, with one's head in the clouds, daydreaming, dreamy, inattentive, thoughtful, pensive, lost in thought, deep in thought, immersed in thought, wool-gathering, in a brown study, musing, brooding, absent, distrait; *informal* miles away.
– OPPOSITES attentive.

abstraction ▶ **noun** ❶ *philosophical abstractions* CONCEPT, idea, notion, thought, theory, hypothesis. ❷ *she sensed his momentary abstraction* ABSENT-MINDEDNESS, distraction, preoccupation, dreaminess, inattentiveness, inattention, wool-gathering; thoughtfulness, pensiveness. ❸ *the abstraction of metal from ore* EXTRACTION, removal, separation.

abstruse ▶ **adjective** OBSCURE, arcane, esoteric, little known, recherché, rarefied, recondite, difficult, hard, puzzling, perplexing, cryptic, Delphic, complex, complicated, involved, over/above one's head, incomprehensible, unfathomable, impenetrable, mysterious.

absurd ▶ **adjective** PREPOSTEROUS, ridiculous, ludicrous, farcical, laughable, risible, idiotic, stupid, foolish, silly, inane, imbecilic, insane, hare-brained; unreasonable, irrational, illogical, nonsensical, pointless, senseless; *informal* crazy; *Brit. informal* barmy, daft.
– OPPOSITES reasonable, sensible.

absurdity ▶ **noun** PREPOSTEROUSNESS, ridiculousness, ludicrousness, risibility, idiocy, stupidity, foolishness, folly, silliness, inanity, insanity; unreasonableness, irrationality, illogicality, pointlessness, senselessness; *informal* craziness.

abundance ▶ **noun** PROFUSION, plentifulness, profuseness, copiousness, amplitude, lavishness, bountifulness; host, cornucopia, riot; plenty, quantities, scores, multitude; *informal* millions, sea, ocean(s), wealth, lot(s), heap(s), mass(es), stack(s), pile(s), load(s), bags, mountain(s), ton(s), oodles, slew, scads; *Brit. informal* shedload; *N. Amer. informal* gobs; *formal* plenitude.
– OPPOSITES lack, scarcity.

abundant ▶ **adjective** *an abundant supply of food* PLENTIFUL, copious, ample, profuse, rich, lavish, liberal, generous, bountiful, large, huge, great, bumper, overflowing, prolific, teeming; in plenty, in abundance; *informal* a gogo, galore; *poetic/literary* plenteous, bounteous.
– OPPOSITES scarce, sparse.

■ **be abundant** ABOUND, be plentiful, be numerous, be in abundance, proliferate, be thick on the ground; *informal* grow on trees, be two/ten a penny.

abuse ▶ **verb** ❶ *the judge abused his power* MISUSE, misapply, misemploy; exploit, take advantage of. ❷ *he was accused of abusing children* MISTREAT, maltreat, ill-treat, treat badly; molest, interfere with, indecently assault, sexually abuse, sexually assault; injure, hurt, harm, damage. ❸ *the referee was abused by players from both teams* INSULT, be rude to, swear at, curse, call someone names, taunt, shout at, revile, inveigh against, vilify, slander, cast aspersions on; *Brit. informal* slag off.

▶ **noun** ❶ *the abuse of power* MISUSE, misapplication, misemployment; exploitation. ❷ *the abuse of children* MISTREATMENT, maltreatment, ill-treatment; molestation, interference, indecent assault, sexual abuse, sexual assault; injury, hurt, harm, damage. ❸ *the scheme is open to administrative abuse* CORRUPTION, injustice, wrongdoing, wrong, misconduct, misdeed(s), offence(s), crime(s), sin(s). ❹ *torrents of abuse* INSULTS, curses, jibes, expletives, swear words; swearing, cursing, name-calling; invective, vilification, vituperation, slander; *Brit. informal* verbal(s); *N. Amer. informal* trash talk; *archaic* contumely.

abusive ▶ **adjective** INSULTING, rude, vulgar, offensive, disparaging, belittling, derogatory, disrespectful, denigratory, uncomplimentary, pejorative, vituperative; defamatory, slanderous, libellous, scurrilous, blasphemous; *informal* bitchy; *archaic* contumelious.

abut ▶ **verb** ADJOIN, be adjacent to, border, neighbour, join, touch, meet, reach, be contiguous with.

abysmal ▶ **adjective** (*informal*) *some of the teaching was abysmal* VERY BAD, dreadful, awful, terrible, frightful, atrocious, disgraceful, deplorable, shameful, hopeless, lamentable, laughable; *informal* rotten, appalling, crummy, pathetic, pitiful, woeful, useless, lousy, dire, poxy, the pits; *Brit. informal* chronic, shocking.

abyss ▶ **noun** CHASM, gorge, ravine, canyon, fissure, rift, crevasse, hole, gulf, pit, cavity, void, bottomless pit.

academic ▶ **adjective** ❶ *an academic institution* EDUCATIONAL, scholastic, instructional, pedagogical. ❷ *his academic turn of mind* SCHOLARLY, studious, literary, well read, intellectual, clever, erudite, learned, educated, cultured, bookish, highbrow, pedantic, donnish, cerebral; *informal* brainy; *dated* lettered. ❸ *the debate has been largely academic* THEORETICAL, conceptual, notional, philosophical, hypothetical, speculative, conjectural, suppositional, putative; impractical, unrealistic, ivory-tower.

▶ **noun** *a group of Russian academics* SCHOLAR, lecturer, don, teacher, tutor, professor, fellow, man/woman of letters, thinker, bluestocking; *informal* egghead, bookworm; *formal* pedagogue.

academy ▶ **noun** EDUCATIONAL INSTITUTION, school, college, university, institute, seminary, conservatory, conservatoire.

accede ▶ **verb** (*formal*) ❶ *he acceded to the government's demands* AGREE TO, consent to, accept, assent to, acquiesce in, comply with, go along with, concur with, surrender to, yield to, give in to, give way to, defer to. ❷ *Elizabeth I acceded to the throne in 1558* SUCCEED TO, come to, assume, inherit, take. ❸ *Albania acceded to the IMF in 1990* JOIN, become a member of, sign up to.

accelerate ▶ **verb** ❶ *the car accelerated down the hill* SPEED UP, go faster, gain momentum, increase speed, pick up speed, gather speed, put on a spurt. ❷ *inflation started to accelerate* INCREASE, rise, go up, leap up, surge, escalate, spiral. ❸ *the university accelerated the planning process* HASTEN, expedite, precipitate, speed up, quicken, make faster, step up, advance, further, forward, promote, give a boost to, stimulate, spur on; *informal* crank up.
– OPPOSITES decelerate, delay.

acceleration ▶ **noun** ❶ *the car's acceleration is sensational* INCREASE IN SPEED, increasing speed, gain in momentum. ❷ *the acceleration of the industrial process* HASTENING, precipitation, speeding up, quickening, stepping up, advancement, furtherance, boost, stimulation, spur. ❸ *an acceleration in the divorce rate* INCREASE, rise, leap, surge, escalation.

accent ▶ **noun** ❶ *a Scottish accent* PRONUNCIATION, intonation, enunciation, articulation, inflection, tone, modulation, cadence, timbre, manner of speaking, delivery; brogue, burr, drawl, twang. ❷ *the accent is on the first syllable* STRESS, emphasis, accentuation, force, prominence; beat; *technical* ictus. ❸ *the accent is on comfort* EMPHASIS, stress, priority; importance, prominence. ❹ *an acute accent* MARK, diacritic, diacritical mark.

▶ **verb** *fabrics which accent the background colours in the room* FOCUS ATTENTION ON, draw attention to, point up, underline, underscore, accentuate, highlight, spotlight, foreground, feature, play up, bring to the fore, heighten, stress, emphasize.

accentuate ▶ **verb** FOCUS ATTENTION ON, draw attention to, point up, underline, underscore, accent, highlight, spotlight, foreground, feature, play up, bring to the fore, heighten, stress, emphasize.

accept ▶ **verb** ❶ *he accepted a pen as a present* RECEIVE, take, get, gain, obtain, acquire. ❷ *he accepted the job immediately* TAKE ON, undertake, assume, take responsibility for. ❸ *she accepted an invitation to lunch* SAY YES TO, reply in the affirmative, agree to. ❹ *she was accepted as one of the family* WELCOME, receive, embrace, adopt.

❺ *he accepted Ellen's explanation* BELIEVE, regard as true, give credence to, credit, trust; *informal* buy, swallow. ❻ *we have agreed to accept his decision* GO ALONG WITH, agree to, consent to, acquiesce in, concur with, assent to, comply with, abide by, follow, adhere to, act in accordance with, defer to, yield to, surrender to, bow to, give in to, submit to, respect; *formal* accede to. ❼ *she will just have to accept the consequences* TOLERATE, endure, put up with, bear, take, submit to, stomach, swallow; reconcile oneself to, resign oneself to, get used to, adjust to, learn to live with, make the best of; face up to.
– OPPOSITES refuse, reject.

acceptable ▶ **adjective** ❶ *an acceptable standard of living* SATISFACTORY, adequate, reasonable, quite good, fair, decent, good enough, sufficient, sufficiently good, fine, not bad, all right, average, tolerable, passable, middling, moderate; *informal* OK, so-so, fair-to-middling. ❷ *a most acceptable present* WELCOME, appreciated; pleasing, agreeable, delightful, desirable, satisfying, gratifying, to one's liking. ❸ *the risk had seemed acceptable at the time* BEARABLE, tolerable, allowable, admissible, sustainable, justifiable, defensible.

acceptance ▶ **noun** ❶ *the acceptance of an award* RECEIPT, receiving, taking, obtaining. ❷ *the acceptance of responsibility* UNDERTAKING, assumption. ❸ *acceptances to an invitation* YES, affirmative reply, confirmation. ❹ *her acceptance as one of the family* WELCOME, favourable reception, adoption. ❺ *his acceptance of Matilda's explanation* BELIEF, credence, trust, faith. ❻ *their acceptance of the decision* COMPLIANCE, acquiescence, agreement, consent, concurrence, assent, adherence, deference, surrender, submission, respect. ❼ *the acceptance of pain* TOLERATION, endurance, forbearance.

accepted ▶ **adjective** RECOGNIZED, acknowledged, established, traditional, orthodox; usual, customary, common, normal, general, prevailing, accustomed, familiar, wonted, popular, expected, routine, standard, stock.

access ▶ **noun** ❶ *the building has a side access* ENTRANCE, entry, way in, means of entry; approach, means of approach. ❷ *they were denied access to the stadium* ADMISSION, admittance, entry, entrée, ingress, right of entry. ❸ *students have access to a photocopier* (THE) USE OF, permission to use. ❹ *an access of rage* FIT, attack, outburst, outpouring, eruption, explosion, burst, outbreak, flare-up, blow-up, blaze, paroxysm, bout, rush; outflow, outflowing, welling up.
▶ **verb** *the program used to access the data* RETRIEVE, gain access to, obtain; read.

accessible ▶ **adjective** ❶ *the village is only accessible on foot* | *an easily accessible reference tool* REACHABLE, attainable, approachable; obtainable, available; *informal* get-at-able. ❷ *his accessible style of writing* UNDERSTANDABLE, comprehensible, easy to understand, intelligible. ❸ *Professor Cooper is very accessible* APPROACHABLE, friendly, agreeable, obliging, congenial, affable, cordial, welcoming, easy-going, pleasant.

accession ▶ **noun** ❶ *the Queen's accession to the throne* SUCCESSION, assumption, inheritance. ❷ *accession to the Treaty of Rome was effected in 1971* ASSENT, consent, agreement; acceptance, acquiescence, compliance, concurrence. ❸ *recent accessions to the museum* ADDITION, acquisition, new item, gift, purchase.

accessorize ▶ **verb** COMPLEMENT, enhance, set off, show off; go with, accompany; decorate, adorn, ornament, trim.

accessory ▶ **noun** ❶ *camera accessories such as tripods and flashguns* ATTACHMENT, extra, addition, add-on, adjunct, appendage, appurtenance, fitment, supplement. ❷ *fashion accessories* ADORNMENT, embellishment, ornament, ornamentation, decoration; frills, trimmings. ❸ *she was charged as an accessory to murder* ACCOMPLICE, partner in crime, associate, collaborator, fellow conspirator; henchman.
▶ **adjective** *an accessory gearbox* ADDITIONAL, extra, supplementary, supplemental, auxiliary, ancillary, secondary, subsidiary, reserve, add-on.

accident ▶ **noun** ❶ *an accident at work* MISHAP, misadventure, unfortunate incident, mischance, misfortune, disaster, tragedy, catastrophe, calamity; *technical* casualty. ❷ *an accident on the motorway* CRASH, collision, smash, bump, car crash, road traffic accident, RTA; derailment; *N. Amer.* wreck; *informal* smash-up, pile-up; *Brit. informal* prang, shunt. ❸ *it is no accident that there is a similarity between them* CHANCE, mere chance, coincidence, twist of fate, freak, hazard; fluke, bit of luck, serendipity; fate, fortuity, fortune, providence, happenstance.

accidental ▶ **adjective** ❶ *an accidental meeting* FORTUITOUS, chance, adventitious, fluky, coincidental, casual, serendipitous, random; unexpected, unforeseen, unanticipated, unlooked-for, unintentional, unintended, inadvertent, unplanned, unpremeditated, unthinking, unwitting. ❷ *the location is accidental and contributes nothing to the poem* INCIDENTAL, unimportant, by the way, by the by, supplementary, subsidiary, subordinate, secondary, accessory, peripheral, tangential, extraneous, extrinsic, irrelevant, non-essential, inessential.
– OPPOSITES intentional, deliberate.

accidentally ▶ **adverb** BY ACCIDENT, by chance, by a mere chance, by a twist of fate, as luck would have it, fortuitously, by a fluke, by happenstance, coincidentally, adventitiously; unexpectedly, unintentionally, inadvertently, unwittingly.

acclaim ▶ **verb** *the booklet has been widely acclaimed by teachers* PRAISE, applaud, cheer, commend, approve, welcome, pay tribute to,

speak highly of, eulogize, compliment, celebrate, sing the praises of, rave about, heap praise on, wax lyrical about, lionize, exalt, admire, hail, extol, honour, hymn; *informal* crack someone/something up; *N. Amer. informal* ballyhoo; *formal* laud.
– OPPOSITES criticize.

▶ **noun** *she has won acclaim for her commitment to democracy* PRAISE, applause, cheers, ovation, tribute, accolade, acclamation, salutes, plaudits, bouquets; approval, approbation, admiration, congratulations, commendation, welcome, homage; compliment, a pat on the back.
– OPPOSITES criticism.

acclaimed ▶ **adjective** CELEBRATED, admired, highly rated, lionized, honoured, esteemed, exalted, well thought of, well received, acknowledged; eminent, great, renowned, distinguished, prestigious, illustrious, preeminent.

acclamation ▶ **noun** PRAISE, applause, cheers, ovation, tribute, accolade, acclaim, salutes, plaudits, bouquets; approval, admiration, approbation, congratulations, commendation, homage; compliment, a pat on the back.
– OPPOSITES criticism.

acclimatization ▶ **noun** ADJUSTMENT, adaptation, accommodation, habituation, acculturation, familiarization, inurement; naturalization; *N. Amer.* acclimation.

acclimatize ▶ **verb** ADJUST, adapt, accustom, accommodate, habituate, acculturate; get used, become inured, reconcile oneself, resign oneself; familiarize oneself; find one's feet, get one's bearings, become seasoned, become naturalized; *N. Amer.* acclimate.

accolade ▶ **noun** ❶ *he received the accolade of knighthood* HONOUR, privilege, award, gift, title; prize, laurels, bays, palm. ❷ *the hotel won a top accolade from the inspectors* TRIBUTE, commendation, praise, testimonial, compliment, pat on the back; salutes, plaudits, congratulations, bouquets; *informal* rave.

accommodate ▶ **verb** ❶ *refugees were accommodated in army camps* LODGE, house, put up, billet, quarter, board, take in, shelter, give someone a roof over their head; harbour. ❷ *the cottages accommodate up to six people* HOLD, take, have room for. ❸ *our staff will make every effort to accommodate you* HELP, assist, aid, oblige; meet the needs/wants of, cater for, fit in with, satisfy. ❹ *she tried to accommodate herself to her new situation* ADJUST, adapt, accustom, habituate, acclimatize, acculturate, get accustomed, get used, come to terms with; *N. Amer.* acclimate. ❺ *the bank would be glad to accommodate you with a loan* PROVIDE, supply, furnish, grant.

accommodating ▶ **adjective** OBLIGING, cooperative, helpful, eager to help, adaptable, amenable, considerate, unselfish, generous, willing, kindly, hospitable, neighbourly, kind, friendly, pleasant, agreeable; *Brit. informal* decent.

accommodation ▶ **noun** ❶ *temporary accommodation* HOUSING, lodging(s), living quarters, quarters, rooms; place to stay, billet; shelter, a roof over one's head; *informal* digs, pad; *formal* abode, residence, place of residence, dwelling, dwelling place, habitation. ❷ *lifeboat accommodation for 1,178 people* SPACE, room, seating; places. ❸ *an accommodation between the two parties was reached* ARRANGEMENT, understanding, settlement, accord, deal, bargain, compromise. ❹ *their accommodation to changing economic circumstances* ADJUSTMENT, adaptation, habituation, acclimatization, acculturation; inurement; *N. Amer.* acclimation.

accompaniment ▶ **noun** ❶ *a musical accompaniment* BACKING, support, background, soundtrack. ❷ *the wine makes a superb accompaniment to cheese* COMPLEMENT, supplement, addition, adjunct, appendage, companion, accessory.

accompany ▶ **verb** ❶ *the driver accompanied her to the door* GO WITH, travel with, keep someone company, tag along with, partner, escort, chaperone, attend, show, see, usher, conduct. ❷ *the illness is often accompanied by nausea* OCCUR WITH, co-occur with, coexist with, go with, go together with, go hand in hand with, appear with, attend by. ❸ *he accompanied the choir on the piano* BACK, play with, play for, support.

accomplice ▶ **noun** PARTNER IN CRIME, associate, accessory, confederate, collaborator, fellow conspirator; henchman; *informal* sidekick.

accomplish ▶ **verb** FULFIL, achieve, succeed in, realize, attain, manage, bring about/off, carry out/through, execute, effect, perform, do, discharge, complete, finish, consummate, conclude; *formal* effectuate.

accomplished ▶ **adjective** EXPERT, skilled, skilful, masterly, virtuoso, master, consummate, complete, proficient, talented, gifted, adept, adroit, deft, dexterous, able, good, competent, capable, efficient, experienced, seasoned, trained, practised, professional, polished, ready, apt; *informal* great, mean, nifty, crack, ace, wizard; *Brit. informal* a dab hand at; *N. Amer. informal* crackerjack.

accomplishment ▶ **noun** ❶ *the reduction of inflation was a remarkable accomplishment* ACHIEVEMENT, act, deed, exploit, performance, attainment, effort, feat, move, coup. ❷ *typing was another of her accomplishments* TALENT, skill, gift, ability, attainment, achievement, forte, knack. ❸ *a poet of considerable accomplishment* EXPERTISE, skill, skilfulness, talent, adeptness, adroitness, deftness, dexterity, ability, prowess, mastery, competence, capability, proficiency, aptitude, artistry, art; *informal* know-how.

accord ▶ verb ❶ *the national assembly accorded him more power* GIVE, grant, present, award, vouchsafe; confer on, bestow on, vest in, invest with. ❷ *his views accorded with mine* CORRESPOND, agree, tally, match, concur, be consistent, harmonize, be in harmony, be compatible, be in tune, correlate; conform to; *informal* square.

– OPPOSITES withhold, disagree, differ.

▶ noun ❶ *a peace accord* PACT, treaty, agreement, settlement, deal, entente, concordat, protocol, contract, convention. ❷ *the two sides failed to reach accord* AGREEMENT, consensus, unanimity, harmony, unison, unity; *formal* concord.

■ **of one's own accord** VOLUNTARILY, of one's own free will, of one's own volition, by choice; willingly, freely, readily.

■ **with one accord** UNANIMOUSLY, in complete agreement, with one mind, without exception, as one, of one voice, to a man.

accordance ▶ noun *a ballot held in accordance with trade union rules* IN AGREEMENT WITH, in conformity with, in line with, true to, in the spirit of, observing, following, heeding.

according ▶ adjective ❶ *she had a narrow escape, according to the doctors* AS STATED BY, as claimed by, on the authority of, in the opinion of. ❷ *cook the rice according to the instructions* AS SPECIFIED BY, as per, in accordance with, in compliance with, in agreement with. ❸ *salary will be fixed according to experience* IN PROPORTION TO, proportional to, commensurate with, in relation to, relative to, in line with, corresponding to.

accordingly ▶ adverb ❶ *they appreciated the danger and acted accordingly* APPROPRIATELY, correspondingly, suitably. ❷ *accordingly, he returned home to Yorkshire* THEREFORE, for that reason, consequently, so, as a result, as a consequence, in consequence, hence, thus, that being the case, ergo.

accost ▶ verb SPEAK TO, call to, shout to, hail, address; approach, confront, detain, stop; *informal* buttonhole, collar; *Brit. informal* nobble.

account ▶ noun ❶ *his account of the incident* DESCRIPTION, report, version, story, narration, narrative, statement, explanation, exposition, delineation, portrayal, tale; chronicle, history, record, log; view, impression. ❷ *a sensitive account of the Debussy Sonata* PERFORMANCE, interpretation, rendering, rendition, execution. ❸ *the firm's quarterly accounts* FINANCIAL RECORD, ledger, balance sheet, financial statement; (**accounts**) books. ❹ *I pay the account off in full each month* BILL, invoice, tally; debt, charges; *N. Amer.* check; *informal* tab. ❺ *his background is of no account* IMPORTANCE, import, significance, consequence, substance, note; *formal* moment.

▶ verb *her visit could not be accounted a success* CONSIDER, regard as, reckon, hold to be, think, look on as, view as, see as, judge, adjudge, count, deem, rate.

■ **account for** ❶ *they must account for the delay* EXPLAIN, answer for, give reasons for, rationalize, justify. ❷ *excise duties account for over half the price of Scotch* CONSTITUTE, make up, comprise, form, compose, represent.

■ **on account of** BECAUSE OF, owing to, due to, as a consequence of, thanks to, by/in virtue of, in view of.

■ **on no account** NEVER, under no circumstances, not for any reason.

accountability ▶ noun RESPONSIBILITY, liability, answerability.

accountable ▶ adjective ❶ *the government was held accountable for the food shortage* RESPONSIBLE, liable, answerable; to blame. ❷ *the game's popularity is barely accountable* EXPLICABLE, explainable; understandable, comprehensible.

accoutrements ▶ plural noun EQUIPMENT, paraphernalia, stuff, things, apparatus, tackle, kit, implements, material(s), rig, outfit, regalia, appurtenances, impedimenta, odds and ends, bits and pieces, bits and bobs, trappings, accessories.

accredit ▶ verb ❶ *he was accredited with being one of the world's fastest sprinters* RECOGNIZE AS, credit with. ❷ *the discovery of distillation is usually accredited to the Arabs* ASCRIBE, attribute. ❸ *professional bodies accredit these research degrees* RECOGNIZE, authorize, approve, certify, license.

accredited ▶ adjective OFFICIAL, appointed, recognized, authorized, approved, certified, licensed.

accretion ▶ noun ❶ *the accretion of sediments* ACCUMULATION, formation, collecting, cumulation, accrual; growth, increase. ❷ *architectural accretions* ADDITION, extension, appendage, add-on, supplement.

accrue ▶ verb ❶ *financial benefits will accrue from restructuring* RESULT, arise, follow, ensue; be caused by. ❷ *interest is added to the account as it accrues* ACCUMULATE, collect, build up, mount up, grow, increase.

accumulate ▶ verb GATHER, collect, amass, stockpile, pile up, heap up, store (up), hoard, cumulate, lay in/up; increase, multiply, accrue; run up.

accumulation ▶ noun MASS, build-up, pile, heap, stack, collection, stock, store, stockpile, reserve, hoard; amassing, gathering, cumulation, accrual, accretion.

accuracy ▶ noun CORRECTNESS, precision, exactness; factuality, literalness, fidelity, faithfulness, truth, truthfulness, veracity, authenticity, realism, verisimilitude.

accurate ▶ adjective ❶ *accurate information | an accurate representation of the situation* CORRECT, precise, exact, right, error-free, perfect; FACTUAL, fact-based, literal, faithful, true, truthful, true to life, authentic, realistic; *informal* on the mark, on the beam, on the nail; *Brit.*

informal spot on, bang on; *N. Amer. informal* on the money, on the button. ❷ *an accurate shot* WELL AIMED, on target, unerring, deadly, lethal, sure, true, on the mark.

accursed ▶ **adjective** ❶ (*dated*) *that accursed woman* HATEFUL, detestable, loathsome, foul, abominable, damnable, odious, obnoxious, despicable, horrible, horrid, ghastly, awful, dreadful, terrible; annoying, irritating, infuriating, exasperating; *informal* damned, damn, blasted, pesky, pestilential, infernal; *Brit. informal* beastly. ❷ (*poetic/literary*) *he and his line are accursed* CURSED, damned, doomed, condemned, ill-fated, ill-omened, jinxed.
– OPPOSITES pleasant, blessed.

accusation ▶ **noun** ALLEGATION, charge, claim, assertion, imputation; indictment, arraignment; suit, lawsuit; *Law, Brit.* plaint; *N. Amer.* impeachment.

accuse ▶ **verb** ❶ *four people were accused of assault* CHARGE WITH, indict for, arraign for; summons, cite, prefer charges against; *N. Amer.* impeach for. ❷ *the companies were accused of causing job losses* BLAME FOR, lay the blame on, hold responsible for, hold accountable for; condemn for, criticize for, denounce for; *informal* lay at the door of, point the finger at, stick on, pin on.
– OPPOSITES absolve, exonerate.

accustom ▶ **verb** ADAPT, adjust, acclimatize, habituate, accommodate, acculturate; reconcile oneself, become reconciled, get used to, come to terms with, learn to live with, become inured; *N. Amer.* acclimate.

accustomed ▶ **adjective** CUSTOMARY, usual, normal, habitual, regular, routine, ordinary, typical, traditional, established, common, general; *poetic/literary* wonted.

ace (*informal*) ▶ **noun** *a rowing ace* EXPERT, master, genius, virtuoso, maestro, adept, past master, doyen, champion, star; *informal* demon, hotshot, wizard, whizz; *Brit. informal* dab hand; *N. Amer. informal* maven, crackerjack.
– OPPOSITES amateur.
▶ **adjective** *an ace tennis player* EXCELLENT, first-rate, first-class, marvellous, wonderful, magnificent, outstanding, superlative, formidable, virtuoso, masterly, expert, champion, consummate, skilful, adept; *informal* great, terrific, tremendous, superb, fantastic, sensational, fabulous, fab, crack, hotshot, A1, mean, demon, awesome, magic, tip-top, top-notch; *Brit. informal* smashing, brilliant, brill.
– OPPOSITES mediocre.

acerbic ▶ **adjective** SHARP, sarcastic, sardonic, mordant, trenchant, cutting, razor-edged, biting, stinging, searing, scathing, caustic, astringent, abrasive; *N. Amer.* acerb; *Brit. informal* sarky; *N. Amer. informal* snarky.

ache ▶ **noun** ❶ *a stomach ache* PAIN, cramp, twinge, pang; gnawing, stabbing, stinging, smarting; soreness, tenderness, irritation, discomfort. ❷ *the ache in her heart* SORROW, sadness, misery, grief, anguish, suffering, pain, agony, torture, hurt.
▶ **verb** ❶ *my legs were aching* HURT, be sore, be painful, be in pain, throb, pound, twinge; smart, burn, sting; *informal* give someone gyp; *Brit. informal* play up. ❷ *her heart ached for poor Philippa* GRIEVE, sorrow, be in distress, be miserable, be in anguish, bleed. ❸ *Marie ached for his affection* LONG, yearn, hunger, thirst, hanker, pine, itch; crave, desire.

achieve ▶ **verb** ATTAIN, reach, arrive at; realize, bring off/about, pull off, accomplish, carry out/through, fulfil, execute, perform, engineer, conclude, complete, finish, consummate; earn, win, gain, acquire, obtain, come by, get, secure, clinch, net; *informal* wrap up, wangle, swing; *formal* effectuate.

achievement ▶ **noun** ❶ *the achievement of a high rate of economic growth* ATTAINMENT, realization, accomplishment, fulfilment, implementation, execution, performance; conclusion, completion, close, consummation. ❷ *they felt justifiably proud of their achievement* ACCOMPLISHMENT, attainment, feat, performance, undertaking, act, action, deed, effort, exploit; work, handiwork.

Achilles' heel ▶ **noun** WEAK SPOT, weak point, weakness, soft underbelly, shortcoming, failing, imperfection, flaw, defect, chink in one's armour.
– OPPOSITES strength.

aching ▶ **adjective** ❶ *his aching back* PAINFUL, achy, sore, stiff, hurt, tender, uncomfortable; hurting, in pain, throbbing, pounding, smarting, burning, stinging. ❷ *her aching heart* SORROWFUL, sad, miserable, grieving, upset, distressed, anguished, grief-stricken, heavy.

acid ▶ **adjective** ❶ *a slightly acid flavour* ACIDIC, SOUR, tart, bitter, sharp, acrid, pungent, acerbic, vinegary, acetic, acetous. ❷ *acid remarks* ACERBIC, sarcastic, sharp, sardonic, scathing, cutting, razor-edged, biting, stinging, caustic, trenchant, mordant, bitter, acrimonious, astringent, harsh, abrasive, wounding, hurtful, unkind, vitriolic, venomous, waspish, spiteful, malicious; *N. Amer.* acerb; *informal* bitchy, catty; *Brit. informal* sarky; *N. Amer. informal* snarky.
– OPPOSITES sweet, pleasant.

acknowledge ▶ **verb** ❶ *the government acknowledged the need to begin talks* ADMIT, accept, grant, allow, concede, confess, own, recognize. ❷ *he did not acknowledge Colin, but hurried past* GREET, salute, address; nod to, wave to, raise one's hat to, say hello to. ❸ *Douglas was glad to acknowledge her help* EXPRESS GRATITUDE FOR, show appreciation for, thank someone for. ❹ *few people acknowledged my letters* ANSWER, reply to, respond to.
– OPPOSITES reject, deny, ignore.

acknowledged ▸ adjective RECOGNIZED, accepted, approved, accredited, confirmed, declared, confessed, avowed.

acknowledgement ▸ noun ❶ *acknowledgement of the need to take new initiatives* ACCEPTANCE, admission, concession, confession, recognition. ❷ *a smile of acknowledgement* GREETING, welcome, salutation. ❸ *she left without a word of acknowledgement* THANKS, gratitude, appreciation, recognition. ❹ *I sent off the form, but there was no acknowledgement* ANSWER, reply, response.

acme ▸ noun PEAK, pinnacle, zenith, height, high point, crown, crest, summit, top, apex, apogee; climax, culmination.
– OPPOSITES nadir.

acolyte ▸ noun ASSISTANT, helper, attendant, minion, underling, lackey, henchman; follower, disciple, supporter, votary; *informal* sidekick, groupie, hanger-on.

acquaint ▸ verb *he will need to acquaint himself with the regulations* FAMILIARIZE, make familiar, make aware of, inform of, advise of, apprise of, let know, get up to date; brief, prime; *informal* fill in on, gen up on, clue in on.

acquaintance ▸ noun ❶ *a business acquaintance* CONTACT, associate, colleague. ❷ *my acquaintance with George* ASSOCIATION, relationship, contact. ❸ *the pupils had little acquaintance with the language* FAMILIARITY WITH, knowledge of, experience of, awareness of, understanding of, comprehension of, grasp of.

acquainted ▸ adjective ❶ *she was well acquainted with Gothic literature* FAMILIAR, conversant, at home, up to date, abreast, au fait, au courant, well versed, knowledgeable, well informed; informed, apprised; *informal* genned up, clued in; *formal* cognizant. ❷ *I am not personally acquainted with him* FRIENDLY, on friendly terms.

acquiesce ▸ verb *he acquiesced in the cover-up* ACCEPT, consent to, agree to, allow, concede, assent to, concur with, give the nod to; comply with, cooperate with, give in to, bow to, yield to, submit to; *informal* go along with.

acquiescence ▸ noun CONSENT, agreement, acceptance, concurrence, assent, leave; compliance, concession, cooperation; submission.

acquiescent ▸ adjective COMPLIANT, cooperative, willing, obliging, agreeable, amenable, tractable, persuadable, pliant, unprotesting; submissive, self-effacing, unassertive, yielding, biddable, docile.

acquire ▸ verb OBTAIN, come by, get, receive, gain, earn, win, come into, be given; buy, purchase, procure, possess oneself of, secure, pick up; *informal* get one's hands on, get hold of, land, bag, score.
– OPPOSITES lose.

acquirement ▸ noun ❶ *her many acquirements* ATTAINMENT, achievement, accomplishment, skill, talent. ❷ *the acquirement of money* ACQUISITION, obtaining, gaining, earning, winning, procurement.

acquisition ▸ noun ❶ *a new acquisition* PURCHASE, buy, gain, accession, addition, investment, possession. ❷ *the acquisition of funds* OBTAINING, acquirement, gaining, earning, winning, procurement, collection.

acquisitive ▸ adjective GREEDY, covetous, avaricious, possessive, grasping, grabbing, predatory, avid, rapacious, mercenary, materialistic; *informal* money-grubbing.

acquisitiveness ▸ noun GREED, greediness, covetousness, cupidity, possessiveness, avarice, avidity, rapaciousness, rapacity, materialism.

acquit ▸ verb ❶ *the jury acquitted her* CLEAR, exonerate, find innocent, absolve; discharge, release, free, set free; *informal* let off (the hook); *formal* exculpate. ❷ *the boys acquitted themselves well* BEHAVE, conduct oneself, perform, act; *formal* comport oneself. ❸ (*archaic*) *they acquitted themselves of their duty* CARRY OUT, perform, discharge, execute.
– OPPOSITES convict.

acquittal ▸ noun ❶ *the acquittal of the defendants* CLEARING, exoneration; discharge, release, freeing; *informal* let-off; *formal* exculpation. ❷ (*archaic*) *the acquittal of these duties* DISCHARGE, carrying out, execution, performance.
– OPPOSITES conviction.

acrid ▸ adjective PUNGENT, bitter, sharp, sour, tart, harsh, acid, acidic, vinegary, acetic, acetous; stinging, burning.

acrimonious ▸ adjective BITTER, angry, rancorous, caustic, acerbic, scathing, sarcastic, acid, harsh, sharp, cutting; virulent, spiteful, vicious, vitriolic, hostile, venomous, nasty, bad-tempered, ill-natured, mean, malign, malicious, malignant, waspish; *informal* bitchy, catty.

acrimony ▸ noun BITTERNESS, anger, rancour, resentment, ill feeling, ill will, bad blood, animosity, hostility, enmity, antagonism, waspishness, spleen, malice, spitefulness, venom.
– OPPOSITES goodwill.

acrobat ▸ noun TUMBLER, gymnast, tightrope walker, wire walker, trapeze artist; *rare* funambulist.

acrobatics ▸ plural noun ❶ *staggering feats of acrobatics* GYMNASTICS, tumbling; agility; *rare* funambulism. ❷ *the acrobatics required to negotiate an international contract* MENTAL AGILITY, skill, quick thinking, alertness, inventiveness.

act ▸ verb ❶ *the Government must act to remedy the situation* TAKE ACTION, take steps, take measures, move, react. ❷ *he was acting on the orders of the party leader* FOLLOW, act in accordance with, obey, heed, comply with; fulfil, meet, discharge. ❸ *an estate agent acting for a prospec-*

tive buyer REPRESENT, act on behalf of; stand in for, fill in for, deputize for, take the place of. ❹ *Alison began to act oddly* BEHAVE, conduct oneself, react; *formal* comport oneself. ❺ *the scents act as a powerful aphrodisiac* OPERATE, work, function, serve. ❻ *the drug acted directly on the blood vessels* AFFECT, have an effect on, work on; have an impact on, impact on, influence. ❼ *he acted in a highly successful film* PERFORM, play a part, take part, appear; *informal* tread the boards. ❽ *we laughed, but most of us were just acting* PRETEND, play-act, put it on, fake it, feign it, dissemble, dissimulate.

▶ **noun** ❶ *acts of kindness | a criminal act* DEED, action, feat, exploit, move, gesture, performance, undertaking, stunt, operation; achievement, accomplishment. ❷ *the act raised the tax on tobacco* LAW, decree, statute, bill, act of Parliament, enactment, resolution, edict, dictum, ruling, measure; *N. Amer. formal* ordinance. ❸ *the first act of the play* DIVISION, section, subsection, part, segment. ❹ *a music hall act* PERFORMANCE, turn, routine, number, sketch, skit. ❺ *it was all just an act* PRETENCE, show, front, facade, masquerade, charade, posture, pose, affectation, sham, fake; *informal* a put-on.

■ **act up** (*informal*) ❶ *all children act up from time to time* MISBEHAVE, behave badly, get up to mischief; *Brit. informal* play up. ❷ *the engine was acting up* MALFUNCTION, go wrong, be defective, be faulty; *informal* be on the blink; *Brit. informal* play up.

acting ▶ **noun** *the theory and practice of acting* DRAMA, the theatre, the stage, the performing arts, thespianism, dramatics, dramaturgy, stagecraft, theatricals; *informal* treading the boards.

▶ **adjective** *the bank's acting governor* TEMPORARY, interim, caretaker, pro tem, provisional, stopgap; deputy, stand-in, fill-in; *N. Amer. informal* pinch-hitting.

– OPPOSITES permanent.

action ▶ **noun** ❶ *there can be no excuse for their actions* DEED, act, move, undertaking, exploit, manoeuvre, endeavour, effort, exertion; behaviour, conduct, activity. ❷ *the need for local community action* MEASURES, steps, activity, movement, work, operation. ❸ *a man of action* ENERGY, vitality, vigour, forcefulness, drive, initiative, spirit, liveliness, vim, pep; activity; *informal* get-up-and-go. ❹ *the action of hormones on the pancreas* EFFECT, influence, working; power. ❺ *he missed all the action while he was away* EXCITEMENT, activity, happenings, events, incidents; *informal* goings-on. ❻ *twenty-nine men died in the action* FIGHTING, hostilities, battle, conflict, combat, warfare; engagement, clash, encounter, skirmish. ❼ *a civil action for damages* LAWSUIT, legal action, suit (at law), case, prosecution, litigation, proceedings.

activate ▶ **verb** OPERATE, switch on, turn on, start (up), set going, trigger (off), set in motion, actuate, energize; trip.

active ▶ **adjective** ❶ *despite her illness she remained active* ENERGETIC, lively, sprightly, spry, mobile, vigorous, vital, dynamic, sporty; busy, occupied; *informal* on the go, full of beans. ❷ *an active member of the union* HARD-WORKING, busy, industrious, diligent, tireless, contributing, effective, enterprising, involved, enthusiastic, keen, committed, devoted, zealous. ❸ *the watermill was active until 1960* OPERATIVE, working, functioning, functional, operating, operational, in action, in operation; live; *informal* up and running.

– OPPOSITES listless, passive.

activity ▶ **noun** ❶ *there was a lot of activity in the area* BUSTLE, hustle and bustle, busyness, action, liveliness, movement, life, stir, flurry; happenings, occurrences, proceedings, events, incidents; *informal* toing and froing, comings and goings. ❷ *a wide range of activities* PURSUIT, occupation, interest, hobby, pastime, recreation, diversion; venture, undertaking, enterprise, project, scheme, business, entertainment; act, action, deed, exploit.

actor, actress ▶ **noun** PERFORMER, player, trouper, thespian; film star, matinee idol, star, starlet; *informal* ham; *Brit. informal* luvvy; *N. Amer. informal* hambone.

– RELATED TERMS histrionic.

actual ▶ **adjective** REAL, true, genuine, authentic, verified, attested, confirmed, definite, hard, plain, veritable; existing, existent, manifest, substantial, factual, de facto, bona fide; *informal* real live.

– OPPOSITES notional.

actuality ▶ **noun** *the journalistic debate about actuality and fiction* REALITY, fact, truth, real life.

■ **in actuality** IN (ACTUAL) FACT, actually, really, in reality, in point of fact, in truth, if truth be told, to tell the truth; *archaic* in sooth.

actually ▶ **adverb** *I looked upset but actually I was terribly excited* REALLY, in (actual) fact, in point of fact, as a matter of fact, in reality, in actuality, in truth, if truth be told, to tell the truth; *archaic* in sooth.

actuate ▶ **verb** ❶ *the sprinkler system was actuated by the fire* ACTIVATE, operate, switch on, turn on, start (up), set going, trigger (off), trip, set in motion, energize. ❷ *the defendant was actuated by malice* MOTIVATE, prompt, stimulate, move, drive, influence, incite, spur on, impel.

acumen ▶ **noun** ASTUTENESS, shrewdness, acuity, sharpness, sharp-wittedness, cleverness, smartness, brains; judgement, understanding, awareness, sense, common sense, canniness, discernment, wisdom, wit, sagacity, perspicacity, insight, perception, penetration; *informal* nous, savvy, know-how, horse sense; *N. Amer. informal* smarts; *formal* perspicuity.

acute ▶ **adjective** ❶ *the acute food shortages* SEVERE, critical, drastic, dire, dreadful, terrible,

awful, grave, bad, serious, desperate, parlous, dangerous. ❷ *acute stomach pains* SHARP, severe, stabbing, excruciating, agonizing, racking, searing. ❸ *his acute mind* ASTUTE, shrewd, sharp, sharp-witted, razor-sharp, rapier-like, quick, quick-witted, agile, nimble, clever, intelligent, brilliant, smart, canny, discerning, perceptive, perspicacious, penetrating, insightful, incisive, piercing, discriminating, sagacious, wise, judicious; *informal* on the ball, quick off the mark, quick on the uptake, streetwise, savvy; *N. Amer. informal* heads-up. ❹ *an acute sense of smell* KEEN, sharp, good, penetrating, discerning, sensitive.
– OPPOSITES mild, dull.

acutely ▶adverb EXTREMELY, exceedingly, very, markedly, severely, intensely, deeply, profoundly, keenly, painfully, desperately, tremendously, enormously, thoroughly, heartily; *informal* awfully, terribly.
– OPPOSITES slightly.

adage ▶noun SAYING, maxim, axiom, proverb, aphorism, apophthegm, saw, dictum, precept, motto, truism, platitude, cliché, commonplace.

adamant ▶adjective UNSHAKEABLE, immovable, inflexible, unwavering, unswerving, uncompromising, resolute, resolved, determined, firm, steadfast; stubborn, unrelenting, unyielding, unbending, rigid, obdurate, inexorable, intransigent, dead set.

adapt ▶verb ❶ *we've adapted the hotels to suit their needs* MODIFY, alter, change, adjust, convert, redesign, restyle, refashion, remodel, reshape, revamp, rework, rejig, redo, reconstruct, reorganize; customize, tailor; improve, amend, refine; *informal* tweak. ❷ *he has adapted well to his new home* ADJUST, acclimatize oneself, accommodate oneself, habituate oneself, become habituated, get used, orient oneself, reconcile oneself, come to terms, get one's bearings, find one's feet, acculturate, assimilate, blend in, fit in; *N. Amer.* acclimate.

adaptable ▶adjective ❶ *competent and adaptable staff* FLEXIBLE, versatile, cooperative, accommodating, amenable. ❷ *an adaptable piece of furniture* VERSATILE, modifiable, convertible, alterable, adjustable, changeable; multipurpose, all-purpose.

adaptation ▶noun ❶ *the adaptation of old buildings* CONVERSION, alteration, modification, redesign, remodelling, revamping, reconstruction. ❷ *the adaptation of an ethnic community to British society* ADJUSTMENT, acclimatization, accommodation, habituation, acculturation, assimilation, integration; *N. Amer.* acclimation.

add ▶verb ❶ *the front porch was added in 1751* ATTACH, build on, join, append, affix, connect, annex; include, incorporate. ❷ *they added all the figures up* TOTAL, count (up), compute, reckon up, tally; *Brit.* tot up. ❸ *the subsidies added up to £1700* AMOUNT TO, come to, run to, make, total, equal, number. ❹ *the recent riots add up to a deepening crisis* AMOUNT TO, constitute; signify, signal, mean, indicate, denote, point to, be evidence of, be symptomatic of; *informal* spell. ❺ *her decision just added to his woe* INCREASE, magnify, amplify, augment, intensify, heighten, deepen; exacerbate, aggravate, compound, reinforce; add fuel to the fire, fan the flames, rub salt on the wound. ❻ *she added that she had every confidence in Laura* GO ON TO SAY, state further, continue, carry on.
– OPPOSITES subtract.
■ **add up** (*informal*) *the situation just didn't add up* MAKE SENSE, stand to reason, hold up, hold water, ring true, be convincing.

addendum ▶noun APPENDIX, codicil, postscript, afterword, tailpiece, rider, coda, supplement; adjunct, appendage, addition, add-on, attachment.

addict ▶noun ❶ *a heroin addict* ABUSER, user; *informal* junkie, druggy, -freak, -head, pill-popper; *N. Amer. informal* hophead. ❷ (*informal*) *skiing addicts* ENTHUSIAST, fan, lover, devotee, aficionado; *informal* freak, nut, fiend, fanatic, maniac.

addicted ▶adjective ❶ *he was addicted to tranquillizers* DEPENDENT ON; *informal* hooked on. ❷ *she became addicted to the theatre* DEVOTED TO, obsessed with, fixated on, fanatical about, passionate about, a slave to; *informal* hooked on, mad on, crazy about.

addiction ▶noun ❶ *his heroin addiction* DEPENDENCY, dependence, habit; *informal* monkey. ❷ *a slavish addiction to fashion* DEVOTION TO, dedication to, obsession with, infatuation with, passion for, love of, mania for, enslavement to.

addictive ▶adjective HABIT-FORMING; compulsive; *Brit. informal* moreish.

addition ▶noun ❶ *the soil is improved by the addition of compost* ADDING, incorporation, inclusion, introduction. ❷ *an addition to the existing regulations* SUPPLEMENT, adjunct, addendum, appendage, add-on, extra; rider.
■ **in addition** ❶ *conditions were harsh and in addition some soldiers fell victim to snipers* ADDITIONALLY, as well, what's more, furthermore, moreover, also, into the bargain, to boot. ❷ *eight presidential candidates in addition to the General* BESIDES, as well as, on top of, plus, over and above.

additional ▶adjective EXTRA, added, supplementary, supplemental, further, auxiliary, ancillary; more, other, another, new, fresh.

additionally ▶adverb ALSO, in addition, as well, too, besides, on top (of that), moreover, further, furthermore, what's more, over and above that, into the bargain, to boot; *archaic* withal.

additive ▶noun ADDED INGREDIENT, addition; preservative, colouring; *Brit. informal* E-number.

addled ▶ **adjective** MUDDLED, confused, muzzy, fuddled, befuddled, dazed, disoriented, disorientated, fuzzy; *informal* woozy.

address ▶ **noun** ❶ *the address on the envelope* inscription, superscription; directions. ❷ *our officers called at the address* HOUSE, flat, apartment, home; *formal* residence, dwelling, dwelling place, habitation, abode, domicile. ❸ *his address to the European Parliament* SPEECH, lecture, talk, monologue, dissertation, discourse, oration, peroration; sermon, homily, lesson.
▶ **verb** ❶ *I addressed the envelope by hand* inscribe, superscribe. ❷ *the preacher addressed a crowded congregation* TALK TO, give a talk to, speak to, make a speech to, give a lecture to, lecture, hold forth to; PREACH TO, give a sermon to. ❸ *the question of how to address one's parents-in-law* CALL, name, designate; speak to, write to; *formal* denominate. ❹ *correspondence should be addressed to the Banking Ombudsman* DIRECT, send, communicate, convey, remit. ❺ *the minister failed to address the issue of subsidies* ATTEND TO, apply oneself to, tackle, see to, deal with, confront, get to grips with, get down to, turn one's hand to, take in hand, undertake, concentrate on, focus on, devote oneself to.

adduce ▶ **verb** CITE, quote, name, mention, instance, point out, refer to; put forward, present, offer, advance, propose, proffer.

adept ▶ **adjective** *an adept negotiator* EXPERT, proficient, accomplished, skilful, talented, masterly, consummate, virtuoso; adroit, dexterous, deft, artful; brilliant, splendid, marvellous, formidable, outstanding, first-rate, first-class, excellent, fine; *informal* great, top-notch, tip-top, A1, ace, mean, hotshot, crack, nifty, deadly; *Brit. informal* a dab hand at; *N. Amer. informal* crackerjack.
– OPPOSITES inept.
▶ **noun** *kung fu adepts* EXPERT, past master, master, genius, maestro, doyen; *informal* wizard, demon, ace, hotshot, whizz; *N. Amer. informal* maven, crackerjack.
– OPPOSITES amateur.

adequacy ▶ **noun** ❶ *the adequacy of the existing services* SATISFACTORINESS, acceptability, acceptableness; sufficiency. ❷ *he had deep misgivings about his own adequacy* CAPABILITY, competence, ability, aptitude, suitability; effectiveness, fitness; *formal* efficacy.

adequate ▶ **adjective** ❶ *he lacked adequate financial resources* SUFFICIENT, enough, requisite. ❷ *the company provides an adequate service* ACCEPTABLE, passable, reasonable, satisfactory, tolerable, fair, decent, quite good, pretty good, goodish, moderate, unexceptional, unremarkable, undistinguished, ordinary, average, not bad, all right, middling; *informal* OK, so-so, fair-to-middling, nothing to write home about. ❸ *the workstations were small but seemed adequate to the task* EQUAL TO, up to, capable of, suitable for, able to do, fit for, sufficient for.

adhere ▶ **verb** ❶ *a dollop of cream adhered to her nose* STICK (FAST), cohere, cling, bond, attach; be stuck, be fixed, be glued. ❷ *they adhere scrupulously to Judaic law* ABIDE BY, stick to, hold to, comply with, act in accordance with, conform to, submit to; follow, obey, heed, observe, respect, uphold, fulfil.
– OPPOSITES flout, ignore.

adherent ▶ **noun** FOLLOWER, supporter, upholder, defender, advocate, disciple, votary, devotee, partisan, member, friend, stalwart, sectary; believer, worshipper.
– OPPOSITES opponent.

adhesion ▶ **noun** ❶ *the adhesion of the gum strip to the paper fibres* STICKING, adherence. ❷ *the front tyres were struggling for adhesion* TRACTION, grip, purchase.

adhesive ▶ **noun** *a spray adhesive* GLUE, fixative, gum, paste, cement; *N. Amer.* mucilage; *N. Amer. informal* stickum.
▶ **adjective** *adhesive mortar* STICKY, tacky, gluey, gummed; viscous, viscid; *technical* adherent; *informal* icky.

adieu ▶ **noun & exclamation** GOODBYE, farewell, until we meet again; *informal* bye-bye, ta-ta, bye, cheerio, cheers, ciao, so long; *informal, dated* toodle-oo, toodle-pip.

ad infinitum ▶ **adverb** FOREVER, for ever and ever, evermore, always, for all time, until the end of time, in perpetuity, until hell freezes over; perpetually, eternally, endlessly, interminably, unceasingly, unendingly; *Brit.* for evermore; *informal* until the cows come home, until the twelfth of never, until doomsday, until kingdom come; *archaic* for aye.

adjacent ▶ **adjective** ADJOINING, neighbouring, next-door, abutting, contiguous, proximate; (**adjacent to**) close to, near, next to, by, by the side of, bordering on, beside, alongside, attached to, touching, cheek by jowl with.

adjoin ▶ **verb** BE NEXT TO, be adjacent to, border (on), abut, be contiguous with, communicate with, extend to; join, conjoin, connect with, touch, meet.

adjoining ▶ **adjective** CONNECTING, connected, interconnecting, adjacent, neighbouring, bordering, next-door; contiguous, proximate; attached, touching.

adjourn ▶ **verb** ❶ *the hearing was adjourned* SUSPEND, break off, discontinue, interrupt, prorogue, stay, recess. ❷ *sentencing was adjourned until June 9* POSTPONE, put off/back, defer, delay, hold over, shelve. ❸ *they adjourned to the sitting room for liqueurs* WITHDRAW, retire, retreat, take oneself; *formal* repair, remove; *poetic/literary* betake oneself.

adjournment ▶ **noun** SUSPENSION, discontinuation, interruption, postponement, deferment, deferral, stay, prorogation; break, pause, recess.

adjudge ▶ verb JUDGE, deem, find, pronounce, proclaim, rule, hold, determine; consider, think, rate, reckon, perceive, regard as, view as, see as, believe to be.

adjudicate ▶ verb JUDGE, try, hear, examine, arbitrate; pronounce on, give a ruling on, pass judgement on, decide, determine, settle, resolve.

adjudication ▶ noun JUDGEMENT, decision, pronouncement, ruling, settlement, resolution, arbitration, finding, verdict, sentence; *Law* determination.

adjudicator ▶ noun JUDGE, arbitrator, arbiter; referee, umpire.

adjunct ▶ noun SUPPLEMENT, addition, extra, add-on, accessory, accompaniment, complement, appurtenance; attachment, appendage, addendum.

adjust ▶ verb ❶ *Kate had adjusted to her new life* ADAPT, become accustomed, get used, accommodate, acclimatize, orient oneself, reconcile oneself, habituate oneself, assimilate; come to terms with, blend in with, fit in with, find one's feet in; *N. Amer.* acclimate. ❷ *he adjusted the brakes* MODIFY, alter, regulate, tune, fine-tune, calibrate, balance; adapt, rearrange, change, rejig, rework, revamp, remodel, reshape, convert, tailor, improve, enhance, customize; repair, fix, correct, rectify, overhaul, put right; *informal* tweak.

adjustable ▶ adjective ALTERABLE, adaptable, modifiable, convertible, variable, multiway, versatile.

adjustment ▶ noun ❶ *a period of adjustment* ADAPTATION, accommodation, acclimatization, habituation, acculturation, naturalization, assimilation; *N. Amer.* acclimation. ❷ *the car will run on unleaded petrol with no adjustment* MODIFICATION, alteration, regulation, adaptation, rearrangement, change, reconstruction, customization, refinement; repair, correction, amendment, overhaul, improvement.

ad-lib ▶ verb *she ad-libbed half the speech* IMPROVISE, extemporize, speak impromptu, play it by ear, make it up as one goes along; *informal* busk it, wing it.
▶ adverb *she spoke ad lib* IMPROMPTU, extempore, without preparation, without rehearsal, extemporaneously; *informal* off the cuff, off the top of one's head.
▶ adjective *a live, ad-lib commentary* IMPROMPTU, extempore, extemporaneous, extemporary, improvised, unprepared, unrehearsed, unscripted; *informal* off-the-cuff, spur-of-the-moment.

administer ▶ verb ❶ *the union is administered by a central executive* MANAGE, direct, control, operate, regulate, conduct, handle, run, organize, supervise, superintend, oversee, preside over, govern, rule, lead, head, steer; be in control of, be in charge of, be responsible for, be at the helm of; *informal* head up. ❷ *the lifeboat crew administered first aid* DISPENSE, issue, give, provide, apply, allot, distribute, hand out, dole out, disburse. ❸ *a gym shoe was used to administer punishment* INFLICT, mete out, deal out, deliver.

administration ▶ noun ❶ *the day-to-day administration of the company* MANAGEMENT, direction, control, command, charge, conduct, operation, running, leadership, government, governing, superintendence, supervision, regulation, overseeing. ❷ *the previous Labour administration* GOVERNMENT, cabinet, ministry, regime, executive, authority, directorate, council, leadership, management; parliament, congress, senate; rule, term of office, incumbency. ❸ *the administration of anti-inflammatory drugs* PROVISION, issuing, issuance, application, dispensing, dispensation, distribution, disbursement.

administrative ▶ adjective MANAGERIAL, management, directorial, executive, organizational, supervisory, regulatory.

administrator ▶ noun MANAGER, director, executive, controller, head, chief, leader, governor, superintendent, supervisor; *informal* boss.

admirable ▶ adjective COMMENDABLE, praiseworthy, laudable, estimable, meritorious, creditable, exemplary, honourable, worthy, deserving, respectable, worthwhile, good, sterling, fine, masterly, great.
–OPPOSITES deplorable.

admiration ▶ noun RESPECT, approval, approbation, appreciation, regard, (high) regard, esteem; commendation, acclaim, applause, praise, compliments, tributes, accolades, plaudits; *formal* laudation.
–OPPOSITES scorn.

admire ▶ verb ❶ *I admire your courage* RESPECT, approve of, esteem, think highly of, rate highly, hold in high regard, applaud, praise, commend, acclaim. ❷ *Simon had admired her for a long time* ADORE, love, worship, dote on, be enamoured of, be infatuated with; be taken with, be attracted to, find attractive; *informal* carry a torch for, have a thing about.
–OPPOSITES despise.

admirer ▶ noun ❶ *a great admirer of Henry James* FAN, devotee, enthusiast, aficionado; supporter, adherent, follower, disciple. ❷ *a handsome admirer of hers* SUITOR, wooer, sweetheart, lover, boyfriend, young man; *poetic/literary* swain; *dated* beau.

admissible ▶ adjective VALID, allowable, allowed, permissible, permitted, acceptable, satisfactory, justifiable, defensible, supportable, well founded, tenable, sound; legitimate, lawful, legal, licit; *informal* OK, legit, kosher, pukka.

admission ▶ noun ❶ *membership entitles you to free admission* ADMITTANCE, entry, entrance, right of entry, access, right of access, ingress; entrée. ❷ *admission is fifty pence* ENTRANCE FEE, entry charge, ticket. ❸ *a written admission of liability* CONFESSION, acknowledgement, acceptance, concession, disclosure, divulgence.

admit ▶ verb ❶ *he unlocked the door to admit her* LET IN, allow entry, permit entry, take in, usher in, show in, receive, welcome. ❷ *he was admitted as a scholar to Winchester College* ACCEPT, take on, receive, enrol, enlist, register, sign up. ❸ *Paul admitted that he was angry* CONFESS, acknowledge, own, concede, grant, accept, allow; reveal, disclose, divulge. ❹ *he admitted three offences of reckless driving* CONFESS (TO), plead guilty to, own up to, make a clean breast of.
– OPPOSITES exclude, deny.

admittance ▶ noun ENTRY, right of entry, admission, entrance, access, right of access, ingress; entrée.
– OPPOSITES exclusion.

admonish ▶ verb ❶ *he was severely admonished by his father* REPRIMAND, rebuke, scold, reprove, reproach, upbraid, chastise, chide, berate, criticize, take to task, pull up, read the Riot Act to, haul over the coals; *informal* tell off, dress down, bawl out, rap over the knuckles, give someone hell; *Brit. informal* tick off, give someone a rocket, have a go at, carpet, tear someone off a strip; *N. Amer. informal* chew out; *formal* castigate; *rare* reprehend. ❷ *she admonished him to drink less* ADVISE, recommend, counsel, urge, exhort, bid, enjoin; *formal* adjure.

admonition ▶ noun ❶ *a breach of the rules which led to an admonition* REPRIMAND, rebuke, reproof, remonstrance, reproach, reproval, stricture, criticism, recrimination, scolding, censure; *informal* telling-off, dressing-down, talking-to, tongue-lashing, rap over the knuckles, slap on the wrist, flea in one's ear, earful; *Brit. informal* rocket, rollicking, wigging, ticking-off; *formal* castigation. ❷ *an admonition to proceed carefully* EXHORTATION, warning, piece of advice, recommendation, counsel.

ado ▶ noun FUSS, trouble, bother, upset, agitation, commotion, stir, hubbub, confusion, excitement, hurly-burly, flurry; palaver, rigmarole, brouhaha; *N. Amer.* fuss and feathers; *informal* hassle, hoo-ha, ballyhoo, to-do, song and dance, performance, kerfuffle; *Brit. informal* carry-on.

adolescence ▶ noun TEENAGE YEARS, teens, youth; pubescence, puberty.

adolescent ▶ noun *an awkward adolescent* TEENAGER, youngster, young person, youth, boy, girl; juvenile, minor; *informal* teen, teenybopper.
▶ adjective ❶ *an adolescent boy* TEENAGE, pubescent, young; juvenile; *informal* teen. ❷ *adolescent silliness* IMMATURE, childish, juvenile, infantile, puerile, jejune.
– OPPOSITES adult, mature.

adopt ▶ verb ❶ *the child was adopted by an American family* take as one's child, be adoptive parents to, take in, take care of. ❷ *they adopted local customs* ESPOUSE, take on/up, embrace, assume; appropriate, arrogate. ❸ *the people adopted him as their patron saint* CHOOSE, select, pick, vote for, elect, settle on, decide on, opt for; name, nominate, appoint.
– OPPOSITES abandon.

adorable ▶ adjective LOVABLE, appealing, charming, cute, sweet, enchanting, bewitching, captivating, engaging, endearing, dear, darling, delightful, lovely, beautiful, attractive, gorgeous, winsome, winning, fetching; *Scottish & N. English* bonny.
– OPPOSITES hateful.

adoration ▶ noun ❶ *the girl gazed at him with adoration* LOVE, devotion, care, fondness; admiration, high regard, awe, idolization, worship, hero-worship, adulation. ❷ *our day of prayer and adoration* WORSHIP, glory, glorification, praise, thanksgiving, homage, exaltation, extolment, veneration, reverence; *archaic* magnification.

adore ▶ verb ❶ *he adored his mother* LOVE DEARLY, love, be devoted to, dote on, hold dear, cherish, treasure, prize, think the world of; admire, hold in high regard, look up to, idolize, worship; *informal* put on a pedestal. ❷ *the people had come to pray and adore God* WORSHIP, glorify, praise, revere, reverence, exalt, extol, venerate, pay homage to; *formal* laud; *archaic* magnify. ❸ (*informal*) *I adore oysters* LIKE, love, be very fond of, be very keen on, be partial to, have a weakness for; delight in, revel in, relish, savour; *informal* be crazy about, be wild about, have a thing about, be hooked on, go a bundle on; *Brit. informal* be potty about.
– OPPOSITES hate.

adorn ▶ verb DECORATE, embellish, ornament, enhance; beautify, prettify, grace, bedeck, deck (out), dress (up), trim, swathe, wreathe, festoon, garland, array, emblazon; *poetic/literary* bedizen, caparison.
– OPPOSITES disfigure.

adornment ▶ noun DECORATION, embellishment, ornamentation, ornament, enhancement; beautification, prettification; frills, accessories, trimmings, finishing touches.

adrift ▶ adjective ❶ *their empty boat was spotted adrift* DRIFTING, unmoored, unanchored. ❷ (*Brit. informal*) *the pipe of my breathing apparatus came adrift* LOOSE, free; detached, unsecured, unfastened, untied, unknotted, undone. ❸ *he was adrift in a strange country* LOST, off course; disorientated, disoriented, confused, (all) at sea; drifting, rootless, unsettled, directionless, aimless, purposeless, without purpose. ❹ (*Brit. informal*) *his instincts were not entirely adrift. See* WRONG adjective sense 1.

adroit ▶ adjective SKILFUL, adept, dexterous,

deft, nimble, able, capable, skilled, expert, masterly, masterful, master, practised, polished, slick, proficient, accomplished, gifted, talented; quick-witted, quick-thinking, clever, smart, sharp, cunning, wily, resourceful, astute, shrewd, canny; *informal* nifty, crack, mean, wizard, demon, ace, A1, on the ball, savvy; *N. Amer. informal* crackerjack.
– OPPOSITES inept, clumsy.

adroitness ▶ noun SKILL, skilfulness, prowess, expertise, adeptness, dexterity, deftness, nimbleness, ability, capability, mastery, proficiency, accomplishment, artistry, art, facility, aptitude, flair, finesse, talent; quick-wittedness, cleverness, sharpness, cunning, astuteness, shrewdness, resourcefulness, savoir faire; *informal* know-how, savvy.

adulation ▶ noun HERO-WORSHIP, worship, idolization, adoration, admiration, veneration, awe, devotion, glorification, praise, flattery, blandishments.

adulatory ▶ adjective FLATTERING, complimentary, highly favourable, enthusiastic, glowing, reverential, rhapsodic, eulogistic, laudatory; fulsome, honeyed.
– OPPOSITES disparaging.

adult ▶ adjective ❶ *an adult woman* MATURE, grown-up, fully grown, full-grown, fully developed, of age. ❷ *an adult movie* SEXUALLY EXPLICIT, pornographic, obscene, smutty, dirty, rude, erotic, sexy, suggestive, titillating; *informal* porn, porno, naughty, blue, X-rated, skin.

adulterate ▶ verb MAKE IMPURE, degrade, debase, spoil, taint, contaminate; doctor, tamper with, dilute, water down, weaken; bastardize, corrupt; *informal* cut, spike, dope.
– OPPOSITES purify.

adulterer ▶ noun PHILANDERER, deceiver, womanizer, ladies' man, Don Juan, Casanova, Lothario; *informal* cheat, two-timer, love rat; *formal* fornicator.

adulterous ▶ adjective UNFAITHFUL, faithless, disloyal, untrue, inconstant, false, false-hearted, deceiving, deceitful, treacherous; extramarital; *informal* cheating, two-timing.
– OPPOSITES faithful.

adultery ▶ noun INFIDELITY, unfaithfulness, falseness, disloyalty, cuckoldry, extramarital sex; affair, liaison, amour; *informal* carryings-on, hanky-panky, a bit on the side, playing around; *formal* fornication.
– OPPOSITES fidelity.

advance ▶ verb ❶ *the battalion advanced rapidly* MOVE FORWARD, proceed, press on, push on, push forward, make progress, make headway, gain ground, approach, come closer, draw nearer, near; *archaic* draw nigh. ❷ *the court may advance the date of the hearing* BRING FORWARD, put forward, move forward. ❸ *the move advanced his career* PROMOTE, further, forward, help, aid, assist, boost, strengthen, improve, benefit, foster. ❹ *our technology has advanced in the last few years* PROGRESS, make progress, make headway, develop, evolve, make strides, move forward (in leaps and bounds), move ahead; improve, thrive, flourish, prosper. ❺ *the hypothesis I wish to advance in this article* PUT FORWARD, present, submit, suggest, propose, introduce, offer, adduce, moot. ❻ *a relative advanced him some money* LEND, loan, put up, come up with; *Brit. informal* sub.
– OPPOSITES retreat, hinder, postpone, retract, borrow.
▶ noun ❶ *the advance of the aggressors* PROGRESS, forward movement; approach. ❷ *a significant medical advance* BREAKTHROUGH, development, step forward, step in the right direction, (quantum) leap; find, finding, discovery, invention. ❸ *share prices showed significant advances* INCREASE, rise, upturn, upsurge, upswing, growth; *informal* hike. ❹ *the writer is going to be given a huge advance* DOWN PAYMENT, retainer, prepayment, deposit, front money, money up front. ❺ *unwelcome sexual advances* PASS, proposition.
▶ adjective ❶ *an advance party of settlers* PRELIMINARY, sent (on) ahead, first, exploratory; pilot, test, trial. ❷ *advance warning* EARLY, prior, beforehand.
■ **in advance** BEFOREHAND, before, ahead of time, earlier, previously; in readiness.

advanced ▶ adjective ❶ *advanced manufacturing techniques* STATE-OF-THE-ART, new, modern, up to date, up to the minute, the newest, the latest; progressive, avant-garde, ahead of the times, pioneering, innovatory, sophisticated. ❷ *advanced further-education courses* HIGHER-LEVEL, higher, tertiary.
– OPPOSITES primitive.

advancement ▶ noun ❶ *the advancement of computer technology* DEVELOPMENT, progress, evolution, growth, improvement, advance, furtherance; headway. ❷ *employees must be offered opportunities for advancement* PROMOTION, preferment, career development, upgrading, a step up the ladder, progress, improvement, betterment, growth.

advantage ▶ noun ❶ *the advantages of belonging to a union* BENEFIT, value, good point, strong point, asset, plus, bonus, boon, blessing, virtue; attraction, beauty, usefulness, helpfulness, convenience, advantageousness, profit. ❷ *they appeared to be gaining the advantage over their opponents* UPPER HAND, edge, lead, whip hand, trump card; superiority, dominance, ascendancy, supremacy, power, mastery. ❸ *there is no advantage to be gained from delaying the process* BENEFIT, profit, gain, good; *informal* mileage, percentage.
– OPPOSITES disadvantage, drawback, detriment.

advantageous ▶ adjective ❶ *an advantageous position* SUPERIOR, dominant, powerful;

good, fortunate, lucky, favourable. ❷ *the arrangement is advantageous to both sides* BENEFICIAL, of benefit, helpful, of assistance, useful, of use, of value, of service, profitable, fruitful; convenient, expedient, in everyone's interests.
– OPPOSITES disadvantageous, detrimental.

advent ▶ noun ARRIVAL, appearance, emergence, materialization, occurrence, dawn, birth, rise, development; approach, coming.
– OPPOSITES disappearance.

adventitious ▶ adjective ❶ *he felt that the conversation was not entirely adventitious* UNPLANNED, unpremeditated, accidental, chance, fortuitous, serendipitous, coincidental, casual, random. ❷ *the adventitious population* FOREIGN, alien, non-native.
– OPPOSITES premeditated.

adventure ▶ noun ❶ *her recent adventures in Italy* EXPLOIT, escapade, deed, feat, experience; stunt. ❷ *they set off in search of adventure* EXCITEMENT, thrill, stimulation; risk, danger, hazard, peril, uncertainty, precariousness.

adventurer ▶ noun DAREDEVIL, hero, heroine; swashbuckler, knight errant.

adventurous ▶ adjective ❶ *an adventurous traveller* DARING, daredevil, intrepid, venturesome, bold, fearless, brave, unafraid, unshrinking, dauntless; *informal* gutsy, spunky. ❷ *adventurous activities* RISKY, dangerous, perilous, hazardous, precarious, uncertain; exciting, thrilling.
– OPPOSITES cautious.

adversary ▶ noun OPPONENT, rival, enemy, antagonist, combatant, challenger, contender, competitor, opposer; opposition, competition; *poetic/literary* foe.
– OPPOSITES ally, supporter.

adverse ▶ adjective ❶ *adverse weather conditions* UNFAVOURABLE, disadvantageous, inauspicious, unpropitious, unfortunate, unlucky, untimely, untoward. ❷ *the drug's adverse side effects* HARMFUL, dangerous, injurious, detrimental, hurtful, deleterious. ❸ *an adverse response from the public* HOSTILE, UNFAVOURABLE, antagonistic, unfriendly, ill-disposed, negative.
– OPPOSITES favourable, auspicious, beneficial.

adversity ▶ noun MISFORTUNE, ill luck, bad luck, trouble, difficulty, hardship, distress, disaster, suffering, affliction, sorrow, misery, tribulation, woe, pain, trauma; mishap, misadventure, accident, upset, reverse, setback, crisis, catastrophe, tragedy, calamity, trial, cross, burden, blow, vicissitude; hard times, trials and tribulations.

advertise ▶ verb PUBLICIZE, make public, make known, announce, broadcast, proclaim, trumpet, call attention to, bill; promote, market, beat/bang the drum for, trail, huckster; *informal* push, plug, hype, boost; *N. Amer. informal* ballyhoo, flack.

advertisement ▶ noun NOTICE, announcement, bulletin; commercial, promotion, blurb, write-up; poster, leaflet, pamphlet, flyer, bill, handbill, handout, circular, brochure, sign, placard; *informal* ad, push, plug, puff, bumph; *Brit. informal* advert.

advice ▶ noun GUIDANCE, counselling, counsel, help, direction; information, recommendations, guidelines, suggestions, hints, tips, pointers, ideas, opinions, views.

advisability ▶ noun WISDOM, desirability, preferability, prudence, sense, appropriateness, aptness, fitness, suitability, judiciousness; expediency, advantageousness, advantage, benefit, profit, profitability.

advisable ▶ adjective WISE, desirable, preferable, well, best, sensible, prudent, proper, appropriate, apt, suitable, fitting, judicious, recommended, suggested; expedient, politic, advantageous, beneficial, profitable, in one's (best) interests.

advise ▶ verb ❶ *her grandmother advised her about marriage* COUNSEL, give guidance, guide, offer suggestions, give hints/tips/pointers. ❷ *he advised caution* ADVOCATE, recommend, suggest, urge, encourage, enjoin. ❸ *you will be advised of the requirements* INFORM, notify, give notice, apprise, warn, forewarn; acquaint with, make familiar with, make known to, update about; *informal* fill in on.

adviser ▶ noun COUNSELLOR, mentor, guide, consultant, confidant, confidante; coach, teacher, tutor, guru.

advisory ▶ adjective CONSULTATIVE, consultatory, advising; recommendatory.
– OPPOSITES executive.

advocacy ▶ noun SUPPORT, backing, promotion, championing; recommendation, prescription; *N. Amer.* boosterism.

advocate ▶ noun *an advocate of children's rights* CHAMPION, upholder, supporter, backer, promoter, proponent, exponent, spokesman, spokeswoman, spokesperson, campaigner, fighter, crusader; propagandist, apostle, apologist; *N. Amer.* booster.
– OPPOSITES critic.
▶ verb *heart specialists advocate a diet low in cholesterol* RECOMMEND, prescribe, advise, urge; support, back, favour, uphold, subscribe to, champion, campaign on behalf of, speak for, argue for, lobby for, promote.

aegis ▶ noun PROTECTION, backing, support, patronage, sponsorship, charge, care, guidance, guardianship, trusteeship, agency, safeguarding, shelter, umbrella, aid, assistance; auspices.

aeon ▶ noun AGES, an age, an eternity, a long time, a lifetime; years; *informal* donkey's years; *Brit. informal* yonks.

aesthetic ▶ adjective ARTISTIC, tasteful, in

good taste; graceful, elegant, exquisite, beautiful, attractive, pleasing, lovely.

affability ▶ noun FRIENDLINESS, amiability, geniality, congeniality, cordiality, warmth, pleasantness, likeability, good humour, good nature, kindliness, kindness, courtesy, courteousness, civility, approachability, amenability, sociability, gregariousness, neighbourliness.

affable ▶ adjective FRIENDLY, amiable, genial, congenial, cordial, warm, pleasant, nice, likeable, personable, charming, agreeable, sympathetic, good-humoured, good-natured, kindly, kind, courteous, civil, gracious, approachable, accessible, amenable, sociable, outgoing, gregarious, clubbable, neighbourly, welcoming, hospitable, obliging; *Scottish* couthy.
– OPPOSITES unfriendly.

affair ▶ noun ❶ *what you do is your affair* BUSINESS, concern, matter, responsibility, province, preserve; problem, worry; *Brit. informal* lookout. ❷ (**affairs**) *his financial affairs* TRANSACTIONS, concerns, matters, activities, dealings, undertakings, ventures, business. ❸ *the board admitted responsibility for the affair* EVENT, incident, happening, occurrence, eventuality, episode; case, matter, business. ❹ *his affair with Anthea was over* RELATIONSHIP, love affair, affaire (de cœur), romance, fling, flirtation, dalliance, liaison, involvement, intrigue, amour; *informal* hanky-panky; *Brit. informal* carry-on.

affect[1] ▶ verb ❶ *this development may have affected the judge's decision* HAVE AN EFFECT ON, influence, act on, work on, have an impact on; change, alter, modify, transform, form, shape, sway, bias. ❷ *he was visibly affected by the experience* MOVE, touch, make an impression on, hit (hard), tug at someone's heartstrings; UPSET, trouble, distress, disturb, agitate, shake (up). ❸ *the disease affected his lungs* ATTACK, infect; hit, strike.

affect[2] ▶ verb ❶ *he deliberately affected a republican stance* ASSUME, take on, adopt, embrace, espouse. ❷ *Paul affected an air of injured innocence* PRETEND, feign, fake, simulate, make a show of, make a pretence of, sham; *informal* put on; *N. Amer. informal* make like.

affectation ▶ noun ❶ *George had always abhorred affectation* PRETENSION, pretentiousness, affectedness, artificiality, posturing, posing; airs (and graces); *informal* la-di-da; *Brit. informal* side. ❷ *an affectation of calm* FACADE, front, show, appearance, pretence, simulation, posture, pose.

affected ▶ adjective PRETENTIOUS, artificial, contrived, unnatural, stagy, studied, mannered, ostentatious; insincere, unconvincing, feigned, false, fake, sham, simulated; *informal* la-di-da, phoney, pretend, put on.
– OPPOSITES natural, unpretentious, genuine.

affecting ▶ adjective TOUCHING, moving, emotive, emotional; stirring, soul-stirring, heartwarming; poignant, pathetic, pitiful, piteous, tear-jerking, heart-rending, heartbreaking, disturbing, distressing, upsetting, sad, haunting.

affection ▶ noun FONDNESS, love, liking, tenderness, warmth, devotion, endearment, care, caring, attachment, friendship; warm feelings.

affectionate ▶ adjective LOVING, fond, adoring, devoted, caring, doting, tender, warm, warm-hearted, soft-hearted, friendly; demonstrative, cuddly; *informal* touchy-feely, lovey-dovey.
– OPPOSITES cold.

affianced ▶ adjective (*poetic/literary*). *See* ENGAGED sense 2.

affiliate ▶ verb ASSOCIATE WITH, unite with, combine with, join (up) with, join forces with, link up with, ally with, align with, federate with, amalgamate with, merge with; attach to, annex to, incorporate into, integrate into.

affiliated ▶ adjective ASSOCIATED, allied, related, federated, confederated, amalgamated, unified, connected, linked; in league, in partnership.

affiliation ▶ noun ASSOCIATION, connection, alliance, alignment, link, attachment, tie, relationship, fellowship, partnership, coalition, union; amalgamation, incorporation, integration, federation, confederation.

affinity ▶ noun ❶ *her affinity with animals and birds* EMPATHY, rapport, sympathy, accord, harmony, relationship, bond, fellow feeling, like-mindedness, closeness, understanding; liking, fondness; *informal* chemistry. ❷ *the semantic affinity between the two words* SIMILARITY, resemblance, likeness, kinship, relationship, association, link, analogy, similitude, correspondence.
– OPPOSITES aversion, dislike, dissimilarity.

affirm ▶ verb ❶ *he affirmed that they would lend military assistance* DECLARE, state, assert, proclaim, pronounce, attest, swear, avow, guarantee, pledge, give an undertaking; *formal* aver; *rare* asseverate. ❷ *the referendum affirmed the republic's right to secede* UPHOLD, support, confirm, ratify, endorse.
– OPPOSITES deny.

affirmation ▶ noun ❶ *an affirmation of faith* DECLARATION, statement, assertion, proclamation, pronouncement, attestation; oath, avowal, guarantee, pledge; deposition; *formal* averment; *rare* asseveration. ❷ *the poem ends with an affirmation of pastoral values* CONFIRMATION, ratification, endorsement.
– OPPOSITES denial.

affirmative ▶ adjective *an affirmative answer* POSITIVE, assenting, consenting, corroborative, favourable.
– OPPOSITES negative.

▶ **noun** *she took his grunt as an affirmative* AGREEMENT, acceptance, assent, acquiescence, concurrence; OK, yes.
– OPPOSITES disagreement.

affix ▶ **verb** ❶ *he affixed a stamp to the envelope* STICK, glue, paste, gum; attach, fasten, fix; clip, tack, pin; tape. ❷ (*formal*) *affix your signature to the document* APPEND, add, attach.
– OPPOSITES detach.

afflict ▶ **verb** TROUBLE, burden, distress, cause suffering to, beset, harass, worry, oppress; torment, plague, blight, bedevil, rack, smite, curse; *archaic* ail.

affliction ▶ **noun** ❶ *a herb reputed to cure a variety of afflictions* DISORDER, disease, malady, complaint, ailment, illness, indisposition, handicap; scourge, plague, trouble. ❷ *he bore his affliction with great dignity* SUFFERING, distress, pain, trouble, misery, wretchedness, hardship, misfortune, adversity, sorrow, torment, tribulation, woe.

affluence ▶ **noun** WEALTH, prosperity, fortune; riches, money, resources, assets, possessions, property, substance, means.
– OPPOSITES poverty.

affluent ▶ **adjective** WEALTHY, rich, prosperous, well off, moneyed, well-to-do; propertied, substantial, of means, of substance, plutocratic; *informal* well heeled, rolling in it, made of money, filthy rich, stinking rich, loaded, on easy street, worth a packet.
– OPPOSITES poor, impoverished.

afford ▶ **verb** ❶ *I can't afford a new car* PAY FOR, bear the expense of, have the money for, spare the price of; run to, stretch to, manage. ❷ *it took more time than he could afford* SPARE, allow (oneself). ❸ *the rooftop terrace affords beautiful views* PROVIDE, supply, furnish, offer, give, make available, yield.

affray ▶ **noun** (*Law, dated*) FIGHT, brawl, confrontation, clash, skirmish, scuffle, tussle; fracas, altercation, disturbance, breach of the peace; *informal* scrap, dust-up, punch-up, set-to, shindig, free-for-all.

affront ▶ **noun** *an affront to public morality* INSULT, offence, indignity, slight, snub, put-down, provocation, injury; outrage, atrocity, scandal; *informal* slap in the face, kick in the teeth.
▶ **verb** *she was affronted by his familiarity* INSULT, offend, mortify, provoke, pique, wound, hurt; put out, irk, displease, bother, rankle, vex, gall; outrage, scandalize, disgust; *informal* needle, put someone's back up.

aficionado ▶ **noun** CONNOISSEUR, expert, authority, specialist, pundit; enthusiast, devotee; *informal* buff, freak, nut, fiend, maniac, fanatic, addict.

aflame ▶ **adjective** BURNING, ablaze, alight, on fire, in flames, blazing; *poetic/literary* afire.

afloat ▶ **adverb & adjective** BUOYANT, floating, buoyed up, on/above the surface, (keeping one's head) above water.

afoot ▶ **adjective & adverb** GOING ON, happening, around, about, abroad, stirring, circulating, in circulation, at large, in the air/wind; brewing, looming, in the offing, on the horizon.

aforesaid ▶ **adjective** PREVIOUSLY MENTIONED, aforementioned, aforenamed; foregoing, preceding, earlier, previous; above.

afraid ▶ **adjective** ❶ *they ran away because they were afraid* FRIGHTENED, scared, terrified, fearful, petrified, scared witless, scared to death, terror-stricken, terror-struck, frightened/scared out of one's wits, shaking in one's shoes, shaking like a leaf; intimidated, alarmed, panicky; faint-hearted, cowardly; *informal* scared stiff, in a (blue) funk, in a cold sweat; *N. Amer. informal* spooked; *archaic* afeared, affrighted. ❷ *don't be afraid to ask awkward questions* RELUCTANT, hesitant, unwilling, disinclined, loath, slow, chary, shy. ❸ *I'm afraid that your daughter is ill* SORRY, sad, distressed, regretful, apologetic.
– RELATED TERMS -phobe.
– OPPOSITES brave, confident.

afresh ▶ **adverb** ANEW, again, over/once again, once more, another time.

after ▶ **preposition** ❶ *he made a speech after the performance* FOLLOWING, subsequent to, at the close/end of, in the wake of; *formal* posterior to. ❷ *Guy shut the door after them* BEHIND, following. ❸ *after the way he treated my sister I never want to speak to him again* BECAUSE OF, as a result/consequence of, in view of, owing to, on account of. ❹ *is he still going to marry her, after all that's happened?* DESPITE, in spite of, regardless of, notwithstanding. ❺ *the policeman ran after him* IN PURSUIT OF, in someone's direction, following. ❻ *I'm after information, and I'm willing to pay for it* IN SEARCH OF, in quest/pursuit of, trying to find, looking for. ❼ *they asked after Dad* ABOUT, concerning, regarding, with regard/respect/reference to. ❽ *the village was named after a Roman officer* IN HONOUR OF, as a tribute to; with the name of. ❾ *animal studies after Bandinelli* IN THE STYLE OF, in the manner of, in imitation of; similar to, like, characteristic of.
– RELATED TERMS post-.
– OPPOSITES before, preceding.
▶ **adverb** ❶ *the week after, we went to Madrid* LATER, afterwards, after this/that, subsequently. ❷ *porters were following on after with their bags* BEHIND, in the rear, at the back, in someone's wake.
– OPPOSITES previously, before, ahead, in front.
■ **after all** MOST IMPORTANTLY, above all, beyond everything, ultimately; *informal* when all's said and done, at the end of the day, when push comes to shove.

after-effect ▶noun REPERCUSSION, aftermath, consequence; *Medicine* sequela.

afterlife ▶noun LIFE AFTER DEATH, the next world, the hereafter, the afterworld; immortality.

aftermath ▶noun REPERCUSSIONS, after-effects, consequences, effects, results, fruits.

afterwards ▶adverb LATER, later on, subsequently, then, next, after this/that; at a later time/date, in due course.

again ▶adverb ❶ *her spirits lifted again* ONCE MORE, another time, afresh, anew. ❷ *this can add half as much again to the price* EXTRA, in addition, additionally, on top. ❸ *again, evidence was not always consistent* ALSO, furthermore; moreover, besides.

■ **again and again** REPEATEDLY, over and over (again), time and (time) again, many times, many a time; often, frequently, continually, constantly.

against ▶preposition ❶ *a number of delegates were against the motion* OPPOSED TO, in opposition to, hostile to, averse to, antagonistic towards, inimical to, unsympathetic to, resistant to, at odds with, in disagreement with, dead set against; *informal* anti, agin. ❷ *he was swimming against the tide* IN OPPOSITION TO, counter to, contrary to, in the opposite direction to. ❸ *his age is against him* DISADVANTAGEOUS TO, unfavourable to, damaging to, detrimental to, prejudicial to, deleterious to, harmful to, injurious to, a drawback for. ❹ *she leaned against the wall* TOUCHING, in contact with, up against, on.

– RELATED TERMS anti-.

– OPPOSITES in favour of, pro.

age ▶noun ❶ *he is 35 years of age* NUMBER OF YEARS, length of life; stage of life, generation, age group. ❷ *her hearing had deteriorated with age* ELDERLINESS, old age, oldness, senescence, seniority, maturity; one's advancing/advanced/declining years; *poetic/literary* eld; *archaic* caducity. ❸ *the Elizabethan age* ERA, epoch, period, time. ❹ (*informal*) *you haven't been in touch with me for ages* A LONG TIME, days/months/years on end, an eternity; *informal* ages and ages, donkey's years, a month of Sundays; *Brit. informal* yonks.

▶verb *Cabernet Sauvignon ages well* | *the experience has aged her* MATURE, mellow, ripen; grow/become/make old, (cause to) decline.

aged ▶adjective ELDERLY, old, mature, older, senior, ancient, senescent, advanced in years, in one's dotage, long in the tooth, as old as the hills, past one's prime, not as young as one used to be; *informal* getting on, over the hill, no spring chicken.

– OPPOSITES young.

agency ▶noun ❶ *an advertising agency* BUSINESS, organization, company, firm, office, bureau. ❷ *the infection is caused by the agency of insects* ACTION, activity, means, effect, influence, force, power, vehicle, medium. ❸ *regional policy was introduced through the agency of the Board of Trade* INTERVENTION, intercession, involvement, good offices; auspices, aegis.

agenda ▶noun LIST OF ITEMS, schedule, programme, timetable, line-up, list, plan.

agent ▶noun ❶ *the sale was arranged through an agent* REPRESENTATIVE, emissary, envoy, go-between, proxy, negotiator, broker, spokesperson, spokesman, spokeswoman; *informal* rep. ❷ *a travel agent* AGENCY, business, organization, company, firm, bureau. ❸ *a CIA agent* SPY, secret agent, undercover agent, operative, fifth columnist, mole, Mata Hari; *N. Amer. informal* spook, G-man; *archaic* intelligencer. ❹ *the agents of destruction* PERFORMER, author, executor, perpetrator, producer, instrument, catalyst. ❺ *a cleansing agent* MEDIUM, means, instrument, vehicle.

agglomeration ▶noun COLLECTION, mass, cluster, lump, clump, pile, heap; accumulation, build-up; miscellany, jumble, hotchpotch, mixed bag.

aggravate ▶verb ❶ *the new law could aggravate the situation* WORSEN, make worse, exacerbate, inflame, compound; add fuel to the fire/flames, add insult to injury, rub salt in the wound. ❷ (*informal*) *you don't have to aggravate people to get what you want* ANNOY, irritate, exasperate, put out, nettle, provoke, antagonize, get on someone's nerves, ruffle (someone's feathers), try someone's patience; *Brit.* rub up the wrong way; *informal* peeve, needle, bug, miff, hack off, get someone's goat, get under someone's skin, get up someone's nose; *Brit. informal* wind up, nark, get at, get across, get on someone's wick; *N. Amer. informal* tick off.

– OPPOSITES alleviate, improve.

aggravation ▶noun ❶ *the recession led to the aggravation of unemployment problems* WORSENING, exacerbation, compounding. ❷ (*informal*) *no amount of money is worth the aggravation* NUISANCE, annoyance, irritation, hassle, trouble, difficulty, inconvenience, bother; *informal* aggro.

aggregate ▶noun ❶ *the specimen is an aggregate of rock and mineral fragments* COLLECTION, mass, agglomeration, assemblage; mixture, mix, combination, blend; compound, alloy, amalgam. ❷ *he won with an aggregate of 325* TOTAL, sum total, sum, grand total.

▶adjective *an aggregate score* TOTAL, combined, gross, overall, composite.

aggression ▶noun ❶ *an act of aggression* HOSTILITY, aggressiveness, belligerence, bellicosity, force, violence; pugnacity, pugnaciousness, militancy, warmongering. ❷ *he played the game with unceasing aggression* CONFIDENCE, self-confidence, boldness, determination, forcefulness, vigour, energy, dynamism, zeal.

aggressive ▶adjective ❶ *aggressive and dis-*

ruptive behaviour VIOLENT, confrontational, antagonistic, truculent, pugnacious, macho; quarrelsome, argumentative. ❷ *aggressive foreign policy* WARMONGERING, warlike, warring, belligerent, bellicose, hawkish, militaristic; offensive, expansionist; *informal* gung-ho. ❸ *an aggressive promotional drive* ASSERTIVE, pushy, forceful, vigorous, energetic, dynamic; bold, audacious; *informal* in-your-face, feisty.
– OPPOSITES peaceable, peaceful.

aggressor ▶ **noun** ATTACKER, assaulter, assailant; invader.

aggrieved ▶ **adjective** ❶ *the manager looked aggrieved at the suggestion* RESENTFUL, affronted, indignant, disgruntled, discontented, upset, offended, piqued, riled, nettled, vexed, irked, irritated, annoyed, put out, chagrined; *informal* peeved, miffed, in a huff; *Brit. informal* cheesed off; *N. Amer. informal* sore, steamed. ❷ *the aggrieved party* WRONGED, injured, harmed.
– OPPOSITES pleased.

aghast ▶ **adjective** HORRIFIED, appalled, dismayed, thunderstruck, stunned, shocked, staggered; *informal* flabbergasted; *Brit. informal* gobsmacked.

agile ▶ **adjective** ❶ *she was as agile as a monkey* NIMBLE, lithe, supple, limber, acrobatic, fleet-footed, light-footed, light on one's feet; *informal* nippy, twinkle-toed; *poetic/literary* fleet, lightsome. ❷ *an agile mind* ALERT, sharp, acute, shrewd, astute, perceptive, quick-witted.
– OPPOSITES clumsy, stiff.

agitate ▶ **verb** ❶ *any mention of Clare agitates my grandmother* UPSET, perturb, fluster, ruffle, disconcert, unnerve, disquiet, disturb, distress, unsettle; *informal* rattle, faze; *N. Amer. informal* discombobulate. ❷ *she agitated for the appointment of more women* CAMPAIGN, strive, battle, fight, struggle, push, press. ❸ *agitate the water to disperse the oil* STIR, whisk, beat.

agitated ▶ **adjective** UPSET, perturbed, flustered, ruffled, disconcerted, unnerved, disquieted, disturbed, distressed, unsettled; nervous, jumpy, on edge, tense, keyed up; *informal* rattled, fazed, in a dither, in a flap, in a state, in a lather, jittery, in a tizz/tizzy; *Brit. informal* having kittens, in a (flat) spin; *N. Amer. informal* discombobulated.
– OPPOSITES calm, relaxed.

agitation ▶ **noun** ❶ *Freddie gritted his teeth in agitation* ANXIETY, perturbation, disquiet, distress, concern, alarm, worry; *rare* disconcertment. ❷ *an upsurge in nationalist agitation* CAMPAIGNING, striving, battling, fighting, struggling. ❸ *the vigorous agitation of the components* STIRRING, whisking, beating.

agitator ▶ **noun** TROUBLEMAKER, rabble-rouser, agent provocateur, demagogue, incendiary; revolutionary, firebrand, rebel, insurgent, subversive; *informal* stirrer.

agnostic ▶ **noun** SCEPTIC, doubter, doubting Thomas; unbeliever, disbeliever, non-believer; rationalist; *rare* nullifidian.
– OPPOSITES believer, theist.

ago ▶ **adverb** IN THE PAST, before, earlier, back, since, previously; *formal* heretofore.

agog ▶ **adverb** EAGER, excited, impatient, keen, anxious, avid, in suspense, on tenterhooks, on the edge of one's seat, on pins and needles, waiting with bated breath.

agonize ▶ **verb** WORRY, fret, fuss, brood, upset oneself, rack one's brains, wrestle with oneself, be worried/anxious, feel uneasy, exercise oneself; *informal* stew; *archaic* pore on.

agonizing ▶ **adjective** EXCRUCIATING, harrowing, racking, searing, extremely painful, acute, severe, torturous, tormenting, piercing; *informal* hellish, killing; *formal* grievous.

agony ▶ **noun** PAIN, hurt, suffering, torture, torment, anguish, affliction, trauma; pangs, throes; *rare* excruciation.

agrarian ▶ **adjective** AGRICULTURAL, rural, rustic, pastoral, countryside, farming; *poetic/literary* georgic, sylvan, Arcadian, agrestic.

agree ▶ **verb** ❶ *I agree with you* CONCUR, be of the same mind/opinion, see eye to eye, be in sympathy, be united, be as one man. ❷ *they had agreed to a ceasefire* CONSENT, assent, acquiesce, accept, approve, say yes, give one's approval, give the nod; *formal* accede. ❸ *the plan and the drawing do not agree with each other* MATCH (UP), accord, correspond, conform, coincide, fit, tally, be in harmony/agreement, be consistent/equivalent; *informal* square. ❹ *they agreed on a price* SETTLE, decide, arrive at, negotiate, reach an agreement, come to terms, strike a bargain, make a deal, shake hands.
– OPPOSITES differ, contradict, reject.

agreeable ▶ **adjective** ❶ *an agreeable atmosphere of rural tranquillity* PLEASANT, pleasing, enjoyable, pleasurable, nice, to one's liking, appealing, charming, delightful. ❷ *an agreeable fellow* LIKEABLE, charming, amiable, affable, pleasant, nice, friendly, good-natured, sociable, genial, congenial. ❸ *we should get together for a talk, if you're agreeable* WILLING, amenable, in accord/agreement.
– OPPOSITES unpleasant.

agreement ▶ **noun** ❶ *all heads nodded in agreement* ACCORD, concurrence, consensus; assent, acceptance, consent, acquiescence, endorsement. ❷ *an agreement on military cooperation* CONTRACT, compact, treaty, covenant, pact, accord, concordat, protocol. ❸ *there is some agreement between my view and that of the author* CORRESPONDENCE, consistency, compatibility, accord; similarity, resemblance, likeness, similitude.
– OPPOSITES discord.

agricultural ▶ **adjective** ❶ *an agricultural labourer* FARM, farming, agrarian; rural, rustic, pastoral, countryside; *poetic/literary* georgic,

sylvan, Arcadian, agrestic. ❷ *agricultural land* FARMED, farm, agrarian, cultivated, tilled.
– OPPOSITES urban.

agriculture ▶ **noun** FARMING, cultivation, tillage, tilling, husbandry, land/farm management; agribusiness, agronomy.
– RELATED TERMS agri-, agro-.

aground ▶ **adverb & adjective** GROUNDED, ashore, beached, stuck, shipwrecked, high and dry, on the rocks, on the ground/bottom.

ahead ▶ **adverb** ❶ *he peered ahead, but could see nothing* FORWARD(S), towards the front, frontwards. ❷ *he had ridden on ahead* IN FRONT, at the head, in the lead, at the fore, in the vanguard, in advance. ❸ *she was preparing herself for what lay ahead* IN THE FUTURE, in time, in time to come, in the fullness of time, at a later date, after this, henceforth, later on, in due course, next. ❹ *they are ahead by six points* LEADING, winning, in the lead, (out) in front, first, coming first.
– OPPOSITES behind, at the back, in the past.
■ **ahead of** ❶ *Blanche went ahead of the others* IN FRONT OF, before. ❷ *we have a demanding trip ahead of us* IN STORE FOR, waiting for. ❸ *two months ahead of schedule* IN ADVANCE OF, before, earlier than. ❹ *in terms of these amenities, Britain is ahead of other European countries* MORE ADVANCED THAN, further on than, superior to, surpassing, exceeding, better than.

aid ▶ **noun** ❶ *with the aid of his colleagues he prepared a manifesto* ASSISTANCE, support, help, backing, cooperation, succour; a helping hand. ❷ *humanitarian aid* RELIEF, charity, financial assistance, donations, contributions, subsidies, handouts, subvention; debt remission; *historical* alms. ❸ *a hospital aid* HELPER, assistant, girl/man Friday.
– OPPOSITES hindrance.
▶ **verb** ❶ *he provided an army to aid the King of England* HELP, assist, abet, come to someone's aid, give assistance, lend a hand, be of service; avail, succour, sustain. ❷ *essences can aid restful sleep* FACILITATE, promote, encourage, help, further, boost; speed up, hasten, accelerate, expedite.
– OPPOSITES hinder.

aide ▶ **noun** ASSISTANT, helper, adviser, right-hand man, man/girl Friday, adjutant, deputy, second (in command); subordinate, junior, underling, acolyte; *N. Amer.* cohort.

ail ▶ **verb** (*archaic*) TROUBLE, afflict, pain, distress, bother, worry, be the matter with.

ailing ▶ **adjective** ❶ *his ailing mother* ILL, unwell, sick, sickly, poorly, weak, indisposed, in poor/bad health, infirm, debilitated, delicate, valetudinarian, below par; *Brit* off colour; *informal* laid up, under the weather. ❷ *the country's ailing economy* FAILING, in poor condition, weak, poor, deficient.
– OPPOSITES healthy.

ailment ▶ **noun** ILLNESS, disease, disorder, affliction, malady, complaint, infirmity; *informal* bug, virus; *Brit. informal* lurgy.

aim ▶ **verb** ❶ *he aimed the rifle* POINT, direct, train, sight, line up. ❷ *she aimed at the target* TAKE AIM, fix on, zero in on, draw a bead on. ❸ *undergraduates aiming for a first degree* WORK TOWARDS, be after, set one's sights on, try for, strive for, aspire to, endeavour to achieve; *formal* essay. ❹ *this system is aimed at the home entertainment market* TARGET, intend, destine, direct, design, tailor, market, pitch. ❺ *we aim to give you the best possible service* INTEND, mean, have in mind/view; plan, resolve, propose, design.
▶ **noun** *our aim is to develop gymnasts to the top level* OBJECTIVE, object, goal, end, target, design, desire, desired result, intention, intent, plan, purpose, object of the exercise; ambition, aspiration, wish, dream, hope, raison d'être.

aimless ▶ **adjective** ❶ *Flavia set out on an aimless walk* PURPOSELESS, objectless, goalless, without purpose, without goal. ❷ *aimless men standing outside the bars* UNOCCUPIED, idle, at a loose end; purposeless, undirected.
– OPPOSITES purposeful.

air ▶ **noun** ❶ *hundreds of birds hovered in the air* SKY, atmosphere; heavens, ether. ❷ *open the windows to get some air into the room* BREEZE, draught, wind; breath/blast of air, gust/puff of wind. ❸ *an air of defiance* EXPRESSION, appearance, look, impression, aspect, aura, mien, countenance, manner, bearing, tone. ❹ *women putting on airs* AFFECTATIONS, pretension, pretentiousness, affectedness, posing, posturing, airs and graces; *Brit. informal* side. ❺ *a traditional Scottish air* TUNE, melody, song; *poetic/literary* lay.
– RELATED TERMS aerial, aero-.
▶ **verb** ❶ *a chance to air your views* EXPRESS, voice, make public, ventilate, articulate, state, declare, give expression/voice to; have one's say. ❷ *the windows were opened to air the room* VENTILATE, freshen, refresh, cool. ❸ *the film was aired nationwide* BROADCAST, transmit, screen, show, televise, telecast.

airborne ▶ **adjective** FLYING, in flight, in the air, on the wing.

airily ▶ **adverb** LIGHTLY, breezily, flippantly, casually, nonchalantly, heedlessly, without consideration.
– OPPOSITES seriously.

airing ▶ **noun** ❶ *give the bedroom a good airing* VENTILATING, ventilation, freshening, refreshing, cooling. ❷ *they went to the park for an airing* STROLL, walk, saunter, turn, amble, promenade; *dated* constitutional. ❸ *the airing of different views* EXPRESSION, voicing, venting, ventilation, articulation, stating, declaration, communication. ❹ *I hope the BBC gives the play another airing* BROADCAST, transmission, screening, showing, televising, telecast.

airless ▶ **adjective** STUFFY, close, stifling, suffocating, oppressive; unventilated, badly/poorly ventilated.
– OPPOSITES airy, ventilated.

airport ▶ **noun** *Brit.* aerodrome; *N. Amer.* airdrome; *informal* drome.

airtight ▶ **adjective** ❶ *an airtight container* SEALED, hermetically sealed, closed/shut tight. ❷ *an airtight alibi* INDISPUTABLE, unquestionable, incontrovertible, undeniable, incontestable, irrefutable, watertight, beyond dispute/question/doubt.

airy ▶ **adjective** ❶ *the conservatory is light and airy* WELL VENTILATED, fresh; spacious, uncluttered; light, bright. ❷ *an airy gesture* NONCHALANT, casual, breezy, flippant, insouciant, heedless. ❸ *airy clouds* DELICATE, soft, fine, feathery, insubstantial.
– OPPOSITES stuffy.

airy-fairy ▶ **adjective** (*informal*) IMPRACTICAL, unrealistic, idealistic, fanciful.
– OPPOSITES practical.

aisle ▶ **noun** PASSAGE, passageway, gangway, walkway.

ajar ▶ **adjective & adverb** SLIGHTLY OPEN, half open, agape.
– OPPOSITES closed, wide open.

akin ▶ **adjective** SIMILAR, related, close, near, corresponding, comparable, equivalent; connected, alike, analogous.
– OPPOSITES unlike.

alacrity ▶ **noun** EAGERNESS, willingness, readiness; enthusiasm, ardour, fervour, keenness; promptness, haste, swiftness, dispatch, speed.

alarm ▶ **noun** ❶ *the girl spun round in alarm* FEAR, anxiety, apprehension, trepidation, nervousness, unease, distress, agitation, consternation, disquiet, perturbation, fright, panic. ❷ *a smoke alarm* SIREN, warning sound, danger/distress signal; warning device, alarm bell; *archaic* tocsin.
– OPPOSITES calmness, composure.
▶ **verb** *the news had alarmed her* FRIGHTEN, scare, panic, unnerve, distress, agitate, upset, disconcert, shock, dismay, disturb; *informal* rattle, spook, scare the living daylights out of; *Brit. informal* put the wind up.

alarming ▶ **adjective** FRIGHTENING, unnerving, shocking; distressing, upsetting, disconcerting, perturbing, dismaying, disquieting, disturbing; *informal* scary.
– OPPOSITES reassuring.

alarmist ▶ **noun** SCAREMONGER, gloom-monger, doom-monger, doomster, doomsayer, Cassandra; *informal* doom and gloom merchant.
– OPPOSITES optimist.

alchemy ▶ **noun** CHEMISTRY; magic, sorcery, witchcraft.

alcohol ▶ **noun** LIQUOR, intoxicating liquor, strong/alcoholic drink, drink, spirits; *informal* booze, hooch, the hard stuff, firewater, rotgut, moonshine, grog, tipple, the demon drink, the bottle; *Brit. informal* gut-rot; *N. Amer. informal* juice; *technical* ethyl alcohol, ethanol.

alcoholic ▶ **adjective** *alcoholic drinks* INTOXICATING, inebriating, containing alcohol; strong, hard, stiff; *formal* spirituous.
▶ **noun** *he is an alcoholic* DIPSOMANIAC, drunk, drunkard, heavy/hard/serious drinker, problem drinker, alcohol-abuser, person with a drink problem; tippler, sot, inebriate; *informal* boozer, lush, alky, dipso, soak, tosspot, wino, sponge, barfly; *Austral./NZ informal* hophead; *archaic* toper.

alcove ▶ **noun** RECESS, niche, nook, inglenook, bay.

alert ▶ **adjective** ❶ *police have asked neighbours to keep alert* VIGILANT, watchful, attentive, observant, wideawake, circumspect; on the lookout, on one's guard/toes, on the qui vive; *informal* keeping one's eyes open/peeled. ❷ *mentally alert* QUICK-WITTED, sharp, bright, quick, keen, perceptive, wideawake, on one's toes; *informal* on the ball, quick on the uptake, all there, with it.
– OPPOSITES inattentive.
▶ **noun** ❶ *a state of alert* VIGILANCE, watchfulness, attentiveness, alertness, circumspection. ❷ *a flood alert* WARNING, notification, notice; siren, alarm, signal, danger/distress signal.
▶ **verb** *police were alerted by a phone call* WARN, notify, apprise, forewarn, put on one's guard, put on the qui vive; *informal* tip off, clue in.

alias ▶ **noun** *he is known under several aliases* ASSUMED NAME, false name, pseudonym, sobriquet, incognito; pen/stage name, nom de plume/guerre.
▶ **adverb** *Cassius Clay, alias Muhammed Ali* ALSO KNOWN AS, aka, also called, otherwise known as.

alibi ▶ **noun** *we've both got a good alibi for last night* DEFENCE, justification, explanation, reason; *informal* story, line.
▶ **verb** (*informal*) *her brother agreed to alibi her* COVER FOR, give an alibi to, provide with an alibi.

alien ▶ **adjective** ❶ *alien cultures* FOREIGN, overseas, non-native. ❷ *an alien landscape* UNFAMILIAR, unknown, strange, peculiar; exotic, foreign. ❸ *a vicious role alien to his nature* INCOMPATIBLE, opposed, conflicting, contrary, in conflict, at variance; *rare* oppugnant. ❹ *alien beings* EXTRATERRESTRIAL, unearthly; Martian.
– OPPOSITES native, familiar, earthly.
▶ **noun** ❶ *an illegal alien* FOREIGNER, non-native, immigrant, emigrant, émigré, incomer. ❷ *the alien's spaceship crashed* EXTRATERRESTRIAL, ET; Martian; *informal* little green man.

alienate ▶ **verb** ❶ *his homosexuality alienated him from his conservative father* ESTRANGE, divide, distance, put at a distance, isolate, cut off; set against, turn away, drive apart, disunite, set at variance/odds, drive a wedge between. ❷ (*Law*) *they tried to prevent the land from being alienated*

TRANSFER, pass on, hand over; *Law* convey, devolve.

alienation ▶ **verb** ❶ *she also shared my deep sense of alienation* ISOLATION, detachment, estrangement, distance, separation, division; cutting off, turning away. ❷ (*Law*) *most leases contain restrictions against alienation* TRANSFER, passing on, handing over; *Law* conveyance, devolution.

alight[1] ▶ **verb** ❶ *he alighted from the train* GET OFF, step off, disembark, pile out; detrain, deplane. ❷ *a swallow alighted on a branch* LAND, come to rest, settle, perch; *archaic* light.
– OPPOSITES get on, board.

alight[2] ▶ **adjective** ❶ *the bales of hay were alight* BURNING, ablaze, aflame, on fire, in flames, blazing; *poetic/literary* afire. ❷ *her face was alight with laughter* LIT UP, gleaming, glowing, aglow, ablaze, bright, shining, radiant.

align ▶ **verb** ❶ *the desks are aligned in straight rows* LINE UP, put in order, put in rows/columns, place, position, situate, set, range. ❷ *he aligned himself with the workers* ALLY, affiliate, associate, join, side, unite, combine, join forces, form an alliance, team up, band together, throw in one's lot, make common cause.

alike ▶ **adjective** *all the doors looked alike* SIMILAR, (much) the same, indistinguishable, identical, uniform, interchangeable, cut from the same cloth, like (two) peas in a pod, (like) Tweedledum and Tweedledee; *informal* much of a muchness.
– OPPOSITES different.
▶ **adverb** *great minds think alike* SIMILARLY, (just) the same, in the same way/manner/fashion, identically.

alimony ▶ **noun** FINANCIAL SUPPORT, maintenance, support; child support.

alive ▶ **adjective** ❶ *he was last seen alive on Boxing Day* LIVING, live, breathing, animate, sentient; *informal* alive and kicking; *archaic* quick. ❷ *the synagogue has kept the Jewish faith alive* ACTIVE, existing, in existence, existent, functioning, in operation; on the map. ❸ *the thrills that kept him really alive* ANIMATED, lively, full of life, alert, active, energetic, vigorous, spry, sprightly, vital, vivacious, buoyant, exuberant, ebullient, zestful, spirited; *informal* full of beans, bright-eyed and bushy-tailed, chirpy, chipper, peppy, full of vim and vigour. ❹ *teachers need to be alive to their pupils' backgrounds* ALERT, awake, aware, conscious, mindful, heedful, sensitive, familiar; *informal* wise; *formal* cognizant. ❺ *the place was alive with mice* TEEMING, swarming, overrun, crawling, bristling, infested; crowded, packed; *informal* lousy.
– OPPOSITES dead, inanimate, inactive, lethargic.

all ▶ **determiner** ❶ *all the children went | all creatures need sleep* EACH OF, each/every one of, every single one of; every (single), each and every. ❷ *the sun shone all week* THE WHOLE OF THE, every bit of the, the complete, the entire. ❸ *in all honesty | with all speed* COMPLETE, entire, total, full; greatest (possible), maximum.
– RELATED TERMS omni-, pan-, panto-.
– OPPOSITES no, none of.
▶ **pronoun** ❶ *all are welcome* EVERYONE, everybody, each/every person. ❷ *all of the cups were broken* EACH ONE, the sum, the total, the whole lot. ❸ *they took all of it* EVERYTHING, every part, the whole/total amount, the (whole) lot, the entirety.
– OPPOSITES none, nobody, nothing.
▶ **adverb** *he was dressed all in black* COMPLETELY, fully, entirely, totally, wholly, absolutely, utterly; in every respect, in all respects, without reservation/exception.
– OPPOSITES partly.

allay ▶ **verb** REDUCE, diminish, decrease, lessen, assuage, alleviate, ease, relieve, soothe, soften, calm, take the edge off.
– OPPOSITES increase, intensify.

allegation ▶ **noun** CLAIM, assertion, charge, accusation, declaration, statement, contention, argument, affirmation, attestation; *formal* averment.

allege ▶ **verb** CLAIM, assert, charge, accuse, declare, state, contend, argue, affirm, attest, testify, swear; *formal* aver.

alleged ▶ **adjective** SUPPOSED, so-called, claimed, professed, purported, ostensible, putative, unproven.

allegedly ▶ **adverb** REPORTEDLY, supposedly, reputedly, purportedly, ostensibly, apparently, putatively, by all accounts, so the story goes.

allegiance ▶ **noun** LOYALTY, faithfulness, fidelity, obedience, adherence, homage, devotion; *formal* troth; *historical* fealty.
– OPPOSITES disloyalty, treachery.

allegorical ▶ **adjective** SYMBOLIC, metaphorical, figurative, representative, emblematic.

allegory ▶ **noun** PARABLE, analogy, metaphor, symbol, emblem.

allergic ▶ **adjective** ❶ *she was allergic to nuts* HYPERSENSITIVE, sensitive, sensitized. ❷ (*informal*) AVERSE, opposed, hostile, inimical, antagonistic, antipathetic, resistant, (dead) set against.

allergy ▶ **noun** ❶ *an allergy to feathers* HYPERSENSITIVITY, sensitivity, allergic reaction. ❷ (*informal*) *their allergy to free enterprise* AVERSION, antipathy, opposition, hostility, antagonism, dislike, distaste.

alleviate ▶ **verb** REDUCE, ease, relieve, take the edge off, deaden, dull, diminish, lessen, weaken, lighten, attenuate, allay, assuage, palliate, damp, soothe, help, soften, temper.
– OPPOSITES aggravate.

alley ▶ **noun** PASSAGE, passageway, alleyway, back alley, backstreet, lane, path, pathway, walk, allée.

alliance ▶ noun ❶ *a defensive alliance* ASSOCIATION, union, league, confederation, federation, confederacy, coalition, consortium, affiliation, partnership. ❷ *an alliance between medicine and morality* RELATIONSHIP, affinity, association, connection.

allied ▶ adjective ❶ *a group of allied nations* FEDERATED, confederated, associated, in alliance, in league, in partnership; unified, united, amalgamated, integrated. ❷ *agricultural and allied industries* ASSOCIATED, related, connected, interconnected, linked; similar, like, comparable, equivalent.
– OPPOSITES independent, unrelated.

all-important ▶ adjective VITAL, essential, indispensable, crucial, key, vitally important, of the utmost importance; critical, life-and-death, paramount, pre-eminent, high-priority; urgent, pressing, burning.
– OPPOSITES inessential.

allocate ▶ verb ALLOT, assign, distribute, apportion, share out, portion out, deal out, dole out, give out, dish out, parcel out, ration out, divide out/up; *informal* divvy up.

allocation ▶ noun ❶ *the efficient allocation of resources* ALLOTMENT, assignment, distribution, apportionment, sharing out, handing out, dealing out, doling out, giving out, dishing out, parcelling out, rationing out, dividing out/up; *informal* divvying up. ❷ *our annual allocation of funds* ALLOWANCE, allotment, quota, share, ration, grant, slice; *informal* cut; *Brit. informal* whack.

allot ▶ verb ALLOCATE, assign, apportion, distribute, issue, grant; earmark for, designate for, set aside for; hand out, deal out, dish out, dole out, give out; *informal* divvy up.

allotment ▶ noun ❶ *the allotment of shares by a company* ALLOCATION, assignment, distribution, apportionment, issuing, sharing out, handing out, dealing out, doling out, giving out, dishing out, parcelling out, rationing out, dividing out/up; *informal* divvying up. ❷ *each member received an allotment of new shares* QUOTA, share, ration, grant, allocation, allowance, slice; *informal* cut; *Brit. informal* whack.

all out ▶ adverb *I'm working all out to finish my novel* STRENUOUSLY, energetically, vigorously, hard, with all one's might (and main), eagerly, enthusiastically, industriously, diligently, assiduously, sedulously, indefatigably, with application/perseverance; *informal* like mad, like crazy; *Brit. informal* like billy-o.
– OPPOSITES lackadaisically.
▶ adjective *an all-out attack* STRENUOUS, energetic, vigorous, forceful, forcible; spirited, mettlesome, plucky, determined, resolute, aggressive, eager, keen, enthusiastic, zealous, ardent, fervent.
– OPPOSITES half-hearted.

allow ▶ verb ❶ *the police allowed him to go home* PERMIT, let, authorize, give permission/authorization/leave, sanction, grant someone the right, license, enable, entitle; consent, assent, give one's consent/assent/blessing, give the nod, acquiesce, agree, approve; *informal* give the go-ahead, give the thumbs up, OK, give the OK, give the green light; *formal* accede. ❷ *allow an hour or so for driving* SET ASIDE, allocate, allot, earmark, designate, assign. ❸ *the house was demolished to allow for road widening* PROVIDE, get ready, cater, take into consideration, take into account, make provision, make preparations, prepare, plan, make plans. ❹ *she allowed that all people had their funny little ways* ADMIT, acknowledge, recognize, agree, accept, concede, grant.
– OPPOSITES prevent, forbid.

allowable ▶ adjective *the maximum allowable number of users* PERMISSIBLE, permitted, allowed, admissible, acceptable, legal, lawful, legitimate, licit, authorized, sanctioned, approved, in order; *informal* OK, legit.
– OPPOSITES forbidden.

allowance ▶ noun ❶ *your baggage allowance* PERMITTED AMOUNT/QUANTITY, allocation, allotment, quota, share, ration, grant, limit, portion, slice. ❷ *her father gave her an allowance* PAYMENT, pocket money, sum of money, contribution, grant, subsidy, maintenance, financial support. ❸ *a tax allowance* CONCESSION, reduction, decrease, discount.
■ **make allowance(s) for** ❶ *you must make allowances for delays* TAKE INTO CONSIDERATION, take into account, bear in mind, have regard to, provide for, plan for, make plans for, get ready for, cater for, allow for, make provision for, make preparations for, prepare for. ❷ *she made allowances for his faults* EXCUSE, make excuses for, forgive, pardon, overlook.

alloy ▶ noun MIXTURE, mix, amalgam, fusion, meld, blend, compound, combination, composite, union; *technical* admixture.

all-powerful ▶ adjective OMNIPOTENT, almighty, supreme, pre-eminent; dictatorial, despotic, totalitarian, autocratic.
– OPPOSITES powerless.

all right ▶ adjective ❶ *the tea was all right* SATISFACTORY, acceptable, adequate, fairly good, passable, reasonable; *informal* so-so, OK. ❷ *are you all right?* UNHURT, uninjured, unharmed, unscathed, in one piece, safe (and sound); well, fine, alive and well; *informal* OK. ❸ *it's all right for you to go now* PERMISSIBLE, permitted, allowed, allowable, admissible, acceptable, legal, lawful, legitimate, licit, authorized, sanctioned, approved, in order; *informal* OK, legit.
– OPPOSITES unsatisfactory, hurt, forbidden.
▶ adverb ❶ *the system works all right* SATISFACTORILY, adequately, fairly well, passably, acceptably, reasonably; *informal* OK. ❷ *it's him all right* DEFINITELY, certainly, unquestionably, undoubtedly, indubitably, undeniably, as-

suredly, without (a) doubt, beyond (any) doubt, beyond the shadow of a doubt; *archaic* in sooth, verily.

▶ **exclamation** *all right, I'll go* VERY WELL (THEN), right (then), fine, good, yes, agreed, wilco; *informal* OK, okey-dokey, roger; *Brit. informal* righto.

allude ▶ **verb** REFER, touch on, suggest, hint, imply, mention (in passing), make an allusion to; *formal* advert.

allure ▶ **noun** *the allure of Paris* ATTRACTION, lure, draw, pull, appeal, allurement, enticement, temptation, charm, seduction, fascination.

▶ **verb** *will sponsors be allured by such opportunities?* ATTRACT, lure, entice, tempt, appeal to, captivate, draw, win over, charm, seduce, fascinate, whet the appetite of, make someone's mouth water.

–OPPOSITES repel.

alluring ▶ **adjective** ENTICING, tempting, attractive, appealing, inviting, captivating, fetching, seductive; enchanting, charming, fascinating; *informal* come-hither.

allusion ▶ **noun** REFERENCE, mention, suggestion, hint, comment, remark.

ally ▶ **noun** *close political allies* ASSOCIATE, colleague, friend, confederate, partner, supporter.

–OPPOSITES enemy, opponent.

▶ **verb** ❶ *he allied his racing experience with business acumen* COMBINE, marry, couple, merge, amalgamate, join, fuse. ❷ *the Catholic powers allied with Philip II* UNITE, combine, join (up), join forces, band together, team up, collaborate, side, align oneself, form an alliance, throw in one's lot, make common cause.

–OPPOSITES split.

almanac ▶ **noun** YEARBOOK, calendar, register, annual; manual, handbook.

almighty ▶ **adjective** ❶ *I swear by almighty God* ALL-POWERFUL, omnipotent, supreme, preeminent. ❷ (*informal*) *an almighty explosion* VERY GREAT, huge, enormous, immense, colossal, massive, prodigious, stupendous, tremendous, monumental, mammoth, vast, gigantic, giant, mighty, Herculean, epic; very loud, deafening, ear-splitting, ear-piercing, booming, thundering, thunderous; *informal* whopping, thumping, astronomical, mega, monster, humongous, jumbo; *Brit. informal* whacking, ginormous.

–OPPOSITES powerless, insignificant.

almost ▶ **adverb** NEARLY, (just) about, more or less, practically, virtually, all but, as good as, close to, near, not quite, not far from/off, to all intents and purposes; approaching, bordering on, verging on; *informal* pretty nearly/much/well; *poetic/literary* well-nigh, nigh on.

–RELATED TERMS quasi-.

alms ▶ **plural noun** (*historical*) GIFT(S), donation(s), handout(s), offering(s), charity, baksheesh, largesse; *rare* donative.

aloft ▶ **adjective & adverb** ❶ *he hoisted the Cup aloft* UPWARDS, up, high, into the air/sky, skyward, heavenward. ❷ *the airships stayed aloft for many hours* IN THE AIR, in the sky, high up, up (above), on high, overhead.

–OPPOSITES down.

alone ▶ **adjective & adverb** ❶ *she was alone in the house* BY ONESELF, on one's own, all alone, solitary, single, singly, solo, solus; unescorted, partnerless, companionless; *Brit. informal* on one's tod, on one's lonesome, on one's Jack Jones; *Austral./NZ informal* on one's Pat Malone. ❷ *he managed alone* UNAIDED, unassisted, without help/assistance, single-handedly, solo, on one's own. ❸ *she felt terribly alone* LONELY, isolated, solitary, deserted, abandoned, forlorn, friendless. ❹ *a house standing alone* APART, by itself/oneself, separate, detached, isolated. ❺ *you alone can inspire me* ONLY, solely, just; and no one else, and nothing else, no one but, nothing but.

–OPPOSITES in company, with help, among others.

along ▶ **preposition** ❶ *she walked along the corridor* DOWN, from one end of —— to the other. ❷ *trees grew along the river bank* BESIDE, by the side of, on the edge of, alongside. ❸ *they'll stop along the way* ON, at a point on, in the course of.

▶ **adverb** ❶ *Maurice moved along past the other exhibits* ONWARDS, on, ahead, forward(s). ❷ *I invited a friend along* AS COMPANY, with one, to accompany one, as a partner.

■ **along with** TOGETHER WITH, accompanying, accompanied by; at the same time as; as well as, in addition to, plus, besides.

aloof ▶ **adjective** DISTANT, detached, unfriendly, unsociable, remote, unapproachable, formal, stiff, austere, withdrawn, reserved, unforthcoming, uncommunicative; *informal* standoffish.

–OPPOSITES familiar, friendly.

aloud ▶ **adverb** AUDIBLY, out loud, for all to hear.

–OPPOSITES silently.

alphabet ▶ **noun** ABC, letters, writing system, syllabary.

already ▶ **adverb** ❶ *Anna had suffered a great deal already* BY THIS/THAT TIME, by now/then, thus/so far, before now/then, until now/then, up to now/then. ❷ *is it 3 o'clock already?* AS EARLY AS THIS/THAT, as soon as this/that, so soon.

also ▶ **adverb** TOO, as well, besides, in addition, additionally, furthermore, further, moreover, into the bargain, on top (of that), what's more, to boot, equally; *informal* and all; *archaic* withal, forbye.

alter ▶ **verb** ❶ *Eliot was persuaded to alter the passage* CHANGE, make changes to, make different, make alterations to, adjust, make adjustments to, adapt, amend, modify, revise,

revamp, rework, redo, refine, vary, transform; *informal* tweak; *technical* permute. ❷ *the state of affairs has altered* CHANGE, become different, undergo a (sea) change, adjust, adapt, transform, evolve.
– OPPOSITES preserve, stay the same.

alteration ▶noun CHANGE, adjustment, adaptation, modification, variation, revision, amend-ment; rearrangement, reordering, restyling, rejigging, reworking, revamping; sea change, transformation; *humorous* transmogrification.

altercation ▶noun ARGUMENT, quarrel, squabble, fight, shouting match, disagreement, difference of opinion, falling-out, dispute, disputation, wrangle, war of words; *informal* tiff, run-in, slanging match, spat, scrap; *Brit. informal* row, barney, ding-dong, bust-up, bit of argy-bargy; *N. Amer. informal* rhubarb; *archaic* broil, miff.

alternate ▶verb ❶ *rows of trees alternate with dense shrub* BE INTERSPERSED, occur in turn/rotation, rotate, follow one another; take turns, take it in turns, work/act in sequence. ❷ *we could alternate the groups so that no one felt they had been left out* GIVE TURNS TO, take in turn, rotate, take in rotation; swap, exchange, interchange.
▶adjective ❶ *she attended on alternate days* EVERY OTHER, every second. ❷ *place the leeks and noodles in alternate layers* ALTERNATING, interchanging, following in sequence, sequential, occurring in turns. ❸ (*N. Amer.*) *an alternate plan.* See ALTERNATIVE adjective sense 1.

alternative ▶adjective ❶ *an alternative route* DIFFERENT, other, another, second, possible, substitute, replacement; standby, emergency, reserve, back-up, auxiliary, fallback; *N. Amer.* alternate. ❷ *an alternative lifestyle* UNORTHODOX, unconventional, non-standard, unusual, uncommon, out of the ordinary, radical, revolutionary, nonconformist, avant-garde; *informal* off the wall, oddball, offbeat, way-out.
▶noun *we have no alternative* OPTION, choice, other possibility; substitute, replacement.

alternatively ▶adverb ON THE OTHER HAND, as an alternative, or; otherwise, instead, if not, then again; *N. Amer.* alternately.

although ▶conjunction IN SPITE OF THE FACT THAT, despite the fact that, notwithstanding (the fact) that, even though/if, for all that, while, whilst.

altitude ▶noun HEIGHT, elevation, distance above the sea/ground.

altogether ▶adverb ❶ *he wasn't altogether happy* COMPLETELY, totally, entirely, absolutely, wholly, fully, thoroughly, utterly, perfectly, one hundred per cent, in all respects. ❷ *we have five offices altogether* IN ALL, all told, in toto. ❸ *altogether it was a great evening* ON THE WHOLE, overall, all in all, all things considered, on balance, on average, for the most part, in the main, in general, generally, by and large.

altruism ▶noun UNSELFISHNESS, selflessness, compassion, kindness, public-spiritedness; charity, benevolence, beneficence, philanthropy, humanitarianism; *poetic/literary* bounty, bounteousness.
– OPPOSITES selfishness.

always ▶adverb ❶ *he's always late* EVERY TIME, each time, at all times, all the time, without fail, consistently, invariably, regularly, habitually, unfailingly. ❷ *she's always complaining* CONTINUALLY, continuously, constantly, forever, perpetually, incessantly, ceaselessly, unceasingly, endlessly, the entire time; *informal* 24-7. ❸ *the place will always be dear to me* FOREVER, for always, for good (and all), for evermore, for ever and ever, until the end of time, eternally, for eternity, until hell freezes over; *informal* for keeps, until the cows come home; *archaic* for aye. ❹ *you can always take it back to the shop* AS A LAST RESORT, no matter what, in any event/case, come what may.
– OPPOSITES never, seldom, sometimes.

amalgamate ▶verb COMBINE, merge, unite, fuse, blend, meld; join (together), join forces, band (together), link (up), team up, go into partnership; *poetic/literary* commingle.
– OPPOSITES separate.

amalgamation ▶noun COMBINATION, union, blend, mixture, fusion, coalescence, synthesis, composite, amalgam.

amass ▶verb GATHER, collect, assemble; accumulate, stockpile, store (up), cumulate, accrue, lay in/up, garner; *informal* stash (away).
– OPPOSITES dissipate.

amateur ▶noun ❶ *the crew were all amateurs* NON-PROFESSIONAL, non-specialist, layman, layperson; dilettante. ❷ *what a bunch of amateurs* BUNGLER, incompetent, bumbler; *Brit. informal* bodger.
– OPPOSITES professional, expert.
▶adjective ❶ *an amateur sportsman* NON-PROFESSIONAL, non-specialist, lay; dilettante. ❷ *their amateur efforts* INCOMPETENT, inept, unskilful, inexpert, amateurish, clumsy, maladroit, bumbling; *Brit. informal* bodged.

amateurish ▶adjective. See AMATEUR adjective sense 2.

amatory ▶adjective SEXUAL, erotic, amorous, romantic, sensual, passionate, sexy; *informal* randy, steamy, naughty.

amaze ▶verb ASTONISH, astound, surprise, stun, stagger, nonplus, shock, startle, stupefy, stop someone in their tracks, leave open-mouthed, leave aghast, take someone's breath away, dumbfound; *informal* bowl over, flabbergast; *Brit. informal* knock for six; (**amazed**) thunderstruck, at a loss for words, speechless; *Brit. informal* gobsmacked.

amazement ▶ **noun** ASTONISHMENT, surprise, shock, stupefaction, incredulity, disbelief, speechlessness, awe, wonder, wonderment.

amazing ▶ **adjective** ASTONISHING, astounding, surprising, stunning, staggering, shocking, startling, stupefying, breathtaking; awesome, awe-inspiring, sensational, remarkable, spectacular, stupendous, phenomenal, extraordinary, incredible, unbelievable; *informal* mind-blowing, flabbergasting; *poetic/literary* wondrous.

ambassador ▶ **noun** ❶ *the American ambassador* ENVOY, plenipotentiary, emissary, (papal) nuncio, representative, diplomat; *archaic* legate. ❷ *a great ambassador for the sport* CAMPAIGNER, representative, promoter, champion, supporter, backer; *N. Amer.* booster.

ambience ▶ **noun** ATMOSPHERE, air, aura, climate, mood, feel, feeling, vibrations, character, quality, impression, flavour, look, tone; *informal* vibes.

ambiguity ▶ **noun** AMBIVALENCE, equivocation; obscurity, vagueness, abstruseness, doubtfulness, uncertainty; *formal* dubiety.

ambiguous ▶ **adjective** EQUIVOCAL, ambivalent, open to debate/argument, arguable, debatable; obscure, unclear, vague, abstruse, doubtful, dubious, uncertain.
– OPPOSITES clear.

ambit ▶ **noun** SCOPE, extent, range, breadth, width, reach, sweep; terms of reference, field of reference, jurisdiction, remit; area, sphere, field, realm, compass.

ambition ▶ **noun** ❶ *young people with ambition* DRIVE, determination, enterprise, initiative, eagerness, motivation, enthusiasm, zeal, commitment, a sense of purpose; *informal* get-up-and-go. ❷ *her ambition was to become a model* ASPIRATION, intention, goal, aim, objective, object, purpose, intent, plan, desire, wish, design, target, dream.

ambitious ▶ **adjective** ❶ *an energetic and ambitious politician* ASPIRING, determined, forceful, pushy, enterprising, motivated, enthusiastic, energetic, zealous, committed, purposeful, power-hungry; *informal* go-ahead, go-getting. ❷ *he was ambitious to make it to the top* EAGER, determined, intent on, enthusiastic, anxious, hungry, impatient, striving. ❸ *an ambitious task* DIFFICULT, exacting, demanding, formidable, challenging, hard, arduous, onerous, tough; *archaic* toilsome.
– OPPOSITES laid-back.

ambivalent ▶ **adjective** EQUIVOCAL, uncertain, unsure, doubtful, indecisive, inconclusive, irresolute, in two minds, undecided, torn, in a dilemma, on the horns of a dilemma, in a quandary, on the fence, hesitating, wavering, vacillating, equivocating, blowing hot and cold; *informal* iffy.
– OPPOSITES unequivocal, certain.

amble ▶ **verb** STROLL, saunter, wander, ramble, promenade, walk, go for a walk, take a walk; *informal* mosey, tootle; *Brit. informal* pootle, mooch; *formal* perambulate.

ambush ▶ **noun** *the soldiers were killed in an ambush* SURPRISE ATTACK, trap; *archaic* ambuscade.
▶ **verb** *twenty youths ambushed their patrol car* ATTACK BY SURPRISE, surprise, pounce on, lay a trap for, set an ambush for, lie in wait for, waylay; *N. Amer.* bushwhack; *archaic* ambuscade.

ameliorate ▶ **verb** IMPROVE, make better, better, make improvements to, enhance, help, benefit, boost, amend; relieve, ease, mitigate; *informal* tweak, patch up.
– OPPOSITES worsen.

amenable ▶ **adjective** ❶ *an amenable child* COMPLIANT, acquiescent, biddable, manageable, controllable, governable, persuadable, tractable, responsive, pliant, malleable, complaisant, easily handled; *rare* persuasible. ❷ *many cancers are amenable to treatment* SUSCEPTIBLE, receptive, responsive; *archaic* susceptive.
– OPPOSITES uncooperative.

amend ▶ **verb** REVISE, alter, change, modify, qualify, adapt, adjust; edit, copy-edit, rewrite, redraft, rephrase, reword, rework, revamp.

amends ▶ **plural noun** *I wanted to make amends* COMPENSATION, recompense, reparation, restitution, redress, atonement, expiation.
■ **make amends** COMPENSATE, recompense, indemnify, make it up to; atone for, make up for, make good, expiate.

amenity ▶ **noun** ❶ *basic amenities* FACILITY, service, convenience, resource, appliance, aid, comfort, benefit, advantage. ❷ *a loss of amenity* PLEASANTNESS, agreeableness, niceness.

America ▶ **noun.** *See* UNITED STATES OF AMERICA.

amiable ▶ **adjective** FRIENDLY, affable, amicable, cordial; warm, warm-hearted, good-natured, nice, pleasant, agreeable, likeable, genial, good-humoured, charming, easy to get on/along with, companionable, sociable, personable; *informal* chummy; *Brit. informal* matey; *N. Amer. informal* regular.
– OPPOSITES unfriendly, disagreeable.

amicable ▶ **adjective** FRIENDLY, good-natured, cordial, easy, easy-going, neighbourly, harmonious, cooperative, civilized.
– OPPOSITES unfriendly.

amid ▶ **preposition** ❶ *the jeep was concealed amid pine trees* IN THE MIDDLE OF, surrounded by, among, amongst; *poetic/literary* amidst, in the midst of. ❷ *the truce collapsed amid fears of a revolt* AT A TIME OF, in an atmosphere of, against a background of; as a result of.

amiss ▶ **adjective** *an inspection revealed nothing amiss* WRONG, awry, faulty, out of order, defective, unsatisfactory, incorrect; inappropriate, improper.
– OPPOSITES right, in order.

■ **not come/go amiss** BE WELCOME, be appropriate, be useful.

■ **take something amiss** BE OFFENDED, take offence, be upset.

amity ▶ noun FRIENDSHIP, friendliness, harmony, harmoniousness, understanding, accord, cooperation, amicableness, goodwill, cordiality, warmth; *formal* concord.
– OPPOSITES animosity, enmity.

ammunition ▶ noun *police seized arms and ammunition* BULLETS, shells, projectiles, missiles, rounds, shot, slugs, cartridges, munitions; *informal* ammo.

amnesty ▶ noun *an amnesty for political prisoners* PARDON, pardoning, reprieve; release, discharge; *informal* let-off.
▶ verb *the guerrillas were amnestied* PARDON, grant an amnesty to, reprieve; release, discharge, liberate, free, spare; *informal* let off, let off the hook.

amok
■ **run amok** GO BERSERK, get out of control, rampage, riot, run riot, go on the rampage, behave like a maniac, behave wildly/uncontrollably, become violent/destructive; *informal* raise hell.

among, amongst ▶ preposition ❶ *you're among friends* SURROUNDED BY, in the company of, amongst, amid, in the middle of; *poetic/literary* amidst, in the midst of. ❷ *a child was among the injured* INCLUDED IN, one/some of, in the group/number of. ❸ *he distributed the proceeds among his creditors* BETWEEN, to each of.
– RELATED TERMS inter-.
■ **between ourselves/yourselves/themselves** JOINTLY, with one another, together, mutually, reciprocally.

amoral ▶ adjective UNPRINCIPLED, without standards/morals/scruples, unethical.
– OPPOSITES principled.

amorous ▶ adjective LUSTFUL, sexual, erotic, amatory, ardent, passionate, impassioned; in love, enamoured, lovesick; *informal* lovey-dovey, kissy, smoochy, goo-goo, hot; *Brit. informal* randy; *archaic* sportive.
– OPPOSITES unloving.

amorphous ▶ adjective SHAPELESS, formless, structureless, indeterminate.
– OPPOSITES shaped, definite.

amount ▶ noun QUANTITY, number, total, aggregate, sum, quota, group, size, mass, weight, volume, bulk, quantum.
■ **amount to** ❶ *the bill amounted to £50* ADD UP TO, come to, run to, be, make, total; *Brit.* tot up to. ❷ *the delays amounted to maladministration* CONSTITUTE, comprise, be tantamount, come down, boil down; signify, signal, mean, indicate, suggest, denote, point to, be evidence, be symptomatic; *poetic/literary* betoken. ❸ *her relationships had never amounted to anything significant* BECOME, grow/develop into, prove to be, turn out to be.
■ **the full amount** THE GRAND TOTAL, the total, the aggregate; *informal* the whole caboodle/shebang, the full nine yards.

ample ▶ adjective ❶ *there is ample time for discussion* ENOUGH, sufficient, adequate, plenty of, more than enough, enough and to spare. ❷ *an ample supply of wine* PLENTIFUL, abundant, copious, profuse, rich, lavish, liberal, generous, bountiful, large, huge, great, bumper; *informal* a gogo, galore; *poetic/literary* plenteous. ❸ *his ample tunic* SPACIOUS, capacious, roomy, sizeable; voluminous, loose-fitting, baggy, sloppy; *formal* commodious.
– OPPOSITES insufficient, meagre.

amplify ▶ verb ❶ *many frogs amplify their voices* MAKE LOUDER, louden, turn up, magnify, intensify, increase, boost, step up, raise. ❷ *these notes amplify our statement* EXPAND, enlarge on, elaborate on, add to, supplement, develop, flesh out, add detail to, go into detail about.
– OPPOSITES reduce, quieten.

amplitude ▶ noun MAGNITUDE, size, volume; extent, range, compass; breadth, width.

amputate ▶ verb CUT OFF, sever, remove (surgically), saw/chop off.

amulet ▶ noun LUCKY CHARM, charm, talisman, fetish, mascot, totem, idol, juju; *archaic* periapt.

amuse ▶ verb ❶ *her annoyance simply amused him* ENTERTAIN, make laugh, delight, divert, cheer (up), please, charm, tickle; *informal* tickle pink, crack up; *Brit. informal* crease up. ❷ *he amused himself by writing poetry* OCCUPY, engage, busy, employ, distract, absorb, engross, hold someone's attention; interest, entertain, divert.
– OPPOSITES bore.

amusement ▶ noun ❶ *we looked with amusement at the cartoon* MIRTH, merriment, lightheartedness, hilarity, glee, delight, gaiety, joviality, fun; enjoyment, pleasure, high spirits, cheerfulness. ❷ *I read the book for amusement* ENTERTAINMENT, pleasure, leisure, relaxation, fun, enjoyment, interest, diversion; *informal* R and R; *N. Amer. informal* rec; *archaic* disport. ❸ *a wide range of amusements* ACTIVITY, entertainment, diversion; game, sport.

amusing ▶ adjective ENTERTAINING, funny, comical, humorous, light-hearted, jocular, witty, mirthful, hilarious, droll, diverting; *informal* wacky, side-splitting, rib-tickling.
– OPPOSITES boring, solemn.

anaemic ▶ adjective ❶ *his anaemic face* COLOURLESS, bloodless, pale, pallid, wan, ashen, grey, sallow, pasty-faced, whey-faced, peaky, sickly, etiolated. ❷ *an anaemic description of her feelings* FEEBLE, weak, insipid, wishy-washy, vapid, bland; lame, tame, lacklustre, spiritless, lifeless, ineffective, ineffectual, etiolated; *informal* pathetic.

anaesthetic ▶ noun NARCOTIC, painkiller, painkilling drug, pain reliever, sedative, anodyne, analgesic; general, local.

analgesic ▶ adjective PAINKILLING, pain-relieving, anodyne, narcotic, palliative.

analogous ▶ adjective COMPARABLE, parallel, similar, like, corresponding, related, kindred, equivalent; *formal* cognate.
– OPPOSITES unrelated.

analogy ▶ noun SIMILARITY, parallel, correspondence, likeness, resemblance, correlation, relation, kinship, equivalence, similitude.
– OPPOSITES dissimilarity.

analyse ▶ verb EXAMINE, inspect, survey, study, scrutinize, look over; investigate, explore, probe, research, go over (with a fine-tooth comb), review, evaluate, break down, dissect, anatomize.

analysis ▶ noun EXAMINATION, investigation, inspection, survey, study, scrutiny; exploration, probe, research, review, evaluation, interpretation, anatomization, dissection.

analytical, analytic ▶ adjective SYSTEMATIC, logical, scientific, methodical, (well) organized, ordered, orderly, meticulous, rigorous.
– OPPOSITES unsystematic.

anarchic ▶ adjective LAWLESS, without law and order, in disorder/turmoil, unruly, chaotic, turbulent.
– OPPOSITES ordered.

anarchist ▶ noun NIHILIST, insurgent, agitator, subversive, terrorist, revolutionary, revolutionist, insurrectionist.

anarchy ▶ noun LAWLESSNESS, nihilism, mobocracy, revolution, insurrection, disorder, chaos, tumult, turmoil.
– OPPOSITES government, order.

anathema ▶ noun ❶ *racial hatred was anathema to her* ABHORRENT, hateful, repugnant, repellent, offensive; ABOMINATION, outrage, bane, bugbear, bête noire. ❷ *the Vatican Council issued an anathema* CURSE, ban, excommunication, proscription, debarment, denunciation.

anatomy ▶ noun ❶ *a cat's anatomy* STRUCTURE, make-up, composition, constitution, form. ❷ *an anatomy of society* ANALYSIS, examination, inspection, survey, study, investigation, review, evaluation.

ancestor ▶ noun ❶ *he could trace his ancestors back to King James I* FOREBEAR, forefather, predecessor, antecedent, progenitor, primogenitor. ❷ *the instrument is an ancestor of the lute* FORERUNNER, precursor, predecessor.
– OPPOSITES descendant, successor.

ancestral ▶ adjective INHERITED, hereditary, familial.

ancestry ▶ noun ANCESTORS, forebears, forefathers, progenitors, antecedents; family tree; lineage, genealogy, roots.

anchor ▶ noun ❶ *the anchor of the new coalition* MAINSTAY, cornerstone, linchpin, bulwark, foundation. ❷ *a CBS news anchor* PRESENTER, announcer, anchorman, anchorwoman, broadcaster.
▶ verb ❶ *the ship was anchored in the bay* MOOR, berth, be at anchor; *archaic* harbour. ❷ *the fish anchors itself to the coral* SECURE, fasten, attach, affix, fix.

anchorage ▶ noun MOORINGS, moorage, roads, roadstead, harbourage.

anchorite ▶ noun (*historical*) HERMIT, recluse, ascetic; *historical* stylite; *archaic* eremite.

ancient ▶ adjective ❶ *ancient civilizations* OF LONG AGO, early, prehistoric, primeval, primordial, primitive; *poetic/literary* of yore; *archaic* foregone. ❷ *an ancient custom* OLD, very old, age-old, archaic, antediluvian, time-worn, time-honoured. ❸ *I feel positively ancient* ANTIQUATED, aged, elderly, decrepit, antediluvian, in one's dotage; old-fashioned, out of date, outmoded, démodé, passé; *informal* out of the ark; *Brit. informal* past its/one's sell-by date.
– RELATED TERMS archaeo-, palaeo-.
– OPPOSITES recent, contemporary.

ancillary ▶ adjective ADDITIONAL, auxiliary, supporting, helping, extra, supplementary, accessory; *Medicine* adjuvant; *rare* adminicular.
– RELATED TERMS para-.

and ▶ conjunction TOGETHER WITH, along with, with, as well as, in addition to, also, too; besides, furthermore; *informal* plus.

anecdotal ▶ adjective ❶ *anecdotal evidence* UNSCIENTIFIC, unreliable, based on hearsay. ❷ *her book is anecdotal and chatty* NARRATIVE, full of stories.

anecdote ▶ noun STORY, tale, narrative; urban myth; *informal* yarn.

anew ▶ adverb AGAIN, afresh, once more/again, over again.

angel ▶ noun ❶ *God sent an angel* MESSENGER OF GOD, divine/heavenly messenger, divine being. ❷ *she's an absolute angel* PARAGON OF VIRTUE, saint; gem, treasure, darling, dear; *informal* star; *Brit. informal, dated* brick. ❸ (*informal*) *a financial angel* BACKER, sponsor, benefactor, promoter, patron.
– OPPOSITES devil.

angelic ▶ adjective ❶ *angelic beings* DIVINE, heavenly, celestial, holy, seraphic; *poetic/literary* empyrean. ❷ *Sophie's angelic appearance* INNOCENT, pure, virtuous, good, saintly, wholesome.
– OPPOSITES demonic, infernal.

anger ▶ noun *his face was livid with anger* ANNOYANCE, vexation, exasperation, crossness, irritation, irritability, indignation, pique; rage, fury, wrath, outrage, irascibility, ill temper/humour; *informal* aggravation; *poetic/literary* ire, choler.
– RELATED TERMS irascible.

– OPPOSITES pleasure, good humour.

▶ **verb** *she was angered by his terse reply* ANNOY, irritate, exasperate, irk, vex, put out; enrage, incense, infuriate, make someone's hackles rise; *Brit.* rub up the wrong way; *informal* make someone's blood boil, get someone's back up, make someone see red, get someone's dander up, rattle someone's cage; aggravate, get someone, rile, hack off; *Brit. informal* wind up, nark; *N. Amer. informal* tee off, tick off, burn up, gravel; *informal, dated* give someone the pip.
– OPPOSITES pacify, placate.

angle[1] ▶ **noun** ❶ *the wall is sloping at an angle of 33°* GRADIENT, slant, inclination. ❷ *the angle of the roof* CORNER, intersection, point, apex. ❸ *consider the problem from a different angle* PERSPECTIVE, point of view, viewpoint, standpoint, position, aspect, slant, direction.

▶ **verb** ❶ *Anna angled her camera towards the tree* TILT, slant, direct, turn. ❷ *angle your answer so that it is relevant* PRESENT, slant, orient, twist, bias.

angle[2] ▶ **verb** *he was angling for an invitation* TRY TO GET, seek to obtain, fish for, hope for, be after.

angler ▶ **noun** FISHERMAN, rod; *archaic* fisher.

angry ▶ **adjective** ❶ *Vivienne got angry* IRATE, annoyed, cross, vexed, irritated, indignant, irked; furious, enraged, infuriated, in a temper, incensed, raging, incandescent, fuming, seething, beside oneself, outraged; *informal* (hopping) mad, wild, livid, apoplectic, as cross as two sticks, hot under the collar, up in arms, foaming at the mouth, steamed up, in a lather/paddy, fit to be tied; *Brit. informal* aerated, shirty; *N. Amer. informal* sore, bent out of shape, teed off, ticked off; *Austral./NZ informal* ropeable, snaky; *poetic/literary* wrathful; *archaic* wroth. ❷ *an angry debate* HEATED, passionate, stormy, 'lively'; bad-tempered, ill-tempered, acrimonious, bitter. ❸ *angry sores* INFLAMED, red, swollen, sore, painful.
– OPPOSITES pleased, good-humoured.

■ **get angry** LOSE ONE'S TEMPER, become enraged, go into a rage, go berserk, flare up; *informal* go mad/crazy/wild, go bananas, hit the roof, go through the roof, go up the wall, see red, go off the deep end, fly off the handle, blow one's top, blow a fuse/gasket, lose one's rag, flip (one's lid), foam at the mouth, have a fit, explode, go non-linear, go ballistic; *Brit. informal* go spare, do one's nut; *N. Amer. informal* flip one's wig, blow one's lid/stack, have a conniption fit.

angst ▶ **noun** ANXIETY, fear, apprehension, worry, foreboding, trepidation, malaise, disquiet, disquietude, unease, uneasiness.

anguish ▶ **noun** AGONY, pain, torment, torture, suffering, distress, angst, misery, sorrow, grief, heartache, desolation, despair; *poetic/literary* dolour.
– OPPOSITES happiness.

anguished ▶ **adjective** AGONIZED, tormented, tortured; grief-stricken, wretched, heartbroken, desolate, devastated; *informal* cut up; *poetic/literary* dolorous.

angular ▶ **adjective** ❶ *an angular shape* SHARP-CORNERED, pointed, V-shaped, Y-shaped. ❷ *an angular face* BONY, raw-boned, lean, rangy, spare, thin, gaunt.
– OPPOSITES rounded, curving.

animal ▶ **noun** ❶ *endangered animals* CREATURE, beast, living thing; (**animals**) wildlife, fauna; *N. Amer. informal* critter. ❷ *the man was an animal* BRUTE, beast, monster, devil, demon, fiend; *informal* swine, bastard, pig.
– RELATED TERMS ZOO-.

▶ **adjective** ❶ *animal life* ZOOLOGICAL, animalistic; *rare* zoic. ❷ *a grunt of animal passion* CARNAL, fleshly, bodily, physical; brutish, unrefined, uncultured, coarse.

animate ▶ **verb** *a sense of excitement animated the whole school* ENLIVEN, vitalize, breathe (new) life into, energize, invigorate, revive, vivify, liven up; inspire, inspirit, exhilarate, thrill, excite, fire, arouse, rouse; *N. Amer.* light a fire under; *informal* buck up, pep up, give someone a buzz.
– OPPOSITES depress.

▶ **adjective** *an animate being* LIVING, alive, live, breathing; *archaic* quick.
– OPPOSITES inanimate.

animated ▶ **adjective** LIVELY, spirited, high-spirited, energetic, full of life, excited, enthusiastic, eager, alive, active, vigorous, vibrant, vital, vivacious, buoyant, exuberant, ebullient, effervescent, bouncy, bubbly, perky; *informal* bright-eyed and bushy-tailed, full of beans, bright and breezy, chirpy, chipper, peppy.
– OPPOSITES lethargic, lifeless.

animosity ▶ **noun** ANTIPATHY, hostility, friction, antagonism, enmity, animus, bitterness, rancour, resentment, dislike, ill feeling/will, bad blood, hatred, hate, loathing; malice, spite, spitefulness.
– OPPOSITES goodwill, friendship.

annals ▶ **plural noun** RECORDS, archives, chronicles, accounts, registers; *Law* muniments.

annex ▶ **verb** ❶ *ten amendments were annexed to the constitution* ADD, append, attach, tack on, tag on. ❷ *Charlemagne annexed northern Italy* TAKE OVER, take possession of, appropriate, seize, conquer, occupy.

▶ **noun** (also **annexe**) EXTENSION, addition; wing; *N. Amer.* ell.

annexation ▶ **noun** SEIZURE, occupation, invasion, conquest, takeover, appropriation.

annihilate ▶ **verb** DESTROY, wipe out, obliterate, wipe off the face of the earth; kill, slaughter, exterminate, eliminate, liquidate; *informal* take out, rub out, snuff out, waste.
– OPPOSITES create.

annotate ▶ verb COMMENT ON, add notes/footnotes to, gloss, interpret; *archaic* margin.

annotation ▶ noun NOTE, notation, comment, gloss, footnote; commentary, explanation, interpretation.

announce ▶ verb ❶ *their financial results were announced* MAKE PUBLIC, make known, report, declare, state, give out, notify, publicize, broadcast, publish, advertise, circulate, proclaim, blazon abroad. ❷ *Victor announced the guests* INTRODUCE, present, name. ❸ *strains of music announced her arrival* SIGNAL, indicate, give notice of, herald, proclaim; *poetic/literary* betoken.

announcement ▶ noun ❶ *an announcement by the Minister* STATEMENT, report, declaration, proclamation, pronouncement, rescript; bulletin, communiqué; *N. Amer.* advisory. ❷ *the announcement of the decision* DECLARATION, notification, reporting, publishing, broadcasting, proclamation; *archaic* annunciation.

announcer ▶ noun PRESENTER, anchorman, anchorwoman, anchor; newsreader, newscaster, broadcaster.

annoy ▶ verb IRRITATE, vex, make angry/cross, anger, exasperate, irk, gall, pique, put out, antagonize, get on someone's nerves, ruffle someone's feathers, make someone's hackles rise, nettle; *Brit.* rub up the wrong way; *informal* aggravate, peeve, hassle, miff, rile, needle, get (to), bug, hack off, get up someone's nose, get someone's goat, get someone's back up, give someone the hump, drive mad/crazy, drive round the bend/twist, drive up the wall, get someone's dander up; *Brit. informal* wind up, nark, get on someone's wick; *N. Amer. informal* tee off, tick off, burn up, rankle, gravel; *informal, dated* give someone the pip.
– OPPOSITES please, gratify.

annoyance ▶ noun ❶ *much to his annoyance, Louise didn't even notice* IRRITATION, exasperation, vexation, indignation, anger, displeasure, chagrin; *informal* aggravation. ❷ *they found him an annoyance* NUISANCE, pest, bother, irritant, inconvenience, thorn in one's flesh; *informal* pain (in the neck), bind, bore, hassle; *N. Amer. informal* nudnik, burr in/under someone's saddle; *Austral./NZ informal* nark.

annoyed ▶ adjective IRRITATED, cross, angry, vexed, exasperated, irked, piqued, displeased, put out, disgruntled, nettled, in a bad mood, in a temper; *informal* aggravated, peeved, miffed, miffy, riled, hacked off, hot under the collar; *Brit. informal* narked, shirty; *N. Amer. informal* teed off, ticked off, sore, bent out of shape; *Austral./NZ informal* snaky, crook; *archaic* wroth.

annoying ▶ adjective IRRITATING, infuriating, exasperating, maddening, trying, tiresome, troublesome, bothersome, irksome, vexing, vexatious, galling; *informal* aggravating, pesky.

annual ▶ adjective YEARLY, once-a-year; year-long, twelve-month.

annually ▶ adverb YEARLY, once a year, each year, per annum.

annul ▶ verb DECLARE INVALID, declare null and void, nullify, invalidate, void; repeal, reverse, rescind, revoke; *Law* vacate; *formal* abrogate; *archaic* recall.
– OPPOSITES restore, enact.

anodyne ▶ noun PAINKILLER, painkilling drug, pain reliever, analgesic, narcotic.
▶ adjective *the conversation was anodyne* BLAND, inoffensive, innocuous, neutral, unobjectionable.

anoint ▶ verb ❶ *the head of the infant was anointed* SMEAR/RUB WITH OIL; *archaic* anele. ❷ *he was anointed and crowned* CONSECRATE, bless, ordain; *formal* hallow.

anomalous ▶ adjective ABNORMAL, atypical, irregular, aberrant, exceptional, freak, freakish, odd, bizarre, peculiar, unusual, out of the ordinary.
– OPPOSITES normal, typical.

anomaly ▶ noun ODDITY, peculiarity, abnormality, irregularity, inconsistency, incongruity, aberration, quirk.

anon ▶ adverb (*informal*) SOON, shortly, in a little while, presently, before long, by and by; *dated* directly; *poetic/literary* ere long.

anonymous ▶ adjective ❶ *an anonymous donor* UNNAMED, of unknown name, nameless, incognito, unidentified, unknown; *rare* innominate. ❷ *an anonymous letter* UNSIGNED, unattributed. ❸ *an anonymous housing estate* CHARACTERLESS, nondescript, impersonal, faceless.
– OPPOSITES known, identified.

another ▶ determiner ❶ *have another drink* ONE MORE, a further, an additional; an extra, a spare. ❷ *she left him for another man* A DIFFERENT, some other, an alternative.
– OPPOSITES the same.

answer ▶ noun ❶ *her answer was unequivocal* REPLY, response, rejoinder, reaction; retort, riposte; *informal* comeback. ❷ *the answer is 150* SOLUTION, key. ❸ *a new filter is the answer* SOLUTION, remedy, way out.
– OPPOSITES question.
▶ verb ❶ *Steve was about to answer* REPLY, respond, make a rejoinder, rejoin; retort, riposte. ❷ *he has yet to answer the charges* REBUT, refute, defend oneself against. ❸ *a man answering this description* MATCH, fit, correspond to, be similar to. ❹ *we're trying to answer the needs of our audience* SATISFY, meet, fulfil, fill, measure up to. ❺ *I answer to the Commissioner* REPORT, work for/under, be subordinate, be accountable, be answerable, be responsible.
■ **answer someone back** RESPOND CHEEKILY TO, be cheeky to, be impertinent to, talk back to, cheek; *N. Amer. informal* sass.

■ **answer for** ❶ *he will answer for his crime* PAY FOR, be punished for, suffer for; make amends for, make reparation for, atone for. ❷ *the government has a lot to answer for* BE ACCOUNTABLE FOR, be responsible for, be liable for, take the blame for; *informal* take the rap for.

answerable ▶ **adjective** ACCOUNTABLE, responsible, liable; subject.

ant
– RELATED TERMS formic.

antagonism ▶ **noun** HOSTILITY, friction, enmity, antipathy, animus, opposition, dissension, rivalry; acrimony, bitterness, rancour, resentment, aversion, dislike, ill/bad feeling, ill will; *Brit. informal* needle.
– OPPOSITES rapport, friendship.

antagonist ▶ **noun** ADVERSARY, opponent, enemy, rival; (**antagonists**) opposition, competition.
– OPPOSITES ally.

antagonistic ▶ **adjective** ❶ *he was antagonistic to the reforms* HOSTILE, against, (dead) set against, opposed, inimical, antipathetic, ill-disposed, resistant, in disagreement; *informal* anti. ❷ *an antagonistic group of bystanders* HOSTILE, aggressive, belligerent, bellicose, pugnacious; *rare* oppugnant.
– OPPOSITES pro.

antagonize ▶ **verb** AROUSE HOSTILITY IN, alienate; anger, annoy, provoke, vex, irritate; *Brit.* rub up the wrong way; *informal* aggravate, rile, needle, rattle someone's cage, get someone's back up, get someone's dander up; *Brit. informal* nark, get on someone's wick.
– OPPOSITES pacify, placate.

antecedent ▶ **noun** ❶ *her antecedents have been traced* ANCESTOR, forefather, forebear, progenitor, primogenitor; (**antecedents**) ancestry, family tree, lineage, genealogy, roots. ❷ *the guitar's antecedent* PRECURSOR, forerunner, predecessor.
– OPPOSITES descendant.
▶ **adjective** *antecedent events* PREVIOUS, earlier, prior, preceding, precursory; *formal* anterior.
– OPPOSITES subsequent.

antedate ▶ **verb** PRECEDE, predate, come/go before.

antediluvian ▶ **adjective** ❶ *antediluvian animals* PREHISTORIC, primeval, primordial, primal, ancient, early. ❷ *his antediluvian attitudes* OUT OF DATE, outdated, outmoded, old-fashioned, antiquated, behind the times, passé.

ante-room ▶ **noun** ANTECHAMBER, vestibule, lobby, foyer; *Architecture* narthex.

anthem ▶ **noun** HYMN, song, chorale, psalm, paean.

anthology ▶ **noun** COLLECTION, selection, compendium, treasury, miscellany; *archaic* garland.

anticipate ▶ **verb** ❶ *the police did not anticipate trouble* EXPECT, foresee, predict, be prepared for, bargain on, reckon on; *N. Amer. informal* figure on. ❷ *Elaine anticipated her meeting with Will* LOOK FORWARD TO, await, lick one's lips over. ❸ *warders can't always anticipate the actions of prisoners* PRE-EMPT, forestall, second-guess; *informal* beat someone to the punch. ❹ *her plays anticipated her film work* FORESHADOW, precede, antedate, come/go before.

anticipation ▶ **noun** ❶ *my anticipation is that we will see a rise in rates* EXPECTATION, prediction, forecast. ❷ *her eyes sparkled with anticipation* EXPECTANCY, expectation, excitement, suspense.
■ **in anticipation of** IN THE EXPECTATION OF, in preparation for, ready for.

anticlimax ▶ **noun** LET-DOWN, disappointment, comedown, non-event; disillusionment; *Brit.* damp squib; *informal* washout.

antics ▶ **plural noun** CAPERS, pranks, larks, high jinks, skylarking; *Brit. informal* monkey tricks.

antidote ▶ **noun** ❶ *the antidote to this poison* ANTITOXIN, antiserum, antivenin. ❷ *laughter is a good antidote to stress* REMEDY, cure, nostrum.

antipathetic ▶ **adjective** HOSTILE, against, (dead) set against, opposed, antagonistic, ill-disposed, unsympathetic; *informal* anti, down on.
– OPPOSITES pro.

antipathy ▶ **noun** HOSTILITY, antagonism, animosity, aversion, animus, enmity, dislike, distaste, hatred, hate, abhorrence, loathing.
– OPPOSITES liking, affinity.

antiquated ▶ **adjective** OUTDATED, out of date, outmoded, outworn, behind the times, old-fashioned, anachronistic, old-fangled, passé, démodé; *informal* out of the ark, mouldy; *N. Amer. informal* horse and buggy, mossy, clunky.
– OPPOSITES modern, up to date.

antique ▶ **noun** COLLECTOR'S ITEM, period piece, antiquity, object of virtu, objet d'art.
▶ **adjective** ❶ *antique furniture* OLD, antiquarian, collectable. ❷ *statues of antique gods* ANCIENT, of long ago; *poetic/literary* of yore. ❸ *antique work practices.* See ANTIQUATED.
– OPPOSITES modern, state-of-the-art.

antiquity ▶ **noun** ❶ *the civilizations of antiquity* ANCIENT TIMES, the ancient past, classical times, the distant past. ❷ *Islamic antiquities* ANTIQUE, period piece, collector's item. ❸ *a church of great antiquity* AGE, oldness, ancientness.

antiseptic ▶ **adjective** ❶ *an antiseptic substance* DISINFECTANT, germicidal, bactericidal. ❷ *antiseptic bandages* STERILE, aseptic, germ-free, uncontaminated, disinfected. ❸ *their antiseptic surroundings* CHARACTERLESS, colourless, soulless; clinical, institutional.
– OPPOSITES contaminated.
▶ **noun** DISINFECTANT, germicide, bactericide.

antisocial ▶ **adjective** ❶ *antisocial behaviour* OBJECTIONABLE, offensive, unacceptable, distasteful, disruptive; sociopathic. ❷ *I'm feeling* *a bit antisocial* UNSOCIABLE, unfriendly, uncommunicative, reclusive, misanthropic.

antithesis ▶ **noun** (DIRECT) OPPOSITE, converse, reverse, inverse, obverse, the other side of the coin; *informal* the flip side.

antithetical ▶ **adjective** (DIRECTLY) OPPOSED, contrasting, contrary, contradictory, conflicting, incompatible, irreconcilable, inconsistent, poles apart, at variance/odds; *rare* oppugnant.
– OPPOSITES identical, like.

anxiety ▶ **noun** ❶ *his anxiety grew* WORRY, concern, apprehension, apprehensiveness, uneasiness, unease, fearfulness, fear, disquiet, disquietude, perturbation, agitation, angst, nervousness, nerves, tension, tenseness; *informal* butterflies (in one's stomach), jitteriness, twitchiness, collywobbles, jim-jams. ❷ *an anxiety to please* EAGERNESS, keenness, desire.
– OPPOSITES serenity.

anxious ▶ **adjective** ❶ *I'm anxious about her* WORRIED, concerned, apprehensive, fearful, uneasy, perturbed, troubled, bothered, disturbed, distressed, fretful, agitated, nervous, edgy, unquiet, on edge, tense, overwrought, worked up, keyed up, jumpy, worried sick, with one's stomach in knots, with one's heart in one's mouth; *informal* uptight, on tenterhooks, with butterflies in one's stomach, like a cat on a hot tin roof, jittery, twitchy, in a stew/twitter, all of a dither/lather, in a tizz/tizzy, het up; *Brit. informal* strung up, windy, having kittens, in a (flat) spin, like a cat on hot bricks; *N. Amer. informal* antsy, spooky, squirrelly, in a twit; *Austral./NZ informal* toey; *dated* overstrung. ❷ *she was anxious for news* EAGER, keen, desirous, impatient.
– OPPOSITES carefree, unconcerned.

any ▶ **determiner** ❶ *is there any cake left?* SOME, a piece/part/bit of. ❷ *it doesn't make any difference* THE SLIGHTEST BIT OF, a scrap/shred/jot/whit of, an iota of. ❸ *any job will do* WHICHEVER, no matter which, never mind which; *informal* any old.
▶ **pronoun** *you don't know any of my friends* A SINGLE ONE, (even) one; anyone, anybody.
▶ **adverb** *is your father any better?* AT ALL, in the least, to any extent, in any degree.

anyhow ▶ **adverb** ❶ *anyhow, it doesn't really matter* ANYWAY, in any case/event, at any rate; however, be that as it may; *N. Amer. informal* anyways. ❷ *her clothes were strewn about anyhow* HAPHAZARDLY, carelessly, heedlessly, negligently, in a muddle; *informal* all over the place; *Brit. informal* all over the shop; *N. Amer. informal* all over the lot.

apace ▶ **adverb** (*poetic/literary*) QUICKLY, fast, swiftly, rapidly, speedily, briskly, without delay, post-haste, expeditiously.
– OPPOSITES slowly.

apart ▶ **adverb** ❶ *the villages are two miles apart* AWAY/DISTANT FROM EACH OTHER. ❷ *Isabel stood apart* TO ONE SIDE, aside, separately, alone, by oneself/itself. ❸ *his parents are living apart* SEPARATELY, independently, on one's own. ❹ *the car was blown apart* TO PIECES/BITS, up; *poetic/literary* asunder.
■ **apart from** EXCEPT FOR, but for, aside from, with the exception of, excepting, excluding, bar, barring, besides, other than; *informal* outside of; *formal* save.

apartment ▶ **noun** ❶ *a rented apartment* FLAT, penthouse; *Austral.* home unit; *N. Amer. informal* crib. ❷ *the royal apartments* SUITE (OF ROOMS), rooms, living quarters, accommodation.

apathetic ▶ **adjective** UNINTERESTED, indifferent, unconcerned, unmoved, uninvolved, unemotional, emotionless, dispassionate, lukewarm, unmotivated; *informal* couldn't-care-less; *rare* Laodicean.

apathy ▶ **noun** INDIFFERENCE, lack of interest/enthusiasm/concern, unconcern, uninterestedness, unresponsiveness, impassivity, dispassion, dispassionateness, lethargy, languor, ennui, accidie.
– OPPOSITES enthusiasm, passion.

ape ▶ **noun** PRIMATE, simian; monkey; *technical* anthropoid.
▶ **verb** *he aped Barbara's accent* IMITATE, mimic, copy, do an impression of; *informal* take off, send up; *archaic* monkey.

aperture ▶ **noun** OPENING, hole, gap, slit, slot, vent, crevice, chink, crack, interstice; *technical* orifice, foramen.

apex ▶ **noun** ❶ *the apex of a pyramid* TIP, peak, summit, pinnacle, top, vertex. ❷ *the apex of his career* CLIMAX, culmination, apotheosis; peak, pinnacle, zenith, acme, apogee, high(est) point.
– RELATED TERMS apical.
– OPPOSITES bottom, nadir.

aphorism ▶ **noun** SAYING, maxim, axiom, adage, epigram, dictum, gnome, proverb, saw, tag, apophthegm.

aphrodisiac ▶ **noun** LOVE POTION, philtre.
▶ **adjective** EROTIC, sexy, sexually arousing.

apiece ▶ **adverb** EACH, respectively, per item; *informal* a throw.

aplenty ▶ **adjective** IN ABUNDANCE, in profusion, galore, in large quantities/numbers, by the dozen; *informal* a gogo, by the truckload.

aplomb ▶ **noun** POISE, self-assurance, self-confidence, calmness, composure, collectedness, level-headedness, sangfroid, equilibrium, equanimity; *informal* unflappability.

apocryphal ▶ **adjective** FICTITIOUS, made-up, untrue, fabricated, false, spurious; unverified, unauthenticated, unsubstantiated.
– OPPOSITES authentic.

apologetic ▶ **adjective** REGRETFUL, sorry, contrite, remorseful, penitent, repentant; conscience-stricken, shamefaced, ashamed.
– OPPOSITES unrepentant.

apologia ▶ noun DEFENCE, justification, vindication, explanation; argument, case.

apologist ▶ noun DEFENDER, supporter, upholder, advocate, proponent, exponent, propagandist, champion, campaigner.
– OPPOSITES critic.

apologize ▶ verb SAY SORRY, express regret, be apologetic, make an apology, ask forgiveness, ask for pardon, eat humble pie.

apology ▶ noun ❶ *I owe you an apology* EXPRESSION OF REGRET, one's regrets; *Austral./NZ informal* beg-pardon; *poetic/literary* amende honorable. ❷ (*informal*) *an apology for a flat* TRAVESTY, inadequate/poor example; *informal* excuse.

apoplectic ▶ adjective (*informal*) FURIOUS, enraged, infuriated, incensed, raging; incandescent, fuming, seething; *informal* (hopping) mad, livid, as cross as two sticks, foaming at the mouth, fit to be tied; *poetic/literary* wrathful.

apostate ▶ noun DISSENTER, heretic, defector, turncoat; *archaic* recreant; *rare* tergiversator.
– OPPOSITES follower.

apostle ▶ noun ❶ *the 12 apostles* DISCIPLE, follower. ❷ *the apostles of the Slavs* MISSIONARY, evangelist, proselytizer. ❸ *an apostle of capitalism* ADVOCATE, apologist, proponent, exponent, promoter, supporter, upholder, champion; *N. Amer.* booster.

apotheosis ▶ noun CULMINATION, climax, peak, pinnacle, zenith, acme, apogee, high(est) point.
– OPPOSITES nadir.

appal ▶ verb HORRIFY, shock, dismay, distress, outrage, scandalize; disgust, repel, revolt, sicken, nauseate, offend, make someone's blood run cold.

appalling ▶ adjective ❶ *an appalling crime* SHOCKING, horrific, horrifying, horrible, terrible, awful, dreadful, ghastly, hideous, horrendous, frightful, atrocious, abominable, abhorrent, outrageous, gruesome, grisly, monstrous, heinous, egregious. ❷ (*informal*) *your schoolwork is appalling* DREADFUL, awful, terrible, frightful, atrocious, disgraceful, deplorable, hopeless, lamentable; *informal* rotten, crummy, pathetic, pitiful, woeful, useless, lousy, abysmal, dire; *Brit. informal* chronic, shocking.

apparatus ▶ noun ❶ *laboratory apparatus* EQUIPMENT, gear, rig, tackle, gadgetry; appliance, instrument, machine, mechanism, device, contraption. ❷ *the apparatus of government* STRUCTURE, system, framework, organization, network.

apparel ▶ noun (*formal*) CLOTHES, clothing, garments, dress, attire, wear, garb; *informal* gear, togs, duds; *Brit. informal* clobber, kit; *N. Amer. informal* threads; *archaic* raiment, habit, habiliments.

apparent ▶ adjective ❶ *their relief was all too apparent* EVIDENT, plain, obvious, clear, manifest, visible, discernible, perceptible; unmistakable, crystal clear, palpable, patent, blatant, as plain as a pikestaff, writ large; *informal* as plain as the nose on one's face, written all over one's face. ❷ *his apparent lack of concern* SEEMING, ostensible, outward, superficial; supposed, alleged, professed.
– OPPOSITES unclear.

apparently ▶ adverb SEEMINGLY, evidently, it seems/appears (that), as far as one knows, by all accounts; ostensibly, outwardly, on the face of it, so the story goes, so I'm told; allegedly, reputedly.

apparition ▶ noun ❶ *a monstrous apparition* GHOST, phantom, spectre, spirit, wraith; vision, hallucination; *informal* spook; *poetic/literary* phantasm, revenant, shade, visitant, wight; *rare* eidolon. ❷ *the apparition of a strange man* APPEARANCE, manifestation, materialization, emergence; visitation.

appeal ▶ verb ❶ *police are appealing for information* ASK URGENTLY/EARNESTLY, make an urgent/earnest request, call, make a plea, plead. ❷ *Andrew appealed to me to help them* IMPLORE, beg, entreat, call on, plead with, exhort, ask, request, petition; *formal* adjure; *poetic/literary* beseech. ❸ *the thought of travelling appealed to me* ATTRACT, be attractive to, interest, take someone's fancy, fascinate, tempt, entice, allure, lure, draw, whet someone's appetite; *informal* float someone's boat.
▶ noun ❶ *an appeal for help* PLEA, urgent/earnest request, entreaty, cry, call, petition, supplication, cri de cœur; *rare* obsecration. ❷ *the cultural appeal of the island* ATTRACTION, attractiveness, allure, charm; fascination, magnetism, drawing power, pull. ❸ *the court allowed the appeal* RETRIAL, re-examination.

appealing ▶ adjective ATTRACTIVE, engaging, alluring, enchanting, captivating, bewitching, fascinating, tempting, enticing, seductive, irresistible, winning, winsome, charming, desirable; *Brit. informal* tasty; *dated* taking.
– OPPOSITES disagreeable, off-putting.

appear ▶ verb ❶ *a cloud of dust appeared on the horizon* BECOME VISIBLE, come into view/sight, materialize, pop up. ❷ *fundamental differences were beginning to appear* BE REVEALED, emerge, surface, manifest itself, become apparent/evident, come to light; arise, crop up. ❸ (*informal*) *Bill still hadn't appeared* ARRIVE, turn up, put in an appearance, come, get here/there; *informal* show (up), pitch up, fetch up, roll in, blow in. ❹ *they appeared to be completely devoted* SEEM, look, give the impression, come across as, strike someone as. ❺ *the paperback edition didn't appear for two years* BECOME AVAILABLE, come on the market, go on sale, come out, be published, be produced. ❻ *he appeared on Broadway* PERFORM, play, act.
– OPPOSITES vanish.

appearance ▶ noun ❶ *her dishevelled appearance* LOOK(S), air, aspect, mien. ❷ *an appearance of respectability* IMPRESSION, air, (outward) show; semblance, facade, veneer, front, pretence. ❸ *the sudden appearance of her daughter* ARRIVAL, advent, coming, emergence, materialization. ❹ *the appearance of these symptoms* OCCURRENCE, manifestation, development.

appease ▶ verb ❶ *an attempt to appease his critics* CONCILIATE, placate, pacify, propitiate, reconcile, win over; *informal* sweeten. ❷ *I'd wasted a lot of money to appease my vanity* SATISFY, fulfil, gratify, indulge; assuage, relieve, take the edge off.
–OPPOSITES provoke, inflame.

appeasement ▶ noun ❶ *a policy of appeasement* CONCILIATION, placation, pacification, propitiation, reconciliation; peacemaking, peace-mongering. ❷ *appeasement for battered consciences* SATISFACTION, fulfilment, gratification, indulgence; assuagement, relief.
–OPPOSITES provocation.

appellation ▶ noun (*formal*) NAME, title, designation, tag, sobriquet, byname, nickname, cognomen; *informal* moniker, handle; *formal* denomination.

append ▶ verb ADD, attach, affix, tack on, tag on; *formal* subjoin.

appendage ▶ noun ❶ *I am not just an appendage to the family* ADDITION, attachment, adjunct, addendum, appurtenance, accessory. ❷ *a pair of feathery appendages* PROTUBERANCE, projection; *technical* process.

appendix ▶ noun SUPPLEMENT, addendum, postscript, codicil; coda, epilogue, afterword, tailpiece, back matter.

appertain
■ **appertain to** PERTAIN TO, be pertinent to, apply to, relate to, concern, be concerned with, have to do with, be relevant to, have reference to, have a bearing on, bear on; *archaic* regard.

appetite ▶ noun ❶ *a walk sharpens the appetite* HUNGER, ravenousness, hungriness; taste, palate; *rare* edacity. ❷ *my appetite for learning* CRAVING, longing, yearning, hankering, hunger, thirst, passion; enthusiasm, keenness, eagerness, desire; *informal* yen; *archaic* appetency.

appetizer ▶ noun STARTER, first course, hors d'oeuvre, amuse-gueule, antipasto.

appetizing ▶ adjective ❶ *an appetizing lunch* MOUTH-WATERING, inviting, tempting; tasty, delicious, flavoursome, toothsome, delectable; *informal* scrumptious, scrummy, yummy, moreish. ❷ *the least appetizing part of election campaigns* APPEALING, attractive, inviting, alluring.
–OPPOSITES bland, unappealing.

applaud ▶ verb ❶ *the audience applauded* CLAP, give a standing ovation, put one's hands together; show one's appreciation; *informal* give someone a big hand. ❷ *police have applauded the decision* PRAISE, commend, acclaim, salute, welcome, celebrate, express admiration for, express approval of, look on with favour, approve of, sing the praises of, pay tribute to, speak highly of, take one's hat off to, express respect for.
–OPPOSITES boo, criticize.

applause ▶ noun ❶ *a massive round of applause* CLAPPING, handclapping, (standing) ovation; acclamation. ❷ *the museum's design won general applause* PRAISE, acclaim, acclamation, admiration, commendation, adulation, favour, approbation, approval, respect; compliments, accolades, tributes.

appliance ▶ noun ❶ *domestic appliances* DEVICE, machine, instrument, gadget, contraption, apparatus, utensil, implement, tool, mechanism, contrivance, labour-saving device; *informal* gizmo, mod con. ❷ *the appliance of science* APPLICATION, use, exercise, employment, implementation, utilization, practice, applying, discharge, execution, prosecution, enactment; *formal* praxis.

applicable ▶ adjective *the laws applicable to the dispute* RELEVANT, appropriate, pertinent, appurtenant, apposite, germane, material, significant, related, connected; fitting, suitable, apt, befitting, to the point, useful, helpful; *formal* ad rem.
–OPPOSITES inappropriate, irrelevant.

applicant ▶ noun CANDIDATE, interviewee, competitor, contestant, contender, entrant; claimant, suppliant, supplicant, petitioner, postulant; prospective student/employee, jobseeker, job-hunter, auditioner.

application ▶ noun ❶ *an application for an overdraft* REQUEST, appeal, petition, entreaty, plea, solicitation, supplication, requisition, suit, approach, claim, demand. ❷ *the application of anti-inflation policies* IMPLEMENTATION, use, exercise, employment, utilization, practice, applying, discharge, execution, prosecution, enactment; *formal* praxis. ❸ *the argument is clearest in its application to the theatre* RELEVANCE, relevancy, bearing, significance, pertinence, aptness, appositeness, germaneness, importance. ❹ *the application of make-up* PUTTING ON, rubbing in, applying. ❺ *an application to relieve muscle pain* OINTMENT, lotion, cream, rub, salve, emollient, preparation, liniment, embrocation, balm, unguent, poultice. ❻ *the job takes a great deal of application* DILIGENCE, industriousness, industry, assiduity, commitment, dedication, devotion, conscientiousness, perseverance, persistence, tenacity, doggedness, sedulousness; concentration, attention, attentiveness, steadiness, patience, endurance; effort, hard work, labour, endeavour. ❼ *a vector graphics application* PROGRAM, software, routine.

apply ▸ verb ❶ *300 people applied for the job* PUT IN AN APPLICATION, put in, try, bid, appeal, petition, sue, register, audition; request, seek, solicit, claim, ask, try to obtain. ❷ *the Act did not apply to Scotland* BE RELEVANT, have relevance, have a bearing, appertain, pertain, relate, concern, affect, involve, cover, deal with, touch; be pertinent, be appropriate, be significant. ❸ *she applied some ointment* PUT ON, rub in, work in, spread, smear. ❹ *a steady pressure should be applied* EXERT, administer, implement, use, exercise, employ, utilize, bring to bear.

■ **apply oneself** BE DILIGENT, be industrious, be assiduous, show commitment, show dedication; work hard, exert oneself, make an effort, try hard, do one's best, give one's all, buckle down, put one's shoulder to the wheel, keep one's nose to the grindstone; strive, endeavour, struggle, labour, toil; pay attention, commit oneself, devote oneself; persevere, persist; *informal* put one's back in it, knuckle down, get stuck in.

appoint ▸ verb ❶ *he was appointed chairman* NOMINATE, name, designate, install as, commission, engage, co-opt; select, choose, elect, vote in; *Military* detail. ❷ *the arbitrator shall appoint a date for the meeting* SPECIFY, determine, assign, designate, allot, set, fix, arrange, choose, decide on, establish, settle, ordain, prescribe, decree.
– OPPOSITES reject.

appointed ▸ adjective ❶ *at the appointed time* SCHEDULED, arranged, pre-arranged, specified, decided, agreed, determined, assigned, designated, allotted, set, fixed, chosen, established, settled, preordained, ordained, prescribed, decreed. ❷ *a well appointed room* FURNISHED, decorated, outfitted, fitted out, provided, supplied.

appointment ▸ noun ❶ *a six o'clock appointment* MEETING, engagement, interview, arrangement, consultation, session; date, rendezvous, assignation; commitment, fixture; *poetic/literary* tryst. ❷ *the appointment of directors* NOMINATION, naming, designation, installation, commissioning, engagement, co-option; selection, choosing, election, voting in; *Military* detailing. ❸ *he held an appointment at the university* JOB, post, position, situation, employment, place, office; *dated* station.

apportion ▸ verb SHARE, divide, allocate, distribute, allot, assign, give out, hand out, mete out, deal out, dish out, dole out; ration, measure out; split; *informal* divvy up.

apposite ▸ adjective APPROPRIATE, suitable, fitting, apt, befitting; relevant, pertinent, appurtenant, to the point, applicable, germane, material, congruous, felicitous; *formal* ad rem.
– OPPOSITES inappropriate.

appraisal ▸ noun ❶ *an objective appraisal of the book* ASSESSMENT, evaluation, estimation, judgement, rating, gauging, sizing up, summing-up, consideration. ❷ *a free insurance appraisal* VALUATION, estimate, estimation, quotation, pricing; survey.

appraise ▸ verb ❶ *they appraised their handiwork* ASSESS, evaluate, judge, rate, gauge, review, consider; *informal* size up. ❷ *his goods were appraised at £1,800* VALUE, price, estimate, quote; survey.

appreciable ▸ adjective CONSIDERABLE, substantial, significant, sizeable, goodly, fair, reasonable, marked; perceptible, noticeable, visible; *informal* tidy.
– OPPOSITES negligible.

appreciate ▸ verb ❶ *I'd appreciate your advice* BE GRATEFUL, be thankful, be obliged, be indebted, be in your debt, be appreciative. ❷ *the college appreciated her greatly* VALUE, treasure, admire, respect, hold in high regard, think highly of, think much of. ❸ *we appreciate the problems* RECOGNIZE, acknowledge, realize, know, be aware of, be conscious of, be sensitive to, understand, comprehend; *informal* be wise to. ❹ *a home that will appreciate in value* INCREASE, gain, grow, rise, go up, escalate, soar, rocket.
– OPPOSITES disparage, depreciate, decrease.

appreciation ▸ noun ❶ *he showed his appreciation* GRATITUDE, thanks, gratefulness, thankfulness, recognition, sense of obligation. ❷ *her appreciation of literature* VALUING, treasuring, admiration, respect, regard, esteem, high opinion. ❸ *an appreciation of the value of teamwork* ACKNOWLEDGEMENT, recognition, realization, knowledge, awareness, consciousness, understanding, comprehension. ❹ *the appreciation of the franc against the pound* INCREASE, gain, growth, rise, inflation, escalation. ❺ *an appreciation of the professor's work* REVIEW, critique, criticism, critical analysis, assessment, evaluation, judgement, rating; *Brit. informal* crit.
– OPPOSITES ingratitude, unawareness, depreciation, decrease.

appreciative ▸ adjective ❶ *we are appreciative of all your efforts* GRATEFUL, thankful, obliged, indebted, in someone's debt. ❷ *an appreciative audience* SUPPORTIVE, encouraging, sympathetic, responsive; enthusiastic, admiring, approving, complimentary.
– OPPOSITES ungrateful, disparaging.

apprehend ▸ verb ❶ *the thieves were quickly apprehended* ARREST, catch, capture, seize; take prisoner, take into custody, detain, put in jail, put behind bars, imprison, incarcerate; *informal* collar, nab, nail, run in, pinch, bust, pick up, pull in, feel someone's collar; *Brit. informal* nick, do. ❷ *they are slow to apprehend danger* APPRECIATE, recognize, discern, perceive, make out, take in, realize, grasp, understand, comprehend; *informal* get the picture; *Brit. informal* twig, suss (out).

apprehension ▸ noun ❶ *he was filled with*

apprehension ANXIETY, worry, unease, nervousness, nerves, misgivings, disquiet, concern, tension, trepidation, perturbation, consternation, angst, dread, fear, foreboding; *informal* butterflies, the willies, the heebie-jeebies. ❷ *her quick apprehension of their wishes* APPRECIATION, recognition, discernment, perception, realization, grasp, understanding, comprehension, awareness. ❸ *the apprehension of a perpetrator* ARREST, capture, seizure; detention, imprisonment, incarceration; *informal* collar, nabbing, bust; *Brit. informal* nick.
– OPPOSITES confidence.

apprehensive ▶ **adjective** ANXIOUS, worried, uneasy, nervous, concerned, agitated, tense, afraid, scared, frightened, fearful; *informal* on tenterhooks.
– OPPOSITES confident.

apprentice ▶ **noun** TRAINEE, learner, probationer, novice, beginner, starter; pupil, student; *N. Amer.* tenderfoot; *informal* rookie; *N. Amer. informal* greenhorn.
– OPPOSITES veteran.

apprenticeship ▶ **noun** TRAINEESHIP, training period, studentship, novitiate; *historical* indentureship.

apprise ▶ **verb** INFORM, tell, notify, advise, brief, make aware, enlighten, update, keep posted; *informal* clue in, fill in, put wise, put in the picture.

approach ▶ **verb** ❶ *she approached the altar* MOVE TOWARDS, come/go towards, advance towards, go/come/draw/move nearer, go/come/draw/move closer, near; close in, gain on; reach, arrive at. ❷ *the trade deficit is approaching £20 million* BORDER ON, verge on, approximate, touch, nudge, get on for, near, come near to, come close to. ❸ *she approached him about leaving his job* SPEAK TO, talk to; make advances, make overtures, make a proposal, sound out, proposition. ❹ *he approached the problem in the best way* TACKLE, set about, address oneself to, undertake, get down to, launch into, embark on, go about, get to grips with.
– OPPOSITES leave.

▶ **noun** ❶ *the traditional British approach* METHOD, procedure, technique, modus operandi, MO, style, way, manner; strategy, tactic, system, means, line of action. ❷ *he considered an approach to the High Court* PROPOSAL, proposition, submission, application, appeal, plea, request. ❸ (*dated*) *his approaches were repulsed* ADVANCES, overtures, suggestions, attentions; suit. ❹ *the dog barked at the approach of any intruder* ADVANCE, coming, nearing; arrival, appearance; advent. ❺ *the approach to the castle* DRIVEWAY, drive, access road, road, avenue; way.

approachable ▶ **adjective** ❶ *students found the staff approachable* FRIENDLY, welcoming, pleasant, agreeable, congenial, affable, cordial; obliging, communicative, helpful. ❷ *the south landing is approachable by boat* ACCESSIBLE, attainable, reachable; *informal* get-at-able.
– OPPOSITES aloof, inaccessible.

approbation ▶ **noun** APPROVAL, acceptance, endorsement, appreciation, respect, admiration, commendation, praise, congratulations, acclaim, esteem, applause.
– OPPOSITES criticism.

appropriate ▶ **adjective** *this isn't the appropriate time* SUITABLE, proper, fitting, apt, right; relevant, pertinent, apposite; convenient, opportune; seemly, befitting; *formal* ad rem; *archaic* meet.
– OPPOSITES unsuitable.

▶ **verb** ❶ *the barons appropriated church lands* SEIZE, commandeer, expropriate, annex, arrogate, sequestrate, sequester, take over, hijack; steal, take; *informal* swipe, nab, bag; *Brit. informal* pinch, half-inch, nick. ❷ *his images have been appropriated by advertisers* PLAGIARIZE, copy; poach, steal, 'borrow'; *informal* rip off. ❸ *we are appropriating funds for these expenses* ALLOCATE, assign, allot, earmark, set aside, devote, apportion.

approval ▶ **noun** ❶ *their proposals went to the ministry for approval* ACCEPTANCE, agreement, consent, assent, permission, leave, the nod; rubber stamp, sanction, endorsement, ratification, authorization, validation; support, backing; *informal* the go-ahead, the green light, the OK, the thumbs up. ❷ *Lily looked at him with approval* APPROBATION, appreciation, favour, liking, admiration, regard, esteem, respect, praise. ❸ *we will send you the goods on approval* TRIAL, sale or return; *Brit. informal* appro.
– OPPOSITES refusal, dislike.

approve ▶ **verb** ❶ *his boss doesn't approve of his lifestyle* AGREE WITH, hold with, endorse, support, back, uphold, subscribe to, recommend, advocate, be in favour of, favour, think well of, like, appreciate, take kindly to; be pleased with, admire, applaud, praise. ❷ *the government approved the proposals* ACCEPT, agree to, consent to, assent to, give one's blessing to, bless, rubber-stamp, give the nod; ratify, sanction, endorse, authorize, validate, pass; support, back; *informal* give the go-ahead, give the green light, give the OK, give the thumbs-up.
– OPPOSITES condemn, refuse.

approximate ▶ **adjective** *all measurements are approximate* ESTIMATED, rough, imprecise, inexact, indefinite, broad, loose; *N. Amer. informal* ballpark.
– OPPOSITES precise.

▶ **verb** *this scenario probably approximates to the truth* BE/COME CLOSE TO, be/come near to, approach, border on, verge on; resemble, be similar to, be not unlike.

approximately ▶ **adverb** ROUGHLY, about, around, circa, round about, more or less, in the neighbourhood of, in the region of, of the

order of, something like, give or take (a few); near to, close to, nearly, almost, approaching; *Brit.* getting on for; *informal* pushing; *N. Amer. informal* in the ballpark of.
– OPPOSITES precisely.

approximation ▶ noun ❶ *the figure is only an approximation* ESTIMATE, estimation, guess, rough calculation; *informal* guesstimate; *N. Amer. informal* ballpark figure. ❷ *an approximation to the truth* SEMBLANCE, resemblance, likeness, similarity, correspondence.

appurtenances ▶ plural noun ACCESSORIES, trappings, appendages, accoutrements, equipment, paraphernalia, impedimenta, bits and pieces, things; *informal* stuff.

a priori ▶ adjective *a priori reasoning* THEORETICAL, deduced, deductive, inferred, postulated, suppositional; scientific.
– OPPOSITES empirical.
▶ adverb *the results cannot be predicted a priori* THEORETICALLY, deductively, scientifically.

apron ▶ noun PINAFORE, overall; *informal* pinny.

apropos ▶ preposition *he was asked a question apropos his resignation* WITH REFERENCE TO, with regard to, with respect to, regarding, concerning, on the subject of, connected with, about, re.
▶ adjective *the word 'conglomerate' was decidedly apropos* APPROPRIATE, pertinent, relevant, apposite, apt, applicable, suitable, germane, material.
– OPPOSITES inappropriate.
■ **apropos of nothing** IRRELEVANTLY, arbitrarily, at random, for no reason, illogically.

apt ▶ adjective ❶ *a very apt description of how I felt* SUITABLE, fitting, appropriate, befitting, relevant, applicable, apposite; *Brit. informal* spot on. ❷ *they are apt to get a mite slipshod* INCLINED, given, likely, liable, disposed, predisposed, prone. ❸ *an apt pupil* CLEVER, quick, bright, sharp, smart, intelligent, able, gifted, adept, astute.
– OPPOSITES inappropriate, unlikely, slow.

aptitude ▶ noun TALENT, gift, flair, bent, skill, knack, facility, ability, capability, potential, capacity, faculty, genius.

aquatic ▶ adjective MARINE, water, saltwater, freshwater, seawater, sea, oceanic, river; *technical* pelagic, thalassic.

aqueduct ▶ noun CONDUIT, race, channel, watercourse, sluice, sluiceway, spillway; bridge, viaduct.

aquiline ▶ adjective HOOKED, curved, bent, angular; beak-like.

arable ▶ adjective FARMABLE, cultivable, cultivatable; fertile, productive, fecund.

arbiter ▶ noun ❶ *an arbiter between Moscow and Washington. See* ARBITRATOR. ❷ *the great arbiter of fashion* AUTHORITY, judge, controller, director; master, expert, pundit.

arbitrary ▶ adjective ❶ *an arbitrary decision* CAPRICIOUS, whimsical, random, chance, unpredictable; casual, wanton, unmotivated, motiveless, unreasoned, unsupported, irrational, illogical, groundless, unjustified. ❷ *the arbitrary power of a prince* AUTOCRATIC, dictatorial, autarchic, undemocratic, despotic, tyrannical, authoritarian; absolute, uncontrolled, unlimited, unrestrained.
– OPPOSITES reasoned, democratic.

arbitrate ▶ verb ADJUDICATE, judge, referee, umpire; mediate, conciliate, intervene, intercede; settle, decide, resolve, pass judgement.

arbitration ▶ noun ADJUDICATION, judgement, arbitrament; mediation, mediatorship, conciliation, intervention, interposition.

arbitrator ▶ noun ADJUDICATOR, arbiter, judge, referee, umpire; mediator, conciliator, intervenor, intercessor, go-between.

arbour ▶ noun BOWER, alcove, grotto, recess, pergola, gazebo.

arc ▶ noun *the arc of a circle* CURVE, arch, crescent, semicircle, half-moon; curvature, convexity.
▶ verb *I sent the ball arcing out over the river* CURL, curve; arch.

arcade ▶ noun ❶ *a classical arcade* GALLERY, colonnade, cloister, loggia, portico, peristyle, stoa. ❷ *she went to a cafe in the arcade* (*Brit.*) SHOPPING CENTRE, shopping precinct; *N. Amer.* plaza, mall, shopping mall.

arcane ▶ adjective MYSTERIOUS, secret, covert, clandestine; enigmatic, esoteric, obscure, abstruse, recondite, recherché, impenetrable, opaque.

arch[1] ▶ noun ❶ *a stone arch* ARCHWAY, vault, span, dome. ❷ *the arch of his spine* CURVE, bow, bend, arc, curvature, convexity; hunch, crook.
▶ verb *she arched her eyebrows* CURVE, arc; raise.

arch[2] ▶ adjective *an arch grin* MISCHIEVOUS, teasing, saucy, knowing, playful, roguish, impish, cheeky, tongue-in-cheek.

arch- ▶ combining form *his arch-enemy* CHIEF, principal, foremost, leading, main, major, prime, premier, greatest; *informal* number-one.
– OPPOSITES minor.

archaic ▶ adjective OBSOLETE, out of date, old-fashioned, outmoded, behind the times, bygone, anachronistic, antiquated, superannuated, antediluvian, olde worlde, old-fangled; ancient, old, extinct, defunct; *informal* out of the arc; *poetic/literary* of yore.
– OPPOSITES modern.

arched ▶ adjective VAULTED, domed, curved, bowed; *poetic/literary* embowed.

archer ▶ noun BOWMAN.
– RELATED TERMS toxophily.

archetypal ▶ adjective QUINTESSENTIAL, clas-

sic, most typical, representative, model, exemplary, textbook, copybook; stock, stereotypical, prototypical.
– OPPOSITES atypical.

archetype ▶ noun QUINTESSENCE, essence, typification, representative, model, embodiment, prototype, stereotype; original, pattern, standard, paradigm.

architect ▶ noun ❶ *the architect of Durham Cathedral* DESIGNER, planner, draughtsman. ❷ *the architect of the National Health Service* ORIGINATOR, author, creator, founder, (founding) father; engineer, inventor, mastermind; *poetic/literary* begetter.

architecture ▶ noun ❶ *modern architecture* BUILDING DESIGN, building style, planning, building, construction; *formal* architectonics. ❷ *the architecture of a computer system* STRUCTURE, construction, organization, layout, design, build, anatomy, make-up; *informal* set-up.

archive ▶ noun ❶ *she delved into the family archives* RECORDS, annals, chronicles, accounts; papers, documents, files; history; *Law* muniments. ❷ *the National Sound Archive* RECORD OFFICE, registry, repository, museum, chancery.
▶ verb *the videos are archived for future use* FILE, log, catalogue, document, record, register; store, cache.

arctic ▶ adjective ❶ *Arctic waters* POLAR, far northern; *poetic/literary* hyperborean; *technical* boreal. ❷ *arctic weather conditions* (BITTERLY) COLD, wintry, freezing, frozen, icy, glacial, gelid, sub-zero, polar, Siberian.
– OPPOSITES Antarctic, tropical.
▶ noun FAR NORTH, North Pole, Arctic circle.
– OPPOSITES Antarctic.

ardent ▶ adjective PASSIONATE, fervent, zealous, wholehearted, vehement, intense, fierce; enthusiastic, keen, eager, avid, committed, dedicated.
– OPPOSITES apathetic.

ardour ▶ noun PASSION, fervour, zeal, vehemence, intensity, fire, emotion; enthusiasm, eagerness, gusto, keenness, dedication.

arduous ▶ adjective ONEROUS, taxing, difficult, hard, heavy, laborious, burdensome, strenuous, vigorous, back-breaking; demanding, tough, challenging, formidable; exhausting, tiring, punishing, gruelling; *informal* killing; *Brit. informal* knackering; *archaic* toilsome.
– OPPOSITES easy.

area ▶ noun ❶ *an inner-city area* DISTRICT, region, zone, sector, quarter; locality, locale, neighbourhood, parish, patch; tract, belt; *informal* neck of the woods; *Brit. informal* manor; *N. Amer. informal* turf. ❷ *specific areas of scientific knowledge* FIELD, sphere, discipline, realm, domain, sector, province, territory, line. ❸ *the dining area* SECTION, space; place, room. ❹ *the area of a circle* EXPANSE, extent, size, scope, compass; dimensions, proportions.

arena ▶ noun ❶ *an ice-hockey arena* STADIUM, amphitheatre, coliseum; ground, field, ring, rink, pitch, court; *N. Amer.* bowl, park; *historical* circus. ❷ *the political arena* SCENE, sphere, realm, province, domain, sector, forum, territory, world.

argot ▶ noun JARGON, slang, idiom, cant, parlance, vernacular, patois; dialect, speech, language; *informal* lingo.

arguable ▶ adjective ❶ *he had an arguable claim for asylum* TENABLE, defendable, defensible, supportable, sustainable, able to hold water; reasonable, viable, acceptable. ❷ *it is arguable whether these routes are worthwhile* DEBATABLE, questionable, open to question, controversial, contentious, doubtful, uncertain, moot.
– OPPOSITES untenable, certain.

arguably ▶ adverb POSSIBLY, conceivably, feasibly, plausibly, probably, maybe, perhaps.

argue ▶ verb ❶ *they argued that the government was to blame* CONTEND, assert, maintain, insist, hold, claim, reason, swear, allege; *Law* depose; *formal* aver, represent, opine. ❷ *the children are always arguing* QUARREL, disagree, row, squabble, fall out, bicker, fight, wrangle, dispute, feud, have words, cross swords, lock horns, be at each other's throats; *informal* argufy, spat; *archaic* altercate. ❸ *it is hard to argue the point* DISPUTE, debate, discuss, controvert.

argument ▶ noun ❶ *he had an argument with Tony* QUARREL, disagreement, squabble, fight, dispute, wrangle, clash, altercation, feud, contretemps, falling-out, disputation; *informal* tiff, barney, slanging match; *Brit. informal* row. ❷ *arguments for the existence of God* REASONING, justification, explanation, rationalization; case, defence, vindication; evidence, reasons, grounds. ❸ (*archaic*) *the argument of the book* THEME, topic, subject matter; summary, synopsis, precis, gist, outline.

argumentative ▶ adjective QUARRELSOME, disputatious, captious, contrary, cantankerous, contentious; belligerent, bellicose, combative, antagonistic, truculent, pugnacious; *rare* oppugnant.

arid ▶ adjective ❶ *an arid landscape* DRY, dried up, waterless, moistureless, parched, scorched, baked, thirsty, droughty, desert; BARREN, infertile. ❷ *this town has an arid, empty feel* DREARY, dull, drab, dry, sterile, colourless, unstimulating, uninspiring, flat, boring, uninteresting, lifeless.
– OPPOSITES wet, fertile, vibrant.

aright ▶ adverb (*dated*) CORRECTLY, rightly, right, all right; accurately, properly, precisely, perfectly; *informal* OK.

arise ▶ verb ❶ *many problems arose* COME TO LIGHT, become apparent, appear, emerge, crop up, turn up, surface, spring up; occur; *poetic/literary* befall, come to pass. ❷ *injuries arising from defective products* RESULT, proceed, follow, ensue, derive, stem, originate; be caused by. ❸ (*formal*) *the beast arose* STAND UP, rise, get to one's feet, get up.

aristocracy ▶ noun NOBILITY, peerage, gentry, upper class, ruling class, elite, high society, establishment, haut monde; aristocrats, lords, ladies, peers (of the realm), nobles, noblemen, noblewomen; *informal* upper crust, top drawer, aristos; *Brit. informal* nobs, toffs.
– OPPOSITES working class.

aristocrat ▶ noun NOBLEMAN, noblewoman, lord, lady, peer (of the realm), peeress, grandee; *informal* aristo; *Brit. informal* toff, nob.
– OPPOSITES commoner.

aristocratic ▶ adjective ❶ *an aristocratic family* NOBLE, titled, upper-class, blue-blooded, high-born, well born, elite; *Brit.* upmarket; *informal* upper crust, top drawer; *Brit. informal* posh; *archaic* gentle. ❷ *an aristocratic manner* REFINED, polished, courtly, dignified, decorous, gracious, fine, gentlemanly, ladylike; haughty, proud.
– OPPOSITES working-class, vulgar.

arm[1] ▶ noun ❶ *the arm of her jacket* SLEEVE. ❷ *an arm of the sea* INLET, creek, cove, fjord, bay, voe; estuary, firth, strait(s), sound, channel. ❸ *the political arm of the group* BRANCH, section, department, division, wing, sector, detachment, offshoot, extension. ❹ *the long arm of the law* REACH, power, authority, influence.

arm[2] ▶ verb ❶ *he armed himself with a revolver* EQUIP, provide, supply, furnish, issue, fit out. ❷ *arm yourself against criticism* PREPARE, forearm, make ready, brace, steel, fortify.

armada ▶ noun FLEET, flotilla, squadron; *poetic/literary* navy.

armaments ▶ plural noun ARMS, weapons, weaponry, firearms, guns, ordnance, artillery, munitions, materiel.

armistice ▶ noun TRUCE, ceasefire, peace, suspension of hostilities.

armour ▶ noun PROTECTIVE COVERING, armour plate; *historical* chain mail, coat of mail, panoply.

armoured ▶ adjective ARMOUR-PLATED, steel-plated, ironclad; bulletproof, bombproof; reinforced, toughened.

armoury ▶ noun ARSENAL, arms depot, arms cache, ordnance depot, magazine, ammunition dump.

arms ▶ plural noun ❶ *the illegal export of arms* WEAPONS, weaponry, firearms, guns, ordnance, artillery, armaments, munitions, materiel. ❷ *the family arms* CREST, emblem, coat of arms, heraldic device, insignia, escutcheon, shield.
– RELATED TERMS heraldic.

army ▶ noun ❶ *the invading army* ARMED FORCE, military force, land force, military, soldiery, infantry, militia; troops, soldiers; *archaic* host. ❷ *an army of tourists* CROWD, swarm, multitude, horde, mob, gang, throng, mass, flock, herd, pack.
– RELATED TERMS military, martial.

aroma ▶ noun SMELL, odour, fragrance, scent, perfume, bouquet, nose; *poetic/literary* redolence.

aromatic ▶ adjective FRAGRANT, scented, perfumed, fragranced, odoriferous; *poetic/literary* redolent.

around ▶ adverb ❶ *there were houses scattered around* ON EVERY SIDE, on all sides, throughout, all over (the place), everywhere; about, here and there. ❷ *he turned around* IN THE OPPOSITE DIRECTION, to face the other way, backwards, to the rear. ❸ *there was no one around* NEARBY, near, about, close by, close (at hand), at hand, in the vicinity, at close range.
▶ preposition ❶ *the palazzo is built around a courtyard* ON ALL SIDES OF, about, encircling, surrounding. ❷ *they drove around town* ABOUT, all over, in/to all parts of. ❸ *around three miles* APPROXIMATELY, about, round about, circa, roughly, something like, more or less, in the region of, in the neighbourhood of, give or take (a few); nearly, close to, approaching; *Brit.* getting on for; *N. Amer. informal* in the ballpark of.

arouse ▶ verb ❶ *they had aroused his suspicion* INDUCE, prompt, trigger, stir up, bring out, kindle, fire, spark off, provoke, engender, cause, foster; *poetic/literary* enkindle. ❷ *his ability to arouse the masses* STIR UP, rouse, galvanize, excite, electrify, stimulate, inspire, inspirit, move, fire up, whip up, get going, inflame, agitate, goad, incite. ❸ *his touch aroused her* EXCITE, stimulate (sexually), titillate; *informal* turn on, get going, give a thrill to, light someone's fire. ❹ *she was aroused from her sleep* WAKE (UP), awaken, bring to/round, rouse; *Brit. informal* knock up; *poetic/literary* waken.
– OPPOSITES allay, pacify, turn off.

arraign ▶ verb ❶ *he was arraigned for murder* INDICT, prosecute, put on trial, bring to trial, take to court, lay/file/prefer charges against, summons, cite; accuse of, charge with; *N. Amer.* impeach; *informal* do; *archaic* inculpate. ❷ *they bitterly arraigned the government* CRITICIZE, censure, attack, condemn, chastise, lambaste, rebuke, admonish, remonstrate with, take to task, berate, reproach; *informal* knock, slam, blast, lay into; *Brit. informal* slate, slag off; *formal* castigate, excoriate.
– OPPOSITES acquit, praise.

arrange ▶ verb ❶ *she arranged the flowers* ORDER, set out, lay out, array, position, dispose, present, display, exhibit; group, sort, organize, tidy. ❷ *they hoped to arrange a meeting* ORGANIZE, fix, plan, schedule, pencil in, contrive, fix up, settle on, decide, determine, agree. ❸ *he arranged the piece for a full orchestra* ADAPT, set, score, orchestrate, instrument.

arrangement ▶ noun ❶ *the arrangement of*

the furniture POSITIONING, disposition, order, presentation, display; grouping, organization, alignment. ❷ *the arrangements for my trip* PREPARATION, plan, provision; planning, groundwork. ❸ *we had an arrangement* AGREEMENT, deal, understanding, bargain, settlement, pact, modus vivendi. ❹ *an arrangement of Beethoven's symphonies* ADAPTATION, orchestration, instrumentation.

arrant ▶ **adjective** *what arrant nonsense!* UTTER, complete, total, absolute, downright, outright, thorough, out-and-out, sheer, pure, unmitigated, unqualified; blatant, flagrant; *Brit. informal* right.

array ▶ **noun** ❶ *a huge array of cars* RANGE, collection, selection, assortment, diversity, variety; arrangement, assemblage, line-up, formation; display, exhibition, exposition. ❷ *she arrived in silken array* DRESS, attire, clothing, garb, garments; finery; *formal* apparel.
▶ **verb** ❶ *a buffet was arrayed on the table* ARRANGE, assemble, group, order, range, place, position, set out, lay out, dispose; display. ❷ *he was arrayed in grey flannel* DRESS, attire, clothe, garb, deck (out), outfit, get up, turn out; *archaic* apparel, habit.

arrears ▶ **plural noun** *rent arrears* MONEY OWING, outstanding payment(s), debt(s), liabilities, dues.
– OPPOSITES credit.
■ **in arrears** BEHIND, behindhand, late, overdue, in the red, in debt.

arrest ▶ **verb** ❶ *police arrested him for murder* APPREHEND, take into custody, take prisoner, detain, put in jail; *informal* pick up, pull in, pinch, bust, nab, do, collar; *Brit. informal* nick. ❷ *the spread of the disease can be arrested* STOP, halt, check, block, hinder, restrict, limit, inhibit, impede, curb; prevent, obstruct; *poetic/literary* stay. ❸ *she tried to arrest his attention* ATTRACT, capture, catch, hold, engage; absorb, occupy, engross.
– OPPOSITES release, start.
▶ **noun** ❶ *a warrant for your arrest* DETENTION, apprehension, seizure, capture. ❷ *a cardiac arrest* STOPPAGE, halt, interruption.

arresting ▶ **adjective** *an arresting image* STRIKING, eye-catching, conspicuous, engaging, impressive, imposing, spectacular, dramatic, breathtaking, dazzling, stunning, awe-inspiring; remarkable, outstanding, distinctive.
– OPPOSITES inconspicuous.

arrival ▶ **noun** ❶ *they awaited Ruth's arrival* COMING, appearance, entrance, entry, approach. ❷ *staff greeted the late arrivals* COMER, entrant, incomer; visitor, caller, guest. ❸ *the arrival of democracy* EMERGENCE, appearance, advent, coming, dawn, onset, inauguration, origin, birth.
– OPPOSITES departure, end.

arrive ▶ **verb** ❶ *more police arrived* COME, turn up, get here/there, make it, appear, enter, present oneself, come along, materialize; *informal* show (up), roll in/up, blow in, show one's face. ❷ *we arrived at his house* REACH, get to, come to, make, make it to, gain, end up at; *informal* wind up at. ❸ *they arrived at an agreement* REACH, achieve, attain, gain, accomplish; work out, draw up, put together, strike, settle on; *informal* clinch. ❹ *the wedding finally arrived* HAPPEN, occur, take place, come about; present itself, crop up; *poetic/literary* come to pass. ❺ *quadraphony had arrived* EMERGE, appear, surface, dawn, be born, come into being, arise. ❻ (*informal*) *their Rolls Royce proved that they had arrived* SUCCEED, be a success, do well, reach the top, make good, prosper, thrive; *informal* make it, make one's mark, do all right for oneself.
– OPPOSITES depart, leave.

arriviste ▶ **noun** SOCIAL CLIMBER, status seeker, would-be, self-seeker; upstart, parvenu(e), vulgarian; (**arrivistes**) nouveau riche, new money; *informal* go-getter.

arrogant ▶ **adjective** HAUGHTY, conceited, self-important, egotistic, full of oneself, superior; overbearing, pompous, bumptious, imperious, overweening; proud, immodest; *informal* high and mighty, too big for one's boots, big-headed; *rare* hubristic.
– OPPOSITES modest.

arrogate ▶ **verb** ASSUME, take, claim, appropriate, seize, expropriate, wrest, usurp, commandeer.

arrow ▶ **noun** ❶ *a bow and arrow* SHAFT, bolt, dart; *historical* quarrel. ❷ *the arrow pointed right* POINTER, indicator, marker, needle.

arsenal ▶ **noun** ❶ *Britain's nuclear arsenal* WEAPONS, weaponry, arms, armaments. ❷ *mutineers broke into the arsenal* ARMOURY, arms depot, arms cache, ordnance depot, magazine, ammunition dump.

arson ▶ **noun** INCENDIARISM, pyromania; *Brit.* fire-raising.

arsonist ▶ **noun** INCENDIARY, pyromaniac; *Brit.* fire-raiser; *informal* firebug, pyro; *N. Amer. informal* torch.

art ▶ **noun** ❶ *he studied art* FINE ART, artwork, design. ❷ *the art of writing* SKILL, craft, technique, knack, facility, ability. ❸ *she uses art to achieve her aims* CUNNING, artfulness, slyness, craftiness, guile; deceit, duplicity, artifice, wiles.

artery ▶ **noun** *the main arteries out of town* MAIN ROAD, trunk road, high road, highway.

artful ▶ **adjective** SLY, crafty, cunning, wily, scheming, devious, Machiavellian, sneaky, tricky, conniving, designing, calculating; canny, shrewd; deceitful, duplicitous, disingenuous, underhand; *informal* foxy, shifty; *archaic* subtle.
– OPPOSITES ingenuous.

article ▶ noun ❶ *small household articles* OBJECT, thing, item, artefact, commodity, product. ❷ *an article in The Times* REPORT, account, story, write-up, feature, item, piece (of writing), column, review, commentary. ❸ *the crucial article of the treaty* CLAUSE, section, subsection, point, item, paragraph, division, subdivision, part, portion.

articulate ▶ adjective *an articulate speaker* ELOQUENT, fluent, effective, persuasive, lucid, expressive, silver-tongued; intelligible, comprehensible, understandable.
– OPPOSITES unintelligible.
▶ verb *they were unable to articulate their emotions* EXPRESS, voice, vocalize, put in words, communicate, state; air, ventilate, vent, pour out; utter, say, speak, enunciate, pronounce; *informal* come out with.

articulated ▶ adjective HINGED, jointed, segmented; *technical* articulate.

artifice ▶ noun TRICKERY, deceit, deception, duplicity, guile, cunning, artfulness, wiliness, craftiness, slyness, chicanery; fraud, fraudulence.

artificial ▶ adjective ❶ *artificial flowers* SYNTHETIC, fake, imitation, mock, ersatz, substitute, replica, reproduction; man-made, manufactured, fabricated; plastic; *informal* pretend. ❷ *an artificial smile* INSINCERE, feigned, false, unnatural, contrived, put-on, exaggerated, forced, laboured, strained, hollow; *informal* pretend, phoney.
– OPPOSITES natural, genuine.

artillery ▶ noun ORDNANCE, (big) guns, cannon(s), cannonry.

artisan ▶ noun CRAFTSMAN, craftswoman, craftsperson; skilled worker, technician; smith, wright, journeyman; *archaic* artificer.

artist ▶ noun ❶ *a Belfast mural artist* DESIGNER, creator, originator, producer; old master. ❷ *the surgeon is an artist with the knife* EXPERT, master, maestro, past master, virtuoso, genius; *informal* pro, ace; *Brit. informal* dab hand.
– OPPOSITES novice.

artiste ▶ noun ENTERTAINER, performer, showman, artist; player, musician, singer, dancer, actor, actress; star.

artistic ▶ adjective ❶ *he's very artistic* CREATIVE, imaginative, inventive, expressive; sensitive, perceptive, discerning. ❷ *artistic dances* AESTHETIC, aesthetically pleasing, beautiful, attractive, fine; decorative, ornamental; tasteful, stylish, elegant, exquisite.
– OPPOSITES unimaginative, inelegant.

artistry ▶ noun CREATIVE SKILL, creativity, art, skill, talent, genius, brilliance, flair, proficiency, virtuosity, finesse, style; craftsmanship, workmanship.

artless ▶ adjective NATURAL, ingenuous, naive, simple, innocent, childlike, guileless; candid, open, sincere, unaffected.
– OPPOSITES scheming.

as ▶ conjunction ❶ *she saw him as he disappeared* WHILE, just as, even as, just when, at the time that, at the moment that. ❷ *we all felt as Frank did* IN THE (SAME) WAY THAT, the (same) way; *informal* like. ❸ *do as you're told* WHAT, that which. ❹ *they were free, as the case had not been proved* BECAUSE, since, seeing that/as, in view of the fact that, owing to the fact that; *informal* on account of; *poetic/literary* for. ❺ *try as she did, she couldn't smile* THOUGH, although, even though, in spite of the fact that, despite the fact that, notwithstanding that, for all that, albeit, however. ❻ *relatively short distances, as Paris to Lyons* SUCH AS, like, for instance, for example, e.g. ❼ *I'm away a lot, as you know* WHICH, a fact which.
▶ preposition ❶ *he was dressed as a policeman* LIKE, in the guise of, so as to appear to be. ❷ *I'm speaking to you as your friend* IN THE ROLE OF, being, acting as.
■ **as for/as to** CONCERNING, with respect to, on the subject of, in the matter of, as regards, with regard to, regarding, with reference to, re, in re, apropos, vis-à-vis.
■ **as it were** SO TO SPEAK, in a manner of speaking, to some extent, so to say; *informal* sort of.
■ **as yet** SO FAR, thus far, yet, still, up till now, up to now.

ascend ▶ verb CLIMB, go up/upwards, move up/upwards, rise (up); mount, scale, conquer; take to the air, take off.
– OPPOSITES descend.

ascendancy ▶ noun DOMINANCE, domination, supremacy, superiority, paramountcy, predominance, primacy, dominion, hegemony, authority, control, command, power, rule, sovereignty, lordship, leadership, influence.
– OPPOSITES subordination.

ascendant ▶ adjective RISING (IN POWER), on the rise, on the way up, up-and-coming, flourishing, prospering, burgeoning.
– OPPOSITES declining.

ascent ▶ noun ❶ *the first ascent of the Matterhorn* CLIMB, scaling, conquest. ❷ *a balloon ascent* RISE, climb, launch, take-off, lift-off, blast-off. ❸ *the ascent grew steeper* (UPWARD) SLOPE, incline, rise, upward gradient, inclination, acclivity.
– OPPOSITES descent, drop.

ascertain ▶ verb FIND OUT, discover, get to know, work out, make out, fathom (out), learn, deduce, divine, discern, see, understand, comprehend; establish, determine, verify, confirm; *informal* figure out; *Brit. informal* suss (out).

ascetic ▶ adjective *an ascetic life* AUSTERE, self-denying, abstinent, abstemious, self-disciplined, self-abnegating; simple, puritanical, monastic; reclusive, eremitic, hermitic; celibate, chaste.
– OPPOSITES sybaritic.

▶ **noun** *a desert ascetic* ABSTAINER, puritan, recluse, hermit, solitary; fakir, Sufi, dervish, sadhu, muni; *historical* anchorite; *archaic* eremite.
– OPPOSITES sybarite.

ascribe ▶ **verb** ATTRIBUTE, assign, put down, accredit, credit, chalk up, impute; blame on, lay at the door of; connect with, associate with.

ash ▶ **noun** CINDERS, ashes, clinker.

ashamed ▶ **adjective** ❶ *the poor are made to feel ashamed* SORRY, shamefaced, abashed, sheepish, guilty, contrite, remorseful, repentant, penitent, regretful, rueful, apologetic; embarrassed, mortified. ❷ *he was ashamed to admit it* RELUCTANT, loath, unwilling, disinclined, indisposed, afraid.
– OPPOSITES proud, pleased.

ashen ▶ **adjective** PALE, wan, pasty, grey, colourless, pallid, white, waxen, ghostly, bloodless.

ashore ▶ **adverb** ON TO (THE) LAND, on to the shore; shorewards, landwards; on the shore, on (dry) land.

aside ▶ **adverb** ❶ *they stood aside* TO ONE SIDE, to the side, on one side; apart, away, separately. ❷ *that aside, he seemed a nice man* APART, notwithstanding.
▶ **noun** *'Her parents died,' said Mrs Manton in an aside* WHISPERED REMARK, confidential remark, stage whisper; digression, incidental remark, obiter dictum, deviation.
■ **aside from** APART FROM, besides, in addition to, not counting, barring, other than, but (for), excluding, not including, except (for), excepting, leaving out, save (for).

asinine ▶ **adjective** FOOLISH, stupid, brainless, mindless, senseless, idiotic, imbecilic, ridiculous, ludicrous, absurd, nonsensical, fatuous, silly, inane, witless, empty-headed; *informal* half-witted, dumb, moronic; *Brit. informal* daft; *Scottish & N. English informal* glaikit.
– OPPOSITES intelligent, sensible.

ask ▶ **verb** ❶ *he asked what time we opened* ENQUIRE, query, want to know; question, interrogate, quiz. ❷ *they want to ask a few questions* PUT (FORWARD), pose, raise, submit. ❸ *don't be afraid to ask for advice* REQUEST, demand; solicit, seek, crave, apply, petition, call, appeal, sue. ❹ *let's ask them to dinner* INVITE, bid, summon, have someone over/round.
– OPPOSITES answer.

askance ▶ **adverb** *they look askance at anything foreign* SUSPICIOUSLY, sceptically, cynically, mistrustfully, distrustfully, doubtfully, dubiously; disapprovingly, contemptuously, scornfully, disdainfully.
– OPPOSITES approvingly.

askew ▶ **adjective** CROOKED, lopsided, tilted, angled, at an angle, skew, skewed, slanted, aslant, awry, squint, out of true, to/on one side, uneven, off centre, asymmetrical; *informal* cock-eyed, wonky; *Brit. informal* skew-whiff.
– OPPOSITES straight.

asleep ▶ **adjective** ❶ *she was asleep in bed* SLEEPING, in a deep sleep, napping, catnapping, dozing, drowsing; *informal* snoozing, dead to the world; *Brit. informal* kipping; *humorous* in the land of Nod; *poetic/literary* slumbering. ❷ *my leg's asleep* NUMB, with no feeling, numbed, benumbed, dead, insensible, insensate, unfeeling.
– OPPOSITES awake.

aspect ▶ **noun** ❶ *the photos depict every aspect of life* FEATURE, facet, side, characteristic, particular, detail; angle, slant. ❷ *his face had a sinister aspect* APPEARANCE, look, air, cast, mien, demeanour, expression; atmosphere, mood, quality, ambience, feeling. ❸ *a summer house with a southern aspect* OUTLOOK, view, exposure; situation, position, location. ❹ *the front aspect of the hotel* FACE, elevation, facade, side.

asperity ▶ **noun** HARSHNESS, sharpness, abrasiveness, severity, acerbity, astringency, tartness, sarcasm.

aspersions ▶ **plural noun** VILIFICATION, disparagement, denigration, defamation, condemnation, criticism, denunciation, slander, libel, calumny; slurs, smears, insults, slights; *informal* mud-slinging, bad-mouthing; *Brit. informal* slagging off; *formal* castigation.
■ **cast aspersions on** VILIFY, disparage, denigrate, defame, run down, impugn, belittle, criticize, condemn, decry, denounce, pillory; malign, slander, libel, discredit; *informal* pull apart, throw mud at, knock, bad-mouth; *Brit. informal* rubbish, slate, slag off.

asphyxiate ▶ **verb** CHOKE (TO DEATH), suffocate, smother, stifle; throttle, strangle.

aspiration ▶ **noun** DESIRE, hope, dream, wish, longing, yearning; aim, ambition, expectation, goal, target.

aspire ▶ **verb** DESIRE, hope, dream, long, yearn, set one's heart on, wish, want, be desirous of; aim, seek, pursue, set one's sights on.

aspiring ▶ **adjective** WOULD-BE, aspirant, hopeful, budding; potential, prospective, future; ambitious, determined; *informal* wannabe.

ass ▶ **noun** ❶ *he rode on an ass* DONKEY, jackass, jenny; *Scottish* cuddy; *Brit. informal* moke, neddy. ❷ (*informal*) *don't be a silly ass* FOOL, idiot, dolt, simpleton, imbecile; *informal* ninny, nincompoop, dimwit, donkey, chump, halfwit, dumdum, loon, jackass, cretin, jerk, nerd, fathead, blockhead, numbskull, dunce, dipstick, lamebrain, pea-brain, thickhead, woodenhead, pinhead, airhead, birdbrain; *Brit. informal* nitwit, twit, clot, plonker, berk, prat, pillock, wally, twerp, charlie; *Scottish informal* nyaff, balloon, gowk; *N. Amer. informal* schmuck, bozo, turkey, goofball, putz, wiener, weeny; *Austral./NZ informal* drongo, galah; *dated* tomfool, muttonhead.

assail ▶ **verb** ❶ *the army moved in to assail the enemy* ATTACK, assault, pounce on, set upon/about, fall on, charge, rush, storm; *informal* lay into, tear into, pitch into. ❷ *she was assailed by doubts* PLAGUE, torment, rack, beset, dog, trouble, disturb, worry, bedevil, nag, vex. ❸ *critics assailed the policy* CRITICIZE, censure, attack, condemn, pillory, revile; *informal* knock, slam; *Brit. informal* slate, slag off; *formal* castigate.

assailant ▶ **noun** ATTACKER, mugger, assaulter; *rare* assailer.

assassin ▶ **noun** MURDERER, killer, gunman; executioner; *informal* hit man, hired gun; *poetic/literary* slayer; *dated* homicide.

assassinate ▶ **verb** MURDER, kill, slaughter; eliminate, execute; *N. Amer.* terminate; *informal* hit; *poetic/literary* slay.

assassination ▶ **noun** MURDER, killing, slaughter, homicide; political execution, elimination; *N. Amer.* termination; *informal* hit; *poetic/literary* slaying.

assault ▶ **verb** ❶ *he assaulted a police officer* ATTACK, hit, strike, punch, beat up, thump; pummel, pound, batter; *informal* clout, wallop, belt, clobber, bop, biff, sock, deck, slug, plug, lay into, do over, rough up; *Austral. informal* quilt; *poetic/literary* smite. ❷ *they left to assault the hill* ATTACK, assail, pounce on, set upon, strike, fall on, swoop on, rush, storm, besiege. ❸ *he first assaulted then murdered her* RAPE, sexually assault, molest, interfere with.

▶ **noun** ❶ *he was charged with assault* BATTERY, violence; sexual assault, rape; *Brit.* grievous bodily harm, GBH, actual bodily harm, ABH. ❷ *an assault on the city* ATTACK, strike, onslaught, offensive, charge, push, thrust, invasion, bombardment, sortie, incursion, raid, blitz, campaign.

assay ▶ **noun** *new plate was brought for assay* EVALUATION, assessment, appraisal, analysis, examination, tests, inspection, scrutiny.

▶ **verb** *gold is assayed to determine its purity* EVALUATE, assess, appraise, analyse, examine, test, inspect, scrutinize, probe.

assemblage ▶ **noun** COLLECTION, accumulation, conglomeration, gathering, group, grouping, cluster, aggregation, mass, number; assortment, selection, array.

assemble ▶ **verb** ❶ *a crowd had assembled* GATHER, collect, get together, congregate, convene, meet, muster, rally; *formal* foregather. ❷ *he assembled the suspects* BRING/CALL TOGETHER, gather, collect, round up, marshal, muster, summon; *formal* convoke. ❸ *how to assemble the kite* CONSTRUCT, build, fabricate, manufacture, erect, set up, put/piece together, connect, join.
– OPPOSITES disperse, dismantle.

assembly ▶ **noun** ❶ *an assembly of dockers* GATHERING, meeting, congregation, convention, rally, convocation, assemblage, group, body, crowd, throng, company; *informal* get-together. ❷ *the labour needed in car assembly* CONSTRUCTION, manufacture, building, fabrication, erection.

assent ▶ **noun** *they are likely to give their assent* AGREEMENT, acceptance, approval, approbation, consent, acquiescence, compliance, concurrence, the nod; sanction, endorsement, confirmation; permission, leave, blessing; *informal* the go-ahead, the green light, the OK, the thumbs up.
– OPPOSITES dissent, refusal.

▶ **verb** *he assented to the change* AGREE TO, accept, approve, consent to, acquiesce in, concur in, give one's blessing to, give the nod; sanction, endorse, confirm; *informal* give the go-ahead, give the green light, give the OK, OK, give the thumbs up; *formal* accede to.
– OPPOSITES refuse.

assert ▶ **verb** ❶ *they asserted that all aboard were safe* DECLARE, maintain, contend, argue, state, claim, propound, proclaim, announce, pronounce, swear, insist, avow; *formal* aver, opine; *rare* asseverate. ❷ *we find it difficult to assert our rights* INSIST ON, stand up for, uphold, defend, contend, establish, press/push for, stress.

■ **assert oneself** BEHAVE/SPEAK CONFIDENTLY, be assertive, put oneself forward, make one's presence felt; *informal* put one's foot down.

assertion ▶ **noun** ❶ *I questioned his assertion* DECLARATION, contention, statement, claim, opinion, proclamation, announcement, pronouncement, protestation, avowal; *formal* averment; *rare* asseveration. ❷ *an assertion of the right to march* DEFENCE, upholding; insistence on.

assertive ▶ **adjective** CONFIDENT, self-confident, bold, decisive, assured, self-assured, self-possessed; authoritative, strong-willed, forceful, insistent, determined, commanding, pushy; *informal* feisty; *dated* pushful.
– OPPOSITES timid.

assess ▶ **verb** ❶ *the committee's power is hard to assess* EVALUATE, judge, gauge, rate, estimate, appraise, get the measure of, determine, weigh up, analyse; *informal* size up. ❷ *the damage was assessed at £5 billion* VALUE, calculate, work out, determine, fix, cost, price, estimate.

assessment ▶ **noun** ❶ *a teacher's assessment of the pupil's abilities* EVALUATION, judgement, rating, estimation, appraisal, analysis, opinion. ❷ *some assessments valued the estate at £2 million* VALUATION, calculation, costing, pricing, estimate.

asset ▶ **noun** ❶ *he sees his age as an asset* BENEFIT, advantage, blessing, good point, strong point, strength, forte, virtue, recommendation, attraction, resource, boon, merit, bonus, plus, pro. ❷ *the seizure of all their assets* PROPERTY, resources, estate, holdings, possessions, effects, goods, valuables, belongings, chattels.
– OPPOSITES liability.

assiduous ▶ adjective DILIGENT, careful, meticulous, thorough, sedulous, attentive, conscientious, punctilious, painstaking, rigorous, particular; persevering.

assign ▶ verb ❶ *a young doctor was assigned the task* ALLOCATE, allot, give, set; charge with, entrust with. ❷ *she was assigned to a new post* APPOINT, promote, delegate, commission, post, co-opt; select for, choose for, install in; *Military* detail. ❸ *we assign large sums of money to travel budgets* EARMARK, designate, set aside, reserve, appropriate, allot, allocate, apportion. ❹ *he assigned the opinion to the Prince* ASCRIBE, attribute, put down, accredit, credit, chalk up, impute; pin on, lay at the door of. ❺ *he may assign the money to a third party* TRANSFER, make over, give, pass, hand over/down, convey, consign; *Law* attorn, devise.

assignation ▶ noun RENDEZVOUS, date, appointment, meeting; *poetic/literary* tryst.

assignment ▶ noun ❶ *I'm going to finish this assignment tonight* TASK, piece of work, job, duty, chore, mission, errand, undertaking, exercise, business, endeavour, enterprise; project, homework. ❷ *the assignment of tasks* ALLOCATION, allotment, issuance, designation; sharing out, apportionment, distribution, handing out, dispensation. ❸ *the assignment of property* TRANSFER, making over, giving, hand down, consignment; *Law* conveyance, devise, attornment.

assimilate ▶ verb ❶ *the amount of information he can assimilate* ABSORB, take in, acquire, pick up, grasp, comprehend, understand, learn, master; digest, ingest. ❷ *many tribes were assimilated by Turkic peoples* SUBSUME, incorporate, integrate, absorb, engulf, acculturate; co-opt, adopt, embrace, admit.

assist ▶ verb ❶ *I spend my time assisting the chef* HELP, aid, abet, lend a (helping) hand to, oblige, accommodate, serve; collaborate with, work with; support, back (up), second; *informal* pitch in with; *Brit. informal* muck in with. ❷ *the exchange rates assisted the firm's expansion* FACILITATE, aid, ease, expedite, spur, promote, boost, benefit, foster, encourage, stimulate, precipitate, accelerate, advance, further, forward.
– OPPOSITES hinder, impede.

assistance ▶ noun HELP, aid, support, backing, reinforcement, succour, relief, intervention, cooperation, collaboration; a (helping) hand, a good turn; *informal* a break, a leg up.
– OPPOSITES hindrance.

assistant ▶ noun ❶ *a photographer's assistant* SUBORDINATE, deputy, second (in command), number two, right-hand man/woman, aide, personal assistant, PA, attendant, mate, apprentice, junior, auxiliary; hired hand, hired help, helper, man/girl Friday; *informal* sidekick, gofer; *Brit. informal* skivvy, dogsbody. ❷ *an assistant in the local shop* SALES ASSISTANT, salesperson, saleswoman/girl, salesman, server, checkout operator; seller, vendor; *N. Amer.* clerk; *informal* counter-jumper; *dated* shop boy/girl.

associate ▶ verb ❶ *the colours that we associate with fire* LINK, connect, relate, identify, equate, bracket, set side by side. ❷ *I was forced to associate with them* MIX, keep company, mingle, socialize, go around, rub shoulders, fraternize, consort, have dealings; *N. Amer.* rub elbows; *informal* hobnob, hang out/around/round, be thick with; *Brit. informal* hang about. ❸ *the firm is associated with a local charity* AFFILIATE, align, connect, join, attach, team up, be in league, ally; merge, integrate, confederate.
▶ noun *his business associate* PARTNER, colleague, coworker, workmate, comrade, ally, confederate; connection, contact, acquaintance; collaborator, partner; *informal* crony; *Brit. informal* oppo; *Austral./NZ informal* offsider.

associated ▶ adjective ❶ *salaries and associated costs* RELATED, connected, linked, correlated, similar, corresponding; attendant, accompanying, incidental. ❷ *their associated company* AFFILIATED, allied, integrated, amalgamated, federated, confederated, syndicated, connected, related.
– OPPOSITES unrelated.

association ▶ noun ❶ *a trade association* ALLIANCE, consortium, coalition, union, league, guild, syndicate, federation, confederation, confederacy, conglomerate, cooperative, partnership, affiliation. ❷ *the association between man and environment* RELATIONSHIP, relation, interrelation, connection, interconnection, link, bond, union, tie, attachment, interdependence, affiliation.

assorted ▶ adjective VARIOUS, miscellaneous, mixed, varied, varying, diverse, eclectic, multifarious, sundry; *poetic/literary* divers.

assortment ▶ noun MIXTURE, variety, array, mixed bag, mix, miscellany, selection, medley, diversity, ragbag, pot-pourri, salmagundi, farrago, gallimaufry, omnium gatherum.

assuage ▶ verb ❶ *a pain that could never be assuaged* RELIEVE, ease, alleviate, soothe, mitigate, allay, palliate, abate, suppress, subdue, tranquillize; moderate, lessen, diminish, reduce. ❷ *her hunger was quickly assuaged* SATISFY, gratify, appease, fulfil, indulge, relieve, slake, sate, satiate, quench, check.
– OPPOSITES aggravate, intensify.

assume ▶ verb ❶ *I assumed he wanted me to keep the book* PRESUME, suppose, take it (as given), take for granted, take as read, conjecture, surmise, conclude, deduce, infer, reckon, reason, think, fancy, believe, understand, gather; *N. Amer.* figure; *archaic* ween. ❷ *he assumed a Southern accent* AFFECT, adopt, impersonate, put on, simulate, feign, fake. ❸ *the* *disease may assume epidemic proportions* ACQUIRE, take on, come to have. ❹ *they are to assume more responsibility* ACCEPT, shoulder, bear, undertake, take on/up, manage, handle, deal with. ❺ *he assumed control of their finances* SEIZE, take (over), appropriate, commandeer, expropriate, hijack, wrest, usurp.

assumed ▸ adjective FALSE, fictitious, invented, made-up, fake, bogus, sham, spurious, make-believe, improvised, adopted; *informal* pretend, phoney; *Brit. informal* cod.
– OPPOSITES genuine.

assumption ▸ noun ❶ *an informed assumption* SUPPOSITION, presumption, belief, expectation, conjecture, speculation, surmise, guess, premise, hypothesis; conclusion, deduction, inference, notion, impression. ❷ *her assumption of ease* PRETENCE, simulation, affectation. ❸ *the early assumption of community obligation* ACCEPTANCE, shouldering, tackling, undertaking. ❹ *the assumption of power by revolutionaries* SEIZURE, arrogation, appropriation, expropriation, commandeering, confiscation, hijacking, wresting.

assurance ▸ noun ❶ *her calm assurance* SELF-CONFIDENCE, confidence, self-assurance, self-possession, nerve, poise, aplomb, level-headedness; calmness, composure, sangfroid, equanimity; *informal* cool, unflappability. ❷ *you have my assurance* WORD (OF HONOUR), promise, pledge, vow, avowal, oath, bond, undertaking, guarantee, commitment. ❸ *there is no assurance of getting one's money back* GUARANTEE, certainty, certitude, surety, confidence, expectation. ❹ *life assurance* INSURANCE, indemnity, indemnification, protection, security, cover.
– OPPOSITES self-doubt, uncertainty.

assure ▸ verb ❶ *we must assure him of our loyal support* REASSURE, convince, satisfy, persuade, guarantee, promise, tell; affirm, pledge, swear, vow. ❷ *he wants to assure a favourable vote* ENSURE, secure, guarantee, seal, clinch, confirm; *informal* sew up. ❸ *they guarantee to assure your life* INSURE, provide insurance, cover, indemnify.

assured ▸ adjective ❶ *an assured voice* CONFIDENT, self-confident, self-assured, self-possessed, poised, phlegmatic, level-headed; calm, composed, equanimous, imperturbable, unruffled; *informal* unflappable, together. ❷ *an assured supply of weapons* GUARANTEED, certain, sure, secure, reliable, dependable, sound; infallible, unfailing; *informal* sure-fire.
– OPPOSITES doubtful, uncertain.

astonish ▸ verb AMAZE, astound, stagger, surprise, startle, stun, confound, dumbfound, stupefy, daze, nonplus, take aback, leave open-mouthed, leave aghast; *informal* flabbergast, bowl over; *Brit. informal* knock for six.

astonished ▸ adjective AMAZED, astounded, staggered, surprised, startled, stunned, thunderstruck, aghast, taken aback, dumbfounded, dumbstruck, stupefied, dazed, nonplussed, awestruck; *informal* flabbergasted; *Brit. informal* gobsmacked.

astonishing ▸ adjective AMAZING, astounding, staggering, surprising, breathtaking; remarkable, extraordinary, incredible, unbelievable, phenomenal; *informal* mind-boggling.

astonishment ▸ noun AMAZEMENT, surprise, stupefaction, incredulity, disbelief, speechlessness, awe, wonder.

astound ▸ verb AMAZE, astonish, stagger, surprise, startle, stun, confound, dumbfound, stupefy, daze, nonplus, take aback, leave open-mouthed, leave aghast; *informal* flabbergast, bowl over; *Brit. informal* knock for six.

astounding ▸ adjective AMAZING, astonishing, staggering, surprising, breathtaking, remarkable, extraordinary, incredible, unbelievable, phenomenal; *informal* mind-boggling.

astray ▸ adverb ❶ *the shots went astray* OFF TARGET, wide of the mark, awry, off course. ❷ *the older boys lead him astray* INTO WRONGDOING, into sin, into iniquity, away from the straight and narrow.

astringent ▸ adjective ❶ *the lotion has an astringent effect on pores* CONSTRICTING, constrictive, contracting; styptic. ❷ *her astringent words* SEVERE, sharp, stern, harsh, acerbic, acidulous, caustic, mordant, trenchant; scathing, cutting, incisive, waspish; *N. Amer.* acerb.

astrology ▸ noun HOROSCOPY; horoscopes; *rare* astromancy.

astronaut ▸ noun SPACEMAN/WOMAN, cosmonaut, space traveller, space cadet; *N. Amer. informal* jock.

astronomical ▸ adjective ❶ *astronomical alignments* PLANETARY, stellar; celestial. ❷ (*informal*) *the sums he has paid are astronomical* HUGE, enormous, very large, prodigious, monumental, colossal, vast, gigantic, massive; substantial, considerable, sizeable, hefty; inordinate; *informal* astronomic, whopping, humongous; *Brit. informal* ginormous.
– OPPOSITES tiny.

astute ▸ adjective SHREWD, sharp, acute, quick, clever, intelligent, bright, smart, canny, intuitive, perceptive, insightful, incisive, sagacious, wise; *informal* on the ball, quick on the uptake, savvy; *Brit. informal* suss; *N. Amer. informal* heads-up; *rare* argute.
– OPPOSITES stupid.

asunder ▸ adverb (*poetic/literary*) *the fabric of society may be torn asunder* APART, up, in two; to pieces, to shreds.

asylum ▸ noun ❶ *he appealed for political asylum* REFUGE, sanctuary, shelter, safety, protection, security, immunity; a safe haven. ❷ *his father was confined to an asylum* PSYCHIATRIC HOSPITAL, mental hospital, mental institution, mental asylum; *informal* madhouse, loony bin, funny farm; *N. Amer. informal* bughouse; *dated* lunatic asylum; *archaic* bedlam.

asymmetrical ▶ **adjective** LOPSIDED, unsymmetrical, uneven, unbalanced, crooked, awry, askew, skew, squint, misaligned; disproportionate, unequal, irregular; *informal* cock-eyed; *Brit. informal* skew-whiff, wonky.

atheism ▶ **noun** NON-BELIEF, disbelief, unbelief, scepticism, doubt, agnosticism; nihilism.

atheist ▶ **noun** NON-BELIEVER, disbeliever, unbeliever, sceptic, doubter, doubting Thomas, agnostic; nihilist; *rare* nullifidian.
–OPPOSITES believer.

athlete ▶ **noun** SPORTSMAN, sportswoman, sportsperson; Olympian; runner; *N. Amer. informal* jock.

athletic ▶ **adjective** ❶ *his athletic physique* MUSCULAR, muscly, sturdy, strapping, well built, strong, powerful, robust, able-bodied, vigorous, hardy, lusty, hearty, brawny, burly, broad-shouldered, Herculean; FIT, in good shape, in trim; *informal* sporty, husky, hunky, beefy; *poetic/literary* thewy, stark. ❷ *athletic events* SPORTING, sports; Olympic.
–OPPOSITES puny.

athletics ▶ **plural noun** TRACK AND FIELD EVENTS, sporting events, sports, games, races; contests.

atmosphere ▶ **noun** ❶ *the gases present in the atmosphere* AIR, aerospace; sky; *poetic/literary* the heavens, the firmament, the blue, the azure, the ether. ❷ *the hotel has a relaxed atmosphere* AMBIENCE, air, mood, feel, feeling, character, tone, tenor, aura, quality, undercurrent, flavour; *informal* vibe.

atom ▶ **noun** ❶ *they build tiny circuits atom by atom* PARTICLE, molecule, bit, piece, fragment, fraction. ❷ *there wasn't an atom of truth in the allegations* GRAIN, iota, jot, whit, mite, scrap, shred, ounce, scintilla; *Irish* stim; *informal* smidgen.

atone ▶ **verb** MAKE AMENDS, make reparation, make up for, compensate, pay, recompense, expiate, make good, offset; do penance.

atrocious ▶ **adjective** ❶ *atrocious cruelties* BRUTAL, barbaric, barbarous, savage, vicious; wicked, cruel, nasty, heinous, monstrous, vile, inhuman, black-hearted, fiendish, ghastly, horrible; abominable, outrageous, hateful, disgusting, despicable, contemptible, loathsome, odious, abhorrent, sickening, horrifying, unspeakable, execrable, egregious. ❷ *the weather was atrocious* APPALLING, dreadful, terrible, very bad, unpleasant, miserable; *informal* abysmal, dire, rotten, lousy, God-awful; *Brit. informal* shocking, chronic.
–OPPOSITES admirable, superb.

atrocity ▶ **noun** ❶ *press reports detailed a number of atrocities* ABOMINATION, cruelty, enormity, outrage, horror, monstrosity, obscenity, violation, crime, abuse. ❷ *conflict and atrocity around the globe* BARBARITY, barbarism, brutality, savagery, inhumanity, cruelty, wickedness, evil, iniquity, horror.

atrophy ▶ **verb** ❶ *muscles atrophy in microgravity* WASTE AWAY, become emaciated, wither, shrivel (up), shrink; decay, decline, deteriorate, degenerate, weaken. ❷ *the Labour campaign atrophied* DWINDLE, deteriorate, decline, wane, fade, peter out, crumble, disintegrate, collapse, slump, go downhill.
–OPPOSITES strengthen, flourish.
▶ **noun** *muscular atrophy* WASTING, emaciation, withering, shrivelling, shrinking; decay, decline, deterioration, degeneration, weakening, debilitation, enfeeblement.
–OPPOSITES strengthening.

attach ▶ **verb** ❶ *a lead weight is attached to the cord* FASTEN, fix, affix, join, connect, link, secure, make fast, tie, bind, chain; stick, adhere, glue, fuse; append. ❷ *he attached himself to the Liberal Party* AFFILIATE, associate, align, ally, unite, integrate, join; be in league with, form an alliance with. ❸ *they attached importance to research* ASCRIBE, assign, attribute, accredit, impute. ❹ *the medical officer attached to HQ* ASSIGN, appoint, allocate, second; *Military* detail.
–OPPOSITES detach, separate.

attached ▶ **adjective** ❶ *I'm not interested in you—I'm attached* MARRIED, engaged, promised in marriage; going out, spoken for, involved; *informal* hitched, spliced, shackled, going steady; *dated* betrothed; *formal* wed, wedded; *poetic/literary* affianced; *archaic* espoused. ❷ *she was very attached to her brother* FOND OF, devoted to; *informal* mad about, crazy about.
–OPPOSITES single.

attachment ▶ **noun** ❶ *he has a strong attachment to his mother* BOND, closeness, devotion, loyalty; fondness for, love for, affection for, feeling for; relationship with. ❷ *the shower had a massage attachment* ACCESSORY, fitting, fitment, extension, add-on, appendage. ❸ *the attachment of safety restraints* FIXING, fastening, linking, coupling, connection. ❹ *he was on attachment from another regiment* ASSIGNMENT, appointment, secondment, transfer; *Military* detail. ❺ *his family's Conservative attachment* AFFILIATION, association, alliance, alignment, connection; links, ties, sympathies.

attack ▶ **verb** ❶ *Chris had been brutally attacked* ASSAULT, assail, set upon, beat up; batter, pummel, punch; *N. Amer.* beat up on; *informal* do over, work over, rough up; *Brit. informal* duff up. ❷ *the French had still not attacked* STRIKE, charge, pounce; bombard, shell, blitz, strafe, fire. ❸ *the clergy attacked government policies* CRITICIZE, censure, condemn, pillory, savage, revile, vilify; *informal* knock, slam, bash, lay into; *Brit. informal* slate, slag off, rubbish; *N. Amer. informal* pummel. ❹ *they have to attack the problem soon*

ADDRESS, attend to, deal with, confront, apply oneself to, get to work on, undertake, embark on; *informal* get stuck into, get cracking on, get weaving on. ❺ *the virus attacks the liver* AFFECT, have an effect on, strike; infect, damage, injure.
– OPPOSITES defend, praise, protect.
▶ **noun** ❶ *an attack on their home* ASSAULT, onslaught, offensive, strike, blitz, raid, charge, rush, invasion, incursion. ❷ *she wrote a hostile attack on him* CRITICISM, censure, rebuke, admonishment, reprimand, reproval; condemnation, denunciation, revilement, vilification; tirade, diatribe, polemic; *informal* roasting, caning; *Brit. informal* slating, rollicking, blast. ❸ *an asthmatic attack* FIT, seizure, spasm, convulsion, paroxysm, outburst, bout.
– OPPOSITES defence, commendation.

attacker ▶ **noun** ASSAILANT, assaulter, aggressor; mugger, rapist, killer, murderer.

attain ▶ **verb** ACHIEVE, accomplish, reach, obtain, gain, procure, secure, get, hook, net, win, earn, acquire; realize, fulfil; *informal* clinch, bag, wrap up.

attainable ▶ **adjective** ACHIEVABLE, obtainable, accessible, within reach, securable, realizable; practicable, workable, realistic, reasonable, viable, feasible, possible; *informal* doable, get-at-able.

attainment ▶ **noun** ❶ *the attainment of common goals* ACHIEVEMENT, accomplishment, realization, fulfilment, completion; *formal* effectuation, reification. ❷ *educational attainment* ACHIEVEMENT, accomplishment, proficiency, competence; qualification; skill, aptitude, ability.

attempt ▶ **verb** *I attempted to answer the question* TRY, strive, aim, venture, endeavour, seek, undertake, make an effort; have a go at, try one's hand at; *informal* go all out, bend over backwards, bust a gut, have a crack at, have a shot at, have a stab at; *formal* essay; *archaic* assay.
▶ **noun** *an attempt to put the economy to rights* EFFORT, endeavour, try, venture, trial; *informal* crack, go, shot, stab; *formal* essay; *archaic* assay.

attend ▶ **verb** ❶ *they attended a carol service* BE PRESENT AT, sit in on, take part in; appear at, present oneself at, turn up at, visit, go to; *informal* show up at, show one's face at. ❷ *he had not attended to the regulations* PAY ATTENTION, pay heed, be attentive, listen; concentrate, take note, bear in mind, take into consideration, heed, observe, mark. ❸ *the wounded were attended to nearby* CARE FOR, look after, minister to, see to; tend, treat, nurse, help, aid, assist, succour; *informal* doctor. ❹ *he attended to the boy's education* DEAL WITH, see to, manage, organize, sort out, handle, take care of, take charge of, take in hand, tackle. ❺ *the queen was attended by an usher* ESCORT, accompany, chaperone, squire, guide, lead, conduct, usher, shepherd; assist, help, serve, wait on. ❻ *her giddiness was attended with a fever* BE ACCOMPANIED BY, occur with, coexist with, be associated with, connected with, be linked with; be produced by, originate from/in, stem from, result from, arise from.
– OPPOSITES miss, disregard, ignore, neglect.

attendance ▶ **noun** ❶ *you requested the attendance of a doctor* PRESENCE, appearance; attention. ❷ *their gig attendances grew* AUDIENCE, turnout, house, gate; crowd, congregation, gathering; *Austral. informal* muster.
– OPPOSITES absence.
■ **in attendance** PRESENT, here, there, near, nearby, at hand, available; assisting, supervising.

attendant ▶ **noun** ❶ *a sleeping car attendant* STEWARD, waiter, waitress, garçon, porter, servant; *N. Amer.* waitperson. ❷ *a royal attendant* ESCORT, companion, retainer, aide, lady in waiting, equerry, chaperone; servant, manservant, valet, gentleman's gentleman, maidservant, maid; *N. Amer.* houseman; *Brit. informal* skivvy; *Military, dated* batman.
▶ **adjective** *new discoveries and the attendant excitement* ACCOMPANYING, associated, related, connected, concomitant; resultant, resulting, consequent.

attention ▶ **noun** ❶ *the issue needs further attention* CONSIDERATION, contemplation, deliberation, thought, study, observation, scrutiny, investigation, action. ❷ *he tried to attract the attention of a policeman* AWARENESS, notice, observation, heed, regard, scrutiny, surveillance. ❸ *adequate medical attention* CARE, treatment, ministration, succour, relief, aid, help, assistance. ❹ *he was effusive in his attentions* OVERTURES, approaches, suit, wooing, courting; compliments, flattery.

attentive ▶ **adjective** ❶ *a bright and attentive scholar* PERCEPTIVE, observant, alert, acute, aware, heedful, vigilant; intent, focused, committed, studious, diligent, conscientious, earnest; *informal* not missing a trick, on the ball. ❷ *the most attentive of husbands* CONSCIENTIOUS, considerate, thoughtful, kind, caring, solicitous, understanding, sympathetic, obliging, accommodating, gallant, chivalrous; dutiful, responsible.
– OPPOSITES inconsiderate.

attenuated ▶ **adjective** ❶ *attenuated fingers* THIN, slender, narrow, slim, skinny, spindly, bony; *poetic/literary* extenuated; *rare* attenuate. ❷ *his muscle activity was much attenuated* WEAKENED, reduced, lessened, decreased, diminished, impaired.
– OPPOSITES plump, broad, strengthened.

attest ▶ **verb** CERTIFY, corroborate, confirm, verify, substantiate, authenticate, evidence, demonstrate, show, prove; endorse, support, affirm, bear out, give credence to, vouch for; *formal* evince.
– OPPOSITES disprove.

attic ▶ **noun** LOFT, roof space, cock loft; garret, mansard.

attire ▶ **noun** *Thomas preferred formal attire* CLOTHING, clothes, garments, dress, wear, outfits, garb, costume; *informal* gear, togs, duds, get-up; *Brit. informal* clobber; *N. Amer. informal* threads; *formal* apparel; *archaic* raiment, habiliments.
▶ **verb** *she was attired in black crêpe* DRESS (UP), clothe, garb, robe, array, costume, swathe, deck (out), turn out, fit out, trick out/up, rig out; *informal* get up; *archaic* apparel, invest, habit.

attitude ▶ **noun** ❶ *you seem ambivalent in your attitude* VIEW, viewpoint, outlook, perspective, stance, standpoint, position, inclination, orientation, approach, reaction; opinion, ideas, convictions, feelings, thinking. ❷ *an attitude of prayer* POSITION, posture, pose, stance.

attorney ▶ **noun** LAWYER, legal practitioner, legal executive, legal representative, member of the bar, counsel; *Brit.* barrister, Queen's counsel, QC; *Scottish* advocate; *N. Amer.* counselor(-at-law); *informal* brief.

attract ▶ **verb** ❶ *positive ions are attracted to the negatively charged terminal* DRAW, pull, magnetize. ❷ *he was attracted by her smile* ENTICE, allure, lure, tempt, charm, win over, woo, engage, enchant, entrance, captivate, beguile, bewitch, seduce; excite, titillate, arouse; *informal* turn on.
– OPPOSITES repel.

attraction ▶ **noun** ❶ *the stars are held together by gravitational attraction* PULL, draw; magnetism. ❷ *she had lost whatever attraction she had ever had* APPEAL, attractiveness, desirability, seductiveness, seduction, allure, animal magnetism; charisma, charm, beauty, good looks; *informal* come-on. ❸ *the fair offers sideshows and other attractions* ENTERTAINMENT, activity, diversion, interest.
– OPPOSITES repulsion.

attractive ▶ **adjective** ❶ *a more attractive career* APPEALING, inviting, tempting, irresistible; agreeable, pleasing, interesting. ❷ *she has no idea how attractive she is* GOOD-LOOKING, beautiful, pretty, handsome, lovely, stunning, striking, arresting, gorgeous, prepossessing, fetching, captivating, bewitching, beguiling, engaging, charming, enchanting, appealing, delightful; sexy, seductive, alluring, tantalizing, irresistible, ravishing, desirable; *Scottish & N. English* bonny; *informal* fanciable, tasty, hot, easy on the eye, drop-dead gorgeous; *Brit. informal* fit; *N. Amer. informal* cute, foxy; *Austral./NZ informal* spunky; *poetic/literary* beauteous; *archaic* comely, fair.
– OPPOSITES uninviting, ugly.

attribute ▶ **verb** *they attributed their success to him* ASCRIBE, assign, accredit, credit, impute; put down, chalk up, hold responsible, pin on; connect with, associate with.
▶ **noun** ❶ *he has all the attributes of a top player* QUALITY, characteristic, trait, feature, element, aspect, property, sign, hallmark, mark, distinction. ❷ *the hourglass is the attribute of Father Time* SYMBOL, mark, sign, hallmark, trademark.

attrition ▶ **noun** ❶ *a gradual attrition of the market economy* WEARING DOWN/AWAY, weakening, debilitation, enfeebling, sapping, attenuation. ❷ *the attrition of the edges of the teeth* ABRASION, friction, erosion, corrosion, grinding, wearing (away); deterioration, damaging; *rare* detrition.

attune ▶ **verb** ACCUSTOM, adjust, adapt, acclimatize, condition, accommodate, assimilate; *N. Amer.* acclimate.

atypical ▶ **adjective** UNUSUAL, untypical, uncommon, unconventional, unorthodox, irregular, abnormal, aberrant, deviant, unrepresentative; strange, odd, peculiar, bizarre, weird, queer, freakish; exceptional, singular, rare, out of the way, out of the ordinary, extraordinary; *Brit.* out of the common; *informal* funny, freaky.
– OPPOSITES normal.

auburn ▶ **adjective** REDDISH-BROWN, red-brown, Titian (red), tawny, russet, chestnut, copper, coppery, rufous.

au courant ▶ **adjective** UP TO DATE, au fait, in touch, familiar, at home, acquainted, conversant; abreast, apprised, in the know, well informed, knowledgeable, well versed, enlightened; *informal* clued up, wise to, hip to.

audacious ▶ **adjective** ❶ *his audacious exploits* BOLD, daring, fearless, intrepid, brave, courageous, valiant, heroic, plucky; daredevil, devil-may-care, death-or-glory, reckless, madcap; venturesome, mettlesome; *informal* gutsy, spunky, ballsy; *poetic/literary* temerarious. ❷ *an audacious remark* IMPUDENT, impertinent, insolent, presumptuous, cheeky, irreverent, discourteous, disrespectful, insubordinate, ill-mannered, unmannerly, rude, brazen, shameless, pert, defiant, cocky, bold (as brass); *informal* brass-necked, fresh, lippy, mouthy, saucy; *N. Amer. informal* sassy, nervy; *archaic* malapert, contumelious.
– OPPOSITES timid, polite.

audacity ▶ **noun** ❶ *a traveller of extraordinary audacity* BOLDNESS, daring, fearlessness, intrepidity, bravery, courage, heroism, pluck, grit; recklessness; spirit, mettle; *informal* guts, gutsiness, spunk; *Brit. informal* bottle; *N. Amer. informal* moxie. ❷ *he had the audacity to contradict me* IMPUDENCE, impertinence, insolence, presumption, cheek, bad manners, effrontery, nerve, gall, defiance, temerity; *informal* brass (neck), chutzpah; *Brit. informal* sauce; *N. Amer. informal* sass.

audible ▶ **adjective** HEARABLE, perceptible, discernible, detectable, appreciable; clear, distinct, loud.
– OPPOSITES faint.

audience ▶ **noun** ❶ *the audience applauded* SPECTATORS, LISTENERS, viewers, onlookers, patrons; crowd, throng, congregation, turnout; house, gallery, stalls; *Brit. informal* punters. ❷ *the radio station has a teenage audience* MARKET, PUBLIC, following, fans; listenership, viewership. ❸ *an audience with the Pope* MEETING, consultation, conference, hearing, reception, interview.

audit ▶ **noun** *an audit of the party accounts* INSPECTION, examination, scrutiny, probe, investigation, assessment, appraisal, evaluation, review, analysis; *informal* going-over, once-over.
▶ **verb** *we audited their accounts* INSPECT, examine, survey, go through, scrutinize, check, probe, vet, investigate, enquire into, assess, appraise, evaluate, review, analyse, study; *informal* give something a/the once-over, give something a going-over.

auditorium ▶ **noun** THEATRE, hall, assembly room; chamber, room.

au fait ▶ **adjective** FAMILIAR, acquainted, conversant, at home, up to date, au courant, in touch; abreast, apprised, in the know, well informed, knowledgeable, well versed, enlightened; *informal* clued up, wise to, hip to.

augment ▶ **verb** INCREASE, add to, supplement, top up, build up, enlarge, expand, extend, raise, multiply, swell; magnify, amplify, escalate; improve, boost; *informal* up, jack up, hike up, bump up.
– OPPOSITES decrease.

augur ▶ **verb** *these successes augur well for the future* BODE, portend, herald, be a sign, warn, forewarn, foreshadow, be an omen, presage, indicate, signify, signal, promise, threaten, spell, denote; predict, prophesy; *poetic/literary* betoken, foretoken, forebode.

august ▶ **adjective** DISTINGUISHED, respected, eminent, venerable, hallowed, illustrious, prestigious, renowned, celebrated, honoured, acclaimed, esteemed, exalted; great, important, lofty, noble; imposing, impressive, awe-inspiring, stately, grand, dignified.

aura ▶ **noun** ATMOSPHERE, ambience, air, quality, character, mood, feeling, feel, flavour, tone, tenor; emanation, vibration; *informal* vibe.

auspices ▶ **plural noun** PATRONAGE, aegis, umbrella, protection, keeping, care; support, backing, guardianship, trusteeship, guidance, supervision.

auspicious ▶ **adjective** FAVOURABLE, propitious, promising, rosy, good, encouraging; opportune, timely, lucky, fortunate, providential, felicitous, advantageous.

austere ▶ **adjective** ❶ *an outwardly austere man* SEVERE, stern, strict, harsh, steely, flinty, dour, grim, cold, frosty, unemotional, unfriendly; formal, stiff, reserved, aloof, forbidding; grave, solemn, serious, unsmiling, unsympathetic, unforgiving; hard, unyielding, unbending, inflexible, illiberal; *informal* hard-boiled. ❷ *an austere life* ASCETIC, self-denying, self-disciplined, non-indulgent, frugal, spartan, puritanical, abstemious, abstinent, self-sacrificing, strict, temperate, sober, simple, restrained; celibate, chaste. ❸ *the buildings were austere* PLAIN, simple, basic, functional, modest, unadorned, unembellished, unfussy, restrained; stark, bleak, bare, clinical, spartan, ascetic; *informal* no frills.
– OPPOSITES genial, immoderate, ornate.

Australia ▶ **noun** *informal* Oz, Aussie, down under.

authentic ▶ **adjective** ❶ *an authentic document* GENUINE, real, bona fide, true, veritable, simon-pure; legitimate, lawful, legal, valid; *informal* the real McCoy, the real thing, pukka, kosher; *Austral./NZ informal* dinkum. ❷ *an authentic depiction of the situation* RELIABLE, dependable, trustworthy, authoritative, honest, faithful; accurate, factual, true, truthful; *formal* veridical, veracious.
– OPPOSITES fake, unreliable.

authenticate ▶ **verb** ❶ *the evidence will authenticate his claim* VERIFY, validate, prove, substantiate, corroborate, confirm, support, back up, attest to, give credence to. ❷ *a mandate authenticated by the popular vote* VALIDATE, ratify, confirm, seal, sanction, endorse.

authenticity ▶ **noun** ❶ *the authenticity of the painting* GENUINENESS, bona fides; legitimacy, legality, validity. ❷ *the authenticity of this account* RELIABILITY, dependability, trustworthiness, credibility; accuracy, truth, veracity, fidelity.

author ▶ **noun** ❶ *modern Canadian authors* WRITER, wordsmith; novelist, playwright, poet, essayist, biographer; columnist, reporter; *informal* penman, penwoman, scribe, scribbler. ❷ *the author of the peace plan* ORIGINATOR, creator, instigator, founder, father, architect, designer, deviser, producer; cause, agent.
– RELATED TERMS auctorial.

authoritarian ▶ **adjective** *his authoritarian manner* AUTOCRATIC, dictatorial, despotic, tyrannical, draconian, oppressive, repressive, illiberal, undemocratic; disciplinarian, domineering, overbearing, high-handed, peremptory, imperious, strict, rigid, inflexible; *informal* bossy.
– OPPOSITES democratic, liberal.
▶ **noun** *the army is dominated by authoritarians* AUTOCRAT, despot, dictator, tyrant; disciplinarian, martinet.

authoritative ▶ **adjective** ❶ *authoritative information* RELIABLE, dependable, trustworthy, sound, authentic, valid, attested, verifiable; accurate. ❷ *the authoritative edition* DEFINITIVE, most reliable, best; authorized, accredited, recognized, accepted, approved. ❸ *his authoritative manner* ASSURED, confident, assertive; commanding, masterful, lordly; domineering, imperious, overbearing, authoritarian; *informal* bossy.
– OPPOSITES unreliable, timid.

authority ▸ noun ❶ *a rebellion against those in authority* POWER, jurisdiction, command, control, charge, dominance, rule, sovereignty, supremacy; influence; *informal* clout. ❷ *the authority to arrest drug traffickers* AUTHORIZATION, right, power, mandate, prerogative, licence. ❸ *the money was spent without parliamentary authority* AUTHORIZATION, permission, consent, leave, sanction, licence, dispensation, assent, acquiescence, agreement, approval, endorsement, clearance; *informal* the go-ahead, the thumbs up, the OK, the green light. ❹ *the authorities* OFFICIALS, officialdom; government, administration, establishment; police; *informal* the powers that be. ❺ *an authority on the stock market* EXPERT, specialist, aficionado, pundit, doyen(ne), guru, sage; *informal* boffin. ❻ *he cites the nuns' testimony as an authority* SOURCE, reference, citation, quotation, passage. ❼ *on good authority* EVIDENCE, testimony, witness, attestation, word, avowal; *Law* deposition.

authorization ▸ noun PERMISSION, consent, leave, sanction, licence, dispensation, clearance, the nod; assent, agreement, approval, endorsement; authority, right, power, mandate; *informal* the go-ahead, the thumbs up, the OK, the green light.
– OPPOSITES refusal.

authorize ▸ verb ❶ *they authorized further action* SANCTION, permit, allow, approve, consent to, assent to; ratify, endorse, validate; *informal* give the green light, give the go-ahead, OK, give the thumbs up. ❷ *the troops were authorized to fire* EMPOWER, mandate, commission; entitle.
– OPPOSITES forbid.

authorized ▸ adjective APPROVED, recognized, sanctioned; accredited, licensed, certified; official, lawful, legal, legitimate.
– OPPOSITES unofficial.

autobiography ▸ noun MEMOIRS, life story, personal history.

autocracy ▸ noun ABSOLUTISM, totalitarianism, dictatorship, despotism, tyranny, monocracy, autarchy.
– OPPOSITES democracy.

autocrat ▸ noun ABSOLUTE RULER, dictator, despot, tyrant, monocrat.

autocratic ▸ adjective DESPOTIC, tyrannical, dictatorial, totalitarian, autarchic; undemocratic, one-party, monocratic; domineering, draconian, overbearing, high-handed, peremptory, imperious; harsh, rigid, inflexible, illiberal, oppressive.

autograph ▸ noun *fans pestered him for his autograph* SIGNATURE; *N. Amer. informal* John Hancock.
▸ verb *Jack autographed copies of his book* SIGN.

automatic ▸ adjective ❶ *automatic garage doors* MECHANIZED, mechanical, automated, computerized, electronic, robotic; self-activating. ❷ *an automatic reaction* INSTINCTIVE, involuntary, unconscious, reflex, knee-jerk, instinctual, subconscious; spontaneous, impulsive, unthinking; mechanical; *informal* gut. ❸ *he is the automatic choice for the team* INEVITABLE, unavoidable, inescapable, mandatory, compulsory; certain, definite, undoubted, assured.
– OPPOSITES manual, deliberate.

autonomous ▸ adjective SELF-GOVERNING, self-ruling, self-determining, independent, sovereign, free.

autonomy ▸ noun SELF-GOVERNMENT, self-rule, home rule, self-determination, independence, sovereignty, freedom.

autopsy ▸ noun POST-MORTEM, PM, necropsy.

auxiliary ▸ adjective ❶ *an auxiliary power source* ADDITIONAL, supplementary, supplemental, extra, reserve, back-up, emergency, fall-back, other. ❷ *auxiliary nursing staff* ANCILLARY, assistant, support.
▸ noun *a nursing auxiliary* ASSISTANT, helper, ancillary.

avail ▸ verb ❶ *guests can avail themselves of the facilities* USE, take advantage of, utilize, employ. ❷ *his arguments cannot avail him* HELP, aid, assist, benefit, profit, be of service.
■ **to no avail** IN VAIN, without success, unsuccessfully, fruitlessly, for nothing.

available ▸ adjective ❶ *refreshments will be available* OBTAINABLE, accessible, to/at hand, at one's disposal, handy, convenient; on sale, procurable; untaken, unengaged, unused; *informal* up for grabs, on tap, gettable. ❷ *I'll see if he's available* FREE, unoccupied; present, in attendance; contactable.
– OPPOSITES busy, engaged.

avalanche ▸ noun ❶ SNOWSLIDE, icefall; rockslide, landslide, landslip; *Brit.* snow-slip. ❷ *an avalanche of press comment* BARRAGE, volley, flood, deluge, torrent, tide, shower, wave.

avant-garde ▸ adjective INNOVATIVE, innovatory, original, experimental, left-field, inventive, ahead of the times, new, modern, advanced, forward-looking, state-of-the-art, trendsetting, pioneering, progressive, groundbreaking, trailblazing, revolutionary; unfamiliar, unorthodox, unconventional; *informal* offbeat, way-out.
– OPPOSITES conservative.

avarice ▸ noun GREED, acquisitiveness, cupidity, covetousness, rapacity, materialism, mercenariness, Mammonism; *informal* money-grubbing.
– OPPOSITES generosity.

avenge ▸ verb REQUITE, punish, repay, pay back, take revenge for, get even for.

avenue ▸ noun ❶ *tree-lined avenues* ROAD, street, drive, parade, boulevard, broadway, thoroughfare. ❷ *possible avenues of research* LINE, path; method, approach.

aver ▶ **verb** (*formal*) DECLARE, maintain, claim, assert, state, swear, avow, vow; *rare* asseverate.

average ▶ **noun** *the price is above the national average* MEAN, median, mode; norm, standard, rule, par.
▶ **adjective** ❶ *the average temperature in May* MEAN, median, modal. ❷ *a woman of average height* ORDINARY, standard, normal, typical, regular. ❸ *a very average director* MEDIOCRE, second-rate, undistinguished, ordinary, middle-of-the-road, unexceptional, unexciting, unremarkable, unmemorable, indifferent, pedestrian, lacklustre, forgettable, amateurish; *informal* OK, so-so, fair-to-middling, no great shakes, not up to much; *Brit. informal* not much cop; *N. Amer. informal* bush-league; *NZ informal* half-pie.
– OPPOSITES outstanding, exceptional.
■ **on average** NORMALLY, usually, ordinarily, generally, in general, for the most part, as a rule, typically; overall, by and large, on the whole.

averse ▶ **adjective** OPPOSED, against, antipathetic, hostile, ill-disposed, resistant; disinclined, reluctant, loath; *informal* anti.
– OPPOSITES keen.

aversion ▶ **noun** DISLIKE, antipathy, distaste, abhorrence, hatred, loathing, detestation, hostility; reluctance, disinclination; *archaic* disrelish.
– OPPOSITES liking.

avert ▶ **verb** ❶ *she averted her head* TURN ASIDE, turn away. ❷ *an attempt to avert political chaos* PREVENT, avoid, stave off, ward off, forestall, preclude.

aviator ▶ **noun** (*dated*) PILOT, airman/woman, flyer; *dated* aeronaut.

avid ▶ **adjective** KEEN, eager, enthusiastic, ardent, passionate, zealous; devoted, dedicated, wholehearted, earnest; *Brit. informal* as keen as mustard.
– OPPOSITES apathetic.

avoid ▶ **verb** ❶ *I avoid situations that stress me* KEEP AWAY FROM, steer clear of, give a wide berth to, fight shy of. ❷ *he is trying to avoid responsibility* EVADE, dodge, sidestep, escape, run away from; *informal* duck, wriggle out of, get out of, cop out of; *Austral./NZ informal* duck-shove. ❸ *she moved to avoid a blow* DODGE, duck, get out of the way of. ❹ *you've been avoiding me all evening* SHUN, stay away from, evade, keep one's distance, elude, hide from; ignore. ❺ *he should avoid drinking alcohol* REFRAIN FROM, abstain from, desist from, eschew.
– OPPOSITES confront, face up to, seek out.

avoidable ▶ **adjective** PREVENTABLE, stoppable, avertable, escapable.
– OPPOSITES inescapable.

avow ▶ **verb** ASSERT, declare, state, maintain, swear, vow, insist; *rare* asseverate; *formal* aver.

avowed ▶ **adjective** SELF-CONFESSED, self-declared, acknowledged, admitted; open, overt.

await ▶ **verb** ❶ *Peter was awaiting news* WAIT FOR, expect, anticipate. ❷ *many dangers await them* BE IN STORE FOR, lie ahead of, lie in wait for, be waiting for.

awake ▶ **verb** ❶ *she awoke the following morning* WAKE (UP), awaken, stir, come to, come round; *poetic/literary* waken. ❷ *the alarm awoke him at 7.30* WAKE (UP), awaken, rouse, arouse; *Brit. informal* knock up. ❸ *they finally awoke to the extent of the problem* REALIZE, become aware of, become conscious of; *informal* get wise to.
▶ **adjective** ❶ *she was still awake* WAKEFUL, sleepless, restless, restive; *archaic* watchful; *rare* insomnolent. ❷ *too few are awake to the dangers* AWARE OF, conscious of, mindful of, alert to; *formal* cognizant of; *archaic* ware of.
– OPPOSITES asleep, oblivious.

awaken ▶ **verb** ❶ *I awakened early | the jolt awakened her. See* AWAKE senses 1, 2. ❷ *he had awakened strong emotions in her* AROUSE, rouse, bring out, engender, evoke, trigger, stir up, stimulate, kindle; revive; *poetic/literary* enkindle.

award ▶ **verb** *the society awarded him a silver medal* GIVE, grant, accord, assign; confer on, bestow on, present to, endow with, decorate with.
▶ **noun** ❶ *an award for high-quality service* PRIZE, trophy, medal, decoration; reward; *informal* gong. ❷ *a libel award* PAYMENT, settlement, compensation. ❸ *the Arts Council gave him an award of £1,500* GRANT, scholarship, endowment; *Brit.* bursary. ❹ *the award of an honorary doctorate* CONFERRAL, conferment, bestowal, presentation.

aware ▶ **adjective** ❶ *she is aware of the dangers* CONSCIOUS OF, mindful of, informed about, acquainted with, familiar with, alive to, alert to; *informal* wise to, in the know about, hip to; *formal* cognizant of; *archaic* ware of. ❷ *we need to be more environmentally aware* KNOWLEDGEABLE, enlightened, well informed, au fait; *informal* clued up, genned up; *Brit. informal* switched-on.
– OPPOSITES ignorant.

awareness ▶ **noun** CONSCIOUSNESS, recognition, realization; understanding, grasp, appreciation, knowledge, insight; familiarity; *formal* cognizance.

awash ▶ **adjective** ❶ *the road was awash* FLOODED, under water, submerged, submersed. ❷ *the city was awash with journalists* INUNDATED, flooded, swamped, teeming, overflowing, overrun; *informal* knee-deep in.

away ▶ **adverb** ❶ *she began to walk away* OFF, from here, from there. ❷ *stay away from the trouble* AT A DISTANCE FROM, apart from. ❸ *Bernice pushed him away* ASIDE, off, to one side. ❹ *we'll be away for two weeks* ELSEWHERE, abroad; gone, absent; on holiday, on vacation.

awe ▶ **noun** WONDER, wonderment; admiration, reverence, respect; dread, fear.

awe-inspiring ▶ **adjective.** *See* AWESOME.

awesome ▶ adjective BREATHTAKING, awe-inspiring, magnificent, amazing, stunning, staggering, imposing, stirring, impressive; formidable, fearsome; *informal* mind-boggling, mind-blowing; *poetic/literary* wondrous; *archaic* awful.
– OPPOSITES unimpressive.

awestruck ▶ adjective AWED, wonderstruck, amazed, lost for words, open-mouthed; reverential; terrified, afraid, fearful.

awful ▶ adjective ❶ *the place smelled awful* DISGUSTING, nasty, terrible, dreadful, ghastly, horrible, vile, foul, revolting, repulsive, repugnant, odious, sickening, nauseating; *informal* yucky, sick-making, gross; *Brit. informal* beastly; *poetic/literary* noisome. ❷ *an awful book* DREADFUL, terrible, frightful, atrocious, execrable; inadequate, inferior, substandard, lamentable; *informal* crummy, pathetic, rotten, woeful, lousy, appalling, abysmal, dire, poxy; *Brit. informal* duff, rubbish. ❸ *an awful accident* SERIOUS, grave, bad, terrible, dreadful. ❹ *you look awful—go and lie down* ILL, unwell, sick, peaky, queasy, nauseous; *Brit.* off colour, poorly; *informal* rough, lousy, rotten, terrible, dreadful; *Brit. informal* grotty, ropy; *Scottish informal* wabbit, peely-wally; *Austral./NZ informal* crook; *dated* queer, seedy. ❺ *I felt awful for getting so angry* REMORSEFUL, guilty, ashamed, contrite, sorry, regretful, repentant, self-reproachful. ❻ (*archaic*) *the awful sights of nature* AWE-INSPIRING, awesome, impressive; dread, fearful.
– OPPOSITES wonderful.

awfully ▶ adverb ❶ (*informal*) *an awfully nice man* VERY, extremely, really, immensely, exceedingly, thoroughly, dreadfully, exceptionally, remarkably, extraordinarily; *N. English* right; *informal* terrifically, terribly, devilishly, seriously, majorly; *Brit. informal* jolly, ever so, dead, well; *N. Amer. informal* real, mighty, awful; *informal, dated* frightfully; *archaic* exceeding. ❷ (*informal*) *thanks awfully* VERY MUCH, a lot; *informal* a million. ❸ *we played awfully* VERY BADLY, terribly, dreadfully, atrociously, appallingly, execrably; *informal* abysmally, pitifully, diabolically.

awhile ▶ adverb FOR A MOMENT, for a (little) while, for a short time; *informal* for a bit.

awkward ▶ adjective ❶ *the box was awkward to carry* DIFFICULT, tricky; cumbersome, lumbersome, unwieldy; *Brit. informal* fiddly. ❷ *an awkward time* INCONVENIENT, inappropriate, inopportune, unseasonable, difficult. ❸ *he put her in a very awkward position* EMBARRASSING, uncomfortable, unpleasant, delicate, tricky, problematic(al), troublesome, thorny; humiliating, compromising; *informal* sticky, dicey, hairy; *Brit. informal* dodgy. ❹ *she felt awkward alone with him* UNCOMFORTABLE, uneasy, tense, nervous, edgy, unquiet; self-conscious, embarrassed. ❺ *his awkward movements* CLUMSY, ungainly, uncoordinated, graceless, inelegant, gauche, gawky, wooden, stiff; unskilful, maladroit, inept, blundering; *informal* clodhopping, ham-fisted, ham-handed, cack-handed; *Brit. informal* all (fingers and) thumbs. ❻ (*Brit.*) *you're being damned awkward* UNREASONABLE, uncooperative, unhelpful, disobliging, difficult, obstructive; contrary, perverse; stubborn, obstinate; *Brit. informal* bloody-minded, bolshie; *N. Amer. informal* balky; *formal* refractory.
– OPPOSITES easy, convenient, at ease, graceful, amenable.

awning ▶ noun CANOPY, shade, sunshade, shelter, cover; *Brit.* blind, sunblind.

awry ▶ adjective ❶ *something was awry* AMISS, wrong; *informal* up. ❷ *his wig looked awry* ASKEW, crooked, lopsided, tilted, skewed, skew, squint, to one side, off-centre, uneven; *informal* cock-eyed; *Brit. informal* skew-whiff, wonky.
– OPPOSITES straight.

axe ▶ noun HATCHET, cleaver, tomahawk, adze, poleaxe; *Brit.* chopper; *historical* battleaxe.
▶ verb ❶ *the show was axed* CANCEL, withdraw, drop, scrap, discontinue, terminate, end; *informal* ditch, dump, pull the plug on. ❷ *500 staff were axed* DISMISS, make redundant, lay off, let go, discharge, get rid of; *informal* sack, fire, give someone the sack, give someone the bullet, give someone their marching orders; *Brit. informal* give someone their cards.

axiom ▶ noun ACCEPTED TRUTH, general truth, dictum, truism; maxim, adage, aphorism, apophthegm, gnome.

axis ▶ noun ❶ *the earth revolves on its axis* CENTRE LINE, vertical, horizontal. ❷ *the Anglo-American axis* ALLIANCE, coalition, bloc, union, confederation, confederacy, league.

axle ▶ noun SHAFT, spindle, rod, arbor, mandrel, pivot.

azure ▶ adjective SKY-BLUE, bright blue, blue; *poetic/literary* cerulean; *rare* cyanic.

Bb

babble ▶ **verb** ❶ *Betty babbled away* PRATTLE, rattle on, gabble, chatter, jabber, twitter, go on, run on, prate, ramble, burble, blather, blether; *informal* gab, yak, yabber, yatter, yammer, blabber, jaw, gas, shoot one's mouth off; *Brit. informal* witter, rabbit, chunter, natter, waffle; *N. Amer. informal* run off at the mouth. ❷ *a brook babbled gently* BURBLE, murmur, gurgle, purl, tinkle; *poetic/literary* plash.
▶ **noun** *his inarticulate babble* PRATTLE, gabble, chatter, jabber, prating, rambling, blather, blether; *informal* gab, yak, yabbering, yatter; *Brit. informal* wittering, waffle, natter, chuntering.

babe ▶ **noun** (*poetic/literary*). See BABY noun.

babel ▶ **noun** CLAMOUR, din, racket, confused noise, tumult, uproar, hubbub; babble, babbling, shouting, yelling, screaming; *informal* hullabaloo; *Brit. informal* row.

baby ▶ **noun** *a newborn baby* INFANT, newborn, child, tot, little one; *Scottish & N. English* bairn; *informal* sprog, tiny; *poetic/literary* babe, babe in arms; *technical* neonate.
– RELATED TERMS infantile.
▶ **adjective** *baby carrots* MINIATURE, mini, little, small, small-scale, scaled-down, toy, pocket, midget, dwarf; *Scottish* wee; *N. Amer.* vest-pocket; *informal* teeny, teeny-weeny, teensy, teensy-weensy, itsy-bitsy, itty-bitty, tiddly, bite-sized; *Brit. informal* titchy; *N. Amer. informal* little-bitty.
– OPPOSITES large.
▶ **verb** *her aunt babied her* PAMPER, mollycoddle, spoil, cosset, coddle, indulge, overindulge, pet, nanny, pander to.

babyish ▶ **adjective** CHILDISH, immature, infantile, juvenile, puerile, adolescent.
– OPPOSITES mature.

back ▶ **noun** ❶ *she's broken her back* SPINE, backbone, spinal column, vertebral column. ❷ *the back of the house* REAR, rear side, other side; *Nautical* stern. ❸ *the back of the queue* END, tail end, rear end, tail; *N. Amer.* tag end. ❹ *the back of a postcard* REVERSE, other side, underside; verso; *informal* flip side.
– RELATED TERMS dorsal, lumbar.
– OPPOSITES front, head, face.
▶ **adverb** ❶ *he pushed his chair back* BACKWARDS, behind one, to one's rear, rearwards; away, off. ❷ *a few months back* AGO, earlier, previously, before, in the past.
– OPPOSITES forward.
▶ **verb** ❶ *the record companies backed the scheme with a few hundred pounds* SPONSOR, finance, put up the money for, fund, subsidize, underwrite, be a patron of, act as guarantor of; *informal* foot the bill for, pick up the tab for; *N. Amer. informal* bankroll, stake. ❷ *most people backed the idea* SUPPORT, endorse, sanction, approve of, give one's blessing to, smile on, favour, advocate, promote, uphold, champion; vote for, ally oneself with, stand behind, side with, be on the side of, defend, take up the cudgels for; second; *informal* throw one's weight behind. ❸ *he backed the horse at 33–1* BET ON, gamble on, stake money on. ❹ *he backed away* REVERSE, draw back, step back, move backwards, back off, pull back, retreat, withdraw, give ground, backtrack, retrace one's steps.
– OPPOSITES oppose, advance.
▶ **adjective** ❶ *the back seats* REAR, rearmost, hind, hindmost, hinder, posterior. ❷ *a back copy* PAST, old, previous, earlier, former, out of date.
– OPPOSITES front, future.
■ **back down** GIVE IN, concede defeat, surrender, yield, submit, climb down, concede, reconsider; backtrack, back-pedal.
■ **back out of** RENEGE ON, go back on, withdraw from, pull out of, retreat from, fail to honour, abandon, default on, repudiate, back-pedal on.
■ **back something up** SUBSTANTIATE, corroborate, confirm, support, bear out, endorse, bolster, reinforce, lend weight to.
■ **back someone up** SUPPORT, stand by, give one's support to, side with, be on someone's side, take someone's side, take someone's part; vouch for.
■ **behind someone's back** SECRETLY, without someone's knowledge, on the sly, slyly, sneakily, covertly, surreptitiously, furtively.

backbiting ▶ **noun** MALICIOUS TALK, spiteful talk, slander, libel, defamation, abuse, character assassination, disparagement, denigration; slurs, aspersions; *informal* bitching, bitchiness, cattiness, mud-slinging, bad-mouthing; *Brit. informal* slagging off, rubbishing.

backbone ▶ **noun** ❶ *an injured backbone* SPINE, spinal column, vertebral column, vertebrae; back; *Anatomy* dorsum, rachis. ❷ *infantry are the backbone of most armies* MAINSTAY, cornerstone, foundation, chief support, buttress, pillar. ❸ *he has enough backbone to see us through* STRENGTH OF CHARACTER, strength of will, firmness of purpose, firmness, resolution, resolve, grit, determination, fortitude, mettle, spirit;

informal guts, spunk; *Brit. informal* bottle.
– RELATED TERMS spinal.

back-breaking ▶ **adjective** GRUELLING, arduous, strenuous, onerous, punishing, crushing, demanding, exacting, taxing, exhausting, draining; *informal* killing; *Brit. informal* knackering; *archaic* toilsome.
– OPPOSITES easy.

backchat ▶ **noun** (*Brit. informal*) IMPUDENCE, impertinence, cheek, cheekiness, effrontery, insolence, rudeness, rude retorts; answering back, talking back; *informal* mouth, lip; *N. Amer. informal* sass, smart mouth, back talk; *rare* contumely.

backer ▶ **noun** ❶ *£3 million was provided by the project's backers* SPONSOR, investor, underwriter, financier, patron, benefactor, benefactress; *informal* angel. ❷ *the backers of the proposition* SUPPORTER, defender, advocate, promoter, proponent; seconder; *N. Amer.* booster.

backfire ▶ **verb** *Bernard's plan backfired on him* REBOUND, boomerang, come back; fail, miscarry, go wrong; *informal* blow up in someone's face; *archaic* redound on.

background ▶ **noun** ❶ *a background of palm trees* BACKDROP, backcloth, surrounding(s), setting, scene. ❷ *students from many different backgrounds* SOCIAL CIRCUMSTANCES, family circumstances; environment, class, culture, tradition; upbringing. ❸ *her nursing background* EXPERIENCE, record, history, past, training, education, grounding, knowledge. ❹ *the political background* CIRCUMSTANCES, context, conditions, situation, environment, milieu, scene, scenario.
– OPPOSITES foreground.
■ **in the background** *maybe there was a sugar daddy in the background* BEHIND THE SCENES, out of the public eye, out of the spotlight, out of the limelight, backstage; inconspicuous, unobtrusive, unnoticed.

backhanded ▶ **adjective** INDIRECT, ambiguous, oblique, equivocal; double-edged, two-edged; tongue-in-cheek.
– OPPOSITES direct.

backing ▶ **noun** ❶ *he has the backing of his colleagues* SUPPORT, help, assistance, aid; approval, endorsement, sanction, blessing. ❷ *financial backing* SPONSORSHIP, funding, patronage; money, investment, funds, finance; grant, contribution, subsidy. ❸ *musical backing* ACCOMPANIMENT; harmony, obbligato.

backlash ▶ **noun** ADVERSE REACTION, adverse response, counterblast, comeback; retaliation, reprisal.

backlog ▶ **noun** ACCUMULATION, logjam, pile-up.

back-pedal ▶ **verb** *the government has back-pedalled on its plans* CHANGE ONE'S MIND, go into reverse, backtrack, back down, climb down, do an about-face, do a U-turn, renege, go back on, back out of, fail to honour, withdraw, take back, default on; *Brit.* do an about-turn.

backslide ▶ **verb** *many things can cause slimmers to backslide* RELAPSE, lapse, regress, retrogress, weaken, lose one's resolve, give in to temptation, go astray, leave the straight and narrow.
– OPPOSITES persevere.

backslider ▶ **noun** RECIDIVIST, regressor; apostate, fallen angel.

back-up ▶ **noun** HELP, support, assistance, aid; reinforcements, reserves, additional resources.

backward ▶ **adjective** ❶ *a backward look* REARWARD, to/towards the rear, to/towards the back, behind one, reverse. ❷ *the decision was a backward step* RETROGRADE, retrogressive, regressive, for the worse, in the wrong direction, downhill, negative. ❸ *an economically backward country* UNDERDEVELOPED, undeveloped; primitive, benighted. ❹ *he was not backward in displaying his talents* HESITANT, reticent, reluctant; shy, diffident, bashful, timid; unwilling, afraid, loath, averse.
– OPPOSITES forward, progressive, advanced, confident.
▶ **adverb** *the car rolled slowly backward. See* BACKWARDS.

backwards ▶ **adverb** ❶ *Penny glanced backwards* TOWARDS THE REAR, rearwards, backward, behind one. ❷ *count backwards from twenty to ten* IN REVERSE, in reverse order.
– OPPOSITES forwards.

backwash ▶ **noun** ❶ *a ship's backwash* WAKE, wash, slipstream, backflow. ❷ *the backwash of the Cuban missile crisis* REPERCUSSIONS, reverberations, after-effects, aftermath, fallout.

backwoods ▶ **plural noun** THE BACK OF BEYOND, remote areas, the wilds, the hinterlands, a backwater; *N. Amer.* the backcountry, the backland; *informal* the middle of nowhere, the sticks; *N. Amer. informal* the boondocks, the boonies; *Austral./NZ informal* beyond the black stump.

bacteria ▶ **plural noun** MICRO-ORGANISMS, microbes, germs, bacilli, pathogens; *informal* bugs.

bad ▶ **adjective** ❶ *bad workmanship* SUBSTANDARD, poor, inferior, second-rate, second-class, unsatisfactory, inadequate, unacceptable, not up to scratch, not up to par, deficient, imperfect, defective, faulty, shoddy, amateurish, careless, negligent, miserable, sorry; incompetent, inept, inexpert, ineffectual; *informal* crummy, rotten, pathetic, useless, woeful, bum, lousy, ropy, not up to snuff; *Brit. informal* duff, rubbish. ❷ *the alcohol had a really bad effect on me* HARMFUL, damaging, detrimental, injurious, hurtful, inimical, destructive, ruinous, deleterious; unhealthy, unwholesome. ❸ *the bad guys* WICKED, sinful, immoral, evil, morally wrong, corrupt, base, black-hearted, reprobate, amoral; criminal, villainous, nefarious, iniquitous, dishonest, dishonourable, unscrupulous, unprincipled; *informal* crooked, bent, dirty; *dated* dastardly. ❹ *you bad girl!* NAUGHTY, badly behaved, disobedient, wayward, wilful, self-willed, defiant, unruly, insubordinate, undisciplined. ❺ *bad news* UNPLEASANT, disagreeable, unwelcome; unfortunate, unlucky, unfavourable; terrible, dreadful, awful, grim, distressing. ❻ *a bad time to arrive* INAUSPICIOUS, unfavourable, inopportune, unpropitious, unfortunate, disadvantageous, adverse, inappropriate, unsuitable, untoward. ❼ *a bad accident* SEVERE, serious, grave, critical, acute; *formal* grievous. ❽ *the meat's bad* ROTTEN, off, decayed, decomposed, decomposing, putrid, putrefied, mouldy, mouldering; sour, rancid, rank, unfit for human consumption; addled. ❾ *if you still feel bad, stay in bed. See* ILL adjective sense 1. ❿ *a bad knee* INJURED, wounded, diseased; *Brit. informal* gammy, knackered; *Austral./NZ informal* crook. ⓫ *I felt bad about leaving them* GUILTY, conscience-stricken, remorseful, guilt-ridden, ashamed, contrite, sorry, full of regret, regretful, shamefaced. ⓬ *a bad cheque* INVALID, worthless; counterfeit, fake, false, bogus, fraudulent; *informal* phoney, dud. ⓭ *bad language* OFFENSIVE, vulgar, crude, foul, obscene, rude, coarse, smutty, dirty, filthy, indecent, indecorous; blasphemous, profane.

– OPPOSITES good, beneficial, virtuous, well behaved, minor, slight, fresh, unrepentant.

■ **not bad** ALL RIGHT, adequate, good enough, reasonable, fair, decent, average, tolerable, acceptable, passable, middling, moderate, fine; *informal* OK, so-so, fair-to-middling.

badge ▶ **noun** ❶ *a name badge* pin, brooch; *N. Amer.* button. ❷ *a badge of success* SIGN, symbol, indication, signal, mark; hallmark, trademark.

badger ▶ **verb** PESTER, harass, bother, plague, torment, hound, nag, chivvy, harry, keep on at, go on at; *informal* hassle, bug.

badinage ▶ **noun** BANTER, repartee, witty conversation, raillery, wordplay, cut and thrust; witticisms, bons mots, ripostes, sallies, quips; *N. Amer. informal* josh.

badly ▶ **adverb** ❶ *the job had been very badly done* POORLY, incompetently, ineptly, inexpertly, inefficiently, imperfectly, deficiently, defectively, unsatisfactorily, inadequately, incorrectly, faultily, shoddily, amateurishly, carelessly, negligently; *informal* crummily, pitifully, woefully. ❷ *try not to think badly of me* UNFAVOURABLY, ill, critically, disapprovingly. ❸ *stop behaving badly* NAUGHTILY, disobediently, wilfully, reprehensibly, mischievously. ❹ *he had been badly treated* CRUELLY, wickedly, unkindly, harshly, shamefully; unfairly, unjustly, wrongly, improperly. ❺ *it turned out badly* UNSUCCESSFULLY, unfavourably, adversely, unfortunately, unhappily, unluckily. ❻ *some of the victims are badly hurt* SEVERELY, seriously, gravely, acutely, critically; *formal* grievously. ❼ *she badly needs help* DESPERATELY, sorely, intensely, seriously, very much, greatly, exceedingly.

– OPPOSITES well, slightly.

bad-tempered ▶ **adjective** IRRITABLE, irascible, tetchy, testy, grumpy, grouchy, crotchety, in a (bad) mood, cantankerous, curmudgeonly, ill-tempered, ill-humoured, peevish, having got out of bed on the wrong side, cross, as cross as two sticks, fractious, pettish, crabby; *informal* snappish, on a short fuse; *Brit. informal* shirty, stroppy, ratty; *N. Amer. informal* cranky, ornery; *Austral./NZ informal* snaky; *informal, dated* miffy.

– OPPOSITES good-humoured, affable.

baffle ▶ **verb** PERPLEX, puzzle, bewilder, mystify, bemuse, confuse, confound, nonplus; *informal* flummox, faze, stump, beat, fox, make someone scratch their head, be all Greek to, floor; *N. Amer. informal* discombobulate, buffalo.

– OPPOSITES enlighten.

baffling ▶ **adjective** PUZZLING, BEWILDERING, perplexing, mystifying, bemusing, confusing, unclear; inexplicable, incomprehensible, impenetrable, cryptic, opaque.

– OPPOSITES clear, comprehensible.

bag ▶ **noun** ❶ *I dug around in my bag for my lipstick* HANDBAG, shoulder bag, clutch bag, evening bag, pochette; *N. Amer.* pocketbook, purse; *historical* reticule, scrip. ❷ *she began to unpack her bags* SUITCASE, case, valise, portmanteau, holdall, grip, overnighter; backpack, rucksack, knapsack, haversack, kitbag, duffel bag; satchel; (**bags**) luggage, baggage.

▶ **verb** ❶ *locals bagged the most fish* CATCH, land, capture, trap, snare, ensnare; kill, shoot. ❷ *he bagged seven medals* GET, secure, obtain, acquire, pick up; win, achieve, attain; commandeer, grab, appropriate, take; *informal* get one's hands on, land, net.

baggage ▶ **noun** LUGGAGE, suitcases, cases, bags.

baggy ▶ **adjective** LOOSE-FITTING, loose, roomy, generously cut, full, ample, voluminous, billowing; oversized, shapeless, ill-fitting, tent-like, sack-like.

– OPPOSITES tight.

bail ▶ **noun** *he was released on bail* SURETY, security, assurance, indemnity, indemnification; bond, guarantee, pledge; *archaic* gage.

■ **bail out** *the pilot bailed out* EJECT, parachute to safety.

■ **bail someone/something out** RESCUE, save, relieve; finance, help (out), assist, aid; *informal* save someone's bacon/neck/skin.

bait ▶ **noun** ❶ *the fish let go of the bait* LURE, decoy, fly, troll, jig, plug. ❷ *was she the bait to lure him into a trap?* ENTICEMENT, lure, decoy, snare, trap, siren, carrot, attraction, draw, magnet, incentive, temptation, inducement; *informal* come-on.

▶ **verb** *he was baited at school* TAUNT, tease, goad, pick on, torment, persecute, plague, harry, harass, hound; *informal* needle; *Brit. informal* wind up, nark.

bake ▶ **verb** ❶ *bake the fish for 15–20 minutes* COOK, oven-bake, roast, dry-roast, pot-roast; *rare* oven. ❷ *the earth was baked by the sun* SCORCH, burn, sear, parch, dry (up), desiccate.

balance ▶ **noun** ❶ *I tripped and lost my balance* STABILITY, equilibrium, steadiness, footing. ❷ *political balance in broadcasting* FAIRNESS, justice, impartiality, egalitarianism, equal opportunity; parity, equity, equilibrium, equipoise, evenness, symmetry, correspondence, uniformity, equality, equivalence, comparability. ❸ *this stylistic development provides a balance to the rest of the work* COUNTERBALANCE, counterweight, stabilizer, compensation. ❹ *the food was weighed on a balance* SCALE(S), weighing machine, weighbridge. ❺ *the balance of the rent* REMAINDER, outstanding amount, rest, residue, difference, remaining part.
–OPPOSITES instability.

▶ **verb** ❶ *she balanced the book on her head* STEADY, stabilize, poise, level. ❷ *he balanced his radical remarks with more familiar declarations* COUNTERBALANCE, balance out, offset, even out/up, counteract, compensate for, make up for. ❸ *their income and expenditure do not balance* CORRESPOND, agree, tally, match up, concur, coincide, be in agreement, be consistent, equate, be equal. ❹ *you need to balance cost against benefit* WEIGH, weigh up, compare, evaluate, consider, assess, appraise, judge.

■ **in the balance** UNCERTAIN, undetermined, unsettled, unresolved, unsure, pending, in limbo, up in the air, at a turning point, critical, at a critical stage, at a crisis.

■ **on balance** OVERALL, all in all, all things considered, taking everything into consideration/account, by and large, on average.

balanced ▶ **adjective** ❶ *a balanced view* FAIR, equitable, just, unbiased, unprejudiced, objective, impartial, dispassionate. ❷ *a balanced diet* MIXED, varied; healthy, sensible. ❸ *a balanced individual* LEVEL-HEADED, well balanced, well adjusted, mature, stable, sensible, practical, realistic, with both feet on the ground, pragmatic, reasonable, rational, sane, even-tempered, commonsensical, full of common sense; *informal* together.
–OPPOSITES partial, unhealthy, neurotic.

balcony ▶ **noun** ❶ *the balcony of the villa* veranda, loggia, terrace, patio. ❷ *the applause from the balcony* GALLERY, upper circle; *informal* the gods.

bald ▶ **adjective** ❶ *a bald head* HAIRLESS, smooth, shaven, depilated; bald-headed. ❷ *a few bald bushes* LEAFLESS, bare, uncovered. ❸ *a bald statement* PLAIN, simple, unadorned, unvarnished, unembellished, undisguised, unveiled, stark, severe, austere, brutal, harsh; blunt, direct, forthright, plain-spoken, straight, straightforward, candid, honest, truthful, realistic, frank, outspoken; *informal* upfront.
–OPPOSITES hairy, lush, vague.

balderdash ▶ **noun**. *See* NONSENSE sense 1.

baldness ▶ **noun** HAIR LOSS, hairlessness; *Medicine* alopecia.

bale[1] ▶ **noun** *a bale of cotton* BUNDLE, truss, bunch, pack, package, parcel.

bale[2]

■ **bale out**. *See* BAIL.

baleful ▶ **adjective** MENACING, threatening, unfriendly, hostile, antagonistic, evil, evil-intentioned, vindictive, malevolent, malicious, malignant, malign, sinister; harmful, injurious, dangerous, noxious, pernicious, deadly, venomous, poisonous; *poetic/literary* malefic, maleficent.
–OPPOSITES benevolent, friendly.

balk ▶ **verb**. *See* BAULK.

ball[1] ▶ **noun** ❶ *a ball of dough* SPHERE, globe, orb, globule, spherule, spheroid, ovoid. ❷ *a musket ball* BULLET, pellet, slug, projectile.

ball[2] ▶ **noun** *a fancy-dress ball* DANCE, dinner dance, masked ball, masquerade; *N. Amer.* hoedown, prom; *informal* hop, disco, bop.

ballad ▶ **noun** SONG, folk song, shanty, ditty, canzone; poem, tale, saga.

balloon ▶ **noun** hot-air balloon, barrage balloon; airship, dirigible, Zeppelin; envelope, gasbag; *informal* blimp.

▶ **verb** ❶ *her long skirt ballooned in the wind* SWELL (OUT), puff out/up, bulge (out), bag, belly (out), fill (out), billow (out). ❷ *the company's debt has ballooned* INCREASE RAPIDLY, soar, rocket, shoot up, escalate, mount, surge, spiral; *informal* go through the roof, skyrocket.
–OPPOSITES plummet.

ballot ▶ **noun** VOTE, poll, election, referendum, plebiscite, show of hands.

ballyhoo ▶ **noun** (*informal*) PUBLICITY, advertising, promotion, marketing, propaganda, push, puffery, build-up, boosting; fuss, excitement; *informal* hype, spiel, hoo-ha, hullabaloo, splash.

balm ▶ **noun** ❶ *a skin balm* OINTMENT, lotion, cream, salve, liniment, embrocation, rub, gel, emollient, unguent, balsam, moisturizer; *dated* pomade; *technical* demulcent, humectant; *archaic* unction. ❷ *balm for troubled spirits* RELIEF, comfort, ease, succour, consolation, cheer, solace; *poetic/literary* easement.
–OPPOSITES astringent, misery.

balmy ▶ **adjective** MILD, gentle, temperate, summery, calm, tranquil, clement, fine, pleasant, benign, soothing, soft.
–OPPOSITES harsh, wintry.

bamboozle ▶ **verb** (*informal*). *See* TRICK verb.

ban ▶ **verb** ❶ *smoking was banned* PROHIBIT, forbid, veto, proscribe, disallow, outlaw, make illegal, embargo, bar, debar, block, stop, suppress, interdict; *Law* enjoin, restrain. ❷ *Gary was banned from the playground* EXCLUDE, banish, expel, eject, evict, drive out, force out, oust, remove, get rid of; *informal* boot out, kick out; *Brit. informal* turf out.
– OPPOSITES permit, admit.
▶ **noun** ❶ *a ban on smoking* PROHIBITION, veto, proscription, embargo, bar, suppression, stoppage, interdict, interdiction, moratorium, injunction. ❷ *a ban from international football* EXCLUSION, banishment, expulsion, ejection, eviction, removal.
– OPPOSITES permission, admission.

banal ▶ **adjective** TRITE, hackneyed, clichéd, platitudinous, vapid, commonplace, ordinary, common, stock, conventional, stereotyped, overused, overdone, overworked, stale, worn out, time-worn, tired, threadbare, hoary, hack, unimaginative, unoriginal, uninteresting, dull; *informal* old hat, corny, played out; *N. Amer. informal* cornball, dime-store.
– OPPOSITES original.

banality ▶ **noun** ❶ *the banality of most sitcoms* TRITENESS, platitudinousness, vapidity, staleness, unimaginativeness, lack of originality, prosaicness, dullness; *informal* corniness. ❷ *they exchanged banalities* PLATITUDE, cliché, truism, commonplace, old chestnut, bromide.
– OPPOSITES originality, epigram, witticism.

band[1] ▶ **noun** ❶ *a band round her waist* BELT, sash, girdle, strap, tape, ring, hoop, loop, circlet, circle, cord, tie, string, thong, ribbon, fillet, strip; *poetic/literary* cincture. ❷ *the green band round his pullover* STRIPE, strip, streak, line, bar, belt, swathe; *technical* stria, striation.

band[2] ▶ **noun** ❶ *a band of robbers* GROUP, gang, mob, pack, troop, troupe, company, party, crew, body, working party, posse; team, side, line-up; association, society, club, circle, fellowship, partnership, guild, lodge, order, fraternity, confraternity, sodality, brotherhood, sisterhood, sorority, union, alliance, affiliation, institution, league, federation, clique, set, coterie; *informal* bunch. ❷ *the band played on* (MUSICAL) GROUP, pop group, ensemble, orchestra; *informal* combo.
▶ **verb** *local people banded together* JOIN (UP), team up, join forces, pool resources, club together, get together; amalgamate, unite, form an alliance, form an association, affiliate, federate.
– OPPOSITES split up.

bandage ▶ **noun** *she had a bandage on her foot* DRESSING, covering, gauze, compress, plaster, tourniquet; *trademark* Elastoplast, Band-Aid.
▶ **verb** *she bandaged my knee* BIND, bind up, dress, cover, wrap, swaddle, strap (up).

bandit ▶ **noun** *they were robbed by bandits* ROBBER, thief, raider, mugger; freebooter, outlaw, hijacker, looter, marauder, gangster; *dated* desperado; *poetic/literary* brigand; *historical* rustler, highwayman, footpad, reaver; *Scottish historical* mosstrooper.

bandy[1] ▶ **adjective** *bandy legs* BOWED, curved, bent; bow-legged, bandy-legged.
– OPPOSITES straight.

bandy[2] ▶ **verb** ❶ *lots of figures were bandied about* SPREAD (ABOUT/AROUND), put about, toss about, discuss, rumour, mention, repeat; *poetic/literary* bruit about/abroad. ❷ *I'm not going to bandy words with you* EXCHANGE, swap, trade.

bane ▶ **noun** SCOURGE, plague, curse, blight, pest, nuisance, headache, nightmare, trial, hardship, cross to bear, burden, thorn in one's flesh/side, bitter pill, affliction, trouble, misery, woe, tribulation, misfortune; *informal* pain.

bang ▶ **noun** ❶ *the door slammed with a bang* THUD, thump, bump, crack, crash, smack, boom, clang, clap, knock, tap, clunk, clonk; stamp, stomp, clump, clomp; report, explosion, detonation; *informal* wham, whump, whomp. ❷ *a nasty bang on the head* BLOW, knock, thump, bump, hit, smack, crack; *informal* bash, whack, thwack.
▶ **verb** ❶ *he banged the table with his fist* HIT, strike, beat, thump, hammer, knock, rap, pound, thud, punch, bump, smack, crack, slap, slam, welt, cuff, pummel, buffet; *informal* bash, whack, thwack, clobber, clout, clip, wallop, belt, biff, bop, sock, lam, whomp; *Brit. informal* slosh; *N. Amer. informal* boff, bust, slug, whale. ❷ *fireworks banged in the air* GO BANG, thud, thump, boom, clap, pound, crack, crash, explode, detonate, burst, blow up.
▶ **adverb** (*informal*) ❶ *bang in the middle of town* | *bang on time* PRECISELY, exactly, right, directly, immediately, squarely, dead; promptly, prompt, dead on, on the stroke of ——, on the dot of ——; sharp, on the dot; *informal* smack, slap, slap bang, plumb; *N. Amer. informal* on the button, on the nose, smack dab, spang. ❷ *bang up to date* COMPLETELY, absolutely, totally, entirely, wholly, fully, thoroughly, in all respects, utterly, perfectly, quite, altogether, one hundred per cent.

bangle ▶ **noun** BRACELET, wristlet, anklet, armlet.

banish ▶ **verb** ❶ *he was banished for his crime* EXILE, expel, deport, eject, expatriate, extradite, repatriate, transport; cast out, oust, evict, throw out, exclude, shut out, ban. ❷ *he tried to banish his fear* DISPEL, dismiss, disperse, scatter, dissipate, drive away, chase away, shut out, quell, allay.
– OPPOSITES admit, engender.

banister ▶ **noun** HANDRAIL, railing, rail; baluster; balustrade.

bank[1] ▶ **noun** ❶ *the banks of Lake Michigan* EDGE,

side, embankment, levee, border, verge, boundary, margin, rim, fringe; *poetic/literary* marge, bourn, skirt. ❷ *a grassy bank* SLOPE, rise, incline, gradient, ramp; mound, ridge, hillock, hummock, knoll; bar, reef, shoal, shelf; accumulation, pile, heap, mass, drift. ❸ *a bank of switches* ARRAY, row, line, tier, group, series.

– RELATED TERMS riparian, riverain.

▶ **verb** ❶ *they banked up the earth* PILE (UP), heap (up), stack (up); accumulate, amass, assemble, put together. ❷ *the aircraft banked* TILT, LEAN, tip, slant, incline, angle, slope, list, camber, pitch, dip, cant.

bank² ▶ **noun** ❶ *money in the bank* FINANCIAL INSTITUTION, merchant bank, savings bank, finance company, finance house; *Brit.* building society; *N. Amer.* savings and loan (association), thrift. ❷ *a blood bank* STORE, reserve, accumulation, stock, stockpile, supply, pool, fund, cache, hoard, deposit; storehouse, reservoir, repository, depository.

▶ **verb** ❶ *I banked the money* DEPOSIT, pay in. ❷ *they bank with Barclays* HAVE AN ACCOUNT AT, deposit one's money with, use, be a customer of.

■ **bank on** RELY ON, depend on, count on, place reliance on, bargain on, plan on, reckon on, calculate on; anticipate, expect; be confident of, be sure of, pin one's hopes/faith on; *N. Amer. informal* figure on.

banknote ▶ **noun** NOTE; *N. Amer.* bill; *US informal* greenback; *US & historical* Treasury note; (**banknotes**) paper money.

bankrupt ▶ **adjective** ❶ *the company was declared bankrupt* INSOLVENT, failed, ruined, in debt, owing money, in the red, in arrears; *Brit.* in administration, in receivership; *informal* bust, belly up, gone to the wall, broke, flat broke; *informal, dated* smashed; *Brit. informal* skint, stony broke, in Queer Street; *Brit. informal, dated* in Carey Street. ❷ *this government is bankrupt of ideas* BEREFT, devoid, empty, destitute; completely lacking, without, in need of, wanting; *informal* minus, sans.

– OPPOSITES solvent, teeming with.

▶ **verb** *the strike nearly bankrupted the union* RUIN, impoverish, reduce to penury/destitution, bring to ruin, bring someone to their knees, wipe out, break, pauperize; *rare* beggar.

bankruptcy ▶ **noun** *many companies were facing bankruptcy* INSOLVENCY, liquidation, failure, (financial) ruin; *Brit.* administration, receivership.

– OPPOSITES solvency.

banner ▶ **noun** ❶ *students waved banners* PLACARD, sign, poster, notice. ❷ *banners fluttered above the troops* FLAG, standard, ensign, colour(s), pennant, banderole, guidon; *Brit.* pendant; *Nautical* burgee.

banquet ▶ **noun** FEAST, dinner; *informal* spread, blowout; *Brit. informal* nosh-up, slap-up meal; *Brit. informal, dated* tuck-in.

– OPPOSITES snack.

banter ▶ **noun** *a brief exchange of banter* REPARTEE, witty conversation, raillery, wordplay, cut and thrust, badinage; *N. Amer. informal* josh.

▶ **verb** *sightseers were bantering with the guards* JOKE, jest, quip; *informal* josh, wisecrack.

baptism ▶ **noun** ❶ *the baptism ceremony* CHRISTENING, naming; *rare* lustration. ❷ *his baptism as a politician* INITIATION, debut, introduction, inauguration, launch, rite of passage.

baptize ▶ **verb** ❶ *he was baptized as a baby* CHRISTEN; *rare* lustrate. ❷ *they were baptized into the church* ADMIT, initiate, enrol, recruit, convert. ❸ *he was baptized Enoch* NAME, give the name, call, dub; *formal* denominate.

bar ▶ **noun** ❶ *an iron bar* ROD, pole, stick, batten, shaft, rail, paling, spar, strut, crosspiece, beam. ❷ *a bar of chocolate* BLOCK, slab, cake, tablet, brick, loaf, wedge, ingot. ❸ *your drinks are on the bar* COUNTER, table, buffet, stand. ❹ *she had a drink in a bar* HOSTELRY, tavern, inn, taproom; *Brit.* pub, public house; *informal* watering hole; *Brit. informal* local, boozer; *historical* alehouse; *N. Amer. historical* saloon. ❺ *a bar to promotion* OBSTACLE, impediment, hindrance, obstruction, block, hurdle, barrier, stumbling block. ❻ (*Brit.*) *members of the Bar* BARRISTERS, advocates, counsel. ❼ *the bar across the river mouth* SANDBANK, shoal, shallow, reef.

– OPPOSITES aid.

▶ **verb** ❶ *they have barred the door* BOLT, lock, fasten, secure, block, barricade, obstruct. ❷ *I was barred from entering* PROHIBIT, debar, preclude, forbid, ban, interdict, inhibit; exclude, keep out; obstruct, hinder, block; *Law* enjoin.

– OPPOSITES open, admit.

▶ **preposition** *everyone bar me.* See EXCEPT preposition.

barb ▶ **noun** ❶ *the hook has a nasty barb* SPIKE, prong, spur, thorn, needle, prickle, spine, quill. ❷ *the barbs from his critics* INSULT, sneer, jibe, cutting remark, shaft, slight, brickbat, slur, jeer, taunt; (**barbs**) abuse, disparagement, scoffing, scorn, sarcasm, goading; *informal* dig, put-down.

barbarian ▶ **noun** *the city was besieged by barbarians* SAVAGE, heathen, brute, beast, wild man/woman; ruffian, thug, lout, vandal, hoodlum, hooligan; *informal* roughneck; *Brit. informal* yobbo, yob, lager lout.

▶ **adjective** *the barbarian hordes* SAVAGE, uncivilized, barbaric, primitive, heathen, wild, brutish, Neanderthal.

– OPPOSITES civilized.

barbaric ▶ **adjective** ❶ *barbaric crimes* BRUTAL, barbarous, brutish, bestial, savage, vicious, wicked, cruel, ruthless, merciless, villainous, murderous, heinous, monstrous, vile, inhuman, infernal, dark, fiendish, diabolical. ❷ *barbaric cultures* SAVAGE, barbarian, primitive, heathen, wild, brutish, Neanderthal.

– OPPOSITES civilized.

barbarity ▶ **noun** ❶ *the barbarity of slavery* BRUTALITY, brutalism, cruelty, bestiality, barbarism, barbarousness, savagery, viciousness, wickedness, villainy, baseness, inhumanity. ❷ *the barbarities of the last war* ATROCITY, act of brutality, act of savagery, crime, outrage, enormity.
– OPPOSITES benevolence.

barbarous ▶ **adjective.** *See* BARBARIC sense 1.

barbecue ▶ **noun** *she held a barbecue* MEAL COOKED OUTDOORS, —— roast; *N. Amer.* cookout; *informal* barbie, BBQ.
▶ **verb** *they barbecued some steaks* COOK OUTDOORS, grill, spit-roast; *N. Amer.* broil, charbroil.

barbed ▶ **adjective** HURTFUL, wounding, cutting, stinging, mean, spiteful, nasty, cruel, vicious, unkind, snide, scathing, pointed, bitter, acid, caustic, sharp, vitriolic, venomous, poisonous, hostile, malicious, malevolent, vindictive; *informal* bitchy, catty.
– OPPOSITES kindly.

bard ▶ **noun** (*poetic/literary*). *See* POET.

bare ▶ **adjective** ❶ *he was bare to the waist* NAKED, unclothed, undressed, uncovered, stripped, having nothing on, nude, in the nude, stark naked; *informal* without a stitch on, in one's birthday suit, in the raw, in the altogether, in the buff; *Brit. informal* starkers; *Scottish informal* in the scud; *N. Amer. informal* buck naked. ❷ *a bare room* EMPTY, unfurnished, cleared; stark, austere, spartan, unadorned, unembellished, unornamented, plain. ❸ *a cupboard bare of food* EMPTY, devoid, bereft; without, lacking, wanting, free from. ❹ *a bare landscape* BARREN, bleak, exposed, desolate, stark, arid, desert, lunar; treeless, deforested. ❺ *the bare facts* BASIC, essential, fundamental, plain, straightforward, simple, pure, stark, bald, cold, hard, brutal, harsh. ❻ *a bare minimum* MERE, no more than, simple; slim, slight, slender, paltry, minimum.
– OPPOSITES clothed, furnished, embellished, lush.
▶ **verb** *he bared his arm* UNCOVER, strip, lay bare, undress, unclothe, denude, expose.
– OPPOSITES cover.

barefaced ▶ **adjective** FLAGRANT, blatant, glaring, obvious, undisguised, unconcealed, naked; shameless, unabashed, unashamed, impudent, audacious, unblushing, brazen, brass-necked.

barely ▶ **adverb** HARDLY, scarcely, just, only just, narrowly, by the skin of one's teeth, by a hair's breadth; almost not; *informal* by a whisker.
– OPPOSITES easily.

bargain ▶ **noun** ❶ *I'll make a bargain with you* AGREEMENT, arrangement, understanding, deal; contract, pact, compact; pledge, promise. ❷ *this binder is a bargain at £1.98* GOOD BUY, cheap buy; (good) value for money, surprisingly cheap; *informal* snip, steal, giveaway.
– OPPOSITES rip-off.
▶ **verb** *they bargained over the contract* HAGGLE, negotiate, discuss terms, hold talks, deal, barter, dicker; *formal* treat.
■ **bargain for/on** EXPECT, anticipate, be prepared for, allow for, plan for, reckon with, take into account/consideration, contemplate, imagine, envisage, foresee, predict; count on, rely on, depend on, bank on, plan on, reckon on; *N. Amer. informal* figure on.
■ **into the bargain** ALSO, as well, in addition, additionally, besides, on top (of that), over and above that, to boot, for good measure; *N. Amer.* in the bargain.

barge ▶ **noun** lighter, canal boat; *Brit.* narrowboat, wherry; *N. Amer.* scow.
▶ **verb** *he barged us out of the way* PUSH, shove, force, elbow, shoulder, jostle, bulldoze, muscle.
■ **barge in** BURST IN, break in, butt in, cut in, interrupt, intrude, encroach; gatecrash; *informal* horn in.

bark[1] ▶ **noun** *the bark of a dog* WOOF, yap, yelp, bay.
▶ **verb** ❶ *the dog barked* WOOF, yap, yelp, bay. ❷ *'Okay, outside!' he barked* SAY BRUSQUELY, say abruptly, say angrily, snap; shout, bawl, cry, yell, roar, bellow, thunder; *informal* holler.
– OPPOSITES whisper.

bark[2] ▶ **noun** *the bark of a tree* RIND, skin, peel, covering; integument; cork; *technical* cortex.
– RELATED TERMS corticate.
▶ **verb** *he barked his shin* SCRAPE, graze, scratch, abrade, scuff, rasp, skin.

barmy ▶ **adjective** (*Brit. informal*). *See* FOOLISH.

barn ▶ **noun** OUTBUILDING, shed, outhouse, shelter; stable, stall; *Brit.* byre; *archaic* grange, garner.

baron ▶ **noun** ❶ *he was created a baron* LORD, noble, nobleman, aristocrat, peer. ❷ *a press baron* MAGNATE, tycoon, mogul, captain of industry, nabob, mandarin.

baroque ▶ **adjective** ❶ *the baroque exuberance of his printed silk shirts* ORNATE, fancy, over-elaborate, extravagant, rococo, fussy, busy, ostentatious, showy. ❷ *baroque prose* FLOWERY, florid, flamboyant, high-flown, high-sounding, magniloquent, grandiloquent, orotund, overblown, convoluted, pleonastic; *informal* highfalutin, purple; *rare* fustian.
– OPPOSITES plain.

barrack ▶ **verb** (*Brit. & Austral./NZ*) JEER, heckle, shout at/down; interrupt, boo, hiss.
– OPPOSITES applaud.

barracks ▶ **plural noun** GARRISON, camp, encampment, depot, billet, quarters, fort, cantonment.

barrage ▶ **noun** ❶ *an artillery barrage* BOMBARDMENT, cannonade; gunfire, shelling; salvo, volley, fusillade; *historical* broadside. ❷ *a barrage of* *criticism* DELUGE, stream, storm, torrent, onslaught, flood, spate, tide, avalanche, hail, blaze; abundance, mass, profusion. ❸ *a barrage across the river* DAM, barrier, weir, dyke, embankment, wall.

barrel ▶ **noun** CASK, keg, butt, vat, tun, drum, hogshead, kilderkin, pin, pipe; *historical* firkin.
– RELATED TERMS cooper, stave, hoop.

barren ▶ **adjective** ❶ *barren land* UNPRODUCTIVE, infertile, unfruitful, sterile, arid, desert. ❷ (*archaic*) *a barren woman* INFERTILE, sterile, childless; *technical* infecund. ❸ *a barren exchange of courtesies* POINTLESS, futile, worthless, profitless, valueless, unrewarding, purposeless, useless, vain, aimless, hollow, empty, vacuous, vapid.
– OPPOSITES fertile.

barricade ▶ **noun** *a barricade across the street* BARRIER, roadblock, blockade; obstacle, obstruction.
▶ **verb** *they barricaded the building* SEAL (UP), close up, block off, shut off/up; defend, protect, fortify, occupy.

barrier ▶ **noun** ❶ *the barrier across the entrance* FENCE, railing, barricade, hurdle, bar, blockade, roadblock. ❷ *a barrier to international trade* OBSTACLE, obstruction, hurdle, stumbling block, bar, block, impediment, hindrance, curb.

barring ▶ **preposition** EXCEPT FOR, with the exception of, excepting, if there is/are no, bar, discounting, short of, apart from, but for, other than, aside from, excluding, omitting, leaving out, save for, saving; *informal* outside of.

barrister ▶ **noun** COUNSEL, Queen's Counsel, QC, lawyer; *Scottish* advocate; *N. Amer.* attorney, counselor(-at-law); *informal* brief; (**barristers**) *Brit.* the Bar.

barter ▶ **verb** ❶ *they bartered grain for salt* TRADE, swap, exchange, sell. ❷ *you can barter for souvenirs* HAGGLE, bargain, negotiate, discuss terms, deal, dicker; *formal* treat.
▶ **noun** *an economy based on barter* TRADING, trade, exchange, business, commerce, buying and selling, dealing.

base[1] ▶ **noun** ❶ *the base of the tower* FOUNDATION, bottom, foot, support, stand, pedestal, plinth. ❷ *the system uses existing technology as its base* BASIS, foundation, bedrock, starting point, source, origin, root(s), core, key component, heart, backbone. ❸ *the troops returned to their base* HEADQUARTERS, camp, site, station, settlement, post, centre, starting point.
– OPPOSITES top.
▶ **verb** ❶ *he based his idea on a movie* FOUND, build, construct, form, ground, root; use as a basis; (**be based on**) derive from, spring from, stem from, originate in, have its origin in, issue from. ❷ *the company was based in London* LOCATE, situate, position, install, station, site, establish; garrison.

base[2] ▶ **adjective** *base motives* SORDID, ignoble, low, low-minded, mean, immoral, improper, unseemly, unscrupulous, unprincipled, dishonest, dishonourable, shameful, bad, wrong, evil, wicked, iniquitous, sinful.
– OPPOSITES noble.

baseless ▶ **adjective** *baseless accusations* GROUNDLESS, unfounded, ill-founded, without foundation; unsubstantiated, unproven, unsupported, uncorroborated, unconfirmed, unverified, unattested; unjustified, unwarranted; speculative, conjectural; unsound, unreliable, spurious, specious, trumped up, fabricated, untrue.
– OPPOSITES valid.

basement ▶ **noun** CELLAR, vault, crypt, undercroft; *Brit.* lower ground floor; *Scottish* dunny.

bash (*informal*) ▶ **verb** ❶ *she bashed him with her stick* STRIKE, hit, beat, thump, slap, smack, clip, bang, knock, batter, pound, pummel; *informal* wallop, clout, belt, whack, thwack, clobber, bop, biff, sock; *archaic* smite. ❷ *they bashed into one another* CRASH, run, bang, smash, slam, cannon, knock, bump; collide with, hit, meet head-on.
▶ **noun** ❶ *a bash on the head* BLOW, rap, hit, knock, bang, slap, crack, thump, tap, clip; *informal* wallop, clout, belt, whack, thwack, bop, biff, sock; *archaic* smite. ❷ *Harry's birthday bash. See* PARTY noun sense 1. ❸ (*Brit.*) *I'll have a bash at it. See* ATTEMPT.

bashful ▶ **adjective** SHY, reserved, diffident, inhibited, retiring, reticent, reluctant, shrinking; hesitant, timid, apprehensive, nervous, wary.
– OPPOSITES bold, confident.

basic ▶ **adjective** ❶ *basic human rights* FUNDAMENTAL, essential, primary, principal, cardinal, elementary, elemental, quintessential, intrinsic, central, pivotal, critical, key, focal; vital, necessary, indispensable. ❷ *basic cooking facilities* PLAIN, simple, unsophisticated, straightforward, adequate; unadorned, undecorated, unornamented, without frills; spartan, stark, severe, austere, limited, meagre, rudimentary, patchy, sketchy, minimal; unfussy, homely, homespun; rough (and ready), crude, makeshift; *informal* bog-standard.
– OPPOSITES secondary, unimportant, elaborate.

basically ▶ **adverb** FUNDAMENTALLY, essentially, in essence; firstly, first of all, first and foremost, primarily; at heart, at bottom, au fond; principally, chiefly, above all, most of all, mostly, mainly, on the whole, by and large, substantially; intrinsically, inherently; *informal* at the end of the day, when all is said and done.

basics ▶ **plural noun** FUNDAMENTALS, essentials, rudiments, (first) principles, foundations, preliminaries, groundwork; essence, basis, core;

informal nitty-gritty, brass tacks, nuts and bolts, ABC.

basin ▶ **noun** ❶ *she poured water into the basin* BOWL, dish, pan. ❷ *a basin among low hills* VALLEY, hollow, dip, depression.

basis ▶ **noun** ❶ *the basis of his method* FOUNDATION, support, base; reasoning, rationale, defence; reason, grounds, justification, motivation. ❷ *the basis of discussion* STARTING POINT, base, point of departure, beginning, premise, fundamental point/principle, principal constituent, main ingredient, cornerstone, core, heart, thrust, essence, kernel, nub. ❸ *on a part-time basis* FOOTING, condition, status, position; arrangement, system, method.

bask ▶ **verb** ❶ *I basked in the sun* LAZE, lie, lounge, relax, sprawl, loll; sunbathe, sun oneself. ❷ *she's basking in all the glory* REVEL, delight, luxuriate, wallow, take pleasure, rejoice, glory, indulge oneself; enjoy, relish, savour, lap up.

basket ▶ **noun** WICKERWORK BOX, hamper, creel, pannier, punnet, trug.

bass ▶ **adjective** LOW, deep, low-pitched, resonant, sonorous, rumbling, booming, resounding; baritone.
– OPPOSITES high.

bastard ▶ **noun** ❶ (*archaic*) *he had fathered a bastard* ILLEGITIMATE CHILD, child born out of wedlock; *dated* love child; *Brit. dated* by-blow; *archaic* natural child/son/daughter. ❷ (*informal*) *he's a real bastard. See* SCOUNDREL.
▶ **adjective** ❶ (*archaic*) *a bastard child* ILLEGITIMATE, born out of wedlock; *archaic* natural. ❷ *a bastard Darwinism* ADULTERATED, alloyed, impure, inferior; hybrid, mongrel, patchwork.

bastardize ▶ **verb** ADULTERATE, corrupt, contaminate, weaken, dilute, taint, pollute, debase, distort.

bastion ▶ **noun** ❶ *the town wall and bastions* PROJECTION, outwork, breastwork, barbican; *Architecture* bartizan. ❷ *a bastion of respectability* STRONGHOLD, bulwark, defender, support, supporter, guard, protection, protector, defence, prop, mainstay.

batch ▶ **noun** GROUP, quantity, lot, bunch, mass, cluster, raft, set, collection, bundle, pack; consignment, shipment.

bath ▶ **noun** ❶ *he lay soaking in the bath* BATHTUB, tub, hot tub, whirlpool, sauna, steam bath, Turkish bath; *trademark* jacuzzi. ❷ *she had a quick bath* WASH, soak, dip; shower.
– RELATED TERMS balneal, balneary.
▶ **verb** *have you bathed?* | *he would bath the baby* BATHE, have/take a bath, give someone a bath, wash, shower.

bathe ▶ **verb** ❶ *she bathed and dressed. See* BATH verb. ❷ *I bathed in the local swimming pool* SWIM, go swimming, take a dip. ❸ *they bathed his wounds* CLEAN, wash, rinse, wet, soak, immerse. ❹ *the room was bathed in light* SUFFUSE, permeate, pervade, envelop, flood, cover, wash, fill.
▶ **noun** *we had a bathe* SWIM, dip, paddle.

bathing costume (*Brit.*) ▶ **noun** SWIMSUIT, bathing suit; swimming trunks, bikini; swimwear; *Brit.* swimming costume; *informal* cossie; *Austral./NZ informal* bathers.

bathos ▶ **noun** ANTICLIMAX, let-down, disappointment, disillusionment; absurdity; *informal* comedown.

baton ▶ **noun** ❶ *the conductor's baton* STICK, rod, staff, wand. ❷ *police batons* TRUNCHEON, club, cudgel, bludgeon, stick, mace, shillelagh; *N. Amer.* nightstick, blackjack; *Brit. informal* cosh.

battalion ▶ **noun** ❶ *an infantry battalion* regiment, brigade, force, division, squadron, squad, company, section, detachment, contingent, legion, corps, cohort. ❷ *a battalion of supporters. See* CROWD noun sense 1.

batten ▶ **noun** *a timber batten* BAR, bolt, rail, shaft; board, strip.
▶ **verb** *Stephen was battening down the shutters* FASTEN, fix, secure, clamp, lash, make fast, nail, seal.

batter ▶ **verb** PUMMEL, pound, hit repeatedly, rain blows on, buffet, belabour, thrash, beat up; *informal* knock about/around, beat the living daylights out of, give someone a good hiding, lay into, lace into, do over, rough up.

battered ▶ **adjective** DAMAGED, shabby, run down, worn out, falling to pieces, falling apart, dilapidated, rickety, ramshackle, crumbling, the worse for wear, on its last legs.

battery ▶ **noun** ❶ *a flat battery* CELL, accumulator. ❷ *a gun battery* EMPLACEMENT, artillery unit; cannonry, ordnance. ❸ *a battery of equipment* ARRAY, set, bank, group, row, line, lineup, collection. ❹ *a battery of tests* SERIES, sequence, cycle, string, succession. ❺ *assault and battery* VIOLENCE, assault, mugging; *Brit.* grievous bodily harm, GBH, actual bodily harm, ABH.

battle ▶ **noun** ❶ *he was killed in the battle* FIGHT, armed conflict, clash, struggle, skirmish, engagement, fray, duel; war, campaign, crusade; fighting, warfare, combat, action, hostilities; *informal* scrap, dogfight, shoot-out. ❷ *a legal battle* CONFLICT, clash, contest, competition, struggle; disagreement, argument, altercation, dispute, controversy.
▶ **verb** ❶ *he has been battling against illness* FIGHT, combat, contend with; resist, withstand, stand up to, confront; war, feud; struggle, strive, work. ❷ *Mark battled his way to the bar* FORCE, push, elbow, shoulder, fight; struggle, labour.

battleaxe ▶ **noun** ❶ *a severe blow from a battleaxe* POLEAXE, axe, pike, halberd, tomahawk, war mattock. ❷ (*informal*) *she's a real battleaxe. See* HARRIDAN.

battle cry ▶ **noun** ❶ *the army's battle cry* WAR

CRY, war whoop, rallying call/cry. ❷ *the battle cry of the feminist movement* SLOGAN, motto, watchword, catchphrase.

battlefield ▶ noun BATTLEGROUND, field of battle, field of operations, combat zone, theatre (of war), front.

battlement ▶ noun CASTELLATION, crenellation, parapet, rampart, wall.

batty ▶ adjective (*informal*). *See* MAD sense 1.

bauble ▶ noun TRINKET, knick-knack, ornament, frippery, gewgaw, gimcrack, bibelot; *N. Amer.* kickshaw; *N. Amer. informal* tchotchke.

baulk ▶ verb ❶ *I baulk at paying that much* BE UNWILLING TO, draw the line at, jib at, be reluctant to, hesitate over; eschew, resist, scruple to, refuse to, take exception to; draw back from, flinch from, shrink from, recoil from, demur from, not like to, hate to. ❷ *they were baulked by traffic* IMPEDE, obstruct, thwart, hinder, prevent, check, stop, curb, halt, bar, block, forestall, frustrate.
–OPPOSITES accept, assist.

bawdy ▶ adjective RIBALD, indecent, risqué, racy, rude, spicy, sexy, suggestive, titillating, naughty, improper, indelicate, indecorous, off colour, earthy, broad, locker-room, Rabelaisian; pornographic, obscene, vulgar, crude, coarse, gross, lewd, dirty, filthy, smutty, unseemly, salacious, prurient, lascivious, licentious, near the bone, near the knuckle; *informal* X-rated, blue, raunchy, nudge-nudge; *euphemistic* adult.
–OPPOSITES clean, innocent.

bawl ▶ verb ❶ *'Come on!' he bawled* SHOUT, yell, roar, bellow, screech, scream, shriek, howl, whoop, bark, trumpet, thunder; *informal* yammer, holler. ❷ *the children continued to bawl* CRY, sob, weep, shed tears, wail, whine, howl, squall, ululate; *Scottish informal* greet.
–OPPOSITES whisper.
▶ noun *a terrifying bawl* SHOUT, yell, roar, bellow, screech, scream, howl, whoop; *informal* holler.
–OPPOSITES whisper.
■ **bawl someone out** (*informal*). *See* REPRIMAND verb.

bay[1] ▶ noun *ships were anchored in the bay* COVE, inlet, indentation, gulf, bight, basin, fjord, arm; natural harbour, anchorage.

bay[2] ▶ noun *there was a bay let into the wall* ALCOVE, recess, niche, nook, opening, hollow, cavity, inglenook.

bay[3] ▶ verb ❶ *the hounds bayed* HOWL, bark, yelp, yap, cry, bellow, roar. ❷ *the crowd bayed for an encore* CLAMOUR, shout, call, press, yell, scream, shriek, roar; demand, insist on.
■ **at bay** AT A DISTANCE, away, off, at arm's length.

bayonet ▶ noun *a man armed with a bayonet* sword, knife, blade, spear, lance, pike, javelin; *poetic/literary* brand.
▶ verb *stragglers were bayoneted* STAB, spear, knife, gore, spike, stick, impale, run through, transfix, gash, slash.

bazaar ▶ noun ❶ *a Turkish bazaar* MARKET, market place, souk, mart, exchange. ❷ *the church bazaar* FÊTE, fair, jumble sale, bring-and-buy sale, car boot sale, carnival; fund-raiser, charity event; *N. Amer.* tag sale.

be ▶ verb ❶ *there was once a king* EXIST, have being, have existence; live, be alive, have life, breathe, draw breath, be extant. ❷ *is there a cafe here?* BE PRESENT, be around, be available, be near, be nearby, be at hand. ❸ *the trial is tomorrow at half past one* OCCUR, happen, take place, come about, arise, crop up, transpire, fall, materialize, ensue; *poetic/literary* come to pass, befall, betide. ❹ *the bed is over there* BE SITUATED, be located, be found, be present, be set, be positioned, be placed, be installed. ❺ *it has been like this for hours* REMAIN, stay, last, continue, survive, endure, persist, prevail; wait, linger, hold on, hang on; *formal* obtain. ❻ *I'm at college* ATTEND, go to, be present at, take part in; frequent, haunt, patronize.

beach ▶ noun *a sandy beach* SEASIDE, seashore, shore, coast, coastline, coastal region, littoral, seaboard, foreshore, water's edge; sands, lido; *dated* plage; *poetic/literary* strand.
▶ verb *they beached the boat* LAND, ground, strand, run aground, run ashore.

beachcomber ▶ noun SCAVENGER, forager, collector; *informal* scrounger.

beached ▶ adjective STRANDED, grounded, aground, ashore, marooned, high and dry, stuck.

beacon ▶ noun WARNING LIGHT/FIRE, signal (light/fire), danger signal, bonfire; lighthouse, light-tower.

bead ▶ noun ❶ *a string of beads* BALL, pellet, pill, globule, sphere, spheroid, oval, ovoid, orb, round; (**beads**) necklace, rosary, chaplet. ❷ *beads of sweat* DROPLET, drop, blob, dot, dewdrop, teardrop.
■ **draw/get a bead on** AIM AT, fix on, focus on, zero in on, sight.

beak ▶ noun ❶ *a bird's beak* BILL, nib, mandible; *Scottish & N. English* neb. ❷ (*informal*) *he blew his beak loudly. See* NOSE noun sense 1.

beaker ▶ noun CUP, tumbler, glass, mug; drinking vessel.

beam ▶ noun ❶ *an oak beam* JOIST, lintel, rafter, purlin; spar, girder, baulk, timber, plank; support, strut; scantling, transom, stringer. ❷ *a beam of light coming from the window* RAY, shaft, stream, streak, pencil, finger; flash, gleam, glow, glimmer, glint, flare. ❸ *the beam on her face* GRIN, smile, happy expression, bright look.
–OPPOSITES frown.
▶ verb ❶ *the signal is beamed out* BROADCAST, trans-

mit, relay, send/put out, disseminate; direct, aim. ❷ *the sun beamed down* SHINE, radiate, give off light, glare, gleam. ❸ *he beamed broadly* GRIN, smile, smirk; *informal* be all smiles.
– OPPOSITES frown.

■ **off beam** (*informal*) MISTAKEN, incorrect, inaccurate, wrong, erroneous, off target, out, on the wrong track, wide of the mark, awry.

■ **on the beam** (*informal*) CORRECT, right, accurate, true, on the straight and narrow, on the right track, on the right lines; *informal* on the money, on the mark; *Brit. informal* spot on.

bear ▶ **verb** ❶ *she was bearing a box of cookies* CARRY, bring, transport, move, convey, take, fetch, deliver; *informal* tote. ❷ *the bag bore my name* DISPLAY, exhibit, be marked with, show, carry, have. ❸ *will it bear his weight?* SUPPORT, carry, hold up, prop up. ❹ *they can't bear the cost alone* SUSTAIN, carry, support, shoulder, absorb, take on. ❺ *she bore no grudge* HARBOUR, foster, entertain, cherish, nurse, nurture, brood over. ❻ *such a solution does not bear close scrutiny* WITHSTAND, stand up to, stand, put up with, take, cope with, handle, sustain, accept. ❼ *I can't bear having him around* ENDURE, tolerate, put up with, stand, abide, submit to, experience, undergo, go through, countenance, brave, weather, stomach, support; *Scottish* thole; *informal* hack, swallow; *Brit. informal* stick, wear, be doing with; *formal* brook; *archaic* suffer. ❽ *she bore a son* GIVE BIRTH TO, bring forth, deliver, be delivered of, have, produce, spawn; *N. Amer.* birth; *informal* drop; *poetic/literary* beget. ❾ *a shrub that bears yellow berries* PRODUCE, yield, give forth, give, grow, provide, supply. ❿ *bear left at the junction* VEER, curve, swerve, fork, diverge, deviate, turn, bend.

■ **bear oneself** CONDUCT ONESELF, carry oneself, acquit oneself, act, behave, perform; *formal* comport oneself.

■ **bear down on** ADVANCE ON, close in on, move in on, converge on.

■ **bear fruit** YIELD RESULTS, get results, succeed, meet with success, be successful, be effective, be profitable, work, go as planned; *informal* pay off, come off, pan out, do the trick, do the business.

■ **bear something in mind** TAKE INTO ACCOUNT, take into consideration, remember, consider, be mindful, mind, mark, heed.

■ **bear on** BE RELEVANT TO, appertain to, pertain to, relate to, have a bearing on, have relevance to, apply to, be pertinent to.

■ **bear something out** CONFIRM, corroborate, substantiate, endorse, vindicate, give credence to, support, ratify, warrant, uphold, justify, prove, authenticate, verify.

■ **bear up** REMAIN CHEERFUL, grin and bear it; cope, manage, get by, muddle through; *informal* hack it.

■ **bear with** BE PATIENT WITH, show forbearance towards, make allowances for, tolerate, put up with, endure.

■ **bear witness/testimony to** TESTIFY TO, be evidence of, be proof of, attest to, evidence, prove, vouch for; demonstrate, show, establish, indicate, reveal, bespeak.

bearable ▶ **adjective** TOLERABLE, endurable, supportable, sustainable.

beard ▶ **noun** *a black beard* FACIAL HAIR, whiskers, stubble, designer stubble, five o'clock shadow, bristles; goatee, imperial, Vandyke.
▶ **verb** *I bearded him when he was on his own* CONFRONT, face, challenge, brave, come face to face with, meet head on; defy, oppose, stand up against, square up to, dare, throw down the gauntlet to.

bearded ▶ **adjective** UNSHAVEN, whiskered, whiskery, bewhiskered; stubbly, bristly.
– OPPOSITES clean shaven.

bearer ▶ **noun** ❶ *a lantern-bearer* CARRIER, porter. ❷ *the bearer of bad news* MESSENGER, agent, conveyor, carrier, emissary. ❸ *the bearer of the documents* HOLDER, possessor, owner.

bearing ▶ **noun** ❶ *a man of military bearing* POSTURE, stance, carriage, gait; *Brit.* deportment; *formal* comportment. ❷ *a rather regal bearing* DEMEANOUR, manner, air, aspect, attitude, behaviour, mien, style. ❸ *this has no bearing on the matter* RELEVANCE, pertinence, connection, appositeness, germaneness, importance, significance, application. ❹ *a bearing of 015°* DIRECTION, orientation, course, trajectory, heading, tack, path, line, run. ❺ *he tormented her beyond bearing* ENDURANCE, tolerance, toleration. ❻ *I lost my bearings* ORIENTATION, sense of direction; whereabouts, location, position.

beast ▶ **noun** ❶ *the beasts of the forest* ANIMAL, creature, brute; *N. Amer. informal* critter. ❷ *he is a cruel beast* MONSTER, brute, savage, barbarian, animal, swine, pig, ogre, fiend, sadist, demon, devil.
– RELATED TERMS bestial.

beastly ▶ **adjective** (*Brit. informal*) ❶ *politics is a beastly profession* AWFUL, horrible, rotten, nasty, foul, objectionable, unpleasant, disagreeable, offensive, vile, hateful, detestable; *informal* terrible, God-awful. ❷ *he was beastly to her* UNKIND, malicious, mean, nasty, unpleasant, unfriendly, spiteful, cruel, vicious, base, foul, malevolent, despicable, contemptible; *informal* horrible, horrid, rotten.
– OPPOSITES pleasant, kind.

beat ▶ **verb** ❶ *they were beaten with truncheons* HIT, strike, batter, thump, bang, hammer, punch, knock, thrash, pound, pummel, slap, rain blows on; assault, attack, abuse; cudgel, club, birch; *informal* wallop, belt, bash, whack, thwack, clout, clobber, slug, tan, biff, bop, sock, deck, plug, beat the living daylights out of, give someone a good hiding. ❷ *the waves beat all along the shore* BREAK ON/AGAINST, dash against; lash, strike, lap, wash; splash, ripple, roll; *poetic/literary* plash, lave. ❸ *the metal is* *beaten into a die* HAMMER, forge, form, shape, mould, work, stamp, fashion, model. ❹ *her heart was still beating* PULSATE, pulse, palpitate, vibrate, throb; pump, pound, thump, thud, hammer, drum; pitter-patter, go pit-a-pat. ❺ *the eagle beat its wings* FLAP, flutter, thresh, thrash, wave, vibrate, oscillate. ❻ *beat the cream into the mixture* WHISK, mix, blend, whip. ❼ *she beat a path through the grass* TREAD, tramp, trample, wear, flatten, press down. ❽ *the team they need to beat* DEFEAT, conquer, win against, get the better of, vanquish, trounce, rout, overpower, overcome, subdue; *informal* lick, thrash, whip, wipe the floor with, clobber. ❾ *he beat the record* SURPASS, exceed, better, improve on, go one better than, eclipse, transcend, top, trump, cap.

▶ **noun** ❶ *the song has a good beat* RHYTHM, pulse, metre, time, measure, cadence; stress, accent. ❷ *the beat of hooves* POUNDING, banging, thumping, thudding, booming, hammering, battering, crashing. ❸ *the beat of her heart* PULSE, pulsating, vibration, throb, palpitation, reverberation; pounding, thump, thud, hammering, drumming; pit-a-pat. ❹ *a policeman on his beat* CIRCUIT, round, route, way, path.

▶ **adjective** (*informal*) *phew, I'm beat! See* EXHAUSTED sense 1.

■ **beat a (hasty) retreat**. *See* RETREAT verb sense 1.

■ **beat it** (*informal*). *See* RUN verb sense 2.

■ **beat someone/something off** REPEL, fight off, fend off, stave off, repulse, drive away/back, force back, beat back, push back, put to flight.

■ **beat someone up** ASSAULT, attack, mug, thrash; *informal* knock about/around, do over, work over, rough up, fill in, lay into, lace into, sail into, beat the living daylights out of, let someone have it; *Brit. informal* duff someone up; *N. Amer. informal* beat up on.

beatific ▶ **adjective** ❶ *a beatific smile* RAPTUROUS, joyful, ecstatic, seraphic, blissful, serene, happy, beaming. ❷ *a beatific vision* BLESSED, exalted, sublime, heavenly, holy, divine, celestial, paradisical, glorious.

beatify ▶ **verb** CANONIZE, bless, sanctify, hallow, consecrate, make holy.

beatitude ▶ **noun** BLESSEDNESS, benediction, grace; bliss, ecstasy, exaltation, supreme happiness, divine joy/rapture; saintliness, sainthood.

beau ▶ **noun** (*dated*) ❶ *Sally and her beau* BOYFRIEND, sweetheart, lover, darling, partner, significant other, escort, young man, admirer, suitor. ❷ *an eighteenth-century beau* DANDY, fop, man about town; *informal, dated* swell; *archaic* coxcomb, popinjay.

beautiful ▶ **adjective** ATTRACTIVE, pretty, handsome, good-looking, alluring, prepossessing; lovely, charming, delightful, appealing, engaging, winsome; ravishing, gorgeous, stunning, arresting, glamorous, bewitching, beguiling; graceful, elegant, exquisite, aesthetic, artistic, decorative, magnificent; *Scottish & N. English* bonny; *informal* tasty, divine, knockout, drop-dead gorgeous, fanciable; *Brit. informal* smashing; *N. Amer. informal* cute, foxy; *Austral./NZ informal* beaut, spunky; *formal* beauteous; *archaic* comely, fair.

– OPPOSITES ugly.

beautify ▶ **verb** ADORN, embellish, enhance, decorate, ornament, garnish, gild, smarten, prettify, enrich, glamorize, spruce up, deck (out), trick out, grace; *informal* get up, do up, do out, tart up.

– OPPOSITES spoil, uglify.

beauty ▶ **noun** ❶ *the great beuty of the scenery* ATTRACTIVENESS, prettiness, good looks, comeliness, allure; loveliness, charm, appeal, heavenliness; winsomeness, grace, elegance, exquisiteness; splendour, magnificence, grandeur, impressiveness, artistry, decorativeness; gorgeousness, glamour; *Scottish & N. English* bonniness; *poetic/literary* beauteousness, pulchritude. ❷ *she is a beauty* BEAUTIFUL WOMAN, belle, vision, Venus, goddess, beauty queen, English rose, picture; *informal* looker, good looker, lovely, stunner, knockout, bombshell, dish, cracker, peach, eyeful, bit of all right; *Brit. informal* smasher. ❸ *the beauty of this plan* ADVANTAGE, attraction, strength, benefit, boon, blessing, good thing, strong point, virtue, merit, selling point.

– OPPOSITES ugliness, drawback.

beaver

■ **beaver away** (*informal*). *See* SLOG verb sense 1.

becalmed ▶ **adjective** MOTIONLESS, still, at a standstill, at a halt, unmoving, stuck.

because ▶ **conjunction** SINCE, as, in view of the fact that, owing to the fact that, seeing that/as; *informal* on account of; *poetic/literary* for.

– OPPOSITES despite.

■ **because of** ON ACCOUNT OF, as a result of, as a consequence of, owing to, due to; thanks to, by/in virtue of; *formal* by reason of.

beckon ▶ **verb** ❶ *the guard beckoned to Benny* GESTURE, signal, wave, gesticulate, motion. ❷ *the countryside beckons you* ENTICE, invite, tempt, coax, lure, charm, attract, draw, call.

become ▶ **verb** ❶ *she became rich* GROW, get, turn, come to be, get to be; *poetic/literary* wax. ❷ *he became a tyrant* TURN INTO, change into, be transformed into, be converted into. ❸ *he became Foreign Secretary* BE APPOINTED (AS), be assigned as, be nominated, be elected (as), be made. ❹ *the dress becomes her* SUIT, flatter, look good on; set off, show to advantage; *informal* do something for. ❺ *it ill becomes him to preach the gospel* BEFIT, suit; *formal* behove.

■ **become of** HAPPEN TO, be the fate of, be the lot of, overtake; *poetic/literary* befall, betide.

becoming ▶ **adjective** FLATTERING, fetching;

attractive, lovely, pretty, handsome; stylish, elegant, chic, fashionable, tasteful; *archaic* comely.

bed ▶ **noun** ❶ *she got into bed* couch, cot, cradle, berth, billet; *informal* the sack, the hay; *Brit. informal* one's pit; *Scottish informal* one's kip. ❷ *a flower bed* PATCH, plot, border, strip. ❸ *built on a bed of stones* BASE, foundation, support, prop, substructure, substratum. ❹ *a river bed* BOTTOM, floor, ground.

▶ **verb** ❶ *the tiles are bedded in mortar* EMBED, set, fix, insert, inlay, implant, bury, base, plant, settle. ❷ *time to bed out the seedlings* PLANT (OUT), transplant.

■ **bed down**. *See* GO TO BED.

■ **go to bed** RETIRE, call it a day; go to sleep, have/take a nap, have a doze, get some sleep; *informal* hit the sack, hit the hay, turn in, snatch forty winks, get some shut-eye; *Brit. informal* have a kip, get some kip, hit the pit; *N. Amer. informal* catch some Zs.

bedaub ▶ **verb** (*poetic/literary*) SMEAR, daub, bespatter, spatter, splatter, cover, coat; *poetic/literary* besmirch, begrime.

bedclothes ▶ **plural noun** BEDDING, sheets and blankets; bed linen; bedcovers, covers.

bedding ▶ **noun**. *See* BEDCLOTHES.

bedeck ▶ **verb** DECORATE, adorn, ornament, embellish, furnish, garnish, trim, deck, grace, enrich, dress up, trick out; swathe, wreathe, festoon; *informal* get up, do out; *poetic/literary* furbelow.

bedevil ▶ **verb** AFFLICT, torment, beset, assail, beleaguer, plague, blight, rack, oppress, harry, curse, dog; harass, distress, trouble, worry, torture.

bedlam ▶ **noun** UPROAR, pandemonium, commotion, mayhem, confusion, disorder, chaos, anarchy, lawlessness; furore, upheaval, hubbub, hurly-burly, turmoil, riot, ruckus, rumpus, tumult; *informal* hullabaloo, ructions, snafu.
– OPPOSITES calm.

bedraggled ▶ **adjective** DISHEVELLED, disordered, untidy, unkempt, tousled, disarranged, in a mess; *N. Amer. informal* mussed.
– OPPOSITES neat, clean, dry.

bedridden ▶ **adjective** CONFINED TO BED, immobilized; *informal* laid up, flat on one's back.

bedrock ▶ **noun** *this fact is the bedrock of our authority* CORE, basis, base, foundation, roots, heart, backbone, principle, essence, nitty-gritty; *informal* nuts and bolts.

bedspread ▶ **noun** BEDCOVER, coverlet, quilt, throwover, blanket; *Brit.* eiderdown; *N. Amer.* throw, spread, comforter; *dated* counterpane.

bee
– RELATED TERMS apian.

beef (*informal*) ▶ **noun** ❶ *there's plenty of beef on him* MUSCLE, brawn, bulk; strength, power. ❷ *his beef was about the cost* COMPLAINT, criticism, objection, cavil, quibble, grievance, grumble, grouse; *informal* gripe, grouch, moan, whinge.

▶ **verb** *security was being beefed up* TOUGHEN UP, strengthen, build up, reinforce, consolidate, invigorate, improve.

beefy ▶ **adjective** (*informal*) MUSCULAR, brawny, hefty, burly, hulking, strapping, well built, solid, strong, powerful, heavy, robust, sturdy; *informal* hunky, husky.
– OPPOSITES puny.

beer ▶ **noun** ALE, brew; *Brit. informal* wallop, pint, jar; *Austral./NZ informal* hop, sherbet.

beetle ▶ **noun**
– RELATED TERMS coleopteran, coleopterous.

▶ **verb** (*informal*) *he beetled past* SCURRY, scamper, scuttle, bustle, hurry, hasten, rush, dash; *informal* scoot, zip.

beetling ▶ **adjective** PROJECTING, protruding, prominent, overhanging, sticking out, jutting out.

befall ▶ **verb** (*poetic/literary*) ❶ *the same fate befell him* HAPPEN TO, overtake, come upon, be visited on. ❷ *tell us what befell* HAPPEN, occur, take place, come about, transpire, materialize; ensue, follow, result; *N. Amer. informal* go down; *poetic/literary* come to pass, betide; *formal* eventuate.

befitting ▶ **preposition** IN KEEPING WITH, as befits, appropriate to, fit for, suitable for, suited to, proper to, right for, compatible with, consistent with, in character with; *archaic* meet for.

befogged ▶ **adjective** CONFUSED, muddled, fuddled, befuddled, groggy, dizzy, muzzy; *informal* dopey, woozy, not with it.
– OPPOSITES lucid.

before ▶ **preposition** ❶ *he dressed up before going out* PRIOR TO, previous to, earlier than, preparatory to, in preparation for, preliminary to, in anticipation of, in expectation of; in advance of, ahead of, leading up to, on the eve of; *rare* anterior to. ❷ *he appeared before the judge* IN FRONT OF, in the presence of, in the sight of. ❸ *death before dishonour* IN PREFERENCE TO, rather than, sooner than.
– RELATED TERMS pre-.
– OPPOSITES after.

▶ **adverb** ❶ *she has ridden before* PREVIOUSLY, before now/then, until now/then, up to now/then; earlier, formerly, hitherto, in the past, in days gone by; *formal* heretofore. ❷ *a small party went on before* AHEAD, in front, in advance.
– OPPOSITES behind.

beforehand ▶ **adverb** IN ADVANCE, in readiness, ahead of time; before, before now/then, earlier (on), previously, already, sooner.
– OPPOSITES afterwards.

befriend ▶ **verb** MAKE FRIENDS WITH, make a friend of; look after, help, protect, stand by.

befuddled ▶ **adjective** CONFUSED, muddled, addled, bewildered, disorientated, all at sea, fazed, perplexed, dazed, dizzy, stupefied, groggy, muzzy, foggy, fuzzy, dopey, woozy; *informal* mixed up; *N. Amer. informal* discombobulated.

– OPPOSITES clear.

beg ▶ **verb** ❶ *he begged on the streets* ASK FOR MONEY, seek charity, seek alms; *informal* sponge, cadge, scrounge, bum; *Brit. informal* scab; *N. Amer. informal* mooch; *Austral./NZ informal* bludge. ❷ *we begged for mercy* ASK FOR, request, plead for, appeal for, call for, sue for, solicit, seek, press for. ❸ *he begged her not to go* IMPLORE, entreat, plead with, appeal to, supplicate, pray to, importune; ask, request, call on, petition; *poetic/literary* beseech.

beget ▶ **verb** (*poetic/literary*) ❶ *he begat a son* FATHER, sire, have, bring into the world, give life to, bring into being, spawn. ❷ *violence begets violence* CAUSE, give rise to, lead to, result in, bring about, create, produce, generate, engender, spawn, occasion, bring on, precipitate, prompt, provoke, kindle, trigger, spark off, touch off, stir up, whip up, induce, inspire, promote; *poetic/literary* enkindle.

beggar ▶ **noun** ❶ *he never turned any beggar from his kitchen door* TRAMP, beggarman, beggarwoman, vagrant, vagabond, mendicant; *N. Amer.* hobo; *informal* scrounger, sponger, cadger, freeloader; *Brit. informal* dosser; *N. Amer. informal* bum, moocher, mooch, schnorrer; *Austral./NZ informal* bagman, bludger; *rare* clochard. ❷ (*informal*) *the lucky beggar!* See PERSON.

▶ **verb** *the fare beggared her for a week* IMPOVERISH, make poor, reduce to penury, bankrupt, make destitute, pauperize, ruin, wipe out, break, cripple; bring someone to their knees.

beggarly ▶ **adjective** ❶ *a beggarly sum* MEAGRE, paltry, pitiful, miserable, miserly, ungenerous, scant, scanty, skimpy, puny, inadequate, insufficient, insubstantial; *informal* measly, stingy, pathetic, piddling, piffling, mingy; *formal* exiguous. ❷ *in beggarly circumstances* WRETCHED, miserable, sordid, squalid, shabby, mean; poor, poverty-stricken, impoverished, distressed, needy, destitute.

– OPPOSITES considerable, affluent.

beggary ▶ **noun** POVERTY, penury, destitution, ruin, ruination, indigence, impecuniousness, impoverishment, need, privation, pauperism, mendicity, want, hardship, reduced circumstances, straitened circumstances, debt, financial ruin; *rare* pauperdom.

begin ▶ **verb** ❶ *we began work* START, commence, set about, go about, embark on, launch into, get down to, take up; initiate, set in motion, institute, inaugurate, get ahead with; *informal* get cracking on, get going on. ❷ *he began by saying hello* OPEN, lead off, get under way, get going, get off the ground, start (off), go ahead, commence; *informal* start the ball rolling, kick off, get the show on the road, fire away, take the plunge. ❸ *when did the illness begin?* APPEAR, arise, become apparent, make an appearance, spring up, crop up, turn up, come into existence, come into being, originate, start, commence, develop; *poetic/literary* come to pass.

– RELATED TERMS incipient, inceptive, inchoate, embryonic.

– OPPOSITES finish, end, disappear.

beginner ▶ **noun** NOVICE, starter, (raw) recruit, newcomer, tyro, fledgling, neophyte, initiate, fresher, freshman, cub, probationer; postulant, novitiate; *N. Amer.* tenderfoot; *informal* rookie, new kid (on the block), newie, newbie; *N. Amer. informal* greenhorn, probie.

– OPPOSITES expert, veteran.

beginning ▶ **noun** ❶ *the beginning of socialism* DAWN, birth, inception, conception, origination, genesis, emergence, rise, start, commencement, starting point, launch, onset, outset; day one; *informal* kick-off. ❷ *the beginning of the article* OPENING, start, commencement, first part, introduction, preamble, opening statement. ❸ *the therapy has its beginnings in China* ORIGIN, source, roots, starting point, birthplace, fons et origo, cradle, spring, early stages, fountainhead; genesis, creation; *poetic/literary* fount, well spring.

– OPPOSITES end, conclusion.

begrime ▶ **verb** (*poetic/literary*) DIRTY, soil, sully, stain, mark, muddy; smear, daub, spatter, bespatter, splatter; *poetic/literary* besmirch, bedaub.

begrudge ▶ **verb** ❶ *she begrudged Brian his affluence* ENVY, grudge; resent, be jealous of, be envious of. ❷ *don't begrudge the cost* RESENT, feel aggrieved about, feel bitter about, be annoyed about, be resentful of, grudge, mind, object to, take exception to, regret; give unwillingly, give reluctantly.

beguile ▶ **verb** ❶ *she was beguiled by its beauty* CHARM, attract, enchant, entrance, win over, woo, captivate, bewitch, spellbind, dazzle, hypnotize, mesmerize, seduce. ❷ *the programme has been beguiling children for years* ENTERTAIN, amuse, delight, please, occupy, absorb, engage, distract, divert, fascinate, enthral, engross.

– OPPOSITES repel, bore.

beguiling ▶ **adjective** CHARMING, enchanting, entrancing, charismatic, captivating, bewitching, spellbinding, hypnotizing, mesmerizing, magnetic, alluring, enticing, tempting, inviting, seductive, irresistible; *informal* come-hither.

– OPPOSITES unappealing.

behalf

■ **on behalf of/on someone's behalf** ❶ *I am writing on behalf of my client* AS A REPRESENTATIVE OF, as a spokesperson for, for, in the name of, in place of, on the authority of, at the behest of. ❷ *a campaign on behalf of cycling* IN THE INTERESTS OF, in support of, for, for the benefit of, for the good of, for the sake of.

behave ▶ verb ❶ *she behaved badly* CONDUCT ONESELF, act, acquit oneself, bear oneself; *formal* comport oneself; *archaic* deport oneself. ❷ *the children behaved themselves* ACT CORRECTLY, act properly, conduct oneself well, be well behaved, be good; be polite, show good manners, mind one's manners, mind one's Ps and Qs.
– OPPOSITES misbehave.

behaviour ▶ noun ❶ *his behaviour was inexcusable* CONDUCT, deportment, bearing, etiquette; actions, doings; manners, ways; *formal* comportment. ❷ *the behaviour of these organisms* FUNCTIONING, action, performance, operation, working, reaction, response.

behead ▶ verb DECAPITATE, cut someone's head off, guillotine.

behest ▶ noun (*poetic/literary*) INSTRUCTION, requirement, demand, insistence, bidding, request, wish, desire, will; command, order, decree, ruling, directive; *informal* say-so.

behind ▶ preposition ❶ *he hid behind a tree* AT THE BACK/REAR OF, beyond, on the far/other side of; *N. Amer.* in back of. ❷ *a guard ran behind him* AFTER, following, at the back/rear of, hard on the heels of, in the wake of. ❸ *you are behind the rest of the class* LESS ADVANCED THAN, slower than, weaker than, inferior to. ❹ *he was behind the bombings* RESPONSIBLE FOR, at the bottom of, the cause of, the source of, the organizer of; to blame for, culpable of, guilty of. ❺ *they have the nation behind them* SUPPORTING, backing, for, on the side of, in agreement with; financing; *informal* rooting for.
– OPPOSITES in front of, ahead of.
▶ adverb ❶ *a man followed behind* AFTER, afterwards, at the back/end, in the rear. ❷ *I looked behind* OVER ONE'S SHOULDER, to/towards the back, to/towards the rear, backwards. ❸ *we're behind, so don't stop* (RUNNING) LATE, behind schedule, behindhand, not on time, behind time. ❹ *he was behind with his subscription* IN ARREARS, overdue; late, unpunctual, behindhand.
– OPPOSITES in front, ahead.
▶ noun (*informal*) *he sat on his behind.* See BOTTOM noun sense 6.
■ **put something behind one** CONSIGN TO THE PAST, put down to experience, regard as water under the bridge, forget about, ignore.

behindhand ▶ adverb BEHIND, behind schedule/time; late, belated, unpunctual, slow.
– OPPOSITES ahead.

behold ▶ verb (*poetic/literary*) *no eyes beheld them* SEE, observe, view, look at, watch, survey, gaze at/upon, regard, contemplate, inspect, eye; catch sight of, glimpse, spot, spy, notice; *informal* clap eyes on, have/take a gander at, get a load of; *Brit. informal* have/take a dekko at, have/take a butcher's at, have/take a shufti at, clock; *N. Amer. informal* eyeball; *poetic/literary* espy, descry.
▶ exclamation (*archaic*) *behold, here I am!* LOOK, see; *archaic* lo.

beholden ▶ adjective INDEBTED, in someone's debt, obligated, under an obligation; grateful, owing a debt of gratitude.

behove ▶ verb ❶ *it behoves me to go* BE INCUMBENT ON, be obligatory for, be required of, be expected of, be appropriate for. ❷ *it ill behoves them to comment* BEFIT, become, suit.

beige ▶ adjective FAWN, pale brown, buff, sand, sandy, oatmeal, biscuit, coffee, coffee-coloured, café au lait, camel, ecru.

being ▶ noun ❶ *she is warmed by his very being* EXISTENCE, living, life, reality, actuality, essential nature, lifeblood, vital force; *Philosophy* esse. ❷ *God is alive in the being of man* SOUL, spirit, nature, essence, inner being, inner self, psyche; heart, bosom, breast; *Philosophy* quiddity, pneuma. ❸ *an enlightened being* CREATURE, life form, living entity, living thing, (living) soul, individual, person, human (being).

belabour ▶ verb ❶ *he belaboured the driver about the head* BEAT, hit, strike, smack, batter, pummel, pound, buffet, rain blows on, thrash; *N. Amer.* beat up on; *informal* wallop, whack, clout, clobber, bop, biff, sock, plug; *N. Amer. informal* whale; *archaic* smite. ❷ *he was belaboured in the press* CRITICIZE, attack, berate, censure, condemn, denounce, denigrate, revile, pillory, flay, lambaste, savage, tear/pull to pieces, run down; *informal* knock, slam, pan, bash, take apart, crucify, hammer, lay into, roast; *Brit. informal* slate, rubbish, slag off; *N. Amer. informal* pummel, cut up; *formal* castigate, excoriate. ❸ *don't belabour the point* OVER-ELABORATE, labour, dwell on, harp on about, hammer away at; overdo, overplay, over-dramatize, make too much of, place too much emphasis on; *informal* flog to death, drag out, make a big thing of, blow out of all proportion.
– OPPOSITES praise, understate.

belated ▶ adjective LATE, overdue, behindhand, behind time, behind schedule, delayed, tardy, unpunctual.
– OPPOSITES early.

belch ▶ verb ❶ *onions make me belch* bring up wind; *informal* BURP; *Scottish & N. English informal* rift. ❷ *the furnace belched flames* EMIT, give off, give out, pour out, discharge, disgorge, spew out, spit out, vomit, cough up; *poetic/literary* disembogue.
▶ noun *he gave a loud belch informal* BURP; *Scottish & N. English informal* rift; *formal* eructation.

beleaguered ▶ adjective ❶ *the beleaguered garrison* BESIEGED, under siege, blockaded, surrounded, encircled, hemmed in, under attack. ❷ *a beleaguered government* HARD-PRESSED, troubled, in difficulties, under pressure, under stress, with one's back to the wall, in a tight corner, in a tight spot; *informal* up against it.

belie ▶ verb ❶ *his eyes belied his words* CONTRADICT, be at odds with, call into question, give the lie to, show/prove to be false, disprove,

debunk, discredit, controvert, negative; *formal* confute. ❷ *his image belies his talent* CONCEAL, cover, disguise; misrepresent, falsify, give a false idea/account of.
– OPPOSITES testify to, reveal.

belief ▶ **noun** ❶ *it's my belief that age is irrelevant* OPINION, view, conviction, judgement, thinking, way of thinking, idea, impression, theory, conclusion, notion. ❷ *belief in God* FAITH, trust, reliance, confidence, credence. ❸ *traditional beliefs* IDEOLOGY, principle, ethic, tenet, canon; doctrine, teaching, dogma, article of faith, creed, credo.
– OPPOSITES disbelief, doubt.

believable ▶ **adjective** CREDIBLE, plausible, tenable, able to hold water, conceivable, likely, probable, possible, feasible, reasonable, with a ring of truth.
– OPPOSITES inconceivable.

believe ▶ **verb** ❶ *I don't believe you* BE CONVINCED BY, trust, have confidence in, consider honest, consider truthful. ❷ *do you believe that story?* REGARD AS TRUE, accept, be convinced by, give credence to, credit, trust, put confidence in; *informal* swallow, buy, go for. ❸ *I believe he worked for you* THINK, be of the opinion that, have an idea that, imagine, suspect, suppose, assume, presume, take it, conjecture, surmise, conclude, deduce, understand, be given to understand, gather, fancy, guess, dare say; *informal* reckon, figure; *archaic* ween.
– OPPOSITES doubt.

■ **believe in** ❶ *she believed in God* BE CONVINCED OF THE EXISTENCE OF, be sure of the existence of. ❷ *I believe in lots of exercise* HAVE FAITH IN, pin one's faith on, trust in, have every confidence in, cling to, set (great) store by, value, be convinced by, be persuaded by; subscribe to, approve of; *informal* swear by, rate.

believer ▶ **noun** DEVOTEE, adherent, disciple, follower, supporter, upholder, worshipper.
– OPPOSITES infidel, sceptic.

belittle ▶ **verb** DISPARAGE, denigrate, run down, deprecate, depreciate, downgrade, play down, trivialize, minimize, make light of, treat lightly; *informal* do down, pooh-pooh; *formal* derogate; *rare* misprize.
– OPPOSITES praise, magnify.

belle ▶ **noun** BEAUTY, vision, picture, pin-up, beauty queen, English rose, goddess, Venus; *informal* looker, good looker, lovely, stunner, knockout, bombshell, dish, cracker, bobby-dazzler, peach, honey, eyeful, sight for sore eyes, bit of all right; *Brit. informal* smasher.

bellicose ▶ **adjective** BELLIGERENT, aggressive, hostile, antagonistic, pugnacious, truculent, confrontational, contentious, militant, combative; *informal* spoiling for a fight; *Brit. informal* stroppy, bolshie; *N. Amer. informal* scrappy; *rare* oppugnant.
– OPPOSITES peaceable.

belligerent ▶ **adjective** ❶ *a belligerent stare* HOSTILE, aggressive, threatening, antagonistic, pugnacious, bellicose, truculent, confrontational, contentious, militant, combative; *informal* spoiling for a fight; *Brit. informal* stroppy, bolshie; *N. Amer. informal* scrappy; *rare* oppugnant. ❷ *the belligerent states* WARRING, at war, combatant, fighting, battling.
– OPPOSITES peaceable, neutral.

bellow ▶ **verb** *she bellowed in his ear* ROAR, shout, bawl, thunder, trumpet, boom, bark, yell, shriek, howl, scream; raise one's voice; *informal* holler.
– OPPOSITES whisper.

▶ **noun** *a bellow of pain* ROAR, shout, bawl, bark, yell, yelp, shriek, howl, scream; *informal* holler.
– OPPOSITES whisper.

belly ▶ **noun** *he scratched his belly* STOMACH, abdomen, paunch, middle, midriff, girth; *informal* tummy, tum, gut, guts, insides, pot, pot belly, beer belly, beer gut, bread basket; *Scottish informal* kyte; *N. Amer. informal* bay window; *dated* corporation.

▶ **verb** *her skirt bellied out* BILLOW (OUT), bulge (out), balloon (out), bag (out), fill (out); distend.
– OPPOSITES sag, flap.

belong ▶ **verb** ❶ *the house belongs to his mother* BE OWNED BY, be the property of, be the possession of, be held by, be in the hands of. ❷ *I belong to a trade union* BE A MEMBER OF, be in, be affiliated to, be allied to, be associated with, be linked to, be an adherent of. ❸ *the garden belongs to the basement flat* BE PART OF, be attached to, be an adjunct of, go with. ❹ *these creatures belong with bony fish* BE CLASSED, be classified, be categorized, be included, have a place, be located, be situated, be found, lie. ❺ *she doesn't belong here* FIT IN, be suited to, have a rightful place, have a home; *informal* go, click.

belonging ▶ **noun** AFFILIATION, acceptance, association, attachment, integration, closeness; rapport, fellow feeling, fellowship.
– OPPOSITES alienation.

belongings ▶ **plural noun** POSSESSIONS, effects, worldly goods, chattels, property; *informal* gear, tackle, kit, things, stuff, bits and pieces, bits and bobs; *Brit. informal* clobber, gubbins.

beloved ▶ **adjective** *her beloved brother* DARLING, dear, dearest, precious, adored, much loved, cherished, treasured, prized, highly regarded, admired, esteemed, worshipped, revered, venerated, idolized.
– OPPOSITES hated.

▶ **noun** *he watched his beloved* SWEETHEART, love, darling, dearest, lover, girlfriend, boyfriend, young lady, young man, lady friend, man friend; *informal* steady, baby, angel, honey, pet; *poetic/literary* swain; *dated* beau; *archaic* paramour, doxy.

below ▶ preposition ❶ *the water rushed below them* BENEATH, under, underneath, further down than, lower than. ❷ *the sum is below average* LESS THAN, lower than, under, not as much as, smaller than. ❸ *a captain is below a major* LOWER THAN, under, inferior to, subordinate to, subservient to.
– RELATED TERMS hypo-, sub-.
– OPPOSITES above, over, more than.
▶ adverb ❶ *I could see what was happening below* FURTHER DOWN, lower down, in a lower position, underneath, beneath. ❷ *the statements below* UNDERNEATH, following, further on, at a later point.

belt ▶ noun ❶ *the belt of her coat* GIRDLE, sash, strap, cummerbund, band; *poetic/literary* cincture; *historical* baldric. ❷ *farmers in the cotton belt* REGION, area, district, zone, sector, territory; tract, strip, stretch. ❸ (*informal*) *a belt across the face* BLOW, punch, smack, crack, slap, bang, thump, knock, box; *informal* clout, bash, clip, biff, whack, thwack, wallop, sock, swipe; *Brit. informal* slosh; *N. Amer. informal* boff, bust, slug, whale; *archaic* smite.
▶ verb ❶ *she belted the children in* FASTEN, tie, bind; *poetic/literary* gird. ❷ (*informal*) *a guy belted him in the face* HIT, strike, smack, slap, bang, beat, punch, thump, welt; *informal* clout, bash, biff, whack, thwack, wallop, sock, slog, clobber, bop, lam, larrup; *N. Amer. informal* boff, bust, slug, whale; *archaic* smite. ❸ (*informal*) *he belted down the hill. See* SPEED verb sense 1.
■ **below the belt** UNFAIR, unjust, unacceptable, inequitable; unethical, unprincipled, immoral, unscrupulous, unsporting, sneaky, dishonourable, dishonest, underhand; *informal* low-down, dirty; *Brit. informal* out of order, off, a bit thick, not cricket.
■ **belt up** (*informal*) BE QUIET, quieten down, be silent, fall silent, hush, stop talking, hold your tongue; *informal* shut up, shut your face/mouth/trap, button your lip, pipe down, cut the cackle, put a sock in it; *Brit. informal* shut your gob, wrap up; *N. Amer. informal* save it.

bemoan ▶ verb LAMENT, bewail, mourn, grieve over, sorrow over, cry over; deplore, complain about; *archaic* plain over.
– OPPOSITES rejoice at, applaud.

bemused ▶ adjective BEWILDERED, confused, puzzled, perplexed, baffled, mystified, nonplussed, muddled, dumbfounded, at sea, at a loss, taken aback, disoriented, disconcerted; *informal* flummoxed, bamboozled, clueless, fazed; *N. Amer. informal* discombobulated.

bemusement ▶ noun BEWILDERMENT, confusion, puzzlement, perplexity, bafflement, befuddlement, stupefaction, mystification, disorientation; *informal* bamboozlement; *N. Amer. informal* discombobulation.

bench ▶ noun ❶ *he sat on a bench* PEW, form, stall, settle. ❷ *a laboratory bench* WORKBENCH, work table, worktop, work surface, counter. ❸ *the bench heard the evidence* JUDGES, magistrates, judiciary; court.

benchmark ▶ noun STANDARD, point of reference, gauge, criterion, specification, canon, convention, guide, guideline, guiding principle, norm, touchstone, yardstick, barometer, indicator, measure, model, exemplar, pattern.

bend ▶ verb ❶ *the frames can be bent to fit your face* CURVE, crook, flex, angle, hook, bow, arch, buckle, warp, contort, distort, deform. ❷ *the highway bent to the left* TURN, curve, incline, swing, veer, deviate, diverge, fork, change course, curl, loop. ❸ *he bent down to tie his shoe* STOOP, bow, crouch, hunch, lean down/over. ❹ *they want to bend me to their will* MOULD, shape, manipulate, direct, force, press, influence, incline, sway. ❺ *he bent his mind to the question* DIRECT, turn, train, steer, set.
– OPPOSITES straighten.
▶ noun *he came to a bend in the road* CURVE, turn, corner, kink, angle, arc, crescent, twist, crook, deviation, deflection, loop; dogleg, oxbow, zigzag; *Brit.* hairpin bend, hairpin turn, hairpin; *rare* incurvation.
– OPPOSITES straight.
■ **bend over backwards** (*informal*) TRY ONE'S HARDEST, do one's best, do one's utmost, do all one can, give one's all, make every effort; *informal* do one's damnedest, go all out, pull out all the stops, bust a gut, move heaven and earth.

beneath ▶ preposition ❶ *we sat beneath the trees* UNDER, underneath, below, at the foot of, at the bottom of; lower than. ❷ *the rank beneath theirs* INFERIOR TO, below, not so important as, lower in status than, subordinate to, subservient to. ❸ *such an attitude was beneath her* UNWORTHY OF, unbecoming to, degrading to, below.
– OPPOSITES above.
▶ adverb *sand with rock beneath* UNDERNEATH, below, further down, lower down.
– OPPOSITES above.

benediction ▶ noun ❶ *the priest said a benediction* BLESSING, prayer, invocation; grace. ❷ *filled with heavenly benediction* BLESSEDNESS, beatitude, bliss, grace.

benefactor, benefactress ▶ noun PATRON, supporter, backer, sponsor; donor, contributor, subscriber; *informal* angel.

beneficent ▶ adjective BENEVOLENT, charitable, altruistic, humanitarian, neighbourly, public-spirited, philanthropic; generous, magnanimous, munificent, unselfish, unstinting, open-handed, liberal, lavish, bountiful; *poetic/literary* bounteous.
– OPPOSITES unkind, mean.

beneficial ▶ adjective ADVANTAGEOUS, favourable, helpful, useful, of use, of benefit, of assistance, valuable, of value, profitable, rewarding, gainful.
– OPPOSITES disadvantageous.

beneficiary ▶ noun HEIR, heiress, inheritor,

legatee; recipient; *Law* devisee, cestui que trust; *Scottish Law* heritor.

benefit ▶ **noun** ❶ *for the benefit of others* GOOD, sake, welfare, well-being, advantage, comfort, ease, convenience; help, aid, assistance, service. ❷ *the benefits of working for a large firm* ADVANTAGE, reward, merit, boon, blessing, virtue; bonus; value; *informal* perk; *formal* perquisite. ❸ *state benefit* SOCIAL SECURITY PAYMENTS, public assistance allowance, welfare; charity, donations, gifts, financial assistance; *informal* the dole; *Scottish informal* the buroo, the broo.
– OPPOSITES detriment, disadvantage.
▶ **verb** ❶ *the deal benefited them both* BE ADVANTAGEOUS TO, be beneficial to, be of advantage to, be to the advantage of, profit, do good to, be of service to, serve, be useful to, be of use to, be helpful to, be of help to, help, aid, assist, be of assistance to; better, improve, strengthen, boost, advance, further. ❷ *they may benefit from drugs* PROFIT, gain, reap benefits, reap reward, make money; make the most of, exploit, turn to one's advantage, put to good use, do well out of; *informal* cash in, make a killing.
– OPPOSITES damage, suffer.

benevolence ▶ **noun** KINDNESS, kind-heartedness, big-heartedness, goodness, goodwill, charity, altruism, humanitarianism, compassion, philanthropism; generosity, magnanimity, munificence, unselfishness, open-handedness, beneficence; *poetic/literary* bounty, bounteousness.
– OPPOSITES spite, miserliness.

benevolent ▶ **adjective** ❶ *a benevolent patriarch* KIND, kindly, kind-hearted, big-hearted, good-natured, good, benign, compassionate, caring, altruistic, humanitarian, philanthropic; generous, magnanimous, munificent, unselfish, open-handed, beneficent; *poetic/literary* bounteous. ❷ *a benevolent institution* CHARITABLE, non-profit-making, non-profit, not-for-profit; *formal* eleemosynary.
– OPPOSITES unkind, tight-fisted.

benighted ▶ **adjective** IGNORANT, unenlightened, uneducated, uninformed, backward, simple; primitive, uncivilized, unsophisticated, philistine, barbarian, barbaric, barbarous; *poetic/literary* nescient; *archaic* rude.
– OPPOSITES enlightened.

benign ▶ **adjective** ❶ *a benign grandfatherly role* KINDLY, kind, warm-hearted, good-natured, friendly, warm, affectionate, agreeable, genial, congenial, cordial, approachable, tender-hearted, gentle, sympathetic, compassionate, caring, well disposed, benevolent. ❷ *a benign climate* TEMPERATE, mild, gentle, balmy, soft, pleasant; healthy, wholesome, salubrious. ❸ (*Medicine*) *a benign tumour* HARMLESS, non-malignant, non-cancerous, innocent; *Medicine* benignant.
– OPPOSITES unfriendly, hostile, unhealthy, unfavourable, malignant.

bent ▶ **adjective** ❶ *the bucket had a bent handle* TWISTED, crooked, warped, contorted, deformed, misshapen, out of shape, irregular; bowed, arched, curved, angled, hooked, kinked; *N. Amer. informal* pretzeled. ❷ (*Brit. informal*) *a bent policeman. See* CORRUPT adjective sense 1. ❸ (*Brit. informal*). *See* HOMOSEXUAL adjective.
– OPPOSITES straight, law-abiding, heterosexual.
▶ **noun** *an artistic bent* INCLINATION, leaning, tendency; talent, gift, flair, aptitude, facility, skill, capability, capacity; predisposition, disposition, instinct, orientation, predilection, proclivity, propensity.
■ **bent on** INTENT ON, determined on, set on, insistent on, resolved on, hell-bent on; committed to, single-minded about, obsessed with, fanatical about, fixated on.

benumbed ▶ **adjective** NUMB, unfeeling, insensible, stupefied, groggy, foggy, fuzzy, muzzy, dazed, dizzy; befuddled, fuddled, disoriented, confused, bewildered, all at sea; *informal* dopey, woozy, mixed up; *N. Amer. informal* discombobulated.
– OPPOSITES perceptive.

bequeath ▶ **verb** LEAVE (IN ONE'S WILL), will, make over, pass on, hand on/down, entrust, grant, transfer; donate, give; endow on, bestow on, confer on; *Law* demise, devise, convey.

bequest ▶ **noun** LEGACY, inheritance, endowment, settlement; estate, heritage; bestowal, bequeathal; *Law* devise; *Law, dated* hereditament.

berate ▶ **verb** SCOLD, rebuke, reprimand, reproach, reprove, admonish, chide, criticize, upbraid, take to task, pull up, read someone the Riot Act, haul over the coals; *informal* tell off, give someone a talking-to, give someone a telling-off, give someone a dressing-down, give someone a roasting, rap over the knuckles, send someone away with a flea in their ear, bawl out, come down on, tear into, put on the mat, slap down, blast; *Brit. informal* tick off, have a go at, carpet, give someone a rocket, give someone a rollicking, tear someone off a strip; *Brit. informal, dated* give someone a wigging; *N. Amer. informal* chew out, ream out, take to the woodshed; *Austral. informal* monster; *formal* castigate; *dated* call down, rate; *rare* reprehend, objurgate.
– OPPOSITES praise.

bereaved ▶ **adjective** orphaned, widowed; mourning, grieving.

bereavement ▶ **noun** DEATH IN THE FAMILY, loss, passing (away), demise; *formal* decease.

bereft ▶ **adjective** DEPRIVED, robbed, stripped, devoid, bankrupt; wanting, in need of, lacking, without; *informal* minus, sans, clean out of.

berry ▶ **noun** FRUIT, currant.

berserk ▶ **adjective** MAD, crazy, insane, out of one's mind, hysterical, frenzied, crazed, demented, maniacal, manic, frantic, raving, wild, out of control, amok, on the rampage; *informal* off one's head, off the deep end, ape, bananas, bonkers, nuts, hyper; *Brit. informal* spare, crackers, barmy; *N. Amer. informal* postal.

berth ▶ **noun** ❶ *a 4-berth cabin* BUNK, bed, cot, couch, hammock. ❷ *the vessel left its berth* MOORING, dock.

▶ **verb** ❶ *the ship berthed in London Docks* DOCK, moor, land, tie up, make fast. ❷ *the boats each berth six* ACCOMMODATE, sleep.

■ **give someone/something a wide berth** AVOID, shun, keep away from, stay away from, steer clear of, keep at arm's length, have nothing to do with; dodge, sidestep, circumvent, skirt round.

beseech ▶ **verb** (*poetic/literary*) IMPLORE, beg, entreat, plead with, appeal to, call on, supplicate, importune, pray to, ask, request, petition.

beset ▶ **verb** ❶ *he is beset by fears* PLAGUE, bedevil, assail, beleaguer, afflict, torment, rack, oppress, trouble, worry, harass, dog. ❷ *they were beset by enemy forces* SURROUND, besiege, hem in, shut in, fence in, box in, encircle, ring round.

beside ▶ **preposition** ❶ *Kate walked beside him* ALONGSIDE, by/at the side of, next to, parallel to, abreast of, at someone's elbow; adjacent to, next door to, cheek by jowl with; bordering, abutting, neighbouring. ❷ *beside Paula, she felt clumsy* COMPARED WITH/TO, in comparison with/to, by comparison with, next to, against, contrasted with, in contrast to/with.

– RELATED TERMS para-.

■ **beside oneself** DISTRAUGHT, overcome, out of one's mind, frantic, desperate, distracted, at one's wits' end, frenzied, wound up, worked up; hysterical, unhinged, mad, crazed, berserk, demented.

■ **beside the point**. *See* POINT[1].

besides ▶ **preposition** *who did you ask besides Mary?* IN ADDITION TO, as well as, over and above, above and beyond, on top of; apart from, other than, aside from, but for, save for, not counting, excluding, not including, except, with the exception of, excepting, leaving aside; *N. Amer. informal* outside of; *archaic* forbye.

▶ **adverb** ❶ *there's a lot more besides* IN ADDITION, as well, too, also, into the bargain, on top of that, to boot; *archaic* therewithal. ❷ *besides, he's a man* FURTHERMORE, moreover, further; anyway, anyhow, in any case, be that as it may; *informal* what's more; *N. Amer. informal* anyways.

besiege ▶ **verb** ❶ *the English army besieged Leith* LAY SIEGE TO, beleaguer, blockade, surround; *archaic* invest. ❷ *fans besieged his hotel* SURROUND, mob, crowd round, swarm round, throng round, ring round, encircle. ❸ *guilt besieged him* OPPRESS, torment, torture, rack, plague, afflict, haunt, harrow, beset, beleaguer, trouble, bedevil, prey on. ❹ *he was besieged with requests* OVERWHELM, inundate, deluge, flood, swamp, snow under; bombard.

besmirch ▶ **verb** (*poetic/literary*) SULLY, tarnish, blacken, drag through the mud/mire, stain, taint, smear, disgrace, dishonour, bring discredit to, damage, ruin.

– OPPOSITES honour, enhance.

besotted ▶ **adjective** INFATUATED, smitten, in love, head over heels in love, obsessed; doting on, greatly enamoured of; *informal* bowled over by, swept off one's feet by, struck on, crazy about, mad about, wild about, gone on, carrying a torch for; *Brit. informal* potty about.

bespatter ▶ **verb** SPLATTER, spatter, splash, speck, fleck, spot; dirty, soil; *Scottish & Irish* slabber; *informal* splotch, splodge, splosh.

bespeak ▶ **verb** ❶ *a tree-lined road which bespoke money* INDICATE, be evidence of, be a sign of, denote, point to, testify to, evidence, reflect, demonstrate, show, manifest, display, signify; reveal, betray; *informal* spell; *poetic/literary* betoken. ❷ *he had bespoken a room* ORDER, reserve, book; *informal* bag.

– OPPOSITES belie.

best ▶ **adjective** ❶ *the best hotel in Paris* FINEST, greatest, top, foremost, leading, pre-eminent, premier, prime, first, chief, principal, supreme, of the highest quality, superlative, par excellence, unrivalled, second to none, without equal, nonpareil, unsurpassed, peerless, matchless, unparalleled, unbeaten, unbeatable, optimum, optimal, ultimate, incomparable, ideal, perfect; highest, record-breaking; *informal* star, number-one, a cut above the rest, top-drawer; *formal* unexampled. ❷ *do whatever you think best* MOST ADVANTAGEOUS, most useful, most suitable, most fitting, most appropriate; most prudent, most sensible, most advisable.

– OPPOSITES worst.

▶ **adverb** ❶ *the best-dressed man* TO THE HIGHEST STANDARD, in the best way. ❷ *the food he liked best* MOST, to the highest/greatest degree. ❸ *this is best done at home* MOST ADVANTAGEOUSLY, most usefully, most suitably, most fittingly, most appropriately; most sensibly, most prudently, most wisely; better.

– OPPOSITES worst, least.

▶ **noun** ❶ *only the best will do* FINEST, choicest, top, cream, choice, prime, elite, crème de la crème, flower, jewel in the crown, nonpareil; *informal* tops, pick of the bunch. ❷ *she dressed in her best* BEST CLOTHES, finery, Sunday best; *informal* best bib and tucker, glad rags. ❸ *give her my best* BEST WISHES, regards, kind/kindest regards, greetings, compliments, felicitations, respects; love.

▶ **verb** (*informal*) *she was not to be bested* DEFEAT, beat, get the better of, outdo, outwit, outsmart, worst, be more than a match for, prevail over, vanquish, trounce, triumph over; surpass, outclass, outshine, put someone in the shade, overshadow, eclipse; *informal* lick, get one over on.

■ **at one's best** ON TOP FORM, at one's peak, in one's prime, in the pink, in the best of health.

■ **do one's best** DO ONE'S UTMOST, try one's hardest, make every effort, do all one can, give one's all; *informal* bend over backwards, do one's damnedest, go all out, pull out all the stops, bust a gut, break one's neck, move heaven and earth.

■ **had best** OUGHT TO, should.

bestial ▶ **adjective** ❶ *Stanley's bestial behaviour* SAVAGE, brutish, brutal, barbarous, barbaric, cruel, vicious, violent, inhuman, subhuman; depraved, degenerate, perverted, immoral, warped. ❷ *man's bestial ancestors* ANIMAL, beast-like, animalistic; *rare* zoic.

– OPPOSITES civilized, humane.

bestir

■ **bestir oneself** EXERT ONESELF, make an effort, rouse oneself, get going, get moving, get on with it; *informal* shake a leg, look lively, get cracking, get weaving, get one's finger out, get off one's backside; *Brit. informal, dated* stir one's stumps.

bestow ▶ **verb** CONFER ON, grant, accord, afford, endow someone with, vest in, present, award, give, donate, entrust with, vouchsafe.

bestride ▶ **verb** ❶ *the oilfield bestrides the border* EXTEND ACROSS, lie on both sides of, straddle, span, bridge. ❷ *he bestrode his horse* STRADDLE, sit/stand astride. ❸ *Italy bestrode Europe in opera* DOMINATE, tower over/above.

best-seller ▶ **noun** great success, brand leader; *informal* hit, smash (hit), blockbuster, chart-topper, chartbuster.

– OPPOSITES failure, flop.

best-selling ▶ **adjective** VERY SUCCESSFUL, very popular; *informal* number-one, chart-topping, hit, smash.

bet ▶ **verb** ❶ *he bet £10 on the favourite* WAGER, gamble, stake, risk, venture, hazard, chance; put/lay money, speculate; *informal* punt; *Brit. informal* have a flutter, chance one's arm. ❷ (*informal*) *I bet it was your idea* BE CERTAIN, be sure, be convinced, be confident; expect, predict, forecast, guess; *Brit. informal* put one's shirt on.

▶ **noun** ❶ *a £20 bet* WAGER, gamble, stake, ante; *Brit. informal* flutter, punt. ❷ (*informal*) *my bet is that they'll lose* PREDICTION, forecast, guess; opinion, belief, feeling, view, theory. ❸ (*informal*) *your best bet is to go early* OPTION, choice, alternative, course of action, plan.

bête noire ▶ **noun** BUGBEAR, pet hate, bogey; a thorn in one's flesh/side, the bane of one's life; *N. Amer.* bugaboo.

– OPPOSITES favourite.

betide ▶ **verb** (*poetic/literary*) HAPPEN, occur, take place, come about, transpire, arise, chance; result, ensue, follow, develop, supervene; *N. Amer. informal* go down; *formal* eventuate; *poetic/literary* come to pass, befall; *archaic* hap, bechance.

betoken ▶ **verb** (*poetic/literary*) ❶ *a small gift betokening regret* INDICATE, be a sign of, be evidence of, evidence, manifest, mean, signify, denote, represent, show, demonstrate, bespeak; *informal* spell. ❷ *the blue sky betokened a day of good weather* FORETELL, signal, give notice of, herald, proclaim, prophesy, foreshadow, presage, be a harbinger of, portend, augur, be an omen of, be a sign of, be a warning of, warn of, bode; *poetic/literary* foretoken, forebode.

betray ▶ **verb** ❶ *he betrayed his own brother* BREAK ONE'S PROMISE TO, be disloyal to, be unfaithful to, break faith with, play someone false; inform on/against, give away, denounce, sell out, stab in the back; *informal* split on, rat on, peach on, stitch up, do the dirty on, sell down the river, squeal on; *Brit. informal* grass on, shop, sneak on; *N. Amer. informal* rat out, drop a/the dime on, finger; *Austral./NZ informal* dob on, point the bone at. ❷ *he betrayed a secret* REVEAL, disclose, divulge, tell, give away, leak; unmask, expose, bring out into the open; let slip, let out, let drop, blurt out; *informal* blab, spill.

– OPPOSITES be loyal to, hide.

betrayal ▶ **noun** DISLOYALTY, treachery, bad faith, faithlessness, falseness, Punic faith; duplicity, deception, double-dealing; breach of faith, breach of trust, stab in the back; double-cross, sell-out; *poetic/literary* perfidy.

– OPPOSITES loyalty.

betrayer ▶ **noun** TRAITOR, back-stabber, Judas, double-crosser; renegade, quisling, double agent, collaborator, informer, mole, stool pigeon; turncoat, defector; *informal* snake in the grass, rat, scab, stoolie; *Brit. informal* grass, supergrass, nark; *N. Amer. informal* fink.

betrothal ▶ **noun** (*dated*) ENGAGEMENT, marriage contract; *archaic* espousal.

betrothed ▶ **adjective** (*dated*) ENGAGED (TO BE MARRIED), promised/pledged in marriage, attached; *informal* spoken for; *poetic/literary* affianced; *archaic* plighted, espoused.

– OPPOSITES unattached.

better ▶ **adjective** ❶ *better facilities* SUPERIOR, finer, of higher quality; preferable; *informal* a cut above, streets ahead, head and shoulders above, ahead of the pack/field. ❷ *there couldn't be a better time* MORE ADVANTAGEOUS, more suitable, more fitting, more appropriate, more useful, more valuable, more desirable. ❸ *are you better?* HEALTHIER, fitter, stronger; well, cured, healed, recovered; recovering, on the road to recovery, making progress, improving; *informal* on the mend.

– OPPOSITES worse, inferior.

▶ **adverb** ❶ *I played better today* TO A HIGHER STANDARD, in a superior/finer way. ❷ *this may suit you better* MORE, to a greater degree/extent. ❸ *the* *money could be better spent* MORE WISELY, more sensibly, more suitably, more fittingly, more advantageously.

▶ **verb** ❶ *he bettered the record* SURPASS, improve on, beat, exceed, top, cap, trump, eclipse. ❷ *refugees who want to better their lot* IMPROVE, ameliorate, raise, advance, further, lift, upgrade, enhance.
– OPPOSITES worsen.

betterment ▶ **noun** IMPROVEMENT, amelioration, advancement, furtherance, upgrading, enhancement.

between ▶ **preposition** ❶ *Philip stood between his parents* IN THE SPACE SEPARATING, in the middle of, with one on either side; *archaic* betwixt. ❷ *the bond between her and her mother* CONNECTING, linking, joining; uniting, allying.
– RELATED TERMS inter-.

bevel ▶ **noun** SLOPE, slant, angle, cant, chamfer.

beverage ▶ **noun** DRINK, liquid refreshment; *humorous* libation; *archaic* potation.

bevy ▶ **noun** GROUP, crowd, herd, flock, horde, army, galaxy, assemblage, gathering, band, body, pack; knot, cluster; *informal* bunch, gaggle, posse.

bewail ▶ **verb** LAMENT, bemoan, mourn, grieve over, sorrow over, cry over; deplore, complain about; *archaic* plain over.
– OPPOSITES rejoice at, applaud.

beware ▶ **verb** BE ON YOUR GUARD, watch out, look out, mind out, be alert, be on the lookout, keep your eyes open/peeled, keep an eye out, keep a sharp lookout, be on the qui vive; take care, be careful, be cautious, have a care, watch your step; *Brit. school slang, dated* cave; *Golf* fore; *Hunting* ware.

bewilder ▶ **verb** BAFFLE, mystify, bemuse, perplex, puzzle, confuse, confound, nonplus; *informal* flummox, faze, stump, beat, fox, make someone scratch their head, be all Greek to, floor; *N. Amer. informal* discombobulate, buffalo.
– OPPOSITES enlighten.

bewildered ▶ **adjective** BAFFLED, mystified, bemused, perplexed, puzzled, confused, nonplussed, at sea, at a loss, disorientated, taken aback; *informal* flummoxed, bamboozled; *N. Amer. informal* discombobulated.

bewitch ▶ **verb** ❶ *that evil woman bewitched him* CAST/PUT A SPELL ON, enchant; possess, witch, curse; *N. Amer.* hex, hoodoo; *Austral.* point the bone at. ❷ *she was bewitched by her surroundings* CAPTIVATE, enchant, entrance, enrapture, charm, beguile, delight, fascinate, enthral.
– OPPOSITES repel.

beyond ▶ **preposition** ❶ *beyond the trees* ON THE FAR SIDE OF, on the other side of, further away than, behind, past, after. ❷ *beyond six o'clock* LATER THAN, past, after. ❸ *inflation beyond 10 per cent* GREATER THAN, more than, exceeding, in excess of, above, over and above, above and beyond, upwards of. ❹ *little beyond food was provided* APART FROM, except, other than, besides; *informal* outside of; *formal* save.

▶ **adverb** *a house with a garden beyond* FURTHER AWAY, further off.

bias ▶ **noun** ❶ *he accused the media of bias* PREJUDICE, partiality, partisanship, favouritism, unfairness, one-sidedness; bigotry, intolerance, discrimination, a jaundiced eye; leaning, tendency, inclination, predilection. ❷ *a dress cut on the bias* DIAGONAL, cross, slant, angle.
– OPPOSITES impartiality.

▶ **verb** *this may have biased the result* PREJUDICE, influence, colour, sway, weight, predispose; distort, skew, slant.

biased ▶ **adjective** PREJUDICED, partial, partisan, one-sided, blinkered; bigoted, intolerant, discriminatory; jaundiced, distorted, warped, twisted, skewed.
– OPPOSITES impartial.

Bible ▶ **noun** ❶ *he read the Bible* THE (HOLY) SCRIPTURES, Holy Writ, the Good Book, the Book of Books. ❷ (*informal*) *the taxi driver's bible* HANDBOOK, manual, ABC, companion, guide, vade mecum.

bibliophile ▶ **noun** BOOK LOVER, avid reader; *informal* book worm; *rare* bibliomaniac.

bicker ▶ **verb** SQUABBLE, argue, quarrel, wrangle, fight, disagree, dispute, spar, have words, be at each other's throats, lock horns; *informal* scrap, argufy, spat; *archaic* altercate.
– OPPOSITES agree.

bicycle ▶ **noun** CYCLE, two-wheeler, pedal cycle; *informal* bike, pushbike.

bid[1] ▶ **verb** ❶ *United bid £1 million for the striker* OFFER, make an offer of, put in a bid of, put up, tender, proffer, propose. ❷ *she is bidding for a place in the England team* TRY TO OBTAIN, try to get, make a pitch for, make a bid for.

▶ **noun** ❶ *a bid of £3,000* OFFER, tender, proposal. ❷ *a bid to cut crime* ATTEMPT, effort, endeavour, try; *informal* crack, go, shot, stab; *formal* essay.

bid[2] ▶ **verb** ❶ *she bid him farewell* WISH; utter. ❷ (*poetic/literary*) *I did as he bade me* ORDER, command, tell, instruct, direct, enjoin, charge. ❸ (*poetic/literary*) *he bade his companions enter* INVITE TO, ask to, request to.

biddable ▶ **adjective** OBEDIENT, acquiescent, compliant, tractable, amenable, complaisant, cooperative, dutiful, submissive; *rare* persuasible.
– OPPOSITES disobedient, uncooperative.

bidding ▶ **noun** COMMAND, order, instruction, decree, injunction, demand, mandate, direction, summons, call; wish, desire; request; *poetic/literary* behest; *archaic* hest.

big ▶ **adjective** ❶ *a big building* LARGE, sizeable, substantial, great, huge, immense, enormous,

extensive, colossal, massive, mammoth, vast, tremendous, gigantic, giant, monumental, mighty, gargantuan, elephantine, titanic, mountainous, Brobdingnagian; towering, tall, high, lofty; outsize, oversized; goodly; capacious, voluminous, spacious; king-size(d), man-size, family-size(d), economy-size(d); *informal* jumbo, whopping, thumping, bumper, mega, humongous, monster, astronomical, almighty, dirty great, socking great; *Brit. informal* whacking, ginormous; *formal* commodious. ❷ *a big man* WELL BUILT, sturdy, brawny, burly, broad-shouldered, muscular, muscly, rugged, lusty, Herculean, bulky, hulking, strapping, thickset, stocky, solid, hefty; tall, huge, gigantic; fat, stout, portly, plump, fleshy, paunchy, corpulent, obese; *informal* hunky, beefy, husky; *poetic/literary* thewy, stark. ❸ *my big brother* GROWN-UP, adult, mature, grown; elder, older. ❹ *a big decision* IMPORTANT, significant, major, momentous, weighty, consequential, far-reaching, key, vital, critical, crucial. ❺ (*informal*) POWERFUL, important, prominent, influential, high-powered, leading; *N. Amer.* major-league. ❻ (*informal*) *he has big plans* AMBITIOUS, far-reaching, grandiose, on a grand scale. ❼ *she's got a big heart* GENEROUS, kind, kindly, caring, compassionate, loving. ❽ (*informal*) *African bands are big in Britain* POPULAR, successful, in demand, sought-after, all the rage; *informal* hot, in, cool, trendy, now, hip; *Brit. informal, dated* all the go.
– OPPOSITES small, minor, modest.

■ **too big for one's boots** (*informal*) CONCEITED, full of oneself, cocky, arrogant, cocksure, above oneself, self-important; vain, self-satisfied, pleased with oneself, smug, complacent; *informal* big-headed, swollen-headed; *poetic/literary* vainglorious.

big-headed ▶ adjective (*informal*) CONCEITED, full of oneself, cocky, arrogant, cocksure, above oneself, self-important; vain, self-satisfied, pleased with oneself, smug, complacent; *informal* swollen-headed, too big for one's boots; *poetic/literary* vainglorious.
– OPPOSITES modest.

big-hearted ▶ adjective GENEROUS, magnanimous, munificent, open-handed, bountiful, unstinting, unselfish, altruistic, charitable, philanthropic, benevolent; kind, kindly, kind-hearted; *poetic/literary* bounteous.
– OPPOSITES mean.

bigot ▶ noun DOGMATIST, partisan, sectarian; racist, sexist, chauvinist, jingoist.

bigoted ▶ adjective PREJUDICED, biased, partial, one-sided, sectarian, discriminatory; opinionated, dogmatic, intolerant, narrow-minded, blinkered, illiberal; racist, sexist, chauvinistic, jingoistic; jaundiced, warped, twisted, distorted.
– OPPOSITES open-minded.

bigotry ▶ noun PREJUDICE, bias, partiality, partisanship, sectarianism, discrimination; dogmatism, intolerance, narrow-mindedness; racism, sexism, chauvinism, jingoism.
– OPPOSITES open-mindedness.

bigwig ▶ noun (*informal*) VIP, important person, notable, dignitary, grandee; celebrity; *informal* somebody, heavyweight, big shot, big noise, big gun, big cheese, big fish; *Brit. informal* brass hat; *N. Amer. informal* big wheel.
– OPPOSITES nonentity.

bijou ▶ adjective SMALL, little, compact, snug, cosy.

bilge ▶ noun (*informal*). *See* NONSENSE sense 1.

bilious ▶ adjective ❶ *I felt bilious* NAUSEOUS, sick, queasy, nauseated, green about the gills; *N. Amer. informal* barfy. ❷ *his bilious disposition* BAD-TEMPERED, irritable, irascible, tetchy, testy, crotchety, ill-tempered, ill-natured, ill-humoured, peevish, fractious, pettish, crabby, waspish, prickly, crusty, shrewish, quick-tempered; *N. Amer. informal* cranky, ornery. ❸ *a bilious green and pink colour scheme* LURID, garish, loud, violent; sickly, nauseating.
– OPPOSITES well, good-humoured, muted.

bilk ▶ verb (*informal*). *See* SWINDLE verb.

bill[1] ▶ noun ❶ *a bill for £6* INVOICE, account, statement, list of charges; *N. Amer.* check; *informal, humorous* the damage; *N. Amer. informal* tab; *archaic* reckoning, score. ❷ *a parliamentary bill* DRAFT LAW, proposed piece of legislation, proposal, measure. ❸ *she was top of the bill* PROGRAMME (OF ENTERTAINMENT), line-up; *N. Amer.* playbill. ❹ (*N. Amer.*) *a $10 bill* BANKNOTE, note; *US informal* greenback; *US & historical* Treasury note. ❺ *he had been posting bills* POSTER, advertisement, public notice, announcement; flyer, leaflet, handbill; *Brit.* fly-poster; *N. Amer.* dodger; *informal* ad; *Brit. informal* advert.

▶ verb ❶ *please bill me for the work* INVOICE, charge, debit, send a statement to. ❷ *the concert went ahead as billed* ADVERTISE, announce; schedule, programme, timetable; *N. Amer.* slate. ❸ *he was billed as the new Sean Connery* DESCRIBE, call, style, label, dub; promote, publicize, talk up; *informal* hype.

bill[2] ▶ noun *a bird's bill* BEAK; *Scottish & N. English* neb; *technical* mandibles.

billet ▶ noun *the troops' billets* QUARTERS, rooms; accommodation, lodging, housing; barracks, cantonment.

▶ verb *two soldiers were billeted here* ACCOMMODATE, quarter, put up, lodge, house; station, garrison.

billow ▶ noun ❶ *billows of smoke* CLOUD, mass. ❷ (*archaic*) *the billows that break upon the shore* WAVE, roller, boomer, breaker.

▶ verb ❶ *her dress billowed around her* PUFF UP/OUT, balloon (out), swell, fill (out), belly out. ❷ *smoke billowed from the chimney* SWIRL, spiral, roll, undulate, eddy; pour, flow.

billowing ▶ adjective ROLLING, swirling, undulating, surging, heaving, billowy, swelling, rippling.

bin ▶ **noun** CONTAINER, receptacle, holder; drum, canister, caddy, can, tin.

bind ▶ **verb** ❶ *they bound her hands and feet* TIE (UP), fasten (together), hold together, secure, make fast, attach; rope, strap, lash, truss, tether. ❷ *Shelley bound up the wound with a clean dressing* BANDAGE, dress, cover, wrap; strap up, tape up. ❸ *the experience had bound them together* UNITE, join, bond, knit together, draw together, yoke together. ❹ *we have not bound ourselves to join* COMMIT ONESELF, undertake, pledge, vow, promise, swear, give one's word. ❺ *the edges are bound in a contrasting colour* TRIM, hem, edge, border, fringe; finish. ❻ *they are bound by the agreement* CONSTRAIN, restrict, restrain, trammel, tie hand and foot, tie down, shackle; hamper, hinder, inhibit.
– OPPOSITES untie, separate.
▶ **noun** (*informal*) ❶ *starting so early is a bind* NUISANCE, annoyance, inconvenience, bore, bother, source of irritation, irritant, trial; *informal* pain, pain in the neck/backside, headache, hassle, drag; *N. Amer. informal* pain in the butt. ❷ *he is in a political bind* PREDICAMENT, difficult/awkward situation, quandary, dilemma, plight, cleft stick; *informal* spot, tight spot, hole.

binding ▶ **adjective** IRREVOCABLE, unalterable, inescapable, unbreakable, contractual; compulsory, obligatory, mandatory, incumbent.

binge ▶ **noun** (*informal*) DRINKING BOUT, debauch; *informal* bender, session, sesh, booze-up, blind; *Scottish informal* skite; *N. Amer. informal* jag, toot; *dated* souse; *poetic/literary* bacchanal, bacchanalia; *archaic* wassail.

biography ▶ **noun** LIFE STORY, life history, life, memoir; *informal* bio, biog.

bird ▶ **noun** fowl; chick, fledgling, nestling; (**birds**) avifauna; *informal* feathered friend, birdie.
– RELATED TERMS avian, ornith-.

birth ▶ **noun** ❶ *the birth of a child* CHILDBIRTH, delivery, nativity, birthing; *formal* parturition; *dated* confinement; *archaic* accouchement, childbed. ❷ *the birth of science* BEGINNING(S), emergence, genesis, dawn, dawning, rise, start. ❸ *he is of noble birth* ANCESTRY, lineage, blood, descent, parentage, family, extraction, origin, genealogy, heritage, stock, kinship.
– RELATED TERMS natal.
– OPPOSITES death, demise, end.
■ **give birth to** HAVE, bear, produce, be delivered of, bring into the world; *N. Amer.* birth; *informal* drop; *dated* mother; *archaic* bring forth.

birthmark ▶ **noun** NAEVUS, mole, blemish.

birthright ▶ **noun** PATRIMONY, inheritance, heritage; right, due, prerogative, privilege; primogeniture.

biscuit ▶ **noun** (*Brit.*) CRACKER, wafer; *N. Amer.* cookie; *informal* bicky.

bisect ▶ **verb** CUT IN HALF, halve, divide/cut/split in two, split down the middle; cross, intersect.

bisexual ▶ **adjective** ❶ *bisexual crustaceans* HERMAPHRODITE, hermaphroditic, intersex; androgynous, epicene; *technical* monoclinous, gynandrous, gynandromorphic. ❷ *a bisexual actor* AMBISEXUAL; *informal* AC/DC, bi, swinging both ways, ambidextrous; *N. Amer. informal* switch-hitting.

bishop ▶ **noun** diocesan, metropolitan, suffragan; *formal* prelate.
– RELATED TERMS episcopal.

bishopric ▶ **noun** DIOCESE, see.

bit ▶ **noun** ❶ *a bit of bread* PIECE, portion, segment, section, part; chunk, lump, hunk, slice; fragment, scrap, shred, crumb, grain, speck; spot, drop, pinch, dash, soupçon, modicum; morsel, mouthful, bite, sample; iota, jot, tittle, whit, atom, particle, trace, touch, suggestion, hint, tinge; snippet, snatch; *informal* smidgen, tad. ❷ *wait a bit* MOMENT, minute, second, (little) while; *informal* sec, jiffy; *Brit. informal* mo, tick.
– OPPOSITES lot.
■ **a bit** RATHER, fairly, slightly, somewhat, quite, moderately; *informal* pretty, sort of, kind of.
■ **bit by bit** GRADUALLY, little by little, in stages, step by step, piecemeal, slowly.
■ **in a bit** SOON, in a (little) while, in a second, in a minute, in a moment, shortly; *informal* anon, in a jiffy, in two shakes; *Brit. informal* in a tick, in two ticks, in a mo; *N. Amer. informal* in a snap; *dated* directly; *poetic/literary* ere long.

bitch ▶ **noun** (*informal*) ❶ *she's such a bitch* SHREW, vixen, she-devil, hellcat; *informal* cow, cat; *archaic* grimalkin. ❷ *a bitch of a job* NIGHTMARE; *informal* bastard, bummer, —— from hell, swine, pig, stinker.
▶ **verb** ❶ *big men bitched about the price of oil* COMPLAIN, whine, grumble, grouse; *informal* whinge, moan, grouch, gripe. ❷ *he's always bitching about colleagues* BE SPITEFUL ABOUT, criticize, run down, speak ill of, slander, malign; *informal* knock, pull to pieces, take apart, bad-mouth, do a hatchet job on; *N. Amer. informal* trash; *Brit. informal* slag off.
■ **bitch something up** (*informal*) MAKE A MESS OF, mess up, spoil, ruin, wreck; bungle; *informal* botch, muck up, make a hash of, screw up, louse up, muff; *Brit. informal* make a pig's ear of, cock up; *N. Amer. informal* flub, goof up.

bitchy ▶ **adjective** (*informal*). *See* SPITEFUL.

bite ▶ **verb** ❶ *the dog bit his arm* SINK ONE'S TEETH INTO, chew, munch, crunch, champ, tear at. ❷ *the acid bites into the copper* CORRODE, eat into, eat away at, burn (into), etch, dissolve. ❸ *my boots failed to bite* GRIP, hold, get a purchase. ❹ *the measures begin to bite* TAKE EFFECT, have an effect, be effective, work, act, have results. ❺ *a hundred or so retailers should bite* ACCEPT, agree, respond; be lured, be enticed, be tempted; take the bait.

▶ **noun** ❶ *he took a bite at his sandwich* CHEW, munch, nibble, gnaw, nip, snap. ❷ *he ate it in two bites* MOUTHFUL, piece, bit, morsel. ❸ *do you fancy a bite?* SNACK, light meal, mouthful, soupçon; refreshments; *informal* a little something. ❹ *the appetizer had a fiery bite* PIQUANCY, pungency, spiciness, strong flavour, tang, zest, sharpness, tartness; *informal* kick, punch, zing.

biting ▶ **adjective** ❶ *biting comments* VICIOUS, harsh, cruel, savage, cutting, sharp, bitter, scathing, caustic, acid, acrimonious, acerbic, stinging; vitriolic, hostile, spiteful, venomous, mean, nasty; *informal* bitchy, catty. ❷ *the biting wind* FREEZING, icy, arctic, glacial; bitter, piercing, penetrating, raw, wintry.
– OPPOSITES mild.

bitter ▶ **adjective** ❶ *bitter coffee* SHARP, acid, acidic, acrid, tart, sour, biting, unsweetened, vinegary; *N. Amer.* acerb; *technical* acerbic. ❷ *a bitter woman* RESENTFUL, embittered, aggrieved, grudge-bearing, begrudging, rancorous, spiteful, jaundiced, ill-disposed, sullen, sour, churlish, morose, petulant, peevish, with a chip on one's shoulder. ❸ *a bitter blow* PAINFUL, unpleasant, disagreeable, nasty, cruel, awful, distressing, upsetting, harrowing, heartbreaking, heart-rending, agonizing, traumatic, tragic, chilling; *formal* grievous. ❹ *a bitter wind* FREEZING, icy, arctic, glacial; biting, piercing, penetrating, raw, wintry. ❺ *a bitter row* ACRIMONIOUS, virulent, angry, rancorous, spiteful, vicious, vitriolic, savage, ferocious, hate-filled, venomous, poisonous, acrid, nasty, ill-natured.
– OPPOSITES sweet, magnanimous, content, welcome, warm, amicable.

bitterness ▶ **noun** ❶ *the bitterness of the medicine* SHARPNESS, acidity, acridity, tartness, sourness, harshness, vinegariness; *technical* acerbity. ❷ *his bitterness grew* RESENTMENT, rancour, indignation, grudge, spite, sullenness, sourness, churlishness, moroseness, petulance, pique, peevishness. ❸ *the bitterness of war* TRAUMA, pain, agony, grief; unpleasantness, disagreeableness, nastiness; heartache, heartbreak, distress, desolation, despair, tragedy. ❹ *there was no bitterness between them* ACRIMONY, hostility, antipathy, antagonism, enmity, animus, friction, rancour, vitriol, hatred, loathing, venom, poison, nastiness, ill feeling, ill will, bad blood.
– OPPOSITES sweetness, magnanimity, contentment, warmth, goodwill.

bitty ▶ **adjective** (*informal*) DISJOINTED, incoherent, fragmented, fragmentary, scrappy, piecemeal; inconsistent, unsystematic, jumbled; uneven, erratic, patchy.
– OPPOSITES coherent.

bizarre ▶ **adjective** STRANGE, peculiar, odd, funny, curious, outlandish, outré, eccentric, unconventional, unorthodox, queer, extraordinary; *informal* weird, wacky, oddball, way out, freaky, off the wall, offbeat; *Brit. informal* rum; *N. Amer. informal* wacko.
– OPPOSITES normal.

blab ▶ **verb** (*informal*) ❶ *she blabbed to the press* TALK, give the game away; *informal* let the cat out of the bag, spill the beans; *Brit. informal* blow the gaff, cough. ❷ *I do not blab secrets* BLURT OUT, let slip, let out, tell, reveal, betray, disclose, give away, divulge, leak; *informal* let on, spill.

blabber ▶ **verb** (*informal*). *See* CHAT verb.

blabbermouth ▶ **noun** (*informal*) TALKER, chatterer, prattler; *N. Amer.* blatherskite; *informal* chatterbox, windbag, gasbag; *Brit. informal* natterer.

black ▶ **adjective** ❶ *a black horse* DARK, pitch-black, jet-black, coal-black, inky; *Heraldry* sable; *rare* nigrescent. ❷ *a black night* UNLIT, dark, starless, moonless; *poetic/literary* tenebrous, Stygian. ❸ *the blackest day of the war* TRAGIC, disastrous, calamitous, catastrophic, cataclysmic, fateful, wretched, woeful, awful, terrible; *formal* grievous. ❹ *Mary was in a black mood* MISERABLE, unhappy, sad, wretched, broken-hearted, heartbroken, grief-stricken, grieving, sorrowful, sorrowing, anguished, desolate, despairing, disconsolate, downcast, dejected, cheerless, melancholy, morose, gloomy, glum, mournful, doleful, funereal, dismal, forlorn, woeful, abject; *informal* blue; *poetic/literary* dolorous. ❺ *black humour* CYNICAL, macabre, weird, unhealthy, ghoulish, morbid, perverted, gruesome; *informal* sick. ❻ *a black look. See* ANGRY sense 1. ❼ (*archaic*) *a black deed. See* WICKED sense 1.
– RELATED TERMS melan-.
– OPPOSITES white, clear, bright, joyful.

▶ **verb** ❶ *the steps of the houses were neatly blacked* BLACKEN, darken; dirty, make sooty, make smoky, stain, grime, soil. ❷ *she blacked his eye* BRUISE, contuse; hit, punch, injure. ❸ (*Brit. dated*) *trade union members blacked the work* BOYCOTT, embargo, blacklist, proscribe.

■ **black out** FAINT, lose consciousness, pass out, swoon; *informal* flake out, go out.

■ **black something out** DARKEN, shade, turn off the lights in; keep the light out of.

■ **in the black** IN CREDIT, in funds, debt-free, out of debt, solvent, financially sound, able to pay one's debts, creditworthy; *rare* unindebted.

■ **black and white** ❶ *a black-and-white picture* MONOCHROME, greyscale. ❷ *I wish to see the proposals in black and white* IN PRINT, printed, written down, set down, on paper, recorded, on record, documented. ❸ *in black-and-white terms* CATEGORICAL, unequivocal, absolute, uncompromising, unconditional, unqualified, unambiguous, clear, clear-cut.

blackball ▶ **verb** REJECT, debar, bar, ban, vote

against, blacklist, exclude, shut out.
– OPPOSITES admit.

blacken ▸ verb ❶ *they blackened their faces* BLACK, darken; dirty, make sooty, make smoky, stain, grime, soil. ❷ *the sky blackened* GROW/BECOME BLACK, darken, dim, grow dim, cloud over. ❸ *someone has blackened my name* SULLY, tarnish, besmirch, drag through the mud/mire, stain, taint, smear, disgrace, dishonour, bring discredit to, damage, ruin; slander, defame.
– OPPOSITES whiten, clean, lighten, brighten, clear.

blackguard ▸ noun (*archaic*). *See* VILLAIN.

blacklist ▸ verb BOYCOTT, ostracize, avoid, embargo, steer clear of, ignore; refuse to employ; *Brit. dated* black.

black magic ▸ noun SORCERY, witchcraft, wizardry, necromancy, the black arts, devilry; malediction, voodoo, witching, witchery.

blackmail ▸ noun *he was accused of blackmail* EXTORTION, demanding money with menaces; *informal* hush money; *formal* exaction.
▸ verb ❶ *he was blackmailing the murderer* EXTORT MONEY FROM, threaten, hold to ransom; *informal* demand hush money from. ❷ *she blackmailed me to work for her* COERCE, pressurize, pressure, force; *informal* lean on, put the screws on, twist someone's arm.

blackout ▸ noun ❶ *a power blackout* POWER CUT, power failure, failure of the electricity supply; brown-out. ❷ *a news blackout* SUPPRESSION, silence, censorship, reporting restrictions. ❸ *he had a blackout* FAINTING FIT, faint, loss of consciousness, passing out, swoon, collapse; *Medicine* syncope.

blame ▸ verb ❶ *he always blames others* HOLD RESPONSIBLE, hold accountable, condemn, accuse, find/consider guilty, assign fault/liability/guilt to; *archaic* inculpate. ❷ *they blame youth crime on unemployment* ASCRIBE TO, attribute to, impute to, lay at the door of, put down to; *informal* pin.
– OPPOSITES absolve.
▸ noun *he was cleared of all blame* RESPONSIBILITY, guilt, accountability, liability, culpability, fault.

blameless ▸ adjective INNOCENT, guiltless, above reproach, irreproachable, unimpeachable, in the clear, exemplary, perfect, virtuous, pure, impeccable; *informal* squeaky clean.
– OPPOSITES blameworthy.

blameworthy ▸ adjective CULPABLE, reprehensible, indefensible, inexcusable, guilty, criminal, delinquent, wrong, evil, wicked; to blame, at fault, reproachable, responsible, answerable, erring, errant, in the wrong.
– OPPOSITES blameless.

blanch ▸ verb ❶ *the moon blanches her hair* TURN PALE, whiten, lighten, wash out, fade, blench, etiolate. ❷ *his face blanched* PALE, turn pale, turn white, whiten, lose its colour, lighten, fade, blench. ❸ *blanch the spinach leaves* SCALD, boil briefly.
– OPPOSITES colour, darken.

bland ▸ adjective ❶ *bland food* TASTELESS, flavourless, insipid, weak, watery, spiceless, wishy-washy. ❷ *a bland film* UNINTERESTING, dull, boring, tedious, monotonous, dry, drab, dreary, wearisome; unexciting, unimaginative, uninspiring, uninspired, lacklustre, vapid, flat, stale, trite, vacuous, wishy-washy. ❸ *a bland expression* UNEMOTIONAL, emotionless, dispassionate, passionless; unexpressive, cool, impassive; expressionless, blank, wooden, stony, deadpan, hollow, undemonstrative, imperturbable.
– OPPOSITES tangy, interesting, emotional.

blandishments ▸ plural noun FLATTERY, cajolery, coaxing, wheedling, persuasion, honeyed words, smooth talk, blarney; *informal* sweet talk, soft soap, buttering up.

blank ▸ adjective ❶ *a blank sheet of paper* EMPTY, unmarked, unused, clear, free, bare, clean, plain. ❷ *a blank face* EXPRESSIONLESS, deadpan, wooden, stony, impassive, unresponsive, poker-faced, vacuous, empty, glazed, fixed, lifeless, inscrutable. ❸ *'What?' said Maxim, looking blank* BAFFLED, mystified, puzzled, perplexed, stumped, at a loss, stuck, bewildered, nonplussed, bemused, lost, uncomprehending, (all) at sea, confused; *informal* flummoxed, bamboozled. ❹ *a blank refusal* OUTRIGHT, absolute, categorical, unqualified, complete, flat, straight, positive, certain, explicit, unequivocal, clear, clear-cut.
– OPPOSITES full, expressive, qualified.
▸ noun SPACE, gap, lacuna.

blanket ▸ noun *a blanket of cloud* COVERING, layer, coating, carpet, overlay, cloak, mantle, veil, pall, shroud.
▸ adjective *blanket coverage* complete, total, comprehensive, overall, general, mass, umbrella, inclusive, all-inclusive, all-round, wholesale, outright, across the board, sweeping, indiscriminate, thorough; universal, global, worldwide, international, nationwide, countrywide, coast-to-coast.
– OPPOSITES partial, piecemeal.
▸ verb ❶ *snow blanketed the mountains* COVER, coat, carpet, overlay; cloak, shroud, swathe, envelop; *poetic/literary* mantle. ❷ *double glazing blankets the noise a bit* MUFFLE, deaden, soften, mute, silence, quieten, smother, dampen.
– OPPOSITES amplify.

blare ▸ verb *sirens blared* BLAST, sound loudly, trumpet, clamour, boom, roar, thunder, bellow, resound.
– OPPOSITES murmur.
▸ noun *the blare of the siren* BLAST, trumpeting, clamour, boom, roar, thunder, bellow.
– OPPOSITES murmur.

blarney ▶ noun BLANDISHMENTS, honeyed words, smooth talk, flattery, cajolery, coaxing, wheedling, persuasion; charm offensive; *informal* sweet talk, soft soap, smarm, buttering up.

blasé ▶ adjective INDIFFERENT, unconcerned, uncaring, casual, nonchalant, offhand, uninterested, apathetic, unimpressed, unmoved, unresponsive, phlegmatic; *informal* laid-back; *rare* pococurante.
– OPPOSITES concerned, responsive.

blaspheme ▶ verb SWEAR, curse, take the Lord's name in vain; *informal* cuss; *archaic* execrate.

blasphemous ▶ adjective SACRILEGIOUS, profane, irreligious, irreverent, impious, ungodly, godless.
– OPPOSITES reverent.

blasphemy ▶ noun PROFANITY, sacrilege, irreligion, irreverence, taking the Lord's name in vain, swearing, curse, cursing, impiety, desecration; *archaic* execration.
– OPPOSITES reverence.

blast ▶ noun ❶ *the blast from the bomb* SHOCK WAVE, pressure wave. ❷ *Friday's blast killed two people* EXPLOSION, detonation, discharge, burst. ❸ *a sudden blast of cold air* GUST, rush, gale, squall, wind, draught, waft, puff, flurry. ❹ *the shrill blast of the trumpets* BLARE, wail, roar, screech, shriek, hoot, honk, beep. ❺ (*informal*) *I braced myself for the inevitable blast. See* REPRIMAND noun.
▶ verb ❶ *bombers were blasting enemy airfields* BLOW UP, bomb, blow (to pieces), dynamite, explode. ❷ *guns were blasting away* FIRE, shoot, blaze, let fly, discharge. ❸ *he blasted his horn* HONK, beep, toot, sound. ❹ *radios blasting out pop music* BLARE, boom, roar, thunder, bellow, pump, shriek, screech. ❺ *Fowler was blasted with an air gun* SHOOT, gun down, mow down, cut down, put a bullet in; *informal* pot, plug. ❻ (*informal*) *he blasted the pupils for being late. See* REPRIMAND verb.
■ **blast off** BE LAUNCHED, take off, lift off, leave the ground, become airborne, take to the air.

blasted ▶ adjective (*informal*). *See* DAMNED sense 2.

blast-off ▶ noun LAUNCH, lift-off, take-off, ascent, firing.
– OPPOSITES touchdown.

blatant ▶ adjective FLAGRANT, glaring, obvious, undisguised, unconcealed, open; shameless, barefaced, unabashed, unashamed, unblushing, brazen, brass-necked.
– OPPOSITES inconspicuous, shamefaced.

blather ▶ verb *he just blathered on* PRATTLE, babble, chatter, twitter, prate, go on, run on, rattle on, yap, jibber-jabber, maunder, ramble, burble, drivel; *informal* yak, yatter; *Brit. informal* witter, rabbit, chunter, waffle.
▶ noun *mindless blather* PRATTLE, chatter, twitter, babble, prating, gabble, jabber, rambling; *informal* yatter, twaddle; *Brit. informal* wittering, chuntering.

blaze ▶ noun ❶ *firemen fought the blaze* FIRE, flames, conflagration, inferno, holocaust. ❷ *a blaze of light* GLARE, gleam, flash, burst, flare, streak, radiance, brilliance, beam. ❸ *a blaze of anger* OUTBURST, burst, eruption, flare-up, explosion, outbreak; blast, attack, fit, spasm, paroxysm, access, rush, storm.
▶ verb ❶ *the fire blazed merrily* BURN, be alight, be on fire, be in flames, flame. ❷ *headlights blazed* SHINE, flash, flare, glare, gleam, glint, dazzle, glitter, glisten. ❸ *soldiers blazed away* FIRE, shoot, blast, let fly.

blazon ▶ verb ❶ *their name is blazoned across the sails* DISPLAY, exhibit, present, spread, emblazon, plaster. ❷ *the newspapers blazoned the news abroad* PUBLICIZE, make known, make public, announce, report, communicate, spread, circulate, give out, publish, broadcast, trumpet, proclaim, promulgate.

bleach ▶ verb ❶ *the blinds had been bleached by the sun* TURN WHITE, whiten, turn pale, blanch, lighten, fade, decolour, decolorize, peroxide. ❷ *they saw bones bleaching in the sun* TURN WHITE, whiten, turn pale, pale, blanch, lose its colour, lighten, fade.
– OPPOSITES darken.

bleak ▶ adjective ❶ *a bleak landscape* BARE, exposed, desolate, stark, desert, lunar, open, empty, windswept; treeless, without vegetation, denuded. ❷ *the future is bleak* UNPROMISING, unfavourable, unpropitious, inauspicious; discouraging, disheartening, depressing, dim, gloomy, black, dark, grim, hopeless.
– OPPOSITES lush, promising.

bleary ▶ adjective BLURRED, blurry, unfocused; fogged, clouded, dull, misty, watery, rheumy; *archaic* blear.
– OPPOSITES clear.

bleat ▶ verb ❶ *the sheep were bleating* BAA; *N. Amer. informal* blat. ❷ *don't bleat to me about fairness* COMPLAIN, grouse, carp, fuss, snivel; *Scottish & Irish* girn; *informal* gripe, beef, whinge, bellyache, moan, go on; *N. English informal* mither; *N. Amer. informal* kvetch.

bleed ▶ verb ❶ *his arm was bleeding* LOSE BLOOD, haemorrhage. ❷ *the doctor bled him* DRAW BLOOD FROM; *Medicine* exsanguinate; *archaic* phlebotomize. ❸ *one colour bled into another* FLOW, run, seep, filter, percolate, leach. ❹ *sap was bleeding from the trunk* FLOW, run, ooze, seep, exude, weep. ❺ *the country was bled dry by poachers* DRAIN, sap, deplete, milk, exhaust. ❻ *my heart bleeds for them* GRIEVE, ache, sorrow, mourn, lament, feel, suffer; sympathize with, pity.

blemish ▶ noun ❶ *not a blemish marred her skin* IMPERFECTION, flaw, defect, fault, deformity, discoloration, disfigurement; bruise, scar, pit, pock, scratch, cut, gash; mark, streak, spot,

smear, speck, blotch, smudge, smut; birthmark; *Medicine* stigma. ❷ *government is not without blemish* DEFECT, fault, failing, flaw, imperfection, foible, vice; shortcoming, weakness, deficiency, limitation; taint, stain, dishonour, disgrace.
– OPPOSITES virtue.
▶ **verb** ❶ *nothing blemished the coast* MAR, spoil, impair, disfigure, blight, deface, mark, scar; ruin. ❷ *his reign has been blemished by controversy* SULLY, tarnish, besmirch, blacken, blot, taint; spoil, mar, ruin, disgrace, damage, undermine, degrade, dishonour; *formal* vitiate.
– OPPOSITES enhance.

blench ▶ **verb** FLINCH, start, shy (away), recoil, shrink, pull back, cringe, wince, quail, cower.

blend ▶ **verb** ❶ *blend the ingredients until smooth* MIX, mingle, combine, merge, fuse, meld, coalesce, integrate, intermix; stir, whisk, fold in; *technical* admix; *poetic/literary* commingle. ❷ *the new buildings blend with the older ones* HARMONIZE, go (well), fit (in), be in tune, be compatible, coordinate; match, complement.
▶ **noun** *a blend of bananas, raisins, and ginger* MIXTURE, mix, combination, amalgamation, amalgam, union, marriage, fusion, meld, synthesis; *technical* admixture.

bless ▶ **verb** ❶ *the chaplain blessed the couple* ASK/INVOKE GOD'S FAVOUR FOR, give a benediction for. ❷ *the Cardinal blessed the memorial plaque* CONSECRATE, sanctify, dedicate (to God), make holy, make sacred; *formal* hallow. ❸ *bless the name of the Lord* PRAISE, worship, glorify, honour, exalt, pay homage to, venerate, reverence, hallow; *archaic* magnify. ❹ *the gods blessed us with magical voices* ENDOW, bestow, furnish, accord, give, favour, grace; confer on; *poetic/literary* endue. ❺ *I bless the day you came here* GIVE THANKS FOR, be grateful for, thank; appreciate. ❻ *the government refused to bless the undertaking* SANCTION, consent to, endorse, agree to, approve, back, support; *informal* give the thumbs up to, give the green light to, OK.
– OPPOSITES curse, trouble, rue, oppose.

blessed ▶ **adjective** ❶ *a blessed place* HOLY, sacred, hallowed, consecrated, sanctified; ordained, canonized, beatified. ❷ *blessed are the meek* FAVOURED, fortunate, lucky, privileged, enviable. ❸ *the fresh air made a blessed change* WELCOME, pleasant, agreeable, refreshing, favourable, gratifying, heartening, much needed.
– OPPOSITES cursed, wretched, unwelcome.

blessing ▶ **noun** ❶ *may God give us his blessing* PROTECTION, favour. ❷ *a special blessing from the priest* BENEDICTION, invocation, prayer, intercession; grace. ❸ *she gave the plan her blessing* SANCTION, endorsement, approval, approbation, favour, consent, assent, agreement; backing, support; *informal* the thumbs up. ❹ *it was a blessing they didn't have far to go* BOON, godsend, advantage, benefit, help, bonus, plus; stroke of luck, windfall; *poetic/literary* benison.
– OPPOSITES condemnation, affliction.

blight ▶ **noun** ❶ *potato blight* DISEASE, canker, infestation, fungus, mildew, mould. ❷ *the blight of aircraft noise* AFFLICTION, scourge, bane, curse, plague, menace, misfortune, woe, trouble, ordeal, trial, nuisance, pest.
– OPPOSITES blessing.
▶ **verb** ❶ *a tree blighted by leaf curl* INFECT, mildew; kill, destroy. ❷ *scandal blighted the careers of several politicians* RUIN, wreck, spoil, mar, frustrate, disrupt, undo, end, scotch, destroy, shatter, devastate, demolish; *informal* mess up, foul up, put paid to, put the kibosh on, stymie; *Brit. informal* scupper; *archaic* bring to naught.

blind ▶ **adjective** ❶ *he has been blind since birth* SIGHTLESS, unsighted, visually impaired, visionless, unseeing; partially sighted, purblind; *informal* as blind as a bat. ❷ *she was ignorant, but not blind* IMPERCEPTIVE, unperceptive, insensitive, slow, obtuse, uncomprehending; stupid, unintelligent; *informal* dense, dim, thick, dumb, dopey; *Brit. informal* dozy; *Scottish & N. English informal* glaikit. ❸ *you should be blind to failure* UNMINDFUL OF, mindless of, careless of, heedless of, oblivious to, insensible to, unconcerned about, indifferent to. ❹ *blind acceptance of conventional opinion* UNCRITICAL, unreasoned, unthinking, unconsidered, mindless, undiscerning, indiscriminate. ❺ *a blind rage* IMPETUOUS, impulsive, uncontrolled, uncontrollable, unrestrained, immoderate, intemperate, wild, irrational, unbridled. ❻ *a blind alley* WITHOUT EXIT, blocked, closed, barred, impassable; dead end.
– OPPOSITES sighted, perceptive, mindful, discerning.
▶ **verb** ❶ *he was blinded in a car crash* MAKE BLIND, deprive of sight, render sightless; put someone's eyes out. ❷ *scaffolding blinded the windows* OBSCURE, cover, blot out, mask, shroud, block, eclipse, obstruct. ❸ *he was blinded by his faith* DEPRIVE OF JUDGEMENT, deprive of perception, deprive of reason, deprive of sense. ❹ *they try to blind you with science* OVERAWE, intimidate, daunt, deter, discourage, cow, abash, subdue, dismay; disquiet, discomfit, unsettle, disconcert; confuse, bewilder, confound, perplex, overwhelm; *informal* faze, psych out.
▶ **noun** ❶ *a window blind* SCREEN, shade, sunshade, curtain, awning, canopy; louvre, jalousie, shutter. ❷ *some crook had sent the card as a blind* DECEPTION, camouflage, smokescreen, front, facade, cover, pretext, masquerade, feint; trick, ploy, ruse, machination.

blindly ▶ **adverb** ❶ *he stared blindly ahead* SIGHTLESSLY, unseeingly. ❷ *he ran blindly upstairs* IMPETUOUSLY, impulsively, recklessly, heedlessly, uncontrolledly. ❸ *they blindly followed US policy* UNCRITICALLY, unthinkingly, mindlessly, indiscriminately.

blink ▶ **verb** ❶ *his eyes did not blink* flutter, flicker, wink, bat; *technical* nictitate, nictate.

❷ *several red lights began to blink* FLASH, flicker, wink. ❸ *no one even blinks at the 'waitresses' in drag* BE SURPRISED, look twice; *informal* boggle.

blinkered ▶ **adjective** NARROW-MINDED, inward-looking, parochial, provincial, insular, small-minded, close-minded, short-sighted; hidebound, inflexible, entrenched, prejudiced, bigoted; *Brit.* parish-pump.
– OPPOSITES broad-minded.

bliss ▶ **noun** ❶ *she gave a sigh of bliss* JOY, happiness, pleasure, delight, ecstasy, elation, rapture, euphoria. ❷ *religions promise perfect bliss after death* BLESSEDNESS, benediction, beatitude, glory, heavenly joy, divine happiness; heaven, paradise.
– OPPOSITES misery, hell.

blissful ▶ **adjective** ECSTATIC, euphoric, joyful, elated, rapturous, on cloud nine, in seventh heaven; delighted, thrilled, overjoyed, joyous; *informal* over the moon, on top of the world; *Austral. informal* wrapped.

blister ▶ **noun** ❶ *a blister on each heel* bleb; *Medicine* bulla, pustule, vesicle, vesication. ❷ *check for blisters in the roofing felt* BUBBLE, swelling, bulge, protuberance.

blistering ▶ **adjective** ❶ *blistering heat* INTENSE, extreme, ferocious, fierce; SCORCHING, searing, blazing, burning, fiery; *informal* boiling, baking, roasting, sweltering. ❷ *a blistering attack on the government* SAVAGE, vicious, fierce, bitter, harsh, scathing, devastating, caustic, searing, vitriolic. ❸ *a blistering pace* VERY FAST, breakneck; *informal* blinding.
– OPPOSITES mild, leisurely.

blithe ▶ **adjective** ❶ *a blithe disregard for the rules* CASUAL, indifferent, unconcerned, unworried, untroubled, uncaring, careless, heedless, thoughtless; nonchalant, blasé. ❷ (*poetic/literary*) HAPPY, cheerful, jolly, merry, joyful, joyous, blissful, ecstatic, euphoric, elated; *poetic/literary* blithesome; *dated* gay.
– OPPOSITES thoughtful, sad.

blitz ▶ **noun** *the 1940 blitz on London* BOMBARDMENT, bombing, onslaught, barrage; attack, assault, raid, strike, blitzkrieg.
▶ **verb** *the town was blitzed in the war* BOMBARD, attack, bomb, shell, torpedo, strafe; destroy, devastate, ravage.

blizzard ▶ **noun** SNOWSTORM, white-out.

bloated ▶ **adjective** SWOLLEN, distended, tumefied, bulging, inflated, enlarged, expanded, dilated.

blob ▶ **noun** ❶ *a blob of cold gravy* DROP, droplet, globule, bead, bubble; *informal* glob. ❷ *a blob of ink* SPOT, dab, blotch, blot, dot, smudge; *informal* splotch, splodge.
▶ **verb** *masking fluid is blobbed on freely* DAUB, dab, spot, slop.

bloc ▶ **noun** ALLIANCE, coalition, federation, confederation, league, union, partnership, axis, body, association, group.

block ▶ **noun** ❶ *a block of cheese* CHUNK, hunk, lump, wedge, cube, brick, slab, piece; *Brit. informal* wodge. ❷ *an apartment block* BUILDING, complex, structure, development. ❸ *a block of shares* BATCH, group, set, quantity. ❹ *a sketching block* PAD, notepad, sketchpad, jotter, tablet. ❺ *a block to Third World development* OBSTACLE, bar, barrier, impediment, hindrance, check, hurdle, stumbling block, handicap, deterrent. ❻ *a block in the pipe* BLOCKAGE, obstruction, stoppage, congestion, occlusion, clot.
– OPPOSITES aid.
▶ **verb** ❶ *weeds can block drainage ditches* CLOG (UP), stop up, choke, plug, obstruct, gum up, dam up, congest, jam, close; *informal* bung up; *Brit. informal* gunge up; *technical* occlude. ❷ *picket lines blocked access to the factory* HINDER, hamper, obstruct, impede, inhibit, restrict, limit; halt, stop, bar, check, prevent. ❸ *he blocked a shot on the goal line* PARRY, stop, deflect, fend off, hold off, repel, repulse.
– OPPOSITES facilitate.
■ **block something off** CLOSE UP, shut off, seal off, barricade, bar, obstruct.
■ **block something out** ❶ *trees blocked out the light* CONCEAL, keep out, blot out, exclude, obliterate, blank out, stop. ❷ *block out an area in charcoal* ROUGH OUT, sketch out, outline, delineate, draft.

blockade ▶ **noun** ❶ *a naval blockade of the island* SIEGE; *rare* besiegement. ❷ *they erected blockades in the streets* BARRICADE, barrier, roadblock; obstacle, obstruction.
▶ **verb** *rebels blockaded the capital* BARRICADE, block off, shut off, seal; BESIEGE, surround.

blockage ▶ **noun** OBSTRUCTION, stoppage, block, occlusion, congestion.

bloke ▶ **noun** (*Brit. informal*). *See* FELLOW sense 1.

blonde, masc. **blond** ▶ **adjective** FAIR, light, yellow, flaxen, tow-coloured, golden, platinum, ash blonde, strawberry blonde; bleached, peroxide.
– OPPOSITES dark.

blood ▶ **noun** ❶ *he had lost too much blood* gore, vital fluid; *poetic/literary* lifeblood, ichor. ❷ *a woman of noble blood* ANCESTRY, lineage, bloodline, descent, parentage, family, birth, extraction, origin, genealogy, heritage, stock, kinship.
– RELATED TERMS haemal, haemic, haematic, sanguineous.

blood-curdling ▶ **adjective** TERRIFYING, frightening, spine-chilling, chilling, hair-raising, horrifying, alarming; eerie, sinister, horrible; *Scottish* eldritch; *informal* scary.

bloodless ▶ **adjective** ❶ *a bloodless revolution* NON-VIOLENT, peaceful, peaceable, pacifist. ❷ *his face was bloodless* ANAEMIC, pale, wan, pallid, ashen, colourless, chalky, waxen, white, grey, pasty, drained, drawn, deathly. ❸ *a bloodless Hollywood mogul* HEARTLESS, unfeeling,

cruel, ruthless, merciless, pitiless, uncharitable; cold, hard, stony-hearted, cold-blooded, callous. ❹ *a bloodless chorus* FEEBLE, spiritless, lifeless, listless, half-hearted, unenthusiastic, lukewarm.
– OPPOSITES bloody, ruddy, charitable, powerful.

bloodshed ▶ noun SLAUGHTER, massacre, killing, wounding; carnage, butchery, bloodletting, bloodbath; violence, fighting, warfare, battle; *poetic/literary* slaying.

bloodthirsty ▶ adjective MURDEROUS, homicidal, violent, vicious, barbarous, barbaric, savage, brutal, cut-throat; fierce, ferocious, inhuman.

bloody ▶ adjective ❶ *his bloody nose* BLEEDING. ❷ *bloody medical waste* BLOODSTAINED, blood-soaked, gory; *archaic* sanguinary. ❸ *a bloody civil war* VICIOUS, ferocious, savage, fierce, brutal, murderous, gory; *archaic* sanguinary. ❹ (*Brit. informal*) *what a bloody nuisance!* See DAMNED sense 2.

bloody-minded ▶ adjective (*Brit. informal*) UNCOOPERATIVE, awkward, disobliging, recalcitrant, unaccommodating, inflexible, uncompromising, contrary, perverse, obstinate, stubborn; difficult; *informal* pig-headed; *Brit. informal* bolshie, stroppy.
– OPPOSITES compliant.

bloom ▶ noun ❶ *orchid blooms* FLOWER, blossom, floweret, floret. ❷ *a girl in the bloom of youth* PRIME, perfection, acme, peak, height, heyday; salad days. ❸ *the bloom of her skin* RADIANCE, lustre, sheen, glow, freshness; BLUSH, rosiness, pinkness, colour.
▶ verb ❶ *the geraniums bloomed* FLOWER, blossom, open; mature. ❷ *the children bloomed in the Devonshire air* FLOURISH, thrive, prosper, progress, burgeon; *informal* be in the pink.
– OPPOSITES wither, decline.

blossom ▶ noun *pink blossoms* FLOWER, bloom, floweret, floret.
▶ verb ❶ *the snowdrops have blossomed* BLOOM, flower, open, unfold; mature. ❷ *the whole region had blossomed* DEVELOP, grow, mature, progress, evolve; flourish, thrive, prosper, bloom, burgeon.
– OPPOSITES fade, decline.
■ **in blossom** IN FLOWER, flowering, blossoming, blooming, in (full) bloom, open, out.

blot ▶ noun ❶ *an ink blot* SPOT, dot, mark, blotch, smudge, patch, dab; *informal* splotch; *Brit. informal* splodge. ❷ *the only blot on a clean campaign* BLEMISH, taint, stain, blight, flaw, fault; disgrace, dishonour. ❸ *a blot on the landscape* EYESORE, monstrosity, carbuncle, mess; *informal* sight.
▶ verb ❶ *blot the excess water* SOAK UP, absorb, sponge up, mop up; dry up/out; dab, pat. ❷ *the writing was messy and blotted* SMUDGE, smear, blotch, mark. ❸ *he had blotted our name forever* TARNISH, taint, stain, blacken, sully, mar; dishonour, disgrace, besmirch.
– OPPOSITES honour.
■ **blot something out** ❶ *Mary blotted out her picture* ERASE, obliterate, delete, efface, rub out, blank out, expunge; cross out, strike out. ❷ *clouds were starting to blot out the stars* CONCEAL, hide, obscure, exclude, obliterate; shadow, eclipse. ❸ *he urged her to blot out the memory* ERASE, efface, eradicate, expunge, wipe out.

blotch ▶ noun ❶ *pink flowers with dark blotches* PATCH, smudge, dot, spot, blot, dab, daub; *informal* splotch; *Brit. informal* splodge. ❷ *his face was covered in blotches* PATCH, mark, freckle, birthmark, discoloration, eruption, naevus.
▶ verb *her face was blotched and swollen* SPOT, mark, smudge, streak, blemish.

blotchy ▶ adjective MOTTLED, dappled, blotched, patchy, spotty, spotted, smudged, marked; *informal* splotchy; *Brit. informal* splodgy.

blow[1] ▶ verb ❶ *the icy wind blew around us* GUST, puff, flurry, blast, roar, bluster, rush, storm. ❷ *his ship was blown on to the rocks* SWEEP, carry, toss, drive, push, force. ❸ *leaves blew across the road* DRIFT, flutter, waft, float, glide, whirl, move. ❹ *he blew a smoke ring* EXHALE, puff; emit, expel, discharge, issue. ❺ *Uncle Albert was puffing and blowing* WHEEZE, puff, pant, gasp. ❻ *he blew a trumpet* SOUND, blast, toot, pipe, trumpet; play. ❼ *a rear tyre had blown* BURST, explode, blow out, split, rupture, puncture. ❽ *the bulb had blown* FUSE, short-circuit, burn out, break, go. ❾ (*informal*) *he blew his money on gambling* SQUANDER, waste, misspend, throw away, fritter away, go through, lose, lavish, dissipate, use up; spend recklessly; *informal* splurge; *Brit. informal, dated* blue. ❿ (*informal*) *don't blow this opportunity* SPOIL, ruin, bungle, mess up, fudge, muff; WASTE, lose, squander; *informal* botch, screw up, foul up; *Brit. informal* cock up, bodge. ⓫ *his cover was blown* EXPOSE, reveal, uncover, disclose, divulge, unveil, betray, leak.
▶ noun ❶ *a severe blow* GALE, storm, tempest, hurricane; wind, breeze, gust, draught, flurry. ❷ *a blow on the guard's whistle* TOOT, blast, blare; whistle.
■ **blow out** ❶ *the matches will not blow out in a strong wind* BE EXTINGUISHED, go out, be put out, stop burning. ❷ *the front tyre blew out.* See BLOW[1] verb sense 7. ❸ *the windows blew out* SHATTER, rupture, crack, smash, splinter, disintegrate; burst, explode, fly apart; *informal* bust.
■ **blow something out** EXTINGUISH, put out, snuff, douse, quench, smother.
■ **blow over** ABATE, subside, drop off, lessen, ease (off), let up, diminish, fade, dwindle, slacken, recede, tail off, peter out, pass, die down, fizzle out.
■ **blow up** ❶ *a lorryload of shells blew up* EXPLODE, detonate, go off, ignite, erupt. ❷ *he blows up at whoever's in his way* LOSE ONE'S TEM-

PER, get angry, rant and rave, go berserk, flare up, erupt; *informal* go mad, go crazy, go wild, go ape, hit the roof, fly off the handle. ❸ *a crisis blew up* BREAK OUT, erupt, flare up, boil over; emerge, arise.

■ **blow something up** ❶ *they blew the plane up* BOMB, blast, destroy; explode, detonate. ❷ *blow up the balloons* INFLATE, pump up, fill up, puff up, swell, expand, aerate. ❸ *things get blown up out of all proportion* EXAGGERATE, overstate, overstress, overestimate, magnify, amplify; aggrandize, embellish, elaborate. ❹ *I blew the picture up on a photocopier* ENLARGE, magnify, expand, increase.

blow² ▶ noun ❶ *a blow on the head* KNOCK, BANG, hit, punch, thump, smack, crack, rap; *informal* whack, thwack, bash, clout, sock, wallop. ❷ *losing his wife must have been a blow* SHOCK, surprise, bombshell, thunderbolt, jolt; calamity, catastrophe, disaster, upset, setback.

blowout ▶ noun ❶ *the steering is automatic in the event of blowouts* PUNCTURE, flat tyre, burst tyre; *informal* flat. ❷ (*informal*) *this meal is our last real blowout* FEAST, banquet, celebration, party; *informal* shindig, do, binge; *Brit. informal* beanfeast, bunfight, nosh-up.

blowsy ▶ adjective UNTIDY, sloppy, scruffy, messy, dishevelled, unkempt, frowzy, slovenly; coarse; RED-FACED, ruddy, florid, raddled.
–OPPOSITES tidy, respectable.

blowy ▶ adjective WINDY, windswept, blustery, gusty, breezy; stormy, squally.
–OPPOSITES still.

blubber¹ ▶ noun *whale blubber* FAT, fatty tissue.

blubber² ▶ verb (*informal*) *she started to blubber* CRY, sob, weep, howl, snivel; *informal* blub, boohoo.

bludgeon ▶ noun *hooligans wielding bludgeons* CUDGEL, club, stick, truncheon, baton; *N. Amer.* nightstick, blackjack; *Brit. informal* cosh.
▶ verb ❶ *he was bludgeoned to death* BATTER, cudgel, club, beat, thrash; *informal* clobber. ❷ *I let him bludgeon me into marriage* COERCE, force, compel, pressurize, pressure, bully, browbeat, hector, dragoon, steamroller; *informal* strong-arm, railroad.

blue ▶ adjective ❶ *bright blue eyes* sky-blue, azure, cobalt, sapphire, navy, Oxford blue, Cambridge blue, ultramarine, aquamarine, cyan; *poetic/literary* cerulean. ❷ (*informal*) *Mum was feeling a bit blue* DEPRESSED, down, sad, unhappy, melancholy, miserable, gloomy, dejected, downhearted, downcast, despondent, low, glum; *informal* down in the dumps, down in the mouth, fed up. ❸ (*informal*) *a blue movie* PORNOGRAPHIC, racy, risqué, naughty, spicy; indecent, dirty, lewd, smutty, filthy, obscene, sordid; erotic, arousing, sexy, titillating, explicit; *informal* porn, porno, X-rated, raunchy; *euphemistic* adult.
–OPPOSITES happy, clean.

blueprint ▶ noun ❶ *blueprints of the aircraft* PLAN, design, diagram, drawing, sketch, map, layout, representation. ❷ *a blueprint for similar measures in other countries* MODEL, plan, template, framework, pattern, example, guide, prototype, pilot.

blues ▶ plural noun (*informal*) *a fit of blues* DEPRESSION, sadness, unhappiness, melancholy, misery, sorrow, gloom, dejection, despondency, despair; the doldrums.

bluff¹ ▶ noun *this offer was denounced as a bluff* DECEPTION, subterfuge, pretence, sham, fake, deceit, feint, hoax, fraud, charade; trick, ruse, scheme, machination; *informal* put-on.
▶ verb ❶ *they are bluffing to hide their guilt* PRETEND, sham, fake, feign, lie, hoax, pose, posture, masquerade, dissemble. ❷ *I managed to bluff the board into believing me* DECEIVE, delude, mislead, trick, fool, hoodwink, dupe, hoax, beguile, gull; *informal* con, kid, have on.

bluff² ▶ adjective *a bluff man* PLAIN-SPOKEN, straightforward, blunt, direct, no-nonsense, frank, open, candid, forthright, unequivocal; hearty, genial, good-natured; *informal* upfront.

bluff³ ▶ noun *an impregnable high bluff* CLIFF, promontory, headland, crag, bank, peak, escarpment, scarp.

blunder ▶ noun *he shook his head at his blunder* MISTAKE, error, gaffe, slip, oversight, faux pas; *informal* botch, slip-up, boo-boo; *Brit. informal* clanger, boob; *N. Amer. informal* blooper.
▶ verb ❶ *the government admitted it had blundered* MAKE A MISTAKE, err, miscalculate, bungle, trip up, be wrong; *informal* slip up, screw up, blow it, goof; *Brit. informal* boob. ❷ *she blundered down the steps* STUMBLE, lurch, stagger, flounder, struggle, fumble, grope.

blunt ▶ adjective ❶ *a blunt knife* UNSHARPENED, dull, worn, edgeless. ❷ *the leaf is broad with a blunt tip* ROUNDED, flat, obtuse, stubby. ❸ *a blunt message* STRAIGHTFORWARD, frank, plain-spoken, candid, direct, bluff, forthright, unequivocal; BRUSQUE, abrupt, curt, terse, bald, brutal, harsh; stark, undisguised, unvarnished; *informal* upfront.
–OPPOSITES sharp, pointed, subtle.
▶ verb ❶ *ebony blunts tools very rapidly* DULL, make less sharp. ❷ *age hasn't blunted my passion for life* DULL, deaden, dampen, numb, weaken, sap, cool, temper, allay, abate; diminish, reduce, decrease, lessen, deplete.
–OPPOSITES sharpen, intensify.

blur ▶ verb ❶ *she felt tears blur her vision* CLOUD, fog, obscure, dim, make hazy, unfocus, soften; *poetic/literary* bedim; *archaic* blear. ❷ *films blur the difference between villains and victims* OBSCURE, make vague, confuse, muddle, muddy, obfuscate, cloud, weaken. ❸ *memories of the picnic had blurred* BECOME DIM, dull, numb, deaden, mute; lessen, decrease, diminish.
–OPPOSITES sharpen, focus.

▶ **noun** *a blur on the horizon* INDISTINCT SHAPE, smudge; haze, cloud, mist.

blurred ▶ **adjective** INDISTINCT, blurry, fuzzy, hazy, misty, foggy, shadowy, faint; unclear, vague, indefinite, unfocused, obscure, nebulous.

blurt
■ **blurt something out** BURST OUT WITH, exclaim, call out; DIVULGE, disclose, reveal, betray, let slip, give away; *informal* blab, gush, let on, spill the beans, let the cat out of the bag; *dated* ejaculate.

blush ▶ **verb** *Joan blushed at the compliment* REDDEN, turn/go pink, turn/go red, flush, colour, burn up; feel shy, feel embarrassed.
▶ **noun** *the darkness hid her fiery blush* FLUSH, rosiness, pinkness, bloom, high colour.

bluster ▶ **verb** ❶ *he started blustering about the general election* RANT, thunder, bellow, sound off; be overbearing; *informal* throw one's weight about/around. ❷ *storms bluster in from the sea* BLAST, gust, storm, roar, rush.
▶ **noun** *his bluster turned to cooperation* RANTING, thundering, hectoring, bullying; bombast, bumptiousness, braggadocio.

blustery ▶ **adjective** STORMY, gusty, blowy, windy, squally, wild, tempestuous, turbulent; howling, roaring.
– OPPOSITES calm.

board ▶ **noun** ❶ *a wooden board* PLANK, beam, panel, slat, batten, timber, lath. ❷ *the board of directors* COMMITTEE, council, panel, directorate, commission, group. ❸ *your room and board will be free* FOOD, meals, provisions, refreshments, diet, table, bread; keep, maintenance; *informal* grub, nosh, eats, chow; *Brit. informal* scoff.
▶ **verb** ❶ *he boarded the aircraft* GET ON, go aboard, enter, mount, ascend; embark, emplane, entrain; catch; *informal* hop on. ❷ *a number of students boarded with them* LODGE, live, reside, be housed; *N. Amer.* room; *informal* put up, have digs. ❸ *they run a facility for boarding dogs* ACCOMMODATE, lodge, take in, put up, house; keep, feed, cater for.
■ **board something up/over** COVER UP/OVER, close up, shut up, seal.

boast ▶ **verb** ❶ *his mother had been boasting about him* BRAG, crow, swagger, swank, gloat, show off; exaggerate, overstate; *informal* talk big, lay it on thick; *Austral./NZ informal* skite. ❷ *the hotel boasts a fine restaurant* POSSESS, have, own, enjoy, pride oneself/itself on.
▶ **noun** ❶ *the government's main boast seemed undone* BRAG, self-praise; exaggeration, overstatement, fanfaronade; *informal* swank; *Austral./NZ informal* skite. ❷ *the hall is the boast of the county* PRIDE, joy, wonder, delight, treasure, gem.

boastful ▶ **adjective** BRAGGING, swaggering, bumptious, puffed up, full of oneself; cocky, conceited, arrogant, egotistical; *informal* swanky, big-headed; *N. Amer. informal* blowhard; *poetic/literary* vainglorious.
– OPPOSITES modest.

boat ▶ **noun** *a rowing boat* VESSEL, craft, watercraft, ship; *poetic/literary* keel, barque.
▶ **verb** *he insisted on boating into the lake* SAIL, yacht, cruise.

bob ▶ **verb** ❶ *their yacht bobbed about* MOVE UP AND DOWN, bounce, toss, skip, dance, jounce; wobble, jiggle, joggle, jolt, jerk. ❷ *the bookie's head bobbed* NOD, incline, dip; wag, waggle. ❸ *the maid bobbed and left the room* CURTSY, bow.
▶ **noun** ❶ *a bob of his head* NOD, inclination, dip; wag, waggle. ❷ *the maid scurried away with a bob* CURTSY, bow, obeisance.

bode ▶ **verb** AUGUR, portend, herald, be a sign of, warn of, foreshadow, be an omen of, presage, indicate, signify, promise, threaten, spell, denote, foretell; prophesy, predict; *poetic/literary* betoken, forebode.

bodily ▶ **adjective** *bodily sensations* PHYSICAL, corporeal, corporal, somatic, fleshly; concrete, real, actual, tangible.
– OPPOSITES spiritual, mental.
▶ **adverb** *he hauled her bodily from the van* FORCEFULLY, forcibly, violently; wholly, completely, entirely.

body ▶ **noun** ❶ *the human body* FIGURE, frame, form, physique, anatomy, skeleton; soma; *informal* bod. ❷ *he was hit by shrapnel in the head and body* TORSO, trunk. ❸ *the bodies were put in the fire* CORPSE, carcass, skeleton, remains; *informal* stiff; *Medicine* cadaver. ❹ *the body of the article* MAIN PART, central part, core, heart, hub. ❺ *the body of the ship* BODYWORK, hull; fuselage. ❻ *a body of water* EXPANSE, mass, area, stretch, tract, sweep, extent. ❼ *a growing body of evidence* QUANTITY, amount, volume, collection, mass, corpus. ❽ *the representative body of the employers* ASSOCIATION, organization, group, party, company, society, circle, syndicate, guild, corporation, contingent. ❾ *a heavenly body* OBJECT, entity. ❿ *add body to your hair* FULLNESS, thickness, substance, bounce, lift, shape.
■ **body and soul** COMPLETELY, entirely, totally, utterly, fully, thoroughly, wholeheartedly, unconditionally, to the hilt.

bodyguard ▶ **noun** MINDER, guard, protector, guardian, defender; *informal* heavy.

boffin ▶ **noun** (*Brit. informal*) EXPERT, specialist, authority, genius, mastermind; SCIENTIST, technician, inventor; *informal* egghead, Einstein.

bog ▶ **noun** MARSH, swamp, mire, quagmire, morass, slough, fen, wetland; *Brit.* carr; *Scottish & N. English* moss.
■ **bog someone/something down** MIRE, stick, entangle, ensnare, embroil; hamper, hinder, impede, delay, stall, detain; swamp, overwhelm.

bogey ▶ **noun** ❶ *water bogies frighten children from pools* EVIL SPIRIT, bogle, spectre, phantom, hobgoblin, demon; *informal* spook. ❷ *the guild is* *the bogey of bankers* BUGBEAR, pet hate, bane, anathema, abomination, nightmare, horror, dread, curse; *N. Amer.* bugaboo.

boggle ▶ verb (*informal*) ❶ *this data makes the mind boggle* MARVEL, wonder, be astonished, be overwhelmed, be staggered; gape, goggle; *informal* gawk. ❷ *you never boggle at plain speaking* DEMUR, baulk; shrink from, shy away from, be shy about; hesitate, waver, falter; *informal* be cagey about.

boggy ▶ adjective MARSHY, swampy, miry, fenny, muddy, waterlogged, wet, soggy, sodden, squelchy; spongy, heavy, sloughy.

bogus ▶ adjective FAKE, spurious, false, fraudulent, sham, deceptive; COUNTERFEIT, forged, feigned; make-believe, dummy, pseudo; *informal* phoney, pretend.
– OPPOSITES genuine.

bohemian ▶ noun *he is an artist and a real bohemian* NONCONFORMIST, avant-gardist, free spirit, dropout; hippy, beatnik.
– OPPOSITES conservative.
▶ adjective *a bohemian student life* UNCONVENTIONAL, nonconformist, unorthodox, avant-garde, irregular, alternative; artistic; *informal* arty-farty, way-out, offbeat.
– OPPOSITES conventional.

boil[1] ▶ verb ❶ *boil the potatoes* BRING TO THE BOIL, simmer; cook. ❷ *the soup is boiling* SIMMER, bubble, stew. ❸ *a huge cliff with the sea boiling below* CHURN, seethe, froth, foam; *poetic/literary* roil. ❹ *she boiled at his lack of consideration* FUME, seethe, rage, smoulder, bristle, be angry, be furious; get worked up; *informal* see red, get steamed up.
▶ noun *bring the stock to the boil* BOILING POINT, 100 degrees centigrade.
■ **boil something down** CONDENSE, reduce, concentrate, thicken.
■ **boil down to** COME DOWN TO, amount to, add up to, be in essence.

boil[2] ▶ noun *a boil on her neck* SWELLING, SPOT, pimple, blister, pustule, eruption, carbuncle, wen, abscess, ulcer; *technical* furuncle.

boiling ▶ adjective ❶ *boiling water* AT BOILING POINT, at 100 degrees centigrade; very hot, piping hot; bubbling. ❷ (*informal*) *it was a boiling day* VERY HOT, scorching, blistering, sweltering, sultry, torrid; *informal* roasting, baking.
– OPPOSITES freezing.

boisterous ▶ adjective ❶ *a boisterous game of handball* LIVELY, animated, exuberant, spirited; rowdy, unruly, wild, uproarious, unrestrained, undisciplined, uninhibited, uncontrolled, rough, disorderly, riotous; noisy, loud, clamorous; *Brit. informal* rumbustious. ❷ *a boisterous wind* BLUSTERY, gusty, windy, stormy, wild, squally, tempestuous; howling, roaring; *informal* blowy.
– OPPOSITES restrained, calm.

bold ▶ adjective ❶ *bold adventurers* DARING, intrepid, brave, courageous, valiant, valorous, fearless, dauntless, audacious, daredevil; adventurous, heroic, plucky, spirited, confident, assured; *informal* gutsy, spunky, feisty. ❷ *a bold pattern* STRIKING, vivid, bright, strong, eye-catching, prominent; gaudy, lurid, garish. ❸ *departure times are in bold type* HEAVY, thick, pronounced.
– OPPOSITES timid, pale.

bolshie ▶ adjective (*Brit. informal*) UNCOOPERATIVE, awkward, disobliging, unhelpful, recalcitrant, contrary, perverse, obstinate, stubborn, difficult, unreasonable, exasperating, trying; *Brit. informal* bloody-minded, stroppy.
– OPPOSITES compliant.

bolster ▶ noun *the bed was strewn with bolsters* PILLOW, cushion, pad.
▶ verb *a break would bolster her morale* STRENGTHEN, reinforce, boost, fortify, renew; support, buoy up, shore up, maintain, aid, help; augment, increase.
– OPPOSITES undermine.

bolt ▶ noun ❶ *the bolt on the shed door* BAR, LOCK, catch, latch, fastener. ❷ *nuts and bolts* RIVET, pin, peg, screw. ❸ *a bolt whirred over my head* ARROW, quarrel, dart, shaft; *poetic/literary* reed. ❹ *a bolt of lightning* FLASH, shaft, streak, burst, flare. ❺ *Mark made a bolt for the door* DASH, dart, run, sprint, leap, bound. ❻ *a bolt of cloth* ROLL, reel, spool; quantity, amount.
▶ verb ❶ *he bolted the door* LOCK, bar, latch, fasten, secure. ❷ *the lid was bolted down* RIVET, pin, peg, screw; fasten, fix. ❸ *Anna bolted from the room* DASH, dart, run, sprint, hurtle, rush, fly, shoot, bound; flee; *informal* tear, scoot, leg it. ❹ *he bolted down his breakfast* GOBBLE, gulp, wolf, guzzle, devour; *informal* demolish, polish off, shovel down; *Brit. informal* shift, gollop, scoff; *N. Amer. informal* scarf, snarf.
■ **a bolt from/out of the blue** SHOCK, surprise, bombshell, thunderbolt, revelation; *informal* turn-up for the books.
■ **bolt upright** STRAIGHT, rigidly, stiffly.

bomb ▶ noun ❶ *they saw bombs bursting on the runway* EXPLOSIVE, incendiary (device); missile, projectile; *dated* blockbuster, bombshell. ❷ *the world has lived with the bomb* NUCLEAR WEAPONS, nuclear bombs, atom bombs, A-bombs. ❸ (*Brit. informal*) *a new superstore will cost a bomb. See* FORTUNE sense 5.
▶ verb ❶ *their headquarters were bombed* BOMBARD, blast, shell, blitz, strafe, pound; attack, assault; blow up, destroy, demolish, flatten, devastate. ❷ (*Brit. informal*) *she bombed across Texas. See* SPEED verb sense 1. ❸ (*informal*) *the film bombed at the box office. See* FAIL sense 1.

bombard ▶ verb ❶ *gun batteries bombarded the islands* SHELL, pound, blitz, strafe, bomb; assail, attack, assault, batter, blast, pelt. ❷ *we were bombarded with information* INUNDATE, swamp, flood, deluge, snow under; besiege, overwhelm.

bombast ▶ noun BLUSTER, pomposity, empty talk, humbug, turgidity, verbosity, verbiage; pretentiousness, ostentation, grandiloquence; *informal* hot air; *rare* fustian.

bombastic ▶ adjective POMPOUS, blustering, turgid, verbose, orotund, high-flown, high-sounding, overwrought, pretentious, ostentatious, grandiloquent; *informal* highfalutin; *rare* fustian.

bona fide ▶ adjective AUTHENTIC, genuine, real, true, actual; legal, legitimate, lawful, valid, proper; *informal* legit, pukka, the real McCoy.
– OPPOSITES bogus.

bonanza ▶ noun WINDFALL, godsend, boon, blessing, bonus, stroke of luck; *informal* jackpot.

bond ▶ noun ❶ *the women forged a close bond* FRIENDSHIP, relationship, fellowship, partnership, association, affiliation, alliance, attachment. ❷ *the prisoner struggled with his bonds* CHAINS, fetters, shackles, manacles, irons, restraints. ❸ *I've broken my bond* PROMISE, pledge, vow, oath, word (of honour), guarantee, assurance; agreement, contract, pact, bargain, deal.
▶ verb *the extensions are bonded to your hair* JOIN, fasten, fix, affix, attach, secure, bind, stick, fuse.

bondage ▶ noun SLAVERY, enslavement, servitude, subjugation, subjection, oppression, domination, exploitation, persecution; *historical* serfdom, vassalage; *archaic* enthralment.
– OPPOSITES liberty.

bonhomie ▶ noun GENIALITY, affability, conviviality, cordiality, amiability, sociability, friendliness, warmth, joviality.
– OPPOSITES coldness.

bon mot ▶ noun WITTICISM, quip, pun, pleasantry, jest, joke; *informal* wisecrack, one-liner.

bonny ▶ adjective (*Scottish & N. English*) BEAUTIFUL, attractive, pretty, gorgeous, fetching, prepossessing; lovely, nice, sweet, cute, appealing, endearing, adorable, lovable, charming, winsome; *informal* divine; *Austral./NZ informal* beaut; *poetic/literary* beauteous; *archaic* fair, comely.
– OPPOSITES unattractive.

bonus ▶ noun ❶ *the extra work's a real bonus* BENEFIT, advantage, boon, blessing, godsend, stroke of luck, asset, plus, pro, attraction; *informal* perk; *formal* perquisite. ❷ *she's on a good salary and she gets a bonus* GRATUITY, handout, gift, present, reward, prize; incentive, inducement; *informal* perk, sweetener; *formal* perquisite.
– OPPOSITES disadvantage.

bon viveur, bon vivant ▶ noun HEDONIST, pleasure-seeker, sensualist, sybarite, voluptuary; epicure, gourmet, gastronome.
– OPPOSITES puritan.

bony ▶ adjective GAUNT, ANGULAR, skinny, thin, lean, spare, spindly, skin-and-bones, skeletal, emaciated, underweight; *informal* like a bag of bones.
– OPPOSITES plump.

booby ▶ noun *See* IDIOT.

book ▶ noun ❶ *he published his first book in 1610* VOLUME, tome, publication, title; novel, storybook, treatise, manual; paperback, hardback, softback. ❷ *he scribbled in his book* NOTEPAD, notebook, pad, memo pad, exercise book; logbook, ledger, journal, diary; *Brit.* jotter, pocketbook; *N. Amer.* scratch pad. ❸ *the council had to balance its books* ACCOUNTS, records; account book, record book, ledger, balance sheet.
▶ verb ❶ *she booked a table at the restaurant* RESERVE, make a reservation for, pre-arrange, order; *informal* bag; *formal* bespeak. ❷ *we booked a number of events in the Festival* ARRANGE, programme, schedule, timetable, line up, lay on; *N. Amer.* slate.
■ **by the book** ACCORDING TO THE RULES, within the law, lawfully, legally, legitimately; honestly, fairly; *informal* on the level, fair and square.
■ **book in** REGISTER, check in, enrol.

booking ▶ noun RESERVATION, pre-arrangement; appointment, date.

bookish ▶ adjective STUDIOUS, scholarly, academic, intellectual, highbrow, erudite, learned, educated, knowledgeable; cerebral, serious, earnest, thoughtful.

booklet ▶ noun PAMPHLET, brochure, leaflet, handbill, flyer, tract; *N. Amer.* folder, mailer.

boom ▶ noun ❶ *the boom of the waves on the rocks* REVERBERATION, resonance, thunder, echoing, crashing, drumming, pounding, roar, rumble. ❷ *an unprecedented boom in sales* UPTURN, upsurge, upswing, increase, advance, growth, boost, escalation, improvement.
– OPPOSITES slump.
▶ verb ❶ *thunder boomed overhead* REVERBERATE, resound, resonate; rumble, thunder, blare, echo; crash, roll, clap, explode, bang. ❷ *a voice boomed at her* BELLOW, roar, thunder, shout, bawl; *informal* holler. ❸ *the market continued to boom* FLOURISH, burgeon, thrive, prosper, progress, improve, pick up, expand, mushroom, snowball.
– OPPOSITES whisper, slump.

boomerang ▶ verb BACKFIRE, recoil, reverse, rebound, come back, ricochet; be self-defeating; *informal* blow up in one's face.

booming ▶ adjective ❶ *a booming voice* RESONANT, sonorous, ringing, resounding, reverberating, carrying, thunderous; strident, stentorian, strong, powerful. ❷ *booming business* FLOURISHING, burgeoning, thriving, prospering, prosperous, successful, strong, buoyant; profitable, fruitful, lucrative; expanding.

boon[1] ▶ noun *their help was such a boon* BLESSING, godsend, bonus, plus, benefit, advantage, help, aid, asset; stroke of luck; *informal* perk;

formal perquisite.
– OPPOSITES curse.

boon[2] ▶ **adjective** *a boon companion* CLOSE, intimate, bosom, inseparable, faithful; favourite, best.

boor ▶ **noun** LOUT, oaf, ruffian, thug, yahoo, barbarian, Neanderthal, brute, beast; *informal* clod, roughneck, peasant, pig; *Brit. informal* yobbo, yob, oik.

boorish ▶ **adjective** COARSE, uncouth, rude, ill-bred, ill-mannered, uncivilized, unrefined, common, rough, thuggish, loutish; vulgar, unsavoury, gross, brutish, Neanderthal; *informal* cloddish, plebby; *Brit. informal* yobbish; *Austral. informal* ocker.
– OPPOSITES refined.

boost ▶ **noun** ❶ *a boost to one's morale* UPLIFT, lift, spur, encouragement, help, inspiration, stimulus, fillip. ❷ *a boost in sales* INCREASE, expansion, upturn, upsurge, upswing, rise, escalation, improvement, advance, growth, boom; *informal* hike.
– OPPOSITES decrease.
▶ **verb** ❶ *he phones her to boost her morale* IMPROVE, raise, uplift, increase, enhance, encourage, heighten, help, promote, foster, stimulate, invigorate, revitalize; *informal* buck up. ❷ *they used advertising to boost sales* INCREASE, raise, escalate, improve, strengthen, inflate, push up, promote, advance, foster, stimulate; facilitate, help, assist, aid; *informal* hike, bump up.
– OPPOSITES decrease.

boot[1] ▶ **noun** ❶ *muddy boots* GUMBOOT, wellington, wader, walking boot, riding boot, moon boot, thigh boot, ankle boot, pixie boot, desert boot; *informal* welly; *trademark* Doc Martens; *historical* top boot. ❷ (*informal*) *a boot in the stomach* KICK, blow, knock.
▶ **verb** ❶ *his shot was booted away by the goalkeeper* KICK, punt, bunt, tap; propel, drive, knock. ❷ *boot up your computer* START UP, fire up.
■ **boot someone out** (*informal*). *See* DISMISS sense 1.
■ **give someone the boot** (*informal*). *See* DISMISS sense 1.

boot[2]
■ **to boot** AS WELL, also, too, besides, into the bargain, in addition, additionally, on top, what's more, moreover, furthermore; *informal* and all.

booth ▶ **noun** ❶ *booths for different traders* STALL, stand, kiosk. ❷ *a phone booth* CUBICLE, kiosk, box, enclosure, cabin.

bootleg ▶ **adjective** ILLEGAL, illicit, unlawful, unauthorized, unlicensed, pirated; contraband, smuggled, black-market.

bootless ▶ **adjective** (*archaic*). *See* FRUITLESS.

bootlicker ▶ **noun** (*informal*) SYCOPHANT, toady, fawner, flatterer, creep, crawler, lickspittle, truckler, groveller, kowtower; *informal* yes-man; *archaic* toad-eater.

booty ▶ **noun** LOOT, plunder, pillage, haul, spoils, stolen goods, ill-gotten gains, pickings; *informal* swag.

booze (*informal*) ▶ **noun** *fill him up with food and booze* ALCOHOL, alcoholic drink, (intoxicating) liquor, drink, spirits, intoxicants; *informal* grog, firewater, rotgut, the hard stuff, the bottle, Dutch courage, hooch, moonshine; *Brit. informal* bevvies; *N. Amer. informal* juice, the sauce.
▶ **verb** *I was boozing with my mates* DRINK (ALCOHOL), tipple, imbibe, indulge; *informal* hit the bottle, knock a few back, swill; *Brit. informal* bevvy; *N. Amer. informal* bend one's elbow.

boozer ▶ **noun** ❶ (*informal*) *he's a notorious boozer* DRINKER, drunk, drunkard, alcoholic, dipsomaniac, tippler, imbiber, sot, inebriate; *informal* lush, alky, dipso, soak, tosspot, wino, sponge, barfly; *Austral./NZ informal* hophead; *archaic* toper. ❷ (*Brit. informal*) *I'm off down the boozer* BAR, wine bar, inn, roadhouse; *Brit.* pub, public house; *N. Amer.* tavern; *informal* watering hole; *Brit. informal* local; *dated* alehouse; *N. Amer. historical* saloon; *archaic* hostelry.

bop ▶ **noun** (*Brit. informal*) ❶ *I fancy a bop* DANCE; *informal* boogie, jive. ❷ *a college bop* DISCOTHEQUE; *informal* disco, hop.
▶ **verb** (*informal*) *they were bopping to disco music* DANCE, jig; *informal* boogie, jive, groove, disco, rock, stomp, hoof it; *N. Amer. informal* get down, cut a/the rug.

bordello ▶ **noun** (*N. Amer.*) BROTHEL, whorehouse; *Law* disorderly house; *Brit. informal* knocking shop; *N. Amer. informal* cathouse; *euphemistic* massage parlour; *archaic* bawdy house, house of ill fame, house of ill repute.

border ▶ **noun** ❶ *the border of a medieval manuscript* EDGE, MARGIN, perimeter, circumference, periphery; rim, fringe, verge; sides. ❷ *the Soviet border* FRONTIER, boundary, borderline, perimeter; marches, bounds.
▶ **verb** ❶ *the fields were bordered by hedges* SURROUND, enclose, encircle, circle, edge, fringe, bound, flank. ❷ *the straps are bordered with gold braid* EDGE, fringe, hem; trim, pipe, finish. ❸ *the forest bordered on Broadmoor* ADJOIN, abut, be next to, be adjacent to, be contiguous with, touch, join, meet, reach.
■ **border on** VERGE ON, approach, come close to, be comparable to, approximate to, be tantamount to, be similar to, resemble.

borderline ▶ **noun** *the borderline between old and antique* DIVIDING LINE, divide, division, demarcation line, line, cut-off point; threshold, margin, border, boundary.
▶ **adjective** *borderline cases* MARGINAL, uncertain, indefinite, unsettled, undecided, doubtful, indeterminate, unclassifiable, equivocal; questionable, debatable, controversial, contentious, problematic; *informal* iffy.

bore[1] ▶ **verb** *bore a hole in the ceiling* DRILL, pierce, perforate, puncture, punch, cut; tunnel,

burrow, mine, dig, gouge, sink.
▶ **noun** ❶ *a well bore* BOREHOLE, hole, well, shaft, pit. ❷ *the canon has a bore of 890 millimetres* CALIBRE, diameter, gauge.

bore² ▶ **verb** *the television news bored Philip* STULTIFY, pall on, stupefy, weary, tire, fatigue, send to sleep, leave cold; bore to death, bore to tears; *informal* turn off.
– OPPOSITES interest.
▶ **noun** *you can be such a bore* TEDIOUS PERSON/THING, tiresome person/thing, bother, nuisance, pest, annoyance, trial, vexation, thorn in one's flesh/side; *informal* drag, pain (in the neck), headache, hassle; *N. Amer. informal* nudnik.

boredom ▶ **noun** WEARINESS, ennui, apathy, unconcern, accidie; frustration, dissatisfaction, restlessness, restiveness; tedium, dullness, monotony, repetitiveness, flatness, dreariness; *informal* deadliness.

boring ▶ **adjective** TEDIOUS, dull, monotonous, repetitive, unrelieved, unvaried, unimaginative, uneventful; characterless, featureless, colourless, lifeless, insipid, uninteresting, unexciting, uninspiring, unstimulating, jejune, flat, bland, dry, stale, tired, banal, lacklustre, stodgy, dreary, humdrum, mundane; mind-numbing, soul-destroying, wearisome, tiring, tiresome, irksome, trying, frustrating; *informal* deadly, not up to much; *Brit. informal* samey; *N. Amer. informal* dullsville.

borrow ▶ **verb** ❶ *we borrowed a lot of money* LOAN, take as a loan; lease, hire; *informal* cadge, scrounge, bum; *Brit. informal* scab; *N. Amer. informal* mooch; *Austral./NZ informal* bludge. ❷ (*informal*) *they 'borrowed' all of his tools* TAKE, help oneself to, appropriate, commandeer, abscond with, carry off; steal, purloin; *informal* filch, rob, swipe, nab, rip off, lift, 'liberate', snaffle; *Brit. informal* nick, pinch, half-inch, whip, knock off; *N. Amer. informal* heist, glom. ❸ *adventurous chefs borrow foreign techniques* ADOPT, take on, acquire, embrace.
– OPPOSITES lend.

bosom ▶ **noun** ❶ *the gown was set low over her bosom* BUST, chest; breasts, mammary glands, mammae; *informal* boobs, knockers, bubbies; *Brit. informal* bristols, charlies; *N. Amer. informal* bazooms; *archaic* embonpoint. ❷ (*poetic/literary*) *the family took Gill into its bosom* PROTECTION, shelter, safety, refuge; heart, core; *poetic/literary* midst. ❸ *love was kindled within his bosom* HEART, breast, soul, core, spirit.
▶ **adjective** *bosom friends* CLOSE, boon, intimate, inseparable, faithful, constant, devoted; good, best, firm, favourite.

boss (*informal*) ▶ **noun** *the boss of a large company* HEAD, chief, principal, director, president, chief executive, chair, manager(ess); supervisor, foreman, overseer, controller; employer, owner, proprietor, patron; *informal* number one, kingpin, top dog, bigwig; *Brit. informal* gaffer, governor; *N. Amer. informal* head honcho, padrone, sachem, big kahuna.
▶ **verb** *you have no right to boss me about* ORDER ABOUT/AROUND, dictate to, lord it over, bully, push around/about, domineer, dominate, pressurize, browbeat; call the shots, lay down the law; *informal* bulldoze, walk all over, railroad.

bossy ▶ **adjective** (*informal*) DOMINEERING, pushy, overbearing, imperious, officious, high-handed, authoritarian, dictatorial, controlling; *informal* high and mighty.
– OPPOSITES submissive.

botch (*informal*) ▶ **verb** *examiners botched the marking* BUNGLE, mismanage, mishandle, make a mess of; *informal* mess up, make a hash of, muff, fluff, foul up, screw up; *Brit. informal* bodge, cock up; *N. Amer. informal* flub.
▶ **noun** *I've made a botch of things* MESS, blunder, failure, wreck, fiasco, debacle; *informal* hash; *Brit. informal* bodge, cock-up, pig's ear.
– OPPOSITES success.

bother ▶ **verb** ❶ *no one bothered her* DISTURB, trouble, inconvenience, pester, badger, harass, molest, plague, nag, hound, harry, annoy, upset, irritate; *informal* hassle, bug, get up someone's nose, get in someone's hair; *N. English informal* mither; *N. Amer. informal* ride. ❷ *the incident was too small to bother about* MIND, care, concern oneself, trouble oneself, worry oneself; *informal* give a damn, give a hoot. ❸ *there was something bothering him* WORRY, trouble, concern, perturb, disturb, disquiet, disconcert, unnerve; fret, upset, distress, agitate, gnaw at, weigh down; *informal* rattle.
▶ **noun** ❶ *I don't want to put you to any bother* TROUBLE, effort, exertion, inconvenience, fuss, pains; *informal* hassle. ❷ *the food was such a bother to cook* NUISANCE, pest, palaver, rigmarole, job, trial, bind, bore, drag, inconvenience, trouble, problem; *informal* hassle, headache, pain (in the neck). ❸ *a spot of bother in the public bar* DISORDER, fighting, trouble, ado, disturbance, agitation, commotion, uproar; *NZ* bobsy-die; *informal* hoo-ha, aggro, argy-bargy, kerfuffle.

bothersome ▶ **adjective** ANNOYING, irritating, vexatious, maddening, exasperating; tedious, wearisome, tiresome; troublesome, trying, taxing, awkward; *informal* aggravating, pesky, pestilential.

bottle ▶ **noun** ❶ *a bottle of whisky* carafe, flask, decanter, pitcher, flagon, carboy, demijohn. ❷ (*informal*) *a world blurred by the bottle. See* ALCOHOL. ❸ (*Brit. informal*) *no one had the bottle to stand up to McGregor* COURAGE, bravery, valour, nerve, confidence, daring, audacity, pluck, spirit, grit, mettle, spine, backbone; *informal* guts, spunk, gumption; *N. Amer. informal* moxie.
■ **bottle something up** SUPPRESS, repress, restrain, withhold, hold in, rein in, inhibit, smother, stifle, contain, conceal, hide; *informal* keep a lid on.

bottleneck ▶ **noun** TRAFFIC JAM, jam, congestion, hold-up, gridlock, tailback; constriction, narrowing, restriction, obstruction, blockage; *informal* snarl-up.

bottom ▶ **noun** ❶ *the bottom of the stairs* FOOT, lowest part, lowest point, base; foundation, substructure, underpinning. ❷ *the bottom of the car* UNDERSIDE, underneath, undersurface, undercarriage, underbelly. ❸ *the bottom of Lake Ontario* FLOOR, bed, depths. ❹ *the bottom of his garden* FARTHEST POINT, far end, extremity. ❺ *the bottom of his class* LOWEST LEVEL, lowest position. ❻ (*Brit.*) *I've got a tattoo on my bottom* REAR (END), rump, backside, seat; buttocks, cheeks; *informal* behind, BTM, sit-upon, derrière; *Brit. informal* bum, botty, jacksie; *N. Amer. informal* butt, fanny, tush, tail, buns, booty, heinie; *humorous* fundament, posterior, stern; *Anatomy* nates. ❼ *police got to the bottom of the mystery* ORIGIN, cause, root, source, basis, foundation; heart, kernel; reality, essence.
– OPPOSITES top, surface.
▶ **adjective** *she sat on the bottom step* LOWEST, last, bottommost; *technical* basal.
– OPPOSITES top.
■ **from top to bottom** THOROUGHLY, fully, extensively, completely, comprehensively, rigorously, exhaustively, scrupulously, meticulously.

bottomless ▶ **adjective** ❶ *the bottomless pits of hell* FATHOMLESS, unfathomable, endless, infinite, immeasurable. ❷ *George's appetite was bottomless* UNLIMITED, limitless, boundless, infinite, inexhaustible, endless, never-ending, everlasting; vast, huge, enormous.
– OPPOSITES limited.

bough ▶ **noun** BRANCH, limb, arm, offshoot.

boulder ▶ **noun** ROCK, stone; *Austral./NZ* gibber.

boulevard ▶ **noun** AVENUE, street, road, drive, lane, parade, broadway, thoroughfare.

bounce ▶ **verb** ❶ *the ball bounced* REBOUND, spring back, ricochet, jounce; *N. Amer.* carom. ❷ *William bounced down the stairs* BOUND, leap, jump, spring, bob, hop, skip, trip, prance.
▶ **noun** ❶ *he reached the door in a single bounce* BOUND, leap, jump, spring, hop, skip. ❷ *the pitch's uneven bounce* SPRINGINESS, resilience, elasticity, give. ❸ *she had lost her bounce* VITALITY, vigour, energy, vivacity, liveliness, animation, sparkle, verve, spirit, enthusiasm, dynamism; cheerfulness, happiness, buoyancy, optimism; *informal* get-up-and-go, pep, zing.
■ **bounce back** RECOVER, revive, rally, pick up, be on the mend; perk up, cheer up, brighten up, liven up; *informal* buck up.

bouncing ▶ **adjective** VIGOROUS, thriving, flourishing, blooming; HEALTHY, strong, robust, fit, in fine fettle; *informal* in the pink.

bouncy ▶ **adjective** ❶ *a bouncy bridge* SPRINGY, flexible, resilient, elastic, stretchy, rubbery. ❷ *a rather bouncy ride* BUMPY, jolting, jerky, jumpy, jarring, rough. ❸ *she was always bouncy* LIVELY, energetic, perky, frisky, jaunty, dynamic, vital, vigorous, vibrant, animated, spirited, buoyant, bubbly, sparkling, vivacious; enthusiastic, upbeat; *informal* peppy, zingy, chirpy.

bound[1] ▶ **adjective** ❶ *he raised his bound ankles* TIED, chained, fettered, shackled, secured. ❷ *she seemed bound to win* CERTAIN, sure, very likely, destined. ❸ *you're bound by the Official Secrets Act to keep quiet* OBLIGATED, obliged, compelled, required, constrained. ❹ *religion and morality are bound up with one another* CONNECTED, linked, tied, united, allied.

bound[2] ▶ **verb** *hares bound in the fields* LEAP, jump, spring, bounce, hop; skip, bob, dance, prance, gambol, gallop.
▶ **noun** *he crossed the room with a single bound* LEAP, jump, spring, bounce, hop.

bound[3] ▶ **verb** ❶ *corporate freedom is bounded by law* LIMIT, restrict, confine, circumscribe, demarcate, delimit. ❷ *the heath is bounded by a hedge* ENCLOSE, surround, encircle, circle, border; close in/off, hem in. ❸ *the garden was bounded by Mill Lane* BORDER, adjoin, abut; be next to, be adjacent to.

boundary ▶ **noun** ❶ *the boundary between Israel and Jordan* BORDER, frontier, borderline, partition. ❷ *the boundary between art and advertising* DIVIDING LINE, divide, division, borderline, cut-off point. ❸ *the boundary of his estate* BOUNDS, confines, limits, margins, edges, fringes; border, periphery, perimeter. ❹ *the boundaries of accepted behaviour* LIMITS, parameters, bounds, confines; ambit, compass.

boundless ▶ **adjective** LIMITLESS, unlimited, unbounded, untold, immeasurable, abundant; inexhaustible, endless, infinite, interminable, unfailing, ceaseless, everlasting.
– OPPOSITES limited.

bounds ▶ **plural noun** ❶ *we keep rents within reasonable bounds* LIMITS, confines, proportions. ❷ *land within the forest bounds* BORDERS, boundaries, confines, limits, margins, edges; periphery, perimeter.
■ **out of bounds** OFF LIMITS, restricted; forbidden, banned, proscribed, illegal, illicit, unlawful, unacceptable, taboo; *informal* no go.

bountiful ▶ **adjective** ❶ *their bountiful patron* GENEROUS, magnanimous, munificent, open-handed, unselfish, unstinting, lavish; benevolent, beneficent, charitable. ❷ *a bountiful supply of fresh food* ABUNDANT, plentiful, ample, copious, bumper, superabundant, inexhaustible, prolific, profuse; lavish, generous, handsome, rich; *informal* whopping; *poetic/literary* plenteous.
– OPPOSITES mean, meagre.

bounty ▶ **noun** ❶ *a bounty for each man killed* REWARD, prize, award, commission, premium, dividend, bonus, gratuity, tip, donation, handout; incentive, inducement; money; *informal* perk, sweetener; *formal* perquisite. ❷ (*poetic/literary*) *I thank the Lord for all his bounty* GENEROSITY, magnanimity, munificence, bountifulness, largesse, lavishness; benevolence, beneficence, charity, goodwill; blessings, favours.

bouquet ▶ **noun** ❶ *her bridal bouquet* BUNCH OF FLOWERS, posy, nosegay, tussie-mussie, spray, corsage. ❷ *bouquets go to Ann for a well-planned event* COMPLIMENT, commendation, tribute, accolade; praise, congratulations, applause. ❸ *the Chardonnay has a fine bouquet* AROMA, nose, smell, fragrance, perfume, scent, odour.

bourgeois ▶ **adjective** ❶ *a bourgeois family* MIDDLE-CLASS, propertied; CONVENTIONAL, conservative, conformist; provincial, suburban, small-town. ❷ *bourgeois decadence* CAPITALISTIC, materialistic, money-oriented, commercial.
–OPPOSITES proletarian, communist.
▶ **noun** *a proud bourgeois* MEMBER OF THE MIDDLE CLASS, property owner.

bout ▶ **noun** ❶ *a short bout of exercise* SPELL, period, time, stretch, stint, session; burst, flurry, spurt. ❷ *a coughing bout* ATTACK, fit, spasm, paroxysm, convulsion, eruption, outburst. ❸ *he is fighting only his fifth bout* CONTEST, match, round, heat, competition, event, meeting, fixture; fight, prizefight.

bovine ▶ **adjective** ❶ *large, bovine eyes* COW-LIKE, calf-like, taurine. ❷ *an expression of bovine amazement* STUPID, slow, ignorant, unintelligent, imperceptive, half-baked, vacuous, mindless, witless, doltish; *informal* dumb, dense, dim, dim-witted, dopey, birdbrained, pea-brained; *Brit. informal* dozy, daft; *Scottish & N. English informal* glaikit.
▶ **noun** cow, heifer, bull, bullock, calf, ox; *N. Amer. informal* boss, bossy; *Farming* beef.

bow[1] ▶ **verb** ❶ *the officers bowed* INCLINE THE BODY, incline the head, nod, salaam, curtsy, bob. ❷ *the mast quivered and bowed* BEND, buckle, stoop, curve, flex, deform. ❸ *the government bowed to foreign pressure* YIELD, submit, give in, surrender, succumb, capitulate, defer, conform; comply with, accept, heed, observe. ❹ *a footman bowed her in* USHER, conduct, show, lead, guide, direct, steer, shepherd.
▶ **noun** *a perfunctory bow* OBEISANCE, salaam, bob, curtsy, nod; *archaic* reverence.
■ **bow out** WITHDRAW, resign, retire, step down, pull out, back out; give up, quit, leave; *informal* pack in, chuck (in); *Brit. informal* jack in.

bow[2] ▶ **noun** *the bow of the tanker* PROW, front, stem, nose, head, cutwater; *Brit. humorous* sharp end.

bow[3] ▶ **noun** ❶ *she tied a bow in her hair* LOOP, knot; ribbon. ❷ *he bent the rod into a bow* ARC, curve, bend; crescent, half-moon. ❸ *an archer's bow* longbow, crossbow; *Archery* recurve.

bowdlerize ▶ **verb** EXPURGATE, censor, blue-pencil, cut, edit; sanitize, water down, emasculate.

bowel ▶ **noun** ❶ *a disorder of the bowels* INTESTINE(S), small intestine, large intestine, colon; *informal* guts, insides. ❷ *the bowels of the ship* INTERIOR, inside, core, belly; depths, recesses; *informal* innards.

bower ▶ **noun** ❶ *a rose-scented bower* ARBOUR, pergola, grotto, alcove, sanctuary. ❷ (*poetic/literary*) *the lady's bower* BEDROOM; *historical* boudoir; *archaic* bedchamber, chamber.

bowl[1] ▶ **verb** ❶ *he bowled a hundred or so balls* PITCH, throw, propel, hurl, toss, lob, loft, fling, launch, deliver; spin, roll; *informal* chuck, sling, bung, heave, buzz; *dated* shy. ❷ *the car bowled along the roads* HURTLE, speed, shoot, sweep, career, hare, fly; *informal* belt, tear, scoot; *Brit. informal* bomb; *N. Amer. informal* clip.
■ **bowl someone over** ❶ *the explosion bowled us over* KNOCK DOWN/OVER, fell, floor, prostrate. ❷ (*informal*) *I have been bowled over by your generosity* OVERWHELM, astound, astonish, overawe, dumbfound, stagger, stun, daze, shake, take aback, leave aghast; *informal* knock sideways, flabbergast, blow away; *Brit. informal* knock for six.

bowl[2] ▶ **noun** ❶ *she cracked two eggs into a bowl* DISH, basin, pot, crock, crucible, mortar; container, vessel, receptacle; *historical* jorum, porringer. ❷ *the town lay in a shallow bowl* VALLEY, hollow, dip, depression, trough, crater. ❸ (*N. Amer.*) *the Hollywood Bowl* STADIUM, arena, amphitheatre, colosseum; enclosure, ground; *informal* park.

box[1] ▶ **noun** ❶ *a box of cigars* CARTON, pack, packet; case, crate, chest, coffer, casket; container, receptacle. ❷ *a telephone box* BOOTH, cubicle, kiosk, cabin, hut; compartment, carrel, alcove, bay, recess.
▶ **verb** *Muriel boxed up his clothes* PACKAGE, pack, parcel, wrap, bundle, bale, crate.
■ **box something/someone in** HEM IN, fence in, close in, shut in; trap, confine, imprison, intern; surround, enclose, encircle, circle.

box[2] ▶ **verb** ❶ *he began boxing professionally* FIGHT, prizefight, spar; battle, brawl; *informal* scrap. ❷ *he boxed my ears* CUFF, smack, strike, hit, thump, slap, swat, punch, jab, wallop; *Scottish & N. English* skelp; *informal* belt, bop, biff, sock, clout, clobber, whack, plug, slug; *Brit. informal* slosh, dot; *N. Amer. informal* boff, bust.
▶ **noun** *a box on the ear* CUFF, hit, thump, slap, smack, swat, punch, jab, hook; *Scottish & N. English* skelp; *informal* belt, bop, biff, sock, clout, whack, plug, slug.

boxer ▶ **noun** FIGHTER, pugilist, ringster, prizefighter, kick-boxer; *informal* bruiser, scrapper.

boxing ▶ **noun** PUGILISM, the noble art, fighting, sparring, fisticuffs; kick-boxing, prizefighting, the (prize) ring.

boy ▶ **noun** LAD, schoolboy, male child, youth,

young man, stripling; *Scottish & N. English* laddie; *derogatory* brat. *See also* CHILD.

boycott ▶ **verb** *they boycotted the elections* SPURN, snub, shun, avoid, abstain from, wash one's hands of, turn one's back on, reject, veto.
– OPPOSITES support.
▶ **noun** *a boycott on the use of tropical timbers* BAN, veto, embargo, prohibition, sanction, restriction; avoidance, rejection, refusal.

boyfriend ▶ **noun** LOVER, sweetheart, beloved, darling, dearest, young man, man friend, man, escort, suitor; PARTNER, significant other; *informal* fella, flame, fancy man, toy boy, sugar daddy; *N. Amer. informal* squeeze; *poetic/literary* swain; *dated* beau; *archaic* paramour.

boyish ▶ **adjective** YOUTHFUL, young, childlike, adolescent, teenage; immature, juvenile, infantile, childish, babyish, puerile.

brace ▶ **noun** ❶ *the saw is best used with a brace* VICE, clamp, press. ❷ *power drills run faster than a brace* DRILL, boring tool, rotary tool. ❸ *the aquarium is supported by wooden braces* PROP, beam, joist, batten, rod, post, strut, stay, support, stanchion, bracket. ❹ *a brace on his right leg* SUPPORT, caliper. ❺ *a brace of partridges* PAIR, couple, duo, twosome; two. ❻ (*Printing*) *the term within braces* BRACKET, parenthesis.
▶ **verb** ❶ *the plane's wing is braced by a system of rods* SUPPORT, shore up, prop up, hold up, buttress, underpin; strengthen, reinforce. ❷ *he braced his hand on the railing* STEADY, secure, stabilize, fix, poise; tense, tighten. ❸ *brace yourself for disappointment* PREPARE, get ready, gear up, nerve, steel, galvanize, gird, strengthen, fortify; *informal* psych oneself up.

bracelet ▶ **noun** BANGLE, band, circlet, armlet, wristlet; manilla, rakhi, kara.

bracing ▶ **adjective** INVIGORATING, refreshing, stimulating, energizing, exhilarating, reviving, restorative, rejuvenating, revitalizing, rousing, fortifying, strengthening; FRESH, brisk, keen.

bracket ▶ **noun** ❶ *each speaker is fixed on a separate bracket* SUPPORT, prop, stay, batten, joist; rest, mounting, rack, frame. ❷ *put the words in brackets* PARENTHESIS; *Printing* brace. ❸ *a higher tax bracket* GROUP, category, grade, classification, set, division, order.
▶ **verb** *women were bracketed with minors* GROUP, CLASSIFY, class, categorize, grade, list, sort, place, assign; couple, pair, twin; liken, compare.

brackish ▶ **adjective** SLIGHTLY SALTY, saline, salt.

brag ▶ **verb** BOAST, crow, swagger, swank, bluster, gloat, show off; blow one's own trumpet, sing one's own praises; *informal* talk big, lay it on thick; *Austral./NZ informal* skite.

braggart ▶ **noun** *he was a prodigious braggart and a liar* BOASTER, bragger, swaggerer, poser, poseur, egotist; *informal* big-head, loudmouth, show-off, swank; *N. Amer. informal* showboat, blowhard; *Austral./NZ informal* skite; *Brit. informal, dated* swankpot.

braid ▶ **noun** ❶ *straps bordered with gold braid* CORD, bullion, thread, tape, binding, rickrack, ribbon; cordon, torsade; *Military slang* scrambled egg. ❷ *his hair is in braids* PLAIT, pigtail, twist; cornrows, dreadlocks.
▶ **verb** ❶ *she began to braid her hair* PLAIT, entwine, intertwine, interweave, weave, twist, twine. ❷ *the sleeves are braided in scarlet* TRIM, edge, border, pipe, hem, fringe.

brain ▶ **noun** ❶ *the disease attacks certain cells in the brain* CEREBRUM, cerebral matter, encephalon. ❷ *success requires brains as well as brawn* INTELLIGENCE, intellect, brainpower, cleverness, wit(s), reasoning, wisdom, acumen, discernment, judgement, understanding, sense; *informal* nous, grey matter, savvy; *N. Amer. informal* smarts. ❸ (*informal*) *Janice is the brains of the family* CLEVER PERSON, intellectual, intellect, thinker, mind, scholar; genius, Einstein; *informal* egghead, bright spark; *Brit. informal* brainbox, clever clogs; *N. Amer. informal* brainiac, rocket scientist.
– RELATED TERMS cerebral, encephalic.
– OPPOSITES dunce.

brainless ▶ **adjective** STUPID, FOOLISH, witless, unintelligent, ignorant, idiotic, simple-minded, empty-headed, half-baked; *informal* dumb, half-witted, brain-dead, moronic, cretinous, thick, dopey, dozy, birdbrained, pea-brained, dippy, wooden-headed; *Brit. informal* divvy; *Scottish & N. English informal* glaikit; *N. Amer. informal* dumb-ass, chowderheaded.
– OPPOSITES clever.

brain-teaser ▶ **noun** (*informal*) PUZZLE, problem, riddle, conundrum, poser.

brainwash ▶ **verb** INDOCTRINATE, condition, re-educate, persuade, influence.

brainy ▶ **adjective** (*informal*) CLEVER, intelligent, bright, brilliant, gifted; intellectual, erudite, academic, scholarly, studious, bookish; *informal* smart; *Brit. informal* swotty.
– OPPOSITES stupid.

brake ▶ **noun** *a brake on research* CURB, check, restraint, restriction, constraint, control, limitation.
▶ **verb** *she braked at the traffic lights* SLOW (DOWN), decelerate, reduce speed.
– OPPOSITES accelerate.

branch ▶ **noun** ❶ *the branches of a tree* BOUGH, limb, arm, offshoot. ❷ *a branch of the river* TRIBUTARY, feeder, side stream. ❸ *the judicial branch of government* DIVISION, subdivision, section, subsection, department, sector, part, side, wing. ❹ *the corporation's New York branch* OFFICE, bureau, agency; subsidiary, offshoot, satellite.
▶ **verb** ❶ *the place where the road branches* FORK,

bifurcate, divide, subdivide, split. ❷ *narrow paths branched off the road* DIVERGE FROM, deviate from, split off from; fan out from, radiate from.

■ **branch out** EXPAND, open up, extend; diversify, broaden one's horizons.

brand ▶ **noun** ❶ *a new brand of margarine* MAKE, line, label, marque; type, kind, sort, variety; trade name, trademark, proprietary name. ❷ *her particular brand of humour* TYPE, kind, sort, variety, class, category, genre, style, ilk; *N. Amer.* stripe. ❸ *the brand on a sheep* IDENTIFICATION, marker, earmark. ❹ *the brand of dipsomania* STIGMA, shame, disgrace; taint, blot, mark.

▶ **verb** ❶ *the letter M was branded on each animal* MARK, stamp, burn, sear. ❷ *the scene was branded on her brain* ENGRAVE, stamp, etch, imprint. ❸ *the media branded us as communists* STIGMATIZE, mark out; denounce, discredit, vilify; label.

brandish ▶ **verb** FLOURISH, wave, shake, wield; swing, swish; display, flaunt.

brash ▶ **adjective** ❶ *a brash man* SELF-ASSERTIVE, pushy, cocksure, cocky, self-confident, arrogant, bold, audacious, brazen; forward, impudent, insolent, rude. ❷ *brash colours* GARISH, gaudy, loud, flamboyant, showy, tasteless; *informal* flashy, tacky.
– OPPOSITES meek, muted.

brassy ▶ **adjective** ❶ BRAZEN, forward, bold, self-assertive, pushy, cocksure, cocky, brash; shameless, immodest; loud, vulgar, showy, ostentatious; *informal* flashy. ❷ *brassy music* LOUD, blaring, noisy, deafening, strident; raucous, harsh, dissonant, discordant, cacophonous; tinny.
– OPPOSITES demure, soft.

brat ▶ **noun** (*derogatory*) RASCAL, wretch, imp; minx, chit; *informal* monster, horror, whippersnapper.

bravado ▶ **noun** BOLDNESS, swaggering, bluster; machismo; boasting, bragging, bombast, braggadocio; *informal* showing off.

brave ▶ **adjective** ❶ *they put up a brave fight* COURAGEOUS, plucky, valiant, valorous, intrepid, heroic, lionhearted, bold, fearless, daring, audacious; unflinching, unshrinking, unafraid, dauntless, doughty, mettlesome, stout-hearted, spirited; *informal* game, gutsy, spunky. ❷ (*poetic/literary*) *his medals made a brave show* SPLENDID, magnificent, impressive, fine, handsome.
– OPPOSITES cowardly.

▶ **noun** (*dated*) *an Indian brave* WARRIOR, soldier, fighter.

▶ **verb** *fans braved freezing temperatures to see them play* ENDURE, put up with, bear, withstand, weather, suffer, go through; face, confront, defy.

bravery ▶ **noun** COURAGE, pluck, valour, intrepidity, nerve, daring, fearlessness, audacity, boldness, dauntlessness, stout-heartedness, heroism; backbone, grit, spine, spirit, mettle; *informal* guts, spunk; *Brit. informal* bottle; *N. Amer. informal* moxie.

bravo ▶ **exclamation** WELL DONE, congratulations; encore.

bravura ▶ **noun** *a display of bravura* SKILL, brilliance, virtuosity, expertise, artistry, talent, ability, flair.

▶ **adjective** *a bravura performance* VIRTUOSO, masterly, outstanding, excellent, superb, brilliant, first-class; *informal* mean, ace, A1.

brawl ▶ **noun** *a drunken brawl* FIGHT, skirmish, scuffle, tussle, fray, melee, free-for-all, scrum; fisticuffs; *informal* scrap, dust-up, set-to; *Brit. informal* punch-up, ruck; *Scottish informal* rammy; *N. Amer. informal* rough house, brannigan; *Law, dated* affray.

▶ **verb** *he ended up brawling with photographers* FIGHT, skirmish, scuffle, tussle, exchange blows, grapple, wrestle; *informal* scrap; *N. Amer. informal* rough-house.

brawn ▶ **noun** PHYSICAL STRENGTH, muscle(s), burliness, huskiness, toughness, power, might; *informal* beef, beefiness.

brawny ▶ **adjective** STRONG, muscular, muscly, well built, powerful, mighty, Herculean, strapping, burly, sturdy, husky, rugged; bulky, hefty, meaty, solid; *informal* beefy, hunky, hulking.
– OPPOSITES puny, weak.

bray ▶ **verb** ❶ *a donkey brayed* NEIGH, whinny, hee-haw. ❷ *Billy brayed with laughter* ROAR, bellow, trumpet.

brazen ▶ **adjective** ❶ *brazen defiance* BOLD, SHAMELESS, unashamed, unabashed, unembarrassed; defiant, impudent, impertinent, cheeky; barefaced, blatant, flagrant; *Brit. informal* saucy. ❷ (*poetic/literary*) *brazen objects* BRASS.
– OPPOSITES timid.

■ **brazen it out** PUT ON A BOLD FRONT, stand one's ground, be defiant, be unrepentant, be unabashed.

breach ▶ **noun** ❶ *a clear breach of the regulations* CONTRAVENTION, violation, infringement, infraction, transgression, neglect; *Law* delict. ❷ *a breach between government and Church* RIFT, schism, division, gulf, chasm; disunion, estrangement, discord, dissension, disagreement; split, break, rupture, scission; *Brit. informal* bust-up. ❸ *a breach in the sea wall* BREAK, rupture, split, crack, fracture; opening, gap, hole, fissure.

▶ **verb** ❶ *the river breached its bank* BREAK (THROUGH), burst, rupture; *informal* bust. ❷ *the changes breached union rules* BREAK, contravene, violate, infringe; defy, disobey, flout, fly in the face of; *Law* infract.

bread ▶ **noun** ❶ (*informal*) *his job puts bread on the table. See* FOOD sense 1. ❷ (*informal*) *I hate doing this, but I need the bread. See* MONEY sense 1.

breadth ▶ noun ❶ *a breadth of 100 metres* WIDTH, broadness, wideness, thickness; span; diameter. ❷ *the breadth of his knowledge* RANGE, extent, scope, depth, reach, compass, scale, degree.

break ▶ verb ❶ *the mirror broke* SHATTER, smash, crack, snap, fracture, fragment, splinter, fall to bits, fall to pieces; split, burst; *informal* bust. ❷ *she had broken her leg* FRACTURE, crack. ❸ *the bite had barely broken the skin* PIERCE, puncture, penetrate, perforate; cut. ❹ *the coffee machine has broken* STOP WORKING, break down, give out, go wrong, malfunction, crash; *informal* go kaput, conk out, be on the blink, give up the ghost; *Brit. informal* pack up. ❺ *traders who break the law* CONTRAVENE, violate, infringe, breach; defy, flout, disobey, fly in the face of. ❻ *his concentration was broken* INTERRUPT, disturb, interfere with. ❼ *they broke for coffee* STOP, pause, have a rest; *N. Amer.* recess; *informal* knock off, take five. ❽ *a pile of carpets broke his fall* CUSHION, soften the impact of, take the edge off. ❾ *the film broke box-office records* EXCEED, surpass, beat, better, cap, top, outdo, outstrip, eclipse; *informal* leave standing. ❿ *habits are very difficult to break* GIVE UP, relinquish, drop; *informal* kick, shake, pack in, quit. ⓫ *the strategies used to break the union* DESTROY, crush, quash, defeat, vanquish, overcome, overpower, overwhelm, suppress, cripple; weaken, subdue, cow, undermine. ⓬ *her self-control finally broke* GIVE WAY, crack, cave in, yield, go to pieces. ⓭ *four thousand pounds wouldn't break him* BANKRUPT, ruin, pauperize. ⓮ *he tried to break the news gently* REVEAL, disclose, divulge, impart, tell; announce, release. ⓯ *he broke the encryption code* DECIPHER, decode, decrypt, unravel, work out; *informal* figure out. ⓰ *the day broke fair and cloudless* DAWN, begin, start, emerge, appear. ⓱ *a political scandal broke* ERUPT, break out. ⓲ *the weather broke* CHANGE, alter, shift. ⓳ *waves broke against the rocks* CRASH, dash, beat, pound, lash. ⓴ *her voice broke as she relived the experience* FALTER, quaver, quiver, tremble, shake.
–OPPOSITES repair, keep, resume.

▶ noun ❶ *the magazine has been published without a break since 1950* INTERRUPTION, interval, gap, hiatus; discontinuation, suspension, disruption, cut-off; stop, stoppage, cessation. ❷ *a break in the weather* CHANGE, alteration, variation. ❸ *let's have a break* REST, respite, recess; stop, pause; interval, intermission; *informal* breather, time out, down time. ❹ *a weekend break* HOLIDAY; *N. Amer.* vacation; *Brit. informal* vac. ❺ *a break in diplomatic relations* RIFT, schism, split, break-up, severance, rupture; *Brit. informal* bust-up. ❻ *a break in the wall* GAP, opening, space, hole, breach, chink, crack, fissure; tear, split. ❼ (*informal*) *the actress got her first break in 1951* OPPORTUNITY, chance, opening.

■ **break away** ❶ *she attempted to break away from his grip* ESCAPE, get away, run away, flee, make off; break free, break loose, get out of someone's clutches; *informal* leg it, cut and run. ❷ *a group broke away from the main party* LEAVE, secede from, split off from, separate from, part company with, defect from; form a splinter group.

■ **break down** ❶ *his van broke down. See* BREAK verb sense 4. ❷ *pay negotiations broke down* FAIL, collapse, founder, fall through, disintegrate; *informal* fizzle out. ❸ *Vicky broke down, sobbing loudly* BURST INTO TEARS; lose control, be overcome, go to pieces, crumble, disintegrate; *informal* crack up, lose it.

■ **break something down** ❶ *the police broke the door down* KNOCK DOWN, kick down, smash in, pull down, tear down, demolish. ❷ *break big tasks down into smaller parts* DIVIDE, separate. ❸ *graphs show how the information can be broken down* ANALYSE, categorize, classify, sort out, itemize, organize; dissect.

■ **break in** ❶ *thieves broke in and took her cheque book* COMMIT BURGLARY, break and enter; force one's way in, burst in. ❷ *'I don't want to interfere,' Mrs Hendry broke in* INTERRUPT, butt in, cut in, interject, interpose, intervene, chime in; *Brit. informal* chip in.

■ **break someone in** TRAIN, initiate; *informal* show someone the ropes.

■ **break into** ❶ *thieves broke into a house in Perth Street* BURGLE, rob; force one's way into, burst into. ❷ *Phil broke into the discussion* INTERRUPT, butt into, cut in on, intervene in. ❸ *he broke into a song* BURST INTO, launch into.

■ **break off** SNAP OFF, come off, become detached, become separated.

■ **break something off** ❶ *I broke off a branch from the tree* SNAP OFF, pull off, sever, detach. ❷ *they threatened to break off diplomatic relations* END, terminate, stop, cease, call a halt to, finish, dissolve; SUSPEND, discontinue; *informal* pull the plug on.

■ **break out** ❶ *he broke out of the detention centre* ESCAPE FROM, abscond from, flee from; get free. ❷ *fighting broke out* FLARE UP, start suddenly, erupt, burst out.

■ **break up** ❶ *the meeting broke up* END, finish, stop, terminate; adjourn; *N. Amer.* recess. ❷ *the crowd began to break up* DISPERSE, scatter, disband, part company. ❸ *Danny and I broke up last year* SPLIT UP, separate, part (company); divorce. ❹ (*informal*) *the whole cast broke up* BURST OUT LAUGHING, dissolve into laughter; *informal* fall about, crack up, crease up; *theatrical slang* corpse.

■ **break something up** ❶ *police tried to break up the crowd* DISPERSE, scatter, disband. ❷ *I'm not going to let you break up my marriage* WRECK, ruin, destroy.

breakable ▶ adjective FRAGILE, delicate, flimsy, insubstantial; destructible; *formal* frangible.

breakaway ▶ adjective *a breakaway group* SEP-

ARATIST, secessionist, schismatic, splinter; rebel, renegade.

breakdown ▶ noun ❶ *the breakdown of the negotiations* FAILURE, collapse, disintegration, foundering. ❷ *on the death of her father she suffered a breakdown* NERVOUS BREAKDOWN; *informal* crack-up. ❸ *the breakdown of the computer system* MALFUNCTION, failure, crash. ❹ *a breakdown of the figures* ANALYSIS, classification, examination, investigation, dissection.

breaker ▶ noun WAVE, roller, comber, white horse; *informal* boomer; *N. Amer. informal* kahuna.

break-in ▶ noun BURGLARY, robbery, theft, raid; *informal* smash-and-grab.

breakneck ▶ adjective *the breakneck pace of change* EXTREMELY FAST, rapid, speedy, high-speed, lightning, whirlwind.

■ **at breakneck speed** DANGEROUSLY FAST, at full tilt, flat out, ventre à terre; *informal* hell for leather, like the wind, like a bat out of hell, like greased lightning; *Brit. informal* like the clappers.

breakthrough ▶ noun ADVANCE, development, step forward, success, improvement; discovery, innovation, revolution.
– OPPOSITES setback.

break-up ▶ noun ❶ *the break-up of negotiations* END, dissolution; breakdown, failure, collapse, disintegration. ❷ *their break-up was very amicable* SEPARATION, split, parting, divorce; estrangement, rift; *Brit. informal* bust-up. ❸ *the break-up of the Soviet Union* DIVISION, partition.

breakwater ▶ noun SEA WALL, jetty, mole, groyne, pier.

breast ▶ noun ❶ *the curve of her breasts* mammary gland, mamma; (**breasts**) BOSOM(S), bust, chest; *informal* boobs, knockers, bubbies; *Brit. informal* bristols, charlies; *N. Amer. informal* bazooms. ❷ *feelings of frustration were rising up in his breast* HEART, bosom, soul, core.

breath ▶ noun ❶ *I took a deep breath* INHALATION, inspiration, gulp of air; exhalation, expiration; *Medicine* respiration. ❷ *I had barely enough breath to reply* wind; *informal* puff. ❸ *a breath of wind* PUFF, waft, faint breeze. ❹ *a breath of scandal* HINT, suggestion, trace, touch, whisper, suspicion, whiff, undertone. ❺ (*archaic*) *there was no breath left in him* LIFE (FORCE).
– RELATED TERMS respiratory.

■ **take someone's breath away** ASTONISH, astound, amaze, stun, startle, stagger, shock, take aback, dumbfound, jolt, shake up; awe, overawe, thrill; *informal* knock sideways, flabbergast, blow away, bowl over; *Brit. informal* knock for six.

breathe ▶ verb ❶ *she breathed deeply* inhale and exhale, respire, draw breath; puff, pant, blow, gasp, wheeze; *Medicine* inspire, expire; *poetic/literary* suspire. ❷ *at least I'm still breathing* BE ALIVE, be living, live. ❸ *he would breathe new life into his firm* INSTIL, infuse, inject, impart. ❹ *'Together at last,' she breathed* WHISPER, murmur, purr, sigh, say. ❺ *the room breathed an air of hygiene* SUGGEST, indicate, have all the hallmarks of.

breather ▶ noun (*informal*) BREAK, REST, respite, breathing space, pause, interval, recess.

breathless ▶ adjective ❶ *Will arrived flushed and breathless* OUT OF BREATH, panting, puffing, gasping, wheezing; winded, puffed out, short of breath; *informal* out of puff. ❷ *the crowd were breathless with anticipation* AGOG, open-mouthed, waiting with bated breath, on the edge of one's seat, on tenterhooks, in suspense; excited, impatient.

breathtaking ▶ adjective SPECTACULAR, magnificent, wonderful, awe-inspiring, awesome, astounding, astonishing, amazing, stunning, incredible; thrilling, exciting; *informal* sensational, out of this world; *poetic/literary* wondrous.

breed ▶ verb ❶ *elephants breed readily in captivity* REPRODUCE, produce offspring, procreate, multiply; mate. ❷ *she was born and bred in the village* BRING UP, rear, raise, nurture. ❸ *the political system bred discontent* CAUSE, bring about, give rise to, lead to, produce, generate, foster, result in; stir up; *poetic/literary* beget.
▶ noun ❶ *a breed of cow* VARIETY, stock, strain; type, kind, sort. ❷ *a new breed of journalist* TYPE, kind, sort, variety, class, genre, generation; *N. Amer.* stripe.

breeding ▶ noun ❶ *individual birds pair for breeding* REPRODUCTION, procreation; mating. ❷ *the breeding of rats* REARING, raising, nurturing. ❸ *her aristocratic breeding* UPBRINGING, rearing; parentage, family, pedigree, blood, birth. ❹ *people of rank and breeding* (GOOD) MANNERS, gentility, refinement, cultivation, polish, urbanity; *informal* class.

breeding ground ▶ noun *the school is a breeding ground for communists* NURSERY, cradle, nest, den; hotbed.

breeze ▶ noun ❶ *a breeze ruffled the leaves* GENTLE WIND, puff of air, gust; *Meteorology* light air(s); *poetic/literary* zephyr. ❷ (*informal*) *travelling through London was a breeze* EASY TASK, five-finger exercise, walkover; child's play, nothing; *informal* doddle, piece of cake, cinch, kids' stuff, cakewalk; *N. Amer. informal* duck soup, snap; *Austral./NZ informal* bludge; *dated* snip.
▶ verb (*informal*) *Roger breezed into her office* SAUNTER, stroll, sail, cruise.

breezy ▶ adjective ❶ *a bright, breezy day* WINDY, fresh, brisk, airy; blowy, blustery, gusty. ❷ *his breezy manner* JAUNTY, CHEERFUL, cheery, brisk, carefree, easy, casual, relaxed, informal, light-hearted, lively, buoyant, sunny; *informal* upbeat, bright-eyed and bushy-tailed; *dated* gay.

brevity ▶ noun ❶ *the report is notable for its*

brevity CONCISENESS, concision, succinctness, economy of language, pithiness, incisiveness, shortness, compactness. ❷ *the brevity of human life* SHORTNESS, briefness, transience, ephemerality, impermanence.
– OPPOSITES verbosity.

brew ▶ verb ❶ *this beer is brewed in Frankfurt* FERMENT, make. ❷ *I'll brew some tea* PREPARE, infuse, make, stew; *Brit. informal* mash. ❸ *there's trouble brewing* DEVELOP, loom, impend, be imminent, be on the horizon, be in the offing, be just around the corner.
▶ noun ❶ *home brew* BEER, ale. ❷ *a hot reviving brew* DRINK, beverage; tea, coffee. ❸ *a dangerous brew of political turmoil and violent conflict* MIXTURE, mix, blend, combination, amalgam.

bribe ▶ verb *he used his wealth to bribe officials* BUY OFF, pay off, suborn; *informal* grease someone's palm, keep someone sweet, fix, square; *Brit. informal* nobble.
▶ noun *he accepted bribes* INDUCEMENT, incentive, douceur; *informal* backhander, pay-off, kickback, sweetener, carrot; *Brit. informal* bung; *N. Amer. informal* schmear.

bribery ▶ noun SUBORNATION; *N. Amer.* payola; *informal* palm-greasing, graft, hush money.

bric-a-brac ▶ noun ORNAMENTS, knickknacks, trinkets, bibelots, gewgaws, gimcracks; bits and pieces, bits and bobs, odds and ends, things, stuff; *informal* junk.

brick ▶ noun ❶ *bricks and mortar* breeze block, adobe, clinker; header, stretcher, bondstone; *Brit.* airbrick. ❷ *a brick of ice cream* BLOCK, cube, bar, cake.

bridal ▶ adjective *the bridal party* WEDDING, nuptial, marriage, matrimonial, marital, conjugal.

bride ▶ noun WIFE, marriage partner; newlywed.

bridge ▶ noun ❶ *a bridge over the river* VIADUCT, flyover, overpass, aqueduct. ❷ *a bridge between rival groups* LINK, connection, bond, tie.
▶ verb ❶ *a walkway bridged the motorway* SPAN, cross (over), extend across, traverse, arch over. ❷ *an attempt to bridge the gap between cultures* JOIN, link, connect, unite; straddle; overcome, reconcile.

bridle ▶ noun *a horse's bridle* HARNESS, headgear.
▶ verb ❶ *she bridled at his tone* BRISTLE, take offence, take umbrage, be affronted, be offended, get angry. ❷ *he bridled his indignation* CURB, restrain, hold back, control, check, rein in/back; suppress, stifle; *informal* keep a/the lid on.

brief ▶ adjective ❶ *a brief account* CONCISE, succinct, short, pithy, incisive, abridged, condensed, compressed, abbreviated, compact, thumbnail, potted; *formal* compendious. ❷ *a brief visit* SHORT, flying, fleeting, hasty, hurried, quick, cursory, perfunctory; temporary, short-lived, momentary, transient; *informal* quickie. ❸ *a pair of brief shorts* SKIMPY, scanty, short; revealing. ❹ *the boss was rather brief with him* BRUSQUE, abrupt, curt, short, blunt, sharp.
– OPPOSITES lengthy.
▶ noun ❶ *a barrister's brief* SUMMARY, case, argument, contention; dossier. ❷ (*informal*) *his brief's eloquence saved him. See* LAWYER. ❸ *a brief of our requirements* OUTLINE, summary, synopsis, precis, sketch, digest.
▶ verb *employees were briefed about the decision* INFORM, tell, update, notify, advise, apprise; prepare, prime, instruct; *informal* fill in, clue in, put in the picture.

briefing ▶ noun ❶ *a press briefing* CONFERENCE, meeting, interview; *N. Amer.* backgrounder. ❷ *this briefing explains the systems* INFORMATION, rundown, guidance; instructions, directions, guidelines.

briefly ▶ adverb ❶ *Henry paused briefly* MOMENTARILY, temporarily, for a moment, fleetingly. ❷ *briefly, the plot is as follows* IN SHORT, in brief, to cut a long story short, in a word, in sum, in a nutshell, in essence.

briefs ▶ plural noun UNDERPANTS, pants, knickers, Y-fronts, G-string, thong; *N. Amer.* shorts, undershorts; *informal* panties, undies, frillies; *Brit. informal* kecks, smalls.

brigade ▶ noun ❶ *a brigade of soldiers* UNIT, contingent, battalion, regiment, division, squadron, company, platoon, section, corps, troop. ❷ *the volunteer ambulance brigade* SQUAD, team, group, band, party, crew, force, outfit.

brigand ▶ noun (*poetic/literary*). *See* BANDIT.

bright ▶ adjective ❶ *the bright surface of the metal* SHINING, brilliant, dazzling, beaming, glaring; sparkling, flashing, glittering, scintillating, gleaming, glowing, luminous, radiant; shiny, lustrous, glossy. ❷ *a bright morning* SUNNY, sunshiny, cloudless, clear, fair, fine. ❸ *bright colours* VIVID, brilliant, intense, strong, bold, glowing, rich; gaudy, lurid, garish. ❹ *bright flowers* COLOURFUL, brightly-coloured, vivid, vibrant; *dated* gay. ❺ *a bright guitar sound* CLEAR, vibrant, pellucid; high-pitched. ❻ *a bright young graduate* CLEVER, intelligent, quick-witted, smart, canny, astute, intuitive, perceptive; ingenious, resourceful; gifted, brilliant; *informal* brainy. ❼ *a bright smile* HAPPY, cheerful, cheery, jolly, merry, sunny, beaming; lively, exuberant, buoyant, bubbly, bouncy, perky, chirpy; *dated* gay. ❽ *a bright future* PROMISING, rosy, optimistic, hopeful, favourable, propitious, auspicious, encouraging, good, golden.
– OPPOSITES dull, dark, stupid.
▶ adverb (*poetic/literary*) *the moon shone bright* BRIGHTLY, brilliantly, intensely.

brighten ▶ verb ❶ *sunshine brightened the room* ILLUMINATE, light up, lighten, make bright, make brighter, cast/shed light on. ❷ *you can brighten up the shadiest of corners* ENHANCE, embellish, enrich, dress up, prettify, beautify; *informal* jazz up. ❸ *Sarah brightened up as she thought of Emily's words* CHEER UP, perk up, rally; be enlivened, feel heartened, be uplifted, be encouraged, take heart; *informal* buck up, pep up.

brilliance ▶ **noun** ❶ *a philosopher of great brilliance* GENIUS, talent, ability, prowess, skill, expertise, aptitude, flair, finesse, panache; greatness, distinction; intelligence, wisdom, sagacity, intellect. ❷ *the brilliance and beauty of Paris* SPLENDOUR, magnificence, grandeur, resplendence. ❸ *the brilliance of the sunshine* BRIGHTNESS, vividness, intensity; sparkle, glitter, glittering, glow, blaze, beam, luminosity, radiance.

brilliant ▶ **adjective** ❶ *a brilliant student* GIFTED, talented, able, adept, skilful; bright, intelligent, clever, smart, astute, intellectual; elite, superior, first-class, first-rate, excellent; *informal* brainy. ❷ *his brilliant career* SUPERB, glorious, illustrious, impressive, remarkable, exceptional. ❸ (*Brit. informal*) *we had a brilliant time* EXCELLENT, marvellous, superb, very good, first-rate, first-class, wonderful, splendid; *informal* great, terrific, tremendous, fantastic, sensational, fabulous, fab, ace, cool, awesome, magic, wicked; *Brit. informal* smashing, brill; *Austral./NZ informal* bonzer. ❹ *a shaft of brilliant light* BRIGHT, shining, blazing, dazzling, vivid, intense, gleaming, glaring, luminous, radiant; *poetic/literary* irradiant, coruscating. ❺ *brilliant green* VIVID, intense, bright, bold, dazzling.
– OPPOSITES stupid, bad, dark.

brim ▶ **noun** ❶ *the brim of his hat* peak, visor, shield, shade. ❷ *the cup was filled to its brim* RIM, lip, brink, edge.
▶ **verb** ❶ *the pan was brimming with water* BE FULL (UP), be filled to the top; overflow, run over. ❷ *her eyes were brimming with tears* FILL, fill up; overflow.

brimful ▶ **adjective** FULL (UP), brimming, filled/full to the brim, filled to capacity, overfull, running over; *informal* chock-full.
– OPPOSITES empty.

brindle, brindled ▶ **adjective** TAWNY, brownish, brown; DAPPLED, streaked, mottled, speckled, flecked.

bring ▶ **verb** ❶ *he brought over a tray* CARRY, fetch, bear, take; convey, transport; move, haul, shift. ❷ *Philip brought his bride to his mansion* ESCORT, conduct, guide, lead, usher, show, shepherd. ❸ *the wind changed and brought rain* CAUSE, produce, create, generate, precipitate, lead to, give rise to, result in; stir up, whip up, promote; *poetic/literary* beget. ❹ *the police contemplated bringing charges* PUT FORWARD, prefer, lay, submit, present, initiate, institute. ❺ *this job brings him a regular salary* EARN, make, fetch, bring in, yield, net, gross, return, produce; command, attract.

■ **bring something about** ❶ *the affair that brought about her death* CAUSE, produce, give rise to, result in, lead to, occasion, bring to pass; provoke, generate, engender, precipitate; *formal* effectuate. ❷ *he brought the ship about* TURN (ROUND/AROUND), reverse, change the direction of.

■ **bring something back** ❶ *the smell brought back memories* REMIND ONE OF, put one in mind of, bring/call to mind, conjure up, evoke, summon up; take one back. ❷ *bring back capital punishment* REINTRODUCE, reinstate, re-establish, revive, resurrect.

■ **bring someone down** ❶ *he was brought down by a clumsy challenge* TRIP, knock over/down; foul. ❷ *I couldn't bear to bring her down* DEPRESS, sadden, upset, get down, dispirit, dishearten, discourage.

■ **bring something down** ❶ *we will bring down the price* DECREASE, reduce, lower, cut, drop; *informal* slash. ❷ *the unrest brought down the government* UNSEAT, overturn, topple, overthrow, depose, oust.

■ **bring something forward** PROPOSE, suggest, advance, raise, table, present, move, submit, lodge.

■ **bring someone in** INVOLVE, include, count in.

■ **bring something in** ❶ *he brought in a private member's bill* INTRODUCE, launch, inaugurate, initiate, institute. ❷ *the event brings in one million pounds each year. See* BRING sense 5.

■ **bring something off** ACHIEVE, accomplish, attain, bring about, pull off, manage, realize, complete, finish; execute, perform, discharge; *formal* effectuate.

■ **bring something on**. *See* BRING SOMETHING ABOUT sense 1.

■ **bring something out** ❶ *they were bringing out a new magazine* LAUNCH, establish, begin, start, found, set up, instigate, inaugurate, market; publish, print, issue, produce. ❷ *the shawl brings out the colour of your eyes* ACCENTUATE, highlight, emphasize, accent, set off.

■ **bring someone round** ❶ *she administered artificial respiration and brought him round* WAKE UP, return to consciousness, rouse, bring to. ❷ *we would have brought him round, given time* PERSUADE, convince, talk round, win over, sway, influence.

■ **bring oneself to** *she could not bring herself to complain* FORCE ONESELF TO, make oneself, bear to.

■ **bring someone up** REAR, raise, care for, look after, nurture, provide for.

■ **bring something up** MENTION, allude to, touch on, raise, broach, introduce; voice, air, suggest, propose, submit, put forward, bring forward, table.

brink ▶ **noun** ❶ *the brink of the abyss* EDGE, verge, margin, rim, lip; border, boundary, perimeter, periphery, limit(s). ❷ *two countries on the brink of war* VERGE, threshold, point, edge.

brio ▶ **noun** VIGOUR, vivacity, gusto, verve, zest, enthusiasm, vitality, dynamism, animation, spirit, energy; *informal* pep, vim, get-up-and-go.

brisk ▶ **adjective** ❶ *a brisk pace* QUICK, rapid, fast, swift, speedy, hurried; energetic, lively, vigorous; *informal* nippy. ❷ *the bar was doing a brisk trade* BUSY, bustling, lively, hectic; good. ❸ *his tone became brisk* NO-NONSENSE, decisive, businesslike; brusque, abrupt, short, sharp, curt, blunt, terse, gruff; *informal* snappy. ❹ *a brisk breeze* BRACING, fresh, crisp, invigorating, refreshing, stimulating, energizing; biting, keen, chilly, cold; *informal* nippy.
– OPPOSITES slow, quiet.

bristle ▶ **noun** ❶ *the bristles on his chin* HAIR, whisker; (**bristles**) stubble, five o'clock shadow; *Zoology* seta. ❷ *a hedgehog's bristles* SPINE, prickle, quill, barb.
▶ **verb** ❶ *the hair on the back of his neck bristled* RISE, stand up, stand on end; *poetic/literary* horripilate. ❷ *she bristled at his tone* BRIDLE, take offence, take umbrage, be affronted, be offended; get angry, be irritated. ❸ *the roof bristled with antennae* ABOUND, overflow, be full, be packed, be crowded, be jammed, be covered; *informal* be thick, be jam-packed, be chock-full.

bristly ▶ **adjective** ❶ *bristly little bushes* PRICKLY, spiky, thorny, scratchy, brambly. ❷ *the bristly skin of his cheek* STUBBLY, hairy, fuzzy, unshaven, whiskered, whiskery; scratchy, rough, coarse, prickly; *Zoology* hispid.
– OPPOSITES smooth.

Britain ▶ **noun** THE UNITED KINGDOM, the UK, Great Britain, the British Isles; *Brit. informal* Blighty; *poetic/literary* Albion.

brittle ▶ **adjective** ❶ *glass is a brittle material* BREAKABLE, fragile, delicate; splintery; *formal* frangible. ❷ *a brittle laugh* HARSH, hard, sharp, grating. ❸ *a brittle young woman* EDGY, nervy, anxious, unstable, highly strung, tense, excitable, jumpy, skittish, neurotic; *informal* uptight.
– OPPOSITES flexible, resilient, soft, relaxed.

broach ▶ **verb** ❶ *I broached the matter with my parents* BRING UP, raise, introduce, talk about, mention, touch on, air. ❷ *he broached a barrel of beer* PIERCE, puncture, tap; OPEN, uncork; *informal* crack open.

broad ▶ **adjective** ❶ *a broad flight of steps* WIDE. ❷ *the leaves are two inches broad* WIDE, across, in breadth, in width. ❸ *a broad expanse of prairie* EXTENSIVE, vast, immense, great, spacious, expansive, sizeable, sweeping, rolling. ❹ *a broad range of opportunities* COMPREHENSIVE, inclusive, extensive, wide, all-embracing, eclectic, unlimited. ❺ *this report gives a broad outline* GENERAL, non-specific, unspecific, rough, approximate, basic; loose, vague. ❻ *a broad hint* OBVIOUS, unsubtle, explicit, direct, plain, clear, straightforward, bald, patent, transparent, undisguised, overt. ❼ *his broad humour has been toned down* INDECENT, coarse, indelicate, ribald, risqué, racy, rude, suggestive, naughty, off colour, earthy, smutty, dirty, filthy, vulgar; *informal* blue, near the knuckle. ❽ *a broad Somerset accent* PRONOUNCED, noticeable, strong, thick. ❾ *he was attacked in broad daylight* FULL, complete, total; clear, bright.
– OPPOSITES narrow, limited, detailed, subtle.

broadcast ▶ **verb** ❶ *the show will be broadcast worldwide* TRANSMIT, relay, air, beam, show, televise, telecast, screen. ❷ *the result was broadcast far and wide* REPORT, announce, publicize, proclaim; spread, circulate, air, blazon, trumpet. ❸ *don't broadcast too much seed* SCATTER, sow, disperse, sprinkle, spread, distribute.
▶ **noun** *radio and television broadcasts* PROGRAMME, show, production, transmission, telecast, screening; *informal* prog.

broaden ▶ **verb** ❶ *her smile broadened* WIDEN, expand, stretch (out), draw out, spread; deepen. ❷ *the government tried to broaden its political base* EXPAND, enlarge, extend, widen, swell; increase, augment, add to, amplify; develop, enrich, improve, build on.

broadly ▶ **adverb** ❶ *the pattern is broadly similar for men and women* IN GENERAL, on the whole, as a rule, in the main, mainly, predominantly; loosely, roughly, approximately. ❷ *he was smiling broadly now* WIDELY, openly.

broad-minded ▶ **adjective** LIBERAL, tolerant, open-minded, free-thinking, indulgent, progressive, permissive, unshockable; unprejudiced, unbiased, unbigoted.
– OPPOSITES intolerant.

broadside ▶ **noun** ❶ (*historical*) *the gunners fired broadsides* SALVO, volley, cannonade, barrage, blast, fusillade. ❷ *a broadside against the economic reforms* CRITICISM, censure, polemic, diatribe, tirade; attack, onslaught; *poetic/literary* philippic.

brochure ▶ **noun** BOOKLET, prospectus, catalogue; pamphlet, leaflet, handbill, handout; *N. Amer.* folder.

broil ▶ **verb** (*N. Amer.*) GRILL, toast, barbecue, bake; cook.

broke ▶ **adjective** (*informal*). *See* PENNILESS.

broken ▶ **adjective** ❶ *a broken bottle* SMASHED, shattered, fragmented, splintered, crushed, snapped; in bits, in pieces; destroyed, disintegrated; cracked, split; *informal* in smithereens. ❷ *a broken arm* FRACTURED, damaged, injured. ❸ *his video's broken* DAMAGED, faulty, defective, not working, malfunctioning, in disrepair, inoperative, out of order, broken-down, down; *informal* on the blink, kaput, bust, busted, conked out, acting up, done for; *Brit. informal* knackered. ❹ *broken skin* CUT, ruptured, punctured, perforated. ❺ *a broken marriage* FAILED, ended. ❻ *broken promises* FLOUTED, violated, infringed, contravened, disregarded, ignored. ❼ *he was left a broken man* DEFEATED, beaten, subdued; DEMORALIZED, dispirited, discouraged, crushed, humbled; dishonoured, ruined. ❽ *a*

night of broken sleep INTERRUPTED, disturbed, fitful, disrupted, discontinuous, intermittent, unsettled, troubled. ❾ *he pressed on over the broken ground* UNEVEN, rough, irregular, bumpy; rutted, pitted. ❿ *she spoke in broken English* HALTING, hesitating, disjointed, faltering, imperfect.
– OPPOSITES whole, working, uninterrupted, smooth, perfect.

broken-down ▶ adjective ❶ *a broken-down hotel* DILAPIDATED, run down, ramshackle, tumbledown, in disrepair, battered, crumbling, deteriorated, gone to rack and ruin. ❷ *a broken-down car* DEFECTIVE, broken, faulty; not working, malfunctioning, inoperative, non-functioning; *informal* kaput, conked out, clapped out, done for; *Brit. informal* knackered.
– OPPOSITES smart.

broken-hearted ▶ adjective HEARTBROKEN, grief-stricken, desolate, devastated, inconsolable, miserable, depressed, melancholy, wretched, sorrowful, forlorn, heavy-hearted, woeful, doleful, downcast, woebegone, sad, down; *informal* down in the mouth; *poetic/literary* heartsick.
– OPPOSITES overjoyed.

broker ▶ noun *a top City broker* DEALER, broker-dealer, agent; middleman, intermediary, mediator; factor, liaison; stockbroker.
▶ verb *an agreement brokered by the secretariat* ARRANGE, organize, orchestrate, work out, settle, clinch, bring about; negotiate, mediate.

bronze ▶ noun *Scotland won the bronze* BRONZE MEDAL, third prize.

bronzed ▶ adjective TANNED, suntanned, tan, bronze, brown, reddish-brown.

brooch ▶ noun BREASTPIN, pin, clip, badge.

brood ▶ noun ❶ *the bird flew to feed its brood* OFFSPRING, young, progeny; family, hatch, clutch; *formal* progeniture. ❷ (*informal*) *Gill was the youngest of the brood* FAMILY; children, offspring, youngsters, progeny; *informal* kids.
▶ verb ❶ *once the eggs are laid the male broods them* INCUBATE, hatch. ❷ *he slumped in his armchair, brooding* WORRY, fret, agonize, mope, sulk; think, ponder, contemplate, meditate, muse, ruminate.

brook[1] ▶ noun *a babbling brook* STREAM, streamlet, rill, brooklet, runnel, runlet, gill; *N. English* beck; *Scottish & N. English* burn; *S. English* bourn; *N. Amer. & Austral./NZ* creek.

brook[2] ▶ verb (*formal*) *we brook no violence* TOLERATE, allow, stand, bear, abide, put up with, endure; accept, permit, countenance; *informal* stomach, stand for, hack; *Brit. informal* stick; *archaic* suffer.

brothel ▶ noun WHOREHOUSE; *N. Amer.* bordello; *Brit. informal* knocking shop; *N. Amer. informal* cathouse, creepjoint; *euphemistic* massage parlour; *Law* disorderly house; *archaic* bawdy house, house of ill fame, house of ill repute.

brother ▶ noun ❶ *she had a younger brother informal* bro. ❷ *they were brothers in crime* COLLEAGUE, associate, partner, comrade, fellow, friend; *informal* pal, chum; *Brit. informal* mate. ❸ *a brother of the Order* MONK, cleric, friar, religious, monastic.
– RELATED TERMS fraternal.

brotherhood ▶ noun ❶ *the ideals of justice and brotherhood* COMRADESHIP, fellowship, brotherliness, fraternalism, kinship; camaraderie, friendship. ❷ *a masonic brotherhood* SOCIETY, fraternity, association, alliance, union, league, guild, order, body, community, club, lodge, circle.

brotherly ▶ adjective ❶ *brotherly rivalry* FRATERNAL, sibling. ❷ *brotherly love* FRIENDLY, comradely; affectionate, amicable, kind, devoted, loyal.

brow ▶ noun ❶ *the doctor wiped his brow* FOREHEAD, temple; *Zoology* frons. ❷ *heavy black brows* EYEBROW. ❸ *the brow of the hill* SUMMIT, peak, top, crest, crown, head, pinnacle, apex.

browbeat ▶ verb BULLY, hector, intimidate, force, coerce, compel, dragoon, bludgeon, pressure, pressurize, tyrannize, terrorize, menace; harass, harry, hound; *informal* bulldoze, railroad.

brown ▶ adjective ❶ *she has brown eyes* hazel, chocolate-coloured, coffee-coloured, cocoa-coloured, nut-brown; brunette; sepia, mahogany, umber, burnt sienna; beige, buff, tan, fawn, camel, café au lait, caramel, chestnut. ❷ *his skin was brown* TANNED, suntanned, browned, bronze, bronzed; dark, swarthy, dusky. ❸ *brown bread* WHOLEMEAL.
▶ verb *the grill browns food evenly* GRILL, toast, singe, sear, crisp (up); barbecue, bake, cook.

browned off ▶ adjective (*informal*) FED UP, irritated, annoyed, irked, put out, peeved, disgruntled; disheartened, depressed; *informal* hacked off; *Brit. informal* brassed off, cheesed off, narked.

browse ▶ verb ❶ *I browsed among the little shops* LOOK AROUND/ROUND, window-shop, peruse. ❷ *she browsed through the newspaper* SCAN, skim, glance, look, peruse; thumb, leaf, flick; dip into. ❸ *three cows were browsing in the meadow* GRAZE, feed, crop; ruminate.
▶ noun *this brochure is well worth a browse* SCAN, read, skim, glance, look.

bruise ▶ noun *a bruise across her forehead* CONTUSION, lesion, mark, injury; swelling, lump, bump, welt; *Medicine* ecchymosis.
▶ verb ❶ *her face was badly bruised* CONTUSE, injure, mark, discolour. ❷ *every one of the apples is bruised* MARK, discolour, blemish; damage, spoil. ❸ *Eric's ego was bruised* UPSET, offend, insult, affront, hurt, wound, injure, crush.

brunette ▶ adjective BROWN-HAIRED, dark, dark-haired.

brunt ▶ **noun** (FULL) FORCE, impact, shock, burden, pressure, weight; effect, repercussions, consequences.

brush[1] ▶ **noun** ❶ *a dustpan and brush* BROOM, sweeper, besom, whisk. ❷ *he gave the seat a brush with his hand* CLEAN, sweep, wipe, dust. ❸ *a fox's brush* TAIL. ❹ *the brush of his lips against her cheek* TOUCH, stroke, skim, graze, nudge, contact; kiss. ❺ *a brush with the law* ENCOUNTER, clash, confrontation, conflict, altercation, incident; *informal* run-in, to-do; *Brit. informal* spot of bother.

▶ **verb** ❶ *he spent his day brushing the floors* SWEEP, clean, buff, scrub. ❷ *she brushed her hair* GROOM, comb, neaten, tidy, smooth, arrange, fix, do; curry. ❸ *she felt his lips brush her cheek* TOUCH, stroke, caress, skim, sweep, graze, contact; kiss. ❹ *she brushed a wisp of hair away* PUSH, move, sweep, clear.

■ **brush something aside** DISREGARD, ignore, dismiss, shrug off, wave aside; overlook, pay no attention to, take no notice of, neglect, forget about, turn a blind eye to; reject, spurn; laugh off, make light of, trivialize; *informal* pooh-pooh.

■ **brush someone off** REBUFF, dismiss, spurn, reject; slight, scorn, disdain; ignore, disregard, snub, cut, turn one's back on, give someone the cold shoulder, freeze out; jilt, cast aside, discard, throw over, drop, leave; *informal* knock back.

■ **brush up (on)** REVISE, read up, go over, relearn, cram, study; improve, sharpen (up), polish up; hone, refine, perfect; *informal* bone up; *Brit. informal* swot up, gen up.

brush[2] ▶ **noun** *an area covered in dense brush* UNDERGROWTH, underwood, scrub, brushwood, shrubs, bushes; *N. Amer.* underbrush, chaparral.

brush-off ▶ **noun** (*informal*) REJECTION, refusal, rebuff, repulse; snub, slight, cut; *informal* knock-back; *N. Amer. informal* kiss-off.

brusque ▶ **adjective** CURT, abrupt, blunt, short, sharp, terse, brisk, peremptory, gruff, bluff; offhand, discourteous, impolite, rude; *informal* snappy.

– OPPOSITES polite.

brutal ▶ **adjective** ❶ *a brutal attack* SAVAGE, cruel, vicious, ferocious, barbaric, barbarous, wicked, murderous, bloodthirsty, cold-blooded, callous, heartless, merciless, sadistic; heinous, monstrous, abominable, atrocious. ❷ *brutal honesty* UNSPARING, unstinting, unembellished, unvarnished, bald, naked, stark, blunt, direct, straightforward, frank, outspoken, forthright, plain-spoken; complete, total.

– OPPOSITES gentle.

brutalize ▶ **verb** ❶ *the men were brutalized by life in the trenches* DESENSITIZE, dehumanize, harden, toughen, inure. ❷ *they were brutalized by the police* ATTACK, assault, beat, batter; abuse.

brute ▶ **noun** ❶ *a callous brute* SAVAGE, beast, monster, animal, barbarian, fiend, ogre; sadist; thug, lout, ruffian; *informal* swine, pig. ❷ *the alsatian was a vicious-looking brute* ANIMAL, beast, creature; *N. Amer. informal* critter.

▶ **adjective** *brute strength* PHYSICAL, bodily; crude, violent.

bubble ▶ **noun** ❶ *the bubbles in his mineral water* globule, bead, blister; air pocket; (**bubbles**) sparkle, fizz, effervescence, froth. ❷ *a bubble of confidence* ILLUSION, delusion, fantasy, dream, chimera, castle in the air; *informal* pie in the sky.

▶ **verb** ❶ *this wine bubbled nicely on the tongue* SPARKLE, fizz, effervesce, foam, froth. ❷ *the milk was bubbling above the flame* BOIL, simmer, seethe, gurgle. ❸ *she was bubbling over with enthusiasm* OVERFLOW, brim over, be filled, gush.

bubbly ▶ **adjective** ❶ *a bubbly wine* SPARKLING, bubbling, fizzy, effervescent, gassy, aerated, carbonated; spumante, pétillant, mousseux; frothy, foamy. ❷ *she was bubbly and full of life* VIVACIOUS, animated, ebullient, lively, high-spirited, zestful; sparkling, bouncy, buoyant, carefree; merry, happy, cheerful, perky, sunny, bright; *informal* upbeat, chirpy.

– OPPOSITES still, listless.

▶ **noun** (*informal*) *a bottle of bubbly* CHAMPAGNE, sparkling wine; mousseux, spumante, cava; *informal* champers, fizz.

buccaneer ▶ **noun** (*archaic*) PIRATE, marauder, raider, freebooter, plunderer, cut-throat, privateer.

buck ▶ **verb** *it takes guts to buck the system* RESIST, oppose, defy, fight, kick against.

■ **buck up** (*informal*) CHEER UP, perk up, take heart, pick up, bounce back.

■ **buck someone up** (*informal*) CHEER UP, buoy up, ginger up, perk up, hearten, uplift, encourage, enliven, give someone a lift; *informal* pep up.

bucket ▶ **noun** ❶ *a bucket of cold water* PAIL, scuttle, can, tub. ❷ (*informal*) *everyone wept buckets* FLOODS, gallons, oceans.

▶ **verb** (*Brit. informal*) ❶ *it was bucketing down* RAIN HEAVILY, rain cats and dogs, rain hard, pour, pelt, lash, teem; *Brit.* tip. ❷ *the car came bucketing out of a side road. See* SPEED verb sense 1.

buckle ▶ **noun** *a belt buckle* CLASP, clip, catch, hasp, fastener.

▶ **verb** ❶ *he buckled the belt round his waist* FASTEN, do up, hook, strap, secure, clasp, clip. ❷ *the front axle buckled* WARP, bend, twist, curve, distort, contort, deform; bulge, arc, arch; crumple, collapse, give way.

■ **buckle down** GET (DOWN) TO WORK, set to work, get down to business; work hard, apply oneself, make an effort, be industrious, be diligent, focus; *informal* pull one's finger out; *Brit. informal* get stuck in.

bucolic ▶ **adjective** RUSTIC, rural, pastoral, country, countryside; *poetic/literary* Arcadian, sylvan, georgic.

bud ▶ noun *fresh buds* SPROUT, shoot; *Botany* plumule.
▶ verb *trees began to bud* SPROUT, shoot, germinate, swell; *dated* vegetate.

budding ▶ adjective PROMISING, up-and-coming, rising, in the making, aspiring, future, prospective, potential, fledgling, developing; *informal* would-be, wannabe.

budge ▶ verb ❶ *the horses wouldn't budge* MOVE, shift, stir, go. ❷ *I couldn't budge the door* DISLODGE, shift, move, reposition. ❸ *they refuse to budge on the issue* GIVE WAY, give in, yield, change one's mind, acquiesce, compromise, do a U-turn. ❹ *our customers won't be budged on price alone* INFLUENCE, sway, convince, persuade, induce, entice, tempt, lure, cajole, bring round.
■ **budge up/over** (*informal*) MOVE UP/OVER, shift up/over, make room, make space.

budget ▶ noun ❶ *your budget for the week* FINANCIAL PLAN, forecast; accounts, statement. ❷ *the defence budget* ALLOWANCE, allocation, quota; grant, award, funds, resources, capital.
▶ verb ❶ *we have to budget £7,000 for the work* ALLOCATE, allot, allow, earmark, designate, set aside. ❷ *budget your finances* SCHEDULE, plan, cost, estimate; ration.
▶ adjective *a budget hotel* CHEAP, inexpensive, economy, low-cost, low-price, cut-price, discount, bargain.
– OPPOSITES expensive.

buff[1] ▶ adjective *a plain buff envelope* BEIGE, yellowish, yellowish-brown, light brown, fawn, sandy, wheaten, biscuit, camel.
▶ verb *he buffed the glass* POLISH, burnish, shine, clean, rub.
■ **in the buff** (*informal*). *See* NAKED sense 1.

buff[2] ▶ noun (*informal*) *a film buff* ENTHUSIAST, fan, devotee, lover, admirer; expert, aficionado, authority, pundit; *informal* freak, nut, fanatic, addict.

buffer ▶ noun *a buffer against market fluctuations* CUSHION, bulwark, shield, barrier, guard, safeguard.
▶ verb *a massage helped to buffer the strain* CUSHION, absorb, soften, lessen, diminish, moderate, allay.
– OPPOSITES intensify.

buffet[1] ▶ noun ❶ *a sumptuous buffet* COLD TABLE, self-service meal, smorgasbord. ❷ *a station buffet* CAFE, cafeteria, snack bar, canteen, restaurant. ❸ *the plates are kept in the buffet* SIDEBOARD, cabinet, cupboard.

buffet[2] ▶ verb ❶ *rough seas buffeted the coast* BATTER, pound, lash, strike, hit. ❷ *he has been buffeted by bad publicity* AFFLICT, trouble, harm, burden, bother, beset, harass, torment, blight, bedevil.
▶ noun ❶ (*dated*) *I rained buffets on the door* BLOW, punch, thump, box, knock, rap; *informal* whack, wallop, clout. ❷ *all the buffets of this world* SHOCK, upset, setback, crisis, blow; misfortune, trouble, problem, hardship, adversity; affliction, sorrow, tribulation, tragedy, vicissitude.

buffoon ▶ noun *he regarded the chaplain as a buffoon* FOOL, idiot, dunce, ignoramus, simpleton, jackass; *informal* chump, blockhead, nincompoop, numbskull, dope, twit, nitwit, halfwit, clot, birdbrain, twerp.

bug ▶ noun ❶ *bugs were crawling everywhere* INSECT, mite; *informal* creepy-crawly, beastie. ❷ (*informal*) *a stomach bug* ILLNESS, ailment, disorder, infection, disease, sickness, complaint, upset, condition; bacterium, germ, virus; *Brit. informal* lurgy. ❸ (*informal*) *he caught the journalism bug* OBSESSION, enthusiasm, craze, fad, mania, passion, fixation. ❹ *the bug planted on his phone* LISTENING DEVICE, hidden microphone, wire, wiretap, tap. ❺ *the program developed a bug* FAULT, error, defect, flaw; virus; *informal* glitch, gremlin.
▶ verb ❶ *her conversations were bugged* RECORD, eavesdrop on, spy on, overhear; wiretap, tap, monitor. ❷ (*informal*) *she really bugs me. See* ANNOY.

bugbear ▶ noun PET HATE, bête noire, bogey; bane, irritation, vexation, anathema, thorn in one's flesh/side; nightmare, horror; *informal* peeve, pain (in the neck), hang-up; *N. Amer.* bugaboo.

build ▶ verb ❶ *a supermarket had been built* CONSTRUCT, erect, put up, assemble. ❷ *they were building a snowman* MAKE, construct, form, create, fashion, model, shape. ❸ *they are building a business strategy* ESTABLISH, found, set up, institute, inaugurate, initiate.
▶ noun *a man of slim build* PHYSIQUE, frame, body, figure, form, shape, stature, proportions; *informal* vital statistics.
■ **build something in/into** INCORPORATE IN/INTO, include in, absorb into, subsume into, assimilate into.
■ **build on** EXPAND ON, enlarge on, develop, elaborate, flesh out, embellish, amplify; refine, improve, perfect.
■ **build up** INCREASE, grow, mount up, intensify, escalate; strengthen.
■ **build something up** ❶ *he built up a huge business* ESTABLISH, set up, found, institute, start, create; develop, expand, enlarge. ❷ *he built up his stamina* BOOST, strengthen, increase, improve, augment, raise, enhance, swell; *informal* beef up. ❸ *I have built up a collection of prints* ACCUMULATE, amass, collect, gather; stockpile, hoard.

builder ▶ noun ❶ *a canal builder* DESIGNER, planner, architect, deviser, creator, maker, constructor. ❷ *the builders must finish the job in time* CONSTRUCTION WORKER, bricklayer, labourer; *Brit.* ganger; *Brit. dated* navvy.

building ▶ noun ❶ *a brick building* STRUCTURE, construction, edifice, erection, pile; property, premises, establishment. ❷ *the building of*

power stations CONSTRUCTION, erection, fabrication, assembly.
– RELATED TERMS tectonic.

build-up ▸ **noun** ❶ *the build-up of military strength* INCREASE, growth, expansion, escalation, development, proliferation. ❷ *the build-up of carbon dioxide* ACCUMULATION, accretion. ❸ *the build-up for the World Cup* PUBLICITY, promotion, advertising, marketing; *informal* hype, ballyhoo.

built-in ▸ **adjective** ❶ *a built-in cupboard* FITTED, integral, integrated, incorporated. ❷ *built-in advantages* INHERENT, intrinsic, inbuilt; essential, implicit, basic, fundamental, deep-rooted.

bulb ▸ **noun** TUBER, corm, rhizome.

bulbous ▸ **adjective** BULGING, protuberant, round, fat, rotund; swollen, tumid, distended, bloated.

bulge ▸ **noun** ❶ *a bulge in his pocket* SWELLING, bump, lump, protuberance, prominence. ❷ (*informal*) *a bulge in the population* SURGE, upsurge, rise, increase, escalation.
▸ **verb** *his eyes were bulging* SWELL, stick out, puff out, balloon (out), fill out, belly, distend; project, protrude, stand out.

bulk ▸ **noun** ❶ *the sheer bulk of the bags* SIZE, volume, dimensions, proportions, mass, scale, magnitude, immensity, vastness. ❷ *the bulk of entrants were British* MAJORITY, generality, main part, major part, lion's share, preponderance; most, almost all.
– OPPOSITES minority.
▸ **verb** *some meals are bulked out with fat* EXPAND, pad out, fill out, eke out; augment, increase.
■ **bulk large** BE IMPORTANT, loom large, dominate; be significant, be influential, be of consequence, carry weight; count, matter, signify.

bulky ▸ **adjective** ❶ *bulky items of refuse* LARGE, big, huge, sizeable, substantial, massive; king-size, outsize, oversized, considerable; CUMBERSOME, unmanageable, unwieldy, ponderous, heavy, weighty; *informal* jumbo, whopping, hulking; *Brit. informal* ginormous. ❷ *a bulky man* HEAVILY BUILT, stocky, thickset, sturdy, well built, burly, strapping, solid, heavy, hefty, meaty; stout, fat, plump, chubby, portly, rotund, round, chunky; overweight, obese, fleshy, corpulent; *informal* tubby, pudgy, roly-poly, beefy, porky, blubbery; *Brit. informal* podgy.
– OPPOSITES small, slight.

bulldoze ▸ **verb** ❶ *they plan to bulldoze the park* DEMOLISH, knock down, tear down, pull down, flatten, level, raze, clear. ❷ *he bulldozed his way through* FORCE, push, shove, barge, elbow, shoulder, jostle; plunge, crash, sweep, bundle. ❸ (*informal*) *she tends to bulldoze everyone* BULLY, hector, browbeat, intimidate, steamroller, dragoon, bludgeon, domineer, pressurize, tyrannize, strong-arm; *informal* railroad, lean on, boss.

bullet ▸ **noun** ball, shot; *informal* slug; (**bullets**) lead.

bulletin ▸ **noun** ❶ *a news bulletin* REPORT, dispatch, story, press release, newscast, flash; statement, announcement, message, communication, communiqué. ❷ *the society's monthly bulletin* NEWSLETTER, news-sheet, proceedings; newspaper, magazine, digest, gazette, review.

bullish ▸ **adjective** CONFIDENT, positive, assertive, self-assertive, assured, self-assured, bold, determined; optimistic, buoyant, sanguine; *informal* feisty, upbeat.

bully ▸ **noun** *the village bully* PERSECUTOR, oppressor, tyrant, tormentor, intimidator; tough guy, bully boy, thug.
▸ **verb** ❶ *the others bully him* PERSECUTE, oppress, tyrannize, browbeat, intimidate, strong-arm, dominate; *informal* push around/about. ❷ *she was bullied into helping* COERCE, pressure, pressurize, press, push; force, compel; badger, goad, prod, browbeat, bludgeon, intimidate, dragoon, strong-arm; *informal* bulldoze, railroad, lean on.

bulwark ▸ **noun** ❶ *ancient bulwarks* WALL, rampart, fortification, parapet, stockade, palisade, barricade, embankment, earthwork. ❷ *a bulwark of liberty* PROTECTOR, defender, protection, guard, defence, supporter, buttress; mainstay, bastion, stronghold.

bum[1] ▸ **noun** (*Brit. informal*). *See* BOTTOM noun sense 6.

bum[2] (*informal*) ▸ **noun** ❶ (*N. Amer.*) *the bums sleeping on the sidewalk. See* TRAMP noun sense 1. ❷ *you lazy bum* IDLER, loafer, good-for-nothing, ne'er-do-well, layabout, lounger, shirker; *informal* waster, loser, scrounger.
▸ **verb** ❶ *he bummed around Florida* LOAF, lounge, idle, moon, amble, wander, drift, meander, dawdle; *informal* mooch; *N. Amer. informal* lollygag. ❷ *they bummed money off him* BEG, borrow; *informal* scrounge, cadge, sponge; *Brit. informal* scab; *N. Amer. informal* mooch; *Austral./NZ informal* bludge.
▸ **adjective** *a bum deal* BAD, poor, second-rate, third-rate, second-class, unsatisfactory, inadequate, unacceptable; dreadful, awful, terrible, deplorable, lamentable; *informal* crummy, rotten, pathetic, lousy, pitiful, dire, poxy; *Brit. informal* duff, rubbish.
– OPPOSITES excellent.

bumble ▸ **verb** ❶ *they bumbled around the house* BLUNDER, lurch, stumble, stagger, lumber, flounder, totter. ❷ *the speakers bumbled* MUTTER, mumble, stumble, babble, burble, drivel, gibber.

bumbling ▸ **adjective** BLUNDERING, bungling, inept, clumsy, maladroit, awkward, muddled; oafish, clodhopping, lumbering; crude; *informal* botched, ham-fisted, cack-handed.
– OPPOSITES efficient.

bump ▸ **noun** ❶ *I landed with a bump* JOLT, crash, smash, smack, crack, bang, thud, thump; *informal* whack, thwack, bash, wallop. ❷ *I was woken by a bump* BANG, crack, boom, clang, knock, thud, thump, clunk, crash, smash; stomp, clump, clomp; *informal* whump. ❸ *a bump in the road* HUMP, lump, ridge, bulge, knob, protuberance. ❹ *a bump on his head* SWELLING, lump, bulge, injury, contusion; outgrowth, growth, carbuncle, protuberance; *Anatomy* bulla.

▸ **verb** ❶ *cars bumped into each other* HIT, crash, smash, slam, bang, knock, run, plough; ram, collide with, strike; *N. Amer.* impact. ❷ *a cart bumping along the road* BOUNCE, jolt, jerk, rattle, shake.

■ **bump into** (*informal*) MEET (BY CHANCE), encounter, run into/across, come across, chance on, happen on.

■ **bump someone off** (*informal*). *See* KILL verb sense 1.

bumper ▸ **adjective** ABUNDANT, rich, bountiful, good, fine; large, big, huge, plentiful, profuse, copious; *informal* whopping; *poetic/literary* plenteous, bounteous.

– OPPOSITES meagre.

bumpkin ▸ **noun** YOKEL, peasant, provincial, rustic, country cousin, countryman/woman; *N. Amer. informal* hayseed, hillbilly, hick; *Austral. informal* bushy; *Irish informal* culchie.

bumptious ▸ **adjective** SELF-IMPORTANT, conceited, arrogant, self-assertive, pushy, swollen-headed, pompous, overbearing, cocky, swaggering; proud, haughty, overweening, egotistical; *informal* snooty, uppity.

– OPPOSITES modest.

bumpy ▸ **adjective** ❶ *a bumpy road* UNEVEN, rough, rutted, pitted, potholed, holey; lumpy, rocky. ❷ *a bumpy ride* BOUNCY, rough, uncomfortable, jolting, lurching, jerky, jarring, boneshaking. ❸ *a bumpy start* INCONSISTENT, variable, irregular, fluctuating, intermittent, erratic, patchy; rocky, unsettled, unstable, turbulent, chaotic, full of ups and downs.

– OPPOSITES smooth.

bunch ▸ **noun** ❶ *a bunch of flowers* BOUQUET, posy, nosegay, tussie-mussie, spray, corsage; wreath, garland. ❷ *a bunch of keys* CLUSTER, clump, knot; group. ❸ (*informal*) *a great bunch of people* GROUP, set, circle, company, collection, bevy, band; *informal* gang, crowd, load. ❹ (*N. Amer. informal*) *a whole bunch of things. See* LOT pronoun.

▸ **verb** ❶ *he bunched the reins in his hand* BUNDLE, clump, cluster, group, gather; pack. ❷ *his trousers bunched around his ankles* GATHER, ruffle, pucker, fold, pleat. ❸ *the runners bunched up behind him* CLUSTER, huddle, gather, congregate, collect, amass, group, crowd.

bundle ▸ **noun** *a bundle of clothes* BUNCH, roll, clump, wad, parcel, sheaf, bale, bolt; pile, stack, heap, mass; *informal* load, wodge.

▸ **verb** ❶ *she bundled up her things* TIE, pack, parcel, wrap, roll, fold, bind, truss, bale. ❷ *she was bundled in furs* WRAP, envelop, clothe, cover, muffle, swathe, swaddle, shroud, drape, enfold. ❸ (*informal*) *he was bundled into a van* HUSTLE, manhandle, frogmarch, hurry, rush; shove, push, thrust.

bung ▸ **noun** STOPPER, plug, cork, spigot, spile, seal; *N. Amer.* stopple.

bungle ▸ **verb** MISHANDLE, mismanage, mess up, spoil, ruin; *informal* botch, muff, fluff, make a hash of, foul up, screw up; *Brit. informal* make a pig's ear of, cock up; *N. Amer. informal* flub, goof up.

bungler ▸ **noun** BLUNDERER, incompetent, amateur, bumbler, clown; *informal* botcher, butterfingers; *Brit. informal* bodger; *N. Amer. informal* jackleg.

bungling ▸ **adjective** INCOMPETENT, blundering, amateurish, inept, unskilful, clumsy, awkward, bumbling; *informal* ham-fisted, cack-handed.

bunk[1] ▸ **noun** BERTH, cot, bed.

bunk[2] (*Brit. informal*) ▸ **verb** *he bunked off school* (PLAY) TRUANT FROM, skip, avoid, shirk; *Brit. informal* skive off; *N. Amer. informal* play hookey from, goof off, cut; *Austral./NZ informal* wag.

■ **do a bunk**. *See* ABSCOND.

bunk[3] ▸ **noun** (*informal*). *See* NONSENSE sense 1.

bunkum ▸ **noun** (*informal, dated*). *See* NONSENSE sense 1.

buoy ▸ **noun** *a mooring buoy* FLOAT, marker, beacon.

▸ **verb** *the party was buoyed by an election victory* CHEER (UP), hearten, rally, invigorate, uplift, lift, encourage, stimulate, inspirit; *informal* pep up, perk up, buck up.

– OPPOSITES depress.

buoyancy ▸ **noun** ❶ *the drum's buoyancy* ABILITY TO FLOAT, lightness, floatability. ❷ *her natural buoyancy* CHEERFULNESS, happiness, lightheartedness, joy, bounce, sunniness, breeziness, jollity; liveliness, ebullience, high spirits, vivacity, vitality, verve, sparkle, zest; optimism; *informal* pep. ❸ *the buoyancy of the market* VIGOUR, strength, resilience, growth, improvement, expansion.

buoyant ▸ **adjective** ❶ *a buoyant substance* ABLE TO FLOAT, floating, floatable. ❷ *a buoyant mood* CHEERFUL, cheery, happy, light-hearted, carefree, bright, merry, joyful, bubbly, bouncy, sunny, jolly; lively, jaunty, high-spirited, perky; optimistic, confident, positive; *informal* peppy, upbeat. ❸ *sales were buoyant* BOOMING, strong, vigorous, thriving; improving, expanding, mushrooming, snowballing.

burble ▸ **verb** ❶ *the exhaust was burbling* GURGLE, bubble, murmur, purr, whirr, drone, hum, rumble. ❷ *he burbled on* PRATTLE, blather, blether, babble, gabble, prate, drivel, rattle, ramble, maunder, go on, run on; *informal* jabber, blabber, yatter, gab; *Brit. informal* rabbit, witter, waffle, chunter; *N. Amer. informal* run off at the mouth.

burden ▶ **noun** ❶ *they shouldered their burdens* LOAD, cargo, weight; pack, bundle. ❷ *a financial burden* RESPONSIBILITY, onus, charge, duty, obligation, liability; trouble, care, problem, worry, difficulty, strain, encumbrance. ❸ *the burden of his message* GIST, substance, drift, thrust, meaning, significance, essence, import, message.

▶ **verb** ❶ *he was burdened with a heavy pack* LOAD, charge, weigh down, encumber, hamper; overload, overburden. ❷ *avoid burdening them with guilt* OPPRESS, trouble, worry, harass, upset, distress; haunt, afflict, strain, stress, tax, overwhelm.

burdensome ▶ **adjective** ONEROUS, oppressive, troublesome, weighty, worrisome, stressful; vexatious, irksome, trying, difficult; arduous, strenuous, hard, laborious, exhausting, tiring, taxing, demanding, punishing, gruelling.

bureau ▶ **noun** ❶ *an oak bureau* DESK, writing table, secretaire, escritoire; *Brit.* davenport. ❷ *a marriage bureau* AGENCY, service, office, business, company, firm. ❸ *the intelligence bureau* DEPARTMENT, division, branch, section.

bureaucracy ▶ **noun** ❶ *the ranks of the bureaucracy* CIVIL SERVICE, government, administration; establishment, system, powers that be; ministries, authorities. ❷ *unnecessary bureaucracy* RED TAPE, rules and regulations, protocol, officialdom, paperwork.

bureaucrat ▶ **noun** OFFICIAL, administrator, civil servant, minister, functionary, mandarin; *Brit.* jack-in-office; *derogatory* apparatchik.

bureaucratic ▶ **adjective** ❶ *bureaucratic structure* ADMINISTRATIVE, official, governmental, ministerial, state, civic. ❷ *current practice is far too bureaucratic* RULE-BOUND, rigid, inflexible, complicated.

burgeon ▶ **verb** FLOURISH, thrive, prosper, improve; expand, escalate, swell, grow, boom, mushroom, snowball, rocket.

burglar ▶ **noun** HOUSEBREAKER, robber, cat burglar, thief, raider, looter, safe-breaker/cracker; intruder; *N. Amer. informal* yegg; *informal, dated* cracksman.

burglary ▶ **noun** ❶ *a sentence for burglary* HOUSEBREAKING, breaking and entering, theft, stealing, robbery, larceny, thievery, looting. ❷ *a series of burglaries* BREAK-IN, theft, robbery, raid; *informal* smash and grab; *N. Amer. informal* heist.

burgle ▶ **verb** ROB, loot, steal from, plunder, rifle, pillage; break into; *informal* do.

burial ▶ **noun** BURYING, interment, committal, inhumation, entombment; funeral, obsequies; *formal* exequies; *archaic* sepulture.

– RELATED TERMS funerary, sepulchral.

– OPPOSITES exhumation.

burial ground ▶ **noun** CEMETERY, graveyard, churchyard, necropolis, garden of remembrance; *Scottish* kirkyard; *N. Amer.* memorial park; *informal* boneyard; *archaic* God's acre; *historical* potter's field.

burlesque ▶ **noun** PARODY, caricature, satire, lampoon, skit; *informal* send-up, take-off, spoof.

burly ▶ **adjective** STRAPPING, well built, sturdy, brawny, strong, muscular, muscly, thickset, big, hefty, bulky, stocky, Herculean; *informal* hunky, beefy, husky, hulking.

– OPPOSITES puny.

burn ▶ **verb** ❶ *the coal was burning* BE ON FIRE, be alight, be ablaze, blaze, go up (in smoke), be in flames, be aflame; smoulder, glow. ❷ *he burned the letters* SET FIRE TO, set on fire, set alight, set light to, light, ignite, touch off; incinerate; *informal* torch. ❸ *I burned my dress with the iron* SCORCH, singe, sear, char, blacken, brand; scald. ❹ *her face burned* BE HOT, be warm, be feverish, be on fire; blush, redden, go red, flush, colour. ❺ *she was burning with curiosity* BE CONSUMED, be eaten up, be obsessed, be tormented, be beside oneself. ❻ *Meredith burned to know the secret* YEARN, long, ache, desire, want, wish, hanker, crave, hunger, thirst; *informal* have a yen, yen, itch, be dying. ❼ *the energy they burn up* CONSUME, use up, expend, get/go through, eat up; dissipate.

burning ▶ **adjective** ❶ *burning coals* BLAZING, flaming, fiery, ignited, glowing, red-hot, smouldering; raging, roaring. ❷ *burning desert sands* EXTREMELY HOT, red-hot, fiery, blistering, scorching, searing, sweltering, torrid; *informal* baking, boiling (hot), roasting, sizzling. ❸ *a burning desire* INTENSE, passionate, deep-seated, profound, wholehearted, strong, ardent, fervent, urgent, fierce, eager, frantic, consuming, uncontrollable. ❹ *burning issues* IMPORTANT, crucial, significant, vital, essential, pivotal; urgent, pressing, compelling, critical.

burnish ▶ **verb** POLISH (UP), shine, buff (up), rub (up).

burp (*informal*) ▶ **verb** BELCH, bring up wind; *Scottish & N. English informal* rift.

▶ **noun** BELCH; wind; *Scottish & N. English informal* rift; *formal* eructation.

burrow ▶ **noun** *a rabbits' burrow* WARREN, tunnel, hole, dugout; lair, set, den, earth.

▶ **verb** *the mouse burrows a hole* TUNNEL, dig (out), excavate, grub, mine, bore, channel; hollow out, gouge out.

burst ▶ **verb** ❶ *one balloon burst* SPLIT (OPEN), rupture, break, tear. ❷ *a shell burst* EXPLODE, blow up, detonate, go off. ❸ *smoke burst through the hole* BREAK, erupt, surge, gush, rush, stream, flow, pour, spill; spout, spurt, jet, spew. ❹ *he burst into the room* PLUNGE, charge, barge, plough, hurtle, career, rush, dash, tear. ❺ *she burst into tears* BREAK OUT IN, erupt in, have a fit of.

▶ **noun** ❶ *a burst in the tyre* RUPTURE, puncture, breach, split, blowout. ❷ *mortar bursts* EXPLOSION, detonation, blast, eruption, bang. ❸ *a burst of gunfire* VOLLEY, salvo, fusillade, barrage, discharge; hail, rain. ❹ *a burst of activity* OUTBREAK, eruption, flare-up, blaze, attack, fit, rush, gale, storm, surge, upsurge, spurt; *informal* splurt.

■ **burst out** ❶ *'I don't care!' she burst out* EXCLAIM, blurt, cry, shout, yell; *dated* ejaculate. ❷ *he burst out crying* SUDDENLY START.

bury ▶ **verb** ❶ *the dead were buried* INTER, lay to rest, entomb; *informal* put six feet under, plant; *poetic/literary* inhume. ❷ *she buried her face in her hands* HIDE, conceal, cover, enfold, engulf, tuck, cup, sink. ❸ *the bullet buried itself in the wood* EMBED, sink, implant, submerge; drive into. ❹ *he buried himself in his work* ABSORB, engross, immerse, occupy, engage, busy, involve.

– OPPOSITES exhume.

bush ▶ **noun** ❶ *a rose bush* SHRUB; (**bushes**) undergrowth, shrubbery. ❷ *the bush* WILDS, wilderness; backwoods, hinterland(s); *N. Amer.* backcountry, backland(s); *Austral./NZ* outback, backblocks, booay; *N. Amer. informal* boondocks, tall timbers; *Austral./NZ informal* Woop Woop, beyond the black stump.

bushy ▶ **adjective** THICK, shaggy, fuzzy, bristly, fluffy, woolly; luxuriant; *informal* jungly.

– OPPOSITES sleek, wispy.

busily ▶ **adverb** ACTIVELY, energetically, vigorously, enthusiastically; industriously, purposefully, diligently.

business ▶ **noun** ❶ *she has to smile in her business* WORK, line of work, occupation, profession, career, employment, job, position; vocation, calling; field, sphere, trade, craft; *informal* racket, game; *archaic* employ. ❷ *who do you do business with?* TRADE, trading, commerce, dealing, traffic, merchandising; dealings, transactions, negotiations. ❸ *her own business* FIRM, company, concern, enterprise, venture, organization, operation, undertaking; office, agency, franchise, practice; *informal* outfit, set-up. ❹ *none of your business* CONCERN, affair, responsibility, duty, function, obligation; problem, worry; *informal* pigeon, bailiwick; *Brit. informal* lookout. ❺ *an odd business* AFFAIR, matter, thing, case, circumstance, situation, event, incident, happening, occurrence; episode.

– RELATED TERMS corporate.

businesslike ▶ **adjective** PROFESSIONAL, efficient, slick, competent, methodical, disciplined, systematic, orderly, organized, structured, practical, pragmatic.

businessman, businesswoman ▶ **noun** ENTREPRENEUR, business person, industrialist, manufacturer, tycoon, magnate, employer; dealer, trader, broker, merchant, buyer, seller, marketeer, merchandiser, vendor, tradesman, retailer, supplier.

bust[1] ▶ **noun** ❶ *her large bust* CHEST, bosom; breasts, mammary glands, mammae; *informal* boobs, knockers, bubbies; *Brit. informal* bristols, charlies; *N. Amer. informal* bazooms. ❷ *a bust of Caesar* SCULPTURE, carving, effigy, statue; head and shoulders.

bust[2] (*informal*) ▶ **verb** ❶ *the lock has bust* BREAK, crack, snap, smash, fracture, shatter, disintegrate; split, burst. ❷ *he promised to bust the mafia* OVERTHROW, destroy, topple, bring down, ruin, break, overturn, overcome, defeat, get rid of, oust, dislodge. ❸ *they were busted for drugs. See* ARREST verb sense 1. ❹ (*N. Amer.*) *my apartment got busted. See* RAID verb sense 3.

■ **go bust** FAIL, collapse, fold, go under, founder; go bankrupt, go into receivership, go into liquidation, be wound up; *informal* crash, go broke, go to the wall, go belly up, flop.

bustle ▶ **verb** ❶ *people bustled about* RUSH, dash, hurry, scurry, scuttle, scamper, scramble; run, tear, charge; *informal* scoot, beetle, buzz, zoom. ❷ *she bustled us into the kitchen* HUSTLE, bundle, sweep, push, whisk.

▶ **noun** *the bustle of the market* ACTIVITY, action, liveliness, hustle and bustle, excitement; tumult, hubbub, whirl; *informal* toing and froing, comings and goings.

bustling ▶ **adjective** BUSY, crowded, swarming, teeming, thronged; buzzing, hectic, lively.

– OPPOSITES deserted.

busy ▶ **adjective** ❶ *they are busy raising money* OCCUPIED (IN), engaged in, involved in, employed in, working at, hard at work (on); rushed off one's feet, hard-pressed; on the job, absorbed, engrossed, immersed, preoccupied; *informal* (as) busy as a bee, on the go, hard at it; *Brit. informal* on the hop. ❷ *she is busy at the moment* UNAVAILABLE, engaged, occupied; working, in a meeting, on duty; *informal* tied up. ❸ *a busy day* HECTIC, active, lively, full, eventful; energetic, tiring. ❹ *the town was busy* CROWDED, bustling, hectic, swarming, teeming, full, thronged. ❺ *a busy design* ORNATE, over-elaborate, overblown, overwrought, overdone, fussy, cluttered, overworked.

– OPPOSITES idle, free, quiet.

▶ **verb** *he busied himself with paperwork* OCCUPY, involve, engage, concern, absorb, engross, immerse, preoccupy; distract, divert.

busybody ▶ **noun** MEDDLER, interferer, mischief-maker, troublemaker; gossip, scandalmonger; eavesdropper, gawker; *informal* nosy parker, snoop, snooper, rubberneck; *Brit. informal* gawper; *informal, dated* Paul Pry.

but ▶ **conjunction** ❶ *he stumbled but didn't fall* YET, nevertheless, nonetheless, even so, however, still, notwithstanding, despite that, in spite of that, for all that, all the same, just the same; though, although. ❷ *I am clean but you aren't* WHEREAS, conversely, but then, then again, on the other hand, by/in contrast, on the contrary. ❸ *one cannot but sympathize* (DO) OTHER THAN, (do) otherwise than; except.

▶ **preposition** *everyone but him* EXCEPT (FOR), apart from, other than, besides, aside from, with the exception of, bar, excepting, excluding, leaving out, save (for), saving.

▶ **adverb** *he is but a shadow of his former self* ONLY, just, simply, merely, no more than, nothing but; a mere; *N. English* nobbut.

■ **but for** EXCEPT FOR, if it were not for, were it not for, barring, notwithstanding.

butch ▶ **adjective** (*informal*) MASCULINE, manly; mannish, manlike, unfeminine, unladylike; *informal* macho.
– OPPOSITES effeminate.

butcher ▶ **noun** ❶ *a butcher's shop* MEAT SELLER, meat trader; slaughterer; *Scottish* flesher. ❷ *a Nazi butcher* MURDERER, slaughterer, killer, assassin; *N. Amer.* terminator; *poetic/literary* slayer; *dated* cut-throat, homicide.

▶ **verb** ❶ *the goat was butchered* SLAUGHTER, cut up, carve up, joint. ❷ *they butchered 150 people* MASSACRE, murder, slaughter, kill, dispose of, destroy, exterminate, assassinate; *N. Amer.* terminate; *poetic/literary* slay. ❸ *the studio butchered the film* SPOIL, ruin, mutilate, mangle, mess up, wreck; *informal* make a hash of, screw up.

butchery ▶ **noun** ❶ *the butchery trade* MEAT SELLING. ❷ (*Brit.*) *the cattle went to the butchery* ABATTOIR, slaughterhouse. ❸ (*Brit.*) *a butchery* BUTCHER'S (SHOP), meat market, meat counter. ❹ *the butchery in the war* SLAUGHTER, massacre, mass murder; *poetic/literary* slaying.

butt[1] ▶ **verb** *she butted him* RAM, headbutt, bunt; bump, buffet, push, shove; *N. English* tup.

■ **butt in** INTERRUPT, break in, cut in, chime in, interject, intervene, interfere; *informal* poke one's nose in, put one's oar in; *Brit. informal* chip in.

butt[2] ▶ **noun** *the butt of a joke* TARGET, victim, object, subject; laughing stock.

butt[3] ▶ **noun** ❶ *the butt of a gun* STOCK, end, handle, hilt, haft, helve. ❷ *a cigarette butt* STUB, end, tail end, stump, remnant; *informal* fag end, dog end. ❸ (*N. Amer. informal*) *sitting on his butt. See* BOTTOM noun sense 6.

▶ **verb** *the shop butts up against the house* ADJOIN, abut, be next to, be adjacent to, border (on), neighbour, be connected to; join, touch.

butt[4] ▶ **noun** *a brandy butt* BARREL, cask, keg, vat, tun; tub, bin, drum, canister.

butter

■ **butter someone up** (*informal*) FLATTER, court, wheedle, persuade, blarney, coax, get round, prevail on; be obsequious towards, be sycophantic towards, toady to, fawn on, make up to, play up to, ingratiate oneself with, rub up the right way, curry favour with; *informal* suck up to, be all over, keep someone sweet, sweet-talk, soft-soap.

butterfly ▶ **noun** LEPIDOPTERAN.

buttocks ▶ **plural noun** CHEEKS; rear (end), rump, backside, seat; *Brit.* bottom; *informal* behind, BTM, sit-upon, derrière; *Brit. informal* bum, botty, jacksie; *N. Amer. informal* butt, fanny, tush, tail, buns, booty, heinie; *humorous* fundament, posterior, stern; *Anatomy* nates.

button ▶ **noun** ❶ *shirt buttons* FASTENER, stud, toggle; hook, catch, clasp. ❷ *press the button* SWITCH, knob, control; lever, handle.

buttonhole ▶ **verb** (*informal*). *See* ACCOST.

buttress ▶ **noun** ❶ *stone buttresses* PROP, support, abutment, shore, pier, reinforcement, stanchion. ❷ *a buttress against social collapse* SAFEGUARD, defence, protection, guard; support, prop; bulwark.

▶ **verb** *authority was buttressed by religion* STRENGTHEN, reinforce, fortify, support, bolster, shore up, underpin, cement, uphold, defend, back up.

buxom ▶ **adjective** LARGE-BREASTED, big-breasted, bosomy, big-bosomed; shapely, ample, plump, rounded, full-figured, voluptuous, curvaceous, Rubenesque; *informal* busty, chesty, well endowed, curvy.

buy ▶ **verb** ❶ *they bought a new house* PURCHASE, acquire, obtain, get, pick up, snap up; take, procure, pay for; invest in; *informal* get hold of, score. ❷ *he could not be bought* BRIBE, buy off, suborn, corrupt; *informal* grease someone's palm, give a backhander to, get at, fix, square; *Brit. informal* nobble.
– OPPOSITES sell.

▶ **noun** (*informal*) *a good buy* PURCHASE, investment, acquisition, gain; deal, bargain.

buyer ▶ **noun** PURCHASER, customer, consumer, shopper, investor; (**buyers**) clientele, patronage, market; *Law* vendee.

buzz ▶ **noun** ❶ *the buzz of the bees* HUM, humming, buzzing, murmur, drone; *Brit. informal* zizz. ❷ *an insistent buzz from her control panel* WARNING SOUND, purr, ring, note, tone, beep, bleep, warble, alarm. ❸ (*informal*) *give me a buzz. See* CALL noun sense 3. ❹ (*informal*) *the buzz is that he's gone. See* RUMOUR. ❺ (*informal*) *get a buzz out of flying* THRILL, stimulation, glow, tingle; *informal* kick; *N. Amer. informal* charge.

▶ **verb** ❶ *bees buzzed* HUM, drone, bumble, murmur; *Brit. informal* zizz. ❷ *the intercom soon buzzed* PURR, warble, sound, ring, beep, bleep. ❸ (*informal*) *he buzzed around* BUSTLE, scurry, scuttle, hurry, rush, race, dash, tear, chase; *informal* scoot, beetle, whizz, zoom, zip. ❹ *the club is buzzing with excitement* HUM, throb, vibrate, pulse, bustle.

by ▶ **preposition** ❶ *I broke it by forcing the lid* THROUGH, as a result of, because of, by dint of, by way of, via, by means of; with the help of, with the aid of, by virtue of. ❷ *be there by midday* NO LATER THAN, in good time for, at, before. ❸ *a house by the lake* NEXT TO, beside, alongside, by/at the side of, adjacent to, side by side with; near, close to, neighbouring, adjoining, bordering, overlooking; connected to, contiguous with, attached to. ❹ *go by the building* PAST, in front of, beyond. ❺ *all right by me* ACCORDING TO, with, as far as —— is concerned.

▶ **adverb** *people hurried by* PAST, on, along.

■ **by and by** EVENTUALLY, ultimately, finally, in the end, one day, some day, sooner or later, in time, in a while, in the long run, in the fullness of time, in time to come, at length, in the future, in due course.

■ **by oneself** ALONE, on one's own, singly, separately, solitarily, unaccompanied, companionless, unattended, unescorted, solo; unaided, unassisted, without help, by one's own efforts, under one's own steam, independently, single-handed(ly), off one's own bat, on one's own initiative; *informal* by one's lonesome; *Brit. informal* on one's tod, on one's Jack Jones.

bygone ▶ **adjective** PAST, former, olden, earlier, previous, one-time, long-ago, of old, ancient, antiquated; departed, dead, extinct, defunct, out of date, outmoded; *poetic/literary* of yore.

– OPPOSITES present, recent.

by-law ▶ **noun** (*Brit.*) LOCAL LAW, regulation, rule.

bypass ▶ **noun** RING ROAD, detour, diversion, alternative route; *Brit.* relief road.

▶ **verb** ❶ *bypass the farm* GO ROUND, go past, make a detour round; avoid. ❷ *an attempt to bypass the problem* AVOID, evade, dodge, escape, elude, circumvent, get round, skirt, sidestep, steer clear of; *informal* duck. ❸ *they bypassed the regulations* IGNORE, pass over, omit, neglect, go over the head of; *informal* short-circuit.

by-product ▶ **noun** SIDE EFFECT, consequence, entailment, corollary; ramification, repercussion, spin-off, fallout; fruits; *Brit.* knock-on effect.

bystander ▶ **noun** ONLOOKER, looker-on, passer-by, non-participant, observer, spectator, eyewitness, witness, watcher; *informal* gawper, rubberneck.

byword ▶ **noun** ❶ *the office was a byword for delay* PERFECT EXAMPLE, classic case, model, exemplar, embodiment, incarnation, personification, epitome, typification. ❷ *reality was his byword* SLOGAN, motto, maxim, mantra, catchword, watchword, formula; middle name.

Cc

cab ▶ **noun** ❶ *she hailed a cab* TAXI, taxi cab; *Brit* minicab, hackney carriage; *N. Amer.* hack; *historical* fiacre. ❷ *a truck driver's cab* (DRIVER'S) COMPARTMENT, cabin.

cabal ▶ **noun** CLIQUE, faction, coterie, cell, sect, camarilla; pressure group; *Brit.* ginger group.

cabaret ▶ **noun** ❶ *the evening's cabaret* ENTERTAINMENT, (floor) show, performance. ❷ *the cabarets of Montreal* NIGHTCLUB, club, boîte; *N. Amer.* cafe; *informal* nightspot, niterie, clip joint; *N. Amer. informal* honky-tonk.

cabin ▶ **noun** ❶ *a first-class cabin* BERTH, stateroom, deckhouse; *historical* roundhouse. ❷ *a cabin by the lake* HUT, log cabin, shanty, shack; chalet; *Scottish* bothy; *N. Amer.* cabana; *Austral.* mia-mia; *archaic* cot; *N. Amer. archaic* shebang. ❸ *the driver's cabin* CAB, compartment.

cabinet ▶ **noun** ❶ *a walnut cabinet* CUPBOARD, bureau, chest of drawers. ❷ *the new cabinet* SENIOR MINISTERS, ministry, council, executive.

cable ▶ **noun** ❶ *a thick cable moored the ship* ROPE, cord, line, guy; *Nautical* hawser, stay, bridle, topping lift; *N. Amer.* choker. ❷ *electric cables* WIRE, lead; power line; *Brit.* flex. ❸ (*historical*) *he immediately sent a cable* TELEGRAM, telemessage, radiogram; *informal* wire; *historical* cablegram.

▶ **verb** *the secretariat cabled a reply* RADIO, send, transmit; *informal* wire.

cache ▶ **noun** ❶ *a cache of arms* HOARD, store, stockpile, stock, supply, reserve; arsenal; *informal* stash. ❷ *a niche used as a cache* HIDING PLACE, secret place; *informal* hidey-hole; *informal, dated* stash.

cachet ▶ **noun** PRESTIGE, prestigiousness, status, standing, kudos, snob value, stature, pre-eminence, eminence; street credibility.

cackle ▶ **verb** ❶ *the geese cackled at him* SQUAWK, cluck. ❷ *Noel cackled with glee* LAUGH LOUDLY, guffaw, crow, chortle, chuckle.

cacophonous ▶ **adjective** LOUD, noisy, ear-splitting, raucous, discordant, dissonant, inharmonious, unmelodious, unmusical, tuneless; *archaic* absonant.

– OPPOSITES harmonious.

cacophony ▶ **noun** DIN, racket, noise, discord, dissonance, discordance.

cad ▶ **noun** (*dated*). *See* SCOUNDREL.

cadaver ▶ **noun** (*Medicine*) CORPSE, (dead) body, remains, carcass; *informal* stiff; *archaic* corse.

cadaverous ▶ **adjective** (DEATHLY) PALE, pallid, ashen, grey, whey-faced, etiolated, corpse-like; as thin as a rake, bony, skeletal, emaciated, skin-and-bones, haggard, gaunt, drawn, pinched, hollow-cheeked, hollow-eyed; *informal* like a bag of bones, anorexic; *archaic* starveling.
– OPPOSITES rosy, plump.

cadence ▶ **noun** RHYTHM, tempo, metre, beat, pulse; intonation, modulation, lilt.

cadge ▶ **verb** (*informal*) SCROUNGE, borrow; *informal* bum, touch someone for, sponge; *Brit. informal* scab; *N. Amer. informal* mooch; *Austral./NZ informal* bludge.

cadre ▶ **noun** CORPS, body, team, group.

cafe ▶ **noun** SNACK BAR, cafeteria, buffet; coffee bar/shop, tea room/shop; bistro, brasserie; *N. Amer.* diner; *informal* eatery, noshery; *Brit. informal* caff.

cafeteria ▶ **noun** SELF-SERVICE RESTAURANT, canteen, cafe, buffet.

cage ▶ **noun** *animals in cages* ENCLOSURE, pen, pound; coop, hutch; birdcage, aviary; *N. Amer.* corral.
▶ **verb** *many animals are caged* CONFINE, shut in/up, pen, coop up, immure, impound; *N. Amer.* corral.

cagey ▶ **adjective** (*informal*) SECRETIVE, guarded, non-committal, tight-lipped, reticent, evasive; *informal* playing one's cards close to one's chest.
– OPPOSITES open.

cahoots
■ **in cahoots** (*informal*) IN LEAGUE, colluding, in collusion, conspiring, collaborating, hand in glove.

cajole ▶ **verb** PERSUADE, wheedle, coax, talk into, prevail on, blarney; *informal* sweet-talk, soft-soap, twist someone's arm; *archaic* blandish.

cajolery ▶ **noun** PERSUASION, wheedling, coaxing, inveiglement, cajolement; blandishments, blarney; *informal* sweet talk, soft soap, arm-twisting; *formal* suasion.

cake ▶ **noun** ❶ *cream cakes* BUN, pastry, gateau. ❷ *a cake of soap* BAR, tablet, block, slab, lump.
▶ **verb** ❶ *boots caked with mud* COAT, encrust, plaster, cover. ❷ *the blood was beginning to cake* CLOT, congeal, coagulate, solidify, set, inspissate.

calamitous ▶ **adjective** DISASTROUS, catastrophic, cataclysmic, devastating, dire, tragic; *poetic/literary* direful.

calamity ▶ **noun** DISASTER, catastrophe, tragedy, cataclysm, adversity, tribulation, affliction, misfortune, misadventure.
– OPPOSITES godsend.

calculate ▶ **verb** ❶ *the interest is calculated on a daily basis* COMPUTE, work out, reckon, figure; add up/together, count up, tally, total; *Brit.* tot up. ❷ *his words were calculated to wound her* INTEND, mean, design. ❸ *we had calculated on a quiet Sunday* EXPECT, anticipate, reckon, bargain; *N. Amer. informal* figure on.

calculated ▶ **adjective** DELIBERATE, premeditated, planned, pre-planned, preconceived, intentional, intended; *Law, dated* prepense.
– OPPOSITES unintentional.

calculating ▶ **adjective** CUNNING, crafty, wily, shrewd, scheming, devious, designing, Machiavellian; *informal* foxy; *archaic* subtle.
– OPPOSITES ingenuous.

calculation ▶ **noun** ❶ *the calculation of the overall cost* COMPUTATION, reckoning, adding up, counting up, working out, figuring; *Brit.* totting up. ❷ *political calculations* ASSESSMENT, judgement; forecast, projection, prediction.

calendar ▶ **noun** ❶ ALMANAC. ❷ *my social calendar* SCHEDULE, programme, diary.

calibre ▶ **noun** ❶ *a man of his calibre* QUALITY, merit, distinction, stature, excellence, pre-eminence; ability, expertise, talent, capability, capacity, proficiency. ❷ *rugby of this calibre* STANDARD, level, quality. ❸ *the calibre of a gun* BORE, diameter, gauge.

call ▶ **verb** ❶ *'Wait for me!' she called* CRY (OUT), shout, yell, bellow, roar, bawl, scream, vociferate; *informal* holler. ❷ *Mum called me in the morning* WAKE (UP), awaken, rouse; *Brit. informal* knock up; *poetic/literary* waken. ❸ *I'll call you tomorrow* PHONE, telephone, get someone on the phone, give someone a call; *Brit.* ring (up), give someone a ring; *informal* call up, give someone a buzz; *Brit. informal* give someone a bell/tinkle, get someone on the blower; *N. Amer. informal* get someone on the horn. ❹ *Rose called a taxi* SUMMON, send for, order. ❺ *he called at Ashgrove Cottage* PAY A (BRIEF) VISIT TO, visit, pay a call on, call/drop/look in on, drop/stop by, pop into. ❻ *the prime minister called a meeting* CONVENE, summon, assemble; *formal* convoke. ❼ *they called their daughter Hannah* NAME, christen, baptize; designate, style, term, dub; *formal* denominate. ❽ *I would call him a friend* DESCRIBE AS, regard as, look on as, consider to be.
▶ **noun** ❶ *I heard calls from the auditorium* CRY, shout, yell, roar, scream, exclamation, vociferation; *informal* holler. ❷ *the call of the water rail* CRY, song, sound. ❸ *I'll give you a call tomorrow* PHONE CALL, telephone call; *Brit.* ring; *informal* buzz; *Brit. informal* bell, tinkle. ❹ *he paid a call on Harold* VISIT, social call. ❺ *a call for party unity* APPEAL, request, plea, entreaty. ❻ *the last call for passengers on flight BA701* SUMMONS, request. ❼ *there's no call for that kind of language*

NEED, necessity, reason, justification, excuse. ❸ *there's no call for expensive wine here* DEMAND, desire, market. ❾ *the call of the Cairngorms* ATTRACTION, appeal, lure, allure, spell, pull, draw.

■ **call for** ❶ *desperate times call for desperate measures* REQUIRE, need, necessitate; justify, warrant. ❷ *I'll call for you around seven* PICK UP, collect, fetch.

■ **call something off** CANCEL, abandon, scrap, drop, axe; *informal* scrub, nix; *N. Amer. informal* redline.

■ **call on** ❶ *I might call on her later* VISIT, pay a call on, go and see, look/drop in on; *N. Amer.* visit with; *informal* look up, pop in on. ❷ *he called on the government to hold a plebiscite* APPEAL TO, ask, request, petition, urge. ❸ *we are able to call on qualified staff* HAVE RECOURSE TO, avail oneself of, draw on, make use of.

■ **call the shots** BE IN CHARGE, be in control, be at the helm/wheel, be in the driving seat, pull the strings; *informal* run the show, be the boss.

■ **call to mind** ❶ *this calls to mind Cézanne's works* EVOKE, bring to mind, call up, conjure up. ❷ *I cannot call to mind where I have seen you* REMEMBER, recall, recollect.

■ **call someone up** ❶ (*informal*) *Roland called me up. See* CALL verb sense 3. ❷ *they called up the reservists* ENLIST, recruit, conscript; *US* draft. ❸ *he was called up for the England team* SELECT, pick, choose; *Brit.* cap.

■ **on call** ON DUTY, on standby, available.

call girl ▶ **noun** PROSTITUTE, whore, sex worker, fille de joie; *informal* tart, pro, working girl; *N. Amer. informal* hooker, hustler; *euphemistic* escort, masseuse; *dated* woman of the streets; *archaic* strumpet, harlot, trollop.

calling ▶ **noun** PROFESSION, occupation, vocation, career, work, employment, job, business, trade, craft, line (of work); *archaic* employ.

callous ▶ **adjective** HEARTLESS, unfeeling, uncaring, cold, cold-hearted, hard, as hard as nails, hard-hearted, stony-hearted, insensitive, lacking compassion, hardbitten, unsympathetic.
– OPPOSITES kind, compassionate.

callow ▶ **adjective** IMMATURE, inexperienced, juvenile, adolescent, naive, green, raw, untried, unworldly, unsophisticated; *informal* wet behind the ears.
– OPPOSITES mature.

calm ▶ **adjective** ❶ *she seemed very calm* SERENE, tranquil, relaxed, unruffled, unperturbed, unflustered, untroubled; equable, even-tempered; placid, unexcitable, unemotional, phlegmatic; composed, {cool, calm, and collected}, cool-headed, self-possessed; *informal* unflappable, unfazed. ❷ *the night was calm* WINDLESS, still, tranquil, quiet. ❸ *the calm waters of the lake* TRANQUIL, still, smooth, glassy, like a millpond; *poetic/literary* stilly.
– OPPOSITES excited, nervous, stormy.
▶ **noun** ❶ *calm prevailed* TRANQUILLITY, stillness, calmness, quiet, quietness, quietude, peace, peacefulness. ❷ *his usual calm deserted him* COMPOSURE, coolness, calmness, self-possession, sangfroid; serenity, tranquillity, equanimity, equability, placidness, placidity; *informal* cool, unflappability.
▶ **verb** ❶ *I tried to calm him down* SOOTHE, pacify, placate, mollify, appease, conciliate; *Brit.* quieten (down); *Austral.* square off; *poetic/literary* dulcify. ❷ *she forced herself to calm down* COMPOSE ONESELF, recover/regain one's composure, control oneself, pull oneself together, simmer down, cool down/off, take it easy; *Brit.* quieten down; *informal* get a grip, keep one's shirt on, wind down; *N. Amer. informal* chill out, hang/stay loose, decompress.
– OPPOSITES excite, upset.

calumny ▶ **noun** SLANDER, defamation (of character), character assassination, calumniation, libel; vilification, traducement, obloquy, verbal abuse, revilement, scurrility; *informal* mud-slinging; *archaic* contumely.

camaraderie ▶ **noun** FRIENDSHIP, comradeship, fellowship, companionship; mutual support, team spirit, esprit de corps.

camouflage ▶ **noun** ❶ *pieces of turf served for camouflage* DISGUISE, concealment. ❷ *her indifference was merely camouflage* FACADE, (false) front, smokescreen, cover-up, mask, blind, screen, masquerade, dissimulation, pretence.
▶ **verb** *the caravan was camouflaged with branches* DISGUISE, hide, conceal, keep hidden, mask, screen, cover (up).

camp[1] ▶ **noun** ❶ *an army camp* BIVOUAC, encampment; campsite, camping ground. ❷ *the liberal and conservative camps* FACTION, wing, group, lobby, caucus, bloc, coterie, sect, cabal.
▶ **verb** *they camped in a field* PITCH TENTS, set up camp, encamp, bivouac.

camp[2] (*informal*) ▶ **adjective** ❶ *a highly camp actor* EFFEMINATE, effete, mincing; *informal* campy, limp-wristed; *Brit. informal* poncey. ❷ *camp humour* EXAGGERATED, theatrical, affected; *informal* over the top, OTT, camped up.
– OPPOSITES macho.

■ **camp it up** POSTURE, behave theatrically/affectedly, overact; *informal* ham it up.

campaign ▶ **noun** ❶ *Napoleon's Russian campaign* MILITARY OPERATION(S), manoeuvre(s); crusade, war, battle, offensive, attack. ❷ *the campaign to reduce vehicle emissions* CRUSADE, drive, push, struggle; operation, strategy, battle plan.
▶ **verb** ❶ *they are campaigning for political reform* CRUSADE, fight, battle, push, press, strive, struggle, lobby. ❷ *she campaigned as a political outsider*

RUN/STAND FOR OFFICE, canvass, electioneer; *N. Amer.* stump.

campaigner ▶ noun CRUSADER, fighter, activist; champion, advocate, promoter.

can ▶ noun TIN, canister; jerrycan, oilcan.

canal ▶ noun ❶ *barges chugged up the canal* INLAND WATERWAY, watercourse. ❷ *the ear canal* DUCT, tube, passage.

cancel ▶ verb ❶ *the match was cancelled* CALL OFF, abandon, scrap, drop, axe; *informal* scrub, nix; *N. Amer. informal* redline. ❷ *his visa has been cancelled* ANNUL, invalidate, nullify, declare null and void, void; revoke, rescind, retract, countermand, withdraw; *Law* vacate, discharge. ❸ *rising unemployment cancelled out earlier economic gains* NEUTRALIZE, counterbalance, counteract, balance (out), countervail; negate, nullify, wipe out, negative.

cancer ▶ noun ❶ *most skin cancers are curable* MALIGNANT GROWTH, cancerous growth, tumour, malignancy; *technical* carcinoma, sarcoma, melanoma, lymphoma, myeloma. ❷ *racism is a cancer* EVIL, blight, scourge, poison, canker, plague; *archaic* pestilence.
– RELATED TERMS carcinomatous, carcin-.

candid ▶ adjective ❶ *his responses were remarkably candid* FRANK, outspoken, forthright, blunt, open, honest, truthful, sincere, direct, plain-spoken, bluff; *informal* upfront, on the level; *N. Amer. informal* on the up and up; *archaic* round, free-spoken. ❷ *candid shots* UNPOSED, informal, uncontrived, impromptu, natural.
– OPPOSITES guarded.

candidate ▶ noun ❶ *candidates should be computer-literate* (JOB) APPLICANT, job-seeker, interviewee; contender, nominee, possible; *Brit. informal* runner. ❷ *A-level candidates* EXAMINEE, entrant.

candour ▶ noun FRANKNESS, openness, honesty, candidness, truthfulness, sincerity, forthrightness, directness, plain-spokenness, bluffness, bluntness, outspokenness; *informal* telling it like it is.

candy ▶ noun (*N. Amer.*). *See* CONFECTIONERY.

cane ▶ noun ❶ *a silver-topped cane* (WALKING) STICK, staff; alpenstock; crook; *Austral./NZ* waddy. ❷ *tie the shoot to a cane* STICK, stake, upright, pole. ❸ *he was been beaten with a cane* STICK, rod, birch; *N. Amer. informal* paddle; *historical* ferule.
▶ verb *Matthew was caned for bullying* BEAT, strike, hit, flog, thrash, lash, birch, flagellate; *informal* give someone a hiding, larrup; *N. Amer. informal* whale.

canker ▶ noun ❶ *this plant is susceptible to canker* FUNGAL DISEASE, plant rot; blight. ❷ *ear cankers* ULCER, ulceration, infection, sore, abscess. ❸ *racism remains a canker. See* CANCER sense 2.

cannabis ▶ noun MARIJUANA, hashish, bhang, hemp, kif, ganja, sinsemilla, skunkweed; *informal* hash, dope, grass, skunk, pot, blow, draw, the weed, reefer; *Brit. informal* wacky baccy; *N. Amer. informal* locoweed.

cannibal ▶ noun MANEATER, people-eater.

cannon ▶ noun MOUNTED GUN, field gun, piece of artillery; mortar, howitzer; *historical* carronade, bombard, culverin, falconet, serpentine; *Brit. historical* pom-pom.
▶ verb *the couple behind cannoned into us* COLLIDE WITH, hit, run into, crash into, plough into.

cannonade ▶ noun BOMBARDMENT, shelling, gunfire, artillery fire, barrage, pounding.

canny ▶ adjective SHREWD, astute, smart, sharp, sharp-witted, discerning, penetrating, discriminating, perceptive, perspicacious, wise, sagacious; cunning, crafty, wily; *N. Amer.* as sharp as a tack; *informal* savvy; *Brit. informal* suss, sussed; *N. Amer. informal* heads-up; *dated* long-headed; *rare* argute.
– OPPOSITES foolish.

canoe ▶ noun KAYAK, dugout, outrigger, bidarka, pirogue, waka.

canon[1] ▶ noun ❶ *the canons of fair play and equal opportunity* PRINCIPLE, rule, law, tenet, precept; standard, convention, criterion, measure. ❷ *a set of ecclesiastical canons* LAW, decree, edict, statute, dictate, decretal. ❸ *the Shakespeare canon* (LIST OF) WORKS, writings, oeuvre.

canon[2] ▶ noun *a canon assists the bishop* PREBENDARY, minor canon.

canonical ▶ adjective ❶ *the canonical method* RECOGNIZED, authoritative, authorized, accepted, sanctioned, approved, established, orthodox. ❷ *canonical rites* ACCORDING TO ECCLESIASTICAL LAW, official, sanctioned.
– OPPOSITES unorthodox.

canonize ▶ verb ❶ *the saint was canonized* BEATIFY, declare to be a saint. ❷ *we canonize freedom of speech* GLORIFY, acclaim, regard as sacred; enshrine.

canopy ▶ noun AWNING, shade, sunshade; baldachin, tester, chuppah, velarium.

cant[1] ▶ noun ❶ *religious cant* HYPOCRISY, sanctimoniousness, sanctimony, humbug, pietism. ❷ *thieves' cant* SLANG, jargon, idiom, argot, patois, speech, terminology, language; *informal* lingo, -speak, -ese.

cant[2] ▶ verb *the deck canted some twenty degrees* TILT, lean, slant, slope, incline; tip, list, bank, heel.
▶ noun *the cant of the walls* SLOPE, slant, tilt, angle, inclination.

cantankerous ▶ adjective BAD-TEMPERED, irascible, irritable, grumpy, grouchy, crotchety, tetchy, testy, crusty, curmudgeonly, ill-

tempered, ill-humoured, peevish, cross, fractious, pettish, crabbed, crabby, prickly, touchy; *informal* snappish, snappy, chippy; *Brit. informal* shirty, stroppy, narky, ratty; *N. Amer. informal* cranky, ornery; *Austral./NZ informal* snaky; *informal, dated* miffy.
– OPPOSITES affable.

canteen ▶ noun ❶ *the staff canteen* RESTAURANT, cafeteria, refectory, mess hall; *Brit. Military* NAAFI; *N. Amer.* lunchroom. ❷ *a canteen of water* CONTAINER, flask, bottle.

canvass ▶ verb ❶ *he's canvassing for the Green Party* CAMPAIGN, electioneer; *N. Amer.* stump; *Brit. informal* doorstep. ❷ *they promised to canvass all members* POLL, question, ask, survey, interview. ❸ *they're canvassing support* SEEK, try to obtain. ❹ *early retirement was canvassed as a solution* PROPOSE, suggest, discuss, debate, consider.

canyon ▶ noun RAVINE, gorge, gully, defile, couloir; chasm, abyss, gulf; *N. Amer.* gulch, coulee.

cap ▶ noun ❶ *a white plastic cap* LID, top, stopper, cork, bung, spile; *N. Amer.* stopple. ❷ *cap and gown* MORTAR BOARD, academic cap; *Brit.* square; *dated* trencher. ❸ *the cap on spending* (UPPER) LIMIT, ceiling; curb, check.
▶ verb ❶ *mountains capped with snow* TOP, crown, cover, coat. ❷ *his innings capped a great day* ROUND OFF, crown, be a fitting climax to. ❸ *they tried to cap each other's stories* BEAT, better, improve on, surpass, outdo, outshine, top, upstage. ❹ (*Brit.*) *he was capped for England* CHOOSE, select, pick, give someone the nod. ❺ *budgets will be capped* SET A LIMIT ON, limit, restrict; curb, control, peg.

capability ▶ noun ABILITY, capacity, power, potential; competence, proficiency, accomplishment, adeptness, aptitude, faculty, experience, skill, skilfulness, talent, flair; *informal* know-how.

capable ▶ adjective *a very capable young woman* COMPETENT, able, efficient, effective, proficient, accomplished, adept, handy, experienced, skilful, skilled, talented, gifted; *informal* useful; *rare* habile.
– OPPOSITES incompetent.
■ **be capable of** ❶ *I'm quite capable of looking after myself* HAVE THE ABILITY TO, be equal to (the task of), be up to; *informal* have what it takes to. ❷ *the strange events are capable of rational explanation* BE OPEN/SUSCEPTIBLE TO, admit of, allow of.

capacious ▶ adjective ROOMY, spacious, ample, big, large, sizeable, generous; *formal* capacious.
– OPPOSITES cramped, small.

capacity ▶ noun ❶ *the capacity of the freezer* VOLUME, size, magnitude, dimensions, measurements, proportions. ❷ *his capacity to inspire trust.* See CAPABILITY. ❸ *in his capacity as Commander-in-Chief* POSITION, post, job, office; role, function.

cape[1] ▶ noun *a woollen cape* CLOAK, mantle, cope, wrap, stole, tippet, poncho; *historical* pelisse, pelerine, mantlet.

cape[2] ▶ noun *the ship rounded the cape* HEADLAND, promontory, point, head, foreland; horn, hook, bill, ness, mull.

caper ▶ verb *children were capering about* SKIP, dance, romp, frisk, gambol, cavort, prance, frolic, leap, hop, jump; *rare* curvet, rollick.
▶ noun ❶ *she did a little caper* DANCE, skip, hop, leap, jump, curvet, gambado. ❷ (*informal*) *I'm too old for this kind of caper* ESCAPADE, stunt, prank, trick, mischief, antics, high jinks, skylarking; *informal* lark, shenanigans.

capital ▶ noun ❶ *Warsaw is the capital of Poland* FIRST CITY, seat of government, metropolis. ❷ *he had enough capital to pull off the deal* MONEY, finance(s), funds, the wherewithal, the means, assets, wealth, resources, investment capital; *informal* dough, bread, loot; *Brit. informal* dosh, brass, lolly, spondulicks; *US informal* greenbacks; *N. Amer. informal* bucks; *Austral./NZ informal* Oscar. ❸ *he wrote the name in capitals* CAPITAL LETTER, upper-case letter, block capital; *informal* cap.
▶ adjective ❶ *capital letters* UPPER-CASE, block. ❷ (*informal, dated*) *he's a really capital fellow.* See SPLENDID sense 2.

capitalism ▶ noun PRIVATE ENTERPRISE, free enterprise, the free market.
– OPPOSITES communism.

capitalist ▶ noun FINANCIER, investor, industrialist; magnate, tycoon.

capitalize ▶ verb *the capacity to capitalize new ventures* FINANCE, fund, underwrite, provide capital for, back; *N. Amer. informal* bankroll, stake.
■ **capitalize on** TAKE ADVANTAGE OF, profit from, make the most of, exploit; *informal* cash in on.

capitulate ▶ verb SURRENDER, give in, yield, concede defeat, give up the struggle, submit; lay down one's arms, raise/show the white flag, throw in the towel/sponge.
– OPPOSITES resist, hold out.

caprice ▶ noun ❶ *his wife's caprices* WHIM, whimsy, vagary, fancy, fad, quirk, eccentricity, foible. ❷ *the staff tired of his caprice* FICKLENESS, changeableness, volatility, capriciousness, unpredictability.

capricious ▶ adjective FICKLE, inconstant, changeable, variable, mercurial, volatile, unpredictable, temperamental; whimsical, fanciful, flighty, quirky, faddish.
– OPPOSITES consistent.

capsize ▶ verb OVERTURN, turn over, turn up-

side down, upend, flip/tip/keel over, turn turtle; *Nautical* pitchpole; *archaic* overset.
– OPPOSITES right.

capsule ▶ **noun** ❶ *he swallowed a capsule* PILL, tablet, lozenge, pastille, drop; *informal* tab. ❷ *the bottle's capsule* COVER, seal, cap, top. ❸ *a space capsule* MODULE, craft, probe.

captain ▶ **noun** ❶ *the ship's captain* COMMANDER, master; *informal* skipper. ❷ *the team's captain* LEADER, head; *informal* boss, skipper. ❸ *a captain of industry* MAGNATE, tycoon, industrialist; chief, head, leader, principal; *informal* boss, number one, bigwig, big shot/gun, honcho, top dog; *N. Amer. informal* kahuna, top banana.
▶ **verb** *a vessel captained by a cut-throat* COMMAND, run, be in charge of, control, manage, govern; *informal* skipper.

caption ▶ **noun** TITLE, heading, wording, head, legend, rubric, slogan.

captious ▶ **adjective** CRITICAL, fault-finding, quibbling, cavilling; hypercritical, pedantic, hair-splitting; *informal* nit-picking, pernickety.
– OPPOSITES forgiving.

captivate ▶ **verb** ENTHRAL, charm, enchant, bewitch, fascinate, beguile, entrance, enrapture, delight, attract, allure.
– OPPOSITES repel, bore.

captive ▶ **noun** *release the captives* PRISONER, convict, detainee, inmate; prisoner of war, POW, internee; *informal* jailbird, con; *Brit. informal* (old) lag; *N. Amer. informal* yardbird.
▶ **adjective** *captive wild animals* CONFINED, caged, incarcerated, locked up; jailed, imprisoned, in prison, interned, detained, in captivity, under lock and key, behind bars.

captivity ▶ **noun** IMPRISONMENT, confinement, internment, incarceration, detention; *archaic* duress, durance.
– OPPOSITES freedom.

captor ▶ **noun** JAILER, guard, incarcerator, keeper.

capture ▶ **verb** ❶ *the spy was captured in Moscow* CATCH, apprehend, seize, arrest; take prisoner/captive, imprison, detain, put/throw in jail, put behind bars, put under lock and key, incarcerate; *informal* nab, collar, lift, pick up, pull in; *Brit. informal* nick. ❷ *guerrillas captured a strategic district* OCCUPY, invade, conquer, seize, take (possession of). ❸ *the music captured the atmosphere of a summer morning* EXPRESS, reproduce, represent, encapsulate. ❹ *the tales of pirates captured the children's imaginations* ENGAGE, attract, catch, seize, hold.
– OPPOSITES free.
▶ **noun** *he tried to evade capture* ARREST, apprehension, seizure, being taken prisoner/captive, imprisonment.

car ▶ **noun** ❶ *he drove up in his car* MOTOR (CAR), automobile; *informal* wheels; *N. Amer. informal* auto. ❷ *the dining car* CARRIAGE, coach; *Brit.* saloon.

carafe ▶ **noun** FLASK, jug, pitcher, decanter, flagon.

caravan ▶ **noun** ❶ *a fishing holiday in a caravan* MOBILE HOME, camper, caravanette; *N. Amer.* trailer; *Brit. trademark* Dormobile. ❷ *a gypsy caravan* WAGON, covered cart. ❸ *a refugee caravan* CONVOY, procession, column, train.

carbuncle ▶ **noun** BOIL, sore, abscess, pustule, wen, whitlow; *technical* furuncle.

carcass ▶ **noun** ❶ *a lamb carcass* CORPSE, (dead) body, remains; *Medicine* cadaver; *informal* stiff; *archaic* corse. ❷ (*informal*) *shift your carcass* BODY, self; backside; *N. Amer. informal* butt.

card ▶ **noun** ❶ *a piece of stiff card* CARDBOARD, pasteboard, board. ❷ *I'll send her a card* GREETINGS CARD, postcard. ❸ *she produced her card* IDENTIFICATION, ID, credentials; business card. ❹ *she paid with her card* CREDIT CARD; debit card, cash card, swipe card; *informal* plastic. ❺ *the cards were dealt* PLAYING CARD; (**cards**) pack of cards. ❻ (*informal, dated*) *he said she was a card* ECCENTRIC, character; JOKER, wit, wag, jester, clown; *informal* laugh, scream, hoot, riot; *informal, dated* caution.
■ **give someone their cards** (*Brit. informal*) DISMISS, get rid of, lay off, make redundant, let someone go, discharge; *informal* sack, fire, kick/boot out, give someone their marching orders, give someone the (old) heave-ho, give someone the elbow/push.
■ **on the cards** (*informal*) LIKELY, possible, probable, expected, in the wind, in the offing.

cardinal ▶ **adjective** FUNDAMENTAL, basic, main, chief, primary, prime, principal, paramount, pre-eminent, highest, key, essential.
– OPPOSITES unimportant.

care ▶ **noun** ❶ *the care of the child* SAFE KEEPING, supervision, custody, charge, protection, control, responsibility; guardianship, wardship. ❷ *handle with care* CAUTION, carefulness, heedfulness, heed, attention, attentiveness. ❸ *she chose her words with care* DISCRETION, judiciousness, forethought, thought, regard, heed, mindfulness; accuracy, precision. ❹ *the cares of the day* WORRY, anxiety, trouble, concern, stress, pressure, strain; sorrow, woe, hardship. ❺ *constant care for others* CONCERN, consideration, thought, regard, solicitude.
– OPPOSITES neglect, carelessness.
▶ **verb** *the teachers didn't care about our work* BE CONCERNED, worry (oneself), trouble/concern oneself, bother, mind, be interested; *informal* give a damn/hoot/rap.
■ **care for** ❶ *he cares for his children* LOVE, be fond of, be devoted to, treasure, adore, dote on, think the world of, worship, idolize.

❷ *would you care for a cup of coffee?* LIKE, want, desire, fancy, feel like. ❸ *the hospice cares for the terminally ill* LOOK AFTER, take care of, tend, attend to, minister to, nurse; be responsible for, keep safe, keep an eye on.

career ▶ **noun** ❶ *a business career* PROFESSION, occupation, vocation, calling, employment, line (of work), walk of life, métier. ❷ *a chequered career* EXISTENCE, life, course, passage, path.

▶ **adjective** *a career politician* PROFESSIONAL, permanent, full-time.

▶ **verb** *they careered down the hill* RUSH, hurtle, streak, shoot, race, bolt, dash, speed, run, whizz, zoom, flash, blast, charge, hare, fly, pelt, go like the wind; *informal* belt, scoot, tear, zap, zip, whip, go like a bat out of hell; *Brit. informal* bomb, bucket; *N. Amer. informal* hightail, clip.

carefree ▶ **adjective** UNWORRIED, untroubled, blithe, airy, nonchalant, insouciant, happy-go-lucky, free and easy, easy-going, relaxed; *informal* laid back.
– OPPOSITES careworn.

careful ▶ **adjective** ❶ *be careful when you go up the stairs* CAUTIOUS, heedful, alert, attentive, watchful, vigilant, wary, on guard, circumspect. ❷ *Roland was careful of his reputation* MINDFUL, heedful, protective. ❸ *careful with money* PRUDENT, thrifty, economical, sparing, frugal, scrimping, abstemious; *informal* stingy. ❹ *careful consideration of the facts* ATTENTIVE, conscientious, painstaking, meticulous, diligent, assiduous, sedulous, scrupulous, punctilious, methodical; *informal* pernickety; *archaic* nice.
– OPPOSITES careless, extravagant.

careless ▶ **adjective** ❶ *careless motorists* INATTENTIVE, incautious, negligent, remiss; heedless, irresponsible, impetuous, reckless. ❷ *careless work* SHODDY, slapdash, slipshod, scrappy, slovenly, negligent, lax, slack, disorganized, hasty, hurried; *informal* sloppy, slaphappy. ❸ *a careless remark* THOUGHTLESS, insensitive, indiscreet, unguarded, incautious, inadvertent. ❹ *she was very careless of investments* NEGLIGENT, heedless, improvident, unconcerned, indifferent, oblivious. ❺ *careless masculine grace* UNSTUDIED, artless, casual, effortless, nonchalant, insouciant, languid.
– OPPOSITES careful, meticulous.

caress ▶ **verb** STROKE, touch, fondle, brush, skim, nuzzle.

caretaker ▶ **noun** JANITOR, attendant, porter, custodian, concierge; *N. Amer.* superintendent.

▶ **adjective** *the caretaker manager* TEMPORARY, short-term, provisional, substitute, acting, interim, pro tem, stand-in, fill-in, stopgap; *N. Amer. informal* pinch-hitting.
– OPPOSITES permanent.

careworn ▶ **adjective** WORRIED, anxious, harassed, strained, stressed; drained, drawn, gaunt, haggard; *informal* hassled.
– OPPOSITES carefree.

cargo ▶ **noun** FREIGHT, load, haul, consignment, delivery, shipment; goods, merchandise; *archaic* lading.

caricature ▶ **noun** *a caricature of the Prime Minister* CARTOON, parody, satire, lampoon, burlesque; *informal* send-up, take-off.

▶ **verb** *she has turned to caricaturing her fellow actors* PARODY, satirize, lampoon, make fun of, burlesque; *informal* send up, take off.

caring ▶ **adjective** KIND, kind-hearted, warm-hearted, tender; concerned, attentive, thoughtful, solicitous, considerate; affectionate, loving, doting, fond; sympathetic, understanding, compassionate, feeling.
– OPPOSITES cruel.

carnage ▶ **noun** SLAUGHTER, massacre, mass murder, butchery, bloodbath, bloodletting; holocaust, pogrom, ethnic cleansing.

carnal ▶ **adjective** SEXUAL, sensual, erotic, lustful, lascivious, libidinous, lecherous, licentious; physical, bodily, corporeal, fleshly.
– OPPOSITES spiritual.

carnival ▶ **noun** ❶ *the town's carnival* FESTIVAL, fiesta, fête, gala, jamboree, celebration. ❷ (*N. Amer.*) *he worked at a carnival* FUNFAIR, circus, fair, amusement show.

carnivorous ▶ **adjective** MEAT-EATING, predatory, of prey.
– OPPOSITES herbivorous.

carol ▶ **noun** *children sang carols* CHRISTMAS SONG, hymn, canticle.

▶ **verb** *Boris carolled happily* SING, trill, warble, chirp; *archaic* wassail.

carouse ▶ **verb** DRINK AND MAKE MERRY, go on a drinking bout, go on a spree; revel, celebrate, roister; *informal* booze, go boozing, binge, go on a binge, go on a bender, paint the town red, party, rave, make whoopee, whoop it up; *Brit. informal* go on the bevvy; *archaic* wassail.

carp ▶ **verb** COMPLAIN, cavil, grumble, grouse, whine, bleat, nag; *informal* gripe, grouch, beef, bellyache, moan, bitch, whinge; *Brit. informal* be on at someone; *N. English informal* mither; *N. Amer. informal* kvetch.
– OPPOSITES praise.

carpenter ▶ **noun** WOODWORKER, joiner, cabinet-maker; *Brit. informal* chippy.

carpet ▶ **noun** ❶ *a Turkish carpet* RUG, mat, matting, floor covering. ❷ *a carpet of wild flowers* COVERING, blanket, layer, cover, cloak, mantle.

▶ **verb** ❶ *the gravel was carpeted in moss* COVER, coat, overlay, overspread, blanket. ❷ (*Brit. informal*) *an officer was carpeted for leaking information.* See REPRIMAND verb.

carriage ▶ noun ❶ *a railway carriage* COACH, car; *Brit.* saloon. ❷ *a horse and carriage* WAGON, hackney, hansom, gig, landau, trap. ❸ *the carriage of bikes on trains* TRANSPORT, transportation, conveyance, carrying, movement, shipment. ❹ *an erect carriage* POSTURE, bearing, stance, gait; attitude, manner, demeanour; *Brit.* deportment.

carrier ▶ noun BEARER, conveyor, transporter; porter, courier, haulier.

carry ▶ verb ❶ *she carried the box into the kitchen* CONVEY, transfer, move, take, bring, bear, lug, fetch; *informal* cart, hump. ❷ *a coach operator carrying 12 million passengers a year* TRANSPORT, convey, move, handle. ❸ *satellites carry the signal over the Atlantic* TRANSMIT, conduct, relay, communicate, convey, dispatch, beam. ❹ *the dinghy can carry the weight of the baggage* SUPPORT, sustain, stand; prop up, shore up, bolster. ❺ *managers carry most responsibility* UNDERTAKE, accept, assume, bear, shoulder, take on (oneself). ❻ *she was carrying his baby* BE PREGNANT WITH, bear, expect; *technical* be gravid with. ❼ *she carried herself with assurance* CONDUCT, bear, hold; act, behave, acquit; *formal* comport; *archaic* deport. ❽ *a resolution was carried* APPROVE, vote for, accept, endorse, ratify; agree to, assent to, rubber-stamp; *informal* OK, give the thumbs up to. ❾ *I carried the whole audience* WIN OVER, sway, convince, persuade, influence; motivate, stimulate. ❿ *today's paper carried an article on housing policy* PUBLISH, print, communicate, distribute; broadcast, transmit. ⓫ *we carry a wide range* SELL, stock, keep (in stock), offer, have (for sale), retail, supply. ⓬ *most toxins carry warnings* DISPLAY, bear, exhibit, show, be marked with. ⓭ *it carries a penalty of two years' imprisonment* ENTAIL, involve, result in, occasion, have as a consequence. ⓮ *his voice carried across the quay* BE AUDIBLE, travel, reach.

■ **be/get carried away** LOSE SELF-CONTROL, get overexcited, go too far; *informal* flip, lose it.

■ **carry someone off** KILL (OFF), cause the death of, take/end the life of, finish off; *informal* do in.

■ **carry something off** ❶ *she carried off four awards* WIN, secure, gain, achieve, collect; *informal* land, net, bag, scoop. ❷ *he has carried it off* SUCCEED, triumph, be victorious, be successful, do well, make good; *informal* crack it.

■ **carry on** ❶ *they carried on arguing* CONTINUE, keep (on), go on; persist in, persevere in; *informal* stick with/at. ❷ (*informal*) *the English way of carrying on* BEHAVE, act, conduct oneself, acquit oneself; *formal* comport oneself; *archaic* deport oneself. ❸ (*informal*) *she was carrying on with other men* HAVE AN AFFAIR, commit adultery, have a fling; *informal* play around, mess about/around; *Brit. informal* play away; *N. Amer. informal* fool around. ❹ (*informal*) *I was always carrying on* MISBEHAVE, behave badly, get up to mischief, cause trouble, get up to no good, be naughty; clown about/around, fool about/around, mess about/around; *informal* act up; *Brit. informal* muck about/around, play up.

■ **carry something on** ENGAGE IN, conduct, undertake, be involved in, carry out, perform.

■ **carry something out** ❶ *they carried out a Caesarean* CONDUCT, perform, implement, execute. ❷ *I carried out my promise to her* FULFIL, carry through, honour, redeem, make good; keep, observe, abide by, comply with, adhere to, stick to, keep faith with.

carry-on ▶ noun (*Brit. informal*) FUSS, commotion, trouble, bother, excitement, palaver; *informal* hoo-ha, ballyhoo, song and dance, performance, kerfuffle.

cart ▶ noun ❶ *a horse-drawn cart* WAGON, carriage, dray; *archaic* wain. ❷ *a man with a cart took their luggage* HANDCART, pushcart, trolley, barrow.

▶ verb (*informal*) *he had the wreckage carted away* TRANSPORT, convey, haul, move, shift, take; carry, lug, heft; *informal* hump.

carton ▶ noun BOX, package, cardboard box, container, pack, packet.

cartoon ▶ noun ❶ *a cartoon of the Prime Minister* CARICATURE, parody, lampoon, satire; *informal* take-off, send-up. ❷ *he was reading cartoons* COMIC STRIP, comic, graphic novel. ❸ *they watched cartoons on television* ANIMATED FILM, animation. ❹ *detailed cartoons for a full-size portrait* SKETCH, rough, outline, preliminary drawing, underdrawing; *Computing* wireframe.

cartridge ▶ noun ❶ *a toner cartridge* CASSETTE, magazine, canister, container. ❷ *a rifle cartridge* BULLET, round, shell, charge, shot.

carve ▶ verb ❶ *he carved horn handles* SCULPT, sculpture; cut, hew, whittle; form, shape, fashion. ❷ *I carved my initials on the tree* ENGRAVE, etch, incise, score. ❸ *he carved the roast chicken* SLICE, cut up, chop.

■ **carve something up** DIVIDE, partition, apportion, subdivide, split up, break up; share out, dole out; *informal* divvy up.

carving ▶ noun SCULPTURE, model, statue, statuette, figure, figurine.

– RELATED TERMS glyptic.

cascade ▶ noun WATERFALL, cataract, falls, rapids, white water.

▶ verb *rain cascaded from the roof* POUR, gush, surge, spill, stream, flow, issue, spurt, jet.

case[1] ▶ noun ❶ *a classic case of overreaction* INSTANCE, occurrence, manifestation, demonstration, exposition, exhibition; example, illustration, specimen, sample, exemplification. ❷ *if that is the case I will have to find some-*

body else SITUATION, position, state of affairs, the lie of the land; circumstances, conditions, facts, how things stand; *Brit.* state of play; *informal* score. ❸ *the officers on the case* INVESTIGATION, enquiry, examination, exploration, probe, search, inquest. ❹ *urgent cases* PATIENT, sick person, invalid, sufferer, victim. ❺ *he lost his case* LAWSUIT, (legal) action, legal dispute, suit, trial, legal/judicial proceedings, litigation. ❻ *a strong case* ARGUMENT, contention, reasoning, logic, defence, justification, vindication, exposition, thesis.

case² ▶ **noun** ❶ *a cigarette case* CONTAINER, box, canister, receptacle, holder; *dated* etui. ❷ *a seed case* CASING, cover, covering, sheath, sheathing, envelope, sleeve, jacket, integument. ❸ (*Brit.*) *she threw some clothes into a case* SUITCASE, (travelling) bag, valise, portmanteau; (**cases**) luggage, baggage. ❹ *a case of wine* CRATE, box, pack. ❺ *a glass display case* CABINET, cupboard.

▶ **verb** ❶ *the rifle is cased in wood* COVER, surround, encase, sheathe, envelop. ❷ (*informal*) *a thief casing the joint* RECONNOITRE, inspect, examine, survey, explore; *informal* recce, check out.

cash ▶ **noun** ❶ *a wallet stuffed with cash* MONEY, currency, hard cash; (bank) notes, coins, change; *N. Amer.* bills; *informal* dough, bread, loot, readies, moolah; *Brit. informal* dosh, brass, lolly, spondulicks; *US informal* greenbacks; *N. Amer. informal* bucks, dinero; *Austral./NZ informal* Oscar; *Brit. dated* l.s.d. ❷ *a lack of cash* FINANCE, money, resources, funds, assets, the means, the wherewithal.

– OPPOSITES cheque, credit.

▶ **verb** *the bank cashed her cheque* EXCHANGE, change, convert into cash/money; honour, pay, accept; *Brit.* encash.

■ **cash in on** TAKE ADVANTAGE OF, exploit, milk; make money from, profit from; *informal* make a killing out of.

cashier¹ ▶ **noun** *the cashier took the cheque* CLERK, bank clerk, teller, banker, treasurer, bursar, purser.

cashier² ▶ **verb** (*Military*) *he was found guilty and cashiered* DISMISS, discharge, expel, throw/cast out, get rid of; *informal* sack, fire, kick/boot out, give someone their marching orders, give someone the bullet, give someone the elbow/push.

casing ▶ **noun** COVER, case, shell, envelope, sheath, sheathing, sleeve, jacket, housing.

casino ▶ **noun** GAMBLING HOUSE, gambling club, gambling den; *dated* gaming house.

cask ▶ **noun** BARREL, keg, butt, tun, vat, drum, hogshead; *historical* puncheon, firkin.

casket ▶ **noun** ❶ *a small casket* BOX, chest, case, container, receptacle. ❷ (*N. Amer.*) *the casket of a dead soldier* COFFIN; *informal* box; *humorous* wooden overcoat.

cast ▶ **verb** ❶ *he cast the stone into the stream* THROW, toss, fling, pitch, hurl, lob; *informal* chuck, sling, bung; *dated* shy. ❷ *fishermen cast their nets* SPREAD, throw, open out. ❸ *she cast a fearful glance over her shoulder* DIRECT, shoot, throw, send. ❹ *each citizen cast a vote* REGISTER, record, enter, file, vote. ❺ *the fire cast a soft light* EMIT, give off, send out, radiate. ❻ *the figures cast shadows* FORM, create, produce; project, throw. ❼ *the stags' antlers are cast each year* SHED, lose, discard, slough off. ❽ *a figure cast by hand* MOULD, fashion, form, shape, model; sculpt, sculpture, forge. ❾ *they were cast as extras* CHOOSE, select, pick, name, nominate.

▶ **noun** ❶ *a cast of the writer's hand* MOULD, die, matrix, shape, casting, model. ❷ *a cast of the dice* THROW, toss, fling, pitch, hurl, lob; *informal* chuck, sling, bung; *dated* shy. ❸ *an enquiring cast of mind* TYPE, sort, kind, character, variety, class, style, stamp, nature. ❹ *a cast in one eye* SQUINT, strabismus. ❺ *the cast of 'The Barber of Seville'* ACTORS, performers, players, company; dramatis personae, characters.

■ **cast something aside** DISCARD, reject, throw away/out, get rid of, dispose of, abandon.

■ **cast someone away** SHIPWRECK, wreck; strand, leave stranded, maroon.

■ **cast down** DEPRESSED, downcast, unhappy, sad, miserable, gloomy, down, low; dejected, dispirited, discouraged, disheartened, downhearted, demoralized, disconsolate, crestfallen, despondent; *informal* blue.

caste ▶ **noun** (SOCIAL) CLASS, social order, rank, level, stratum, echelon, status; *dated* estate, station.

castigate (*formal*) ▶ **verb** REPRIMAND, rebuke, admonish, chastise, chide, upbraid, reprove, reproach, scold, berate, take to task, lambaste, give someone a piece of one's mind, haul over the coals, censure; *informal* tell off, give someone an earful, give someone a roasting, rap someone on the knuckles, slap someone's wrist, dress down, bawl out, give someone hell, blow up at, pitch into, lay into, blast; *Brit. informal* tick off, have a go at, carpet, tear someone off a strip, give someone what for, give someone a rocket; *N. Amer. informal* chew out, ream out; *Austral. informal* monster; *dated* give someone a rating; *rare* reprehend, objurgate.

– OPPOSITES praise, commend.

castle ▶ **noun** FORTRESS, fort, stronghold, fortification, keep, citadel.

castrate ▶ **verb** NEUTER, geld, cut, desex, sterilize, fix; *N. Amer. & Austral.* alter; *Brit. informal* doctor; *archaic* emasculate.

casual ▶ **adjective** ❶ *a casual attitude to life* INDIFFERENT, apathetic, uncaring, unconcerned; lackadaisical, blasé, nonchalant, insouciant, offhand, flippant; easy-going, free and easy, blithe, carefree, devil-may-care; *informal* laid-back. ❷ *a casual remark* OFFHAND, spontaneous, unpremeditated, unthinking, unconsidered, impromptu, throwaway, unguarded; *informal* off-the-cuff. ❸ *a casual glance* CURSORY, perfunctory, superficial, passing, fleeting; hasty, brief, quick. ❹ *a casual acquaintance* SLIGHT, superficial. ❺ *casual work* TEMPORARY, part-time, freelance, impermanent, irregular, occasional. ❻ *casual sex* PROMISCUOUS, recreational, extramarital, free. ❼ *a casual meeting changed his life* CHANCE, accidental, unplanned, unintended, unexpected, unforeseen, unanticipated, fortuitous, serendipitous, adventitious. ❽ *a casual shirt* INFORMAL, comfortable, leisure, sportif, everyday; *informal* sporty. ❾ *the inn's casual atmosphere* RELAXED, friendly, informal, unceremonious, easy-going, free and easy; *informal* laid-back.

–OPPOSITES careful, planned, formal.

▶ **noun** *we employ ten casuals* TEMPORARY WORKER, part-timer, freelance, freelancer; *informal* temp.

casualty ▶ **noun** VICTIM, fatality, loss, MIA; (**casualties**) dead and injured, missing (in action).

casuistry ▶ **noun** SOPHISTRY, specious reasoning, speciousness.

cat ▶ **noun** FELINE, tomcat, tom, kitten, mouser; *informal* pussy (cat), puss; *Brit. informal* moggie, mog; *archaic* grimalkin.

cataclysm ▶ **noun** DISASTER, catastrophe, calamity, tragedy, devastation, holocaust, ruin, ruination, upheaval, convulsion.

cataclysmic ▶ **adjective** DISASTROUS, catastrophic, calamitous, tragic, devastating, ruinous, terrible, violent, awful.

catacombs ▶ **plural noun** UNDERGROUND CEMETERY, crypt, vault, tomb, ossuary.

catalogue ▶ **noun** ❶ *a library catalogue* DIRECTORY, register, index, list, listing, record, archive, inventory. ❷ *a mail-order catalogue* BROCHURE, magalogue, mailer; *N. Amer. informal* wish book.

▶ **verb** *the collection is fully catalogued* CLASSIFY, categorize, systematize, index, list, archive, make an inventory of, inventory, record, itemize.

catapult ▶ **noun** *a boy fired the catapult* SLING, slingshot; *Austral./NZ* shanghai; *historical* ballista, trebuchet.

▶ **verb** *Sam was catapulted into the sea* PROPEL, launch, hurl, fling, send flying, fire, blast, shoot.

cataract ▶ **noun** WATERFALL, cascade, falls, rapids, white water.

catastrophe ▶ **noun** DISASTER, calamity, cataclysm, holocaust, ruin, ruination, tragedy; adversity, blight, trouble, trial, tribulation.

catastrophic ▶ **adjective** DISASTROUS, calamitous, cataclysmic, ruinous, tragic, fatal, dire, awful, terrible, dreadful; *poetic/literary* direful.

catcall ▶ **noun** WHISTLE, boo, hiss, jeer, raspberry, hoot, taunt; (**catcalls**) scoffing, abuse, taunting, derision.

catch ▶ **verb** ❶ *he caught the ball* SEIZE, grab, snatch, seize/grab/take hold of, grasp, grip, clutch, clench; receive, get, intercept. ❷ *we've caught the thief* CAPTURE, seize; apprehend, arrest, take prisoner/captive, take into custody; trap, snare, ensnare; net, hook, land; *informal* nab, collar, run in, bust; *Brit. informal* nick. ❸ *her heel caught in a hole* BECOME TRAPPED, become entangled, snag. ❹ *she caught the 7.45 bus* BE IN TIME FOR, make, get; board, get on, step aboard. ❺ *they were caught siphoning petrol* DISCOVER, find, come upon/across, stumble on, chance on; surprise, catch red-handed, catch in the act. ❻ *it caught his imagination* ENGAGE, capture, attract, draw, grab, grip, seize; hold, absorb, engross. ❼ *she caught a trace of aftershave* PERCEIVE, notice, observe, discern, detect, note, make out; *Brit. informal* clock. ❽ *I couldn't catch what she was saying* HEAR, perceive, discern, make out; understand, comprehend, grasp, apprehend; *informal* get, get the drift of, figure out; *Brit. informal* twig, suss (out). ❾ *it caught the flavour of the sixties* EVOKE, conjure up, call to mind, recall, encapsulate, capture. ❿ *the blow caught her on the side of her face* HIT, strike, slap, smack, bang. ⓫ *he caught malaria* BECOME INFECTED WITH, contract, get, be taken ill with, develop, come down with, be struck down with; *Brit.* go down with; *informal* take ill with; *N. Amer. informal* take sick with. ⓬ *the kindling wouldn't catch* IGNITE, start burning, catch fire, kindle. ⓭ *the generator caught immediately* START (RUNNING), fire, begin working.

–OPPOSITES drop, release, miss.

▶ **noun** ❶ *he inspected the catch* HAUL, net, bag, yield. ❷ (*informal*) *Giles is a good catch* ELIGIBLE MAN/WOMAN, marriage prospect. ❸ *he slipped the catch* LATCH, lock, fastener, clasp, hasp. ❹ *he is always looking for the catch* SNAG, disadvantage, drawback, stumbling block, hitch, fly in the ointment, pitfall, complication, problem, hiccup, difficulty; trap, trick, snare; *informal* con. ❺ *a catch in her voice* TREMOR, unevenness, shake, quiver, wobble.

■ **catch it** (*informal*) BE REPRIMANDED, be scolded, be rebuked, be taken to task, be chastised, get into trouble, be hauled over the coals; *informal* be told off, be for the high jump, be in hot water, get a dressing-down, get an earful, get a roasting, get a rap over the knuckles, get a slap on the wrist; *Brit. informal* be for it; *formal* be castigated.

■ **catch on** ❶ *radio soon caught on* BECOME POPULAR/FASHIONABLE, take off, boom, flourish, thrive. ❷ *I caught on fast* UNDERSTAND, comprehend, learn, see the light; *informal* cotton on, latch on, get the picture/message, get wise.

■ **catch (someone) up** DRAW LEVEL (WITH), reach; gain on.

catching ▶ adjective (*informal*) INFECTIOUS, contagious, communicable, transmittable, transmissible; *dated* infective.

catchphrase ▶ noun SAYING, quotation, quote, slogan, catchword; *N. Amer. informal* tag line.

catchword ▶ noun MOTTO, watchword, slogan, byword, catchphrase; *informal* buzzword.

catchy ▶ adjective MEMORABLE, unforgettable; appealing, popular; singable, melodious, tuneful.

catechize ▶ verb INTERROGATE, question, cross-examine, cross-question, quiz, sound out, give the third degree to; *informal* grill, pump.

categorical ▶ adjective UNQUALIFIED, unconditional, unequivocal, absolute, explicit, unambiguous, definite, direct, downright, outright, emphatic, positive, point-blank, conclusive, without reservations, out-and-out; *formal* apodictic.
– OPPOSITES qualified, equivocal.

categorize ▶ verb CLASSIFY, class, group, grade, rate, designate; order, arrange, sort, rank; file, catalogue, list, index.

category ▶ noun CLASS, classification, group, grouping, bracket, heading, set; type, sort, kind, variety, species, breed, brand, make, model; grade, order, rank.

cater

■ **cater for** ❶ *we cater for vegetarians* PROVIDE FOOD FOR, feed, serve, cook for; *dated* victual. ❷ *a resort catering for older holidaymakers* SERVE, provide for, meet the needs/wants of, accommodate. ❸ *he seemed to cater for all tastes* TAKE INTO ACCOUNT/CONSIDERATION, allow for, consider, bear in mind, make provision for, have regard for.

■ **cater to** SATISFY, indulge, pander to, gratify, accommodate, minister to, give in to, fulfil.

caterwaul ▶ verb HOWL, wail, bawl, cry, yell, scream, screech, yowl, ululate.

catharsis ▶ noun PURGING, purgation, purification, cleansing, (emotional) release, relief; *Psychoanalysis* abreaction.

catholic ▶ adjective DIVERSE, diversified, wide, broad, broad-based, eclectic, liberal; comprehensive, all-encompassing, all-embracing, all-inclusive.
– OPPOSITES narrow.

cattle ▶ plural noun COWS, bovines, oxen, bulls; stock, livestock.
– RELATED TERMS bovine.

catty ▶ adjective (*informal*) *a catty remark. See* SPITEFUL.

caucus ▶ noun ❶ (*in North America & NZ*) *caucuses will be held in eleven states* MEETING, assembly, gathering, congress, conference, convention, rally, convocation. ❷ (*in the UK*) *the right-wing caucus* FACTION, camp, bloc, group, set, band, ring, cabal, coterie, pressure group; *Brit.* ginger group.

cause ▶ noun ❶ *the cause of the fire* SOURCE, root, origin, beginning(s), starting point; mainspring, base, basis, foundation, fountainhead; originator, author, creator, producer, agent; *formal* radix. ❷ *there is no cause for alarm* REASON, grounds, justification, call, need, necessity, occasion, excuse, pretext. ❸ *the cause of human rights | a good cause* PRINCIPLE, ideal, belief, conviction; object, end, aim, objective, purpose; charity. ❹ *he went to plead his cause* CASE, suit, lawsuit, action, dispute.
– RELATED TERMS -genic, -facient.
– OPPOSITES effect, result.

▶ verb *this disease can cause blindness* BRING ABOUT, give rise to, lead to, result in, create, produce, generate, engender, spawn, bring on, precipitate, prompt, provoke, trigger, make happen, induce, inspire, promote, foster; *poetic/literary* beget, enkindle.
– OPPOSITES result from.

caustic ▶ adjective ❶ *a caustic cleaner* CORROSIVE, corroding, mordant, acid. ❷ *a caustic comment* SARCASTIC, cutting, biting, mordant, sharp, bitter, scathing, derisive, sardonic, ironic, scornful, trenchant, acerbic, vitriolic, acidulous; *Brit. informal* sarky; *formal* mordacious.

cauterize ▶ verb (*Medicine*) BURN, sear, singe, scorch; disinfect, sterilize.

caution ▶ noun ❶ *proceed with caution* CARE, carefulness, heedfulness, heed, attention, attentiveness, alertness, watchfulness, vigilance, circumspection, discretion, prudence. ❷ *a first offender may receive a caution* WARNING, admonishment, injunction; reprimand, rebuke, reproof, scolding; *informal* telling-off, dressing-down, talking-to; *Brit. informal* ticking-off, carpeting. ❸ (*informal, dated*) *her uncle's a caution. See* CLOWN noun sense 2.

▶ verb ❶ *advisers cautioned against tax increases* ADVISE, warn, counsel, urge. ❷ *he was cautioned by the police* WARN, admonish; reprimand, rebuke, reprove, scold; *informal* tell off, give someone a dressing-down, give someone a talking-to; *Brit. informal* give someone a ticking-off, carpet.

cautious ▶ adjective CAREFUL, heedful, attentive, alert, watchful, vigilant, circumspect, prudent.
– OPPOSITES reckless.

cavalcade ▶ noun PROCESSION, parade, motorcade, cortège; *Brit.* march past.

cavalier ▶ noun ❶ (*historical*) *Cavaliers dying for King Charles* ROYALIST, king's man. ❷ (*archaic*) *the lady and her cavalier* ESCORT, gentleman; *dated* beau. ❸ (*archaic*) *foot soldiers and cavaliers* HORSEMAN, equestrian; cavalryman, trooper, knight.
– OPPOSITES Roundhead.
▶ adjective *a cavalier disregard for danger* OFFHAND, indifferent, casual, dismissive, insouciant, unconcerned; supercilious, patronizing, condescending, disdainful, scornful, contemptuous; *informal* couldn't-care-less.

cavalry ▶ plural noun (*historical*) MOUNTED TROOPS, cavalrymen, troopers, horse; *historical* dragoons, lancers, hussars.

cave ▶ noun CAVERN, grotto, pothole, underground chamber.
– RELATED TERMS speleology, speleologist; *N. Amer.* spelunking.
■ **cave in** ❶ *the roof caved in* COLLAPSE, fall in/down, give (way), crumble, subside. ❷ *the manager caved in to their demands* YIELD, surrender, capitulate, give in, back down, make concessions, throw in the towel/sponge.

caveat ▶ noun WARNING, caution, admonition; proviso, condition, stipulation, provision, clause, rider, qualification.

caveman, cavewoman ▶ noun CAVE-DWELLER, troglodyte, primitive man/woman, prehistoric man/woman.

cavern ▶ noun LARGE CAVE, grotto, underground chamber/gallery.

cavernous ▶ adjective VAST, huge, large, immense, spacious, roomy, airy, capacious, voluminous, extensive, deep; hollow, gaping, yawning; *formal* commodious.
– OPPOSITES small.

cavil ▶ verb COMPLAIN, carp, grumble, grouse, whine, bleat, quibble, niggle; *informal* gripe, grouch, beef, bellyache, moan, bitch, whinge, kick up a fuss; *Brit. informal* chunter, create; *N. English informal* mither; *N. Amer. informal* kvetch.

cavity ▶ noun SPACE, chamber, hollow, hole, pocket, pouch; orifice, aperture; socket, gap, crater, pit.

cavort ▶ verb SKIP, dance, romp, jig, caper, frisk, gambol, prance, frolic, lark; bounce, trip, leap, jump, bound, spring, hop; *rare* rollick.

cease ▶ verb ❶ *hostilities had ceased* COME TO AN END, come to a halt, end, halt, stop, conclude, terminate, finish, draw to a close, be over. ❷ *they ceased all military activity* BRING TO AN END, bring to a halt, end, halt, stop, conclude, terminate, finish, wind up, discontinue, suspend, break off; *informal* leave off.
– OPPOSITES start, continue.
■ **without cease** CONTINUOUSLY, incessantly, unendingly, unremittingly, without a pause/break, on and on.

ceaseless ▶ adjective CONTINUAL, constant, continuous; incessant, unceasing, unending, endless, never-ending, interminable, nonstop, uninterrupted, unremitting, relentless, unrelenting, unrelieved, sustained, persistent, eternal, perpetual.
– OPPOSITES intermittent.

cede ▶ verb SURRENDER, concede, relinquish, yield, part with, give up; hand over, deliver up, give over, make over, transfer; abandon, forgo, sacrifice; *poetic/literary* forsake.

ceiling ▶ noun UPPER LIMIT, maximum, limitation.

celebrate ▶ verb ❶ *they were celebrating their wedding anniversary* COMMEMORATE, observe, mark, keep, honour, remember, memorialize. ❷ *let's all celebrate!* ENJOY ONESELF, make merry, have fun, have a good time, have a party, revel, roister, carouse; *N. Amer.* step out; *informal* party, go out on the town, paint the town red, whoop it up, make whoopee, live it up, have a ball. ❸ *the priest celebrated mass* PERFORM, observe, officiate at. ❹ *he was celebrated for his achievements* PRAISE, extol, glorify, eulogize, reverence, honour, pay tribute to; *formal* laud; *archaic* emblazon.

celebrated ▶ adjective ACCLAIMED, admired, highly rated, lionized, revered, honoured, esteemed, exalted, vaunted, well thought of; eminent, great, distinguished, prestigious, illustrious, pre-eminent, estimable, notable, of note, of repute; *formal* lauded.
– OPPOSITES unsung.

celebration ▶ noun ❶ *the celebration of his 50th birthday* COMMEMORATION, observance, marking, keeping. ❷ *a cause for celebration* JOLLIFICATION, merrymaking, enjoying oneself, carousing, revelry, revels, festivities; *informal* partying. ❸ *a birthday celebration* PARTY, function, gathering, festivities, festival, fête, carnival, jamboree; *informal* do, bash, rave; *Brit. informal* rave-up, knees-up, beanfeast, bunfight, beano. ❹ *the celebration of the Eucharist* OBSERVANCE, performance, officiation, solemnization.

celebrity ▶ noun ❶ *his celebrity grew* FAME, prominence, renown, eminence, pre-eminence, stardom, popularity, distinction, note, notability, prestige, stature, repute, reputation. ❷ *a sporting celebrity* FAMOUS PERSON, VIP, very important person, personality, (big) name, famous/household name, star, superstar; *informal* celeb, somebody, someone, megastar.
– OPPOSITES obscurity.

celestial ▶ adjective ❶ *a celestial body* (IN) SPACE, heavenly, astronomical, extraterrestrial, stellar, planetary. ❷ *celestial beings* HEAVENLY, holy, saintly, divine, godly, godlike,

ethereal; immortal, angelic, seraphic, cherubic.
– OPPOSITES earthly, hellish.

celibate ▶ adjective UNMARRIED, single, unwed, spouseless; chaste, virginal, virgin, maidenly, maiden, intact, abstinent, self-denying.

cell ▶ noun ❶ *a prison cell* ROOM, cubicle, chamber; dungeon, oubliette, lock-up. ❷ *each cell of the honeycomb* COMPARTMENT, cavity, hole, hollow, section. ❸ *terrorist cells* UNIT, faction, arm, section, coterie, group.

cellar ▶ noun BASEMENT, vault, underground room, lower ground floor; crypt, undercroft.
– OPPOSITES attic.

cement ▶ noun *polystyrene cement* ADHESIVE, glue, fixative, gum, paste; superglue, epoxy resin; *N. Amer.* mucilage; *N. Amer. informal* stickum.
▶ verb *he cemented the sample to a microscope slide* STICK, bond; fasten, fix, affix, attach, secure, bind, glue, gum, paste.

cemetery ▶ noun GRAVEYARD, churchyard, burial ground, necropolis; *informal* boneyard; *historical* potter's field; *archaic* God's acre.

censor ▶ noun *the film censors* EXPURGATOR, bowdlerizer; examiner, inspector, editor.
▶ verb *letters home were censored* CUT, delete parts of, make cuts in, blue-pencil; edit, expurgate, bowdlerize, sanitize; *informal* clean up.

censorious ▶ adjective HYPERCRITICAL, overcritical, disapproving, condemnatory, denunciatory, deprecatory, disparaging, reproachful, reproving, censuring, captious; *formal* castigatory.
– OPPOSITES complimentary.

censure ▶ verb *he was censured for his conduct.* See REPRIMAND verb.
▶ noun *a note of censure* CONDEMNATION, criticism, attack, abuse; reprimand, rebuke, admonishment, reproof, reproval, upbraiding, disapproval, reproach, reprehension, obloquy; *formal* excoriation, castigation; *rare* objurgation.
– OPPOSITES approval.

central ▶ adjective ❶ *occupying a central position* MIDDLE, centre, halfway, midway, mid, median, medial, mean; *Anatomy* mesial. ❷ *central London* INNER, innermost, middle, mid. ❸ *their central campaign issue* MAIN, chief, principal, primary, leading, foremost, first, most important, predominant, dominant, key, crucial, vital, essential, basic, fundamental, core, prime, premier, paramount, major, overriding; *informal* number-one.
– OPPOSITES side, outer, subordinate.

centralize ▶ verb CONCENTRATE, consolidate, amalgamate, condense, unify, streamline, focus, rationalize.
– OPPOSITES devolve.

centre ▶ noun *the centre of the town* MIDDLE, nucleus, heart, core, hub; middle point, midpoint, halfway point, mean, median.
– OPPOSITES edge.
▶ verb *the story centres on a doctor* FOCUS, concentrate, pivot, revolve, be based.

centrepiece ▶ noun HIGHLIGHT, main feature, high point/spot, best part, climax; focus of attention, focal point, centre of attention/interest, magnet, cynosure.

ceramics ▶ plural noun POTTERY, pots, china.

ceremonial ▶ adjective *a ceremonial occasion* FORMAL, official, state, public; ritual, ritualistic, prescribed, stately, courtly, solemn.
– OPPOSITES informal.
▶ noun *diplomatic ceremonial* RITUAL, ceremony, rite, formality, pomp, protocol; *formal* praxis.

ceremonious ▶ adjective DIGNIFIED, majestic, imposing, impressive, solemn, stately, formal, courtly; regal, imperial, elegant, grand, glorious, splendid, magnificent, resplendent, portentous; *informal* starchy.

ceremony ▶ noun ❶ *a wedding ceremony* RITE, ritual, ceremonial, observance; service, sacrament, liturgy, worship, celebration. ❷ *the new Queen was proclaimed with due ceremony* POMP, protocol, formalities, niceties, decorum, etiquette, punctilio, politesse.

certain ▶ adjective ❶ *I'm certain he's guilty* SURE, confident, positive, convinced, in no doubt, satisfied, assured, persuaded. ❷ *it is certain that more changes are in the offing* UNQUESTIONABLE, sure, definite, beyond question, not in doubt, indubitable, undeniable, irrefutable, indisputable; obvious, evident, recognized, confirmed, accepted, acknowledged, undisputed, undoubted, unquestioned, as sure as eggs is eggs. ❸ *they are certain to win* SURE, very likely, bound, destined. ❹ *certain defeat* INEVITABLE, assured, destined, predestined; unavoidable, inescapable, inexorable, ineluctable. ❺ *there is no certain cure for this* RELIABLE, dependable, trustworthy, foolproof, tried and tested, effective, guaranteed, sure, unfailing, infallible; *informal* sure-fire; *dated* sovereign. ❻ *a certain sum of money* DETERMINED, definite, fixed, established, precise. ❼ *a certain lady* PARTICULAR, specific, individual, special. ❽ *to a certain extent that is true* MODERATE, modest, medium, middling; limited, small.
– OPPOSITES doubtful, possible, unlikely.

certainly ▶ adverb ❶ *this is certainly a late work* UNQUESTIONABLY, surely, assuredly, definitely, beyond/without question, without doubt, indubitably, undeniably, irrefutably, indisputably; obviously, patently, evidently, plainly, clearly, unmistakably, undisputedly, undoubtedly, as sure as eggs is eggs. ❷ *our revenues are certainly lower* ADMITTEDLY, without question,

definitely, undoubtedly, without a doubt.
– OPPOSITES possibly.
▶ **exclamation** *'Shall we eat now?' 'Certainly.'* YES, definitely, absolutely, sure, by all means, indeed, of course, naturally; affirmative; *Brit. dated* rather.

certainty ▶ **noun** ❶ *she knew with certainty that he was telling the truth* CONFIDENCE, sureness, positiveness, conviction, certitude, assurance. ❷ *he accepted defeat as a certainty* INEVITABILITY, foregone conclusion; *informal* sure thing; *Brit. informal* cert, dead cert.
– OPPOSITES doubt, possibility.

certificate ▶ **noun** GUARANTEE, certification, document, authorization, authentication, credentials, accreditation, licence, diploma.

certify ▶ **verb** ❶ *the aircraft was certified as airworthy* VERIFY, guarantee, attest, validate, confirm, substantiate, endorse, vouch for, testify to; provide evidence, give proof, prove, demonstrate. ❷ *a certified hospital* ACCREDIT, recognize, license, authorize, approve, warrant.

certitude ▶ **noun** CERTAINTY, confidence, sureness, positiveness, conviction, assurance.
– OPPOSITES doubt.

cessation ▶ **noun** END, ending, termination, stopping, halting, ceasing, finish, finishing, stoppage, conclusion, winding up, discontinuation, abandonment, suspension, breaking off, cutting short.
– OPPOSITES start, resumption.

cession ▶ **noun** SURRENDER, surrendering, ceding, concession, relinquishment, yielding, giving up; handing over, transfer; abandonment, sacrifice; *poetic/literary* forsaking.

chafe ▶ **verb** ❶ *the collar chafed his neck* ABRADE, graze, rub against, gall, scrape, scratch; *Medicine* excoriate. ❷ *I chafed her feet* RUB, warm (up). ❸ *material chafed by the rock* WEAR AWAY/DOWN, erode, abrade, scour, scrape away. ❹ *the bank chafed at the restrictions* BE ANGRY, be annoyed, be irritated, fume, be exasperated, be frustrated.

chaff[1] ▶ **noun** ❶ *separating the chaff from the grain* HUSKS, hulls, pods, shells, bran; *N. Amer.* shucks. ❷ *the proposals were so much chaff* RUBBISH, dross; *N. Amer.* garbage, trash; *Austral./NZ* mullock; *informal* junk.

chaff[2] ▶ **noun** *good-natured chaff* BANTER, repartee, teasing, ragging, joking, jesting, raillery, badinage, wisecracks, witticism(s); *informal* kidding, ribbing; *formal* persiflage.
▶ **verb** *the pleasures of chaffing your mates* TEASE, make fun of, poke fun at, rag; *informal* take the mickey out of, rib, josh, kid, wind up, have on, pull someone's leg; *N. Amer. informal* goof on, rag on, razz; *Austral./NZ informal* poke mullock at, poke borak at; *informal, dated* twit; *archaic* make sport of.

chagrin ▶ **noun** ANNOYANCE, irritation, vexation, exasperation, displeasure, dissatisfaction, discontent; anger, rage, fury, wrath, indignation, resentment; embarrassment, mortification, humiliation, shame.
– OPPOSITES delight.

chain ▶ **noun** ❶ *he was held in chains* FETTERS, shackles, irons, leg-irons, manacles, handcuffs; *informal* cuffs, bracelets; *Brit. archaic, informal* darbies; *historical* bilboes; *archaic* gyves. ❷ *a chain of events* SERIES, succession, string, sequence, train, course. ❸ *a chain of shops* GROUP, multiple shop/store, multiple.
▶ **verb** *she chained her bicycle to the railings* SECURE, fasten, tie, tether, hitch; restrain, shackle, fetter, manacle, handcuff.

chair ▶ **noun** ❶ *he sat down on a chair* SEAT. ❷ *the chair of the committee. See* CHAIRMAN. ❸ *a university chair* PROFESSORSHIP. ❹ (*N. Amer.*) *he was sent to the chair* ELECTRIC CHAIR, electrocution, execution.
▶ **verb** *she chairs the economic committee* PRESIDE OVER, take the chair of; lead, direct, run, manage, control, be in charge of.

chairman, chairwoman ▶ **noun** CHAIR, chairperson, president, leader, convener; spokesperson, spokesman, spokeswoman.

chalk
– RELATED TERMS calcareous.
■ **chalk something up** ❶ *he has chalked up another success* ACHIEVE, attain, accomplish, gain, earn, win, succeed in making, make, get, obtain, notch up, rack up. ❷ *I forgot completely—chalk it up to age* ATTRIBUTE, assign, ascribe, put down; blame on, pin on, lay at the door of.

chalky ▶ **adjective** ❶ *chalky skin* PALE, bloodless, pallid, colourless, wan, ashen, white, pasty. ❷ *chalky bits at the bottom of the glass* POWDERY, gritty, granular; *archaic* pulverulent.

challenge ▶ **noun** ❶ *he accepted the challenge* DARE, provocation; summons. ❷ *a challenge to his leadership* TEST, questioning, dispute, stand, opposition, confrontation. ❸ *it was proving quite a challenge* PROBLEM, difficult task, test, trial.
▶ **verb** ❶ *we challenged their statistics* QUESTION, disagree with, dispute, take issue with, protest against, call into question, object to. ❷ *he challenged one of my men to a duel* DARE, summon, throw down the gauntlet to. ❸ *changes that would challenge them* TEST, tax, strain, make demands on; stretch, stimulate, inspire, excite.

challenging ▶ **adjective** DEMANDING, testing, taxing, exacting; stretching, exciting, stimulating, inspiring; difficult, tough, hard, formidable, onerous, arduous, strenuous, gruelling; *formal* exigent.
– OPPOSITES easy, uninspiring.

chamber ▶ **noun** ❶ *a debating chamber* ROOM, hall, assembly room, auditorium. ❷ (*archaic*) *we slept safely in our chamber* BEDROOM, room; *poetic/literary* bower; *historical* boudoir; *archaic* bedchamber. ❸ *the left chamber of the heart* COMPARTMENT, cavity; *Anatomy* auricle, ventricle.

champagne ▶ **noun** SPARKLING WINE; mousseux, spumante, cava; *informal* champers, bubbly, fizz.

champion ▶ **noun** ❶ *the world champion* WINNER, title-holder, defending champion, gold medallist; prizewinner, victor (ludorum); *informal* champ, number one. ❷ *a champion of change* ADVOCATE, proponent, promoter, supporter, defender, upholder, backer, exponent; campaigner, lobbyist, crusader, apologist; *N. Amer.* booster. ❸ (*historical*) *the king's champion* KNIGHT, man-at-arms, warrior.

▶ **verb** *championing the rights of tribal peoples* ADVOCATE, promote, defend, uphold, support, back, stand up for, take someone's part; campaign for, lobby for, fight for, crusade for, stick up for.

– OPPOSITES oppose.

chance ▶ **noun** ❶ *there was a chance he might be released* POSSIBILITY, prospect, probability, likelihood, likeliness, expectation, anticipation; risk, threat, danger. ❷ *I gave her a chance to answer* OPPORTUNITY, opening, occasion, turn, time, window (of opportunity); *N. Amer. & Austral./NZ* show; *informal* shot, look-in. ❸ *Nigel took an awful chance* RISK, gamble, venture, speculation, long shot, leap in the dark. ❹ *pure chance* ACCIDENT, coincidence, serendipity, fate, destiny, fortuity, providence, happenstance; good fortune, (good) luck, fluke.

▶ **adjective** *a chance discovery* ACCIDENTAL, fortuitous, adventitious, fluky, coincidental, serendipitous; unintentional, unintended, inadvertent, unplanned.

– OPPOSITES intentional.

▶ **verb** ❶ *I chanced to meet him* HAPPEN. ❷ (*informal*) *she chanced another look* RISK, hazard, venture, try; *formal* essay.

■ **by chance** FORTUITOUSLY, by accident, accidentally, coincidentally, serendipitously; unintentionally, inadvertently.

■ **chance on/upon** COME ACROSS/UPON, run across/into, happen on, light on, stumble on, find by chance, meet (by chance); *informal* bump into; *archaic* run against.

chancy ▶ **adjective** (*informal*) RISKY, unpredictable, uncertain, precarious; unsafe, insecure, tricky, high-risk, hazardous, perilous, parlous; *informal* dicey, hairy; *Brit. informal* dodgy.

– OPPOSITES predictable.

change ▶ **verb** ❶ *this could change the face of Britain | things have changed* ALTER, make/become different, adjust, adapt, amend, modify, revise, refine; reshape, refashion, redesign, restyle, revamp, rework, remodel, reorganize, reorder; vary, transform, transfigure, transmute, metamorphose, evolve; *informal* tweak; *technical* permute. ❷ *he's changed his job* EXCHANGE, substitute, swap, switch, replace, alternate, interchange.

– OPPOSITES preserve, keep.

▶ **noun** ❶ *a change of plan* ALTERATION, modification, variation, revision, amendment, adjustment, adaptation; remodelling, reshaping, rearrangement, reordering, restyling, reworking; metamorphosis, transformation, evolution, mutation; *humorous* transmogrification. ❷ *a change of government* EXCHANGE, substitution, swap, switch, replacement, alternation, interchange. ❸ *I've no change* COINS, loose/small change, (hard) cash, silver, coppers, specie.

■ **have a change of heart**. *See* HEART.

changeable ▶ **adjective** ❶ *the weather will be changeable | changeable moods* VARIABLE, inconstant, varying, changing, fluctuating, irregular; erratic, inconsistent, unstable, unsettled, turbulent, changeful, protean; fickle, capricious, temperamental, volatile, mercurial, unpredictable, blowing hot and cold; *informal* up and down; *poetic/literary* fluctuant. ❷ *the colours are changeable* ALTERABLE, adjustable, modifiable, variable, mutable, exchangeable, interchangeable, replaceable.

– OPPOSITES constant.

changeless ▶ **adjective** UNCHANGING, unvarying, timeless, static, fixed, permanent, constant, unchanged, consistent, uniform, undeviating; stable, steady, unchangeable, unalterable, invariable, immutable.

– OPPOSITES variable.

channel ▶ **noun** ❶ *the English Channel* STRAIT(S), sound, narrows, (sea) passage. ❷ *the water ran down a channel* DUCT, gutter, conduit, trough, culvert, sluice, spillway, race, drain. ❸ *a channel for their extraordinary energy* USE, medium, vehicle, way of harnessing; release (mechanism), safety valve, vent. ❹ *a channel of communication* MEANS, medium, instrument, mechanism, agency, vehicle, route, avenue.

▶ **verb** ❶ *she channelled out a groove* HOLLOW OUT, gouge (out), cut (out). ❷ *many countries channel their aid through charities* CONVEY, transmit, conduct, direct, guide, relay, pass on, transfer.

chant ▶ **noun** ❶ *the protesters' chants* SHOUT, cry, (rallying) call, slogan. ❷ *the melodious chant of the monks* INCANTATION, intonation, singing, song, recitative; *rare* cantillation.

▶ **verb** ❶ *protesters were chanting slogans* SHOUT, chorus, repeat. ❷ *the choir chanted Psalm 118* SING, intone, incant; *rare* cantillate.

chaos ▶ **noun** DISORDER, disarray, disorganization, confusion, mayhem, bedlam, pandemo-

nium, havoc, turmoil, tumult, commotion, disruption, upheaval, uproar; a muddle, a mess, a shambles; anarchy, lawlessness; *informal* hullabaloo, all hell broken loose.
–OPPOSITES order.

chaotic ▶ **adjective** DISORDERLY, disordered, in disorder, in chaos, in disarray, disorganized, topsy-turvy, in pandemonium, in turmoil, in uproar; in a muddle, in a mess, messy, in a shambles; anarchic, lawless; *Brit. informal* shambolic.

chap[1] ▶ **verb** *my skin chapped in the wind* BECOME RAW, become sore, become inflamed, chafe, crack.

chap[2] ▶ **noun** (*Brit. informal*) *he's a nice chap* MAN, boy, character; *informal* fellow, guy, geezer; *Brit. informal* bloke, lad, bod; *N. Amer. informal* dude, hombre; *Brit. informal, dated* cove.

chaperone ▶ **noun** *Aunt Millie went as chaperone* COMPANION, duenna, escort, protectress, protector, minder.
▶ **verb** *she was chaperoned by her mother* ACCOMPANY, escort, attend, watch over, keep an eye on, protect, mind.

chapter ▶ **noun** ❶ *the first chapter of the book* SECTION, division, part, portion. ❷ *a new chapter in our history* PERIOD, phase, page, stage, epoch, era. ❸ (*N. Amer.*) *a local chapter of the American Cancer Society* BRANCH, division, subdivision, section, department, lodge, wing, arm. ❹ *the cathedral chapter* GOVERNING BODY, council, assembly, convocation, synod, consistory.

char ▶ **verb** SCORCH, burn, singe, sear, blacken; *informal* toast.

character ▶ **noun** ❶ *a forceful character | the character of a town* PERSONALITY, nature, disposition, temperament, temper, mentality, make-up; features, qualities, properties, traits; spirit, essence, identity, ethos, complexion, tone, feel, feeling. ❷ *a woman of character* INTEGRITY, honour, moral strength/fibre, rectitude, uprightness; fortitude, strength, backbone, resolve, grit, will power; *informal* guts, gutsiness; *Brit. informal* bottle. ❸ *a stain on his character* REPUTATION, (good) name, standing, stature, position, status. ❹ (*informal*) *a bit of a character* ECCENTRIC, oddity, madcap, crank, individualist, nonconformist, rare bird; *informal* oddball; *Brit. informal* odd bod; *informal, dated* card, caution. ❺ *a boorish character* PERSON, man, woman, soul, creature, individual, customer; *informal* cookie; *Brit. informal* bod, guy; *informal, dated* body, dog. ❻ *the characters develop throughout the play* PERSONA, role, part; (**characters**) dramatis personae. ❼ *thirty characters* LETTER, figure, symbol, sign, mark.

characteristic ▶ **noun** *interesting characteristics* ATTRIBUTE, feature, (essential) quality, property, trait, aspect, element, facet; mannerism, habit, custom, idiosyncrasy, peculiarity, quirk, oddity, foible.
▶ **adjective** *his characteristic eloquence* TYPICAL, usual, normal, predictable, habitual; distinctive, particular, special, especial, peculiar, idiosyncratic, singular, unique.

characterize ▶ **verb** ❶ *the period was characterized by scientific advancement* DISTINGUISH, make distinctive, mark, typify, set apart. ❷ *the women are characterized as prophets of doom* PORTRAY, depict, present, represent, describe; categorize, class, style, brand.

charade ▶ **noun** FARCE, pantomime, travesty, mockery, parody, act, masquerade.

charge ▶ **verb** ❶ *he didn't charge much* ASK (IN PAYMENT), levy, demand, exact; bill, invoice. ❷ *the subscription will be charged to your account* BILL, debit from, take from. ❸ *two men were charged with affray* ACCUSE, indict, arraign; prosecute, try, put on trial; *N. Amer.* impeach; *archaic* inculpate. ❹ *they charged him with reforming the system* ENTRUST, burden, encumber, saddle, tax. ❺ *the cavalry charged the tanks* ATTACK, storm, assault, assail, fall on, swoop on, descend on; *informal* lay into, tear into. ❻ *riot police charged into the crowd* RUSH, storm, stampede, push, plough, launch oneself, go headlong; *informal* steam; *N. Amer. informal* barrel. ❼ *charge your glasses! | the guns were charged* FILL (UP), top up; load (up), arm, prepare to fire. ❽ *his work was charged with energy* SUFFUSE, pervade, permeate, saturate, infuse, imbue, fill. ❾ *I charge you to stop* ORDER, command, direct, instruct, enjoin; *formal* adjure; *poetic/literary* bid.
▶ **noun** ❶ *all customers pay a charge* FEE, payment, price, tariff, amount, sum, fare, levy. ❷ *he pleaded guilty to the charge* ACCUSATION, allegation, indictment, arraignment; *N. Amer.* impeachment; *archaic* inculpation. ❸ *an infantry charge* ATTACK, assault, offensive, onslaught, drive, push, thrust. ❹ *the child was in her charge* CARE, protection, safe keeping, control; custody, guardianship, wardship; hands; *archaic* ward. ❺ *his charge was to save the business* DUTY, responsibility, task, job, assignment, mission, function; *Brit. informal* pigeon. ❻ *the safety of my charge* WARD, protégé, dependant. ❼ *the judge gave a careful charge to the jury* INSTRUCTION, direction, directive, order, command, dictate, exhortation. ❽ (*N. Amer. informal*) *I get a real charge out of working hard* THRILL, tingle, glow; excitement, stimulation, enjoyment, pleasure; *informal* kick, buzz.
■ **in charge of** RESPONSIBLE FOR, in control of, at the helm/wheel of; MANAGING, running, administering, directing, supervising, overseeing, controlling; *informal* running the show.

charisma ▶ **noun** CHARM, presence, (force of) personality, strength of character; (animal) magnetism, attractiveness, appeal, allure.

charismatic ▶ adjective CHARMING, fascinating, strong in character; magnetic, captivating, beguiling, attractive, appealing, alluring.

charitable ▶ adjective ❶ *charitable activities* PHILANTHROPIC, humanitarian, altruistic, benevolent, public-spirited; non-profit-making; *formal* eleemosynary. ❷ *charitable people* BIG-HEARTED, generous, open-handed, free-handed, munificent, bountiful, beneficent; *poetic/literary* bounteous. ❸ *he was charitable in his judgements* MAGNANIMOUS, generous, liberal, tolerant, easy-going, broad-minded, considerate, sympathetic, lenient, indulgent, forgiving.

charity ▶ noun ❶ *an AIDS charity* NON-PROFIT-MAKING ORGANIZATION, voluntary organization, charitable institution; fund, trust, foundation. ❷ *we don't need charity* FINANCIAL ASSISTANCE, aid, welfare, (financial) relief; handouts, gifts, presents, largesse; *historical* alms. ❸ *his actions are motivated by charity* PHILANTHROPY, humanitarianism, humanity, altruism, public-spiritedness, social conscience, benevolence, beneficence, munificence. ❹ *show a bit of charity* GOODWILL, compassion, consideration, concern, kindness, kind-heartedness, tenderness, tender-heartedness, sympathy, indulgence, tolerance, leniency, caritas; *poetic/literary* bounteousness.

charlatan ▶ noun QUACK, mountebank, sham, fraud, fake, impostor, hoodwinker, hoaxer, cheat, deceiver, double-dealer, (confidence) trickster, swindler, fraudster; *informal* phoney, shark, con man/artist, flimflammer; *Brit. informal* twister; *N. Amer. informal* bunco artist, gold brick, chiseller; *Austral. informal* magsman, illywhacker; *dated* confidence man/woman.

charm ▶ noun ❶ *people were captivated by her charm* ATTRACTIVENESS, beauty, glamour, loveliness; appeal, allure, desirability, seductiveness, sexual/animal magnetism, charisma; *informal* pulling power. ❷ *these traditions retain a lot of charm* APPEAL, drawing power, attraction, allure, fascination. ❸ *magical charms* SPELL, incantation, conjuration, rune, magic formula/word; *N. Amer.* mojo, hex. ❹ *a lucky charm* TALISMAN, fetish, amulet, mascot, totem, juju; *archaic* periapt.

▶ verb ❶ *he charmed them with his singing* DELIGHT, please, win (over), attract, captivate, allure, lure, dazzle, fascinate, enchant, enthral, enrapture, seduce, spellbind. ❷ *he charmed his mother into agreeing* COAX, cajole, wheedle; *informal* sweet-talk, soft-soap; *archaic* blandish.

charming ▶ adjective DELIGHTFUL, pleasing, pleasant, agreeable, likeable, endearing, lovely, lovable, adorable, appealing, attractive, good-looking, prepossessing; alluring, delectable, ravishing, winning, winsome, fetching, captivating, enchanting, entrancing, fascinating, seductive; *informal* heavenly, divine, gorgeous, easy on the eye; *Brit. informal* smashing; *poetic/literary* beauteous; *archaic* fair, comely.
– OPPOSITES repulsive.

chart ▶ noun ❶ *check your ideal weight on the chart* GRAPH, table, diagram, histogram; bar chart, pie chart, flow chart; *Computing* graphic. ❷ *the pop charts* TOP TWENTY, list, listing; *dated* hit parade.

▶ verb ❶ *the changes were charted accurately* TABULATE, plot, graph, record, register, represent; make a chart/diagram of. ❷ *the book charted his progress* FOLLOW, trace, outline, describe, detail, record, document, chronicle, log.

charter ▶ noun ❶ *a Royal charter* AUTHORITY, authorization, sanction, dispensation, consent, permission; permit, licence, warrant, franchise. ❷ *the UN Charter* CONSTITUTION, code, canon; fundamental principles, rules, laws. ❸ *the charter of a yacht* HIRE, hiring, lease, leasing, rent, rental, renting; booking, reservation, reserving.

▶ verb *they chartered a bus* HIRE, lease, rent; book, reserve.

chary ▶ adjective WARY, cautious, circumspect, heedful, careful, on one's guard; distrustful, mistrustful, sceptical, suspicious, dubious, hesitant, reluctant, leery, nervous, apprehensive, uneasy; *informal* cagey, iffy.

chase[1] ▶ verb ❶ *the dogs chased the fox* PURSUE, run after, give chase to, follow; hunt, track, trail; *informal* tail. ❷ *chasing young girls* WOO, pursue, run after, make advances to, flirt with, pay court to; *informal* chat up, come on to; *dated* court, romance, set one's cap at, make love to. ❸ *she chased away the donkeys* DRIVE, send, scare; *informal* send packing. ❹ *she chased away all thoughts of him* DISPEL, banish, dismiss, drive away, shut out, put out of one's mind. ❺ *photographers chased on to the runway* RUSH, dash, race, speed, streak, shoot, charge, scramble, scurry, hurry, fly, pelt; *informal* scoot, belt, tear, zip, whip; *N. Amer. informal* boogie, hightail, clip; *archaic* hie.

▶ noun *they gave up the chase* PURSUIT, hunt, trail.

■ **chase someone/something up** PESTER, harass, harry, nag; seek out, find, go after; *informal* hassle.

chase[2] ▶ verb *the figures are chased on the dish* ENGRAVE, etch, carve, inscribe, cut, chisel.

chasm ▶ noun ❶ *a deep chasm* GORGE, abyss, canyon, ravine, gully, gulf, defile, couloir, crevasse, fissure, crevice; *N. Amer.* gulch, coulee. ❷ *the chasm between their views* BREACH, gulf, rift; difference, separation, division, dissension, schism, scission.

chassis ▶ noun FRAMEWORK, frame, structure, substructure, shell, casing, bodywork, body.

chaste ▶ adjective ❶ *chaste girlhood* VIRGINAL, virgin, intact, maidenly, unmarried, unwed; celibate, abstinent, self-restrained, self-denying, continent; innocent, virtuous, pure (as the driven snow), sinless, undefiled, unsullied; *Christianity* immaculate; *poetic/literary* vestal. ❷ *a chaste kiss on the cheek* NON-SEXUAL, platonic, innocent. ❸ *the dark, chaste interior* PLAIN, simple, bare, unadorned, undecorated, unornamented, unembellished, functional, no-frills, austere.

– OPPOSITES promiscuous, passionate.

chasten ▶ verb ❶ *both men were chastened* SUBDUE, humble, cow, squash, deflate, flatten, take down a peg or two, put someone in their place; *informal* cut down to size, settle someone's hash. ❷ (*archaic*) *the Heaven that chastens us. See* CHASTISE sense 1.

chastise ▶ verb ❶ *the staff were chastised for arriving late* SCOLD, upbraid, berate, reprimand, reprove, rebuke, admonish, chide, censure, lambaste, lecture, give someone a piece of one's mind, take to task, haul over the coals; *informal* tell off, dress down, bawl out, blow up at, give someone an earful, give someone a roasting, come down on someone like a ton of bricks, have someone's guts for garters, slap someone's wrist, rap over the knuckles, give someone hell; *Brit. informal* carpet, tick off, have a go at, tear someone off a strip, give someone what for, give someone a rocket; *N. Amer. informal* chew out, ream out; *Austral. informal* monster; *dated* give someone a rating; *formal* castigate; *archaic* chasten; *rare* reprehend, objurgate. ❷ (*dated*) *her mistress chastised her with a whip. See* BEAT verb sense 1.

– OPPOSITES praise.

chastity ▶ noun CELIBACY, chasteness, virginity, abstinence, self-restraint, self-denial, continence; singleness, maidenhood; innocence, purity, virtue, morality; *Christianity* immaculateness.

chat ▶ noun *I popped in for a chat* TALK, conversation, gossip, chatter, heart-to-heart, tête-à-tête, blather; *informal* jaw, gas, confab; *Brit. informal* natter, chinwag, rabbit; *N. Amer. informal* rap, bull session; *formal* confabulation, colloquy.

▶ verb *they chatted with their guests* TALK, gossip, chatter, speak, converse, engage in conversation, tittle-tattle, prattle, jabber, babble; *informal* gas, jaw, chew the rag/fat, yap, yak, yabber, yatter, yammer; *Brit. informal* natter, rabbit, chunter, have a chinwag; *N. Amer. informal* shoot the breeze/bull, visit; *Austral./NZ informal* mag; *formal* confabulate; *archaic* clack.

■ **chat someone up** (*informal*) FLIRT WITH, make advances to; *informal* come on to; *dated* make love to, set one's cap at, romance.

chatter ▶ noun *she tired him with her chatter* CHAT, talk, gossip, chit-chat, patter, jabbering, jabber, prattling, prattle, babbling, babble, tittle-tattle, blathering, blather; *informal* yabbering, yammering, yattering, yapping, jawing, chewing the rag/fat; *Brit. informal* nattering, chuntering, rabbiting on; *formal* confabulation, colloquy; *archaic* clack.

▶ verb *they chattered excitedly. See* CHAT verb.

chatterbox ▶ noun (*informal*) TALKER, chatterer, prattler; *N. Amer.* blatherskite; *informal* windbag, gasbag, blabbermouth; *Brit. informal* natterer.

chatty ▶ adjective ❶ *he was a chatty person* TALKATIVE, communicative, expansive, unreserved, gossipy, gossiping, garrulous, loquacious, voluble, verbose; *informal* mouthy, gabby, gassy; *Brit. informal* able to talk the hind legs off a donkey. ❷ *a chatty letter* CONVERSATIONAL, gossipy, informal, casual, familiar, friendly; *informal* newsy.

– OPPOSITES taciturn.

chauvinist ▶ adjective *chauvinist sentiments* JINGOISTIC, chauvinistic, excessively patriotic, excessively nationalistic, flag-waving, xenophobic, racist, racialist, ethnocentric; sexist, male chauvinist, anti-feminist, misogynist, woman-hating.

▶ noun *he's a chauvinist* SEXIST, anti-feminist, misogynist, woman-hater; *informal* male chauvinist pig, MCP.

cheap ▶ adjective ❶ *cheap tickets* INEXPENSIVE, low-priced, low-cost, economical, competitive, affordable, reasonable, reasonably priced, budget, economy, bargain, cut-price, reduced, discounted, discount, rock-bottom, giveaway, bargain-basement; *informal* dirt cheap. ❷ *plain without looking cheap* POOR-QUALITY, second-rate, third-rate, substandard, low-grade, inferior, vulgar, shoddy, trashy, tawdry, meretricious, cheap and nasty, cheapjack, gimcrack, Brummagem, pinchbeck; *informal* rubbishy, cheapo, junky, tacky, kitsch; *Brit. informal* naff, duff, ropy, grotty; *N. Amer. informal* two-bit, dime-store. ❸ *the cheap exploitation of suffering* DESPICABLE, contemptible, immoral, unscrupulous, unprincipled, unsavoury, distasteful, vulgar, ignoble, shameful; *archaic* scurvy. ❹ *he made me feel cheap* ASHAMED, humiliated, mortified, debased, degraded. ❺ (*N. Amer. informal*) *he made the other guests look cheap. See* MEAN² sense 1.

– OPPOSITES expensive.

cheapen ▶ verb ❶ *cheapening the cost of exports* REDUCE, lower (in price), cut, mark down, discount; *informal* slash. ❷ *Hetty never cheapened herself* DEMEAN, debase, degrade, lower, humble, devalue, abase, discredit, disgrace, dishonour, shame, humiliate, mortify, prostitute.

cheat ▶ verb ❶ *customers were cheated* SWINDLE, defraud, deceive, trick, dupe, hoodwink, double-cross, gull; *informal* diddle, rip off, con, fleece, shaft, sting, bilk, rook, gyp, finagle, flimflam, put one over on, pull a fast one on; *N. Amer. informal* sucker, gold-brick, stiff; *Austral. informal* pull a swifty on; *formal* mulct; *poetic/literary* cozen; *archaic* chicane. ❷ *she cheated Ryan out of his fortune* DEPRIVE OF, deny, prevent from gaining; *informal* do out of. ❸ *the boy cheated death* AVOID, escape, evade, elude; foil, frustrate, thwart. ❹ *cheating husbands* COMMIT ADULTERY, be unfaithful, stray; *informal* two-time, play about/around; *Brit. informal* play away.

▶ **noun** ❶ *a liar and a cheat* SWINDLER, cheater, fraudster, (confidence) trickster, deceiver, hoaxer, hoodwinker, double-dealer, double-crosser, sham, fraud, fake, charlatan, quack, mountebank; *informal* con man/artist, shark, sharper, phoney, flimflammer; *Brit. informal* twister; *N. Amer. informal* grifter, bunco artist, gold brick, chiseller; *Austral. informal* magsman, illywhacker; *dated* confidence man, confidence woman. ❷ *a sure cheat for generating cash* SWINDLE, fraud, deception, deceit, hoax, sham, trick, ruse; *informal* con.

check ▶ **verb** ❶ *troops checked all vehicles | I checked her background* EXAMINE, inspect, look at/over, scrutinize, survey; study, investigate, research, probe, look into, enquire into; *informal* check out, give something a/the once-over. ❷ *he checked that the gun was cocked* MAKE SURE, confirm, verify. ❸ *two defeats checked their progress* HALT, stop, arrest, cut short; bar, obstruct, hamper, impede, inhibit, frustrate, foil, thwart, curb, block, stall, hold up, retard, delay, slow down; *poetic/literary* stay. ❹ *her tears could not be checked* SUPPRESS, repress, restrain, control, curb, rein in, stifle, hold back, choke back; *informal* keep a lid on.

▶ **noun** ❶ *a check of the records* EXAMINATION, inspection, scrutiny, scrutinization, perusal, study, investigation, probe, analysis; test, trial, monitoring; check-up; *informal* once-over, look-see. ❷ *a check on the abuse of authority* CONTROL, restraint, constraint, curb, limitation. ❸ (*N. Amer.*) *the waitress arrived with the check* BILL, account, invoice, statement; *N. Amer. informal* tab; *archaic* reckoning.

■ **check in** REPORT (ONE'S ARRIVAL), book in, register.

■ **check out** LEAVE, vacate, depart; pay the bill, settle up.

■ **check something out** (*informal*) ❶ *the police checked out dozens of leads* INVESTIGATE, look into, enquire into, probe, research, examine, go over; assess, weigh up, analyse, evaluate; follow up; *informal* give something a/the once-over; *N. Amer. informal* scope out. ❷ *she checked herself out in the mirror* LOOK AT, survey, regard, inspect, contemplate; *informal* have a gander/squint at; *Brit. informal* have a dekko/butcher's at, clock; *N. Amer. informal* eyeball.

■ **keep something in check** CURB, restrain, hold back, keep a tight rein on, rein in/back; control, govern, master, suppress, stifle; *informal* keep a lid on.

check-up ▶ **noun** EXAMINATION, inspection, evaluation, analysis, survey, probe, test, appraisal; check, health check; *informal* once-over, going-over.

cheek ▶ **noun** *that's enough of your cheek!* IMPUDENCE, impertinence, insolence, cheekiness, presumption, effrontery, gall, pertness, impoliteness, disrespect, bad manners, overfamiliarity, cockiness; answering back, talking back; *informal* brass (neck), lip, mouth, chutzpah; *Brit. informal* sauce, backchat; *N. Amer. informal* sass, sassiness, nerviness, back talk; *archaic* assumption.

▶ **verb** *they were cheeking the dinner lady* ANSWER BACK, talk back, be cheeky, be impertinent; *Brit. informal* backchat; *N. Amer. informal* sass, be sassy.

cheeky ▶ **adjective** IMPUDENT, impertinent, insolent, presumptuous, forward, pert, bold (as brass), brazen, cocky, overfamiliar, discourteous, disrespectful, impolite, bad-mannered; *informal* brass-necked, lippy, mouthy, fresh, saucy; *N. Amer. informal* sassy, nervy; *archaic* assumptive.

– OPPOSITES respectful, polite.

cheep ▶ **verb** CHIRP, chirrup, twitter, tweet, peep, chitter, chirr, trill, warble, sing.

cheer ▶ **noun** ❶ *the cheers of the crowd* HURRAH, hurray, whoop, bravo, shout; hosanna, alleluia; (**cheers**) acclaim, acclamation, clamour, applause, ovation. ❷ *a time of cheer* HAPPINESS, joy, joyousness, cheerfulness, cheeriness, gladness, merriment, gaiety, jubilation, jollity, jolliness, high spirits, joviality, jocularity, conviviality, light-heartedness; merrymaking, pleasure, rejoicing, revelry. ❸ *Christmas cheer* FARE, food, foodstuffs, eatables, provender; drink, beverages; *informal* eats, nibbles, nosh, grub, chow; *Brit. informal* scoff; *dated* victuals; *formal* comestibles; *poetic/literary* viands.

– OPPOSITES boo, sadness.

▶ **verb** ❶ *they cheered their team* ACCLAIM, hail, salute, shout for, hurrah, hurray, applaud, clap, put one's hands together for; bring the house down; *informal* holler for, give someone a big hand; *N. Amer. informal* ballyhoo. ❷ *the bad weather did little to cheer me* RAISE SOMEONE'S SPIRITS, make happier, brighten, buoy up, enliven, exhilarate, hearten, gladden, uplift, perk up, encourage, inspirit; *informal* buck up.

– OPPOSITES boo, depress.

■ **cheer someone on** ENCOURAGE, urge on, spur on, drive on, motivate, inspire, fire (up), inspirit; *N. Amer.* light a fire under.

■ **cheer up** PERK UP, brighten (up), become more cheerful, liven up, rally, revive, bounce back, take heart; *informal* buck up.

■ **cheer someone up**. *See* CHEER verb sense 2.

cheerful ▶ adjective ❶ *he arrived looking cheerful* HAPPY, jolly, merry, bright, glad, sunny, joyful, joyous, light-hearted, in good/high spirits, full of the joys of spring, sparkling, bubbly, exuberant, buoyant, ebullient, cock-a-hoop, elated, gleeful, breezy, cheery, jaunty, animated, radiant, smiling; jovial, genial, good-humoured; carefree, unworried, untroubled, without a care in the world; *informal* upbeat, chipper, chirpy, peppy, bright-eyed and bushy-tailed, full of beans; *dated* gay; *formal* jocund; *poetic/literary* gladsome, blithe, blithesome. ❷ *a cheerful room* PLEASANT, attractive, agreeable, cheering, bright, sunny, happy, friendly, welcoming.
–OPPOSITES sad.

cheerio ▶ exclamation (*Brit. informal*) GOODBYE, farewell, adieu, au revoir, ciao, adios, auf Wiedersehen, sayonara; *Austral./NZ* hooray; *informal* bye, bye-bye, so long, see you (later), later(s); *Brit. informal* cheers, ta-ta, ta-ra; *informal, dated* pip pip, toodle-oo.

cheerless ▶ adjective GLOOMY, dreary, dull, dismal, bleak, drab, sombre, dark, dim, dingy, funereal; austere, stark, bare, comfortless, unwelcoming, uninviting; miserable, wretched, joyless, depressing, disheartening, dispiriting.

cheers ▶ exclamation ❶ (*informal*) *he raised his glass and said 'Cheers!'* HERE'S TO YOU, good health, your health, skol, prosit, salut; *informal* bottoms up, down the hatch; *Brit. informal* here's mud in your eye; *Brit. informal, dated* cheerio, chin-chin. ❷ (*Brit. informal*) *cheers, see you later! See* CHEERIO. ❸ (*Brit. informal*) *cheers, mate* (MANY) THANKS, thanks a lot, thank you (kindly), much obliged; *informal* thanks a million; *Brit. informal* ta.

cheery ▶ adjective. *See* CHEERFUL sense 1.

chef ▶ noun COOK, cordon bleu cook, food preparer; chef de cuisine, chef de partie; pastry cook, saucier; *N. Amer. informal* short-order cook.

chef-d'œuvre ▶ noun MASTERPIECE, masterwork, finest work, magnum opus, pièce de résistance, tour de force.

chequered ▶ adjective ❶ *a chequered tablecloth* CHECKED, multicoloured, many-coloured. ❷ *a chequered history* VARIED, mixed, full of ups and downs, vicissitudinous; unstable, irregular, erratic, inconstant; *informal* up and down.

cherish ▶ verb ❶ *a woman he could cherish* ADORE, hold dear, love, dote on, be devoted to, revere, esteem, admire; think the world of, set great store by, hold in high esteem; care for, look after, protect, preserve, keep safe. ❷ *I cherish her letters* TREASURE, prize, value highly, hold dear. ❸ *they cherished dreams of glory* HARBOUR, entertain, possess, hold (on to), cling to, keep in one's mind, foster, nurture.

cherub ▶ noun ❶ *she was borne up to heaven by cherubs* ANGEL, seraph. ❷ *a cherub of 18 months* BABY, infant, toddler; pretty/loveable child, innocent child, little angel; *informal* (tiny) tot, tiny; *poetic/literary* babe (in arms).

cherubic ▶ adjective ANGELIC, sweet, cute, adorable, appealing, loveable; innocent, seraphic, saintly.

chest ▶ noun ❶ *a bullet wound in the chest* BREAST, upper body, torso, trunk; *technical* thorax. ❷ *a large chest* BUST, bosom; *archaic* embonpoint. ❸ *an oak chest* BOX, case, casket, crate, trunk, coffer, strongbox.
–RELATED TERMS pectoral, thoracic.

■ **get something off one's chest** (*informal*) CONFESS, disclose, divulge, reveal, make known, make public, make a clean breast of, bring into the open, tell all about, get a load off one's mind.

chew ▶ verb *Carolyn chewed a mouthful of toast* MASTICATE, munch, champ, crunch, nibble, gnaw, eat, consume; *formal* manducate.

■ **chew something over** MEDITATE ON, ruminate on, think about/over/through, mull over, consider, weigh up, ponder on, deliberate on, reflect on, muse on, dwell on, give thought to, turn over in one's mind; brood over, puzzle over, rack one's brains about; *N. Amer.* think on; *informal* kick around/about, bat around/about; *formal* cogitate about; *archaic* pore on.

■ **chew the fat/rag** (*informal*). *See* CHAT verb.

chic ▶ adjective STYLISH, smart, elegant, sophisticated, dressy, dapper, dashing, trim; fashionable, high-fashion, in vogue, up to date, up to the minute, contemporary, à la mode; *informal* trendy, with it, snappy, snazzy, natty, swish; *N. Amer. informal* fly, spiffy, kicky, tony.
–OPPOSITES unfashionable.

chicanery ▶ noun TRICKERY, deception, deceit, deceitfulness, duplicity, dishonesty, deviousness, unscrupulousness, underhandedness, subterfuge, fraud, fraudulence, sharp practice, skulduggery, swindling, cheating, duping, hoodwinking; *informal* crookedness, monkey business, hanky-panky, shenanigans; *Brit. informal* jiggery-pokery; *N. Amer. informal* monkeyshines; *archaic* management, knavery.

chide ▶ verb SCOLD, chastise, upbraid, berate, reprimand, reprove, rebuke, admonish, censure, lambaste, lecture, give someone a piece of one's mind, take to task, haul over the coals; *informal* tell off, dress down, bawl out, blow up at, give someone an earful, give someone a roasting, come down on someone like a ton

of bricks, have someone's guts for garters, slap someone's wrist, rap over the knuckles, give someone hell; *Brit. informal* carpet, tick off, have a go at, tear someone off a strip, give someone what for, give someone a rocket; *N. Amer. informal* chew out, ream out; *Austral. informal* monster; *formal* castigate; *dated* give someone a rating; *archaic* chasten; *rare* reprehend, objurgate.
– OPPOSITES praise.

chief ▶ **noun** ❶ *a Highland chief* LEADER, chieftain, head, headman, ruler, overlord, master, commander, seigneur, liege (lord), potentate. ❷ *the chief of the central bank* HEAD, principal, chief executive, president, chair, chairman, chairwoman, chairperson, governor, director, manager, manageress; employer, proprietor; *N. Amer.* chief executive officer, CEO; *informal* skipper, numero uno, (head) honcho, boss; *Brit. informal* gaffer, guv'nor; *N. Amer. informal* padrone, sachem.
▶ **adjective** ❶ *the chief rabbi* HEAD, leading, principal, premier, highest, foremost, supreme, arch. ❷ *their chief aim* MAIN, principal, most important, primary, prime, first, cardinal, central, key, crucial, essential, predominant, preeminent, paramount, overriding; *informal* number-one.
– RELATED TERMS arch-.
– OPPOSITES subordinate, minor.

chiefly ▶ **adverb** MAINLY, in the main, primarily, principally, predominantly, mostly, for the most part; usually, habitually, typically, commonly, generally, on the whole, largely, by and large, as a rule, almost always.

child ▶ **noun** YOUNGSTER, little one, boy, girl; baby, newborn, infant, toddler; schoolboy, schoolgirl, minor, junior; son, daughter, descendant; (**children**) offspring, progeny; *Scottish & N. English* bairn, laddie, lassie, lass; *informal* kid, kiddie, kiddiewink, nipper, tiny, (tiny) tot, shaver, young 'un, lad; *Brit. informal* sprog; *N. Amer. informal* rug rat; *Austral./NZ informal* anklebiter; *derogatory* brat, guttersnipe; *poetic/literary* babe (in arms).
– RELATED TERMS paedo-.

childbirth ▶ **noun** LABOUR, delivery, giving birth, birthing; *formal* parturition; *dated* confinement; *poetic/literary* travail; *archaic* lying-in, accouchement, childbed.
– RELATED TERMS obstetric, puerperal.

childhood ▶ **noun** YOUTH, early years/life, infancy, babyhood, boyhood, girlhood, preteens, pre-pubescence, minority; the springtime of life, one's salad days; *formal* nonage, juvenescence.
– OPPOSITES adulthood.

childish ▶ **adjective** ❶ *childish behaviour* IMMATURE, babyish, infantile, juvenile, puerile; silly, inane, jejune, foolish, irresponsible. ❷ *a round childish face* CHILDLIKE, youthful, young, young-looking, girlish, boyish.
– OPPOSITES mature, adult.

childlike ▶ **adjective** ❶ *grandmother looked almost childlike* YOUTHFUL, young, young-looking, girlish, boyish. ❷ *geniuses tend to be rather childlike* INNOCENT, artless, guileless, unworldly, unsophisticated, naive, ingenuous, trusting, unsuspicious, unwary, credulous, gullible; unaffected, without airs, uninhibited, natural, spontaneous; *informal* wet behind the ears.

chill ▶ **noun** ❶ *a chill in the air* COLDNESS, chilliness, coolness, iciness, rawness, bitterness, nip. ❷ *he had a chill* COLD, dose of flu/influenza; *archaic* grippe. ❸ *the chill in their relations* UNFRIENDLINESS, lack of warmth/understanding, chilliness, coldness, coolness.
– OPPOSITES warmth.
▶ **verb** ❶ *the dessert is best chilled* MAKE COLD, make colder, cool (down/off); refrigerate, ice. ❷ *his quiet tone chilled Ruth* SCARE, frighten, petrify, terrify, alarm; make someone's blood run cold, chill to the bone/marrow, make someone's flesh crawl; *informal* scare the pants off; *Brit. informal* put the wind up; *archaic* affright.
– OPPOSITES warm.
▶ **adjective** *a chill wind* COLD, chilly, cool, fresh; wintry, frosty, icy, ice-cold, icy-cold, glacial, polar, arctic, raw, bitter, bitterly cold, biting, freezing, frigid, gelid; *informal* nippy; *Brit. informal* parky.
■ **chill out** (*N. Amer. informal*) *a place to chill out. See* RELAX sense 1.

chilly ▶ **adjective** ❶ *the weather had turned chilly* COLD, cool, crisp, fresh, wintry, frosty, icy, ice-cold, icy-cold, chill, glacial, polar, arctic, raw, bitter, bitterly cold, freezing, frigid, gelid; *informal* nippy; *Brit. informal* parky. ❷ *I woke up feeling chilly* COLD, frozen (stiff), frozen to the marrow/core/bone, freezing (cold), bitterly cold, shivery, chilled. ❸ *a chilly reception* UNFRIENDLY, unwelcoming, cold, cool, frosty, gelid; *informal* stand-offish, offish.
– OPPOSITES warm.

chime ▶ **verb** ❶ *the bells began to chime* RING, peal, toll, sound; ding, dong, clang, boom; *poetic/literary* knell. ❷ *the clock chimed eight o'clock* STRIKE, sound.
▶ **noun** *the chimes of the bells* PEAL, pealing, ringing, carillon, toll, tolling; ding-dong, clanging, tintinnabulation; *poetic/literary* knell.
■ **chime in** ❶ *'Yes, you do that,' Doreen chimed in* INTERJECT, interpose, interrupt, butt in, cut in, join in; *Brit. informal* chip in. ❷ *his remarks chimed in with the ideas of Adam Smith* ACCORD, correspond, be consistent, be compatible, agree, be in agreement, fit in, be in tune, be consonant; *informal* square.

chimera ▶ **noun** ILLUSION, fantasy, delusion, dream, fancy.

chimney ▶ **noun** STACK, smokestack; flue, funnel, vent.

china ▶ **noun** ❶ *a china cup* PORCELAIN. ❷ *a table laid with the best china* DISHES, plates, cups and saucers, crockery, tableware, dinner service, tea service.

chink[1] ▶ **noun** *a chink in the curtains* OPENING, gap, space, hole, aperture, crack, fissure, crevice, cranny, cleft, split, slit, slot.

chink[2] ▶ **verb** *the glasses chinked* JINGLE, jangle, clink, tinkle.

chip ▶ **noun** ❶ *wood chips* FRAGMENT, sliver, splinter, spell, shaving, paring, flake. ❷ *a chip in the glass* NICK, crack, scratch; flaw, fault. ❸ *fish and chips* chipped potatoes, potato chips; *Brit.* French fried potatoes; *N. Amer.* French fries. ❹ *gambling chips* COUNTER, token, jetton; *N. Amer.* check.

▶ **verb** ❶ *the teacup was chipped* NICK, crack, scratch; damage. ❷ *the plaster had chipped* BREAK (OFF), crack, crumble. ❸ *chip the flint to the required shape* WHITTLE, hew, chisel.

■ **chip in** ❶ *'He's right,' Gloria chipped in* INTERRUPT, interject, interpose, cut in, chime in, butt in. ❷ *parents and staff chipped in to raise the cash* CONTRIBUTE, make a contribution/donation, club together, pay; *informal* fork out, shell out, cough up; *Brit. informal* stump up; *N. Amer. informal* kick in.

chirp ▶ **verb** TWEET, twitter, chirrup, cheep, peep, chitter, chirr; sing, warble, trill.

chirpy ▶ **adjective** (*informal*) *a chirpy mood. See* CHEERFUL sense 2.

chit-chat ▶ **noun** (*informal*) SMALL TALK, chat, chatting, chatter, prattle; *Brit. informal* nattering, chuntering.

chivalrous ▶ **adjective** ❶ *his chivalrous treatment of women* GALLANT, gentlemanly, honourable, respectful, considerate; courteous, polite, gracious, well mannered, mannerly; *archaic* gentle. ❷ *chivalrous pursuits* KNIGHTLY, noble, chivalric; brave, courageous, bold, valiant, valorous, heroic, daring, intrepid.
– OPPOSITES rude, cowardly.

chivalry ▶ **noun** ❶ *acts of chivalry* GALLANTRY, gentlemanliness, considerateness; courtesy, courteousness, politeness, graciousness, mannerliness, good manners. ❷ *the values of chivalry* KNIGHT ERRANTRY, courtly manners, knightliness, courtliness, nobility; bravery, courage, boldness, valour, heroism, daring, intrepidity.
– OPPOSITES rudeness.

chivvy ▶ **verb** NAG, badger, hound, harass, harry, pester, keep on at, go on at; *informal* hassle, bug, breathe down someone's neck; *N. Amer. informal* ride.

choice ▶ **noun** ❶ *their choice of candidate | freedom of choice* SELECTION, election, choosing, picking; decision, say, vote. ❷ *you have no other choice* OPTION, alternative, possible course of action. ❸ *an extensive choice of wines* RANGE, variety, selection, assortment. ❹ *the perfect choice* APPOINTEE, nominee, candidate, selection.

▶ **adjective** ❶ *choice plums* SUPERIOR, first-class, first-rate, prime, premier, grade A, best, finest, excellent, select, quality, high-quality, top, top-quality, high-grade, prize, fine, special; hand-picked, carefully chosen; *informal* tip-top, A1, top-notch. ❷ *a few choice words* RUDE, abusive, insulting, offensive.
– OPPOSITES inferior.

choir ▶ **noun** SINGERS, chorus, chorale.
– RELATED TERMS choral.

choke ▶ **verb** ❶ *Christopher started to choke* GAG, retch, cough, fight for breath. ❷ *thick dust choked her* SUFFOCATE, asphyxiate, smother, stifle. ❸ *she had been choked to death* STRANGLE, throttle; asphyxiate, suffocate; *informal* strangulate. ❹ *the guttering was choked with leaves* CLOG (UP), bung up, stop up, block, obstruct, plug; *technical* occlude.

■ **choke something back** SUPPRESS, hold back, fight back, bite back, swallow, check, restrain, control, repress, smother, stifle; *informal* keep a/the lid on.

choleric ▶ **adjective** BAD-TEMPERED, irascible, irritable, grumpy, grouchy, crotchety, tetchy, testy, crusty, cantankerous, curmudgeonly, ill-tempered, peevish, cross, fractious, crabbed, crabby, waspish, prickly, peppery, touchy, short-tempered; *informal* snappish, snappy, chippy, short-fused; *Brit. informal* shirty, stroppy, narky, ratty; *N. Amer. informal* cranky, ornery, soreheaded; *Austral./NZ informal* snaky.
– OPPOSITES good-natured, affable.

choose ▶ **verb** ❶ *we chose a quiet country hotel* SELECT, pick (out), opt for, plump for, settle on, decide on, fix on; appoint, name, nominate, vote for. ❷ *I'll stay as long as I choose* WISH, want, desire, feel/be inclined, please, like, see fit.

choosy ▶ **adjective** (*informal*) FUSSY, finicky, fastidious, over-particular, difficult/hard to please, exacting, demanding; *informal* picky, pernickety; *N. Amer. informal* persnickety; *archaic* nice.

chop ▶ **verb** ❶ *chop the potatoes into pieces* CUT UP, cut into pieces, chop up, cube, dice; *N. Amer.* hash. ❷ *chopping wood* CHOP UP, cut up, cut into pieces, hew, split. ❸ *four fingers were chopped off* SEVER, cut off, hack off, slice off, lop off, saw off, shear off. ❹ *they chopped down large areas of rainforest* CUT DOWN, fell, hack down. ❺ (*informal*) *their training courses were chopped* REDUCE DRASTICALLY, cut; abolish, axe, scrap; *informal* slash.

■ **the chop** (*Brit. informal*) NOTICE; *informal* the sack, the boot, the elbow, the push, one's marching orders; *Brit. informal* one's cards.

chopper ▶ **noun** (*Brit.*) AXE, cleaver, hatchet.

choppy ▶ **adjective** ROUGH, turbulent, heavy, heaving, stormy, tempestuous, squally.
– OPPOSITES calm.

chore ▶ **noun** TASK, job, duty, errand; (domestic) work.

chortle ▶ **verb** CHUCKLE, laugh, giggle, titter, tee-hee, snigger.

chorus ▶ **noun** ❶ *the chorus sang powerfully* CHOIR, ensemble, choral group, choristers, (group of) singers. ❷ *they sang the chorus* REFRAIN.
■ **in chorus** IN UNISON, together, simultaneously, as one; in concert, in harmony.

Christ ▶ **noun** JESUS (CHRIST), the Messiah, the Son of God, the Lamb of God, the Prince of Peace, the Nazarene, the Galilean.

christen ▶ **verb** ❶ *she was christened Sara* BAPTIZE, name, give the name of, call. ❷ *a group who were christened 'The Magic Circle'* CALL, name, dub, style, term, designate, label, nickname, give the name of; *formal* denominate.

Christmas ▶ **noun** NOEL; *informal* Xmas; *Brit. informal* Chrimbo, Chrissie; *archaic* Yule, Yuletide.

chronic ▶ **adjective** ❶ *a chronic illness* PERSISTENT, long-standing, long-term; incurable. ❷ *chronic economic problems* CONSTANT, continuing, ceaseless, unabating, unending, persistent, long-lasting; severe, serious, acute, grave, dire. ❸ *a chronic liar* INVETERATE, hardened, dyed-in-the-wool, incorrigible; compulsive; *informal* pathological. ❹ (*Brit. informal*) *the film was chronic. See* SUBSTANDARD.
– OPPOSITES acute, temporary.

chronicle ▶ **noun** *a chronicle of the region's past* RECORD, written account, history, annals, archive(s); log, diary, journal.
▶ **verb** *the events that followed have been chronicled* RECORD, put on record, write down, set down, document, register, report.

chronicler ▶ **noun** ANNALIST, historian, archivist, diarist, recorder, reporter.

chronological ▶ **adjective** SEQUENTIAL, consecutive, in sequence, in order (of time).

chubby ▶ **adjective** PLUMP, tubby, fat, rotund, portly, dumpy, chunky, well upholstered, well covered, well rounded; *informal* roly-poly, pudgy, blubbery; *Brit. informal* podgy; *N. Amer. informal* zaftig, corn-fed; *archaic* pursy.
– OPPOSITES skinny.

chuck ▶ **verb** (*informal*) ❶ *he chucked the letter onto the table* THROW, toss, fling, hurl, pitch, cast, lob; *informal* sling, bung, buzz; *Austral. informal* hoy; *NZ informal* bish. ❷ *I chucked the rubbish* THROW AWAY/OUT, discard, dispose of, get rid of, dump, bin, scrap, jettison; *informal* ditch, junk; *N. Amer. informal* trash. ❸ *I've chucked my job* GIVE UP, leave, resign from; *informal* quit, pack in; *Brit. informal* jack in. ❹ *Mary chucked him for another guy* LEAVE, throw over, finish with, break off with, jilt; *informal* dump, ditch, give someone the elbow; *Brit. informal* give someone the push give someone the big E.

chuckle ▶ **verb** CHORTLE, giggle, titter, tee-hee, snicker, snigger.

chum ▶ **noun** (*informal*) FRIEND, companion, intimate; playmate, classmate, schoolmate, workmate; *informal* pal, spar, crony; *Brit. informal* mate, oppo, china, mucker; *N. Amer. informal* buddy, amigo, compadre, homeboy.
– OPPOSITES enemy, stranger.

chummy ▶ **adjective** (*informal*) FRIENDLY, on good terms, close, familiar, intimate; *informal* thick, matey, pally, buddy-buddy, palsy-walsy.

chunk ▶ **noun** LUMP, hunk, wedge, block, slab, square, nugget, brick, cube, bar, cake; *informal* wodge; *N. Amer. informal* gob.

chunky ▶ **adjective** ❶ *a chunky young man* STOCKY, sturdy, thickset, heavily built, well built, burly, bulky, brawny, solid, heavy; *Austral./NZ* nuggety; *Brit. informal* fubsy. ❷ *a chunky sweater* THICK, bulky, heavy-knit.
– OPPOSITES slight, light.

church ▶ **noun** ❶ *a village church* PLACE OF WORSHIP, house of God; cathedral, minster, abbey, chapel, basilica; *Scottish & N. English* kirk. ❷ *the Methodist Church* DENOMINATION, sect, creed; faith.
– RELATED TERMS ecclesiastical.

churchyard ▶ **noun** GRAVEYARD, cemetery, necropolis, burial ground, garden of remembrance; *Scottish* kirkyard; *N. Amer.* memorial park; *archaic* God's acre.

churlish ▶ **adjective** RUDE, ill-mannered, ill-bred, discourteous, impolite, unmannerly, uncivil, unchivalrous; inconsiderate, uncharitable, surly, sullen; *informal* ignorant.
– OPPOSITES polite.

churn ▶ **verb** ❶ *village girls churned the milk* STIR, agitate, beat, whip, whisk. ❷ *the sea churned* HEAVE, boil, swirl, toss, seethe; *poetic/literary* roil. ❸ *the propellers churned up the water* DISTURB, stir up, agitate; *poetic/literary* roil.
■ **churn something out** PRODUCE, make, turn out; *informal* crank out, bang out.

chute ▶ **noun** ❶ *a refuse chute* CHANNEL, slide, shaft, funnel, conduit. ❷ *water chutes* (WATER) SLIDE, flume.

cigarette ▶ **noun** filter tip, king-size; *informal* ciggy, cig, smoke, cancer stick, coffin nail; *Brit. informal* fag, snout, roll-up.

cinch ▶ **noun** (*informal*) ❶ *it's a cinch* EASY TASK, child's play, five-finger exercise, gift, walk-

over; *informal* doddle, piece of cake, picnic, breeze, kids' stuff, cakewalk, pushover; *Brit. informal* doss; *N. Amer. informal* duck soup, snap; *Austral./NZ informal* bludge, snack; *dated* snip. ❷ *he was a cinch to take a prize* CERTAINTY, sure thing; *Brit. informal* (dead) cert.
– OPPOSITES challenge.

cinders ▶ **plural noun** ASHES, ash, embers.

cinema ▶ **noun** ❶ *the local cinema* multiplex, cinematheque; *N. Amer.* movie theatre/house; *dated* picture palace/theatre; *historical* nickelodeon. ❷ *I hardly ever go to the cinema* THE PICTURES, the movies; *informal* the flicks. ❸ *British cinema* FILMS, movies, pictures, motion pictures.

cipher ▶ **noun** ❶ *information in cipher* CODE, secret writing; cryptograph. ❷ *working as a cipher* NOBODY, nonentity, unimportant person. ❸ (*dated*) *a row of ciphers* ZERO, nought, nil, 0.

circa ▶ **preposition** APPROXIMATELY, (round) about, around, in the region of, roughly, something like, of the order of, or so, or thereabouts, more or less; *informal* as near as dammit; *N. Amer. informal* in the ballpark of.
– OPPOSITES exactly.

circle ▶ **noun** ❶ *a circle of gold stars* RING, band, hoop, circlet; halo, disc; *technical* annulus. ❷ *her circle of friends* GROUP, set, company, coterie, clique; crowd, band; *informal* gang, bunch, crew. ❸ *illustrious circles* SPHERE, world, milieu; society.
▶ **verb** ❶ *seagulls circled above* WHEEL, move round, revolve, rotate, whirl, spiral. ❷ *satellites circling the earth* GO ROUND, travel round, circumnavigate; orbit, revolve round. ❸ *the abbey was circled by a wall* SURROUND, encircle, ring, enclose, encompass; *poetic/literary* gird.

circuit ▶ **noun** ❶ *two circuits of the village green* LAP, turn, round, circle. ❷ (*Brit.*) *a racing circuit* TRACK, racetrack, running track, course. ❸ *the judge's circuit* TOUR (OF DUTY), rounds.

circuitous ▶ **adjective** ❶ *a circuitous route* ROUNDABOUT, indirect, winding, meandering, serpentine. ❷ *a circuitous discussion* INDIRECT, oblique, roundabout, circumlocutory, periphrastic.
– OPPOSITES direct.

circular ▶ **adjective** *a circular window* ROUND, disc-shaped, ring-shaped, annular.
▶ **noun** *a free circular* LEAFLET, pamphlet, handbill, flyer; *N. Amer.* mailer, folder, dodger.

circulate ▶ **verb** ❶ *the news was widely circulated* SPREAD (ABOUT/AROUND), communicate, disseminate, make known, make public, broadcast, publicize, advertise; distribute, give out, pass around. ❷ *fresh air circulates freely* FLOW, course, move round. ❸ *they circulated among their guests* SOCIALIZE, mingle.

circumference ▶ **noun** ❶ *the circumference of the pit* PERIMETER, border, boundary; edge, rim, verge, margin, fringe; *poetic/literary* marge, bourn. ❷ *the circumference of his arm* GIRTH, width.

circumlocution ▶ **noun** PERIPHRASIS, discursiveness, long-windedness, verbosity, verbiage, wordiness, prolixity, redundancy, pleonasm, tautology, repetitiveness, repetitiousness.

circumscribe ▶ **verb** RESTRICT, limit, keep within bounds, curb, confine, restrain; regulate, control.

circumspect ▶ **adjective** CAUTIOUS, wary, careful, chary, guarded, on one's guard; watchful, alert, attentive, heedful, vigilant, leery; *informal* cagey, playing one's cards close to one's chest.
– OPPOSITES unguarded.

circumstances ▶ **plural noun** ❶ *favourable economic circumstances* SITUATION, conditions, state of affairs, position; (turn of) events, incidents, occurrences, happenings; factors, context, background, environment; *informal* circs. ❷ *Jane explained the circumstances to him* THE FACTS, the details, the particulars, how things stand, the lie of the land; *Brit.* the state of play; *N. Amer.* the lay of the land; *informal* what's what, the score. ❸ *reduced circumstances* FINANCIAL POSITION, lot, lifestyle; resources, means, finances, income; *dated* station in life.

circumstantial ▶ **adjective** ❶ *they have only circumstantial evidence* INDIRECT, inferred, deduced, conjectural; inconclusive, unprovable. ❷ *the picture was so circumstantial that it began to be convincing* DETAILED, particularized, comprehensive, thorough, exhaustive; explicit, specific.

circumvent ▶ **verb** AVOID, get round/past, evade, bypass, sidestep, dodge; *N. Amer.* end-run; *informal* duck.

cistern ▶ **noun** TANK, reservoir, container, butt.

citadel ▶ **noun** FORTRESS, fort, stronghold, fortification, castle, burg; *archaic* hold.

citation ▶ **noun** ❶ *a citation from an eighteenth-century text* QUOTATION, quote, extract, excerpt, passage, line; reference, allusion; *N. Amer.* cite. ❷ *a citation for gallantry* COMMENDATION, (honourable) mention. ❸ (*Law*) *a traffic citation* SUMMONS, subpoena, writ, court order.

cite ▶ **verb** ❶ *cite the passage in full* QUOTE, reproduce. ❷ *he cited the case of Leigh v. Gladstone* REFER TO, make reference to, mention, allude to, adduce, instance; specify, name. ❸ *he has been cited many times* COMMEND, pay tribute to, praise. ❹ (*Law*) *the writ cited four of the signatories* SUMMON, summons, serve with a summons/writ, subpoena.

citizen ▶ **noun** ❶ *a British citizen* SUBJECT, national, passport holder, native. ❷ *the citizens of Edinburgh* INHABITANT, resident, native, townsman, townswoman; *formal* denizen; *archaic* burgher; *Brit. archaic* burgess.

city ▶ **noun** TOWN, municipality, metropolis, megalopolis; conurbation, urban area, metropolitan area; *Scottish* burgh; *informal* big smoke; *N. Amer. informal* burg.
– RELATED TERMS urban, civic.

civic ▶ **adjective** MUNICIPAL, city, town, urban, metropolitan; public, civil, community.

civil ▶ **adjective** ❶ *a civil marriage* SECULAR, non-religious, lay; *formal* laic. ❷ *civil aviation* NON-MILITARY, civilian. ❸ *a civil war* INTERNAL, domestic, interior, national. ❹ *he behaved in a civil manner* POLITE, courteous, well mannered, well bred, gentlemanly, chivalrous, gallant, ladylike; cordial, genial, pleasant, affable.
– OPPOSITES religious, military, rude, international.

civilian ▶ **noun** NON-MILITARY PERSON, non-combatant person, ordinary/private citizen; *informal* civvy.

civility ▶ **noun** ❶ *he treated me with civility* COURTESY, courteousness, politeness, good manners, graciousness, consideration, respect, politesse, comity. ❷ *she didn't waste time on civilities* POLITE REMARK, politeness, courtesy; formality.
– OPPOSITES rudeness.

civilization ▶ **noun** ❶ *a higher stage of civilization* HUMAN DEVELOPMENT, advancement, progress, enlightenment, culture, refinement, sophistication. ❷ *ancient civilizations* CULTURE, society, nation, people.

civilize ▶ **verb** ENLIGHTEN, edify, improve, educate, instruct, refine, cultivate, polish, socialize, humanize.

civilized ▶ **adjective** POLITE, courteous, well mannered, civil, gentlemanly, ladylike, mannerly; cultured, cultivated, refined, polished, sophisticated; enlightened, educated, advanced, developed.
– OPPOSITES rude, unsophisticated.

civil servant ▶ **noun** PUBLIC SERVANT, government official; bureaucrat, mandarin, official, administrator, functionary.

clad ▶ **adjective** DRESSED, clothed, attired, got up, garbed, rigged out, costumed; wearing, sporting; *archaic* apparelled.

claim ▶ **verb** ❶ *Davies claimed that she was lying* ASSERT, declare, profess, maintain, state, hold, affirm, avow; argue, contend, allege; *formal* aver; *archaic* avouch. ❷ *no one claimed the items* LAY CLAIM TO, assert ownership of, formally request. ❸ *you can claim compensation* REQUEST, ask for, apply for; demand, exact. ❹ *the fire claimed four lives* TAKE, cause/result in the loss of.

▶ **noun** ❶ *her claims that she was raped* ASSERTION, declaration, profession, affirmation, avowal, protestation; contention, allegation. ❷ *a claim for damages* REQUEST, application; demand, petition. ❸ *we have first claim on their assets* ENTITLEMENT TO, title to, right to.

claimant ▶ **noun** APPLICANT, candidate, supplicant; petitioner, plaintiff, litigant, appellant.

clairvoyance ▶ **noun** SECOND SIGHT, psychic powers, ESP, extrasensory perception, sixth sense; telepathy.

clairvoyant ▶ **noun** PSYCHIC, fortune teller, crystal-gazer; medium, spiritualist; telepathist, telepath, mind-reader.

▶ **adjective** *I'm not clairvoyant* PSYCHIC, having second sight, having a sixth sense; telepathic.

clamber ▶ **verb** SCRAMBLE, climb, scrabble, claw one's way.

clammy ▶ **adjective** ❶ *his clammy hands* MOIST, damp, sweaty, sticky; slimy, slippery. ❷ *the clammy atmosphere* DAMP, dank, wet; humid, close, muggy, heavy.
– OPPOSITES dry.

clamorous ▶ **adjective** NOISY, loud, vocal, vociferous, raucous, rowdy; importunate, demanding, insistent, vehement.
– OPPOSITES quiet.

clamour ▶ **noun** ❶ *her voice rose above the clamour* DIN, racket, rumpus, loud noise, uproar, tumult, shouting, yelling, screaming, baying, roaring; commotion, brouhaha, hue and cry, hubbub; *informal* hullabaloo; *Brit. informal* row. ❷ *the clamour for her resignation* DEMAND(S), call(s), urging. ❸ *the clamour of protectionists* PROTESTS, complaints, outcry.

▶ **verb** ❶ *clamouring crowds* YELL, shout loudly, bay, scream, roar. ❷ *scientists are clamouring for a ban* DEMAND, call, press, push, lobby.

clamp ▶ **noun** ❶ *a clamp was holding the wood* BRACE, vice, press, clasp; *Music* capo (tasto); *Climbing* jumar. ❷ *clamps had been fitted to the car* IMMOBILIZER, wheel clamp; *N. Amer.* boot.

▶ **verb** ❶ *the sander is clamped on to the workbench* FASTEN, secure, fix, attach; screw, bolt. ❷ *a pipe was clamped between his teeth* CLENCH, grip, hold, press, clasp. ❸ *his car was clamped* IMMOBILIZE, wheel-clamp; *N. Amer.* boot.

■ **clamp down on** SUPPRESS, prevent, stop, put a stop/end to, stamp out; crack down on, limit, restrict, control, keep in check.

clampdown ▶ **noun** (*informal*) SUPPRESSION, prevention, stamping out; crackdown, restriction, restraint, curb, check.

clan ▶ **noun** ❶ *the Macleod clan* GROUP OF FAMILIES, sept; family, house, dynasty, tribe; *Anthropology* sib, kinship group. ❷ *a clan of art collectors* GROUP, set, circle, clique, coterie; crowd, band; *informal* gang, bunch.

clandestine ▶ adjective SECRET, covert, furtive, surreptitious, stealthy, cloak-and-dagger, hole-and-corner, closet, backstairs, hugger-mugger; *informal* hush-hush.

clang ▶ noun *the clang of the church bells* REVERBERATION, ringing, ring, ding-dong, bong, peal, chime, toll.
▶ verb *the huge bells clanged* REVERBERATE, resound, ring, bong, peal, chime, toll.

clanger ▶ noun (*Brit. informal*). *See* BLUNDER noun.

clank ▶ noun *the clank of rusty chains* JANGLING, clanging, rattling, clinking, jingling; clang, jangle, rattle, clangour, clink, jingle.
▶ verb *I could hear the chain clanking* JANGLE, rattle, clink, clang, jingle.

clannish ▶ adjective CLIQUEY, cliquish, insular, exclusive; unfriendly, unwelcoming.

clap ▶ verb ❶ *the audience clapped* APPLAUD, clap one's hands, give someone a round of applause, put one's hands together; *informal* give someone a (big) hand; *N. Amer. informal* give it up. ❷ *he clapped Owen on the back* SLAP, strike, hit, smack, thump; pat; *informal* whack, thwack. ❸ *the dove clapped its wings* FLAP, beat, flutter.
▶ noun ❶ *everybody gave him a clap* ROUND OF APPLAUSE, handclap; *informal* hand. ❷ *a clap on the shoulder* SLAP, blow, smack, thump; pat; *informal* whack, thwack. ❸ *a clap of thunder* CRACK, crash, bang, boom; thunderclap.

claptrap ▶ noun *sentimental claptrap. See* NONSENSE sense 1.

clarify ▶ verb ❶ *their report clarified the situation* MAKE CLEAR, shed/throw light on, elucidate, illuminate; EXPLAIN, explicate, define, spell out, clear up. ❷ *clarified butter* PURIFY, refine; filter, fine.
– OPPOSITES confuse.

clarity ▶ noun ❶ *the clarity of his account* LUCIDITY, lucidness, clearness, coherence; *formal* perspicuity. ❷ *the clarity of the image* SHARPNESS, clearness, crispness, definition. ❸ *the crystal clarity of the water* LIMPIDITY, limpidness, clearness, transparency, translucence, pellucidity.
– OPPOSITES vagueness, blurriness, opacity.

clash ▶ noun ❶ *clashes between armed gangs* CONFRONTATION, skirmish, fight, battle, engagement, encounter, conflict. ❷ *an angry clash* ARGUMENT, altercation, confrontation, shouting match; contretemps, quarrel, disagreement, dispute; *informal* run-in, slanging match. ❸ *a clash of tweeds and a striped shirt* MISMATCH, discordance, discord, lack of harmony. ❹ *a clash of dates* COINCIDENCE, concurrence; conflict. ❺ *the clash of cymbals* STRIKING, bang, clang, crash.
▶ verb ❶ *protesters clashed with police* FIGHT, skirmish, contend, come to blows, come into conflict; do battle. ❷ *the prime minister clashed with union leaders* DISAGREE, differ, wrangle, dispute, cross swords, lock horns, be at loggerheads. ❸ *her red coat clashed with her hair* BE INCOMPATIBLE, not match, not go, be discordant. ❹ *the dates clash* CONFLICT, coincide, occur simultaneously. ❺ *she clashed the cymbals together* BANG, strike, clang, crash.

clasp ▶ verb ❶ *Ruth clasped his hand* GRASP, grip, clutch, hold tightly; take hold of, seize, grab. ❷ *he clasped Joanne in his arms* EMBRACE, hug, enfold, fold, envelop; hold, squeeze.
▶ noun ❶ *a gold clasp* FASTENER, fastening, catch, clip, pin; buckle, hasp. ❷ *his tight clasp* EMBRACE, hug, cuddle; grip, grasp.

class ▶ noun ❶ *a hotel of the first class* CATEGORY, grade, rating, classification, group, grouping. ❷ *a new class of heart drug* KIND, sort, type, variety, genre, brand; species, genus, breed, strain; *N. Amer.* stripe. ❸ *the middle class* SOCIAL DIVISION, social stratum, rank, level, echelon, group, grouping; social status; *dated* estate; *archaic* condition. ❹ *there are 30 pupils in the class* FORM, study group, set, stream. ❺ *a Maths class* LESSON, period; seminar, tutorial, workshop. ❻ (*informal*) *a woman of class* STYLE, stylishness, elegance, chic, sophistication, taste, refinement, quality, excellence.
▶ verb *the 12-seater is classed as a commercial vehicle* CLASSIFY, categorize, group, grade; order, sort, codify; bracket, designate, label, pigeonhole.
▶ adjective (*informal*) *a class player. See* EXCELLENT.

classic ▶ adjective ❶ *the classic work on the subject* DEFINITIVE, authoritative; outstanding, first-rate, first-class, best, finest, excellent, superior, masterly. ❷ *a classic example of Norman design* TYPICAL, archetypal, quintessential, vintage; model, representative, perfect, prime, textbook. ❸ *a classic style* SIMPLE, elegant, understated; traditional, timeless, ageless.
– OPPOSITES atypical.
▶ noun *a classic of the genre* DEFINITIVE EXAMPLE, model, epitome, paradigm, exemplar; great work, masterpiece.

classical ▶ adjective ❶ *classical mythology* ancient Greek, Hellenic, Attic; Latin, ancient Roman. ❷ *classical music* TRADITIONAL, long-established; serious, highbrow, heavyweight. ❸ *a classical style* SIMPLE, pure, restrained, plain, austere; well proportioned, harmonious, balanced, symmetrical, elegant.
– OPPOSITES modern.

classification ▶ noun ❶ *the classification of diseases* CATEGORIZATION, categorizing, classifying, grouping, grading, ranking, organization, sorting, codification, systematization. ❷ *a series of classifications* CATEGORY, class, group, grouping, grade, grading, ranking, bracket.

classify ▶ verb *we can classify the students into*

two groups CATEGORIZE, group, grade, rank, rate, order, organize, range, sort, type, codify, bracket, systematize, systemize; catalogue, list, file, index; *archaic* assort.

classy ▶ **adjective** (*informal*) *a classy hotel* STYLISH, high-class, superior, exclusive, chic, elegant, smart, sophisticated; *Brit.* upmarket; *N. Amer.* high-toned; *informal* posh, ritzy, plush, swanky; *Brit. informal* swish.

clatter ▶ **verb** *the cups clattered on the tray* RATTLE, clank, clink, clunk, clang.

clause ▶ **noun** *a new clause in the treaty* SECTION, paragraph, article, subsection; stipulation, condition, proviso, rider.

claw ▶ **noun** ❶ *a bird's claw* TALON, nail; *technical* unguis. ❷ *a crab's claw* PINCER, nipper; *technical* chela.

▶ **verb** *her fingers clawed his shoulders* SCRATCH, lacerate, tear, rip, scrape, graze, dig into.

clay ▶ **noun** ❶ *the soil is mainly clay* EARTH, soil, loam. ❷ *potter's clay* argil, china clay, kaolin, adobe, ball clay, pug; fireclay.

clean ▶ **adjective** ❶ *keep the wound clean* WASHED, scrubbed, cleansed, cleaned; spotless, unsoiled, unstained, unsullied, unblemished, immaculate, pristine, dirt-free, as clean as a whistle; hygienic, sanitary, disinfected, sterilized, sterile, aseptic, decontaminated; laundered; *informal* squeaky clean. ❷ *a clean sheet of paper* BLANK, empty, clear, plain; unused, new, pristine, fresh, unmarked. ❸ *clean air* PURE, clear, fresh, crisp, refreshing; unpolluted, uncontaminated. ❹ *a clean life* VIRTUOUS, good, upright, upstanding; honourable, respectable, reputable, decent, righteous, moral, exemplary; innocent, pure, chaste; *informal* squeaky clean. ❺ *the firm is clean* INNOCENT, guiltless, blameless, guilt-free, crime-free, above suspicion; *informal* squeaky clean. ❻ *a good clean fight* FAIR, honest, sporting, sportsmanlike, honourable, according to the rules; *informal* on the level. ❼ (*informal*) *they are trying to stay clean* SOBER, teetotal, dry, non-drinking; DRUG-FREE, off drugs; *informal* on the wagon. ❽ *a clean cut* NEAT, smooth, crisp, straight, precise. ❾ *a clean break* COMPLETE, thorough, total, absolute, conclusive, decisive, final, irrevocable. ❿ *clean lines* SIMPLE, elegant, graceful, streamlined, smooth.

– OPPOSITES dirty, polluted.

▶ **adverb** (*informal*) *I clean forgot* COMPLETELY, entirely, totally, fully, quite, utterly, absolutely.

▶ **verb** ❶ *Dad cleaned the windows* WASH, cleanse, wipe, sponge, scrub, mop, rinse, scour, swab, hose down, sluice (down), disinfect; shampoo; *poetic/literary* lave. ❷ *I got my clothes cleaned* LAUNDER, dry-clean. ❸ *she cleaned the fish* GUT, draw, dress; *formal* eviscerate.

– OPPOSITES dirty.

■ **clean someone out** (*informal*) BANKRUPT, ruin, make insolvent, make penniless, wipe out.

■ **come clean** (*informal*) TELL THE TRUTH, tell all, make a clean breast of it; confess, own up, admit guilt, admit to one's crimes/sins; *informal* fess up.

cleanse ▶ **verb** ❶ *the wound was cleansed* CLEAN (UP), wash, bathe, rinse, disinfect. ❷ *cleansing the environment of traces of lead* RID, clear, free, purify, purge. ❸ *only God can cleanse us from sin* PURIFY, purge, absolve, free; deliver.

clear ▶ **adjective** ❶ *clear instructions* UNDERSTANDABLE, comprehensible, intelligible, plain, uncomplicated, explicit, lucid, coherent, simple, straightforward, unambiguous, clear-cut, crystal clear; *formal* perspicuous. ❷ *a clear case of harassment* OBVIOUS, evident, plain, crystal clear; sure, definite, unmistakable, manifest, indisputable, patent, incontrovertible, irrefutable, beyond doubt, beyond question; palpable, visible, discernible, conspicuous, overt, blatant, glaring; as plain as a pikestaff, as plain as day; *informal* as plain as the nose on one's face. ❸ *clear water* TRANSPARENT, limpid, pellucid, translucent, crystal clear; unclouded. ❹ *a clear blue sky* BRIGHT, cloudless, unclouded, without a cloud in the sky. ❺ *her clear complexion* UNBLEMISHED, spot-free. ❻ *Rosa's clear voice* DISTINCT, bell-like, as clear as a bell. ❼ *the road was clear | a clear view* UNOBSTRUCTED, unblocked, passable, open; unrestricted, unhindered. ❽ *the algae were clear of toxins* FREE, devoid, without, unaffected by; rid, relieved. ❾ *a clear conscience* UNTROUBLED, undisturbed, unperturbed, unconcerned, having no qualms; peaceful, at peace, tranquil, serene, calm, easy. ❿ *two clear days' notice* WHOLE, full, entire, complete.

– OPPOSITES vague, opaque, cloudy, obstructed.

▶ **adverb** ❶ *stand clear of the doors* AWAY FROM, apart from, at a (safe) distance from, out of contact with. ❷ *Tommy's voice came loud and clear* DISTINCTLY, clearly, as clear as a bell, plainly, audibly. ❸ *he has time to get clear away* COMPLETELY, entirely, fully, wholly, totally, utterly; *informal* clean.

▶ **verb** ❶ *the sky cleared briefly* BRIGHTEN (UP), lighten, clear up, become bright/brighter/lighter, become fine/sunny. ❷ *the drizzle had cleared* DISAPPEAR, go away, end; peter out, fade, wear off, decrease, lessen, diminish. ❸ *together they cleared the table* EMPTY, unload, unburden, strip. ❹ *clearing drains* UNBLOCK, unstop. ❺ *staff cleared the building* EVACUATE, empty; leave. ❻ *Karen cleared the dirty plates* REMOVE, take away, carry away, tidy away/up. ❼ *I'm clearing my debts* PAY (OFF), repay, settle, discharge. ❽ *I cleared the bar at my first attempt*

GO OVER, pass over, sail over; jump (over), vault (over), leap (over), hurdle. ❾ *he was cleared by an appeal court* ACQUIT, declare innocent, find not guilty; absolve, exonerate; *informal* let off (the hook); *formal* exculpate. ❿ *I was cleared to work on the atomic project* AUTHORIZE, give permission, permit, allow, pass, accept, endorse, license, sanction, give approval/consent to; *informal* OK, give the OK, give the thumbs up, give the green light, give the go-ahead. ⓫ *I cleared £50,000 profit* NET, make/realize a profit of, take home, pocket; gain, earn, make, get, bring in, pull in.

■ **clear off** (*informal*) GO AWAY, get out, leave; be off with you, shoo, on your way; *informal* beat it, push off, shove off, scram, scoot, buzz off, clear out; *Brit. informal* hop it, sling your hook; *Austral./NZ informal* rack off; *N. Amer. informal* bug off, take a hike; *poetic/literary* begone.

■ **clear out** (*informal*). *See* LEAVE[1] sense 1.

■ **clear something out** ❶ *we cleared out the junk room* EMPTY (OUT); tidy (up), clear up. ❷ *clear out the rubbish* GET RID OF, throw out/away, discard, dispose of, dump, bin, scrap, jettison; *informal* chuck (out/away), ditch, get shut of; *Brit. informal* get shot of; *N. Amer. informal* trash.

■ **clear up**. *See* CLEAR verb sense 1.

■ **clear something up** ❶ *clear up the garden* TIDY (UP), put in order, straighten up, clean up, spruce up. ❷ *we've cleared up the problem* SOLVE, resolve, straighten out, find an/the answer to; get to the bottom of, explain; *informal* crack, figure out, suss out.

clearance ▶ noun ❶ *slum clearance* REMOVAL, clearing, demolition. ❷ *you must have Home Office clearance* AUTHORIZATION, permission, consent, approval, blessing, leave, sanction, licence, dispensation, assent, agreement, endorsement; *informal* the green light, the go-ahead, the thumbs up, the OK, the say-so. ❸ *the clearance of a debt* REPAYMENT, payment, paying (off), settling, discharge. ❹ *there is plenty of clearance* SPACE, room (to spare), margin, leeway.

clear-cut ▶ adjective DEFINITE, distinct, clear, well defined, precise, specific, explicit, unambiguous, unequivocal, black and white, cut and dried.
– OPPOSITES vague.

clearing ▶ noun GLADE, dell, gap, opening.

clearly ▶ adverb ❶ *write clearly* INTELLIGIBLY, plainly, distinctly, comprehensibly, with clarity; legibly, audibly; *formal* perspicuously. ❷ *clearly, substantial changes are needed* OBVIOUSLY, evidently, patently, unquestionably, undoubtedly, without doubt, indubitably, plainly, undeniably, incontrovertibly, irrefutably, doubtless, it goes without saying, needless to say.

cleave[1] ▶ verb ❶ *cleaving wood for the fire* SPLIT (OPEN), cut (up), hew, hack, chop up; *poetic/literary* sunder; *archaic* rive. ❷ *cleaving a path through the traffic* PLOUGH, drive, bulldoze, carve.

cleave[2]

■ **cleave to** (*poetic/literary*) ❶ *her tongue clove to the roof of her mouth* STICK (FAST) TO, adhere to, be attached to. ❷ *cleaving too closely to Moscow's line* ADHERE TO, hold to, abide by, be loyal/faithful to.

cleaver ▶ noun CHOPPER, hatchet, axe, knife; butcher's knife, kitchen knife.

cleft ▶ noun ❶ *a deep cleft in the rocks* SPLIT, slit, crack, fissure, crevice, rift, break, fracture, rent, breach. ❷ *the cleft in his chin* DIMPLE.
▶ adjective *a cleft tail* SPLIT, divided, cloven.

clemency ▶ noun MERCY, mercifulness, leniency, lenience, mildness, indulgence, quarter; compassion, humanity, pity, sympathy.
– OPPOSITES ruthlessness.

clench ▶ verb ❶ *he stood there clenching his hands* SQUEEZE TOGETHER, clamp together, close/shut tightly; make into a fist. ❷ *he clenched the back of chair* GRIP, grasp, grab, clutch, clasp, hold tightly, seize, press, squeeze.
▶ noun *the clench of his fists* CONTRACTION, tightening, tensing, constricting.

clergy ▶ noun CLERGYMEN, clergywomen, churchmen, churchwomen, clerics, priests, ecclesiastics, men/women of God; ministry, priesthood, holy orders, the church, the cloth.
– RELATED TERMS clerical.
– OPPOSITES laity.

clergyman, clergywoman ▶ noun PRIEST, churchman, churchwoman, man/woman of the cloth, man/woman of God; cleric, minister, preacher, chaplain, father, ecclesiastic, bishop, pastor, vicar, rector, parson, curate, deacon, deaconess; *Scottish* kirkman; *N. Amer.* dominie; *informal* reverend, padre, Holy Joe, sky pilot; *Austral. informal* josser.

clerical ▶ adjective ❶ *clerical jobs* OFFICE, desk, back-room; administrative, secretarial; white-collar. ❷ *a clerical minister* ECCLESIASTICAL, church, priestly, religious, spiritual, sacerdotal; holy, divine.
– OPPOSITES secular.

clerk ▶ noun OFFICE WORKER, clerical worker, administrator; bookkeeper; cashier, teller; *informal* pen-pusher; *historical* scrivener.

clever ▶ adjective ❶ *a clever young woman* INTELLIGENT, bright, smart, astute, quick-witted, shrewd; talented, gifted, brilliant, capable, able, competent, apt; educated, learned, knowledgeable, wise; *informal* brainy, savvy. ❷ *a clever scheme* INGENIOUS, canny, cunning, crafty, artful, slick, neat. ❸ *she was clever with*

her hands SKILFUL, dexterous, adroit, adept, deft, nimble, handy; skilled, talented, gifted. ❹ *a clever remark* WITTY, amusing, droll, humorous, funny.
– OPPOSITES stupid.

cliché ▸noun PLATITUDE, hackneyed phrase, commonplace, banality, truism, stock phrase, trite phrase; *informal* old chestnut; *dated* bromide.

click ▸noun CLACK, snick, snap, pop, tick; clink.
▸verb ❶ *cameras clicked* CLACK, snap, snick, tick, pop; clink. ❷ (*informal*) *that night it clicked* BECOME CLEAR, fall into place, come home, make sense, dawn, register, get through, sink in. ❸ (*informal*) *we just clicked* TAKE TO EACH OTHER, get along, be compatible, be like-minded, feel a rapport, see eye to eye; *informal* hit it off, get on like a house on fire, be on the same wavelength. ❹ (*informal*) *this issue hasn't clicked with the voters* GO DOWN WELL, prove popular, be a hit, succeed.

client ▸noun CUSTOMER, buyer, purchaser, shopper, consumer, user; patient; patron, regular; (**clients**) clientele, patronage, public, market; *Brit. informal* punter; *Law* vendee.

clientele ▸noun CLIENTS. *See* CLIENT.

cliff ▸noun PRECIPICE, rock face, crag, bluff, ridge, escarpment, scar, scarp, overhang.

climactic ▸adjective FINAL, ending, closing, concluding, ultimate; exciting, thrilling, gripping, riveting, dramatic, hair-raising; crucial, decisive, critical.

climate ▸noun ❶ *a mild climate* WEATHER CONDITIONS, weather; atmospheric conditions. ❷ *they come from colder climates* REGION, area, zone, country, place; *poetic/literary* clime. ❸ *the political climate* ATMOSPHERE, mood, feeling, ambience, tenor; tendency, ethos, attitude; milieu; *informal* vibe(s).

climax ▸noun ❶ *the climax of his career* PEAK, pinnacle, height, high(est) point, top; acme, zenith; culmination, crowning point, crown, crest; highlight, high spot, high water mark. ❷ ORGASM; ejaculation.
– OPPOSITES nadir.
▸verb ❶ *the event will climax with a concert* CULMINATE, peak, reach a pinnacle, come to a crescendo, come to a head. ❷ ORGASM; ejaculate; *informal* come, feel the earth move; *poetic/literary* die.

climb ▸verb ❶ *we climbed the hill* ASCEND, mount, scale, scramble up, clamber up, shin up; go up, walk up; conquer, gain. ❷ *the plane climbed* RISE, ascend, go up, gain altitude. ❸ *the road climbs steeply* SLOPE UPWARDS, rise, go uphill, incline upwards. ❹ *the shares climbed to 550 pence* INCREASE, rise, go up; shoot up, soar, rocket. ❺ *he climbed through the ranks* ADVANCE, rise, move up, progress, work one's way. ❻ *he climbed out of his car* CLAMBER, scramble; step.
– OPPOSITES descend, drop, fall.
▸noun *a steep climb* ASCENT, clamber.
– OPPOSITES descent.
■ **climb down** ❶ *Sandy climbed down the ladder* DESCEND, go/come down, move down, shin down. ❷ *the Government had to climb down* BACK DOWN, admit defeat, surrender, capitulate, yield, give in, give way, submit; retreat, backtrack; eat one's words, eat humble pie; do a U-turn; *Brit.* do an about-turn; *N. Amer. informal* eat crow.

clinch ▸verb ❶ *he clinched the deal* SECURE, settle, conclude, close, pull off, bring off, complete, confirm, seal, finalize; *informal* sew up, wrap up. ❷ *these findings clinched the matter* SETTLE, decide, determine; resolve; *informal* sort out. ❸ *they clinched the title* WIN, secure; be victorious, come first, triumph, prevail. ❹ *they clinch every nail* SECURE, fasten, fix, pinion. ❺ *the boxers clinched* GRAPPLE, wrestle, struggle, scuffle.
– OPPOSITES lose.
▸noun *a passionate clinch* EMBRACE, hug, cuddle, squeeze, hold, clasp.

cling ▸verb *rice grains tend to cling together* STICK, adhere, hold, cohere, bond, bind.
■ **cling (on) to** ❶ *she clung to him* HOLD ON, clutch, grip, grasp, clasp, attach oneself to, hang on; embrace, hug. ❷ *they clung to their beliefs* ADHERE TO, hold to, stick to, stand by, abide by, cherish, remain true to, have faith in; *informal* swear by, stick with.

clinic ▸noun MEDICAL CENTRE, health centre, outpatients' department, surgery, doctor's.

clinical ▸adjective ❶ *he seemed so clinical* DETACHED, impersonal, dispassionate, objective, uninvolved, distant, remote, aloof, removed, cold, indifferent, neutral, unsympathetic, unfeeling, unemotional. ❷ *the room was clinical* PLAIN, simple, unadorned, unembellished, stark, austere, spartan, bleak, bare; clean; functional, basic, institutional, impersonal, characterless.
– OPPOSITES emotional, luxurious.

clip[1] ▸noun ❶ *a briefcase clip* FASTENER, clasp, hasp, catch, hook, buckle, lock. ❷ *a diamanté clip* BROOCH, pin, badge. ❸ *his clip was empty* MAGAZINE, cartridge, cylinder.
▸verb *he clipped the pages together* FASTEN, attach, fix, join; pin, staple, tack.

clip[2] ▸verb ❶ *I clipped the hedge* TRIM, prune, cut, snip, shorten, crop, shear, pare; lop; neaten, shape. ❷ *clip the coupon below* REMOVE, cut out, snip out, tear out, detach. ❸ *his lorry clipped a van* HIT, strike, touch, graze, glance off, run into. ❹ *Mum clipped his ear* HIT, cuff, strike, smack, slap, box; *informal* clout, whack, wallop, clobber, biff, sock.

▶ **noun** ❶ *I gave the dog a clip* TRIM, cut, crop, haircut; shear. ❷ *a film clip* EXTRACT, excerpt, snippet, cutting, fragment; trailer. ❸ (*informal*) *a clip round the ear* SMACK, cuff, slap, box; *informal* clout, whack, wallop, biff, sock. ❹ (*informal*) *the truck went at a good clip* SPEED, rate, pace, velocity; *informal* lick.

■ **clip someone's wings** RESTRICT SOMEONE'S FREEDOM, impose limits on, keep under control, stand in the way of; obstruct, impede, frustrate, thwart, fetter, hamstring.

clipping ▶ **noun** CUTTING, snippet, extract, excerpt.

clique ▶ **noun** COTERIE, set, circle, ring, in-crowd, group; club, society, fraternity, sorority; cabal, caucus; *informal* gang.

cloak ▶ **noun** ❶ *the cloak over his shoulders* CAPE, robe, mantle, shawl, wrap, stole, tippet; poncho, serape, djellaba; cope; *historical* pelisse. ❷ *a cloak of secrecy* COVER, veil, mantle, shroud, screen, mask, shield, blanket.

▶ **verb** *a peak cloaked in mist* CONCEAL, hide, cover, veil, shroud, mask, obscure, cloud; envelop, swathe, surround.

clobber[1] ▶ **noun** (*Brit. informal*) *get your clobber on. See* CLOTHES.

clobber[2] ▶ **verb** (*informal*) *I'll clobber him. See* HIT verb sense 1.

clock ▶ **noun** ❶ *a grandfather clock* TIMEPIECE, timekeeper, timer; chronometer, chronograph. ❷ (*informal*) *the car had 50,000 miles on the clock* MILOMETER, counter; taximeter.

▶ **verb** (*informal*) ❶ *the UK clocked up record exports* REGISTER, record, log, notch up; achieve, attain, accomplish, make; *informal* chalk up, bag. ❷ (*Brit.*) *Liz soon clocked the change. See* NOTICE verb.

clod ▶ **noun** ❶ *clods of earth* LUMP, clump, chunk, hunk, wedge. ❷ (*informal*) *an insensitive clod. See* IDIOT sense 1.

clog ▶ **noun** *a wooden clog* sabot.

▶ **verb** *the pipes were clogged* BLOCK, obstruct, congest, jam, choke, bung up, plug, stop up, fill up; *Brit. informal* gunge up.

cloister ▶ **noun** ❶ *the convent cloisters* WALKWAY, covered walk, arcade, loggia, gallery. ❷ *I was educated in the cloister* ABBEY, monastery, friary, convent, priory, nunnery.

▶ **verb** *they were cloistered at home* CONFINE, isolate, shut away, sequester, seclude, closet.

cloistered ▶ **adjective** SECLUDED, sequestered, sheltered, protected, insulated; shut off, isolated, confined; solitary, monastic, reclusive.

close[1] ▶ **adjective** ❶ *the town is close to Leeds* NEAR, adjacent; in the vicinity of, in the neighbourhood of, within reach of; neighbouring, adjoining, abutting, alongside, on the doorstep, a stone's throw away; nearby, at hand, at close quarters; *informal* within spitting distance; *archaic* nigh. ❷ *flying in close formation* DENSE, compact, tight, close-packed, packed, solid; crowded, cramped, congested. ❸ *I was close to tears* NEAR, on the verge of, on the brink of, on the point of. ❹ *a very close match* EVENLY MATCHED, even, with nothing to choose between them, neck and neck; *informal* fifty-fifty, even-steven(s). ❺ *close relatives* IMMEDIATE, direct, near. ❻ *close friends* INTIMATE, dear, bosom; close-knit, inseparable, attached, devoted, faithful; special, good, best, fast, firm; *informal* (as) thick as thieves. ❼ *a close resemblance* STRONG, marked, distinct, pronounced. ❽ *a close examination* CAREFUL, detailed, thorough, minute, searching, painstaking, meticulous, rigorous, scrupulous, conscientious; attentive, focused. ❾ *keep a close eye on them* VIGILANT, watchful, keen, alert. ❿ *a close translation* STRICT, faithful, exact, precise, literal; word for word, verbatim. ⓫ *he's close about his deals* RETICENT, secretive, uncommunicative, unforthcoming, tight-lipped, guarded, evasive. ⓬ *Sylvie was close with money* MEAN, miserly, niggardly, parsimonious, penny-pinching; *informal* tight-fisted, stingy, tight. ⓭ *the weather was close* HUMID, muggy, stuffy, airless, heavy, sticky, sultry, oppressive, stifling.

– OPPOSITES far, distant, one-sided, slight, loose, generous, fresh.

▶ **noun** (*Brit.*) *a small close of houses* CUL-DE-SAC, street, road; courtyard, quadrangle, enclosure.

close[2] ▶ **verb** ❶ *she closed the door* SHUT, pull to, push to, slam; fasten, secure. ❷ *close the hole* BLOCK (UP/OFF), stop up, plug, seal (up/off), shut up/off, cork, stopper, bung (up); clog (up), choke, obstruct. ❸ *the enemy were closing fast* CATCH UP, creep up, near, approach, gain on someone. ❹ *the gap is closing* NARROW, reduce, shrink, lessen, get smaller, diminish, contract. ❺ *his arms closed around her* MEET, join, connect; form a circle. ❻ *he closed the meeting* END, conclude, finish, terminate, wind up, break off, halt, discontinue, dissolve; adjourn, suspend. ❼ *the factory is to close* SHUT DOWN, close down, cease production, cease trading, be wound up, go out of business, go bankrupt, go into receivership, go into liquidation; *informal* fold, go to the wall, go bust. ❽ *he closed a deal* CLINCH, settle, secure, seal, confirm, establish; transact, pull off; complete, conclude, fix, agree, finalize; *informal* wrap up.

– OPPOSITES open, widen, begin.

▶ **noun** *the close of the talks* END, finish, conclusion, termination, cessation, completion, resolution; climax, denouement.

– OPPOSITES beginning.

■ **close down**. *See* CLOSE[2] verb sense 7.

closet ▶ **noun** *a clothes closet* CUPBOARD, wardrobe, cabinet, locker.

▶ **adjective** *a closet gay* SECRET, covert, private; surreptitious, clandestine, underground, furtive.

▶ **verb** *David was closeted in his den* SHUT AWAY, sequester, seclude, cloister, confine, isolate.

closure ▶ **noun** CLOSING DOWN, shutdown, winding up; termination, discontinuation, cessation, finish, conclusion; failure; *informal* folding.

clot ▶ **noun** ❶ *blood clots* LUMP, clump, mass; thrombus, thrombosis, embolus; *informal* glob; *Brit. informal* gob. ❷ (*Brit. informal*) *a clumsy clot. See* FOOL noun sense 1.

▶ **verb** *the blood is likely to clot* COAGULATE, set, congeal, curdle, thicken, solidify.

cloth ▶ **noun** ❶ *a maker of cloth* FABRIC, material, textile(s); *Brit.* soft goods. ❷ *a cloth to wipe the table* RAG, wipe, duster, sponge; flannel, towel; *Austral.* washer; *UK trademark* J-cloth. ❸ *a gentleman of the cloth* THE CLERGY, the church, the priesthood, the ministry; clergymen, clerics, priests.

clothe ▶ **verb** ❶ *they were clothed in silk* DRESS, attire, robe, garb, array, costume, swathe, deck (out), turn out, fit out, rig (out); *informal* get up; *archaic* apparel, habit, invest. ❷ *a valley clothed in conifers* COVER, blanket, carpet; envelop, swathe.

clothes ▶ **plural noun** CLOTHING, garments, attire, garb, dress, wear, costume; *informal* gear, togs, duds, get-up; *Brit. informal* clobber; *N. Amer. informal* threads; *formal* apparel; *archaic* raiment, habiliments, vestments.

– RELATED TERMS sartorial.

clothing ▶ **noun.** *See* CLOTHES.

cloud ▶ **noun** ❶ *dark clouds* storm cloud, cloudbank; mackerel sky. ❷ *a cloud of exhaust smoke* MASS, billow; pall, mantle, blanket. ❸ *a cloud of rooks* FLOCK, swarm, mass, multitude, host, throng, crowd.

▶ **verb** ❶ *the sky clouded* BECOME CLOUDY, cloud over, become overcast, lour, blacken, darken. ❷ *the sand is churned up, clouding the water* MAKE CLOUDY, make murky, dirty, darken, blacken. ❸ *anger clouded my judgement* CONFUSE, muddle, obscure, fog, muddy, mar.

■ **on cloud nine** ECSTATIC, rapturous, joyful, elated, blissful, euphoric, in seventh heaven, walking on air, transported, in raptures, delighted, thrilled, overjoyed, very happy; *informal* over the moon, on top of the world; *Austral. informal* wrapped.

cloudy ▶ **adjective** ❶ *a cloudy sky* OVERCAST, clouded; dark, grey, black, leaden, murky; sombre, dismal, heavy, gloomy; sunless, starless; hazy, misty, foggy. ❷ *cloudy water* MURKY, muddy, milky, dirty, opaque, turbid. ❸ *his eyes grew cloudy* TEARFUL, teary, weepy, lachrymose; moist, watery; misty, blurred. ❹ *avoid cloudy phrases* VAGUE, imprecise, foggy, hazy, confused, muddled, nebulous, obscure.

– OPPOSITES clear.

clout (*informal*) ▶ **noun** ❶ *a clout on the ear* SMACK, slap, thump, punch, blow, hit, cuff, box, clip; *informal* whack, wallop. ❷ *his clout in the business world* INFLUENCE, power, weight, sway, leverage, control, say; dominance, authority; *informal* teeth, muscle.

▶ **verb** *he clouted me* HIT, strike, punch, smack, slap, cuff, thump, buffet; *informal* wallop, belt, whack, clobber, sock, bop, biff.

cloven ▶ **adjective** SPLIT, divided, cleft.

clown ▶ **noun** ❶ *a circus clown* COMIC ENTERTAINER, comedian; *historical* jester, fool, zany; *archaic* merry andrew. ❷ *the class clown* JOKER, comedian, comic, humorist, wag, wit, prankster, jester, buffoon; *informal* laugh, kidder, wisecracker; *Austral./NZ informal* hard case. ❸ *bureaucratic clowns* FOOL, idiot, dolt, ass, simpleton, ignoramus; bungler, blunderer; *informal* moron, jackass, chump, numbskull, nincompoop, halfwit, bonehead, fathead, birdbrain; *Brit. informal* prat, berk, twit, nitwit, twerp.

▶ **verb** *Harvey clowned around* FOOL AROUND/ABOUT, play the fool, play about/around, monkey about/around; joke, jest; *informal* mess about/around, lark (about/around), horse about/around; *Brit. informal* muck about/around; *dated* play the giddy goat.

cloy ▶ **verb** SICKEN, disgust; become sickening, become nauseating, pall; be excessive.

cloying ▶ **adjective** SICKLY, syrupy, saccharine, oversweet; sickening, nauseating; mawkish, sentimental; *Brit.* twee; *informal* over the top, OTT, mushy, slushy, sloppy, gooey, cheesy, corny; *N. Amer. informal* cornball, sappy.

club[1] ▶ **noun** ❶ *a canoeing club* SOCIETY, association, organization, institution, group, circle, band, body, ring, crew; alliance, league, union. ❷ *the city has great clubs* NIGHTCLUB, disco, discotheque, bar; *informal* niterie. ❸ *the top club in the league* TEAM, squad, side, line-up.

■ **club together** POOL RESOURCES, join forces, team up, band together, get together, pull together, collaborate, ally; *informal* have a whip-round.

club[2] ▶ **noun** *a wooden club* CUDGEL, truncheon, bludgeon, baton, stick, mace, bat; *N. Amer.* blackjack, nightstick; *Brit. informal* cosh.

▶ **verb** *he was clubbed with an iron bar* CUDGEL, bludgeon, bash, beat, hit, strike, batter, belabour; *informal* clout, clobber; *Brit. informal* cosh.

clue ▶ **noun** ❶ *police are searching for clues* HINT, indication, sign, signal, pointer, trace, indicator; lead, tip, tip-off; evidence, information. ❷ *a crossword clue* QUESTION, problem, puzzle, riddle, poser, conundrum.

■ **clue someone in/up** (*informal*) INFORM, notify, make aware, prime; keep up to date, keep posted; *informal* tip off, give the gen, give the low-down, fill in on, gen up on, put in the picture, put wise, keep up to speed.

■ **not have a clue** (*informal*) HAVE NO IDEA, be ignorant, not have an inkling; be baffled, be mystified, be at a loss; *informal* be clueless, not have the faintest.

clump ▶ **noun** ❶ *a clump of trees* CLUSTER, thicket, group, bunch, assemblage. ❷ *a clump of earth* LUMP, clod, mass, gobbet, wad; *informal* glob; *Brit. informal* gob.

▶ **verb** ❶ *galaxies clump together* CLUSTER, group, collect, gather, assemble, congregate, mass. ❷ *they were clumping around upstairs* STAMP, stomp, clomp, tramp, lumber; thump, thud, bang; *informal* galumph.

clumsy ▶ **adjective** ❶ *she was terribly clumsy* AWKWARD, uncoordinated, ungainly, graceless, inelegant; inept, maladroit, unskilful, unhandy, accident-prone, like a bull in a china shop, all fingers and thumbs; *informal* cack-handed, ham-fisted, butterfingered, having two left feet; *N. Amer. informal* klutzy. ❷ *a clumsy contraption* UNWIELDY, cumbersome, bulky, awkward. ❸ *a clumsy remark* GAUCHE, awkward, graceless; unsubtle, uncouth, boorish, crass; tactless, insensitive, thoughtless, undiplomatic, indelicate, ill-judged.

– OPPOSITES graceful, elegant, tactful.

cluster ▶ **noun** ❶ *clusters of berries* BUNCH, clump, mass, knot, group, clutch, bundle, truss. ❷ *a cluster of spectators* CROWD, group, knot, huddle, bunch, throng, flock, pack, band; *informal* gang, gaggle.

▶ **verb** *they clustered around the television* CONGREGATE, gather, collect, group, assemble; huddle, crowd, flock.

clutch[1] ▶ **verb** *she clutched his arm* GRIP, grasp, clasp, cling to, hang on to, clench, hold.

■ **clutch at** REACH FOR, snatch at, make a grab for, catch at, claw at.

clutch[2] ▶ **noun** ❶ *a clutch of eggs* GROUP, batch. ❷ *a clutch of awards* GROUP, collection; raft, armful; *informal* load, bunch.

clutches ▶ **plural noun** POWER, control, domination, command, rule, tyranny; hands, hold, grip, grasp, claws, jaws; custody.

clutter ▶ **noun** ❶ *a clutter of toys* MESS, jumble, litter, heap, tangle, muddle, hotchpotch. ❷ *a desk full of clutter* DISORDER, chaos, disarray, untidiness, mess, confusion; litter, rubbish.

▶ **verb** *the garden was cluttered with tools* LITTER, mess up, disarrange; be strewn, be scattered; *poetic/literary* bestrew.

coach[1] ▶ **noun** ❶ *a journey by coach* BUS, minibus; *dated* omnibus, charabanc. ❷ *a railway coach* CARRIAGE, wagon, compartment, van, Pullman; *N. Amer.* car. ❸ *a coach and horses* HORSE-DRAWN CARRIAGE, trap, hackney, hansom, gig, landau, brougham.

coach[2] ▶ **noun** *a football coach* INSTRUCTOR, trainer; teacher, tutor, mentor, guru.

▶ **verb** *he coached Richard in maths* INSTRUCT, teach, tutor, school, educate; drill, cram; train.

coagulate ▶ **verb** CONGEAL, clot, thicken, gel; solidify, harden, set, dry.

coalesce ▶ **verb** MERGE, unite, join together, combine, fuse, mingle, blend; amalgamate, consolidate, integrate, homogenize, converge.

coalition ▶ **noun** ALLIANCE, union, partnership, bloc, caucus; federation, league, association, confederation, consortium, syndicate, combine; amalgamation, merger.

coarse ▶ **adjective** ❶ *coarse blankets* ROUGH, scratchy, prickly, wiry. ❷ *his coarse features* LARGE, rough, rough-hewn, heavy; ugly. ❸ *a coarse boy* OAFISH, loutish, boorish, uncouth, rude, impolite, ill-mannered, uncivil; vulgar, common, rough, uncultured, crass. ❹ *a coarse innuendo* VULGAR, crude, rude, off colour, dirty, filthy, smutty, indelicate, improper, unseemly, crass, tasteless, lewd, prurient; *informal* blue, farmyard.

– OPPOSITES soft, delicate, refined.

coarsen ▶ **verb** ❶ *hands coarsened by work* ROUGHEN, toughen, harden. ❷ *I had been coarsened by the army* DESENSITIZE, dehumanize; dull, deaden.

– OPPOSITES soften, refine.

coast ▶ **noun** *the west coast* SEABOARD, coastal region, coastline, seashore, shore, foreshore, shoreline, seaside, waterfront, littoral; *poetic/literary* strand.

▶ **verb** *the car coasted down a hill* FREEWHEEL, cruise, taxi, drift, glide, sail.

coat ▶ **noun** ❶ *a winter coat* OVERCOAT, jacket. ❷ *a dog's coat* FUR, hair, wool, fleece; hide, pelt, skin. ❸ *a coat of paint* LAYER, covering, coating, skin, film, wash; plating, glaze, varnish, veneer, patina; deposit.

▶ **verb** *the tube was coated with wax* COVER, paint, glaze, varnish, wash; surface, veneer, laminate, plate, face; daub, smear, cake, plaster.

coating ▶ **noun**. *See* COAT noun sense 3.

coax ▶ **verb** PERSUADE, wheedle, cajole, get round; beguile, seduce, inveigle, manoeuvre; *informal* sweet-talk, soft-soap, butter up, twist someone's arm.

cobble

■ **cobble something together** PREPARE ROUGHLY/HASTILY, make roughly/hastily, throw together; improvise, contrive, rig (up), whip up; *informal* rustle up; *Brit. informal* knock up.

cock ▶ **noun** ROOSTER, cockerel, capon.

▶ **verb** ❶ *he cocked his head* TILT, tip, angle, incline, dip. ❷ *she cocked her little finger* BEND, flex, crook, curve. ❸ *the dog cocked its leg* LIFT, raise, hold up.

cock-eyed ▶ **adjective** (*informal*) ❶ *that picture is cock-eyed* CROOKED, awry, askew, lopsided, tilted, off-centre, skewed, skew, squint, misaligned; *Brit. informal* skew-whiff, wonky. ❷ *a cock-eyed scheme* ABSURD, preposterous, ridiculous, ludicrous, farcical, laughable, risible, idiotic, stupid, foolish, silly, inane, imbecilic, half-baked, hare-brained; impractical, unfeasible; irrational, illogical, nonsensical; *informal* crazy; *Brit. informal* barmy, daft.

cocksure ▶ **adjective** ARROGANT, conceited, overweening, overconfident, cocky, proud, vain, self-important, swollen-headed, egotistical, presumptuous; smug, patronizing, pompous; *informal* high and mighty.
– OPPOSITES modest.

cocky ▶ **adjective** ARROGANT, conceited, overweening, overconfident, cocksure, swollen-headed, self-important, egotistical, presumptuous, boastful, self-assertive; bold, forward, insolent, cheeky.
– OPPOSITES modest.

cocoon ▶ **verb** ❶ *he cocooned her in a towel* WRAP, swathe, swaddle, muffle, cloak, enfold, envelop, cover, fold. ❷ *he was cocooned in the upper classes* PROTECT, shield, shelter, screen, cushion, insulate, isolate, cloister.

coddle ▶ **verb** PAMPER, cosset, mollycoddle; spoil, indulge, overindulge, pander to; wrap in cotton wool; baby, mother, wait on hand and foot.
– OPPOSITES neglect.

code ▶ **noun** ❶ *a secret code* CIPHER, key, hieroglyphics; cryptogram. ❷ *a strict social code* MORALITY, convention, etiquette, protocol. ❸ *the penal code* LAW(S), rules, regulations; constitution, system.

codify ▶ **verb** SYSTEMATIZE, systemize, organize, arrange, order, structure; tabulate, catalogue, list, sort, index, classify, categorize, file, log.

coerce ▶ **verb** PRESSURE, pressurize, press, push, constrain; force, compel, oblige, browbeat, bludgeon, bully, threaten, intimidate, dragoon, twist someone's arm; *informal* railroad, squeeze, lean on.

coercion ▶ **noun** FORCE, compulsion, constraint, duress, oppression, enforcement, harassment, intimidation, threats, arm-twisting, pressure.

coffee ▶ **noun** *N. Amer. informal* joe, java.

coffer ▶ **noun** ❶ *every church had a coffer* STRONGBOX, money box, cash box, money chest, treasure chest, safe; casket, box. ❷ *the Imperial coffers* FUND(S), reserves, resources, money, finances, wealth, cash, capital, purse; treasury, exchequer.

coffin ▶ **noun** sarcophagus; *N. Amer.* casket; *informal* box; *humorous* wooden overcoat.

cogent ▶ **adjective** CONVINCING, compelling, strong, forceful, powerful, potent, weighty, effective; valid, sound, plausible, telling; impressive, persuasive, eloquent, credible, influential; conclusive, authoritative; logical, reasoned, rational, reasonable, lucid, coherent, clear.

cogitate ▶ **verb** (*formal*) THINK (ABOUT), contemplate, consider, mull over, meditate, muse, ponder, reflect, deliberate, ruminate; dwell on, brood on, chew over, weigh up; *informal* put on one's thinking cap.

cognate ▶ **adjective** (*formal*) ASSOCIATED, related, connected, allied, linked; similar, like, alike, akin, kindred, comparable, parallel, corresponding, analogous.

cognition ▶ **noun** PERCEPTION, discernment, apprehension, learning, understanding, comprehension, insight; reasoning, thinking, thought.

cognizance ▶ **noun** (*formal*). *See* AWARENESS.

cognizant ▶ **adjective** (*formal*). *See* AWARE sense 1.

cohabit ▶ **verb** LIVE TOGETHER, live with; *informal* shack up (with); *informal, dated* live in sin.

cohere ▶ **verb** ❶ *the stories cohere into a convincing whole* STICK TOGETHER, hold together, be united, bind, fuse. ❷ *this view does not cohere with others* BE CONSISTENT, hang together.

coherent ▶ **adjective** LOGICAL, reasoned, reasonable, rational, sound, cogent, consistent; clear, lucid, articulate; intelligible, comprehensible.
– OPPOSITES muddled.

cohesion ▶ **noun** UNITY, togetherness, solidarity, bond, coherence; connection, linkage.

cohort ▶ **noun** ❶ *a Roman army cohort* UNIT, force, corps, division, brigade, battalion, regiment, squadron, company, troop, contingent, legion. ❷ *the 1940–4 birth cohort of women* GROUP, grouping, category, class, set, division, batch, list; age group, generation.

coil ▶ **noun** *coils of rope* LOOP, twist, turn, curl, convolution; spiral, helix, corkscrew.
▶ **verb** *he coiled her hair around his finger* WIND, loop, twist, curl, curve, bend, twine, entwine; spiral, corkscrew.

coin ▶ **noun** ❶ *a gold coin* PIECE. ❷ *large amounts of coin* COINAGE, coins, specie; (loose) change, small change, silver, copper(s), gold.
– RELATED TERMS numismatic.
▶ **verb** ❶ *guineas were coined* MINT, stamp, strike, cast, punch, die, mould, forge, make. ❷ *he*

coined the term INVENT, create, make up, conceive, originate, think up, dream up.

coincide ▶ verb ❶ *the events coincided* OCCUR SIMULTANEOUSLY, happen together, be concurrent, concur, coexist. ❷ *their interests do not always coincide* TALLY, correspond, agree, accord, concur, match, fit, be consistent, equate, harmonize, be compatible, dovetail, correlate; *informal* square.
– OPPOSITES differ.

coincidence ▶ noun ❶ *too close to be mere coincidence* ACCIDENT, chance, serendipity, fortuity, providence, happenstance, fate; a fluke. ❷ *the coincidence of inflation and unemployment* CO-OCCURRENCE, coexistence, conjunction, simultaneity, contemporaneity, concomitance. ❸ *a coincidence of interests* CORRESPONDENCE, agreement, accord, concurrence, consistency, conformity, harmony, compatibility.

coincident ▶ adjective ❶ *algae blooms coincident with dolphin deaths* CONCURRENT, coinciding, simultaneous, contemporaneous, concomitant, coexistent. ❷ *their aims are coincident* IN AGREEMENT, in harmony, in accord, consistent, compatible, congruent, in step, in tune; the same.

coincidental ▶ adjective ❶ *a coincidental resemblance* ACCIDENTAL, chance, fluky, random; fortuitous, adventitious, serendipitous; unexpected, unforeseen, unintentional, inadvertent, unplanned. ❷ *the coincidental disappearance of the two men* SIMULTANEOUS, concurrent, coincident, contemporaneous, concomitant.

coitus ▶ noun (*technical*). *See* SEX noun sense 1.

cold ▶ adjective ❶ *a cold day* CHILLY, chill, cool, freezing, icy, snowy, wintry, frosty, frigid, gelid; bitter, biting, raw; *informal* nippy, brass monkeys, arctic; *Brit. informal* parky. ❷ *I'm very cold* CHILLY, chilled, cool, freezing, frozen, shivery, numb, benumbed; hypothermic. ❸ *a cold reception* UNFRIENDLY, inhospitable, unwelcoming, forbidding, cool, frigid, frosty, glacial, lukewarm, indifferent, unfeeling, unemotional, formal, stiff.
– OPPOSITES hot, warm.

cold-blooded ▶ adjective CRUEL, callous, sadistic, inhuman, inhumane, pitiless, merciless, ruthless, unforgiving, unfeeling, uncaring, heartless; savage, brutal, barbaric, barbarous; cold, cold-hearted, unemotional.

cold-hearted ▶ adjective UNFEELING, unloving, uncaring, unsympathetic, unemotional, unfriendly, uncharitable, unkind, insensitive; hard-hearted, stony-hearted, heartless, hard, cold.

collaborate ▶ verb ❶ *they collaborated on the project* COOPERATE, join forces, team up, band together, work together, participate, combine, ally; pool resources, club together. ❷ *they collaborated with the enemy* FRATERNIZE, conspire, collude, cooperate, consort, sympathize.

collaborator ▶ noun ❶ *his collaborator on the book* CO-WORKER, partner, associate, colleague, confederate; assistant. ❷ *a wartime collaborator* QUISLING, fraternizer, collaborationist, colluder, (enemy) sympathizer; traitor, fifth columnist.

collapse ▶ verb ❶ *the roof collapsed* CAVE IN, fall in, subside, fall down, give (way), crumple, sag, slump. ❷ *he collapsed last night* FAINT, pass out, black out, lose consciousness, keel over, swoon; *informal* flake out, conk out. ❸ *she collapsed in tears* BREAK DOWN, go to pieces, lose control, be overcome, crumble; *informal* crack up. ❹ *peace talks collapsed* BREAK DOWN, fail, fall through, fold, founder, miscarry, come to grief, be unsuccessful; end; *informal* flop, fizzle out.
▶ noun ❶ *the collapse of the roof* CAVE-IN, subsidence. ❷ *her collapse on stage* FAINTING FIT, faint, blackout, loss of consciousness, swoon; *Medicine* syncope. ❸ *the collapse of the talks* BREAKDOWN, failure, disintegration; end. ❹ *he suffered a collapse* (NERVOUS) BREAKDOWN, personal crisis, psychological trauma; *informal* crack-up.

collar ▶ noun ❶ *a shirt collar* NECKBAND, choker; *historical* ruff, gorget, bertha. ❷ *a collar round the pipe* RING, band, collet, sleeve, flange.
▶ verb (*informal*) ❶ *he collared a thief* APPREHEND, arrest, catch, capture, seize; take prisoner, take into custody, detain; *informal* nab, pinch, bust, pick up, pull in, feel someone's collar; *Brit. informal* nick. ❷ *she collared me in the street* ACCOST, waylay, hail, approach, detain, stop, halt, catch, confront, importune; *informal* buttonhole; *Brit. informal* nobble.

collate ▶ verb ❶ *the system is used to collate information* COLLECT, gather, accumulate, assemble; combine, aggregate, put together; arrange, organize. ❷ *we must collate these two sources* COMPARE, contrast, set side by side, juxtapose, weigh against.

collateral ▶ noun SECURITY, surety, guarantee, guaranty, insurance, indemnity, indemnification; backing.

colleague ▶ noun CO-WORKER, fellow worker, workmate, teammate, associate, partner, collaborator, ally, confederate; *Brit. informal* oppo.

collect ▶ verb ❶ *he collected the rubbish* GATHER, accumulate, assemble; amass, stockpile, pile up, heap up, store (up), hoard, save; mass, accrue. ❷ *a crowd soon collected* GATHER, assemble, meet, muster, congregate, convene, converge, flock together. ❸ *I must collect the children* FETCH, go/come to get, call for, meet. ❹ *they*

collect money for charity RAISE, appeal for, ask for, solicit; obtain, acquire, gather. ❺ *he paused to collect himself* RECOVER, regain one's composure, pull oneself together, steady oneself; *informal* get a grip (on oneself). ❻ *she collected her thoughts* MUSTER, summon (up), gather, get together, marshal.
–OPPOSITES disperse, distribute.

collected ▸ **adjective** CALM, cool, self-possessed, self-controlled, composed, poised; serene, tranquil, relaxed, unruffled, unperturbed, untroubled; placid, quiet, sedate, phlegmatic; *informal* unfazed, together, laid-back.
–OPPOSITES excited, hysterical.

collection ▸ **noun** ❶ *a collection of stolen items* HOARD, pile, heap, stack, stock, store, stockpile; accumulation, reserve, supply, bank, pool, fund, mine, reservoir. ❷ *a collection of shoppers* GROUP, crowd, body, assemblage, gathering, throng; knot, cluster; multitude, bevy, party, band, horde, pack, flock, swarm, mob; *informal* gang, load, gaggle. ❸ *a collection of Victorian dolls* SET, series; array, assortment. ❹ *a collection of short stories* ANTHOLOGY, selection, compendium, treasury, compilation, miscellany, pot-pourri. ❺ *a collection for the poor* DONATIONS, contributions, gifts, subscription(s); *informal* whip-round; *historical* alms. ❻ *a church collection* OFFERING, offertory, tithe.

collective ▸ **adjective** COMMON, shared, joint, combined, mutual, communal, pooled; united, allied, cooperative, collaborative.
–OPPOSITES individual.

college ▸ **noun** ❶ *a college of technology* SCHOOL, academy, university, polytechnic, institute, seminary, conservatoire, conservatory. ❷ *the College of Heralds* ASSOCIATION, society, club, institute, body, fellowship, guild, lodge, order, fraternity, league, union, alliance.

collide ▸ **verb** ❶ *the trains collided with each other* CRASH, impact; hit, strike, run into, bump into, meet head-on, cannon into, plough into; *N. Amer. informal* barrel into. ❷ *politics and metaphysics collide* CONFLICT, clash; differ, diverge, disagree, be at odds, be incompatible.

collision ▸ **noun** ❶ *a collision on the ring road* CRASH, accident, impact, smash, bump, hit; *Brit.* RTA (road traffic accident); *N. Amer.* wreck; *informal* pile-up; *Brit. informal* prang, shunt. ❷ *a collision between two ideas* CONFLICT, clash; disagreement, incompatibility, contradiction.

colloquial ▸ **adjective** INFORMAL, conversational, everyday, non-literary; unofficial, idiomatic, slangy, vernacular, popular, demotic.
–OPPOSITES formal.

collude ▸ **verb** CONSPIRE, connive, collaborate, plot, scheme; *informal* be in cahoots.

colonist ▸ **noun** SETTLER, colonizer, colonial, pioneer; immigrant, incomer, newcomer; *N. Amer. historical* homesteader.
–OPPOSITES native.

colonize ▸ **verb** SETTLE (IN), people, populate; occupy, take over, seize, capture, subjugate.

colonnade ▸ **noun** ROW OF COLUMNS; portico, stoa, peristyle.

colony ▸ **noun** ❶ *a French colony* TERRITORY, dependency, protectorate, satellite, settlement, outpost, province. ❷ *the British colony in New York* POPULATION, community. ❸ *an artists' colony* COMMUNITY, commune; quarter, district, ghetto.

colossal ▸ **adjective** HUGE, massive, enormous, gigantic, very big, giant, mammoth, vast, immense, monumental, prodigious, mountainous, titanic, towering, king-size(d); *informal* monster, whopping, humongous, jumbo; *Brit. informal* ginormous.
–OPPOSITES tiny.

colour ▸ **noun** ❶ *the lights changed colour* HUE, shade, tint, tone, coloration. ❷ *oil colour* PAINT, pigment, colourant, dye, stain, tint, wash. ❸ *the colour in her cheeks* REDNESS, pinkness, rosiness, ruddiness, blush, flush, bloom. ❹ *people of every colour* SKIN COLOURING, skin tone, colouring; race, ethnic group. ❺ *anecdotes add colour to the text* VIVIDNESS, life, liveliness, vitality, excitement, interest, richness, zest, spice, piquancy, impact, force; *informal* oomph, pizzazz, punch, kick; *poetic/literary* salt. ❻ *the colours of the Oxford City club* STRIP, kit, uniform, costume, livery, regalia. ❼ *the regimental colours. See* FLAG[1] noun.
–RELATED TERMS chromatic.
▸ **verb** ❶ *the wood was coloured blue* TINT, dye, stain, paint, pigment, wash. ❷ *she coloured up* BLUSH, redden, go pink, go red, flush. ❸ *the experience coloured her outlook* INFLUENCE, affect, taint, warp, skew, distort, bias, prejudice. ❹ *they colour evidence to make a story saleable* EXAGGERATE, overstate, embroider, embellish, dramatize, enhance, varnish; falsify, misreport, manipulate.

colourful ▸ **adjective** ❶ *a colourful picture* BRIGHTLY COLOURED, vivid, vibrant, brilliant, radiant, rich; gaudy, glaring, garish; multicoloured, multicolour, rainbow, varicoloured, harlequin, polychromatic, psychedelic; *informal* jazzy. ❷ *a colourful account* VIVID, graphic, lively, animated, dramatic, fascinating, interesting, stimulating, scintillating, evocative.

colourless ▸ **adjective** ❶ *a colourless liquid* UNCOLOURED, white, bleached; *poetic/literary* achromatic. ❷ *her colourless face* PALE, pallid, wan, anaemic, bloodless, ashen, white, waxen, pasty, peaky, sickly, drained, drawn, ghostly, deathly. ❸ *a colourless personality* UNINTERESTING,

dull, boring, tedious, dry, dreary; unexciting, bland, weak, insipid, vapid, vacuous, feeble, wishy-washy, lame, lifeless, spiritless, anaemic, bloodless; nondescript, characterless.
– OPPOSITES colourful, rosy.

column ▶ noun ❶ *arches supported by massive columns* PILLAR, post, support, upright, baluster, pier, pile, pilaster, stanchion; obelisk, monolith. ❷ *a column in the paper* ARTICLE, piece, item, story, report, account, write-up, feature, review, notice, editorial, leader. ❸ *we walked in a column* LINE, file, queue, procession, train, cavalcade, convoy; *informal* crocodile.

columnist ▶ noun WRITER, contributor, journalist, correspondent, newspaperman, newspaperwoman, newsman, newswoman; wordsmith, penman; critic, reviewer, commentator; *informal* scribbler, pen-pusher, hack(ette), journo.

coma ▶ noun STATE OF UNCONSCIOUSNESS; *Medicine* persistent vegetative state, PVS.

comatose ▶ adjective ❶ *he was comatose after the accident* UNCONSCIOUS, in a coma, insensible, insensate. ❷ (*informal*) *she lay comatose in the sun* INERT, inactive, lethargic, sluggish, torpid, languid; somnolent, sleeping, dormant.

comb ▶ verb ❶ *she combed her hair* GROOM, brush, untangle, smooth, straighten, neaten, tidy, arrange; curry. ❷ *the wool was combed* SEPARATE, dress, card, tease, hackle, heckle. ❸ *police combed the area* SEARCH, scour, explore, sweep, probe, hunt through, forage through, poke about/around in, go over, go over with a fine-tooth comb; leave no stone unturned.

combat ▶ noun *he was killed in combat* BATTLE, fighting, action, hostilities, conflict, war, warfare.
▶ verb *they tried to combat the disease* FIGHT, battle, tackle, attack, counter, resist, withstand; impede, block, thwart, inhibit; stop, halt, prevent, check, curb.

combatant ▶ noun ❶ *a combatant in the war* FIGHTER, soldier, serviceman/woman, warrior, trooper. ❷ *combatants in the computer market* CONTENDER, adversary, opponent, competitor, challenger, rival.
▶ adjective *combatant armies* WARRING, at war, opposing, belligerent, fighting, battling.

combative ▶ adjective PUGNACIOUS, aggressive, antagonistic, quarrelsome, argumentative, contentious, hostile, truculent, belligerent, bellicose, militant; *informal* spoiling for a fight.
– OPPOSITES conciliatory.

combination ▶ noun ❶ *a combination of ancient and modern* AMALGAMATION, amalgam, merge, blend, mixture, mix, fusion, marriage, coalition, integration, incorporation, synthesis, composite. ❷ *he acted in combination with his brother* COOPERATION, collaboration, association, union, partnership, league.

combine ▶ verb ❶ *he combines comedy with tragedy* AMALGAMATE, integrate, incorporate, merge, mix, fuse, blend; bind, join, marry, unify. ❷ *teachers combined to tackle the problem* COOPERATE, collaborate, join forces, get together, club together, unite, team up, throw in one's lot; *informal* gang up.

combustible ▶ adjective INFLAMMABLE, flammable, incendiary, ignitable.

combustion ▶ noun BURNING; kindling, ignition.

come ▶ verb ❶ *come and listen* MOVE NEARER, move closer, approach, advance, draw close/closer, draw near/nearer; proceed; *archaic* draw nigh. ❷ *they came last night* ARRIVE, get here/there, make it, appear, come on the scene; approach, enter, turn up, come along, materialize; *informal* show (up), roll in/up, blow in, show one's face. ❸ *they came to a stream* REACH, arrive at, get to, make it to, make, gain; come across, run across, happen on, chance on, come upon, stumble on; end up at; *informal* wind up at. ❹ *the dress comes to her ankles* EXTEND, stretch, reach, come as far as. ❺ *she comes from Belgium* BE FROM, be a native of, hail from, originate in; live in, reside in. ❻ *attacks came without warning* HAPPEN, occur, take place, come about, transpire, fall, present itself, crop up, materialize, arise, arrive, appear; ensue, follow; *poetic/literary* come to pass, befall. ❼ *the car does not come in red* BE AVAILABLE, be for sale; be made, be produced. ❽ (*informal*) CLIMAX, orgasm.
– OPPOSITES go, leave.

■ **come about** HAPPEN, occur, take place, transpire, fall; crop up, materialize, arise, arrive, appear, surface; ensue, follow; *poetic/literary* come to pass, befall.

■ **come across** ❶ *they came across his friends* MEET/FIND BY CHANCE, meet, run into, run across, come upon, chance on, stumble on, happen on; discover, encounter, find, locate; *informal* bump into. ❷ *the emotion comes across* BE COMMUNICATED, be perceived, get across, be clear, be understood, register, sink in, strike home. ❸ *she came across as cool* SEEM, appear, look, sound, look to be; *Brit.* come over; *N. Amer.* come off. ❹ (*informal*) *she had come across with more information* HAND OVER, give, deliver, produce, part with; *informal* come up with, cough up; *N. Amer. informal* ante up.

■ **come along** ❶ *the puppies are coming along nicely* PROGRESS, develop, shape up; come on, turn out; improve, get better, pick up, rally, recover. ❷ *Come along!* HURRY (UP), be quick, get a move on, come along, look lively, speed up, move faster; *informal* get moving, get cracking,

step on it, move it, buck up, shake a leg, make it snappy; *Brit. informal* get your skates on; *N. Amer. informal* get a wiggle on; *dated* make haste.
■ **come apart** BREAK UP, fall to bits, fall to pieces, disintegrate, come unstuck, separate, split, tear.
■ **come back** RETURN, get back, arrive home, come home; come again.
■ **come between** ALIENATE, estrange, separate, divide, split up, break up, disunite, set at odds.
■ **come by** OBTAIN, acquire, gain, get, find, pick up, procure, secure; buy, purchase; *informal* get one's hands on, get hold of, bag, score, swing.
■ **come down** DECIDE, conclude, settle; choose, opt, plump.
■ **come down on**. *See* REPRIMAND verb.
■ **come down to** AMOUNT TO, add up to, constitute, boil down to, be equivalent to.
■ **come down with** FALL ILL WITH, fall sick with, be taken ill with, show symptoms of, become infected with, get, catch, develop, contract, fall victim to; *Brit.* go down with.
■ **come forward** VOLUNTEER, offer one's services, make oneself available.
■ **come in** ENTER, gain admission, cross the threshold.
■ **come into** INHERIT, be left, be willed, be bequeathed.
■ **come in for** RECEIVE, experience, sustain, undergo, go through, encounter, face, be subjected to, bear, suffer.
■ **come off** ❶ *this soufflé rarely comes off* SUCCEED, work, turn out well, work out, go as planned, produce the desired result, get results. ❷ *she always came off worse* END UP, finish up.
■ **come on** PROGRESS, develop, shape up, take shape, come along, turn out; improve.
■ **come out** ❶ *it came out that he'd been to Rome* BECOME KNOWN, become apparent, come to light, emerge, transpire; get out, be discovered, be uncovered, be revealed, leak out, be disclosed. ❷ *my book is coming out* BE PUBLISHED, be issued, be released, be brought out, be printed, go on sale. ❸ *the flowers have come out* BLOOM, flower, open. ❹ *it will come out all right* END, finish, conclude, work out, turn out; *informal* pan out. ❺ *the MP came out voluntarily* declare that one is homosexual, come out of the closet. ❻ (*Brit. dated*) *she came out in 1929* ENTER SOCIETY, make one's debut in society.
■ **come out with** UTTER, say, let out, blurt out, burst out with.
■ **come round** ❶ *he has just come round from anaesthetic* REGAIN CONSCIOUSNESS, come to, come to one's senses, recover, revive, awake, wake up. ❷ *I came round to her view* BE CONVERTED, be won over (by), agree (with), change one's mind, be persuaded (by); give way, yield, relent. ❸ *Friday the 13th comes round every few months* OCCUR, take place, happen, come up, crop up, arise; recur, reoccur, return, reappear. ❹ *come round for a drink* VISIT, call (in/round), look in, stop by, drop by/in/round/over, come over; *informal* pop in/round/over.
■ **come through** SURVIVE, get through, ride out, weather, live through, pull through; withstand, stand up to, endure, surmount, overcome; *informal* stick out.
■ **come to** ❶ *the bill came to* £17.50 AMOUNT TO, add up to, run to, total, equal; *Brit.* tot up to. ❷ *I came to in the hospital* REGAIN CONSCIOUSNESS, come round, come to one's senses, recover, revive, awake, wake up.
■ **come up** ARISE, occur, happen, come about, transpire, emerge, surface, crop up, turn up, pop up.
■ **come up to** ❶ *she came up to his shoulder* REACH, come to, be as tall as, extend to. ❷ *he never came up to her expectations* MEASURE UP TO, match up to, live up to, fulfil, satisfy, meet, equal, compare with; be good enough; *informal* hold a candle to.
■ **come up with** PRODUCE, devise, think up; propose, put forward, submit, suggest, recommend, advocate, introduce, moot.

comeback ▶ **noun** ❶ *he made a determined comeback* RESURGENCE, recovery, return, rally, upturn; *Brit.* fightback. ❷ (*informal*) *one of my best comebacks* RETORT, riposte, return, rejoinder; answer, reply, response.

comedian ▶ **noun** ❶ *a famous comedian* COMIC, comedienne, funny man/woman, humorist, gagster, stand-up; *N. Amer.* tummler. ❷ *Dad was such a comedian* JOKER, jester, wit, wag, comic, wisecracker, jokester; prankster, clown, fool, buffoon; *informal* laugh, hoot, case; *informal, dated* card, caution.

comedienne ▶ **noun**. *See* COMEDIAN sense 1.

comedown ▶ **noun** (*informal*) ❶ *a bit of a comedown for a sergeant* LOSS OF STATUS, loss of face, humiliation, belittlement, demotion, degradation, disgrace. ❷ *it's such a comedown after Christmas* ANTICLIMAX, let-down, disappointment, disillusionment, deflation, decline.

comedy ▶ **noun** ❶ *he excels in comedy* LIGHT ENTERTAINMENT, comic play, comic film, farce, situation comedy, satire, pantomime, comic opera; burlesque, slapstick; *informal* sitcom. ❷ *the comedy in their work* HUMOUR, fun, funny side, comical aspect, absurdity, drollness, farce.
– OPPOSITES tragedy, gravity.

comely ▶ **adjective** (*archaic*). *See* ATTRACTIVE sense 2.

come-on ▶ **noun** (*informal*) INDUCEMENT, incentive, attraction, lure, pull, draw, enticement, bait, carrot, temptation; fascination, charm, appeal, allure.

comeuppance ▶ **noun** (*informal*) JUST DESERTS, just punishment, due, retribution, requital.

comfort ▶ **noun** ❶ *travel in comfort* EASE, relaxation, repose, serenity, tranquillity, contentment, cosiness; luxury, opulence, prosperity; bed of roses. ❷ *words of comfort* CONSOLATION, solace, condolence, sympathy, commiseration; support, reassurance, cheer.
▶ **verb** *a friend tried to comfort her* CONSOLE, solace, condole with, commiserate with, sympathize with; support, succour, ease, reassure, soothe, calm; cheer, hearten, uplift; *informal* buck up.
– OPPOSITES distress, depress.

comfortable ▶ **adjective** ❶ *a comfortable lifestyle* PLEASANT, free from hardship; affluent, well-to-do, luxurious, opulent. ❷ *a comfortable room* COSY, snug, warm, pleasant, agreeable; restful, homelike, homely; *informal* comfy. ❸ *comfortable clothes* LOOSE, loose-fitting, casual; *informal* comfy. ❹ *a comfortable pace* LEISURELY, unhurried, relaxed, easy, gentle, sedate, undemanding, slow; *informal* laid-back. ❺ *they feel comfortable with each other* AT EASE, relaxed, secure, safe, unworried, contented, happy.
– OPPOSITES hard, spartan, tense.

comforting ▶ **adjective** CONSOLING, sympathetic, compassionate, solicitous, tender, warm, caring, loving; supportive, reassuring, soothing, calming; cheering, heartening, encouraging.

comfortless ▶ **adjective** ❶ *a comfortless house* GLOOMY, dreary, dismal, bleak, grim, sombre; joyless, cheerless, depressing, disheartening, dispiriting, unwelcoming, uninviting; austere, spartan, institutional. ❷ *he left her comfortless* MISERABLE, heartbroken, grief-stricken, unhappy, sad, distressed, desolate, devastated, inconsolable, disconsolate, downcast, downhearted, dejected, cheerless, depressed, melancholy, gloomy, glum; *informal* blue, down in the mouth, down in the dumps.
– OPPOSITES cosy, happy.

comic ▶ **adjective** *a comic play* HUMOROUS, funny, droll, amusing, hilarious, uproarious; comical, farcical, silly, slapstick, zany; witty, jocular; *informal* priceless, side-splitting, rib-tickling; *informal, dated* killing.
– OPPOSITES serious.
▶ **noun** ❶ *a music hall comic* COMEDIAN, comedienne, funny man/woman, comedy actor/actress, humorist, wit; joker, clown; *informal* kidder, wisecracker. ❷ *Tony read his comic* CARTOON PAPER, comic paper, comic book, graphic novel; *informal* funny.

comical ▶ **adjective** ❶ *he could be quite comical* FUNNY, comic, humorous, droll, witty, jocular, hilarious, amusing, diverting, entertaining; *informal* jokey, wacky, waggish, side-splitting, rib-tickling, priceless, a scream, a laugh; *informal, dated* killing, a card, a caution. ❷ *they look comical in those suits* SILLY, absurd, ridiculous, laughable, risible, ludicrous, preposterous, foolish; *informal* wacky, crazy.
– OPPOSITES sensible.

coming ▶ **adjective** *the coming election* FORTHCOMING, imminent, impending, approaching; future, expected, anticipated; close, at hand, in store, in the offing, in the pipeline, on the horizon, on the way; *informal* on the cards.
▶ **noun** *the coming of spring* APPROACH, advance, advent, arrival, appearance, emergence, onset.

command ▶ **verb** ❶ *he commanded his men to retreat* ORDER, tell, direct, instruct, call on, require; *poetic/literary* bid. ❷ *Jones commanded a tank squadron* BE IN CHARGE OF, be in command of, be the leader of; head, lead, control, direct, manage, supervise, oversee; *informal* head up. ❸ *they command great respect* RECEIVE, get, gain, secure.
▶ **noun** ❶ *officers shouted commands* ORDER, instruction, directive, direction, commandment, injunction, demand, stipulation, requirement, exhortation, bidding, request. ❷ *he had 160 men under his command* AUTHORITY, control, charge, power, direction, dominion, guidance; leadership, rule, government, management, supervision, jurisdiction. ❸ *a brilliant command of English* KNOWLEDGE, mastery, grasp, comprehension, understanding.

commandeer ▶ **verb** SEIZE, take, requisition, appropriate, expropriate, sequestrate, sequester, confiscate, annex, take over, claim, pre-empt; hijack, arrogate, help oneself to; *informal* walk off with; *Law* distrain; *Scottish Law* poind.

commander ▶ **noun** LEADER, head, chief, overseer, controller; commander-in-chief, C in C, commanding officer, CO, officer; *informal* boss, boss man, skipper, numero uno, number one, top dog, kingpin, head honcho; *Brit. informal* gaffer, guv'nor.

commanding ▶ **adjective** ❶ *a commanding position* DOMINANT, dominating, controlling, superior, powerful, prominent, advantageous, favourable. ❷ *a commanding voice* AUTHORITATIVE, masterful, assertive, firm, emphatic, insistent, imperative; peremptory, imperious, dictatorial; *informal* bossy.

commemorate ▶ **verb** CELEBRATE, pay tribute to, pay homage to, honour, salute, toast; remember, recognize, acknowledge, observe, mark.

commemorative ▶ **adjective** MEMORIAL, remembrance; celebratory.

commence ▶ **verb** BEGIN, start; get the ball rolling, get going, get under way, get off the

ground, set about, embark on, launch into, lead off; open, initiate, inaugurate; *informal* kick off, get the show on the road.
– OPPOSITES conclude.

commencement ▶ **noun** BEGINNING, start, opening, outset, onset, launch, initiation, inception, origin; *informal* kick-off.

commend ▶ **verb** ❶ *we should commend him* PRAISE, compliment, congratulate, applaud, salute, honour; sing the praises of, pay tribute to, take one's hat off to, pat on the back; *formal* laud. ❷ *I commend her to you without reservation* RECOMMEND, suggest, propose; endorse, advocate, vouch for, speak for, support, back. ❸ (*formal*) *I commend them to your care* ENTRUST, trust, deliver, commit, hand over, give, turn over, consign, assign.
– OPPOSITES criticize.

commendable ▶ **adjective** ADMIRABLE, praiseworthy, creditable, laudable, estimable, meritorious, exemplary, noteworthy, honourable, respectable, fine, excellent.
– OPPOSITES reprehensible.

commendation ▶ **noun** ❶ *letters of commendation* PRAISE, congratulation, appreciation; acclaim, credit, recognition, respect, esteem, admiration, homage, tribute. ❷ *a commendation for bravery* AWARD, accolade, prize, honour, (honourable) mention, citation.

commensurate ▶ **adjective** ❶ *they had privileges but commensurate duties* EQUIVALENT, equal, corresponding, correspondent, comparable, proportionate, proportional. ❷ *a salary commensurate with your qualifications* APPROPRIATE TO, in keeping with, in line with, consistent with, corresponding to, according to, relative to; dependent on, based on.

comment ▶ **noun** ❶ *their comments on her appearance* REMARK, observation, statement, utterance; pronouncement, judgement, reflection, opinion, view; criticism. ❷ *a great deal of comment* DISCUSSION, debate; interest. ❸ *a comment in the margin* NOTE, annotation, footnote, gloss, commentary, explanation.
▶ **verb** ❶ *they commented on the food* REMARK ON, speak about, talk about, discuss, mention. ❷ *'It will soon be night,' he commented* REMARK, observe, reflect, say, state, declare, announce; interpose, interject.

commentary ▶ **noun** ❶ *the test match commentary* NARRATION, description, account, report, review. ❷ *textual commentary* EXPLANATION, elucidation, interpretation, exegesis, analysis; assessment, appraisal, criticism; notes, comments.

commentator ▶ **noun** ❶ *a television commentator* NARRATOR, announcer, presenter, anchor, anchorman, anchorwoman; reporter, journalist, newscaster, sportscaster; *informal* talking head. ❷ *a political commentator* ANALYST, pundit, monitor, observer; writer, speaker.

commerce ▶ **noun** ❶ *eastern commerce* TRADE, trading, buying and selling, business, dealing, traffic; (financial) transactions, dealings. ❷ (*dated*) *human commerce* RELATIONS, dealings, socializing, communication, association, contact, intercourse.

commercial ▶ **adjective** ❶ *a vessel built for commercial purposes* TRADE, trading, business, private enterprise, mercantile, sales. ❷ *we turn good ideas into commercial products* LUCRATIVE, moneymaking, money-spinning, profitable, remunerative, fruitful, gainful; viable, successful. ❸ *public opinion was commercial* PROFIT-ORIENTATED, money-orientated, materialistic, mercenary.
▶ **noun** *a TV commercial* ADVERTISEMENT, promotion, display; *informal* ad, plug; *Brit. informal* advert.

commercialized ▶ **adjective** PROFIT-ORIENTATED, money-orientated, commercial, materialistic, mercenary.

commiserate ▶ **verb** (**commiserate with**) OFFER SYMPATHY TO, be sympathetic to, offer condolences to, condole with, sympathize with, empathize with, feel pity for, feel sorry for, feel for; comfort, console.

commiseration ▶ **noun** CONDOLENCE(S), sympathy, pity, comfort, solace, consolation; compassion, understanding.

commission ▶ **noun** ❶ *the dealer's commission* PERCENTAGE, brokerage, share, portion, dividend, premium, fee, consideration, bonus; *informal* cut, take, rake-off, slice; *Brit. informal* whack, divvy. ❷ *the commission of building a palace* TASK, employment, job, project, mission, assignment, undertaking; duty, charge, responsibility. ❸ *items made under royal commission* WARRANT, licence, sanction, authority. ❹ *an independent commission* COMMITTEE, board, council, panel, directorate, delegation. ❺ *the commission of an offence* PERPETRATION, committing, committal, execution.
▶ **verb** ❶ *he was commissioned to paint a portrait* ENGAGE, contract, charge, employ, hire, recruit, retain, appoint, enlist, co-opt, book, sign up. ❷ *they commissioned a sculpture* ORDER; authorize; *formal* bespeak.
■ **in commission** IN SERVICE, in use; working, functional, operative, up and running, in operation, in working order.
■ **out of commission** NOT IN SERVICE, not in use, unserviceable; not working, inoperative, out of order; down.

commit ▶ **verb** ❶ *he committed a murder* CARRY OUT, do, perpetrate, engage in, enact, execute, effect, accomplish; be responsible for; *informal* pull off. ❷ *she was committed to their care* EN-

TRUST, consign, assign, deliver, give, hand over, relinquish; *formal* commend. ❸ *they committed themselves to the project* PLEDGE, devote, apply, give, dedicate. ❹ *the judge committed him to prison* CONSIGN, send, deliver, confine. ❺ *her husband had her committed* HOSPITALIZE, confine, institutionalize, put away; certify.

commitment ▶ noun ❶ *the pressure of his commitments* RESPONSIBILITY, obligation, duty, tie, liability; task; engagement, arrangement. ❷ *her commitment to her students* DEDICATION, devotion, allegiance, loyalty, faithfulness, fidelity. ❸ *he made a commitment* VOW, promise, pledge, oath; contract, pact, deal; decision, resolution.

committed ▶ adjective DEVOUT, devoted, dedicated, loyal, faithful, staunch, firm, steadfast, unwavering, wholehearted, keen, passionate, ardent, fervent, sworn, pledged; dutiful, diligent; *informal* card-carrying, true blue, deep-dyed.
– OPPOSITES apathetic.

commodious ▶ adjective (*formal*) ROOMY, capacious, spacious, ample, generous, sizeable, large, big, extensive.
– OPPOSITES cramped.

commodity ▶ noun ITEM, material, product, article, object; import, export.

common ▶ adjective ❶ *the common folk* ORDINARY, normal, average, unexceptional; simple. ❷ *a very common art form* USUAL, ordinary, familiar, regular, frequent, recurrent, everyday; standard, typical, conventional, stock, commonplace, run-of-the-mill. ❸ *a common belief* WIDESPREAD, general, universal, popular, mainstream, prevalent, prevailing, rife, established, conventional, traditional, orthodox, accepted. ❹ *the common good* COLLECTIVE, communal, community, public, popular, general; shared, combined. ❺ *they are far too common* UNCOUTH, vulgar, coarse, rough, boorish, unladylike, ungentlemanly, ill-bred, uncivilized, unsophisticated, unrefined; lowly, low-born, low-class, inferior, proletarian, plebeian; *informal* plebby; *Brit. informal* common as muck.
– OPPOSITES unusual, rare, individual, refined.
▶ noun (*Brit. informal*) *use your common! See* COMMON SENSE.

commonly ▶ adverb OFTEN, frequently, regularly, repeatedly, time and (time) again, all the time, routinely, habitually, customarily; *N. Amer.* oftentimes; *informal* lots.

commonplace ▶ adjective ❶ *a commonplace writing style* ORDINARY, run-of-the-mill, unremarkable, unexceptional, average, mediocre, pedestrian, prosaic, lacklustre, dull, bland, uninteresting, mundane; hackneyed, trite, banal, clichéd, predictable, stale, tired, unoriginal; *informal* (plain) vanilla, bog-standard, a dime a dozen; *Brit. informal* common or garden; *N. Amer. informal* ornery, bush-league. ❷ *a commonplace occurrence* COMMON, normal, usual, ordinary, familiar, routine, standard, everyday, daily, regular, frequent, habitual, typical.
– OPPOSITES original, unusual.
▶ noun ❶ *early death was a commonplace* EVERYDAY EVENT, routine. ❷ *a great store of commonplaces* PLATITUDE, cliché, truism, hackneyed phrase, trite phrase, old chestnut, banality; *dated* bromide.

common sense ▶ noun SENSIBLENESS, (good) sense, (native) wit, judgement, level-headedness, prudence, discernment, canniness, astuteness, shrewdness, wisdom, insight, perception, perspicacity; practicality, capability, resourcefulness, enterprise; *informal* horse sense, gumption, nous, savvy; *Brit. informal* common; *N. Amer. informal* smarts.
– OPPOSITES folly.

commotion ▶ noun DISTURBANCE, uproar, tumult, rumpus, ruckus, brouhaha, furore, hue and cry, fuss, stir, storm; turmoil, disorder, confusion, chaos, mayhem, havoc, pandemonium; unrest, fracas, riot, breach of the peace; *Irish, N. Amer., & Austral.* donnybrook; *informal* ruction(s), ballyhoo, kerfuffle, hoo-ha, to-do, hullabaloo; *Brit. informal* carry-on, row, aggro, argy-bargy; *Law, dated* affray.

communal ▶ adjective ❶ *the kitchen was communal* SHARED, joint, common. ❷ *they farm on a communal basis* COLLECTIVE, cooperative, community, communalist, combined.
– OPPOSITES private, individual.

commune ▶ noun *she lives in a commune* COLLECTIVE, cooperative, communal settlement, kibbutz.
▶ verb ❶ *we pray to commune with God* COMMUNICATE, speak, talk, converse, interface. ❷ *she likes to commune with nature* EMPATHIZE, identify, have a rapport, feel at one; relate to, feel close to.

communicable ▶ adjective CONTAGIOUS, INFECTIOUS, transmittable, transmissible, transferable, spreadable; *informal* catching; *dated* infective.

communicate ▶ verb ❶ *he communicated the news to his boss* CONVEY, tell, impart, relay, transmit, pass on, announce, report, recount, relate, present; divulge, disclose, mention; spread, disseminate, promulgate, broadcast. ❷ *they communicate daily* LIAISE, be in touch, be in contact, have dealings, interface, commune, meet; talk, speak, converse; *informal* have a confab, powwow. ❸ *learn how to communicate better* GET ONE'S MESSAGE ACROSS, explain oneself, be understood, get through to someone. ❹ *the disease is communicated easily* TRANS-

MIT, transfer, spread, carry, pass on. ❺ *each bedroom communicates with a bathroom* CONNECT WITH, join up with, open on to, lead into.

communication ▶ noun ❶ *the communication of news* TRANSMISSION, conveyance, divulgence, divulgation, disclosure; dissemination, promulgation, broadcasting. ❷ *there was no communication between them* CONTACT, dealings, relations, connection, association, socializing, intercourse; correspondence, dialogue, talk, conversation, discussion; *dated* commerce. ❸ *an official communication* MESSAGE, statement, announcement, report, dispatch, communiqué, letter, bulletin, correspondence. ❹ *road and rail communications* LINKS, connections; services, routes.

communicative ▶ adjective FORTHCOMING, expansive, expressive, unreserved, uninhibited, vocal, outgoing, frank, open, candid; talkative, chatty, loquacious; *informal* gabby.

communion ▶ noun ❶ *a sense of communion with others* AFFINITY, fellowship, kinship, friendship, fellow feeling, togetherness, closeness, harmony, understanding, rapport, connection, communication, empathy, accord, unity. ❷ *Christ's presence at Communion* EUCHARIST, Holy Communion, Lord's Supper, Mass.

communiqué ▶ noun OFFICIAL COMMUNICATION, press release, bulletin, message, missive, dispatch, statement, report, announcement, declaration, proclamation; *N. Amer.* advisory; *informal* memo.

communism ▶ noun COLLECTIVISM, state ownership, (radical) socialism; Sovietism, Bolshevism, Marxism, Leninism, Trotskyism, Maoism.

communist ▶ noun & adjective COLLECTIVIST, leftist, (radical) socialist; Soviet, Bolshevik, Bolshevist, Marxist, Leninist, Trotskyist, Trotskyite, Maoist; *informal, derogatory* Commie, Bolshie, red, lefty.

community ▶ noun ❶ *work done for the community* POPULATION, populace, people, citizenry, (general) public, collective; residents, inhabitants, citizens. ❷ *a rural community* DISTRICT, region, zone, area, locality, locale, neighbourhood; *informal* neck of the woods, turf; *Brit. informal* manor; *N. Amer. informal* hood, nabe. ❸ *gays are not one homogenous community* GROUP, body, set, circle, clique, faction; *informal* gang, bunch. ❹ *a monastic community* BROTHERHOOD, sisterhood, fraternity, sorority, sodality; colony, order. ❺ *community of interests* SIMILARITY, likeness, comparability, correspondence, agreement, closeness, affinity. ❻ *the community of goods* JOINT OWNERSHIP, common ownership, shared possession.

commute ▶ verb ❶ *they commute on a train* TRAVEL TO AND FROM WORK, travel to and fro, travel back and forth. ❷ *his sentence was commuted* REDUCE, lessen, lighten, shorten, cut, attenuate, moderate. ❸ *knight service was commuted for a payment* EXCHANGE, change, substitute, swap, trade, switch.
– OPPOSITES increase.

commuter ▶ noun (DAILY) TRAVELLER, traveller, passenger; *informal* straphanger.

compact[1] ▶ adjective ❶ *a compact rug* DENSE, close-packed, tightly packed; thick, tight, firm. ❷ *a compact camera* SMALL, little, petite, miniature, mini, small-scale; *Scottish* wee; *informal* teeny, teeny-weeny; *Brit. informal* dinky; *N. Amer.* little-bitty. ❸ *her tale is compact* CONCISE, succinct, condensed, brief, pithy; short and sweet; *informal* snappy; *formal* compendious.
– OPPOSITES loose, large, rambling.
▶ verb *the snow has been compacted* COMPRESS, condense, pack down, press down, tamp (down), flatten.

compact[2] ▶ noun *the warring states signed a compact* TREATY, pact, accord, agreement, contract, bargain, deal, settlement, covenant, concordat; pledge, promise, bond.

companion ▶ noun ❶ *Harry and his companion* ASSOCIATE, partner, escort, compatriot, confederate; friend, intimate, confidant(e), comrade; *informal* pal, chum, crony, sidekick; *Brit. informal* mate, oppo, china, mucker; *N. Amer. informal* buddy, amigo, compadre; *Austral./NZ informal* offsider. ❷ *a lady's companion* ATTENDANT, aide, helper, assistant, valet, equerry, lady in waiting; chaperone; carer, minder. ❸ *the tape is a companion to the book* COMPLEMENT, counterpart, twin, match; accompaniment, supplement, addition, adjunct, accessory. ❹ *The Gardener's Companion* HANDBOOK, manual, guide, reference book, ABC, primer, vade mecum; *informal* bible.

companionable ▶ adjective FRIENDLY, affable, cordial, genial, congenial, amiable, easy-going, good-natured, comradely; sociable, convivial, outgoing, gregarious; *informal* chummy, pally; *Brit. informal* matey; *N. Amer. informal* buddy-buddy, clubby.

companionship ▶ noun FRIENDSHIP, fellowship, closeness, togetherness, amity, intimacy, rapport, camaraderie, brotherhood, sisterhood; company, society, social contact.

company ▶ noun ❶ *an oil company* FIRM, business, corporation, establishment, agency, office, bureau, institution, organization, concern, enterprise; conglomerate, consortium, syndicate, multinational; *informal* outfit. ❷ *I enjoy his company* COMPANIONSHIP, friendship, fellowship, amity, camaraderie; society, association. ❸ *I'm expecting company* GUESTS, visitors, callers, people; someone. ❹ *a company of poets* GROUP, crowd, party, band, assembly, cluster,

flock, herd, troupe, throng, congregation; *informal* bunch, gang. ❺ *a company of infantry* UNIT, section, detachment, troop, corps, squad, squadron, platoon, battalion, division.
– RELATED TERMS corporate.

comparable ▶ adjective ❶ *comparable incomes* SIMILAR, close, near, approximate, akin, equivalent, commensurate, proportional, proportionate; like, matching. ❷ *nobody is comparable with him* EQUAL TO, as good as, in the same league as, able to hold a candle to, on a par with, on a level with; a match for.

comparative ▶ adjective RELATIVE; in/by comparison.

compare ▶ verb ❶ *we compared the data sets* CONTRAST, juxtapose, collate, differentiate, weigh up. ❷ *he was compared to Wagner* LIKEN, equate, analogize; class with, bracket with, set side by side with. ❸ *the porcelain compares with Dresden's fine china* BE AS GOOD AS, be comparable to, bear comparison with, be the equal of, match up to, be on a par with, be in the same league as, come close to, hold a candle to, be not unlike; match, resemble, emulate, rival, approach.
■ **beyond compare** WITHOUT EQUAL, second to none, in a class of one's own; peerless, matchless, unmatched, incomparable, inimitable, supreme, outstanding, consummate, unique, singular, perfect.

comparison ▶ noun ❶ *a comparison of the results* JUXTAPOSITION, collation, differentiation. ❷ *there's no comparison between them* RESEMBLANCE, likeness, similarity, correspondence, correlation, parallel, parity, comparability.

compartment ▶ noun ❶ *a secret compartment* SECTION, part, bay, recess, chamber, cavity; pocket. ❷ *they put science and religion in separate compartments* DOMAIN, field, sphere, department; category, pigeonhole, bracket, group, set.

compartmentalize ▶ verb CATEGORIZE, pigeonhole, bracket, group, classify, characterize, stereotype, label, brand; sort, rank, rate.

compass ▶ noun SCOPE, range, extent, reach, span, breadth, ambit, limits, parameters, bounds.

compassion ▶ noun PITY, sympathy, empathy, fellow feeling, care, concern, solicitude, sensitivity, warmth, love, tenderness, mercy, leniency, tolerance, kindness, humanity, charity.
– OPPOSITES indifference, cruelty.

compassionate ▶ adjective SYMPATHETIC, empathetic, understanding, caring, solicitous, sensitive, warm, loving; merciful, lenient, tolerant, considerate, kind, humane, charitable, big-hearted.

compatibility ▶ noun LIKE-MINDEDNESS, similarity, affinity, closeness, fellow feeling, harmony, rapport, empathy, sympathy.

compatible ▶ adjective ❶ *they were never compatible* (WELL) SUITED, well matched, like-minded, in tune, in harmony; reconcilable. ❷ *her bruising is compatible with a fall* CONSISTENT, congruous, congruent; in keeping.

compatriot ▶ noun FELLOW COUNTRYMAN/WOMAN, countryman, countrywoman, fellow citizen.

compel ▶ verb ❶ *he compelled them to leave their land* FORCE, pressurize, pressure, press, push, urge; dragoon, browbeat, bully, intimidate; oblige, require, make; *informal* lean on, put the screws on. ❷ *they can compel compliance* EXACT, extort, demand, insist on, force, necessitate.

compelling ▶ adjective ❶ *a compelling performance* ENTHRALLING, captivating, gripping, riveting, spellbinding, mesmerizing, absorbing, irresistible. ❷ *a compelling argument* CONVINCING, persuasive, cogent, irresistible, powerful, strong, weighty, plausible, credible, sound, valid, telling, conclusive, irrefutable, unanswerable.
– OPPOSITES boring, weak.

compendious ▶ adjective (*formal*) SUCCINCT, pithy, short and to the point, concise, compact, condensed, compressed, abridged, summarized, synoptic; *informal* snappy.
– OPPOSITES expanded.

compendium ▶ noun COLLECTION, compilation, anthology, treasury, digest; summary, synopsis, precis, outline.

compensate ▶ verb ❶ *you must compensate for what you did* MAKE AMENDS, make up, make reparation, recompense, atone, requite, pay; expiate, make good, rectify. ❷ *we agreed to compensate him for his loss* RECOMPENSE, repay, pay back, reimburse, remunerate, recoup, requite, indemnify. ❸ *his flair compensated for his faults* BALANCE (OUT), counterbalance, counteract, offset, make up for, cancel out, neutralize, negative.

compensation ▶ noun RECOMPENSE, repayment, reimbursement, remuneration, requital, indemnification, indemnity, redress; damages; *N. Amer. informal* comp.

compère ▶ noun HOST, presenter, anchor, anchorman/woman, master of ceremonies, MC, announcer; *N. Amer. informal* emcee.

compete ▶ verb ❶ *they competed in a tennis tournament* TAKE PART, participate, play, be a competitor, be involved; enter, go in for. ❷ *they had to compete with other firms* CONTEND, vie, battle, wrangle, jockey, go head to head; strive against, pit oneself against; challenge, take on. ❸ *no one can compete with him* RIVAL, challenge, keep up with, keep pace with, compare with, match, be in the same league as, come near to, come close to, touch; *informal* hold a candle to.

competence ▶ noun ❶ *my technical competence* CAPABILITY, ability, competency, proficiency, accomplishment, expertise, adeptness, skill, prowess, mastery, talent; *informal* savvy, know-how. ❷ *the competence of the system* ADEQUACY, appropriateness, suitability, fitness; effectiveness; *formal* efficacy. ❸ *matters within the competence of the courts* AUTHORITY, power, control, jurisdiction, ambit, scope, remit.

competent ▶ adjective ❶ *a competent carpenter* CAPABLE, able, proficient, adept, adroit, accomplished, complete, skilful, skilled, gifted, talented, expert; good, excellent; *informal* great, mean, wicked, nifty, ace. ❷ *she spoke competent French* ADEQUATE, acceptable, satisfactory, reasonable, fair, decent, not bad, all right, average, tolerable, passable, moderate, middling; *informal* OK, okay, so-so. ❸ *the court was not competent to hear the case* FIT, suitable, suited, appropriate; qualified, empowered, authorized.
– OPPOSITES inadequate, unfit.

competition ▶ noun ❶ *Stephanie won the competition* CONTEST, tournament, match, game, heat, fixture, event; trials, stakes. ❷ *I'm not interested in competition* RIVALRY, competitiveness, vying; conflict, feuding, fighting; *informal* keeping up with the Joneses. ❸ *we must stay ahead of the competition* OPPOSITION, other side, field; enemy; challengers, opponents, rivals, adversaries; *poetic/literary* foe.

competitive ▶ adjective ❶ *a competitive player* AMBITIOUS, zealous, keen, pushy, combative, aggressive; *informal* go-ahead. ❷ *a highly competitive industry* RUTHLESS, aggressive, fierce; *informal* dog-eat-dog, cut-throat. ❸ *competitive prices* REASONABLE, moderate, keen; low, inexpensive, cheap, budget, bargain, reduced, discount; rock-bottom, bargain-basement.
– OPPOSITES apathetic, exorbitant.

competitor ▶ noun ❶ *the competitors in the race* CONTESTANT, contender, challenger, participant, entrant; runner, player. ❷ *our European competitors* RIVAL, challenger, opponent, adversary; competition, opposition.
– OPPOSITES ally.

compilation ▶ noun COLLECTION, selection, anthology, treasury, compendium, album, corpus, collectanea; pot-pourri.

compile ▶ verb ASSEMBLE, put together, make up, collate, compose, organize, arrange; gather, collect.

complacency ▶ noun SMUGNESS, self-satisfaction, self-congratulation, self-regard; gloating, triumph, pride; satisfaction, contentment.

complacent ▶ adjective SMUG, self-satisfied, self-congratulatory, self-regarding; gloating, triumphant, proud; pleased, satisfied, content, contented; *informal* like the cat that got the cream, I'm-all-right-Jack; *N. Amer. informal* wisenheimer.

complain ▶ verb PROTEST, grumble, whine, bleat, carp, cavil, grouse, make a fuss; object to, speak out against, oppose, criticize, find fault with; *informal* whinge, kick up a fuss, bellyache, moan, beef, bitch, sound off; *Brit. informal* gripe, chunter, create; *N. Amer. informal* kvetch.

complaint ▶ noun ❶ *they lodged a complaint* PROTEST, objection, grievance, grouse, cavil, quibble, grumble; charge, accusation, criticism; *informal* beef, gripe, whinge; *Law, Brit.* plaint. ❷ *little cause for complaint* PROTESTATION, objection, exception, grievance, grumbling; criticism, fault-finding, condemnation, disapproval, dissatisfaction; *informal* whingeing, grousing, bellyaching, nit-picking. ❸ *a kidney complaint* DISORDER, disease, infection, affliction, illness, ailment, sickness; condition, problem, upset, trouble; *informal* bug, virus.

complaisant ▶ adjective WILLING, acquiescent, agreeable, amenable, cooperative, accommodating, obliging; biddable, compliant, docile, obedient.

complement ▶ noun ❶ *the perfect complement to the food* ACCOMPANIMENT, companion, addition, supplement, accessory, trimming. ❷ *a full complement of lifeboats* AMOUNT, total, contingent, capacity, allowance, quota.
▶ verb *this sauce complements the dessert* ACCOMPANY, go with, round off, set off, suit, harmonize with; enhance, complete.

complementary ▶ adjective HARMONIOUS, compatible, corresponding, matching, twin, complemental; supportive, reciprocal, interdependent.
– OPPOSITES incompatible.

complete ▶ adjective ❶ *the complete interview* ENTIRE, whole, full, total; uncut, unabridged. ❷ *their research was complete* FINISHED, ended, concluded, completed, finalized; accomplished, achieved, discharged, settled, done; *informal* wrapped up, sewn up, polished off. ❸ *a complete fool* ABSOLUTE, out-and-out, utter, total, real, downright, thoroughgoing, veritable, prize, perfect, unqualified, unmitigated, sheer, arrant; *N. Amer.* full-bore; *Brit. informal* right.
– OPPOSITES partial, unfinished.
▶ verb ❶ *he had to complete his training* FINISH, end, conclude, finalize, wind up; *informal* wrap up, sew up, polish off. ❷ *the outfit was completed with a veil* FINISH OFF, round off, top off, crown, cap, complement. ❸ *complete the application form* FILL IN/OUT, answer.

completely ▶ adverb TOTALLY, entirely, wholly, thoroughly, fully, utterly, absolutely, perfectly, unreservedly, unconditionally, quite, altogether, downright; in every way, in every respect, one hundred per cent, every inch, to the hilt; *informal* dead, deadly.

completion ▶ noun REALIZATION, accomplishment, achievement, fulfilment, consummation, finalization, resolution; finish, end, conclusion, close, cessation.

complex ▶ adjective ❶ *a complex situation* COMPLICATED, involved, intricate, convoluted, elaborate, impenetrable, Gordian; difficult, knotty, tricky, thorny; *Brit. informal* fiddly. ❷ *a complex structure* COMPOUND, composite, multiplex.
– OPPOSITES simple.
▶ noun ❶ *a complex of roads* NETWORK, system, nexus, web, tissue; combination, aggregation. ❷ (*informal*) *he had a complex about losing his hair* OBSESSION, fixation, preoccupation; neurosis; *informal* hang-up, thing, bee in one's bonnet.

complexion ▶ noun ❶ *a pale complexion* SKIN, skin colour, skin tone; pigmentation. ❷ *this puts an entirely new complexion on things* PERSPECTIVE, angle, slant, interpretation; appearance, light, look. ❸ *governments of all complexions* TYPE, kind, sort; nature, character, stamp, ilk, kidney.

complexity ▶ noun COMPLICATION, problem, difficulty; twist, turn, intricacy.

compliance ▶ noun ❶ *compliance with international law* OBEDIENCE TO, observance of, adherence to, conformity to, respect for. ❷ *he mistook her silence for compliance* ACQUIESCENCE, agreement, assent, consent, acceptance; complaisance, pliability, docility, meekness, submission.
– OPPOSITES violation, defiance.

compliant ▶ adjective ACQUIESCENT, amenable, biddable, tractable, complaisant, accommodating, cooperative; obedient, docile, malleable, pliable, submissive, tame, yielding, controllable, unresisting, persuadable, persuasible.
– OPPOSITES recalcitrant.

complicate ▶ verb MAKE (MORE) DIFFICULT, make complicated, mix up, confuse, muddle; *informal* mess up, screw up, snarl up.
– OPPOSITES simplify.

complicated ▶ adjective COMPLEX, intricate, involved, convoluted, tangled, impenetrable, knotty, tricky, thorny, labyrinthine, tortuous, Gordian; confusing, bewildering, perplexing; *Brit. informal* fiddly.
– OPPOSITES straightforward.

complication ▶ noun ❶ *a complication concerning ownership* DIFFICULTY, problem, obstacle, hurdle, stumbling block; drawback, snag, catch, hitch; *informal* fly in the ointment, prob, headache, facer; *Brit. informal* spanner in the works. ❷ *the complication of life in our society* COMPLEXITY, complicatedness, intricacy, convolutedness.

complicity ▶ noun COLLUSION, involvement, collaboration, connivance; conspiracy; *informal* being in cahoots.

compliment ▶ noun ❶ *an unexpected compliment* FLATTERING REMARK, tribute, accolade, commendation, bouquet, pat on the back; (**compliments**) praise, acclaim, admiration, flattery, blandishments, honeyed words. ❷ *my compliments on your cooking* CONGRATULATIONS, commendations, praise. ❸ *Margaret sends her compliments* GREETINGS, regards, respects, good wishes, best wishes, salutations, felicitations.
– OPPOSITES insult.
▶ verb *they complimented his performance* PRAISE, pay tribute to, speak highly/well of, flatter, wax lyrical about, make much of, commend, acclaim, applaud, salute, honour; congratulate, pat on the back.
– OPPOSITES criticize.

complimentary ▶ adjective ❶ *complimentary remarks* FLATTERING, appreciative, congratulatory, admiring, approving, commendatory, favourable, glowing, adulatory; *informal* rave. ❷ *complimentary tickets* FREE (OF CHARGE), gratis, for nothing; courtesy; *informal* on the house.
– OPPOSITES derogatory.

comply ▶ verb *Myra complied with his wishes* ABIDE BY, observe, obey, adhere to, conform to, follow, respect; agree to, assent to, go along with, yield to, submit to, defer to; satisfy, fulfil.
– OPPOSITES ignore, disobey.

component ▶ noun *the components of electronic devices* PART, piece, bit, element, constituent, ingredient; unit, module, section.
▶ adjective *the molecule's component elements* CONSTITUENT, integral; basic, essential.

comport
■ **comport oneself** (*formal*) BEHAVE, conduct oneself, act, acquit oneself; *archaic* deport oneself.

compose ▶ verb ❶ *a poem composed by Shelley* WRITE, formulate, devise, make up, think up, produce, invent, concoct; pen, author, draft; *poetic/literary* rhyme. ❷ *compose a still life* ORGANIZE, arrange, set out. ❸ *the congress is composed of ten senators* MAKE UP, constitute, form, comprise.
■ **compose oneself** CALM DOWN, control oneself, regain one's composure, pull oneself together, collect oneself, steady oneself, keep one's head; *informal* get a grip, keep one's cool; *N. Amer. informal* decompress.

composed ▶ adjective CALM, collected, cool (as a cucumber), self-controlled, self-possessed; serene, tranquil, relaxed, at ease, unruffled, unperturbed, untroubled; equable, even-tempered, imperturbable; *informal* unflappable, together, laid-back.
– OPPOSITES excited.

composer ▶ noun melodist, symphonist, songwriter, songster, writer; *informal* tunesmith, songsmith.

composite ▶ adjective *a composite structure* COMPOUND, complex; combined, blended, mixed.
▶ noun *a composite of plastic and metal* AMALGAMATION, amalgam, combination, compound, fusion, synthesis, mixture, blend; alloy.

composition ▶ noun ❶ *the composition of the council* MAKE-UP, constitution, configuration, structure, formation, form, framework, fabric, anatomy, organization; *informal* set-up. ❷ *a literary composition* WORK (OF ART), creation, opus, oeuvre, piece, arrangement. ❸ *the composition of a poem* WRITING, creation, formulation, invention, concoction, compilation. ❹ *a school composition* ESSAY, paper, study, piece of writing; *N. Amer.* theme. ❺ *the composition of the painting* ARRANGEMENT, disposition, layout; proportions, balance, symmetry. ❻ *an adhesive composition* MIXTURE, compound, amalgam, blend, mix.

compost ▶ noun FERTILIZER, mulch, manure, bonemeal, fishmeal, guano; humus, peat; plant food, top-dressing.

composure ▶ noun SELF-CONTROL, self-possession, calm, equanimity, equilibrium, serenity, tranquillity; aplomb, poise, presence of mind, sangfroid; imperturbability, placidness, impassivity; *informal* cool.

compound ▶ noun *a compound of two elements* AMALGAM, amalgamation, combination, composite, blend, mixture, mix, fusion, synthesis; alloy.
▶ adjective *a compound substance* COMPOSITE, complex; blended, fused, combined.
– OPPOSITES simple.
▶ verb ❶ *a smell compounded of dust and mould* BE COMPOSED OF, be made up of, be formed from. ❷ *soap compounded with disinfectant* MIX, combine, blend, amalgamate, fuse, synthesize. ❸ *his illness compounds their problems* AGGRAVATE, exacerbate, worsen, add to, augment, intensify, heighten, increase, magnify; complicate.
– OPPOSITES alleviate.

comprehend ▶ verb ❶ *Katie couldn't comprehend his message* UNDERSTAND, grasp, take in, see, apprehend, follow, make sense of, fathom, get to the bottom of; unravel, decipher, interpret; *informal* work out, figure out, make head or tail of, get one's head around, take on board, get the drift of, catch on to, get; *Brit. informal* twig, suss (out). ❷ (*formal*) *a divine order comprehending all men* COMPRISE, include, encompass, embrace, involve, contain.
– OPPOSITES exclude.

comprehensible ▶ adjective INTELLIGIBLE, understandable, accessible; lucid, coherent, clear, plain, explicit, unambiguous, straightforward, fathomable.
– OPPOSITES opaque.

comprehension ▶ noun UNDERSTANDING, grasp, conception, apprehension, cognition, ken, knowledge, awareness, perception; interpretation.
– OPPOSITES ignorance.

comprehensive ▶ adjective INCLUSIVE, all-inclusive, complete; thorough, full, extensive, all-embracing, exhaustive, detailed, in-depth, encyclopedic, universal, catholic; far-reaching, radical, sweeping, across the board, wholesale; broad, wide-ranging; *informal* wall-to-wall.
– OPPOSITES limited.

compress ▶ verb ❶ *the skirt can be compressed into a bag* SQUEEZE, press, squash, crush, cram, jam, stuff; tamp, pack, compact; constrict; *informal* scrunch. ❷ *Polly compressed her lips* PURSE, press together, pucker. ❸ *the text was compressed* ABRIDGE, condense, shorten, cut, abbreviate, truncate; summarize, precis.
– OPPOSITES expand.

comprise ▶ verb ❶ *the country comprises twenty states* CONSIST OF, be made up of, be composed of, contain, encompass, incorporate; include; *formal* comprehend. ❷ *this breed comprises half the herd* MAKE UP, constitute, form, compose; account for.

compromise ▶ noun ❶ *they reached a compromise* AGREEMENT, understanding, settlement, terms, deal, trade-off, bargain; middle ground, happy medium, balance. ❷ *a happy marriage needs compromise* GIVE AND TAKE, concession, cooperation.
– OPPOSITES intransigence.
▶ verb ❶ *we compromised* MEET EACH OTHER HALFWAY, come to an understanding, make a deal, make concessions, find a happy medium, strike a balance; give and take. ❷ *his actions could compromise his reputation* UNDERMINE, weaken, damage, harm; jeopardize, prejudice; discredit, dishonour, shame, embarrass.

compulsion ▶ noun ❶ *he is under no compulsion to go* OBLIGATION, constraint, coercion, duress, pressure, intimidation. ❷ *a compulsion to tell the truth* URGE, impulse, need, desire, drive; obsession, fixation, addiction; temptation.

compulsive ▶ adjective ❶ *a compulsive desire* IRRESISTIBLE, uncontrollable, compelling, overwhelming, urgent; obsessive. ❷ *compulsive eating* OBSESSIVE, obsessional, addictive, uncontrollable. ❸ *a compulsive liar* INVETERATE, chronic, incorrigible, incurable, hardened, hopeless, persistent; obsessive, addicted, habitual; *informal* pathological, hooked. ❹ *it's compulsive viewing* FASCINATING, compelling, gripping, riveting, engrossing, enthralling, captivating.

compulsory ▶ **adjective** OBLIGATORY, mandatory, required, requisite, necessary, essential; imperative, unavoidable, enforced, demanded, prescribed.
– OPPOSITES optional.

compunction ▶ **noun** SCRUPLES, misgivings, qualms, worries, unease, uneasiness, doubts, reluctance, reservations; guilt, regret, contrition, self-reproach.

compute ▶ **verb** CALCULATE, work out, reckon, determine, evaluate, quantify; add up, count up, tally, total, totalize; *Brit.* tot up.

comrade ▶ **noun** COMPANION, friend; colleague, associate, partner, co-worker, workmate; *informal* pal, crony; *Brit. informal* mate, chum, oppo; *N. Amer. informal* buddy.

con (*informal*) ▶ **verb & noun.** *See* SWINDLE.

concatenation ▶ **noun** SERIES, sequence, succession, chain.

concave ▶ **adjective** INCURVED, curved inwards, hollow, depressed, sunken; indented, recessed.
– OPPOSITES convex.

conceal ▶ **verb** ❶ *clouds concealed the sun* HIDE, screen, cover, obscure, block out, blot out, mask, shroud, secrete. ❷ *he concealed his true feelings* HIDE, cover up, disguise, mask, veil; keep secret, keep dark, draw a veil over; suppress, repress, bottle up; *informal* keep a/the lid on, keep under one's hat.
– OPPOSITES reveal, confess.

concealed ▶ **adjective** HIDDEN, not visible, out of sight, invisible, covered, disguised, camouflaged, obscured; private, secret.

concealment ▶ **noun** ❶ *the concealment of his weapon* HIDING, secretion. ❷ *the concealment of the bushes* COVER, shelter, protection, screen; privacy, seclusion; secrecy. ❸ *the deliberate concealment of facts* SUPPRESSION, hiding, cover-up, hushing up; whitewash.

concede ▶ **verb** ❶ *I had to concede that I'd overreacted* ADMIT, acknowledge, accept, allow, grant, recognize, own, confess; agree. ❷ *he conceded the Auvergne to the king* SURRENDER, yield, give up, relinquish, cede, hand over.
– OPPOSITES deny, retain.
■ **concede defeat** CAPITULATE, give in, surrender, yield, give up, submit, raise the white flag; back down, climb down, throw in the towel.

conceit ▶ **noun** ❶ *his extraordinary conceit* VANITY, narcissism, conceitedness, egotism, self-admiration, self-regard; pride, arrogance, hubris, self-importance; self-satisfaction, smugness; *informal* big-headedness, swollen-headedness; *poetic/literary* vainglory. ❷ *the conceits of Shakespeare's verse* IMAGE, imagery, metaphor, simile, trope. ❸ *the conceit of time travel* IDEA, notion, fancy.
– OPPOSITES humility.

conceited ▶ **adjective** VAIN, narcissistic, self-centred, egotistic, egotistical, egocentric; proud, arrogant, boastful, full of oneself, self-important, immodest, swaggering; self-satisfied, smug; supercilious, haughty, snobbish; *informal* big-headed, too big for one's boots, stuck-up, high and mighty, uppity, snotty; *Brit. informal* toffee-nosed; *N. Amer. informal* chesty; *poetic/literary* vainglorious.

conceivable ▶ **adjective** IMAGINABLE, possible; plausible, tenable, credible, believable, thinkable, feasible; understandable, comprehensible.

conceive ▶ **verb** ❶ *she was unable to conceive* BECOME PREGNANT, become impregnated. ❷ *the project was conceived in 1977* THINK UP, think of, dream up, devise, formulate, design, originate, create, develop; hatch; *informal* cook up. ❸ *I could hardly conceive what it must be like* IMAGINE, envisage, visualize, picture, think, envision; grasp, appreciate, apprehend.

concentrate ▶ **verb** ❶ *the government concentrated its efforts* FOCUS, direct, centre, centralize. ❷ *she concentrated on the film* FOCUS ON, pay attention to, keep one's mind on, devote oneself to; be absorbed in, be engrossed in, be immersed in; *informal* get stuck into. ❸ *troops concentrated on the horizon* COLLECT, gather, congregate, converge, mass, cluster, rally. ❹ *the liquid is filtered and concentrated* CONDENSE, boil down, reduce, thicken.
– OPPOSITES disperse, dilute.
▶ **noun** *a fruit concentrate* EXTRACT, decoction, distillation.

concentrated ▶ **adjective** ❶ *a concentrated effort* STRENUOUS, concerted, intensive, intense; *informal* all-out. ❷ *a concentrated solution* CONDENSED, reduced, evaporated, thickened; undiluted, strong.
– OPPOSITES half-hearted, diluted.

concentration ▶ **noun** ❶ *a task requiring concentration* CLOSE ATTENTION, attentiveness, application, single-mindedness, absorption. ❷ *the concentration of effort* FOCUSING, centralization. ❸ *concentrations of barnacle geese* GATHERING, cluster, mass, flock, congregation, assemblage.
– OPPOSITES inattention.

concept ▶ **noun** IDEA, notion, conception, abstraction; theory, hypothesis; belief, conviction, opinion; image, impression, picture.

conception ▶ **noun** ❶ *the fertility treatment*

resulted in conception INCEPTION OF PREGNANCY, conceiving, fertilization, impregnation, insemination. ❷ *the product's conception* INCEPTION, genesis, origination, creation, invention; beginning, origin. ❸ *his original conception* PLAN, scheme, project, proposal; intention, aim, idea. ❹ *my conception of democracy* IDEA, concept, notion, understanding, abstraction; theory, hypothesis; perception, image, impression. ❺ *they had no conception of our problems* UNDERSTANDING, comprehension, appreciation, grasp, knowledge; idea, inkling; *informal* clue.

concern ▶ **verb** ❶ *the report concerns the war* BE ABOUT, deal with, cover; discuss, go into, examine, study, review, analyse; relate to, pertain to. ❷ *that doesn't concern you* AFFECT, involve, be relevant to, apply to, have a bearing on, impact on; be important to, interest. ❸ *I won't concern myself with your affairs* INVOLVE ONESELF IN, take an interest in, busy oneself with, devote one's time to, bother oneself with. ❹ *one thing still concerns me* WORRY, disturb, trouble, bother, perturb, unsettle, make anxious.
▶ **noun** ❶ *a voice full of concern* ANXIETY, worry, disquiet, apprehensiveness, unease, consternation. ❷ *his concern for others* SOLICITUDE, solicitousness, consideration, care, sympathy, regard. ❸ *housing is the concern of the council* RESPONSIBILITY, business, affair, charge, duty, job; province, preserve; problem, worry; *informal* pigeon, bag, bailiwick; *Brit. informal* lookout. ❹ *issues that are of concern to women* INTEREST, importance, relevance, significance. ❺ *Aboriginal concerns* AFFAIR, issue, matter, question, consideration. ❻ *a publishing concern* COMPANY, business, firm, organization, operation, corporation, establishment, house, office, agency; *informal* outfit, set-up.
– OPPOSITES indifference.

concerned ▶ **adjective** ❶ *her mother looked concerned* WORRIED, anxious, upset, perturbed, troubled, distressed, uneasy, apprehensive, agitated. ❷ *he is concerned about your welfare* SOLICITOUS, caring; attentive to, considerate of. ❸ *all concerned parties* INTERESTED, involved, affected; connected, related, implicated.

concerning ▶ **preposition** ABOUT, regarding, relating to, with reference to, referring to, with regard to, as regards, with respect to, respecting, dealing with, on the subject of, in connection with, re, apropos of.

concert ▶ **noun** MUSICAL PERFORMANCE, show, production, presentation; recital; *informal* gig.
■ **in concert** TOGETHER, jointly, in combination, in collaboration, in cooperation, in league, side by side; in unison.

concerted ▶ **adjective** ❶ *make a concerted effort* STRENUOUS, vigorous, intensive, intense, concentrated; *informal* all-out. ❷ *concerted action* JOINT, united, collaborative, collective, combined, cooperative.
– OPPOSITES half-hearted, individual.

concession ▶ **noun** ❶ *the government made several concessions* COMPROMISE, allowance, exception, sop. ❷ *a concession of failure* ADMISSION, acknowledgement, acceptance, recognition, confession. ❸ *the concession of territory* SURRENDER, relinquishment, sacrifice, handover. ❹ *tax concessions* REDUCTION, cut, discount, deduction, decrease; rebate; *informal* break. ❺ *a logging concession* RIGHT, privilege; licence, permit, franchise, warrant, authorization.
– OPPOSITES denial, acquisition.

conciliate ▶ **verb** ❶ *he tried to conciliate the peasantry* APPEASE, placate, pacify, mollify, assuage, soothe, humour, reconcile, win over, make peace with. ❷ *he conciliated in the dispute* MEDIATE, act as peacemaker, arbitrate; pour oil on troubled waters.
– OPPOSITES provoke.

conciliator ▶ **noun** PEACEMAKER, mediator, go-between, middleman, intermediary, intercessor; dove.
– OPPOSITES troublemaker.

conciliatory ▶ **adjective** PROPITIATORY, placatory, appeasing, pacifying, pacific, mollifying, peacemaking.

concise ▶ **adjective** SUCCINCT, pithy, incisive, brief, short and to the point, short and sweet; abridged, condensed, compressed, abbreviated, compact, potted; *informal* snappy.
– OPPOSITES lengthy, wordy.

conclave ▶ **noun** (PRIVATE) MEETING, gathering, assembly, conference, council, summit; *informal* parley, powwow, get-together.

conclude ▶ **verb** ❶ *the meeting concluded at ten* FINISH, end, draw to a close, be over, stop, cease. ❷ *he concluded the press conference* BRING TO AN END, close, wind up, terminate, dissolve; round off; *informal* wrap up. ❸ *an attempt to conclude a ceasefire* NEGOTIATE, broker, agree, come to terms on, settle, clinch, finalize, tie up; bring about, arrange, effect, engineer; *informal* sew up. ❹ *I concluded that he was rather unpleasant* DEDUCE, infer, gather, judge, decide, conjecture, surmise; *N. Amer.* figure; *informal* reckon.
– OPPOSITES commence.

conclusion ▶ **noun** ❶ *the conclusion of his speech* END, ending, finish, close, termination, wind-up, cessation; culmination, denouement, coda. ❷ *the conclusion of a trade agreement* NEGOTIATION, brokering, settlement, completion, arrangement, resolution. ❸ *his conclusions have been verified* DEDUCTION, inference, interpretation, reasoning; opinion, judgement, verdict; assumption, presumption, supposition.
– OPPOSITES beginning.

■ **in conclusion** FINALLY, in closing, to conclude, last but not least; to sum up, in short.

conclusive ▶ adjective ❶ *conclusive proof* INCONTROVERTIBLE, undeniable, indisputable, irrefutable, unquestionable, unassailable, convincing, certain, decisive, definitive, definite, positive, categorical, unequivocal; airtight, watertight. ❷ *a conclusive win* EMPHATIC, resounding, convincing.
– OPPOSITES unconvincing.

concoct ▶ verb ❶ *she began to concoct her dinner* PREPARE, make, assemble; *informal* fix, rustle up; *Brit. informal* knock up. ❷ *this story she has concocted* MAKE UP, dream up, fabricate, invent, trump up; formulate, hatch, brew; *informal* cook up.

concoction ▶ noun ❶ *a concoction containing gin and vodka* MIXTURE, brew, preparation, potion. ❷ *a strange concoction of styles* BLEND, mixture, mix, combination, hybrid. ❸ *her story is an improbable concoction* FABRICATION, invention, falsification; *informal* fairy story, fairy tale.

concomitant ▶ adjective (*formal*) ATTENDANT, accompanying, associated, related, connected; resultant, consequent.
– OPPOSITES unrelated.

concord ▶ noun (*formal*) ❶ *council meetings rarely ended in concord* AGREEMENT, harmony, accord, consensus, concurrence, unity. ❷ *a concord was to be drawn up* TREATY, agreement, accord, pact, compact, settlement.
– OPPOSITES discord.

concourse ▶ noun ❶ *the station concourse* ENTRANCE, foyer, lobby, hall. ❷ (*formal*) *a vast concourse of onlookers* CROWD, group, gathering, assembly, body, company, throng, flock, mass.

concrete ▶ adjective ❶ *concrete objects* SOLID, material, real, physical, tangible, palpable, substantial, visible, existing. ❷ *concrete proof* DEFINITE, firm, positive, conclusive, definitive; real, genuine, bona fide.
– OPPOSITES abstract, imaginary.

concubine ▶ noun (*archaic*) MISTRESS, kept woman; lover; *informal* fancy woman, bit on the side; *archaic* paramour.

concupiscence ▶ noun (*formal*). *See* LUST noun sense 1.

concur ▶ verb ❶ *we concur with this view* AGREE, be in agreement, go along, fall in, be in sympathy; see eye to eye, be of the same mind, be of the same opinion. ❷ *the two events concurred* COINCIDE, be simultaneous, be concurrent, coexist.
– OPPOSITES disagree.

concurrent ▶ adjective ❶ *nine concurrent life sentences* SIMULTANEOUS, coincident, contemporaneous, parallel. ❷ *concurrent lines* CONVERGENT, converging, meeting, intersecting.

concussion ▶ noun ❶ *he suffered concussion* temporary unconsciousness; brain injury. ❷ *the concussion of the blast* FORCE, impact, shock, jolt.

condemn ▶ verb ❶ *he condemned the suspended players* CENSURE, criticize, denounce, revile, blame, chastise, berate, reprimand, rebuke, reprove, take to task, find fault with; *informal* slam, blast, lay into; *Brit. informal* slate, slag off, have a go at; *formal* castigate. ❷ *he was condemned to death* SENTENCE; convict, find guilty. ❸ *the house has been condemned* DECLARE UNFIT, declare unsafe. ❹ *her mistake had condemned her* INCRIMINATE, implicate; *archaic* inculpate. ❺ *his illness condemned him to a lonely life* DOOM, destine, damn; consign, assign.
– OPPOSITES praise.

condemnation ▶ noun CENSURE, criticism, strictures, denunciation, vilification; reproof, disapproval; *informal* flak, a bad press; *formal* castigation.

condemnatory ▶ adjective CENSORIOUS, critical, damning; reproving, reproachful, deprecatory, disapproving, unfavourable; *formal* castigatory.

condensation ▶ noun ❶ *windows misty with condensation* MOISTURE, water droplets, steam. ❷ *the condensation of the vapour* PRECIPITATION, liquefaction, deliquescence. ❸ *a condensation of recent literature* ABRIDGEMENT, summary, synopsis, precis, digest. ❹ *the condensation of the report* SHORTENING, abridgement, abbreviation, summarization.

condense ▶ verb ❶ *the water vapour condenses* PRECIPITATE, liquefy, become liquid, deliquesce. ❷ *he condensed the play* ABRIDGE, shorten, cut, abbreviate, compact; summarize, synopsize, precis; truncate, curtail.
– OPPOSITES vaporize, expand.

condensed ▶ adjective ❶ *a condensed text* ABRIDGED, shortened, cut, compressed, abbreviated, reduced, truncated, concise; outline, thumbnail; *informal* potted. ❷ *condensed soup* CONCENTRATED, evaporated, reduced; strong, undiluted.
– OPPOSITES diluted.

condescend ▶ verb ❶ *don't condescend to your reader* PATRONIZE, talk down to, look down one's nose at, look down on, put down. ❷ *he condescended to see us* DEIGN, stoop, descend, lower oneself, demean oneself; vouchsafe, see fit, consent.

condescending ▶ adjective PATRONIZING, supercilious, superior, snobbish, snobby, disdainful, lofty, haughty; *informal* snooty, stuck-up; *Brit. informal* toffee-nosed.

condition ▶ noun ❶ *check the condition of your wiring* STATE, shape, order; *Brit. informal* nick.

❷ *they lived in appalling conditions* CIRCUMSTANCES, surroundings, environment, situation, set-up, setting, habitat; *informal* circs. ❸ *she was in tip-top condition* FITNESS, health, form, shape, trim, fettle. ❹ *a liver condition* DISORDER, problem, complaint, illness, disease, ailment, sickness, affliction, infection, upset; *informal* bug, virus; *Brit. informal* lurgy. ❺ *a condition of employment* STIPULATION, constraint, prerequisite, precondition, requirement, rule, term, specification, provision, proviso.

▶ **verb** ❶ *their choices are conditioned by the economy* CONSTRAIN, control, govern, determine, decide; affect, touch, impact on; form, shape, guide, sway, bias. ❷ *our minds are conditioned by habit* TRAIN, teach, educate, guide; accustom, adapt, habituate, mould, inure. ❸ *condition the boards with water* TREAT, prepare, prime, temper, process, acclimatize, acclimate, season. ❹ *a product to condition your skin* IMPROVE, nourish, tone (up), moisturize.

conditional ▶ **adjective** ❶ *their approval is conditional on success* SUBJECT TO, dependent on, contingent on, based on, determined by, controlled by, tied to. ❷ *a conditional offer* CONTINGENT, dependent, qualified, with reservations, limited, provisional, provisory.

condolences ▶ **plural noun** SYMPATHY, commiseration(s), compassion, pity, support, comfort, consolation, understanding.

condom ▶ **noun** CONTRACEPTIVE, sheath; *N. Amer.* prophylactic; *Brit. trademark* Durex, Femidom; *Brit. informal* johnny; *N. Amer. informal* rubber, safe; *Brit. informal, dated* French letter; *dated* protective.

condone ▶ **verb** DISREGARD, accept, allow, let pass, turn a blind eye to, overlook, forget; forgive, pardon, excuse, let go.
– OPPOSITES condemn.

conducive ▶ **adjective** FAVOURABLE, beneficial, advantageous, opportune, propitious, encouraging, promising, convenient, good, helpful, instrumental, productive, useful.
– OPPOSITES unfavourable.

conduct ▶ **noun** ❶ *they complained about her conduct* BEHAVIOUR, performance, demeanour; actions, activities, deeds, doings, exploits; habits, manners; *formal* comportment. ❷ *the conduct of the elections* MANAGEMENT, running, direction, control, supervision, regulation, administration, organization, coordination, orchestration, handling.

▶ **verb** ❶ *the election was conducted lawfully* MANAGE, direct, run, administer, organize, coordinate, orchestrate, handle, control, oversee, supervise, regulate, carry out/on. ❷ *he was conducted through the corridors* ESCORT, guide, lead, usher, show; shepherd, see, bring, take, help. ❸ *aluminium conducts heat* TRANSMIT, convey, carry, transfer, impart, channel, relay; disseminate, diffuse, radiate.

■ **conduct oneself** BEHAVE, act, acquit oneself, bear oneself; *formal* comport oneself; *archaic* deport oneself.

conduit ▶ **noun** CHANNEL, duct, pipe, tube, gutter, trench, culvert, cut, sluice, spillway, flume, chute.

confectionery ▶ **noun** SWEETS, chocolates, bonbons; *N. Amer.* candy; *informal* sweeties; *archaic* sweetmeats.

confederacy ▶ **noun** FEDERATION, confederation, alliance, league, association, coalition, consortium, syndicate, group, circle; bloc, axis.

confederate ▶ **adjective** *confederate councils* FEDERAL, confederated, federated, allied, associated, united.
– OPPOSITES split.

▶ **noun** *he met his confederate in the street* ASSOCIATE, partner, accomplice, helper, assistant, ally, collaborator, colleague; *Brit. informal* oppo; *Austral./NZ informal* offsider.

confederation ▶ **noun** ALLIANCE, league, confederacy, federation, association, coalition, consortium, conglomerate, cooperative, syndicate, group, circle; society, union.

confer ▶ **verb** ❶ *she conferred a knighthood on him* BESTOW ON, present to, grant to, award to, decorate with, honour with, give to, endow with, extend to, vouchsafe to. ❷ *she went to confer with her colleagues* CONSULT, talk, speak, converse, have a chat, have a tête-à-tête, parley; *informal* have a confab, powwow.

conference ▶ **noun** ❶ *an international conference* CONGRESS, meeting, convention, seminar, colloquium, symposium, forum, summit. ❷ *he gathered them for a conference* DISCUSSION, consultation, debate, talk, conversation, dialogue, chat, tête-à-tête, parley; *informal* confab; *formal* confabulation.

confess ▶ **verb** ❶ *he confessed that he had done it* ADMIT, acknowledge, reveal, disclose, divulge, avow, declare, profess; own up, tell all. ❷ *they could not make him confess* OWN UP, plead guilty, accept the blame; tell the truth, tell all, make a clean breast of it; *informal* come clean, spill the beans, let the cat out of the bag, get something off one's chest, let on; *Brit. informal* cough. ❸ *I confess I don't know* ACKNOWLEDGE, admit, concede, grant, allow, own, declare, affirm.
– OPPOSITES deny.

confession ▶ **noun** ADMISSION, acknowledgement, profession; revelation, disclosure, divulgence, avowal; guilty plea.

confidant, fem. **confidante** ▶ **noun** CLOSE FRIEND, bosom friend, best friend; intimate, familiar; *informal* chum, pal, crony; *Brit. informal* mate, oppo, mucker; *N. Amer. informal* buddy.

confide ▸ verb ❶ *he confided his fears to his mother* REVEAL, disclose, divulge, lay bare, betray, impart, declare, intimate, uncover, expose, vouchsafe, tell; confess, admit, give away; *informal* blab, spill. ❷ *I need him to confide in* OPEN ONE'S HEART TO, unburden oneself to, confess to, tell all to.

confidence ▸ noun ❶ *I have little confidence in these figures* TRUST, belief, faith, credence, conviction. ❷ *she's brimming with confidence* SELF-ASSURANCE, self-confidence, self-possession, assertiveness; poise, aplomb, phlegm; courage, boldness, mettle, nerve. ❸ *the girls exchanged confidences* SECRET, confidentiality, intimacy.
– OPPOSITES scepticism, doubt.

confident ▸ adjective ❶ *we are confident that business will improve* OPTIMISTIC, hopeful, sanguine; sure, certain, positive, convinced, in no doubt, satisfied, assured, persuaded. ❷ *a confident girl* SELF-ASSURED, assured, self-confident, positive, assertive, self-possessed, self-reliant, poised; cool-headed, phlegmatic, level-headed, unperturbed, imperturbable, unruffled, at ease; *informal* together.

confidential ▸ adjective ❶ *a confidential chat* PRIVATE, personal, intimate, quiet; secret, sensitive, classified, restricted, unofficial, unrevealed, undisclosed, unpublished; *informal* hush-hush, mum; *formal* sub rosa; *archaic* privy. ❷ *a confidential friend* TRUSTED, trustworthy, trusty, faithful, reliable, dependable; close, bosom, intimate.

confidentially ▸ adverb PRIVATELY, in private, in confidence, between ourselves/themselves, off the record, quietly, secretly, in secret, behind closed doors; *formal* sub rosa.

configuration ▸ noun ARRANGEMENT, layout, geography, design, organization, order, grouping, positioning, disposition, alignment; shape, form, appearance, formation, structure, format.

confine ▸ verb ❶ *they were confined in the house* ENCLOSE, incarcerate, imprison, intern, impound, hold captive, trap; shut in/up, keep, lock in/up, coop (up); fence in, hedge in, wall in/up. ❷ *he confined his remarks to the weather* RESTRICT, limit.

confined ▸ adjective CRAMPED, constricted, restricted, limited, small, narrow, compact, tight, poky, uncomfortable, inadequate.
– OPPOSITES roomy.

confinement ▸ noun ❶ *solitary confinement* IMPRISONMENT, internment, incarceration, custody, captivity, detention, restraint; house arrest. ❷ *the confinement of an animal* CAGING, enclosure; quarantine. ❸ (*dated*) *she went to hospital for her confinement* LABOUR, delivery, birthing; birth, childbirth; *formal* parturition; *archaic* lying-in, childbed.

confines ▸ plural noun LIMITS, margins, extremities, edges, borders, boundaries, fringes, marches; periphery, perimeter.

confirm ▸ verb ❶ *records confirm the latest evidence* CORROBORATE, verify, prove, validate, authenticate, substantiate, justify, vindicate; support, uphold, back up. ❷ *he confirmed that help was on the way* AFFIRM, reaffirm, assert, assure someone, repeat; promise, guarantee. ❸ *his appointment was confirmed by the President* RATIFY, validate, sanction, endorse, formalize, authorize, warrant, accredit, approve, accept.
– OPPOSITES contradict, deny.

confirmation ▸ noun ❶ *independent confirmation of the deaths* CORROBORATION, verification, proof, testimony, endorsement, authentication, substantiation, evidence. ❷ *confirmation of your appointment* RATIFICATION, approval, authorization, validation, sanction, endorsement, formalization, accreditation, acceptance.

confirmed ▸ adjective ESTABLISHED, long-standing, committed, dyed-in-the-wool, through and through; staunch, loyal, faithful, devoted, dedicated, steadfast; habitual, compulsive, persistent; unapologetic, unashamed, inveterate, chronic, incurable; *informal* deep-dyed, card-carrying.

confiscate ▸ verb IMPOUND, seize, commandeer, requisition, appropriate, expropriate, sequester, sequestrate, take (away); *Law* distrain; *Scottish Law* poind.
– OPPOSITES return.

confiscation ▸ noun SEIZURE, requisition, appropriation, expropriation, sequestration; *Law* distraint, distrainment; *Scottish Law* poind.

conflagration ▸ noun FIRE, blaze, flames, inferno, firestorm.

conflict ▸ noun ❶ *industrial conflicts* DISPUTE, quarrel, squabble, disagreement, dissension, clash; discord, friction, strife, antagonism, hostility, disputation, contention; feud, schism. ❷ *the Vietnam conflict* WAR, campaign, battle, fighting, (armed) confrontation, engagement, encounter, struggle, hostilities; warfare, combat. ❸ *a conflict between his business and domestic life* CLASH, incompatibility, incongruity, friction; mismatch, variance, difference, divergence, contradiction, inconsistency.
– OPPOSITES agreement, peace, harmony.
▸ verb *their interests sometimes conflict* CLASH, be incompatible, vary, be at odds, be in conflict, differ, diverge, disagree, contrast, collide.

conflicting ▸ adjective CONTRADICTORY, incompatible, inconsistent, irreconcilable, incongruous, contrary, opposite, opposing, antithetical, clashing, discordant, divergent; at odds.

confluence ▶ noun CONVERGENCE, meeting, junction, conflux, watersmeet.

conform ▶ verb ❶ *visitors have to conform to our rules* COMPLY WITH, abide by, obey, observe, follow, keep to, stick to, adhere to, uphold, heed, accept, go along with, fall in with, respect, defer to; satisfy, meet, fulfil. ❷ *they refuse to conform* FOLLOW CONVENTION, be conventional, fit in, adapt, adjust, follow the crowd; comply, acquiesce, toe the line, follow the rules; submit, yield; *informal* play it by the book, play by the rules. ❸ *goods must conform to their description* MATCH, fit, suit, answer, agree with, be like, correspond to, be consistent with, measure up to, tally with, square with.
– OPPOSITES flout, rebel.

conformist ▶ noun CONVENTIONALIST, traditionalist, conservative, stickler, formalist, diehard, reactionary; *informal* stick-in-the-mud, stuffed shirt.
– OPPOSITES eccentric, rebel.

confound ▶ verb ❶ *the figures confounded analysts* AMAZE, astonish, dumbfound, stagger, surprise, startle, stun, nonplus; throw, shake, discompose, bewilder, baffle, mystify, bemuse, perplex, puzzle, confuse; take aback, shake up, catch off balance; *informal* flabbergast, blow someone's mind, blow away, flummox, faze, stump, beat, fox; *N. Amer. informal* discombobulate. ❷ *he has always confounded expectations* CONTRADICT, counter, invalidate, negate, go against, drive a coach and horses through; quash, explode, demolish, shoot down, destroy, disprove; *informal* shoot full of holes.

confront ▶ verb ❶ *Jones confronted the burglar* CHALLENGE, square up to, face (up to), come face to face with, meet, accost, waylay; stand up to, brave, beard, tackle; *informal* collar; *Brit. informal* nobble. ❷ *the problems that confront us* TROUBLE, bother, burden, distress, worry, oppress, annoy, strain, stress, tax, torment, plague, blight, curse; face, beset. ❸ *they must confront their problems* TACKLE, address, face, get to grips with, grapple with, take on, attend to, see to, deal with, take care of, handle, manage; *informal* get stuck into. ❹ *she confronted him with the evidence* PRESENT, face.
– OPPOSITES avoid.

confrontation ▶ noun CONFLICT, clash, fight, battle, encounter, head-to-head, face-off, engagement, skirmish; hostilities, fighting; *informal* set-to, run-in, dust-up, showdown.

confuse ▶ verb ❶ *don't confuse students with too much detail* BEWILDER, baffle, mystify, bemuse, perplex, puzzle, confound, nonplus; *informal* flummox, faze, stump, fox; *N. Amer. informal* discombobulate. ❷ *the authors have confused the issue* COMPLICATE, muddle, jumble, garble, blur, obscure, cloud. ❸ *some confuse strokes with heart attacks* MIX UP, muddle up, confound; mistake for.
– OPPOSITES enlighten, simplify.

confused ▶ adjective ❶ *they are confused about what is going on* BEWILDERED, bemused, puzzled, perplexed, baffled, mystified, nonplussed, muddled, dumbfounded, at sea, at a loss, taken aback, disoriented, disconcerted; *informal* flummoxed, bamboozled, clueless, fazed; *N. Amer. informal* discombobulated. ❷ *her confused elderly mother* DEMENTED, bewildered, muddled, addled, befuddled, disoriented, disorientated; unbalanced, unhinged; senile. ❸ *a confused recollection* VAGUE, unclear, indistinct, imprecise, blurred, hazy, woolly, shadowy, dim; imperfect, sketchy. ❹ *a confused mass of bones* DISORDERLY, disordered, disorganized, disarranged, out of order, untidy, muddled, jumbled, mixed up, chaotic, topsy-turvy; *informal* higgledy-piggledy; *Brit. informal* shambolic.
– OPPOSITES lucid, clear, precise, neat.

confusing ▶ adjective BEWILDERING, baffling, unclear, perplexing, puzzling, mystifying, disconcerting; ambiguous, misleading, inconsistent, contradictory; unaccountable, inexplicable, impenetrable, unfathomable; complex, complicated.

confusion ▶ noun ❶ *there is confusion about the new system* UNCERTAINTY, incertitude, unsureness, doubt, ignorance; *formal* dubiety. ❷ *she stared in confusion* BEWILDERMENT, bafflement, perplexity, puzzlement, mystification, befuddlement; shock, daze, wonder, wonderment, astonishment; *informal* bamboozlement; *N. Amer. informal* discombobulation. ❸ *her life was in utter confusion* DISORDER, disarray, disorganization, untidiness, chaos, mayhem; turmoil, tumult, disruption, upheaval, uproar, hurly-burly, muddle, mess; *informal* shambles. ❹ *a confusion of boxes* JUMBLE, muddle, mess, heap, tangle; *informal* shambles.
– OPPOSITES certainty, order.

confute ▶ verb (*formal*) DISPROVE, contradict, controvert, refute, deny, rebut, belie, negate, invalidate, explode, discredit, debunk, quash, drive a coach and horses through; *informal* shoot full of holes; *formal* gainsay.
– OPPOSITES prove.

congeal ▶ verb COAGULATE, clot, thicken, gel, inspissate, cake, set, curdle.

congenial ▶ adjective ❶ *very congenial people* LIKE-MINDED, compatible, kindred, well suited; companionable, sociable, sympathetic, comradely, convivial, hospitable, genial, personable, agreeable, friendly, pleasant, likeable, amiable, nice. ❷ *a congenial environment* PLEASANT, pleasing, agreeable, enjoyable, pleasurable, nice, appealing, satisfying, gratifying,

delightful, relaxing, welcoming, hospitable; suitable, well suited, favourable.
– OPPOSITES unpleasant.

congenital ▶ adjective ❶ *congenital defects* INBORN, inherited, hereditary, innate, inbred, constitutional, inbuilt, natural, inherent. ❷ *a congenital liar* INVETERATE, compulsive, persistent, chronic, regular, habitual, obsessive, confirmed; incurable, incorrigible, irredeemable, hopeless; unashamed, shameless; *informal* pathological.
– OPPOSITES acquired.

congested ▶ adjective CROWDED, overcrowded, full, overflowing, packed, jammed, thronged, teeming, swarming; obstructed, blocked, clogged, choked; *informal* snarled up, gridlocked, jam-packed; *Brit. informal* like Piccadilly Circus.
– OPPOSITES clear.

congestion ▶ noun CROWDING, overcrowding; obstruction, blockage; traffic jam, bottleneck; *informal* snarl-up, gridlock.

conglomerate ▶ noun ❶ *the conglomerate was broken up* CORPORATION, combine, group, consortium, partnership; firm, company, business, multinational. ❷ *a conglomerate of disparate peoples* MIXTURE, mix, combination, amalgamation, union, marriage, fusion, composite, synthesis; miscellany, hotchpotch.
▶ adjective *a conglomerate mass* AGGREGATE, agglomerate, amassed, combined.
▶ verb *the debris conglomerated into planets* COALESCE, unite, join, combine, merge, fuse, consolidate, amalgamate, integrate, mingle, intermingle.

congratulate ▶ verb ❶ *she congratulated him on his marriage* SEND ONE'S BEST WISHES, wish someone good luck, wish someone joy; drink someone's health, toast. ❷ *they are to be congratulated* PRAISE, commend, applaud, salute, honour; pay tribute to, regard highly, pat on the back, take one's hat off to.
– OPPOSITES criticize.
■ **congratulate oneself** TAKE PRIDE, feel proud, flatter oneself, preen oneself, pat oneself on the back; feel satisfaction, take pleasure, glory, bask, delight.

congratulations ▶ plural noun ❶ *her congratulations on their wedding* GOOD WISHES, best wishes, compliments, felicitations. ❷ *you all deserve congratulations* PRAISE, commendation, applause, salutes, honour, acclaim, cheers, bouquets; approval, admiration, compliments, kudos, adulation; a pat on the back.

congregate ▶ verb ASSEMBLE, gather, collect, come together, convene, rally, rendezvous, muster, meet, cluster, group.
– OPPOSITES disperse.

congregation ▶ noun ❶ *the chapel congregation* PARISHIONERS, parish, churchgoers, flock, faithful, followers, believers, fellowship, communicants, laity, brethren; throng, company, assemblage, audience. ❷ *congregations of birds* GATHERING, assembly, flock, swarm, bevy, pack, group, body, crowd, mass, multitude, horde, host, mob, throng.

congress ▶ noun ❶ *a congress of mathematicians* CONFERENCE, convention, seminar, colloquium, symposium, forum, meeting, assembly, gathering, rally, summit. ❷ *elections for the new Congress* LEGISLATURE, legislative assembly, parliament, convocation, diet, council, senate, chamber, house.

congruence ▶ noun COMPATIBILITY, consistency, conformity, match, balance, consonance, congruity; agreement, accord, consensus, harmony, unity; *formal* concord.
– OPPOSITES conflict.

conical ▶ adjective CONE-SHAPED, tapered, tapering, pointed, funnel-shaped; *informal* pointy; *Zoology* conoid.

conjectural ▶ adjective SPECULATIVE, suppositional, suppositious, theoretical, hypothetical, putative, notional; postulated, inferred, presumed, assumed, presupposed, tentative.

conjecture ▶ noun *the information is merely conjecture* SPECULATION, guesswork, surmise, fancy, presumption, assumption, theory, postulation, supposition; inference, extrapolation; estimate; *informal* guesstimate, a shot in the dark.
– OPPOSITES fact.
▶ verb *I conjectured that the game was over* GUESS, speculate, surmise, infer, fancy, imagine, believe, think, suspect, presume, assume, hypothesize, suppose.
– OPPOSITES know.

conjugal ▶ adjective MARITAL, matrimonial, nuptial, marriage, bridal; *Law* spousal; *poetic/literary* connubial.

conjunction ▶ noun CO-OCCURRENCE, concurrence, coincidence, coexistence, simultaneity, contemporaneity, concomitance, synchronicity, synchrony.

conjure ▶ verb ❶ *he conjured a cigarette out of the air* PRODUCE, make something appear, materialize, magic, summon. ❷ *the picture that his words conjured up* BRING TO MIND, call to mind, evoke, summon up, recall, recreate; echo, allude to, suggest, awaken.

conjuring ▶ noun MAGIC, illusion, sleight of hand, legerdemain; *formal* prestidigitation.

conjuror ▶ noun MAGICIAN, illusionist; *formal* prestidigitator.

connect ▶ verb ❶ *electrodes were connected to the device* ATTACH, join, fasten, fix, affix, couple, link, secure, hitch; stick, adhere, fuse, pin, screw, bolt, clamp, clip, hook (up); add, append. ❷ *customs connected with Easter* ASSOCIATE, link, couple; identify, equate, bracket, relate to.

connection ▶ **noun** ❶ *the connection between commerce and art* LINK, relationship, relation, interconnection, interdependence, association; bond, tie, tie-in, correspondence, parallel, analogy. ❷ *a poor connection in the plug* ATTACHMENT, joint, fastening, coupling. ❸ *he has the right connections* CONTACT, friend, acquaintance, ally, colleague, associate; relation, relative, kin.

■ **in connection with** REGARDING, concerning, with reference to, with regard to, with respect to, respecting, relating to, in relation to, on, connected with, on the subject of, in the matter of, apropos, re, in re.

connivance ▶ **noun** COLLUSION, complicity, collaboration, involvement, assistance; tacit consent, conspiracy, intrigue.

connive ▶ **verb** ❶ *wardens connived at offences* DELIBERATELY IGNORE, overlook, disregard, pass over, take no notice of, make allowances for, turn a blind eye to, wink at, excuse, condone, let go; look the other way, let something ride. ❷ *the government connived with security forces* CONSPIRE, collude, collaborate, intrigue, be hand in glove, plot, scheme; *informal* be in cahoots.

conniving ▶ **adjective** SCHEMING, cunning, crafty, calculating, devious, wily, sly, tricky, artful, guileful; manipulative, Machiavellian, disingenuous, deceitful, underhand, treacherous; *informal* foxy.

connoisseur ▶ **noun** EXPERT, authority, specialist, pundit, savant; arbiter of taste, aesthete; gourmet, epicure, gastronome; *informal* buff; *N. Amer. informal* maven.

connotation ▶ **noun** OVERTONE, undertone, undercurrent, implication, hidden meaning, nuance, hint, echo, vibrations, association, intimation, suggestion, suspicion, insinuation.

connote ▶ **verb** IMPLY, suggest, indicate, signify, hint at, give the impression of, smack of, be associated with, allude to.

conquer ▶ **verb** ❶ *the Franks conquered the Visigoths* DEFEAT, beat, vanquish, trounce, triumph over, be victorious over, get the better of, worst; overcome, overwhelm, overpower, overthrow, subdue, subjugate, quell, quash, crush, rout; *informal* lick, best, hammer, clobber, thrash, paste, demolish, annihilate, wipe the floor with, walk all over, make mincemeat of, massacre, slaughter; *Brit. informal* stuff; *N. Amer. informal* cream, shellac, skunk. ❷ *Peru was conquered by Spain* SEIZE, take (over), appropriate, subjugate, capture, occupy, invade, annex, overrun. ❸ *the first men to conquer Mount Everest* CLIMB, ascend, mount, scale, top, crest. ❹ *the way to conquer fear* OVERCOME, get the better of, control, master, get a grip on, deal with, cope with, surmount, rise above, get over; quell, quash, beat, triumph over; *informal* lick.
– OPPOSITES lose.

conqueror ▶ **noun** VANQUISHER, conquistador; victor, winner, champion, conquering hero.

conquest ▶ **noun** ❶ *the conquest of the Aztecs* DEFEAT, vanquishment, annihilation, overthrow, subjugation, rout, mastery, crushing; victory over, triumph over. ❷ *their conquest of the valley* SEIZURE, takeover, capture, occupation, invasion, acquisition, appropriation, subjugation, subjection. ❸ *the conquest of Everest* ASCENT. ❹ *she's his latest conquest* CATCH, acquisition, prize, slave; admirer, fan, worshipper; lover, boyfriend, girlfriend; *informal* fancy man, fancy woman.
– OPPOSITES victory, surrender.

conscience ▶ **noun** SENSE OF RIGHT AND WRONG, moral sense, inner voice; morals, standards, values, principles, ethics, beliefs; compunction, scruples, qualms.

conscience-stricken ▶ **adjective** GUILT-RIDDEN, remorseful, ashamed, shamefaced, apologetic, sorry; chastened, contrite, guilty, regretful, rueful, repentant, penitent, self-reproachful, abashed, sheepish, compunctious.
– OPPOSITES unrepentant.

conscientious ▶ **adjective** DILIGENT, industrious, punctilious, painstaking, sedulous, assiduous, dedicated, careful, meticulous, thorough, attentive, hard-working, studious, rigorous, particular; religious, strict.
– OPPOSITES casual.

conscious ▶ **adjective** ❶ *the patient was conscious* AWARE, awake, alert, responsive, sentient, compos mentis. ❷ *he became conscious of people talking* AWARE OF, alert to, mindful of, sensible of; *formal* cognizant of; *archaic* ware of. ❸ *a conscious effort* DELIBERATE, intentional, intended, purposeful, purposive, knowing, considered, calculated, wilful, premeditated, planned, volitional; *Law, dated* prepense.
– OPPOSITES unaware.

conscript ▶ **verb** *they were conscripted into the army* CALL UP, enlist, recruit; *US* draft; *historical* press, impress.
▶ **noun** *an army conscript* compulsorily enlisted soldier, recruit; *US* draftee.
– OPPOSITES volunteer.

consecrate ▶ **verb** SANCTIFY, bless, make holy, make sacred; dedicate to God, devote, reserve, set apart; anoint, ordain; *formal* hallow.

consecutive ▶ **adjective** SUCCESSIVE, succeeding, following, in succession, running, in a row, one after the other, back-to-back, continuous, straight, uninterrupted; *informal* on the trot.

consensus ▶ **noun** ❶ *there was consensus among delegates* AGREEMENT, harmony, concurrence, accord, unity, unanimity, solidarity; *formal* concord. ❷ *the consensus was that they should act* GENERAL OPINION, majority opinion, common view.
– OPPOSITES disagreement.

consent ▶ **noun** *the consent of all members* AGREEMENT, assent, acceptance, approval, approbation; permission, authorization, sanction, leave; backing, endorsement, support; *informal* go-ahead, thumbs up, green light, OK.
– OPPOSITES dissent.
▶ **verb** *she consented to surgery* AGREE, assent, yield, give in, submit; allow, give permission for, sanction, accept, approve, go along with.
– OPPOSITES forbid.

consequence ▶ **noun** ❶ *a consequence of inflation* RESULT, upshot, outcome, out-turn, effect, repercussion, ramification, corollary, concomitant, aftermath; fruit(s), product, by-product, end result; *informal* pay-off; *Medicine* sequela. ❷ *the past is of no consequence* IMPORTANCE, import, significance, account, substance, note, mark, prominence, value, concern, interest; *formal* moment.
– OPPOSITES cause.

consequent ▶ **adjective** RESULTING, resultant, ensuing, consequential; following, subsequent, successive; attendant, accompanying, concomitant; collateral, associated, related.

consequential ▶ **adjective** ❶ *a fire and the consequential smoke damage* RESULTING, resultant, ensuing, consequent; following, subsequent; attendant, accompanying, concomitant; collateral, associated, related. ❷ *one of his more consequential initiatives* IMPORTANT, significant, major, momentous, weighty, material, appreciable, memorable, far-reaching, serious.
– OPPOSITES insignificant.

consequently ▶ **adverb** AS A RESULT, as a consequence, so, thus, therefore, ergo, accordingly, hence, for this/that reason, because of this/that, on this/that account; inevitably, necessarily.

conservation ▶ **noun** PRESERVATION, protection, safeguarding, safe keeping; care, guardianship, husbandry, supervision; upkeep, maintenance, repair, restoration; ecology, environmentalism.

conservative ▶ **adjective** ❶ *the conservative wing of the party* RIGHT-WING, reactionary, traditionalist; *Brit.* Tory, blimpish; *US* Republican; *informal* true blue. ❷ *the conservative trade-union movement* TRADITIONALIST, traditional, conventional, orthodox, old-fashioned, dyed-in-the-wool, hidebound, unadventurous, set in one's ways; moderate, middle-of-the-road; *informal* stick in the mud. ❸ *a conservative suit* CONVENTIONAL, sober, modest, plain, unobtrusive, restrained, subtle, low-key, demure; *informal* square, straight. ❹ *a conservative estimate* LOW, cautious, understated, moderate, reasonable.
– OPPOSITES socialist, radical, ostentatious.
▶ **noun** *liberals and conservatives have found common ground* RIGHT-WINGER, reactionary, rightist, die-hard; *Brit.* Tory, blimp; *US* Republican.

conservatory ▶ **noun** ❶ *a frost-free conservatory* SUMMER HOUSE, belvedere; glasshouse, greenhouse, hothouse. ❷ *a teaching job at the conservatory* CONSERVATOIRE, music school, drama school.

conserve ▶ **verb** *fossil fuel should be conserved* PRESERVE, protect, save, safeguard, keep, look after; sustain, prolong, perpetuate; store, reserve, husband.
– OPPOSITES squander.
▶ **noun** *cherry conserve* JAM, preserve, jelly, marmalade, confiture.

consider ▶ **verb** ❶ *Isabel considered her choices* THINK ABOUT, contemplate, reflect on, examine, review; mull over, ponder, deliberate on, chew over, meditate on, ruminate on; assess, evaluate, weigh up, appraise; *informal* size up. ❷ *I consider him irresponsible* DEEM, think, believe, judge, adjudge, rate, count, find; regard as, hold to be, reckon to be, view as, see as. ❸ *he considered the ceiling* LOOK AT, contemplate, observe, regard, survey, view, scrutinize, scan, examine, inspect; *informal* check out; *N. Amer. informal* eyeball. ❹ *the inquiry will consider those issues* TAKE INTO CONSIDERATION, take account of, make allowances for, bear in mind, be mindful of, remember, mind, mark, respect, heed, note, make provision for.
– OPPOSITES ignore.

considerable ▶ **adjective** ❶ *a considerable amount of money* SIZEABLE, substantial, appreciable, significant; goodly, fair, hefty, handsome, decent, worthwhile; ample, plentiful, abundant, great, large, generous; *informal* tidy, not to be sneezed at. ❷ *considerable success* MUCH, great, a lot of, lots of, a great deal of, plenty of, a fair amount of. ❸ *a considerable cricketer* DISTINGUISHED, noteworthy, important, significant, prominent, eminent, influential, illustrious; renowned, celebrated, acclaimed.
– OPPOSITES paltry, minor.

considerably ▶ **adverb** GREATLY, (very) much, a great deal, a lot, lots; significantly, substantially, appreciably, markedly, noticeably; *informal* plenty, seriously.

considerate ▶ **adjective** ATTENTIVE, thoughtful, solicitous, mindful, heedful; obliging, accommodating, helpful, cooperative, patient;

kind, unselfish, compassionate, sympathetic, caring, charitable, altruistic, generous; polite, sensitive, tactful.

consideration ▶ noun ❶ *your case needs careful consideration* THOUGHT, deliberation, reflection, contemplation, rumination, meditation; examination, inspection, scrutiny, analysis, discussion; attention, regard; *formal* cogitation. ❷ *his health is the prime consideration* FACTOR, issue, matter, concern, detail, aspect, feature. ❸ *firms should show more consideration* ATTENTIVENESS, concern, care, thoughtfulness, solicitude; kindness, understanding, respect, sensitivity, tact, discretion; compassion, charity, benevolence. ❹ *I might do it, for a consideration* PAYMENT, fee, premium, remuneration, compensation; commission, percentage, dividend; *informal* cut, slice, piece of the action; *formal* emolument.

■ **take something into consideration** CONSIDER, give thought to, take into account, allow for, provide for, plan for, make provision for, accommodate, bargain for, reckon with; foresee, anticipate.

considering ▶ preposition *considering his size he was speedy* BEARING IN MIND, taking into consideration, taking into account, keeping in mind, in view of, in the light of.

▶ adverb (*informal*) *he'd been lucky, considering* ALL THINGS CONSIDERED, all in all, on the whole, at the end of the day, when all's said and done.

consign ▶ verb ❶ *he was consigned to prison* SEND, deliver, hand over, turn over, sentence; confine in, imprison in, incarcerate in, lock up in; *informal* put away, put behind bars; *Brit. informal* bang up. ❷ *the picture was consigned for sale* ASSIGN, allocate, place, put, remit, hand down. ❸ *the package was consigned by a local company* SEND (OFF), dispatch, transmit, convey, post, mail, ship. ❹ *I consigned her picture to the bin* DEPOSIT, commit, banish, relegate.

consignment ▶ noun DELIVERY, shipment, load, boatload, truckload, cargo; batch; goods.

consist ▶ verb ❶ *the exhibition consists of 180 drawings* BE COMPOSED, be made up, be formed; comprise, contain, include, incorporate. ❷ *style consists in the choices that writers make* BE INHERENT, lie, reside, be present, be contained; be expressed by.

consistency ▶ noun ❶ *the trend shows a degree of consistency* UNIFORMITY, constancy, regularity, evenness, steadiness, stability, equilibrium; dependability, reliability. ❷ *cream of pouring consistency* THICKNESS, density, viscosity, heaviness, texture; firmness, solidity.

consistent ▶ adjective ❶ *consistent opinion-poll evidence* CONSTANT, regular, uniform, steady, stable, even, unchanging, undeviating, unfluctuating; dependable, reliable, predictable. ❷ *her injuries were consistent with a knife attack* COMPATIBLE, congruous, consonant, in tune, in line, reconcilable; corresponding to, conforming to.

– OPPOSITES irregular, incompatible.

consolation ▶ noun COMFORT, solace, sympathy, compassion, pity, commiseration; relief, help, (moral) support, encouragement, reassurance.

console[1] ▶ verb *she tried to console him* COMFORT, solace, condole with, sympathize with, commiserate with, show compassion for; help, support, cheer (up), hearten, encourage, reassure, soothe.

– OPPOSITES upset.

console[2] ▶ noun *a digital console* CONTROL PANEL, instrument panel, dashboard, keyboard, keypad; *informal* dash.

consolidate ▶ verb ❶ *we consolidated our position in the market* STRENGTHEN, secure, stabilize, reinforce, fortify; enhance, improve. ❷ *consolidate the results into an action plan* COMBINE, unite, merge, integrate, amalgamate, fuse, synthesize, bring together, unify.

consonance ▶ noun AGREEMENT, accord, harmony, unison; compatibility, congruity, congruence; *formal* concord.

consonant

■ **consonant with** IN AGREEMENT WITH, consistent with, in accordance with, in harmony with, compatible with, congruous with, in tune with.

consort ▶ noun *the queen and her consort* PARTNER, companion, mate; spouse, husband, wife.

▶ verb *he consorted with other women* ASSOCIATE, keep company, mix, go around, spend time, socialize, fraternize, have dealings; *informal* run around, hang around/round, hang out, be thick; *Brit. informal* hang about.

conspicuous ▶ adjective EASILY SEEN, clear, visible, noticeable, discernible, perceptible, detectable; obvious, manifest, evident, apparent, marked, pronounced, prominent, patent, crystal clear; striking, eye-catching, overt, blatant, writ large; distinct, recognizable, unmistakable, inescapable; *informal* as plain as the nose on one's face, standing out like a sore thumb, standing out a mile.

conspiracy ▶ noun ❶ *a conspiracy to manipulate the race results* PLOT, scheme, plan, machination, ploy, trick, ruse, subterfuge; *informal* racket. ❷ *conspiracy to murder* PLOTTING, collusion, intrigue, connivance, machination, collaboration; treason.

conspirator ▶ noun PLOTTER, schemer, intriguer, colluder, collaborator, conniver, machinator.

conspire ▶ verb ❶ *they admitted conspiring to steal cars* PLOT, scheme, plan, intrigue, machinate, collude, connive, collaborate, work hand in glove; *informal* be in cahoots. ❷ *circumstances conspired against them* ACT TOGETHER, work together, combine, unite, join forces; *informal* gang up.

constancy ▶ **noun** ❶ *constancy between lovers* FIDELITY, faithfulness, loyalty, commitment, dedication, devotion; dependability, reliability, trustworthiness. ❷ *the constancy of Henry's views* STEADFASTNESS, resolution, resolve, firmness, fixedness; determination, perseverance, tenacity, doggedness, staunchness, staying power, obstinacy. ❸ *a constancy of human motive* CONSISTENCY, permanence, persistence, durability, endurance; uniformity, immutability, regularity, stability, steadiness.

constant ▶ **adjective** ❶ *the constant background noise* CONTINUAL, continuous, persistent, sustained, round-the-clock; ceaseless, unceasing, perpetual, incessant, never-ending, eternal, endless, unabating, non-stop, unrelieved; interminable, unremitting, relentless. ❷ *a constant speed* CONSISTENT, regular, steady, uniform, even, invariable, unvarying, unchanging, undeviating, unfluctuating. ❸ *a constant friend* FAITHFUL, loyal, devoted, true, fast, firm, unswerving; steadfast, staunch, dependable, trustworthy, trusty, reliable, dedicated, committed. ❹ *constant vigilance* STEADFAST, steady, resolute, determined, tenacious, dogged, unwavering, unflagging.
– OPPOSITES fitful, variable, fickle.
▶ **noun** *dread of cancer has been a constant* UNCHANGING FACTOR, given.

constantly ▶ **adverb** ALWAYS, all the time, continually, continuously, persistently; round-the-clock, night and day, {morning, noon, and night}; endlessly, non-stop, incessantly, unceasingly, perpetually, eternally, forever; interminably, unremittingly, relentlessly; *Scottish* aye; *informal* 24-7.
– OPPOSITES occasionally.

consternation ▶ **noun** DISMAY, perturbation, distress, disquiet, discomposure; surprise, amazement, astonishment; alarm, panic, fear, fright, shock.
– OPPOSITES satisfaction.

constituent ▶ **adjective** *constituent parts* COMPONENT, integral; elemental, basic, essential, inherent.
▶ **noun** ❶ *MPs must listen to their constituents* VOTER, elector, member of a constituency. ❷ *the constituents of tobacco* COMPONENT, ingredient, element; part, piece, bit, unit; section, portion.

constitute ▶ **verb** ❶ *farmers constituted 10 per cent of the population* AMOUNT TO, add up to, account for, form, make up, compose, comprise. ❷ *this constitutes a breach of copyright* BE EQUIVALENT TO, be, embody, be tantamount to, be regarded as. ❸ *the courts were constituted in 1875* INAUGURATE, establish, initiate, found, create, set up, start, form, organize, develop; commission, charter, invest, appoint, install, empower.

constitution ▶ **noun** ❶ *the constitution guarantees our rights* CHARTER, social code, law; bill of rights; rules, regulations, fundamental principles. ❷ *the chemical constitution of the dye* COMPOSITION, make-up, structure, construction, arrangement, configuration, formation, anatomy; *informal* set-up. ❸ *she has the constitution of an ox* HEALTH, physique, physical condition, shape, fettle.

constitutional ▶ **adjective** ❶ *constitutional powers* LEGAL, lawful, legitimate, authorized, permitted; sanctioned, ratified, warranted, constituted, statutory, chartered, vested, official; by law. ❷ *a constitutional weakness* INHERENT, intrinsic, innate, fundamental, essential, organic; congenital, inborn, inbred.
▶ **noun** (*dated*) *she went out for a constitutional. See* WALK noun sense 1.

constrain ▶ **verb** ❶ *he felt constrained to explain* COMPEL, force, drive, impel, oblige, coerce, prevail on, require; press, push, pressure, pressurize. ❷ *prices were constrained by state controls* RESTRICT, limit, curb, check, restrain, contain, rein in, hold back, keep down.

constrained ▶ **adjective** *his constrained manner* UNNATURAL, awkward, self-conscious, forced, stilted, strained; restrained, reserved, reticent, guarded.
– OPPOSITES relaxed.

constraint ▶ **noun** ❶ *financial constraints* RESTRICTION, limitation, curb, check, restraint, control, damper, rein; hindrance, impediment, obstruction, handicap. ❷ *they were able to talk without constraint* INHIBITION, uneasiness, embarrassment; restraint, reticence, guardedness, formality; self-consciousness, forcedness, awkwardness, stiltedness.

constrict ▶ **verb** ❶ *fat constricts the blood vessels* NARROW, make narrower, tighten, compress, contract, squeeze, strangle, strangulate; *archaic* straiten. ❷ *fear of crime constricts many people's lives* RESTRICT, impede, limit, inhibit, obstruct, interfere with, hinder, hamper.
– OPPOSITES expand, dilate.

constriction ▶ **noun** TIGHTNESS, pressure, compression, contraction; obstruction, blockage, impediment; *Medicine* stricture, stenosis.

construct ▶ **verb** ❶ *a new motorway was being constructed* BUILD, erect, put up, set up, raise, establish, assemble, manufacture, fabricate, create, make. ❷ *he constructed a faultless argument* FORMULATE, form, put together, create, devise, design, compose, work out; fashion, mould, shape, frame.
– OPPOSITES demolish.

construction ▶ noun ❶ *the construction of a new airport* BUILDING, erection, putting up, setting up, establishment; assembly, manufacture, fabrication, creation. ❷ *the station was a spectacular construction* STRUCTURE, building, edifice, pile. ❸ *you could put an honest construction on their conduct* INTERPRETATION, reading, meaning, explanation, explication, construal; *informal* take.

constructive ▶ adjective USEFUL, helpful, productive, positive, encouraging; practical, valuable, profitable, worthwhile.

construe ▶ verb INTERPRET, understand, read, see, take, take to mean, regard.

consul ▶ noun AMBASSADOR, diplomat, chargé d'affaires, attaché, envoy, emissary, plenipotentiary; *archaic* legate.

consult ▶ verb ❶ *you need to consult a solicitor* SEEK ADVICE FROM, ask, take counsel from, call on/upon, speak to, turn to, have recourse to; *informal* pick someone's brains. ❷ *the government must consult with interested parties* CONFER, have discussions, talk things over, exchange views, communicate, parley, deliberate; *informal* put their heads together. ❸ *she consulted her diary* REFER TO, turn to, look at.

consultant ▶ noun ❶ *an engineering consultant* ADVISER, expert, specialist, authority, pundit. ❷ *a consultant at Guy's hospital* SENIOR DOCTOR, specialist.

consultation ▶ noun ❶ *the need for further consultation with industry* DISCUSSION, dialogue, discourse, debate, negotiation, deliberation. ❷ *a 30-minute consultation* MEETING, talk, discussion, interview, audience, hearing; appointment, session; *formal* confabulation, colloquy.

consume ▶ verb ❶ *vast amounts of food and drink were consumed* EAT, devour, ingest, swallow, gobble up, wolf down, guzzle, feast on, snack on; DRINK, gulp down, imbibe, sup; *informal* tuck into, put away, polish off, dispose of, pig oneself on, down, neck, sink, swill; *Brit. informal* scoff, gollop, shift; *N. Amer. informal* scarf (down/up), snarf (down/up). ❷ *natural resources are being consumed at an alarming rate* USE (UP), utilize, expend; deplete, exhaust; waste, squander, drain, dissipate, fritter away. ❸ *the fire consumed fifty houses* DESTROY, demolish, lay waste, wipe out, annihilate, devastate, gut, ruin, wreck. ❹ *Carolyn was consumed with guilt* EAT UP, devour, obsess, grip, overwhelm; absorb, preoccupy.

consumer ▶ noun PURCHASER, buyer, customer, shopper; user, end-user; client; (**the consumer** or **consumers**) the public, the market.

consuming ▶ adjective ABSORBING, compelling, compulsive, besetting, obsessive, overwhelming; intense, ardent, strong, powerful, burning, raging, fervid, profound, deep-seated.

consummate ▶ verb *the deal was finally consummated* COMPLETE, conclude, finish, accomplish, achieve; execute, carry out, perform; *informal* sew up, wrap up; *formal* effectuate.
▶ adjective *his consummate skill | a consummate politician* SUPREME, superb, superlative, superior, accomplished, expert, proficient, skilful, skilled, masterly, master, first-class, talented, gifted, polished, practised, perfect, ultimate; complete, total, utter, absolute, pure.

consumption ▶ noun ❶ *food unfit for human consumption* EATING, drinking, ingestion. ❷ *the consumption of fossil fuels* USE, using up, utilization, expending, depletion; waste, squandering, dissipation.

contact ▶ noun ❶ *a disease transmitted through direct contact with rats* TOUCH, touching; proximity, exposure. ❷ *foreign diplomats were asked to avoid all contact with him* COMMUNICATION, correspondence, touch; association, connection, intercourse, relations, dealings; *archaic* traffic. ❸ *he had many contacts in Germany* CONNECTION, acquaintance, associate, friend.
▶ verb *anyone with information should contact the police* GET IN TOUCH WITH, communicate with, make contact with, approach, notify; telephone, phone, call, ring up, speak to, talk to, write to; *informal* get hold of.

contagion ▶ noun (*dated*) DISEASE, infection, illness, plague, blight; *informal* bug, virus; *archaic* pestilence.

contagious ▶ adjective INFECTIOUS, communicable, transmittable, transmissible, spreadable; *informal* catching; *dated* infective.

contain ▶ verb ❶ *the archive contains much unpublished material* INCLUDE, comprise, take in, incorporate, involve, encompass, embrace; consist of, be made up of, be composed of. ❷ *the boat contained four people* HOLD, carry, accommodate, seat. ❸ *he must contain his anger* RESTRAIN, curb, rein in, suppress, repress, stifle, subdue, quell, swallow, bottle up, hold in, keep in check; control, master.

container ▶ noun RECEPTACLE, vessel, holder, repository.

contaminate ▶ verb POLLUTE, adulterate; defile, debase, corrupt, taint, infect, foul, spoil, soil, stain, sully; poison; *poetic/literary* befoul.
– OPPOSITES purify.

contemplate ▶ verb ❶ *she contemplated her image in the mirror* LOOK AT, view, regard, examine, inspect, observe, survey, study, scrutinize, scan, stare at, gaze at, eye. ❷ *he contemplated his fate* THINK ABOUT, ponder, reflect on, consider, mull over, muse on, dwell on, deliberate over, meditate on, ruminate on, chew over, brood on/about, turn over in one's mind; *formal* cogitate. ❸ *he was contemplating action for damages* CONSIDER, think about, have in mind, intend, plant, propose; envisage, foresee.

contemplation ▶ **noun** ❶ *the contemplation of beautiful objects* VIEWING, examination, inspection, observation, survey, study, scrutiny. ❷ *the monks sat in quiet contemplation* THOUGHT, reflection, meditation, consideration, rumination, deliberation, reverie, introspection, brown study; *formal* cogitation, cerebration.

contemplative ▶ **adjective** THOUGHTFUL, pensive, reflective, meditative, musing, ruminative, introspective, brooding, deep/lost in thought, in a brown study.

contemporary ▶ **adjective** ❶ *contemporary sources* OF THE TIME, of the day, contemporaneous, concurrent, coeval, coexisting, coexistent. ❷ *contemporary society* MODERN, present-day, present, current, present-time. ❸ *a very contemporary design* MODERN, up to date, up to the minute, fashionable; modish, latest, recent; *informal* trendy, with it.
– OPPOSITES old-fashioned, out of date.

▶ **noun** *Chaucer's contemporaries* PEER, fellow; *formal* compeer.

contempt ▶ **noun** ❶ *she regarded him with contempt* SCORN, disdain, disrespect, scornfulness, contemptuousness, derision; disgust, loathing, hatred, abhorrence; *archaic* despite. ❷ *he is guilty of contempt of court* DISRESPECT, disregard, slighting.
– OPPOSITES respect.

contemptible ▶ **adjective** DESPICABLE, detestable, hateful, reprehensible, deplorable, unspeakable, disgraceful, shameful, ignominious, abject, low, mean, cowardly, unworthy, discreditable, petty, worthless, shabby, cheap, beyond contempt, beyond the pale, sordid; *archaic* scurvy.
– OPPOSITES admirable.

contemptuous ▶ **adjective** SCORNFUL, disdainful, disrespectful, insulting, insolent, derisive, mocking, sneering, scoffing, withering, scathing, snide; condescending, supercilious, haughty, proud, superior, arrogant, dismissive, aloof; *informal* high and mighty, snotty, sniffy; *archaic* contumelious.
– OPPOSITES respectful.

contend ▶ **verb** ❶ *the pilot had to contend with torrential rain* COPE WITH, face, grapple with, deal with, take on, pit oneself against. ❷ *three main groups were contending for power* COMPETE, vie, contest, fight, battle, tussle, go head to head; strive, struggle. ❸ *he contends that the judge was wrong* ASSERT, maintain, hold, claim, argue, insist, state, declare, profess, affirm; allege; *formal* aver.

content[1] ▶ **adjective** *she seemed content with life* CONTENTED, satisfied, pleased, gratified, fulfilled, happy, cheerful, glad; unworried, untroubled, at ease, at peace, tranquil, serene.
– OPPOSITES discontented, dissatisfied.

▶ **verb** *her reply seemed to content him* SATISFY, please; soothe, pacify, placate, appease, mollify.

▶ **noun** *a time of content. See* CONTENTMENT.

content[2] ▶ **noun** ❶ *foods with a high fibre content* AMOUNT, proportion, quantity. ❷ (**contents**) *the contents of a vegetarian sausage* CONSTITUENTS, ingredients, components, elements. ❸ (**contents**) *the book's list of contents* CHAPTERS, sections, divisions. ❹ *the content of the essay* SUBJECT MATTER, subject, theme, argument, thesis, message, thrust, substance, matter, material, text, ideas.

contented ▶ **adjective** *a contented man. See* CONTENT[1] adjective.

contention ▶ **noun** ❶ *a point of contention* DISAGREEMENT, dispute, disputation, argument, discord, conflict, friction, strife, dissension, disharmony. ❷ *the Marxist contention that capitalism equals exploitation* ARGUMENT, claim, plea, submission, allegation, assertion, declaration; opinion, stand, position, view, belief, thesis, case.
– OPPOSITES agreement.

■ **in contention** IN COMPETITION, competing, contesting, contending, vying; striving, struggling.

contentious ▶ **adjective** ❶ *a contentious issue* CONTROVERSIAL, disputable, debatable, disputed, open to debate, moot, vexed. ❷ *a contentious debate* HEATED, vehement, fierce, violent, intense, impassioned. ❸ *contentious people. See* QUARRELSOME.

contentment ▶ **noun** CONTENTEDNESS, content, satisfaction, gratification, fulfilment, happiness, pleasure, cheerfulness; ease, comfort, well-being, peace, equanimity, serenity, tranquillity.

contest ▶ **noun** ❶ *a boxing contest* COMPETITION, match, tournament, game, meet, event, trial, bout, heat, fixture, tie, race. ❷ *the contest for the party leadership* FIGHT, battle, tussle, struggle, competition, race.

▶ **verb** ❶ *he intended to contest the seat* COMPETE FOR, contend for, vie for, fight for, try to win, go for, throw one's hat in the ring. ❷ *we contested the decision* OPPOSE, object to, challenge, take a stand against, take issue with, question, call into question. ❸ *the issues have been hotly contested* DEBATE, argue about, dispute, quarrel over.

contestant ▶ **noun** COMPETITOR, participant, player, contender, candidate, aspirant, entrant; rival, opponent, adversary, antagonist.

context ▶ **noun** ❶ *the wider historical context*

CIRCUMSTANCES, conditions, factors, state of affairs, situation, background, scene, setting. ❷ *a quote taken out of context* FRAME OF REFERENCE, contextual relationship; text, subject, theme, topic.

contiguous ▶ **adjective** ADJACENT, neighbouring, adjoining, bordering, next-door; abutting, connecting, touching, in contact, proximate.

continent ▶ **adjective** SELF-RESTRAINED, self-disciplined, abstemious, abstinent, self-denying, ascetic; chaste, celibate, monkish, monastic, virginal.

contingency ▶ **noun** EVENTUALITY, (chance) event, incident, happening, occurrence, juncture, possibility, fortuity, accident, chance, emergency.

contingent ▶ **adjective** ❶ *the merger is contingent on government approval* DEPENDENT ON, conditional on, subject to, determined by, hinging on, resting on. ❷ *contingent events* CHANCE, accidental, fortuitous, possible, unforeseeable, unpredictable, random, haphazard.

▶ **noun** ❶ *a contingent of Japanese businessmen* GROUP, party, body, band, company, cohort, deputation, delegation; *informal* bunch, gang. ❷ *a contingent of marines* DETACHMENT, unit, group.

continual ▶ **adjective** ❶ *a service disrupted by continual breakdowns* FREQUENT, repeated, constant, recurrent, recurring, regular. ❷ *she was in continual pain* CONSTANT, continuous, unending, never-ending, unremitting, unabating, relentless, unrelenting, unrelieved, chronic, uninterrupted, unbroken, round-the-clock.
– OPPOSITES occasional, temporary.

continuance ▶ **noun.** *See* CONTINUATION.

continuation ▶ **noun** CARRYING ON, continuance, extension, prolongation, protraction, perpetuation.
– OPPOSITES end.

continue ▶ **verb** ❶ *he was unable to continue with his job* CARRY ON, proceed, pursue, go on, keep on, persist, press on, persevere, keep at; *informal* stick at, soldier on. ❷ *discussions continued throughout the year* GO ON, carry on, last, extend, be prolonged, run on, drag on. ❸ *we are keen to continue this relationship* MAINTAIN, keep up, sustain, keep going, keep alive, preserve. ❹ *his willingness to continue in office* REMAIN, stay, carry on, keep going. ❺ *we continued our conversation after supper* RESUME, pick up, take up, carry on with, return to, recommence.
– OPPOSITES stop, break off.

continuing ▶ **adjective** ONGOING, continuous, sustained, persistent, steady, relentless, uninterrupted, unabating, unremitting, unrelieved, unceasing.
– OPPOSITES sporadic.

continuity ▶ **noun** CONTINUOUSNESS, uninterruptedness, flow, progression.

continuous ▶ **adjective** CONTINUAL, uninterrupted, unbroken, constant, ceaseless, incessant, steady, sustained, solid, continuing, ongoing, unceasing, without a break, non-stop, round-the-clock, persistent, unremitting, relentless, unrelenting, unabating, unrelieved, without respite, endless, unending, never-ending, perpetual, everlasting, eternal, interminable; consecutive, running; *N. Amer.* without surcease.
– OPPOSITES intermittent.

contort ▶ **verb** TWIST, bend out of shape, distort, misshape, warp, buckle, deform.

contour ▶ **noun** OUTLINE, shape, form; lines, curves, figure; silhouette, profile.

contraband ▶ **noun** *contraband was suspected* SMUGGLING, illegal traffic, black marketeering, bootlegging; the black market.

▶ **adjective** *contraband goods* SMUGGLED, black-market, bootleg, under the counter, illegal, illicit, unlawful; prohibited, banned, proscribed, forbidden; *informal* hot.

contract ▶ **noun** *a legally binding contract* AGREEMENT, commitment, arrangement, settlement, understanding, compact, covenant, bond; deal, bargain; *Law* indenture.

▶ **verb** ❶ *the market for such goods began to contract* SHRINK, get smaller, decrease, diminish, reduce, dwindle, decline. ❷ *her stomach muscles contracted* TIGHTEN, tense, flex, constrict, draw in, narrow. ❸ *she contracted her brow* WRINKLE, knit, crease, purse, pucker. ❹ *his name was soon contracted to 'Jack'* SHORTEN, abbreviate, cut, reduce; elide. ❺ *the company contracted to rebuild the stadium* UNDERTAKE, pledge, promise, covenant, commit oneself, engage, agree, enter an agreement, make a deal. ❻ *she contracted German measles* DEVELOP, catch, get, pick up, come down with, be struck down by, be stricken with, succumb to; *Brit.* go down with. ❼ *he contracted a debt of £3,300* INCUR, run up.
– OPPOSITES expand, relax, lengthen.

■ **contract something out** SUBCONTRACT, outsource, farm out.

contraction ▶ **noun** ❶ *the contraction of the industry* SHRINKING, shrinkage, decline, decrease, diminution, dwindling. ❷ *the contraction of muscles* TIGHTENING, tensing, flexing. ❸ *my contractions started at midnight* LABOUR PAINS, labour; cramps; *poetic/literary* travail. ❹ *'goodbye' is a contraction of 'God be with you'* ABBREVIATION, short form, shortened form, elision, diminutive.

contradict ▶ **verb** ❶ *he contradicted the government's account of the affair* DENY, refute, rebut, dispute, challenge, counter, controvert; *formal* gainsay. ❷ *nobody dared to contradict him* ARGUE

[illegible], go against, challenge, oppose; *formal* gainsay. ❸ *this research contradicts previous computer models* CONFLICT WITH, be at odds with, be at variance with, be inconsistent with, run counter to, disagree with.
– OPPOSITES confirm, agree with.

contradiction ▶ **noun** ❶ *the contradiction between his faith and his lifestyle* CONFLICT, clash, disagreement, opposition, inconsistency, mismatch, variance. ❷ *a contradiction of his statement* DENIAL, refutation, rebuttal, countering, counterstatement.
– OPPOSITES confirmation, agreement.

contradictory ▶ **adjective** OPPOSED, in opposition, opposite, antithetical, contrary, contrasting, conflicting, at variance, at odds, opposing, clashing, divergent, discrepant, different; inconsistent, incompatible, irreconcilable.

contraption ▶ **noun** DEVICE, gadget, apparatus, machine, appliance, mechanism, invention, contrivance; *informal* gizmo, widget; *Brit. informal* gubbins; *Austral. informal* bitzer.

contrary ▶ **adjective** ❶ *contrary views* OPPOSITE, opposing, opposed, contradictory, clashing, conflicting, antithetical, incompatible, irreconcilable. ❷ *she was sulky and contrary* PERVERSE, awkward, difficult, uncooperative, unhelpful, obstructive, disobliging, recalcitrant, wilful, self-willed, stubborn, obstinate, mulish, pig-headed, intractable; *informal* cussed; *Brit. informal* bloody-minded, bolshie, stroppy; *N. Amer. informal* balky; *formal* refractory; *archaic* froward.
– OPPOSITES compatible, accommodating.
▶ **noun** *in fact, the contrary is true* OPPOSITE, reverse, converse, antithesis.
■ **contrary to** IN CONFLICT WITH, against, at variance with, at odds with, in opposition to, counter to, incompatible with.

contrast ▶ **noun** ❶ *the contrast between rural and urban trends* DIFFERENCE, dissimilarity, disparity, distinction, contradistinction, divergence, variance, variation, differentiation; contradiction, incongruity, opposition, polarity; *formal* dissimilitude. ❷ *Jane was a complete contrast to Sarah* OPPOSITE, antithesis; foil, complement.
– OPPOSITES similarity.
▶ **verb** ❶ *a view which contrasts with his earlier opinion* DIFFER FROM, be at variance with, be contrary to, conflict with, go against, be at odds with, be in opposition to, disagree with, clash with. ❷ *people contrasted her with her sister* COMPARE, set side by side, juxtapose; measure against; distinguish from, differentiate from.
– OPPOSITES resemble, liken.

contravene ▶ **verb** ❶ *he contravened the Official Secrets Act* BREAK, breach, violate, infringe; defy, disobey, flout. ❷ *the prosecution contravened the rights of the individual* CONFLICT WITH, be in conflict with, be at odds with, be at variance with, run counter to.
– OPPOSITES comply with.

contravention ▶ **noun** BREACH, violation, infringement, neglect, dereliction.

contretemps ▶ **noun** ARGUMENT, quarrel, squabble, disagreement, difference of opinion, dispute; *informal* tiff, set-to, run-in, spat; *Brit. informal* row, barney; *Scottish informal* rammy.

contribute ▶ **verb** ❶ *the government contributed a million pounds* GIVE, donate, put up, subscribe, hand out, grant, bestow, present, provide, supply, furnish; *informal* chip in, pitch in, fork out, shell out, cough up; *Brit. informal* stump up; *N. Amer. informal* kick in, ante up, pony up. ❷ *an article contributed by Dr Clouson* SUPPLY, provide, submit. ❸ *numerous factors contribute to job satisfaction* PLAY A PART IN, be instrumental in, be a factor in, have a hand in, be conducive to, make for, lead to, cause; *formal* conduce to.

contribution ▶ **noun** ❶ *voluntary financial contributions* DONATION, gift, offering, present, handout, grant, subsidy, allowance, endowment, subscription; *formal* benefaction; *historical* alms. ❷ *contributions from local authors* ARTICLE, piece, story, item, chapter, paper, essay.

contributor ▶ **noun** ❶ *the magazine's regular contributors* WRITER, columnist, correspondent. ❷ *campaign contributors* DONOR, benefactor, subscriber, supporter, backer, subsidizer, patron, sponsor.

contrite ▶ **adjective** REMORSEFUL, repentant, penitent, regretful, sorry, apologetic, rueful, sheepish, hangdog, ashamed, chastened, shamefaced, conscience-stricken, guilt-ridden, in sackcloth and ashes.

contrition ▶ **noun** REMORSE, remorsefulness, repentance, penitence, sorrow, sorrowfulness, regret, ruefulness, pangs of conscience; shame, guilt, compunction; *archaic* rue.

contrivance ▶ **noun** ❶ *a mechanical contrivance* DEVICE, gadget, machine, appliance, contraption, apparatus, mechanism, implement, tool, invention; *informal* gizmo, widget; *Austral. informal* bitzer. ❷ *her matchmaking contrivances* SCHEME, stratagem, tactic, manoeuvre, move, plan, ploy, gambit, wile, trick, ruse, plot, machination.

contrive ▶ **verb** BRING ABOUT, engineer, manufacture, orchestrate, stage-manage, create, devise, concoct, construct, plan, fabricate, plot, hatch; *informal* wangle, set up.

contrived ▶ **adjective** FORCED, strained, studied, artificial, affected, put-on, pretended, false, feigned, manufactured, unnatural; la-

boured, overdone, elaborate.
– OPPOSITES natural.

control ▶ noun ❶ *China retained control over the region* JURISDICTION, sway, power, authority, command, dominance, government, mastery, leadership, rule, sovereignty, supremacy, ascendancy; charge, management, direction, supervision, superintendence. ❷ *strict import controls* RESTRAINT, constraint, limitation, restriction, check, curb, brake, rein; regulation. ❸ *her control deserted her* SELF-CONTROL, self-restraint, self-possession, composure, calmness; *informal* cool. ❹ *easy-to-use controls* SWITCH, knob, button, dial, handle, lever. ❺ *mission control* HEADQUARTERS, HQ, base, centre of operations, command post.
▶ verb ❶ *one family had controlled the company since its formation* BE IN CHARGE OF, run, manage, direct, administer, head, preside over, supervise, superintend, steer; command, rule, govern, lead, dominate, hold sway over, be at the helm; *informal* head up, be in the driving seat, run the show. ❷ *she struggled to control her temper* RESTRAIN, keep in check, curb, check, contain, hold back, bridle, rein in, suppress, repress, master. ❸ *public spending was controlled* LIMIT, restrict, curb, cap, constrain; *informal* put the brakes on.

controversial ▶ adjective CONTENTIOUS, disputed, at issue, moot, disputable, debatable, arguable, vexed, tendentious.

controversy ▶ noun DISAGREEMENT, dispute, argument, debate, dissension, contention, disputation, altercation, wrangle, wrangling, quarrel, quarrelling, war of words, storm; cause célèbre; *Brit. informal* row.

contusion ▶ noun BRUISE, discoloration, black-and-blue mark, injury; *Medicine* ecchymosis.

conundrum ▶ noun ❶ *the conundrums facing policy-makers in the 1980s* PROBLEM, difficult question, vexed question, difficulty, quandary, dilemma; *informal* poser, facer. ❷ *Roderick enjoyed conundrums and crosswords* RIDDLE, puzzle, wordgame; *informal* brain-teaser.

convalesce ▶ verb RECUPERATE, get better, recover, get well, get back on one's feet.

convalescence ▶ noun RECUPERATION, recovery, return to health, rehabilitation, improvement.

convalescent ▶ adjective RECUPERATING, recovering, getting better, on the road to recovery, improving; *informal* on the mend.

convene ▶ verb ❶ *he convened a secret meeting* SUMMON, call, call together, order; *formal* convoke. ❷ *the committee convened for its final session* ASSEMBLE, gather, meet, come together, congregate; *formal* foregather.

convenience ▶ noun ❶ *the convenience of the arrangement* EXPEDIENCE, advantageousness, advantage, opportuneness, propitiousness, timeliness; suitability, appropriateness. ❷ *for convenience, the handset is wall-mounted* EASE OF USE, usability, usefulness, utility, serviceability, practicality. ❸ *the kitchen has all the modern conveniences* APPLIANCE, (labour-saving) device, gadget; amenity, facility; *informal* gizmo, mod con.

convenient ▶ adjective ❶ *a convenient time* SUITABLE, appropriate, fitting, fit, suited, opportune, timely, well timed, favourable, advantageous, seasonable, expedient. ❷ *a hotel that's convenient for the beach* NEAR (TO), close to, within easy reach of, well situated for, handy for, not far from, just round the corner from; *informal* a stone's throw from, within spitting distance of.

convent ▶ noun NUNNERY, priory, abbey, religious community.

convention ▶ noun ❶ *social conventions* CUSTOM, usage, practice, tradition, way, habit, norm; rule, code, canon, punctilio; propriety, etiquette, protocol; *formal* praxis; (**conventions**) mores. ❷ *a convention signed by 74 countries* AGREEMENT, accord, protocol, compact, pact, treaty, concordat, entente; contract, bargain, deal. ❸ *the party's biennial convention* CONFERENCE, meeting, congress, assembly, gathering, summit, convocation, synod, conclave.

conventional ▶ adjective ❶ *the conventional wisdom of the day* ORTHODOX, traditional, established, accepted, received, mainstream, prevailing, prevalent, accustomed, customary. ❷ *a conventional railway* NORMAL, standard, regular, ordinary, usual, traditional, typical, common. ❸ *a very conventional woman* CONSERVATIVE, traditional, traditionalist, conformist, bourgeois, old-fashioned, of the old school, small-town, suburban; *informal* straight, square, stick-in-the-mud, fuddy-duddy. ❹ *a conventional piece of work* UNORIGINAL, formulaic, predictable, stock, unadventurous, unremarkable.
– OPPOSITES unorthodox, original.

converge ▶ verb ❶ *Oxford Circus, a station where three lines converge* MEET, intersect, cross, connect, link up, coincide, join, unite, merge. ❷ *90,000 fans converged on Wembley* CLOSE IN ON, bear down on, approach, move towards.
– OPPOSITES diverge, leave.

conversant ▶ adjective FAMILIAR, acquainted, au fait, au courant, at home, well versed, well informed, knowledgeable, informed, abreast, up to date; *informal* up to speed, clued up, genned up; *formal* cognizant.

conversation ▶ noun DISCUSSION, talk, chat, gossip, tête-à-tête, heart-to-heart, head-to-

…ge, dialogue; *informal* confab, jaw, …t, *Brit. informal* chinwag, natter; *N. Amer.* …ormal gabfest, schmooze; *Austral./NZ informal* yarn; *formal* confabulation, colloquy.

conversational ▶ **adjective** ❶ *conversational English* INFORMAL, chatty, relaxed, friendly; colloquial, idiomatic. ❷ *a conversational man* TALKATIVE, chatty, communicative, forthcoming, expansive, loquacious, garrulous.

converse¹ ▶ **verb** *they conversed in low voices* TALK, speak, chat, have a conversation, discourse, communicate; *informal* chew the fat/rag, jaw; *Brit. informal* natter; *N. Amer. informal* visit, shoot the breeze/bull; *Austral./NZ informal* mag; *formal* confabulate.

converse² ▶ **noun** *the converse is also true* OPPOSITE, reverse, obverse, contrary, antithesis, other side of the coin; *informal* flip side.

conversion ▶ **noun** ❶ *the conversion of waste into energy* CHANGE, changing, transformation, metamorphosis, transfiguration, transmutation, sea change; *humorous* transmogrification. ❷ *the conversion of the building* ADAPTATION, alteration, modification, reconstruction, rebuilding, redevelopment, redesign, renovation, rehabilitation. ❸ *his religious conversion* REBIRTH, regeneration, reformation.

convert ▶ **verb** ❶ *plants convert the sun's energy into chemical energy* CHANGE, turn, transform, metamorphose, transfigure, transmute; *humorous* transmogrify; *technical* permute. ❷ *the factory was converted into flats* ADAPT, turn, change, alter, modify, rebuild, reconstruct, redevelop, refashion, redesign, restyle, revamp, renovate, rehabilitate; *N. Amer.* bring up to code; *informal* do up; *N. Amer. informal* rehab. ❸ *they sought to convert sinners* PROSELYTIZE, evangelize, bring to God, redeem, save, reform, re-educate, cause to see the light.

▶ **noun** *Christian converts* PROSELYTE, neophyte, new believer; *Christianity* catechumen.

convey ▶ **verb** ❶ *taxis conveyed guests to the station* TRANSPORT, carry, bring, take, fetch, bear, move, ferry, shuttle, shift, transfer. ❷ *he conveyed the information to me* COMMUNICATE, pass on, make known, impart, relay, transmit, send, hand on, relate, tell, reveal, disclose. ❸ *it's impossible to convey how I felt* EXPRESS, communicate, get across/over, put across/over, indicate, say. ❹ *he conveys an air of competence* PROJECT, exude, emit, emanate.

conveyance ▶ **noun** ❶ *the conveyance of agricultural produce* TRANSPORTATION, transport, carriage, carrying, transfer, movement, delivery; haulage, portage, cartage, shipment, freightage. ❷ (*formal*) *three-wheeled conveyances* VEHICLE, means/method of transport; car, bus, coach, van, lorry, truck, bicycle, motorbike, motorcycle.

convict ▶ **verb** *he was convicted of indecent assault* FIND GUILTY, sentence; *Brit. informal* be done for.
– OPPOSITES acquit.

▶ **noun** *two escaped convicts* PRISONER, inmate; trusty; criminal, offender, lawbreaker, felon; *informal* jailbird, con, (old) lag, crook; *N. Amer. informal* yardbird.

conviction ▶ **noun** ❶ *his conviction for murder* DECLARATION OF GUILT, sentence, judgement. ❷ *his political convictions* BELIEF, opinion, view, thought, persuasion, idea, position, stance, article of faith. ❸ *she spoke with conviction* CERTAINTY, certitude, assurance, confidence, sureness, no shadow of a doubt.
– OPPOSITES acquittal, uncertainty.

convince ▶ **verb** ❶ *he convinced me that I was wrong* MAKE CERTAIN, persuade, satisfy, prove to; assure, put/set someone's mind at rest. ❷ *I convinced her to marry me* PERSUADE, induce, prevail on, get, talk into, win over, cajole, inveigle.

convincing ▶ **adjective** ❶ *a convincing argument* COGENT, persuasive, plausible, powerful, potent, strong, forceful, compelling, irresistible, telling, conclusive. ❷ *a convincing 5–0 win* RESOUNDING, emphatic, decisive, conclusive.

convivial ▶ **adjective** FRIENDLY, genial, affable, amiable, congenial, agreeable, good-humoured, cordial, warm, sociable, outgoing, gregarious, clubbable, companionable, hail-fellow-well-met, cheerful, jolly, jovial, lively; enjoyable, festive; *Scottish* couthy.

conviviality ▶ **noun** FRIENDLINESS, geniality, affability, amiability, bonhomie, congeniality, cordiality, warmth, good nature, sociability, gregariousness, cheerfulness, good cheer, joviality, jollity, gaiety, liveliness.

convocation ▶ **noun** ASSEMBLY, gathering, meeting, conference, convention, congress, council, symposium, colloquium, conclave, synod.

convoke ▶ **verb** (*formal*) CONVENE, summon, call together, call.

convoluted ▶ **adjective** COMPLICATED, complex, involved, elaborate, serpentine, labyrinthine, tortuous, tangled, Byzantine; confused, confusing, bewildering, baffling.
– OPPOSITES straightforward.

convolution ▶ **noun** ❶ *crosses adorned with elaborate convolutions* TWIST, turn, coil, spiral, twirl, curl, helix, whorl, loop, curlicue; *Architecture* volute. ❷ *the convolutions of the plot* COMPLEXITY, intricacy, complication, twist, turn, entanglement.

convoy ▶ **noun** *a convoy of vehicles* GROUP, fleet, cavalcade, motorcade, cortège, caravan, line, train.

▶ **verb** *the ship was convoyed by army gunboats* ESCORT, accompany, attend, flank; protect, defend, guard.

convulse ▶ **verb** SHAKE UNCONTROLLABLY, go into spasms, shudder, jerk, thrash about.

convulsion ▶ **noun** ❶ *she had convulsions* FIT, seizure, paroxysm, spasm, attack; throes; *Medicine* ictus. ❷ (**convulsions**) *the audience collapsed in convulsions* FITS OF LAUGHTER, paroxysms of laughter, uncontrollable laughter; *informal* hysterics. ❸ *the political convulsions of the period* UPHEAVAL, eruption, cataclysm, turmoil, turbulence, tumult, disruption, agitation, disturbance, unrest, disorder.

convulsive ▶ **adjective** SPASMODIC, jerky, paroxysmal, violent, uncontrollable.

cook ▶ **verb** ❶ *Iris had cooked dinner* PREPARE, make, put together; *informal* fix, rustle up; *Brit. informal* knock up. ❷ (*informal*) *he'd been cooking the books* FALSIFY, alter, doctor, tamper with, interfere with, massage, manipulate; *Brit. informal* fiddle. ❸ (*informal*) *what's cooking? See* HAPPEN sense 1.

■ **cook something up** (*informal*) CONCOCT, devise, contrive, fabricate, trump up, hatch, plot, plan, invent, make up, think up, dream up.

cooking ▶ **noun** CUISINE, cookery, baking; food.
– RELATED TERMS culinary.

cool ▶ **adjective** ❶ *a cool breeze* CHILLY, chill, cold, bracing, brisk, crisp, fresh, refreshing, invigorating; draughty; *informal* nippy; *Brit. informal* parky. ❷ *a cool response* UNENTHUSIASTIC, lukewarm, tepid, indifferent, uninterested, apathetic, half-hearted; unfriendly, distant, remote, aloof, cold, chilly, frosty, unwelcoming, unresponsive, offhand, uncommunicative, undemonstrative; *informal* stand-offish. ❸ *his ability to keep cool in a crisis* CALM, {cool, calm, and collected}, composed, as cool as a cucumber, collected, cool-headed, level-headed, self-possessed, controlled, self-controlled, poised, serene, tranquil, unruffled, unperturbed, unmoved, untroubled, imperturbable, placid, phlegmatic; *informal* unflappable, together, laid-back. ❹ *a cool lack of morality* BOLD, audacious, nerveless; brazen, shameless, unabashed. ❺ (*informal*) *she thinks she's so cool* FASHIONABLE, stylish, chic, up to the minute, sophisticated; *informal* trendy, funky, with it, hip, big, happening, groovy; *N. Amer. informal* kicky, tony, fly. ❻ (*informal*) *a really cool song. See* EXCELLENT.
– OPPOSITES warm, enthusiastic, agitated.

▶ **noun** ❶ *the cool of the evening* CHILL, chilliness, coldness, coolness. ❷ *Ken lost his cool* SELF-CONTROL, control, composure, self-possession, calmness, equilibrium, calm; aplomb, poise, sangfroid, presence of mind.
– OPPOSITES warmth.

▶ **verb** ❶ *cool the sauce in the fridge* CHILL, refrigerate. ❷ *her reluctance did nothing to cool his interest* LESSEN, moderate, diminish, reduce, dampen. ❸ *Simpson's ardour had cooled* SUBSIDE, lessen, diminish, decrease, abate, moderate, die down, fade, dwindle, wane. ❹ *after a while, she cooled off* CALM DOWN, recover/regain one's composure, compose oneself, control oneself, pull oneself together, simmer down.
– OPPOSITES heat, inflame, intensify.

coop ▶ **noun** *a hen coop* PEN, run, cage, hutch, enclosure.

▶ **verb** *he hates being cooped up at home* CONFINE, shut in/up, cage (in), pen up/in, keep, detain, trap, incarcerate, immure.

cooperate ▶ **verb** ❶ *police and social services cooperated in the operation* COLLABORATE, work together, work side by side, pull together, band together, join forces, team up, unite, combine, pool resources, make common cause, liaise. ❷ *he was happy to cooperate* BE OF ASSISTANCE, assist, help, lend a hand, be of service, do one's bit; *informal* play ball.

cooperation ▶ **noun** ❶ *cooperation between management and workers* COLLABORATION, joint action, combined effort, teamwork, partnership, coordination, liaison, association, synergy, give and take, compromise. ❷ *thank you for your cooperation* ASSISTANCE, helpfulness, help, helping hand, aid.

cooperative ▶ **adjective** ❶ *a cooperative effort* COLLABORATIVE, collective, combined, common, joint, shared, mutual, united, concerted, coordinated. ❷ *pleasant and cooperative staff* HELPFUL, eager to help, glad to be of assistance, obliging, accommodating, willing, amenable, adaptable.

coordinate ▶ **verb** ❶ *exhibitions coordinated by a team of international scholars* ORGANIZE, arrange, order, systematize, harmonize, correlate, synchronize, bring together, fit together, dovetail. ❷ *care workers coordinate at a local level* COOPERATE, liaise, collaborate, work together, negotiate, communicate, be in contact. ❸ *floral designs coordinate with the decor* MATCH, complement, set off; harmonize, blend, fit in, go.

cop (*informal*) ▶ **noun** *a traffic cop. See* POLICE OFFICER.

▶ **verb** *he tried to cop out of his responsibilities. See* AVOID sense 2.

cope ▶ **verb** ❶ *she couldn't cope on her own* MANAGE, survive, subsist, look after oneself, fend for oneself, shift for oneself, carry on, get by/through, bear up, hold one's own, keep one's end up, keep one's head above water; *informal* make it, hack it. ❷ *his inability to cope with the situation* DEAL WITH, handle, manage, address, face (up to), confront, tackle, get to grips with, get through, weather, come to terms with.

copious ▶ adjective ABUNDANT, superabundant, plentiful, ample, profuse, full, extensive, generous, bumper, lavish, fulsome, liberal, overflowing, in abundance, many, numerous; *informal* a gogo, galore; *poetic/literary* plenteous.
– OPPOSITES sparse.

copse ▶ noun THICKET, grove, wood, coppice, stand, clump, brake; *Brit.* spinney; *N. Amer. & Austral./NZ* brush; *archaic* hurst, holt, boscage.

copulate ▶ verb. *See* HAVE SEX at SEX.

copulation ▶ noun. *See* SEX sense 1.

copy ▶ noun ❶ *a copy of the report* DUPLICATE, facsimile, photocopy, carbon (copy), mimeograph, mimeo; transcript; reprint; *trademark* Xerox, photostat. ❷ *a copy of a sketch by Leonardo da Vinci* REPLICA, reproduction, replication, print, imitation, likeness; counterfeit, forgery, fake; *informal* knock-off.
▶ verb ❶ *each form had to be copied* DUPLICATE, photocopy, xerox, photostat, mimeograph, run off, reproduce. ❷ *portraits copied from original paintings by Reynolds* REPRODUCE, replicate; forge, fake, counterfeit. ❸ *their sound was copied by a lot of jazz players* IMITATE, reproduce, emulate, follow, echo, mirror, parrot, mimic, ape; plagiarize, steal; *informal* rip off.

coquettish ▶ adjective FLIRTATIOUS, flirty, provocative, seductive, inviting, kittenish, coy, arch, teasing, playful; *informal* come-hither, vampish.

cord ▶ noun STRING, thread, thong, lace, ribbon, strap, tape, tie, line, rope, cable, wire, ligature; twine, yarn, elastic, braid, braiding.

cordial ▶ adjective *a cordial welcome* FRIENDLY, warm, genial, affable, amiable, pleasant, fond, affectionate, warm-hearted, good-natured, gracious, hospitable, welcoming, hearty.
▶ noun *fruit cordial* SQUASH, crush, concentrate.

cordon ▶ noun *a cordon of 500 police* BARRIER, line, row, chain, ring, circle; picket line.
▶ verb *troops cordoned off the area* CLOSE OFF, shut off, seal off, fence off, separate off, isolate, enclose, surround.

core ▶ noun ❶ *the earth's core* CENTRE, interior, middle, nucleus; recesses, bowels, depths; *informal* innards; *poetic/literary* midst. ❷ *the core of the argument* HEART, heart of the matter, nucleus, nub, kernel, marrow, meat, essence, quintessence, crux, gist, pith, substance, basis, fundamentals; *informal* nitty-gritty, brass tacks, nuts and bolts.
▶ adjective *the core issue* CENTRAL, key, basic, fundamental, principal, primary, main, chief, crucial, vital, essential; *informal* number-one.
– OPPOSITES peripheral.

cork ▶ noun STOPPER, stop, plug, bung, peg, spigot, spile; *N. Amer.* stopple.

corn ▶ noun GRAIN, cereal (crop); wheat, barley, oats, rye.

corner ▶ noun ❶ *the cart lurched round the corner* BEND, curve, crook, dog-leg; turn, turning, junction, fork, intersection; *Brit.* hairpin bend. ❷ *a charming corner of Italy* DISTRICT, region, area, section, quarter, part; *informal* neck of the woods. ❸ *he found himself in a tight corner* PREDICAMENT, plight, tight spot, mess, muddle, difficulty, problem, dilemma, quandary; *informal* pickle, jam, stew, fix, hole, hot water, bind.
▶ verb ❶ *he was eventually cornered by police dogs* DRIVE INTO A CORNER, run to earth, bring to bay, cut off, block off, trap, hem in, pen in, surround, enclose; capture, catch. ❷ *crime syndicates have cornered the stolen car market* GAIN CONTROL OF, take over, control, dominate, monopolize; capture; *informal* sew up.

cornerstone ▶ noun FOUNDATION, basis, keystone, mainspring, mainstay, linchpin, bedrock, base, backbone, key, centrepiece, core, heart, centre, crux.

corny ▶ adjective (*informal*) BANAL, trite, hackneyed, commonplace, clichéd, predictable, stereotyped, platitudinous, tired, stale, overworked, overused, well worn; mawkish, sentimental, cloying, syrupy, sugary, saccharine; *Brit.* twee; *informal* cheesy, schmaltzy, mushy, slushy, sloppy, cutesy, toe-curling; *Brit. informal* soppy; *N. Amer. informal* cornball, hokey.

corollary ▶ noun CONSEQUENCE, (end) result, upshot, effect, repercussion, product, by-product; *Brit.* knock-on effect.

coronet ▶ noun. *See* CROWN noun sense 1.

corporal ▶ adjective BODILY, fleshly, corporeal, somatic, carnal, physical, material.
– OPPOSITES spiritual.

corporation ▶ noun ❶ *the chairman of the corporation* COMPANY, firm, business, concern, operation, house, organization, agency, trust, partnership; conglomerate, group, chain, multinational; *informal* outfit, set-up. ❷ (*Brit.*) *the corporation refused two planning applications* COUNCIL, town council, municipal authority.

corporeal ▶ adjective BODILY, fleshly, carnal, corporal, human, mortal, earthly, physical, material, tangible, concrete, real, actual.

corps ▶ noun ❶ *an army corps* UNIT, division, detachment, section, company, contingent, squad, squadron, regiment, battalion, brigade, platoon. ❷ *a corps of trained engineers* GROUP, body, band, cohort, party, gang, pack; team, crew.

corpse ▶ noun DEAD BODY, body, carcass, skeleton, remains; *informal* stiff; *Medicine* cadaver; *archaic* corse.
– RELATED TERMS necro-.

corpulent ▶ adjective FAT, obese, overweight,

plump, portly, stout, chubby, paunchy, beer-bellied, heavy, bulky, chunky, well upholstered, well padded, well covered, meaty, fleshy, rotund, broad in the beam; *informal* tubby, pudgy, beefy, porky, roly-poly, blubbery; *Brit. informal* podgy, fubsy; *N. Amer. informal* corn-fed; *rare* abdominous.
– OPPOSITES thin.

correct ▶ **adjective** ❶ *the correct answer* RIGHT, accurate, true, exact, precise, unerring, faithful, strict, faultless, flawless, error-free, perfect, word-perfect; *informal* on the mark, on the beam, on the nail; *Brit. informal* spot on, bang on; *N. Amer. informal* on the money, on the button. ❷ *correct behaviour* PROPER, seemly, decorous, decent, respectable, right, suitable, fit, fitting, befitting, appropriate, apt; approved, accepted, conventional, customary, traditional, orthodox, comme il faut.
– OPPOSITES wrong, improper.
▶ **verb** ❶ *proof-read your work and correct any mistakes* RECTIFY, put right, set right, right, amend, emend, remedy, repair. ❷ *an attempt to correct the trade imbalance* COUNTERACT, offset, counterbalance, compensate for, make up for, neutralize. ❸ *the brakes need correcting* ADJUST, regulate, fix, set, standardize, normalize, calibrate, fine-tune.

correction ▶ **noun** RECTIFICATION, rectifying, righting, amendment, emendation, repair, remedy; *archaic* reparation.

corrective ▶ **adjective** REMEDIAL, therapeutic, restorative, curative, reparatory, reparative, rehabilitative.

correctly ▶ **adverb** ❶ *the questions were answered correctly* ACCURATELY, right, unerringly, precisely, faultlessly, flawlessly, perfectly, without error; *dated* aright. ❷ *she behaved correctly at all times* PROPERLY, decorously, with decorum, decently, suitably, fittingly, appropriately, well.

correlate ▶ **verb** ❶ *socio-economic status often correlates with educational achievement* CORRESPOND, match, parallel, agree, tally, tie in, be consistent, be compatible, be consonant, coordinate, dovetail, relate, conform; *informal* square; *N. Amer. informal* jibe. ❷ *consumption of such foods was correlated with a decreased risk for certain cancers* CONNECT, establish a relationship/connection between, associate, relate.
– OPPOSITES contrast.

correlation ▶ **noun** CONNECTION, association, link, tie-in, tie-up, relation, relationship, interrelationship, interdependence, interconnection, interaction; correspondence, parallel.

correspond ▶ **verb** ❶ *their policies do not correspond with their statements* CORRELATE, agree, be in agreement, be consistent, be compatible, be consonant, accord, be in tune, concur, coincide, tally, tie in, dovetail, fit in; match, parallel; *informal* square; *N. Amer. informal* jibe. ❷ *a rank corresponding to the British rank of sergeant* BE EQUIVALENT, be analogous, be comparable, equate. ❸ *Debbie and I corresponded for years* EXCHANGE LETTERS, write, communicate, keep in touch/contact.

correspondence ▶ **noun** ❶ *there is some correspondence between the two variables* CORRELATION, agreement, consistency, compatibility, consonance, conformity, similarity, resemblance, parallel, comparability, accord, concurrence, coincidence. ❷ *his private correspondence* LETTERS, messages, missives, mail, post; communication.

correspondent ▶ **noun** *the paper's foreign correspondent* REPORTER, journalist, columnist, writer, contributor, newspaperman, newspaperwoman, commentator; *Brit.* pressman; *informal* stringer, news hound, journo.
▶ **adjective** *a correspondent improvement in quality* CORRESPONDING, parallel, matching, equivalent, comparable, similar, analogous, commensurate.

corresponding ▶ **adjective** COMMENSURATE, parallel, correspondent, matching, correlated, relative, proportional, proportionate, comparable, equivalent, analogous.

corridor ▶ **noun** PASSAGE, passageway, aisle, gangway, hall, hallway, gallery, arcade.

corroborate ▶ **verb** CONFIRM, verify, endorse, ratify, authenticate, validate, certify; support, back up, uphold, bear out, bear witness to, attest to, testify to, vouch for, give credence to, substantiate, sustain.
– OPPOSITES contradict.

corrode ▶ **verb** ❶ *the iron had corroded* RUST, become rusty, tarnish; wear away, disintegrate, crumble, perish, spoil; oxidize. ❷ *acid rain corrodes buildings* WEAR AWAY, eat away (at), gnaw away (at), erode, abrade, consume, destroy.

corrosive ▶ **adjective** CAUSTIC, corroding, erosive, abrasive, burning, stinging; destructive, damaging, harmful, harsh.

corrugated ▶ **adjective** RIDGED, fluted, grooved, furrowed, crinkled, crinkly, puckered, creased, wrinkled, wrinkly, crumpled; *technical* striate, striated.

corrupt ▶ **adjective** ❶ *a corrupt official | corrupt practices* DISHONEST, unscrupulous, dishonourable, unprincipled, unethical, amoral, untrustworthy, venal, underhand, double-dealing, fraudulent, bribable, buyable; criminal, illegal, unlawful, nefarious; *informal* crooked, shady, dirty, mucky, sleazy; *Brit. informal* bent, dodgy. ❷ *the earth was corrupt in God's sight* IMMORAL, depraved, degenerate, reprobate, vice-

ridden, perverted, debauched, dissolute, dissipated, bad, wicked, evil, base, sinful, ungodly, unholy, irreligious, profane, impious, impure; *informal* warped. ❸ *a corrupt text* IMPURE, bastardized, debased, adulterated.
– OPPOSITES honest, ethical, pure.
▶ **verb** ❶ *the fear of firms corrupting politicians in the search for contracts* BRIBE, suborn, buy (off), pay off; *informal* grease someone's palm, give someone a backhander/sweetener, get at, square; *Brit. informal* nobble. ❷ *a book that might corrupt its readers* DEPRAVE, pervert, debauch, degrade, warp, lead astray, defile, pollute, sully; *archaic* demoralize. ❸ *the apostolic writings had been corrupted* ALTER, tamper with, interfere with, bastardize, debase, adulterate.

corruption ▶ **noun** ❶ *political corruption* DISHONESTY, unscrupulousness, double-dealing, fraud, fraudulence, misconduct, crime, criminality, wrongdoing; bribery, subornation, venality, extortion, profiteering, jobbery; *N. Amer.* payola; *informal* graft, crookedness, sleaze; *formal* malversation. ❷ *his fall into corruption* IMMORALITY, depravity, vice, degeneracy, perversion, pervertedness, debauchery, dissoluteness, decadence, wickedness, evil, sin, sinfulness, ungodliness; *formal* turpitude. ❸ *these figures have been subject to corruption* ALTERATION, bastardization, debasement, adulteration.
– OPPOSITES honesty, morality, purity.

corsair ▶ **noun** (*archaic*). *See* PIRATE noun sense 1.

corset ▶ **noun** GIRDLE, panty girdle, foundation (garment), corselette; *Brit.* roll-on; *informal, dated* waspie; *historical* stays.

cortège ▶ **noun** ❶ *the funeral cortège* PROCESSION, parade, cavalcade, motorcade, convoy, caravan, train, column, file, line. ❷ *the prince's cortège* ENTOURAGE, retinue, train, suite; attendants, companions, followers, retainers.

cosmetic ▶ **adjective** *most of the changes were merely cosmetic* SUPERFICIAL, surface, skin-deep, outward, exterior, external.
– OPPOSITES fundamental.
▶ **noun** (**cosmetics**) *a new range of cosmetics* MAKE-UP, beauty products, maquillage, face paint; *informal* warpaint, paint, slap.

cosmic ▶ **adjective** ❶ *cosmic bodies* EXTRATERRESTRIAL, in space, from space. ❷ *an epic of cosmic dimensions* VAST, huge, immense, enormous, massive, colossal, prodigious, immeasurable, incalculable, unfathomable, fathomless, measureless, infinite, limitless, boundless.

cosmonaut ▶ **noun** ASTRONAUT, spaceman/woman, space traveller, space cadet; *N. Amer. informal* jock.

cosmopolitan ▶ **adjective** ❶ *the student body has a cosmopolitan character* MULTICULTURAL, multiracial, international, worldwide, global. ❷ *a cosmopolitan audience* WORLDLY, worldly-wise, well travelled, experienced, unprovincial, cultivated, cultured, sophisticated, suave, urbane, glamorous, fashionable; *informal* jet-setting, cool.

cosset ▶ **verb** PAMPER, indulge, overindulge, mollycoddle, coddle, baby, pet, mother, nanny, nursemaid, pander to, feather-bed, spoil; wrap in cotton wool, wait on someone hand and foot.

cost ▶ **noun** ❶ *the cost of the equipment* PRICE, asking price, market price, selling price, fee, tariff, fare, toll, levy, charge, rental; value, valuation, quotation, rate, worth; *informal, humorous* damage. ❷ *the human cost of the conflict* SACRIFICE, loss, expense, penalty, toll, price. ❸ (**costs**) *we need to make £10,000 to cover our costs* EXPENSES, outgoings, disbursements, overheads, running costs, operating costs, fixed costs; expenditure, spending, outlay.
▶ **verb** ❶ *the chair costs £186* BE PRICED AT, sell for, be valued at, fetch, come to, amount to; *informal* set someone back, go for; *Brit. informal* knock someone back. ❷ *the proposal has not yet been costed* PUT A PRICE ON, price, value, put a value on, put a figure on.

costly ▶ **adjective** ❶ *costly machinery* EXPENSIVE, dear, high-cost, highly priced, overpriced; *Brit.* over the odds; *informal* steep, pricey. ❷ *a costly mistake* CATASTROPHIC, disastrous, calamitous, ruinous; damaging, harmful, injurious, deleterious, woeful, awful, terrible, dreadful; *formal* grievous.
– OPPOSITES cheap.

costume ▶ **noun** ❶ *Elizabethan costumes* (SET OF) CLOTHES, garments, robes, outfit, ensemble; dress, clothing, attire, garb, uniform, livery; *informal* get-up, gear, togs; *Brit. informal* clobber, kit; *N. Amer. informal* threads; *formal* apparel; *archaic* habit, habiliments, raiment. ❷ (*Brit.*) *if you'd like a dip, we can lend you a costume. See* SWIMSUIT.

cosy ▶ **adjective** ❶ *a cosy country cottage* SNUG, comfortable, warm, homelike, homey, homely, welcoming; safe, sheltered, secure; *N. Amer.* down-home, homestyle; *informal* comfy, snug as a bug (in a rug). ❷ *a cosy chat* INTIMATE, relaxed, informal, friendly.

coterie ▶ **noun** CLIQUE, set, circle, inner circle, crowd, in-crowd, band, community; *informal* gang.

cottage ▶ **noun** SMALL HOUSE, lodge, chalet, cabin; shack, shanty; (*in Russia*) dacha; *Scottish* bothy, but and ben; *Austral. informal* weekender; *poetic/literary* bower; *archaic* cot.

couch ▶ **noun** *she seated herself on the couch* SETTEE, sofa, divan, chaise longue, chesterfield, love seat, settle, ottoman; *Brit.* put-you-up; *N. Amer.* daybed, davenport, studio couch.

▶ **verb** *his reply was couched in deferential terms* EXPRESS, phrase, word, frame, put, formulate, style, convey, say, state, utter.

cough ▶ **verb** *he coughed loudly* HACK, hawk, bark, clear one's throat, hem.

▶ **noun** *a loud cough* HACK, bark; *informal* frog in one's throat.

– RELATED TERMS tussive.

■ **cough something up** PAY (UP), come up with, hand over, dish out, part with; *informal* fork out, shell out, lay out; *Brit. informal* stump up; *N. Amer. informal* ante up, pony up.

council ▶ **noun** ❶ *the town council* LOCAL AUTHORITY, local government, municipal authority, administration, executive, chamber, assembly; *Brit.* corporation. ❷ *the Schools Council* ADVISORY BODY, board, committee, commission, assembly, panel; synod, convocation. ❸ *that evening, she held a family council* meeting, gathering, conference, conclave, assembly.

counsel ▶ **noun** ❶ *his wise counsel* ADVICE, guidance, counselling, direction, information; recommendations, suggestions, guidelines, hints, tips, pointers, warnings. ❷ *the counsel for the defence* BARRISTER, lawyer; *Scottish* advocate; *N. Amer.* attorney, counselor(-at-law); *informal* brief.

▶ **verb** *he counselled the team to withdraw from the deal* ADVISE, recommend, direct, advocate, encourage, urge, warn, caution; guide, give guidance.

counsellor ▶ **noun** ADVISER, consultant, guide, mentor; expert, specialist.

count ▶ **verb** ❶ *she counted the money again* ADD UP, add together, reckon up, figure up, total, tally, calculate, compute; *Brit.* tot up; *formal* enumerate; *dated* cast up. ❷ *a company with 250 employees, not counting overseas staff* INCLUDE, take into account, take account of, take into consideration, allow for. ❸ *I count it a privilege to be asked* CONSIDER, think, feel, regard, look on as, view as, hold to be, judge, deem, account. ❹ *it's your mother's feelings that count* MATTER, be of consequence, be of account, be significant, signify, be important, carry weight; *informal* cut any ice.

▶ **noun** ❶ *at the last count, the committee had 579 members* CALCULATION, computation, reckoning, tally; *formal* enumeration. ❷ *her white blood cell count* AMOUNT, number, total.

■ **count on/upon** ❶ *you can count on me* RELY ON, depend on, bank on, trust (in), be sure of, have (every) confidence in, believe in, put one's faith in, take for granted, take as read. ❷ *they hadn't counted on Rangers' indomitable spirit* EXPECT, reckon on, anticipate, envisage, allow for, be prepared for, bargain for/on; *N. Amer. informal* figure on.

■ **out for the count** (*informal*). *See* UNCONSCIOUS adjective sense 1.

countenance ▶ **noun** *his strikingly handsome countenance* FACE, features, physiognomy, profile; (facial) expression, look, appearance, aspect, mien; *informal* mug; *Brit. informal* mush, phizog, phiz, clock, boat race; *N. Amer. informal* puss; *poetic/literary* visage, lineaments.

▶ **verb** *he would not countenance the use of force* TOLERATE, permit, allow, agree to, consent to, give one's blessing to, go along with, hold with, put up with, endure, stomach, swallow; *Scottish* thole; *informal* stand for; *formal* brook.

counter[1] ▶ **noun** *a pile of counters* TOKEN, chip, disc, jetton, plaque; piece, man, marker; *N. Amer.* check.

counter[2] ▶ **verb** ❶ *workers countered accusations of dishonesty with claims of oppression* RESPOND TO, parry, hit back at, answer, retort to. ❷ *the second argument is more difficult to counter* OPPOSE, dispute, argue against/with, contradict, controvert, negate, counteract; challenge, contest; *formal* gainsay, confute.

– OPPOSITES support.

▶ **adjective** *a counter bid* OPPOSING, opposed, opposite.

■ **counter to** AGAINST, in opposition to, contrary to, at variance with, in defiance of, in contravention of, in conflict with, at odds with, against.

counteract ▶ **verb** ❶ *new measures to counteract drug trafficking* PREVENT, thwart, frustrate, foil, impede, curb, hinder, hamper, check, put a stop/end to, defeat. ❷ *a drug to counteract the possible effect on her heart* OFFSET, counterbalance, balance (out), cancel out, even out, counterpoise, countervail, compensate for, make up for, remedy; neutralize, nullify, negate, invalidate.

– OPPOSITES encourage, exacerbate.

counterbalance ▶ **verb** COMPENSATE FOR, make up for, offset, balance (out), even out, counterpoise, counteract, equalize, neutralize; nullify, negate, undo.

counterfeit ▶ **adjective** *counterfeit cassettes* FAKE, faked, bogus, forged, imitation, spurious, substitute, ersatz; *informal* phoney.

– OPPOSITES genuine.

▶ **noun** *the notes were counterfeits* FAKE, forgery, copy, reproduction, imitation; fraud, sham; *informal* phoney, knock-off.

– OPPOSITES original.

▶ **verb** ❶ *his signature was hard to counterfeit* FAKE, forge, copy, reproduce, imitate. ❷ *he grew tired of counterfeiting interest* FEIGN, simulate, pretend, fake, sham.

countermand ▶ **verb** REVOKE, rescind, reverse, undo, repeal, retract, withdraw, quash, overturn, overrule, cancel, annul, invalidate, nullify, negate; *Law* disaffirm, discharge, vacate; *formal* abrogate; *archaic* recall.

– OPPOSITES uphold.

counterpane ▶ noun (*dated*). *See* BEDSPREAD.

counterpart ▶ noun EQUIVALENT, opposite number, peer, equal, coequal, parallel, complement, analogue, match, twin, mate, fellow, brother, sister; *formal* compeer.

countless ▶ adjective INNUMERABLE, numerous, untold, legion, without number, numberless, unnumbered, limitless, multitudinous, incalculable; *informal* umpteen, no end of, a slew of, loads of, stacks of, heaps of, masses of, oodles of, zillions of; *N. Amer. informal* gazillions of; *poetic/literary* myriad.
–OPPOSITES few.

countrified ▶ adjective RURAL, rustic, pastoral, bucolic, country; idyllic, unspoilt; *poetic/literary* Arcadian, sylvan, georgic.
–OPPOSITES urban.

country ▶ noun ❶ *foreign countries* NATION, (sovereign) state, kingdom, realm, territory, province, principality, palatinate, duchy. ❷ *he risked his life for his country* HOMELAND, native land, fatherland, motherland, the land of one's fathers. ❸ *the whole country took to the streets* PEOPLE, public, population, populace, citizenry, nation, body politic; electors, voters, taxpayers, grass roots; *Brit. informal* Joe Public. ❹ *thickly forested country* TERRAIN, land, territory, parts; landscape, scenery, setting, surroundings, environment. ❺ *she hated living in the country* COUNTRYSIDE, green belt, great outdoors; provinces, rural areas, backwoods, back of beyond, hinterland; *Austral. NZ* outback, bush, back country, backblocks, booay; *informal* sticks, middle of nowhere; *N. Amer. informal* boondocks, boonies, tall timbers; *Austral. informal* beyond the black stump.
▶ adjective *country pursuits* RURAL, countryside, outdoor, rustic, pastoral, bucolic; *poetic/literary* sylvan, Arcadian, georgic.
–OPPOSITES urban.

countryman, countrywoman ▶ noun ❶ *the traditions of his countrymen* COMPATRIOT, fellow citizen. ❷ *the countryman takes a great interest in the weather* COUNTRY DWELLER, country cousin, son/daughter of the soil, farmer; rustic, yokel, bumpkin, peasant, provincial; *Irish informal* culchie; *N. Amer. informal* hayseed, hick, hillbilly, rube; *Austral. informal* bushy; *archaic* swain, hind, kern, carl, cottier.

countryside ▶ noun ❶ *beautiful unspoilt countryside* LANDSCAPE, scenery, surroundings, setting, environment; country, terrain, land. ❷ *I was brought up in the countryside. See* COUNTRY noun sense 5.

county ▶ noun *the northern counties* SHIRE, province, territory, administrative unit, region, district, area.
▶ adjective (*Brit.*) *a county lady* UPPER-CLASS, aristocratic, landed, landowning; *informal* upper-crust, top-drawer, {huntin', shootin', and fishin'}, tweedy.

coup ▶ noun ❶ *a violent military coup* SEIZURE OF POWER, coup d'état, putsch, overthrow, takeover, deposition; (palace) revolution, rebellion, revolt, insurrection, mutiny, insurgence, uprising. ❷ *a major publishing coup* SUCCESS, triumph, feat, accomplishment, achievement, scoop, master stroke, stroke of genius.

coup de grâce ▶ noun DEATH BLOW, finishing blow, kiss of death; *informal* KO, kayo.

coup d'état ▶ noun. *See* COUP sense 1.

couple ▶ noun ❶ *a couple of girls* PAIR, duo, twosome, two, brace, span, yoke; *archaic* twain. ❷ *a honeymoon couple* HUSBAND AND WIFE, twosome, partners, lovers; *informal* item.
▶ verb ❶ *a sense of hope is coupled with a sense of loss* COMBINE, accompany, mix, incorporate, link, associate, connect, ally; add to, join to; *formal* conjoin. ❷ *a cable is coupled to one of the wheels* CONNECT, attach, join, fasten, fix, link, secure, tie, bind, strap, rope, tether, truss, lash, hitch, yoke, chain, hook (up).
–OPPOSITES detach.

coupon ▶ noun ❶ *money-off coupons* VOUCHER, token, ticket, slip; *N. Amer. informal* ducat, comp, rain check. ❷ *fill in the coupon below* FORM, tear-off slip.

courage ▶ noun BRAVERY, courageousness, pluck, pluckiness, valour, fearlessness, intrepidity, nerve, daring, audacity, boldness, grit, hardihood, heroism, gallantry; *informal* guts, spunk; *Brit. informal* bottle; *N. Amer. informal* moxie, cojones, sand.
–OPPOSITES cowardice.

courageous ▶ adjective BRAVE, plucky, fearless, valiant, valorous, intrepid, heroic, lionhearted, bold, daring, daredevil, audacious, undaunted, unflinching, unshrinking, unafraid, dauntless, indomitable, doughty, mettlesome, venturesome, stout-hearted, gallant, death-or-glory; *N. Amer.* rock-ribbed; *informal* game, gutsy, spunky, ballsy, have-a-go.
–OPPOSITES cowardly.

courier ▶ noun ❶ *the documents were sent by courier* MESSENGER, dispatch rider, runner. ❷ *a courier for a package holiday company* REPRESENTATIVE, (tour) guide; dragoman; *N. Amer.* tour director; *informal* rep.

course ▶ noun ❶ *the island was not far off our course* ROUTE, way, track, direction, tack, path, line, trail, trajectory, bearing, heading, orbit. ❷ *the course of history* PROGRESSION, development, progress, advance, evolution, flow, movement, sequence, order, succession, rise, march, passage, passing. ❸ *what is the best course to adopt?* PROCEDURE, plan (of action), course/line of action, MO, modus operandi, practice, approach, technique, way, means, policy, strategy, programme; *formal* praxis. ❹ *a waterlogged course* RACECOURSE, racetrack, track, ground. ❺ *a French course* PROGRAMME/COURSE OF STUDY, curriculum, syllabus; classes, lectures, studies. ❻ *a course of antibiotics* PROGRAMME, series, sequence, system, schedule, regimen.

▶ **verb** *tears coursed down her cheeks* FLOW, pour, stream, run, rush, gush, cascade, flood, roll.

■ **in due course** AT THE APPROPRIATE TIME, when the time is ripe, in time, in the fullness of time, in the course of time, at a later date, by and by, sooner or later, in the end, eventually.

■ **of course** NATURALLY, as might be expected, as you/one would expect, needless to say, certainly, to be sure, as a matter of course, obviously, it goes without saying; *informal* natch.

court ▶ **noun** ❶ *the court found him guilty* COURT OF LAW, law court, bench, bar, judicature, tribunal, chancery, assizes. ❷ *walking in the castle court* COURTYARD, quadrangle, square, close, enclosure, plaza, piazza, cloister; *informal* quad. ❸ *the King's's court* ROYAL HOUSEHOLD, retinue, entourage, train, suite, courtiers, attendants. ❹ *she made her way to the queen's court* ROYAL RESIDENCE, palace, castle, chateau.

▶ **verb** ❶ *a newspaper editor who was courted by senior politicians* CURRY FAVOUR WITH, cultivate, try to win over, make up to, ingratiate oneself with; *informal* suck up to, butter up; *N. Amer. informal* shine up to; *archaic* blandish. ❷ *he was busily courting public attention* SEEK, pursue, go after, strive for, solicit. ❸ *he's often courted controversy* RISK, invite, attract, bring on oneself. ❹ (*dated*) *he's courting her sister* WOO, go out with, pursue, run after, chase, pay court to; *informal* date, see, go steady with; *Austral. informal* track (square) with; *dated* set one's cap at, romance, seek the hand of, make love to.

courteous ▶ **adjective** POLITE, well mannered, civil, respectful, well behaved, well bred, well spoken, mannerly; gentlemanly, chivalrous, gallant; gracious, obliging, considerate, pleasant, cordial, urbane, polished, refined, courtly, civilized; *archaic* fair-spoken.

– OPPOSITES rude.

courtesan ▶ **noun** (*archaic*). *See* PROSTITUTE noun.

courtesy ▶ **noun** POLITENESS, courteousness, good manners, civility, respect, respectfulness; chivalry, gallantry; graciousness, consideration, thought, thoughtfulness, cordiality, urbanity, courtliness.

courtier ▶ **noun** ATTENDANT, lord, lady, lady-in-waiting, steward, equerry, page, squire; *historical* liegeman.

courtly ▶ **adjective** REFINED, polished, suave, cultivated, civilized, elegant, urbane, debonair; polite, civil, courteous, gracious, well mannered, well bred, chivalrous, gallant, gentlemanly, ladylike, aristocratic, dignified, decorous, formal, ceremonious, stately.

– OPPOSITES uncouth.

courtship ▶ **noun** ❶ *a whirlwind courtship* ROMANCE, (love) affair; engagement. ❷ *his courtship of Emma* WOOING, courting, suit, pursuit; *archaic* addresses.

courtyard ▶ **noun** QUADRANGLE, cloister, square, plaza, piazza, close, enclosure, yard; *informal* quad.

cove[1] ▶ **noun** *a small sandy cove* BAY, inlet, fjord, anchorage; *Scottish* (sea) loch; *Irish* lough.

cove[2] ▶ **noun** (*informal, dated*) *he's a funny cove. See* FELLOW sense 1.

covenant ▶ **noun** *a breach of the covenant* CONTRACT, agreement, undertaking, commitment, guarantee, warrant, pledge, promise, bond, indenture; pact, deal, settlement, arrangement, understanding.

▶ **verb** *the landlord covenants to repair the property* UNDERTAKE, contract, guarantee, pledge, promise, agree, engage, warrant, commit oneself, bind oneself.

cover ▶ **verb** ❶ *she covered face with a towel* PROTECT, shield, shelter; hide, conceal, veil. ❷ *his car was covered in mud* CAKE, coat, encrust, plaster, smother, daub, bedaub. ❸ *snow covered the fields* BLANKET, overlay, overspread, carpet, coat; *poetic/literary* mantle. ❹ *a course covering all aspects of the business* DEAL WITH, consider, take in, include, involve, comprise, incorporate, embrace. ❺ *the trial was covered by a range of newspapers* REPORT ON, write about, describe, commentate on, publish/broadcast details of. ❻ *he turned on the radio to cover their conversation* MASK, disguise, hide, camouflage, muffle, stifle, smother. ❼ *I'm covering for Jill* STAND IN FOR, fill in for, deputize for, take over from, relieve, take the place of, sit in for, understudy, hold the fort; *informal* sub for; *N. Amer. informal* pinch-hit for. ❽ *can you make enough to cover your costs?* PAY (FOR), be enough for, fund, finance; pay back, make up for, offset. ❾ *your home is covered against damage and loss* INSURE, protect, secure, underwrite, assure, indemnify. ❿ *we covered ten miles each day* TRAVEL, journey, go, do, traverse.

– OPPOSITES expose.

▶ **noun** ❶ *a protective cover* COVERING, sleeve, wrapping, wrapper, envelope, sheath, housing, jacket, casing, cowling; awning, canopy, tarpaulin. ❷ *a manhole cover* LID, top, cap. ❸ *a book cover* BINDING, jacket, dust jacket, dust cover, wrapper. ❹ (**covers**) *she pulled the covers over her head* BEDCLOTHES, bedding, sheets, blankets. ❺ *a thick cover of snow* COATING, coat, covering, layer, carpet, blanket, overlay, dusting, film, sheet, veneer, crust, skin, cloak, mantle, veil, pall, shroud. ❻ *panicking onlookers ran for cover* SHELTER, protection, refuge, sanctuary, haven, hiding place. ❼ *there is considerable game cover around the lake* UNDERGROWTH, vegetation, greenery, woodland, trees, bushes, brush, scrub, plants; covert, thicket, copse, coppice. ❽ *the company was a cover for an international swindle* FRONT, facade, smokescreen, screen, blind, camouflage, disguise, mask, cloak. ❾ (*Brit.*) *your policy provides cover against damage by subsidence* INSURANCE, protection, security, assurance, indemnification, indemnity, compensation.

■ **cover something up** CONCEAL, hide, keep secret/dark, hush up, draw a veil over, suppress, sweep under the carpet, gloss over; *informal* whitewash, keep a/the lid on.

coverage ▶ **noun** REPORTAGE, reporting, description, treatment, handling, presentation, investigation, commentary; reports, articles, pieces, stories.

covering ▶ **noun** ❶ *a canvas covering* AWNING, canopy, tarpaulin, cowling, casing, housing; wrapping, wrapper, cover, envelope, sheath, sleeve, jacket, lid, top, cap. ❷ *a covering of snow* LAYER, coating, coat, carpet, blanket, overlay, topping, dusting, film, sheet, veneer, crust, skin, cloak, mantle, veil.

▶ **adjective** *a covering letter* ACCOMPANYING, explanatory, introductory, prefatory.

coverlet ▶ **noun** BEDSPREAD, bedcover, cover, throw, duvet, quilt; *Brit.* eiderdown; *N. Amer.* spread, comforter; *dated* counterpane.

covert ▶ **adjective** SECRET, furtive, clandestine, surreptitious, stealthy, cloak-and-dagger, hole-and-corner, backstairs, hidden, under-the-table, hugger-mugger, concealed, private, undercover, underground; *informal* hush-hush.
–OPPOSITES overt.

cover-up ▶ **noun** WHITEWASH, concealment, false front, facade, camouflage, disguise, mask.
–OPPOSITES exposé.

covet ▶ **verb** DESIRE, yearn for, crave, have one's heart set on, want, wish for, long for, hanker after/for, hunger after/for, thirst for.

covetous ▶ **adjective** GRASPING, greedy, acquisitive, desirous, possessive, envious, green with envy, green-eyed.

covey ▶ **noun** GROUP, gang, troop, troupe, party, company, band, bevy, flock; knot, cluster; *informal* bunch, gaggle, posse, crew.

cow ▶ **verb** INTIMIDATE, daunt, browbeat, bully, tyrannize, scare, terrorize, frighten, dishearten, unnerve, subdue; *informal* psych out, bulldoze.

coward ▶ **noun** WEAKLING, milksop, namby-pamby, mouse; *informal* chicken, scaredy-cat, yellow-belly, sissy, baby; *Brit. informal* big girl's blouse; *N. Amer. informal* candy-ass, pussy; *Austral./NZ informal* dingo, sook; *archaic* poltroon, caitiff.
–OPPOSITES hero.

cowardly ▶ **adjective** FAINT-HEARTED, lily-livered, spineless, chicken-hearted, craven, timid, timorous, fearful, pusillanimous; *informal* yellow, chicken, weak-kneed, gutless, yellow-bellied, wimpish, wimpy; *Brit. informal* wet; *archaic* recreant.
–OPPOSITES brave.

cowboy ▶ **noun** ❶ *cowboys on horseback* CATTLEMAN, cowhand, cowman, cowherd, herder, herdsman, drover, stockman, rancher, gaucho, vaquero; *N. Amer. informal* cowpuncher, cowpoke, broncobuster; *N. Amer. dated* buckaroo. ❷ (*informal*) *the builders were complete cowboys* ROGUE, rascal, scoundrel, cheat, swindler, fraudster, fly-by-night.

cower ▶ **verb** CRINGE, shrink, crouch, recoil, flinch, pull back, draw back, tremble, shake, quake, blench, quail, grovel.

coy ▶ **adjective** ARCH, simpering, coquettish, flirtatious, kittenish, skittish; demure, shy, modest, bashful, reticent, diffident, self-effacing, shrinking, timid.
–OPPOSITES brazen.

cozen ▶ **verb** (*poetic/literary*). *See* TRICK verb.

crabbed ▶ **adjective** ❶ *her crabbed handwriting* CRAMPED, ill-formed, bad, illegible, unreadable, indecipherable; shaky, spidery. ❷ *a crabbed old man. See* CRABBY.

crabby ▶ **adjective** IRRITABLE, cantankerous, irascible, bad-tempered, grumpy, grouchy, crotchety, tetchy, testy, crusty, curmudgeonly, ill-tempered, ill-humoured, peevish, cross, fractious, pettish, crabbed, prickly, waspish; *informal* snappish, snappy, chippy; *Brit. informal* shirty, stroppy, narky, ratty; *N. Amer. informal* cranky, ornery; *Austral./NZ informal* snaky.
–OPPOSITES affable.

crack ▶ **noun** ❶ *a crack in the glass* SPLIT, break, chip, fracture, rupture; crazing. ❷ *a crack between two rocks* SPACE, gap, crevice, fissure, cleft, breach, rift, cranny, chink, interstice. ❸ *the crack of a rifle* BANG, report, explosion, detonation, pop; clap, crash. ❹ *a crack on the head* BLOW, bang, hit, knock, rap, punch, thump, bump, smack, slap; *informal* bash, whack, thwack, clout, wallop, clip, biff, bop. ❺ (*informal*) *we'll have a crack at it* ATTEMPT, try; *informal* go, shot, stab, whack; *formal* essay. ❻ (*informal*) *cheap cracks about her clothes* JOKE, witticism, quip; jibe, barb, taunt, sneer, insult; *informal* gag, wisecrack, funny, dig.

▶ **verb** ❶ *the glass cracked in the heat* BREAK, split, fracture, rupture, snap. ❷ *she cracked him across* *the forehead* HIT, strike, smack, slap, beat, thump, knock, rap, punch; *informal* bash, whack, thwack, clobber, clout, clip, wallop, belt, biff, bop, sock; *Brit. informal* slosh; *N. Amer. informal* boff, bust, slug. ❸ *the witnesses cracked* BREAK DOWN, give way, cave in, go to pieces, crumble, lose control, yield, succumb. ❹ (*informal*) *the naval code proved harder to crack* DECIPHER, interpret, decode, break, solve, resolve, work out, find the key to; *informal* figure out, suss out.

▶ **adjective** *a crack shot* EXPERT, skilled, skilful, formidable, virtuoso, masterly, consummate, excellent, first-rate, first-class, marvellous, wonderful, magnificent, outstanding, superlative; deadly; *informal* great, superb, fantastic, ace, hotshot, mean, demon; *Brit. informal* brilliant; *N. Amer. informal* crackerjack.

– OPPOSITES incompetent.

■ **crack down on** SUPPRESS, prevent, stop, put a stop to, put an end to, stamp out, eliminate, eradicate; clamp down on, get tough on, come down hard on, limit, restrain, restrict, check, keep in check, control, keep under control.

■ **crack up** (*informal*) BREAK DOWN, have a breakdown, lose control, go to pieces, go out of one's mind, go mad; *informal* lose it, fall/come apart at the seams, go crazy, freak out.

cracked ▶ **adjective** ❶ *a cracked cup* CHIPPED, broken, crazed, fractured, splintered, split; damaged, defective, flawed, imperfect. ❷ (*informal*) *you're cracked! See* MAD sense 1.

crackle ▶ **verb** SIZZLE, fizz, hiss, crack, snap, sputter, crepitate; *technical* decrepitate.

cradle ▶ **noun** ❶ *the baby's cradle* CRIB, bassinet, Moses basket, cot, carrycot. ❷ *the cradle of democracy* BIRTHPLACE, fount, fountainhead, source, spring, fountain, origin, place of origin, seat; *poetic/literary* wellspring.

▶ **verb** *she cradled his head in her arms* HOLD, support, pillow, cushion, shelter, protect; rest, prop (up).

craft ▶ **noun** ❶ *a player with plenty of craft* SKILL, skilfulness, ability, capability, competence, art, talent, flair, artistry, dexterity, craftsmanship, expertise, proficiency, adroitness, adeptness, deftness, virtuosity. ❷ *the historian's craft* ACTIVITY, occupation, profession, work, line of work, pursuit. ❸ *she used craft and diplomacy* CUNNING, craftiness, guile, wiliness, artfulness, deviousness, slyness, trickery, duplicity, dishonesty, deceit, deceitfulness, deception, intrigue, subterfuge; wiles, ploys, ruses, schemes, stratagems, tricks. ❹ *a sailing craft* VESSEL, ship, boat; *poetic/literary* barque.

craftsman, craftswoman ▶ **noun** ARTISAN, artist, skilled worker; expert, master; *archaic* artificer, mechanic.

craftsmanship ▶ **noun** WORKMANSHIP, artistry, craft, art, handiwork, work; skill, skilfulness, expertise, technique.

crafty ▶ **adjective** CUNNING, wily, guileful, artful, devious, sly, tricky, scheming, calculating, designing, sharp, shrewd, astute, canny; duplicitous, dishonest, deceitful; *informal* foxy; *archaic* subtle.

– OPPOSITES honest.

crag ▶ **noun** CLIFF, bluff, ridge, precipice, height, peak, tor, escarpment, scarp.

craggy ▶ **adjective** ❶ *the craggy cliffs* STEEP, precipitous, sheer, perpendicular; rocky, rugged, ragged. ❷ *his craggy face* RUGGED, rough-hewn, strong, manly; weather-beaten, weathered.

cram ▶ **verb** ❶ *wardrobes crammed with clothes* FILL, stuff, pack, jam, fill to overflowing, fill to the brim, overload; crowd, throng, overcrowd. ❷ *they all crammed into the car* CROWD, pack, pile, squash, wedge oneself, force one's way. ❸ *he crammed his clothes into a suitcase* THRUST, push, shove, force, ram, jam, stuff, pack, pile, squash, compress, squeeze, wedge. ❹ *most of the students are cramming for exams* REVISE; *informal* swot, mug up, bone up.

cramp ▶ **noun** *stomach cramps* MUSCLE/MUSCULAR SPASM, pain, shooting pain, pang, stitch; *Medicine* clonus, hyperkinesis.

▶ **verb** *tighter rules will cramp economic growth* HINDER, impede, inhibit, hamper, constrain, hamstring, interfere with, restrict, limit, shackle; slow down, check, arrest, curb, retard.

cramped ▶ **adjective** ❶ *cramped accommodation* POKY, uncomfortable, confined, restricted, constricted, small, tiny, narrow; crowded, packed, congested; *archaic* strait. ❷ *cramped handwriting* SMALL, crabbed, illegible, unreadable, indecipherable.

– OPPOSITES spacious.

crane ▶ **noun** DERRICK, winch, hoist, davit, windlass; block and tackle.

cranium ▶ **noun** SKULL, head; *N. Amer. informal* brainpan.

crank[1] ▶ **verb** *you crank the engine by hand* START, turn (over), get going.

■ **crank something up** (*informal*) INCREASE, intensify, amplify, heighten, escalate, add to, augment, build up, expand, extend, raise; speed up, accelerate; *informal* up, jack up, hike up, step up, bump up, pump up.

crank[2] ▶ **noun** *they're nothing but a bunch of cranks* ECCENTRIC, oddity, madman/madwoman, lunatic; *informal* oddball, freak, weirdo, crackpot, loony, nut, nutcase, head case, maniac; *Brit. informal* nutter; *N. Amer. informal* screwball, kook.

cranky ▶ **adjective** ❶ (*informal*) *a cranky diet* ECCENTRIC, bizarre, weird, peculiar, odd, strange, unconventional, left-field, unorthodox, outlandish; silly, stupid, mad, crazy, idiotic; *informal* wacky, crackpot, nutty; *Brit. informal* daft, potty; *N. Amer. informal* wacko. ❷ (*N. Amer. informal*) *the children were tired and cranky.* See IRRITABLE.

cranny ▶ **noun** CHINK, crack, crevice, slit, split, fissure, rift, cleft, opening, gap, aperture, cavity, hole, hollow, niche, corner, nook, interstice.

crash ▶ **verb** ❶ *the car crashed into a tree* SMASH INTO, collide with, be in collision with, hit, strike, ram, cannon into, plough into, meet head-on, run into; *N. Amer.* impact. ❷ *he crashed his car* SMASH, wreck; *Brit.* write off; *Brit. informal* prang; *N. Amer. informal* total. ❸ *waves crashed against the shore* DASH, batter, pound, lash, slam, be hurled. ❹ *thunder crashed overhead* BOOM, crack, roll, clap, explode, bang, blast, blare, resound, reverberate, rumble, thunder, echo. ❺ (*informal*) *his clothing company crashed* COLLAPSE, fold, fail, go under, go bankrupt, become insolvent, cease trading, go into receivership, go into liquidation, be wound up; *informal* go broke, go bust, go to the wall, go belly up.

▶ **noun** ❶ *a crash on the motorway* ACCIDENT, collision, smash, road traffic accident, RTA; derailment; *N. Amer.* wreck; *informal* pile-up; *Brit. informal* prang, shunt. ❷ *a loud crash* BANG, smash, smack, crack, bump, thud, clatter, clunk, clonk, clang; report, detonation, explosion; noise, racket, clangour, din. ❸ *the crash of her company* COLLAPSE, failure, bankruptcy, insolvency, liquidation.

▶ **adjective** *a crash course* INTENSIVE, concentrated, rapid, short; accelerated-learning, total-immersion.

crass ▶ **adjective** STUPID, insensitive, mindless, thoughtless, witless, oafish, boorish, asinine, coarse, gross, graceless, tasteless, tactless, clumsy, heavy-handed, blundering; *informal* ignorant, pig-ignorant.

–OPPOSITES intelligent.

crate ▶ **noun** CASE, packing case, chest, tea chest, box; container, receptacle.

crater ▶ **noun** HOLLOW, bowl, basin, hole, cavity, depression; *Geology* caldera, maar, solfatara.

crave ▶ **verb** LONG FOR, yearn for, desire, want, wish for, hunger for, thirst for, sigh for, pine for, hanker after, covet, lust after, ache for, set one's heart on, dream of, be bent on; *informal* have a yen for, itch for, be dying for; *archaic* desiderate.

craven ▶ **adjective** COWARDLY, lily-livered, faint-hearted, chicken-hearted, spineless, timid, timorous, fearful, pusillanimous, weak, feeble; *informal* yellow, chicken, weak-kneed, gutless, yellow-bellied, wimpish; contemptible, abject, ignominious; *Brit. informal* wet; *archaic* recreant.

–OPPOSITES brave.

craving ▶ **noun** LONGING, yearning, desire, want, wish, hankering, hunger, thirst, appetite, greed, lust, ache, need, urge; *informal* yen, itch.

crawl ▶ **verb** ❶ *they crawled under the table* CREEP, worm one's way, go on all fours, go on hands and knees, wriggle, slither, squirm, scrabble. ❷ (*informal*) *I'm not going to go crawling to him* GROVEL TO, ingratiate oneself with, be obsequious to, kowtow to, pander to, toady to, truckle to, bow and scrape to, dance attendance on, curry favour with, make up to, fawn on/over; *informal* suck up to, lick someone's boots, butter up. ❸ *the place was crawling with soldiers* BE FULL OF, overflow with, teem with, be packed with, be crowded with, be alive with, be overrun with, swarm with, be bristling with, be infested with, be thick with; *informal* be lousy with, be stuffed with, be jam-packed with, be chock-a-block with, be chock-full of.

craze ▶ **noun** FAD, fashion, trend, vogue, enthusiasm, mania, passion, rage, obsession, compulsion, fixation, fetish, fancy, taste, fascination, preoccupation; *informal* thing.

crazed ▶ **adjective** MAD, insane, out of one's mind, deranged, demented, certifiable, lunatic, psychopathic; wild, raving, berserk, manic, maniac, frenzied; *informal* crazy, mental, off one's head, out of one's head, raving mad. *See also* CRAZY sense 1.

–OPPOSITES sane.

crazy ▶ **adjective** (*informal*) ❶ *a crazy old man* MAD, insane, out of one's mind, deranged, demented, not in one's right mind, crazed, lunatic, non compos mentis, unhinged, mad as a hatter, mad as a March hare; *informal* mental, off one's head, nutty (as a fruitcake), off one's rocker, not right in the head, round the bend, raving mad, bats, batty, bonkers, cuckoo, loopy, loony, bananas, loco, with a screw loose, touched, gaga, doolally, not all there, out to lunch, away with the fairies; *Brit. informal* barmy, crackers, barking, potty, round the twist, off one's trolley, not the full shilling; *N. Amer. informal* nutso, out of one's tree, meshuga, wacko, gonzo; *Austral./NZ informal* bushed. ❷ *a crazy idea* STUPID, foolish, idiotic, silly, absurd, ridiculous, ludicrous, preposterous, farcical, laughable, risible, nonsensical, imbecilic, hare-brained, half-baked, impracticable, unworkable, ill-conceived, senseless; *informal* cock-eyed; *Brit. informal* barmy, daft. ❸ *he's crazy about her* PASSIONATE ABOUT, very keen on, enamoured of, infatuated with, smitten with, devoted to; very enthusiastic about, fanatical about; *informal* wild/mad/nuts about, gone on; *Brit. informal* potty about.

–OPPOSITES sane, sensible, apathetic.

creak ▶ **verb** SQUEAK, grate, rasp; groan, complain.

cream ▶ **noun** ❶ *skin creams* LOTION, ointment, moisturizer, emollient, unguent, cosmetic; salve, rub, embrocation, balm, liniment. ❷ *the cream of the world's photographers* BEST, finest, pick, flower, crème de la crème, elite.
– OPPOSITES dregs.
▶ **adjective** *a cream dress* OFF-WHITE, whitish, cream-coloured, creamy, ivory, yellowish-white.

creamy ▶ **adjective** ❶ *a creamy paste* SMOOTH, thick, velvety, whipped; rich, buttery. ❷ *creamy flowers* OFF-WHITE, whitish, cream-coloured, cream, ivory, yellowish-white.
– OPPOSITES lumpy.

crease ▶ **noun** ❶ *trousers with knife-edge creases* FOLD, line, ridge; pleat, tuck; furrow, groove, corrugation. ❷ *the creases at the corners of her eyes* WRINKLE, line, crinkle, pucker; (**creases**) crow's feet.
▶ **verb** *her skirt was creased and stained* CRUMPLE, wrinkle, crinkle, line, scrunch up, rumple, ruck up.

create ▶ **verb** ❶ *she has created a work of stunning originality* PRODUCE, generate, bring into being, make, fabricate, fashion, build, construct; design, devise, originate, frame, develop, shape, form, forge. ❷ *regular socializing creates a good team spirit* BRING ABOUT, give rise to, lead to, result in, cause, breed, generate, engender, produce, make for, promote, foster, sow the seeds of, contribute to. ❸ *the governments planned to create a free-trade zone* ESTABLISH, found, initiate, institute, constitute, inaugurate, launch, set up, form, organize, develop. ❹ *she was created a life peer in 1990* APPOINT, make; invest as, install as.
– OPPOSITES destroy.

creation ▶ **noun** ❶ *the creation of a coalition government* ESTABLISHMENT, formation, foundation, initiation, institution, inauguration, constitution; production, generation, fabrication, fashioning, building, construction, origination, development. ❷ *the whole of creation* THE WORLD, the universe, the cosmos; the living world, the natural world, nature, life, living things. ❸ *Dickens's literary creations* WORK, work of art, production, opus, oeuvre; achievement.
– OPPOSITES destruction.

creative ▶ **adjective** INVENTIVE, imaginative, innovative, innovatory, experimental, original; artistic, expressive, inspired, visionary; enterprising, resourceful.

creativity ▶ **noun** INVENTIVENESS, imagination, imaginativeness, innovation, innovativeness, originality, individuality; artistry, inspiration, vision; enterprise, initiative, resourcefulness.

creator ▶ **noun** ❶ *the creator of the series* AUTHOR, writer, designer, deviser, maker, producer; originator, inventor, architect, mastermind, prime mover; *poetic/literary* begetter. ❷ *the Sabbath is kept to honour the Creator. See* GOD sense 1.

creature ▶ **noun** ❶ *the earth and its creatures* ANIMAL, beast, brute; living thing, living being; *N. Amer. informal* critter. ❷ *you're such a lazy creature!* PERSON, individual, human being, character, soul, wretch, customer; *informal* devil, beggar, sort, type; *Brit. informal* bod; *archaic* wight. ❸ *she was denounced as a creature of the liberals* LACKEY, minion, hireling, servant, puppet, tool, cat's paw, pawn; *informal* stooge, yes-man; *Brit. informal* poodle.

credence ▶ **noun** ❶ *the government placed little credence in the scheme* BELIEF, faith, trust, confidence, reliance. ❷ *later reports lent credence to this view* CREDIBILITY, plausibility; *archaic* credit.

credentials ▶ **plural noun** DOCUMENTS, documentation, papers, identity papers, bona fides, ID, ID card, identity card, passport, proof of identity; certificates, diplomas, certification.

credibility ▶ **noun** ❶ *the whole tale lacks credibility* PLAUSIBILITY, believability, tenability, probability, feasibility, likelihood, credence; authority, cogency; *archaic* credit. ❷ *the party lacked moral credibility* TRUSTWORTHINESS, reliability, dependability, integrity.

credible ▶ **adjective** BELIEVABLE, plausible, tenable, able to hold water, conceivable, likely, probable, possible, feasible, reasonable, with a ring of truth, persuasive.

credit ▶ **noun** ❶ *he never got much credit for the show's success* PRAISE, commendation, acclaim, acknowledgement, recognition, kudos, glory, esteem, respect, admiration, tributes, thanks, gratitude, appreciation; *informal* bouquets, brownie points. ❷ *the speech did his credit no good in the House of Commons* REPUTATION, repute, image, (good) name, character, prestige, standing, status, estimation, credibility. ❸ (*archaic*) *his theory has been given very little credit* CREDENCE, belief, faith, trust, reliance, confidence.
▶ **verb** ❶ *the wise will seldom credit all they hear* BELIEVE, accept, give credence to, trust, have faith in; *informal* buy, swallow, fall for, take something as gospel. ❷ *the scheme's success can be credited to the team's frugality* ASCRIBE, attribute, assign, accredit, chalk up, put down.
■ **on credit** ON HIRE PURCHASE, on (the) HP, by instalments, on account; *informal* on tick, on the slate; *Brit. informal* on the never-never.

creditable ▶ **adjective** COMMENDABLE, praiseworthy, laudable, admirable, honourable, estimable, meritorious, worthy, deserving, respectable.
– OPPOSITES deplorable.

credulous ▶ **adjective** GULLIBLE, naive, over-trusting, over-trustful, easily taken in, impressionable, unsuspecting, unsuspicious, unwary, unquestioning; innocent, ingenuous, inexperienced, unsophisticated, unworldly, wide-eyed; *informal* born yesterday, wet behind the ears.
– OPPOSITES suspicious.

creed ▶ **noun** ❶ *people of many creeds and cultures* FAITH, religion, religious belief, religious persuasion, Church, denomination, sect. ❷ *his political creed* SYSTEM OF BELIEF, (set of) beliefs, principles, articles of faith, ideology, credo, doctrine, teaching, dogma, tenets, canons.

creek ▶ **noun** INLET, arm of the sea, bay, estuary, bight, fjord, sound; *Scottish* firth, frith; (*in Orkney & Shetland*) voe.

creep ▶ **verb** ❶ *Tim crept out of the house* TIPTOE, steal, sneak, slip, slink, sidle, pad, edge, inch; skulk, prowl. ❷ (*informal*) *they're always creeping to the boss* GROVEL TO, ingratiate oneself with, curry favour with, toady to, truckle to, kowtow to, bow and scrape to, pander to, fawn on/over, make up to; *informal* crawl to, suck up to, lick someone's boots, butter up.

creeper ▶ **noun** CLIMBING PLANT, trailing plant; vine, climber, rambler.

creeps
■ **give someone the creeps** (*informal*) REPEL, repulse, revolt, disgust, sicken, nauseate, make someone's flesh creep, make someone's skin crawl; scare, frighten, terrify, horrify; *N. Amer. informal* gross out.

creepy ▶ **adjective** (*informal*) FRIGHTENING, eerie, disturbing, sinister, weird, hair-raising, menacing, threatening; *Scottish* eldritch; *informal* spooky, scary.

crescent ▶ **noun** HALF-MOON, sickle-shape, demilune, lunula, lunette; arc, curve, bow.

crest ▶ **noun** ❶ *the bird's crest* COMB, plume, tuft of feathers. ❷ *the crest of the hill* SUMMIT, peak, top, tip, pinnacle, brow, crown, apex. ❸ *the Duke of Wellington's crest* INSIGNIA, regalia, badge, emblem, heraldic device, coat of arms, arms; *Heraldry* bearing, charge.

crestfallen ▶ **adjective** DOWNHEARTED, downcast, despondent, disappointed, disconsolate, disheartened, discouraged, dispirited, dejected, depressed, desolate, in the doldrums, sad, glum, gloomy, dismayed, doleful, miserable, unhappy, woebegone, forlorn; *informal* blue, down in the mouth, down in the dumps.
– OPPOSITES cheerful.

crevasse ▶ **noun** CHASM, abyss, fissure, cleft, crack, split, breach, rift, hole, cavity.

crevice ▶ **noun** CRACK, fissure, cleft, chink, interstice, cranny, nook, slit, split, rift, fracture, breach; opening, gap, hole.

crew ▶ **noun** ❶ *the ship's crew* SAILORS, mariners, hands, ship's company, ship's complement. ❷ *a crew of cameramen and sound engineers* TEAM, group, company, unit, corps, party, gang. ❸ (*informal*) *a crew of inebriated locals* CROWD, group, band, gang, mob, pack, troop, swarm, herd, posse; *informal* bunch, gaggle.

crib ▶ **noun** ❶ *the baby's crib* COT, cradle, bassinet, Moses basket, carrycot. ❷ *the oxen's cribs* MANGER, stall, feeding trough, fodder rack.
▶ **verb** (*informal*) *she cribbed the plot from a Shakespeare play* COPY, plagiarize, poach, appropriate, steal, 'borrow'; *informal* rip off, lift; *Brit. informal* nick, pinch.

crick ▶ **verb** STRAIN, twist, rick, sprain, pull, wrench; injure, hurt, damage.

crime ▶ **noun** ❶ *kidnapping is a very serious crime* OFFENCE, unlawful act, illegal act, felony, misdemeanour, misdeed, wrong; *Law* tort. ❷ *the increase in crime* LAWBREAKING, delinquency, wrongdoing, criminality, misconduct, illegality, villainy; *informal* crookedness; *Law* malfeasance. ❸ *a crime against humanity* SIN, evil, immoral act, wrong, atrocity, abomination, disgrace, outrage.

criminal ▶ **noun** *a convicted criminal* LAWBREAKER, offender, villain, delinquent, felon, convict, malefactor, wrongdoer, culprit, miscreant; thief, burglar, robber, armed robber, gunman, gangster, terrorist; *informal* crook, con, jailbird, (old) lag; *N. Amer. informal* hood, yardbird; *Austral./NZ informal* crim; *Law* malfeasant.
▶ **adjective** ❶ *criminal conduct* UNLAWFUL, illegal, illicit, lawless, felonious, delinquent, fraudulent, actionable, culpable; villainous, nefarious, corrupt, wrong, bad, evil, wicked, iniquitous; *informal* crooked; *Brit. informal* bent; *Law* malfeasant. ❷ (*informal*) *a criminal waste of taxpayer's money* DEPLORABLE, shameful, reprehensible, disgraceful, inexcusable, unforgivable, unpardonable, outrageous, monstrous, shocking, scandalous, wicked.
– OPPOSITES lawful.

crimp ▶ **verb** PLEAT, flute, corrugate, ruffle, fold, crease, crinkle, pucker, gather; pinch, compress, press together, squeeze together.

crimped ▶ **adjective** *crimped blonde hair* CURLY, wavy, curled, frizzy, ringlety.

cringe ▶ **verb** ❶ *she cringed as he bellowed in her ear* COWER, shrink, recoil, shy away, flinch, blench, draw back; shake, tremble, quiver, quail, quake. ❷ *it makes me cringe when I think of it* WINCE, shudder, squirm, feel embarrassed/mortified.

crinkle ▶ **verb** WRINKLE, crease, pucker, furrow, corrugate, line; rumple, scrunch up, ruck up.

crinkly ▶ **adjective** WRINKLED, wrinkly, crinkled,

creased, crumpled, rumpled, crimped, corrugated, fluted, puckered, furrowed; wavy.

cripple ▶ verb ❶ *the accident crippled her* DISABLE, paralyse, immobilize, lame, incapacitate, handicap. ❷ *the company had been crippled by the recession* DEVASTATE, ruin, destroy, wipe out; paralyse, hamstring, bring to a standstill, put out of action, put out of business, bankrupt, break, bring someone to their knees.

crippled ▶ adjective DISABLED, paralysed, incapacitated, physically handicapped, lame, immobilized, bedridden, confined to a wheelchair; *euphemistic* physically challenged; *archaic* halt.

crisis ▶ noun ❶ *the situation had reached a crisis* CRITICAL POINT, turning point, crossroads, climacteric, head, moment of truth, zero hour, point of no return, Rubicon, doomsday; *informal* crunch. ❷ *the current economic crisis* EMERGENCY, disaster, catastrophe, calamity; predicament, plight, mess, trouble, dire straits, difficulty, extremity.

crisp ▶ adjective ❶ *crisp bacon* CRUNCHY, crispy, brittle, crumbly, friable, breakable; firm, dry. ❷ *a crisp autumn day* INVIGORATING, bracing, brisk, fresh, refreshing, exhilarating, tonic, energizing; cool, chill, chilly, cold; *informal* nippy; *Brit. informal* parky. ❸ *her answer was crisp* BRISK, decisive, businesslike, no-nonsense, incisive, to the point, matter of fact, brusque; terse, succinct, concise, brief, short, short and sweet, laconic; *informal* snappy. ❹ *crisp white bedlinen* SMOOTH, uncreased, ironed; starched.
– OPPOSITES soft, sultry, rambling.

criterion ▶ noun STANDARD, specification, measure, gauge, test, scale, benchmark, yardstick, touchstone, barometer; principle, rule, law, canon.

critic ▶ noun ❶ *a literary critic* REVIEWER, commentator, evaluator, analyst, judge, pundit. ❷ *critics of the government* DETRACTOR, attacker, fault-finder.

critical ▶ adjective ❶ *a highly critical report* CENSORIOUS, condemnatory, condemning, denunciatory, disparaging, disapproving, scathing, fault-finding, judgemental, negative, unfavourable; *informal* nit-picking, picky. ❷ *a critical essay* EVALUATIVE, analytical, interpretative, expository, explanatory. ❸ *the situation is critical* GRAVE, serious, dangerous, risky, perilous, hazardous, precarious, touch-and-go, in the balance, uncertain, parlous, desperate, dire, acute, life-and-death. ❹ *the choice of materials is critical for product safety* CRUCIAL, vital, essential, of the essence, all-important, paramount, fundamental, key, pivotal, decisive, deciding, climacteric.
– OPPOSITES complimentary, unimportant.

criticism ▶ noun ❶ *she was stung by his criticism* CENSURE, condemnation, denunciation, disapproval, disparagement, opprobrium, fault-finding, attack, broadside, brickbats, stricture, recrimination; *informal* flak, a bad press, panning; *Brit. informal* stick, slating; *formal* excoriation. ❷ *literary criticism* EVALUATION, assessment, appraisal, analysis, judgement; commentary, interpretation, explanation, explication, elucidation.

criticize ▶ verb FIND FAULT WITH, censure, denounce, condemn, attack, lambaste, pillory, rail against, inveigh against, arraign, cast aspersions on, pour scorn on, disparage, denigrate, give a bad press to, run down; *informal* knock, pan, slam, hammer, lay into, pull to pieces, pick holes in; *Brit. informal* slag off, slate, rubbish; *N. Amer. informal* pummel, trash; *Austral./NZ informal* bag, monster; *formal* excoriate.
– OPPOSITES praise.

critique ▶ noun ANALYSIS, evaluation, assessment, appraisal, appreciation, criticism, review, study, commentary, exposition, exegesis.

crock ▶ noun ❶ *a crock of honey* POT, jar; jug, pitcher, ewer; container, receptacle, vessel. ❷ (**crocks**) *a pile of dirty crocks. See* CROCKERY. ❸ (*informal*) *he's a bit of an old crock* INVALID, valetudinarian; geriatric, dotard; *informal* crumbly, wrinkly.

crockery ▶ noun DISHES, crocks, china, tableware; plates, bowls, cups, saucers.

crony ▶ noun (*informal*) FRIEND, companion, bosom friend, intimate, confidant(e), familiar, associate, comrade; *informal* pal, chum, sidekick; *Brit. informal* mate; *N. Amer. informal* buddy, amigo, compadre; *archaic* compeer.

crook ▶ noun ❶ (*informal*) *a small-time crook* CRIMINAL, lawbreaker, offender, villain, delinquent, felon, convict, malefactor, culprit, wrongdoer; rogue, scoundrel, cheat, swindler, racketeer, confidence trickster; thief, robber, burglar; *informal* (old) lag, shark, con man, con, jailbird; *N. Amer. informal* hood, yardbird; *Austral./NZ informal* crim; *Law* malfeasant. ❷ *the crook of a tree branch* BEND, fork, curve, angle.
▶ verb *he crooked his finger and called the waiter* COCK, flex, bend, curve, curl.

crooked ▶ adjective ❶ *narrow, crooked streets* WINDING, twisting, zigzag, meandering, tortuous, serpentine. ❷ *a crooked spine* BENT, twisted, misshapen, deformed, malformed, contorted, out of shape, wry, warped, bowed, distorted; *Scottish* thrawn. ❸ *the picture over the bed looked crooked* LOPSIDED, askew, awry, off-centre, uneven, out of true, out of line, asymmetrical, tilted, at an angle, aslant, slanting, squint; *Scottish* agley; *informal* cock-eyed; *Brit. informal* skew-whiff, wonky. ❹ (*informal*) *a crooked cop* | *crooked deals* DISHONEST, unscrupulous, unprin-

cipled, untrustworthy, corrupt, corruptible, buyable, venal; criminal, illegal, unlawful, nefarious, fraudulent; *Brit. informal* bent, dodgy.
– OPPOSITES straight, honest.

croon ▶ verb SING SOFTLY, hum, warble, trill.

crop ▶ noun ❶ *some farmers lost their entire crop* HARVEST, year's growth, yield; fruits, produce. ❷ *a bumper crop of mail* BATCH, lot, assortment, selection, collection, supply, intake. ❸ *the bird's crop* CRAW; gullet, throat. ❹ *a rider's crop* WHIP, switch, cane, stick.
▶ verb ❶ *she's had her hair cropped* CUT SHORT, cut, clip, shear, shave, lop off, chop off, hack off; dock. ❷ *a flock of sheep were cropping the turf* GRAZE ON, browse on, feed on, nibble, eat. ❸ *the hay was cropped several times this summer* HARVEST, reap, mow; gather (in), collect, pick, bring home.
■ **crop up** HAPPEN, occur, arise, turn up, spring up, pop up, emerge, materialize, surface, appear, come to light, present itself; *poetic/literary* come to pass, befall; *archaic* hap.

cross ▶ noun ❶ *a bronze cross* CRUCIFIX, rood. ❷ *we all have our crosses to bear* BURDEN, trouble, worry, trial, tribulation, affliction, curse, bane, misfortune, adversity, hardship, vicissitude; millstone, albatross, thorn in one's flesh/side; misery, woe, pain, sorrow, suffering; *informal* hassle, headache. ❸ *a cross between a yak and a cow* HYBRID, hybridization, cross-breed, half-breed, mongrel; mixture, amalgam, blend, combination.
▶ verb ❶ *they crossed the hills on foot* TRAVEL ACROSS, traverse, range over; negotiate, navigate, cover. ❷ *a lake crossed by a fine stone bridge* SPAN, bridge; extend/stretch across, pass over. ❸ *the point where the two roads cross* INTERSECT, meet, join, connect, criss-cross. ❹ *no one dared cross him* OPPOSE, resist, defy, obstruct, impede, hinder, hamper; contradict, argue with, quarrel with, stand up to, take a stand against, take issue with; *formal* gainsay. ❺ *the breed was crossed with the similarly coloured Friesian* HYBRIDIZE, cross-breed, interbreed, cross-fertilize, cross-pollinate.
▶ adjective *Jane was getting cross* ANGRY, annoyed, irate, irritated, in a bad mood, peeved, vexed, irked, piqued, out of humour, put out, displeased; irritable, short-tempered, bad-tempered, snappish, crotchety, grouchy, grumpy, fractious, testy, tetchy, crabby; *informal* mad, hot under the collar, riled, snappy, on the warpath, up in arms, steamed up, in a paddy; *Brit. informal* aerated, shirty, stroppy, ratty; *N. Amer. informal* sore, bent out of shape, teed off, ticked off; *Austral./NZ informal* ropeable, snaky, crook.
– OPPOSITES pleased.
■ **cross something out** DELETE, strike out, ink out, score out, edit out, blue-pencil, cancel, obliterate; *Printing* dele.

cross-examine ▶ verb INTERROGATE, question, cross-question, quiz, catechize, give someone the third degree; *informal* grill, pump, put someone through the wringer/mangle.

cross-grained ▶ adjective BAD-TEMPERED, cantankerous, irascible, grumpy, grouchy; awkward, perverse, contrary, uncooperative, unhelpful, obstructive, disobliging, recalcitrant, stubborn, obstinate, mulish, pigheaded, intractable; *informal* cussed; *Brit. informal* bloody-minded, bolshie, stroppy; *N. Amer. informal* balky; *formal* refractory.
– OPPOSITES good-humoured.

crossing ▶ noun ❶ *a busy road crossing* JUNCTION, crossroads, intersection, interchange; level crossing. ❷ *a short ferry crossing* JOURNEY, passage, voyage.

crosswise, crossways ▶ adverb DIAGONALLY, obliquely, transversely, aslant, cornerwise, at an angle, on the bias; *N. Amer.* catercornered, kitty-corner.

crotch ▶ noun GROIN, crutch; lap.

crotchet ▶ noun WHIM, whimsy, fancy, notion, vagary, caprice; foible, quirk, eccentricity; *archaic* megrim.

crotchety ▶ adjective BAD-TEMPERED, irascible, irritable, grumpy, grouchy, cantankerous, short-tempered, tetchy, testy, curmudgeonly, ill-tempered, ill-humoured, peevish, cross, fractious, pettish, waspish, crabbed, crabby, crusty, prickly, touchy; *informal* snappish, snappy, chippy; *Brit. informal* shirty, stroppy, narky, ratty; *N. Amer. informal* cranky, ornery; *Austral./NZ informal* snaky.
– OPPOSITES good-humoured.

crouch ▶ verb SQUAT, bend (down), hunker down, hunch over, stoop, kneel (down); duck, cower.

crow ▶ verb ❶ *a cock crowed* CRY, squawk, screech, caw. ❷ *try to avoid crowing about your success* BOAST, brag, trumpet, swagger, swank, gloat, show off, preen oneself, sing one's own praises; *informal* talk big, blow one's own trumpet, lay it on thick; *Austral./NZ informal* skite.

crowd ▶ noun ❶ *a crowd of people* THRONG, horde, mass, multitude, host, army, herd, flock, drove, swarm, sea, troupe, pack, press, crush, mob, rabble; collection, company, gathering, assembly, assemblage, congregation; *informal* gaggle, bunch, gang, posse; *archaic* rout. ❷ *she wanted to stand out from the crowd* MAJORITY, multitude, common people, populace, general public, masses, rank and file; *Brit. informal* Joe Public. ❸ *he's been hanging round with Hurley's crowd* SET, group, circle, clique, coterie; camp; *informal* gang, crew, lot. ❹ *the final attracted a capacity crowd* AUDIENCE, spectators, listeners, viewers; house, turnout, attendance, gate; congregation; *Brit. informal* punters.

▶ verb ❶ *reporters crowded round her* CLUSTER, flock, swarm, mill, throng, huddle, gather, assemble, congregate, converge. ❷ *the guests all crowded into the dining room* SURGE, push one's way, jostle, elbow one's way; squeeze, pile, cram. ❸ *the quayside was crowded with holidaymakers* THRONG, pack, jam, cram, fill. ❹ *stop crowding me* PRESSURIZE, pressure; harass, hound, pester, harry, badger, nag; *informal* hassle, lean on.

crowded ▶ adjective PACKED, full, filled to capacity, full to bursting, congested, overcrowded, overflowing, teeming, swarming, thronged, populous, overpopulated; busy; *informal* jam-packed, stuffed, chock-a-block, chock-full, bursting at the seams, full to the gunwales, wall-to-wall; *Austral./NZ informal* chocker.
– OPPOSITES deserted.

crown ▶ noun ❶ *a jewelled crown* CORONET, diadem, circlet; *poetic/literary* coronal; *historical* taj. ❷ *the world heavyweight crown* TITLE, award, accolade, distinction; trophy, cup, medal, plate, shield, belt, prize; laurels, bays, palm. ❸ *his family were loyal servants of the Crown* MONARCH, sovereign, king, queen, emperor, empress; monarchy, royalty; *informal* royals. ❹ *the crown of the hill* TOP, crest, summit, peak, pinnacle, tip, head, brow, apex.
▶ verb ❶ *David II was crowned in 1331* ENTHRONE, install; invest, induct. ❷ *a teaching post at Harvard crowned his career* ROUND OFF, cap, be the climax of, be the culmination of, top off, consummate, perfect, complete, put the finishing touch(es) to. ❸ *a steeple crowned by a gilded weathercock* TOP, cap, tip, head, surmount. ❹ (*informal*) *someone crowned him with a poker. See* HIT verb sense 1.

crucial ▶ adjective ❶ *negotiations were at a crucial stage* PIVOTAL, critical, key, climacteric, decisive, deciding; life-and-death. ❷ *confidentiality is crucial in this case* ALL-IMPORTANT, of the utmost importance, of the essence, critical, pre-eminent, paramount, essential, vital.
– OPPOSITES unimportant.

crucify ▶ verb ❶ *two thieves were crucified with Jesus* NAIL TO A CROSS; execute, put to death, kill. ❷ *she had been crucified by his departure* DEVASTATE, crush, shatter, cut to the quick, wound, pain, harrow, torture, torment, agonize. ❸ (*informal*) *the fans would crucify us if we lost. See* CRITICIZE.

crude ▶ adjective ❶ *crude oil* UNREFINED, unpurified, unprocessed, untreated; unmilled, unpolished; coarse, raw, natural. ❷ *a crude barricade* PRIMITIVE, simple, basic, homespun, rudimentary, rough, rough and ready, rough-hewn, make-do, makeshift, improvised, unfinished; *dated* rude. ❸ *crude jokes* VULGAR, rude, naughty, suggestive, bawdy, off colour, indecent, obscene, offensive, lewd, salacious, licentious, ribald, coarse, uncouth, indelicate, tasteless, crass, smutty, dirty, filthy, scatological; *informal* blue.
– OPPOSITES refined, sophisticated.

cruel ▶ adjective ❶ *a cruel man* BRUTAL, savage, inhuman, barbaric, barbarous, brutish, bloodthirsty, murderous, vicious, sadistic, wicked, evil, fiendish, diabolical, monstrous, abominable; callous, ruthless, merciless, pitiless, remorseless, uncaring, heartless, stony-hearted, hard-hearted, cold-blooded, cold-hearted, unfeeling, unkind, inhumane; *dated* dastardly; *poetic/literary* fell. ❷ *her death was a cruel blow* HARSH, severe, bitter, harrowing, heartbreaking, heart-rending, painful, agonizing, traumatic; *formal* grievous.
– OPPOSITES compassionate.

cruelty ▶ noun BRUTALITY, savagery, inhumanity, barbarity, barbarousness, brutishness, bloodthirstiness, viciousness, sadism, wickedness; callousness, ruthlessness, lack of compassion.

cruise ▶ noun *a cruise down the Nile* BOAT TRIP, sea trip; voyage, journey.
▶ verb ❶ *she cruised across the Atlantic* SAIL, voyage, journey. ❷ *a taxi cruised past* DRIVE SLOWLY, drift; *informal* mosey, tootle; *Brit. informal* pootle.

crumb ▶ noun FRAGMENT, bit, morsel, particle, speck, scrap, shred, sliver, atom, grain, trace, tinge, mite, iota, jot, whit, ounce, scintilla, soupçon; *informal* smidgen, tad.

crumble ▶ verb DISINTEGRATE, fall apart, fall to pieces, fall down, break up, collapse, fragment; decay, fall into decay, deteriorate, degenerate, go to rack and ruin, decompose, rot, moulder, perish.

crumbly ▶ adjective BRITTLE, breakable, friable, powdery, granular; short; crisp, crispy.

crumple ▶ verb ❶ *she crumpled the note in her fist* CRUSH, scrunch up, screw up, squash, squeeze; *Brit.* scrumple. ❷ *his trousers were dirty and crumpled* CREASE, wrinkle, crinkle, rumple, ruck up. ❸ *her resistance crumpled* COLLAPSE, give way, cave in, go to pieces, break down, crumble, be overcome.

crunch ▶ verb *she crunched the biscuit with relish* MUNCH, chomp, champ, scrunch, bite into.
▶ noun (*informal*) *when the crunch comes, she'll be forced to choose* MOMENT OF TRUTH, critical point, crux, crisis, decision time, zero hour, point of no return; showdown.

crusade ▶ noun ❶ *the medieval crusades* HOLY WAR; *Islam* jihad. ❷ *a crusade against crime* CAMPAIGN, drive, push, movement, effort, struggle; battle, war, offensive.
▶ verb *she likes crusading for the cause of the underdog* CAMPAIGN, fight, do battle, battle, take up arms, take up the cudgels, work, strive, struggle, agitate, lobby, champion, promote.

crusader ▶ **noun** CAMPAIGNER, fighter, champion, advocate; reformer.

crush ▶ **verb** ❶ *essential oils are released when the herbs are crushed* SQUASH, squeeze, press, compress; pulp, mash, macerate, mangle; flatten, trample on, tread on; *informal* squidge, splat; *N. Amer. informal* smush. ❷ *your dress will get crushed* CREASE, crumple, rumple, wrinkle, crinkle, scrunch up, ruck up; *Brit.* scrumple up. ❸ *crush the biscuits with a rolling pin* PULVERIZE, pound, grind, break up, smash, crumble; mill; *technical* triturate, comminute; *archaic* bray, levigate. ❹ *he crushed her in his arms* HUG, squeeze, hold tight, embrace, enfold. ❺ *the new regime crushed all popular uprisings* SUPPRESS, put down, quell, quash, stamp out, put an end to, overcome, overpower, defeat, triumph over, break, repress, subdue, extinguish. ❻ *Alan was crushed by her words* MORTIFY, humiliate, abash, chagrin, deflate, demoralize, flatten, squash; devastate, shatter, put someone in their place; *informal* shoot down in flames, cut down to size, knock the stuffing out of.

▶ **noun** ❶ *the crush of people* CROWD, throng, horde, swarm, sea, mass, pack, press, mob; *archaic* rout. ❷ (*informal*) *a teenage crush* INFATUATION, obsession, love, passion; *informal* pash, puppy love, calf love. ❸ *lemon crush* SQUASH, fruit juice, cordial, drink.

crust ▶ **noun** ❶ *a crust of ice* COVERING, layer, coating, cover, coat, sheet, thickness, film, skin, topping; incrustation, scab. ❷ (*informal*) *I'm just trying to earn an honest crust* LIVING, livelihood, income, daily bread, means of subsistence; *informal* bread and butter.

crusty ▶ **adjective** ❶ *crusty French bread* CRISP, crispy, well baked; crumbly, brittle, friable. ❷ *a crusty old man* IRRITABLE, cantankerous, irascible, bad-tempered, ill-tempered, grumpy, grouchy, crotchety, short-tempered, tetchy, testy, crabby, curmudgeonly, peevish, cross, fractious, pettish, crabbed, prickly, waspish, peppery, cross-grained; *informal* snappish, snappy, chippy; *Brit. informal* stroppy, narky, ratty; *N. Amer. informal* cranky, ornery; *Austral./NZ informal* snaky.

–OPPOSITES soft, good-natured.

crux ▶ **noun** NUB, heart, essence, central point, main point, core, centre, nucleus, kernel; *informal* the bottom line.

cry ▶ **verb** ❶ *Mandy started to cry* WEEP, shed tears, sob, wail, cry one's eyes out, bawl, howl, snivel, whimper, squall, mewl, bleat; lament, grieve, mourn, keen; *Scottish* greet; *informal* boohoo, blub, blubber, turn on the waterworks; *Brit. informal* grizzle; *poetic/literary* pule. ❷ *'Wait!' he cried* CALL, shout, exclaim, sing out, yell, shriek, scream, screech, bawl, bellow, roar, vociferate, squeal, yelp; *informal* holler; *dated* ejaculate.

–OPPOSITES laugh, whisper.

▶ **noun** ❶ *Leonora had a good cry* SOB, weep, crying fit. ❷ *a cry of despair* CALL, shout, exclamation, yell, shriek, scream, screech, bawl, bellow, roar, howl, yowl, squeal, yelp, interjection; *informal* holler; *dated* ejaculation. ❸ *fund-raisers have issued a cry for help* APPEAL, plea, entreaty, cry from the heart, cri de cœur.

■ **cry someone/something down** (*dated*) DISPARAGE, run down, belittle, make light of, denigrate, decry, deprecate, depreciate, play down, trivialize, minimize; *archaic* hold cheap.

■ **cry off** (*informal*) BACK OUT, pull out, cancel, withdraw, beg off, excuse oneself, change one's mind; *informal* get cold feet, cop out.

crypt ▶ **noun** TOMB, vault, mausoleum, burial chamber, sepulchre, catacomb, ossuary, undercroft.

cryptic ▶ **adjective** ENIGMATIC, mysterious, confusing, mystifying, perplexing, puzzling, obscure, abstruse, arcane, oracular, Delphic, ambiguous, elliptical, oblique; *informal* as clear as mud.

–OPPOSITES clear.

cub ▶ **noun** ❶ *a lioness and her cubs* (**cubs**) YOUNG, offspring, pups; *archaic* whelps. ❷ *a cub reporter* TRAINEE, apprentice, probationer, novice, tyro, learner, beginner; *N. Amer.* tenderfoot; *informal* rookie, newbie; *N. Amer. informal* greenhorn, probie.

–OPPOSITES veteran.

cubbyhole ▶ **noun** SMALL ROOM, booth, cubicle; den, snug; *N. Amer.* cubby.

cube ▶ **noun** ❶ *a shape that was neither a cube nor a sphere* HEXAHEDRON, cuboid, parallelepiped. ❷ *a cube of soap* BLOCK, lump, chunk, brick.

cuddle ▶ **verb** ❶ *she picked up the baby and cuddled her* HUG, embrace, clasp, hold tight, hold/fold in one's arms. ❷ *the pair were kissing and cuddling* EMBRACE, hug, caress, pet, fondle; *informal* canoodle, smooch; *informal, dated* spoon, bill and coo. ❸ *I cuddled up to him* SNUGGLE, nestle, curl, nuzzle, burrow against.

cuddly ▶ **adjective** HUGGABLE, cuddlesome; plump, curvaceous, rounded, buxom, soft, warm; attractive, endearing, lovable; *N. Amer. informal* zaftig.

cudgel ▶ **noun** *a thick wooden cudgel* CLUB, bludgeon, stick, truncheon, baton, blackthorn, shillelagh, mace; *Brit.* life preserver; *N. Amer.* blackjack, billy, nightstick; *Brit. informal* cosh.

▶ **verb** *she was cudgelled to death* BLUDGEON, club, beat, batter, bash; *Brit. informal* cosh.

cue ▶ **noun** SIGNAL, sign, indication, prompt, reminder; nod, word, gesture.

cuff ▶ **verb** *Cullam cuffed him on the head* HIT, strike, slap, smack, thump, beat, punch; *informal* clout, wallop, belt, whack, thwack, bash, clobber, bop, biff, sock; *Brit. informal* slosh; *N. Amer. informal* boff, slug; *archaic* smite.

■ **off the cuff** (*informal*) ❶ *an off-the-cuff remark* IMPROMPTU, extempore, ad lib; unrehearsed, unscripted, unprepared, improvised, spontaneous, unplanned. ❷ *I spoke off the cuff* WITHOUT PREPARATION, without rehearsal, impromptu, ad lib; *informal* off the top of one's head.

cuisine ▶ noun COOKING, cookery; haute cuisine, cordon bleu, nouvelle cuisine.

cul-de-sac ▶ noun NO THROUGH ROAD, blind alley, dead end.

cull ▶ verb ❶ *anecdotes culled from Greek history* SELECT, choose, pick, take, obtain, glean. ❷ *he sees culling deer as a necessity* SLAUGHTER, kill, destroy.

culminate ▶ verb *the festival culminated in a dramatic fire-walking ceremony* COME TO A CLIMAX, come to a head, peak, climax, reach a pinnacle; build up to, lead up to; end with, finish with, conclude with.

culmination ▶ noun CLIMAX, pinnacle, peak, high point, highest point, height, high water mark, top, summit, crest, zenith, crowning moment, apotheosis, apex, apogee; consummation, completion, finish, conclusion.
–OPPOSITES nadir.

culpable ▶ adjective TO BLAME, guilty, at fault, in the wrong, answerable, accountable, responsible, blameworthy, censurable.
–OPPOSITES innocent.

culprit ▶ noun GUILTY PARTY, offender, wrongdoer, miscreant; criminal, malefactor, lawbreaker, felon, delinquent; *informal* baddy, crook.

cult ▶ noun ❶ *a religious cult* SECT, denomination, group, movement, church, persuasion, body, faction. ❷ *the cult of youth in Hollywood* OBSESSION WITH, fixation on, mania for, passion for, idolization of, devotion to, worship of, veneration of.

cultivate ▶ verb ❶ *the peasants cultivated the land* TILL, plough, dig, hoe, farm, work, fertilize, mulch. ❷ *they were encouraged to cultivate basic food crops* GROW, raise, rear, plant, sow. ❸ *Tessa tried to cultivate her* WIN SOMEONE'S FRIENDSHIP, woo, court, pay court to, keep sweet, curry favour with, ingratiate oneself with; *informal* get in someone's good books, butter up, suck up to; *N. Amer. informal* shine up to. ❹ *he wants to cultivate his mind* IMPROVE, better, refine, elevate; educate, train, develop, enrich.

cultivated ▶ adjective CULTURED, educated, well read, civilized, enlightened, discerning, discriminating, refined, polished; sophisticated, urbane, cosmopolitan.

cultural ▶ adjective ❶ *cultural differences* ETHNIC, racial, folk; societal, lifestyle. ❷ *cultural achievements* AESTHETIC, artistic, intellectual; educational, edifying, civilizing.

culture ▶ noun ❶ *20th century popular culture* THE ARTS, the humanities, intellectual achievement; literature, music, painting, philosophy. ❷ *a man of culture* INTELLECTUAL/ARTISTIC AWARENESS, education, cultivation, enlightenment, discernment, discrimination, good taste, taste, refinement, polish, sophistication. ❸ *Afro-Caribbean culture* CIVILIZATION, society, way of life, lifestyle; customs, traditions, heritage, habits, ways, mores, values. ❹ *the culture of crops* CULTIVATION, farming; agriculture, husbandry, agronomy.

cultured ▶ adjective CULTIVATED, intellectually/artistically aware, artistic, enlightened, civilized, educated, well educated, well read, well informed, learned, knowledgeable, discerning, discriminating, refined, polished, sophisticated; *informal* arty.
–OPPOSITES ignorant.

culvert ▶ noun CHANNEL, conduit, watercourse, trough; drain, gutter.

cumbersome ▶ adjective ❶ *a cumbersome diving suit* UNWIELDY, unmanageable, awkward, clumsy, inconvenient, incommodious; bulky, large, heavy, hefty, weighty, burdensome; *informal* hulking, clunky. ❷ *cumbersome procedures* COMPLICATED, complex, involved, inefficient, unwieldy, slow.
–OPPOSITES manageable, straightforward.

cumulative ▶ adjective INCREASING, accumulative, growing, mounting; collective, aggregate, amassed; *Brit.* knock-on.

cunning ▶ adjective *a cunning scheme* CRAFTY, wily, artful, guileful, devious, sly, scheming, designing, calculating, Machiavellian; shrewd, astute, clever, canny; deceitful, deceptive, duplicitous; *informal* foxy; *archaic* subtle.
–OPPOSITES honest.
▶ noun *his political cunning* GUILE, craftiness, deviousness, slyness, trickery, duplicity; shrewdness, astuteness.

cup ▶ noun ❶ *a cup and saucer* teacup, coffee cup, demitasse; mug, beaker; *historical* chalice. ❷ *the winner was presented with a silver cup* TROPHY, award, prize.

cupboard ▶ noun CABINET, sideboard, dresser, armoire, credenza, buffet; *Brit.* chiffonier; *informal* glory hole.

Cupid ▶ noun EROS, the god of love; amoretto.

cupidity ▶ noun GREED, avarice, avariciousness, acquisitiveness, covetousness, rapacity, materialism, mercenariness, Mammonism; *informal* money-grubbing, an itching palm.
–OPPOSITES generosity.

cur ▶ noun ❶ *a mangy cur* MONGREL, tyke; *N. Amer.*

yellow dog; *NZ* kuri; *informal* mutt; *Austral. informal* mong, bitzer. ❷ (*informal*) *Neil was beginning to feel like a cur. See* SCOUNDREL.

curable ▶ **adjective** REMEDIABLE, treatable, medicable, operable.

curative ▶ **adjective** HEALING, therapeutic, medicinal, remedial, corrective, restorative, tonic, health-giving; *archaic* sanative.

curator ▶ **noun** CUSTODIAN, keeper, conservator, guardian, caretaker, steward.

curb ▶ **noun** *a curb on public spending* RESTRAINT, restriction, check, brake, rein, control, limitation, limit, constraint; *informal* crackdown; *poetic/literary* trammel.

▶ **verb** *he tried to curb his temper* RESTRAIN, hold back/in, keep back, repress, suppress, fight back, bite back, keep in check, check, control, rein in, contain, bridle, subdue; *informal* keep a/the lid on.

curdle ▶ **verb** CLOT, coagulate, congeal, solidify, thicken; turn, sour, ferment.

cure ▶ **verb** ❶ *he was cured of the disease* HEAL, restore to health, make well/better; *archaic* cleanse. ❷ *economic equality cannot cure all social ills* RECTIFY, remedy, put/set right, right, fix, mend, repair, heal, make better; solve, sort out, be the answer/solution to; eliminate, end, put an end to. ❸ *some farmers cured their own bacon* PRESERVE, smoke, salt, dry, pickle.

▶ **noun** ❶ *a cure for cancer* REMEDY, medicine, medication, medicament, antidote, antiserum; treatment, therapy; *archaic* physic. ❷ *interest rate cuts are not the cure for the problem* SOLUTION, answer, antidote, nostrum, panacea, cure-all; *informal* quick fix, magic bullet.

cure-all ▶ **noun** PANACEA, cure for all ills, sovereign remedy, heal-all, nostrum; *informal* magic bullet.

curio ▶ **noun** TRINKET, knick-knack, bibelot, ornament, bauble; objet d'art, collector's item, object of virtu, rarity, curiosity; *N. Amer.* kickshaw.

curiosity ▶ **noun** ❶ *his evasiveness roused my curiosity* INTEREST, spirit of inquiry, inquisitiveness. ❷ *the shop is a treasure trove of curiosities* ODDITY, curio, conversation piece, object of virtu, collector's item.

curious ▶ **adjective** ❶ *she was curious to know what had happened* INTRIGUED, interested, eager/dying to know, agog; inquisitive. ❷ *her curious behaviour* STRANGE, odd, peculiar, funny, unusual, bizarre, weird, eccentric, queer, unexpected, unfamiliar, extraordinary, abnormal, out of the ordinary, anomalous, surprising, incongruous, unconventional, unorthodox; *informal* offbeat; *Brit.* out of the common; *Scottish* unco; *Brit. informal* rum.

– OPPOSITES uninterested, ordinary.

curl ▶ **verb** ❶ *smoke curled up from his cigarette* SPIRAL, coil, wreathe, twirl, swirl; wind, curve, bend, twist (and turn), loop, meander, snake, corkscrew, zigzag. ❷ *Ruth curled her arms around his neck* WIND, twine, entwine, wrap. ❸ *she washed and curled my hair* CRIMP, perm, tong. ❹ *they curled up together on the sofa* NESTLE, snuggle, cuddle; *N. Amer.* snug down.

▶ **noun** ❶ *the tangled curls of her hair* RINGLET, corkscrew, kink; kiss-curl. ❷ *a curl of smoke* SPIRAL, coil, twirl, swirl, twist, corkscrew, curlicue, helix.

curly ▶ **adjective** WAVY, curling, curled, ringlety, crimped, permed, frizzy, kinky, corkscrew.

– OPPOSITES straight.

currency ▶ **noun** ❶ *foreign currency* MONEY, legal tender, cash, banknotes, notes, coins, coinage, specie; *N. Amer.* bills. ❷ *a term which has gained new currency* PREVALENCE, circulation, exposure; acceptance, popularity.

current ▶ **adjective** ❶ *current events* CONTEMPORARY, present-day, modern, present, contemporaneous; topical, in the news, live, burning. ❷ *the idea is still current* PREVALENT, prevailing, common, accepted, in circulation, circulating, on everyone's lips, popular, widespread. ❸ *a current driving licence* VALID, usable, up to date. ❹ *the current prime minister* INCUMBENT, present, in office, in power; reigning.

– OPPOSITES past, out of date, former.

▶ **noun** ❶ *a current of air* FLOW, stream, backdraught, slipstream; airstream, thermal, updraught, draught; undercurrent, undertow, tide. ❷ *the current of human life* COURSE, progress, progression, flow, tide, movement. ❸ *the current of opinion* TREND, drift, direction, tendency.

curriculum ▶ **noun** SYLLABUS, course/programme of study, subjects, modules.

curse ▶ **noun** ❶ *she put a curse on him* MALEDICTION, the evil eye; *N. Amer.* hex; *Irish* cess; *informal* jinx; *formal* imprecation; *poetic/literary* anathema. ❷ *the curse of racism* EVIL, blight, scourge, plague, cancer, canker, poison. ❸ *the curse of unemployment* AFFLICTION, burden, cross to bear, bane. ❹ *muffled curses* SWEAR WORD, expletive, oath, profanity, four-letter word, dirty word, obscenity, blasphemy; *informal* cuss, cuss word; *formal* imprecation.

▶ **verb** ❶ *it seemed as if the family had been cursed* PUT A CURSE ON, put the evil eye on, hoodoo, anathematize, damn; *N. Amer.* hex; *informal* jinx; *archaic* imprecate. ❷ *she was cursed with feelings of inadequacy* AFFLICT, trouble, plague, bedevil. ❸ *drivers cursed and sounded their horns* SWEAR, blaspheme, take the Lord's name in vain; *informal* cuss, turn the air blue, eff and blind; *archaic* execrate.

cursed ▶ **adjective** ❶ *a cursed city* UNDER A

CURSE, damned, doomed, ill-fated, ill-starred; *informal* jinxed; *poetic/literary* accursed, star-crossed. ❷ (*informal, dated*) *those cursed children.* *See* ANNOYING.

cursory ▶ **adjective** PERFUNCTORY, desultory, casual, superficial, token; hasty, quick, hurried, rapid, brief, passing, fleeting.
– OPPOSITES thorough.

curt ▶ **adjective** TERSE, brusque, abrupt, clipped, blunt, short, monosyllabic, summary; snappish, sharp, tart; gruff, offhand, unceremonious, ungracious, rude, impolite, discourteous, uncivil; *informal* snappy.
– OPPOSITES expansive.

curtail ▶ **verb** ❶ *economic policies designed to curtail spending* REDUCE, cut, cut down, decrease, lessen, pare down, trim, retrench; restrict, limit, curb, rein in/back; *informal* slash. ❷ *his visit was curtailed* SHORTEN, cut short, truncate.
– OPPOSITES increase, lengthen.

curtain ▶ **noun** *he drew the curtains* WINDOW HANGING, screen, blind; *N. Amer.* drape.
▶ **verb** *the bed was curtained off from the rest of the room* CONCEAL, hide, screen, shield; separate, isolate.

curtsy ▶ **verb** *she curtsied to the king* BEND ONE'S KNEE, drop/bob a curtsy, genuflect.
▶ **noun** *she made a curtsy* BOB, genuflection, obeisance.

curvaceous ▶ **adjective** SHAPELY, voluptuous, sexy, full-figured, buxom, full-bosomed, bosomy, Junoesque; cuddly; *informal* curvy, well endowed, pneumatic, busty; *archaic* comely.
– OPPOSITES skinny.

curve ▶ **noun** *the serpentine curves of the river* BEND, turn, loop, curl, twist, hook; arc, arch, bow, half-moon, undulation, curvature.
– RELATED TERMS sinuous.
▶ **verb** *the road curved back on itself* BEND, turn, loop, wind, meander, undulate, snake, spiral, twist, coil, curl; arc, arch.

curved ▶ **adjective** BENT, arched, bowed, crescent, curving, wavy, sinuous, serpentine, meandering, undulating, curvilinear, curvy.
– OPPOSITES straight.

cushion ▶ **noun** *a cushion against inflation* PROTECTION, buffer, shield, defence, bulwark.
▶ **verb** ❶ *she cushioned her head on her arms* SUPPORT, cradle, prop (up), rest. ❷ *to cushion the blow, wages and pensions were increased* SOFTEN, lessen, diminish, decrease, mitigate, temper, allay, alleviate, take the edge off, dull, deaden. ❸ *residents are cushioned from the outside world* PROTECT, shield, shelter, cocoon.

cushy ▶ **adjective** (*informal*) *a cushy job* EASY, undemanding; comfortable, secure; *Brit. informal* jammy.
– OPPOSITES difficult.

custodian ▶ **noun** CURATOR, keeper, conservator, guardian, overseer, superintendent; caretaker, steward, protector.

custody ▶ **noun** *the parent who has custody of the child* CARE, guardianship, charge, keeping, safe keeping, wardship, responsibility, protection, tutelage; custodianship, trusteeship; *archaic* ward.
■ **in custody** IN PRISON, in jail, imprisoned, incarcerated, locked up, under lock and key, interned, detained; on remand; *informal* behind bars, doing time, inside; *Brit. informal* banged up.

custom ▶ **noun** ❶ *his unfamiliarity with the local customs* TRADITION, practice, usage, observance, way, convention, formality, ceremony, ritual; shibboleth, sacred cow, unwritten rule; mores; *formal* praxis. ❷ *it is our custom to visit the Lake District in October* HABIT, practice, routine, way, wont; policy, rule. ❸ (*Brit.*) *if you keep me waiting I will take my custom elsewhere* BUSINESS, patronage, trade.

customarily ▶ **adverb** USUALLY, traditionally, normally, as a rule, generally, ordinarily, commonly; habitually, routinely.
– OPPOSITES occasionally.

customary ▶ **adjective** ❶ *customary social practices* USUAL, traditional, normal, conventional, familiar, accepted, routine, established, time-honoured, regular, prevailing. ❷ *her customary good sense* USUAL, accustomed, habitual, wonted.
– OPPOSITES unusual.

customer ▶ **noun** CONSUMER, buyer, purchaser, patron, client; shopper; *Brit. informal* punter.

customs ▶ **plural noun**. *See* TAX noun sense 1.

cut ▶ **verb** ❶ *the knife slipped and cut his finger* GASH, slash, lacerate, sever, slit, pierce, penetrate, wound, injure; scratch, graze, nick, snick, incise, score; lance. ❷ *cut the pepper into small pieces* CHOP, cut up, slice, dice, cube, mince; carve; *N. Amer.* hash. ❸ *cut back the new growth to about half its length* TRIM, snip, clip, crop, barber, shear, shave; pare; prune, pollard, poll, lop, dock; mow. ❹ *I went to cut some flowers* PICK, pluck, gather; *poetic/literary* cull. ❺ *lettering had been cut into the stonework* CARVE, engrave, incise, etch, score; chisel, whittle. ❻ *the government cut public expenditure* REDUCE, cut back/down on, decrease, lessen, retrench, trim, slim down; rationalize, downsize, slenderize; mark down, discount, lower; *informal* slash. ❼ *the text has been substantially cut* SHORTEN, abridge, condense, abbreviate, truncate; edit; bowdlerize, expurgate. ❽ *you need to cut at least ten lines per page* DELETE, remove, take out, excise, blue-pencil. ❾ *oil supplies to the area had been cut* DISCONTINUE, break off, suspend, interrupt; stop, end, put an end to. ❿ *the point where the line cuts the vertical axis* CROSS, intersect, bisect; meet, join. ⓫ (*dated*) *the bank-*

er's wife cut her at church SNUB, ignore, shun, give someone the cold shoulder, cold-shoulder, cut dead, look right through, rebuff, turn one's back on; *informal* freeze out.

▶ **noun** ❶ *a cut on his jaw* GASH, slash, laceration, incision, wound, injury; scratch, graze, nick, snick. ❷ *a cut of beef* JOINT, piece, section. ❸ (*informal*) *the directors are demanding their cut* SHARE, portion, bit, quota, percentage; *informal* slice of the cake, rake-off, piece of the action; *Brit. informal* whack. ❹ *his hair was in need of a cut* HAIRCUT, trim, clip, crop. ❺ *a smart cut of the whip* BLOW, slash, stroke. ❻ *he followed this with the unkindest cut of all* INSULT, slight, affront, slap in the face, jibe, barb, cutting remark; *informal* put-down, dig. ❼ *a cut in interest rates* REDUCTION, cutback, decrease, lessening; *N. Amer.* rollback. ❽ *the elegant cut of his jacket* STYLE, design; tailoring, lines, fit.

■ **cut back** *companies cut back on foreign investment* REDUCE, cut, cut down on, decrease, lessen, retrench, economize on, trim, slim down, scale down; rationalize, downsize, pull/draw in one's horns, tighten one's belt; *informal* slash.

■ **cut someone/something down** ❶ *24 hectares of trees were cut down* FELL, chop down, hack down, saw down, hew. ❷ *he was cut down in his prime* KILL, slaughter, shoot down, mow down, gun down; *informal* take out, blow away; *poetic/*literary slay.

■ **cut and dried** DEFINITE, decided, settled, explicit, specific, precise, unambiguous, clear-cut, unequivocal, black and white, hard and fast.

■ **cut in** INTERRUPT, butt in, break in, interject, interpose, chime in; *Brit. informal* chip in.

■ **cut someone/something off** ❶ *they cut off his finger* SEVER, chop off, hack off; amputate. ❷ *oil and gas supplies were cut off* DISCONTINUE, break off, disconnect, suspend; stop, end, bring to an end. ❸ *a community cut off from the mainland by the flood waters* ISOLATE, separate, keep apart; seclude, closet, cloister, sequester.

■ **cut out** STOP WORKING, stop, fail, give out, break down; *informal* die, give up the ghost, conk out; *Brit. informal* pack up.

■ **cut someone/something out** ❶ *cut out all the diseased wood* REMOVE, take out, excise, extract; snip out, clip out. ❷ *it's best to cut out alcohol altogether* GIVE UP, refrain from, abstain from, go without; *informal* quit, leave off, pack in, lay off, knock off. ❸ *his mother cut him out of her will* EXCLUDE, leave out, omit, eliminate.

■ **cut something short** BREAK OFF, shorten, truncate, curtail, terminate, end, stop, abort, bring to an untimely end.

■ **cut someone short** INTERRUPT, cut off, butt in on, break in on.

cutback ▶ **noun** REDUCTION, cut, decrease; economy, saving; *N. Amer.* rollback.
– OPPOSITES increase.

cute ▶ **adjective** ENDEARING, adorable, lovable, sweet, lovely, appealing, engaging, delightful, dear, darling, winning, winsome, attractive, pretty; *informal* cutesy, twee; *Brit. informal* dinky.

cut-price ▶ **adjective** CHEAP, marked down, reduced, on (special) offer, discount; *N. Amer.* cut-rate.

cut-throat ▶ **noun** (*dated*) *a band of robbers and cut-throats* MURDERER, killer, assassin; *informal* hit-man; *dated* homicide.

▶ **adjective** *cut-throat competition between rival firms* RUTHLESS, merciless, fierce, intense, aggressive, dog-eat-dog.

cutting ▶ **noun** ❶ *a newspaper cutting* CLIPPING, clip, snippet; article, piece, column, paragraph. ❷ *plant cuttings* SCION, slip; graft. ❸ *fabric cuttings* PIECE, bit, fragment; trimming.

▶ **adjective** ❶ *a cutting remark* HURTFUL, wounding, barbed, pointed, scathing, acerbic, mordant, caustic, acid, sarcastic, sardonic, snide, spiteful, malicious, mean, nasty, cruel, unkind; *informal* bitchy, catty; *Brit. informal* sarky; *N. Amer. informal* snarky. ❷ *cutting winter winds* ICY, icy-cold, freezing, arctic, Siberian, glacial, bitter, chilling, chilly, chill; biting, piercing, penetrating, raw, keen, sharp.
– OPPOSITES friendly, warm.

cut up ▶ **adjective** (*informal*) *he's pretty cut up about it. See* UPSET adjective sense 1.

cycle ▶ **noun** ❶ *the cycle of birth, death, and rebirth* ROUND, rotation; pattern, rhythm. ❷ *the painting is one of a cycle of seven* SERIES, sequence, succession, run; set. ❸ *cycles may be hired from the station. See* BICYCLE.

cyclical ▶ **adjective** RECURRENT, recurring, regular, repeated; periodic, seasonal, circular.

cyclone ▶ **noun** HURRICANE, typhoon, tropical storm, storm, tornado, windstorm, whirlwind, tempest; *Austral.* willy-willy; *N. Amer. informal* twister.

cynic ▶ **noun** SCEPTIC, doubter, doubting Thomas; pessimist, prophet of doom, doomsayer, Cassandra; *informal* doom (and gloom) merchant.
– OPPOSITES idealist.

cynical ▶ **adjective** SCEPTICAL, doubtful, distrustful, suspicious, disbelieving; pessimistic, negative, world-weary, disillusioned, disenchanted, jaundiced, sardonic.
– OPPOSITES idealistic.

cynicism ▶ **noun** SCEPTICISM, doubt, distrust, mistrust, suspicion, disbelief; pessimism, negativity, world-weariness, disenchantment.
– OPPOSITES idealism.

cyst ▶ **noun** GROWTH, lump; abscess, wen, boil, carbuncle.

Dd

dab ▶ verb *she dabbed disinfectant on the cut* PAT, press, touch, blot, mop, swab; daub, apply, wipe, stroke.
▶ noun ❶ *a dab of glue* DROP, spot, smear, splash, speck, taste, trace, touch, hint, bit; *informal* smidgen, tad, lick. ❷ *apply concealer with light dabs* PAT, touch, blot, wipe.

dabble ▶ verb ❶ *they dabbled their feet in rock pools* SPLASH, dip, paddle, trail; immerse. ❷ *he dabbled in politics* TOY WITH, dip into, flirt with, tinker with, trifle with, play with, dally with.

dabbler ▶ noun AMATEUR, dilettante, layman, layperson; tinkerer, trifler.
– OPPOSITES professional.

daemon ▶ noun NUMEN, genius (loci), attendant spirit, tutelary spirit.

daft ▶ adjective (*Brit. informal*) ❶ *a daft idea* ABSURD, preposterous, ridiculous, ludicrous, farcical, laughable; idiotic, stupid, foolish, silly, inane, fatuous, hare-brained, half-baked; *informal* crazy, cock-eyed; *Brit. informal* barmy. ❷ *are you daft?* SIMPLE-MINDED, stupid, idiotic, slow, witless, feeble-minded, empty-headed, vacuous, vapid; unhinged, insane, mad; *informal* thick, dim, dopey, dumb, dim-witted, half-witted, birdbrained, pea-brained, slow on the uptake, soft in the head, brain-dead, not all there, touched, crazy, mental, nuts, batty, bonkers; *Brit. informal* potty, not the full shilling, barmy, crackers; *N. Amer. informal* dumb-ass. ❸ *she's daft about him* INFATUATED WITH, enamoured of, smitten with, besotted by, very fond of; *informal* crazy, mad, nuts; *Brit. informal* potty; *informal, dated* sweet on.
– OPPOSITES sensible.

daily ▶ adjective *a daily event* EVERYDAY, day-to-day, quotidian, diurnal, circadian.
▶ adverb *the museum is open daily* EVERY DAY, once a day, day after day, diurnally.

dainty ▶ adjective ❶ *a dainty china cup* DELICATE, fine, neat, elegant, exquisite; *Brit. informal* dinky. ❷ *a dainty morsel* TASTY, delicious, choice, palatable, luscious, mouth-watering, delectable, toothsome; appetizing, inviting, tempting; *informal* scrumptious, yummy, scrummy, finger-licking, moreish. ❸ *a dainty eater* FASTIDIOUS, fussy, finicky, finical, faddish; particular, discriminating; *informal* choosy, pernickety, picky; *Brit. informal* faddy.
– OPPOSITES unwieldy, unpalatable, undiscriminating.
▶ noun *home-made dainties* DELICACY, titbit, fancy, luxury, treat; nibble, savoury, appetizer, confection, bonbon; *informal* goody; *archaic* sweetmeat.

dais ▶ noun PLATFORM, stage, podium, rostrum, stand, apron; soapbox, stump.

dale ▶ noun VALLEY, vale; hollow, basin, gully, gorge, ravine; *Brit.* dene, combe; *N. English* clough; *Scottish* glen, strath; *poetic/literary* dell.

dally ▶ verb ❶ *don't dally on the way to work* DAWDLE, delay, loiter, linger, waste time; lag, trail, straggle, fall behind; amble, meander, drift; *informal* dilly-dally; *archaic* tarry. ❷ *he likes dallying with film stars* TRIFLE, toy, amuse oneself, flirt, play fast and loose, philander, carry on; *informal* play around.
– OPPOSITES hurry.

dam ▶ noun *the dam burst* BARRAGE, barrier, wall, embankment, barricade, obstruction.
▶ verb *the river was dammed* BLOCK (UP), obstruct, bung up, close; *technical* occlude.

damage ▶ noun ❶ *did the thieves do any damage?* HARM, destruction, vandalism; injury, impairment, desecration, vitiation, detriment; ruin, havoc, devastation. ❷ (*informal, humorous*) *what's the damage?* COST, price, expense, charge, total. ❸ *she won £4,300 damages* COMPENSATION, recompense, restitution, redress, reparation(s); indemnification, indemnity; *N. Amer. informal* comp.
▶ verb *the parcel had been damaged* HARM, deface, mutilate, mangle, impair, injure, disfigure, vandalize; tamper with, sabotage; ruin, destroy, wreck; *N. Amer. informal* trash; *formal* vitiate.
– OPPOSITES repair.

damaging ▶ adjective HARMFUL, detrimental, injurious, hurtful, inimical, dangerous, destructive, ruinous, deleterious; bad, malign, adverse, undesirable, prejudicial, unfavourable; unhealthy, unwholesome.
– OPPOSITES beneficial.

damn ▶ verb ❶ *they were all were damning him* CURSE, put the evil eye on, hoodoo; anathematize; *N. Amer.* hex; *informal* jinx; *archaic* imprecate. ❷ *we are not going to damn the new product* CONDEMN, censure, criticize, attack, denounce, revile; find fault with, give something a bad press, deprecate, disparage; *informal* slam, lay into, blast; *Brit. informal* slate, slag off, have a go at.
– OPPOSITES bless, praise.
▶ noun (*informal*) *I don't care a damn* JOT, whit, iota, rap, scrap, bit; *informal* hoot, two hoots.

damnable ▶ adjective ❶ *a damnable nuisance* UNPLEASANT, disagreeable, objectionable, horrible, horrid, awful, nasty, dreadful, terrible; annoying, irritating, maddening, exasperating; hateful, detestable, loathsome, abominable; *Brit. informal* beastly. ❷ *suicide was thought damnable* SINFUL, wicked, evil, iniquitous, heinous, base, execrable.

damnation ▶ noun CONDEMNATION TO HELL, eternal punishment, perdition, doom, hellfire; curse, anathema; *N. Amer.* hex; *formal* imprecation; *archaic* execration.

damned ▶ adjective ❶ *damned souls* CURSED, doomed, lost, condemned to hell; anathematized; *poetic/literary* accursed. ❷ (*informal*) *this damned car won't start* BLASTED, damn, damnable, flaming, confounded, rotten, wretched; *Brit. informal* blessed, flipping, blinking, blooming, bloody, bleeding, ruddy; *dated* accursed.

damning ▶ adjective INCRIMINATING, condemnatory, damnatory; damaging, derogatory; conclusive, strong.

damp ▶ adjective *her hair was damp* MOIST, moistened, wettish, dampened, dampish; humid, steamy, muggy, clammy, sweaty, sticky, dank, moisture-laden, wet, wetted, rainy, drizzly, showery, misty, foggy, vaporous, dewy.
– OPPOSITES dry.

▶ noun *the damp in the air* MOISTURE, dampness, humidity, wetness, wet, water, condensation, steam, vapour; clamminess, dankness; rain, dew, drizzle, precipitation, spray; perspiration, sweat.
– OPPOSITES dryness.

▶ verb ❶ *sweat damped his hair. See* DAMPEN sense 1. ❷ *nothing damped my enthusiasm. See* DAMPEN sense 2.

dampen ▶ verb ❶ *the rain dampened her face* MOISTEN, damp, wet, dew, water; *poetic/literary* bedew. ❷ *nothing could dampen her enthusiasm* LESSEN, decrease, diminish, reduce, moderate, damp, put a damper on, throw cold water on, cool, discourage; suppress, extinguish, quench, stifle, curb, limit, check, restrain, inhibit, deter.
– OPPOSITES dry, heighten.

damper ▶ noun CURB, check, restraint, restriction, limit, limitation, constraint, rein, brake, control, impediment; chill, pall, gloom.

dampness ▶ noun. *See* DAMP noun.

damsel ▶ noun (*poetic/literary*). *See* GIRL sense 2.

dance ▶ verb ❶ *he danced with her* sway, trip, twirl, whirl, pirouette, gyrate; *informal* bop, disco, shake a leg, hoof it, cut a rug, trip the light fantastic; *N. Amer. informal* get down. ❷ *little girls danced round me* CAPER, cavort, frisk, frolic, skip, prance, gambol, jig; leap, jump, hop, bounce. ❸ *flames danced in the fireplace* FLICKER, leap, dart, play, flit, quiver; twinkle, shimmer.

▶ noun *the school dance* BALL, discotheque; masquerade; *N. Amer.* prom, hoedown; *informal* disco, hop, bop.

dancer ▶ noun danseur, danseuse; *informal* bopper, hoofer.

dandle ▶ verb BOUNCE, jiggle, dance, rock.

dandy ▶ noun *he became something of a dandy* FOP, man about town, bright young thing, glamour boy, rake; *informal* sharp dresser, snappy dresser, trendy, dude, pretty boy; *informal, dated* swell; *dated* beau; *archaic* buck, coxcomb, popinjay.

▶ adjective (*N. Amer. informal*) *our trip was dandy. See* EXCELLENT.

danger ▶ noun ❶ *an element of danger* PERIL, hazard, risk, jeopardy; perilousness, riskiness, precariousness, uncertainty, instability, insecurity. ❷ *he is a danger to society* MENACE, hazard, threat, risk. ❸ *a serious danger of fire* POSSIBILITY, chance, risk, probability, likelihood, fear, prospect.
– OPPOSITES safety.

dangerous ▶ adjective ❶ *a dangerous animal* MENACING, threatening, treacherous; savage, wild, vicious, murderous, desperate; *rare* minacious. ❷ *dangerous wiring* HAZARDOUS, perilous, risky, high-risk, unsafe, unpredictable, precarious, insecure, touch-and-go, chancy, treacherous; *informal* dicey, hairy; *Brit. informal* dodgy.
– OPPOSITES harmless, safe.

dangle ▶ verb ❶ *a chain dangled from his belt* HANG (DOWN), droop, swing, sway, wave, trail, stream. ❷ *he dangled the keys* WAVE, swing, jiggle, brandish, flourish. ❸ *he dangled money in front of the locals* OFFER, hold out; entice someone with, tempt someone with.

dangling ▶ adjective HANGING, drooping, droopy, suspended, pendulous, pendent, trailing, flowing, tumbling.

dank ▶ adjective DAMP, musty, chilly, clammy, moist, wet, unaired, humid.
– OPPOSITES dry.

dapper ▶ adjective SMART, spruce, trim, debonair, neat, well dressed, well groomed, well turned out, elegant, chic, dashing; *informal* snazzy, snappy, natty, sharp; *N. Amer. informal* spiffy, fly.
– OPPOSITES scruffy.

dapple ▶ verb DOT, spot, fleck, streak, speck, speckle, mottle, marble.

dappled ▶ adjective SPECKLED, blotched, blotchy, spotted, spotty, dotted, mottled, marbled, flecked, freckled; piebald, pied, brindle, pinto, tabby; patchy, variegated; *informal* splotchy, splodgy.

dare ▶ verb ❶ *nobody dared to say a word* BE BRAVE ENOUGH, have the courage; venture, have the nerve, have the temerity, be so bold as, have the audacity; risk, hazard, take the liberty of; *N. Amer.* take a flyer; *informal* stick one's neck out, go out on a limb. ❷ *she dared* *him to go* CHALLENGE, defy, invite, bid, provoke, goad; throw down the gauntlet.

▶ **noun** *she accepted the dare* CHALLENGE, provocation, goad; gauntlet, invitation.

daredevil ▶ **noun** *a young daredevil crashed his car* MADCAP, hothead, adventurer, exhibitionist, swashbuckler; stuntman; *Brit.* tearaway; *informal* show-off.

▶ **adjective** *a daredevil skydiver* DARING, bold, audacious, intrepid, fearless, madcap, death-or-glory, dauntless; heedless, reckless, rash, impulsive, impetuous, foolhardy, incautious, imprudent; *Brit.* tearaway, harum-scarum.

– OPPOSITES cowardly, cautious.

daring ▶ **adjective** *a daring attack* BOLD, audacious, intrepid, venturesome, fearless, brave, unafraid, undaunted, dauntless, valiant, valorous, heroic, dashing; madcap, rash, reckless, heedless; *informal* gutsy, spunky.

▶ **noun** *his sheer daring* BOLDNESS, audacity, temerity, fearlessness, intrepidity, bravery, courage, valour, heroism, pluck, spirit, mettle; recklessness, rashness, foolhardiness; *informal* nerve, guts, spunk, grit; *Brit. informal* bottle; *N. Amer. informal* moxie, sand.

dark ▶ **adjective** ❶ *a dark night* BLACK, pitch-black, jet-black, inky; unlit, unilluminated; starless, moonless; dingy, gloomy, dusky, shadowy, shady; *poetic/literary* Stygian. ❷ *a dark secret* MYSTERIOUS, secret, hidden, concealed, veiled, covert, clandestine; enigmatic, arcane, esoteric, obscure, abstruse, impenetrable, incomprehensible, cryptic. ❸ *dark hair* BRUNETTE, dark brown, chestnut, sable, jet-black, ebony. ❹ *dark skin* SWARTHY, dusky, olive, black, ebony; tanned, bronzed. ❺ *dark days* TRAGIC, disastrous, calamitous, catastrophic, cataclysmic; dire, awful, terrible, dreadful, horrible, horrendous, atrocious, nightmarish, harrowing; wretched, woeful. ❻ *dark thoughts* GLOOMY, dismal, pessimistic, negative, downbeat, bleak, grim, fatalistic, black, sombre; despairing, despondent, hopeless, cheerless, melancholy, glum, grave, morose, mournful, doleful. ❼ *a dark look* MOODY, brooding, sullen, dour, scowling, glowering, angry, forbidding, threatening, ominous. ❽ *dark deeds* EVIL, wicked, sinful, immoral, bad, iniquitous, ungodly, unholy, base; vile, unspeakable, foul, monstrous, shocking, atrocious, abominable, hateful, despicable, odious, horrible, heinous, execrable, diabolical, fiendish, murderous, barbarous, black; sordid, degenerate, depraved; dishonourable, dishonest, unscrupulous; *informal* low-down, dirty, crooked, shady.

– OPPOSITES bright, blonde, pale, happy, good.

▶ **noun** ❶ *he's afraid of the dark* DARKNESS, blackness, gloom, murkiness, shadow, shade; dusk, twilight, gloaming. ❷ *she went out after dark* NIGHT, night-time, darkness; nightfall, evening, twilight, sunset.

– OPPOSITES light, day.

■ **in the dark** (*informal*) UNAWARE, ignorant, oblivious, uninformed, unenlightened, unacquainted, unconversant.

darken ▶ **verb** ❶ *the sky darkened* GROW DARK, blacken, dim, cloud over, lour; shade, fog. ❷ *his mood darkened* BLACKEN, become angry, become annoyed; sadden, become gloomy, become unhappy, become depressed, become dejected, become dispirited, become troubled.

darkness ▶ **noun** ❶ *lights shone in the darkness* DARK, blackness, gloom, dimness, murkiness, shadow, shade; dusk, twilight, gloaming. ❷ *darkness fell* NIGHT, night-time, dark. ❸ *the forces of darkness* EVIL, wickedness, sin, iniquity, immorality; devilry, the Devil.

darling ▶ **noun** ❶ *good night, darling* DEAR, dearest, love, lover, sweetheart, sweet, beloved; *informal* honey, angel, pet, sweetie, sugar, babe, baby, poppet, treasure. ❷ *the darling of the media* FAVOURITE, pet, idol, hero, heroine; *informal* blue-eyed boy/girl.

▶ **adjective** ❶ *his darling wife* DEAR, dearest, precious, adored, loved, beloved, cherished, treasured, esteemed, worshipped. ❷ *a darling little hat* ADORABLE, appealing, charming, cute, sweet, enchanting, bewitching, endearing, dear, delightful, lovely, beautiful, attractive, gorgeous, fetching; *Scottish & N. English* bonny.

darn ▶ **verb** *he was darning his socks* MEND, repair, reinforce; sew up, stitch, patch.

▶ **noun** *a sweater with darns in the elbows* PATCH, repair, reinforcement, stitch.

dart ▶ **noun** ❶ *a poisoned dart* SMALL ARROW, flechette, bolt; missile, projectile. ❷ *she made a dart for the door* DASH, rush, run, bolt, break, start, charge, sprint, bound, leap, dive; scurry, scamper, scramble.

▶ **verb** ❶ *Karl darted across the road* DASH, rush, tear, run, bolt, fly, shoot, charge, race, sprint, bound, leap, dive, gallop, scurry, scamper, scramble; *informal* scoot. ❷ *he darted a glance at her* DIRECT, cast, throw, shoot, send, flash.

dash ▶ **verb** ❶ *he dashed home* RUSH, race, run, sprint, bolt, dart, gallop, career, charge, shoot, hurtle, hare, fly, speed, zoom, scurry, scuttle, scamper; *informal* tear, belt, pelt, scoot, zip, whip, hotfoot it, leg it; *Brit. informal* bomb, go like the clappers; *N. Amer. informal* barrel. ❷ *he dashed the glass to the ground* HURL, smash, crash, slam, throw, toss, fling, pitch, cast, project, propel, send; *informal* chuck, heave, sling, bung; *N. Amer. informal* peg; *dated* shy. ❸ *rain dashed against the walls* BE HURLED, crash, smash; batter, strike, beat, pound, lash. ❹ *her hopes were dashed* SHATTER, destroy, wreck, ruin, crush, devastate, demolish, blight, overturn, scotch, spoil, frustrate, thwart, check; *informal* banjax, do for, blow a hole in, put paid to; *Brit. informal* scupper.

– OPPOSITES dawdle, raise.

▶ **noun** ❶ *a dash for the door* RUSH, race, run, sprint, bolt, dart, leap, charge, bound, break; scramble. ❷ *a dash of salt* PINCH, touch, sprinkle, taste, spot, drop, dab, speck, smattering, sprinkling, splash, bit, modicum, little; *informal* smidgen, tad, lick. ❸ *he led off with such dash* VERVE, style, flamboyance, gusto, zest, confidence, self-assurance, elan, flair, vigour, vivacity, sparkle, brio, panache, éclat, vitality, dynamism; *informal* pizzazz, pep, oomph.

dashing ▶ **adjective** ❶ *a dashing pilot* DEBONAIR, devil-may-care, raffish, sporty, spirited, lively, dazzling, energetic, animated, exuberant, flamboyant, dynamic, bold, intrepid, daring, adventurous, plucky, swashbuckling; romantic, attractive, gallant. ❷ *he looked exceptionally dashing* STYLISH, smart, elegant, chic, dapper, spruce, trim, debonair; fashionable, modish, voguish; *informal* trendy, with it, hip, sharp, snazzy, classy, natty, swish; *N. Amer. informal* fly, spiffy.

dastardly ▶ **adjective** (*dated*) WICKED, evil, heinous, villainous, diabolical, fiendish, barbarous, cruel, black, dark, rotten, vile, monstrous, abominable, despicable, degenerate, sordid; bad, base, mean, low, dishonourable, dishonest, unscrupulous, unprincipled; *informal* low-down, dirty, shady, rascally, scoundrelly, crooked; *Brit. informal* beastly.
– OPPOSITES noble.

data ▶ **noun** FACTS, figures, statistics, details, particulars, specifics; information, intelligence, material, input; *informal* info, gen.

date ▶ **noun** ❶ *the only date he has to remember* DAY (OF THE MONTH), occasion, time; year; anniversary. ❷ *a later date is suggested for this bridge* AGE, time, period, era, epoch, century, decade, year. ❸ *a lunch date* APPOINTMENT, meeting, engagement, rendezvous, assignation; commitment. ❹ (*informal*) *a date for tonight* PARTNER, escort, girlfriend, boyfriend; *informal* steady, bird, fella.
▶ **verb** ❶ *the sculpture can be dated accurately* ASSIGN A DATE TO, ascertain the date of, put a date on. ❷ *the building dates from the 16th century* WAS MADE IN, was built in, originates in, comes from, belongs to, goes back to. ❸ *the best films don't date* BECOME OLD-FASHIONED, become outmoded, become dated, show its age. ❹ (*informal*) *he's dating Jill* GO OUT WITH, take out, go around with, be involved with, see, woo; *informal* go steady with; *dated* court.
■ **to date** SO FAR, thus far, yet, as yet, up to now, till now, until now, up to the present (time), hitherto.

dated ▶ **adjective** OLD-FASHIONED, outdated, outmoded, passé, behind the times, archaic, obsolete, antiquated; unfashionable, unstylish; crusty, olde worlde, prehistoric, antediluvian; *informal* old hat, out, out of the ark.
– OPPOSITES modern.

daub ▶ **verb** *he daubed a rock with paint* SMEAR, bedaub, plaster, splash, spatter, splatter, cake, cover, smother, coat.
▶ **noun** *daubs of paint* SMEAR, smudge, splash, blot, spot, patch, blotch; *informal* splodge, splotch.

daughter ▶ **noun** FEMALE CHILD, girl.

daunt ▶ **verb** DISCOURAGE, deter, demoralize, put off, dishearten, dispirit; intimidate, abash, take aback, throw, cow, overawe, awe, frighten, scare, unman, dismay, disconcert, discompose, perturb, unsettle, unnerve; throw off balance; *informal* rattle, faze, shake up.
– OPPOSITES hearten.

dauntless ▶ **adjective** FEARLESS, determined, resolute, indomitable, intrepid, doughty, plucky, spirited, mettlesome; undaunted, undismayed, unflinching, unshrinking, bold, audacious, valiant, brave, courageous, daring; *informal* gutsy, spunky, feisty.

dawdle ▶ **verb** ❶ *they dawdled over breakfast* LINGER, dally, take one's time, be slow, waste time, idle; delay, procrastinate, stall; *informal* dilly-dally; *archaic* tarry. ❷ *Ruth dawdled home* AMBLE, stroll, trail, walk slowly, move at a snail's pace; *informal* mosey, tootle; *Brit. informal* pootle, mooch.
– OPPOSITES hurry.

dawn ▶ **noun** ❶ *we got up at dawn* DAYBREAK, sunrise, first light, daylight, cockcrow; first thing in the morning; *N. Amer.* sunup. ❷ *the dawn of civilization* BEGINNING, start, birth, inception, origination, genesis, emergence, advent, appearance, arrival, dawning, rise, origin, onset; unfolding, development, infancy; *informal* kick-off.
– OPPOSITES dusk, end.
▶ **verb** ❶ *Thursday dawned crisp and sunny* BEGIN, break, arrive, emerge. ❷ *a bright new future has dawned* BEGIN, start, commence, be born, appear, arrive, emerge; arise, rise, break, unfold, develop. ❸ *the reality dawned on him* OCCUR TO, come to, strike, hit, enter someone's mind, register with, enter someone's consciousness, cross someone's mind, suggest itself.
– OPPOSITES end.

day ▶ **noun** ❶ *I stayed for a day* TWENTY-FOUR-HOUR PERIOD, twenty-four hours. ❷ *enjoy the beach during the day* DAYTIME, daylight; waking hours. ❸ *the leading architect of the day* PERIOD, time, age, era, generation. ❹ *in his day he had great influence* HEYDAY, prime, time; peak, height, zenith, ascendancy; youth, springtime, salad days.
– RELATED TERMS diurnal.
– OPPOSITES night, decline.
■ **day after day** REPEATEDLY, again and again, over and over (again), time and (time) again, frequently, often, time after time; {day in, day out}, night and day, all the time; persistently, recurrently, constantly, continuously, continually, relentlessly, regularly, habitually, un-

failingly, always; *N. Amer.* oftentimes; *informal* 24-7; *poetic/literary* oft, oft-times.

■ **day by day** ❶ *day by day they were forced to retreat* GRADUALLY, slowly, progressively; bit by bit, inch by inch, little by little, inchmeal. ❷ *they follow the news day by day* DAILY, every day, day after day; diurnally.

■ **day in, day out**. *See* DAY AFTER DAY.

daybreak ▶ **noun** DAWN, crack of dawn, sunrise, first light, first thing in the morning, cockcrow; daylight; *N. Amer.* sunup.
– OPPOSITES nightfall.

daydream ▶ **noun** ❶ *she was lost in a daydream* REVERIE, trance, fantasy, vision, fancy, brown study; inattentiveness, wool-gathering, preoccupation, absorption, self-absorption, absent-mindedness, abstraction. ❷ *a big house was one of her daydreams* DREAM, pipe dream, fantasy, castle in the air, castle in Spain, fond hope; wishful thinking; *informal* pie in the sky.
▶ **verb** *stop daydreaming!* DREAM, muse, stare into space; fantasize, be in cloud cuckoo land, build castles in the air, build castles in Spain.

daydreamer ▶ **noun** DREAMER, fantasist, fantasizer, romantic, wishful thinker, idealist; visionary, theorizer, utopian, Walter Mitty.

daylight ▶ **noun** ❶ *do the test in daylight* NATURAL LIGHT, sunlight. ❷ *she only went there in daylight* DAYTIME, day; broad daylight. ❸ *police moved in at daylight* DAWN, daybreak, break of day, crack of dawn, sunrise, first light, first thing in the morning, early morning, cockcrow; *N. Amer.* sunup.
– OPPOSITES darkness, night-time, nightfall.

■ **see daylight** ❶ *Sam finally saw daylight* UNDERSTAND, comprehend, realize, see the light; *informal* cotton on, catch on, latch on, get the picture, get the message, get it; *Brit. informal* twig. ❷ *his project never saw daylight* BE COMPLETED, be accomplished, see (the) light of day.

day-to-day ▶ **adjective** REGULAR, everyday, daily, routine, habitual, frequent, normal, standard, usual, typical.

daze ▶ **verb** ❶ *he was dazed by his fall* STUN, stupefy; knock unconscious, knock out; *informal* knock the stuffing out of. ❷ *she was dazed by the revelations* ASTOUND, amaze, astonish, startle, dumbfound, stupefy, overwhelm, stagger, shock, confound, bewilder, take aback, nonplus, shake up; *informal* flabbergast, knock sideways, bowl over, blow away; *Brit. informal* knock for six.
▶ **noun** *she is in a daze* STUPOR, trance, haze; spin, whirl, muddle, jumble.

dazzle ▶ **verb** ❶ *she was dazzled by the headlights* BLIND TEMPORARILY, deprive of sight. ❷ *I was dazzled by the exhibition* OVERWHELM, overcome, impress, move, stir, affect, touch, awe, overawe, leave speechless, take someone's breath away; spellbind, hypnotize; *informal* bowl over, blow away, knock out.
▶ **noun** ❶ *dazzle can be a problem to sensitive eyes* GLARE, brightness, brilliance, shimmer, radiance, shine. ❷ *the dazzle of the limelight* SPARKLE, glitter, brilliance, glory, splendour, magnificence, glamour; attraction, lure, allure, draw, appeal; *informal* razzle-dazzle, razzmatazz.

dazzling ▶ **adjective** ❶ *the sunlight was dazzling* BRIGHT, blinding, glaring, brilliant. ❷ *a dazzling performance* IMPRESSIVE, remarkable, extraordinary, outstanding, exceptional; incredible, amazing, astonishing, phenomenal, breathtaking, thrilling; excellent, wonderful, magnificent, marvellous, superb, first-rate, superlative, matchless; *informal* mind-blowing, out of this world, fabulous, fab, super, sensational, ace, A1, cool, awesome; *Brit. informal* smashing, brill.

dead ▶ **adjective** ❶ *my parents are dead* PASSED ON/AWAY, expired, departed, gone, no more; late, lost, lamented; perished, fallen, slain, slaughtered, killed, murdered; lifeless, extinct; *informal* (as) dead as a doornail, six feet under, pushing up daisies; *formal* deceased; *euphemistic* with God, asleep. ❷ *patches of dead ground* BARREN, lifeless, bare, desolate, sterile. ❸ *a dead language* OBSOLETE, extinct, defunct, disused, abandoned, discarded, superseded, vanished, forgotten; archaic, antiquated, ancient; *poetic/literary* of yore. ❹ *the phone was dead* NOT WORKING, out of order, inoperative, inactive, in disrepair, broken, malfunctioning, defective; *informal* kaput, conked out, on the blink, bust; *Brit. informal* knackered. ❺ *a dead leg* NUMB, numbed, deadened, desensitized, unfeeling; paralysed, crippled, incapacitated, immobilized, frozen. ❻ *she has dead eyes* EMOTIONLESS, unemotional, unfeeling, impassive, unresponsive, indifferent, dispassionate, inexpressive, wooden, stony, cold; deadpan, flat; blank, vacant. ❼ *his affection for her was dead* EXTINGUISHED, quashed, stifled; finished, over, gone, no more; ancient history. ❽ *a dead town* UNEVENTFUL, uninteresting, unexciting, uninspiring, dull, boring, flat, quiet, sleepy, slow, lacklustre, lifeless; *informal* one-horse, dead-and-alive; *N. Amer. informal* dullsville. ❾ *dead silence* COMPLETE, absolute, total, utter, out-and-out, thorough, unmitigated. ❿ *a dead shot* UNERRING, unfailing, impeccable, sure, true, accurate, precise; deadly, lethal; *Brit. informal* spot on, bang on.
– OPPOSITES alive, fertile, modern, lively, poor.
▶ **adverb** ❶ *he was dead serious* COMPLETELY, absolutely, totally, utterly, deadly, perfectly, entirely, quite, thoroughly; definitely, certainly, positively, categorically, unquestionably, undoubtedly, surely; in every way, one hundred per cent. ❷ *flares were seen dead ahead* DIRECTLY, exactly, precisely, immediately, right, straight, due, squarely; *informal* bang, slap bang. ❸ (*Brit. informal*) *it's dead easy. See* VERY.

deadbeat ▶ noun (*informal*) LAYABOUT, loafer, idler, good-for-nothing; *informal* waster; *Brit. informal* skiver; *N. Amer. informal* bum; *poetic/literary* wastrel.

deaden ▶ verb ❶ *surgeons tried to deaden the pain* NUMB, dull, blunt, suppress; alleviate, mitigate, diminish, reduce, lessen, ease, soothe, relieve, assuage. ❷ *the wood panelling deadened any noise* MUFFLE, mute, smother, stifle, dull, damp (down); silence, quieten, soften; cushion, buffer, absorb. ❸ *laughing might deaden us to the moral issue* DESENSITIZE, numb, anaesthetize; harden (one's heart), toughen.
– OPPOSITES intensify, amplify, sensitize.

deadline ▶ noun TIME LIMIT, limit, finishing date, target date, cut-off point.

deadlock ▶ noun ❶ *the strike reached a deadlock* STALEMATE, impasse, checkmate, stand-off; standstill, halt, (full) stop, dead end. ❷ (*Brit.*) *the deadlock is opened with a key* BOLT, lock, latch, catch; *Scottish* sneck, snib.

deadly ▶ adjective ❶ *these drugs can be deadly* FATAL, lethal, mortal, death-dealing, life-threatening; dangerous, injurious, harmful, detrimental, deleterious, unhealthy; noxious, toxic, poisonous; *poetic/literary* deathly. ❷ *deadly enemies* MORTAL, irreconcilable, implacable, unappeasable, unforgiving, remorseless, merciless, pitiless; bitter, hostile, antagonistic. ❸ *deadly seriousness* INTENSE, great, marked, extreme. ❹ *he was deadly pale* DEATHLY, ghostly, ashen, white, pallid, wan, pale; ghastly. ❺ *his aim is deadly* UNERRING, unfailing, impeccable, perfect, flawless, faultless; sure, true, precise, accurate, exact; *Brit. informal* spot on, bang on. ❻ (*informal*) *life here can be deadly. See* BORING.
– OPPOSITES harmless, mild, inaccurate, exciting.
▶ adverb *deadly calm* COMPLETELY, absolutely, totally, utterly, perfectly, entirely, wholly, quite, dead, thoroughly; in every way, one hundred per cent, to the hilt.

deadpan ▶ adjective BLANK, expressionless, unexpressive, impassive, inscrutable, poker-faced, straight-faced; stony, wooden, vacant, fixed, lifeless.
– OPPOSITES expressive.

deaf ▶ adjective ❶ *she is deaf and blind* HARD OF HEARING, having impaired hearing; *informal* deaf as a post. ❷ *she was deaf to their pleading* UNMOVED BY, untouched by, unaffected by, indifferent to, unresponsive to, unconcerned by; unaware of, oblivious to, impervious to.

deafen ▶ verb MAKE DEAF, deprive of hearing, impair someone's hearing.

deafening ▶ adjective VERY LOUD, very noisy, ear-splitting, ear-shattering, overwhelming, almighty, mighty, tremendous; booming, thunderous, roaring, resounding, resonant, reverberating.
– OPPOSITES quiet.

deal ▶ noun *completion of the deal* AGREEMENT, understanding, pact, bargain, covenant, contract, treaty; arrangement, compromise, settlement; terms; transaction, sale, account; *Law* indenture.
▶ verb ❶ *how to deal with difficult children* COPE WITH, handle, manage, treat, take care of, take charge of, take in hand, sort out, tackle, take on; control; act towards, behave towards. ❷ *the article deals with advances in chemistry* CONCERN, be about, have to do with, discuss, consider, cover, pertain to; tackle, study, explore, investigate, examine, review, analyse. ❸ *the company deals in high-tech goods* TRADE IN, buy and sell; sell, purvey, supply, stock, market, merchandise; traffic, smuggle; *informal* push; *Brit. informal* flog. ❹ *the cards were dealt* DISTRIBUTE, give out, share out, divide out, hand out, pass out, pass round, dole out, dispense, allocate; *informal* divvy up. ❺ *the court dealt a blow to government reforms* DELIVER, administer, dispense, inflict, give, impose; aim.
■ **a great deal/a good deal** A LOT, a large amount, a fair amount, much, plenty; *informal* lots, loads, heaps, bags, masses, tons; *Brit. informal* a shedload.

dealer ▶ noun ❶ *an antique dealer* TRADER, tradesman, tradesperson, merchant, salesman/woman, seller, vendor, purveyor, pedlar, hawker; buyer, merchandiser, distributor, supplier, shopkeeper, retailer, wholesaler; *Brit.* stockist. ❷ *a dealer in a bank* STOCKBROKER, broker-dealer, broker, agent.

dealing ▶ noun ❶ *dishonest dealing* BUSINESS METHODS, business practices, business, commerce, trading, transactions; behaviour, conduct, actions. ❷ *the UK's dealings with China* RELATIONS, relationship, association, connections, contact, intercourse; negotiations, bargaining, transactions; trade, trading, business, commerce, traffic; *informal* truck, doings.

dean ▶ noun ❶ *student must have the consent of the dean* FACULTY HEAD, department head, college head, provost, university official; chief, director, principal, president, governor. ❷ *the dean of St Patrick's Cathedral* CHAPTER HEAD, supervisor.

dear ▶ adjective ❶ *a dear friend* BELOVED, loved, adored, cherished, precious; esteemed, respected, worshipped; close, intimate, bosom, boon, best. ❷ *her pictures were too dear to part with* PRECIOUS, treasured, valued, prized, cherished, special. ❸ *such a dear man* ENDEARING, adorable, lovable, appealing, engaging, charming, captivating, winsome, lovely, nice, pleasant, delightful, sweet, darling. ❹ *rather dear meals* EXPENSIVE, costly, high-priced, overpriced, exorbitant, extortionate; *Brit.* over the odds; *informal* pricey, steep, stiff.
– OPPOSITES hated, disagreeable, cheap.
▶ noun ❶ *don't worry, my dear* DARLING, dearest, love, beloved, sweetheart, sweet, precious,

treasure; *informal* sweetie, sugar, honey, baby, pet, sunshine, poppet. ❷ *he's such a dear* LOVABLE PERSON; darling, sweetheart, pet, angel, gem, treasure; *informal* star.

▶ **adverb** *they buy cheaply and sell dear* AT A HIGH PRICE, at an exorbitant price, at high cost.

dearly ▶ **adverb** ❶ *I love my son dearly* VERY MUCH, a great deal, greatly, deeply, profoundly, extremely; fondly, devotedly, tenderly. ❷ *our freedom has been bought dearly* AT GREAT COST, at a high price, with much suffering, with much sacrifice.

dearth ▶ **noun** LACK, scarcity, shortage, shortfall, want, deficiency, insufficiency, inadequacy, paucity, sparseness, scantiness, rareness; absence.
– OPPOSITES surfeit.

death ▶ **noun** ❶ *her father's death* DEMISE, dying, end, passing, loss of life; eternal rest, quietus; murder, assassination, execution, slaughter, massacre; *informal* curtains; *formal* decease; *archaic* expiry. ❷ *the death of their dream* END, finish, termination, extinction, extinguishing, collapse, destruction, eradication, obliteration. ❸ *Death gestured towards a grave* THE GRIM REAPER, the Dark Angel, the Angel of Death.
– OPPOSITES life, birth.

■ **put someone to death** EXECUTE, hang, behead, guillotine, decapitate, electrocute, shoot, gas, crucify, stone; kill, murder, assassinate, eliminate, terminate, exterminate, destroy; *informal* bump off, polish off, do away with, do in, knock off, top, string up, take out, croak, stiff, blow away; *N. Amer. informal* ice, rub out, waste, whack, smoke; *poetic/literary* slay.

deathless ▶ **adjective** IMMORTAL, undying, imperishable, indestructible; enduring, everlasting, eternal; timeless, ageless.
– OPPOSITES mortal, ephemeral.

deathly ▶ **adjective** ❶ *a deathly pallor* DEATHLIKE, deadly, ghostly, ghastly; ashen, chalky, white, pale, pallid, bloodless, wan, anaemic, pasty. ❷ (*poetic/literary*) *the eagle's deathly grasp* DEADLY, fatal, lethal, mortal, death-dealing; terrible, baleful, dangerous, perilous.

debacle ▶ **noun** FIASCO, failure, catastrophe, disaster, mess, ruin; downfall, collapse, defeat; *informal* foul-up, screw-up, hash, botch, washout; *Brit. informal* cock-up, pig's ear, bodge; *N. Amer. informal* snafu.

debar ▶ **verb** ❶ *women were debarred from the club* EXCLUDE, ban, bar, disqualify, declare ineligible, preclude, shut out, lock out, keep out, reject, blackball; *N. Amer.* disfellowship. ❷ *the unions were debarred from striking* PREVENT, prohibit, proscribe, disallow, ban, interdict, block, stop; forbid to; *Law* enjoin, estop.
– OPPOSITES admit, allow.

debase ▶ **verb** ❶ *the moral code has been debased* DEGRADE, devalue, demean, cheapen, prostitute, discredit, drag down, tarnish, blacken, blemish; disgrace, dishonour, shame; damage, harm, undermine. ❷ *the added copper debases the silver* REDUCE IN VALUE, reduce in quality, depreciate; contaminate, adulterate, pollute, taint, sully, corrupt; dilute, alloy.
– OPPOSITES enhance.

debased ▶ **adjective** ❶ *their debased amusements* IMMORAL, debauched, dissolute, perverted, degenerate, wicked, sinful, vile, base, iniquitous, corrupt; lewd, lascivious, lecherous, prurient, indecent. ❷ *the myth lives on in a debased form* CORRUPT, corrupted, bastardized, adulterated, diluted, tainted, sullied.
– OPPOSITES honourable, original.

debatable ▶ **adjective** ARGUABLE, disputable, questionable, open to question, controversial, contentious; doubtful, dubious, uncertain, unsure, unclear; borderline, inconclusive, moot, unsettled, unresolved, unconfirmed, undetermined, undecided, up in the air; *informal* iffy.

debate ▶ **noun** *a debate on the reforms* DISCUSSION, discourse, parley, dialogue; argument, dispute, wrangle, war of words; argumentation, disputation, dissension, disagreement, contention, conflict; negotiations, talks; *informal* confab, powwow.

▶ **verb** ❶ *MPs will debate our future* DISCUSS, talk over/through, talk about, thrash out, argue, dispute; *informal* kick around/about, bat around/about. ❷ *he debated whether to call her* CONSIDER, think over/about, chew over, mull over, weigh up, ponder, deliberate, contemplate, muse, meditate; *formal* cogitate.

debauch ▶ **verb** ❶ *public morals have been debauched* CORRUPT, debase, deprave, warp, pervert, lead astray, ruin. ❷ (*dated*) *he debauched six schoolgirls* SEDUCE, deflower, defile, violate; *poetic/literary* ravish.

debauched ▶ **adjective** DISSOLUTE, dissipated, degenerate, corrupt, depraved, sinful, unprincipled, immoral; lascivious, lecherous, lewd, lustful, libidinous, licentious, promiscuous, loose, wanton, abandoned; decadent, profligate, intemperate, sybaritic.
– OPPOSITES wholesome.

debauchery ▶ **noun** DISSIPATION, degeneracy, corruption, vice, depravity; immodesty, indecency, perversion, iniquity, wickedness, sinfulness, impropriety, immorality; lasciviousness, salaciousness, lechery, lewdness, lust, promiscuity, wantonness, profligacy; decadence, intemperance, sybaritism; *formal* turpitude.

debilitate ▶ **verb** WEAKEN, enfeeble, enervate, devitalize, sap, drain, exhaust, weary, fatigue, prostrate; undermine, impair, indispose, incapacitate, cripple, disable, paralyse, immobilize, lay low; *informal* knock out, do in.
– OPPOSITES invigorate.

debility ▶ **noun** FRAILTY, weakness, enfeeblement, enervation, devitalization, lassitude, exhaustion, weariness, fatigue, prostration; incapacity, indisposition, infirmity, illness, sickness, sickliness; *informal* weediness; *Medicine* asthenia.

debonair ▶ **adjective** SUAVE, urbane, sophisticated, cultured, self-possessed, self-assured, confident, charming, gracious, courteous, gallant, chivalrous, gentlemanly, refined, polished, well bred, genteel, dignified, courtly; well groomed, elegant, stylish, smart, dashing; *informal* smooth, swish, sharp, cool.
– OPPOSITES unsophisticated.

debrief ▶ **verb** QUESTION, quiz, interview, examine, cross-examine, interrogate, probe, sound out; *informal* grill, pump.

debris ▶ **noun** DETRITUS, refuse, rubbish, waste, litter, scrap, dross, chaff, flotsam and jetsam; lumber, rubble, wreckage; remains, scraps, dregs; *N. Amer.* trash, garbage; *Austral./NZ* mullock; *informal* dreck, junk.

debt ▶ **noun** ❶ *he couldn't pay his debts* BILL, account, dues, arrears, charges; financial obligation, outstanding payment, money owing; *N. Amer.* check; *informal* tab. ❷ *his debt to the author* INDEBTEDNESS, obligation; gratitude, appreciation, thanks.
■ **in debt** OWING MONEY, in arrears, behind with payments, overdrawn; insolvent, bankrupt, ruined; *Brit.* in liquidation; *informal* in the red, in Queer Street, on the rocks.
■ **in someone's debt** INDEBTED TO, beholden to, obliged to, duty-bound to, honour-bound to, obligated to; grateful, thankful, appreciative.

debtor ▶ **noun** BORROWER, mortgagor; bankrupt, insolvent, defaulter.
– OPPOSITES creditor.

debunk ▶ **verb** EXPLODE, deflate, quash, drive a coach and horses through, discredit, disprove, contradict, controvert, invalidate, negate; challenge, call into question; *informal* shoot full of holes, blow sky-high; *formal* confute.
– OPPOSITES confirm.

debut ▶ **noun** FIRST APPEARANCE, first performance, launch, coming out, entrance, premiere, introduction, inception, inauguration; *informal* kick-off.

decadence ▶ **noun** ❶ *the decadence of modern society* DISSIPATION, degeneracy, debauchery, corruption, depravity, vice, sin, moral decay, immorality; immoderateness, intemperance, licentiousness, self-indulgence, hedonism. ❷ *the decadence of nations* DECLINE, fall, decay, degeneration, deterioration, degradation, retrogression.
– OPPOSITES morality, rise.

decadent ▶ **adjective** ❶ *decadent city life* DISSOLUTE, dissipated, degenerate, corrupt, depraved, sinful, unprincipled, immoral; licentious, abandoned, profligate, intemperate; sybaritic, hedonistic, pleasure-seeking, self-indulgent. ❷ *the decadent empire* DECLINING, decaying, ebbing, degenerating, deteriorating.

decamp ▶ **verb** ❶ *he decamped with the profits* ABSCOND, make off, run off/away, flee, bolt, take flight, disappear, vanish, steal away, sneak away, escape, make a run for it, leave, depart; *informal* split, scram, vamoose, cut and run, do a disappearing act, head for the hills, go AWOL; *Brit. informal* do a bunk, do a runner, scarper; *N. Amer. informal* take a powder, go on the lam. ❷ (*archaic*) *the armies decamped* STRIKE ONE'S TENTS, break camp, move on.

decant ▶ **verb** POUR OUT/OFF, draw off, siphon off, drain, tap; transfer.

decapitate ▶ **verb** BEHEAD, guillotine; *archaic* decollate.

decay ▶ **verb** ❶ *the corpses had decayed* DECOMPOSE, rot, putrefy, go bad, go off, spoil, fester, perish, deteriorate; degrade, break down, moulder, mortify, shrivel, wither. ❷ *the cities continue to decay* DETERIORATE, degenerate, decline, go downhill, slump, slide, go to rack and ruin, go to seed; disintegrate, fall to pieces, fall into disrepair; fail, collapse; *informal* go to pot, go to the dogs, go down the toilet; *Austral./NZ informal* go to the pack.
▶ **noun** ❶ *signs of decay* DECOMPOSITION, putrefaction, festering; rot, mould, mildew, fungus. ❷ *tooth decay* ROT, corrosion, decomposition; caries, cavities, holes. ❸ *the decay of American values* DETERIORATION, degeneration, debasement, degradation, decline, weakening, atrophy; crumbling, disintegration, collapse.

decayed ▶ **adjective** DECOMPOSED, decomposing, rotten, putrescent, putrid, bad, off, spoiled, perished; mouldy, festering, fetid, rancid, rank; maggoty, wormy, flyblown.

decaying ▶ **adjective** ❶ *decaying fish* DECOMPOSING, decomposed, rotting, rotten, putrescent, putrid, bad, off, perished; mouldy, festering, fetid, rancid, rank; maggoty, wormy, flyblown. ❷ *a decaying city* DECLINING, degenerating, dying, crumbling; run down, tumbledown, ramshackle, shabby, decrepit; in decline, in ruins; *informal* on the way out.

decease ▶ **noun** (*formal*) *her decease was imminent* DEATH, dying, demise, end, passing, loss of life, quietus; *informal* curtains, croaking, snuffing; *archaic* expiry.
▶ **verb** (*archaic*) *he deceased at his palace. See* DIE sense 1.

deceased ▶ **adjective** (*formal*) DEAD, expired, departed, gone, no more, passed on/away; late, lost, lamented; perished, fallen, slain, slaughtered, killed, murdered; lifeless, extinct; *informal* (as) dead as a doornail, six feet under, pushing up daisies; *euphemistic* with God, asleep.

deceit ▶ **noun** ❶ *her endless deceit* DECEPTION, deceitfulness, duplicity, double-dealing, fraud, cheating, trickery, chicanery, deviousness, slyness, wiliness, guile, bluff, lying, pretence, treachery; *informal* crookedness, monkey business, jiggery-pokery; *N. Amer. informal* monkeyshines. ❷ *their life is a deceit* SHAM, fraud, pretence, hoax, fake, blind, artifice; trick, stratagem, device, ruse, scheme, dodge, machination, deception, subterfuge; cheat, swindle; *informal* con, set-up, scam, flimflam; *N. Amer. informal* bunco.

– OPPOSITES honesty.

deceitful ▶ **adjective** ❶ *a deceitful woman* DISHONEST, untruthful, mendacious, insincere, false, disingenuous, untrustworthy, unscrupulous, unprincipled, two-faced, duplicitous, double-dealing, underhand, crafty, cunning, sly, scheming, calculating, treacherous, Machiavellian; *informal* sneaky, tricky, foxy, crooked; *Brit. informal* bent. ❷ *a deceitful allegation* FRAUDULENT, counterfeit, fabricated, invented, concocted, made up, trumped up, untrue, false, bogus, fake, spurious, fallacious, deceptive, misleading; *euphemistic* economical with the truth.

deceive ▶ **verb** ❶ *she was deceived by a con man* SWINDLE, defraud, cheat, trick, hoodwink, hoax, dupe, take in, mislead, delude, fool, outwit, lead on, inveigle, beguile, double-cross, gull; *informal* con, bamboozle, do, gyp, diddle, swizzle, rip off, shaft, pull a fast one on, take for a ride, pull the wool over someone's eyes, sell a pup to; *N. Amer. informal* sucker, snooker, stiff. ❷ *he deceived her with another woman* BE UNFAITHFUL TO, cheat on, betray, play someone false; *informal* two-time.

decelerate ▶ **verb** SLOW DOWN/UP, ease up, slack up, reduce speed, brake.

decency ▶ **noun** ❶ *standards of taste and decency* PROPRIETY, decorum, good taste, respectability, dignity, correctness, good form, etiquette; morality, virtue, modesty, delicacy. ❷ *he didn't have the decency to tell me* COURTESY, politeness, good manners, civility, respect; consideration, thoughtfulness, tact, diplomacy.

decent ▶ **adjective** ❶ *a decent Christian burial* PROPER, correct, appropriate, apt, fitting, suitable; respectable, dignified, decorous, seemly; nice, tasteful; conventional, accepted, standard, traditional, orthodox; comme il faut; *informal* pukka. ❷ (*Brit. informal*) *a very decent chap* HONOURABLE, honest, trustworthy, dependable; respectable, upright, clean-living, virtuous, good; obliging, helpful, accommodating, unselfish, generous, kind, thoughtful, considerate; neighbourly, hospitable, pleasant, agreeable, amiable. ❸ *a job with decent pay* SATISFACTORY, reasonable, fair, acceptable, adequate, sufficient, ample; not bad, all right, tolerable, passable, suitable; *informal* OK, okay, up to snuff.

– OPPOSITES unpleasant, unsatisfactory.

deception ▶ **noun** ❶ *they obtained money by deception* DECEIT, deceitfulness, duplicity, double-dealing, fraud, cheating, trickery, chicanery, deviousness, slyness, wiliness, guile, bluff, lying, pretence, treachery; *informal* crookedness, monkey business, jiggery-pokery; *N. Amer. informal* monkeyshines. ❷ *it was all a deception* TRICK, deceit, sham, fraud, pretence, hoax, fake, blind, artifice; stratagem, device, ruse, scheme, dodge, machination, subterfuge; cheat, swindle; *informal* con, set-up, scam, flimflam; *N. Amer. informal* bunco.

deceptive ▶ **adjective** ❶ *distances are very deceptive* MISLEADING, illusory, illusionary, specious; ambiguous; distorted; *poetic/literary* illusive. ❷ *deceptive practices* DECEITFUL, duplicitous, fraudulent, counterfeit, underhand, cunning, crafty, sly, guileful, scheming, treacherous, Machiavellian; disingenuous, untrustworthy, unscrupulous, unprincipled, dishonest, insincere, false; *informal* crooked, sharp, shady, sneaky, tricky, foxy; *Brit. informal* bent.

decide ▶ **verb** ❶ *she decided to become a writer* RESOLVE, determine, make up one's mind, make a decision; elect, choose, opt, plan, aim, have the intention, have in mind, set one's sights on. ❷ *research to decide a variety of questions* SETTLE, resolve, determine, work out, answer; *informal* sort out, figure out. ❸ *the court is to decide the case* ADJUDICATE, arbitrate, adjudge, judge; hear, try, examine; sit in judgement on, pronounce on, give a verdict on, rule on.

decided ▶ **adjective** ❶ *they have a decided advantage* DISTINCT, clear, marked, pronounced, obvious, striking, noticeable, unmistakable, patent, manifest; definite, certain, positive, emphatic, undeniable, indisputable, unquestionable; assured, guaranteed. ❷ *he was very decided* DETERMINED, resolute, firm, strong-minded, strong-willed, emphatic, dead set, unwavering, unyielding, unbending, inflexible, unshakeable, unrelenting, obstinate, stubborn; *N. Amer.* rock-ribbed. ❸ *our future is decided* SETTLED, established, resolved, determined, agreed, designated, chosen, ordained, prescribed; set, fixed; *informal* sewn up, wrapped up.

decidedly ▶ **adverb** DISTINCTLY, clearly, markedly, obviously, noticeably, unmistakably, patently, manifestly; definitely, certainly, positively, absolutely, downright, undeniably, unquestionably; extremely, exceedingly, exceptionally, particularly, especially, very; *N. English* right; *informal* terrifically, devilishly, ultra, mega, majorly; *Brit. informal* jolly, ever so, dead, well; *N. Amer. informal* real, mighty, awful; *archaic* exceeding.

deciding ▶ **adjective** DETERMINING, decisive, conclusive, key, pivotal, crucial, critical, significant, major, chief, principal, prime.

decipher ▶ verb ❶ *he deciphered the code* DECODE, decrypt, break, work out, solve, interpret, translate; make sense of, get to the bottom of, unravel; *informal* crack, figure out; *Brit. informal* twig, suss (out). ❷ *the writing was hard to decipher* MAKE OUT, discern, perceive, read, follow, fathom, make sense of, interpret, understand, comprehend, grasp.
– OPPOSITES encode.

decision ▶ noun ❶ *they came to a decision* RESOLUTION, conclusion, settlement, commitment, resolve, determination; choice, option, selection. ❷ *the judge's decision* VERDICT, finding, ruling, recommendation, judgement, pronouncement, adjudication, arbitrament; order, rule; findings, results; *Law* determination; *N. Amer.* resolve. ❸ *his order had a ring of decision* DECISIVENESS, determination, resolution, resolve, firmness; strong-mindedness, purpose, purposefulness.

decisive ▶ adjective ❶ *a decisive man* RESOLUTE, firm, strong-minded, strong-willed, determined; purposeful, forceful, dead set, unwavering, unyielding, unbending, inflexible, unshakeable, obstinate, stubborn; *N. Amer.* rock-ribbed. ❷ *the decisive factor* DECIDING, conclusive, determining; key, pivotal, critical, crucial, significant, influential, major, chief, principal, prime.

deck ▶ verb ❶ *the street was decked with bunting* DECORATE, bedeck, adorn, ornament, trim, trick out, garnish, cover, hang, festoon, garland, swathe, wreathe; embellish, beautify, prettify, enhance, grace, set off; *informal* get up, do up, do out, tart up; *poetic/literary* bejewel, bedizen, caparison, furbelow. ❷ *Ingrid was decked out in blue* DRESS (UP), clothe, attire, garb, robe, drape, turn out, fit out, rig out, outfit, costume; *informal* doll up, get up, do up.

declaim ▶ verb ❶ *a preacher declaiming from the pulpit* MAKE A SPEECH, give an address, give a lecture, deliver a sermon; speak, hold forth, orate, preach, lecture, sermonize, moralize; *informal* sound off, spout, speechify, preachify. ❷ *they loved to hear him declaim poetry* RECITE, read aloud, read out loud, read out; deliver; *informal* spout. ❸ *he declaimed against the evils of society* SPEAK OUT, rail, inveigh, fulminate, rage, thunder; rant, expostulate; condemn, criticize, attack, decry, disparage.

declamation ▶ noun SPEECH, address, lecture, sermon, homily, discourse, oration, recitation, disquisition, monologue.

declaration ▶ noun ❶ *they issued a declaration* ANNOUNCEMENT, statement, communication, pronouncement, proclamation, communiqué, edict; *N. Amer.* advisory. ❷ *the declaration of war* PROCLAMATION, notification, announcement, revelation, disclosure, broadcasting. ❸ *a declaration of faith* ASSERTION, profession, affirmation, acknowledgement, revelation, disclosure, manifestation, confirmation, testimony, validation, certification, attestation; pledge, avowal, vow, oath, protestation.

declare ▶ verb ❶ *she declared her political principles* PROCLAIM, announce, state, reveal, air, voice, articulate, express, vent, set forth, publicize, broadcast; *informal* come out with, shout from the rooftops. ❷ *he declared that they were guilty* ASSERT, maintain, state, affirm, contend, argue, insist, hold, profess, claim, avow, swear; *formal* aver. ❸ *his speech declared him a gentleman* SHOW TO BE, reveal as, confirm as, prove to be, attest to someone's being.

decline ▶ verb ❶ *she declined all invitations* TURN DOWN, reject, brush aside, refuse, rebuff, spurn, repulse, dismiss; forgo, deny oneself, pass up; abstain from, say no; *informal* give the thumbs down to, give something a miss, give someone the brush-off; *Brit. informal* knock back. ❷ *the number of traders has declined* DECREASE, reduce, lessen, diminish, dwindle, contract, shrink, fall off, tail off; drop, fall, go down, slump, plummet; *informal* nosedive, take a header, crash. ❸ *standards steadily declined* DETERIORATE, degenerate, decay, crumble, collapse, slump, slip, slide, go downhill, worsen; weaken, wane, ebb; *informal* go to pot, go to the dogs, go down the toilet; *Austral./NZ informal* go to the pack.
– OPPOSITES accept, increase, rise.
▶ noun ❶ *a decline in profits* REDUCTION, decrease, downturn, downswing, devaluation, depreciation, diminution, ebb, drop, slump, plunge; *informal* nosedive, crash. ❷ *forest decline* DETERIORATION, degeneration, degradation, shrinkage; death, decay.
■ **in decline** DECLINING, decaying, crumbling, collapsing, failing; disappearing, dying, moribund; *informal* on its last legs, on the way out.

decode ▶ verb DECIPHER, decrypt, work out, solve, interpret, translate; make sense of, get to the bottom of, unravel, find the key to; *informal* crack, figure out; *Brit. informal* twig, suss (out).

decompose ▶ verb ❶ *the chemical prevents corpses decomposing* DECAY, rot, putrefy, go bad, go off, spoil, fester, perish, deteriorate; degrade, break down, moulder, mortify, shrivel, wither. ❷ *some minerals decompose rapidly* BREAK UP, fragment, disintegrate, crumble, dissolve; break down, decay. ❸ *decompose words into simpler elements* SEPARATE, divide, break down, dissect, resolve, reduce.

decomposition ▶ noun ❶ *an advanced state of decomposition* DECAY, putrefaction, putrescence, putridity. ❷ *the decomposition of granite* DISINTEGRATION, dissolution; breaking down, decay. ❸ *the decomposition of a sentence* SEPARATION, division, breakdown; dissection, dissolution, resolution, analysis, reduction.

decontaminate ▶ verb SANITIZE, sterilize, disinfect, clean, cleanse, purify; fumigate.

decor ▶ noun DECORATION, furnishing, ornamentation; colour scheme.

decorate ▶ verb ❶ *the door was decorated with a wreath* ORNAMENT, adorn, trim, embellish, garnish, furnish, enhance, grace, prettify; festoon, garland, bedeck. ❷ *he started to decorate his home* PAINT, WALLPAPER, paper; refurbish, furbish, renovate, redecorate; *informal* do up, spruce up, do over, fix up, give something a facelift. ❸ *he was decorated for courage* GIVE A MEDAL TO, honour, cite, reward.

decoration ▶ noun ❶ *a ceiling with rich decoration* ORNAMENTATION, adornment, trimming, embellishment, garnishing, gilding; beautification, prettification; enhancements, enrichments, frills, accessories, trimmings, finery, frippery. ❷ *internal decoration. See* DECOR. ❸ *a Christmas tree decoration* ORNAMENT, bauble, trinket, knick-knack, spangle; trimming, tinsel. ❹ *a decoration won on the battlefield* MEDAL, award, star, ribbon; laurel, trophy, prize; *Military slang* fruit salad; *Brit. informal* gong.

decorative ▶ adjective ORNAMENTAL, embellishing, garnishing; fancy, ornate, attractive, pretty, showy.
– OPPOSITES functional.

decorous ▶ adjective PROPER, seemly, decent, becoming, befitting, tasteful, correct, appropriate, suitable, fitting; tactful, polite, well mannered, genteel, respectable; formal, restrained, modest, demure, gentlemanly, ladylike.
– OPPOSITES unseemly.

decorum ▶ noun ❶ *he had acted with decorum* PROPRIETY, seemliness, decency, good taste, correctness; politeness, courtesy, good manners; dignity, respectability, modesty, demureness. ❷ *a breach of decorum* ETIQUETTE, protocol, good form, custom, convention; formalities, niceties, punctilios, politeness.
– OPPOSITES impropriety.

decoy ▶ noun *a decoy to distract their attention* LURE, bait, red herring; enticement, inducement, temptation, attraction, carrot; snare, trap.
▶ verb *he was decoyed to the mainland* LURE, entice, tempt; entrap, snare, trap.

decrease ▶ verb ❶ *pollution levels decreased* LESSEN, reduce, drop, diminish, decline, dwindle, fall off; die down, abate, subside, tail off, ebb, wane; plummet, plunge. ❷ *decrease the amount of fat in your body* REDUCE, lessen, lower, cut, curtail; slim down, tone down, deplete, minimize; *informal* slash.
– OPPOSITES increase.
▶ noun *a decrease in crime* REDUCTION, drop, decline, downturn, cut, cutback, diminution, ebb, wane.
– OPPOSITES increase.

decree ▶ noun ❶ *a presidential decree* ORDER, edict, command, commandment, mandate, proclamation, dictum, fiat; law, statute, act; *formal* ordinance. ❷ *a court decree* JUDGEMENT, verdict, adjudication, ruling, resolution, decision.
▶ verb *he decreed that a stadium should be built* ORDER, command, rule, dictate, pronounce, proclaim, ordain; direct, decide, determine.

decrepit ▶ adjective ❶ *a decrepit old man* FEEBLE, infirm, weak, weakly, frail; disabled, incapacitated, crippled, doddering, tottering; old, elderly, aged, ancient, senile; *informal* past it, over the hill, no spring chicken. ❷ *a decrepit house* DILAPIDATED, rickety, run down, tumbledown, ramshackle, derelict, ruined, in (a state of) disrepair, gone to rack and ruin; battered, decayed, crumbling, deteriorating.
– OPPOSITES strong, sound.

decry ▶ verb DENOUNCE, condemn, criticize, censure, attack, rail against, run down, pillory, lambaste, vilify, revile; disparage, deprecate, cast aspersions on; *informal* slam, blast, knock; *Brit. informal* slate.
– OPPOSITES praise.

dedicate ▶ verb ❶ *she dedicated her life to the sick* DEVOTE, commit, pledge, give, surrender, sacrifice; set aside, allocate, consign. ❷ *a book dedicated to a noblewoman* INSCRIBE, address; assign. ❸ *the chapel was dedicated to the Virgin Mary* DEVOTE, assign; bless, consecrate, sanctify; *formal* hallow.

dedicated ▶ adjective ❶ *a dedicated socialist* COMMITTED, devoted, staunch, firm, steadfast, resolute, unwavering, loyal, faithful, true, dyed-in-the-wool; wholehearted, single-minded, enthusiastic, keen, earnest, zealous, ardent, passionate, fervent; *informal* card-carrying, deep-dyed. ❷ *data is accessed by a dedicated machine* EXCLUSIVE, custom built, customized.
– OPPOSITES indifferent.

dedication ▶ noun ❶ *sport requires dedication* COMMITMENT, application, diligence, industry, resolve, enthusiasm, zeal, conscientiousness, perseverance, persistence, tenacity, drive, staying power; hard work, effort. ❷ *her dedication to the job* DEVOTION, commitment, loyalty, adherence, allegiance. ❸ *the book has a dedication to his wife* INSCRIPTION, address, message. ❹ *the dedication of the church* BLESSING, consecration, sanctification, benediction.
– OPPOSITES apathy.

deduce ▶ verb CONCLUDE, reason, work out, infer; glean, divine, intuit, understand, assume, presume, conjecture, surmise, reckon; *informal* figure out; *Brit. informal* suss out.

deduct ▶ verb SUBTRACT, take away, take off, debit, dock, discount; abstract, remove; *informal* knock off.
– OPPOSITES add.

deduction ▶ noun ❶ *the deduction of tax* SUBTRACTION, removal, debit, abstraction. ❷ *gross pay, before deductions* STOPPAGE, subtraction. ❸ *she was right in her deduction* CONCLUSION, inference, supposition, hypothesis, assumption, presumption; suspicion, conviction, belief, reasoning.

deed ▶ noun ❶ *knightly deeds* ACT, action; feat, exploit, achievement, accomplishment, endeavour, undertaking, enterprise. ❷ *unity must be established in deed and word* FACT, reality, actuality. ❸ *mortgage deeds* LEGAL DOCUMENT, contract, indenture, instrument.

deem ▶ verb CONSIDER, regard as, judge, adjudge, hold to be, view as, see as, take for, class as, count, find, esteem, suppose, reckon; think, believe, feel.

deep ▶ adjective ❶ *a deep ravine* CAVERNOUS, yawning, gaping, huge, extensive; bottomless, fathomless, unfathomable; *archaic* profound. ❷ *two inches deep* IN DEPTH, downwards, inwards, in vertical extent. ❸ *deep affection* INTENSE, heartfelt, wholehearted, deep-seated, deep-rooted; sincere, genuine, earnest, enthusiastic, great. ❹ *a deep sleep* SOUND, heavy, intense. ❺ *a deep thinker* PROFOUND, serious, philosophical, complex, weighty; abstruse, esoteric, recondite, mysterious, obscure; intelligent, intellectual, learned, wise, scholarly; discerning, penetrating, perceptive, insightful. ❻ *he was deep in concentration* RAPT, absorbed, engrossed, preoccupied, immersed, lost, gripped, intent, engaged. ❼ *a deep mystery* OBSCURE, mysterious, secret, unfathomable, opaque, abstruse, recondite, esoteric, enigmatic, arcane; puzzling, baffling, mystifying, inexplicable. ❽ *his deep voice* LOW-PITCHED, low, bass, rich, powerful, resonant, booming, sonorous. ❾ *a deep red* DARK, intense, rich, strong, bold, warm.
– OPPOSITES shallow, superficial, high, light.
▶ noun ❶ (*poetic/literary*) *creatures of the deep* THE SEA, the ocean; *informal* the drink; *Brit. informal* the briny; *poetic/literary* the profound. ❷ *the deep of night* THE MIDDLE, the midst; the depths, the dead, the thick.
▶ adverb ❶ *I dug deep* FAR DOWN, way down, to a great depth. ❷ *he brought them deep into woodland* FAR, a long way, a great distance.

deepen ▶ verb ❶ *his love for her had deepened* GROW, increase, intensify, strengthen, heighten, amplify, augment; *informal* step up; *Brit. informal* hot up. ❷ *they deepened the hole* DIG OUT, dig deeper, excavate.

deeply ▶ adverb PROFOUNDLY, greatly, enormously, extremely, very much; strongly, powerfully, intensely, keenly, acutely; thoroughly, completely, entirely; *informal* well, seriously, majorly.

deep-rooted ▶ adjective DEEP-SEATED, deep, profound, fundamental, basic; established, ingrained, entrenched, unshakeable, inveterate, inbuilt; secure; persistent, abiding, lingering.
– OPPOSITES superficial.

deep-seated ▶ adjective. *See* DEEP-ROOTED.

deface ▶ verb VANDALIZE, disfigure, mar, spoil, ruin, sully, damage, blight, impair; *N. Amer. informal* trash.

de facto ▶ adverb *the republic is de facto two states* IN PRACTICE, in effect, in fact, in reality, really, actually.
– OPPOSITES de jure.
▶ adjective *de facto control* ACTUAL, real, effective.
– OPPOSITES de jure.

defamation ▶ noun LIBEL, slander, calumny, character assassination, vilification; scandalmongering, malicious gossip, aspersions, muckraking, abuse; disparagement, denigration; smear, slur; *informal* mud-slinging.

defamatory ▶ adjective LIBELLOUS, slanderous, calumnious, calumniatory, scandalmongering, malicious, vicious, backbiting, muckraking; abusive, disparaging, denigratory, insulting; *informal* mud-slinging, bitchy, catty.

defame ▶ verb LIBEL, slander, malign, cast aspersions on, smear, traduce, give someone a bad name, run down, speak ill of, vilify, besmirch, stigmatize, disparage, denigrate, discredit, decry; *informal* do a hatchet job on, drag through the mud; *N. Amer.* slur; *informal* bad-mouth; *Brit. informal* slag off; *formal* calumniate.
– OPPOSITES compliment.

default ▶ noun ❶ *the incidence of defaults on loans* NON-PAYMENT, failure to pay, non-remittance. ❷ *I became a teacher by default* INACTION, omission, lapse, neglect, negligence, disregard; absence, non-appearance.
▶ verb ❶ *the customer defaulted* FAIL TO PAY, not pay, renege, back out; go back on one's word; *informal* welsh, bilk. ❷ *the program will default to its own style* REVERT, select automatically.

defaulter ▶ noun ❶ *a mortgage defaulter* NON-PAYER, debt-dodger; tax-dodger; *N. Amer.* delinquent. ❷ (*Brit. Military*) *the defaulters' room* OFFENDER, wrongdoer, felon, delinquent.

defeat ▶ verb ❶ *the army which defeated the Scots* BEAT, conquer, win against, triumph over, get the better of, vanquish; rout, trounce, overcome, overpower, crush, subdue; *informal* lick, thrash, whip, wipe the floor with, make mincemeat of, clobber, slaughter, demolish, cane; *Brit. informal* stuff; *N. Amer. informal* cream, skunk. ❷ *these complex plans defeat their purpose* THWART, frustrate, foil, ruin, scotch, debar, snooker, derail; obstruct, impede, hinder, hamper; *informal* put the kibosh on, put paid to, stymie; *Brit. informal* scupper, nobble. ❸ *the motion was defeated* REJECT, overthrow, throw out, dismiss, outvote, turn down; *informal* give the thumbs down. ❹ *how to make it work defeats me* BAFFLE, perplex, bewilder, mystify, bemuse, confuse, confound, throw; *informal* beat, flummox, faze, stump, fox.
▶ noun ❶ *a crippling defeat* LOSS, conquest, vanquishment; rout, trouncing; downfall; *informal*

thrashing, hiding, drubbing, licking, pasting, massacre, slaughter. ❷ *the defeat of his plans* FAILURE, downfall, collapse, ruin; rejection, frustration, abortion, miscarriage; undoing, reverse.
– OPPOSITES victory, success.

defeatist ▶ adjective *a defeatist attitude* PESSIMISTIC, fatalistic, negative, cynical, despondent, despairing, hopeless, bleak, gloomy.
– OPPOSITES optimistic.
▶ noun PESSIMIST, fatalist, cynic, prophet of doom, doomster; misery, killjoy, worrier; *informal* quitter, wet blanket.
– OPPOSITES optimist.

defecate ▶ verb EXCRETE (FAECES), have a bowel movement, evacuate one's bowels, void excrement, relieve oneself, go to the lavatory; *informal* do number two, do a pooh.

defect[1] ▶ noun *he spotted a defect in my work* FAULT, flaw, imperfection, deficiency, weakness, weak spot, inadequacy, shortcoming, limitation, failing; kink, deformity, blemish; mistake, error; *informal* glitch, gremlin; *Computing* bug.

defect[2] ▶ verb *his chief intelligence officer defected* DESERT, change sides, turn traitor, rebel, renege; abscond, quit, escape; break faith; secede from, revolt against; *informal* rat on; *Military* go AWOL; *poetic/literary* forsake; *rare* tergiversate.

defection ▶ noun DESERTION, absconding, decamping, flight; apostasy, secession; treason, betrayal, disloyalty; *poetic/literary* perfidy; *rare* tergiversation.

defective ▶ adjective ❶ *a defective seat belt* FAULTY, flawed, imperfect, shoddy, inoperative, malfunctioning, out of order, unsound; in disrepair, broken; *informal* on the blink; *Brit. informal* knackered, duff. ❷ *these methods are defective* LACKING, wanting, deficient, inadequate, insufficient. ❸ (*dated*) *a mentally defective child* IMPAIRED, slow, simple, backward, retarded; *dated* deficient, subnormal, educationally subnormal, ESN.
– OPPOSITES perfect.

defector ▶ noun DESERTER, turncoat, traitor, renegade, Judas, quisling; *informal* rat; *rare* tergiversator.

defence ▶ noun ❶ *the defence of the fortress* PROTECTION, guarding, security, fortification; resistance, deterrent. ❷ *the enemy's defences* BARRICADE, fortification; fortress, keep, rampart, bulwark, bastion. ❸ *he spoke in defence of his boss* VINDICATION, justification, support, advocacy, endorsement; apology, explanation, exoneration. ❹ *more spending on defence* ARMAMENTS, weapons, weaponry, arms; the military, the armed forces. ❺ *the prisoner's defence* VINDICATION, explanation, mitigation, justification, rationalization, excuse, alibi, reason; plea, pleading; testimony, declaration, case.

defenceless ▶ adjective ❶ *defenceless animals* VULNERABLE, helpless, powerless, impotent, weak, susceptible. ❷ *the country is wholly defenceless* UNDEFENDED, unprotected, unguarded, unshielded, unarmed; vulnerable, assailable, exposed, insecure, pregnable.
– OPPOSITES resilient.

defend ▶ verb ❶ *a fort built to defend Ireland* PROTECT, guard, safeguard, secure, shield; fortify, garrison, barricade; uphold, support, watch over. ❷ *he defended his policy* JUSTIFY, vindicate, argue for, support, make a case for, plead for; excuse, explain. ❸ *the manager defended his players* SUPPORT, back, stand by, stick up for, stand up for, argue for, champion, endorse; *informal* throw one's weight behind.
– OPPOSITES attack, criticize.

defendant ▶ noun ACCUSED, prisoner (at the bar); appellant, litigant, respondent; suspect.
– OPPOSITES plaintiff.

defender ▶ noun ❶ *defenders of the environment* PROTECTOR, guard, guardian, preserver; custodian, watchdog, keeper, overseer, superintendent, caretaker. ❷ *a defender of colonialism* SUPPORTER, upholder, backer, champion, advocate, apologist, proponent, exponent, promoter; adherent, believer. ❸ *he passed two defenders and scored* FULLBACK, back, sweeper; (**defenders**) back four.

defensible ▶ adjective ❶ *a defensible attitude* JUSTIFIABLE, arguable, tenable, defendable, supportable; plausible, sound, sensible, reasonable, rational, logical; acceptable, valid, legitimate; excusable, pardonable, understandable. ❷ *a defensible territory* SECURE, safe, fortified; invulnerable, impregnable, impenetrable, unassailable.
– OPPOSITES untenable, vulnerable.

defensive ▶ adjective ❶ *troops in defensive positions* DEFENDING, protective; wary, watchful. ❷ *a defensive response* SELF-JUSTIFYING, oversensitive, prickly, paranoid, neurotic; *informal* uptight, twitchy.

defer[1] ▶ verb *the committee will defer their decision* POSTPONE, put off, delay, hold over/off, put back; shelve, suspend, stay, mothball; *N. Amer.* put over, table, take a rain check on; *informal* put on ice, put on the back burner, put in cold storage.

defer[2] ▶ verb *they deferred to Joseph's judgement* YIELD, submit, give way, give in, surrender, capitulate, acquiesce; respect, honour.

deference ▶ noun RESPECT, respectfulness, dutifulness; submissiveness, submission, obedience, surrender, accession, capitulation, acquiescence, complaisance, obeisance.
– OPPOSITES disrespect.

deferential ▶ adjective RESPECTFUL, humble, obsequious; dutiful, obedient, submissive, subservient, yielding, acquiescent, complaisant, compliant, tractable, biddable, docile.

deferment ▶ **noun** POSTPONEMENT, deferral, suspension, delay, adjournment, interruption, pause; respite, stay, moratorium, reprieve, grace.

defiance ▶ **noun** RESISTANCE, opposition, noncompliance, disobedience, insubordination, dissent, recalcitrance, subversion, rebellion; contempt, disregard, scorn, insolence, truculence.
– OPPOSITES obedience.

defiant ▶ **adjective** INTRANSIGENT, resistant, obstinate, uncooperative, non-compliant, recalcitrant; obstreperous, truculent, dissenting, disobedient, insubordinate, subversive, rebellious, mutinous; *informal* feisty; *Brit. informal* stroppy, bolshie.
– OPPOSITES cooperative.

deficiency ▶ **noun** ❶ *a vitamin deficiency* INSUFFICIENCY, lack, shortage, want, dearth, inadequacy, deficit, shortfall; scarcity, paucity, absence, undersupply, deprivation, shortness. ❷ *the team's big deficiency* DEFECT, fault, flaw, imperfection, weakness, weak point, inadequacy, shortcoming, limitation, failing.
– OPPOSITES surplus, strength.

deficient ▶ **adjective** ❶ *a diet deficient in vitamin A* LACKING, wanting, inadequate, insufficient, limited, poor, scant; short of/on, low on. ❷ *deficient leadership* DEFECTIVE, faulty, flawed, inadequate, imperfect, shoddy, weak, inferior, unsound, substandard, second-rate, poor; *Brit. informal* duff.

deficit ▶ **noun** SHORTFALL, deficiency, shortage, undersupply; debt, arrears; negative amount, loss.
– OPPOSITES surplus.

defile ▶ **verb** ❶ *her capacity for love had been defiled* SPOIL, sully, mar, impair, debase, degrade; poison, taint, tarnish; destroy, ruin. ❷ *the sacred bones were defiled* DESECRATE, profane, violate; contaminate, pollute, debase, degrade, dishonour. ❸ (*archaic*) *she was defiled by a married man* RAPE, violate; *poetic/literary* ravish; *dated* deflower.
– OPPOSITES sanctify.

definable ▶ **adjective** DETERMINABLE, ascertainable, known, definite, clear-cut, precise, exact, specific.

define ▶ **verb** ❶ *the dictionary defines it succinctly* EXPLAIN, expound, interpret, elucidate, describe, clarify; give the meaning of, put into words. ❷ *he defined the limits of the middle class* DETERMINE, establish, fix, specify, designate, decide, stipulate, set out; demarcate, delineate. ❸ *the farm buildings defined against the fields* OUTLINE, delineate, silhouette.

definite ▶ **adjective** ❶ *a definite answer* EXPLICIT, specific, express, precise, exact, clear-cut, direct, plain, outright; fixed, established, confirmed, concrete. ❷ *definite evidence* CERTAIN, sure, positive, conclusive, decisive, firm, concrete, unambiguous, unequivocal, clear, unmistakable, proven; guaranteed, assured, cut and dried. ❸ *she had a definite dislike for Robert* UNMISTAKABLE, unequivocal, unambiguous, certain, undisputed, decided, marked, distinct. ❹ *a definite geographical area* FIXED, marked, demarcated, delimited, stipulated, particular.
– OPPOSITES vague, ambiguous, indeterminate.

definitely ▶ **adverb** CERTAINLY, surely, for sure, unquestionably, without doubt, without question, undoubtedly, indubitably, positively, absolutely; undeniably, unmistakably, plainly, clearly, obviously, patently, palpably, transparently, unequivocally, as sure as eggs is eggs.

definition ▶ **noun** ❶ *the definition of 'intelligence'* MEANING, denotation, sense; interpretation, explanation, elucidation, description, clarification, illustration. ❷ *the definition of the picture* CLARITY, visibility, sharpness, crispness, acuteness; resolution, focus, contrast.

definitive ▶ **adjective** ❶ *a definitive decision* CONCLUSIVE, final, ultimate; unconditional, unqualified, absolute, categorical, positive, definite. ❷ *the definitive guide* AUTHORITATIVE, exhaustive, best, finest, consummate; classic, standard, recognized, accepted, official.

deflate ▶ **verb** ❶ *he deflated the tyres* LET DOWN, flatten, void; puncture. ❷ *the balloon deflated* GO DOWN, collapse, shrink, contract. ❸ *the news had deflated him* SUBDUE, humble, cow, chasten; dispirit, dismay, discourage, dishearten; squash, crush, bring down, take the wind out of someone's sails; *informal* knock the stuffing out of. ❹ *the budget deflated the economy* REDUCE, slow down, diminish; devalue, depreciate, depress.
– OPPOSITES inflate.

deflect ▶ **verb** ❶ *she wanted to deflect attention from herself* TURN ASIDE/AWAY, divert, avert, sidetrack; distract, draw away; block, parry, fend off, stave off. ❷ *the ball deflected off the wall* BOUNCE, glance, ricochet; diverge, deviate, veer, swerve, slew.

deform ▶ **verb** DISFIGURE, bend out of shape, contort, buckle, warp; damage, impair.

deformed ▶ **adjective** MISSHAPEN, distorted, malformed, contorted, out of shape; twisted, crooked, warped, buckled, gnarled; crippled, humpbacked, hunchbacked, disfigured, grotesque; injured, damaged, mutilated, mangled.

deformity ▶ **noun** MALFORMATION, misshapenness, distortion, crookedness; imperfection, abnormality, irregularity; disfigurement; defect, flaw, blemish.

defraud ▶ **verb** SWINDLE, cheat, rob; deceive, dupe, hoodwink, double-cross, trick; *informal* con, do, sting, diddle, rip off, shaft, bilk, rook, gyp, pull a fast one on, put one over on, sell a pup to; *N. Amer. informal* sucker, snooker, stiff; *Austral. informal* pull a swifty on.

defray ▸ **verb** PAY (FOR), cover, meet, square, settle, clear, discharge; foot the bill for; *N. Amer. informal* pick up the tab for.

deft ▸ **adjective** SKILFUL, adept, adroit, dexterous, agile, nimble, handy; able, capable, skilled, proficient, accomplished, expert, polished, slick, professional, masterly; clever, shrewd, astute, canny, sharp; *informal* nifty, nippy.
– OPPOSITES clumsy.

defunct ▸ **adjective** DISUSED, unused, inoperative, non-functioning, unusable, obsolete; no longer existing, discontinued; extinct.
– OPPOSITES working, extant.

defuse ▸ **verb** ❶ *he tried to defuse the grenade* DEACTIVATE, disarm, disable, make safe. ❷ *an attempt to defuse the tension* REDUCE, lessen, diminish, lighten, relieve, ease, alleviate, moderate, mitigate.
– OPPOSITES activate, intensify.

defy ▸ **verb** ❶ *he defied European law* DISOBEY, go against, flout, fly in the face of, disregard, ignore; break, violate, contravene, breach, infringe; *informal* cock a snook at. ❷ *his actions defy belief* ELUDE, escape, defeat; frustrate, thwart, baffle. ❸ *he glowered, defying her to mock him* CHALLENGE, dare.
– OPPOSITES obey.

degeneracy ▸ **noun** CORRUPTION, decadence, moral decay, dissipation, dissolution, profligacy, vice, immorality, sin, sinfulness, ungodliness; debauchery; *formal* turpitude.

degenerate ▸ **adjective** ❶ *a degenerate form of classicism* DEBASED, degraded, corrupt, impure; *formal* vitiated. ❷ *her degenerate brother* CORRUPT, decadent, dissolute, dissipated, debauched, reprobate, profligate; sinful, ungodly, immoral, unprincipled, amoral, dishonourable, disreputable, unsavoury, sordid, low, ignoble.
– OPPOSITES pure, moral.
▸ **noun** *a group of degenerates* REPROBATE, debauchee, profligate, libertine, roué, loose-liver.
▸ **verb** ❶ *their quality of life had degenerated* DETERIORATE, decline, slip, slide, worsen, lapse, slump, go downhill, regress, retrogress; go to rack and ruin; *informal* go to pot, go to the dogs, hit the skids, go down the toilet. ❷ *the muscles started to degenerate* WASTE (AWAY), atrophy, weaken.
– OPPOSITES improve.

degradation ▸ **noun** ❶ *poverty brings with it degradation* HUMILIATION, shame, loss of self-respect, abasement, indignity, ignominy. ❷ *the degradation of women* DEMEANING, debasement, discrediting. ❸ *the degradation of the tissues* DETERIORATION, degeneration, atrophy, decay; breakdown.

degrade ▸ **verb** ❶ *prisons should not degrade prisoners* DEMEAN, debase, cheapen, devalue; shame, humiliate, humble, mortify, abase, dishonour; dehumanize, brutalize. ❷ *the polymer will not degrade* BREAK DOWN, deteriorate, degenerate, decay.
– OPPOSITES dignify.

degraded ▸ **adjective** ❶ *I feel so degraded* HUMILIATED, demeaned, cheapened, cheap, ashamed. ❷ *his degraded sensibilities* DEGENERATE, corrupt, depraved, dissolute, dissipated, debauched, immoral, base, sordid.
– OPPOSITES proud, moral.

degrading ▸ **adjective** HUMILIATING, demeaning, shameful, mortifying, ignominious, undignified, inglorious, wretched; *informal* infra dig.

degree ▸ **noun** LEVEL, standard, grade, mark; amount, extent, measure; magnitude, intensity, strength; proportion, ratio.
■ **by degrees** GRADUALLY, little by little, bit by bit, inch by inch, step by step, slowly; piecemeal.
■ **to a degree** TO SOME EXTENT, to a certain extent, up to a point.

dehydrate ▸ **verb** ❶ *alcohol dehydrates the skin* DRY (OUT), desiccate, dehumidify, effloresce. ❷ *frogs can dehydrate quickly* DRY UP/OUT, lose water.
– OPPOSITES hydrate.

deify ▸ **verb** ❶ *she was deified by the early Romans* WORSHIP, revere, venerate, reverence, hold sacred; immortalize. ❷ *he was deified by the press* IDOLIZE, lionize, hero-worship, extol; idealize, glorify, aggrandize; *informal* put on a pedestal.
– OPPOSITES demonize.

deign ▸ **verb** CONDESCEND, stoop, lower oneself, demean oneself, humble oneself; consent, vouchsafe; *informal* come down from one's high horse.

deity ▸ **noun** GOD, goddess, divine being, supreme being, divinity, immortal; creator, demiurge; godhead.

dejected ▸ **adjective** DOWNCAST, downhearted, despondent, disconsolate, dispirited, crestfallen, disheartened; depressed, crushed, desolate, heartbroken, in the doldrums, sad, unhappy, doleful, melancholy, miserable, woebegone, forlorn, fed up, wretched, glum, gloomy; *informal* blue, down in the mouth, down in the dumps; *Brit. informal* brassed off, cheesed off.
– OPPOSITES cheerful.

de jure ▸ **adverb & adjective** BY RIGHT, rightfully, legally, according to the law; rightful, legal.
– OPPOSITES de facto.

delay ▸ **verb** ❶ *we were delayed by the traffic* DETAIN, hold up, make late, slow up/down, bog down; hinder, hamper, impede, obstruct.

❷ *they delayed no longer* LINGER, dally, drag one's feet, be slow, hold back, dawdle, waste time; procrastinate, stall, hang fire, mark time, temporize, hesitate, dither, shilly-shally; *informal* dilly-dally; *archaic* tarry. ❸ *he may delay the cut in interest rates* POSTPONE, put off, defer, hold over, shelve, suspend, stay; reschedule; *N. Amer.* put over, table; *informal* put on ice, put on the back burner, put in cold storage.
–OPPOSITES hurry, advance.
▶ noun ❶ *drivers will face lengthy delays* HOLD-UP, wait, detainment; hindrance, impediment, obstruction, setback. ❷ *the delay of his trial* POSTPONEMENT, deferral, deferment, stay, respite; adjournment. ❸ *I set off without delay* PROCRASTINATION, stalling, hesitation, dithering, dallying, dawdling.

delectable ▶ adjective ❶ *a delectable meal* DELICIOUS, mouth-watering, appetizing, flavoursome, flavourful, toothsome, palatable; succulent, luscious, tasty; *informal* scrumptious, delish, scrummy, yummy; *Brit. informal* moreish; *N. Amer. informal* finger-licking, nummy. ❷ *the delectable Ms Davis* DELIGHTFUL, lovely, captivating, charming, enchanting, appealing, beguiling; beautiful, attractive, ravishing, gorgeous, stunning, alluring, sexy, seductive, desirable, luscious; *informal* divine, heavenly, dreamy; *Brit. informal* tasty.
–OPPOSITES unpalatable, unattractive.

delectation ▶ noun (*humorous*) ENJOYMENT, gratification, delight, pleasure, satisfaction, relish; entertainment, amusement, titillation.

delegate ▶ noun *trade union delegates* REPRESENTATIVE, envoy, emissary, commissioner, agent, deputy, commissary; spokesperson, spokesman/woman; ambassador, plenipotentiary.
▶ verb ❶ *she must delegate routine tasks* ASSIGN, entrust, pass on, hand on/over, turn over, devolve, depute, transfer. ❷ *they were delegated to negotiate with the States* AUTHORIZE, commission, depute, appoint, nominate, mandate, empower, charge, choose, designate, elect.

delegation ▶ noun ❶ *the delegation from South Africa* DEPUTATION, delegacy, legation, (diplomatic) mission, commission; delegates, representatives, envoys, emissaries, deputies. ❷ *the delegation of tasks to others* ASSIGNMENT, entrusting, giving, devolution, deputation, transference.

delete ▶ verb REMOVE, cut out, take out, edit out, expunge, excise, eradicate, cancel; cross out, strike out, blue-pencil, ink out, scratch out, obliterate, white out; rub out, erase, efface, wipe out, blot out; *Printing* dele.
–OPPOSITES add.

deleterious ▶ adjective HARMFUL, damaging, detrimental, injurious; bad, adverse, disadvantageous, unfavourable, unfortunate, undesirable.
–OPPOSITES beneficial.

deliberate ▶ adjective ❶ *a deliberate attempt to provoke him* INTENTIONAL, calculated, conscious, intended, planned, studied, knowing, wilful, wanton, purposeful, purposive, premeditated, pre-planned; voluntary, volitional; *Law, dated* prepense. ❷ *small, deliberate steps* CAREFUL, cautious; measured, regular, even, steady. ❸ *a deliberate worker* METHODICAL, systematic, careful, painstaking, meticulous, thorough.
–OPPOSITES accidental, hasty, careless.
▶ verb *she deliberated on his words* THINK ABOUT/OVER, ponder, consider, contemplate, reflect on, muse on, meditate on, ruminate on, mull over, give thought to, weigh up; brood over, dwell on; *N. Amer.* think on.

deliberately ▶ adverb ❶ *he deliberately hurt me* INTENTIONALLY, on purpose, purposely, by design, knowingly, wittingly, consciously, purposefully; wilfully, wantonly; *Law* with malice aforethought. ❷ *he walked deliberately down the aisle* CAREFULLY, cautiously, slowly, steadily, evenly.

deliberation ▶ noun ❶ *after much deliberation, I accepted* THOUGHT, consideration, reflection, contemplation, meditation, rumination; *formal* cogitation. ❷ *he replaced the glass with deliberation* CARE, carefulness, caution, steadiness.

delicacy ▶ noun ❶ *the fabric's delicacy* FINENESS, exquisiteness, delicateness, daintiness, airiness; flimsiness, gauziness, floatiness, silkiness. ❷ *the children's delicacy* SICKLINESS, ill health, frailty, fragility, weakness, debility; infirmity, valetudinarianism. ❸ *the delicacy of the situation* DIFFICULTY, trickiness; sensitivity, ticklishness, awkwardness. ❹ *treat this matter with delicacy* CARE, sensitivity, tact, discretion, diplomacy, subtlety, sensibility. ❺ *an Australian delicacy* CHOICE FOOD, gourmet food, dainty, treat, luxury, bonne bouche; speciality.

delicate ▶ adjective ❶ *delicate embroidery* FINE, exquisite, intricate, dainty; flimsy, gauzy, filmy, floaty, diaphanous, wispy, insubstantial. ❷ *a delicate shade of blue* SUBTLE, soft, muted; pastel, pale, light. ❸ *delicate china cups* FRAGILE, breakable, frail; *formal* frangible. ❹ *his wife is delicate* SICKLY, unhealthy, frail, feeble, weak, debilitated; unwell, infirm; *formal* valetudinarian. ❺ *a delicate issue* DIFFICULT, tricky, sensitive, ticklish, awkward, problematical, touchy, prickly; embarrassing; *informal* sticky, dicey. ❻ *the matter required delicate handling* CAREFUL, sensitive, tactful, diplomatic, discreet, kid-glove, softly-softly. ❼ *his delicate palate* DISCRIMINATING, discerning; FASTIDIOUS, fussy, finicky, dainty; *informal* picky, choosy, pernickety. ❽ *a delicate mechanism* SENSITIVE, precision, precise.
–OPPOSITES coarse, lurid, strong, robust, clumsy.

delicious ▶ adjective ❶ *a delicious meal* DELECTABLE, mouth-watering, appetizing, tasty, fla-

voursome, flavourful, toothsome, palatable; succulent, luscious; *informal* scrumptious, delish, scrummy, yummy; *Brit. informal* moreish; *N. Amer. informal* finger-licking, nummy. ❷ *a delicious languor stole over her* DELIGHTFUL, exquisite, lovely, pleasurable, pleasant; *informal* heavenly, divine.
– OPPOSITES unpalatable, unpleasant.

delight ▶ **verb** ❶ *her manners delighted him* PLEASE GREATLY, charm, enchant, captivate, entrance, thrill; gladden, gratify, appeal to; entertain, amuse, divert; *informal* send, tickle pink, bowl over. ❷ *Fabia delighted in his touch* TAKE PLEASURE, revel, luxuriate, wallow, glory; adore, love, relish, savour, lap up; *informal* get a kick out of, get a buzz out of, get a thrill out of, dig; *N. Amer. informal* get a charge out of.
– OPPOSITES dismay, disgust, dislike.
▶ **noun** *she squealed with delight* PLEASURE, happiness, joy, glee, gladness; excitement, amusement, bliss, rapture, elation, euphoria.
– OPPOSITES displeasure.

delighted ▶ **adjective** PLEASED, glad, happy, thrilled, overjoyed, ecstatic, elated; on cloud nine, walking on air, in seventh heaven, jumping for joy; enchanted, charmed; amused, diverted; gleeful, cock-a-hoop; *informal* over the moon, tickled pink, as pleased as Punch, on top of the world, as happy as Larry, blissed out; *Brit. informal* chuffed; *N. English informal* made up; *Austral. informal* wrapped.

delightful ▶ **adjective** ❶ *a delightful evening* PLEASANT, lovely, pleasurable, enjoyable; amusing, entertaining, diverting; gratifying, satisfying; marvellous, wonderful, splendid, sublime, thrilling; *informal* great, super, fabulous, fab, terrific, heavenly, divine, grand; *Brit. informal* brilliant, brill, smashing; *N. Amer. informal* peachy, ducky; *Austral./NZ informal* beaut, bonzer. ❷ *the delightful Sally* CHARMING, enchanting, captivating, bewitching, appealing; sweet, endearing, cute, lovely, adorable, delectable, delicious, gorgeous, ravishing, beautiful, pretty; *Scottish & N. English* bonny; *informal* dreamy, divine.

delimit ▶ **verb** DETERMINE, establish, set, fix, demarcate, define, delineate.

delineate ▶ **verb** ❶ *the aims of the study as delineated by the boss* DESCRIBE, set forth/out, present, outline, depict, represent; map out, define, specify, identify. ❷ *a section delineated in red marker pen* OUTLINE, trace, block in, mark (out/off), delimit.

delinquency ▶ **noun** ❶ *teenage delinquency* CRIME, wrongdoing, lawbreaking, lawlessness, misconduct, misbehaviour; misdemeanours, offences, misdeeds. ❷ (*formal*) *grave delinquency on the host's part* NEGLIGENCE, dereliction of duty, irresponsibility.

delinquent ▶ **adjective** ❶ *delinquent teenagers* LAWLESS, lawbreaking, criminal; errant, badly behaved, troublesome, difficult, unruly, disobedient, uncontrollable. ❷ (*formal*) *delinquent parents face tough penalties* NEGLIGENT, neglectful, remiss, irresponsible, lax, slack; *N. Amer.* derelict.
– OPPOSITES dutiful.
▶ **noun** *teenage delinquents* OFFENDER, wrongdoer, malefactor, lawbreaker, culprit, criminal; hooligan, vandal, ruffian, hoodlum; young offender; *informal* tearaway.

delirious ▶ **adjective** ❶ *she was delirious but had lucid intervals* INCOHERENT, raving, babbling, irrational; feverish, frenzied; deranged, demented, unhinged, mad, insane, out of one's mind. ❷ *the delirious crowd* ECSTATIC, euphoric, elated, thrilled, overjoyed, beside oneself, walking on air, on cloud nine, in seventh heaven, carried away, transported, rapturous; hysterical, wild, frenzied; *informal* blissed out, over the moon, on a high.

delirium ▶ **noun** ❶ *she had fits of delirium* DERANGEMENT, dementia, madness, insanity; incoherence, irrationality, hysteria, feverishness, hallucination. ❷ *the delirium of desire* ECSTASY, rapture, transports, wild emotion, passion, wildness, excitement, frenzy, feverishness, fever; euphoria, elation.
– OPPOSITES lucidity.

deliver ▶ **verb** ❶ *the parcel was delivered to his house* BRING, take, convey, carry, transport; send, dispatch, remit. ❷ *the money was delivered up to the official* HAND OVER, turn over, make over, sign over; surrender, give up, yield, cede; consign, commit, entrust, trust. ❸ *he was delivered from his enemies* SAVE, rescue, free, liberate, release, extricate, emancipate, redeem. ❹ *the court delivered its verdict* UTTER, give, make, read, broadcast; pronounce, announce, declare, proclaim, hand down, return, set forth. ❺ *she delivered a blow to his head* ADMINISTER, deal, inflict, give; *informal* land. ❻ *he delivered the first ball* BOWL, pitch, hurl, throw, cast, lob. ❼ *the trip delivered everything she wanted* PROVIDE, supply, furnish. ❽ *we must deliver on our commitments* FULFIL, live up to, carry out, carry through, make good; *informal* deliver the goods, come across. ❾ *she returned home to deliver her child* GIVE BIRTH TO, bear, be delivered of, have, bring into the world; *N. Amer.* birth; *informal* drop.

deliverance ▶ **noun** ❶ *their deliverance from prison* LIBERATION, release, delivery, discharge, rescue, emancipation; salvation. ❷ *the tone he adopted for such deliverances* UTTERANCE, statement, announcement, pronouncement, declaration, proclamation; lecture, speech.

delivery ▶ **noun** ❶ *the delivery of the goods* CONVEYANCE, carriage, transportation, transport, distribution; dispatch, remittance; freightage, haulage, shipment. ❷ *we get several deliveries a day* CONSIGNMENT, load, shipment. ❸ *the deliv-*

eries take place in hospital BIRTH, childbirth; *formal* parturition. ❹ *her delivery was stilted* SPEECH, pronunciation, enunciation, articulation, elocution; utterance, recitation, recital, execution.

delude ▶ verb MISLEAD, deceive, fool, take in, trick, dupe, hoodwink, gull, lead on; *informal* con, pull the wool over someone's eyes, lead up the garden path, take for a ride; *N. Amer. informal* sucker, snooker; *Austral. informal* pull a swifty on.

deluge ▶ noun ❶ *homes were swept away by the deluge* FLOOD, torrent; *Brit.* spate. ❷ *the deluge turned the pitch into a swamp* DOWNPOUR, torrential rain; thunderstorm, rainstorm, cloudburst. ❸ *a deluge of complaints* BARRAGE, volley; flood, torrent, avalanche, stream, spate, rush, outpouring.

▶ verb ❶ *homes were deluged by the rains* FLOOD, inundate, submerge, swamp, drown. ❷ *we have been deluged with calls* INUNDATE, overwhelm, overrun, flood, swamp, snow under, engulf, bombard.

delusion ▶ noun ❶ *a common male delusion* MISAPPREHENSION, misconception, misunderstanding, mistake, error, misinterpretation, misconstruction, misbelief; fallacy, illusion, fantasy. ❷ *a web of delusion* DECEPTION, trickery.

de luxe ▶ adjective LUXURIOUS, luxury, sumptuous, palatial, opulent, lavish; grand, high-class, quality, exclusive, choice, fancy; expensive, costly; *Brit.* upmarket; *informal* plush, posh, classy, ritzy, swanky, pricey; *Brit. informal* swish; *N. Amer. informal* swank.
–OPPOSITES basic, cheap.

delve ▶ verb ❶ *she delved in her pocket* RUMMAGE, search, hunt, scrabble about/around, root about/around, ferret, fish about/around in, dig; go through, rifle through; *Brit. informal* rootle around in. ❷ *we must delve deeper into the matter* INVESTIGATE, enquire, probe, explore, research, look into, go into.

demagogue ▶ noun RABBLE-ROUSER, political agitator, soapbox orator, firebrand; *informal* tub-thumper.

demand ▶ noun ❶ *I gave in to her demands* REQUEST, call, command, order, dictate, ultimatum, stipulation. ❷ *the demands of a young family* REQUIREMENT, need, desire, wish, want; claim, imposition. ❸ *the big demand for such toys* MARKET, call, appetite, desire; run on, rush on.

▶ verb ❶ *workers demanded wage increases* CALL FOR, ask for, request, push for, hold out for; insist on, claim. ❷ *Harvey demanded that I tell him the truth* ORDER, command, enjoin, urge; *poetic/literary* bid. ❸ *'Where is she?' he demanded* ASK, inquire, question, interrogate; challenge. ❹ *an activity demanding detailed knowledge* REQUIRE, need, necessitate, call for, involve, entail. ❺ *they demanded complete anonymity* INSIST ON, stipulate, make a condition of; expect, look for.
■ **in demand** SOUGHT-AFTER, desired, coveted, wanted, requested; marketable, desirable, popular, all the rage, at a premium, like gold dust; *informal* big, trendy, hot.

demanding ▶ adjective ❶ *a demanding task* DIFFICULT, challenging, taxing, exacting, tough, hard, onerous, burdensome, formidable; arduous, uphill, rigorous, gruelling, back-breaking, punishing. ❷ *a demanding child* NAGGING, clamorous, importunate, insistent; trying, tiresome, hard to please.
–OPPOSITES easy.

demarcate ▶ verb SEPARATE, divide, mark (out/off), delimit, delineate; bound.

demarcation ▶ noun ❶ *clear demarcation of function* SEPARATION, distinction, differentiation, division, delimitation, definition. ❷ *territorial demarcations* BOUNDARY, border, borderline, frontier; dividing line, divide.

demean ▶ verb DISCREDIT, lower, degrade, debase, devalue; cheapen, abase, humble, humiliate, disgrace, dishonour.
–OPPOSITES dignify.

demeaning ▶ adjective DEGRADING, humiliating, shameful, mortifying, abject, ignominious, undignified, inglorious; *informal* infra dig.

demeanour ▶ noun MANNER, air, attitude, appearance, look; bearing, carriage; behaviour, conduct; *formal* comportment.

demented ▶ adjective MAD, insane, deranged, out of one's mind, crazed, lunatic, unbalanced, unhinged, disturbed, non compos mentis; *informal* crazy, mental, off one's head, off one's rocker, nutty, round the bend, raving mad, batty, cuckoo, loopy, loony, bananas, screwy, touched, gaga, not all there, out to lunch; *Brit. informal* barmy, bonkers, crackers, barking, round the twist, off one's trolley, not the full shilling; *N. Amer. informal* buggy, nutso, squirrelly, wacko.
–OPPOSITES sane.

dementia ▶ noun MENTAL ILLNESS, madness, insanity, derangement, lunacy; Alzheimer's (disease).

demise ▶ noun ❶ *her tragic demise* DEATH, dying, passing, loss of life, end, quietus; *formal* decease; *archaic* expiry. ❷ *the demise of the Ottoman empire* END, break-up, disintegration, fall, downfall, collapse.
–OPPOSITES birth.

demobilize ▶ verb DISBAND, decommission, discharge; *Brit. informal* demob.

democracy ▶ noun REPRESENTATIVE GOVERNMENT, elective government, constitutional government; self-government, autonomy; republic, commonwealth.
–OPPOSITES dictatorship.

democratic ▶ adjective ELECTED, representative, parliamentary, popular; egalitarian, classless; self-governing, autonomous, republican.

demolish ▶ verb ❶ *they demolished a block of flats* KNOCK DOWN, pull down, tear down, bring down, destroy, flatten, raze (to the ground), level, bulldoze, topple; blow up; dismantle, disassemble. ❷ *he demolished her credibility* DESTROY, ruin, wreck; refute, disprove, discredit, overturn, explode, drive a coach and horses through; *informal* shoot full of holes, do for. ❸ (*informal*) *our team were demolished.* See TROUNCE. ❹ (*informal*) *she demolished a sausage roll.* See DEVOUR sense 1.
– OPPOSITES construct, strengthen.

demolition ▶ noun ❶ *the demolition of the building* DESTRUCTION, levelling, bulldozing, clearance; obliteration. ❷ *the demolition of his theory* DESTRUCTION, refutation. ❸ (*informal*) *New Zealand's demolition of England.* See DEFEAT noun sense 1.

demon ▶ noun ❶ *the demons from hell* DEVIL, fiend, evil spirit, cacodemon; incubus, succubus; hellhound. ❷ *the man was a demon* MONSTER, ogre, fiend, devil, brute, savage, beast, barbarian, animal. ❸ *Surrey's fast-bowling demon* GENIUS, expert, master, virtuoso, maestro, past master, marvel; star; *informal* hotshot, whizz, buff, pro, ace. ❹ *the demon of creativity.* See DAEMON.
– OPPOSITES angel, saint.

demonic, demoniac, demoniacal ▶ adjective ❶ *demonic powers* DEVILISH, fiendish, diabolical, satanic, Mephistophelean, hellish, infernal; evil, wicked. ❷ *the demonic intensity of his playing* FRENZIED, wild, feverish, frenetic, frantic, furious, manic, like one possessed.

demonstrable ▶ adjective VERIFIABLE, provable, attestable; verified, proven, confirmed; obvious, clear, clear-cut, evident, apparent, manifest, patent, distinct, noticeable; unmistakable, undeniable.

demonstrate ▶ verb ❶ *his findings demonstrate that boys commit more crimes* SHOW, indicate, determine, establish, prove, confirm, verify, corroborate, substantiate. ❷ *she was asked to demonstrate quilting* GIVE A DEMONSTRATION OF, show how something is done; display, show, illustrate, exemplify. ❸ *his work demonstrated an analytical ability* REVEAL, bespeak, indicate, signify, signal, denote, show, display, exhibit; bear witness to, testify to; imply, intimate, give away. ❹ *they demonstrated against the Government* PROTEST, rally, march; stage a sit-in, picket, strike, walk out; mutiny, rebel.

demonstration ▶ noun ❶ *there is no demonstration of God's existence* PROOF, substantiation, confirmation, affirmation, corroboration, verification, validation; evidence, indication, witness, testament. ❷ *a demonstration of woodcarving* EXHIBITION, presentation, display, exposition, teach-in; *informal* demo, expo, taster. ❸ *his paintings are a demonstration of his talent* MANIFESTATION, indication, sign, mark, token, embodiment; expression. ❹ *an anti-racism demonstration* PROTEST, march, rally, lobby, sit-in; stoppage, strike, walkout, picket (line); *informal* demo.

demonstrative ▶ adjective ❶ *a very demonstrative family* EXPRESSIVE, open, forthcoming, communicative, unreserved, emotional, effusive, gushing; affectionate, cuddly, loving, warm, friendly, approachable; *informal* touchy-feely, lovey-dovey. ❷ *the successes are demonstrative of their skill* INDICATIVE, indicatory, suggestive, illustrative. ❸ *demonstrative evidence of his theorem* CONVINCING, definite, positive, telling, conclusive, certain, decisive; incontrovertible, irrefutable, undeniable, indisputable, unassailable.
– OPPOSITES reserved, inconclusive.

demoralize ▶ verb DISHEARTEN, dispirit, deject, cast down, depress, dismay, daunt, discourage, unman, unnerve, crush, shake, throw, cow, subdue; break someone's spirit; *informal* knock the stuffing out of, knock sideways; *Brit. informal* knock for six.
– OPPOSITES hearten.

demoralized ▶ adjective DISPIRITED, disheartened, downhearted, dejected, downcast, low, depressed, despairing; disconsolate, crestfallen, disappointed, dismayed, daunted, discouraged; crushed, humbled, subdued.

demote ▶ verb DOWNGRADE, relegate, declass, reduce in rank; depose, unseat, displace, oust; *Military* cashier, disrate.
– OPPOSITES promote.

demotic ▶ adjective POPULAR, vernacular, colloquial, idiomatic, vulgar, common; informal, everyday, slangy.
– OPPOSITES formal.

demur ▶ verb *Steed demurred when the suggestion was made* OBJECT, take exception, take issue, protest, cavil, dissent; voice reservations, be unwilling, be reluctant, baulk, think twice; drag one's heels, refuse; *informal* boggle, kick up a fuss.
▶ noun *they accepted without demur* OBJECTION, protest, protestation, complaint, dispute, dissent, opposition, resistance; reservation, hesitation, reluctance, disinclination; doubts, qualms, misgivings, second thoughts; a murmur, a word.

demure ▶ adjective MODEST, unassuming, meek, mild, reserved, retiring, quiet, shy, bashful, diffident, reticent, timid, shrinking, coy; decorous, decent, seemly, ladylike, respectable, proper, virtuous, pure, innocent, chaste; sober, sedate, staid, prim, goody-goody, strait-laced; *informal* butter-wouldn't-melt.
– OPPOSITES brazen.

den ▶ noun ❶ *the mink left its den* LAIR, sett, earth, drey, burrow, hole, dugout, covert, shelter, hiding place, hideout. ❷ *a notorious drinking den* HAUNT, site, hotbed, nest, pit, hole; *informal* joint, dive. ❸ *the poet scribbled in his den* STUDY, studio, library; sanctum, retreat, sanctuary, hideaway, snug, cubbyhole; *informal* hidey-hole.

denial ▶ noun ❶ *the reports met with a denial* CONTRADICTION, refutation, rebuttal, repudiation, disclaimer; negation, dissent; *Law* disaffirmation. ❷ *the denial of insurance to certain people* REFUSAL, withholding; rejection, rebuff, repulse, veto, turndown; *informal* knock-back; *N. Amer. formal* declination. ❸ *the denial of worldly values* RENUNCIATION, eschewal, repudiation, disavowal, rejection, abandonment, surrender, relinquishment.

denigrate ▶ verb DISPARAGE, belittle, deprecate, decry, cast aspersions on, criticize, attack; speak ill of, give someone a bad name, defame, slander, libel; run down, abuse, insult, revile, malign, vilify; *N. Amer.* slur; *informal* bad-mouth, pull to pieces; *Brit. informal* rubbish, slate, slag off; *formal* calumniate.
– OPPOSITES extol.

denizen ▶ noun (*formal*) INHABITANT, resident, townsman/woman, native, local; occupier, occupant, dweller; *archaic* burgher.

denominate ▶ verb (*formal*) CALL, name, term, designate, style, dub, label, entitle.

denomination ▶ noun ❶ *a Christian denomination* RELIGIOUS GROUP, sect, cult, movement, body, branch, persuasion, order, school; Church. ❷ *banknotes in a number of denominations* VALUE, unit, size. ❸ (*formal*) *the invention's denomination still stands today* NAME, title, term, designation, epithet, label, tag; *informal* handle, moniker; *formal* appellation.

denote ▶ verb ❶ *the headdresses denoted warriors* DESIGNATE, indicate, be a mark of, signify, signal, symbolize, represent, mean; typify, characterize, distinguish, mark, identify. ❷ *his manner denoted an inner strength* SUGGEST, point to, smack of, indicate, show, reveal, intimate, imply, convey, betray, bespeak; *informal* spell.

denouement ▶ noun ❶ *the film's denouement* FINALE, final scene, epilogue, coda, end, ending, finish, close; culmination, climax, conclusion, resolution, solution. ❷ *the debate had an unexpected denouement* OUTCOME, upshot, consequence, result, end; *informal* pay-off.
– OPPOSITES beginning, origin.

denounce ▶ verb ❶ *the pope denounced abortion* CONDEMN, criticize, attack, censure, decry, revile, vilify, discredit, damn, reject; proscribe; malign, rail against, run down; *N. Amer.* slur; *informal* knock, slam, hit out at, lay into; *Brit. informal* slate, slag off; *formal* castigate. ❷ *he was denounced as a traitor* EXPOSE, betray, inform on; incriminate, implicate, cite, name, accuse; *archaic* inculpate.
– OPPOSITES praise.

dense ▶ adjective ❶ *a dense forest* THICK, close-packed, tightly packed, closely set, crowded, compact, solid, tight; overgrown, jungly, impenetrable, impassable. ❷ *dense smoke* THICK, heavy, opaque, soupy, murky, smoggy; concentrated, condensed. ❸ (*informal*) *they were dense enough to believe me* STUPID, unintelligent, ignorant, brainless, mindless, foolish, slow, witless, simple-minded, empty-headed, vacuous, vapid, idiotic, imbecilic; *informal* thick, dim, moronic, dumb, dopey, dozy, wooden-headed, lamebrained, birdbrained, pea-brained; *Brit. informal* daft.
– OPPOSITES sparse, thin, clever.

density ▶ noun SOLIDITY, solidness, denseness, thickness, substance, mass; compactness, tightness, hardness.

dent ▶ noun ❶ *I made a dent in his car* INDENTATION, dint, dimple, dip, depression, hollow, crater, pit, trough. ❷ *a nasty dent in their finances* REDUCTION, depletion, deduction, cut.
– OPPOSITES increase.
▶ verb ❶ *Jamie dented his bike* DINT, indent, mark. ❷ *the experience dented her confidence* DIMINISH, reduce, lessen, shrink, weaken, erode, undermine, sap, shake, damage, impair.

dentist ▶ noun DENTAL SURGEON, orthodontist, periodontist, paedodontist.

denude ▶ verb STRIP, clear, deprive, bereave, rob; lay bare, uncover, expose; deforest, defoliate; *dated* divest.
– OPPOSITES cover.

deny ▶ verb ❶ *the report was denied by witnesses* CONTRADICT, repudiate, challenge, contest, oppose; disprove, debunk, explode, discredit, refute, rebut, invalidate, negate, nullify, quash; *informal* shoot full of holes; *formal* gainsay; *Law* disaffirm. ❷ *he denied the request* REFUSE, turn down, reject, rebuff, repulse, decline, veto, dismiss; *informal* knock back, give the thumbs down to, give the red light to. ❸ *she had to deny her parents* RENOUNCE, eschew, repudiate, disavow, disown, wash one's hands of, reject, discard, cast aside, abandon, give up; *formal* forswear; *poetic/literary* forsake.
– OPPOSITES confirm, accept.

deodorant ▶ noun *an underarm deodorant* ANTIPERSPIRANT, body spray, perfume, scent.

deodorize ▶ verb FRESHEN, sweeten, purify, disinfect, sanitize, sterilize; fumigate, aerate, air, ventilate.

depart ▶ verb ❶ *James departed after lunch* LEAVE, go (away), withdraw, absent oneself, abstract oneself, quit, exit, decamp, retreat, retire; make off, run off/away; set off/out, get under way, be on one's way; *informal* make tracks, up sticks, clear off/out, take off, split; *Brit. informal* sling one's hook. ❷ *the budget departed from the norm* DEVIATE, diverge, digress, drift, stray, veer; differ, vary; contrast with.
– OPPOSITES arrive.

departed ▶ adjective DEAD, expired, gone, no

more, passed on/away; perished, fallen; *informal* six feet under, pushing up daisies; *formal* deceased; *euphemistic* with God, asleep.

department ▶ noun ❶ *the public health department* DIVISION, section, sector, unit, branch, arm, wing; office, bureau, agency, ministry. ❷ *rural departments* DISTRICT, canton, province, territory, state, county, shire, parish; region, area. ❸ *the food is Kay's department* DOMAIN, territory, province, area, line; responsibility, duty, function, business, affair, charge, task, concern; *informal* pigeon, baby, bag, bailiwick.

departure ▶ noun ❶ *he tried to delay her departure* LEAVING, going, leave-taking, withdrawal, exit, egress, retreat. ❷ *a departure from normality* DEVIATION, divergence, digression, shift; variation, change. ❸ *an exciting departure for film-makers* CHANGE, innovation, novelty, rarity.

depend ▶ verb ❶ *her career depends on a good reference* BE CONTINGENT ON, be conditional on, be dependent on, hinge on, hang on, rest on, rely on; be decided by. ❷ *my family depends on me* RELY ON, lean on; count on, bank on, trust (in), have faith in, believe in; pin one's hopes on.

dependable ▶ adjective RELIABLE, trustworthy, trusty, faithful, loyal, unfailing, sure, steadfast, stable; honourable, sensible, responsible.

dependant ▶ noun CHILD, minor; ward, charge, protégé; relative; (**dependants**) offspring, progeny.

dependence ▶ noun. *See* DEPENDENCY senses 1, 2, 3.

dependency ▶ noun ❶ *her dependency on her husband* DEPENDENCE, reliance; need for. ❷ *the association of retirement with dependency* HELPLESSNESS, dependence, weakness, defencelessness, vulnerability. ❸ *drug dependency* ADDICTION, dependence, reliance; craving, compulsion, fixation, obsession; abuse. ❹ *a British dependency* COLONY, protectorate, province, outpost, satellite state; holding, possession. ❺ *a dependency of the firm* SUBSIDIARY, adjunct, offshoot, auxiliary, attachment, satellite, derivative.
– OPPOSITES independence.

dependent ▶ adjective ❶ *your placement is dependent on her decision* CONDITIONAL, contingent, based; subject to, determined by, influenced by. ❷ *the army is dependent on volunteers* RELIANT ON, relying on, counting on; sustained by. ❸ *she is dependent on drugs* ADDICTED TO, reliant on; *informal* hooked on. ❹ *he is ill and dependent* RELIANT, needy; helpless, weak, infirm, invalid, incapable; debilitated, disabled. ❺ *a UK dependent territory* SUBSIDIARY, subject; satellite, ancillary; puppet.

depict ▶ verb ❶ *the painting depicts the Last Supper* PORTRAY, represent, picture, illustrate, delineate, reproduce, render; draw, paint. ❷ *the process depicted by Darwin's theory* DESCRIBE, detail, relate; present, set forth, set out, outline, delineate; represent, portray, characterize.

depiction ▶ noun ❶ *a depiction of Aphrodite* PICTURE, painting, portrait, drawing, sketch, study, illustration; image, likeness. ❷ *the film's depiction of women* PORTRAYAL, representation, presentation, characterization.

deplete ▶ verb EXHAUST, use up, consume, expend, drain, empty, milk; reduce, decrease, diminish; slim down, cut back.
– OPPOSITES augment.

depletion ▶ noun EXHAUSTION, use, consumption, expenditure; reduction, decrease, diminution; impoverishment.

deplorable ▶ adjective ❶ *your conduct is deplorable* DISGRACEFUL, shameful, dishonourable, unworthy, inexcusable, unpardonable, unforgivable; reprehensible, despicable, abominable, contemptible, execrable, heinous, beyond the pale. ❷ *the garden is in a deplorable state* LAMENTABLE, regrettable, unfortunate, wretched, atrocious, awful, terrible, dreadful, diabolical; sorry, poor, inadequate; *informal* appalling, dire, abysmal, woeful, lousy; *formal* grievous.
– OPPOSITES admirable.

deplore ▶ verb ❶ *we deplore violence* ABHOR, find unacceptable, frown on, disapprove of, take a dim view of, take exception to, detest, despise; condemn, denounce. ❷ *he deplored their lack of flair* REGRET, lament, mourn, rue, bemoan, bewail, complain about, grieve over, sigh over.
– OPPOSITES applaud.

deploy ▶ verb ❶ *forces were deployed at strategic points* POSITION, station, post, place, install, locate, situate, site, establish; base; distribute, dispose. ❷ *she deployed all her skills* USE, utilize, employ, take advantage of, exploit; bring into service, call on, turn to, resort to.

deport ▶ verb ❶ *they were fined and deported* EXPEL, banish, exile, transport, expatriate, extradite, repatriate; evict, oust, throw out; *informal* kick out, boot out, send packing; *Brit. informal* turf out. ❷ (*archaic*) *he deported himself with dignity. See* BEHAVE sense 1.
– OPPOSITES admit.

deportment ▶ noun ❶ (*Brit.*) *poise is concerned with good deportment* POSTURE, carriage, bearing, stance, gait; *formal* comportment. ❷ (*N. Amer.*) *unprofessional deportment* BEHAVIOUR, conduct, performance; manners, practices, actions.

depose ▶ verb ❶ *the president was deposed* OVERTHROW, unseat, dethrone, topple, remove, supplant, displace; dismiss, oust, drum out, throw out, expel, eject; *informal* chuck out, boot out, get rid of, show someone the door; *Brit. informal* turf out. ❷ (*Law*) *a witness deposed that he had seen me* SWEAR, testify, attest, assert, declare, claim; *rare* asseverate.

deposit ▶ **noun** ❶ *a thick deposit of ash* ACCUMULATION, sediment; layer, covering, coating, blanket. ❷ *a copper deposit* SEAM, vein, lode, layer, stratum, bed. ❸ *they paid a deposit* DOWN PAYMENT, advance payment, prepayment, instalment, retainer, stake.
▶ **verb** ❶ *she deposited her books on the table* PUT (DOWN), place, set (down), unload, rest; drop; *informal* dump, park, plonk; *N. Amer. informal* plunk. ❷ *the silt deposited by flood water* LEAVE (BEHIND), precipitate, dump; wash up, cast up. ❸ *the gold was deposited at the bank* LODGE, bank, house, store, stow, put away; *informal* stash, squirrel away.

deposition ▶ **noun** ❶ *the King's deposition* OVERTHROW, downfall, removal, dethronement, displacement, dismissal, expulsion, ejection; *N. Amer.* ouster. ❷ (*Law*) *depositions from witnesses* STATEMENT, affidavit, attestation, affirmation, assertion; allegation, declaration; testimony, evidence; *rare* asseveration. ❸ *the deposition of calcium* DEPOSITING, accumulation, build-up, precipitation.

depository ▶ **noun** REPOSITORY, cache, store, storeroom, storehouse, warehouse; vault, strongroom, safe, treasury; container, receptacle; *informal* lock-up.

depot ▶ **noun** ❶ *the bus depot* TERMINAL, terminus, station, garage; headquarters, base. ❷ *an arms depot* STOREHOUSE, warehouse, store, repository, depository, cache; arsenal, magazine, armoury, ammunition dump.

deprave ▶ **verb** CORRUPT, lead astray, warp, subvert, pervert, debauch, debase, degrade, defile, sully, pollute.

depraved ▶ **adjective** CORRUPT, perverted, deviant, degenerate, debased, immoral, unprincipled; debauched, dissolute, licentious, lecherous, prurient, indecent, sordid; wicked, sinful, vile, iniquitous, nefarious; *informal* warped, twisted, pervy, sick.

depravity ▶ **noun** CORRUPTION, vice, perversion, deviance, degeneracy, immorality, debauchery, dissipation, profligacy, licentiousness, lechery, prurience, obscenity, indecency; wickedness, sin, iniquity; *informal* perviness; *formal* turpitude.

deprecate ▶ **verb** ❶ *the school deprecates this behaviour* DEPLORE, abhor, disapprove of, frown on, take a dim view of, take exception to, detest, despise; criticize, censure. ❷ *he deprecates the value of television* BELITTLE, disparage, denigrate, run down, discredit, decry, play down, trivialize, underrate, undervalue, underestimate, depreciate; scoff at, sneer at, scorn, disdain; *informal* pooh-pooh.
– OPPOSITES praise, overrate.

deprecatory ▶ **adjective** ❶ *deprecatory remarks* DISAPPROVING, censorious, critical, scathing, damning, condemnatory, denunciatory, disparaging, denigratory, derogatory, negative, unflattering; disdainful, derisive, snide. ❷ *a deprecatory smile* APOLOGETIC, rueful, regretful, sorry, remorseful, contrite, penitent, repentant; shamefaced, sheepish.

depreciate ▶ **verb** ❶ *these cars will depreciate* DECREASE IN VALUE, lose value, fall in price. ❷ *the decision to depreciate property* DEVALUE, cheapen, reduce, lower in price, mark down, cut, discount; *informal* slash. ❸ *they depreciate the importance of art* BELITTLE, disparage, denigrate, decry, deprecate, underrate, undervalue, underestimate, diminish, trivialize; disdain, sneer at, scoff at, scorn; *informal* knock, bad-mouth, sell short, pooh-pooh, do down; *Brit. informal* rubbish.

depredation ▶ **noun** PLUNDERING, plunder, looting, pillaging, robbery; devastation, destruction, damage, rape; ravages, raids.

depress ▶ **verb** ❶ *the news depressed him* SADDEN, dispirit, cast down, get down, dishearten, demoralize, crush, shake, desolate, weigh down, oppress; upset, distress, grieve, haunt, harrow; *informal* give someone the blues, make someone fed up. ❷ *new economic policies depressed sales* SLOW DOWN, reduce, lower, weaken, impair; limit, check, inhibit, restrict. ❸ *imports will depress farm prices* REDUCE, lower, cut, cheapen, keep down, discount, deflate, depreciate, devalue, diminish, axe; *informal* slash. ❹ *depress each key in turn* PRESS, push, hold down; thumb, tap; operate, activate.
– OPPOSITES encourage, raise.

depressant ▶ **noun** SEDATIVE, tranquillizer, calmative, sleeping pill, soporific, opiate, hypnotic; *informal* downer, trank, sleeper, dope; *Medicine* neuroleptic.
– OPPOSITES stimulant.

depressed ▶ **adjective** ❶ *he felt lonely and depressed* SAD, unhappy, miserable, gloomy, glum, melancholy, dejected, disconsolate, downhearted, downcast, down, despondent, dispirited, low, heavy-hearted, morose, dismal, desolate; tearful, upset; *informal* blue, down in the dumps, down in the mouth, fed up. ❷ *a depressed economy* WEAK, enervated, devitalized, impaired; inactive, flat, slow, slack, sluggish, stagnant. ❸ *depressed prices* REDUCED, low, cut, cheap, marked down, discounted, discount; *informal* slashed. ❹ *a depressed town* POVERTY-STRICKEN, poor, disadvantaged, deprived, needy, distressed; run down; *informal* slummy. ❺ *a depressed fracture* SUNKEN, hollow, concave, indented, recessed.
– OPPOSITES cheerful, strong, inflated, prosperous, raised.

depressing ▶ **adjective** ❶ *depressing thoughts* UPSETTING, distressing, painful, heartbreaking; dismal, bleak, black, sombre, gloomy, grave, unhappy, melancholy, sad; wretched, doleful; *informal* morbid, blue. ❷ *a depressing room* GLOOMY, bleak, dreary, grim, drab, sombre, dark, dingy, funereal, cheerless, joyless, comfortless, uninviting.

depression ▶ noun ❶ *she ate to ease her depression* UNHAPPINESS, sadness, melancholy, melancholia, misery, sorrow, woe, gloom, despondency, low spirits, heavy heart, despair, desolation, hopelessness; upset, tearfulness; *informal* the dumps, the doldrums, the blues, one's black dog, a (blue) funk; *Psychiatry* dysthymia. ❷ *an economic depression* RECESSION, slump, decline, downturn, standstill; stagnation; *Economics* stagflation. ❸ *a depression in the ground* HOLLOW, indentation, dent, dint, cavity, concavity, dip, pit, hole, sinkhole, trough, crater; basin, bowl.

deprivation ▶ noun ❶ *unemployment and deprivation* POVERTY, impoverishment, penury, privation, hardship, destitution; need, want, distress, indigence, beggary, ruin; straitened circumstances; *rare* pauperdom. ❷ *deprivation of political rights* DISPOSSESSION, withholding, withdrawal, removal, divestment, expropriation, seizure, confiscation; denial, forfeiture, loss; absence, lack.
– OPPOSITES wealth.

deprive ▶ verb DISPOSSESS, strip, divest, relieve, bereave, deny, rob; cheat out of; *informal* do out of.

deprived ▶ adjective DISADVANTAGED, underprivileged, poverty-stricken, impoverished, poor, destitute, needy, unable to make ends meet; *Brit.* on the bread line.

depth ▶ noun ❶ *the depth of the caves* DEEPNESS, distance downwards, distance inwards; drop, vertical extent; *archaic* profundity. ❷ *the depth of his knowledge* EXTENT, range, scope, breadth, width; magnitude, scale, degree. ❸ *her lack of depth* PROFUNDITY, deepness, wisdom, understanding, intelligence, sagacity, discernment, penetration, insight, astuteness, acumen, shrewdness; *formal* perspicuity. ❹ *a work of great depth* COMPLEXITY, intricacy; profundity, gravity, weight. ❺ *depth of colour* INTENSITY, richness, deepness, vividness, strength, brilliance. ❻ *the depths of the sea* DEEPEST PART, bottom, floor, bed; abyss.
– OPPOSITES shallowness, triviality, surface.
■ **in depth** THOROUGHLY, extensively, comprehensively, rigorously, exhaustively, completely, fully; meticulously, scrupulously, painstakingly.

deputation ▶ noun DELEGATION, delegacy, legation, commission, committee, (diplomatic) mission; contingent, group, party.

depute ▶ verb ❶ *he was deputed to handle negotiations* APPOINT, designate, nominate, assign, commission, charge, choose, select, elect; empower, authorize. ❷ *the judge deputed smaller cases to others* DELEGATE, transfer, hand over, pass on, consign, assign, entrust, give.

deputize ▶ verb STAND IN, sit in, fill in, cover, substitute, replace, take someone's place, understudy, be a locum, relieve, take over; hold the fort, step into the breach; act for, act on behalf of; *informal* sub.

deputy ▶ noun *he handed over to his deputy* SECOND (IN COMMAND), number two, subordinate, junior, assistant, personal assistant, PA, aide, helper, right-hand man/woman, underling, man/girl Friday; substitute, stand-in, fill-in, relief, understudy, locum tenens; representative, proxy, agent, spokesperson; *Scottish* depute; *informal* sidekick, locum, temp.
▶ adjective *her deputy editor* ASSISTANT, substitute, stand-in, acting, reserve, fill-in, caretaker, temporary, provisional, stopgap, surrogate; pro tempore, ad interim; *informal* second-string.

deranged ▶ adjective INSANE, mad, disturbed, unbalanced, unhinged, unstable, irrational; crazed, demented, berserk, frenzied, lunatic, certifiable; non compos mentis; *informal* touched, crazy, mental; *Brit. informal* barmy, barking (mad), round the twist.
– OPPOSITES rational.

derelict ▶ adjective ❶ *a derelict building* DILAPIDATED, ramshackle, run down, tumbledown, in ruins, falling apart; rickety, creaky, deteriorating, crumbling; neglected, untended, gone to rack and ruin. ❷ *a derelict airfield* DISUSED, abandoned, deserted, discarded, rejected, neglected, untended. ❸ (*N. Amer.*) *he was derelict in his duty* NEGLIGENT, neglectful, remiss, lax, careless, sloppy, slipshod, slack, irresponsible, delinquent.
▶ noun *the derelicts who survive on the streets* TRAMP, vagrant, vagabond, down and out, homeless person, drifter; beggar, mendicant; outcast; *informal* dosser, bag lady; *N. Amer. informal* hobo, bum.

dereliction ▶ noun ❶ *buildings were reclaimed from dereliction* DILAPIDATION, disrepair, deterioration, ruin, rack and ruin; abandonment, neglect, disuse. ❷ *dereliction of duty* NEGLIGENCE, neglect, delinquency, failure; carelessness, laxity, sloppiness, slackness, irresponsibility; oversight, omission.

deride ▶ verb RIDICULE, mock, scoff at, jibe at, make fun of, poke fun at, laugh at, hold up to ridicule, pillory; disdain, disparage, denigrate, dismiss, slight; sneer at, scorn, insult; *informal* knock, pooh-pooh, take the mickey out of.
– OPPOSITES praise.

de rigueur ▶ adjective ❶ *straight hair was de rigueur* FASHIONABLE, in fashion, in vogue, modish, up to date, up to the minute, all the rage; *informal* trendy, with it. ❷ *an address is de rigueur for business cards* CUSTOMARY, standard, conventional, normal, orthodox, usual, comme il faut; compulsory; *informal* done.

derision ▶ noun MOCKERY, ridicule, jeers, sneers, taunts; disdain, disparagement, denigration, disrespect, insults; scorn, contempt; lampooning, satire.

derisive ▶ adjective MOCKING, jeering, scoffing, teasing, derisory, snide, sneering; disdainful, scornful, contemptuous, taunting, insulting; scathing, sarcastic; *informal* snidey; *Brit. informal* sarky.

derisory ▶ adjective ❶ *a derisory sum* INADEQUATE, insufficient, tiny, small; trifling, paltry, pitiful, miserly, miserable; negligible, token, nominal; ridiculous, laughable, ludicrous, preposterous, insulting; *informal* measly, stingy, lousy, pathetic, piddling, piffling, mingy, poxy. ❷ *derisory calls from the crowd. See* DERISIVE.

derivation ▶ noun ❶ *the derivation of theories from empirical observation* DERIVING, induction, deduction, inference; extraction, eliciting. ❷ *the derivation of a word* ORIGIN, etymology, root, etymon, provenance, source; origination, beginning, foundation, basis, cause; development, evolution.

derivative ▶ adjective *her poetry was derivative* IMITATIVE, unoriginal, uninventive, unimaginative, uninspired; copied, plagiarized, plagiaristic, second-hand; trite, hackneyed, clichéd, stale, stock, banal; *informal* copycat, cribbed, old hat.
– OPPOSITES original.
▶ noun ❶ *a derivative of opium* BY-PRODUCT, subsidiary product; spin-off. ❷ *a derivative of a verb* DERIVED WORD.

derive ▶ verb ❶ *he derives consolation from his poetry* OBTAIN, get, take, gain, acquire, procure, extract, attain, glean. ❷ *'coffee' derives from the Turkish 'kahveh'* ORIGINATE IN, stem from, descend from, spring from, be taken from. ❸ *his fortune derives from property* ORIGINATE IN, be rooted in; stem from, come from, spring from, proceed from, issue from.

derogate ▶ verb (*formal*) ❶ *his contribution was derogated by critics* DISPARAGE, denigrate, belittle, deprecate, deflate; decry, discredit, cast aspersions on, run down, criticize; defame, vilify, abuse, insult, attack, pour scorn on; *informal* pull apart, drag through the mud, knock, slam, bash, bad-mouth; *Brit. informal* rubbish, slate, slag off. ❷ *the act would derogate from the king's majesty* DETRACT FROM, devalue, diminish, reduce, lessen, depreciate; demean, cheapen. ❸ *rules which derogate from an Act of Parliament* DEVIATE, diverge, depart, digress, stray; differ, vary; conflict with, be incompatible with.
– OPPOSITES praise, increase.

derogatory ▶ adjective DISPARAGING, denigratory, deprecatory, disrespectful, demeaning; critical, pejorative, negative, unfavourable, uncomplimentary, unflattering, insulting; offensive, personal, abusive, rude, nasty, mean, hurtful; defamatory, slanderous, libellous; *informal* bitchy, catty.
– OPPOSITES complimentary.

descend ▶ verb ❶ *the plane started descending* GO DOWN, come down; drop, fall, sink, dive, plummet, plunge, nosedive. ❷ *she descended the stairs* CLIMB DOWN, go down, come down; shin down. ❸ *the road descends to a village* SLOPE, dip, slant, go down, fall away. ❹ *she saw Leo descend from the bus* ALIGHT, disembark, get down, get off, dismount. ❺ *they would not to descend to such mean tricks* STOOP, lower oneself, demean oneself, debase oneself; resort, be reduced, go as far as. ❻ *the army descended into chaos* DEGENERATE, deteriorate, decline, sink, slide, fall. ❼ *they descended on the pub* COME IN FORCE, arrive in hordes; attack, assail, assault, storm, invade, swoop on, charge. ❽ *he is descended from a Flemish family* BE A DESCENDANT OF, originate from, issue from, spring from, derive from. ❾ *his estates descended to his son* BE HANDED DOWN, be passed down; be inherited by.
– OPPOSITES ascend, climb, board.

descendant ▶ noun SUCCESSOR, scion; heir; (**descendants**) offspring, progeny, family, lineage; *Law* issue; *archaic* seed, fruit of one's loins.
– OPPOSITES ancestor.

descent ▶ noun ❶ *the plane began its descent* DIVE, drop; fall, pitch. ❷ *their descent of the mountain* DOWNWARD CLIMB. ❸ *a steep descent* SLOPE, incline, dip, drop, gradient, declivity, slant; hill. ❹ *his descent into alcoholism* DECLINE, slide, fall, degeneration, deterioration, regression. ❺ *she is of Italian descent* ANCESTRY, parentage, ancestors, family, antecedents; extraction, origin, derivation, birth; lineage, line, genealogy, heredity, stock, pedigree, blood, bloodline; roots, origins. ❻ *the descent of property* INHERITANCE, succession. ❼ *the sudden descent of the cavalry* ATTACK, assault, raid, onslaught, charge, thrust, push, drive, incursion, foray.

describe ▶ verb ❶ *he described his experiences* REPORT, recount, relate, tell of, set out, chronicle; detail, catalogue, give a rundown of; explain, illustrate, discuss, comment on. ❷ *she described him as a pathetic figure* DESIGNATE, pronounce, call, label, style, dub; characterize, class; portray, depict, brand, paint. ❸ *the pen described a circle* DELINEATE, mark out, outline, trace, draw.

description ▶ noun ❶ *a description of my travels* ACCOUNT, report, rendition, explanation, illustration; chronicle, narration, narrative, story, commentary; portrayal, portrait; details. ❷ *the description of coal as 'bottled sunshine'* DESIGNATION, labelling, naming, dubbing, pronouncement; characterization, classification, branding; portrayal, depiction. ❸ *vehicles of every description* SORT, variety, kind, type, category, order, breed, class, designation, specification, genre, genus, brand, make, character, ilk; *N. Amer.* stripe.

descriptive ▶ adjective ILLUSTRATIVE, expressive, graphic, detailed, lively, vivid, striking; explanatory, elucidatory, explicative.

descry ▶ verb (*poetic/literary*). *See* NOTICE verb.

desecrate ▶ verb VIOLATE, profane, defile, debase, degrade, dishonour; vandalize, damage, destroy, deface.

desert¹ ▶ verb ❶ *his wife deserted him* ABANDON, leave, turn one's back on; throw over, jilt, break up with; leave high and dry, leave in the lurch, leave behind, strand, maroon; *informal* walk out on, run out on, drop, dump, ditch; *poetic/literary* forsake. ❷ *his allies were deserting the cause* RENOUNCE, repudiate, relinquish, wash one's hands of, abandon, turn one's back on, betray, disavow; *formal* abjure; *poetic/literary* forsake. ❸ *soldiers deserted in droves* ABSCOND, defect, run away, make off, decamp, flee, turn tail, take French leave, depart, quit; *Military* go AWOL.

desert² ▶ noun *an African desert* WASTELAND, wastes, wilderness, wilds, barren land; dust bowl.

▶ adjective ❶ *desert conditions* ARID, dry, moistureless, parched, scorched, hot; barren, bare, stark, infertile, unfruitful, dehydrated, sterile. ❷ *a desert island* UNINHABITED, empty, lonely, desolate, bleak; wild, uncultivated.
– OPPOSITES fertile.

deserted ▶ adjective ❶ *a deserted wife* ABANDONED, thrown over, jilted, cast aside; neglected, stranded, marooned; forlorn, bereft; *informal* dumped, ditched, dropped; *poetic/literary* forsaken. ❷ *a deserted village* EMPTY, uninhabited, unoccupied, unpeopled, abandoned, evacuated, vacant; untenanted, tenantless, neglected; desolate, lonely, godforsaken.
– OPPOSITES populous.

deserter ▶ noun ABSCONDER, runaway, fugitive, truant, escapee; renegade, defector, turncoat, traitor.

desertion ▶ noun ❶ *his wife's desertion of him* ABANDONMENT, leaving, jilting. ❷ *the desertion of the president's colleagues* DEFECTION; betrayal, renunciation, repudiation, apostasy; *formal* abjuration. ❸ *soldiers were executed for desertion* ABSCONDING, running away, truancy, going absent without leave, taking French leave, escape; defection, treason; *Military* going AWOL.

deserve ▶ verb MERIT, earn, warrant, rate, justify, be worthy of, be entitled to, have a right to, be qualified for.

deserved ▶ adjective WELL EARNED, merited, warranted, justified, justifiable; rightful, due, right, just, fair, fitting, appropriate, suitable, proper, apt; *archaic* meet.

deserving ▶ adjective ❶ *the deserving poor* WORTHY, meritorious, commendable, praiseworthy, admirable, estimable, creditable; respectable, decent, honourable, righteous. ❷ *a lapse deserving of punishment* MERITING, warranting, justifying, suitable for, worthy of.

desiccated ▶ adjective DRIED, dry, dehydrated, powdered.
– OPPOSITES moist.

desideratum ▶ noun REQUIREMENT, prerequisite, need, indispensable thing, sine qua non, essential, requisite, necessary.

design ▶ noun ❶ *a design for the offices* PLAN, blueprint, drawing, sketch, outline, map, plot, diagram, draft, representation, scheme, model. ❷ *tableware with a gold design* PATTERN, motif, device; style, composition, make-up, layout, construction, shape, form. ❸ *his design of reaching the top* INTENTION, aim, purpose, plan, intent, objective, object, goal, end, target; hope, desire, wish, dream, aspiration, ambition.

▶ verb ❶ *the church was designed by Hicks* PLAN, outline, map out, draft, draw. ❷ *they designed a new engine* INVENT, originate, create, think up, come up with, devise, formulate, conceive; make, produce, develop, fashion; *informal* dream up. ❸ *this paper is designed to provoke discussion* INTEND, aim; devise, contrive, purpose, plan; tailor, fashion, adapt, gear; mean, destine.

■ **by design** DELIBERATELY, intentionally, on purpose, purposefully; knowingly, wittingly, consciously, calculatedly.

designate ▶ verb ❶ *some firms designate a press officer* APPOINT, nominate, depute, delegate; select, choose, pick, elect, name, identify, assign. ❷ *the rivers are designated 'Sites of Special Scientific Interest'* CLASSIFY, class, label, tag; name, call, entitle, term, dub; *formal* denominate.

designation ▶ noun ❶ *the designation of a leader* APPOINTMENT, nomination, naming, selection, election. ❷ *the designation of nature reserves* CLASSIFICATION, specification, definition, earmarking, pinpointing. ❸ *the designation 'Generalissimo'* TITLE, name, epithet, tag; nickname, byname, sobriquet; *informal* moniker, handle; *formal* denomination, appellation.

designer ▶ noun ❶ *a designer of farmhouses* CREATOR, planner, deviser, inventor, originator; maker; architect, builder. ❷ *young designers made the dress* COUTURIER, tailor, costumier, dressmaker.

designing ▶ adjective SCHEMING, calculating, conniving; cunning, crafty, artful, wily, devious, guileful, manipulative; treacherous, sly, underhand, deceitful, double-dealing; *informal* crooked, foxy.

desirability ▶ noun ❶ *the desirability of the property* APPEAL, attractiveness, allure; agreeableness, worth, excellence. ❷ *the desirability of a different economy* ADVISABILITY, advantage, expedience, benefit, merit, value, profit, profitability. ❸ *her obvious desirability* ATTRACTIVENESS, sexual attraction, beauty, good looks; charm, seductiveness; *informal* sexiness.

desirable ▶ adjective ❶ *a desirable location* ATTRACTIVE, sought-after, in demand, popular,

desired, covetable, enviable; appealing, agreeable, pleasant; valuable, good, excellent; *informal* to die for. ❷ *it is desirable that they should meet* ADVANTAGEOUS, advisable, wise, sensible, recommendable; helpful, useful, beneficial, worthwhile, profitable, preferable. ❸ *a very desirable woman* (SEXUALLY) ATTRACTIVE, beautiful, pretty, appealing; seductive, alluring, enchanting, beguiling, captivating, bewitching, irresistible; *informal* sexy, beddable.
– OPPOSITES unattractive, unwise, ugly.

desire ▶ noun ❶ *a desire to see the world* WISH, want, aspiration, fancy, inclination, impulse; yearning, longing, craving, hankering, hunger; eagerness, enthusiasm, determination; *informal* yen, itch. ❷ *his eyes glittered with desire* LUST, sexual attraction, passion, sensuality, sexuality; lasciviousness, lechery, salaciousness, libidinousness; *informal* the hots, raunchiness, horniness; *Brit. informal* randiness.
▶ verb ❶ *they desired peace* WANT, wish for, long for, yearn for, crave, hanker after, be desperate for, be bent on, covet, aspire to; fancy; *informal* have a yen for, yen for. ❷ *she desired him* BE ATTRACTED TO, lust after, burn for, be infatuated by; *informal* fancy, have the hots for, have a crush on, be mad about.

desired ▶ adjective ❶ *cut the cloth to the desired length* REQUIRED, necessary, proper, right, correct; appropriate, suitable; preferred, chosen, selected. ❷ *the desired results* WISHED FOR, wanted, coveted; sought-after, longed for, yearned for.

desirous ▶ adjective EAGER, desiring, anxious, keen, craving, yearning, longing, hungry; ambitious, aspiring; covetous, envious; *informal* dying, itching.

desist ▶ verb ABSTAIN, refrain, forbear, hold back, keep; stop, cease, discontinue, suspend, give up, break off, drop, dispense with, eschew; *informal* lay off, give over, quit, pack in.
– OPPOSITES continue.

desk ▶ noun WRITING TABLE, bureau, escritoire, secretaire; *Brit.* davenport.

desolate ▶ adjective ❶ *desolate moorlands* BLEAK, stark, bare, dismal, grim; wild, inhospitable; deserted, uninhabited, godforsaken, abandoned, unpeopled, untenanted, empty; unfrequented, unvisited, isolated, remote. ❷ *she is desolate* MISERABLE, despondent, depressed, disconsolate, devastated, despairing, inconsolable, broken-hearted, grief-stricken, crushed, bereft; sad, unhappy, downcast, down, dejected, forlorn, upset, distressed; *informal* blue, cut up.
– OPPOSITES populous, joyful.
▶ verb ❶ *droughts desolated the plains* DEVASTATE, ravage, ruin, lay waste to; level, raze, demolish, wipe out, obliterate. ❷ *she was desolated by the loss of her husband* DISHEARTEN, depress, sadden, cast down, make miserable, weigh down, crush, upset, distress; *informal* shatter.

desolation ▶ noun ❶ *the desolation of the Gobi desert* BLEAKNESS, starkness, barrenness, sterility; wildness; isolation, loneliness, remoteness. ❷ *a feeling of utter desolation* MISERY, sadness, unhappiness, despondency, sorrow, depression, grief, woe; broken-heartedness, wretchedness, dejection, devastation, despair, anguish, distress.

despair ▶ noun HOPELESSNESS, disheartenment, discouragement, desperation, distress, anguish, unhappiness; despondency, depression, disconsolateness, melancholy, misery, wretchedness; defeatism, pessimism.
– OPPOSITES hope, joy.
▶ verb LOSE HOPE, abandon hope, give up, lose heart, be discouraged, be despondent, be demoralized, resign oneself; be pessimistic, look on the black side.
■ **be the despair of** BE THE BANE OF, be the scourge of, be a burden on, be a trial to, be a thorn in the flesh/side of.

despairing ▶ adjective HOPELESS, in despair, dejected, depressed, despondent, disconsolate, gloomy, miserable, wretched, desolate, inconsolable; disheartened, discouraged, demoralized, devastated; defeatist, pessimistic.

despatch ▶ verb & noun. *See* DISPATCH.

desperado ▶ noun (*dated*) BANDIT, criminal, outlaw, lawbreaker, villain, renegade; robber, cut-throat, gangster, pirate.

desperate ▶ adjective ❶ *a desperate look* DESPAIRING, hopeless; anguished, distressed, wretched, desolate, forlorn, distraught, fraught; out of one's mind, at one's wits' end, beside oneself, at the end of one's tether. ❷ *a desperate attempt to escape* LAST-DITCH, last-gasp, eleventh-hour, do-or-die, final; frantic, frenzied, wild; futile, hopeless, doomed. ❸ *a desperate shortage of teachers* GRAVE, serious, critical, acute, risky, precarious; dire, awful, terrible, dreadful; urgent, pressing, crucial, vital, drastic, extreme; *informal* chronic. ❹ *they were desperate for food* IN GREAT NEED OF, urgently requiring, in want of; eager, longing, yearning, hungry, crying out; *informal* dying. ❺ *a desperate act* VIOLENT, dangerous, lawless; reckless, rash, hasty, impetuous, foolhardy, incautious, hazardous, risky; death-or-glory, do-or-die.

desperately ▶ adverb ❶ *he screamed desperately for help* IN DESPERATION, in despair, despairingly, in anguish, in distress; wretchedly, hopelessly, desolately, forlornly. ❷ *they are desperately ill* SERIOUSLY, critically, gravely, severely, acutely, dangerously, perilously; very, extremely, dreadfully; hopelessly, irretrievably; *informal* terribly. ❸ *he desperately wanted to talk* URGENTLY, pressingly; intensely, eagerly.

desperation ▶ noun HOPELESSNESS, despair, distress; anguish, agony, torment, misery, wretchedness; disheartenment, discouragement.

despicable ▶ adjective CONTEMPTIBLE, loathsome, hateful, detestable, reprehensible, abhorrent, abominable, awful, heinous; odious, vile, low, mean, abject, shameful, ignominious, shabby, ignoble, disreputable, discreditable, unworthy; *informal* dirty, rotten, low-down; *Brit. informal* beastly; *archaic* scurvy.
– OPPOSITES admirable.

despise ▶ verb DETEST, hate, loathe, abhor, execrate, deplore, dislike; scorn, disdain, look down on, deride, sneer at, revile; spurn, shun; *formal* abominate.
– OPPOSITES adore.

despite ▶ preposition IN SPITE OF, notwithstanding, regardless of, in the face of, for all, even with.

despoil ▶ verb ❶ *a village despoiled by invaders* PLUNDER, pillage, rob, ravage, raid, ransack, rape, loot, sack; devastate, lay waste, ruin. ❷ *the robbers despoiled him of all he had* ROB, strip, deprive, dispossess, denude, divest, relieve, clean out.

despondency ▶ noun HOPELESSNESS, despair, disheartenment, discouragement, low spirits, wretchedness; melancholy, gloom, misery, desolation, disappointment, dejection, sadness, unhappiness; *informal* the blues, heartache.

despondent ▶ adjective DISHEARTENED, discouraged, dispirited, downhearted, downcast, crestfallen, down, low, disconsolate, despairing, wretched; melancholy, gloomy, morose, dismal, woebegone, miserable, depressed, dejected, sad; *informal* blue, down in the mouth, down in the dumps.
– OPPOSITES hopeful, cheerful.

despot ▶ noun TYRANT, oppressor, dictator, absolute ruler, totalitarian, autocrat.

despotic ▶ adjective AUTOCRATIC, dictatorial, totalitarian, absolutist, undemocratic, unaccountable; one-party, autarchic, monocratic; tyrannical, tyrannous, oppressive, repressive, draconian, illiberal.
– OPPOSITES democratic.

despotism ▶ noun TYRANNY, dictatorship, totalitarianism, absolute rule, absolutism; oppression, repression; autocracy, monocracy, autarchy.

dessert ▶ noun PUDDING, sweet, second course, last course; *Brit. informal* afters, pud.

destabilize ▶ verb UNDERMINE, weaken, damage, subvert, sabotage, unsettle, upset, disrupt.
– OPPOSITES strengthen.

destination ▶ noun JOURNEY'S END, end of the line; terminus, stop, stopping place, port of call; goal, target, end.

destined ▶ adjective ❶ *he is destined to lead a troubled life* FATED, ordained, predestined, meant; certain, sure, bound, assured, likely; doomed. ❷ *computers destined for Pakistan* HEADING, bound, en route, scheduled; intended, meant, designed, designated, allotted, reserved.

destiny ▶ noun ❶ *master of his own destiny* FUTURE, fate, fortune, doom; lot; *archaic* portion. ❷ *she was sent by destiny* FATE, providence; predestination; divine decree, God's will, kismet, the stars; luck, fortune, chance; karma.

destitute ▶ adjective ❶ *she was left destitute* PENNILESS, poor, impoverished, poverty-stricken, impecunious, without a penny to one's name; needy, in straitened circumstances, distressed, badly off; *Brit.* on the breadline; *informal* hard up, (flat) broke, strapped (for cash), without a brass farthing, without two pennies to rub together, without a bean; *Brit. informal* stony broke, skint; *N. Amer. informal* stone broke, without a red cent. ❷ *we were destitute of clothing* DEVOID, bereft, deprived, in need; lacking, without, deficient in, wanting.
– OPPOSITES rich.

destitution ▶ noun POVERTY, impoverishment, penury, pennilessness, privation, pauperism; hardship, need, want, straitened circumstances, dire straits, deprivation, (financial) distress.

destroy ▶ verb ❶ *their offices were destroyed by bombing* DEMOLISH, knock down, level, raze (to the ground), fell; wreck, ruin, shatter; blast, blow up, dynamite, explode, bomb. ❷ *traffic would destroy the conservation area* SPOIL, ruin, wreck, disfigure, blight, mar, impair, deface, scar, injure, harm, devastate, damage, wreak havoc on. ❸ *illness destroyed his career chances* WRECK, ruin, spoil, disrupt, undo, upset, put an end to, put a stop to, terminate, frustrate, blight, crush, quash, dash, scotch; devastate, demolish, sabotage; *informal* mess up, muck up, foul up, put paid to, put the kibosh on, do for, queer, blow a hole in; *Brit. informal* scupper, throw a spanner in the works of; *archaic* bring to naught. ❹ *the horse had to be destroyed* KILL, put down, put to sleep, slaughter, terminate, exterminate. ❺ *we had to destroy the enemy* ANNIHILATE, wipe out, obliterate, wipe off the face of the earth, eliminate, eradicate, liquidate, finish off, erase; kill, slaughter, massacre, exterminate; *informal* take out, rub out, snuff out; *N. Amer. informal* waste.
– OPPOSITES build, preserve, raise, spare.

destruction ▶ noun ❶ *the destruction by allied bombers* DEMOLITION, wrecking, ruination, blasting, bombing; wreckage, ruins. ❷ *the destruction of the countryside* SPOLIATION, devastation, ruination, blighting, disfigurement, impairment, scarring, harm, desolation. ❸ *the destruction of cattle* SLAUGHTER, killing, putting down, extermination, termination. ❹ *the destruction of the enemies' forces* ANNIHILATION, obliteration, elimination, eradication, liquidation; killing, slaughter, massacre, extermination.

destructive ▶ adjective ❶ *the most destructive war* DEVASTATING, ruinous, disastrous, catastrophic, calamitous, cataclysmic; harmful, damaging, detrimental, deleterious, injurious, crippling; violent, savage, fierce, brutal, deadly, lethal. ❷ *destructive criticism* NEGATIVE, hostile, vicious, unfriendly; unhelpful, obstructive, discouraging.

desultory ▶ adjective CASUAL, cursory, superficial, token, perfunctory, half-hearted, lukewarm; random, aimless, erratic, unmethodical, unsystematic, chaotic, inconsistent, irregular, intermittent, sporadic, fitful.
– OPPOSITES keen.

detach ▶ verb ❶ *he detached the lamp from its bracket* UNFASTEN, disconnect, disengage, separate, uncouple, remove, loose, unhitch, unhook, free, disunite; pull off, cut off, break off. ❷ *he detached himself from the crowd* FREE, separate, segregate; move away, split off; leave, abandon. ❸ *he has detached himself from his family* DISSOCIATE, divorce, alienate, separate, segregate, isolate, cut off; break away, disaffiliate, defect; leave, quit, withdraw from, break with.
– OPPOSITES attach, join.

detached ▶ adjective ❶ *a detached collar* UNFASTENED, disconnected, separated, separate, loosened; untied, unhitched, undone, unhooked, unbuttoned; free, severed, cut off. ❷ *a detached observer* DISPASSIONATE, disinterested, objective, uninvolved, outside, neutral, unbiased, unprejudiced, impartial, nonpartisan; indifferent, aloof, remote, distant, impersonal. ❸ *a detached house* STANDING ALONE, separate.

detachment ▶ noun ❶ *she looked on everything with detachment* OBJECTIVITY, dispassion, disinterest, open-mindedness, neutrality, impartiality; indifference, aloofness. ❷ *a detachment of soldiers* UNIT, detail, squad, troop, contingent, outfit, task force, patrol, crew; platoon, company, corps, regiment, brigade, battalion. ❸ *the detachment of the wallpaper* LOOSENING, disconnection, disengagement, separation; removal.

detail ▶ noun ❶ *the picture is correct in every detail* PARTICULAR, respect, feature, characteristic, attribute, specific, aspect, facet, part, unit, component, constituent; fact, piece of information, point, element, circumstance, consideration. ❷ *that's just a detail* UNIMPORTANT POINT, trivial fact, triviality, technicality, nicety, subtlety, trifle, fine point, incidental, inessential, nothing. ❸ *records with a considerable degree of detail* PRECISION, exactness, accuracy, thoroughness, carefulness, scrupulousness, particularity. ❹ *a guard detail* UNIT, detachment, squad, troop, contingent, outfit, task force, patrol. ❺ *I got the toilet detail* DUTY, task, job, chore, charge, responsibility, assignment, function, mission, engagement, occupation, undertaking, errand.
▶ verb ❶ *the report details our objections* DESCRIBE, explain, expound, relate, catalogue, list, spell out, itemize, particularize, identify, specify; state, declare, present, set out, frame; cite, quote, instance, mention, name. ❷ *troops were detailed to prevent the escape* ASSIGN, allocate, appoint, delegate, commission, charge; send, post; nominate, vote, elect, co-opt.
■ **in detail** THOROUGHLY, in depth, exhaustively, minutely, closely, meticulously, rigorously, scrupulously, painstakingly, carefully; completely, comprehensively, fully, extensively.

detailed ▶ adjective COMPREHENSIVE, full, complete, thorough, exhaustive, all-inclusive; elaborate, minute, intricate; explicit, specific, precise, exact, accurate, meticulous, painstaking; itemized, blow-by-blow.
– OPPOSITES general.

detain ▶ verb ❶ *they were detained for questioning* HOLD, take into custody, take (in), confine, imprison, lock up, put in jail, intern; arrest, apprehend, seize; *informal* pick up, run in, haul in, nab, collar; *Brit. informal* nick. ❷ *don't let me detain you* DELAY, hold up, make late, keep, slow up/down; hinder, hamper, impede, obstruct.
– OPPOSITES release.

detect ▶ verb ❶ *no one detected the smell of diesel* NOTICE, perceive, discern, be aware of, note, make out, spot, recognize, distinguish, remark, identify, diagnose; catch, sense, see, smell, scent, taste; *Brit. informal* clock. ❷ *they are responsible for detecting fraud* DISCOVER, uncover, find out, turn up, unearth, dig up, root out, expose, reveal. ❸ *help the police to detect crime* SOLVE, clear up, get to the bottom of, find the person behind; *informal* crack. ❹ *the hackers were detected* CATCH, hunt down, track down, find, expose, reveal, unmask, smoke out; apprehend, arrest; *informal* nail.

detection ▶ noun ❶ *the detection of methane* DISCERNMENT, perception, awareness, recognition, identification, diagnosis; sensing, sight, smelling, tasting. ❷ *the detection of insider dealing* DISCOVERY, uncovering, unearthing, exposure, revelation. ❸ *the detection rate for burglary* SOLVING, clear-up. ❹ *he managed to escape detection* CAPTURE, identification, exposure; apprehension, arrest.

detective ▶ noun INVESTIGATOR, private investigator, private detective, operative; *Brit.* enquiry agent; *informal* private eye, PI, sleuth, snoop; *N. Amer. informal* shamus, gumshoe; *informal, dated* dick.

detention ▶ noun CUSTODY, imprisonment, confinement, incarceration, internment, detainment, captivity; arrest, house arrest; quarantine.

deter ▶ verb ❶ *the high cost deterred many* DISCOURAGE, dissuade, put off, scare off; dis-

hearten, demoralize, daunt, intimidate. ❷ *the presence of a caretaker deters crime* PREVENT, stop, avert, fend off, stave off, ward off, block, halt, check; hinder, impede, hamper, obstruct, foil, forestall, counteract, inhibit, curb.
– OPPOSITES encourage.

detergent ▶ noun *washing detergent* CLEANER, cleanser; washing powder, washing-up liquid; soap.
▶ adjective *detergent action* CLEANING, cleansing; surface-active.

deteriorate ▶ verb ❶ *his health deteriorated* WORSEN, decline, degenerate; fail, slump, slip, go downhill, go backwards, wane, ebb; *informal* go to pot. ❷ *these materials deteriorate if stored wrongly* DECAY, degrade, degenerate, break down, decompose, rot, go off, spoil, perish; break up, disintegrate, crumble, fall apart.
– OPPOSITES improve.

deterioration ▶ noun ❶ *a deterioration in law and order* DECLINE, collapse, failure, drop, downturn, slump, slip, retrogression. ❷ *deterioration of the roof structure* DECAY, degradation, degeneration, breakdown, decomposition, rot; atrophy, weakening; break-up, disintegration, dilapidation.

determinate ▶ adjective FIXED, settled, specified, established, defined, explicit, known, determined, definitive, conclusive, express, precise, categorical, positive, definite.

determination ▶ noun ❶ *it took great determination to win* RESOLUTION, resolve, will power, strength of character, single-mindedness, purposefulness, intentness; staunchness, perseverance, persistence, tenacity, staying power; strong-mindedness, backbone; stubbornness, doggedness, obstinacy; spirit, courage, pluck, grit, stout-heartedness; *informal* guts, spunk; *formal* pertinacity. ❷ *the determination of the rent* SETTING, specification, settlement, designation, arrangement, establishment, prescription. ❸ *the determination of the speed of light* CALCULATION, discovery, ascertainment, establishment, deduction, divination, diagnosis, discernment, verification, confirmation.

determine ▶ verb ❶ *chromosomes determine the sex of the embryo* CONTROL, decide, regulate, direct, dictate, govern; affect, influence, mould. ❷ *he determined to sell up* RESOLVE, decide, make up one's mind, choose, elect, opt; *formal* purpose. ❸ *the rent shall be determined by an accountant* SPECIFY, set, fix, decide on, settle, assign, designate, arrange, choose, establish, ordain, prescribe, decree. ❹ *determine the composition of the fibres* ASCERTAIN, find out, discover, learn, establish, calculate, work out, make out, deduce, diagnose, discern; check, verify, confirm; *informal* figure out.

determined ▶ adjective ❶ *he was determined to have his way* INTENT ON, bent on, set on, insistent on, resolved to, firm about, committed to; single-minded about, obsessive about. ❷ *a very determined man* RESOLUTE, purposeful, purposive, adamant, single-minded, unswerving, unwavering, undaunted, intent, insistent; steadfast, staunch, stalwart; persevering, persistent, indefatigable, tenacious; strong-minded, strong-willed, unshakeable, steely, four-square, dedicated, committed; stubborn, dogged, obstinate, inflexible, intransigent, unyielding, immovable; *N. Amer.* rock-ribbed; *formal* pertinacious.

determining ▶ adjective DECIDING, decisive, conclusive, final, definitive, key, pivotal, crucial, critical, major, chief, prime.

deterrent ▶ noun DISINCENTIVE, discouragement, damper, curb, check, restraint; obstacle, hindrance, impediment, obstruction, block, barrier, inhibition.
– OPPOSITES incentive.

detest ▶ verb ABHOR, hate, loathe, despise, shrink from, be unable to bear, find intolerable, dislike, disdain, have an aversion to; *formal* abominate.
– OPPOSITES love.

detestable ▶ adjective ABHORRENT, hateful, loathsome, despicable, abominable, execrable, repellent, repugnant, repulsive, revolting, disgusting, distasteful, horrible, horrid, awful; heinous, reprehensible, obnoxious, odious, offensive, contemptible.

dethrone ▶ verb DEPOSE, unseat, uncrown, oust, topple, overthrow, bring down, dislodge, displace, supplant, usurp, eject, drum out.
– OPPOSITES crown.

detonate ▶ verb ❶ *the charge detonated under the engine* EXPLODE, go off, blow up, shatter, erupt; ignite; bang, blast, boom. ❷ *they detonated the bomb* SET OFF, explode, discharge, let off, touch off, trigger; ignite, kindle.

detonation ▶ noun EXPLOSION, discharge, blowing up, ignition; blast, bang, report.

detour ▶ noun DIVERSION, roundabout route, indirect route, scenic route; bypass, ring road; digression, deviation; *Brit.* relief road.

detract ▶ verb ❶ *my reservations should not detract from the book's excellence* BELITTLE, take away from, diminish, reduce, lessen, minimize, play down, trivialize, decry, depreciate, devalue, deprecate. ❷ *the patterns will detract attention from each other* DIVERT, distract, draw away, deflect, avert, shift one's attention.

detractor ▶ noun CRITIC, disparager, denigrator, deprecator, belittler, attacker, faultfinder, backbiter; slanderer, libeller; *informal* knocker.

detriment ▶ noun HARM, damage, injury, hurt, impairment, loss, disadvantage, disservice, mischief.
– OPPOSITES benefit.

detrimental ▶ adjective HARMFUL, damaging,

injurious, hurtful, inimical, deleterious, destructive, ruinous, disastrous, bad, malign, adverse, undesirable, unfavourable, unfortunate; unhealthy, unwholesome.
–OPPOSITES benign.

detritus ▶ noun DEBRIS, waste, refuse, rubbish, litter, scrap, flotsam and jetsam, lumber, rubble; remains, remnants, fragments, scraps, dregs, leavings, sweepings, dross, scum; *N. Amer.* trash, garbage; *Austral./NZ* mullock; *informal* dreck.

devalue ▶ verb BELITTLE, depreciate, disparage, denigrate, decry, deprecate, treat lightly, discredit, underrate, undervalue, underestimate, deflate, diminish, trivialize, run down; *informal* knock, sell short, put down, pooh-pooh, do down, pick holes in; *Brit. informal* rubbish.

devastate ▶ verb ❶ *the city was devastated by an earthquake* DESTROY, ruin, wreck, lay waste, ravage, demolish, raze (to the ground), level, flatten. ❷ *he was devastated by the news* SHATTER, shock, stun, daze, dumbfound, traumatize, crush, overwhelm, overcome, distress; *informal* knock sideways; *Brit. informal* knock for six.

devastating ▶ adjective ❶ *a devastating cyclone* DESTRUCTIVE, ruinous, disastrous, catastrophic, calamitous, cataclysmic; harmful, damaging, injurious, detrimental; crippling, violent, savage, fierce, dangerous, fatal, deadly, lethal. ❷ *devastating news* SHATTERING, shocking, traumatic, overwhelming, crushing, distressing, terrible. ❸ (*informal*) *he presented devastating arguments* INCISIVE, highly effective, penetrating, cutting; withering, blistering, searing, scathing, fierce, savage, stinging, biting, caustic, harsh, unsparing.

devastation ▶ noun ❶ *the hurricane left a trail of devastation* DESTRUCTION, ruin, desolation, havoc, wreckage; ruins, ravages. ❷ *the devastation of Prussia* DESTRUCTION, wrecking, ruination, despoliation; demolition, annihilation. ❸ *the devastation you have caused the family* SHOCK, trauma, distress, stress, strain, pain, anguish, suffering, upset, agony, misery, heartache.

develop ▶ verb ❶ *the industry developed rapidly* GROW, expand, spread; advance, progress, evolve, mature; prosper, thrive, flourish, blossom. ❷ *a plan was developed* INITIATE, instigate, set in motion; originate, invent, form, establish, generate. ❸ *children should develop their talents* EXPAND, augment, broaden, supplement, reinforce; enhance, refine, improve, polish, perfect. ❹ *a row developed* START, begin, emerge, erupt, break out, burst out, arise, break, unfold, happen. ❺ *he developed the disease last week* FALL ILL WITH, be stricken with, succumb to; contract, catch, get, pick up, come down with, become infected with.

development ▶ noun ❶ *the development of the firm* EVOLUTION, growth, maturation, expansion, enlargement, spread, progress; success. ❷ *the development of an idea* FORMING, establishment, initiation, instigation, origination, invention, generation. ❸ *keep abreast of developments* EVENT, occurrence, happening, circumstance, incident, situation, issue. ❹ *a housing development* ESTATE, complex, site.

deviant ▶ adjective *deviant behaviour* ABERRANT, abnormal, atypical, anomalous, irregular, non-standard; nonconformist, perverse, uncommon, unusual; freakish, strange, odd, peculiar, bizarre, eccentric, idiosyncratic, unorthodox, exceptional; warped, perverted; *informal* kinky, quirky.
–OPPOSITES normal.
▶ noun *we were seen as deviants* NONCONFORMIST, eccentric, maverick, individualist; outsider, misfit; *informal* oddball, weirdo, freak; *N. Amer. informal* screwball, kook.

deviate ▶ verb DIVERGE, digress, drift, stray, slew, veer, swerve; get sidetracked, branch off; differ, vary, run counter to, contrast with.

deviation ▶ noun DIVERGENCE, digression, departure; difference, variation, variance; aberration, abnormality, irregularity, anomaly, inconsistency, discrepancy.

device ▶ noun ❶ *a device for measuring pressure* IMPLEMENT, gadget, utensil, tool, appliance, apparatus, instrument, machine, mechanism, contrivance, contraption; *informal* gizmo, widget. ❷ *an ingenious legal device* PLOY, tactic, move, stratagem, scheme, plot, trick, ruse, manoeuvre, machination, contrivance, expedient, dodge, wile; *Brit. informal* wheeze. ❸ *their shields bear his device* EMBLEM, symbol, logo, badge, crest, insignia, coat of arms, escutcheon, seal, mark, design, motif; monogram, hallmark, trademark.

devil ▶ noun ❶ *God and the Devil* SATAN, Beelzebub, Lucifer, the Lord of the Flies, the Prince of Darkness; *informal* Old Nick. ❷ *they drove out the devils from their bodies* EVIL SPIRIT, demon, cacodemon, fiend, bogie; *informal* spook. ❸ *look what the cruel devil has done* BRUTE, beast, monster, fiend; villain, sadist, barbarian, ogre. ❹ *he's a naughty little devil* RASCAL, rogue, imp, fiend, monkey, wretch; *informal* monster, horror, scamp, tyke; *Brit. informal* perisher; *N. Amer. informal* varmint. ❺ (*informal*) *the poor devils looked ill* WRETCH, unfortunate, creature, soul, person, fellow; *informal* thing, beggar.

devilish ▶ adjective ❶ *a devilish grin* DIABOLICAL, fiendish, demonic, satanic, demoniac, demoniacal; hellish, infernal. ❷ *a devilish torture* WICKED, evil, iniquitous, vile, foul, abominable, unspeakable, loathsome, monstrous, atrocious, heinous, hideous, odious, horrible, appalling, dreadful, awful, terrible, ghastly, abhorrent, despicable, depraved, dark, black, immoral; vicious, cruel, savage, barbaric. ❸ *a devilish job* DIFFICULT, tricky, ticklish, troublesome, thorny, awkward, problematic.

devil-may-care ▶ adjective RECKLESS, rash, incautious, heedless, impetuous, impulsive, daredevil, hot-headed, wild, foolhardy, audacious, death-or-glory; nonchalant, casual, breezy, flippant, insouciant, happy-go-lucky, easy-going, unworried, untroubled, unconcerned, harum-scarum; *Brit.* tearaway.

devilment ▶ noun. *See* DEVILRY sense 2.

devilry, deviltry ▶ noun ❶ *some devilry was afoot* WICKEDNESS, evil, sin, iniquity, vileness, badness, wrongdoing, dishonesty, unscrupulousness, villainy, delinquency, devilishness, fiendishness; *informal* crookedness, shadiness. ❷ *she had a perverse sense of devilry* MISCHIEF, mischievousness, naughtiness, badness, perversity, impishness; misbehaviour, troublemaking, misconduct; pranks, tricks, roguery, devilment; *informal* monkey business, shenanigans. ❸ *they dabbled in devilry* BLACK MAGIC, sorcery, witchcraft, wizardry, necromancy, enchantment, spell-working, incantation; the supernatural, occultism, the occult, the black arts, divination, voodoo, witchery; *N. Amer.* mojo, orenda.

devious ▶ adjective ❶ *the devious ways in which they bent the rules* UNDERHAND, deceitful, dishonest, dishonourable, unethical, unprincipled, immoral, unscrupulous, fraudulent, dubious, unfair, treacherous, duplicitous; crafty, cunning, calculating, artful, conniving, scheming, sly, wily; sneaky, furtive, secret, clandestine, surreptitious, covert; *N. Amer.* snide, snidey; *informal* crooked, shady, dirty, low-down; *Brit. informal* dodgy. ❷ *a devious route around the coast* CIRCUITOUS, roundabout, indirect, meandering, tortuous.

devise ▶ verb CONCEIVE, think up, dream up, work out, formulate, concoct; design, invent, coin, originate; compose, construct, fabricate, create, produce, develop; discover, hit on; hatch, contrive; *informal* cook up.

devitalize ▶ verb WEAKEN, enfeeble, debilitate, enervate, sap, drain, tax, exhaust, weary, tire (out), fatigue, wear out, prostrate; indispose, incapacitate, lay low; *informal* knock out, do in, shatter, whack, bush, frazzle, poop; *Brit. informal* knacker.
–OPPOSITES strengthen.

devoid ▶ adjective FREE, empty, vacant, bereft, denuded, deprived, destitute, bankrupt; (**devoid of**) lacking, without, wanting; *informal* minus.

devolution ▶ noun DECENTRALIZATION, delegation; redistribution, transfer; surrender, relinquishment.

devolve ▶ verb DELEGATE, depute, pass (down/on), hand down/over/on, transfer, transmit, assign, consign, convey, entrust, turn over, give, cede, surrender, relinquish, deliver; bestow, grant.

devote ▶ verb ALLOCATE, assign, allot, commit, give (over), apportion, consign, pledge; dedicate, consecrate; set aside, earmark, reserve, designate.

devoted ▶ adjective LOYAL, faithful, true (blue), staunch, steadfast, constant, committed, dedicated, devout; fond, loving, affectionate, caring, admiring.

devotee ▶ noun ❶ *a devotee of rock music* ENTHUSIAST, fan, lover, aficionado, admirer; *informal* buff, freak, nut, fiend, fanatic, addict, maniac. ❷ *devotees thronged the temple* FOLLOWER, adherent, supporter, advocate, disciple, votary, member, stalwart, fanatic, zealot; believer, worshipper.

devotion ▶ noun ❶ *her devotion to her husband* LOYALTY, faithfulness, fidelity, constancy, commitment, adherence, allegiance, dedication; fondness, love, admiration, affection, care. ❷ *a life of devotion* DEVOUTNESS, piety, religiousness, spirituality, godliness, holiness, sanctity. ❸ *morning devotions* (RELIGIOUS) WORSHIP, religious observance; prayers, vespers, matins; prayer meeting, church service.

devotional ▶ adjective RELIGIOUS, sacred, spiritual, divine, church, ecclesiastical.
–OPPOSITES secular.

devour ▶ verb ❶ *he devoured his meal* EAT HUNGRILY, eat greedily, gobble (up/down), guzzle, gulp (down), bolt (down), cram down, gorge oneself on, wolf (down), feast on, consume, eat up; *informal* pack away, demolish, dispose of, make short work of, polish off, shovel down, stuff oneself with, pig oneself on, put away, get outside of; *Brit. informal* scoff. ❷ *flames devoured the house* CONSUME, engulf, envelop; destroy, demolish, lay waste, devastate; gut, ravage, ruin, wreck. ❸ *he was devoured by remorse* AFFLICT, plague, bedevil, trouble, harrow, rack; consume, swallow up, overcome, overwhelm.

devout ▶ adjective ❶ *a devout Christian* PIOUS, religious, devoted, dedicated, reverent, God-fearing; holy, godly, saintly, faithful, dutiful, righteous, churchgoing, orthodox. ❷ *a devout soccer fan* DEDICATED, devoted, committed, loyal, faithful, staunch, genuine, firm, steadfast, unwavering, sincere, wholehearted, keen, enthusiastic, zealous, passionate, ardent, fervent, active, sworn, pledged; *informal* card-carrying, true blue, deep-dyed.

dexterity ▶ noun ❶ *painting china demanded dexterity* DEFTNESS, adeptness, adroitness, agility, nimbleness, handiness, ability, talent, skill, proficiency, expertise, experience, efficiency, mastery, delicacy, knack, artistry, finesse. ❷ *his political dexterity* SHREWDNESS, astuteness, sharp-wittedness, acumen, acuity, intelligence; ingenuity, inventiveness, cleverness, smartness; canniness, sense, discernment, insight, understanding, penetration, perception, perspicacity, discrimination; cunning, artfulness, craftiness; *informal* nous, horse sense, savvy.

dexterous ▶ adjective ❶ *a dexterous flick of the wrist* DEFT, adept, adroit, agile, nimble, neat, handy, able, capable, skilful, skilled, proficient, expert, practised, polished; efficient, effortless, slick, professional, masterly; *informal* nifty, mean, ace. ❷ *his dexterous accounting abilities* SHREWD, ingenious, inventive, clever, intelligent, brilliant, smart, sharp, acute, astute, canny, intuitive, discerning, perceptive, insightful, incisive, judicious; cunning, artful, crafty, wily; *informal* on the ball, quick off the mark, quick on the uptake, brainy, savvy; *Brit. informal* suss.
– OPPOSITES clumsy, stupid.

diabolical, diabolic ▶ adjective ❶ *his diabolical skill* DEVILISH, fiendish, satanic, demonic, demoniacal, hellish, infernal, evil, wicked, ungodly, unholy. ❷ (*informal*) *a diabolical performance* VERY BAD, dreadful, awful, terrible, disgraceful, shameful, lamentable, deplorable, appalling, atrocious; inferior, substandard, unsatisfactory, inadequate, second-rate, third-rate, shoddy, inept; *informal* crummy, dire, dismal, God-awful, abysmal, rotten, pathetic, pitiful, lousy; *Brit. informal* duff, rubbish, ropy. ❸ (*informal*) *a diabolical liberty* EXTREME, excessive, undue, inordinate, immoderate, unconscionable, outrageous; intolerable, unacceptable, unreasonable, unjustifiable, unwarrantable, inexcusable, unpardonable.

diadem ▶ noun CROWN, coronet, tiara, circlet, chaplet; *poetic/literary* coronal; *historical* taj.

diagnose ▶ verb IDENTIFY, determine, distinguish, recognize, detect, pinpoint.

diagnosis ▶ noun ❶ *the diagnosis of coeliac disease* IDENTIFICATION, detection, recognition, determination, discovery, pinpointing. ❷ *the results confirmed his diagnosis* OPINION, judgement, verdict, conclusion.

diagonal ▶ adjective CROSSWISE, crossways, slanting, slanted, aslant, squint, oblique, angled, at an angle, cornerways, cornerwise; *N. Amer.* cater-cornered, kitty-cornered.

diagram ▶ noun DRAWING, line drawing, sketch, representation, draft, illustration, picture, plan, outline, delineation, figure; *Computing* graphic.

diagrammatic ▶ adjective GRAPHIC, graphical, representational, representative, schematic, simplified.

dial ▶ verb PHONE, telephone, call, ring, make/place a call (to); *informal* buzz; *Brit. informal* get on the blower; *N. Amer. informal* get someone on the horn.

dialect ▶ noun REGIONAL LANGUAGE, local language, local speech, vernacular, patois, idiom; regionalisms, localisms; *informal* lingo.

dialectic ▶ noun DISCUSSION, debate, dialogue, logical argument, reasoning, argumentation, polemics; *formal* ratiocination.

dialogue ▶ noun ❶ *a book consisting of a series of dialogues* CONVERSATION, talk, discussion, interchange, discourse; chat, tête à tête; *informal* confab; *formal* colloquy, confabulation; *archaic* converse. ❷ *they called for a serious political dialogue* DISCUSSION, exchange, debate, exchange of views, talk, head-to-head, consultation, conference, parley; talks, negotiations; *informal* powwow; *N. Amer. informal* skull session.

diameter ▶ noun BREADTH, width, thickness; calibre, bore, gauge.

diametrical, diametric ▶ adjective DIRECT, absolute, complete, exact, extreme, polar, antipodal.

diaphanous ▶ adjective SHEER, fine, delicate, light, thin, insubstantial, floaty, flimsy, filmy, silken, chiffony, gossamer, gossamer-thin, gauzy; translucent, transparent, see-through.
– OPPOSITES thick, opaque.

diarrhoea ▶ noun loose motions; *informal* the runs, the trots, gippy tummy, holiday tummy, Delhi belly, Montezuma's revenge; *Brit. informal* the squits; *N. Amer. informal* turista; *archaic* the flux.
– OPPOSITES constipation.

diary ▶ noun ❶ *he put the date in his diary* APPOINTMENT BOOK, engagement book, personal organizer; *trademark* Filofax. ❷ *her World War II diaries* JOURNAL, memoir, chronicle, log, logbook, history, annal, record; *N. Amer.* daybook.

diatribe ▶ noun TIRADE, harangue, onslaught, attack, polemic, denunciation, broadside, fulmination, condemnation, censure, criticism; *informal* blast; *poetic/literary* philippic.

dicey ▶ adjective (*informal*) RISKY, uncertain, unpredictable, touch-and-go, precarious, unsafe, dangerous, fraught with danger, hazardous, perilous, high-risk, difficult; *informal* chancy, hairy, iffy; *Brit. informal* dodgy; *N. Amer. informal* gnarly.
– OPPOSITES safe.

dichotomy ▶ noun CONTRAST, difference, polarity, conflict; gulf, chasm, division, separation, split; *rare* contrariety.

dicky ▶ adjective (*Brit. informal*) WEAK, unhealthy, ailing, poorly, sickly, frail; unsound, unreliable, unsteady.
– OPPOSITES robust.

dictate ▶ verb ❶ *the tsar's attempts to dictate policy* PRESCRIBE, lay down, impose, set down, order, command, decree, ordain, direct, determine, decide, control, govern. ❷ *you are in no position to dictate to me* GIVE ORDERS TO, order about/around, lord it over; lay down the law; *informal* boss about/around, push around/about, throw one's weight about/around. ❸ *choice is often dictated by availability* DETERMINE, control, govern, decide, influence, affect.

▶ **noun** *the dictates of his superior* ORDER, command, commandment, decree, edict, ruling, dictum, diktat, directive, direction, instruction, pronouncement, mandate, requirement, stipulation, injunction, demand; *formal* ordinance; *poetic/literary* behest.

dictator ▶ **noun** AUTOCRAT, absolute ruler, despot, tyrant, oppressor, autarch.

dictatorial ▶ **adjective** ❶ *a dictatorial regime* AUTOCRATIC, undemocratic, totalitarian, authoritarian, autarchic, despotic, tyrannical, tyrannous, absolute, unrestricted, unlimited, unaccountable, arbitrary. ❷ *his dictatorial manner* DOMINEERING, autocratic, authoritarian, oppressive, imperious, officious, overweening, overbearing, peremptory, dogmatic, high and mighty; severe, strict; *informal* bossy, high-handed.
– OPPOSITES democratic, meek.

dictatorship ▶ **noun** ABSOLUTE RULE, undemocratic rule, despotism, tyranny, autocracy, autarchy, authoritarianism, totalitarianism, Fascism; oppression, repression.
– OPPOSITES democracy.

diction ▶ **noun** ❶ *his careful diction* ENUNCIATION, articulation, elocution, locution, pronunciation, speech, intonation, inflection; delivery. ❷ *the need for contemporary diction in poetry* PHRASEOLOGY, phrasing, turn of phrase, wording, language, usage, vocabulary, terminology, expressions, idioms.

dictionary ▶ **noun** LEXICON, wordbook, word list, glossary.
– RELATED TERMS lexicographic.

dictum ▶ **noun** ❶ *he received the head's dictum with evident reluctance* PRONOUNCEMENT, proclamation, direction, injunction, dictate, command, commandment, order, decree, edict, mandate, diktat. ❷ *the old dictum 'might is right'* SAYING, maxim, axiom, proverb, adage, aphorism, saw, precept, epigram, motto, truism, commonplace; expression, phrase, tag.

didactic ▶ **adjective** INSTRUCTIVE, instructional, educational, educative, informative, informational, edifying, improving, preceptive, pedagogic, moralistic.

die ▶ **verb** ❶ *her father died last year* PASS AWAY, pass on, lose one's life, expire, breathe one's last, meet one's end, meet one's death, lay down one's life, perish, go the way of all flesh, go to one's last resting place, go to meet one's maker, cross the great divide; *informal* give up the ghost, kick the bucket, croak, buy it, turn up one's toes, cash in one's chips, shuffle off this mortal coil; *Brit. informal* snuff it, peg out, pop one's clogs; *N. Amer. informal* bite the big one, buy the farm; *archaic* decease, depart this life. ❷ *the wind had died down* ABATE, subside, drop, lessen, ease (off), let up, moderate, fade, dwindle, peter out, wane, ebb, relent, weaken; melt away, dissolve, vanish, disappear; *archaic* remit. ❸ (*informal*) *the engine died* FAIL, cut out, give out, stop, break down, stop working; *informal* conk out, go kaput, give up the ghost; *Brit. informal* pack up. ❹ (*informal*) *she's dying to meet you* LONG, yearn, burn, ache; *informal* itch.
– OPPOSITES live, intensify.

diehard ▶ **adjective** HARD-LINE, reactionary, ultra-conservative, conservative, traditionalist, dyed-in-the-wool, deep-dyed, intransigent, inflexible, uncompromising, rigid, entrenched, set in one's ways; staunch, steadfast; *informal* blimpish.

diet[1] ▶ **noun** *health problems related to your diet* SELECTION OF FOOD, food, foodstuffs; *informal* grub, nosh.
▶ **verb** *she dieted for most of her life* BE ON A DIET, eat sparingly; slim, lose weight, watch one's weight; *N. Amer.* reduce; *informal* weight-watch; *N. Amer. informal* slenderize.

diet[2] ▶ **noun** *the diet's lower house* LEGISLATIVE ASSEMBLY, legislature, parliament, congress, senate, council, assembly.

differ ▶ **verb** ❶ *the second set of data differed from the first* CONTRAST WITH, be different/dissimilar to, be unlike, vary from, diverge from, deviate from, conflict with, run counter to, be incompatible with, be at odds with, go against, contradict. ❷ *the two sides differed over this issue* DISAGREE, conflict, be at variance/odds, be in dispute, not see eye to eye.
– OPPOSITES resemble, agree.

difference ▶ **noun** ❶ *the difference between the two sets of data* DISSIMILARITY, contrast, distinction, differentiation, variance, variation, divergence, disparity, deviation, polarity, gulf, gap, imbalance, contradiction, contradistinction; *formal* dissimilitude. ❷ *we've had our differences in the past* DISAGREEMENT, difference of opinion, dispute, argument, quarrel, wrangle, contretemps, altercation; *informal* tiff, set-to, run-in, spat; *Brit. informal* row. ❸ *I am willing to pay the difference* BALANCE, remainder, rest, remaining amount, residue.
– OPPOSITES similarity.

different ▶ **adjective** ❶ *people with different lifestyles* DISSIMILAR, unalike, unlike, contrasting, contrastive, divergent, differing, varying, disparate; poles apart, incompatible, mismatched, conflicting, clashing; *informal* like chalk and cheese. ❷ *suddenly everything in her life was different* CHANGED, altered, transformed, new, unfamiliar, unknown, strange. ❸ *two different occasions* DISTINCT, separate, individual, discrete, independent. ❹ (*informal*) *he wanted to try something different* UNUSUAL, out of the ordinary, unfamiliar, unusual, novel, new, fresh, original, unconventional, exotic, uncommon.
– OPPOSITES similar, related, ordinary.

differential ▶ **adjective** (*technical*) ❶ *the differential achievements of boys and girls* DIFFERENT,

dissimilar, contrasting, unalike, divergent, disparate, contrastive. ❷ *the differential features between benign and malignant tumours* DISTINCTIVE, distinguishing.
– OPPOSITES similar.

differentiate ▶ verb ❶ *he unable to differentiate between fantasy and reality* DISTINGUISH, discriminate, make/draw a distinction, tell the difference, tell apart. ❷ *this differentiates their business from all other booksellers* MAKE DIFFERENT, distinguish, set apart, single out, separate, mark off.

differentiation ▶ noun DISTINCTION, distinctness, difference; separation, demarcation, delimitation.

difficult ▶ adjective ❶ *a very difficult job* HARD, strenuous, arduous, laborious, tough, onerous, burdensome, demanding, punishing, gruelling, back-breaking, exhausting, tiring, fatiguing, wearisome; *informal* hellish, killing, no picnic; *archaic* toilsome. ❷ *she found maths very difficult* HARD, complicated, complex, involved, impenetrable, unfathomable, over/above one's head, beyond one, puzzling, baffling, perplexing, confusing, mystifying; problematic, intricate, knotty, thorny, ticklish. ❸ *a difficult child* TROUBLESOME, tiresome, trying, exasperating, awkward, demanding, perverse, contrary, recalcitrant, unmanageable, obstreperous, unaccommodating, unhelpful, uncooperative, disobliging; hard to please, fussy, finicky; *formal* refractory. ❹ *you've come at a difficult time* INCONVENIENT, awkward, inopportune, unfavourable, unfortunate, inappropriate, unsuitable, untimely, ill-timed. ❺ *the family have been through very difficult times* BAD, tough, grim, dark, black, hard, adverse, distressing; straitened, hard-pressed.
– OPPOSITES easy, simple, accommodating.

difficulty ▶ noun ❶ *the difficulty of balancing motherhood with a career* STRAIN, trouble, problems, toil, struggle, laboriousness, arduousness; *informal* hassle, stress. ❷ *practical difficulties* PROBLEM, complication, snag, hitch, pitfall, handicap, impediment, hindrance, obstacle, hurdle, stumbling block, obstruction, barrier; *informal* fly in the ointment, headache, hiccup; *Brit. informal* spanner in the works. ❸ *Charles got into difficulties* TROUBLE, predicament, plight, hard times, dire straits; quandary, dilemma; *informal* deep water, a fix, a jam, a spot, a scrape, a stew, a hole, a pickle.
– OPPOSITES ease.

diffidence ▶ noun SHYNESS, bashfulness, modesty, self-effacement, meekness, unassertiveness, timidity, humility, hesitancy, reticence, insecurity, self-doubt, uncertainty, self-consciousness.

diffident ▶ adjective SHY, bashful, modest, self-effacing, unassuming, meek, unconfident, unassertive, timid, timorous, humble, shrinking, reticent, hesitant, insecure, self-doubting, doubtful, uncertain, unsure, self-conscious; *informal* mousy.
– OPPOSITES confident.

diffuse ▶ verb *such ideas were diffused widely in the 1970s* SPREAD, spread around, send out, disseminate, scatter, disperse, distribute, put about, circulate, communicate, purvey, propagate, transmit, broadcast, promulgate.
▶ adjective ❶ *a diffuse community centred on the church* SPREAD OUT, scattered. ❷ *a diffuse narrative* VERBOSE, wordy, prolix, long-winded, long-drawn-out, discursive, rambling, wandering, meandering, maundering, digressive, circuitous, roundabout, circumlocutory, periphrastic; *Brit. informal* waffly.

diffusion ▶ noun SPREAD, dissemination, scattering, dispersal, distribution, circulation, propagation, transmission, broadcasting, promulgation.

dig ▶ verb ❶ *she began to dig the heavy clay soil* TURN OVER, work, break up; till, harrow, plough. ❷ *he took a spade and dug a hole* EXCAVATE, dig out, quarry, hollow out, scoop out, gouge out; cut, bore, tunnel, burrow, mine. ❸ *the bodies were hastily dug up* EXHUME, disinter, unearth. ❹ *Winnie dug her elbow into his ribs* POKE, prod, jab, stab, shove, ram, push, thrust, drive. ❺ *he'd been digging into my past* DELVE, probe, search, inquire, look, investigate, research, examine, scrutinize, check up on; *informal* check out. ❻ *I dug up some disturbing information* UNCOVER, discover, find (out), unearth, dredge up, root out, ferret out, turn up, reveal, bring to light, expose. ❼ (*informal, dated*) *I dig talking with him. See* ENJOY verb sense 1.
▶ noun ❶ *a dig in the ribs* POKE, prod, jab, stab, shove, push. ❷ (*informal*) *they're always making digs at each other* SNIDE REMARK, cutting remark, jibe, jeer, taunt, sneer, insult, barb, insinuation; *informal* wisecrack, crack, put-down.

digest ▶ verb *Liz digested this information* ASSIMILATE, absorb, take in, understand, comprehend, grasp; consider, think about, reflect on, ponder, contemplate, mull over.
▶ noun *a digest of their findings* SUMMARY, synopsis, abstract, precis, résumé, summation; compilation; *N. Amer. informal* wrap-up.

digit ▶ noun ❶ *the door code has ten digits* NUMERAL, number, figure, integer. ❷ *our frozen digits* FINGER, thumb, toe; extremity.

dignified ▶ adjective STATELY, noble, courtly, majestic, distinguished, proud, august, lofty, exalted, regal, lordly, imposing, impressive, grand; solemn, serious, grave, formal, proper, ceremonious, decorous, reserved, composed, sedate.

dignify ▶ verb ENNOBLE, enhance, distinguish, add distinction to, honour, grace, exalt, magnify, glorify, elevate.

dignitary ▶ noun WORTHY, personage, VIP,

grandee, notable, notability, pillar of society, luminary, leading light, big name; *informal* heavyweight, bigwig, top brass, top dog, big gun, big shot, big noise, big cheese, big chief, supremo; *N. Amer. informal* big wheel, big kahuna, big enchilada, top banana.

dignity ▶ **noun** ❶ *the dignity of the Crown* STATELINESS, nobility, majesty, regality, courtliness, augustness, loftiness, lordliness, grandeur; solemnity, gravity, gravitas, formality, decorum, propriety, sedateness. ❷ *he had lost his dignity* SELF-RESPECT, pride, self-esteem, self-worth, amour propre. ❸ *Cnut promised dignities to the noblemen* HIGH RANK, high standing, high station, status, elevation, eminence, honour, glory, greatness.

digress ▶ **verb** DEVIATE, go off at a tangent, get off the subject, get sidetracked, lose the thread, diverge, turn aside/away, depart, drift, stray, wander.

digression ▶ **noun** DEVIATION, detour, diversion, departure, divergence, excursus; aside, incidental remark.

digs ▶ **plural noun** (*informal*) LODGINGS, rooms, accommodation, living quarters; bedsit, flat, house, home; *informal* pad, place; *formal* abode, dwelling, dwelling place, residence, domicile, habitation.

dilapidated ▶ **adjective** RUN DOWN, tumbledown, ramshackle, broken-down, in disrepair, shabby, battered, rickety, shaky, unsound, crumbling, in ruins, ruined, decayed, decaying, decrepit; neglected, uncared-for, untended, the worse for wear, falling to pieces, falling apart, gone to rack and ruin, gone to seed.

dilate ▶ **verb** ❶ *her nostrils dilated* ENLARGE, widen, expand, distend. ❷ *Diane dilated on the joys of her married life* EXPATIATE, expound, enlarge, elaborate, speak/write at length.
– OPPOSITES contract.

dilatory ▶ **adjective** ❶ *he had been dilatory in appointing a solicitor* SLOW, tardy, unhurried, sluggish, sluggardly, snail-like, tortoise-like, lazy. ❷ *dilatory procedural tactics* DELAYING, stalling, temporizing, procrastinating, time-wasting, Fabian.
– OPPOSITES fast.

dilemma ▶ **noun** QUANDARY, predicament, catch-22, vicious circle, plight, mess, muddle; difficulty, problem, trouble, perplexity, confusion, conflict; *informal* no-win situation, fix, tight spot/corner; *Brit. informal* sticky wicket.
■ **on the horns of a dilemma** BETWEEN THE DEVIL AND THE DEEP BLUE SEA, between Scylla and Charybdis; *informal* between a rock and a hard place.

dilettante ▶ **noun** DABBLER, amateur, nonprofessional, non-specialist, layman, layperson.
– OPPOSITES professional.

diligence ▶ **noun** CONSCIENTIOUSNESS, assiduousness, assiduity, hard work, application, concentration, effort, care, industriousness, rigour, meticulousness, thoroughness; perseverance, persistence, tenacity, dedication, commitment, tirelessness, indefatigability, doggedness.

diligent ▶ **adjective** INDUSTRIOUS, hard-working, assiduous, conscientious, particular, punctilious, meticulous, painstaking, rigorous, careful, thorough, sedulous, earnest; persevering, persistent, tenacious, zealous, dedicated, committed, unflagging, untiring, tireless, indefatigable, dogged; *archaic* laborious.
– OPPOSITES lazy.

dilly-dally ▶ **verb** (*informal*) WASTE TIME, dally, dawdle, loiter, linger, take one's time, delay, temporize, stall, procrastinate, pussyfoot around, drag one's feet; dither, hesitate, falter, vacillate, waver; *Brit.* haver, hum and haw; *informal* shilly-shally, let the grass grow under one's feet; *archaic* tarry.
– OPPOSITES hurry.

dilute ▶ **verb** ❶ *strong bleach can be diluted with water* MAKE WEAKER, weaken, water down; thin out, thin; doctor, adulterate; *informal* cut. ❷ *the original plans have been diluted* WEAKEN, moderate, tone down, water down.
▶ **adjective** *a dilute acid.* See DILUTED.

diluted ▶ **adjective** WEAK, dilute, thin, watered down, watery; adulterated.
– OPPOSITES concentrated.

dim ▶ **adjective** ❶ *the dim light* FAINT, weak, feeble, soft, pale, dull, subdued, muted, wishy-washy. ❷ *long dim corridors* DARK, badly lit, ill-lit, dingy, dismal, gloomy, murky; *poetic/literary* tenebrous. ❸ *a dim figure* INDISTINCT, ill-defined, unclear, vague, shadowy, nebulous, obscured, blurred, blurry, fuzzy. ❹ *dim memories* VAGUE, imprecise, imperfect, unclear, indistinct, sketchy, hazy, blurred, shadowy. ❺ (*informal*) *I'm awfully dim.* See STUPID sense 1. ❻ *their prospects for the future looked dim* GLOOMY, unpromising, unfavourable, discouraging, disheartening, depressing, dispiriting, hopeless.
– OPPOSITES bright, distinct, encouraging.
▶ **verb** ❶ *the lights were dimmed* TURN DOWN, lower, dip, soften, subdue, mute; *poetic/literary* bedim. ❷ *my memories have not dimmed with time* FADE, become vague, dwindle, blur. ❸ *the fighting dimmed hopes of peace* DIMINISH, reduce, lessen, weaken, undermine.
– OPPOSITES brighten, sharpen, intensify.

dimension ▶ **noun** ❶ *the dimensions of the room* SIZE, measurements, proportions, extent; length, width, breadth, depth, area, volume, capacity; footage, acreage. ❷ *the dimension of the problem* SIZE, scale, extent, scope, magnitude; importance, significance. ❸ *the cultural dimensions of the problem* ASPECT, feature, element, facet, side.

diminish ▶ verb ❶ *the pain will gradually diminish* DECREASE, lessen, decline, reduce, subside, die down, abate, dwindle, fade, slacken off, moderate, let up, ebb, wane, recede, die away/out, peter out; *archaic* remit. ❷ *new legislation diminished the courts' authority* REDUCE, decrease, lessen, curtail, cut, cut down/back, constrict, restrict, limit, curb, check; weaken, blunt, erode, undermine, sap. ❸ *she lost no opportunity to diminish him* BELITTLE, disparage, denigrate, defame, deprecate, run down; decry, demean, cheapen, devalue; *formal* derogate.
– OPPOSITES increase.

diminution ▶ noun REDUCTION, decrease, lessening, decline, dwindling, moderation, fading, weakening, ebb.

diminutive ▶ adjective TINY, small, little, petite, elfin, minute, miniature, mini, minuscule, compact, pocket, toy, midget, undersized, short; *Scottish* wee; *informal* teeny, weeny, teeny-weeny, teensy-weensy, itty-bitty, itsy-bitsy, tiddly, dinky, baby, pint-sized, knee-high to a grasshopper; *Brit. informal* titchy; *N. Amer. informal* little-bitty.
– OPPOSITES enormous.

dimple ▶ noun INDENTATION, hollow, cleft, dint.

dimwit ▶ noun (*informal*). *See* FOOL noun sense 1.

dim-witted ▶ adjective (*informal*). *See* STUPID senses 1, 2.

din ▶ noun *he shouted above the din* NOISE, racket, rumpus, cacophony, babel, hubbub, tumult, uproar, commotion, clangour, clatter; shouting, yelling, screaming, caterwauling, clamour, outcry; *Scottish & N. English* stramash; *informal* hullabaloo; *Brit. informal* row.
– OPPOSITES silence.

▶ verb ❶ *she had had the evils of drink dinned into her* INSTIL, inculcate, drive, drum, hammer, drill, ingrain; indoctrinate, brainwash. ❷ *the sound dinning in my ears* BLARE, blast, clang, clatter, crash, clamour.

dine ▶ verb ❶ *we dined at a restaurant* HAVE DINNER, have supper, eat; *dated* sup, break bread. ❷ *they dined on lobster* EAT, feed on, feast on, banquet on, partake of; *informal* tuck into.

dingle ▶ noun (*poetic/literary*) VALLEY, dale, vale, hollow; *Brit.* dene; *Scottish* glen, strath; *poetic/literary* dell.

dingy ▶ adjective GLOOMY, dark, dull, badly/poorly lit, murky, dim, dismal, dreary, drab, sombre, grim, cheerless; dirty, grimy, shabby, faded, worn, dowdy, seedy, run down.
– OPPOSITES bright.

dinky ▶ adjective (*Brit. informal*) SMALL, little, petite, dainty, neat, diminutive, mini, miniature; sweet, cute, dear, adorable; *Scottish* wee; *informal* teeny, teeny-weeny, teensy-weensy; *N. Amer. informal* little-bitty.

dinner ▶ noun EVENING MEAL, supper, main meal; lunch; feast, banquet, dinner party; *Brit.* tea; *informal* spread, blowout; *Brit. informal* nosh-up, slap-up meal; *formal* repast.
– RELATED TERMS prandial.

dint ▶ noun DENT, indentation, hollow, depression, dip, dimple, cleft, pit.
■ **by dint of** BY MEANS OF, by virtue of, on account of, as a result of, as a consequence of, owing to, on the strength of, due to, thanks to, by; *formal* by reason of.

diocese ▶ noun BISHOPRIC, see.

dip ▶ verb ❶ *he dipped a rag in the water* IMMERSE, submerge, plunge, duck, dunk, lower, sink. ❷ *the sun dipped below the horizon* SINK, set, drop, go/drop down, fall, descend; disappear, vanish. ❸ *the president's popularity has dipped* DECREASE, fall, drop, fall off, decline, diminish, dwindle, slump, plummet, plunge; *informal* hit the floor. ❹ *the road dipped* SLOPE DOWN, descend, go down; drop away, fall, sink. ❺ *he dipped his headlights* DIM, LOWER, turn down. ❻ *you might have to dip into your savings* DRAW ON, use, make use of, have recourse to, spend. ❼ *an interesting book to dip into* BROWSE THROUGH, skim through, look through, flick through, glance at, peruse, run one's eye over.
– OPPOSITES rise, increase.

▶ noun ❶ *a relaxing dip in the pool* SWIM, bathe; paddle. ❷ *give the fish a ten-minute dip in a salt bath* IMMERSION, plunge, ducking, dunking. ❸ *chicken satay with peanut dip* SAUCE, relish, dressing. ❹ *the hedge at the bottom of the dip* SLOPE, incline, decline, descent; hollow, concavity, depression, basin, indentation. ❺ *a dip in sales* DECREASE, fall, drop, downturn, decline, falling-off, slump, reduction, diminution, ebb.

diplomacy ▶ noun ❶ *diplomacy failed to win them independence* STATESMANSHIP, statecraft, negotiation(s), discussion(s), talks, dialogue; international relations, foreign affairs. ❷ *Jack's quiet diplomacy* TACT, tactfulness, sensitivity, discretion, subtlety, finesse, delicacy, savoir faire, politeness, thoughtfulness, care, judiciousness, prudence.

diplomat ▶ noun AMBASSADOR, attaché, consul, chargé d'affaires, envoy, emissary, plenipotentiary; *archaic* legate.

diplomatic ▶ adjective ❶ *diplomatic activity* AMBASSADORIAL, consular, foreign-office. ❷ *he tried to be diplomatic* TACTFUL, sensitive, subtle, delicate, polite, discreet, thoughtful, careful, judicious, prudent, politic, clever, skilful.
– OPPOSITES tactless.

dire ▶ adjective ❶ *the dire economic situation* TERRIBLE, dreadful, appalling, frightful, awful, atrocious, grim, alarming; grave, serious, disastrous, ruinous, hopeless, irretrievable, wretched, desperate, parlous; *formal* grievous. ❷ *he was in dire need of help* URGENT, desperate, pressing, crying, sore, grave, serious, extreme, acute, drastic. ❸ *dire warnings of fuel shortages* OMINOUS, gloomy, grim, dismal, unpropitious, inauspicious, unfavourable, pessimistic. ❹ (*informal*) *the concert was dire. See* AWFUL sense 2.

direct ▶ **adjective** ❶ *the most direct route* STRAIGHT, undeviating, unswerving; shortest, quickest. ❷ *a direct flight* NON-STOP, unbroken, uninterrupted, through. ❸ *he is very direct* FRANK, candid, straightforward, honest, open, blunt, plain-spoken, outspoken, forthright, downright, no-nonsense, matter-of-fact, not afraid to call a spade a spade; *informal* upfront. ❹ *direct contact with the president* FACE TO FACE, personal, head-on, immediate, first-hand, tête-à-tête. ❺ *a direct quotation* VERBATIM, word for word, to the letter, faithful, exact, precise, accurate, correct. ❻ *the direct opposite* EXACT, absolute, complete, diametrical.

▶ **verb** ❶ *an economic elite directed the nation's affairs* MANAGE, govern, run, administer, control, conduct, handle, be in charge/control of, preside over, lead, head, rule, be at the helm of; supervise, superintend, oversee, regulate, orchestrate, coordinate; *informal* run the show, call the shots/tune, be in the driving seat. ❷ *was that remark directed at me?* AIM AT, target at, address to, intend for, mean for, design for. ❸ *a man in uniform directed them to the hall* GIVE DIRECTIONS, show the way, guide, lead, conduct, accompany, usher, escort ❹ *the judge directed the jury to return a not guilty verdict* INSTRUCT, tell, command, order, charge, require; *poetic/literary* bid.

direction ▶ **noun** ❶ *a northerly direction* WAY, route, course, line, run, bearing, orientation. ❷ *the newspaper's political direction* ORIENTATION, inclination, leaning, tendency, bent, bias, preference; drift, tack, attitude, tone, tenor, mood, current, trend. ❸ *his direction of the project* ADMINISTRATION, management, conduct, handling, running, supervision, superintendence, regulation, orchestration; control, command, rule, leadership, guidance. ❹ *explicit directions about nursing care* INSTRUCTION, order, command, prescription, rule, regulation, requirement.

directive ▶ **noun** INSTRUCTION, direction, command, order, charge, injunction, prescription, rule, ruling, regulation, law, dictate, decree, dictum, edict, mandate, fiat; *formal* ordinance.

directly ▶ **adverb** ❶ *they flew directly to New York* STRAIGHT, right, as the crow flies, by a direct route. ❷ *I went directly after breakfast* IMMEDIATELY, at once, instantly, right away, straight away, post-haste, without delay, without hesitation, forthwith; quickly, speedily, promptly; *informal* pronto. ❸ *the houses directly opposite* EXACTLY, right, immediately; diametrically; *informal* bang. ❹ *she spoke simply and directly* FRANKLY, candidly, openly, bluntly, forthrightly, without beating around the bush.

director ▶ **noun** ADMINISTRATOR, manager, chairman, chairwoman, chairperson, chair, head, chief, principal, leader, governor, president; managing director, MD, chief executive, CEO; supervisor, controller, overseer; *informal* boss, kingpin, top dog, gaffer, head honcho, numero uno; *N. Amer. informal* Mister Big.

directory ▶ **noun** INDEX, list, listing, register, catalogue, record, archive, inventory.

dirge ▶ **noun** ELEGY, lament, threnody, requiem, dead march; *Irish* keen; *Irish & Scottish* coronach.

dirt ▶ **noun** ❶ *his face was streaked with dirt* GRIME, filth; dust, soot, smut; muck, mud, mire, sludge, slime, ooze, dross; smudges, stains; *informal* crud, yuck, grunge; *Brit. informal* grot, gunge. ❷ *the packed dirt of the road* EARTH, soil, loam, clay, silt; ground. ❸ (*informal*) *dog dirt. See* EXCREMENT. ❹ (*informal*) *they tried to dig up dirt on the President* SCANDAL, gossip, revelations, rumour(s); information.

dirty ▶ **adjective** ❶ *a dirty sweatshirt | dirty water* SOILED, grimy, grubby, filthy, mucky, stained, unwashed, greasy, smeared, smeary, spotted, smudged, cloudy, muddy, dusty, sooty; unclean, sullied, impure, tarnished, polluted, contaminated, defiled, foul, unhygienic, insanitary, unsanitary; *informal* cruddy, yucky, icky; *Brit. informal* manky, gungy, grotty; *poetic/literary* befouled, besmirched, begrimed. ❷ *a dirty joke* INDECENT, obscene, rude, naughty, vulgar, smutty, coarse, crude, filthy, bawdy, suggestive, ribald, racy, salacious, risqué, offensive, off colour, lewd, pornographic, explicit, X-rated; *informal* blue; *euphemistic* adult. ❸ *dirty tricks* DISHONEST, deceitful, unscrupulous, dishonourable, unsporting, ungentlemanly, below the belt, unfair, unethical, unprincipled; crooked, double-dealing, underhand, sly, crafty, devious, sneaky; *Brit. informal* out of order, not cricket. ❹ (*informal*) *a dirty cheat* DESPICABLE, contemptible, hateful, vile, low, mean, unworthy, worthless, beyond contempt, sordid; *informal* rotten; *archaic* scurvy. ❺ *a dirty look* MALEVOLENT, resentful, hostile, black, dark; angry, cross, indignant, annoyed, disapproving; *informal* peeved. ❻ *dirty weather* UNPLEASANT, nasty, foul, inclement, bad; rough, stormy, squally, gusty, windy, blowy, rainy; murky, overcast, louring.

–OPPOSITES clean, innocent, honourable, pleasant.

▶ **verb** *the dog had dirtied her dress* SOIL, stain, muddy, blacken, mess up, mark, spatter, bespatter, smudge, smear, splatter; sully, pollute, foul, defile; *poetic/literary* befoul, besmirch, begrime.

–OPPOSITES clean.

disability ▶ **noun** HANDICAP, disablement, incapacity, impairment, infirmity, defect, abnormality; condition, disorder, affliction.

disable ▶ **verb** ❶ *an injury that could disable somebody for life* INCAPACITATE, put out of action, debilitate; handicap, cripple, lame, maim, immobilize, paralyse. ❷ *the bomb squad disabled the device* DEACTIVATE, defuse, disarm. ❸ *he was disabled from holding public office* DISQUALIFY, prevent, preclude.

disabled ▶ adjective HANDICAPPED, incapacitated; debilitated, infirm, out of action; crippled, lame, paralysed, immobilized, bedridden; *euphemistic* physically challenged, differently abled.
– OPPOSITES able-bodied.

disabuse ▶ verb DISILLUSION, set straight, open someone's eyes, correct, enlighten, disenchant, shatter someone's illusions.

disadvantage ▶ noun DRAWBACK, snag, downside, stumbling block, fly in the ointment, catch, hindrance, obstacle, impediment; flaw, defect, weakness, fault, handicap, con, trouble, difficulty, problem, complication, nuisance; *Brit.* disbenefit; *informal* minus, spanner in the works.
– OPPOSITES benefit.

disadvantaged ▶ adjective DEPRIVED, underprivileged, depressed, in need, needy, poor, impoverished, indigent, hard up; *Brit.* on the breadline.

disadvantageous ▶ adjective UNFAVOURABLE, adverse, unfortunate, unlucky, bad; detrimental, prejudicial, deleterious, harmful, damaging, injurious, hurtful; inconvenient, inopportune, ill-timed, untimely, inexpedient.

disaffected ▶ adjective DISSATISFIED, disgruntled, discontented, malcontent, frustrated, alienated; disloyal, rebellious, mutinous, seditious, dissident, up in arms; hostile, antagonistic, unfriendly.
– OPPOSITES contented.

disagree ▶ verb ❶ *no one was willing to disagree with him* TAKE ISSUE, challenge, contradict, oppose; be at variance/odds, not see eye to eye, differ, dissent, be in dispute, debate, argue, quarrel, wrangle, clash, be at loggerheads, cross swords, lock horns; *formal* gainsay. ❷ *their accounts disagree on details* DIFFER, be dissimilar, be different, vary, diverge; contradict each other, conflict, clash, contrast. ❸ *the spicy food disagreed with her* MAKE ILL, make unwell, nauseate, sicken, upset.

disagreeable ▶ adjective ❶ *a disagreeable smell* UNPLEASANT, displeasing, nasty, offensive, off-putting, obnoxious, objectionable, horrible, horrid, dreadful, frightful, abominable, odious, repugnant, repulsive, repellent, revolting, disgusting, foul, vile, nauseating, sickening, unpalatable. ❷ *a disagreeable man* BAD-TEMPERED, ill-tempered, curmudgeonly, cross, crabbed, irritable, grumpy, peevish, sullen, prickly; unfriendly, unpleasant, nasty, mean, mean-spirited, rude, surly, discourteous, impolite, brusque, abrupt, churlish, disobliging.
– OPPOSITES pleasant.

disagreement ▶ noun ❶ *there was some disagreement over possible solutions* DISSENT, dispute, difference of opinion, variance, controversy, disaccord, discord, contention, division. ❷ *a heated disagreement* ARGUMENT, debate, quarrel, wrangle, squabble, falling-out, altercation, dispute, disputation, war of words, contretemps; *informal* tiff, barney, set-to, spat, dingdong; *Brit. informal* row; *Scottish informal* rammy. ❸ *the disagreement between the results of the two assessments* DIFFERENCE, dissimilarity, variation, variance, discrepancy, disparity, divergence, deviation, nonconformity; incompatibility, contradiction, conflict, clash, contrast; *formal* dissimilitude.

disallow ▶ verb REJECT, refuse, dismiss, say no to; ban, bar, block, debar, forbid, prohibit; cancel, invalidate, overrule, quash, overturn, countermand, reverse, throw out, set aside; *informal* give the thumbs down to.

disappear ▶ verb ❶ *by 4 o'clock the mist had disappeared* VANISH, pass from sight, be lost to view/sight, recede from view; fade (away), melt away, clear, dissolve, disperse, evaporate, dematerialize; *poetic/literary* evanesce. ❷ *this way of life has disappeared* DIE OUT, die, cease to exist, come to an end, end, pass away, pass into oblivion, perish, vanish.
– OPPOSITES materialize.

disappoint ▶ verb ❶ *I'm sorry to have disappointed you* LET DOWN, fail, dissatisfy, dash someone's hopes; upset, dismay, sadden, disenchant, disillusion, shatter someone's illusions, disabuse. ❷ *his hopes were disappointed* THWART, frustrate, foil, dash, put a/the damper on; *informal* throw cold water on.
– OPPOSITES fulfil.

disappointed ▶ adjective UPSET, saddened, let down, cast down, disheartened, downhearted, downcast, depressed, dispirited, discouraged, despondent, dismayed, crestfallen, distressed, chagrined; disenchanted, disillusioned; displeased, discontented, dissatisfied, frustrated, disgruntled; *informal* choked, miffed, cut up; *Brit. informal* gutted, as sick as a parrot.
– OPPOSITES pleased.

disappointing ▶ adjective REGRETTABLE, unfortunate, sorry, discouraging, disheartening, dispiriting, depressing, dismaying, upsetting, saddening; dissatisfactory, unsatisfactory; *informal* not all it's cracked up to be.

disappointment ▶ noun ❶ *she tried to hide her disappointment* SADNESS, regret, dismay, sorrow; dispiritedness, despondency, distress, chagrin; disenchantment, disillusionment; displeasure, dissatisfaction, disgruntlement. ❷ *the trip was a bit of a disappointment* LET-DOWN, non-event, anticlimax; *Brit.* damp squib; *informal* washout, lead balloon.
– OPPOSITES satisfaction.

disapprobation ▶ noun. *See* DISAPPROVAL.

disapproval ▶ noun DISAPPROBATION, objection, dislike; dissatisfaction, disfavour, displeasure, distaste, exception; criticism, censure, condemnation, denunciation, deprecation; *informal* the thumbs down.

disapprove ▶ **verb** ❶ *he disapproved of gamblers* OBJECT TO, have a poor opinion of, look down one's nose at, take exception to, dislike, take a dim view of, look askance at, frown on, be against, not believe in; deplore, criticize, censure, condemn, denounce, decry, deprecate. ❷ *the board disapproved the plan* REJECT, veto, refuse, turn down, disallow, throw out, dismiss, rule against; *informal* give the thumbs down to.

disapproving ▶ **adjective** REPROACHFUL, reproving, critical, censorious, condemnatory, disparaging, denigratory, deprecatory, unfavourable; dissatisfied, displeased, hostile.

disarm ▶ **verb** ❶ *the UN must disarm the country* DEMILITARIZE, demobilize. ❷ *the militia refused to disarm* LAY DOWN ONE'S ARMS, demilitarize; *poetic/literary* turn swords into ploughshares. ❸ *police disarmed the bomb* DEFUSE, disable, deactivate, put out of action, make harmless. ❹ *the warmth in his voice disarmed her* WIN OVER, charm, persuade, thaw; mollify, appease, placate, pacify, conciliate, propitiate.

disarmament ▶ **noun** DEMILITARIZATION, demobilization, decommissioning; arms reduction, arms limitation, arms control; the zero option.

disarming ▶ **adjective** WINNING, charming, irresistible, persuasive, beguiling; conciliatory, mollifying.

disarrange ▶ **verb** DISORDER, throw into disarray/disorder, put out of place, disorganize, disturb, displace; mess up, make untidy, make a mess of, jumble, mix up, muddle, turn upside-down, scatter; dishevel, tousle, rumple; *informal* turn topsy-turvy, make a shambles of; *N. Amer. informal* muss up.

disarray ▶ **noun** *the room was in disarray* DISORDER, confusion, chaos, untidiness, disorganization, dishevelment, mess, muddle, clutter, jumble, tangle, hotchpotch, shambles.
– OPPOSITES tidiness.
▶ **verb** *her clothes were disarrayed. See* DISARRANGE.

disassemble ▶ **verb** DISMANTLE, take apart, take to pieces, take to bits, deconstruct, break up, strip down.

disaster ▶ **noun** ❶ *a railway disaster* CATASTROPHE, calamity, cataclysm, tragedy, act of God, holocaust; accident. ❷ *a string of personal disasters* MISFORTUNE, mishap, misadventure, mischance, setback, reversal, stroke of bad luck, blow. ❸ (*informal*) *the film was a disaster* FAILURE, fiasco, catastrophe, debacle; *informal* flop, dud, washout, dead loss.
– OPPOSITES success.

disastrous ▶ **adjective** CATASTROPHIC, calamitous, cataclysmic, tragic; devastating, ruinous, harmful, dire, terrible, awful, shocking, appalling, dreadful; black, dark, unfortunate, unlucky, ill-fated, ill-starred, inauspicious; *formal* grievous.

disavow ▶ **verb** DENY, disclaim, disown, wash one's hands of, repudiate, reject, renounce.

disavowal ▶ **noun** DENIAL, rejection, repudiation, renunciation, disclaimer.

disband ▶ **verb** BREAK UP, disperse, demobilize, dissolve, scatter, separate, go separate ways, part company.
– OPPOSITES assemble.

disbelief ▶ **noun** ❶ *she stared at him in disbelief* INCREDULITY, incredulousness, scepticism, doubt, doubtfulness, dubiousness; cynicism, suspicion, distrust, mistrust; *formal* dubiety. ❷ *I'll burn in hell for disbelief* ATHEISM, unbelief, godlessness, irreligion, agnosticism, nihilism.

disbelieve ▶ **verb** NOT BELIEVE, give no credence to, discredit, discount, doubt, distrust, mistrust, be incredulous, be unconvinced; reject, repudiate, question, challenge; *informal* take with a pinch of salt.

disbeliever ▶ **noun** UNBELIEVER, non-believer, atheist, irreligionist, nihilist; sceptic, doubter, agnostic, doubting Thomas, cynic; *rare* nullifidian.

disbelieving ▶ **adjective** INCREDULOUS, doubtful, dubious, unconvinced; distrustful, mistrustful, suspicious, cynical, sceptical.

disburden ▶ **verb** RELIEVE, free, liberate, unburden, disencumber, discharge, excuse, absolve.

disburse ▶ **verb** PAY OUT, spend, expend, dole out, dish out, hand out, part with, donate, give; *informal* fork out, shell out, lay out; *Brit. informal* stump up; *N. Amer. informal* ante up, pony up.

disc, disk ▶ **noun** ❶ *the sun was a huge scarlet disc* CIRCLE, round, saucer, discus, ring. ❷ *computer disks* DISKETTE, floppy disk, floppy; hard disk; CD-ROM. ❸ (*dated*) *an old T-Rex disc* RECORD, gramophone record, album, LP, vinyl.

discard ▶ **verb** DISPOSE OF, throw away/out, get rid of, toss out, jettison, scrap, dispense with, cast aside/off, throw on the scrap heap; reject, repudiate, abandon, drop, have done with, shed; *informal* chuck (away/out), dump, ditch, bin, junk, get shut of; *Brit. informal* get shot of; *N. Amer. informal* trash.
– OPPOSITES keep.

discern ▶ **verb** PERCEIVE, make out, pick out, detect, recognize, notice, observe, see, spot; identify, determine, distinguish; *poetic/literary* descry, espy.

discernible ▶ **adjective** VISIBLE, detectable, noticeable, perceptible, observable, distinguishable, recognizable, identifiable; apparent, evident, distinct, appreciable, clear, obvious, manifest, conspicuous.

discerning ▶ adjective DISCRIMINATING, judicious, shrewd, clever, astute, intelligent, sharp, selective, sophisticated, tasteful, sensitive, perceptive, percipient, perspicacious, wise, aware, knowing.

discharge ▶ verb ❶ *he was discharged from the RAF* DISMISS, eject, expel, throw out, give someone notice, make redundant; release, let go; *Military* cashier; *informal* sack, give someone the sack, fire, boot out, give someone the boot, turf out, give someone their cards, give someone their marching orders, give someone the push. ❷ *he was discharged from prison* RELEASE, free, set free, let go, liberate, let out. ❸ *oil is routinely discharged from ships* SEND OUT, release, eject, let out, pour out, void, give off. ❹ *the swelling will burst and discharge pus* EMIT, exude, ooze, leak. ❺ *he accidentally discharged a pistol* FIRE, shoot, let off; set off, loose off, trigger, explode, detonate. ❻ *the ferry was discharging passengers* UNLOAD, offload, put off; remove; *archaic* unlade. ❼ *they discharged their duties efficiently* CARRY OUT, perform, execute, conduct, do; fulfil, accomplish, achieve, complete. ❽ *the executor must discharge the funeral expenses* PAY, pay off, settle, clear, honour, meet, liquidate, defray, make good; *informal* square.
–OPPOSITES recruit, imprison, absorb.
▶ noun ❶ *his discharge from the service* DISMISSAL, release, removal, ejection, expulsion, congé; *Military* cashiering; *informal* the sack, the boot. ❷ *her discharge from prison* RELEASE, liberation. ❸ *a discharge of diesel oil into the river* LEAK, leakage, emission, release, flow. ❹ *a watery discharge from the eyes* EMISSION, secretion, excretion, seepage, suppuration; pus, matter; *Medicine* exudate. ❺ *a single discharge of his gun* SHOT, firing, blast; explosion, detonation. ❻ *the discharge of their duties* CARRYING OUT, performance, performing, execution, conduct; fulfilment, accomplishment, completion. ❼ *the discharge of all debts* PAYMENT, repayment, settlement, clearance, meeting, liquidation, defrayal.

disciple ▶ noun ❶ *the disciples of Jesus* APOSTLE, follower. ❷ *a disciple of Rousseau* FOLLOWER, adherent, believer, admirer, devotee, acolyte, votary; pupil, student, learner; upholder, supporter, advocate, proponent, apologist.

disciplinarian ▶ noun MARTINET, hard taskmaster, authoritarian, stickler for discipline; tyrant, despot; *N. Amer.* ramrod; *informal* slave-driver.

discipline ▶ noun ❶ *a lack of proper parental discipline* CONTROL, training, teaching, instruction, regulation, direction, order, authority, rule, strictness, a firm hand; routine, regimen, drill, drilling. ❷ *he was able to maintain discipline among his men* GOOD BEHAVIOUR, orderliness, control, obedience; self-control, self-discipline, self-government, self-restraint. ❸ *sociology is a fairly new discipline* FIELD (OF STUDY), branch of knowledge, subject, area; speciality, specialty.
▶ verb ❶ *she had disciplined herself to ignore the pain* TRAIN, drill, teach, school, coach; regiment. ❷ *she learned to discipline her emotions* CONTROL, restrain, regulate, govern, keep in check, check, curb, keep a tight rein on, rein in, bridle, tame, bring into line. ❸ *he was disciplined by the management* PUNISH, penalize, bring to book; reprimand, rebuke, reprove, chastise, upbraid; *informal* dress down, give someone a dressing-down, rap over the knuckles, give someone a roasting; *Brit. informal* carpet; *formal* castigate.

disclaim ▶ verb ❶ *the school disclaimed responsibility for his death* DENY, refuse to accept/acknowledge, reject, wash one's hands of. ❷ (*Law*) *the earl disclaimed his title* RENOUNCE, relinquish, resign, give up, abandon.
–OPPOSITES accept.

disclose ▶ verb ❶ *the information must not be disclosed to anyone* REVEAL, make known, divulge, tell, impart, communicate, pass on, vouchsafe; release, make public, broadcast, publish, report, unveil; leak, betray, let slip, let drop, give away; *informal* let on, blab, spill the beans, let the cat out of the bag; *Brit. informal* blow the gaff; *archaic* discover, unbosom. ❷ *exploratory surgery disclosed an aneurysm* UNCOVER, reveal, show, bring to light.
–OPPOSITES conceal.

disclosure ▶ noun ❶ *she was embarrassed by this unexpected disclosure* REVELATION, declaration, announcement, news, report; exposé, leak. ❷ *the disclosure of official information* PUBLISHING, broadcasting; revelation, communication, release, uncovering, unveiling, exposure; leakage.

discoloration ▶ noun STAIN, mark, patch, soiling, streak, spot, blotch, tarnishing; blemish, flaw, defect, bruise, contusion; birthmark, naevus; liver spot, age spot; *informal* splodge, splotch; *Medicine* ecchymosis.

discolour ▶ verb STAIN, mark, soil, dirty, streak, smear, spot, tarnish, sully, spoil, mar, blemish; blacken, char; fade, bleach.

discoloured ▶ adjective STAINED, marked, spotted, dirty, soiled, tarnished, blackened; bleached, faded, yellowed.

discomfit ▶ verb EMBARRASS, abash, disconcert, nonplus, discompose, discomfort, take aback, set someone back on their heels, unsettle, unnerve, put someone off their stroke, ruffle, confuse, fluster, agitate, disorientate, upset, disturb, perturb, distress; chagrin, mortify; *informal* faze, rattle; *N. Amer. informal* discombobulate.

discomfiture ▶ noun EMBARRASSMENT, unease, uneasiness, awkwardness, discomfort, discomposure, abashment, confusion, agitation, nervousness, disorientation, perturbation, distress; chagrin, mortification, shame, humiliation; *N. Amer. informal* discombobulation.

discomfort ▶ **noun** ❶ *abdominal discomfort* PAIN, aches and pains, soreness, tenderness, irritation, stiffness; ache, twinge, pang, throb, cramp; *Brit. informal* gyp. ❷ *the discomforts of life at sea* INCONVENIENCE, difficulty, bother, nuisance, vexation, drawback, disadvantage, trouble, problem, trial, tribulation, hardship; *informal* hassle. ❸ *Ruth flushed and Thomas noticed her discomfort* EMBARRASSMENT, discomfiture, unease, uneasiness, awkwardness, discomposure, confusion, nervousness, flusteredness, perturbation, distress, anxiety; chagrin, mortification, shame, humiliation.

▶ **verb** *his purpose was to discomfort the Prime Minister. See* DISCOMFIT.

discomposure ▶ **noun** AGITATION, discomfiture, discomfort, uneasiness, unease, confusion, disorientation, perturbation, distress, nervousness; anxiety, worry, consternation, disquiet, disquietude; embarrassment, abashment, chagrin, loss of face; *N. Amer. informal* discombobulation.

disconcert ▶ **verb** UNSETTLE, nonplus, discomfit, throw/catch off balance, take aback, rattle, set someone back on their heels, unnerve, disorient, perturb, disturb, perplex, confuse, bewilder, baffle, fluster, ruffle, shake, upset, agitate, worry, dismay, discountenance; surprise, take by surprise, startle, put someone off (their stroke/stride), distract; *informal* throw, faze; *N. Amer. informal* discombobulate.

disconcerting ▶ **adjective** UNSETTLING, unnerving, discomfiting, disturbing, perturbing, troubling, upsetting, worrying, alarming, distracting, off-putting; confusing, bewildering, perplexing.

disconnect ▶ **verb** ❶ *the trucks were disconnected from the train* DETACH, disengage, uncouple, decouple, unhook, unhitch, undo, unfasten, unyoke. ❷ *she felt as if she had been disconnected from the real world* SEPARATE, cut off, divorce, sever, isolate, divide, part, disengage, dissociate, remove. ❸ *an engineer disconnected the appliance* DEACTIVATE, shut off, turn off, switch off, unplug.

– OPPOSITES attach.

disconnected ▶ **adjective** ❶ *a world that seemed disconnected from reality* DETACHED, separate, separated, divorced, cut off, isolated, dissociated, disengaged; apart. ❷ *a disconnected narrative* DISJOINTED, incoherent, garbled, confused, jumbled, mixed up, rambling, wandering, disorganized, uncoordinated, ill-thought-out.

disconsolate ▶ **adjective** SAD, unhappy, doleful, woebegone, dejected, downcast, downhearted, despondent, dispirited, crestfallen, cast down, depressed, down, fed up, disappointed, disheartened, discouraged, demoralized, low-spirited, forlorn, in the doldrums, melancholy, miserable, long-faced, glum, gloomy; *informal* blue, choked, down in the mouth, down in the dumps; *poetic/literary* dolorous.

– OPPOSITES cheerful.

discontent ▶ **noun** DISSATISFACTION, disaffection, discontentment, discontentedness, disgruntlement, grievances, unhappiness, displeasure, bad feelings, resentment, envy; restlessness, unrest, uneasiness, unease, frustration, irritation, annoyance; *informal* a chip on one's shoulder.

– OPPOSITES satisfaction.

discontented ▶ **adjective** DISSATISFIED, disgruntled, fed up, disaffected, discontent, malcontent, unhappy, aggrieved, displeased, resentful, envious; restless, frustrated, irritated, annoyed; *informal* fed up to the (back) teeth, browned off, hacked off; *Brit. informal* cheesed off, brassed off; *N. Amer. informal* teed off, ticked off.

– OPPOSITES satisfied.

discontinue ▶ **verb** STOP, end, terminate, put an end to, put a stop to, wind up, finish, call a halt to, cancel, drop, abandon, dispense with, do away with, get rid of, axe, abolish; suspend, interrupt, break off, withdraw; *informal* cut, pull the plug on, scrap, knock something on the head.

discontinuity ▶ **noun** DISCONNECTEDNESS, disconnection, break, disruption, interruption, disjointedness.

discontinuous ▶ **adjective** INTERMITTENT, sporadic, broken, fitful, interrupted, on and off, disrupted, erratic, disconnected.

discord ▶ **noun** ❶ *stress resulting from family discord* STRIFE, conflict, friction, hostility, antagonism, antipathy, enmity, bad feeling, ill feeling, bad blood, argument, quarrelling, squabbling, bickering, wrangling, feuding, contention, disagreement, dissension, dispute, difference of opinion, disunity, division, opposition. ❷ *the music faded in discord* DISSONANCE, discordance, disharmony, cacophony, jangling.

– OPPOSITES accord, harmony.

discordant ▶ **adjective** ❶ *the messages from Washington and London were discordant* DIFFERENT, in disagreement, at variance, at odds, divergent, discrepant, contradictory, contrary, in conflict, conflicting, opposite, opposed, opposing, clashing; incompatible, inconsistent, irreconcilable. ❷ *discordant sounds* INHARMONIOUS, tuneless, off-key, dissonant, harsh, jarring, grating, jangling, jangly, strident, shrill, screeching, screechy, cacophonous; sharp, flat.

– OPPOSITES harmonious.

discount ▶ **noun** *students get a 10 per cent discount* REDUCTION, deduction, markdown, price cut, cut, concession; rebate.

▶ **verb** ❶ *I'd heard rumours, but discounted them* DISREGARD, pay no attention to, take no notice of, take no account of, dismiss, ignore, overlook, disbelieve, reject; *informal* take with a pinch of salt, pooh-pooh. ❷ *the RRP is discounted in many stores* REDUCE, mark down, cut, lower; *informal* knock down. ❸ *top Paris hotels discounted 20 per cent off published room rates* DEDUCT, take off, rebate; *informal* knock off, slash.
– OPPOSITES believe, increase.

discountenance ▶ **verb** ❶ *she was not discountenanced by the accusation* DISCONCERT, discomfit, unsettle, nonplus, throw/catch off balance, take aback, unnerve, disorient, perturb, disturb, perplex, fluster, ruffle, shake, upset, agitate, worry, dismay, discompose, abash; *informal* throw, faze, rattle; *N. Amer. informal* discombobulate. ❷ *a family environment in which alcohol consumption is discountenanced* DISAPPROVE OF, frown on, take a dim view of, object to.

discourage ▶ **verb** ❶ *we want to discourage children from smoking* DETER, dissuade, disincline, put off, talk out of; advise against, urge against. ❷ *she was discouraged by his hostile tone* DISHEARTEN, dispirit, demoralize, cast down, depress, disappoint, dash someone's hopes; put off, unnerve, daunt, intimidate, cow, crush. ❸ *he sought to discourage further conversation* PREVENT, stop, put a stop to, avert, fend off, stave off, ward off; inhibit, hinder, check, curb, put a damper on, throw cold water on.
– OPPOSITES encourage.

discouraged ▶ **adjective** DISHEARTENED, dispirited, demoralized, deflated, disappointed, let down, disconsolate, despondent, fed up, dejected, cast down, downcast, depressed, crestfallen, dismayed, low-spirited, gloomy, glum, pessimistic, unenthusiastic; put off, daunted, intimidated, cowed, crushed; *informal* down in the mouth, down in the dumps, unenthused; *archaic* chap-fallen.

discouraging ▶ **adjective** DEPRESSING, demoralizing, disheartening, dispiriting, disappointing, gloomy, off-putting; unfavourable, unpromising, inauspicious.
– OPPOSITES encouraging.

discourse ▶ **noun** ❶ *they prolonged their discourse outside the door* DISCUSSION, conversation, talk, dialogue, conference, debate, consultation; parley, powwow, chat; *informal* confab; *formal* confabulation, colloquy; *archaic* converse. ❷ *a discourse on critical theory* ESSAY, treatise, dissertation, paper, study, critique, monograph, disquisition, tract; lecture, address, speech, oration; sermon, homily.

▶ **verb** ❶ *he discoursed at length on his favourite topic* HOLD FORTH, expatiate, pontificate; talk, give a talk, give a speech, lecture, sermonize, preach; *informal* spout, sound off; *formal* perorate. ❷ *Edward was discoursing with his friends* CONVERSE, talk, speak, debate, confer, consult, parley, chat; *formal* confabulate.

discourteous ▶ **adjective** RUDE, impolite, ill-mannered, bad-mannered, disrespectful, uncivil, unmannerly, unchivalrous, ungentlemanly, unladylike, ill-bred, churlish, boorish, crass, ungracious, graceless, uncouth; insolent, impudent, cheeky, audacious, presumptuous; curt, brusque, blunt, offhand, unceremonious, short, sharp; *informal* ignorant; *archaic* malapert.
– OPPOSITES polite.

discourtesy ▶ **noun** RUDENESS, impoliteness, ill manners, bad manners, incivility, disrespect, ungraciousness, churlishness, boorishness, ill breeding, uncouthness, crassness; insolence, impudence, impertinence; curtness, brusqueness, abruptness.

discover ▶ **verb** ❶ *firemen discovered a body in the debris* FIND, locate, come across/upon, stumble on, chance on, light on, bring to light, uncover, unearth, turn up; track down, run to earth, run to ground. ❷ *eventually, I discovered the truth* FIND OUT, learn, realize, recognize, see, ascertain, work out, fathom out, dig up/out, ferret out, root out; *informal* figure out, tumble to; *Brit. informal* twig, rumble, suss out; *N. Amer. informal* dope out. ❸ *scientists discovered a new way of dating fossil crustaceans* HIT ON, come up with, invent, originate, devise, design, contrive, conceive of; pioneer, develop.

discoverer ▶ **noun** ORIGINATOR, inventor, creator, deviser, designer; pioneer.

discovery ▶ **noun** ❶ *the discovery of the body* FINDING, location, uncovering, unearthing. ❷ *the discovery that she was pregnant* REALIZATION, recognition; revelation, disclosure. ❸ *the discovery of new drugs* INVENTION, origination, devising; pioneering. ❹ *he failed to take out a patent on his discoveries* FIND, finding; invention, breakthrough, innovation.

discredit ▶ **verb** ❶ *an attempt to discredit him and his company* BRING INTO DISREPUTE, disgrace, dishonour, damage the reputation of, blacken the name of, put/show in a bad light, reflect badly on, compromise, stigmatize, smear, tarnish, taint; *N. Amer.* slur. ❷ *that theory has been discredited* DISPROVE, invalidate, explode, drive a coach and horses through, refute; *informal* debunk, shoot full of holes, blow sky-high; *formal* confute.

▶ **noun** ❶ *crimes which brought discredit on the administration* DISHONOUR, disrepute, disgrace, shame, humiliation, ignominy, infamy, notoriety; censure, blame, reproach, opprobrium; stigma; *dated* disesteem. ❷ *the ships were a discredit to the country* DISGRACE, source of shame, reproach, blot on the escutcheon.
– OPPOSITES honour, glory.

discreditable ▶ **adjective** DISHONOURABLE, reprehensible, shameful, deplorable, disgrace-

ful, disreputable, blameworthy, ignoble, shabby, objectionable, regrettable, unacceptable, unworthy.
– OPPOSITES praiseworthy.

discreet ▶ **adjective** ❶ *discreet enquiries* CAREFUL, circumspect, cautious, wary, chary, guarded; tactful, diplomatic, prudent, judicious, strategic, politic, delicate, sensitive, kid-glove; *informal* softly-softly. ❷ *discreet lighting* UNOBTRUSIVE, inconspicuous, subtle, low-key, understated, subdued, muted, soft, restrained.

discrepancy ▶ **noun** DIFFERENCE, disparity, variance, variation, deviation, divergence, disagreement, inconsistency, dissimilarity, mismatch, discordance, incompatibility, conflict; *formal* dissimilitude.
– OPPOSITES correspondence.

discrete ▶ **adjective** SEPARATE, distinct, individual, detached, unattached, disconnected, discontinuous, disjunct, disjoined.
– OPPOSITES connected.

discretion ▶ **noun** ❶ *you can rely on his discretion* CIRCUMSPECTION, carefulness, caution, wariness, chariness, guardedness; TACT, tactfulness, diplomacy, delicacy, sensitivity, prudence, judiciousness. ❷ *honorary fellowships awarded at the discretion of the council* CHOICE, option, preference, disposition, volition; pleasure, liking, wish, will, inclination, desire.

discretionary ▶ **adjective** OPTIONAL, voluntary, at one's discretion, elective; *Law* permissive.
– OPPOSITES compulsory.

discriminate ▶ **verb** ❶ *he cannot discriminate between fact and opinion* DIFFERENTIATE, distinguish, draw a distinction, tell the difference, tell apart; separate, separate the sheep from the goats, separate the wheat from the chaff. ❷ *existing employment policies discriminate against women* BE BIASED, be prejudiced; treat differently, treat unfairly, put at a disadvantage, disfavour; victimize.

discriminating ▶ **adjective** DISCERNING, perceptive, astute, shrewd, judicious, perspicacious, insightful, keen; selective, fastidious, tasteful, refined, sensitive, cultivated, cultured, artistic, aesthetic.
– OPPOSITES indiscriminate.

discrimination ▶ **noun** ❶ *racial discrimination* PREJUDICE, bias, bigotry, intolerance, narrow-mindedness, unfairness, inequity, favouritism, one-sidedness, partisanship; sexism, chauvinism, racism, racialism, anti-Semitism, heterosexism, ageism, classism; positive discrimination; (*in S. Africa, historical*) apartheid. ❷ *a man with no discrimination* DISCERNMENT, judgement, perception, perceptiveness, perspicacity, acumen, astuteness, shrewdness, judiciousness, insight; selectivity, (good) taste, fastidiousness, refinement, sensitivity, cultivation, culture.
– OPPOSITES impartiality.

discriminatory ▶ **adjective** PREJUDICIAL, biased, prejudiced, preferential, unfair, unjust, invidious, inequitable, weighted, one-sided, partisan; sexist, chauvinistic, chauvinist, racist, racialist, anti-Semitic, ageist, classist.
– OPPOSITES impartial.

discursive ▶ **adjective** ❶ *dull, discursive prose* RAMBLING, digressive, meandering, wandering, maundering, diffuse, long, lengthy, wordy, verbose, long-winded, prolix; circuitous, roundabout, circumlocutory; *Brit. informal* waffly. ❷ *an elegant discursive style* FLUENT, flowing, fluid, eloquent, expansive.
– OPPOSITES concise, terse.

discuss ▶ **verb** ❶ *I discussed the matter with my wife* TALK OVER, talk about, talk through, converse about, debate, confer about, deliberate about, chew over, consider, weigh up, consider the pros and cons of, thrash out; *informal* kick around/about, bat around/about. ❷ *chapter three discusses this topic in detail* EXAMINE, explore, study, analyse, go into, deal with, treat, consider, concern itself with, tackle.

discussion ▶ **noun** ❶ *a long discussion with her husband* CONVERSATION, talk, dialogue, discourse, conference, debate, exchange of views, consultation, deliberation; powwow, chat, tête-à-tête, heart-to-heart; negotiations, parley; *informal* confab, chit-chat, rap; *N. Amer. informal* skull session, bull session; *formal* confabulation, colloquy; *archaic* converse. ❷ *the book's candid discussion of sexual matters* EXAMINATION, exploration, analysis, study; treatment, consideration.

disdain ▶ **noun** *she looked at him with disdain* CONTEMPT, scorn, scornfulness, contemptuousness, derision, disrespect; disparagement, condescension, superciliousness, hauteur, haughtiness, arrogance, snobbishness, indifference, dismissiveness; distaste, dislike, disgust; *archaic* despite.
– OPPOSITES respect.
▶ **verb** ❶ *she disdained such vulgar exhibitionism* SCORN, deride, pour scorn on, regard with contempt, sneer at, sniff at, curl one's lip at, look down one's nose at, look down on; despise; *informal* turn up one's nose at, pooh-pooh; *archaic* contemn. ❷ *she disdained his invitation* SPURN, reject, refuse, rebuff, disregard, ignore, snub; decline, turn down, brush aside.

disdainful ▶ **adjective** CONTEMPTUOUS, scornful, derisive, sneering, withering, slighting, disparaging, disrespectful, condescending, patronizing, supercilious, haughty, superior, arrogant, proud, snobbish, lordly, aloof, indifferent, dismissive; *informal* high and mighty, hoity-toity, sniffy, snotty; *archaic* contumelious.
– OPPOSITES respectful.

disease ▶ noun ILLNESS, sickness, ill health; infection, ailment, malady, disorder, complaint, affliction, condition, indisposition, upset, problem, trouble, infirmity, disability, defect, abnormality; pestilence, plague, cancer, canker, blight; *informal* bug, virus; *Brit. informal* lurgy; *dated* contagion.
– RELATED TERMS pathological.

diseased ▶ adjective UNHEALTHY, ill, sick, unwell, ailing, sickly, unsound; infected, septic, contaminated, blighted, rotten, bad, abnormal.

disembark ▶ verb GET OFF, step off, leave, pile out; go ashore, debark, detrain; land, arrive; *Brit.* alight; *N. Amer.* deplane.

disembodied ▶ adjective BODILESS, incorporeal, discarnate, spiritual; intangible, insubstantial, impalpable; ghostly, spectral, phantom, wraithlike.

disembowel ▶ verb GUT, draw, remove the guts from; *formal* eviscerate.

disenchanted ▶ adjective DISILLUSIONED, disappointed, disabused, let down, fed up, dissatisfied, discontented; cynical, soured, jaundiced, sick, out of love, indifferent.

disenchantment ▶ noun DISILLUSIONMENT, disappointment, dissatisfaction, discontent, discontentedness, rude awakening; cynicism.

disengage ▶ verb ❶ *I disengaged his hand from mine* REMOVE, detach, disentangle, extricate, separate, release, free, loosen, loose, disconnect, unfasten, unclasp, uncouple, undo, unhook, unhitch, untie, unyoke, disentwine. ❷ *American forces disengaged from the country* WITHDRAW, leave, pull out of, quit, retreat from.
– OPPOSITES attach, enter.

disentangle ▶ verb ❶ *Allen was disentangling a coil of rope* UNTANGLE, unravel, untwist, unwind, undo, untie, straighten out, smooth out; comb, card. ❷ *he disentangled his fingers from her hair* EXTRICATE, extract, free, remove, disengage, untwine, disentwine, release, loosen, detach, unfasten, unclasp, disconnect.

disfavour ▶ noun DISAPPROVAL, disapprobation; dislike, displeasure, distaste, dissatisfaction, low opinion; *dated* disesteem; *archaic* disrelish.

disfigure ▶ verb MAR, spoil, deface, scar, blemish, uglify; damage, injure, impair, blight, mutilate, deform, maim, ruin; vandalize.
– OPPOSITES adorn.

disfigurement ▶ noun ❶ *the disfigurement of Victorian buildings* DEFACEMENT, spoiling, scarring, uglification, mutilation, damage, vandalizing, ruin. ❷ *a permanent facial disfigurement* BLEMISH, flaw, defect, imperfection, discoloration, blotch; scar, pockmark; deformity, malformation, abnormality, injury, wound.

disgorge ▶ verb ❶ *the combine disgorged a stream of grain* POUR OUT, discharge, eject, throw out, emit, expel, spit out, spew out, belch forth, spout; vomit, regurgitate. ❷ *they were made to disgorge all the profits* SURRENDER, relinquish, hand over, give up, turn over, yield.

disgrace ▶ noun ❶ *he brought disgrace on the family* DISHONOUR, shame, discredit, ignominy, degradation, disrepute, ill-repute, infamy, scandal, stigma, opprobrium, obloquy, condemnation, vilification, contempt, disrespect; humiliation, embarrassment, loss of face; *Austral.* strife; *dated* disesteem. ❷ *the unemployment figures are a disgrace* SCANDAL, outrage; discredit, reproach, affront, insult; stain, blemish, blot, blot on the escutcheon, black mark; *informal* crime, sin.
– OPPOSITES honour.

▶ verb ❶ *you have disgraced the family name* BRING SHAME ON, shame, dishonour, discredit, bring into disrepute, degrade, debase, defame, stigmatize, taint, sully, tarnish, besmirch, stain, blacken, drag through the mud/mire. ❷ *he was publicly disgraced* DISCREDIT, dishonour, stigmatize; humiliate, cause to lose face, chasten, humble, demean, put someone in their place, take down a peg or two, cut down to size.
– OPPOSITES honour.

■ **in disgrace** OUT OF FAVOUR, unpopular, in bad odour, under a cloud, disgraced; *informal* in someone's bad/black books, in the doghouse; *NZ informal* in the dogbox.

disgraceful ▶ adjective SHAMEFUL, shocking, scandalous, deplorable, despicable, contemptible, beyond contempt, beyond the pale, dishonourable, discreditable, reprehensible, base, mean, low, blameworthy, unworthy, ignoble, shabby, inglorious, outrageous, abominable, atrocious, appalling, dreadful, terrible, disgusting, shameless, vile, odious, monstrous, heinous, iniquitous, unspeakable, loathsome, sordid, nefarious; *archaic* scurvy.
– OPPOSITES admirable.

disgruntled ▶ adjective DISSATISFIED, discontented, aggrieved, resentful, fed up, displeased, unhappy, disappointed, disaffected; angry, irate, annoyed, cross, exasperated, indignant, vexed, irritated, piqued, irked, put out; *informal* peeved, miffed, aggravated, hacked off, browned off, riled, peed off, hot under the collar, in a huff; *Brit. informal* cheesed off, shirty, narked; *N. Amer. informal* sore, teed off, ticked off.

disguise ▶ verb *his controlled voice disguised his true feelings* CAMOUFLAGE, conceal, hide, cover up, dissemble, mask, screen, shroud, veil, cloak; paper over, gloss over, put up a smokescreen.
– OPPOSITES expose.

■ **disguise oneself as** DRESS UP AS, pretend to be, pass oneself of as, impersonate, pose as; *formal* personate.

disguised ▶ adjective IN DISGUISE, camouflaged; incognito, under cover.

disgust ▶ **noun** *a look of disgust* REVULSION, repugnance, aversion, distaste, nausea, abhorrence, loathing, detestation, odium, horror; contempt, outrage; *archaic* disrelish.
– OPPOSITES delight.
▶ **verb** ❶ *the hospital food disgusted me* REVOLT, repel, repulse, sicken, nauseate, turn someone's stomach, make someone's gorge rise; *informal* turn off; *N. Amer. informal* gross out. ❷ *Toby's behaviour disgusted her* OUTRAGE, shock, horrify, appal, scandalize, offend.

disgusting ▶ **adjective** ❶ *the food was disgusting* REVOLTING, repellent, repulsive, sickening, nauseating, stomach-churning, stomach-turning, off-putting, unpalatable, distasteful, foul, nasty; *N. Amer.* vomitous; *informal* yucky, icky, gross, sick-making. ❷ *I find racism disgusting* ABHORRENT, loathsome, offensive, appalling, outrageous, objectionable, shocking, horrifying, scandalous, monstrous, unspeakable, shameful, vile, odious, obnoxious, detestable, hateful, sickening, contemptible, despicable, deplorable, abominable, beyond the pale; *informal* gross, ghastly, sick.
– OPPOSITES delicious, appealing.

dish ▶ **noun** ❶ *a china dish* BOWL, plate, platter, salver, paten; container, receptacle; *archaic* trencher, charger; *historical* porringer. ❷ *vegetarian dishes* RECIPE, meal, course; (**dishes**) food, fare. ❸ (*informal*) *she's quite a dish. See* BEAUTY sense 2.
■ **dish something out** DISTRIBUTE, dispense, issue, hand out/round, give out, pass out/round; deal out, dole out, share out, allocate, allot, apportion.
■ **dish something up** SERVE (UP), spoon out, ladle out, scoop out.

disharmony ▶ **noun** DISCORD, friction, strife, conflict, hostility, acrimony, bad blood, bad feeling, enmity, dissension, disagreement, feuding, quarrelling; disunity, division, divisiveness.

dishearten ▶ **verb** DISCOURAGE, dispirit, demoralize, cast down, depress, disappoint, dismay, dash someone's hopes; put off, deter, unnerve, daunt, intimidate, cow, crush.
– OPPOSITES encourage.

disheartened ▶ **adjective** DISCOURAGED, dispirited, demoralized, deflated, disappointed, let down, disconsolate, despondent, fed up, dejected, cast down, downcast, depressed, crestfallen, dismayed, low-spirited, gloomy, glum, pessimistic, unenthusiastic; daunted, intimidated, cowed, crushed; *informal* down in the mouth, down in the dumps, unenthused; *archaic* chap-fallen.

dishevelled ▶ **adjective** UNTIDY, unkempt, scruffy, messy, in a mess, disordered, disarranged, rumpled, bedraggled; uncombed, tousled, tangled, tangly, knotted, knotty, shaggy, straggly, windswept, wind-blown, wild; slovenly, slatternly, blowsy, frowzy; *informal* ratty; *N. Amer. informal* mussed (up); *archaic* draggle-tailed.
– OPPOSITES tidy.

dishonest ▶ **adjective** FRAUDULENT, corrupt, swindling, cheating, double-dealing; underhand, crafty, cunning, devious, treacherous, unfair, unjust, dirty, unethical, immoral, dishonourable, untrustworthy, unscrupulous, unprincipled, amoral; criminal, illegal, unlawful; false, untruthful, deceitful, deceiving, lying, mendacious; *informal* crooked, shady, tricky, sharp, shifty; *Brit. informal* bent, dodgy; *Austral./NZ informal* shonky; *poetic/literary* perfidious.

dishonesty ▶ **noun** FRAUD, fraudulence, sharp practice, corruption, cheating, chicanery, double-dealing, deceit, deception, duplicity, lying, falseness, falsity, falsehood, untruthfulness; craft, cunning, trickery, artifice, underhandedness, subterfuge, skulduggery, treachery, untrustworthiness, unscrupulousness, criminality, misconduct; *informal* crookedness, dirty tricks, shenanigans; *Brit. informal* jiggery-pokery; *poetic/literary* perfidy.
– OPPOSITES probity.

dishonour ▶ **noun** *the incident brought dishonour upon the police profession* DISGRACE, shame, discredit, humiliation, degradation, ignominy, scandal, infamy, disrepute, ill repute, loss of face, disfavour, ill favour, debasement, opprobrium, obloquy; stigma; *dated* disesteem.
▶ **verb** *his family name has been dishonoured* DISGRACE, shame, discredit, bring into disrepute, humiliate, degrade, debase, lower, cheapen, drag down, drag through the mud, blacken the name of, give a bad name to; sully, stain, taint, besmirch, smear, mar, blot, stigmatize.

dishonourable ▶ **adjective** DISGRACEFUL, shameful, disreputable, discreditable, degrading, ignominious, ignoble, blameworthy, contemptible, despicable, reprehensible, shabby, shoddy, sordid, sorry, base, low, improper, unseemly, unworthy; unprincipled, unscrupulous, corrupt, untrustworthy, treacherous, traitorous; *informal* shady, dirty; *poetic/literary* perfidious; *archaic* scurvy.

disillusion ▶ **verb** DISABUSE, enlighten, set straight, open someone's eyes; disenchant, shatter someone's illusions, disappoint, make sadder and wiser.
– OPPOSITES deceive.

disillusioned ▶ **adjective** DISENCHANTED, disabused, disappointed, let down, discouraged; cynical, sour, negative, world-weary.

disincentive ▶ **noun** DETERRENT, discouragement, damper, brake, curb, check, restraint, inhibitor; obstacle, impediment, hindrance, obstruction, block, barrier.

disinclination ▶ **noun** RELUCTANCE, unwillingness, lack of enthusiasm, indisposition, hesitancy; aversion, dislike, distaste; objection, demur, resistance, opposition; *archaic* disrelish.
– OPPOSITES enthusiasm.

disinclined ▸ adjective RELUCTANT, unwilling, unenthusiastic, unprepared, indisposed, ill-disposed, not in the mood, hesitant; loath, averse, antipathetic, resistant, opposed.
– OPPOSITES willing.

disinfect ▸ verb STERILIZE, sanitize, clean, cleanse, purify, decontaminate; fumigate.
– OPPOSITES contaminate.

disinfectant ▸ noun ANTISEPTIC, bactericide, germicide, sterilizer, cleanser, decontaminant; fumigant.

disingenuous ▸ adjective INSINCERE, dishonest, untruthful, false, deceitful, duplicitous, lying, mendacious; hypocritical; *archaic* hollow-hearted.

disinherit ▸ verb CUT SOMEONE OUT OF ONE'S WILL, cut off, dispossess; disown, repudiate, reject, cast off/aside, wash one's hands of, have nothing more to do with, turn one's back on; *informal* cut off without a penny.

disintegrate ▸ verb BREAK UP, break apart, fall apart, fall to pieces, fragment, fracture, shatter, splinter; explode, blow up, blow apart, fly apart; crumble, deteriorate, decay, decompose, rot, moulder, perish, dissolve, collapse, go to rack and ruin, degenerate; *informal* bust, be smashed to smithereens.

disinter ▸ verb EXHUME, unearth, dig up, disentomb.

disinterest ▸ noun ❶ *scholarly disinterest* IMPARTIALITY, neutrality, objectivity, detachment, disinterestedness, lack of bias, lack of prejudice; open-mindedness, fairness, fair-mindedeness, equity, balance, even-handedness. ❷ *he looked at us with complete disinterest* INDIFFERENCE, lack of interest, unconcern, impassivity; boredom, apathy.
– OPPOSITES bias.

disinterested ▸ adjective ❶ *disinterested advice* UNBIASED, unprejudiced, impartial, neutral, non-partisan, detached, uninvolved, objective, dispassionate, impersonal, clinical; open-minded, fair, just, equitable, balanced, even-handed, with no axe to grind, without fear or favour. ❷ *he looked at her with disinterested eyes* UNINTERESTED, indifferent, incurious, unconcerned, unmoved, unresponsive, impassive, passive, detached, unenthusiastic, lukewarm, bored, apathetic; *informal* couldn't-care-less.

disjointed ▸ adjective UNCONNECTED, disconnected, disunited, discontinuous, fragmented, disorganized, disordered, muddled, mixed up, jumbled, garbled, incoherent, confused; rambling, wandering.

dislike ▸ verb *a man she had always disliked* FIND DISTASTEFUL, regard with distaste, be averse to, have an aversion to, have no liking/taste for, disapprove of, object to, take exception to; hate, detest, loathe, abhor, despise, be unable to bear/stand, shrink from, shudder at, find repellent; *informal* be unable to stomach; *formal* abominate; *archaic* disrelish.
▸ noun *she viewed the other woman with dislike* DISTASTE, aversion, disfavour, disapproval, disapprobation, enmity, animosity, hostility, antipathy, antagonism; hate, hatred, detestation, loathing, disgust, repugnance, abhorrence, disdain, contempt; *archaic* disrelish.

dislocate ▸ verb ❶ *she dislocated her hip* PUT OUT OF JOINT; *informal* put out; *Medicine* luxate. ❷ *trade was dislocated by a famine* DISRUPT, disturb, throw into disarray, throw into confusion, play havoc with, interfere with, disorganize, upset; *informal* mess up.

dislodge ▸ verb ❶ *replace any stones you dislodge* DISPLACE, knock out of place/position, move, shift; knock over, upset. ❷ *economic sanctions failed to dislodge the dictator* REMOVE, force out, drive out, oust, eject, get rid of, evict, unseat, depose, topple, drum out; *informal* kick out, boot out; *Brit. informal* turf out.

disloyal ▸ adjective UNFAITHFUL, faithless, false, false-hearted, untrue, inconstant, untrustworthy, unreliable, undependable, fickle; treacherous, traitorous, subversive, seditious, unpatriotic, two-faced, double-dealing, double-crossing, deceitful; dissident, renegade; adulterous; *informal* back-stabbing, two-timing; *poetic/literary* perfidious; *archaic* hollow-hearted.

disloyalty ▸ noun UNFAITHFULNESS, infidelity, inconstancy, faithlessness, fickleness, unreliability, untrustworthiness, betrayal, falseness; duplicity, double-dealing, treachery, treason, subversion, sedition, dissidence; adultery; *informal* back-stabbing, two-timing; *poetic/literary* perfidy, perfidiousness.

dismal ▸ adjective ❶ *a dismal look* GLOOMY, glum, melancholy, morose, doleful, woebegone, forlorn, dejected, depressed, dispirited, downcast, despondent, disconsolate, miserable, sad, unhappy, sorrowful, desolate, wretched; *informal* blue, fed up, down in the dumps/mouth; *poetic/literary* dolorous. ❷ *a dismal hall* DINGY, dim, dark, gloomy, dreary, drab, dull, bleak, cheerless, depressing, uninviting, unwelcoming. ❸ (*informal*) *a dismal performance*. See POOR sense 2.
– OPPOSITES cheerful, bright.

dismantle ▸ verb TAKE APART, take to pieces/bits, pull apart, pull to pieces, disassemble, break up, strip (down); knock down, pull down, demolish.
– OPPOSITES assemble, build.

dismay ▸ verb *he was dismayed by the change in his friend* APPAL, horrify, shock, shake (up); disconcert, take aback, alarm, unnerve, unsettle, throw off balance, discompose; disturb, upset, distress; *informal* rattle, faze, knock sideways; *Brit. informal* knock for six.
– OPPOSITES encourage, please.
▸ noun *they greeted his decision with dismay* ALARM,

shock, surprise, consternation, concern, perturbation, disquiet, discomposure, distress.
– OPPOSITES pleasure, relief.

dismember ▶ verb DISJOINT, joint; pull apart, cut up, chop up, butcher.

dismiss ▶ verb ❶ *the president dismissed five ministers* GIVE SOMEONE THEIR NOTICE, get rid of, discharge; lay off, make redundant; *informal* sack, give someone the sack, fire, boot out, give someone the boot/elbow/push, give someone their marching orders, show someone the door; *Brit. informal* give someone their cards; *Military* cashier. ❷ *the guards were dismissed* SEND AWAY, let go; disband, dissolve, discharge. ❸ *he dismissed all morbid thoughts* BANISH, set aside, disregard, brush off, shrug off, put out of one's mind; reject, deny, repudiate, spurn.
– OPPOSITES engage.

dismissal ▶ noun ❶ *the threat of dismissal* ONE'S NOTICE, discharge; redundancy, laying off; *informal* the sack, sacking, firing, the push, the boot, the axe, the elbow, one's marching orders; *Brit. informal* one's cards, the chop; *Military* cashiering. ❷ *a condescending dismissal* REJECTION, repudiation, repulse, non-acceptance.
– OPPOSITES recruitment.

dismissive ▶ adjective CONTEMPTUOUS, disdainful, scornful, sneering, snide, disparaging, negative; *informal* sniffy.
– OPPOSITES admiring.

dismount ▶ verb ❶ *the cyclist dismounted* ALIGHT, get off/down. ❷ *the horse dismounted the trooper* UNSEAT, dislodge, throw, unhorse.

disobedient ▶ adjective INSUBORDINATE, unruly, wayward, badly behaved, naughty, delinquent, disruptive, troublesome, rebellious, defiant, mutinous, recalcitrant, uncooperative, wilful, intractable, obstreperous; *Brit. informal* bolshie; *archaic* contumacious.

disobey ▶ verb DEFY, go against, flout, contravene, infringe, transgress, violate; disregard, ignore, pay no heed to.

disobliging ▶ adjective UNHELPFUL, uncooperative, unaccommodating, unamenable, unreasonable, awkward, difficult; discourteous, uncivil, unfriendly.
– OPPOSITES helpful.

disorder ▶ noun ❶ *he hates disorder* UNTIDINESS, disorderliness, mess, disarray, chaos, confusion; clutter, jumble; a muddle, a shambles. ❷ *incidents of public disorder* UNREST, disturbance, disruption, upheaval, turmoil, mayhem, pandemonium; violence, fighting, rioting, lawlessness, anarchy; breach of the peace, fracas, rumpus, melee; *Law, dated* affray; *informal* aggro. ❸ *a blood disorder* DISEASE, infection, complaint, condition, affliction, malady, sickness, illness, ailment, infirmity, irregularity.
– OPPOSITES tidiness, peace.

disordered ▶ adjective ❶ *her grey hair was disordered* UNTIDY, unkempt, messy, in a mess; disorganized, chaotic, confused, jumbled, muddled; *N. Amer. informal* mussed (up); *Brit. informal* shambolic. ❷ *a disordered digestive system* DYSFUNCTIONAL, disturbed, unsettled, unbalanced, upset, poorly.

disorderly ▶ adjective ❶ *a disorderly desk* UNTIDY, disorganized, messy, cluttered; in disarray, in a mess, in a jumble, in a muddle, at sixes and sevens; *informal* like a bomb's hit it, higgledy-piggledy; *Brit. informal* shambolic. ❷ *disorderly behaviour* UNRULY, boisterous, rough, rowdy, wild, riotous; disruptive, troublesome, undisciplined, lawless, unmanageable, uncontrollable, out of hand, out of control.
– OPPOSITES tidy, peaceful.

disorganized ▶ adjective ❶ *a disorganized tool box* DISORDERLY, disordered, unorganized, jumbled, muddled, untidy, messy, chaotic, topsy-turvy, haphazard; in disorder, in disarray, in a mess, in a muddle, in a shambles; *informal* higgledy-piggledy; *Brit. informal* shambolic. ❷ *muddled and disorganized* UNMETHODICAL, unsystematic, undisciplined, badly organized, inefficient; haphazard, careless, slapdash; *informal* sloppy, hit-or-miss.
– OPPOSITES orderly.

disorientated, disoriented ▶ adjective CONFUSED, bewildered, (all) at sea; lost, adrift, off-course, having lost one's bearings; *informal* not knowing whether one is coming or going; *archaic* mazed.

disown ▶ verb REJECT, cast off/aside, abandon, renounce, deny; turn one's back on, wash one's hands of, have nothing more to do with; *poetic/literary* forsake.

disparage ▶ verb BELITTLE, denigrate, deprecate, play down, trivialize, make light of, undervalue, underrate; ridicule, deride, mock, scorn, scoff at, sneer at; run down, defame, discredit, speak badly of, cast aspersions on, impugn, vilify, traduce, criticize; *N. Amer.* slur; *informal* do down, pick holes in, knock, slam, pan, bad-mouth, pooh-pooh; *Brit. informal* rubbish, slate; *formal* calumniate, derogate.
– OPPOSITES praise, overrate.

disparaging ▶ adjective DEROGATORY, deprecatory, denigratory, belittling; critical, scathing, negative, unfavourable, uncomplimentary, uncharitable; contemptuous, scornful, snide, disdainful; *informal* bitchy, catty; *archaic* contumelious.
– OPPOSITES complimentary.

disparate ▶ adjective CONTRASTING, different, differing, dissimilar, unalike, poles apart; varying, various, diverse, diversified, heterogeneous, distinct, separate, divergent; *poetic/literary* divers.
– OPPOSITES homogen(e)ous.

disparity ▶ noun DISCREPANCY, inconsistency,

imbalance; variance, variation, divergence, gap, gulf; difference, dissimilarity, contrast; *formal* dissimilitude.
– OPPOSITES similarity.

dispassionate ▶ adjective ❶ *a calm, dispassionate manner* UNEMOTIONAL, emotionless, impassive, cool, calm, {cool, calm, and collected}, unruffled, unperturbed, composed, self-possessed, self-controlled, unexcitable; *informal* laid-back. ❷ *a dispassionate analysis* OBJECTIVE, detached, neutral, disinterested, impartial, non-partisan, unbiased, unprejudiced; scientific, analytical.
– OPPOSITES emotional, biased.

dispatch ▶ verb ❶ *all the messages were dispatched* SEND (OFF), post, mail, forward, transmit. ❷ *the business was dispatched in the morning* DEAL WITH, finish, conclude, settle, discharge, perform; expedite, push through; *informal* make short work of. ❸ *the good guy dispatched a host of villains* KILL, put to death, take/end the life of; slaughter, butcher, massacre, wipe out, exterminate, eliminate; murder, assassinate, execute; *informal* bump off, do in, do away with, top, take out, blow away; *N. Amer. informal* ice, rub out, waste; *poetic/literary* slay.
▶ noun ❶ *goods ready for dispatch* SENDING, posting, mailing. ❷ *efficiency and dispatch* PROMPTNESS, speed, speediness, swiftness, rapidity, briskness, haste, hastiness; *poetic/literary* fleetness, celerity; *formal* expedition. ❸ *the latest dispatch from the front* COMMUNICATION, communiqué, bulletin, report, statement, letter, message; news, intelligence; *informal* memo, info, low-down; *poetic/literary* tidings. ❹ *the capture and dispatch of the wolf* KILLING, slaughter, massacre, extermination, elimination; murder, assassination, execution; *poetic/literary* slaying.

dispel ▶ verb BANISH, eliminate, drive away/off, get rid of; relieve, allay, ease, quell.

dispensable ▶ adjective EXPENDABLE, disposable, replaceable, inessential, non-essential; unnecessary, redundant, superfluous, surplus to requirements.

dispensation ▶ noun ❶ *the dispensation of supplies* DISTRIBUTION, supply, supplying, issue, issuing, handing out, doling out, dishing out, sharing out, dividing out; division, allocation, allotment, apportionment. ❷ *the dispensation of justice* ADMINISTRATION, administering, delivery, discharge, dealing out, meting out. ❸ *dispensation from National Insurance contributions* EXEMPTION, immunity, exception, exoneration, reprieve, remission; *informal* a let-off. ❹ *the new constitutional dispensation* SYSTEM, order, arrangement, organization.

dispense ▶ verb ❶ *servants dispensed the drinks* DISTRIBUTE, pass round, hand out, dole out, dish out, share out; allocate, supply, allot, apportion. ❷ *the soldiers dispensed summary justice* ADMINISTER, deliver, issue, discharge, deal out, mete out. ❸ *dispensing medicines* PREPARE, make up; supply, provide, sell. ❹ *the pope dispensed him from his impediment* EXEMPT, excuse, except, release, let off, reprieve, absolve.
■ **dispense with** ❶ *let's dispense with the formalities* WAIVE, omit, drop, leave out, forgo; do away with; *informal* give something a miss. ❷ *he dispensed with his crutches* GET RID OF, throw away/out, dispose of, discard; manage without, cope without; *informal* ditch, scrap, dump, chuck out/away, get shut of; *Brit. informal* get shot of.

disperse ▶ verb ❶ *the crowd began to disperse | police dispersed the demonstrators* BREAK UP, split up, disband, scatter, leave, go their separate ways; drive away/off, chase away. ❷ *the fog finally dispersed* DISSIPATE, dissolve, melt away, fade away, clear, lift. ❸ *seeds dispersed by birds* SCATTER, disseminate, distribute, spread, broadcast.
– OPPOSITES assemble, gather.

dispirited ▶ adjective DISHEARTENED, discouraged, demoralized, downcast, low, low-spirited, dejected, downhearted, depressed, disconsolate; *informal* fed up; *Brit. informal* cheesed off.
– OPPOSITES heartened.

dispiriting ▶ adjective DISHEARTENING, depressing, discouraging, daunting, demoralizing.

displace ▶ verb ❶ *roof tiles displaced by gales* DISLODGE, dislocate, move, shift, reposition; move out of place, knock out of place/position. ❷ *the minister was displaced* DEPOSE, dislodge, unseat, remove (from office), dismiss, eject, oust, expel, force out, drive out; overthrow, topple, bring down; *informal* boot out, give someone the boot, show someone the door; *Brit. informal* turf out; *dated* out. ❸ *English displaced the local language* REPLACE, take the place of, supplant, supersede.
– OPPOSITES replace, reinstate.

display ▶ noun ❶ *a display of dolls and puppets | a motorcycle display* EXHIBITION, exposition, array, arrangement, presentation, demonstration; spectacle, show, parade, pageant. ❷ *they vied to outdo each other in display* OSTENTATION, ostentatiousness, showiness, extravagance, flamboyance, lavishness, splendour; *informal* swank, flashiness, glitziness. ❸ *his display of concern* MANIFESTATION, expression, show.
▶ verb ❶ *the Crown Jewels are displayed in London* EXHIBIT, show, put on show/view; arrange, array, present, lay out, set out. ❷ *the play displays his many theatrical talents* SHOW OFF, parade, flaunt, reveal; publicize, make known, call/draw attention to; *informal* hype. ❸ *she displayed a vein of sharp humour* MANIFEST, show evidence of, reveal; demonstrate, show; *formal* evince.
– OPPOSITES conceal.

displease ▶ verb ANNOY, irritate, anger, irk, vex, pique, gall, nettle; put out, upset; *informal* aggravate, peeve, needle, bug, rile, miff, hack off; *N. Amer. informal* tee off, tick off.

displeasure ▶ noun ANNOYANCE, irritation, crossness, anger, vexation, pique, rancour; dissatisfaction, discontent, discontentedness, disgruntlement, disapproval; *informal* aggravation.
– OPPOSITES satisfaction.

disposable ▶ adjective ❶ *disposable plates* THROWAWAY, expendable, one-use. ❷ *disposable income* AVAILABLE, usable, spendable.

disposal ▶ noun ❶ *rubbish ready for disposal* THROWING AWAY, discarding, jettisoning, scrapping; *informal* dumping, ditching, chucking (out/away). ❷ *we have twenty copies for disposal* DISTRIBUTION, handing out, giving out/away, allotment, allocation. ❸ *the disposal of the troops in two lines* ARRANGEMENT, arranging, positioning, placement, lining up, disposition, grouping; *Military* dressing.
■ **at someone's disposal** FOR USE BY, in reserve for, in the hands of, in the possession of.

dispose ▶ verb ❶ *he disposed his attendants in a circle* ARRANGE, place, put, position, array, set up, form; marshal, gather, group; *Military* dress. ❷ *the experience disposed him to be kind* INCLINE, encourage, persuade, predispose, make willing, prompt, lead, motivate; sway, influence.
■ **dispose of** ❶ *the waste was disposed of* THROW AWAY/OUT, get rid of, discard, jettison, scrap; *informal* dump, ditch, chuck (out/away), get shut of; *Brit. informal* get shot of; *N. Amer. informal* trash. ❷ *he had disposed of all his assets* PART WITH, give away, hand over, deliver up, transfer; sell, auction; *informal* get shut of; *Brit. informal* get shot of. ❸ (*informal*) *she disposed of a fourth cake. See* CONSUME sense 1. ❹ (*informal*) *he robbed her and then disposed of her. See* KILL verb sense 1.

disposed ▶ adjective ❶ *they are philanthropically disposed* INCLINED, predisposed, minded. ❷ *we are not disposed to argue* WILLING, inclined, prepared, ready, minded, in the mood. ❸ *he was disposed to be cruel* LIABLE, apt, inclined, likely, predisposed, prone, tending; capable of.

disposition ▶ noun ❶ *a nervous disposition* TEMPERAMENT, nature, character, constitution, make-up, mentality. ❷ *his disposition to clemency* INCLINATION, tendency, proneness, propensity, proclivity. ❸ *the disposition of the armed forces* ARRANGEMENT, positioning, placement, configuration; set-up, line-up, layout, array; marshalling, mustering, grouping; *Military* dressing. ❹ (*Law*) *the disposition of the company's property* DISTRIBUTION, disposal, allocation, transfer; sale, auction.
■ **at someone's disposition** AT THE DISPOSAL OF, for use by, in reserve for, in the hands of, in the possession of.

dispossess ▶ verb DIVEST, strip, rob, cheat out of, deprive; *informal* do out of; *archaic* reave.

disproportionate ▶ adjective OUT OF PROPORTION TO, not appropriate to, not commensurate with, relatively too large/small for; inordinate, unreasonable, excessive, undue.

disprove ▶ verb REFUTE, prove false, rebut, falsify, debunk, negate, invalidate, contradict, confound, controvert, negative, discredit; *informal* shoot full of holes, blow out of the water; *formal* confute, gainsay.

disputable ▶ adjective DEBATABLE, open to debate/question, arguable, contestable, moot, questionable, doubtful, controvertible; *informal* iffy.

disputation ▶ noun DEBATE, discussion, dispute, argument, arguing, altercation, dissension, disagreement, controversy; polemics.

dispute ▶ noun ❶ *a subject of dispute* DEBATE, discussion, disputation, argument, controversy, disagreement, quarrelling, dissension, conflict, friction, strife, discord. ❷ *they have settled their dispute* QUARREL, argument, altercation, squabble, falling-out, disagreement, difference of opinion, clash, wrangle; *informal* tiff, spat, scrap; *Brit. informal* row, barney, ding-dong; *N. Amer. informal* rhubarb; *archaic* broil.
– OPPOSITES agreement.
▶ verb ❶ *George disputed with him* DEBATE, discuss, exchange views; quarrel, argue, disagree, clash, fall out, wrangle, bicker, squabble; *informal* have words, have a tiff/spat; *archaic* altercate. ❷ *they disputed his proposals* CHALLENGE, contest, question, call into question, impugn, quibble over, contradict, controvert, argue about, disagree with, take issue with; *formal* gainsay.
– OPPOSITES accept.

disqualified ▶ adjective BANNED, barred, debarred; ineligible.
– OPPOSITES allowed.

disquiet ▶ noun *grave public disquiet* UNEASE, uneasiness, worry, anxiety, anxiousness, concern, disquietude; perturbation, consternation, upset, malaise, angst; agitation, restlessness, fretfulness; *informal* jitteriness.
– OPPOSITES calm.
▶ verb *I was disquieted by the news* PERTURB, agitate, upset, disturb, unnerve, unsettle, discompose, disconcert; make uneasy, worry, make anxious; trouble, concern, make fretful, make restless.

disquisition ▶ noun ESSAY, dissertation, treatise, paper, tract, article; discussion, lecture, address, presentation, speech, talk.

disregard ▶ verb *Annie disregarded the remark* IGNORE, take no notice of, pay no attention/heed to; overlook, turn a blind eye to, turn a deaf ear to, shut one's eyes to, gloss over, brush off/aside, shrug off.
– OPPOSITES heed.
▶ noun *blithe disregard for the rules* INDIFFERENCE, non-observance, inattention, heedlessness, neglect.
– OPPOSITES attention.

disrepair ▶ **noun** DILAPIDATION, decrepitude, shabbiness, ricketiness, collapse, ruin; abandonment, neglect, disuse.

disreputable ▶ **adjective** ❶ *he fell into disreputable company* OF BAD REPUTATION, infamous, notorious, louche; dishonourable, dishonest, untrustworthy, unwholesome, villainous, corrupt, immoral; unsavoury, slippery, seedy, sleazy; *informal* crooked, shady, shifty; *Brit. informal* dodgy. ❷ *filthy and disreputable* SCRUFFY, shabby, down at heel, seedy, untidy, unkempt, dishevelled.
– OPPOSITES respectable, smart.

disrepute ▶ **noun** DISGRACE, shame, dishonour, infamy, notoriety, ignominy, bad reputation; humiliation, discredit, ill repute, low esteem, opprobrium, obloquy.
– OPPOSITES honour.

disrespect ▶ **noun** ❶ *disrespect for authority* CONTEMPT, lack of respect, scorn, disregard, disdain. ❷ *he meant no disrespect to anybody* DISCOURTESY, rudeness, impoliteness, incivility, ill/bad manners; insolence, impudence, impertinence.
– OPPOSITES esteem.

disrespectful ▶ **adjective** DISCOURTEOUS, rude, impolite, uncivil, ill-mannered, bad-mannered; insolent, impudent, impertinent, cheeky, flippant, insubordinate.
– OPPOSITES polite.

disrobe ▶ **verb** UNDRESS, strip, take off one's clothes, remove one's clothes; *Brit. informal* peel off.

disrupt ▶ **verb** ❶ *the strike disrupted public transport* THROW INTO CONFUSION/DISORDER/DISARRAY, cause confusion/turmoil in, play havoc with; disturb, interfere with, upset, unsettle; obstruct, impede, hold up, delay, interrupt, suspend; *Brit. informal* throw a spanner in the works of; *N. Amer. informal* throw a monkey wrench in the works of. ❷ *the explosion disrupted the walls of the crater* DISTORT, damage, buckle, warp; shatter; *poetic/literary* sunder.

disruptive ▶ **adjective** TROUBLESOME, unruly, badly behaved, rowdy, disorderly, undisciplined, wild; unmanageable, uncontrollable, uncooperative, out of control/hand, obstreperous, truculent; *formal* refractory.
– OPPOSITES well behaved.

dissatisfaction ▶ **noun** DISCONTENT, discontentment, disaffection, disquiet, unhappiness, malaise, disgruntlement, vexation, annoyance, irritation, anger; disapproval, disapprobation, disfavour, displeasure.

dissatisfied ▶ **adjective** DISCONTENTED, malcontent, unsatisfied, disappointed, disaffected, unhappy, displeased; disgruntled, aggrieved, vexed, annoyed, irritated, angry, exasperated, fed up; *informal* cheesed off; *Brit. informal* brassed off.
– OPPOSITES contented.

dissect ▶ **verb** ❶ *the body was dissected* ANATOMIZE, cut up/open, dismember; vivisect. ❷ *the text of the gospels was dissected* ANALYSE, examine, study, scrutinize, pore over, investigate, go over with a fine-tooth comb.

dissection ▶ **noun** ❶ *the dissection of corpses* CUTTING UP/OPEN, dismemberment; autopsy, post-mortem, necropsy, anatomy, vivisection. ❷ *a thorough dissection of their policies* ANALYSIS, examination, study, scrutiny, scrutinization, investigation; evaluation, assessment.

dissemble ▶ **verb** DISSIMULATE, pretend, feign, act, masquerade, sham, fake, bluff, posture, hide one's feelings, put on a false front.

dissembler ▶ **noun** LIAR, dissimulator; humbug, bluffer, fraud, impostor, actor, hoaxer, charlatan.

disseminate ▶ **verb** SPREAD, circulate, distribute, disperse, promulgate, propagate, publicize, communicate, pass on, put about, make known.

dissension ▶ **noun** DISAGREEMENT, difference of opinion, dispute, dissent, conflict, friction, strife, discord, antagonism; argument, debate, controversy, disputation, contention.

dissent ▶ **verb** *two members dissented* DIFFER, disagree, demur, fail to agree, be at variance/odds, take issue; decline/refuse to support, protest, object, dispute, challenge, quibble.
– OPPOSITES agree, accept.
▶ **noun** *murmurs of dissent* DISAGREEMENT, difference of opinion, argument, dispute; disapproval, objection, protest, opposition, defiance; conflict, friction, strife.
– OPPOSITES agreement.

dissenter ▶ **noun** DISSIDENT, dissentient, objector, protester, disputant; rebel, renegade, maverick, independent; apostate, heretic.

dissentient ▶ **adjective** *dissentient voices* DISSENTING, dissident, disagreeing, differing, discordant, contradicting, contrary, anti-; opposing, objecting, protesting, complaining, rebellious, revolutionary; nonconformist, recusant, unorthodox, heterodox, heretical.
▶ **noun** *a dissentient spoke up. See* DISSENTER.

dissertation ▶ **noun** ESSAY, thesis, treatise, paper, study, discourse, disquisition, tract, monograph.

disservice ▶ **noun** UNKINDNESS, bad/ill turn, disfavour; injury, harm, hurt, damage, wrong, injustice.
– OPPOSITES favour.

dissidence ▶ **noun** DISAGREEMENT, dissent, discord, discontent; opposition, resistance, protest, sedition.

dissident ▶ **noun** *a jailed dissident* DISSENTER, objector, protester; rebel, revolutionary, recusant, subversive, agitator, insurgent, insurrectionist, refusenik.
– OPPOSITES conformist.

▶ adjective *dissident intellectuals* DISSENTIENT, dissenting, disagreeing; opposing, objecting, protesting, rebellious, rebelling, revolutionary, recusant, nonconformist.
– OPPOSITES conforming.

dissimilar ▶ adjective DIFFERENT, differing, unalike, variant, diverse, divergent, heterogeneous, disparate, unrelated, distinct, contrasting; *poetic/literary* divers.

dissimilarity ▶ noun DIFFERENCE(S), variance, diversity, heterogeneity, disparateness, disparity, distinctness, contrast, non-uniformity, divergence; *formal* dissimilitude.

dissimilitude ▶ noun (*formal*). *See* DISSIMILARITY.

dissimulate ▶ verb PRETEND, deceive, feign, act, dissemble, masquerade, pose, posture, sham, fake, bluff, hide one's feelings, be dishonest, put on a false front, lie.

dissimulation ▶ noun PRETENCE, dissembling, deceit, dishonesty, duplicity, lying, guile, subterfuge, feigning, shamming, faking, bluff, bluffing, posturing, hypocrisy.

dissipate ▶ verb ❶ *his anger dissipated* DISAPPEAR, vanish, evaporate, dissolve, melt away, melt into thin air, be dispelled; disperse, scatter; *poetic/literary* evanesce. ❷ *he dissipated his fortune* SQUANDER, fritter (away), misspend, waste, be prodigal with, spend recklessly/freely, spend like water; expend, use up, consume, run through, go through; *informal* blow, splurge.

dissipated ▶ adjective DISSOLUTE, debauched, decadent, intemperate, profligate, self-indulgent, wild, depraved; licentious, promiscuous; drunken.
– OPPOSITES ascetic.

dissipation ▶ noun ❶ *drunken dissipation* DEBAUCHERY, decadence, dissoluteness, dissolution, intemperance, excess, profligacy, self-indulgence, wildness; depravity, degeneracy; licentiousness, promiscuity; drunkenness. ❷ *the dissipation of our mineral wealth* SQUANDERING, frittering (away), waste, misspending; expenditure, draining, depletion.
– OPPOSITES asceticism.

dissociate ▶ verb *the word 'spiritual' has become dissociated from religion* SEPARATE, detach, disconnect, sever, cut off, divorce; isolate, alienate.
– OPPOSITES relate.
■ **dissociate oneself from** ❶ *he dissociated himself from the Church of England* BREAK AWAY FROM, end relations with, sever connections with; withdraw from, quit, leave, disaffiliate from, resign from, pull out of, drop out of, defect from. ❷ *he dissociated himself from the statement* DISOWN, reject, disagree with, distance oneself from.

dissociation ▶ noun SEPARATION, disconnection, detachment, severance, divorce, split; segregation, division; *poetic/literary* sundering.
– OPPOSITES union.

dissolute ▶ adjective DISSIPATED, debauched, decadent, intemperate, profligate, self-indulgent, wild, depraved; licentious, promiscuous; drunken.
– OPPOSITES ascetic.

dissolution ▶ noun ❶ *the dissolution of parliament* CESSATION, conclusion, end, ending, termination, winding up/down, discontinuation, suspension, disbanding; prorogation, recess. ❷ (*technical*) *the dissolution of a polymer in a solvent* DISSOLVING, liquefaction, melting, deliquescence; breaking up, decomposition, disintegration. ❸ *the dissolution of the empire* DISINTEGRATION, breaking up; decay, collapse, demise, extinction. ❹ *a life of dissolution. See* DISSIPATION sense 1.

dissolve ▶ verb ❶ *sugar dissolves in water* GO INTO SOLUTION, break down; liquefy, deliquesce, disintegrate. ❷ *his hopes dissolved* DISAPPEAR, vanish, melt away, evaporate, disperse, dissipate, disintegrate; dwindle, fade (away), wither; *poetic/literary* evanesce. ❸ *the crowd dissolved* DISPERSE, disband, break up, scatter, go in different directions. ❹ *the assembly was dissolved* DISBAND, disestablish, bring to an end, end, terminate, discontinue, close down, wind up/down, suspend; prorogue, adjourn. ❺ *their marriage was dissolved* ANNUL, nullify, void, invalidate, overturn, revoke.
■ **dissolve into/in** BURST INTO, break (down) into, be overcome with.

dissonant ▶ adjective ❶ *dissonant sounds* INHARMONIOUS, discordant, unmelodious, atonal, off-key, cacophonous. ❷ *harmonious and dissonant colours* INCONGRUOUS, anomalous, clashing; disparate, different, dissimilar.
– OPPOSITES harmonious.

dissuade ▶ verb DISCOURAGE, deter, prevent, divert, stop; talk out of, persuade against, advise against, argue out of.
– OPPOSITES encourage.

distance ▶ noun ❶ *they measured the distance* INTERVAL, space, span, gap, extent; length, width, breadth, depth; range, reach. ❷ *our perception of distance* REMOTENESS; closeness. ❸ *a mix of warmth and distance* ALOOFNESS, remoteness, detachment, unfriendliness; reserve, reticence, restraint, formality; *informal* stand-offishness.
▶ verb *he distanced himself from her* WITHDRAW, detach, separate, dissociate, isolate, put at a distance.
■ **in the distance** FAR AWAY/OFF, afar, just in view; on the horizon; *archaic* yonder.

distant ▶ adjective ❶ *distant parts of the world* FARAWAY, far-off, far-flung, remote, out of the way, outlying. ❷ *the distant past* LONG AGO, bygone, olden; ancient, prehistoric; *poetic/literary* of yore. ❸ *half a mile distant* AWAY, off, apart.

❹ *a distant memory* VAGUE, faint, dim, indistinct, unclear, indefinite, sketchy, hazy. ❺ *a distant family connection* REMOTE, indirect, slight. ❻ *father was always distant* ALOOF, reserved, remote, detached, unapproachable; withdrawn, reticent, taciturn, uncommunicative, undemonstrative, unforthcoming, unresponsive, unfriendly; *informal* stand-offish. ❼ *a distant look in his eyes* DISTRACTED, absent-minded, faraway, detached, distrait, vague.
– OPPOSITES near, close, recent.

distaste ▶ noun DISLIKE, aversion, disinclination, disapproval, disapprobation, disdain, repugnance, hatred, loathing; *archaic* disrelish.
– OPPOSITES liking.

distasteful ▶ adjective ❶ *distasteful behaviour* UNPLEASANT, disagreeable, displeasing, undesirable; objectionable, offensive, unsavoury, unpalatable, obnoxious; disgusting, repellent, repulsive, revolting, repugnant, abhorrent, loathsome, vile. ❷ *their eggs are distasteful to predators* UNPALATABLE, unsavoury, unappetizing, inedible, disgusting.
– OPPOSITES agreeable, tasty.

distended ▶ adjective SWOLLEN, bloated, dilated, engorged, enlarged, inflated, expanded, extended, bulging, protuberant.

distil ▶ verb ❶ *the water was distilled* PURIFY, refine, filter, treat, process; evaporate and condense. ❷ *oil distilled from marjoram* EXTRACT, press out, squeeze out, express. ❸ *whisky is distilled from barley* BREW, ferment. ❹ *the solvent is distilled to leave the oil* BOIL DOWN, reduce, concentrate, condense; purify, refine.

distinct ▶ adjective ❶ *two distinct categories* DISCRETE, separate, different, unconnected; precise, specific, distinctive, contrasting. ❷ *the tail has distinct black tips* CLEAR, well defined, unmistakable, easily distinguishable; recognizable, visible, obvious, pronounced, prominent, striking.
– OPPOSITES overlapping, indefinite.

distinction ▶ noun ❶ *class distinctions* DIFFERENCE, contrast, dissimilarity, variance, variation; division, differentiation, dividing line, gulf, gap; *formal* dissimilitude. ❷ *a painter of distinction* IMPORTANCE, significance, note, consequence; renown, fame, celebrity, prominence, eminence, pre-eminence, repute, reputation; merit, worth, greatness, excellence, quality. ❸ *he had served with distinction* HONOUR, credit, excellence, merit.
– OPPOSITES similarity, mediocrity.

distinctive ▶ adjective DISTINGUISHING, characteristic, typical, individual, particular, peculiar, unique, exclusive, special.
– OPPOSITES common.

distinctly ▶ adverb ❶ *there's something distinctly odd about him* DECIDEDLY, markedly, definitely; clearly, noticeably, obviously, plainly, evidently, unmistakably, manifestly, patently; *Brit. informal* dead. ❷ *Laura spoke quite distinctly* CLEARLY, plainly, intelligibly, audibly, unambiguously.

distinguish ▶ verb ❶ *distinguishing reality from fantasy* DIFFERENTIATE, tell apart, discriminate between, tell the difference between. ❷ *he could distinguish shapes in the dark* DISCERN, see, perceive, make out; detect, recognize, identify; *poetic/literary* descry, espy. ❸ *this is what distinguishes history from other disciplines* SEPARATE, set apart, make distinctive, make different; single out, mark off, characterize.
■ **distinguish oneself** ATTAIN DISTINCTION, be successful, bring fame/honour to oneself, become famous.

distinguishable ▶ adjective DISCERNIBLE, recognizable, identifiable, detectable.

distinguished ▶ adjective EMINENT, famous, renowned, prominent, well known; esteemed, respected, illustrious, acclaimed, celebrated, great; notable, important, influential.
– OPPOSITES unknown, obscure.

distinguishing ▶ adjective DISTINCTIVE, differentiating, characteristic, typical, peculiar, singular, unique.

distorted ▶ adjective ❶ *a distorted face* TWISTED, warped, contorted, buckled, deformed, malformed, misshapen, disfigured, crooked, awry, out of shape. ❷ *a distorted version* MISREPRESENTED, perverted, twisted, falsified, misreported, misstated, garbled, inaccurate; biased, prejudiced, slanted, coloured, loaded, weighted, altered, changed.

distract ▶ verb DIVERT, sidetrack, draw away, disturb, put off.

distracted ▶ adjective PREOCCUPIED, inattentive, vague, abstracted, distrait, absent-minded, faraway, in a world of one's own; bemused, confused, bewildered; troubled, harassed, worried; *informal* miles away, not with it.
– OPPOSITES attentive.

distracting ▶ adjective DISTURBING, unsettling, intrusive, disconcerting, bothersome, off-putting.

distraction ▶ noun ❶ *a distraction from the real issues* DIVERSION, interruption, disturbance, interference, hindrance. ❷ *frivolous distractions* AMUSEMENT, entertainment, diversion, recreation, leisure pursuit, divertissement. ❸ *he was driven to distraction* FRENZY, hysteria, mental distress, madness, insanity, mania; agitation, perturbation.

distrait, fem. **distraite** ▶ adjective DISTRACTED, preoccupied, absorbed, abstracted, distant, faraway; absent-minded, vague, inattentive, in a brown study, wool-gathering, with one's head in the clouds, in a world of one's own; *informal* miles away, not with it.
– OPPOSITES alert.

distraught ▶ adjective WORRIED, upset, distressed, fraught; overcome, overwrought, beside oneself, out of one's mind, desperate, hysterical, worked up, at one's wits' end; *informal* in a state.

distress ▶ **noun** ❶ *she concealed her distress* ANGUISH, suffering, pain, agony, torment, heartache, heartbreak; misery, wretchedness, sorrow, grief, woe, sadness, unhappiness, desolation, despair. ❷ *a ship in distress* DANGER, peril, difficulty, trouble, jeopardy, risk. ❸ *the poor in distress* HARDSHIP, adversity, poverty, deprivation, privation, destitution, indigence, impoverishment, penury, need, dire straits.
– OPPOSITES happiness, safety, prosperity.
▶ **verb** *he was distressed by the trial* CAUSE ANGUISH/SUFFERING TO, pain, upset, make miserable; trouble, worry, bother, perturb, disturb, disquiet, agitate, harrow, torment; *informal* cut up.
– OPPOSITES calm, please.

distressing ▶ **adjective** UPSETTING, worrying, disturbing, disquieting, painful, traumatic, agonizing, harrowing; sad, saddening, heartbreaking, heart-rending.
– OPPOSITES comforting.

distribute ▶ **verb** ❶ *the were proceeds distributed among his creditors* GIVE OUT, deal out, dole out, dish out, hand out/round; allocate, allot, apportion, share out, divide out/up, parcel out. ❷ *the newsletter is distributed free* CIRCULATE, issue, hand out, deliver. ❸ *a hundred and thirty different species are distributed worldwide* DISPERSE, scatter, spread.
– OPPOSITES collect.

distribution ▶ **noun** ❶ *the distribution of charity* GIVING OUT, dealing out, doling out, handing out/round, issue, issuing, dispensation; allocation, allotment, apportioning, sharing out, dividing up/out, parcelling out. ❷ *the geographical distribution of plants* DISPERSAL, dissemination, spread; placement, position, location, disposition. ❸ *centres of food distribution* SUPPLY, supplying, delivery, transport, transportation. ❹ *the statistical distribution of the problem* FREQUENCY, prevalence, incidence, commonness.

district ▶ **noun** NEIGHBOURHOOD, area, region, locality, locale, community, quarter, sector, zone, territory; administrative division, ward, parish; *informal* neck of the woods.

distrust ▶ **noun** *the general distrust of authority* MISTRUST, suspicion, wariness, chariness, leeriness, lack of trust, lack of confidence; scepticism, doubt, doubtfulness, cynicism; misgivings, qualms, disbelief; *formal* dubiety.
▶ **verb** *Louise distrusted him* MISTRUST, be suspicious of, be wary/chary of, be leery of, regard with suspicion, suspect; be sceptical of, have doubts about, doubt, be unsure of/about, have misgivings about, wonder about, disbelieve (in).

disturb ▶ **verb** ❶ *somewhere where we won't be disturbed* INTERRUPT, intrude on, butt in on, barge in on; distract, disrupt, bother, trouble, pester, harass; *informal* hassle. ❷ *don't disturb his papers* DISARRANGE, muddle, rearrange, disorganize, disorder, mix up, interfere with, throw into disorder/confusion, turn upside down. ❸ *waters disturbed by winds* AGITATE, churn up, stir up; *poetic/literary* roil. ❹ *he wasn't disturbed by the allegations* PERTURB, trouble, concern, worry, upset; agitate, fluster, discomfit, disconcert, dismay, distress, discompose, unsettle, ruffle.

disturbance ▶ **noun** ❶ *a disturbance to local residents* DISRUPTION, distraction, interference; bother, trouble, inconvenience, upset, annoyance, irritation, intrusion, harassment; *informal* hassle. ❷ *disturbances among the peasantry* RIOT, fracas, upheaval, brawl, street fight, melee, free-for-all, ruckus, rumpus; *Law, dated* affray; *informal* ruction. ❸ *emotional disturbance* TROUBLE, perturbation, distress, worry, upset, agitation, discomposure, discomfiture; neurosis, illness, sickness, disorder, complaint.

disturbed ▶ **adjective** ❶ *disturbed sleep* DISRUPTED, interrupted, fitful, intermittent, broken. ❷ *disturbed children* TROUBLED, distressed, upset, distraught; unbalanced, unstable, disordered, dysfunctional, maladjusted, neurotic, unhinged; *informal* screwed up, mixed up.

disturbing ▶ **adjective** WORRYING, perturbing, troubling, upsetting; distressing, discomfiting, disconcerting, disquieting, unsettling, dismaying, alarming, frightening.

disunion ▶ **noun** BREAKING UP, separation, dissolution, partition.
– OPPOSITES federation.

disunite ▶ **verb** BREAK UP, separate, divide, split up, partition, dismantle; *poetic/literary* sunder.
– OPPOSITES unify.

disunity ▶ **noun** DISAGREEMENT, dissent, dissension, argument, arguing, quarrelling, feuding; conflict, strife, friction, discord.

disuse ▶ **noun** NON-USE, non-employment, lack of use; neglect, abandonment, desertion, obsolescence; *formal* desuetude.

disused ▶ **adjective** UNUSED, no longer in use, unemployed, idle; abandoned, deserted, vacated, unoccupied, uninhabited.

ditch ▶ **noun** *she rescued an animal from a ditch* TRENCH, trough, channel, dyke, drain, gutter, gully, watercourse, conduit; *Archaeology* fosse.
▶ **verb** ❶ *they started ditching the coastal areas* DIG A DITCH IN, trench, excavate, drain. ❷ (*informal*) *she ditched her old curtains. See* THROW SOMETHING AWAY sense 1 at THROW. ❸ (*informal*) *she ditched her husband. See* THROW SOMEONE OVER at THROW.

dither ▶ **verb** HESITATE, falter, waver, vacillate, change one's mind, be in two minds, be indecisive, be undecided; *Brit.* haver; *informal* shilly-shally, dilly-dally.

diurnal ▶ **adjective** DAILY, everyday, quotidian, occurring every/each day.

divan ▶ noun SETTEE, sofa, couch; sofa bed; *Brit.* put-you-up; *N. Amer.* studio couch.

dive ▶ verb ❶ *they dived into the clear water | the plane was diving towards the ground* PLUNGE, nosedive, jump head first, bellyflop; plummet, fall, drop, pitch. ❷ *the islanders dive for oysters* SWIM UNDER WATER; snorkel, scuba dive. ❸ *they dived for cover* LEAP, jump, lunge, launch oneself, throw oneself, go headlong, duck.

▶ noun ❶ *a dive into the pool* PLUNGE, nosedive, jump, bellyflop; plummet, fall, drop, swoop, pitch. ❷ *a sideways dive* LUNGE, spring, jump, leap. ❸ (*informal*) *John got into a fight in some dive* SLEAZY BAR/NIGHTCLUB, seedy bar/nightclub, drinking den; *informal* drinking joint.

diverge ▶ verb ❶ *the two roads diverged* SEPARATE, part, fork, divide, split, bifurcate, go in different directions. ❷ *areas where our views diverge* DIFFER, be different, be dissimilar; disagree, be at variance/odds, conflict, clash. ❸ *he diverged from his text* DEVIATE, digress, depart, veer, stray; stray from the point, get off the subject.
– OPPOSITES converge, agree.

divergence ▶ noun ❶ *the divergence of the human and ape lineages* SEPARATION, dividing, parting, forking, bifurcation. ❷ *a marked political divergence* DIFFERENCE, dissimilarity, variance, disparity; disagreement, incompatibility, mismatch; *formal* dissimilitude. ❸ *divergence from standard behaviour* DEVIATION, digression, departure, shift, straying; variation, change, alteration.

divergent ▶ adjective DIFFERING, varying, different, dissimilar, unalike, disparate, contrasting, contrastive; conflicting, incompatible, contradictory, at odds, at variance.
– OPPOSITES similar.

divers ▶ adjective (*poetic/literary*) SEVERAL, many, numerous, multiple, manifold, multifarious, multitudinous; sundry, miscellaneous, assorted, various; *poetic/literary* myriad.

diverse ▶ adjective VARIOUS, sundry, manifold, multiple; varied, varying, miscellaneous, assorted, mixed, diversified, divergent, heterogeneous, a mixed bag of; different, differing, distinct, unlike, dissimilar; *poetic/literary* divers, myriad.

diversify ▶ verb ❶ *farmers looking for ways to diversify* BRANCH OUT, expand, extend operations. ❷ *a plan aimed at diversifying the economy* VARY, bring variety to; modify, alter, change, transform; expand, enlarge.

diversion ▶ noun ❶ *the diversion of 19 rivers* REROUTING, redirection, deflection, deviation, divergence. ❷ *traffic diversions* DETOUR, deviation, alternative route. ❸ *the noise created a diversion* DISTRACTION, disturbance, smokescreen. ❹ *a city full of diversions* ENTERTAINMENT, amusement, pastime, delight, divertissement; fun, recreation, rest and relaxation, pleasure; *informal* R and R; *dated* sport.

diversity ▶ noun VARIETY, miscellany, assortment, mixture, mix, melange, range, array, multiplicity; variation, variance, diverseness, diversification, heterogeneity, difference, contrast; *formal* dissimilitude.
– OPPOSITES uniformity.

divert ▶ verb ❶ *a plan to divert Siberia's rivers* REROUTE, redirect, change the course of, deflect, channel. ❷ *he diverted her from her studies* DISTRACT, sidetrack, disturb, draw away, be a distraction, put off. ❸ *the story diverted them* AMUSE, entertain, distract, delight, enchant, interest, fascinate, absorb, engross, rivet, grip, hold the attention of.

diverting ▶ adjective ENTERTAINING, amusing, enjoyable, pleasing, agreeable, delightful, appealing; interesting, fascinating, intriguing, absorbing, riveting, compelling; humorous, funny, witty, comical.
– OPPOSITES boring.

divest ▶ verb DEPRIVE, strip, dispossess, rob, cheat/trick out of; *archaic* reave.

divide ▶ verb ❶ *he divided his kingdom into four* SPLIT (UP), cut up, carve up; dissect, bisect, halve, quarter; *poetic/literary* sunder. ❷ *a curtain divided her cabin from the galley* SEPARATE, segregate, partition, screen off, section off, split off. ❸ *the stairs divide at the mezzanine* DIVERGE, separate, part, branch (off), fork, split (in two), bifurcate. ❹ *Jack divided up the cash* SHARE OUT, allocate, allot, apportion, portion out, ration out, parcel out, deal out, dole out, dish out, distribute, dispense; *informal* divvy up. ❺ *he aimed to divide his opponents* DISUNITE, drive apart, break up, split up, set at variance/odds; separate, isolate, estrange, alienate; *poetic/literary* tear asunder. ❻ *living things are divided into three categories* CLASSIFY, sort (out), categorize, order, group, grade, rank.
– RELATED TERMS schizo-.
– OPPOSITES unify, join, converge.

▶ noun *the sectarian divide* BREACH, gulf, gap, split; borderline, boundary, dividing line.

dividend ▶ noun ❶ *an annual dividend* SHARE, portion, premium, return, gain, profit; *informal* cut, rake-off; *Brit. informal* divvy. ❷ *the research will produce dividends in the future* BENEFIT, advantage, gain; bonus, extra, plus.

divination ▶ noun FORTUNE TELLING, divining, prophecy, prediction, soothsaying, augury; clairvoyance, second sight.
– RELATED TERMS mantic, -mancy.

divine[1] ▶ adjective ❶ *a divine being* GODLY, angelic, seraphic, saintly, beatific; heavenly, celestial, holy. ❷ *divine worship* RELIGIOUS, holy, sacred, sanctified, consecrated, blessed, devotional. ❸ (*informal*) *divine food. See* LOVELY sense 3.

– OPPOSITES mortal.

▶ **noun** (*dated*) *puritan divines* THEOLOGIAN, clergyman, clergywoman, member of the clergy, churchman, churchwoman, cleric, minister, man/woman of the cloth, preacher, priest; *informal* reverend.

divine² ▶ **verb** ❶ *Fergus divined how afraid she was* GUESS, surmise, conjecture, deduce, infer; discern, intuit, perceive, recognize, see, realize, appreciate, understand, grasp, comprehend; *informal* figure (out), savvy; *Brit. informal* twig, suss. ❷ *they divined that this was an auspicious day* FORETELL, predict, prophesy, forecast, foresee, prognosticate; *rare* vaticinate. ❸ *he divined water supplies* DOWSE, find by dowsing.

diviner ▶ **noun** FORTUNE TELLER, clairvoyant, crystal-gazer, psychic, seer, soothsayer, prognosticator, prophesier, oracle, sibyl; *rare* vaticinator.

divinity ▶ **noun** ❶ *they denied Christ's divinity* DIVINE NATURE, divineness, godliness, deity, godhead, holiness. ❷ *the study of divinity* THEOLOGY, religious studies, religion, scripture. ❸ *a female divinity* DEITY, god, goddess, divine/supreme being.

division ▶ **noun** ❶ *the division of the island | cell division* DIVIDING (UP), breaking up, break up, carving up, splitting, dissection, bisection; partitioning, separation, segregation. ❷ *the division of his estates* SHARING OUT, dividing up, parcelling out, dishing out, allocation, allotment, apportionment; splitting up, carving up; *informal* divvying up. ❸ *the division between nomadic and urban cultures* DIVIDING LINE, divide, boundary, borderline, border, demarcation line. ❹ *each class is divided into nine divisions* SECTION, subsection, subdivision, category, class, group, grouping, set, family. ❺ *an independent division of the executive* DEPARTMENT, branch, arm, wing, sector, section, subsection, subdivision, subsidiary. ❻ *the causes of social division* DISUNITY, disunion, conflict, discord, disagreement, dissension, disaffection, estrangement, alienation, isolation.

divisive ▶ **adjective** ALIENATING, estranging, isolating, schismatic.
– OPPOSITES unifying.

divorce ▶ **noun** ❶ *she wants a divorce* DISSOLUTION, annulment, (official/judicial) separation. ❷ *a growing divorce between the church and people* SEPARATION, division, split, disunity, estrangement, alienation; schism, gulf, chasm.
– OPPOSITES marriage, unity.

▶ **verb** ❶ *her parents have divorced* DISSOLVE ONE'S MARRIAGE, annul one's marriage, end one's marriage, get a divorce. ❷ *religion cannot be divorced from morality* SEPARATE, disconnect, divide, dissociate, detach, isolate, alienate, set apart, cut off.

divulge ▶ **verb** DISCLOSE, reveal, tell, communicate, pass on, publish, broadcast, proclaim; expose, uncover, make public, give away, let slip; *informal* spill the beans about, let on about.
– OPPOSITES conceal.

dizzy ▶ **adjective** ❶ *she felt dizzy* GIDDY, light-headed, faint, unsteady, shaky, muzzy, wobbly; *informal* woozy. ❷ *dizzy heights* CAUSING DIZZINESS, causing giddiness, vertiginous. ❸ (*informal*) *a dizzy blond. See* EMPTY-HEADED.

do ▶ **verb** ❶ *she does most of the manual work* CARRY OUT, undertake, discharge, execute, perform, accomplish, achieve; bring about, engineer; *informal* pull off; *formal* effectuate. ❷ *they can do as they please* ACT, behave, conduct oneself, acquit oneself; *formal* comport oneself. ❸ *regular coffee will do* SUFFICE, be adequate, be satisfactory, fill/fit the bill, serve one's purpose, meet one's needs. ❹ *the boys will do the dinner* PREPARE, make, get ready, see to, arrange, organize, be responsible for, be in charge of; *informal* fix. ❺ *the company are doing a new range | a portrait I am doing* MAKE, create, produce, turn out, design, manufacture; paint, draw, sketch; *informal* knock up/off. ❻ *each room was done in a different colour* DECORATE, furnish, ornament, deck out, trick out; *informal* do up. ❼ *her maid did her hair* STYLE, arrange, adjust; brush, comb, wash, dry, cut; *informal* fix. ❽ *I am doing a show to raise money* PUT ON, present, produce; perform in, act in, take part in, participate in. ❾ *you've done me a favour* GRANT, pay, render, give. ❿ *show me how to do these equations* WORK OUT, figure out, calculate; solve, resolve. ⓫ *she's doing archaeology* STUDY, read, learn, take a course in. ⓬ *what does he do?* HAVE AS A JOB, have as a profession, be employed at, earn a living at. ⓭ *he is doing well at college* GET ON/ALONG, progress, fare, manage, cope; succeed, prosper. ⓮ *he was doing 80mph* DRIVE AT, travel at, move at. ⓯ *the cyclists do 30 miles per day* TRAVEL (OVER), journey, cover, traverse, achieve, notch up, log; *informal* chalk up. ⓰ (*informal*) *we're doing Scotland this summer* VISIT, tour, sightsee in.

▶ **noun** (*Brit. informal*) *he invited us to a grand do* PARTY, reception, gathering, celebration, function, social event/occasion, social, soirée; *informal* bash, shindig; *Brit. informal* knees-up, beanfeast, bunfight; *Austral./NZ informal* rage, jollo.

■ **do away with** ❶ *they want to do away with the old customs* ABOLISH, get rid of, discard, remove, eliminate, discontinue, stop, end, terminate, put an end/stop to, dispense with, drop, abandon, give up; *informal* scrap, ditch, dump. ❷ (*informal*) *she tried to do away with her husband. See* KILL verb sense 1.

■ **do someone/something down** (*informal*) BELITTLE, disparage, denigrate, run down, deprecate, cast aspersions on, discredit, vilify, defame, criticize, malign; *N. Amer.* slur; *informal* have a go at, hit out at, knock, slam, pan, badmouth; *Brit. informal* rubbish, slag off.

■ **do someone/something in** (*informal*) ❶ *the poor devil's been done in. See* KILL verb sense 1. ❷ *the long walk home did me in* WEAR OUT, tire out, exhaust, fatigue, weary, overtire, drain; *informal* shatter, take it out of; *Brit. informal* knacker. ❸ *I did my back in* INJURE, hurt, damage.

■ **do something out** (*Brit. informal*) DECORATE, furnish, ornament, deck out, trick out; *informal* do up.

■ **do someone out of something** (*informal*) SWINDLE OUT OF, cheat out of, trick out of, deprive of; *informal* con out of, diddle out of.

■ **do something up** ❶ *she did her bootlace up* FASTEN, tie (up), lace, knot; make fast, secure. ❷ (*informal*) *he's had his house done up* RENOVATE, refurbish, refit, redecorate, decorate, revamp, make over, modernize, improve, spruce up, smarten up; *informal* give something a facelift; *N. Amer. informal* rehab.

■ **do without** FORGO, dispense with, abstain from, refrain from, eschew, give up, cut out, renounce, manage without; *formal* forswear.

docile ▶ **adjective** COMPLIANT, obedient, pliant, dutiful, submissive, deferential, unassertive, cooperative, amenable, accommodating, biddable, malleable.

– OPPOSITES disobedient, wilful.

dock[1] ▶ **noun** *his boat was moored at the dock* HARBOUR, marina, port, anchorage; wharf, quay, pier, jetty, landing stage.

▶ **verb** *the ship docked* MOOR, berth, put in, tie up, anchor.

dock[2] ▶ **verb** ❶ *they docked the money from his salary* DEDUCT, subtract, remove, debit, take off/away; *informal* knock off. ❷ *workers had their pay docked* REDUCE, cut, decrease. ❸ *the dog's tail was docked* CUT OFF, cut short, shorten, crop, lop; remove, amputate, detach, sever, chop off, take off.

docket (*Brit.*) ▶ **noun** *a docket for every transaction* DOCUMENT, chit, coupon, voucher, certificate, counterfoil, bill, receipt; *Brit. informal* chitty.

▶ **verb** *docket the package* DOCUMENT, record, register; label, tag, tab, mark.

doctor ▶ **noun** *Tim went to see a doctor* PHYSICIAN, medical practitioner, clinician; general practitioner, GP, consultant, registrar, medical officer, MO; *Brit.* house officer, houseman; *N. Amer.* intern, extern; *informal* doc, medic, medico; *Brit. informal* quack.

▶ **verb** ❶ (*informal*) *he doctored their wounds* TREAT, medicate, cure, heal; tend, attend to, minister to, care for, nurse. ❷ *he doctored Stephen's drinks* ADULTERATE, contaminate, tamper with, lace; *informal* spike, dope. ❸ *the reports have been doctored* FALSIFY, tamper with, interfere with, alter, change; forge, fake; *informal* cook; *Brit. informal* fiddle (with).

doctrinaire ▶ **adjective** DOGMATIC, rigid, inflexible, uncompromising; authoritarian, intolerant, fanatical, zealous, extreme.

doctrine ▶ **noun** CREED, credo, dogma, belief, teaching, ideology; tenet, maxim, canon, principle, precept.

document ▶ **noun** *their solicitor drew up a document* (OFFICIAL/LEGAL) PAPER, certificate, deed, contract, legal agreement; *Law* instrument, indenture.

▶ **verb** *many aspects of school life have been documented* RECORD, register, report, log, chronicle, archive, put on record, write down; detail, note, describe.

documentary ▶ **adjective** ❶ *documentary evidence* RECORDED, documented, registered, written, chronicled, archived, on record/paper, in writing. ❷ *a documentary film* FACTUAL, non-fictional.

▶ **noun** *a documentary about rural England* FACTUAL PROGRAMME/FILM; programme, film, broadcast.

dodder ▶ **verb** TOTTER, teeter, toddle, hobble, shuffle, shamble, falter.

doddery ▶ **adjective** TOTTERING, tottery, staggering, shuffling, shambling, faltering, shaky, unsteady, wobbly; feeble, frail, weak.

dodge ▶ **verb** ❶ *she dodged into a telephone booth* DART, bolt, dive, lunge, leap, spring. ❷ *he could easily dodge the two coppers* ELUDE, evade, avoid, escape, run away from, lose, shake (off); *informal* give someone the slip. ❸ *the minister tried to dodge the debate* AVOID, evade, get out of, back out of, sidestep; *N. Amer.* end-run; *informal* duck, wriggle out of; *Austral./NZ informal* duck-shove.

▶ **noun** ❶ *a dodge to the right* DART, bolt, dive, lunge, leap, spring. ❷ *a clever dodge | a tax dodge* RUSE, ploy, scheme, tactic, stratagem, subterfuge, trick, hoax, wile, cheat, deception, blind; swindle, fraud; *informal* scam, con (trick); *Brit. informal* wheeze; *N. Amer. informal* bunco, grift; *Austral. informal* lurk, rort.

dodgy ▶ **adjective** (*Brit. informal*) ❶ *a dodgy second-hand car salesman. See* DISHONEST. ❷ *the champagne was dodgy* SECOND-RATE, third-rate, substandard, low-quality; awful, terrible, dreadful, dire; *N. Amer.* cheapjack; *informal* not up to much, woeful; *Brit. informal* ropy, grotty.

doer ▶ **noun** ❶ *the doer of unspeakable deeds* PERFORMER, perpetrator, executor, accomplisher, agent. ❷ *Daniel is a thinker more than a doer* WORKER, organizer, man/woman of action; *informal* mover and shaker, busy bee.

doff ▶ **verb** (*dated*) TAKE OFF, remove, strip off, pull off; raise, lift, tip; *dated* divest oneself of.

– OPPOSITES don.

dog ▶ **noun** ❶ *she went for a walk with her dog* HOUND, canine, mongrel; pup, puppy; *informal* doggy, pooch; *Austral. informal* bitzer. ❷ (*informal*) *you black-hearted dog! See* SCOUNDREL. ❸ (*informal, dated*) *you're a lucky dog! See* FELLOW sense 1.

▶ **verb** ❶ *they dogged him the length of the country* PURSUE, follow, track, trail, shadow, hound; *informal* tail. ❷ *the scheme was dogged by bad* *weather* PLAGUE, beset, bedevil, beleaguer, blight, trouble.

dogged ▶ **adjective** TENACIOUS, determined, resolute, resolved, purposeful, persistent, persevering, single-minded, tireless; strong-willed, steadfast, staunch; *formal* pertinacious.
– OPPOSITES half-hearted.

dogma ▶ **noun** TEACHING, belief, tenet, principle, precept, maxim, article of faith, canon; creed, credo, set of beliefs, doctrine, ideology.

dogmatic ▶ **adjective** OPINIONATED, peremptory, assertive, insistent, emphatic, adamant, doctrinaire, authoritarian, imperious, dictatorial, uncompromising, unyielding, inflexible, rigid.

dogsbody ▶ **noun** (*Brit. informal*) DRUDGE, menial (worker), factotum, servant, slave, lackey, minion, man/girl Friday; *informal* gofer; *Brit. informal* skivvy; *N. Amer. informal* peon; *archaic* scullion.

doing ▶ **noun** ❶ *the doing of the act constitutes the offence* PERFORMANCE, performing, carrying out, execution, implementation, implementing, achievement, accomplishment, realization, completion; *formal* effectuation. ❷ *an account of his doings in Paris* EXPLOIT, activity, act, action, deed, feat, achievement, accomplishment; *informal* caper. ❸ *that would take some doing* EFFORT, exertion, (hard) work, application, labour, toil, struggle. ❹ (*Brit. informal*) *the drawer where he kept the doings* THING, so-and so; *informal* whatsit, whatnot, doodah, thingummy, thingamajig, thingamabob, what's-its-name, what-d'you-call-it, oojamaflip, oojah; *Brit. informal* gubbins; *N. Amer. informal* doohickey, doojigger, dingus.

doldrums ▶ **plural noun** *winter doldrums* DEPRESSION, melancholy, gloom, gloominess, downheartedness, dejection, despondency, low spirits, despair; inertia, apathy, listlessness; *N. Amer.* blahs; *informal* blues.
■ **in the doldrums** INACTIVE, quiet, slow, slack, sluggish, stagnant.

dole ▶ **noun** ❶ (*dated*) *the customary dole was a tumblerful of rice* HANDOUT, charity; gift, donation; *historical* alms. ❷ (*Brit. informal*) *he was on the dole* (UNEMPLOYMENT/STATE) BENEFIT, benefit payments, social security, welfare.
■ **dole something out** DEAL OUT, share out, divide up, allocate, allot, distribute, dispense, hand out, give out, dish out/up; *informal* divvy up.

doleful ▶ **adjective** MOURNFUL, woeful, sorrowful, sad, unhappy, depressed, gloomy, morose, melancholy, miserable, forlorn, wretched, woebegone, despondent, dejected, disconsolate, downcast, crestfallen, downhearted; *informal* blue, down in the mouth/dumps; *poetic/literary* dolorous, heartsick.
– OPPOSITES cheerful.

doll ▶ **noun** ❶ *the child was hugging a doll* FIGURE, figurine, model; toy, plaything; *informal* dolly. ❷ (*informal*) *she was quite a doll. See* BEAUTY sense 1.
■ **doll oneself up** (*informal*) DRESS UP; *informal* get/do oneself up, dress up to the nines, put on one's glad rags; *Brit. informal* tart oneself up.

dollop (*informal*) ▶ **noun** BLOB, gobbet, lump, ball; *informal* glob; *Brit. informal* gob, wodge.

dolorous ▶ **adjective** (*poetic/literary*). *See* DOLEFUL.

dolour ▶ **noun** (*poetic/literary*). *See* MISERY sense 1.

dolt ▶ **noun**. *See* IDIOT.

doltish ▶ **adjective**. *See* STUPID sense 1.

domain ▶ **noun** ❶ *they extended their domain* REALM, kingdom, empire, dominion, province, territory, land. ❷ *the domain of art* FIELD, area, sphere, discipline, province, world.

dome ▶ **noun** CUPOLA, vault, arched roof.

domestic ▶ **adjective** ❶ *domestic commitments* FAMILY, home, household. ❷ *she was not at all domestic* HOUSEWIFELY, domesticated, homely. ❸ *small domestic animals* DOMESTICATED, tame, pet, household. ❹ *the domestic car industry* NATIONAL, state, home, internal. ❺ *domestic plants* NATIVE, indigenous.
▶ **noun** *they worked as domestics* SERVANT, domestic worker/help, home help, maid, housemaid, cleaner, housekeeper; *Brit. dated* charwoman, charlady, char; *Brit. informal* daily (help).

domesticated ▶ **adjective** ❶ *domesticated animals* TAME, tamed, pet, domestic, trained. ❷ *domesticated crops* CULTIVATED, naturalized. ❸ *I'm quite domesticated really* HOUSEWIFELY, home-loving, homely.
– OPPOSITES wild.

domicile (*formal*) ▶ **noun** *changes of domicile* RESIDENCE, home, house, address, residency, lodging, accommodation; *informal* digs; *formal* dwelling (place), abode, habitation.
▶ **verb** *he is now domiciled in Australia* SETTLE, live, make one's home, take up residence; move to, emigrate to.

dominance ▶ **noun** SUPREMACY, superiority, ascendancy, pre-eminence, predominance, domination, dominion, mastery, power, authority, rule, command, control, sway; *poetic/literary* puissance.

dominant ▶ **adjective** ❶ *the dominant classes* PRESIDING, ruling, governing, controlling, commanding, ascendant, supreme, authoritative. ❷ *he has a dominant personality* ASSERTIVE, authoritative, forceful, domineering, commanding, controlling, pushy; *dated* pushful. ❸ *the dominant issues in psychology* MAIN, principal, prime, premier, chief, foremost, primary, predominant, paramount, prominent; central, key, crucial, core; *informal* number-one.
– OPPOSITES subservient.

dominate ▶ **verb** ❶ *the Russians dominated Iran in the nineteenth century* CONTROL, influence, exercise control over, command, be in command of, be in charge of, rule, govern, direct, have ascendancy over, have mastery over; *informal* head up, be in the driver's seat, be at the helm, rule the roost; *Brit. informal* wear the trousers; *N. Amer. informal* have someone in one's hip pocket; *poetic/literary* sway. ❷ *the Puritan work ethic still dominates* PREDOMINATE, prevail, reign, be prevalent, be paramount, be pre-eminent. ❸ *the village is dominated by the viaduct* OVERLOOK, command, tower above/over, loom over.

domination ▶ **noun** RULE, government, sovereignty, control, command, authority, power, dominion, dominance, mastery, supremacy, superiority, ascendancy, sway.

domineer ▶ **verb** BROWBEAT, bully, intimidate, push around/about, order about/around, lord it over; dictate to, be overbearing, have under one's thumb, rule with a rod of iron; *informal* boss about/around, walk all over.

domineering ▶ **adjective** OVERBEARING, authoritarian, imperious, high-handed, autocratic; masterful, dictatorial, despotic, oppressive, iron-fisted, strict, harsh; *informal* bossy.

dominion ▶ **noun** ❶ *France had dominion over Laos* SUPREMACY, ascendancy, dominance, domination, superiority, predominance, pre-eminence, hegemony, authority, mastery, control, command, power, sway, rule, government, jurisdiction, sovereignty, suzerainty. ❷ *a British dominion* DEPENDENCY, colony, protectorate, territory, province, possession; *historical* tributary.

don[1] ▶ **noun** *an Oxford don* UNIVERSITY TEACHER, (university) lecturer, fellow, professor, reader, academic, scholar.

don[2] ▶ **verb** *he donned an overcoat* PUT ON, get dressed in, dress (oneself) in, get into, slip into/on.

donate ▶ **verb** GIVE, give/make a donation of, contribute, make a contribution of, gift, subscribe, grant, bestow; *informal* chip in, pitch in; *Brit. informal* stump up; *N. Amer. informal* kick in.

donation ▶ **noun** GIFT, contribution, subscription, present, handout, grant, offering; charity; *formal* benefaction; *historical* alms.

done ▶ **adjective** ❶ *the job is done* FINISHED, ended, concluded, complete, completed, accomplished, achieved, fulfilled, discharged, executed; *informal* wrapped up, sewn up, polished off. ❷ *is the meat done?* COOKED (THROUGH), ready. ❸ *those days are done* OVER (AND DONE WITH), at an end, finished, ended, concluded, terminated, no more, dead, gone, in the past. ❹ (*informal*) *that's just not done* PROPER, seemly, decent, respectable, right, correct, in order, fitting, appropriate, acceptable, the done thing.

– OPPOSITES incomplete, underdone, ongoing.

▶ **exclamation** *Done!* AGREED, all right, very well; *informal* you're on, OK, okey-dokey; *Brit. informal* righto, righty-ho.

■ **be/have done with** BE/HAVE FINISHED WITH, be through with, want no more to do with.

■ **done for** (*informal*) RUINED, finished, destroyed, undone, doomed, lost; *informal* washed-up.

■ **done in** (informal). *See* EXHAUSTED sense 1.

Don Juan ▶ **noun** WOMANIZER, philanderer, Casanova, Lothario, flirt, ladies' man, playboy, seducer, rake, roué, libertine; *informal* skirt-chaser, ladykiller, wolf.

donkey ▶ **noun** ❶ *the cart was drawn by a donkey* ASS, jackass, jenny; mule, hinny; *Brit. informal* moke. ❷ (*informal*) *you silly donkey! See* FOOL noun sense 1.

– RELATED TERMS asinine.

donnish ▶ **adjective** SCHOLARLY, studious, academic, bookish, intellectual, learned, highbrow; *informal* egghead; *dated* lettered.

donor ▶ **noun** GIVER, contributor, benefactor, benefactress, subscriber; supporter, backer, patron, sponsor; *informal* angel.

doom ▶ **noun** ❶ *his impending doom* DESTRUCTION, downfall, ruin, ruination; extinction, annihilation, death. ❷ (*archaic*) *the day of doom* JUDGEMENT DAY, the Last Judgement, doomsday, Armageddon.

▶ **verb** *we were doomed to fail* DESTINE, fate, predestine, preordain, foredoom, mean; condemn, sentence.

doomed ▶ **adjective** ILL-FATED, ill-starred, cursed, jinxed, foredoomed, damned; *poetic/literary* star-crossed.

door ▶ **noun** DOORWAY, portal, opening, entrance, entry, exit.

■ **out of doors** OUTSIDE, outdoors, in/into the open air, alfresco.

doorkeeper ▶ **noun** DOORMAN, commissionaire, concierge.

dope ▶ **noun** (*informal*) ❶ *he was caught smuggling dope* (ILLEGAL) DRUGS, narcotics; cannabis, heroin. ❷ *what a dope! See* FOOL noun sense 1. ❸ *they had plenty of dope on Mr Dixon. See* INTELLIGENCE sense 2.

▶ **verb** ❶ *the horse was doped* DRUG, administer drugs/narcotics to, tamper with, interfere with; sedate; *Brit. informal* nobble. ❷ *they doped his drink* ADD DRUGS TO, tamper with, adulterate, contaminate, lace; *informal* spike, doctor.

dopey ▶ **adjective** (*informal*) STUPEFIED, confused, muddled, befuddled, disorientated, groggy, muzzy; *informal* woozy, not with it.

– OPPOSITES alert.

dormant ▶ **adjective** ASLEEP, sleeping, resting; INACTIVE, passive, inert, latent, quiescent.

– OPPOSITES awake, active.

dose ▶ **noun** MEASURE, portion, dosage, drench; *informal* hit.

dossier ▶ **noun** FILE, report, case history; account, notes, document(s), documentation, data, information, evidence.

dot ▸ **noun** *a pattern of tiny dots* SPOT, speck, fleck, speckle; full stop, decimal point.

▸ **verb** ❶ *spots of rain dotted his shirt* SPOT, fleck, mark, stipple, freckle, sprinkle; *poetic/literary* bestrew, besprinkle. ❷ *restaurants are dotted around the site* SCATTER, pepper, sprinkle, strew; spread, disperse, distribute.

■ **on the dot** (*informal*) PRECISELY, exactly, sharp, prompt, dead on, on the stroke of ——; *informal* bang on; *N. Amer. informal* on the button, on the nose.

dotage ▸ **noun** DECLINING YEARS, winter/autumn of one's life; advanced years, old age; *poetic/literary* eld.

dote

■ **dote on** ADORE, love dearly, be devoted to, idolize, treasure, cherish, worship, hold dear; indulge, spoil, pamper.

doting ▸ **adjective** ADORING, loving, besotted, infatuated; affectionate, fond, devoted, caring.

dotty ▸ **adjective** (*informal*). *See* MAD sense 1.

double ▸ **adjective** ❶ *a double garage | double yellow lines* DUAL, duplex, twin, binary, duplicate, in pairs, coupled, twofold. ❷ *a double helping* DOUBLED, twofold. ❸ *a double meaning* AMBIGUOUS, equivocal, dual, two-edged, double-edged, ambivalent, cryptic, enigmatic. ❹ *a double life* DECEITFUL, double-dealing, two-faced, dual; hypocritical, false, duplicitous, insincere, deceiving, dissembling, dishonest.

– RELATED TERMS di-, diplo-.

– OPPOSITES single, unambiguous.

▸ **adverb** *we had to pay double* TWICE (OVER), twice the amount, doubly.

▸ **noun** ❶ *if it's not her, it's her double* LOOKALIKE, twin, clone, duplicate, exact likeness, replica, copy, facsimile, Doppelgänger; *informal* spitting image, dead ringer, dead spit. ❷ *she used a double for the stunts* STAND-IN, substitute.

▸ **verb** ❶ *they doubled his salary* MULTIPLY BY TWO, increase twofold. ❷ *the bottom sheet had been doubled up* FOLD (BACK/UP/DOWN/OVER/UNDER), turn back/up/down/over/under, tuck back/up/down/under. ❸ *the kitchen doubles as a dining room* FUNCTION, do, (also) serve.

■ **at/on the double** VERY QUICKLY, as fast as one's legs can carry one, at a run, at a gallop, fast, swiftly, rapidly, speedily, at (full) speed, at full tilt, as fast as possible; *informal* double quick, like (greased) lightning, like the wind, like a scalded cat, like a bat out of hell; *Brit. informal* like the clappers, at a rate of knots; *N. Amer. informal* lickety-split.

double-cross ▸ **verb** BETRAY, cheat, defraud, trick, hoodwink, mislead, deceive, swindle, be disloyal to, be unfaithful to, play false; *informal* do the dirty on, sell down the river.

double-dealing ▸ **noun** DUPLICITY, treachery, betrayal, double-crossing, unfaithfulness, untrustworthiness, infidelity, bad faith, disloyalty, breach of trust, fraud, underhandedness, cheating, dishonesty, deceit, deceitfulness, deception, falseness; *informal* crookedness.

– OPPOSITES honesty.

double entendre ▸ **noun** AMBIGUITY, double meaning, innuendo, play on words.

doubly ▸ **adverb** TWICE AS, in double measure, even more, especially, extra.

doubt ▸ **noun** ❶ *there was some doubt as to the caller's identity* UNCERTAINTY, unsureness, indecision, hesitation, dubiousness, suspicion, confusion; queries, questions; *formal* dubiety. ❷ *a weak leader racked by doubt* INDECISION, hesitation, uncertainty, insecurity, unease, uneasiness, apprehension; hesitancy, vacillation, irresolution. ❸ *there is doubt about their motives* SCEPTICISM, distrust, mistrust, doubtfulness, suspicion, cynicism, uneasiness, apprehension, wariness, chariness, leeriness; reservations, misgivings, suspicions; *formal* dubiety.

– OPPOSITES certainty, conviction.

▸ **verb** ❶ *they doubted my story* DISBELIEVE, distrust, mistrust, suspect, have doubts about, be suspicious of, have misgivings about, feel uneasy about, feel apprehensive about, query, question, challenge. ❷ *I doubt whether he will come* THINK SOMETHING UNLIKELY, have (one's) doubts about, question, query, be dubious. ❸ *stop doubting and believe!* BE UNDECIDED, have doubts, be irresolute, be ambivalent, be doubtful, be unsure, be uncertain, be in two minds, hesitate, shilly-shally, waver, vacillate.

– OPPOSITES trust.

■ **in doubt** ❶ *the issue was in doubt* DOUBTFUL, uncertain, open to question, unconfirmed, unknown, undecided, unresolved, in the balance, up in the air; *informal* iffy. ❷ *if you are in doubt, ask for advice* IRRESOLUTE, hesitant, vacillating, dithering, wavering, ambivalent; doubtful, unsure, uncertain, in two minds, shilly-shallying, undecided, in a quandary/dilemma; *informal* sitting on the fence.

■ **no doubt** DOUBTLESS, undoubtedly, indubitably, doubtlessly, without (a) doubt; unquestionably, undeniably, incontrovertibly, irrefutably; unequivocally, clearly, plainly, obviously, patently.

doubter ▸ **noun** SCEPTIC, doubting Thomas, non-believer, unbeliever, disbeliever, cynic, scoffer, questioner, challenger, dissenter.

– OPPOSITES believer.

doubtful ▸ **adjective** ❶ *I was doubtful about going* IRRESOLUTE, hesitant, vacillating, dithering, wavering, in doubt, unsure, uncertain, in two minds, shilly-shallying, undecided, in a quandary/dilemma, blowing hot and cold. ❷ *it is doubtful whether he will come* IN DOUBT, uncertain, open to question, unsure, unconfirmed, not definite, unknown, undecided, unresolved, debatable, in the balance, up in the air; *informal* iffy. ❸ *the whole trip is looking rather doubtful* UNLIKELY, improbable, dubious, impossible. ❹ *they are doubtful of the methods used* DIS-

TRUSTFUL, mistrustful, suspicious, wary, chary, leery, apprehensive; sceptical, unsure, ambivalent, dubious, cynical. ❺ *this decision is of doubtful validity* QUESTIONABLE, arguable, debatable, controversial, contentious; *informal* iffy; *Brit. informal* dodgy.
– OPPOSITES confident, certain, probable, trusting.

doubtless ▶ **adverb** UNDOUBTEDLY, indubitably, doubtlessly, no doubt; unquestionably, indisputably, undeniably, incontrovertibly, irrefutably; certainly, surely, of course, indeed.

doughty ▶ **adjective** FEARLESS, dauntless, determined, resolute, indomitable, intrepid, plucky, spirited, bold, valiant, brave, stout-hearted, courageous; *informal* gutsy, spunky, feisty.

dour ▶ **adjective** STERN, unsmiling, unfriendly, severe, forbidding, gruff, surly, grim, sullen, solemn, austere, stony.
– OPPOSITES cheerful, friendly.

douse ▶ **verb** ❶ *a mob doused the thieves with petrol* DRENCH, soak, saturate, wet, splash, slosh. ❷ *a guard doused the flames* EXTINGUISH, put out, quench, smother, dampen down.

dovetail ▶ **verb** ❶ *the ends of the logs were dovetailed* JOINT, join, fit together, splice, mortise, tenon. ❷ *this will dovetail well with the division's existing activities* FIT IN, go together, be consistent, match, conform, harmonize, be in tune, correspond; *informal* square; *N. Amer. informal* jibe.

dowdy ▶ **adjective** UNFASHIONABLE, frumpy, old-fashioned, inelegant, shabby, scruffy, frowzy; *Brit. informal* mumsy; *Austral./NZ informal* daggy.
– OPPOSITES fashionable.

down[1] ▶ **adverb** ❶ *they went down in the lift* TOWARDS A LOWER POSITION, downwards, downstairs. ❷ *she fell down* TO THE GROUND/FLOOR, over.
– OPPOSITES up.

▶ **preposition** ❶ *the lift plunged down the shaft* TO A LOWER POSITION IN, to the bottom of. ❷ *I walked down the street* ALONG, to the other end of, from one end of —— to the other. ❸ *down the years* THROUGHOUT, through, during.

▶ **adjective** ❶ *I'm feeling a bit down* DEPRESSED, sad, unhappy, melancholy, miserable, wretched, sorrowful, gloomy, dejected, downhearted, despondent, dispirited, low; *informal* blue, down in the dumps/mouth, fed up. ❷ *the computer is down* NOT WORKING, inoperative, malfunctioning, out of order, broken; not in service, out of action, out of commission; *informal* conked out, bust, (gone) kaput; *N. Amer. informal* on the fritz.
– OPPOSITES elated, working.

▶ **verb** (*informal*) ❶ *he struck Slater, downing him* KNOCK DOWN/OVER, knock to the ground, bring down, topple; *informal* deck, floor, flatten. ❷ *he downed his beer* DRINK (UP/DOWN), gulp (down), guzzle, quaff, drain, toss off, slug, finish off; *informal* sink, knock back, put away; *N. Amer. informal* scarf (down/up), snarf (down/up).

▶ **noun** ❶ *the ups and downs of running a business* SETBACKS, upsets, reverses, reversals, mishaps, vicissitudes; *informal* glitches. ❷ (*informal*) *he's having a bit of a down* FIT OF DEPRESSION; *informal* the blues, the dumps, a low; *N. Amer. informal* the blahs.

■ **have a down on** (informal) DISAPPROVE OF, be against, feel antagonism to, be hostile to, feel ill will towards; *informal* have it in for, be down on.

down[2] ▶ **noun** *goose down* SOFT FEATHERS, fine hair; fluff, fuzz, floss, lint.

down and out ▶ **adjective** DESTITUTE, poverty-stricken, impoverished, penniless, insolvent, impecunious; needy, in straitened circumstances, distressed, badly off; homeless, on the streets, vagrant, sleeping rough; *informal* hard up, (flat) broke, strapped (for cash), without a brass farthing, without two pennies to rub together; *Brit. informal* stony broke, skint; *N. Amer. informal* without a red cent, on skid row.
– OPPOSITES wealthy.

▶ **noun** (**down-and-out**) POOR PERSON, pauper, indigent; beggar, homeless person, vagrant, tramp, drifter, derelict, vagabond; *N. Amer.* hobo; *Austral.* bagman; *informal* have-not, dosser, bag lady; *N. Amer. informal* bum.

down at heel ▶ **adjective** ❶ *the resort looks down at heel* RUN DOWN, dilapidated, neglected, uncared-for; seedy, insalubrious, squalid, slummy, wretched; *informal* scruffy, scuzzy; *Brit. informal* grotty; *N. Amer. informal* shacky. ❷ *a down-at-heel labourer* SCRUFFY, shabby, ragged, tattered, mangy, sorry; unkempt, bedraggled, dishevelled, ungroomed, seedy, untidy, slovenly; *informal* tatty, scuzzy, grungy; *Brit. informal* grotty; *N. Amer. informal* raggedy.
– OPPOSITES smart.

downbeat ▶ **adjective** ❶ *the mood is decidedly downbeat* PESSIMISTIC, gloomy, negative, defeatist, cynical, bleak, fatalistic, dark, black; despairing, despondent, depressed, dejected, demoralized, hopeless, melancholy, glum. ❷ *his downbeat joviality* RELAXED, easy-going, easy, casual, informal, nonchalant, insouciant; low-key, subtle, unostentatious, cool; *informal* laid-back.

downcast ▶ **adjective** DESPONDENT, disheartened, discouraged, dispirited, downhearted, crestfallen, down, low, disconsolate, despairing; sad, melancholy, gloomy, glum, morose, doleful, dismal, woebegone, miserable, depressed, dejected; *informal* blue, down in the mouth, down in the dumps.
– OPPOSITES elated.

downfall ▶ **noun** UNDOING, ruin, ruination; defeat, conquest, deposition, overthrow; nemesis, destruction, annihilation, elimination; end, collapse, fall, crash, failure; debasement, degradation, disgrace; Waterloo.
– OPPOSITES rise.

downgrade ▶ verb ❶ *plans to downgrade three workers* DEMOTE, lower, reduce/lower in rank; relegate. ❷ *I won't downgrade their achievement* DISPARAGE, denigrate, detract from, run down, belittle; *informal* bad-mouth.
– OPPOSITES promote, praise.

downhearted ▶ adjective DESPONDENT, disheartened, discouraged, dispirited, downcast, crestfallen, down, low, disconsolate, wretched; melancholy, gloomy, glum, morose, doleful, dismal, woebegone, miserable, depressed, dejected, sorrowful, sad; *informal* blue, down in the mouth, down in the dumps.
– OPPOSITES elated.

downmarket ▶ adjective (*Brit.*) CHEAP, cheap and nasty, inferior; low-class, lowbrow, unsophisticated, rough, insalubrious; *informal* tacky, rubbishy, dumbed down.

downpour ▶ noun RAINSTORM, cloudburst, deluge; thunderstorm; torrential/pouring rain.

downright ▶ adjective ❶ *downright lies* COMPLETE, total, absolute, utter, thorough, out-and-out, outright, sheer, arrant, pure, real, veritable, categorical, unmitigated, unadulterated, unalloyed, unequivocal; *Brit. informal* proper. ❷ *her downright attitude* FRANK, straightforward, direct, blunt, plain-spoken, forthright, uninhibited, unreserved; no-nonsense, matter-of-fact, bluff, undiplomatic; explicit, clear, plain, unequivocal, unambiguous; honest, candid, open, sincere; *informal* upfront.
▶ adverb *that's downright dangerous* THOROUGHLY, utterly, positively, profoundly, really, completely, totally, entirely; unquestionably, undeniably, in every respect, through and through; *informal* plain.

downside ▶ noun DRAWBACK, disadvantage, snag, stumbling block, catch, pitfall, fly in the ointment; handicap, limitation, trouble, difficulty, problem, complication, nuisance; hindrance; weak spot/point; *informal* minus, flip side.
– OPPOSITES advantage.

down-to-earth ▶ adjective PRACTICAL, sensible, realistic, matter-of-fact, responsible, reasonable, rational, logical, balanced, sober, pragmatic, level-headed, commonsensical, sane.
– OPPOSITES idealistic.

downtrodden ▶ adjective OPPRESSED, subjugated, persecuted, repressed, tyrannized, crushed, enslaved, exploited, victimized, bullied; disadvantaged, underprivileged, powerless, helpless; abused, maltreated.

downward ▶ adjective DESCENDING, downhill, falling, sinking, dipping; earthbound, earthward.

downy ▶ adjective SOFT, velvety, smooth, fleecy, fluffy, fuzzy, feathery, furry, woolly, silky.

dowry ▶ noun MARRIAGE SETTLEMENT, (marriage) portion; *archaic* dot.

doze ▶ verb CATNAP, nap, drowse, sleep lightly, rest; *informal* snooze, snatch forty winks, get some shut-eye; *Brit. informal* kip; *N. Amer. informal* catch some Zs; *poetic/literary* slumber.
▶ noun CATNAP, nap, siesta, light sleep, drowse, rest; *informal* snooze, forty winks; *Brit. informal* kip, zizz; *poetic/literary* slumber.
■ **doze off** FALL ASLEEP, go to sleep, drop off; *informal* nod off, drift off; *N. Amer. informal* sack out, zone out.

dozy ▶ adjective DROWSY, sleepy, half asleep, heavy-eyed, somnolent; lethargic, listless, enervated, inactive, languid, weary, tired, fatigued; *N. Amer.* logy; *informal* dopey, yawny.

drab ▶ adjective ❶ *a drab interior* COLOURLESS, grey, dull, washed out, muted, lacklustre; dingy, dreary, dismal, cheerless, gloomy, sombre. ❷ *a drab existence* UNINTERESTING, dull, boring, tedious, monotonous, dry, dreary; unexciting, unimaginative, uninspiring, insipid, lacklustre, flat, stale, wishy-washy, colourless, lame, tired, sterile, anaemic, barren, tame; middle-of-the-road, run-of-the-mill, mediocre, nondescript, characterless, mundane, unremarkable, humdrum.
– OPPOSITES bright, cheerful, interesting.

draconian ▶ adjective HARSH, severe, strict, extreme, drastic, stringent, tough; cruel, oppressive, ruthless, relentless, punitive; authoritarian, despotic, tyrannical, repressive; *Brit.* swingeing.
– OPPOSITES lenient.

draft ▶ noun ❶ *the draft of his speech* PRELIMINARY VERSION, rough outline, plan, skeleton, abstract; main points, bare bones. ❷ *a draft of the building* PLAN, blueprint, design, diagram, drawing, sketch, map, layout, representation. ❸ *a banker's draft* CHEQUE, order, money order, bill of exchange, postal order.

drag ▶ verb ❶ *she dragged the chair backwards* HAUL, pull, tug, heave, lug, draw; trail, trawl, tow; *informal* yank. ❷ *the day dragged* BECOME TEDIOUS, pass slowly, creep along, hang heavy, wear on, go on too long, go on and on.
▶ noun ❶ *the drag of the air brakes* PULL, resistance, tug. ❷ (*informal*) *work can be a drag* BORE, nuisance, bother, trouble, pest, annoyance, trial, vexation; *informal* pain (in the neck), bind, headache, hassle.
■ **drag on** PERSIST, continue, go on, carry on, extend, run on, be protracted, endure, prevail.
■ **drag something out** PROLONG, protract, draw out, spin out, string out, extend, lengthen, carry on, keep going, continue.

dragoon ▶ noun (*historical*) *the dragoons charged* CAVALRYMAN, mounted soldier; *historical* knight, chevalier, hussar; *archaic* cavalier.
▶ verb *he dragooned his friends into participating* COERCE, pressure, pressurize, press, push;

force, compel, impel; hound, harass, nag, harry, badger, goad, pester; browbeat, bludgeon, bully, twist someone's arm, strong-arm; *informal* railroad.

drain ▶ **verb** ❶ *a valve for draining the tank* EMPTY (OUT), void, clear (out), evacuate, unload. ❷ *drain off any surplus liquid* DRAW OFF, extract, withdraw, remove, siphon off, pour out, pour off; milk, bleed, tap, void, filter, discharge. ❸ *the water drained away to the sea* FLOW, pour, trickle, stream, run, rush, gush, flood, surge; leak, ooze, seep, dribble, issue, filter, bleed, leach. ❹ *more people would just drain our resources* USE UP, exhaust, deplete, consume, expend, get through, sap, strain, tax; milk, bleed. ❺ *he drained his drink* DRINK (UP/DOWN), gulp (down), guzzle, quaff, down, imbibe, sup, swallow, finish off, toss off, slug; *informal* sink, swig, swill (down), polish off, knock back, put away.
– OPPOSITES fill.

▶ **noun** ❶ *the drain filled with water* SEWER, channel, conduit, ditch, culvert, duct, pipe, gutter, trough; sluice, spillway, race, flume, chute. ❷ *a drain on the battery* STRAIN, pressure, burden, load, tax, demand.

dram ▶ **noun** DRINK, nip, tot, sip, drop, finger, splash, little, spot, taste.

drama ▶ **noun** ❶ *a television drama* PLAY, show, piece, theatrical work, dramatization. ❷ *he is studying drama* ACTING, the theatre, the stage, the performing arts, dramatic art, stagecraft. ❸ *she liked to create a drama* INCIDENT, scene, spectacle, crisis; excitement, thrill, sensation; disturbance, row, commotion, turmoil; dramatics, theatrics.

dramatic ▶ **adjective** ❶ *dramatic art* THEATRICAL, theatric, thespian, stage, dramaturgical; *formal* histrionic. ❷ *a dramatic increase* CONSIDERABLE, substantial, sizeable, goodly, fair, marked, noticeable, measurable, perceptible, obvious, appreciable; significant, notable, noteworthy, remarkable, extraordinary, exceptional, phenomenal; *informal* tidy. ❸ *there were dramatic scenes in the city* EXCITING, stirring, action-packed, sensational, spectacular; startling, unexpected, tense, gripping, riveting, fascinating, thrilling, hair-raising; rousing, lively, electrifying, impassioned, moving. ❹ *dramatic headlands* STRIKING, impressive, imposing, spectacular, breathtaking, dazzling, sensational, awesome, awe-inspiring, remarkable, outstanding, incredible, phenomenal. ❺ *a dramatic gesture* EXAGGERATED, theatrical, ostentatious, actressy, stagy, showy, melodramatic, overdone, histrionic, affected, mannered, artificial; *informal* hammy, ham, campy.
– OPPOSITES insignificant, boring.

dramatist ▶ **noun** PLAYWRIGHT, writer, scriptwriter, screenwriter, scenarist, dramaturge.

dramatize ▶ **verb** ❶ *the novel was dramatized for television* TURN INTO A PLAY/FILM, adapt for the stage/screen. ❷ *the tabloids dramatized the event* EXAGGERATE, overdo, overstate, hyperbolize, magnify, amplify, inflate; sensationalize, embroider, colour, aggrandize, embellish, elaborate; *informal* blow up (out of all proportion).

drape ▶ **verb** ❶ *she draped a shawl round her* WRAP, wind, swathe, sling, hang. ❷ *the chair was draped with blankets* COVER, envelop, swathe, shroud, deck, festoon, overlay, cloak, wind, enfold, sheathe. ❸ *he draped one leg over the arm of his chair* DANGLE, hang, suspend, droop, drop.

drastic ▶ **adjective** EXTREME, serious, desperate, radical, far-reaching, momentous, substantial; heavy, severe, harsh, rigorous; oppressive, draconian.
– OPPOSITES moderate.

draught ▶ **noun** ❶ *the draught made Robyn shiver* CURRENT OF AIR, rush of air; waft, wind, breeze, gust, puff, blast; *informal* blow. ❷ *a deep draught of beer* GULP, drink, swallow, mouthful, slug; *informal* swig, swill.

draw ▶ **verb** ❶ *he drew the house* SKETCH, make a drawing (of), delineate, outline, draft, rough out, illustrate, render, represent, trace; portray, depict. ❷ *she drew her chair in to the table* PULL, haul, drag, tug, heave, lug, trail, tow; *informal* yank. ❸ *the train drew into the station* MOVE, go, come, proceed, progress, travel, advance, pass, drive; inch, roll, glide, cruise; forge, sweep; back. ❹ *she drew the curtains* CLOSE, shut, pull to, lower; open, part, pull back, pull open, fling open, raise. ❺ *he drew some fluid off the knee joint* DRAIN, extract, withdraw, remove, suck, pump, siphon, milk, bleed, tap. ❻ *he drew his gun* PULL OUT, take out, produce, fish out, extract, withdraw; unsheathe. ❼ *I drew £50 out of the bank* WITHDRAW, take out. ❽ *while I draw breath* BREATHE IN, inhale, inspire, respire. ❾ *she was drawing huge audiences* ATTRACT, interest, win, capture, catch, engage, lure, entice; absorb, occupy, rivet, engross, fascinate, mesmerize, spellbind, captivate, enthral, grip. ❿ *what conclusion can we draw?* DEDUCE, infer, conclude, derive, gather, glean.

▶ **noun** ❶ *she won the Christmas draw* RAFFLE, lottery, sweepstake, sweep, tombola, ballot; *N. Amer.* lotto. ❷ *the match ended in a draw* TIE, dead heat, stalemate. ❸ *the draw of central London* ATTRACTION, lure, allure, pull, appeal, glamour, enticement, temptation, charm, seduction, fascination, magnetism.

■ **draw on** CALL ON, have recourse to, avail oneself of, turn to, look to, fall back on, rely on, exploit, use, employ, utilize, bring into play.

■ **draw something out** ❶ *he drew out a gun.* See DRAW verb sense 6. ❷ *they always drew their parting out* PROLONG, protract, drag out, spin out, string out, extend, lengthen.

■ **draw someone out** ENCOURAGE TO TALK, put at ease.

■ **draw up** STOP, pull up, halt, come to a standstill, brake, park; arrive.

■ **draw something up** ❶ *we drew up a list* COMPOSE, formulate, frame, write down, draft, prepare, think up, devise, work out; create, invent, design. ❷ *he drew up his forces in battle array* ARRANGE, marshal, muster, assemble, group, order, range, rank, line up, dispose, position, array.

drawback ▶ noun DISADVANTAGE, snag, downside, stumbling block, catch, hitch, pitfall, fly in the ointment; weak spot/point, weakness, imperfection; handicap, limitation, trouble, difficulty, problem, complication; hindrance, obstacle, impediment, obstruction, inconvenience, discouragement, deterrent; *informal* minus, hiccup; *Brit. informal* spanner in the works.

– OPPOSITES benefit.

drawing ▶ noun SKETCH, picture, illustration, representation, portrayal, delineation, depiction, composition, study, diagram, outline, design, plan.

– RELATED TERMS graphic.

drawl ▶ verb SAY SLOWLY, speak slowly; drone.

drawn ▶ adjective *she looked pale and drawn* PINCHED, haggard, drained, wan, hollow-cheeked; fatigued, tired, exhausted; tense, stressed, strained, worried, anxious, harassed, fraught; *informal* hassled.

dread ▶ verb *I used to dread going to school* FEAR, be afraid of, worry about, be anxious about, have forebodings about; be terrified by, tremble/shudder at, shrink from, quail from, flinch from; *informal* get cold feet about.

▶ noun *she was filled with dread* FEAR, apprehension, trepidation, anxiety, worry, concern, foreboding, disquiet, unease, angst; fright, panic, alarm; terror, horror; *informal* the jitters, the heebie-jeebies.

– OPPOSITES confidence.

▶ adjective *a dread secret* AWFUL, frightful, terrible, horrible, dreadful; feared, frightening, alarming, terrifying, dire, dreaded.

dreadful ▶ adjective ❶ *a dreadful accident* TERRIBLE, frightful, horrible, grim, awful, dire; horrifying, alarming, shocking, distressing, appalling, harrowing; ghastly, fearful, horrendous; tragic, calamitous; *formal* grievous. ❷ *a dreadful meal* UNPLEASANT, disagreeable, nasty; frightful, shocking, awful, abysmal, atrocious, disgraceful, deplorable, very bad, repugnant; poor, inadequate, inferior, unsatisfactory, distasteful; *informal* pathetic, woeful, crummy, rotten, sorry, third-rate, lousy, ropy, God-awful; *Brit. informal* duff, chronic, rubbish. ❸ *you're a dreadful flirt* OUTRAGEOUS, shocking; inordinate, immoderate, unrestrained.

– OPPOSITES pleasant, agreeable.

dreadfully ▶ adverb ❶ *I'm dreadfully hungry* EXTREMELY, very, really, exceedingly, tremendously, exceptionally, extraordinarily; decidedly, most, particularly; *N. English* right; *informal* terrifically, terribly, desperately, awfully, devilishly, mega, seriously, majorly; *Brit. informal* jolly, ever so, dead, well; *N. Amer. informal* real, mighty, awful; *informal, dated* frightfully. ❷ *she missed James dreadfully* VERY MUCH, much, lots, a lot, a great deal, intensely, desperately. ❸ *the company performed dreadfully* TERRIBLY, awfully, very badly, atrociously, appallingly, abominably, poorly; *informal* abysmally, pitifully, diabolically.

dream ▶ noun ❶ *I awoke from my dreams* REM sleep; nightmare; vision, fantasy, hallucination. ❷ *she went around in a dream* DAYDREAM, reverie, trance, daze, stupor, haze; *Scottish* dwam. ❸ *he realized his childhood dream* AMBITION, aspiration, hope; goal, aim, objective, grail, intention, intent, target; desire, wish, yearning; daydream, fantasy, pipe dream. ❹ *he's an absolute dream* DELIGHT, joy, marvel, wonder, gem, treasure; beauty, vision.

▶ verb ❶ *she dreamed of her own funeral* HAVE A DREAM, have a nightmare. ❷ *I dream of making the Olympic team* FANTASIZE ABOUT, daydream about; WISH FOR, hope for, long for, yearn for, hanker after, set one's heart on; aspire to, aim for, set one's sights on. ❸ *she's always dreaming* DAYDREAM, be in a trance, be lost in thought, be preoccupied, be abstracted, stare into space, be in cloud cuckoo land; muse. ❹ *I wouldn't dream of being late* THINK, consider, contemplate, conceive.

▶ adjective *his dream home* IDEAL, perfect, fantasy.

■ **dream something up** THINK UP, invent, concoct, devise, hatch, contrive, create, work out, come up with; *informal* cook up.

dreamer ▶ noun FANTASIST, daydreamer; romantic, sentimentalist, idealist, wishful thinker, Don Quixote; Utopian, visionary.

– OPPOSITES realist.

dreamland ▶ noun ❶ *I drift off to dreamland* SLEEP; *humorous* the land of Nod. ❷ *they must be living in dreamland* THE LAND OF MAKE-BELIEVE, fairyland, cloud cuckoo land; paradise, Utopia, heaven, Shangri-La.

dreamlike ▶ adjective UNREAL, illusory, imaginary, unsubstantial, chimerical, ethereal, phantasmagorical, trance-like; surreal; nightmarish, Kafkaesque; hazy, shadowy, faint, indistinct, unclear; *poetic/literary* illusive.

dreamy ▶ adjective ❶ *a dreamy expression* DAYDREAMING, dreaming; pensive, thoughtful, reflective, meditative, ruminative; lost in thought, preoccupied, distracted, rapt, inattentive, wool-gathering, vague, absorbed, absent-minded, with one's head in the clouds, in a world of one's own; *informal* miles away. ❷ *he was dreamy as a child* IDEALISTIC, romantic, starry-eyed, impractical, unrealistic, Utopian, quixotic; *Brit. informal* airy-fairy. ❸ *a dreamy recollection* DREAMLIKE, vague, dim,

hazy, shadowy, faint, indistinct, unclear. ❹ (*informal*) *the prince was really dreamy* ATTRACTIVE, handsome, good-looking; appealing, lovely, delightful; *informal* heavenly, divine, gorgeous, hot, cute.
– OPPOSITES alert, practical, clear, ugly.

dreary ▶ **adjective** ❶ *a dreary day at school* DULL, drab, uninteresting, flat, tedious, wearisome, boring, unexciting, unstimulating, uninspiring, soul-destroying; humdrum, monotonous, uneventful, unremarkable, featureless. ❷ *she thought of dreary things* SAD, miserable, depressing, gloomy, sombre, grave, mournful, melancholic, joyless, cheerless. ❸ *a dreary day* GLOOMY, dismal, dull, dark, dingy, murky, overcast; depressing, sombre.
– OPPOSITES exciting, cheerful, bright.

dregs ▶ **plural noun** ❶ *the dregs from a bottle of wine* SEDIMENT, deposit, residue, accumulation, sludge, lees, grounds, settlings; remains; *technical* residuum; *archaic* grouts. ❷ *the dregs of humanity* SCUM, refuse, riff-raff, outcasts, deadbeats; the underclass, the untouchables, the lowest of the low, the great unwashed, the hoi polloi; *informal* trash, dossers.

drench ▶ **verb** SOAK, saturate, wet through, permeate, douse, souse; drown, swamp, inundate, flood; steep, bathe.

dress ▶ **verb** ❶ *he dressed quickly* PUT ON CLOTHES, clothe oneself, get dressed. ❷ *she was dressed in a suit* CLOTHE, attire, garb, deck out, trick out/up, costume, array, robe; *informal* get up, doll up; *archaic* apparel. ❸ *they dress for dinner every day* WEAR FORMAL CLOTHES, wear evening dress, dress up. ❹ *she enjoyed dressing the tree* DECORATE, trim, deck, adorn, ornament, embellish, beautify, prettify; festoon, garland, garnish. ❺ *they dressed his wounds* BANDAGE, cover, bind, wrap, swathe. ❻ *she had to dress the chickens* PREPARE, get ready; clean. ❼ *the field was dressed with manure* FERTILIZE, enrich, manure, mulch, compost, top-dress. ❽ *he dressed Michelle's hair* STYLE, groom, arrange, do; comb, brush; preen, primp; *informal* fix. ❾ (*Military*) *the battalion dressed its ranks* LINE UP, align, straighten, arrange, order, dispose; fall in.
▶ **noun** ❶ *a long blue dress* FROCK, gown, robe, shift. ❷ *full evening dress* CLOTHES, clothing, garments, attire; costume, outfit, ensemble, garb, turnout; *informal* gear, get-up, togs, duds, glad rags; *Brit. informal* clobber; *N. Amer. informal* threads; *formal* apparel; *archaic* raiment.
– RELATED TERMS sartorial.
■ **dress down** DRESS INFORMALLY, dress casually; *informal* slob around.
■ **dress someone down** (*informal*). *See* REPRIMAND verb.
■ **dress up** ❶ *Angela loved dressing up* DRESS SMARTLY, dress formally, wear evening dress; *informal* doll oneself up, put on one's glad rags. ❷ *Hugh dressed up as Santa Claus* DISGUISE ONESELF, dress; put on fancy dress, put on a costume.
■ **dress something up** PRESENT, represent, portray, depict, characterize; embellish, enhance, touch up, embroider.

dressing ▶ **noun** ❶ *salad dressing* SAUCE, relish, condiment, dip. ❷ *they put fresh dressings on her burns* BANDAGE, covering, plaster, gauze, lint, compress. ❸ *a soil dressing* FERTILIZER, mulch; manure, compost, dung, bonemeal, fishmeal, guano; top-dressing.

dressmaker ▶ **noun** TAILOR, seamstress, needlewoman; outfitter, costumier, clothier; couturier, designer; *dated* modiste.
– RELATED TERMS sartorial.

dressy ▶ **adjective** SMART, formal; elaborate, ornate; stylish, elegant, chic, fashionable; *informal* snappy, snazzy, natty, trendy.
– OPPOSITES casual.

dribble ▶ **verb** ❶ *the baby started to dribble* DROOL, slaver, slobber, salivate, drivel, water at the mouth; *Scottish & Irish* slabber. ❷ *rainwater dribbled down her face* TRICKLE, drip, fall, drizzle; ooze, seep.
▶ **noun** ❶ *there was dribble on his chin* SALIVA, spittle, spit, slaver, slobber, drool. ❷ *a dribble of sweat* TRICKLE, drip, driblet, stream, drizzle; drop, splash.

dried ▶ **adjective** DEHYDRATED, desiccated, dry, dried up, moistureless.

drift ▶ **verb** ❶ *his raft drifted down the river* BE CARRIED, be borne; float, bob, waft, meander. ❷ *the guests drifted away* WANDER, meander, stray, potter, dawdle; *Brit. informal* mooch. ❸ *don't allow your attention to drift* STRAY, digress, deviate, diverge, veer, get sidetracked. ❹ *snow drifted over the path* PILE UP, bank up, heap up, accumulate, gather, amass.
▶ **noun** ❶ *a drift from the country to urban areas* MOVEMENT, shift, flow, transfer, relocation, gravitation. ❷ *the pilot had not noticed any drift* DEVIATION, digression. ❸ *he caught the drift of her thoughts* GIST, essence, meaning, sense, substance, significance; thrust, import, tenor; implication, intention; direction, course. ❹ *a drift of deep snow* PILE, heap, bank, mound, mass, accumulation.

drifter ▶ **noun** WANDERER, traveller, transient, roamer, tramp, vagabond, vagrant; *N. Amer.* hobo.

drill ▶ **noun** ❶ *a hydraulic drill* DRILLING TOOL, boring tool, auger, (brace and) bit, gimlet, awl, bradawl. ❷ *they learned military discipline and drill* TRAINING, instruction, coaching, teaching; (physical) exercises, workout; *informal* square-bashing. ❸ *Estelle knew the drill* PROCEDURE, routine, practice, regimen, programme, schedule; method, system.
▶ **verb** ❶ *drill the piece of wood* BORE A HOLE IN, make a hole in; bore, pierce, puncture, perforate. ❷ *a sergeant drilling new recruits* TRAIN, instruct,

coach, teach, discipline; exercise, put someone through their paces. ❸ *his mother had drilled politeness into him* INSTIL, hammer, drive, drum, din, implant, ingrain; teach, indoctrinate, brainwash.

drink ▶ **verb** ❶ *she drank her coffee* SWALLOW, gulp down, quaff, guzzle, sup; imbibe, sip, consume; drain, toss off, slug; *informal* swig, down, knock back, put away, neck, sink, swill. ❷ *he never drank* DRINK ALCOHOL, tipple, indulge; carouse; *informal* hit the bottle, booze, knock a few back, have one over the eight, get tanked up, go on a bender; *Brit. informal* bevvy; *N. Amer. informal* bend one's elbow. ❸ *let's drink to success* TOAST, salute.

▶ **noun** ❶ *he took a sip of his drink* BEVERAGE, liquid refreshment; dram, bracer, nightcap, nip, tot; pint; *Brit. informal* bevvy; *humorous* libation; *archaic* potation. ❷ *she turned to drink* ALCOHOL, (intoxicating) liquor, alcoholic drink; *informal* booze, hooch, the hard stuff, firewater, rotgut, moonshine, the bottle, the sauce, grog, Dutch courage. ❸ *she took a drink of her wine* SWALLOW, gulp, sip, draught, slug; *informal* swig, swill. ❹ *a drink of orange juice* GLASS, cup, mug. ❺ (*informal*) *he fell into the drink* THE SEA, the ocean, the water; *informal* the briny, Davy Jones's locker; *poetic/literary* the deep.

■ **drink something in** ABSORB, assimilate, digest, ingest, take in; be rapt in, be lost in, be fascinated by, pay close attention to.

drinkable ▶ **adjective** FIT TO DRINK, palatable; pure, clean, safe, unpolluted, untainted, uncontaminated; *formal* potable.

drinker ▶ **noun** DRUNKARD, drunk, inebriate, imbiber, tippler, sot; alcoholic, dipsomaniac, alcohol-abuser; *informal* boozer, soak, lush, wino, alky, sponge, barfly; *Austral./NZ informal* hophead; *archaic* toper.
– OPPOSITES teetotaller.

drip ▶ **verb** ❶ *there was a tap dripping* DRIBBLE, drop, leak. ❷ *sweat dripped from his chin* DROP, dribble, trickle, drizzle, run, splash, plop; leak, emanate, issue.

▶ **noun** ❶ *a bucket to catch the drips* DROP, dribble, spot, trickle, splash. ❷ (*informal*) *that drip who fancies you* WEAKLING, ninny, milksop, namby-pamby, crybaby, softie, doormat; *informal* wimp, weed, sissy, wuss; *Brit. informal* wet, big girl's blouse; *N. Amer. informal* candy-ass, pantywaist, pussy.

drive ▶ **verb** ❶ *I can't drive a car* OPERATE, handle, manage; pilot, steer. ❷ *he drove to the police station* TRAVEL BY CAR, motor. ❸ *I'll drive you to the airport* CHAUFFEUR, run, give someone a lift, take, ferry, transport, convey, carry. ❹ *the engine drives the front wheels* POWER, propel, move, push. ❺ *he drove a nail into the boot* HAMMER, screw, ram, sink, plunge, thrust, propel, knock. ❻ *she drove her cattle to market* IMPEL, urge; herd, round-up, shepherd. ❼ *a desperate mother driven to crime* FORCE, compel, prompt, precipitate; oblige, coerce, pressure, goad, spur, prod. ❽ *he drove his staff extremely hard* WORK, push, tax, exert.

▶ **noun** ❶ *an afternoon drive* EXCURSION, outing, trip, jaunt, tour; ride, run, journey; *informal* spin. ❷ *the house has a long drive* DRIVEWAY, approach, access road. ❸ *sexual drive* URGE, appetite, desire, need; impulse, instinct. ❹ *she lacked the drive to succeed* MOTIVATION, ambition, single-mindedness, will power, dedication, doggedness, tenacity; enthusiasm, zeal, commitment, aggression, spirit; energy, vigour, verve, vitality, pep; *informal* get-up-and-go. ❺ *an anti-corruption drive* CAMPAIGN, crusade, movement, effort, push, appeal. ❻ (*Brit.*) *a whist drive* TOURNAMENT, competition, contest, event, match.

■ **drive at** SUGGEST, imply, hint at, allude to, intimate, insinuate, indicate; refer to, mean, intend; *informal* get at.

drivel ▶ **noun** *he was talking complete drivel* NONSENSE, twaddle, claptrap, balderdash, gibberish, rubbish, mumbo-jumbo; *N. Amer.* garbage; *informal* rot, poppycock, phooey, piffle, tripe, bosh, bull, hogwash, baloney; *Brit. informal* cobblers, codswallop, waffle, tosh, double Dutch; *N. Amer. informal* flapdoodle, bushwa; *informal, dated* tommyrot, bunkum.

▶ **verb** *you always drivel on* TALK NONSENSE, talk rubbish, babble, ramble, gibber, blather, blether, prattle, gabble; *Brit. informal* waffle, witter.

driver ▶ **verb** MOTORIST, chauffeur; pilot, operator.

drizzle ▶ **noun** ❶ *they shivered in the drizzle* FINE RAIN, light shower, spray; *N. English* mizzle. ❷ *a drizzle of sour cream* TRICKLE, dribble, drip, stream, rivulet; sprinkle, sprinkling.

▶ **verb** ❶ *it's beginning to drizzle* RAIN LIGHTLY, shower, spot; *Brit.* spit; *N. English* mizzle; *N. Amer.* sprinkle. ❷ *drizzle the cream over the jelly* TRICKLE, drip, dribble, pour, splash, sprinkle.

droll ▶ **adjective** FUNNY, humorous, amusing, comic, comical, mirthful, hilarious; clownish, farcical, zany, quirky; jocular, light-hearted, facetious, witty, whimsical, wry, tongue-in-cheek; *informal* waggish, wacky, side-splitting, rib-tickling.
– OPPOSITES serious.

drone ▶ **verb** ❶ *a plane droned overhead* HUM, buzz, whirr, vibrate, murmur, rumble, purr. ❷ *he droned on about right and wrong* SPEAK BORINGLY, go on and on, talk at length; intone, pontificate; *informal* spout, sound off, jaw, spiel, speechify.

▶ **noun** ❶ *the drone of aircraft taking off* HUM, buzz, whirr, vibration, murmur, purr. ❷ *drones supported by tax-payers' money* HANGER-ON, parasite, leech, passenger; idler, loafer, layabout, good-for-nothing, do-nothing; *informal* lazybones, scrounger, sponger, cadger, freeloader, bloodsucker, waster, slacker.

drool ▶ **verb** *his mouth was drooling* SALIVATE, dribble, slaver, slobber; *Scottish & Irish* slabber.
▶ **noun** *a fine trickle of drool* SALIVA, spit, spittle, dribble, slaver, slobber.

droop ▶ **verb** ❶ *the dog's tail is drooping* HANG (DOWN), dangle, sag, flop; wilt, sink, slump, drop, drape. ❷ *his eyelids were drooping* CLOSE, shut, fall. ❸ *the news made her droop* BE DESPONDENT, lose heart, give up hope, become dispirited, become dejected; flag, languish, wilt.

droopy ▶ **adjective** HANGING (DOWN), dangling, falling, dropping, draped; bent, bowed, stooping; sagging, flopping, wilting.

drop ▶ **verb** ❶ *Eric dropped the box* LET FALL, let go of, lose one's grip on; release, unhand, relinquish. ❷ *water drops from the cave roof* DRIP, fall, dribble, trickle, run, plop, leak. ❸ *a plane dropped out of the sky* FALL, descend, plunge, plummet, dive, nosedive, tumble, pitch. ❹ *she dropped to her knees* FALL, sink, collapse, slump, tumble. ❺ (*informal*) *I was dropping with exhaustion* COLLAPSE, faint, pass out, black out, swoon, keel over; *informal* flake out, conk out. ❻ *the track dropped from the ridge* SLOPE DOWNWARDS, slant downwards, descend, go down, fall away, sink, dip. ❼ *the exchange rate dropped* DECREASE, lessen, reduce, diminish, depreciate; fall, decline, dwindle, sink, slump, plunge, plummet. ❽ *pupils can drop history if they wish* GIVE UP, finish with, withdraw from; discontinue, end, stop, cease, halt; abandon, forgo, relinquish, dispense with, have done with; *informal* pack in, quit. ❾ *he was dropped from the team* EXCLUDE, discard, expel, oust, throw out, leave out; dismiss, discharge, let go; *informal* boot out, kick out, turf out. ❿ *he dropped his unsuitable friends* ABANDON, desert, throw over; renounce, disown, turn one's back on, wash one's hands of; reject, give up, cast off; neglect, shun; *poetic/literary* forsake. ⓫ *he dropped all reference to compensation* OMIT, leave out, eliminate, take out, miss out, delete, cut, erase. ⓬ *the taxi dropped her off* DELIVER, bring, take, convey, carry, transport; leave, unload. ⓭ *drop the gun on the ground* PUT, place, deposit, set, lay, leave; *informal* pop, plonk. ⓮ *she dropped names* MENTION, refer to, hint at; bring up, raise, broach, introduce; show off. ⓯ *the team has yet to drop a point* LOSE, concede, give away.
– OPPOSITES lift, rise, increase, keep, win.
▶ **noun** ❶ *a drop of water* DROPLET, blob, globule, bead, bubble, tear, dot; *informal* glob. ❷ *it needs a drop of oil* SMALL AMOUNT, little, bit, dash, spot; dribble, driblet, sprinkle, trickle, splash; dab, speck, smattering, sprinkling, modicum; *informal* smidgen, tad. ❸ *an acid drop* SWEET, lozenge, pastille, bonbon; *N. Amer.* candy. ❹ *a small drop in profits* DECREASE, reduction, decline, fall-off, downturn, slump; cut, cutback, curtailment; depreciation. ❺ *I walked to the edge of the drop* CLIFF, abyss, chasm, gorge, gully, precipice; slope, descent, incline. ❻ *the hangman measured her for the drop* HANGING, gibbeting; execution; *informal* stringing up.
– OPPOSITES increase.
■ **drop back/behind** FALL BACK/BEHIND, get left behind, lag behind; straggle, linger, dawdle, dally, hang back, loiter, bring/take up the rear; *informal* dilly-dally.
■ **drop off** ❶ *trade dropped off sharply. See* DROP verb sense 7. ❷ *she kept dropping off* FALL ASLEEP, doze (off), nap, catnap, drowse; *informal* nod off, drift off, snooze, take forty winks.
■ **drop out of** *he dropped out of his studies. See* DROP verb sense 8.

dropout ▶ **noun** NONCONFORMIST, hippy, beatnik, bohemian, free spirit, rebel; idler, layabout, loafer; *informal* oddball, deadbeat, waster.

droppings ▶ **plural noun** EXCREMENT, excreta, faeces, stools, dung, ordure, manure; *informal* pooh.

dross ▶ **noun** RUBBISH, junk; debris, chaff, detritus, flotsam and jetsam; *N. Amer.* garbage, trash; *informal* dreck.

drought ▶ **noun** DRY SPELL, lack of rain, shortage of water.

drove ▶ **noun** ❶ *a drove of cattle* HERD, flock, pack. ❷ *they came in droves* CROWD, swarm, horde, multitude, mob, throng, host, mass, army, herd.

drown ▶ **verb** ❶ *he nearly drowned* SUFFOCATE IN WATER, inhale water; go to a watery grave. ❷ *the valleys were drowned* FLOOD, submerge, immerse, inundate, deluge, swamp, engulf. ❸ *his voice was drowned out by the footsteps* MAKE INAUDIBLE, overpower, overwhelm, override; muffle, deaden, stifle, extinguish.

drowse ▶ **verb** *they like to drowse in the sun* DOZE, nap, catnap, rest; *informal* snooze, get forty winks, get some shut-eye; *Brit. informal* kip; *N. Amer. informal* catch some Zs.
▶ **noun** *she had been woken from her drowse* DOZE, light sleep, nap, catnap, rest; *informal* snooze, forty winks, shut-eye; *Brit. informal* kip.

drowsy ▶ **adjective** ❶ *the tablet made her drowsy* SLEEPY, dozy, heavy-eyed, groggy, somnolent; tired, weary, fatigued, exhausted, yawning, nodding; lethargic, sluggish, torpid, listless, languid; *informal* snoozy, dopey, yawny, dead beat, all in, dog-tired; *Brit. informal* knackered. ❷ *a drowsy afternoon* SOPORIFIC, sleep-inducing, sleepy, somniferous; narcotic, sedative, tranquillizing; lulling, soothing.
– OPPOSITES alert, invigorating.

drubbing ▶ **noun** ❶ *I gave him a good drubbing* BEATING, thrashing, walloping, thumping, battering, pounding, pummelling, slapping, punching, pelting; *informal* hammering, licking, clobbering, belting, bashing, pasting, tanning, hiding, kicking. ❷ (*informal*) *Scotland's 3-0 drubbing by France. See* DEFEAT noun sense 1.

drudge ▶ **noun** *a household drudge* MENIAL WORKER, slave, lackey, servant, labourer, worker, maid/man of all work; *informal* dogsbody, gofer, runner; *Brit. informal* skivvy; *Brit. dated* charwoman, charlady, char.
▶ **verb** (*archaic*) *he drudged in the fields. See* TOIL verb sense 1.

drudgery ▶ **noun** HARD WORK, menial work, donkey work, toil, labour; chores; *informal* skivvying; *Brit. informal* graft; *Austral./NZ informal* (hard) yakka.

drug ▶ **noun** ❶ *drugs prescribed by doctors* MEDICINE, medication, medicament; remedy, cure, antidote. ❷ *she was under the influence of drugs* NARCOTIC, stimulant, hallucinogen; *informal* dope, gear, downer, upper.
▶ **verb** ❶ *he was drugged* ANAESTHETIZE, narcotize; poison; knock out, stupefy; *informal* dope. ❷ *she drugged his coffee* ADD DRUGS TO, tamper with, adulterate, contaminate, lace, poison; *informal* dope, spike, doctor.

drugged ▶ **adjective** STUPEFIED, insensible, befuddled; delirious, hallucinating, narcotized; anaesthetized, knocked out; *informal* stoned, high (as a kite), doped, tripping, spaced out, wasted, wrecked, off one's head.
– OPPOSITES sober.

drum ▶ **noun** ❶ *the beat of a drum* percussion instrument; bongo, tom-tom, snare drum, kettledrum; *historical* tambour. ❷ *the steady drum of raindrops* BEAT, rhythm, patter, tap, pounding, thump, thud, rattle, pitter-patter, pit-a-pat, rat-a-tat, thrum. ❸ *a drum of radioactive waste* CANISTER, barrel, cylinder, tank, bin, can; container.
▶ **verb** ❶ *she drummed her fingers on the desk* TAP, beat, rap, thud, thump; tattoo, thrum. ❷ *the rules were drummed into us at school* INSTIL, drive, din, hammer, drill, drub, implant, ingrain, inculcate.
■ **drum someone out** EXPEL, dismiss, throw out, oust; drive out, get rid of; exclude, banish; *informal* give someone the boot, boot out, kick out, give someone their marching orders, give someone the push, show someone the door, send packing; *Military* cashier.
■ **drum something up** ROUND UP, gather, collect; summon, attract; canvass, solicit, petition.

drunk ▶ **adjective** INTOXICATED, inebriated, drunken, incapable, tipsy, the worse for drink, under the influence; *informal* tight, merry, in one's cups, three sheets to the wind, pie-eyed, plastered, smashed, wrecked, wasted, sloshed, soused, sozzled, blotto, stewed, pickled, tanked (up), off one's face, out of one's head, ratted; *Brit. informal* legless, bevvied, paralytic, Brahms and Liszt, half cut, out of it, bladdered, trolleyed, squiffy, tiddly; *N. Amer. informal* loaded, trashed, juiced, sauced, out of one's gourd, in the bag, zoned; *euphemistic* tired and emotional; *informal, dated* lit up.
– OPPOSITES sober.
▶ **noun** DRUNKARD, inebriate, drinker, tippler, imbiber, sot; heavy drinker, problem drinker, alcoholic, dipsomaniac; *informal* boozer, soak, lush, wino, alky, sponge, barfly, tosspot; *Austral./NZ informal* hophead, metho; *archaic* toper.
– OPPOSITES teetotaller.

drunken ▶ **adjective** ❶ *a drunken driver. See* DRUNK adjective. ❷ *a drunken all-night party* DEBAUCHED, dissipated, carousing, roistering, intemperate, unrestrained, uninhibited, abandoned; bacchanalian, bacchic; *informal* boozy.

drunkenness ▶ **noun** INTOXICATION, inebriation, insobriety, tipsiness; intemperance, overindulgence, debauchery; heavy drinking, alcoholism, alcohol abuse, dipsomania.

dry ▶ **adjective** ❶ *the dry desert* ARID, parched, droughty, scorched, baked; waterless, moistureless, rainless; dehydrated, desiccated, thirsty, bone dry. ❷ *dry leaves* PARCHED, dried, withered, shrivelled, wilted, wizened; crisp, crispy, brittle; dehydrated, desiccated. ❸ *the hamburgers were dry* HARD, stale, old, past its best; off. ❹ *a dry well* WATERLESS, empty. ❺ *I'm really dry* THIRSTY, dehydrated; *informal* parched, gasping. ❻ *it was dry work* THIRSTY, thirst-making; hot; strenuous, arduous. ❼ *dry toast* UNBUTTERED, butterless, plain. ❽ *the dry facts* BARE, simple, basic, fundamental, stark, bald, hard, straightforward. ❾ *a dry debate* DULL, uninteresting, boring, unexciting, tedious, tiresome, wearisome, dreary, monotonous; unimaginative, sterile, flat, bland, lacklustre, stodgy, prosaic, humdrum, mundane; *informal* deadly. ❿ *a dry sense of humour* WRY, subtle, laconic, sharp; ironic, sardonic, sarcastic, cynical; satirical, mocking, droll; *informal* waggish; *Brit. informal* sarky. ⓫ *a dry response to his cordial advance* UNEMOTIONAL, indifferent, impassive, cool, cold, emotionless; reserved, restrained, impersonal, formal, stiff, wooden. ⓬ *this is a dry state* TEETOTAL, prohibitionist, alcohol-free, non-drinking, abstinent, sober; *informal* on the wagon. ⓭ *dry white wine* CRISP, sharp, piquant, tart, bitter.
– OPPOSITES wet, moist, fresh, lively, emotional, sweet.
▶ **verb** ❶ *the sun dried the ground* PARCH, scorch, bake; dehydrate, desiccate, dehumidify. ❷ *dry the leaves completely* DEHYDRATE, desiccate; wither, shrivel. ❸ *he dried the dishes* TOWEL, rub; mop up, blot up, soak up, absorb. ❹ *she dried her eyes* WIPE, rub, dab. ❺ *methods of drying meat* DESICCATE, dehydrate; preserve, cure, smoke.
– OPPOSITES moisten.
■ **dry out** GIVE UP DRINKING, give up alcohol, become teetotal, take the pledge; *informal* go on the wagon.
■ **dry up** ❶ (*informal*) *he dried up and didn't say another thing* STOP SPEAKING, stop talking, fall silent, shut up; forget one's words. ❷ *investment may dry up* DWINDLE, subside, peter out,

wane, taper off, ebb, come to a halt/end, run out, give out, disappear, vanish.

dual ▶ **adjective** DOUBLE, twofold, binary; duplicate, twin, matching, paired, coupled.
– OPPOSITES single.

dub ▶ **verb** ❶ *he was dubbed 'the world's sexiest man'* NICKNAME, call, name, label, christen, term, tag, entitle, style; designate, characterize, nominate; *formal* denominate. ❷ *she dubbed a new knight* KNIGHT, invest.

dubiety ▶ **noun** (*formal*) DOUBTFULNESS, uncertainty, unsureness, incertitude; ambiguity, ambivalence, confusion; hesitancy, doubt.

dubious ▶ **adjective** ❶ *I was rather dubious about the idea* DOUBTFUL, uncertain, unsure, hesitant; undecided, indefinite, unresolved, up in the air; vacillating, irresolute; sceptical, suspicious; *informal* iffy. ❷ *a dubious businessman* SUSPICIOUS, suspect, untrustworthy, unreliable, questionable; *informal* shady, fishy; *Brit. informal* dodgy.
– OPPOSITES certain, trustworthy.

duck ▶ **verb** ❶ *he ducked behind the wall* BOB DOWN, bend (down), stoop (down), crouch (down), squat (down), hunch down, hunker down; cower, cringe. ❷ *she was ducked in the river* DIP, dunk, plunge, immerse, submerge, lower, sink. ❸ (*informal*) *they cannot duck the issue forever* SHIRK, dodge, evade, avoid, elude, escape, back out of, shun, eschew, sidestep, bypass, circumvent; *informal* cop out of, get out of, wriggle out of, funk; *Austral./NZ informal* duck-shove.

duct ▶ **noun** TUBE, channel, canal, vessel; conduit, culvert; pipe, pipeline, outlet, inlet, flue, shaft, vent; *Anatomy* ductus, ductule.

ductile ▶ **adjective** ❶ *ductile metals* PLIABLE, pliant, flexible, supple, plastic, tensile; soft, malleable, workable, bendable; *informal* bendy. ❷ *a way to make people ductile* DOCILE, obedient, submissive, meek, mild, lamblike; willing, accommodating, amenable, cooperative, compliant, malleable, tractable, biddable, persuadable.
– OPPOSITES brittle, intransigent.

dud (*informal*) ▶ **noun** *their new product is a dud* FAILURE, flop, let-down, disappointment; *Brit.* damp squib; *informal* washout, lemon, no-hoper, non-starter, dead loss, lead balloon; *N. Amer. informal* clinker.
– OPPOSITES success.
▶ **adjective** ❶ *a dud typewriter* DEFECTIVE, faulty, unsound, inoperative, broken, malfunctioning; *informal* bust, busted, kaput, conked out; *Brit. informal* duff, knackered. ❷ *a dud £50 note* COUNTERFEIT, fraudulent, forged, fake, faked, false, bogus; invalid, worthless; *informal* phoney.
– OPPOSITES sound, genuine.

dudgeon
■ **in high dudgeon** INDIGNANTLY, resentfully, angrily, furiously; in a temper, in anger, with displeasure; *informal* in a huff, in a paddy, as cross as two sticks, seeing red; *Brit. informal, dated* in a bate, in a wax.

due ▶ **adjective** ❶ *their fees were due* OWING, owed, payable; outstanding, overdue, unpaid, unsettled, undischarged; *N. Amer.* delinquent. ❷ *the chancellor's statement is due today* EXPECTED, anticipated, scheduled for, awaited; required. ❸ *the respect due to a great artist* DESERVED BY, merited by, warranted by; appropriate to, fit for, fitting for, right for, proper to. ❹ *he drove without due care* PROPER, correct, rightful, suitable, appropriate, apt; adequate, sufficient, enough, satisfactory, requisite.
▶ **noun** ❶ *he attracts more criticism than is his due* RIGHTFUL TREATMENT, fair treatment, just punishment; right, entitlement; just deserts; *informal* comeuppance. ❷ *members have paid their dues* FEE, subscription, charge; payment, contribution.
▶ **adverb** *he hiked due north* DIRECTLY, straight, exactly, precisely, dead.
■ **due to** ❶ *her death was due to an infection* ATTRIBUTABLE TO, caused by, ascribed to, because of, put down to. ❷ *the train was cancelled due to staff shortages* BECAUSE OF, owing to, on account of, as a consequence of, as a result of, thanks to, in view of; *formal* by reason of.

duel ▶ **noun** ❶ *he was killed in a duel* MANO-A-MANO, single combat; fight, confrontation, head-to-head; *informal* face-off, shoot-out; *archaic* rencounter. ❷ *a snooker duel* CONTEST, match, game, meet, encounter.
▶ **verb** *they duelled with swords* FIGHT A DUEL, fight, battle, combat, contend.

duff ▶ **adjective** (*Brit. informal*). *See* BAD sense 1.

duffer ▶ **noun** (*informal*). *See* DUNCE.

dulcet ▶ **adjective** SWEET, soothing, mellow, honeyed, mellifluous, euphonious, pleasant, agreeable; melodious, melodic, lilting, lyrical, silvery, golden.
– OPPOSITES harsh.

dull ▶ **adjective** ❶ *a dull novel* UNINTERESTING, boring, tedious, monotonous, unrelieved, unvaried, unimaginative, uneventful; characterless, featureless, colourless, lifeless, insipid, unexciting, uninspiring, unstimulating, jejune, flat, bland, dry, stale, tired, banal, lacklustre, stodgy, dreary, humdrum, mundane; mind-numbing, soul-destroying, wearisome, tiring, tiresome, irksome; *informal* deadly, not up to much; *Brit. informal* samey; *N. Amer. informal* dullsville. ❷ *a dull morning* OVERCAST, cloudy, gloomy, dark, dismal, dreary, sombre, grey, murky, sunless. ❸ *dull colours* DRAB, dreary, sombre, dark, subdued, muted, lacklustre, faded, washed out, muddy. ❹ *a dull sound* MUFFLED, muted, quiet, soft, faint, indistinct; stifled, suppressed. ❺ *the chisel became dull* BLUNT, unsharpened, edgeless, worn down. ❻ *a rather dull child* UNINTELLIGENT, stupid, slow, witless, vacuous, empty-headed, brain-

less, mindless, foolish, idiotic; *informal* dense, dim, moronic, cretinous, half-witted, thick, dumb, dopey, dozy, bovine, slow on the uptake, wooden-headed, fat-headed. ❼ *her cold made her feel dull* SLUGGISH, lethargic, enervated, listless, languid, torpid, slow, sleepy, drowsy, weary, tired, fatigued; apathetic; *informal* dozy, dopey, yawny.
– OPPOSITES interesting, bright, loud, resonant, sharp, clever.
▶ **verb** ❶ *the pain was dulled by drugs* LESSEN, decrease, diminish, reduce, dampen, blunt, deaden, allay, ease, soothe, assuage, alleviate. ❷ *sleep dulled her mind* NUMB, benumb, deaden, desensitize, stupefy, daze. ❸ *the leaves are dulled by mildew* FADE, bleach, decolorize, decolour, etiolate. ❹ *rain dulled the sky* DARKEN, blacken, dim, veil, obscure, shadow, fog. ❺ *the sombre atmosphere dulled her spirit* DAMPEN, lower, depress, crush, sap, extinguish, smother, stifle.
– OPPOSITES intensify, enliven, enhance, brighten.

dullard ▶ **noun** IDIOT, fool, stupid person, simpleton, ignoramus, oaf, dunce, dolt; *informal* duffer, moron, cretin, imbecile, nincompoop, dope, chump, nitwit, dimwit, birdbrain, pea-brain, numbskull, fathead, dumbo, dumdum, donkey; *Brit. informal* wally, berk, divvy; *N. Amer. informal* doofus, goof, bozo, dummy; *Austral./NZ informal* galah.

duly ▶ **adverb** ❶ *the document was duly signed* PROPERLY, correctly, appropriately, suitably, fittingly. ❷ *he duly arrived to collect Alice* AT THE RIGHT TIME, on time, punctually.

dumb ▶ **adjective** ❶ *she stood dumb while he shouted* MUTE, speechless, tongue-tied, silent, at a loss for words; taciturn, uncommunicative, untalkative, tight-lipped, close-mouthed; *informal* mum. ❷ (*informal*) *he is not as dumb as you'd think* STUPID, unintelligent, ignorant, dense, brainless, mindless, foolish, slow, dull, simple, empty-headed, vacuous, vapid, idiotic, half-baked, imbecilic, bovine; *informal* thick, dim, moronic, cretinous, dopey, dozy, thick-headed, wooden-headed, fat-headed, bird-brained, pea-brained; *Brit. informal* daft.
– OPPOSITES clever.

dumbfound ▶ **verb** ASTONISH, astound, amaze, stagger, surprise, startle, stun, confound, stupefy, daze, nonplus, take aback, stop someone in their tracks, strike dumb, leave open-mouthed, leave aghast; *informal* flabbergast, floor, knock sideways, bowl over; *Brit. informal* knock for six.

dumbfounded ▶ **adjective** ASTONISHED, astounded, amazed, staggered, surprised, startled, stunned, confounded, nonplussed, stupefied, dazed, dumbstruck, open-mouthed, speechless, thunderstruck; taken aback, disconcerted; *informal* flabbergasted, flummoxed; *Brit. informal* gobsmacked.

dummy ▶ **noun** ❶ *a shop-window dummy* MANNEQUIN, model, figure. ❷ *the book is just a dummy* MOCK-UP, imitation, likeness, lookalike, representation, substitute, sample; replica, reproduction; counterfeit, sham, fake, forgery; *informal* dupe. ❸ (*informal*) *you're a dummy. See* IDIOT.
▶ **adjective** *a dummy attack on the airfield* SIMULATED, feigned, pretended, practice, trial, mock, make-believe; *informal* pretend, phoney.
– OPPOSITES real.

dump ▶ **noun** ❶ *take the rubbish to the dump* TIP, rubbish dump, rubbish heap, dumping ground; dustheap, slag heap. ❷ (*informal*) *the house is a dump* HOVEL, shack, slum; mess; *informal* hole, pigsty.
▶ **verb** ❶ *he dumped his bag on the table* PUT DOWN, set down, deposit, place, shove, unload; drop, throw down; *informal* stick, park, plonk; *Brit. informal* bung; *N. Amer. informal* plunk. ❷ *they will dump asbestos at the site* DISPOSE OF, get rid of, throw away/out, discard, bin, jettison; *informal* ditch, junk. ❸ (*informal*) *he dumped her* ABANDON, desert, leave, jilt, break up with, finish with, throw over; *informal* walk out on, rat on, drop, ditch, chuck, give someone the elbow; *Brit. informal* give someone the big E.

dumps
■ **down in the dumps** (*informal*) UNHAPPY, sad, depressed, gloomy, glum, melancholy, miserable, dejected, despondent, dispirited, downhearted, downcast, down, low, heavy-hearted, dismal, desolate; tearful, upset; *informal* blue, down in the mouth, fed up.

dumpy ▶ **adjective** SHORT, squat, stubby; PLUMP, stout, chubby, chunky, portly, fat, bulky; *informal* tubby, roly-poly, pudgy, porky; *Brit. informal* podgy.
– OPPOSITES tall, slender.

dun[1] ▶ **adjective** *a dun cow* GREYISH-BROWN, brownish, mousy, muddy, khaki, umber.

dun[2] ▶ **verb** *you can't dun me for her debts* IMPORTUNE, press, plague, pester, nag, harass, hound, badger; *informal* hassle, bug; *N. English informal* mither.

dunce ▶ **noun** FOOL, idiot, stupid person, simpleton, ignoramus, dullard; *informal* dummy, dumbo, clot, thickhead, nitwit, dimwit, halfwit, moron, cretin, imbecile, dope, duffer, booby, chump, numbskull, nincompoop, fathead, airhead, birdbrain, pea-brain, ninny, ass; *Brit. informal* wally, berk, divvy; *N. Amer. informal* doofus, goof, schmuck, bozo, lummox; *Austral./NZ informal* galah.
– OPPOSITES genius.

dune ▶ **noun** BANK, mound, hillock, hummock, knoll, ridge, heap, drift.

dung ▶ **noun** MANURE, muck; excrement, faeces, droppings, ordure, cowpats.

dungeon ▶ **noun** UNDERGROUND PRISON, oubliette; cell, jail, lock-up.

dupe ▶ **verb** *they were duped by a con man* DECEIVE, trick, hoodwink, hoax, swindle, defraud, cheat, double-cross; gull, mislead, take in, fool, inveigle; *informal* con, do, rip off, diddle, shaft, bilk, rook, pull the wool over someone's eyes, pull a fast one on, sell a pup to; *N. Amer. informal* sucker, snooker; *Austral. informal* pull a swifty on.

▶ **noun** *an innocent dupe in her game* VICTIM, gull, pawn, puppet, instrument; fool, innocent; *informal* sucker, stooge, sitting duck, muggins, fall guy; *Brit. informal* mug; *N. Amer. informal* pigeon, patsy, sap.

duplicate ▶ **noun** *a duplicate of the invoice* COPY, carbon copy, photocopy, facsimile, mimeograph, reprint; replica, reproduction, clone; *informal* dupe; *trademark* Xerox, photostat.

▶ **adjective** *duplicate keys* MATCHING, identical, twin, corresponding, equivalent.

▶ **verb** ❶ *she will duplicate the newsletter* COPY, photocopy, photostat, xerox, mimeograph, reproduce, replicate, reprint, run off. ❷ *a feat difficult to duplicate* REPEAT, do again, redo, replicate.

duplicity ▶ **noun** DECEITFULNESS, deceit, deception, double-dealing, underhandedness, dishonesty, fraud, fraudulence, sharp practice, chicanery, trickery, subterfuge, skulduggery, treachery; *informal* crookedness, shadiness, dirty tricks, shenanigans, monkey business; *poetic/literary* perfidy.
– OPPOSITES honesty.

durability ▶ **noun** IMPERISHABILITY, durableness, longevity; resilience, strength, sturdiness, toughness, robustness.
– OPPOSITES fragility.

durable ▶ **adjective** ❶ *durable carpets* HARD-WEARING, long-lasting, heavy-duty, tough, resistant, imperishable, indestructible, strong, sturdy. ❷ *a durable peace* LASTING, long-lasting, long-term, enduring, persistent, abiding; stable, secure, firm, deep-rooted, permanent, undying, everlasting.
– OPPOSITES delicate, short-lived.

duration ▶ **noun** FULL LENGTH, time, time span, time scale, period, term, span, fullness, length, extent, continuation.

duress ▶ **noun** COERCION, compulsion, force, pressure, intimidation, constraint; threats; *informal* arm-twisting.

during ▶ **conjunction** THROUGHOUT, through, in, in the course of, for the time of.

dusk ▶ **noun** TWILIGHT, nightfall, sunset, sundown, evening, close of day; semi-darkness, gloom, murkiness; *poetic/literary* gloaming, eventide.
– OPPOSITES dawn.

dusky ▶ **adjective** ❶ *the dusky countryside* SHADOWY, dark, dim, gloomy, murky, shady; unlit, unilluminated; sunless, moonless. ❷ (*dated*) *a dusky maiden* DARK-SKINNED, dark, olive-skinned, swarthy, ebony, black; tanned, bronzed, brown.
– OPPOSITES bright, fair.

dust ▶ **noun** ❶ *the desk was covered in dust* DIRT, grime, filth, smut, soot; fine powder. ❷ *they fought in the dust* EARTH, soil, dirt; ground.

▶ **verb** ❶ *she dusted her mantelpiece* WIPE, clean, brush, sweep, mop. ❷ *dust the cake with icing sugar* SPRINKLE, scatter, powder, dredge, sift, cover, strew.

dust-up ▶ **noun** (*informal*). *See* SCRAP[2] noun.

dusty ▶ **adjective** ❶ *the floor was dusty* DIRTY, grimy, grubby, unclean, soiled, mucky, sooty; undusted; *informal* grungy, cruddy; *Brit. informal* grotty. ❷ *dusty sandstone* POWDERY, crumbly, chalky, friable; granular, gritty, sandy. ❸ *a dusty pink* MUTED, dull, faded, pale, pastel, subtle; greyish, darkish, dirty. ❹ (*Brit.*) *a dusty answer* CURT, abrupt, terse, brusque, blunt, short, sharp, tart, gruff, offhand; *informal* snippy, snappy.
– OPPOSITES clean, bright.

dutiful ▶ **adjective** CONSCIENTIOUS, responsible, dedicated, devoted, attentive; obedient, compliant, submissive, biddable; deferential, reverent, reverential, respectful, good.
– OPPOSITES remiss.

duty ▶ **noun** ❶ *she was free of any duty* RESPONSIBILITY, obligation, commitment; allegiance, loyalty, faithfulness, fidelity, homage. ❷ *it was his duty to attend the king* JOB, task, assignment, mission, function, charge, place, role, responsibility, obligation; *dated* office. ❸ *the duty was raised on alcohol* TAX, levy, tariff, excise, toll, fee, payment, rate; dues.

■ **off duty** NOT WORKING, at leisure, on holiday, on leave, off (work), free.

■ **on duty** WORKING, at work, busy, occupied, engaged; *informal* on the job, tied up.

dwarf ▶ **noun** ❶ PERSON OF RESTRICTED GROWTH, small person, short person; midget, pygmy, manikin, homunculus. ❷ *the wizard captured the dwarf* GNOME, goblin, hobgoblin, troll, imp, elf, brownie, leprechaun.

▶ **adjective** *dwarf conifers* MINIATURE, small, little, tiny, toy, pocket, diminutive, baby, pygmy, stunted, undersized, undersize; *Scottish* wee; *informal* mini, teeny, teeny-weeny, itsy-bitsy, tiddly, pint-sized; *Brit. informal* titchy; *N. Amer. informal* little-bitty.
– OPPOSITES giant.

▶ **verb** ❶ *the buildings dwarf the trees* DOMINATE, tower over, loom over, overshadow, overtop. ❷ *her progress was dwarfed by her sister's success* OVERSHADOW, outshine, surpass, exceed, outclass, outstrip, outdo, top, trump, transcend; diminish, minimize.

dwell ▶ **verb** (*formal*) *gypsies dwell in these caves* RESIDE, live, be settled, be housed, lodge, stay; *informal* put up; *formal* abide, be domiciled.

■ **dwell on** LINGER OVER, mull over, muse on,

brood about/over, think about; be preoccupied by, be obsessed by, eat one's heart out over; harp on about, discuss at length.

dwelling ▶ noun (*formal*) RESIDENCE, home, house, accommodation, lodging place; lodgings, quarters, rooms; *informal* place, pad, digs; *formal* abode, domicile, habitation.

dwindle ▶ verb ❶ *the population dwindled* DIMINISH, decrease, reduce, lessen, shrink; fall off, tail off, drop, fall, slump, plummet; disappear, vanish, die out; *informal* nosedive. ❷ *her career dwindled* DECLINE, deteriorate, fail, slip, slide, fade, go downhill, go to rack and ruin; *informal* go to pot, go to the dogs, hit the skids, go down the toilet; *Austral./NZ informal* go to the pack.
– OPPOSITES increase, flourish.

dye ▶ noun *a blue dye* COLOURANT, colouring, colour, dyestuff, pigment, tint, stain, wash.
▶ verb *the gloves were dyed* COLOUR, tint, pigment, stain, wash.

dyed-in-the-wool ▶ adjective INVETERATE, confirmed, entrenched, established, longstanding, deep-rooted, diehard; complete, absolute, thorough, thoroughgoing, out-and-out, true blue; firm, unshakeable, staunch, steadfast, committed, devoted, dedicated, loyal, unswerving; *N. Amer.* full-bore; *informal* deep-dyed, card-carrying.

dying ▶ adjective ❶ *his dying aunt* TERMINALLY ILL, at death's door, on one's deathbed, near death, fading fast, expiring, moribund, not long for this world, in extremis; *informal* on one's last legs, having one foot in the grave. ❷ *a dying art form* DECLINING, vanishing, fading, ebbing, waning; *informal* on the way out. ❸ *her dying words* FINAL, last; deathbed.
– OPPOSITES thriving, first.
▶ noun *he took her dying very hard* DEATH, demise, passing, loss of life, quietus; *formal* decease; *archaic* expiry.

dynamic ▶ adjective ENERGETIC, spirited, active, lively, zestful, vital, vigorous, forceful, powerful, positive; high-powered, aggressive, bold, enterprising; magnetic, passionate, fiery, high-octane; *informal* go-getting, peppy, full of get-up-and-go, full of vim and vigour, gutsy, spunky, feisty, go-ahead.
– OPPOSITES half-hearted.

dynamism ▶ noun ENERGY, spirit, liveliness, zestfulness, vitality, vigour, forcefulness, power, potency, positivity; aggression, drive, ambition, enterprise; magnetism, passion, fire; *informal* pep, get-up-and-go, vim and vigour, guts, feistiness.

dynasty ▶ noun BLOODLINE, line, ancestral line, lineage, house, family, ancestry, descent, succession, genealogy, family tree; regime, rule, reign, empire, sovereignty.

dyspeptic ▶ adjective BAD-TEMPERED, short-tempered, irritable, snappish, testy, tetchy, touchy, crabby, crotchety, grouchy, cantankerous, peevish, cross, disagreeable, waspish, prickly; *informal* snappy, on a short fuse; *Brit. informal* stroppy, ratty, eggy, like a bear with a sore head; *N. Amer. informal* cranky, ornery.

Ee

each ▶ pronoun *there are 5000 books and each must be cleaned* EVERY ONE, each one, each and every one, all, the whole lot.
▶ determiner *he visited each month* EVERY, each and every, every single.
▶ adverb *they gave a tenner each* APIECE, per person, per capita, from each, individually, respectively, severally.

eager ▶ adjective ❶ *small eager faces* KEEN, enthusiastic, avid, fervent, ardent, motivated, wholehearted, dedicated, committed, earnest; *informal* mad keen, (as) keen as mustard. ❷ *we were eager for news* ANXIOUS, impatient, longing, yearning, wishing, hoping, hopeful; desirous of, hankering after; on the edge of one's seat, on tenterhooks, on pins and needles; *informal* itching, gagging, dying.
– OPPOSITES apathetic.

eagerness ▶ noun KEENNESS, enthusiasm, avidity, fervour, zeal, wholeheartedness, earnestness, commitment, dedication; impatience, desire, longing, yearning, hunger, appetite, ambition; *informal* yen.

ear ▶ noun ❶ *an infection of the ear* inner ear, middle ear, outer ear. ❷ *he had the ear of the president* ATTENTION, notice, heed, regard, consideration. ❸ *he has an ear for a good song* APPRECIATION, discrimination, perception.
– RELATED TERMS aural, auricular.
■ **play it by ear** IMPROVISE, extemporize, ad lib; make it up as one goes along, think on one's feet; *informal* busk it, wing it.

early ▶ adjective ❶ *early copies of the book* ADVANCE, forward; initial, preliminary, first; pilot, trial. ❷ *an early death* UNTIMELY, premature, unseasonable, before time. ❸ *early man* PRIMITIVE, ancient, prehistoric, primeval; *poetic/literary* of yore. ❹ *an early official statement* PROMPT, timely, quick, speedy, rapid, fast.
– OPPOSITES late, modern, overdue.
▶ adverb ❶ *Rachel has to get up early* IN THE EARLY MORNING; at dawn, at daybreak, at cockcrow, with the lark. ❷ *they hoped to leave school early* BEFORE THE USUAL TIME; prematurely, too soon, ahead of time, ahead of schedule.
– OPPOSITES late.

earmark ▶ verb *the cash had been earmarked for the firm* SET ASIDE, keep (back), reserve; designate, assign, mark; allocate, allot, devote, pledge, give over.
▶ noun *he has all the earmarks of a leader* CHARACTERISTICS, attribute, feature, hallmark, quality.

earn ▶ verb ❶ *they earned £20,000* BE PAID, take home, gross; receive, get, make, obtain, collect, bring in; *informal* pocket, bank, rake in, net, bag. ❷ *he has earned their trust* DESERVE, merit, warrant, justify, be worthy of; gain, win, secure, establish, obtain, procure, get, acquire; *informal* clinch.
– OPPOSITES lose.

earnest[1] ▶ adjective ❶ *he is dreadfully earnest* SERIOUS, solemn, grave, sober, humourless, staid, intense; committed, dedicated, keen, diligent, zealous; thoughtful, cerebral, deep, profound. ❷ *earnest prayer* DEVOUT, heartfelt, wholehearted, sincere, impassioned, fervent, ardent, intense, urgent.
– OPPOSITES frivolous, half-hearted.
■ **in earnest** ❶ *we are in earnest about stopping burglaries* SERIOUS, sincere, wholehearted, genuine; committed, firm, resolute, determined. ❷ *he started writing in earnest* ZEALOUSLY, purposefully, determinedly, resolutely; passionately, wholeheartedly.

earnest[2] ▶ noun *an earnest of a good harvest* SIGN, token, promise, guarantee, pledge, assurance; security, surety, deposit.

earnestly ▶ adverb SERIOUSLY, solemnly, gravely, intently; sincerely, resolutely, firmly, ardently, fervently, eagerly.

earnings ▶ plural noun INCOME, wages, salary, stipend, pay, payment, fees; revenue, yield, profit, takings, proceeds, dividends, return, remuneration.

earth ▶ noun ❶ *the moon orbits the earth* WORLD, globe, planet. ❷ *a trembling of the earth* LAND, ground, terra firma; floor. ❸ *he ploughed the earth* SOIL, clay, loam; dirt, sod, turf; ground. ❹ *the fox's earth* DEN, lair, sett, burrow, warren, hole; retreat, shelter, hideout, hideaway; *informal* hidey-hole.
– RELATED TERMS terrestrial, telluric.

earthenware ▶ noun POTTERY, crockery, stoneware; china, porcelain; pots.

earthly ▶ adjective ❶ *the earthly environment* TERRESTRIAL, telluric. ❷ *the promise of earthly delights* WORLDLY, temporal, mortal, human; material; carnal, fleshly, bodily, physical, corporeal, sensual. ❸ (*informal*) *there is no earthly explanation for this* FEASIBLE, possible, likely, conceivable, imaginable.
– OPPOSITES extraterrestrial, heavenly.

earthquake ▶ noun (EARTH) TREMOR, shock, foreshock, aftershock, convulsion; *informal* quake, shake, trembler.
– RELATED TERMS seismic.

earthy ▶ adjective ❶ *an earthy smell* SOIL-LIKE, dirt-like. ❷ *the earthy Calvinistic tradition* DOWN-TO-EARTH, unsophisticated, unrefined, simple, plain, unpretentious, natural. ❸ *Emma's earthy language* BAWDY, ribald, off colour, racy, rude, vulgar, lewd, crude, foul, coarse, uncouth, unseemly, indelicate, indecent, obscene; *informal* blue, locker-room, X-rated; *Brit. informal* fruity, near the knuckle.

ease ▶ noun ❶ *he defeated them all with ease* EFFORTLESSNESS, no trouble, simplicity; deftness, adroitness, proficiency, mastery. ❷ *his ease of manner* NATURALNESS, casualness, informality, amiability, affability; unconcern, composure, nonchalance, insouciance. ❸ *he couldn't find any ease* PEACE, calm, tranquillity, serenity; repose, restfulness, quiet, security, comfort. ❹ *a life of ease* AFFLUENCE, wealth, prosperity, luxury, plenty; comfort, contentment, enjoyment, well-being.
– OPPOSITES difficulty, formality, trouble, hardship.
▶ verb ❶ *the alcohol eased his pain* RELIEVE, alleviate, mitigate, soothe, palliate, moderate, dull, deaden, numb; reduce, lighten, diminish. ❷ *the rain eased off* ABATE, subside, die down, let up, slacken off, diminish, lessen, peter out, relent, come to an end. ❸ *work helped to ease her mind* CALM, quieten, pacify, soothe, comfort, console; hearten, gladden, uplift, encourage. ❹ *we want to ease their adjustment* FACILITATE, expedite, assist, help, aid, advance, further, forward, simplify. ❺ *he eased out the cork* GUIDE, manoeuvre, inch, edge; slide, slip, squeeze.
– OPPOSITES aggravate, worsen, hinder.
■ **at ease/at one's ease** RELAXED, calm, serene, tranquil, unworried, contented, content, happy; comfortable.

easily ▶ adverb ❶ *I overcame this problem easily* EFFORTLESSLY, comfortably, simply; with ease, without difficulty, without a hitch, smoothly; skilfully, deftly, smartly; *informal* no sweat. ❷ *he's easily the best* UNDOUBTEDLY, without doubt, without question, indisputably, undeniably, definitely, certainly, clearly, obviously, patently; by far, far and away, by a mile.

east ▶ adjective EASTERN, easterly, oriental.

easy ▶ adjective ❶ *the task was very easy* UNCOMPLICATED, undemanding, unchallenging, effortless, painless, trouble-free, facile, simple, straightforward, elementary, plain sailing; *informal* easy as pie, a piece of cake, child's play, kids' stuff, a cinch, no sweat, a doddle, a breeze; *Brit. informal* easy-peasy; *N. Amer. informal* duck soup, a snap; *dated* a snip. ❷ *easy babies* DOCILE, manageable, amenable, tractable, compliant, pliant, acquiescent, obliging, cooperative, easy-going. ❸ *an easy target* VULNERABLE, susceptible, defenceless; naive, gullible, trusting. ❹ *Vic's easy manner* NATURAL, casual, informal, unceremonious, unreserved, uninhibited, unaffected, easy-going, amiable, affable, genial, good-humoured; carefree, nonchalant, unconcerned; *informal* laid-back. ❺ *an easy life* CALM, tranquil, serene, quiet, peaceful, untroubled, contented, relaxed, comfortable, secure, safe; *informal* cushy. ❻ *an easy pace* LEISURELY, unhurried, comfortable, undemanding, easy-going, gentle, sedate, moderate, steady. ❼ (*informal*) *people think she's easy* PROMISCUOUS, free with one's favours, unchaste, loose, wanton, abandoned, licentious, debauched; *informal* sluttish, whorish, tarty; *N. Amer. informal* roundheeled.
– OPPOSITES difficult, demanding, formal, chaste.

easy-going ▶ adjective RELAXED, even-tempered, placid, mellow, mild, happy-go-lucky, carefree, free and easy, nonchalant, insouciant, imperturbable; amiable, considerate, undemanding, patient, tolerant, lenient, broad-minded, understanding; good-natured, pleasant, agreeable; *informal* laid-back, unflappable.
– OPPOSITES intolerant.

eat ▶ verb ❶ *we ate a hearty breakfast* CONSUME, devour, ingest, partake of; gobble (up/down), bolt (down), wolf (down); swallow, chew, munch, chomp; *informal* guzzle, nosh, put away, tuck into, demolish, dispose of, polish off, get stuck into, pig out on, get outside of; *Brit. informal* scoff, gollop; *N. Amer. informal* scarf, snarf. ❷ *we ate at a local restaurant* HAVE A MEAL, consume food, feed, snack; breakfast, lunch, dine; feast, banquet; *informal* graze, nosh. ❸ *acidic water can eat away at pipes* ERODE, corrode, wear away/down/through, burn through, consume, dissolve, disintegrate, crumble, decay; damage, destroy.

eatable ▶ adjective EDIBLE, palatable, digestible; fit to eat, fit for consumption.

eats ▶ plural noun (*informal*) FOOD, sustenance, nourishment, fare; eatables, snacks, titbits; *informal* nosh, grub, chow; *Brit. informal* scoff, tuck; *N. Amer. informal* chuck.

eavesdrop ▶ verb LISTEN IN, spy; monitor, tap, wiretap, record, overhear; *informal* snoop, bug.

ebb ▶ verb ❶ *the tide ebbed* RECEDE, go out, retreat, flow back, fall back/away, subside. ❷ *his courage began to ebb* DIMINISH, dwindle, wane, fade away, peter out, decline, flag, let up, decrease, weaken, disappear.
– OPPOSITES increase.
▶ noun ❶ *the ebb of the tide* RECEDING, retreat, subsiding. ❷ *the ebb of the fighting* ABATEMENT, subsiding, easing, dying down, de-escalation, decrease, decline, diminution.

ebony ▶ adjective BLACK, jet black, pitch black, coal black, sable, inky, sooty, raven, dark.

ebullience ▶ noun EXUBERANCE, buoyancy, cheerfulness, cheeriness, merriment, jollity, sunniness, jauntiness, light-heartedness, high spirits, elation, euphoria, jubilation; animation, sparkle, vivacity, enthusiasm, perkiness; *informal* bubbliness, chirpiness, bounciness, pep.

ebullient ▶ adjective EXUBERANT, buoyant, cheerful, joyful, cheery, merry, jolly, sunny, jaunty, light-hearted, elated; animated, sparkling, vivacious, irrepressible; *informal* bubbly, bouncy, peppy, upbeat, chirpy, smiley, full of beans; *dated* gay.
– OPPOSITES depressed.

eccentric ▶ adjective *eccentric behaviour* UNCONVENTIONAL, uncommon, abnormal, irregular, aberrant, anomalous, odd, queer, strange, peculiar, weird, bizarre, outlandish, freakish, extraordinary; idiosyncratic, quirky, nonconformist, outré; *informal* way out, offbeat, freaky, oddball, wacky, cranky; *Brit. informal* rum; *N. Amer. informal* kooky, wacko.
– OPPOSITES conventional.
▶ noun *he was something of an eccentric* ODDITY, odd fellow, character, individualist, individual, free spirit; misfit; *informal* oddball, queer fish, weirdo, freak, nut, head case, crank; *Brit. informal* one-off, odd bod, nutter; *N. Amer. informal* wacko, screwball.

eccentricity ▶ noun UNCONVENTIONALITY, singularity, oddness, strangeness, weirdness, quirkiness, freakishness; peculiarity, foible, idiosyncrasy, caprice, whimsy, quirk; *informal* nuttiness, screwiness, freakiness; *N. Amer. informal* kookiness.

ecclesiastic ▶ noun *a high ecclesiastic* CLERGYMAN, clergywoman, priest, churchman/woman, man/woman of the cloth, man/woman of God, cleric, minister, preacher, chaplain, father; bishop, vicar, rector, parson, curate, deacon; *Scottish* kirkman; *N. Amer.* dominie; *informal* reverend, padre, Holy Joe, Bible-basher.
▶ adjective *ecclesiastic embroidery. See* ECCLESIASTICAL.

ecclesiastical ▶ adjective PRIESTLY, ministerial, clerical, ecclesiastic, canonical, sacerdotal; church, churchly, religious, spiritual, holy, divine; *informal* churchy.

echelon ▶ noun LEVEL, rank, grade, step, rung, tier, position, order.

echo ▶ noun ❶ *a faint echo of my shout* REVERBERATION, reflection, ringing, repetition, repeat. ❷ *the scene she described was an echo of the photograph* DUPLICATE, copy, replica, imitation, mirror image, double, match, parallel; *informal* lookalike, spitting image, dead ringer. ❸ *an echo of their love* TRACE, vestige, remnant, ghost, memory, recollection, remembrance; reminder, sign, mark, token, indication, suggestion, hint; evidence.

▶ verb ❶ *his laughter echoed round the room* REVERBERATE, resonate, resound, reflect, ring, vibrate. ❷ *Bill echoed Rex's words* REPEAT, restate, reiterate; copy, imitate, parrot, mimic; reproduce, recite, quote, regurgitate; *informal* recap.

éclat ▶ noun STYLE, flamboyance, confidence, elan, dash, flair, vigour, gusto, verve, zest, sparkle, brio, panache, dynamism, spirit; *informal* pizzazz, pep, oomph.

eclectic ▶ adjective WIDE-RANGING, broad-based, extensive, comprehensive, encyclopedic; varied, diverse, catholic, all-embracing, multifaceted, multifarious, heterogeneous, miscellaneous, assorted.

eclipse ▶ noun ❶ *the eclipse of the sun* BLOTTING OUT, blocking, covering, obscuring, concealing, darkening; *Astronomy* occultation. ❷ *the eclipse of the empire* DECLINE, fall, failure, decay, deterioration, degeneration, weakening, collapse.

▶ verb ❶ *the sun was eclipsed by the moon* BLOT OUT, block, cover, obscure, hide, conceal, obliterate, darken; shade; *Astronomy* occult. ❷ *the system was eclipsed by new methods* OUTSHINE, overshadow, surpass, exceed, outclass, outstrip, outdo, top, trump, transcend, upstage.

economic ▶ adjective ❶ *economic reform* FINANCIAL, monetary, budgetary, fiscal; commercial. ❷ *the firm cannot remain economic* PROFITABLE, moneymaking, lucrative, remunerative, fruitful, productive; solvent, viable, cost-effective. ❸ *an economic alternative to carpeting* CHEAP, inexpensive, low-cost, budget, economy, economical, cut-price, discount, bargain.
– OPPOSITES unprofitable, expensive.

economical ▶ adjective ❶ *an economical car* CHEAP, inexpensive, low-cost, budget, economy, economic; cut-price, discount, bargain. ❷ *a very economical shopper* THRIFTY, provident, prudent, sensible, frugal, sparing, abstemious; mean, parsimonious, penny-pinching, miserly; *N. Amer.* forehanded; *informal* stingy.
– OPPOSITES expensive, spendthrift.

economize ▶ verb SAVE (MONEY), cut costs; cut back, make cutbacks, retrench, budget, make economies, be thrifty, be frugal, scrimp, cut corners, tighten one's belt, draw in one's horns, watch the/your pennies.

economy ▶ noun ❶ *the nation's economy* WEALTH, (financial) resources; financial system, financial management. ❷ *one can combine good living with economy* THRIFT, thriftiness, providence, prudence, careful budgeting, economizing, saving, scrimping, restraint, frugality, abstemiousness; *N. Amer.* forehandedness.
– OPPOSITES extravagance.

ecstasy ▶ noun RAPTURE, bliss, elation, euphoria, transports, rhapsodies; joy, jubilation, exultation.
– OPPOSITES misery.

ecstatic ▶ adjective ENRAPTURED, elated, in raptures, euphoric, rapturous, joyful, overjoyed, blissful; on cloud nine, in seventh heaven, beside oneself with joy, jumping for joy, delighted, thrilled, exultant; *informal* over the moon, on top of the world, blissed out.

ecumenical ▶ adjective NON-DENOMINATIONAL, universal, catholic, all-embracing, all-inclusive.
– OPPOSITES denominational.

eddy ▶ noun *small eddies at the river's edge* SWIRL, whirlpool, vortex, maelstrom.

▶ verb *cold air eddied around her* SWIRL, whirl, spiral, wind, circulate, twist; flow, ripple, stream, surge, billow.

edge ▶ noun ❶ *the edge of the lake* BORDER, boundary, extremity, fringe, margin, side; lip, rim, brim, brink, verge; perimeter, circumference, periphery, limits, bounds. ❷ *she had an edge in her voice* SHARPNESS, severity, bite, sting, asperity, acerbity, acidity, trenchancy; sarcasm, acrimony, malice, spite, venom. ❸ *they have an edge over their rivals* ADVANTAGE, lead, head start, the whip hand, the upper hand; superiority, dominance, ascendancy, supremacy, primacy.
– OPPOSITES middle, disadvantage.

▶ verb ❶ *poplars edged the orchard* BORDER, fringe, verge, skirt; surround, enclose, encircle, circle, encompass, bound. ❷ *a frock edged with lace* TRIM, pipe, band, decorate, finish; border, fringe; bind, hem. ❸ *he edged closer to the fire* CREEP, inch, work one's way, pick one's way, ease oneself; sidle, steal, slink.

■ **on edge** TENSE, nervous, edgy, anxious, apprehensive, uneasy, unsettled; twitchy, jumpy, nervy, keyed up, restive, skittish, neurotic, insecure; *informal* uptight, wired; *Brit. informal* strung up.

edgy ▶ adjective TENSE, nervous, on edge, anxious, apprehensive, uneasy, unsettled; twitchy, jumpy, nervy, keyed up, restive, skittish, neurotic, insecure; irritable, touchy, tetchy, testy, crotchety, prickly; *informal* uptight, wired, snappy; *Brit. informal* strung up.
– OPPOSITES calm.

edible ▶ adjective SAFE TO EAT, fit for human consumption, wholesome, good to eat; consumable, digestible, palatable; *formal* comestible.

edict ▶ **noun** DECREE, order, command, commandment, mandate, proclamation, pronouncement, dictate, fiat, promulgation; law, statute, act, bill, ruling, injunction; *formal* ordinance.

edification ▶ **noun** (*formal*) EDUCATION, instruction, tuition, teaching, training, tutelage, guidance; enlightenment, cultivation, information; improvement, development.

edifice ▶ **noun** BUILDING, structure, construction, erection, pile, complex; property, development, premises.

edify ▶ **verb** (*formal*) EDUCATE, instruct, teach, school, tutor, train, guide; enlighten, inform, cultivate, develop, improve, better.

edit ▶ **verb** ❶ *she edited the text* CORRECT, check, copy-edit, improve, emend, polish; modify, adapt, revise, rewrite, reword, rework, redraft; shorten, condense, cut, abridge; *informal* clean up. ❷ *this volume was edited by a consultant* SELECT, choose, assemble, organize, put together. ❸ *he edited The Times* BE THE EDITOR OF, direct, run, manage, head, lead, supervise, oversee, preside over; *informal* be the boss of.

edition ▶ **noun** ISSUE, number, volume, impression, publication; version, revision.

educate ▶ **verb** TEACH, school, tutor, instruct, coach, train, drill; guide, inform, enlighten; inculcate, indoctrinate; *formal* edify.

educated ▶ **adjective** INFORMED, literate, schooled, tutored, well read, learned, knowledgeable, enlightened; intellectual, academic, erudite, scholarly, cultivated, cultured; *dated* lettered.

education ▶ **noun** ❶ *the education of young children* TEACHING, schooling, tuition, tutoring, instruction, coaching, training, tutelage, guidance; indoctrination, inculcation, enlightenment; *formal* edification. ❷ *a woman of some education* LEARNING, knowledge, literacy, scholarship, enlightenment.
–RELATED TERMS pedagogic.

educational ▶ **adjective** ❶ *an educational establishment* ACADEMIC, scholastic, school, learning, teaching, pedagogic, tuitional, instructional. ❷ *an educational experience* INSTRUCTIVE, instructional, educative, informative, illuminating, pedagogic, enlightening, didactic, heuristic; *formal* edifying.

educative ▶ **adjective**. *See* EDUCATIONAL sense 2.

educator ▶ **noun** TEACHER, tutor, instructor, schoolteacher, schoolmaster, schoolmistress; educationalist, educationist; lecturer, professor; guide, mentor, guru; *N. Amer. informal* schoolmarm; *Brit. informal* beak; *formal* pedagogue; *archaic* schoolman.

eerie ▶ **adjective** UNCANNY, sinister, ghostly, unnatural, unearthly, supernatural, otherworldly; strange, abnormal, odd, weird, freakish; frightening, spine-chilling, hair-raising, blood-curdling, terrifying; *informal* creepy, scary, spooky, freaky.

efface ▶ **verb** ❶ *the words were effaced by the rain* ERASE, eradicate, expunge, blot out, rub out, wipe out, remove, eliminate; delete, cancel, obliterate, blank out. ❷ *he attempted to efface himself* MAKE ONESELF INCONSPICUOUS, keep out of sight, keep out of the limelight, lie low, keep a low profile, withdraw.

effect ▶ **noun** ❶ *the effect of these changes* RESULT, consequence, upshot, outcome, out-turn, repercussions, ramifications; end result, conclusion, culmination, corollary, concomitant, aftermath; fruit(s), product, by-product; *informal* pay-off; *Medicine* sequela. ❷ *the effect of the drug* IMPACT, action, effectiveness, influence; power, potency, strength; success; *formal* efficacy. ❸ *with effect from tomorrow* FORCE, operation, enforcement, implementation, effectiveness; validity, lawfulness, legality, legitimacy. ❹ *some words to that effect* SENSE, meaning, theme, drift, import, intent, intention, tenor, significance, message; gist, essence, spirit. ❺ *the dead man's effects* BELONGINGS, possessions, (worldly) goods, chattels; property, paraphernalia; *informal* gear, tackle, things, stuff, bits and pieces; *Brit. informal* clobber.
–OPPOSITES cause.
▶ **verb** *they effected many changes* ACHIEVE, accomplish, carry out, realize, manage, bring off, execute, conduct, engineer, perform, do, perpetrate, discharge, complete, consummate; cause, bring about, create, produce, make; provoke, occasion, generate, engender, actuate, initiate; *formal* effectuate.
■ **in effect** REALLY, in reality, in truth, in (actual) fact, effectively, essentially, in essence, practically, to all intents and purposes, all but, as good as, more or less, almost, nearly, just about; *informal* pretty much; *poetic/literary* well nigh, nigh on.
■ **take effect** ❶ *these measures will take effect in May* COME INTO FORCE, come into operation, begin, become valid, become law, apply, be applied. ❷ *the drug started to take effect* WORK, act, be effective, produce results.

effective ▶ **adjective** ❶ *an effective treatment* SUCCESSFUL, effectual, potent, powerful; helpful, beneficial, advantageous, valuable, useful; *formal* efficacious. ❷ *a more effective argument* CONVINCING, compelling, strong, forceful, potent, weighty, sound, valid; impressive, persuasive, plausible, credible, authoritative; logical, reasonable, lucid, coherent, cogent, eloquent; *formal* efficacious. ❸ *the new law will be effective next week* OPERATIVE, in force, in effect; valid, official, lawful, legal, binding; *Law* effectual. ❹ *Korea was under effective Japanese control* VIRTUAL, practical, essential, actual, implicit, tacit.
–OPPOSITES weak, invalid, theoretical.

effectiveness ▶ noun SUCCESS, productiveness, potency, power; benefit, advantage, value, virtue, usefulness; *formal* efficacy.

effectual ▶ adjective ❶ *effectual political action* EFFECTIVE, successful, productive, constructive; worthwhile, helpful, beneficial, advantageous, valuable, useful; *formal* efficacious. ❷ (*Law*) *an effectual document* VALID, authentic, bona fide, genuine, official; lawful, legal, legitimate, (legally) binding, contractual.

effeminate ▶ adjective WOMANISH, effete, foppish, mincing; *informal* camp, campy, limp-wristed.
– OPPOSITES manly.

effervesce ▶ verb ❶ *heat the mixture until it effervesces* FIZZ, sparkle, bubble; froth, foam. ❷ *managers must effervesce with praise* SPARKLE, be vivacious, be animated, be ebullient, be exuberant, be bubbly, be effervescent.

effervescence ▶ noun ❶ *wines of uniform effervescence* FIZZ, fizziness, sparkle, gassiness, carbonation, aeration, bubbliness. ❷ *his cheeky effervescence* VIVACITY, liveliness, animation, high spirits, ebullience, exuberance, buoyancy, sparkle, gaiety, jollity, cheerfulness, perkiness, breeziness, enthusiasm, irrepressibility, vitality, zest, energy, dynamism; *informal* pep, bounce.

effervescent ▶ adjective ❶ *an effervescent drink* FIZZY, sparkling, carbonated, aerated, gassy, bubbly; mousseux, pétillant, spumante. ❷ *effervescent young people* VIVACIOUS, lively, animated, high-spirited, bubbly, ebullient, buoyant, sparkling, scintillating, light-hearted, jaunty, happy, jolly, cheery, cheerful, perky, sunny, enthusiastic, irrepressible, vital, zestful, energetic, dynamic; *informal* bright-eyed and bushy-tailed, peppy, bouncy, upbeat, chirpy, full of beans.
– OPPOSITES still, depressed.

effete ▶ adjective ❶ *effete trendies* AFFECTED, pretentious, precious, mannered, over-refined; ineffectual; *informal* la-di-da, pseud; *Brit. informal* poncey. ❷ *an effete young man* EFFEMINATE, unmanly, girlish, feminine; soft, timid, cowardly, lily-livered, spineless, pusillanimous; *informal* sissy, wimpish, wimpy. ❸ *the fabric of society is effete* WEAK, enfeebled, enervated, worn out, exhausted, finished, drained, spent, powerless, ineffectual.
– OPPOSITES manly, powerful.

efficacious ▶ adjective (*formal*) EFFECTIVE, effectual, successful, productive, constructive, potent; helpful, beneficial, advantageous, valuable, useful.

efficacy ▶ noun (*formal*) EFFECTIVENESS, success, productiveness, potency, power; benefit, advantage, value, virtue, usefulness.

efficiency ▶ noun ❶ *we need reforms to bring efficiency* ORGANIZATION, order, orderliness, regulation, coherence; productivity, effectiveness. ❷ *I compliment you on your efficiency* COMPETENCE, capability, ability, proficiency, adeptness, expertise, professionalism, skill, effectiveness.

efficient ▶ adjective ❶ *efficient techniques* ORGANIZED, methodical, systematic, logical, orderly, businesslike, streamlined, productive, effective, cost-effective. ❷ *an efficient secretary* COMPETENT, capable, able, proficient, adept, skilful, skilled, effective, productive, organized, businesslike.
– OPPOSITES disorganized, incompetent.

effigy ▶ noun STATUE, statuette, sculpture, model, dummy, figurine; guy; likeness, image; bust.

effluent ▶ noun (LIQUID) WASTE, sewage, effluvium, outflow, discharge, emission.

effort ▶ noun ❶ *they made an effort to work together* ATTEMPT, try, endeavour; *informal* crack, shot, stab, bash; *formal* essay. ❷ *his score was a fine effort* ACHIEVEMENT, accomplishment, attainment, result, feat; undertaking, enterprise, work; triumph, success, coup. ❸ *the job requires little effort* EXERTION, energy, work, endeavour, application, labour, power, muscle, toil, strain; *informal* sweat, elbow grease; *Brit. informal* graft; *Austral./NZ informal* (hard) yakka.

effortless ▶ adjective EASY, undemanding, unchallenging, painless, simple, uncomplicated, straightforward, elementary; fluent, natural; *informal* as easy as pie, child's play, kids' stuff, a cinch, no sweat, a doddle, a breeze; *Brit. informal* easy-peasy; *N. Amer. informal* duck soup, a snap.
– OPPOSITES difficult.

effrontery ▶ noun IMPUDENCE, impertinence, cheek, insolence, cockiness, audacity, temerity, presumption, nerve, gall, shamelessness, impoliteness, disrespect, bad manners; *informal* brass (neck), face, chutzpah; *Brit. informal* sauce; *N. Amer. informal* sass.

effusion ▶ noun ❶ *an effusion of poisonous gas* OUTFLOW, outpouring, rush, current, flood, deluge, emission, discharge, emanation; spurt, surge, jet, stream, torrent, gush, flow. ❷ *reporters' flamboyant effusions* OUTBURST, outpouring, gushing; wordiness, verbiage.

effusive ▶ adjective GUSHING, gushy, unrestrained, extravagant, fulsome, demonstrative, lavish, enthusiastic, lyrical; expansive, wordy, verbose; *informal* over the top, OTT.
– OPPOSITES restrained.

egg ▶ noun OVUM; gamete, germ cell; (**eggs**) roe, spawn, seed.
– RELATED TERMS ovoid.
■ **egg someone on** URGE, goad, incite, provoke, push, drive, prod, prompt, induce, impel, spur on; encourage, exhort, motivate, galvanize.

egghead ▶ noun (*informal*) INTELLECTUAL, think-

er, academic, scholar, sage; bookworm, highbrow; expert, genius, Einstein, mastermind; *informal* brain, whizz; *Brit. informal* brainbox, boffin; *N. Amer. informal* brainiac, rocket scientist.
– OPPOSITES dunce.

ego ▶ **noun** SELF-ESTEEM, self-importance, self-worth, self-respect, self-image, self-confidence.

egocentric ▶ **adjective** SELF-CENTRED, egomaniacal, self-interested, selfish, self-seeking, self-absorbed, self-obsessed; narcissistic, vain, self-important.
– OPPOSITES altruistic.

egotism, egoism ▶ **noun** SELF-CENTREDNESS, egomania, egocentricity, self-interest, selfishness, self-seeking, self-serving, self-regard, self-obsession; self-love, narcissism, self-admiration, vanity, conceit, self-importance; boastfulness.

egotist, egoist ▶ **noun** SELF-SEEKER, egocentric, egomaniac, narcissist; boaster, brag, braggart; *informal* swank, show-off, big-head; *N. Amer. informal* showboat.

egotistic, egoistic ▶ **adjective** SELF-CENTRED, selfish, egocentric, egomaniacal, self-interested, self-seeking, self-absorbed, self-obsessed; narcissistic, vain, conceited, self-important; boastful.

egregious ▶ **adjective** SHOCKING, appalling, terrible, awful, horrendous, frightful, atrocious, abominable, abhorrent, outrageous; monstrous, heinous, dire, unspeakable, shameful, unforgivable, intolerable, dreadful; *formal* grievous.
– OPPOSITES marvellous.

egress ▶ **noun** ❶ *the egress from the gallery was blocked* EXIT, way out, escape route. ❷ *a means of egress* DEPARTURE, exit, withdrawal, retreat, exodus; escape; vacation.
– OPPOSITES entrance.

eight ▶ **cardinal number** OCTET, eightsome, octuplets; *technical* octad.
– RELATED TERMS octo-.

ejaculate ▶ **verb** ❶ EMIT SEMEN, climax, orgasm; *informal* come. ❷ *the sperm is ejaculated* EMIT, eject, discharge, release, expel, disgorge; shoot out, squirt out, spurt out. ❸ (*dated*) *'What?' he ejaculated* EXCLAIM, cry out, call out, yell, blurt out, come out with.

ejaculation ▶ **noun** ❶ *the ejaculation of fluid* EMISSION, ejection, discharge, release, expulsion. ❷ *premature ejaculation* EMISSION OF SEMEN, climax, orgasm. ❸ (*dated*) *the conversation consisted of ejaculations* EXCLAMATION, interjection; call, shout, yell.

eject ▶ **verb** ❶ *the volcano ejected ash* EMIT, spew out, discharge, give off, send out, belch, vent; expel, release, disgorge, spout, vomit, throw up. ❷ *the pilot had time to eject* BAIL OUT, escape, get out. ❸ *they were ejected from the hall* EXPEL, throw out, turn out, cast out, remove, oust; evict, banish; *informal* chuck out, kick out, turf out, boot out; *N. Amer. informal* give someone the bum's rush. ❹ *he was ejected from the job* DISMISS, remove, discharge, oust, expel, axe, throw out, force out, drive out; *informal* sack, fire, send packing, boot out, chuck out, kick out, give someone their marching orders, give someone the push, show someone the door; *Brit. informal* give someone their cards, turf out; *Military* cashier.
– OPPOSITES admit, appoint.

ejection ▶ **noun** ❶ *the ejection of electrons* EMISSION, discharge, expulsion, release; elimination. ❷ *their ejection from the ground* EXPULSION, removal; eviction, banishment, exile. ❸ *his ejection from office* DISMISSAL, removal, discharge, expulsion; *informal* the sack, the boot, the push, the (old) heave-ho, the bullet; *Brit. informal* the chop.

eke ▶ **verb** *I had to eke out my remaining funds* HUSBAND, use sparingly, be thrifty with, be frugal with, be sparing with, use economically; *informal* go easy on.
– OPPOSITES squander.
■ **eke out a living** SUBSIST, survive, get by, scrape by, make ends meet, keep body and soul together, keep the wolf from the door, keep one's head above water.

elaborate ▶ **adjective** ❶ *an elaborate plan* COMPLICATED, complex, intricate, involved, detailed, painstaking, careful; tortuous, convoluted, serpentine, Byzantine. ❷ *an elaborate plasterwork ceiling* ORNATE, decorated, embellished, adorned, ornamented, fancy, fussy, busy, ostentatious, extravagant, showy, baroque, rococo, florid, wedding-cake.
– OPPOSITES simple, plain.
▶ **verb** *both sides refused to elaborate on their reasons* EXPAND ON, enlarge on, add to, flesh out, put flesh on the bones of, add detail to, expatiate on; develop, fill out, embellish, embroider, enhance, amplify.

elan ▶ **noun** FLAIR, style, panache, confidence, dash, éclat; energy, vigour, vitality, liveliness, brio, esprit, animation, vivacity, zest, verve, spirit, pep, sparkle, enthusiasm, gusto, eagerness, feeling, fire; *informal* pizzazz, zing, zip, vim, oomph.

elapse ▶ **verb** PASS, go by/past, wear on, slip by/away/past, roll by/past, slide by/past, steal by/past, tick by/past.

elastic ▶ **adjective** ❶ *elastic material* STRETCHY, elasticated, stretchable, springy, flexible, pliant, pliable, supple, yielding, plastic, resilient. ❷ *an elastic concept of nationality* ADAPTABLE, flexible, adjustable, accommodating, variable, fluid, versatile.
– OPPOSITES rigid.

elasticity ▶ **noun** ❶ *the skin's natural elasticity* STRETCHINESS, flexibility, pliancy, suppleness, plasticity, resilience, springiness; *informal* give.

❷ *the elasticity of the term* ADAPTABILITY, flexibility, adjustability, fluidity, versatility.

elated ▶ adjective THRILLED, delighted, overjoyed, ecstatic, euphoric, very happy, joyous, gleeful, jubilant, beside oneself, exultant, rapturous, in raptures, walking on air, on cloud nine/seven, in seventh heaven, jumping for joy, in transports of delight; *informal* on top of the world, over the moon, on a high, tickled pink; *Austral. informal* wrapped.
– OPPOSITES miserable.

elation ▶ noun EUPHORIA, ecstasy, happiness, delight, transports of delight, joy, joyousness, glee, jubilation, exultation, bliss, rapture.

elbow ▶ verb *he elbowed his way through the crowd* PUSH, shove, force, shoulder, jostle, barge, muscle, bulldoze.

elbow room ▶ noun ROOM TO MANOEUVRE, room, space, Lebensraum, breathing space, scope, freedom, play, free rein, licence, latitude, leeway.

elder ▶ adjective *his elder brother* OLDER, senior, big.
▶ noun *the church elders* LEADER, senior figure, patriarch, father.

elderly ▶ adjective *her elderly mother* AGED, old, advanced in years, ageing, long in the tooth, past one's prime; grey-haired, grey-bearded, grizzled, hoary; in one's dotage, decrepit, doddering, doddery, senescent; *informal* getting on, past it, over the hill, no spring chicken.
– OPPOSITES youthful.
▶ noun (**the elderly**) OLD PEOPLE, senior citizens, (old-age) pensioners, OAPs, retired people; geriatrics; *N. Amer.* seniors, retirees, golden agers; *informal* (golden) oldies, wrinklies; *N. Amer. informal* oldsters, woopies.

elect ▶ verb ❶ *a new president was elected* VOTE FOR, VOTE IN, return, cast one's vote for; choose, pick, select. ❷ *she elected to stay behind* CHOOSE, decide, opt, vote.
▶ adjective *the president elect* FUTURE, -to-be, designate, chosen, elected, coming, next, appointed, presumptive.
▶ noun (**the elect**) THE CHOSEN, the elite, the favoured; the crème de la crème.

election ▶ noun BALLOT, vote, popular vote; poll; *Brit.* by-election; *US* primary.
– RELATED TERMS psephology.

electioneer ▶ verb CAMPAIGN, canvass, go on the hustings, doorstep; *Brit. informal* go out on the knocker.

elector ▶ noun VOTER, member of the electorate, constituent; selector.

electric ▶ adjective ❶ *an electric kettle* ELECTRIC-POWERED, electrically operated, mains-operated, battery-operated. ❷ *the atmosphere was electric* EXCITING, charged, electrifying, thrilling, heady, dramatic, intoxicating, dynamic, stimulating, galvanizing, rousing, stirring, moving; tense, knife-edge, explosive, volatile.

electricity ▶ noun POWER, electric power, energy, current, static; *Brit.* mains; *Canadian* hydro; *Brit. informal* leccy; *historical* galvanism.

electrify ▶ verb EXCITE, thrill, stimulate, arouse, rouse, inspire, stir (up), exhilarate, intoxicate, galvanize, move, fire (with enthusiasm), fire someone's imagination, invigorate, animate; startle, jolt, shock; *N. Amer.* light a fire under; *informal* give someone a buzz, give someone a kick; *N. Amer. informal* give someone a charge.

elegance ▶ noun ❶ *he was attracted by her elegance* STYLE, stylishness, grace, gracefulness, taste, tastefulness, sophistication; refinement, dignity, beauty, poise, charm, culture; suaveness, urbanity, panache. ❷ *the elegance of the idea* NEATNESS, simplicity; ingenuity, cleverness, inventiveness.

elegant ▶ adjective ❶ *an elegant black outfit* STYLISH, graceful, tasteful, sophisticated, classic, chic, smart, fashionable, modish; refined, dignified, poised, beautiful, lovely, charming, artistic, aesthetic; cultivated, polished, cultured; dashing, debonair, suave, urbane. ❷ *an elegant solution* NEAT, simple, effective; ingenious, clever, deft, intelligent, inventive.
– OPPOSITES gauche.

elegiac ▶ adjective MOURNFUL, melancholic, melancholy, plaintive, sorrowful, sad, lamenting, doleful; funereal, dirgelike; nostalgic, valedictory, poignant; *poetic/literary* dolorous.
– OPPOSITES cheerful.

elegy ▶ noun LAMENT, requiem, funeral poem/song, threnody, dirge, plaint; *Irish* keen; *Irish & Scottish* coronach.

element ▶ noun ❶ *an essential element of the local community* COMPONENT, constituent, part, section, portion, piece, segment, bit; aspect, factor, feature, facet, ingredient, strand, detail, point; member, unit, module, item. ❷ *there is an element of truth in this stereotype* TRACE, touch, hint, smattering, soupçon. ❸ (**elements**) *the elements of political science* BASICS, essentials, principles, first principles; foundations, fundamentals, rudiments; *informal* nuts and bolts, ABC. ❹ *I braved the elements* THE WEATHER, the climate, meteorological conditions, atmospheric conditions; the wind, the rain.

elemental ▶ adjective ❶ *the elemental principles of accountancy* BASIC, primary, fundamental, essential, root, underlying; rudimentary. ❷ *elemental forces* NATURAL, atmospheric, meteorological, environmental.

elementary ▶ adjective ❶ *an elementary astronomy course* BASIC, rudimentary, fundamental; preparatory, introductory, initiatory. ❷ *a lot of the work is elementary* EASY, simple, straightforward, uncomplicated, undemand-

ing, painless, child's play, plain sailing; *informal* as easy as falling off a log, as easy as pie, as easy as ABC, a piece of cake, no sweat, kids' stuff; *Brit. informal* easy-peasy.
– OPPOSITES advanced, difficult.

elephantine ▶ **adjective** ENORMOUS, huge, gigantic, very big, massive, giant, immense, tremendous, colossal, mammoth, gargantuan, vast, prodigious, monumental, titanic; hulking, bulky, heavy, weighty, ponderous, lumbering; *informal* jumbo, whopping, humongous, monster; *Brit. informal* whacking, ginormous.
– OPPOSITES tiny.

elevate ▶ **verb** ❶ *we need a breeze to elevate the kite* RAISE, lift (up), raise up/aloft, upraise; hoist, hike up, haul up. ❷ *he was elevated to Secretary of State* PROMOTE, upgrade, advance, move up, raise, prefer; ennoble, exalt, aggrandize; *informal* kick upstairs, move up the ladder.
– OPPOSITES lower, demote.

elevated ▶ **adjective** ❶ *an elevated motorway* RAISED, upraised, high up, aloft; overhead. ❷ *elevated language* LOFTY, grand, exalted, fine, sublime; inflated, pompous, bombastic, orotund. ❸ *the gentry's elevated status* HIGH, higher, high-ranking, of high standing, lofty, superior, exalted, eminent; grand, noble.
– OPPOSITES lowly.

elevation ▶ **noun** ❶ *his elevation to the peerage* PROMOTION, upgrading, advancement, advance, preferment, aggrandizement; ennoblement; *informal* step up the ladder, kick upstairs. ❷ *1500 to 3,00 metres in elevation* ALTITUDE, height. ❸ *elevations in excess of 3000 metres* HEIGHT, hill, mountain, mount; *formal* eminence. ❹ *elevation of thought* GRANDEUR, greatness, nobility, loftiness, majesty, sublimity.

elf ▶ **noun** PIXIE, fairy, sprite, imp, brownie; dwarf, gnome, goblin, hobgoblin; leprechaun, puck, troll.

elfin ▶ **adjective** ELFLIKE, elfish, elvish, pixie-like; puckish, impish, playful, mischievous; dainty, delicate, small, petite, slight, little, tiny, diminutive.

elicit ▶ **verb** OBTAIN, draw out, extract, bring out, evoke, call forth, bring forth, induce, prompt, generate, engender, trigger, provoke; *formal* educe.

eligible ▶ **adjective** ❶ *those people eligible to vote* ENTITLED, permitted, allowed, qualified, able. ❷ *an eligible bachelor* DESIRABLE, suitable; available, single, unmarried, unattached, unwed.

eliminate ▶ **verb** ❶ *a policy that would eliminate inflation* REMOVE, get rid of, put an end to, do away with, end, stop, terminate, eradicate, destroy, annihilate, stamp out, wipe out, extinguish; *informal* knock something on the head. ❷ *he was eliminated from the title race* KNOCK OUT, beat; exclude, rule out, disqualify.

elite ▶ **noun** BEST, pick, cream, crème de la crème, flower, nonpareil, elect; high society, jet set, beautiful people, beau monde, haut monde; aristocracy, nobility, upper class; *N. Amer.* four hundred.
– OPPOSITES dregs.

elixir ▶ **noun** POTION, concoction, brew, philtre, decoction, mixture; medicine, tincture; extract, essence, concentrate, distillate, distillation; *poetic/literary* draught; *archaic* potation.

elliptical ▶ **adjective** ❶ *an elliptical shape* OVAL, egg-shaped, elliptic, ovate, ovoid, oviform, ellipsoidal; *Botany* obovate. ❷ *elliptical phraseology* CRYPTIC, abstruse, ambiguous, obscure, oblique, Delphic; terse, concise, succinct, compact, economic, laconic, sparing.

elocution ▶ **noun** PRONUNCIATION, enunciation, articulation, diction, speech, intonation, vocalization, modulation; phrasing, delivery, public speaking.

elongate ▶ **verb** ❶ *an exercise that elongates the muscles* LENGTHEN, extend, stretch (out). ❷ *the high notes were elongated* PROLONG, protract, draw out, sustain.
– OPPOSITES shorten.

eloquence ▶ **noun** FLUENCY, articulacy, articulateness, expressiveness, silver tongue, persuasiveness, forcefulness, power, potency, effectiveness; oratory, rhetoric, grandiloquence, magniloquence; *informal* gift of the gab, way with words, blarney.

eloquent ▶ **adjective** ❶ *an eloquent speaker* FLUENT, articulate, expressive, silver-tongued; persuasive, strong, forceful, powerful, potent, well expressed, effective, lucid, vivid, graphic; smooth-tongued, glib. ❷ *her glance was more eloquent than words* EXPRESSIVE, meaningful, suggestive, revealing, telling, significant, indicative.
– OPPOSITES inarticulate.

elsewhere ▶ **adverb** SOMEWHERE ELSE, in/at/to another place, in/at/to a different place, hence; not here, not present, absent, away, abroad, out.
– OPPOSITES here.

elucidate ▶ **verb** EXPLAIN, make clear, illuminate, throw/shed light on, clarify, clear up, sort out, unravel, spell out; interpret, explicate; gloss.
– OPPOSITES confuse.

elucidation ▶ **noun** EXPLANATION, clarification, illumination; interpretation, explication; gloss.

elude ▶ **verb** EVADE, avoid, get away from, dodge, escape from, run (away) from; lose, shake off, give the slip to, slip away from, throw off the scent; *informal* slip through someone's fingers, slip through the net; *archaic* bilk.

elusive ▶ **adjective** ❶ *her elusive husband* DIFFICULT TO FIND; evasive, slippery; *informal* always on the move. ❷ *an elusive quality* INDEFINABLE, intangible, impalpable, unanalysable; fugitive; ambiguous.

Elysian ▶ adjective HEAVENLY, paradisal, paradisiacal, celestial, superlunary, divine; *poetic/literary* empyrean.

Elysium ▶ noun (*Greek Mythology*) HEAVEN, paradise, the Elysian fields; eternity, the afterlife, the next world, the hereafter; *Scandinavian Mythology* Valhalla; *Classical Mythology* the Islands of the Blessed; *Arthurian Legend* Avalon.

emaciated ▶ adjective THIN, skeletal, bony, gaunt, wasted, thin as a rake; scrawny, skinny, scraggy, skin and bones, raw-boned, stick-like; starved, underfed, undernourished, underweight, half-starved; cadaverous, shrivelled, shrunken, withered; *informal* anorexic, like a bag of bones.
– OPPOSITES fat.

emanate ▶ verb ❶ *warmth emanated from the fireplace* ISSUE, spread, radiate, be sent forth/out. ❷ *the proposals emanated from a committee* ORIGINATE, stem, derive, proceed, spring, issue, emerge, flow, come. ❸ *he emanated an air of power* EXUDE, emit, radiate, give off/out, send out/forth.

emanation ▶ noun ❶ *an emanation of his tortured personality* PRODUCT, consequence, result, fruit. ❷ *radon gas emanation* DISCHARGE, emission, radiation, effusion, outflow, outpouring, flow, leak; *technical* efflux.

emancipate ▶ verb FREE, liberate, set free, release, deliver, discharge; unchain, unfetter, unshackle, untie, unyoke; *historical* manumit; *rare* disenthral.
– OPPOSITES enslave.

emancipated ▶ adjective LIBERATED, independent, unconstrained, uninhibited; free.

emasculate ▶ verb ❶ *an Act which emasculated the House of Lords* WEAKEN, enfeeble, debilitate, erode, undermine, cripple; remove the sting from, pull the teeth of; *informal* water down. ❷ (*archaic*) *young cocks should be emasculated at three months. See* CASTRATE.

embalm ▶ verb ❶ *his body had been embalmed* PRESERVE, mummify, lay out. ❷ *the poem ought to embalm his memory* PRESERVE, conserve, enshrine, immortalize.

embankment ▶ noun BANK, mound, ridge, earthwork, causeway, barrier, levee, dam, dyke.

embargo ▶ noun *an embargo on oil sales* BAN, bar, prohibition, stoppage, interdict, proscription, veto, moratorium; restriction, restraint, block, barrier, impediment, obstruction; boycott.
▶ verb *arms sales were embargoed* BAN, bar, prohibit, stop, interdict, debar, proscribe, outlaw; restrict, restrain, block, obstruct; boycott.
– OPPOSITES allow.

embark ▶ verb ❶ *he embarked at Dover* BOARD SHIP, go on board, go aboard, take ship; emplane; *informal* hop on, jump on; *dated* ship. ❷ *he embarked on a new career* BEGIN, start, commence, undertake, set about, take up, turn one's hand to, get down to; enter into, venture into, launch into, plunge into, engage in, settle down to; *informal* get cracking on, get going on, have a go/crack/shot at.

embarrass ▶ verb MORTIFY, shame, put someone to shame, humiliate, abash, chagrin, make uncomfortable, make self-conscious; discomfit, disconcert, discompose, upset, discountenance, distress; *informal* show up.

embarrassed ▶ adjective MORTIFIED, red-faced, blushing, abashed, shamed, ashamed, shamefaced, humiliated, chagrined, awkward, self-conscious, uncomfortable, not knowing where to look, sheepish; discomfited, disconcerted, upset, discomposed, flustered, agitated, discountenanced, distressed; shy, bashful, tongue-tied; *informal* with egg on one's face, wishing the earth would swallow one up.

embarrassing ▶ adjective HUMILIATING, shaming, shameful, mortifying, ignominious; awkward, uncomfortable, compromising; disconcerting, discomfiting, upsetting, distressing; *informal* blush-making, cringeworthy, cringe-making, toe-curling.

embarrassment ▶ noun ❶ *he was scarlet with embarrassment* MORTIFICATION, humiliation, shame, shamefacedness, chagrin, awkwardness, self-consciousness, sheepishness, discomfort, discomfiture, discomposure, agitation, distress; ignominy; shyness, bashfulness. ❷ *his current financial embarrassment* DIFFICULTY, predicament, plight, problem, mess; *informal* bind, jam, pickle, fix, scrape. ❸ *an embarrassment of riches* SURPLUS, excess, overabundance, superabundance, glut, surfeit, superfluity; abundance, profusion, plethora.

embassy ▶ noun ❶ *the Italian embassy* CONSULATE, legation, ministry. ❷ (*historical*) *Charles sent an embassy to the Lombards* ENVOY, representative, delegate, emissary; delegation, deputation, legation, (diplomatic) mission; *archaic* embassage, legate.

embed, imbed ▶ verb IMPLANT, plant, set, fix, lodge, root, insert, place; sink, drive in, hammer in, ram in.

embellish ▶ verb ❶ *weapons embellished with precious metal* DECORATE, adorn, ornament; beautify, enhance, grace; trim, garnish, gild; deck, bedeck, festoon, emblazon; *poetic/literary* bejewel, bedizen. ❷ *the legend was embellished by an American academic* ELABORATE, embroider, expand on, exaggerate.

embellishment ▶ noun ❶ *architectural embellishments* DECORATION, ornamentation, adornment; beautification, enhancement, trimming, trim, garnishing, gilding. ❷ *we wanted the* *truth, not romantic embellishments* ELABORATION, addition, exaggeration.

ember ▶ noun GLOWING COAL, live coal; cinder; (**embers**) ashes, residue.

embezzle ▶ verb MISAPPROPRIATE, steal, thieve, pilfer, purloin, appropriate, abstract, defraud someone of, siphon off, pocket, help oneself to; put one's hand in the till; *informal* rob, rip off, skim, line one's pockets; *Brit. informal* pinch, nick, half-inch; *formal* peculate.

embezzlement ▶ noun MISAPPROPRIATION, theft, stealing, robbery, thieving, pilfering, purloining, pilferage, appropriation, swindling; fraud, larceny; *formal* peculation.

embittered ▶ adjective BITTER, resentful, grudge-bearing, rancorous, jaundiced, aggrieved, sour, frustrated, dissatisfied, alienated, disaffected.

emblazon ▶ verb ❶ *shirts emblazoned with the company name* ADORN, decorate, ornament, embellish; inscribe. ❷ *a flag with a hammer and sickle emblazoned on it* DISPLAY, depict, show.

emblem ▶ noun SYMBOL, representation, token, image, figure, mark, sign; crest, badge, device, insignia, stamp, seal, heraldic device, coat of arms, shield; logo, trademark.

emblematic, emblematical ▶ adjective ❶ *a situation emblematic of the industrialized twentieth century* SYMBOLIC, representative, demonstrative, suggestive, indicative. ❷ *emblematic works of art* ALLEGORICAL, symbolic, metaphorical, parabolic, figurative.

embodiment ▶ noun PERSONIFICATION, incarnation, realization, manifestation, expression, representation, actualization, symbol, symbolization; paradigm, epitome, paragon, soul, model; type, essence, quintessence, exemplification, example, exemplar, ideal; *formal* reification.

embody ▶ verb ❶ *Gradgrind embodies the spirit of industrial capitalism* PERSONIFY, realize, manifest, symbolize, represent, express, concretize, incarnate, epitomize, stand for, typify, exemplify; *formal* reify. ❷ *the changes in law embodied in the Children Act* INCORPORATE, include, contain, encompass; assimilate, consolidate, integrate, organize, systematize; combine.

embolden ▶ verb FORTIFY, make brave/braver, encourage, hearten, strengthen, brace, stiffen the resolve of, lift the morale of; rouse, stir, stimulate, cheer, rally, fire, animate, inspirit, invigorate; *informal* buck up.
– OPPOSITES dishearten.

embrace ▶ verb ❶ *he embraced her warmly* HUG, take/hold in one's arms, hold, cuddle, clasp to one's bosom, clasp, squeeze, clutch; caress; enfold, enclasp, encircle, envelop, entwine oneself around; *informal* canoodle, smooch; *poetic/literary* embosom. ❷ *most western European countries have embraced the concept* WELCOME, welcome with open arms, accept, take up, take to one's heart, adopt; espouse, support, back, champion. ❸ *the faculty embraces a wide range of departments* INCLUDE, take in, comprise, contain, incorporate, encompass, cover, involve, embody, subsume, comprehend.
▶ noun *a fond embrace* HUG, cuddle, squeeze, clinch, caress; bear hug.

embrocation ▶ noun OINTMENT, lotion, cream, rub, salve, emollient, liniment, balm, unguent.

embroider ▶ verb ❶ *a cushion embroidered with a pattern of golden keys* SEW, stitch; DECORATE, adorn, ornament, embellish. ❷ *she embroidered her stories with colourful detail* ELABORATE, embellish, enlarge on, exaggerate, touch up, dress up, gild, colour; *informal* jazz up.

embroidery ▶ noun ❶ *the girls were taught embroidery* NEEDLEWORK, needlepoint, needlecraft, sewing, tatting, crewel work, tapestry. ❷ *fanciful embroidery of the facts* ELABORATION, embellishment, adornment, ornamentation, colouring, enhancement; exaggeration, overstatement, hyperbole.

embroil ▶ verb INVOLVE, entangle, ensnare, enmesh, catch up, mix up, bog down, mire.

embryo ▶ noun ❶ *a human embryo* FETUS, fertilized egg, unborn child/baby. ❷ *the embryo of a capitalist economy* GERM, nucleus, seed; rudimentary version, rudiments, basics, beginning, start.

embryonic ▶ adjective ❶ *an embryonic chick* FETAL, unborn, unhatched. ❷ *an embryonic prodemocracy movement* RUDIMENTARY, undeveloped, unformed, immature, incomplete, incipient, inchoate; fledgling, budding, nascent, emerging, developing, early, germinal.
– OPPOSITES mature.

emend ▶ verb CORRECT, rectify, repair, fix; improve, enhance, polish, refine, amend; edit, rewrite, revise, copy-edit, subedit, redraft, recast, rephrase, reword, rework, alter, change, modify; *rare* redact.

emerge ▶ verb ❶ *a policeman emerged from the alley* COME OUT, appear, come into view, become visible, surface, materialize, manifest oneself, issue, come forth. ❷ *several unexpected facts emerged* BECOME KNOWN, become apparent, be revealed, come to light, come out, turn up, transpire, unfold, turn out, prove to be the case.

emergence ▶ noun APPEARANCE, arrival, coming, materialization; advent, inception, dawn, birth, origination, start, development, rise.

emergency ▶ noun *a military emergency* CRISIS, urgent situation, extremity, exigency; accident, disaster, catastrophe, calamity; difficulty, plight, predicament, danger; *informal* panic stations.

▶ **adjective** ❶ *an emergency meeting* URGENT, crisis; impromptu, extraordinary. ❷ *emergency supplies* RESERVE, standby, back-up, fallback, in reserve.

emergent ▶ **adjective** EMERGING, developing, rising, dawning, budding, embryonic, infant, fledgling, nascent, incipient.

emigrate ▶ **verb** MOVE ABROAD, move overseas, leave one's country, migrate; relocate, resettle; defect.
– OPPOSITES immigrate.

emigration ▶ **noun** MOVING ABROAD, moving overseas, expatriation, migration; exodus, diaspora; relocation, resettling; defection.

eminence ▶ **noun** ❶ *his eminence as a scientist* FAME, celebrity, illustriousness, distinction, renown, pre-eminence, notability, greatness, prestige, importance, reputation, repute, note; prominence, superiority, stature, standing. ❷ *various legal eminences* IMPORTANT PERSON, dignitary, luminary, worthy, grandee, notable, notability, personage, leading light, VIP; *informal* somebody, someone, big shot, big noise, big gun, heavyweight. ❸ (*formal*) *the hotel's eminence above the sea* ELEVATION, height, rise.

eminent ▶ **adjective** ❶ *an eminent man of letters* ILLUSTRIOUS, distinguished, renowned, esteemed, pre-eminent, notable, noteworthy, great, prestigious, important, influential, outstanding, noted, of note; famous, celebrated, prominent, well known, lionized, acclaimed, exalted, revered, august, venerable. ❷ *the eminent reasonableness of their claims* OBVIOUS, clear, conspicuous, marked, singular, signal; total, complete, utter, absolute, thorough, perfect, downright, sheer.
– OPPOSITES unknown.

eminently ▶ **adverb** VERY, greatly, highly, exceedingly, extremely, particularly, exceptionally, supremely, uniquely; obviously, clearly, conspicuously, markedly, singularly, signally, outstandingly, strikingly, notably, surpassingly; totally, completely, utterly, absolutely, thoroughly, perfectly, downright.

emissary ▶ **noun** ENVOY, ambassador, delegate, attaché, consul, plenipotentiary; agent, representative, deputy; messenger, courier; nuncio; *archaic* legate.

emission ▶ **noun** DISCHARGE, release, outpouring, outflow, outrush, leak, excretion, secretion, ejection; emanation, radiation, effusion, ejaculation, disgorgement, issuance.

emit ▶ **verb** ❶ *the hydrocarbons emitted from vehicle exhausts* DISCHARGE, release, give out/off, pour out, send forth, throw out, void, vent, issue; leak, ooze, excrete, disgorge, secrete, eject, ejaculate; spout, belch, spew out; emanate, radiate, exude. ❷ *he emitted a loud cry* UTTER, voice, let out, produce, give vent to, come out with, vocalize.
– OPPOSITES absorb.

emollient ▶ **adjective** ❶ *a rich emollient shampoo* MOISTURIZING, soothing, softening. ❷ *an emollient response* CONCILIATORY, conciliating, appeasing, soothing, calming, pacifying, assuaging, placating, mollifying, propitiatory.
▶ **noun** *she applied an emollient* MOISTURIZER, cream, lotion, oil, rub, salve, unguent, balm; *technical* humectant.

emolument ▶ **noun** (*formal*) SALARY, pay, payment, wage(s), earnings, allowance, stipend, honorarium, reward, premium; fee, charge, consideration; income, profit, gain, return.

emotion ▶ **noun** ❶ *she was good at hiding her emotions* FEELING, sentiment; reaction, response. ❷ *overcome by emotion, she turned away* PASSION, strength of feeling, warmth of feeling. ❸ *responses based purely on emotion* INSTINCT, intuition, gut feeling; sentiment, the heart.

emotional ▶ **adjective** ❶ *an emotional young man* PASSIONATE, hot-blooded, ardent, fervent, excitable, temperamental, melodramatic, tempestuous; demonstrative, responsive, tender, loving, feeling, sentimental, sensitive. ❷ *he paid an emotional tribute to his wife* POIGNANT, moving, touching, affecting, powerful, stirring, emotive, heart-rending, heart-warming, impassioned, dramatic; haunting, pathetic, sentimental; *informal* tear-jerking.
– OPPOSITES unfeeling.

emotionless ▶ **adjective** UNEMOTIONAL, unfeeling, dispassionate, passionless, unexpressive, cool, cold, cold-blooded, impassive, indifferent, detached, remote, aloof; toneless, flat, dead, expressionless, blank, wooden, stony, deadpan, vacant.

emotive ▶ **adjective** CONTROVERSIAL, contentious, inflammatory; sensitive, delicate, difficult, problematic, touchy, awkward, prickly, ticklish.

empathize ▶ **verb** IDENTIFY, sympathize, be in sympathy, understand, share someone's feelings, be in tune; be on the same wavelength as, talk the same language as; relate to, feel for, have insight into; *informal* put oneself in someone else's shoes.

emperor ▶ **noun** RULER, sovereign, king, monarch, potentate; *historical* tsar, kaiser, mikado.
– RELATED TERMS imperial.

emphasis ▶ **noun** ❶ *the curriculum gave more emphasis to reading and writing* PROMINENCE, importance, significance, value; stress, weight, accent, attention, priority, pre-eminence, urgency, force. ❷ *the emphasis is on the word 'little'* STRESS, accent, accentuation, weight, prominence; beat; *Prosody* ictus.

emphasize ▶ **verb** STRESS, underline, highlight, focus attention on, point up, lay stress on, draw attention to, spotlight, foreground, play up, make a point of; bring to the fore, insist on, belabour; accent, accentuate, underscore; *informal* press home, rub it in.

– OPPOSITES understate.

emphatic ▶ adjective ❶ *an emphatic denial* VEHEMENT, firm, wholehearted, forceful, forcible, energetic, vigorous, direct, assertive, insistent; certain, definite, out-and-out, one hundred per cent; decided, determined, categorical, unqualified, unconditional, unequivocal, unambiguous, absolute, explicit, downright, outright, clear. ❷ *an emphatic victory* CONCLUSIVE, decisive, decided, unmistakable; resounding, telling; *informal* thumping, thundering.
– OPPOSITES hesitant, narrow.

empire ▶ noun ❶ *the Ottoman Empire* KINGDOM, realm, domain, territory; commonwealth; power, world power, superpower. ❷ *a worldwide shipping empire* ORGANIZATION, corporation, multinational, conglomerate, consortium, company, business, firm, operation. ❸ *his dream of empire* POWER, rule, ascendancy, supremacy, command, control, authority, sway, dominance, domination, dominion.
– RELATED TERMS imperial.

empirical ▶ adjective EXPERIENTIAL, practical, heuristic, first-hand, hands-on; observed, seen.
– OPPOSITES theoretical.

employ ▶ verb ❶ *she employed a chauffeur* HIRE, engage, recruit, take on, secure the services of, sign up, sign, put on the payroll, enrol, appoint; retain; indenture, apprentice. ❷ *Sam was employed in carving a stone figure* OCCUPY, engage, involve, keep busy, tie up; absorb, engross, immerse. ❸ *the team employed subtle psychological tactics* USE, utilize, make use of, avail oneself of; apply, exercise, practise, put into practice, exert, bring into play, bring to bear; draw on, resort to, turn to, have recourse to.
– OPPOSITES dismiss.

employed ▶ adjective WORKING, in work, in employment, holding down a job; earning, waged, breadwinning.

employee ▶ noun WORKER, member of staff; blue-collar worker, white-collar worker, workman, labourer, (hired) hand; wage-earner, breadwinner; (**employees**) personnel, staff, workforce; *informal* liveware.

employer ▶ noun ❶ *his employer gave him a glowing reference* MANAGER, manageress, proprietor, director, head man, head woman; *informal* boss, boss man, skipper; *Brit. informal* gaffer, governor, guv'nor; *N. Amer. informal* padrone, sachem. ❷ *the largest private sector employer in Sheffield* FIRM, company, business, organization, manufacturer.

employment ▶ noun ❶ *she found employment as a clerk* WORK, labour, service; job, post, position, situation, occupation, profession, trade, métier, business, line, line of work, calling, vocation, craft, pursuit; *archaic* employ. ❷ *the employment of children* HIRING, hire, engagement, taking on; apprenticing. ❸ *the employment of nuclear weapons* USE, utilization, application, exercise.

emporium ▶ noun SHOP, store, outlet, retail outlet; department store, chain store, supermarket, hypermarket, superstore, megastore; establishment.

empower ▶ verb ❶ *the act empowered Henry to punish heretics* AUTHORIZE, entitle, permit, allow, license, sanction, warrant, commission, delegate, qualify, enable, equip. ❷ *movements to empower the poor* EMANCIPATE, unshackle, set free, liberate.
– OPPOSITES forbid.

empress ▶ noun RULER, sovereign, queen, monarch, potentate; *historical* tsarina.

emptiness ▶ noun *she had filled an emptiness in his life* VOID, vacuum, empty space, vacuity, gap, vacancy, hole.

empty ▶ adjective ❶ *an empty house* VACANT, unoccupied, uninhabited, untenanted, bare, desolate, deserted, abandoned; clear, free. ❷ *an empty threat* MEANINGLESS, hollow, idle, vain, futile, worthless, useless, insubstantial, ineffective, ineffectual. ❸ *without her my life is empty* FUTILE, pointless, purposeless, worthless, meaningless, valueless, of no value, useless, of no use, aimless, senseless, hollow, barren, insignificant, inconsequential, trivial. ❹ *his eyes were empty* BLANK, expressionless, vacant, deadpan, wooden, stony, impassive, absent, glazed, fixed, lifeless, emotionless, unresponsive.
– OPPOSITES full, serious, worthwhile.
▶ verb ❶ *I emptied the dishwasher* UNLOAD, unpack, void; clear, evacuate; *archaic* unlade. ❷ *he emptied out the contents of the case* REMOVE, take out, extract, tip out, pour out.
– OPPOSITES fill.

empty-headed ▶ adjective STUPID, foolish, silly, unintelligent, idiotic, brainless, witless, vacuous, vapid, feather-brained, birdbrained, scatterbrained, scatty, thoughtless; *informal* half-witted, dumb, dim, airheaded, brain-dead, dippy, dizzy, dopey, dozy, soft in the head, slow on the uptake; *Brit. informal* daft; *N. Amer. informal* ditsy, dumb-ass.
– OPPOSITES intelligent.

empyrean (*poetic/literary*) ▶ adjective *the empyrean regions* HEAVENLY, celestial, ethereal; upper.
▶ noun (**the empyrean**) HEAVEN, the heavens, the sky, the upper regions, the stratosphere; *poetic/literary* the ether, the wide blue yonder, the firmament, the welkin.

emulate ▶ verb IMITATE, copy, mirror, echo, follow, model oneself on, take a leaf out of someone's book; match, equal, parallel, be on a par with, be in the same league as, come close to; compete with, contend with, rival, surpass.

enable ▶ verb ALLOW, permit, let, give the means to, equip, empower, make able, fit; authorize, entitle, qualify; *formal* capacitate.
– OPPOSITES prevent.

enact ▶ verb ❶ *the Bill was enacted in 1963* PASS, make law, legislate; approve, ratify, sanction, authorize; impose, lay down. ❷ *members of the church enacted a nativity play* ACT OUT, act, perform, appear in, stage, mount, put on, present.
– OPPOSITES repeal.

enactment ▶ noun ❶ *the enactment of a Bill of Rights* PASSING; ratification, sanction, approval, authorization; imposition. ❷ *parliamentary enactments* ACT, law, by-law, ruling, rule, regulation, statute, measure; *N. Amer. formal* ordinance; (**enactments**) legislation. ❸ *the enactment of the play* ACTING, performing, performance, staging, presentation.

enamoured ▶ adjective IN LOVE, infatuated, besotted, smitten, captivated, enchanted, fascinated, bewitched, beguiled; keen on, taken with; *informal* mad about, crazy about, wild about, bowled over by, struck on, sweet on, carrying a torch for; *poetic/literary* ensorcelled by.

encampment ▶ noun CAMP, military camp, bivouac, cantonment; campsite, camping ground; tents.

encapsulate ▶ verb ❶ *their conclusions are encapsulated in one sentence* SUMMARIZE, sum up, give the gist of, put in a nutshell; capture, express. ❷ *seeds encapsulated in resin* ENCLOSE, encase, contain, envelop, enfold, sheath, cocoon, surround.

enchant ▶ verb CAPTIVATE, charm, delight, enrapture, entrance, enthral, beguile, bewitch, spellbind, fascinate, hypnotize, mesmerize, rivet, grip, transfix; *informal* bowl someone over.
– OPPOSITES bore.

enchanter ▶ noun WIZARD, witch, sorcerer, warlock, magician, necromancer, magus; witch doctor, medicine man, shaman; *archaic* mage; *rare* thaumaturge.

enchanting ▶ adjective CAPTIVATING, charming, delightful, bewitching, beguiling, adorable, lovely, attractive, appealing, engaging, winning, fetching, winsome, alluring, disarming, irresistible, fascinating; *dated* taking.

enchantment ▶ noun ❶ *a race of giants skilled in enchantment* MAGIC, witchcraft, sorcery, wizardry, necromancy; charms, spells, incantations; *N. Amer.* mojo; *rare* thaumaturgy. ❷ *the enchantment of the garden by moonlight* ALLURE, delight, charm, beauty, attractiveness, appeal, fascination, irresistibility, magnetism, pull, draw, lure. ❸ *being with him was sheer enchantment* BLISS, ecstasy, heaven, rapture, joy.

enchantress ▶ noun WITCH, sorceress, magician, fairy; Circe, siren.

encircle ▶ verb SURROUND, enclose, circle, girdle, ring, encompass; close in, shut in, fence in, wall in, hem in, confine; *poetic/literary* gird, engirdle.

enclose ▶ verb ❶ *tall trees enclosed the garden* SURROUND, circle, ring, girdle, encompass, encircle; confine, close in, shut in, fence in, wall in, hedge in, hem in; *poetic/literary* gird, engirdle. ❷ *please enclose a stamped addressed envelope* INCLUDE, insert, put in; send.

enclosure ▶ noun PADDOCK, fold, pen, compound, stockade, ring, yard; sty, coop; *N. Amer.* corral.

encomium ▶ noun (*formal*) EULOGY, panegyric, paean, accolade, tribute, testimonial; praise, acclaim, acclamation, homage; *formal* laudation.

encompass ▶ verb ❶ *the monument is encompassed by Hunsbury Park* CONTAIN, have within; surround, enclose, encircle. ❷ *debates encompassing a vast range of subjects* COVER, embrace, include, incorporate, take in, contain, comprise, involve, deal with; *formal* comprehend.

encounter ▶ verb ❶ *I encountered a girl I used to know* MEET, meet by chance, run into, come across/upon, stumble across/on, chance on, happen on; *informal* bump into; *archaic* run against, rencounter. ❷ *we encountered a slight problem* EXPERIENCE, run into, come up against, face, be faced with, confront.
▶ noun ❶ *an unexpected encounter* MEETING, chance meeting; *archaic* rencounter. ❷ *a violent encounter between police and demonstrators* BATTLE, fight, clash, confrontation, struggle, skirmish, engagement; *informal* run-in, set-to, dust-up, scrap.

encourage ▶ verb ❶ *the players were encouraged by the crowd's response* HEARTEN, cheer, buoy up, uplift, inspire, motivate, spur on, stir, stir up, fire up, stimulate, invigorate, vitalize, revitalize, embolden, fortify, rally; *informal* buck up, pep up, give a shot in the arm to. ❷ *she had encouraged him to go* PERSUADE, coax, urge, press, push, pressure, pressurize, prod, goad, egg on, prompt, influence, sway. ❸ *the Government was keen to encourage local businesses* SUPPORT, back, champion, promote, further, foster, nurture, cultivate, strengthen, stimulate; help, assist, aid, boost, fuel.
– OPPOSITES discourage, dissuade, hinder.

encouragement ▶ noun ❶ *she needed a bit of encouragement* HEARTENING, cheering up, inspiration, motivation, stimulation, fortification; morale-boosting; *informal* a shot in the arm. ❷ *they required no encouragement to get back to work* PERSUASION, coaxing, urging, pressure, pressurization, prodding, prompting; spur, goad, inducement, incentive, bait, motive; *informal* carrot. ❸ *the encouragement of foreign investment* SUPPORT, backing, championship, championing, sponsoring, promotion, furtherance, furthering, fostering, nurture, cultivation; help, assistance; *N. Amer.* boosterism.

encouraging ▶ adjective ❶ *an encouraging start* PROMISING, hopeful, auspicious, propitious, favourable, bright, rosy; heartening, reassuring, cheering, comforting, welcome, pleasing, gratifying. ❷ *my parents were very encouraging* SUPPORTIVE, understanding, helpful; positive, responsive, enthusiastic.

encroach ▶ verb INTRUDE, trespass, impinge, obtrude, impose oneself, invade, infiltrate, interrupt, infringe, violate, interfere with, disturb; tread/step on someone's toes; *informal* horn in on, muscle in on; *archaic* entrench on.

encroachment ▶ noun INTRUSION, trespass, invasion, infiltration, incursion, obtrusion, infringement, impingement.

encumber ▶ verb ❶ *her movements were encumbered by her heavy skirts* HAMPER, hinder, obstruct, impede, cramp, inhibit, restrict, limit, constrain, restrain, bog down, retard, slow (down); inconvenience, disadvantage, handicap. ❷ *they are encumbered with debt* BURDEN, load, weigh down, saddle; overwhelm, tax, stress, strain, overload, overburden; *Brit. informal* lumber.

encumbrance ▶ noun ❶ *he soon found the old equipment a great encumbrance* HINDRANCE, obstruction, obstacle, impediment, constraint, handicap, inconvenience, nuisance, disadvantage, drawback; *poetic/literary* trammel; *archaic* cumber. ❷ *she knew she was an encumbrance to him* BURDEN, responsibility, obligation, liability, weight, load, stress, strain, pressure, trouble, worry; millstone, albatross, cross to bear.

encyclopedic ▶ adjective COMPREHENSIVE, complete, thorough, thoroughgoing, full, exhaustive, in-depth, wide-ranging, all-inclusive, all-embracing, all-encompassing, universal, vast; *formal* compendious.

end ▶ noun ❶ *the end of the road* EXTREMITY, furthermost part, limit; margin, edge, border, boundary, periphery; point, tip, tail end; *N. Amer.* tag end. ❷ *the end of the novel* CONCLUSION, termination, ending, finish, close, resolution, climax, finale, culmination, denouement; epilogue, coda, peroration. ❸ *a cigarette end* BUTT, stub, stump, remnant; *informal* fag end, dog end. ❹ *wealth is a means and not an end in itself* AIM, goal, purpose, objective, object, holy grail, target; intention, intent, design, motive; aspiration, wish, desire, ambition. ❺ *the commercial end of the business* ASPECT, side, section, area, field, part, share, portion, segment, province. ❻ *his end might come at any time* DEATH, dying, demise, passing, expiry, quietus; doom, extinction, annihilation, extermination, destruction; downfall, ruin, ruination, Waterloo; *informal* curtains; *formal* decease.
– OPPOSITES beginning.

▶ verb ❶ *the show ended with a wedding scene* FINISH, conclude, terminate, come to an end, draw to a close, close, stop, cease; culminate, climax. build up to, lead up to, come to a head. ❷ *she ended their relationship* BREAK OFF, call off, bring to an end, put an end to, stop, finish, terminate, discontinue; dissolve, cancel, annul.
– OPPOSITES begin.

endanger ▶ verb IMPERIL, jeopardize, risk, put at risk, put in danger; threaten, pose a threat to, be a danger to, be detrimental to, damage, injure, harm; *archaic* peril.

endearing ▶ adjective LOVABLE, adorable, cute, sweet, dear, delightful, lovely, charming, appealing, attractive, engaging, winning, captivating, enchanting, beguiling, winsome; *dated* taking.

endearment ▶ noun ❶ *his murmured endearments* TERM OF AFFECTION, term of endearment, pet name; (**endearments**) sweet nothings, sweet talk. ❷ *he spoke to her without endearment* AFFECTION, fondness, tenderness, feeling, sentiment, warmth, love, liking, care.

endeavour ▶ verb *the company endeavoured to expand its activities* TRY, attempt, seek, undertake, aspire, aim, set out; strive, struggle, labour, toil, work, exert oneself, apply oneself, do one's best, do one's utmost, give one's all, be at pains; *informal* have a go/shot/stab, give something one's best shot, do one's damnedest, go all out, bend over backwards; *formal* essay.

▶ noun ❶ *an endeavour to build a more buoyant economy* ATTEMPT, try, bid, effort, venture; *informal* go, crack, shot, stab, bash; *formal* essay. ❷ *several days of endeavour* EFFORT, exertion, striving, struggling, labouring, struggle, labour, hard work, application, industry; pains; *informal* sweat, {blood, sweat, and tears}, elbow grease; *Brit. informal* graft; *Austral./NZ informal* (hard) yakka; *poetic/literary* travail. ❸ *an extremely unwise endeavour* UNDERTAKING, enterprise, venture, exercise, activity, exploit, deed, act, action, move; scheme, plan, project; *informal* caper.

ending ▶ noun END, finish, close, closing, conclusion, resolution, summing-up, denouement, finale; cessation, stopping, termination, discontinuation.
– OPPOSITES beginning.

endless ▶ adjective ❶ *a woman with endless energy* UNLIMITED, limitless, infinite, inexhaustible, boundless, unbounded, untold, immeasurable, measureless, incalculable; abundant, abounding, great; ceaseless, unceasing, unending, without end, everlasting, constant, continuous, continual, interminable, unfading, unfailing, perpetual, eternal, enduring, lasting. ❷ *as children we played endless games* COUNTLESS, innumerable, untold, legion, numberless, unnumbered, numerous, very many, manifold, multitudinous, multifarious; a great number of, infinite numbers of, a multitude of; *informal* umpteen, no end of, loads of, stacks of, heaps of, masses of, oodles of, scads of, zillions of; *N. Amer. informal* gazillions of; *poetic/literary* myriad, divers.
– OPPOSITES limited, few.

endorse ▸ verb SUPPORT, back, agree with, approve (of), favour, subscribe to, recommend, champion, stick up for, uphold, affirm, sanction; *informal* throw one's weight behind.
– OPPOSITES oppose.

endorsement ▸ noun SUPPORT, backing, approval, seal of approval, agreement, recommendation, championship, patronage, affirmation, sanction.

endow ▸ verb ❶ *Henry II endowed a hospital for poor pilgrims* FINANCE, fund, pay for, subsidize, support financially, settle money on; establish, found, set up, institute. ❷ *nature endowed the human race with intelligence* PROVIDE, supply, furnish, equip, invest, favour, bless, grace, gift; give, bestow; *poetic/literary* endue.

endowment ▸ noun ❶ *the endowment of a Chair of Botany* FUNDING, financing, subsidizing; establishment, foundation, institution. ❷ *a generous endowment* BEQUEST, legacy, inheritance; gift, present, grant, award, donation, contribution, subsidy, settlement; *formal* benefaction. ❸ *his natural endowments* QUALITY, characteristic, feature, attribute, facility, faculty, ability, talent, gift, strength, aptitude, capability, capacity.

endurable ▸ adjective BEARABLE, tolerable, supportable, manageable, sustainable.
– OPPOSITES unbearable.

endurance ▸ noun ❶ *she pushed him beyond the limit of his endurance* TOLERATION, tolerance, sufferance, forbearance, patience, acceptance, resignation, stoicism. ❷ *the race is a test of endurance* STAMINA, staying power, fortitude, perseverance, persistence, tenacity, doggedness, grit, indefatigability, resolution, determination; *informal* stickability; *formal* pertinacity.

endure ▸ verb ❶ *he endured years of pain* UNDERGO, go through, live through, experience, meet, encounter; cope with, deal with, face, suffer, tolerate, put up with, brave, bear, withstand, sustain, weather; *Scottish* thole. ❷ *I cannot endure such behaviour* TOLERATE, bear, put up with, suffer, take; *informal* hack, stand for, stomach, swallow, abide, hold with; *Brit. informal* stick, wear, be doing with; *formal* brook. ❸ *God's love will endure for ever* LAST, live, live on, go on, survive, abide, continue, persist, remain, stay.
– OPPOSITES fade.

enduring ▸ adjective LASTING, long-lasting, abiding, durable, continuing, persisting, eternal, perennial, permanent, unending, everlasting; constant, stable, steady, steadfast, fixed, firm, unwavering, unfaltering, unchanging.
– OPPOSITES short-lived.

enemy ▸ noun OPPONENT, adversary, rival, antagonist, combatant, challenger, competitor, opposer, opposition, competition, other side; *poetic/literary* foe.
– OPPOSITES ally.

energetic ▸ adjective ❶ *an energetic woman* ACTIVE, lively, dynamic, zestful, spirited, animated, vital, vibrant, bouncy, bubbly, exuberant, perky, frisky, sprightly, tireless, indefatigable, enthusiastic; *informal* peppy, sparky, feisty, full of beans, full of the joys of spring, bright-eyed and bushy-tailed. ❷ *energetic exercises* VIGOROUS, strenuous, brisk; hard, arduous, demanding, taxing, tough, rigorous. ❸ *an energetic advertising campaign* FORCEFUL, vigorous, high-powered, all-out, determined, bold, powerful, potent; intensive, hard-hitting, pulling no punches, aggressive, high-octane; *informal* punchy, in-your-face.
– OPPOSITES lethargic, gentle, half-hearted.

energize ▸ verb ❶ *people are energized by his ideas* ENLIVEN, liven up, animate, vitalize, invigorate, perk up, excite, electrify, stimulate, stir up, fire up, rouse, motivate, move, drive, spur on, encourage, galvanize; *informal* pep up, buck up, give a shot in the arm to. ❷ *floor sensors energized by standing passengers* ACTIVATE, trigger, trip, operate, actuate, switch on, turn on, start, start up, power.

energy ▸ noun VITALITY, vigour, life, liveliness, animation, vivacity, spirit, spiritedness, verve, enthusiasm, zest, vibrancy, spark, sparkle, effervescence, exuberance, buoyancy, sprightliness; strength, stamina, forcefulness, power, dynamism, drive; fire, passion, ardour, zeal; *informal* zip, zing, pep, pizzazz, punch, bounce, oomph, go, get-up-and-go, vim and vigour; *N. Amer. informal* feistiness.

enervate ▸ verb EXHAUST, tire, fatigue, weary, wear out, devitalize, drain, sap, weaken, enfeeble, debilitate, incapacitate, prostrate; *informal* knock out, do in, shatter, fag out; *Brit. informal* knacker.
– OPPOSITES invigorate.

enervation ▸ noun FATIGUE, exhaustion, tiredness, weariness, lassitude, weakness, feebleness, debilitation, indisposition, prostration.

enfeeble ▸ verb WEAKEN, debilitate, incapacitate, indispose, lay low; drain, sap, exhaust, tire, fatigue, devitalize.
– OPPOSITES strengthen.

enfold ▸ verb ❶ *the summit was enfolded in white cloud* ENVELOP, engulf, sheathe, swathe, swaddle, cocoon, shroud, veil, cloak, drape, cover; surround, enclose, encase, encircle; *poetic/literary* enshroud, mantle. ❷ *he enfolded her in his arms* CLASP, hold, fold, wrap, squeeze, clutch, gather; embrace, hug, cuddle; *poetic/literary* embosom.

enforce ▸ verb ❶ *the sheriff enforced the law* IMPOSE, apply, administer, implement, bring to bear, discharge, execute, prosecute. ❷ *they cannot enforce cooperation between the parties* FORCE, compel, coerce, exact, extort; *archaic* constrain.

enforced ▸ adjective COMPULSORY, obligatory,

mandatory, involuntary, forced, imposed, required, requisite, stipulated, prescribed, contractual, binding, necessary, unavoidable, inescapable.
– OPPOSITES voluntary.

enfranchise ▶ verb ❶ *women over thirty were enfranchised in 1918* GIVE THE VOTE TO, give/grant suffrage to. ❷ (*historical*) *he enfranchised his slaves* EMANCIPATE, liberate, free, set free, release; unchain, unyoke, unfetter, unshackle; *historical* manumit.

engage ▶ verb ❶ *tasks which engage children's interest* CAPTURE, catch, arrest, grab, draw, attract, gain, win, hold, grip, captivate, engross, absorb, occupy. ❷ *he engaged a nursemaid* EMPLOY, hire, recruit, take on, secure the services of, put on the payroll, enrol, appoint. ❸ (*dated*) *she engaged a room in the boarding house* BOOK, reserve; rent, hire; *formal* bespeak. ❹ *he engaged to pay them £10,000* CONTRACT, promise, agree, pledge, vow, covenant, commit oneself, bind oneself, undertake, enter into an agreement. ❺ *the chance to engage in many social activities* PARTICIPATE IN, take part in, join in, become involved in, go in for, partake in/of, share in, play a part/role in; have a hand in, be a party to, enter into. ❻ *infantry units engaged the enemy* FIGHT, do battle with, wage war on/against, attack, take on, set upon, clash with, skirmish with; encounter, meet.
– OPPOSITES lose, dismiss.

engaged ▶ adjective ❶ *he's otherwise engaged* BUSY, occupied, unavailable; *informal* tied up. ❷ *she's engaged to an American guy* promised/pledged in marriage; attached; *informal* spoken for; *dated* betrothed; *poetic/literary* affianced; *archaic* plighted, espoused.
– OPPOSITES free, unattached.

engagement ▶ noun ❶ *they broke off their engagement* MARRIAGE CONTRACT; *dated* betrothal; *archaic* espousal. ❷ *a business engagement* APPOINTMENT, meeting, arrangement, commitment; date, assignation, rendezvous; *poetic/literary* tryst. ❸ *Britain's continued engagement in open trading* PARTICIPATION, involvement, association. ❹ *his engagement as a curate* EMPLOYMENT, appointment; work, job, post, situation. ❺ *the first engagement of the war* BATTLE, fight, clash, confrontation, encounter, conflict, skirmish; warfare, action, combat, hostilities; *informal* dogfight.

engaging ▶ adjective CHARMING, appealing, attractive, pretty, delightful, lovely, pleasing, pleasant, agreeable, likeable, lovable, sweet, winning, winsome, fetching, captivating, enchanting, bewitching; *Scottish & N. English* bonny; *dated* taking; *archaic* comely, fair.
– OPPOSITES unappealing.

engender ▶ verb ❶ *his works engendered considerable controversy* CAUSE, be the cause of, give rise to, bring about, occasion, lead to, result in, produce, create, generate, arouse, rouse, inspire, provoke, kindle, trigger, spark, stir up, whip up, induce, incite, instigate, foment; *poetic/literary* beget, enkindle. ❷ (*archaic*) *he engendered six children* FATHER, sire, bring into the world, spawn, breed; *poetic/literary* beget.

engine ▶ noun ❶ *a car engine* MOTOR, machine, mechanism. ❷ *the main engine of change* CAUSE, agent, instrument, originator, initiator, generator. ❸ (*historical*) *engines of war* DEVICE, contraption, apparatus, machine, appliance, mechanism, implement, instrument, tool.

engineer ▶ noun ❶ *a structural engineer* designer, planner, builder. ❷ *the ship's engineer* OPERATOR, driver, controller. ❸ *the prime engineer of the approach* ORIGINATOR, deviser, designer, architect, inventor, developer, creator; mastermind.
▶ verb *he engineered a takeover deal* BRING ABOUT, arrange, pull off, bring off, contrive, manoeuvre, manipulate, negotiate, organize, orchestrate, choreograph, mount, stage, mastermind, originate, manage, stage-manage, coordinate, control, superintend, direct, conduct; *informal* wangle.

England ▶ noun *Brit. informal* Blighty; *Austral./NZ informal* Old Dart; *poetic/literary* Albion.

engrained ▶ adjective. *See* INGRAINED.

engrave ▶ verb ❶ *my name was engraved on the ring* CARVE, inscribe, cut (in), incise, chisel, chase, score, notch, etch, imprint, impress. ❷ *the image was engraved in his memory* FIX, set, imprint, stamp, brand, impress, embed, etch.

engraving ▶ noun ETCHING, print, impression, lithograph; plate, dry point, woodcut, linocut.

engross ▶ verb ABSORB, engage, rivet, grip, hold, interest, involve, occupy, preoccupy; fascinate, captivate, enthral, intrigue.

engrossed ▶ adjective ABSORBED, involved, interested, occupied, preoccupied, immersed, caught up, riveted, gripped, rapt, fascinated, intent, captivated, enthralled, intrigued.

engrossing ▶ adjective ABSORBING, interesting, riveting, gripping, captivating, compelling, compulsive, fascinating, intriguing, enthralling; *informal* unputdownable.

engulf ▶ verb INUNDATE, flood, deluge, immerse, swamp, swallow up, submerge; bury, envelop, overwhelm.

enhance ▶ verb INCREASE, add to, intensify, heighten, magnify, amplify, inflate, strengthen, build up, supplement, augment, boost, raise, lift, elevate, exalt; improve, enrich, complement.
– OPPOSITES diminish.

enigma ▶ noun MYSTERY, puzzle, riddle, conundrum, paradox, problem; a closed book; *informal* poser.

enigmatic ▶ adjective MYSTERIOUS, inscrutable, puzzling, mystifying, baffling, perplexing, impenetrable, unfathomable, sphinx-like, Delphic, oracular; cryptic, elliptical, ambiguous, equivocal, paradoxical, obscure, oblique, secret.

enjoin ▶ verb URGE, encourage, admonish, press; instruct, direct, require, order, command, tell, call on, demand, charge; *formal* adjure; *poetic/literary* bid.

enjoy ▶ verb ❶ *he enjoys playing the piano* LIKE, love, be fond of, be entertained by, take pleasure in, be keen on, delight in, appreciate, relish, revel in, adore, lap up, savour, luxuriate in, bask in; *informal* get a kick out of, get a thrill out of, get a buzz out of, go a bundle on. ❷ *she had always enjoyed good health* BENEFIT FROM, have the benefit of; be blessed with, be favoured with, be endowed with, be possessed of, possess, own, boast.
– OPPOSITES dislike, lack.
■ **enjoy oneself** HAVE FUN, have a good time, have the time of one's life; make merry, celebrate, revel; *informal* party, have a ball, have a whale of a time, whoop it up, let one's hair down.

enjoyable ▶ adjective ENTERTAINING, amusing, diverting, delightful, to one's liking, pleasant, congenial, convivial, lovely, fine, good, great, agreeable, pleasurable, delicious, delectable, satisfying, gratifying; marvellous, wonderful, magnificent, splendid; *informal* super, fantastic, fabulous, fab, terrific, grand, magic; *Brit. informal* brilliant, brill, smashing.

enjoyment ▶ noun PLEASURE, fun, entertainment, amusement, diversion, recreation, relaxation; delight, happiness, merriment, joy, gaiety, jollity; satisfaction, gratification, liking, relish, gusto; *humorous* delectation; *dated* sport.

enlarge ▶ verb ❶ *they enlarged the scope of their research* EXTEND, expand, grow, add to, amplify, augment, magnify, build up, supplement; widen, broaden, stretch, lengthen; elongate, deepen, thicken. ❷ *the lymph glands had enlarged* SWELL, distend, bloat, bulge, dilate, tumefy, blow up, puff up, balloon. ❸ *he enlarged on this subject* ELABORATE ON, expand on, add to, build on, flesh out, put flesh on the bones of, add detail to, expatiate on; develop, fill out, embellish, embroider.
– OPPOSITES reduce, shrink.

enlargement ▶ noun EXPANSION, extension, growth, amplification, augmentation, addition, magnification, widening, broadening, lengthening; elongation, deepening, thickening; swelling, distension, dilation, tumefaction.

enlighten ▶ verb INFORM, tell, make aware, open someone's eyes, notify, illuminate, apprise, brief, update, bring up to date; disabuse, set straight; *informal* put in the picture, clue in, fill in, put wise, bring up to speed.

enlightened ▶ adjective INFORMED, well informed, aware, sophisticated, advanced, developed, liberal, open-minded, broad-minded, educated, knowledgeable, wise; civilized, refined, cultured, cultivated.
– OPPOSITES benighted.

enlightenment ▶ noun INSIGHT, understanding, awareness, wisdom, education, learning, knowledge; illumination, awakening, instruction, teaching; sophistication, advancement, development, open-mindedness, broad-mindedness; culture, refinement, cultivation, civilization.

enlist ▶ verb ❶ *he enlisted in the Royal Engineers* JOIN UP, join, enrol in, sign up for, volunteer for; *Brit. archaic* take the King's shilling. ❷ *he was enlisted in the army* RECRUIT, call up, enrol, sign up; conscript; *US* draft, induct; *archaic* levy. ❸ *he enlisted the help of a friend* OBTAIN, engage, secure, win, get, procure.

enliven ▶ verb ❶ *a meeting enlivened by her wit and vivacity* LIVEN UP, spice up, add spice to, ginger up, vitalize, leaven; *informal* perk up, pep up. ❷ *the visit had enlivened my mother* CHEER UP, brighten up, liven up, raise someone's spirits, uplift, gladden, buoy up, animate, vivify, vitalize, invigorate, restore, revive, refresh, stimulate, rouse, boost, exhilarate; *N. Amer.* light a fire under; *informal* perk up, buck up, pep up.

en masse ▶ adverb (ALL) TOGETHER, as a group, as one, en bloc, as a whole, in a body, wholesale.

enmesh ▶ verb EMBROIL, entangle, ensnare, snare, trap, entrap, ensnarl, involve, catch up, mix up, bog down, mire.

enmity ▶ noun HOSTILITY, animosity, antagonism, friction, antipathy, animus, acrimony, bitterness, rancour, resentment, aversion, ill feeling, bad feeling, ill will, bad blood, hatred, hate, loathing, odium; malice, spite, spitefulness, venom, malevolence; *Brit. informal* needle.
– OPPOSITES friendship.

ennoble ▶ verb DIGNIFY, honour, exalt, elevate, raise, enhance, add dignity to, distinguish; magnify, glorify, aggrandize.
– OPPOSITES demean.

ennui ▶ noun BOREDOM, tedium, listlessness, lethargy, lassitude, languor, weariness, enervation; malaise, dissatisfaction, melancholy, world-weariness, depression, Weltschmerz.

enormity ▶ noun ❶ *the enormity of the task* IMMENSITY, hugeness; size, extent, magnitude, greatness. ❷ *the enormity of his crimes* WICKEDNESS, evil, vileness, baseness, depravity; outrageousness, monstrousness, hideousness, heinousness, horror, atrocity; villainy, cruelty, inhumanity, mercilessness, brutality, savagery, viciousness. ❸ *the enormities of the regime* OUTRAGE, horror, evil, atrocity, barbarity, abomination, monstrosity, obscenity, iniquity; crime, sin, violation, wrong, offence, disgrace, injustice, abuse.

enormous ▶ **adjective** HUGE, vast, immense, gigantic, very big, great, giant, massive, colossal, mammoth, tremendous, mighty, monumental, epic, prodigious, mountainous, king-size(d), titanic, towering, elephantine, gargantuan; *informal* mega, monster, whopping (great), humongous, jumbo, astronomical; *Brit. informal* whacking (great), ginormous.
– OPPOSITES tiny.

enormously ▶ **adverb** ❶ *an enormously important factor* VERY, extremely, really, exceedingly, exceptionally, tremendously, immensely, hugely; singularly, particularly, eminently; *informal* terrifically, awfully, terribly, seriously, desperately, ultra, damn, damned; *Brit. informal* ever so, well, dead, jolly; *N. Amer. informal* real, mighty, darned; *informal, dated* frightfully. ❷ *prices vary enormously* CONSIDERABLY, greatly, very much, a great deal, a lot.
– OPPOSITES slightly.

enough ▶ **determiner** *they had enough food* SUFFICIENT, adequate, ample, the necessary; *informal* plenty of.
– OPPOSITES insufficient.
▶ **pronoun** *there's enough for everyone* SUFFICIENT, plenty, a sufficient amount, an adequate amount, as much as necessary; a sufficiency, an ample supply; one's fill.

en passant ▶ **adverb** IN PASSING, incidentally, by the way, parenthetically, while on the subject, apropos.

enquire, inquire ▶ **verb** ❶ *I enquired about part-time training courses* ASK, make enquiries, question someone, request information. ❷ *the commission is to enquire into alleged illegal payments* INVESTIGATE, conduct an enquiry, probe, look into; research, examine, explore, delve into; *informal* check out.

enquiring, inquiring ▶ **adjective** INQUISITIVE, curious, interested, questioning, probing, searching; investigative.

enquiry, inquiry ▶ **noun** ❶ *telephone enquiries* QUESTION, query. ❷ *an enquiry into alleged security leaks* INVESTIGATION, probe, examination, exploration; inquest, hearing.

enrage ▶ **verb** ANGER, infuriate, incense, madden, inflame; antagonize, provoke, exasperate; *informal* drive mad/crazy, drive up the wall, make someone see red, make someone's blood boil, make someone's hackles rise, get someone's back up, get someone's dander up; *N. Amer. informal* burn up.
– OPPOSITES placate.

enraged ▶ **adjective** FURIOUS, infuriated, very angry, irate, incensed, raging, incandescent, fuming, ranting, raving, seething, beside oneself; *informal* mad, hopping mad, wild, livid, boiling, apoplectic, hot under the collar, on the warpath, foaming at the mouth, steamed up, in a paddy, fit to be tied; *poetic/literary* wrathful.
– OPPOSITES calm.

enrapture ▶ **verb** DELIGHT, enchant, captivate, charm, enthral, entrance, bewitch, beguile, transport, thrill, excite, exhilarate, intoxicate, take someone's breath away; *informal* bowl someone over, blow someone's mind; *poetic/literary* ravish.

enrich ▶ **verb** ENHANCE, improve, better, add to, augment; supplement, complement; boost, elevate, raise, lift, refine.
– OPPOSITES spoil.

enrol ▶ **verb** ❶ *they both enrolled for the course* REGISTER, sign on/up, put one's name down, apply, volunteer; matriculate; enter, join. ❷ *280 new members were enrolled* ACCEPT, admit, take on, register, sign on/up, recruit, engage; matriculate; impanel.

en route ▶ **adverb** ON THE WAY, in transit, during the journey, along/on the road, on the move; coming, going, proceeding, travelling.

ensconce ▶ **verb** SETTLE, install, plant, position, seat, sit, sit down; establish; *informal* park, plonk.

ensemble ▶ **noun** ❶ *a Bulgarian folk ensemble* GROUP, band; company, troupe, cast, chorus, corps; *informal* combo. ❷ *the buildings present a charming provincial ensemble* WHOLE, entity, unit, body, set, combination, composite, package; sum, total, totality, entirety, aggregate. ❸ *a pink and black ensemble* OUTFIT, costume, suit; separates, coordinates; *informal* get-up.

enshrine ▶ **verb** SET DOWN, set out, spell out, express, lay down, set in stone, embody, realize, manifest, incorporate, represent, contain, include, preserve, treasure, immortalize, cherish.

enshroud ▶ **verb** (*poetic/literary*) ENVELOP, veil, shroud, swathe, cloak, cloud, enfold, surround, bury; cover, conceal, obscure, blot out, hide, mask; *poetic/literary* mantle.

ensign ▶ **noun** FLAG, standard, colour(s), banner, pennant, pennon, streamer, banderole.

enslavement ▶ **noun** SLAVERY, servitude, bondage, forced labour; exploitation, oppression, bonds, chains, fetters, shackles, yoke; *historical* thraldom.
– OPPOSITES liberation.

ensnare ▶ **verb** CAPTURE, catch, trap, entrap, snare, net; entangle, embroil, enmesh.

ensue ▶ **verb** RESULT, follow, be consequent on, develop, proceed, succeed, emerge, stem, arise, derive, issue; occur, happen, take place, come next/after, transpire, supervene; *formal* eventuate; *poetic/literary* come to pass, befall.

ensure ▶ **verb** ❶ *ensure that the surface is com-*

pletely clean MAKE SURE, make certain, see to it; check, confirm, establish, verify. ❷ *legislation to ensure equal opportunities for all* SECURE, guarantee, assure, certify, set the seal on, clinch.

entail ▸ **verb** INVOLVE, necessitate, require, need, demand, call for; mean, imply; cause, produce, result in, lead to, give rise to, occasion.

entangle ▸ **verb** ❶ *their parachutes became entangled* TWIST, intertwine, entwine, tangle, ravel, snarl, knot, coil, mat. ❷ *the fish are easily entangled in fine nets* CATCH, capture, trap, snare, ensnare, entrap, enmesh. ❸ *he was entangled in a lawsuit* INVOLVE, implicate, embroil, mix up, catch up, bog down, mire.

entanglement ▸ **noun** ❶ *their entanglement in the war* INVOLVEMENT, embroilment. ❷ *romantic entanglements* AFFAIR, relationship, love affair, romance, amour, fling, dalliance, liaison, involvement, intrigue; complication.

entente ▸ **noun** UNDERSTANDING, agreement, arrangement, entente cordiale, settlement, deal; alliance, treaty, pact, accord, convention, concordat.

enter ▸ **verb** ❶ *police entered the house* GO IN/INTO, come in/into, get in/into, set foot in, cross the threshold of, gain access to. ❷ *a bullet entered his chest* PENETRATE, pierce, puncture, perforate; *poetic/literary* transpierce. ❸ *he entered politics in 1979* GET INVOLVED IN, join, throw oneself into, engage in, embark on, take up; participate in, take part in, play a part/role in, contribute to. ❹ *the planning entered a new phase* REACH, move into, get to, begin, start, commence. ❺ *they entered the Army at eighteen* JOIN, become a member of, enrol in/for, enlist in, volunteer for, sign up for; take up. ❻ *she entered a cookery competition* GO IN FOR, put one's name down for, register for, enrol for, sign on/up for; compete in, take part in, participate in. ❼ *the cashier entered the details in a ledger* RECORD, write, set down, put down, take down, note, jot down; put on record, minute, register, log. ❽ *please enter your password* KEY (IN), type (in), tap in. ❾ *(Law) he entered a plea of guilty* SUBMIT, register, lodge, record, file, put forward, present.
– OPPOSITES leave.

enterprise ▸ **noun** ❶ *a joint enterprise* UNDERTAKING, endeavour, venture, exercise, activity, operation, task, business, proceeding; project, scheme, plan, programme, campaign. ❷ *a woman with enterprise* INITIATIVE, resourcefulness, entrepreneurialism, imagination, ingenuity, inventiveness, originality, creativity; quick-wittedness, native wit, cleverness; enthusiasm, dynamism, drive, ambition, energy; boldness, daring, courage; *informal* gumption, get-up-and-go, oomph. ❸ *a profit-making enterprise* BUSINESS, company, firm, venture, organization, operation, concern, corporation, establishment, partnership; *informal* outfit, set-up.

enterprising ▸ **adjective** RESOURCEFUL, entrepreneurial, imaginative, ingenious, inventive, creative; quick-witted, clever, bright, sharp, sharp-witted; enthusiastic, dynamic, ambitious, energetic; bold, daring, courageous, adventurous; *informal* go-ahead.
– OPPOSITES unimaginative.

entertain ▸ **verb** ❶ *he wrote stories to entertain them* AMUSE, divert, delight, please, charm, cheer, interest; engage, occupy, absorb, engross. ❷ *he entertains foreign visitors* RECEIVE, play host/hostess to, invite (round/over), throw a party for; wine and dine, feast, cater for, feed, treat, welcome, fête. ❸ *we don't entertain much* RECEIVE GUESTS, have people round/over, have company, hold/throw a party. ❹ *I would never entertain such an idea* CONSIDER, give consideration to, contemplate, think about, give thought to; countenance, tolerate, support; *formal* brook.
– OPPOSITES bore, reject.

entertainer ▸ **noun** PERFORMER, artiste, artist.

entertaining ▸ **adjective** DELIGHTFUL, enjoyable, diverting, amusing, pleasing, agreeable, appealing, engaging, interesting, fascinating, absorbing, compelling; humorous, funny, comical; *informal* fun.

entertainment ▸ **noun** ❶ *he read for entertainment* AMUSEMENT, pleasure, leisure, recreation, relaxation, fun, enjoyment, interest, diversion; *N. Amer. informal* rec. ❷ *an entertainment for the emperor* SHOW, performance, presentation, production, extravaganza, spectacle.

enthral ▸ **verb** CAPTIVATE, charm, enchant, bewitch, fascinate, beguile, entrance, delight; win, ensnare, absorb, engross, rivet, grip, transfix, hypnotize, mesmerize, spellbind.
– OPPOSITES bore.

enthralling ▸ **adjective** FASCINATING, entrancing, enchanting, bewitching, captivating, charming, beguiling, delightful; absorbing, engrossing, compelling, riveting, gripping, exciting, spellbinding; *informal* unputdownable.

enthuse ▸ **verb** ❶ *I enthused about the idea* RAVE, be enthusiastic, gush, wax lyrical, be effusive, get all worked up, rhapsodize; praise to the skies; *informal* go wild/mad/crazy; *N. Amer. informal* ballyhoo. ❷ *he enthuses people* MOTIVATE, inspire, stimulate, encourage, spur (on), galvanize, rouse, excite, stir (up), fire, inspirit.

enthusiasm ▸ **noun** ❶ *she worked with enthusiasm* EAGERNESS, keenness, ardour, fervour, passion, zeal, zest, gusto, energy, verve, vigour, vehemence, fire, spirit, avidity; wholeheartedness, commitment, willingness, devotion, earnestness; *informal* get-up-and-go. ❷ *they put their enthusiasms to good use* INTEREST, passion, obsession, mania; inclination, preference, penchant, predilection, fancy; pastime,

hobby, recreation, pursuit.
– OPPOSITES apathy.

enthusiast ▶ noun FAN, devotee, aficionado, lover, admirer, follower; expert, connoisseur, authority, pundit; *informal* buff, freak, fanatic, nut, fiend, addict, maniac.

enthusiastic ▶ adjective EAGER, keen, avid, ardent, fervent, passionate, zealous, vehement; excited, wholehearted, committed, devoted, fanatical, earnest.

entice ▶ verb TEMPT, lure, attract, appeal to; invite, persuade, convince, beguile, coax, woo; seduce, lead on; *informal* sweet-talk.

enticement ▶ noun LURE, temptation, allure, attraction, appeal, draw, pull, bait; charm, seduction, fascination; *informal* come-on.

enticing ▶ adjective TEMPTING, alluring, attractive, appealing, inviting, seductive, beguiling, charming; magnetic, irresistible.

entire ▶ adjective ❶ *I devoted my entire life to him* WHOLE, complete, total, full; undivided. ❷ *only one of the gates is entire* INTACT, unbroken, undamaged, unimpaired, unscathed, unspoiled, perfect, in one piece. ❸ *they are in entire agreement* ABSOLUTE, total, utter, out-and-out, thorough, wholehearted; unqualified, unreserved, outright.
– OPPOSITES partial, broken.

entirely ▶ adverb ❶ *that's entirely out of the question* ABSOLUTELY, completely, totally, wholly, utterly, quite; altogether, in every respect, thoroughly, downright, one hundred per cent. ❷ *a gift entirely for charitable purposes* SOLELY, only, exclusively, purely, merely, just, alone.

entirety ▶ noun WHOLE, total, aggregate, totality, sum total.
– OPPOSITES part.
■ **in its entirety** COMPLETELY, entirely, totally, fully, wholly; in every respect, in every way, one hundred per cent, all the way, every inch, to the hilt, to the core.

entitle ▶ verb ❶ *this pass entitles you to visit the museum* QUALIFY, make eligible, authorize, allow, permit; enable, empower. ❷ *a chapter entitled 'Comedy and Tragedy'* TITLE, name, call, label, designate, dub; *formal* denominate.

entitlement ▶ noun ❶ *their entitlement to benefits* RIGHT, prerogative, claim; permission, dispensation, privilege. ❷ *your holiday entitlement* ALLOWANCE, allocation, quota, ration, limit.

entity ▶ noun ❶ *a single entity* BEING, creature, individual, organism, life form; person; body, object, article, thing. ❷ *the distinction between entity and nonentity* EXISTENCE, being; life, living, animation; substance, essence, reality, actuality.

entomb ▶ verb INTER, lay to rest, bury; *informal* plant; *poetic/literary* inhume, sepulchre.

entourage ▶ noun RETINUE, escort, cortège, train, suite; court, staff, bodyguard; attendants, companions, retainers.

entrails ▶ plural noun INTESTINES, bowels, guts, viscera, internal organs, vital organs; offal; *informal* insides, innards.

entrance[1] ▶ noun ❶ *the main entrance* ENTRY, way in, access, ingress, approach; door, portal, gate; opening, mouth; entrance hall, foyer, lobby, porch; *N. Amer.* entryway. ❷ *the entrance of Mrs Knight* APPEARANCE, arrival, entry, ingress, coming. ❸ *he was refused entrance* ADMISSION, admittance, (right of) entry, access, ingress.
– OPPOSITES exit, departure.

entrance[2] ▶ verb ❶ *I was entranced by her beauty* ENCHANT, bewitch, beguile, captivate, mesmerize, hypnotize, spellbind; enthral, engross, absorb, fascinate; stun, overpower, electrify; charm, delight; *informal* bowl over, knock out. ❷ *Orpheus entranced the wild beasts* CAST A SPELL ON, bewitch, hex, spellbind, hypnotize, mesmerize.

entrant ▶ noun ❶ *university entrants* NEW MEMBER, new arrival, beginner, newcomer, fresher, freshman, recruit; novice, neophyte; *N. Amer.* tenderfoot, greenhorn; *informal* rookie. ❷ *a prize will be awarded to the best entrant* COMPETITOR, contestant, contender, participant; candidate, applicant.

entrap ▶ verb ❶ *fishing lines can entrap wildlife* TRAP, snare, ensnare, entangle, enmesh; catch, capture. ❷ *he was entrapped by an undercover policeman* ENTICE, lure, inveigle; bait, decoy, trap; lead on, trick, deceive, dupe, hoodwink; *informal* set up, frame; *Brit. informal* fit up.

entreat ▶ verb IMPLORE, beg, plead with, pray, ask, request; bid, enjoin, appeal to, call on, petition, solicit; *poetic/literary* beseech.

entreaty ▶ noun PLEA, appeal, request, petition; suit, application, claim; solicitation, supplication; prayer.

entrée ▶ noun ❶ *there are a dozen entrées on the menu* MAIN COURSE, main dish. ❷ *an excellent entrée into the profession* (MEANS OF) ENTRY, entrance, ingress; route, path, avenue, way, key, passport.

entrench, intrench ▶ verb ESTABLISH, settle, lodge, set, root, install, plant, embed, seat; *informal* dig in.

entrenched, intrenched ▶ adjective INGRAINED, established, confirmed, fixed, firm, deep-seated, deep-rooted; unshakeable, indelible, ineradicable, inexorable.

entre nous ▶ adverb BETWEEN OURSELVES, between us, between you and me, in confidence, confidentially, privately, off the record; *informal* between you and me and the gatepost.

entrepreneur ▶ noun BUSINESSMAN/WOMAN, enterpriser, speculator, tycoon, magnate, mogul; dealer, trader; promoter, impresario;

informal wheeler-dealer, whizz-kid, mover and shaker, go-getter, high-flyer.

entrust ▶ **verb** ❶ *he was entrusted with the task* CHARGE, invest, endow; burden, encumber, saddle. ❷ *the powers entrusted to the Home Secretary* ASSIGN, confer on, bestow on, vest in, consign; delegate, depute, devolve; give, grant, vouchsafe. ❸ *she entrusted them to the hospital* HAND OVER, give custody of, turn over, commit, consign, deliver; *formal* commend.

entry ▶ **noun** ❶ *my moment of entry* APPEARANCE, arrival, entrance, ingress, coming. ❷ *the entry to the flats* ENTRANCE, way in, access, ingress, approach; door, portal, gate; entrance hall, foyer, lobby; *N. Amer.* entryway. ❸ *he was refused entry* ADMISSION, admittance, entrance, access, ingress. ❹ *entries in the cash book* ITEM, record, note, listing; memo, memorandum; account. ❺ *data entry* RECORDING, archiving, logging, documentation, capture. ❻ *we must pick a winner from the entries* CONTESTANT, competitor, contender, entrant, participant; candidate, applicant; submission, entry form, application.
–OPPOSITES departure, exit.

entwine ▶ **verb** WIND ROUND, twist round, coil round; weave, intertwine, interlace, interweave; entangle, tangle; twine, braid, plait, knit.

enumerate ▶ **verb** ❶ *he enumerated four objectives* LIST, itemize, set out, give; cite, name, specify, identify, spell out, detail, particularize. ❷ (*formal*) *they enumerated hospital readmission rates* CALCULATE, compute, count, add up, tally, total, number, quantify; reckon, work out; *Brit.* tot up.

enunciate ▶ **verb** ❶ *she enunciated each word slowly* PRONOUNCE, articulate; say, speak, utter, voice, vocalize, sound, mouth. ❷ *a document enunciating the policy* EXPRESS, state, put into words, declare, profess, set forth, assert, affirm; put forward, air, proclaim.

envelop ▶ **verb** SURROUND, cover, enfold, engulf, encircle, encompass, cocoon, sheathe, swathe, enclose; cloak, screen, shield, veil, shroud.

envelope ▶ **noun** WRAPPER, wrapping, sleeve, cover, covering, casing.

envenom ▶ **verb** ❶ (*archaic*) *the arrows are envenomed* POISON. ❷ *incidents which envenom international relations* EMBITTER, sour, poison, jaundice, taint; antagonize.

enviable ▶ **adjective** DESIRABLE, desired, favoured, sought-after, admirable, covetable, attractive; fortunate, lucky; *informal* to die for.

envious ▶ **adjective** JEALOUS, covetous, desirous; grudging, begrudging, resentful; bitter, green-eyed.

environ ▶ **verb** (*formal*) SURROUND, encircle, enclose, ring, envelop.

environment ▶ **noun** ❶ *birds from many environments* HABITAT, territory, domain; surroundings, conditions. ❷ *the hospital environment* SITUATION, SETTING, milieu, background, backdrop, scene, location; context, framework; sphere, world, realm; ambience, atmosphere. ❸ *the impact of pesticides on the environment* THE NATURAL WORLD, nature, the earth, the ecosystem, the biosphere, Mother Nature; wildlife, flora and fauna, the countryside.

environmentalist ▶ **noun** CONSERVATIONIST, preservationist, ecologist, nature-lover; *informal* ecofreak, tree hugger.

environs ▶ **plural noun** SURROUNDINGS, surrounding area, vicinity; locality, neighbourhood, district, region; precincts; *N. Amer.* vicinage.

envisage ▶ **verb** ❶ *it was envisaged that the hospital would open soon* FORESEE, predict, forecast, anticipate, expect, think likely. ❷ *I cannot envisage what the future holds* IMAGINE, contemplate, visualize, envision, picture; conceive of, think of.

envision ▶ **verb** VISUALIZE, imagine, envisage, picture; conceive of, think of, see; intend, mean.

envoy ▶ **noun** AMBASSADOR, emissary, diplomat, consul, attaché, chargé d'affaires, plenipotentiary; nuncio; representative, delegate, proxy, surrogate, liaison, spokesperson; agent, intermediary, mediator; *informal* go-between; *historical* legate.

envy ▶ **noun** ❶ *a pang of envy* JEALOUSY, covetousness; resentment, bitterness, discontent; the green-eyed monster. ❷ *the firm is the envy of Europe* FINEST, best, pride, top, cream, jewel, flower, leading light, the crème de la crème.
▶ **verb** ❶ *I admired and envied her* BE ENVIOUS OF, be jealous of; begrudge, be resentful of. ❷ *we envied her lifestyle* COVET, desire, aspire to, wish for, want, long for, yearn for, hanker after, crave.

ephemeral ▶ **adjective** TRANSITORY, transient, fleeting, passing, short-lived, momentary, brief, short; temporary, impermanent, short-term; fly-by-night.
–OPPOSITES permanent.

epic ▶ **noun** ❶ *the epics of Homer* HEROIC POEM; story, saga, legend, romance, chronicle, myth, fable, tale. ❷ *a big Hollywood epic* long film; *informal* blockbuster.
▶ **adjective** ❶ *a traditional epic poem* HEROIC, long, grand, monumental, Homeric, Miltonian. ❷ *their epic journey* AMBITIOUS, heroic, grand, great, Herculean; very long, monumental.

epicene ▶ **adjective** ❶ *a sort of epicene beauty* SEXLESS, asexual, neuter; androgynous. ❷ *he gave an epicene titter* EFFEMINATE, unmanly, unmasculine, girly, girlish; *informal* camp, campy.
–OPPOSITES macho.

epicure ▶ **noun** GOURMET, gastronome, gourmand, connoisseur; *informal* foodie.

epicurean ▶ noun HEDONIST, sensualist, pleasure-seeker, sybarite, voluptuary, bon viveur; epicure, gourmet, gastronome, connoisseur, gourmand.
▶ adjective HEDONISTIC, sensualist, pleasure-seeking, self-indulgent, sybaritic, voluptuary, lotus-eating; decadent, unrestrained, extravagant, intemperate, immoderate; gluttonous, gourmandizing.

epidemic ▶ noun ❶ *an epidemic of typhoid* OUTBREAK, plague, pandemic, epizootic. ❷ *a joyriding epidemic* SPATE, rash, wave, eruption, outbreak, craze; flood, torrent; upsurge, upturn, increase, growth, rise.
▶ adjective *the craze is now epidemic* RIFE, rampant, widespread, wide-ranging, extensive, pervasive; global, universal, ubiquitous; endemic, pandemic, epizootic.

epigram ▶ noun WITTICISM, quip, jest, pun, bon mot; saying, maxim, adage, aphorism, apophthegm, epigraph; *informal* one-liner, wisecrack, (old) chestnut.

epigrammatic ▶ adjective CONCISE, succinct, pithy, aphoristic; incisive, short and sweet; witty, clever, quick-witted, piquant, sharp; *informal* snappy.
– OPPOSITES expansive.

epilogue ▶ noun AFTERWORD, postscript, PS, coda, codicil, appendix, tailpiece, supplement, addendum, postlude, rider, back matter; conclusion.
– OPPOSITES prologue.

episode ▶ noun ❶ *the best episode of his career* INCIDENT, event, occurrence, happening; occasion, interlude, chapter, experience, adventure, exploit; matter, affair, thing. ❷ *the final episode of the series* INSTALMENT, chapter, passage; part, portion, section, component; programme, show. ❸ *an episode of illness* PERIOD, spell, bout, attack, phase; *informal* dose.

episodic ▶ adjective ❶ *episodic wheezing* INTERMITTENT, sporadic, periodic, fitful, irregular, spasmodic, occasional. ❷ *an episodic account of the war* IN EPISODES, in instalments, in sections, in parts.
– OPPOSITES continuous.

epistle ▶ noun (*formal*) LETTER, missive, communication, dispatch, note, line; correspondence, news.

epitaph ▶ noun ELEGY, commemoration, obituary; inscription, legend.

epithet ▶ noun SOBRIQUET, nickname, byname, title, name, label, tag; description, designation; *informal* moniker, handle; *formal* appellation, denomination.

epitome ▶ noun ❶ *he was the epitome of respectability* PERSONIFICATION, embodiment, incarnation, paragon; essence, quintessence, archetype, paradigm, typification; exemplar, model, soul, example; height. ❷ *an epitome of a larger work* SUMMARY, abstract, synopsis, precis, résumé, outline, digest, summation; abridgement, abbreviation, condensation.

epitomize ▶ verb ❶ *the town epitomizes the pioneer spirit* EMBODY, encapsulate, typify, exemplify, represent, manifest, symbolize, illustrate, sum up; personify; *formal* reify. ❷ (*archaic*) *we will epitomize the pamphlet. See* SUMMARIZE.

epoch ▶ noun ERA, age, period, time, span, stage; aeon.

equable ▶ adjective ❶ *an equable man* EVEN-TEMPERED, calm, composed, collected, self-possessed, relaxed, easy-going; nonchalant, insouciant, mellow, mild, tranquil, placid, stable, level-headed; imperturbable, unexcitable, untroubled, well balanced; *informal* unflappable, together, laid-back. ❷ *an equable climate* STABLE, constant, uniform, unvarying, consistent, unchanging, changeless; moderate, temperate.
– OPPOSITES temperamental, extreme.

equal ▶ adjective ❶ *lines of equal length* IDENTICAL, uniform, alike, like, the same, equivalent; matching, comparable, similar, corresponding. ❷ *fares equal to a fortnight's wages* EQUIVALENT, identical, amounting; proportionate to, commensurate with, on a par with. ❸ *equal treatment before the law* UNBIASED, impartial, non-partisan, fair, just, equitable; unprejudiced, non-discriminatory, egalitarian; neutral, objective, disinterested. ❹ *an equal contest* EVENLY MATCHED, even, balanced, level; on a par, on an equal footing; *informal* fifty-fifty, level pegging, neck and neck.
– OPPOSITES different, discriminatory.
▶ noun *they did not treat him as their equal* EQUIVALENT, peer, fellow, coequal, like; counterpart, match, parallel.
▶ verb ❶ *two plus two equals four* BE EQUAL TO, be equivalent to, be the same as; come to, amount to, make, total, add up to. ❷ *he equalled the world record* MATCH, reach, parallel, be level with, measure up to. ❸ *the fable equals that of any other poet* BE AS GOOD AS, be a match for, measure up to, equate with; be in the same league as, rival, compete with.
■ **equal to** CAPABLE OF, fit for, up to, good/strong enough for; suitable for, suited to, appropriate for; *informal* having what it takes.

equality ▶ noun ❶ *we promote equality for women* FAIRNESS, equal rights, equal opportunities, equitability, egalitarianism; impartiality, even-handedness; justice. ❷ *equality between supply and demand* PARITY, similarity, comparability, correspondence; likeness, resemblance; uniformity, evenness, balance, equilibrium, consistency, agreement, congruence, symmetry.

equalize ▶ verb ❶ *attempts to equalize their earnings* MAKE EQUAL, make even, even out/up, level, regularize, standardize, balance, square, match; bring into line. ❷ *Villa equalized in the second half* LEVEL THE SCORE, draw.

equanimity ▶ noun COMPOSURE, calm, level-headedness, self-possession, cool-headedness, presence of mind; serenity, tranquillity, phlegm, imperturbability, equilibrium; poise, assurance, self-confidence, aplomb, sangfroid, nerve; *informal* cool.
– OPPOSITES anxiety.

equate ▶ verb ❶ *he equates criticism with treachery* IDENTIFY, compare, bracket, class, associate, connect, link, relate, ally. ❷ *the rent equates to £24 per square foot* CORRESPOND, be equivalent, amount; equal. ❸ *moves to equate supply and demand* EQUALIZE, balance, even out/up, level, square, tally, match; make equal, make even, make equivalent.

equation ▶ noun ❶ *a quadratic equation* MATHEMATICAL PROBLEM, sum, calculation, question. ❷ *the equation of success with riches* IDENTIFICATION, association, connection, matching; equivalence, correspondence, agreement, comparison. ❸ *other factors came into the equation* SITUATION, problem, case, question; quandary, predicament.

equatorial ▶ adjective TROPICAL, hot, humid, sultry.
– OPPOSITES polar.

equestrian ▶ adjective *an equestrian statue* ON HORSEBACK, mounted, riding.
▶ noun *tracks for equestrians* (HORSE) RIDER, horseman, horsewoman, jockey.

equilibrium ▶ noun ❶ *the equilibrium of the economy* BALANCE, symmetry, equipoise, parity, equality; stability. ❷ *his equilibrium was never shaken* COMPOSURE, calm, equanimity, sangfroid; level-headedness, cool-headedness, imperturbability, poise, presence of mind; self-possession, self-command; impassivity, placidity, tranquillity, serenity; *informal* cool.
– OPPOSITES imbalance, agitation.

equip ▶ verb ❶ *the boat was equipped with a flare gun* PROVIDE, furnish, supply, issue, kit out, stock, provision, arm, endow. ❷ *the course will equip them for the workplace* PREPARE, qualify, suit.

equipment ▶ noun APPARATUS, paraphernalia, articles, appliances, impedimenta; tools, utensils, implements, instruments, hardware, gadgets, gadgetry; stuff, things; kit, tackle; resources, supplies; trappings, appurtenances, accoutrements; *informal* gear; *Military* materiel, baggage.

equipoise ▶ noun ❶ *an equipoise of power* EQUILIBRIUM, balance, evenness, symmetry, parity, equality, equity; stability. ❷ *an equipoise to imbalances in savings* COUNTERWEIGHT, counterbalance, counterpoise, balance; stabilizer.
– OPPOSITES imbalance.

equitable ▶ adjective FAIR, just, impartial, even-handed, unbiased, unprejudiced, egalitarian; disinterested, objective, neutral, non-partisan, open-minded; *informal* fair and square.
– OPPOSITES unfair.

equity ▶ noun ❶ *the equity of Finnish society* FAIRNESS, justness, impartiality, egalitarianism; objectivity, balance, open-mindedness. ❷ *he owns 25% of the equity in the property* VALUE, worth; ownership, rights, proprietorship.

equivalence ▶ noun EQUALITY, sameness, interchangeability, comparability, correspondence; uniformity, similarity, likeness, nearness.

equivalent ▶ adjective *a degree or equivalent qualification* EQUAL, identical; similar, parallel, analogous, comparable, corresponding, commensurate; approximate, near.
▶ noun *Denmark's equivalent of the Daily Mirror* COUNTERPART, parallel, alternative, match, analogue, twin, opposite number; equal, peer.

equivocal ▶ adjective AMBIGUOUS, indefinite, non-committal, vague, imprecise, inexact, inexplicit, hazy; unclear, cryptic, enigmatic; ambivalent, uncertain, unsure, indecisive.
– OPPOSITES definite.

equivocate ▶ verb PREVARICATE, be evasive, be non-committal, be vague, be ambiguous, dodge the issue, beat about the bush, hedge one's bets, pussyfoot around; vacillate, shilly-shally, waver; temporize, hesitate, stall; *Brit.* hum and haw; *informal* sit on the fence, duck the issue; *rare* tergiversate.

era ▶ noun EPOCH, age, period, time, span, aeon; generation.

eradicate ▶ verb ELIMINATE, get rid of, remove, obliterate; exterminate, destroy, annihilate, kill, wipe out; abolish, stamp out, extinguish, quash; erase, efface, excise, expunge.

erase ▶ verb ❶ *they erased his name from all lists* DELETE, rub out, wipe off, blot out, blank out, cancel; efface, expunge, excise, remove, obliterate, eliminate. ❷ *the old differences in style were erased* DESTROY, wipe out, obliterate, eradicate, abolish, stamp out, quash.

erect ▶ adjective ❶ *she held her body erect* UPRIGHT, straight, vertical, perpendicular; standing. ❷ *an erect penis* ENGORGED, enlarged, swollen, tumescent; hard, stiff. ❸ *the dog's fur was erect* BRISTLING, standing on end, upright.
– OPPOSITES bent, flaccid, flat.
▶ verb ❶ *the bridge was erected in 1973* BUILD, construct, put up; assemble, put together, fabricate. ❷ *the party that erected the welfare state* ESTABLISH, form, set up, found, institute, initiate, create, organize.
– OPPOSITES demolish, dismantle, lower.

erection ▶ noun ❶ *the erection of a house* CONSTRUCTION, building, assembly, fabrication, elevation. ❷ *a bleak concrete erection* BUILDING, structure, edifice, construction, pile. ❸ ERECT PENIS, phallus; tumescence, tumidity.

eremite ▶ noun (*archaic*) HERMIT, recluse, solitary, ascetic; *historical* anchorite, anchoress.

ergo ▶ adverb THEREFORE, consequently, so, as a result, hence, thus, accordingly, for that reason, that being the case, on that account; *formal* whence; *archaic* wherefore.

erode ▶ verb WEAR AWAY/DOWN, abrade, grind down, crumble; weather; eat away at, dissolve, corrode, rot, decay; undermine, weaken, deteriorate, destroy.

erosion ▶ noun WEARING AWAY, abrasion, attrition; weathering; dissolution, corrosion, decay; deterioration, disintegration, destruction; *rare* detrition.

erotic ▶ adjective SEXUALLY AROUSING, sexually stimulating, titillating, suggestive; pornographic, sexually explicit, lewd, smutty, hardcore, soft-core, dirty, racy, risqué, ribald, naughty; sexual, sexy, sensual, amatory; seductive, alluring, tantalizing; *informal* blue, X-rated, steamy, raunchy; *euphemistic* adult.

err ▶ verb ❶ *the judge had erred* MAKE A MISTAKE, be wrong, be in error, be mistaken, blunder, be incorrect, miscalculate, get it wrong; *informal* slip up, screw up, foul up, goof, make a booboo, bark up the wrong tree, get the wrong end of the stick; *Brit. informal* boob. ❷ *she struck them when they erred* MISBEHAVE, be bad, be naughty, get up to mischief, cause trouble; sin, transgress, lapse; clown about/around, fool about/around, act the goat; *informal* mess about/around, act up; *Brit. informal* play up.

errand ▶ noun TASK, job, chore, assignment; collection, delivery; mission, undertaking.

errant ▶ adjective ❶ *he fined the errant councillors* OFFENDING, guilty, culpable, misbehaving, delinquent, lawbreaking; troublesome, unruly, disobedient. ❷ (*archaic*) *a knight errant* TRAVELLING, wandering, itinerant, roaming, roving, voyaging.
–OPPOSITES innocent.

erratic ▶ adjective UNPREDICTABLE, inconsistent, changeable, variable, inconstant, irregular, fitful, unstable, turbulent, unsettled, changing, varying, fluctuating, mutable; unreliable, undependable, volatile, mercurial, capricious, fickle, temperamental, moody.
–OPPOSITES consistent.

erring ▶ adjective OFFENDING, guilty, culpable, misbehaving, errant, delinquent, lawbreaking, aberrant, deviant.

erroneous ▶ adjective WRONG, incorrect, mistaken, in error, inaccurate, untrue, false, fallacious; unsound, specious, faulty, flawed; *informal* off beam, way out, full of holes.
–OPPOSITES correct.

error ▶ noun MISTAKE, inaccuracy, miscalculation, blunder, oversight; fallacy, misconception, delusion; misprint, erratum; *informal* slip-up, bloomer, boo-boo; *Brit. informal* boob.
■ **in error** WRONGLY, by mistake, mistakenly, incorrectly; accidentally, by accident, inadvertently, unintentionally, by chance.

ersatz ▶ adjective ARTIFICIAL, substitute, imitation, synthetic, fake, false, mock, simulated; pseudo, sham, bogus, spurious, counterfeit; manufactured, man-made; *informal* phoney.
–OPPOSITES genuine.

erstwhile ▶ adjective FORMER, old, past, one-time, sometime, ex-, late, then; previous; *formal* quondam.
–OPPOSITES present.

erudite ▶ adjective LEARNED, scholarly, educated, knowledgeable, well read, well informed, intellectual; intelligent, clever, academic, literary; bookish, highbrow, cerebral; *informal* brainy; *dated* lettered.
–OPPOSITES ignorant.

erupt ▶ verb ❶ *the volcano erupted* EMIT LAVA, become active, flare up; explode. ❷ *lava was erupted* EMIT, discharge, eject, expel, spew out, pour out, disgorge. ❸ *fighting erupted* BREAK OUT, flare up, start suddenly; ensue, arise, happen. ❹ *a boil erupted on her temple* APPEAR, break out, flare up, come to a head, emerge.

eruption ▶ noun ❶ *a volcanic eruption* DISCHARGE, ejection, emission; explosion. ❷ *an eruption of violence* OUTBREAK, flare-up, upsurge, outburst, breakout, explosion; wave, spate. ❸ *a skin eruption* RASH, outbreak, inflammation.

escalate ▶ verb ❶ *prices have escalated* INCREASE RAPIDLY, soar, rocket, shoot up, mount, spiral, climb, go up; *informal* go through the roof, skyrocket. ❷ *the dispute escalated* GROW, develop, mushroom, increase, heighten, intensify, accelerate.
–OPPOSITES plunge, shrink.

escalation ▶ noun ❶ *an escalation in oil prices* INCREASE, rise, hike, growth, leap, upsurge, upturn, climb. ❷ *an escalation of the conflict* INTENSIFICATION, aggravation, exacerbation, magnification, amplification, augmentation; expansion, build-up; deterioration.

escapade ▶ noun EXPLOIT, stunt, caper, antic(s), spree; adventure, venture, mission; deed, feat, trial, experience; incident, occurrence, event.

escape ▶ verb ❶ *he escaped from prison* RUN AWAY/OFF, get out, break out, break free, make a break for it, bolt, flee, take flight, make off, take off, abscond, take to one's heels, make one's getaway, make a run for it; disappear, vanish, slip away, sneak away; *informal* cut and run, skedaddle, scarper, vamoose, do a vanishing act, fly the coop, take French leave, leg it; *Brit. informal* do a bunk, do a runner; *N. Amer. informal* go on the lam. ❷ *he escaped his pursuers* GET AWAY FROM, escape from, elude, avoid, dodge, shake off; *informal* give someone the slip. ❸ *they escaped injury* AVOID, evade, dodge, elude, miss, cheat, sidestep, circumvent, steer clear of; shirk; *informal* duck. ❹ *lethal gas escaped* LEAK (OUT), seep (out), discharge, emanate, issue, flow (out), pour (out), gush (out), spurt (out), spew (out).

▶ **noun** ❶ *his escape from prison* GETAWAY, breakout, bolt, flight; disappearance, vanishing act; *Brit. informal* flit; *informal, dated* spring. ❷ *a narrow escape from death* AVOIDANCE OF, evasion of, circumvention of. ❸ *a gas escape* LEAK, leakage, spill, seepage, discharge, emanation, outflow, outpouring; gush, stream, spurt. ❹ *an escape from boredom* DISTRACTION, diversion.

escapee ▶ **noun** RUNAWAY, escaper, absconder; jailbreaker, fugitive; truant; deserter, defector.

escapism ▶ **noun** FANTASY, fantasizing, daydreaming, daydreams, reverie; imagination, flight(s) of fancy, pipe dreams, wishful thinking, wool-gathering; *informal* pie in the sky.
– OPPOSITES realism.

eschew ▶ **verb** ABSTAIN FROM, refrain from, give up, forgo, shun, renounce, steer clear of, have nothing to do with, fight shy of; relinquish, reject, disavow, abandon, spurn, wash one's hands of, drop; *informal* kick, pack in; *Brit. informal* jack in; *formal* forswear, abjure.

escort ▶ **noun** ❶ *a police escort* GUARD, bodyguard, protector, minder, custodian; attendant, chaperone; entourage, retinue, cortège; protection, defence, convoy. ❷ *her escort for the evening* COMPANION, partner; *informal* date. ❸ *an agency dealing with escorts* PAID COMPANION, hostess, geisha; gigolo.

▶ **verb** ❶ *he was escorted home by the police* CONDUCT, accompany, guide, usher, shepherd, take. ❷ *he escorted her in to dinner* ACCOMPANY, partner, take, bring.

esoteric ▶ **adjective** ABSTRUSE, obscure, arcane, recherché, rarefied, recondite, abstract; enigmatic, inscrutable, cryptic, Delphic; complex, complicated, incomprehensible, opaque, impenetrable, mysterious.

especial ▶ **adjective** ❶ *especial care is required* PARTICULAR, (extra) special, superior, exceptional, extraordinary; unusual, out of the ordinary, uncommon, remarkable, singular. ❷ *her especial brand of charm* DISTINCTIVE, individual, special, particular, distinct, peculiar, personal, own, unique, specific.

especially ▶ **adverb** ❶ *work poured in, especially from Kent* MAINLY, mostly, chiefly, principally, largely; substantially, particularly, primarily, generally, usually, typically. ❷ *a committee especially for the purpose* EXPRESSLY, specially, specifically, exclusively, just, particularly, explicitly. ❸ *he is especially talented* EXCEPTIONALLY, particularly, specially, very, extremely, singularly, distinctly, unusually, extraordinarily, uncommonly, uniquely, remarkably, outstandingly, really; *informal* seriously, majorly; *Brit. informal* jolly, dead, well.

espionage ▶ **noun** SPYING, infiltration; eavesdropping, surveillance, reconnaissance, intelligence.

espousal ▶ **noun** ADOPTION, embracing, acceptance; support, championship, encouragement, defence; sponsorship, promotion, endorsement, advocacy, approval.

espouse ▶ **verb** ADOPT, embrace, take up, accept, welcome; support, back, champion, favour, prefer, encourage; promote, endorse, advocate.
– OPPOSITES reject.

espy ▶ **verb** (*poetic/literary*) CATCH SIGHT OF, glimpse, see, spot, spy, notice, observe, discern, pick out, detect; *poetic/literary* behold, descry.

essay ▶ **noun** ❶ *he wrote an essay* ARTICLE, composition, study, paper, dissertation, thesis, discourse, treatise, disquisition, monograph; commentary, critique; *N. Amer.* theme. ❷ (*formal*) *his first essay in telecommunications* ATTEMPT, effort, endeavour, try, venture, trial, experiment, undertaking.

▶ **verb** (*formal*) *many essayed to travel that way* ATTEMPT, try, strive, venture, endeavour, seek, undertake.

essence ▶ **noun** ❶ *the very essence of economics* QUINTESSENCE, soul, spirit, nature; core, heart, crux, nucleus, substance; principle, fundamental quality, sum and substance, reality, actuality; *informal* nitty-gritty. ❷ *essence of ginger* EXTRACT, concentrate, distillate, elixir, decoction, juice, tincture; scent, perfume, oil.

■ **in essence** ESSENTIALLY, basically, fundamentally, primarily, principally, chiefly, predominantly, substantially; above all, first and foremost; effectively, virtually, to all intents and purposes; intrinsically, inherently.

■ **of the essence**. *See* ESSENTIAL adjective sense 1.

essential ▶ **adjective** ❶ *it is essential to remove the paint* CRUCIAL, necessary, key, vital, indispensable, important, all-important, of the essence, critical, imperative, mandatory, compulsory, obligatory; urgent, pressing, paramount, pre-eminent, high-priority. ❷ *the essential simplicity of his style* BASIC, inherent, fundamental, quintessential, intrinsic, underlying, characteristic, innate, primary, elementary, elemental; central, pivotal, vital. ❸ *the essential English gentleman* IDEAL, absolute, complete, perfect, quintessential.
– OPPOSITES unimportant, optional, secondary.

▶ **noun** ❶ *an essential for broadcasters* NECESSITY, prerequisite, requisite, requirement, need; condition, precondition, stipulation; sine qua non; *informal* must. ❷ *the essentials of the job* FUNDAMENTALS, basics, rudiments, first principles, foundations, bedrock; essence, basis, core, kernel, crux, sine qua non; *informal* nitty-gritty, brass tacks, nuts and bolts.

establish ▶ verb ❶ *they established an office in Moscow* SET UP, start, initiate, institute, form, found, create, inaugurate; build, construct, install. ❷ *evidence to establish his guilt* PROVE, demonstrate, show, indicate, signal, exhibit, manifest, attest to, evidence, determine, confirm, verify, certify, substantiate.

established ▶ adjective ❶ *established practice* ACCEPTED, traditional, orthodox, habitual, set, fixed, official; usual, customary, common, normal, general, prevailing, accustomed, familiar, expected, routine, typical, conventional, standard. ❷ *an established composer* WELL KNOWN, recognized, esteemed, respected, famous, prominent, noted, renowned.

establishment ▶ noun ❶ *the establishment of a democracy* FOUNDATION, institution, formation, inception, creation, installation; inauguration, start, initiation. ❷ *a dressmaking establishment* BUSINESS, firm, company, concern, enterprise, venture, organization, operation; factory, plant, shop, office, practice; *informal* outfit, set-up. ❸ *educational establishments* INSTITUTION, place, premises, foundation, institute. ❹ *they dare to poke fun at the Establishment* THE AUTHORITIES, the powers that be, the system, the ruling class; *informal* Big Brother.

estate ▶ noun ❶ *the Balmoral estate* PROPERTY, grounds, garden(s), park, parkland, land(s), landholding, manor, territory. ❷ *a housing estate* AREA, site, development, complex. ❸ *a coffee estate* PLANTATION, farm, holding; forest, vineyard; *N. Amer.* ranch. ❹ *he left an estate worth £610,000* ASSETS, capital, wealth, riches, holdings, fortune; property, effects, possessions, belongings; *Law* goods and chattels. ❺ (*dated*) *the estate of matrimony* STATE, condition, situation, position, circumstance.

estate agent ▶ noun PROPERTY AGENT; *Brit.* house agent; *N. Amer.* realtor.

esteem ▶ noun *she was held in high esteem* RESPECT, admiration, acclaim, approbation, appreciation, favour, recognition, honour, reverence; estimation, regard, opinion.

▶ verb ❶ *such ceramics are highly esteemed* RESPECT, ADMIRE, value, regard, acclaim, appreciate, like, prize, treasure, favour, revere. ❷ (*formal*) *I would esteem it a favour if you could speak to him.* See DEEM.

estimate ▶ verb ❶ *estimate the cost* CALCULATE ROUGHLY, approximate, guess; evaluate, judge, gauge, reckon, rate, determine; *informal* guesstimate. ❷ *we estimate it to be worth £50,000* CONSIDER, believe, reckon, deem, judge, rate, gauge; *formal* opine.

▶ noun ❶ *an estimate of the cost* ROUGH CALCULATION, approximation, estimation, rough guess; costing, quotation, valuation, evaluation; *informal* guesstimate. ❷ *his estimate of Paul's integrity* EVALUATION, estimation, judgement, rating, appraisal, opinion, view.

estimation ▶ noun ❶ *an estimation of economic growth* ESTIMATE, approximation, rough calculation, rough guess, evaluation; *informal* guesstimate. ❷ *he rated highly in Carl's estimation* ASSESSMENT, evaluation, judgement; esteem, opinion, view.

estrange ▶ verb ALIENATE, antagonize, turn away, drive away, distance; sever, set at odds with, drive a wedge between.

estrangement ▶ noun ALIENATION, antagonism, antipathy, disaffection, hostility, unfriendliness; variance, difference; parting, separation, divorce, break-up, split, breach, schism.

estuary ▶ noun (RIVER) MOUTH, firth; delta.

et cetera ▶ adverb AND SO ON, and so forth, and the rest, and/or the like, and suchlike, among others, et al., etc.; *informal* and what have you, and whatnot.

etch ▶ verb ❶ *the metal is etched with acid* CORRODE, burn into; mark. ❷ *a stone etched with tiny designs* ENGRAVE, carve, inscribe, incise, chase, score, print, mark.

etching ▶ noun ENGRAVING, print, impression, block, plate; woodcut, linocut.

eternal ▶ adjective ❶ *eternal happiness* EVERLASTING, never-ending, endless, perpetual, undying, immortal, abiding, permanent, enduring, infinite, boundless, timeless. ❷ *eternal vigilance* CONSTANT, continual, continuous, perpetual, persistent, sustained, unremitting, relentless, unrelieved, uninterrupted, unbroken, never-ending, non-stop, round-the-clock, endless, ceaseless.
– OPPOSITES transient, intermittent.

eternally ▶ adverb ❶ *I shall be eternally grateful* FOREVER, permanently, perpetually, (for) evermore, for ever and ever, for eternity, in perpetuity, enduringly; *N. Amer.* forevermore; *informal* until doomsday, until the cows come home; *archaic* for aye. ❷ *the tenants complain eternally* CONSTANTLY, continually, continuously, always, all the time, persistently, repeatedly, regularly; day and night, non-stop; endlessly, incessantly, perpetually; interminably, relentlessly; *informal* 24-7.

eternity ▶ noun ❶ *the memory will remain for eternity* EVER, all time, perpetuity. ❷ (*Theology*) *souls destined for eternity* THE AFTERLIFE, everlasting life, life after death, the hereafter, the afterworld, the next world; heaven, paradise, immortality. ❸ (*informal*) *I waited an eternity for you* A LONG TIME, an age, ages, a lifetime; hours, years, aeons; forever; *informal* donkey's years, a month of Sundays; *Brit. informal* yonks.

ethereal ▶ adjective ❶ *her ethereal beauty* DELICATE, exquisite, dainty, elegant, graceful; fragile, airy, fine, subtle. ❷ *theologians discuss ethereal ideas* CELESTIAL, heavenly, spiritual, other-worldly, paradisal, Elysian.
– OPPOSITES substantial, earthly.

ethical ▶ adjective ❶ *an ethical dilemma* MORAL, social, behavioural. ❷ *an ethical investment policy* MORALLY CORRECT, right-minded, principled, irreproachable; righteous, high-minded, virtuous, good, moral; clean, lawful, just, honourable, reputable, respectable, noble, worthy; praiseworthy, commendable, admirable, laudable; whiter than white, saintly, impeccable; *informal* squeaky clean.

ethics ▶ plural noun MORAL CODE, morals, morality, values, rights and wrongs, principles, ideals, standards (of behaviour), virtues.

ethnic ▶ adjective RACIAL, race-related, ethnological; cultural, national, tribal, ancestral, traditional.

ethos ▶ noun SPIRIT, character, atmosphere, climate, mood, feeling, tenor, essence; disposition, rationale, morality, moral code, principles, standards, ethics.

etiquette ▶ noun PROTOCOL, manners, accepted behaviour, rules of conduct, decorum, good form; courtesy, propriety, formalities, niceties, punctilios; custom, convention; *informal* the done thing; *formal* politesse.

etymology ▶ noun DERIVATION, word history, development, origin, source.

eulogize ▶ verb EXTOL, acclaim, sing the praises of, praise to the skies, wax lyrical about, rhapsodize about, rave about, enthuse about; *N. Amer. informal* ballyhoo.
– OPPOSITES criticize.

eulogy ▶ noun ACCOLADE, panegyric, paean, tribute, compliment, commendation; praise, acclaim; plaudits, bouquets; *formal* encomium.
– OPPOSITES attack.

euphemism ▶ noun POLITE TERM, indirect term, substitute, alternative, understatement, genteelism.

euphemistic ▶ adjective POLITE, substitute, mild, understated, indirect, neutral, evasive; diplomatic, inoffensive, genteel.

euphonious ▶ adjective PLEASANT-SOUNDING, sweet-sounding, mellow, mellifluous, dulcet, sweet, honeyed, lyrical, silvery, golden, lilting, soothing; harmonious, melodious; *informal* easy on the ear.
– OPPOSITES cacophonous.

euphoria ▶ noun ELATION, happiness, joy, delight, glee; excitement, exhilaration, jubilation, exultation; ecstasy, bliss, rapture.
– OPPOSITES misery.

euphoric ▶ adjective ELATED, happy, joyful, delighted, gleeful; excited, exhilarated, jubilant, exultant; ecstatic, blissful, rapturous, transported, on cloud nine, in seventh heaven; *informal* on the top of the world, over the moon, on a high.

euthanasia ▶ noun MERCY KILLING, assisted suicide.

evacuate ▶ verb ❶ *local residents were evacuated* REMOVE, clear, move out, take away. ❷ *they evacuated the bombed town* LEAVE, vacate, abandon, desert, move out of, quit, withdraw from, retreat from, decamp from, flee, depart from, escape from. ❸ *police evacuated the area* CLEAR, empty, depopulate. ❹ *patients couldn't evacuate their bowels* EMPTY (OUT), void, open, move, purge; defecate. ❺ *he evacuated the contents of his stomach* EXPEL, eject, discharge, excrete, void, empty (out).

evacuation ▶ noun ❶ *the evacuation of civilians* REMOVAL, clearance, shifting; eviction, deportation. ❷ *the evacuation of military bases* CLEARANCE, depopulation; abandonment, vacation, desertion. ❸ *involuntary evacuation of the bowels* EMPTYING (OUT), voidance, opening, purging; defecation. ❹ *dysenteric evacuations* BOWEL MOVEMENT/MOTION, stools, excrement, excreta, faeces, waste.

evade ▶ verb ❶ *they evaded the guards* ELUDE, avoid, dodge, escape (from), steer clear of, keep at arm's length, sidestep; lose, leave behind, shake off; *N. Amer.* end-run; *informal* give someone the slip. ❷ *he evaded the question* AVOID, dodge, sidestep, bypass, hedge, fence, skirt round, fudge, be evasive about; *informal* duck, cop out of.
– OPPOSITES confront.

evaluate ▶ verb ASSESS, judge, gauge, rate, estimate, appraise, analyse, weigh up, get the measure of; *informal* size up, check out.

evaluation ▶ noun ASSESSMENT, appraisal, judgement, gauging, rating, estimation, consideration, analysis.

evanescent ▶ adjective (*poetic/literary*) VANISHING, fading, evaporating, melting away, disappearing; ephemeral, fleeting, short-lived, short-term, transitory, transient, fugitive, temporary.
– OPPOSITES permanent.

evangelical ▶ adjective ❶ *evangelical Christianity* SCRIPTURAL, biblical; fundamentalist, orthodox. ❷ *an evangelical preacher* EVANGELISTIC, evangelizing, missionary, crusading, propagandist, propagandizing, proselytizing.

evangelist ▶ noun PREACHER, missionary, gospeller, proselytizer, crusader, propagandist.

evangelistic ▶ adjective. *See* EVANGELICAL sense 2.

evangelize ▶ verb CONVERT, proselytize, redeem, save, preach to, recruit; act as a missionary, crusade, campaign.

evaporate ▶ verb ❶ *the water evaporated* VAPORIZE, become vapour, volatilize; dry up. ❷ *the rock salt is washed and evaporated* DRY OUT, dehydrate, desiccate, dehumidify. ❸ *the feeling has evaporated* END, pass (away), fizzle out, peter out, wear off, vanish, fade, disappear, melt away.
– OPPOSITES condense, wet, materialize.

evasion ▶ **noun** ❶ *the evasion of immigration control* AVOIDANCE, elusion, circumvention, dodging, sidestepping. ❷ *she grew tired of all the evasion* PREVARICATION, evasiveness, beating about the bush, hedging, pussyfooting, equivocation, vagueness, temporization; *Brit.* humming and hawing; *rare* tergiversation.

evasive ▶ **adjective** EQUIVOCAL, prevaricating, elusive, ambiguous, non-committal, vague, inexplicit, unclear; roundabout, indirect; *informal* cagey.

eve ▶ **noun** ❶ *the eve of the election* DAY BEFORE, evening before, night before; the run-up to. ❷ (*poetic/literary*) *a winter's eve* EVENING, night; *poetic/literary* eventide.
– OPPOSITES morning.

even ▶ **adjective** ❶ *an even surface* FLAT, smooth, uniform, featureless; unbroken, undamaged; level, plane. ❷ *an even temperature* UNIFORM, constant, steady, stable, consistent, unvarying, unchanging, regular. ❸ *they all have an even chance* EQUAL, the same, identical, like, alike, similar, comparable, parallel. ❹ *the score was even* LEVEL, drawn, tied, all square, balanced; neck and neck; *Brit.* level pegging; *informal* even-steven(s). ❺ *an even disposition* EVEN-TEMPERED, balanced, stable, equable, placid, calm, composed, poised, cool, relaxed, easy, imperturbable, unexcitable, unruffled, untroubled; *informal* together, laid-back, unflappable.
– OPPOSITES bumpy, irregular, unequal, moody.
▶ **verb** ❶ *the canal bottom was evened out* FLATTEN, level (off/out), smooth (off/out), plane; make uniform, make regular. ❷ *the union wants to even up our wages* EQUALIZE, make equal, level up, balance, square; standardize, regularize.
▶ **adverb** ❶ *it got even colder* STILL, yet, more, all the more. ❷ *even the best hitters missed the ball* SURPRISINGLY, unexpectedly, paradoxically. ❸ *she is afraid, even ashamed, to ask for help* INDEED, you could say, veritably, in truth, actually, or rather, nay. ❹ *she couldn't even afford food* SO MUCH AS.
■ **even as** WHILE, whilst, as, just as, at the very time that, during the time that.
■ **even so** NEVERTHELESS, nonetheless, all the same, just the same, anyway, anyhow, still, yet, however, notwithstanding, despite that, in spite of that, for all that, be that as it may, in any event, at any rate.
■ **get even** HAVE ONE'S REVENGE, avenge oneself, take vengeance, even the score, settle the score, hit back, give as good as one gets, pay someone back, repay someone, reciprocate, retaliate, take reprisals, exact retribution; give someone their just deserts; *informal* get one's own back, give someone a taste of their own medicine, settle someone's hash; *poetic*/literary be revenged.

even-handed ▶ **adjective** FAIR, just, equitable, impartial, unbiased, unprejudiced, non-partisan, non-discriminatory; disinterested, detached, objective, neutral.
– OPPOSITES biased.

evening ▶ **noun** NIGHT, late afternoon, end of day, close of day; twilight, dusk, nightfall, sunset, sundown; *poetic/literary* eve, eventide.

event ▶ **noun** ❶ *an annual event* OCCURRENCE, happening, proceeding, incident, affair, circumstance, occasion, phenomenon; function, gathering; *informal* bash, do. ❷ *the team lost the event* COMPETITION, contest, tournament, round, heat, match, fixture; race, game, bout.
■ **in any event/at all events** REGARDLESS, whatever happens, come what may, no matter what, at any rate, in any case, anyhow, anyway, even so, still, nevertheless, nonetheless; *N. Amer. informal* anyways.
■ **in the event** AS IT TURNED OUT, as it happened, in the end; as a result, as a consequence.

even-tempered ▶ **adjective** SERENE, calm, composed, tranquil, relaxed, easy-going, mellow, unworried, untroubled, unruffled, imperturbable, placid, equable, stable, level-headed; *informal* unflappable, together, laid-back.
– OPPOSITES excitable.

eventful ▶ **adjective** BUSY, action-packed, full, lively, active, hectic, strenuous; momentous, significant, important, historic, consequential, fateful.
– OPPOSITES dull.

eventual ▶ **adjective** FINAL, ultimate, concluding, closing, end; resulting, ensuing, consequent, subsequent.

eventuality ▶ **noun** EVENT, incident, occurrence, happening, development, phenomenon, situation, circumstance, case, contingency, chance, likelihood, possibility, probability; outcome, result.

eventually ▶ **adverb** IN THE END, in due course, by and by, in time, after some time, after a bit, finally, at last; ultimately, in the long run, at the end of the day, one day, some day, sometime, sooner or later.

eventuate ▶ **verb** (*formal*) ❶ *you never know what might eventuate. See* HAPPEN *sense 1.* ❷ *the fight eventuated in his death* RESULT IN, end in, lead to, give rise to, bring about, cause.

ever ▶ **adverb** ❶ *the best I've ever done* AT ANY TIME, at any point, on any occasion, under any circumstances, on any account; up till now, until now. ❷ *he was ever the optimist* ALWAYS, forever, eternally, until hell freezes over; *informal* until the twelfth of never, until the cows come home, until doomsday. ❸ *an ever increasing rate of crime* CONTINUALLY, constantly, always, endlessly, perpetually, incessantly, unremittingly. ❹ *will she ever learn?* AT ALL, in any way.
■ **ever so** (*Brit. informal*) VERY, extremely, exceedingly, especially, immensely, particularly, really, truly; *N. English* right; *informal* awfully, terribly, desperately, mega, ultra; *Brit. informal*

well, dead, jolly; *N. Amer. informal* real, mighty, awful.

everlasting ▶ **adjective** ❶ *everlasting love* ETERNAL, endless, never-ending, perpetual, undying, abiding, enduring, infinite, boundless, timeless. ❷ *his everlasting complaints* CONSTANT, continual, continuous, persistent, relentless, unrelieved, uninterrupted, unabating, endless, interminable, never-ending, non-stop, incessant.
– OPPOSITES transient, occasional.

evermore ▶ **adverb** ALWAYS, forever, ever, for always, for all time, until hell freezes over, eternally, in perpetuity; ever after, henceforth; *Brit.* for evermore, forever more; *N. Amer.* forevermore; *informal* until the cows come home, until the twelfth of never.

every ▶ **determiner** ❶ *he exercised every day* EACH, each and every, every single. ❷ *we make every effort to satisfy our clients* ALL POSSIBLE, the utmost.

everybody ▶ **pronoun** EVERYONE, every person, each person, all, one and all, all and sundry, the whole world, the public; *informal* {every Tom, Dick, and Harry}, every man jack, every mother's son.

everyday ▶ **adjective** ❶ *the everyday demands of a baby* DAILY, day-to-day, quotidian. ❷ *everyday drugs like aspirin* COMMONPLACE, ordinary, common, usual, regular, familiar, conventional, run-of-the-mill, standard, stock; household, domestic; *Brit.* common or garden; *informal* bog-standard.
– OPPOSITES unusual.

everyone ▶ **pronoun** EVERYBODY, every person, each person, all, one and all, all and sundry, the whole world, the public; *informal* {every Tom, Dick, and Harry}, every man jack, every mother's son.

everything ▶ **pronoun** EACH ITEM, each thing, every single thing, the (whole) lot; all; *informal* the whole caboodle, the whole shebang; *N. Amer. informal* the whole ball of wax.
– OPPOSITES nothing.

everywhere ▶ **adverb** ALL OVER, all around, in every nook and cranny, far and wide, near and far, high and low, {here, there, and everywhere}; throughout the land, the world over, worldwide; *informal* all over the place; *Brit. informal* all over the shop; *N. Amer. informal* all over the map.
– OPPOSITES nowhere.

evict ▶ **verb** EXPEL, eject, oust, remove, dislodge, turn out, throw out, drive out; dispossess, expropriate; *informal* chuck out, kick out, boot out, bounce, give someone the (old) heave-ho, throw someone out on their ear; *Brit. informal* turf out; *N. Amer. informal* give someone the bum's rush; *dated* out.

eviction ▶ **noun** EXPULSION, ejection, ousting, removal, dislodgement, displacement, banishment; dispossession, expropriation; *Law* ouster.

evidence ▶ **noun** ❶ *they found evidence of his plotting* PROOF, confirmation, verification, substantiation, corroboration, affirmation, attestation. ❷ *the court accepted her evidence* TESTIMONY, statement, attestation, declaration, avowal, submission, claim, contention, allegation; *Law* deposition, representation, affidavit. ❸ *evidence of a struggle* SIGNS, indications, pointers, marks, traces, suggestions, hints; manifestation.
▶ **verb** *the rise of racism is evidenced here* INDICATE, show, reveal, display, exhibit, manifest; testify to, confirm, prove, substantiate, endorse, bear out; *formal* evince.
– OPPOSITES disprove.
■ **in evidence** NOTICEABLE, conspicuous, obvious, perceptible, visible, on view, plain to see; palpable, tangible, unmistakable, undisguised, prominent, striking, glaring; *informal* as plain as the nose on your face, sticking out like a sore thumb, sticking out a mile, staring someone in the face.

evident ▶ **adjective** OBVIOUS, apparent, noticeable, conspicuous, perceptible, visible, discernible, clear, plain, manifest, patent; palpable, tangible, distinct, pronounced, marked, striking, glaring, blatant; unmistakable, indisputable; *informal* as plain as the nose on your face, sticking out like a sore thumb, sticking out a mile, as clear as day.

evidently ▶ **adverb** ❶ *he was evidently dismayed* OBVIOUSLY, clearly, plainly, visibly, manifestly, patently, distinctly, markedly; unmistakably, undeniably, undoubtedly, as sure as eggs is eggs. ❷ *evidently, she believed herself superior* SEEMINGLY, apparently, as far as one can tell, from all appearances, on the face of it; it seems (that), it appears (that).

evil ▶ **adjective** ❶ *an evil deed* WICKED, bad, wrong, immoral, sinful, foul, vile, dishonourable, corrupt, iniquitous, depraved, villainous, nefarious, vicious, malicious; malevolent, sinister, demonic, devilish, diabolical, fiendish, dark; monstrous, shocking, despicable, atrocious, heinous, odious, contemptible, horrible, execrable; *informal* low-down, dirty. ❷ *an evil spirit* HARMFUL, hurtful, injurious, detrimental, deleterious, inimical, bad, mischievous, pernicious, malignant, malign, baleful; destructive, ruinous. ❸ *evil weather* UNPLEASANT, disagreeable, nasty, horrible, foul, filthy, vile, inclement.
– OPPOSITES good, beneficial, pleasant.
▶ **noun** ❶ *the evil in our midst* WICKEDNESS, bad, badness, wrongdoing, sin, immorality, vice, iniquity, degeneracy, corruption, depravity, villainy, nefariousness, malevolence; *formal* turpitude. ❷ *nothing but evil would ensue* HARM, pain, misery, sorrow, suffering, trouble, disas-

ter, misfortune, catastrophe, affliction, woe, hardship. ❸ *the evils of war* ABOMINATION, atrocity, obscenity, outrage, enormity, crime, monstrosity, barbarity.

evince ▶ verb (*formal*) REVEAL, show, make plain, manifest, indicate, display, exhibit, demonstrate, evidence, attest to; convey, communicate, proclaim, bespeak.
– OPPOSITES conceal.

eviscerate ▶ verb (*formal*) DISEMBOWEL, gut, draw, dress.

evocative ▶ adjective REMINISCENT, suggestive, redolent; expressive, vivid, graphic, powerful, haunting, moving, poignant.

evoke ▶ verb BRING TO MIND, put one in mind of, conjure up, summon (up), invoke, elicit, induce, kindle, stimulate, stir up, awaken, arouse; recall, echo, capture.

evolution ▶ noun ❶ *the evolution of Bolshevism* DEVELOPMENT, advancement, growth, rise, progress, expansion, evolvement; transformation, adaptation, modification, revision. ❷ *his interest in evolution* DARWINISM, natural selection.

evolve ▶ verb DEVELOP, progress, advance; mature, grow, expand, spread; alter, change, transform, adapt, metamorphose; *humorous* transmogrify.

exacerbate ▶ verb AGGRAVATE, worsen, inflame, compound; intensify, increase, heighten, magnify, add to, amplify, augment; *informal* add fuel to the fire/flames.
– OPPOSITES reduce.

exact ▶ adjective ❶ *an exact description* PRECISE, accurate, correct, faithful, close, true; literal, strict, faultless, perfect, impeccable; explicit, detailed, minute, meticulous, thorough; *informal* on the nail, on the mark; *Brit. informal* spot on, bang on; *N. Amer. informal* on the money, on the button. ❷ *an exact manager* CAREFUL, meticulous, painstaking, punctilious, conscientious, scrupulous, exacting; methodical, organized, orderly.
– OPPOSITES inaccurate, careless.
▶ verb ❶ *she exacted high standards from them* DEMAND, require, insist on, request, impose, expect; extract, compel, force, squeeze. ❷ *they exacted a terrible vengeance on him* INFLICT, impose, administer, apply.

exacting ▶ adjective ❶ *an exacting training routine* DEMANDING, stringent, testing, challenging, onerous, arduous, laborious, taxing, gruelling, punishing, hard, tough. ❷ *an exacting boss* STRICT, stern, firm, demanding, tough, harsh; inflexible, uncompromising, unyielding, unsparing.
– OPPOSITES easy, easy-going.

exactly ▶ adverb ❶ *it's exactly as I expected it to be* PRECISELY, entirely, absolutely, completely, totally, just, quite, in every way, in every respect, one hundred per cent, every inch, to the hilt; *informal* to a T; *N. Amer. informal* on the money. ❷ *write the quotation out exactly* ACCURATELY, precisely, correctly, unerringly, faultlessly, perfectly; verbatim, word for word, letter for letter, to the letter, faithfully.
▶ exclamation *'She escaped?' 'Exactly.'* PRECISELY, yes, that's right, just so, quite (so), indeed, absolutely; *informal* you got it.
■ **not exactly** BY NO MEANS, not at all, in no way, certainly not; not really.

exaggerate ▶ verb OVERSTATE, overemphasize, overestimate, magnify, amplify, aggrandize, inflate; embellish, embroider, elaborate, overplay, dramatize; hyperbolize, stretch the truth; *Brit.* overpitch; *informal* lay it on thick, make a mountain out of a molehill, blow out of all proportion, make a big thing of.
– OPPOSITES understate.

exaggerated ▶ adjective OVERSTATED, inflated, magnified, amplified, aggrandized, excessive; hyperbolic, elaborate, overdone, overplayed, over-dramatized, highly coloured, melodramatic, sensational; *informal* over the top, OTT.

exaggeration ▶ noun OVERSTATEMENT, overemphasis, magnification, amplification, aggrandizement; dramatization, elaboration, embellishment, embroidery, hyperbole, overkill, gilding the lily.

exalt ▶ verb ❶ *they exalted their hero* EXTOL, praise, acclaim, esteem; pay homage to, revere, venerate, worship, lionize, idolize, look up to; *informal* put on a pedestal; *formal* laud. ❷ *this power exalts the peasant* ELEVATE, promote, raise, advance, upgrade, ennoble, dignify, aggrandize. ❸ *his works exalt the emotions* UPLIFT, elevate, inspire, excite, stimulate, enliven, exhilarate.
– OPPOSITES disparage, lower, depress.

exaltation ▶ noun ❶ *a heart full of exaltation* ELATION, joy, rapture, ecstasy, bliss, happiness, delight, gladness. ❷ *their exaltation of Shakespeare* PRAISE, extolment, acclamation, reverence, veneration, worship, adoration, idolization, lionization; *formal* laudation. ❸ *the exaltation of Jesus to God's right hand* ELEVATION, rise, promotion, advancement, ennoblement.

exalted ▶ adjective ❶ *his exalted office* HIGH, high-ranking, elevated, superior, lofty, eminent, prestigious, illustrious, distinguished, esteemed. ❷ *his exalted aims* NOBLE, lofty, high-minded, elevated; inflated, pretentious. ❸ *she felt spiritually exalted* ELATED, exultant, jubilant, joyful, rapturous, ecstatic, blissful, transported, happy, exuberant, exhilarated; *informal* high.

exam ▶ noun TEST, examination, assessment; paper, oral, practical; *Brit.* viva (voce); *N. Amer.* quiz.

examination ▶ noun ❶ *artefacts spread out for examination* SCRUTINY, inspection, perusal, study, investigation, consideration, analysis, appraisal, evaluation. ❷ *a medical examination* INSPECTION, check-up, assessment, appraisal; probe, test, scan; *informal* once-over, overhaul. ❸ *a school examination* TEST, exam, assessment; paper, oral, practical; *Brit.* viva (voce); *N. Amer.* quiz. ❹ (*Law*) *the examination of witnesses* INTERROGATION, questioning, cross-examination, inquisition.

examine ▶ **verb** ❶ *they examined the bank records* INSPECT, scrutinize, investigate, look at, study, scan, sift, probe, appraise, analyse, review, survey; *informal* check out. ❷ *students were examined after a year* TEST, quiz, question; assess, appraise. ❸ (*Law*) *name the witnesses to be examined* INTERROGATE, question, quiz, cross-examine; catechize, give the third degree to, probe, sound out; *informal* grill, pump.

examiner ▶ **noun** TESTER, questioner, interviewer, assessor, appraiser, marker, inspector; auditor, analyst; adjudicator, judge, scrutineer.

example ▶ **noun** ❶ *a fine example of Chinese porcelain* SPECIMEN, sample, exemplar, exemplification, instance, case, illustration. ❷ *we must follow their example* PRECEDENT, lead, model, pattern, exemplar, ideal, standard; role model. ❸ *he was hanged as an example to others* WARNING, caution, lesson, deterrent, admonition; moral.
■ **for example** FOR INSTANCE, e.g., by way of illustration, such as, as, like; in particular, namely, viz.

exasperate ▶ **verb** INFURIATE, incense, anger, annoy, irritate, madden, enrage, antagonize, provoke, irk, vex, get on someone's nerves, ruffle someone's feathers; *Brit.* rub up the wrong way; *informal* aggravate, rile, bug, needle, hack off, get up someone's nose, get someone's back up, get someone's goat, give someone the hump; *Brit. informal* nark, wind up, get on someone's wick; *N. Amer. informal* tee off, tick off.
– OPPOSITES please.

exasperating ▶ **adjective** INFURIATING, annoying, irritating, maddening, provoking, irksome, vexatious, trying, displeasing; *informal* aggravating.

exasperation ▶ **noun** IRRITATION, annoyance, vexation, anger, fury, rage, ill humour, crossness, tetchiness, testiness; disgruntlement, discontent, displeasure; *informal* aggravation.

excavate ▶ **verb** ❶ *she excavated a narrow tunnel* DIG (OUT), bore, hollow out, scoop out; burrow, tunnel, sink, gouge. ❷ *numerous artefacts have been excavated* UNEARTH, dig up, uncover, reveal; disinter, exhume.

excavation ▶ **noun** ❶ *the excavation of a grave* UNEARTHING, digging up; disinterment, exhumation. ❷ *the excavation of a moat* DIGGING, hollowing out, boring, channelling. ❸ *implements found in the excavations* HOLE, pit, trench, trough; archaeological site.

exceed ▶ **verb** ❶ *the cost will exceed £400* BE MORE THAN, be greater than, be over, go beyond, overreach, top. ❷ *Brazil exceeds America in fertile land* SURPASS, outdo, outstrip, outshine, outclass, transcend, top, beat, better, eclipse, overshadow; *informal* best, leave standing, be head and shoulders above.

exceeding (*archaic*) ▶ **adjective** *his exceeding kindness* GREAT, considerable, exceptional, tremendous, immense, extreme, supreme, outstanding.
▶ **adverb** *the Lord has been exceeding gracious. See* EXCEEDINGLY.

exceedingly ▶ **adverb** EXTREMELY, exceptionally, especially, tremendously, very, really, truly, most; *informal* terribly, awfully, seriously, mega, ultra; *Brit. informal* ever so, well, dead, jolly; *N. Amer. informal* real, mighty; *archaic* exceeding.

excel ▶ **verb** ❶ *he excelled at football* SHINE, be excellent, be outstanding, be skilful, be talented, be pre-eminent, reign supreme; stand out, be the best, be unparalleled, be unequalled, be second to none, be unsurpassed. ❷ *she excelled him in her work* SURPASS, outdo, outshine, outclass, outstrip, beat, top, transcend, better, pass, eclipse, overshadow; *informal* best, be head and shoulders above, be a cut above.

excellence ▶ **noun** DISTINCTION, quality, superiority, brilliance, greatness, merit, calibre, eminence, pre-eminence, supremacy, peerlessness; skill, talent, virtuosity, accomplishment, mastery.

excellent ▶ **adjective** VERY GOOD, superb, outstanding, exceptional, marvellous, wonderful; pre-eminent, perfect, matchless, peerless, supreme, first-rate, first-class, superlative, splendid, fine; *informal* A1, ace, great, terrific, tremendous, fantastic, fabulous, fab, top-notch, class, awesome, magic, wicked, cool, out of this world; *Brit. informal* brilliant, brill, smashing; *Austral. informal* bonzer; *informal, dated* spiffing, capital.
– OPPOSITES inferior.

except ▶ **preposition** *every day except Monday* EXCLUDING, not including, excepting, omitting, not counting, but, besides, apart from, aside from, barring, bar, other than, saving; with the exception of; *informal* outside of; *formal* save.
– OPPOSITES including.
▶ **verb** *you're all crooks, present company excepted* EXCLUDE, omit, leave out, count out, disregard.
– OPPOSITES include.

exception ▶ **noun** *this case is an exception* ANOMALY, irregularity, deviation, special case, peculiarity, abnormality, oddity; misfit; *informal* freak.
■ **take exception** OBJECT, take offence, take umbrage, demur, disagree; resent, argue against, protest against, oppose, complain

about; *informal* kick up a fuss, kick up a stink.

■ **with the exception of.** *See* EXCEPT preposition.

exceptionable ▶ **adjective** (*formal*). *See* OBJECTIONABLE.

exceptional ▶ **adjective** ❶ *the drought was exceptional* UNUSUAL, uncommon, abnormal, atypical, extraordinary, out of the ordinary, rare, unprecedented, unexpected, surprising; strange, odd, freakish, anomalous, peculiar; *Brit.* out of the common; *informal* weird, freaky, something else. ❷ *her exceptional ability* OUTSTANDING, extraordinary, remarkable, special, excellent, phenomenal, prodigious; unequalled, unparalleled, unsurpassed, peerless, matchless, first-rate, first-class; *informal* A1, top-notch.

–OPPOSITES normal, average.

exceptionally ▶ **adverb** ❶ *it was exceptionally cold* UNUSUALLY, uncommonly, abnormally, atypically, extraordinarily, unexpectedly, surprisingly; strangely, oddly; *informal* weirdly, freakily. ❷ *an exceptionally acute mind* EXCEEDINGLY, outstandingly, extraordinarily, remarkably, especially, phenomenally, prodigiously.

excerpt ▶ **noun** EXTRACT, part, section, piece, portion, snippet, clip, bit; reading, citation, quotation, quote, line, passage; *N. Amer.* cite.

excess ▶ **noun** ❶ *an excess of calcium* SURPLUS, surfeit, overabundance, superabundance, superfluity, glut; too much. ❷ *the excess is turned into fat* REMAINDER, rest, residue; leftovers, remnants; surplus, extra, difference. ❸ *a life of excess* OVERINDULGENCE, intemperance, immoderation, profligacy, lavishness, extravagance, decadence, self-indulgence.

–OPPOSITES lack, restraint.

▶ **adjective** *excess skin oils* SURPLUS, superfluous, redundant, unwanted, unneeded, excessive; extra.

■ **in excess of** MORE THAN, over, above, upwards of, beyond.

excessive ▶ **adjective** ❶ *excessive alcohol consumption* IMMODERATE, intemperate, imprudent, overindulgent, unrestrained, uncontrolled, lavish, extravagant; superfluous. ❷ *the cost is excessive* EXORBITANT, extortionate, unreasonable, outrageous, undue, uncalled for, extreme, inordinate, unwarranted, disproportionate, too much; *informal* over the top, OTT.

excessively ▶ **adverb** INORDINATELY, unduly, unnecessarily, unreasonably, ridiculously, overly; very, extremely, exceedingly, exceptionally, impossibly; immoderately, intemperately, too much.

exchange ▶ **noun** ❶ *the exchange of ideas* INTERCHANGE, trade, trading, swapping, traffic, trafficking; *archaic* truck. ❷ *a broker on the exchange* STOCK EXCHANGE, money market, bourse. ❸ *an acrimonious exchange* CONVERSATION, dialogue, chat, talk, discussion; debate, argument, altercation; *Brit. informal* confab, row, barney; *formal* confabulation, colloquy.

▶ **verb** *we exchanged shirts* TRADE, swap, switch, change, interchange; *archaic* truck.

■ **exchange blows** FIGHT, brawl, scuffle, tussle, engage in fisticuffs; *informal* scrap, have a set-to; *Brit. informal* have a punch-up.

■ **exchange words** ARGUE, quarrel, squabble, have an argument/disagreement; *informal* have a slanging match.

excise[1] ▶ **noun** *the excise on spirits* DUTY, tax, levy, tariff.

excise[2] ▶ **verb** ❶ *the tumours were excised* CUT OUT/OFF/AWAY, take out, extract, remove; *technical* resect. ❷ *all unnecessary detail should be excised* DELETE, cross out/through, strike out, score out, cancel, put a line through; erase; *Computing, informal* kill; *Printing* dele.

excitable ▶ **adjective** TEMPERAMENTAL, mercurial, volatile, emotional, sensitive, highly strung, unstable, nervous, tense, edgy, jumpy, twitchy, uneasy, neurotic; *informal* uptight, wired.

–OPPOSITES placid.

excite ▶ **verb** ❶ *the prospect of a holiday excited me* THRILL, exhilarate, animate, enliven, rouse, stir, stimulate, galvanize, electrify, inspirit; *informal* buck up, pep up, ginger up, give someone a buzz/kick; *N. Amer. informal* give someone a charge. ❷ *she wore a chiffon nightgown to excite him* AROUSE (SEXUALLY), stimulate, titillate, inflame; *informal* turn someone on, get someone going, float someone's boat. ❸ *his clothes excited envy* PROVOKE, stir up, rouse, arouse, kindle, trigger (off), spark off, incite, cause; *poetic/literary* enkindle.

–OPPOSITES bore, depress.

excited ▶ **adjective** ❶ *they were excited about the prospect* THRILLED, exhilarated, animated, enlivened, electrified; enraptured, intoxicated, feverish, enthusiastic; *informal* high (as a kite), fired up. ❷ (SEXUALLY) AROUSED, stimulated, titillated, inflamed; *informal* turned on, hot, horny, sexed up; *Brit. informal* randy; *N. Amer. informal* squirrelly.

excitement ▶ **noun** ❶ *the excitement of seeing a leopard in the wild* THRILL, pleasure, delight, joy; *informal* kick, buzz; *N. Amer. informal* charge. ❷ *excitement in her eyes* EXHILARATION, elation, animation, enthusiasm, eagerness, anticipation, feverishness; *informal* pep, vim, zing. ❸ (SEXUAL) AROUSAL, passion, stimulation, titillation.

exciting ▶ **adjective** ❶ *an exciting story* THRILLING, exhilarating, stirring, rousing, stimulating, intoxicating, electrifying, invigorating; gripping, compelling, powerful, dramatic. ❷ (SEXUALLY) AROUSING, (sexually) stimulating, titillating, erotic, sexual, sexy; *informal* raunchy, steamy.

exclaim ▶ **verb** CRY (OUT), declare, blurt out; call (out), shout, yell; *dated* ejaculate.

exclamation ▶noun CRY, call, shout, yell, interjection; *dated* ejaculation.

exclude ▶verb ❶ *women were excluded from many scientific societies* KEEP OUT, deny access to, shut out, debar, disbar, bar, ban, prohibit. ❷ *the clause excluded any judicial review* ELIMINATE, rule out, preclude; *formal* except. ❸ *the price excludes postage* BE EXCLUSIVE OF, not include. ❹ *he excluded his name from the list* LEAVE OUT, omit, miss out.
–OPPOSITES admit, include.

exclusion ▶noun ❶ *the exclusion of women from the society* BARRING, keeping out, debarment, debarring, disbarring, banning, prohibition. ❷ *the exclusion of other factors* ELIMINATION, ruling out, precluding. ❸ *the exclusion of pupils* EXPULSION, ejection, throwing out; suspension.
–OPPOSITES acceptance, inclusion.

exclusive ▶adjective ❶ *an exclusive club* SELECT, chic, high-class, elite, fashionable, stylish, elegant, premier, grade A; expensive; *Brit.* upmarket; *N. Amer.* high-toned; *informal* posh, ritzy, classy; *Brit. informal* swish; *N. Amer. informal* tony. ❷ *a room for your exclusive use* SOLE, unshared, unique, only, individual, personal, private. ❸ *prices exclusive of VAT* NOT INCLUDING, excluding, leaving out, omitting, excepting. ❹ *mutually exclusive alternatives* INCOMPATIBLE, irreconcilable.
–OPPOSITES inclusive.
▶noun *a six-page exclusive* SCOOP, exposé, special, coup.

excoriate ▶verb ❶ (*Medicine*) *the skin had been excoriated* ABRADE, rub away/raw, scrape, scratch, chafe; strip away, skin. ❷ (*formal*) *he was excoriated in the press. See* CRITICIZE.

excrement ▶noun FAECES, excreta, stools, droppings; waste matter, ordure, dung; *informal* pooh, doings; *Brit. informal* cack, whoopsies, jobbies; *N. Amer. informal* poop.
–RELATED TERMS copro-, scato-.

excrescence ▶noun ❶ *an excrescence on his leg* GROWTH, lump, swelling, nodule, outgrowth. ❷ *the new buildings were an excrescence* EYESORE, blot on the landscape, monstrosity.

excrete ▶verb EXPEL, pass, void, discharge, eject, evacuate; defecate, urinate.
–OPPOSITES ingest.

excruciating ▶adjective AGONIZING, severe, acute, intense, violent, racking, searing, piercing, stabbing, raging; unbearable, unendurable; *informal* splitting, killing.

excursion ▶noun TRIP, outing, jaunt, expedition, journey, tour; day trip/out, drive, run, ride; *informal* junket, spin.

excusable ▶adjective FORGIVABLE, pardonable, defensible, justifiable; venial.
–OPPOSITES unforgivable.

excuse ▶verb ❶ *eventually she excused him* FORGIVE, pardon, absolve, exonerate, acquit; *informal* let someone off (the hook); *formal* exculpate. ❷ *such conduct can never be excused* JUSTIFY, defend, condone, vindicate; forgive, overlook, disregard, ignore, tolerate, sanction. ❸ *she has been excused from her duties* LET OFF, release, relieve, exempt, absolve, free.
–OPPOSITES punish, blame, condemn.
▶noun ❶ *that's no excuse for stealing* JUSTIFICATION, defence, reason, explanation, mitigating circumstances, mitigation, vindication. ❷ *an excuse to get away* PRETEXT, ostensible reason, pretence; *Brit.* get-out; *informal* story, alibi. ❸ (*informal*) *that pathetic excuse for a man!* TRAVESTY OF, poor specimen of; *informal* apology for.

execrable ▶adjective APPALLING, awful, dreadful, terrible, frightful, atrocious, lamentable, egregious; disgusting, deplorable, disgraceful, reprehensible, abhorrent, loathsome, odious, hateful, vile; *informal* abysmal, diabolical, lousy, God-awful; *Brit. informal* chronic, shocking.
–OPPOSITES admirable.

execrate ▶verb ❶ *the men were execrated as corrupt* REVILE, denounce, decry, condemn, vilify; detest, loathe, abhor, despise; *formal* abominate, excoriate. ❷ (*archaic*) *he execrated aloud. See* SWEAR sense 3.

execute ▶verb ❶ *he was convicted and executed* PUT TO DEATH, kill; hang, behead, guillotine, electrocute, shoot, put before a firing squad; *N. Amer.* send to the (electric) chair; *informal* string up; *N. Amer. informal* fry. ❷ *the corporation executed a series of financial deals* CARRY OUT, accomplish, bring off/about, achieve, complete, engineer; *informal* pull off; *formal* effectuate. ❸ *a well-executed act* PERFORM, present, render; stage.

execution ▶noun ❶ *the execution of the plan* IMPLEMENTATION, carrying out, accomplishment, bringing off/about, engineering, attainment, realization. ❷ *the execution of the play* PERFORMANCE, presentation, rendition, rendering, staging. ❸ *thousands were sentenced to execution* CAPITAL PUNISHMENT, the death penalty; the gibbet, the gallows, the noose, the rope, the scaffold, the guillotine, the firing squad; *N. Amer.* the (electric) chair.

executioner ▶noun HANGMAN, official killer; *historical* headsman.

executive ▶adjective *executive powers* ADMINISTRATIVE, decision-making, managerial; law-making.
▶noun ❶ *top-level bank executives* CHIEF, head, director, senior official, senior manager, CEO, chief executive officer; *informal* boss, exec, suit. ❷ *the executive has increased in number* ADMINISTRATION, management, directorate; government, legislative body.

exegesis ▶noun INTERPRETATION, explanation, exposition, explication.

exemplar ▶noun EPITOME, perfect example,

model, paragon, ideal, exemplification, textbook example, embodiment, essence, quintessence.

exemplary ▶ adjective ❶ *her exemplary behaviour* PERFECT, ideal, model, faultless, flawless, impeccable, irreproachable; excellent, outstanding, admirable, commendable, laudable, above/beyond reproach. ❷ *exemplary jail sentences* SERVING AS A DETERRENT, cautionary, warning, admonitory; *rare* monitory. ❸ *her works are exemplary of certain feminist arguments* TYPICAL, characteristic, representative, illustrative.
– OPPOSITES deplorable.

exemplify ▶ verb ❶ *this story exemplifies current trends* TYPIFY, epitomize, be a typical example of, be representative of, symbolize. ❷ *he exemplified his point with an anecdote* ILLUSTRATE, give an example of, demonstrate.

exempt ▶ adjective *they are exempt from all charges* FREE, not liable/subject, exempted, excepted, excused, absolved.
– OPPOSITES subject to.
▶ verb *he had been exempted from military service* EXCUSE, free, release, exclude, give/grant immunity, spare, absolve; *informal* let off (the hook); *N. Amer. informal* grandfather.

exemption ▶ noun IMMUNITY, exception, dispensation, indemnity, exclusion, freedom, release, relief, absolution; *informal* let-off.

exercise ▶ noun ❶ *exercise improves your heart* PHYSICAL ACTIVITY, a workout, working-out; gymnastics, sports, games, physical education, PE, physical training, PT, aerobics, jogging, running; *Brit. informal* physical jerks. ❷ *translation exercises* TASK, piece of work, problem, assignment; *Music* étude. ❸ *the exercise of professional skill* USE, utilization, employment; practice, application. ❹ *military exercises* MANOEUVRES, operations; war games.
▶ verb ❶ *she exercised every day* WORK OUT, do exercises, train; *informal* pump iron. ❷ *he must learn to exercise patience* USE, employ, make use of, utilize; practise, apply. ❸ *the problem continued to exercise him* WORRY, trouble, concern, make anxious, bother, disturb, perturb, distress, preoccupy, prey on someone's mind, make uneasy; *informal* bug, do someone's head in.

exert ▶ verb ❶ *he exerted considerable pressure on me* BRING TO BEAR, apply, exercise, employ, use, utilize, deploy. ❷ *he had been exerting himself* MAKE AN/EVERY EFFORT, try hard, strive, endeavour, do one's best/utmost, give one's all, push oneself, drive oneself, work hard; *informal* go all out, pull out all the stops, bend/lean over backwards, do one's damnedest, move heaven and earth, work one's socks off; *N. Amer. informal* do one's darnedest, bust one's chops; *Austral. informal* go for the doctor.

exertion ▶ noun ❶ *she was panting with the exertion* EFFORT, strain, struggle, toil, endeavour, hard work, labour; *Brit. informal* graft; *Austral./NZ informal* yakka; *poetic/literary* travail. ❷ *the exertion of pressure* USE, application, exercise, employment, utilization.

exhale ▶ verb ❶ *she exhaled her cigarette smoke* BREATHE OUT, blow out, puff out. ❷ *the jungle exhaled mists of early morning* GIVE OFF, emanate, send forth, emit.
– OPPOSITES inhale.

exhaust ▶ verb ❶ *the effort had exhausted him* TIRE (OUT), wear out, overtire, fatigue, weary, drain, run someone into the ground; *informal* do in, take it out of one, wipe out, knock out, shatter; *Brit. informal* knacker; *N. Amer. informal* poop, tucker out. ❷ *the country has exhausted its reserves* USE UP, run through, go through, consume, finish, deplete, spend, empty, drain; *informal* blow. ❸ *we've exhausted the subject* TREAT THOROUGHLY, do to death, study in great detail.
– OPPOSITES invigorate, replenish.

exhausted ▶ adjective ❶ *I'm exhausted* TIRED OUT, worn out, weary, dog-tired, bone-tired, ready to drop, drained, fatigued, enervated; *informal* done in, all in, dead beat, shattered, bushed, knocked out, wiped out, bushwhacked; *Brit. informal* knackered, whacked (out), jiggered; *N. Amer. informal* pooped, tuckered out, fried, whipped; *Austral./NZ informal* stonkered. ❷ *exhausted reserves* USED UP, consumed, finished, spent, depleted; empty, drained.

exhausting ▶ adjective TIRING, wearying, taxing, fatiguing, wearing, enervating, draining; arduous, strenuous, onerous, demanding, gruelling; *informal* killing, murderous; *Brit. informal* knackering.

exhaustion ▶ noun ❶ *sheer exhaustion forced Paul to give up* EXTREME TIREDNESS, overtiredness, fatigue, weariness. ❷ *the exhaustion of fuel reserves* CONSUMPTION, depletion, using up, expenditure; draining, emptying.

exhaustive ▶ adjective COMPREHENSIVE, all-inclusive, complete, full, encyclopedic, thorough, in-depth; detailed, meticulous, painstaking.
– OPPOSITES perfunctory.

exhibit ▶ verb ❶ *the paintings were exhibited at Sotheby's* PUT ON DISPLAY/SHOW, display, show, put on public view, showcase; set out, lay out, array, arrange. ❷ *Luke exhibited signs of jealousy* SHOW, reveal, display, manifest; express, indicate, demonstrate, present; *formal* evince.
▶ noun ❶ *an exhibit at the British Museum* OBJECT ON DISPLAY, item, piece. ❷ (*N. Amer.*) *people flocked to the exhibit. See* EXHIBITION sense 1.

exhibition ▶ noun ❶ *an exhibition of French sculpture* (PUBLIC) DISPLAY, show, showing, presentation, demonstration, exposition, showcase; *N. Amer.* exhibit. ❷ *a convincing exhibition of concern* DISPLAY, show, demonstration, manifestation, expression.

exhibitionist ▶ noun POSTURER, poser, self-publicist; extrovert; *informal* show-off; *N. Amer. informal* showboat.

exhilarate ▶ verb THRILL, excite, intoxicate, elate, delight, enliven, animate, invigorate, energize, stimulate; *informal* give someone a thrill/buzz; *N. Amer. informal* give someone a charge.

exhilaration ▶ noun ELATION, euphoria, exultation, exaltation, joy, happiness, delight, joyousness, jubilation, rapture, ecstasy.

exhort ▶ verb URGE, encourage, call on, enjoin, charge, press; bid, appeal to, entreat, implore; *formal* adjure; *poetic/literary* beseech.

exhortation ▶ noun ❶ *no amount of exhortation had any effect* URGING, encouragement, persuasion, pressure; admonishment, warning. ❷ *the government's exhortations* ENTREATY, appeal, call, charge, injunction; admonition, warning.

exhume ▶ verb DISINTER, dig up, disentomb.
– OPPOSITES bury.

exigency ▶ noun ❶ *the exigencies of the continuing war* NEED, demand, requirement, necessity. ❷ *financial exigency* URGENCY, crisis, difficulty, pressure.

exiguous ▶ adjective (*formal*) MEAGRE, inadequate, insufficient, small, scanty, paltry, negligible, modest, deficient, miserly, niggardly, beggarly; *informal* measly, stingy, piddling.
– OPPOSITES ample, generous.

exile ▶ noun ❶ *his exile from the land of his birth* BANISHMENT, expulsion, expatriation, deportation. ❷ *political exiles* ÉMIGRÉ, expatriate; displaced person, DP, refugee, deportee; *informal* expat.
▶ verb *he was exiled from his country* EXPEL, banish, expatriate, deport, drive out, throw out, outlaw.

exist ▶ verb ❶ *animals existing in the distant past* LIVE, be alive, be living; be, have being, have existence. ❷ *the liberal climate that existed during his presidency* PREVAIL, occur, be found, be in existence; be the case. ❸ *she had to exist on a low income* SURVIVE, subsist, live, support oneself; manage, make do, get by, scrape by, make ends meet.

existence ▶ noun ❶ *the industry's continued existence* ACTUALITY, being, existing, reality; survival, continuation. ❷ *her suburban existence* WAY OF LIFE/LIVING, life, lifestyle. ❸ (*archaic*) *malevolent existences* BEING, entity, creation.
■ **in existence** ❶ *there are several million unidentified species in existence* ALIVE, existing, extant, existent. ❷ *the only copy still in existence* SURVIVING, remaining, undestroyed, in circulation.

existent ▶ adjective IN EXISTENCE, alive, existing, living, extant; surviving, remaining, undestroyed.

exit ▶ noun ❶ *the fire exit* WAY OUT, door, egress, escape route; doorway, gate, gateway, portal. ❷ *take the second exit* TURNING, turn-off, turn; *N. Amer.* turnout. ❸ *his sudden exit* DEPARTURE, leaving, withdrawal, going, decamping, retreat; flight, exodus, escape.
– OPPOSITES entrance, arrival.
▶ verb *the doctor had just exited* LEAVE, go (out), depart, withdraw, retreat.
– OPPOSITES enter.

exodus ▶ noun MASS DEPARTURE, withdrawal, evacuation, leaving; migration, emigration; flight, escape, fleeing.

exonerate ▶ verb ❶ *the inquiry exonerated them* ABSOLVE, clear, acquit, find innocent, discharge; *formal* exculpate. ❷ *the pope exonerated the king from his oath* RELEASE, discharge, free, liberate; excuse, exempt, except, dispense; *informal* let off.
– OPPOSITES convict.

exorbitant ▶ adjective EXTORTIONATE, excessively high, excessive, prohibitive, outrageous, unreasonable, inflated, unconscionable, huge, enormous; *Brit.* over the odds; *informal* steep, stiff, over the top, a rip-off; *Brit. informal* daylight robbery.
– OPPOSITES reasonable.

exorcize ▶ verb ❶ *exorcizing an spirit* DRIVE OUT, cast out, expel. ❷ *they exorcized the house* PURIFY, cleanse, purge; *rare* lustrate.

exordium ▶ noun (*formal*) INTRODUCTION, opening, preface, prelude, foreword, preamble, prologue; *informal* intro; *formal* proem, prolegomenon.
– OPPOSITES conclusion.

exotic ▶ adjective ❶ *exotic birds* FOREIGN, non-native, tropical. ❷ *exotic places* FOREIGN, faraway, far-off, far-flung, distant. ❸ *Linda's exotic appearance* STRIKING, colourful, eye-catching; unusual, unconventional, out of the ordinary, foreign-looking, extravagant, outlandish; *informal* offbeat, off the wall.
– OPPOSITES native, nearby, conventional.

expand ▶ verb ❶ *metals expand when heated* INCREASE IN SIZE, become larger, enlarge; swell, dilate, inflate; lengthen, stretch, thicken, fill out; *rare* intumesce. ❷ *the company is expanding* GROW, become/make larger, become/make bigger, increase in size/scope; extend, augment, broaden, widen, develop, diversify, build up; branch out, spread, proliferate. ❸ *the minister expanded on the proposals* ELABORATE ON, enlarge on, go into detail about, flesh out, develop, expatiate on. ❹ *she expanded and flourished* RELAX, unbend, become relaxed, grow friendlier, loosen up.
– OPPOSITES shrink, contract.

expanse ▶ noun AREA, stretch, sweep, tract, swathe, belt, region; sea, carpet, blanket, sheet.

expansion ▶ noun ❶ *expansion and contraction* ENLARGEMENT, increase in size, swelling, dila-

tion; lengthening, elongation, stretching, thickening. ❷ *the expansion of the company* GROWTH, increase in size, enlargement, extension, development; spread, proliferation, multiplication. ❸ *an expansion of a lecture given last year* ELABORATION, enlargement, amplification, development.
–OPPOSITES contraction.

expansive ▶ adjective ❶ *expansive moorland* EXTENSIVE, sweeping, rolling. ❷ *expansive coverage* WIDE-RANGING, extensive, broad, wide, comprehensive, thorough. ❸ *Cara became engagingly expansive* COMMUNICATIVE, forthcoming, sociable, friendly, outgoing, affable, chatty, talkative, garrulous, loquacious, voluble.

expatiate ▶ verb SPEAK/WRITE AT LENGTH, go into detail, expound, dwell, dilate, expand, enlarge, elaborate; *formal* perorate.

expatriate ▶ noun *expatriates working overseas* EMIGRANT, non-native, émigré, (economic) migrant; *informal* expat.
–OPPOSITES national.
▶ adjective *expatriate workers* EMIGRANT, living abroad, non-native, émigré; *informal* expat.
–OPPOSITES indigenous.
▶ verb ❶ *he was not tempted to expatriate himself* SETTLE ABROAD, live abroad. ❷ *he was expatriated* EXILE, deport, banish, expel.

expect ▶ verb ❶ *I expect she'll be late* SUPPOSE, presume, think, believe, imagine, assume, surmise; *informal* guess, reckon; *N. Amer. informal* figure. ❷ *a 10 per cent rise was expected* ANTICIPATE, await, look for, hope for, look forward to; contemplate, bargain for/on, bank on; predict, forecast, envisage, envision. ❸ *we expect total loyalty* REQUIRE, ask for, call for, want, insist on, demand.

expectancy ▶ noun ❶ *feverish expectancy* ANTICIPATION, expectation, eagerness, excitement. ❷ *life expectancy* LIKELIHOOD, probability, outlook, prospect.

expectant ▶ adjective ❶ *expectant fans* EAGER, excited, agog, waiting with bated breath, hopeful; in suspense, on tenterhooks. ❷ *an expectant mother* PREGNANT; *informal* expecting, in the family way, preggers; *Brit. informal* up the duff/spout, in the (pudding) club; *technical* gravid; *archaic* with child, in a delicate/interesting condition.

expectation ▶ noun ❶ *her expectations were unrealistic* SUPPOSITION, assumption, presumption, conjecture, surmise, calculation, prediction. ❷ *tense with expectation* ANTICIPATION, expectancy, eagerness, excitement, suspense.

expecting ▶ adjective (*informal*). *See* EXPECTANT sense 2.

expedient ▶ adjective *a politically expedient strategy* CONVENIENT, advantageous, in one's own interests, useful, of use, beneficial, of benefit, helpful; practical, pragmatic, politic, prudent, wise, judicious, sensible.
▶ noun *a temporary expedient* MEASURE, means, method, stratagem, scheme, plan, move, tactic, manoeuvre, device, contrivance, ploy, machination, dodge; *Austral. informal* lurk.

expedite ▶ verb SPEED UP, accelerate, hurry, hasten, step up, quicken, precipitate, dispatch; advance, facilitate, ease, make easier, further, promote, aid, push through, urge on, boost, stimulate, spur on, help along.
–OPPOSITES delay.

expedition ▶ noun ❶ *an expedition to the South Pole* JOURNEY, voyage, tour, odyssey; exploration, safari, trek, hike. ❷ (*informal*) *a shopping expedition* TRIP, excursion, outing, jaunt. ❸ *all members of the expedition* GROUP, team, party, crew, band, squad. ❹ (*formal*) *use all expedition possible* SPEED, haste, swiftness, quickness, rapidity, briskness; *poetic/literary* fleetness, celerity.

expeditious ▶ adjective SPEEDY, swift, quick, rapid, fast, brisk, efficient; prompt, punctual, immediate, instant; *poetic/literary* fleet.
–OPPOSITES slow.

expel ▶ verb ❶ *she was expelled from her party* THROW OUT, bar, ban, debar, drum out, oust, remove, get rid of, dismiss; *Military* cashier; *informal* chuck out, sling out, kick/boot out; *Brit. informal* turf out; *N. Amer. informal* give someone the bum's rush; *dated* out. ❷ *he was expelled from the country* BANISH, exile, deport, evict, expatriate, drive out, throw out. ❸ *Dolly expelled a hiss* LET OUT, discharge, eject, issue, send forth.
–OPPOSITES admit.

expend ▶ verb ❶ *they had already expended $75,000* SPEND, pay out, disburse, dole out, dish out, get through, waste, fritter (away), dissipate; *informal* fork out, shell out, lay out, cough up, blow, splurge; *Brit. informal* splash out, stump up; *N. Amer. informal* ante up. ❷ *children expend a lot of energy* USE (UP), utilize, consume, eat up, deplete, get through.
–OPPOSITES save, conserve.

expendable ▶ adjective ❶ *an accountant decided he was expendable* DISPENSABLE, replaceable, non-essential, inessential, unnecessary, not required, superfluous, disposable. ❷ *an expendable satellite launcher* DISPOSABLE, throwaway, one-use, single-use.
–OPPOSITES indispensable.

expenditure ▶ noun ❶ *the expenditure of funds* SPENDING, paying out, outlay, disbursement, doling out, waste, wasting, frittering (away), dissipation. ❷ *reducing public expenditure* OUTGOINGS, costs, payments, expenses, overheads, spending.
–OPPOSITES saving, income.

expense ▶ noun ❶ *Nigel resented the expense* COST, price, charge, outlay, fee, tariff, levy, payment; *informal, humorous* damage. ❷ *regular expenses* OUTGOING, payment, outlay, expenditure, charge, bill, overhead. ❸ *pollution controls come at the expense of jobs* SACRIFICE, cost, loss.

expensive ▶ adjective COSTLY, dear, high-priced, overpriced, exorbitant, extortionate; *informal* steep, pricey, costing an arm and a leg, costing the earth, costing a bomb.
– OPPOSITES cheap, economical.

experience ▶ noun ❶ *qualifications and experience* SKILL, (practical) knowledge, understanding; background, record, history; maturity, worldliness, sophistication; *informal* know-how. ❷ *an enjoyable experience* INCIDENT, occurrence, event, happening, episode; adventure, exploit, escapade. ❸ *his first experience of business* INVOLVEMENT IN, participation in, contact with, acquaintance with, exposure to, observation of, awareness of, insight into.
▶ verb *some police officers experience harassment* UNDERGO, encounter, meet, come into contact with, come across, come up against, face, be faced with.

experienced ▶ adjective ❶ *an experienced pilot* KNOWLEDGEABLE, skilful, skilled, expert, accomplished, adept, adroit, master, consummate; proficient, trained, competent, capable, well trained, well versed; seasoned, practised, mature, veteran. ❷ *she deluded herself that she was experienced* WORLDLY (WISE), sophisticated, suave, urbane, mature, knowing; *informal* streetwise.
– OPPOSITES novice, naive.

experiment ▶ noun ❶ *carrying out experiments* TEST, investigation, trial, examination, observation; assessment, evaluation, appraisal, analysis, study. ❷ *these results have been established by experiment* RESEARCH, experimentation, observation, analysis, testing.
– RELATED TERMS empirical.
▶ verb *they experimented with new ideas* CONDUCT EXPERIMENTS, carry out trials/tests, conduct research; test, trial, do tests on, try out, assess, appraise, evaluate.

experimental ▶ adjective ❶ *the experimental stage* EXPLORATORY, investigational, trial, test, pilot; speculative, conjectural, hypothetical, tentative, preliminary, untested, untried. ❷ *experimental music* INNOVATIVE, innovatory, new, original, radical, avant-garde, alternative, unorthodox, unconventional, left-field; *informal* way-out.

expert ▶ noun *he is an expert in kendo* SPECIALIST, authority, pundit; adept, maestro, virtuoso, (past) master, wizard; connoisseur, aficionado; *informal* ace, buff, pro, whizz, hotshot; *Brit. informal* dab hand; *N. Amer. informal* maven, crackerjack.
▶ adjective *an expert chess player* SKILFUL, skilled, adept, accomplished, talented, fine; master, masterly, brilliant, virtuoso, magnificent, outstanding, great, exceptional, excellent, first-class, first-rate, superb; proficient, good, able, capable, experienced, practised, knowledgeable; *informal* wizard, ace, crack, mean.
– OPPOSITES incompetent.

expertise ▶ noun SKILL, skilfulness, expertness, prowess, proficiency, competence; knowledge, mastery, ability, aptitude, facility, capability; *informal* know-how.

expiate ▶ verb ATONE FOR, make amends for, make up for, do penance for, pay for, redress, redeem, offset, make good.

expire ▶ verb ❶ *my contract has expired* RUN OUT, become invalid, become void, lapse; END, finish, stop, come to an end, terminate. ❷ *the spot where he expired* DIE, pass away/on, breathe one's last; *informal* kick the bucket, bite the dust, croak, buy it; *Brit. informal* snuff it, peg out, pop one's clogs; *archaic* decease, depart this life. ❸ (*technical*) *afterwards the breath is expired* BREATHE OUT, exhale, blow out, expel.

expiry ▶ noun ❶ *the expiry of the lease* LAPSE, expiration. ❷ *the expiry of his term of office* END, finish, termination, conclusion. ❸ (*archaic*) *the sad expiry of their friend* DEATH, demise, passing (away/on), dying; *formal* decease.

explain ▶ verb ❶ *a technician explained the procedure* DESCRIBE, give an explanation of, make clear/intelligible, spell out, put into words; elucidate, expound, explicate, clarify, throw light on; gloss, interpret. ❷ *nothing could explain his new-found wealth* ACCOUNT FOR, give an explanation for, give a reason for; justify, give a justification for, give an excuse for, vindicate, legitimize.

explanation ▶ noun ❶ *an explanation of the ideas contained in the essay* CLARIFICATION, simplification; description, report, statement; elucidation, exposition, expounding, explication; gloss, interpretation, commentary, exegesis. ❷ *I owe you an explanation* ACCOUNT, reason; justification, excuse, alibi, defence, vindication.

explanatory ▶ adjective EXPLAINING, descriptive, describing, illustrative, illuminative, elucidatory.

expletive ▶ noun SWEAR WORD, oath, curse, obscenity, profanity, four-letter word, dirty word; *informal* cuss word, cuss; *formal* imprecation; (**expletives**) bad language, foul language, strong language, swearing.

explicable ▶ adjective EXPLAINABLE, understandable, comprehensible, accountable, intelligible, interpretable.

explicate ▶ verb EXPLAIN, make explicit, clarify, make plain/clear, spell out; interpret, elucidate, expound, illuminate, throw light on.

explicit ▶ adjective ❶ *explicit instructions* CLEAR, plain, straightforward, crystal clear, easily understandable; precise, exact, specific, unequivocal, unambiguous; detailed, comprehensive, exhaustive. ❷ *sexually explicit material* UNCENSORED, graphic, candid, full-frontal.
– OPPOSITES vague.

explode ▶ verb ❶ *a bomb has exploded* BLOW UP, detonate, go off, burst (apart), fly apart. ❷ *ex-*

ploding the first atomic device DETONATE, set off, let off, discharge. ❸ *he exploded in anger* LOSE ONE'S TEMPER, blow up, get angry, become enraged; *informal* fly off the handle, hit the roof, blow one's cool/top, go wild, go bananas, see red, go off the deep end; *Brit. informal* go spare, go crackers; *N. Amer. informal* blow one's lid/stack. ❹ *the city's exploding population* INCREASE SUDDENLY/RAPIDLY, mushroom, snowball, escalate, multiply, burgeon, rocket. ❺ *exploding the myths about men* DISPROVE, refute, rebut, invalidate, negate, negative, controvert, repudiate, discredit, debunk, belie, give the lie to; *informal* shoot full of holes, blow out of the water; *formal* confute.
– OPPOSITES defuse.

exploit ▶ **verb** ❶ *we should exploit this new technology* UTILIZE, use, make use of, turn/put to good use, make the most of, capitalize on, benefit from; *informal* cash in on. ❷ *exploiting the workers* TAKE ADVANTAGE OF, abuse, impose on, treat unfairly, misuse, ill-treat; *informal* walk (all) over, take for a ride, rip off.
▶ **noun** *his exploits brought him notoriety* FEAT, deed, act, adventure, stunt, escapade; achievement, accomplishment, attainment; *informal* lark, caper.

exploitation ▶ **noun** ❶ *the exploitation of mineral resources* UTILIZATION, use, making use of, making the most of, capitalization on; *informal* cashing in on. ❷ *the exploitation of the poor* TAKING ADVANTAGE, abuse, misuse, ill-treatment, unfair treatment, oppression.

exploration ▶ **noun** ❶ *the exploration of space* INVESTIGATION, study, survey, research, inspection, examination, scrutiny, observation; consideration, analysis, review. ❷ *explorations into the mountains* EXPEDITION, trip, journey, voyage; *archaic* peregrination; (**explorations**) travels.

exploratory ▶ **adjective** INVESTIGATIVE, investigational, explorative, probing, fact-finding; experimental, trial, test, preliminary, provisional.

explore ▶ **verb** ❶ *they explored all the possibilities* INVESTIGATE, look into, consider; examine, research, survey, scrutinize, study, review, go over with a fine-tooth comb; *informal* check out. ❷ *exploring Iceland's north-west* TRAVEL OVER, tour, range over; survey, take a look at, inspect, investigate, reconnoitre; *informal* recce, give something a/the once-over.

explorer ▶ **noun** TRAVELLER, discoverer, voyager, adventurer; surveyor, scout, prospector.

explosion ▶ **noun** ❶ *Edward heard the explosion* DETONATION, eruption, blowing up; bang, blast, boom. ❷ *an explosion of anger* OUTBURST, flare-up, outbreak, eruption, storm, rush, surge; fit, paroxysm, attack. ❸ *the explosion of human populations* SUDDEN/RAPID INCREASE, mushrooming, snowballing, escalation, multiplication, burgeoning, rocketing.

explosive ▶ **adjective** ❶ *explosive gases* VOLATILE, inflammable, flammable, combustible, incendiary. ❷ *Marco's explosive temper* FIERY, stormy, violent, volatile, angry, passionate, tempestuous, turbulent, touchy, irascible, hot-headed, short-tempered. ❸ *an explosive situation* TENSE, (highly) charged, overwrought; dangerous, perilous, hazardous, sensitive, delicate, unstable, volatile. ❹ *explosive population growth* SUDDEN, dramatic, rapid; mushrooming, snowballing, escalating, rocketing, accelerating.
▶ **noun** *stocks of explosives* BOMB, incendiary (device).

exponent ▶ **noun** ❶ *an exponent of free-trade policies* ADVOCATE, supporter, proponent, upholder, backer, defender, champion; promoter, propagandist, campaigner, fighter, crusader, enthusiast, apologist. ❷ *a karate exponent* PRACTITIONER, performer, player.
– OPPOSITES critic, opponent.

export ▶ **verb** ❶ *exporting raw materials* SELL OVERSEAS/ABROAD, send overseas/abroad, trade internationally. ❷ *he is trying to export his ideas to America* TRANSMIT, spread, disseminate, circulate, communicate, pass on; *poetic/literary* bruit about/abroad.
– OPPOSITES import.

expose ▶ **verb** ❶ *at low tide the sands are exposed* REVEAL, uncover, lay bare. ❷ *he was exposed to asbestos* MAKE VULNERABLE, subject, lay open, put at risk, put in jeopardy. ❸ *they were exposed to liberal ideas* INTRODUCE TO, bring into contact with, make aware of, familiarize with, acquaint with. ❹ *he was exposed as a liar* UNCOVER, reveal, unveil, unmask, detect, find out; discover, bring to light, bring into the open, make known; denounce, condemn; *informal* spill the beans on, blow the whistle on.
– OPPOSITES cover.
■ **expose oneself** REVEAL ONE'S GENITALIA; *informal* flash.

exposé ▶ **noun** REVELATION, disclosure, exposure; report, feature, piece, column; *informal* scoop.
– OPPOSITES cover-up.

exposed ▶ **adjective** UNPROTECTED, unsheltered, open to the elements/weather; vulnerable, defenceless, undefended, pregnable.
– OPPOSITES sheltered.

exposition ▶ **noun** ❶ *a lucid exposition* EXPLANATION, description, elucidation, explication, interpretation; account, commentary, appraisal, assessment, discussion, exegesis. ❷ *the exposition will feature 200 exhibits* EXHIBITION, (trade) fair, display, show, presentation, demonstration; *N. Amer.* exhibit.

expository ▶ **adjective** EXPLANATORY, descriptive, describing, elucidatory, explicatory, explicative, interpretative, exegetic.

expostulate ▶ **verb** REMONSTRATE, disagree,

argue, take issue, protest, reason, express disagreement, raise objections.

exposure ▶ **noun** ❶ *the exposure of the lizard's vivid blue tongue* REVEALING, revelation, uncovering, baring, laying bare. ❷ *exposure to harmful chemicals* SUBJECTION, vulnerability, laying open. ❸ *suffering from exposure* FROSTBITE, cold, hypothermia. ❹ *exposure to great literature* INTRODUCTION TO, experience of, contact with, familiarity with, acquaintance with, awareness of. ❺ *the exposure of a banking scandal* UNCOVERING, revelation, disclosure, unveiling, unmasking, discovery, detection; denunciation, condemnation. ❻ *we're getting a lot of exposure* PUBLICITY, publicizing, advertising, public interest/attention, media interest/attention; *informal* hype. ❼ *the exposure is perfect* OUTLOOK, aspect, view; position, setting, location.

expound ▶ **verb** ❶ *he expounded his theories* PRESENT, put forward, set forth, propose, propound; explain, give an explanation of, detail, spell out, describe. ❷ *a treatise expounding Paul's teachings* EXPLAIN, interpret, explicate, elucidate; comment on, give a commentary on.

■ **expound on** ELABORATE ON, expand on, expatiate on, discuss at length.

express[1] ▶ **verb** ❶ *community leaders expressed their anger* COMMUNICATE, convey, indicate, show, demonstrate, reveal, make manifest, put across/over, get across/over; articulate, put into words, utter, voice, give voice to; state, assert, proclaim, profess, air, make public, give vent to; *formal* evince. ❷ *all the juice is expressed* SQUEEZE OUT, press out, extract.

■ **express oneself** COMMUNICATE ONE'S VIEWS/OPINIONS/THOUGHTS, put thoughts into words, speak one's mind, say what's on one's mind.

express[2] ▶ **adjective** *an express bus* RAPID, swift, fast, quick, speedy, high-speed; non-stop, direct.

– OPPOSITES slow.

▶ **noun** *an overnight express* EXPRESS TRAIN, fast train, direct train.

express[3] ▶ **adjective** ❶ *express reference to confidential matters* EXPLICIT, clear, direct, obvious, plain, distinct, unambiguous, unequivocal; specific, precise, crystal clear, certain, categorical. ❷ *one express purpose* SOLE, specific, particular, exclusive, specified, fixed.

– OPPOSITES implied.

expression ▶ **noun** ❶ *the free expression of opposition views* UTTERANCE, uttering, voicing, pronouncement, declaration, articulation, assertion, setting forth; dissemination, circulation, communication, spreading, promulgation. ❷ *an expression of sympathy* INDICATION, demonstration, show, exhibition, token; communication, illustration, revelation. ❸ *an expression of harassed fatigue* LOOK, appearance, air, manner, countenance, mien. ❹ *a time-worn expression* IDIOM, phrase, idiomatic expression; proverb, saying, adage, maxim, axiom, aphorism, saw, motto, platitude, cliché. ❺ *these pieces are very different in expression* EMOTION, feeling, spirit, passion, intensity; style, intonation, tone. ❻ *essential oils obtained by expression* SQUEEZING, pressing, extraction, extracting.

expressionless ▶ **adjective** ❶ *his face was expressionless* INSCRUTABLE, deadpan, poker-faced; blank, vacant, emotionless, unemotional, inexpressive; glazed, stony, wooden, impassive. ❷ *a flat, expressionless tone* DULL, dry, toneless, monotonous, boring, tedious, flat, wooden, unmodulated, unvarying, devoid of feeling/emotion.

– OPPOSITES expressive, lively.

expressive ▶ **adjective** ❶ *an expressive shrug* ELOQUENT, meaningful, demonstrative, suggestive. ❷ *an expressive song* EMOTIONAL, full of emotion/feeling, passionate, poignant, moving, stirring, evocative, powerful, emotionally charged. ❸ *his diction is very expressive of his Englishness* INDICATIVE, demonstrative, demonstrating, showing, suggesting.

– OPPOSITES expressionless, unemotional.

expressly ▶ **adverb** ❶ *he was expressly forbidden to discuss the matter* EXPLICITLY, clearly, directly, plainly, distinctly, unambiguously, unequivocally; absolutely; specifically, categorically, pointedly, emphatically. ❷ *a machine expressly built for spraying paint* SOLELY, specifically, particularly, specially, exclusively, just, only, explicitly.

expropriate ▶ **verb** SEIZE, take (away/over), appropriate, take possession of, requisition, commandeer, claim, acquire, sequestrate, confiscate; *Law* distrain.

expulsion ▶ **noun** ❶ *expulsion from the party* REMOVAL, debarment, dismissal, exclusion, discharge, ejection, drumming out. ❷ *the expulsion of bodily wastes* DISCHARGE, ejection, excretion, voiding, evacuation, elimination, passing.

– OPPOSITES admission.

expunge ▶ **verb** ERASE, remove, delete, rub out, wipe out, efface; cross out, strike out, blot out, blank out; destroy, obliterate, eradicate, eliminate.

expurgate ▶ **verb** CENSOR, bowdlerize, blue-pencil, cut, edit; clean up, sanitize, make acceptable, make palatable, water down.

exquisite ▶ **adjective** ❶ *exquisite antique glass* BEAUTIFUL, lovely, elegant, fine; magnificent, superb, excellent, wonderful, well-crafted, well-made, perfect; delicate, fragile, dainty, subtle. ❷ *exquisite taste* DISCRIMINATING, discerning, sensitive, selective, fastidious; refined, cultivated, cultured, educated. ❸ *exquisite agony* INTENSE, acute, keen, piercing, sharp, severe, racking, excruciating, agonizing, harrowing, searing; unbearable, unendurable.

▶ **noun** (*dated*) *even among these snappy dressers, he*

was an exquisite DANDY, fop, glamour boy; *informal* dude, snappy dresser, natty dresser; *informal, dated* swell, blade; *dated* beau.

extant ▶ **adjective** STILL EXISTING, in existence, existent, surviving, remaining, undestroyed.

extemporary, extemporaneous ▶ **adjective** *an extemporaneous address. See* EXTEMPORE.

extempore ▶ **adjective** *an extempore speech* IMPROMPTU, spontaneous, unscripted, ad lib, extemporary, extemporaneous; improvised, unrehearsed, unplanned, unprepared, off the top of one's head; *informal* off-the-cuff; *formal* ad libitum.
– OPPOSITES rehearsed.
▶ **adverb** *he was speaking extempore* SPONTANEOUSLY, extemporaneously, ad lib, without preparation, without rehearsal, off the top of one's head; *informal* off the cuff; *formal* ad libitum.

extemporize ▶ **verb** IMPROVISE, ad lib, play it by ear, think on one's feet, do something off the top of one's head; *informal* busk it, wing it, do something off the cuff.

extend ▶ **verb** ❶ *he attempted to extend his dominions* EXPAND, enlarge, increase, make larger/bigger; lengthen, widen, broaden. ❷ *the garden extends down to the road* CONTINUE, carry on, run on, stretch (out), reach, lead. ❸ *we have extended our range of services* WIDEN, expand, broaden; augment, supplement, increase, add to, enhance, develop. ❹ *extending the life of parliament* PROLONG, lengthen, increase; stretch out, protract, spin out, string out. ❺ *extend your arms and legs* STRETCH OUT, spread out, reach out, straighten out. ❻ *he extended a hand in greeting* HOLD OUT, reach out, hold forth; offer, give, outstretch, proffer. ❼ *we wish to extend our thanks to Mr Bayes* OFFER, proffer, give, grant, bestow, accord.
– OPPOSITES reduce, narrow, shorten.
■ **extend to** INCLUDE, take in, incorporate, encompass.

extended ▶ **adjective** PROLONGED, protracted, long-lasting, long-drawn-out, spun out, long, dragged out, strung out, lengthy.

extension ▶ **noun** ❶ *they are planning a new extension* ADDITION, add-on, adjunct, annexe, wing, supplementary building; *N. Amer.* ell. ❷ *an extension of knowledge* EXPANSION, increase, enlargement, widening, broadening, deepening; augmentation, enhancement, development, growth, continuation. ❸ *an extension of opening hours* PROLONGATION, lengthening, increase. ❹ *I need an extension of time* POSTPONEMENT, deferral, delay, more/extra time.

extensive ▶ **adjective** ❶ *a mansion with extensive grounds* LARGE, large-scale, sizeable, substantial, considerable, ample, expansive, great, vast. ❷ *extensive knowledge* COMPREHENSIVE, thorough, exhaustive; broad, wide, wide-ranging, catholic.

extent ▶ **noun** ❶ *two acres in extent* AREA, size, expanse, length; proportions, dimensions. ❷ *the full extent of her father's illness* DEGREE, scale, level, magnitude, scope; size, breadth, width, reach, range.

extenuate ▶ **verb** EXCUSE, mitigate, palliate, make allowances/excuses for, defend, vindicate, justify; diminish, lessen, moderate, qualify, play down.

extenuating ▶ **adjective** MITIGATING, excusing, exonerative, palliating, palliative, justifying, justificatory, vindicating; *formal* exculpatory.

exterior ▶ **adjective** *the exterior walls* OUTER, outside, outermost, outward, external.
– RELATED TERMS ecto-, exo-.
– OPPOSITES interior.
▶ **noun** *the exterior of the building* OUTSIDE, outer surface, external surface, outward appearance, facade.

exterminate ▶ **verb** KILL, put to death, take/end the life of, dispatch; slaughter, butcher, massacre, wipe out, eliminate, eradicate, annihilate; murder, assassinate, execute; *informal* do away with, bump off, do in, top, take out, blow away; *N. Amer. informal* ice, rub out, waste; *poetic/literary* slay.

extermination ▶ **noun** KILLING, murder, assassination, putting to death, execution, dispatch, slaughter, massacre, liquidation, elimination, eradication, annihilation; *poetic/literary* slaying.

external ▶ **adjective** ❶ *an external wall* OUTER, outside, outermost, outward, exterior. ❷ *an external examiner* OUTSIDE, independent, non-resident, from elsewhere.
– RELATED TERMS ecto-, exo-.
– OPPOSITES internal, in-house.

extinct ▶ **adjective** ❶ *an extinct species* VANISHED, lost, died out, no longer existing, no longer extant, wiped out, destroyed, gone. ❷ *an extinct volcano* INACTIVE.
– OPPOSITES extant, dormant.

extinction ▶ **noun** DYING OUT, disappearance, vanishing; extermination, destruction, elimination, eradication, annihilation.

extinguish ▶ **verb** ❶ *the fire was extinguished* DOUSE, put out, stamp out, smother, beat out, dampen down. ❷ *all hope was extinguished* DESTROY, end, finish off, put an end to, bring to an end, terminate, remove, annihilate, wipe out, erase, eliminate, eradicate, obliterate; *informal* take out, rub out.
– OPPOSITES light.

extirpate ▶ **verb** WEED OUT, destroy, eradicate, stamp out, root out, wipe out, eliminate, suppress, crush, put down, put an end to, get rid of.

extol ▶ **verb** PRAISE ENTHUSIASTICALLY, go into raptures about/over, wax lyrical about, sing the praises of, praise to the skies, acclaim,

eulogize, rhapsodize over, rave about, enthuse about/over; *informal* go wild about, go on about; *N. Amer. informal* ballyhoo; *formal* laud; *archaic* panegyrize.
–OPPOSITES criticize.

extort ▶ verb OBTAIN BY FORCE, obtain by threat(s), blackmail someone for, extract, exact, wring, wrest, screw, squeeze; *N. Amer. & Austral. informal* put the bite on someone for.

extortion ▶ noun DEMANDING MONEY WITH MENACES, blackmail, extraction; *N. Amer. informal* shakedown; *formal* exaction.

extortionate ▶ adjective ❶ *extortionate prices* EXORBITANT, excessively high, excessive, outrageous, unreasonable, inordinate, inflated; *informal* over the top, OTT. ❷ *an extortionate clause* GRASPING, bloodsucking, avaricious, greedy; exacting, harsh, severe, oppressive; *informal* money-grubbing.

extortionist ▶ noun RACKETEER, extortioner, extorter, blackmailer; *informal* bloodsucker.

extra ▶ adjective *extra income* ADDITIONAL, more, added, supplementary, further, auxiliary, ancillary, subsidiary, secondary.
▶ adverb ❶ *working extra hard* EXCEPTIONALLY, particularly, specially, especially, very, extremely; unusually, extraordinarily, remarkably, uncommonly, outstandingly, amazingly, incredibly, really; *informal* seriously, mucho, awfully, terribly; *Brit.* jolly, dead, well; *informal, dated* frightfully. ❷ *postage is charged extra* IN ADDITION, additionally, as well, also, too, besides, on top (of that); *archaic* withal.
▶ noun ❶ *an optional extra* ADDITION, supplement, adjunct, addendum, add-on. ❷ *a film extra* WALK-ON, supernumerary, spear-carrier.

extract ▶ verb ❶ *he extracted the cassette* TAKE OUT, draw out, pull out, remove, withdraw; free, release, extricate. ❷ *extracting money* WREST, exact, wring, screw, squeeze, obtain by force, obtain by threat(s), extort, blackmail someone for; *N. Amer. & Austral. informal* put the bite on someone for. ❸ *the roots are crushed to extract the juice* SQUEEZE OUT, express, press out, obtain. ❹ *the table is extracted from the report* EXCERPT, select, reproduce, copy, take. ❺ *ideas extracted from a variety of theories* DERIVE, develop, evolve, deduce, infer, obtain; *formal* educe.
–OPPOSITES insert.
▶ noun ❶ *an extract from his article* EXCERPT, passage, citation, quotation; (**excerpts**) analects. ❷ *an extract of the ginseng root* DECOCTION, distillation, distillate, abstraction, concentrate, essence, juice.

extraction ▶ noun ❶ *the extraction of gall bladder stones* REMOVAL, taking out, drawing out, pulling out, withdrawal; freeing, release, extrication. ❷ *the extraction of grape juice* SQUEEZING, expressing, pressing, obtaining. ❸ *a man of Irish extraction* DESCENT, ancestry, parentage, ancestors, family, antecedents; lineage, line, origin, derivation, birth; genealogy, heredity, stock, pedigree, blood, bloodline; roots, origins.
–OPPOSITES insertion.

extradite ▶ verb ❶ *the government extradited him to Germany* DEPORT, send back, send home, repatriate. ❷ *the government attempted to extradite suspects from Belgium* HAVE SOMEONE DEPORTED, have someone sent home, bring back.

extradition ▶ noun DEPORTATION, repatriation, expulsion.

extraneous ▶ adjective ❶ *extraneous considerations* IRRELEVANT, immaterial, beside the point, unrelated, unconnected, inapposite, inapplicable. ❷ *extraneous noise* EXTERNAL, outside, exterior.

extraordinary ▶ adjective ❶ *an extraordinary coincidence* REMARKABLE, exceptional, amazing, astonishing, astounding, sensational, stunning, incredible, unbelievable, phenomenal; striking, outstanding, momentous, impressive, singular, memorable, unforgettable, unique, noteworthy; out of the ordinary, unusual, uncommon, rare, surprising; *informal* fantastic, terrific, tremendous, stupendous, awesome; *poetic/literary* wondrous. ❷ *extraordinary speed* VERY GREAT, tremendous, enormous, immense, prodigious, stupendous, monumental; *informal* almighty.

extravagance ▶ noun ❶ *a fit of extravagance* PROFLIGACY, unthriftiness, improvidence, wastefulness, prodigality, lavishness. ❷ *the costliest brands are an extravagance* LUXURY, indulgence, self-indulgence, treat, extra, non-essential. ❸ *the extravagance of the decor* ORNATENESS, elaborateness, embellishment, ornamentation; ostentation, over-elaborateness. ❹ *the extravagance of his compliments* EXCESSIVENESS, exaggeration, outrageousness, immoderation, excess.

extravagant ▶ adjective ❶ *an extravagant lifestyle* SPENDTHRIFT, profligate, unthrifty, improvident, wasteful, prodigal, lavish. ❷ *extravagant gifts* EXPENSIVE, costly, dear, high-priced, high-cost; valuable, precious; *informal* pricey, costing the earth, costing a bomb. ❸ *extravagant prices* EXORBITANT, extortionate, excessive, high, unreasonable. ❹ *extravagant praise* EXCESSIVE, immoderate, exaggerated, gushing, unrestrained, effusive, fulsome. ❺ *decorated in an extravagant style* ORNATE, elaborate, decorated, ornamented, fancy; over-elaborate, ostentatious, exaggerated, baroque, rococo; *informal* flash, flashy.
–OPPOSITES thrifty, cheap, plain.

extravaganza ▶ noun SPECTACULAR, display, spectacle, show, pageant.

extreme ▶ adjective ❶ *extreme danger* UTMOST, very great, greatest (possible), maximum, maximal, highest, supreme, great, acute, enor-

mous, severe, high, exceptional, extraordinary. ❷ *extreme measures* DRASTIC, serious, desperate, dire, radical, far-reaching, momentous, consequential; heavy, sharp, severe, austere, harsh, tough, strict, rigorous, oppressive, draconian; *Brit.* swingeing. ❸ *extreme views* RADICAL, extremist, immoderate, fanatical, revolutionary, rebel, subversive, militant. ❹ *extreme sports* DANGEROUS, hazardous, risky, high-risk, adventurous. ❺ *the extreme northwest* FURTHEST, farthest, furthermost, farthermost, very, utmost; *archaic* outmost.
– RELATED TERMS ultra-.
– OPPOSITES slight, moderate.
▶ **noun** ❶ *the two extremes* OPPOSITE, antithesis, side of the coin, (opposite) pole, antipode. ❷ *this attitude is taken to its extreme in the following quote* LIMIT, extremity, highest/greatest degree, maximum, height, top, zenith, peak.
■ **in the extreme**. *See* EXTREMELY.

extremely ▶ **adverb** VERY, exceedingly, exceptionally, especially, extraordinarily, in the extreme, tremendously, immensely, vastly, hugely, intensely, acutely, singularly, uncommonly, unusually, decidedly, particularly, supremely, highly, remarkably, really, truly, mightily; *informal* terrifically, awfully, fearfully, terribly, devilishly, majorly, seriously, mega, ultra, damn, damned; *Brit. informal* ever so, well, hellish, dead, jolly; *N. Amer. informal* real, mighty, awful, darned; *informal, dated* devilish, frightfully; *archaic* exceeding.
– OPPOSITES slightly.

extremist ▶ **noun** FANATIC, radical, zealot, fundamentalist, hardliner, militant, activist; *informal* ultra.
– OPPOSITES moderate.

extremity ▶ **noun** ❶ *the eastern extremity* LIMIT, end, edge, side, farthest point, boundary, border, frontier; perimeter, periphery, margin; *poetic/literary* bourn, marge. ❷ *she lost feeling in her extremities* HANDS AND FEET, fingers and toes, limbs. ❸ *the extremity of the violence* INTENSITY, magnitude, acuteness, ferocity, vehemence, fierceness, violence, severity, seriousness, strength, power, powerfulness, vigour, force, forcefulness. ❹ *in extremity he will send for her* DIRE STRAITS, trouble, difficulty, hard times, hardship, adversity, misfortune, distress; crisis, emergency, disaster, catastrophe, calamity; predicament, plight, mess, dilemma; *informal* fix, pickle, jam, spot, bind, scrape, hole, sticky situation, hot/deep water.

extricate ▶ **verb** EXTRACT, free, release, disentangle, get out, remove, withdraw, disengage; *informal* get someone/oneself off the hook.

extrinsic ▶ **adjective** EXTERNAL, extraneous, exterior, outside, outward.
– OPPOSITES intrinsic.

extrovert ▶ **noun** *like most extroverts he was a good dancer* OUTGOING PERSON, sociable person, socializer, life and soul of the party.
– OPPOSITES introvert.
▶ **adjective** *his extrovert personality* OUTGOING, extroverted, sociable, gregarious, genial, affable, friendly, unreserved.
– OPPOSITES introverted.

extrude ▶ **verb** FORCE OUT, thrust out, express, eject, expel, release, emit.

exuberant ▶ **adjective** ❶ *exuberant guests dancing on the terrace* EBULLIENT, buoyant, cheerful, jaunty, light-hearted, high-spirited, exhilarated, excited, elated, exultant, euphoric, joyful, cheery, merry, jubilant, vivacious, enthusiastic, irrepressible, energetic, animated, full of life, lively, vigorous; *informal* bubbly, bouncy, chipper, chirpy, full of beans; *poetic/literary* blithe, blithesome. ❷ *an exuberant coating of mosses* LUXURIANT, lush, rich, dense, thick, abundant, profuse, plentiful, prolific. ❸ *an exuberant welcome* EFFUSIVE, extravagant, fulsome, expansive, gushing, gushy, demonstrative.
– OPPOSITES gloomy, restrained.

exude ▶ **verb** ❶ *milkweed exudes a milky sap* GIVE OFF/OUT, discharge, release, emit, issue; ooze, weep, secrete, excrete. ❷ *slime exudes from the fungus* OOZE, seep, issue, escape, discharge, flow, leak. ❸ *he exuded self-confidence* EMANATE, radiate, ooze, emit; display, show, exhibit, manifest, transmit, embody.

exult ▶ **verb** ❶ *her opponents exulted when she left* REJOICE, be joyful, be happy, be delighted, be elated, be ecstatic, be overjoyed, be cock-a-hoop, be jubilant, be rapturous, be in raptures, be thrilled, jump for joy, be on cloud nine, be in seventh heaven; celebrate, cheer; *informal* be over the moon, be on top of the world; *Austral. informal* be wrapped; *poetic/literary* joy; *archaic* jubilate. ❷ *he exulted in his triumph* REJOICE AT/IN, take delight in, find/take pleasure in, find joy in, enjoy, revel in, glory in, delight in, relish, savour; be/feel proud of, congratulate oneself on; *archaic* pique oneself on/in.
– OPPOSITES sorrow.

exultant ▶ **adjective** JUBILANT, thrilled, triumphant, delighted, exhilarated, happy, overjoyed, joyous, joyful, gleeful, cock-a-hoop, excited, rejoicing, ecstatic, euphoric, elated, rapturous, in raptures, enraptured, on cloud nine/seven, in seventh heaven; *informal* over the moon; *N. Amer. informal* wigged out.

exultation ▶ **noun** JUBILATION, rejoicing, happiness, pleasure, joy, gladness, delight, glee, elation, cheer, euphoria, exhilaration, delirium, ecstasy, rapture, exuberance.

eye ▶ **noun** ❶ *he rubbed his eyes* EYEBALL; *informal* peeper; *poetic/literary* orb. ❷ *sharp eyes* EYESIGHT, vision, sight, powers of observation, (visual) perception. ❸ *an eye for a bargain* APPRECIATION, awareness, alertness, perception, consciousness, feeling, instinct, intuition, nose. ❹ *his watchful eye* WATCH, observance, gaze, stare, regard; observation, surveillance, vigilance, contemplation, scrutiny. ❺ *to desert was despicable in their eyes* OPINION, (way of) thinking, mind, view, viewpoint, attitude, standpoint, perspective, belief, judgement, assessment, analysis, estimation. ❻ *the eye of a needle* HOLE, opening, aperture, eyelet, slit, slot. ❼ *the eye of the storm* CENTRE, middle, heart, core, hub, thick.

– RELATED TERMS ocular, ophthalmic.

▶ **verb** ❶ *he eyed the stranger suspiciously* LOOK AT, observe, view, gaze at, stare at, regard, contemplate, survey, scrutinize, consider, glance at; watch, keep an eye on, keep under observation; *informal* have/take a gander at, check out, size up; *Brit. informal* have/take a butcher's at, have/take a dekko at, have/take a shufti at, clock; *N. Amer. informal* eyeball; *poetic/literary* behold. ❷ *eyeing young women in the street* OGLE, leer at, stare at, make eyes at; *informal* eye up, give someone the glad eye; *Brit. informal* gawp at, gawk at; *Austral./NZ informal* perv on.

■ **clap/lay/set eyes on** (*informal*) SEE, observe, notice, spot, spy, catch sight of, glimpse, catch/get a glimpse of; *poetic/literary* behold, espy, descry.

■ **see eye to eye** AGREE, concur, be in agreement, be of the same mind/opinion, be in accord, think as one; be on the same wavelength, get on/along.

■ **up to one's eyes** (informal) VERY BUSY, fully occupied; overloaded, overburdened, overworked, under pressure, hard-pressed, run/rushed off one's feet; *informal* pushed, up against it.

eye-catching ▶ **adjective** STRIKING, arresting, conspicuous, dramatic, impressive, spectacular, breathtaking, dazzling, amazing, stunning, sensational, remarkable, distinctive, unusual, out of the ordinary.

eyeful ▶ **noun** (*informal*) ❶ *did you get an eyeful of that?* LOOK, peep, peek, glimpse, view, gaze, glance, sight; *informal* gander, squint; *Brit. informal* dekko, shufti, butcher's; *Austral./NZ informal* geek, squiz. ❷ *she was quite an eyeful* BEAUTIFUL SIGHT, vision, picture, dream, sensation, beauty, dazzler; *informal* stunner, looker, knockout, sight for sore eyes, bombshell, dish, cracker, good-looker; *Brit. informal* smasher.

eyelash ▶ **noun** LASH; *Anatomy* cilium.

eyesight ▶ **noun** SIGHT, vision, faculty of sight, ability to see, (visual) perception.

eyesore ▶ **noun** UGLY SIGHT, blot (on the landscape), mess, scar, blight, disfigurement, blemish, monstrosity; *informal* sight.

eyewitness ▶ **noun** OBSERVER, onlooker, witness, bystander, spectator, watcher, viewer, passer-by; *poetic/literary* beholder.

fable ▶ **noun** ❶ *the fable of the wary fox* MORAL TALE, parable, apologue, allegory. ❷ *the fables of ancient Greece* MYTH, legend, saga, epic, folk tale, folk story, fairy tale, mythos, mythus; folklore, mythology. ❸ *it's a fable that I have a taste for fancy restaurants* FALSEHOOD, fib, fabrication, made-up story, invention, fiction, falsification, fairy story/tale, cock-and-bull story; lie, untruth, half-truth, exaggeration; story, rumour, myth; *informal* tall story; *Brit. informal* porky (pie).

fabled ▶ **adjective** ❶ *a fabled god-giant of Irish myth* LEGENDARY, mythical, mythic, mythological, fabulous, folkloric, fairy-tale; fictitious, imaginary, imagined, made up. ❷ *the fabled quality of French wine* CELEBRATED, renowned, famed, famous, well known, prized, noted, notable, acclaimed, esteemed, prestigious, of repute, of high standing.

fabric ▶ **noun** ❶ *the finest silk fabric* CLOTH, material, textile, tissue. ❷ *the fabric of the building* STRUCTURE, framework, frame, form, composition, construction, foundations.

fabricate ▶ **verb** ❶ *he fabricated research data* FALSIFY, fake, counterfeit; invent, make up. ❷ *fabricating a pack of lies* CONCOCT, make up, dream up, invent, trump up; *informal* cook up. ❸ *you will have to fabricate an exhaust system* MAKE, create, manufacture, produce; construct, build, assemble, put together, form, fashion.

fabrication ▶ **noun** ❶ *the story was a complete fabrication* INVENTION, concoction, (piece of) fiction, falsification, lie, untruth, falsehood, fib, myth, made-up story, fairy story/tale, cock-and-bull story; white lie, half-truth, exaggeration; *informal* tall story, whopper; *Brit. informal* porky (pie). ❷ *the lintels are galvanized after fabrication* MANUFACTURE, creation, production; construction, building, assembly, forming, fashioning.

fabulous ▶ adjective ❶ *fabulous salaries* TREMENDOUS, stupendous, prodigious, phenomenal, remarkable, exceptional; astounding, amazing, fantastic, breathtaking, staggering, unthinkable, unimaginable, incredible, unbelievable, unheard of, untold, undreamed of, beyond one's wildest dreams; *informal* mind-boggling, mind-blowing. ❷ (*informal*) *we had a fabulous time. See* EXCELLENT. ❸ *a fabulous horse-like beast* MYTHICAL, legendary, mythic, mythological, fabled, folkloric, fairy-tale; fictitious, imaginary, imagined, made up.

facade ▶ noun ❶ *a half-timbered facade* FRONT, frontage, face, elevation, exterior, outside. ❷ *a facade of bonhomie* SHOW, front, appearance, pretence, simulation, affectation, semblance, illusion, act, masquerade, charade, mask, cloak, veil, veneer.

face ▶ noun ❶ *a beautiful face* COUNTENANCE, physiognomy, features; *informal* mug; *Brit. informal* mush, dial, clock, phiz, boat race; *N. Amer. informal* puss, pan; *poetic/literary* visage; *archaic* front. ❷ *her face grew sad* (FACIAL) EXPRESSION, look, appearance, air, manner, bearing, countenance, mien. ❸ *he made a face at the sourness of the drink* GRIMACE, scowl, wry face, wince, frown, glower, pout, moue. ❹ *a cube has six faces* SIDE, aspect, flank, surface, plane, facet, wall, elevation. ❺ *a watch face* DIAL, display. ❻ *changing the face of the industry* (OUTWARD) APPEARANCE, aspect, nature, image. ❼ *he put on a brave face* FRONT, show, display, act, appearance, facade, exterior, mask, masquerade, pretence, pose, veneer. ❽ *criticism should never cause the recipient to lose face* RESPECT, honour, esteem, regard, admiration, approbation, acclaim, approval, favour, appreciation, popularity, prestige, standing, status, dignity; self-respect, self-esteem. ❾ (*informal*) *they had the face to upbraid others. See* EFFRONTERY.
– RELATED TERMS facial.

▶ verb ❶ *the hotel faces the sea* LOOK OUT ON, front on to, look towards, be facing, look over/across, overlook, give on to, be opposite (to). ❷ *you'll just have to face facts* ACCEPT, become reconciled to, get used to, become accustomed to, adjust to, acclimatize oneself to; learn to live with, cope with, deal with, come to terms with, become resigned to. ❸ *he faces a humiliating rejection* BE CONFRONTED BY, be faced with, encounter, experience, come into contact with, come up against. ❹ *the problems facing our police force* BESET, worry, distress, trouble, bother, confront; harass, oppress, vex, irritate, exasperate, strain, stress, tax; torment, plague, blight, bedevil, curse; *formal* discommode. ❺ *he faced the challenge boldly* BRAVE, face up to, encounter, meet (head-on), confront; oppose, resist, withstand. ❻ *a wall faced with flint* COVER, clad, veneer, overlay, surface, dress, put a facing on, laminate, coat, line.

■ **face to face** FACING (EACH OTHER), opposite (each other), across from each other.

■ **on the face of it** OSTENSIBLY, to all appearances, to all intents and purposes, at first glance, on the surface, superficially; apparently, seemingly, outwardly, it seems (that), it would seem (that), it appears (that), it would appear (that), as far as one can see/tell, by all accounts.

facelift ▶ noun ❶ *she's planning to have a facelift* COSMETIC SURGERY, plastic surgery. ❷ (*informal*) *the theatre is reopening after a facelift* RENOVATION, redecoration, refurbishment, revamp, revamping, makeover, reconditioning, overhauling, modernization, restoration, repair, redevelopment, rebuilding, reconstruction, refit.

facet ▶ noun ❶ *the many facets of the gem* SURFACE, face, side, plane. ❷ *other facets of his character* ASPECT, feature, side, dimension, characteristic, detail, point, ingredient, strand; component, constituent, element.

facetious ▶ adjective FLIPPANT, flip, glib, frivolous, tongue-in-cheek, joking, jokey, jocular, playful, sportive, teasing, mischievous; witty, amusing, funny, droll, comic, comical, light-hearted; *formal* jocose.
– OPPOSITES serious.

facile ▶ adjective ❶ *a facile explanation* SIMPLISTIC, superficial, oversimplified; shallow, glib, jejune, naive; *N. Amer.* dime-store. ❷ *he achieved a facile victory* EFFORTLESS, easy, undemanding, unexacting, painless, trouble-free; *Brit. informal* easy-peasy.

facilitate ▶ verb MAKE EASY/EASIER, ease, make possible, make smooth/smoother, smooth the way for; enable, assist, help (along), aid, oil the wheels of, expedite, speed up, accelerate, forward, advance, promote, further, encourage.
– OPPOSITES impede.

facility ▶ noun ❶ *car-parking facilities* PROVISION, space, means, potential, equipment. ❷ *the camera has a zoom facility* POSSIBILITY, feature. ❸ *a wealth of local facilities* AMENITY, resource, service, advantage, convenience, benefit. ❹ *a medical facility* ESTABLISHMENT, centre, place, station, location, premises, site, post, base; *informal* joint, outfit, set-up. ❺ *his facility for drawing* APTITUDE, talent, gift, flair, bent, skill, knack, genius; ability, proficiency, competence, capability, capacity, faculty; expertness, adeptness, prowess, mastery, artistry. ❻ *I was turning out poetry with facility* EASE, effortlessness, no difficulty, no trouble, facileness; deftness, adroitness, dexterity, proficiency, mastery.

facing ▶ noun ❶ *green velvet facings* COVERING, trimming, lining, interfacing. ❷ *brick facing on a concrete core* CLADDING, veneer, skin, surface, facade, front, coating, covering, dressing, overlay, lamination, plating; *N. Amer.* siding.

facsimile ▶ noun COPY, reproduction, duplicate, photocopy, mimeograph, replica, like-

ness, carbon copy, print, reprint, offprint, autotype; fax, telefax; *trademark* Xerox, photostat.
– OPPOSITES original.

fact ▶ **noun** ❶ *it is a fact that the water is polluted* REALITY, actuality, certainty; truth, verity, gospel. ❷ *every fact was double-checked* DETAIL, piece of information, particular, item, specific, element, point, factor, feature, characteristic, ingredient, circumstance, aspect, facet; (**facts**) information. ❸ *an accessory after the fact* EVENT, happening, occurrence, incident, act, deed.
– OPPOSITES lie, fiction.
■ **in fact** ACTUALLY, in actuality, in actual fact, really, in reality, in point of fact, as a matter of fact, in truth, to tell the truth; *archaic* in sooth, verily.

faction ▶ **noun** ❶ *a faction of the Liberal Party* CLIQUE, coterie, caucus, cabal, bloc, camp, group, grouping, sector, section, wing, arm, branch, set; ginger group, pressure group. ❷ *the council was split by faction* INFIGHTING, dissension, dissent, dispute, discord, strife, conflict, friction, argument, disagreement, controversy, quarrelling, wrangling, bickering, squabbling, disharmony, disunity, schism.

factious ▶ **adjective** DIVIDED, split, schismatic, discordant, conflicting, argumentative, disagreeing, disputatious, quarrelling, quarrelsome, clashing, warring, at loggerheads, at odds, rebellious, mutinous.
– OPPOSITES harmonious.

factitious ▶ **adjective** BOGUS, fake, specious, false, counterfeit, fraudulent, spurious, sham, mock, feigned, affected, pretended, contrived, engineered; *informal* phoney, pseudo, pretend; *Brit. informal* cod.
– OPPOSITES genuine.

factor ▶ **noun** ELEMENT, part, component, ingredient, strand, constituent, point, detail, item, feature, facet, aspect, characteristic, consideration, influence, circumstance.

factory ▶ **noun** WORKS, plant, yard, mill, industrial unit; workshop, shop; *archaic* manufactory.

factotum ▶ **noun** ODD-JOB MAN, handyman, man/maid of all work, jack of all trades, man/girl Friday; *Austral.* knockabout; *informal* (Mr) Fixit.

factual ▶ **adjective** TRUTHFUL, true, accurate, authentic, historical, genuine, fact-based; true-to-life, correct, exact, honest, faithful, literal, verbatim, word for word, unbiased, objective, unvarnished; *formal* veridical.
– OPPOSITES fictitious.

faculty ▶ **noun** ❶ *the faculty of speech* POWER, capability, capacity, facility, wherewithal, means; (**faculties**) senses, wits, reason, intelligence. ❷ *an unusual faculty for unearthing contributors* ABILITY, proficiency, competence, capability, potential, capacity, facility; aptitude, talent, gift, flair, bent, skill, knack, genius; expertise, expertness, adeptness, adroitness, dexterity, prowess, mastery, artistry. ❸ *the arts faculty* DEPARTMENT, school, division, section. ❹ *the vicar introduced certain ornaments without the faculty to do so* AUTHORIZATION, authority, power, right, permission, consent, leave, sanction, licence, dispensation, assent, acquiescence, agreement, approval, endorsement, clearance; *informal* the go-ahead, the thumbs up, the OK, the green light, say-so.

fad ▶ **noun** CRAZE, vogue, trend, fashion, mode, enthusiasm, passion, obsession, mania, rage, compulsion, fixation, fetish, fancy, whim, fascination; *informal* thing.

faddy ▶ **adjective** (*Brit. informal*) FUSSY, finicky, faddish, over-particular, over-fastidious, dainty; *informal* picky, pernickety; *N. Amer. informal* persnickety; *archaic* nice.

fade ▶ **verb** ❶ *the paintwork has faded* BECOME PALE, become bleached, become washed out, lose colour, discolour; grow dull, grow dim, lose lustre. ❷ *sunlight had faded the picture* BLEACH, wash out, make pale, blanch, whiten. ❸ *remove the flower heads as they fade* WITHER, wilt, droop, shrivel, die. ❹ *the afternoon light began to fade* (GROW) DIM, grow faint, fail, dwindle, die away, wane, disappear, vanish, decline, melt away; *poetic/literary* evanesce. ❺ *the Communist movement was fading away* DECLINE, die out, diminish, deteriorate, decay, crumble, collapse, fail, fall, sink, slump, go downhill; *informal* go to pot, go to the dogs; *archaic* retrograde.
– OPPOSITES brighten, increase.

faeces ▶ **plural noun** EXCREMENT, bodily waste, waste matter, ordure, dung, manure; excreta, stools, droppings; dirt, filth, muck, mess, night soil; *informal* pooh, doo-doo, doings, turds; *Brit. informal* cack, whoopsies, jobbies; *N. Amer. informal* poop.
– RELATED TERMS copro-.

fag[1] (*Brit. informal*) ▶ **noun** *it's too much of a fag!* CHORE, slog, grind, bother, bore; *informal* pain, sweat.
– OPPOSITES pleasure.
▶ **verb** *we fagged away all day* TOIL, slave, slog, labour, grind, work hard; *informal* work one's socks off; *Brit. informal* graft; *Austral./NZ informal* bullock; *poetic/literary* travail.
■ **fag someone out** EXHAUST, tire (out), wear out, fatigue, overtire, weary; *informal* do in, wipe out, knock out, shatter; *Brit. informal* knacker; *N. Amer. informal* poop, tucker out.

fag[2] ▶ **noun** (*Brit. informal*) *he was smoking a fag* CIGARETTE, filter tip, king-size; *informal* ciggy, cig, smoke, cancer stick, coffin nail; *Brit. informal* snout, roll-up.

fagged ▶ **adjective** (*informal*) EXHAUSTED, tired (out), worn out, fatigued, weary, drained, washed out; *informal* done in, all in, dead beat, dead on one's feet, shattered, bushed; *Brit.*

informal knackered; *N. Amer. informal* tuckered, pooped.

fail ▶ **verb** ❶ *the enterprise had failed* BE UNSUCCESSFUL, not succeed, fall through, fall flat, collapse, founder, backfire, meet with disaster, come to nothing/naught; *informal* flop, bomb. ❷ *he failed his examination* BE UNSUCCESSFUL IN, not pass; not make the grade; *informal* flunk. ❸ *his friends had failed him* LET DOWN, disappoint; desert, abandon, betray, be disloyal to; *poetic/literary* forsake. ❹ *the crops failed* BE DEFICIENT, be insufficient, be inadequate; wither. ❺ *the daylight failed* FADE, dim, die away, wane, disappear, vanish. ❻ *the ventilation system failed* BREAK (DOWN), stop working, cut out, crash; malfunction, go wrong, develop a fault; *informal* conk out, go on the blink; *Brit. informal* pack up, play up. ❼ *Ceri's health was failing* DETERIORATE, degenerate, decline, fade, wane, ebb. ❽ *900 businesses are failing a week* COLLAPSE, crash, go under, go bankrupt, go into receivership, go into liquidation, cease trading, be wound up; *informal* fold, flop, go bust, go broke, go to the wall.

– OPPOSITES succeed, pass, thrive, work.

■ **without fail** WITHOUT EXCEPTION, unfailingly, regularly, invariably, predictably, conscientiously, religiously, whatever happened.

failing ▶ **noun** *Jeanne accepted him despite his failings* FAULT, shortcoming, weakness, imperfection, defect, flaw, frailty, foible, idiosyncrasy, vice.

– OPPOSITES strength.

▶ **preposition** *failing financial assistance, you will be bankrupt* IN THE ABSENCE OF, lacking, notwithstanding.

failure ▶ **noun** ❶ *the failure of the assassination attempt* LACK OF SUCCESS, non-fulfilment, defeat, collapse, foundering. ❷ *all his schemes had been a failure* FIASCO, debacle, catastrophe, disaster; *informal* flop, washout, dead loss; *N. Amer. informal* snafu, clinker. ❸ *she was regarded as a failure* LOSER, underachiever, ne'er-do-well, disappointment; *informal* no-hoper, dead loss. ❹ *a failure in duty* NEGLIGENCE, remissness, dereliction; omission, oversight. ❺ *a crop failure* INADEQUACY, insufficiency, deficiency. ❻ *the failure of the camera* BREAKING DOWN, breakdown, malfunction; crash. ❼ *company failures* COLLAPSE, crash, bankruptcy, insolvency, liquidation, closure.

– OPPOSITES success.

faint ▶ **adjective** ❶ *a faint mark* INDISTINCT, vague, unclear, indefinite, ill-defined, imperceptible, unobtrusive; pale, light, faded. ❷ *a faint cry* QUIET, muted, muffled, stifled; feeble, weak, whispered, murmured, indistinct; low, soft, gentle. ❸ *a faint possibility* SLIGHT, slender, slim, small, tiny, negligible, remote, vague, unlikely, improbable; *informal* minuscule. ❹ *faint praise* UNENTHUSIASTIC, half-hearted, weak, feeble. ❺ *I suddenly felt faint* DIZZY, giddy, light-headed, unsteady; *informal* woozy.

– OPPOSITES clear, loud, strong.

▶ **verb** *she thought he would faint* PASS OUT, lose consciousness, black out, keel over, swoon; *informal* flake out, conk out, zonk out, go out like a light.

▶ **noun** *a dead faint* BLACKOUT, fainting fit, loss of consciousness, swoon; *Medicine* syncope.

faint-hearted ▶ **adjective** TIMID, timorous, nervous, nervy, easily scared, fearful, afraid; cowardly, craven, spineless, pusillanimous, lily-livered; *informal* chicken-hearted, yellow-bellied, gutless, sissy, wimpy, wimpish; *archaic* recreant.

– OPPOSITES brave.

faintly ▶ **adverb** ❶ *Maria called his name faintly* INDISTINCTLY, softly, gently, weakly; in a whisper, in a murmur, in a low voice. ❷ *he looked faintly bewildered* SLIGHTLY, vaguely, somewhat, quite, fairly, rather, a little, a bit, a touch, a shade; *informal* sort of, kind of.

– OPPOSITES loudly, extremely.

fair[1] ▶ **adjective** ❶ *the courts were generally fair* JUST, equitable, honest, upright, honourable, trustworthy; impartial, unbiased, unprejudiced, non-partisan, neutral, even-handed; lawful, legal, legitimate; *informal* legit, on the level; *N. Amer. informal* on the up and up. ❷ *fair weather* FINE, dry, bright, clear, sunny, cloudless; warm, balmy, clement, benign, pleasant. ❸ *fair winds* FAVOURABLE, advantageous, benign; on one's side, in one's favour. ❹ *fair hair* BLOND(E), yellowish, golden, flaxen, light, light brown, tow-coloured, ash blonde; fair-haired, light-haired, golden-haired. ❺ *fair skin* PALE, light, light-coloured, white, creamy. ❻ (*archaic*) *the fair maiden's heart. See* BEAUTIFUL. ❼ *a fair achievement* REASONABLE, passable, tolerable, satisfactory, acceptable, respectable, decent, all right, good enough, pretty good, not bad, average, middling; *informal* OK, so-so.

– OPPOSITES inclement, unfavourable, dark.

■ **fair and square** HONESTLY, fairly, without cheating, without foul play, by the book; lawfully, legally, legitimately; *informal* on the level; *N. Amer. informal* on the up and up.

fair[2] ▶ **noun** ❶ *a country fair* FÊTE, gala, festival, carnival. ❷ *an antiques fair* MARKET, bazaar, mart, exchange, sale; *archaic* emporium. ❸ *a new art fair* EXHIBITION, display, show, presentation, exposition; *N. Amer.* exhibit.

fairly ▶ **adverb** ❶ *all pupils were treated fairly* JUSTLY, equitably, impartially, without bias, without prejudice, even-handedly; lawfully, legally, legitimately, by the book; equally, the same. ❷ *the pipes are in fairly good condition* REASONABLY, passably, tolerably, adequately, moderately, quite, relatively, comparatively; *informal* pretty, kind of, sort of. ❸ *he fairly hauled her along the street* POSITIVELY, really, veritably, simply, actually, absolutely; practically, almost, nearly, all but; *informal* plain.

fair-minded ▶ adjective FAIR, just, even-handed, equitable, impartial, non-partisan, unbiased, unprejudiced; honest, honourable, trustworthy, upright, decent; *informal* on the level; *N. Amer. informal* on the up and up.

fairy ▶ noun SPRITE, pixie, elf, imp, brownie, puck, leprechaun, pishogue, nixie; *poetic/literary* faerie, fay.

fairy tale, fairy story ▶ noun ❶ *the film was inspired by a fairy tale* FOLK TALE, folk story, traditional story, myth, legend, fantasy, fable. ❷ (*informal*) *she accused him of telling fairy tales* (WHITE) LIE, fib, half-truth, untruth, falsehood, (tall) story, fabrication, invention, piece of fiction; *informal* whopper, cock-and-bull story; *Brit. informal* porky (pie).

faith ▶ noun ❶ *he justified his boss's faith in him* TRUST, belief, confidence, conviction; optimism, hopefulness, hope. ❷ *she gave her life for her faith* RELIGION, church, sect, denomination, (religious) persuasion, (religious) belief, ideology, creed, teaching, doctrine.
– OPPOSITES mistrust.

■ **break faith with** BE DISLOYAL TO, be unfaithful to, be untrue to, betray, play someone false, break one's promise to, fail, let down; double-cross, deceive, cheat, stab in the back; *informal* do the dirty on.

■ **keep faith with** BE LOYAL TO, be faithful to, be true to, stand by, stick by, keep one's promise to.

faithful ▶ adjective ❶ *his faithful assistant* LOYAL, constant, true, devoted, true-blue, unswerving, staunch, steadfast, dedicated, committed; trusty, trustworthy, dependable, reliable. ❷ *a faithful copy* ACCURATE, precise, exact, errorless, unerring, faultless, true, close, strict; realistic, authentic; *informal* on the mark, on the nail; *Brit. informal* spot on, bang on; *N. Amer. informal* on the money.
– OPPOSITES inaccurate.

faithless ▶ adjective ❶ *her faithless lover* UNFAITHFUL, disloyal, inconstant, false, untrue, adulterous, traitorous; fickle, flighty, untrustworthy, unreliable, undependable; deceitful, two-faced, double-crossing; *informal* cheating, two-timing, back-stabbing; *poetic/literary* perfidious. ❷ *the natives were faithless* UNBELIEVING, non-believing, irreligious, disbelieving, agnostic, atheistic; pagan, heathen; *rare* nullifidian.

fake ▶ noun ❶ *the sculpture was a fake* FORGERY, counterfeit, copy, pirate(d) copy, sham, fraud, hoax, imitation, mock-up, dummy, reproduction; *informal* phoney, rip-off, dupe. ❷ *that doctor is a fake* CHARLATAN, quack, mountebank, sham, fraud, humbug, impostor, hoaxer, cheat, (confidence) trickster, fraudster; *informal* phoney, con man, con artist.
▶ adjective ❶ *fake banknotes* COUNTERFEIT, forged, fraudulent, sham, imitation, pirate(d), false, bogus; invalid; *informal* phoney, dud. ❷ *fake diamonds* IMITATION, artificial, synthetic, simulated, reproduction, replica, ersatz, man-made, dummy, false, mock, bogus; *informal* pretend, phoney, pseudo. ❸ *a fake accent* FEIGNED, faked, put-on, assumed, invented, affected, pseudo; unconvincing, artificial, mock; *informal* phoney, pseud; *Brit. informal* cod.
– OPPOSITES genuine, authentic.
▶ verb ❶ *the certificate was faked* FORGE, counterfeit, falsify, mock up, copy, pirate, reproduce, replicate; doctor, alter, tamper with. ❷ *he faked a yawn* FEIGN, pretend, simulate, put on, make-believe, affect.

fall ▶ verb ❶ *bombs began to fall* DROP, descend, come down, go down; plummet, plunge, sink, dive, tumble; cascade. ❷ *he tripped and fell* TOPPLE OVER, tumble over, keel over, fall down/over, go head over heels, go headlong, collapse, take a spill, pitch forward; trip (over), stumble, slip; *informal* come a cropper; *Brit. informal* go for six. ❸ *the river began to fall* SUBSIDE, recede, ebb, flow back, fall away, go down, sink. ❹ *inflation will fall* DECREASE, decline, diminish, fall off, drop off, lessen, dwindle; plummet, plunge, slump, sink; depreciate, cheapen, devalue; *informal* go through the floor, nosedive, take a header, crash. ❺ *the Mogul empire fell* DECLINE, deteriorate, degenerate, go downhill, go to rack and ruin; decay, wither, fade, fail; *informal* go to the dogs, go to pot, go down the toilet; *Austral./NZ informal* go to the pack. ❻ *those who fell in the war* DIE, perish, lose one's life, be killed, be slain, be lost, meet one's death; *informal* bite the dust, croak, buy it; *Brit. informal* snuff it; *archaic* decease. ❼ *the town fell to the barbarians* SURRENDER, yield, submit, give in, capitulate, succumb; be taken by, be defeated by, be conquered by, be overwhelmed by. ❽ *Easter falls on 23rd April* OCCUR, take place, happen, come about; arise; *poetic/literary* come to pass. ❾ *night fell* COME, arrive, appear, arise, materialize. ❿ *she fell ill* BECOME, grow, get, turn. ⓫ *more tasks may fall to him* BE THE RESPONSIBILITY OF, be the duty of, be borne by, be one's job; come someone's way.
– OPPOSITES rise, flood, increase, flourish.
▶ noun ❶ *an accidental fall* TUMBLE, trip, spill, topple, slip; collapse; *informal* nosedive, header, cropper. ❷ *a fall in sales* DECLINE, fall-off, drop, decrease, cut, dip, reduction, downswing; plummet, plunge, slump; *informal* nosedive, crash. ❸ *the fall of the Roman Empire* DOWNFALL, collapse, ruin, ruination, failure, decline, deterioration, degeneration; destruction, overthrow, demise. ❹ *the fall of the city* SURRENDER, capitulation, yielding, submission; defeat. ❺ *a steep fall down to the ocean* DESCENT, declivity, slope, slant, incline; *N. Amer.* downgrade. ❻ *the fall of man* SIN, wrongdoing, transgression, error, offence, lapse, fall from grace. ❼ *rafting trips below the falls* WATERFALL, cascade, cataract; rapids, white water.
– OPPOSITES increase, rise, ascent.

■ **fall apart** FALL/COME TO PIECES, fall/come to bits, come apart (at the seams); disintegrate, fragment, break up, break apart, crumble, decay, perish; *informal* bust.

■ **fall asleep** DOZE OFF, drop off, go to sleep; *informal* nod off, go off, drift off, crash (out), flake out, conk out, go out like a light; *N. Amer. informal* sack out.

■ **fall away** SLOPE (DOWN), slant down, go down, drop (away), descend, dip, sink, plunge.

■ **fall back** RETREAT, withdraw, back off, draw back, pull back, pull away, move away.

■ **fall back on** RESORT TO, turn to, look to, call on, have recourse to; rely on, depend on, lean on.

■ **fall behind** ❶ *the other walkers fell behind* LAG (BEHIND), trail (behind), be left behind, drop back, bring up the rear; straggle, dally, dawdle, hang back. ❷ *they fell behind on their payments* GET INTO DEBT, get into arrears, default, be in the red.

■ **fall down** ❶ *I spin round till I fall down.* See FALL verb sense 2. ❷ *his work fell down in some areas* FAIL, be unsuccessful, not succeed, not make the grade, fall short, fall flat, disappoint; miss the mark; *informal* come a cropper, flop.

■ **fall for** ❶ *she fell for John* FALL IN LOVE WITH, become infatuated with, lose one's heart to, take a fancy to, be smitten by, be attracted to; *informal* fancy, have the hots for. ❷ *she won't fall for that trick* BE DECEIVED BY, be duped by, be fooled by, be taken in by, believe, trust, be convinced by; *informal* go for, buy, swallow (hook, line, and sinker).

■ **fall in** ❶ *the roof fell in* COLLAPSE, cave in, crash in, fall down; give way, crumble, disintegrate. ❷ *the troops fell in* GET IN FORMATION, get in line, line up, take one's position; *Military* dress.

■ **fall in with** ❶ *he fell in with a bad crowd* GET INVOLVED WITH, take up with, join up with, go around with, string along with, make friends with; *informal* hang out/about with. ❷ *he won't fall in with their demands* COMPLY WITH, go along with, support, cooperate with, obey, yield to, submit to, bow to, defer to, adhere to, conform to; agree to, agree with, accept, concur with.

■ **fall off**. *See* FALL verb sense 4.

■ **fall on** ATTACK, assail, assault, fly at, set about, set upon; pounce upon, ambush, surprise, rush, storm, charge; *informal* jump, lay into, pitch into, beat someone up; *Brit. informal* have a go at.

■ **fall out** ❶ *let's not fall out* QUARREL, argue, row, fight, squabble, bicker, have words, disagree, be at odds, clash, wrangle, cross swords, lock horns, be at loggerheads, be at each other's throats; *informal* scrap, argufy, argy-bargy. ❷ *the soldiers fell out* MOVE OUT OF FORMATION, move out of line; stand at ease.

■ **fall short of** FAIL TO MEET, fail to reach, fail to live up to; be deficient, be inadequate, be insufficient, be wanting, be lacking, disappoint; *informal* not come up to scratch.

■ **fall through** FAIL, be unsuccessful, come to nothing, miscarry, abort, go awry, collapse, founder, come to grief; *informal* fizzle out, flop, fold, come a cropper, go down like a lead balloon.

fallacious ▶ **adjective** ERRONEOUS, false, untrue, wrong, incorrect, flawed, inaccurate, mistaken, misinformed, misguided; specious, spurious, bogus, fictitious, fabricated, made up; groundless, unfounded, unproven, unsupported, uncorroborated; *informal* phoney, full of holes, off beam.
– OPPOSITES correct.

fallacy ▶ **noun** MISCONCEPTION, misbelief, delusion, mistaken impression, misapprehension, misinterpretation, misconstruction, error, mistake; untruth, inconsistency, myth.

fallen ▶ **adjective** ❶ *fallen heroes* DEAD, perished, killed, slain, slaughtered, murdered; lost, late, lamented, departed, gone; *formal* deceased; *rare* demised. ❷ (*dated*) *fallen women* IMMORAL, loose, promiscuous, unchaste, sinful, impure, sullied, tainted, dishonoured, ruined.

fallible ▶ **adjective** ERROR-PRONE, errant, liable to err, open to error; imperfect, flawed, weak.

fallow ▶ **adjective** ❶ *fallow farmland* UNCULTIVATED, unploughed, untilled, unplanted, unsown; unused, dormant, resting, empty, bare. ❷ *a fallow trading period* INACTIVE, dormant, quiet, slack, slow, stagnant; barren, unproductive.
– OPPOSITES cultivated, busy.

false ▶ **adjective** ❶ *a false report* INCORRECT, untrue, wrong, erroneous, fallacious, flawed, distorted, inaccurate, imprecise; untruthful, fictitious, concocted, fabricated, invented, made up, trumped up, unfounded, spurious; counterfeit, forged, fraudulent. ❷ *a false friend* FAITHLESS, unfaithful, disloyal, untrue, inconstant, treacherous, traitorous, two-faced, double-crossing, deceitful, dishonest, duplicitous, untrustworthy, unreliable; untruthful; *informal* cheating, two-timing, back-stabbing; *poetic/literary* perfidious. ❸ *false pearls* FAKE, artificial, imitation, synthetic, simulated, reproduction, replica, ersatz, man-made, dummy, mock; *informal* phoney, pretend, pseudo.
– OPPOSITES correct, truthful, faithful, genuine.

falsehood ▶ **noun** ❶ *a downright falsehood* LIE, untruth, fib, falsification, fabrication, invention, fiction, story, cock and bull story, flight of fancy; half truth; *informal* tall story, tall tale, fairy story, fairy tale, whopper; *Brit. informal* porky (pie); *humorous* terminological inexactitude. ❷ *he accused me of falsehood* LYING, mendacity, untruthfulness, fibbing, fabrication, invention, perjury, telling stories; deceit, deception, pretence, artifice, double-crossing, treachery; *poetic/literary* perfidy.
– OPPOSITES truth, honesty.

falsify ▶ verb ❶ *she falsified the accounts* FORGE, fake, counterfeit, fabricate; alter, change, doctor, tamper with, fudge, manipulate, adulterate, corrupt, misrepresent, misreport, distort, warp, embellish, embroider. ❷ *the theory is falsified by the evidence* DISPROVE, refute, rebut, deny, debunk, negate, negative, invalidate, contradict, controvert, confound, demolish, discredit; *informal* shoot full of holes, blow out of the water; *formal* confute, gainsay.

falsity ▶ noun UNTRUTHFULNESS, untruth, fallaciousness, falseness, falsehood, fictitiousness, inaccuracy; mendacity, fabrication, dishonesty, deceit.

falter ▶ verb ❶ *the government faltered* HESITATE, delay, drag one's feet, stall; waver, vacillate, be indecisive, be irresolute, blow hot and cold; *Brit.* haver, hum and haw; *informal* sit on the fence, dilly-dally, shilly-shally. ❷ *she faltered over his name* STAMMER, stutter, stumble; hesitate, flounder.

fame ▶ noun RENOWN, celebrity, stardom, popularity, prominence; note, distinction, esteem, importance, account, consequence, greatness, eminence, prestige, stature, repute; notoriety, infamy.
– OPPOSITES obscurity.

famed ▶ adjective FAMOUS, celebrated, well known, prominent, noted, notable, renowned, respected, esteemed, acclaimed; notorious, infamous.
– OPPOSITES unknown.

familiar ▶ adjective ❶ *a familiar task* WELL KNOWN, recognized, accustomed; common, commonplace, everyday, day-to-day, ordinary, habitual, usual, customary, routine, standard, stock, mundane, run-of-the-mill; *poetic/literary* wonted. ❷ *are you familiar with the subject?* ACQUAINTED, conversant, versed, knowledgeable, well informed; skilled, proficient; at home with, no stranger to, au fait with, au courant with; *informal* well up on, in the know about, genned up on, clued up on. ❸ *a familiar atmosphere* INFORMAL, casual, relaxed, easy, comfortable; friendly, unceremonious, unreserved, open, natural, unpretentious. ❹ *he is too familiar with the teachers* OVERFAMILIAR, presumptuous, disrespectful, forward, bold, impudent, impertinent.
– OPPOSITES formal.

familiarity ▶ noun ❶ *he wants greater familiarity with politics* ACQUAINTANCE WITH, awareness of, experience of, insight into, conversancy with, conversance with; knowledge of, understanding of, comprehension of, grasp of, skill in, proficiency in. ❷ *she was affronted by his familiarity* OVERFAMILIARITY, presumption, presumptuousness, forwardness, boldness, audacity, cheek, impudence, impertinence, disrespect; liberties. ❸ *our familiarity allows us to tease each other* CLOSENESS, intimacy, attachment, affinity, friendliness, friendship, amity; *informal* chumminess, palliness; *Brit. informal* mateyness.

familiarize ▶ verb MAKE CONVERSANT, make familiar, acquaint; accustom to, habituate to, instruct in, teach in, educate in, school in, prime in, introduce to; *informal* gen up on, clue up on, put in the picture about, give the gen about, give the low-down on, fill in on.

family ▶ noun ❶ *I met his family* RELATIVES, relations, (next of) kin, kinsfolk, kindred, one's (own) flesh and blood, nearest and dearest, people, connections; extended family; clan, tribe; *informal* folks. ❷ *he had the right kind of family* ANCESTRY, parentage, pedigree, genealogy, background, family tree, descent, lineage, bloodline, blood, extraction, stock; forebears, forefathers, antecedents, roots, origins. ❸ *she is married with a family* CHILDREN, little ones, youngsters; offspring, progeny, descendants, scions, heirs; brood; *Law* issue; *informal* kids, kiddies, tots. ❹ *the weaver bird family* TAXONOMIC GROUP, order, class, genus, species; stock, strain, line; *Zoology* phylum.

family tree ▶ noun ANCESTRY, genealogy, descent, lineage, line, bloodline, pedigree, background, extraction, derivation; family, dynasty, house; forebears, forefathers, antecedents, roots, origins.

famine ▶ noun ❶ *a nation threatened by famine* SCARCITY OF FOOD, food shortages. ❷ *the cotton famine* SHORTAGE, scarcity, lack, dearth, deficiency, insufficiency, shortfall, scantiness, paucity, poverty, drought.
– OPPOSITES plenty.

famished ▶ adjective RAVENOUS, hungry, starving, starved, empty, unfed; *informal* peckish.
– OPPOSITES full.

famous ▶ adjective WELL KNOWN, prominent, famed, popular; renowned, noted, eminent, distinguished, esteemed, celebrated, respected; of distinction, of repute; illustrious, acclaimed, great, legendary, lionized; notorious, infamous.
– OPPOSITES unknown.

fan[1] ▶ noun *a ceiling fan* AIR-COOLER, air conditioner, ventilator, blower, aerator.
▶ verb ❶ *she fanned her face* COOL, aerate, ventilate; freshen, refresh. ❷ *they fanned public fears* INTENSIFY, increase, agitate, inflame, exacerbate; stimulate, stir up, whip up, fuel, kindle, spark, arouse. ❸ *the police squad fanned out* SPREAD, branch; outspread.

fan[2] ▶ noun *a basketball fan* ENTHUSIAST, devotee, admirer, lover; supporter, follower, disciple, adherent, zealot; expert, connoisseur, aficionado; *informal* buff, fiend, freak, nut, addict, fanatic, groupie; *N. Amer. informal* jock.

fanatic ▶ noun ❶ *a religious fanatic* ZEALOT, extremist, militant, dogmatist, devotee, adherent; sectarian, bigot, partisan, radical, diehard, ultra; *informal* maniac. ❷ (*informal*) *a keep-fit fanatic. See* FAN[2].

fanatical ▶ adjective ❶ *they are fanatical about their faith* ZEALOUS, extremist, extreme, militant, dogmatic, radical, diehard; intolerant, single-minded, blinkered, inflexible, uncompromising. ❷ *he was fanatical about tidiness* ENTHUSIASTIC, eager, keen, fervent, ardent, passionate; obsessive, obsessed, fixated, compulsive; *informal* wild, gung-ho, nuts, crazy; *Brit. informal* potty.

fancier ▶ noun *a pigeon fancier* ENTHUSIAST, lover, hobbyist; expert, connoisseur, aficionado; breeder; *informal* buff.

fanciful ▶ adjective ❶ *a fanciful story* FANTASTIC, far-fetched, unbelievable, extravagant; ridiculous, absurd, preposterous; imaginary, made-up, make-believe, mythical, fabulous; *informal* tall, hard to swallow. ❷ *a fanciful girl* IMAGINATIVE, inventive; whimsical, impractical, dreamy, quixotic; out of touch with reality, in a world of one's own. ❸ *a fanciful building* ORNATE, exotic, fancy, imaginative, extravagant, fantastic; curious, bizarre, eccentric, unusual.
–OPPOSITES literal, practical.

fancy ▶ verb ❶ (*Brit. informal*) *I fancied a change of scene* WISH FOR, want, desire; long for, yearn for, crave, thirst for, hanker after, dream of, covet; *informal* have a yen for; *archaic* be desirous of. ❷ (*Brit. informal*) *she fancied him* BE ATTRACTED TO, find attractive, be infatuated with, be taken with, desire; lust after, burn for; *informal* have a crush on, have the hots for, be crazy about, have a thing about, have a soft spot for, carry a torch for. ❸ *I fancied I could see lights* THINK, imagine, believe, be of the opinion, be under the impression; *informal* reckon.
▶ adjective *fancy clothes* ELABORATE, ornate, ornamental, decorative, adorned, embellished, intricate; ostentatious, showy, flamboyant; luxurious, lavish, extravagant, expensive; *informal* flash, flashy, jazzy, ritzy, snazzy, posh, classy; *Brit. informal* swish.
–OPPOSITES plain.
▶ noun ❶ *his fancy to own a farm* DESIRE, urge, wish; inclination, whim, impulse, notion, whimsy; yearning, longing, hankering, craving; *informal* yen, itch. ❷ *I've a fancy they want to be alone* IDEA, notion, thought, supposition, opinion, belief, impression, understanding; feeling, suspicion, hunch, inkling.

fanfare ▶ noun ❶ *a fanfare announced her arrival* TRUMPET CALL, flourish, fanfaronade; *archaic* trump. ❷ *the project was greeted with great fanfare* FUSS, commotion, show, display, ostentation, flashiness, pageantry, splendour; *informal* ballyhoo, hype, pizzazz, razzle-dazzle, glitz.

fantasize ▶ verb DAYDREAM, dream, muse, make-believe, pretend, imagine; build castles in the air, build castles in Spain, live in a dream world.

fantastic ▶ adjective ❶ *a fantastic notion* FANCIFUL, extravagant, extraordinary, irrational, wild, absurd, far-fetched, nonsensical, incredible, unbelievable, unthinkable, implausible, improbable, unlikely, doubtful, dubious; strange, peculiar, odd, queer, weird, eccentric, whimsical, capricious; visionary, romantic; *informal* crazy, cock-eyed, off the wall. ❷ *his fantastic accuracy* TREMENDOUS, remarkable, great, terrific, impressive, outstanding, phenomenal. ❸ *fantastic shapes* STRANGE, weird, bizarre, outlandish, queer, peculiar, grotesque, freakish, surreal, exotic; elaborate, ornate, intricate. ❹ (*informal*) *a fantastic car* MARVELLOUS, wonderful, sensational, outstanding, superb, excellent, first-rate, first-class, dazzling, out of this world, breathtaking; *informal* great, terrific, fabulous, fab, mega, super, ace, magic, cracking, cool, wicked, awesome; *Brit. informal* brilliant, brill, smashing; *Austral./NZ informal* bonzer; *Brit. informal, dated* spiffing.
–OPPOSITES rational, ordinary.

fantasy ▶ noun ❶ *a mix of fantasy and realism* IMAGINATION, fancy, invention, make-believe; creativity, vision; daydreaming, reverie. ❷ *his fantasy about being famous* DREAM, daydream, pipe dream, fanciful notion, wish; fond hope, chimera, delusion, illusion; *informal* pie in the sky.
–OPPOSITES realism.

far ▶ adverb ❶ *we are far from the palace* A LONG WAY, a great distance, a good way; afar. ❷ *her charm far outweighs any flaws* MUCH, considerably, markedly, immeasurably, greatly, significantly, substantially, appreciably, noticeably; to a great extent, by a long way, by far, by a mile, easily.
–OPPOSITES near.
▶ adjective ❶ *far places* DISTANT, faraway, far-off, remote, out of the way, far-flung, outlying. ❷ *the far side of the campus* FURTHER, more distant; opposite.
–OPPOSITES near.
■ **by far** BY A GREAT AMOUNT, by a good deal, by a long way, by a mile, far and away; undoubtedly, without doubt, without question, positively, absolutely, easily; significantly, substantially, appreciably, much; *Brit.* by a long chalk.
■ **far and away**. *See* BY FAR.
■ **far and near** EVERYWHERE, {here, there, and everywhere}, all over (the world), throughout the land, worldwide; *informal* all over the place; *Brit. informal* all over the shop; *N. Amer. informal* all over the map.
■ **far and wide**. *See* FAR AND NEAR.
■ **far from** *staff were far from happy* NOT, not at all, nowhere near; the opposite of.
■ **go far** BE SUCCESSFUL, succeed, prosper, flourish, thrive, get on (in the world), make good, set the world on fire; *informal* make a name for oneself, make one's mark, go places, do all right for oneself, find a place in the sun.
■ **go too far** GO OVER THE TOP, go to extremes, go overboard.

■ **so far** ❶ *nobody has noticed so far* UNTIL NOW, up to now, up to this point, as yet, thus far, hitherto, up to the present, to date. ❷ *his liberalism only extends so far* TO A CERTAIN EXTENT, up to a point, to a degree, within reason, within limits.

faraway ▶ adjective ❶ *faraway places* DISTANT, far off, far, remote, far-flung, outlying; obscure, out of the way, off the beaten track. ❷ *a faraway look in her eyes* DREAMY, daydreaming, abstracted, absent-minded, distracted, preoccupied, vague; lost in thought, somewhere else, not with us, in a world of one's own; *informal* miles away.
– OPPOSITES nearby.

farce ▶ noun ❶ *the stories approach farce* SLAPSTICK (COMEDY), burlesque, vaudeville, buffoonery. ❷ *the trial was a farce* MOCKERY, travesty, absurdity, sham, pretence, masquerade, charade, joke, waste of time; *informal* shambles.
– OPPOSITES tragedy.

farcical ▶ adjective ❶ *the idea is farcical* RIDICULOUS, preposterous, ludicrous, absurd, laughable, risible, nonsensical; senseless, pointless, useless; silly, foolish, idiotic, stupid, harebrained; *informal* crazy; *Brit. informal* barmy, daft. ❷ *farcical goings-on* MADCAP, zany, slapstick, comic, comical, clownish, amusing; hilarious, uproarious; *informal* wacky.

fare ▶ noun ❶ *we paid the fare* TICKET PRICE, transport cost; price, cost, charge, fee, toll, tariff. ❷ *the taxi picked up a fare* PASSENGER, traveller, customer; *Brit. informal* punter. ❸ *they eat simple fare* FOOD, meals, sustenance, nourishment, nutriment, foodstuffs, provender, eatables, provisions; cooking, cuisine; diet, table; *informal* grub, nosh, eats, chow; *Brit. informal* scoff; *formal* comestibles, victuals.
▶ verb *how are you faring?* GET ON, get along, cope, manage, do, muddle through/along, survive; *informal* make out.

farewell ▶ exclamation *farewell, Patrick!* GOODBYE, so long, adieu; au revoir, ciao; *informal* bye, bye-bye, cheerio, see you (later), later(s); *Brit. informal* ta-ta, cheers; *informal, dated* toodle-oo, toodle-pip.
▶ noun *an emotional farewell* GOODBYE, valediction, adieu; leave-taking, parting, departure; send-off.

far-fetched ▶ adjective IMPROBABLE, unlikely, implausible, unconvincing, dubious, doubtful, incredible, unbelievable, unthinkable; contrived, fanciful, unrealistic, ridiculous, absurd, preposterous; *informal* hard to swallow, fishy.
– OPPOSITES likely.

farm ▶ noun *a farm of 100 acres* SMALLHOLDING, farmstead, plantation, estate; farmland; *Brit.* grange, croft; *Scottish* steading; *N. Amer.* ranch; *Austral./NZ* station.
▶ verb ❶ *he farmed locally* BE A FARMER, cultivate the land, work the land; rear livestock. ❷ *they farm the land* CULTIVATE, till, work, plough, dig, plant. ❸ *the family farms sheep* BREED, rear, keep, raise, tend.
■ **farm something out** CONTRACT OUT, outsource, subcontract, delegate.

farmer ▶ noun AGRICULTURALIST, agronomist, smallholder, grazier; farmhand; *Brit.* crofter; *N. Amer.* rancher; *historical* yeoman.

farming ▶ noun AGRICULTURE, cultivation, land management, farm management; husbandry; agriscience, agronomy, agribusiness; *Brit.* crofting.

far out ▶ adjective (*informal*). *See* UNCONVENTIONAL.

farrago ▶ noun HOTCHPOTCH, mishmash, ragbag, pot-pourri, jumble, mess, confusion, melange, gallimaufry, hash, assortment, miscellany, mixture, conglomeration, medley; *N. Amer.* hodgepodge.

far-reaching ▶ adjective EXTENSIVE, wide-ranging, comprehensive, widespread, all-embracing, overarching, across the board, sweeping, blanket, wholesale; important, significant, radical, major, consequential.
– OPPOSITES limited.

far-sighted ▶ adjective PRESCIENT, visionary, percipient, shrewd, discerning, judicious, canny, prudent.

farther ▶ adverb & adjective. *See* FURTHER.

farthest ▶ adjective. *See* FURTHEST.

fascinate ▶ verb INTEREST, captivate, engross, absorb, enchant, enthral, entrance, transfix, rivet, mesmerize, engage, compel; lure, tempt, entice, draw; charm, attract, intrigue, divert, entertain.
– OPPOSITES bore.

fascinating ▶ adjective INTERESTING, captivating, engrossing, absorbing, enchanting, enthralling, spellbinding, riveting, engaging, compelling, compulsive, gripping, thrilling; alluring, tempting, irresistible; charming, attractive, intriguing, diverting, entertaining.

fascination ▶ noun INTEREST, preoccupation, passion, obsession, compulsion; allure, lure, charm, attraction, intrigue, appeal, pull, draw.

fascism ▶ noun AUTHORITARIANISM, totalitarianism, dictatorship, despotism, autocracy; Nazism, rightism; nationalism, xenophobia, racism, anti-Semitism, jingoism, isolationism; neo-fascism, neo-Nazism.

fascist ▶ noun *he was branded a fascist* AUTHORITARIAN, totalitarian, autocrat, extreme right-winger, rightist; Nazi, blackshirt; nationalist, xenophobe, racist, anti-Semite, jingoist; neo-fascist, neo-Nazi.
– OPPOSITES liberal.
▶ adjective *a fascist regime* AUTHORITARIAN, totalitarian, dictatorial, despotic, autocratic, undemocratic, illiberal; Nazi, extreme right-wing, rightist, militarist; nationalist(ic), xenophobic,

racist, jingoistic.
– OPPOSITES democratic.

fashion ▶ noun ❶ *the fashion for tight clothes* VOGUE, trend, craze, rage, mania, fad; style, look; tendency, convention, custom, practice; *informal* thing. ❷ *the world of fashion* CLOTHES, clothing design, couture; *informal* the rag trade. ❸ *it needs to be run in a sensible fashion* MANNER, way, method, mode, style; system, approach.
▶ verb *the model was fashioned from lead* CONSTRUCT, build, make, manufacture, fabricate, contrive; cast, shape, form, mould, sculpt; forge, hew.
■ **after a fashion** TO A CERTAIN EXTENT, in a way, somehow (or other), in a manner of speaking, in its way.
■ **in fashion** FASHIONABLE, in vogue, up to date, up to the minute, all the rage, chic, à la mode; *informal* trendy, with it, cool, in, the in thing, hot, big, hip, happening, now, sharp, groovy; *N. Amer.* tony, fly; *Brit. informal, dated* all the go.
■ **out of fashion** UNFASHIONABLE, dated, old-fashioned, out of date, outdated, outmoded, behind the times; unstylish, unpopular, passé, démodé; *informal* old hat, out, square, out of the ark.

fashionable ▶ adjective IN VOGUE, voguish, in fashion, popular, (bang) up to date, up to the minute, modern, all the rage, modish, à la mode, trendsetting; stylish, chic; *informal* trendy, classy, with it, cool, in, the in thing, hot, big, hip, happening, now, sharp, groovy, snazzy; *N. Amer. informal* tony, fly; *Brit. informal, dated* all the go.

fast[1] ▶ adjective ❶ *a fast pace* SPEEDY, quick, swift, rapid; fast-moving, high-speed, turbo, sporty; accelerated, express, blistering, breakneck, pell-mell; hasty, hurried; *informal* nippy, zippy, scorching, blinding, supersonic; *Brit. informal* cracking; *poetic/literary* fleet. ❷ *he held the door fast* SECURE, fastened, tight, firm, closed, shut, to; immovable, unbudgeable. ❸ *a fast colour* INDELIBLE, lasting, permanent, stable. ❹ *fast friends* LOYAL, devoted, faithful, firm, steadfast, staunch, true, boon, bosom, inseparable; constant, enduring, unswerving. ❺ *a fast woman* PROMISCUOUS, licentious, dissolute, debauched, impure, unchaste, wanton, abandoned, of easy virtue; sluttish, whorish; intemperate, immoderate, shameless, sinful, immoral; *informal* easy, tarty; *Brit. informal* slaggy; *N. Amer. informal* roundheeled; *dated* loose.
– OPPOSITES slow, loose, temporary, chaste.
▶ adverb ❶ *she drove fast* QUICKLY, rapidly, swiftly, speedily, briskly, at speed, at full tilt; hastily, hurriedly, in a hurry, post-haste, pell-mell; like a shot, like a flash, on the double, at the speed of light; *informal* double quick, p.d.q. (pretty damn quick), nippily, like (greased) lightning, hell for leather, like mad, like the wind, like a scalded cat, like a bat out of hell; *Brit. informal* like the clappers, at a rate of knots, like billy-o; *N. Amer. informal* lickety-split; *poetic/literary* apace. ❷ *his wheels were stuck fast* SECURELY, firmly, immovably, fixedly. ❸ *he's fast asleep* DEEPLY, sound, completely. ❹ *she lived fast and dangerously* WILDLY, dissolutely, intemperately, immoderately, recklessly, self-indulgently, extravagantly.
– OPPOSITES slowly.

fast[2] ▶ verb *we must fast and pray* EAT NOTHING, abstain from food, refrain from eating, go without food, go hungry, starve oneself; go on hunger strike.
– OPPOSITES eat.
▶ noun *a five-day fast* PERIOD OF FASTING, period of abstinence; hunger strike; diet.
– OPPOSITES feast.

fasten ▶ verb ❶ *he fastened the door* BOLT, lock, secure, make fast, chain, seal. ❷ *they fastened splints to his leg* ATTACH, fix, affix, clip, pin, tack; stick, bond, join. ❸ *he fastened his horse to a tree* TIE (UP), bind, tether, truss, fetter, lash, hitch, anchor, strap, rope. ❹ *the dress fastens at the front* BUTTON (UP), zip (up), do up, close. ❺ *his gaze fastened on me* FOCUS, fix, be riveted, concentrate, zero in, zoom in, direct at. ❻ *blame had been fastened on some nutter* ASCRIBE TO, attribute to, assign to, chalk up to; pin on, lay at the door of. ❼ *critics fastened on the end of the report* SINGLE OUT, concentrate on, focus on, pick out, fix on, seize on.
– OPPOSITES unlock, remove, open, untie, undo.

fastidious ▶ adjective SCRUPULOUS, punctilious, painstaking, meticulous; perfectionist, fussy, finicky, over-particular; critical, over-critical, hypercritical, hard to please, exacting, demanding; *informal* pernickety, nit-picking, choosy, picky; *N. Amer. informal* persnickety.
– OPPOSITES lax.

fat ▶ adjective ❶ *a fat man* PLUMP, stout, overweight, large, chubby, portly, flabby, paunchy, pot-bellied, beer-bellied, meaty, of ample proportions; obese, corpulent, gross, fleshy; *informal* tubby, roly-poly, beefy, porky, blubbery, chunky; *Brit. informal* podgy, fubsy; *archaic* pursy. ❷ *fat bacon* FATTY, greasy, oily, oleaginous; *formal* pinguid. ❸ *a fat book* THICK, big, chunky, substantial; long. ❹ (*informal*) *a fat salary* LARGE, substantial, sizeable, considerable; generous, lucrative.
– OPPOSITES thin, lean, small, good.
▶ noun ❶ *whale fat* BLUBBER, fatty tissue, adipose tissue. ❷ *he was running to fat* FATNESS, plumpness, stoutness, chubbiness, tubbiness, portliness, podginess, flabbiness; obesity, corpulence; *informal* flab, blubber. ❸ *eggs in sizzling fat* COOKING OIL, grease; lard, suet, butter, margarine.

fatal ▶ adjective ❶ *a fatal disease* DEADLY, lethal, mortal, death-dealing; terminal, incurable, untreatable, inoperable, malignant; *poetic/literary* deathly. ❷ *a fatal mistake* DISASTROUS, devastating, ruinous, catastrophic, calamitous, dire;

costly; *formal* grievous.
– OPPOSITES harmless, beneficial.

fatalism ▶ noun PASSIVE ACCEPTANCE, resignation, stoicism; fate.

fatality ▶ noun DEATH, casualty, mortality, victim; fatal accident.

fate ▶ noun ❶ *what has fate in store for me?* DESTINY, providence, the stars, chance, luck, serendipity, fortune, kismet, karma. ❷ *my fate was in their hands* FUTURE, destiny, outcome, end, lot. ❸ *a similar fate would befall other killers* DEATH, demise, end; retribution, sentence. ❹ *the Fates will decide* the weird sisters, the Parcae, the Moirai.
▶ verb *his daughter was fated to face the same problem* BE PREDESTINED, be preordained, be destined, be meant, be doomed; be sure, be certain, be bound, be guaranteed.

fateful ▶ adjective ❶ *that fateful day* DECISIVE, critical, crucial, pivotal; momentous, important, key, significant, historic, portentous. ❷ *the fateful defeat of 1402* DISASTROUS, ruinous, calamitous, devastating, tragic, terrible.
– OPPOSITES unimportant.

father ▶ noun ❶ *his mother and father* MALE PARENT, patriarch, paterfamilias; *informal* dad, daddy, pop, pa, old man; *Brit. informal, dated* pater. ❷ (*poetic/literary*) *the religion of my fathers* ANCESTOR, forefather, forebear, predecessor, antecedent, progenitor, primogenitor. ❸ *the father of democracy* ORIGINATOR, initiator, founder, inventor, creator, maker, author, architect. ❹ *the city fathers* LEADER, elder, patriarch, official. ❺ *our heavenly Father* GOD, Lord (God). ❻ *pray for me, Father* PRIEST, pastor, parson, clergyman, cleric, minister, preacher; *informal* reverend, padre.
– RELATED TERMS paternal, patri-.
– OPPOSITES child, mother, descendant.
▶ verb ❶ *he fathered six children* BE THE FATHER OF, sire, bring into the world, spawn, breed; *poetic/literary* beget; *archaic* engender. ❷ *he fathered a strand of applied economics* ESTABLISH, institute, originate, initiate, invent, found, create.

fatherland ▶ noun NATIVE LAND, native country, homeland, mother country, motherland, land of one's birth.

fatherly ▶ adjective PATERNAL, fatherlike; protective, supportive, encouraging, affectionate, caring, sympathetic, indulgent.

fathom ▶ verb ❶ *Charlie tried to fathom her expression* UNDERSTAND, comprehend, work out, make sense of, grasp, divine, puzzle out, get to the bottom of; interpret, decipher, decode; *informal* make head or tail of, tumble to, crack; *Brit. informal* twig, suss (out), savvy. ❷ *fathoming the ocean* MEASURE THE DEPTH OF, sound, plumb.

fatigue ▶ noun ❶ *his face was grey with fatigue* TIREDNESS, weariness, exhaustion, enervation, prostration. ❷ (*Military*) *kitchen fatigues* MENIAL WORK, drudgery, chores; *informal* skivvying.
– OPPOSITES energy.
▶ verb *the troops were fatigued* TIRE (OUT), exhaust, wear out, drain, weary, wash out, overtire, prostrate, enervate; *informal* knock out, take it out of, do in, fag out, whack, poop, shatter, bush, wear to a frazzle; *Brit. informal* knacker.
– OPPOSITES invigorate.

fatness ▶ noun PLUMPNESS, stoutness, heaviness, chubbiness, portliness, rotundity, flabbiness, paunchiness; obesity, corpulence; *informal* tubbiness, podginess.
– OPPOSITES thinness.

fatten ▶ verb ❶ *fattening livestock* MAKE FAT/FATTER, feed (up), build up. ❷ *we're sending her home to fatten up* PUT ON WEIGHT, gain weight, get heavier, grow fatter, fill out.
– OPPOSITES slim.

fatty ▶ adjective GREASY, oily, fat, oleaginous.
– OPPOSITES lean.

fatuous ▶ adjective SILLY, foolish, stupid, inane, idiotic, vacuous, asinine; pointless, senseless, ridiculous, ludicrous, absurd; *informal* dumb, gormless; *Brit. informal* daft.
– OPPOSITES sensible.

fault ▶ noun ❶ *he has his faults* DEFECT, failing, imperfection, flaw, blemish, shortcoming, weakness, frailty, foible, vice. ❷ *engineers have located the fault* DEFECT, flaw, imperfection, bug; error, mistake, inaccuracy; *informal* glitch, gremlin. ❸ *it was not my fault* RESPONSIBILITY, liability, culpability, blameworthiness, guilt. ❹ *don't blame one child for another's faults* MISDEED, wrongdoing, offence, misdemeanour, misconduct, indiscretion, peccadillo, transgression.
– OPPOSITES merit, strength.
▶ verb *you couldn't fault any of the players* FIND FAULT WITH, criticize, attack, censure, condemn, reproach; complain about, quibble about, moan about; *informal* knock, slam, gripe about, beef about, pick holes in; *Brit. informal* slag off, have a go at, slate.
■ **at fault** TO BLAME, blameworthy, culpable; responsible, guilty, in the wrong.
■ **to a fault** EXCESSIVELY, unduly, immoderately, overly, needlessly.

fault-finding ▶ noun CRITICISM, captiousness, cavilling, quibbling; complaining, grumbling, carping, moaning; *informal* griping, grousing, bellyaching.
– OPPOSITES praise.

faultless ▶ adjective PERFECT, flawless, without fault, error-free, impeccable, accurate, precise, exact, correct, exemplary.
– OPPOSITES flawed.

faulty ▶ adjective ❶ *a faulty electric blanket* MALFUNCTIONING, broken, damaged, defective, not working, out of order; *informal* on the blink, acting up, kaput, bust; *Brit. informal* knackered, playing up, duff; *N. Amer. informal* on the fritz. ❷ *her logic is faulty* DEFECTIVE, flawed, unsound,

inaccurate, incorrect, erroneous, fallacious, wrong.
– RELATED TERMS dys-.
– OPPOSITES working, sound.

faux pas ▶ noun GAFFE, blunder, mistake, indiscretion, impropriety, solecism; *informal* boo-boo; *Brit. informal* boob; *N. Amer. informal* blooper.

favour ▶ noun ❶ *will you do me a favour?* GOOD TURN, service, good deed, (act of) kindness, courtesy. ❷ *she looked on him with favour* APPROVAL, approbation, goodwill, kindness, benevolence. ❸ *they showed favour to one of the players* FAVOURITISM, bias, partiality, partisanship. ❹ *you shall receive the king's favour* PATRONAGE, backing, support, assistance. ❺ (*archaic*) *you shall wear my favours* RIBBON, rosette, badge, token; keepsake, souvenir, memento.
– OPPOSITES disservice, disapproval.
▶ verb ❶ *the party favours electoral reform* ADVOCATE, recommend, approve of, be in favour of, support, back, champion; campaign for, stand up for, press for, lobby for, promote; *informal* plug, push for. ❷ *Robyn favours loose clothes* PREFER, go (in) for, choose, opt for, select, pick, plump for, be partial to, like. ❸ *father always favoured George* SHOW FAVOURITISM TOWARDS, have a bias towards, think more highly of. ❹ *the conditions favoured the other team* BENEFIT, be to the advantage of, help, assist, aid, be of service to, do someone a favour. ❺ *he favoured Lucy with a smile* OBLIGE, honour, gratify, humour, indulge. ❻ (*informal*) *Travis favours our father* RESEMBLE, look like, be similar to, bear a resemblance to, remind one of, take after; *informal* be the spitting image of, be a dead ringer for.
– OPPOSITES oppose, dislike, hinder.
■ **in favour of** ON THE SIDE OF, pro, (all) for, giving support to, approving of, sympathetic to.

favourable ▶ adjective ❶ *a favourable assessment of his ability* APPROVING, commendatory, complimentary, flattering, glowing, enthusiastic; good, pleasing, positive; *informal* rave. ❷ *conditions are favourable* ADVANTAGEOUS, beneficial, in one's favour, good, right, suitable, fitting, appropriate; propitious, auspicious, promising, encouraging. ❸ *a favourable reply* POSITIVE, affirmative, assenting, agreeing, approving; encouraging, reassuring.
– OPPOSITES critical, disadvantageous, negative.

favourably ▶ adverb POSITIVELY, approvingly, sympathetically, enthusiastically, appreciatively.

favoured ▶ adjective PREFERRED, favourite, recommended, chosen, choice.

favourite ▶ adjective *his favourite aunt* BEST-LOVED, most-liked, favoured, dearest; preferred, chosen, choice.
▶ noun ❶ *Brutus was Caesar's favourite* (FIRST) CHOICE, pick, preference, pet, darling, the apple of one's eye; *informal* blue-eyed boy, golden boy; *N. Amer. informal* fair-haired boy. ❷ *the favourite fell at the first fence* EXPECTED WINNER, front runner.

favouritism ▶ noun PARTIALITY, partisanship, unfair preference, preferential treatment, favour, prejudice, bias, inequality, unfairness, discrimination.

fawn[1] ▶ adjective *a fawn carpet* BEIGE, yellowish-brown, pale brown, buff, sand, oatmeal, café au lait, camel, ecru, taupe, stone, mushroom.

fawn[2] ▶ verb *they were fawning over the President* BE OBSEQUIOUS TO, be sycophantic to, curry favour with, pay court to, play up to, crawl to, ingratiate oneself with, dance attendance on; *informal* suck up to, make up to, be all over; *Austral./NZ informal* smoodge to.

fawning ▶ adjective OBSEQUIOUS, servile, sycophantic, flattering, ingratiating, unctuous, oleaginous, grovelling, crawling; *informal* boot-licking, smarmy.

fear ▶ noun ❶ *she felt fear at entering the house* TERROR, fright, fearfulness, horror, alarm, panic, agitation, trepidation, dread, consternation, dismay, distress; anxiety, worry, angst, unease, uneasiness, apprehension, apprehensiveness, nervousness, nerves, perturbation, foreboding; *informal* the creeps, the willies, the heebie-jeebies, jitteriness, twitchiness, butterflies (in the stomach), (blue) funk. ❷ *she overcame her fears* PHOBIA, aversion, antipathy, dread, bugbear, bogey, nightmare, horror, terror; anxiety, neurosis; *informal* hang-up. ❸ (*archaic*) *the love and fear of God* AWE, wonder, wonderment; reverence, veneration, respect. ❹ *there's no fear of me leaving you alone* LIKELIHOOD, likeliness, prospect, possibility, chance, probability; risk, danger.
▶ verb ❶ *she feared her husband* BE AFRAID OF, be fearful of, be scared of, be apprehensive of, dread, live in fear of, be terrified of; be anxious about, worry about, feel apprehensive about. ❷ *he fears heights* HAVE A PHOBIA ABOUT, have a horror of, take fright at. ❸ *he feared to tell them* BE TOO AFRAID, be too scared, hesitate, dare not. ❹ *they feared for his health* WORRY ABOUT, feel anxious about, feel concerned about, have anxieties about. ❺ (*archaic*) *all who fear the Lord* STAND IN AWE OF, revere, reverence, venerate, respect. ❻ *I fear that you may be right* SUSPECT, have a (sneaking) suspicion, be inclined to think, be afraid, have a hunch, think it likely.

fearful ▶ adjective ❶ *they are fearful of being overheard* AFRAID, frightened, scared (stiff), scared to death, terrified, petrified; alarmed, panicky, nervy, nervous, tense, apprehensive, uneasy, worried (sick), anxious; *informal* jittery, jumpy; *Brit. informal* in a (blue) funk; *archaic* afeared, affrighted. ❷ *the guards were fearful* NERVOUS, trembling, quaking, cowed, daunted; timid, timorous, faint-hearted; *Brit.* nervy; *informal* jittery, jumpy, twitchy, keyed up, in a cold sweat, a bundle of nerves, like a cat on a hot tin roof; *Brit. informal* having kittens, like a cat on hot bricks; *N. Amer. informal* spooky. ❸ *a fearful accident* TERRIBLE, dreadful, awful, appalling, frightful, ghastly, horrific, horrible, horrifying, horrendous, terribly bad, shocking, atrocious, abominable, hideous, monstrous, gruesome. ❹ (*informal*) *he was in a fearful hurry* (VERY) GREAT, extreme, real, dreadful; *informal* terrible.

fearfully ▸ **adverb** ❶ *she opened the door fearfully* APPREHENSIVELY, uneasily, nervously, timidly, timorously, hesitantly, with one's heart in one's mouth. ❷ (*informal*) *Stephanie looked fearfully glamorous* EXTREMELY, exceedingly, exceptionally, remarkably, uncommonly, extraordinarily, tremendously, incredibly, very, really; *Scottish* unco; *informal* awfully, terribly, dreadfully; *Brit.* well, ever so, dead; *N. Amer. informal* real, mighty, awful; *dated* frightfully.

fearless ▸ **adjective** BOLD, brave, courageous, intrepid, valiant, valorous, gallant, plucky, lionhearted, heroic, daring, audacious, indomitable, doughty; unafraid, undaunted, unflinching; *informal* gutsy, spunky, ballsy, feisty.
– OPPOSITES timid, cowardly.

fearsome ▸ **adjective** FRIGHTENING, horrifying, terrifying, menacing, chilling, spine-chilling, hair-raising, alarming, unnerving, daunting, formidable, forbidding, dismaying, disquieting, disturbing; *informal* scary.

feasible ▸ **adjective** PRACTICABLE, practical, workable, achievable, attainable, realizable, viable, realistic, sensible, reasonable, within reason; suitable, possible, expedient, constructive; *informal* doable.
– OPPOSITES impractical.

feast ▸ **noun** ❶ *a wedding feast* BANQUET, celebration meal, lavish dinner; treat, entertainment; revels, festivities; *informal* blowout, spread; *Brit. informal* nosh-up, beanfeast, bunfight, beano, slap-up meal. ❷ *the feast of St Stephen* (RELIGIOUS) FESTIVAL, feast day, saint's day, holy day, holiday. ❸ *a feast for the eyes* TREAT, delight, joy, pleasure.
▸ **verb** ❶ *they feasted on lobster* GORGE ON, dine on, eat one's fill of, overindulge in, binge on; eat, devour, consume, partake of; *informal* stuff one's face with, stuff oneself with, pig oneself on, pig out on. ❷ *they feasted the deputation* HOLD A BANQUET FOR, throw a feast/party for, wine and dine, entertain lavishly, regale, treat, fête.

feat ▸ **noun** ACHIEVEMENT, accomplishment, attainment, coup, triumph; undertaking, enterprise, venture, operation, exercise, endeavour, effort, performance, exploit.

feather ▸ **noun** PLUME, quill, flight feather, tail feather; *Ornithology* covert, plumule; (**feathers**) plumage, feathering, down.

feature ▸ **noun** ❶ *a typical feature of French music* CHARACTERISTIC, attribute, quality, property, trait, hallmark, trademark; aspect, facet, factor, ingredient, component, element, theme; peculiarity, idiosyncrasy, quirk. ❷ *her delicate features* FACE, countenance, physiognomy; *informal* mug, kisser; *Brit. informal* mush, phiz; *N. Amer. informal* puss, pan; *poetic/literary* visage, lineaments. ❸ *she made a feature of her garden sculptures* CENTREPIECE, (special) attraction, highlight, focal point, focus (of attention). ❹ *a series of short features* ARTICLE, piece, item, report, story, column, review, commentary, write-up.
▸ **verb** ❶ *Radio Ulster is featuring a week of live concerts* PRESENT, promote, make a feature of, give prominence to, focus attention on, spotlight, highlight. ❷ *she is to feature in a major advertising campaign* STAR, appear, participate, play a part.

febrile ▸ **adjective** FEVERISH, hot, burning, flushed, sweating; *informal* having a temperature; *rare* pyretic.

feckless ▸ **adjective** USELESS, worthless, incompetent, inept, good-for-nothing, ne'er-do-well; lazy, idle, slothful, indolent, shiftless; *informal* no-good, no-account.

fecund ▸ **adjective** FERTILE, fruitful, productive, high-yielding; rich, lush, flourishing, thriving; *formal* fructuous.
– OPPOSITES barren.

federal ▸ **adjective** CONFEDERATE, federated, federative; combined, allied, united, amalgamated, integrated.

federate ▸ **verb** CONFEDERATE, combine, unite, unify, merge, amalgamate, integrate, join (up), band together, team up.

federation ▸ **noun** CONFEDERATION, confederacy, federacy, league; combination, alliance, coalition, union, syndicate, guild, consortium, partnership, cooperative, association, amalgamation.

fee ▸ **noun** PAYMENT, wage, salary, allowance; price, cost, charge, tariff, rate, amount, sum, figure; (**fees**) remuneration, dues, earnings, pay; *formal* emolument.

feeble ▸ **adjective** ❶ *he was very old and feeble* WEAK, weakly, weakened, frail, infirm, delicate, sickly, ailing, unwell, poorly, enfeebled, enervated, debilitated, incapacitated, decrepit. ❷ *a feeble argument* INEFFECTIVE, ineffectual, inadequate, unconvincing, implausible, unsatisfactory, poor, weak, flimsy. ❸ *he's too feeble to stand up to his boss* COWARDLY, craven, faint-hearted, spineless, spiritless, lily-livered; timid, timorous, fearful, unassertive, weak, ineffectual; *informal* wimpy, sissy, sissified, gutless, chicken; *Brit. informal* wet. ❹ *a feeble light* FAINT, dim, weak, pale, soft, subdued, muted.
– OPPOSITES strong, brave.

feeble-minded ▸ **adjective** ❶ *don't be so feeble-minded* STUPID, idiotic, imbecilic, foolish,

witless, doltish, empty-headed, vacuous; *informal* half-witted, moronic, dumb, dim, dopey, dozy, dotty, dippy; *Brit. informal* daft. ❷ (*dated*) *the segregation of the feeble-minded* HAVING LEARNING DIFFICULTIES, having special (educational) needs, backward, simple, slow, (mentally) retarded; *dated* educationally subnormal, ESN; *informal* mental.
– OPPOSITES clever, gifted.

feed ▶ **verb** ❶ *a large family to feed* GIVE FOOD TO, provide (food) for, cater for, cook for; suckle, breastfeed, bottle-feed; *dated* victual. ❷ *the baby spends all day feeding* EAT, consume food, have a meal, snack; *informal* nosh, graze. ❸ *too many cows feeding in a small area* GRAZE, browse, crop, pasture. ❹ *the birds feed on a varied diet* LIVE ON/OFF, exist on, subsist on, eat, consume. ❺ *feeding one's self-esteem* STRENGTHEN, fortify, support, bolster, reinforce, boost, fuel, encourage. ❻ *she fed secrets to the Russians* SUPPLY, provide, give, deliver, furnish, issue.
▶ **noun** ❶ *feed for goats and sheep* FODDER, food, forage, pasturage, herbage, provender; *formal* comestibles. ❷ (*informal*) *they halted for their feed* MEAL, lunch, dinner, supper; *Brit.* tea; *informal* nosh; *Brit. informal* scoff; *formal* repast.

feel ▶ **verb** ❶ *she felt the fabric* TOUCH, stroke, caress, fondle, finger, thumb, handle. ❷ *she felt a breeze on her back* PERCEIVE, sense, detect, discern, notice, be aware of, be conscious of. ❸ *the patient does not feel pain* EXPERIENCE, undergo, go through, bear, endure, suffer. ❹ *he felt his way towards the door* GROPE, fumble, scrabble, pick. ❺ *feel the temperature of the water* TEST, try (out), assess. ❻ *he feels that he should go to the meeting* BELIEVE, think, consider (it right), be of the opinion, hold, maintain, judge; *informal* reckon, figure. ❼ *I feel that he is only biding his time* SENSE, have a (funny) feeling, get the impression, have a hunch, intuit. ❽ *the air feels damp* SEEM, appear, strike one as.
▶ **noun** ❶ *the divers worked by feel* (SENSE OF) TOUCH, tactile sense, feeling (one's way). ❷ *the feel of the paper* TEXTURE, surface, finish; weight, thickness, consistency, quality. ❸ *the feel of a room* ATMOSPHERE, ambience, aura, mood, feeling, air, impression, character, tenor, spirit, flavour; *informal* vibrations, vibes. ❹ *a feel for languages* APTITUDE, knack, flair, bent, talent, gift, faculty, ability.

■ **feel for** SYMPATHIZE WITH, be sorry for, pity, feel pity for, feel sympathy for, feel compassion for, be moved by; commiserate with, condole with.

■ **feel like** WANT, would like, wish for, desire, fancy, feel in need of, long for; *informal* yen for, be dying for.

feeler ▶ **noun** ❶ *the fish has two feelers on its head* ANTENNA, tentacle, tactile/sensory organ; *Zoology* antennule. ❷ *the minister put out feelers* TENTATIVE ENQUIRY/PROPOSAL, advance, approach, overture, probe.

feeling ▶ **noun** ❶ *assess the fabric by feeling* (SENSE OF) TOUCH, feel, tactile sense, using one's hands. ❷ *a feeling of nausea* SENSATION, sense, consciousness. ❸ *I had a feeling that I would win* (SNEAKING) SUSPICION, notion, inkling, hunch, funny feeling, feeling in one's bones, fancy, idea; presentiment, premonition; *informal* gut feeling. ❹ *the strength of her feeling* LOVE, affection, fondness, tenderness, warmth, warmness, emotion, sentiment; passion, ardour, desire. ❺ *out of touch with public feeling* SENTIMENT, emotion; opinion, attitude, belief, ideas, views. ❻ *a rush of feeling* COMPASSION, sympathy, empathy, fellow feeling, concern, solicitude, solicitousness, tenderness, (brotherly) love; pity, sorrow, commiseration. ❼ *he had hurt her feelings* SENSIBILITIES, sensitivities, self-esteem, pride. ❽ *my feeling is that it is true* OPINION, belief, view, impression, intuition, instinct, hunch, estimation, guess. ❾ *a feeling of peace* ATMOSPHERE, ambience, aura, air, feel, mood, impression, spirit, quality, flavour; *informal* vibrations, vibes. ❿ *a remarkable feeling for language* APTITUDE, knack, flair, bent, talent, gift, faculty, ability.
▶ **adjective** *a feeling man* SENSITIVE, warm, warm-hearted, tender, tender-hearted, caring, sympathetic, kind, compassionate, understanding, thoughtful.

feign ▶ **verb** ❶ *she lay still and feigned sleep* SIMULATE, fake, sham, affect, give the appearance of, make a pretence of. ❷ *he's not really ill, he's only feigning* PRETEND, put it on, fake, sham, bluff, masquerade, play-act; *informal* kid.

feigned ▶ **adjective** PRETENDED, simulated, affected, artificial, insincere, put-on, fake, false, sham; *informal* pretend, phoney.
– OPPOSITES sincere.

feint ▶ **noun** BLUFF, blind, ruse, deception, subterfuge, hoax, trick, ploy, device, dodge, sham, pretence, cover, smokescreen, distraction, contrivance; *informal* red herring.

felicitations ▶ **plural noun** CONGRATULATIONS, good/best wishes, (kind) regards, blessings, compliments, respects.

felicitous ▶ **adjective** ❶ *his nickname was particularly felicitous* APT, well chosen, fitting, suitable, appropriate, apposite, pertinent, germane, relevant. ❷ *the room's only felicitous feature* FAVOURABLE, advantageous, good, pleasing.
– OPPOSITES inappropriate, unfortunate.

felicity ▶ **noun** ❶ *domestic felicity* HAPPINESS, joy, joyfulness, joyousness, bliss, delight, cheerfulness; contentedness, satisfaction, pleasure. ❷ *David expressed his feelings with his customary felicity* ELOQUENCE, aptness, appropriateness, suitability, suitableness, applicability, fitness, relevance, pertinence.
– OPPOSITES unhappiness, inappropriateness.

feline ▶ **adjective** *she moved with feline grace* CATLIKE, graceful, sleek, sinuous.

▶ **noun** *her pet feline* CAT, kitten; *informal* puss, pussy (cat); *Brit. informal* moggie, mog; *archaic* grimalkin.

fell[1] ▶ **verb** ❶ *all the dead sycamores had to be felled* CUT DOWN, chop down, hack down, saw down, clear. ❷ *she felled him with one punch* KNOCK DOWN/OVER, knock to the ground, strike down, bring down, bring to the ground, prostrate; knock out, knock unconscious; *informal* deck, floor, flatten, down, lay out, KO; *Brit. informal* knock for six.

fell[2] ▶ **adjective** (*poetic/literary*) *a fell intent* MURDEROUS, savage, violent, vicious, fierce, ferocious, barbarous, barbaric, monstrous, cruel, ruthless; *archaic* sanguinary.

■ **at/in one fell swoop** ALL AT ONCE, together, at the same time, in one go.

fellow ▶ **noun** ❶ (*informal*) *he's a decent sort of fellow* MAN, boy; person, individual, soul; *informal* guy, geezer, lad, fella, character, customer, devil, bastard; *Brit. informal* chap, bloke; *N. Amer. informal* dude, hombre; *Austral./NZ informal* digger; *informal, dated* body, dog, cove. ❷ (*informal*) *she longed to have a fellow* BOYFRIEND, lover. ❸ *he exchanged glances with his fellows* COMPANION, friend, comrade, partner, associate, co-worker, colleague; *informal* chum, pal, buddy; *Brit. informal* mate. ❹ *some peasants were wealthier than their fellows* PEER, equal, contemporary, confrère; *archaic* compeer.

■ **fellow feeling** SYMPATHY, empathy, feeling, compassion, care, concern, solicitude, solicitousness, warmth, tenderness, (brotherly) love; pity, sorrow, commiseration.

fellowship ▶ **noun** ❶ *a community bound together in fellowship* COMPANIONSHIP, companionability, sociability, comradeship, camaraderie, friendship, mutual support; togetherness, solidarity; *informal* chumminess, palliness; *Brit. informal* mateyness. ❷ *the church fellowship* ASSOCIATION, society, club, league, union, guild, affiliation, alliance, fraternity, brotherhood, sorority, sodality.

female ▶ **adjective** *typical female attributes* FEMININE, womanly, ladylike; *archaic* feminal.

▶ **noun** *the author was a female. See* WOMAN sense 1.

– RELATED TERMS gynaeco-.

– OPPOSITES male.

feminine ▶ **adjective** ❶ *a very feminine young woman* WOMANLY, ladylike, girlish, girly; *archaic* feminal. ❷ *he seemed slightly feminine* EFFEMINATE, womanish, unmanly, effete; *informal* sissy, wimpy, limp-wristed.

– OPPOSITES masculine, manly.

femininity ▶ **noun** WOMANLINESS, feminineness, womanly/feminine qualities.

feminism ▶ **noun** THE WOMEN'S MOVEMENT, the feminist movement, women's liberation, female emancipation, women's rights; *informal* women's lib.

femme fatale ▶ **noun** SEDUCTRESS, temptress, siren; *informal* vamp.

fen ▶ **noun** MARSH, marshland, salt marsh, fenland, wetland, (peat) bog, swamp, swampland; *N. Amer.* moor.

fence ▶ **noun** ❶ *a gap in the fence* BARRIER, paling, railing, enclosure, barricade, stockade, palisade. ❷ (*informal*) *a fence dealing mainly in jewellery* RECEIVER (OF STOLEN GOODS), dealer.

▶ **verb** ❶ *they fenced off many acres* ENCLOSE, surround, circumscribe, encircle, circle, encompass; *poetic/literary* engirdle; *archaic* compass. ❷ *he fenced in his chickens* CONFINE, pen in, coop up, shut in/up, separate off; enclose, surround; *N. Amer.* corral. ❸ *he fences as a hobby* FIGHT WITH SWORDS, sword-fight. ❹ *the man fenced but Jim persisted* BE EVASIVE, be vague, be non-committal, equivocate, prevaricate, stall, vacillate, hedge, pussyfoot around, sidestep the issue; *informal* duck the question/issue, flannel, shilly-shally; *Brit. informal* waffle; *rare* palter.

■ **(sitting) on the fence** (*informal*) UNDECIDED, uncommitted, uncertain, unsure, vacillating, wavering, dithering, hesitant, doubtful, ambivalent, in two minds, in a quandary; neutral, impartial, non-partisan, open-minded; *Brit.* humming and hawing.

fend ▶ **verb** *they were unable to fend off the invasion* WARD OFF, head off, stave off, hold off, repel, repulse, resist, fight off, defend oneself against, prevent, stop, block, intercept, hold back.

■ **fend for oneself** TAKE CARE OF ONESELF, look after oneself, provide for oneself, shift for oneself, manage by oneself, cope alone, stand on one's own two feet.

feral ▶ **adjective** ❶ *feral dogs* WILD, untamed, undomesticated, untrained. ❷ *a feral snarl* FIERCE, ferocious, vicious, savage, predatory, menacing, bloodthirsty.

– OPPOSITES tame, pet.

ferment ▶ **verb** ❶ *the beer continues to ferment* UNDERGO FERMENTATION, brew; effervesce, fizz, foam, froth. ❷ *an environment that ferments disorder* CAUSE, bring about, give rise to, generate, engender, spawn, instigate, provoke, incite, excite, stir up, whip up, foment; *poetic/literary* beget, enkindle.

▶ **noun** ❶ *a ferment of revolutionary upheaval* FEVER, furore, frenzy, tumult, storm, rumpus; turmoil, upheaval, unrest, disquiet, uproar, agitation, turbulence, disruption, confusion, disorder, chaos, mayhem; *informal* kerfuffle, hoo-ha, to-do; *Brit. informal* aggro. ❷ (*archaic*) *the action of a ferment* FERMENTING AGENT/SUBSTANCE, enzyme; yeast, bacteria, leaven.

ferocious ▶ **adjective** ❶ *ferocious animals* FIERCE, savage, wild, predatory, aggressive, dangerous. ❷ *a ferocious attack* BRUTAL, vicious, violent, bloody, barbaric, savage, sadistic, ruthless, cruel, merciless, heartless, bloodthirsty, murderous; *poetic/literary* fell; *archaic* sanguinary. ❸ (*informal*) *a ferocious headache* INTENSE, strong, powerful, fierce, severe, extreme,

acute, unbearable; *informal* hellish.
– OPPOSITES gentle, mild.

ferocity ▶ **noun** SAVAGERY, brutality, barbarity, fierceness, violence, bloodthirstiness, murderousness; ruthlessness, cruelty, pitilessness, mercilessness, heartlessness.

ferret ▶ **verb** ❶ *she ferreted in her handbag* RUMMAGE, feel around, grope around, forage around, fish about/around, poke about/around; search through, hunt through, rifle through; *Austral./NZ informal* fossick through. ❷ *ferreting out misdemeanours* UNEARTH, uncover, discover, detect, search out, bring to light, track down, dig up, root out, nose out; *informal* get wise to; *Brit. informal* rumble.

ferry ▶ **noun** *the ferry from Dover to Calais* PASSENGER BOAT/SHIP, ferry boat, car ferry; ship, boat, vessel; *dated* packet (boat).
▶ **verb** ❶ *ferrying passengers to and from the Continent* TRANSPORT, convey, carry, ship, run, take, bring, shuttle. ❷ *the boat ferried hourly across the river* GO BACK AND FORTH, shuttle, run.

fertile ▶ **adjective** ❶ *the soil is fertile* FECUND, fruitful, productive, high-yielding, rich, lush; *formal* fructuous. ❷ *fertile couples* ABLE TO CONCEIVE, able to have children; *technical* fecund. ❸ *a fertile brain* IMAGINATIVE, inventive, innovative, creative, visionary, original, ingenious; productive, prolific.
– OPPOSITES barren.

fertilization ▶ **noun** CONCEPTION, impregnation, insemination; pollination, propagation.

fertilize ▶ **verb** ❶ *the field was fertilized* ADD FERTILIZER TO, feed, mulch, compost, manure, dress, top-dress. ❷ *these orchids are fertilized by insects* POLLINATE, cross-pollinate, cross-fertilize.

fertilizer ▶ **noun** MANURE, plant food, compost, dressing, top dressing, dung.

fervent ▶ **adjective** IMPASSIONED, passionate, intense, vehement, ardent, sincere, fervid, heartfelt; enthusiastic, zealous, fanatical, wholehearted, avid, eager, keen, committed, dedicated, devout; *informal* mad keen; *poetic/literary* perfervid.
– OPPOSITES apathetic.

fervid ▶ **adjective** FERVENT, ardent, passionate, impassioned, intense, vehement, wholehearted, heartfelt, sincere, earnest; *poetic/literary* perfervid.

fervour ▶ **noun** PASSION, ardour, intensity, zeal, vehemence, emotion, warmth, earnestness, avidity, eagerness, keenness, enthusiasm, excitement, animation, vigour, energy, fire, spirit, zest, fervency, ardency.
– OPPOSITES apathy.

fester ▶ **verb** ❶ *his deep wound festered* SUPPURATE, become septic, form pus, weep; *Medicine* maturate, be purulent; *archaic* rankle. ❷ *rubbish festered* ROT, moulder, decay, decompose, putrefy, go bad/off, spoil, deteriorate. ❸ *their resentment festered* RANKLE, eat/gnaw away at one's mind, brew, smoulder.

festival ▶ **noun** ❶ *the town's autumn festival* FÊTE, fair, gala (day), carnival, fiesta, jamboree, celebrations, festivities, eisteddfod. ❷ *fasting precedes the festival* HOLY DAY, feast day, saint's day, commemoration, day of observance.

festive ▶ **adjective** JOLLY, merry, joyous, joyful, happy, jovial, light-hearted, cheerful, jubilant, convivial, high-spirited, mirthful, uproarious; celebratory, holiday, carnival; Christmassy; *archaic* festal.

festivity ▶ **noun** ❶ *food plays an important part in the festivities* CELEBRATION, festival, entertainment, party, jamboree; merrymaking, feasting, revelry, jollification; revels, fun and games; *informal* bash, shindig, shindy; *Brit. informal* rave-up, knees-up, beanfeast, bunfight, beano. ❷ *the festivity of the Last Night of the Proms* JOLLITY, merriment, gaiety, cheerfulness, cheer, joyfulness, jubilance, conviviality, high spirits, revelry.

festoon ▶ **noun** *festoons of paper flowers* GARLAND, chain, lei, swathe, swag, loop.
▶ **verb** *the room was festooned with streamers* DECORATE, adorn, ornament, trim, deck (out), hang, loop, drape, swathe, garland, wreathe, bedeck; *informal* do up/out, get up, trick out; *poetic/literary* bedizen, furbelow.

fetch ▶ **verb** ❶ *he went to fetch a doctor* (GO AND) GET, go for, call for, summon, pick up, collect, bring, carry, convey, transport. ❷ *the land could fetch a million pounds* SELL FOR, bring in, raise, realize, yield, make, command, cost, be priced at; *informal* go for, set one back, pull in; *Brit. informal* knock someone back.
■ **fetch up** (*informal*) END UP, finish up, turn up, appear, materialize, find itself; *informal* wind up, show up.

fetching ▶ **adjective** ATTRACTIVE, appealing, sweet, pretty, lovely, delightful, charming, prepossessing, captivating, enchanting, irresistible; *Scottish & N. English* bonny; *informal* divine, heavenly; *Brit. informal* fit, smashing; *archaic* comely, fair.

fête ▶ **noun** (*Brit.*) GALA (DAY), bazaar, fair, festival, fiesta, jubilee, carnival; fund-raiser, charity event.

fetid ▶ **adjective** STINKING, smelly, foul-smelling, malodorous, reeking, pungent, acrid, high, rank, foul, noxious; *Brit. informal* niffy, pongy, whiffy, humming; *N. Amer. informal* funky; *poetic/literary* noisome, miasmic, miasmal.
– OPPOSITES fragrant.

fetish ▶ **noun** ❶ *he developed a rubber fetish* FIXATION, obsession, compulsion, mania; weakness, fancy, fascination, fad; *informal* thing, hang-up. ❷ *an African fetish* JUJU, talisman, charm, amulet; totem, idol, image, effigy; *archaic* periapt.

fetter ▶ verb ❶ *the captive was fettered* SHACKLE, manacle, handcuff, clap in irons, put in chains, chain (up); *informal* cuff; *poetic/literary* enfetter. ❷ *these obligations fetter the company's powers* RESTRICT, restrain, constrain, limit; hinder, hamper, impede, obstruct, hamstring, inhibit, check, curb, trammel.

fetters ▶ plural noun SHACKLES, manacles, handcuffs, irons, leg-irons, chains, restraints; *informal* cuffs, bracelets; *historical* bilboes.

fettle ▶ noun SHAPE, trim, (physical) fitness, (state of) health; condition, form, (state of) repair, (working) order; *Brit. informal* nick.

fetus ▶ noun EMBRYO, fertilized egg, unborn baby/child.

feud ▶ noun *tribal feuds* VENDETTA, conflict; rivalry, hostility, enmity, strife, discord; quarrel, argument, falling-out.

▶ verb *he feuded with his teammates* QUARREL, fight, argue, bicker, squabble, fall out, dispute, clash, differ, be at odds; *informal* scrap.

fever ▶ noun ❶ *he developed fever* FEVERISHNESS, high temperature, febrility; *Medicine* pyrexia; *informal* temperature. ❷ *a fever of excitement* FERMENT, frenzy, furore; ecstasy, rapture. ❸ *World Cup fever* EXCITEMENT, frenzy, agitation, passion.
– RELATED TERMS febrile.

fevered ▶ adjective ❶ *her fevered brow* FEVERISH, febrile, hot, burning; *rare* pyretic. ❷ *a fevered imagination* EXCITED, agitated, frenzied, overwrought, fervid.

feverish ▶ adjective ❶ *she's really feverish* FEBRILE, fevered, hot, burning; *informal* having a temperature; *rare* pyretic. ❷ *feverish excitement* FRENZIED, frenetic, hectic, agitated, excited, restless, nervous, worked up, overwrought, frantic, furious, hysterical, wild, uncontrolled, unrestrained.

few ▶ determiner *police are revealing few details* NOT MANY, hardly any, scarcely any; a small number of, a small amount of, one or two, a handful of; little.
– OPPOSITES many.

▶ adjective *comforts here are few* SCARCE, scant, meagre, insufficient, in short supply; thin on the ground, few and far between, infrequent, uncommon, rare.
– OPPOSITES plentiful.

■ **a few** A SMALL NUMBER, a handful, one or two, a couple, two or three; not many, hardly any.

fiancée, masc. **fiancé** ▶ noun BETROTHED, wife-to-be, husband-to-be, bride-to-be, future wife/husband, prospective spouse; *informal* intended.

fiasco ▶ noun FAILURE, disaster, catastrophe, debacle, shambles, farce, mess, wreck; *informal* flop, washout; *Brit. informal* cock-up; *N. Amer. informal* snafu; *Austral./NZ informal* fizzer.
– OPPOSITES success.

fiat ▶ noun DECREE, edict, order, command, commandment, injunction, proclamation, mandate, dictum, diktat.

fib ▶ noun *you're telling a fib* LIE, untruth, falsehood, made-up story, invention, fabrication, deception, (piece of) fiction; (little) white lie, half-truth; *informal* tall story/tale, whopper; *Brit. informal* porky (pie).
– OPPOSITES truth.

▶ verb *she had bunked off school, fibbing about a sore throat* LIE, tell a fib, tell a lie, invent a story, make up a story; *informal* kid.

fibre ▶ noun ❶ *fibres from the murderer's jumper* THREAD, strand, filament; *technical* fibril. ❷ *natural fibres* MATERIAL, cloth, fabric. ❸ *a man with no fibre. See* MORAL FIBRE. ❹ *fibre in the diet* ROUGHAGE, bulk.

fickle ▶ adjective CAPRICIOUS, changeable, variable, volatile, mercurial; inconstant, undependable, unsteady, unfaithful, faithless, flighty, giddy, skittish; *technical* labile; *poetic/literary* mutable.
– OPPOSITES constant.

fiction ▶ noun ❶ *the traditions of British fiction* NOVELS, stories, creative writing, prose literature. ❷ *the president dismissed the allegation as absolute fiction* FABRICATION, invention, lies, fibs, untruth, falsehood, fantasy, nonsense.
– OPPOSITES fact.

fictional ▶ adjective FICTITIOUS, invented, imaginary, made up, make-believe, unreal, fabricated, mythical.
– OPPOSITES real.

fictitious ▶ adjective ❶ *a fictitious name* FALSE, fake, fabricated, sham; bogus, spurious, assumed, affected, adopted, feigned, invented, made up; *informal* pretend, phoney. ❷ *a fictitious character. See* FICTIONAL.
– OPPOSITES genuine.

fiddle (*informal*) ▶ noun ❶ *she played the fiddle* VIOLIN, viola. ❷ *a VAT fiddle* FRAUD, swindle, confidence trick; *informal* racket, con trick, flimflam.

▶ verb ❶ *he fiddled with a beer mat* FIDGET, play, toy, twiddle, fuss, fool about/around; finger, thumb, handle; *informal* mess about/around; *Brit. informal* muck about/around. ❷ *he fiddled with the dials* ADJUST, tinker, play about/around, meddle, interfere. ❸ *fiddling the figures* FALSIFY, manipulate, massage, rig, distort, misrepresent, doctor, alter, tamper with, interfere with; *informal* fix, flimflam, cook (the books).

fiddling ▶ adjective (*informal*) TRIVIAL, petty, trifling, insignificant, unimportant, inconsequential, negligible, paltry, footling, minor, small, incidental, of little/no account; *informal* piddling, piffling.
– OPPOSITES important.

fidelity ▶ noun ❶ *fidelity to her husband* FAITHFULNESS, loyalty, constancy; true-heartedness, trustworthiness, dependability, reliability; *formal* troth. ❷ *fidelity to your king* LOYALTY, allegiance, obedience, constancy, homage; *historical*

fealty. ❸ *the fidelity of the reproduction* ACCURACY, exactness, precision, preciseness, correctness; strictness, closeness, faithfulness, authenticity.
– OPPOSITES disloyalty.

fidget ▶ verb ❶ *the audience began to fidget* MOVE RESTLESSLY, wriggle, squirm, twitch, jiggle, shuffle, be agitated; *informal* be jittery. ❷ *she fidgeted with her scarf* PLAY, fuss, toy, twiddle, fool about/around; *informal* fiddle, mess about/around. ❸ *she seemed to fidget him* MAKE UNEASY, worry, agitate, bother, upset, ruffle.
▶ noun ❶ *his convulsive fidgets* TWITCH, wriggle, squirm, jiggle, shuffle, tic, spasm. ❷ *what a fidget you are!* RESTLESS PERSON, bundle of nerves. ❸ *that woman gives me the fidgets* RESTLESSNESS, nervousness, fidgetiness; *informal* the jitters, twitchiness.

fidgety ▶ adjective RESTLESS, restive, on edge, uneasy, nervous, nervy, keyed up, anxious, agitated; *informal* jittery, twitchy.

field ▶ noun ❶ *a large ploughed field* MEADOW, pasture, paddock, grassland, pastureland, sward; *poetic/literary* lea, mead; *archaic* glebe. ❷ *a football field* PITCH, ground, sports field, playing field, recreation ground. ❸ *the field of biotechnology* AREA, sphere, discipline, province, department, domain, sector, branch, subject; *informal* bailiwick. ❹ *your field of vision* SCOPE, range, sweep, reach, extent. ❺ *she is well ahead of the field* COMPETITORS, entrants, competition; applicants, candidates, possibles.
▶ verb ❶ *he was fielding* ACT AS A FIELDER, play in outfield. ❷ *she fielded the ball* CATCH, stop, retrieve; return, throw back. ❸ *fielding an ineligible player* PUT IN THE TEAM, send out, play, put up. ❹ *they can field an army of about one million* DEPLOY, position, range, dispose. ❺ *he fielded some awkward questions* DEAL WITH, handle, cope with, answer, reply to, respond to.
▶ adjective ❶ *field experience* PRACTICAL, hands-on, applied, experiential, empirical. ❷ *field artillery* MOBILE, portable, transportable, movable, manoeuvrable, light.
– OPPOSITES theoretical.

fiend ▶ noun ❶ *a fiend had taken possession of him* DEMON, devil, evil spirit, bogie, cacodemon; *informal* spook. ❷ *a fiend bent on global evil-doing* BRUTE, beast, villain, barbarian, monster, ogre, sadist, evil-doer; *informal* swine. ❸ (*informal*) *a drug fiend* ADDICT, abuser, user; *informal* junkie, —head/freak. ❹ (*informal*) *I'm a fiend for Mexican food* ENTHUSIAST, maniac; devotee, fan, lover; *informal* fanatic, addict, buff, freak, nut.

fiendish ▶ adjective ❶ *a fiendish torturer* WICKED, cruel, vicious, evil, malevolent, villainous; brutal, savage, barbaric, barbarous, inhuman, murderous, ruthless, merciless; *dated* dastardly. ❷ *a fiendish plot* CUNNING, clever, ingenious, crafty, canny, wily, devious, shrewd; *informal* foxy, sneaky. ❸ *a fiendish puzzle* DIFFICULT, complex, challenging, complicated, intricate, involved, knotty, thorny.

fierce ▶ adjective ❶ *a fierce black mastiff* FEROCIOUS, savage, vicious, aggressive. ❷ *fierce competition* AGGRESSIVE, cut-throat, competitive; keen, intense, strong, relentless. ❸ *fierce, murderous jealousy* INTENSE, powerful, vehement, passionate, impassioned, fervent, fervid, ardent. ❹ *a fierce wind* POWERFUL, strong, violent, forceful; stormy, blustery, gusty, tempestuous. ❺ *a fierce pain* SEVERE, extreme, intense, acute, awful, dreadful; excruciating, agonizing, piercing.
– OPPOSITES gentle, mild.

fiery ▶ adjective ❶ *fiery breath* BURNING, blazing, flaming; on fire, ablaze; *poetic/literary* afire. ❷ *a fiery red* BRIGHT, brilliant, vivid, intense, deep, rich. ❸ *her fiery spirit* PASSIONATE, impassioned, ardent, fervent, fervid, spirited; quick-tempered, volatile, explosive, aggressive, determined, resolute.

fiesta ▶ noun FESTIVAL, carnival, holiday, celebration, party.

fight ▶ verb ❶ *two men were fighting* BRAWL, exchange blows, attack/assault each other, hit/punch each other; struggle, grapple, wrestle; *informal* scrap, have a dust-up, have a set-to; *Brit. informal* have a punch-up; *N. Amer. informal* roughhouse; *Austral./NZ informal* stoush, go the knuckle. ❷ *he fought in the First World War* (DO) BATTLE, go to war, take up arms, be a soldier; engage, meet, clash, skirmish. ❸ *a war fought for freedom* ENGAGE IN, wage, conduct, prosecute, undertake. ❹ *they are always fighting* QUARREL, argue, row, bicker, squabble, fall out, have a row/fight, wrangle, be at odds, disagree, differ, have words, bandy words, be at each other's throats, be at loggerheads; *informal* scrap; *archaic* altercate. ❺ *fighting against wage reductions* CAMPAIGN, strive, battle, struggle, contend, crusade, agitate, lobby, push, press. ❻ *they will fight the decision* OPPOSE, contest, contend with, confront, challenge, combat, dispute, quarrel with, argue against/with, strive against, struggle against. ❼ *Donaldson fought the urge to put his tongue out* REPRESS, restrain, suppress, stifle, smother, hold back, fight back, keep in check, curb, control, rein in, choke back; *informal* keep the lid on, cork up.
▶ noun ❶ *a fight outside a club* BRAWL, fracas, melee, rumpus, skirmish, sparring match, struggle, scuffle, altercation, scrum, clash, disturbance; fisticuffs; *informal* scrap, dust-up, set-to, shindy, shindig; *Brit. informal* punch-up, bust-up, ruck; *N. Amer. informal* rough house, brannigan; *Austral./NZ informal* stoush; *Law, dated* affray; *rare* broil. ❷ *a heavyweight fight* BOXING MATCH, bout, match. ❸ *Britain's fight against Germany* BATTLE, engagement, clash, conflict, struggle; war, campaign, crusade, action, hostilities. ❹ *a fight with my girlfriend* ARGUMENT, quarrel, squabble, row, wrangle, disagree-

ment, falling-out, contretemps, altercation, dispute; *informal* tiff, spat, scrap, slanging match; *Brit. informal* barney, ding-dong, bust-up. ❺ *their fight for control of the company* STRUGGLE, battle, campaign, push, effort. ❻ *she had no fight left in her* WILL TO RESIST, resistance, spirit, courage, pluck, pluckiness, grit, strength, backbone, determination, resolution, resolve, resoluteness, aggression, aggressiveness; *informal* guts, spunk; *Brit. informal* bottle; *N. Amer. informal* sand, moxie.

■ **fight back** ❶ *use your pent-up anger to fight back* RETALIATE, counter-attack, strike back, hit back, respond, reciprocate, return fire, give tit for tat; *formal* requite something. ❷ *she fought back tears. See* FIGHT verb sense 7.

■ **fight someone/something off** REPEL, repulse, beat off/back, ward off, fend off, keep/hold at bay, drive away/back, force back.

■ **fight shy of** FLINCH FROM, demur from, recoil from; have scruples about, have misgivings about, have qualms about, be averse to, be chary of, be loath to, be reluctant to, be disinclined to, be afraid to, hesitate to, baulk at; *informal* boggle at; *archaic* disrelish.

fightback ▶ noun (*Brit.*) COUNTER-ATTACK, counter-offensive; rally, recovery; *informal* comeback.

fighter ▶ noun ❶ *a guerrilla fighter* SOLDIER, fighting man/woman, warrior, combatant, serviceman, servicewoman, trooper; *Brit. informal* squaddie; *archaic* man-at-arms. ❷ *the fighter was knocked to the ground* BOXER, pugilist, prizefighter; wrestler; *informal* scrapper, pug. ❸ *enemy fighters* WARPLANE, armed aircraft.

fighting ▶ adjective *a fighting man* VIOLENT, combative, aggressive, pugnacious, truculent, belligerent, bellicose.

– OPPOSITES peaceful.

▶ noun *200 were injured in the fighting* VIOLENCE, hostilities, conflict, action, combat; warfare, war, battles, skirmishing, rioting; *Law, dated* affray.

– OPPOSITES peace.

figment ▶ noun INVENTION, creation, fabrication; hallucination, illusion, delusion, fancy, vision.

figurative ▶ adjective METAPHORICAL, non-literal, symbolic, allegorical, representative, emblematic.

– OPPOSITES literal.

figure ▶ noun ❶ *the production figure* STATISTIC, number, quantity, amount, level, total, sum; (**figures**) data, information. ❷ *the second figure was 9* DIGIT, numeral, numerical symbol. ❸ *he can't put a figure on it* PRICE, cost, amount, value, valuation. ❹ *I'm good at figures* ARITHMETIC, mathematics, sums, calculations, computation, numbers; *Brit. informal* maths; *N. Amer. informal* math. ❺ *her petite figure* PHYSIQUE, build, frame, body, proportions, shape, form. ❻ *a dark figure emerged* SILHOUETTE, outline, shape, form. ❼ *a figure of authority* PERSON, personage, individual, man, woman, character, personality; representative, embodiment, personification, epitome. ❽ *life-size figures* HUMAN REPRESENTATION, effigy. ❾ *geometrical figures* SHAPE, pattern, design, motif. ❿ *see figure 4* DIAGRAM, illustration, drawing, picture, plate.

▶ verb ❶ *a beast figuring in Egyptian legend* FEATURE, appear, be featured, be mentioned, be referred to, have prominence. ❷ *a way to figure the values* CALCULATE, work out, total, reckon, compute, determine, assess, put a figure on; *Brit.* tot up. ❸ (*informal*) *I figured that I didn't have a chance* SUPPOSE, think, believe, consider, expect, take it, suspect, sense; assume, dare say, conclude, take it as read, presume, deduce, infer, gather; *N. Amer.* guess. ❹ (*informal*) *'Rosemary's away.' 'That figures.'* MAKE SENSE, seem reasonable, stand to reason, be to be expected, be logical, follow, ring true.

■ **figure on** (*N. Amer. informal*) *they figured on paying about $100* PLAN ON, count on, rely on, bank on, bargain on, depend on, pin one's hopes on; anticipate, expect to.

■ **figure something out** (*informal*) *he tried to figure out how to switch on the lamp* WORK OUT, fathom, puzzle out, decipher, ascertain, make sense of, think through, get to the bottom of; understand, comprehend, see, grasp, get the hang of, get the drift of; *informal* twig, crack; *Brit. informal* suss out.

filament ▶ noun FIBRE, thread, strand; *technical* fibril.

file[1] ▶ noun ❶ *he opened the file* FOLDER, portfolio, binder, document case. ❷ *we have files on all the major companies* DOSSIER, document, record, report; data, information, documentation, annals, archives. ❸ *the computer file was searched* DATA, document, text.

▶ verb ❶ *file the documents correctly* CATEGORIZE, classify, organize, put in place/order, order, arrange, catalogue, record, store, archive. ❷ *Debbie has filed for divorce* APPLY, register, ask. ❸ *two women have filed a civil suit against him* BRING, press, lodge, place; *formal* prefer.

file[2] ▶ noun *a file of boys* LINE, column, row, string, chain, procession; *Brit. informal* crocodile.

▶ verb *we filed out into the car park* WALK IN A LINE, march, parade, troop.

file[3] ▶ verb *she filed her nails* SMOOTH, buff, rub (down), polish, shape; scrape, abrade, rasp, sandpaper.

filial ▶ adjective DUTIFUL, devoted, compliant, respectful, affectionate, loving.

filibuster ▶ noun *many hours in committee are characterized by filibuster* DELAYING TACTICS, stonewalling, procrastination, obstruction, temporizing.

▶ verb *the opposition are filibustering* WASTE TIME, stall, play for time, stonewall, procrastinate, buy time, employ delaying tactics.

filigree ▶ noun TRACERY, fretwork, latticework, scrollwork, lacework.

fill ▶ verb ❶ *he filled a bowl with cereal* MAKE/BECOME FULL, fill up, fill to the brim, top up, charge. ❷ *guests filled the parlour* CROWD INTO, throng, pack (into), occupy, squeeze into, cram (into); overcrowd, overfill. ❸ *he began filling his shelves* STOCK, pack, load, supply, replenish, restock, refill. ❹ *fill all the holes with a wood-repair compound* BLOCK UP, stop (up), plug, seal, caulk. ❺ *the perfume filled the room* PERVADE, permeate, suffuse, be diffused through, penetrate, infuse, perfuse. ❻ *he was going to fill a government post* OCCUPY, hold, take up; *informal* hold down. ❼ *we had just filled a big order* CARRY OUT, complete, fulfil, execute, discharge; *formal* effectuate.

– OPPOSITES empty.

■ **fill in** SUBSTITUTE, deputize, stand in, cover, take over, act as stand-in, take the place of; *informal* sub, step into someone's shoes/boots; *N. Amer. informal* pinch-hit.

■ **fill someone in** INFORM OF, advise of, tell about, acquaint with, apprise of, brief on, update with; *informal* put in the picture about, bring up to speed on.

■ **fill something in** (*Brit.*) COMPLETE, answer, fill up; *N. Amer.* fill out.

■ **fill out** GROW FATTER, become plumper, flesh out, put on weight, get heavier.

■ **fill something out** ❶ *this account needs to be filled out* EXPAND, enlarge, add to, elaborate on, flesh out; supplement, extend, develop, amplify. ❷ (*N. Amer.*) *he filled out the forms. See* FILL SOMETHING IN.

filling ▶ noun *filling for cushions* STUFFING, padding, wadding, filler.

▶ adjective *a filling meal* SUBSTANTIAL, hearty, ample, satisfying, square; heavy, stodgy.

fillip ▶ noun STIMULUS, stimulation, boost, incentive, impetus; tonic, spur, push, aid, help; *informal* shot in the arm.

film ▶ noun ❶ *a film of sweat* LAYER, coat, coating, covering, cover, sheet, patina, skin, overlay. ❷ *Emma was watching a film* MOVIE, picture, feature (film), motion picture; *informal* flick, pic, talkie; *dated* moving picture. ❸ *she would like to work in film* CINEMA, movies, the pictures.

– RELATED TERMS cinematic.

▶ verb ❶ *he immediately filmed the next scene* RECORD (ON FILM), shoot, capture on film, video. ❷ *his eyes had filmed over* CLOUD, mist, haze; become blurred, blur; *archaic* blear.

film star ▶ noun (FILM) ACTOR/ACTRESS, movie star, leading man/woman, leading lady, lead; celebrity, star, starlet, superstar; *informal* celeb; *informal, dated* matinee idol.

filmy ▶ adjective DIAPHANOUS, transparent, see-through, translucent, sheer, gossamer; delicate, fine, light, thin, silky.

– OPPOSITES thick, opaque.

filter ▶ noun *a carbon filter* STRAINER, sifter; sieve, riddle; gauze, netting.

▶ verb ❶ *the farmers filter the water* SIEVE, strain, sift, filtrate, riddle; clarify, purify, refine, treat. ❷ *the rain had filtered through her jacket* SEEP, percolate, leak, trickle, ooze.

filth ▶ noun ❶ *stagnant pools of filth* DIRT, muck, grime, mud, mire, sludge, slime, ooze; excrement, excreta, dung, manure, ordure, sewage; rubbish, refuse, dross; pollution, contamination, filthiness, uncleanness, foulness, nastiness; *N. Amer.* garbage; *informal* crud, grunge; *Brit. informal* grot, gunge; *N. Amer. informal* trash. ❷ *I felt sick after reading that filth* PORNOGRAPHY, pornographic literature/films, dirty books, smut, obscenity, indecency; *informal* porn, porno.

filthy ▶ adjective ❶ *the room was filthy* DIRTY, mucky, grimy, muddy, slimy, unclean; foul, squalid, sordid, nasty, soiled, sullied; polluted, contaminated, unhygienic, unsanitary; *informal* cruddy, grungy; *Brit. informal* grotty; *poetic/literary* besmirched. ❷ *his face was filthy* UNWASHED, unclean, dirty, grimy, smeared, grubby, muddy, mucky, black, blackened, stained; *poetic/literary* begrimed. ❸ *filthy jokes* OBSCENE, indecent, dirty, smutty, rude, improper, coarse, bawdy, vulgar, lewd, racy, off colour, earthy, ribald, risqué, 'adult', pornographic, explicit; *informal* blue, porn, porno, X-rated; *N. Amer. informal* raw. ❹ *you filthy brute!* DESPICABLE, contemptible, nasty, low, base, mean, vile, obnoxious; *informal* dirty (rotten), low-down, no-good. ❺ *he was in a filthy mood* BAD, foul, bad-tempered, ill-tempered, irritable, grumpy, grouchy, cross, fractious, peevish; *informal* snappish, snappy; *Brit. informal* shirty, stroppy, narky, ratty; *N. Amer. informal* cranky, ornery.

– OPPOSITES clean.

▶ adverb *filthy rich* VERY, extremely, tremendously, immensely, remarkably, excessively, exceedingly; *informal* stinking, awfully, terribly, seriously, mega, ultra, damn.

final ▶ adjective ❶ *the final year of study* LAST, closing, concluding, finishing, end, terminating, ultimate, eventual. ❷ *their decisions are final* IRREVOCABLE, unalterable, absolute, conclusive, irrefutable, incontrovertible, indisputable, unchallengeable, binding.

– OPPOSITES first, provisional.

▶ noun *the FA Cup final* DECIDER, final game/match.

– OPPOSITES qualifier.

finale ▶ noun CLIMAX, culmination; end, ending, finish, close, conclusion, termination; denouement, last act, final scene.

– OPPOSITES beginning.

finality ▶ noun CONCLUSIVENESS, decisiveness, decision, definiteness, definitiveness, certainty, certitude; irrevocability, irrefutability, incontrovertibility.

finalize ▶ verb CONCLUDE, complete, clinch, settle, work out, secure, wrap up, wind up, put the finishing touches to; reach an agreement on, agree on, come to terms on; *informal* sew up.

finally ▶ **adverb** ❶ *she finally got her man to the altar* EVENTUALLY, ultimately, in the end, after a long time, at (long) last; in the long run, in the fullness of time. ❷ *finally, wrap the ribbon round the edge* LASTLY, last, in conclusion, to conclude, to end. ❸ *this should finally dispel that common misconception* CONCLUSIVELY, irrevocably, decisively, definitively, for ever, for good, once and for all.

finance ▶ **noun** ❶ *he knows about finance* FINANCIAL AFFAIRS, money matters, fiscal matters, economics, money management, commerce, business, investment. ❷ *short-term finance* FUNDS, assets, money, capital, resources, cash, reserves, revenue, income; funding, backing, sponsorship.
▶ **verb** *the project was financed by grants* FUND, pay for, back, capitalize, endow, subsidize, invest in; underwrite, guarantee, sponsor, support; *N. Amer. informal* bankroll.

financial ▶ **adjective** MONETARY, money, economic, pecuniary, fiscal, banking, commercial, business, investment.

financier ▶ **noun** INVESTOR, speculator, banker, capitalist, industrialist, businessman, businesswoman, stockbroker; *informal* money man.

find ▶ **verb** ❶ *I found the book I wanted* LOCATE, spot, pinpoint, unearth, obtain; search out, nose out, track down, root out; come across/upon, run across/into, chance on, light on, happen on, stumble on, encounter; *informal* bump into; *poetic/literary* espy, descry. ❷ *they have found a cure for rabies* DISCOVER, invent, come up with, hit on. ❸ *the police found her purse* RETRIEVE, recover, get back, regain, repossess. ❹ *I hope you find peace* OBTAIN, acquire, get, procure, come by, secure, gain, earn, achieve, attain. ❺ *I found the courage to speak* SUMMON (UP), gather, muster (up), screw up, call up. ❻ *caffeine is found in coffee and tea* BE (PRESENT), occur, exist, be existent, appear. ❼ *you'll find that it's a lively area* DISCOVER, become aware, realize, observe, notice, note, perceive, learn. ❽ *I find their decision strange* CONSIDER, think, believe to be, feel to be, look on as, view as, see as, judge, deem, regard as. ❾ *he was found guilty* JUDGE, adjudge, adjudicate, deem, rule, declare, pronounce. ❿ *her barb found its mark* ARRIVE AT, reach, attain, achieve; hit, strike.
– OPPOSITES lose.
▶ **noun** ❶ *an archaeological find* DISCOVERY, acquisition, asset. ❷ *this table is a real find* GOOD BUY, bargain; godsend, boon.
■ **find out** DISCOVER, become aware, learn, detect, discern, perceive, observe, notice, note, get/come to know, realize; bring to light, reveal, expose, unearth, disclose; *informal* figure out, cotton on, catch on, tumble, get wise, savvy; *Brit. informal* twig, rumble, suss.

finding ▶ **noun** ❶ *the finding of the leak* DISCOVERY, location, locating, detection, detecting, uncovering. ❷ *the tribunal's findings* CONCLUSION, decision, verdict, pronouncement, judgement, ruling, rule, decree, order, recommendation; *Law* determination; *N. Amer.* resolve.

fine[1] ▶ **adjective** ❶ *fine wines* EXCELLENT, first-class, first-rate, great, exceptional, outstanding, quality, superior, splendid, magnificent, exquisite, choice, select, prime, supreme, superb, wonderful, superlative, of high quality, second to none; *informal* A1, top-notch, splendiferous. ❷ *a fine lady* WORTHY, admirable, praiseworthy, laudable, estimable, upright, upstanding, respectable. ❸ *the initiative is fine, but it's not enough on its own* ALL RIGHT, acceptable, suitable, good (enough), passable, satisfactory, adequate, reasonable, tolerable; *informal* OK. ❹ *I feel fine* IN GOOD HEALTH, well, healthy, all right, (fighting) fit, as fit as a fiddle/flea, blooming, thriving, in good shape/condition, in fine fettle; *informal* OK, in the pink. ❺ *a fine day* FAIR, dry, bright, clear, sunny, without a cloud in the sky, warm, balmy, summery. ❻ *a fine old house* IMPRESSIVE, imposing, striking, splendid, grand, majestic, magnificent, stately. ❼ *fine clothes* ELEGANT, stylish, expensive, smart, chic, fashionable; fancy, sumptuous, lavish, opulent; *informal* flashy, swanky, ritzy, plush. ❽ *a fine mind* KEEN, quick, alert, sharp, bright, brilliant, astute, clever, intelligent, perspicacious. ❾ *fine china* DELICATE, fragile, dainty. ❿ *fine hair* THIN, light, delicate, wispy, flyaway. ⓫ *a fine point* SHARP, keen, acute, sharpened, razor-sharp. ⓬ *fine material* SHEER, light, lightweight, thin, flimsy; diaphanous, filmy, gossamer, silky, transparent, translucent, see-through. ⓭ *a fine gold chain* PURE, sterling, solid, unmixed, unblended, one hundred per cent. ⓮ *fine sand* FINE-GRAINED, powdery, powdered, dusty, ground, crushed; *technical* comminuted; *archaic* pulverulent. ⓯ *fine detailed work* INTRICATE, delicate, detailed, elaborate, dainty, meticulous. ⓰ *a fine distinction* SUBTLE, ultra-fine, nice, hair-splitting. ⓱ *people's finer feelings* ELEVATED, lofty, exalted; refined, sensitive, cultivated, cultured, civilized, sophisticated. ⓲ *fine taste* DISCERNING, discriminating, refined, cultivated, cultured, critical.
– OPPOSITES poor, unsatisfactory, ill, inclement, thick, coarse.
▶ **adverb** (*informal*) *you're doing fine* WELL, all right, not badly, satisfactorily, adequately, nicely, tolerably; *informal* OK, good.
– OPPOSITES badly.
▶ **verb** ❶ *it can be fined right down to the required shape* THIN, make/become thin, narrow, taper, attenuate. ❷ *additives for fining wine* CLARIFY, clear, purify, refine, filter.

fine[2] ▶ **noun** *heavy fines* (FINANCIAL) PENALTY, sanction, fee, charge; *formal* mulct; *Brit. historical* amercement.

▶ **verb** *they were fined for breaking environmental laws* PENALIZE, impose a fine on, charge; *formal* mulct; *Brit. historical* amerce.

finery ▶ **noun** REGALIA, best clothes, (Sunday) best; *informal* glad rags, best bib and tucker.

finesse ▶ **noun** ❶ *masterly finesse* SKILL, skilfulness, expertise, subtlety, flair, panache, elan, polish, artistry, virtuosity, mastery. ❷ *a modicum of finesse* TACT, tactfulness, discretion, diplomacy, delicacy, sensitivity, perceptiveness, savoir faire. ❸ *a clever finesse* WINNING MOVE, trick, stratagem, ruse, manoeuvre, artifice, machination.

finger ▶ **noun** *he wagged his finger at her* DIGIT, thumb, index finger, forefinger; *informal* pinkie.
– RELATED TERMS digital.

▶ **verb** ❶ *she fingered her brooch uneasily* TOUCH, feel, handle, stroke, rub, caress, fondle, toy with, play (about/around) with, fiddle with. ❷ (*N. Amer. informal*) *no one fingered the culprit* IDENTIFY, recognize, pick out, spot; inform on, point the finger at; *informal* rat on, squeal on, tell on, blow the whistle on, snitch on, peach on; *Brit. informal* grass on.

finicky ▶ **adjective** FUSSY, fastidious, punctilious, over-particular, difficult, exacting, demanding; *informal* picky, choosy, pernickety; *N. Amer. informal* persnickety; *archaic* nice.

finish ▶ **verb** ❶ *Mrs Porter had just finished the task* COMPLETE, end, conclude, stop, cease, terminate, bring to a conclusion/end/close, wind up; crown, cap, round off, put the finishing touches to; accomplish, discharge, carry out, do, get done, fulfil; *informal* wrap up, sew up, polish off. ❷ *Sarah has finished school* LEAVE, give up, drop; stop, discontinue, have done with, complete; *informal* pack in, quit. ❸ *Hitch finished his dinner* CONSUME, eat, devour, drink, finish off, polish off, gulp (down); use (up), exhaust, empty, drain, get through, run through; *informal* down. ❹ *the programme has finished* END, come to an end, stop, conclude, come to a conclusion/end/close, cease. ❺ *some items were finished in a black lacquer* VARNISH, lacquer, veneer, coat, stain, wax, shellac, enamel, glaze.
– OPPOSITES start, begin, continue.

▶ **noun** ❶ *the finish of filming* END, ending, completion, conclusion, close, closing, cessation, termination; final part/stage, finale, denouement; *informal* sewing up, polishing off. ❷ *a gallop to the finish* FINISHING LINE/POST, tape. ❸ *an antiquated paint finish* VENEER, lacquer, lamination, glaze, coating, covering; surface, texture.
– OPPOSITES start, beginning.

■ **finish someone/something off** ❶ *the executioners finished them off* KILL, take/end the life of, execute, terminate, exterminate, liquidate, get rid of; *informal* wipe out, do in, bump off, take out, dispose of, do away with; *N. Amer. informal* ice, rub out, waste. ❷ *financial difficulties finished off the business* OVERWHELM, overcome, defeat, get the better of, worst, bring down; *informal* drive to the wall, best.

finished ▶ **adjective** ❶ *the finished job* COMPLETED, concluded, terminated, over (and done with), at an end; accomplished, executed, discharged, fulfilled, done; *informal* wrapped up, sewn up, polished off; *formal* effectuated. ❷ *a finished performance* ACCOMPLISHED, polished, flawless, faultless, perfect; expert, proficient, masterly, impeccable, virtuoso, skilful, skilled, professional. ❸ *he was finished* RUINED, defeated, beaten, wrecked, doomed, bankrupt, broken; *informal* washed up, through.
– OPPOSITES incomplete.

finite ▶ **adjective** LIMITED, restricted, determinate, fixed.

fire ▶ **noun** ❶ *a fire broke out* BLAZE, conflagration, inferno; flames, burning, combustion. ❷ *an electric fire* HEATER, radiator, convector. ❸ *he lacked fire* DYNAMISM, energy, vigour, animation, vitality, vibrancy, exuberance, zest, elan; passion, ardour, zeal, spirit, verve, vivacity, vivaciousness; enthusiasm, eagerness, gusto, fervour, fervency; *informal* pep, vim, go, get-up-and-go, oomph. ❹ *rapid machine-gun fire* GUNFIRE, firing, flak, bombardment. ❺ *they directed their fire at the prime minister* CRITICISM, censure, condemnation, denunciation, opprobrium, admonishments, brickbats; hostility, antagonism, animosity; *informal* flak.
– RELATED TERMS pyro-.

▶ **verb** ❶ *howitzers firing shells* LAUNCH, shoot, discharge, let fly with. ❷ *someone fired a gun* SHOOT, discharge, let off, set off. ❸ (*informal*) *he was fired* DISMISS, discharge, give someone their notice, lay off, let go, get rid of, axe, cashier; *informal* sack, give someone the sack, boot out, give someone the boot/bullet, give someone the elbow/push, give someone their marching orders; *Brit. informal* give someone their cards. ❹ *the engine fired* START, get started, get going. ❺ (*archaic*) *I fired the straw* LIGHT, ignite, set fire to, set on fire, set alight, set ablaze; *informal* torch; *poetic/literary* enkindle, inflame. ❻ *the stories fired my imagination* STIMULATE, stir up, excite, awaken, arouse, rouse, inflame, animate, inspire, motivate.

■ **catch fire** IGNITE, catch light, burst into flames, go up in flames.

■ **on fire** ❶ *the restaurant was on fire* BURNING, alight, ablaze, blazing, aflame, in flames; *poetic/literary* afire. ❷ *she was on fire with passion* ARDENT, passionate, fervent, excited, eager, enthusiastic.

firearm ▶ **noun** GUN, weapon; *informal* shooter; *N. Amer. informal* piece, rod, shooting iron.

firebrand ▶ **noun** RADICAL, revolutionary, agitator, rabble-rouser, incendiary, subversive, troublemaker.

fireproof ▶ **adjective** NON-FLAMMABLE, incombustible, fire resistant, flame resistant, flame retardant, heatproof.

– OPPOSITES inflammable.

fireworks ▶ plural noun ❶ *firework displays* PYROTECHNICS, feux d'artifice. ❷ *his stubbornness has produced some fireworks* UPROAR, trouble, mayhem, fuss; tantrums, hysterics.

firm[1] ▶ adjective ❶ *the ground is fairly firm* HARD, solid, unyielding, resistant; solidified, hardened, compacted, compressed, dense, stiff, rigid, frozen, set. ❷ *firm foundations* SECURE, secured, stable, steady, strong, fixed, fast, set, taut, tight; immovable, irremovable, stationary, motionless. ❸ *a firm handshake* STRONG, vigorous, sturdy, forceful. ❹ *I was very firm about what I wanted | a firm supporter* RESOLUTE, determined, decided, resolved, steadfast; adamant, emphatic, insistent, single-minded, in earnest, whole-hearted; unfaltering, unwavering, unflinching, unswerving, unbending; hard-line, committed, dyed-in-the-wool. ❺ *firm friends* CLOSE, good, boon, intimate, inseparable, dear, special, fast; constant, devoted, loving, faithful, long-standing, steady, steadfast. ❻ *firm plans* DEFINITE, fixed, settled, decided, established, confirmed, agreed; unalterable, unchangeable, irreversible.
– OPPOSITES soft, unstable, limp, indefinite.

firm[2] ▶ noun *an accountancy firm* COMPANY, business, concern, enterprise, organization, corporation, conglomerate, office, bureau, agency, consortium; *informal* outfit, set-up.

firmament ▶ noun (*poetic/literary*) THE SKY, heaven; the heavens, the skies; *poetic/literary* the empyrean, the welkin.

first ▶ adjective ❶ *the first chapter* EARLIEST, initial, opening, introductory. ❷ *first principles* FUNDAMENTAL, basic, rudimentary, primary; key, cardinal, central, chief, vital, essential. ❸ *our first priority* FOREMOST, principal, highest, greatest, paramount, top, uppermost, prime, chief, leading, main, major; overriding, predominant, prevailing, central, core, dominant; *informal* number-one. ❹ *first prize* TOP, best, prime, premier, winner's, winning.
– OPPOSITES last, closing.
▶ adverb ❶ *the room they had first entered* AT FIRST, to begin with, first of all, at the outset, initially. ❷ *she would eat first* BEFORE ANYTHING ELSE, first and foremost, now. ❸ *she wouldn't go—she'd die first!* IN PREFERENCE, sooner, rather.
▶ noun ❶ *from the first, surrealism was theatrical* THE (VERY) BEGINNING, the start, the outset, the commencement; *informal* the word go, the off. ❷ (*informal*) *it was a first for both of us* NOVELTY, new/first experience.

first-class ▶ adjective SUPERIOR, first-rate, high-quality, top-quality, high-grade, five-star; prime, premier, premium, grade A, best, finest, select, exclusive, excellent, superb; *informal* tip-top, A1, top-notch.
– OPPOSITES poor.

first-hand ▶ adjective DIRECT, immediate, personal, hands-on, experiential, empirical.
– OPPOSITES vicarious, indirect.

first name ▶ noun FORENAME, Christian name, given name.
– OPPOSITES surname.

first-rate ▶ adjective TOP-QUALITY, high-quality, top-grade, first-class, second to none, fine; superlative, excellent, superb, outstanding, exceptional, exemplary, marvellous, magnificent, splendid; *informal* tip-top, top-notch, ace, A1, super, great, terrific, tremendous, fantastic; *Brit. informal* top-hole, smashing; *informal, dated* capital.

fiscal ▶ adjective TAX, budgetary; financial, economic, monetary, money.

fish ▶ verb ❶ *some people were fishing in the lake* GO FISHING, angle, trawl. ❷ *she fished for her purse* SEARCH, delve, look, hunt; grope, fumble, ferret (about/around), root about/around, rummage (about/around/round). ❸ *I'm not fishing for compliments* TRY TO GET, seek to obtain, solicit, angle, aim, hope, cast about/around/round, be after.
■ **fish someone/something out** PULL OUT, haul out, remove, extricate, extract, retrieve; rescue from, save from.

fisherman ▶ noun ANGLER, rod; *archaic* fisher.

fishing ▶ noun ANGLING, trawling, catching fish.

fishy ▶ adjective ❶ *a fishy smell* FISHLIKE, piscine. ❷ *round fishy eyes* EXPRESSIONLESS, inexpressive, vacant, lacklustre, glassy. ❸ (*informal*) *there was something fishy going on* SUSPICIOUS, questionable, dubious, doubtful, suspect; odd, queer, peculiar, strange; *informal* funny, shady, crooked, bent; *Brit. informal* dodgy; *Austral./NZ informal* shonky.

fission ▶ noun SPLITTING, division, dividing, rupture, breaking, severance.
– OPPOSITES fusion.

fissure ▶ noun OPENING, crevice, crack, cleft, breach, crevasse, chasm; break, fracture, fault, rift, rupture, split.

fist ▶ noun CLENCHED HAND; *informal* duke, meat hook; *Brit. informal* bunch of fives.

fit[1] ▶ adjective ❶ *fit for human habitation | he is a fit subject for such a book* SUITABLE, good enough; relevant, pertinent, apt, appropriate, suited, apposite, fitting; *archaic* meet. ❷ *is he fit to look after a child?* COMPETENT, able, capable; ready, prepared, qualified, trained, equipped. ❸ (*informal*) *you look fit to commit murder!* READY, prepared, all set, in a fit state, likely, about; *informal* psyched up. ❹ *he looked tanned and fit* HEALTHY, well, in good health, in (good) shape, in (good) trim, in good condition, fighting fit, as fit as a fiddle/flea; athletic, muscular, strong, robust, hale and hearty.
– OPPOSITES unsuitable, incapable, unwell.
▶ verb ❶ *my overcoat should fit you* BE THE RIGHT/COR-

RECT SIZE (FOR), be big/small enough (for), fit like a glove. ❷ *have your carpets fitted professionally* LAY, put in place/position, position, place, fix. ❸ *cameras fitted with a backlight button* EQUIP, provide, supply, fit out, furnish. ❹ *concrete slabs were fitted together* JOIN, connect, put together, piece together, attach, unite, link. ❺ *a sentence that fits his crimes* BE APPROPRIATE TO, suit, match, correspond to, tally with, go with, accord with, correlate to, be congruous with, be congruent with, be consonant with. ❻ *an MSc fits you for a professional career* QUALIFY, prepare, make ready, train, groom.

▶ **noun** *the degree of fit between a school's philosophy and practice* CORRELATION, correspondence, agreement, consistency, equivalence, match, similarity, compatibility, concurrence.

■ **fit in** CONFORM, be in harmony, blend in, be in line, be assimilated into.

■ **fit someone/something out/up** EQUIP, provide, supply, furnish, kit out, rig out.

■ **fit someone up** (*Brit. informal*) FALSELY INCRIMINATE; *informal* frame, set up.

fit² ▶ **noun** ❶ *an epileptic fit* CONVULSION, spasm, paroxysm, seizure, attack; *Medicine* ictus. ❷ *a fit of the giggles* OUTBREAK, outburst, attack, bout, spell. ❸ *my mother would have a fit if she knew* TANTRUM, fit of temper, outburst of anger/rage, frenzy; *informal* paddy, stress; *N. Amer. informal* blowout; *formal* boutade.

■ **in/by fits and starts** SPASMODICALLY, intermittently, sporadically, erratically, irregularly, fitfully, haphazardly.

fitful ▶ **adjective** INTERMITTENT, sporadic, spasmodic, broken, disturbed, disrupted, patchy, irregular, uneven, unsettled.

fitness ▶ **noun** ❶ *polo requires tremendous fitness* GOOD HEALTH, strength, robustness, vigour, athleticism, toughness, physical fitness, muscularity; good condition, good shape, well-being. ❷ *his fitness for active service* SUITABILITY, capability, competence, ability, aptitude; readiness, preparedness, eligibility.

fitted ▶ **adjective** ❶ *a fitted sheet* SHAPED, contoured, fitting tightly/well. ❷ *a fitted wardrobe* BUILT-IN, integral, integrated, fixed. ❸ *he wasn't fitted for the job* (WELL) SUITED, right, suitable; equipped, fit; *informal* cut out.

fitting ▶ **noun** ❶ *a light fitting* ATTACHMENT, connection, part, piece, component, accessory. ❷ *bathroom fittings* FURNISHINGS, furniture, fixtures, fitments, equipment, appointments, appurtenances. ❸ *the fitting of catalytic converters* INSTALLATION, installing, putting in, fixing.

▶ **adjective** *a fitting conclusion* APT, appropriate, suitable, apposite; fit, proper, right, seemly, correct; *archaic* meet.

– OPPOSITES unsuitable.

five ▶ **cardinal number** QUINTET, fivesome; quintuplets; *technical* pentad.

– RELATED TERMS quin-, quinque-, penta-.

fix ▶ **verb** ❶ *signs were fixed to lamp posts* FASTEN, attach, affix, secure; join, connect, couple, link; install, implant, embed; stick, glue, pin, nail, screw, bolt, clamp, clip. ❷ *his words are fixed in my memory* STICK, lodge, embed. ❸ *his eyes were fixed on the ground* FOCUS, direct, level, point, train. ❹ *techniques of fixing audience's attention* ATTRACT, draw; hold, grip, engage, captivate, rivet. ❺ *he fixed my washing machine* REPAIR, mend, put right, put to rights, get working, restore (to working order); overhaul, service, renovate, recondition. ❻ *James fixed it for his parents to watch the show from the wings* ARRANGE, organize, contrive, manage, engineer; *informal* swing, wangle. ❼ (*informal*) *Laura was fixing her hair* ARRANGE, put in order, adjust; style, groom, comb, brush; *informal* do. ❽ (*informal*) *Chris will fix supper* PREPARE, cook, make, get; *informal* rustle up; *Brit. informal* knock up. ❾ *let's fix a date for the meeting* DECIDE ON, select, choose, resolve on; determine, settle, set, arrange, establish, allot; designate, name, appoint, specify. ❿ *chemicals are used to fix the dye* MAKE PERMANENT, make fast, set. ⓫ (*informal*) *the fight was fixed* RIG, arrange fraudulently; tamper with, influence; *informal* fiddle. ⓬ (*informal*) *don't tell anybody, or I'll fix you!* GET ONE'S REVENGE ON, avenge oneself on, get even with, get back at, take reprisals against, punish, deal with; *informal* get one's own back on, sort someone out, settle someone's hash. ⓭ (*informal*) *a place where they can fix* INJECT DRUGS, take drugs; *informal* shoot up, mainline. ⓮ *the cat has been fixed* CASTRATE, neuter, geld, spay, desex, sterilize; *N. Amer. & Austral.* alter; *Brit. informal* doctor; *archaic* emasculate.

– OPPOSITES remove.

▶ **noun** (*informal*) ❶ *they are in a bit of a fix* PREDICAMENT, plight, difficulty, awkward situation, corner, tight spot; mess, mare's nest, dire straits; *informal* pickle, jam, hole, scrape, bind, sticky situation. ❷ *he needed his fix* DOSE; *informal* hit. ❸ *a quick fix for the coal industry* SOLUTION, answer, resolution, way out, remedy, cure; *informal* magic bullet. ❹ *the result was a complete fix* FRAUD, swindle, trick, charade, sham; *informal* set-up, fiddle.

■ **fix someone up** (*informal*) PROVIDE, supply, furnish.

■ **fix something up** ORGANIZE, arrange, make arrangements for, fix, sort out.

fixated ▶ **adjective** OBSESSED, preoccupied, obsessive; focussed, keen, gripped, engrossed, immersed, wrapped up, enthusiastic, fanatical; *informal* hooked, wild, nuts, crazy; *Brit. informal* potty.

fixation ▶ **noun** OBSESSION, preoccupation, mania, addiction, compulsion; *informal* thing, bug, craze, fad.

fixed ▶ **adjective** ❶ *there are fixed ropes on the rock face* FASTENED, secure, fast, firm; riveted, moored, anchored. ❷ *a fixed period of time* PRE-

DETERMINED, set, established, arranged, specified, decided, agreed, determined, confirmed, prescribed, definite, defined, explicit, precise.

fixture ▶ **noun** ❶ *fixtures and fittings* FIXED APPLIANCE, installation, unit. ❷ (*Brit.*) *their first fixture of the season* MATCH, race, game, competition, contest, sporting event.

fizz ▶ **verb** ❶ *the mixture fizzed like mad* EFFERVESCE, sparkle, bubble, froth; *poetic/literary* spume. ❷ *all the screens were fizzing* CRACKLE, buzz, hiss, fizzle, crepitate.

▶ **noun** ❶ *the fizz in champagne* EFFERVESCENCE, sparkle, fizziness, bubbles, bubbliness, gassiness, carbonation, froth. ❷ (*informal*) *they all had another glass of fizz* SPARKLING WINE, champagne; *informal* bubbly, champers, sparkler. ❸ (*informal*) *their set is a little lacking in fizz* EBULLIENCE, exuberance, liveliness, life, vivacity, animation, vigour, energy, verve, dash, spirit, sparkle, zest; *informal* pizzazz, pep, zip, oomph. ❹ *the fizz of the static* CRACKLE, crackling, buzz, buzzing, hiss, hissing, white noise; *poetic/literary* susurration.

fizzle ▶ **verb** *the loudspeaker fizzled* CRACKLE, buzz, hiss, fizz, crepitate.

▶ **noun** ❶ *electric fizzle. See* FIZZ noun sense 4. ❷ *the whole thing turned out to be a fizzle* FAILURE, fiasco, debacle, disaster; *Brit.* damp squib; *informal* flop, washout, let-down, dead loss; *N. Amer. informal* snafu.

■ **fizzle out** PETER OUT, die off, ease off, cool off; tail off, wither away.

fizzy ▶ **adjective** EFFERVESCENT, sparkling, carbonated, gassy, bubbly, frothy; mousseux, pétillant, spumante, frizzante.

– OPPOSITES still, flat.

flab ▶ **noun** (*informal*) FAT, excessive weight, fatness, plumpness; paunch, pot belly, beer gut.

flabbergast ▶ **verb** (*informal*). *See* ASTONISH.

flabbiness ▶ **noun** FAT, fatness, fleshiness, plumpness, chubbiness, portliness, obesity, corpulence; softness, looseness, flaccidity, droopiness, sag; *informal* flab, tubbiness.

flabby ▶ **adjective** ❶ *his flabby stomach* SOFT, loose, flaccid, slack, untoned, drooping, sagging. ❷ *a flabby woman* FAT, fleshy, overweight, plump, chubby, portly, rotund, broad in the beam, of ample proportions, obese, corpulent; *informal* tubby, roly-poly, well covered, well upholstered.

– OPPOSITES firm, thin.

flaccid ▶ **adjective** ❶ *your muscles are sagging, they're flaccid* SOFT, loose, flabby, slack, lax; drooping, sagging. ❷ *his play seemed flaccid* LACKLUSTRE, lifeless, listless, uninspiring, unanimated, tame.

– OPPOSITES firm, spirited.

flag[1] ▶ **noun** *the Irish flag* BANNER, standard, ensign, pennant, banderole, streamer, jack, gonfalon; colours; *Brit.* pendant.

– RELATED TERMS vexillary.

▶ **verb** *flag the misspelt words* INDICATE, identify, point out, mark, label, tag.

■ **flag someone/something down** HAIL, wave down, signal to stop, stop, halt.

flag[2] ▶ **noun** *stone flags. See* FLAGSTONE.

flag[3] ▶ **verb** ❶ *they were flagging towards the finish* TIRE, grow tired/weary, weaken, grow weak, wilt, droop. ❷ *my energy flags in the afternoon* FADE, decline, wane, ebb, diminish, decrease, lessen, dwindle; wither, melt away, peter out, die away/down.

– OPPOSITES revive.

flagellate ▶ **verb** FLOG, whip, beat, scourge, lash, birch, strap, belt, cane, thrash, horsewhip, tan/whip someone's hide, give someone a hiding.

flagon ▶ **noun** JUG, vessel, bottle, carafe, flask, decanter, tankard, ewer, pitcher.

flagrant ▶ **adjective** BLATANT, glaring, obvious, overt, conspicuous, barefaced, shameless, brazen, undisguised, unconcealed; outrageous, scandalous, shocking, disgraceful, dreadful, terrible, gross.

flagstone ▶ **noun** PAVING SLAB, paving stone, slab, flag, sett.

flail ▶ **verb** ❶ *he fell headlong, his arms flailing* WAVE, swing, thrash about, flap about. ❷ *I was flailing about in the water* FLOUNDER, struggle, thrash, writhe, splash. ❸ *he flailed their shoulders with his cane* THRASH, beat, strike, flog, whip, lash, scourge, cane; *informal* wallop, whack.

flair ▶ **noun** ❶ *a flair for publicity* APTITUDE, talent, gift, instinct, (natural) ability, facility, skill, bent, feel. ❷ *she dressed with flair* STYLE, stylishness, panache, dash, elan, poise, elegance; (good) taste, discernment, discrimination; *informal* class.

flak ▶ **noun** ❶ *my aircraft had been damaged by flak* ANTI-AIRCRAFT FIRE, shelling, gunfire; bombardment, barrage, salvo, volley. ❷ (*informal*) *he has come in for a lot of flak* CRITICISM, censure, disapproval, disapprobation, hostility, complaints; opprobrium, obloquy, calumny, calumniation, vilification, abuse, brickbats; *Brit. informal* stick, verbal; *formal* castigation, excoriation.

flake[1] ▶ **noun** *flakes of pastry* SLIVER, wafer, shaving, paring; chip, scale, spillikin; fragment, scrap, shred; *technical* lamina.

▶ **verb** *the paint was flaking* PEEL (OFF), chip, blister, come off (in layers).

flake[2]

■ **flake out** (*informal*) *she flaked out in her chair* FALL ASLEEP, go to sleep, drop off; collapse, faint, pass out, lose consciousness, black out, swoon; *informal* conk out, nod off; *N. Amer. informal* sack out, zone out.

flaky ▶ **adjective** FLAKING, peeling, scaly, blistering, scabrous.

flamboyant ▶ **adjective** ❶ *her flamboyant personality* OSTENTATIOUS, exuberant, confident, lively, animated, vibrant, vivacious. ❷ *a flamboyant cravat* COLOURFUL, brightly coloured, bright, vibrant, vivid; dazzling, eye-catching, bold; showy, gaudy, garish, lurid, loud; *informal* jazzy, flashy; *dated* gay. ❸ *a flamboyant architectural style* ELABORATE, ornate, fancy; baroque, rococo.
– OPPOSITES restrained.

flame ▶ **noun** ❶ *a sheet of flames* FIRE, blaze, conflagration, inferno. ❷ *the flames of her anger* PASSION, warmth, ardour, fervour, fervency, fire, intensity. ❸ (*informal*) *an old flame* SWEETHEART, boyfriend, girlfriend, lover, partner; *informal* steady; *dated* beau.
▶ **verb** ❶ *logs crackled and flamed* BURN, blaze, be ablaze, be alight, be on fire, be in flames, be aflame. ❷ *pour the whisky over the lobster and flame it* IGNITE, light, set light to, set fire to, set on fire, set alight, touch off; *informal* set/put a match to. ❸ *Erica's cheeks flamed* BECOME RED, go red, blush, flush, redden, grow pink/crimson/scarlet, colour, glow.
– OPPOSITES extinguish.
■ **in flames** ON FIRE, burning, alight, flaming, blazing, ignited; *poetic/literary* afire.

flameproof ▶ **adjective** NON-FLAMMABLE, non-inflammable, flame-resistant, fire-resistant, flame-retardant, uninflammable.
– OPPOSITES flammable.

flaming ▶ **adjective** ❶ *a flaming bonfire* BLAZING, ablaze, burning, on fire, in flames, aflame; *poetic/literary* afire. ❷ *flaming hair* BRIGHT, brilliant, vivid; red, reddish-orange, ginger. ❸ *a flaming row* FURIOUS, violent, vehement, frenzied, angry, passionate. ❹ *in a flaming temper* FURIOUS, enraged, fuming, seething, incensed, infuriated, angry, raging; *informal* livid; *poetic/literary* wrathful. ❺ (*informal*) *where's that flaming ambulance?* WRETCHED; *informal* damned, damnable, blasted, blessed, confounded; *Brit. informal* flipping, blinking, blooming, bleeding, effing; *Brit. informal, dated* bally, ruddy; *dated* cursed, accursed.

flammable ▶ **adjective** INFLAMMABLE, burnable, combustible.

flank ▶ **noun** ❶ *the horse's flanks* SIDE, haunch, quarter, thigh. ❷ *the southern flank of the Eighth Army* SIDE, wing; face, aspect.
▶ **verb** *the garden is flanked by two rivers* EDGE, bound, line, border, fringe.

flannel ▶ **noun** ❶ (*Brit.*) *she dabbed her face with a flannel* FACECLOTH, cloth; *N. Amer.* washcloth, washrag; *Austral.* washer. ❷ (*Brit. informal*) *don't accept any flannel from salespeople* SMOOTH TALK, flattery, blarney, blandishments, honeyed words; prevarication, equivocation, evasion, doublespeak; *informal* spiel, soft soap, sweet talk, baloney, hot air; *Brit. informal* waffle; *Austral./NZ informal* guyver.
▶ **verb** (*Brit. informal*) *she can tell if you're flannelling* USE FLATTERY, talk blarney; prevaricate, equivocate, be evasive, blather, stall; *Brit.* hum and haw; *informal* soft-soap, sweet-talk; *Brit. informal* waffle; *N. Amer. informal* fast-talk; *rare* tergiversate.

flap ▶ **verb** ❶ *the mallards flapped their wings* BEAT, flutter, agitate, wave, wag, swing. ❷ *the flag flapped in the breeze* FLUTTER, fly, blow, swing, sway, ripple, stir. ❸ (*informal*) *a deliberate ploy to make us flap* PANIC, go into a panic, become flustered, be agitated, fuss; *informal* be in a state, be in a tizzy.
▶ **noun** ❶ *pockets with buttoned flaps* FOLD, overlap, covering; lappet. ❷ *a few flaps of the wing* FLUTTER, fluttering, beat, beating, waving. ❸ (*informal*) *I'm in a frightful flap* PANIC, fluster; *informal* state, dither, twitter, blue funk, stew, tizzy; *N. Amer. informal* twit. ❹ (*informal*) *she created a flap with her controversial statement* FUSS, commotion, stir, hubbub, storm, uproar; controversy, brouhaha, furore; *informal* to-do, ballyhoo, hoo-ha, kerfuffle.

flare ▶ **noun** ❶ *the flare of the match* BLAZE, flash, dazzle, burst, flicker. ❷ *a flare set off by the crew* DISTRESS SIGNAL, rocket, Very light, beacon, light, signal. ❸ *a flare of anger* BURST, rush, eruption, explosion, spasm, access.
▶ **verb** ❶ *the match flared* BLAZE, flash, flare up, flame, burn; glow, flicker. ❷ *her nostrils flared* SPREAD, broaden, widen; dilate.
■ **flare up** ❶ *the wooden houses flared up like matchsticks* BURN, blaze, go up in flames. ❷ *his injury has flared up again* RECUR, reoccur, reappear; break out, start suddenly, erupt. ❸ *I flared up at him* LOSE ONE'S TEMPER, become enraged, fly into a temper, go berserk; *informal* blow one's top, fly off the handle, go mad, go bananas, hit the roof, go up the wall, go off the deep end, lose one's rag, flip (one's lid), explode, have a fit; *Brit. informal* go spare, go crackers, do one's nut; *N. Amer. informal* flip one's wig, blow one's lid/stack, have a conniption fit.

flash ▶ **verb** ❶ *a torch flashed* LIGHT UP, shine, flare, blaze, gleam, glint, sparkle, burn; blink, wink, flicker, shimmer, twinkle, glimmer, glisten, scintillate; *poetic/literary* glister, coruscate. ❷ (*informal*) *he was flashing his money about* SHOW OFF, flaunt, flourish, display, parade. ❸ (*informal*) *he flashed at me* EXPOSE ONESELF. ❹ *racing cars flashed past* ZOOM, streak, tear, shoot, dash, dart, fly, whistle, hurtle, rush, bolt, race, speed, career, whizz, whoosh, buzz; *informal* belt, zap; *Brit. informal* bomb, bucket; *N. Amer. informal* barrel.
▶ **noun** ❶ *a flash of light* FLARE, blaze, burst; gleam, glint, sparkle, flicker, shimmer, twinkle, glimmer. ❷ *a basic uniform with no flashes* EMBLEM, insignia, badge; stripe, bar, chevron. ❸ *a sudden flash of inspiration* BURST, outburst, wave, rush, surge, flush.
▶ **adjective** (*informal*) *a flash sports car*. *See* FLASHY.

■ **in/like a flash** INSTANTLY, suddenly, abruptly, immediately, all of a sudden; quickly, rapidly, swiftly, speedily; in an instant/moment, in a (split) second, in a trice, in the blink of an eye; *informal* in a jiffy, before you can say Jack Robinson.

flashy ▶ **adjective** (*informal*) OSTENTATIOUS, flamboyant, showy, conspicuous, extravagant, expensive; vulgar, tasteless, brash, lurid, garish, loud, gaudy; *informal* snazzy, fancy, swanky, flash, jazzy, glitzy.
– OPPOSITES understated.

flask ▶ **noun** BOTTLE, container; hip flask, vacuum flask; *trademark* Thermos.

flat[1] ▶ **adjective** ❶ *a flat surface* LEVEL, horizontal; smooth, even, uniform, regular, plane. ❷ *the sea was flat* CALM, still, pacific, glassy, undisturbed, without waves, like a millpond. ❸ *a flat wooden box* SHALLOW, low-sided. ❹ *flat sandals* LOW, low-heeled, without heels. ❺ *his voice was flat* MONOTONOUS, toneless, droning, boring, dull, tedious, uninteresting, unexciting, soporific; bland, dreary, colourless, featureless, emotionless, expressionless, lifeless, spiritless, lacklustre. ❻ *he felt flat and weary* DEPRESSED, dejected, dispirited, despondent, downhearted, disheartened, low, low-spirited, down, unhappy, blue; without energy, enervated, sapped, weary, tired out, worn out, exhausted, drained; *informal* down in the mouth/dumps. ❼ *the market was flat* SLOW, inactive, sluggish, slack, quiet, depressed. ❽ (*Brit.*) *a flat battery* EXPIRED, dead, finished, used up, run out. ❾ *a flat tyre* DEFLATED, punctured, burst. ❿ *a flat fee* FIXED, set, regular, unchanging, unvarying, invariable. ⓫ *a flat denial* OUTRIGHT, direct, absolute, definite, positive, straight, plain, explicit; firm, resolute, adamant, assertive, emphatic, categorical, unconditional, unqualified, unequivocal.
– OPPOSITES vertical, uneven.
▶ **adverb** ❶ *she lay down flat on the floor* STRETCHED OUT, outstretched, spreadeagled, sprawling, prone, supine, prostrate, recumbent. ❷ (*informal*) *she turned me down flat* OUTRIGHT, absolutely, firmly, resolutely, adamantly, emphatically, insistently, categorically, unconditionally, unequivocally.
■ **flat out** HARD, as hard as possible, for all one's worth, to the full/limit, all out; at full speed, as fast as possible, at full tilt; *informal* like crazy, like mad, like the wind, like a bomb; *Brit. informal* like billy-o, like the clappers.

flat[2] ▶ **noun** *a two-bedroom flat* APARTMENT, set of rooms, penthouse; rooms; *Austral.* home unit; *N. Amer. informal* crib.

flatten ▶ **verb** ❶ *Tom flattened the crumpled paper* MAKE/BECOME FLAT, make/become even, smooth (out/off), level (out/off). ❷ *the cows flattened the grass* COMPRESS, press down, crush, squash, compact, trample. ❸ *tornadoes can flatten buildings in seconds* DEMOLISH, raze (to the ground), tear down, knock down, destroy, wreck, devastate, obliterate; *N. Amer. informal* total. ❹ (*informal*) *Flynn flattened him with a single punch* KNOCK DOWN/OVER, knock to the ground, fell, prostrate; *informal* floor, deck; *Brit. informal* knock for six. ❺ *I flattened a drunken heckler* HUMILIATE, crush, quash, squash, take down a peg or two, put someone in their place; *informal* put down, cut down to size.

flatter ▶ **verb** ❶ *it amused him to flatter her* COMPLIMENT, praise, express admiration for, say nice things about, pay court to, fawn on; cajole, humour, flannel, blarney; *informal* sweet-talk, soft-soap, butter up, play up to; *formal* laud. ❷ *I was flattered to be asked* HONOUR, gratify, please, delight; *informal* tickle pink. ❸ *a hairstyle that flattered her* SUIT, become, look good on, go well with; *informal* do something for.
– OPPOSITES insult, offend.

flatterer ▶ **noun** SYCOPHANT, groveller, fawner, lackey; *informal* crawler, toady, bootlicker, yes man, lickspittle; *formal* encomiast.

flattering ▶ **adjective** ❶ *flattering remarks* COMPLIMENTARY, praising, favourable, commending, admiring, applauding, appreciative, good; honeyed, sugary, cajoling, flannelling, silver-tongued, honey-tongued; fawning, oily, obsequious, ingratiating, servile, sycophantic; *informal* sweet-talking, soft-soaping, crawling, boot-licking; *formal* encomiastic. ❷ *it was very flattering to be nominated* PLEASING, gratifying, honouring, gladdening. ❸ *her most flattering dress* BECOMING, enhancing.

flattery ▶ **noun** PRAISE, adulation, compliments, blandishments, honeyed words; fawning, blarney, cajolery; *informal* sweet talk, soft soap, buttering up, toadying; *Brit. informal* flannel; *formal* laudation.

flatulence ▶ **noun** ❶ *medications that help with flatulence* (INTESTINAL) GAS, wind; *informal* farting; *formal* flatus. ❷ *the flatulence of his latest recordings* POMPOSITY, pompousness, pretension, pretentiousness, grandiloquence, bombast, turgidity.

flaunt ▶ **verb** SHOW OFF, display ostentatiously, make a (great) show of, put on show/display, parade; brag about, crow about, vaunt; *informal* flash.

flavour ▶ **noun** ❶ *the flavour of prosciutto* TASTE, savour, tang. ❷ *salami can give extra flavour* FLAVOURING, seasoning, tastiness, tang, relish, bite, piquancy, pungency, spice, spiciness, zest; *informal* zing, zip. ❸ *a strong international flavour* CHARACTER, quality, feel, feeling, ambience, atmosphere, aura, air, mood, tone; spirit, essence, nature. ❹ *this excerpt will give a flavour of the report* IMPRESSION, suggestion, hint, taste.
– RELATED TERMS gustative, gustatory.
▶ **verb** *spices for flavouring food* ADD FLAVOUR TO, add flavouring to, season, spice (up), add piquancy to, ginger up, enrich; *informal* pep up.
■ **flavour of the month** (*informal*) ALL THE RAGE,

the latest thing, the fashion, in vogue; *informal* hot, in; *Brit. informal, dated* all the go.

flavouring ▶ **noun** ❶ *this cheese is often combined with other flavourings* SEASONING, spice, herb, additive; condiment, dressing. ❷ *vanilla flavouring* ESSENCE, extract, concentrate, distillate.

flaw ▶ **noun** DEFECT, blemish, fault, imperfection, deficiency, weakness, weak spot/point, inadequacy, shortcoming, limitation, failing, foible; *Computing* bug; *informal* glitch.
–OPPOSITES strength.

flawed ▶ **adjective** ❶ *a flawed mirror* FAULTY, defective, unsound, imperfect; broken, cracked, torn, scratched, deformed, distorted, warped, buckled; *Brit. informal* duff. ❷ *the findings were flawed* UNSOUND, defective, faulty, distorted, inaccurate, incorrect, erroneous, imprecise, fallacious, misleading.
–OPPOSITES flawless, sound.

flawless ▶ **adjective** PERFECT, unblemished, unmarked, unimpaired; whole, intact, sound, unbroken, undamaged, mint, pristine; impeccable, immaculate, consummate, accurate, correct, faultless, error-free, unerring; exemplary, model, ideal, copybook.
–OPPOSITES flawed.

flay ▶ **verb** ❶ *the saint was flayed alive* SKIN, strip the skin off; *Medicine* excoriate. ❷ *he flayed his critics. See* CRITICIZE.

fleck ▶ **noun** *flecks of pale blue* SPOT, mark, dot, speck, speckle, freckle, patch, smudge, streak, blotch, dab; *informal* splosh, splodge; *rare* macula.
▶ **verb** *the deer's flanks were flecked with white* SPOT, mark, dot, speckle, bespeckle, freckle, stipple, stud, bestud, blotch, mottle, streak, splash, spatter, bespatter, scatter, sprinkle; *Scottish & Irish* slabber; *informal* splosh, splodge.

fledgling ▶ **noun** *a woodpecker fledgling* CHICK, baby bird, nestling.
▶ **adjective** *fledgling industries* EMERGING, emergent, sunrise, dawning, embryonic, infant, nascent; developing, in the making, budding, up-and-coming, rising.
–OPPOSITES declining, mature.

flee ▶ **verb** ❶ *she fled to her room* RUN (AWAY/OFF), run for it, make a run for it, take flight, be gone, make off, take off, take to one's heels, make a break for it, bolt, beat a (hasty) retreat, make a quick exit, make one's getaway, escape; *informal* beat it, clear off/out, vamoose, skedaddle, split, leg it, turn tail, scram; *Brit. informal* scarper; *N. Amer. informal* light out, bug out, cut out, peel out; *Austral. informal* shoot through; *archaic* fly. ❷ *they fled the country* RUN AWAY FROM, leave hastily, escape from; *informal* skip; *archaic* fly.

fleece ▶ **noun** *a sheep's fleece* WOOL, coat.
▶ **verb** (*informal*) *we were fleeced by a ticket tout. See* SWINDLE verb.

fleecy ▶ **adjective** FLUFFY, woolly, downy, soft, fuzzy, furry, velvety, shaggy; *technical* floccose, pilose.
–OPPOSITES coarse.

fleet[1] ▶ **noun** *the fleet set sail* NAVY, naval force, (naval) task force, armada, flotilla, squadron, convoy.

fleet[2] ▶ **adjective** (*poetic/literary*) *as fleet as a greyhound* NIMBLE, agile, lithe, lissom, acrobatic, supple, light-footed, light on one's feet, spry, sprightly; quick, fast, swift, rapid, speedy, brisk, smart; *informal* nippy, zippy, twinkle-toed.

fleeting ▶ **adjective** BRIEF, short, short-lived, quick, momentary, cursory, transient, ephemeral, fugitive, passing, transitory; *poetic/literary* evanescent.
–OPPOSITES lasting.

flesh ▶ **noun** ❶ *you need more flesh on your bones* MUSCLE, meat, tissue, brawn; *informal* beef. ❷ *she carries too much flesh* FAT, weight; *Anatomy* adipose tissue; *informal* blubber, flab. ❸ *a fruit with juicy flesh* PULP, soft part, marrow, meat. ❹ *the pleasures of the flesh* THE BODY, human nature, physicality, carnality, animality; sensuality, sexuality.
–RELATED TERMS carn-.
■ **one's (own) flesh and blood** FAMILY, relative(s), relation(s), blood relation(s), kin, kinsfolk, kinsman, kinsmen, kinswoman, kinswomen, kindred, nearest and dearest, people; *informal* folks.
■ **flesh out** PUT ON WEIGHT, gain weight, get heavier, grow fat/fatter, fatten up, get fat, fill out.
■ **flesh something out** EXPAND (ON), elaborate on, add to, build on, add flesh to, put flesh on (the bones of), add detail to, expatiate on, supplement, reinforce, augment, fill out, enlarge on.
■ **in the flesh** IN PERSON, before one's (very) eyes, in front of one; in real life, live; physically, bodily, in bodily/human form, incarnate.

fleshly ▶ **adjective** CARNAL, physical, animal, bestial; sexual, sensual, erotic, lustful.
–OPPOSITES spiritual, noble.

fleshy ▶ **adjective** PLUMP, chubby, portly, fat, obese, overweight, stout, corpulent, paunchy, well padded, well covered, well upholstered, rotund; *informal* tubby, pudgy, beefy, porky, roly-poly, blubbery; *Brit. informal* podgy, fubsy; *N. Amer. informal* corn-fed; *Austral./NZ* nuggety; *rare* abdominous.
–OPPOSITES thin.

flex[1] ▶ **verb** ❶ *you must flex your elbow* BEND, crook, hook, cock, angle, double up. ❷ *Rachel flexed her cramped muscles* TIGHTEN, tauten, tense (up), tension, contract.
–OPPOSITES straighten, relax.

flex[2] ▶ **noun** (*Brit.*) *an electric flex* CABLE, wire, lead; *N. Amer.* cord.

flexibility ▶ **noun** ❶ *the flexibility of wood*

PLIABILITY, suppleness, pliancy, plasticity; elasticity, stretchiness, springiness, spring, resilience, bounce; *informal* give. ❷ *the flexibility of an endowment loan* ADAPTABILITY, adjustability, variability, versatility, open-endedness, freedom, latitude. ❸ *the flexibility shown by the local authority* WILLINGNESS TO COMPROMISE, accommodation, amenability, cooperation, tolerance.

–OPPOSITES rigidity, inflexibility, intransigence.

flexible ▶ adjective ❶ *flexible tubing* PLIABLE, supple, bendable, pliant, plastic; elastic, stretchy, whippy, springy, resilient, bouncy; *informal* bendy; *archaic* flexile. ❷ *a flexible arrangement* ADAPTABLE, adjustable, variable, versatile, open-ended, open, free. ❸ *the need to be flexible towards tenants* ACCOMMODATING, amenable, willing to compromise, cooperative, tolerant, easy-going.

–OPPOSITES rigid, inflexible, intransigent.

flick ▶ noun *a flick of the wrist* JERK, snap, flip, whisk.

▶ verb ❶ *he flicked the switch* CLICK, snap, flip, jerk. ❷ *the horse flicked its tail* SWISH, twitch, wave, wag, waggle, shake.

■ **flick through** THUMB (THROUGH), leaf through, flip through, skim through, scan, look through, browse through, dip into, glance at/through, peruse, run one's eye over.

flicker ▶ verb ❶ *the lights flickered* GLIMMER, glint, flare, dance, gutter; twinkle, sparkle, blink, wink, flash, scintillate; *poetic/literary* glister, coruscate. ❷ *his eyelids flickered* FLUTTER, quiver, tremble, shiver, shudder, spasm, jerk, twitch.

flight ▶ noun ❶ *the history of flight* AVIATION, flying, air transport, aerial navigation, aeronautics. ❷ *a flight to Rome* PLANE TRIP/JOURNEY, air trip/journey, trip/journey by air. ❸ *the flight of a cricket ball* TRAJECTORY, path through the air, track, orbit. ❹ *a flight of birds* FLOCK, skein, covey, swarm, cloud. ❺ *his headlong flight from home* ESCAPE, getaway, hasty departure, exit, exodus, decamping, breakout, bolt, disappearance; *Brit informal* flit. ❻ *a flight of stairs* STAIRCASE, set of steps/stairs.

■ **put someone to flight** CHASE AWAY/OFF, drive back/away/off/out, scatter (to the four winds), disperse, repel, repulse, rout, stampede, scare off; *Brit.* see off; *informal* send packing.

■ **take flight** FLEE, run (away/off), run for it, make a run for it, be gone, make off, take off, take to one's heels, make a break for it, bolt, beat a (hasty) retreat, make a quick exit, make one's getaway, escape; *informal* beat it, clear off/out, vamoose, skedaddle, split, leg it, turn tail, scram; *Brit. informal* scarper; *N. Amer. informal* light out, bug out, cut out, peel out; *Austral. informal* shoot through; *archaic* fly.

flighty ▶ adjective FICKLE, inconstant, mercurial, whimsical, capricious, skittish, volatile, impulsive; irresponsible, giddy, reckless, wild, careless, thoughtless.

–OPPOSITES steady, responsible.

flimsy ▶ adjective ❶ *a flimsy building* INSUBSTANTIAL, fragile, breakable, frail, shaky, unstable, wobbly, tottery, rickety, ramshackle, makeshift; jerry-built, badly built, shoddy, gimcrack. ❷ *a flimsy garment* THIN, light, fine, filmy, floaty, diaphanous, sheer, delicate, insubstantial, wispy, gossamer, gauzy. ❸ *flimsy evidence* WEAK, feeble, poor, inadequate, insufficient, thin, unsubstantial, unconvincing, implausible, unsatisfactory.

–OPPOSITES sturdy, thick, sound.

flinch ▶ verb ❶ *he flinched at the noise* WINCE, start, shudder, quiver, jerk, shy. ❷ *he never flinched from his duty* SHRINK FROM, recoil from, shy away from, swerve from, demur from; dodge, evade, avoid, duck, baulk at, jib at, quail at, fight shy of.

fling ▶ verb *he flung the axe into the river* THROW, toss, sling, hurl, cast, pitch, lob; *informal* chuck, heave, bung, buzz; *dated* shy.

▶ noun ❶ *a birthday fling* GOOD TIME, spree, bit of fun, night on the town; fun and games, revels, larks; *informal* binge. ❷ *she had a brief fling with him* AFFAIR, love affair, relationship, romance, affaire (de cœur), amour, flirtation, dalliance, liaison, entanglement, involvement, attachment.

flip ▶ verb ❶ *the wave flipped the dinghy over | the plane flipped on to its back* OVERTURN, turn over, tip over, roll (over), upturn, capsize; upend, invert, knock over; keel over, topple over, turn turtle; *archaic* overset. ❷ *he flipped the key through the air* THROW, flick, toss, fling, sling, pitch, cast, spin, lob; *informal* chuck, bung; *dated* shy. ❸ *I flipped the transmitter switch* FLICK, click, snap.

■ **flip through** THUMB (THROUGH), leaf through, flick through, skim through, scan, look through, browse through, dip into, glance at/through, peruse, run one's eye over.

flippancy ▶ noun FRIVOLITY, levity, facetiousness; disrespect, irreverence, cheek, impudence, impertinence; *Brit. informal* sauce; *N. Amer. informal* sassiness; *dated* waggery.

–OPPOSITES seriousness, respect.

flippant ▶ adjective FRIVOLOUS, facetious, tongue-in-cheek; disrespectful, irreverent, cheeky, impudent, impertinent; *informal* flip, saucy, waggish; *N. Amer. informal* sassy.

–OPPOSITES serious, respectful.

flirt ▶ verb ❶ *it amused him to flirt with her* TRIFLE WITH, toy with, tease, lead on. ❷ *those conservatives who flirted with fascism* DABBLE IN, toy with, trifle with, amuse oneself with, play with, tinker with, dip into, scratch the surface of. ❸ *he is flirting with danger* DICE WITH, court, risk, not fear.

▶ **noun** *Anna was quite a flirt* TEASE, trifler, philanderer, coquette, heartbreaker; *archaic* fizgig.

flirtation ▶ **noun** COQUETRY, teasing, trifling.

flirtatious ▶ **adjective** COQUETTISH, flirty, kittenish, teasing.

flit ▶ **verb** DART, dance, skip, play, dash, trip, flutter, bob, bounce.

float ▶ **verb** ❶ *oil floats on water* STAY AFLOAT, stay on the surface, be buoyant, be buoyed up. ❷ *the balloon floated in the air* HOVER, levitate, be suspended, hang, defy gravity. ❸ *a cloud floated across the moon* DRIFT, glide, sail, slip, slide, waft. ❹ *they have just floated that idea* SUGGEST, put forward, come up with, submit, moot, propose, advance, test the popularity of; *informal* run something up the flagpole (to see who salutes). ❺ *the company was floated on the Stock Exchange* LAUNCH, get going, get off the ground, offer, sell, introduce.
– OPPOSITES sink, rush, withdraw.

floating ▶ **adjective** ❶ *floating seaweed* BUOYANT, on the surface, afloat, drifting. ❷ *floating gas balloons* HOVERING, levitating, suspended, hanging, defying gravity. ❸ *floating voters* UNCOMMITTED, undecided, in two minds, torn, split, uncertain, unsure, wavering, vacillating, indecisive, blowing hot and cold, undeclared; *informal* sitting on the fence. ❹ *a floating population* UNSETTLED, transient, temporary, variable, fluctuating; migrant, wandering, nomadic, on the move, migratory, travelling, drifting, roving, roaming, itinerant, vagabond. ❺ *a floating exchange rate* VARIABLE, changeable, changing, fluid, fluctuating.
– OPPOSITES sunken, grounded, committed, settled, fixed.

flock ▶ **noun** ❶ *a flock of sheep* HERD, drove. ❷ *a flock of birds* FLIGHT, congregation, covey, clutch. ❸ *flocks of people* CROWD, throng, horde, mob, rabble, mass, multitude, host, army, pack, swarm, sea; *informal* gaggle.
▶ **verb** ❶ *people flocked around Jesus* GATHER, collect, congregate, assemble, converge, mass, crowd, throng, cluster, swarm; *formal* foregather. ❷ *tourists flock to the place* STREAM, go in large numbers, swarm, crowd, troop.

flog ▶ **verb** ❶ *the thief was flogged* WHIP, scourge, flagellate, lash, birch, switch, cane, thrash, beat, tan/whip someone's hide. ❷ (*Brit. informal*) *he is flogging his old car* SELL, put on sale, put up for sale, offer for sale, trade in, deal in, peddle; *informal* push.

flood ▶ **noun** ❶ *a flood warning* INUNDATION, swamping, deluge; torrent, overflow, flash flood, freshet; *Brit.* spate. ❷ *a flood of tears* OUTPOURING, torrent, rush, stream, gush, surge, cascade. ❸ *a flood of complaints* SUCCESSION, series, string, chain; barrage, volley, battery; avalanche, torrent, stream, tide, spate, storm, shower, cascade.
– OPPOSITES trickle.
▶ **verb** ❶ *the whole town was flooded* INUNDATE, swamp, deluge, immerse, submerge, drown, engulf. ❷ *the river could flood* OVERFLOW, burst its banks, brim over, run over. ❸ *imports are flooding the domestic market* GLUT, swamp, saturate, oversupply. ❹ *refugees flooded in* POUR, stream, flow, surge, swarm, pile, crowd.
– OPPOSITES trickle.

floor ▶ **noun** ❶ *he sat on the floor* GROUND, flooring. ❷ *the second floor* STOREY, level, deck, tier.
▶ **verb** ❶ *he floored his attacker* KNOCK DOWN, knock over, bring down, fell, prostrate; *informal* lay out. ❷ (*informal*) *the question floored him* BAFFLE, defeat, confound, perplex, puzzle, nonplus, mystify; *informal* beat, flummox, stump, fox, make someone scratch their head; *N. Amer. informal* buffalo; *archaic* pose.

flop ▶ **verb** ❶ *he flopped into a chair* COLLAPSE, slump, crumple, subside, sink, drop. ❷ *his hair flopped over his eyes* HANG (DOWN), dangle, droop, sag, loll. ❸ (*informal*) *the play flopped* BE UNSUCCESSFUL, fail, not work, fall flat, founder, misfire, backfire, be a disappointment, do badly, lose money, be a disaster; *informal* bomb, go to the wall, come a cropper, bite the dust, blow up in someone's face; *N. Amer. informal* tank.
– OPPOSITES succeed.
▶ **noun** (*informal*) *the play was a flop* FAILURE, disaster, debacle, catastrophe, loser; *Brit.* damp squib; *informal* flopperoo, washout, also-ran, dog, lemon, non-starter; *N. Amer. informal* clinker.
– OPPOSITES success.

floppy ▶ **adjective** LIMP, flaccid, slack, flabby, relaxed; drooping, droopy; loose, flowing.
– OPPOSITES erect, stiff.

florid ▶ **adjective** ❶ *a florid complexion* RUDDY, red, red-faced, rosy, rosy-cheeked, pink; flushed, blushing, high-coloured; *archaic* sanguine. ❷ *florid plasterwork* ORNATE, fancy, elaborate, embellished, curlicued, extravagant, flamboyant, baroque, rococo, fussy, busy. ❸ *florid English* FLOWERY, flamboyant, high-flown, high-sounding, grandiloquent, ornate, fancy, bombastic, elaborate, turgid, pleonastic; *informal* highfalutin; *rare* fustian.
– OPPOSITES pale, plain.

flotsam ▶ **noun** WRECKAGE, lost cargo, floating remains; rubbish, debris, detritus, waste, dross, refuse, scrap; *N. Amer.* trash, garbage; *informal* dreck, junk; *Brit. informal* grot.

flounce[1] ▶ **verb** *she flounced off to her room* STORM, stride angrily, sweep, stomp, stamp, march, strut, stalk.

flounce[2] ▶ **noun** *a lace flounce* FRILL, ruffle, ruff, peplum, jabot, furbelow, ruche.

flounder ▶ **verb** ❶ *people were floundering in the water* STRUGGLE, thrash, flail, twist and turn, splash, stagger, stumble, reel, lurch, blunder, squirm, writhe. ❷ *she floundered, not knowing quite what to say* STRUGGLE MENTALLY, be out of

one's depth, have difficulty, be confounded, be confused; *informal* scratch one's head, be flummoxed, be clueless, be foxed, be fazed, be floored, be beaten. ❸ *more firms are floundering* STRUGGLE FINANCIALLY, be in dire straits, face financial ruin, be in difficulties, face bankruptcy/insolvency.
– OPPOSITES prosper.

flourish ▶ verb ❶ *ferns flourish in the shade* GROW, thrive, prosper, do well, burgeon, increase, multiply, proliferate; spring up, shoot up, bloom, blossom, bear fruit, burst forth, run riot. ❷ *the arts flourished* THRIVE, prosper, bloom, be in good health, be vigorous, be in its heyday; progress, make progress, advance, make headway, develop, improve; evolve, make strides, move forward (in leaps and bounds), expand; *informal* be in the pink, go places, go great guns, get somewhere. ❸ *he flourished the sword at them* BRANDISH, wave, shake, wield; swing, twirl, swish; display, exhibit, flaunt, show off.
– OPPOSITES die, wither, decline.

flout ▶ verb DEFY, refuse to obey, disobey, break, violate, fail to comply with, fail to observe, contravene, infringe, breach, commit a breach of, transgress against; ignore, disregard; *informal* cock a snook at.
– OPPOSITES observe.

flow ▶ verb ❶ *the water flowed down the channel* RUN, course, glide, drift, circulate; trickle, seep, ooze, dribble, drip, drizzle, spill; stream, swirl, surge, sweep, gush, cascade, pour, roll, rush. ❷ *many questions flow from today's announcement* RESULT, proceed, arise, follow, ensue, derive, stem, accrue; originate, emanate, spring, emerge; be caused by, be brought about by, be produced by, be consequent on.
▶ noun *a good flow of water* MOVEMENT, motion, current, flux, circulation; trickle, ooze, percolation, drip; stream, swirl, surge, gush, rush, spate, tide.

flower ▶ noun ❶ *blue flowers* BLOOM, blossom, floweret, floret. ❷ *the flower of the nation's youth* BEST, finest, pick, choice, cream, the crème de la crème, elite.
– RELATED TERMS floral, flor-.
– OPPOSITES dregs.

flowery ▶ adjective ❶ *flowery fabrics* FLORAL, flower-patterned. ❷ *flowery language* FLORID, flamboyant, ornate, fancy, convoluted; high-flown, high-sounding, magniloquent, grandiloquent, baroque, orotund, overblown, pleonastic; *informal* highfalutin, purple; *rare* fustian.
– OPPOSITES plain.

flowing ▶ adjective ❶ *long flowing hair* LOOSE, free, unconfined, draping. ❷ *the new model will have soft, flowing lines* SLEEK, streamlined, aerodynamic, smooth, clean; elegant, graceful; *technical* faired. ❸ *he writes in an easy, flowing style* FLUENT, fluid, free-flowing, effortless, easy, natural, smooth.
– OPPOSITES stiff, curly, jagged, halting.

fluctuate ▶ verb VARY, change, differ, shift, alter, waver, swing, oscillate, alternation, rise and fall, go up and down, see-saw, yo-yo, be unstable.

fluctuation ▶ noun VARIATION, change, shift, alteration, swing, movement, oscillation, alternation, rise and fall, see-sawing, yo-yoing, instability, unsteadiness.
– OPPOSITES stability.

flue ▶ noun DUCT, tube, shaft, vent, pipe, passage, channel, conduit; funnel, chimney, smokestack.

fluent ▶ adjective ❶ *a fluent speech* ARTICULATE, eloquent, expressive, communicative, coherent, cogent, illuminating, vivid. ❷ *fluent in French* ARTICULATE; (**be fluent in**) have a (good) command of. ❸ *a very fluent running style* FREE-FLOWING, smooth, effortless, easy, natural, fluid; graceful, elegant; regular, rhythmic.
– OPPOSITES inarticulate, jerky.

fluff ▶ noun ❶ *fluff on her sleeve* FUZZ, lint, dust; *N. Amer.* dustballs, dust bunnies. ❷ (*informal*) *he only made a few fluffs* MISTAKE, error, slip, slip of the tongue; wrong note; *informal* slip-up; *formal* lapsus linguae.
▶ verb (*informal*) *Penney fluffed the shot | he fluffed his only line* BUNGLE, make a mess of, fumble, miss, deliver badly, muddle up, forget; *informal* mess up, make a hash of, make a botch of, foul up, bitch up, screw up; *Brit. informal* make a muck of, make a pig's ear of, cock up, make a Horlicks of; *N. Amer. informal* flub, goof up.
– OPPOSITES succeed in.

fluffy ▶ adjective FLEECY, woolly, fuzzy, hairy, feathery, downy, furry; soft.
– OPPOSITES rough.

fluid ▶ noun *the fluid seeps up the tube* LIQUID, watery substance, solution; GAS, gaseous substance, vapour.
– OPPOSITES solid.
▶ adjective ❶ *a fluid substance* FREE-FLOWING; liquid, liquefied, melted, molten, runny, running; gaseous, gassy. ❷ *his plans were still fluid* ADAPTABLE, flexible, adjustable, open-ended, open, open to change, changeable, variable. ❸ *the fluid state of affairs* FLUCTUATING, changeable, subject/likely to change, (ever-)shifting, inconstant; unstable, unsettled, turbulent, volatile, mercurial, protean. ❹ *he stood up in one fluid movement* SMOOTH, fluent, flowing, effortless, easy, continuous; graceful, elegant.
– OPPOSITES solid, firm, static, jerky.

fluke ▶ noun CHANCE, coincidence, accident, twist of fate; piece of luck, stroke of good luck/fortune.

fluky ▶ adjective LUCKY, fortunate, providential, timely, opportune, serendipitous, expedient, heaven-sent, auspicious, propitious, felicitous; chance, fortuitous, accidental, unintended;

Brit. informal jammy.
– OPPOSITES planned.

flummox ▶ verb (*informal*) BAFFLE, perplex, puzzle, bewilder, mystify, bemuse, confuse, confound, nonplus; *informal* faze, stump, beat, fox, make someone scratch their head, be all Greek to, floor; *N. Amer. informal* discombobulate, buffalo.

flunkey ▶ noun ❶ *a flunkey brought us drinks* LIVERIED SERVANT, lackey, steward, butler, footman, valet, attendant, page. ❷ *government flunkeys searched his offices* MINION, lackey, hireling, subordinate, underling, servant; creature, instrument, cat's paw; *informal* stooge, gofer; *Brit. informal* poodle, dogsbody, skivvy.

flurried ▶ adjective AGITATED, flustered, ruffled, in a panic, worked up, beside oneself, overwrought, perturbed, frantic; *informal* in a flap, in a state, in a twitter, in a fluster, in a dither, all of a dither, all of a lather, in a tizz/tizzy, in a tiz-woz; *Brit. informal* in a (flat) spin, having kittens; *N. Amer. informal* in a twit.
– OPPOSITES calm.

flurry ▶ noun ❶ *a flurry of snow* SWIRL, whirl, eddy, billow, shower, gust. ❷ *a flurry of activity* BURST, outbreak, spurt, fit, spell, bout, rash, eruption; fuss, stir, bustle, hubbub, commotion, disturbance, furore; *informal* to-do, flap. ❸ *a flurry of imports* SPATE, wave, flood, deluge, torrent, stream, tide, avalanche; series, succession, string, outbreak, rash, explosion, run, rush.
– OPPOSITES dearth, trickle.
▶ verb *snow flurried through the door* SWIRL, whirl, eddy, billow, gust, blast, blow, rush.

flush[1] ▶ verb ❶ *she flushed in embarrassment* BLUSH, redden, go pink, go red, go crimson, go scarlet, colour (up); *archaic* mantle. ❷ *fruit helps to flush toxins from the body* RINSE, wash, sluice, swill, cleanse, clean; *Brit. informal* sloosh. ❸ *they flushed out the snipers* DRIVE, chase, force, dislodge, expel, frighten, scare.
– OPPOSITES pale.
▶ noun ❶ *a flush crept over her face* BLUSH, reddening, high colour, colour, rosiness, pinkness, ruddiness, bloom. ❷ *the first flush of manhood* BLOOM, glow, freshness, radiance, vigour, rush.
– OPPOSITES paleness.

flush[2] ▶ adjective (*informal*) ❶ *the company was flush with cash* WELL SUPPLIED, well provided, well stocked, replete, overflowing, bursting, brimful, brimming, loaded, overloaded, teeming, stuffed, swarming, thick, solid; full of, abounding in, rich in, abundant in; *informal* awash, jam-packed, chock-full of; *Austral./NZ informal* chocker. ❷ *the years when cash was flush* PLENTIFUL, abundant, in abundance, copious, ample, profuse, superabundant; *informal* a gogo, galore; *poetic/literary* plenteous, bounteous.
– OPPOSITES lacking, low (on).

flushed ▶ adjective ❶ *flushed faces* RED, pink, ruddy, glowing, reddish, pinkish, rosy, florid, high-coloured, healthy-looking, aglow, burning, feverish; blushing, red-faced, embarrassed, shamefaced. ❷ *flushed with success* ELATED, excited, thrilled, exhilarated, happy, delighted, overjoyed, joyous, gleeful, jubilant, exultant, ecstatic, euphoric, rapturous; *informal* blissed out, over the moon, high, on a high; *N. Amer. informal* wigged out.
– OPPOSITES pale, dismayed.

fluster ▶ verb *she was flustered by his presence* UNSETTLE, make nervous, unnerve, agitate, ruffle, upset, bother, put on edge, disquiet, disturb, worry, perturb, disconcert, confuse, throw off balance, confound, nonplus; *informal* rattle, faze, put into a flap, throw into a tizzy; *Brit. informal* send into a spin; *N. Amer. informal* discombobulate.
– OPPOSITES calm.
▶ noun *I was in a terrible fluster* STATE OF AGITATION, state of anxiety, nervous state, panic, frenzy, fret; *informal* dither, flap, tizz, tizzy, tiz-woz, twitter, state, sweat; *N. Amer. informal* twit.
– OPPOSITES state of calm.

fluted ▶ adjective GROOVED, channelled, furrowed, ribbed, corrugated, ridged.
– OPPOSITES smooth, plain.

flutter ▶ verb ❶ *butterflies fluttered around* FLIT, hover, flitter, dance. ❷ *a tern was fluttering its wings* FLAP, move up and down, beat, quiver, agitate, vibrate. ❸ *she fluttered her eyelashes* FLICKER, bat. ❹ *flags fluttered* FLAP, wave, ripple, undulate, quiver; fly. ❺ *her heart fluttered* BEAT WEAKLY, beat irregularly, palpitate, miss/skip a beat, quiver, go pit-a-pat; *Medicine* exhibit arrhythmia; *rare* quop.
▶ noun ❶ *the flutter of wings* BEATING, flapping, quivering, agitation, vibrating. ❷ *a flutter of dark eyelashes* FLICKER, bat. ❸ *the flutter of the flags* FLAPPING, waving, rippling. ❹ *a flutter of nervousness* TREMOR, wave, rush, surge, flash, stab, flush, tremble, quiver, shiver, frisson, chill, thrill, tingle, shudder, ripple, flicker. ❺ (*Brit. informal*) *he enjoys a flutter on the horses* BET, wager, gamble; *Brit. informal* punt.

flux ▶ noun CONTINUOUS CHANGE, changeability, variability, inconstancy, fluidity, instability, unsteadiness, fluctuation, variation, shift, movement, oscillation, alternation, rise and fall, see-sawing, yo-yoing.
– OPPOSITES stability.

fly[1] ▶ verb ❶ *a bird flew overhead* TRAVEL THROUGH THE AIR, wing its way, wing, glide, soar, wheel; hover, hang; take wing, take to the air, mount. ❷ *they flew to Paris* TRAVEL BY PLANE/AIR, jet. ❸ *military planes flew in food supplies* TRANSPORT BY PLANE/AIR, airlift, lift, jet. ❹ *he could fly a plane* PILOT, operate, control, manoeuvre, steer. ❺ *the ship was flying a quarantine flag* DISPLAY, show, exhibit; have hoisted, have run up. ❻ *flags flew in the town* FLUTTER, flap, wave.

❼ *doesn't time fly?* GO QUICKLY, fly by/past, pass swiftly, slip past, rush past. ❽ *the runners flew by. See* SPEED verb sense 1. ❾ (*archaic*) *the beaten army had to fly. See* FLEE sense 1. ❿ (*dated*) *they had to fly the country. See* FLEE sense 2.

■ **fly at** ATTACK, assault, pounce on, set upon, set about, weigh into, let fly at, turn on, round on, lash out at, hit out at, belabour, fall on; *informal* lay into, tear into, lace into, sail into, pitch into, wade into, let someone have it, jump; *Brit. informal* have a go at; *N. Amer. informal* light into.

■ **let fly**. *See* LET.

fly[2] ▶ **adjective** (*Brit. informal*) *she's fly enough not to get conned* SHREWD, sharp, astute, acute, canny, worldly-wise, knowing, clever; *informal* streetwise, not born yesterday, smart, no fool, nobody's fool; *Brit. informal* suss, knowing how many beans make five; *Scottish & N. English informal* pawky.

– OPPOSITES naive.

fly-by-night ▶ **adjective** UNRELIABLE, undependable, untrustworthy, disreputable; DISHONEST, deceitful, dubious, unscrupulous; *informal* iffy, shady, shifty, slippery, crooked; *Brit. informal* dodgy, bent; *Austral./NZ informal* shonky.

– OPPOSITES reliable, honest.

flyer, flier ▶ **noun** ❶ *frequent flyers* AIR TRAVELLER, air passenger, airline customer. ❷ *flyers killed in the war* PILOT, airman, airwoman; *N. Amer. informal* jock; *dated* aviator, aeronaut. ❸ *flyers promoting a new sandwich bar* HANDBILL, bill, handout, leaflet, circular, advertisement; *N. Amer.* dodger.

flying ▶ **adjective** ❶ *a flying beetle* WINGED; AIRBORNE, in the air, in flight. ❷ *a flying visit* BRIEF, short, lightning, fleeting, hasty, rushed, hurried, quick, whistle-stop, cursory, perfunctory; *informal* quickie.

– OPPOSITES long.

foam ▶ **noun** *the foam on the waves* FROTH, spume, surf; fizz, effervescence, bubbles, head; lather, suds.

▶ **verb** *the water foamed* FROTH, spume; fizz, effervesce, bubble; lather; ferment, rise; boil, seethe, simmer.

foamy ▶ **adjective** FROTHY, foaming, spumy, bubbly, aerated, bubbling; sudsy; whipped, whisked.

fob

■ **fob someone off** *I wasn't going to be fobbed off with excuses* PUT OFF, stall, give someone the runaround, deceive; placate, appease.

■ **fob something off on** *he fobbed off the chairmanship on Clifford* IMPOSE, palm off, unload, dump, get rid of, foist, offload; saddle someone with something, land someone with something, lumber someone with something.

focus ▶ **noun** ❶ *schools are a focus of community life* CENTRE, focal point, central point, centre of attention, hub, pivot, nucleus, heart, cornerstone, linchpin, cynosure. ❷ *the focus is on helping people* EMPHASIS, accent, priority, attention, concentration. ❸ *the main focus of this chapter* SUBJECT, theme, concern, subject matter, topic, issue, thesis, point, thread; substance, essence, gist, matter. ❹ *the resulting light beams are brought to a focus at the eyepiece* FOCAL POINT, point of convergence.

▶ **verb** ❶ *he focused his binoculars on the tower* BRING INTO FOCUS; aim, point, turn. ❷ *the investigation will focus on areas of social need* CONCENTRATE, centre, zero in, zoom in; address itself to, pay attention to, pinpoint, revolve around, have as its starting point.

■ **in focus** SHARP, crisp, distinct, clear, well defined, well focused.

■ **out of focus** BLURRED, unfocused, indistinct, blurry, fuzzy, hazy, misty, cloudy, lacking definition, nebulous.

foe ▶ **noun** (*poetic/literary*) ENEMY, adversary, opponent, rival, antagonist, combatant, challenger, competitor, opposer, opposition, competition, other side.

– OPPOSITES friend.

fog ▶ **noun** MIST, smog, murk, haze, haar; *N. English* (sea) fret; *informal* pea-souper; *poetic/literary* brume, fume.

▶ **verb** ❶ *the windscreen fogged up | his breath fogged the glass* STEAM UP, mist over, cloud over, film over, make/become misty. ❷ *his brain was fogged with sleep* MUDDLE, daze, stupefy, fuddle, befuddle, bewilder, confuse, befog; *poetic/literary* bedim, becloud.

– OPPOSITES demist, clear.

foggy ▶ **adjective** ❶ *the weather was foggy* MISTY, smoggy, hazy, murky. ❷ *she was foggy with sleep | a foggy memory* MUDDLED, fuddled, befuddled, confused, at sea, bewildered, dazed, stupefied, numb, groggy, fuzzy, bleary; dark, dim, hazy, shadowy, cloudy, blurred, obscure, vague, indistinct, unclear; *informal* dopey, woolly, woozy, out of it.

– OPPOSITES clear.

foible ▶ **noun** WEAKNESS, failing, shortcoming, flaw, imperfection, blemish, fault, defect, limitation; quirk, kink, idiosyncrasy, eccentricity, peculiarity.

– OPPOSITES strength.

foil[1] ▶ **verb** *their escape attempt was foiled* THWART, frustrate, counter, baulk, impede, obstruct, hamper, hinder, snooker, cripple, scotch, derail, smash; stop, block, prevent, defeat; *informal* do for, put paid to, stymie, cook someone's goose; *Brit. informal* scupper, nobble, queer, put the mockers on.

– OPPOSITES assist.

foil[2] ▶ **noun** *the wine was a perfect foil to pasta* CONTRAST, complement, antithesis, relief.

foist ▶ **verb** IMPOSE, force, thrust, offload, unload, dump, palm off, fob off; pass off, get rid of; saddle someone with, land someone with, lumber someone with.

fold[1] ▶ **verb** ❶ *I folded the cloth* DOUBLE (OVER/UP), crease, turn under/up/over, bend; tuck, gather, pleat. ❷ *fold the cream into the chocolate mixture* MIX, blend, stir gently. ❸ *he folded her in his arms* ENFOLD, wrap, envelop; take, gather, clasp, squeeze, clutch; embrace, hug, cuddle, cradle. ❹ *the firm folded last year* FAIL, collapse, founder; go bankrupt, become insolvent, cease trading, go into receivership, go into liquidation, be wound up, be closed (down), be shut (down); *informal* crash, go bust, go broke, go under, go to the wall, go belly up.
▶ **noun** *there was a fold in the paper* CREASE, knife-edge; wrinkle, crinkle, pucker, furrow; pleat, gather.

fold[2] ▶ **noun** ❶ *the sheep were in their fold* ENCLOSURE, pen, paddock, pound, compound, ring; *N. Amer.* corral. ❷ *Lloyd George returned to the Liberal fold* COMMUNITY, group, body, company, mass, throng, flock, congregation, assembly.

folder ▶ **noun** FILE, binder, ring binder, portfolio, document case, envelope, sleeve, wallet.

foliage ▶ **noun** LEAVES, leafage; greenery, vegetation, verdure.

folk ▶ **noun** (*informal*) ❶ *the local folk* PEOPLE, individuals, {men, women, and children}, (living) souls, mortals; citizenry, inhabitants, residents, populace, population; *informal* peeps; *formal* denizens. ❷ *my folks came from the north* RELATIVES, relations, blood relations, family, nearest and dearest, people, kinsfolk, kinsmen, kinswomen, kin, kith and kin, kindred, flesh and blood.

folklore ▶ **noun** MYTHOLOGY, lore, oral history, tradition, folk tradition; legends, fables, myths, folk tales, folk stories, old wives' tales; mythos.

follow ▶ **verb** ❶ *we'll let the others follow* COME BEHIND, come after, go behind, go after, walk behind. ❷ *he was expected to follow his father in the business* TAKE THE PLACE OF, replace, succeed, take over from; *informal* step into someone's shoes, fill someone's shoes/boots. ❸ *people used to follow the band around* ACCOMPANY, go along with, go around with, travel with, escort, attend, trail around with, string along with; *informal* tag along with. ❹ *the KGB man followed her everywhere* SHADOW, trail, stalk, track, dog, hound; *informal* tail. ❺ *do follow the instructions* OBEY, comply with, conform to, adhere to, stick to, keep to, act in accordance with, abide by, observe, heed, pay attention to. ❻ *penalties may follow from such behaviour* RESULT, arise, be a consequence of, be caused by, be brought about by, be a result of, come after, develop, ensue, emanate, issue, proceed, spring, flow, originate, stem. ❼ *I couldn't follow what he said* UNDERSTAND, comprehend, apprehend, take in, grasp, fathom, appreciate, see; *informal* make head or tail of, get, figure out, savvy, get one's head around, get one's mind around, get the drift of; *Brit. informal* suss out. ❽ *he followed his master in his poetic style* IMITATE, copy, mimic, ape, reproduce, mirror, echo; emulate, take as a pattern, take as an example, take as a model, adopt the style of, model oneself on, take a leaf out of someone's book. ❾ *he follows Manchester United* BE A FAN OF, be a supporter of, support, be a follower of, be an admirer of, be a devotee of, be devoted to.
– OPPOSITES lead, flout, misunderstand.
■ **follow something through** COMPLETE, bring to completion, see something through; continue with, carry on with, keep on with, keep going with, stay with; *informal* stick something out.
■ **follow something up** INVESTIGATE, research, look into, dig into, delve into, make enquiries into, enquire about, ask questions about, pursue, chase up; *informal* check out; *N. Amer. informal* scope out.

follower ▶ **noun** ❶ *the president's closest followers* ACOLYTE, assistant, attendant, companion, henchman, minion, lackey, servant; *informal* hanger-on, sidekick; *archaic* liegeman. ❷ *a follower of Caravaggio* IMITATOR, emulator, copier, mimic; pupil, disciple; *informal* copycat. ❸ *a follower of Christ* DISCIPLE, apostle, supporter, defender, champion; believer, worshipper. ❹ *followers of Scottish football* FAN, enthusiast, admirer, devotee, lover, supporter, adherent; *N. Amer. informal* rooter.
– OPPOSITES leader, opponent.

following ▶ **noun** *his devoted following* ADMIRERS, supporters, backers, fans, adherents, devotees, advocates, patrons, public, audience, circle, retinue, train.
– OPPOSITES opposition.
▶ **adjective** ❶ *the following day* NEXT, ensuing, succeeding, subsequent. ❷ *the following questions* below, further on, underneath; these; *formal* hereunder, hereinafter.
– OPPOSITES preceding, aforementioned.

folly ▶ **noun** FOOLISHNESS, foolhardiness, stupidity, idiocy, lunacy, madness, rashness, recklessness, imprudence, injudiciousness, irresponsibility, thoughtlessness, indiscretion; *informal* craziness; *Brit. informal* daftness.
– OPPOSITES wisdom.

foment ▶ **verb** INSTIGATE, incite, provoke, agitate, excite, stir up, whip up, encourage, urge, fan the flames of.

fond ▶ **adjective** ❶ *she was fond of dancing* KEEN ON, partial to, addicted to, enthusiastic about, passionate about; attached to, attracted to, enamoured of, in love with, having a soft spot for; *informal* into, hooked on, gone on, sweet on, struck on. ❷ *his fond father* ADORING, devoted, doting, loving, caring, affectionate, warm, tender, kind, attentive. ❸ *a fond hope* UNREALISTIC, naive, foolish, over-optimistic, deluded, delusory, absurd, vain, Panglossian.

– OPPOSITES indifferent, unfeeling, realistic.

fondle ▶ verb CARESS, stroke, pat, pet, finger, tickle, play with; maul, molest; *informal* paw, grope, feel up, touch up, cop a feel of.

fondness ▶ noun ❶ *they look at each other with such fondness* AFFECTION, love, liking, warmth, tenderness, kindness, devotion, endearment, attachment, friendliness. ❷ *a fondness for spicy food* LIKING, love, taste, partiality, keenness, inclination, penchant, predilection, relish, passion, appetite; weakness, soft spot; *informal* thing, yen.

– OPPOSITES hatred.

food ▶ noun ❶ *French food* NOURISHMENT, sustenance, nutriment, fare, bread, daily bread; cooking, cuisine; foodstuffs, edibles, provender, refreshments, meals, provisions, rations; solids; *informal* eats, eatables, nosh, grub, chow, nibbles; *Brit. informal* scoff, tuck; *N. Amer. informal* chuck; *formal* comestibles; *poetic/literary* viands; *dated* victuals; *archaic* commons, meat, aliment. ❷ *food for the cattle* FODDER, feed, provender, forage.

– RELATED TERMS alimentary, culinary.

foodie ▶ noun (*informal*) GOURMET, epicure, gastronome, gourmand.

fool ▶ noun ❶ *you've acted like a complete fool* IDIOT, ass, halfwit, blockhead, dunce, dolt, dullard, simpleton, clod; *informal* dope, ninny, nincompoop, chump, dimwit, coot, goon, dumbo, dummy, dum-dum, fathead, numbskull, dunderhead, pudding-head, thickhead, airhead, lamebrain, cretin, moron, nerd, imbecile, pea-brain, birdbrain, jerk, dipstick, donkey, noodle; *Brit. informal* nit, nitwit, twit, clot, goat, plonker, berk, prat, pillock, wally, git, dork, twerp, charlie, mug; *Scottish informal* nyaff, balloon, sumph, gowk; *N. Amer. informal* schmuck, bozo, boob, turkey, schlepper, chowderhead, dumbhead, goofball, goof, goofus, galoot, lummox, klutz, putz, schlemiel, sap, meatball; *Austral./NZ informal* drongo, dill, alec, galah, boofhead. ❷ *she made a fool of me* LAUGHING STOCK, dupe, butt, gull; *informal* stooge, sucker, mug, fall guy; *N. Amer. informal* sap. ❸ (*historical*) *the fool in King James's court* JESTER, court jester, clown, buffoon, joker, zany, merry andrew; wearer of the motley.

▶ verb ❶ *he'd been fooled by a schoolboy* DECEIVE, trick, hoax, dupe, take in, mislead, delude, hoodwink, bluff, gull; swindle, defraud, cheat, double-cross; *informal* con, bamboozle, pull a fast one on, take for a ride, pull the wool over someone's eyes, put one over on, have on, diddle, fiddle, rip off, do, sting, shaft; *Brit. informal* sell a pup to; *N. Amer. informal* sucker, snooker, stiff, euchre, hornswoggle; *Austral. informal* pull a swifty on; *poetic/literary* cozen. ❷ *I'm not fooling, I promise* PRETEND, make believe, feign, put on an act, act, sham, fake; joke, jest; *informal* kid; *Brit. informal* have someone on.

■ **fool around** ❶ *someone's been fooling around with the controls* FIDDLE, play (about/around), toy, trifle, meddle, tamper, interfere, monkey about/around; *informal* mess about/around; *Brit. informal* muck about/around. ❷ (*N. Amer. informal*) *my husband's been fooling around* PHILANDER, womanize, flirt, have an affair, commit adultery; *informal* play around, mess about/around, carry on, play the field, sleep around; *Brit. informal* play away.

foolery ▶ noun CLOWNING, fooling, tomfoolery, buffoonery, silliness, foolishness, stupidity, idiocy; antics, capers; *informal* larking around, larks, shenanigans; *Brit. informal* monkey tricks; *N. Amer. informal* didoes; *archaic* harlequinade.

foolhardy ▶ adjective RECKLESS, rash, irresponsible, impulsive, hot-headed, impetuous, daredevil, devil-may-care, death-or-glory, madcap, hare-brained, precipitate, hasty, overhasty; *poetic/literary* temerarious.

– OPPOSITES prudent.

foolish ▶ adjective STUPID, silly, idiotic, witless, brainless, mindless, unintelligent, thoughtless, half-baked, imprudent, incautious, injudicious, unwise; ill-advised, ill-considered, impolitic, rash, reckless, foolhardy; *informal* dumb, dim, dim-witted, half-witted, thick, gormless, hare-brained, crackbrained, peabrained, wooden-headed; *Brit. informal* barmy, daft; *Scottish & N. English informal* glaikit; *N. Amer. informal* dumb-ass, chowderheaded.

– OPPOSITES sensible, wise.

foolishness ▶ noun FOLLY, stupidity, idiocy, imbecility, silliness, inanity, thoughtlessness, imprudence, injudiciousness, lack of caution/foresight/sense, irresponsibility, indiscretion, foolhardiness, rashness, recklessness; *Brit. informal* daftness.

– OPPOSITES sense, wisdom.

foolproof ▶ adjective INFALLIBLE, dependable, reliable, trustworthy, certain, sure, guaranteed, safe, sound, tried and tested; watertight, airtight, flawless, perfect; *informal* sure-fire; *formal* efficacious.

– OPPOSITES flawed.

foot ▶ noun ❶ *my feet hurt informal* tootsies, trotters, plates of meat; *N. Amer. informal* dogs. ❷ *the animal's foot* paw, hoof, trotter, pad. ❸ *the foot of the hill* BOTTOM, base, lowest part; end; foundation.

– RELATED TERMS pedi-, -pod(e).

■ **foot the bill** (*informal*) PAY (THE BILL), settle up; *informal* pick up the tab, cough up, fork out, shell out, come across; *N. Amer. informal* pick up the check.

football ▶ noun (*Brit.*) SOCCER, Association Football.

footing ▶ noun ❶ *Jenny lost her footing* FOOTHOLD, toehold, grip, purchase. ❷ *a solid financial footing* BASIS, base, foundation. ❸ *on an equal* *footing* STANDING, status, position; condition, arrangement, basis; relationship, terms.

footling ▶ adjective TRIVIAL, trifling, petty, insignificant, inconsequential, unimportant, minor, small, time-wasting; *informal* piddling, piffling, fiddling.
– OPPOSITES important, large.

footnote ▶ noun NOTE, marginal note, annotation, comment, gloss; aside, incidental remark, digression.

footprint ▶ noun FOOTMARK, footstep, mark, impression; pug, slot; (**footprints**) track(s), spoor.

footstep ▶ noun ❶ *he heard a footstep* FOOTFALL, step, tread, stomp, stamp. ❷ *footsteps in the sand* FOOTPRINT, footmark, mark, impression; (**footsteps**) track(s), spoor.

footwear ▶ noun BOOTS AND SHOES, footgear.

fop ▶ noun DANDY, poseur, man about town; *informal* snappy dresser, natty dresser, trendy; *informal, dated* swell; *dated* beau; *archaic* coxcomb, popinjay.

foppish ▶ adjective DANDYISH, dandified, dapper, dressy; affected, preening, vain; effeminate, girly, niminy-piminy, mincing; *informal* natty, sissy, camp, campy; *Brit. informal* poncey.

forage ▶ verb HUNT, search, look, rummage (about/around/round), ferret (about/around), root about/around, scratch about/around, nose around/about/round, scavenge; *Brit. informal* rootle around.
▶ noun ❶ *forage for the horses* FODDER, feed, food, provender. ❷ *a nightly forage for food* HUNT, search, look, quest, rummage, scavenge.

foray ▶ noun RAID, attack, assault, incursion, swoop, strike, onslaught, sortie, sally, push, thrust; *archaic* onset.

forbear ▶ verb REFRAIN, abstain, desist, keep, restrain oneself, stop oneself, hold back, withhold; resist the temptation to; eschew, avoid, decline to.
– OPPOSITES persist.

forbearance ▶ noun TOLERANCE, patience, resignation, endurance, fortitude, stoicism; leniency, clemency, indulgence; restraint, self-restraint, self-control.

forbearing ▶ adjective PATIENT, tolerant, easygoing, lenient, clement, forgiving, understanding, accommodating, indulgent; long-suffering, resigned, stoic; restrained, self-controlled.
– OPPOSITES impatient, intolerant.

forbid ▶ verb PROHIBIT, ban, outlaw, make illegal, veto, proscribe, disallow, embargo, bar, debar, interdict; *Law* enjoin, restrain.
– OPPOSITES permit.

forbidding ▶ adjective ❶ *a forbidding manner* HOSTILE, unwelcoming, unfriendly, off-putting, unsympathetic, unapproachable, grim, stern, hard, tough, frosty. ❷ *the dark castle looked forbidding* THREATENING, ominous, menacing, sinister, brooding, daunting, fearsome, frightening, chilling, disturbing, disquieting.
– OPPOSITES friendly, inviting.

force ▶ noun ❶ *he pushed with all his force* STRENGTH, power, energy, might, effort, exertion; impact, pressure, weight, impetus. ❷ *they used force to achieve their aims* COERCION, compulsion, constraint, duress, oppression, harassment, intimidation, threats; *informal* arm-twisting. ❸ *the force of the argument* COGENCY, weight, effectiveness, soundness, validity, strength, power, significance, influence, authority; *informal* punch; *formal* efficacy. ❹ *a force for good* AGENCY, power, influence, instrument, vehicle, means. ❺ *a peace-keeping force* BODY, body of people, group, outfit, party, team; detachment, unit, squad; *informal* bunch.
– OPPOSITES weakness.
▶ verb ❶ *he was forced to pay* COMPEL, coerce, make, constrain, oblige, impel, drive, pressurize, pressure, press, push, press-gang, bully, dragoon, bludgeon; *informal* put the screws on, lean on, twist someone's arm. ❷ *the door had to be forced* BREAK OPEN, burst open, knock down, smash down, kick in. ❸ *water was forced through a hole* PROPEL, push, thrust, shove, drive, press, pump. ❹ *they forced a confession out of the kids* EXTRACT, elicit, exact, extort, wrest, wring, drag, screw, squeeze.
■ **in force** ❶ *the law is now in force* EFFECTIVE, in operation, operative, operational, in action, valid. ❷ *her fans were out in force* IN GREAT NUMBERS, in hordes, in full strength.

forced ▶ adjective ❶ *forced entry* VIOLENT, forcible. ❷ *forced repatriation* ENFORCED, compulsory, obligatory, mandatory, involuntary, imposed, required, stipulated, dictated, ordained, prescribed. ❸ *a forced smile* STRAINED, unnatural, artificial, false, feigned, simulated, contrived, laboured, stilted, studied, mannered, affected, unconvincing, insincere, hollow; *informal* phony, pretend, put on.
– OPPOSITES voluntary, natural.

forceful ▶ adjective ❶ *a forceful personality* DYNAMIC, energetic, assertive, authoritative, vigorous, powerful, strong, pushy, driving, determined, insistent, commanding, dominant, domineering; *informal* bossy, in-your-face, go-ahead, feisty. ❷ *a forceful argument* COGENT, convincing, compelling, strong, powerful, potent, weighty, effective, well founded, telling, persuasive, irresistible, eloquent, coherent.
– OPPOSITES weak, submissive, unconvincing.

forcible ▶ adjective ❶ *forcible entry* FORCED, violent. ❷ *forcible repatriation. See* FORCED sense 2. ❸ *a forcible argument. See* FORCEFUL sense 2.

forebear ▶ noun ANCESTOR, forefather, antecedent, progenitor, primogenitor.
– OPPOSITES descendant.

forebode ▶ verb (*poetic/literary*) PRESAGE, augur, portend, herald, warn of, forewarn of, foreshadow, be an omen of, indicate, signify, signal, promise, threaten, spell, denote; *poetic/literary* betoken, foretoken.

foreboding ▶ noun ❶ *a feeling of foreboding* APPREHENSION, anxiety, trepidation, disquiet, unease, uneasiness, misgiving, suspicion, worry, fear, fearfulness, dread, alarm; *informal* the willies, the heebie-jeebies, the jitters. ❷ *their forebodings proved justified* PREMONITION, presentiment, bad feeling, sneaking suspicion, funny feeling, intuition; *archaic* presage.
– OPPOSITES calm.

forecast ▶ verb *they forecast record profits* PREDICT, prophesy, prognosticate, foretell, foresee, forewarn of.
▶ noun *a gloomy forecast* PREDICTION, prophecy, forewarning, prognostication, augury, divination, prognosis.

forefather ▶ noun FOREBEAR, ancestor, antecedent, progenitor, primogenitor.
– OPPOSITES descendant.

forefront ▶ noun VANGUARD, van, spearhead, head, lead, front, fore, front line, cutting edge.
– OPPOSITES rear, background.

forego ▶ verb. *See* FORGO.

foregoing ▶ adjective PRECEDING, aforesaid, aforementioned, previously mentioned, earlier, above; previous, prior, antecedent.
– OPPOSITES following.

foregone
■ **a foregone conclusion** CERTAINTY, inevitability, matter of course, predictable result; *informal* sure thing; *Brit. informal* cert, dead cert.

foreground ▶ noun ❶ *the foreground of the picture* FRONT, fore. ❷ *in the foreground of the political drama* FOREFRONT, vanguard, van, spearhead, head, lead, front, fore, front line, cutting edge.

forehead ▶ noun BROW, temple.
– RELATED TERMS frontal, metopic.

foreign ▶ adjective ❶ *foreign branches of UK banks* OVERSEAS, exotic, distant, external, alien, non-native. ❷ *the concept is very foreign to us* UNFAMILIAR, unknown, unheard of, strange, alien; novel, new.
– RELATED TERMS xeno-.
– OPPOSITES domestic, native, familiar.

foreigner ▶ noun ALIEN, non-native, stranger, outsider; immigrant, settler, newcomer, incomer.
– OPPOSITES native.

foreman, forewoman ▶ noun SUPERVISOR, overseer, superintendent, team leader; foreperson; *Brit.* chargehand, captain, ganger; *Scottish* grieve; *N. Amer. informal* ramrod, straw boss; *Austral. informal* pannikin boss; *Mining* overman.

foremost ▶ adjective LEADING, principal, premier, prime, top, top-level, greatest, best, supreme, pre-eminent, outstanding, most important, most prominent, most influential, most illustrious, most notable; *N. Amer.* ranking; *informal* number-one.
– OPPOSITES minor.

foreordained ▶ adjective PREDETERMINED, preordained, ordained, predestined, destined, fated.

forerunner ▶ noun ❶ *archosaurs were the forerunners of dinosaurs* PREDECESSOR, precursor, antecedent, ancestor, forebear; prototype. ❷ *headache may be the forerunner of other complaints* PRELUDE, herald, harbinger, precursor, sign, signal, indication, warning.
– OPPOSITES descendant.

foresee ▶ verb ANTICIPATE, predict, forecast, expect, envisage, envision, see; foretell, prophesy, prognosticate; *Scottish* spae; *poetic/literary* foreknow.

foreshadow ▶ verb SIGNAL, indicate, signify, mean, be a sign of, suggest, herald, be a harbinger of, warn of, portend, prefigure, presage, promise, point to, anticipate; *informal* spell; *poetic/literary* forebode, foretoken, betoken; *archaic* foreshow.

foresight ▶ noun FORETHOUGHT, planning, far-sightedness, vision, anticipation, prudence, care, caution, precaution, readiness, preparedness; *N. Amer.* forehandedness.
– OPPOSITES hindsight.

forest ▶ noun WOOD(S), woodland, trees, plantation; jungle; *archaic* greenwood.
– RELATED TERMS sylvan.

forestall ▶ verb PRE-EMPT, get in before, steal a march on; anticipate, second-guess; nip in the bud, thwart, frustrate, foil, stave off, ward off, fend off, avert, preclude, obviate, prevent; *informal* beat someone to it.

forestry ▶ noun FOREST MANAGEMENT, tree growing, agroforestry; *technical* arboriculture, silviculture.

foretaste ▶ noun SAMPLE, taster, taste, preview, specimen, example; indication, suggestion, hint, whiff; warning, forewarning, omen; *informal* try-out.

foretell ▶ verb ❶ *the locals can foretell a storm* PREDICT, forecast, prophesy, prognosticate; foresee, anticipate, envisage, envision, see; *Scottish* spae. ❷ *dreams can foretell the future* INDICATE, foreshadow, prefigure, anticipate, warn of, point to, signal, portend, augur, presage, be an omen of; *poetic/literary* forebode, foretoken, betoken; *archaic* foreshow.

forethought ▶ noun ANTICIPATION, planning, forward planning, provision, precaution, prudence, care, caution; foresight, far-sightedness, vision.
– OPPOSITES impulse, recklessness.

forever ▶ adverb ❶ *their love would last forever* FOR ALWAYS, evermore, for ever and ever, for good, for all time, until the end of time, until

hell freezes over, eternally; *Brit.* for evermore; *N. Amer.* forevermore; *informal* until the cows come home, until doomsday, until kingdom come; *archaic* for aye. ❷ *he was forever banging into things* ALWAYS, continually, constantly, perpetually, incessantly, endlessly, persistently, repeatedly, regularly; non-stop, day and night, {morning, noon, and night}; all the time, the entire time; *Scottish* aye; *informal* 24-7.
– OPPOSITES never, occasionally.

forewarn ▶ verb WARN, warn in advance, give advance warning, give fair warning, give notice, apprise, inform; alert, caution, put someone on their guard; *informal* tip off; *Brit. informal* tip someone the wink.

forewarning ▶ noun OMEN, sign, indication, portent, presage, warning, harbinger, foreshadowing, augury, signal, promise, threat, straw in the wind, writing on the wall, hint; *poetic/literary* foretoken.

foreword ▶ noun PREFACE, introduction, prologue, preamble; *informal* intro; *formal* exordium, prolegomenon, proem.
– OPPOSITES conclusion.

forfeit ▶ verb *latecomers will forfeit their places* LOSE, be deprived of, surrender, relinquish, sacrifice, give up, yield, renounce, forgo; *informal* pass up, lose out on.
– OPPOSITES retain.
▶ noun *they are liable to a forfeit* PENALTY, sanction, punishment, penance; fine; confiscation, loss, relinquishment, forfeiture, surrender; *Law* sequestration.

forfeiture ▶ noun CONFISCATION, loss; relinquishment, giving up, surrender, sacrifice; *Law* sequestration; *historical* attainder.

forge[1] ▶ verb ❶ *a smith forged swords* HAMMER OUT, beat into shape, fashion. ❷ *they forged a partnership* BUILD, construct, form, create, establish, set up. ❸ *he forged her signature* FAKE, falsify, counterfeit, copy, imitate, reproduce, replicate, simulate; *informal* pirate.

forge[2] ▶ verb *they forged through swamps* ADVANCE STEADILY, advance gradually, press on, push on, soldier on, march on, push forward, make progress, make headway.
■ **forge ahead** ADVANCE RAPIDLY, progress quickly, make rapid progress, increase speed, put a spurt on.

forged ▶ adjective FAKE, faked, false, counterfeit, imitation, copied, pirate(d); sham, bogus; *informal* phoney, dud.
– OPPOSITES genuine.

forger ▶ noun COUNTERFEITER, faker, copyist, imitator, pirate.

forgery ▶ noun ❶ *guilty of forgery* COUNTERFEITING, falsification, faking, copying, pirating. ❷ *the painting was a forgery* FAKE, counterfeit, fraud, sham, imitation, replica, copy, pirate copy; *informal* phoney.

forget ▶ verb ❶ *he forgot where he was* FAIL TO REMEMBER, fail to recall, fail to think of. ❷ *I never forget my briefcase* LEAVE BEHIND, fail to take/bring. ❸ *I forgot to close the door* NEGLECT, fail, omit. ❹ *you can forget that idea* STOP THINKING ABOUT, put out of one's mind, shut out, blank out, pay no heed to, not worry about, ignore, overlook, take no notice of.
– OPPOSITES remember.
■ **forget oneself** MISBEHAVE, behave badly, be naughty, be disobedient, get up to mischief, get up to no good; be bad-mannered, be rude; *informal* carry on, act up.

forgetful ▶ adjective ❶ *I'm so forgetful these days* ABSENT-MINDED, amnesic, amnesiac, vague, disorganized, dreamy, abstracted, with a mind/memory like a sieve; *informal* scatterbrained, scatty. ❷ *forgetful of the time* HEEDLESS, careless, unmindful; inattentive to, negligent about, oblivious to, unconcerned about, indifferent to, not bothered about.
– OPPOSITES reliable, heedful.

forgetfulness ▶ noun ❶ *his excuse was forgetfulness* ABSENT-MINDEDNESS, amnesia, poor memory, a lapse of memory, vagueness, abstraction; *informal* scattiness. ❷ *a forgetfulness of God* NEGLECT, heedlessness, carelessness, disregard; inattention, obliviousness, lack of concern, indifference.
– OPPOSITES reliability, heed.

forgivable ▶ adjective PARDONABLE, excusable, condonable, understandable, tolerable, permissible, allowable, justifiable.

forgive ▶ verb ❶ *she would not forgive him* PARDON, excuse, exonerate, absolve; make allowances for, feel no resentment/malice towards, harbour no grudge against, bury the hatchet with; let bygones be bygones; *informal* let off (the hook); *formal* exculpate. ❷ *you must forgive his rude conduct* EXCUSE, overlook, disregard, ignore, pass over, make allowances for, allow; turn a blind eye to, turn a deaf ear to, wink at, blink at, indulge, tolerate.
– OPPOSITES blame, resent, punish.

forgiveness ▶ noun PARDON, absolution, exoneration, remission, dispensation, indulgence, clemency, mercy; reprieve, amnesty; *informal* let-off; *archaic* shrift.
– OPPOSITES mercilessness, punishment.

forgiving ▶ adjective MERCIFUL, lenient, compassionate, magnanimous, humane, soft-hearted, forbearing, tolerant, indulgent, understanding.
– OPPOSITES merciless, vindictive.

forgo, forego ▶ verb DO WITHOUT, go without, give up, waive, renounce, surrender, relinquish, part with, drop, sacrifice, abstain from, refrain from, eschew, cut out; *informal* swear off; *formal* forswear, abjure.
– OPPOSITES keep.

forgotten ▶ adjective UNREMEMBERED, out of

mind, gone clean out of someone's mind, past recollection, beyond/past recall, consigned to oblivion; left behind; neglected, overlooked, ignored, disregarded, unrecognized.
– OPPOSITES remembered.

fork ▶ verb SPLIT, branch (off), divide, subdivide, separate, part, diverge, go in different directions, bifurcate; *technical* furcate, divaricate, ramify.

forked ▶ adjective SPLIT, branching, branched, bifurcate(d), Y-shaped, V-shaped, pronged, divided; *technical* divaricate.
– OPPOSITES straight.

forlorn ▶ adjective ❶ *he sounded forlorn* UNHAPPY, sad, miserable, sorrowful, dejected, despondent, disconsolate, wretched, abject, down, downcast, dispirited, downhearted, crestfallen, depressed, melancholy, gloomy, glum, mournful, despairing, doleful, woebegone; *informal* blue, down in the mouth, down in the dumps, fed up; *rare* lachrymose. ❷ *a forlorn garden* DESOLATE, deserted, abandoned, forsaken, forgotten, neglected. ❸ *a forlorn attempt* HOPELESS, with no chance of success; useless, futile, pointless, purposeless, vain, unavailing, nugatory; *archaic* bootless.
– OPPOSITES happy, busy, cared for, hopeful, sure-fire.

form ▶ noun ❶ *the general form of the landscape | form is less important than content* SHAPE, configuration, formation, structure, construction, arrangement, appearance, exterior, outline, format, layout, design. ❷ *the human form* BODY, shape, figure, stature, build, frame, physique, anatomy; *informal* vital statistics. ❸ *the infection takes different forms* MANIFESTATION, appearance, embodiment, incarnation, semblance, shape, guise. ❹ *sponsorship is a form of advertising* KIND, sort, type, class, classification, category, variety, genre, brand, style; species, genus, family. ❺ *put the mixture into a form* MOULD, cast, shape, matrix, die. ❻ *what is the form here?* ETIQUETTE, social practice, custom, usage, use, modus operandi, habit, wont, protocol, procedure, rules, convention, tradition, fashion, style; *formal* praxis. ❼ *you have to fill in a form* QUESTIONNAIRE, document, coupon, tear-off slip, paper. ❽ *what form is your daughter in?* CLASS, year; *N. Amer.* grade. ❾ *in top form* FITNESS, condition, fettle, shape, trim, health; *Brit. informal* nick. ❿ (*Brit.*) *a wooden form* BENCH, pew, stall.
– OPPOSITES content.

▶ verb ❶ *the pads are formed from mild steel* MAKE, construct, build, manufacture, fabricate, assemble, put together; create, produce, concoct, devise, contrive, frame, fashion, shape. ❷ *he formed a plan* FORMULATE, devise, conceive, work out, think up, lay, draw up, put together, produce, fashion, concoct, forge, hatch, develop; *informal* dream up. ❸ *they plan to form a company* SET UP, establish, found, launch, float, create, bring into being, institute, start, get going, initiate, bring about, inaugurate. ❹ *a mist was forming* MATERIALIZE, come into being/existence, crystallize, emerge, spring up, develop; take shape, appear, loom, show up, become visible. ❺ *the horse may form bad habits* ACQUIRE, develop, get, pick up, contract, slip into, get into. ❻ *his men formed themselves into an arrowhead* ARRANGE, draw up, line up, assemble, organize, sort, order, range, array, dispose, marshal, deploy. ❼ *the parts of society form an integrated whole* COMPRISE, make, make up, constitute, compose, add up to. ❽ *the city formed a natural meeting point* CONSTITUTE, serve as, act as, function as, perform the function of, do duty for, make. ❾ *natural objects are most important in forming the mind of the child* DEVELOP, mould, shape, train, teach, instruct, educate, school, drill, discipline, prime, prepare, guide, direct, inform, enlighten, inculcate, indoctrinate, edify.
– OPPOSITES dissolve, disappear, break.

■ **good form** GOOD MANNERS, manners, polite behaviour, correct behaviour, convention, etiquette, protocol; *informal* the done thing.

formal ▶ adjective ❶ *a formal dinner* CEREMONIAL, ceremonious, ritualistic, ritual, conventional, traditional; stately, courtly, solemn, dignified; elaborate, ornate, dressy. ❷ *a very formal manner* ALOOF, reserved, remote, detached, unapproachable; stiff, prim, stuffy, staid, ceremonious, correct, proper, decorous, conventional, precise, exact, punctilious, unbending, inflexible, strait-laced; *informal* standoffish. ❸ *a formal garden* SYMMETRICAL, regular, orderly, arranged, methodical, systematic. ❹ *formal permission* OFFICIAL, legal, authorized, approved, validated, certified, endorsed, documented, sanctioned, licensed, recognized, authoritative. ❺ *formal education* CONVENTIONAL, mainstream; school, institutional.
– OPPOSITES informal, casual, colloquial, unofficial.

formality ▶ noun ❶ *the formality of the occasion* CEREMONY, ceremoniousness, ritual, conventionality, red tape, protocol, decorum; stateliness, courtliness, solemnity. ❷ *his formality was off-putting* ALOOFNESS, reserve, remoteness, detachment, unapproachability; stiffness, primness, stuffiness, staidness, correctness, decorum, punctiliousness, inflexibility; *informal* stand-offishness. ❸ *we keep the formalities to a minimum* OFFICIAL PROCEDURE, bureaucracy, red tape, paperwork. ❹ *the medical examination is just a formality* ROUTINE, routine practice, normal procedure. ❺ *promotion looks a formality* MATTER OF COURSE, foregone conclusion, inevitability, certainty; *informal* sure thing.
– OPPOSITES informality.

format ▶ noun DESIGN, style, presentation, appearance, look; form, shape, size; arrangement, plan, structure, scheme, composition, configuration.

formation ▶ noun ❶ *the formation of the island's sand ridges* EMERGENCE, coming into being, genesis, development, evolution, shaping, origination. ❷ *the formation of a new government* ESTABLISHMENT, setting up, start, initiation, institution, foundation, inception, creation, inauguration, launch, flotation. ❸ *the aircraft were flying in tight formation* CONFIGURATION, arrangement, pattern, array, alignment, positioning, disposition, order.
– OPPOSITES destruction, disappearance, dissolution.

formative ▶ adjective ❶ *at a formative stage* DEVELOPMENTAL, developing, growing, malleable, impressionable, susceptible. ❷ *a formative influence* DETERMINING, controlling, influential, guiding, decisive, forming, shaping, determinative.

former ▶ adjective ❶ *the former bishop* ONE-TIME, erstwhile, sometime, ex-, late; PREVIOUS, foregoing, preceding, earlier, prior, past, last. ❷ *in former times* EARLIER, old, past, bygone, olden, long-ago, gone by, long past, of old; *poetic/literary* of yore. ❸ *the former view* FIRST-MENTIONED, first.
– OPPOSITES future, next, latter.

formerly ▶ adverb PREVIOUSLY, earlier, before, until now/then, hitherto, née, once, once upon a time, at one time, in the past; *formal* heretofore.

formidable ▶ adjective ❶ *a formidable curved dagger* INTIMIDATING, forbidding, daunting, disturbing, alarming, frightening, disquieting, brooding, awesome, fearsome, ominous, foreboding, sinister, menacing, threatening, dangerous. ❷ *a formidable task* ONEROUS, arduous, taxing, difficult, hard, heavy, laborious, burdensome, strenuous, back-breaking, uphill, Herculean, monumental, colossal; demanding, tough, challenging, exacting; *formal* exigent; *archaic* toilsome. ❸ *a formidable pianist* CAPABLE, able, proficient, adept, adroit, accomplished, seasoned, skilful, skilled, gifted, talented, masterly, virtuoso, expert, knowledgeable, qualified; impressive, powerful, mighty, terrific, tremendous, great, complete, redoubtable; *informal* mean, wicked, deadly, nifty, crack, ace, wizard, magic; *N. Amer. informal* crackerjack.
– OPPOSITES pleasant-looking, comforting, easy, poor, weak.

formless ▶ adjective SHAPELESS, amorphous, unshaped, indeterminate; structureless, unstructured.
– OPPOSITES shaped, definite.

formula ▶ noun ❶ *a legal formula* FORM OF WORDS, set expression, phrase, saying, aphorism. ❷ *a peace formula* RECIPE, prescription, blueprint, plan, method, procedure, technique, system. ❸ *a formula for removing grease* PREPARATION, concoction, mixture, compound, creation, substance.

formulate ▶ verb ❶ *the miners formulated a plan* DEVISE, conceive, work out, think up, lay, draw up, put together, form, produce, fashion, concoct, contrive, forge, hatch, prepare, develop; *informal* dream up. ❷ *this is how Marx formulated his question* EXPRESS, phrase, word, put into words, frame, couch, put, articulate, convey, say, state, utter.

fornication ▶ noun (*formal*) EXTRAMARITAL SEX, extramarital relations, adultery, infidelity, unfaithfulness, cuckoldry; *informal* hanky-panky, a bit on the side.

forsake ▶ verb (*poetic/literary*) ❶ *he forsook his wife* ABANDON, desert, leave, leave high and dry, turn one's back on, cast aside, break (up) with; jilt, strand, leave stranded, leave in the lurch, throw over; *informal* walk out on, run out on, dump, ditch. ❷ *I won't forsake my vegetarian principles* RENOUNCE, abandon, relinquish, dispense with, disclaim, disown, disavow, discard, wash one's hands of; give up, drop, jettison, do away with, axe; *informal* ditch, scrap, scrub, junk; *formal* forswear.
– OPPOSITES keep to, adopt.

forswear ▶ verb (*formal*) RENOUNCE, relinquish, reject, forgo, disavow, abandon, deny, repudiate, give up, wash one's hands of; eschew, abstain from, refrain from; *informal* kick, pack in, quit, swear off; *Law* disaffirm; *poetic/literary* forsake; *formal* abjure, abnegate.
– OPPOSITES adhere to, persist with, take up.

fort ▶ noun FORTRESS, castle, citadel, blockhouse, burg; stronghold, redoubt, fortification, bastion; fastness.

forte ▶ noun STRENGTH, strong point, speciality, strong suit, talent, special ability, skill, bent, gift, métier; *informal* thing.
– OPPOSITES weakness.

forth ▶ adverb ❶ *smoke billowed forth* OUT, outside, away, off, ahead, forward, into view; into existence. ❷ *from that day forth* ONWARDS, onward, on, forward; for ever, into eternity; until now.

forthcoming ▶ adjective ❶ *forthcoming events* IMMINENT, impending, coming, upcoming, approaching, future; close, (close) at hand, in store, in the wind, in the air, in the offing, in the pipeline, on the horizon, on the way, on us, about to happen. ❷ *no reply was forthcoming* AVAILABLE, ready, at hand, accessible, obtainable, at someone's disposal, on offer; obtained, given, vouchsafed to someone; *informal* up for grabs, on tap. ❸ *he was not very forthcoming about himself* COMMUNICATIVE, talkative, chatty, loquacious, vocal; expansive, expressive, unreserved, uninhibited, outgoing, frank, open, candid; *informal* gabby.
– OPPOSITES past, current, unavailable, uncommunicative.

forthright ▶ adjective FRANK, direct, straightforward, honest, candid, open, sincere, outspoken, straight, blunt, plain-spoken, no-

nonsense, bluff, matter-of-fact, to the point; *informal* upfront.
– OPPOSITES secretive, evasive.

forthwith ▸ **adverb** IMMEDIATELY, at once, instantly, directly, right away, straight away, post-haste, without delay, without hesitation; quickly, speedily, promptly; *informal* pronto.
– OPPOSITES sometime.

fortification ▸ **noun** ❶ RAMPART, wall, defence, bulwark, palisade, stockade, redoubt, earthwork, bastion, parapet, barricade.

fortify ▸ **verb** ❶ *the knights fortified their citadel* BUILD DEFENCES ROUND, strengthen, secure, protect. ❷ *the wall had been fortifed* STRENGTHEN, reinforce, toughen, consolidate, bolster, shore up, brace, buttress. ❸ *I'll have a drink to fortify me* INVIGORATE, strengthen, energize, enliven, liven up, animate, vitalize, rejuvenate, restore, revive, refresh; *informal* pep up, buck up, give a shot in the arm to.
– OPPOSITES weaken, sedate, subdue.

fortitude ▸ **noun** COURAGE, bravery, endurance, resilience, mettle, moral fibre, strength of mind, strength of character, strong-mindedness, backbone, spirit, grit, doughtiness, steadfastness; *informal* guts; *Brit. informal* bottle.
– OPPOSITES faint-heartedness.

fortress ▸ **noun** FORT, castle, citadel, blockhouse, burg; stronghold, redoubt, fortification, bastion; fastness.

fortuitous ▸ **adjective** ❶ *a fortuitous resemblance* CHANCE, adventitious, unexpected, unanticipated, unpredictable, unforeseen, unlooked-for, serendipitous, casual, incidental, coincidental, random, accidental, inadvertent, unintentional, unintended, unplanned, unpremeditated. ❷ *United were saved by a fortuitous penalty* LUCKY, fluky, fortunate, providential, advantageous, timely, opportune, serendipitous, heaven-sent; *Brit. informal* jammy.
– OPPOSITES predictable, unlucky.

fortunate ▸ **adjective** ❶ *he was fortunate that the punishment was so slight* LUCKY, favoured, blessed, blessed with good luck, in luck, having a charmed life, charmed; *informal* sitting pretty; *Brit. informal* jammy. ❷ *in a fortunate position* FAVOURABLE, advantageous, providential, auspicious, welcome, heaven-sent, beneficial, propitious, fortuitous, opportune, happy, felicitous. ❸ *the society gives generously to less fortunate people* WEALTHY, rich, affluent, prosperous, well off, moneyed, well-to-do, well heeled, opulent, comfortable; favoured, privileged.
– OPPOSITES unfortunate, unfavourable, underprivileged.

fortunately ▸ **adverb** LUCKILY, by good luck, by good fortune, as luck would have it, propitiously; mercifully, thankfully; thank goodness, thank God, thank heavens, thank the stars.

fortune ▸ **noun** ❶ *fortune favoured him* CHANCE, accident, coincidence, serendipity, destiny, fortuity, providence; *N. Amer.* happenstance. ❷ *a change of fortune* LUCK, fate, destiny, predestination, the stars, serendipity, karma, kismet, lot. ❸ *an upswing in Sheffield's fortunes* CIRCUMSTANCES, state of affairs, condition, position, situation; plight, predicament. ❹ *he made his fortune in steel* WEALTH, riches, substance, property, assets, resources, means, possessions, treasure, estate. ❺ (*informal*) *this dress cost a fortune* HUGE AMOUNT, vast sum, king's ransom, millions, billions; *informal* small fortune, packet, mint, bundle, pile, wad, arm and a leg, pretty penny, tidy sum, killing, big money; *Brit. informal* bomb, loadsamoney, shedloads; *N. Amer. informal* big bucks, gazillions.
– OPPOSITES pittance.

fortune teller ▸ **noun** CLAIRVOYANT, crystal-gazer, psychic, prophet, seer, oracle, soothsayer, augur, diviner, sibyl; palmist, palm-reader; *Scottish* spaewife.

forum ▸ **noun** ❶ *forums were held for staff to air grievances* MEETING, assembly, gathering, rally, conference, seminar, convention, symposium, colloquium; *N. Amer. & NZ* caucus; *informal* get-together; *formal* colloquy. ❷ *a forum for discussion* SETTING, place, scene, context, stage, framework, backdrop; medium, means, apparatus, auspices. ❸ *the Roman forum* PUBLIC MEETING PLACE, marketplace, agora.

forward ▸ **adverb** ❶ *the traffic moved forward* AHEAD, forwards, onwards, onward, on, further. ❷ *the winner stepped forward* TOWARDS THE FRONT, out, forth, into view. ❸ *from that day forward* ONWARD, onwards, on, forth; for ever, into eternity; until now.
– OPPOSITES backwards.

▸ **adjective** ❶ *in a forward direction* MOVING FORWARDS, moving ahead, onward, advancing, progressing, progressive. ❷ *the fortress served as the Austrian army's forward base against the Russians* FRONT, advance, foremost, head, leading, frontal. ❸ *forward planning* FUTURE, forward-looking, for the future, prospective. ❹ *the girls seemed very forward* BOLD, BRAZEN, brazen-faced, barefaced, brash, shameless, immodest, audacious, daring, presumptuous, familiar, overfamiliar, pert; *informal* brass-necked, fresh.
– OPPOSITES backward, rear, shy, late.

▸ **verb** ❶ *my mother forwarded me your letter* SEND ON, post on, redirect, readdress, pass on. ❷ *the goods were forwarded by sea* SEND, dispatch, transmit, carry, convey, deliver, ship. ❸ *Sir William forwarded his plan* ADVANCE, further, promote, assist, carry forward, hasten, hurry along, expedite, accelerate, speed up.

forward-looking ▸ **adjective** PROGRESSIVE, enlightened, dynamic, pushing, bold, enterprising, ambitious, pioneering, innovative, modern, avant-garde, positive, reforming, radical; *informal* go-ahead, go-getting.

–OPPOSITES backward-looking.

forwards ▶ adverb. *See* FORWARD adverb.

fossil ▶ noun PETRIFIED REMAINS, petrified impression, remnant, relic; *Geology* reliquiae.

fossilized ▶ adjective ❶ *fossilized remains* petrified, ossified. ❷ *a fossilized idea* ARCHAIC, antiquated, antediluvian, old-fashioned, quaint, outdated, outmoded, behind the times, anachronistic, stuck in time; *informal* prehistoric.

foster ▶ verb ❶ *he fostered the arts* ENCOURAGE, promote, further, stimulate, advance, forward, cultivate, nurture, strengthen, enrich; help, aid, abet, assist, contribute to, support, back. ❷ *they started fostering children* BRING UP, rear, raise, care for, take care of, look after, nurture, provide for; mother, parent.
–OPPOSITES neglect, suppress.

foul ▶ adjective ❶ *a foul stench* DISGUSTING, revolting, repulsive, repugnant, abhorrent, loathsome, offensive, sickening, nauseating, nauseous, stomach-churning, stomach-turning, distasteful, obnoxious, objectionable, odious, noxious; *N. Amer.* vomitous; *informal* ghastly, gruesome, gross, putrid, yucky, skanky, sick-making; *Brit. informal* beastly; *Austral. informal* on the nose; *poetic/literary* miasmic, noisome, mephitic. ❷ *a foul mess* DIRTY, filthy, mucky, grimy, grubby, muddy, muddied, unclean, unwashed; squalid, sordid, soiled, sullied, scummy; rotten, defiled, decaying, putrid, putrefied, smelly, fetid; *informal* cruddy, yucky, icky; *Brit. informal* manky, gungy, grotty; *rare* feculent. ❸ *he had been foul to her* UNKIND, malicious, mean, nasty, unpleasant, unfriendly, spiteful, cruel, vicious, base, malevolent, despicable, contemptible; *informal* horrible, horrid, rotten; *Brit. informal* beastly. ❹ *foul weather* INCLEMENT, unpleasant, disagreeable, bad; rough, stormy, squally, gusty, windy, blustery, wild, blowy, rainy, wet; *Brit. informal* filthy. ❺ *foul drinking water* CONTAMINATED, polluted, infected, tainted, impure, filthy, dirty, unclean; *rare* feculent. ❻ *a foul deed* EVIL, wicked, bad, wrong, immoral, sinful, vile, dishonourable, corrupt, iniquitous, depraved, villainous, nefarious, vicious, malicious; malevolent, sinister, demonic, devilish, diabolical, fiendish, dark; monstrous, shocking, despicable, atrocious, heinous, odious, contemptible, horrible, execrable; *informal* low-down, dirty. ❼ *foul language* VULGAR, crude, coarse, filthy, dirty, obscene, indecent, indelicate, naughty, lewd, suggestive, smutty, ribald, salacious, scatological, offensive, abusive; *informal* blue. ❽ *a foul tackle* UNFAIR, illegal, unsporting, unsportsmanlike, below the belt, dirty.
–OPPOSITES pleasant, kind, fair, clean, righteous, mild, fair.
▶ verb ❶ *the river had been fouled with waste* DIRTY, infect, pollute, contaminate, poison, taint, sully, soil, stain, blacken, muddy, splash, spatter, smear, blight, defile, make filthy. ❷ *the vessel had fouled her nets* TANGLE UP, entangle, snarl, catch, entwine, enmesh, twist.
–OPPOSITES clean up, disentangle.

foul-mouthed ▶ adjective VULGAR, crude, coarse; obscene, rude, smutty, dirty, filthy, indecent, indelicate, offensive, lewd, X-rated, scatological, foul, abusive; *informal* blue.

found ▶ verb ❶ *he founded his company in 1989* ESTABLISH, set up, start, begin, get going, institute, inaugurate, launch, float, form, create, bring into being, originate, develop. ❷ *they founded a new city* BUILD, construct, erect, put up; plan, lay plans for. ❸ *their relationship was founded on trust* BASE, build, construct; ground in, root in; rest, hinge, depend.
–OPPOSITES dissolve, liquidate, abandon, demolish.

foundation ▶ noun ❶ *the foundations of a wall* FOOTING, foot, base, substructure, underpinning; bottom, bedrock, substratum. ❷ *the report has a scientific foundation* BASIS, starting point, base, point of departure, beginning, premise; principles, fundamentals, rudiments; cornerstone, core, heart, thrust, essence, kernel. ❸ *there was no foundation for the claim* JUSTIFICATION, grounds, defence, reason, rationale, cause, basis, motive, excuse, call, pretext, provocation. ❹ *an educational foundation* ENDOWED INSTITUTION, charitable body, funding agency, source of funds.

founder[1] ▶ noun *the founder of modern physics* ORIGINATOR, creator, (founding) father, prime mover, architect, engineer, designer, developer, pioneer, author, planner, inventor, mastermind; *poetic/literary* begetter.

founder[2] ▶ verb ❶ *the ship foundered* SINK, go to the bottom, go down, be lost at sea; *informal* go to Davy Jones's locker. ❷ *the scheme foundered* FAIL, be unsuccessful, not succeed, fall flat, fall through, collapse, backfire, meet with disaster, come to nothing/naught; *informal* flop, bomb. ❸ *their horses foundered in the river bed* STUMBLE, trip, trip up, lose one's balance, lose/miss one's footing, slip, stagger, lurch, totter, fall, tumble, topple, sprawl, collapse.
–OPPOSITES succeed.

foundling ▶ noun ABANDONED INFANT, waif, stray, orphan, outcast; *archaic* wastrel.

fountain ▶ noun ❶ *a fountain of water* JET, spray, spout, spurt, well, fount, cascade. ❷ *a fountain of knowledge* SOURCE, fount, well; reservoir, fund, mass, mine.

four ▶ cardinal number QUARTET, foursome, tetralogy, quadruplets; *technical* tetrad; *rare* quadrumvirate.
–RELATED TERMS quadri-, tetra-.

foxy ▶ adjective (*informal*) CRAFTY, wily, artful, guileful, devious, sly, scheming, designing, calculating, Machiavellian; shrewd, astute, clever, canny; deceitful, deceptive, duplicitous; *archaic* subtle.

foyer ▶ noun ENTRANCE HALL, hall, hallway, entrance, entry, porch, reception area, atrium, concourse, lobby; *N. Amer.* entryway.

fracas ▶ noun DISTURBANCE, brawl, melee, rumpus, skirmish, struggle, scuffle, scrum, clash, fisticuffs, altercation; *informal* scrap, dust-up, set-to, shindy, shindig; *Brit. informal* punch-up, bust-up, ruck; *N. Amer. informal* rough house, brannigan; *Austral./NZ informal* stoush; *Law, dated* affray.

fraction ▶ noun ❶ *a fraction of the population* PART, subdivision, division, portion, segment, slice, section, sector; proportion, percentage, ratio, measure. ❷ *only a fraction of the collection* TINY PART, fragment, snippet, snatch, smattering, selection. ❸ *he moved a fraction closer* TINY AMOUNT, little, bit, touch, soupçon, trifle, mite, shade, jot; *informal* smidgen, smidge, tad.
– OPPOSITES whole.

fractious ▶ adjective ❶ *fractious children* GRUMPY, bad-tempered, irascible, irritable, crotchety, grouchy, cantankerous, short-tempered, tetchy, testy, curmudgeonly, ill-tempered, ill-humoured, peevish, cross, pettish, waspish, crabbed, crabby, crusty, prickly, touchy; *informal* snappish, snappy, chippy; *Brit. informal* shirty, stroppy, narky, ratty; *N. Amer. informal* cranky, ornery; *Austral./NZ informal* snaky. ❷ *the fractious parliamentary party* WAYWARD, unruly, uncontrollable, unmanageable, out of hand, obstreperous, difficult, headstrong, recalcitrant, intractable; disobedient, insubordinate, disruptive, disorderly, undisciplined; contrary, wilful; *formal* refractory; *archaic* contumacious.
– OPPOSITES contented, affable, dutiful.

fracture ▶ noun ❶ *the risk of vertebral fracture* BREAKING, breakage, cracking, fragmentation, splintering, rupture. ❷ *tiny fractures in the rock* CRACK, split, fissure, crevice, break, rupture, breach, rift, cleft, chink, interstice; crazing.
▶ verb *the glass fractured* BREAK, crack, shatter, splinter, split, rupture; *informal* bust.

fragile ▶ adjective ❶ *fragile porcelain* BREAKABLE, easily broken; delicate, dainty, fine, flimsy; eggshell; *formal* frangible. ❷ *the fragile ceasefire* TENUOUS, shaky, insecure, unreliable, vulnerable, flimsy. ❸ *she is still very fragile* WEAK, delicate, frail, debilitated; ill, unwell, ailing, poorly, sickly, infirm, enfeebled.
– OPPOSITES strong, durable, robust.

fragment ▶ noun ❶ *meteorite fragments* PIECE, bit, particle, speck; chip, shard, sliver, splinter; shaving, paring, snippet, scrap, offcut, flake, shred, wisp, morsel; *Scottish* skelf. ❷ *a fragment of conversation* SNATCH, snippet, scrap, bit.
▶ verb *explosions caused the chalk to fragment* BREAK UP, break, break into pieces, crack open/apart, shatter, splinter, fracture; disintegrate, fall to pieces, fall apart.

fragmentary ▶ adjective INCOMPLETE, fragmented, disconnected, disjointed, broken, discontinuous, piecemeal, scrappy, bitty, sketchy, uneven, patchy.

fragrance ▶ noun ❶ *the fragrance of spring flowers* SWEET SMELL, scent, perfume, bouquet; aroma, redolence, nose. ❷ *a bottle of fragrance* PERFUME, scent, eau de toilette, toilet water; eau de cologne, cologne; aftershave.

fragrant ▶ adjective SWEET-SCENTED, sweet-smelling, scented, perfumed, aromatic, perfumy; *poetic/literary* redolent.
– OPPOSITES smelly.

frail ▶ adjective ❶ *a frail old lady* WEAK, delicate, feeble, enfeebled, debilitated; infirm, ill, ailing, unwell, sickly, poorly, in poor health. ❷ *a frail structure* FRAGILE, breakable, easily damaged, delicate, flimsy, insubstantial, unsteady, unstable, rickety; *formal* frangible.
– OPPOSITES strong, robust.

frailty ▶ noun ❶ *the frailty of old age* INFIRMITY, weakness, enfeeblement, debility; fragility, delicacy; ill health, sickliness. ❷ *his many frailties* WEAKNESS, fallibility; weak point, flaw, imperfection, defect, failing, fault, shortcoming, deficiency, inadequacy, limitation.
– OPPOSITES strength.

frame ▶ noun ❶ *a tubular metal frame* FRAMEWORK, structure, substructure, skeleton, chassis, shell, casing, body, bodywork; support, scaffolding, foundation. ❷ *his tall, slender frame* BODY, figure, form, shape, physique, build, size, proportions. ❸ *a photograph frame* SETTING, mount, mounting.
▶ verb ❶ *he had the picture framed* MOUNT, set in a frame. ❷ *the legislators who frame the regulations* FORMULATE, draw up, draft, plan, shape, compose, put together, form, devise, create, establish, conceive, think up, originate; *informal* dream up.
■ **frame of mind** MOOD, state of mind, humour, temper, disposition.

frame-up ▶ noun (*informal*) CONSPIRACY, plot; trick, trap, entrapment; *informal* put-up job, fit-up, set-up.

framework ▶ noun ❶ *a metal framework* FRAME, substructure, structure, skeleton, chassis, shell, body, bodywork; support, scaffolding, foundation. ❷ *the framework of society* STRUCTURE, shape, fabric, order, scheme, system, organization, construction, configuration, composition; *informal* make-up.

franchise ▶ noun ❶ *the extension of the franchise to women* SUFFRAGE, the vote, the right to vote, voting rights, enfranchisement. ❷ *the company lost its TV franchise* WARRANT, charter, licence, permit, authorization, permission, sanction.

frank[1] ▶ adjective ❶ *he was quite frank with me* CANDID, direct, forthright, plain, plain-spoken, straight, straightforward, straight from the

shoulder, explicit, to the point, matter-of-fact; open, honest, truthful, sincere; outspoken, bluff, blunt, unsparing, not afraid to call a spade a spade; *informal* upfront. ❷ *she looked at Sam with frank admiration* OPEN, undisguised, unconcealed, naked, unmistakable, clear, obvious, transparent, patent, manifest, evident, perceptible, palpable; blatant, barefaced, flagrant.
– OPPOSITES evasive.

frank² ▶ **verb** *the envelope had not been franked* STAMP, postmark; imprint, print, mark.

frankly ▶ **adverb** ❶ *frankly, I'm not very interested* TO BE FRANK, to be honest, to tell you the truth, to be truthful, in all honesty, as it happens. ❷ *he stated the case quite frankly* CANDIDLY, directly, plainly, straightforwardly, straight from the shoulder, forthrightly, openly, honestly, without beating about the bush, without mincing one's words, without prevarication, point-blank; bluntly, outspokenly, with no holds barred.

frantic ▶ **adjective** PANIC-STRICKEN, panic-struck, panicky, beside oneself, at one's wits' end, distraught, overwrought, worked up, agitated, distressed; frenzied, wild, frenetic, fraught, feverish, hysterical, desperate; *informal* in a state, in a tizzy/tizz, wound up, het up, in a flap, tearing one's hair out; *Brit. informal* having kittens, in a flat spin.
– OPPOSITES calm.

fraternity ▶ **noun** ❶ *a spirit of fraternity* BROTHERHOOD, fellowship, kinship, friendship, (mutual) support, solidarity, community, union, togetherness; sisterhood. ❷ *the teaching fraternity* PROFESSION, body of workers; band, group, set, circle. ❸ (*N. Amer.*) *a college fraternity* SOCIETY, club, association; group, set.

fraternize ▶ **verb** ASSOCIATE, mix, consort, socialize, keep company, rub shoulders; *N. Amer.* rub elbows; *informal* hang around/round, hang out, run around, knock about/around, hobnob, be thick with.

fraud ▶ **noun** ❶ *he was arrested for fraud* FRAUDULENCE, sharp practice, cheating, swindling, embezzlement, deceit, deception, double-dealing, chicanery. ❷ *social security frauds* SWINDLE, racket, deception, trick, cheat, hoax; *informal* scam, con, con trick, rip-off, sting, gyp, diddle, fiddle; *N. Amer. informal* bunco, hustle, grift. ❸ *they exposed him as a fraud* IMPOSTOR, fake, sham, charlatan, quack, mountebank; swindler, fraudster, racketeer, cheat, confidence trickster; *informal* phoney, con man, con artist.

fraudulent ▶ **adjective** DISHONEST, cheating, swindling, corrupt, criminal, illegal, unlawful, illicit; deceitful, double-dealing, duplicitous, dishonourable, unscrupulous, unprincipled; *informal* crooked, shady, dirty; *Brit. informal* bent, dodgy; *Austral./NZ informal* shonky.
– OPPOSITES honest.

fraught ▶ **adjective** ❶ *their world is fraught with danger* FULL OF, filled with, rife with; attended by, accompanied by. ❷ *she sounded a bit fraught* ANXIOUS, worried, stressed, upset, distraught, overwrought, worked up, agitated, distressed, distracted, desperate, frantic, panic-stricken, panic-struck, panicky; beside oneself, at one's wits' end, at the end of one's tether; *informal* wound up, in a state, in a flap, in a cold sweat, tearing one's hair out; *Brit. informal* having kittens, in a flat spin.

fray¹ ▶ **verb** ❶ *cheap fabric soon frays* UNRAVEL, wear, wear thin, wear out/through, become worn. ❷ *her nerves were frayed* STRAIN, tax, overtax, put on edge.

fray² ▶ **noun** *two men started the fray* BATTLE, fight, engagement, conflict, clash, skirmish, altercation, tussle, struggle, scuffle, melee, brawl; *informal* scrap, dust-up, set-to; *Brit. informal* punch-up, bust-up; *Scottish informal* rammy; *Law, dated* affray.

frayed ▶ **adjective** ❶ *a frayed shirt collar* WORN, well worn, threadbare, tattered, ragged, holey, moth-eaten, in holes, the worse for wear; *informal* tatty; *N. Amer. informal* raggedy. ❷ *his frayed nerves* STRAINED, fraught, tense, edgy, stressed.

freak ▶ **noun** ❶ *a genetically engineered freak* ABERRATION, abnormality, irregularity, oddity; monster, monstrosity, mutant; freak of nature. ❷ *the accident was a complete freak* ANOMALY, aberration, rarity, oddity, unusual occurrence; fluke, twist of fate. ❸ (*informal*) *they were dismissed as a bunch of freaks* ODDITY, eccentric, misfit; crank, lunatic; *informal* oddball, weirdo, nutcase, nut; *Brit. informal* nutter; *N. Amer. informal* wacko, kook. ❹ (*informal*) *a fitness freak* ENTHUSIAST, fan, devotee, lover, aficionado; *informal* fiend, nut, fanatic, addict, maniac.

▶ **adjective** *a freak storm | a freak result* UNUSUAL, anomalous, aberrant, atypical, unrepresentative, irregular, fluky, exceptional, unaccountable, bizarre, queer, peculiar, odd, freakish; unpredictable, unforeseeable, unexpected, unanticipated, surprising; rare, singular, isolated.
– OPPOSITES normal.

▶ **verb** (*informal*) *he freaked out* GO CRAZY, go mad, go out of one's mind, go to pieces, crack, snap, lose control; panic, become hysterical; *informal* lose it, lose one's cool, crack up; *N. Amer. informal* go ape, go postal.

freakish ▶ **adjective** *freakish weather. See* FREAK adjective.

freaky ▶ **adjective** (*informal*). *See* ODD senses 1, 2.

free ▶ **adjective** ❶ *admission is free* WITHOUT CHARGE, free of charge, for nothing; complimentary, gratis; *informal* for free, on the house. ❷ *she was free of any pressures* UNENCUMBERED BY, unaffected by, clear of, without, rid of; exempt from, not liable to, safe from, immune to, excused of; *informal* sans, minus. ❸ *I'm free this afternoon* UNOCCUPIED, not busy, available, between appointments; off duty, off work, off, on holiday, on leave; at leisure, with time on one's hands, with time to spare. ❹ *the bathroom's free now* VACANT, empty, available, unoccupied, not taken, not in use. ❺ *a citizen of a proud free nation* INDEPENDENT, self-governing, self-governed, self-ruling, self-determining, non-aligned, sovereign, autonomous; democratic. ❻ *the killer is still free* ON THE LOOSE, at liberty, at large; loose, unconfined, unbound, untied, unchained, untethered, unshackled, unfettered, unrestrained. ❼ *you are free to leave* ABLE TO, in a position to, capable of; ALLOWED, permitted. ❽ *the free flow of water* UNIMPEDED, unobstructed, unrestricted, unhampered, clear, open, unblocked. ❾ *she was free with her money* GENEROUS, liberal, open-handed, unstinting, bountiful; lavish, extravagant, prodigal. ❿ *his free and hearty manner* FRANK, open, candid, direct, plain-spoken; unrestrained, unconstrained, free and easy, uninhibited.

– OPPOSITES busy, occupied, captive, mean.

▸ **verb** ❶ *three of the hostages were freed* RELEASE, set free, let go, liberate, discharge, deliver; set loose, let loose, turn loose, untie, unchain, unfetter, unshackle, unleash; *poetic/literary* disenthral; *historical* manumit. ❷ *the victims were freed by firefighters* EXTRICATE, release, get out, pull out, pull free; rescue, set free. ❸ *they wish to be freed from all legal ties* EXEMPT, except, excuse, relieve, unburden, disburden.

– OPPOSITES confine, trap.

■ **free and easy** EASY-GOING, relaxed, casual, informal, unceremonious, unforced, natural, open, spontaneous, uninhibited, friendly; tolerant, liberal; *informal* laid-back.

■ **a free hand** FREE REIN, carte blanche, freedom, liberty, licence, latitude, leeway.

freebooter ▸ **noun** PIRATE, marauder, raider; bandit, robber; adventurer, swashbuckler; *historical* privateer; *archaic* buccaneer, corsair.

freedom ▸ **noun** ❶ *a desperate bid for freedom* LIBERTY, liberation, release, deliverance, delivery, discharge; *poetic/literary* disenthralment; *historical* manumission. ❷ *national revolution was the only path to freedom* INDEPENDENCE, self-government, self-determination, self rule, home rule, sovereignty, non-alignment, autonomy; democracy. ❸ *freedom from local political accountability* EXEMPTION, immunity, dispensation; impunity. ❹ *patients have more freedom to choose who treats them* RIGHT, entitlement, privilege, prerogative; scope, latitude, leeway, flexibility, space, breathing space, room, elbow room; licence, leave, free rein, a free hand, carte blanche.

– OPPOSITES captivity, subjection, liability.

free-for-all ▸ **noun** BRAWL, fight, scuffle, tussle, struggle, confrontation, clash, altercation, fray, fracas, melee, rumpus, disturbance; breach of the peace; *informal* dust-up, scrap, set-to, shindy; *Brit. informal* punch-up, bust-up, barney; *Scottish informal* rammy; *Law, dated* affray.

freely ▸ **adverb** ❶ *may I speak freely?* OPENLY, candidly, frankly, directly, without constraint, without inhibition; truthfully, honestly, without beating about the bush, without mincing one's words, without prevarication. ❷ *they gave their time and labour freely* VOLUNTARILY, willingly, readily; of one's own volition, of one's own accord, of one's own free will, without compulsion.

freethinker ▸ **noun** NONCONFORMIST, individualist, independent, maverick; agnostic, atheist, non-believer, unbeliever.

– OPPOSITES conformist.

free will ▸ **noun** SELF-DETERMINATION, freedom of choice, autonomy, liberty, independence.

■ **of one's own free will** VOLUNTARILY, willingly, readily, freely, without reluctance, without compulsion, of one's own accord, of one's own volition, of one's own choosing.

freeze ▸ **verb** ❶ *the stream had frozen* ICE OVER, ice up, solidify. ❷ *the campers stifled in summer and froze in winter* BE VERY COLD, be numb with cold, turn blue with cold, shiver, be chilled to the bone/marrow. ❸ *she froze in horror* STOP DEAD, stop in one's tracks, stop, stand (stock) still, go rigid, become motionless, become paralysed. ❹ *the prices of basic foodstuffs were frozen* FIX, hold, peg, set; limit, restrict, cap, confine, regulate; hold/keep down.

– OPPOSITES thaw.

■ **freeze someone out** (*informal*) EXCLUDE, leave out, shut out, cut out, ignore, ostracize, spurn, snub, shun, cut, cut dead, turn one's back on, cold-shoulder, give someone the cold shoulder, leave out in the cold; *Brit.* send to Coventry; *Brit. informal* blank.

freezing ▸ **adjective** ❶ *a freezing wind* BITTER, bitterly cold, icy, chill, frosty, glacial, wintry, sub-zero; raw, biting, piercing, penetrating, cutting, numbing; arctic, polar, Siberian. ❷ *you must be freezing* FROZEN, extremely cold, numb with cold, chilled to the bone/marrow, frozen stiff, shivery, shivering; *informal* frozen to death.

– OPPOSITES balmy, hot.

freight ▸ **noun** ❶ *freight carried by rail* GOODS, cargo, freightage; load, consignment, delivery, shipment; merchandise. ❷ *the importance of air freight* TRANSPORTATION, transport, conveyance, freightage, carriage, portage, haulage.

frenetic ▸ **adjective** FRANTIC, wild, frenzied, hectic, fraught, feverish, fevered, mad, manic, hyperactive, energetic, intense, fast and furious, turbulent, tumultuous.

– OPPOSITES calm.

frenzied ▸ **adjective** FRANTIC, wild, frenetic, hectic, fraught, feverish, fevered, mad, crazed, manic, intense, furious, uncontrolled, out of control.

– OPPOSITES calm.

frenzy ▶ **noun** ❶ *the crowd worked themselves into a state of frenzy* HYSTERIA, madness, mania, dementedness, delirium, feverishness, fever, wildness, agitation, turmoil, tumult; wild excitement, euphoria, elation, ecstasy. ❷ *a frenzy of anger* FIT, paroxysm, spasm, bout.

frequency ▶ **noun** RATE OF OCCURRENCE, incidence, amount, commonness, prevalence; *Statistics* distribution.

frequent ▶ **adjective** ❶ *frequent bouts of chest infection* RECURRENT, recurring, repeated, periodic, continual, one after another, successive; many, numerous, lots of, several. ❷ *a frequent business traveller* HABITUAL, regular.
– OPPOSITES occasional.
▶ **verb** *he frequented chic supper clubs* VISIT, patronize, spend time in, visit regularly, be a regular visitor to, haunt; *informal* hang out at.

frequenter ▶ **noun** HABITUÉ, patron, regular, regular visitor, regular customer, regular client, familiar face.

frequently ▶ **adverb** REGULARLY, often, very often, all the time, habitually, customarily, routinely; many times, many a time, lots of times, again and again, time and again, over and over again, repeatedly, recurrently, continually; *N. Amer.* oftentimes; *poetic/literary* oft, oft times.

fresh ▶ **adjective** ❶ *fresh fruit* NEWLY PICKED, garden-fresh, crisp, unwilted; raw, natural, unprocessed. ❷ *a fresh sheet of paper* CLEAN, blank, empty, clear, white; unused, new, pristine, unmarked, untouched. ❸ *a fresh approach* NEW, recent, latest, up-to-date, modern, modernistic, ultra-modern, newfangled; original, novel, different, innovative, unusual, unconventional, unorthodox; radical, revolutionary; *informal* offbeat. ❹ *fresh recruits* YOUNG, youthful; new, inexperienced, naive, untrained, unqualified, untried, raw; *informal* wet behind the ears. ❺ *he felt fresh and happy to be alive* REFRESHED, rested, restored, revived; (as) fresh as a daisy, energetic, vigorous, invigorated, full of vim and vigour, lively, vibrant, spry, sprightly, bright, alert, perky; *informal* full of beans, raring to go, bright-eyed and bushy-tailed, chirpy, chipper. ❻ *her fresh complexion* HEALTHY, healthy-looking, clear, bright, youthful, blooming, glowing, unblemished; fair, rosy, rosy-cheeked, pink, ruddy. ❼ *the night air was fresh* COOL, crisp, refreshing, invigorating, tonic; pure, clean, clear, uncontaminated, untainted. ❽ *a fresh wind* CHILLY, chill, cool, cold, brisk, bracing, invigorating; strong; *informal* nippy; *Brit. informal* parky. ❾ (*informal*) *that young man has been getting a little too fresh* IMPUDENT, impertinent, insolent, presumptuous, forward, cheeky, disrespectful, rude, brazen, shameless, pert, bold, (as) bold as brass; *informal* brass-necked, lippy, mouthy, saucy; *N. Amer. informal* sassy.
– OPPOSITES stale, old, tired, warm.

freshen ▶ **verb** ❶ *the cold water freshened him* REFRESH, revitalize, restore, revive, wake up, rouse, enliven, liven up, energize, brace, invigorate; *informal* buck up, pep up. ❷ *he opened a window to freshen the room* VENTILATE, air, aerate, oxygenate; deodorize, purify, cleanse; refresh, cool. ❸ *she went to freshen up before dinner* HAVE A WASH, wash oneself, bathe, shower; tidy oneself (up), spruce oneself up, smarten oneself up, groom oneself, primp oneself; *N. Amer.* wash up; *informal* titivate oneself, do oneself up, doll oneself up; *Brit. informal* tart oneself up; *formal or humorous* perform one's ablutions. ❹ (*N. Amer.*) *the waitress freshened their coffee* REFILL, top up, fill up, replenish.

freshman, freshwoman ▶ **noun** FIRST YEAR STUDENT, undergraduate; newcomer, new recruit, starter, probationer; beginner, learner, novice; *N. Amer.* tenderfoot; *informal* undergrad, rookie; *Brit. informal* fresher; *N. Amer. informal* greenhorn.

fret ▶ **verb** ❶ *she was fretting about Jonathan* WORRY, be anxious, feel uneasy, be distressed, be upset, upset oneself, concern oneself; agonize, sigh, pine, brood, eat one's heart out. ❷ *his absence began to fret her* TROUBLE, bother, concern, perturb, disturb, disquiet, disconcert, distress, upset, alarm, panic, agitate; *informal* eat away at.

fretful ▶ **adjective** DISTRESSED, upset, miserable, unsettled, uneasy, ill at ease, uncomfortable, edgy, agitated, worked up, tense, stressed, restive, fidgety; querulous, irritable, cross, fractious, peevish, petulant, out of sorts, bad-tempered, irascible, grumpy, crotchety, captious, testy, tetchy; *N. Amer. informal* cranky; *informal* het up, uptight, twitchy, crabby.

friable ▶ **adjective** CRUMBLY, easily crumbled, powdery, dusty, chalky, soft; dry, crisp, brittle.

friar ▶ **noun** MONK, brother, religious, coenobite, contemplative; prior, abbot.

friction ▶ **noun** ❶ *a lubrication system which reduces friction* ABRASION, rubbing, chafing, grating, rasping, scraping; resistance, drag. ❷ *there was considerable friction between father and son* DISCORD, strife, conflict, disagreement, dissension, dissent, opposition, contention, dispute, disputation, arguing, argument, quarrelling, bickering, squabbling, wrangling, fighting, feuding, rivalry; hostility, animosity, antipathy, enmity, antagonism, resentment, acrimony, bitterness, bad feeling, ill feeling, ill will, bad blood.
– OPPOSITES harmony.

friend ▶ **noun** ❶ *a close friend* COMPANION, boon companion, bosom friend, best friend, intimate, confidante, confidant, familiar, soul mate, alter ego, second self, playmate, playfellow, classmate, schoolmate, workmate; ally, associate; sister, brother; *informal* pal,

chum, sidekick, crony, main man; *Brit. informal* mate, china, mucker; *N. English informal* marrow, marra; *N. Amer. informal* buddy, amigo, compadre, homeboy; *archaic* compeer. ❷ *the friends of the Royal Botanic Garden* PATRON, backer, supporter, benefactor, benefactress, sponsor; well-wisher, defender, champion; *informal* angel.
– OPPOSITES enemy.

friendless ▶ **adjective** ALONE, all alone, by oneself, solitary, lonely, with no one to turn to, lone, without friends, companionless, unbefriended, unpopular, unwanted, unloved, abandoned, rejected, forsaken, shunned, spurned, forlorn; *N. Amer.* lonesome.
– OPPOSITES popular.

friendliness ▶ **noun** AFFABILITY, amiability, geniality, congeniality, bonhomie, cordiality, good nature, good humour, warmth, affection, demonstrativeness, conviviality, joviality, companionability, sociability, gregariousness, camaraderie, neighbourliness, hospitableness, approachability, accessibility, openness, kindness, kindliness, sympathy, amenability, benevolence.

friendly ▶ **adjective** ❶ *a friendly woman* AFFABLE, amiable, genial, congenial, cordial, warm, affectionate, demonstrative, convivial, companionable, sociable, gregarious, outgoing, clubbable, comradely, neighbourly, hospitable, approachable, easy to get on with, accessible, communicative, open, unreserved, easygoing, good-natured, kindly, benign, amenable, agreeable, obliging, sympathetic, well disposed, benevolent; *Scottish* couthy; *informal* chummy, pally, clubby; *Brit. informal* matey; *N. Amer. informal* buddy-buddy. ❷ *friendly conversation* AMICABLE, congenial, cordial, pleasant, easy, relaxed, casual, informal, unceremonious; close, intimate, familiar. ❸ *a friendly wind swept the boat to the shore* FAVOURABLE, advantageous, helpful; lucky, providential.
– OPPOSITES hostile.

friendship ▶ **noun** ❶ *lasting friendships* RELATIONSHIP, close relationship, attachment, mutual attachment, association, bond, tie, link, union. ❷ *old ties of love and friendship* AMITY, camaraderie, friendliness, comradeship, companionship, fellowship, fellow feeling, closeness, affinity, rapport, understanding, harmony, unity; intimacy, mutual affection.
– OPPOSITES enmity.

fright ▶ **noun** ❶ *she was paralysed with fright* FEAR, fearfulness, terror, horror, alarm, panic, dread, trepidation, dismay, nervousness, apprehension, apprehensiveness, perturbation, disquiet; *informal* jitteriness, twitchiness. ❷ *the experience gave everyone a fright* SCARE, shock, surprise, turn, jolt, start; the shivers, the shakes; *informal* the jitters, the heebie-jeebies, the willies, the creeps, the collywobbles, a cold sweat; *Brit. informal* the (screaming) abdabs, butterflies (in one's stomach). ❸ (*informal*) *she looked an absolute fright* UGLY SIGHT, eyesore, monstrosity; *informal* mess, sight, state, blot on the landscape.

frighten ▶ **verb** SCARE, startle, alarm, terrify, petrify, shock, chill, panic, shake, disturb, dismay, unnerve, unman, intimidate, terrorize, cow, daunt; strike terror into, put the fear of God into, chill someone to the bone/marrow, make someone's blood run cold; *informal* scare the living daylights out of, scare stiff, scare someone out of their wits, scare witless, scare to death, scare the pants off, spook, make someone's hair stand on end, throw into a blue funk, make someone jump out of their skin; *Brit. informal* put the wind up, give someone the heebie-jeebies, make someone's hair curl; *Irish informal* scare the bejesus out of; *archaic* affright.

frightening ▶ **adjective** TERRIFYING, horrifying, alarming, startling, chilling, spine-chilling, hair-raising, blood-curdling, disturbing, unnerving, intimidating, daunting, dismaying, upsetting, harrowing, traumatic; eerie, sinister, fearsome, nightmarish, macabre, menacing; *Scottish* eldritch; *informal* scary, spooky, creepy, hairy.

frightful ▶ **adjective** ❶ *a frightful accident* HORRIBLE, horrific, ghastly, horrendous, serious, awful, dreadful, terrible, nasty, grim, dire, unspeakable; alarming, shocking, terrifying, harrowing, appalling, fearful; hideous, gruesome, grisly; *informal* horrid; *formal* grievous. ❷ (*informal*) *a frightful racket* AWFUL, very bad, terrible, dreadful, appalling, ghastly, abominable; unpleasant, disagreeable, lamentable, deplorable, insufferable, unbearable; *informal* God-awful; *Brit. informal* beastly.

frigid ▶ **adjective** ❶ *a frigid January night* VERY COLD, bitterly cold, bitter, freezing, frozen, frosty, icy, gelid, chilly, chill, wintry, bleak, sub-zero, arctic, Siberian, polar, glacial; *informal* nippy; *Brit. informal* parky. ❷ *frigid politeness* STIFF, formal, stony, wooden, unemotional, passionless, unfeeling, indifferent, unresponsive, unenthusiastic, austere, distant, aloof, remote, reserved, unapproachable; frosty, cold, icy, cool, unsmiling, forbidding, unfriendly, unwelcoming, hostile; *informal* offish, stand-offish.
– OPPOSITES hot, friendly.

frill ▶ **noun** ❶ *a full skirt with a wide frill* RUFFLE, flounce, ruff, furbelow, jabot, peplum, ruche, ruching, fringe; *archaic* purfle. ❷ *a comfortable flat with no frills* OSTENTATION, ornamentation, decoration, embellishment, fanciness, fuss, chichi, gilding, excess; trimmings, extras, additions, non-essentials, luxuries, extravagances, superfluities.

frilly ▶ **adjective** RUFFLED, flounced, frilled, crimped, ruched, trimmed, lacy, frothy; fancy, ornate.

fringe ▶ noun ❶ *the city's northern fringe* PERIMETER, periphery, border, borderline, margin, rim, outer edge, edge, extremity, limit; outer limits, limits, borders, bounds, outskirts, marches; *poetic/literary* marge, bourn. ❷ *blue curtains with a yellow fringe* EDGING, edge, border, trimming, frill, flounce, ruffle; tassels; *archaic* purfle.
– OPPOSITES middle.
▶ adjective *fringe theatre* UNCONVENTIONAL, unorthodox, alternative, avant-garde, experimental, innovative, left-field, innovatory, radical, extreme; peripheral; off Broadway; *informal* offbeat, way out.
– OPPOSITES mainstream.
▶ verb ❶ *a robe of gold, fringed with black velvet* TRIM, edge, hem, border, bind, braid; decorate, adorn, ornament, embellish, finish; *archaic* purfle. ❷ *the lake is fringed by a belt of trees* BORDER, edge, bound, skirt, line, surround, enclose, encircle, circle, girdle, encompass, ring; *poetic/literary* gird.

fringe benefit ▶ noun EXTRA, added extra, additional benefit, privilege; *informal* perk; *formal* perquisite.

frippery ▶ noun ❶ *a functional building with not a hint of frippery* OSTENTATION, showiness, embellishment, adornment, ornamentation, ornament, decoration, trimming, gilding, prettification, gingerbread; finery; *informal* bells and whistles. ❷ *stalls full of fripperies* TRINKET, bauble, knick-knack, gewgaw, gimcrack, bibelot, ornament, novelty, trifle; *N. Amer.* kickshaw; *archaic* gaud.

frisk ▶ verb ❶ *the spaniels frisked around my ankles* FROLIC, gambol, cavort, caper, cut capers, scamper, skip, dance, romp, trip, prance, leap, spring, hop, jump, bounce. ❷ *the officer frisked him* SEARCH, body-search, check.

frisky ▶ adjective LIVELY, bouncy, bubbly, perky, active, energetic, animated, zestful, full of vim and vigour; playful, coltish, skittish, spirited, high-spirited, in high spirits, exuberant; *informal* full of beans, sparky, zippy, peppy, bright-eyed and bushy-tailed; *poetic/literary* frolicsome.

fritter ▶ verb SQUANDER, waste, misuse, misspend, dissipate; overspend, spend like water, be prodigal with, run through, get through; *informal* blow, splurge, pour/chuck something down the drain; *Brit. informal, dated* blue.
– OPPOSITES save.

frivolity ▶ noun LIGHT-HEARTEDNESS, levity, joking, jocularity, gaiety, fun, frivolousness, silliness, foolishness, flightiness, skittishness; superficiality, shallowness, vacuity, empty-headedness.

frivolous ▶ adjective ❶ *a frivolous girl* SKITTISH, flighty, giddy, silly, foolish, superficial, shallow, light-minded, irresponsible, thoughtless, feather-brained, empty-headed, pea-brained, birdbrained, vacuous, vapid; *informal* dizzy, dippy; *N. Amer. informal* ditsy. ❷ *frivolous remarks* FLIPPANT, glib, facetious, joking, jokey, light-hearted; fatuous, inane, senseless, thoughtless; *informal* flip. ❸ *new rules to stop frivolous lawsuits* TIME-WASTING, pointless, trivial, trifling, minor, petty, insignificant, unimportant.
– OPPOSITES sensible, serious.

frizzle[1] ▶ verb *a hamburger frizzled in the pan* SIZZLE, crackle, fizz, hiss, spit, sputter, crack, snap; fry, cook.

frizzle[2] ▶ verb *their hair was powdered and frizzled* CURL, coil, crimp, crinkle, kink, wave, frizz.
– OPPOSITES straighten.

frizzy ▶ adjective CURLY, curled, corkscrew, ringlety, crimped, crinkly, kinky, frizzed; permed; *N. Amer. informal* nappy.
– OPPOSITES straight.

frock ▶ noun DRESS, gown, robe, shift; garment, costume.

frolic ▶ verb *children frolicked on the sand* PLAY, amuse oneself, romp, disport oneself, frisk, gambol, cavort, caper, cut capers, scamper, skip, dance, prance, leap about, jump about; *dated* sport.
▶ noun *the youngsters enjoyed their frolic* ANTIC, caper, game, romp, escapade; (**frolics**) fun (and games), high jinks, merrymaking, amusement, skylarking.

frolicsome ▶ adjective (*poetic/literary*) PLAYFUL, frisky, fun-loving, jolly, merry, gleeful, light-hearted, exuberant, high-spirited, spirited, lively, perky, skittish, coltish, kittenish; mischievous, impish, roguish; *informal* peppy, zippy, full of beans.

front ▶ noun ❶ *the front of the boat* FORE, foremost part, forepart, anterior, forefront, nose, head; bow, prow; foreground. ❷ *a shop front* FRONTAGE, face, facing, facade; window. ❸ *the battlefield surgeons who work at the front* FRONT LINE, firing line, vanguard, van; trenches. ❹ *the front of the queue* HEAD, beginning, start, top, lead. ❺ *she kept up a brave front* APPEARANCE, air, face, manner, demeanour, bearing, pose, exterior, veneer, (outward) show, act, pretence, affectation. ❻ *the shop was a front for his real business* COVER, cover-up, false front, blind, disguise, facade, mask, cloak, screen, smokescreen, camouflage. ❼ (*informal*) *he's got a lot of front* SELF-CONFIDENCE, boldness, forwardness, pushiness, audacity, temerity, presumption, presumptuousness, cockiness, daring; *informal* nerve, face, neck, brass neck.
– OPPOSITES rear, back.
▶ adjective *the front runners* LEADING, lead, first, foremost; in first place.
– OPPOSITES last.
▶ verb *the houses fronted on a reservoir* OVERLOOK, look out on/over, face (towards), lie opposite (to); have a view of, command a view of.

■ **in front** AHEAD, to/at the fore, at the head, up ahead, in the vanguard, in the van, in the lead, leading, coming first; at the head of the queue; *informal* up front.

frontier ▶ **noun** BORDER, boundary, borderline, dividing line, demarcation line; perimeter, limit, edge, rim; marches, bounds.

frost ▶ **noun** ❶ *hedges covered with frost* ICE CRYSTALS, ice, rime, verglas; hoar frost, ground frost, black frost; *informal* Jack Frost; *archaic* hoar. ❷ *there was frost in his tone* COLDNESS, coolness, frostiness, ice, iciness, frigidity; hostility, unfriendliness, stiffness; *informal* stand-offishness.

frosty ▶ **adjective** ❶ *a frosty morning* FREEZING, cold, icy-cold, bitter, bitterly cold, chill, wintry, frigid, glacial, arctic; frozen, icy, gelid; *informal* nippy; *Brit. informal* parky; *poetic/literary* frore, rimy. ❷ *her frosty gaze* COLD, frigid, icy, glacial, unfriendly, inhospitable, unwelcoming, forbidding, hostile, stony, stern, hard.

froth ▶ **noun** *the froth on top of the beer* FOAM, head; bubbles, frothiness, fizz, effervescence; lather, suds; scum; *poetic/literary* spume.

▶ **verb** *the liquid frothed up* BUBBLE, fizz, effervesce, foam, lather; churn, seethe; *poetic/literary* spume.

frothy ▶ **adjective** ❶ *a frothy liquid* FOAMING, foamy, bubbling, bubbly, fizzy, sparkling, effervescent, gassy, carbonated; sudsy; *poetic/literary* spumy, spumous. ❷ *a frothy pink evening dress* FRILLY, flouncy, lacy. ❸ *a frothy woman's magazine* LIGHTWEIGHT, light, superficial, shallow, slight, insubstantial; trivial, trifling, frivolous.

frown ▶ **verb** ❶ *she frowned at him* SCOWL, glower, glare, lour, make a face, look daggers, give someone a black look; knit/furrow one's brows; *informal* give someone a dirty look. ❷ *public displays of affection were frowned on* DISAPPROVE OF, view with disfavour, dislike, look askance at, not take kindly to, take a dim view of, take exception to, object to, have a low opinion of.
– OPPOSITES smile.

frowsty ▶ **adjective** (*Brit.*) STUFFY, airless, unventilated, fusty, close, muggy, stifling; stale, musty, smelly; *N. Amer.* funky.
– OPPOSITES airy.

frowzy ▶ **adjective** ❶ *a frowzy old biddy* SCRUFFY, unkempt, untidy, messy, dishevelled, slovenly, slatternly, bedraggled, down at heel, badly dressed, dowdy; *N. Amer. informal* raggedy. ❷ *a frowzy room* DINGY, gloomy, dull, drab, dark, dim; stuffy, close, musty, stale, stifling; shabby, seedy, run down; *Brit.* frowsty, fuggy.

frozen ▶ **adjective** ❶ *the frozen ground* ICY, ice-covered, ice-bound, frosty, frosted, gelid; frozen solid, hard, (as) hard as iron; *poetic/literary* rimy. ❷ *his hands were frozen* FREEZING, icy, very cold, chilled to the bone/marrow, numb, numbed, frozen stiff; *informal* frozen to death.
– OPPOSITES boiling.

frugal ▶ **adjective** ❶ *a hard-working, frugal man* THRIFTY, economical, careful, cautious, prudent, provident, unwasteful, sparing, scrimping; abstemious, abstinent, austere, self-denying, ascetic, monkish, spartan; parsimonious, miserly, niggardly, cheese-paring, penny-pinching, close-fisted; *N. Amer.* forehanded; *informal* tight-fisted, tight, stingy. ❷ *their frugal breakfast* MEAGRE, scanty, scant, paltry, skimpy; plain, simple, spartan, inexpensive, cheap, economical.
– OPPOSITES extravagant, lavish.

fruit ▶ **noun** *the fruits of their labours* REWARD, benefit, profit, product, return, yield, legacy, issue; result, outcome, upshot, consequence, effect.

fruitful ▶ **adjective** ❶ *a fruitful tree* FERTILE, fecund, prolific, high-yielding; fruit-bearing, fruiting. ❷ *fruitful discussions* PRODUCTIVE, constructive, useful, of use, worthwhile, helpful, beneficial, valuable, rewarding, profitable, advantageous, gainful, successful, effective, effectual, well spent.
– OPPOSITES barren, futile.

fruition ▶ **noun** FULFILMENT, realization, actualization, materialization, achievement, attainment, accomplishment, resolution; success, completion, consummation, conclusion, close, finish, perfection, maturity, maturation, ripening, ripeness; implementation, execution, performance.

fruitless ▶ **adjective** FUTILE, vain, in vain, to no avail, to no effect, idle; pointless, useless, worthless, wasted, hollow; ineffectual, ineffective, inefficacious; unproductive, unrewarding, profitless, unsuccessful, unavailing, barren, for naught; abortive; *archaic* bootless.
– OPPOSITES productive.

fruity ▶ **adjective** ❶ *his fruity voice* DEEP, rich, resonant, full, mellow, clear, strong, vibrant. ❷ (*Brit. informal*) *a fruity story* BAWDY, racy, risqué, naughty, spicy, earthy, ribald, suggestive, titillating; rude, indelicate, vulgar, indecent, improper, dirty, smutty, coarse, off colour; *N. Amer.* gamy; *euphemistic* adult; *informal* blue, near the knuckle, nudge-nudge, raunchy; *Brit. informal* saucy.

frumpy ▶ **adjective** DOWDY, frumpish, unfashionable, old-fashioned; drab, dull, shabby, scruffy; *Brit. informal* mumsy.
– OPPOSITES fashionable.

frustrate ▶ **verb** ❶ *his plans were frustrated* THWART, defeat, foil, block, stop, put a stop to, counter, spoil, check, baulk, disappoint, forestall, dash, scotch, quash, crush, derail, snooker; obstruct, impede, hamper, hinder, hamstring, stand in the way of, spike someone's guns; *informal* stymie, foul up, screw up, put the kibosh on, banjax, do for; *Brit. informal* scupper. ❷ *the delays frustrated him* EXASPERATE, infuriate, annoy, anger, vex, irritate, irk, try

someone's patience; disappoint, discontent, dissatisfy, discourage, dishearten, dispirit; *informal* aggravate, bug, miff, hack off.
–OPPOSITES help, facilitate.

frustration ▶ **noun** ❶ *he clenched his fists in frustration* EXASPERATION, annoyance, anger, vexation, irritation; disappointment, dissatisfaction, discontentment, discontent; *informal* aggravation. ❷ *the frustration of his attempts to introduce changes* THWARTING, defeat, prevention, foiling, blocking, spoiling, circumvention, forestalling, disappointment, derailment; obstruction, hampering, hindering; failure, collapse.

fuddled ▶ **adjective** STUPEFIED, addled, befuddled, confused, muddled, bewildered, dazed, stunned, muzzy, groggy, foggy, fuzzy, vague, disorientated, disoriented, all at sea; *informal* dopey, woozy, woolly-minded, fazed, not with it; *N. Amer. informal* discombobulated.

fuddy-duddy ▶ **noun** (*informal*) (OLD) FOGY, conservative, traditionalist, conformist; fossil, dinosaur, troglodyte; *Brit.* museum piece; *informal* stick-in-the-mud, square, stuffed shirt, dodo.

fudge ▶ **verb** ❶ *the minister tried to fudge the issue* EVADE, avoid, dodge, skirt, duck, gloss over; hedge, prevaricate, vacillate, be non-committal, stall, beat about the bush, equivocate; *Brit.* hum and haw; *informal* cop out, sit on the fence; *rare* tergiversate. ❷ *the government has been fudging figures* ADJUST, manipulate, massage, put a spin on, juggle, misrepresent, misreport, bend; tamper with, tinker with, interfere with, doctor, falsify, distort; *informal* cook, fiddle with.
▶ **noun** *the latest proposals are a fudge* COMPROMISE, cover-up; spin, casuistry, sophistry; *informal* cop-out.

fuel ▶ **noun** ❶ *the car ran out of fuel* PETROL, diesel; power source; *N. Amer.* gasoline, gas. ❷ *she added more fuel to the fire* FIREWOOD, wood, kindling, logs; coal, coke, anthracite; oil, paraffin, kerosene; heat source. ❸ *we all need fuel to keep our bodies going* NOURISHMENT, food, sustenance, nutriment, nutrition. ❹ *his antics added fuel to the Republican cause* ENCOURAGEMENT, ammunition, stimulus, incentive; provocation, goading.
▶ **verb** ❶ *power stations fuelled by low-grade coal* POWER, fire, charge. ❷ *the rumours fuelled anxiety among opposition backbenchers* FAN, feed, stoke up, inflame, intensify, stimulate, encourage, provoke, incite, whip up; sustain, keep alive.

fug ▶ **noun** (*Brit. informal*) STUFFINESS, fustiness, frowstiness, staleness, stuffy atmosphere.

fuggy ▶ **adjective** (*Brit. informal*) STUFFY, smoky, close, muggy, stale, fusty, unventilated, airless, stifling, heavy.
–OPPOSITES airy.

fugitive ▶ **noun** *a hunted fugitive* ESCAPEE, runaway, deserter, absconder; refugee.
▶ **adjective** ❶ *a fugitive criminal* ESCAPED, runaway, on the run, on the loose, at large; wanted; *informal* AWOL; *N. Amer. informal* on the lam. ❷ *the fugitive nature of life* FLEETING, transient, transitory, ephemeral, fading, momentary, short-lived, short, brief, passing, impermanent, here today and gone tomorrow; *poetic/literary* evanescent.

fulfil ▶ **verb** ❶ *he fulfilled a lifelong ambition to visit Israel* ACHIEVE, attain, realize, actualize, make happen, succeed in, bring to completion, bring to fruition, satisfy. ❷ *she failed to fulfil her duties* CARRY OUT, perform, accomplish, execute, do, discharge, conduct; complete, finish, conclude, perfect. ❸ *they fulfilled the criteria* MEET, satisfy, comply with, conform to, fill, answer.

fulfilled ▶ **adjective** SATISFIED, content, contented, happy, pleased; serene, placid, untroubled, at ease, at peace.
–OPPOSITES discontented.

full ▶ **adjective** ❶ *her glass was full* FILLED, filled up, filled to capacity, filled to the brim, brimming, brimful. ❷ *streets full of people* CROWDED, packed, crammed, congested; teeming, swarming, thick, thronged, overcrowded, overrun; abounding, bursting, overflowing; *informal* jam-packed, wall-to-wall, stuffed, chock-a-block, chock-full, bursting at the seams, packed to the gunwales, awash. ❸ *all the seats were full* OCCUPIED, taken, in use, unavailable. ❹ *I'm full* REPLETE, full up, satisfied, well fed, sated, satiated, surfeited; gorged, glutted; *informal* stuffed. ❺ *she'd had a full life* EVENTFUL, interesting, exciting, lively, action-packed, busy, energetic, active. ❻ *a full list of available facilities* COMPREHENSIVE, thorough, exhaustive, all-inclusive, all-encompassing, all-embracing, in depth; complete, entire, whole, unabridged, uncut. ❼ *a fire engine driven at full speed* MAXIMUM, top, greatest, highest. ❽ *she had a full figure* PLUMP, well rounded, rounded, buxom, shapely, ample, curvaceous, voluptuous, womanly, Junoesque; *informal* busty, curvy, well upholstered, well endowed; *N. Amer. informal* zaftig. ❾ *a full skirt* LOOSE-FITTING, loose, baggy, voluminous, roomy, capacious, billowing. ❿ *his full baritone voice* RESONANT, rich, sonorous, deep, vibrant, full-bodied, strong, fruity, clear. ⓫ *the full flavour of a Bordeaux* RICH, intense, full-bodied, strong, deep.
–OPPOSITES empty, hungry, selective, thin.
▶ **adverb** ❶ *she looked full into his face* DIRECTLY, right, straight, squarely, square, dead, point-blank; *informal* bang, slap (bang), plumb. ❷ *you knew full well I was leaving* VERY, perfectly, quite; *informal* darn, damn, damned; *Brit. informal* jolly, bloody; *N. Amer. informal* darned.
■ **in full** IN ITS ENTIRETY, in toto, in total, unabridged, uncut.
■ **to the full** FULLY, thoroughly, completely, to the utmost, to the limit, to the maximum, for all one's worth.

full-blooded ▶ adjective *a full-blooded price war* UNCOMPROMISING, all-out, out and out, committed, vigorous, strenuous, intense; unrestrained, uncontrolled, unbridled, hard-hitting, pulling no punches.
– OPPOSITES half-hearted.

full-blown ▶ adjective FULLY DEVELOPED, full-scale, full-blooded, fully fledged, complete, total, thorough, entire; advanced.

full-bodied ▶ adjective FULL-FLAVOURED, flavourful, flavoursome, full of flavour, rich, mellow, fruity, robust, strong, well-matured.
– OPPOSITES tasteless.

full-grown ▶ adjective ADULT, mature, grown-up, of age; fully grown, fully developed, fully fledged, in one's prime, in full bloom, ripe.
– OPPOSITES infant.

fullness ▶ noun ❶ *the fullness of the information they provide* COMPREHENSIVENESS, completeness, thoroughness, exhaustiveness, all-inclusiveness. ❷ *the fullness of her body* PLUMPNESS, roundedness, roundness, shapeliness, curvaceousness, voluptuousness, womanliness; *informal* curviness. ❸ *the recording has a fullness and warmth* RESONANCE, richness, intensity, depth, vibrancy, strength, clarity.
■ **in the fullness of time** IN DUE COURSE, when the time is ripe, eventually, in time, in time to come, one day, some day, sooner or later; ultimately, finally, in the end.

full-scale ▶ adjective ❶ *a full-scale model* FULL-SIZE, unreduced. ❷ *a full-scale public inquiry* THOROUGH, comprehensive, extensive, exhaustive, complete, all-out, all-encompassing, all-inclusive, all-embracing, thoroughgoing, wide-ranging, sweeping, in-depth, far-reaching.
– OPPOSITES small-scale.

fully ▶ adverb ❶ *I fully agree with him* COMPLETELY, entirely, wholly, totally, quite, utterly, perfectly, altogether, thoroughly, in all respects, in every respect, without reservation, without exception, to the hilt. ❷ *fully two minutes must have passed* AT LEAST, no less than, no fewer than, easily, without exaggeration.
– OPPOSITES partly, nearly.

fully fledged ▶ adjective TRAINED, qualified, proficient, experienced; mature, fully developed, full grown; *Brit.* time-served.
– OPPOSITES novice.

fulminate ▶ verb PROTEST, rail, rage, rant, thunder, storm, vociferate, declaim, inveigh, speak out, make/take a stand; denounce, decry, condemn, criticize, censure, disparage, attack, execrate, arraign; *informal* mouth off about, kick up a stink about; *formal* excoriate.

fulmination ▶ noun PROTEST, objection, complaint, rant, tirade, diatribe, harangue, invective, railing, obloquy; denunciation, condemnation, criticism, censure, attack, broadside, brickbats; *formal* excoriation; *poetic/literary* philippic.

fulsome ▶ adjective EXCESSIVE, extravagant, overdone, immoderate, inordinate, over-appreciative, flattering, adulatory, fawning, unctuous, ingratiating, cloying, saccharine; enthusiastic, effusive, rapturous, glowing, gushing, profuse, generous, lavish; *informal* over the top, OTT, smarmy.

fumble ▶ verb ❶ *he fumbled for his keys* GROPE, fish, search blindly, scrabble around. ❷ *he fumbled about in the dark* STUMBLE, blunder, flounder, lumber, stagger, totter, lurch; feel one's way, grope one's way. ❸ *the keeper fumbled the ball* MISS, drop, mishandle; misfield. ❹ *he fumbled his lines* MESS UP, make a mess of, bungle, mismanage, mishandle, spoil; *informal* make a hash of, fluff, botch, muff; *Brit. informal* cock up; *N. Amer. informal* flub.
▶ noun *a fumble from the goalkeeper* SLIP, mistake, error, gaffe; *informal* slip-up, boo-boo; *Brit. informal* cock-up, boob.

fume ▶ noun ❶ *a fire giving off toxic fumes* SMOKE, vapour, gas, effluvium; exhaust; pollution. ❷ *stale wine fumes* SMELL, odour, stink, reek, stench; *Brit. informal* pong, niff; *Scottish informal* guff; *N. Amer. informal* funk; *poetic/literary* miasma.
▶ verb ❶ *fragments of lava were fuming and sizzling* EMIT SMOKE, emit gas, smoke; *archaic* reek. ❷ *Ella was still fuming at his arrogance* BE FURIOUS, be enraged, be very angry, seethe, be livid, be incensed, boil, be beside oneself, spit; rage, rant and rave; *informal* be hot under the collar, foam at the mouth, see red.

fumigate ▶ verb DISINFECT, purify, sterilize, sanitize, decontaminate, cleanse, clean out.
– OPPOSITES soil.

fun ▶ noun ❶ *I joined in with the fun* ENJOYMENT, entertainment, amusement, pleasure; jollification, merrymaking; recreation, diversion, leisure, relaxation; good time, great time; *informal* R and R (rest and recreation), living it up, a ball, beer and skittles. ❷ *she's full of fun* MERRIMENT, cheerfulness, cheeriness, jollity, joviality, jocularity, high spirits, gaiety, mirth, laughter, hilarity, glee, gladness, light-heartedness, levity. ❸ *he became a figure of fun* RIDICULE, derision, mockery, laughter, scorn, contempt, jeering, sneering, jibing, teasing, taunting.
– OPPOSITES boredom, misery.
▶ adjective (*informal*) *a fun evening* ENJOYABLE, entertaining, amusing, diverting, pleasurable, pleasing, agreeable, interesting.
■ **in fun** PLAYFUL, in jest, as a joke, tongue in cheek, light-hearted, for a laugh, to tease, teasing.
■ **make fun of** TEASE, poke fun at, chaff, rag; ridicule, mock, laugh at, taunt, jeer at, scoff at, deride; parody, lampoon, caricature, satirize; *informal* take the mickey out of, rib, kid, have on, pull someone's leg, send up; *Brit. informal* wind up; *N. Amer. informal* goof on, rag on, razz.

function ▶ noun ❶ *the main function of the ma-*

chine PURPOSE, task, use, role. ❷ *my function was to select and train the recruits* RESPONSIBILITY, duty, role, concern, province, activity, assignment, obligation, charge; task, job, mission, undertaking, commission; capacity, post, situation, office, occupation, employment, business. ❸ *a function attended by local dignitaries* SOCIAL EVENT, party, social occasion, affair, gathering, reception, soirée, jamboree, gala; *N. Amer.* levee; *informal* do, bash, shindig; *Brit. informal* jolly, beanfeast.

▶ **verb** ❶ *the electrical system had ceased to function* WORK, go, run, be in working/running order, operate, be operative. ❷ *the museum functions as an educational and study centre* ACT, serve, operate; perform, work, play the role of, do duty as.

functional ▶ **adjective** ❶ *a small functional kitchen* PRACTICAL, useful, utilitarian, utility, workaday, serviceable; minimalist, plain, simple, basic, modest, unadorned, unostentatious, no-frills, without frills; impersonal, characterless, soulless, institutional, clinical. ❷ *the machine is now fully functional* WORKING, in working order, functioning, in service, in use; going, running, operative, operating, in operation, in commission, in action; *informal* up and running.

functionary ▶ **noun** OFFICIAL, office-holder, public servant, civil servant, bureaucrat, administrator, apparatchik; *Brit.* jack-in-office.

fund ▶ **noun** ❶ *an emergency fund for refugees* COLLECTION, kitty, reserve, pool, purse; endowment, foundation, trust, grant, investment; savings, nest egg; *informal* stash. ❷ *I was very short of funds* MONEY, cash, ready money; wealth, means, assets, resources, savings, capital, reserves, the wherewithal; *informal* dough, bread, loot, dosh, the ready; *Brit. informal* lolly, spondulicks. ❸ *his fund of stories* STOCK, store, supply, accumulation, collection, bank, pool; mine, reservoir, storehouse, treasury, treasure house, hoard, repository.

▶ **verb** *the agency was funded by the Treasury* FINANCE, pay for, back, capitalize, sponsor, put up the money for, subsidize, underwrite, endow, support, maintain; *informal* foot the bill for, pick up the tab for; *N. Amer. informal* bankroll, stake.

fundamental ▶ **adjective** BASIC, underlying, core, foundational, rudimentary, elemental, elementary, basal, root; primary, prime, cardinal, first, principal, chief, key, central, vital, essential, important, indispensable, necessary, crucial, pivotal, critical; structural, organic, constitutional, inherent, intrinsic.

– OPPOSITES secondary, unimportant.

fundamentally ▶ **adverb** *she was, fundamentally, a good person* ESSENTIALLY, in essence, basically, at heart, at bottom, deep down, au fond; primarily, above all, first and foremost, first of all; *informal* at the end of the day, when all is said and done, when you get right down to it.

fundamentals ▶ **plural noun** BASICS, essentials, rudiments, foundations, basic principles, first principles, preliminaries; crux, crux of the matter, heart of the matter, essence, core, heart, base, bedrock; *informal* nuts and bolts, nitty-gritty, brass tacks, ABC.

funeral ▶ **noun** ❶ *he'd attended a funeral* BURIAL, interment, entombment, committal, inhumation, laying to rest; cremation; obsequies, last offices; *formal* exequies; *archaic* sepulture. ❷ (*informal*) *remember, it was you who asked—it's your funeral* RESPONSIBILITY, problem, worry, concern, business, affair; *informal* headache; *Brit. informal* lookout.

funereal ▶ **adjective** ❶ *the funereal atmosphere* SOMBRE, gloomy, mournful, melancholy, lugubrious, sepulchral, miserable, doleful, woeful, sad, sorrowful, cheerless, joyless, bleak, dismal, depressing, dreary; grave, solemn, serious; *poetic/literary* dolorous. ❷ *funereal colours* DARK, black, drab.

– OPPOSITES cheerful.

fungus ▶ **noun** MUSHROOM, toadstool; mould, mildew, rust; *Biology* saprophyte.

– RELATED TERMS myco-

funk (*informal*) ▶ **noun** ❶ *he put us all into a funk* PANIC, state of fear, fluster; *informal* cold sweat, state, stew, flap, tizzy, tizz; *Brit. informal* blue funk, heebie-jeebies; *N. Amer. informal* twit.

▶ **verb** *I'm certain he funked it* AVOID, evade, dodge, run away from, baulk at, flinch from; *informal* chicken out of, duck out of, wriggle out of, cop out of, get out of.

funnel ▶ **noun** ❶ *fluid was poured through the funnel* TUBE, pipe, channel, conduit. ❷ *smoke poured from the ship's funnels* CHIMNEY, flue, vent.

▶ **verb** *the money was funnelled back into Europe* CHANNEL, feed, direct, convey, move, pass; pour, filter.

funny ▶ **adjective** ❶ *a very funny film* AMUSING, humorous, witty, comic, comical, droll, facetious, jocular, jokey; hilarious, hysterical, riotous, uproarious; entertaining, diverting, sparkling, scintillating; silly, farcical, slapstick; *informal* side-splitting, rib-tickling, laugh-a-minute, wacky, zany, waggish, off the wall, a scream, rich, priceless; *informal, dated* killing. ❷ *a funny coincidence* STRANGE, peculiar, odd, queer, weird, bizarre, curious, freakish, freak, quirky; mysterious, mystifying, puzzling, perplexing; unusual, uncommon, anomalous, irregular, abnormal, exceptional, singular, out of the ordinary, extraordinary; *Brit. informal, dated* rum. ❸ *there's something funny about him* SUSPICIOUS, suspect, dubious, untrustworthy, questionable; *informal* shady, fishy; *Brit. informal* dodgy.

– OPPOSITES serious, unsurprising, trustworthy.

fur ▶ **noun** HAIR, wool; coat, fleece, pelt; *Zoology* pelage.

furious ▶ **adjective** ❶ *he was furious when he*

learned about it ENRAGED, infuriated, very angry, irate, incensed, raging, incandescent, fuming, ranting, raving, seething, beside oneself, outraged; *informal* mad, hopping mad, wild, livid, boiling, apoplectic, hot under the collar, on the warpath, foaming at the mouth, steamed up, in a paddy, fit to be tied; *poetic/literary* wrathful. ❷ *a furious debate* HEATED, hot, passionate, fiery, 'lively'; fierce, vehement, violent, wild, unrestrained, tumultuous, turbulent, tempestuous, stormy.
– OPPOSITES calm.

furnish ▶ **verb** ❶ *the bedrooms are elegantly furnished* FIT OUT, provide with furniture, appoint, outfit; *Brit. informal* do out. ❷ *grooms furnished us with horses for our journey* SUPPLY, provide, equip, provision, issue, kit out, present, give, offer, afford, purvey, bestow; *informal* fix up.

furniture ▶ **noun** FURNISHINGS, fittings, fitments, movables, appointments, effects; *Law* chattels; *informal* stuff, things.

furore ▶ **noun** COMMOTION, uproar, outcry, fuss, upset, brouhaha, palaver, pother, tempest, agitation, pandemonium, disturbance, hubbub, rumpus, tumult, turmoil; stir, excitement; *informal* song and dance, to-do, hoo-ha, hullabaloo, ballyhoo, kerfuffle, flap, stink; *Brit. informal* carry-on.

furrow ▶ **noun** ❶ *furrows in a ploughed field* GROOVE, trench, rut, trough, channel, hollow. ❷ *the furrows on either side of her mouth* WRINKLE, line, crease, crinkle, crow's foot, corrugation.
▶ **verb** *his brow furrowed* WRINKLE, crease, line, crinkle, pucker, screw up, scrunch up, corrugate.

furry ▶ **adjective** COVERED WITH FUR, hairy, downy, fleecy, soft, fluffy, fuzzy, woolly.

further ▶ **adverb** *further, it gave him an excellent excuse not to attend* FURTHERMORE, moreover, what's more, also, additionally, in addition, besides, as well, too, to boot, on top of that, over and above that, into the bargain, by the same token; *archaic* withal.
▶ **adjective** ❶ *the further side of the field* MORE DISTANT, more remote, remoter, further away/off, farther (away/off); far, other, opposite. ❷ *further information* ADDITIONAL, more, extra, supplementary, supplemental, other; new, fresh.
▶ **verb** *an attempt to further his career* PROMOTE, advance, forward, develop, facilitate, aid, assist, help, help along, lend a hand to, abet; expedite, hasten, speed up, accelerate, step up, spur on, oil the wheels of, give a push to, boost, encourage, cultivate, nurture, foster.
– OPPOSITES impede.

furtherance ▶ **noun** PROMOTION, furthering, advancement, forwarding, development, facilitation, aiding, assisting, helping, abetting; hastening, acceleration, boosting, encouragement, cultivation, nurturing, fostering.
– OPPOSITES hindrance.

furthermore ▶ **adverb** MOREOVER, further, what's more, also, additionally, in addition, besides, as well, too, to boot, on top of that, over and above that, into the bargain, by the same token; *archaic* withal.

furthest ▶ **adjective** MOST DISTANT, most remote, remotest, furthest/farthest away, farthest, furthermost, farthermost; outlying, outer, outermost, extreme, uttermost, ultimate; *archaic* outmost.
– OPPOSITES nearest.

furtive ▶ **adjective** SECRETIVE, secret, surreptitious, clandestine, hidden, covert, conspiratorial, cloak-and-dagger, hole-and-corner, backstairs, hugger-mugger; sly, sneaky, under-the-table; sidelong, sideways, oblique, indirect; *informal* hush-hush, shifty.
– OPPOSITES open.

fury ▶ **noun** ❶ *she exploded with fury* RAGE, anger, wrath, outrage, spleen, temper; crossness, indignation, umbrage, annoyance, exasperation; *poetic/literary* ire, choler. ❷ *the fury of the storm* FIERCENESS, ferocity, violence, turbulence, tempestuousness, savagery; severity, intensity, vehemence, force, forcefulness, power, strength. ❸ *she turned on Mother like a fury* VIRAGO, hellcat, termagant, spitfire, vixen, shrew, harridan, dragon, gorgon; (**Furies**) *Greek Mythology* Eumenides.
– OPPOSITES good humour, mildness.

fuse ▶ **verb** ❶ *a band which fuses rap with rock* COMBINE, amalgamate, put together, join, unite, marry, blend, merge, meld, mingle, integrate, intermix, intermingle, synthesize; coalesce, compound, alloy; *technical* admix; *poetic/literary* commingle. ❷ *metal fused to a base of coloured glass* BOND, stick, bind, weld, solder; melt, smelt. ❸ (*Brit.*) *a light had fused* SHORT-CIRCUIT, stop working, trip; *informal* go, blow.
– OPPOSITES separate.

fusillade ▶ **noun** SALVO, volley, barrage, bombardment, cannonade, battery, burst, blast, hail, shower, rain, stream; *historical* broadside.

fusion ▶ **noun** BLEND, blending, combination, amalgamation, joining, union, marrying, bonding, merging, melding, mingling, integration, intermixture, intermingling, synthesis; coalescence.

fuss ▶ **noun** ❶ *what's all the fuss about?* ADO, excitement, agitation, pother, stir, commotion, confusion, disturbance, brouhaha, uproar, furore, palaver, storm in a teacup, much ado about nothing; bother, fluster, flurry, bustle; *informal* hoo-ha, to-do, ballyhoo, song and dance, performance, pantomime, kerfuffle; *Brit. informal* carry-on; *N. Amer. informal* fuss and feathers. ❷ *they settled in with very little fuss* BOTHER, trouble, inconvenience, effort, exertion, labour; *informal* hassle. ❸ *he didn't put up a fuss* PROTEST, complaint, objection, grumble, grouse; *informal* gripe.

▶ **verb** *he was still fussing about his clothes* WORRY, fret, be anxious, be agitated, make a big thing out of; make a mountain out of a molehill; *informal* flap, be in a tizzy, be in a stew, make a meal of.

fussy ▶ **adjective** ❶ *he's very fussy about what he eats* FINICKY, particular, over-particular, fastidious, discriminating, selective, dainty; hard to please, difficult, exacting, demanding; faddish; *informal* pernickety, choosy, picky, old womanish; *Brit. informal* faddy; *N. Amer. informal* persnickety. ❷ *a fussy, frilly bridal gown* OVER-ELABORATE, over-decorated, ornate, fancy, overdone; busy, cluttered.

fusty ▶ **adjective** ❶ *the room smelt fusty* STALE, musty, dusty; stuffy, airless, unventilated; damp, mildewed, mildewy; *Brit.* frowsty. ❷ *a fusty conservative* OLD-FASHIONED, out of date, outdated, behind the times, antediluvian, backward-looking; fogeyish; *informal* square, out of the ark.
– OPPOSITES fresh.

futile ▶ **adjective** FRUITLESS, vain, pointless, useless, ineffectual, ineffective, inefficacious, to no effect, of no use, in vain, to no avail, unavailing; unsuccessful, failed, thwarted; unproductive, barren, unprofitable, abortive; impotent, hollow, empty, forlorn, idle, hopeless; *archaic* bootless.
– OPPOSITES useful.

futility ▶ **noun** FRUITLESSNESS, pointlessness, uselessness, vanity, ineffectiveness, inefficacy; failure, barrenness, unprofitability; impotence, hollowness, emptiness, forlornness, hopelessness; *archaic* bootlessness.

future ▶ **noun** ❶ *his plans for the future* TIME TO COME, time ahead; what lies ahead, coming times. ❷ *she knew her future lay in acting* DESTINY, fate, fortune; prospects, expectations, chances.
– OPPOSITES past.
▶ **adjective** ❶ *a future date* LATER, to come, following, ensuing, succeeding, subsequent, coming. ❷ *his future wife* TO BE, destined; intended, planned, prospective.
■ **in future** FROM NOW ON, after this, in the future, from this day forward, hence, henceforward, subsequently, in time to come; *formal* hereafter.

fuzz[1] ▶ **noun** *the soft fuzz on his cheeks* HAIR, down; fur, fluff, fleeciness.

fuzz[2] ▶ **noun** (*informal*) *we'd better call the fuzz.* See POLICE noun.

fuzzy ▶ **adjective** ❶ *her fuzzy hair* FRIZZY, fluffy, woolly; downy, soft; *N. Amer. informal* nappy. ❷ *a fuzzy picture* BLURRY, blurred, indistinct, unclear, bleary, misty, distorted, out of focus, unfocused, lacking definition, nebulous; ill-defined, indefinite, vague, hazy, imprecise, inexact, loose, woolly. ❸ *my mind was fuzzy* CONFUSED, muddled, addled, fuddled, befuddled, groggy, disoriented, disorientated, mixed up, fazed, foggy, dizzy, stupefied, benumbed.

gab (*informal*) ▶ **verb** *they were all gabbing away like crazy* CHATTER, chitter-chatter, chat, talk, gossip, gabble, babble, prattle, jabber, blather, blab; *informal* yak, yackety-yak, yabber, yatter, yammer, blabber, blah-blah, jaw, gas, shoot one's mouth off; *Brit. informal* witter, rabbit, chunter, natter; *N. Amer. informal* run off at the mouth.
■ **the gift of the gab** ELOQUENCE, fluency, expressiveness, a silver tongue; persuasiveness; *informal* a way with words, blarney.

gabble ▶ **verb** *he gabbled on in a panicky way* JABBER, babble, prattle, rattle, blabber, gibber, blab, drivel, twitter, splutter; *Brit. informal* waffle, chunter, witter.
▶ **noun** *the boozy gabble of the crowd* JABBERING, babbling, chattering, gibbering, babble, chatter, rambling; *Brit. informal* waffle, waffling, chuntering, wittering.

gabby ▶ **adjective** (*informal*). *See* TALKATIVE.

gad ▶ **verb** (*informal*) *she's been gadding about in Italy* GALLIVANT, flit around, run around, travel around, roam (around); *Brit. informal* swan about.

gadabout ▶ **noun** (*informal*) PLEASURE-SEEKER; traveller, globetrotter, wanderer, drifter, bird of passage; *informal* gallivanter.

gadget ▶ **noun** APPLIANCE, apparatus, instrument, implement, tool, utensil, contrivance, contraption, machine, mechanism, device, labour-saving device, convenience, invention; *informal* gizmo, gimmick, widget, mod con.

gaffe ▶ **noun** BLUNDER, mistake, error, slip, faux pas, indiscretion, impropriety, miscalculation, gaucherie, solecism; *informal* slip-up, howler, boo-boo, boner, fluff; *Brit. informal* boob, bloomer, clanger; *N. Amer. informal* blooper, goof.

gaffer ▶ **noun** ❶ (*Brit. informal*) *being the gaffer's gone to her head* MANAGER, manageress, foreman, forewoman, overseer, supervisor, superintendent; *informal* boss, boss man, head honcho, numero uno, number one, kingpin, top dog, big chief, skipper; *Brit. informal* governor, guv'nor; *N. Amer. informal* padrone, sachem, big kahuna. ❷ (*informal*) *an old gaffer* OLD MAN, elderly man, senior citizen, pensioner, OAP; *informal* old boy, old codger, old-timer, greybeard, grandad, wrinkly; *Brit. informal* buffer.

gag[1] ▶ **verb** ❶ *a dirty rag was used to gag her mouth* STOP UP, block, plug, stifle, smother, muffle. ❷ *the government tried to gag its critics* SILENCE, muzzle, mute, muffle, suppress, stifle; censor, curb, check, restrain, fetter, shackle, restrict. ❸ *the stench made her gag* RETCH, heave, dry-heave; *informal* keck.

▶ **noun** *his scream was muffled by the gag* MUZZLE, tie, restraint.

gag[2] ▶ **noun** (*informal*) *he told a few gags* JOKE, jest, witticism, quip, pun, play on words, double entendre; *informal* crack, wisecrack, one-liner, funny.

gaiety ▶ **noun** ❶ *I was struck by her gaiety* CHEERFULNESS, light-heartedness, happiness, merriment, glee, gladness, joy, joie de vivre, joyfulness, joyousness, delight, high spirits, good spirits, good humour, cheeriness, jollity, mirth, joviality, exuberance, elation; liveliness, vivacity, animation, effervescence, sprightliness, zest, zestfulness; *informal* chirpiness, bounce, pep; *poetic/literary* blitheness. ❷ *the hotel restaurant was a scene of gaiety* MERRYMAKING, festivity, fun, fun and games, frolics, revelry, jollification, celebration, pleasure; *informal* partying.
– OPPOSITES misery.

gaily ▶ **adverb** ❶ *she skipped gaily along the path* MERRILY, cheerfully, cheerily, happily, joyfully, joyously, light-heartedly, blithely, jauntily, gleefully. ❷ *gaily painted boats* BRIGHTLY, colourfully, brilliantly. ❸ *she plunged gaily into speculation on the stock market* HEEDLESSLY, unthinkingly, thoughtlessly, without thinking, carelessly; casually, nonchalantly, airily, breezily, lightly.

gain ▶ **verb** ❶ *he gained a scholarship to the college* OBTAIN, get, secure, acquire, come by, procure, attain, achieve, earn, win, capture, clinch, pick up, carry off, reap; *informal* land, net, bag, scoop, wangle, swing, walk away/off with. ❷ *they stood to gain from the deal* PROFIT, make money, reap benefits, benefit, do well out of; *informal* make a killing, milk. ❸ *she had gained weight* PUT ON, increase in. ❹ *the others were gaining on us* CATCH UP WITH/ON, catch someone up, catch, close in on, near. ❺ *we gained the ridge* REACH, arrive at, get to, come to, make, attain, set foot on; *informal* hit.
– OPPOSITES lose.

▶ **noun** ❶ *his gain from the deal* PROFIT, advantage, benefit, reward; percentage, takings, yield, return, winnings, receipts, proceeds, dividend, interest; *informal* pickings, cut, take, rake-off, slice of the cake; *Brit. informal* whack. ❷ *a price gain of 7.5 per cent* INCREASE, rise, increment, augmentation, addition.
– OPPOSITES loss, decrease.

■ **gain time** PLAY FOR TIME, stall, procrastinate, delay, temporize, hold back, hang back, hang fire, dally, drag one's feet.

gainful ▶ **adjective** PROFITABLE, paid, well paid, remunerative, lucrative, moneymaking; rewarding, fruitful, worthwhile, useful, productive, constructive, beneficial, advantageous, valuable.

gainsay ▶ **verb** (*formal*) DENY, dispute, disagree with, argue with, dissent from, contradict, repudiate, challenge, oppose, contest, counter, controvert, refute, rebut; *formal* confute.
– OPPOSITES confirm.

gait ▶ **noun** WALK, step, stride, pace, tread, way of walking; bearing, carriage; *Brit.* deportment; *formal* comportment.

gala ▶ **noun** *the annual summer gala* FÊTE, fair, festival, carnival, pageant, jubilee, jamboree, party, garden party, celebration; festivities.

▶ **adjective** *a gala occasion* FESTIVE, celebratory, merry, joyous, joyful; diverting, entertaining, enjoyable, spectacular.

galaxy ▶ **noun** ❶ *a distant galaxy* STAR SYSTEM, solar system, constellation; stars, heavens. ❷ *a galaxy of the rock world's biggest stars* HOST, multitude, array, gathering, assemblage, assembly, throng, crowd, company, flock, group.

gale ▶ **noun** ❶ *a howling gale* STRONG WIND, high wind, hurricane, tornado, cyclone, whirlwind; storm, squall, tempest, typhoon; *N. Amer.* windstorm; *informal* burster, buster. ❷ *gales of laughter* PEAL, howl, hoot, shriek, scream, roar; outburst, burst, fit, paroxysm, explosion.

gall[1] ▶ **noun** ❶ *she had the gall to ask for money* EFFRONTERY, impudence, impertinence, cheek, cheekiness, insolence, audacity, temerity, presumption, cockiness, nerve, shamelessness, disrespect, bad manners; *informal* brass neck, face, chutzpah; *Brit. informal* sauce; *N. Amer. informal* sass. ❷ *scholarly gall was poured on this work* BITTERNESS, resentment, rancour, bile, spleen, malice, spite, spitefulness, malignity, venom, vitriol, poison.

gall[2] ▶ **noun** ❶ *this was a gall that she frequently had to endure* IRRITATION, irritant, annoyance, vexation, nuisance, provocation, bother, torment, plague, thorn in one's side/flesh; *informal* aggravation, pain, pain in the neck, bore, headache, hassle; *N. Amer. informal* pain in the butt. ❷ *a bay horse with a gall on its side* SORE, ulcer, ulceration; abrasion, scrape, scratch, graze, chafe.

▶ **verb** ❶ *it galled him to have to sit in silence* IRRITATE, annoy, vex, anger, infuriate, exasperate, irk, pique, nettle, put out, displease, antagonize, get on someone's nerves, make someone's hackles rise; *Brit.* rub up the wrong way; *informal* aggravate, peeve, miff, rile, needle, get (to), bug, hack off, get up someone's nose, get someone's goat, get/put someone's back up, get someone's dander up, drive mad/crazy, drive round the bend/twist, drive up the wall; *Brit. informal* wind up, nark, get on someone's wick, give someone the hump; *N. Amer. informal* tee off, tick off, rankle; *informal, dated* give someone the pip. ❷ *the straps galled their shoulders* CHAFE, abrade, rub (against), rub raw, scrape, graze, skin, scratch, rasp, bark.

gallant ▶ **adjective** ❶ *his gallant countrymen* BRAVE, courageous, valiant, valorous, bold, plucky, daring, fearless, intrepid, heroic, lionhearted, stout-hearted, doughty, mettlesome, death-or-glory, dauntless, undaunted, unflinching, unafraid; *informal* gutsy, spunky. ❷ *her gallant companion* CHIVALROUS, gentlemanly, honourable, courteous, polite, mannerly, attentive, respectful, gracious, considerate, thoughtful.
– OPPOSITES cowardly, discourteous.
▶ **noun** (*archaic*) ❶ *a young gallant in red and white silks* MAN ABOUT TOWN, ladies' man, man of the world, dandy, fop; *informal* ladykiller; *informal, dated* gay dog, blade, swell, blood; *archaic* coxcomb. ❷ *her amorous gallant* SUITOR, wooer, admirer; sweetheart, lover, love, beloved, boyfriend, young man; *poetic/literary* swain; *dated* beau.

gallantry ▶ **noun** ❶ *he received medals for gallantry* BRAVERY, courage, courageousness, valour, pluck, pluckiness, nerve, daring, boldness, fearlessness, dauntlessness, intrepidity, heroism, stout-heartedness, mettle, grit; *informal* guts, spunk; *Brit. informal* bottle; *N. Amer. informal* moxie. ❷ *she acknowledged his selfless gallantry* CHIVALRY, chivalrousness, gentlemanliness, courtesy, courteousness, politeness, good manners, attentiveness, graciousness, respectfulness, respect, considerateness.

gallery ▶ **noun** ❶ *the National Gallery* ART GALLERY, museum; exhibition room, display room. ❷ *they sat up in the gallery* BALCONY, circle, upper circle; *informal* gods. ❸ *a long gallery with doors along each side* PASSAGE, passageway, corridor, walkway, arcade.

galling ▶ **adjective** ANNOYING, irritating, vexing, vexatious, infuriating, maddening, irksome, provoking, exasperating, trying, tiresome, troublesome, bothersome, displeasing, disagreeable; *informal* aggravating.

gallivant ▶ **verb** FLIT, jaunt, run; roam, wander, travel, rove; *informal* gad.

gallop ▶ **verb** *Paul galloped across the clearing* RUSH, race, run, sprint, bolt, dart, dash, career, charge, shoot, hurtle, hare, fly, speed, zoom, streak; *informal* tear, belt, pelt, scoot, zip, whip, hotfoot it, leg it; *Brit. informal* bomb, go like the clappers; *N. Amer. informal* barrel.
– OPPOSITES amble.

gallows ▶ **plural noun** ❶ *the wooden gallows* GIBBET, scaffold, gallows tree, Tyburn tree. ❷ *they were condemned to the gallows* HANGING, being hanged, the noose, the rope, the gibbet, the scaffold, execution; *informal* the drop.

galore ▶ **adjective** APLENTY, in abundance, in profusion, in great quantities, in large numbers, by the dozen; to spare; everywhere, all over (the place); *informal* a gogo, by the truckload; *Brit. informal* by the shedload.

galvanize ▶ **verb** JOLT, shock, startle, impel, stir, spur, prod, urge, motivate, stimulate, electrify, excite, rouse, arouse, awaken; invigorate, fire, animate, vitalize, energize, exhilarate, thrill, dynamize, inspire; *N. Amer.* light a fire under; *informal* give someone a shot in the arm.

gambit ▶ **noun** STRATAGEM, scheme, plan, tactic, manoeuvre, move, course/line of action, device; machination, ruse, trick, ploy; *Brit. informal* wheeze, wangle.

gamble ▶ **verb** ❶ *he started to gamble more often* BET, place/lay a bet on something, stake money on something, back the horses, game; *informal* play the ponies; *Brit. informal* punt, have a flutter. ❷ *investors are gambling that the pound will fall* TAKE A CHANCE, take a risk; *N. Amer.* take a flier; *informal* stick one's neck out, go out on a limb; *Brit. informal* chance one's arm.
▶ **noun** ❶ *his grandfather enjoyed a gamble* BET, wager, speculation; game of chance; *Brit. informal* flutter, punt. ❷ *I took a gamble and it paid off* RISK, chance, hazard, leap in the dark; pig in a poke, pot luck.

gambol ▶ **verb** FROLIC, frisk, cavort, caper, skip, dance, romp, prance, leap, hop, jump, spring, bound, bounce; play; *dated* sport.

game ▶ **noun** ❶ *the children invented a new game* PASTIME, diversion, entertainment, amusement, distraction, divertissement, recreation, sport, activity. ❷ *the club haven't lost a game all season* MATCH, contest, fixture, tie, tournament; cup tie, final, cup final, play-off. ❸ *we were only playing a game on him* PRACTICAL JOKE, prank, jest, trick, hoax; *informal* lark. ❹ *he's in the banking game* BUSINESS, profession, occupation, trade, industry, line, line of work/business; *informal* racket. ❺ *I spoiled his little game* SCHEME, plot, ploy, stratagem, strategy, gambit, cunning plan, tactics; trick, device, manoeuvre, wile, dodge, ruse, machination, contrivance, subterfuge; *informal* scam; *Brit. informal* wheeze; *archaic* shift. ❻ *he hunted game in Africa* WILD ANIMALS, wild fowl, big game.
▶ **adjective** ❶ *they weren't game enough to join in* BRAVE, courageous, plucky, bold, daring, intrepid, valiant, stout-hearted, mettlesome;

fearless, dauntless, undaunted, unflinching; *informal* gutsy, spunky. ❷ *I need a bit of help—are you game?* WILLING, prepared, ready, disposed, of a mind; eager, keen, enthusiastic.

▶ **verb** *they were drinking and gaming all evening* GAMBLE, bet, place/lay bets.

gamin, fem. **gamine** ▶ **noun** (*dated*) URCHIN, ragamuffin, waif, stray; *derogatory* guttersnipe; *archaic* mudlark, street Arab.

gamut ▶ **noun** RANGE, spectrum, span, scope, sweep, compass, area, breadth, reach, extent, catalogue, scale; variety.

gang ▶ **noun** ❶ *a gang of teenagers* BAND, group, crowd, pack, horde, throng, mob, herd, swarm, troop, cluster; company, gathering; *informal* posse, bunch, gaggle, load. ❷ (*informal*) *John was one of our gang* CIRCLE, social circle, social set, group, clique, in-crowd, coterie, lot, ring; *informal* crew. ❸ *a gang of workmen* CREW, team, group, squad, shift, detachment, unit.

▶ **verb** *they all ganged up to put me down* CONSPIRE, cooperate, work together, act together, combine, join forces, team up, get together, unite, ally.

gangling, gangly ▶ **adjective** LANKY, rangy, tall, thin, skinny, spindly, stringy, bony, angular, scrawny, spare; awkward, uncoordinated, ungainly, gawky, inelegant, graceless, ungraceful; *dated* spindle-shanked.

– OPPOSITES squat.

gangster ▶ **noun** HOODLUM, gang member, racketeer, robber, ruffian, thug, tough, villain, lawbreaker, criminal; gunman, terrorist; Mafioso; *informal* mobster, crook, hit man; *N. Amer. informal* hood; *dated* desperado.

gaol ▶ **noun** (*Brit. dated*). *See* JAIL.

gaoler ▶ **noun** (*Brit. dated*). *See* JAILER.

gap ▶ **noun** ❶ *a gap in the shutters* OPENING, aperture, space, breach, chink, slit, slot, vent, crack, crevice, cranny, cavity, hole, orifice, interstice, perforation, break, fracture, rift, rent, fissure, cleft, divide. ❷ *a gap between meetings* PAUSE, intermission, interval, interlude, break, breathing space, breather, respite, hiatus; *N. Amer.* recess. ❸ *a gap in our records* OMISSION, blank, lacuna, void, vacuity. ❹ *the gap between rich and poor* CHASM, gulf, rift, split, separation, breach; contrast, difference, disparity, divergence, imbalance.

gape ▶ **verb** ❶ *she gaped at him in astonishment* STARE, stare open-mouthed, stare in wonder, goggle, gaze, ogle; *informal* rubberneck; *Brit. informal* gawk, gawp. ❷ *a leather jerkin which gaped at every seam* OPEN WIDE, open up, yawn; part, split.

gaping ▶ **adjective** *a gaping hole* CAVERNOUS, yawning, wide, broad; vast, huge, enormous, immense, extensive.

garb ▶ **noun** *men and women in riding garb* CLOTHES, clothing, garments, attire, costume, outfit, wear, uniform, livery, regalia; *informal* gear, get-up, togs, rig-out, duds; *Brit. informal* clobber; *formal* apparel; *archaic* raiment, habiliment, vestments.

▶ **verb** *both men were garbed in black* DRESS, clothe, attire, fit out, turn out, deck (out), kit out, costume, robe; *informal* get up; *archaic* apparel.

garbage (*N. Amer.*) ▶ **noun** ❶ *the garbage is taken to landfill sites* RUBBISH, refuse, waste, detritus, litter, junk, scrap; scraps, scourings, leftovers, remains, slops; *N. Amer.* trash; *Austral./NZ* mullock. ❷ *most of what he says is garbage* RUBBISH, nonsense, balderdash, claptrap, twaddle, blather; dross; *informal* hogwash, baloney, tripe, bilge, bull, bunk, poppycock, rot, bosh, piffle, dreck; *Brit. informal* tosh, codswallop, cobblers, stuff and nonsense; *informal, dated* tommyrot, bunkum.

garble ▶ **verb** MIX UP, muddle, jumble, confuse, obscure, distort; misstate, misquote, misreport, misrepresent, mistranslate, misinterpret, misconstrue, twist.

garden ▶ **noun** cottage garden, flower garden, rock garden, walled garden, knot garden; vegetable garden, kitchen garden, potager; (**gardens**) park, estate, grounds.

– RELATED TERMS horticultural.

■ **lead someone up the garden path** (*informal*) DECEIVE, mislead, delude, hoodwink, dupe, trick, entrap, beguile, take in, fool, pull the wool over someone's eyes, gull; *informal* con, pull a fast one on, string along, take for a ride, put one over on.

gargantuan ▶ **adjective** HUGE, enormous, vast, gigantic, very big, giant, massive, colossal, mammoth, immense, mighty, monumental, mountainous, titanic, towering, tremendous, elephantine, king-size(d), prodigious; *informal* mega, monster, whopping, humongous, jumbo; *Brit. informal* whacking, ginormous.

– OPPOSITES tiny.

garish ▶ **adjective** GAUDY, lurid, loud, overbright, harsh, glaring, violent, showy, glittering, brassy, brash; tasteless, in bad taste, vulgar, unattractive, bilious; *informal* flash, flashy, tacky.

– OPPOSITES drab.

garland ▶ **noun** *a garland of flowers* FESTOON, lei, wreath, ring, circle, swag; coronet, crown, coronal, chaplet, fillet.

▶ **verb** *gardens garlanded with coloured lights* FESTOON, wreathe, swathe, hang; adorn, ornament, embellish, decorate, deck, trim, dress, bedeck, array; *poetic/literary* bedizen, caparison.

garment ▶ **noun** ITEM OF CLOTHING, article of clothing; (**garments**) clothes, clothing, dress, garb, outfit, costume, attire; *informal* get-up, rig-out, gear, togs, duds; *N. Amer. informal* threads; *formal* apparel.

garner ▶ **verb** *Edward garnered ideas from his*

travels GATHER, collect, accumulate, amass, get together, assemble.

▶ **noun** (*archaic*) *the malt went into a garner* GRANARY, silo, storehouse, store, storeroom, depository.

garnish ▶ **verb** *garnish the dish with chopped parsley* DECORATE, adorn, ornament, trim, dress, embellish; enhance, grace, beautify, prettify, add the finishing touch to.

▶ **noun** *keep a few sprigs for a garnish* DECORATION, adornment, trim, trimming, ornament, ornamentation, embellishment, enhancement, finishing touch; *Cookery* chiffonade.

garret ▶ **noun** ATTIC, loft, roof space, cock loft, mansard.

garrison ▶ **noun** ❶ *the English garrison had been burned alive* TROOPS, militia, soldiers, forces; armed force, military detachment, unit, platoon, brigade, squadron, battalion, corps. ❷ *forces from three garrisons* FORTRESS, fort, fortification, stronghold, citadel, camp, encampment, cantonment, command post, base, station; barracks.

▶ **verb** ❶ *French infantry garrisoned the town* DEFEND, guard, protect, barricade, shield, secure; man, occupy. ❷ *troops were garrisoned in various regions* STATION, post, put on duty, deploy, assign, install; base, site, place, position; billet.

garrulity ▶ **noun** TALKATIVENESS, garrulousness, loquacity, loquaciousness, volubility, verbosity, verboseness, long-windedness, wordiness, chattiness, effusiveness; *informal* the gift of the gab; *Brit. informal* wittering; *rare* logorrhoea.

garrulous ▶ **adjective** ❶ *a garrulous old man* TALKATIVE, loquacious, voluble, verbose, chatty, chattering, gossipy; effusive, expansive, forthcoming, conversational, communicative; *informal* mouthy, gabby, gassy, windy, having the gift of the gab, having kissed the Blarney Stone; *Brit. informal* able to talk the hind legs off a donkey. ❷ *his garrulous reminiscences* LONG-WINDED, wordy, verbose, prolix, long, lengthy, rambling, wandering, maundering, meandering, digressive, diffuse, discursive; gossipy, chatty; *informal* windy, gassy.
– OPPOSITES taciturn, concise.

gash ▶ **noun** *a gash on his forehead* LACERATION, cut, wound, injury, slash, tear, incision; slit, split, rip, rent; scratch, scrape, graze, abrasion; *Medicine* lesion.

▶ **verb** *he gashed his hand on some broken glass* LACERATE, cut (open), wound, injure, hurt, slash, tear, gouge, puncture, slit, split, rend; scratch, scrape, graze, abrade.

gasp ▶ **verb** ❶ *I gasped in surprise* CATCH ONE'S BREATH, draw in one's breath, gulp; exclaim, cry (out). ❷ *he collapsed on the ground, gasping* PANT, puff, puff and pant, puff and blow, wheeze, breathe hard, choke, fight for breath.

▶ **noun** *a gasp of dismay* DRAWING-IN OF BREATH, gulp; exclamation, cry; *dated* ejaculation.

gastric ▶ **adjective** *gastric pain* STOMACH, intestinal, enteric, duodenal, coeliac, abdominal, ventral.

gate ▶ **noun** ❶ *heavy wooden gates* BARRIER, wicket gate, lychgate, five-barred gate, turnstile; *Brit.* kissing gate. ❷ *she went through the gate* GATEWAY, doorway, entrance, exit, egress, opening; door, portal; *N. Amer.* entryway.

gather ▶ **verb** ❶ *we gathered in the hotel lobby* CONGREGATE, assemble, meet, collect, come/get together, convene, muster, rally, converge; cluster together, crowd, mass, flock together; *formal* foregather. ❷ *he gathered his family together* SUMMON, call together, bring together, assemble, convene, rally, round up, muster, marshal. ❸ *knick-knacks she had gathered over the years* COLLECT, accumulate, amass, garner, accrue; store, stockpile, hoard, put by/away, lay by/in; *informal* stash away, squirrel away. ❹ *they gathered corn from the fields* HARVEST, reap, crop; pick, pluck; collect. ❺ *the show soon gathered a fanatical following* ATTRACT, draw, pull, pull in, collect, pick up. ❻ *I gather he's a keen footballer* UNDERSTAND, be given to understand, believe, be led to believe, think, conclude, deduce, infer, assume, take it, surmise, fancy; hear, hear tell, learn, discover. ❼ *he gathered her to his chest* CLASP, clutch, pull, embrace, enfold, hold, hug, cuddle, squeeze; *poetic/literary* embosom; *archaic* strain. ❽ *his tunic was gathered at the waist* PLEAT, shirr, pucker, tuck, fold, ruffle.
– OPPOSITES disperse.

gathering ▶ **noun** ❶ *she rose to address the gathering* ASSEMBLY, meeting, convention, rally, turnout, congress, convocation, conclave, council, synod, forum; congregation, audience, crowd, group, throng, mass, multitude; *informal* get-together; *formal* concourse. ❷ *the gathering of data for a future book* COLLECTING, collection, garnering, amassing, accumulation, accrual, cumulation, building up.

gauche ▶ **adjective** AWKWARD, gawky, inelegant, graceless, ungraceful, ungainly, maladroit, inept; lacking in social grace(s), unsophisticated, uncultured, uncultivated, unrefined, raw, inexperienced, unworldly.
– OPPOSITES elegant, sophisticated.

gaudy ▶ **adjective** GARISH, lurid, loud, overbright, glaring, harsh, violent, showy, glittering, brassy, ostentatious; tasteless, in bad taste, vulgar, unattractive, bilious; *informal* flash, flashy, tacky.
– OPPOSITES drab, tasteful.

gauge ▶ **noun** ❶ *the temperature gauge* MEASURING DEVICE, measuring instrument, meter, measure; indicator, dial, scale, display. ❷ *exports are an important gauge of economic activity* MEASURE, indicator, barometer, point of reference, guide, guideline, touchstone, yardstick, benchmark, criterion, test, litmus test. ❸ *guitar strings of a different gauge* SIZE, diameter, thickness, width, breadth; measure, capacity, magnitude; bore, calibre.

▶ **verb** ❶ *astronomers can gauge the star's intrinsic brightness* MEASURE, calculate, compute, work out, determine, ascertain; count, weigh, quantify, put a figure on. ❷ *it is difficult to gauge how effective the ban was* ASSESS, evaluate, determine, estimate, form an opinion of, appraise, weigh up, get the measure of, judge, guess; *informal* guesstimate, size up.

gaunt ▶ **adjective** ❶ *a gaunt, greying man* HAGGARD, drawn, thin, lean, skinny, spindly, spare, bony, angular, raw-boned, pinched, hollow-cheeked, scrawny, scraggy, as thin as a rake, cadaverous, skeletal, emaciated, skin-and-bones; wasted, withered; *informal* like a bag of bones; *dated* spindle-shanked; *archaic* starveling. ❷ *the gaunt ruin of Pendragon Castle* BLEAK, stark, desolate, bare, gloomy, dismal, sombre, grim, stern, harsh, forbidding, uninviting, cheerless.
– OPPOSITES plump.

gauzy ▶ **adjective** TRANSLUCENT, transparent, sheer, see-through, fine, delicate, flimsy, filmy, gossamer-like, diaphanous, chiffony, wispy, thin, light, insubstantial; *Brit.* floaty.
– OPPOSITES opaque, thick.

gawk ▶ **verb** (*informal*) GAPE, goggle, gaze, ogle, stare, stare open-mouthed; *informal* rubberneck; *Brit. informal* gawp.

gawky ▶ **adjective** AWKWARD, ungainly, gangling, gauche, maladroit, clumsy, inelegant, uncoordinated, graceless, ungraceful; unsophisticated, unconfident.
– OPPOSITES graceful.

gay ▶ **adjective** ❶ *gay men and women* HOMOSEXUAL, lesbian; *informal* queer, camp, pink, swinging the other way, homo, dykey; *Brit. informal* bent, poofy. ❷ (*dated*) *her children all looked chubby and gay* CHEERFUL, cheery, merry, jolly, light-hearted, carefree, jovial, glad, happy, in good/high spirits, joyful, elated, exuberant, animated, lively, sprightly, vivacious, buoyant, bouncy, bubbly, perky, effervescent, playful; *informal* chirpy. ❸ (*dated*) *they were having a gay old time* JOLLY, merry, hilarious, amusing, uproarious, rollicking, entertaining, enjoyable, convivial; festive. ❹ (*dated*) *gay checked curtains* BRIGHT, brightly coloured, vivid, brilliant, vibrant; richly coloured, many-coloured, multicoloured; flamboyant, showy, gaudy.
– OPPOSITES heterosexual, gloomy.

▶ **noun** *in Denmark gays can marry in church* HOMOSEXUAL, lesbian; *informal* queer, homo, queen, friend of Dorothy, pansy, nancy, dyke, les, lezzy, butch, femme; *Brit. informal* poof, ponce, woofter.

gaze ▶ **verb** *he gazed at her* STARE, look fixedly, gape, goggle, eye, look, study, scrutinize, take a good look; ogle, leer; *informal* gawk, rubberneck; *Brit. informal* gawp; *N. Amer. informal* eyeball.

▶ **noun** *his piercing gaze* STARE, fixed look, gape; regard, inspection, scrutiny.

gazebo ▶ **noun** SUMMER HOUSE, pavilion, belvedere; arbour, bower.

gazette ▶ **noun** NEWSPAPER, paper, journal, periodical, organ, news-sheet, newsletter, bulletin; *informal* rag.

gear ▶ **noun** (*informal*) ❶ *his fishing gear* EQUIPMENT, apparatus, paraphernalia, articles, appliances, impedimenta; tools, utensils, implements, instruments, gadgets; stuff, things; kit, rig, tackle, odds and ends, bits and pieces, bits and bobs; trappings, appurtenances, accoutrements, regalia; *Brit. informal* clobber, gubbins, odds and sods; *archaic* equipage. ❷ *I'll go back to my hotel and pick up my gear* BELONGINGS, possessions, effects, personal effects, property, paraphernalia, odds and ends, bits and pieces, bits and bobs, bags, baggage; *Law* chattels; *informal* things, stuff, kit; *Brit. informal* clobber. ❸ *the best designer gear* CLOTHES, clothing, garments, outfits, attire, garb; dress, wear; *informal* togs, duds, get-up; *Brit. informal* clobber, kit; *N. Amer. informal* threads; *formal* apparel.

gel, jell ▶ **verb** ❶ *leave the mixture to gel* SET, stiffen, solidify, thicken, harden; cake, congeal, coagulate, clot. ❷ *things started to gel very quickly* TAKE SHAPE, fall into place, come together, take form, work out; crystallize.

gelatinous ▶ **adjective** JELLY-LIKE, glutinous, viscous, viscid, mucilaginous, ropy, sticky, gluey, gummy, slimy; *informal* gooey, gunky.

geld ▶ **verb** CASTRATE, neuter, desex, fix; *N. Amer. & Austral.* alter; *Brit. informal* doctor.

gelid ▶ **adjective** FROZEN, freezing, icy, glacial, frosty, wintry, snowy; arctic, polar, Siberian.

gem ▶ **noun** ❶ *rubies and other gems* JEWEL, precious stone, semi-precious stone, stone; solitaire, brilliant, cabochon; *archaic* bijou. ❷ *the gem of the collection* BEST, finest, pride, prize, treasure, flower, pearl, the jewel in the crown; pick, choice, cream, the crème de la crème, elite, acme; *informal* one in a million, the bee's knees.

genealogy ▶ **noun** LINEAGE, line (of descent), family tree, bloodline; pedigree, ancestry, extraction, heritage, parentage, birth, family, dynasty, house, stock, blood, roots.

general ▶ **adjective** ❶ *this is suitable for general use* WIDESPREAD, common, extensive, universal, wide, popular, public, mainstream; established, conventional, traditional, orthodox, accepted. ❷ *a general pay increase* COMPREHENSIVE, overall, across the board, blanket, umbrella, mass, wholesale, sweeping, broad-ranging, inclusive, company-wide; universal, global, worldwide, nationwide. ❸ *general knowledge* MISCELLANEOUS, mixed, assorted, diversified, composite, heterogeneous. ❹ *the*

general practice USUAL, customary, habitual, traditional, normal, conventional, typical, standard, regular; familiar, accepted, prevailing, routine, run-of-the-mill, established, everyday, ordinary, common. ❺ *a general description* BROAD, imprecise, inexact, rough, loose, approximate, unspecific, vague, woolly, indefinite; *N. Amer. informal* ballpark.
– OPPOSITES restricted, localized, specialist, exceptional, detailed.

generality ▶ noun ❶ *the debate has moved on from generalities* GENERALIZATION, general statement, general principle, sweeping statement; abstraction, extrapolation. ❷ *the generality of this principle* UNIVERSALITY, comprehensiveness, all-inclusiveness, broadness. ❸ *the generality of people are kind* MAJORITY, greater part/number, best/better part; bulk, mass, preponderance, predominance; most.
– OPPOSITES specific, minority.

generally ▶ adverb ❶ *summers were generally hot* NORMALLY, in general, as a rule, by and large, more often than not, almost always, mainly, mostly, for the most part, predominantly, on the whole; usually, habitually, customarily, typically, ordinarily, commonly. ❷ *France was moving generally to the left* OVERALL, in general terms, generally speaking, all in all, broadly, on average, basically, effectively. ❸ *the method was generally accepted* WIDELY, commonly, extensively, universally, popularly.

generate ▶ verb ❶ *moves to generate extra business* CAUSE, give rise to, lead to, result in, bring about, create, make, produce, engender, spawn, precipitate, prompt, provoke, trigger, spark off, stir up, induce, promote, foster. ❷ *the male most likely to generate offspring* PROCREATE, breed, father, sire, spawn, create, produce, have; *poetic/literary* beget; *archaic* engender.

generation ▶ noun ❶ *people of the same generation* AGE, age group, peer group. ❷ *generations ago* AGES, years, aeons, a long time, an eternity; *informal* donkey's years; *Brit. informal* yonks. ❸ *the next generation of computers* CROP, batch, wave, range. ❹ *the generation of novel ideas* CREATION, production, initiation, origination, inception, inspiration. ❺ *human generation* PROCREATION, reproduction, breeding; creation.

generic ▶ adjective ❶ *a generic term for two separate offences* GENERAL, common, collective, non-specific, inclusive, all-encompassing, broad, comprehensive, blanket, umbrella. ❷ *generic drugs are cheaper than branded ones* UNBRANDED, non-proprietary.
– OPPOSITES specific.

generosity ▶ noun ❶ *the generosity of our host* LIBERALITY, lavishness, magnanimity, munificence, open-handedness, free-handedness, unselfishness; kindness, benevolence, altruism, charity, big-heartedness, goodness; *poetic/literary* bounteousness. ❷ *the generosity of the food portions* ABUNDANCE, plentifulness, copiousness, lavishness, liberality, largeness.

generous ▶ adjective ❶ *she is generous with money* LIBERAL, lavish, magnanimous, munificent, giving, open-handed, free-handed, bountiful, unselfish, ungrudging, free, indulgent, prodigal; *poetic/literary* bounteous. ❷ *it was generous of them to offer* MAGNANIMOUS, kind, benevolent, altruistic, charitable, noble, big-hearted, honourable, good; unselfish, self-sacrificing. ❸ *a generous amount of fabric* LAVISH, plentiful, copious, ample, liberal, large, great, abundant, profuse, bumper, opulent, prolific; *informal* a gogo, galore.
– OPPOSITES mean, selfish, meagre.

genesis ▶ noun ❶ *the hatred had its genesis in something dark* ORIGIN, source, root, beginning, start. ❷ *the genesis of neurosis* FORMATION, development, evolution, emergence, inception, origination, creation, formulation, propagation.

genial ▶ adjective FRIENDLY, affable, cordial, amiable, warm, easy-going, approachable, sympathetic; good-natured, good-humoured, cheerful; neighbourly, hospitable, companionable, comradely, sociable, convivial, outgoing, gregarious; *informal* chummy, pally; *Brit. informal* matey.
– OPPOSITES unfriendly.

genitals ▶ plural noun PRIVATE PARTS, genitalia, sexual organs, reproductive organs, pudenda; crotch, groin; *informal* naughty bits, privates; *euphemistic* nether regions.

genius ▶ noun ❶ *the world knew of his genius* BRILLIANCE, intelligence, intellect, ability, cleverness, brains, erudition, wisdom, fine mind; artistry, flair. ❷ *he has a genius for organization* TALENT, gift, flair, aptitude, facility, knack, bent, ability, expertise, capacity, faculty; strength, forte, brilliance, skill, artistry. ❸ *he is a genius* BRILLIANT PERSON, gifted person, mastermind, Einstein, intellectual, great intellect, brain; prodigy; *informal* egghead, bright spark; *Brit. informal* brainbox, clever clogs; *N. Amer. informal* brainiac, rocket scientist.
– OPPOSITES stupidity, dunce.

genocide ▶ noun MASS MURDER, mass homicide, massacre; annihilation, extermination, elimination, liquidation, eradication, decimation, butchery, bloodletting; pogrom, ethnic cleansing, holocaust.

genre ▶ noun CATEGORY, class, classification, group, set, list; type, sort, kind, variety, style, model, school, stamp, cast, ilk.

genteel ▶ adjective REFINED, respectable, decorous, mannerly, well mannered, courteous, polite, proper, correct, seemly; well bred, cultured, sophisticated, ladylike, gentlemanly, dignified, gracious; affected; *Brit. informal* posh.
– OPPOSITES uncouth.

gentility ▶ **noun** SOCIAL SUPERIORITY, respectability, punctiliousness, decorum, good manners, politeness, civility, courtesy, correctness; refinement, distinction, breeding, sophistication; graciousness, affectation, ostentation.

gentle ▶ **adjective** ❶ *his manner was gentle* KIND, tender, sympathetic, considerate, understanding, compassionate, benevolent, good-natured; humane, lenient, merciful, clement; mild, placid, serene, sweet-tempered. ❷ *a gentle breeze* LIGHT, soft. ❸ *a gentle slope* GRADUAL, slight, easy. ❹ (*archaic*) *a woman of gentle birth. See* NOBLE adjective sense 1.
– OPPOSITES brutal, strong, steep, low.

gentleman ▶ **noun** MAN; nobleman, honnête homme; *informal* gent; *archaic* cavalier.

gentlemanly ▶ **adjective** CHIVALROUS, gallant, honourable, noble, courteous, civil, mannerly, polite, gracious, considerate, thoughtful; well bred, cultivated, cultured, refined, suave, urbane.
– OPPOSITES rude.

gentry ▶ **noun** UPPER CLASSES, privileged classes, elite, high society, haut monde, smart set; establishment; *informal* upper crust, top drawer; *Brit. informal* nobs, toffs.

genuine ▶ **adjective** ❶ *a genuine Picasso* AUTHENTIC, real, actual, original, bona fide, true, veritable; attested, undisputed; *informal* pukka, the real McCoy, the real thing, kosher; *Austral./NZ informal* dinkum. ❷ *a very genuine person* SINCERE, honest, truthful, straightforward, direct, frank, candid, open; artless, natural, unaffected; *informal* straight, upfront, on the level; *N. Amer. informal* on the up and up.
– OPPOSITES bogus, insincere.

genus ▶ **noun** ❶ (*Biology*) *a large genus of plants* subdivision, division, group, subfamily. ❷ *a new genus of music* TYPE, sort, kind, genre, style, variety, category, class; breed, brand, family, stamp, cast, ilk.

germ ▶ **noun** ❶ *this detergent kills germs* MICROBE, micro-organism, bacillus, bacterium, virus; *informal* bug. ❷ *a fertilized germ* EMBRYO, bud; seed, spore, ovule; egg, ovum. ❸ *the germ of an idea* START, beginning(s), seed, embryo, bud, root, rudiment; origin, source, potential; core, nucleus, kernel, essence.

germane ▶ **adjective** RELEVANT, pertinent, applicable, apposite, material; apropos, to the point, appropriate, apt, fitting, suitable; connected, related, akin; *formal* ad rem.
– OPPOSITES irrelevant.

germinate ▶ **verb** ❶ *the grain is allowed to germinate* SPROUT, shoot (up), bud; develop, grow, spring up; *dated* vegetate. ❷ *the idea began to germinate* DEVELOP, take root, grow, emerge, evolve, mature, expand, advance, progress.

gestation ▶ **noun** ❶ *a gestation of thirty days* PREGNANCY, incubation; development, maturation. ❷ *the law underwent a period of gestation* DEVELOPMENT, evolution, formation, emergence, origination.

gesticulate ▶ **verb** GESTURE, signal, motion, wave, sign.

gesticulation ▶ **noun** GESTURING, gesture, hand movement, signals, signs; wave, indication; body language.

gesture ▶ **noun** ❶ *a gesture of surrender* SIGNAL, sign, motion, indication, gesticulation. ❷ *a symbolic gesture* ACTION, act, deed, move.
▶ **verb** *he gestured to her* SIGNAL, motion, gesticulate, wave, indicate, give a sign.

get ▶ **verb** ❶ *where did you get that hat?* ACQUIRE, obtain, come by, receive, gain, earn, win, come into, take possession of, be given; buy, purchase, procure, secure; gather, collect, pick up, hook, net, land; achieve, attain; *informal* get one's hands on, get one's mitts on, get hold of, grab, bag, score. ❷ *I got your letter* RECEIVE, be sent, be in receipt of, be given. ❸ *your tea's getting cold* BECOME, grow, turn, go. ❹ *get the children from school* FETCH, collect, go for, call for, pick up, bring, deliver, convey, ferry, transport. ❺ *the chairman gets £650,000 a year* EARN, be paid, take home, bring in, make, receive, collect, gross; *informal* pocket, bank, rake in, net, bag. ❻ *have the police got their man?* APPREHEND, catch, arrest, capture, seize; take prisoner, take into custody, detain, put in jail, put behind bars, imprison, incarcerate; *informal* collar, grab, nab, nail, run in, pinch, bust, pick up, pull in, do, feel someone's collar; *Brit. informal* nick. ❼ *I got a taxi* TRAVEL BY/ON/IN; take, catch, use. ❽ *she got flu* SUCCUMB TO, develop, go/come down with, sicken for, fall victim to, be struck down with, be afflicted by/with; become infected with, catch, contract, fall ill with, be taken ill with; *Brit.* go down with; *informal* take ill with; *N. Amer. informal* take sick with. ❾ *I got a pain in my arm* EXPERIENCE, suffer, be afflicted with, sustain, feel, have. ❿ *I got him on the radio* CONTACT, get in touch with, communicate with, make contact with, reach; phone, call, radio; speak to, talk to; *Brit.* get on to; *informal* get hold of. ⓫ *I didn't get what he said* HEAR, discern, distinguish, make out, perceive, follow, take in. ⓬ *I don't get the joke* UNDERSTAND, comprehend, grasp, see, fathom, follow, perceive, apprehend, unravel, decipher; *informal* get the drift of, catch on to, latch on to, figure out; *Brit. informal* twig, suss. ⓭ *we got there early* ARRIVE, reach, come, make it, turn up, appear, come on the scene, approach, enter, present oneself, come along, materialize, show one's face; *informal* show (up), roll in/up, blow in. ⓮ *we got her to go* PERSUADE, induce, prevail on, influence; wheedle into, talk into, cajole into. ⓯ *I'd like to get to meet him* CONTRIVE, arrange, find a way, manage; succeed in, organize; *informal* work it, fix it. ⓰ *I'll get supper* PREPARE, get ready, cook, make, assemble, muster, concoct; *informal* fix, rustle up; *Brit. informal* knock up. **17** (*informal*) *I'll get him for that* TAKE REVENGE ON, exact/wreak revenge on, get one's revenge on, avenge oneself on, take vengeance on, get even with, pay back, get back at, exact retribution on, give someone their just deserts; *Brit. informal* get one's own back on. **18** *He scratched his head. 'You've got me there.'* BAFFLE, nonplus, perplex, puzzle, bewilder, mystify, bemuse, confuse, confound; *informal* flummox, faze, stump, beat, fox; *N. Amer. informal* discombobulate. **19** *what gets me is how neurotic she is* ANNOY, irritate, exasperate, anger, irk, vex, provoke, incense, infuriate, madden, try someone's patience, ruffle someone's feathers; *informal* aggravate, peeve, miff, rile, get to, needle, hack off, get someone's back up, get on someone's nerves, get up someone's nose, get someone's goat, drive mad, make someone see red; *Brit. informal* wind up, nark, get someone's wick; *N. Amer. informal* tee off, tick off.

– OPPOSITES give, send, take, leave.

■ **get about** MOVE ABOUT, move around, travel.

■ **get something across** COMMUNICATE, get over, impart, convey, transmit, make clear, express.

■ **get ahead** PROSPER, flourish, thrive, do well; succeed, make it, advance, get on in the world, go up in the world, make good, become rich; *informal* go places, get somewhere, make the big time.

■ **get along** **1** *does he get along with his family?* BE FRIENDLY, be compatible, get on; agree, see eye to eye, concur, be in accord; *informal* hit it off, be on the same wavelength. **2** *he was getting along well at school* FARE, manage, progress, advance, get on, get by, do, cope; succeed.

■ **get around** TRAVEL, circulate, socialize, do the rounds.

■ **get at** **1** *it's difficult to get at the pipes* ACCESS, get to, reach, touch. **2** *he had been got at by enemy agents* CORRUPT, suborn, influence, bribe, buy off, pay off; *informal* fix, square; *Brit. informal* nobble. **3** (*informal*) *what are you getting at?* IMPLY, suggest, intimate, insinuate, hint, mean, drive at, allude to. **4** (*Brit. informal*) *I don't like being got at* CRITICIZE, pick on, find fault with, nag; BULLY, victimize, persecute, discriminate against.

■ **get away** ESCAPE, run away/off, break out, break free, break loose, bolt, flee, take flight, make off, take off, decamp, abscond, make a run for it; slip away, sneak away; *informal* cut and run, skedaddle, do a disappearing act, scarper, leg it; *Brit. informal* do a bunk, do a runner.

■ **get away with** ESCAPE BLAME FOR, escape punishment for.

■ **get back** RETURN, come home, come back.

■ **get something back** RETRIEVE, regain, win back, recover, recoup, reclaim, repossess, recapture, redeem; find (again), trace.

■ **get back at** TAKE REVENGE ON, exact/wreak revenge on, avenge oneself on, take vengeance on, get even with, pay back, retaliate on/against, exact retribution on, give someone their just deserts; *Brit. informal* get one's own back on.

■ **get someone down** DEPRESS, sadden, make unhappy, make gloomy, dispirit, dishearten, demoralize, discourage, crush, weigh down, oppress; upset, distress; *informal* give someone the blues, make someone fed up.

■ **get by** MANAGE, cope, survive, exist, subsist, muddle through/along, scrape by, make ends meet, make do, keep the wolf from the door; *informal* make out.

■ **get off** **1** *Sally got off the bus* ALIGHT (FROM), step off, dismount (from), descend (from), disembark (from), leave, exit. **2** (*informal*) *he was arrested but got off* ESCAPE PUNISHMENT, be acquitted, be absolved, be cleared, be exonerated.

■ **get on** **1** *we got on the train* BOARD, enter, step aboard, climb on, mount, ascend, catch; *informal* hop on, jump on. **2** *how are you getting on?* FARE, manage, progress, get along, do, cope, get by, survive, muddle through/along; succeed, prosper; *informal* make out. **3** *he got on with his job* CONTINUE, proceed, go ahead, carry on, go on, press on, persist, persevere; keep at; *informal* stick with/at. **4** *we don't get on. See* GET ALONG sense 1.

■ **get out** **1** *the prisoners got out. See* GET AWAY. **2** *the news got out* BECOME KNOWN, become common knowledge, come to light, emerge, transpire; come out, be uncovered, be revealed, be divulged, be disclosed, be reported, be released, leak out.

■ **get out of** EVADE, dodge, shirk, avoid, escape, sidestep; *informal* duck (out of), wriggle out of, cop out of; *Austral./NZ informal* duckshove.

■ **get over** **1** *I have just got over flu* RECOVER FROM, recuperate from, get better after, shrug off, survive. **2** *we tried to get over this problem* OVERCOME, surmount, get the better of, master, get round, find an/the answer to, get a grip on, deal with, cope with, sort out, take care of, crack, rise above; *informal* lick.

■ **get something over**. *See* GET SOMETHING ACROSS.

■ **get round someone** CAJOLE, persuade, wheedle, coax, prevail on, win over, bring round, sway, beguile, charm, inveigle, influence, woo; *informal* sweet-talk, soft-soap, butter up, twist someone's arm.

■ **get together** **1** *get together the best writers* COLLECT, gather, assemble, bring together, rally, muster, marshal, congregate, convene, amass; *formal* convoke. **2** *we must get together soon* MEET (UP), rendezvous, see each other, socialize.

■ **get up** GET OUT OF BED, rise, stir, rouse oneself; *informal* surface; *formal* arise.

■ **get someone up** (*informal*) DRESS, clothe, attire, garb, fit out, turn out, deck (out), trick out/up, costume, array, robe; *informal* doll up; *archaic* apparel.

getaway ▶ **noun** ESCAPE, breakout, bolt for freedom, flight; disappearance, vanishing act; *Brit. informal* flit.

get-together ▶ **noun** PARTY, meeting, gathering, social event; *informal* do, bash; *Brit. informal* rave-up, knees-up, jolly, bunfight, beano.

get-up ▶ **noun** (*informal*) OUTFIT, clothes, costume, ensemble, suit, clothing, dress, attire, garments, garb; *informal* gear, togs, duds; *Brit. informal* clobber, rig-out; *N. Amer. informal* threads; *formal* apparel.

get-up-and-go ▶ **noun** (*informal*) DRIVE, initiative, enterprise, enthusiasm, eagerness, ambition, motivation, dynamism, energy, gusto, vigour, vitality, verve, fire, fervour, zeal, commitment, spirit; *informal* gumption, oomph, vim, pep.
– OPPOSITES apathy.

ghastly ▶ **adjective** ❶ *a ghastly stabbing* TERRIBLE, frightful, horrible, grim, awful, dire; frightening, terrifying, horrifying, alarming; distressing, shocking, appalling, harrowing; dreadful, horrendous, monstrous, gruesome, grisly. ❷ (*informal*) *a ghastly building* UNPLEASANT, objectionable, disagreeable, distasteful, awful, terrible, dreadful, frightful, detestable, insufferable, vile; *informal* horrible, horrid. ❸ *the patient feels ghastly* ILL, unwell, peaky, poorly; sick, queasy, nauseous; *Brit.* off colour; *informal* rough, lousy, rotten, terrible, awful, dreadful; *Brit. informal* grotty, ropy; *Scottish informal* peely-wally; *Austral./NZ informal* crook. ❹ *a ghastly pallor* PALE, white, pallid, pasty, wan, bloodless, peaky, ashen, grey, waxy, blanched, drained, pinched, green, sickly; *informal* like death warmed up.
– OPPOSITES pleasant, charming, healthy, fine.

ghost ▶ **noun** ❶ *his ghost haunts the crypt* SPECTRE, phantom, wraith, spirit, presence; apparition; *informal* spook. ❷ *the ghost of a smile* TRACE, hint, suggestion, impression, suspicion, tinge; glimmer, semblance, shadow, whisper.

ghostly ▶ **adjective** SPECTRAL, ghostlike, phantom, wraithlike, phantasmal, phantasmic; unearthly, unnatural, supernatural; insubstantial, shadowy; eerie, weird, uncanny; frightening, spine-chilling, hair-raising, blood-curdling, terrifying, chilling, sinister; *informal* creepy, scary, spooky.

ghoulish ▶ **adjective** MACABRE, grisly, gruesome, grotesque, ghastly; unhealthy, horrible, unwholesome.

giant ▶ **noun** *the forest giant had died* COLOSSUS, man mountain, behemoth, Brobdingnagian, mammoth, monster; *informal* jumbo.
– OPPOSITES dwarf.

▶ **adjective** *a giant vacuum cleaner* HUGE, colossal, massive, enormous, gigantic, very big, mammoth, vast, immense, monumental, mountainous, titanic, towering, elephantine, king-size(d), gargantuan, Brobdingnagian; substantial, hefty; *informal* mega, monster, whopping, humongous, jumbo, hulking, bumper; *Brit. informal* ginormous.
– OPPOSITES miniature.

gibber ▶ **verb** PRATTLE, babble, ramble, drivel, jabber, gabble, burble, twitter, flannel, mutter, mumble; *informal* yammer, blabber, jibber-jabber, blather, blether; *Brit. informal* witter, chunter.

gibberish ▶ **noun** NONSENSE, rubbish, balderdash, blather, blether; *informal* drivel, gobbledegook, mumbo-jumbo, tripe, hogwash, baloney, bilge, bosh, bull, bunk, guff, eyewash, piffle, twaddle, poppycock; *Brit. informal* cobblers, codswallop, double Dutch, tosh, cack; *N. Amer. informal* garbage, blathers, applesauce.

gibe ▶ **noun & verb.** *See* JIBE.

giddiness ▶ **noun** DIZZINESS, light-headedness; faintness, unsteadiness, shakiness, wobbliness; *informal* wooziness, legs like jelly.

giddy ▶ **adjective** ❶ *she felt giddy* DIZZY, light-headed, faint, weak, vertiginous; unsteady, shaky, wobbly, reeling; *informal* woozy. ❷ *she was young and giddy* FLIGHTY, silly, frivolous, skittish, irresponsible, flippant, whimsical, capricious; feather-brained, scatty, thoughtless, heedless, carefree; *informal* dippy; *N. Amer. informal* ditsy.
– OPPOSITES steady, sensible.

gift ▶ **noun** ❶ *he gave the staff a gift* PRESENT, handout, donation, offering, bestowal, bonus, award, endowment; tip, gratuity, baksheesh; largesse; *informal* prezzie, freebie, perk; *formal* benefaction. ❷ *a gift for melody* TALENT, flair, aptitude, facility, knack, bent, ability, expertise, capacity, capability, faculty; endowment, strength, genius, brilliance, skill, artistry.

▶ **verb** *he gifted a composition to the orchestra* PRESENT, give, bestow, confer, donate, endow, award, accord, grant; hand over, make over.

gifted ▶ **adjective** TALENTED, skilful, skilled, accomplished, expert, consummate, master(ly), first-rate, able, apt, adept, proficient; intelligent, clever, bright, brilliant; precocious; *informal* crack, top-notch, ace.
– OPPOSITES inept.

gigantic ▶ **adjective** HUGE, enormous, vast, extensive, very big, very large, giant, massive, colossal, mammoth, immense, monumental, mountainous, titanic, towering, elephantine, king-size(d), gargantuan; *informal* mega, monster, whopping, humongous, jumbo, hulking, bumper; *Brit. informal* ginormous.
– OPPOSITES tiny.

giggle ▶ **verb** *he giggled at the picture* TITTER,

snigger, snicker, tee-hee, chuckle, chortle, laugh.

▶ **noun** *she suppressed a giggle* TITTER, snigger, snicker, tee-hee, chuckle, chortle, laugh.

gigolo ▶ **noun** PLAYBOY, (male) escort; admirer, lover; *informal* fancy man; *Brit. informal* toy boy.

gild ▶ **verb** ❶ *a gilded weathercock* COVER WITH GOLD, paint gold. ❷ *he tends to gild the truth* ELABORATE, embellish, embroider; camouflage, disguise, dress up, colour, exaggerate, expand on; *informal* jazz up.

gimcrack ▶ **adjective** SHODDY, jerry-built, flimsy, insubstantial, thrown together, make-shift; inferior, poor-quality, second-rate, cheap, cheapjack, tawdry, kitschy, trashy; *informal* tacky, junky, rubbishy.

gimmick ▶ **noun** PUBLICITY DEVICE, stunt, contrivance, scheme, stratagem, ploy; *informal* shtick.

gingerly ▶ **adverb** CAUTIOUSLY, carefully, with care, warily, charily, circumspectly, delicately; heedfully, watchfully, vigilantly, attentively; hesitantly, timidly.
– OPPOSITES recklessly.

gird ▶ **verb** (*poetic/literary*) ❶ *Sir Hector girded on his sword* FASTEN, belt, bind, tie. ❷ *the island was girded by rocks* SURROUND, enclose, encircle, circle, encompass, border, bound, edge, skirt, fringe; close in, confine. ❸ *they girded themselves for war* PREPARE, get ready, gear up; nerve, steel, galvanize, brace, fortify; *informal* psych oneself up.

girdle ▶ **noun** ❶ *a diamond-studded girdle* BELT, sash, cummerbund, waistband, strap, band, girth, cord. ❷ *her stockings were held up by her girdle* CORSET, corselet, foundation garment, panty girdle; truss.

▶ **verb** *a garden girdled the house* SURROUND, enclose, encircle, circle, encompass, circumscribe, border, bound, skirt, edge; (*poetic/literary*) gird.

girl ▶ **noun** ❶ *a five-year-old girl* FEMALE CHILD, daughter; schoolgirl; *Scottish & N. English* lass, lassie; *derogatory* chit. *See also* CHILD. ❷ *a tall dark girl* YOUNG WOMAN, young lady, miss, mademoiselle; *Scottish* lass, lassie; *Irish* colleen; *informal* chick, girlie, filly; *Brit. informal* bird, bint; *N. Amer. informal* gal, broad, dame, jane, babe; *Austral./NZ informal* sheila; *poetic/literary* maid, damsel; *archaic* wench. ❸ *his girl left him. See* GIRLFRIEND.

girlfriend ▶ **noun** SWEETHEART, lover, partner, significant other, girl, woman; fiancée; *informal* steady; *Brit. informal* bird; *N. Amer. informal* squeeze; *dated* lady (friend), lady love, betrothed; *archaic* leman.

girlish ▶ **adjective** GIRLY, youthful, childlike, childish, immature; feminine.

girth ▶ **noun** ❶ *a tree ten feet in girth* CIRCUMFERENCE, perimeter; width, breadth. ❷ *he tied the towel around his girth* STOMACH, midriff, middle, abdomen, belly, gut; *informal* tummy, tum. ❸ *a horse's girth N. Amer.* cinch.

gist ▶ **noun** ESSENCE, substance, central theme, heart of the matter, nub, kernel, marrow, meat, burden, crux; thrust, drift, sense, meaning, significance, import; *informal* nitty-gritty.

give ▶ **verb** ❶ *he gave them £2000* PRESENT WITH, provide with, supply with, furnish with, let someone have; hand (over), offer, proffer; award, grant, bestow, accord, confer, make over; donate, contribute, put up. ❷ *can I give him a message?* CONVEY, pass on, impart, communicate, transmit; send, deliver, relay; tell. ❸ *a baby given into their care* ENTRUST, commit, consign, assign; *formal* commend. ❹ *he gave his life for them* SACRIFICE, give up, relinquish; devote, dedicate. ❺ *he gave her time to think* ALLOW, permit, grant, accord; offer. ❻ *this leaflet gives our opening times* SHOW, display, set out, indicate, detail, list. ❼ *they gave no further trouble* CAUSE, make, create, occasion. ❽ *garlic gives flavour* PRODUCE, yield, afford, impart, lend. ❾ *he gave a party* ORGANIZE, arrange, lay on, throw, host, hold, have, provide. ❿ *Dominic gave a bow* PERFORM, execute, make, do. ⓫ *she gave a shout* UTTER, let out, emit, produce, make. ⓬ *he gave Harry a beating* ADMINISTER, deliver, deal, inflict, impose. ⓭ *the door gave* GIVE WAY, cave in, collapse, break, fall apart; bend, buckle.
– OPPOSITES receive, take.

▶ **noun** (*informal*) *there isn't enough give in the jacket* ELASTICITY, flexibility, stretch, stretchiness; slack, play.

■ **give someone away** BETRAY, inform on; *informal* split on, rat on, peach on, do the dirty on, blow the whistle on, sell down the river; *Brit. informal* grass on, shop; *N. Amer. informal* rat out, finger; *Austral./NZ informal* dob on; *English Law* turn Queen's/King's evidence.

■ **give something away** REVEAL, disclose, divulge, let slip, leak, let out.

■ **give in** CAPITULATE, concede defeat, admit defeat, give up, surrender, yield, submit, back down, give way, defer, relent, throw in the towel/sponge.

■ **give something off/out** EMIT, produce, send out, throw out; discharge, release, exude, vent.

■ **give out** RUN OUT, be used up, be consumed, be exhausted, be depleted; fail, flag; dry up.

■ **give something out** DISTRIBUTE, issue, hand out, pass round, dispense; dole out, dish out, mete out; allocate, allot, share out.

■ **give up**. *See* GIVE IN.

■ **give something up** STOP, cease, discontinue, desist from, abstain from, cut out, renounce, forgo; resign from, stand down from; *informal* quit, kick, swear off, leave off, pack in, lay off; *Brit. informal* jack in.

give and take ▶ **noun** COMPROMISE, concession; cooperation, reciprocity, teamwork, interplay.

given ▶ **adjective** ❶ *a given number of years* SPECIFIED, stated, designated, set, particular, specific; prescribed, agreed, appointed, prearranged, predetermined. ❷ *she was given to fits of temper* PRONE, liable, inclined, disposed, predisposed, apt, likely.
– OPPOSITES unspecified.
▶ **preposition** *given the issue's complexity, a summary is difficult* CONSIDERING, in view of, bearing in mind, in the light of; assuming.
▶ **noun** *his aggression is taken as a given* ESTABLISHED FACT, reality, certainty.

giver ▶ **noun** DONOR, contributor, donator, benefactor, benefactress, provider; supporter, backer, patron, sponsor, subscriber.

glacial ▶ **adjective** ❶ *glacial conditions* FREEZING, cold, icy, ice-cold, sub-zero, frozen, gelid, wintry; arctic, polar, Siberian; bitter, biting, raw, chill. ❷ *Polly's tone was glacial* UNFRIENDLY, hostile, unwelcoming; frosty, icy, cold, chilly.
– OPPOSITES tropical, hot, friendly.

glad ▶ **adjective** ❶ *I'm really glad you're coming* PLEASED, happy, delighted, thrilled, overjoyed, cock-a-hoop, elated, gleeful; gratified, grateful, thankful; *informal* tickled pink, over the moon; *Brit. informal* chuffed; *N. English informal* made up; *Austral. informal* wrapped. ❷ *I'd be glad to help* WILLING, eager, happy, pleased, delighted; ready, prepared. ❸ *glad tidings* PLEASING, welcome, happy, joyful, cheering, heartening, gratifying; *poetic/literary* gladsome.
– OPPOSITES dismayed, reluctant, distressing.

gladden ▶ **verb** DELIGHT, please, make happy, elate; cheer (up), hearten, buoy up, give someone a lift, uplift; gratify; *informal* give someone a kick, tickle someone pink, buck up.
– OPPOSITES sadden.

gladly ▶ **adverb** WITH PLEASURE, happily, cheerfully; willingly, readily, eagerly, freely, ungrudgingly; *archaic* fain, lief.

glamorous ▶ **adjective** ❶ *a glamorous woman* BEAUTIFUL, attractive, lovely, bewitching, enchanting, beguiling; elegant, chic, stylish, fashionable; charming, charismatic, appealing, alluring, seductive; *informal* classy, glam. ❷ *a glamorous lifestyle* EXCITING, thrilling, stimulating; dazzling, glittering, glossy, colourful, exotic; *informal* ritzy, glitzy, jet-setting.
– OPPOSITES dowdy, dull.

glamour ▶ **noun** ❶ *she had undeniable glamour* BEAUTY, allure, attractiveness; elegance, chic, style; charisma, charm, magnetism, desirability. ❷ *the glamour of show business* ALLURE, attraction, fascination, charm, magic, romance, mystique, exoticism, spell; excitement, thrill; glitter, the bright lights; *informal* glitz, glam.

glance ▶ **verb** ❶ *Rachel glanced at him* LOOK BRIEFLY, look quickly, peek, peep; glimpse; *Scottish* keek; *informal* have a gander; *Brit. informal* take a dekko, have a shufti, have a butcher's; *Austral./NZ informal* squiz. ❷ *I glanced through the report* READ QUICKLY, scan, skim, leaf, flick, flip, thumb, browse; dip into. ❸ *a bullet glanced off the ice* RICOCHET, rebound, be deflected, bounce; graze, clip. ❹ *sunlight glanced off her hair* REFLECT, flash, gleam, glint, glitter, glisten, glimmer, shimmer.
▶ **noun** ❶ *a glance at his watch* PEEK, peep, brief look, quick look, glimpse; *Scottish* keek; *informal* gander; *Brit. informal* dekko, shufti, butcher's; *Austral./NZ informal* squiz, geek.
■ **at first glance** ON THE FACE OF IT, on the surface, at first sight, to the casual eye, to all appearances; apparently, seemingly, outwardly, superficially, it would seem, it appears, as far as one can see/tell, by all accounts.

glare ▶ **verb** ❶ *she glared at him* SCOWL, glower, stare angrily, look daggers, frown, lour, give someone a black look, look threateningly; *informal* give someone a dirty look. ❷ *the sun glared out of the sky* BLAZE, beam, shine brightly, be dazzling, be blinding.
▶ **noun** ❶ *a cold glare* SCOWL, glower, angry stare, frown, black look, threatening look; *informal* dirty look. ❷ *the harsh glare of the lights* BLAZE, dazzle, shine, beam; radiance, brilliance, luminescence.

glaring ▶ **adjective** ❶ *glaring lights* DAZZLING, blinding, blazing, strong, bright, harsh. ❷ *a glaring omission* OBVIOUS, conspicuous, unmistakable, inescapable, unmissable, striking; flagrant, blatant, outrageous, gross; overt, patent, transparent, manifest; *informal* standing/sticking out like a sore thumb.
– OPPOSITES soft, minor.

glass ▶ **noun** ❶ *a glass of water* TUMBLER, drinking vessel; flute, schooner, balloon, goblet, chalice. ❷ *we sell china and glass* GLASSWARE, crystal, crystalware. ❸ (*Brit.*) *she looked in the glass* MIRROR, looking glass.
– RELATED TERMS vitreous.

glasses ▶ **plural noun** SPECTACLES; *N. Amer.* eyeglasses; *informal* specs.

glasshouse ▶ **noun** GREENHOUSE, hothouse, conservatory.

glassy ▶ **adjective** ❶ *the glassy surface of the lake* SMOOTH, mirror-like, gleaming, shiny, glossy, polished, vitreous; slippery, icy; clear, transparent, translucent; calm, still, flat. ❷ *a glassy stare* EXPRESSIONLESS, glazed, blank, vacant, fixed, motionless; emotionless, impassive, lifeless, wooden, vacuous.
– OPPOSITES rough, expressive.

glaze ▶ **verb** ❶ *the pots are glazed when dry* VARNISH, enamel, lacquer, japan, shellac, paint; gloss. ❷ *pastry glazed with caramel* COVER, coat; ice, frost. ❸ *his eyes glazed over* BECOME GLASSY, go blank; mist over, film over.
▶ **noun** ❶ *pottery with a blue glaze* VARNISH, enamel, lacquer, finish, coating; lustre, shine, gloss. ❷ *a cake with an apricot glaze* COATING, topping; icing, frosting.

gleam ▶ verb SHINE, glimmer, glint, glitter, shimmer, sparkle, twinkle, flicker, wink, glisten, flash; *poetic/literary* glister.
▶ noun ❶ *a gleam of light* GLIMMER, glint, shimmer, twinkle, sparkle, flicker, flash; beam, ray, shaft. ❷ *the gleam of brass* SHINE, lustre, gloss, sheen; glint, glitter, glimmer, sparkle; brilliance, radiance, glow; *poetic/literary* glister. ❸ *a gleam of hope* GLIMMER, flicker, ray, spark, trace, suggestion, hint, sign.

glean ▶ verb OBTAIN, get, take, draw, derive, extract, cull, garner, gather; learn, find out.

glee ▶ noun DELIGHT, pleasure, happiness, joy, gladness, elation, euphoria; amusement, mirth, merriment; excitement, gaiety, exuberance; triumph, jubilation, relish, satisfaction, gratification.
– OPPOSITES disappointment.

gleeful ▶ adjective DELIGHTED, pleased, joyful, happy, glad, overjoyed, elated, euphoric; amused, mirthful, merry, exuberant; cock-a-hoop, jubilant; *informal* over the moon.

glib ▶ adjective SLICK, pat, plausible; smooth-talking, fast-talking, silver-tongued, smooth, urbane, having kissed the Blarney Stone; disingenuous, insincere, facile, shallow, superficial, flippant; *informal* flip, sweet-talking.
– OPPOSITES sincere.

glide ▶ verb ❶ *a gondola glided past* SLIDE, slip, sail, float, drift, flow; coast, freewheel, roll; skim, skate. ❷ *seagulls gliding over the waves* SOAR, wheel, plane; fly. ❸ *he glided out of the door* SLIP, steal, slink.

glimmer ▶ verb *moonlight glimmered on the lawn* GLEAM, shine, glint, flicker, shimmer, glisten, glow, twinkle, sparkle, glitter, wink, flash; *poetic/literary* glister.
▶ noun ❶ *a glimmer of light* GLEAM, glint, flicker, shimmer, glow, twinkle, sparkle, flash, ray. ❷ *a glimmer of hope* GLEAM, flicker, ray, trace, sign, suggestion, hint.

glimpse ▶ noun *a glimpse of her face* BRIEF LOOK, quick look; glance, peek, peep; sight, sighting.
▶ verb *he glimpsed a figure* CATCH SIGHT OF, notice, discern, spot, spy, sight, pick out, make out; *Brit. informal* clock; *poetic/literary* espy, descry.

glint ▶ verb *the diamond glinted* SHINE, gleam, catch the light, glitter, sparkle, twinkle, wink, glimmer, shimmer, glisten, flash; *poetic/literary* glister.
▶ noun *the glint of the silver* GLITTER, gleam, sparkle, twinkle, glimmer, flash.

glisten ▶ verb SHINE, sparkle, twinkle, glint, glitter, glimmer, shimmer, wink, flash; *poetic/literary* glister.

glitter ▶ verb *crystal glittered in the candlelight* SHINE, sparkle, twinkle, glint, gleam, shimmer, glimmer, wink, flash, catch the light; *poetic/literary* glister.
▶ noun ❶ *the glitter of light on the water* SPARKLE, twinkle, glint, gleam, shimmer, glimmer, flicker, flash; brilliance, luminescence. ❷ *the glitter of show business* GLAMOUR, excitement, thrills, attraction, appeal; dazzle; *informal* razzle-dazzle, razzmatazz, glitz, ritziness.

gloat ▶ verb DELIGHT, relish, take great pleasure, revel, rejoice, glory, exult, triumph, crow; boast, brag, be smug, congratulate oneself, preen oneself, pat oneself on the back; rub one's hands together; *informal* rub it in.

global ▶ adjective ❶ *the global economy* WORLDWIDE, international, world, intercontinental. ❷ *a global view of the problem* COMPREHENSIVE, overall, general, all-inclusive, all-encompassing, encyclopedic, universal, blanket; broad, far-reaching, extensive, sweeping.

globe ▶ noun ❶ *every corner of the globe* WORLD, earth, planet. ❷ *the sun is a globe* SPHERE, orb, ball, spheroid, round.

globular ▶ adjective SPHERICAL, spheric, spheroidal, round, globe-shaped, ball-shaped, orb-shaped, rounded, bulbous.

globule ▶ noun DROPLET, drop, bead, tear, ball, bubble, pearl; *informal* blob, glob.

gloom ▶ noun ❶ *she peered into the gloom* DARKNESS, dark, dimness, blackness, murkiness, shadows, shade; dusk, twilight, gloaming. ❷ *his gloom deepened* DESPONDENCY, depression, dejection, downheartedness, melancholy, melancholia, unhappiness, sadness, glumness, gloominess, misery, sorrow, woe, wretchedness; despair, pessimism, hopelessness; *informal* the blues, the dumps.
– OPPOSITES light, happiness.

gloomy ▶ adjective ❶ *a gloomy room* DARK, shadowy, sunless, dim, sombre, dingy, dismal, dreary, murky, unwelcoming, cheerless, comfortless, funereal; *poetic/literary* Stygian. ❷ *Joanna looked gloomy* DESPONDENT, downcast, downhearted, dejected, dispirited, disheartened, discouraged, demoralized, crestfallen; depressed, desolate, low, sad, unhappy, glum, melancholy, miserable, fed up, woebegone, mournful, forlorn, morose; *informal* blue, down in the mouth, down in the dumps. ❸ *gloomy forecasts about the economy* PESSIMISTIC, depressing, downbeat, disheartening, disappointing; unfavourable, bleak, bad, black, sombre, grim, cheerless, hopeless.
– OPPOSITES bright, cheerful, optimistic.

glorify ▶ verb ❶ *they gather to glorify God* PRAISE, extol, exalt, worship, revere, reverence, venerate, pay homage to, honour, adore, thank, give thanks to; *formal* laud; *archaic* magnify. ❷ *a poem to glorify the memory of the dead* ENNOBLE, exalt, elevate, dignify, enhance, augment, promote; praise, celebrate, honour, extol, lionize, acclaim, applaud, hail; glamorize, idealize, romanticize, enshrine, immortalize; *formal* laud.
– OPPOSITES dishonour.

glorious ▶ **adjective** ❶ *a glorious victory* ILLUSTRIOUS, celebrated, famous, acclaimed, distinguished, honoured; outstanding, great, magnificent, noble, triumphant. ❷ *glorious views* WONDERFUL, marvellous, magnificent, superb, sublime, spectacular, lovely, fine, delightful; *informal* super, great, stunning, fantastic, terrific, tremendous, sensational, heavenly, divine, gorgeous, fabulous, fab, awesome, ace; *informal, dated* capital, spiffing; *Brit. informal* smashing; *poetic/literary* wondrous, beauteous.
– OPPOSITES undistinguished, horrid.

glory ▶ **noun** ❶ *a sport that won him glory* RENOWN, fame, prestige, honour, distinction, kudos, eminence, acclaim, praise; celebrity, recognition, reputation; *informal* bouquets. ❷ *glory be to God* PRAISE, worship, adoration, veneration, honour, reverence, exaltation, extolment, homage, thanksgiving, thanks. ❸ *a house restored to its former glory* MAGNIFICENCE, splendour, resplendence, grandeur, majesty, greatness, nobility; opulence, beauty, elegance. ❹ *the glories of Vermont* WONDER, beauty, delight, marvel, phenomenon; sight, spectacle.
– OPPOSITES shame, obscurity, modesty.
▶ **verb** *we gloried in our independence* TAKE PLEASURE IN, revel in, rejoice in, delight in; relish, savour; congratulate oneself on, be proud of; boast about; *informal* get a kick out of, get a thrill out of.

gloss[1] ▶ **noun** ❶ *the gloss of her hair* SHINE, sheen, lustre, gleam, patina, brilliance, shimmer. ❷ *beneath the gloss of success* FACADE, veneer, surface, show, camouflage, disguise, mask, smokescreen; window dressing.
▶ **verb** ❶ *she glossed her lips* MAKE GLOSSY, shine; glaze, polish, burnish. ❷ *he tried to gloss over his problems* CONCEAL, cover up, hide, disguise, mask, veil; shrug off, brush aside, play down, minimize, understate, make light of; *informal* brush under the carpet.

gloss[2] ▶ **noun** *glosses in the margin* EXPLANATION, interpretation, exegesis, explication, elucidation; annotation, note, footnote, commentary, comment; translation; *historical* scholium.
▶ **verb** *difficult words are glossed in a footnote* EXPLAIN, interpret, explicate, elucidate; annotate; translate, paraphrase.

glossy ▶ **adjective** ❶ *a glossy wooden floor* SHINY, gleaming, lustrous, brilliant, shimmering, glistening, satiny, sheeny, smooth, glassy; polished, lacquered, glazed. ❷ *a glossy magazine* EXPENSIVE, high-quality; stylish, fashionable, glamorous; attractive, artistic; *Brit.* upmarket, coffee-table; *informal* classy, ritzy, glitzy.
– OPPOSITES dull, cheap.

glove ▶ **noun** MITTEN, mitt, gauntlet.

glow ▶ **verb** ❶ *lights glowed from the windows* SHINE, radiate, gleam, glimmer, flicker, flare; luminesce. ❷ *a fire glowed in the hearth* RADIATE HEAT, smoulder, burn. ❸ *she glowed with embarrassment* FLUSH, blush, redden, colour (up), go pink, go scarlet; burn. ❹ *she glowed with pride* TINGLE, thrill; beam.
▶ **noun** ❶ *the glow of the fire* RADIANCE, light, shine, gleam, glimmer, incandescence, luminescence; warmth, heat. ❷ *a glow spread over her face* FLUSH, blush, rosiness, pinkness, redness, high colour; bloom, radiance. ❸ *a warm glow deep inside her* HAPPINESS, contentment, pleasure, satisfaction.
– OPPOSITES pallor.

glower ▶ **verb** *she glowered at him* SCOWL, glare, look daggers, frown, lour, give a someone black look; *informal* give someone a dirty look.
▶ **noun** *the glower on his face* SCOWL, glare, frown, black look; *informal* dirty look.

glowing ▶ **adjective** ❶ *glowing coals* BRIGHT, shining, radiant, glimmering, flickering, twinkling, incandescent, luminous, luminescent; lit (up), lighted, illuminated, ablaze; aglow, smouldering. ❷ *his glowing cheeks* ROSY, pink, red, flushed, blushing; radiant, blooming, ruddy, florid; hot, burning. ❸ *glowing colours* VIVID, vibrant, bright, brilliant, rich, intense, strong, radiant, warm. ❹ *a glowing report* COMPLIMENTARY, favourable, enthusiastic, commendatory, admiring, lionizing, rapturous, rhapsodic, adulatory; fulsome; *informal* rave.

glue ▶ **noun** *a tube of glue* ADHESIVE, fixative, gum, paste, cement; epoxy (resin), size; *N. Amer.* mucilage; *N. Amer. informal* stickum.
▶ **verb** ❶ *the planks were glued together* STICK, gum, paste; affix, fix, cement. ❷ (*informal*) *she was glued to the television* BE RIVETED TO, be gripped by, be hypnotized by, be mesmerized by.

glum ▶ **adjective** GLOOMY, downcast, downhearted, dejected, despondent, crestfallen, disheartened; depressed, desolate, unhappy, doleful, melancholy, miserable, woebegone, mournful, forlorn, fed up, in the doldrums, morose; *informal* blue, down in the mouth, down in the dumps.
– OPPOSITES cheerful.

glut ▶ **noun** *a glut of cars* SURPLUS, excess, surfeit, superfluity, overabundance, superabundance, oversupply, plethora.
– OPPOSITES dearth.
▶ **verb** *the factories are glutted* CRAM FULL, overfill, overload, oversupply, saturate, flood, inundate, deluge, swamp; *informal* stuff.

glutinous ▶ **adjective** STICKY, viscous, viscid, tacky, gluey, gummy, treacly; adhesive; *informal* gooey, gloopy, cloggy; *N. Amer. informal* gloppy.

glutton ▶ **noun** GOURMAND, overeater, big eater, gorger, gobbler; *informal* (greedy) pig, gannet, greedy guts, gutbucket, guzzler.

gluttonous ▶ **adjective** GREEDY, gourmandizing, voracious, insatiable, wolfish; *informal* piggish, piggy.

gluttony ▶ **noun** GREED, greediness, overeating, gourmandism, gourmandizing, voracity, insatiability; *informal* piggishness.

gnarled ▶ **adjective** ❶ *a gnarled tree trunk* KNOBBLY, knotty, knotted, gnarly, lumpy, bumpy, nodular; twisted, bent, crooked, distorted, contorted. ❷ *gnarled hands* TWISTED, bent, misshapen; arthritic; rough, wrinkled, wizened.

gnash ▶ **verb** GRIND, grate, rasp, grit.

gnaw ▶ **verb** ❶ *the dog gnawed at a bone* CHEW, champ, chomp, bite, munch, crunch; nibble, worry. ❷ *the pressures are gnawing away their independence* ERODE, wear away, wear down, eat away (at); consume, devour. ❸ *the doubts gnawed at her* NAG, plague, torment, torture, trouble, distress, worry, haunt, oppress, burden, hang over, bother, fret; niggle.

go ▶ **verb** ❶ *he's gone into town* MOVE, proceed, make one's way, advance, progress, pass; walk, travel, journey; *poetic/literary* betake oneself. ❷ *the road goes to London* EXTEND, stretch, reach; lead. ❸ *the money will go to charity* BE GIVEN, be donated, be granted, be presented, be awarded; be devoted; be handed (over). ❹ *it's time to go* LEAVE, depart, take oneself off, go away, withdraw, absent oneself, make an exit, exit; set off, start out, get under way, be on one's way; decamp, retreat, retire, make off, clear out, run off/away, flee; *Brit.* make a move; *informal* make tracks, push off, beat it, take off, skedaddle, scram, split, scoot; *Brit. informal* sling one's hook. ❺ *three years went past* PASS, elapse, slip by/past, roll by/past, tick away; fly by/past. ❻ *a golden age that has gone for good* DISAPPEAR, vanish, be no more, be over, run its course, fade away; finish, end, cease. ❼ *all our money had gone* BE USED UP, be spent, be exhausted, be consumed, be drained, be depleted. ❽ *I'd like to see my grandchildren before I go* DIE, pass away, pass on, lose one's life, expire, breathe one's last, perish, go to meet one's maker; *informal* give up the ghost, kick the bucket, croak, buy it, turn up one's toes; *Brit. informal* snuff it, pop one's clogs; *N. Amer. informal* bite the big one, buy the farm; *archaic* decease, depart this life. ❾ *the bridge went suddenly* COLLAPSE, give way, fall down, cave in, crumble, disintegrate. ❿ *his hair had gone grey* BECOME, get, turn, grow. ⓫ *he heard the bell go* MAKE A SOUND, sound, reverberate, resound; ring, chime, peal, toll, clang. ⓬ *everything went well* TURN OUT, work out, develop, come out; result, end (up); *informal* pan out. ⓭ *those colours don't go* MATCH, be harmonious, harmonize, blend, be suited, be complementary, coordinate, be compatible. ⓮ *my car won't go* FUNCTION, work, run, operate. ⓯ *where does the cutlery go?* BELONG, be kept, be found, be located, be situated. ⓰ *this all goes to prove my point* CONTRIBUTE, help, serve; incline, tend.
– OPPOSITES arrive, come, return, clash.

▶ **noun** ❶ *his second go* ATTEMPT, try, effort, bid, endeavour; *informal* shot, stab, crack, bash, whirl, whack; *formal* essay. ❷ *he has plenty of go in him* ENERGY, vigour, vitality, life, liveliness, spirit, verve, enthusiasm, zest, vibrancy, sparkle; stamina, dynamism, drive, push, determination; *informal* pep, punch, oomph, get-up-and-go.

■ **go about** SET ABOUT, begin, embark on, start, commence, address oneself to, get down to, get to work on, get going on, undertake; approach, tackle, attack; *informal* get cracking on/with.

■ **go along with** AGREE TO/WITH, fall in with, comply with, cooperate with, acquiesce in, assent to, follow; submit to, yield to, defer to.

■ **go away**. *See* GO verb sense 4.

■ **go back on** RENEGE ON, break, fail to honour, default on, repudiate, retract; do an about-face; *informal* cop out (of), rat on.

■ **go by** *we have to go by his decision* OBEY, abide by, comply with, keep to, conform to, follow, heed, defer to, respect.

■ **go down** ❶ *the ship went down* SINK, founder, go under. ❷ *interest rates are going down* DECREASE, get lower, fall, drop, decline; plummet, plunge, slump. ❸ (*informal*) *they went down in the first leg* LOSE, be beaten, be defeated, come to grief. ❹ *his name will go down in history* BE REMEMBERED, be recorded, be commemorated, be immortalized.

■ **go down with** (*Brit.*) FALL ILL WITH, get, develop, contract, pick up, succumb to, fall victim to, be struck down with, become infected with.

■ **go far** BE SUCCESSFUL, succeed, be a success, do well, get on, get somewhere, get ahead, make good; *informal* make a name for oneself, make one's mark.

■ **go for** ❶ *I went for the tuna* CHOOSE, pick, opt for, select, plump for, decide on. ❷ *the man went for her* ATTACK, assault, hit, strike, beat up, assail, set upon, rush at, lash out at; *informal* lay into, rough up; *Brit. informal* have a go at, duff up; *N. Amer. informal* beat up on. ❸ *he goes for older women* BE ATTRACTED TO, like, fancy; prefer, favour, choose; *informal* have a thing about.

■ **go in for** TAKE PART IN, participate in, engage in, get involved in, join in, enter into, undertake; practise, pursue; espouse, adopt, embrace.

■ **go into** INVESTIGATE, examine, enquire into, look into, research, probe, explore, delve into; consider, review, analyse.

■ **go off** ❶ *the bomb went off* EXPLODE, detonate, blow up. ❷ (*Brit.*) *the milk's gone off* GO BAD, go stale, go sour, turn, spoil, go rancid; decompose, go mouldy.

■ **go on** ❶ *the lecture went on for hours* LAST, continue, carry on, run on, proceed; endure, persist; take. ❷ *she went on about the sea* TALK AT LENGTH, ramble, rattle on, chatter, prattle, gabble, blether, blather, twitter; *informal* gab, yak, yabber, yatter; *Brit. informal* witter, rabbit, natter, waffle, chunter; *N. Amer. informal* run off at the mouth. ❸ *I'm not sure what went on* HAPPEN, take place, occur, transpire; *N. Amer. informal* go down; *poetic/literary* come to pass, betide; *archaic* hap.

■ **go out** ❶ *the lights went out* BE TURNED OFF, be extinguished; stop burning. ❷ *he's going out with Kate* SEE, take out, be someone's boyfriend/girlfriend, be involved with; *informal* date, go steady with, go with; *N. Amer. informal, dated* step out with; *dated* court, woo.

■ **go over** ❶ *go over the figures* EXAMINE, study, scrutinize, inspect, look at/over, scan, check; analyse, appraise, review. ❷ *we are going over our lines* REHEARSE, practise, read through, run through.

■ **go round** ❶ *the wheels were going round* SPIN, revolve, turn, rotate, whirl. ❷ *a nasty rumour going round* BE SPREAD, be circulated, be put about, circulate, pass round, be broadcast.

■ **go through** ❶ *the terrible things she has gone through* UNDERGO, experience, face, suffer, be subjected to, live through, endure, brave, bear, tolerate, withstand, put up with, cope with, weather. ❷ *he went through hundreds of pounds* SPEND, use up, run through, get through, expend, deplete; waste, squander, fritter away. ❸ *he went through Susie's bag* SEARCH, look, hunt, rummage, rifle; *informal* frisk. ❹ *I have to go through the report* EXAMINE, study, scrutinize, inspect, look over, scan, check; analyse, appraise, review. ❺ *the deal has gone through* BE COMPLETED, be concluded, be brought off; be approved, be signed, be rubber-stamped.

■ **go under** GO BANKRUPT, cease trading, go into receivership, go into liquidation, become insolvent, be liquidated, be wound up, be shut (down); fail; *informal* go broke, go to the wall, go belly up, fold.

■ **go without** ❶ *I went without breakfast* ABSTAIN FROM, refrain from, forgo, do without, deny oneself. ❷ *the children did not go without* BE DEPRIVED, be in want, go short, go hungry, be in need.

goad ▶ **noun** ❶ *he applied his goad to the cows* PROD, spike, staff, crook, rod. ❷ *a goad to political change* STIMULUS, incentive, encouragement, inducement, fillip, spur, prod, prompt; motive, motivation.

▶ **verb** *we were goaded into action* PROVOKE, spur, prod, egg on, hound, badger, incite, rouse, stir, move, stimulate, motivate, prompt, induce, encourage, urge, inspire; impel, pressure, pressurize, dragoon.

go-ahead (*informal*) ▶ **noun** *they gave the go-ahead for the scheme* PERMISSION, consent, leave, licence, dispensation, warrant, clearance; authorization, assent, agreement, approval, endorsement, sanction, blessing, the nod; *informal* the thumbs up, the OK, the green light.

▶ **adjective** *go-ahead companies* ENTERPRISING, resourceful, innovative, ingenious, original, creative; progressive, pioneering, modern, forward-looking, enlightened; enthusiastic, ambitious, entrepreneurial, high-powered; bold, daring, audacious, adventurous, dynamic; *informal* go-getting.

goal ▶ **noun** OBJECTIVE, aim, end, target, design, intention, intent, plan, purpose; (holy) grail; ambition, aspiration, wish, dream, desire, hope.

goat ▶ **noun** ❶ *a herd of goats* billy (goat), nanny (goat), kid. ❷ (*Brit. informal*) *she's always playing the goat. See* FOOL noun sense 1. ❸ *be careful of that old goat* LECHER, libertine, womanizer, seducer, Don Juan, Casanova, Lothario, Romeo; pervert, debauchee, rake; *informal* lech, dirty old man, ladykiller.

– RELATED TERMS caprine.

gobble ▶ **verb** GUZZLE, bolt, gulp, devour, wolf, cram, gorge (oneself) on; *informal* tuck into, put away, demolish, polish off, shovel down, stuff one's face (with), pig oneself (on); *Brit. informal* scoff, gollop, shift; *N. Amer. informal* scarf (down/up).

gobbledegook ▶ **noun** (*informal*) GIBBERISH, claptrap, nonsense, rubbish, balderdash, mumbo-jumbo, blather, blether; *N. Amer.* garbage; *informal* drivel, tripe, hogwash, baloney, bilge, bosh, bull, bunk, guff, eyewash, piffle, twaddle, poppycock, phooey, hooey; *Brit. informal* cobblers, codswallop, double Dutch, tosh; *N. Amer. informal* bushwa, applesauce.

go-between ▶ **noun** INTERMEDIARY, middleman, agent, broker, liaison, linkman, contact; negotiator, interceder, intercessor, mediator.

goblet ▶ **noun** WINE GLASS, chalice; glass, beaker, tumbler, cup.

goblin ▶ **noun** HOBGOBLIN, gnome, dwarf, troll, imp, elf, brownie, fairy, pixie, leprechaun.

god ▶ **noun** ❶ *a gift from God* THE LORD, the Almighty, the Creator, the Maker, the Godhead; Allah, Jehovah, Yahweh; (God) the Father, (God) the Son, the Holy Ghost/Spirit, the Holy Trinity. ❷ *sacrifices to appease the gods* DEITY, goddess, divine being, celestial being, divinity, immortal, avatar. ❸ *wooden gods* IDOL, graven image, icon, totem, talisman, fetish, juju.

godforsaken ▶ **adjective** WRETCHED, miserable, dreary, dismal, depressing, grim, cheerless, bleak, desolate, gloomy; deserted, neglected, isolated, remote, backward; *Brit. informal* grotty.

– OPPOSITES charming.

godless ▶ **adjective** ❶ *a godless society* ATHEISTIC, unbelieving, agnostic, sceptical, heretical, faithless, irreligious, ungodly, unholy, impious, profane; infidel, heathen, idolatrous, pagan; satanic, devilish. ❷ *godless pleasures* IMMORAL, wicked, sinful, wrong, evil, bad, iniquitous, corrupt; irreligious, sacrilegious, profane,

blasphemous, impious; depraved, degenerate, debauched, perverted, decadent; impure.
– OPPOSITES religious, virtuous.

godlike ▶ adjective DIVINE, godly, superhuman; angelic, seraphic; spiritual, heavenly, celestial; sacred, holy, saintly.

godly ▶ adjective RELIGIOUS, devout, pious, reverent, believing, God-fearing, saintly, holy, prayerful, churchgoing.
– OPPOSITES irreligious.

godsend ▶ noun BOON, blessing, bonus, plus, benefit, advantage, help, aid, asset; stroke of luck; *informal* perk; *formal* perquisite.
– OPPOSITES curse.

goggle ▶ verb STARE, gape, gaze, ogle; *informal* gawk, rubberneck; *Brit. informal* gawp.

going-over ▶ noun (*informal*) ❶ *his work was subjected to a going-over* EXAMINATION, inspection, investigation, probe, check-up; assessment, review, analysis, appraisal, critique; *informal* once-over. ❷ *the flat needs a going-over* CLEAN, dust, mop, scrub; *informal* vacuum, once-over. ❸ *the thugs gave him a going-over* BEATING, thrashing, thumping, pummelling, battering, pelting; assault, attack; *informal* doing-over, belting, bashing, pasting, walloping, clobbering, hiding.

goings-on ▶ plural noun EVENTS, happenings, affairs, business; mischief, misbehaviour, misconduct, funny business; *informal* monkey business, hanky-panky, shenanigans; *Brit. informal* jiggery-pokery, carry-on; *N. Amer. informal* monkeyshines.

gold ▶ noun *she won the gold* GOLD MEDAL, first prize.
– RELATED TERMS auric, aurous.

golden ▶ adjective ❶ *her golden hair* BLOND(E), yellow, fair, flaxen, tow-coloured. ❷ *a golden time* SUCCESSFUL, prosperous, flourishing, thriving; favourable, providential, lucky, fortunate; happy, joyful, glorious. ❸ *a golden opportunity* EXCELLENT, fine, superb, splendid; special, unique; favourable, opportune, promising, bright, full of promise; advantageous, profitable, valuable, providential. ❹ *the golden girl of tennis* FAVOURITE, favoured, popular, admired, beloved, pet; acclaimed, applauded, praised; brilliant, consummate, gifted; *informal* blue-eyed; *formal* lauded.
– OPPOSITES dark, unhappy.

gone ▶ adjective ❶ *I wasn't gone long* AWAY, absent, off, out; missing, unavailable. ❷ *those days are gone* PAST, over (and done with), no more, done, finished, ended; forgotten, dead and buried. ❸ *the milk's all gone* USED UP, consumed, finished, spent, depleted; at an end. ❹ *an aunt of mine, long since gone* DEAD, expired, departed, no more, passed on/away; late, lost, lamented; perished, fallen; defunct, extinct; *informal* six feet under, pushing up daisies; *formal* deceased; *euphemistic* with God, asleep, at peace.
– OPPOSITES present, here, alive.

goo ▶ noun (*informal*) STICKY SUBSTANCE, ooze, sludge, muck; *informal* gunk, crud, gloop; *Brit. informal* gunge; *N. Amer. informal* glop.

good ▶ adjective ❶ *a good product* FINE, superior, quality; excellent, superb, outstanding, magnificent, exceptional, marvellous, wonderful, first-rate, first-class, sterling; satisfactory, acceptable, up to scratch, up to standard, not bad, all right; *informal* great, OK, A1, ace, terrific, fantastic, fabulous, fab, top-notch, class, awesome, wicked; *informal, dated* capital; *Brit. informal* smashing, brilliant, brill; *Austral. informal* beaut, bonzer; *Brit. informal, dated* spiffing, top hole. ❷ *a good person* VIRTUOUS, righteous, upright, upstanding, moral, ethical, high-minded, principled; exemplary, law-abiding, irreproachable, blameless, guiltless, unimpeachable, honourable, scrupulous, reputable, decent, respectable, noble, trustworthy; meritorious, praiseworthy, admirable; whiter than white, saintly, saintlike, angelic; *informal* squeaky clean. ❸ *the children are good at school* WELL BEHAVED, obedient, dutiful, polite, courteous, respectful, deferential, compliant. ❹ *a good thing to do* RIGHT, correct, proper, decorous, seemly; appropriate, fitting, apt, suitable; convenient, expedient, favourable, opportune, felicitous, timely. ❺ *a good driver* CAPABLE, able, proficient, adept, adroit, accomplished, skilful, skilled, talented, masterly, expert; *informal* great, mean, wicked, nifty, ace; *N. Amer. informal* crackerjack. ❻ *a good friend* CLOSE, intimate, dear, bosom, special, best, firm, valued, treasured; loving, devoted, loyal, faithful, constant, reliable, dependable, trustworthy, trusty, true, unfailing, staunch. ❼ *the dogs are in good condition* HEALTHY, fine, sound, tip-top, hale and hearty, fit, robust, sturdy, strong, vigorous. ❽ *a good time was had by all* ENJOYABLE, pleasant, agreeable, pleasurable, delightful, great, nice, lovely; amusing, diverting, jolly, merry, lively; *informal* super, fantastic, fabulous, fab, terrific, grand; *Brit. informal* brilliant, brill, smashing; *N. Amer. informal* peachy, ducky; *Austral./NZ informal* beaut, bonzer. ❾ *it was good of you to come* KIND, kind-hearted, good-hearted, generous, charitable, magnanimous, gracious; altruistic, unselfish, selfless. ❿ *a good time to call* CONVENIENT, suitable, appropriate, fitting, fit; opportune, timely, favourable, advantageous, expedient, felicitous, happy, providential. ⓫ *milk is good for you* WHOLESOME, healthy, healthful, nourishing, nutritious, nutritional, beneficial, salubrious. ⓬ *are these eggs good?* EDIBLE, safe to eat, fit for human consumption; fresh, wholesome, consumable; *formal* comestible. ⓭ *good food* DELICIOUS, tasty, mouth-watering, appetizing, flavoursome, flavourful, delectable, toothsome, palatable; succulent, luscious; *informal* scrumptious, delish, scrummy, yummy; *Brit. informal* moreish; *N. Amer. informal* finger-licking, nummy. ⓮ *a good reason* VALID, genuine, authentic, legitimate, sound, bona fide; convincing, persuasive, telling, potent, cogent, compelling. ⓯ *we waited a good hour* WHOLE, full, entire, complete, solid. ⓰ *a good number of them* CONSIDERABLE, sizeable, substantial, appreciable, significant; goodly, fair, reasonable; plentiful, abundant, great, large, generous; *informal* tidy. ⓱ *wear your good clothes* BEST, smart, smartest, finest, nicest; special, party, Sunday, formal, dressy. ⓲ *good weather* FINE, fair, dry; bright, clear, sunny, cloudless; calm, windless; warm, mild, balmy, clement, pleasant, nice.

–OPPOSITES bad, wicked, naughty, poor, terrible, inconvenient, small, scruffy.

▶ **noun** ❶ *issues of good and evil* VIRTUE, righteousness, goodness, morality, integrity, rectitude; honesty, truth, honour, probity; propriety, worthiness, merit; blamelessness, purity. ❷ *it's all for your good* BENEFIT, advantage, profit, gain, interest, welfare, well-being; enjoyment, comfort, ease, convenience; help, aid, assistance, service; behalf.

–OPPOSITES wickedness, disadvantage.

▶ **exclamation** *good, that's settled* FINE, very well, all right, right, right then, yes, agreed; *informal* okay, OK, okey-dokey, roger; *Brit. informal* righto, righty-ho.

■ **for good** *those days are gone for good* FOREVER, permanently, for always, (for) evermore, for ever and ever, for eternity, until hell freezes over, never to return; *N. Amer.* forevermore; *informal* for keeps, until doomsday, until the cows come home; *archaic* for aye.

■ **in good part** *she took the joke in good part* GOOD-NATUREDLY, good-humouredly, without offence, amicably, favourably, tolerantly, indulgently, cheerfully, well.

■ **make good** SUCCEED, be successful, be a success, do well, get ahead, reach the top; prosper, flourish, thrive; *informal* make it, make the grade, make a name for oneself, make one's mark, get somewhere, arrive.

■ **make something good** ❶ *he promised to make good any damage* REPAIR, mend, fix, put right, see to; restore, remedy, rectify. ❷ *they made good their escape* EFFECT, conduct, perform, implement, execute, carry out; achieve, accomplish, succeed in, realize, attain, engineer, bring about, bring off. ❸ *he will make good his promise* FULFIL, carry out, implement, discharge, honour, redeem; keep, observe, abide by, comply with, stick to, heed, follow, be bound by, live up to, stand by, adhere to.

goodbye ▶ **exclamation** FAREWELL, adieu, au revoir, ciao, auf Wiedersehen, adios; *Austral./NZ* hooray; *informal* bye, bye-bye, so long, see you (later), later(s); *Brit. informal* cheers, cheerio, ta-ta; *N. English informal* ta-ra; *informal, dated* toodle-oo, toodle-pip.

good-for-nothing ▶ **adjective** *a good-for-nothing layabout* USELESS, worthless, incompetent, inefficient, inept, ne'er-do-well; lazy, idle, slothful, indolent, shiftless; *informal* no-good, lousy.

–OPPOSITES worthy.

▶ **noun** *lazy good-for-nothings* NE'ER-DO-WELL, layabout, do-nothing, idler, loafer, lounger, sluggard, shirker; *informal* waster, slacker, lazybones, couch potato; *Brit. informal* skiver.

good-humoured ▶ **adjective** GENIAL, affable, cordial, friendly, amiable, easy-going, approachable, good-natured, cheerful, cheery; companionable, comradely, sociable, convivial, company-loving; *informal* chummy, pally; *Brit. informal* matey; *N. Amer. informal* clubby.

–OPPOSITES grumpy.

good-looking ▶ **adjective** ATTRACTIVE, beautiful, pretty, handsome, lovely, stunning, striking, arresting, gorgeous, prepossessing, fetching, captivating, bewitching, beguiling, engaging, charming, enchanting, appealing, delightful; sexy, seductive, alluring, tantalizing, irresistible, ravishing, desirable; *Scottish & N. English* bonny; *informal* fanciable, tasty, hot, easy on the eye, drop-dead gorgeous; *Brit. informal* fit; *N. Amer. informal* cute, foxy; *Austral./NZ informal* spunky; *poetic/literary* beauteous; *archaic* comely, fair.

–OPPOSITES ugly.

goodly ▶ **adjective** LARGE, largish, sizeable, substantial, considerable, respectable, significant, decent, generous, handsome; *informal* tidy, serious.

–OPPOSITES paltry.

good-natured ▶ **adjective** WARM-HEARTED, friendly, amiable; neighbourly, benevolent, kind, kind-hearted, generous, unselfish, considerate, thoughtful, obliging, helpful, supportive, charitable; understanding, sympathetic, easy-going, accommodating; *Brit. informal* decent.

–OPPOSITES malicious.

goodness ▶ **noun** ❶ *he had some goodness in him* VIRTUE, good, righteousness, morality, integrity, rectitude; honesty, truth, truthfulness, honour, probity; propriety, decency, respectability, nobility, worthiness, worth, merit, trustworthiness; blamelessness, purity. ❷ *God's goodness towards us* KINDNESS, kindliness, tender-heartedness, humanity, mildness, benevolence, graciousness; tenderness, warmth, affection, love, goodwill; sympathy, compassion, care, concern, understanding, tolerance, generosity, charity, leniency, clemency, magnanimity. ❸ *slow cooking retains the food's goodness* NUTRITIONAL VALUE, nutrients, wholesomeness, nourishment.

goods ▶ **plural noun** ❶ *he dispatched the goods* MERCHANDISE, wares, stock, commodities, produce, products, articles; imports, exports. ❷ *the dead man's goods* PROPERTY, possessions, effects, chattels, valuables; *informal* things, stuff, junk, gear, kit, bits and pieces; *Brit. infor-*

mal clobber. ❸ (*Brit.*) *most goods went by train* FREIGHT, cargo; load, consignment, delivery, shipment.

good-tempered ▶ **adjective** EQUABLE, even-tempered, imperturbable; unruffled, unflustered, untroubled, well balanced; easy-going, mellow, mild, calm, relaxed, cool, at ease; placid, stable, level-headed; cheerful, upbeat; *informal* unflappable, laid-back.
– OPPOSITES moody.

goodwill ▶ **noun** BENEVOLENCE, compassion, goodness, kindness, consideration, charity; co-operation, collaboration; friendliness, amity, thoughtfulness, decency, sympathy, understanding, neighbourliness.
– OPPOSITES hostility.

goody-goody ▶ **adjective** (*informal*) SELF-RIGHTEOUS, sanctimonious, pious; prim and proper, strait-laced, prudish, priggish, puritanical, moralistic; *informal* starchy, square.

gooey ▶ **adjective** (*informal*) ❶ *a gooey mess* STICKY, viscous, viscid; gluey, tacky, gummy, treacly, syrupy; *Brit.* claggy; *informal* gloopy, gungy, icky; *N. Amer. informal* gloppy. ❷ *a gooey film* SENTIMENTAL, mawkish, cloying, sickly, saccharine, sugary, syrupy; romantic; *Brit.* twee; *informal* slushy, sloppy, mushy, schmaltzy, lovey-dovey, cheesy, corny, sick-making; *Brit. informal* soppy; *N. Amer. informal* cornball, sappy.

goose ▶ **noun** gander, gosling.

gore[1] ▶ **noun** *the film's gratuitous gore* BLOOD, bloodiness; bloodshed, slaughter, carnage, butchery.

gore[2] ▶ **verb** *he was gored by a bull* PIERCE, stab, stick, impale, spear, horn.

gorge ▶ **noun** *the river runs through a gorge* RAVINE, canyon, gully, defile, couloir; chasm, gulf; *N. English* clough, gill; *N. Amer.* gulch, coulee.
▶ **verb** ❶ *they gorged themselves on cakes* STUFF, cram, fill; glut, satiate, overindulge, overfill; *informal* pig. ❷ *vultures gorged on the flesh* DEVOUR, guzzle, gobble, gulp (down), wolf; *informal* tuck into, demolish, polish off, scoff (down), down, stuff one's face (with); *Brit. informal* gollop; *N. Amer. informal* scarf (down/up).

gorgeous ▶ **adjective** ❶ *a gorgeous girl* GOOD-LOOKING, attractive, beautiful, pretty, handsome, lovely, stunning, striking, arresting, prepossessing, fetching, captivating, bewitching, charming, enchanting, appealing, delightful; sexy, seductive, alluring, tantalizing, irresistible, ravishing, desirable; *Scottish & N. English* bonny; *informal* fanciable, tasty, hot, easy on the eye, drop-dead gorgeous; *Brit. informal* fit; *N. Amer. informal* cute, foxy; *Austral./NZ informal* spunky; *poetic/literary* beauteous; *archaic* comely, fair. ❷ *a gorgeous view* SPECTACULAR, splendid, superb, wonderful, grand, impressive, awe-inspiring, awesome, amazing, stunning, breathtaking, incredible; *informal* sensational, fabulous, fantastic. ❸ *gorgeous uniforms* RESPLENDENT, magnificent, sumptuous, luxurious, elegant, opulent; dazzling, brilliant. ❹ (*informal*) *gorgeous weather* EXCELLENT, marvellous, superb, very good, first-rate, first-class, wonderful, magnificent, splendid; *informal* great, glorious, terrific, fantastic, fabulous, fab, ace; *Brit. informal* smashing, brilliant, brill; *Austral./NZ informal* bonzer.
– OPPOSITES ugly, drab, terrible.

gory ▶ **adjective** ❶ *a gory ritual slaughter* GRISLY, gruesome, violent, bloody, brutal, savage; ghastly, frightful, horrid, fearful, hideous, macabre, horrible, horrific; shocking, appalling, monstrous, unspeakable; *informal* blood-and-guts, sick-making. ❷ *gory pieces of flesh* BLOODY, bloodstained, bloodsoaked.

gospel ▶ **noun** ❶ *the Gospel was spread by missionaries* CHRISTIAN TEACHING, Christian doctrine, Christ's teaching; the word of God, the New Testament. ❷ *don't treat this as gospel* THE TRUTH; fact, actual fact, reality, actuality, factuality, the case, a certainty. ❸ *his gospel of non-violence* DOCTRINE, dogma, teaching, principle, ethic, creed, credo, ideology, ideal; belief, tenet, canon.

gossamer ▶ **noun** *her dress swirled like gossamer* COBWEBS; silk, gauze, chiffon.
▶ **adjective** *a gossamer veil* GAUZY, gossamery, fine, diaphanous, delicate, filmy, floaty, chiffony, cobwebby, wispy, thin, light, insubstantial, flimsy; translucent, transparent, see-through, sheer.

gossip ▶ **noun** ❶ *tell me all the gossip* TITTLE-TATTLE, tattle, rumour(s), whispers, canards, titbits; scandal, hearsay; *informal* dirt, buzz; *Brit. informal* goss; *N. Amer. informal* scuttlebutt. ❷ *they went for a gossip* CHAT, talk, conversation, chatter, heart-to-heart, tête-à-tête, blether, blather; discussion, dialogue; *informal* chit-chat, jaw, gas, confab, goss; *Brit. informal* natter, chinwag; *N. Amer. informal* gabfest; *Austral./NZ informal* yarn; *formal* confabulation. ❸ *she's such a gossip* SCANDALMONGER, gossipmonger, tattler, busybody, muckraker.
▶ **verb** ❶ *she gossiped about his wife* SPREAD RUMOURS, spread gossip, tittle-tattle, tattle, talk, whisper, tell tales; *informal* dish the dirt. ❷ *people sat around gossiping* CHAT, talk, converse, speak to each other, discuss things; *informal* gas, chew the fat, chew the rag, jaw, yak, yap; *Brit. informal* natter, chinwag; *N. Amer. informal* shoot the breeze, shoot the bull; *formal* confabulate.

gouge ▶ **verb** SCOOP OUT, hollow out, excavate; cut (out), dig (out), scrape (out), scratch (out).

gourmand ▶ **noun** GLUTTON, overeater, big eater, gobbler, gorger; *informal* (greedy) pig, gannet, greedy guts, gutbucket, guzzler.

gourmet ▶ **noun** GASTRONOME, epicure, epicurean; connoisseur; *informal* foodie.

govern ▶ verb ❶ *he governs the province* RULE, preside over, reign over, control, be in charge of, command, lead, dominate; run, head, administer, manage, regulate, oversee, supervise; *informal* be in the driving seat. ❷ *the rules governing social behaviour* DETERMINE, decide, control, regulate, direct, rule, dictate, shape; affect, influence, sway, act on, mould, modify, impact on.

governess ▶ noun TUTOR, instructress, duenna; teacher.

government ▶ noun ❶ *the government announced cuts* ADMINISTRATION, executive, regime, authority, powers that be, directorate, council, leadership; cabinet, ministry; *informal* top brass. ❷ *they help him in the government of the country* RULE, running, leadership, control, administration, regulation, management, supervision.

governor ▶ noun LEADER, ruler, chief, head; premier, president, viceroy, chancellor; administrator, principal, director, chairman/woman, chair, superintendent, commissioner, controller; *informal* boss.

gown ▶ noun DRESS, frock, shift, robe.

grab ▶ verb ❶ *Dot grabbed his arm* SEIZE, grasp, snatch, take hold of, grip, clasp, clutch; take. ❷ (*informal*) *I'll grab another drink* OBTAIN, acquire, get; buy, purchase, procure, secure, snap up; gather, collect; achieve, attain; *informal* get one's hands on, get one's mitts on, get hold of, bag, score, nab.

▶ noun *she made a grab for his gun* LUNGE, snatch.

■ **up for grabs** (*informal*) AVAILABLE, obtainable, to be had, for the taking; for sale, on the market; *informal* for the asking, on tap, gettable.

grace ▶ noun ❶ *the grace of a ballerina* ELEGANCE, poise, gracefulness, finesse; suppleness, agility, nimbleness, light-footedness. ❷ *he had the grace to look sheepish* COURTESY, decency, (good) manners, politeness, decorum, respect, tact. ❸ *he fell from grace* FAVOUR, approval, approbation, acceptance, esteem, regard, respect; goodwill. ❹ *he lived there by grace of the king* FAVOUR, goodwill, generosity, kindness, indulgence; *formal* benefaction. ❺ *they have five days' grace to decide* DEFERMENT, deferral, postponement, suspension, adjournment, delay, pause; respite, stay, moratorium, reprieve. ❻ *say grace* PRAYER OF THANKS, thanksgiving, blessing, benediction.

– OPPOSITES inelegance, effrontery, disfavour.

▶ verb ❶ *the occasion was graced by the prince* DIGNIFY, distinguish, honour, favour; enhance, ennoble, glorify, elevate, aggrandize, upgrade. ❷ *a mosaic graced the floor* ADORN, embellish, decorate, ornament, enhance; beautify, prettify, enrich, bedeck.

graceful ▶ adjective ELEGANT, fluid, fluent, natural, neat; agile, supple, nimble, light-footed.

graceless ▶ adjective GAUCHE, maladroit, inept, awkward, unsure, unpolished, unsophisticated, uncultured, unrefined; clumsy, ungainly, ungraceful, inelegant, uncoordinated, gawky, gangling, bumbling; tactless, thoughtless, inconsiderate; *informal* cack-handed, ham-handed, ham-fisted.

gracious ▶ adjective ❶ *a gracious hostess* COURTEOUS, polite, civil, chivalrous, well mannered, mannerly, decorous; tactful, diplomatic; kind, benevolent, considerate, thoughtful, obliging, accommodating, indulgent, magnanimous; friendly, amiable, cordial, hospitable. ❷ *gracious colonial buildings* ELEGANT, stylish, tasteful, graceful; comfortable, luxurious, sumptuous, opulent, grand, high-class; *informal* swanky, plush. ❸ *God's gracious intervention* MERCIFUL, compassionate, kind; forgiving, lenient, clement, forbearing, humane, tender-hearted, sympathetic; indulgent, generous, magnanimous, benign, benevolent.

– OPPOSITES rude, crude, cruel.

gradation ▶ noun ❶ *a gradation of ability* RANGE, scale, spectrum, compass, span; progression, hierarchy, ladder, pecking order. ❷ *each pay band has a number of gradations* LEVEL, grade, rank, position, status, stage, standard, echelon, rung, step, notch; class, stratum, group, grouping, set.

grade ▶ noun ❶ *hotels within the same grade* CATEGORY, set, class, classification, grouping, group, bracket. ❷ *his job is of the lowest grade* RANK, level, echelon, standing, position, class, status, order; step, rung, stratum, tier. ❸ (*N. Amer.*) *the best grades in the school* MARK, score; assessment, evaluation, appraisal. ❹ (*N. Amer.*) *the fifth grade* YEAR, form, class.

▶ verb ❶ *eggs are graded by size* CLASSIFY, class, categorize, bracket, sort, group, arrange, pigeonhole; rank, evaluate, rate, value. ❷ (*N. Amer.*) *the essays have been graded* ASSESS, mark, score, judge, evaluate, appraise. ❸ *the colours grade into one another* PASS, shade, merge, blend.

■ **make the grade** (*informal*) COME UP TO STANDARD, come up to scratch, qualify, pass, pass muster, measure up; succeed, win through; *informal* be up to snuff, cut it, cut the mustard.

gradient ▶ noun ❶ *a steep gradient* SLOPE, incline, hill, rise, ramp, bank; acclivity, declivity; *N. Amer.* grade. ❷ *the gradient of the line* STEEPNESS, angle, slant, slope, inclination.

gradual ▶ adjective ❶ *a gradual transition* SLOW, measured, unhurried, cautious; piecemeal, step-by-step, little-by-little, bit-by-bit; progressive, continuous, systematic, steady. ❷ *a gradual slope* GENTLE, moderate, slight, easy.

– OPPOSITES abrupt, steep.

gradually ▶ adverb SLOWLY, slowly but surely, cautiously, gently, gingerly; piecemeal, little by little, bit by bit, inch by inch, by degrees; progressively, systematically; regularly, steadily.

graduate ▶ verb ❶ *he wants to teach when he graduates* QUALIFY, pass one's exams, get one's degree, complete one's studies. ❷ *she wants to graduate to serious drama* PROGRESS, advance, move up. ❸ *a proposal to graduate income tax* RANK, grade, order, group, classify, categorize. ❹ *a thermometer graduated in Fahrenheit* CALIBRATE, mark off, measure out, grade.

graft¹ ▶ noun ❶ *grafts may die from lack of water* SCION, cutting, shoot, offshoot, bud, sprout, sprig. ❷ *a skin graft* TRANSPLANT, implant.
▶ verb ❶ *graft a bud onto the stem* AFFIX, join, insert, splice. ❷ *tissue is grafted on to the cornea* TRANSPLANT, implant. ❸ *a mansion grafted on to a farmhouse* ATTACH, add, join.

graft² (*Brit. informal*) ▶ noun *hard graft*. See WORK noun sense 1.
▶ verb *they often graft for each other*. See WORK verb sense 1.

graft³ ▶ noun *sweeping measures to curb official graft* CORRUPTION, bribery, subornation, dishonesty, deceit, fraud, unlawful practices, illegal means; *N. Amer.* payola; *informal* palm-greasing, hush money, kickbacks, crookedness, sharp practices.
– OPPOSITES honesty.

grain ▶ noun ❶ *the local farmers grow grain* CEREAL, cereal crops. ❷ *a grain of corn* KERNEL, seed, grist. ❸ *grains of sand* GRANULE, particle, speck, mote, mite; bit, piece; scrap, crumb, fragment, morsel. ❹ *a grain of truth* TRACE, hint, tinge, suggestion, shadow; bit, soupçon; scintilla, ounce, iota, jot, whit, scrap, shred; *informal* smidgen, smidge, tad. ❺ *the grain of the timber* TEXTURE, surface, finish; weave, pattern.

grammar ▶ noun SYNTAX, rules of language, morphology; linguistics.

grammatical ▶ adjective ❶ *the grammatical structure of a sentence* SYNTACTIC, morphological; linguistic. ❷ *a grammatical sentence* WELL FORMED, correct, proper; acceptable, allowable.

grand ▶ adjective ❶ *a grand hotel* MAGNIFICENT, imposing, impressive, awe-inspiring, splendid, resplendent, majestic, monumental; palatial, stately, large; luxurious, sumptuous, lavish, opulent; *Brit.* upmarket; *N. Amer.* upscale; *informal* fancy, posh, plush, classy, swanky; *Brit. informal* swish. ❷ *a grand scheme* AMBITIOUS, bold, epic, big, extravagant. ❸ *a grand old lady* AUGUST, distinguished, illustrious, eminent, esteemed, honoured, venerable, dignified, respectable; pre-eminent, prominent, notable, renowned, celebrated, famous; aristocratic, noble, regal, blue-blooded, high-born, patrician; *informal* upper-crust; *Brit. informal* posh, upmarket. ❹ *a grand total of £2,000* COMPLETE, comprehensive, all-inclusive, inclusive; final. ❺ *the grand staircase* MAIN, principal, central, prime; biggest, largest. ❻ (*informal*) *you're doing a grand job* EXCELLENT, very good, marvellous, splendid, first-class, first-rate, wonderful, outstanding, sterling, fine; *informal* superb, terrific, great, super, ace; *Brit. informal* smashing, brilliant, brill.
– OPPOSITES inferior, humble, minor, poor.
▶ noun (*informal*) *a cheque for ten grand* THOUSAND POUNDS/DOLLARS; *informal* thou, K; *N. Amer. informal* G, gee.

grandeur ▶ noun SPLENDOUR, magnificence, impressiveness, glory, resplendence, majesty, greatness; stateliness, pomp, ceremony.

grandfather ▶ noun ❶ *his grandfather lives here informal* grandad, grandpa, gramps, grampy, grandaddy. ❷ *the grandfather of modern liberalism* FOUNDER, inventor, originator, creator, initiator; father, founding father, pioneer. ❸ *our Victorian grandfathers* FOREFATHER, forebear, ancestor, progenitor, antecedent.
▶ verb (*N. Amer. informal*) *some smokers have been grandfathered* EXEMPT, excuse, free, exclude, grant immunity, spare, absolve; *informal* let off (the hook).

grandiloquent ▶ adjective POMPOUS, bombastic, magniloquent, pretentious, ostentatious, high-flown, orotund, florid, flowery; overwrought, overblown, overdone; *informal* highfalutin, purple.
– OPPOSITES understated.

grandiose ▶ adjective ❶ *the court's grandiose facade* MAGNIFICENT, impressive, grand, imposing, awe-inspiring, splendid, resplendent, majestic, glorious, elaborate; palatial, stately, luxurious, opulent; *informal* plush, swanky, flash. ❷ *a grandiose plan* AMBITIOUS, bold, overambitious, extravagant, high-flown, flamboyant; *informal* over the top, OTT.
– OPPOSITES humble, modest.

grandmother ▶ noun *informal* grandma, granny, gran, nan, nanna.

grant ▶ verb ❶ *he granted them leave of absence* ALLOW, accord, permit, afford, vouchsafe. ❷ *he granted them £20,000* GIVE, award, bestow on, confer on, present with, provide with, endow with, supply with. ❸ *I grant that the difference is not absolute* ADMIT, accept, concede, yield, allow, appreciate, recognize, acknowledge, confess; agree.
– OPPOSITES refuse, deny.
▶ noun *a grant from the council* ENDOWMENT, subvention, award, donation, bursary, allowance, subsidy, contribution, handout, allocation, gift; scholarship.

granular ▶ adjective POWDER, powdered, powdery, grainy, granulated, gritty.

granulated ▶ adjective POWDERED, crushed, crumbed, ground, minced, grated, pulverized.

granule ▶ noun GRAIN, particle, fragment, bit, crumb, morsel, mote, speck.

graph ▶ noun *use graphs to analyse your data* CHART, diagram; histogram, bar chart, pie chart, scatter diagram.

▸ **verb** *we graphed the new prices* PLOT, trace, draw up, delineate.

graphic ▸ **adjective** ❶ *a graphic representation of language* VISUAL, symbolic, pictorial, illustrative, diagrammatic; drawn, written. ❷ *a graphic account* VIVID, explicit, expressive, detailed; uninhibited, powerful, colourful, rich, lurid, shocking; realistic, descriptive, illustrative; telling, effective.
– OPPOSITES vague.
▸ **noun** (*Computing*) *this printer's good enough for graphics* PICTURE, illustration, image; diagram, graph, chart.

grapple ▸ **verb** ❶ *the policemen grappled with him* WRESTLE, struggle, tussle; brawl, fight, scuffle, battle. ❷ *he grappled his prey* SEIZE, grab, catch (hold of), take hold of, grasp. ❸ *she is grappling with the problems of exile* TACKLE, confront, face, deal with, cope with, get to grips with; apply oneself to, devote oneself to.

grasp ▸ **verb** ❶ *she grasped his hands* GRIP, clutch, clasp, hold, clench; catch, seize, grab, snatch, latch on to. ❷ *everybody grasped the important points* UNDERSTAND, comprehend, follow, take in, perceive, see, apprehend, assimilate, absorb; *informal* get, catch on to, figure out, get one's head around, take on board; *Brit. informal* twig, suss (out). ❸ *he grasped the opportunity* TAKE ADVANTAGE OF, act on; seize, leap at, snatch, jump at, pounce on.
– OPPOSITES release, overlook.
▸ **noun** ❶ *his grasp on her hand* GRIP, hold; clutch, clasp, clench. ❷ *his domineering mother's grasp* CONTROL, power, clutches, command, domination, rule, tyranny. ❸ *a prize lay within their grasp* REACH, scope, power, limits, range; sights. ❹ *your grasp of history* UNDERSTANDING, comprehension, perception, apprehension, awareness, grip, knowledge; mastery, command.

grasping ▸ **adjective** AVARICIOUS, acquisitive, greedy, rapacious, mercenary, materialistic; mean, miserly, parsimonious, niggardly, hoarding, selfish, possessive, close; *informal* tight-fisted, tight, stingy, money-grubbing; *N. Amer. informal* cheap, grabby.

grass ▸ **noun** ❶ *he sat down on the grass* TURF, sod; lawn, green. ❷ (*informal*) *they smoked grass.* See CANNABIS. ❸ (*Brit. informal*) *few clubs were without a grass* INFORMER, mole, stool pigeon; *informal* snitch, snout, whistle-blower, rat; *Brit. informal* supergrass, nark; *N. Amer. informal* fink, stoolie.
▸ **verb** ❶ *the hill is completely grassed* GRASS OVER, turf. ❷ (*Brit. informal*) *he grassed on the robbers* INFORM, tell; give away, betray, sell out; *informal* split, blow the whistle, rat, peach, squeal, do the dirty, stitch up, sell down the river; *Brit. informal* shop; *N. Amer. informal* finger; *Austral./NZ informal* dob, pimp.

grate ▸ **verb** ❶ *she grated the cheese* SHRED, pulverize, mince, grind, granulate, crush, crumble. ❷ *her bones grated together* GRIND, rub, rasp, scrape, jar, grit, creak. ❸ *the tune grates slightly* IRRITATE, set someone's teeth on edge, jar; annoy, nettle, chafe, fret; *informal* aggravate, get on someone's nerves, get under someone's skin, get someone's goat.

grateful ▸ **adjective** THANKFUL, appreciative; indebted, obliged, obligated, in your debt, beholden.

gratification ▸ **noun** SATISFACTION, fulfilment, indulgence, relief, appeasement; pleasure, enjoyment, relish.

gratify ▸ **verb** ❶ *it gratified him to be seen with her* PLEASE, gladden, make happy, delight, make someone feel good, satisfy; *informal* tickle pink, give someone a kick, buck up. ❷ *he gratified his desires* SATISFY, fulfil, indulge, comply with, pander to, cater to, give in to, satiate, feed, accommodate.
– OPPOSITES displease, frustrate.

grating[1] ▸ **adjective** ❶ *the chair made a grating noise* SCRAPING, scratching, grinding, rasping, jarring. ❷ *a grating voice* HARSH, raucous, strident, piercing, shrill, screechy; discordant, cacophonous; hoarse, rough, gravelly. ❸ *it's written in grating language* IRRITATING, annoying, infuriating, irksome, maddening, displeasing, tiresome; jarring, discordant, inharmonious, unsuitable, inappropriate; *informal* aggravating.
– OPPOSITES harmonious, pleasing, appropriate.

grating[2] ▸ **noun** *a strong iron grating* GRID, grate, grille, lattice, trellis, mesh.

gratis ▸ **adverb** FREE (OF CHARGE), without charge, for nothing, at no cost, gratuitously; *informal* on the house, for free.

gratitude ▸ **noun** GRATEFULNESS, thankfulness, thanks, appreciation, indebtedness; recognition, acknowledgement, credit.

gratuitous ▸ **adjective** ❶ *gratuitous violence* UNJUSTIFIED, uncalled for, unwarranted, unprovoked, undue; indefensible, unjustifiable; needless, unnecessary, inessential, unmerited, groundless, senseless, wanton, indiscriminate; excessive, immoderate, inordinate, inappropriate. ❷ *they offer gratuitous advice* FREE, gratis, complimentary, voluntary, unpaid; free of charge, for nothing; *Law* pro bono (publico); *informal* for free, on the house; *Brit. informal* buckshee.
– OPPOSITES necessary, paid.

gratuity ▸ **noun** (*formal*) TIP, pourboire, baksheesh, gift, present, donation, reward, handout; bonus, extra; *informal* perk; *formal* perquisite.

grave[1] ▸ **noun** *she left flowers at his grave* BURYING PLACE, tomb, sepulchre, vault, burial chamber, mausoleum, crypt; last resting place.

grave[2] ▸ **adjective** ❶ *a grave matter* SERIOUS, important, weighty, profound, significant,

momentous; critical, acute, urgent, pressing; dire, terrible, awful, dreadful; *formal* exigent. ❷ *Jackie looked grave* SOLEMN, serious, sober, unsmiling, grim, sombre; severe, stern, dour.
– OPPOSITES trivial, cheerful.

gravel ▸ **noun** SHINGLE, grit, pebbles, stones.

gravelly ▸ **adjective** ❶ *a gravelly beach* SHINGLY, pebbly, stony, gritty. ❷ *his gravelly voice* HUSKY, gruff, throaty, deep, croaky, rasping, grating, harsh, rough.

gravestone ▸ **noun** HEADSTONE, tombstone, stone, monument, memorial.

graveyard ▸ **noun** CEMETERY, churchyard, burial ground, necropolis; *informal* boneyard; *historical* potter's field; *archaic* God's acre.

gravitas ▸ **noun** DIGNITY, seriousness, solemnity, gravity, sobriety.
– OPPOSITES frivolity.

gravitate ▸ **verb** MOVE, head, drift, be drawn, be attracted; tend, lean, incline.

gravity ▸ **noun** ❶ *the gravity of the situation* SERIOUSNESS, importance, significance, weight, consequence, magnitude; acuteness, urgency, exigence; awfulness, dreadfulness; *formal* moment. ❷ *the gravity of his demeanour* SOLEMNITY, seriousness, sombreness, sobriety, soberness, severity, grimness, humourlessness, dourness; gloominess.

graze[1] ▸ **verb** *the deer grazed* FEED, eat, crop, nibble, browse.

graze[2] ▸ **verb** ❶ *he grazed his knuckles on the box* SCRAPE, abrade, skin, scratch, chafe, bark, scuff, rasp; cut, nick. ❷ *his shot grazed the far post* TOUCH, brush, shave, skim, kiss, scrape, clip, glance off.
▸ **noun** *grazes on the skin* SCRATCH, scrape, abrasion, cut; *Medicine* trauma.

grease ▸ **noun** ❶ *guns packed in grease* OIL, lubricant, lubricator, lubrication. ❷ *the kitchen was filmed with grease* FAT, oil, cooking oil, animal fat; lard, suet. ❸ *his hair was smothered with grease* GEL, lotion, cream; *trademark* Brylcreem.
▸ **verb** *grease a baking dish* LUBRICATE, oil, smear with oil.

greasy ▸ **adjective** ❶ *a greasy supper* FATTY, oily, buttery, oleaginous; *formal* pinguid. ❷ *greasy hair* OILY. ❸ *the pitch was very greasy* SLIPPERY, slick, slimy, slithery, oily; *informal* slippy, skiddy. ❹ *a greasy little man* INGRATIATING, obsequious, sycophantic, fawning, toadying, grovelling; effusive, gushing, gushy; unctuous, oily; *informal* smarmy, slimy, bootlicking, sucky.
– OPPOSITES lean, dry.

great ▸ **adjective** ❶ *they showed great interest* CONSIDERABLE, substantial, significant, appreciable, special, serious; exceptional, extraordinary. ❷ *a great expanse of water* LARGE, big, extensive, expansive, broad, wide, sizeable, ample; vast, immense, huge, enormous, massive; *informal* humongous, whopping; *Brit. informal* ginormous. ❸ *a great big house* VERY, extremely, exceedingly, exceptionally, especially, really; *informal* dirty. ❹ *you great fool!* ABSOLUTE, total, utter, out-and-out, downright, thoroughgoing, complete; perfect, positive, prize, sheer, arrant, unqualified, consummate, veritable; *informal* thundering; *Brit. informal* right, proper. ❺ *great writers* PROMINENT, eminent, important, distinguished, illustrious, celebrated, honoured, acclaimed, admired, esteemed, revered, renowned, notable, famous, famed, well known; leading, top, major, principal, first-rate, matchless, peerless, star. ❻ *the country is now a great power* POWERFUL, dominant, influential, strong, potent, formidable, redoubtable; leading, important, foremost, major, chief, principal. ❼ *a great castle* MAGNIFICENT, imposing, impressive, awe-inspiring, grand, splendid, majestic, sumptuous, resplendent. ❽ *a great sportsman* EXPERT, skilful, skilled, adept, accomplished, talented, fine, masterly, master, brilliant, virtuoso, marvellous, outstanding, first class, superb; *informal* crack, ace, A1, class. ❾ *a great fan of rugby* ENTHUSIASTIC, eager, keen, zealous, devoted, ardent, fanatical, passionate, dedicated, committed. ❿ *we had a great time* ENJOYABLE, delightful, lovely, pleasant, congenial; exciting, thrilling; excellent, marvellous, wonderful, fine, splendid, very good; *informal* terrific, fantastic, fabulous, fab, super, grand, cool; *Brit. informal* smashing, brilliant, brill; *Austral./NZ informal* bonzer, beaut; *Brit. informal, dated* spiffing; *N. Amer. informal, dated* swell.
– OPPOSITES little, small, minor, modest, poor, unenthusiastic, bad.

greatly ▸ **adverb** VERY MUCH, considerably, substantially, appreciably, significantly, markedly, sizeably, seriously, materially, profoundly; enormously, vastly, immensely, tremendously, mightily, abundantly, extremely, exceedingly; *informal* plenty, majorly.
– OPPOSITES slightly.

greatness ▸ **noun** ❶ *a woman destined for greatness* EMINENCE, distinction, illustriousness, repute, high standing; importance, significance; celebrity, fame, prominence, renown. ❷ *his greatness as a writer* BRILLIANCE, genius, prowess, talent, expertise, mastery, artistry, virtuosity, skill, proficiency; flair, finesse; calibre, distinction.

greed, greediness ▸ **noun** ❶ *human greed* AVARICE, cupidity, acquisitiveness, covetousness, rapacity; materialism, mercenariness, Mammonism; *informal* money-grubbing, money-grabbing. ❷ *her mouth watered with greed* GLUTTONY, hunger, voracity, insatiability; gourmandism, intemperance, overeating, self-indulgence; *informal* piggishness. ❸ *their greed for power* DESIRE, appetite, hunger, thirst, craving, longing, yearning, hankering; avidity, eagerness; *informal* yen, itch.

– OPPOSITES generosity, temperance, indifference.

greedy ▶ adjective ❶ *a greedy eater* GLUTTONOUS, ravenous, voracious, intemperate, self-indulgent, insatiable, wolfish; *informal* piggish, piggy. ❷ *a greedy millionaire* AVARICIOUS, acquisitive, covetous, grasping, materialistic, mercenary, possessive; *informal* money-grubbing, money-grabbing; *N. Amer. informal* grabby. ❸ *she is greedy for a title* EAGER, avid, hungry, craving, longing, yearning, hankering; impatient, anxious; *informal* dying, itching, gagging.

green ▶ adjective ❶ *a green scarf* viridescent; olive green, pea green, emerald green, lime green, bottle green, Lincoln green, sea green, eau de Nil; *poetic/literary* virescent, glaucous. ❷ *a green island* VERDANT, grassy, leafy, verdurous. ❸ *he promotes Green issues* ENVIRONMENTAL, ecological, conservation, eco-. ❹ *a green alternative to diesel* ENVIRONMENTALLY FRIENDLY, non-polluting; ozone-friendly. ❺ *green bananas* UNRIPE, immature. ❻ *green timber* UNSEASONED, not aged, unfinished; pliable, supple. ❼ *green bacon* RAW, fresh, unsmoked, uncured. ❽ *the new lieutenant was very green* INEXPERIENCED, unversed, callow, immature; new, raw, unseasoned, untried; inexpert, untrained, unqualified, ignorant; simple, unsophisticated, unpolished; naive, innocent, ingenuous, credulous, gullible, unworldly; *informal* wet behind the ears, born yesterday. ❾ *he went green* PALE, wan, pallid, ashen, ashen-faced, pasty, pasty-faced, grey, whitish, washed out, whey-faced, waxen, waxy, blanched, drained, pinched, sallow; sickly, nauseous, ill, sick, unhealthy.
– OPPOSITES barren, dry, cured, experienced, ruddy.

▶ noun ❶ *a canopy of green over the road* FOLIAGE, greenery, plants, leaves, leafage, vegetation. ❷ *a village green* LAWN, common, grassy area, sward. ❸ *they had roast beef and greens* VEGETABLES, leaf vegetables; *informal* veg, veggies. ❹ *Greens are against multinationals* ENVIRONMENTALIST, conservationist, preservationist, nature-lover, eco-activist.

greenery ▶ noun FOLIAGE, vegetation, plants, green, leaves, leafage, undergrowth, plant life, flora, herbage, verdure.

greenhorn ▶ noun (*N. Amer. informal*). *See* NOVICE sense 1.

greenhouse ▶ noun HOTHOUSE, glasshouse, conservatory.

greet ▶ verb ❶ *she greeted Hank cheerily* SAY HELLO TO, address, salute, hail, halloo; welcome, meet, receive. ❷ *the decision was greeted with outrage* RECEIVE, acknowledge, respond to, react to, take.

greeting ▶ noun ❶ *he shouted a greeting* HELLO, salute, salutation, address; welcome; acknowledgement. ❷ *birthday greetings* BEST WISHES, good wishes, congratulations, felicitations; compliments, regards, respects.
– OPPOSITES farewell.

gregarious ▶ adjective ❶ *he was fun-loving and gregarious* SOCIABLE, company-loving, convivial, companionable, outgoing, friendly, affable, amiable, genial, warm, comradely, clubbable; *Scottish* couthy; *informal* chummy, pally; *Brit. informal* matey. ❷ *gregarious fish* SOCIAL, living in groups.
– OPPOSITES unsociable.

grey ▶ adjective ❶ *a grey suit* silvery, silver-grey, gunmetal, slate, charcoal, smoky. ❷ *his grey hair* WHITE, silver, hoary. ❸ *a grey day* CLOUDY, overcast, dull, sunless, gloomy, dreary, dismal, sombre, bleak, murky. ❹ *her face looked grey* ASHEN, wan, pale, pasty, pallid, colourless, bloodless, white, waxen; sickly, peaky, drained, drawn, deathly. ❺ *the grey daily routine* CHARACTERLESS, colourless, nondescript, unremarkable, insipid, jejune, flat, bland, dry, stale; dull, uninteresting, boring, tedious, monotonous. ❻ *a grey area* AMBIGUOUS, doubtful, unclear, uncertain, indefinite, open to question, debatable. ❼ *the grey economy* UNOFFICIAL, informal, irregular, back-door.
– OPPOSITES sunny, ruddy, lively, certain.

▶ verb *the population greyed* AGE, grow old, mature.

grid ▶ noun ❶ *a metal grid* GRATING, mesh, grille, gauze, lattice. ❷ *the grid of streets* NETWORK, matrix, reticulation.

grief ▶ noun ❶ *he was overcome with grief* SORROW, misery, sadness, anguish, pain, distress, heartache, heartbreak, agony, torment, affliction, suffering, woe, desolation, dejection, despair; mourning, mournfulness, bereavement, lamentation; *poetic/literary* dolour, dole. ❷ (*informal*) *the police gave me loads of grief* TROUBLE, annoyance, bother, irritation, vexation, harassment; *informal* aggravation, aggro, hassle.
– OPPOSITES joy.

■ **come to grief** FAIL, meet with disaster, miscarry, go wrong, go awry, fall through, fall flat, founder, come to nothing, come to naught; *informal* come unstuck, come a cropper, flop, go phut; *Brit. informal* go pear-shaped.

grief-stricken ▶ adjective SORROWFUL, sorrowing, miserable, sad, heartbroken, broken-hearted, anguished, pained, distressed, tormented, suffering, woeful, doleful, desolate, despairing, devastated, upset, inconsolable, wretched; mourning, grieving, mournful, bereaved, lamenting; *poetic/literary* dolorous, heartsick.
– OPPOSITES joyful.

grievance ▶ noun ❶ *social and economic grievances* INJUSTICE, wrong, injury, ill, unfairness; affront, insult, indignity. ❷ *students voiced their grievances* COMPLAINT, criticism, objection, grumble, grouse; ill feeling, bad feeling, resentment, bitterness, pique; *informal* gripe, whinge, moan, grouch, niggle, beef, bone to pick.

grieve ▶ **verb** ❶ *she grieved for her father* MOURN, lament, sorrow, be sorrowful; cry, sob, weep, shed tears, keen, weep and wail, beat one's breast. ❷ *it grieved me to leave her* SADDEN, upset, distress, pain, hurt, wound, break someone's heart, make someone's heart bleed.
– OPPOSITES rejoice, please.

grievous (*formal*) ▶ **adjective** ❶ *his death was a grievous blow* SERIOUS, severe, grave, bad, critical, dreadful, terrible, awful, crushing, calamitous; painful, agonizing, traumatic, wounding, damaging, injurious; sharp, acute. ❷ *a grievous sin* HEINOUS, grave, deplorable, shocking, appalling, atrocious, gross, dreadful, egregious, iniquitous.
– OPPOSITES slight, trivial.

grim ▶ **adjective** ❶ *his grim expression* STERN, forbidding, uninviting, unsmiling, dour, formidable, harsh, steely, flinty, stony; cross, churlish, crabbed, surly, sour, ill-tempered; fierce, ferocious, threatening, menacing, implacable, ruthless, merciless. ❷ *grim humour* BLACK, dark, mirthless, bleak, cynical. ❸ *the asylum holds some grim secrets* DREADFUL, dire, ghastly, horrible, horrendous, horrid, terrible, awful, appalling, frightful, shocking, unspeakable, grisly, gruesome, hideous, macabre; depressing, distressing, upsetting, worrying, unpleasant. ❹ *a grim little hovel* BLEAK, dreary, dismal, dingy, wretched, miserable, depressing, cheerless, comfortless, joyless, gloomy, uninviting; *informal* God-awful. ❺ *grim determination* RESOLUTE, determined, firm, decided, steadfast, dead set; obstinate, stubborn, obdurate, unyielding, intractable, uncompromising, unshakeable, unrelenting, relentless, dogged, tenacious.
– OPPOSITES amiable, pleasant.

grimace ▶ **noun** *his mouth twisted into a grimace* SCOWL, frown, sneer; face.
▶ **verb** *Nina grimaced at Joe* SCOWL, frown, sneer, glower, lour; make a face, make faces, pull a face; *Brit.* girn.
– OPPOSITES smile.

grime ▶ **noun** *her skirt was smeared with grime* DIRT, smut, soot, dust, mud, filth, mire; *informal* muck, yuck, crud; *Brit. informal* grot, gunge.
▶ **verb** *concrete grimed by diesel exhaust* BLACKEN, dirty, stain, soil; *poetic/literary* begrime, besmirch.

grimy ▶ **adjective** DIRTY, grubby, mucky, soiled, stained, smeared, filthy, smutty, sooty, dusty, muddy; *informal* yucky, cruddy; *Brit. informal* manky, grotty, gungy; *Austral./NZ* scungy; *poetic/literary* besmirched, begrimed.
– OPPOSITES clean.

grin ▶ **verb** *he grinned at her* SMILE, smile broadly, beam, smile from ear to ear, grin like a Cheshire cat; smirk; *informal* be all smiles.
▶ **noun** *a silly grin* SMILE, broad smile; smirk.
– OPPOSITES frown, scowl.

grind ▶ **verb** ❶ *the sandstone is ground into powder* CRUSH, pound, pulverize, mill, granulate, crumble, smash, press; *technical* triturate, comminute; *archaic* levigate, bray. ❷ *a knife being ground on a wheel* SHARPEN, whet, hone, file, strop; smooth, polish, sand, sandpaper. ❸ *one tectonic plate grinds against another* RUB, grate, scrape, rasp.
▶ **noun** *the daily grind* DRUDGERY, toil, hard work, labour, donkey work, exertion, chores, slog; *informal* fag, sweat; *poetic/literary* travail.
■ **grind away** LABOUR, toil, work hard, slave (away), work one's fingers to the bone, work like a Trojan, work like a dog; *informal* slog, plug away, beaver away, work one's socks off; *Brit. informal* graft; *poetic*/literary travail; *archaic* drudge.
■ **grind someone down** OPPRESS, crush, persecute, tyrannize, ill-treat, maltreat.

grip ▶ **verb** ❶ *she gripped the edge of the table* GRASP, clutch, hold, clasp, take hold of, clench, grab, seize, cling to; squeeze, press. ❷ *Harry was gripped by a sneezing fit* AFFLICT, affect, take over, beset, rack, convulse. ❸ *we were gripped by the drama* ENGROSS, enthral, absorb, rivet, spellbind, hold spellbound, bewitch, fascinate, hold, mesmerize, enrapture; interest.
– OPPOSITES release.
▶ **noun** ❶ *a tight grip* GRASP, hold. ❷ *the wheels lost their grip on the road* TRACTION, purchase, friction, adhesion, resistance. ❸ *he was in the grip of an obsession* CONTROL, power, hold, stranglehold, clutches, command, mastery, influence. ❹ *I had a pretty good grip on the situation* UNDERSTANDING, comprehension, grasp, perception, awareness, apprehension, conception; *formal* cognizance. ❺ *a leather grip* TRAVELLING BAG, bag, holdall, overnight bag, flight bag, kitbag, Gladstone bag.
■ **come/get to grips with** DEAL WITH, cope with, handle, grasp, grasp the nettle of, tackle, undertake, take on, grapple with, face, face up to, confront.

gripe (*informal*) ▶ **verb** *he's always griping about something* COMPLAIN, grumble, grouse, protest, whine, bleat; *informal* moan, bellyache, beef, bitch, whinge; *Brit. informal* chunter; *N. Amer. informal* kvetch.
▶ **noun** *employees' gripes* COMPLAINT, grumble, grouse, grievance, objection; cavil, quibble, niggle; *informal* moan, beef, whinge; *N. Amer. informal* kvetch.

gripping ▶ **adjective** ENGROSSING, enthralling, absorbing, riveting, captivating, spellbinding, bewitching, fascinating, compulsive, compelling, mesmerizing; thrilling, exciting, action-packed, dramatic, stimulating; *informal* unputdownable, page-turning.
– OPPOSITES boring.

grisly ▶ **adjective** GRUESOME, ghastly, frightful, horrid, horrifying, fearful, hideous, macabre, spine-chilling, horrible, horrendous, grim, awful, dire, dreadful, terrible, horrific, shocking, appalling, abominable, loathsome, abhorrent, odious, monstrous, unspeakable, disgusting, repulsive, repugnant, revolting, repellent, sickening; *informal* sick-making, gross; *archaic* disgustful.

gristly ▶ **adjective** STRINGY, sinewy, fibrous; tough, leathery, chewy.

grit ▶ **noun** ❶ *the grit from the paths* GRAVEL, pebbles, stones, shingle, sand; dust, dirt. ❷ *the true grit of a seasoned campaigner* COURAGE, bravery, pluck, mettle, backbone, spirit, strength of character, strength of will, moral fibre, steel, nerve, fortitude, toughness, hardiness, resolve, resolution, determination, tenacity, perseverance, endurance; *informal* guts, spunk; *Brit. informal* bottle.

▶ **verb** *Gina gritted her teeth* CLENCH, clamp together, shut tightly; grind, gnash.

gritty ▶ **adjective** ❶ *a gritty floor* SANDY, gravelly, pebbly, stony; powdery, dusty. ❷ *a gritty performance* COURAGEOUS, brave, plucky, mettlesome, stout-hearted, valiant, bold, spirited, intrepid, tough, determined, resolute, purposeful, dogged, tenacious; *informal* gutsy, spunky.

grizzle ▶ **verb** (*Brit. informal*) CRY, whimper, mewl, snivel, sob, wail; *Scottish* greet.

grizzled ▶ **adjective** GREY, greying, silver, silvery, snowy, white, salt-and-pepper; grey-haired, hoary.

groan ▶ **verb** ❶ *she groaned and rubbed her stomach* MOAN, whimper, cry, call out. ❷ *they were groaning about the management* COMPLAIN, grumble, grouse; *informal* moan, niggle, beef, bellyache, bitch, whinge, gripe. ❸ *the old wooden door groaned* CREAK, squeak; grate, rasp.

▶ **noun** ❶ *a groan of anguish* MOAN, cry, whimper. ❷ *their moans and groans* COMPLAINT, grumble, grouse, objection, protest, grievance; *informal* grouch, moan, beef, whinge; *informal* gripe. ❸ *the groan of the elevator* CREAKING, creak, squeak, grating, grinding.

groggy ▶ **adjective** DAZED, muzzy, stupefied, in a stupor, befuddled, fuddled, disoriented, disorientated, dizzy, punch-drunk, shaky, unsteady, wobbly, weak, faint; *informal* dopey, woozy, not with it.

groin ▶ **noun** CROTCH, crutch, genitals.
– RELATED TERMS inguinal.

groom ▶ **verb** ❶ *she groomed her pony* CURRY, brush, comb, clean, rub down. ❷ *his dark hair was carefully groomed* BRUSH, comb, arrange, do; tidy, spruce up, smarten up, preen, primp; *informal* fix. ❸ *they were groomed for stardom* PREPARE, prime, ready, condition, tailor; coach, train, instruct, drill, teach, school.

▶ **noun** ❶ *a groom took his horse* STABLE HAND, stableman, stable lad, stable boy, stable girl; *historical* equerry. ❷ *the bride and groom* BRIDEGROOM; newly-married man, newly-wed.

groove ▶ **noun** FURROW, channel, trench, trough, canal, gouge, hollow, indentation, rut, gutter, cutting, cut, fissure; *Carpentry* rebate.

grooved ▶ **adjective** FURROWED, fluted, corrugated, ribbed, ridged.

grope ▶ **verb** ❶ *she groped for her glasses* FUMBLE, scrabble, fish, ferret, rummage, feel, search, hunt; *Brit. informal* rootle. ❷ (*informal*) *one of the men started groping her* FONDLE, touch; *informal* paw, maul, feel up, touch up.

gross ▶ **adjective** ❶ *the man was pale and gross* OBESE, corpulent, overweight, fat, big, large, fleshy, flabby, portly, bloated; *informal* porky, pudgy, tubby, blubbery, roly-poly; *Brit. informal* podgy, fubsy. ❷ *men of gross natures* BOORISH, coarse, vulgar, loutish, oafish, thuggish, brutish, philistine, uncouth, crass, common, unrefined, unsophisticated, uncultured, uncultivated; *informal* cloddish; *Brit. informal* yobbish. ❸ (*informal*) *the place smelled gross* DISGUSTING, repellent, repulsive, abhorrent, loathsome, foul, nasty, obnoxious, sickening, nauseating, stomach-churning, unpalatable; *N. Amer.* vomitous; *informal* yucky, icky, sick-making, gut-churning; *archaic* disgustful. ❹ *a gross distortion of the truth* FLAGRANT, blatant, glaring, obvious, overt, naked, barefaced, shameless, brazen, audacious, brass-necked, undisguised, unconcealed, patent, transparent, manifest, palpable; out and out, utter, complete. ❺ *their gross income* TOTAL, whole, entire, complete, full, overall, combined, aggregate; before deductions, before tax.
– OPPOSITES slender, refined, pleasant, net.

▶ **verb** *he grosses over a million dollars a month* EARN, make, bring in, take, get, receive, collect; *informal* rake in.

grotesque ▶ **adjective** ❶ *a grotesque creature* MALFORMED, deformed, misshapen, misproportioned, distorted, twisted, gnarled, mangled, mutilated; ugly, unsightly, hideous, freakish, unnatural, abnormal, strange, odd, peculiar; *informal* weird, freaky. ❷ *grotesque mismanagement of funds* OUTRAGEOUS, monstrous, shocking, appalling, preposterous; ridiculous, ludicrous, farcical, unbelievable, incredible.
– OPPOSITES normal.

grotto ▶ **noun** CAVE, cavern, hollow; pothole, underground chamber.

grouch ▶ **noun** (*informal*) *an ill-mannered grouch* GRUMBLER, complainer, moaner; *informal* grump, sourpuss, crosspatch, whinger; *Brit. informal* misery, bear with a sore head; *N. Amer. informal* sorehead, kvetch.

▶ **verb** (*informal*) *there's not a lot to grouch about* GRUMBLE, complain, grouse, whine, bleat, carp, cavil; *informal* moan, whinge, gripe, beef, bellyache, bitch, sound off; *Brit. informal* chunter; *N. Amer. informal* kvetch.

grouchy ▶ **adjective** GRUMPY, cross, irritable, bad-tempered, crotchety, crabby, crabbed, cantankerous, curmudgeonly, testy, tetchy, huffy, snappish, waspish, prickly; *informal* snappy; *Brit. informal* narky, ratty, like a bear with a sore head, whingy; *N. Amer. informal* cranky, soreheaded; *informal, dated* miffy.

ground ▶ **noun** ❶ *she collapsed on the ground* FLOOR, earth, terra firma; flooring; *informal* deck. ❷ *the soggy ground* EARTH, soil, dirt, clay, loam, turf, clod, sod; land, terrain. ❸ *the team's home ground* STADIUM, pitch, field, arena, track; *N. Amer.* bowl; *Brit. informal* park. ❹ *the mansion's grounds* ESTATE, gardens, lawns, park, parkland, land, acres, property, surroundings, holding, territory; *archaic* demesne. ❺ *grounds for dismissal* REASON, cause, basis, base, foundation, justification, rationale, argument, premise, occasion, excuse, pretext, motive, motivation. ❻ *coffee grounds* SEDIMENT, precipitate, settlings, dregs, lees, deposit, residue; *archaic* grouts.

▶ **verb** ❶ *the boat grounded on a mud bank* RUN AGROUND, run ashore, beach, land. ❷ *an assertion grounded on results of several studies* BASE, found, establish, root, build, construct, form. ❸ *they were grounded in classics and history* INSTRUCT, coach, teach, tutor, educate, school, train, drill, prime, prepare; familiarize with, acquaint with.

groundless ▶ **adjective** BASELESS, without basis, without foundation, ill-founded, unfounded, unsupported, uncorroborated, unproven, empty, idle, unsubstantiated, unwarranted, unjustified, unjustifiable, without cause, without reason, without justification, unreasonable, irrational, illogical, misguided.

groundwork ▶ **noun** PRELIMINARY WORK, preliminaries, preparations, spadework, legwork, donkey work; planning, arrangements, organization, homework; basics, essentials, fundamentals, underpinning, foundation.

group ▶ **noun** ❶ *the exhibits were divided into three distinct groups* CATEGORY, class, classification, grouping, set, lot, batch, bracket, type, sort, kind, variety, family, species, genus, breed; grade, grading, rank, status. ❷ *a group of tourists* CROWD, party, body, band, company, gathering, congregation, assembly, collection, cluster, flock, pack, troop, gang; *informal* bunch. ❸ *a coup attempt by a group within the parliament* FACTION, division, section, clique, coterie, circle, set, ring, camp, bloc, caucus, cabal, fringe movement, splinter group. ❹ *the women's group* ASSOCIATION, club, society, league, guild, circle, union. ❺ *a small group of trees* CLUSTER, knot, collection, mass, clump. ❻ *a local folk group* BAND, ensemble, act; *informal* line-up, combo, outfit.

▶ **verb** ❶ *patients were grouped according to their symptoms* CATEGORIZE, classify, class, catalogue, sort, bracket, pigeonhole, grade, rate, rank. ❷ *wooden chairs were grouped round the table* PLACE, arrange, assemble, organize, range, line up, dispose. ❸ *the two parties grouped together* UNITE, join together/up, team up, join forces, get together, ally, form an alliance, affiliate, combine; collaborate, work together, pull together, cooperate.

grouse ▶ **verb** *she groused about the food* GRUMBLE, complain, protest, whine, bleat, carp, cavil, make a fuss; *informal* moan, bellyache, gripe, beef, bitch, grouch, whinge, sound off; *Brit. informal* chunter, create; *N. Amer. informal* kvetch.

▶ **noun** *our biggest grouse was about the noise* GRUMBLE, complaint, grievance, objection, cavil, quibble; *informal* moan, beef, gripe, grouch.

grove ▶ **noun** COPSE, wood, thicket, coppice; orchard, plantation; *Brit.* spinney; *archaic* hurst, holt.

grovel ▶ **verb** ❶ *George grovelled at his feet* PROSTRATE ONESELF, lie, kneel, cringe. ❷ *she was not going to grovel to him* BE OBSEQUIOUS, fawn on, kowtow, bow and scrape, toady, truckle, abase oneself, humble oneself; curry favour with, flatter, dance attendance on, make up to, play up to, ingratiate oneself with; *informal* crawl, creep, suck up to, lick someone's boots.

grow ▶ **verb** ❶ *the boys had grown* GET BIGGER, get taller, get larger, increase in size. ❷ *sales and profits continue to grow* INCREASE, swell, multiply, snowball, mushroom, balloon, build up, mount up, pile up; *informal* skyrocket. ❸ *flowers grew among the rocks* SPROUT, germinate, shoot up, spring up, develop, bud, burst forth, bloom, flourish, thrive, run riot. ❹ *he grew vegetables* CULTIVATE, produce, propagate, raise, rear, nurture, tend; farm. ❺ *the family business grew* EXPAND, extend, develop, progress, make progress; flourish, thrive, burgeon, prosper, succeed, boom. ❻ *the fable grew from an ancient Indian source* ORIGINATE, stem, spring, arise, emerge, issue; develop, evolve. ❼ *Leonora grew bored* BECOME, get, turn, begin to feel.

– OPPOSITES shrink, decline.

growl ▶ **verb** SNARL, bark, yap, bay.

grown-up ▶ **noun** *she wanted to be treated like a grown-up* ADULT, (grown) woman, (grown) man, mature woman, mature man.

– OPPOSITES child.

▶ **adjective** *she has two grown-up daughters* ADULT, mature, of age; fully grown, full-grown, fully developed.

growth ▶ **noun** ❶ *population growth* INCREASE, expansion, augmentation, proliferation, multiplication, enlargement, mushrooming, snowballing, rise, escalation, build-up. ❷ *the growth of plants* DEVELOPMENT, maturation, growing, germination, sprouting; blooming. ❸ *the marked growth of local enterprises* EXPANSION, extension, development, progress, advance, advancement, headway, spread; rise, success, boom, upturn, upswing. ❹ *a growth on his jaw* TUMOUR, malignancy, cancer; lump, excrescence, outgrowth, swelling, nodule; cyst, polyp.

– OPPOSITES decrease, decline.

grub ▶ noun ❶ *a small black grub* LARVA; maggot; caterpillar. ❷ (*informal*) *pub grub.* *See* FOOD sense 1.
▶ verb ❶ *kids grubbing around in the dirt* DIG, poke, scratch. ❷ *they grubbed up the old trees* DIG UP, unearth, uproot, root up/out, pull up/out, tear out. ❸ *he began grubbing about in the bin* RUMMAGE, search, hunt, delve, dig, scrabble, ferret, root, rifle, fish, poke; *Brit. informal* rootle; *Austral./NZ informal* fossick through.

grubby ▶ adjective DIRTY, grimy, filthy, mucky, unwashed, stained, soiled, smeared, spotted, muddy, dusty, sooty; unhygienic, insanitary; *informal* cruddy, yucky; *Brit. informal* manky, grotty, gungy; *poetic/literary* befouled, begrimed.
– OPPOSITES clean.

grudge ▶ noun *a former employee with a grudge* GRIEVANCE, resentment, bitterness, rancour, pique, umbrage, dissatisfaction, disgruntlement, bad feelings, hard feelings, ill feelings, ill will, animosity, antipathy, antagonism, enmity, animus; *informal* a chip on one's shoulder.
▶ verb ❶ *he grudged the time that the meetings involved* BEGRUDGE, resent, feel aggrieved about, be resentful of, mind, object to, take exception to. ❷ *I don't grudge you your success* ENVY, begrudge, resent, be jealous of, be envious of, be resentful of.

grudging ▶ adjective RELUCTANT, unwilling, forced, half-hearted, unenthusiastic, hesitant; begrudging, resentful.
– OPPOSITES eager.

gruelling ▶ adjective EXHAUSTING, tiring, fatiguing, wearying, taxing, draining, debilitating; demanding, exacting, difficult, hard, arduous, strenuous, laborious, back-breaking, harsh, severe, stiff, punishing, crippling; *informal* killing, murderous, hellish; *Brit. informal* knackering.

gruesome ▶ adjective GRISLY, ghastly, frightful, horrid, horrifying, hideous, horrible, horrendous, grim, awful, dire, dreadful, terrible, horrific, shocking, appalling, disgusting, repulsive, repugnant, revolting, repellent, sickening; loathsome, abhorrent, odious, monstrous, unspeakable; *informal* sick, sick-making, gross; *archaic* disgustful.
– OPPOSITES pleasant.

gruff ▶ adjective ❶ *a gruff reply | his gruff exterior* ABRUPT, brusque, curt, short, blunt, bluff, no-nonsense; laconic, taciturn; surly, churlish, grumpy, crotchety, crabby, crabbed, cross, bad-tempered, short-tempered, ill-natured, crusty, tetchy, bearish, ungracious, unceremonious; *informal* grouchy. ❷ *a gruff voice* ROUGH, guttural, throaty, gravelly, husky, croaking, rasping, raspy, growly, hoarse, harsh; low, thick.
– OPPOSITES friendly, soft.

grumble ▶ verb *they grumbled about the disruption* COMPLAIN, grouse, whine, mutter, bleat, carp, cavil, protest, make a fuss; *informal* moan, bellyache, beef, bitch, grouch, whinge, sound off; *Brit. informal* gripe, chunter, create; *N. English informal* mither; *N. Amer. informal* kvetch.
▶ noun *his customers' grumbles* COMPLAINT, grouse, grievance, protest, cavil, quibble, criticism; *informal* grouch, moan, whinge, beef, bitch, gripe.

grumpy ▶ adjective BAD-TEMPERED, crabby, ill-tempered, short-tempered, crotchety, tetchy, testy, crabbed, waspish, prickly, touchy, irritable, irascible, crusty, cantankerous, curmudgeonly, bearish, surly, ill-natured, churlish, ill-humoured, peevish, cross, fractious, disagreeable, pettish; *informal* grouchy, snappy, snappish; *Brit. informal* shirty, stroppy, narky, ratty, eggy, like a bear with a sore head; *N. Amer. informal* cranky, ornery, soreheaded; *informal, dated* miffy.
– OPPOSITES good-humoured.

guarantee ▶ noun ❶ *all repairs have a one-year guarantee* WARRANTY, warrant. ❷ *a guarantee that the hospital will stay open* PROMISE, assurance, word (of honour), pledge, vow, oath, bond, commitment, covenant. ❸ *banks usually demand a personal guarantee for loans* COLLATERAL, security, surety, guaranty, earnest.
▶ verb ❶ *he agreed to guarantee the loan* UNDERWRITE, put up collateral for. ❷ *can you guarantee he wasn't involved?* PROMISE, swear, swear to the fact, pledge, vow, undertake, give one's word, give an assurance, give an undertaking, take an oath, cross one's heart (and hope to die); *archaic* plight.

guard ▶ verb ❶ *infantry guarded the barricaded bridge* PROTECT, stand guard over, watch over, keep an eye on; cover, patrol, police, defend, shield, safeguard, keep safe, secure. ❷ *the prisoners were guarded by armed men* KEEP UNDER SURVEILLANCE, keep under guard, keep watch over, mind. ❸ *forest wardens must guard against poachers* BEWARE OF, keep watch for, be alert to, keep an eye out for, be on the alert/lookout for.
▶ noun ❶ *border guards* SENTRY, sentinel, security guard, nightwatchman; protector, defender, guardian; lookout, watch; garrison; *archaic* watchman. ❷ *her prison guard* WARDER, warden, keeper; jailer; *informal* screw; *archaic* turnkey. ❸ *he let his guard slip and they escaped* VIGILANCE, vigil, watch, surveillance, watchfulness, caution, heed, attention, care, wariness. ❹ *a metal guard* SAFETY GUARD, safety device, protective device, shield, screen, fender; bumper, buffer.
■ **off (one's) guard** UNPREPARED, unready, inattentive, unwary, with one's defences down, cold, unsuspecting; *informal* napping, asleep at the wheel, on the hop.
■ **on one's guard** VIGILANT, alert, on the alert, wary, watchful, cautious, careful, heedful, chary, circumspect, on the lookout, on the qui vive, on one's toes, prepared, ready, wide-

awake, attentive, observant, keeping one's eyes peeled; *informal* keeping a weather eye out.

guarded ▶ adjective CAUTIOUS, careful, circumspect, wary, chary, on one's guard, reluctant, non-committal, reticent, restrained, reserved; *informal* cagey.

guardian ▶ noun PROTECTOR, defender, preserver, custodian, warden, guard, keeper; conservator, curator, caretaker, steward, trustee.
– RELATED TERMS tutelary.

guerrilla ▶ noun FREEDOM FIGHTER, irregular, member of the resistance, partisan; rebel, radical, revolutionary, revolutionist; terrorist.

guess ▶ verb ❶ *he guessed she was about 40* ESTIMATE, hazard a guess, reckon, gauge, judge, calculate; hypothesize, postulate, predict, speculate, conjecture, surmise; *informal* guesstimate. ❷ (*informal*) *I guess I owe you an apology* SUPPOSE, think, imagine, expect, suspect, dare say; *informal* reckon, figure.
▶ noun *my guess was right* HYPOTHESIS, theory, prediction, postulation, conjecture, surmise, estimate, belief, opinion, reckoning, judgement, supposition, speculation, suspicion, impression, feeling; *informal* guesstimate.

guesswork ▶ noun GUESSING, conjecture, surmise, supposition, assumptions, presumptions, speculation, hypothesizing, theorizing, prediction; approximations, rough calculations; hunches; *informal* guesstimates.

guest ▶ noun ❶ *I have two guests coming to dinner* VISITOR, caller; company; *archaic* visitant. ❷ *hotel guests* RESIDENT, boarder, lodger, paying guest, PG; patron, client; *N. Amer.* roomer.
– OPPOSITES host.

guest house ▶ noun BOARDING HOUSE, bed and breakfast, B&B, hotel; pension, pensione.

guff ▶ noun (*informal*). *See* NONSENSE sense 1.

guffaw ▶ verb ROAR WITH LAUGHTER, laugh heartily/loudly, roar, bellow, cackle; *informal* laugh like a drain.

guidance ▶ noun ❶ *she looked to her father for guidance* ADVICE, counsel, direction, instruction, enlightenment, information; recommendations, suggestions, tips, hints, pointers, guidelines. ❷ *work continued under the guidance of a project supervisor* DIRECTION, control, leadership, management, supervision, superintendence, charge; handling, conduct, running, overseeing.

guide ▶ noun ❶ *our guide took us back to the hotel* ESCORT, attendant, courier, cicerone, dragoman; usher; chaperone. ❷ *he is my inspiration and my guide* ADVISER, mentor, counsellor; guru. ❸ *the light acted as a guide for shipping* POINTER, marker, indicator, signpost, mark, landmark; guiding light, sign, signal, beacon. ❹ *the techniques outlined are meant as a guide* MODEL, pattern, blueprint, template, example, exemplar; standard, touchstone, measure, benchmark, yardstick, gauge. ❺ *a pocket guide of Paris* GUIDEBOOK, travelogue, vade mecum; companion, handbook, directory, A to Z; *informal* bible.
▶ verb ❶ *he guided her to her seat* LEAD, lead the way, conduct, show, show someone the way, usher, shepherd, direct, steer, pilot, escort, accompany, attend; see, take, help, assist. ❷ *the chairman must guide the meeting* DIRECT, steer, control, manage, command, lead, conduct, run, be in charge of, have control of, govern, preside over, superintend, supervise, oversee; handle, regulate. ❸ *he was always there to guide me* ADVISE, counsel, give advice to, direct, give direction to.

guidebook ▶ noun GUIDE, travel guide, travelogue, vade mecum; companion, handbook, directory, A to Z; *informal* bible.

guideline ▶ noun RECOMMENDATION, instruction, direction, suggestion, advice; regulation, rule, principle, guiding principle; standard, criterion, measure, gauge, yardstick, benchmark, touchstone; procedure, parameter.

guild ▶ noun ASSOCIATION, society, union, league, organization, company, cooperative, fellowship, club, order, lodge, brotherhood, fraternity, sisterhood, sorority.

guile ▶ noun CUNNING, craftiness, craft, artfulness, art, artifice, wiliness, slyness, deviousness; wiles, ploys, schemes, stratagems, manoeuvres, subterfuges, tricks, ruses; deception, deceit, duplicity, underhandedness, double-dealing, trickery.
– OPPOSITES honesty.

guileless ▶ adjective ARTLESS, ingenuous, naive, open, genuine, natural, simple, childlike, innocent, unsophisticated, unworldly, unsuspicious, trustful, trusting; honest, truthful, sincere, straightforward.
– OPPOSITES scheming.

guilt ▶ noun ❶ *the proof of his guilt* CULPABILITY, guiltiness, blameworthiness; wrongdoing, wrong, criminality, misconduct, sin. ❷ *a terrible feeling of guilt* SELF-REPROACH, self-condemnation, shame, a guilty conscience, pangs of conscience; remorse, remorsefulness, regret, contrition, contriteness, compunction.
– OPPOSITES innocence.

guiltless ▶ adjective INNOCENT, blameless, not to blame, without fault, above reproach, above suspicion, in the clear, unimpeachable, irreproachable, faultless, sinless, spotless, immaculate, unsullied, uncorrupted, undefiled, untainted, unblemished, untarnished, impeccable; *informal* squeaky clean, whiter than white, as pure as the driven snow.
– OPPOSITES guilty.

guilty ▶ adjective ❶ *the guilty party* CULPABLE, to blame, at fault, in the wrong, blameworthy, responsible; erring, errant, delinquent, offending, sinful, criminal; *archaic* peccant. ❷ *I still feel guilty about it* ASHAMED, guilt-ridden,

conscience-stricken, remorseful, sorry, contrite, repentant, penitent, regretful, rueful, abashed, shamefaced, sheepish, hangdog; in sackcloth and ashes.
– OPPOSITES innocent, unrepentant.

guise ▶ noun ❶ *the god appeared in the guise of a swan* LIKENESS, outward appearance, appearance, semblance, form, shape, image; disguise. ❷ *additional sums paid under the guise of consultancy fees* PRETENCE, disguise, front, facade, cover, blind, screen, smokescreen.

gulf ▶ noun ❶ *our ship sailed into the gulf* INLET, bay, creek, bight, cove, fjord, estuary, sound, arm of the sea; *Scottish* firth, frith. ❷ *the ice gave way and a gulf widened slowly* HOLE, crevasse, fissure, cleft, split, rift, pit, cavity, chasm, abyss, void; ravine, gorge, canyon, gully. ❸ *a growing gulf between rich and poor* DIVIDE, division, separation, gap, breach, rift, split, chasm, abyss; difference, contrast, polarity.

gull ▶ verb HOODWINK, fool, dupe, deceive, delude, hoax, trick, mislead, lead on, take in, swindle, cheat, double-cross; *informal* pull the wool over someone's eyes, pull a fast one on, put one over on, sell a pup to, bamboozle, con, do; *N. Amer. informal* sucker, snooker; *Austral. informal* pull a swifty on; *poetic/literary* cozen.

gullet ▶ noun OESOPHAGUS, throat, maw, pharynx; crop, craw; *archaic* throttle, gorge.

gullible ▶ adjective CREDULOUS, naive, overtrusting, over-trustful, easily deceived, easily taken in, exploitable, dupable, impressionable, unsuspecting, unsuspicious, unwary, ingenuous, innocent, inexperienced, unworldly, green; *informal* wet behind the ears, born yesterday.
– OPPOSITES suspicious.

gully ▶ noun ❶ *a steep icy gully* RAVINE, canyon, gorge, pass, defile, couloir; *S. English* chine; *N. English* clough, gill; *N. Amer.* gulch, coulee. ❷ *water runs from the drainpipe into a gully* CHANNEL, conduit, trench, ditch, drain, culvert, cut, gutter.

gulp ▶ verb ❶ *she gulped her juice* SWALLOW, quaff, swill down, down; *informal* swig, knock back. ❷ *he gulped down the rest of his meal* GOBBLE, guzzle, devour, bolt, wolf, cram, stuff; *informal* put away, demolish, polish off, shovel down; *Brit. informal* scoff. ❸ *Jenny gulped back her tears* CHOKE BACK, fight back, hold back/in, suppress, stifle, smother.
– OPPOSITES sip.
▶ noun *a gulp of cold beer* MOUTHFUL, swallow, draught; *informal* swig.

gum[1] ▶ noun *photographs stuck down with gum* GLUE, adhesive, fixative, paste, epoxy resin; *N. Amer.* mucilage.
▶ verb *the receipts were gummed into a book* STICK, glue, paste; fix, affix, attach, fasten.
■ **gum something up** CLOG (UP), choke (up), stop up, plug; obstruct; *informal* bung up; *Brit. informal* gunge up; *technical* occlude.

gummy ▶ adjective STICKY, tacky, gluey, adhesive, resinous, viscous, viscid, glutinous, mucilaginous; *informal* gooey.

gumption ▶ noun (*informal*) INITIATIVE, resourcefulness, enterprise, ingenuity, imagination; astuteness, shrewdness, acumen, sense, common sense, wit, mother wit, native wit, practicality; spirit, backbone, pluck, mettle, nerve, courage; *informal* get-up-and-go, spunk, oomph, nous, savvy, horse sense; *N. Amer. informal* smarts.

gun ▶ noun FIREARM, pistol, revolver, rifle, shotgun, automatic, handgun, machine gun; weapon; *informal* shooter; *N. Amer. informal* piece, shooting iron.

gunfire ▶ noun GUNSHOTS, shots, shooting, firing, sniping; artillery fire, strafing, shelling.

gunman ▶ noun ARMED ROBBER, gangster, terrorist; sniper, gunfighter; assassin, murderer, killer; *informal* hit man, hired gun, gunslinger, mobster; *N. Amer. informal* shootist, hood.

gurgle ▶ verb *the water swirled and gurgled* BABBLE, burble, tinkle, bubble, ripple, murmur, purl, splash; *poetic/literary* plash.
▶ noun *the gurgle of a small brook* BABBLING, tinkling, bubbling, rippling, trickling, murmur, murmuring, purling, splashing; *poetic/literary* plashing.

guru ▶ noun ❶ *a Hindu guru and mystic* SPIRITUAL TEACHER, teacher, tutor, sage, mentor, spiritual leader, leader, master; *Hinduism* swami, Maharishi. ❷ *a management guru* EXPERT, authority, pundit, leading light, master, specialist; *informal* whizz.
– OPPOSITES disciple.

gush ▶ verb ❶ *water gushed through the weir* SURGE, burst, spout, spurt, jet, stream, rush, pour, spill, well out, cascade, flood; flow, run, issue; *Brit. informal* sloosh. ❷ *everyone gushed about the script* ENTHUSE, rave, be enthusiastic, be effusive, rhapsodize, go into raptures, wax lyrical, praise to the skies; *informal* go mad/wild/crazy, go over the top; *N. Amer. informal* ballyhoo.
▶ noun *a gush of water* SURGE, stream, spurt, jet, spout, outpouring, outflow, burst, rush, cascade, flood, torrent; *technical* efflux.

gushing, gushy ▶ adjective EFFUSIVE, enthusiastic, over-enthusiastic, unrestrained, extravagant, fulsome, lavish, rhapsodic, lyrical; *informal* over the top, OTT, laid on with a trowel.
– OPPOSITES restrained.

gust ▶ noun ❶ *a sudden gust of wind* FLURRY, blast, puff, blow, rush; squall. ❷ *gusts of laughter* OUTBURST, burst, eruption, fit, paroxysm; gale, peal, howl, hoot, shriek, roar.
▶ verb *wind gusted around the chimneys* BLOW, bluster, flurry, roar.

gusto ▶ noun ENTHUSIASM, relish, appetite, enjoyment, delight, glee, pleasure, satisfaction, appreciation, liking; zest, zeal, fervour, verve, keenness, avidity.

– OPPOSITES apathy, distaste.

gusty ▶ **adjective** BLUSTERY, windy, breezy; squally, stormy, tempestuous, wild, turbulent; *informal* blowy.
– OPPOSITES calm.

gut ▶ **noun** ❶ *he had an ache in his gut* STOMACH, belly, abdomen, solar plexus; intestines, bowels; *informal* tummy, tum, insides, innards. ❷ *fish heads and guts* ENTRAILS; intestines, viscera; offal; *informal* insides, innards; *Brit. archaic* numbles. ❸ (*informal*) *Nicola had the guts to say what she felt* COURAGE, bravery, backbone, nerve, pluck, spirit, boldness, audacity, daring, grit, fearlessness, toughness, determination; *informal* spunk; *Brit. informal* bottle; *N. Amer. informal* moxie.
– RELATED TERMS visceral, enteric.
▶ **adjective** (*informal*) *a gut feeling* INSTINCTIVE, instinctual, intuitive, deep-seated; knee-jerk, automatic, involuntary, spontaneous, unthinking.
▶ **verb** ❶ *clean, scale, and gut the sardines* REMOVE THE GUTS FROM, disembowel, draw; *formal* eviscerate. ❷ *the church was gutted by fire* DEVASTATE, destroy, demolish, wipe out, lay waste, ravage, consume, ruin, wreck.

gutless ▶ **adjective** (*informal*). *See* COWARDLY.

gutsy ▶ **adjective** (*informal*) BRAVE, courageous, plucky, bold, daring, fearless, adventurous, audacious, valiant, intrepid, heroic, lionhearted, undaunted, unflinching, unshrinking, unafraid, dauntless, indomitable, doughty, stouthearted; spirited, determined, resolute, death-or-glory; *informal* spunky, ballsy, have-a-go.

gutter ▶ **noun** DRAIN, sluice, sluiceway, culvert, spillway, sewer; channel, conduit, pipe; trough, trench, ditch, furrow, cut.

guttersnipe ▶ **noun** (*derogatory*) URCHIN, ragamuffin, waif, stray; *dated* gamin; *archaic* mudlark, street Arab.

guttural ▶ **adjective** THROATY, husky, gruff, gravelly, growly, growling, croaky, croaking, harsh, rough, rasping, raspy; deep, low, thick.

guy ▶ **noun** (*informal*) *he's a handsome guy* MAN, fellow, gentleman; youth, boy; *informal* lad, fella, geezer, gent; *Brit. informal* chap, bloke; *N. Amer. informal* dude, hombre; *Brit. informal, dated* cove.
▶ **verb** *she guyed him about his weight* MAKE FUN OF, poke fun at, laugh at, mock, ridicule, jeer at, scoff at; satirize, lampoon; *informal* send up, take the mickey out of; *N. Amer. informal* goof on.

guzzle ▶ **verb** ❶ *he guzzled his burger* GOBBLE, bolt, wolf, devour; *informal* tuck into, put away, pack away, demolish, polish off, stuff one's face with, pig oneself on, shovel down; *Brit. informal* scoff, shift; *N. Amer. informal* snarf down/up, scarf down/up. ❷ *she guzzled down the orange juice* GULP DOWN, swallow, quaff, down, swill; *informal* knock back, swig, slug down.

gypsy, gipsy ▶ **noun** ROMANY, Rom, chal, gitano, gitana, tzigane; traveller, nomad, rover, roamer, wanderer; *dialect* didicoi; *Brit. derogatory* tinker.

gyrate ▶ **verb** ROTATE, revolve, wheel, turn round, whirl, circle, pirouette, twirl, swirl, spin, swivel.

habit ▶ **noun** ❶ *it was his habit to go for a run every morning* CUSTOM, practice, routine, wont, pattern, convention, way, norm, tradition, matter of course, rule, usage. ❷ *her many irritating habits* MANNERISM, way, quirk, foible, trick, trait, idiosyncrasy, peculiarity, singularity, oddity, eccentricity, feature; tendency, propensity, inclination, bent, proclivity, disposition, predisposition. ❸ *a scientific habit of mind* DISPOSITION, temperament, character, nature, make-up, constitution, frame of mind, bent. ❹ (*informal*) *his cocaine habit* ADDICTION, dependence, dependency, craving, fixation, compulsion, obsession, weakness; *informal* monkey on one's back; *N. Amer. informal* jones. ❺ *a monk's habit* GARMENTS, dress, garb, clothes, clothing, attire, outfit, costume; *informal* gear; *formal* apparel.

■ **in the habit of** ACCUSTOMED TO, used to, given to, wont to, inclined to.

habitable ▶ **adjective** FIT TO LIVE IN, inhabitable, fit to occupy, in good repair, liveable-in; *formal* tenantable.

habitat ▶ **noun** NATURAL ENVIRONMENT, natural surroundings, home, domain, haunt; *formal* habitation.

habitation ▶ **noun** ❶ *a house fit for human habitation* OCCUPANCY, occupation, residence, residency, living in, tenancy; *archaic* inhabitancy. ❷ (*formal*) *his main habitation* RESIDENCE, place of residence, house, home, seat, lodging place, billet, quarters, living quarters, rooms, accommodation; *informal* pad, digs; *formal* dwelling, dwelling place, abode, domicile.

habitual ▶ adjective ❶ *her father's habitual complaints* CONSTANT, persistent, continual, continuous, perpetual, non-stop, recurrent, repeated, frequent; interminable, incessant, ceaseless, endless, never-ending; *informal* eternal. ❷ *habitual drinkers* INVETERATE, confirmed, compulsive, obsessive, incorrigible, hardened, ingrained, dyed-in-the-wool, chronic, regular; addicted; *informal* pathological. ❸ *his habitual secretiveness* CUSTOMARY, accustomed, regular, usual, normal, set, fixed, established, routine, common, ordinary, familiar, traditional, typical, general, characteristic, standard, time-honoured; *poetic/literary* wonted.
– OPPOSITES occasional, unaccustomed.

habituate ▶ verb ACCUSTOM, make used, familiarize, adapt, adjust, attune, acclimatize, acculturate, condition; inure, harden; *N. Amer.* acclimate.

habitué ▶ noun FREQUENT VISITOR, regular visitor/customer/client, familiar face, regular, patron, frequenter, haunter.

hack[1] ▶ verb *I hacked the padlock off* CUT, chop, hew, lop, saw; slash.
■ **hack it** (*informal*) COPE, manage, get on/by, carry on, come through, muddle along/through; stand it, tolerate it, bear it, endure it, put up with it; *informal* handle it, abide it, stick it; *Brit. informal* be doing with it.
■ **hack someone off** (*informal*). *See* ANNOY.

hack[2] ▶ noun ❶ *a tabloid hack* JOURNALIST, reporter, newspaperman, newspaperwoman, writer, Grub Street writer; *informal* journo, scribbler, hackette; *archaic* penny-a-liner. ❷ *office hacks* DRUDGE, menial, menial worker, factotum; *informal* dogsbody, gofer; *Brit. informal* skivvy. ❸ *a riding-school hack* HORSE, pony; *informal* nag; *N. Amer. informal* plug; *Austral./NZ informal* moke.

hackle
■ **make someone's hackles rise** ANNOY, irritate, exasperate, anger, incense, infuriate, irk, nettle, vex, put out, provoke, gall, antagonize, get on someone's nerves, ruffle someone's feathers, rankle with; *Brit.* rub up the wrong way; *informal* aggravate, peeve, needle, rile, make someone see red, make someone's blood boil, hack off, get someone's back up, get someone's goat, get up someone's nose, get someone's dander up, bug, miff; *Brit. informal* wind up, nark, get on someone's wick; *N. Amer. informal* tee off, tick off, burn up; *informal, dated* give someone the pip.

hackneyed ▶ adjective OVERUSED, overdone, overworked, worn out, time-worn, platitudinous, vapid, stale, tired, threadbare; trite, banal, hack, clichéd, hoary, commonplace, common, ordinary, stock, conventional, stereotyped, predictable; unimaginative, unoriginal, uninspired, prosaic, dull, boring, pedestrian, run-of-the-mill, routine; *informal* old hat, corny, played out.
– OPPOSITES original.

Hades ▶ noun. *See* HELL sense 1.

haft ▶ noun HANDLE, shaft, hilt, butt, stock, grip, handgrip, helve, shank.

hag ▶ noun CRONE, old woman, gorgon; *informal* witch, crow, cow, old bag, old boot; *archaic* beldam.

haggard ▶ adjective DRAWN, tired, exhausted, drained, careworn, unwell, unhealthy, spent, washed out, rundown; gaunt, pinched, peaked, peaky, hollow-cheeked, hollow-eyed, thin, emaciated, wasted, cadaverous; pale, wan, grey, ashen.
– OPPOSITES healthy.

haggle ▶ verb BARTER, bargain, negotiate, dicker, quibble, wrangle; beat someone down, drive a hard bargain; *archaic* chaffer.

hail[1] ▶ verb ❶ *a friend hailed him from the upper deck* CALL OUT TO, shout to, halloo, address; greet, say hello to, salute. ❷ *he hailed a cab* FLAG DOWN, wave down, signal to. ❸ *critics hailed the film as a masterpiece* ACCLAIM, praise, applaud, rave about, extol, eulogize, hymn, lionize, sing the praises of, make much of, glorify, cheer, salute, toast; *N. Amer. informal* ballyhoo; *black English* big up; *formal* laud. ❹ *Rick hails from Australia* COME FROM, be from, be a native of, have one's roots in.

hail[2] ▶ noun *a hail of bullets* BARRAGE, volley, shower, rain, torrent, burst, stream, storm, avalanche, onslaught; bombardment, cannonade, battery, blast, salvo; *historical* broadside.
▶ verb *tons of dust hailed down on us* BEAT, shower, rain, fall, pour; pelt, pepper, batter, bombard, assail.

hail-fellow-well-met ▶ adjective CONVIVIAL, sociable, outgoing, gregarious, companionable, friendly, genial, affable, amiable, congenial, agreeable, good-humoured; extrovert, uninhibited; *Scottish* couthy; *informal* backslapping, chummy, pally, clubbable, clubby, buddy-buddy; *Brit. informal* matey.
– OPPOSITES unsociable.

hair ▶ noun ❶ *her thick black hair* HEAD OF HAIR, shock of hair, mane, mop; locks, tresses, curls, ringlets. ❷ *I like your hair* HAIRSTYLE, haircut, cut, coiffure; *informal* hairdo, do, coif. ❸ *a dog with short, blue-grey hair* FUR, wool; coat, fleece, pelt; mane.
– RELATED TERMS tricho-.
■ **a hair's breadth** THE NARROWEST OF MARGINS, a narrow margin, the skin of one's teeth, a split second, a nose; *informal* a whisker.
■ **let one's hair down** (*informal*) ENJOY ONESELF, have a good time, have fun, make merry, let oneself go; *informal* have a ball, whoop it up, paint the town red, live it up, have a whale of a time, let it all hang out.
■ **make someone's hair stand on end** HORRIFY, shock, appal, scandalize, stun; make

someone's blood run cold; *informal* make someone's hair curl.

■ **split hairs** QUIBBLE, cavil, carp, niggle, chop logic; *informal* nit-pick; *archaic* pettifog.

hairdo ▶ noun (*informal*). *See* HAIRSTYLE.

hairdresser ▶ noun HAIRSTYLIST, stylist, coiffeur, coiffeuse; barber; *informal* crimper.

hairless ▶ adjective BALD, bald-headed; shaven, shaved, shorn, clean-shaven, beardless, smooth, smooth-faced, depilated; tonsured; *informal* baldy; *technical* glabrous; *archaic* baldpated.
– OPPOSITES hairy.

hairpiece ▶ noun WIG, toupee, periwig; merkin; *informal* rug.

hair-raising ▶ adjective TERRIFYING, frightening, petrifying, alarming, chilling, horrifying, shocking, spine-chilling, blood-curdling, fearsome, nightmarish; eerie, sinister, weird, ghostly, unearthly; *Scottish* eldritch; *informal* hairy, spooky, scary, creepy.

hair-splitting ▶ adjective PEDANTIC, pettifogging; quibbling, niggling, cavilling, carping, critical, overcritical, hypercritical; *informal* nitpicking, pernickety, picky; *N. Amer. informal* persnickety.

hairstyle ▶ noun HAIRCUT, cut, style, hair, coiffure; *informal* hairdo, do, coif.

hairy ▶ adjective ❶ *animals with hairy coats* SHAGGY, bushy, long-haired; woolly, furry, fleecy, fuzzy; *Botany & Zoology* pilose. ❷ *his hairy face* BEARDED, bewhiskered, moustachioed; unshaven, stubbly, bristly; *formal* hirsute. ❸ (*informal*) *a hairy situation* RISKY, dangerous, perilous, hazardous, touch-and-go; tricky, ticklish, difficult, awkward; *informal* dicey, sticky; *Brit. informal* dodgy.

halcyon ▶ adjective HAPPY, golden, idyllic, palmy, carefree, blissful, joyful, joyous, contented; flourishing, thriving, prosperous, successful; serene, calm, tranquil, peaceful.

hale ▶ adjective HEALTHY, fit, fighting fit, well, in good health, bursting with health, in fine fettle, as fit as a fiddle/flea; strong, robust, vigorous, hardy, sturdy, hearty, lusty, able-bodied; *informal* in the pink, as right as rain.
– OPPOSITES unwell.

half ▶ adjective *a half grapefruit* HALVED, divided in two.
– OPPOSITES whole.
▶ adverb ❶ *half-cooked chicken* PARTIALLY, partly, incompletely, inadequately, insufficiently; in part, part, slightly. ❷ *I'm half inclined to believe you* TO A CERTAIN EXTENT/DEGREE, to some extent/degree, (up) to a point, in part, partly, in some measure.
– OPPOSITES fully.

half-baked ▶ adjective ❶ *half-baked theories* ILL-CONCEIVED, hare-brained, ill-judged, impractical, unrealistic, unworkable, ridiculous, absurd; *informal* crazy, crackpot, cock-eyed. ❷ *her half-baked young nephew* FOOLISH, stupid, silly, idiotic, simple-minded, feeble-minded, empty-headed, feather-brained, featherheaded, brainless, witless, unintelligent, ignorant; *informal* dim, dopey, dumb, thick, halfwitted, dim-witted, birdbrained; *Brit. informal* gormless, daft, divvy, dozy.
– OPPOSITES sensible.

half-hearted ▶ adjective UNENTHUSIASTIC, cool, lukewarm, tepid, apathetic, indifferent, uninterested, unconcerned, languid, listless; perfunctory, cursory, superficial, desultory, feeble, lacklustre.
– OPPOSITES enthusiastic.

halfway ▶ adjective *the halfway point* MIDWAY, middle, mid, central, centre, intermediate; *Anatomy* medial, mesial.
▶ adverb ❶ *he stopped halfway down the passage* MIDWAY, in the middle, in the centre; part of the way, part-way. ❷ *he seemed halfway friendly* TO SOME EXTENT/DEGREE, in some measure, relatively, comparatively, moderately, somewhat, (up) to a point; just about, almost, nearly.

■ **meet someone halfway** COMPROMISE, come to terms, reach an agreement, make a deal, make concessions, find the middle ground, strike a balance; give and take.

halfwit ▶ noun (*informal*). *See* FOOL noun sense 1.

half-witted ▶ adjective (*informal*). *See* STUPID senses 1, 2.

hall ▶ noun ❶ *hang your coat in the hall* ENTRANCE HALL, hallway, entry, entrance, lobby, foyer, vestibule; atrium, concourse; passageway, passage, corridor; *N. Amer.* entryway. ❷ *the village hall* ASSEMBLY ROOM, meeting room, chamber; auditorium, concert hall, theatre.

hallmark ▶ noun ❶ *the hallmark on silver* ASSAY MARK, official mark, stamp of authenticity. ❷ *the tiny bubbles are the hallmark of fine champagnes* MARK, distinctive feature, characteristic, sign, sure sign, telltale sign, badge, stamp, trademark, indication, indicator.

halloo ▶ verb CALL OUT, shout, cry out, yell, bawl, bellow, roar, whoop; hail, greet; *informal* holler, yoo-hoo, cooee.

hallowed ▶ adjective HOLY, sacred, consecrated, sanctified, blessed; revered, venerated, honoured, sacrosanct, worshipped, divine, inviolable.

hallucinate ▶ verb HAVE HALLUCINATIONS, see things, be delirious, fantasize; *informal* trip, see pink elephants.

hallucination ▶ noun DELUSION, illusion, figment of the imagination, vision, apparition, mirage, chimera, fantasy; (**hallucinations**) delirium, phantasmagoria; *informal* trip, pink elephants.

halo ▶ noun RING OF LIGHT, nimbus, aureole, glory, crown of light, corona; *technical* halation; *rare* gloriole.

halt ▶ verb ❶ *Len halted and turned round* STOP, come to a halt, come to a stop, come to a standstill; pull up, draw up. ❷ *a further strike has halted production* STOP, bring to a stop, put a stop to, bring to an end, put an end to, terminate, end, wind up; suspend, break off, arrest; impede, check, curb, stem, staunch, block, stall, hold back; *informal* pull the plug on, put the kibosh on.
– OPPOSITES start, continue.
▶ noun ❶ *the car drew to a halt* STOP, standstill. ❷ *a halt in production* STOPPAGE, stopping, discontinuation, break, suspension, pause, interval, interruption, hiatus; cessation, termination, close, end.

halter ▶ noun HARNESS, head collar, bridle; *N. Amer.* headstall.

halting ▶ adjective ❶ *a halting conversation | halting English* HESITANT, faltering, hesitating, stumbling, stammering, stuttering; broken, imperfect. ❷ *his halting gait* UNSTEADY, awkward, faltering, stumbling, limping, hobbling.
– OPPOSITES fluent.

ham-fisted ▶ adjective CLUMSY, bungling, incompetent, amateurish, inept, unskilful, inexpert, maladroit, gauche, awkward, inefficient, bumbling, useless; *informal* cack-handed, ham-handed; *Brit. informal* all fingers and thumbs.
– OPPOSITES expert.

hammer ▶ noun *a hammer and chisel* mallet, beetle, gavel, sledgehammer.
▶ verb ❶ *the alloy is hammered into a circular shape* BEAT, forge, shape, form, mould, fashion, make. ❷ *Sally hammered at the door* BATTER, pummel, beat, bang, pound; strike, hit, knock on, thump on; cudgel, bludgeon, club; *informal* bash, wallop, clobber, whack, thwack. ❸ *they hammered away at their non-smoking campaign* WORK HARD, labour, slog away, plod away, grind away, slave away, work like a Trojan, work like a dog, keep one's nose to the grindstone; persist with, persevere with, press on with; *informal* stick at, peg away, beaver away, plug away, work one's socks off, soldier on; *Brit. informal* graft away. ❹ *anti-racism had been hammered into her* DRUM, instil, inculcate, knock, drive, din; drive home to, impress upon; ingrain. ❺ (*informal*) *he got hammered for an honest mistake. See* CHASTISE sense 1. ❻ (*informal*) *we've hammered them twice this season. See* TROUNCE.
■ **hammer something out** THRASH OUT, work out, agree on, sort out, decide on, bring about, effect, produce, broker, negotiate, reach an agreement on.

hamper[1] ▶ noun *a picnic hamper* BASKET, pannier, wickerwork basket; box, container, holder.

hamper[2] ▶ verb *the search was hampered by fog* HINDER, obstruct, impede, inhibit, retard, baulk, thwart, foil, curb, delay, set back, slow down, hold up, interfere with; restrict, constrain, trammel, block, check, curtail, frustrate, cramp, bridle, handicap, cripple, hamstring, shackle, fetter; *informal* stymie; *Brit. informal* throw a spanner in the works of; *N. Amer. informal* bork, throw a monkey wrench in the works of.
– OPPOSITES help.

hamstring ▶ verb ❶ *cattle were killed or hamstrung* CRIPPLE, lame, disable, incapacitate. ❷ *manufacturing companies were hamstrung by the economic chaos* HANDICAP, constrain, restrict, cripple, shackle, fetter, encumber, block, frustrate; hamper, hinder, obstruct, impede, trammel, inhibit, baulk, thwart, foil; *informal* stymie; *N. Amer. informal* bork.
– OPPOSITES help.

hand ▶ noun ❶ *big, strong hands* palm, fist; *informal* paw, mitt, duke, hook, meat hook; *Zoology* manus. ❷ *the clock's second hand* POINTER, indicator, needle, arrow, marker. ❸ *the frontier posts remained in government hands* CONTROL, power, charge, authority; command, responsibility, guardianship, management, care, supervision, jurisdiction; possession, keeping, custody; clutches, grasp, thrall; disposal; *informal* say-so. ❹ *let me give you a hand* HELP, a helping hand, assistance, aid, support, succour, relief; a good turn, a favour. ❺ (*informal*) *his fans gave him a big hand* ROUND OF APPLAUSE, clap, handclap, ovation, standing ovation; applause, handclapping. ❻ *a document written in his own hand* HANDWRITING, writing, script, calligraphy. ❼ *a factory hand* WORKER, factory worker, manual worker, unskilled worker, blue-collar worker, workman, labourer, operative, hired hand, roustabout; *N. Amer.* peon; *Austral./NZ* rouseabout.
– RELATED TERMS manual.
▶ verb ❶ *he handed each man a glass* PASS, give, reach, let someone have, throw, toss; present to; *informal* chuck, bung. ❷ *he handed him into a carriage* ASSIST, help, give someone a hand; guide.
■ **at hand** ❶ *keep the manual close at hand* READILY AVAILABLE, available, handy, to hand, within reach, accessible, close (by), near, nearby, at the ready, at one's fingertips, at one's disposal, convenient; *informal* get-at-able. ❷ *the time for starting the campaign is at hand* IMMINENT, approaching, coming, about to happen, on the horizon; impending.
■ **hand something down** PASS ON, pass down; bequeath, will, leave, make over, give, gift, transfer; *Law* demise, devise.
■ **hand in glove** IN CLOSE COLLABORATION, in close association, in close cooperation, very closely, in partnership, in league, in collusion; *informal* in cahoots.
■ **hand something on** GIVE, pass, hand, transfer, grant, cede, surrender, relinquish, yield; part with, let go of; bequeath, will, leave.
■ **hand something out** DISTRIBUTE, hand round, give out/round, pass out/round, share

out, dole out, dish out, deal out, mete out, issue, dispense; allocate, allot, apportion, disburse; circulate, disseminate.

■ **hand something over** YIELD, give, give up, pass, grant, entrust, surrender, relinquish, cede, turn over, deliver up, forfeit, sacrifice.

■ **hands down** EASILY, effortlessly, with ease, with no trouble, without effort; *informal* by a mile, no sweat.

■ **to hand** READILY AVAILABLE, available, handy, at hand, within reach, accessible, ready, close (by), near, nearby, at the ready, at one's fingertips, at one's disposal, convenient; *informal* get-at-able.

■ **try one's hand** HAVE A GO, make an attempt, have a shot; attempt, try, try out, give something a try; *informal* have a stab, have a bash, give something a whirl; *formal* essay.

handbag ▶ **noun** BAG, shoulder bag, clutch bag, evening bag, pochette; *N. Amer.* purse, pocketbook; *historical* reticule.

handbill ▶ **noun** NOTICE, advertisement, flyer, leaflet, circular, handout, pamphlet, brochure; *N. Amer.* dodger; *informal* ad; *Brit. informal* advert.

handbook ▶ **noun** MANUAL, instructions, instruction manual, ABC, A to Z; almanac, companion, directory, compendium; guide, guidebook, vade mecum.

handcuff ▶ **verb** MANACLE, shackle, fetter; restrain, clap/put someone in irons; *informal* cuff.

handcuffs ▶ **plural noun** MANACLES, shackles, irons, fetters, bonds, restraints; *informal* cuffs, bracelets; *archaic* darbies, gyves.

handful ▶ **noun** ❶ *a handful of British firms* A FEW, a small number, a small amount, a small quantity, one or two, some, not many, a scattering, a trickle. ❷ (*informal*) *the child is a real handful* NUISANCE, problem, bother, irritant, thorn in someone's flesh/side; *informal* pest, headache, pain, pain in the neck/backside; *Scottish informal* nyaff, skelf; *N. Amer. informal* pain in the butt.

handgun ▶ **noun** PISTOL, revolver, gun, side arm, six-shooter, thirty-eight, derringer; *N. Amer. informal* piece, shooting iron, Saturday night special, rod; *trademark* Colt.

handicap ▶ **noun** ❶ *a visual handicap* DISABILITY, physical/mental abnormality, defect, impairment, affliction, deficiency. ❷ *a handicap to the competitiveness of the industry* IMPEDIMENT, hindrance, obstacle, barrier, bar, obstruction, encumbrance, constraint, restriction, check, block, curb; disadvantage, drawback, stumbling block, difficulty, shortcoming, limitation; ball and chain, albatross, millstone round someone's neck; *poetic/literary* trammel.
– OPPOSITES benefit, advantage.

▶ **verb** *lack of funding handicapped the research* HAMPER, impede, hinder, impair, hamstring; restrict, check, obstruct, block, curb, bridle, hold back, constrain, trammel, limit, encumber; *informal* stymie; *N. Amer. informal* bork.
– OPPOSITES help.

handicapped ▶ **adjective** DISABLED, incapacitated, disadvantaged; infirm, invalid; *euphemistic* physically challenged, differently abled.

handicraft ▶ **noun** CRAFT, handiwork, craftwork; craftsmanship, workmanship, artisanship, art, skill.

handiwork ▶ **noun** *jewellery which is the handiwork of Chinese smiths* CREATION, product, work, achievement; handicraft, craft, craftwork.

handkerchief ▶ **noun** pocket handkerchief, tissue, paper handkerchief; *trademark* Kleenex; *informal* hanky, nose rag, snot rag; *poetic/literary* kerchief.

handle ▶ **verb** ❶ *the equipment must be handled with care* HOLD, pick up, grasp, grip, lift; feel, touch, finger; *informal* paw. ❷ *a car which is easy to handle* CONTROL, drive, steer, operate, manoeuvre, manipulate. ❸ *she handled the job formidably* DEAL WITH, manage, tackle, take care of, take charge of, attend to, see to, sort out, apply oneself to, take in hand. ❹ *the advertising company that is handling the account* ADMINISTER, manage, control, conduct, direct, guide, supervise, oversee, be in charge of, take care of, look after. ❺ *the traders handled goods manufactured in the Rhineland* TRADE IN, deal in, buy, sell, supply, peddle, traffic in, purvey, hawk, tout, market.

▶ **noun** *the knife's handle* HAFT, shank, stock, shaft, grip, handgrip, hilt, helve, butt; knob.

hand-me-down ▶ **adjective** SECOND-HAND, used, nearly new, handed-down, passed-on, cast-off, worn, old, pre-owned; *Brit. informal* reach-me-down.
– OPPOSITES new.

handout ▶ **noun** ❶ *she existed on handouts* CHARITY, aid, benefit, financial support, donations, subsidies; *historical* alms. ❷ *a xeroxed handout* LEAFLET, pamphlet, brochure; handbill, flyer, notice, circular, mailshot.

hand-picked ▶ **adjective** SPECIALLY CHOSEN, selected, invited; select, elite; choice.

handsome ▶ **adjective** ❶ *a handsome man* GOOD-LOOKING, attractive, personable, striking; *informal* hunky, dishy, tasty, fanciable; *Brit. informal* fit; *N. Amer. informal* cute; *Austral./NZ informal* spunky. ❷ *a handsome woman of 30* STRIKING, imposing, prepossessing, elegant, stately, dignified, statuesque, good-looking, attractive, personable. ❸ *a handsome profit* SUBSTANTIAL, considerable, sizeable, princely, large, big, ample, bumper; *informal* tidy, whopping, not to be sneezed at; *Brit. informal* whacking, ginormous.
– OPPOSITES ugly, meagre.

handwriting ▶ **noun** WRITING, script, hand, pen; penmanship, calligraphy, chirography; *informal* scrawl, scribble.

handy ▶ adjective ❶ *a handy reference tool* USEFUL, convenient, practical, easy-to-use, well-designed, user-friendly, user-oriented, helpful, functional, serviceable. ❷ *keep your credit card handy* READILY AVAILABLE, available, at hand, to hand, near at hand, within reach, accessible, ready, close (by), near, nearby, at the ready, at one's fingertips; *informal* get-at-able. ❸ *he's handy with a needle* SKILFUL, skilled, dexterous, deft, nimble-fingered, adroit, able, adept, proficient, capable; good with one's hands; *informal* nifty.
– OPPOSITES inconvenient, inept.

handyman ▶ noun ODD-JOB MAN, odd-jobber, factotum, jack of all trades, man of all work; DIY'er; *informal* Mr Fixit.

hang ▶ verb ❶ *lights hung from the trees* BE SUSPENDED, hang down, be pendent, dangle, swing, sway; *archaic* depend. ❷ *hang your pictures at eye level* PUT UP, fix, attach, affix, fasten, post, display, suspend, pin up, nail up. ❸ *the room was hung with streamers* DECORATE, adorn, drape, festoon, deck out, trick out, bedeck, array, garland, swathe, cover, ornament; *poetic/literary* bedizen. ❹ *he was hanged for murder* HANG BY THE NECK, send to the gallows; *informal* string up. ❺ *a pall of smoke hung over the city* HOVER, float, drift, be suspended. ❻ *the threat of budget cuts is hanging over us* BE IMMINENT, threaten, be close, be impending, impend, loom, be on the horizon.

■ **hang about** (*Brit. informal*). *See* HANG AROUND.

■ **hang around/round** (*informal*) ❶ *they spent their time hanging around in bars* LOITER, linger, wait around, waste time, kill time, mark time, while away the/one's time, kick/cool one's heels, twiddle one's thumbs; frequent, be a regular visitor to, haunt; *informal* hang out in. ❷ *hang about, what's this? See* HANG ON sense 4. ❸ *she's hanging around with a bunch of hippies* ASSOCIATE, mix, keep company, socialize, fraternize, consort, rub shoulders; *N. Amer.* rub elbows; *informal* hang out, run around, knock about/around, be thick, hobnob.

■ **hang fire** DELAY, hang back, hold back, hold on, stall, pause; procrastinate, vacillate, adopt Fabian tactics; *informal* hang about/around, sit tight, hold one's horses.

■ **hang on** ❶ *he hung on to her coat* HOLD ON, hold fast, grip, clutch, grasp, hold tightly, cling. ❷ *her future hung on his decision* DEPEND ON, be dependent on, turn on, hinge on, rest on, be contingent on, be determined by, be decided by. ❸ *I'll hang on as long as I can* PERSEVERE, hold out, hold on, go on, carry on, keep on, keep going, keep at it, continue, persist, stay with it, struggle on, plod on, plough on; *informal* soldier on, stick at it, stick it out, hang in there. ❹ (*informal*) *hang on, let me think* WAIT, wait a minute, hold on, stop; hold the line; *informal* hold your horses, sit tight; *Brit. informal* hang about.

hangdog ▶ adjective SHAMEFACED, sheepish, abashed, ashamed, guilty-looking, abject, cowed, dejected, downcast, crestfallen, woebegone, disconsolate.
– OPPOSITES unabashed.

hanger-on ▶ noun FOLLOWER, flunkey, toady, camp follower, sycophant, parasite, leech; henchman, minion, lackey, vassal, dependant, retainer; acolyte; *N. Amer.* cohort; *informal* groupie, sponger, freeloader, passenger, sidekick.

hanging ▶ noun *silk wall hangings* DRAPE, curtain; drapery.
▶ adjective *hanging fronds of honeysuckle* PENDENT, dangling, trailing, tumbling; suspended.

hang-out ▶ noun HAUNT, stamping ground, favourite spot, meeting place, territory; den, refuge, retreat; *N. Amer.* stomping ground.

hang-up ▶ noun NEUROSIS, phobia, preoccupation, fixation, obsession, idée fixe; inhibition, mental block, psychological block, block, difficulty; *informal* complex, thing, bee in one's bonnet.

hank ▶ noun COIL, skein, length, roll, loop, twist, piece; lock, ringlet, curl.

hanker ▶ verb YEARN, long, crave, desire, wish, want, hunger, thirst, lust, ache, pant, be eager, be desperate, be eating one's heart out; fancy, pine for, have one's heart set on; *informal* be dying, have a yen, itch.

hankering ▶ noun LONGING, yearning, craving, desire, wish, hunger, thirst, urge, ache, lust, appetite, fancy; *informal* yen, itch; *archaic* appetency.
– OPPOSITES aversion.

hanky-panky ▶ noun (*informal*) GOINGS-ON, funny business, mischief, misbehaviour, misconduct, chicanery, dishonesty, deception, deceit, trickery, intrigue, skulduggery, subterfuge, machinations; infidelity, unfaithfulness, adultery; *informal* monkey business, shenanigans, carryings-on; *Brit. informal* jiggery-pokery.

haphazard ▶ adjective RANDOM, unplanned, unsystematic, unmethodical, disorganized, disorderly, irregular, indiscriminate, chaotic, hit-and-miss, arbitrary, aimless, careless, casual, slapdash, slipshod; chance, accidental; *informal* higgledy-piggledy.
– OPPOSITES methodical.

hapless ▶ adjective UNFORTUNATE, unlucky, luckless, out of luck, ill-starred, ill-fated, jinxed, cursed, doomed; unhappy, forlorn, wretched, miserable, woebegone; *informal* down on one's luck; *poetic/literary* star-crossed.
– OPPOSITES lucky.

happen ▶ verb ❶ *remember what happened last time he was here* OCCUR, take place, come about; ensue, result, transpire, materialize, arise, crop up, come up, present itself, supervene; *N. Amer. informal* go down; *formal* eventuate; *poetic/*

literary come to pass, betide; *archaic* hap. ❷ *I wonder what happened to Susie?* BECOME OF; *poetic/literary* befall, betide. ❸ *they happened to be in London* CHANCE, have the good/bad luck. ❹ *he happened on a linnet's nest* DISCOVER, find, find by chance, come across, chance on, stumble on, hit on.

happening ▶ **noun** *bizarre happenings* OCCURRENCE, event, incident, proceeding, affair, circumstance, phenomenon, episode, experience, occasion, development, eventuality.

▶ **adjective** (*informal*) *a happening nightspot* FASHIONABLE, modern, popular, new, latest, up to date, up to the minute, in fashion, in vogue, le dernier cri; *informal* trendy, funky, hot, cool, with it, hip, in, big, now, groovy; *N. Amer. informal* kicky, tony.
– OPPOSITES old-fashioned.

happily ▶ **adverb** ❶ *he smiled happily* CONTENTEDLY, cheerfully, cheerily, merrily, delightedly, joyfully, joyously, gaily, gleefully. ❷ *I will happily do as you ask* GLADLY, willingly, readily, freely, cheerfully, ungrudgingly, with pleasure; *archaic* fain. ❸ *happily, we are living in enlightened times* FORTUNATELY, luckily, thankfully, mercifully, by good luck, by good fortune, as luck would have it; thank goodness, thank God, thank heavens, thank the stars.

happiness ▶ **noun** PLEASURE, contentment, satisfaction, cheerfulness, merriment, gaiety, joy, joyfulness, joviality, jollity, glee, delight, good spirits, light-heartedness, well-being, enjoyment; exuberance, exhilaration, elation, ecstasy, jubilation, rapture, bliss, blissfulness, euphoria, transports of delight.

happy ▶ **adjective** ❶ *Melissa looked happy and excited* CHEERFUL, cheery, merry, joyful, jovial, jolly, jocular, gleeful, carefree, untroubled, delighted, smiling, beaming, grinning, in good spirits, in a good mood, light-hearted, pleased, contented, content, satisfied, gratified, buoyant, radiant, sunny, blithe, joyous, beatific; thrilled, elated, exhilarated, ecstatic, blissful, euphoric, overjoyed, exultant, rapturous, in seventh heaven, on cloud nine, walking on air, jumping for joy, cock-a-hoop, jubilant; *informal* chirpy, over the moon, on top of the world, as happy as a sandboy, tickled pink, like a dog with two tails, as pleased as Punch, on a high; *Brit. informal* chuffed, as happy as Larry; *N. English informal* made up; *N. Amer. informal* as happy as a clam; *Austral. informal* wrapped; *formal* jocund; *dated* gay. ❷ *we will be happy to advise you* GLAD, pleased, delighted; willing, ready, disposed. ❸ *a happy coincidence* FORTUNATE, lucky, favourable, advantageous, opportune, timely, well-timed, convenient.
– OPPOSITES sad, unwilling, unfortunate.

happy-go-lucky ▶ **adjective** EASY-GOING, carefree, casual, free and easy, devil-may-care, blithe, nonchalant, insouciant, blasé, unconcerned, untroubled, unworried, light-hearted; *informal* laid-back.
– OPPOSITES anxious.

harangue ▶ **noun** *a ten-minute harangue* TIRADE, diatribe, lecture, polemic, rant, fulmination, broadside, attack, onslaught; criticism, condemnation, censure, admonition; declamation, speech; *informal* blast; *poetic/literary* philippic.

▶ **verb** *he harangued his erstwhile colleagues* RANT AT, hold forth to, lecture, shout at; berate, criticize, attack; *informal* earbash, sound off at, mouth off at.

harass ▶ **verb** ❶ *council tenants who harass their neighbours* PERSECUTE, intimidate, hound, harry, plague, torment, bedevil, pressurize; pester, bother, worry, disturb, trouble, provoke, stress; *informal* hassle, bug, give someone a hard time; *N. English informal* mither; *N. Amer. informal* devil, ride. ❷ *they were sent to harass the enemy flanks* HARRY, attack, beleaguer, set upon, assail.

harassed ▶ **adjective** STRESSED, strained, worn out, hard-pressed, careworn, worried, troubled, beleaguered, under pressure, at the end of one's tether; *N. Amer.* at the end of one's rope; *informal* hassled.
– OPPOSITES carefree.

harassment ▶ **noun** PERSECUTION, intimidation, pressure, pressurization, force, coercion; *informal* hassle.

harbinger ▶ **noun** HERALD, sign, indication, signal, portent, omen, augury, forewarning, presage; forerunner, precursor, messenger; *poetic/literary* foretoken.

harbour ▶ **noun** ❶ *a picturesque harbour* PORT, dock, haven, marina; mooring, moorage, anchorage, harbourage; waterfront. ❷ *a safe harbour for me* REFUGE, haven, safe haven, shelter, sanctuary, retreat, place of safety, port in a storm.

▶ **verb** ❶ *he is harbouring a dangerous criminal* SHELTER, conceal, hide, shield, protect, give sanctuary to; take in, put up, accommodate, house. ❷ *Rose had harboured a grudge against him* BEAR, nurse, nurture, cherish, entertain, foster, hold on to, cling to.

hard ▶ **adjective** ❶ *hard ground* FIRM, solid, rigid, stiff, resistant, unbreakable, inflexible, impenetrable, unyielding, solidified, hardened, compact, compacted, dense, close-packed, compressed; steely, tough, strong, stony, rock-like, flinty, as hard as iron, as hard as stone; frozen; *poetic/literary* adamantine. ❷ *hard physical work* ARDUOUS, strenuous, tiring, fatiguing, exhausting, wearying, back-breaking, gruelling, heavy, laborious; difficult, taxing, exacting, testing, challenging, demanding, punishing, tough, formidable, onerous, rigorous, uphill, Herculean; *informal* murderous, killing, hellish; *Brit. informal* knackering; *formal* exigent; *archaic* toilsome. ❸ *hard workers* DILI-

GENT, hard-working, industrious, sedulous, assiduous, conscientious, energetic, keen, enthusiastic, zealous, earnest, persevering, persistent, unflagging, untiring, indefatigable; studious. ❹ *a hard problem* DIFFICULT, puzzling, perplexing, baffling, bewildering, mystifying, knotty, thorny, problematic, complicated, complex, intricate, involved; insoluble, unfathomable, impenetrable, incomprehensible, unanswerable. ❺ *times are hard* HARSH, grim, difficult, bad, bleak, dire, tough, austere, unpleasant, uncomfortable, straitened, spartan; dark, distressing, painful, awful. ❻ *a hard taskmaster* STRICT, harsh, firm, severe, stern, tough, rigorous, demanding, exacting; callous, unkind, unsympathetic, cold, heartless, hard-hearted, unfeeling; intransigent, unbending, uncompromising, inflexible, implacable, stubborn, obdurate, unyielding, unrelenting, unsparing, grim, ruthless, merciless, pitiless, cruel; standing no nonsense, ruling with a rod of iron. ❼ *a hard winter* BITTERLY COLD, cold, bitter, harsh, severe, bleak, freezing, icy, icy-cold, arctic. ❽ *a hard blow* FORCEFUL, heavy, strong, sharp, smart, violent, powerful, vigorous, mighty, hefty, tremendous. ❾ *hard facts* RELIABLE, definite, true, confirmed, substantiated, undeniable, indisputable, unquestionable, verifiable. ❿ *hard liquor* ALCOHOLIC, strong, intoxicating, potent; *formal* spirituous. ⓫ *hard drugs* ADDICTIVE, habit-forming; strong, harmful.

–OPPOSITES soft, easy lazy, gentle.

▶ **adverb** ❶ *George pushed her hard* FORCEFULLY, forcibly, roughly, powerfully, strongly, heavily, sharply, vigorously, energetically, with all one's might, with might and main. ❷ *they worked hard* DILIGENTLY, industriously, assiduously, conscientiously, sedulously, busily, enthusiastically, energetically, doggedly, steadily; *informal* like mad, like crazy; *Brit. informal* like billy-o. ❸ *this prosperity has been hard won* WITH DIFFICULTY, with effort, after a struggle, painfully, laboriously. ❹ *her death hit him hard* SEVERELY, badly, acutely, deeply, keenly, seriously, profoundly, gravely; *formal* grievously. ❺ *it was raining hard* HEAVILY, strongly, in torrents, in sheets, cats and dogs; steadily. ❻ *my mother looked hard at me* CLOSELY, attentively, intently, critically, carefully, keenly, searchingly, earnestly, sharply.

■ **hard and fast** DEFINITE, fixed, set, strict, rigid, binding, clear-cut, cast-iron; inflexible, immutable, unchangeable, incontestable.

■ **hard by** CLOSE TO, right by, beside, near (to), nearby, not far from, a stone's throw from, on the doorstep of; *informal* within spitting distance of, {a hop, skip, and jump away from}.

■ **hard feelings** RESENTMENT, animosity, ill feeling, ill will, bitterness, bad blood, resentfulness, rancour, malice, acrimony, antagonism, antipathy, animus, friction, anger, hostility, hate, hatred.

■ **hard up** (informal) POOR, short of money, badly off, impoverished, impecunious, in reduced circumstances, unable to make ends meet; penniless, destitute, poverty-stricken; *informal* broke, strapped (for cash); *Brit. informal* skint.

hardbitten ▶ **adjective** HARDENED, tough, cynical, unsentimental, hard-headed, case-hardened, as hard as nails; *informal* hard-nosed, hard-boiled.

–OPPOSITES sentimental.

hard-boiled ▶ **adjective** (*informal*) *a hard-boiled undercover agent. See* HARDBITTEN.

hard-core ▶ **adjective** DIEHARD, staunch, dedicated, committed, steadfast, dyed-in-the-wool, long-standing; hard-line, extreme, entrenched, radical, intransigent, uncompromising, rigid; *informal* deep-dyed.

harden ▶ **verb** ❶ *this glue will harden in four hours* SOLIDIFY, set, congeal, clot, coagulate, stiffen, thicken, cake, inspissate; freeze, crystallize; ossify, petrify. ❷ *their suffering had hardened them* TOUGHEN, desensitize, inure, case-harden, harden someone's heart; deaden, numb, benumb, anaesthetize; brutalize.

–OPPOSITES liquefy, soften.

hardened ▶ **adjective** ❶ *he was hardened to the violence he had seen* INURED, desensitized, deadened; accustomed, habituated, acclimatized, used. ❷ *a hardened criminal* INVETERATE, seasoned, habitual, chronic, compulsive, confirmed, dyed-in-the-wool; incorrigible, incurable, irredeemable, unregenerate. ❸ *the silos are hardened against air attack* STRENGTHENED, fortified, reinforced, toughened.

hard-headed ▶ **adjective** UNSENTIMENTAL, practical, pragmatic, businesslike, realistic, sensible, rational, clear-thinking, cool-headed, down-to-earth, matter-of-fact, no-nonsense, with one's/both feet on the ground; tough, hardbitten; shrewd, astute, sharp, sharp-witted; *informal* hard-nosed, hard-boiled.

–OPPOSITES idealistic.

hard-hearted ▶ **adjective** UNFEELING, heartless, cold, hard, callous, unsympathetic, uncaring, unloving, unconcerned, indifferent, unmoved, unkind, uncharitable, unemotional, cold-hearted, cold-blooded, mean-spirited, stony-hearted, having a heart of stone, as hard as nails, cruel.

–OPPOSITES compassionate.

hard-hitting ▶ **adjective** UNCOMPROMISING, blunt, forthright, frank, honest, direct, tough; critical, unsparing, strongly worded, straight-talking, pulling no punches, not mincing one's words, not beating about the bush.

hardihood ▶ **noun** BRAVERY, courage, pluck, valour, intrepidity, nerve, daring, fearlessness, audacity, boldness, dauntlessness, stout-heartedness, heroism; backbone, grit, spine, spirit, mettle; *informal* guts, spunk; *Brit. informal* bottle;

N. Amer. informal moxie.
– OPPOSITES timidity.

hardiness ▶ noun ROBUSTNESS, strength, toughness, ruggedness, sturdiness, resilience, stamina, vigour; healthiness, good health.
– OPPOSITES frailty.

hard-line ▶ adjective UNCOMPROMISING, strict, extreme, tough, diehard, inflexible, intransigent, intractable, unyielding, single-minded, not giving an inch.
– OPPOSITES moderate.

hardly ▶ adverb *we hardly know each other* SCARCELY, barely, only just, slightly.

hard-nosed ▶ adjective (*informal*) TOUGH-MINDED, unsentimental, no-nonsense, hard-headed, hardbitten, pragmatic, realistic, down-to-earth, practical, rational, shrewd, astute, businesslike; *informal* hard-boiled.
– OPPOSITES sentimental.

hard-pressed ▶ adjective ❶ *the hard-pressed infantry* UNDER ATTACK, hotly pursued, harried. ❷ *the hard-pressed construction industry* IN DIFFICULTIES, under pressure, troubled, beleaguered, harassed, with one's back to/against the wall, in a tight corner, in a tight spot, between a rock and a hard place; overburdened, overworked, overloaded, rushed off one's feet; *informal* pushed, up against it.

hardship ▶ noun PRIVATION, deprivation, destitution, poverty, austerity, penury, want, need, neediness, impecuniousness; misfortune, distress, suffering, affliction, trouble, pain, misery, wretchedness, tribulation, adversity, trials, trials and tribulations, dire straits; *poetic/literary* travails.
– OPPOSITES prosperity, ease.

hardware ▶ noun EQUIPMENT, apparatus, gear, paraphernalia, tackle, kit, machinery; tools, articles, implements, instruments, appliances.

hard-wearing ▶ adjective DURABLE, strong, tough, resilient, lasting, long-lasting, made to last, stout, well made, rugged, heavy-duty.
– OPPOSITES flimsy.

hard-working ▶ adjective DILIGENT, industrious, conscientious, assiduous, sedulous, painstaking, persevering, unflagging, untiring, tireless, indefatigable, studious; keen, enthusiastic, zealous, busy, with one's shoulder to the wheel, with one's nose to the grindstone.
– OPPOSITES lazy.

hardy ▶ adjective ROBUST, healthy, fit, strong, sturdy, tough, rugged, hearty, lusty, vigorous, hale and hearty, fit as a fiddle, fighting fit, in fine fettle, in good health, in good condition; *Brit.* in rude health; *dated* stalwart.
– OPPOSITES delicate.

hare-brained ▶ adjective ❶ *a hare-brained scheme* ILL-JUDGED, rash, foolish, foolhardy, reckless, madcap, wild, silly, stupid, ridiculous, absurd, idiotic, asinine, imprudent, impracticable, unworkable, unrealistic, unconsidered, half-baked, ill-thought-out, ill-advised, ill-conceived; *informal* crackpot, crackbrained, cock-eyed, crazy; *Brit. informal* daft, barmy. ❷ *a hare-brained young girl* FOOLISH, silly, idiotic, unintelligent, empty-headed, scatterbrained, feather-brained, birdbrained, pea-brained, brainless, giddy; *informal* dippy, dizzy, dopey, dotty, airheaded.
– OPPOSITES sensible, intelligent.

harem ▶ noun SERAGLIO, zenana; *historical* gynaeceum.

hark ▶ verb (*poetic/literary*) *hark, I hear a warning note* LISTEN, lend an ear, pay attention, attend, mark; *archaic* hearken, give ear.
■ **hark back to** RECALL, call/bring to mind, evoke, put one in mind of.

harlequin ▶ noun JESTER, joker, merry andrew.
▶ adjective *a harlequin pattern* MULTICOLOURED, many-coloured, colourful, particoloured, varicoloured, many-hued, rainbow, variegated, jazzy, kaleidoscopic, psychedelic, polychromatic, chequered; *archaic* motley.

harlot ▶ noun (*archaic*) PROSTITUTE, whore, fille de joie, call girl; promiscuous woman, slut; *informal* tart, pro, member of the oldest profession; *Brit. informal* scrubber, slag, slapper; *N. Amer. informal* hooker, hustler, tramp, roundheel; *dated* streetwalker, hussy, woman of the streets, woman of the night, scarlet woman, loose woman, fallen woman, cocotte, wanton; *archaic* strumpet, courtesan, trollop, doxy, drab, trull.

harm ▶ noun ❶ *the voltage is not sufficient to cause harm* INJURY, hurt, pain, trauma; damage, impairment, mischief. ❷ *I can't see any harm in it* EVIL, wrong, ill, wickedness, iniquity, sin.
– OPPOSITES benefit.
▶ verb ❶ *he's never harmed anybody in his life* INJURE, hurt, wound, lay a finger on, maltreat, mistreat, misuse, ill-treat, ill-use, abuse, molest. ❷ *this could harm his World Cup prospects* DAMAGE, spoil, mar, do mischief to, impair.

harmful ▶ adjective DAMAGING, injurious, detrimental, dangerous, deleterious, unfavourable, negative, disadvantageous, unhealthy, unwholesome, hurtful, baleful, destructive; noxious, hazardous, poisonous, toxic, deadly, lethal; bad, evil, malign, malignant, malevolent, corrupting, subversive, pernicious.
– OPPOSITES beneficial.

harmless ▶ adjective ❶ *a harmless substance* SAFE, innocuous, benign, gentle, mild, wholesome, non-toxic, non-poisonous, non-irritant; non-addictive. ❷ *he seems harmless enough* INOFFENSIVE, innocuous, unobjectionable, unexceptionable.
– OPPOSITES dangerous.

harmonious ▶ adjective ❶ *harmonious music* TUNEFUL, melodious, melodic, sweet-sounding,

mellifluous, dulcet, lyrical; euphonious, euphonic, harmonic, polyphonic; *informal* easy on the ear. ❷ *their harmonious relationship* FRIENDLY, amicable, cordial, amiable, congenial, easy, peaceful, peaceable, cooperative; compatible, sympathetic, united, attuned, in harmony, in rapport, in tune, in accord, of one mind, seeing eye to eye. ❸ *a harmonious blend of traditional and modern* CONGRUOUS, coordinated, balanced, in proportion, compatible, well matched, well balanced.
– OPPOSITES discordant, hostile, incongruous.

harmonize ▶ **verb** ❶ *colours which harmonize in a pleasing way* COORDINATE, go together, match, blend, mix, balance, tone in; be compatible, be harmonious, suit each other, set each other off. ❷ *the need to harmonize tax laws across Europe* COORDINATE, systematize, correlate, integrate, synchronize, make consistent, bring in line, bring in tune.
– OPPOSITES clash.

harmony ▶ **noun** ❶ *musical harmony* EUPHONY, polyphony; tunefulness, melodiousness, mellifluousness. ❷ *the harmony of the whole structure* BALANCE, symmetry, congruity, consonance, coordination, compatibility. ❸ *the villagers live together in harmony* ACCORD, agreement, peace, peacefulness, amity, amicability, friendship, fellowship, cooperation, understanding, consensus, unity, sympathy, rapport, like-mindedness; unison, union, concert, oneness, synthesis; *formal* concord.
– OPPOSITES dissonance, disagreement.

harness ▶ **noun** *a horse's harness* TACK, tackle, equipment; trappings; yoke; *archaic* equipage.
▶ **verb** ❶ *he harnessed his horse* HITCH UP, put in harness, yoke, couple. ❷ *attempts to harness solar energy* CONTROL, exploit, utilize, use, employ, make use of, put to use; channel, mobilize, apply, capitalize on.

harp ▶ **noun** lyre, aeolian harp, wind harp, Jew's harp, Celtic harp, clarsach, triple harp, Welsh harp; *historical* trigon.
■ **harp on about** KEEP ON ABOUT, go on about, keep talking about, dwell on, make an issue of; labour the point.

harpoon ▶ **noun** SPEAR, trident, dart, barb, gaff, leister.

harridan ▶ **noun** SHREW, termagant, virago, harpy, vixen, nag, hag, crone, dragon, ogress; fishwife, hellcat, she-devil, gorgon; martinet, tartar; *informal* old bag, old bat, old cow, bitch, battleaxe, witch; *archaic* scold.

harried ▶ **adjective** HARASSED, beleaguered, flustered, agitated, bothered, vexed, beset, plagued; *informal* hassled, up against it.

harrow ▶ **verb** DISTRESS, trouble, bother, afflict, grieve, torment, pain, hurt, mortify.
– OPPOSITES comfort.

harrowing ▶ **adjective** DISTRESSING, distressful, traumatic, upsetting; shocking, disturbing, painful, haunting, appalling, horrifying.

harry ▶ **verb** ❶ *they harried the retreating enemy* ATTACK, assail, assault; charge, rush, strike, set upon; bombard, shell, strafe. ❷ *the government was harried by a new lobby* HARASS, hound, pressurize, bedevil, torment, pester, bother, worry, badger, nag, plague; *informal* hassle, bug, lean on, give someone a hard time, get on someone's back.

harsh ▶ **adjective** ❶ *a harsh voice* GRATING, jarring, rasping, strident, raucous, brassy, discordant, unharmonious, unmelodious; screeching, shrill; rough, coarse, hoarse, gruff, croaky. ❷ *harsh colours* GLARING, bright, dazzling; loud, garish, gaudy, lurid, bold. ❸ *his harsh rule over them* CRUEL, savage, barbarous, despotic, dictatorial, tyrannical, tyrannous; ruthless, merciless, pitiless, relentless, unmerciful; severe, strict, intolerant, illiberal; hard-hearted, heartless, unkind, inhuman, inhumane. ❹ *they took harsh measures to end the crisis* SEVERE, stringent, firm, stiff, hard, stern, rigorous, grim, uncompromising; punitive, cruel, brutal. ❺ *harsh words* RUDE, discourteous, uncivil, impolite; unfriendly, sharp, bitter, abusive, unkind, disparaging; abrupt, brusque, curt, gruff, short, surly, offhand. ❻ *harsh conditions* AUSTERE, grim, spartan, hard, comfortless, inhospitable, stark, bleak, desolate. ❼ *a harsh winter* HARD, severe, cold, bitter, bleak, freezing, icy; arctic, polar, Siberian. ❽ *harsh cream cleaners* ABRASIVE, strong, caustic; coarse, rough.
– OPPOSITES soft, subdued, kind, friendly, comfortable, balmy, mild.

harum-scarum ▶ **adjective** RECKLESS, impetuous, impulsive, imprudent, rash, wild; daredevil, madcap, hot-headed, hare-brained, foolhardy, incautious, careless, heedless; *informal* devil-may-care; *poetic/literary* temerarious.
– OPPOSITES cautious.

harvest ▶ **noun** ❶ *we all helped with the harvest* HARVESTING, reaping, picking, collecting; *formal* ingathering. ❷ *a poor harvest* YIELD, crop, vintage; fruits, produce. ❸ *the experiment yielded a meagre harvest* RETURN, result, fruits; product, output, effect; consequence.
▶ **verb** ❶ *he harvested the wheat* GATHER (IN), bring in, reap, pick, collect; *formal* ingather. ❷ *he harvested many honours* ACQUIRE, obtain, gain, get, earn; accumulate, amass, gather, collect; *informal* land, net, bag, scoop.

hash[1] ▶ **noun** *a whole hash of excuses* MIXTURE, assortment, variety, array, mix, miscellany, selection, medley, mishmash, hotchpotch, ragbag, gallimaufry, pot-pourri; *N. Amer.* hodgepodge.
■ **make a hash of** (*informal*) BUNGLE, fluff, mess up, make a mess of; mismanage, mishandle, ruin, wreck; *informal* botch, muff, muck up, foul up, screw up, blow; *Brit. informal* make a pig's ear of, cock up; *N. Amer. informal* flub.

hash² ▶ noun (*informal*) *she smokes a lot of hash.* See CANNABIS.

hassle (*informal*) ▶ noun ❶ *parking is such a hassle* INCONVENIENCE, bother, nuisance, problem, trouble, struggle, difficulty, annoyance, irritation, thorn in one's flesh/side, fuss; *informal* aggravation, aggro, stress, headache, pain (in the neck). ❷ (*N. Amer.*) *she got into a hassle with that guy.* See QUARREL noun.

▶ verb *they were hassling him to pay up* HARASS, pester, nag, keep on at, badger, hound, harry, chivvy, bother, torment, plague; *informal* bug, give someone a hard time, get on someone's back, breathe down someone's neck; *N. English informal* mither.

hassled ▶ adjective (*informal*) HARASSED, agitated, stressed (out), harried, frayed, flustered; beleaguered, hounded, plagued, bothered, beset, tormented; under pressure, hot and bothered; *informal* up against it.
– OPPOSITES calm.

haste ▶ noun *working with feverish haste* SPEED, hastiness, hurriedness, swiftness, rapidity, quickness, briskness; *formal* expedition.
– OPPOSITES delay.
■ **in haste** QUICKLY, rapidly, fast, speedily, with urgency, in a rush, in a hurry.

hasten ▶ verb ❶ *we hastened back home* HURRY, rush, dash, race, fly, shoot; scurry, scramble, dart, bolt, sprint, run, gallop; go fast, go quickly, go like lightning, go hell for leather; *informal* tear, hare, pelt, scoot, zip, zoom, belt, hotfoot it, leg it; *Brit. informal* bomb, bucket; *N. Amer. informal* hightail, barrel; *dated* make haste. ❷ *chemicals can hasten ageing* SPEED UP, accelerate, quicken, precipitate, advance, hurry on, step up, spur on; facilitate, aid, assist, boost.
– OPPOSITES dawdle, delay.

hastily ▶ adverb ❶ *Meg retreated hastily* QUICKLY, hurriedly, fast, swiftly, rapidly, speedily, briskly, without delay, post-haste; with all speed, as fast as possible, at breakneck speed, at a run, hotfoot, on the double; *informal* double quick, p.d.q. (pretty damn quick), nippily, like (greased) lightning, like the wind, like a scalded cat, like a bat out of hell; *Brit. informal* at a rate of knots, like the clappers; *N. Amer. informal* lickety-split. ❷ *an agreement was hastily drawn up* HURRIEDLY, speedily, quickly; on the spur of the moment, prematurely.

hasty ▶ adjective ❶ *hasty steps* QUICK, hurried, fast, swift, rapid, speedy, brisk; *poetic/literary* fleet. ❷ *hasty decisions* RASH, impetuous, impulsive, reckless, precipitate, spur-of-the-moment, premature, unconsidered, unthinking; *poetic/literary* temerarious.
– OPPOSITES slow, considered.

hat ▶ noun CAP, beret, bonnet; *Brit. informal* titfer.

hatch ▶ verb ❶ *the duck hatched her eggs* INCUBATE, brood, sit on. ❷ *the plot that you hatched up last night* DEVISE, conceive, concoct, brew, invent, plan, design, formulate; think up, dream up; *informal* cook up.

hatchet ▶ noun AXE, cleaver, mattock, tomahawk; *Brit.* chopper.

hate ▶ verb ❶ *they hate each other* LOATHE, detest, despise, dislike, abhor, execrate; be repelled by, be unable to bear/stand, find intolerable, recoil from, shrink from; *formal* abominate; *archaic* disrelish. ❷ *I hate to bother you* BE SORRY, be reluctant, be loath, be unwilling, be disinclined; regret, dislike.
– OPPOSITES love.

▶ noun ❶ *feelings of hate* HATRED, loathing, detestation, dislike, distaste, abhorrence, abomination, execration, aversion; hostility, enmity, animosity, antipathy, revulsion, disgust, contempt, odium; *archaic* disrelish. ❷ *his pet hate is filling in forms* BUGBEAR, bane, bête noire, bogey, aversion, thorn in one's flesh/side; *N. Amer.* bugaboo.
– OPPOSITES love.

hateful ▶ adjective DETESTABLE, horrible, horrid, unpleasant, awful, nasty, disagreeable, despicable, objectionable, insufferable, revolting, loathsome, abhorrent, abominable, execrable, odious, disgusting, distasteful, obnoxious, offensive, vile, heinous; *informal* ghastly; *Brit. informal* beastly, God-awful.
– OPPOSITES delightful.

hatred ▶ noun LOATHING, hate, detestation, dislike, distaste, abhorrence, abomination, execration; aversion, hostility, ill will, ill feeling, enmity, animosity, antipathy; revulsion, disgust, contempt, odium; *archaic* disrelish.

haughtiness ▶ noun ARROGANCE, conceit, pride, hubris, hauteur, vanity, self-importance, pomposity, condescension, disdain, contempt; snobbishness, snobbery, superciliousness; *informal* snootiness.
– OPPOSITES modesty.

haughty ▶ adjective PROUD, arrogant, vain, conceited, snobbish, superior, self-important, pompous, supercilious, condescending, patronizing; scornful, contemptuous, disdainful; full of oneself, above oneself; *informal* stuck-up, snooty, hoity-toity, uppity, uppish, bigheaded, high and mighty, la-di-da; *Brit. informal* toffee-nosed; *N. Amer. informal* chesty.
– OPPOSITES humble.

haul ▶ verb ❶ *she hauled the basket along* DRAG, pull, tug, heave, lug, hump, draw, tow; *informal* yank. ❷ *a contract to haul coal* TRANSPORT, convey, carry, ship, ferry, move, shift.

▶ noun *the thieves abandoned their haul* BOOTY, loot, plunder; spoils, stolen goods, ill-gotten gains; *informal* swag, boodle.

haunches ▶ plural noun RUMP, hindquarters, rear (end), seat; buttocks, thighs, derrière; *Brit.* bottom; *Anatomy* nates; *informal* behind, backside; *Brit. informal* bum, botty; *N. Amer. informal* butt, fanny, tush, heinie; *humorous* fundament, posterior, stern.

haunt ▶ **verb** ❶ *a ghost haunts this house* APPEAR IN, materialize in; visit. ❷ *he haunts street markets* FREQUENT, patronize, visit regularly; loiter in, linger in; *informal* hang out in. ❸ *the sight haunted me for years* TORMENT, disturb, trouble, worry, plague, burden, beset, beleaguer; prey on, weigh on, gnaw at, nag at, weigh heavily on, obsess; *informal* bug.

▶ **noun** *a favourite haunt of artists* HANG-OUT, stamping ground, meeting place; territory, domain, resort, retreat, spot; *N. Amer.* stomping ground; *Brit. informal* patch.

haunted ▶ **adjective** ❶ *a haunted house* POSSESSED, cursed; ghostly, eerie; *informal* spooky, scary. ❷ *his haunted eyes* TORMENTED, anguished, troubled, tortured, worried, disturbed.

haunting ▶ **adjective** EVOCATIVE, emotive, affecting, moving, touching, stirring, powerful; poignant, nostalgic, wistful; memorable, unforgettable, indelible.

hauteur ▶ **noun** HAUGHTINESS, superciliousness, arrogance, pride, conceit, snobbery, snobbishness, superiority, self-importance; disdain, condescension; airs and graces; *informal* snootiness, uppishness; *Brit. informal* side.

have ▶ **verb** ❶ *he had a new car* POSSESS, own, be in possession of, be the owner of; be blessed with, boast, enjoy; keep, retain, hold, occupy. ❷ *the flat has five rooms* COMPRISE, consist of, contain, include, incorporate, be composed of, be made up of; encompass; *formal* comprehend. ❸ *they had tea together* EAT, consume, devour, partake of; drink, imbibe, quaff; *informal* demolish, dispose of, put away, get outside of, scoff (down); sink, knock back; *N. Amer. informal* scarf (down/up). ❹ *she had a letter from Mark* RECEIVE, get, be given, be sent, obtain, acquire, come by, take receipt of. ❺ *we've decided to have a party* ORGANIZE, arrange, hold, give, host, throw, put on, lay on, set up, fix up. ❻ *she's going to have a baby* GIVE BIRTH TO, bear, be delivered of, bring into the world; *informal* drop; *archaic* be brought to bed of, beget. ❼ *we are having guests for dinner* ENTERTAIN, be host to, cater for, receive; invite round/over, ask round/over, wine and dine; accommodate, put up. ❽ *he had trouble finding the restaurant* EXPERIENCE, encounter, face, meet, find, run into, go through, undergo. ❾ *I have a headache* BE SUFFERING FROM, be afflicted by, be affected by, be troubled with; *informal* be a martyr to. ❿ *I had a good time* EXPERIENCE; enjoy. ⓫ *many of them have doubts* HARBOUR, entertain, feel, nurse, nurture, sustain, maintain. ⓬ *he had little patience* MANIFEST, show, display, exhibit, demonstrate. ⓭ *he had them throw Chris out* MAKE, ask to, request to, get to, tell to, require to, induce to, prevail upon someone to; order to, command to, direct to, force to. ⓮ *I can't have you insulting me* TOLERATE, endure, bear, support, accept, put up with, go along with, take, countenance; permit to, allow to; *informal* stand, abide, stomach; *Brit. informal* stick, be doing with; *formal* brook. ⓯ *I have to get up at six* MUST, be obliged to, be required to, be compelled to, be forced to, be bound to. ⓰ (*informal*) *I'd been had* TRICK, fool, deceive, cheat, dupe, take in, hoodwink, swindle; *informal* do, con, diddle, rip off, shaft; *N. Amer. informal* sucker, snooker.

–OPPOSITES send, give, visit.

■ **have done with** HAVE FINISHED WITH, be done with, be through with, want no more to do with; have given up, have turned one's back on, have washed one's hands of, have no more truck with.

■ **have had it** (*informal*) ❶ *they admit that they've had it* HAVE NO CHANCE, have no hope, have failed, be finished, be defeated, have lost; *informal* have flopped, have come a cropper. ❷ *if you tell anyone, you've had it* BE IN TROUBLE, be in for a scolding; *informal* be for the high jump, be in hot water, be in (deep) shtook; *Brit. informal* be for it.

■ **have nothing on someone** (*informal*) HAVE NO EVIDENCE AGAINST, know nothing bad about, know nothing incriminating about.

■ **have someone on** (*Brit. informal*) PLAY A TRICK ON, play a joke on, joke with, trick, tease, rag, make a monkey (out) of, pull someone's leg; *informal* kid, rib, take for a ride, lead up the garden path; *Brit. informal* wind up; *N. Amer. informal* put on.

■ **have something on** ❶ *she had a blue dress on* BE WEARING, be dressed in, be clothed in, be attired in, be decked out in, be robed in. ❷ (*Brit.*) *I have got a lot on at the moment* BE COMMITTED TO, have arranged, have planned, have organized, have fixed up, have on the agenda.

haven ▶ **noun** ❶ *they stopped in a small haven* ANCHORAGE, harbour, harbourage, port, moorage, mooring; road, roadstead; cove, inlet, bay. ❷ *a safe haven* REFUGE, retreat, shelter, sanctuary, asylum; port in a storm, oasis, sanctum.

haversack ▶ **noun** KNAPSACK, rucksack, backpack, pack.

havoc ▶ **noun** ❶ *the hurricane caused havoc* DEVASTATION, destruction, damage, desolation, ruination, ruin; disaster, catastrophe. ❷ *hyperactive children create havoc* DISORDER, chaos, disruption, mayhem, bedlam, pandemonium, turmoil, tumult, uproar; commotion, furore; *N. Amer.* a three-ring circus; *informal* hullabaloo.

hawk ▶ **verb** PEDDLE, sell, tout, vend, trade in, traffic in, push; *Brit. informal* flog.

hawker ▶ **noun** PEDLAR, trader, seller, dealer, purveyor, vendor, huckster, travelling salesman; *Brit.* barrow boy, tout; *informal* pusher.

hawk-eyed ▶ **adjective** VIGILANT, observant, alert, sharp-eyed, keen-eyed, eagle-eyed; on the alert, on the lookout, with one's eyes skinned/peeled; *informal* beady-eyed, not miss-

ing a trick, on the ball.
– OPPOSITES inattentive.

hay ▶ **noun** FORAGE, dried grass, herbage, silage, fodder, straw.
■ **make hay while the sun shines** make the most of an opportunity, take advantage of something, strike while the iron is hot, seize the day, carpe diem.

haywire ▶ **adjective** (*informal*) OUT OF CONTROL, erratic, faulty, malfunctioning, out of order; chaotic, confused, disorganized, disordered, topsy-turvy; *informal* on the blink; *Brit. informal* up the spout, shambolic.

hazard ▶ **noun** ❶ *the hazards of radiation* DANGER, risk, peril, threat, menace; problem, pitfall. ❷ (*poetic/literary*) *the laws of hazard* CHANCE, probability, fortuity, luck, fate, destiny, fortune, providence.
▶ **verb** ❶ *he hazarded a guess* VENTURE, advance, put forward, volunteer; conjecture, speculate, surmise; *formal* opine. ❷ *it's too risky to hazard money on* RISK, jeopardize, gamble, stake, bet, chance; endanger, imperil.

hazardous ▶ **adjective** RISKY, dangerous, unsafe, perilous, precarious, fraught with danger; unpredictable, uncertain, chancy, high-risk, insecure, touch-and-go; *informal* dicey, hairy; *Brit. informal* dodgy.
– OPPOSITES safe, certain.

haze ▶ **noun** ❶ *a thick haze on the sea* MIST, fog, cloud; smoke, vapour, steam. ❷ *a haze of euphoria* BLUR, daze, confusion, muddle, befuddlement.

hazy ▶ **adjective** ❶ *a hazy day* MISTY, foggy, cloudy, overcast; smoggy, murky. ❷ *hazy memories* VAGUE, indistinct, unclear, faint, dim, nebulous, shadowy, blurred, fuzzy, confused.

head ▶ **noun** ❶ *her head hit the wall* skull, cranium, crown; *informal* nut, noodle, noggin, dome; *Brit. informal* bonce; *informal, dated* conk, noddle. ❷ *he had to use his head* BRAIN(S), brainpower, intellect, intelligence; wit(s), wisdom, mind, sense, reasoning, common sense; *informal* nous, savvy, grey matter; *Brit. informal* loaf; *N. Amer. informal* smarts. ❸ *she had a good head for business* APTITUDE, faculty, talent, gift, capacity, ability; mind, brain. ❹ *the head of the church* LEADER, chief, controller, governor, superintendent, headman; commander, captain; director, manager; principal, president, premier; *informal* boss, boss man, kingpin, top dog, Mr Big, skipper, numero uno, head honcho; *Brit. informal* gaffer, guv'nor; *N. Amer. informal* sachem, big kahuna. ❺ *the head of the queue* FRONT, beginning, start, fore, forefront; top. ❻ *the head of the river* SOURCE, origin, well head, headspring, headwater; *poetic/literary* wellspring. ❼ *beer with a head* FROTH, foam, bubbles, spume, fizz, effervescence; suds.
– OPPOSITES back, mouth.
▶ **adjective** *the head waiter* CHIEF, principal, leading, main, first, prime, premier, top, highest, supreme, top-ranking; *N. Amer.* ranking; *informal* top-notch.
– OPPOSITES subordinate.
▶ **verb** ❶ *the procession was headed by the mayor* LEAD, be at the front of; be first, lead the way. ❷ *a team headed by a line manager* COMMAND, control, lead, run, manage, direct, supervise, superintend, oversee, preside over, rule, govern, captain; *informal* be the boss of. ❸ *he was heading for the exit* MOVE TOWARDS, make for, aim for, go in the direction of, be bound for, make a beeline for; set out for, start out for.
■ **at the head of** IN CHARGE OF, controlling, commanding, leading, managing, running, directing, supervising, overseeing; at the wheel of, at the helm of.
■ **come to a head** REACH A CRISIS, come to a climax, reach a critical point, reach a crossroads; *informal* come to the crunch.
■ **go to someone's head** ❶ *the wine has gone to my head* INTOXICATE, befuddle, make drunk; *informal* make woozy; *formal* inebriate. ❷ *her victory went to her head* MAKE CONCEITED, make someone full of themselves, turn someone's head, puff someone up.
■ **head someone/something off** ❶ *he went to head off the cars* INTERCEPT, divert, deflect, redirect, re-route, draw away, turn away. ❷ *they headed off a row* FORESTALL, avert, ward off, fend off, stave off, hold off, nip in the bud, keep at bay; prevent, avoid, stop.
■ **keep one's head** KEEP/STAY CALM, keep one's self-control, maintain one's composure; *informal* keep one's cool, keep one's shirt on.
■ **lose one's head** LOSE CONTROL, lose one's composure, lose one's equilibrium, go to pieces; panic, get flustered, get confused, get hysterical; *informal* lose one's cool, freak out, crack up; *Brit. informal* go into a (flat) spin, throw a wobbly.

headache ▶ **noun** ❶ *I've got a headache* PAIN IN THE HEAD, sore head, migraine; neuralgia; *informal* head. ❷ (*informal*) *their behaviour was a headache for Mr Jones* NUISANCE, trouble, problem, bother, bugbear, pest, worry, inconvenience, vexation, irritant, thorn in one's flesh; *informal* aggravation, hassle, pain (in the neck), bind.

head case ▶ **noun** (*informal*) MANIAC, lunatic, madman, madwoman; *informal* loony, nut, nutcase, fruitcake, crank, crackpot; *Brit. informal* nutter; *N. Amer. informal* screwball, crazy, kook, wacko; *N. Amer. & Austral./NZ informal* dingbat.

head first ▶ **adjective & adverb** ❶ *she dived head first into the water* HEADLONG, on one's head. ❷ *don't plunge head first into a relationship* WITHOUT THINKING, without forethought, precipitously, impetuously, rashly, recklessly, heedlessly, hastily, headlong.
– OPPOSITES cautiously.

heading ▶ **noun** ❶ *chapter headings* TITLE, caption, legend, subtitle, sub-heading, rubric, headline. ❷ *this topic falls under four main headings* CATEGORY, division, classification, class, section, group, grouping, subject, topic.

headland ▶ noun CAPE, promontory, point, head, foreland, peninsula, ness, bluff; *Scottish* mull.

headlong ▶ adverb ❶ *he fell headlong into the tent* HEAD FIRST, on one's head. ❷ *she rushed headlong to join the craze* WITHOUT THINKING, without forethought, precipitously, impetuously, rashly, recklessly, carelessly, heedlessly, hastily.
– OPPOSITES cautiously.
▶ adjective *a headlong dash* BREAKNECK, whirlwind; reckless, precipitate, precipitous, hasty, careless, heedless.
– OPPOSITES cautious.

headman ▶ noun CHIEF, chieftain, leader, head, ruler, overlord, master, commander; lord, potentate; *N. Amer.* sachem.
– OPPOSITES underling.

head-on ▶ adjective ❶ *a head-on collision* DIRECT, front-to-front. ❷ *a head-on confrontation* DIRECT, face to face, eyeball to eyeball, personal.

headquarters ▶ plural noun HEAD OFFICE, main office, HQ, base, nerve centre, mission control, command post.

headstone ▶ noun GRAVESTONE, tombstone, stone, monument, memorial.

headstrong ▶ adjective WILFUL, strong-willed, stubborn, obstinate, unyielding, obdurate; contrary, perverse, wayward, unruly; *formal* refractory.
– OPPOSITES tractable.

head teacher ▶ noun HEAD, headmaster, headmistress, principal, director, president, governor; *Brit.* master.

headway
■ **make headway** MAKE PROGRESS, progress, make strides, gain ground, advance, proceed, move, get ahead, come along, take shape.

heady ▶ adjective ❶ *heady wine* POTENT, intoxicating, strong; alcoholic, vinous; *formal* spirituous. ❷ *the heady days of my youth* EXHILARATING, exciting, thrilling, stimulating, invigorating, electrifying, rousing; *informal* mind-blowing.
– OPPOSITES boring.

heal ▶ verb ❶ *he heals sick people* MAKE BETTER, make well, cure, treat, restore to health. ❷ *his knee had healed* GET BETTER, get well, be cured, recover, mend, improve. ❸ *time will heal the pain of grief* ALLEVIATE, ease, assuage, palliate, relieve, help, lessen, mitigate, attenuate, allay. ❹ *we tried to heal the rift* PUT RIGHT, set right, repair, remedy, resolve, correct, settle; conciliate, reconcile, harmonize; *informal* patch up.
– OPPOSITES aggravate, worsen.

healing ▶ adjective CURATIVE, therapeutic, medicinal, remedial, corrective, reparative; restorative, tonic, health-giving, healthful, beneficial.
– OPPOSITES harmful.

health ▶ noun ❶ *he was restored to health* WELL-BEING, healthiness, fitness, good condition, good shape, fine fettle; strength, vigour. ❷ *bad health forced him to retire* PHYSICAL STATE, physical shape, condition, constitution.
– OPPOSITES illness.

healthful ▶ adjective HEALTHY, health-giving, beneficial, good for one, salubrious; wholesome, nourishing, nutritious.
– OPPOSITES unhealthy.

healthy ▶ adjective ❶ *a healthy baby* WELL, in good health, fine, fit, in good trim, in good shape, in fine fettle, in tip-top condition; blooming, thriving, hardy, robust, strong, vigorous, fighting fit, fit as a fiddle, the picture of health; *Brit.* in rude health; *informal* OK, in the pink, right as rain. ❷ *a healthy diet* HEALTH-GIVING, healthful, good for one; wholesome, nutritious, nourishing; beneficial, salubrious.
– OPPOSITES ill, unwholesome.

heap ▶ noun ❶ *a heap of boxes* PILE, stack, mound, mountain, mass, quantity, load, lot, jumble; collection, accumulation, assemblage, store, hoard. ❷ (*informal*) *we have heaps of room* A LOT, a fair amount, much, plenty, a good deal, a great deal, an abundance, a wealth, a profusion; (a great) many, a large number, numerous, scores; *informal* hundreds, thousands, millions, a load, loads, loadsa, a pile, piles, oodles, stacks, lots, masses, scads, reams, wads, pots, oceans, miles, tons, zillions; *Brit. informal* a shedload, lashings.
▶ verb *she heaped logs on the fire* PILE (UP), stack (up), make a mound of; assemble, collect.
■ **heap something on/upon** *they heaped praise on her* SHOWER ON, lavish on, load on; bestow on, confer on, give, grant, vouchsafe, favour with.

hear ▶ verb ❶ *she can't hear* PERCEIVE SOUND; have hearing. ❷ *she could hear men's voices* PERCEIVE, make out, discern, catch, get, apprehend; overhear. ❸ *they heard that I had moved* BE INFORMED, be told, find out, discover, learn, gather, glean, ascertain, get word, get wind. ❹ *a jury heard the case* TRY, judge; adjudicate (on), adjudge, pass judgement on.

hearing ▶ noun ❶ *acute hearing* ABILITY TO HEAR, auditory perception, sense of hearing, aural faculty. ❷ *she moved out of hearing* EARSHOT, hearing distance, hearing range, auditory range. ❸ *I had a fair hearing* CHANCE TO SPEAK, opportunity to be heard; interview, audience. ❹ *he gave evidence at the hearing* TRIAL, court case, inquiry, inquest, tribunal; investigation, inquisition.
– RELATED TERMS acoustic, auditory, aural.

hearsay ▶ noun RUMOUR, gossip, tittle-tattle, tattle, idle talk; stories, tales, on dit; *informal* the grapevine; *Brit. informal* goss; *N. Amer. informal* scuttlebutt.

heart ▶ **noun** ❶ *his heart stopped beating informal* ticker. ❷ *he poured out his heart* EMOTIONS, feelings, sentiments; soul, mind, bosom, breast; love, affection, passion. ❸ *he has no heart* COMPASSION, sympathy, humanity, feeling(s), fellow feeling, brotherly love, tenderness, empathy, understanding; kindness, goodwill. ❹ *they may lose heart* ENTHUSIASM, keenness, eagerness, spirit, determination, resolve, purpose, courage, nerve, will power, fortitude; *informal* guts, spunk; *Brit. informal* bottle. ❺ *the heart of the city* CENTRE, middle, hub, core, nucleus, eye, bosom. ❻ *the heart of the matter* ESSENCE, crux, core, nub, root, gist, meat, marrow, pith, substance, kernel; *informal* nitty-gritty.
– RELATED TERMS cardiac, coronary.
– OPPOSITES edge.
■ **after one's own heart** LIKE-MINDED, of the same mind, kindred, compatible, congenial, sharing one's tastes; *informal* on the same wavelength.
■ **at heart** DEEP DOWN, basically, fundamentally, essentially, in essence, intrinsically, really, actually, truly, in fact; *informal* when you get right down to it.
■ **(off) by heart** FROM MEMORY, off pat, by rote, word for word, verbatim, parrot-fashion, word-perfect.
■ **do one's heart good** CHEER (UP), please, gladden, make one happy, delight, hearten, gratify, make one feel good, give one a lift; *informal* give someone a buzz, tickle someone pink, buck up.
■ **eat one's heart out** PINE, long, ache, brood, mope, fret, sigh, sorrow, yearn, agonize; grieve, mourn, lament.
■ **from the (bottom of one's) heart** SINCERELY, earnestly, fervently, passionately, truly, genuinely, heartily, with all sincerity.
■ **give/lose one's heart to** FALL IN LOVE WITH, fall for, be smitten by; *informal* fall head over heels for, be swept off one's feet by, develop a crush on.
■ **have a change of heart** CHANGE ONE'S MIND, change one's tune, have second thoughts, have a rethink, think again, think twice; *informal* get cold feet.
■ **have a heart** BE COMPASSIONATE, be kind, be merciful, be lenient, be sympathetic, be considerate, have mercy.
■ **heart and soul** WHOLEHEARTEDLY, enthusiastically, eagerly, zealously; absolutely, completely, entirely, fully, utterly, to the hilt, one hundred per cent.
■ **take heart** BE ENCOURAGED, be heartened, be comforted; cheer up, brighten up, perk up, liven up, revive; *informal* buck up.
■ **with one's heart in one's mouth** IN ALARM, in fear, fearfully, apprehensively, on edge, with trepidation, in suspense, in a cold sweat, with bated breath, on tenterhooks; *informal* with butterflies in one's stomach, in a state, in a stew, in a sweat; *Brit. informal* having kittens; *N. Amer. informal* in a twit.

heartache ▶ **noun** ANGUISH, grief, suffering, distress, unhappiness, misery, sorrow, sadness, heartbreak, pain, hurt, agony, angst, despondency, despair, woe, desolation.
– OPPOSITES happiness.

heartbreak ▶ **noun**. *See* HEARTACHE.

heartbreaking ▶ **adjective** DISTRESSING, upsetting, disturbing, heart-rending, sad, tragic, painful, traumatic, agonizing, harrowing; pitiful, poignant, plaintive, moving, tear-jerking.
– OPPOSITES comforting.

heartbroken ▶ **adjective** ANGUISHED, devastated, broken-hearted, heavy-hearted, grieving, grief-stricken, inconsolable, crushed, shattered, desolate, despairing; upset, distressed, miserable, sorrowful, sad, downcast, disconsolate, crestfallen, despondent; *informal* choked, down in the mouth, down in the dumps, cut up.

heartburn ▶ **noun** INDIGESTION, dyspepsia, pyrosis.

hearten ▶ **verb** CHEER (UP), encourage, raise someone's spirits, boost, buoy up, perk up, ginger up, inspirit, uplift, elate; comfort, reassure; *informal* buck up, pep up.

heartfelt ▶ **adjective** SINCERE, genuine, from the heart; earnest, profound, deep, wholehearted, ardent, fervent, passionate, enthusiastic, eager; honest, bona fide.
– OPPOSITES insincere.

heartily ▶ **adverb** ❶ *we heartily welcome the changes* WHOLEHEARTEDLY, sincerely, genuinely, warmly, profoundly, with all one's heart; eagerly, enthusiastically, earnestly, ardently. ❷ *they were heartily sick of her* VERY, extremely, thoroughly, completely, absolutely, really, exceedingly, immensely, most, downright; *N. Amer.* quite; *informal* right, seriously; *Brit. informal* jolly, dead, well; *N. Amer. informal* real, mighty.

heartless ▶ **adjective** UNFEELING, unsympathetic, unkind, uncaring, unconcerned, insensitive, inconsiderate, hard-hearted, stony-hearted, cold-hearted, mean-spirited; cold, callous, cruel, merciless, pitiless, inhuman.
– OPPOSITES compassionate.

heart-rending ▶ **adjective** DISTRESSING, upsetting, disturbing, heartbreaking, sad, tragic, painful, traumatic, harrowing; pitiful, poignant, plaintive, moving, tear-jerking.

heartsick ▶ **adjective** (*poetic/literary*) DESPONDENT, dejected, depressed, desolate, downcast, forlorn, unhappy, sad, upset, miserable, wretched, woebegone, inconsolable, grieving, grief-stricken, heavy-hearted, broken-hearted.
– OPPOSITES happy.

heart-throb ▶ **noun** (*informal*) IDOL, pin-up, star, superstar, hero; *informal* dreamboat.

heart-to-heart ▶ **adjective** *a heart-to-heart*

chat INTIMATE, personal, man-to-man, woman-to-woman; candid, honest, truthful, sincere.
▶ **noun** *they had a long heart-to-heart* PRIVATE CONVERSATION, tête-à-tête, one-to-one, head-to-head; chat, talk, word; *informal* confab, chinwag; *Brit. informal* natter.

heart-warming ▶ **adjective** TOUCHING, moving, heartening, stirring, uplifting, pleasing, cheering, gladdening, encouraging, gratifying.
– OPPOSITES distressing.

hearty ▶ **adjective** ❶ *a hearty character* EXUBERANT, jovial, ebullient, cheerful, uninhibited, effusive, lively, loud, animated, vivacious, energetic, spirited, dynamic, enthusiastic, eager; warm, cordial, friendly, affable, amiable, good natured. ❷ *hearty congratulations* WHOLEHEARTED, heartfelt, sincere, genuine, real, true; earnest, fervent, ardent, enthusiastic. ❸ *a hearty woman of sixty-five* ROBUST, healthy, hardy, fit, flourishing, blooming, fighting fit, fit as a fiddle; vigorous, sturdy, strong; *Brit.* in rude health; *informal* full of vim. ❹ *a hearty meal* SUBSTANTIAL, large, ample, sizeable, filling, generous, square, solid; healthy.
– OPPOSITES introverted, half-hearted, frail, light.

heat ▶ **noun** ❶ *a plant sensitive to heat* WARMTH, hotness, warmness, high temperature; hot weather, warm weather, sultriness, mugginess, humidity; heatwave, hot spell. ❷ *he took the heat out of the dispute* PASSION, intensity, vehemence, warmth, fervour, fervency, ardency; enthusiasm, excitement, agitation; anger, fury.
– RELATED TERMS thermal.
– OPPOSITES cold, apathy.
▶ **verb** ❶ *the food was heated* WARM (UP), heat up, make hot, make warm; reheat, cook; *Brit. informal* hot up. ❷ *the pipes expand as they heat up* BECOME HOT, become warm, get hotter, get warmer, increase in temperature; *Brit. informal* hot up. ❸ *he calmed down as quickly as he had heated up* BECOME IMPASSIONED, become excited, become animated; get angry, become enraged.
– OPPOSITES cool.

heated ▶ **adjective** ❶ *a heated swimming pool* MADE WARM, made hot, warmed up; reheated; hot, piping hot. ❷ *a heated argument* VEHEMENT, passionate, impassioned, animated, spirited, 'lively', intense, fiery; angry, bitter, furious, fierce, stormy, tempestuous. ❸ *Robert grew heated as he spoke of the risks* EXCITED, animated, inflamed, worked up, wound up, keyed up; *informal* het up, in a state.

heater ▶ **noun** RADIATOR, convector, fire, brazier, warmer.

heath ▶ **noun** (*Brit.*) MOOR, heathland, moorland, scrub; common land.

heathen ▶ **noun** ❶ *bringing Christianity to the heathens* PAGAN, infidel, idolater, idolatress; unbeliever, non-believer, disbeliever, atheist, agnostic, sceptic, heretic; *archaic* paynim. ❷ *heathens who spoil good whisky with ice* PHILISTINE, boor, oaf, ignoramus, lout, yahoo, vulgarian, plebeian; *informal* pleb, peasant, oik.
– OPPOSITES believer.
▶ **adjective** *a heathen practice* PAGAN, infidel, idolatrous, heathenish; unbelieving, non-believing, atheistic, agnostic, heretical, faithless, godless, irreligious, ungodly, unholy; barbarian, barbarous, uncivilized, uncultured, primitive, ignorant, philistine.

heave ▶ **verb** ❶ *she heaved the sofa backwards* HAUL, pull, lug, drag, draw, tug, heft; *informal* hump, yank. ❷ (*informal*) *she heaved a brick at him* THROW, fling, cast, toss, hurl, lob, pitch; *informal* chuck, sling; *Brit. informal* bung; *N. English & Austral. informal* hoy; *NZ informal* bish. ❸ *he heaved a sigh of relief* LET OUT, breathe, give, sigh; emit, utter. ❹ *the sea heaved* RISE AND FALL, roll, swell, surge, churn, seethe, swirl. ❺ *she heaved into the sink* RETCH, gag; vomit, bring up, cough up; *Brit.* be sick; *N. Amer.* get sick; *informal* throw up, puke, chunder, chuck up, hurl, spew; *Brit. informal* sick up; *Scottish informal* boke; *N. Amer. informal* barf, upchuck.

heaven ▶ **noun** ❶ *the good will have a place in heaven* PARADISE, nirvana, Zion; the hereafter, the next world, the next life, the afterworld; Elysium, the Elysian Fields, Valhalla; *poetic/literary* the empyrean. ❷ *a good book is my idea of heaven* BLISS, ecstasy, rapture, contentment, happiness, delight, joy, seventh heaven; paradise, Utopia, nirvana. ❸ *he observed the heavens* THE SKY, the skies, the upper atmosphere, the stratosphere; *poetic/literary* the firmament, the vault of heaven, the blue, the (wide) blue yonder, the welkin, the empyrean, the azure, the upper regions, the sphere.
– RELATED TERMS celestial.
– OPPOSITES hell, misery.
■ **in seventh heaven** ECSTATIC, euphoric, thrilled, elated, delighted, overjoyed, on cloud nine, walking on air, jubilant, rapturous, jumping for joy, transported, delirious, blissful; *informal* over the moon, on top of the world, on a high, tickled pink, as pleased as Punch, cock-a-hoop, as happy as a sandboy; *Brit. informal* as happy as Larry; *N. Amer. informal* as happy as a clam; *Austral. informal* wrapped.
■ **move heaven and earth** TRY ONE'S HARDEST, do one's best, do one's utmost, do all one can, give one's all, spare no effort, put oneself out; strive, exert oneself, work hard; *informal* bend over backwards, do one's damnedest, go all out, bust a gut.

heavenly ▶ **adjective** ❶ *heavenly choirs* DIVINE, holy, celestial; angelic, seraphic, cherubic; *poetic/literary* empyrean. ❷ *heavenly constellations* CELESTIAL, cosmic, stellar; planetary; extraterrestrial, superterrestrial. ❸ (*informal*) *a heavenly morning* DELIGHTFUL, wonderful, glorious, perfect, excellent, sublime, idyllic, first-class,

first-rate; blissful, pleasurable, enjoyable; exquisite, beautiful, lovely, gorgeous, enchanting; *informal* divine, super, great, fantastic, fabulous, terrific.
–OPPOSITES mortal, infernal, terrestrial, dreadful.

heaven-sent ▶ **adjective** AUSPICIOUS, providential, propitious, felicitous, opportune, golden, favourable, advantageous, serendipitous, lucky, happy, good, fortunate.
–OPPOSITES inopportune.

heavily ▶ **adverb** ❶ *Dad walked heavily* LABORIOUSLY, slowly, ponderously, woodenly, stiffly; with difficulty, painfully, awkwardly, clumsily. ❷ *we were heavily defeated* DECISIVELY, conclusively, roundly, soundly; utterly, completely, thoroughly. ❸ *he drank heavily* EXCESSIVELY, to excess, immoderately, copiously, inordinately, intemperately, a great deal, too much, overmuch. ❹ *the area is heavily planted with trees* DENSELY, closely, thickly. ❺ *I became heavily involved* DEEPLY, very, extremely, greatly, exceedingly, tremendously, profoundly; *informal* terribly, seriously; *Brit. informal* jolly, ever so.
–OPPOSITES easily, narrowly, moderately.

heavy ▶ **adjective** ❶ *a heavy box* WEIGHTY, hefty, substantial, ponderous; solid, dense, leaden; burdensome; *informal* hulking, weighing a ton. ❷ *a heavy man* OVERWEIGHT, fat, obese, corpulent, large, bulky, stout, stocky, portly, plump, paunchy, fleshy; *informal* hulking, tubby, beefy, porky; *Brit. informal* podgy. ❸ *a heavy blow to the head* FORCEFUL, hard, strong, violent, powerful, vigorous, mighty, hefty, sharp, smart, severe. ❹ *a gardener did the heavy work for me* ARDUOUS, hard, physical, laborious, difficult, strenuous, demanding, tough, onerous, back-breaking, gruelling; *archaic* toilsome. ❺ *a heavy burden of responsibility* ONEROUS, burdensome, demanding, challenging, difficult, formidable, weighty; worrisome, stressful, trying, crushing, oppressive. ❻ *heavy fog* DENSE, thick, soupy, murky, impenetrable. ❼ *a heavy sky* OVERCAST, cloudy, clouded, grey, dull, gloomy, murky, dark, black, stormy, leaden, louring. ❽ *heavy rain* TORRENTIAL, relentless, copious, teeming, severe. ❾ *heavy soil* CLAY, clayey, muddy, sticky, wet; *Brit.* claggy; *informal* cloggy. ❿ *a heavy fine* SIZEABLE, hefty, substantial, colossal, big, considerable; stiff; *informal* tidy, whopping, steep, astronomical. ⓫ *heavy seas* TEMPESTUOUS, turbulent, rough, wild, stormy, choppy, squally. ⓬ *heavy fighting* INTENSE, fierce, vigorous, relentless, all-out, severe, serious. ⓭ *a heavy drinker* IMMODERATE, excessive, intemperate, overindulgent, unrestrained, uncontrolled. ⓮ *a heavy meal* SUBSTANTIAL, filling, hearty, large, big, ample, sizeable, generous, square, solid. ⓯ *their diet is heavy on vegetables* ABOUNDING IN, abundant in, lavish with, profuse with, unstinting with, using a lot of. ⓰ *he felt heavy and very tired* LETHARGIC, listless, sluggish, torpid, languid, apathetic. ⓱ *a heavy heart* SAD, sorrowful, melancholy, gloomy, downcast, downhearted, heartbroken, dejected, disconsolate, demoralized, despondent, depressed, crestfallen, desolate, down; *informal* blue; *poetic/literary* dolorous. ⓲ *these poems are rather heavy* TEDIOUS, difficult, dull, dry, serious, heavy going, dreary, boring, turgid, uninteresting; *informal* deadly. ⓳ *branches heavy with blossoms* LADEN, loaded, covered, filled, groaning, bursting, teeming, abounding. ⓴ *a heavy crop* BOUNTIFUL, plentiful, abundant, large, bumper, rich, copious, considerable, sizeable, profuse; *informal* whopping; *poetic/literary* plenteous. ㉑ *he has heavy features* COARSE, rough, rough-hewn, unrefined; rugged, craggy.
–OPPOSITES light, thin, gentle, easy, bright, friable, small, calm, moderate, energetic, cheerful, meagre, delicate.

heavy-handed ▶ **adjective** ❶ *they are heavy-handed with the equipment* CLUMSY, awkward, maladroit, unhandy, inept, unskilful; *informal* ham-handed, ham-fisted, cack-handed; *Brit. informal* all (fingers and) thumbs. ❷ *heavy-handed policing* INSENSITIVE, oppressive, overbearing, high-handed, harsh, stern, severe, tyrannical, despotic, ruthless, merciless; tactless, undiplomatic, inept.
–OPPOSITES dexterous, sensitive.

heavy-hearted ▶ **adjective** MELANCHOLY, sad, sorrowful, mournful, gloomy, depressed, desolate, despondent, dejected, downhearted, downcast, crestfallen, disconsolate, glum, miserable, wretched, dismal, morose, woeful, woebegone, doleful, unhappy; *informal* down in the dumps, down in the mouth, blue; *poetic/literary* dolorous.
–OPPOSITES cheerful.

heckle ▶ **verb** JEER, taunt, jibe at, shout down, boo, hiss, harass; *Brit. & Austral./NZ* barrack; *informal* give someone a hard time.
–OPPOSITES cheer.

hectic ▶ **adjective** FRANTIC, frenetic, frenzied, feverish, manic, busy, active, fast and furious; lively, brisk, bustling, buzzing.
–OPPOSITES leisurely.

hector ▶ **verb** BULLY, intimidate, browbeat, harass, torment, plague; coerce, pressurize, strong-arm; threaten, menace; *informal* bulldoze; *N. Amer. informal* bullyrag.

hedge ▶ **noun** ❶ *high hedges* HEDGEROW, bushes, fence; windbreak; *Brit.* quickset. ❷ *an excellent hedge against a fall in sterling* SAFEGUARD, protection, shield, screen, guard, buffer, cushion; insurance, security. ❸ *his analysis is full of hedges* EQUIVOCATION, evasion, fudge, quibble, qualification; temporizing, uncertainty, prevarication, vagueness.
▶ **verb** ❶ *fields hedged with hawthorn* SURROUND, enclose, encircle, ring, border, edge, bound. ❷ *she was hedged in by her education* CONFINE, restrict, limit, hinder, obstruct, impede, con-

strain, trap; hem in. ❸ *he hedged at every new question* PREVARICATE, equivocate, vacillate, quibble, hesitate, stall, dodge the issue, be non-committal, be evasive, be vague, beat about the bush, pussyfoot around, mince one's words; *Brit.* hum and haw; *informal* sit on the fence, duck the question. ❹ *the company hedged its position on the market* SAFEGUARD, protect, shield, guard, cushion; cover, insure.

hedonism ▶ **noun** SELF-INDULGENCE, pleasure-seeking, self-gratification, lotus-eating, sybaritism; intemperance, immoderation, extravagance, luxury, high living.
– OPPOSITES self-restraint.

hedonist ▶ **noun** SYBARITE, sensualist, voluptuary, pleasure-seeker, bon viveur, bon vivant; epicure, gastronome.
– OPPOSITES ascetic.

hedonistic ▶ **adjective** SELF-INDULGENT, pleasure-seeking, sybaritic, lotus-eating, epicurean; unrestrained, intemperate, immoderate, extravagant, decadent.

heed ▶ **verb** *heed the warnings* PAY ATTENTION TO, take notice of, take note of, pay heed to, attend to, listen to; bear in mind, be mindful of, mind, mark, consider, take into account, follow, obey, adhere to, abide by, observe, take to heart, be alert to.
– OPPOSITES disregard.
▶ **noun** *he paid no heed* ATTENTION, notice, note, regard; consideration, thought, care.

heedful ▶ **adjective** ATTENTIVE, careful, mindful, cautious, prudent, circumspect; alert, aware, wary, chary, watchful, vigilant, on guard, on the alert.

heedless ▶ **adjective** UNMINDFUL, taking no notice, paying no heed, unheeding, disregardful, neglectful, oblivious, inattentive, blind, deaf; incautious, imprudent, rash, reckless, foolhardy, improvident, unwary.

heel[1] ▶ **noun** ❶ *shoes with low heels* heel piece; wedge, stiletto. ❷ *the heel of a loaf* TAIL END, end, crust, remnant, remainder, remains. ❸ (*informal, dated*) *you're such a heel* SCOUNDREL, rogue, rascal, reprobate, miscreant; *informal* beast, rat, louse, swine, snake, scumbag, stinker; *Brit. informal, dated* rotter, bounder, blighter; *dated* cad, blackguard.
■ **take to one's heels** RUN AWAY, run off, make a run for it, take flight, take off, make a break for it, flee, make one's getaway, escape; *informal* beat it, clear off, vamoose, skedaddle, split, cut and run, leg it, hotfoot it, show a clean pair of heels, scram; *Brit. informal* do a runner, scarper, do a bunk; *N. Amer. informal* light out, bug out; *Austral. informal* shoot through.

heel[2] ▶ **verb** *the ship heeled to starboard* LEAN OVER, list, careen, tilt, tip, incline, keel over.

heft ▶ **verb** LIFT (UP), raise (up), heave, hoist, haul; carry, lug, tote; *informal* cart, hump.

hefty ▶ **adjective** ❶ *a hefty young man* BURLY, heavy, sturdy, strapping, bulky, brawny, husky, strong, muscular, large, big, solid, well built; portly, stout; *informal* hulking, hunky, beefy. ❷ *a hefty kick* POWERFUL, violent, hard, forceful, heavy, mighty. ❸ *hefty loads of timber* HEAVY, weighty, bulky, big, large, substantial, massive, ponderous; unwieldy, cumbersome, burdensome; *informal* hulking. ❹ *a hefty fine* SUBSTANTIAL, sizeable, considerable, stiff, extortionate, large, excessive; *informal* steep, astronomical, whopping.
– OPPOSITES slight, feeble, light, small.

hegemony ▶ **noun** LEADERSHIP, dominance, dominion, supremacy, authority, mastery, control, power, sway, rule, sovereignty.

height ▶ **noun** ❶ *the height of the wall* HIGHNESS, tallness, extent upwards, vertical measurement, elevation, stature, altitude. ❷ *the mountain heights* SUMMIT, top, peak, crest, crown, tip, cap, pinnacle, apex, brow, ridge. ❸ *the height of their fame* HIGHEST POINT, crowning moment, peak, acme, zenith, apogee, pinnacle, climax, high water mark. ❹ *the height of bad manners* EPITOME, acme, zenith, quintessence, very limit; ultimate, utmost. ❺ *he is terrified of heights* HIGH PLACES, high ground; precipices, cliffs.
– OPPOSITES width, nadir.

heighten ▶ **verb** ❶ *the roof had to be heightened* MAKE HIGHER, raise, lift (up), elevate. ❷ *her pleasure was heightened by guilt* INTENSIFY, increase, enhance, add to, augment, boost, strengthen, deepen, magnify, amplify, reinforce.
– OPPOSITES lower, reduce.

heinous ▶ **adjective** ODIOUS, wicked, evil, atrocious, monstrous, abominable, detestable, contemptible, reprehensible, despicable, egregious, horrific, terrible, awful, abhorrent, loathsome, hideous, unspeakable, execrable; iniquitous, villainous, beyond the pale.
– OPPOSITES admirable.

heir, heiress ▶ **noun** SUCCESSOR, next in line, inheritor, beneficiary, legatee; descendant, scion; *Law* devisee; *English Law* coparcener; *Scottish Law* heritor.

helix ▶ **noun** SPIRAL, coil, corkscrew, curl, twist, gyre, whorl, convolution.

hell ▶ **noun** ❶ *they feared hell* THE NETHERWORLD, the Inferno, the infernal regions, the abyss; eternal damnation, perdition; hellfire, fire and brimstone; Hades, Acheron, Gehenna, Tophet, Sheol; *poetic/literary* the pit. ❷ *he made her life hell* A MISERY, torture, agony, a torment, a nightmare, an ordeal; anguish, wretchedness, woe.
– RELATED TERMS infernal.
– OPPOSITES heaven, paradise.
■ **give someone hell** (*informal*) ❶ *when I found out I gave him hell* REPRIMAND SEVERELY, rebuke, admonish, chastise, chide, upbraid, reprove, scold, berate, remonstrate with, reprehend,

take to task, lambaste; read someone the Riot Act, give someone a piece of one's mind, haul over the coals; *informal* tell off, dress down, give someone an earful, give someone a roasting, rap over the knuckles, let someone have it, bawl out, come down hard on, lay into, blast; *Brit. informal* tick off, have a go at, carpet, give someone a rollicking, give someone a mouthful, tear someone off a strip, give someone what for; *N. Amer. informal* chew out; *formal* castigate. ❷ *she gave me hell when I was her junior* HARASS, hound, plague, harry, bother, trouble, bully, intimidate, pick on, victimize, terrorize; *informal* hassle, give someone a hard time.

■ **hell for leather** VERY FAST, very quickly, rapidly, speedily, swiftly, hurriedly, at full tilt, at full pelt, headlong, hotfoot, post-haste, helter-skelter, at the speed of light, at breakneck speed; *informal* like a bat out of hell, like the wind, like greased lightning, like a bomb; *Brit. informal* like the clappers, at a rate of knots; *N. Amer. informal* lickety-split.

■ **raise hell** (*informal*) ❶ *they were hollering and raising hell* CAUSE A DISTURBANCE, cause a commotion, be noisy, run riot, run wild, go on the rampage, be out of control; *informal* raise the roof. ❷ *he raised hell with the planners* REMONSTRATE, expostulate, be angry, be furious; argue; *informal* kick up a fuss, kick up a stink.

hell-bent ▶ **adjective** INTENT, bent, determined, (dead) set, insistent, fixed, resolved; single-minded, fixated.
– OPPOSITES half-hearted.

hellish ▶ **adjective** ❶ *the hellish face of Death* INFERNAL, Hadean; diabolical, fiendish, satanic, demonic; evil, wicked. ❷ (*informal*) *a hellish week* HORRIBLE, rotten, awful, terrible, dreadful, ghastly, horrid, vile, foul, appalling, atrocious, horrendous, frightful; difficult, unpleasant, nasty, disagreeable; stressful, taxing, tough, hard, frustrating, fraught, traumatic, gruelling; *informal* murderous, lousy; *Brit. informal* beastly; *N. Amer. informal* hellacious.
– OPPOSITES angelic, wonderful.
▶ **adverb** (*Brit. informal*) *it's hellish hard work* EXTREMELY, very, exceedingly, exceptionally, tremendously, immensely, intensely, unusually, decidedly, particularly, really, truly, mightily; most, so; *N. English* right; *informal* terrifically, awfully, fearfully, terribly, devilishly, majorly, seriously, ultra, oh-so, damn, damned; *Brit. informal* ever so, well, bloody, dead; *N. Amer. informal* real, mighty, awful; *informal, dated* devilish; *archaic* exceeding.
– OPPOSITES moderately.

helm ▶ **noun** *he took the helm* TILLER, wheel; steering gear, rudder.

■ **at the helm** IN CHARGE, in command, in control, responsible, in authority, at the wheel, in the driving seat, in the saddle; *informal* holding the reins, running the show, calling the shots.

help ▶ **verb** ❶ *can you help me please?* ASSIST, aid, lend a (helping) hand to, give assistance to, come to the aid of; be of service to, be of use to; do someone a favour, do someone a service, do someone a good turn, bail someone out, come to the rescue, give someone a leg up; rally round, pitch in; *informal* get someone out of a tight spot, save someone's bacon, save someone's skin. ❷ *this credit card helps cancer research* SUPPORT, contribute to, give money to, donate to; promote, boost, back; further the interests of; *N. Amer. informal* bankroll. ❸ *sore throats are helped by lozenges* RELIEVE, soothe, ease, alleviate, make better, improve, assuage, lessen; remedy, cure, heal.
– OPPOSITES hinder, impede, worsen.
▶ **noun** ❶ *this could be of help to you* ASSISTANCE, aid, a helping hand, support, succour, advice, guidance; benefit, use, advantage, service, comfort; *informal* a shot in the arm. ❷ *he sought help for his eczema* RELIEF, alleviation, improvement, assuagement, healing; a remedy, a cure, a restorative. ❸ *they treated the help badly* DOMESTIC WORKER, domestic servant, cleaner, cleaning lady, home help, maid, housemaid, hired help, helper; *Brit. informal* daily (woman), skivvy, Mrs Mop; *Brit. dated* charwoman, charlady, char.

■ **cannot help** *he could not help laughing* BE UNABLE TO STOP, be unable to refrain from, be unable to keep from.

■ **help oneself to** STEAL, take, appropriate, 'borrow', 'liberate', pocket, purloin, commandeer; *informal* swipe, nab, filch, snaffle, walk off with, run off with; *Brit. informal* nick, pinch, whip, knock off.

helper ▶ **noun** ASSISTANT, aide, helpmate, helpmeet, deputy, auxiliary, second, right-hand man/woman, attendant, acolyte; co-worker, workmate, teammate, associate, colleague, partner; *informal* sidekick.

helpful ▶ **adjective** ❶ *the staff are helpful* OBLIGING, eager to please, kind, accommodating, supportive, cooperative; sympathetic, neighbourly, charitable. ❷ *we found your comments helpful* USEFUL, of use, beneficial, valuable, profitable, fruitful, advantageous, worthwhile, constructive; informative, instructive. ❸ *a helpful new tool* HANDY, useful, convenient, practical, easy-to-use, functional, serviceable; *informal* neat, nifty.
– OPPOSITES unsympathetic, useless, inconvenient.

helping ▶ **noun** PORTION, serving, piece, slice, share, ration, allocation; *informal* dollop.

helpless ▶ **adjective** DEPENDENT, incapable, powerless, impotent, weak; defenceless, vulnerable, exposed, unprotected, open to attack; paralysed, disabled.
– OPPOSITES independent.

helpmate, helpmeet ▶ **noun** HELPER, assistant, attendant; supporter, friend, companion; spouse, partner, mate, husband, wife.

helter-skelter ▶ **adverb** *they ran helter-skelter down the hill* HEADLONG, pell-mell, hotfoot, post-haste, hastily, hurriedly, at full pelt, at full tilt, hell for leather; recklessly, precipitately, heedlessly, wildly; *informal* like a bat out of hell, like the wind, like greased lightning, like a bomb; *Brit. informal* like the clappers, at a rate of knots; *N. Amer. informal* lickety-split.

▶ **adjective** *a helter-skelter collection of houses* DISORDERED, disorderly, chaotic, muddled, jumbled, untidy, haphazard, disorganized, topsy-turvy; *informal* higgledy-piggledy; *Brit. informal* shambolic.

– OPPOSITES orderly.

hem ▶ **noun** *the hem of her dress* EDGE, edging, border, trim, trimming.

▶ **verb** *Nan taught me to hem skirts* EDGE, trim.

■ **hem someone/something in** ❶ *a bay hemmed in by pine trees* SURROUND, border, edge, encircle, circle, ring, enclose, skirt, fringe, encompass. ❷ *we were hemmed in by the rules* RESTRICT, confine, trap, hedge in, fence in; constrain, restrain, limit, curb, check.

he-man ▶ **noun** (*informal*) MUSCLEMAN, strongman, macho man, iron man; Hercules, Samson, Tarzan; *informal* hunk, tough guy, beefcake, bruiser.

– OPPOSITES wimp.

hence ▶ **adverb** CONSEQUENTLY, as a consequence, for this reason, therefore, ergo, thus, so, accordingly, as a result, because of that, that being so.

henceforth, henceforward ▶ **adverb** FROM NOW ON, as of now, in (the) future, hence, subsequently, from this day on, from this day forth; *formal* hereafter.

henchman ▶ **noun** RIGHT-HAND MAN, assistant, aide, helper; underling, minion, man Friday, lackey, flunkey, stooge; bodyguard, minder; *informal* sidekick, crony, heavy.

henpecked ▶ **adjective** BROWBEATEN, downtrodden, bullied, dominated, subjugated, oppressed, intimidated; meek, timid, cringing; *informal* under someone's thumb, led by the nose.

– OPPOSITES domineering.

herald ▶ **noun** ❶ (*historical*) *a herald announced the armistice* MESSENGER, courier; proclaimer, announcer, crier. ❷ *the first herald of spring* HARBINGER, sign, indicator, indication, signal, prelude, portent, omen; forerunner, precursor; *poetic/literary* foretoken.

▶ **verb** ❶ *shouts heralded their approach* PROCLAIM, announce, broadcast, publicize, declare, trumpet, blazon, advertise. ❷ *the speech heralded a policy change* SIGNAL, indicate, announce, spell, presage, augur, portend, promise, foretell; usher in, pave the way for, be a harbinger of; *poetic/literary* foretoken, betoken.

Herculean ▶ **adjective** ❶ *a Herculean task* ARDUOUS, gruelling, laborious, back-breaking, onerous, strenuous, difficult, formidable, hard, tough, huge, massive, uphill; demanding, exhausting, taxing; *archaic* toilsome. ❷ *his Herculean build* STRONG, muscular, muscly, powerful, robust, solid, strapping, brawny, burly; *informal* hunky, beefy, hulking.

– OPPOSITES easy, puny.

herd ▶ **noun** ❶ *a herd of cows* drove, flock, pack, fold; group, collection. ❷ *a herd of actors* CROWD, group, bunch, horde, mob, host, pack, multitude, throng, swarm, company. ❸ *they consider themselves above the herd* THE COMMON PEOPLE, the masses, the rank and file, the crowd, the commonality, the commonalty, the plebeians; the hoi polloi, the mob, the proletariat, the rabble, the riff-raff, the great unwashed; *informal* the proles, the plebs.

▶ **verb** ❶ *we herded the sheep into the pen* DRIVE, shepherd, guide; round up, gather, collect. ❷ *we all herded into the room* CROWD, pack, flock; cluster, huddle. ❸ *they herd reindeer* TEND, look after, keep, watch (over), mind, guard.

herdsman, herdswoman ▶ **noun** STOCKMAN, herder, drover, cattleman, cowherd, cowhand, cowman, cowboy, rancher, shepherd; *N. Amer.* ranchero; *N. Amer. informal* cowpuncher, cowpoke; *archaic* herd.

here ▶ **adverb** ❶ *they lived here* AT/IN THIS PLACE, at/in this spot, at/in this location. ❷ *I am here now* PRESENT, in attendance, attending, at hand; available. ❸ *come here tomorrow* TO THIS PLACE, to this spot, to this location, over here, nearer, closer; *poetic/literary* hither. ❹ *here is your opportunity* NOW, at this moment, at this point (in time), at this juncture, at this stage.

– OPPOSITES absent.

■ **here and there** ❶ *clumps of heather here and there* IN VARIOUS PLACES, in different places; at random. ❷ *they darted here and there* HITHER AND THITHER, around, about, to and fro, back and forth, in all directions.

hereafter ▶ **adverb** (*formal*) *nothing I say hereafter is intended to offend* FROM NOW ON, after this, as of now, from this moment forth, from this day forth, from this day forward, subsequently, in (the) future, hence, henceforth, henceforward; *formal* hereinafter.

▶ **noun** *our preparation for the hereafter* LIFE AFTER DEATH, the afterlife, the afterworld, the next world; eternity, heaven, paradise.

hereditary ▶ **adjective** ❶ *a hereditary right* INHERITED; bequeathed, willed, handed-down, passed-down, passed-on, transferred; ancestral, family, familial. ❷ *a hereditary disease* GENETIC, genetical, congenital, inborn, inherited, inbred, innate; in the family, in the blood, in the genes.

heredity ▶ **noun** CONGENITAL TRAITS, genetic make-up, genes; ancestry, descent, extraction, parentage.

heresy ▶ **noun** DISSENSION, dissent, nonconformity, heterodoxy, unorthodoxy, apostasy, blasphemy, freethinking; agnosticism, atheism, non-belief; idolatry, paganism.

heretic ▶ **noun** DISSENTER, nonconformist, apostate, freethinker, iconoclast; agnostic, atheist, non-believer, unbeliever, idolater, idolatress, pagan, heathen; *archaic* paynim.
– OPPOSITES conformist, believer.

heritage ▶ **noun** ❶ *they stole his heritage* INHERITANCE, birthright, patrimony; legacy, bequest; *Law, dated* hereditament. ❷ *Europe's cultural heritage* TRADITION, history, past, background; culture, customs. ❸ *his Greek heritage* ANCESTRY, lineage, descent, extraction, parentage, roots, background, heredity.

hermaphrodite ▶ **noun** ANDROGYNE, intersex, epicene; *Biology* bisexual, gynandromorph.
▶ **adjective** *hermaphrodite creatures* ANDROGYNOUS, intersex, hermaphroditic, hermaphroditical, epicene; *Biology* bisexual, gynandrous, gynandromorphic.

hermetic ▶ **adjective** AIRTIGHT, tight, sealed; watertight, waterproof.

hermit ▶ **noun** RECLUSE, solitary, loner, ascetic; *historical* anchorite, anchoress; *archaic* eremite.

hermitage ▶ **noun** RETREAT, refuge, hideaway, hideout, shelter; *informal* hidey-hole.

hero ▶ **noun** ❶ *a war hero* BRAVE MAN, man of courage, man of the hour, lionheart, warrior; champion, victor, conqueror. ❷ *a football hero* STAR, superstar, megastar, idol, celebrity, luminary; ideal, paragon, shining example; favourite, darling; *informal* celeb. ❸ *the hero of the film* MALE PROTAGONIST, principal male character/role, starring role, star part; male lead, lead (actor), leading man.
– OPPOSITES coward, loser, villain.

heroic ▶ **adjective** ❶ *heroic rescuers* BRAVE, courageous, valiant, valorous, lionhearted, intrepid, bold, fearless, daring, audacious; unafraid, undaunted, dauntless, doughty, plucky, stout-hearted, mettlesome; gallant, chivalrous, noble; *informal* gutsy, spunky. ❷ *obelisks on a heroic scale* PRODIGIOUS, grand, enormous, huge, massive, titanic, colossal, monumental; epic; *informal* mega.

heroine ▶ **noun** ❶ *she's a heroine—she saved my baby* BRAVE WOMAN, hero, woman of courage, woman of the hour; victor, winner, conqueror. ❷ *the literary heroine of Moscow* STAR, superstar, megastar, idol, celebrity, luminary; ideal, paragon, shining example; favourite, darling; *informal* celeb. ❸ *the film's heroine* FEMALE PROTAGONIST, principal female character/role; female lead, lead (actress), leading lady; prima donna, diva.

heroism ▶ **noun** BRAVERY, courage, valour, intrepidity, boldness, daring, audacity, fearlessness, dauntlessness, pluck, stout-heartedness, lionheartedness; backbone, spine, grit, spirit, mettle; gallantry, chivalry; *informal* guts, spunk; *Brit. informal* bottle; *N. Amer. informal* moxie.

hero-worship ▶ **noun** IDOLIZATION, adulation, admiration, lionization, idealization, worship, adoration, veneration.

hesitancy ▶ **noun**. *See* HESITATION.

hesitant ▶ **adjective** ❶ *she is hesitant about buying* UNCERTAIN, undecided, unsure, doubtful, dubious, sceptical; tentative, nervous, reluctant; indecisive, irresolute, hesitating, dithering, vacillating, blowing hot and cold; ambivalent, in two minds; *Brit.* havering, humming and hawing; *informal* iffy. ❷ *a hesitant child* LACKING CONFIDENCE, diffident, timid, shy, bashful, insecure.
– OPPOSITES certain, decisive, confident.

hesitate ▶ **verb** ❶ *she hesitated, unsure of what to say* PAUSE, delay, wait, shilly-shally, dither, stall, temporize; be in two minds, be uncertain, be unsure, be doubtful, be indecisive, equivocate, vacillate, waver, blow hot and cold, have second thoughts; *Brit.* haver, hum and haw; *informal* dilly-dally. ❷ *don't hesitate to contact me* BE RELUCTANT, be unwilling, be disinclined, scruple; have misgivings about, have qualms about, shrink from, demur from, think twice about, baulk at.

hesitation ▶ **noun** HESITANCY, hesitance, uncertainty, unsureness, doubt, doubtfulness, dubiousness; irresolution, irresoluteness, indecision, indecisiveness; equivocation, vacillation, second thoughts; dithering, stalling, temporization, delay; reluctance, disinclination, unease, ambivalence; *formal* dubiety.

heterodox ▶ **adjective** UNORTHODOX, nonconformist, dissenting, dissident, rebellious, renegade; heretical, blasphemous, apostate, sceptical.
– OPPOSITES orthodox.

heterogeneous ▶ **adjective** DIVERSE, varied, varying, miscellaneous, assorted, mixed, sundry, disparate, different, differing, unrelated; motley; *poetic/literary* divers.
– OPPOSITES homogeneous.

heterosexual ▶ **adjective** *informal* STRAIGHT, hetero, het.
– OPPOSITES homosexual, gay.

hew ▶ **verb** CHOP, hack, cut, lop, axe, cleave; fell; carve, shape, fashion, sculpt, model.

heyday ▶ **noun** PRIME, peak, height, pinnacle, acme, zenith; day, time, bloom; prime of life, salad days.

hiatus ▶ **noun** PAUSE, break, gap, lacuna, interval, intermission, interlude, interruption, suspension, lull, respite, time out; *N. Amer.* recess; *informal* breather, let-up.

hibernate ▶ **verb** LIE DORMANT, lie torpid, sleep; overwinter.

hidden ▶ **adjective** ❶ *a hidden camera* CON-

CEALED, secret, invisible, unseen, out of sight; camouflaged, disguised, masked. ❷ *a hidden meaning* OBSCURE, unclear, concealed, indistinct, indefinite, vague, unfathomable, inexplicable; cryptic, mysterious, secret, covert, abstruse, arcane; ulterior, deep, subliminal, coded.
– OPPOSITES visible, obvious.

hide[1] ▶ **verb** ❶ *he hid the money* CONCEAL, secrete, put out of sight; camouflage; lock up, stow away, cache; *informal* stash. ❷ *they hid in an air vent* CONCEAL ONESELF, secrete oneself, hide out, take cover, keep out of sight; lie low, go to ground, go to earth; *informal* hole up; *Brit. informal, dated* lie doggo. ❸ *clouds hid the moon* OBSCURE, block out, blot out, obstruct, cloud, shroud, veil, blanket, envelop, eclipse. ❹ *he could not hide his dislike* CONCEAL, keep secret, cover up, keep dark, keep quiet about, hush up, bottle up, suppress; disguise, mask, camouflage; *informal* keep under one's hat, keep a/the lid on.
– OPPOSITES flaunt, reveal.

hide[2] ▶ **noun** *the hide should be tanned quickly* SKIN, pelt, coat; leather.

hideaway ▶ **noun** RETREAT, refuge, hiding place, hideout, den, bolt-hole, shelter, sanctuary, sanctum; hermitage; *informal* hidey-hole.

hidebound ▶ **adjective** CONSERVATIVE, reactionary, conventional, orthodox; fundamentalist, diehard, hard-line, dyed-in-the-wool, set in one's ways; narrow-minded, small-minded, intolerant, uncompromising, rigid; prejudiced, bigoted; *Brit.* blimpish.
– OPPOSITES liberal.

hideous ▶ **adjective** ❶ *a hideous smile* UGLY, repulsive, repellent, unsightly, revolting, gruesome, grotesque, monstrous, ghastly, reptilian; *informal* as ugly as sin. ❷ *hideous cases of torture* HORRIFIC, terrible, appalling, awful, dreadful, frightful, horrible, horrendous, horrifying, shocking, sickening, gruesome, ghastly, unspeakable, abhorrent, monstrous, heinous, abominable, foul, vile, odious, execrable.
– OPPOSITES beautiful, pleasant.

hideout ▶ **noun** HIDING PLACE, hideaway, retreat, refuge, shelter, bolt-hole, safe house, sanctuary, sanctum; *informal* hidey-hole.

hiding[1] ▶ **noun** (*informal*) *they gave him a hiding* BEATING, battering, thrashing, thumping, drubbing, pelting; flogging, whipping, caning, birching; *informal* licking, belting, bashing, pasting, walloping, clobbering, tanning.

hiding[2]
■ **in hiding** *the fugitive is in hiding* HIDDEN, concealed, lying low, gone to ground, gone to earth, in a safe house; *Brit. informal, dated* lying doggo.

hiding place ▶ **noun** HIDEAWAY, hideout, retreat, refuge, shelter, sanctuary, sanctum, bolt-hole, safe house; *informal* hidey-hole.

hie ▶ **verb** (*archaic*). *See* HURRY verb sense 1.

hierarchy ▶ **noun** PECKING ORDER, ranking, grading, ladder, scale.

hieroglyphic ▶ **noun** ❶ *hieroglyphics on a stone monument* SYMBOLS, signs, ciphers, code; cryptograms. ❷ *notebooks filled with hieroglyphics* SCRIBBLE, scrawl, illegible writing; shorthand.
▶ **adjective** ❶ *hieroglyphic brass ornamentation* SYMBOLIC, stylized, emblematic. ❷ *hieroglyphic handwriting* ILLEGIBLE, indecipherable, unreadable, scribbled, scrawled.

higgledy-piggledy (*informal*) ▶ **adjective** *a higgledy-piggledy pile of papers* DISORDERED, disorderly, disorganized, untidy, messy, chaotic, jumbled, muddled, confused, unsystematic, irregular; out of order, in disarray, in a mess, in a muddle, haphazard; *informal* all over the place; *Brit. informal* shambolic.
– OPPOSITES tidy.
▶ **adverb** *the cars were parked higgledy-piggledy* IN DISORDER, in a muddle, in a jumble, in disarray, untidily, haphazardly, anyhow; *informal* all over the place, topsy-turvy, every which way, any old how; *Brit. informal* all over the shop; *N. Amer. informal* all over the map, all over the lot.

high ▶ **adjective** ❶ *a high mountain* TALL, lofty, towering, elevated, giant, big; multi-storey, high-rise. ❷ *a high position in the government* HIGH-RANKING, high-level, leading, top, top-level, prominent, pre-eminent, foremost, senior; influential, powerful, important, elevated, prime, premier, exalted; *N. Amer.* ranking; *informal* top-notch. ❸ *high principles* HIGH-MINDED, noble, lofty, moral, ethical, honourable, admirable, upright, honest, virtuous, righteous. ❹ *high prices* INFLATED, excessive, unreasonable, expensive, dear, costly, exorbitant, extortionate, prohibitive; *Brit.* over the odds; *informal* steep, stiff, pricey. ❺ *high standards* EXCELLENT, outstanding, exemplary, exceptional, admirable, fine, good, first-class, first-rate, superior, superlative, superb; impeccable, irreproachable, unimpeachable, perfect, flawless; *informal* A1, top-notch. ❻ *high winds* STRONG, powerful, violent, intense, extreme, forceful, stiff; blustery, gusty, squally, tempestuous, turbulent. ❼ *the high life* LUXURIOUS, lavish, extravagant, grand, opulent; sybaritic, hedonistic; *Brit.* upmarket; *N. Amer.* upscale; *informal* fancy, classy, swanky. ❽ *I have a high opinion of you* FAVOURABLE, good, positive, approving, admiring, complimentary, commendatory, flattering, glowing, adulatory, rapturous. ❾ *a high note* HIGH-PITCHED, high-frequency; soprano, treble, falsetto, shrill, sharp, piercing, penetrating. ❿ (*informal*) *they are high on drugs* INTOXICATED, inebriated, drugged, stupefied, befuddled, delirious, hallucinating; *informal* high as a kite, stoned, tripping, hyped up, spaced out, wasted, wrecked, off one's head. ⓫ *the partridges were high* GAMY, smelly, strong-smelling; stinking, reeking, rank, mal-

odorous, bad, off, rotting; *Brit. informal* pongy, niffy, whiffy; *N. Amer. informal* funky.
– OPPOSITES short, lowly, amoral, cheap, low, light, abstemious, unfavourable, deep, sober, fresh.

▶ **noun** *prices were at a rare high* HIGH LEVEL, high point, peak, high water mark; pinnacle, zenith, acme, height.
– OPPOSITES low.

▶ **adverb** *a jet flew high overhead* AT GREAT HEIGHT, high up, far up, way up, at altitude; in the air, in the sky, on high, aloft, overhead.
– OPPOSITES low.

■ **high and dry** DESTITUTE, bereft, helpless, in the lurch, in difficulties; abandoned, stranded, marooned.

■ **high and low** EVERYWHERE, all over, all around, far and wide, {here, there, and everywhere}, extensively, thoroughly, widely, in every nook and cranny; *informal* all over the place; *Brit. informal* all over the shop; *N. Amer. informal* all over the map.

■ **high and mighty** (informal) SELF-IMPORTANT, condescending, patronizing, disdainful, supercilious, superior, snobbish, snobby, haughty, conceited, above oneself; *informal* stuck-up, snooty, hoity-toity, la-di-da, uppity; *Brit. informal* toffee-nosed.

■ **on a high** (informal) ECSTATIC, euphoric, delirious, elated, thrilled, overjoyed, beside oneself, walking on air, on cloud nine, in seventh heaven, jumping for joy, in raptures, exultant, jubilant; excited, overexcited; *informal* blissed out, over the moon, on top of the world; *Austral./NZ informal* wrapped.

high-born ▶ **adjective** NOBLE, aristocratic, well born, titled, patrician, blue-blooded, upper-class; *informal* upper-crust, top-drawer; *Brit. informal* posh; *archaic* gentle.
– OPPOSITES lowly.

highbrow ▶ **adjective** *his work has a highbrow following* INTELLECTUAL, scholarly, bookish, academic, educated, donnish, bluestocking; sophisticated, erudite, learned; *informal* brainy, egghead.
– OPPOSITES lowbrow.

▶ **noun** *highbrows who hate pop music* INTELLECTUAL, scholar, academic, bluestocking, bookish person, thinker; *informal* egghead, brain, bookworm; *Brit. informal* brainbox, boffin; *N. Amer. informal* brainiac.

high-class ▶ **adjective** SUPERIOR, upper-class, first-rate; excellent, select, elite, choice, premier, top, top-flight; luxurious, de luxe, high-quality, top-quality; *Brit.* upmarket; *informal* top-notch, top-drawer, A1, classy, posh.

highfalutin ▶ **adjective** (*informal*). *See* PRETENTIOUS.

high-flown ▶ **adjective** GRAND, extravagant, elaborate, flowery, ornate, overblown, overdone, overwrought, grandiloquent, magniloquent, grandiose, inflated, affected, pretentious, turgid; *informal* windy, purple, highfalutin, la-di-da.
– OPPOSITES plain.

high-handed ▶ **adjective** IMPERIOUS, arbitrary, peremptory, arrogant, haughty, domineering, pushy, overbearing, heavy-handed, lordly; inflexible, rigid; autocratic, authoritarian, dictatorial, tyrannical; *informal* bossy, high and mighty.
– OPPOSITES liberal.

high jinks ▶ **plural noun** ANTICS, pranks, larks, escapades, stunts, practical jokes, tricks; fun (and games), skylarking, mischief, horseplay, tomfoolery, clowning; *informal* shenanigans, capers, monkey business; *Brit. informal* monkey tricks.

highland ▶ **noun** UPLANDS, highlands, mountains, hills, heights, moors; upland, tableland, plateau; *Brit.* wolds.

highlight ▶ **noun** *the highlight of his career* HIGH POINT, high spot, best part, climax, peak, pinnacle, height, acme, zenith, summit, crowning moment, high water mark.
– OPPOSITES nadir.

▶ **verb** *he has highlighted shortcomings in the plan* SPOTLIGHT, call attention to, focus on, underline, feature, play up, show up, bring out, accentuate, accent, give prominence to, zero in on, stress, emphasize.

highly ▶ **adverb** ❶ *a highly dangerous substance* VERY, extremely, exceedingly, particularly, most, really, thoroughly, decidedly, distinctly, exceptionally, immensely, inordinately, singularly, extraordinarily; *N. English* right; *informal* terrifically, awfully, terribly, majorly, seriously, desperately, mega, ultra, oh-so, damn, damned; *Brit. informal* ever so, well, dead, jolly; *N. Amer. informal* real, mighty, awful; *dated* frightfully. ❷ *he was highly regarded* FAVOURABLY, well, appreciatively, admiringly, approvingly, positively, glowingly, enthusiastically.
– OPPOSITES slightly, unfavourably.

highly strung ▶ **adjective** NERVOUS, nervy, excitable, temperamental, sensitive, unstable; brittle, on edge, edgy, jumpy, restless, anxious, tense, stressed, overwrought, neurotic; *informal* uptight, twitchy, wired, wound up, het up.
– OPPOSITES easy-going.

high-minded ▶ **adjective** HIGH-PRINCIPLED, principled, honourable, moral, upright, upstanding, right-minded, noble, good, honest, decent, ethical, righteous, virtuous, worthy, idealistic.
– OPPOSITES unprincipled.

high-pitched ▶ **adjective** HIGH, high-frequency, shrill, sharp, piping, piercing; soprano, treble, falsetto.
– OPPOSITES deep.

high-powered ▶ **adjective** DYNAMIC, ambitious, energetic, assertive, enterprising, vigorous; forceful, aggressive, pushy, high-octane;

informal go-ahead, go-getting; *N. Amer. informal* go-go.

high-pressure ▶ **adjective** FORCEFUL, insistent, persistent, pushy; intensive, high-powered, aggressive, coercive, compelling, thrusting, not taking no for an answer.

high-priced ▶ **adjective** EXPENSIVE, costly, dear; overpriced, exorbitant, extortionate; *Brit.* over the odds; *informal* pricey, steep, stiff.

high-sounding ▶ **adjective** GRAND, high-flown, extravagant, elaborate, flowery, ornate, overblown, overdone, overwrought, grandiloquent, magniloquent, grandiose, inflated, affected, pretentious, turgid; *informal* windy, purple, highfalutin, la-di-da.
– OPPOSITES plain.

high-speed ▶ **adjective** FAST, quick, rapid, speedy, swift, breakneck, lightning, brisk; express, non-stop, whistle-stop; *informal* nippy, zippy, supersonic; *poetic/literary* fleet.
– OPPOSITES slow.

high-spirited ▶ **adjective** LIVELY, spirited, full of fun, fun-loving, animated, zestful, bouncy, bubbly, sparkling, vivacious, buoyant, cheerful, joyful, exuberant, ebullient, jaunty, irrepressible; *informal* chirpy, peppy, sparky, bright and breezy, full of beans; *poetic/literary* frolicsome.

high spirits ▶ **plural noun** LIVELINESS, vitality, spirit, zest, energy, bounce, sparkle, vivacity, buoyancy, cheerfulness, good humour, joy, joyfulness, exuberance, ebullience, joie de vivre; *informal* pep, zing.

highwayman ▶ **noun** (*historical*) BANDIT, robber, outlaw, ruffian, marauder, raider; *historical* footpad; *poetic/literary* brigand.

hijack ▶ **verb** COMMANDEER, seize, take over; skyjack; appropriate, expropriate, confiscate; *informal* snatch.

hike ▶ **noun** *a five-mile hike* WALK, trek, tramp, trudge, slog, footslog, march; ramble; *Brit. informal* yomp.
▶ **verb** *they hiked across the moors* WALK, trek, tramp, trudge, slog, footslog, march; ramble; *informal* hoof it, leg it; *Brit. informal* yomp.
■ **hike something up** ❶ *Roy hiked up his trousers* HITCH UP, pull up, hoist, lift, raise; *informal* yank up. ❷ *they hiked up the price* INCREASE, raise, up, put up, mark up, push up, inflate; *informal* jack up, bump up.

hilarious ▶ **adjective** ❶ *a hilarious story* VERY FUNNY, hysterically funny, hysterical, uproarious, riotous, farcical, rib-tickling; humorous, comic, amusing, entertaining; *informal* side-splitting, priceless, a scream, a hoot. ❷ *a hilarious evening* AMUSING, entertaining, animated, high-spirited, lively, funny, merry, jolly, mirthful, cheerful, uproarious, boisterous; *informal* wacky.
– OPPOSITES sad, serious.

hilarity ▶ **noun** AMUSEMENT, mirth, laughter, merriment, light-heartedness, levity, fun, humour, jocularity, jollity, gaiety, delight, glee, exuberance, high spirits; comedy.

hill ▶ **noun** ❶ *the top of the hill* HIGH GROUND, prominence, hillock, foothill, hillside, rise, mound, mount, knoll, hummock, tor, tump, fell, pike, mesa; bank, ridge, slope, incline, gradient; (**hills**) heights, downs; *Scottish & Irish* drum; *Scottish* brae; *Geology* drumlin; *formal* eminence. ❷ *a hill of rubbish* HEAP, pile, stack, mound, mountain, mass; *Scottish, Irish, & N. English* rickle.

hillock ▶ **noun** MOUND, small hill, prominence, elevation, rise, knoll, hummock, hump, tump, dune; bank, ridge; *N. English* howe; *N. Amer.* knob; *formal* eminence.

hilt ▶ **noun** HANDLE, haft, handgrip, grip, shaft, shank, stock, helve.
■ **to the hilt** COMPLETELY, fully, wholly, totally, entirely, utterly, unreservedly, unconditionally, in every respect, in all respects, one hundred per cent, every inch, to the full, to the maximum extent, all the way, body and soul, heart and soul.

hind ▶ **adjective** BACK, rear, hinder, hindmost, posterior.
– OPPOSITES fore, front.

hinder ▶ **verb** HAMPER, obstruct, impede, inhibit, retard, baulk, thwart, foil, curb, delay, arrest, interfere with, set back, slow down, hold back, hold up, stop, halt; restrict, restrain, constrain, block, check, curtail, frustrate, cramp, handicap, cripple, hamstring; *informal* stymie; *Brit. informal* throw a spanner in the works.
– OPPOSITES facilitate.

hindmost ▶ **adjective** FURTHEST BACK, last, rear, rearmost, end, endmost, final, tail.
– OPPOSITES leading.

hindrance ▶ **noun** IMPEDIMENT, obstacle, barrier, bar, obstruction, handicap, block, hurdle, restraint, restriction, limitation, encumbrance; complication, delay, drawback, setback, difficulty, inconvenience, snag, catch, hitch, stumbling block; *informal* fly in the ointment, hiccup, facer; *Brit. informal* spanner in the works.
– OPPOSITES help.

hinge ▶ **verb** *our future hinges on the election* DEPEND, hang, rest, turn, centre, be contingent, be dependent, be conditional; be determined by, be decided by, revolve around.

hint ▶ **noun** ❶ *a hint that he would leave* CLUE, inkling, suggestion, indication, indicator, sign, signal, pointer, intimation, insinuation, innuendo, mention, whisper. ❷ *handy hints about painting* TIP, suggestion, pointer, clue, guideline, recommendation; advice, help; *informal* how-to, wrinkle. ❸ *a hint of mint* TRACE, touch, suspicion, suggestion, dash, soupçon, tinge, modicum, whiff, taste, undertone; *informal* smidgen, tad.

▶ **verb** *what are you hinting at?* IMPLY, insinuate, intimate, suggest, indicate, signal; allude to, refer to, drive at, mean; *informal* get at.

hinterland ▶ **noun** THE BACKWOODS, a backwater, the wilds, the bush, the back of beyond; *Austral./NZ* the outback, the backblocks, the booay; *informal* the sticks, the middle of nowhere; *N. Amer. informal* the boondocks, the tall timbers.

hip ▶ **adjective** (*informal*). *See* FASHIONABLE.

hippy ▶ **noun** FLOWER CHILD, bohemian, dropout, free spirit, nonconformist.

hips ▶ **plural noun** PELVIS, hindquarters, haunches, thighs.
– RELATED TERMS sciatic.

hire ▶ **verb** ❶ *we hired a car* RENT, lease, charter. ❷ *they hire labour in line with demand* EMPLOY, engage, recruit, appoint, take on, sign up, enrol, commission, enlist.
– OPPOSITES dismiss.

▶ **noun** *the hire of the machine* RENTAL, rent, hiring, lease, leasing, charter.

hire purchase ▶ **noun** INSTALMENT PLAN, deferred payment, HP, credit, finance, easy terms; *Brit. informal* the never-never.

hirsute ▶ **adjective** (*formal*) HAIRY, shaggy, bushy, hair-covered; woolly, furry, fleecy, fuzzy; bearded, unshaven, bristly.

hiss ▶ **verb** ❶ *the escaping gas hissed* FIZZ, fizzle, whistle, wheeze; *rare* sibilate. ❷ *the audience hissed* JEER, catcall, whistle, hoot; scoff, jibe.

▶ **noun** ❶ *the hiss of the steam* FIZZ, fizzing, whistle, hissing, sibilance, wheeze; *rare* sibilation. ❷ *the speaker received hisses* JEER, catcall, whistle; abuse, scoffing, taunting, derision.

historian ▶ **noun** CHRONICLER, annalist, archivist, recorder; historiographer, antiquarian, chronologist.

historic ▶ **adjective** SIGNIFICANT, notable, important, momentous, consequential, memorable, unforgettable, remarkable; famous, famed, celebrated, renowned; landmark, ground-breaking, epoch-making, red-letter, earth-shattering.
– OPPOSITES insignificant.

historical ▶ **adjective** ❶ *historical evidence* DOCUMENTED, recorded, chronicled, archival; authentic, factual, actual, true. ❷ *historical figures* PAST, bygone, ancient, old, former; *poetic/literary* of yore.
– OPPOSITES contemporary.

history ▶ **noun** ❶ *my interest in history* THE PAST, former times, historical events, the olden days, the old days, bygone days, yesterday, antiquity; *poetic/literary* days of yore, yesteryear. ❷ *a history of the Civil War* CHRONICLE, archive, record, report, narrative, account, study, tale; memoir. ❸ *she gave details of her history* BACKGROUND, past, life story, experiences; antecedents.

histrionic ▶ **adjective** MELODRAMATIC, theatrical, dramatic, exaggerated, actressy, stagy, showy, affected, artificial, overacted, overdone; *informal* hammy, ham, camp.

histrionics ▶ **plural noun** DRAMATICS, theatricals, theatrics, tantrums; affectation, staginess, artificiality.

hit ▶ **verb** ❶ *she hit her child* STRIKE, slap, smack, cuff, punch, thump, swat; beat, thrash, batter, belabour, pound, welt, pummel, box someone's ears; whip, flog, cane; *informal* whack, wallop, bash, biff, bop, lam, clout, clip, clobber, sock, swipe, crown, beat the living daylights out of, give someone a (good) hiding, belt, tan, lay into, let someone have it, deck, floor; *Brit. informal* stick one on, dot, slosh; *N. Amer. informal* slug, boff; *Austral./NZ informal* dong; *poetic/literary* smite. ❷ *a car hit the barrier* CRASH INTO, run into, smash into, smack into, knock into, bump into, cannon into, plough into, collide with, meet head-on; *N. Amer.* impact. ❸ *the tragedy hit her hard* DEVASTATE, affect badly, hurt, harm, leave a mark on; upset, shatter, crush, shock, overwhelm, traumatize; *informal* knock sideways, knock the stuffing out of; *Brit. informal* knock for six. ❹ (*informal*) *spending will hit £1,800 million* REACH, touch, arrive at, rise to, climb to. ❺ *it hit me that I had forgotten* OCCUR TO, strike, dawn on, come to; enter one's head, cross one's mind, come to mind, spring to mind.

▶ **noun** ❶ *he received a hit from behind* BLOW, thump, punch, knock, bang, box, cuff, slap, smack, tap, crack, stroke, welt; impact, collision, bump, crash; *informal* whack, thwack, wallop, bash, belt, biff, clout, sock, swipe, clip; *Brit. informal* slosh; *N. Amer. informal* boff, slug; *Austral./NZ* dong. ❷ *a hit at his friend's religion* JIBE, taunt, jeer, sneer, barb; *informal* dig, crack, wisecrack, put-down. ❸ *he directed many big hits* SUCCESS, box-office success, sell-out, winner, triumph, sensation; best-seller; *informal* smash (hit), knockout, crowd-puller, wow, biggie; *Brit. informal* smasher.
– OPPOSITES compliment, failure.

■ **hit back** RETALIATE, respond, reply, react, counter, defend oneself.

■ **hit home** HAVE THE INTENDED EFFECT, strike home, hit the mark, register, be understood, get through, sink in.

■ **hit it off** (informal) GET ON (WELL), get along, be friends, be friendly, be compatible, feel a rapport, see eye to eye, take to each other, warm to each other; *informal* click, get on like a house on fire, be on the same wavelength.

■ **hit on/upon** DISCOVER, come up with, think of, conceive of, dream up, work out, invent, create, devise, design, pioneer; uncover, stumble on, chance on, light on, come upon.

■ **hit out at** CRITICIZE, attack, censure, denounce, condemn, lambaste, pillory, rail against, inveigh against, arraign, cast aspersions on, pour scorn on, disparage, denigrate, give a bad press to, run down; *informal* knock, pan, slam, hammer, lay into, pull to pieces, pick holes in; *Brit. informal* slag off, slate, rubbish; *N. Amer. informal* pummel, trash; *formal* excoriate.

hitch ▶ **verb** ❶ *she hitched the blanket around her* PULL, jerk, hike, lift, raise; *informal* yank. ❷ *Tom hitched the pony to his cart* HARNESS, yoke, couple, fasten, connect, attach, tether. ❸ (*informal*) *they hitched to college* HITCH-HIKE; *informal* thumb a lift, hitch a lift.

▶ **noun** *it went without a hitch* PROBLEM, difficulty, snag, setback, hindrance, obstacle, obstruction, complication, impediment, stumbling block, barrier; hold-up, interruption, delay; *informal* headache, glitch, hiccup.

hither ▶ **adverb** (*poetic/literary*) HERE, to this place, to here, over here, near, nearer, close, closer.

hitherto ▶ **adverb** PREVIOUSLY, formerly, earlier, before, beforehand; so far, thus far, to date, as yet, until now, until then, till now, till then, up to now, up to then; *formal* heretofore.

hit-or-miss, hit-and-miss ▶ **adjective** ERRATIC, haphazard, disorganized, undisciplined, unmethodical, uneven; careless, slapdash, slipshod, casual, cursory, lackadaisical, perfunctory, random, aimless, undirected, indiscriminate; *informal* sloppy, slap-happy.
– OPPOSITES meticulous.

hoard ▶ **noun** *a secret hoard of gold* CACHE, stockpile, stock, store, collection, supply, reserve, reservoir, fund, accumulation; treasure house, treasure trove; *informal* stash.

▶ **verb** *they hoarded rations* STOCKPILE, store (up), stock up on, put aside, put by, lay by, lay up, set aside, stow away, buy up; cache, amass, collect, save, gather, garner, accumulate, squirrel away, put aside for a rainy day; *informal* stash away, salt away.
– OPPOSITES squander.

hoarse ▶ **adjective** ROUGH, harsh, croaky, throaty, gruff, husky, guttural, growly, gravelly, grating, rasping.
– OPPOSITES mellow, clear.

hoary ▶ **adjective** ❶ *hoary cobwebs* GREYISH-WHITE, grey, white, silver, silvery; frosty; *poetic/literary* rimy. ❷ *a hoary ancient* GREY-HAIRED, white-haired, silver-haired, grizzled; elderly, aged, old, long in the tooth; *informal* getting on, over the hill. ❸ *a hoary old adage* TRITE, hackneyed, clichéd, banal, commonplace, predictable, overused, stale, time-worn, tired, unimaginative, unoriginal, uninspired; *informal* old hat, corny; *N. Amer. informal* cornball.
– OPPOSITES young, original.

hoax ▶ **noun** *the call was a hoax* PRACTICAL JOKE, joke, jest, prank, trick; ruse, deception, fraud, bluff, humbug, confidence trick; *informal* con, spoof, scam.

▶ **verb** *the DJ hoaxed his listeners* PLAY A (PRACTICAL) JOKE ON, play a prank on, trick, fool; deceive, hoodwink, delude, dupe, take in, lead on, bluff, gull, humbug; *informal* con, kid, have on, pull a fast one on, put one over on, take for a ride, lead up the garden path; *N. Amer. informal* sucker, snooker.

hoaxer ▶ **noun** (PRACTICAL) JOKER, prankster, trickster; fraudster, hoodwinker, swindler; *informal* spoofer, con man.

hobble ▶ **verb** LIMP, walk with difficulty, move unsteadily, walk haltingly; shamble, totter, dodder, stagger, stumble; *Scottish* hirple.

hobby ▶ **noun** PASTIME, leisure activity, leisure pursuit; sideline, diversion, avocation; recreation, entertainment, amusement, enthusiasm.

hobgoblin ▶ **noun** GOBLIN, imp, sprite, elf, brownie, pixie, leprechaun, gnome; *Scottish* kelpie.

hobnob ▶ **verb** (*informal*) ASSOCIATE, mix, fraternize, socialize, keep company, spend time, go around, mingle, consort, rub shoulders; *N. Amer.* rub elbows; *informal* hang around/round/out, knock about/around, be thick with.

hocus-pocus ▶ **noun** JARGON, mumbo-jumbo, argle-bargle, gibberish, balderdash, claptrap, nonsense, rubbish, twaddle, garbage; *informal* gobbledegook, double Dutch, hokum; *N. Amer. informal* flapdoodle; *informal, dated* bunkum.

hodgepodge ▶ **noun** (*N. Amer.*). *See* HOTCHPOTCH.

hog ▶ **noun** PIG, sow, swine, porker, piglet, boar; *informal* piggy.

▶ **verb** (*informal*) *he hogged the limelight* MONOPOLIZE, dominate, take over, corner, control.
– OPPOSITES share.

hogwash ▶ **noun** (*informal*). *See* NONSENSE sense 1.

hoi polloi ▶ **noun** THE MASSES, the common people, the populace, the public, the multitude, the rank and file, the lower orders, the commonality, the commonalty, the third estate, the plebeians, the proletariat; the mob, the herd, the rabble, the riff-raff, the great unwashed; *informal* the plebs, the proles.

hoist ▶ **verb** *we hoisted the mainsail* RAISE, lift (up), haul up, heave up, jack up, hike up, winch up, pull up, upraise, uplift, elevate, erect.
– OPPOSITES lower.

▶ **noun** *a mechanical hoist* LIFTING GEAR, crane, winch, block and tackle, pulley, windlass, derrick.

hoity-toity ▶ **adjective** (*informal*) SNOBBISH, snobby, haughty, disdainful, conceited, proud, arrogant, supercilious, superior, imperious, above oneself, self-important; *informal* high and mighty, snooty, uppity, uppish, la-di-da; *Brit. informal* toffee-nosed.

hold ▶ verb ❶ *she held a suitcase* CLASP, clutch, grasp, grip, clench, cling to, hold on to; carry, bear. ❷ *I wanted to hold her* EMBRACE, hug, clasp, cradle, enfold, squeeze, fold in one's arms. ❸ *do you hold a driving licence?* POSSESS, have, own, bear, carry, have to one's name. ❹ *the branch held my weight* SUPPORT, bear, carry, take, keep up, sustain, prop up, shore up. ❺ *the police were holding him* DETAIN, hold in custody, imprison, lock up, put behind bars, put in prison, put in jail, incarcerate, keep under lock and key, confine, intern; *informal* put away, put inside. ❻ *try to hold the audience's attention* MAINTAIN, keep, occupy, engross, absorb, interest, captivate, fascinate, enthral, rivet; engage, catch, capture, arrest. ❼ *he held a senior post* OCCUPY, have, fill; *informal* hold down. ❽ *the tank held 250 gallons* TAKE, contain, accommodate, fit; have a capacity of, have room for. ❾ *the court held that there was no evidence* MAINTAIN, consider, take the view, believe, think, feel, deem, be of the opinion; judge, rule, decide; *informal* reckon; *formal* opine. ❿ *let's hope the weather holds* PERSIST, continue, carry on, go on, hold out, keep up, last, endure, stay, remain. ⓫ *the offer still holds* BE AVAILABLE, be valid, hold good, stand, apply, remain, exist, be the case, be in force, be in effect. ⓬ *they held a meeting* CONVENE, call, summon; conduct, have, organize, run; *formal* convoke.

– OPPOSITES release, lose, end.

▶ noun ❶ *she kept a hold on my hand* GRIP, grasp, clasp, clutch. ❷ *Tom had a hold over his father* INFLUENCE, power, control, dominance, authority, leverage, sway, mastery. ❸ *the military tightened their hold on the capital* CONTROL, grip, power, stranglehold, dominion, authority.

■ **get hold of** (*informal*) ❶ *I just can't get hold of saffron* OBTAIN, acquire, get, find, come by, pick up, procure; buy, purchase; *informal* get one's hands on. ❷ *I'll try to get hold of Mark* CONTACT, get in touch with, communicate with, make contact with, reach, notify; phone, call, speak to, talk to; *Brit.* ring (up), get on to.

■ **hold back** HESITATE, pause, stop oneself, desist, forbear.

■ **hold someone back** HINDER, hamper, impede, obstruct, check, curb, block, thwart, baulk, hamstring, restrain, frustrate, stand in someone's way.

■ **hold something back** ❶ *Jane held back the tears* SUPPRESS, fight back, choke back, stifle, smother, subdue, rein in, repress, curb, control, keep a tight rein on; *informal* keep a/the lid on. ❷ *don't hold anything back from me* WITHHOLD, hide, conceal, keep secret, keep hidden, keep quiet about, hush up; *informal* sit on, keep under one's hat.

■ **hold someone/something dear** CHERISH, treasure, prize, appreciate, value highly, care for/about, set great store by; *informal* put on a pedestal.

■ **hold someone down** OPPRESS, repress, suppress, subdue, subjugate, keep down, keep under, tyrannize, dominate.

■ **hold something down** ❶ *they will hold down inflation* KEEP DOWN, keep low, freeze, fix. ❷ (*informal*) *she held down two jobs* OCCUPY, hold, have, do, fill.

■ **hold forth** SPEAK AT LENGTH, talk at length, go on, sound off; declaim, spout, pontificate, orate, preach, sermonize; *informal* speechify, preachify, drone on.

■ **hold off** *the rain held off* STAY AWAY, keep off, not come.

■ **hold something off** RESIST, repel, repulse, rebuff, parry, deflect, fend off, stave off, ward off, keep at bay.

■ **hold on** ❶ *hold on a minute* WAIT (A MINUTE), just a moment, just a second; stay here, stay put; hold the line; *informal* hang on, sit tight, hold your horses; *Brit. informal* hang about. ❷ *if only they could hold on a while* KEEP GOING, persevere, survive, last, continue, struggle on, carry on, go on, hold out, see it through, stay the course; *informal* soldier on, stick at it, hang in there.

■ **hold on to** ❶ *he held on to the chair* CLUTCH, hold, hang on to, clasp, grasp, grip, cling to. ❷ *they can't hold on to their staff* RETAIN, keep, hang on to.

■ **hold one's own**. *See* OWN.

■ **hold out** ❶ *we held out against the attacks* RESIST, withstand, hold off, fight off, fend off, keep off, keep at bay, stand up to, stand firm against. ❷ *our supplies will hold out* LAST, remain, be extant, continue.

■ **hold something out** EXTEND, proffer, offer, present; outstretch, reach out, stretch out, put out.

■ **hold something over** POSTPONE, put off, put back, delay, defer, suspend, shelve, hold in abeyance; *N. Amer.* put over, table, take a rain check on; *informal* put on ice, put on the back burner, put in cold storage, mothball.

■ **hold up** *the argument doesn't hold up* BE CONVINCING, be logical, hold water, bear examination, be sound.

■ **hold something up** ❶ *they held up the trophy* DISPLAY, hold aloft, exhibit, show (off), flourish, brandish; *informal* flash. ❷ *concrete pillars hold up the bridge* SUPPORT, hold, bear, carry, take, keep up, prop up, shore up, buttress. ❸ *our flight was held up for hours* DELAY, detain, make late, set back, keep back, retard, slow up. ❹ *a lack of cash has held up progress* OBSTRUCT, impede, hinder, hamper, inhibit, baulk, thwart, curb, hamstring, frustrate, foil, interfere with, stop; *informal* stymie; *Brit. informal* throw a spanner in the works of. ❺ *a raider held up the bank* ROB; *informal* stick up, mug.

■ **hold water**. *See* WATER.

■ **hold with** APPROVE OF, agree with, be in favour of, endorse, accept, countenance, support, subscribe to, give one's blessing to, take kindly to; *informal* stand for; *Brit. informal* be doing with.

holder ▶ noun ❶ *a knife holder* CONTAINER, receptacle, case, casing, cover, covering, housing, sheath; stand, rest, rack. ❷ *a British passport holder* BEARER, owner, possessor, keeper; custodian.

holdings ▶ plural noun ASSETS, funds, capital, resources, savings, investments, securities, equities, bonds, stocks and shares, reserves; property, possessions.

hold-up ▶ noun ❶ *I ran into a series of hold-ups* DELAY, setback, hitch, snag, difficulty, problem, trouble; traffic jam, tailback, gridlock; *informal* snarl-up, glitch, hiccup. ❷ *a bank hold-up* (ARMED) ROBBERY, (armed) raid; theft, burglary, mugging; *informal* stick-up; *N. Amer. informal* heist.

hole ▶ noun ❶ *a hole in the roof* OPENING, aperture, gap, space, orifice, vent, chink, breach; crack, leak, rift, rupture; puncture, perforation, cut, split, gash, slit, crevice, fissure. ❷ *a hole in the ground* PIT, ditch, trench, cavity, crater, depression, hollow; well, borehole, excavation, dugout; cave, cavern, pothole. ❸ *the badger's hole* BURROW, lair, den, earth, sett; retreat, shelter. ❹ *there are holes in their argument* FLAW, fault, defect, weakness, shortcoming, inconsistency, discrepancy, loophole; error, mistake. ❺ (*informal*) *I was living in a real hole* HOVEL, slum, shack, mess; *informal* dump, dive, pigsty, tip. ❻ (*informal*) *they steal when they are in a hole* PREDICAMENT, difficult situation, awkward situation, (tight) corner, quandary, dilemma; crisis, emergency, difficulty, trouble, plight, dire straits; *informal* fix, jam, bind, (tight) spot, pickle, sticky situation, hot water; *Brit. informal* spot of bother.

▶ verb *a fuel tank was holed by the attack* PUNCTURE, perforate, pierce, penetrate, rupture, split, rent, lacerate, gash.

■ **hole up** ❶ *the bears hole up in winter* HIBERNATE, lie dormant. ❷ (*informal*) *the snipers holed up in a farmhouse* HIDE (OUT), conceal oneself, secrete oneself, shelter, take cover, lie low, go to ground, go to earth; *Brit. informal, dated* lie doggo.

■ **pick holes in** (*informal*). *See* CRITICIZE.

hole-and-corner ▶ adjective SECRET, secretive, clandestine, covert, furtive, surreptitious; underhand, devious, stealthy, sneaky, backstairs, hugger-mugger, cloak-and-dagger, under-the-counter; *informal* hush-hush.

holiday ▶ noun ❶ *a ten-day holiday* VACATION, break, rest, recess; time off, time out, leave, furlough, sabbatical; trip, tour, journey, voyage; *informal* hols, vac; *formal* sojourn. ❷ *the twenty-fourth of May is a holiday* PUBLIC HOLIDAY, bank holiday, festival, feast day, fête, fiesta, celebration, anniversary, jubilee; saint's day, holy day.

holier-than-thou ▶ adjective SANCTIMONIOUS, self-righteous, smug, self-satisfied; priggish, pious, pietistic, Pharisaic; *informal* goody-goody, preachy.
– OPPOSITES humble.

holler (*informal*) ▶ verb *he hollers when he wants feeding* SHOUT, yell, cry (out), vociferate, call (out), roar, bellow, bawl, bark, howl; boom, thunder.
– OPPOSITES whisper.

▶ noun *a euphoric holler* SHOUT, cry, yell, roar, bellow, bawl, howl; whoop.
– OPPOSITES whisper.

hollow ▶ adjective ❶ *each fibre has a hollow core* EMPTY, void, unfilled, vacant. ❷ *hollow cheeks* SUNKEN, deep-set, concave, depressed, indented. ❸ *a hollow voice* DULL, low, flat, toneless, expressionless; muffled, muted. ❹ *a hollow victory* MEANINGLESS, empty, valueless, worthless, useless, pyrrhic, futile, fruitless, profitless, pointless. ❺ *a hollow promise* INSINCERE, hypocritical, feigned, false, sham, deceitful, cynical, spurious, untrue, two-faced; *informal* phoney, pretend.
– OPPOSITES solid, worthwhile, sincere.

▶ noun ❶ *a hollow under the tree* HOLE, pit, cavity, crater, trough, cave, cavern; depression, indentation, dip; niche, nook, cranny, recess. ❷ *the village lay in a hollow* VALLEY, vale, dale; *Brit.* dene, combe; *N. English* clough; *Scottish* glen, strath; *poetic/literary* dell.

▶ verb *a tunnel hollowed out of a mountain* GOUGE, scoop, dig, cut; excavate, channel.

■ **beat someone hollow** TROUNCE, defeat utterly, crush, rout, overwhelm, outclass; *informal* annihilate, drub, hammer, clobber, thrash, lick, paste, crucify, slaughter, massacre, flatten, demolish, destroy, walk over, wipe the floor with, make mincemeat of; *Brit. informal* stuff; *N. Amer. informal* shellac, cream, skunk.

holocaust ▶ noun CATACLYSM, disaster, catastrophe; destruction, devastation, annihilation; massacre, slaughter, mass murder, carnage, butchery; genocide, ethnic cleansing.

holy ▶ adjective ❶ *holy men* SAINTLY, godly, saintlike, pious, pietistic, religious, devout, God-fearing, spiritual; righteous, good, virtuous, sinless, pure; canonized, beatified, ordained. ❷ *a Jewish holy place* SACRED, consecrated, hallowed, sanctified, venerated, revered, divine, religious, blessed, dedicated.
– OPPOSITES sinful, irreligious, cursed.

homage ▶ noun RESPECT, honour, reverence, worship, admiration, esteem, adulation, acclaim; tribute, acknowledgement, recognition; accolade, panegyric, paean, salute.

■ **pay homage to** HONOUR, acclaim, applaud, salute, praise, commend, pay tribute to, take one's hat off to; *formal* laud.

home ▶ noun ❶ *they fled their homes* RESIDENCE, place of residence, house, flat, apartment, bungalow, cottage; accommodation, property, quarters, lodgings, rooms; a roof over one's head; address, place; *informal* pad, digs, semi; *formal* domicile, abode, dwelling (place), habitation. ❷ *I am far from my home* HOMELAND, native land, home town, birthplace, roots, fatherland, motherland, mother country, country of origin, the old country. ❸ *a home for the elderly* INSTITUTION, nursing home, retirement home, rest home, children's home; hospice, shelter, refuge, retreat, asylum, hostel. ❹ *the home of fine wines* DOMAIN, realm, origin, source, cradle, fount, fountainhead.

▶ **adjective** ❶ *the UK home market* DOMESTIC, internal, local, national, interior. ❷ *home produce* HOME-MADE, home-grown, local, family.
– OPPOSITES foreign, international.

■ **at home** ❶ *I was at home all day* IN, in one's house, present, available, indoors, inside, here. ❷ *she felt very much at home* AT EASE, comfortable, relaxed, content; in one's element. ❸ *he is at home with mathematics* CONFIDENT WITH, conversant with, proficient in; used to, familiar with, au fait with, au courant with, skilled in, experienced in, well versed in; *informal* well up on. ❹ *she was not at home to friends* ENTERTAINING, receiving; playing host to.

■ **bring something home to someone** MAKE SOMEONE REALIZE, make someone understand, make someone aware, make something clear to someone; drive home, press home, impress upon someone, draw attention to, focus attention on, underline, highlight, spotlight, emphasize, stress.

■ **hit home**. *See* HIT.

■ **home in on** FOCUS ON, concentrate on, zero in on, centre on, fix on; highlight, spotlight, underline, pinpoint; *informal* zoom in on.

■ **nothing to write home about** (informal) UNEXCEPTIONAL, mediocre, ordinary, commonplace, indifferent, average, middle-of-the-road, run-of-the-mill; tolerable, passable, adequate, fair; *informal* OK, so-so, bog-standard, (plain) vanilla, no great shakes, not so hot, not up to much; *Brit. informal* common or garden; *N. Amer. informal* ornery.

homeland ▶ **noun** NATIVE LAND, country of origin, home, fatherland, motherland, mother country, land of one's fathers, the old country.

homeless ▶ **adjective** *homeless people* OF NO FIXED ABODE, without a roof over one's head, on the streets, vagrant, sleeping rough; destitute, down and out.

▶ **noun** *charities for the homeless* PEOPLE OF NO FIXED ABODE, vagrants, down-and-outs, tramps, vagabonds, itinerants, transients, migrants, derelicts, drifters; *N. Amer.* hoboes; *Austral.* bagmen; *informal* bag ladies; *Brit. informal* dossers; *N. Amer. informal* bums.

homely ▶ **adjective** ❶ *a homely atmosphere* COSY, homelike, homey, comfortable, snug, welcoming, friendly, congenial, intimate, warm, hospitable, informal, relaxed, pleasant, cheerful; *informal* comfy. ❷ *homely pursuits* UNSOPHISTICATED, everyday, ordinary, domestic, simple, modest, unpretentious, unassuming; homespun, folksy. ❸ (*N. Amer.*) *she's rather homely* UNATTRACTIVE, plain, unprepossessing, unlovely, ill-favoured, ugly; *informal* not much to look at; *Brit. informal* no oil painting.
– OPPOSITES uncomfortable, formal, sophisticated, attractive.

homespun ▶ **adjective** UNSOPHISTICATED, plain, simple, unpolished, unrefined, rustic, folksy; coarse, rough, crude, rudimentary.
– OPPOSITES sophisticated.

homey ▶ **adjective** ❶ *the house is homey yet elegant* COSY, homelike, homely, comfortable, snug, welcoming, informal, relaxed, intimate, warm, pleasant, cheerful; *informal* comfy. ❷ *peasant life was simple and homey* UNSOPHISTICATED, homely, unrefined, unpretentious, plain, simple, modest.
– OPPOSITES uncomfortable, formal, sophisticated.

homicidal ▶ **adjective** MURDEROUS, violent, brutal, savage, ferocious, vicious, bloody, bloodthirsty, barbarous, barbaric; deadly, lethal, mortal, death-dealing; *poetic/literary* fell; *archaic* sanguinary.

homicide ▶ **noun** ❶ *he was charged with homicide* MURDER, killing, slaughter, butchery, massacre; assassination, execution, extermination; patricide, matricide, infanticide; *poetic/literary* slaying. ❷ (*dated*) *a convicted homicide* KILLER, assassin, serial killer, butcher, slaughterer; patricide, matricide, infanticide; *informal* hit man, hired gun; *dated* cut-throat; *poetic/literary* slayer.

homily ▶ **noun** SERMON, lecture, discourse, address, lesson, talk, speech, oration.

homogeneous ▶ **adjective** ❶ *a homogeneous group* UNIFORM, identical, unvaried, consistent, undistinguishable; alike, similar, (much) the same, all of a piece; *informal* much of a muchness. ❷ *we have to compete with homogeneous products* SIMILAR, comparable, equivalent, like, analogous, corresponding, parallel, matching, related; *formal* cognate.
– OPPOSITES different.

homogenize ▶ **verb** MAKE UNIFORM, make similar, unite, integrate, fuse, merge, blend, meld, coalesce, amalgamate, combine.
– OPPOSITES diversify.

homogenous ▶ **adjective**. *See* HOMOGENEOUS.

homologous ▶ **adjective** SIMILAR, comparable, equivalent, like, analogous, corresponding, correspondent, parallel, matching, related, congruent; *formal* cognate.
– OPPOSITES different.

homosexual ▶ **adjective** GAY, lesbian; *informal* queer, camp, pink, swinging the other way, homo, dykey; *Brit. informal* bent, poofy.
– OPPOSITES heterosexual.

▶ noun GAY, lesbian; *informal* queer, homo, queen, friend of Dorothy, pansy, nancy, dyke, les, lezzy, butch, femme; *Brit. informal* poof, ponce, woofter.
– OPPOSITES heterosexual.

hone ▶ verb SHARPEN, whet, strop, grind, file.
– OPPOSITES blunt.

honest ▶ adjective ❶ *an honest man* UPRIGHT, honourable, moral, ethical, principled, righteous, right-minded, respectable; virtuous, good, decent, law-abiding, high-minded, upstanding, incorruptible, truthful, trustworthy, trusty, reliable, conscientious, scrupulous, reputable; *informal* on the level. ❷ *I haven't been honest with you* TRUTHFUL, sincere, candid, frank, open, forthright, straight; straightforward, plain-speaking, matter-of-fact; *informal* upfront. ❸ *an honest mistake* GENUINE, real, authentic, actual, true, bona fide, legitimate, fair and square; *informal* legit, kosher, on the level, honest-to-goodness.
– OPPOSITES unscrupulous, insincere.

honestly ▶ adverb ❶ *he earned the money honestly* FAIRLY, lawfully, legally, legitimately, honourably, decently, ethically, in good faith, by the book; *informal* on the level. ❷ *we honestly believe this is for the best* SINCERELY, genuinely, truthfully, truly, wholeheartedly; really, actually, to be honest, to tell you the truth, to be frank, in all honesty, in all sincerity; *informal* Scouts' honour.

honesty ▶ noun ❶ *I can attest to his honesty* INTEGRITY, uprightness, honourableness, honour, morality, morals, ethics, (high) principles, righteousness, right-mindedness; virtue, goodness, probity, high-mindedness, fairness, incorruptibility, truthfulness, trustworthiness, reliability, dependability. ❷ *they spoke with honesty about their fears* SINCERITY, candour, frankness, directness, truthfulness, truth, openness, straightforwardness.

honeyed ▶ adjective SWEET, sugary, saccharine, pleasant, flattering, adulatory, unctuous; dulcet, soothing, soft, mellow, mellifluous.
– OPPOSITES harsh.

honorarium ▶ noun FEE, payment, consideration, allowance; remuneration, pay, expenses, compensation, recompense, reward; *formal* emolument.

honorary ▶ adjective ❶ *an honorary doctorate* TITULAR, nominal, in name only, unofficial, token. ❷ (*Brit.*) *an honorary treasurer* UNPAID, unsalaried, voluntary, volunteer; *N. Amer.* pro bono (publico).

honour ▶ noun ❶ *a man of honour* INTEGRITY, honesty, uprightness, ethics, morals, morality, (high) principles, righteousness, high-mindedness; virtue, goodness, decency, probity, scrupulousness, worth, fairness, justness, trustworthiness, reliability, dependability. ❷ *a mark of honour* DISTINCTION, privilege, glory, kudos, cachet, prestige, merit, credit; importance, illustriousness, notability; respect, esteem, approbation. ❸ *our honour is at stake* REPUTATION, (good) name, character, repute, image, kudos, standing, stature, status. ❹ *he was welcomed with honour* ACCLAIM, acclamation, applause, accolades, tributes, compliments, salutes, bouquets; homage, praise, glory, reverence, adulation, exaltation. ❺ *she had the honour of meeting the Queen* PRIVILEGE, pleasure, pride, joy; compliment, favour. ❻ *military honours* ACCOLADE, award, reward, prize, decoration, distinction, medal, ribbon, star, laurel; *Military, informal* fruit salad; *Brit. informal* gong. ❼ (*dated*) *she died defending her honour* CHASTITY, virginity, maidenhead, purity, innocence, modesty; *informal* cherry; *archaic* virtue, maidenhood.
– OPPOSITES unscrupulousness, shame.

▶ verb ❶ *we should honour our parents* ESTEEM, respect, admire, defer to, look up to; appreciate, value, cherish; reverence, revere, venerate, worship; *informal* put on a pedestal. ❷ *they were honoured at a special ceremony* APPLAUD, acclaim, praise, salute, recognize, celebrate, commemorate, commend, hail, lionize, exalt, eulogize, pay homage to, pay tribute to, sing the praises of; *formal* laud. ❸ *he honoured the contract* FULFIL, observe, keep, obey, heed, follow, carry out, discharge, implement, execute, effect; keep to, abide by, adhere to, comply with, conform to, be true to, live up to. ❹ *the cheque was not honoured* ACCEPT, take, clear, pass, cash; *Brit.* encash.
– OPPOSITES disgrace, criticize, disobey.

honourable ▶ adjective ❶ *an honourable man* HONEST, moral, ethical, principled, righteous, right-minded; decent, respectable, virtuous, good, upstanding, upright, worthy, noble, fair, just, truthful, trustworthy, trusty, law-abiding, reliable, reputable, dependable. ❷ *an honourable career* ILLUSTRIOUS, distinguished, eminent, great, glorious, prestigious, noble, creditable.
– OPPOSITES crooked, deplorable.

hoodlum ▶ noun HOOLIGAN, thug, lout, delinquent, tearaway, vandal, ruffian; gangster, mobster, criminal, Mafioso; *Austral.* larrikin; *informal* tough, bruiser, roughneck, heavy, hit man; *Brit. informal* yob, yobbo, bovver boy, lager lout; *N. Amer. informal* hood.

hoodoo ▶ noun WITCHCRAFT, magic, black magic, sorcery, wizardry, devilry, voodoo, necromancy; *N. Amer.* mojo.

hoodwink ▶ verb DECEIVE, trick, dupe, outwit, fool, delude, cheat, take in, hoax, mislead, lead on, defraud, double-cross, swindle, gull; *informal* con, bamboozle, do, have, sting, gyp, diddle, shaft, rip off, lead up the garden path, pull a fast one on, put one over on, take for a ride, pull the wool over someone's eyes; *N. Amer. informal* sucker, snooker;

Austral. informal pull a swifty on; *poetic/literary* cozen.

hoof ▶ **noun** trotter, foot; *Zoology* ungula.

hook ▶ **noun** ❶ *she hung her jacket on the hook* PEG. ❷ *the dress has six hooks* FASTENER, fastening, catch, clasp, hasp, clip, pin. ❸ *I had a fish on the end of my hook* FISH-HOOK, barb, snare. ❹ *a right hook to the chin* PUNCH, blow, hit, cuff, thump, smack; *Scottish & N. English* skelp; *informal* belt, bop, biff, sock, clout, whack, wallop, slug; *N. Amer. informal* boff.

▶ **verb** ❶ *they hooked baskets onto the ladder* ATTACH, hitch, fasten, fix, secure, clasp. ❷ *he hooked his thumbs in his belt* CURL, bend, crook, loop, curve. ❸ *he hooked a 24 lb pike* CATCH, land, net, take, bag, snare, trap.

■ **by hook or by crook** BY ANY MEANS, somehow (or other), no matter how, in one way or another, by fair means or foul.

■ **hook, line, and sinker** COMPLETELY, totally, utterly, entirely, wholly, absolutely, through and through, one hundred per cent, {lock, stock, and barrel}.

■ **off the hook** (*informal*) OUT OF TROUBLE, in the clear, free; acquitted, cleared, reprieved, exonerated, absolved; *informal* let off.

hooked ▶ **adjective** ❶ *a hooked nose* CURVED, hook-shaped, hook-like, aquiline, angular, bent; *Biology* falcate, falciform, uncinate. ❷ (*informal*) *they are hooked on cocaine* ADDICTED TO, dependent on; *informal* using; *N. Amer. informal* have a jones for. ❸ (*informal*) *he is hooked on crosswords* KEEN ON, enthusiastic about, addicted to, obsessed with, fixated on, fanatical about; *informal* mad about, crazy about, wild about, nuts about; *Brit. informal* potty about.

– OPPOSITES straight.

hooligan ▶ **noun** HOODLUM, thug, lout, delinquent, tearaway, vandal, ruffian, troublemaker; *Austral.* larrikin; *informal* tough, rough, bruiser, roughneck; *Brit. informal* yob, yobbo, bovver boy, lager lout; *Scottish informal* ned.

hoop ▶ **noun** RING, band, circle, circlet, loop; *technical* annulus.

hoot ▶ **noun** ❶ *the hoot of an owl* SCREECH, shriek, call, cry; tu-whit tu-whoo. ❷ *the hoot of a horn* BEEP, honk, toot, blast, blare. ❸ *hoots of derision* SHOUT, yell, cry, howl, shriek, whoop, whistle; boo, hiss, jeer, catcall. ❹ (*informal*) *your mum's a real hoot* AMUSING PERSON, character, clown; *informal* scream, laugh, card, case, one, riot, giggle, barrel of laughs; *informal, dated* caution.

▶ **verb** ❶ *an owl hooted* SCREECH, shriek, cry, call; tu-whit tu-whoo. ❷ *a car horn hooted* BEEP, honk, toot, blare, blast, sound. ❸ *they hooted in disgust* SHOUT, yell, cry, howl, shriek, whistle; boo, hiss, jeer, catcall.

■ **give a hoot** (*informal*) CARE, be concerned, mind, be interested, be bothered, get worked up; *informal* give a damn, give a rap, give a monkey's.

hop ▶ **verb** ❶ *he hopped along the road* JUMP, bound, spring, bounce, skip, jig, leap; prance, dance, frolic, gambol. ❷ (*informal*) *she hopped over the Atlantic* GO, dash; travel; *informal* pop, whip; *Brit. informal* nip.

▶ **noun** ❶ *the rabbit had a hop around* JUMP, bound, bounce, prance, leap, spring, gambol. ❷ (*informal*) *a short hop by taxi* JOURNEY, distance, ride, drive, run, trip; flight. ❸ (*informal*) *come to the hop on Saturday* DANCE, social, party, disco; *informal* bash, bop, shindig, do; *Brit. informal* rave-up, knees-up.

■ **on the hop** (*Brit. informal*) ❶ *he was caught on the hop* UNPREPARED, unready, off guard, unawares, by surprise, with one's defences down; *informal* napping; *Brit. informal* with one's trousers down. ❷ *we were always kept on the hop* BUSY, occupied, employed, working, at work, on the job; rushed off one's feet; *informal* on the go.

hope ▶ **noun** ❶ *I had high hopes* ASPIRATION, desire, wish, expectation, ambition, aim, plan; dream, daydream, pipe dream. ❷ *a life filled with hope* HOPEFULNESS, optimism, expectation, expectancy; confidence, faith, trust, belief, conviction, assurance; promise.

– OPPOSITES pessimism.

▶ **verb** ❶ *he's hoping for a medal* EXPECT, anticipate, look for, be hopeful of, pin one's hopes on, want; wish for, dream of. ❷ *we're hoping to address the issue* AIM, intend, be looking, have the intention, have in mind, plan, aspire.

hopeful ▶ **adjective** ❶ *he remained hopeful* OPTIMISTIC, full of hope, confident, positive, buoyant, sanguine, bullish, cheerful; *informal* upbeat. ❷ *hopeful signs* PROMISING, encouraging, heartening, reassuring, auspicious, favourable, optimistic, propitious, bright, rosy.

hopefully ▶ **adverb** ❶ *he rode on hopefully* OPTIMISTICALLY, full of hope, confidently, buoyantly, sanguinely; expectantly. ❷ *hopefully it should finish soon* ALL BEING WELL, if all goes well, God willing, with luck; most likely, probably; conceivably, feasibly; *informal* touch wood, fingers crossed.

hopeless ▶ **adjective** ❶ *her hopeless appeal* DESPAIRING, desperate, wretched, forlorn, pessimistic, defeatist, resigned; dejected, downhearted, despondent, demoralized. ❷ *a hopeless case* IRREMEDIABLE, beyond hope, lost, beyond repair, irreparable, irreversible; past cure, incurable; impossible, no-win, futile, forlorn, unworkable, impracticable; *archaic* bootless. ❸ *Joseph was hopeless at maths* BAD, poor, awful, terrible, dreadful, appalling, atrocious; inferior, incompetent, unskilled; *informal* pathetic, useless, lousy, rotten; *Brit. informal* duff, rubbish.

hopelessly ▶ **adverb** ❶ *she began to cry hopelessly* DESPAIRINGLY, in despair, in distress, desperately; dejectedly, downheartedly, despondently, wretchedly, miserably, forlornly. ❷ *she was hopelessly lost* UTTERLY, completely, irretrievably, impossibly; extremely, very, desperately, totally, dreadfully; *informal* terribly.

horde ▶ **noun** CROWD, mob, pack, gang, troop, army, swarm, mass; throng, multitude, host, band, flock; *informal* crew, tribe, load.

horizon ▶ **noun** ❶ *the sun rose above the horizon* SKYLINE. ❷ *she wanted to broaden her horizons* OUTLOOK, perspective, perception; range of experience, scope, ambit, orbit.
■ **on the horizon** IMMINENT, impending, close, near, approaching, coming, forthcoming, in prospect, at hand, on the way, about to happen, upon us, in the offing, in the pipeline, in the air, just around the corner; brewing, looming, threatening, menacing; *informal* on the cards.

horizontal ▶ **adjective** ❶ *a horizontal surface* level, flat, plane, smooth, even; straight, parallel. ❷ *she was stretched horizontal on a sunbed* FLAT, supine, prone, prostrate.
– OPPOSITES vertical.

horny ▶ **adjective** (*informal*) (SEXUALLY) AROUSED, excited, stimulated, titillated, inflamed; *informal* turned on, hot, sexed up; *Brit. informal* randy.

horrendous ▶ **adjective.** *See* HORRIBLE sense 1.

horrible ▶ **adjective** ❶ *a horrible murder* DREADFUL, awful, terrible, shocking, appalling, horrifying, horrific, horrendous, grisly, ghastly, gruesome, harrowing, heinous, vile, unspeakable; nightmarish, macabre, spine-chilling; loathsome, monstrous, abhorrent, hateful, execrable, abominable, atrocious, sickening. ❷ (*informal*) *a horrible little man* NASTY, horrid, disagreeable, unpleasant, awful, dreadful, terrible, appalling, foul, repulsive, repellent, ghastly; obnoxious, hateful, odious, objectionable, insufferable, vile, loathsome, abhorrent; *informal* frightful, God-awful; *Brit. informal* beastly.
– OPPOSITES pleasant, agreeable.

horrid ▶ **adjective** ❶ *horrid apparitions. See* HORRIBLE sense 1. ❷ (*informal*) *the teachers were horrid. See* HORRIBLE sense 2.

horrific ▶ **adjective** DREADFUL, horrendous, horrible, frightful, awful, terrible, atrocious; horrifying, shocking, appalling, harrowing, gruesome; hideous, grisly, ghastly, unspeakable, monstrous, nightmarish, sickening.

horrify ▶ **verb** ❶ *she horrified us with ghastly tales* FRIGHTEN, scare, terrify, petrify, alarm, panic, terrorize, fill with fear, scare someone out of their wits, frighten the living daylights out of, make someone's hair stand on end, make someone's blood run cold; *informal* scare the pants off; *Brit. informal* put the wind up; *N. Amer. informal* spook; *archaic* affright. ❷ *he was horrified by her remarks* SHOCK, appal, outrage, scandalize, offend; disgust, revolt, nauseate, sicken.

horror ▶ **noun** ❶ *children screamed in horror* TERROR, fear, fright, alarm, panic; dread, trepidation. ❷ *to her horror she found herself alone* DISMAY, consternation, perturbation, alarm, distress; disgust, outrage, shock. ❸ *the horror of the tragedy* AWFULNESS, frightfulness, savagery, barbarity, hideousness; atrocity, outrage. ❹ (*informal*) *he's a little horror* RASCAL, devil, imp, monkey; *informal* terror, scamp, scallywag, tyke; *Brit. informal* perisher; *N. Amer. informal* varmint.
– OPPOSITES delight, satisfaction.
■ **have a horror of** HATE, detest, loathe, abhor; *formal* abominate.

horror-struck, horror-stricken ▶ **adjective** HORRIFIED, terrified, petrified, frightened, afraid, fearful, scared, panic-stricken, scared/frightened to death, scared witless; *informal* scared stiff.

horse ▶ **noun** MOUNT, charger, cob, nag, hack; pony, foal, yearling, colt, stallion, gelding, mare, filly; *N. Amer.* bronco; *Austral./NZ* moke, yarraman; *informal* gee-gee; *archaic* steed.
– RELATED TERMS equine.
■ **horse around/about** (*informal*) FOOL AROUND/ABOUT, play the fool, act the clown, clown about/around, monkey about/around; *informal* mess about/around, lark about/around; *Brit. informal* muck about/around; *dated* play the giddy goat.

horseman, horsewoman ▶ **noun** RIDER, equestrian, jockey; cavalryman, trooper; *historical* hussar, dragoon; *archaic* cavalier.

horseplay ▶ **noun** TOMFOOLERY, fooling around, foolish behaviour, clowning, buffoonery; pranks, antics, high jinks; *informal* shenanigans, monkey business; *Brit. informal* monkey tricks.

horse sense ▶ **noun** (*informal*). *See* COMMON SENSE.

horticulture ▶ **noun** GARDENING, floriculture, arboriculture, agriculture, cultivation.

hosanna ▶ **noun** SHOUT OF PRAISE, alleluia, hurrah, hurray, cheer, paean; *formal* laudation.

hose ▶ **noun** ❶ *a garden hose* PIPE, piping, tube, tubing, duct, outlet, pipeline, siphon. ❷ *her hose had laddered. See* HOSIERY.

hosiery ▶ **noun** STOCKINGS, tights, stay-ups, nylons, hose; socks; *N. Amer.* pantyhose.

hospitable ▶ **adjective** WELCOMING, friendly, congenial, genial, sociable, convivial, cordial; gracious, well disposed, amenable, helpful, obliging, accommodating, neighbourly, warm, kind, generous, bountiful.

hospital ▶ **noun** INFIRMARY, sanatorium, hospice, medical centre, health centre, clinic; *Brit.* cottage hospital; *Military* field hospital.

hospitality ▶ **noun** ❶ *he is renowned for his hospitality* FRIENDLINESS, hospitableness, warm reception, helpfulness, neighbourliness, warmth, kindness, congeniality, geniality, cordiality, amenability, generosity. ❷ *corporate hospitality* entertainment; catering, food.

host[1] ▶ noun ❶ *the host greeted the guests* PARTY-GIVER, hostess, entertainer. ❷ *the host of a TV series* PRESENTER, compère, anchor, anchorman, anchorwoman, announcer.
– OPPOSITES guest.
▶ verb ❶ *the Queen hosted a dinner* GIVE, have, hold, throw, put on, provide, arrange, organize. ❷ *the show is hosted by Angus* PRESENT, introduce, compère, front, anchor.

host[2] ▶ noun ❶ *a host of memories* MULTITUDE, lot, abundance, wealth, profusion; *informal* load, heap, mass, pile, ton; *Brit. informal* shedload; *poetic/literary* myriad. ❷ *a host of film stars* CROWD, throng, flock, herd, swarm, horde, mob, army, legion; assemblage, gathering.

hostage ▶ noun CAPTIVE, prisoner, detainee, internee.

hostel ▶ noun CHEAP HOTEL, YMCA, YWCA, bed and breakfast, B&B, boarding house, guest house, pension.

hostile ▶ adjective ❶ *a hostile attack* UNFRIENDLY, unkind, bitter, unsympathetic, malicious, vicious, rancorous, venomous; antagonistic, aggressive, confrontational, belligerent, truculent. ❷ *hostile climatic conditions* UNFAVOURABLE, adverse, bad, harsh, grim, hard, tough, inhospitable, forbidding. ❸ *they are hostile to the idea* OPPOSED, averse, antagonistic, ill-disposed, unsympathetic, antipathetic; opposing, against; *informal* anti, down on.
– OPPOSITES friendly, favourable.

hostility ▶ noun ❶ *he glared at her with hostility* ANTAGONISM, unfriendliness, malevolence, malice, unkindness, rancour, venom, hatred; aggression, belligerence. ❷ *their hostility to the present regime* OPPOSITION, antagonism, animosity, antipathy, ill will, ill feeling, resentment, aversion, enmity. ❸ *a cessation of hostilities* FIGHTING, (armed) conflict, combat, warfare, war, bloodshed, violence.

hot ▶ adjective ❶ *hot food* HEATED, piping (hot), sizzling, steaming, roasting, boiling (hot), searing, scorching, scalding, red-hot. ❷ *a hot day* VERY WARM, balmy, summery, tropical, scorching, searing, blistering; sweltering, torrid, sultry, humid, muggy, close; *informal* boiling, baking, roasting. ❸ *she felt very hot* FEVERISH, fevered, febrile; burning, flushed. ❹ *a hot chilli* SPICY, spiced, highly seasoned, peppery, fiery, strong; piquant, pungent, aromatic. ❺ *the competition was too hot* FIERCE, intense, keen, competitive, cut-throat, dog-eat-dog, ruthless, aggressive, strong. ❻ (*informal*) *the hottest story in Fleet Street* NEW, fresh, recent, late, up to date, up to the minute; just out, hot off the press. ❼ (*informal*) *this band is hot* POPULAR, in demand, sought-after, in favour; fashionable, in vogue, all the rage; *informal* big, in, now, hip, trendy, cool. ❽ (*informal*) *she is hot on local history* KNOWLEDGEABLE ABOUT, well informed about, au fait with, up on, well versed in, au courant with; *informal* clued up about, genned up about. ❾ (*informal*) *hot goods* STOLEN, illegally obtained, illegal, illicit, unlawful; smuggled, bootleg, contraband; *Brit. informal* dodgy.
– OPPOSITES cold, chilly, mild, dispassionate, weak, old, lawful.
■ **blow hot and cold** VACILLATE, dither, shilly-shally, waver, be indecisive, change one's mind, be undecided, be uncertain, be unsure; *Brit.* haver, hum and haw; *Scottish* swither.
■ **hot on the heels of** CLOSE BEHIND, directly after, right after, straight after, hard on the heels of, following closely.
■ **hot under the collar** (*informal*). *See* ANGRY sense 1.
■ **make it/things hot for someone** (*informal*) HARASS, hound, plague, badger, harry; bully, intimidate, pick on, persecute, victimize, terrorize; *N. Amer.* devil; *informal* hassle, give someone a hard time, get on someone's back.

hot air ▶ noun (*informal*) NONSENSE, rubbish, garbage, empty talk, wind, blather, claptrap, drivel, balderdash, gibberish; pomposity, bombast; *informal* guff, bosh, hogwash, poppycock, bilge, twaddle; *Brit. informal* cobblers, codswallop, tosh; *N. Amer. informal* flapdoodle.

hotbed ▶ noun *a hotbed of crime* BREEDING GROUND, den, cradle, nest.

hot-blooded ▶ adjective PASSIONATE, amorous, amatory, ardent, lustful, libidinous, lecherous, sexy; *informal* horny, randy.
– OPPOSITES cold.

hotchpotch ▶ noun MIXTURE, mix, mixed bag, assortment, random collection, jumble, ragbag, miscellany, medley, pot-pourri; melange, mishmash, confusion, farrago, gallimaufry; *N. Amer.* hodgepodge.

hotel ▶ noun INN, motel, boarding house, guest house, bed and breakfast, B&B, hostel; pension, auberge.

hotfoot ▶ adverb HASTILY, hurriedly, speedily, quickly, fast, rapidly, swiftly, without delay; at top speed, at full tilt, headlong, post-haste, pell-mell, helter-skelter; *informal* like the wind, like greased lightning, like blazes; *Brit. informal* like the clappers, like billy-o; *N. Amer. informal* lickety-split.
– OPPOSITES slowly.
■ **hotfoot it** (*informal*) HURRY, dash, run, race, sprint, bolt, dart, career, charge, shoot, hurtle, hare, fly, speed, zoom, streak; *informal* tear, belt, pelt, scoot, clip, leg it, go like a bat out of hell; *Brit. informal* bomb; *N. Amer. informal* hightail it.

hot-headed ▶ adjective IMPETUOUS, impulsive, headstrong, reckless, rash, irresponsible, foolhardy, madcap; excitable, volatile, fiery, hot-tempered, quick-tempered, unruly, harum-scarum.

hothouse ▶ noun GREENHOUSE, glasshouse, conservatory, orangery, vinery, winter garden.
▶ adjective *the school has a hothouse atmosphere*

INTENSE, oppressive, stifling; overprotected, pampered, shielded.

hotly ▶ **adverb** ❶ *the rumours were hotly denied* VEHEMENTLY, vigorously, strenuously, fiercely, passionately, heatedly; angrily, indignantly. ❷ *he was hotly pursued by Boris* CLOSELY, swiftly, quickly, hotfoot; eagerly, enthusiastically.
– OPPOSITES calmly.

hot-tempered ▶ **adjective** IRASCIBLE, quick-tempered, short-tempered, irritable, fiery, bad-tempered; touchy, volatile, testy, tetchy, fractious, prickly, peppery; *informal* snappish, snappy, chippy, on a short fuse; *Brit. informal* narky, ratty, like a bear with a sore head; *N. Amer. informal* soreheaded.
– OPPOSITES easy-going.

hound ▶ **noun** ❶ (HUNTING) DOG, canine, mongrel, cur; *informal* doggy, pooch, mutt; *Austral./NZ informal* mong, bitzer. ❷ (*informal, dated*) *you monstrous hound! See* SCOUNDREL.
▶ **verb** ❶ *she was hounded by the press* PURSUE, chase, follow, shadow, be hot on someone's heels, hunt (down), stalk, track, trail; harass, persecute, harry, pester, bother, badger, torment, bedevil; *informal* hassle, bug, give someone a hard time; *N. Amer. informal* devil. ❷ *they hounded him out of office* FORCE, drive, pressure, pressurize, push, urge, coerce, impel, dragoon, strong-arm; nag, bully, browbeat, chivvy; *informal* bulldoze, railroad; *Brit. informal* bounce; *N. Amer. informal* hustle.

house ▶ **noun** ❶ *an estate of 200 houses* RESIDENCE, home, place of residence; homestead; a roof over one's head; *formal* habitation, dwelling (place), abode, domicile. ❷ *you'll wake the whole house!* HOUSEHOLD, family, clan, tribe; *informal* brood. ❸ *the house of Stewart* FAMILY, clan, tribe; dynasty, line, bloodline, lineage, ancestry, family tree. ❹ *a printing house* FIRM, business, company, corporation, enterprise, establishment, institution, concern, organization, operation; *informal* outfit, set-up. ❺ *the country's upper house* LEGISLATIVE ASSEMBLY, legislative body, chamber, council, parliament, congress, senate, diet. ❻ *the house applauded* AUDIENCE, crowd, spectators, viewers; congregation; gallery, stalls; *Brit. informal* punters.
▶ **verb** ❶ *they can house twelve employees* ACCOMMODATE, provide accommodation for, give someone a roof over their head, lodge, quarter, board, billet, take in, sleep, put up; harbour, shelter. ❷ *this panel houses the main switch* CONTAIN, hold, store; cover, protect, enclose.
■ **on the house** (*informal*) FREE (OF CHARGE), without charge, at no cost, for nothing, gratis; courtesy, complimentary; *informal* for free; *N. Amer. informal* comp.

household ▶ **noun** *the household was asleep* FAMILY, house, occupants; clan, tribe; *informal* brood.
▶ **adjective** *household goods* DOMESTIC, family; everyday, workaday.

householder ▶ **noun** HOMEOWNER, owner, occupant, resident; tenant, leaseholder; proprietor, landlady, landlord, freeholder; *Brit.* occupier, owner-occupier.

housekeeping ▶ **noun** HOUSEHOLD MANAGEMENT, domestic work, home-making, housewifery; home economics; *Brit.* housecraft.

houseman ▶ **noun** (*Brit.*) JUNIOR DOCTOR, house doctor, newly qualified doctor; *Brit.* house officer; *N. Amer.* intern, resident.

house-trained ▶ **adjective** (*Brit.*) DOMESTICATED, trained; *N. Amer.* housebroken.

housing ▶ **noun** ❶ *they invested in housing* HOUSES, homes, residences, buildings; accommodation, living quarters; *formal* dwellings, dwelling places, habitations. ❷ *the housing for the antennae* CASING, covering, case, cover, holder, sheath, jacket, shell, capsule.

hovel ▶ **noun** SHACK, slum, shanty, hut; *informal* dump, hole.

hover ▶ **verb** ❶ *helicopters hovered overhead* BE SUSPENDED, be poised, hang, levitate; fly. ❷ *she hovered anxiously nearby* LINGER, loiter, wait about; *informal* hang around, stick around; *Brit. informal* hang about.

however ▶ **adverb** ❶ *however, gaining weight is not inevitable* NEVERTHELESS, nonetheless, but, still, yet, though, although, even so, for all that, despite that, in spite of that; anyway, anyhow, be that as it may, having said that, notwithstanding; *informal* still and all. ❷ *however you look at it* IN WHATEVER WAY, regardless of how, no matter how.

howl ▶ **noun** ❶ *the howl of a wolf* BAYING, howling, bay, cry, yowl, bark, yelp. ❷ *a howl of anguish* WAIL, cry, yell, yelp, yowl; bellow, roar, shout, shriek, scream, screech.
▶ **verb** ❶ *dogs howled in the distance* BAY, cry, yowl, bark, yelp. ❷ *a baby started to howl* WAIL, cry, yell, yowl, bawl, bellow, shriek, scream, screech, caterwaul; *informal* holler. ❸ *we howled with laughter* LAUGH, guffaw, roar; be creased up, be doubled up, split one's sides; *informal* fall about, crack up, be in stitches, be rolling in the aisles.

howler ▶ **noun** (*informal*) MISTAKE, error, blunder, fault, gaffe, slip; *informal* slip-up, boo-boo, botch, clanger; *Brit. informal* boob; *N. Amer. informal* blooper.

hub ▶ **noun** ❶ *the hub of the wheel* PIVOT, axis, fulcrum, centre, middle. ❷ *the hub of family life* CENTRE, core, heart, focus, focal point, nucleus, kernel, nerve centre.
– OPPOSITES periphery.

hubbub ▶ **noun** ❶ *her voice was lost in the hubbub* NOISE, din, racket, commotion, clamour, cacophony, babel, rumpus; *Brit. informal* row. ❷ *she fought through the hubbub* CONFUSION, chaos, pandemonium, bedlam, mayhem, disorder, turmoil, tumult, fracas, hurly-burly.

hubris ▶ noun ARROGANCE, conceit, haughtiness, hauteur, pride, self-importance, pomposity, superciliousness, superiority; *informal* bigheadedness.
– OPPOSITES humility.

huckster ▶ noun TRADER, dealer, seller, purveyor, vendor, salesman, pedlar, hawker; *informal* pusher.

huddle ▶ verb ❶ *they huddled together* CROWD, cluster, gather, bunch, throng, flock, herd, collect, group, congregate; press, pack, squeeze. ❷ *he huddled beneath the sheets* CURL UP, snuggle, nestle, hunch up.
– OPPOSITES disperse.
▶ noun ❶ *a huddle of passengers* CROWD, cluster, bunch, knot, group, throng, flock, press, pack; collection, assemblage; *informal* gaggle. ❷ *the team went into a huddle* CONSULTATION, discussion, debate, talk, parley, meeting, conference; *informal* confab, powwow.

hue ▶ noun ❶ *paints in a variety of hues* COLOUR, shade, tone, tint. ❷ *men of all political hues* COMPLEXION, type, kind, sort, cast, stamp, character, nature.

hue and cry ▶ noun COMMOTION, outcry, uproar, fuss, clamour, storm, stir, furore, ruckus, brouhaha, palaver, rumpus; *informal* hoo-ha, hullabaloo, ballyhoo, kerfuffle, to-do, song and dance; *Brit. informal* row, stink.

huff ▶ noun BAD MOOD, sulk, fit of pique, pet; temper, tantrum, rage; *informal* grump; *Brit. informal* strop, paddy; *N. Amer. informal* snit; *Brit. informal, dated* bate, wax.

huffy ▶ adjective IRRITABLE, irritated, annoyed, cross, grumpy, bad-tempered, crotchety, crabby, cantankerous, moody, petulant, sullen, surly; touchy, testy, tetchy, snappish; *informal* snappy, cranky; *Brit. informal* narky, miffed, ratty, eggy, shirty, like a bear with a sore head; *N. Amer. informal* soreheaded.

hug ▶ verb ❶ *they hugged each other* EMBRACE, cuddle, squeeze, clasp, clutch, cling to, hold close, hold tight, take someone in one's arms, clasp someone to one's bosom; *poetic/literary* embosom. ❷ *our route hugged the coastline* FOLLOW CLOSELY, keep close to, stay near to, follow the course of. ❸ *we hugged the comforting thought* CLING TO, hold on to, cherish, harbour, nurse, foster, retain, keep in mind.
▶ noun *there were hugs as we left* EMBRACE, cuddle, squeeze, bear hug, clinch.

huge ▶ adjective ENORMOUS, vast, immense, large, big, great, massive, colossal, prodigious, gigantic, gargantuan, mammoth, monumental; giant, towering, elephantine, mountainous, titanic; epic, Herculean, Brobdingnagian; *informal* jumbo, mega, monster, whopping, humongous, hulking, bumper, astronomical; *Brit. informal* ginormous.
– OPPOSITES tiny.

hugely ▶ adverb VERY, extremely, exceedingly, most, really, particularly, tremendously, greatly, decidedly, exceptionally, immensely, inordinately, extraordinarily, vastly; very much, to a great extent; *N. English* right; *informal* terrifically, awfully, terribly, majorly, seriously, mega, ultra, oh-so, damn, damned; *Brit. informal* ever so, well, dead, jolly; *N. Amer. informal* real, mighty, awful; *informal, dated* devilish, frightfully; *archaic* exceeding.

hugger-mugger ▶ adjective ❶ *at home, all was hugger-mugger* DISORDERLY, confused, disorganized, chaotic, muddled, haphazard, in a mess, in disarray, topsy-turvy; *informal* higgledy-piggledy; *Brit. informal* shambolic. ❷ *hugger-mugger dealings* CLANDESTINE, secret, covert, furtive, cloak-and-dagger, hole-and-corner, sneaky, sly, underhand; undercover, underground; *informal* hush-hush.
– OPPOSITES orderly, overt.

hulk ▶ noun ❶ *the rusting hulks of ships* WRECK, shipwreck, ruin, derelict; shell, skeleton, hull. ❷ *a great hulk of a man* GIANT, lump; oaf; *informal* clodhopper, ape, gorilla; *N. Amer. informal* lummox.

hulking ▶ adjective (*informal*) LARGE, big, heavy, sturdy, burly, brawny, hefty, strapping; bulky, weighty, massive, ponderous; clumsy, awkward, ungainly, lumbering, lumpish, oafish; *informal* hunky, beefy, clodhopping.
– OPPOSITES small.

hull[1] ▶ noun *the ship's hull* FRAMEWORK, body, shell, frame, skeleton, structure.

hull[2] ▶ noun *seed hulls* SHELL, husk, pod, case, covering, integument, shuck; *Botany* pericarp, legume.
▶ verb *the bird uses its beak to hull seeds* SHELL, husk, peel, pare, skin, shuck; *technical* decorticate.

hullabaloo ▶ noun (*informal*) FUSS, commotion, hue and cry, uproar, outcry, clamour, storm, furore, hubbub, ruckus, brouhaha; pandemonium, mayhem, tumult, turmoil, hurly-burly; *informal* hoo-ha, to-do, kerfuffle, song and dance; *Brit. informal* carry-on, row, stink.

hum ▶ verb ❶ *the engine was humming* PURR, drone, murmur, buzz, thrum, whirr, throb, vibrate; *poetic/literary* bombinate. ❷ *she hummed a tune* sing, croon, murmur, drone. ❸ *the workshops are humming* BE BUSY, be active, be lively, buzz, bustle, be a hive of activity, throb. ❹ (*Brit. informal*) *this stuff really hums.* See REEK verb.
▶ noun *a low hum of conversation* MURMUR, drone, purr, buzz; *poetic/literary* bombination.
■ **hum and haw** (*Brit.*) HESITATE, dither, vacillate, be indecisive, equivocate, prevaricate, waver, blow hot and cold; *Brit.* haver; *Scottish* swither; *informal* shilly-shally.

human ▶ adjective ❶ *the human race* anthropoid. ❷ *they're only human* MORTAL, flesh and blood; fallible, weak, frail, imperfect, vulnerable, susceptible, erring, error-prone; phys-

ical, bodily, fleshly. ❸ *the human side of politics* COMPASSIONATE, humane, kind, considerate, understanding, sympathetic, tolerant; approachable, accessible.
–OPPOSITES infallible.
▶ **noun** *the link between humans and animals* PERSON, human being, personage, mortal, member of the human race; man, woman; individual, (living) soul, being; Homo sapiens; earthling.

humane ▶ **adjective** COMPASSIONATE, kind, considerate, understanding, sympathetic, tolerant; lenient, forbearing, forgiving, merciful, mild, tender, clement, benign, humanitarian, benevolent, charitable.
–OPPOSITES cruel.

humanitarian ▶ **adjective** ❶ *a humanitarian act* COMPASSIONATE, humane; unselfish, altruistic, generous, magnanimous, benevolent, merciful, kind, sympathetic. ❷ *a humanitarian organization* CHARITABLE, philanthropic, public-spirited, socially concerned, welfare.
–OPPOSITES selfish.
▶ **noun** PHILANTHROPIST, altruist, benefactor, social reformer, good Samaritan; do-gooder; *archaic* philanthrope.

humanities ▶ **plural noun** (LIBERAL) ARTS, literature; classics, classical studies, classical literature.

humanity ▶ **noun** ❶ *humanity evolved from the apes* HUMANKIND, mankind, man, people, the human race; Homo sapiens. ❷ *the humanity of Christ* HUMAN NATURE, humanness, mortality. ❸ *he praised them for their humanity* COMPASSION, brotherly love, fellow feeling, humaneness, kindness, consideration, understanding, sympathy, tolerance; leniency, mercy, mercifulness, pity, tenderness; benevolence, charity.

humanize ▶ **verb** CIVILIZE, improve, better; educate, enlighten, instruct; sophisticate, socialize, refine, polish; *formal* edify.

humankind ▶ **noun** THE HUMAN RACE, the human species, humanity, human beings, mankind, man, people, mortals; Homo sapiens.

humble ▶ **adjective** ❶ *her bearing was humble* MEEK, deferential, respectful, submissive, self-effacing, unassertive; unpresuming, modest, unassuming, self-deprecating; *Scottish* mim. ❷ *a humble background* LOWLY, working-class, lower-class, poor, undistinguished, mean, ignoble, low-born; common, ordinary, simple, inferior, unremarkable, insignificant, inconsequential; *informal* plebby. ❸ *my humble abode* MODEST, plain, simple, ordinary, unostentatious, unpretentious.
–OPPOSITES proud, noble, grand.
▶ **verb** ❶ *he humbled himself to ask for help* HUMILIATE, abase, demean, lower, degrade, debase; mortify, shame, eat humble pie; take someone down a peg or two; *informal* cut down to size, settle someone's hash; *N. Amer. informal* make someone eat crow. ❷ *Wales were humbled by Romania* DEFEAT, beat, trounce, rout, overwhelm, get the better of, bring to one's knees; *informal* lick, clobber, slaughter, massacre, crucify, walk all over; *N. Amer. informal* shellac, cream.

humbug ▶ **noun** ❶ *that is sheer humbug* HYPOCRISY, hypocritical talk, sanctimoniousness, posturing, cant, empty talk; insincerity, dishonesty, falseness, deceit, deception, fraud. ❷ *you see what a humbug I am?* HYPOCRITE, fraud, fake, plaster saint; charlatan, cheat, deceiver, dissembler; *informal* phoney; *poetic/literary* whited sepulchre.
▶ **verb** *Dave is easily humbugged* DECEIVE, trick, delude, mislead, fool, hoodwink, dupe, take in, beguile, bamboozle, gull; *informal* con, kid, have on, put one over on someone.

humdrum ▶ **adjective** MUNDANE, dull, dreary, boring, tedious, monotonous, prosaic; unexciting, uninteresting, uneventful, unvaried, unremarkable; routine, ordinary, everyday, day-to-day, quotidian, run-of-the-mill, commonplace, workaday, pedestrian; *informal* (plain) vanilla.
–OPPOSITES remarkable, exciting.

humid ▶ **adjective** MUGGY, close, sultry, sticky, steamy, oppressive, airless, stifling, suffocating, stuffy, clammy, heavy.
–OPPOSITES fresh.

humiliate ▶ **verb** EMBARRASS, mortify, humble, shame, put to shame, disgrace; discomfit, chasten, abash, deflate, crush, squash; abase, debase, demean, degrade; cause to feel small, cause to lose face, take down a peg or two; *informal* show up, put down, cut down to size, settle someone's hash; *N. Amer. informal* make someone eat crow.

humiliating ▶ **adjective** EMBARRASSING, mortifying, humbling, ignominious, inglorious, shameful; discreditable, undignified, chastening, demeaning, degrading, deflating.

humiliation ▶ **noun** EMBARRASSMENT, mortification, shame, indignity, ignominy, disgrace, dishonour, degradation, discredit, obloquy, opprobrium; loss of pride, loss of face; blow to one's pride, slap in the face, kick in the teeth.
–OPPOSITES honour.

humility ▶ **noun** MODESTY, humbleness, meekness, diffidence, unassertiveness; lack of pride, lack of vanity.
–OPPOSITES pride.

hummock ▶ **noun** HILLOCK, hump, mound, knoll, tump, prominence, elevation, rise, dune; *N. Amer.* knob; *formal* eminence.

humorist ▶ **noun** COMIC WRITER, wit, wag; comic, funny man/woman, comedian, comedienne, joker, jokester; clown.

humorous ▶ **adjective** AMUSING, funny, comic,

comical, entertaining, diverting, witty, jocular, light-hearted, tongue-in-cheek, wry; hilarious, uproarious, riotous, zany, farcical, droll; *informal* priceless, side-splitting, rib-tickling, a scream, a hoot, a barrel of laughs, waggish; *informal, dated* killing.
–OPPOSITES serious.

humour ▶ **noun** ❶ *the humour of the situation* COMEDY, comical aspect, funny side, funniness, hilarity; absurdity, ludicrousness, drollness; satire, irony. ❷ *the stories are spiced up with humour* JOKES, jests, jesting, quips, witticisms, funny remarks, puns; wit, wittiness, comedy, drollery; *informal* gags, wisecracks, cracks, waggishness, one-liners. ❸ *his good humour was infectious* MOOD, temper, disposition, temperament, state of mind; spirits.
▶ **verb** *she was always humouring him* INDULGE, accommodate, pander to, cater to, yield to, give way to, give in to, go along with; pamper, spoil, overindulge, mollify, placate, gratify, satisfy.

humourless ▶ **adjective** SERIOUS, solemn, sober, sombre, grave, grim, dour, unsmiling, stony-faced; gloomy, glum, sad, melancholy, dismal, joyless, cheerless, lugubrious; boring, tedious, dull, dry.
–OPPOSITES jovial.

hump ▶ **noun** *a hump at the base of the spine* PROTUBERANCE, prominence, lump, bump, knob, protrusion, projection, bulge, swelling, hunch; growth, outgrowth.
▶ **verb** ❶ *he humped his body to avoid a blow* ARCH, hunch, bend, bow, curve. ❷ (*informal*) *he humped boxes up the stairs* HEAVE, carry, lug, lift, hoist, heft, tote; *informal* schlep.
–OPPOSITES straighten.
■ **give someone the hump** (*informal*). *See* ANNOY.

hunch ▶ **verb** ❶ *he hunched his shoulders* ARCH, curve, hump, bow. ❷ *I hunched up as small as I could* CROUCH, huddle, curl; hunker down, bend, stoop, squat.
–OPPOSITES straighten.
▶ **noun** ❶ *the hunch on his back* PROTUBERANCE, hump, lump, bump, knob, protrusion, prominence, bulge, swelling; growth, outgrowth. ❷ *my hunch is that he'll be back* FEELING, feeling in one's bones, guess, suspicion, impression, inkling, idea, notion, fancy, intuition; *informal* gut feeling.

hundred ▶ **cardinal number** century; *informal* ton.
–RELATED TERMS centi-, hecto-, centenary, centennial.

hunger ▶ **noun** ❶ *she was faint with hunger* LACK OF FOOD, hungriness, ravenousness, emptiness; starvation, malnutrition, malnourishment, undernourishment. ❷ *a hunger for news* DESIRE, craving, longing, yearning, hankering, appetite, thirst; want, need; *informal* itch, yen.
■ **hunger after/for** DESIRE, crave; long for, yearn for, pine for, ache for, hanker after, thirst for, lust for; want, need; *informal* have a yen for, itch for, be dying for, be gagging for.

hungry ▶ **adjective** ❶ *I was really hungry* RAVENOUS, empty, in need of food, hollow, faint from hunger; starving, starved, famished; malnourished, undernourished, underfed; *informal* peckish, able to eat a horse; *archaic* esurient. ❷ *they are hungry for success* EAGER, keen, avid, longing, yearning, aching, greedy; craving, desirous of, hankering after; *informal* itching, dying, gagging, hot.
–OPPOSITES full.

hunk ▶ **noun** ❶ *a hunk of bread* CHUNK, wedge, block, slab, lump, square, gobbet; *Brit. informal* wodge. ❷ (*informal*) *he's such a hunk* MUSCLEMAN, strongman, macho man, iron man, Hercules; *informal* tough guy, he-man, beefcake, stud; *N. Amer. informal* studmuffin.
–OPPOSITES wimp.

hunt ▶ **verb** ❶ *they hunted deer* CHASE, stalk, pursue, course, run down; track, trail, follow, shadow; *informal* tail. ❷ *police are hunting for her* SEARCH, look (high and low), scour the area; seek, try to find; cast about/around/round, rummage (about/around/round), root about/around, fish about/around.
▶ **noun** ❶ *the thrill of the hunt* CHASE, pursuit. ❷ *police have stepped up their hunt* SEARCH, look, quest.

hunted ▶ **adjective** HARASSED, persecuted, harried, hounded, beleaguered, troubled, stressed, tormented; careworn, haggard; distraught, desperate; *informal* hassled.
–OPPOSITES carefree.

hunter ▶ **noun** HUNTSMAN, huntswoman, trapper, stalker, woodsman; nimrod; predator.

hunting ▶ **noun** BLOOD SPORTS, field sports, coursing, fox-hunting; trapping; the chase.

hurdle ▶ **noun** ❶ *his leg hit a hurdle* FENCE, jump, barrier, barricade, bar, railing, rail. ❷ *the final hurdle to overcome* OBSTACLE, difficulty, problem, barrier, bar, snag, stumbling block, impediment, obstruction, complication, hindrance; *informal* headache, fly in the ointment; *Brit. informal* spanner in the works.

hurl ▶ **verb** THROW, toss, fling, pitch, cast, lob, bowl, launch, catapult; project, propel, let fly; *informal* chuck, heave, sling, buzz, bung; *N. Amer. informal* peg; *Austral. & N. English informal* hoy; *NZ informal* bish; *dated* shy.

hurly-burly ▶ **noun** BUSTLE, hustle and bustle, hubbub, confusion, disorder, uproar, tumult, pandemonium, mayhem, rumpus; *informal* hoo-ha, hullabaloo, ballyhoo, kerfuffle.
–OPPOSITES calm, order.

hurricane ▶ **noun** CYCLONE, typhoon, tornado, storm, tempest, windstorm, whirlwind, gale; *N. Amer. informal* twister; *Austral.* willy-willy.

hurried ▶ adjective ❶ *hurried glances* QUICK, fast, swift, rapid, speedy, brisk, hasty; cursory, perfunctory, brief, short, fleeting, passing, superficial. ❷ *a hurried decision* HASTY, rushed, speedy, quick; impetuous, impulsive, precipitate, precipitous, rash, incautious, imprudent, spur-of-the-moment.
– OPPOSITES slow, considered.

hurriedly ▶ adverb HASTILY, speedily, quickly, fast, rapidly, swiftly, briskly; without delay, at top speed, at full tilt, at the double; headlong, hotfoot, post-haste; *informal* like the wind, like greased lightning, in double quick time; *Brit. informal* like the clappers, at a rate of knots, like billy-o; *N. Amer. informal* lickety-split.

hurry ▶ verb ❶ *hurry or you'll be late* BE QUICK, hurry up, hasten, speed up, press on, push on; run, dash, rush, race, fly; scurry, scramble, scuttle, sprint; *informal* get a move on, step on it, get cracking, get moving, shake a leg, tear, hare, zip, zoom, hotfoot it, leg it; *Brit. informal* shift, get one's skates on, stir one's stumps; *N. Amer. informal* get the lead out, get a wiggle on; *dated* make haste; *archaic* hie. ❷ *she hurried him out* HUSTLE, hasten, push, urge, drive, spur, goad, prod; *informal* gee up.
– OPPOSITES dawdle, delay.
▶ noun *in all the hurry, we forgot* RUSH, haste, flurry, hustle and bustle, confusion, commotion, hubbub, turmoil; race, scramble, scurry.

hurt ▶ verb ❶ *my back hurts* BE PAINFUL, be sore, be tender, cause pain, cause discomfort; ache, smart, sting, burn, throb; *informal* be killing; *Brit. informal* be playing up. ❷ *Dad hurt his leg* INJURE, wound, damage, disable, incapacitate, maim, mutilate; bruise, cut, gash, graze, scrape, scratch, lacerate. ❸ *his words hurt her* DISTRESS, pain, wound, sting, upset, sadden, devastate, grieve, mortify; cut to the quick. ❹ *high interest rates are hurting the economy* HARM, damage, be detrimental to, weaken, blight, impede, jeopardize, undermine, ruin, wreck, sabotage, cripple.
– OPPOSITES heal, comfort, benefit.
▶ noun ❶ *falling properly minimizes hurt* HARM, injury, wounding, pain, suffering, discomfort, soreness; aching, smarting, stinging, throbbing. ❷ *all the hurt he had caused* DISTRESS, pain, suffering, grief, misery, anguish, trauma, woe, upset, sadness, sorrow; harm, damage, trouble.
– OPPOSITES joy.
▶ adjective ❶ *my hurt hand* INJURED, wounded, bruised, grazed, cut, gashed, sore, painful, aching, smarting, throbbing. ❷ *Anne's hurt expression* PAINED, distressed, anguished, upset, sad, mortified, offended; *informal* miffed, peeved, sore.
– OPPOSITES pleased.

hurtful ▶ adjective ❶ *hurtful words* UPSETTING, distressing, wounding, painful; unkind, cruel, nasty, mean, malicious, spiteful; cutting, barbed; *informal* catty, bitchy. ❷ *this is hurtful to the interests of women* DETRIMENTAL, harmful, damaging, injurious, disadvantageous, unfavourable, prejudicial, deleterious, ruinous.

hurtle ▶ verb SPEED, rush, run, race, bolt, dash, career, whizz, zoom, charge, shoot, streak, gallop, hare, fly, scurry, go like the wind; *informal* belt, pelt, tear, scoot, go like a bat out of hell; *Brit. informal* bomb, bucket, go like the clappers; *N. Amer. informal* hightail, barrel.

husband ▶ noun SPOUSE, partner, mate, consort, man, helpmate, helpmeet; groom, bridegroom; *informal* hubby, old man, one's better half; *Brit. informal* other half.
▶ verb *oil reserves should be husbanded* CONSERVE, preserve, save, safeguard, save for a rainy day, put aside, put by, lay in, reserve, stockpile, hoard; use economically, use sparingly, be frugal with.
– OPPOSITES squander.

husbandry ▶ noun ❶ *farmers have new methods of husbandry* FARM MANAGEMENT, land management, farming, agriculture, agronomy; cultivation; animal husbandry. ❷ *the careful husbandry of their resources* CONSERVATION, management; economy, thrift, thriftiness, frugality.

hush ▶ verb ❶ *he tried to hush her* SILENCE, quieten (down), shush; gag, muzzle; *informal* shut up. ❷ *the crowd hushed* FALL SILENT, stop talking, quieten down; *informal* pipe down, shut up. ❸ *they hushed up the dangers* KEEP SECRET, conceal, hide, suppress, cover up, keep dark, keep quiet about; obscure, veil, sweep under the carpet; *informal* sit on, keep under one's hat.
– OPPOSITES disclose.
▶ exclamation *Hush! Someone will hear you* BE QUIET, keep quiet, quieten down, be silent, stop talking, hold your tongue; *informal* shut up, shut your mouth, shut your face, shut your trap, button your lip, pipe down, put a sock in it, give it a rest, save it, not another word; *Brit. informal* shut your gob.
▶ noun *a hush descended* SILENCE, quiet, quietness; stillness, peace, peacefulness, calm, tranquillity.
– OPPOSITES noise.

hush-hush ▶ adjective (*informal*). *See* SECRET adjective sense 1.

husk ▶ noun SHELL, hull, pod, case, covering, integument, shuck; *Botany* pericarp, legume.

husky ▶ adjective ❶ *a husky voice* THROATY, gruff, gravelly, hoarse, croaky, rough, guttural, harsh, rasping, raspy. ❷ *Paddy was a husky guy* STRONG, muscular, muscly, muscle-bound, brawny, hefty, burly, hulking, chunky, strapping, thickset, solid, powerful, heavy, robust, sturdy, Herculean, well built; *informal* beefy, hunky.
– OPPOSITES shrill, soft, puny.

hussy ▶ noun (*dated*) MINX, coquette, tease, seductress, Lolita, Jezebel; slut, loose woman;

informal floozie, tart, vamp; *Brit. informal* scrubber, slapper, slag; *N. Amer. informal* tramp; *dated* trollop; *archaic* jade, strumpet.

hustle ▶ verb ❶ *they were hustled as they went* JOSTLE, shove, push, bump, knock, nudge, elbow, shoulder. ❷ *I was hustled away* MANHANDLE, push, shove, thrust, frogmarch; rush, hurry, whisk; *informal* bundle. ❸ (*informal*) *don't be hustled into anything* COERCE, force, pressure, pressurize, badger, pester, hound, nag, goad, prod; browbeat, bulldoze, steamroller, dragoon; *informal* railroad, fast-talk.

■ **hustle and bustle** HURLY-BURLY, bustle, tumult, hubbub, activity, action, liveliness, animation, excitement, agitation, flurry, whirl; *informal* toing and froing, comings and goings, ballyhoo, hoo-ha, hullabaloo.

hut ▶ noun SHACK, shanty, (log) cabin, shelter, shed, lean-to; hovel; *Scottish* bothy, shieling; *N. Amer.* cabana.

hybrid ▶ noun *a hybrid between a brown and albino mouse* CROSS, cross-breed, mixed-breed, half-breed, half-blood; mixture, blend, amalgamation, combination, composite, fusion.

▶ adjective *hybrid roses* COMPOSITE, cross-bred, interbred, mongrel; mixed, blended, compound.

hybridize ▶ verb CROSS-BREED, cross, interbreed, cross-fertilize, cross-pollinate; mix, blend, combine, amalgamate.

hygiene ▶ noun CLEANLINESS, sanitation, sterility, purity, disinfection; public health, environmental health.

hygienic ▶ adjective SANITARY, clean, germ-free, disinfected, sterilized, sterile, antiseptic, aseptic, unpolluted, uncontaminated, salubrious, healthy, wholesome; *informal* squeaky clean.

– OPPOSITES insanitary.

hymn ▶ noun RELIGIOUS SONG, song of praise, anthem, canticle, chorale, psalm, carol; spiritual.

hype (*informal*) ▶ noun *her work relies on hype and headlines* PUBLICITY, advertising, promotion, marketing, propaganda, exposure; *informal* plugging, ballyhoo; *Brit. informal* puff.

▶ verb *a stunt to hype a new product* PUBLICIZE, advertise, promote, push, puff, boost, merchandise, build up, bang the drum for; *informal* plug.

hyperbole ▶ noun EXAGGERATION, overstatement, magnification, embroidery, embellishment, excess, overkill; *informal* purple prose, puffery.

– OPPOSITES understatement.

hypercritical ▶ adjective OVERCRITICAL, fault-finding, hair-splitting, carping, cavilling, captious, niggling, quibbling, pedantic, pettifogging, fussy, finicky; *informal* picky, nit-picking, pernickety; *N. Amer. informal* persnickety; *archaic* nice.

hypnosis ▶ noun MESMERISM, hypnotism, hypnotic suggestion, auto-suggestion.

hypnotic ▶ adjective MESMERIZING, mesmeric, spellbinding, entrancing, bewitching, irresistible, compelling; soporific, sedative, numbing; *Medicine* stupefacient.

hypnotism ▶ noun MESMERISM, hypnosis, hypnotic suggestion, auto-suggestion.

hypnotize ▶ verb ❶ *he had been hypnotized* MESMERIZE, put into a trance. ❷ *they were hypnotized by the dancers* ENTRANCE, spellbind, enthral, transfix, captivate, bewitch, enrapture, grip, rivet, absorb, magnetize.

hypochondria ▶ noun VALETUDINARIANISM, imagined ill health, health obsession; neurosis; *technical* hypochondriasis.

hypochondriac ▶ noun *a hypochondriac who depends on her pills* VALETUDINARIAN, valetudinary; neurotic.

▶ adjective *her hypochondriac husband* VALETUDINARIAN, valetudinary, hypochondriacal, malingering, health-obsessed, neurotic.

hypocrisy ▶ noun SANCTIMONIOUSNESS, sanctimony, pietism, piousness, false virtue, cant, posturing, speciousness, empty talk; insincerity, falseness, deceit, dishonesty, dissimulation, duplicity; *informal* phoneyness.

– OPPOSITES sincerity.

hypocrite ▶ noun SANCTIMONIOUS PERSON, pietist, plaster saint, humbug, pretender, deceiver, dissembler; *informal* phoney; *poetic/literary* whited sepulchre.

hypocritical ▶ adjective SANCTIMONIOUS, pietistic, pious, self-righteous, holier-than-thou, superior; insincere, specious, false; deceitful, dishonest, dissembling, two-faced; *informal* phoney.

hypodermic ▶ noun NEEDLE, syringe; *informal* hype, spike.

hypothesis ▶ noun THEORY, theorem, thesis, conjecture, supposition, postulation, postulate, proposition, premise, assumption; notion, concept, idea.

hypothetical ▶ adjective THEORETICAL, speculative, conjectured, notional, suppositional, supposed, assumed; academic.

– OPPOSITES actual.

hysteria ▶ noun FRENZY, feverishness, hysterics, fit of madness, derangement, mania; panic, alarm, distress; *Brit. informal* the screaming abdabs.

– OPPOSITES calm.

hysterical ▶ adjective ❶ *Janet became hysterical* OVERWROUGHT, overemotional, out of control, frenzied, frantic, wild, feverish; beside oneself, driven to distraction, agitated, berserk, manic, delirious, unhinged, deranged, out of one's mind, raving; *informal* in a state. ❷ (*informal*) *her attempts to dance were hysterical* HILARIOUS, uproarious, very funny, very amusing, comical, farcical; *informal* hysterically funny, side-splitting, rib-tickling, a scream, a hoot, a barrel of laughs; *dated* killing.

hysterics ▶ **plural noun** (*informal*) ❶ *a fit of hysterics* HYSTERIA, wildness, feverishness, irrationality, frenzy, loss of control, delirium, derangement, mania; *Brit. informal* the screaming abdabs. ❷ *the girls collapsed in hysterics* FITS OF LAUGHTER, gales of laughter, uncontrollable laughter, convulsions, fits; *informal* stitches.

Ii

ice ▶ **noun** ❶ *a lake covered with ice* FROZEN WATER, icicles; black ice, verglas, frost, rime; *N. Amer.* glaze. ❷ *assorted ices* ICE CREAM, water ice, sorbet; *N. Amer.* sherbet. ❸ *the ice in her voice* COLDNESS, coolness, frostiness, iciness; hostility, unfriendliness.

– RELATED TERMS gelid, glacial.

▶ **verb** ❶ *the lake has iced over* FREEZE (OVER), turn into ice, harden, solidify. ❷ *I'll ice the drinks* COOL, chill, refrigerate. ❸ *she had iced the cake* COVER WITH ICING, glaze; *N. Amer.* frost.

– OPPOSITES thaw, heat.

■ **on ice** (*informal*). *See* PENDING adjective sense 1.

ice-cold ▶ **adjective** ICY, freezing, glacial, gelid, sub-zero, frozen, wintry; arctic, polar, Siberian; bitter, biting, raw, chilly; *poetic/literary* frore, rimy.

– OPPOSITES hot.

icing ▶ **noun** GLAZE, sugar paste; *N. Amer.* frosting.

icon ▶ **noun** IMAGE, idol, portrait, representation, symbol; figure, statue.

iconoclast ▶ **noun** CRITIC, sceptic; heretic, unbeliever, dissident, dissenter; rebel, renegade, mutineer.

icy ▶ **adjective** ❶ *icy roads* FROSTY, frozen (over), iced over, ice-bound, ice-covered, iced up; slippery; *poetic/literary* rimy. ❷ *an icy wind* FREEZING, chill, chilly, biting, bitter, raw, arctic, glacial, Siberian, polar, gelid. ❸ *an icy voice* UNFRIENDLY, hostile, forbidding; cold, cool, chilly, frigid, frosty, glacial, gelid; haughty, stern, hard.

idea ▶ **noun** ❶ *the idea of death scares her* CONCEPT, notion, conception, thought; image, visualization; hypothesis, postulation. ❷ *our idea is to open a new shop* PLAN, scheme, design, proposal, proposition, suggestion; aim, intention, objective, object, goal, target. ❸ *Liz had other ideas on the subject* THOUGHT, theory, view, opinion, feeling, belief, conclusion. ❹ *I had an idea that it might happen* SENSE, feeling, suspicion, fancy, inkling, hunch, theory, notion, impression. ❺ *an idea of the cost* ESTIMATE, estimation, approximation, guess, conjecture, rough calculation; *informal* guesstimate.

ideal ▶ **adjective** ❶ *ideal flying weather* PERFECT, best possible, consummate, supreme, flawless, faultless, exemplary, classic, model, ultimate, quintessential. ❷ *an ideal concept* ABSTRACT, theoretical, conceptual, notional; hypothetical, speculative, conjectural, suppositional. ❸ *an ideal world* UNATTAINABLE, unachievable, impracticable; unreal, fictitious, hypothetical, theoretical, ivory-towered, imaginary, idealized, Utopian, fairy-tale.

– OPPOSITES bad, concrete, real.

▶ **noun** ❶ *she tried to be his ideal* PERFECTION, paragon, epitome, ne plus ultra, nonpareil, dream; *informal* one in a million, the tops, the bee's knees. ❷ *an ideal to aim at* MODEL, pattern, exemplar, example, paradigm, archetype; yardstick. ❸ *liberal ideals* PRINCIPLE, standard, value, belief, conviction, persuasion; (**ideals**) morals, morality, ethics, ideology, creed.

idealist ▶ **noun** UTOPIAN, visionary, fantasist, romantic, romanticist, dreamer, daydreamer; Walter Mitty, Don Quixote; *N. Amer.* fantast.

– OPPOSITES realist.

idealistic ▶ **adjective** UTOPIAN, visionary, romantic, quixotic, dreamy, unrealistic, impractical.

idealize ▶ **verb** ROMANTICIZE, be unrealistic about, look at something through rose-tinted spectacles, paint a rosy picture of, glamorize.

ideally ▶ **adverb** IN A PERFECT WORLD; preferably, if possible, for preference, by choice, as a matter of choice, (much) rather; all things being equal, theoretically, hypothetically, in theory, in principle, on paper.

idée fixe ▶ **noun** OBSESSION, fixation, (consuming) passion, mania, compulsion, preoccupation, infatuation, addiction, fetish; phobia, complex, neurosis; *informal* bee in one's bonnet, hang-up, thing.

identical ▶ adjective ❶ *identical badges* SIMILAR, (exactly) the same, indistinguishable, uniform, twin, interchangeable, undifferentiated, homogeneous, of a piece, cut from the same cloth; alike, like, matching, like (two) peas in a pod; *informal* much of a muchness. ❷ *I used the identical technique* THE (VERY) SAME, the selfsame, the very, one and the same; aforementioned, aforesaid, aforenamed, above, above-stated; foregoing, preceding.
– OPPOSITES different.

identifiable ▶ adjective DISTINGUISHABLE, recognizable, known; noticeable, perceptible, discernible, appreciable, detectable, observable, perceivable, visible; distinct, marked, conspicuous, unmistakable, clear.
– OPPOSITES unrecognizable.

identification ▶ noun ❶ *the identification of the suspect* RECOGNITION, singling out, pinpointing, naming; discerning, distinguishing; *informal* fingering. ❷ *early identification of problems* DETERMINATION, establishment, ascertainment, discovery, diagnosis, divination; verification, confirmation. ❸ *may I see your identification?* ID, (identity/identification) papers, bona fides, documents, credentials; ID card, identity card, pass, badge, warrant, licence, permit, passport. ❹ *the identification of the party with high taxes* ASSOCIATION, link, linkage, connection, bracketing. ❺ *his identification with the music* EMPATHY, rapport, unity, togetherness, bond, sympathy, understanding.

identify ▶ verb ❶ *Gail identified her attacker* RECOGNIZE, single out, pick out, spot, point out, pinpoint, put one's finger on, put a name to, name, know; discern, distinguish; remember, recall, recollect; *informal* finger. ❷ *I identified four problem areas* DETERMINE, establish, ascertain, make out, diagnose, discern, distinguish; verify, confirm; *informal* figure out, get a fix on. ❸ *we identify sport with glamour* ASSOCIATE, link, connect, relate, bracket, couple; mention in the same breath as, set side by side with. ❹ *Peter identifies with the hero* EMPATHIZE, be in tune, have a rapport, feel at one, sympathize; be on the same wavelength as, speak the same language as; understand, relate to, feel for. ❺ *they identify him with this painter of the same name* EQUATE WITH, identify as, consider to be, regard as being the same as.

identity ▶ noun ❶ *the identity of the owner* NAME; specification. ❷ *she was afraid of losing her identity* INDIVIDUALITY, self, selfhood; personality, character, originality, distinctiveness, singularity, uniqueness. ❸ *a case of mistaken identity* IDENTIFICATION, recognition, naming, singling out. ❹ *we share an identity of interests* CONGRUITY, congruence, sameness, oneness, interchangeability; likeness, uniformity, similarity, closeness, accordance, alignment.

ideology ▶ noun BELIEFS, ideas, ideals, principles, ethics, morals; doctrine, creed, credo, teaching, theory; tenets, canon(s); conviction(s), persuasion.

idiocy ▶ noun STUPIDITY, folly, foolishness, foolhardiness; madness, insanity, lunacy; silliness, brainlessness, thoughtlessness, senselessness, irresponsibility, imprudence, ineptitude, inanity, absurdity, ludicrousness, fatuousness; *informal* craziness; *Brit. informal* daftness.
– OPPOSITES sense.

idiom ▶ noun ❶ *a rather dated idiom* EXPRESSION, phrase, turn of phrase, locution. ❷ *the poet's idiom is terse* LANGUAGE, mode of expression, style, speech, locution, usage, phraseology, phrasing, vocabulary, parlance, jargon, patter; *informal* lingo.

idiomatic ▶ adjective VERNACULAR, colloquial, everyday, conversational; natural, grammatical, correct.

idiosyncrasy ▶ noun PECULIARITY, oddity, eccentricity, mannerism, quirk, whim, vagary, caprice, kink; fetish, foible, crotchet, habit, characteristic; individuality; unconventionality, unorthodoxy; *archaic* megrim, freak.

idiosyncratic ▶ adjective DISTINCTIVE, individual, individualistic, characteristic, peculiar, typical, special, specific, unique, personal; eccentric, unconventional, irregular, anomalous, odd, quirky, queer, strange, weird, bizarre, freakish; *informal* freaky.

idiot ▶ noun FOOL, ass, halfwit, blockhead, dunce, dolt, ignoramus, simpleton; *informal* dope, ninny, nincompoop, chump, dimwit, dumbo, dummy, loon, dork, jackass, bonehead, fathead, numbskull, dunderhead, thickhead, woodenhead, airhead, pinhead, lamebrain, cretin, moron, imbecile, pea-brain, birdbrain, jerk, nerd, donkey; *Brit. informal* nit, nitwit, twit, clot, plonker, berk, prat, pillock, wally, divvy, twerp, charlie; *Scottish informal* nyaff, balloon; *N. Amer. informal* schmuck, bozo, turkey, chowderhead, dingbat; *Austral./NZ informal* drongo, dill, alec, galah.
– OPPOSITES genius.

idiotic ▶ adjective STUPID, silly, foolish, witless, brainless, mindless, thoughtless, unintelligent; imprudent, unwise, ill-advised, ill-considered, half-baked, foolhardy; absurd, senseless, pointless, nonsensical, inane, fatuous, ridiculous; *informal* dumb, dim, dim-witted, half-witted, dopey, gormless, hare-brained, pea-brained, wooden-headed, thickheaded; *Brit. informal* barmy, daft; *Scottish & N. English informal* glaikit; *N. Amer. informal* dumb-ass.

idle ▶ adjective ❶ *an idle fellow* LAZY, indolent, slothful, work-shy, shiftless, inactive, sluggish, lethargic, listless; slack, lax, lackadaisical, good-for-nothing; *informal* bone idle. ❷ *I was bored with being idle* UNEMPLOYED, jobless, out of work, redundant, between jobs, workless, unwaged, unoccupied; *Brit. informal* on the dole, 'resting'. ❸ *they left the machine idle* INACTIVE, unused, unoccupied, unemployed, disused; out of action, inoperative, out of service. ❹ *their idle hours* UNOCCUPIED, spare, empty, vacant, unfilled, available. ❺ *idle remarks* FRIVOLOUS, trivial, trifling, minor, petty, lightweight, shallow, superficial, insignificant, unimportant, worthless, paltry, niggling, peripheral, inane, fatuous; unnecessary, time-wasting. ❻ *idle threats* EMPTY, meaningless, pointless, worthless, vain, insubstantial, futile, ineffective, ineffectual; groundless, baseless.

–OPPOSITES industrious, employed, working, busy, serious.

▶ **verb** ❶ *Lily idled on the window seat* DO NOTHING, be inactive, vegetate, take it easy, mark time, kick one's heels, twiddle one's thumbs, kill time, languish, laze, lounge, loll, loaf, slouch; *informal* hang around, veg out; *Brit. informal* hang about; *N. Amer. informal* bum around, lollygag. ❷ *Rob idled along the pavement* SAUNTER, stroll, dawdle, drift, potter, amble, maunder, wander, straggle; *informal* mosey, tootle; *Brit. informal* pootle, mooch. ❸ *he let the engine idle* TICK OVER.

idler ▶ **noun** LOAFER, layabout, good-for-nothing, ne'er-do-well, lounger, shirker, sluggard; *informal* skiver, waster, slacker, slowcoach, slob, lazybones; *N. Amer. informal* slowpoke; *poetic/literary* wastrel.

–OPPOSITES workaholic.

idol ▶ **noun** ❶ *an idol in a shrine* ICON, effigy, statue, figure, figurine, fetish, totem; graven image, false god, golden calf. ❷ *the pop world's latest idol* HERO, heroine, star, superstar, icon, celebrity; favourite, darling; *informal* pin-up, heart throb, blue-eyed boy/girl, golden boy/girl.

idolatry ▶ **noun** ❶ *he preached against idolatry* IDOL WORSHIP, fetishism, iconolatry; paganism, heathenism. ❷ *our idolatry of art* IDOLIZATION, fetishization, worship, adulation, adoration, reverence, glorification, lionization, hero-worshipping.

idolize ▶ **verb** HERO-WORSHIP, worship, revere, venerate, deify, lionize; stand in awe of, reverence, look up to, admire, exalt; *informal* put on a pedestal.

idyll ▶ **noun** ❶ *an idyll unspoilt by machines* PERFECT TIME, ideal time, moment of bliss; paradise, heaven (on earth), Shangri-La, Utopia; *poetic/literary* Arcadia. ❷ *the poem is a two-part idyll* PASTORAL, eclogue, georgic, rural poem.

idyllic ▶ **adjective** PERFECT, wonderful, blissful, halcyon, happy; ideal, idealized; heavenly, paradisal, Utopian, Elysian; peaceful, picturesque; *poetic/literary* Arcadian.

if ▶ **conjunction** ❶ *if the weather is fine, we can walk* ON CONDITION THAT, provided (that), providing (that), presuming (that), supposing (that), assuming (that), as long as, given that, in the event that. ❷ *if I go out she gets nasty* WHENEVER, every time. ❸ *I wonder if he noticed* WHETHER, whether or not. ❹ *a useful, if unintended innovation* ALTHOUGH, albeit, but, yet, whilst; even though, despite being.

▶ **noun** *there is one if in all this* UNCERTAINTY, doubt; condition, stipulation, provision, proviso, constraint, precondition, requirement, specification, restriction.

iffy ▶ **adjective** (*informal*) ❶ *the windscreen's a bit iffy, but it's a good car* SUBSTANDARD, second-rate, low-grade, low-quality; doubtful, dubious, questionable; *informal* not up to much; *Brit. informal* dodgy, ropy. ❷ *that date is a bit iffy* TENTATIVE, undecided, unsettled, unsure, unresolved, in doubt; *informal* up in the air.

ignite ▶ **verb** ❶ *he got to safety moments before the petrol ignited* CATCH FIRE, burst into flames; be set off, explode. ❷ *a cigarette ignited the fumes* LIGHT, set fire to, set on fire, set alight, kindle, touch off; *informal* set/put a match to. ❸ *the campaign failed to ignite voter interest* AROUSE, kindle, trigger, spark, instigate, excite, provoke, stimulate, stir up, whip up, incite, fuel.

–OPPOSITES go out, extinguish.

ignoble ▶ **adjective** DISHONOURABLE, unworthy, base, shameful, contemptible, despicable, shabby, sordid; improper, unprincipled, discreditable.

ignominious ▶ **adjective** HUMILIATING, undignified, embarrassing, ignoble, inglorious.

–OPPOSITES glorious.

ignominy ▶ **noun** SHAME, humiliation, embarrassment; disgrace, dishonour, discredit, degradation, scandal, infamy, indignity, ignobility, loss of face.

ignoramus ▶ **noun** FOOL, ass, halfwit, blockhead, dunce, simpleton; *informal* dope, ninny, nincompoop, chump, dimwit, imbecile, moron, dumbo, dummy, fathead, numbskull, thickhead, woodenhead, airhead, birdbrain; *Brit. informal* nit, nitwit, twit, clot, plonker, berk, divvy; *Scottish informal* balloon; *N. Amer. informal* schmuck, bozo, turkey; *Austral./NZ informal* drongo.

ignorance ▶ **noun** ❶ *his ignorance of economics* INCOMPREHENSION, unawareness, unconsciousness, unfamiliarity, inexperience, innocence, lack of knowledge; *informal* cluelessness; *poetic/literary* nescience. ❷ *their attitudes are based on ignorance* LACK OF KNOWLEDGE, lack of education; unenlightenment, benightedness; lack of intelligence, stupidity, foolishness, idiocy.

–OPPOSITES knowledge, education.

ignorant ▶ **adjective** ❶ *an ignorant country girl* UNEDUCATED, unknowledgeable, untaught, unschooled, untutored, untrained, illiterate, unlettered, unlearned, unread, uninformed, unenlightened, benighted; inexperienced, unworldly, unsophisticated; *informal* pig-ignorant, thick. ❷ *they were ignorant of working-class life* WITHOUT KNOWLEDGE, unaware, unconscious, unfamiliar, unacquainted, uninformed, un-

enlightened, unconversant, inexperienced, naive, innocent, green; *informal* in the dark, clueless; *poetic/literary* nescient.
– OPPOSITES educated, knowledgeable.

ignore ▶ verb ❶ *he ignored the customers* DISREGARD, take no notice of, pay no attention to, pay no heed to; turn a blind eye to, turn a deaf ear to. ❷ *he was ignored by the countess* SNUB, slight, spurn, shun, look right through, cold-shoulder, freeze out; *Brit.* send to Coventry; *informal* give someone the brush-off, cut (dead); *Brit. informal* blank. ❸ *doctors ignored her husband's instructions* SET ASIDE, pay no attention to, take no account of; break, contravene, fail to comply with, fail to observe, disregard, disobey, breach, defy, flout.
– OPPOSITES acknowledge, obey.

ilk ▶ noun TYPE, sort, class, category, group, set, bracket, genre, vintage, make, model, brand, stamp, variety.

ill ▶ adjective ❶ *she was feeling rather ill* UNWELL, sick, not (very) well, ailing, poorly, sickly, peaky, indisposed, infirm; out of sorts, not oneself, under/below par, bad, in a bad way; bedridden, invalided, on the sick list, valetudinarian; queasy, nauseous, nauseated; *Brit.* off colour; *informal* under the weather, laid up, lousy, rough; *Brit. informal* ropy, grotty; *Austral./NZ informal* crook; *Brit. informal, dated* queer. ❷ *the ill effects of smoking* HARMFUL, damaging, detrimental, deleterious, adverse, injurious, hurtful, destructive, pernicious, dangerous; unhealthy, unwholesome, poisonous, noxious; *poetic/literary* malefic, maleficent, nocuous; *archaic* baneful. ❸ *ill feeling* HOSTILE, antagonistic, acrimonious, inimical, antipathetic; unfriendly, unsympathetic; resentful, spiteful, malicious, vindictive, malevolent, bitter. ❹ *an ill omen* UNLUCKY, adverse, unfavourable, unfortunate, unpropitious, inauspicious, unpromising, infelicitous, ominous, sinister; *poetic/literary* direful. ❺ *ill manners* RUDE, discourteous, impolite; impertinent, insolent, impudent, uncivil, disrespectful; *informal* ignorant. ❻ *ill management* BAD, poor, unsatisfactory, incompetent, deficient, defective, inexpert.
– OPPOSITES well, healthy, beneficial, auspicious, polite.
▶ noun ❶ *the ills of society* PROBLEMS, troubles, difficulties, misfortunes, trials, tribulations; worries, anxieties, concerns; *informal* headaches, hassles. ❷ *he wished them no ill* HARM, hurt, injury, damage, pain, trouble, misfortune, suffering, distress. ❸ *the body's ills* ILLNESSES, ailments, disorders, complaints, afflictions, sicknesses, diseases, maladies, infirmities.
▶ adverb ❶ *such behaviour ill became the king* POORLY, badly, imperfectly. ❷ *the look on her face boded ill* UNFAVOURABLY, adversely, badly, inauspiciously. ❸ *he can ill afford the loss of income* BARELY, scarcely, hardly, only just, just possibly. ❹ *things are going ill* BADLY, adversely, unsuccessfully, unfavourably; unfortunately, unluckily, inauspiciously. ❺ *we are ill prepared* INADEQUATELY, unsatisfactorily, insufficiently, imperfectly, poorly, badly.
– OPPOSITES well, auspiciously, satisfactorily.
■ **ill at ease** AWKWARD, uneasy, uncomfortable, embarrassed, self-conscious, out of place, inhibited, gauche; restless, restive, fidgety, discomfited, worried, anxious, on edge, edgy, nervous, tense; *informal* twitchy, jittery; *N. Amer. informal* discombobulated, antsy.
■ **speak ill of** DENIGRATE, disparage, criticize, be critical of, speak badly of, be malicious about, blacken the name of, run down, insult, abuse, attack, revile, malign, vilify; *N. Amer.* slur; *informal* bad-mouth, bitch about, pull to pieces; *Brit. informal* rubbish, slate, slag off; *formal* derogate; *rare* asperse.

ill-advised ▶ adjective UNWISE, injudicious, misguided, imprudent, ill-considered, ill-judged; foolhardy, hare-brained, rash, reckless; *informal* crazy, crackpot.
– OPPOSITES judicious.

ill-assorted ▶ adjective MISMATCHED, incongruous, ill-matched, incompatible; dissimilar, unalike, varied, disparate.

ill-bred ▶ adjective ILL-MANNERED, bad-mannered, rude, impolite, discourteous, uncivil; boorish, churlish, loutish, vulgar, coarse, crass, uncouth, uncivilized, ungentlemanly, indecorous, unseemly; *informal* ignorant; *Brit. informal* yobbish.

ill-considered ▶ adjective RASH, ill-advised, ill-judged, injudicious, imprudent, unwise, hasty; misjudged, ill-conceived, badly thought out, hare-brained; *poetic/literary* temerarious.
– OPPOSITES judicious.

ill-defined ▶ adjective VAGUE, indistinct, unclear, imprecise; blurred, fuzzy, hazy, woolly.

ill-disposed ▶ adjective HOSTILE, antagonistic, unfriendly, unsympathetic, antipathetic, inimical, unfavourable, averse, at odds; *informal* anti.
– OPPOSITES friendly.

illegal ▶ adjective UNLAWFUL, illicit, illegitimate, criminal, felonious; unlicensed, unauthorized, unsanctioned; outlawed, banned, forbidden, prohibited, proscribed; contraband, black-market, bootleg; *Law* malfeasant; *informal* crooked, shady; *Brit. informal* bent, dodgy.
– OPPOSITES lawful, legitimate.

illegible ▶ adjective UNREADABLE, indecipherable, unintelligible; scrawled, scribbled, crabbed.

illegitimate ▶ adjective ❶ *illegitimate share trading* ILLEGAL, unlawful, illicit, criminal, felonious; unlicensed, unauthorized, unsanctioned; prohibited, outlawed, banned, forbidden, proscribed; fraudulent, corrupt, dishonest; *Law* malfeasant; *informal* crooked, shady; *Brit. informal* bent, dodgy. ❷ *an illegitimate child* BORN

OUT OF WEDLOCK; *dated* born on the wrong side of the blanket, unfathered; *archaic* bastard, natural, misbegotten, baseborn, nameless, spurious.
– OPPOSITES legal, lawful.

ill-fated ▶ adjective DOOMED, blighted, damned, cursed, ill-starred, jinxed; *poetic/literary* star-crossed.

ill-favoured ▶ adjective UNATTRACTIVE, plain, ugly; *N. Amer.* homely; *informal* not much to look at; *Austral./NZ informal* drack.
– OPPOSITES attractive.

ill-founded ▶ adjective BASELESS, groundless, without foundation, unjustified; questionable, misinformed, misguided.

ill humour ▶ noun BAD MOOD, bad temper, irritability, irascibility, cantankerousness, petulance, peevishness, pettishness, pique, crabbiness, testiness, tetchiness, fractiousness, snappishness, waspishness, touchiness, moodiness, sullenness, sulkiness, surliness, annoyance, anger, crossness.

ill-humoured ▶ adjective BAD-TEMPERED, ill-tempered, short-tempered, in a (bad) mood, cross; irritable, irascible, tetchy, testy, crotchety, touchy, cantankerous, curmudgeonly, peevish, fractious, waspish, prickly, pettish; grumpy, grouchy, crabbed, crabby, splenetic, dyspeptic, choleric; *informal* snappish, snappy, chippy, on a short fuse; *Brit. informal* shirty, stroppy, ratty, like a bear with a sore head; *N. Amer. informal* cranky, ornery, peckish; *Austral./NZ informal* snaky; *informal, dated* waxy, miffy.
– OPPOSITES amiable.

illiberal ▶ adjective INTOLERANT, conservative, unenlightened, reactionary, undemocratic, authoritarian, repressive, totalitarian, despotic, tyrannical, oppressive.

illicit ▶ adjective ❶ *illicit drugs* ILLEGAL, unlawful, illegitimate, criminal, felonious; outlawed, banned, forbidden, prohibited, proscribed; unlicensed, unauthorized, unsanctioned; contraband, black-market, bootleg; *Law* malfeasant. ❷ *an illicit love affair* TABOO, forbidden, impermissible, unacceptable, tapu, haram; secret, clandestine.
– OPPOSITES lawful, legal.

illimitable ▶ adjective LIMITLESS, unlimited, unbounded; endless, unending, never-ending, infinite, immeasurable.

illiteracy ▶ noun ❶ *illiteracy was widespread* ILLITERATENESS, inability to read or write. ❷ *economic illiteracy* IGNORANCE, unawareness, inexperience, unenlightenment, lack of knowledge/education; *poetic/literary* nescience.

illiterate ▶ adjective ❶ *an illiterate peasant* UNABLE TO READ OR WRITE, unlettered. ❷ *politically illiterate* IGNORANT, unknowledgeable, uneducated, unschooled, untutored, untrained, uninstructed, uninformed; *poetic/literary* nescient.

ill-judged ▶ adjective ILL-CONSIDERED, unwise, ill-thought-out; imprudent, incautious, injudicious, misguided, ill-advised, impolitic, inexpedient; rash, hasty, thoughtless, careless, reckless.
– OPPOSITES judicious.

ill-mannered ▶ adjective BAD-MANNERED, discourteous, rude, impolite, uncivil, abusive; insolent, impertinent, impudent, cheeky, presumptuous, disrespectful; badly behaved, ill-behaved, loutish, oafish, uncouth, uncivilized, ill-bred; *informal* ignorant.
– OPPOSITES polite.

ill-natured ▶ adjective MEAN, nasty, spiteful, malicious, disagreeable; ill-tempered, bad-tempered, moody, irritable, irascible, surly, sullen, peevish, petulant, fractious, crabbed, crabby, tetchy, testy, grouchy.

illness ▶ noun SICKNESS, disease, ailment, complaint, malady, affliction, infection, indisposition; ill health, poor health, infirmity; *informal* bug, virus; *Brit. informal* lurgy; *Austral. informal* wog; *dated* contagion.
– RELATED TERMS -pathy.
– OPPOSITES good health.

illogical ▶ adjective IRRATIONAL, unreasonable, unsound, unreasoned, unjustifiable; incorrect, erroneous, invalid, spurious, faulty, flawed, fallacious, unscientific; specious, sophistic, casuistic; absurd, preposterous, untenable; *informal* off beam, way out.

ill-starred ▶ adjective ILL-FATED, doomed, ill-omened, blighted, damned, cursed, jinxed; unlucky, luckless, unfortunate, hapless; *poetic/ crossed.*
– OPPOSITES blessed.

ill temper ▶ noun BAD MOOD, irritation, vexation, exasperation, indignation, huff, moodiness, pet, pique; anger, crossness, bad temper; irritability, irascibility, peevishness, tetchiness, testiness; *informal* grump; *Brit. informal* paddy, strop; *N. Amer. informal* blowout, hissy fit; *Brit. informal, dated* bate, wax.

ill-tempered ▶ adjective BAD-TEMPERED, short-tempered, ill-humoured, moody; in a (bad) mood, cross, irritable, irascible, tetchy, testy, crotchety, touchy, cantankerous, curmudgeonly, peevish, fractious, waspish, prickly, pettish; grumpy, grouchy, crabbed, crabby, splenetic, dyspeptic, choleric; *informal* snappish, snappy, chippy, on a short fuse; *Brit. informal* shirty, stroppy, ratty; *N. Amer. informal* cranky, ornery, peckish; *Austral./NZ informal* snaky; *informal, dated* waxy, miffy.

ill-timed ▶ adjective UNTIMELY, mistimed, badly timed; premature, early, hasty, inopportune.
– OPPOSITES timely.

ill-treat ▶ verb ABUSE, mistreat, maltreat, ill-use, misuse; manhandle, handle roughly, molest; harm, injure, damage; *informal* knock about/around.

– OPPOSITES pamper.

ill-treatment ▶ noun ABUSE, mistreatment, maltreatment, ill use, ill usage, misuse; manhandling, rough treatment.

illuminate ▶ verb ❶ *the bundle was illuminated by the torch* LIGHT (UP), throw light on, brighten, shine on; *poetic/literary* illumine. ❷ *the manuscripts were illuminated* DECORATE, illustrate, embellish, adorn, ornament. ❸ *documents often illuminate people's thought processes* CLARIFY, elucidate, explain, reveal, shed light on, give insight into.
– OPPOSITES darken, conceal.

illuminating ▶ adjective INFORMATIVE, enlightening, revealing, explanatory, instructive, helpful, educational.

illumination ▶ noun ❶ *a floodlamp provided illumination* LIGHT, lighting, radiance, gleam, glow, glare; shining, gleaming, glowing; *poetic/literary* illumining, irradiance, lucency, lambency, effulgence, refulgence. ❷ *the illumination of a manuscript* DECORATION, illustration, embellishment, adornment, ornamentation. ❸ *these books give illumination on the subject* CLARIFICATION, elucidation, explanation, revelation, explication. ❹ *moments of real illumination* ENLIGHTENMENT, insight, understanding, awareness; learning, education, edification.

illusion ▶ noun ❶ *he had destroyed her illusions* DELUSION, misapprehension, misconception, false impression; fantasy, fancy, dream, chimera. ❷ *the lighting increases the illusion of depth* APPEARANCE, impression, semblance. ❸ *it's just an illusion* MIRAGE, hallucination, apparition, figment of the imagination, trick of the light. ❹ *magical illusions* (MAGIC) TRICK, conjuring trick; (**illusions**) magic, conjuring, sleight of hand, legerdemain.

illusory ▶ adjective DELUSORY, delusive; illusionary, imagined, imaginary, fanciful, fancied, unreal; sham, false, fallacious, fake, bogus, mistaken, erroneous, misguided, untrue.
– OPPOSITES genuine.

illustrate ▶ verb ❶ *the photographs that illustrate the book* DECORATE, adorn, ornament, accompany; add pictures/drawings to, provide artwork for. ❷ *this can be illustrated through a brief example* EXPLAIN, elucidate, clarify, make plain, demonstrate, show, emphasize; *informal* get across/over. ❸ *his wit was illustrated by his remark to Lucy* EXEMPLIFY, show, demonstrate, display, represent.

illustrated ▶ adjective WITH ILLUSTRATIONS, with pictures, with drawings, pictorial.

illustration ▶ noun ❶ *the illustrations in children's books* PICTURE, drawing, sketch, figure, plate, print. ❷ *by way of illustration* EXEMPLIFICATION, demonstration, showing; example, typical case, case in point, analogy. ❸ *a career in illustration* ARTWORK, (graphic) design; ornamentation, decoration, embellishment.

illustrative ▶ adjective EXEMPLIFYING, explanatory, elucidatory, elucidative, explicative, expository, illuminative, exegetic.

illustrious ▶ adjective EMINENT, distinguished, acclaimed, notable, noteworthy, prominent, pre-eminent, foremost, leading, important, influential; renowned, famous, famed, well known, celebrated; esteemed, honoured, respected, venerable, august, highly regarded, well thought of, of distinction.
– OPPOSITES unknown.

ill will ▶ noun ANIMOSITY, hostility, enmity, acrimony, animus, hatred, hate, loathing, antipathy; ill feeling, bad blood, antagonism, unfriendliness, dislike; spite, spitefulness, resentment, hard feelings, bitterness; *archaic* disrelish.
– OPPOSITES goodwill.

image ▶ noun ❶ *an image of the Madonna* LIKENESS, resemblance; depiction, portrayal, representation; statue, statuette, sculpture, bust, effigy; painting, picture, portrait, drawing, sketch. ❷ *images of the planet Neptune* PICTURE, photograph, snapshot, photo. ❸ *he contemplated his image in the mirror* REFLECTION, mirror image, likeness. ❹ *the image of this country as democratic* CONCEPTION, impression, idea, perception, notion; mental picture, vision. ❺ *biblical images* SIMILE, metaphor, metonymy; figure of speech, trope, turn of phrase. ❻ *his heart-throb image* PUBLIC PERCEPTION, persona, profile, face, front, facade, mask, guise. ❼ *I'm the image of my grandfather* DOUBLE, living image, lookalike, clone, copy, twin, duplicate, exact likeness, mirror-image; *informal* spitting image, dead ringer; *archaic* similitude. ❽ *a graven image* IDOL, icon, fetish, totem.
– RELATED TERMS icono-.
▶ verb *she imaged imposing castles* ENVISAGE, envision, imagine, picture, see in one's mind's eye.

imaginable ▶ adjective THINKABLE, conceivable, supposable, believable, credible, creditable; possible, plausible, feasible; *rare* cogitable.

imaginary ▶ adjective UNREAL, non-existent, fictional, fictitious, pretend, make-believe, mythical, fabulous, fanciful, illusory; made-up, dreamed-up, invented, fancied; *archaic* visionary.
– OPPOSITES real.

imagination ▶ noun ❶ *a vivid imagination* CREATIVE POWER, fancy; *informal* mind's eye. ❷ *you need imagination in dealing with these problems* CREATIVITY, imaginativeness, creativeness; vision, inspiration, inventiveness, invention, resourcefulness, ingenuity; originality, innovation, innovativeness. ❸ *the album captured the public's imagination* INTEREST, fascination, attention, passion, curiosity.

imaginative ▶ adjective CREATIVE, visionary,

inspired, inventive, resourceful, ingenious; original, innovative, innovatory, unorthodox, unconventional; fanciful, whimsical.

imagine ▶ verb ❶ *one can imagine the cloud-capped castle* VISUALIZE, envisage, envision, picture, see in the mind's eye; dream up, think up/of, conceive. ❷ *I imagine he was at home* ASSUME, presume, expect, take it (as read), presuppose; suppose, think (it likely), dare say, surmise, believe, be of the view; *N. Amer.* figure; *informal* guess, reckon; *formal* opine.

imbalance ▶ noun DISPARITY, variance, variation, polarity, contrast, lack of harmony; gulf, breach, gap.

imbed ▶ verb. *See* EMBED.

imbibe ▶ verb (*formal*) ❶ *they'd imbibed too much whisky* DRINK, consume, quaff, guzzle, gulp (down); *informal* knock back, down, sink. ❷ *he had imbibed liberally* DRINK (ALCOHOL), take strong drink, tipple; *informal* booze, knock a few back; *N. Amer. informal* bend one's elbow; *archaic* tope. ❸ *imbibing local history* ASSIMILATE, absorb, soak up, take in, drink in, learn, acquire, grasp, pick up, familiarize oneself with.

imbroglio ▶ noun ❶ *a political imbroglio* COMPLICATED SITUATION, complication, problem, difficulty, predicament, trouble, confusion, entanglement, muddle, mess; *informal* bind, jam, pickle, fix, corner, hole. ❷ (*archaic*) *an imbroglio of papers* JUMBLE, muddle, mess, clutter, hotchpotch, mishmash; *N. Amer.* hodgepodge.

imbue ▶ verb PERMEATE, saturate, diffuse, suffuse, pervade; impregnate, inject, inculcate, ingrain, inspire; fill.

imitate ▶ verb ❶ *other artists have imitated his style* EMULATE, copy, model oneself on, follow, echo, parrot; *informal* rip off. ❷ *he imitated Winston Churchill* MIMIC, do an impression of, impersonate, ape; parody, caricature, burlesque, travesty; *informal* take off, send up; *N. Amer. informal* make like; *formal* personate; *archaic* monkey. ❸ *the tombs imitated houses* RESEMBLE, look like, be like; echo, mirror; bring to mind, remind one of.

imitation ▶ noun ❶ *an imitation of a sailor's hat* COPY, simulation, reproduction, replica. ❷ *learning by imitation* EMULATION, copying, echoing, parroting. ❸ *a perfect imitation of Francis* IMPERSONATION, impression, parody, mockery, caricature, burlesque, travesty, lampoon, pastiche; mimicry, mimicking, imitating, aping; *informal* send-up, take-off, spoof.

▶ adjective *imitation ivory* ARTIFICIAL, synthetic, simulated, man-made, manufactured, ersatz, substitute; mock, sham, fake, bogus; *informal* pseudo, phoney.

– OPPOSITES real, genuine.

imitative ▶ adjective ❶ *imitative crime* SIMILAR, like, mimicking; *informal* copycat. ❷ *I found the film empty and imitative* DERIVATIVE, unoriginal, unimaginative, uninspired, plagiarized, plagiaristic; clichéd, hackneyed, stale, trite, banal; *informal* cribbed, old hat. ❸ *imitative words* ONOMATOPOEIC, echoic.

imitator ▶ noun ❶ *the show's success has sparked off many imitators* COPIER, copyist, emulator, follower, mimic, plagiarist, ape, parrot; *informal* copycat. ❷ *an Elvis imitator* IMPERSONATOR, impressionist, mimicker; parodist, caricaturist, lampooner.

immaculate ▶ adjective ❶ *an immaculate white shirt* CLEAN, spotless, pristine, unsoiled, unstained, unsullied; shining, shiny, gleaming; neat, tidy, spick and span; *informal* squeaky clean. ❷ *immaculate condition* PERFECT, pristine, mint; flawless, faultless, unblemished, unspoiled, undamaged; excellent, impeccable; *informal* tip-top, A1. ❸ *his immaculate record* UNBLEMISHED, spotless, impeccable, unsullied, undefiled, untarnished, stainless; *informal* squeaky clean.

– OPPOSITES dirty, damaged.

immanent ▶ adjective ❶ *the protection of liberties immanent in the constitution* INHERENT, intrinsic, innate, latent, essential, fundamental, basic. ❷ *God is immanent in His creation* PERVASIVE, pervading, permeating; omnipresent.

immaterial ▶ adjective ❶ *the difference in our ages was immaterial* IRRELEVANT, unimportant, inconsequential, insignificant, of no matter/moment, of little account, beside the point, neither here nor there. ❷ *the immaterial soul* INTANGIBLE, incorporeal, bodiless, disembodied, impalpable, ethereal, insubstantial; spiritual, unearthly, supernatural.

– OPPOSITES significant, physical.

immature ▶ adjective ❶ *an immature Stilton* UNRIPE, not mature, unmellowed; undeveloped, unformed, unfinished. ❷ *an extremely immature girl* CHILDISH, babyish, infantile, juvenile, puerile, jejune, callow, green, inexperienced, unsophisticated, unworldly, naive; *informal* wet behind the ears.

– OPPOSITES ripe.

immeasurable ▶ adjective INCALCULABLE, inestimable, innumerable, untold; limitless, boundless, unbounded, unlimited, illimitable, infinite, never-ending, interminable, endless, inexhaustible; vast, immense, great, abundant; *informal* no end of; *poetic/literary* myriad.

immediate ▶ adjective ❶ *the UN called for immediate action* INSTANT, instantaneous, swift, prompt, speedy, rapid, quick, expeditious; sudden, hurried, hasty, precipitate; *informal* snappy; *poetic/literary* rathe. ❷ *their immediate concerns* CURRENT, present, existing, actual; urgent, pressing. ❸ *the immediate past* RECENT, not long past, just gone; occurring recently. ❹ *our immediate neighbours* NEAREST, near, close, closest, next-door; adjacent, adjoining. ❺ *the immediate cause of death* DIRECT, primary.

– OPPOSITES delayed, distant.

immediately ▶ adverb ❶ *it was necessary to make a decision immediately* STRAIGHT AWAY, at once, right away, instantly, now, directly, promptly, forthwith, this/that (very) minute, this/that instant, there and then, here and now, without delay, without further ado, post-haste; quickly, as fast as possible, speedily, as soon as possible, a.s.a.p.; *informal* pronto, in double-quick time, pretty damn quick, p.d.q., toot sweet; *archaic* instanter, forthright. ❷ *I sat immediately behind him* DIRECTLY, right, exactly, precisely, squarely, just, dead; *informal* slap bang; *N. Amer. informal* smack dab.

immemorial ▶ adjective ANCIENT, (very) old, age-old, antediluvian, timeless, archaic, long-standing, time-worn, time-honoured; traditional; *poetic/literary* of yore.

immense ▶ adjective HUGE, vast, massive, enormous, gigantic, colossal, great, very large/big, monumental, towering, tremendous; giant, elephantine, monstrous, mammoth, titanic, king-sized; *informal* mega, monster, whopping (great), thumping (great), humongous, jumbo; *Brit. informal* whacking (great), ginormous.
– OPPOSITES tiny.

immensely ▶ adverb EXTREMELY, very, exceedingly, exceptionally, extraordinarily, tremendously, hugely, singularly, distinctly, outstandingly, uncommonly, unusually, decidedly, particularly, eminently, supremely, highly, remarkably, really, truly, mightily, thoroughly, in the extreme; *informal* terrifically, awfully, fearfully, terribly, devilishly, seriously, mega, damn, damned; *Brit. informal* ever so, well, bloody, hellish, dead, jolly; *N. Amer. informal* real, mighty, powerful, awful, darned; *informal, dated* devilish, frightfully; *archaic* exceeding.
– OPPOSITES slightly.

immerse ▶ verb ❶ *litmus paper turns red on being immersed in acid* SUBMERGE, dip, dunk, duck, sink; soak, drench, saturate, wet. ❷ *new Christians were immersed in the river* BAPTIZE, christen; *informal, dated* dip; *rare* lustrate. ❸ *Elliot was immersed in his work* ABSORB, engross, occupy, engage, involve, bury; busy, employ, preoccupy; *informal* lose oneself in.

immigrant ▶ noun NEWCOMER, settler, incomer, migrant, emigrant; non-native, foreigner, alien.
– OPPOSITES native.

imminent ▶ adjective IMPENDING, close (at hand), near, (fast) approaching, coming, forthcoming, on the way, in the offing, in the pipeline, on the horizon, in the air/wind, expected, anticipated, brewing, looming; *informal* on the cards.

immobile ▶ adjective ❶ *she sat immobile for a long time* MOTIONLESS, without moving, still, stock-still, static, stationary; rooted to the spot, rigid, frozen, transfixed, like a statue, not moving a muscle. ❷ *she dreaded being immobile* UNABLE TO MOVE, immobilized; paralysed, crippled.
– OPPOSITES moving.

immobilize ▶ verb PUT OUT OF ACTION, disable, make inoperative, inactivate, deactivate, paralyse, cripple; bring to a standstill, halt, stop; clamp, wheel-clamp.

immoderate ▶ adjective EXCESSIVE, heavy, intemperate, unrestrained, unrestricted, uncontrolled, unlimited, unbridled, uncurbed, overindulgent, imprudent, reckless; undue, inordinate, unreasonable, unjustified, unwarranted, uncalled for, outrageous; extravagant, lavish, prodigal, profligate.

immodest ▶ adjective INDECOROUS, improper, indecent, indelicate, immoral; forward, bold, brazen, impudent, shameless, loose, wanton; *informal* fresh, cheeky, saucy.

immolate ▶ verb SACRIFICE, offer up; kill, slaughter, burn.

immoral ▶ adjective UNETHICAL, bad, morally wrong, wrongful, wicked, evil, unprincipled, unscrupulous, dishonourable, dishonest, unconscionable, iniquitous, disreputable, corrupt, depraved, vile, villainous, nefarious, base, miscreant; sinful, impure, unchaste, unvirtuous, shameless, degenerate, debauched, dissolute, reprobate, lewd, licentious, wanton, promiscuous; *informal* shady, low-down; *Brit. informal* dodgy, crooked.
– OPPOSITES ethical, chaste.

immorality ▶ noun WICKEDNESS, immoral behaviour, badness, evil, vileness, corruption, dishonesty, dishonourableness; sinfulness, unchastity, sin, depravity, vice, degeneracy, debauchery, dissolution, perversion, lewdness, wantonness, promiscuity; *informal* shadiness; *Brit. informal* crookedness; *formal* turpitude.

immortal ▶ adjective ❶ *our souls are immortal* UNDYING, deathless, eternal, everlasting, never-ending, endless, lasting, enduring; imperishable, indestructible, inextinguishable, immutable. ❷ *an immortal children's classic* TIMELESS, perennial, classic, time-honoured, enduring; famous, famed, renowned, great, eminent, outstanding, acclaimed, celebrated.
▶ noun ❶ *Greek temples of the immortals* GOD, GODDESS, deity, divine being, supreme being, divinity. ❷ *one of the immortals of soccer* GREAT, hero, Olympian.

immortality ▶ noun ❶ *the immortality of the gods* ETERNAL LIFE, everlasting life, deathlessness; indestructibility, imperishability. ❷ *the book has achieved immortality* TIMELESSNESS, legendary status, lasting fame/renown.

immortalize ▶ verb COMMEMORATE, memorialize, eternalize; celebrate, eulogize, pay tribute to, honour, salute, exalt, glorify; *poetic/literary* eternize.

immovable ▶ adjective ❶ *lock your bike to something immovable* FIXED, secure, stable, moored, anchored, braced, set firm, set fast; stuck, jammed, stiff, unbudgeable. ❷ *he sat immovable* MOTIONLESS, unmoving, stationary, still, stock-still, not moving a muscle, rooted to the spot; transfixed, paralysed, frozen. ❸ *she was immovable in her loyalties* STEADFAST, unwavering, unswerving, resolute, determined, firm, unshakeable, unfailing, dogged, tenacious, inflexible, unyielding, unbending, uncompromising, iron-willed; *N. Amer.* rock-ribbed.
– OPPOSITES mobile, moving.

immune ▶ adjective RESISTANT, not subject, not liable, unsusceptible, not vulnerable; protected from, safe from, secure against, not in danger of.
– OPPOSITES susceptible.

immunity ▶ noun ❶ *an immunity to malaria* RESISTANCE, non-susceptibility; ability to fight off, protection against, defences against; immunization against, inoculation against. ❷ *immunity from prosecution* EXEMPTION, exception, freedom, release, dispensation; *informal* a let-off. ❸ *diplomatic immunity* INDEMNITY, privilege, prerogative, right, liberty, licence; legal exemption, impunity, protection.

immunize ▶ verb VACCINATE, inoculate, inject; protect from, safeguard against; *informal* give someone a jab/shot.

immure ▶ verb CONFINE, intern, shut up, lock up, incarcerate, imprison, jail, put behind bars, put under lock and key, hold captive, hold prisoner; detain, hold.

immutable ▶ adjective FIXED, set, rigid, inflexible, permanent, established; unchanging, unchanged, unvarying, unvaried, static, constant, lasting, enduring.
– OPPOSITES variable.

imp ▶ noun ❶ *imps are thought to sprout from Satan* DEMON, devil, fiend; hobgoblin, goblin, elf, sprite, puck, cacodemon; *archaic* bugbear. ❷ *a cheeky young imp* RASCAL, monkey, devil, troublemaker, wretch, urchin, tearaway; *informal* scamp, brat, monster, horror, tyke, whippersnapper; *Brit. informal* perisher; *N. Amer. informal* hellion, varmint; *archaic* scapegrace, rapscallion.

impact ▶ noun ❶ *the force of the impact* COLLISION, crash, smash, bump, bang, knock. ❷ *the job losses will have a major impact* EFFECT, influence; consequences, repercussions, ramifications, reverberations.
▶ verb ❶ (*N. Amer.*) *a comet impacted the earth sixty million years ago* CRASH INTO, smash into, collide with, hit, strike, smack into, bang into. ❷ *high interest rates have impacted on retail spending* AFFECT, influence, have an effect, make an impression; hit, touch, change, alter, modify, transform, shape.

impair ▶ verb HAVE A NEGATIVE EFFECT ON, damage, harm, diminish, reduce, weaken, lessen, decrease, impede, hinder; undermine, compromise; *formal* vitiate.
– OPPOSITES improve, enhance.

impaired ▶ adjective DISABLED, handicapped, incapacitated; *euphemistic* challenged, differently abled.

impairment ▶ noun DISABILITY, handicap, abnormality, defect, dysfunction.

impale ▶ verb STICK, skewer, spear, spike, transfix; pierce, stab, run through; *poetic/literary* transpierce.

impalpable ▶ adjective INTANGIBLE, insubstantial, incorporeal; indefinable, elusive, indescribable.

impart ▶ verb ❶ *she had news to impart* COMMUNICATE, pass on, convey, transmit, relay, relate, recount, tell, make known, make public, report, announce, proclaim, spread, disseminate, circulate, promulgate, broadcast; disclose, reveal, divulge; *informal* let on about, blab; *archaic* discover, unbosom. ❷ *the brush imparts a good sheen* GIVE, bestow, confer, grant, lend, afford, provide, supply.

impartial ▶ adjective UNBIASED, unprejudiced, neutral, non-partisan, disinterested, detached, dispassionate, objective, open-minded, equitable, even-handed, fair, just.
– OPPOSITES biased, partisan.

impassable ▶ adjective UNPASSABLE, unnavigable, untraversable; closed, blocked.

impasse ▶ noun DEADLOCK, dead end, stalemate, checkmate, stand-off; standstill, halt, (full) stop.

impassioned ▶ adjective EMOTIONAL, heartfelt, wholehearted, earnest, sincere, fervent, ardent, passionate, fervid; *poetic/literary* perfervid; *rare* passional.

impassive ▶ adjective EXPRESSIONLESS, inexpressive, inscrutable, blank, deadpan, poker-faced, straight-faced; stony, wooden, unresponsive.
– OPPOSITES expressive.

impatience ▶ noun ❶ *he was shifting in his seat with impatience* RESTLESSNESS, restiveness, agitation, nervousness; eagerness, keenness; *informal* jitteriness. ❷ *a burst of impatience* IRRITABILITY, testiness, tetchiness, irascibility, querulousness, peevishness, frustration, exasperation, annoyance, pique.

impatient ▶ adjective ❶ *Melissa grew impatient* RESTLESS, restive, agitated, nervous, anxious, ill at ease, edgy, jumpy, keyed up; *Brit.* nervy; *informal* twitchy, jittery, uptight. ❷ *they are impatient to get back home* ANXIOUS, eager, keen, yearning, longing, aching; *informal* itching, dying. ❸ *an impatient gesture* IRRITATED, annoyed, angry, testy, tetchy, snappy, cross, querulous, peevish, piqued, short-tempered;

abrupt, curt, brusque, terse, short; *informal* peeved.
– OPPOSITES calm, reluctant.

impeach ▶ verb ❶ (*N. Amer.*) *moves to impeach the president* INDICT, charge, accuse, lay charges against, arraign, take to court, put on trial, prosecute. ❷ *the headlines impeached their clean image* CHALLENGE, question, call into question, raise doubts about.

impeccable ▶ adjective FLAWLESS, faultless, unblemished, spotless, stainless, perfect, exemplary; sinless, irreproachable, blameless, guiltless; *informal* squeaky clean.
– OPPOSITES imperfect, sinful.

impecunious ▶ adjective PENNILESS, poor, impoverished, indigent, insolvent, hard up, poverty-stricken, needy, destitute; in straitened circumstances, unable to make ends meet; *Brit.* on the breadline; *informal* (flat) broke, strapped (for cash), on one's uppers; *Brit. informal* skint, stony broke, in Queer Street; *N. Amer. informal* stone broke; *formal* penurious.
– OPPOSITES wealthy.

impede ▶ verb HINDER, obstruct, hamper, hold back/up, delay, interfere with, disrupt, retard, slow (down); block, check, stop, thwart, frustrate, baulk, foil, derail; *informal* stymie; *Brit. informal* scupper, throw a spanner in the works; *N. Amer. informal* bork, throw a monkey wrench in the works; *dated* cumber.
– OPPOSITES facilitate.

impediment ▶ noun ❶ *an impediment to economic improvement* HINDRANCE, obstruction, obstacle, barrier, bar, block, check, curb, restriction, limitation; setback, difficulty, snag, hitch, stumbling block; *informal* fly in the ointment, hiccup; *Brit. informal* spanner in the works; *N. Amer. informal* monkey wrench in the works; *archaic* cumber. ❷ *a speech impediment* DEFECT; stammer, stutter, lisp.

impedimenta ▶ plural noun PARAPHERNALIA, trappings, equipment, accoutrements, appurtenances, accessories, bits and pieces, tackle; *informal* stuff, gear; *Brit. informal* clobber, gubbins; *archaic* equipage.

impel ▶ verb ❶ *financial difficulties impelled her to seek work* FORCE, compel, constrain, oblige, require, make, urge, press, pressurize, drive, push, spur, prod, goad, incite, prompt, persuade. ❷ *vital energies impel him in unforeseen directions* PROPEL, drive, move, get going, get moving.

impending ▶ adjective IMMINENT, close (at hand), near, nearing, approaching, coming, forthcoming, upcoming, to come, on the way, about to happen, in store, in the offing, on the horizon, in the air/wind, brewing, looming, threatening, menacing.

impenetrable ▶ adjective ❶ *impenetrable armoured plating* UNBREAKABLE, indestructible, solid, thick, unyielding; impregnable, inviolable, unassailable, unpierceable. ❷ *a dark, impenetrable forest* IMPASSABLE, unpassable, inaccessible, unnavigable, untraversable; dense, thick, overgrown. ❸ *an impenetrable clique* EXCLUSIVE, closed, secretive, secret, private; restrictive, restricted, limited. ❹ *impenetrable statistics* INCOMPREHENSIBLE, unfathomable, inexplicable, unintelligible, unclear, baffling, bewildering, puzzling, perplexing, confusing, abstruse, opaque; complex, complicated, difficult; *archaic* wildering.

impenitent ▶ adjective UNREPENTANT, unrepenting, uncontrite, remorseless, unashamed, unapologetic, unabashed.

imperative ▶ adjective ❶ *it is imperative that you find him* VITALLY IMPORTANT, of vital importance, all-important, vital, crucial, critical, essential, necessary, indispensable, urgent. ❷ *the imperative note in her voice* PEREMPTORY, commanding, imperious, authoritative, masterful, dictatorial, assertive, firm, insistent.
– OPPOSITES unimportant, submissive.

imperceptible ▶ adjective UNNOTICEABLE, undetectable, indistinguishable, indiscernible, invisible, inaudible, impalpable, unobtrusive; slight, small, subtle, faint, fine, negligible; indistinct, unclear, obscure, vague, indefinite, hard to make out.
– OPPOSITES noticeable.

imperfect ▶ adjective ❶ *the good were returned as imperfect* FAULTY, flawed, defective, shoddy, unsound, inferior, second-rate, below standard, substandard; damaged, blemished, torn, broken, cracked, scratched; *informal* not up to scratch, tenth-rate, crummy; *Brit. informal* duff. ❷ *an imperfect form of the manuscript* INCOMPLETE, unfinished, half-done; unpolished, unrefined, rough. ❸ *she spoke imperfect Arabic* BROKEN, faltering, halting, hesitant, rudimentary, limited.
– OPPOSITES flawless.

imperfection ▶ noun ❶ *the glass is free from imperfections* DEFECT, fault, flaw, deformity, discoloration, disfigurement; crack, scratch, chip, dent, blemish, stain, spot, mark. ❷ *he was aware of his imperfections* FLAW, fault, failing, deficiency, weakness, weak point, shortcoming, foible, inadequacy, limitation. ❸ *the imperfection of the fossil record* INCOMPLETENESS, patchiness, deficiency; roughness, crudeness.
– OPPOSITES strength.

imperial ▶ adjective ❶ *imperial banners* ROYAL, regal, monarchal, monarchial, monarchical, sovereign, kingly, queenly, princely. ❷ *her imperial bearing* MAJESTIC, grand, dignified, proud, stately, noble, aristocratic, regal; magnificent, imposing, impressive. ❸ *our customers thought we were imperial* IMPERIOUS, high-handed, peremptory, dictatorial, domineering, bossy, arrogant, overweening, overbearing.

imperil ▶ verb ENDANGER, jeopardize, risk, put

in danger, put in jeopardy, expose to danger; threaten, pose a threat to; *archaic* peril.

imperious ▶ adjective PEREMPTORY, high-handed, commanding, imperial, overbearing, overweening, domineering, authoritarian, dictatorial, authoritative, lordly, assertive, bossy, arrogant; *informal* pushy, high and mighty.

imperishable ▶ adjective ENDURING, everlasting, undying, immortal, perennial, long-lasting; indestructible, inextinguishable, ineradicable, unfading, permanent, never-ending, never dying; *poetic/literary* sempiternal, perdurable.

impermanent ▶ adjective TEMPORARY, transient, transitory, passing, fleeting, momentary, ephemeral, fugitive; short-lived, brief, here today and gone tomorrow; *poetic/literary* evanescent.

impermeable ▶ adjective WATERTIGHT, waterproof, damp-proof, airtight, (hermetically) sealed.

impersonal ▶ adjective ❶ *the hand of fate is impersonal* NEUTRAL, unbiased, non-partisan, unprejudiced, objective, detached, disinterested, dispassionate, without favouritism. ❷ *he remained strangely impersonal* ALOOF, distant, remote, reserved, withdrawn, unemotional, unsentimental, dispassionate, cold, cool, indifferent, unconcerned; formal, stiff, businesslike; *informal* starchy, stand-offish.
– OPPOSITES biased, warm.

impersonate ▶ verb IMITATE, mimic, do an impression of, ape; parody, caricature, burlesque, travesty, satirize, lampoon; masquerade as, pose as, pass oneself off as; *informal* take off, send up; *N. Amer. informal* make like; *formal* personate; *archaic* monkey.

impersonation ▶ noun IMPRESSION, imitation; parody, caricature, burlesque, travesty, lampoon, pastiche; *informal* take-off, send-up; *formal* personation.

impertinence ▶ noun RUDENESS, insolence, impoliteness, bad manners, discourtesy, discourteousness, disrespect, incivility; impudence, cheek, cheekiness, audacity, temerity, effrontery, nerve, gall, boldness, cockiness, brazenness; *informal* brass (neck); *Brit. informal* sauce; *N. Amer. informal* sass, sassiness, chutzpah; *archaic* assumption.

impertinent ▶ adjective ❶ *she asked a lot of impertinent questions* RUDE, insolent, impolite, ill-mannered, bad-mannered, uncivil, discourteous, disrespectful; impudent, cheeky, audacious, bold, brazen, brash, presumptuous, forward; tactless, undiplomatic; *informal* brass-necked, saucy; *N. Amer. informal* sassy; *archaic* contumelious. ❷ (*formal*) *talk of 'rhetoric' is impertinent to this process* IRRELEVANT, inapplicable, inapposite, inappropriate, immaterial, unrelated, unconnected, not germane; beside the point, out of place.
– OPPOSITES polite, relevant.

imperturbable ▶ adjective SELF-POSSESSED, composed, {cool, calm, and collected}, cool-headed, self-controlled, serene, relaxed, unexcitable, even-tempered, placid, phlegmatic; unperturbed, unflustered, unruffled; *informal* unflappable, unfazed, laid-back.
– OPPOSITES excitable.

impervious ▶ adjective ❶ *he seemed impervious to the chill wind* UNAFFECTED, untouched, immune, invulnerable, insusceptible, resistant, indifferent, heedless, oblivious; proof against. ❷ *an impervious damp-proof course* IMPERMEABLE, impenetrable, impregnable, waterproof, watertight; (hermetically) sealed.
– OPPOSITES susceptible, permeable.

impetuous ▶ adjective ❶ *an impetuous decision* IMPULSIVE, rash, hasty, overhasty, reckless, heedless, foolhardy, incautious, imprudent, injudicious, ill-considered, unthought-out; spontaneous, impromptu, spur-of-the-moment, precipitate, precipitous, hurried, rushed. ❷ *an impetuous flow of water* TORRENTIAL, powerful, forceful, vigorous, violent, raging, relentless, uncontrolled; rapid, fast, fast-flowing.
– OPPOSITES considered, sluggish.

impetus ▶ noun ❶ *the flywheel lost all its impetus* MOMENTUM, propulsion, impulsion, motive force, driving force, drive, thrust; energy, force, power, push, strength. ❷ *the sales force were given fresh impetus* MOTIVATION, stimulus, incitement, incentive, inducement, inspiration, encouragement, boost; *informal* a shot in the arm.

impiety ▶ noun ❶ *a world of impiety and immorality* GODLESSNESS, ungodliness, unholiness, irreligion, sinfulness, sin, vice, immorality, unrighteousness; apostasy, atheism, agnosticism, paganism, heathenism, non-belief, unbelief. ❷ *one impiety will cost me my eternity in paradise* SIN, transgression, wrongdoing, evil-doing, wrong, misdeed, misdemeanour.
– OPPOSITES faith.

impinge ▶ verb ❶ *these issues impinge on all of us* AFFECT, have an effect, touch, influence, make an impact, leave a mark. ❷ *the proposed fencing would impinge on a public bridleway* ENCROACH, intrude, infringe, invade, trespass, obtrude, cut through, interfere with; violate; *archaic* entrench on. ❸ (*Physics*) *electrically charged particles impinge on the lunar surface* STRIKE, hit, collide with.

impious ▶ adjective GODLESS, ungodly, unholy, irreligious, sinful, immoral, unrighteous, sacrilegious, profane, blasphemous, irreverent; apostate, atheistic, agnostic, pagan, heathen, faithless, non-believing, unbelieving; *rare* nullifidian.

impish ▶ adjective ❶ *he takes an impish delight in shocking the press* MISCHIEVOUS, naughty, wicked, rascally, roguish, playful, sportive; mischief-making, full of mischief. ❷ *an impish grin* ELFIN, elflike, pixie-like, puckish; mischievous, roguish.

implacable ▶ adjective UNAPPEASABLE, unpacifiable, unplacatable, unmollifiable, unforgiving; intransigent, inflexible, unyielding, unbending, uncompromising, unrelenting, ruthless, remorseless, merciless, heartless, pitiless, cruel, hard, harsh, stern, tough.

implant ▶ verb ❶ *the collagen is implanted under the skin* INSERT, embed, bury, lodge, place; graft. ❷ *he implanted the idea in my mind* INSTIL, inculcate, insinuate, introduce, inject, plant, sow, root, lodge.

▶ noun *a silicone implant* TRANSPLANT, graft, implantation, insert.

implausible ▶ adjective UNLIKELY, improbable, questionable, doubtful, debatable; unrealistic, unconvincing, far-fetched, incredible, unbelievable, unimaginable, inconceivable, fantastic, fanciful, ridiculous, absurd, preposterous; *informal* cock and bull.
– OPPOSITES convincing.

implement ▶ noun *garden implements* TOOL, utensil, instrument, device, apparatus, gadget, contraption, appliance, machine, contrivance; *informal* gizmo.

▶ verb *the cost of implementing the new law* EXECUTE, apply, put into effect/action, put into practice, carry out/through, perform, enact; fulfil, discharge, accomplish, bring about, achieve, realize; *formal* effectuate.

implicate ▶ verb ❶ *he had been implicated in a financial scandal* INCRIMINATE, compromise; involve, connect, embroil, enmesh; *archaic* inculpate. ❷ *viruses are implicated in the development of cancer* INVOLVE IN, concern with, associate with, connect with. ❸ *when one asks a question one implicates that one desires an answer.* See IMPLY sense 1.

implication ▶ noun ❶ *he was smarting at their implication* SUGGESTION, inference, insinuation, innuendo, hint, intimation, imputation. ❷ *important political implications* CONSEQUENCE, result, ramification, repercussion, reverberation, effect. ❸ *his implication in the murder case* INCRIMINATION, involvement, connection, entanglement, association; *archaic* inculpation.

implicit ▶ adjective ❶ *implicit assumptions* IMPLIED, inferred, understood, hinted at, suggested, deducible; unspoken, unexpressed, undeclared, unstated, tacit, unacknowledged, taken for granted. ❷ *assumptions implicit in the way questions are asked* INHERENT, latent, underlying, inbuilt, incorporated. ❸ *an implicit trust in human nature* ABSOLUTE, complete, total, wholehearted, perfect, utter; unqualified, unconditional; unshakeable, unquestioning, firm, steadfast.
– OPPOSITES explicit.

implicitly ▶ adverb COMPLETELY, absolutely, totally, wholeheartedly, utterly, unconditionally, unreservedly, without reservation.

implied ▶ adjective IMPLICIT, hinted at, suggested, insinuated, inferred, understood, deducible; unspoken, unexpressed, undeclared, unstated, tacit, unacknowledged, taken for granted.
– OPPOSITES explicit.

implore ▶ verb ❶ *his mother implored him to continue studying* PLEAD WITH, beg, entreat, beseech, appeal to, ask, request, call on; exhort, urge, enjoin, press, push, petition, bid. ❷ (*archaic*) *she implored pity* BEG FOR, plead for, appeal for, call for; ask for, request, sue for.

imply ▶ verb ❶ *are you implying he is mad?* INSINUATE, suggest, hint, intimate, say indirectly, indicate, give someone to understand, make out. ❷ *the forecasted traffic increase implies more roads* INVOLVE, entail; mean, point to, signify, indicate, signal; necessitate, require.

impolite ▶ adjective RUDE, bad-mannered, ill-mannered, discourteous, uncivil, disrespectful, inconsiderate, boorish, churlish, ill-bred, ungentlemanly, unladylike, ungracious; insolent, impudent, impertinent, cheeky; loutish, rough, crude, indelicate, indecorous; *informal* ignorant, lippy; *archaic* malapert, contumelious.

impolitic ▶ adjective IMPRUDENT, unwise, injudicious, incautious, irresponsible; ill-judged, ill-advised, misguided, rash, reckless, foolhardy, foolish, short-sighted; undiplomatic, tactless.
– OPPOSITES prudent.

import ▶ verb *the UK imports iron ore* BUY FROM ABROAD, bring in, buy in, ship in.
– OPPOSITES export.

▶ noun ❶ *a tax on imports* IMPORTED COMMODITY, foreign commodity. ❷ *the import of foreign books* IMPORTATION, importing, bringing in, bringing from abroad, shipping in. ❸ *a matter of great import* IMPORTANCE, significance, consequence, momentousness, magnitude, substance, weight, note, gravity, seriousness; *formal* moment. ❹ *the full import of her words* MEANING, sense, essence, gist, drift, purport, message, thrust, substance, implication.
– OPPOSITES export, insignificance.

importance ▶ noun ❶ *an event of immense importance* SIGNIFICANCE, momentousness, import, consequence, note, noteworthiness, substance; seriousness, gravity, weightiness, urgency. ❷ *she had a fine sense of her own importance* POWER, influence, authority, sway, weight, dominance; prominence, eminence, pre-eminence, notability, worth.
– OPPOSITES insignificance.

important ▶ adjective ❶ *an important meeting* SIGNIFICANT, consequential, momentous, of great import, major; critical, crucial, vital, pivotal, decisive, urgent, historic; serious, grave, weighty, material; *formal* of great moment.

❷ *the important thing is that you do well in your exams* MAIN, chief, principal, key, major, salient, prime, foremost, paramount, overriding, crucial, vital, critical, essential, significant; central, fundamental; *informal* number-one. ❸ *the school was important to the community* OF VALUE, valuable, beneficial, necessary, essential, indispensable, vital; of concern, of interest, relevant, pertinent. ❹ *he was an important man* POWERFUL, influential, of influence, well-connected, high-ranking; prominent, eminent, pre-eminent, notable, noteworthy, of note; distinguished, esteemed, respected, prestigious, celebrated, famous, great; *informal* major league.
– OPPOSITES trivial, insignificant.

importunate ▶ adjective PERSISTENT, insistent, tenacious, persevering, dogged, unrelenting, tireless, indefatigable; aggressive, high-pressure; *informal* pushy; *formal* exigent, pertinacious.

importune ▶ verb ❶ *he importuned her for some spare change* BEG, beseech, entreat, implore, plead with, appeal to, call on; harass, pester, press, badger, bother, nag, harry; *informal* hassle. ❷ *they arrested me for importuning* SOLICIT; *informal* proposition; *N. Amer. informal* hustle.

impose ▶ verb ❶ *he imposed his ideas on the art director* FOIST, force, inflict, press, urge; *informal* saddle someone with, land someone with. ❷ *new taxes will be imposed* LEVY, charge, apply, enforce; set, establish, institute, introduce, bring into effect. ❸ *how dare you impose on me like this!* TAKE ADVANTAGE OF, exploit, take liberties with, treat unfairly; bother, trouble, disturb, inconvenience, put out, put to trouble.
■ **impose oneself** FORCE ONESELF, foist oneself; control, take charge of; *informal* call the shots/tune, be in the driving seat, be in the saddle, run the show.

imposing ▶ adjective IMPRESSIVE, striking, arresting, eye-catching, dramatic, spectacular, stunning, awesome, formidable, splendid, grand, majestic.
– OPPOSITES modest.

imposition ▶ noun ❶ *the imposition of an alien culture* IMPOSING, foisting, forcing, inflicting. ❷ *the imposition of VAT* LEVYING, charging, application, applying, enforcement, enforcing; setting, establishment, introduction, institution. ❸ *it would be no imposition* BURDEN, encumbrance, strain, bother, worry; *informal* hassle. ❹ *the levying of special impositions* TAX, levy, duty, charge, tariff, toll, impost; *formal* mulct, exaction.

impossible ▶ adjective ❶ *gale force winds made fishing impossible* NOT POSSIBLE, out of the question, unfeasible, impractical, impracticable, non-viable, unworkable; unthinkable, unimaginable, inconceivable. ❷ *an impossible dream* UNATTAINABLE, unachievable, unobtainable, hopeless, impractical, implausible, far-fetched, impracticable, unworkable. ❸ *food shortages made life impossible* UNBEARABLE, intolerable, unendurable. ❹ (*informal*) *an impossible woman* UNREASONABLE, objectionable, difficult, awkward; intolerable, unbearable, unendurable; exasperating, maddening, infuriating.
– OPPOSITES attainable, bearable.

impostor ▶ noun IMPERSONATOR, masquerader, pretender, deceiver, hoaxer, trickster, fraudster; fake, fraud, sham; *informal* phoney.

imposture ▶ noun MISREPRESENTATION, pretence, deceit, deception, trickery, artifice, subterfuge; hoax, trick, ruse, dodge; *informal* con (trick), scam, flimflam; *Brit. informal* wheeze.

impotent ▶ adjective ❶ *the legal sanctions are impotent* POWERLESS, ineffective, ineffectual, inadequate, weak, useless, worthless, futile; *poetic/literary* impuissant. ❷ *forces which man is impotent to control* UNABLE, incapable, powerless. ❸ *an impotent opposition party* WEAK, powerless, ineffective, feeble.
– OPPOSITES powerful, effective.

impound ▶ verb ❶ *officials began impounding documents* CONFISCATE, appropriate, take possession of, seize, commandeer, expropriate, requisition, sequester, sequestrate; *Law* distrain. ❷ *the cattle were impounded* PEN IN, shut up/in, fence in, enclose, confine; *N. Amer.* corral. ❸ *unfortunates impounded in prison* LOCK UP, incarcerate, imprison, confine, intern, immure, hold captive, hold prisoner.

impoverish ▶ verb ❶ *the widow had been impoverished* MAKE POOR, make penniless, reduce to penury, bankrupt, ruin, make insolvent, pauperize. ❷ *the trees were impoverishing the soil* WEAKEN, sap, exhaust, deplete.

impoverished ▶ adjective ❶ *an impoverished peasant farmer* POOR, poverty-stricken, penniless, destitute, indigent, impecunious, needy, pauperized, down and out, on the breadline; bankrupt, ruined, insolvent; *informal* (flat) broke, stony broke, on one's uppers, hard up, without a bean, on skid row; *Brit. informal* skint; *N. Amer. informal* stone broke; *formal* penurious. ❷ *the soil is impoverished* WEAKENED, exhausted, drained, sapped, depleted, spent; barren, unproductive, unfertile.
– OPPOSITES rich.

impracticable ▶ adjective UNWORKABLE, unfeasible, non-viable, unachievable, unattainable, unrealizable; impractical.
– OPPOSITES workable, feasible.

impractical ▶ adjective ❶ *an impractical suggestion* UNREALISTIC, unworkable, unfeasible, non-viable, impracticable; ill-thought-out, impossible, absurd, wild; *informal* cock-eyed, crackpot, crazy. ❷ *impractical white ankle boots* UNSUITABLE, not sensible, inappropriate, unserviceable. ❸ *an impractical scholar* IDEALISTIC, unrealistic, romantic, dreamy, fanciful, quixotic; *informal* airy-fairy.

–OPPOSITES practical, sensible.

imprecation ▶ noun (*formal*) ❶ *the most dreadful imprecations* CURSE, malediction; *N. Amer.* hex; *poetic/literary* anathema; *archaic* execration. ❷ *a stream of imprecations* SWEAR WORD, curse, expletive, oath, profanity, four-letter word, obscenity; (**imprecations**) swearing, cursing, foul language, strong language; *N. Amer. informal* cuss word; *archaic* execration.
–OPPOSITES blessing.

imprecise ▶ adjective ❶ *a rather imprecise definition* VAGUE, loose, indefinite, inexplicit, indistinct, non-specific, unspecific, sweeping, broad, general; hazy, fuzzy, woolly, nebulous, ambiguous, equivocal, uncertain. ❷ *an imprecise estimate* INEXACT, approximate, estimated, rough; *N. Amer. informal* ballpark.
–OPPOSITES exact.

impregnable ▶ adjective ❶ *an impregnable castle* INVULNERABLE, impenetrable, unassailable, inviolable, secure, strong, well fortified, well defended; invincible, unconquerable, unbeatable, indestructible. ❷ *an impregnable parliamentary majority* UNASSAILABLE, unbeatable, undefeatable, unshakeable, invincible, unconquerable, invulnerable.
–OPPOSITES vulnerable.

impregnate ▶ verb ❶ *a pad impregnated with natural oils* INFUSE, soak, steep, saturate, drench. ❷ *the woman he had impregnated* MAKE PREGNANT, inseminate, fertilize; *informal* put in the family way; *Brit. informal* get up the duff/spout, put in the club; *N. Amer. informal* knock up; *informal, dated* get into trouble; *archaic* get with child.

impresario ▶ noun ORGANIZER, (stage) manager, producer; promoter, publicist, showman; director, conductor, maestro.

impress ▶ verb ❶ *Hazel had impressed him mightily* MAKE AN IMPRESSION ON, have an impact on, influence, affect, move, stir, rouse, excite, inspire; dazzle, awe, overawe, take someone's breath away, amaze, astonish; *informal* grab, stick in someone's mind. ❷ *goldsmiths impressed his likeness on medallions* IMPRINT, print, stamp, mark, emboss, punch. ❸ *you must impress upon her the need to save* EMPHASIZE TO, stress to, bring home to, instil in, inculcate into, drum into, knock into, din into.
–OPPOSITES disappoint.

impression ▶ noun ❶ *he got the impression that she was hiding something* FEELING, feeling in one's bones, sense, fancy, (sneaking) suspicion, inkling, intuition, hunch; notion, idea, funny feeling; *informal* gut feeling. ❷ *a favourable impression* OPINION, view, image, picture, perception, judgement, verdict, estimation. ❸ *school made a profound impression on me* IMPACT, effect, influence. ❹ *the cap had left a circular impression* INDENTATION, dent, mark, outline, imprint. ❺ *he did a good impression of their science teacher* IMPERSONATION, imitation; parody, caricature, burlesque, travesty, lampoon; *informal* take-off, send-up, spoof; *formal* personation. ❻ *an artist's impression of the gardens* REPRESENTATION, portrayal, depiction, rendition, interpretation, picture, drawing. ❼ *a revised impression of the 1981 edition* PRINT RUN, imprint, reprint, issue, edition.

impressionable ▶ adjective EASILY INFLUENCED, suggestible, susceptible, persuadable, pliable, malleable, pliant, ingenuous, trusting, naive, gullible.

impressive ▶ adjective ❶ *an impressive building* MAGNIFICENT, majestic, imposing, splendid, spectacular, grand, awe-inspiring, stunning, breathtaking; stately, palatial. ❷ *they played some impressive football* ADMIRABLE, masterly, accomplished, expert, skilled, skilful, consummate; excellent, outstanding, first-class, first-rate, fine; *informal* great, mean, nifty, cracking, ace, wizard; *N. Amer. informal* crackerjack.
–OPPOSITES ordinary, mediocre.

imprint ▶ verb ❶ *patterns can be imprinted in the clay* STAMP, print, impress, mark, emboss. ❷ *the image was imprinted on his mind* FIX, establish, stick, lodge, implant, embed.
▶ noun ❶ *her feet left imprints on the floor* IMPRESSION, print, mark, indentation. ❷ *colonialism has left its imprint* IMPACT, lasting effect, influence, impression.

imprison ▶ verb INCARCERATE, send to prison, jail, lock up, put away, intern, detain, hold prisoner, hold captive; *informal* send down, put behind bars, put inside; *Brit. informal* bang up.
–OPPOSITES free, release.

imprisoned ▶ adjective INCARCERATED, in prison, in jail, jailed, locked up, interned, detained, held prisoner, held captive; *informal* sent down, behind bars, doing time, inside; *Brit. informal* doing porridge, doing bird, banged up.

imprisonment ▶ noun INCARCERATION, internment, confinement, detention, captivity; *informal* time; *Brit. informal* porridge, bird; *archaic* durance.

improbability ▶ noun UNLIKELIHOOD, implausibility; doubtfulness, uncertainty, dubiousness.

improbable ▶ adjective ❶ *it seemed improbable that the hot weather should continue* UNLIKELY, doubtful, dubious, debatable, questionable, uncertain; unthinkable, inconceivable, unimaginable, incredible. ❷ *an improbable exaggeration* UNCONVINCING, unbelievable, incredible, ridiculous, absurd, preposterous.
–OPPOSITES certain, believable.

impromptu ▶ adjective *an impromptu lecture* UNREHEARSED, unprepared, unscripted, extempore, extemporized, extemporaneous, improvised, spontaneous, unplanned; *informal* off-the-cuff.

– OPPOSITES prepared, rehearsed.

▶ **adverb** *they played the song impromptu* EXTEMPORE, spontaneously, extemporaneously, without preparation, without rehearsal; *informal* off the cuff, off the top of one's head.

improper ▶ **adjective** ❶ *it is improper for policemen to accept gifts* INAPPROPRIATE, unacceptable, unsuitable, unprofessional, irregular; unethical, corrupt, immoral, dishonest, dishonourable; *informal* not cricket. ❷ *it was improper for young ladies to drive a young man home* UNSEEMLY, indecorous, unfitting, unladylike, ungentlemanly, indelicate, impolite; indecent, immodest, immoral. ❸ *an extremely improper poem* INDECENT, risqué, off colour, suggestive, naughty, ribald, earthy, smutty, dirty, filthy, vulgar, crude, rude, obscene, lewd; *informal* blue, raunchy, steamy; *Brit. informal* fruity, saucy.
– OPPOSITES acceptable, decent.

impropriety ▶ **noun** ❶ *a suggestion of impropriety* WRONGDOING, misconduct, dishonesty, corruption, unscrupulousness, unprofessionalism, irregularity; unseemliness, indecorousness, indelicacy, indecency, immorality. ❷ *fiscal improprieties* TRANSGRESSION, misdemeanour, offence, misdeed, crime; indiscretion, mistake, peccadillo; *archaic* trespass.

improve ▶ **verb** ❶ *ways to improve the service* MAKE BETTER, ameliorate, upgrade, refine, enhance, boost, build on, raise; *informal* tweak; *formal* meliorate. ❷ *communications improved during the 18th century* GET BETTER, advance, progress, develop; make headway, make progress, pick up, look up. ❸ *the dose is not repeated if patient improves* RECOVER, get better, recuperate, gain strength, rally, revive, get back on one's feet, get over something; be on the road to recovery, be on the mend; *informal* turn the corner, take a turn for the better. ❹ *resources are needed to improve the offer* INCREASE, make larger, raise, augment, supplement, top up; *informal* up, hike up, bump up.
– OPPOSITES worsen, deteriorate.
■ **improve on** SURPASS, better, do better than, outdo, exceed, beat, top, cap.

improvement ▶ **noun** ADVANCE, development, upgrade, refinement, enhancement, advancement, upgrading, amelioration; boost, augmentation, raising; rally, recovery, upswing.

improvident ▶ **adjective** SPENDTHRIFT, thriftless, wasteful, prodigal, profligate, extravagant, free-spending, lavish, immoderate, excessive; imprudent, irresponsible, careless, reckless.
– OPPOSITES thrifty.

improvise ▶ **verb** ❶ *she was improvising in front of the cameras* EXTEMPORIZE, ad-lib, speak impromptu; *informal* speak off the cuff, speak off the top of one's head, busk it, wing it. ❷ *she improvised a sandpit* CONTRIVE, devise, throw together, cobble together, rig up; *Brit. informal* knock up; *informal* whip up, rustle up.

improvised ▶ **adjective** ❶ *an improvised speech* IMPROMPTU, unrehearsed, unprepared, unscripted, extempore, extemporized, spontaneous, unplanned; *informal* off-the-cuff. ❷ *an improvised shelter* MAKESHIFT, thrown together, cobbled together, rough and ready, make-do.
– OPPOSITES prepared, rehearsed.

imprudent ▶ **adjective** UNWISE, injudicious, incautious, misguided, ill-advised; thoughtless, unthinking, improvident, irresponsible, short-sighted, foolish.
– OPPOSITES sensible.

impudence ▶ **noun** IMPERTINENCE, insolence, effrontery, cheek, cockiness, brazenness; presumption, presumptuousness, disrespect, flippancy, bumptiousness, brashness; rudeness, impoliteness, ill manners, discourteousness, gall; *informal* brass neck, chutzpah, nerve; *Brit. informal* sauce; *N. Amer. informal* sassiness.

impudent ▶ **adjective** IMPERTINENT, insolent, cheeky, cocky, brazen; presumptuous, forward, disrespectful, insubordinate, flippant, bumptious, brash; rude, impolite, ill-mannered, discourteous, ill-bred; *informal* brass-necked, saucy, lippy; *N. Amer. informal* sassy; *archaic* malapert, contumelious.
– OPPOSITES polite.

impugn ▶ **verb** CALL INTO QUESTION, challenge, question, dispute, query, take issue with.

impulse ▶ **noun** ❶ *she had an impulse to run and hide* URGE, instinct, drive, compulsion, itch; whim, desire, fancy, notion. ❷ *a man of impulse* SPONTANEITY, impetuosity, recklessness, rashness. ❸ *passions provide the main impulse of poetry* INSPIRATION, stimulation, stimulus, incitement, motivation, encouragement, spur, catalyst. ❹ *impulses from the spinal cord to the muscles* PULSE, current, wave, signal.
■ **on (an) impulse** IMPULSIVELY, spontaneously, on the spur of the moment, without forethought, without premeditation.

impulsive ▶ **adjective** ❶ *he had an impulsive nature* IMPETUOUS, spontaneous, hasty, passionate, emotional, uninhibited; rash, reckless, foolhardy, unwise, madcap, devil-may-care, daredevil. ❷ *an impulsive decision* IMPROMPTU, snap, spontaneous, unpremeditated, spur-of-the-moment, extemporaneous; impetuous, precipitate, hasty, rash; sudden, ill-considered, ill-thought- out.
– OPPOSITES cautious, premeditated.

impunity ▶ **noun** *the impunity enjoyed by military officers* IMMUNITY, indemnity, exemption (from punishment), non-liability, licence; privilege, special treatment.
– OPPOSITES liability.
■ **with impunity** WITHOUT PUNISHMENT, scot-free, unpunished.

impure ▶ **adjective** ❶ *impure gold* ADULTERATED,

mixed, combined, blended, alloyed; *technical* admixed. ❷ *the water was impure* CONTAMINATED, polluted, tainted, unwholesome, poisoned; dirty, filthy, foul; unhygienic, unsanitary, insanitary; *poetic/literary* befouled. ❸ *impure thoughts* IMMORAL, sinful, wrongful, wicked; unchaste, lustful, lecherous, lewd, lascivious, prurient, obscene, indecent, ribald, risqué, improper, crude, coarse; *formal* concupiscent.
– OPPOSITES clean, chaste.

impurity ▶ **noun** ❶ *the impurity of the cast iron* ADULTERATION, debasement, degradation. ❷ *the impurity of the air* CONTAMINATION, pollution; dirtiness, filthiness, uncleanliness, foulness, unwholesomeness. ❸ *the impurities in beer* CONTAMINANT, pollutant, foreign body; dross, dirt, filth. ❹ *sin and impurity* IMMORALITY, sin, sinfulness, wickedness; unchastity, lustfulness, lechery, lecherousness, lewdness, lasciviousness, prurience, obscenity, dirtiness, crudeness, indecency, ribaldry, impropriety, vulgarity, coarseness; *formal* concupiscence.

impute ▶ **verb** ATTRIBUTE, ascribe, assign, credit; connect with, associate with.

in ▶ **preposition** ❶ *she was hiding in a wardrobe* INSIDE, within, in the middle of; surrounded by, enclosed by. ❷ *he was covered in mud* WITH, by. ❸ *he put a fruit gum in his mouth* INTO, inside. ❹ *they met in 1921* DURING, in the course of, over. ❺ *I'll see you in half an hour* AFTER, at the end of, following; within, in less than, in under. ❻ *a tax of ten pence in the pound* TO, per, every, each.
– OPPOSITES outside.
▶ **adverb** ❶ *his mum walked in* INSIDE, indoors, into the room, into the house/building. ❷ *the tide's in* HIGH, at its highest level, rising.
– OPPOSITES out.
▶ **adjective** ❶ *there was no one in* PRESENT, (at) home; inside, indoors, in the house/room. ❷ (*informal*) *beards are in* FASHIONABLE, in fashion, in vogue, popular, (bang) up to date, modern, modish, chic, à la mode, de rigueur; *informal* trendy, all the rage, with it, cool, the in thing, hip. ❸ (*informal*) *I was in with all the right people* IN FAVOUR, popular, friendly, friends; liked, admired, accepted; *informal* in someone's good books.
– OPPOSITES out, unfashionable, unpopular.
■ **in for** DUE FOR, in line for; expecting, about to receive.
■ **in for it** IN TROUBLE, about to be punished; *informal* for the high jump, in hot/deep water, in (deep) shtook; *Brit. informal* for it.
■ **in on** PRIVY TO, aware of, acquainted with, informed about/of, apprised of; *informal* wise to, in the know about, hip to; *archaic* ware of.
■ **ins and outs** (*informal*) DETAILS, particulars, facts, features, characteristics, nuts and bolts; *informal* nitty gritty.

inability ▶ **noun** LACK OF ABILITY, incapability, incapacity, powerlessness, impotence, helplessness; incompetence, ineptitude, unfitness.

inaccessible ▶ **adjective** ❶ *an inaccessible woodland site* UNREACHABLE, out of reach; cut-off, isolated, remote, in the back of beyond, out of the way, lonely, godforsaken. ❷ *the book was elitist and inaccessible* ESOTERIC, obscure, abstruse, recondite, arcane; elitist, exclusive, pretentious.

inaccuracy ▶ **noun** ❶ *the inaccuracy of recent opinion polls* INCORRECTNESS, inexactness, imprecision, erroneousness, mistakenness, fallaciousness, faultiness. ❷ *the article contained a number of inaccuracies* ERROR, mistake, fallacy, slip, oversight, fault, blunder, gaffe; erratum; *Brit.* literal; *informal* howler, boo-boo, typo; *Brit. informal* boob; *N. Amer. informal* blooper, goof.
– OPPOSITES correctness.

inaccurate ▶ **adjective** INEXACT, imprecise, incorrect, wrong, erroneous, faulty, imperfect, flawed, defective, unsound, unreliable; fallacious, false, mistaken, untrue; *informal* off beam; *Brit. informal* adrift.

inaction ▶ **noun** INACTIVITY, non-intervention; neglect, negligence, apathy, inertia, indolence.

inactivate ▶ **verb** DISABLE, deactivate, make inoperative, immobilize.

inactive ▶ **adjective** ❶ *over the next few days I was horribly inactive* IDLE, indolent, lazy, lifeless, slothful, lethargic, inert, sluggish, unenergetic, listless, torpid. ❷ *the device remains inactive while the computer is started up* INOPERATIVE, non-functioning, idle; not working, out of service, unused, not in use.

inactivity ▶ **noun** ❶ *years of inactivity* IDLENESS, indolence, laziness, lifelessness, slothfulness, lethargy, inertia, sluggishness, listlessness. ❷ *government inactivity* INACTION, non-intervention; neglect, negligence, apathy.
– OPPOSITES action.

inadequacy ▶ **noun** ❶ *the inadequacy of available resources* INSUFFICIENCY, deficiency, scarcity, scarceness, sparseness, dearth, paucity, shortage, want, lack, undersupply; paltriness, meagreness; *formal* exiguity. ❷ *her feelings of personal inadequacy* INCOMPETENCE, incapability, unfitness, ineffectiveness, inefficiency, inefficacy, inexpertness, ineptness, uselessness, impotence, powerlessness. ❸ *the inadequacies of the present system* SHORTCOMING, defect, fault, failing, weakness, weak point, limitation, flaw, imperfection.
– OPPOSITES abundance, competence.

inadequate ▶ **adjective** ❶ *inadequate water supplies* INSUFFICIENT, deficient, poor, scant, scanty, scarce, sparse, in short supply; paltry, meagre, niggardly, limited; *informal* measly, pathetic; *formal* exiguous. ❷ *inadequate staff* INCOMPETENT, incapable, unsatisfactory, not up to scratch, unfit, ineffective, ineffectual,

inefficient, unskilful, inexpert, inept, amateurish, substandard, poor, useless, inferior; *informal* not up to snuff; *Brit. informal* duff, not much cop, no great shakes.
– OPPOSITES sufficient, competent.

inadmissible ▶ adjective UNALLOWABLE, invalid, unacceptable, impermissible, disallowed, forbidden, prohibited, precluded.

inadvertent ▶ adjective UNINTENTIONAL, unintended, accidental, unpremeditated, unplanned, innocent, uncalculated, unconscious, unthinking, unwitting, involuntary.
– OPPOSITES deliberate.

inadvertently ▶ adverb ACCIDENTALLY, by accident, unintentionally, unwittingly.

inadvisable ▶ adjective UNWISE, ill-advised, imprudent, ill-judged, ill-considered, injudicious, impolitic, foolish, misguided.
– OPPOSITES shrewd.

inalienable ▶ adjective INVIOLABLE, absolute, sacrosanct; untransferable, non-transferable, non-negotiable; *Law* indefeasible.

inane ▶ adjective SILLY, foolish, stupid, fatuous, idiotic, ridiculous, ludicrous, asinine, frivolous, vapid; childish, puerile; *informal* dumb, gormless, moronic; *Brit. informal* daft.
– OPPOSITES sensible.

inanimate ▶ adjective LIFELESS, insentient, without life; dead, defunct.
– OPPOSITES living.

inapplicable ▶ adjective IRRELEVANT, immaterial, not germane, not pertinent, unrelated, unconnected, extraneous, beside the point; *formal* impertinent.
– OPPOSITES relevant.

inapposite ▶ adjective INAPPROPRIATE, unsuitable, inapt, out of place, infelicitous, misplaced, ill-judged, ill-advised.
– OPPOSITES appropriate.

inappreciable ▶ adjective IMPERCEPTIBLE, minute, tiny, slight, small; insignificant, inconsequential, unimportant, negligible, trivial, minor; *informal* piddling, piffling; *formal* exiguous.
– OPPOSITES considerable.

inappropriate ▶ adjective UNSUITABLE, unfitting, unseemly, unbecoming, unbefitting, improper; incongruous, out of place/keeping, inapposite, inapt; *informal* out of order; *formal* malapropos.
– OPPOSITES suitable.

inapt ▶ adjective. *See* INAPPROPRIATE.

inarticulate ▶ adjective ❶ *an inarticulate young man* TONGUE-TIED, lost for words, unable to express oneself; *archaic* mumchance. ❷ *an inarticulate reply* UNINTELLIGIBLE, incomprehensible, incoherent, unclear, indistinct, mumbled, muffled. ❸ *inarticulate rage* UNSPOKEN, silent, unexpressed, wordless, unvoiced.
– OPPOSITES silver-tongued, fluent.

inattention ▶ noun ❶ *a moment of inattention* DISTRACTION, inattentiveness, preoccupation, absent-mindedness, daydreaming, abstraction. ❷ *his inattention to duty* NEGLIGENCE, neglect, disregard; forgetfulness, carelessness, thoughtlessness, heedlessness.
– OPPOSITES concentration.

inattentive ▶ adjective ❶ *an inattentive pupil* DISTRACTED, lacking concentration, preoccupied, absent-minded, daydreaming, dreamy, abstracted, distrait; *informal* miles away. ❷ *inattentive service* NEGLIGENT, neglectful, remiss, slack, sloppy, slapdash, lax; forgetful, careless, thoughtless, heedless.
– OPPOSITES alert.

inaudible ▶ adjective UNHEARD, out of earshot; indistinct, faint, muted, soft, low, muffled, whispered, muttered, murmured, mumbled.

inaugural ▶ adjective FIRST, opening, initial, introductory, initiatory.
– OPPOSITES final.

inaugurate ▶ verb ❶ *he inaugurated a new policy* INITIATE, begin, start, institute, launch, start off, get going, get under way, establish, lay the foundations of; bring in, usher in; *informal* kick off. ❷ *the new President will be inaugurated* ADMIT TO OFFICE, install, instate, swear in; invest, ordain, crown. ❸ *the museum was inaugurated in September* OPEN, declare open, unveil; dedicate, consecrate; *N. Amer.* hansel.

inauspicious ▶ adjective UNPROMISING, unpropitious, unfavourable, unfortunate, infelicitous, ominous; discouraging, disheartening, bleak.
– OPPOSITES promising.

inborn ▶ adjective INNATE, congenital, connate, connatural; inherent, natural, inbred, inherited, hereditary, in one's genes.

inbred ▶ adjective. *See* INBORN.

inbuilt ▶ adjective ❶ *an inbuilt CD-ROM drive* BUILT-IN, integral, incorporated. ❷ *our inbuilt survival instinct* INHERENT, intrinsic, innate, congenital, natural, connatural, connate.

incalculable ▶ adjective INESTIMABLE, indeterminable, untold, immeasurable, incomputable; infinite, endless, limitless, boundless, measureless; enormous, immense, huge, vast, innumerable.

incandescent ▶ adjective ❶ *incandescent fragments of lava* WHITE-HOT, red-hot, burning, fiery, blazing, ablaze, aflame; glowing, aglow, radiant, bright, brilliant, luminous; *poetic/literary* fervid, rutilant, lucent. ❷ *the minister was incandescent* FURIOUS, enraged, raging, very angry, incensed, seething, infuriated, fuming, irate, in a temper, beside oneself; *informal* livid, foaming at the mouth, (hopping) mad, wild, apoplectic, steamed up, in a lather, in a paddy; *poetic/literary* wrathful; *archaic* wroth.

incantation ▶ noun ❶ *he muttered some weird incantations* CHANT, invocation, conjuration, magic spell/formula, rune; *N. Amer.* hex, mojo; *NZ* makutu. ❷ *ritual incantation* CHANTING, intonation, recitation.

incapable ▶ adjective ❶ *an incapable government* INCOMPETENT, inept, inadequate, not good enough, leaving much to be desired, inexpert, unskilful, ineffective, ineffectual, inefficacious, feeble, unfit, unqualified, unequal to the task; *informal* out of one's depth, not up to it, not up to snuff, useless, hopeless, pathetic, a dead loss. ❷ *he was mentally incapable* INCAPACITATED, helpless, powerless, impotent.
– OPPOSITES competent.

incapacitated ▶ adjective DISABLED, debilitated, indisposed, unfit; immobilized, out of action, out of commission, hors de combat; *informal* laid up.
– OPPOSITES fit.

incapacity ▶ noun ❶ *mental incapacity* DISABILITY, incapability, inability, debility, impairment, indisposition; impotence, powerlessness, helplessness; incompetence, inadequacy, ineffectiveness. ❷ *legal incapacity* DISQUALIFICATION, lack of entitlement.
– OPPOSITES capability.

incarcerate ▶ verb IMPRISON, put in prison, send to prison, jail, lock up, put under lock and key, put away, intern, confine, detain, hold, immure, put in chains, clap in irons, hold prisoner, hold captive; *Brit.* detain at Her Majesty's pleasure; *informal* send down, put behind bars, put inside; *Brit. informal* bang someone up.
– OPPOSITES release.

incarceration ▶ noun IMPRISONMENT, internment, confinement, detention, custody, captivity, restraint; *informal* time; *Brit. informal* porridge; *archaic* durance, duress.

incarnate ▶ adjective IN HUMAN FORM, in the flesh, in physical form, in bodily form, made flesh; corporeal, physical, fleshly, embodied.

incarnation ▶ noun ❶ *the incarnation of artistic genius* EMBODIMENT, personification, exemplification, type, epitome; manifestation, bodily form, avatar. ❷ *a previous incarnation* LIFETIME, life, existence.

incautious ▶ adjective RASH, unwise, careless, heedless, thoughtless, reckless, unthinking, imprudent, misguided, ill-advised, ill-judged, injudicious, impolitic, unguarded, foolhardy, foolish; unwary, off-guard, inattentive; *informal* asleep on the job.
– OPPOSITES circumspect.

incendiary ▶ adjective ❶ *an incendiary bomb* COMBUSTIBLE, flammable, inflammable. ❷ *an incendiary speech* INFLAMMATORY, rabble-rousing, provocative, seditious, subversive; contentious, controversial.
▶ noun ❶ *an aircraft loaded with incendiaries* EXPLOSIVE, bomb, incendiary device. ❷ *incendiaries set the village on fire* ARSONIST, fire-bomber, fire-setter; pyromaniac; *Brit.* fire-raiser; *informal* firebug, pyro; *N. Amer. informal* torch. ❸ *a political incendiary* AGITATOR, demagogue, rabble-rouser, firebrand, troublemaker, agent provocateur, revolutionary, insurgent, subversive.

incense[1] ▶ verb *his taunts used to incense me* ENRAGE, infuriate, anger, madden, outrage, inflame, exasperate, antagonize, provoke; *informal* make someone see red, make someone's blood boil, make someone's hackles rise, drive mad/crazy; *N. Amer. informal* burn up.
– OPPOSITES placate, please.

incense[2] ▶ noun *a whiff of incense* PERFUME, fragrance, scent.

incensed ▶ adjective ENRAGED, very angry, furious, infuriated, irate, in a temper, raging, incandescent, fuming, seething, beside oneself, outraged; *informal* mad, hopping mad, wild, livid, apoplectic, hot under the collar, foaming at the mouth, steamed up, in a paddy, fit to be tied; *poetic/literary* wrathful; *archaic* wroth.

incentive ▶ noun INDUCEMENT, motivation, motive, reason, stimulus, stimulant, spur, impetus, encouragement, impulse; incitement, goad, provocation; attraction, lure, bait; *informal* carrot, sweetener, come-on.
– OPPOSITES deterrent.

inception ▶ noun ESTABLISHMENT, institution, foundation, founding, formation, initiation, setting up, origination, constitution, inauguration, opening, day one; beginning, commencement, start, birth, dawn, genesis, origin; *informal* kick-off.
– OPPOSITES end.

incessant ▶ adjective CEASELESS, unceasing, constant, continual, unabating, interminable, endless, unending, never-ending, everlasting, eternal, perpetual, continuous, non-stop, uninterrupted, unbroken, unremitting, persistent, relentless, unrelenting, unrelieved, sustained.
– OPPOSITES intermittent.

incessantly ▶ adverb CONSTANTLY, continually, all the time, non-stop, without stopping, without a break, round the clock, {morning, noon, and night}, interminably, unremittingly, ceaselessly, endlessly; *informal* 24-7.
– OPPOSITES occasionally.

incidence ▶ noun OCCURRENCE, prevalence; rate, frequency; amount, degree, extent.

incident ▶ noun ❶ *incidents in his youth* EVENT, occurrence, episode, experience, happening, occasion, proceeding, eventuality, affair, business; adventure, exploit, escapade; matter, circumstance, fact, development. ❷ *police are investigating the incident* DISTURBANCE, fracas, melee, commotion, rumpus, scene; fight, skirmish, clash, brawl, free-for-all, encounter, conflict, ruckus, confrontation, altercation, contretemps; *informal* ruction; *Law, dated* affray. ❸ *the journey was not without incident* EXCITEMENT, adventure, drama; danger, peril.

incidental ▶ **adjective** ❶ *incidental details* LESS IMPORTANT, secondary, subsidiary; minor, peripheral, background, by-the-way, by-the-by, non-essential, inessential, unimportant, insignificant, inconsequential, tangential, extrinsic, extraneous. ❷ *an incidental discovery* CHANCE, accidental, random; fluky, fortuitous, serendipitous, adventitious, coincidental, unlooked-for. ❸ *the risks incidental to the job* CONNECTED WITH, related to, associated with, accompanying, attending, attendant on, concomitant with.
–OPPOSITES essential, deliberate.

incidentally ▶ **adverb** ❶ *incidentally, I haven't had a reply yet* BY THE WAY, by the by(e), in passing, en passant, speaking of which; parenthetically; *informal* btw, as it happens. ❷ *the infection was discovered incidentally* BY CHANCE, by accident, accidentally, fortuitously, by a fluke, by happenstance; coincidentally, by coincidence.

incinerate ▶ **verb** BURN, reduce to ashes, consume by fire, carbonize; cremate.

incipient ▶ **adjective** DEVELOPING, growing, emerging, emergent, dawning, just beginning, inceptive, initial; nascent, embryonic, fledgling, in its infancy, germinal.
–OPPOSITES full-blown.

incise ▶ **verb** ❶ *the wound was incised* CUT (OPEN), make an incision in, slit (open), lance. ❷ *an inscription incised in Roman letters* ENGRAVE, etch, carve, cut, chisel, inscribe, score, chase.

incision ▶ **noun** ❶ *a surgical incision* CUT, opening, slit. ❷ *incisions on the marble* NOTCH, nick, snick, scratch, scarification.

incisive ▶ **adjective** PENETRATING, acute, sharp, sharp-witted, razor-sharp, keen, astute, trenchant, shrewd, piercing, perceptive, insightful, percipient, perspicacious, discerning, analytical, clever, smart, quick; concise, succinct, pithy, to the point, crisp, clear; *informal* punchy.
–OPPOSITES rambling, vague.

incite ▶ **verb** ❶ *he was arrested for inciting racial hatred* STIR UP, whip up, encourage, fan the flames of, stoke up, fuel, kindle, ignite, inflame, stimulate, instigate, provoke, excite, arouse, awaken, inspire, trigger, spark off, ferment, foment; *poetic/literary* enkindle, waken. ❷ *she incited him to commit murder* EGG ON, encourage, urge, goad, provoke, spur on, drive, stimulate, push, prod, prompt, induce, impel; arouse, rouse, excite, inflame, sting, prick; *informal* put up to.
–OPPOSITES discourage, deter.

incivility ▶ **noun** RUDENESS, discourtesy, discourteousness, impoliteness, bad manners, disrespect, boorishness, ungraciousness; insolence, impertinence, impudence.
–OPPOSITES politeness.

inclement ▶ **adjective** COLD, chilly, bleak, wintry, freezing, snowy, icy; wet, rainy, drizzly, damp; stormy, blustery, wild, rough, squally, windy; unpleasant, bad, foul, nasty, filthy, severe, extreme, harsh.
–OPPOSITES fine.

inclination ▶ **noun** ❶ *his political inclinations* TENDENCY, propensity, proclivity, leaning, predisposition, disposition, predilection, desire, wish, impulse, bent; liking, penchant, partiality, preference, appetite, fancy, interest, affinity; stomach, taste; *informal* yen; *formal* velleity; *archaic* list, humour. ❷ *an inclination of his head* BOWING, bow, bending, nod, nodding, lowering. ❸ *an inclination of ninety degrees. See* INCLINE noun.
–OPPOSITES aversion.

incline ▶ **verb** ❶ *his prejudice inclines him to overlook obvious facts* PREDISPOSE, lead, make, make of a mind to, dispose, prejudice; prompt, induce, influence, sway; persuade, convince. ❷ *I incline to the opposite view* PREFER, favour, go for; tend, lean, swing, veer, gravitate, be drawn. ❸ *he inclined his head* BEND, bow, nod, bob, lower, dip. ❹ *the columns incline away from the vertical* LEAN, tilt, angle, tip, slope, slant, bend, curve, bank, cant, bevel; list, heel.
▶ **noun** *a steep incline* SLOPE, gradient, pitch, ramp, bank, ascent, rise, acclivity, upslope, dip, descent, declivity, downslope; hill; *N. Amer.* grade, downgrade, upgrade.

inclined ▶ **adjective** ❶ *I'm inclined to believe her* DISPOSED, minded, of a mind, willing, ready, prepared; predisposed. ❷ *she's inclined to gossip* PRONE, given, in the habit of, liable, likely, apt, wont.

include ▶ **verb** ❶ *activities include sports, drama, music, and chess* INCORPORATE, comprise, encompass, cover, embrace, involve, take in, number, contain; consist of, be made up of, be composed of; *formal* comprehend. ❷ *don't forget to include the cost of repairs* ALLOW FOR, count, take into account, take into consideration.
–OPPOSITES exclude.

including ▶ **preposition** INCLUSIVE OF, counting; as well as, plus, together with.

inclusive ▶ **adjective** ❶ *an inclusive price | an inclusive definition* ALL-IN, all-inclusive, comprehensive, in toto, overall, full, all-round, umbrella, catch-all, all-encompassing. ❷ *prices are inclusive of VAT* INCLUDING, incorporating, taking in, counting; comprising, covering.

incognito ▶ **adverb & adjective** UNDER AN ASSUMED NAME, under a false name, in disguise, disguised, under cover, in plain clothes, camouflaged; secretly, anonymously.

incoherent ▶ **adjective** ❶ *a long, incoherent speech* UNCLEAR, confused, muddled, unintelli-

gible, incomprehensible, hard to follow, disjointed, disconnected, disordered, mixed up, garbled, jumbled, scrambled; rambling, wandering, discursive, disorganized, illogical; inarticulate, mumbling, slurred. ❷ *she was incoherent and shivering violently* DELIRIOUS, raving, babbling, hysterical, irrational.
– OPPOSITES lucid.

incombustible ▶ adjective NON-FLAMMABLE, non-combustible; fireproof, flameproof, fire/flame resistant, fire/flame retardant; heatproof, ovenproof.
– OPPOSITES flammable, inflammable.

income ▶ noun EARNINGS, salary, pay, remuneration, wages, stipend; revenue, receipts, takings, profits, gains, proceeds, turnover, yield, dividend, incomings; means; *N. Amer.* take; *formal* emolument.
– OPPOSITES expenditure, outgoings.

incoming ▶ adjective ❶ *the incoming train* ARRIVING, entering; approaching, coming (in). ❷ *the incoming president* NEWLY ELECTED, newly appointed, succeeding, new, next, future; elect, to-be, designate.
– OPPOSITES outgoing.

incommensurate ▶ adjective OUT OF PROPORTION, not in proportion, disproportionate, inappropriate, out of keeping; insufficient, inadequate; excessive, inordinate, unreasonable, uncalled for, undue, unfair.
– OPPOSITES proportional.

incommunicable ▶ adjective INDESCRIBABLE, inexpressible, unutterable, unspeakable, undefinable, ineffable, beyond words, beyond description; overwhelming, intense, profound.

incomparable ▶ adjective WITHOUT EQUAL, beyond compare, unparalleled, matchless, peerless, unmatched, without parallel, beyond comparison, second to none, in a class of its own, unequalled, unrivalled, inimitable, nonpareil, par excellence; transcendent, superlative, surpassing, unsurpassed, unsurpassable, supreme, top, outstanding, consummate, singular, unique, rare, perfect; *informal* one-in-a-million; *formal* unexampled.

incomparably ▶ adverb FAR AND AWAY, by far, infinitely, immeasurably, easily; inimitably, supremely, superlatively, uniquely, transcendently.

incompatible ▶ adjective ❶ *she and McBride are totally incompatible* UNSUITED, mismatched, ill-matched, poles apart, worlds apart, like day and night; *Brit.* like chalk and cheese. ❷ *incompatible economic objectives* IRRECONCILABLE, conflicting, opposed, opposite, contradictory, antagonistic, antipathetic; clashing, inharmonious, discordant; mutually exclusive. ❸ *a theory incompatible with that of his predecessor* INCONSISTENT WITH, at odds with, out of keeping with, at variance with, inconsonant with, different to, divergent from, contrary to, in conflict with, in opposition to, (diametrically) opposed to, counter to, irreconcilable with.
– OPPOSITES well matched, harmonious, consistent.

incompetent ▶ adjective INEPT, unskilful, unskilled, inexpert, amateurish, unprofessional, bungling, blundering, clumsy, inadequate, substandard, inferior, ineffective, deficient, inefficient, ineffectual, wanting, lacking, leaving much to be desired; incapable, unfit, unqualified; *informal* useless, pathetic, cack-handed, ham-fisted, not up to it, not up to scratch; *Brit. informal* not much cop.

incomplete ▶ adjective ❶ *the project is still incomplete* UNFINISHED, uncompleted, partial, half-finished, half-done, half-completed. ❷ *inaccurate or incomplete information* DEFICIENT, insufficient, imperfect, defective, partial, patchy, sketchy, fragmentary, fragmented, scrappy, bitty; abridged, shortened; expurgated, bowdlerized.

incomprehensible ▶ adjective UNINTELLIGIBLE, impossible to understand, impenetrable, unclear, indecipherable, beyond one's comprehension, beyond one, beyond one's grasp, complicated, complex, involved, baffling, bewildering, mystifying, puzzling, confusing, perplexing; abstruse, esoteric, recondite, arcane, mysterious, Delphic; *informal* over one's head, all Greek to someone; *Brit. informal* double Dutch.
– OPPOSITES intelligible, clear.

inconceivable ▶ adjective UNBELIEVABLE, beyond belief, incredible, unthinkable, unimaginable, extremely unlikely; impossible, beyond the bounds of possibility, out of the question, preposterous, ridiculous, ludicrous, absurd, incomprehensible; *informal* hard to swallow.
– OPPOSITES likely.

inconclusive ▶ adjective INDECISIVE, proving nothing; indefinite, indeterminate, unresolved, unproved, unsettled, still open to question/doubt, debatable, unconfirmed; moot; vague, ambiguous; *informal* up in the air, left hanging.

incongruous ▶ adjective ❶ *the women looked incongruous in their smart hats and fur coats* OUT OF PLACE, out of keeping, inappropriate, unsuitable, unsuited; wrong, strange, odd, absurd, bizarre, off-key, extraneous. ❷ *an incongruous collection of objects* ILL-MATCHED, ill-assorted, mismatched, unharmonious, discordant, dissonant, conflicting, clashing, jarring, incompatible, different, dissimilar, contrasting, disparate.
– OPPOSITES appropriate, harmonious.

inconsequential ▶ adjective INSIGNIFICANT, unimportant, of little no/consequence, neither here nor there, incidental, inessential, nonessential, immaterial, irrelevant; negligible,

inappreciable, inconsiderable, slight, minor, trivial, trifling, petty; *informal* piddling, piffling.
– OPPOSITES important.

inconsiderable ▶ adjective INSIGNIFICANT, negligible, trifling, small, tiny, little, minuscule, nominal, token, petty, slight, minor, inappreciable, insubstantial, inconsequential; *informal* piffling; *formal* exiguous.

inconsiderate ▶ adjective THOUGHTLESS, unthinking, insensitive, selfish, self-centred, unsympathetic, uncaring, heedless, unmindful, unkind, uncharitable, ungracious, impolite, discourteous, rude, disrespectful; tactless, undiplomatic, indiscreet, indelicate; *informal* ignorant.
– OPPOSITES thoughtful.

inconsistent ▶ adjective ❶ *his inconsistent behaviour* ERRATIC, changeable, unpredictable, variable, varying, changing, changeful, inconstant, unstable, irregular, fluctuating, unsteady, unsettled, uneven; self-contradictory, contradictory, paradoxical; capricious, fickle, flighty, whimsical, unreliable, mercurial, volatile, blowing hot and cold, ever-changing, chameleon-like; *informal* up and down; *technical* labile. ❷ *he had done nothing inconsistent with his morality* INCOMPATIBLE WITH, conflicting with, in conflict with, at odds with, at variance with, differing from, contrary to, in opposition to, (diametrically) opposed to, irreconcilable with, out of keeping with, out of step with; antithetical to.

inconsolable ▶ adjective HEARTBROKEN, broken-hearted, grief-stricken, beside oneself with grief, devastated, wretched, sick at heart, desolate, despairing, distraught, comfortless; miserable, unhappy, sad; *poetic/literary* heartsick.

inconspicuous ▶ adjective UNOBTRUSIVE, unnoticeable, unremarkable, unspectacular, unostentatious, undistinguished, unexceptional, modest, unassuming, discreet, hidden, concealed; unseen, in the background, low-profile.
– OPPOSITES noticeable.

inconstant ▶ adjective FICKLE, faithless, unfaithful, false, false-hearted; wayward, unreliable, untrustworthy, capricious, volatile, flighty, unpredictable, erratic, blowing hot and cold; *informal* cheating, two-timing.
– OPPOSITES faithful.

incontestable ▶ adjective INCONTROVERTIBLE, indisputable, undeniable, irrefutable, unassailable, beyond dispute, unquestionable, beyond question, indubitable, beyond doubt; airtight, watertight, unarguable, undebatable, emphatic, categorical, certain, definite, definitive, proven, demonstrable, decisive, conclusive.
– OPPOSITES questionable.

incontinent ▶ adjective UNRESTRAINED, uncontrolled, lacking self-restraint, unbridled, unchecked; uncontrollable, ungovernable.

incontrovertible ▶ adjective INDISPUTABLE, incontestable, undeniable, irrefutable, unassailable, beyond dispute, unquestionable, beyond question, indubitable, beyond doubt, unarguable, undebatable; certain, sure, definite, definitive, proven, decisive, conclusive, demonstrable, emphatic, categorical, airtight, watertight.
– OPPOSITES questionable.

inconvenience ▶ noun ❶ *we apologize for any inconvenience caused* TROUBLE, bother, problems, disruption, difficulty, disturbance; vexation, irritation, annoyance; *informal* aggravation, hassle. ❷ *his early arrival was clearly an inconvenience* NUISANCE, trouble, bother, problem, vexation, worry, trial, bind, bore, irritant, thorn in someone's flesh; *informal* headache, pain, pain in the neck, pain in the backside, drag, aggravation, hassle; *N. Amer. informal* pain in the butt.
▶ verb *I don't want to inconvenience you* TROUBLE, bother, put out, put to any trouble, disturb, impose on, burden; vex, annoy, irritate; *informal* hassle; *formal* discommode.

inconvenient ▶ adjective AWKWARD, difficult, inopportune, untimely, ill-timed, unsuitable, inappropriate, unfortunate; tiresome, irritating, annoying, vexing, bothersome; *informal* aggravating.

incorporate ▶ verb ❶ *the region was incorporated into Moldavian territory* ABSORB, include, subsume, assimilate, integrate, take in, swallow up. ❷ *the model incorporates some advanced features* INCLUDE, contain, comprise, embody, embrace, build in, encompass. ❸ *a small amount of salt is incorporated with the butter* BLEND, mix, mingle, meld, combine; fold in, stir in.

incorporeal ▶ adjective INTANGIBLE, impalpable, non-physical; bodiless, disembodied, discarnate; spiritual, ethereal, unsubstantial, insubstantial, transcendental; ghostly, spectral, supernatural.
– OPPOSITES tangible.

incorrect ▶ adjective ❶ *an incorrect answer* WRONG, erroneous, in error, mistaken, inaccurate, wide of the mark, off target; untrue, false, fallacious; *informal* off beam, out, way out, full of holes. ❷ *incorrect behaviour* INAPPROPRIATE, wrong, unsuitable, inapt, inapposite; ill-advised, ill-considered, ill-judged, injudicious, unacceptable, unfitting, out of keeping, improper, unseemly, unbecoming, indecorous; *informal* out of order.

incorrigible ▶ adjective INVETERATE, habitual, confirmed, hardened, incurable, irredeemable, hopeless, beyond hope, beyond redemption; impenitent, uncontrite, unrepentant, unapologetic, unashamed.

incorruptible ▶ adjective ❶ *an incorruptible man* HONEST, honourable, trustworthy, prin-

cipled, high-principled, unbribable, moral, ethical, good, virtuous. ❷ *an incorruptible substance* IMPERISHABLE, indestructible, indissoluble, enduring, everlasting.
– OPPOSITES venal.

increase ▶ verb ❶ *demand is likely to increase* GROW, get bigger, get larger, enlarge, expand, swell; rise, climb, escalate, soar, surge, rocket, shoot up, spiral; intensify, strengthen, extend, heighten, stretch, spread, widen; multiply, snowball, mushroom, proliferate, balloon, build up, mount up, pile up, accrue, accumulate; *poetic/literary* wax. ❷ *higher expectations will increase user demand* ADD TO, make larger, make bigger, augment, supplement, top up, build up, extend, raise, swell, inflate; magnify, intensify, strengthen, heighten, amplify; *informal* up, jack up, hike up, bump up, crank up.
– OPPOSITES decrease, reduce.
▶ noun *the increase in size | an increase in demand* GROWTH, rise, enlargement, expansion, extension, multiplication, elevation, inflation; increment, addition, augmentation; magnification, intensification, amplification, step up, climb, escalation, surge, upsurge, upswing, spiral, spurt; *informal* hike.

increasingly ▶ adverb MORE AND MORE, progressively, to an increasing extent, ever more.

incredible ▶ adjective ❶ *I find his story incredible* UNBELIEVABLE, beyond belief, hard to believe, unconvincing, far-fetched, implausible, improbable, highly unlikely, dubious, doubtful; inconceivable, unthinkable, unimaginable, impossible; feeble, weak, thin, lame; *informal* hard to swallow/take, cock-and-bull. ❷ *an incredible feat of engineering* MAGNIFICENT, wonderful, marvellous, spectacular, remarkable, phenomenal, prodigious, breathtaking, extraordinary, unbelievable, amazing, stunning, astounding, astonishing, awe-inspiring, staggering, formidable, impressive, supreme, great, awesome, superhuman; *informal* fantastic, terrific, tremendous, stupendous, mind-boggling, mind-blowing, out of this world; *poetic/literary* wondrous.

incredulity ▶ noun DISBELIEF, incredulousness, scepticism, distrust, mistrust, suspicion, doubt, doubtfulness, dubiousness, lack of conviction; cynicism.

incredulous ▶ adjective DISBELIEVING, sceptical, unbelieving, distrustful, mistrustful, suspicious, doubtful, dubious, unconvinced; cynical.

increment ▶ noun INCREASE, addition, supplement, gain, augmentation, boost; *informal* hike.
– OPPOSITES reduction.

incriminate ▶ verb IMPLICATE, involve, enmesh; blame, accuse, denounce, inform against, point the finger at; entrap; *informal* frame, set up, stick/pin the blame on, rat on; *Brit. informal* fit up, grass on; *archaic* inculpate.

inculcate ▶ verb ❶ *the beliefs inculcated in him by his father* INSTIL, implant, fix, impress, imprint; hammer into, drum into, drive into, drill into, din into. ❷ *they will try to inculcate you with a respect for culture* IMBUE, infuse, inspire, teach.

inculpate ▶ verb (*archaic*). *See* INCRIMINATE.

incumbent ▶ adjective ❶ *it is incumbent on the government to give a clear lead* NECESSARY, essential, required, imperative; compulsory, binding, obligatory, mandatory. ❷ *the incumbent president* CURRENT, present, in office, in power; reigning.
▶ noun *the first incumbent of the post* HOLDER, bearer, occupant.

incur ▶ verb BRING UPON ONESELF, expose oneself to, lay oneself open to; run up; attract, invite, earn, arouse, cause, give rise to, be liable/subject to, meet with, sustain, experience.

incurable ▶ adjective ❶ *an incurable illness* UNTREATABLE, inoperable, irremediable; terminal, fatal, mortal; chronic. ❷ *an incurable romantic* INVETERATE, dyed-in-the-wool, confirmed, established, long-established, long-standing, absolute, complete, utter, thorough, thoroughgoing, out-and-out, through and through; unashamed, unapologetic, unrepentant, incorrigible, hopeless.

incursion ▶ noun ATTACK, assault, raid, invasion, storming, foray, blitz, sortie, sally, advance, push, thrust.
– OPPOSITES retreat.

indebted ▶ adjective BEHOLDEN, under an obligation, obliged, obligated, grateful, thankful, in someone's debt, owing a debt of gratitude.

indecent ▶ adjective ❶ *indecent photographs* OBSCENE, dirty, filthy, rude, coarse, naughty, vulgar, gross, crude, lewd, salacious, improper, smutty, off colour; pornographic, offensive, prurient, sordid, scatological; ribald, risqué, racy; *informal* blue, nudge-nudge, porn, porno, X-rated, raunchy, skin; *Brit. informal* saucy; *euphemistic* adult. ❷ *indecent clothes* REVEALING, short, brief, skimpy, scanty, low-cut, flimsy, thin, see-through; erotic, arousing, sexy, suggestive, titillating. ❸ *indecent haste* UNSEEMLY, improper, indecorous, unceremonious, indelicate, unbecoming, ungentlemanly, unladylike, unfitting, unbefitting; untoward, unsuitable, inappropriate; in bad taste, tasteless, unacceptable, offensive, crass.

indecipherable ▶ adjective ILLEGIBLE, unreadable, hard to read, unintelligible, unclear; scribbled, scrawled, hieroglyphic, squiggly, cramped, crabbed.

indecision ▶ noun INDECISIVENESS, irresolution, hesitancy, hesitation, tentativeness; ambivalence, doubt, doubtfulness, uncertainty, incertitude; vacillation, equivocation, second thoughts; shilly-shallying, dithering, temporizing; *Brit.* humming and hawing; *Scottish* swithering; *informal* dilly-dallying, sitting on the fence; *formal* dubiety.

indecisive ▶ **adjective** ❶ *an indecisive result* INCONCLUSIVE, proving nothing, settling nothing, open, indeterminate, undecided, unsettled, borderline, indefinite, unclear, ambiguous; *informal* up in the air. ❷ *an indecisive leader* IRRESOLUTE, hesitant, tentative, weak; vacillating, equivocating, dithering, wavering, faltering, shilly-shallying; ambivalent, divided, blowing hot and cold, in two minds, in a dilemma, in a quandary, torn; doubtful, unsure, uncertain; undecided, uncommitted; *informal* iffy, sitting on the fence.

indecorous ▶ **adjective** IMPROPER, unseemly, unbecoming, undignified, immodest, indelicate, indecent, unladylike, ungentlemanly; inappropriate, incorrect, unsuitable, undesirable, unfitting, in bad taste, ill-bred.

indecorum ▶ **noun** IMPROPRIETY, unseemliness, immodesty, indecency, indelicacy; inappropriateness, unsuitability, undesirability, unacceptability, bad taste.

indeed ▶ **adverb** ❶ *there was, indeed, quite a furore* AS EXPECTED, to be sure; in fact, in point of fact, as a matter of fact, in truth, actually, as it happens/happened, if truth be told; *archaic* in sooth. ❷ *'May I join you?' 'Indeed you may.'* YES, certainly, assuredly, of course, naturally, without (a) doubt, without question, by all means; *informal* you bet, I'll say. ❸ *Ian's future with us looked rosy indeed* VERY, extremely, exceedingly, tremendously, immensely, singularly, decidedly, particularly, remarkably, really.

indefatigable ▶ **adjective** TIRELESS, untiring, unwearied, unwearying, unflagging; determined, tenacious, dogged, single-minded, assiduous, industrious, unswerving, unfaltering, unshakeable, indomitable; persistent, relentless, unremitting.

indefensible ▶ **adjective** ❶ *indefensible cruelty* INEXCUSABLE, unjustifiable, unjustified, unpardonable, unforgivable; uncalled for, unprovoked, gratuitous, unreasonable, unnecessary. ❷ *an indefensible system of dual justice* UNTENABLE, unsustainable, insupportable, unwarranted, unwarrantable, unjustifiable, unjustified, flawed, unacceptable. ❸ *an indefensible island* DEFENCELESS, vulnerable, exposed, open to attack, pregnable, undefended, unfortified, unguarded, unprotected, unarmed.

indefinable ▶ **adjective** HARD TO DEFINE, hard to describe, indescribable, inexpressible, nameless; vague, obscure, impalpable, elusive.

indefinite ▶ **adjective** ❶ *an indefinite period* INDETERMINATE, unspecified, unlimited, unrestricted, undecided, undetermined, undefined, unfixed, unsettled, unknown, uncertain; limitless, infinite, endless, immeasurable. ❷ *an indefinite meaning* VAGUE, ill-defined, unclear, loose, general, imprecise, inexact, nebulous, blurred, fuzzy, hazy, obscure, ambiguous, equivocal.

– OPPOSITES fixed, clear.

indefinitely ▶ **adverb** FOR AN UNSPECIFIED PERIOD, for an unlimited period, without limit, sine die.

indelible ▶ **adjective** INERADICABLE, permanent, lasting, persisting, enduring, unfading, unforgettable, haunting, never to be forgotten.

indelicate ▶ **adjective** ❶ *an indelicate question* INSENSITIVE, tactless, undiplomatic, impolitic, indiscreet. ❷ *an indelicate sense of humour* VULGAR, rude, crude, bawdy, racy, risqué, ribald, earthy, indecent, improper, naughty, indecorous, off colour, dirty, smutty, salacious; *informal* blue, nudge-nudge, raunchy; *Brit. informal* saucy.

indemnify ▶ **verb** ❶ *he should be indemnified for his losses* REIMBURSE, compensate, recompense, repay, pay back, remunerate, recoup. ❷ *they are indemnified against breach of contract* INSURE, guarantee, protect, secure, underwrite.

indemnity ▶ **noun** ❶ *no indemnity will be given for loss of cash* INSURANCE, assurance, protection, security, indemnification, surety, guarantee, warranty, safeguard. ❷ *indemnity from prosecution* IMMUNITY, exemption, dispensation, freedom; special treatment, privilege. ❸ *the company was paid $100,000 in indemnity* COMPENSATION, reimbursement, recompense, repayment, restitution, payment, redress, reparation(s), damages.

indent ▶ **verb** ❶ *a coastline indented by many fjords* NOTCH, make an indentation in, scallop, groove, furrow. ❷ *you'll have to indent for a new uniform* ORDER, put in an order for, requisition, apply for, put in for, request, ask for, claim, put in a request/claim for, call for.

▶ **noun** (*Brit.*) *an indent for silk scarves* ORDER, requisition, purchase order, request, call, application; claim.

indentation ▶ **noun** HOLLOW, depression, dip, dent, dint, cavity, concavity, pit, trough; dimple, cleft; snick, nick, notch; recess, bay, inlet, cove.

indenture ▶ **noun** CONTRACT, agreement, compact, covenant, bond, warrant; certificate, deed, document, instrument.

independence ▶ **noun** ❶ *the struggle for American independence* SELF-GOVERNMENT, self-rule, home rule, self-determination, sovereignty, autonomy, non-alignment, freedom, liberty. ❷ *he valued his independence* SELF-SUFFICIENCY, self-reliance. ❸ *the adviser's independence* IMPARTIALITY, neutrality, disinterest, disinterestedness, detachment, objectivity. ❹ *independence of spirit* FREEDOM, individualism, unconventionality, unorthodoxy.

independent ▶ adjective ❶ *an independent country* SELF-GOVERNING, self-ruling, self-determining, sovereign, autonomous, autarchic, free, non-aligned. ❷ *two independent groups of biologists verified the results* SEPARATE, different, unconnected, unrelated, dissociated, discrete. ❸ *an independent school* PRIVATE, non-state-run, private-sector, fee-paying; privatized, denationalized. ❹ *her grown-up, independent children* SELF-SUFFICIENT, self-supporting, self-reliant, standing on one's own two feet. ❺ *independent advice* IMPARTIAL, unbiased, unprejudiced, neutral, disinterested, uninvolved, uncommitted, detached, dispassionate, objective, non-partisan, non-discriminatory, with no axe to grind, without fear or favour. ❻ *an independent spirit* FREETHINKING, free, individualistic, unconventional, maverick, bold, unconstrained, unfettered, untrammelled.
–OPPOSITES subservient, related, public, biased.

independently ▶ adverb ALONE, on one's own, separately, unaccompanied, solo; unaided, unassisted, without help, by one's own efforts, under one's own steam, single-handed(ly), off one's own bat, on one's own initiative.

indescribable ▶ adjective INEXPRESSIBLE, indefinable, beyond words/description, incommunicable, ineffable; unutterable, unspeakable; intense, extreme, acute, strong, powerful, profound; incredible, extraordinary, remarkable, prodigious.

indestructible ▶ adjective UNBREAKABLE, shatterproof, durable; lasting, enduring, everlasting, perennial, deathless, undying, immortal, inextinguishable, imperishable; *poetic/literary* adamantine.
–OPPOSITES fragile.

indeterminate ▶ adjective ❶ *an indeterminate period of time* UNDETERMINED, uncertain, unknown, unspecified, unstipulated, indefinite, unfixed. ❷ *some indeterminate background noise* VAGUE, indefinite, unspecific, unclear, nebulous, indistinct; amorphous, shapeless, formless; hazy, faint, shadowy, dim.

index ▶ noun ❶ *the library's subject index* LIST, listing, inventory, catalogue, register, directory. ❷ *literature is an index to the condition of civilization* GUIDE, sign, indication, indicator, measure, signal, mark, evidence, symptom, token; clue, hint. ❸ *the index jumped up the dial* POINTER, indicator, needle, hand, finger, marker.

indicate ▶ verb ❶ *sales indicate a growing market for such art* POINT TO, be a sign of, be evidence of, evidence, demonstrate, show, testify to, bespeak, be a symptom of, be symptomatic of, denote, connote, mark, signal, signify, suggest, imply; manifest, reveal, betray, display, reflect, represent; *formal* evince; *poetic/literary* betoken. ❷ *the president indicated his willingness to use force* STATE, declare, make known, communicate, announce, mention, reveal, divulge, disclose; put it on record; admit. ❸ *please indicate your choice of prize on the form* SPECIFY, designate, stipulate; show. ❹ *he indicated the room with a sweep of his arm* POINT TO, point out, gesture towards.

indicated ▶ adjective *in such cases surgery is indicated* ADVISABLE, recommended, suggested, desirable, preferable, best, sensible, wise, commonsensical, prudent, in someone's (best) interests; necessary, needed, required, called for.

indication ▶ noun SIGN, signal, indicator, symptom, mark, manifestation, demonstration, show, evidence; pointer, guide, hint, clue, intimation, omen, augury, portent, warning, forewarning.

indicative ▶ adjective SYMPTOMATIC, expressive, suggestive, representative, emblematic, symbolic; typical, characteristic; *rare* indicatory.

indicator ▶ noun ❶ *these tests are a reliable indicator of performance* MEASURE, gauge, barometer, guide, index, mark, sign, signal; standard, touchstone, yardstick, benchmark, criterion, point of reference, guideline, test, litmus test. ❷ *the depth indicator* METER, measuring device, measure, gauge, dial. ❸ *a position indicator* POINTER, needle, hand, arrow, marker.

indict ▶ verb CHARGE, accuse, arraign, take to court, put on trial, prosecute; summons, cite, prefer charges against; *N. Amer.* impeach.
–OPPOSITES acquit.

indictment ▶ noun CHARGE, accusation, arraignment; citation, summons; *Brit.* plaint; *N. Amer.* impeachment.

indifference ▶ noun ❶ *his apparent indifference infuriated her* LACK OF CONCERN, unconcern, disinterest, lack of interest, lack of enthusiasm, apathy, nonchalance; boredom, unresponsiveness, impassivity, dispassion, detachment, coolness. ❷ *the indifference of the midfield players* MEDIOCRITY, lack of distinction, amateurism, amateurishness, lack of inspiration.

indifferent ▶ adjective ❶ *an indifferent shrug* UNCONCERNED, uninterested, uncaring, casual, nonchalant, offhand, uninvolved, unenthusiastic, apathetic, lukewarm, phlegmatic; unimpressed, bored, unmoved, unresponsive, impassive, dispassionate, detached, cool. ❷ *an indifferent performance* MEDIOCRE, ordinary, average, middling, middle-of-the-road, uninspired, undistinguished, unexceptional, unexciting, unremarkable, run-of-the-mill, pedestrian, prosaic, lacklustre, forgettable, amateur, amateurish; *informal* OK, so-so, fair-to-middling, no great shakes, not up to much; *Brit. informal* not much cop; *N. Amer. informal* bush-league; *NZ informal* half-pie.
–OPPOSITES enthusiastic, brilliant.

indigenous ▶ adjective NATIVE, original, aboriginal, autochthonous; earliest, first.

indigent ▶ adjective POOR, impecunious, destitute, penniless, impoverished, insolvent, poverty-stricken; needy, in need, hard up, on the breadline, deprived, disadvantaged, badly off; *informal* on one's uppers, broke, flat broke, strapped (for cash), without a brass farthing, without a bean/sou, as poor as a church mouse, on one's beam-ends; *Brit. informal* stony broke, skint, boracic; *N. Amer. informal* on skid row; *formal* penurious.
– OPPOSITES rich.

indigestion ▶ noun DYSPEPSIA, heartburn, pyrosis, acidity, stomach ache; (an) upset stomach, (a) stomach upset; *informal* bellyache, tummy ache, collywobbles.

indignant ▶ adjective AGGRIEVED, resentful, affronted, disgruntled, displeased, cross, angry, annoyed, offended, exasperated, irritated, piqued, nettled, in high dudgeon, chagrined; *informal* peeved, vexed, irked, put out, miffed, aggravated, riled, in a huff; *Brit. informal* narked; *N. Amer. informal* sore.

indignation ▶ noun RESENTMENT, umbrage, affront, disgruntlement, displeasure, anger, annoyance, irritation, exasperation, vexation, offence, pique; *informal* aggravation; *poetic/literary* ire.

indignity ▶ noun SHAME, humiliation, loss of self-respect, loss of pride, loss of face, embarrassment, mortification; disgrace, dishonour, stigma, discredit; affront, insult, abuse, mistreatment, injury, offence, injustice, slight, snub, discourtesy, disrespect; *informal* slap in the face, kick in the teeth.

indirect ▶ adjective ❶ *an indirect effect* INCIDENTAL, accidental, unintended, secondary, subordinate, ancillary, collateral, concomitant, contingent. ❷ *the indirect route* ROUNDABOUT, circuitous, wandering, meandering, serpentine, winding, tortuous, zigzag. ❸ *an indirect attack* OBLIQUE, inexplicit, implicit, implied, allusive.

indirectly ▶ adverb ❶ *I heard of the damage indirectly* SECOND-HAND, at second hand, from others; *informal* on the grapevine, on the bush/jungle telegraph. ❷ *he referred to the subject indirectly* OBLIQUELY, by implication, allusively.

indiscernible ▶ adjective ❶ *an almost indiscernible change* UNNOTICEABLE, imperceptible, invisible, hidden, undetectable, indistinguishable, inappreciable; tiny, minute, minuscule, microscopic, infinitesimal, negligible, inconsequential. ❷ *an indiscernible shape* INDISTINCT, nebulous, unclear, fuzzy, obscure, vague, indefinite, amorphous, shadowy, dim, hard to make out.
– OPPOSITES distinct.

indiscreet ▶ adjective ❶ *an indiscreet remark* IMPRUDENT, unwise, impolitic, injudicious, incautious, irresponsible, ill-judged, ill-advised, misguided, ill-considered, careless, rash, unwary, hasty, reckless, precipitate, impulsive, foolhardy, foolish, short-sighted; undiplomatic, indelicate, tactless, insensitive; inexpedient, untimely, infelicitous. ❷ *her indiscreet behaviour* IMMODEST, indecorous, unseemly, improper, indecent, indelicate.

indiscretion ▶ noun ❶ *he was prone to indiscretion* IMPRUDENCE, injudiciousness, incaution, irresponsibility; carelessness, rashness, recklessness, precipitateness, impulsiveness, foolhardiness, foolishness, folly; tactlessness, insensitivity. ❷ *his past indiscretions* BLUNDER, lapse, gaffe, mistake, faux pas, error, slip, miscalculation, impropriety; misdemeanour, transgression, peccadillo, misdeed; *informal* slip-up.

indiscriminate ▶ adjective NON-SELECTIVE, unselective, undiscriminating, uncritical, aimless, hit-or-miss, haphazard, random, arbitrary, unsystematic, undirected; wholesale, general, sweeping, blanket; thoughtless, unthinking, unconsidered, casual, careless.
– OPPOSITES selective.

indispensable ▶ adjective ESSENTIAL, necessary, all-important, of the utmost importance, of the essence, vital, crucial, key, needed, required, requisite; invaluable.
– OPPOSITES superfluous.

indisposed ▶ adjective ❶ *my wife is indisposed* ILL, unwell, sick, on the sick list, poorly, ailing, not (very) well, out of sorts, under/below par; out of action, hors de combat; *Brit.* off colour; *informal* under the weather. ❷ *she was indisposed to help him* RELUCTANT, unwilling, disinclined, loath, unprepared, not disposed, not minded, averse.
– OPPOSITES well, willing.

indisposition ▶ noun ❶ *a mild indisposition* ILLNESS, malady, ailment, disorder, sickness, disease, infection; condition, complaint, problem; *informal* bug, virus; *Brit. informal* lurgy. ❷ *his indisposition to leave the house* RELUCTANCE, unwillingness, disinclination, aversion.

indisputable ▶ adjective INCONTROVERTIBLE, incontestable, undeniable, irrefutable, beyond dispute, unassailable, unquestionable, beyond question, indubitable, not in doubt, beyond doubt, beyond a shadow of a doubt, unarguable, undebatable, airtight, watertight; unequivocal, unmistakable, certain, sure, definite, definitive, proven, decisive, conclusive, demonstrable, self-evident, clear, clear-cut, plain, obvious, manifest, patent, palpable.
– OPPOSITES questionable.

indistinct ▶ adjective ❶ *the distant shoreline was indistinct* BLURRED, out of focus, fuzzy, hazy, misty, foggy, cloudy, shadowy, dim, nebulous; unclear, obscure, vague, faint, indistinguishable, barely perceptible, hard to see, hard to make out. ❷ *the last two digits are indis-*

tinct INDECIPHERABLE, illegible, unreadable, hard to read. ❸ *indistinct sounds* MUFFLED, muted, low, quiet, soft, faint, inaudible, hard to hear; muttered, mumbled.
– OPPOSITES clear.

indistinguishable ▶ adjective ❶ *the two girls were indistinguishable* IDENTICAL, difficult to tell apart, like (two) peas in a pod, like Tweedledum and Tweedledee, very similar, two of a kind. ❷ *his words were indistinguishable* UNINTELLIGIBLE, incomprehensible, hard to make out, indistinct, unclear; inaudible.
– OPPOSITES unalike, clear.

individual ▶ adjective ❶ *exhibitions devoted to individual artists* SINGLE, separate, discrete, independent; sole, lone, solitary, isolated. ❷ *he had his own individual style of music* CHARACTERISTIC, distinctive, distinct, typical, particular, peculiar, personal, personalized, special. ❸ *a chic and highly individual apartment* ORIGINAL, unique, exclusive, singular, idiosyncratic, different, unusual, novel, unorthodox, atypical, out of the ordinary.
▶ noun ❶ *Peter was a rather stuffy individual* PERSON, human being, mortal, soul, creature; man, boy, woman, girl; character, personage; *informal* type, sort, beggar, cookie, customer, guy, geezer, devil, bastard; *Brit. informal* bod, gent, punter; *informal, dated* body, cove; *archaic* wight. ❷ *she was a real individual* INDIVIDUALIST, free spirit, nonconformist, original, eccentric, character, maverick, rare bird; *Brit. informal* one-off.

individualism ▶ noun INDEPENDENCE, freethinking, freedom of thought, originality; unconventionality, eccentricity.

individualist ▶ noun FREE SPIRIT, individual, nonconformist, original, eccentric, maverick, rare bird; *Brit. informal* one-off.
– OPPOSITES conformist.

individualistic ▶ adjective UNCONVENTIONAL, unorthodox, atypical, singular, unique, original, nonconformist, independent, freethinking; eccentric, maverick, strange, odd, peculiar, idiosyncratic.

individuality ▶ noun DISTINCTIVENESS, distinction, uniqueness, originality, singularity, particularity, peculiarity, differentness, separateness; personality, character, identity, self.

individually ▶ adverb ONE AT A TIME, one by one, singly, separately, severally, independently, apart.
– OPPOSITES together.

indoctrinate ▶ verb BRAINWASH, propagandize, proselytize, inculcate, re-educate, persuade, convince, condition, mould, discipline; instruct, teach, school, drill.

indolence ▶ noun LAZINESS, idleness, slothfulness, sloth, shiftlessness, inactivity, inaction, inertia, sluggishness, lethargy, languor, languidness, torpor; *poetic/literary* hebetude.

indolent ▶ adjective LAZY, idle, slothful, loafing, work-shy, do-nothing, sluggardly, shiftless, lackadaisical, languid, inactive, inert, sluggish, lethargic, torpid; slack, lax, remiss, negligent, good-for-nothing, feckless; *informal* bone idle.
– OPPOSITES industrious, energetic.

indomitable ▶ adjective INVINCIBLE, unconquerable, unbeatable, unassailable, invulnerable, unshakeable; indefatigable, unyielding, unbending, stalwart, stout-hearted, lion-hearted, strong-willed, strong-minded, steadfast, staunch, resolute, firm, determined, intransigent, inflexible, adamant; unflinching, courageous, brave, valiant, heroic, intrepid, fearless, plucky, mettlesome, gritty, steely.
– OPPOSITES submissive.

indubitable ▶ adjective UNQUESTIONABLE, undoubtable, indisputable, unarguable, undebatable, incontestable, undeniable, irrefutable, incontrovertible, unmistakable, unequivocal, certain, sure, positive, definite, absolute, conclusive, watertight; beyond doubt, beyond the shadow of a doubt, beyond dispute, beyond question, not in question, not in doubt.
– OPPOSITES doubtful.

induce ▶ verb ❶ *the pickets induced many workers to stay away* PERSUADE, convince, prevail upon, get, make, prompt, move, inspire, influence, encourage, motivate; coax into, wheedle into, cajole into, talk into, prod into; *informal* twist someone's arm. ❷ *these activities induce a feeling of togetherness* BRING ABOUT, cause, produce, effect, create, give rise to, generate, instigate, engender, occasion, set in motion, lead to, result in, trigger off, spark off, whip up, stir up, kindle, arouse, rouse, foster, promote, encourage; *poetic/literary* beget, enkindle.
– OPPOSITES dissuade, prevent.

inducement ▶ noun INCENTIVE, encouragement, attraction, temptation, stimulus, bait, lure, pull, draw, spur, goad, impetus, motive, motivation, provocation; bribe, reward; *informal* carrot, come-on, sweetener.
– OPPOSITES deterrent.

induct ▶ verb ❶ *the new ministers were inducted into the government* ADMIT TO, allow into, introduce to, initiate into, install in, instate in, swear into; appoint to. ❷ *he inducted me into the skills of magic* INTRODUCE TO, acquaint with, familiarize with, make conversant with; ground in, instruct in, teach in, educate in, school in.

indulge ▶ verb ❶ *Sally indulged her passion for long walks* SATISFY, gratify, fulfil, feed, accommodate; yield to, give in to, give way to. ❷ *she indulged in a fit of sulks* WALLOW IN, give oneself up to, give way to, yield to, abandon oneself to, give free rein to; luxuriate in, revel in, lose oneself in. ❸ *she did not like her children to be indulged* PAMPER, spoil, overindulge, coddle,

mollycoddle, cosset, baby, pet, spoon-feed, feather-bed, wrap in cotton wool; pander to, wait on hand and foot, cater to someone's every whim, kill with kindness; *archaic* cocker.
– OPPOSITES frustrate.
■ **indulge oneself** TREAT ONESELF, give oneself a treat; have a spree, splash out; *informal* go to town, splurge.

indulgence ▶ **noun** ❶ *the indulgence of all his desires* SATISFACTION, gratification, fulfilment. ❷ *excess indulgence contributed to his ill-health* SELF-GRATIFICATION, self-indulgence, overindulgence, intemperance, immoderation, excess, excessiveness, lack of restraint, extravagance, decadence, pleasure-seeking, sybaritism. ❸ *they viewed holidays as an indulgence* EXTRAVAGANCE, luxury, treat, non-essential, extra, frill. ❹ *her indulgence left him spoilt* PAMPERING, coddling, mollycoddling, cosseting, babying. ❺ *his parents view his lapses with indulgence* TOLERANCE, forbearance, understanding, kindess, compassion, sympathy, forgiveness, leniency.

indulgent ▶ **adjective** GENEROUS, permissive, easy-going, liberal, tolerant, forgiving, forbearing, lenient, kind, kindly, soft-hearted, compassionate, understanding, sympathetic; fond, doting, soft; compliant, obliging, accommodating.
– OPPOSITES strict.

industrial ▶ **adjective** ❶ *industrial areas of the city* MANUFACTURING, factory; commercial, business, trade. ❷ (*Brit.*) *industrial action* STRIKE, protest.

industrialist ▶ **noun** MANUFACTURER, producer, factory owner; captain of industry, big businessman, magnate, tycoon, capitalist, financier; *informal, derogatory* fat cat.

industrious ▶ **adjective** HARD-WORKING, diligent, assiduous, conscientious, steady, painstaking, sedulous, persevering, unflagging, untiring, tireless, indefatigable, studious; busy, as busy as a bee, active, bustling, energetic, on the go, vigorous, determined, dynamic, zealous, productive; with one's shoulder to the wheel, with one's nose to the grindstone.
– OPPOSITES indolent.

industry ▶ **noun** ❶ *British industry* MANUFACTURING, production; construction. ❷ *the publishing industry* BUSINESS, trade, field, line (of business); *informal* racket. ❸ *the kitchen was a hive of industry* ACTIVITY, busyness, energy, vigour, productiveness; hard work, industriousness, diligence, application, dedication.

inebriated ▶ **adjective** DRUNK, intoxicated, drunken, incapable, tipsy, the worse for drink, under the influence; *informal* tight, merry, in one's cups, three sheets to the wind, pie-eyed, plastered, smashed, wrecked, wasted, sloshed, soused, sozzled, blotto, stewed, pickled, tanked (up), off one's face, out of one's head, ratted; *Brit. informal* legless, bevvied, paralytic, Brahms and Liszt, half cut, out of it, bladdered, trolleyed, squiffy, tiddly; *N. Amer. informal* loaded, trashed, juiced, sauced, out of one's gourd, in the bag, zoned; *euphemistic* tired and emotional; *informal, dated* lit up.
– OPPOSITES sober.

inedible ▶ **adjective** UNEATABLE, indigestible, unsavoury, unpalatable, unwholesome; stale, rotten, off, bad.

ineffable ▶ **adjective** ❶ *the ineffable beauty of the Everglades* INDESCRIBABLE, inexpressible, beyond words; undefinable, unutterable, untold, unimaginable; overwhelming, breathtaking, awesome, staggering, amazing. ❷ *the ineffable name of God* UNUTTERABLE, unmentionable; taboo, forbidden, off limits; *informal* no go.

ineffective ▶ **adjective** ❶ *an ineffective scheme* UNSUCCESSFUL, unproductive, fruitless, unprofitable, abortive, futile, purposeless, useless, worthless, ineffectual, inefficient, inefficacious, inadequate; feeble, inept, lame; *archaic* bootless. ❷ *an ineffective president* INEFFECTUAL, inefficient, inefficacious, unsuccessful, powerless, impotent, inadequate, incompetent, incapable, unfit, inept, weak, poor; *informal* useless, hopeless.

ineffectual ▶ **adjective.** *See* INEFFECTIVE senses 1, 2.

inefficacious ▶ **adjective.** *See* INEFFECTIVE sense 1.

inefficient ▶ **adjective** ❶ *an inefficient worker* INEFFECTIVE, ineffectual, incompetent, inept, incapable, unfit, unskilful, inexpert, amateurish; disorganized, unprepared; negligent, lax, sloppy, slack, careless; *informal* lousy, useless. ❷ *inefficient processes* UNECONOMICAL, wasteful, unproductive, time-wasting, slow; deficient, disorganized, unsystematic.

inelegant ▶ **adjective** ❶ *an inelegant bellow of laughter* UNREFINED, uncouth, unsophisticated, unpolished, uncultivated; ill-bred, coarse, vulgar, rude, impolite, unmannerly. ❷ *inelegant dancing* GRACELESS, ungraceful, ungainly, uncoordinated, awkward, clumsy, lumbering; inept, unskilful, inexpert; *informal* having two left feet.
– OPPOSITES refined, graceful.

ineligible ▶ **adjective** ❶ *we are ineligible for a grant* UNQUALIFIED, ruled out, disqualified, disentitled; *Law* incompetent. ❷ (*dated*) *she was in love with someone ineligible* UNMARRIAGEABLE, unavailable; unsuitable, unacceptable, undesirable, inappropriate, unworthy.
– OPPOSITES suitable.

inept ▶ **adjective** INCOMPETENT, unskilful, unskilled, inexpert, amateurish; clumsy, awkward, maladroit, unhandy, blundering, bungling; unproductive, unsuccessful, ineffectual, not up to scratch; *informal* cack-handed, hamfisted, butterfingered, klutzy; *Brit. informal* all

(fingers and) thumbs.
– OPPOSITES competent.

inequality ▸ noun IMBALANCE, inequity, inconsistency, variation, variability; divergence, polarity, disparity, discrepancy, dissimilarity, difference; bias, prejudice, discrimination, unfairness.

inequitable ▸ adjective UNFAIR, unjust, unequal, uneven, unbalanced, one-sided, discriminatory, preferential, biased, partisan, partial, prejudiced.
– OPPOSITES fair.

inequity ▸ noun UNFAIRNESS, injustice, unjustness, discrimination, partisanship, partiality, favouritism, bias, prejudice.

inert ▸ adjective UNMOVING, motionless, immobile, inanimate, still, stationary, static; dormant, sleeping; unconscious, comatose, lifeless, insensible, insensate, insentient; idle, inactive, sluggish, lethargic, stagnant, listless, torpid.
– OPPOSITES active.

inertia ▸ noun INACTIVITY, inaction, inertness; apathy, accidie, malaise, stagnation, enervation, lethargy, listlessness, torpor, idleness, sloth; motionlessness, immobility, lifelessness; *formal* stasis.

inescapable ▸ adjective UNAVOIDABLE, inevitable, ineluctable, inexorable; assured, sure, certain; necessary, required, compulsory, mandatory; *rare* ineludible.
– OPPOSITES avoidable.

inessential ▸ adjective UNNECESSARY, nonessential, unwanted, uncalled-for, needless, redundant, superfluous, excessive, surplus, dispensable, expendable; unimportant, peripheral, minor, secondary.

inestimable ▸ adjective IMMEASURABLE, incalculable, innumerable, unfathomable, indeterminable, measureless, untold; limitless, boundless, unlimited, infinite, endless, inexhaustible; *informal* no end of; *poetic/literary* myriad.
– OPPOSITES few.

inevitable ▸ adjective UNAVOIDABLE, inescapable, inexorable, ineluctable; assured, certain, sure; fated, predestined, predetermined; *rare* ineludible.
– OPPOSITES uncertain.

inevitably ▸ adverb NATURALLY, necessarily, automatically, as a matter of course, of necessity, inescapably, unavoidably, certainly, surely, definitely, undoubtedly; *informal* like it or not; *formal* perforce.

inexact ▸ adjective IMPRECISE, inaccurate, approximate, rough, crude, general, vague; incorrect, erroneous, wrong, false; off, out; *N. Amer. informal* ballpark.

inexcusable ▸ adjective INDEFENSIBLE, unjustifiable, unwarranted, unpardonable, unforgivable; blameworthy, censurable, reprehensible, deplorable, unconscionable, unacceptable, unreasonable; uncalled-for, unprovoked, gratuitous.

inexhaustible ▸ adjective ❶ *her patience is inexhaustible* UNLIMITED, limitless, illimitable, infinite, boundless, endless, never-ending, unfailing, everlasting; immeasurable, incalculable, inestimable, untold; copious, abundant. ❷ *the dancers were inexhaustible* TIRELESS, indefatigable, untiring, unfaltering, unflagging, unremitting, persevering, persistent, dogged.
– OPPOSITES limited, weary.

inexorable ▸ adjective ❶ *the inexorable advance of science* RELENTLESS, unstoppable, inescapable, inevitable, unavoidable, irrevocable; persistent, continuous, non-stop, steady, interminable, incessant, unceasing, unremitting, unrelenting. ❷ *inexorable creditors* INTRANSIGENT, unbending, unyielding, inflexible, adamant, obdurate, immovable, unshakeable; implacable, unappeasable, unforgiving, unsparing, uncompromising, ruthless, relentless, pitiless, merciless.

inexpedient ▸ adjective UNADVISABLE, injudicious, unwise, impolitic, imprudent, incautious; irresponsible, foolhardy, foolish, ill-advised, ill-considered, inappropriate; disadvantageous, prejudicial.
– OPPOSITES wise.

inexpensive ▸ adjective CHEAP, low-priced, low-cost, economical, competitive, affordable, reasonable, budget, economy, bargain, cut-price, reduced, discounted, discount, rock-bottom, giveaway, bargain-basement; *informal* dirt cheap.

inexperience ▸ noun IGNORANCE, unworldliness, naivety, naiveness, innocence, greenness, immaturity; *poetic/literary* nescience.

inexperienced ▸ adjective INEXPERT, unpractised, untrained, unschooled, unqualified, unskilled, amateur; ignorant, unversed, unseasoned; naive, unsophisticated, callow, immature, green; *informal* wet behind the ears, wide-eyed.

inexpert ▸ adjective UNSKILLED, unskilful, amateur, amateurish, unprofessional, inexperienced; inept, incompetent, maladroit, clumsy, bungling, blundering, unhandy; *informal* cack-handed, ham-fisted, butterfingered.

inexplicable ▸ adjective UNACCOUNTABLE, unexplainable, incomprehensible, unfathomable, impenetrable, insoluble; baffling, puzzling, perplexing, mystifying, bewildering; mysterious, strange.
– OPPOSITES understandable.

inexpressible ▸ adjective INDESCRIBABLE, undefinable, unutterable, unspeakable, ineffable, beyond words; unimaginable, inconceivable, unthinkable, untold.

inexpressive ▶ adjective EXPRESSIONLESS, impassive, emotionless; inscrutable, unreadable, blank, vacant, glazed, lifeless, deadpan, wooden, stony; poker-faced, straight-faced.

inextinguishable ▶ adjective IRREPRESSIBLE, unquenchable, indestructible, undying, unfailing, unceasing, ceaseless, enduring, everlasting, eternal, persistent.

inextricable ▶ adjective ❶ *our lives are inextricable* INSEPARABLE, indivisible, entangled, tangled, mixed up. ❷ *an inextricable situation* INESCAPABLE, unavoidable, ineluctable.

infallible ▶ adjective ❶ *an infallible sense of timing* UNERRING, unfailing, faultless, flawless, impeccable, perfect, precise, accurate, meticulous, scrupulous; *Brit. informal* spot on. ❷ *infallible cures* UNFAILING, guaranteed, dependable, trustworthy, reliable, sure, certain, safe, foolproof, effective; *informal* sure-fire; *formal* efficacious.

infamous ▶ adjective ❶ *an infamous mass murderer* NOTORIOUS, disreputable; legendary, fabled. ❷ *infamous misconduct* ABOMINABLE, outrageous, shocking, shameful, disgraceful, dishonourable, discreditable, unworthy; monstrous, atrocious, appalling, dreadful, terrible, heinous, egregious, detestable, loathsome, hateful, vile, unspeakable, unforgivable, iniquitous, scandalous; *informal* dirty, filthy, low-down; *Brit. informal* beastly.
– OPPOSITES reputable, honourable.

infamy ▶ noun ❶ *these acts brought him infamy* NOTORIETY, disrepute, ill fame, disgrace, discredit, shame, dishonour, ignominy, scandal, censure, blame, disapprobation, condemnation. ❷ *she was punished for her infamy* WICKEDNESS, evil, vileness, iniquity, depravity, degeneracy, immorality; sin, wrongdoing, offence, abuse; *formal* turpitude.

infancy ▶ noun ❶ *she died in infancy* BABYHOOD, early childhood. ❷ *the infancy of broadcasting* BEGINNINGS, early days, early stages; seeds, roots; start, commencement, launch, debut, rise, emergence, dawn, birth, inception.
– OPPOSITES end.

infant ▶ noun *a fretful infant* BABY, newborn, young child, (tiny) tot, little one; *Medicine* neonate; *Scottish & N. English* bairn, wean; *informal* tiny, sprog; *poetic/literary* babe.
▶ adjective *infant industries* DEVELOPING, emergent, emerging, embryonic, nascent, new, fledgling, budding, up-and-coming.

infantile ▶ adjective CHILDISH, babyish, immature, puerile, juvenile, adolescent; silly, inane, fatuous.

infantry ▶ noun INFANTRYMEN, foot soldiers, foot guards; the ranks; cannon fodder; *US* GIs; *Brit. informal* Tommies; *Military slang* infanteers, grunts; *US informal, dated* dogfaces; *historical* footmen.

infatuated ▶ adjective BESOTTED, in love, head over heels, obsessed, taken; enamoured of, attracted to, devoted to, captivated by, enchanted by, bewitched by, under the spell of; *informal* smitten with, sweet on, keen on, gone on, mad about, crazy about, stuck on, bowled over by, carrying a torch for.

infatuation ▶ noun PASSION, love, adoration, desire, feeling, devotion; obsession, fixation; fancy; *informal* crush, thing, hang-up, pash.

infect ▶ verb ❶ *the ill can infect their partners* PASS INFECTION TO, spread disease to, contaminate. ❷ *nitrates were infecting rivers* CONTAMINATE, pollute, taint, foul, dirty, blight, damage, ruin; poison. ❸ *his high spirits infected everyone* AFFECT, influence, impact on, touch; excite, inspire, stimulate, animate.

infection ▶ noun ❶ *a kidney infection* DISEASE, virus; disorder, condition, affliction, complaint, illness, ailment, sickness, infirmity; *informal* bug; *Brit. informal* lurgy; *dated* contagion. ❷ *the infection in his wounds* CONTAMINATION, poison; septicity, septicaemia, suppuration, inflammation; germs, bacteria; *Medicine* sepsis.

infectious ▶ adjective ❶ *infectious disease* CONTAGIOUS, communicable, transmittable, transmissible, transferable, spreadable; epidemic; *informal* catching; *dated* infective. ❷ *infectious fluids* CONTAMINATING, germ-laden, polluting; poisonous, toxic, noxious. ❸ *her laughter is infectious* IRRESISTIBLE, compelling, contagious, catching.

infelicitous ▶ adjective UNFORTUNATE, unsuitable, inappropriate, inapposite, inapt; untimely, inopportune; injudicious, imprudent, indiscreet, indelicate.
– OPPOSITES appropriate.

infelicity ▶ noun MISTAKE, error, blunder, slip, lapse, solecism.

infer ▶ verb DEDUCE, conclude, conjecture, surmise, reason; gather, understand, presume, assume, take it; read between the lines; *N. Amer.* figure; *Brit. informal* suss (out).

inference ▶ noun DEDUCTION, conclusion, reasoning, conjecture, speculation, presumption, assumption, supposition, reckoning, extrapolation; guesswork.

inferior ▶ adjective ❶ *she regards him as inferior* SECOND-CLASS, lower-ranking, subordinate, second-fiddle, junior, minor, lowly, humble, menial, beneath one. ❷ *inferior accommodation* SECOND-RATE, substandard, low-quality, low-grade, unsatisfactory, shoddy, deficient; poor, bad, awful, dreadful, wretched; *Brit.* downmarket; *informal* crummy, dire, rotten, lousy, third-rate; *Brit. informal* duff, rubbish, ropy, dodgy.
– OPPOSITES superior, luxury.
▶ noun *how dare she treat him as an inferior?* SUBORDINATE, junior, underling, minion.

infernal ▶ adjective ❶ *the infernal regions* HELLISH, lower, nether, subterranean, underworld, chthonic; Hadean, Tartarean. ❷ (*informal*) *an infernal nuisance* DAMNABLE, wretched; annoying, irritating, infuriating, exasperating; *informal* damned, damn, flaming, blasted, blessed, pesky, aggravating; *Brit. informal* blinking, blooming, flipping; *Brit. informal, dated* bally, ruddy.

infertile ▶ adjective ❶ *infertile soil* BARREN, unfruitful, unproductive, uncultivatable; sterile, impoverished, arid. ❷ *she was infertile* STERILE, barren; childless; *Medicine* infecund.

infest ▶ verb OVERRUN, spread through, invade, infiltrate, pervade, permeate, inundate, overwhelm; beset, plague.

infested ▶ adjective OVERRUN, swarming, teeming, crawling, alive, ridden; plagued, beset.

infidel ▶ noun UNBELIEVER, disbeliever, nonbeliever, agnostic, atheist; heathen, pagan, idolater, idolatress, heretic, freethinker, dissenter, nonconformist; *archaic* paynim; *rare* nullifidian.

infidelity ▶ noun UNFAITHFULNESS, adultery, unchastity; faithlessness, disloyalty, treachery, double-dealing, duplicity, deceit; affair; *informal* playing around, fooling around, cheating, two-timing; *formal* fornication; *dated* cuckoldry.

infiltrate ▶ verb ❶ *he infiltrated the smuggling operation* INSINUATE ONESELF INTO, worm one's way into, sneak into, invade, intrude on, butt into; *informal* gatecrash, muscle in on. ❷ *mineral solutions infiltrate the rocks* PERMEATE, penetrate, pervade, seep into/through, soak into, get into, enter.

infiltrator ▶ noun SPY, (secret) agent, plant, intruder, interloper, subversive, informant, informer, mole, entrist, entryist; *N. Amer. informal* spook.

infinite ▶ adjective ❶ *the universe is infinite* BOUNDLESS, unbounded, unlimited, limitless, never-ending, interminable; immeasurable, fathomless; extensive, vast. ❷ *an infinite number of birds* COUNTLESS, uncountable, inestimable, innumerable, numberless, immeasurable, incalculable, untold; great, huge, enormous. ❸ *she bathed him with infinite care* GREAT, immense, supreme, absolute, real; *informal* no end of.
– OPPOSITES limited, small.

infinitesimal ▶ adjective MINUTE, tiny, minuscule, very small; microscopic, imperceptible, indiscernible; *Scottish* wee; *informal* teeny, teeny-weeny, itsy-bitsy, tiddly; *Brit. informal* titchy; *N. Amer. informal* little-bitty.
– OPPOSITES huge.

infinity ▶ noun ❶ *the infinity of space* ENDLESSNESS, infinitude, infiniteness, boundlessness, limitlessness; vastness, immensity. ❷ *an infinity of different molecules* INFINITE NUMBER; abundance, profusion, host, multitude, mass, wealth; *informal* heap, stack.

infirm ▶ adjective ❶ *she cares for infirm people* FRAIL, weak, feeble, debilitated, decrepit, disabled; ill, unwell, sick, sickly, poorly, indisposed, ailing. ❷ (*archaic*) *he was infirm of purpose* WEAK, uncertain, indefinite, indecisive, irresolute, unresolved, undecided; wavering, vacillating.
– OPPOSITES healthy, strong.

infirmity ▶ noun ❶ *they were excused due to infirmity* FRAILTY, weakness, feebleness, delicacy, debility, decrepitude; disability, impairment; illness, sickness, indisposition, poor health. ❷ *the infirmities of old age* AILMENT, malady, illness, disease, disorder, sickness, affliction, complaint, indisposition.

inflame ▶ verb ❶ *the play inflames anti-semitism* INCITE, arouse, rouse, provoke, stir up, whip up, kindle, ignite, touch off, foment, inspire, stimulate, agitate. ❷ *he inflamed a sensitive situation* AGGRAVATE, exacerbate, intensify, worsen, compound. ❸ *his opinions inflamed his rival* ENRAGE, incense, anger, madden, infuriate, exasperate, provoke, antagonize, rile; *informal* make someone see red, make someone's blood boil.
– OPPOSITES calm, soothe, placate.

inflamed ▶ adjective SWOLLEN, puffed up; red, hot, burning, itchy; raw, sore, painful, tender; infected, septic.

inflammable ▶ adjective FLAMMABLE, combustible, incendiary, ignitable; volatile, unstable.
– OPPOSITES fireproof.

inflammation ▶ noun SWELLING, puffiness; redness, heat, burning; rawness, soreness, tenderness; infection, festering, septicity.

inflammatory ▶ adjective ❶ *an inflammatory lung condition* causing inflammation; *Medicine* erythrogenic. ❷ *inflammatory language* PROVOCATIVE, incendiary, stirring, rousing, rabble-rousing, seditious, mutinous; like a red rag to a bull; fiery, passionate; controversial, contentious.

inflate ▶ verb ❶ *the mattress inflated* BLOW UP, fill up, fill with air, aerate, puff up/out, pump up; dilate, distend, swell. ❷ *the demand inflated prices* INCREASE, raise, boost, escalate, put up; *informal* hike up, jack up, bump up. ❸ *the figures were inflated by the press* EXAGGERATE, magnify, overplay, overstate, enhance, embellish, touch up; increase, amplify, augment.
– OPPOSITES decrease, understate.

inflated ▶ adjective ❶ *an inflated balloon* BLOWN UP, aerated, filled, puffed up/out, pumped up; distended, expanded, engorged, swollen. ❷ *inflated prices* HIGH, sky-high, excessive, unreasonable, prohibitive, outrageous, exorbitant, extortionate; *Brit.* over the odds; *informal* steep. ❸ *an inflated opinion of himself* EXAGGER-

ATED, magnified, aggrandized, immoderate, overblown, overstated. ❹ *inflated language* HIGH-FLOWN, extravagant, exaggerated, elaborate, flowery, ornate, overblown, overwrought, grandiloquent, magniloquent, lofty, grandiose; affected, pretentious; *informal* windy, highfalutin.

inflection ▶ noun ❶ (*Grammar*) *verbal inflections* CONJUGATION, declension; form, ending, case. ❷ *his voice was without inflection* STRESS, cadence, rhythm, accentuation, intonation, emphasis, modulation, lilt.

inflexible ▶ adjective ❶ *his inflexible attitude* STUBBORN, obstinate, obdurate, intractable, intransigent, unbending, immovable, unaccommodating; hidebound, single-minded, pigheaded, mulish, uncompromising, adamant, firm, resolute, diehard, dyed-in-the-wool; *formal* refractory. ❷ *inflexible rules* UNALTERABLE, unchangeable, immutable, unvarying; firm, fixed, set, established, entrenched, hard and fast; stringent, strict. ❸ *an inflexible structure* RIGID, stiff, unyielding, unbending, unbendable; hard, firm, inelastic.
– OPPOSITES accommodating, pliable.

inflict ▶ verb ❶ *he inflicted an injury on Frank* IMPOSE, exact, wreak; administer to, deal out to, mete out to, cause to, give to. ❷ *I won't inflict my pain on my children* IMPOSE, force, thrust, foist; saddle someone with, burden someone with.

infliction ▶ noun ❶ *the infliction of pain* ADMINISTRATION, delivery, application; imposition, perpetration; *formal* exaction. ❷ (*informal, dated*) *they bore the infliction with heroism* AFFLICTION, trial, problem, nuisance, trouble, annoyance, bother, irritant; suffering, torment, tribulation.

influence ▶ noun ❶ *the influence of parents on their children* EFFECT, impact; control, sway, hold, power, authority, mastery, domination, supremacy; guidance, direction; pressure. ❷ *a bad influence on young girls* EXAMPLE TO, (role) model for, guide for, inspiration to. ❸ *political influence* POWER, authority, sway, leverage, weight, pull, standing, prestige, stature, rank; *informal* clout, muscle, teeth; *N. Amer. informal* drag.
▶ verb ❶ *bosses can influence our careers* AFFECT, have an impact on, determine, guide, control, shape, govern, decide; change, alter, transform. ❷ *an attempt to influence the jury* SWAY, bias, prejudice, suborn; pressurize, coerce; dragoon, intimidate, browbeat, brainwash; *informal* twist someone's arm, lean on; *Brit. informal* nobble.

influential ▶ adjective ❶ *an influential leader* POWERFUL, dominant, controlling, strong, authoritative; important, prominent, distinguished. ❷ *he was influential in shaping her career* INSTRUMENTAL, significant, important, crucial, pivotal.

influx ▶ noun ❶ *an influx of tourists* INUNDATION, rush, stream, flood, incursion; invasion, intrusion. ❷ *influxes of river water* INFLOW, inrush, flood, inundation.

inform ▶ verb ❶ *she informed him that she was ill* TELL, notify, apprise, advise, impart to, communicate to, let someone know; brief, prime, enlighten, send word to; *informal* fill in, clue in/up. ❷ *he informed on two villains* DENOUNCE, give away, betray, incriminate, inculpate, report; sell out, stab in the back; *informal* rat, squeal, split, tell, blow the whistle, sell down the river, snitch, peach, stitch up; *Brit. informal* grass, shop, sneak; *Scottish informal* clype; *N. Amer. informal* rat out, finger; *Austral./NZ informal* dob. ❸ *the articles were informed by feminism* SUFFUSE, pervade, permeate, infuse, imbue; characterize, typify.

informal ▶ adjective ❶ *an informal discussion* UNOFFICIAL, casual, relaxed, easy-going, unceremonious; open, friendly, intimate; simple, unpretentious, easy, homely, cosy; *informal* unstuffy, laid-back, chummy, pally, matey. ❷ *an informal speech style* COLLOQUIAL, vernacular, idiomatic, demotic, popular; familiar, everyday, unofficial; simple, natural, unpretentious; *informal* slangy, chatty, folksy. ❸ *informal clothes* CASUAL, relaxed, comfortable, everyday, sloppy, leisure; *informal* comfy.
– OPPOSITES formal, official, literary, smart.

informality ▶ noun LACK OF CEREMONY, casualness, unceremoniousness, unpretentiousness; homeliness, cosiness; ease, naturalness, approachability.

information ▶ noun DETAILS, particulars, facts, figures, statistics, data; knowledge, intelligence; instruction, advice, guidance, direction, counsel, enlightenment; news; *informal* info, gen, the low-down, the dope, the inside story.

informative ▶ adjective INSTRUCTIVE, instructional, illuminating, enlightening, revealing, explanatory; factual, educational, educative, edifying, didactic; *informal* newsy.

informed ▶ adjective KNOWLEDGEABLE, enlightened, literate, educated; sophisticated, cultured; briefed, up to date, up to speed, in the picture, in the know, au courant, au fait; *informal* clued up, genned up; *Brit. informal* switched-on, sussed.
– OPPOSITES ignorant.

informer ▶ noun INFORMANT, betrayer, traitor, Judas, collaborator, stool pigeon, fifth columnist, spy, double agent, infiltrator, plant; telltale, taleteller; *N. Amer.* tattletale; *informal* rat, squealer, whistle-blower, snake in the grass, snitch; *Brit. informal* grass, supergrass, nark, snout; *Scottish informal* clype; *N. Amer. informal* fink, stoolie.

infraction ▶ noun INFRINGEMENT, contravention, breach, violation, transgression; neglect, dereliction, non-compliance; *Law* delict, contumacy.

infrequent ▶ adjective RARE, uncommon, unusual, exceptional, few (and far between), like gold dust, as scarce as hens' teeth; unaccustomed, unwonted; isolated, scarce, scattered; sporadic, irregular, intermittent; *informal* once in a blue moon; *dated* seldom.
– OPPOSITES common.

infringe ▶ verb ❶ *the bid infringed EU rules* CONTRAVENE, violate, transgress, break, breach; disobey, defy, flout, fly in the face of; disregard, ignore, neglect; go beyond, overstep, exceed; *Law* infract. ❷ *surveillance could infringe personal liberties* UNDERMINE, erode, diminish, weaken, impair, damage, compromise; limit, curb, check, encroach on.
– OPPOSITES obey, preserve.

infuriate ▶ verb ENRAGE, incense, anger, madden, inflame; exasperate, antagonize, provoke, rile, annoy, irritate, nettle, gall, irk, vex, pique, get on someone's nerves, try someone's patience; *N. Amer.* rankle; *informal* aggravate, make someone see red, get someone's back up, make someone's blood boil, get up someone's nose, needle, hack off, brown off; *Brit. informal* wind up, get to, nark, cheese off; *N. Amer. informal* bug, tick off.
– OPPOSITES please.

infuriating ▶ adjective EXASPERATING, maddening, annoying, irritating, irksome, vexatious, trying, tiresome; *informal* aggravating, pesky.

infuse ▶ verb ❶ *she was infused with a sense of hope* FILL, suffuse, imbue, inspire, charge, pervade, permeate. ❷ *he infused new life into the group* INSTIL, breathe, inject, impart, inculcate, introduce, add. ❸ *infuse the dried leaves* STEEP, brew, stew, soak, immerse, souse; *Brit. informal* mash.

ingenious ▶ adjective INVENTIVE, creative, imaginative, original, innovative, pioneering, resourceful, enterprising, inspired; clever, intelligent, smart, brilliant, masterly, talented, gifted, skilful; astute, sharp-witted, quick-witted, shrewd; elaborate, sophisticated.

ingenuous ▶ adjective NAIVE, innocent, simple, childlike, trusting, trustful, over-trusting, unwary; unsuspicious, unworldly, wide-eyed, inexperienced, green; open, sincere, honest, frank, candid, forthright, artless, guileless, genuine.
– OPPOSITES artful.

inglorious ▶ adjective SHAMEFUL, dishonourable, ignominious, discreditable, disgraceful, scandalous; humiliating, mortifying, demeaning, ignoble, undignified, wretched.

ingrained, engrained ▶ adjective ❶ *ingrained attitudes* ENTRENCHED, established, deep-rooted, deep-seated, fixed, firm, unshakeable, ineradicable; inveterate, dyed-in-the-wool, abiding, enduring, stubborn. ❷ *ingrained dirt* GROUND-IN, fixed, implanted, embedded; permanent, indelible, ineradicable, inexpungible.
– OPPOSITES transient, superficial.

ingratiate
■ **ingratiate oneself** CURRY FAVOUR WITH, cultivate, win over, get in someone's good books; toady to, crawl to, grovel to, fawn over, kowtow to, play up to, pander to, flatter, court; *informal* suck up to, rub up the right way, lick someone's boots.

ingratiating ▶ adjective SYCOPHANTIC, toadying, fawning, unctuous, obsequious; flattering, insincere; smooth-tongued, silver-tongued, slick; greasy, oily, saccharine; *informal* smarmy, slimy, creepy, sucky.

ingratitude ▶ noun UNGRATEFULNESS, thanklessness, unthankfulness, non-recognition.

ingredient ▶ adjective CONSTITUENT, component, element; part, piece, bit, strand, portion, unit, feature, aspect, attribute; (**ingredients**) contents, makings.

ingress ▶ noun ❶ *the doors gave ingress to the station* ENTRY, entrance, access, admittance, admission; way in, approach. ❷ *the ingress of water* SEEPAGE, leakage, inundation, inrush, intrusion, incursion, entry, entrance.
– OPPOSITES exit.

inhabit ▶ verb LIVE IN, occupy; settle (in), people, populate, colonize; dwell in, reside in, tenant, lodge in, have one's home in; *formal* be domiciled in, abide in.

inhabitable ▶ adjective HABITABLE, fit to live in, usable; *informal* liveable-in; *formal* tenantable.

inhabitant ▶ noun RESIDENT, occupant, occupier, dweller, settler; local, native; (**inhabitants**) population, populace, people, public, community, citizenry, townsfolk, townspeople; *formal* denizen; *archaic* burgher, habitant.

inhale ▶ verb BREATHE IN, inspire, draw in, suck in, sniff in, drink in; *poetic/literary* inbreathe.

inharmonious ▶ adjective ❶ *inharmonious sounds* UNMELODIOUS, unharmonious, unmusical, tuneless, discordant, dissonant, off-key; harsh, grating, jarring, cacophonous; *archaic* absonant. ❷ *an inharmonious modern building* OUT OF PLACE, unsuitable, inappropriate, clashing, conflicting, incompatible, mismatched; jarring, discordant. ❸ *his relationships are inharmonious* ANTAGONISTIC, quarrelsome, argumentative, disputatious, cantankerous, confrontational, belligerent.
– OPPOSITES musical, fitting, congenial.

inherent ▶ adjective INTRINSIC, innate, connate, connatural, immanent, built-in, inborn, ingrained, deep-rooted; essential, fundamental,

basic, structural, organic; natural, instinctive, instinctual, congenital, native.
– OPPOSITES acquired.

inherit ▶ **verb** ❶ *she inherited his farm* BECOME HEIR TO, come into/by, be bequeathed, be left, be willed; *Law* be devised. ❷ *Richard inherited the title* SUCCEED TO, assume, take over, come into; *formal* accede to.

inheritance ▶ **noun** ❶ *a comfortable inheritance* LEGACY, bequest, endowment, bestowal, bequeathal, provision; birthright, heritage, patrimony; *Law* devise. ❷ *his inheritance of the title* SUCCESSION TO, accession to, assumption of, elevation to.

inheritor ▶ **noun** HEIR, heiress, legatee; successor, next in line; *Law* devisee, grantee, cestui que trust; *Scottish Law* heritor.

inhibit ▶ **verb** ❶ *the obstacles which inhibit change* IMPEDE, hinder, hamper, hold back, discourage, interfere with, obstruct, slow down, retard; curb, check, suppress, restrict, fetter, cramp, frustrate, stifle, prevent, block, thwart, foil, stop, halt. ❷ *she feels inhibited from taking part* PREVENT, disallow, exclude, forbid, prohibit, preclude, ban, bar, interdict.
– OPPOSITES assist, encourage, allow.

inhibited ▶ **adjective** SHY, reticent, reserved, self-conscious, diffident, bashful, coy; wary, reluctant, hesitant, insecure, unconfident, unassertive, timid; withdrawn, repressed, undemonstrative; *informal* uptight.

inhibition ▶ **noun** ❶ *they overcame their inhibitions* SHYNESS, reticence, self-consciousness, reserve, diffidence; wariness, hesitance, hesitancy, insecurity; unassertiveness, timidity; repression, reservation; psychological block; *informal* hang-up. ❷ *the inhibition of publishing* HINDRANCE, hampering, discouragement, obstruction, impediment, retardation; suppression, repression, restriction, restraint, constraint, cramping, stifling, prevention; curb, check, bar, barrier.

inhospitable ▶ **adjective** ❶ *the inhospitable landscape* UNINVITING, unwelcoming; bleak, forbidding, cheerless, hostile, harsh, inimical; uninhabitable, barren, bare, desolate, stark. ❷ *forgive me if I seem inhospitable* UNWELCOMING, unfriendly, unsociable, unsocial, antisocial, unneighbourly, uncongenial; aloof, cool, cold, frosty, distant, remote, indifferent, offhand; uncivil, discourteous, ungracious; ungenerous, unkind, unsympathetic; *informal* stand-offish.
– OPPOSITES welcoming.

inhuman ▶ **adjective** ❶ *inhuman treatment* CRUEL, harsh, inhumane, brutal, callous, sadistic, severe, savage, vicious, barbaric; monstrous, heinous, egregious; merciless, ruthless, pitiless, remorseless, cold-blooded, heartless, hard-hearted; unkind, inconsiderate, unfeeling, uncaring; *Brit. informal* beastly; *dated* dastardly. ❷ *hellish and inhuman shapes* NON-HUMAN, non-mortal, monstrous, devilish, ghostly; subhuman, animal; strange, odd, unearthly.
– OPPOSITES humane.

inhumane ▶ **adjective.** *See* INHUMAN sense 1.

inhume ▶ **verb** (*poetic/literary*) BURY, inter, lay to rest, entomb; *informal* plant; *poetic/literary* sepulchre.

inimical ▶ **adjective** ❶ *this is inimical to genuine democracy* HARMFUL, injurious, detrimental, deleterious, prejudicial, damaging, hurtful, destructive, ruinous; antagonistic, contrary, antipathetic, unfavourable, adverse, opposed, hostile; *poetic/literary* malefic. ❷ *he fixed her with an inimical gaze* HOSTILE, unfriendly, antagonistic, unkind, unsympathetic, malevolent; unwelcoming, cold, frosty.
– OPPOSITES advantageous, friendly.

inimitable ▶ **adjective** UNIQUE, exclusive, distinctive, individual, special, idiosyncratic; incomparable, unparalleled, unrivalled, peerless, matchless, unequalled, unsurpassable, superlative, supreme, beyond compare, second to none, in a class of one's own; *formal* unexampled.

iniquity ▶ **noun** ❶ *the iniquity of his conduct* WICKEDNESS, sinfulness, immorality, impropriety; vice, evil, sin; villainy, criminality; odiousness, atrocity, egregiousness; outrage, monstrosity, obscenity, reprehensibility. ❷ *I will forgive their iniquity* SIN, crime, transgression, wrongdoing, wrong, violation, offence, vice; atrocity, outrage.
– OPPOSITES goodness, virtue.

initial ▶ **adjective** *the initial stages* BEGINNING, opening, commencing, starting, inceptive, embryonic, fledgling; first, early, primary, preliminary, elementary, foundational, preparatory; introductory, inaugural.
– OPPOSITES final.

▶ **noun** *what do the initials stand for?* INITIAL LETTER; (**initials**) acronym, abbreviation, initialism.

▶ **verb** ❶ *he initialled the warrant* PUT ONE'S INITIALS ON, sign, countersign, autograph, endorse, inscribe, witness. ❷ *they initialled a new agreement* RATIFY, accept, approve, authorize, validate, recognize.

initially ▶ **adverb** AT FIRST, at the start, at the outset, in/at the beginning, to begin with, to start with, originally.

initiate ▶ **verb** ❶ *the government initiated the scheme* BEGIN, start (off), commence; institute, inaugurate, launch, instigate, establish, set up, sow the seeds of, start the ball rolling; originate, pioneer; *informal* kick off. ❷ *he was initiated into a cult* INTRODUCE, admit, induct, install, incorporate, enlist, enrol, recruit, sign up, swear in; ordain, invest. ❸ *they were initiated into the world of maths* TEACH ABOUT, instruct in, tutor in, school in, prime in, ground in; famil-

iarize with, acquaint with; indoctrinate, inculcate; *informal* show someone the ropes.
– OPPOSITES finish, expel.
▶ **noun** *an initiate on the team* NOVICE, starter, beginner, newcomer; learner, student, pupil, trainee, apprentice; new boy, new girl, recruit, tyro, neophyte; postulant, novitiate; *informal* rookie, new kid (on the block), newie, newbie, greenhorn.

initiative ▶ **noun** ❶ *employers are looking for initiative* ENTERPRISE, resourcefulness, inventiveness, imagination, ingenuity, originality, creativity; drive, dynamism, ambition, motivation, spirit, energy, vision; *informal* get-up-and-go, pep, punch. ❷ *he has lost the initiative* ADVANTAGE, upper hand, edge, lead, whip hand, trump card. ❸ *a recent initiative on recycling* PLAN, scheme, strategy, stratagem, measure, proposal, step, action, approach.

inject ▶ **verb** ❶ *he injected a dose of codeine* ADMINISTER, introduce; inoculate, vaccinate; *informal* shoot (up), mainline, fix (up). ❷ *a pump injects air into the valve* INSERT, introduce, feed, push, force, shoot. ❸ *he injected new life into the team* INTRODUCE, instil, infuse, imbue, breathe.

injection ▶ **noun** INOCULATION, vaccination, vaccine, immunization, booster; dose; *informal* jab, shot, hype.

injudicious ▶ **adjective** IMPRUDENT, unwise, inadvisable, ill-advised, misguided; ill-considered, ill-judged, incautious, hasty, rash, foolish, foolhardy, hare-brained; inappropriate, impolitic, inexpedient; *informal* dumb.
– OPPOSITES prudent.

injunction ▶ **noun** ORDER, ruling, direction, directive, command, instruction; decree, edict, dictum, dictate, fiat, mandate.

injure ▶ **verb** ❶ *he injured his foot* HURT, wound, damage, harm; cripple, lame, disable; maim, mutilate, deform, mangle, break; *Brit. informal* knacker; *archaic* scathe. ❷ *a libel injured her reputation* DAMAGE, mar, spoil, ruin, blight, blemish, tarnish, blacken. ❸ (*archaic*) *I have injured no one by my folly* WRONG, do an injustice to, offend against, maltreat, mistreat, ill-use; *informal* do the dirty on.

injured ▶ **adjective** ❶ *his injured arm* HURT, wounded, damaged, sore, bruised; crippled, lame, game, disabled; maimed, mutilated, deformed, mangled, broken, fractured; *Brit. informal* gammy. ❷ *the injured party* WRONGED, offended, maltreated, mistreated, ill-used, harmed; defamed, maligned, insulted, dishonoured. ❸ *an injured tone* UPSET, hurt, wounded, offended, reproachful, pained, aggrieved, unhappy, put out.
– OPPOSITES healthy, offending.

injurious ▶ **adjective** HARMFUL, damaging, deleterious, detrimental, hurtful; disadvantageous, unfavourable, undesirable, adverse, inimical, unhealthy, pernicious; *poetic/literary* malefic.

injury ▶ **noun** ❶ *minor injuries* WOUND, bruise, cut, gash, scratch, graze, abrasion, contusion, lesion; *Medicine* trauma. ❷ *they escaped without injury* HARM, hurt, damage, pain, suffering, impairment, affliction, incapacity. ❸ *the injury to her feelings* OFFENCE, abuse; affront, insult, slight, snub; wrong, wrongdoing, injustice.

injustice ▶ **noun** ❶ *the injustice of the world* UNFAIRNESS, unjustness, inequity; cruelty, tyranny, repression, exploitation, corruption; bias, prejudice, discrimination, intolerance. ❷ *his sacking was an injustice* WRONG, offence, crime, sin, misdeed, outrage, atrocity, scandal, disgrace, affront.

inkling ▶ **noun** IDEA, notion, sense, impression, suggestion, indication, whisper, glimmer, (sneaking) suspicion, fancy, hunch; hint, clue, intimation, sign; *informal* the foggiest (idea), the faintest (idea).

inky ▶ **adjective** ❶ *the inky darkness* BLACK, jet-black, pitch-black; sable, ebony, dark; *poetic/literary* Stygian. ❷ *inky fingers* INK-STAINED, stained, blotchy.

inlaid ▶ **adjective** INSET, set, studded, lined, panelled; ornamented, decorated; mosaic, intarsia, marquetry.

inland ▶ **adjective** ❶ *inland areas* INTERIOR, inshore, central, internal, upcountry. ❷ *inland trade* DOMESTIC, internal, home, local.
– OPPOSITES coastal, international.
▶ **adverb** *the goods were carried inland* UPCOUNTRY, inshore, to the interior.

inlet ▶ **noun** ❶ COVE, bay, bight, creek, estuary, fjord, sound; *Scottish* firth. ❷ *a fresh air inlet* VENT, flue, shaft, duct, channel, pipe, pipeline.

inmate ▶ **noun** ❶ *the inmates of the hospital* PATIENT, inpatient; convalescent; resident, inhabitant, occupant. ❷ *the prison's inmates* PRISONER, convict, captive, detainee, internee; *informal* jailbird, con; *Brit. informal* lag; *N. Amer. informal* yardbird.

inmost ▶ **adjective**. *See* INNERMOST.

inn ▶ **noun** TAVERN, bar, hostelry, taproom; hotel, guest house; *Brit.* pub, public house; *Canadian* beer parlour; *informal* watering hole; *dated* alehouse.

innards ▶ **plural noun** (*informal*) ENTRAILS, internal organs, viscera, intestines, bowels, guts; *informal* insides.

innate ▶ **adjective** INBORN, inbred, congenital, inherent, natural, intrinsic, instinctive, intuitive, unlearned; hereditary, inherited, in the blood, in the family; inbuilt, deep-rooted, deep-seated, connate, connatural.
– OPPOSITES acquired.

inner ▶ **adjective** ❶ *inner London* CENTRAL, innermost, mid, middle. ❷ *the inner gates* INTERNAL, interior, inside, inmost, innermost, intra-

mural. ❸ *the Queen's inner circle* PRIVILEGED, restricted, exclusive, private, confidential, intimate. ❹ *the inner meaning* HIDDEN, secret, deep, underlying, unapparent; veiled, esoteric, unrevealed. ❺ *one's inner life* MENTAL, intellectual, psychological, spiritual, emotional.
– OPPOSITES external, apparent.

innermost ▶ adjective ❶ *the innermost shrine* CENTRAL, middle, internal, interior. ❷ *her innermost feelings* DEEPEST, deep-seated, inward, underlying, intimate, private, personal, secret, hidden, concealed, unexpressed, unrevealed, unapparent; true, real, honest.

innkeeper ▶ noun LANDLORD, landlady, hotelier, hotel owner, proprietor, manager, manageress; licensee, barman, barmaid; *Brit.* publican.

innocence ▶ noun ❶ *he protested his innocence* GUILTLESSNESS, blamelessness, irreproachability. ❷ *the innocence of his bride* VIRGINITY, chastity, chasteness, purity; integrity, morality, decency; *dated* honour; *archaic* virtue. ❸ *she took advantage of his innocence* NAIVETY, ingenuousness, credulity, inexperience, gullibility, simplicity, unworldliness, guilelessness, greenness.

innocent ▶ adjective ❶ *he was entirely innocent* GUILTLESS, blameless, in the clear, unimpeachable, irreproachable, above suspicion, faultless; honourable, honest, upright, law-abiding; *informal* squeaky clean. ❷ *innocent fun* HARMLESS, innocuous, safe, inoffensive. ❸ *nice innocent girls* VIRTUOUS, pure, moral, decent, righteous, upright, wholesome; demure, modest, chaste, virginal; impeccable, spotless, sinless, unsullied, incorrupt, undefiled; *informal* squeaky clean, whiter than white. ❹ *she is innocent of guile* FREE FROM, without, lacking (in), clear of, ignorant of, unaware of, untouched by; *poetic/literary* nescient of. ❺ *innocent foreigners* NAIVE, ingenuous, trusting, credulous, unsuspicious, unwary, unguarded; impressionable, gullible, easily led; inexperienced, unworldly, unsophisticated, green; simple, artless, guileless; *informal* wet behind the ears, born yesterday.
– OPPOSITES guilty, sinful, worldly, malignant.
▶ noun *an innocent in a strange land* INGÉNUE, unworldly person; child; novice; *N. Amer. informal* greenhorn; *poetic/literary* babe in arms.

innocuous ▶ adjective ❶ *an innocuous fungus* HARMLESS, safe, non-toxic, innocent; edible, eatable. ❷ *an innocuous comment* INOFFENSIVE, unobjectionable, unexceptionable, harmless, mild, tame; anodyne, unremarkable, commonplace, run-of-the-mill.
– OPPOSITES harmful, offensive.

innovation ▶ noun CHANGE, alteration, revolution, upheaval, transformation, metamorphosis; reorganization, restructuring, rearrangement, remodelling; new measures, new methods, modernization, modernism; novelty, newness; *informal* a shake up, a shake-down.

innovative ▶ adjective ORIGINAL, innovatory, innovational, new, novel, fresh, unusual, unprecedented, avant-garde, experimental, inventive, ingenious; advanced, modern, state-of-the-art, pioneering, ground-breaking, revolutionary, radical, newfangled.

innovator ▶ noun PIONEER, trailblazer, pathfinder, ground-breaker; developer, modernizer, reformer, reformist, progressive; experimenter, inventor, creator.

innuendo ▶ noun INSINUATION, suggestion, intimation, implication, hint, overtone, undertone, allusion, reference; aspersion, slur.

innumerable ▶ adjective COUNTLESS, numerous, untold, legion, without number, numberless, unnumbered, multitudinous, incalculable, limitless; *informal* umpteen, a slew of, no end of, loads of, stacks of, heaps of, masses of, oodles of, zillions of; *N. Amer. informal* gazillions of; *poetic/literary* myriad.
– OPPOSITES few.

inoculate ▶ verb IMMUNIZE, vaccinate, inject; protect from, safeguard against; *informal* give someone a jab/shot.

inoculation ▶ noun IMMUNIZATION, vaccination, vaccine; injection, booster; *informal* jab, shot.

inoffensive ▶ adjective HARMLESS, innocuous, unobjectionable, unexceptionable; non-violent, non-aggressive, mild, peaceful, peaceable, gentle; tame, innocent.

inoperable ▶ adjective ❶ *an inoperable tumour* UNTREATABLE, incurable, irremediable; malignant; terminal, fatal, deadly, lethal; *archaic* immedicable. ❷ *the airfield was left inoperable* UNUSABLE, out of action, out of service, non-active. ❸ *the agreement is now inoperable* IMPRACTICAL, unworkable, unfeasible, unrealistic, non-viable, impracticable, unsuitable.
– OPPOSITES curable, workable.

inoperative ▶ adjective ❶ *the fan is inoperative* OUT OF ORDER, out of service, broken, out of commission, unserviceable, faulty, defective; down; *informal* bust, kaput, on the blink, acting up, shot; *Brit. informal* knackered. ❷ *the contract is inoperative* VOID, null and void, invalid, ineffective, non-viable; cancelled, revoked, terminated; worthless, valueless, unproductive, abortive.
– OPPOSITES working, valid.

inopportune ▶ adjective INCONVENIENT, unsuitable, inappropriate, unfavourable, unfortunate, infelicitous, inexpedient; untimely, ill-timed, unseasonable; awkward, difficult.
– OPPOSITES convenient.

inordinate ▶ adjective EXCESSIVE, undue, unreasonable, unjustifiable, unwarrantable, dis-

proportionate, unwarranted, unnecessary, needless, uncalled for, exorbitant, extreme; immoderate, extravagant; *informal* over the top, OTT.
– OPPOSITES moderate.

inorganic ▶ adjective INANIMATE, inert; lifeless, dead, defunct, extinct; mineral.

input ▶ noun *an error resulted from invalid input* DATA, details, information, material; facts, figures, statistics, particulars, specifics; *informal* info.
▶ verb *she input data into the file* FEED IN, put in, load, insert; key in, type in; code, store.

inquest ▶ noun INQUIRY, investigation, inquisition, probe, examination, review, analysis; hearing.

inquire ▶ verb. *See* ENQUIRE.

inquiring ▶ adjective. *See* ENQUIRING.

inquiry ▶ noun. *See* ENQUIRY.

inquisition ▶ noun INTERROGATION, questioning, quizzing, cross-examination; investigation, inquiry, inquest; *informal* grilling; *Law* examination.

inquisitive ▶ adjective CURIOUS, interested, intrigued, agog; prying, spying, eavesdropping, intrusive, busybody, meddlesome; inquiring, questioning, probing; *informal* nosy, nosy-parker, snoopy.
– OPPOSITES uninterested.

insalubrious ▶ adjective SEEDY, unsavoury, sordid, seamy, sleazy, unpleasant, dismal, wretched; slummy, squalid, shabby, ramshackle, tumbledown, dilapidated, neglected, crumbling, decaying; *informal* scruffy, scuzzy, crummy; *Brit. informal* grotty; *N. Amer. informal* shacky.
– OPPOSITES smart.

insane ▶ adjective ❶ *she was declared insane* MENTALLY ILL, mentally disordered, of unsound mind, certifiable; psychotic, schizophrenic; mad, deranged, demented, out of one's mind, non compos mentis, sick in the head, unhinged, unbalanced, unstable, disturbed, crazed; *informal* crazy, (stark) raving mad, not all there, bonkers, cracked, batty, cuckoo, loony, loopy, nuts, screwy, bananas, wacko, off one's rocker, off one's head, round the bend; *Brit. informal* crackers, barmy, barking (mad), off one's trolley, round the twist, not the full shilling; *N. Amer. informal* buggy, nutso, out of one's tree; *Austral./NZ informal* bushed. ❷ *an insane suggestion* FOOLISH, idiotic, stupid, silly, senseless, nonsensical, absurd, ridiculous, ludicrous, preposterous, fatuous, inane, asinine, hare-brained, half-baked; impracticable, implausible, irrational, illogical; *informal* crazy, mad, cock-eyed; *Brit. informal* daft, barmy.
– OPPOSITES sensible, calm.

insanitary ▶ adjective UNHYGIENIC, unsanitary, unhealthy, insalubrious, dirty, filthy, unclean, impure, contaminated, polluted, foul; infected, infested, germ-ridden; *informal* germy.
– OPPOSITES hygienic.

insanity ▶ noun ❶ *insanity runs in her family* MENTAL ILLNESS, madness, dementia; lunacy, instability; mania, psychosis; *informal* craziness. ❷ *it would be insanity to take this loan* FOLLY, foolishness, madness, idiocy, stupidity, lunacy, silliness; *informal* craziness.

insatiable ▶ adjective UNQUENCHABLE, unappeasable, uncontrollable; voracious, gluttonous, greedy, hungry, ravenous, wolfish; avid, eager, keen; *informal* piggy; *poetic/literary* insatiate.

inscribe ▶ verb ❶ *his name was inscribed above the door* CARVE, write, engrave, etch, cut; imprint, stamp, impress, mark. ❷ *a book inscribed to him by the author* DEDICATE, address, name, sign.

inscription ▶ noun ❶ *the inscription on the sarcophagus* ENGRAVING, etching; wording, writing, lettering, legend, epitaph, epigraph. ❷ *the book had an inscription* DEDICATION, message; signature, autograph.

inscrutable ▶ adjective ❶ *her inscrutable face* ENIGMATIC, unreadable, mysterious; unexpressive, inexpressive, emotionless, unemotional, expressionless, impassive, blank, vacant, deadpan, dispassionate; *informal* poker-faced. ❷ *God's ways are inscrutable* MYSTERIOUS, inexplicable, unexplainable, incomprehensible, impenetrable, unfathomable, opaque, abstruse, arcane, obscure, cryptic.
– OPPOSITES expressive, transparent.

insecure ▶ adjective ❶ *an insecure young man* UNCONFIDENT, uncertain, unsure, doubtful, hesitant, self-conscious, unassertive, diffident, unforthcoming, shy, timid, retiring, timorous, inhibited, introverted; anxious, fearful, worried; *informal* mousy. ❷ *insecure windows* UNGUARDED, unprotected, vulnerable, defenceless, unshielded, exposed, assailable, pregnable; unlocked, unsecured. ❸ *an insecure footbridge* UNSTABLE, rickety, rocky, wobbly, shaky, unsteady, precarious; weak, flimsy, unsound, unsafe; *informal* jerry-built; *Brit. informal* dicky, dodgy.
– OPPOSITES confident, stable.

insecurity ▶ noun ❶ *he hid his insecurity* LACK OF CONFIDENCE, self-doubt, diffidence, unassertiveness, timidity, uncertainty, nervousness, inhibition; anxiety, worry, unease. ❷ *the insecurity of our situation* VULNERABILITY, defencelessness, peril, danger; instability, fragility, frailty, shakiness, unreliability.

insensate ▶ adjective. *See* INSENSIBLE sense 1.

insensible ▶ adjective ❶ *she was insensible on the floor* UNCONSCIOUS, insensate, senseless, insentient, inert, comatose, knocked out, passed out, blacked out; stunned, numb, numbed; *informal* out (cold), out for the count, out of it,

zonked (out), dead to the world; *Brit. informal* spark out. ❷ *he was insensible to the risks* UNAWARE OF, ignorant of, unconscious of, unmindful of, oblivious to; indifferent to, impervious to, deaf to, blind to, unaffected by; *informal* in the dark about. ❸ *he scared even the most insensible person* INSENSITIVE, dispassionate, cool, emotionless, unfeeling, unconcerned, detached, indifferent, hardened, tough; *informal* hard-boiled.
– OPPOSITES conscious, aware, sensitive.

insensitive ▶ adjective ❶ *an insensitive bully* HEARTLESS, unfeeling, inconsiderate, thoughtless, thick-skinned; hard-hearted, cold-blooded, uncaring, unconcerned, unsympathetic, unkind, callous, cruel, merciless, pitiless. ❷ *he was insensitive to her feelings* IMPERVIOUS TO, oblivious to, unaware of, unresponsive to, indifferent to, unaffected by, unmoved by, untouched by; *informal* in the dark about.
– OPPOSITES compassionate.

insentient ▶ adjective INANIMATE, lifeless, inorganic, inert; insensate, unconscious, comatose, anaesthetized, desensitized, numb; *informal* dead to the world, out (cold).

inseparable ▶ adjective ❶ *inseparable friends* DEVOTED, bosom, close, fast, firm, good, best, intimate, boon, faithful; *informal* as thick as thieves. ❷ *the laws are inseparable* INDIVISIBLE, indissoluble, inextricable, entangled; (one and) the same.

insert ▶ verb ❶ *he inserted a tape in the machine* PUT, place, push, thrust, slide, slip, load, fit, slot, lodge, install; *informal* pop, stick, bung. ❷ *she inserted a clause* ENTER, introduce, incorporate, interpolate, interpose, interject.
– OPPOSITES extract, remove.
▶ noun *the newspaper carried an insert* ENCLOSURE, insertion, inlay, supplement; circular, advertisement, pamphlet, leaflet; *informal* ad.

inside ▶ noun ❶ *the inside of a volcano* INTERIOR, inner part; centre, core, middle, heart. ❷ (*informal*) *my insides are out of order* STOMACH, gut, bowels, intestines; *informal* belly, tummy, guts.
– OPPOSITES exterior.
▶ adjective ❶ *his inside pocket* INNER, interior, internal, innermost. ❷ *inside information* CONFIDENTIAL, classified, restricted, privileged, private, secret, exclusive; *informal* hush-hush.
– OPPOSITES outer, public.
▶ adverb ❶ *she ushered me inside* INDOORS, within, in. ❷ *how do you feel inside?* INWARDLY, within, secretly, privately, deep down, at heart, emotionally, intuitively, instinctively. ❸ (*informal*) *if I burgle again I'll be back inside* IN PRISON, in jail, in custody; locked up, imprisoned, incarcerated; *informal* behind bars, doing time; *Brit. informal* banged up.

insider ▶ noun MEMBER, worker, employee, representative; person in the know.

insidious ▶ adjective STEALTHY, subtle, surreptitious, cunning, crafty, artful, sly, wily, underhand, backhanded, indirect; *informal* sneaky.

insight ▶ noun ❶ *your insight has been invaluable* INTUITION, discernment, perception, awareness, understanding, comprehension, apprehension, appreciation, penetration, acumen, perspicacity, judgement, acuity; vision, prescience, imagination; *informal* nous, savvy. ❷ *an insight into the government* UNDERSTANDING OF, appreciation of, revelation about; introduction to; *informal* eye-opener.

insignia ▶ noun BADGE, crest, emblem, symbol, sign, device, mark, seal, colours.

insignificant ▶ adjective UNIMPORTANT, trivial, trifling, negligible, inconsequential, of no account, inconsiderable; nugatory, paltry, petty, insubstantial, frivolous, pointless, worthless, irrelevant, immaterial, peripheral; *informal* piddling.

insincere ▶ adjective FALSE, fake, hollow, artificial, feigned, pretended, put-on; disingenuous, hypocritical, cynical, deceitful, deceptive, duplicitous, double-dealing, two-faced, lying, untruthful, mendacious; *informal* phoney, pretend, pseud.

insinuate ▶ verb ❶ *he insinuated that she lied* IMPLY, suggest, hint, intimate, indicate, let it be known, give someone to understand; *informal* make out, tip someone the wink. ❷ *he insinuated his hand under hers* SLIDE, slip, manoeuvre, insert, edge.
■ **insinuate oneself into** WORM ONE'S WAY INTO, ingratiate oneself with, curry favour with; foist oneself on, introduce oneself into; infiltrate, invade, sneak into, intrude on, impinge on; *informal* muscle in on.

insinuation ▶ noun IMPLICATION, inference, suggestion, hint, intimation, innuendo, reference, allusion, indication, undertone, overtone; aspersion, slur, allegation.

insipid ▶ adjective ❶ *insipid coffee* TASTELESS, flavourless, savourless, bland, weak, wishy-washy; unappetizing, unpalatable. ❷ *insipid pictures* UNIMAGINATIVE, uninspired, uninspiring, characterless, flat, uninteresting, lacklustre, dull, boring, dry (as dust), jejune, humdrum, run-of-the-mill, commonplace, pedestrian, trite, tired, hackneyed, stale, lame, tame, poor, inadequate, sterile, anaemic.
– OPPOSITES tasty, interesting.

insist ▶ verb ❶ *be prepared to insist* STAND FIRM, stand one's ground, be resolute, be determined, hold out, be emphatic, not take no for an answer; persevere, persist; *informal* stick to one's guns. ❷ *she insisted that they pay up* DEMAND, command, require, dictate; urge, exhort. ❸ *he insisted that he knew nothing* MAINTAIN, assert, hold, contend, argue, protest, claim, vow, swear, declare, stress, repeat, reiterate; *formal* aver.

insistence ▶ noun ❶ *she sat down at Anne's insistence* DEMAND, bidding, command, dictate, instruction, requirement, request, entreaty, exhortation; *informal* say-so; *poetic/literary* behest. ❷ *his insistence that he loved her* ASSERTION, declaration, contention, claim, pronouncement, assurance, affirmation, avowal, profession.

insistent ▶ adjective ❶ *Tony's insistent questioning* PERSISTENT, determined, adamant, importunate, tenacious, unyielding, dogged, unrelenting, inexorable; demanding, pushy, urgent; emphatic, firm, assertive. ❷ *an insistent buzzing* INCESSANT, constant, unremitting, repetitive; obtrusive, intrusive.

insobriety ▶ noun DRUNKENNESS, intoxication, inebriation, tipsiness; *informal* tightness; *poetic/literary* crapulence.

insolent ▶ adjective IMPERTINENT, impudent, cheeky, ill-mannered, bad mannered, unmannerly, rude, impolite, uncivil, discourteous, disrespectful, insubordinate, contemptuous; audacious, bold, cocky, brazen; insulting, abusive; *informal* fresh, flip, lippy, saucy; *N. Amer. informal* sassy; *archaic* contumelious, malapert.
– OPPOSITES polite.

insoluble ▶ adjective ❶ *some problems are insoluble* UNSOLVABLE, unanswerable, unresolvable; unfathomable, impenetrable, unexplainable, inscrutable, inexplicable. ❷ *these minerals are insoluble* INDISSOLUBLE.

insolvency ▶ noun BANKRUPTCY, liquidation, failure, collapse, (financial) ruin; pennilessness, penury; *Brit.* receivership.

insolvent ▶ adjective BANKRUPT, ruined, liquidated, wiped out; penniless, impoverished, impecunious; *Brit.* in receivership, without a penny (to one's name); *informal* bust, (flat) broke, belly-up, gone to the wall, on the rocks, in the red, hard up, strapped for cash; *Brit. informal* skint, in Queer Street, stony broke, cleaned out; *formal* penurious.

insomnia ▶ noun SLEEPLESSNESS, wakefulness, restlessness; *archaic* watchfulness.

insouciance ▶ noun NONCHALANCE, unconcern, indifference, heedlessness, calm, equanimity, composure, ease, airiness; *informal* cool.
– OPPOSITES anxiety.

insouciant ▶ adjective NONCHALANT, untroubled, unworried, unruffled, unconcerned, indifferent, blasé, heedless; relaxed, calm, equable, equanimous, serene, composed, easy, carefree, free and easy, happy-go-lucky, light-hearted; *informal* cool, laid back.

inspect ▶ verb EXAMINE, check, scrutinize, investigate, vet, test, monitor, survey, study, look over, scan, explore, probe; assess, appraise, review; *informal* check out, give something a/the once-over.

inspection ▶ noun EXAMINATION, check-up, survey, scrutiny, probe, exploration, observation, investigation; assessment, appraisal, review, evaluation; *informal* once-over, going-over, look-see, overhaul.

inspector ▶ noun EXAMINER, checker, scrutinizer, scrutineer, investigator, surveyor, assessor, appraiser, reviewer, analyst; observer, overseer, supervisor, monitor, watchdog, ombudsman; auditor.

inspiration ▶ noun ❶ *she's a real inspiration to others* STIMULUS, stimulation, motivation, fillip, encouragement, influence, muse, spur, lift, boost, incentive, impulse, catalyst; example, model. ❷ *his work lacks inspiration* CREATIVITY, inventiveness, innovation, ingenuity, imagination, originality; artistry, creativity, insight, vision; finesse, flair. ❸ *she had a sudden inspiration* BRIGHT IDEA, revelation; *informal* brainwave; *N. Amer. informal* brainstorm. ❹ *inspiration pains her* INHALATION, breathing in; respiration.

inspire ▶ verb ❶ *the landscape inspired him to write* STIMULATE, motivate, encourage, influence, rouse, move, stir, energize, galvanize, incite; animate, fire, inspirit, incentivize. ❷ *the film inspired a musical* GIVE RISE TO, lead to, bring about, cause, prompt, spawn, engender; *poetic/literary* beget. ❸ *Charles inspired awe in her* AROUSE, awaken, prompt, induce, ignite, trigger, kindle, produce, bring out; *poetic/literary* enkindle.

inspired ▶ adjective OUTSTANDING, wonderful, marvellous, excellent, magnificent, fine, exceptional, first-class, first-rate, virtuoso, supreme, superlative; innovative, innovatory, innovational, ingenious, original; *informal* tremendous, superb, super, ace, wicked, awesome, out of this world; *Brit. informal* brilliant, brill.
– OPPOSITES poor.

inspiring ▶ adjective INSPIRATIONAL, encouraging, heartening, uplifting, stirring, rousing, stimulating, electrifying; moving, affecting, influential.

instability ▶ noun ❶ *the instability of political life* UNRELIABILITY, uncertainty, unpredictability, insecurity, perilousness, riskiness; impermanence, inconstancy, changeability, variability, fluctuation, mutability. ❷ *emotional instability* VOLATILITY, unpredictability, variability, capriciousness, vacillation; frailty, infirmity, weakness, irregularity. ❸ *the instability of the foundations* UNSTEADINESS, unsoundness, shakiness, frailty, fragility.
– OPPOSITES steadiness.

install ▶ verb ❶ *a photocopier was installed in the office* PUT, position, place, locate, situate, station, site, lodge; insert. ❷ *they installed a new president* SWEAR IN, induct, instate, inaugurate, invest; appoint, take on; ordain, consecrate, anoint; enthrone, crown. ❸ *she installed herself behind the table* ENSCONCE, establish, position, settle, seat, lodge, plant; sit (down); *informal*

plonk, park; *Brit. informal* take a pew.
– OPPOSITES remove.

installation ▶ **noun** ❶ *the installation of radiators* INSTALLING, fitting, putting in; insertion. ❷ *the installation of the chancellor* SWEARING IN, induction, instatement, inauguration, investiture; ordination, consecration; enthronement, coronation. ❸ *a new computer installation* UNIT, appliance, fixture; equipment, machinery. ❹ *an army installation* BASE, camp, post, depot, centre, facility; premises.

instalment ▶ **noun** ❶ *I pay by monthly instalments* PART PAYMENT; deferred payment; *Brit.* hire purchase, HP; *Brit. informal* the never-never. ❷ *a story published in instalments* PART, portion, section, segment, bit; chapter, episode, volume, issue.

instance ▶ **noun** ❶ *an instance of racism* EXAMPLE, exemplar, occasion, occurrence, case; illustration. ❷ (*formal*) *proceedings began at the instance of the director* INSTIGATION, prompting, suggestion; request, entreaty, demand, insistence; wish, desire.
▶ **verb** *as an example I would instance Jones's work* CITE, quote, refer to, mention, allude to, give; specify, name, identify, draw attention to, put forward, offer, advance.
■ **in the first instance** INITIALLY, at first, at the start, at the outset, in/at the beginning, to begin with, to start with, originally.

instant ▶ **adjective** ❶ *instant access to your money* IMMEDIATE, instantaneous, on-the-spot, prompt, swift, speedy, rapid, quick, express, lightning; sudden, precipitate, abrupt; *informal* snappy, p.d.q. (pretty damn quick). ❷ *instant meals* PRE-PREPARED, pre-cooked, ready mixed, fast; microwaveable, convenience, TV.
– OPPOSITES delayed.
▶ **noun** ❶ *come here this instant!* MOMENT, time, minute, second; juncture, point. ❷ *it all happened in an instant* TRICE, moment, minute, (split) second, twinkling of an eye, flash, no time (at all); *informal* sec, jiffy, the blink of an eye; *Brit. informal* mo; *N. Amer. informal* snap.

instantaneous ▶ **adjective** IMMEDIATE, instant, on-the-spot, prompt, swift, speedy, rapid, quick, express, lightning; sudden, hurried, precipitate; *informal* snappy, p.d.q. (pretty damn quick).
– OPPOSITES delayed.

instantly ▶ **adverb** IMMEDIATELY, at once, straight away, right away, instantaneously; suddenly, abruptly, all of a sudden; forthwith, there and then, here and now, this/that minute, this/that instant; quickly, rapidly, speedily, promptly; in an instant, in a moment, in a (split) second, in a trice, in/like a flash, like a shot, in the twinkling of an eye, in no time (at all), before you know it; *informal* in a jiffy, pronto, before you can say Jack Robinson, double quick, like (greased) lightning; *archaic* instanter.

instead ▶ **adverb** *travel by train instead* AS AN ALTERNATIVE, in lieu, alternatively; rather, by contrast, for preference, by/from choice; on second thoughts, all things being equal, ideally; *N. Amer.* alternately.
■ **instead of** AS AN ALTERNATIVE TO, as a substitute for, as a replacement for, in place of, in lieu of, in preference to; rather than, as opposed to, as against, as contrasted with, before.

instigate ▶ **verb** ❶ *they instigated formal proceedings* SET IN MOTION, get under way, get off the ground, start, commence, begin, initiate, launch, institute, set up, inaugurate, establish, organize; actuate, generate, bring about; start the ball rolling; *informal* kick off. ❷ *he instigated men to refuse allegiance* INCITE, encourage, urge, goad, provoke, spur on, push, press, prompt, induce, prevail upon, motivate, influence, persuade, sway; *informal* put up to.
– OPPOSITES halt, dissuade.

instigation ▶ **noun** ❶ *they became involved at his instigation* PROMPTING, suggestion; request, entreaty, demand, insistence; wish, desire, persuasion; *formal* instance. ❷ *foreign instigation of the disorder* INITIATION, incitement, provocation, fomentation, encouragement, inducement, inception.

instigator ▶ **noun** INITIATOR, prime mover, motivator, architect, designer, planner, inventor, mastermind, originator, author, creator, agent; founder, pioneer, founding father; agitator, fomenter, troublemaker, ringleader.

instil ▶ **verb** ❶ *we instil vigilance in our children* INCULCATE, implant, ingrain, impress, imprint, introduce; engender, produce, generate, induce, inspire, promote, foster; drum into. ❷ *he instilled Monet with a love of nature* IMBUE, inspire, infuse, inculcate; indoctrinate; teach. ❸ *she instilled the eye drops* ADMINISTER, introduce, infuse, inject.

instinct ▶ **noun** ❶ *some instinct told me to be careful* NATURAL TENDENCY, inherent tendency, inclination, urge, drive, compulsion, need; intuition, feeling, sixth sense, insight; nose. ❷ *a good instinct for acting* TALENT, gift, ability, aptitude, skill, flair, feel, genius, knack, bent.

instinctive ▶ **adjective** INTUITIVE, natural, instinctual, innate, inborn, inherent; unconscious, subconscious, intuitional; automatic, reflex, knee-jerk, mechanical, spontaneous, involuntary, impulsive; *informal* gut.
– OPPOSITES learned, voluntary.

institute ▶ **noun** *a research institute* ORGANIZATION, establishment, institution, foundation, centre; academy, school, college, university; society, association, federation, body, guild.
▶ **verb** ❶ *we instituted a search* INITIATE, set in motion, get under way, get off the ground, start, commence, begin, launch; set up, inaugurate, found, establish, organize, generate, bring

about; start the ball rolling; *informal* kick off. ❷ *he will be instituted as vicar* INSTALL, instate, induct, invest, inaugurate, swear in, initiate; ordain, consecrate, anoint; appoint, create.
– OPPOSITES end, dismiss.

institution ▶ **noun** ❶ *an academic institution* ESTABLISHMENT, organization, institute, foundation, centre; academy, school, college, university; society, association, body, guild, consortium. ❷ *they spent their lives in institutions* (RESIDENTIAL) HOME, hospital, asylum. ❸ *the institution of the rector* INSTALLATION, instatement, induction, investiture, inauguration; ordination, consecration, anointing, appointment, creation. ❹ *the institution of adoption* PRACTICE, custom, convention, tradition; phenomenon, fact; procedure, usage, method, system, policy; idea, notion, concept. ❺ *the institution of legal proceedings* INITIATION, instigation, launch, start, commencement, beginning, inauguration, generation, origination.

institutional ▶ **adjective** ❶ *an institutional framework for discussions* ORGANIZED, established, bureaucratic, conventional, procedural, prescribed, set, routine, formal, systematic, systematized, methodical, businesslike, orderly, coherent, structured, regulated. ❷ *the rooms are rather institutional* IMPERSONAL, formal, regimented, uniform, unvaried, monotonous; insipid, bland, uninteresting, dull; unappealing, uninviting, unattractive, unwelcoming, dreary, drab, colourless; stark, spartan, bare, clinical, sterile.

instruct ▶ **verb** ❶ *the union instructed them to strike* ORDER, direct, command, tell, enjoin, require, call on, mandate, charge; *poetic/literary* bid. ❷ *nobody instructed him in how to operate it* TEACH, school, coach, train, enlighten, inform, educate, tutor, guide, prepare, prime. ❸ *she instructed a solicitor of her own choice* EMPLOY, authorize, brief. ❹ *the bank was instructed that money would be withdrawn* INFORM, tell, notify, apprise, advise, brief, prime; *informal* put in the picture, fill in.

instruction ▶ **noun** ❶ *do not disobey my instructions* ORDER, command, directive, direction, decree, edict, injunction, mandate, dictate, commandment, bidding; requirement, stipulation; *informal* say-so; *poetic/literary* behest. ❷ *read the instructions* DIRECTIONS, key, specification; handbook, manual, guide. ❸ *he gave instruction in demolition work* TUITION, teaching, coaching, schooling, tutelage; lessons, classes, lectures; training, drill, preparation, grounding, guidance.

instructive ▶ **adjective** INFORMATIVE, instructional, informational, illuminating, enlightening, explanatory; educational, educative, edifying, didactic, pedagogic, heuristic; improving, moralistic, homiletic; useful, helpful.

instructor ▶ **noun** TRAINER, coach, teacher, tutor; adviser, counsellor, guide; educator; *formal* pedagogue.

instrument ▶ **noun** ❶ *a wound made with a sharp instrument* IMPLEMENT, tool, utensil; device, apparatus, contrivance, gadget. ❷ *check all the cockpit instruments* MEASURING DEVICE, gauge, meter; indicator, dial, display. ❸ *they tuned their instruments* MUSICAL INSTRUMENT. ❹ *an instrument of learning* AGENT, agency, cause, channel, medium, means, mechanism, vehicle, organ. ❺ *a mere instrument acting under coercion* PAWN, puppet, creature, dupe, cog; tool, cat's paw; *informal* stooge.

instrumental ▶ **adjective** INVOLVED, active, influential, contributory; helpful, useful, of service; significant, important; (**be instrumental in**) play a part in, contribute to, be a factor in, have a hand in; add to, help, promote, advance, further; be conducive to, make for, lead to, cause.

insubordinate ▶ **adjective** DISOBEDIENT, unruly, wayward, errant, badly behaved, disorderly, undisciplined, delinquent, troublesome, rebellious, defiant, recalcitrant, uncooperative, wilful, intractable, unmanageable, uncontrollable; awkward, difficult, perverse, contrary; *Brit. informal* bolshie.
– OPPOSITES obedient.

insubordination ▶ **noun** DISOBEDIENCE, unruliness, indiscipline, bad behaviour, misbehaviour, misconduct, delinquency; rebellion, defiance, mutiny, revolt; recalcitrance, wilfulness, awkwardness, perversity; *informal* acting-up; *Law* contumacy.

insubstantial ▶ **adjective** ❶ *an insubstantial structure* FLIMSY, slight, fragile, breakable, weak, frail, unstable, shaky, wobbly, rickety, ramshackle, jerry-built. ❷ *insubstantial evidence* WEAK, flimsy, feeble, poor, inadequate, insufficient, tenuous, insignificant, inconsequential, unsubstantial, unconvincing, implausible, unsatisfactory, paltry. ❸ *the light made her seem insubstantial* INTANGIBLE, impalpable, untouchable, discarnate, unsubstantial, incorporeal; imaginary, unreal, illusory, spectral, ghostlike, vaporous; *Philosophy* immaterial.
– OPPOSITES sturdy, sound, tangible.

insufferable ▶ **adjective** ❶ *the heat was insufferable* INTOLERABLE, unbearable, unendurable, insupportable, unacceptable, oppressive, overwhelming, overpowering; more than flesh and blood can stand; *informal* too much. ❷ *his win made him insufferable* CONCEITED, arrogant, boastful, cocky, cocksure, full of oneself, self-important, swaggering; vain, self-satisfied, self-congratulatory, smug; *informal* swollen-headed, big-headed, too big for one's boots; *poetic/literary* vainglorious.
– OPPOSITES bearable, modest.

insufficient ▶ **adjective** INADEQUATE, deficient, poor, scant, scanty; not enough, too little, too few, too small; scarce, sparse, in short supply, lacking, wanting; paltry, meagre, niggardly; incomplete, restricted, limited; *informal* measly, pathetic, piddling.

insular ▶ adjective ❶ *insular people* NARROW-MINDED, small-minded, blinkered, inward-looking, parochial, provincial, small-town, short-sighted, hidebound, set in one's ways, inflexible, rigid, entrenched; illiberal, intolerant, prejudiced, bigoted, biased, partisan, xenophobic; *Brit.* blimpish. ❷ *an insular existence* ISOLATED, inaccessible, cut off, segregated, detached, solitary, lonely.
– OPPOSITES broad-minded, cosmopolitan.

insulate ▶ verb ❶ *pipes must be insulated* WRAP, sheathe, cover, encase, enclose, envelop; lag, heatproof, soundproof; pad, cushion. ❷ *they were insulated from the impact of the war* PROTECT, save, shield, shelter, screen, cushion, cocoon; isolate, segregate, sequester, detach, cut off.

insulation ▶ noun ❶ *a layer of insulation* LAGGING; blanket, jacket, wrap. ❷ *insulation from the rigours of city life* PROTECTION, defence, shelter, screen, shield; isolation, segregation, separation, sequestration, detachment.

insult ▶ verb *he insulted my wife* ABUSE, be rude to, call someone names, slight, disparage, discredit, libel, slander, malign, defame, denigrate, cast aspersions on; offend, affront, hurt, humiliate, wound; *informal* bad-mouth; *Brit. informal* slag off; *formal* derogate, calumniate; *rare* asperse.
– OPPOSITES compliment.
▶ noun *he hurled insults at us* ABUSIVE REMARK, jibe, affront, slight, barb, slur, indignity; injury, libel, slander, defamation; abuse, disparagement, aspersions; *informal* dig, put-down, slap in the face, kick in the teeth.

insulting ▶ adjective ABUSIVE, rude, offensive, disparaging, belittling, derogatory, deprecatory, disrespectful, denigratory, uncomplimentary, pejorative; disdainful, derisive, scornful, contemptuous; defamatory, slanderous, libellous, scurrilous, blasphemous; *informal* bitchy, catty.

insuperable ▶ adjective INSURMOUNTABLE, invincible, unassailable; overwhelming, hopeless, impossible.

insupportable ▶ adjective ❶ *this view is insupportable* UNJUSTIFIABLE, indefensible, inexcusable, unwarrantable, unreasonable; baseless, groundless, unfounded, unsupported, unsubstantiated, unconfirmed, uncorroborated, invalid, untenable, implausible, weak, flawed, specious, defective. ❷ *the heat was insupportable* INTOLERABLE, insufferable, unbearable, unendurable; oppressive, overwhelming, overpowering, more than flesh and blood can stand; *informal* too much.
– OPPOSITES justified, bearable.

insurance ▶ noun ❶ *insurance for his new car* INDEMNITY, indemnification, assurance, (financial) protection, security, cover. ❷ *insurance against a third World War* PROTECTION, defence, safeguard, security, precaution, provision; immunity; guarantee, warranty; *informal* backstop.

insure ▶ verb PROVIDE INSURANCE FOR, indemnify, cover, assure, protect, underwrite; guarantee, warrant.

insurgent ▶ adjective *insurgent forces* REBELLIOUS, rebel, revolutionary, mutinous, insurrectionist; renegade, seditious, subversive.
– OPPOSITES loyal.
▶ noun *the troops are fighting insurgents* REBEL, revolutionary, revolutionist, mutineer, insurrectionist, agitator, subversive, renegade; guerrilla, freedom fighter, anarchist, terrorist.
– OPPOSITES loyalist.

insurmountable ▶ adjective INSUPERABLE, unconquerable, invincible, unassailable; overwhelming, hopeless, impossible.

insurrection ▶ noun REBELLION, revolt, uprising, mutiny, revolution, insurgence, riot, sedition; civil disorder, unrest, anarchy; coup (d'état).

intact ▶ adjective WHOLE, entire, complete, unbroken, undamaged, unimpaired, faultless, flawless, unscathed, untouched, unspoiled, unblemished, unmarked, perfect, pristine, inviolate, undefiled, unsullied, in one piece; sound, solid.
– OPPOSITES damaged.

intangible ▶ adjective ❶ *the moonlight made things seem intangible* IMPALPABLE, untouchable, incorporeal, discarnate, abstract; ethereal, insubstantial, airy; ghostly, spectral, unearthly, supernatural; *Philosophy* immaterial. ❷ *an intangible atmosphere* INDEFINABLE, indescribable, inexpressible, nameless; vague, obscure, unclear, indefinite, subtle, elusive, fugitive.

integral ▶ adjective ❶ *an integral part of human behaviour* ESSENTIAL, fundamental, basic, intrinsic, inherent, constitutive, innate, structural; vital, necessary, requisite. ❷ *the dryer has integral cord storage* BUILT-IN, inbuilt, integrated, incorporated, fitted. ❸ *an integral approach to learning* UNIFIED, integrated, comprehensive, composite, combined, aggregate; complete, whole.
– OPPOSITES peripheral, fragmented.

integrate ▶ verb COMBINE, amalgamate, merge, unite, fuse, blend, mingle, coalesce, consolidate, meld, intermingle, mix; incorporate, unify, assimilate, homogenize; desegregate.
– OPPOSITES separate.

integrated ▶ adjective ❶ *an integrated package of services* UNIFIED, united, consolidated, amalgamated, combined, merged, fused, homogeneous, assimilated, cohesive. ❷ *an integrated* *school* DESEGREGATED, non-segregated, unsegregated, mixed.

integrity ▶ noun ❶ *I never doubted his integrity* HONESTY, probity, rectitude, honour, good character, principle(s), ethics, morals, righteousness, morality, virtue, decency, fairness, scrupulousness, sincerity, truthfulness, trustworthiness. ❷ *the integrity of the federation* UNITY, unification, coherence, cohesion, togetherness, solidarity. ❸ *the structural integrity of the aircraft* SOUNDNESS, strength, sturdiness, solidity, durability, stability, stoutness, toughness.
– OPPOSITES dishonesty, division, fragility.

intellect ▶ noun ❶ *a film that appeals to the intellect* MIND, brain(s), intelligence, reason, understanding, thought, brainpower, sense, judgement, wisdom, wits; *informal* nous, grey matter, brain cells, upper storey; *Brit. informal* loaf; *N. Amer. informal* smarts. ❷ *one of the finest intellects* THINKER, intellectual, sage; mind, brain.

intellectual ▶ adjective ❶ *his intellectual capacity* MENTAL, cerebral, cognitive, psychological; rational, abstract, conceptual, theoretical, analytical, logical; academic. ❷ *an intellectual man* INTELLIGENT, clever, academic, educated, well read, erudite, cerebral, learned, knowledgeable, literary, bookish, donnish, highbrow, scholarly, studious, enlightened, sophisticated; *informal* brainy.
– OPPOSITES physical, stupid.
▶ noun *intellectuals are appalled by television* HIGHBROW, intelligent person, learned person, academic, bookworm, man/woman of letters, bluestocking; thinker, brain, scholar, sage; genius, Einstein, polymath, mastermind; *informal* egghead, brains; *Brit. informal* brainbox, clever clogs, boffin; *N. Amer. informal* brainiac, rocket scientist.
– OPPOSITES dunce.

intelligence ▶ noun ❶ *a man of great intelligence* INTELLECTUAL CAPACITY, mental capacity, intellect, mind, brain(s), brainpower, judgement, reasoning, understanding, comprehension; acumen, wit, sense, insight, perception, penetration, discernment, quick-wittedness, smartness, canniness, astuteness, intuition, acuity, cleverness, brilliance, ability, talent; *informal* braininess. ❷ *intelligence from our agents* INFORMATION, facts, details, particulars, data, knowledge, reports; *informal* info, gen, dope. ❸ *military intelligence* INFORMATION GATHERING, surveillance, observation, reconnaissance, spying, espionage, infiltration, ELINT, Humint; *informal* recon.

intelligent ▶ adjective ❶ *an intelligent writer* CLEVER, bright, brilliant, quick-witted, quick on the uptake, smart, canny, astute, intuitive, insightful, perceptive, perspicacious, discerning; knowledgeable; able, gifted, talented; *informal* brainy. ❷ *an intelligent being* RATIONAL, higher-order, capable of thought. ❸ *intelligent machines* SELF-REGULATING, capable of learning, smart.

intelligentsia ▶ plural noun INTELLECTUALS, intelligent people, academics, scholars, literati, cognoscenti, illuminati, highbrows, thinkers, brains; the intelligent; *informal* eggheads; *Brit. informal* boffins.

intelligible ▶ adjective COMPREHENSIBLE, understandable; accessible, digestible, user-friendly, penetrable, fathomable; lucid, clear, coherent, plain, explicit, precise, unambiguous, self-explanatory.

intemperance ▶ noun ❶ *they were criticized for intemperance* OVERINDULGENCE, immoderation, excess, extravagance, prodigality, profligacy, lavishness; self-indulgence, self-gratification; debauchery, decadence, dissipation, dissolution. ❷ *he said intemperance was a disease* DRINKING, alcoholism, alcohol abuse, dipsomania; drunkenness, intoxication, inebriation, insobriety, tipsiness; *formal* inebriety; *poetic/literary* crapulence.

intemperate ▶ adjective IMMODERATE, excessive, undue, inordinate, extreme, unrestrained, uncontrolled; self-indulgent, lavish, overindulgent, extravagant, prodigal, profligate; imprudent, reckless, wild; dissolute, debauched, wanton, dissipated.
– OPPOSITES moderate.

intend ▶ verb PLAN, mean, have in mind, have the intention, aim, propose; aspire, hope, expect, be resolved, be determined; want, wish; contemplate, think of, envisage; design, earmark, set aside; *formal* purpose.

intended ▶ adjective *the foul was not intended* DELIBERATE, intentional, calculated, conscious, planned, studied, knowing, wilful, wanton, purposeful, done on purpose, premeditated, pre-planned, preconceived; *Law* aforethought; *Law, dated* prepense.
– OPPOSITES accidental.
▶ noun (*informal*) *do you share everything with your intended?* FIANCÉ(E), betrothed, bride-to-be, wife-to-be, husband-to-be, future wife, future husband, prospective spouse.

intense ▶ adjective ❶ *intense heat* EXTREME, great, acute, fierce, severe, high; exceptional, extraordinary; harsh, strong, powerful, potent, vigorous; *informal* serious. ❷ *a very intense young man* PASSIONATE, impassioned, ardent, fervent, zealous, vehement, fiery, emotional; earnest, eager, animated, spirited, vigorous, energetic, fanatical, committed.
– OPPOSITES mild, apathetic.

intensify ▶ verb ESCALATE, increase, step up, boost, raise, strengthen, augment, reinforce; pick up, build up, heighten, deepen, extend, expand, amplify, magnify; aggravate, exacerbate, worsen, inflame, compound.
– OPPOSITES abate.

intensity ▶ noun ❶ *the intensity of the sun*

STRENGTH, power, potency, force; severity, ferocity, vehemence, fierceness, harshness; magnitude, greatness, acuteness, extremity. ❷ *his eyes had a glowing intensity* PASSION, ardour, fervour, zeal, vehemence, fire, heat, emotion; eagerness, animation, spirit, vigour, strength, energy; fanaticism.

intensive ▶ adjective THOROUGH, thoroughgoing, in-depth, rigorous, exhaustive, all-out; all-embracing, all-inclusive, comprehensive, complete, full; vigorous, strenuous, detailed, minute, close, meticulous, scrupulous, painstaking, methodical, careful; extensive, widespread, sweeping; determined, resolute, persistent.
– OPPOSITES cursory.

intent ▶ noun *he tried to divine his father's intent* AIM, intention, purpose, objective, object, goal, target; design, plan, scheme; wish, desire, ambition, idea, aspiration.
▶ adjective ❶ *he was intent on proving his point* BENT, set, determined, insistent, resolved, hell-bent, keen; committed to, obsessive about, fanatical about; determined to, anxious to, impatient to. ❷ *an intent expression* ATTENTIVE, absorbed, engrossed, fascinated, enthralled, rapt; focused, earnest, concentrating, intense, studious, preoccupied; alert, watchful.
■ **to all intents and purposes** IN EFFECT, effectively, in essence, essentially, virtually, practically; more or less, just about, all but, as good as, in all but name, as near as dammit; almost, nearly; *informal* pretty much, pretty well; *poetic/literary* nigh on.

intention ▶ noun ❶ *it is his intention to be leader* AIM, purpose, intent, objective, object, goal, target; design, plan, scheme; resolve, resolution, determination; wish, desire, ambition, idea, dream, aspiration. ❷ *he managed, without intention, to upset me* INTENT, intentionality, deliberateness, design, calculation; premeditation, forethought, pre-planning; *Law* malice aforethought.

intentional ▶ adjective DELIBERATE, calculated, conscious, intended, planned, meant, studied, knowing, wilful, wanton, purposeful, purposive, done on purpose, premeditated, pre-planned, preconceived; *Law* aforethought; *Law, dated* prepense.

intently ▶ adverb ATTENTIVELY, closely, keenly, earnestly, hard, carefully, fixedly, steadily.

inter ▶ verb BURY, lay to rest, entomb, inurn; *informal* put six feet under, plant; *poetic/literary* sepulchre, inhume.
– OPPOSITES exhume.

intercede ▶ verb MEDIATE, intermediate, arbitrate, conciliate, negotiate, moderate; intervene, interpose, step in, act; plead, petition.

intercept ▶ verb STOP, head off, cut off; catch, seize, grab, snatch; obstruct, impede, interrupt, block, check, detain; ambush, challenge, waylay.

intercession ▶ noun MEDIATION, intermediation, arbitration, conciliation, negotiation; intervention, involvement; pleading, petition, entreaty, agency; diplomacy.

interchange ▶ verb ❶ *they interchange ideas* EXCHANGE, trade, swap, barter, bandy, reciprocate; *archaic* truck. ❷ *the terms are often interchanged* SUBSTITUTE, transpose, exchange, switch, swap (round), change (round), reverse, invert, replace.
▶ noun ❶ *the interchange of ideas* EXCHANGE, trade, swap, barter, give and take, traffic, reciprocation, reciprocity; *archaic* truck. ❷ *a motorway interchange* JUNCTION, intersection, crossing; *N. Amer.* cloverleaf.

interchangeable ▶ adjective ❶ *the gun has interchangeable barrels* EXCHANGEABLE, transposable, replaceable. ❷ *two more or less interchangeable roads* SIMILAR, identical, indistinguishable, alike, the same, uniform, twin, undifferentiated; corresponding, commensurate, equivalent, comparable, equal; *informal* much of a muchness.

intercourse ▶ noun ❶ *social intercourse* DEALINGS, relations, relationships, association, connections, contact; interchange, communication, communion, correspondence; negotiations, bargaining, transactions; trade, traffic; *informal* truck, doings. ❷ *she did not consent to intercourse* SEXUAL INTERCOURSE, sex, lovemaking, sexual relations, intimacy, coupling, mating, copulation; *informal* nooky; *Brit. informal* bonking, rumpy pumpy, how's your father; *technical* coitus, coition; *formal* fornication; *dated* carnal knowledge.

interdict ▶ noun *they breached an interdict* PROHIBITION, ban, bar, veto, proscription, interdiction, embargo, moratorium, injunction.
– OPPOSITES permission.
▶ verb ❶ *they interdicted foreign commerce* PROHIBIT, forbid, ban, bar, veto, proscribe, embargo, disallow, debar, outlaw; stop, suppress; *Law* enjoin, estop. ❷ *efforts to interdict asylum seekers* INTERCEPT, stop, head off, cut off; obstruct, impede, block; detain.
– OPPOSITES permit.

interest ▶ noun ❶ *we listened with interest* ATTENTIVENESS, attention, absorption; heed, regard, notice; curiosity, inquisitiveness; enjoyment, delight. ❷ *places of interest* ATTRACTION, appeal, fascination, charm, beauty, allure. ❸ *this will be of interest to those involved* CONCERN, consequence, importance, import, significance, note, relevance, value, weight; *formal* moment. ❹ *her interests include reading* HOBBY, pastime, leisure pursuit, recreation, diversion, amusement, relaxation; passion, enthusiasm; *informal* thing, bag, cup of tea. ❺ *a financial interest in the firm* STAKE, share, claim, investment,

stock, equity; involvement, concern. ❻ *what is your interest in the case?* INVOLVEMENT, partiality, partisanship, preference, loyalty; bias, prejudice. ❼ *his attorney guarded his interests* CONCERN, business, affair. ❽ *her savings earned interest* DIVIDENDS, profits, returns; a percentage.
– OPPOSITES boredom.
▶ **verb** ❶ *a topic that interests you* APPEAL TO, be of interest to, attract, intrigue, fascinate; absorb, engross, rivet, grip, captivate; amuse, divert, entertain; arouse one's curiosity, whet one's appetite; *informal* float someone's boat, tickle someone's fancy. ❷ *can I interest you in a drink?* persuade to have; sell.
– OPPOSITES bore.
■ **in someone's interests** OF BENEFIT TO, to the advantage of; for the sake of, for the benefit of.

interested ▶ **adjective** ❶ *an interested crowd* ATTENTIVE, intent, absorbed, engrossed, fascinated, riveted, gripped, captivated, rapt, agog; intrigued, inquisitive, curious; keen, eager; *informal* all ears, nosy, snoopy. ❷ *the government consulted with interested bodies* CONCERNED, involved, affected, connected, related. ❸ *no interested party can judge the contest* PARTISAN, partial, biased, prejudiced, one-sided, preferential.

interesting ▶ **adjective** ABSORBING, engrossing, fascinating, riveting, gripping, compelling, compulsive, captivating, engaging, enthralling; appealing, attractive; amusing, entertaining, stimulating, thought-provoking, diverting, intriguing; *informal* unputdownable.

interfere ▶ **verb** ❶ *don't let emotion interfere with duty* IMPEDE, obstruct, stand in the way of, hinder, inhibit, restrict, constrain, hamper, handicap, cramp, check, block; disturb, disrupt, influence, affect, confuse. ❷ *she tried not to interfere in his life* BUTT INTO, barge into, pry into, nose into, intrude into, intervene in, get involved in, encroach on, impinge on; meddle in, tamper with; *informal* poke one's nose into, horn in on, muscle in on, stick one's oar in. ❸ (*Brit. euphemistic*) *he interfered with local children* (SEXUALLY) ABUSE, sexually assault, indecently assault, molest, grope; *informal* feel up, touch up.

interference ▶ **noun** ❶ *they resent state interference* INTRUSION, intervention, intercession, involvement, trespass, obtrusion; meddling, prying. ❷ *radio interference* DISRUPTION, disturbance, static.

interfering ▶ **adjective** MEDDLESOME, meddling, intrusive, prying, inquisitive, overcurious, busybody; *informal* nosy, nosy-parker, snoopy.

interim ▶ **noun** *in the interim they did more research* MEANTIME, meanwhile, intervening time.
▶ **adjective** *an interim advisory body* PROVISIONAL, temporary, pro tem, stopgap, short-term, fill-in, caretaker, acting, intervening, transitional, makeshift, improvised, impromptu.
– OPPOSITES permanent.

interior ▶ **adjective** ❶ *the house has interior panelling* INSIDE, inner, internal, intramural. ❷ *the interior deserts of the US* INLAND, inshore, upcountry, inner, innermost, central. ❸ *the country's interior affairs* INTERNAL, home, domestic, national, state, civil, local. ❹ *an interior monologue* INNER, mental, spiritual, psychological; private, personal, intimate, secret.
– OPPOSITES exterior, outer, foreign.
▶ **noun** ❶ *the interior of the yacht* INSIDE, inner part, depths, recesses, bowels, belly; centre, core, heart. ❷ *the country's interior* CENTRE, heartland, hinterland.
– OPPOSITES exterior, outside.

interject ▶ **verb** ❶ *she interjected a comment* INTERPOSE, introduce, throw in, interpolate, add. ❷ *he interjected before there was a fight* INTERRUPT, intervene, cut in, break in, butt in, chime in; put one's oar in; *Brit. informal* chip in; *N. Amer. informal* put in one's two cents.

interjection ▶ **noun** ❶ *an astonished interjection* EXCLAMATION; cry, shout, vociferation, utterance; *dated* ejaculation. ❷ *the interjection of a question* INTERPOSITION, interpolation, insertion, addition, introduction.

interlock ▶ **verb** INTERCONNECT, interlink, engage, mesh, intermesh, join, unite, connect, couple.

interloper ▶ **noun** INTRUDER, encroacher, trespasser, invader, infiltrator; uninvited guest; outsider, stranger, alien; *informal* gatecrasher.

interlude ▶ **noun** INTERVAL, intermission, break, recess, pause, respite, rest, breathing space, halt, gap, stop, stoppage, hiatus, lull; *informal* breather, let-up, time out, down time.

intermediary ▶ **noun** MEDIATOR, go-between, negotiator, intervenor, interceder, intercessor, arbitrator, arbiter, conciliator, peacemaker; middleman, broker, linkman.

intermediate ▶ **adjective** HALFWAY, in-between, middle, mid, midway, median, medial, intermediary, intervening, transitional.

interment ▶ **noun** BURIAL, burying, committal, entombment, inhumation; funeral; *archaic* sepulture.

interminable ▶ **adjective** (SEEMINGLY) ENDLESS, never-ending, unending, non-stop, everlasting, ceaseless, unceasing, incessant, constant, continual, uninterrupted, sustained; monotonous, long-winded, overlong, rambling.

intermingle ▶ **verb** MIX, intermix, mingle, blend, fuse, merge, combine, amalgamate; unite, affiliate, associate, fraternize; *poetic/literary* commingle.

intermission ▶ **noun** INTERVAL, interlude, entr'acte, break, recess, pause, rest, respite, breathing space, lull, gap, stop, stoppage, halt; cessation, suspension; *informal* let-up, breather, time out, down time.

intermittent ▶ adjective SPORADIC, irregular, fitful, spasmodic, broken, fragmentary, discontinuous, isolated, random, patchy, scattered; occasional, periodic.
– OPPOSITES continuous.

intern ▶ verb *they were interned without trial* IMPRISON, incarcerate, impound, jail, put behind bars, detain, hold (captive), lock up, confine; *informal* put away, put inside, send down; *Brit. informal* bang up.
▶ noun *an intern at a local firm* TRAINEE, apprentice, probationer, student, novice, beginner.

internal ▶ adjective ❶ *an internal courtyard* INNER, interior, inside, intramural; central. ❷ *the state's internal affairs* DOMESTIC, home, interior, civil, local; national, state. ❸ *an internal battle with herself* MENTAL, psychological, emotional; personal, private, secret, hidden.
– OPPOSITES external, foreign.

international ▶ adjective GLOBAL, worldwide, intercontinental, universal; cosmopolitan, multiracial, multinational.
– OPPOSITES national, local.

interplay ▶ noun INTERACTION, interchange; teamwork, cooperation, reciprocation, reciprocity, give and take.

interpolate ▶ verb INSERT, interpose, enter, add, incorporate, inset, put, introduce.

interpose ▶ verb ❶ *he interposed himself between the girls* INSINUATE, place, put. ❷ *I must interpose a note of caution* INTRODUCE, insert, interject, add. ❸ *they interposed to suppress the custom* INTERVENE, intercede, step in, involve oneself; interfere, intrude, butt in, cut in; *informal* barge in, horn in, muscle in.

interpret ▶ verb ❶ *the rabbis interpreted the Jewish laws* EXPLAIN, elucidate, expound, explicate, clarify, illuminate, shed light on. ❷ *the remark was interpreted as an invitation* UNDERSTAND, construe, take (to mean), see, regard. ❸ *the symbols are difficult to interpret* DECIPHER, decode, make intelligible; understand, comprehend, make sense of; *informal* crack.

interpretation ▶ noun ❶ *the interpretation of the Bible's teachings* EXPLANATION, elucidation, expounding, exposition, explication, exegesis, clarification. ❷ *she did not care what interpretation he put on her haste* MEANING, understanding, construal, connotation, explanation, inference. ❸ *the interpretation of experimental findings* ANALYSIS, evaluation, review, study, examination. ❹ *his interpretation of the sonata* RENDITION, rendering, execution, presentation, performance, reading, playing, singing.

interpreter ▶ noun ❶ *a Japanese interpreter* TRANSLATOR, dragoman. ❷ *a vocal interpreter of his music* PERFORMER, presenter, exponent; singer, player. ❸ *interpreters of Soviet history* ANALYST, evaluator, reviewer, commentator.

interrogate ▶ verb QUESTION, cross-question, cross-examine, quiz; interview, examine, debrief, give someone the third degree; *informal* pump, grill.

interrogative ▶ adjective QUESTIONING, inquiring, inquisitive, probing, searching, quizzing, quizzical, curious.

interrupt ▶ verb ❶ *she opened her mouth to interrupt* CUT IN (ON), break in (on), barge in (on), intervene (in), put one's oar in; *Brit.* put one's pennyworth in; *N. Amer.* put one's two cents in; *informal* butt in (on), chime in (on); *Brit. informal* chip in (on). ❷ *the band had to interrupt their tour* SUSPEND, adjourn, discontinue, break off; stop, halt, cease, end, bring to an end/close; *informal* put on ice, put on a back burner. ❸ *the coastal plain is interrupted by large lagoons* BREAK (UP), punctuate; pepper, strew, dot, scatter. ❹ *their view was interrupted by houses* OBSTRUCT, impede, block, restrict.

interruption ▶ noun ❶ *he was not pleased at her interruption* CUTTING IN, barging in, intervention, intrusion; *informal* butting in. ❷ *an interruption of the power supply* DISCONTINUATION, breaking off, suspension, stopping, halting, cessation. ❸ *an interruption in her career* INTERVAL, interlude, break, pause, gap.

intersect ▶ verb ❶ *the lines intersect at right angles* CROSS, criss-cross; *technical* decussate. ❷ *the cornfield is intersected by a track* BISECT, divide, cut in two/half, cut across/through; cross, traverse.

intersection ▶ noun ❶ *the intersection of the two curves* CROSSING, criss-crossing. ❷ *the driver stopped at an intersection* (ROAD) JUNCTION, T-junction, interchange, crossroads; *Brit.* roundabout.

intersperse ▶ verb ❶ *giant lobelia were interspersed among the rocks* SCATTER, disperse, spread, strew, dot, sprinkle, pepper; *poetic/literary* bestrew. ❷ *the beech trees are interspersed with conifers* INTERMIX, mix, mingle, punctuate.

interstice ▶ noun SPACE, gap, aperture, opening, hole, crevice, chink, slit, slot, crack.

intertwine ▶ verb ENTWINE, interweave, interlace, interwind, twist, coil.

interval ▶ noun ❶ *a 15-minute interval* INTERMISSION, interlude, entr'acte, break, recess; half-time. ❷ *Baldwin made two speeches in the interval* INTERIM, interlude, intervening time/period, meantime, meanwhile. ❸ *short intervals of still water* STRETCH, distance, span, area.

intervene ▶ verb ❶ *had the war not intervened, they might have married* OCCUR, happen, take place, arise, crop up, come about; result, ensue, follow; *poetic/literary* come to pass, befall, betide. ❷ *she intervened in the row* INTERCEDE, involve oneself, get involved, interpose oneself, step in; interfere, intrude.

intervention ▶ noun INVOLVEMENT, intercession, interceding, interposing; interference, intrusion.

interview ▶ noun *all applicants will be called for an interview* MEETING, discussion, conference, examination, interrogation; audience, talk, dialogue, exchange; talks.

▶ verb *we interviewed seventy subjects for the survey* TALK TO, have a discussion/dialogue with; question, interrogate, cross-examine; poll, canvass, survey, sound out; *informal* grill, pump; *Law* examine.

interviewer ▶ noun QUESTIONER, interrogator, examiner, assessor, appraiser; journalist, reporter.

interweave ▶ verb ❶ *the threads are interwoven* INTERTWINE, entwine, interlace, splice, braid, plait; twist together, weave together, wind together; *Nautical* marry. ❷ *their fates were interwoven* INTERLINK, link, connect; intermix, mix, merge, blend, interlock, knit/bind together.

intestinal ▶ adjective ENTERIC, gastro-enteric, duodenal, coeliac, gastric, ventral, stomach, abdominal.

intestines ▶ plural noun GUT, guts, entrails, viscera; small intestine, large intestine; *informal* insides, innards.

– RELATED TERMS enteric.

intimacy ▶ noun ❶ *the sisters re-established their old intimacy* CLOSENESS, togetherness, affinity, rapport, attachment, familiarity, friendliness, amity, affection, warmth; *informal* chumminess, palliness; *Brit. informal* mateyness. ❷ *the memory of their intimacy* SEXUAL RELATIONS, (sexual) intercourse, sex, lovemaking, copulation; *technical* coitus.

intimate[1] ▶ adjective ❶ *an intimate friend* CLOSE, bosom, boon, dear, cherished, faithful, fast, firm; *informal* chummy, pally. ❷ *an intimate atmosphere* FRIENDLY, warm, welcoming, hospitable, relaxed, informal; cosy, comfortable, snug; *informal* comfy. ❸ *intimate thoughts* PERSONAL, private, confidential, secret; innermost, inner, inward, unspoken, undisclosed. ❹ *an intimate knowledge of the industry* DETAILED, thorough, exhaustive, deep, in-depth, profound. ❺ *intimate relations* SEXUAL, carnal, amorous, amatory.

– OPPOSITES distant, formal.

▶ noun *his circle of intimates* CLOSE FRIEND, best friend, bosom friend, confidant, confidante; *informal* chum, pal, crony; *Brit. informal* mate; *N. Amer. informal* buddy.

intimate[2] ▶ verb ❶ *he intimated his decision* ANNOUNCE, state, proclaim, make known, make public, disclose, reveal, divulge. ❷ *her feelings were subtly intimated* IMPLY, suggest, hint at, insinuate, indicate, signal, allude to, refer to, convey.

intimation ▶ noun ❶ *the early intimation of session dates* ANNOUNCEMENT, statement, communication, notification, notice, reporting, publishing; disclosure, revelation, divulging. ❷ *the first intimation of discord* SUGGESTION, hint, indication, sign, signal, inkling, suspicion, impression; clue to, undertone of, whisper of.

intimidate ▶ verb FRIGHTEN, menace, terrify, scare, terrorize, cow, subdue; threaten, browbeat, bully, pressure, pressurize, harass, harry, hound; *informal* lean on, bulldoze, steamroller, railroad, use strong-arm tactics on.

intolerable ▶ adjective UNBEARABLE, insufferable, unsupportable, insupportable, unendurable, beyond endurance, more than flesh and blood can stand, too much to bear.

– OPPOSITES bearable.

intolerant ▶ adjective ❶ *intolerant in religious matters* BIGOTED, narrow-minded, small-minded, parochial, provincial, illiberal, uncompromising; prejudiced, biased, partial, partisan, discriminatory. ❷ *foods to which you are intolerant* ALLERGIC, sensitive, hypersensitive.

intonation ▶ noun ❶ *she read the sentence with the wrong intonation* INFLECTION, pitch, tone, timbre, cadence, cadency, lilt, modulation, speech pattern. ❷ *the intonation of hymns* CHANTING, incantation, recitation, singing; *rare* cantillation.

intone ▶ verb CHANT, sing, recite; *rare* cantillate.

intoxicate ▶ verb ❶ *one glass of wine intoxicated him* INEBRIATE, make drunk, make intoxicated, befuddle, go to someone's head; *informal* make legless, make woozy. ❷ *he was intoxicated by cinema* EXHILARATE, thrill, elate, delight, captivate, enthral, entrance, enrapture, excite, stir, rouse, inspire, fire with enthusiasm; *informal* give someone a buzz, give someone a kick; *N. Amer. informal* give someone a charge.

intoxicated ▶ adjective DRUNK, inebriated, inebriate, drunken, tipsy, under the influence; *informal* tight, merry, the worse for wear, pie-eyed, in one's cups, three sheets to the wind, plastered, smashed, sloshed, sozzled, well oiled, wrecked, blotto, stewed, pickled, tanked up, soaked, off one's face, out of one's head/skull; *Brit. informal* paralytic, legless, Brahms and Liszt, half cut, bladdered, trolleyed, tiddly; *N. Amer. informal* loaded, trashed, out of one's gourd; *euphemistic* tired and emotional; *formal* bibulous; *poetic/literary* crapulent.

– OPPOSITES sober.

intoxicating ▶ adjective ❶ *intoxicating drink* ALCOHOLIC, strong, hard, potent, stiff, intoxicant; *formal* spiritous. ❷ *an intoxicating sense of freedom* HEADY, exhilarating, thrilling, exciting, rousing, stirring, stimulating, invigorating, electrifying; strong, powerful, potent; *informal* mind-blowing.

– OPPOSITES non-alcoholic.

intoxication ▶ noun DRUNKENNESS, inebriation, insobriety, tipsiness; *informal* tightness; *poetic/literary* crapulence.

intractable ▶ adjective ❶ *intractable problems* UNMANAGEABLE, uncontrollable, difficult, awkward, troublesome, demanding, burdensome. ❷ *an intractable man* STUBBORN, obstinate, obdurate, inflexible, unadaptable, unbending, unyielding, uncompromising, unaccommodating, uncooperative, difficult, awkward, perverse, contrary, pig-headed; *N. Amer.* rock-ribbed; *informal* stiff-necked.
– OPPOSITES manageable, compliant.

intransigent ▶ adjective UNCOMPROMISING, inflexible, unbending, unyielding, unshakeable, unwavering, resolute, rigid, unaccommodating, uncooperative, stubborn, obstinate, obdurate, pig-headed, single-minded, iron-willed; *informal* stiff-necked.
– OPPOSITES compliant.

intrench ▶ verb. *See* ENTRENCH.

intrenched ▶ adjective. *See* ENTRENCHED.

intrepid ▶ adjective FEARLESS, unafraid, undaunted, unflinching, unshrinking, bold, daring, audacious, adventurous, heroic, dynamic, spirited, indomitable; brave, courageous, valiant, valorous, stout-hearted, stalwart, plucky, doughty; *informal* gutsy, spunky.
– OPPOSITES fearful.

intricate ▶ adjective COMPLEX, complicated, convoluted, tangled, entangled, twisted; elaborate, ornate, detailed, involuted; *Brit. informal* fiddly.

intrigue ▶ verb ❶ *her answer intrigued him* INTEREST, be of interest to, fascinate, arouse someone's curiosity, attract. ❷ *the ministers were intriguing* PLOT, conspire, make secret plans, scheme, manoeuvre, connive, collude, machinate.
▶ noun ❶ *the intrigue that accompanied the selection of a new leader* PLOTTING, conspiracy, collusion, conniving, scheming, machination, trickery, sharp practice, double-dealing, underhandedness, subterfuge; *informal* dirty tricks. ❷ *the king's intrigues with his nobles' wives* (LOVE) AFFAIR, affair of the heart, liaison, amour, fling, flirtation, dalliance; adultery, infidelity, unfaithfulness; *informal* fooling around, playing around, hanky-panky; *Brit. informal* carryings-on.

intriguer ▶ noun CONSPIRATOR, co-conspirator, plotter, schemer, colluder, conniver, machinator, Machiavelli.

intriguing ▶ adjective INTERESTING, fascinating, absorbing, compelling, gripping, riveting, captivating, engaging, enthralling.

intrinsic ▶ adjective INHERENT, innate, inborn, inbred, congenital, connate, connatural, natural; deep-rooted, indelible, ineradicable; integral, basic, fundamental, essential.

introduce ▶ verb ❶ *he has introduced a new system* INSTITUTE, initiate, launch, inaugurate, establish, found; bring in, set in motion, start, begin, commence, get going, get under way, originate, pioneer; *informal* kick off. ❷ *you can introduce new ideas* PROPOSE, put forward, suggest, table; raise, broach, bring up, mention, air, float. ❸ *she introduced Lindsey to the young man* PRESENT (FORMALLY), make known, acquaint with. ❹ *introducing nitrogen into canned beer* INSERT, inject, put, force, shoot, feed. ❺ *she introduced a note of severity into her voice* INSTIL, infuse, inject, add. ❻ *the same presenter introduces the programme each week* ANNOUNCE, present, give an introduction to; start off, begin, open.

introduction ▶ noun ❶ *the introduction of democratic reforms* INSTITUTION, establishment, initiation, launch, inauguration, foundation; start, commencement, inception, origination, pioneering. ❷ *an introduction to the king* (FORMAL) PRESENTATION; meeting, audience. ❸ *an introduction to the catalogue* FOREWORD, preface, preamble, prologue, prelude; opening (statement), beginning; *informal* intro; *formal* proem, prolegomenon. ❹ *an introduction to the history of the period* BASIC EXPLANATION/ACCOUNT OF; the basics, the rudiments, the fundamentals. ❺ *a gentle introduction to the life of the school* INITIATION, induction, inauguration.
– OPPOSITES afterword.

introductory ▶ adjective ❶ *the introductory chapter* OPENING, initial, starting, initiatory, first; prefatory, preliminary. ❷ *an introductory course* ELEMENTARY, basic, rudimentary; initiatory, preparatory.
– OPPOSITES final, advanced.

introspection ▶ noun SELF-ANALYSIS, soul-searching, introversion; contemplation, meditation, thoughtfulness, pensiveness, reflection; *informal* navel-gazing; *formal* cogitation.

introspective ▶ adjective INWARD-LOOKING, self-analysing, introverted, introvert; contemplative, thoughtful, pensive, meditative, reflective; *informal* navel-gazing.

introverted ▶ adjective SHY, reserved, withdrawn, reticent, diffident, retiring, quiet; introspective, introvert, inward-looking, indrawn, self-absorbed; contemplative, thoughtful, pensive, meditative, reflective.
– OPPOSITES extroverted.

intrude ▶ verb ❶ *intruding on people's privacy* ENCROACH, impinge, trespass, infringe, obtrude, invade, violate, disturb, disrupt; *informal* horn in, muscle in. ❷ *he intruded his own personality into his work* FORCE, push, obtrude, impose, thrust.

intruder ▶ noun TRESPASSER, interloper, invader, infiltrator; burglar, housebreaker, thief.

intrusion ▶ noun ENCROACHMENT, obtrusion; invasion, incursion, intervention, disturbance, disruption, infringement, impingement.

intrusive ▶ adjective ❶ *an intrusive journalist* INTRUDING, invasive, obtrusive, unwelcome; inquisitive, prying; *informal* nosy. ❷ *opinion polls play an intrusive role in elections* INVASIVE, high-profile, prominent; *informal* in one's face. ❸ *intrusive questions* PERSONAL, prying, forward, impertinent; *informal* nosy.

intuition ▶ noun ❶ *he works according to intuition* INSTINCT, intuitiveness; sixth sense, clairvoyance, second sight. ❷ *this confirms an intuition I had* HUNCH, feeling (in one's bones), inkling, (sneaking) suspicion; premonition, presentiment; *informal* gut feeling.

intuitive ▶ adjective INSTINCTIVE, intuitional, instinctual; innate, inborn, inherent, natural, congenital; unconscious, subconscious, involuntary; *informal* gut.

intumescence ▶ noun (*rare*) SWELLING, bulging, bloating, distension, dilatation, turgidity.

inundate ▶ verb ❶ *many buildings were inundated* FLOOD, deluge, overrun, swamp, submerge, engulf. ❷ *we have been inundated by complaints* OVERWHELM, overrun, overload, bog down, swamp, besiege, snow under.

inundation ▶ noun FLOOD, deluge, torrent, flash flood, freshet; *Brit.* spate.

inure ▶ verb HARDEN, toughen, season, temper, condition; accustom, habituate, familiarize, acclimatize, adjust, adapt.
– OPPOSITES sensitize.

invade ▶ verb ❶ *the island was invaded* OCCUPY, conquer, capture, seize, take (over), annex, win, gain, secure; march into, overrun, overwhelm, storm. ❷ *someone had invaded our privacy* INTRUDE ON, violate, encroach on, infringe on, trespass on, obtrude on, disturb, disrupt; *informal* horn in on, muscle in on. ❸ *the feeling of betrayal invaded my being* PERMEATE, pervade, spread through/over, diffuse through, imbue.
– OPPOSITES withdraw.

invader ▶ noun ATTACKER, raider, marauder; occupier, conqueror; intruder.

invalid[1] ▶ noun *my mother is an invalid* ILL PERSON, sick person, valetudinarian; patient, convalescent.
▶ adjective *her invalid husband* ILL, sick, ailing, unwell, infirm, valetudinarian, in poor health; incapacitated, bedridden, frail, feeble, weak, debilitated, sickly, poorly.
– OPPOSITES healthy.
▶ verb *an officer invalided by a chest wound* DISABLE, incapacitate, indispose, hospitalize, put out action, lay up; injure, wound, hurt.

invalid[2] ▶ adjective ❶ *the law was invalid* (LEGALLY) VOID, null and void, unenforceable, not binding, illegitimate, inapplicable. ❷ *the whole theory is invalid* FALSE, untrue, inaccurate, faulty, fallacious, spurious, unconvincing, unsound, weak, wrong, wide of the mark, off target; untenable, baseless, ill-founded, groundless; *informal* off beam, full of holes.
– OPPOSITES binding, true.

invalidate ▶ verb ❶ *a low turnout invalidated the ballot* RENDER INVALID, void, nullify, annul, negate, cancel, overturn, overrule. ❷ *this case invalidates the general argument* DISPROVE, refute, explode, contradict, rebut, negate, belie, discredit, debunk; weaken, undermine, compromise; *informal* shoot full of holes; *formal* confute.

invaluable ▶ adjective INDISPENSABLE, crucial, critical, key, vital, irreplaceable, all-important.
– OPPOSITES dispensable.

invariable ▶ adjective UNVARYING, unchanging, unvaried; constant, stable, set, steady, predictable, regular, consistent; unchangeable, unalterable, immutable, fixed.
– OPPOSITES varied.

invariably ▶ adverb ALWAYS, on every occasion, at all times, without fail, without exception; everywhere, in all places, in all cases/instances; regularly, consistently, repeatedly, habitually, unfailingly.
– OPPOSITES sometimes, never.

invasion ▶ noun ❶ *the invasion of the islands* OCCUPATION, conquering, capture, seizure, annexation, annexing, takeover; overrunning, overwhelming, storming. ❷ *an invasion of cars* INFLUX, inundation, inrush, flood, torrent, deluge, avalanche. ❸ *an invasion of my privacy* VIOLATION, infringement, interruption, intrusion, encroachment, obtrusion, disturbance, disruption, breach.
– OPPOSITES withdrawal.

invective ▶ noun ABUSE, insults, vituperation, expletives, swear words, swearing, curses, bad/foul language, obloquy; *archaic* contumely.
– OPPOSITES praise.

inveigh ▶ verb FULMINATE, declaim, protest, rail, rage, remonstrate; denounce, censure, condemn, decry, criticize; disparage, denigrate, run down, abuse, vilify, impugn; *informal* kick up a fuss/stink about, bellyache about, sound off about.
– OPPOSITES support.

inveigle ▶ verb CAJOLE, wheedle, coax, persuade, talk; tempt, lure, entice, seduce, beguile; *informal* sweet-talk, soft-soap, con; *N. Amer. informal* sucker; *archaic* blandish.

invent ▶ verb ❶ *Louis Braille invented an alphabet to help blind people* ORIGINATE, create, innovate, design, devise, contrive, develop; conceive, think up, dream up, come up with, pioneer. ❷ *they invented the story for a laugh* MAKE UP, fabricate, concoct, hatch, dream up; *informal* cook up.

invention ▶ noun ❶ *the invention of the telescope* ORIGINATION, creation, innovation, devising, contriving, development, design. ❷ *medieval inventions* INNOVATION, creation, design, contraption, contrivance, construction, device, gadget; *informal* brainchild. ❸ *his invention was flagging* INVENTIVENESS, originality, creativity, creativeness, imagination, imaginativeness, inspiration. ❹ *a journalistic invention* FABRICATION, concoction, (piece of) fiction, story, tale; lie, untruth, falsehood, fib; myth, fantasy; *informal* tall story, cock-and-bull story.

inventive ▶ adjective ❶ *the most inventive composer of his time* CREATIVE, original, innovational, innovative, imaginative, ingenious, resourceful. ❷ *a fresh, inventive comedy* ORIGINAL, innovative, unusual, fresh, novel, new; experimental, avant-garde, ground-breaking, unorthodox, unconventional.
– OPPOSITES unimaginative, hackneyed.

inventor ▶ noun ORIGINATOR, creator, innovator; designer, deviser, developer, maker, producer; author, architect; pioneer, mastermind, father.

inventory ▶ noun *a complete inventory of all their belongings* LIST, listing, catalogue, record, register, checklist, log, archive.
▶ verb *I inventoried his collection* LIST, catalogue, record, register, log.

inverse ▶ adjective *inverse snobbery* REVERSE, reversed, inverted, opposite, converse, contrary, counter, antithetical.
▶ noun *alkalinity is the inverse of acidity* OPPOSITE, converse, obverse, antithesis; *informal* flip side.

inversion ▶ noun REVERSAL, transposition, turning upside down; reverse, contrary, antithesis, converse.

invert ▶ verb TURN UPSIDE DOWN, upturn, upend, turn around/about, turn inside out, turn back to front, reverse, flip (over).

invest ▶ verb ❶ *he invested in a cotton mill* PUT/PLOUGH MONEY INTO, provide capital for, fund, back, finance, underwrite; buy into, buy shares in. ❷ *they invested £18 million* SPEND, expend, put in, plough in; venture, speculate, risk; *informal* lay out. ❸ *their words were invested with sarcasm* IMBUE, infuse, charge, steep, suffuse, pervade, endow. ❹ *the powers invested in the bishop* VEST IN, confer on, bestow on, grant to, entrust to, put in someone's hands. ❺ *bishops whom the king had invested* ADMIT TO OFFICE, instate, install, induct, swear in; ordain, crown. ❻ (archaic) *invested in the full canonicals of his calling* CLOTHE, attire, dress, garb, robe, deck out, accoutre; *archaic* apparel. ❼ (archiac) *he invested the fort of Arcot* BESIEGE, lay siege to, beleaguer, surround.

investigate ▶ verb ENQUIRE INTO, look into, go into, probe, explore, scrutinize, conduct an investigation into, make inquiries about; inspect, analyse, study, examine, consider, research; *informal* check out, suss out; *N. Amer. informal* scope out.

investigation ▶ noun EXAMINATION, inquiry, study, inspection, exploration, consideration, analysis, appraisal; research, scrutiny, scrutinization, perusal; probe, review, survey.

investigator ▶ noun INSPECTOR, examiner, inquirer, explorer, analyser; researcher, fact-finder, scrutineer, scrutinizer, prober, searcher; detective.

investiture ▶ noun INAUGURATION, appointment, installation, instatement, initiation, swearing in; ordination, consecration, crowning, enthronement.

investment ▶ noun ❶ *you can lose money by bad investment* INVESTING, speculation; funding, backing, financing, underwriting; buying shares. ❷ *it's a good investment* VENTURE, speculation, risk, gamble; asset, acquisition, holding, possession. ❸ *an investment of £305,000* STAKE, share, money/capital invested. ❹ *a substantial investment of time* SACRIFICE, surrender, loss, forfeiture.

inveterate ▶ adjective ❶ *an inveterate gambler* CONFIRMED, hardened, incorrigible, addicted, compulsive, obsessive; *informal* pathological. ❷ *an inveterate Democrat* STAUNCH, steadfast, committed, devoted, dedicated, dyed-in-the-wool, out and out, diehard. ❸ *mankind's inveterate stupidity* INGRAINED, deep-seated, deep-rooted, entrenched, ineradicable, incurable.

invidious ▶ adjective ❶ *that put her in an invidious position* UNPLEASANT, awkward, difficult; undesirable, unenviable. ❷ *an invidious comparison* UNFAIR, unjust, iniquitous, unwarranted; deleterious, detrimental.
– OPPOSITES pleasant, fair.

invigorate ▶ verb REVITALIZE, energize, refresh, revive, vivify, brace, rejuvenate, enliven, liven up, perk up, wake up, animate, galvanize, fortify, stimulate, rouse, exhilarate; *informal* buck up, pep up.
– OPPOSITES tire.

invincible ▶ adjective INVULNERABLE, indestructible, unconquerable, unbeatable, indomitable, unassailable; impregnable, inviolable.
– OPPOSITES vulnerable.

inviolable ▶ adjective INALIENABLE, absolute, unalterable, unchallengeable; sacrosanct, holy, sacred.

inviolate ▶ adjective UNTOUCHED, undamaged, unhurt, unharmed, unscathed; unspoiled, unflawed, unsullied, unstained, undefiled, unprofaned, perfect, pristine, pure; intact, unbroken, whole, entire, complete.

invisible ▶ adjective UNABLE TO BE SEEN, not visible; undetectable, indiscernible, inconspicuous, imperceptible; unseen, unnoticed, unobserved, hidden, obscured, out of sight.

invitation ▶ noun ❶ *an invitation to dinner* request to attend, call, summons; *informal* invite. ❷ *an open door is an invitation to a thief* ENCOURAGEMENT, provocation, temptation, lure, magnet, bait, enticement, attraction, allure; *informal* come-on.

invite ▶ verb ❶ *they invited us to Sunday lunch*

ASK, summon, have someone over/round, request (the pleasure of) someone's company at. ❷ *applications are invited for the posts* ASK FOR, request, call for, appeal for, solicit, seek, summon. ❸ *airing such views invites trouble* CAUSE, induce, provoke, create, generate, engender, foster, encourage, lead to; incite, elicit, bring on oneself, arouse.

▶ **noun** (*informal*) *an invite to a party. See* INVITATION sense 1.

inviting ▶ **adjective** TEMPTING, enticing, alluring, beguiling; attractive, appealing, pleasant, agreeable, delightful; appetizing, mouth-watering; fascinating, enchanting, entrancing, captivating, intriguing, irresistible, seductive.
– OPPOSITES repellent.

invocation ▶ **noun** ❶ *her invocation of new methodologies* CITATION, mention, acknowledgement, reference to, allusion to. ❷ *the invocation of rain by tribal people* SUMMONING, calling up, conjuring up. ❸ *an invocation to the Holy Ghost* PRAYER, intercession, supplication, entreaty, petition, appeal; *archaic* orison.

invoice ▶ **noun** *an invoice for the goods* BILL, account, statement (of charges); *N. Amer.* check; *informal* tab; *archaic* reckoning.

▶ **verb** *we'll invoice you for the damage* BILL, charge, send an invoice/bill to.

invoke ▶ **verb** ❶ *he invoked his statutory rights* CITE, refer to, adduce, instance; resort to, have recourse to, turn to. ❷ *I invoked the Madonna* PRAY TO, call on, appeal to, supplicate, entreat, solicit, beg, implore; *poetic/literary* beseech. ❸ *invoking the spirits* SUMMON, call (up), conjure (up). ❹ *middle-class moralities invoke peculiar anxieties* BRING FORTH, bring out, elicit, induce, cause, kindle.

involuntary ▶ **adjective** ❶ *an involuntary shudder* REFLEX, automatic; spontaneous, instinctive, unconscious, unintentional, uncontrollable. ❷ *involuntary repatriation* COMPULSORY, obligatory, mandatory, forced, coerced, compelled, imposed, required, prescribed; unwilling, unconsenting, against one's will.
– OPPOSITES deliberate, optional.

involve ▶ **verb** ❶ *the inspection involved a lot of work* REQUIRE, necessitate, demand, call for; entail, mean, imply, presuppose. ❷ *I try to involve everyone in key decisions* INCLUDE, count in, bring in, take into account, take note of; cover, incorporate, encompass, touch on, embrace, comprehend. ❸ *many drug addicts involve themselves in crime* IMPLICATE, incriminate, inculpate; associate, connect, concern; embroil, entangle, enmesh; *informal* mix up.
– OPPOSITES preclude, exclude.

involved ▶ **adjective** ❶ *social workers involved in the case* ASSOCIATED, connected, concerned. ❷ *he had been involved in burglaries* IMPLICATED, incriminated, inculpated, embroiled, entangled, caught up, mixed up. ❸ *a long and involved story* COMPLICATED, intricate, complex, elaborate; convoluted, impenetrable, unfathomable. ❹ *they were totally involved in their work* ENGROSSED, absorbed, immersed, caught up, preoccupied, busy, engaged, intent.
– OPPOSITES unconnected, straightforward.

involvement ▶ **noun** ❶ *his involvement in a plot to overthrow the government* PARTICIPATION, action, hand; collaboration, collusion, complicity, implication, incrimination, inculpation; association, connection, attachment, entanglement. ❷ *emotional involvement* ATTACHMENT, friendship, intimacy; relationship, relations, bond.

invulnerable ▶ **adjective** IMPERVIOUS, insusceptible, immune; indestructible, impenetrable, impregnable, unassailable, inviolable, invincible, secure; proof against.

inward ▶ **adjective** ❶ *a small inward indentation* TOWARDS THE INSIDE, going in, ingoing; concave. ❷ *an inward smile* INTERNAL, inner, interior, innermost; private, personal, hidden, secret, veiled, masked, concealed, unexpressed; *archaic* privy.
– OPPOSITES outward.

▶ **adverb** *the door opened inward. See* INWARDS.

inwardly ▶ **adverb** INSIDE, internally, within, deep down (inside), in one's heart (of hearts); privately, secretly, confidentially.

inwards ▶ **adverb** INSIDE, into the interior, inward, within.

iota ▶ **noun** (LITTLE) BIT, mite, speck, scrap, shred, ounce, scintilla, atom, jot (or tittle); *informal* smidgen; *archaic* scruple.

irascible ▶ **adjective** IRRITABLE, quick-tempered, short-tempered, snappish, tetchy, testy, touchy, edgy, crabby, waspish, dyspeptic; crusty, grouchy, cantankerous, curmudgeonly, ill-natured, peevish, querulous, fractious; *informal* prickly, ratty, snappy.

irate ▶ **adjective** ANGRY, furious, infuriated, incensed, enraged, incandescent, fuming, seething, cross, mad; raging, ranting, raving, in a frenzy, beside oneself, outraged, up in arms; indignant, annoyed, irritated, irked, piqued; *informal* foaming at the mouth, hot under the collar; *poetic/literary* wrathful; *archaic* wroth.

ire ▶ **noun** (*poetic/literary*) ANGER, rage, fury, wrath, outrage, temper, crossness, spleen; annoyance, exasperation, irritation, displeasure, indignation; *poetic/literary* choler.

Ireland ▶ **noun** Eire, the Republic of Ireland, the Irish Republic; Hibernia, the Emerald Isle; *poetic/literary* Erin.

iridescent ▶ **adjective** SHIMMERING, glittering, sparkling, dazzling, shining, gleaming, glowing, lustrous, scintillating, opalescent; *poetic/literary* glistering, coruscating, effulgent.

irk ▶ **verb** IRRITATE, annoy, gall, pique, nettle,

exasperate, try someone's patience; anger, infuriate, madden, incense, get on someone's nerves; antagonize, provoke, ruffle someone's feathers, make someone's hackles rise; *Brit.* rub up the wrong way; *informal* get someone's goat, get/put someone's back up, make someone's blood boil, peeve, miff, rile, aggravate, needle, get (to), bug, hack off, brown off, get up someone's nose, give someone the hump, drive mad/crazy, drive up the wall, make someone see red; *Brit. informal* wind up, cheese off, nark, get on someone's wick; *N. Amer. informal* tee off, tick off, rankle, ride, gravel.
– OPPOSITES please.

irksome ▶ **adjective** IRRITATING, annoying, vexing, vexatious, galling, exasperating, disagreeable; tiresome, wearisome, tedious, trying, troublesome, bothersome, awkward, difficult, boring, uninteresting; infuriating, maddening; *informal* infernal.

iron ▶ **noun** ❶ *a ship built of iron* metal, pig iron, cast iron, wrought iron. ❷ *she needed some iron in her soul* STRENGTH, toughness, resilience, firmness, robustness, steel, grit; *informal* guts, spunk. ❸ *a soldering iron* TOOL, implement, utensil, device. ❹ *a hot iron* FLAT IRON, electric iron, steam iron, smoothing iron. ❺ *they were clapped in irons* MANACLES, shackles, fetters, chains, handcuffs; *informal* cuffs, bracelets.
▶ **adjective** ❶ *an iron key* MADE OF IRON, ferric, ferrous. ❷ *an iron law of politics* INFLEXIBLE, unbreakable, absolute, unconditional, categorical, incontrovertible, infallible. ❸ *an iron will* UNCOMPROMISING, unrelenting, unyielding, unbending, resolute, resolved, determined, firm, rigid, steadfast, unwavering.
– OPPOSITES flexible.
▶ **verb** *she irons his shirts* PRESS.
■ **iron something out** ❶ *John had ironed out all the minor snags* RESOLVE, straighten out, sort out, clear up, settle, put right, solve, remedy, rectify; *informal* fix, mend. ❷ *ironing out differences in national systems* ELIMINATE, eradicate, erase, get rid of; harmonize, reconcile.

ironic ▶ **adjective** ❶ *Edward's tone was ironic* SARCASTIC, sardonic, dry, caustic, sharp, stinging, scathing, acerbic, acid, bitter, trenchant, mordant, cynical; mocking, satirical, scoffing, derisory, derisive, scornful; *Brit. informal* sarky. ❷ *it's ironic that I've ended up writing* PARADOXICAL, incongruous, odd, strange, peculiar, unexpected.
– OPPOSITES sincere.

irony ▶ **noun** ❶ *that note of irony in her voice* SARCASM, sardonicism, dryness, causticity, sharpness, acerbity, bitterness, trenchancy, mordancy, cynicism; mockery, satire, ridicule, derision, scorn; *Brit. informal* sarkiness. ❷ *the irony of the situation* PARADOX, incongruity, incongruousness, peculiarity.
– OPPOSITES sincerity.

irradiate ▶ **verb** ILLUMINATE, light (up), cast light upon, brighten, shine on; *poetic/literary* illumine.

irrational ▶ **adjective** UNREASONABLE, illogical, groundless, baseless, unfounded, unjustifiable; absurd, ridiculous, ludicrous, silly, foolish, senseless.
– OPPOSITES logical.

irreconcilable ▶ **adjective** ❶ *irreconcilable views* INCOMPATIBLE, at odds, at variance, conflicting, clashing, antagonistic, mutually exclusive, diametrically opposed; disparate, variant, dissimilar, poles apart; *rare* oppugnant. ❷ *irreconcilable enemies* IMPLACABLE, unappeasable, uncompromising, inflexible; mortal, bitter, deadly, sworn, out-and-out.
– OPPOSITES compatible.

irrecoverable ▶ **adjective** UNRECOVERABLE, unreclaimable, irretrievable, irredeemable, unsalvageable, gone for ever; written off.

irrefutable ▶ **adjective** INDISPUTABLE, undeniable, unquestionable, incontrovertible, incontestable, beyond question, beyond doubt, indisputable; conclusive, definite, definitive, decisive, certain, positive.

irregular ▶ **adjective** ❶ *irregular features | an irregular coastline* ASYMMETRICAL, non-uniform, uneven, crooked, misshapen, lopsided, twisted; jagged, ragged, serrated, indented. ❷ *irregular surfaces* ROUGH, bumpy, uneven, pitted, rutted; lumpy, knobbly, gnarled. ❸ *an irregular heartbeat* INCONSISTENT, unsteady, uneven, fitful, patchy, variable, varying, changeable, changing, inconstant, erratic, unstable, unsettled, spasmodic, intermittent, fluctuating. ❹ *irregular financial dealings* AGAINST THE RULES, out of order, improper, illegitimate, unscrupulous, unethical, unprofessional, unacceptable, beyond the pale; *informal* shady; *Brit. informal* not cricket; *Austral./NZ informal* over the fence. ❺ *an irregular army* GUERRILLA, underground; paramilitary; partisan, mercenary.
– OPPOSITES straight, smooth.
▶ **noun** *gun-toting irregulars* GUERRILLA, underground fighter; paramilitary; resistance fighter, partisan, mercenary.

irregularity ▶ **noun** ❶ *the irregularity of the coastline* ASYMMETRY, non-uniformity, unevenness, crookedness, lopsidedness; jaggedness, raggedness, indentation. ❷ *the irregularity of the surface* ROUGHNESS, bumpiness, unevenness; lumpiness, knobbliness. ❸ *irregularities in the concrete* BUMP, lump, bulge, hump, protuberance, kink; hole, hollow, pit, crater, depression, dip, indentation, dent; crack, chink, fissure, cranny. ❹ *the irregularity of the bus service* INCONSISTENCY, unsteadiness, unevenness, fitfulness, patchiness, inconstancy, instability, variability, changeableness, fluctuation, unpredictability, unreliability. ❺ *financial irregularities* IMPROPRIETY, wrongdoing, misconduct, dishonesty, corruption, immorality; *informal* shadiness, crookedness. ❻ *staff noted any irregularity in operation* ABNORMALITY, unusualness, strangeness, oddness, singularity, atypicality, anomaly, deviation, aberration, peculiarity, idiosyncrasy.

irregularly ▶ adverb ❶ *irregularly hexagonal* ASYMMETRICALLY, unevenly. ❷ *his heart was beating irregularly* ERRATICALLY, intermittently, in/by fits and starts, fitfully, patchily, haphazardly, unsystematically, unmethodically, inconsistently, unsteadily, unevenly, variably, spasmodically, discontinuously, inconstantly.

irrelevance ▶ noun INAPPLICABILITY, unrelatedness, inappropriateness, inappositeness; unimportance, inconsequentiality, insignificance; *formal* impertinence.

irrelevant ▶ adjective BESIDE THE POINT, immaterial, not pertinent, not germane, off the subject, unconnected, unrelated, peripheral, extraneous, inapposite; unimportant, inconsequential, insignificant, trivial; *formal* impertinent.

irreligious ▶ adjective ATHEISTIC, unbelieving, non-believing, agnostic, heretical, faithless, godless, ungodly, impious, profane, infidel, barbarian, heathen, pagan; *rare* nullifidian.
– OPPOSITES pious.

irreparable ▶ adjective IRREVERSIBLE, unrectifiable, irrevocable, unrestorable, irrecoverable, unrepairable, beyond repair.
– OPPOSITES repairable.

irreplaceable ▶ adjective UNIQUE, unrepeatable, incomparable, unparalleled; treasured, prized, cherished.

irrepressible ▶ adjective ❶ *the desire for freedom is irrepressible* INEXTINGUISHABLE, unquenchable, uncontainable, uncontrollable, indestructible, undying, everlasting. ❷ *his irrepressible personality* EBULLIENT, exuberant, buoyant, sunny, breezy, jaunty, light-hearted, high-spirited, vivacious, animated, full of life, lively; *informal* bubbly, bouncy, peppy, chipper, chirpy, full of beans.

irreproachable ▶ adjective IMPECCABLE, exemplary, model, immaculate, outstanding, exceptional, admirable, perfect; above/beyond reproach, blameless, faultless, flawless, unblemished, untarnished, spotless; *informal* squeaky clean, whiter than white.
– OPPOSITES reprehensible.

irresistible ▶ adjective ❶ *her irresistible smile* TEMPTING, enticing, alluring, inviting, seductive; attractive, desirable, fetching, appealing, captivating, beguiling, enchanting. ❷ *an irresistible impulse* UNCONTROLLABLE, overwhelming, overpowering, compelling, compulsive, irrepressible, ungovernable, driving, forceful.

irresolute ▶ adjective INDECISIVE, hesitant, vacillating, equivocating, dithering, wavering, shilly-shallying; ambivalent, blowing hot and cold, in two minds, in a dilemma, in a quandary, torn; doubtful, in doubt, unsure, uncertain, undecided; *informal* sitting on the fence.
– OPPOSITES decisive.

irresolution ▶ noun INDECISIVENESS, indecision, irresoluteness, hesitancy, hesitation; doubt, doubtfulness, unsureness, uncertainty; vacillation, equivocation, wavering, shilly-shallying, blowing hot and cold, dithering, temporizing, temporization; *Brit.* havering, humming and hawing; *informal* dilly-dallying, sitting on the fence.

irrespective ▶ adjective REGARDLESS OF, without regard to/for, notwithstanding, whatever, no matter what, without consideration of; *informal* irregardless of.

irresponsible ▶ adjective ❶ *irresponsible behaviour* RECKLESS, rash, careless, thoughtless, incautious, unwise, imprudent, ill-advised, injudicious, misguided, unheeding, hasty, overhasty, precipitate, precipitous, foolhardy, impetuous, impulsive, devil-may-care, hot-headed, delinquent; *N. Amer.* derelict. ❷ *an irresponsible teenager* IMMATURE, naive, foolish, hare-brained; unreliable, undependable, untrustworthy, flighty, giddy, scatterbrained, harum-scarum.
– OPPOSITES sensible.

irretrievable ▶ adjective IRREVERSIBLE, unrectifiable, irremediable, irrecoverable, irreparable, unrepairable, beyond repair.
– OPPOSITES reversible.

irreverent ▶ adjective DISRESPECTFUL, disdainful, scornful, contemptuous, derisive, disparaging; impertinent, cheeky, flippant, rude, discourteous.
– OPPOSITES respectful.

irreversible ▶ adjective IRREPARABLE, unrepairable, beyond repair, unrectifiable, irremediable, irrevocable, permanent; unalterable, unchangeable, immutable; *Law* peremptory.

irrevocable ▶ adjective IRREVERSIBLE, unalterable, unchangeable, immutable, final, binding, permanent; *Law* peremptory.

irrigate ▶ verb WATER, bring water to, soak, flood, inundate.

irritability ▶ noun IRASCIBILITY, tetchiness, testiness, touchiness, grumpiness, moodiness, grouchiness, a (bad) mood, cantankerousness, curmudgeonliness, bad temper, short temper, ill humour, peevishness, crossness, fractiousness, pettishness, crabbiness, waspishness, prickliness; *Brit. informal* shirtiness, stroppiness, rattiness; *N. Amer. informal* crankiness, orneriness; *Austral./NZ informal* snakiness; *poetic/literary* choler.

irritable ▶ adjective BAD-TEMPERED, short-tempered, irascible, tetchy, testy, touchy, grumpy, grouchy, moody, crotchety, in a (bad) mood, cantankerous, curmudgeonly, ill-tempered, ill-humoured, peevish, cross, fractious, pettish,

crabby, waspish, prickly, splenetic, dyspeptic, choleric; *informal* on a short fuse; *Brit. informal* shirty, stroppy, ratty; *N. Amer. informal* cranky, ornery, peckish; *Austral./NZ informal* snaky.
–OPPOSITES good-humoured.

irritant ▶ **noun** ANNOYANCE, (source of) irritation, thorn in someone's side/flesh, pest, bother, trial, torment, plague, inconvenience, nuisance; *informal* aggravation, peeve, pain (in the neck), headache; *N. Amer. informal* nudnik, burr in/under someone's saddle; *Austral./NZ informal* nark.

irritate ▶ **verb** ❶ *the smallest things may irritate you* ANNOY, vex, make angry, make cross, anger, exasperate, irk, gall, pique, nettle, put out, antagonize, get on someone's nerves, try someone's patience, ruffle someone's feathers, make someone's hackles rise; infuriate, madden, provoke; *Brit.* rub up the wrong way; *informal* aggravate, miff, rile, needle, get to, bug, hack off, get under someone's skin, get/put someone's back up, get up someone's nose, give someone the hump, drive mad/crazy, drive round the bend/twist, drive up the wall; *Brit. informal* wind up, get on someone's wick; *N. Amer. informal* tee off, tick off, rankle, ride, gravel. ❷ *some sand irritated my eyes* INFLAME, aggravate, hurt, chafe, abrade, scratch, scrape, graze.
–OPPOSITES pacify, soothe.

irritated ▶ **adjective** ANNOYED, cross, angry, vexed, exasperated, irked, piqued, nettled, put out, fed up, disgruntled, in a bad mood, in a temper, testy, huffy, in a huff, aggrieved; irate, infuriated, incensed; *informal* aggravated, peeved, miffed, mad, riled, hacked off, browned off, hot under the collar; *Brit. informal* cheesed off, brassed off, ratty, shirty; *N. Amer. informal* teed off, ticked off, sore; *Austral./NZ informal* snaky, crook; *archaic* snuffy, wroth.
–OPPOSITES good-humoured.

irritating ▶ **adjective** ANNOYING, infuriating, exasperating, maddening, trying, tiresome, vexing, vexatious, irksome, galling; *informal* aggravating.

irritation ▶ **noun** ❶ *she tried not to show her irritation* ANNOYANCE, exasperation, vexation, indignation, impatience, crossness, displeasure, chagrin, pique; anger, rage, fury, wrath; *informal* aggravation; *poetic/literary* ire. ❷ *I realize my presence is an irritation for you* IRRITANT, annoyance, thorn in someone's side/flesh, bother, trial, torment, plague, inconvenience, nuisance; *informal* aggravation, pain (in the neck), headache; *N. Amer. informal* nudnik, burr in/under someone's saddle; *Austral./NZ informal* nark.
–OPPOSITES delight.

island ▶ **noun** ISLE, islet; atoll; *Brit.* holm; (**islands**) archipelago.
–RELATED TERMS insular.

isolate ▶ **verb** ❶ *she isolated herself from her family | the contaminated area was isolated* SEPARATE, set/keep apart, segregate, detach, cut off, shut away, divorce, alienate, distance; keep in solitude, cloister, seclude; cordon off, seal off, close off, fence off. ❷ *the laser beam can isolate the offending vehicles* IDENTIFY, single out, pick out, point out, spot, recognize, distinguish, pinpoint, locate.
–OPPOSITES integrate.

isolated ▶ **adjective** ❶ *isolated communities* REMOTE, out of the way, outlying, off the beaten track, secluded, lonely, in the back of beyond, godforsaken, inaccessible, cut-off; *N. Amer.* in the backwoods, lonesome; *Austral./NZ* in the backblocks, in the booay; *informal* in the middle of nowhere, in the sticks; *N. Amer. informal* jerkwater, in the tall timbers; *Austral./NZ informal* Barcoo, beyond the black stump; *archaic* unapproachable. ❷ *he lived a very isolated existence* SOLITARY, lonely, companionless, friendless; secluded, cloistered, segregated, unsociable, reclusive, hermitic; *N. Amer.* lonesome. ❸ *an isolated incident* UNIQUE, lone, solitary; unusual, uncommon, exceptional, anomalous, abnormal, untypical, freak; *informal* one-off.
–OPPOSITES accessible, sociable, common.

isolation ▶ **noun** ❶ *patients who need isolation* SEPARATION, segregation, seclusion, keeping apart. ❷ *their feeling of isolation* SOLITARINESS, loneliness, friendlessness.
–OPPOSITES contact. ❸ *the isolation of some mental hospitals* REMOTENESS, seclusion, inaccessibility.

issue ▶ **noun** ❶ *the committee discussed the issue* MATTER (IN QUESTION), question, point (at issue), affair, case, subject, topic; problem, bone of contention. ❷ *the issue of a special stamp* ISSUING, publication, publishing; circulation, distribution, supplying, appearance. ❸ *the latest issue of our magazine* EDITION, number, instalment, copy. ❹ (*Law*) *she died without issue* OFFSPRING, descendants, heirs, successors, children, progeny, family; *informal* kids; *archaic* seed, fruit (of one's loins). ❺ *an issue of blood* DISCHARGE, emission, release, outflow, outflowing, outflux; secretion, emanation, exudation, effluence; *technical* efflux. ❻ (*dated*) *a favourable issue* (END) RESULT, outcome, consequence, upshot, conclusion, end.
▶ **verb** ❶ *the minister issued a statement* SEND OUT, put out, release, deliver, publish, announce, broadcast, communicate, circulate, distribute, disseminate. ❷ *the captain issued the crew with guns* SUPPLY, provide, furnish, arm, equip, fit out, rig out, kit out; *informal* fix up. ❸ *savoury smells issued from the kitchen* EMANATE, emerge, exude, flow (out/forth), pour (out/forth); be emitted. ❹ *large profits might issue from the deal* RESULT, follow, ensue, stem, spring, arise, proceed; be the result of, be brought on/about by, be produced by.
–OPPOSITES withdraw.
■ **at issue** IN QUESTION, in dispute, under discussion, under consideration, for debate.

■ **take issue** DISAGREE, be in dispute, be in contention, be at variance, be at odds, argue, quarrel; challenge, dispute, (call into) question; *archaic* disaccord.

itch ▶ noun ❶ *I have an itch on my back* tingling, irritation, itchiness. ❷ (*informal*) *the itch to travel* LONGING, yearning, craving, ache, hunger, thirst, urge, hankering; wish, fancy, desire; *informal* yen.

▶ verb ❶ *my chilblains really itch* tingle, be irritated, be itchy. ❷ (*informal*) *he itched to do something to help* LONG, yearn, ache, burn, crave, hanker for/after, hunger, thirst, be eager, be desperate; want, wish, desire, fancy, set one's sights on; *informal* have a yen, be dying, be gagging.

item ▶ noun ❶ *an item of farm equipment* | *the main item in a badger's diet* THING, article, object, artefact, piece, product; element, constituent, component, ingredient. ❷ *the meeting discussed the item* ISSUE, matter, affair, case, situation, subject, topic, question, point. ❸ *a news item* REPORT, story, account, article, piece, write-up, bulletin, feature. ❹ *items in the profit and loss account* ENTRY, record, statement, listing.

itemize ▶ verb ❶ *Steinburg itemized thirty-two design faults* LIST, catalogue, inventory, record, document, register, detail, specify, identify; enumerate, number. ❷ *an itemized bill* ANALYSE, break down, split up.

iterate ▶ verb REPEAT, recapitulate, go over/through again; say again, restate, reiterate; *informal* recap; *archaic* ingeminate.

itinerant ▶ adjective *itinerant traders* TRAVELLING, peripatetic, wandering, roving, roaming, touring, nomadic, gypsy, migrant, vagrant, vagabond, of no fixed address/abode.

▶ noun *an itinerants' lodging house* TRAVELLER, wanderer, roamer, rover, nomad, gypsy, migrant, transient, drifter, vagabond, vagrant, tramp; *dated* bird of passage.

itinerary ▶ noun (PLANNED) ROUTE, journey, way, road; travel plan, schedule, timetable, programme, tour.

Jj

jab ▶ verb *he jabbed the Englishman with his finger* POKE, prod, dig, nudge, butt, ram; thrust, stab, push.

▶ noun *a jab in the ribs* POKE, prod, dig, nudge, butt; thrust, stab, push.

jabber ▶ verb *they jabbered away non-stop* PRATTLE, babble, chatter, twitter, prate, gabble, rattle on/away, blather; *informal* yak, yap, yabber, yatter, blab, blabber; *Brit. informal* witter, rabbit, natter; *archaic* twaddle, clack.

▶ noun *stop your jabber!* PRATTLE, babble, chatter, chattering, twitter, twittering, gabble, blather; *informal* yabbering, yatter, blabber; *Brit. informal* wittering, rabbiting, nattering; *archaic* clack.

jack

■ **jack something up** ❶ *they jacked up the car* RAISE, hoist, lift (up), winch up, lever up, hitch up, elevate. ❷ (*informal*) *he may need to jack up interest rates* INCREASE, raise, put up, up, mark up; *informal* hike (up), bump up.

jacket ▶ noun WRAPPING, wrapper, wrap, sleeve, sheath, sheathing, cover, covering.

jackpot ▶ noun *this week's lottery jackpot* TOP PRIZE, first prize; pool, bonanza.

■ **hit the jackpot** (*informal*) WIN A LARGE PRIZE, win a lot of money, strike it lucky/rich; *informal* clean up, hit the big time.

jaded ▶ adjective ❶ *a jaded palate* SATIATED, sated, surfeited, glutted; dulled, blunted, deadened. ❷ *she felt really jaded* TIRED (OUT), weary, wearied, worn out, exhausted, fatigued, overtired, sapped, drained; *informal* all in, done (in), dead (beat), dead on one's feet, bushed; *Brit. informal* knackered, whacked; *N. Amer. informal* tuckered out.

– OPPOSITES fresh.

jag ▶ noun SHARP PROJECTION, point, barb, thorn.

jagged ▶ adjective SPIKY, barbed, ragged, rough, uneven, irregular, broken; serrated, sawtooth, indented.

– OPPOSITES smooth.

jail ▶ noun *he was thrown into jail* PRISON, penal institution, lock-up, detention centre; *N. Amer.* penitentiary, jailhouse, stockade, correctional facility; *informal* clink, slammer, inside, jug, brig; *Brit. informal* nick; *N. Amer. informal* can, pen, cooler, slam, pokey; *Brit. historical* approved school, borstal, bridewell; *N. Amer. historical* reformatory.

▶ verb *she was jailed for killing her husband* IMPRISON, put in prison, send to prison, incarcerate, lock up, put away, intern, detain, hold (prisoner/captive), put into detention; *informal* send down, put behind bars, put inside; *Brit. informal* bang up.

– OPPOSITES acquit, release.

jailer ▶ noun PRISON OFFICER, warder, wardress, warden, guard, captor; *informal* screw; *archaic* turnkey.

jam¹ ▶ verb ❶ *he jammed a finger in each ear* STUFF, shove, force, ram, thrust, press, push, stick, squeeze, cram. ❷ *hundreds of people jammed into the hall* CROWD, pack, pile, press, squeeze, cram; throng, mob, occupy, fill, overcrowd, obstruct, block, clog, congest. ❸ *the rudder had jammed* STICK, become stuck, catch, seize (up), become trapped. ❹ *dust can jam the mechanism* IMMOBILIZE, paralyse, disable, cripple, put out of action, bring to a standstill.

▶ noun ❶ *a traffic jam* TAILBACK, hold-up, congestion, bottleneck; *N. Amer.* gridlock; *informal* snarl-up. ❷ (*informal*) *we are in a real jam* PREDICAMENT, plight, tricky situation, difficulty, problem, quandary, dilemma, muddle, mess, imbroglio, mare's nest, dire straits; *informal* pickle, stew, fix, hole, scrape, bind, (tight) spot, (tight) corner, hot/deep water; *Brit. informal* spot of bother.

jam² ▶ noun *raspberry jam* PRESERVE, conserve, jelly, marmalade.

jamb ▶ noun POST, doorpost, upright, frame.

jamboree ▶ noun RALLY, gathering, convention, conference; festival, fête, fiesta, gala, carnival, celebration; *informal* bash, shindig, shindy, junket.

jammy ▶ adjective (*Brit. informal*). *See* LUCKY sense 1.

jangle ▶ verb ❶ *keys jangled at his waist* CLANK, clink, jingle, tinkle. ❷ *the noise jangled her nerves* GRATE ON, jar on, irritate, disturb, fray, put/set on edge; *informal* get on.

▶ noun *the jangle of his chains* CLANK, clanking, clink, clinking, jangling, jingle, jingling, tintinnabulation.

janitor ▶ noun CARETAKER, custodian, porter, concierge, doorkeeper, doorman, warden; cleaner, maintenance man; *N. Amer.* superintendent.

jar¹ ▶ noun *a jar of honey* (GLASS) CONTAINER, pot, crock, receptacle.

jar² ▶ verb ❶ *each step jarred my whole body* JOLT, jerk, shake, vibrate. ❷ *her shrill voice jarred on him* GRATE, set someone's teeth on edge, irritate, annoy, irk, exasperate, nettle, disturb, discompose; *informal* rile, aggravate, get on someone's nerves. ❸ *the play's symbolism jarred with the realism of its setting* CLASH, conflict, contrast, be incompatible, be at variance, be at odds, be inconsistent, be discordant; *informal* scream at.

jargon ▶ noun SPECIALIZED LANGUAGE, slang, cant, idiom, argot, patter, gobbledegook; *informal* -speak, -ese.

jarring ▶ adjective CLASHING, conflicting, contrasting, incompatible, incongruous; discordant, dissonant, inharmonious, harsh, grating, strident, shrill, cacophonous.

–OPPOSITES harmonious.

jaundiced ▶ adjective BITTER, resentful, cynical, soured, disenchanted, disillusioned, disappointed, pessimistic, sceptical, distrustful, suspicious, misanthropic.

jaunt ▶ noun (PLEASURE) TRIP, outing, excursion, day trip, day out, mini holiday, short break; tour, drive, ride, run; *informal* spin, tootle.

jaunty ▶ adjective CHEERFUL, cheery, happy, merry, jolly, joyful; lively, perky, bright, buoyant, bubbly, bouncy, breezy, full of the joys of spring, in good spirits, exuberant, ebullient; carefree, blithe, airy, light-hearted, nonchalant, insouciant, happy-go-lucky; *informal* bright-eyed and bushy-tailed, full of beans, chirpy; *poetic/literary* blithesome.

–OPPOSITES depressed, serious.

javelin ▶ noun SPEAR, harpoon, dart, gig, shaft, assegai.

jaw ▶ noun ❶ *a broken jaw* JAWBONE, lower/upper jaw; *Anatomy* mandible, maxilla. ❷ *the whale seized a seal pup in its jaws* MOUTH, maw, muzzle; *informal* chops. ❸ (*informal*) *we ought to have a jaw. See* CHAT noun.

–RELATED TERMS mandibular, maxillary.

▶ verb (*informal*) *Tom was the type to jaw. See* CHAT verb.

jazz

■ **jazz something up** (*informal*) ENLIVEN, liven up, brighten up, make more interesting/exciting, add (some) colour to, ginger up, spice up; *informal* perk up, pep up.

jazzy ▶ adjective BRIGHT, colourful, brightly coloured, striking, eye-catching, vivid, lively, vibrant, bold, flamboyant, showy, gaudy; *informal* flashy.

–OPPOSITES dull.

jealous ▶ adjective ❶ *he was jealous of his brother's popularity* ENVIOUS, covetous, desirous; resentful, grudging, begrudging, green (with envy). ❷ *a jealous lover* SUSPICIOUS, distrustful, mistrustful, doubting, insecure, anxious; possessive, proprietorial, overprotective. ❸ *they are very jealous of their rights* PROTECTIVE, vigilant, watchful, heedful, mindful, careful, solicitous.

–OPPOSITES proud, trusting.

jealousy ▶ noun ❶ *he was consumed with jealousy* ENVY, covetousness; resentment, resentfulness, bitterness, spite; *informal* the green-eyed monster. ❷ *the jealousy of his long-suffering wife* SUSPICION, suspiciousness, distrust, mistrust, insecurity, anxiety; possessiveness, overprotectiveness. ❸ *an intense jealousy of status* PROTECTIVENESS, vigilance, watchfulness, heedfulness, mindfulness, care, solicitousness.

jeans ▶ plural noun DENIMS, blue jeans; *trademark* Levi's, Wranglers.

jeer ▶ verb *the demonstrators jeered the police* TAUNT, mock, scoff at, ridicule, sneer at, deride, insult, abuse, jibe (at), scorn, shout disap-

proval (at); heckle, catcall (at), boo (at), hoot at, whistle at, hiss (at); *archaic* flout at.
– OPPOSITES cheer.
▶ **noun** *the jeers of the crowd* TAUNT, sneer, insult, shout, jibe, boo, hiss, catcall; derision, teasing, scoffing, abuse, scorn, heckling, catcalling; *Brit. & Austral./NZ* barracking.
– OPPOSITES applause.

jejune ▶ **adjective** ❶ *their jejune opinions* NAIVE, innocent, artless, guileless, unworldly, childlike, ingenuous, unsophisticated; credulous, gullible; childish, immature, juvenile, puerile, infantile. ❷ *the following poem is rather jejune* BORING, dull, tedious, dreary; uninteresting, unexciting, uninspiring, unimaginative; humdrum, run-of-the-mill, mundane, commonplace; lacklustre, dry, sterile, lifeless, vapid, flat, bland, banal, trite, prosaic; *Brit. informal* samey; *N. Amer. informal* ornery.
– OPPOSITES sophisticated, fascinating.

jell ▶ **verb**. *See* GEL.

jeopardize ▶ **verb** THREATEN, endanger, imperil, risk, put at risk, put in danger/jeopardy; leave vulnerable; compromise, prejudice, be prejudicial to; be a danger to, pose a threat to; *archaic* peril.
– OPPOSITES safeguard.

jeopardy ▶ **noun** DANGER, peril; at risk.

jerk ▶ **noun** ❶ *she gave the reins a jerk* YANK, tug, pull, wrench, tweak, twitch. ❷ *he let the clutch in with a jerk* JOLT, lurch, bump, start, jar, jog, bang, bounce, shake, shock. ❸ (*informal*) *I felt a complete jerk. See* FOOL noun sense 1.
▶ **verb** ❶ *she jerked her arm free* YANK, tug, pull, wrench, wrest, drag, pluck, snatch, seize, rip, tear. ❷ *the car jerked along* JOLT, lurch, bump, rattle, bounce, shake, jounce.

jerky ▶ **adjective** ❶ *jerky movements* CONVULSIVE, spasmodic, fitful, twitchy, shaky. ❷ *the coach drew to a jerky halt* JOLTING, lurching, bumpy, bouncy, jarring.
– OPPOSITES smooth.

jerry-built ▶ **adjective** SHODDY, badly built, gimcrack, flimsy, insubstantial, rickety, ramshackle, crude, makeshift; inferior, poor-quality, second-rate, third-rate, low-grade.
– OPPOSITES sturdy.

jersey ▶ **noun** PULLOVER, sweater; *Brit.* jumper; *informal* woolly.

jest ▶ **noun** *jests were bandied about freely* JOKE, witticism, funny remark, gag, quip, sally, pun; *informal* crack, wisecrack, one-liner.
▶ **verb** ❶ *surely you are jesting* JOKE, quip, gag, pun; tell jokes, crack jokes; *informal* wisecrack. ❷ *she feared that they had not been jesting* FOOL (ABOUT/AROUND), play a practical joke, tease; *informal* kid, have someone on, pull someone's leg; *N. Amer. informal* pull someone's chain, fun; *Brit. informal* wind someone up.
■ **in jest** IN FUN, as a joke, tongue in cheek, playfully, jokingly, light-heartedly, facetiously, flippantly, frivolously, for a laugh.

jester ▶ **noun** ❶ (*historical*) *a court jester* (COURT) FOOL, court jester, clown; *archaic* merry andrew. ❷ *the class jester* JOKER, comedian, comic, humorist, wag, wit, prankster, jokester, clown, buffoon; *informal* card, case, caution, hoot, scream, laugh, wisecracker, barrel of laughs; *Austral./NZ informal* hard case.

jet[1] ▶ **noun** ❶ *a jet of water* STREAM, spurt, squirt, spray, spout; gush, rush, surge, burst. ❷ *carburettor jets* NOZZLE, head, spout. ❸ *an executive jet* JET PLANE, jetliner; aircraft, plane; *Brit.* aeroplane.
▶ **verb** ❶ *they jetted out of Heathrow* FLY, travel/go by jet, travel/go by plane. ❷ *puffs of gas jetted out* SQUIRT, spurt, shoot, spray; gush, pour, stream, rush, pump, surge, spew, burst.

jet[2] ▶ **adjective** *her glossy jet hair* BLACK, jet-black, pitch-black, ink-black, ebony, raven, sable, sooty.

jettison ▶ **verb** ❶ *six aircraft jettisoned their loads* DUMP, drop, ditch, discharge, throw out, tip out, unload, throw overboard. ❷ *he jettisoned his unwanted papers | the scheme was jettisoned* DISCARD, dispose of, throw away/out, get rid of; reject, scrap, axe, abandon, drop; *informal* chuck (away/out), dump, ditch, bin, junk, get shut of; *Brit. informal* get shot of; *N. Amer. informal* trash.
– OPPOSITES retain.

jetty ▶ **noun** PIER, landing (stage), quay, wharf, dock; breakwater, mole, groyne, dyke; *N. Amer.* dockominium, levee.

jewel ▶ **noun** ❶ *priceless jewels* GEM, gemstone, (precious) stone, brilliant; baguette; *informal* sparkler, rock; *archaic* bijou. ❷ *the jewel of his collection* FINEST EXAMPLE/SPECIMEN, showpiece, pride (and joy), cream, crème de la crème, jewel in the crown, nonpareil, glory, prize, boast, pick, ne plus ultra. ❸ *the girl is a jewel* TREASURE, angel, paragon, marvel, find, godsend; *informal* one in a million, a star, the tops; *archaic* nonsuch.

jewellery ▶ **noun** JEWELS, gems, gemstones, precious stones, bijouterie, costume jewellery, diamanté; *archaic* bijoux.

Jezebel ▶ **noun** IMMORAL WOMAN; seductress, temptress, femme fatale; *informal* tart, vamp, maneater; *N. Amer. informal* tramp; *Brit. informal* scrubber, slapper, slag; *dated* loose woman, trollop, hussy; *archaic* harlot, strumpet.

jib ▶ **verb** ❶ *the horse jibbed at the final fence* STOP (SHORT) AT, baulk at, shy at; refuse. ❷ *some farmers jib at paying large veterinary bills* BAULK AT, fight shy of, recoil from, shrink from; be unwilling, be reluctant, be loath, demur at; *informal* boggle at.
– OPPOSITES clear.

jibe ▶ **noun** *cruel jibes* SNIDE REMARK, cutting remark, taunt, sneer, jeer, insult, barb; *informal* dig, put-down.

▶ **verb** *Simon jibed in a sarcastic way* JEER, taunt, mock, scoff, sneer.

jiffy

■ **in a jiffy** (*informal*) (VERY) SOON, in a second, in a minute, in a moment, in a trice, in a flash, shortly, any second, any minute (now), in no time (at all); *N. Amer.* momentarily; *informal* in a sec, in a jiff, in two shakes (of a lamb's tail), before you can say Jack Robinson; *Brit. informal* in a tick, in two ticks, in a mo; *N. Amer. informal* in a snap, in jig time; *dated* directly.

jig ▶ **verb** BOB, jump, spring, skip, hop, prance, bounce, jounce.

jiggle ▶ **verb** ❶ *Barrett jiggled his foot* SHAKE, joggle, waggle, wiggle. ❷ *Thomas jiggled excitedly* FIDGET, wriggle, squirm.

jilt ▶ **verb** LEAVE, walk out on, throw over, finish with, break up with; *informal* chuck, ditch, dump, drop, run out on, give someone the push/elbow, give someone the old heave-ho, give someone the big E; *poetic/literary* forsake.

jingle ▶ **noun** ❶ *the jingle of money in the till* CLINK, chink, tinkle, jangle. ❷ *the jingle of the bell* TINKLE, ring, ding, ping, ting-a-ling, chime, tintinnabulation. ❸ *advertising jingles* SLOGAN, catchphrase; ditty, song, rhyme, tune; *N. Amer. informal* tag line.

▶ **verb** ❶ *her bracelets jingled noisily* CLINK, chink, tinkle, jangle. ❷ *the bell jingled* TINKLE, ring, ding, ping, chime.

jingoism ▶ **noun** EXTREME PATRIOTISM, chauvinism, extreme nationalism, xenophobia; hawkishness, militarism, belligerence, bellicosity.

jinx ▶ **noun** *the jinx struck six days later* CURSE, spell, hoodoo, malediction; the evil eye, black magic, voodoo, bad luck; *N. Amer.* hex; *archaic* malison.

▶ **verb** *the family is jinxed* CURSE, cast a spell on, put the evil eye on, hoodoo; *Austral.* point the bone at; *N. Amer.* hex; *Austral. informal* mozz, put the mozz on.

jitters ▶ **plural noun** (*informal*) NERVOUSNESS, nerves, edginess, uneasiness, anxiety, anxiousness, tension, agitation, restlessness; stage fright; *informal* butterflies (in one's stomach), the willies, collywobbles, the heebie-jeebies, jitteriness, the jim-jams.

jittery ▶ **adjective** (*informal*) NERVOUS, on edge, edgy, tense, anxious, ill at ease, uneasy, keyed up, overwrought, jumpy, on tenterhooks, worried, apprehensive; *Brit.* nervy; *informal* with butterflies in one's stomach, like a cat on a hot tin roof, twitchy, uptight, het up, in a tizz/tizzy; *Brit. informal* strung up, like a cat on hot bricks; *N. Amer. informal* spooky, squirrelly, antsy; *Austral./NZ informal* toey; *dated* overstrung.
– OPPOSITES calm.

job ▶ **noun** ❶ *my job involves a lot of travelling* POSITION (OF EMPLOYMENT), post, situation, appointment; occupation, profession, trade, career, (line of) work, métier, craft; vocation, calling; vacancy, opening; *Austral. informal* grip; *archaic* employ. ❷ *this job will take three months* TASK, piece of work, assignment, project; chore, errand; undertaking, venture, operation, enterprise, business. ❸ *it's your job to protect her* RESPONSIBILITY, duty, charge, task; role, function, mission; *informal* department, pigeon. ❹ (*informal*) *it was a job to get here on time* DIFFICULT TASK, problem, trouble, struggle, strain, trial, bother; *informal* headache, hassle, pain. ❺ (*informal*) *a bank job* CRIME, felony; raid, robbery, hold-up, burglary, break-in; *informal* stick-up; *N. Amer. informal* heist.
– RELATED TERMS vocational.

■ **just the job** (*Brit. informal*) THE VERY THING, just the thing, exactly what's needed; *informal* just what the doctor ordered, just the ticket.

jobless ▶ **adjective** UNEMPLOYED, out of work, out of a job, unwaged, between jobs, redundant, laid off; *Brit. informal* signing on, on the dole, 'resting'; *Austral./NZ informal* on the wallaby track.
– OPPOSITES employed.

jockey ▶ **noun** RIDER, horseman, horsewoman, equestrian; *Austral. informal* hoop.

▶ **verb** ❶ *he jockeyed himself into the team* MANOEUVRE, ease, edge, work, steer; inveigle, insinuate, ingratiate; *informal* finagle. ❷ *ministers began jockeying for position* COMPETE, contend, vie; struggle, fight, scramble, jostle.

jocular ▶ **adjective** HUMOROUS, funny, witty, comic, comical, amusing, droll, jokey, hilarious, facetious, tongue-in-cheek, teasing, playful; light-hearted, jovial, cheerful, cheery, merry; *formal* jocose, ludic.
– OPPOSITES solemn.

jocund ▶ **adjective** (*formal*). *See* CHEERFUL sense 1.

jog ▶ **verb** ❶ *he jogged along the road* RUN SLOWLY, jogtrot, dogtrot, trot, lope. ❷ *things are jogging along quite nicely* CONTINUE, proceed, go on, carry on. ❸ *a hand jogged his elbow* NUDGE, prod, poke, push, bump, jar. ❹ *something jogged her memory* STIMULATE, prompt, stir, activate, refresh. ❺ *she jogged her foot up and down* JOGGLE, jiggle, bob, bounce, jolt, jerk.

▶ **noun** *he set off along at a jog* RUN, jogtrot, dogtrot, trot, lope.

joie de vivre ▶ **noun** GAIETY, cheerfulness, cheeriness, light-heartedness, happiness, joy, joyfulness, high spirits, jollity, joviality, exuberance, ebullience, liveliness, vivacity, verve, effervescence, buoyancy, zest, zestfulness; *informal* pep, zing; *poetic/literary* blitheness.
– OPPOSITES sobriety.

joint ▶ **noun** ❶ *a leaky joint in the guttering* JOIN, junction, juncture, intersection, link, linkage, connection; weld, seam; *Anatomy* commissure. ❷ *the hip joint* ball-and-socket joint, hinge joint, articulation. ❸ (*informal*) *a classy joint* ESTABLISHMENT, restaurant, bar, club, nightclub. ❹ (*informal*) *he rolled a joint* CANNABIS CIGARETTE, marijuana cigarette; *informal* spliff, reefer, bomb, bomber, stick.

▶ **adjective** *matters of joint interest | a joint effort* COMMON, shared, communal, collective; mutual, cooperative, collaborative, concerted, combined, united.
– OPPOSITES separate.

▶ **verb** *she jointed the carcass* CUT UP, chop up, butcher, carve.

jointly ▶ **adverb** TOGETHER, in partnership, in cooperation, cooperatively, in conjunction, in combination, mutually.

joke ▶ **noun** ❶ *they were telling jokes* FUNNY STORY, jest, witticism, quip; pun, play on words; *informal* gag, wisecrack, crack, funny, one-liner, killer, rib-tickler, knee-slapper, thigh-slapper; *N. Amer. informal* boffola; *rare* blague. ❷ *playing stupid jokes* TRICK, practical joke, prank, stunt, hoax, jape; *informal* leg-pull, spoof. ❸ (*informal*) *he soon became a joke to us* LAUGHING STOCK, figure of fun, object of ridicule; *Brit.* Aunt Sally. ❹ (*informal*) *the present system is a joke* FARCE, travesty, waste of time; *N. Amer. informal* shuck.

▶ **verb** ❶ *she joked with the guests* TELL JOKES, jest, banter, quip; *informal* wisecrack, josh. ❷ *I'm only joking* FOOL (ABOUT/AROUND), play a trick, play a (practical) joke, tease, hoax, pull someone's leg, mess about/around; *informal* kid; *Brit. informal* have someone on, wind someone up; *N. Amer. informal* fun, shuck, pull someone's chain.

joker ▶ **noun** HUMORIST, comedian, comedienne, comic, wit, jester; prankster, practical joker, hoaxer, trickster, clown; *informal* card, wisecracker, wag.

jolly ▶ **adjective** CHEERFUL, happy, cheery, good-humoured, jovial, merry, sunny, joyful, joyous, light-hearted, in high spirits, bubbly, exuberant, ebullient, cock-a-hoop, gleeful, mirthful, genial, fun-loving; *informal* chipper, chirpy, perky, bright-eyed and bushy-tailed; *formal* jocund, jocose; *dated* gay; *poetic/literary* gladsome, blithe, blithesome.
– OPPOSITES miserable.

▶ **verb** (*informal*) *he tried to jolly her along* ENCOURAGE, urge, coax, cajole, persuade.

▶ **adverb** (*Brit. informal*) *a jolly good idea. See* VERY adverb.

jolt ▶ **verb** ❶ *the train jolted the passengers to one side* PUSH, thrust, jar, bump, knock, bang; shake, joggle, jog. ❷ *the car jolted along* BUMP, bounce, jerk, rattle, lurch, shudder, judder, jounce. ❸ *she was jolted out of her reverie* STARTLE, surprise, shock, stun, shake, take aback; astonish, astound, amaze, stagger, stop someone in their tracks; *informal* rock, floor, knock sideways; *Brit. informal* knock for six.

▶ **noun** ❶ *a series of sickening jolts* BUMP, bounce, shake, jerk, lurch. ❷ *he woke up with a jolt* START, jerk, jump. ❸ *the sight of the dagger gave him a jolt* FRIGHT, the fright of one's life, shock, scare, surprise; *informal* turn.

jostle ▶ **verb** ❶ *she was jostled by noisy students* BUMP INTO/AGAINST, knock into/against, bang into, cannon into, plough into, jolt; push, shove, elbow; mob. ❷ *I jostled my way to the exit* PUSH, thrust, barge, shove, force, elbow, shoulder, bulldoze. ❸ *people jostled for the best position* STRUGGLE, vie, jockey, scramble.

jot ▶ **verb** *I've jotted down a few details* WRITE, note, make a note of, take down, put on paper; scribble, scrawl.

▶ **noun** *not a jot of evidence* IOTA, scrap, shred, whit, grain, crumb, ounce, (little) bit, jot or tittle, speck, atom, particle, scintilla, trace, hint; *informal* smidgen, tad; *Austral./NZ informal* skerrick; *archaic* scruple.

journal ▶ **noun** ❶ *a medical journal* PERIODICAL, magazine, gazette, digest, review, newsletter, news-sheet, bulletin; newspaper, paper; daily, weekly, monthly, quarterly. ❷ *he keeps a journal* DIARY, daily record, log, logbook, chronicle; *N. Amer.* daybook.

journalism ▶ **noun** ❶ *a career in journalism* THE NEWSPAPER BUSINESS, the press, the fourth estate; *Brit.* Fleet Street. ❷ *his incisive style of journalism* REPORTING, writing, reportage, feature writing, news coverage; articles, reports, features, pieces, stories.

journalist ▶ **noun** REPORTER, correspondent, newspaperman, newspaperwoman, newsman, newswoman, columnist, writer, commentator, reviewer; investigative journalist; *Brit.* pressman; *N. Amer.* legman, wireman; *Austral.* roundsman; *informal* news hound, hack, hackette, stringer, journo; *N. Amer. informal* newsy.

journey ▶ **noun** *his journey round the world* TRIP, expedition, tour, trek, voyage, cruise, ride, drive; crossing, passage, flight; travels, wandering, globetrotting; odyssey, pilgrimage; *archaic* peregrination.

▶ **verb** *they journeyed south* TRAVEL, go, voyage, sail, cruise, fly, hike, trek, ride, drive, make one's way; go on a trip/expedition, tour; *archaic* peregrinate.

joust (*historical*) ▶ **verb** *knights jousted with lances* TOURNEY; fight, spar, clash; *historical* tilt.

▶ **noun** *a medieval joust* TOURNAMENT, tourney; combat, contest, fight; *historical* tilt.

jovial ▶ **adjective** CHEERFUL, jolly, happy, cheery, good-humoured, convivial, genial, good-natured, friendly, amiable, affable, sociable, outgoing; smiling, merry, sunny, joyful, joyous, high-spirited, exuberant; *informal* chipper, chirpy, perky, bright-eyed and bushy-tailed; *formal* jocund, jocose; *dated* gay; *poetic/literary* gladsome, blithe, blithesome.
– OPPOSITES miserable.

joy ▶ **noun** ❶ *whoops of joy* DELIGHT, great pleasure, joyfulness, jubilation, triumph, exult-

ation, rejoicing, happiness, gladness, glee, exhilaration, exuberance, elation, euphoria, bliss, ecstasy, rapture; enjoyment, felicity, joie de vivre; *formal* jocundity, jouissance. ❷ *it was a joy to be with her* (SOURCE OF) PLEASURE, delight, treat, thrill; *informal* buzz, kick. ❸ (*Brit. informal*) *we still had no joy* SUCCESS, satisfaction, luck, successful result.
– OPPOSITES misery, trial.

joyful ▶ adjective ❶ *his joyful mood* CHEERFUL, happy, jolly, merry, sunny, joyous, light-hearted, in good spirits, bubbly, exuberant, ebullient, cock-a-hoop, cheery, smiling, mirthful, radiant; jubilant, overjoyed, thrilled, ecstatic, euphoric, blissful, on cloud nine/seven, elated, delighted, gleeful; jovial, genial, good-humoured, full of the joys of spring; *informal* chipper, chirpy, peppy, over the moon, on top of the world; *Austral./NZ informal* wrapped; *dated* gay; *formal* jocund; *poetic/literary* gladsome, blithe, blithesome. ❷ *joyful news* PLEASING, happy, good, cheering, gladdening, welcome, heart-warming; *poetic/literary* gladsome. ❸ *a joyful occasion* HAPPY, cheerful, merry, jolly, festive, joyous.
– OPPOSITES sad, distressing.

joyless ▶ adjective ❶ *a joyless man* GLOOMY, melancholy, morose, lugubrious, glum, sombre, saturnine, sullen, dour, humourless. ❷ *a joyless room* DEPRESSING, cheerless, gloomy, dreary, bleak, dispiriting, drab, dismal, desolate, austere, sombre; unwelcoming, uninviting, inhospitable; *poetic/literary* drear.
– OPPOSITES cheerful, welcoming.

joyous ▶ adjective. *See* JOYFUL senses 1, 3.

jubilant ▶ adjective OVERJOYED, exultant, triumphant, joyful, rejoicing, cock-a-hoop, exuberant, elated, thrilled, gleeful, euphoric, ecstatic, enraptured, in raptures, walking on air, in seventh heaven, on cloud nine; *informal* over the moon, on top of the world, on a high; *N. Amer. informal* wigged out; *Austral. informal* wrapped.
– OPPOSITES despondent.

jubilation ▶ noun EXULTATION, joy, joyousness, elation, euphoria, ecstasy, rapture, glee, gleefulness, exuberance.

jubilee ▶ noun ANNIVERSARY, commemoration; celebration, festival, jamboree; festivities, revelry.

Judas ▶ noun TRAITOR, betrayer, back-stabber, double-crosser; turncoat, quisling, renegade.

judge ▶ noun ❶ *the judge sentenced him to five years* JUSTICE, magistrate, recorder, sheriff; *N. Amer.* jurist; *Brit. informal* beak. ❷ *a panel of judges will select the winner* ADJUDICATOR, arbiter, assessor, evaluator, appraiser, examiner, moderator, mediator.
▶ verb ❶ *I judged that she was simply exhausted* FORM THE OPINION, conclude, decide; consider, believe, think, deem, view; deduce, gather, infer, gauge, estimate, guess, surmise, conjecture; regard as, look on as, take to be, rate as, class as; *informal* reckon, figure. ❷ *the case was judged by a tribunal* TRY, hear; adjudicate, decide, give a ruling/verdict on. ❸ *she was judged innocent of murder* ADJUDGE, pronounce, decree, rule, find. ❹ *the competition will be judged by Alan Amey* ADJUDICATE, arbitrate, mediate, moderate. ❺ *entries were judged by a panel of experts* ASSESS, appraise, evaluate; examine, review.

judgement ▶ noun ❶ *his temper could affect his judgement* DISCERNMENT, acumen, shrewdness, astuteness, (common) sense, perception, perspicacity, percipience, acuity, discrimination, wisdom, wit, judiciousness, prudence, canniness, sharpness, sharp-wittedness, powers of reasoning, reason, logic; *informal* nous, savvy, horse sense, gumption; *Brit. informal* common; *N. Amer. informal* smarts. ❷ *a court judgement* VERDICT, decision, adjudication, ruling, pronouncement, decree, finding; sentence. ❸ *critical judgement* ASSESSMENT, evaluation, appraisal; review, analysis, criticism, critique. ❹ *a judgement on them for their wickedness* PUNISHMENT, retribution, penalty.
■ **against one's better judgement** RELUCTANTLY, unwillingly, grudgingly.
■ **in my judgement** IN MY OPINION, to my mind, to my way of thinking, I believe, I think, as I see it, in my estimation.

judgemental ▶ adjective CRITICAL, censorious, condemnatory, disapproving, disparaging, deprecating, negative, overcritical, hypercritical.

judicial ▶ adjective LEGAL, juridical, judicatory; official.

judicious ▶ adjective WISE, sensible, prudent, politic, shrewd, astute, canny, sagacious, commonsensical, sound, well advised, well judged, discerning, percipient, intelligent, smart; *N. Amer. informal* heads-up.
– OPPOSITES ill-advised.

jug ▶ noun PITCHER, ewer, crock, jar, urn; carafe, flask, flagon, decanter; *N. Amer.* creamer; *historical* amphora, jorum.

juggle ▶ verb MISREPRESENT, tamper with, falsify, distort, alter, manipulate, rig, massage, fudge; *informal* fix, doctor; *Brit. informal* fiddle.

juice ▶ noun ❶ *the juice from two lemons* LIQUID, fluid, sap; extract. ❷ *cooking juices* LIQUID, liquor. ❸ (*informal*) *he ran out of juice. See* PETROL.

juicy ▶ adjective ❶ *a juicy peach* SUCCULENT, tender, moist; ripe; *archaic* mellow. ❷ (*informal*) *juicy gossip* VERY INTERESTING, fascinating, sensational, lurid; scandalous, racy, risqué, spicy; *informal* hot. ❸ (*informal*) *juicy profits* LARGE, substantial, sizeable, generous; lucrative, profitable; *informal* fat, tidy.
– OPPOSITES dry, dull.

jumble ▶ noun ❶ *the books were in a jumble* UNTIDY HEAP, clutter, muddle, mess, confusion, disarray, disarrangement, tangle; hotchpotch, mishmash, miscellany, motley collection, mixed bag, medley, farrago; *N. Amer.* hodgepodge. ❷ (*Brit.*) *bags of jumble* JUNK, bric-a-brac; *Brit.* lumber.

▶ **verb** *the photographs are all jumbled up* MIX UP, muddle up, disarrange, disorganize, disorder, put in disarray.

jumbo ▶ **adjective** (*informal*). *See* HUGE.

jump ▶ **verb** ❶ *the cat jumped off his lap* | *Flora began to jump about* LEAP, spring, bound, hop; skip, caper, dance, prance, frolic, cavort. ❷ *he jumped the fence* VAULT (OVER), leap over, clear, sail over, hop over, hurdle. ❸ *pre-tax profits jumped* RISE, go up, shoot up, soar, surge, climb, increase; *informal* skyrocket. ❹ *the noise made her jump* START, jerk, jolt, flinch, recoil; *informal* jump out of one's skin. ❺ *Polly jumped at the chance* ACCEPT EAGERLY, leap at, welcome with open arms, seize on, snap up, grab, pounce on. ❻ (*informal*) *he jumped the red light* IGNORE, disregard, drive through, overshoot; *informal* run.

▶ **noun** ❶ *the short jump across the gully* LEAP, spring, vault, bound, hop. ❷ *the horse cleared the last jump* OBSTACLE, barrier; fence, hurdle. ❸ *a jump in profits* RISE, leap, increase, upsurge, upswing; *informal* hike. ❹ *I woke up with a jump* START, jerk, involuntary movement, spasm.

■ **jump the gun** (*informal*) ACT PREMATURELY, act too soon, be over-hasty, be precipitate; *informal* be ahead of oneself.

■ **jump to it** (*informal*) HURRY UP, get a move on, be quick; *informal* get cracking, shake a leg, look lively, look sharp, pull one's finger out; *Brit. informal* get one's skates on, stir one's stumps; *N. Amer. informal* get a wiggle on; *Austral./NZ informal* get a wriggle on; *dated* make haste.

jumper ▶ **noun** (*Brit.*) SWEATER, pullover, jersey; *informal* woolly.

jumpy ▶ **adjective** ❶ (*informal*) *he was tired and jumpy* NERVOUS, on edge, edgy, tense, anxious, ill at ease, uneasy, restless, fidgety, keyed up, overwrought, on tenterhooks; *Brit.* nervy; *informal* a bundle of nerves, jittery, like a cat on a hot tin roof, uptight, het up, in a tizz/tizzy; *Brit. informal* strung up, like a cat on hot bricks; *N. Amer. informal* spooky, squirrelly, antsy; *Austral./NZ informal* toey. ❷ *jumpy black-and-white footage* JERKY, jolting, lurching, bumpy, jarring; fitful, convulsive.

–OPPOSITES calm.

junction ▶ **noun** ❶ *the junction between the roof and the wall* JOIN, joint, intersection, bond, seam, connection, juncture; *Anatomy* commissure. ❷ *the junction of the two rivers* CONFLUENCE, convergence, meeting point, conflux, juncture. ❸ *turn right at the next junction* CROSSROADS, intersection, interchange, T-junction; turn, turn-off, exit; *Brit.* roundabout; *N. Amer.* turnout, cloverleaf.

juncture ▶ **noun** ❶ *at this juncture, I am unable to tell you* POINT (IN TIME), time, moment (in time); period, phase. ❷ *the juncture of the pipes. See* JUNCTION sense 1. ❸ *the juncture of the rivers. See* JUNCTION sense 2.

jungle ▶ **noun** ❶ *the Amazon jungle* TROPICAL FOREST, (tropical) rainforest. ❷ *a jungle of bureaucracy* COMPLEXITY, confusion, complication, chaos; labyrinth, maze, tangle, web.

junior ▶ **adjective** ❶ *the junior members of the family* YOUNGER, youngest. ❷ *a junior minister* LOW-RANKING, lower-ranking, subordinate, lesser, lower, minor, secondary. ❸ *John White Junior* THE YOUNGER; *Brit.* minor; *N. Amer.* II.

–OPPOSITES senior, older.

junk (*informal*) ▶ **noun** *an attic full of junk* RUBBISH, clutter, odds and ends, bits and pieces, bric-a-brac; refuse, litter, scrap, waste, debris, detritus, dross; *Brit.* lumber; *N. Amer.* garbage, trash; *Austral./NZ* mullock; *Brit. informal* odds and sods.

▶ **verb** *junk all the rubbish* THROW AWAY/OUT, discard, get rid of, dispose of, scrap, toss out, jettison; *informal* chuck (away/out), dump, ditch, bin, get shut of; *Brit. informal* get shot of.

junket ▶ **noun** (*informal*) CELEBRATION, party, jamboree, feast, festivity; spree, excursion, outing, trip, jaunt; *informal* bash, shindy, shindig; *Brit. informal* beanfeast, jolly, bunfight, beano; *Austral. informal* jollo.

junta ▶ **noun** FACTION, cabal, clique, party, set, ring, gang, league, confederacy; *historical* junto.

jurisdiction ▶ **noun** ❶ *an area under French jurisdiction* AUTHORITY, control, power, dominion, rule, administration, command, sway, leadership, sovereignty, hegemony. ❷ *foreign jurisdictions* TERRITORY, region, province, district, area, domain, realm.

just ▶ **adjective** ❶ *a just and democratic society* FAIR, fair-minded, equitable, even-handed, impartial, unbiased, objective, neutral, disinterested, unprejudiced, open-minded, nonpartisan; honourable, upright, decent, honest, righteous, moral, virtuous, principled. ❷ *a just reward* (WELL) DESERVED, (well) earned, merited; rightful, due, fitting, appropriate, suitable; *formal* condign; *archaic* meet. ❸ *just criticism* VALID, sound, well founded, justified, justifiable, warranted, legitimate.

–OPPOSITES unfair, undeserved, unfair.

▶ **adverb** ❶ *I just saw him* A MOMENT/SECOND AGO, a short time ago, very recently, not long ago. ❷ *she's just right for him* EXACTLY, precisely, absolutely, completely, totally, entirely, perfectly, utterly, wholly, thoroughly, in all respects; *informal* down to the ground, to a T, dead. ❸ *we just made it* NARROWLY, only just, by a hair's breadth; barely, scarcely, hardly; *informal* by the skin of one's teeth, by a whisker. ❹ *she's just a child* ONLY, merely, simply, (nothing) but, no more than. ❺ *the colour's just fantastic* REALLY, absolutely, completely, entirely, totally, quite; indeed, truly.

■ **just about** (*informal*) NEARLY, almost, practically, all but, virtually, as good as, more or less, to all intents and purposes; *informal* pretty much; *poetic/literary* well-nigh, nigh on.

justice ▶ **noun** ❶ *I appealed to his sense of justice* FAIRNESS, justness, fair play, fair-mindedness, equity, equitableness, even-handedness, impartiality, objectivity, neutrality, disinterestedness, honesty, righteousness, morals, morality. ❷ *the justice of his case* VALIDITY, justification, soundness, well-foundedness, legitimacy. ❸ *an order made by the justices* JUDGE, magistrate, recorder, sheriff; *N. Amer.* jurist; *Brit. informal* beak.

justifiable ▶ **adjective** VALID, legitimate, warranted, well founded, justified, just, reasonable; defensible, tenable, supportable, acceptable.
– OPPOSITES indefensible.

justification ▶ **noun** GROUNDS, reason, basis, rationale, premise, rationalization, vindication, explanation; defence, argument, apologia, apology, case.

justify ▶ **verb** ❶ *directors must justify the expenditure* GIVE GROUNDS FOR, give reasons for, give a justification for, explain, give an explanation for, account for; defend, answer for, vindicate. ❷ *the situation justified further investigation* WARRANT, be good reason for, be a justification for.

justly ▶ **adverb** ❶ *he is justly proud of his achievement* JUSTIFIABLY, with (good) reason, legitimately, rightly, rightfully, deservedly. ❷ *they were treated justly* FAIRLY, with fairness, equitably, even-handedly, impartially, without bias, objectively, without prejudice; *informal* fairly and squarely.
– OPPOSITES unjustifiably.

jut ▶ **verb** STICK OUT, project, protrude, bulge out, overhang, obtrude; *archaic* be imminent.

juvenile ▶ **adjective** ❶ *juvenile offenders* YOUNG, teenage, adolescent, junior, pubescent, prepubescent. ❷ *juvenile behaviour* CHILDISH, immature, puerile, infantile, babyish; jejune, inexperienced, callow, green, unsophisticated, naive, foolish, silly.
– OPPOSITES adult, mature.
▶ **noun** *many victims are juveniles* YOUNG PERSON, youngster, child, teenager, adolescent, minor, junior; *informal* kid.
– OPPOSITES adult.

juxtapose ▶ **verb** PLACE SIDE BY SIDE, set side by side, mix; compare, contrast.

Kk

kaleidoscopic ▶ **adjective** ❶ *kaleidoscopic shapes* MULTICOLOURED, many-coloured, multicolour, many-hued, variegated, particoloured, varicoloured, psychedelic, rainbow, polychromatic. ❷ *the kaleidoscopic political landscape* EVER-CHANGING, changeable, shifting, fluid, protean, variable, inconstant, fluctuating, unpredictable, impermanent. ❸ *the kaleidoscopic world we are living in* MULTIFACETED, varied; complex, intricate, complicated.
– OPPOSITES monochrome, constant.

kaput (*informal*) ▶ **adjective** *the TV's kaput* BROKEN, malfunctioning, broken-down, inoperative; *informal* conked out.
■ **go kaput** BREAK DOWN, go wrong, stop working; *informal* conk out.

keel ▶ **noun** *the upturned keel of the boat* BASE, bottom (side), underside.
■ **keel over** ❶ *the boat keeled over* CAPSIZE, turn turtle, turn upside down, founder; overturn, turn over, tip over. ❷ *the slightest activity made him keel over* COLLAPSE, faint, pass out, black out, lose consciousness, swoon.

keen[1] ▶ **adjective** ❶ *his publishers were keen to capitalize on his success* EAGER, anxious, intent, impatient, determined, ambitious; *informal* raring, itching, dying. ❷ *a keen birdwatcher* ENTHUSIASTIC, avid, eager, ardent, passionate, fervent, fervid, impassioned; conscientious, committed, dedicated, zealous. ❸ *they are keen on horses | a girl he was keen on* ENTHUSIASTIC, interested, passionate; attracted to, fond of, taken with, smitten with, enamoured of, infatuated with; *informal* struck on, gone on, mad about, crazy about, nuts about. ❹ *a keen cutting edge* SHARP, sharpened, honed, razor-sharp. ❺ *keen eyesight* ACUTE, sharp, discerning, sensitive, perceptive, clear. ❻ *a keen mind* ACUTE, penetrating, astute, incisive, sharp, perceptive, piercing, razor-sharp, perspicacious, shrewd, discerning, clever, intelligent, brilliant, bright, smart, wise, canny, percipient, insightful. ❼ *a keen wind* COLD, icy, freezing, harsh, raw, bitter; penetrating, piercing, biting. ❽ *a keen sense of duty* INTENSE, acute, fierce, passionate, burning, fervent, ardent, strong, powerful.
– OPPOSITES reluctant, unenthusiastic.

keen[2] ▶ **verb** *the bereaved gathered to keen* LAMENT, mourn, weep, cry, sorrow, grieve; wail, ululate; *archaic* plain.

keenness ▶ **noun** ❶ *the company's keenness to sign a deal* EAGERNESS, willingness, readiness, impatience; enthusiasm, fervour, wholeheartedness, zest, zeal, ardour, passion, avidity. ❷ *the keenness of the blade* SHARPNESS, razor-sharpness. ❸ *keenness of hearing* ACUTENESS, sharpness, sensitivity, perceptiveness, clarity. ❹ *the keenness of his mind* ACUITY, sharpness, incisiveness, astuteness, perspicacity, perceptiveness, shrewdness, insight, cleverness, discernment, intelligence, brightness, brilliance, canniness. ❺ *the keenness of his sense of loss* INTENSITY, acuteness, strength, power, ferocity.

keep[1] ▶ **verb** ❶ *you should keep all the old forms* RETAIN (POSSESSION OF), hold on to, keep hold of, not part with; save, store, put by/aside, set aside; *N. Amer.* set by; *informal* hang on to, stash away. ❷ *I tried to keep calm* REMAIN, continue to be, stay, carry on being, persist in being. ❸ *he keeps going on about the murder* PERSIST IN, keep on, carry on, continue, do something constantly. ❹ *I shan't keep you long* DETAIN, keep waiting, delay, hold up, retard, slow down. ❺ *most people kept the rules | he had to keep his promise* COMPLY WITH, obey, observe, conform to, abide by, adhere to, stick to, heed, follow; fulfil, carry out, act on, make good, honour, keep to, stand by. ❻ *keeping the old traditions* PRESERVE, keep alive/up, keep going, carry on, perpetuate, maintain, uphold, sustain. ❼ *the stand where her umbrella was kept* STORE, house, stow, put (away), place, deposit. ❽ *the shop keeps a good stock of parchment* (HAVE IN) STOCK, carry, have (for sale), hold. ❾ *he stole to keep his family* PROVIDE (FOOD) FOR, support, feed, keep alive, maintain, sustain; take care of, look after. ❿ *she keeps rabbits* BREED, rear, raise, farm; own, have as a pet. ⓫ *his parents kept a shop* MANAGE, run, own, be the proprietor of. ⓬ *God keep you* LOOK AFTER, care for, take care of, mind, watch over; protect, keep safe, preserve, defend, guard. ⓭ *today people do not keep the Sabbath* OBSERVE, respect, honour, hold sacred; celebrate, mark, commemorate.
– OPPOSITES throw away, break, abandon.
▶ **noun** *money to pay for his keep* MAINTENANCE, upkeep, sustenance, board (and lodging), food, livelihood.
■ **for keeps** (*informal*) FOREVER, for ever and ever, for evermore, for always, for good (and all), permanently, in perpetuity; *informal* until kingdom come, until doomsday; *archaic* for aye.
■ **keep at** PERSEVERE WITH, persist with, keep going with, carry on with, press on with, work away at, continue with; *informal* stick at, peg away at, plug away at, hammer away at.
■ **keep something back** ❶ *she kept back some of the money* (KEEP IN) RESERVE, put by/aside, set aside; retain, hold back, keep, hold on to, not part with; *N. Amer.* set by; *informal* stash away. ❷ *she kept back the details* CONCEAL, keep secret, keep hidden, withhold, suppress, keep quiet about. ❸ *she could hardly keep back her tears* SUPPRESS, stifle, choke back, fight back, hold back/in, repress, keep in check, contain, smother, swallow, bite back.
■ **keep from** REFRAIN FROM, stop oneself, restrain oneself from, prevent oneself from, forbear from, avoid.
■ **keep someone from something** ❶ *he could hardly keep himself from laughing* PREVENT, stop, restrain, hold back. ❷ *keep them from harm* PRESERVE, protect, keep safe, guard, shield, shelter, safeguard, defend.
■ **keep something from someone** KEEP SECRET, keep hidden, hide, conceal, withhold; *informal* keep dark.
■ **keep off** ❶ *keep off private land* STAY OFF, not enter, keep/stay away from, not trespass on. ❷ *Maud tried to keep off political subjects* AVOID, steer clear of, stay away from, evade, sidestep; *informal* duck. ❸ *you should keep off alcohol* ABSTAIN FROM, do without, refrain from, give up, forgo, not touch; *informal* swear off; *formal* forswear. ❹ *I hope the rain keeps off* STAY AWAY, hold off, not start, not begin.
■ **keep on** ❶ *they kept on working* CONTINUE, go on, carry on, persist in, persevere in; soldier on, struggle on, keep going. ❷ *the commander kept on about vigilance* TALK CONSTANTLY, talk endlessly, keep talking, go on (and on), rant on; *informal* harp on, witter on, rabbit on.
■ **keep someone on** CONTINUE TO EMPLOY, retain in one's service, not dismiss, not sack.
■ **keep on at** NAG, go on at, harp on at, badger, chivvy, harass, hound, pester; *informal* hassle.
■ **keep to** ❶ *I've got to keep to the rules* OBEY, abide by, observe, follow, comply with, adhere to, respect, keep, stick to, be bound by. ❷ *keep to the path* FOLLOW, stick to, stay on. ❸ *please keep to the point* STICK TO, restrict oneself to, confine oneself to.
■ **keep someone under** KEEP IN SUBJECTION, hold down, keep down, subdue, suppress, repress, oppress; *informal* squash, trample on.
■ **keep something up** CONTINUE (WITH), keep on with, keep going, carry on with, persist with, persevere with.
■ **keep up with** ❶ *she walked fast to keep up with him* KEEP PACE WITH, keep abreast of; match, equal. ❷ *he kept up with events at home* KEEP INFORMED ABOUT, keep up to date with, keep abreast of; *informal* keep tabs on. ❸ *they kept up with him by Christmas cards* REMAIN IN CONTACT WITH, stay in touch with, maintain contact with, keep up one's friendship with.

keep[2] ▶ **noun** *the enemy stormed the keep* FORTRESS, fort, stronghold, tower, donjon, castle, citadel, bastion.

keeper ▶ **noun** ❶ *keeper of the archives* CURATOR,

custodian, guardian, administrator, overseer, steward, caretaker. ❷ *the keeper of an inn* PROPRIETOR, owner, master/mistress, landlord/landlady. ❸ *you're not her keeper* GUARDIAN, protector, guard, minder, chaperon/chaperone; carer, nursemaid, nurse.

keeping ▶ noun *the document is in the keeping of the county archivist* SAFE KEEPING, care, custody, charge, possession, trust, protection.

■ **in keeping with** CONSISTENT WITH, in harmony with, in accord with, in agreement with, in line with, in character with, compatible with; appropriate to, befitting, suitable for.

keepsake ▶ noun MEMENTO, souvenir, reminder, remembrance, token.

keg ▶ noun BARREL, cask, vat, butt, tun, hogshead; *historical* firkin.

ken ▶ noun KNOWLEDGE, awareness, perception, understanding, grasp, comprehension, realization, appreciation, consciousness.

kernel ▶ noun ❶ *the kernel of a nut* seed, grain, core; nut. ❷ *the kernel of the argument* ESSENCE, core, heart, essentials, quintessence, fundamentals, basics, nub, gist, substance; *informal* nitty-gritty. ❸ *a kernel of truth* NUCLEUS, germ, grain, nugget.

key ▶ noun ❶ *I put my key in the lock* door key, latchkey, pass key, master key. ❷ *the key to the mystery* | *the key to success* ANSWER, clue, solution, explanation; basis, foundation, requisite, precondition, means, way, route, path, passport, secret, formula. ❸ (*Music*) *a minor key* TONE, pitch, timbre, tone colour. ❹ *an austerely intellectual key* STYLE, character, mood, vein, spirit, feel, feeling, flavour, quality, atmosphere.

▶ adjective *a key figure* CRUCIAL, central, essential, indispensable, pivotal, critical, dominant, vital, principal, prime, chief, major, leading, main, important, significant.

– OPPOSITES peripheral.

keynote ▶ noun THEME, salient point, gist, substance, burden, tenor, pith, marrow, essence, heart, core, basis, essential feature/element.

keystone ▶ noun ❶ *the keystone of the door* CORNERSTONE, central stone, quoin. ❷ *the keystone of the government's policy* FOUNDATION, basis, linchpin, cornerstone, base, (guiding) principle, core, heart, centre, crux, fundament.

kibosh

■ **put the kibosh on** (*informal*) PUT A STOP TO, stop, halt, put an end to, quash, block, cancel, scotch, thwart, prevent, suppress; *informal* put paid to, stymie; *Brit. informal* scupper.

kick ▶ verb ❶ *her attacker kicked her* BOOT, strike with the foot; *Brit. informal* put the boot into. ❷ (*informal*) *he was struggling to kick his drug habit* GIVE UP, break, abandon, end, stop, cease, desist from, renounce; *informal* shake, pack in, leave off, quit. ❸ *the gun kicked hard* RECOIL, spring back.

▶ noun ❶ *a kick on the knee* BLOW WITH THE FOOT; *informal* boot. ❷ (*informal*) *I get a kick out of driving a racing car* THRILL, excitement, stimulation, tingle; fun, enjoyment, amusement, pleasure, gratification; *informal* buzz, high; *N. Amer. informal* charge. ❸ (*informal*) *a drink with a powerful kick* POTENCY, stimulant effect, strength, power; tang, zest, bite, piquancy, edge, pungency; *informal* punch. ❹ (*informal*) *a health kick* CRAZE, enthusiasm, obsession, mania, passion; fashion, vogue, trend; *informal* fad.

■ **kick against** RESIST, rebel against, oppose, struggle/fight against; defy, disobey, reject, spurn.

■ **kick someone/something around** (*informal*) ❶ *we are undervalued and get kicked around* ABUSE, mistreat, maltreat, push around/about, trample on, take for granted; *informal* boss about/around, walk all over. ❷ *they began to kick ideas around* DISCUSS, talk over, debate, thrash out, consider, toy with, play with.

■ **kick back** (*N. Amer. informal*) RELAX, unwind, take it easy, rest, slow down, let up, ease up/off, sit back; *N. Amer. informal* chill out, hang loose.

■ **kick off** (*informal*) START, commence, begin, get going, get off the ground, get under way; open, start off, set in motion, launch, initiate, introduce, inaugurate, usher in.

■ **kick someone out** (*informal*) EXPEL, eject, throw out, oust, evict, get rid of, axe; dismiss, discharge; *informal* chuck out, send packing, boot out, give someone their marching orders, sack, fire; *Brit. informal* turf out; *N. Amer. informal* give someone the bum's rush.

kickback ▶ noun ❶ *the kickback from the gun* RECOIL, kick, rebound. ❷ (*informal*) *they paid kickbacks to politicians* BRIBE, payment, inducement; *N. Amer.* payola; *informal* pay-off, sweetener, backhander.

kick-off ▶ noun (*informal*) BEGINNING, start, commencement, outset, opening.

kid[1] ▶ noun (*informal*) *she has three kids* CHILD, youngster, little one, baby, toddler, tot, infant, boy/girl, young person, minor, juvenile, adolescent, teenager, youth, stripling; offspring, son/daughter; *Scottish* bairn; *informal* kiddie, nipper, kiddiewink, shaver, young 'un; *Brit. informal* sprog; *N. Amer. informal* rug rat; *Austral./NZ* ankle-biter; *derogatory* brat; *poetic/literary* babe.

kid[2] ▶ verb (*informal*) ❶ *I'm not kidding* JOKE, tease, jest, chaff, be facetious, fool about/around; *informal* pull someone's leg, have on, rib; *Brit. informal* wind up; *N. Amer. informal* pull someone's chain, fun, shuck. ❷ *why did I kid myself that I'd succeed?* DELUDE, deceive, fool, trick, hoodwink, hoax, beguile, dupe, gull; *informal* con, pull the wool over someone's eyes; *poetic/literary* cozen.

kidnap ▶ verb ABDUCT, carry off, capture, seize, snatch, take as hostage; *Brit. informal* nobble.

kill ▶ verb ❶ *gangs killed twenty-seven people* MURDER, take/end the life of, make away with, assassinate, eliminate, terminate, dispatch, finish off, put to death, execute; slaughter, butcher, massacre, wipe out, annihilate, exterminate, liquidate, mow down, shoot down, cut down, cut to pieces; *informal* bump off, polish off, do away with, do in, knock off, top, take out, croak, stiff, blow away, dispose of; *N. Amer. informal* ice, rub out, waste, whack, scrag, smoke; *poetic/literary* slay. ❷ *this would kill all hopes of progress* DESTROY, put an end to, end, extinguish, dash, quash, ruin, wreck, shatter, smash, crush, scotch, thwart; *informal* put paid to, put the kibosh on, stymie; *Brit. informal* scupper. ❸ *we had to kill several hours at the airport* WHILE AWAY, fill (up), occupy, beguile, pass, spend, waste. ❹ (*informal*) *you must rest or you'll kill yourself* EXHAUST, wear out, tire out, overtax, overtire, fatigue, weary, sap, drain, enervate, prostrate; *informal* knock out, shatter; *Brit. informal* knacker. ❺ (*informal*) *my feet were killing me* HURT, cause pain to, torture, torment, cause discomfort to; be painful, be sore, be uncomfortable. ❻ (*informal*) *the music kills me every time I hear it* OVERWHELM, take someone's breath away, move, stir, stun, amaze, stagger; *informal* bowl over, blow away, knock sideways, blow someone's mind. ❼ *the engines were at a low rev to kill the noise* MUFFLE, deaden, stifle, dampen, damp down, smother, reduce, diminish, decrease, suppress, tone down, moderate. ❽ *a shot to kill the pain* ALLEVIATE, assuage, soothe, allay, dull, blunt, deaden, stifle, suppress, subdue. ❾ (*informal*) *the message has been killed* DELETE, wipe out, erase, remove, destroy, cut (out), cancel; *informal* zap. ❿ (*informal*) *Congress killed the bill* VETO, defeat, vote down, rule against, reject, throw out, overrule, overturn, put a stop to, quash, squash. ⓫ (*informal*) *Noel killed the engine* TURN OFF, switch off, stop, shut off/down, cut (out).

– RELATED TERMS -cide.

▶ **noun** ❶ *the hunter's kill* PREY, quarry, victim, bag. ❷ *the wolf was moving in for the kill* DEATH BLOW, killing, dispatch, finish, end, coup de grâce.

killer ▶ **noun** ❶ *police are searching for the killer* MURDERER, assassin, slaughterer, butcher, serial killer, gunman; exterminator, terminator, executioner; *informal* hit man; *poetic/literary* slayer; *dated* homicide. ❷ *a major killer* CAUSE OF DEATH, fatal/deadly illness, threat to life.

killing ▶ **noun** *a brutal killing* MURDER, assassination, homicide, manslaughter, elimination, putting/doing to death, execution; slaughter, massacre, butchery, carnage, bloodshed, extermination, annihilation; *poetic/literary* slaying.

▶ **adjective** ❶ *a killing blow* DEADLY, lethal, fatal, mortal, death-dealing; murderous, homicidal; *poetic/literary* deathly. ❷ (*informal*) *a killing schedule* EXHAUSTING, gruelling, punishing, taxing, draining, wearing, prostrating, crushing, tiring, fatiguing, debilitating, enervating, arduous, tough, demanding, onerous, strenuous, rigorous; *informal* murderous; *Brit. informal* knackering. ❸ (*informal*) *the suspense is killing* UNBEARABLE, intolerable, unendurable, insupportable. ❹ (*informal, dated*) *that's absolutely killing* HILARIOUS, hysterically funny, uproarious, riotous, comical, amusing; *informal* priceless, side-splitting.

■ **make a killing** (*informal*) MAKE A LARGE PROFIT, make a/one's fortune, make money; *informal* clean up, make a packet, make a pretty penny; *Brit. informal* make a bomb; *N. Amer. informal* make big bucks.

killjoy ▶ **noun** SPOILSPORT, prophet of doom; *informal* wet blanket, party-pooper, misery; *Austral./NZ informal* wowser.

kilter

■ **out of kilter** AWRY, off balance, unbalanced, out of order, disordered, confused, muddled, out of tune, out of step.

kin ▶ **noun** *their own kin* RELATIVES, relations, family (members), kindred, kith and kin; kinsfolk, kinsmen, kinswomen, people; *informal* folks.

▶ **adjective** *my uncle was kin to the brothers* RELATED, akin, allied, connected with, consanguineous; *formal* cognate.

kind[1] ▶ **noun** ❶ *all kinds of gifts | the kinds of bird that could be seen* SORT, type, variety, style, form, class, category, genre; genus, species, race, breed. ❷ *they were different in kind | the first of its kind* CHARACTER, nature, essence, quality, disposition, make-up; type, style, stamp, manner, description, mould, cast, temperament, ilk; *N. Amer.* stripe.

■ **kind of** (*informal*) RATHER, quite, fairly, somewhat, a little, slightly, a shade; *informal* sort of, a bit, kinda, pretty, a touch, a tad.

kind[2] ▶ **adjective** *she is such a kind and caring person* KINDLY, good-natured, kind-hearted, warm-hearted, caring, affectionate, loving, warm; considerate, helpful, thoughtful, obliging, unselfish, selfless, altruistic, good, attentive; compassionate, sympathetic, understanding, big-hearted, benevolent, benign, friendly, neighbourly, hospitable, well meaning, public-spirited; generous, liberal, open-handed, bountiful, beneficent, munificent, benignant; *Brit. informal* decent.

– OPPOSITES inconsiderate, mean.

kind-hearted ▶ **adjective** KIND, caring, warm-hearted, kindly, benevolent, good-natured, tender, warm, compassionate, sympathetic, understanding; indulgent, altruistic, benign, beneficent, benignant.

kindle ▶ **verb** ❶ *he kindled a fire* LIGHT, ignite, set alight, set light to, set fire to, put a match to. ❷ *Elvis kindled my interest in music* ROUSE, arouse, wake, awaken; stimulate, inspire, stir (up), excite, evoke, provoke, fire, inflame, trigger, activate, spark off; *poetic/literary* waken, enkindle.

– OPPOSITES extinguish.

kindliness ▶**noun** KINDNESS, benevolence, warmth, gentleness, tenderness, care, humanity, sympathy, compassion, understanding; generosity, charity, kind-heartedness, warm-heartedness, thoughtfulness, solicitousness.

kindly ▶**adjective** *a kindly old lady* BENEVOLENT, kind, kind-hearted, warm-hearted, generous, good-natured; gentle, warm, compassionate, caring, loving, benign, well meaning; helpful, thoughtful, considerate, good-hearted, nice, friendly, neighbourly; *Brit. informal* decent.
– OPPOSITES unkind, cruel.
▶**adverb** ❶ *she spoke kindly* BENEVOLENTLY, good-naturedly, warmly, affectionately, tenderly, lovingly, compassionately; considerately, thoughtfully, helpfully, obligingly, generously, selflessly, unselfishly, sympathetically. ❷ *kindly explain what you mean* PLEASE, if you please, if you wouldn't mind, have the goodness to; *archaic* prithee, pray.
– OPPOSITES unkindly, harshly.
■ **not take kindly to** RESENT, object to, take umbrage at, take exception to, take offence at, be annoyed by, be irritated by, feel aggrieved about, be upset by.

kindness ▶**noun** ❶ *he thanked her for her kindness* KINDLINESS, kind-heartedness, warm-heartedness, affection, warmth, gentleness, concern, care; consideration, considerateness, helpfulness, thoughtfulness, unselfishness, selflessness, altruism, compassion, sympathy, understanding, big-heartedness, benevolence benignity, friendliness, neighbourliness, hospitality, public-spiritedness; generosity, magnanimity, charitableness; *Brit. informal* decency. ❷ *she has done us many a kindness* KIND ACT, good deed, good turn, favour, service.

kindred ▶**noun** ❶ *his mother's kindred* FAMILY, relatives, relations, kin, kith and kin, one's own flesh and blood; kinsfolk, kinsmen/kinswomen, people; *informal* folks. ❷ *ties of kindred* KINSHIP, family ties, being related, (blood) relationship, consanguinity, common ancestry.
▶**adjective** ❶ *industrial relations and kindred subjects* RELATED, allied, connected, comparable, similar, like, parallel, associated, analogous; *formal* cognate. ❷ *a kindred spirit* LIKE-MINDED, in sympathy, in harmony, in tune, of one mind, akin, similar, like, compatible; *informal* on the same wavelength.
– OPPOSITES unrelated, alien.

king ▶**noun** ❶ *the king of France* RULER, sovereign, monarch, crowned head, Crown, emperor, prince, potentate, lord. ❷ (*informal*) *the king of world football* STAR, leading light, luminary, superstar, giant, master; *informal* supremo, megastar.
■ **a king's ransom** A HUGE AMOUNT, a vast sum; *informal* a (small) fortune, a mint, a packet, a pretty penny, big money; *Brit. informal* a bomb; *N. Amer. informal* big bucks; *Austral. informal* big bickies.

kingdom ▶**noun** ❶ *his kingdom stretched to the sea* REALM, domain, dominion, country, empire, land, nation, (sovereign) state, province, territory. ❷ *Henry's little kingdom* DOMAIN, province, realm, sphere, dominion, territory, arena, zone. ❸ *the plant kingdom* DIVISION, category, classification, grouping, group.

kingly ▶**adjective** ❶ *kingly power* ROYAL, regal, monarchical, sovereign, imperial, princely. ❷ *kingly robes* REGAL, majestic, stately, noble, lordly, dignified, distinguished, courtly; splendid, magnificent, grand, glorious, rich, gorgeous, resplendent, princely, superb, sumptuous; *informal* splendiferous.

kink ▶**noun** ❶ *your fishing line should have no kinks in it* CURL, twist, twirl, loop, crinkle; knot, tangle, entanglement. ❷ *a kink in the road* BEND, corner, dog-leg, twist, turn, curve; *Brit.* hairpin bend. ❸ *there are still some kinks to iron out* FLAW, defect, imperfection, problem, complication, hitch, snag, shortcoming, weakness; *informal* hiccup, glitch. ❹ *their sartorial kinks* PECULIARITY, quirk, idiosyncrasy, eccentricity, oddity, foible, whim, caprice.

kinky ▶**adjective** ❶ (*informal*) *a kinky relationship* PERVERTED, abnormal, deviant, unnatural, depraved, degenerate, perverse; *informal* pervy. ❷ (*informal*) *kinky underwear* PROVOCATIVE, sexy, sexually arousing, erotic, titillating, naughty, indecent, immodest; *Brit. informal* saucy. ❸ *Catriona's long kinky hair* CURLY, crimped, curled, curling, frizzy, frizzed, wavy.

kinsfolk ▶**noun** RELATIVES, relations, kin, kindred, family, kith and kin, kinsmen/kinswomen, people; *informal* folks.

kinship ▶**noun** ❶ *ties of kinship* RELATIONSHIP, being related, family ties, blood ties, common ancestry, kindred, consanguinity. ❷ *she felt kinship with the others* AFFINITY, sympathy, rapport, harmony, understanding, empathy, closeness, fellow feeling, bond, compatibility; similarity, likeness, correspondence, concordance.

kinsman, kinswoman ▶**noun** RELATIVE, relation, family member; cousin, uncle, aunt, nephew, niece.

kiosk ▶**noun** BOOTH, stand, stall, counter, news-stand.

kismet ▶**noun** FATE, destiny, fortune, providence, God's will, one's lot (in life), karma, predestination, preordination, predetermination; luck, chance; *poetic/literary* one's dole.

kiss ▶**verb** ❶ *he kissed her on the lips* give a kiss to, brush one's lips against, blow a kiss to, air-kiss; *informal* peck, give a smacker to, smooch, canoodle, neck, pet; *Brit. informal* snog; *N. Amer. informal* buss; *informal, dated* spoon; *formal* osculate. ❷ *allow your foot just to kiss the floor* BRUSH

(AGAINST), caress, touch (gently), stroke, skim over.

▶ **noun** ❶ *a kiss on the cheek* air kiss, French kiss; X; *informal* peck, smack, smacker, smooch; *Brit. informal* snog; *N. Amer. informal* buss; *formal* osculation. ❷ *the kiss of the flowers against her cheeks* GENTLE TOUCH, caress, brush, stroke.

kit ▶ **noun** ❶ *his tool kit* EQUIPMENT, tools, implements, instruments, gadgets, utensils, appliances, tools of the trade, gear, tackle, hardware, paraphernalia; *informal* things, stuff, the necessary; *Military* accoutrements. ❷ (*Brit. informal*) *their football kit* CLOTHES, clothing, rig, outfit, dress, costume, garments, attire, garb, gear, get-up, rig-out; *formal* apparel. ❸ *a model aircraft kit* SET (OF PARTS), DIY kit, do-it-yourself kit, self-assembly set, flat-pack. ❹ (*informal*) *we packed up all our kit* BELONGINGS, luggage, baggage, paraphernalia, effects, impedimenta; *informal* things, stuff, gear; *Brit. informal* clobber.

■ **kit someone/something out** EQUIP, fit (out/up), furnish, supply, provide, issue; dress, clothe, array, attire, rig out, deck out; *informal* fix up.

kitchen ▶ **noun** kitchenette, kitchen-diner, cooking area, galley, cookhouse; *N. Amer.* cookery.

kittenish ▶ **adjective** PLAYFUL, light-hearted, skittish, lively; coquettish, flirtatious, frivolous, flippant, superficial, trivial, shallow, silly; *informal* flirty, dizzy; *poetic/literary* frolicsome.

– OPPOSITES serious.

knack ▶ **noun** ❶ *a knack for making money | it takes practice to acquire the knack* GIFT, talent, flair, genius, instinct, faculty, ability, capability, capacity, aptitude, aptness, bent, forte, facility; TECHNIQUE, method, trick, skill, art, expertise; *informal* the hang of something. ❷ *he has a knack of getting injured at the wrong time* TENDENCY, propensity, habit, proneness, liability, predisposition.

knackered ▶ **adjective** (*Brit. informal*) ❶ *you look absolutely knackered. See* EXHAUSTED sense 1. ❷ *the computer was knackered. See* BROKEN sense 3.

knapsack ▶ **noun** RUCKSACK, backpack, haversack, pack, kitbag.

knave ▶ **noun** (*archaic*). *See* SCOUNDREL.

knavery ▶ **noun** (*archaic*). *See* VILLAINY.

knavish ▶ **adjective** (*archaic*). *See* ROGUISH sense 1.

knead ▶ **verb** ❶ *kneading the dough* PUMMEL, work, pound, squeeze, shape, mould. ❷ *she kneaded the base of his neck* MASSAGE, press, manipulate, rub.

kneel ▶ **verb** FALL TO ONE'S KNEES, get down on one's knees, genuflect; *historical* kowtow.

knell ▶ **noun** (*poetic/literary*) ❶ *the knell of the ship's bell* TOLL, tolling, dong, resounding, reverberation; death knell; *archaic* tocsin. ❷ *this sounded the knell for the project* (BEGINNING OF THE) END, death knell, death warrant.

knickers ▶ **plural noun** (*Brit.*) UNDERPANTS, briefs, French knickers, camiknickers; underwear, lingerie, underclothes, undergarments; *Brit.* pants; *informal* panties, undies; *Brit. informal* knicks, smalls; *dated* drawers; *historical* bloomers, pantalettes.

knick-knack ▶ **noun** ORNAMENT, novelty, gewgaw, bibelot, trinket, trifle, bauble, gimcrack, curio; memento, souvenir; *N. Amer.* kickshaw; *N. Amer. informal* tchotchke; *archaic* gaud, whim-wham, bijou.

knife ▶ **noun** *a sharp knife* CUTTING TOOL, blade, cutter, carver.

▶ **verb** *the victims had been knifed* STAB, hack, gash, run through, slash, lacerate, cut, pierce, spike, impale, transfix, bayonet, spear.

knight ▶ **noun** *knights in armour* CAVALIER, cavalryman, horseman; lord, noble, nobleman; *historical* chevalier, paladin, banneret.

■ **knight in shining armour** KNIGHT ON A WHITE CHARGER, rescuer, saviour, champion, hero, defender, protector, guardian (angel).

knightly ▶ **adjective** ❶ *tales of knightly deeds* GALLANT, noble, valiant, heroic, courageous, brave, bold, valorous; chivalrous, courteous, honourable. ❷ *the knightly classes* UPPER-CLASS, well born, noble, aristocratic; *archaic* gentle.

– OPPOSITES ignoble, low-born.

knit ▶ **verb** ❶ *disparate regions began to knit together* UNITE, unify, come together, draw together, become closer, bond, fuse, coalesce, merge, meld, blend. ❷ *we expect broken bones to knit* HEAL, mend, join, fuse. ❸ *Marcus knitted his brows* FURROW, tighten, contract, gather, wrinkle.

▶ **noun** *silky knits in pretty shades* KNITTED GARMENT, woollen; sweater, pullover, jersey, cardigan; *Brit.* jumper; *informal* woolly; *Brit. informal* cardy.

knob ▶ **noun** ❶ *a black bill with a knob at the base* LUMP, bump, protuberance, protrusion, bulge, swelling, knot, node, nodule, ball; *informal* boss. ❷ *the knobs on the radio* DIAL, button. ❸ *she turned the knob on the door* DOORKNOB, (door) handle. ❹ *a few knobs of butter* NUGGET, lump, pat, ball, dollop, piece; *N. Amer. informal* gob.

knock ▶ **verb** ❶ *he knocked on the door* BANG, tap, rap, thump, pound, hammer; strike, hit, beat. ❷ *she knocked her knee on the table* BUMP, bang, hit, strike, crack; injure, hurt, bruise; *informal* bash, thwack. ❸ *he knocked into an elderly man* COLLIDE WITH, bump into, bang into, be in collision with, run into, crash into, smash into, plough into; *N. Amer.* impact; *informal* bash into. ❹ (*informal*) *I'm not knocking the company. See* CRITICIZE.

▶ **noun** ❶ *a sharp knock at the door* TAP, rap, rat-tat, knocking, bang, banging, pounding, hammering, drumming, thump, thud. ❷ *the casing is tough enough to withstand knocks* BUMP, blow, bang, jolt, jar, shock; collision, crash, smash, impact. ❸ *a knock on the ear* BLOW, bang, hit, slap, smack, crack, punch, cuff, thump, box; *informal* clip, clout, wallop, thwack, belt, bash. ❹ (*informal*) *this isn't a knock on Dave. See* CRITICISM sense 1. ❺ *life's hard knocks* SETBACK, reversal, defeat, failure, difficulty, misfortune, bad luck, mishap, (body) blow, disaster, calamity, disappointment, sorrow, trouble, hardship; *informal* kick in the teeth.

■ **knock about/around** (*informal*) ❶ *knocking around the Mediterranean* WANDER AROUND, roam around, rove around, range over, travel around, journey around, voyage around, drift around, gallivant around, potter around; *informal* gad about. ❷ *she knocks around with artists* ASSOCIATE, consort, keep company, go around, mix, socialize, be friends, be friendly; *informal* hobnob, hang out, run around, pal around.

■ **knock someone/something about/around** BEAT (UP), batter, hit, punch, thump, thrash, slap; maltreat, mistreat, abuse, ill-treat, assault, attack; *N. Amer.* beat up on; *informal* rough up, do over, give someone a hiding, clobber, clout, bash, belt, whack, wallop.

■ **knock something back** (*informal*) SWALLOW, gulp down, drink up, quaff, guzzle, slug; *informal* down, swig, swill (down), toss off; *N. Amer. informal* scarf (down/up), snarf (down/up).

■ **knock someone down** FELL, floor, flatten, bring down, knock to the ground; knock over, run over/down.

■ **knock something down** ❶ *the building was knocked down* DEMOLISH, pull down, tear down, destroy; raze (to the ground), level, flatten, bulldoze. ❷ (*informal*) *the firm has knocked down its prices* REDUCE, lower, cut, decrease, drop, put down, mark down; *informal* slash.

■ **knock off** (*informal*) STOP WORK, finish (working), clock off, leave work.

■ **knock someone off** (*informal*). *See* KILL verb sense 1.

■ **knock something off** ❶ (*Brit. informal*) *someone knocked off the video. See* STEAL verb sense 1. ❷ (*informal*) *we expect you to knock off three stories a day* PRODUCE, make, turn out, create, construct, assemble, put together; complete, finish. ❸ (*informal*) *knock off 10% from the bill* DEDUCT, take off/away, subtract, dock.

■ **knock it off!** (*informal*) STOP IT; *informal* cut it out, give it a rest, leave off, pack it in, lay off; *Brit. informal* give over.

■ **knock someone out** ❶ *I hit him and knocked him out* KNOCK UNCONSCIOUS, knock senseless; floor, prostrate; *informal* lay out, put out cold, KO, kayo. ❷ *England was knocked out* ELIMINATE, beat, defeat, vanquish, overwhelm, trounce. ❸ (*informal*) *walking that far knocked her out* EXHAUST, wear out, tire (out), overtire, fatigue, weary, drain; *informal* do in, take it out of, fag out; *Brit. informal* knacker; *N. Amer. informal* poop. ❹ (*informal*) *the view knocked me out* OVERWHELM, stun, stupefy, amaze, astound, astonish, stagger, take someone's breath away; impress, dazzle, enchant, entrance; *informal* bowl over, flabbergast, knock sideways, blow away; *Brit. informal* knock for six.

■ **knock up** (*Brit. informal*) WARM UP, practise, hit a ball around.

■ **knock someone up** ❶ (*Brit. informal*) *we were knocked up at five in the morning* WAKE (UP), awaken, call, rouse, arouse, get out of bed, get up; *poetic/literary* waken. ❷ (*informal*) *he knocked her up* MAKE PREGNANT, impregnate; *informal* put in the family way; *Brit. informal* get in the club; *archaic* get with child.

■ **knock something up** (*Brit. informal*) MAKE QUICKLY, prepare hastily, build rapidly, whip up, rig up, throw together, cobble together, improvise, contrive; *informal* rustle up.

knockout ▶ **noun** ❶ *the match was won by a knockout* STUNNING BLOW, finishing blow, coup de grâce; *informal* KO, kayo. ❷ (*informal*) *she's a knockout!* BEAUTY, vision, picture, sensation, dream; *informal* stunner, dish, looker, good-looker, peach, cracker; *Brit. informal* smasher. ❸ (*informal*) *a technical knockout* MASTERPIECE, sensation, marvel, wonder, triumph, success, feat, coup, master stroke, tour de force.

knoll ▶ **noun** *she walked up the grassy knoll* HILLOCK, mound, rise, hummock, hill, hump, tor, bank, ridge, elevation; *Scottish* brae; *formal* eminence.

knot ▶ **noun** ❶ *tie a small knot* TIE, twist, loop, join, fastening, bond; tangle, entanglement. ❷ *a knot in the wood* NODULE, gnarl, node; lump, knob, swelling, gall, protuberance, bump; *archaic* knar. ❸ *a small knot of people* CLUSTER, group, band, huddle, bunch, circle, ring, gathering, company, crowd, throng.

▶ **verb** *their scarves were knotted round their throats* TIE (UP), fasten, secure, bind, do up.

knotted ▶ **adjective** TANGLED, tangly, knotty, entangled, matted, snarled, unkempt, uncombed, tousled; *informal* mussed up.

knotty ▶ **adjective** ❶ *a knotty legal problem* COMPLEX, complicated, involved, intricate, convoluted, involuted; difficult, hard, thorny, taxing, awkward, tricky, problematic, troublesome. ❷ *knotty roots* GNARLED, knotted, knurled, nodular, knobbly, lumpy, bumpy. ❸ *a knotty piece of thread* KNOTTED, tangled, tangly, twisted, entangled, snarled, matted.

–OPPOSITES straightforward.

know ▶ **verb** ❶ *she doesn't know I'm here* BE AWARE, realize, be conscious, be informed; notice, perceive, see, sense, recognize; *informal* savvy, latch on. ❷ *I don't know his address* HAVE KNOWLEDGE OF, be informed of, be apprised of; *formal* be cognizant of. ❸ *do you know the rules* BE FAMILIAR WITH, be conversant with, be acquainted with, have knowledge of, be versed in, have mastered, have a grasp of, understand, comprehend; have learned, have memorized; *informal* be clued up on. ❹ *I don't know* *many people here* BE ACQUAINTED WITH, have met, be familiar with; be friends with, be friendly with, be on good terms with, be close to, be intimate with; *Scottish* ken; *informal* be thick with. ❺ *he had known better times* EXPERIENCE, go through, live through, undergo, taste. ❻ *my brothers don't know a saucepan from a frying pan* DISTINGUISH, tell (apart), differentiate, discriminate; recognize, pick out, identify.

know-all ▶ **noun** (*informal*) WISEACRE; *informal* smart alec, wise guy, smarty, smarty-pants; *Brit. informal* clever clogs, clever Dick; *N. Amer. informal* know-it-all.

know-how ▶ **noun** (*informal*) KNOWLEDGE, expertise, skill, skilfulness, expertness, proficiency, understanding, mastery, technique; ability, capability, competence, capacity, adeptness, dexterity, deftness, aptitude, adroitness, ingenuity, faculty; *informal* savvy.

knowing ▶ **adjective** ❶ *a knowing smile* SIGNIFICANT, meaningful, eloquent, expressive, suggestive; ARCH, sly, mischievous, impish, teasing, playful. ❷ *she's a very knowing child* SOPHISTICATED, worldly, worldly-wise, urbane, experienced; knowledgeable, well informed, enlightened; shrewd, astute, canny, sharp, wily, perceptive. ❸ *a knowing infringement of the rules* DELIBERATE, intentional, conscious, calculated, wilful, done on purpose, premeditated, preconceived, planned.

knowingly ▶ **adverb** DELIBERATELY, intentionally, consciously, wittingly, on purpose, by design, premeditatedly, wilfully.

knowledge ▶ **noun** ❶ *his knowledge of history | technical knowledge* UNDERSTANDING, comprehension, grasp, command, mastery; expertise, skill, proficiency, expertness, accomplishment, adeptness, capacity, capability; *informal* know-how. ❷ *people anxious to display their knowledge* LEARNING, erudition, education, scholarship, schooling, wisdom. ❸ *he slipped away without my knowledge* AWARENESS, consciousness, realization, cognition, apprehension, perception, appreciation; *formal* cognizance. ❹ *an intimate knowledge of the countryside* FAMILIARITY, acquaintance, conversance, intimacy. ❺ *inform the police of your knowledge* INFORMATION, facts, intelligence, news, reports; *informal* info, gen.
– OPPOSITES ignorance.

knowledgeable ▶ **adjective** ❶ *a knowledgeable old man* WELL INFORMED, learned, well read, (well) educated, erudite, scholarly, cultured, cultivated, enlightened. ❷ *he is knowledgeable about modern art* ACQUAINTED, familiar, conversant, au courant, au fait; having a knowledge of, up on, up to date with, abreast of; *informal* clued up, genned up; *Brit. informal* switched on.
– OPPOSITES ill-informed.

known ▶ **adjective** ❶ *a known criminal* RECOGNIZED, well known, widely known, noted, celebrated, notable, notorious; acknowledged, self-confessed, declared, overt. ❷ *the known world* FAMILIAR, known about, well known; studied, investigated.

knuckle

■ **knuckle under** SURRENDER, submit, capitulate, give in/up, yield, give way, succumb, climb down, back down, admit defeat, lay down one's arms, throw in the towel/sponge; *informal* quit, raise the white flag.

kowtow ▶ **verb** ❶ *they kowtowed to the Emperor* PROSTRATE ONESELF, bow (down before), genuflect, do/make obeisance, fall on one's knees before, kneel before. ❷ *she didn't have to kowtow to a boss* GROVEL, be obsequious, be servile, be sycophantic, fawn on, bow and scrape, toady, truckle, abase oneself, humble oneself; curry favour with, dance attendance on, make up to, ingratiate oneself with; *informal* crawl, creep, suck up, lick someone's boots; *Austral./NZ informal* smoodge to.

kudos ▶ **noun** PRESTIGE, cachet, glory, honour, status, standing, distinction, prestigiousness, fame, celebrity; admiration, respect, esteem, acclaim, praise, credit.

label ▶ **noun** ❶ *the price is clearly stated on the label* TAG, ticket, tab, sticker, marker, docket, chit, chitty. ❷ *a designer label* BRAND (NAME), trade name, trademark, make, logo. ❸ *the label the media came up with for me* DESIGNATION, description, tag; name, epithet, nickname, title, sobriquet, pet name, cognomen; *formal* denomination, appellation.
▶ **verb** ❶ *label each jar with the date* TAG, put labels on, tab, ticket, mark, docket. ❷ *tests labelled him an underachiever* CATEGORIZE, classify, class, describe, designate, identify; mark, stamp, brand, condemn, pigeonhole, stereotype, typecast; call, name, term, dub, nickname.

laborious ▶ adjective ❶ *a laborious job* ARDUOUS, hard, heavy, difficult, strenuous, gruelling, punishing, exacting, tough, onerous, burdensome, back-breaking, trying, challenging; tiring, fatiguing, exhausting, wearying, wearing, taxing, demanding, wearisome; tedious, boring; *archaic* toilsome. ❷ *Doug's laborious style* LABOURED, strained, forced, contrived, affected, stiff, stilted, unnatural, artificial, overwrought, heavy, ponderous, convoluted.
– OPPOSITES easy, effortless.

labour ▶ noun ❶ *manual labour* (HARD) WORK, toil, exertion, industry, drudgery, effort, donkey work, menial work; *informal* slog, grind, sweat, elbow grease; *Brit. informal* graft; *poetic/literary* travail, moil. ❷ *the conflict between capital and labour* WORKERS, employees, workmen, workforce, staff, working people, blue-collar workers, labourers, labour force, proletariat. ❸ *the labours of Hercules* TASK, job, chore, mission, assignment. ❹ *a difficult labour* CHILDBIRTH, birth, delivery, nativity; contractions, labour pains; *formal* parturition; *poetic/literary* travail; *dated* confinement; *archaic* lying-in, accouchement, childbed.
– OPPOSITES rest, management.
▶ verb ❶ *a project on which he had laboured for many years* WORK (HARD), toil, slave (away), grind away, struggle, strive, exert oneself, work one's fingers to the bone, work like a Trojan/slave; *informal* slog away, plug away, peg away; *Brit. informal* graft; *poetic/literary* travail; *archaic* moil. ❷ *Newcastle laboured to break down their defence* STRIVE, struggle, endeavour, work, try hard, make every effort, do one's best, do one's utmost, do all one can, give one's all, go all out, fight, put oneself out, apply oneself, exert oneself; *informal* bend/lean over backwards, pull out all the stops. ❸ *there is no need to labour the point* OVEREMPHASIZE, belabour, overstress, overdo, strain, overplay, make too much of, exaggerate, dwell on, harp on (about). ❹ *Rex was labouring under a misapprehension* SUFFER FROM, be a victim of, be deceived by, be misled by.

laboured ▶ adjective ❶ *laboured breathing* STRAINED, difficult, forced, laborious. ❷ *a rather laboured joke* CONTRIVED, strained, stilted, forced, unnatural, artificial, overdone, ponderous, over-elaborate, laborious, unconvincing, overwrought.

labourer ▶ noun WORKMAN, worker, working man, labouring man, manual worker, unskilled worker, blue-collar worker, (hired) hand, roustabout, drudge, menial, coolie; *Austral./NZ* rouseabout; *Brit. dated* navvy.

labyrinth ▶ noun ❶ *a labyrinth of little streets* MAZE, warren, network, complex, web, entanglement. ❷ *the labyrinth of conflicting regulations* TANGLE, web, morass, jungle, confusion, entanglement, convolution; jumble, mishmash; *archaic* perplexity.

labyrinthine ▶ adjective ❶ *labyrinthine corridors* MAZE-LIKE, winding, twisting, serpentine, meandering, wandering, rambling. ❷ *a labyrinthine system* COMPLICATED, intricate, complex, involved, tortuous, convoluted, involuted, tangled, elaborate; confusing, puzzling, mystifying, bewildering, baffling.

lace ▶ noun ❶ *a dress trimmed with white lace* openwork, lacework, tatting; passementerie, bobbinet, needlepoint (lace), filet, bobbin lace, pillow lace, duchesse lace, guipure, rosaline. ❷ *brown shoes with laces* SHOELACE, bootlace, shoestring, lacing, thong, tie; *archaic* latchet.
▶ verb ❶ *he laced up his running shoes* FASTEN, do up, tie up, secure, knot. ❷ *he laced his fingers into mine* ENTWINE, intertwine, twine, entangle, interweave, link; braid, plait. ❸ *tea laced with rum* FLAVOUR, mix (in), blend, fortify, strengthen, stiffen, season, spice (up), enrich, liven up; doctor, adulterate; *informal* spike. ❹ *her brown hair was laced with grey* STREAK, stripe, striate, line.
– OPPOSITES untie.
■ **lace into** (*informal*) ❶ *Danny laced into him. See* SET ON at SET[1]. ❷ *the newspaper laced into the prime minister. See* CRITICIZE.

lacerate ▶ verb CUT (OPEN), gash, slash, tear, rip, rend, shred, score, scratch, scrape, graze; wound, injure, hurt.

laceration ▶ noun ❶ *the laceration of her hand* CUTTING (OPEN), gashing, slashing, tearing, ripping, scratching, scraping, grazing, wounding, injury. ❷ *a bleeding laceration* GASH, cut, wound, injury, tear, slash, scratch, scrape, abrasion, graze.

lachrymose ▶ adjective ❶ *she gets quite lachrymose at the mention of his name* TEARFUL, weeping, crying, with tears in one's eyes, close to tears, on the verge of tears, sobbing, snivelling, whimpering; emotional, sad, doleful, maudlin, miserable, forlorn; *informal* weepy; *poetic/literary* dolorous. ❷ *a lachrymose novel* TRAGIC, sad, poignant, moving, heart-rending, tear-jerking; mawkish, sentimental; *Brit. informal* soppy.
– OPPOSITES cheerful, comic.

lack ▶ noun *a lack of cash* ABSENCE, want, need, deficiency, dearth, insufficiency, shortage, shortfall, scarcity, paucity, unavailability, scarceness, deficit; *formal* exiguity.
– OPPOSITES abundance.
▶ verb *she's immature and lacks judgement* BE WITHOUT, be in need of, need, be lacking, require, want, be short of, be deficient in, be bereft of, be low on, be pressed for, have insufficient; *informal* be strapped for.
– OPPOSITES have, possess.

lackadaisical ▶ adjective CARELESS, lazy, lax, unenthusiastic, half-hearted, lukewarm, indifferent, unconcerned, casual, offhand,

blasé, insouciant, relaxed; apathetic, lethargic, listless, sluggish, spiritless, passionless; *informal* laid back, couldn't-care-less, easy going.
– OPPOSITES enthusiastic.

lackey ▶ noun ❶ *lackeys helped them from their carriage* SERVANT, flunkey, footman, manservant, valet, steward, butler, equerry, retainer, attendant, houseboy, domestic; *Brit. informal* skivvy; *archaic* scullion. ❷ *a rich man's lackey* TOADY, flunkey, sycophant, flatterer, minion, doormat, stooge, hanger-on, lickspittle; tool, puppet, instrument, pawn, subordinate, underling; *informal* yes-man, bootlicker.

lacking ▶ adjective ❶ *proof was lacking* ABSENT, missing, non-existent, unavailable. ❷ *the advocate general found the government lacking* DEFICIENT, defective, inadequate, wanting, flawed, faulty, insufficient, unacceptable, imperfect, inferior. ❸ *the game was lacking in atmosphere* WITHOUT, devoid of, bereft of; deficient in, low on, short on, in need of.
– OPPOSITES present, plentiful.

lacklustre ▶ adjective UNINSPIRED, uninspiring, unimaginative, dull, humdrum, colourless, characterless, bland, insipid, vapid, flat, dry, lifeless, tame, prosaic, spiritless, lustreless; boring, monotonous, dreary, tedious.
– OPPOSITES inspired.

laconic ▶ adjective ❶ *his laconic comment* BRIEF, concise, terse, succinct, short, pithy; epigrammatic, aphoristic, gnomic. ❷ *their laconic press officer* TACITURN, uncommunicative, reticent, quiet, reserved, silent, unforthcoming, brusque.
– OPPOSITES verbose, loquacious.

lad ▶ noun (*informal*) ❶ *a young lad of eight* BOY, schoolboy, youth, youngster, juvenile, stripling; *informal* kid, nipper, whippersnapper; *Scottish informal* laddie; *derogatory* brat. ❷ *a hard-working lad* (YOUNG) MAN; *informal* guy, fellow, geezer; *Brit. informal* chap, bloke; *N. Amer. informal* dude, hombre; *Austral./NZ informal* digger.

ladder ▶ noun ❶ *she climbed down the ladder* steps, set of steps. ❷ *the academic ladder* HIERARCHY, scale, grading, ranking, pecking order.

laden ▶ adjective LOADED, burdened, weighed down, overloaded, piled high, fully charged; full, filled, packed, stuffed, crammed; *informal* chock-full, chock-a-block.

la-di-da ▶ adjective (*informal*) SNOBBISH, pretentious, affected, mannered, pompous, conceited, haughty; *informal* snooty, stuck-up, high and mighty, hoity-toity, uppity, snotty; *Brit. informal* posh, toffee-nosed.
– OPPOSITES common.

ladle ▶ noun *a soup ladle* SPOON, scoop, dipper, bailer.
▶ verb *he was ladling out the contents of the pot* SPOON OUT, scoop out, dish up/out, serve.

lady ▶ noun ❶ *several ladies were present* WOMAN, female; *Scottish & N. English* lass, lassie; *Brit. informal* bird, bint; *N. Amer. informal* dame, broad, jane; *Austral./NZ informal* sheila; *poetic/literary* maid, damsel; *archaic* wench. ❷ *lords and ladies* NOBLEWOMAN, duchess, countess, peeress, viscountess, baroness; *archaic* gentlewoman.

ladylike ▶ adjective GENTEEL, polite, refined, well bred, cultivated, polished, decorous, proper, respectable, seemly, well mannered, cultured, sophisticated, elegant; *Brit. informal* posh.
– OPPOSITES coarse.

lag ▶ verb FALL BEHIND, straggle, fall back, trail (behind), hang back, not keep pace, bring up the rear.
– OPPOSITES keep up.

laggard ▶ noun STRAGGLER, loiterer, lingerer, dawdler, sluggard, snail, idler, loafer; *informal* lazybones, slacker, slowcoach; *N. Amer. informal* slowpoke.

lagoon ▶ noun inland sea, bay, lake, bight, pool; *Scottish* loch; *Anglo-Irish* lough; *N. Amer.* bayou.

laid-back ▶ adjective (*informal*) RELAXED, easygoing, equable, free and easy, casual, nonchalant, insouciant, unexcitable, imperturbable, unruffled, blasé, cool, calm, {cool, calm, and collected}, unperturbed, unflustered, unworried, unconcerned; leisurely, unhurried; stoical, phlegmatic, tolerant; *informal* unflappable.
– OPPOSITES uptight.

laid up ▶ adjective (*informal*) BEDRIDDEN, confined to bed, on the sick list, housebound, incapacitated, injured, disabled; ill, sick, unwell, poorly, ailing, indisposed.
– OPPOSITES healthy, active.

lair ▶ noun ❶ *the lair of a large python* DEN, burrow, hole, tunnel, cave. ❷ *a villain's lair* HIDEAWAY, hiding place, hideout, refuge, sanctuary, haven, shelter, retreat; *informal* hidey-hole.

laissez-faire ▶ noun *laissez-faire is based on self-interest* FREE ENTERPRISE, free trade, nonintervention, free-market capitalism, market forces.

lake ▶ noun POND, pool, tarn, reservoir, lagoon, waterhole, inland sea; *Scottish* loch, lochan; *Anglo-Irish* lough; *N. Amer.* bayou, pothole (lake); *poetic/literary* mere.
– RELATED TERMS lacustrine.

lam ▶ verb (*informal*). *See* HIT verb sense 1.

lambaste ▶ verb CRITICIZE, chastise, censure, take to task, harangue, rail at, rant at, fulminate against; upbraid, scold, reprimand, rebuke, chide, reprove, admonish, berate; *informal* lay into, pitch into, tear into, give someone a dressing-down, carpet, tell off, bawl out; *Brit. informal* tick off, have a go at; *N. Amer. informal* chew out; *formal* castigate, excoriate.

lame ▶ adjective ❶ *the mare was lame* LIMPING, hobbling; crippled, disabled, incapacitated; *informal* gammy; *dated* game; *archaic* halt. ❷ *a lame*

excuse FEEBLE, weak, thin, flimsy, poor; unconvincing, implausible, unlikely.
–OPPOSITES convincing.

lament ▶ **noun** ❶ *the widow's laments* WAIL, wailing, lamentation, moan, moaning, weeping, crying, sob, sobbing, keening. ❷ *a lament for the dead* DIRGE, requiem, elegy, threnody, monody; *Irish* keen; *Scottish & Irish* coronach; *formal* epicedium.
▶ **verb** ❶ *the mourners lamented* MOURN, grieve, sorrow, wail, weep, cry, sob, keen, beat one's breast; *archaic* plain. ❷ *he lamented the modernization of the buildings* BEMOAN, bewail, complain about, deplore; protest against, object to, oppose, fulminate against, inveigh against, denounce.
–OPPOSITES celebrate.

lamentable ▶ **adjective** DEPLORABLE, regrettable, terrible, awful, wretched, woeful, dire, disastrous, desperate, grave, appalling, dreadful, egregious; intolerable, pitiful, shameful, sorrowful, unfortunate.
–OPPOSITES wonderful.

lamentation ▶ **noun** WEEPING, wailing, crying, sobbing, moaning, lament, keening, grieving, mourning.

lamp ▶ **noun** LIGHT, lantern.

lampoon ▶ **verb** *he was mercilessly lampooned* SATIRIZE, mock, ridicule, make fun of, caricature, burlesque, parody, take off, guy, rag, tease; *informal* send up.
▶ **noun** *a lampoon of student life* SATIRE, burlesque, parody, skit, caricature, impersonation, travesty, mockery, squib, pasquinade; *informal* send-up, take-off, spoof.

lance ▶ **noun** *a knight with a lance* SPEAR, pike, javelin; harpoon.
▶ **verb** *the boil was lanced* CUT (OPEN), slit, incise, puncture, prick, pierce.

land ▶ **noun** ❶ *Lyme Park has 1323 acres of land | publicly owned land* GROUNDS, fields, open space; property, acres, acreage, estate, lands, real estate; countryside, rural area, green belt; *historical* demesne. ❷ *fertile land* SOIL, earth, loam, topsoil, humus. ❸ *many people are leaving the land* THE COUNTRYSIDE, the country, rural areas. ❹ *Tunisia is a land of variety* COUNTRY, nation, (nation) state, realm, kingdom, province; region, area, domain. ❺ *the lookout sighted land to the east* TERRA FIRMA, dry land; coast, coastline, shore.
–RELATED TERMS terrestrial.
▶ **verb** ❶ *Allied troops landed in France* DISEMBARK, go ashore, debark, alight, get off. ❷ *the ship landed at Le Havre* BERTH, dock, moor, (drop) anchor, tie up, put in. ❸ *their plane landed at Chicago* TOUCH DOWN, make a landing, come in to land, come down. ❹ *a bird landed on the branch* PERCH, settle, come to rest, alight. ❺ (*informal*) *Nick landed the job of editor* OBTAIN, get, acquire, secure, be appointed to, gain, net, win, achieve, attain, bag, carry off; *informal* swing; *Brit. informal* blag. ❻ (*informal*) *that habit landed her in trouble* BRING, lead, cause to be in. ❼ (*informal*) *they landed her with the bill* BURDEN, saddle, encumber; *informal* dump something on someone; *Brit. informal* lumber. ❽ (*informal*) *John landed a punch on Brian's chin* INFLICT, deal, deliver, administer, dispense, mete one; *informal* fetch.
–OPPOSITES sail, take off.
■ **land up** FINISH UP, find oneself, end up; *informal* wind up, fetch up, show up, roll up, blow in.

landing ▶ **noun** ❶ *a forced landing* ALIGHTING, touchdown; *informal* greaser. ❷ *the ferry landing* HARBOUR, berth, dock, jetty, landing stage, pier, quay, wharf, slipway.
–OPPOSITES take-off.

landlady, landlord ▶ **noun** ❶ *the landlord of the pub* PUBLICAN, licensee, innkeeper, pub-owner, bar-keeper; hotel-keeper, hotelier, restaurateur; manager, manageress. ❷ *the landlady had objected to the noise* PROPERTY OWNER, proprietor, proprietress, lessor, householder, landowner.
–OPPOSITES tenant.

landmark ▶ **noun** ❶ *the spire is a landmark for ships* MARKER, mark, indicator, beacon. ❷ *one of London's most famous landmarks* MONUMENT, distinctive feature, prominent feature. ❸ (*historical*) *the landmarks which separated the two states* BOUNDARY MARKER, boundary line, boundary fence. ❹ *the ruling was hailed as a landmark* TURNING POINT, milestone, watershed, critical point.

landscape ▶ **noun** SCENERY, countryside, topography, country, terrain; outlook, view, prospect, aspect, vista, panorama; perspective, sweep.

landslide ▶ **noun** ❶ *floods and landslides* LANDSLIP, mudslide; avalanche. ❷ *the Labour landslide* DECISIVE VICTORY, overwhelming majority, triumph.

lane ▶ **noun** ❶ *country lanes* BYROAD, byway, track, road, street; alley, alleyway. ❷ *cycle lanes | a three-lane highway* TRACK, way, course; road division.

language ▶ **noun** ❶ *the structure of language* SPEECH, writing, communication, conversation, speaking, talking, talk, discourse; words, vocabulary; *archaic* converse. ❷ *the English language* TONGUE, mother tongue, native tongue; *informal* lingo. ❸ *the booklet is written in simple, everyday language* WORDING, phrasing, phraseology, style, vocabulary, terminology, expressions, turns of phrase, parlance, form/mode of expression, usages, locutions, idiolect, choice of words; speech, dialect, patois, slang, idioms, jargon, argot, cant; *informal* lingo.
–RELATED TERMS linguistic.

languid ▶ adjective ❶ *a languid wave of the hand* RELAXED, unhurried, languorous, slow; listless, lethargic, sluggish, lazy, idle, indolent, apathetic; *informal* laid back; *archaic* otiose. ❷ *languid days in the sun* LEISURELY, languorous, relaxed, restful, lazy. ❸ *she was pale and languid* SICKLY, weak, faint, feeble, frail, delicate; tired, weary, fatigued.
– OPPOSITES energetic.

languish ▶ verb ❶ *the plants languished and died* WEAKEN, deteriorate, decline; wither, droop, wilt, fade, waste away; *informal* go downhill. ❷ *the general is now languishing in prison* WASTE AWAY, rot, be abandoned, be neglected, be forgotten, suffer, experience hardship. ❸ (*archaic*) *she still languished after Richard* PINE FOR, yearn for, ache for, long for, sigh for; grieve for, mourn.
– OPPOSITES thrive.

languor ▶ noun ❶ *the sultry languor that was stealing over her* LASSITUDE, lethargy, listlessness, torpor, fatigue, weariness, sleepiness, drowsiness; laziness, idleness, indolence, inertia, sluggishness, apathy. ❷ *the languor of a hot day* STILLNESS, tranquillity, calm, calmness; oppressiveness, heaviness.
– OPPOSITES vigour.

lank ▶ adjective ❶ *lank, greasy hair* LIMP, lifeless, lustreless, dull; straggling, straight, long. ❷ *his lank figure. See* LANKY.

lanky ▶ adjective TALL, THIN, slender, slim, lean, lank, skinny, spindly, spare, gangling, gangly, gawky, rangy.
– OPPOSITES stocky.

lap[1] ▶ noun *Henry sat on his gran's lap* KNEE, knees, thighs.
■ **in the lap of the gods** OUT OF ONE'S HANDS, beyond one's control, in the hands of fate.
■ **live in the lap of luxury** BE VERY RICH, want for nothing; *informal* live the life of Riley; *N. Amer. informal* live high on the hog.

lap[2] ▶ noun *a race of eight laps* CIRCUIT, leg, circle, revolution, round.
▶ verb ❶ *she lapped the other runners* OVERTAKE, outstrip, leave behind, pass, go past; catch up with. ❷ (*poetic/literary*) *he was lapped in blankets* WRAP, swathe, envelop, enfold, swaddle.

lap[3] ▶ verb ❶ *waves lapped against the sea wall* SPLASH, wash, swish, slosh, break, beat, strike, dash, roll; *poetic/literary* plash. ❷ *the dog lapped water out of a puddle* DRINK, lick up, sup, swallow, slurp, gulp.
■ **lap something up** RELISH, revel in, savour, delight in, wallow in, glory in, enjoy.

lapse ▶ noun ❶ *a lapse of concentration* FAILURE, failing, slip, error, mistake, blunder, fault, omission; *informal* slip-up. ❷ *his lapse into petty crime* DECLINE, fall, falling, slipping, drop, deterioration, degeneration, backsliding, regression, retrogression, descent, sinking, slide. ❸ *a lapse of time* INTERVAL, gap, pause, interlude, lull, hiatus, break; passage, course, passing.
▶ verb ❶ *the planning permission has lapsed* EXPIRE, become void, become invalid, run out. ❷ *do not let friendships lapse* (COME TO AN) END, cease, stop, terminate, pass, fade, wither, die. ❸ *morality has lapsed* DETERIORATE, decline, fall (off), drop, worsen, degenerate, backslide, regress, retrogress, get worse, sink, wane, slump; *informal* go downhill, go to pot, go to the dogs. ❹ *she lapsed into silence* REVERT, relapse; drift, slide, slip, sink.

lapsed ▶ adjective ❶ *a lapsed Catholic* NON-PRACTISING, backsliding, apostate; *formal* quondam. ❷ *a lapsed season ticket* EXPIRED, void, invalid, out of date.
– OPPOSITES practising, valid.

larceny ▶ noun THEFT, stealing, robbery, pilfering, thieving; burglary, housebreaking, breaking and entering; *informal* filching, swiping; *Brit. informal* nicking, pinching; *formal* peculation.

larder ▶ noun PANTRY, (food) store, (food) cupboard; cooler, scullery; *Brit.* buttery; *archaic* spence.

large ▶ adjective ❶ *a large house | large numbers of people* BIG, great, huge, sizeable, substantial, immense, enormous, colossal, massive, mammoth, vast, prodigious, tremendous, gigantic, giant, monumental, stupendous, gargantuan, elephantine, titanic, mountainous, monstrous; towering, tall, high; mighty, voluminous, king-size, giant-size; *informal* jumbo, whopping (great), thumping (great), mega, humongous, monster, astronomical; *Brit. informal* whacking (great), ginormous. ❷ *a large red-faced man* BIG, burly, heavy, tall, bulky, thickset, chunky, strapping, hulking, hefty, muscular, brawny, solid, powerful, sturdy, strong, rugged; fat, plump, overweight, chubby, stout, meaty, fleshy, portly, rotund, flabby, paunchy, obese, corpulent; *informal* hunky, beefy, tubby, pudgy; *Brit. informal* podgy, fubsy; *N. Amer. informal* zaftig, corn-fed. ❸ *a large supply of wool* ABUNDANT, copious, plentiful, ample, liberal, generous, lavish, bountiful, bumper, boundless, good, considerable, superabundant; *poetic/literary* plenteous. ❹ *the measure has large economic implications* WIDE-REACHING, far-reaching, wide, sweeping, large-scale, broad, extensive, comprehensive, exhaustive.
– RELATED TERMS macro-, mega-.
– OPPOSITES small, meagre.
■ **at large** ❶ *fourteen criminals are still at large* AT LIBERTY, free, (on the) loose, on the run, fugitive; *N. Amer. informal* on the lam. ❷ *society at large* AS A WHOLE, generally, in general. ❸ (*dated*) *he spoke at large* IN DETAIL, exhaustively, at length, extensively.
■ **by and large** ON THE WHOLE, generally, in general, all things considered, all in all, for the most part, in the main, as a rule, overall,

almost always, mainly, mostly; on average, on balance.

largely ▶ **adverb** MOSTLY, mainly, to a large/great extent, chiefly, predominantly, primarily, principally, for the most part, in the main; usually, typically, commonly.

large-scale ▶ **adjective** ❶ *a large-scale programme* EXTENSIVE, wide-ranging, far-reaching, comprehensive, exhaustive; mass, nationwide, global. ❷ *a large-scale map* ENLARGED, blown-up, magnified.

largesse ▶ **noun** ❶ *Tupper took advantage of his friend's largesse* GENEROSITY, liberality, munificence, bounty, bountifulness, beneficence, altruism, charity, philanthropy, magnanimity, benevolence, charitableness, open-handedness, kindness, big-heartedness; *formal* benefaction. ❷ *distributing largesse to the locals* GIFTS, presents, handouts, grants, aid; patronage, sponsorship, backing, help; *historical* alms.
– OPPOSITES meanness.

lark (*informal*) ▶ **noun** ❶ *we were just having a bit of a lark* FUN, amusement, laugh, giggle, joke; escapade, prank, trick, jape, practical joke; *informal* leg-pull; (**larks**) antics, high jinks, horseplay, mischief, tomfoolery; *informal* shenanigans, monkey business; *Brit. informal* monkey tricks; *dated* sport. ❷ *I've got this snowboarding lark sussed* ACTIVITY; hobby, pastime, task; *informal* business, caper.
▶ **verb** *he's always larking about* FOOL ABOUT/AROUND, play tricks, make mischief, monkey about/around, clown about/around, have fun, skylark; *informal* mess about/around; *Brit. informal* muck about/around.

lascivious ▶ **adjective** LECHEROUS, lewd, lustful, licentious, libidinous, salacious, lubricious, prurient, dirty, smutty, naughty, suggestive, indecent, ribald; *informal* horny; *Brit. informal* randy; *formal* concupiscent.

lash ▶ **verb** ❶ *he lashed her repeatedly* WHIP, flog, beat, thrash, horsewhip, scourge, birch, switch, belt, strap, cane; strike, hit; *informal* wallop, whack, lam, larrup, give someone a (good) hiding; *N. Amer. informal* whale. ❷ *rain lashed the window panes* BEAT AGAINST, dash against, pound, batter, strike, hit, knock. ❸ *the tiger began to lash his tail* SWISH, flick, twitch, whip. ❹ *fear lashed them into a frenzy* PROVOKE, incite, arouse, excite, agitate, stir up, whip up, work up. ❺ *two boats were lashed together* FASTEN, bind, tie (up), tether, hitch, knot, rope, make fast.
▶ **noun** ❶ *he brought the lash down upon the prisoner's back* WHIP, horsewhip, switch, scourge, thong, flail, strap, birch, cane; *historical* knout, cat-o'-nine-tails, cat. ❷ *twenty lashes* STROKE, blow, hit, strike, welt, thwack, thump; *informal* wallop, whack; *archaic* stripe.
■ **lash out** ❶ *the president lashed out at the opposition* CRITICIZE, chastise, censure, attack, condemn, denounce, lambaste, harangue, pillory; berate, upbraid, rebuke, reproach; *informal* lay into; *formal* castigate. ❷ *Norman lashed out at Terry with a knife* HIT OUT, strike, let fly, take a swing; set upon/about, turn on, round on, attack; *informal* lay into, tear into, pitch into. ❸ (*informal*) *they lashed out on a taxi* SPEND LAVISHLY, be extravagant; *informal* splash out, splurge, shell out, squander money, waste money, fritter money away.

lass ▶ **noun** (*Scottish & N. English*) GIRL, young woman, young lady; *Scottish* lassie; *Irish* colleen; *informal* chick, girlie; *Brit. informal* bird, bint; *N. Amer. informal* dame, babe, doll, gal, broad; *Austral./NZ informal* sheila; *poetic/literary* maid, maiden, damsel; *archaic* wench.

lassitude ▶ **noun** LETHARGY, listlessness, weariness, languor, sluggishness, tiredness, fatigue, torpor, lifelessness, apathy.
– OPPOSITES vigour.

last[1] ▶ **adjective** ❶ *the last woman in the queue* REARMOST, hindmost, endmost, at the end, at the back, furthest (back), final, ultimate. ❷ *Rembrandt spent his last years in Amsterdam* CLOSING, concluding, final, ending, end, terminal; later, latter. ❸ *I'd be the last person to say anything against him* LEAST LIKELY, most unlikely, most improbable; least suitable, most unsuitable, most inappropriate, least appropriate. ❹ *we met last year* PREVIOUS, preceding; prior, former. ❺ *this was his last chance* FINAL, only remaining.
– OPPOSITES first, early, next.
▶ **adverb** *the candidate coming last is eliminated* AT THE END, at/in the rear.
▶ **noun** *the most important business was left to the last* END, ending, finish, close, conclusion, finale, termination.
– OPPOSITES beginning.
■ **at last** FINALLY, in the end, eventually, ultimately, at long last, after a long time, in (the fullness of) time.
■ **the last word** ❶ *that's my last word* FINAL DECISION, definitive statement, conclusive comment. ❷ *she was determined to have the last word* CONCLUDING REMARK, final say, closing statement. ❸ *the last word in luxury and efficiency* THE BEST, the peak, the acme, the epitome, the latest; the pinnacle, the apex, the apogee, the ultimate, the height, the zenith, the nonpareil, the crème de la crème; *archaic* the nonsuch.

last[2] ▶ **verb** ❶ *the hearing lasted for six days* CONTINUE, go on, carry on, keep on/going, proceed, take; stay, remain, persist. ❷ *how long will he last as manager?* SURVIVE, endure, hold on/out, keep going, persevere; *informal* stick it out, hang on, hack it. ❸ *the car is built to last* ENDURE, wear well, stand up, bear up; *informal* go the distance.

last-ditch ▶ **adjective** LAST-MINUTE, last-chance, eleventh-hour, last-resort, desperate, final; *informal* last-gasp.

lasting ▶ **adjective** ENDURING, long-lasting, long-lived, abiding, continuing, long-term, surviving, persisting, permanent; durable, constant, stable, established, secure, long-standing; unchanging, irreversible, immutable, eternal, undying, everlasting, unending, never-ending, unfading, changeless, indestructible, unceasing, unwavering, unfaltering.
– OPPOSITES ephemeral.

lastly ▶ **adverb** FINALLY, in conclusion, to conclude, to sum up, to end, last, ultimately.
– OPPOSITES firstly.

latch ▶ **noun** *he lifted the latch* FASTENING, catch, fastener, clasp.
▶ **verb** *Jess latched the back door* FASTEN, secure, make fast.

late ▶ **adjective** ❶ *the train was late* BEHIND TIME, behind schedule, behindhand; tardy, running late, overdue, delayed. ❷ *her late husband* DEAD, departed, lamented, passed on/away; *formal* deceased. ❸ *the late government* PREVIOUS, preceding, former, past, prior, earlier, sometime, one-time, ex-, erstwhile; *formal* quondam.
– OPPOSITES punctual, early.
▶ **adverb** ❶ *she had arrived late* BEHIND SCHEDULE, behind time, behindhand, belatedly, tardily, at the last minute. ❷ *I was working late* AFTER (OFFICE) HOURS, overtime. ❸ *I won't have you staying out late* LATE AT NIGHT; *informal* till all hours.
■ **of late** RECENTLY, lately, latterly.

lately ▶ **adverb** RECENTLY, of late, latterly, in recent times.

lateness ▶ **noun** UNPUNCTUALITY, tardiness, delay.

latent ▶ **adjective** DORMANT, untapped, unused, undiscovered, hidden, concealed, invisible, unseen, undeveloped, unrealized, unfulfilled, potential.

later ▶ **adjective** *a later chapter* SUBSEQUENT, following, succeeding, future, upcoming, to come, ensuing, next; *formal* posterior; *archaic* after.
– OPPOSITES earlier.
▶ **adverb** ❶ *later, the film rights were sold* SUBSEQUENTLY, eventually, then, next, later on, after this/that, afterwards, at a later date, in the future, in due course, by and by, in a while, in time. ❷ *two days later a letter arrived* AFTERWARDS, later on, after (that), subsequently, following; *formal* thereafter.

lateral ▶ **adjective** ❶ *lateral movements* SIDEWAYS, sidewise, sideward, edgewise, edgeways, oblique. ❷ *lateral thinking* UNORTHODOX, inventive, creative, imaginative, original, innovative.

latest ▶ **adjective** MOST RECENT, newest, just out, just released, fresh, (bang) up to date, up to the minute, state-of-the-art, current, modern, contemporary, fashionable, in fashion, in vogue; *informal* in, with it, trendy, hip, hot, happening, cool.
– OPPOSITES old.

lather ▶ **noun** ❶ *a rich, soapy lather* FOAM, froth, suds, soapsuds, bubbles; *poetic/literary* spume. ❷ *the mare was covered with lather* SWEAT, perspiration. ❸ (*informal*) *Dad was in a right lather* PANIC, fluster, fret, fuss, fever; *informal* flap, sweat, tizzy, dither, twitter, state, stew; *N. Amer. informal* twit; *poetic/literary* pother.

latitude ▶ **noun** ❶ *Toronto shares the same latitude as Nice* parallel. ❷ *he gave them a lot of latitude* FREEDOM, scope, leeway, (breathing) space, flexibility, liberty, independence, free rein, licence, room to manoeuvre, freedom of action.
– OPPOSITES longitude, restriction.

latter ▶ **adjective** ❶ *the latter half of the season* LATER, closing, end, concluding, final; latest, most recent. ❷ *Russia chose the latter option* LAST-MENTIONED, second, last, later.
– OPPOSITES former.

latter-day ▶ **adjective** MODERN, present-day, current, contemporary.

latterly ▶ **adverb** ❶ *latterly, she had been in more pain* RECENTLY, lately, of late, in recent times. ❷ *latterly he worked as a political editor* ULTIMATELY, finally, towards the end.

lattice ▶ **noun** GRID, latticework, fretwork, open framework, openwork, trellis, trelliswork, network, mesh.

laud ▶ **verb** (*formal*) PRAISE, extol, hail, applaud, acclaim, commend, sing the praises of, speak highly of, lionize, eulogize, rhapsodize over/about; *informal* rave about; *archaic* magnify, panegyrize.
– OPPOSITES criticize.

laudable ▶ **adjective** PRAISEWORTHY, commendable, admirable, meritorious, worthy, deserving, creditable, estimable, exemplary.
– OPPOSITES shameful.

laudation ▶ **noun** (*formal*) PRAISE, honour, applause, acclaim, acclamation, commendation, admiration, homage, distinction, approval, credit, kudos, glory, esteem, approbation, tribute, congratulations, plaudits; *formal* encomium.

laudatory ▶ **adjective** COMPLIMENTARY, congratulatory, praising, extolling, adulatory, commendatory, approbatory, flattering, celebratory, eulogizing, panegyrical; *informal* glowing; *formal* encomiastic.
– OPPOSITES disparaging.

laugh ▶ **verb** ❶ *he started to laugh excitedly* CHUCKLE, chortle, guffaw, giggle, titter, snigger, snicker, tee-hee, burst out laughing, roar/hoot with laughter, dissolve into laughter, split one's sides, be doubled up; *informal* be in stitches, be rolling in the aisles, crease up, fall about, crack up. ❷ *people laughed at his theories* RIDICULE, mock, deride, scoff at, jeer at, sneer at, jibe at, make fun of, poke fun at, scorn; lampoon, satirize, parody; *informal* send up, take the mickey out of, pooh-pooh; *Austral./NZ informal* poke mullock at.

▶ **noun** ❶ *he gave a short laugh* CHUCKLE, chortle, guffaw, giggle, titter, tee-hee, snigger, snicker, roar/hoot of laughter, shriek of laughter, belly laugh. ❷ (*informal*) *he was a right laugh* JOKER, wag, wit, clown, jester, prankster, character; *informal* card, case, caution, hoot, scream, riot, barrel of laughs; *Austral./NZ informal* hard case. ❸ (*informal*) *I entered the contest for a laugh* JOKE, prank, piece of fun, jest, escapade, caper, practical joke; *informal* lark.

■ **laugh something off** DISMISS, make a joke of, make light of, shrug off, brush aside, scoff at; *informal* pooh-pooh.

laughable ▶ **adjective** ❶ *the idea that nuclear power is safe is laughable* RIDICULOUS, ludicrous, absurd, risible, preposterous; foolish, silly, idiotic, stupid, nonsensical, crazy, insane, outrageous; *informal* cock-eyed; *Brit. informal* daft. ❷ *if it wasn't so tragic, it'd be laughable* AMUSING, funny, humorous, hilarious, uproarious, comical, comic, farcical.

laughing stock ▶ **noun** FIGURE OF FUN, dupe, butt, stooge, Aunt Sally; *informal* fall guy.

laughter ▶ **noun** ❶ *the sound of laughter* LAUGHING, chuckling, chortling, guffawing, giggling, tittering, sniggering; *informal* hysterics. ❷ *a source of laughter* AMUSEMENT, entertainment, humour, mirth, merriment, gaiety, hilarity, jollity, jocularity, fun.

launch ▶ **verb** ❶ *he launched the boat* SET AFLOAT, put to sea, put into the water. ❷ *they've launched the shuttle* SEND INTO ORBIT, blast off, take off, lift off. ❸ *a chair was launched at him* THROW, hurl, fling, pitch, lob, let fly; fire, shoot; *informal* chuck, heave, sling. ❹ *the government launched a new campaign* SET IN MOTION, get going, get under way, start, commence, begin, embark on, initiate, inaugurate, set up, organize, introduce, bring into being; *informal* kick off. ❺ *he launched into a tirade* START, commence, burst into.

launder ▶ **verb** WASH (AND IRON), clean; dry-clean.

laundry ▶ **noun** ❶ *a big pile of laundry* (DIRTY) WASHING, dirty clothes. ❷ *the facilities include a laundry* WASHROOM, laundry room, launderette; *N. Amer. trademark* laundromat.

laurels ▶ **plural noun** HONOURS, tributes, praise, plaudits, accolades, kudos, acclaim, acclamation, credit, glory, honour, distinction, fame, renown, prestige, recognition; *informal* brownie points; *formal* laudation.

lavatory ▶ **noun** TOILET, WC, water closet, (public) convenience, cloakroom, powder room, urinal, privy, latrine, jakes; *N. Amer.* washroom, bathroom, rest room, men's/ladies' room, commode, comfort station; *Nautical* head; *informal* little girls'/boys' room, smallest room; *Brit. informal* loo, bog, the Ladies, the Gents, khazi, lav; *N. Amer. informal* can, john; *Austral./NZ informal* dunny; *archaic* closet, garderobe.

lavish ▶ **adjective** ❶ *lavish parties* SUMPTUOUS, luxurious, gorgeous, costly, expensive, opulent, grand, splendid, rich, fancy; *informal* posh. ❷ *he was lavish with his hospitality* GENEROUS, liberal, bountiful, open-handed, unstinting, unsparing, free, munificent, extravagant, prodigal. ❸ *lavish amounts of champagne* ABUNDANT, copious, plentiful, liberal, prolific, generous; *poetic/literary* plenteous.

–OPPOSITES meagre, frugal.

▶ **verb** *she lavished money on her children* GIVE FREELY, spend generously, heap, shower.

law ▶ **noun** ❶ *the law of the land* RULES AND REGULATIONS, body of laws, constitution, legislation, legal code. ❷ *a new law was passed* REGULATION, statute, enactment, act, bill, decree, edict, rule, ruling, resolution, dictum, command, order, directive, pronouncement, proclamation, dictate, diktat, fiat, by-law; *N. Amer. formal* ordinance. ❸ *a career in the law* THE LEGAL PROFESSION, the bar. ❹ *I'll take you to law!* LITIGATION, legal action, lawsuit, justice. ❺ (*informal*) *on the run from the law.* See POLICE noun. ❻ *the laws of the game* RULE, regulation, principle, convention, instruction, guideline. ❼ *a moral law* PRINCIPLE, rule, precept, directive, injunction, commandment, belief, creed, credo, maxim, tenet, doctrine, canon.

–RELATED TERMS legal.

law-abiding ▶ **adjective** HONEST, lawful, righteous, honourable, upright, upstanding, good, decent, virtuous, moral, dutiful, obedient, compliant, disciplined.

–OPPOSITES criminal.

lawbreaker ▶ **noun** CRIMINAL, felon, wrongdoer, malefactor, evil-doer, offender, transgressor, miscreant; villain, rogue, ruffian; *Law* malfeasant, infractor; *informal* crook, con, jailbird.

law court ▶ **noun** COURT, court of law/justice, tribunal.

–RELATED TERMS judicial, juridical.

lawful ▶ **adjective** ❶ *a verdict of lawful killing* LEGITIMATE, legal, licit, just, permissible, permitted, allowable, allowed, rightful, sanctioned, authorized, warranted, within the law; *informal* legit. ❷ *a lawful political organization* LAW-ABIDING, righteous, good, decent, virtuous, moral, orderly, well behaved, peaceful, dutiful, obedient, compliant, disciplined.

–OPPOSITES illegal, criminal.

lawless ▶ **adjective** ❶ *a lawless rabble* ANARCHIC, disorderly, ungovernable, unruly, disruptive, rebellious, insubordinate, riotous, mutinous. ❷ *lawless activities* ILLEGAL, unlawful, lawbreaking, illicit, illegitimate, criminal, felonious, villainous, miscreant; *informal* crooked, shady, bent.

–OPPOSITES orderly, legal.

lawlessness ▶ **noun** ANARCHY, disorder, chaos, unruliness, criminality, crime.

lawsuit ▶ **noun** (LEGAL) ACTION, suit (at law), case, (legal/judicial) proceedings, litigation, trial.

lawyer ▶ **noun** SOLICITOR, legal practitioner, legal adviser, member of the bar, barrister, advocate, counsel, Queen's Counsel, QC; *N. Amer.* attorney, counselor(-at-law); *informal* brief.

lax ▶ **adjective** SLACK, slipshod, negligent, remiss, careless, heedless, unmindful, slapdash, offhand, casual; easy-going, lenient, permissive, liberal, indulgent, overindulgent; *informal* sloppy.
– OPPOSITES strict.

laxative ▶ **noun** PURGATIVE, evacuant; *Medicine* aperient, cathartic.

lay[1] ▶ **verb** ❶ *Curtis laid the newspaper on the table* PUT (DOWN), place, set (down), deposit, rest, situate, locate, position, stow, shove; *informal* stick, dump, park, plonk; *Brit. informal* bung. ❷ *the act laid the foundation for the new system* SET IN PLACE, set out/up, establish. ❸ *I'll lay money that Michelle will be there* BET, wager, gamble, stake, risk, venture; give odds, speculate; *informal* punt. ❹ *they are going to lay charges* BRING (FORWARD), press, prefer, lodge, register, place, file. ❺ *he laid the blame at the Prime Minister's door* ASSIGN, attribute, ascribe, allot, attach; hold someone responsible/accountable, find guilty, pin the blame on. ❻ *we laid plans for the next voyage* DEVISE, arrange, make (ready), prepare, work out, hatch, design, plan, scheme, plot, conceive, put together, draw up, produce, develop, formulate; *informal* cook up. ❼ *this will lay a new responsibility on the court* IMPOSE, apply, entrust, vest, place, put; inflict, encumber, saddle, charge, burden. ❽ *the eagles laid two eggs* PRODUCE; *Zoology* oviposit.
■ **lay something aside** ❶ *farmers laying aside areas for conservation* PUT ASIDE, put to one side, keep, save. ❷ *producers must lay aside their conservatism* ABANDON, cast aside, reject, renounce, repudiate, disregard, forget, discard; *poetic/literary* forsake. ❸ *protesters led the government to lay the plans aside* DEFER, shelve, suspend, put on ice, mothball, set aside, put off/aside; *informal* put on the back burner.
■ **lay something bare** REVEAL, disclose, divulge, show, expose, exhibit, uncover, unveil, unmask, make a clean breast of, make known, make public.
■ **lay something down** ❶ *he laid down his glass* PUT DOWN, set down, place down, deposit, rest; *informal* dump, plonk down; *Brit. informal* bung down. ❷ *they were forced to lay down their weapons* RELINQUISH, surrender, give up, yield, cede; disarm, give in, submit, capitulate. ❸ *the ground rules have been laid down* FORMULATE, stipulate, set down, draw up, frame; prescribe, ordain, dictate, decree; enact, pass, decide, determine, impose, codify. ❹ *laying down wine* STORE, put into store, keep.
■ **lay down the law** ORDER SOMEONE ABOUT/AROUND, tell someone what to do, ride roughshod over someone; *informal* boss someone about/around, throw one's weight about/around, push someone about/around.
■ **lay eyes on** (*informal*) SEE, spot, observe, regard, view, catch sight of; *informal* clap/set eyes on; *poetic*/literary behold, espy, descry.
■ **lay hands on** ❶ *wait till I lay my hands on you!* CATCH, lay/get hold of, get one's hands on, seize, grab, grasp, capture. ❷ *it's not easy to lay your hands on decent champagne* OBTAIN, acquire, get, come by, find, locate, discover, unearth, uncover, pick up, procure, get one's hands on, get possession of, buy, purchase. ❸ *the pastor laid hands on the children* BLESS, consecrate; confirm; ordain.
■ **lay something in** STOCK UP WITH/ON, stockpile, store (up), amass, hoard, stow (away), put aside/away/by, garner, collect, squirrel away; *informal* salt away, stash (away).
■ **lay into** (*informal*) ❶ *a policeman laying into a protestor. See* ASSAULT verb sense 1. ❷ *he laid into her with a string of insults. See* CRITICIZE.
■ **lay it on thick** (*informal*) EXAGGERATE, overdo it, embellish the truth; flatter, praise, soft-soap; *informal* pile it on, sweet-talk.
■ **lay off** (*informal*) GIVE UP, stop, refrain from, abstain from, desist from, cut out; *informal* pack in, leave off, quit.
■ **lay someone off** MAKE REDUNDANT, dismiss, let go, discharge, give notice to; *informal* sack, fire, give someone their cards, give someone their marching orders, give someone the boot/push, give someone the (old) heave-ho.
■ **lay something on** PROVIDE, supply, furnish, line up, organize, prepare, produce, make available; *informal* fix up.
■ **lay someone out** (*informal*) KNOCK OUT/DOWN, knock unconscious, fell, floor, flatten; *informal* KO, kayo; *Brit. informal* knock for six.
■ **lay something out** ❶ *Robyn laid the plans out on the desk* SPREAD OUT, set out, display, exhibit. ❷ *a paper laying out our priorities* OUTLINE, sketch out, rough out, detail, draw up, formulate, work out, frame, draft. ❸ (*informal*) *he had to lay out £70. See* PAY verb sense 2.
■ **lay waste** DEVASTATE, wipe out, destroy, demolish, annihilate, raze, ruin, wreck, level, flatten, ravage, pillage, sack, despoil.

lay[2] ▶ **adjective** ❶ *a lay preacher* NON-CLERICAL, non-ordained, secular, temporal; *formal* laic. ❷ *a lay audience* NON-PROFESSIONAL, amateur, non-specialist, non-technical, untrained, unqualified.

layabout ▶ **noun** IDLER, good-for-nothing, loafer, lounger, shirker, sluggard, laggard, slugabed, malingerer; *informal* skiver, waster, slacker, lazybones; *Austral./NZ informal* bludger; *poetic/literary* wastrel.

layer ▶ **noun** COATING, sheet, coat, film, covering, blanket, skin, thickness.

layman ▶ **noun.** *See* LAYPERSON senses 1, 2.

lay-off ▶ **noun** REDUNDANCY, dismissal, discharge; *informal* sacking, firing, the sack, the boot, the axe, the elbow.
– OPPOSITES recruitment.

layout ▶ **noun** ❶ *the layout of the house* ARRANGEMENT, geography, design, organization; plan, map. ❷ *the magazine's layout* DESIGN, arrangement, presentation, style, format; structure, organization, composition, configuration.

layperson ▶ **noun** ❶ *a prayer book for laypeople* UNORDAINED PERSON, member of the congregation, layman, laywoman. ❷ *engineering sounds highly specialized to the layperson* NON-EXPERT, layman, non-professional, amateur, non-specialist.

laze ▶ **verb** RELAX, unwind, idle, do nothing, loaf (around/about), lounge (around/about), loll (around/about), lie (around/about), take it easy; *informal* hang around/round, veg (out); *N. Amer. informal* bum (around).

lazy ▶ **adjective** (BONE) IDLE, indolent, slothful, work-shy, shiftless, inactive, sluggish, lethargic; remiss, negligent, slack, lax, lackadaisical; *archaic* otiose.
– OPPOSITES industrious.

lazybones ▶ **noun** (*informal*) IDLER, loafer, layabout, lounger, good-for-nothing, do-nothing, shirker, sluggard, laggard, slugabed; *informal* skiver, waster, slacker; *Austral./NZ informal* bludger; *poetic/literary* wastrel.

leach ▶ **verb** DRAIN, filter, percolate, filtrate, strain.

lead[1] ▶ **verb** ❶ *Michelle led them into the house* GUIDE, conduct, show (the way), lead the way, usher, escort, steer, pilot, shepherd; accompany, see, take. ❷ *he led us to believe they were lying* CAUSE, induce, prompt, move, persuade, influence, drive, condition, make; incline, dispose, predispose. ❸ *this might lead to job losses* RESULT IN, cause, bring on/about, give rise to, be the cause of, make happen, create, produce, occasion, effect, generate, contribute to, promote; provoke, stir up, spark off, arouse, foment, instigate; involve, necessitate, entail; *formal* effectuate. ❹ *he led a march to the city centre* BE AT THE HEAD/FRONT OF, head, spearhead. ❺ *she led a coalition of radicals* BE THE LEADER OF, be the head of, preside over, head, command, govern, rule, be in charge of, be in command of, be in control of, run, control, be at the helm of; administer, organize, manage; reign over, be in power over; *informal* head up. ❻ *Rangers were leading at half-time* BE AHEAD, be winning, be (out) in front, be in the lead, be first. ❼ *the champion was leading the field* BE AT THE FRONT OF, be first in, be ahead of, head; outrun, outstrip, outpace, leave behind, draw away from; outdo, outclass, beat; *informal* leave standing. ❽ *I just want to lead a normal life* EXPERIENCE, have, live, spend.
– OPPOSITES follow.

▶ **noun** ❶ *I was in the lead early on* LEADING POSITION, first place, van, vanguard; ahead, in front, winning. ❷ *they took the lead in the personal computer market* FIRST POSITION, forefront, primacy, dominance, superiority, ascendancy; pre-eminence, supremacy, advantage, upper hand, whip hand. ❸ *sixth-formers should give a lead to younger pupils* EXAMPLE, (role) model, exemplar, paradigm. ❹ *playing the lead* LEADING ROLE, star/starring role, title role, principal part; principal character, male lead, female lead, leading man, leading lady. ❺ *a labrador on a lead* LEASH, tether, cord, rope, chain. ❻ *detectives were following up a new lead* CLUE, pointer, hint, tip, tip-off, suggestion, indication, sign; (**leads**) evidence, information.

▶ **adjective** *the lead position* LEADING, first, top, foremost, front, head; chief, principal, premier.

■ **lead something off** BEGIN, start (off), commence, open; *informal* kick off.

■ **lead someone on** DECEIVE, mislead, delude, hoodwink, dupe, trick, fool, pull the wool over someone's eyes; tease, flirt with; *informal* string along, lead up the garden path, take for a ride.

■ **lead the way** ❶ *he led the way to the kitchen* GUIDE, conduct, show the way. ❷ *Britain is leading the way in aerospace technology* TAKE THE INITIATIVE, break (new) ground, blaze a trail, prepare the way.

■ **lead up to** PREPARE THE WAY FOR, pave the way for, lay the groundwork for, set the scene for, work round/up to, approach the subject of.

lead[2] ▶ **noun** *a lead-lined box.*
– RELATED TERMS plumbic, plumbous, plumb-.

leaden ▶ **adjective** ❶ *his eyes were leaden with sleep* DULL, heavy, weighty; listless, lifeless. ❷ *he moved on leaden feet* SLUGGISH, heavy, lumbering, slow. ❸ *leaden prose* BORING, dull, unimaginative, uninspired, monotonous, heavy, laboured, wooden. ❹ *a leaden sky* GREY, greyish, black, dark; cloudy, gloomy, overcast, dull, murky, sunless, louring, oppressive, threatening; *poetic/literary* tenebrous.

leader ▶ **noun** ❶ *the leader of the Democratic Party* CHIEF, head, principal; commander, captain; controller, superior, headman; chairman, chairwoman, chairperson, chair; (managing) director, MD, manager, superintendent, supervisor, overseer, administrator, employer, master, mistress; president, premier, governor; ruler, monarch, king, queen, sovereign, emperor; *informal* boss, skipper, gaffer, guv'nor, number one, numero uno, honcho; *N. Amer. informal* sachem, padrone. ❷ *a world leader in the use of video conferencing* PIONEER, front runner, innovator, trailblazer, ground-breaker, trendsetter, torch-bearer; originator, initiator, founder, architect.
– OPPOSITES follower, supporter.

leadership ▶ **noun** ❶ *the leadership of the*

Conservative Party HEADSHIP, directorship, premiership, governorship, governance, administration, captaincy, control, ascendancy, rule, command, power, dominion. ❷ *firm leadership* GUIDANCE, direction, control, management, superintendence, supervision; organization, government.

leading ▶ adjective ❶ *he played the leading role in his team's victory* MAIN, chief, major, prime, most significant, principal, foremost, key, central, focal, paramount, dominant, essential. ❷ *the leading industrialized countries* MOST POWERFUL, most important, greatest, chief, preeminent, principal, dominant. ❸ *last season's leading scorer* TOP, highest, best, first; front, lead; unparalleled, matchless, star.
– OPPOSITES subordinate, minor.

leaf ▶ noun ❶ *sycamore leaves* FROND, leaflet, flag; *Botany* cotyledon, blade, bract. ❷ *a sheaf of loose leaves* PAGE, sheet, folio.
– RELATED TERMS foliaceous.
▶ verb *he leafed through the documents* FLICK, flip, thumb, skim, browse, glance, riffle; scan, run one's eye over, peruse.
■ **turn over a new leaf** REFORM, improve, mend one's ways, make a fresh start, change for the better; *informal* go straight.

leaflet ▶ noun PAMPHLET, booklet, brochure, handbill, circular, flyer, handout, bulletin; *N. Amer.* folder, dodger.

league ▶ noun ❶ *a league of nations* ALLIANCE, confederation, confederacy, federation, association, union, coalition, consortium, affiliation, guild, cooperative, partnership, fellowship, syndicate, consociation. ❷ *we won the league last year* CHAMPIONSHIP, competition, contest. ❸ *the store is not in the same league* CLASS, group, category, level.
▶ verb *they leagued together with other companies* ALLY, join forces, join together, unite, band together, affiliate, combine, amalgamate, confederate, team up, join up.
■ **in league with** COLLABORATING WITH, cooperating with, in alliance with, allied with, conspiring with, hand in glove with; *informal* in cahoots with.

leak ▶ verb ❶ *oil leaking from the tanker* SEEP (OUT), escape, ooze (out), emanate, issue, drip, dribble, drain, bleed. ❷ *the tanks are leaking gasoline* DISCHARGE, exude, emit, release, drip, dribble, ooze, secrete. ❸ *civil servants leaking information* DISCLOSE, divulge, reveal, make public, tell, impart, pass on, relate, communicate, expose, broadcast, publish, release, let slip, bring into the open; *informal* blab, let the cat out of the bag, spill the beans, blow the gaff.
▶ noun ❶ *check that there are no leaks in the bag* HOLE, opening, puncture, perforation, gash, slit, nick, rent, break, crack, fissure, rupture. ❷ *a gas leak* DISCHARGE, leakage, leaking, oozing, seeping, seepage, drip, escape. ❸ *leaks to the media* DISCLOSURE, revelation, exposé.

leaky ▶ adjective LEAKING, dripping; cracked, split, punctured, perforated.
– OPPOSITES watertight.

lean[1] ▶ verb ❶ *Polly leaned against the door* REST, recline, be supported. ❷ *trees leaning in the wind* SLANT, incline, bend, tilt, be at an angle, slope, tip, list. ❸ *he leans towards existentialist philosophy* TEND, incline, gravitate; have a preference for, have a penchant for, be partial to, have a liking for, have an affinity with. ❹ *a strong shoulder to lean on* DEPEND, be dependent, rely, count, bank, have faith in, trust. ❺ (*informal*) *I got leaned on by villains* INTIMIDATE, coerce, browbeat, bully, pressurize, threaten, put pressure on; *informal* twist someone's arm, put the frighteners on, put the screws on.

lean[2] ▶ adjective ❶ *a tall, lean man* SLIM, thin, slender, spare, wiry, lanky. ❷ *a lean harvest* MEAGRE, sparse, poor, mean, inadequate, insufficient, paltry, deficient, insubstantial. ❸ *lean times* UNPRODUCTIVE, unfruitful, arid, barren; hard, bad, difficult, tough, impoverished, poverty-stricken.
– OPPOSITES fat, abundant, prosperous.

leaning ▶ noun INCLINATION, tendency, bent, proclivity, propensity, penchant, predisposition, predilection, partiality, preference, bias, attraction, liking, fondness, taste.

leap ▶ verb ❶ *he leapt over the gate* JUMP (OVER), vault (over), spring over, bound over, hop (over), hurdle, clear. ❷ *Claudia leapt to her feet* SPRING, jump (up), bound, dart. ❸ *we leapt to the rescue* RUSH, hurry, hasten. ❹ *she leapt at the chance* ACCEPT EAGERLY, grasp (with both hands), grab, take advantage of, seize (on), jump at. ❺ *don't leap to conclusions* FORM HASTILY, reach hurriedly; hurry, hasten, jump, rush. ❻ *profits leapt by 55%* INCREASE RAPIDLY, soar, rocket, skyrocket, shoot up, escalate.
▶ noun ❶ *an easy leap* JUMP, vault, spring, bound, hop, skip. ❷ *a leap of 33%* SUDDEN RISE, surge, upsurge, upswing, upturn.
■ **in/by leaps and bounds** RAPIDLY, swiftly, quickly, speedily.

learn ▶ verb ❶ *learning a foreign language* ACQUIRE A KNOWLEDGE OF, acquire skill in, become competent in, become proficient in, grasp, master, take in, absorb, assimilate, digest, familiarize oneself with; study, read up on, be taught, have lessons in; *informal* get the hang of, get clued up about. ❷ *she learnt the poem by heart* MEMORIZE, learn by heart, commit to memory, learn parrot-fashion, get off/down pat; *archaic* con. ❸ *he learned that the school would shortly be closing* DISCOVER, find out, become aware, be informed, hear (tell); gather, understand, ascertain, establish; *informal* get wind of the fact; *Brit. informal* suss out.

learned ▶ adjective SCHOLARLY, erudite, well educated, knowledgeable, widely read, well informed, lettered, cultured, intellectual,

academic, literary, bookish, highbrow, studious; *informal* brainy; *formal* sapient.
– OPPOSITES ignorant.

learner ▶ **noun** BEGINNER, trainee, apprentice, pupil, student, novice, newcomer, starter, probationer, tyro, fledgling, neophyte; *N. Amer.* tenderfoot; *N. Amer. informal* greenhorn.
– OPPOSITES veteran.

learning ▶ **noun** ❶ *a centre of learning* STUDY, studying, education, schooling, tuition, teaching, academic work; research, investigation. ❷ *the astonishing range of his learning* SCHOLARSHIP, knowledge, education, erudition, intellect, enlightenment, illumination, edification, book learning, information, understanding, wisdom.
– OPPOSITES ignorance.

lease ▶ **noun** *a 15-year lease* LEASEHOLD, rental/hire agreement, charter; rental, tenancy, tenure, period of occupancy.
– RELATED TERMS lessor, lessee.
– OPPOSITES freehold.
▶ **verb** ❶ *the film crew leased a large hangar* RENT, hire, charter. ❷ *they leased the mill to a reputable family* RENT (OUT), let (out), hire (out), sublet, sublease.

leash ▶ **noun** ❶ *keep your dog on a leash* LEAD, tether, rope, chain, strap, restraint. ❷ *he found himself off the parental leash* CONTROL, restraint, check, curb, rein, discipline.
▶ **verb** ❶ *she leashed the dog* PUT THE LEASH ON, put the lead on, tether, tie up, secure, restrain. ❷ *the ire in her face was barely leashed* CURB, control, keep under control, check, restrain, hold back, suppress.
■ **straining at the leash** EAGER, impatient, anxious, enthusiastic; *informal* itching, dying.

least ▶ **determiner** *I have not the least idea what this means* SLIGHTEST, smallest, minutest, tiniest, littlest.
■ **at least** AT THE MINIMUM, no/not less than, more than.

leather ▶ **noun** *a leather jacket* SKIN, hide.
▶ **verb** *he caught me and leathered me* BEAT, strap, belt, thrash, flog, whip, horsewhip, birch, cane, strike, hit; *informal* wallop, whack, tan someone's hide, give someone a (good) hiding.

leathery ▶ **adjective** ❶ *leathery skin* ROUGH, rugged, wrinkled, wrinkly, furrowed, lined, wizened, weather-beaten, callous, gnarled. ❷ *leathery sides of beef* TOUGH, hard, gristly, chewy, stringy.

leave[1] ▶ **verb** ❶ *I left the hotel* DEPART FROM, go (away) from, withdraw from, retire from, take oneself off from, exit from, take one's leave of, pull out of, quit, be gone from, decamp from, disappear from, vacate, absent oneself from; say one's farewells/goodbyes, make oneself scarce; *informal* push off, shove off, clear out/off, cut and run, split, vamoose, scoot, make tracks, up sticks; *Brit. informal* sling one's hook. ❷ *the next morning we left for Leicester* SET OFF, head, make; set sail. ❸ *he's left his wife* ABANDON, desert, cast aside/off, jilt, leave in the lurch, leave high and dry, throw over; *informal* dump, ditch, chuck, drop, walk/run out on; *poetic/literary* forsake. ❹ *he left his job in November* RESIGN FROM, retire from, step down from, withdraw from, pull out of, give up; *informal* quit. ❺ *she left her handbag on a bus* LEAVE BEHIND, forget, lose, mislay. ❻ *I thought I'd leave it to the experts* ENTRUST, hand over, pass on, refer; delegate. ❼ *he left her £100,000* BEQUEATH, will, endow, hand down, make over; *Law* demise, devise. ❽ *the speech left some feelings of disappointment* CAUSE, produce, generate, give rise to.
– OPPOSITES arrive.
■ **leave someone in the lurch** LEAVE IN TROUBLE, let down, leave stranded, leave high and dry, abandon, desert.
■ **leave off** (*informal*) STOP, cease, finish, desist from, keep from, break off, lay off, give up, discontinue, refrain from, eschew; *informal* quit, knock off, jack in, swear off; *formal* forswear.
■ **leave someone/something out** ❶ *Adam left out the address* MISS OUT, omit, fail to include, overlook, forget; skip, miss, jump. ❷ *he was left out of the England squad* EXCLUDE, omit, drop, pass over.

leave[2] ▶ **noun** ❶ *the judge granted leave to appeal* PERMISSION, consent, authorization, sanction, warrant, dispensation, approval, clearance, blessing, agreement, backing, assent, acceptance, licence, acquiescence; *informal* the go-ahead, the green light, the OK, the rubber stamp. ❷ *he was on leave* HOLIDAY, vacation, break, time off, furlough, sabbatical, leave of absence; *informal* hols, vac. ❸ *I will now take my leave of you* DEPARTURE, leaving, leave-taking, parting, withdrawal, exit, farewell, goodbye.

leaven ▶ **noun** *leaven is added to the dough* LEAVENING, fermentation agent, raising agent.
▶ **verb** ❶ *yeast leavens the bread* RAISE, make rise, puff up, expand. ❷ *formal proceedings leavened by humour* PERMEATE, infuse, pervade, imbue, suffuse; enliven, liven up, invigorate, energize, electrify, ginger up, perk up, brighten up, season, spice; *informal* buck up, pep up.

leavings ▶ **plural noun** RESIDUE, remainder, remains, remnants, leftovers, scrapings, scraps, oddments, odds and ends, rejects, dregs, refuse, rubbish.

lecher ▶ **noun** LECHEROUS MAN, libertine, womanizer, debauchee, rake, roué, profligate, wanton, loose-liver, Don Juan, Casanova, Lothario, Romeo; *informal* lech, dirty old man, goat, wolf; *formal* fornicator.

lecherous ▶ **adjective** LUSTFUL, licentious, lascivious, libidinous, prurient, lewd, salacious, lubricious, debauched, dissolute, wanton, dissipated, degenerate, depraved, dirty, filthy; *informal* randy, horny, goatish; *formal* concupiscent.
– OPPOSITES chaste.

lecture ▶ **noun** ❶ *a lecture on children's literature* SPEECH, talk, address, discourse, disquisition, presentation, oration, lesson. ❷ *Dave got a severe lecture* SCOLDING, chiding, reprimand, rebuke, reproof, reproach, upbraiding, berating, admonishment; *informal* dressing-down, telling-off, talking-to, tongue-lashing; *formal* castigation.

▶ **verb** ❶ *lecturing on the dangers of drugs* GIVE A LECTURE/TALK, talk, make a speech, speak, give an address, discourse, hold forth, declaim, expatiate; *informal* spout, sound off. ❷ *she lectures at Dublin University* TEACH, tutor, give instruction, give lessons. ❸ *he was lectured by the headmaster* SCOLD, chide, reprimand, rebuke, reprove, reproach, upbraid, berate, chastise, admonish, lambaste, haul over the coals, take to task; *informal* give someone a dressing-down, give someone a talking-to, tell off; *Brit. informal* tick off, carpet; *N. Amer. informal* bawl out; *formal* castigate.

lecturer ▶ **noun** ❶ *the lecturer is a journalist* (PUBLIC) SPEAKER, speech-maker, orator. ❷ *a lecturer in economics* UNIVERSITY/COLLEGE TEACHER, tutor, reader, scholar, don, professor, fellow; academic, academician, preceptor; *formal* pedagogue.

ledge ▶ **noun** SHELF, sill, mantel, mantelpiece, shelving; projection, protrusion, overhang, ridge, prominence.

ledger ▶ **noun** (ACCOUNT) BOOK, record book, register, log; records, books; balance sheet, financial statement.

lee ▶ **noun** SHELTER, protection, cover, refuge, safety, security.

leech ▶ **noun** PARASITE, bloodsucker, passenger; *informal* scrounger, sponger, freeloader.

leer ▶ **verb** *Henry leered at her* OGLE, look lasciviously, look suggestively, eye; *informal* give someone a/the once-over, lech after/over.

▶ **noun** *a sly leer* LECHEROUS LOOK, lascivious look, ogle; *informal* the once-over.

leery ▶ **adjective** WARY, cautious, careful, guarded, chary, suspicious, distrustful; worried, anxious, apprehensive.

lees ▶ **plural noun** SEDIMENT, dregs, deposit, grounds, residue, remains, silt, sludge; *technical* residuum; *poetic/literary* draff; *archaic* grouts.

leeway ▶ **noun** FREEDOM, scope, latitude, space, room, liberty, flexibility, licence, free hand, free rein.

left ▶ **adjective** LEFT-HAND, sinistral; *Nautical* port; *Nautical, archaic* larboard; *Heraldry* sinister.
– RELATED TERMS laevo-, sinistro-.
– OPPOSITES right, starboard.

left-handed ▶ **adjective** ❶ *a left-handed golfer* sinistral; *informal* southpaw. ❷ *a left-handed compliment* BACKHANDED, ambiguous, equivocal, double-edged; dubious, indirect, cryptic, ironic, sardonic, insincere, hypocritical.
– OPPOSITES right-handed.

leftover ▶ **noun** ❶ *a leftover from the 60s* RESIDUE, survivor, vestige, legacy. ❷ *put the leftovers in the fridge* LEAVINGS, uneaten food, remainder, scraps, remnants, remains; excess, surplus.

▶ **adjective** *leftover food* REMAINING, left, uneaten, unconsumed; excess, surplus, superfluous, unused, unwanted, spare.

left-wing ▶ **adjective** SOCIALIST, communist, leftist, Labour, Marxist–Leninist, Bolshevik, Trotskyite, Maoist; *informal* commie, lefty, red, pink.
– OPPOSITES right-wing, conservative.

leg ▶ **noun** ❶ *Lee broke his leg* (LOWER) LIMB, shank; *informal* peg, pin; *archaic* member. ❷ *a table leg* UPRIGHT, support, prop. ❸ *the first leg of a European tour* PART, stage, portion, segment, section, phase, stretch, lap.

■ **give someone a leg up** HELP/ASSIST SOMEONE, give someone assistance, lend someone a helping hand, give someone a boost, give someone a flying start.

■ **leg it** (*informal*) ❶ *if the dog starts growling, leg it!* RUN (AWAY), flee, make off, make a break for it, escape, hurry; *informal* hightail it, hotfoot it, make a run for it, cut and run, skedaddle, vamoose, show a clean pair of heels, split, scoot, scram; *Brit. informal* scarper. ❷ *legging it around London* WALK, march, tramp, trek, trudge, plod, wander, go on foot, go on Shanks's pony.

■ **on its last legs** ❶ *my car is on its last legs* DILAPIDATED, worn out, rickety, about to fall apart. ❷ *a foundry business on its last legs* FAILING, about to go bankrupt, near to ruin, going to the wall; *informal* going bust.

■ **pull someone's leg** TEASE, rag, make fun of, chaff, jest, joke with, play a (practical) joke on, play a trick on, make a monkey out of; hoax, fool, deceive, lead on, hoodwink, dupe, beguile, gull; *informal* kid, have on, rib, take for a ride, take the mickey out of; *Brit. informal* wind up; *N. Amer. informal* put on.

■ **stretch one's legs** GO FOR A WALK, take a stroll, walk, stroll, move about, get some exercise.

legacy ▶ **noun** ❶ *a legacy from a great aunt* BEQUEST, inheritance, heritage, bequeathal, bestowal, endowment, gift, patrimony, settlement, birthright; *Law, dated* hereditament; *formal* benefaction. ❷ *the rancorous legacy of the war* CONSEQUENCE, effect, upshot, spin-off, repercussion, aftermath, by-product, result.

legal ▶ **adjective** ❶ *all their actions were legal* LAWFUL, legitimate, licit, within the law, legalized, valid; permissible, permitted, allowable, allowed, above board, admissible, acceptable; authorized, sanctioned, licensed, constitutional; *informal* legit. ❷ *the legal profession* JUDICIAL, juridical, judicatory.
– OPPOSITES criminal.

legality ▶ **noun** LAWFULNESS, legitimacy, validity, admissibility, permissibility, constitutionality; justice.

legalize ▸ verb MAKE LEGAL, decriminalize, legitimize, legitimatize, legitimate, permit, allow, authorize, sanction, license; regularize, normalize; *informal* OK, give the go-ahead to, give the thumbs up to, give the green light to.
– OPPOSITES prohibit.

legate ▸ noun ENVOY, emissary, agent, ambassador, representative, nuncio, commissioner, delegate, proxy, deputy, plenipotentiary, messenger.

legatee ▸ noun BENEFICIARY, inheritor, heir, heiress, recipient; *Law* devisee; *Scottish Law* heritor.

legation ▸ noun ❶ *the British legation* (DIPLOMATIC) MISSION, delegation, deputation, contingent; envoys, delegates, diplomats, aides. ❷ *the legations were besieged* EMBASSY, consulate.

legend ▸ noun ❶ *the Arthurian legends* MYTH, saga, epic, (folk) tale, (folk) story, fairy tale, fable, mythos, mythus; folklore, lore, mythology, fantasy, oral history, folk tradition. ❷ *pop legends* CELEBRITY, star, superstar, icon, phenomenon, luminary, giant; *informal* celeb, megastar. ❸ *the wording of the legend* CAPTION, inscription, dedication, slogan, heading, title, subtitle, sub-heading, rubric. ❹ *the legend to Figure 5* EXPLANATION, key, guide.

legendary ▸ adjective ❶ *legendary kings* FABLED, heroic, traditional, fairy-tale, storybook, mythical, mythological. ❷ *a legendary figure in the trade-union movement* FAMOUS, celebrated, famed, renowned, acclaimed, illustrious, esteemed, honoured, exalted, venerable, well known, popular, prominent, distinguished, great, eminent, pre-eminent; *formal* lauded.
– OPPOSITES historical.

legerdemain ▸ noun ❶ *stage magicians practising legerdemain* SLEIGHT OF HAND, conjuring, magic, wizardry; *formal* prestidigitation; *rare* thaumaturgy. ❷ *a piece of management legerdemain* TRICKERY, cunning, artfulness, craftiness, chicanery, skulduggery, deceit, deception, artifice; *Brit. informal* jiggery-pokery.

legibility ▸ noun READABILITY, clarity, clearness, neatness.

legible ▸ adjective READABLE, easy to read, easily deciphered, clear, plain, neat, intelligible.

legion ▸ noun ❶ *a Roman legion* BRIGADE, regiment, battalion, company, troop, division, squadron, squad, platoon, unit. ❷ *the legions of TV cameras* HORDE, throng, multitude, crowd, mass, mob, gang, swarm, flock, herd, score, army.
▸ adjective *her fans are legion* NUMEROUS, countless, innumerable, incalculable, many, abundant, plentiful; *poetic/literary* myriad.

legislate ▸ verb MAKE LAWS, pass laws, enact laws, formulate laws.

legislation ▸ noun LAW, body of laws, rules, rulings, regulations, acts, bills, statutes, enactments; *N. Amer. formal* ordinances.

legislative ▸ adjective LAW-MAKING, judicial, juridical, parliamentary, governmental, policy-making.

legislator ▸ noun LAWMAKER, lawgiver, parliamentarian, Member of Parliament, MP, congressman, congresswoman, senator.

legitimate ▸ adjective ❶ *the only form of legitimate gambling* LEGAL, lawful, licit, legalized, authorized, permitted, permissible, allowable, allowed, admissible, sanctioned, approved, licensed, statutory, constitutional; *informal* legit. ❷ *the legitimate heir* RIGHTFUL, lawful, genuine, authentic, real, true, proper, authorized, sanctioned, acknowledged, recognized. ❸ *legitimate grounds for unease* VALID, sound, admissible, acceptable, well founded, justifiable, reasonable, sensible, just, fair, bona fide.
– OPPOSITES illegal, invalid.

legitimize ▸ verb VALIDATE, legitimate, permit, authorize, sanction, license, condone, justify, endorse, support; legalize.
– OPPOSITES outlaw.

leisure ▸ noun *the balance between leisure and work* FREE TIME, spare time, time off; recreation, relaxation, inactivity, pleasure; *informal* R and R.
– OPPOSITES work.
■ **at your leisure** AT YOUR CONVENIENCE, when it suits you, in your own (good) time, without haste, unhurriedly.

leisurely ▸ adjective UNHURRIED, relaxed, easy, gentle, sedate, comfortable, restful, undemanding, slow, lazy.
– OPPOSITES hurried.

lemon
– RELATED TERMS citrous.

lend ▸ verb ❶ *I'll lend you my towel* LOAN, let someone use; advance; *Brit. informal* sub. ❷ *these examples lend weight to his assertions* ADD, impart, give, bestow, confer, provide, supply, furnish, contribute.
– OPPOSITES borrow.
■ **lend an ear** LISTEN, pay attention, take notice, be attentive, concentrate, (pay) heed; *informal* be all ears; *archaic* hearken.
■ **lend a hand** HELP (OUT), give a helping hand, assist, give assistance, make a contribution, do one's bit; *informal* pitch in, muck in, get stuck in.
■ **lend itself to** BE SUITABLE FOR, be suited to, be appropriate for, be applicable for.

length ▸ noun ❶ *a length of three or four metres* | *the whole length of the valley* EXTENT, distance, linear measure, span, reach; area, expanse, stretch, range, scope. ❷ *a considerable length of time* PERIOD, duration, stretch, span. ❸ *a length of blue silk* PIECE, swatch, measure. ❹ *MPs criticized the length of the speech* PROTRACTEDNESS, lengthiness, extent, extensiveness; prolixity, wordiness, verbosity, verboseness, long-windedness.

■ **at length** ❶ *he spoke at length* FOR A LONG TIME, for ages, for hours, interminably, endlessly, ceaselessly, unendingly. ❷ *he was questioned at length* THOROUGHLY, fully, in detail, in depth, comprehensively, exhaustively, extensively. ❸ *his search led him, at length, to Seattle* AFTER A LONG TIME, eventually, in time, finally, at (long) last, in the end, ultimately.

■ **go to any length(s)** DO ABSOLUTELY ANYTHING, go to any extreme.

lengthen ▶ **verb** ❶ *he lengthened his stride* ELONGATE, make longer, extend; expand, widen, broaden, enlarge. ❷ *the days are lengthening* GROW/GET LONGER, draw out. ❸ *you'll need to lengthen the cooking time* PROLONG, make longer, increase, extend, expand, protract, stretch out.
– OPPOSITES shorten.

lengthy ▶ **adjective** ❶ *a lengthy civil war* (VERY) LONG, long-lasting, prolonged, extended. ❷ *lengthy discussions* PROTRACTED, overlong, long-drawn-out; verbose, wordy, prolix, long-winded; tedious, boring, interminable.
– OPPOSITES short.

leniency ▶ **noun** MERCIFULNESS, mercy, clemency, forgiveness; tolerance, forbearance, humanity, charity, indulgence, mildness; pity, sympathy, compassion, understanding.

lenient ▶ **adjective** MERCIFUL, clement, forgiving, forbearing, tolerant, charitable, humane, indulgent, easy-going, magnanimous, sympathetic, compassionate.
– OPPOSITES severe.

leper ▶ **noun** (SOCIAL) OUTCAST, pariah, undesirable, persona non grata.

leprechaun ▶ **noun** PIXIE, goblin, elf, sprite, fairy, gnome, imp, brownie.

lesbian ▶ **noun** HOMOSEXUAL WOMAN, gay woman; *informal* les, lesbo, lezzy, butch, dyke.
– OPPOSITES heterosexual.
▶ **adjective** HOMOSEXUAL, gay; *informal* les, lesbo, lezzy, butch, dykey, queer, bent.
– OPPOSITES straight.

lesion ▶ **noun** WOUND, injury, bruise, abrasion, contusion; ulcer, ulceration, (running) sore, abscess; *Medicine* trauma.

less ▶ **pronoun** *the fare is less than £1* A SMALLER AMOUNT, not so/as much as, under, below.
– OPPOSITES more.
▶ **determiner** *there was less noise now* NOT SO MUCH, smaller, slighter, shorter, reduced; fewer.
▶ **adverb** *we must use the car less* TO A LESSER DEGREE, to a smaller extent, not so/as much.
▶ **preposition** *list price less 10 per cent* MINUS, subtracting, excepting, without.
– OPPOSITES plus.

lessen ▶ **verb** ❶ *exercise lessens the risk of heart disease* REDUCE, make less/smaller, minimize, decrease; allay, assuage, alleviate, attenuate, palliate, ease, dull, deaden, blunt, moderate, mitigate, dampen, soften, tone down, dilute, weaken. ❷ *the pain began to lessen* GROW LESS, grow smaller, decrease, diminish, decline, subside, abate; fade, die down/off, let up, ease off, tail off, drop (off/away), fall, dwindle, ebb, wane, recede. ❸ *his behaviour lessened him in their eyes* DIMINISH, degrade, discredit, devalue, belittle.
– OPPOSITES increase.

lesser ▶ **adjective** ❶ *a lesser offence* LESS IMPORTANT, minor, secondary, subsidiary, marginal, ancillary, auxiliary, supplementary, peripheral; inferior, insignificant, unimportant, petty. ❷ *you look down at us lesser mortals* SUBORDINATE, minor, inferior, second-class, subservient, lowly, humble.
– OPPOSITES greater, superior.

lesson ▶ **noun** ❶ *a maths lesson* CLASS, session, seminar, tutorial, lecture, period (of instruction/teaching). ❷ *they should be industrious at their lessons* EXERCISES, assignments, schoolwork, homework. ❸ *reading the lesson in assembly* BIBLE READING, scripture, text, reading. ❹ *Stuart's accident should be a lesson to all parents* WARNING, deterrent, caution; example, exemplar, message, moral.

lest ▶ **conjunction** (JUST) IN CASE, for fear that, in order to avoid.

let ▶ **verb** ❶ *let him sleep for now* ALLOW, permit, give permission to, give leave to, authorize, sanction, grant the right to, license, empower, enable, entitle; assent to, consent to, agree to, acquiesce in, tolerate, countenance, give one's blessing to, give assent to, give someone/something the nod; *informal* give the green light to, give the go-ahead to, give the thumbs up to, OK; *formal* accede to; *archaic* suffer. ❷ *Wilcox opened the door to let her through* ALLOW TO GO, permit to pass; make way for. ❸ *they've let their flat* RENT (OUT), let out, lease, hire (out), sublet, sublease.
– OPPOSITES prevent, prohibit.

■ **let someone down** FAIL (TO SUPPORT), fall short of expectation, disappoint, disillusion; abandon, desert, leave stranded, leave in the lurch.

■ **let something down** LENGTHEN, make longer.

■ **let fly** ❶ *he let fly with a brick* HURL, fling, throw, propel, pitch, lob, toss, launch; shoot, fire, blast; *informal* chuck, sling, heave. ❷ *she let fly at Geoffrey* LOSE ONE'S TEMPER WITH, lash out at, scold, chastise, chide, rant at, inveigh against, rail against; explode, burst out, let someone have it; *informal* carpet, give someone a rocket, tear someone off a strip; *formal* excoriate.

■ **let go** RELEASE (ONE'S HOLD ON), loose/loosen one's hold on, relinquish; *archaic* unhand.

■ **let someone go** MAKE REDUNDANT, dismiss, discharge, lay off, give notice to, axe; *informal* sack, fire, give someone their cards, give someone their marching orders, send packing, give someone the boot/push, give someone the (old) heave-ho.

■ **let someone in** ALLOW TO ENTER, allow in, admit, open the door to; receive, welcome, greet.

■ **let someone in on something** INCLUDE, count in, admit, allow to share in, let participate in, inform about, tell about.

■ **let something off** DETONATE, discharge, explode, set off, fire off.

■ **let someone off** ❶ (*informal*) *I'll let you off this time* PARDON, forgive, grant an amnesty to; deal leniently with, be merciful to, have mercy on; acquit, absolve, exonerate, clear, vindicate; *informal* let someone off the hook; *formal* exculpate. ❷ *he let me off work* EXCUSE FROM, exempt from, spare from.

■ **let on** (*informal*) ❶ *I never let on that I felt anxious* REVEAL, make known, tell, disclose, mention, divulge, let slip, give away, make public; blab; *informal* let the cat out of the bag, give the game away. ❷ *they all let on they didn't hear me* PRETEND, feign, affect, make out, make believe, simulate.

■ **let something out** ❶ *I let out a cry of triumph* UTTER, emit, give (vent to), produce, issue, express, voice, release. ❷ *she let out that he'd given her a lift home* REVEAL, make known, tell, disclose, mention, divulge, let slip, give away, let it be known, blurt out.

■ **let someone out** RELEASE, liberate, (set) free, let go, discharge; set/turn loose, allow to leave.

■ **let up** (*informal*) ❶ *the rain has let up* ABATE, lessen, decrease, diminish, subside, relent, slacken, die down/off, ease (off), tail off; ebb, wane, dwindle, fade; stop, cease, finish. ❷ *you never let up, do you?* RELAX, ease up/off, slow down; pause, break (off), take a break, rest, stop; *informal* take a breather. ❸ *I promise I'll let up on him* TREAT LESS SEVERELY, be more lenient with, be kinder to; *informal* go easy on.

let-down ▶ **noun** DISAPPOINTMENT, anticlimax, comedown, non-event, fiasco, setback, blow; *informal* washout, damp squib.

lethal ▶ **adjective** FATAL, deadly, mortal, death-dealing, life-threatening, murderous, killing; poisonous, toxic, noxious, venomous; dangerous, destructive, harmful, pernicious; *poetic/literary* deathly, nocuous; *archaic* baneful.
– OPPOSITES harmless, safe.

lethargic ▶ **adjective** SLUGGISH, inert, inactive, slow, torpid, lifeless; languid, listless, lazy, idle, indolent, shiftless, slothful, apathetic, weary, tired, fatigued.

lethargy ▶ **noun** SLUGGISHNESS, inertia, inactivity, inaction, slowness, torpor, torpidity, lifelessness, listlessness, languor, languidness, laziness, idleness, indolence, shiftlessness, sloth, apathy, passivity, weariness, tiredness, lassitude, fatigue; *poetic/literary* hebetude.
– OPPOSITES vigour, energy.

letter ▶ **noun** ❶ *capital letters* (ALPHABETICAL) CHARACTER, sign, symbol, mark, figure, rune; *Linguistics* grapheme. ❷ *she received a letter* (WRITTEN) MESSAGE, (written) communication, note, line, missive, dispatch; correspondence, news, information, intelligence, word; post, mail; *formal* epistle. ❸ *a man of letters* (BOOK) LEARNING, scholarship, erudition, education, knowledge; intellect, intelligence, enlightenment, wisdom, sagacity, culture.
– RELATED TERMS epistolary.

■ **to the letter** STRICTLY, precisely, exactly, accurately, closely, faithfully, religiously, punctiliously, literally, verbatim, in every detail.

lettered ▶ **adjective** LEARNED, erudite, academic, (well) educated, well read, widely read, knowledgeable, intellectual, well schooled, enlightened, cultured, cultivated, scholarly, bookish, highbrow, studious.
– OPPOSITES ill-educated.

let-up ▶ **noun** (*informal*) ABATEMENT, lessening, decrease, diminishing, diminution, decline, relenting, remission, slackening, weakening, relaxation, dying down, easing off, tailing off, dropping away/off; respite, break, interval, hiatus, suspension, cessation, stop, pause.

level ▶ **adjective** ❶ *a smooth and level surface* FLAT, smooth, even, uniform, plane, flush, plumb. ❷ *he kept his voice level* UNCHANGING, steady, unvarying, even, uniform, regular, constant, invariable, unaltering; calm, unemotional, composed, equable, unruffled, serene, tranquil. ❸ *the scores were level* EQUAL, even, drawn, tied, all square, neck and neck, level pegging, on a par, evenly matched; *informal* even-steven(s). ❹ *his eyes were level with hers* ALIGNED, on the same level as, on a level, at the same height as, in line.
– OPPOSITES uneven, unsteady, unequal.

▶ **noun** ❶ *the post is at research-officer level* RANK, standing, status, position; echelon, degree, grade, gradation, stage, standard, rung; class, stratum, group, grouping, set, classification. ❷ *a high level of employment* QUANTITY, amount, extent, measure, degree, volume, size, magnitude, intensity, proportion. ❸ *the level of water is rising* HEIGHT, highness, altitude, elevation. ❹ *the sixth level* FLOOR, storey, deck.

▶ **verb** ❶ *tilt the tin to level the mixture* MAKE LEVEL, level out/off, make even, even off/out, make flat, flatten, smooth (out), make uniform. ❷ *bulldozers levelled the building* RAZE (TO THE GROUND), demolish, flatten, topple, destroy; tear down, knock down, pull down, bulldoze. ❸ *he levelled his opponent with a single blow* KNOCK DOWN/OUT, knock to the ground, lay out, prostrate, flatten, floor, fell; *informal* KO, kayo. ❹ *Carl levelled the score* EQUALIZE, make equal, equal, even (up), make level. ❺ *he levelled his pistol at me* AIM, point, direct, train, focus, turn. ❻ (*informal*) *I knew you'd level with me* BE FRANK, be open, be honest, be above board, tell the truth, tell all, hide nothing, be straightforward; *informal* be upfront.

■ **on the level** (*informal*) GENUINE, straight, honest, above board, fair, true, sincere, straightforward; *informal* upfront; *N. Amer. informal* on the up and up.

level-headed ▶ **adjective** SENSIBLE, practical, realistic, prudent, pragmatic, wise, reasonable, rational, mature, judicious, sound, sober, businesslike, no-nonsense, composed, calm, {cool, calm, and collected}, confident, well balanced, equable, cool-headed, self-possessed, having one's feet on the ground; *informal* unflappable, together.
– OPPOSITES excitable.

lever ▶ **noun** ❶ *you can insert a lever and prise the rail off* CROWBAR, bar, jemmy. ❷ *he pulled the lever* HANDLE, grip, pull, switch.
▶ **verb** *he levered the door open* PRISE, force, wrench, pull, wrest, heave; *N. Amer.* pry; *informal* jemmy.

leverage ▶ **noun** ❶ *the long handles provide increased leverage* GRIP, purchase, hold; support, anchorage, force, strength. ❷ *they have significant leverage in negotiations* INFLUENCE, power, authority, weight, sway, pull, control, say, dominance, advantage, pressure; *informal* clout, muscle, teeth.

levitate ▶ **noun** FLOAT, rise (into the air), hover, be suspended, glide, hang, fly, soar up.

levity ▶ **noun** LIGHT-HEARTEDNESS, high spirits, vivacity, liveliness, cheerfulness, cheeriness, humour, gaiety, fun, jocularity, hilarity, frivolity, frivolousness, amusement, mirth, laughter, merriment, glee, comedy, wit, wittiness, jollity, joviality.
– OPPOSITES seriousness.

levy ▶ **verb** ❶ *a proposal to levy VAT on fuel* IMPOSE, charge, exact, raise, collect; tax. ❷ (*archaic*) *levying troops* CONSCRIPT, call up, enlist, mobilize, rally, muster, marshal, recruit, raise; *US* draft.
▶ **noun** ❶ *the levy of taxation* IMPOSITION, raising, collection; *formal* exaction. ❷ *the levy on spirits* TAX, tariff, toll, excise, duty, imposition, impost; *formal* mulct. ❸ (*archaic*) *not shire levies, but professional soldiers* CONSCRIPTS, troops, (armed) forces, army, militia.

lewd ▶ **adjective** ❶ *a lewd old man* LECHEROUS, lustful, licentious, lascivious, dirty, prurient, salacious, lubricious, libidinous, lickerish; debauched, depraved, degenerate, decadent, dissipated, dissolute, perverted; *informal* horny; *Brit. informal* randy; *formal* concupiscent. ❷ *a lewd song* VULGAR, crude, smutty, dirty, filthy, obscene, pornographic, coarse, off colour, unseemly, indecent, salacious; rude, racy, risqué, naughty, earthy, spicy, bawdy, ribald; *informal* blue, raunchy, X-rated, nudge-nudge, porno; *N. Amer. informal* raw; *euphemistic* adult.
– OPPOSITES chaste, clean.

lexicon ▶ **noun** DICTIONARY, wordbook, vocabulary list, glossary, word-finder, thesaurus.

liability ▶ **noun** ❶ *journalists' liability for defamation* ACCOUNTABILITY, (legal) responsibility, answerability; blame, blameworthiness, culpability, guilt, fault. ❷ *they have big liabilities* FINANCIAL OBLIGATIONS, debts, arrears, dues. ❸ *an electoral liability* HINDRANCE, encumbrance, burden, handicap, nuisance, inconvenience; obstacle, impediment, disadvantage, weakness, shortcoming; millstone round one's neck, albatross, Achilles heel; *archaic* cumber. ❹ *their liability to the disease* SUSCEPTIBILITY, vulnerability, proneness, tendency, predisposition, propensity.
– OPPOSITES immunity, asset.

liable ▶ **adjective** ❶ *they are liable for negligence* (LEGALLY) RESPONSIBLE, accountable, answerable, chargeable, blameworthy, at fault, culpable, guilty. ❷ *my income is liable to fluctuate wildly* LIKELY, inclined, tending, disposed, apt, predisposed, prone, given. ❸ *areas liable to flooding* EXPOSED, prone, subject, susceptible, vulnerable, in danger of, at risk of.

liaise ▶ **verb** COOPERATE, work together, collaborate; communicate, network, interface, link up.

liaison ▶ **noun** ❶ *the branches work in close liaison* COOPERATION, contact, association, connection, collaboration, communication, alliance, partnership. ❷ *Dave was my White House liaison* INTERMEDIARY, mediator, middleman, contact, link, linkman, linkwoman, linkperson, go-between, representative, agent. ❸ *a secret liaison* (LOVE) AFFAIR, relationship, romance, attachment, fling, amour, affair of the heart, (romantic) entanglement; *informal* hanky-panky.

liar ▶ **noun** FIBBER, deceiver, perjurer, false witness, fabricator; romancer, fabulist; *informal* storyteller.

libation ▶ **noun** ❶ *they pour libations into the holy well* (LIQUID) OFFERING, tribute, oblation. ❷ (*humorous*) *would you like a small libation?* (ALCOHOLIC) DRINK, beverage, liquid refreshment; dram, draught, nip, tot; *informal* tipple; *archaic* potation.

libel ▶ **noun** *she sued two newspapers for libel* DEFAMATION (OF CHARACTER), character assassination, calumny, misrepresentation, scandalmongering; aspersions, denigration, vilification, disparagement, derogation, insult, slander, malicious gossip, traducement; lie, slur, smear, untruth, false report; *informal* mud-slinging, bad-mouthing.
▶ **verb** *she alleged the magazine had libelled her* DEFAME, malign, slander, blacken someone's name, sully someone's reputation, speak ill/evil of, traduce, smear, cast aspersions on, drag someone's name through the mud/mire, besmirch, tarnish, taint, tell lies about, stain, vilify, denigrate, disparage, run down, stigmatize, discredit; *N. Amer.* slur; *formal* derogate, calumniate.

libellous ▶ **adjective** DEFAMATORY, denigratory,

vilifying, disparaging, derogatory, calumnious, slanderous, false, untrue, traducing, maligning, insulting, scurrilous.

liberal ▶ **adjective** ❶ *the values of a liberal society* TOLERANT, unprejudiced, unbigoted, broad-minded, open-minded, enlightened; permissive, free (and easy), easy-going, libertarian, indulgent, lenient. ❷ *a liberal social agenda* PROGRESSIVE, advanced, modern, forward-looking, forward-thinking, progressivist, enlightened, reformist, radical; *informal* go-ahead. ❸ *a liberal education* WIDE-RANGING, broad-based, general. ❹ *a liberal interpretation of divorce laws* FLEXIBLE, broad, loose, rough, free, general, non-literal, non-specific, imprecise, vague, indefinite. ❺ *liberal coatings of paint* ABUNDANT, copious, ample, plentiful, generous, lavish, luxuriant, profuse, considerable, prolific, rich; *poetic/literary* plenteous. ❻ *they were liberal with their cash* GENEROUS, open-handed, unsparing, unstinting, ungrudging, lavish, free, munificent, bountiful, big-hearted, benevolent, beneficent, philanthropic, charitable, altruistic, unselfish; *poetic/literary* bounteous.
–OPPOSITES reactionary, strict, miserly.

liberate ▶ **verb** (SET) FREE, release, let out/go, set/let loose, save, rescue; emancipate, enfranchise; *historical* manumit.
–OPPOSITES imprison, enslave.

liberation ▶ **noun** ❶ *the liberation of prisoners* FREEING, release, rescue, setting free; freedom, liberty; emancipation; *historical* manumission. ❷ *women's liberation* FREEDOM, equality, equal rights, emancipation, enfranchisement.
–OPPOSITES confinement, oppression.

liberator ▶ **noun** RESCUER, saviour, deliverer, emancipator; *historical* manumitter.

libertine ▶ **noun** *an unrepentant libertine* PHILANDERER, playboy, rake, roué, Don Juan, Lothario, Casanova, Romeo; lecher, seducer, womanizer, adulterer, debauchee, profligate, wanton; *informal* skirt-chaser, ladykiller, lech, wolf; *formal* fornicator.
▶ **adjective** *libertine sexual intercourse* LICENTIOUS, lustful, libidinous, lecherous, lascivious, lubricious, dissolute, dissipated, debauched, wanton, degenerate, depraved, promiscuous, lewd, prurient, salacious, intemperate, lickerish; *informal* loose, fast, goatish; *formal* concupiscent.

liberty ▶ **noun** ❶ *personal liberty* FREEDOM, independence, free rein, license, self-determination, free will, latitude. ❷ *the essence of British liberty* INDEPENDENCE, freedom, autonomy, sovereignty, self government, self rule, self determination; civil liberties, human rights. ❸ *the liberty to go where one pleases* RIGHT, birthright, prerogative, entitlement, privilege, permission, sanction, authorization, authority, licence.
–OPPOSITES constraint, slavery.

■ **at liberty** ❶ *he was at liberty for three months* FREE, (on the) loose, at large, unconfined; escaped, out. ❷ *your great aunt was at liberty to divide her estate how she chose* FREE, permitted, allowed, authorized, able, entitled, eligible.

■ **take liberties** ACT WITH FAMILIARITY, show disrespect, act with impropriety, act indecorously, be impudent, act with impertinence; take advantage, exploit.

libidinous ▶ **adjective** LUSTFUL, lecherous, lascivious, lewd, carnal, salacious, prurient, licentious, libertine, lubricious, dissolute, debauched, depraved, degenerate, decadent, dissipated, wanton, promiscuous, lickerish; *informal* horny, goatish, wolfish; *Brit. informal* randy; *formal* concupiscent.

libido ▶ **noun** SEX DRIVE, sexual appetite; (sexual) desire, passion, sexiness, sensuality, sexuality, lust, lustfulness; *informal* horniness; *Brit. informal* randiness; *formal* concupiscence.

licence ▶ **noun** ❶ *a driving licence* PERMIT, certificate, document, documentation, authorization, warrant; certification, credentials; pass, papers. ❷ *teachers had licence to administer beatings* PERMISSION, authority, right, a free hand, leave, authorization, entitlement, privilege, prerogative; liberty, freedom, power. ❸ *they manufacture footwear under licence* FRANCHISE, permission, consent, sanction, warrant, warranty, charter. ❹ *the army have too much licence* FREEDOM, liberty, free rein, latitude, independence, scope, impunity, carte blanche. ❺ *poetic licence* DISREGARD FOR THE FACTS, inventiveness, invention, creativity, imagination, fancy, freedom, looseness. ❻ *the licence of the age* LICENTIOUSNESS, dissoluteness, dissipation, debauchery, immorality, impropriety, decadence, intemperateness, excess, excessiveness, lack of restraint.

license ▶ **verb** PERMIT, allow, authorize, grant/give authority to, grant/give permission to; certify, empower, entitle, enable, give approval to, let, qualify, sanction.
–OPPOSITES ban.

licentious ▶ **adjective** DISSOLUTE, dissipated, debauched, degenerate, immoral, naughty, wanton, decadent, depraved, sinful, corrupt; lustful, lecherous, lascivious, libidinous, prurient, lubricious, lewd, promiscuous, lickerish; *formal* concupiscent.
–OPPOSITES moral.

licit ▶ **adjective** LEGITIMATE, permissible, admissible, allowable; permitted, allowed, sanctioned, authorized, warranted; lawful, legal, statutory, legalized, licensed; *informal* legit.
–OPPOSITES forbidden.

lick ▶ **verb** ❶ *the spaniel licked his face* pass one's tongue over, touch with one's tongue, tongue; lap, slurp. ❷ *flames licking round the coal* FLICKER, play, flit, dance. ❸ (*informal*) *they licked the home side 3-0. See* DEFEAT verb sense 1. ❹ (*informal*) *the* *government have inflation licked* OVERCOME, get the better of, find an answer/solution to, conquer, beat, control, master, curb, check.

▶ **noun** (*informal*) ❶ *a lick of paint* DAB, bit, drop, dash, spot, touch, splash; *informal* smidgen. ❷ *they ran up at a fair lick* SPEED, rate, pace, tempo; *informal* clip.

licking ▶ **noun** (*informal*) ❶ *Arsenal took a licking* DEFEAT, beating, trouncing, thrashing; *informal* hiding, pasting, hammering, drubbing; *N. Amer. informal* shellacking. ❷ *Ray got the worst licking of his life* THRASHING, beating, flogging, whipping; *informal* walloping, hiding, pasting, lathering; *N. Amer. informal* whaling.

lid ▶ **noun** *the lid of a saucepan* COVER, top, cap, covering.

■ **put a/the lid on** (*informal*) STOP, control, end, put an end/stop to, put paid to.

■ **lift the lid off/on** (*informal*) EXPOSE, reveal, make known, make public, bring into the open, disclose, divulge; *informal* spill the beans, blow the gaff, blab.

lie[1] ▶ **noun** *loyalty had made him tell lies* UNTRUTH, falsehood, fib, fabrication, deception, invention, (piece of) fiction, falsification; (little) white lie, half-truth, exaggeration; *informal* tall story, whopper; *Brit. informal* porky (pie).

– RELATED TERMS mendacious.

– OPPOSITES truth.

▶ **verb** *he had lied to the police* TELL AN UNTRUTH/LIE, fib, dissemble, dissimulate, tell a white lie, perjure oneself, commit perjury; *informal* lie through one's teeth; *formal* forswear oneself.

■ **give the lie to** DISPROVE, contradict, negate, deny, refute, rebut, controvert, belie, invalidate, discredit, debunk; challenge, call into question; *informal* shoot full of holes, shoot down (in flames); *formal* confute, gainsay.

lie[2] ▶ **verb** ❶ *he was lying on a bed* RECLINE, lie down/back, be recumbent, be prostrate, be supine, be prone, be stretched out, sprawl, rest, repose, lounge, loll. ❷ *her handbag lay on a chair* BE PLACED, be situated, be positioned, rest. ❸ *lying on the border of Switzerland and Austria* BE SITUATED, be located, be placed, be found, be sited. ❹ *his body lies in a crypt* BE BURIED, be interred, be laid to rest, rest, be entombed. ❺ *the difficulty lies in building real quality into the products* CONSIST, be inherent, be present, be contained, exist, reside.

– OPPOSITES stand.

■ **lie heavy on** TROUBLE, worry, bother, torment, oppress, nag, prey on one's mind, plague, niggle at, gnaw at, haunt; *informal* bug.

■ **lie low** HIDE (OUT), go into hiding, conceal oneself, keep out of sight, go to earth/ground; *informal* hole up; *Brit. informal, dated* lie doggo.

liege ▶ **noun** (LIEGE) LORD, feudal lord, overlord, master, chief, superior, baron, monarch, sovereign; *historical* suzerain, seigneur.

lieutenant ▶ **noun** DEPUTY, second in command, right-hand man/woman, number two, assistant, aide; *informal* sidekick.

life ▶ **noun** ❶ *the joy of giving life to a child* EXISTENCE, being, living, animation; sentience, creation, viability. ❷ *threats to life on the planet* LIVING BEINGS/CREATURES, the living; human/animal/plant life, fauna, flora, ecosystems; human beings, humanity, humankind, mankind, man. ❸ *an easy life* WAY OF LIFE/LIVING, lifestyle, situation, fate, lot. ❹ *the last nine months of his life* LIFETIME, life span, days, time on earth, existence. ❺ *the life of a Parliament* DURATION, lifetime, existence. ❻ *he is full of life* VIVACITY, animation, liveliness, vitality, verve, high spirits, exuberance, zest, buoyancy, enthusiasm, energy, vigour, dynamism, elan, gusto, brio, bounce, spirit, fire; (hustle and) bustle, movement; *informal* oomph, pizzazz, pep, zing, zip, vim. ❼ *the life of the party* MOVING SPIRIT, (vital) spirit, life force, lifeblood, heart, soul. ❽ *more than 1,500 lives were lost in the accident* PERSON, human being, individual, soul. ❾ *a life of Chopin* BIOGRAPHY, autobiography, life story/history, profile, chronicle, account, portrait; *informal* biog, bio. ❿ *I'll miss you, but that's life* THE WAY OF THE WORLD, the way things go, the human condition; fate, destiny, providence, kismet, karma, fortune, luck, chance; *informal* the way the cookie crumbles.

– RELATED TERMS animate, bio-.

– OPPOSITES death.

■ **come to life** ❶ *the sounds of a barracks coming to life* BECOME ACTIVE, come alive, wake up, awaken, arouse, rouse, stir; *poetic/literary* waken. ❷ *the carved angel suddenly came to life* BECOME ANIMATE, come alive.

■ **for dear life** DESPERATELY, with all one's might, with might and main, for all one is worth, as fast/hard as possible, like the devil.

■ **give one's life** ❶ *he would give his life for her* DIE (TO SAVE), lay down one's life, sacrifice oneself, offer one's life. ❷ *he gave his life to the company* DEDICATE ONESELF, devote oneself, give oneself, surrender oneself.

life-and-death ▶ **adjective** VITAL, of vital importance, crucial, critical, urgent, pivotal, momentous, important, key, serious, grave, significant; *informal* earth-shattering; *formal* of great moment.

– OPPOSITES trivial.

lifeblood ▶ **noun** LIFE (FORCE), essential constituent, driving force, vital spark, inspiration, stimulus, essence, crux, heart, soul, core.

life-giving ▶ **adjective** VITALIZING, animating, energizing, invigorating, stimulating; life-preserving, life-sustaining.

lifeless ▶ **adjective** ❶ *a lifeless body* DEAD, departed, perished, gone, no more, passed on/away, stiff, cold, (as) dead as a doornail; *formal* deceased. ❷ *a lifeless rag doll* INANIMATE, without life, inert, insentient. ❸ *a lifeless landscape* BARREN, sterile, bare, desolate, stark, arid,

infertile, uncultivated, uninhabited; bleak, colourless, characterless, soulless. ❹ *a lifeless performance* LACKLUSTRE, spiritless, apathetic, torpid, lethargic; dull, monotonous, boring, tedious, dreary, unexciting, expressionless, emotionless, colourless, characterless. ❺ *lifeless hair* LANK, lustreless.
– OPPOSITES alive, animate, lively.

lifelike ▶ **adjective** REALISTIC, true to life, representational, faithful, exact, precise, detailed, vivid, graphic, natural, naturalistic.
– OPPOSITES unrealistic.

lifelong ▶ **adjective** LASTING, long-lasting, long-term, constant, stable, established, steady, enduring, permanent.
– OPPOSITES ephemeral.

lifestyle ▶ **noun** WAY OF LIFE/LIVING, life, situation, fate, lot; conduct, behaviour, customs, habits, ways, mores.

lifetime ▶ **noun** ❶ *he made an exceptional contribution during his lifetime* LIFESPAN, life, days, duration of life, one's time (on earth), existence, one's career. ❷ *the lifetime of workstations* DURATION, (active) life, life expectancy, functioning period, period of effectiveness/usefulness. ❸ *it would take a lifetime* ALL ONE'S LIFE, a very long time, an eternity, years (on end), aeons; *informal* ages (and ages), an age.

lift ▶ **verb** ❶ *lift the pack on to your back* RAISE, hoist, heave, haul up, uplift, heft, raise up/aloft, upraise, elevate, hold high; pick up, grab, take up, scoop up, snatch up; winch up, jack up, lever up; *informal* hump; *poetic/literary* upheave. ❷ *the news lifted his spirits* BOOST, raise, buoy up, elevate, cheer up, perk up, uplift, brighten up, ginger up, gladden, encourage, stimulate, revive; *informal* buck up. ❸ *they lift their game on big occasions* IMPROVE, boost, enhance, revitalize, upgrade, ameliorate. ❹ *the fog had lifted* CLEAR, rise, disperse, dissipate, disappear, vanish, dissolve. ❺ *the ban has been lifted* CANCEL, remove, withdraw, revoke, rescind, annul, void, discontinue, end, stop, terminate. ❻ *lifting carrots* DIG UP, pick, pull up, root out, unearth. ❼ *the RAF lifted them to safety* AIRLIFT, transport by air, fly. ❽ *he lifted his voice* AMPLIFY, raise, make louder, increase. ❾ (*informal*) *he lifted sections from a 1986 article* PLAGIARIZE, pirate, copy, reproduce, poach; *informal* crib, rip off. ❿ (*informal*) *she lifted a wallet.* See STEAL verb sense 1.
– OPPOSITES drop, put down.
▶ **noun** ❶ *Alice went up in the lift* ELEVATOR, paternoster (lift); dumb waiter. ❷ *give me a lift up* PUSH, hoist, heave, thrust, shove. ❸ *he gave me a lift to the airport* (CAR) RIDE, run, drive. ❹ *that goal will give his confidence a real lift* BOOST, fillip, stimulus, impetus, encouragement, spur, push; improvement, enhancement; *informal* shot in the arm.
■ **lift off** TAKE OFF, become airborne, take to the air, take wing; be launched, blast off.

light[1] ▶ **noun** ❶ *the light of candles* ILLUMINATION, brightness, luminescence, luminosity, shining, gleaming, gleam, brilliance, radiance, lustre, glowing, glow, blaze, glare, dazzle; sunlight, moonlight, starlight, lamplight, firelight; ray of light, beam of light; *poetic/literary* effulgence, refulgence, lambency. ❷ *there was a light on in the hall* LAMP, wall light; headlight, headlamp, sidelight; street light, floodlight; lantern; torch, flashlight. ❸ *have you got a light?* MATCH, (cigarette) lighter. ❹ *we'll be driving in the light* DAYLIGHT (HOURS), daytime, day; natural light, sunlight. ❺ *he saw the problem in a different light* ASPECT, angle, slant, approach, interpretation, viewpoint, standpoint, context, hue, complexion. ❻ *light dawned on Loretta* UNDERSTANDING, enlightenment, illumination, comprehension, insight, awareness, knowledge. ❼ *an eminent legal light* EXPERT, authority, master, leader, guru, leading light, luminary. ❽ *he served his party loyally according to his lights* TALENT, skill, ability; intelligence, intellect, knowledge, understanding.
– RELATED TERMS photo-, lumin-.
– OPPOSITES darkness.
▶ **verb** *Alan lit a fire* SET ALIGHT, set light to, set burning, set on fire, set fire to, put/set a match to, ignite, kindle, spark (off); *archaic* enkindle.
– OPPOSITES extinguish.
▶ **adjective** ❶ *a light breakfast room* BRIGHT, full of light, well lit, well illuminated, sunny. ❷ *light pastel shades* LIGHT-COLOURED, light-toned, pale, pale-coloured, pastel. ❸ *light hair* FAIR, light-coloured, blond(e), golden, flaxen.
– OPPOSITES dark, gloomy.
■ **bring something to light** REVEAL, disclose, expose, uncover, show up, unearth, dig up/out, bring to notice, identify, hunt out, nose out.
■ **come to light** BE DISCOVERED, be uncovered, be unearthed, come out, become known, become apparent, appear, materialize, emerge.
■ **in the light of** TAKING INTO CONSIDERATION/ACCOUNT, considering, bearing in mind, taking note of, in view of.
■ **light up** *the dashboard lit up* BECOME BRIGHT, brighten, lighten, shine, gleam, flare, blaze, glint, sparkle, shimmer, glisten, scintillate.
■ **light something up** ❶ *a flare lit up the night sky* MAKE BRIGHT, brighten, illuminate, lighten, throw/cast light on, shine on, irradiate; *poetic/literary* illumine. ❷ *her enthusiasm lit up her face* ANIMATE, irradiate, brighten, cheer up, enliven.
■ **throw/cast/shed light on** EXPLAIN, elucidate, clarify, clear up, interpret.

light[2] ▶ **adjective** ❶ *it's light and portable* EASY TO LIFT, not heavy, lightweight; easy to carry, portable. ❷ *a light cotton robe* FLIMSY, lightweight, insubstantial, thin; delicate, floaty, gauzy, gossamer, diaphanous. ❸ *she is light on her feet* NIMBLE, agile, lithe, limber, lissom, graceful; light-footed, fleet-footed, quick,

quick-moving, spry, sprightly; *informal* twinkle-toed; *poetic/literary* fleet, lightsome. ❹ *a light soil* FRIABLE, sandy, easily dug, workable, crumbly, loose. ❺ *a light dinner* SMALL, modest, simple, easily digested. ❻ *light duties* EASY, simple, undemanding, untaxing; *informal* cushy. ❼ *his eyes gleamed with light mockery* GENTLE, mild, moderate, slight; playful, light-hearted. ❽ *light reading* ENTERTAINING, lightweight, diverting, undemanding, middle-of-the-road; frivolous, superficial, trivial. ❾ *a light heart* CAREFREE, light-hearted, cheerful, cheery, happy, merry, jolly, blithe, bright, sunny; buoyant, bubbly, jaunty, bouncy, breezy, optimistic, positive, upbeat, ebullient; *dated* gay. ❿ *this is no light matter* UNIMPORTANT, insignificant, trivial, trifling, petty, inconsequential, superficial. ⓫ *light footsteps* GENTLE, delicate, soft, dainty; faint, indistinct. ⓬ *her head felt light* DIZZY, giddy, light-headed, faint, vertiginous; *informal* woozy. ⓭ (*archaic*) *light women* PROMISCUOUS, loose, wanton.
– OPPOSITES heavy.

light[3]
■ **light into** (*N. Amer. informal*) ❶ *we started lighting into our attackers. See* SET ON at SET[1]. ❷ *my father lit into me for being late. See* SCOLD verb.
■ **light on/upon** COME ACROSS, chance on, hit on, happen on, stumble on/across, blunder on, find, discover, uncover, come up with.

lighten[1] ▶ verb ❶ *the sky was beginning to lighten* BECOME/GROW LIGHTER, brighten. ❷ *the first touch of dawn lightened the sky* MAKE LIGHTER, make brighter, brighten, light up, illuminate, throw/cast light on, shine on, irradiate; *poetic/literary* illumine. ❸ *he used lemon juice to lighten his hair* WHITEN, make whiter, bleach, blanch, make paler; fade, wash out, decolorize.
– OPPOSITES darken.

lighten[2] ▶ verb ❶ *lightening the burden of taxation* MAKE LIGHTER, lessen, reduce, decrease, diminish, ease; alleviate, mitigate, allay, relieve, palliate, assuage. ❷ *an attempt to lighten her spirits* CHEER (UP), brighten, gladden, hearten, perk up, lift, ginger up, enliven, boost, buoy (up), uplift, revive, restore, revitalize.
– OPPOSITES increase, depress.

light-fingered ▶ adjective THIEVING, stealing, pilfering, shoplifting, dishonest; *informal* sticky-fingered, crooked.
– OPPOSITES honest.

light-footed ▶ adjective NIMBLE, light on one's feet, agile, graceful, lithe, spry, sprightly, limber, lissom; swift, fast, quick, quick-moving, fleet-footed; *informal* twinkle-toed; *poetic/literary* fleet.
– OPPOSITES clumsy.

light-headed ▶ adjective DIZZY, giddy, faint, light in the head, muzzy, vertiginous; *informal* woozy.

light-hearted ▶ adjective CAREFREE, cheerful, cheery, happy, merry, glad, playful, jolly, jovial, joyful, gleeful, ebullient, high-spirited, lively, blithe, bright, sunny, buoyant, vivacious, bubbly, jaunty, bouncy, breezy; entertaining, amusing, diverting; *informal* chirpy, upbeat; *dated* gay.
– OPPOSITES miserable.

lightly ▶ adverb ❶ *Maisie kissed him lightly on the cheek* SOFTLY, gently, faintly, delicately. ❷ *season very lightly* SPARINGLY, slightly, sparsely, moderately, delicately. ❸ *he has got off lightly* WITHOUT SEVERE PUNISHMENT, easily, leniently, mildly. ❹ *her views are not to be dismissed lightly* CARELESSLY, airily, heedlessly, without consideration, uncaringly, indifferently, unthinkingly, thoughtlessly, flippantly, breezily, frivolously.
– OPPOSITES hard, heavily.

lightweight ▶ adjective ❶ *a lightweight jacket* THIN, light, flimsy, insubstantial; summery. ❷ *lightweight entertainment* TRIVIAL, insubstantial, superficial, shallow, unintellectual, undemanding, frivolous; of little merit/value.
– OPPOSITES heavy.

like[1] ▶ verb ❶ *I rather like Colonel Maitland* BE FOND OF, be attached to, have a soft spot for, have a liking for, have regard for, think well of, admire, respect, esteem; be attracted to, fancy, find attractive, be keen on, be taken with; *informal* take a shine to, rate. ❷ *Maisie likes veal | she likes gardening* ENJOY, have a taste for, have a preference for, have a liking for, be partial to, find/take pleasure in, be keen on, find agreeable, have a penchant/passion for, find enjoyable; appreciate, love, adore, relish; *informal* have a thing about, be into, be mad about/for, be hooked on, go a bundle on. ❸ *feel free to say what you like* CHOOSE, please, wish, want, see/think fit, care to, will. ❹ *how would she like it if someone did that to her?* FEEL ABOUT, regard, think about, consider.
– OPPOSITES hate.

like[2] ▶ preposition ❶ *you're just like a teacher* SIMILAR TO, the same as, identical to. ❷ *the figure landed like a cat* IN THE SAME WAY/MANNER AS, in the manner of, in a similar way to. ❸ *cities like Birmingham* SUCH AS, for example, for instance; in particular, namely, viz. ❹ *Richard sounded mean, which isn't like him* CHARACTERISTIC OF, typical of, in character with.
– RELATED TERMS -esque, -ish.
▶ noun *we shan't see his like again* EQUAL, match, equivalent, counterpart, twin, parallel; *formal* compeer.
▶ adjective *a like situation* SIMILAR, much the same, comparable, corresponding, resembling, alike, analogous, parallel, equivalent, cognate, related, kindred; identical, same, matching.
– OPPOSITES dissimilar.

likeable ▶ adjective PLEASANT, nice, friendly, agreeable, affable, amiable, genial, personable, charming, popular, good-natured, engaging, appealing, endearing, convivial,

congenial, winning, delightful, enchanting, lovable, adorable, sweet; *informal* darling, lovely.
– OPPOSITES unpleasant.

likelihood ▶ **noun** PROBABILITY, chance, prospect, possibility, likeliness, odds, feasibility; risk, threat, danger; hope, promise.

likely ▶ **adjective** ❶ *it seemed likely that a scandal would break* PROBABLE, (distinctly) possible, to be expected, odds-on, plausible, imaginable; expected, anticipated, predictable, predicted, foreseeable; *informal* on the cards. ❷ *a likely explanation* PLAUSIBLE, reasonable, feasible, acceptable, believable, credible, tenable, conceivable. ❸ *a likely story!* UNLIKELY, implausible, unbelievable, incredible, untenable, unacceptable, inconceivable. ❹ *a likely-looking place* SUITABLE, appropriate, apposite, fit, fitting, acceptable, right; promising, hopeful. ❺ *a likely lad* PROMISING, talented, gifted; *informal* up-and-coming.
– OPPOSITES improbable, unbelievable.
▶ **adverb** *he was most likely dead* PROBABLY, in all probability, presumably, no doubt, doubtlessly; *informal* (as) like as not.

liken ▶ **verb** COMPARE, equate, draw an analogy between, draw a parallel between; link, associate, bracket together.
– OPPOSITES contrast.

likeness ▶ **noun** ❶ *her likeness to Anne is quite uncanny* RESEMBLANCE, similarity, correspondence, analogy, uniformity, conformity. ❷ *the likeness of a naked woman* SEMBLANCE, guise, appearance, (outward) form, shape, image. ❸ *a likeness of the last president* REPRESENTATION, image, depiction, portrayal; picture, drawing, sketch, painting, portrait, photograph, study; statue, sculpture.
– OPPOSITES dissimilarity.

likewise ▶ **adverb** ❶ *an ambush was out of the question, likewise poison* ALSO, in addition, too, as well, to boot; besides, moreover, furthermore. ❷ *encourage your family and friends to do likewise* THE SAME, similarly, correspondingly, in the same way, in similar fashion.

liking ▶ **noun** FONDNESS, love, affection, penchant, attachment; enjoyment, appreciation, taste, passion; preference, partiality, predilection; desire, fancy, inclination.

lilt ▶ **noun** CADENCE, rise and fall, inflection, intonation, rhythm, swing, beat, pulse, tempo.

limb ▶ **noun** ❶ *his sore limbs* ARM, LEG, appendage; *archaic* member. ❷ *the limbs of the tree* BRANCH, bough. ❸ *local job centres act as limbs of the Ministry* SECTION, branch, offshoot, arm, wing, subdivision, department, division.
■ **out on a limb** ❶ *the portrayal of Scotland as being out on a limb* ISOLATED, segregated, set apart, separate, cut off, solitary. ❷ *the government would not go out on a limb* IN A PRECARIOUS POSITION, vulnerable; *informal* sticking one's neck out.

limber ▶ **adjective** *I have to practise to keep myself limber* LITHE, supple, nimble, lissom, flexible, fit, agile, acrobatic, loose-jointed, loose-limbed.
– OPPOSITES stiff.
■ **limber up** WARM UP, loosen up, get into condition, get into shape, practise, train, stretch.

limbo ▶ **noun** *unbaptized infants are thought to live in limbo* non-existence, void, oblivion.
■ **in limbo** IN ABEYANCE, unattended to, unfinished; suspended, deferred, postponed, put off, pending, on ice, in cold storage; unresolved, undetermined, up in the air; *informal* on the back burner, on hold.

limelight ▶ **noun** THE FOCUS OF ATTENTION, public attention/interest, media attention, the public eye, the glare of publicity, prominence, the spotlight.
– OPPOSITES obscurity.

limit ▶ **noun** ❶ *the city limits* BOUNDARY (LINE), border, bound, partition line, frontier, edge, demarcation line; perimeter, outside, outline, confine, periphery, margin, rim. ❷ *a limit of 4,500 supporters* MAXIMUM, ceiling, limitation, upper limit; restriction, check, control, restraint. ❸ *resources are stretched to the limit* UTMOST, breaking point, greatest extent. ❹ (*informal*) *that really is the limit!* THE LAST STRAW, (more than) enough; *informal* the end, it.
▶ **verb** *the pressure to limit costs* RESTRICT, curb, cap, (hold in) check, restrain, put a brake on, freeze, peg; regulate, control, govern, delimit.

limitation ▶ **noun** ❶ *a limitation on the number of newcomers* RESTRICTION, curb, restraint, control, check; impediment, obstacle, obstruction, bar, barrier, block, deterrent. ❷ *he is aware of his own limitations* IMPERFECTION, flaw, defect, failing, shortcoming, weak point, deficiency, failure, frailty, weakness, foible.
– OPPOSITES increase, strength.

limited ▶ **adjective** ❶ *limited resources* RESTRICTED, finite, little, tight, slight, in short supply, short; meagre, scanty, sparse, insubstantial, deficient, inadequate, insufficient, paltry, poor, minimal. ❷ *the limited powers of the council* RESTRICTED, curbed, checked, controlled, restrained, delimited, qualified.
– OPPOSITES ample, boundless.

limitless ▶ **adjective** BOUNDLESS, unbounded, unlimited, illimitable; infinite, endless, never-ending, unending, everlasting, untold, immeasurable, bottomless, fathomless; unceasing, interminable, inexhaustible, constant, perpetual.

limp[1] ▶ **verb** *she limped out of the house* HOBBLE, walk with a limp, walk lamely/unevenly, walk haltingly, falter.
▶ **noun** *walking with a limp* LAMENESS, hobble, uneven gait; *Medicine* claudication.

limp[2] ▶ **adjective** ❶ *a limp handshake* SOFT, flaccid, loose, slack, lax; floppy, drooping, droopy, sagging. ❷ *we were all limp with exhaustion* TIRED,

fatigued, weary, exhausted, worn out; lethargic, listless, spiritless, weak. ❸ *a limp and lacklustre speech* UNINSPIRED, uninspiring, insipid, flat, lifeless, vapid.
– OPPOSITES firm, energetic.

limpid ▶ adjective ❶ *a limpid pool* CLEAR, transparent, glassy, crystal clear, crystalline, translucent, pellucid, unclouded. ❷ *his limpid writing* LUCID, clear, plain, understandable, intelligible, comprehensible, coherent, explicit, unambiguous, simple, vivid, sharp, crystal clear; *formal* perspicuous.
– OPPOSITES opaque.

line[1] ▶ noun ❶ *he drew a line through the name* dash, rule, bar, score; underline, underscore, stroke, slash, solidus; stripe, strip, band, belt; *technical* stria, striation; *Brit.* oblique. ❷ *there were lines round her eyes* WRINKLE, furrow, crease, crinkle, crow's foot. ❸ *the classic lines of the exterior* CONTOUR, outline, configuration, shape, figure, delineation, profile. ❹ *he headed the ball over the line | the county line* BOUNDARY (LINE), limit, border, borderline, bounding line, frontier, demarcation line, dividing line, edge, margin, perimeter. ❺ *behind enemy lines* POSITION, formation, front (line); trenches. ❻ *he put the washing on the line* CORD, rope, string, cable, wire, thread, twine, strand. ❼ *a line of soldiers* FILE, rank, column, string, train, procession; row, queue; *Brit. informal* crocodile. ❽ *a line of figures* COLUMN, row. ❾ *a long line of crass decisions* SERIES, sequence, succession, chain, string, set, cycle. ❿ *the line of flight of some bees* COURSE, route, track, path, way, run. ⓫ *they took a very tough line with the industry | the party line* COURSE (OF ACTION), procedure, technique, tactic, tack; policy, practice, approach, plan, programme, position, stance, philosophy. ⓬ *her own line of thought* COURSE, direction, drift, tack, tendency, trend. ⓭ (*informal*) *don't give me that line!* PATTER, story, piece of fiction, fabrication; *informal* spiel. ⓮ *he couldn't remember his lines* WORDS, part, script, speech. ⓯ *their line of work* (LINE OF) BUSINESS, (line of) work, field, trade, occupation, employment, profession, job, career, walk of life; specialty, forte, province, department, sphere, area (of expertise). ⓰ *a new line of cologne* BRAND, kind, sort, type, variety, make. ⓱ *a noble line* ANCESTRY, family, parentage, birth, descent, lineage, extraction, genealogy, roots, origin, background; stock, bloodline, pedigree. ⓲ *the opening line of the poem* SENTENCE, phrase, clause, utterance; passage, extract, quotation, quote, citation. ⓳ *I should drop Ralph a line* NOTE, letter, card, postcard, message, communication, missive, memorandum; correspondence, word; *informal* memo; *formal* epistle.
– RELATED TERMS linear.
▶ verb ❶ *her face was lined with age* FURROW, wrinkle, crease, mark with lines. ❷ *the driveway was lined by poplars* BORDER, edge, fringe, bound, rim.
■ **draw the line at** STOP SHORT OF, refuse to accept, baulk at; object to, take issue with, take exception to.
■ **in line** ❶ *the poor stood in line for food* IN A QUEUE, in a row, in a file. ❷ *the adverts are in line with the editorial style* IN AGREEMENT, in accord, in accordance, in harmony, in step, in compliance. ❸ *in line with the bullseye* IN ALIGNMENT, aligned, level, at the same height; abreast, side by side. ❹ *the referee kept him in line* UNDER CONTROL, in order, in check.
■ **in line for** A CANDIDATE FOR, in the running for, on the shortlist for, being considered for.
■ **lay it on the line** SPEAK FRANKLY/HONESTLY, pull no punches, be blunt, not mince one's words, call a spade a spade; *informal* give it to someone straight.
■ **line up** FORM A QUEUE/LINE, get into rows/columns, queue up, fall in; *Military* dress; *Brit. informal* form a crocodile.
■ **line someone/something up** ❶ *they lined them up and shot them* ARRANGE IN LINES, put in rows, arrange in columns, align, range; *Military* dress. ❷ *we've lined up an all-star cast* ASSEMBLE, get together, organize, prepare, arrange, prearrange, fix up, lay on; book, schedule, timetable.
■ **on the line** AT RISK, in danger, endangered, imperilled.
■ **toe the line** CONFORM, obey/observe the rules, comply with the rules, abide by the rules.

line[2] ▶ verb *a cardboard box lined with a blanket* COVER, put a lining in, interline, face, back, pad.
■ **line one's pockets** (*informal*) MAKE MONEY, accept bribes, embezzle money; *informal* feather one's nest, graft, be on the make.

lineage ▶ noun ANCESTRY, family, parentage, birth, descent, line, extraction, derivation, genealogy, roots, origin, background; stock, bloodline, breeding, pedigree.

lineaments ▶ plural noun (*poetic/literary*) (DISTINCTIVE) FEATURES, distinguishing characteristics, hallmarks, properties, traits; form, outline, configuration, physiognomy.

lined[1] ▶ adjective ❶ *lined paper* RULED, feint, striped, banded. ❷ *his lined face* WRINKLED, wrinkly, furrowed, wizened.
– OPPOSITES plain, smooth.

lined[2] ▶ adjective *lined curtains* COVERED, backed, interlined; faced, padded.

liner ▶ noun ❶ *a luxury liner* SHIP, ocean liner, passenger vessel, boat. ❷ *her eyes were ringed with liner* EYELINER, eye pencil, kohl (pencil); lipliner.

line-up ▶ noun ❶ *a star-studded line-up* LIST OF PERFORMERS, cast, bill, programme. ❷ *United's line-up* LIST OF PLAYERS, team, squad, side. ❸ *a long line-up of customers* QUEUE, line, row, column.

linger ▸ verb ❶ *the crowd lingered for a long time* WAIT (AROUND), stay (put), remain; loiter, dawdle, dally, take one's time; *informal* stick around, hang around/round, hang on; *archaic* tarry. ❷ *the infection can linger for many years* PERSIST, continue, remain, stay, endure, carry on, last, keep on/up.
– OPPOSITES vanish.

lingerie ▸ noun WOMEN'S UNDERWEAR, underclothes, underclothing, undergarments; nightwear, nightclothes; *informal* undies, frillies, underthings, unmentionables; *Brit. informal* smalls.

lingering ▸ adjective ❶ *lingering doubts* REMAINING, surviving, persisting, abiding, nagging, niggling. ❷ *a slow, lingering death* PROTRACTED, prolonged, long-drawn-out, long-lasting.

lingo ▸ noun (*informal*) ❶ *I can't speak the lingo* LANGUAGE, tongue, dialect. ❷ *computer lingo* JARGON, terminology, slang, argot, cant, patter, mumbo-jumbo; *informal* -ese, -speak, gobbledegook.

linguistic ▸ adjective SEMANTIC, lingual, rhetorical, verbal.

lining ▸ noun BACKING, interlining, facing, padding, liner.

link ▸ noun ❶ *a chain of steel links* LOOP, ring, connection, connector, coupling, joint. ❷ *the links between transport and the environment* CONNECTION, relationship, association, linkage, tie-up. ❸ *their links with the labour movement* BOND, tie, attachment, connection, relationship, association, affiliation. ❹ *one of the links in the organization* COMPONENT, constituent, element, part, piece.
▸ verb ❶ *four boxes were linked together* JOIN, connect, fasten, attach, bind, unite, combine, amalgamate; clamp, secure, fix, tie, couple, yoke. ❷ *the evidence linking him with the body* ASSOCIATE, connect, relate, join, bracket.

lion ▸ noun ❶ *a lion ready to attack* big cat, king of the beasts; lioness. ❷ *a lion amongst men* HERO, man of courage, brave man; conqueror, champion, conquering hero. ❸ *the lions of the symphony hall* CELEBRITY, dignitary, VIP, luminary, star, superstar, big name, leading light; *informal* big shot/noise, celeb, megastar.
– RELATED TERMS leonine.
■ **beard the lion in his den** DEFY DANGER, face up to danger, confront/brave danger.
■ **the lion's share** MOST, the majority, the larger part/number, the greater part/number, more than half, the bulk.

lionhearted ▸ adjective BRAVE, courageous, valiant, gallant, intrepid, valorous, fearless, bold, daring; stout-hearted, stalwart, heroic, doughty, plucky; *informal* gutsy, spunky.
– OPPOSITES cowardly.

lionize ▸ verb CELEBRATE, fête, glorify, honour, exalt, acclaim, admire, praise, extol, applaud, hail, venerate, eulogize; *formal* laud; *archaic* panegyrize.
– OPPOSITES vilify.

lip ▸ noun ❶ *the lip of the crater* EDGE, rim, brim, border, verge, brink. ❷ (*informal*) *I'll have no more of your lip!* INSOLENCE, impertinence, impudence, cheek, rudeness, audacity, effrontery, disrespect, presumptuousness; *informal* mouth; *Brit. informal* sauce, backchat.
– RELATED TERMS labial, labio-.
■ **keep a stiff upper lip** KEEP CONTROL OF ONESELF, not show emotion, appear unaffected; *informal* keep one's cool.

liquefy ▸ verb MAKE/BECOME LIQUID, condense, liquidize, melt; deliquesce.

liquid ▸ adjective ❶ *liquid fuels* FLUID, liquefied; melted, molten, thawed, dissolved; *Chemistry* hydrous. ❷ *her liquid eyes* CLEAR, limpid, crystal clear, crystalline, pellucid, unclouded. ❸ *a liquid voice* PURE, clear, mellifluous, dulcet, mellow, sweet, sweet-sounding, soft, melodious, harmonious; *rare* mellifluent. ❹ *liquid assets* CONVERTIBLE, disposable, usable, spendable.
– OPPOSITES solid.
▸ noun *a vat of liquid* FLUID, moisture, wet, wetness; liquor, solution, juice.

liquidate ▸ verb ❶ *the company was liquidated* CLOSE DOWN, wind up, put into liquidation, dissolve, disband. ❷ *he liquidated his share portfolio* CONVERT (TO CASH), cash in, sell off/up. ❸ *liquidating the public debt* PAY (OFF), pay in full, settle, clear, discharge, square, honour. ❹ (*informal*) *they were liquidated in bloody purges. See* KILL verb sense 1.

liquidize ▸ verb PURÉE, cream, liquefy, blend.

liquor ▸ noun ❶ *alcoholic liquor* ALCOHOL, spirits, (alcoholic) drink, intoxicating liquor, intoxicant; *informal* booze, hard stuff, grog, hooch. ❷ *strain the liquor into the sauce* STOCK, broth, bouillon, juice, liquid.

lissom ▸ adjective SUPPLE, lithe, limber, graceful, flexible, loose-limbed, agile, nimble; slim, slender, thin, willowy, sleek, trim.

list[1] ▸ noun *a list of the world's wealthiest people* CATALOGUE, inventory, record, register, roll, file, index, directory, listing, checklist, enumeration.
▸ verb *the accounts are listed alphabetically* RECORD, register, make a list of, enter; itemize, enumerate, catalogue, file, log, minute, categorize, inventory; classify, group, sort, rank, alphabetize, index.

list[2] ▸ verb *the boat listed to one side* LEAN (OVER), tilt, tip, heel (over), careen, cant, pitch, incline, slant, slope, bank.

listen ▸ verb ❶ *are you listening carefully?* HEAR, pay attention, be attentive, attend, concentrate; keep one's ears open, prick up one's ears; *informal* be all ears, pin back one's ears; *poetic/literary* hark; *archaic* hearken. ❷ *policymakers should listen to popular opinion* PAY ATTEN-

TION, take heed, heed, take notice, take note, mind, mark, bear in mind, take into consideration/account.

■ **listen in** EAVESDROP, spy, overhear, tap, wiretap, bug, monitor.

listless ▶ **adjective** LETHARGIC, enervated, spiritless, lifeless, vigourless; languid, languorous, inactive, inert, sluggish, torpid.
– OPPOSITES energetic.

litany ▶ **noun** ❶ *repeating the litany* PRAYER, invocation, supplication, devotion; *archaic* orison. ❷ *a litany of complaints* RECITAL, recitation, repetition, enumeration; list, listing, catalogue, inventory.

literacy ▶ **noun** ABILITY TO READ AND WRITE, reading/writing proficiency; (book) learning, education, scholarship, schooling.

literal ▶ **adjective** ❶ *the literal sense of the word 'dreadful'* STRICT, factual, plain, simple, exact, straightforward; unembellished, undistorted; objective, correct, true, truthful, accurate, genuine, authentic. ❷ *a literal translation* WORD-FOR-WORD, verbatim, letter-for-letter; exact, precise, faithful, close, strict, accurate; *formal* literatim. ❸ *his literal, unrhetorical manner* LITERAL-MINDED, down-to-earth, matter-of-fact, no-nonsense, unsentimental; prosaic, unimaginative, pedestrian, uninspired, uninspiring.
– OPPOSITES figurative, loose.
▶ **noun** (*Brit.*) *William corrected two literals* MISPRINT, error, mistake, (slip) of the pen, typographical/typing error/mistake, corrigendum, erratum; *informal* typo, howler.

literally ▶ **adverb** VERBATIM, word for word, letter for letter; exactly, precisely, faithfully, closely, strictly, accurately; *formal* literatim.

literary ▶ **adjective** ❶ *literary works* WRITTEN, poetic, artistic, dramatic. ❷ *her literary friends* SCHOLARLY, learned, intellectual, cultured, erudite, bookish, highbrow, lettered, academic, cultivated; well read, widely read, (well) educated. ❸ *literary language* FORMAL, written, poetic, dramatic; elaborate, ornate, flowery.

literate ▶ **adjective** (WELL) EDUCATED, well read, widely read, scholarly, learned, knowledgeable, lettered, cultured, cultivated, sophisticated, well informed.
– OPPOSITES ignorant.

literature ▶ **noun** ❶ *English literature* WRITTEN WORKS, writings, (creative) writing, literary texts, compositions. ❷ *the literature on prototype theory* PUBLICATIONS, published writings, texts, reports, studies. ❸ *election literature* PRINTED MATTER, brochures, leaflets, pamphlets, circulars, flyers, handouts, handbills, mailshots, bulletins, documentation, publicity, blurb, notices; *informal* bumf.

lithe ▶ **adjective** AGILE, graceful, supple, limber, lithesome, loose-limbed, nimble, deft, flexible, lissom.
– OPPOSITES clumsy.

litigant ▶ **noun** LITIGATOR, opponent (in law), contender, disputant, plaintiff, claimant, complainant, petitioner, appellant, respondent.

litigation ▶ **noun** (LEGAL/JUDICIAL) PROCEEDINGS, (legal) action, lawsuit, legal dispute, (legal) case, suit (at law), prosecution, indictment.

litter ▶ **noun** ❶ *never drop litter* RUBBISH, refuse, junk, waste, debris, scraps, leavings, fragments, detritus; *N. Amer.* trash, garbage. ❷ *the litter of glasses around her* CLUTTER, jumble, muddle, mess, heap, disorder, untidiness, confusion, disarray; *informal* shambles. ❸ *a litter of kittens* BROOD, family; young, offspring, progeny; *Law* issue. ❹ *straw for use as litter* (ANIMAL) BEDDING, straw. ❺ *a horse-drawn litter* SEDAN CHAIR, palanquin; stretcher.
▶ **verb** *clothes littered the floor* MAKE UNTIDY, mess up, make a mess of, clutter up, be strewn about, be scattered about; *informal* make a shambles of; *poetic/literary* bestrew.

little ▶ **adjective** ❶ *a little writing desk* SMALL, small-scale, compact; mini, miniature, tiny, minute, minuscule; toy, baby, pocket, undersized, dwarf, midget; *Scottish* wee; *informal* teeny-weeny, teensy-weensy, itsy-bitsy, tiddly, half-pint; *Brit. informal* titchy, dinky; *N. Amer. informal* vest-pocket. ❷ *a little man* SHORT, small, slight, petite, diminutive, tiny; elfin, dwarfish, midget, pygmy, Lilliputian; *Scottish* wee; *informal* teeny-weeny, pint-sized. ❸ *my little sister* YOUNG, younger, junior, small, baby, infant. ❹ *I was a bodyguard for a little while* BRIEF, short, short-lived; fleeting, momentary, transitory, transient; fast, quick, hasty, cursory. ❺ *a few little problems* MINOR, unimportant, insignificant, trivial, trifling, petty, paltry, inconsequential, nugatory.
– OPPOSITES big, large, elder, important.
▶ **determiner** *they have little political influence* HARDLY ANY, not much, slight, scant, limited, restricted, modest, little or no, minimal, negligible.
– OPPOSITES considerable.
▶ **adverb** ❶ *he is little known as a teacher* HARDLY, barely, scarcely, not much, (only) slightly. ❷ *this disease is little seen nowadays* RARELY, seldom, infrequently, hardly (ever), scarcely (ever), not much.
– OPPOSITES well, often.

■ **a little** ❶ *add a little water* SOME, a small amount of, a bit of, a touch of, a soupçon of, a dash of, a taste of, a spot of; a shade of, a suggestion of, a trace of, a hint of, a suspicion of; a dribble of, a splash of, a pinch of, a sprinkling of, a speck of; *informal* a smidgen of, a tad of. ❷ *after a little, Oliver came in* A SHORT TIME, a little while, a bit, an interval, a short period; a minute, a moment, a second, an instant; *informal* a sec, a mo, a jiffy. ❸ *this reminds me a little of the Adriatic* SLIGHTLY, faintly, remotely, vaguely; somewhat, a little bit, quite, to some degree.

■ **little by little** GRADUALLY, slowly, by degrees,

by stages, step by step, bit by bit, progressively; subtly, imperceptibly.

liturgical ▶ **adjective** CEREMONIAL, ritual, solemn; church.

liturgy ▶ **noun** RITUAL, worship, service, ceremony, rite, observance, celebration, sacrament; tradition, custom, practice, rubric; *formal* ordinance.

live[1] ▶ **verb** ❶ *the greatest mathematician who ever lived* EXIST, be alive, be, have life; breathe, draw breath, walk the earth. ❷ *I live in London* RESIDE, have one's home, have one's residence, be settled; be housed, lodge; inhabit, occupy, populate; *Scottish* stay; *formal* dwell, be domiciled. ❸ *they lived quietly* PASS/SPEND ONE'S LIFE, have a lifestyle; behave, conduct oneself; *formal* comport oneself. ❹ *she had lived a difficult life* EXPERIENCE, spend, pass, lead, have, go through, undergo. ❺ *Freddy lived by his wits* SURVIVE, make a living, earn one's living, eke out a living; subsist, support oneself, sustain oneself, make ends meet, keep body and soul together. ❻ *you should live a little* ENJOY ONESELF, enjoy life, have fun, live life to the full.
– OPPOSITES die, be dead.

■ **live it up** (*informal*) LIVE EXTRAVAGANTLY, live in the lap of luxury, live in clover; carouse, revel, enjoy oneself, have a good time, go on a spree, roister; *informal* party, push the boat out, paint the town red, have a ball, make whoopee; *N. Amer. informal* live high on/off the hog; *archaic* wassail.

■ **live off/on** SUBSIST ON, feed on/off, eat, consume.

live[2] ▶ **adjective** ❶ *live bait* LIVING, alive, having life, breathing, animate, sentient. ❷ *a live performance* IN THE FLESH, personal, in person, not recorded. ❸ *a live rail* ELECTRIFIED, charged, powered, active; *informal* hot. ❹ *live coals* (RED) HOT, glowing, aglow; burning, alight, flaming, aflame, blazing, ignited, on fire; *poetic/literary* afire. ❺ *a live grenade* UNEXPLODED, explosive, active; unstable, volatile. ❻ *live issue* TOPICAL, current, of current interest, controversial; burning, pressing, important.
– OPPOSITES dead, inanimate, recorded.

■ **live wire** (*informal*) ENERGETIC PERSON; *informal* fireball, human dynamo, powerhouse, life and soul of the party.

livelihood ▶ **noun** (SOURCE OF) INCOME, means of support, living, subsistence, keep, maintenance, sustenance, nourishment, daily bread, bread and butter; job, work, employment, occupation.

livelong ▶ **adjective** (*poetic/literary*) ENTIRE, whole, total, complete, full, continuous.

lively ▶ **adjective** ❶ *a lively young woman* ENERGETIC, active, animated, dynamic, full of life, outgoing, spirited, high-spirited, vivacious, enthusiastic, vibrant, buoyant, exuberant, effervescent, cheerful; bouncy, bubbly, perky, sparkling, zestful; *informal* full of beans, chirpy, chipper, peppy. ❷ *a lively bar* BUSY, crowded, bustling, buzzing; vibrant, boisterous, jolly, festive; *informal* hopping. ❸ *a lively debate* HEATED, vigorous, animated, spirited, enthusiastic, forceful; exciting, interesting, memorable. ❹ *a lively portrait of the local community* VIVID, colourful, striking, graphic, bold, strong. ❺ *he bowled at a lively pace* BRISK, quick, fast, rapid, swift, speedy, smart; *informal* nippy, snappy. ❻ *the press is making things lively for the Government* AWKWARD, tricky, difficult, challenging, eventful, exciting, busy; *informal* hairy.
– OPPOSITES quiet, dull.

liven

■ **liven up** BRIGHTEN UP, cheer up, perk up, revive, rally, pick up, bounce back; *informal* buck up.

■ **liven someone/something up** BRIGHTEN UP, cheer up, enliven, animate, raise someone's spirits, perk up, spice up, ginger up, make lively, wake up, invigorate, revive, refresh, vivify, galvanize, stimulate, stir up, get going; *informal* buck up, pep up.

liver
– RELATED TERMS hepatic.

livery ▶ **noun** UNIFORM, regalia, costume, dress, attire, garb, clothes, clothing, outfit, suit, garments, ensemble; *informal* get-up, gear, kit; *formal* apparel; *archaic* raiment, vestments.

livid ▶ **adjective** ❶ (*informal*) *Mum was absolutely livid. See* FURIOUS sense 1. ❷ *a livid bruise* PURPLISH, bluish, dark, discoloured, purple, greyish-blue; bruised; angry.

living ▶ **noun** ❶ *she cleaned floors for a living* LIVELIHOOD, (source of) income, means of support, subsistence, keep, maintenance, sustenance, nourishment, daily bread, bread and butter; job, work, employment, occupation. ❷ *healthy living* WAY OF LIFE, lifestyle, way of living, life; conduct, behaviour, activities, habits.
▶ **adjective** ❶ *living organisms* ALIVE, live, having life, animate, sentient; breathing, existing, existent; *informal* alive and kicking. ❷ *a living language* CURRENT, contemporary, present; in use, active, surviving, extant, persisting, remaining, existing, in existence. ❸ *a living image of the man* EXACT, faithful, true to life, authentic.
– OPPOSITES dead, extinct.

living room ▶ **noun** SITTING ROOM, lounge, front room, reception room, family room.

lizard
– RELATED TERMS saurian.

load ▶ **noun** ❶ *MacDowell's got a load to deliver* CARGO, freight, consignment, delivery, shipment, goods, merchandise; pack, bundle, parcel; lorryload, truckload, shipload, boatload, vanload; *archaic* lading. ❷ (*informal*) *I bought a load of clothes* A LOT, a great deal, a large amount/quantity, an abundance, a wealth, a mountain; many, plenty; *informal* a heap, a mass, a pile, a stack, a ton, lots, heaps, masses, piles, stacks, tons. ❸ *a heavy teaching load* COMMITMENT, responsibility, duty, obligation, charge, burden; trouble, worry, strain, pressure.

▶ **verb** ❶ *we quickly loaded the van* FILL (UP), pack, lade, charge, stock, stack. ❷ *Larry loaded boxes into the jeep* PACK, stow, store, stack, bundle; place, deposit, put away. ❸ *loading the committee with responsibilities* BURDEN, weigh down, saddle, charge; overburden, overwhelm, encumber, tax, strain, trouble, worry. ❹ *Richard loaded Marshal with honours* REWARD, ply, regale, shower. ❺ *he loaded a gun* PRIME, charge, prepare to fire/use. ❻ *load the cassette into the camcorder* INSERT, put, place, slot. ❼ *the dice are loaded against him* BIAS, rig, fix; weight.

loaded ▶ **adjective** ❶ *a loaded freight train* FULL, filled, laden, packed, stuffed, crammed, brimming, stacked; *informal* chock-full, chock-a-block. ❷ *a loaded gun* PRIMED, charged, ready to fire. ❸ (*informal*) *they are all loaded. See* RICH sense 1. ❹ *loaded dice* BIASED, rigged, fixed; weighted. ❺ *a politically loaded word* CHARGED, emotive, sensitive, delicate.

loaf[1] ▶ **noun** (*Brit. informal*) *use your loaf. See* HEAD noun sense 2.

loaf[2] ▶ **verb** *he was just loafing around* LAZE, lounge, loll, idle, waste time; *informal* hang around/round; *Brit. informal* hang about, mooch about/around; *N. Amer. informal* bum around.

loafer ▶ **noun** IDLER, layabout, good-for-nothing, lounger, shirker, sluggard, laggard, slugabed; *informal* skiver, slacker, slob, lazybones.

loan ▶ **noun** *a loan of £7,000* CREDIT, advance; mortgage, overdraft; lending, moneylending; *Brit. informal* sub.

▶ **verb** ❶ *he loaned me his flat* LEND, advance, give credit; give on loan, lease, charter, hire; *Brit. informal* sub. ❷ *the exhibits have been loaned from a museum* BORROW, receive/take on loan.
– OPPOSITES borrow.

loath ▶ **adjective** RELUCTANT, unwilling, disinclined, ill-disposed; against, averse, opposed, resistant.
– OPPOSITES willing.

loathe ▶ **verb** HATE, detest, abhor, execrate, have a strong aversion to, feel repugnance towards, not be able to bear/stand, be repelled by; *formal* abominate.
– OPPOSITES love.

loathing ▶ **noun** HATRED, hate, detestation, abhorrence, abomination, execration, odium; antipathy, dislike, hostility, animosity, ill feeling, bad feeling, malice, animus, enmity, aversion; repugnance.

loathsome ▶ **adjective** HATEFUL, detestable, abhorrent, repulsive, odious, repugnant, repellent, disgusting, revolting, sickening, abominable, despicable, contemptible, reprehensible, execrable, damnable; vile, horrible, nasty, obnoxious, gross, foul; *informal* horrid, yucky; *poetic/literary* noisome.

lob ▶ **verb** THROW, toss, fling, pitch, hurl, pelt, sling, launch, propel; *informal* chuck, bung, heave.

lobby ▶ **noun** ❶ *the hotel lobby* ENTRANCE (HALL), hallway, hall, vestibule, foyer, reception area. ❷ *the anti-hunt lobby* PRESSURE GROUP, interest group, movement, campaign, crusade, lobbyists, supporters; faction, camp; *Brit.* ginger group.

▶ **verb** ❶ *readers are urged to lobby their MPs* SEEK TO INFLUENCE, try to persuade, bring pressure to bear on, importune, sway; petition, solicit, appeal to, pressurize. ❷ *a group lobbying for better rail services* CAMPAIGN, crusade, press, push, ask, call, demand; promote, advocate, champion.

local ▶ **adjective** ❶ *the local council* COMMUNITY, district, neighbourhood, regional, city, town, municipal, provincial, village, parish. ❷ *a local restaurant* NEIGHBOURHOOD, nearby, near, at hand, close by; accessible, handy, convenient. ❸ *a local infection* CONFINED, restricted, contained, localized.
– OPPOSITES national.

▶ **noun** ❶ *complaints from the locals* LOCAL PERSON, native, inhabitant, resident, parishioner. ❷ (*Brit. informal*) *a pint in the local. See* PUB.
– OPPOSITES outsider.

locale ▶ **noun** PLACE, site, spot, area; position, location, setting, scene, venue, background, backdrop, environment; neighbourhood, district, region, locality.

locality ▶ **noun** ❶ *the locality of the property* POSITION, location, whereabouts, place, situation, spot, point, site, scene, setting. ❷ *other schools in the locality* VICINITY, neighbourhood, area, district, region; *informal* neck of the woods.

localize ▶ **verb** LIMIT, restrict, confine, contain, circumscribe, concentrate, delimit.
– OPPOSITES generalize, globalize.

locate ▶ **verb** ❶ *spotter planes locate the shoals* FIND, discover, pinpoint, detect, track down, run to earth, unearth, sniff out, smoke out, search out, ferret out, uncover. ❷ *a company located near Pittsburgh* SITUATE, site, position, place, base; put, build, establish, found, station, install, settle.

location ▶ **noun** POSITION, place, situation, site, locality, locale, spot, whereabouts, point; scene, setting, area, environment; bearings, orientation; venue, address; *technical* locus.

lock[1] ▶ **noun** *the lock on the door* BOLT, catch, fastener, clasp, bar, hasp, latch.

▶ **verb** ❶ *he locked the door* BOLT, fasten, bar, secure, seal; padlock, latch, chain. ❷ *she locked her wrists together* JOIN, interlock, link, mesh, engage, unite, connect, yoke, mate; couple. ❸ *the wheels locked* BECOME STUCK, stick, jam, become/make immovable, become/make rigid. ❹ *he locked her in an embrace* CLASP,

clench, grasp, embrace, hug, squeeze.
– OPPOSITES unlock, open, separate, divide.
■ **lock someone out** KEEP OUT, shut out, refuse entrance to, deny admittance to; exclude, bar, debar, ban.
■ **lock someone up** IMPRISON, jail, incarcerate, intern, send to prison, put behind bars, put under lock and key, put in chains, clap in irons, cage, pen, coop up; *informal* send down, put away, put inside.

lock[2] ▶ **noun** *a lock of hair* TRESS, tuft, curl, ringlet, hank, strand, wisp, snippet.

locker ▶ **noun** CUPBOARD, cabinet, chest, safe, box, case, coffer; compartment, storeroom.

lock-up ▶ **noun** ❶ *drunks were put in the lock-up overnight* JAIL, prison, cell, detention centre; *N. Amer.* jailhouse; *informal* cooler, slammer, jug, can, nick, stir, clink, quod, chokey. ❷ *they stored spare furniture in a lock-up* STOREROOM, store, warehouse, depository; garage.

locomotion ▶ **noun** MOVEMENT, motion, moving; travel, travelling; mobility, motility; walking, ambulation, running; progress, progression, passage; *formal* perambulation.

lodge ▶ **noun** ❶ *the porter's lodge* GATEHOUSE, cottage. ❷ *a hunting lodge* HOUSE, cottage, cabin, chalet; *Brit.* shooting box. ❸ *a beaver's lodge* DEN, lair, hole, sett; retreat, haunt, shelter. ❹ *a Masonic lodge* SECTION, branch, wing; hall, clubhouse, meeting room; *N. Amer.* chapter.
▶ **verb** ❶ *William lodged at our house* RESIDE, board, stay, live, have lodgings, have rooms, put up, be quartered, stop; *N. Amer.* room; *informal* have digs; *formal* dwell, be domiciled, sojourn; *archaic* abide. ❷ *they were lodged at an inn* ACCOMMODATE, put up, take in, house, board, billet, quarter, shelter. ❸ *the government lodged a protest* SUBMIT, register, enter, put forward, advance, lay, present, tender, proffer, put on record, record, table, file. ❹ *the money was lodged in a bank* DEPOSIT, put, bank; stash, store, stow, put away, squirrel away. ❺ *the bullet lodged in his back* BECOME FIXED, embed itself, become embedded, become implanted, get/become stuck, stick, catch, become caught, wedge.

lodger ▶ **noun** BOARDER, paying guest, PG, tenant; *N. Amer.* roomer.

lodging ▶ **noun** ACCOMMODATION, rooms, chambers, living quarters, place to stay, a roof over one's head, housing, shelter; *informal* digs, pad; *formal* abode, residence, dwelling, dwelling place, habitation.

lofty ▶ **adjective** ❶ *a lofty tower* TALL, high, giant, towering, soaring, sky-scraping. ❷ *lofty ideals* NOBLE, exalted, high, high-minded, worthy, grand, fine, elevated. ❸ *a lofty post in the department* EMINENT, prominent, leading, distinguished, illustrious, celebrated, elevated, esteemed, respected. ❹ *lofty disdain* HAUGHTY, arrogant, disdainful, supercilious, condescending, patronizing, scornful, contemptuous, self-important, conceited, snobbish; *informal* stuck-up, snooty, snotty; *Brit. informal* toffee-nosed.
– OPPOSITES low, short, base, lowly, modest.

log ▶ **noun** ❶ *a fallen log* BRANCH, trunk; piece of wood; (**logs**) timber, firewood. ❷ *a log of phone calls* RECORD, register, logbook, journal, diary, minutes, chronicle, daybook, record book, ledger, account, tally.
▶ **verb** ❶ *all complaints are logged* REGISTER, record, make a note of, note down, write down, jot down, put in writing, enter, file, minute. ❷ *the pilot had logged 95 hours* ATTAIN, achieve, chalk up, make, do, go, cover.

loggerheads
■ **at loggerheads** IN DISAGREEMENT, at odds, at variance, wrangling, quarrelling, locking horns, at daggers drawn, in conflict, fighting, at war; *informal* at each other's throats.

logic ▶ **noun** ❶ *this case appears to defy all logic* REASON, judgement, logical thought, rationality, wisdom, sense, good sense, common sense, sanity; *informal* horse sense. ❷ *the logic of their argument* REASONING, line of reasoning, rationale, argument, argumentation. ❸ *the study of logic* SCIENCE OF REASONING, science of deduction, science of thought, dialectics, argumentation; *formal* ratiocination.

logical ▶ **adjective** ❶ *information displayed in a logical fashion* REASONED, well reasoned, rational, sound, cogent, well thought out, valid; coherent, clear, well organized, systematic, orderly, methodical, analytical, consistent, objective; *informal* joined-up. ❷ *the logical outcome* NATURAL, reasonable, sensible, understandable; predictable, unsurprising, only to be expected, most likely, likeliest, obvious.
– OPPOSITES illogical, irrational, unlikely, surprising.

logistics ▶ **plural noun** ORGANIZATION, planning, plans, management, arrangement, administration, orchestration, coordination, execution, handling, running.

logo ▶ **noun** EMBLEM, trademark, device, symbol, design, sign, mark; insignia, crest, seal, coat of arms, shield, badge, motif, monogram, colophon.

loiter ▶ **verb** ❶ *he loitered at bus stops* LINGER, wait, skulk; loaf, lounge, idle, laze, waste time; *informal* hang around/round; *Brit. informal* hang about, mooch about/around; *archaic* tarry. ❷ *they loitered along the river bank* DAWDLE, dally, stroll, amble, saunter, meander, drift, potter, take one's time; *informal* dilly-dally, mosey, tootle; *Brit. informal* mooch.

loll ▶ **verb** ❶ *he lolled in an armchair* LOUNGE, sprawl, drape oneself, stretch oneself; slouch, slump; laze, luxuriate, put one's feet up, lean back, recline, relax, take it easy. ❷ *her head lolled to one side* HANG (LOOSELY), droop, dangle, sag, drop, flop.

lone ▸ adjective ❶ *a lone police officer* SOLITARY, single, solo, unaccompanied, unescorted, alone, by oneself/itself, sole, companionless; detached, isolated, unique; lonely. ❷ *a lone parent* SINGLE, unmarried, unattached, partnerless, husbandless, wifeless; separated, divorced, widowed.

loneliness ▸ noun ❶ *his loneliness was unbearable* ISOLATION, friendlessness, abandonment, rejection, unpopularity; *N. Amer.* lonesomeness. ❷ *the enforced loneliness of a prison cell* SOLITARINESS, solitude, lack of company, aloneness, separation. ❸ *the loneliness of the village* ISOLATION, remoteness, seclusion.

lonely ▸ adjective ❶ *I felt very lonely* ISOLATED, alone, friendless, with no one to turn to, forsaken, abandoned, rejected, unloved, unwanted; *N. Amer.* lonesome. ❷ *the lonely life of a writer* SOLITARY, unaccompanied, lone, by oneself/itself, companionless. ❸ *a lonely road* DESERTED, uninhabited, unfrequented, unpopulated, desolate, isolated, remote, out of the way, secluded, off the beaten track, in the back of beyond, godforsaken; *informal* in the middle of nowhere.
– OPPOSITES popular, sociable, crowded.

loner ▸ noun RECLUSE, introvert, lone wolf, hermit, solitary, misanthrope, outsider; *historical* anchorite.

long[1] ▸ adjective *a long silence* LENGTHY, extended, prolonged, extensive, protracted, long-lasting, long-drawn(-out), spun out, dragged out, seemingly endless, lingering, interminable.
– OPPOSITES short, brief.
■ **before long** SOON, shortly, presently, in the near future, in a little while, by and by, in a minute, in a moment, in a second; *informal* anon, in a jiffy; *Brit. informal* in a tick, in two ticks, in a mo; *dated* directly; *poetic/literary* ere long.

long[2] ▸ verb *I longed for the holidays* YEARN, pine, ache, hanker for/after, hunger, thirst, itch, be eager, be desperate; crave, dream of, set one's heart on; *informal* have a yen, be dying.

longing ▸ noun *a longing for the countryside* YEARNING, pining, craving, ache, burning, hunger, thirst, hankering; *informal* yen, itch.
▸ adjective *a longing look* YEARNING, pining, craving, hungry, thirsty, hankering, wistful, covetous.

long-lasting ▸ adjective ENDURING, lasting, abiding, long-lived, long-running, long-established, long-standing, lifelong, deep-rooted, time-honoured, traditional, permanent.
– OPPOSITES short-lived, ephemeral.

long-lived ▸ adjective. *See* LONG-LASTING.

long-standing ▸ adjective WELL ESTABLISHED, long-established; time-honoured, traditional, age-old; abiding, enduring, long-lived, surviving, persistent, prevailing, perennial, deep-rooted, long-term, confirmed.
– OPPOSITES new, recent.

long-suffering ▸ adjective PATIENT, forbearing, tolerant, uncomplaining, stoical, resigned; easy-going, indulgent, charitable, accommodating, forgiving.
– OPPOSITES impatient, complaining.

long-winded ▸ adjective VERBOSE, wordy, lengthy, long, overlong, prolix, prolonged, protracted, long-drawn-out, interminable; discursive, diffuse, rambling, tortuous, meandering, repetitious; *informal* windy; *Brit. informal* waffly.
– OPPOSITES concise, succinct, laconic.

look ▸ verb ❶ *Mrs Wright looked at him* GLANCE, gaze, stare, gape, peer; peep, peek, take a look; watch, observe, view, regard, examine, inspect, eye, scan, scrutinize, survey, study, contemplate, consider, take in, ogle; *informal* take a gander, rubberneck, give someone/something a/the once-over, get a load of; *Brit. informal* take a dekko, take a butcher's, take a shufti, clock, gawp; *N. Amer. informal* eyeball; *poetic/literary* behold. ❷ *her room looked out on Broadway* COMMAND A VIEW OF, face, overlook, front. ❸ *they looked shocked* SEEM (TO BE), appear (to be), have the appearance/air of being, give the impression of being, give every appearance/indication of being, strike someone as being.
– OPPOSITES ignore.
▸ noun ❶ *have a look at this report* GLANCE, view, examination, study, inspection, observation, scan, survey, peep, peek, glimpse, gaze, stare; *informal* eyeful, gander, look-see, once-over, squint, recce; *Brit. informal* shufti, dekko, gawp, butcher's. ❷ *the look on her face* EXPRESSION, mien. ❸ *that rustic look* APPEARANCE, air, aspect, bearing, cast, manner, mien, demeanour, facade, impression, effect. ❹ *this season's look* FASHION, style, vogue, mode.
■ **look after** TAKE CARE OF, care for, attend to, minister to, tend, mind, keep an eye on, keep safe, be responsible for, protect; nurse, babysit, childmind.
■ **look back on** REFLECT ON, think back to, remember, recall, reminisce about.
■ **look down on** DISDAIN, scorn, regard with contempt, look down one's nose at, sneer at, despise.
■ **look for** SEARCH FOR, hunt for, try to find, seek, cast about/around/round for, try to track down, forage for, scout out, quest for/after.
■ **look forward to** AWAIT WITH PLEASURE, eagerly anticipate, lick one's lips over, be unable to wait for, count the days until.
■ **look into** INVESTIGATE, enquire into, ask questions about, go into, probe, explore, follow up, research, study, examine; *informal* check out, give something a/the once-over; *N. Amer. informal* scope out.
■ **look like** RESEMBLE, bear a resemblance to, look similar to, take after, have the look of, have the appearance of, remind one of, make one think of; *informal* be the spitting image of, be a dead ringer for.

■ **look on/upon** REGARD, consider, think of, deem, judge, see, view, count, reckon.

■ **look out** BEWARE, watch out, mind out, be on (one's) guard, be alert, be wary, be vigilant, be careful, take care, be cautious, pay attention, take heed, keep one's eyes open/peeled, keep an eye out; watch your step.

■ **look something over** INSPECT, examine, scan, cast an eye over, take stock of, vet, view, look through, peruse, run through, read through; *informal* take a dekko at, give something a/the once-over; *N. Amer.* check out; *N. Amer. informal* eyeball.

■ **look to** ❶ *we must look to the future* CONSIDER, think about, turn one's thoughts to, focus on, take heed of, pay attention to, attend to, address, mind, heed. ❷ *they look to the government for help* TURN TO, resort to, have recourse to, fall back on, rely on.

■ **look up** IMPROVE, get better, pick up, come along/on, progress, make progress, make headway, perk up, rally, take a turn for the better.

■ **look someone up** (*informal*) VISIT, pay a visit to, call on, go to see, look in on; *N. Amer.* visit with, go see; *informal* drop in on.

■ **look up to** ADMIRE, have a high opinion of, think highly of, hold in high regard, regard highly, rate highly, respect, esteem, value.

lookalike ▶ noun DOUBLE, twin, clone, duplicate, exact likeness, replica, copy, facsimile, Doppelgänger; *informal* spitting image, dead ringer, dead spit.

lookout ▶ noun ❶ *he saw the smoke from the lookout* OBSERVATION POST, lookout point, lookout station, lookout tower, watchtower. ❷ *the lookout sighted sails* WATCHMAN, watch, guard, sentry, sentinel, picket; *historical* vedette. ❸ (*informal*) *it would be a poor lookout for her* OUTLOOK, prospect, chance of success, future. ❹ (*Brit. informal*) *that's your lookout* PROBLEM, concern, business, affair, responsibility, worry; *informal* pigeon.

■ **be on the lookout/keep a lookout** KEEP WATCH, keep an eye out, keep one's eyes peeled, keep a vigil, be alert, be on the qui vive.

loom ▶ verb ❶ *ghostly shapes loomed out of the fog* EMERGE, appear, come into view, take shape, materialize, reveal itself. ❷ *the church loomed above him* SOAR, tower, rise, rear up; overhang, overshadow, dominate. ❸ *without reforms, disaster looms* BE IMMINENT, be on the horizon, impend, threaten, brew, be just around the corner.

loop ▶ noun *a loop of rope* COIL, hoop, ring, circle, noose, oval, spiral, curl, bend, curve, arc, twirl, whorl, twist, hook, zigzag, helix, convolution, incurvation.

▶ verb ❶ *Dave looped rope around their hands* COIL, wind, twist, snake, wreathe, spiral, curve, bend, turn. ❷ *he looped the cables together* FASTEN, tie, join, connect, knot, bind.

loophole ▶ noun MEANS OF EVASION, means of avoidance; ambiguity, omission, flaw, inconsistency, discrepancy.

loose ▶ adjective ❶ *a loose floorboard* NOT FIXED IN PLACE, not secure, unsecured, unattached; detached, unfastened; wobbly, unsteady, movable. ❷ *she wore her hair loose* UNTIED, unpinned, unbound, hanging free, down, flowing. ❸ *there's a wolf loose* FREE, at large, at liberty, on the loose, escaped; unconfined, untied, unchained, untethered. ❹ *a loose interpretation* VAGUE, indefinite, inexact, imprecise, approximate; broad, general, rough; liberal. ❺ *a loose jacket* BAGGY, generously cut, slack, roomy; oversized, shapeless, bagging, sagging, sloppy. ❻ (*dated*) *a loose woman* PROMISCUOUS, of easy virtue, fast, wanton, unchaste, immoral; licentious, dissolute; *N. Amer. informal* roundheeled; *dated* fallen; *derogatory* whorish, sluttish.

–OPPOSITES secure, literal, narrow, tight, chaste.

▶ verb ❶ *the hounds have been loosed* FREE, set free, unloose, turn loose, set loose, let loose, let go, release; untie, unchain, unfasten, unleash. ❷ *the fingers loosed their hold* RELAX, slacken, loosen; weaken, lessen, reduce, diminish, moderate. ❸ *Brian loosed off a shot* FIRE, discharge, shoot, let go, let fly with.

–OPPOSITES confine, tighten.

■ **at a loose end** WITH NOTHING TO DO, unoccupied, unemployed, at leisure, idle, adrift, with time to kill; bored, twiddling one's thumbs, kicking one's heels.

■ **break loose** ESCAPE, make one's escape, get away, get free, break free, free oneself.

■ **let loose**. *See* LOOSE verb sense 1.

■ **on the loose** FREE, at liberty, at large, escaped; on the run, fugitive; *N. Amer. informal* on the lam.

loose-limbed ▶ adjective SUPPLE, limber, lithe, lissom, willowy; agile, nimble.

loosen ▶ verb ❶ *you simply loosen two screws* MAKE SLACK, slacken, unstick; unfasten, detach, release, disconnect, undo, unclasp, unlatch, unbolt. ❷ *her fingers loosened* BECOME SLACK, slacken, become loose, let go, ease; work loose, work free. ❸ *Philip loosened his grip* WEAKEN, relax, slacken, loose, lessen, reduce, moderate, diminish. ❹ *you need to loosen up* RELAX, unwind, ease up/off; *informal* let up, hang loose, lighten up, go easy.

–OPPOSITES tighten.

loot ▶ noun *a bag full of loot* BOOTY, spoils, plunder, stolen goods, contraband, pillage; *informal* swag, hot goods, ill-gotten gains, boodle.

▶ verb *troops looted the cathedral* PLUNDER, pillage, despoil, ransack, sack, raid, rifle, rob, burgle; strip, clear out.

lop ▶ verb CUT, chop, hack, saw, hew, slash, axe; prune, sever, clip, trim, snip, dock, crop.

lope ▶ verb STRIDE, run, bound; lollop.

lopsided ▶ adjective CROOKED, askew, awry, off-centre, uneven, out of true, out of line, asymmetrical, tilted, at an angle, aslant, slanting, squint; *Scottish* agley; *informal* cock-eyed; *Brit. informal* skew-whiff, wonky.
– OPPOSITES even, level, balanced.

loquacious ▶ adjective TALKATIVE, voluble, communicative, expansive, garrulous, unreserved, chatty, gossipy, gossiping; *informal* having the gift of the gab, gabby, gassy; *Brit. informal* able to talk the hind legs off a donkey.
– OPPOSITES reticent, taciturn.

loquacity ▶ noun TALKATIVENESS, volubility, expansiveness, garrulousness, garrulity, chattiness; *informal* the gift of the gab.
– OPPOSITES reticence, taciturnity.

lord ▶ noun ❶ *lords and ladies* NOBLE, nobleman, peer, aristocrat, patrician, grandee, seigneur. ❷ *it is my duty to obey my lord's wishes* MASTER, ruler, leader, chief, superior, monarch, sovereign, king, emperor, prince, governor, commander, suzerain, liege, liege lord. ❸ *let us pray to our Lord* GOD, the Father, the Almighty, Jehovah, the Creator; JESUS CHRIST, the Messiah, the Saviour, the Son of God, the Redeemer, the Lamb of God, the Prince of Peace, the King of Kings. ❹ *a press lord* MAGNATE, tycoon, mogul, captain, baron, king; industrialist, proprietor; *informal* big shot, honcho; *derogatory* fat cat.
– OPPOSITES commoner, servant, inferior.
■ **lord it over someone** ORDER ABOUT/AROUND, dictate to, ride roughshod over, pull rank on, tyrannize, have under one's thumb; be overbearing, put on airs, swagger; *informal* boss about/around, walk all over, push around, throw one's weight about/around.

lordly ▶ adjective ❶ *lordly titles* NOBLE, aristocratic, princely, kingly, regal, royal, imperial, courtly, stately; magnificent, majestic, grand, august. ❷ *in lordly tones* IMPERIOUS, arrogant, haughty, self-important, swaggering; supercilious, disdainful, scornful, contemptuous, condescending, patronizing, superior; dictatorial, authoritarian, peremptory, autocratic; *informal* bossy, high and mighty, snooty, uppity, hoity-toity; *Brit. informal* toffee-nosed.
– OPPOSITES lowly, humble.

lore ▶ noun ❶ *Arthurian legend and lore* MYTHOLOGY, myths, legends, stories, traditions, folklore, oral tradition, mythos, mythus. ❷ *cricket lore* KNOWLEDGE, learning, wisdom; *informal* know-how, how-tos.

lorry ▶ noun TRUCK, wagon, van, juggernaut, trailer; articulated lorry, heavy-goods vehicle, HGV; *dated* pantechnicon.

lose ▶ verb ❶ *I've lost my watch* MISLAY, misplace, be unable to find, lose track of, leave (behind), fail to keep/retain, fail to keep sight of. ❷ *he's lost a lot of blood* BE DEPRIVED OF, suffer the loss of; no longer have. ❸ *he lost his pursuers* ESCAPE FROM, evade, elude, dodge, avoid, give someone the slip, shake off, throw off, throw off the scent; leave behind, outdistance, outstrip, outrun. ❹ *their lost their way* STRAY FROM, wander from, depart from, go astray from, fail to keep to. ❺ *you've lost your opportunity* NEGLECT, waste, squander, fail to grasp, fail to take advantage of, let pass, miss, forfeit; *informal* pass up, lose out on. ❻ *they always lose at football* BE DEFEATED, be beaten, suffer defeat, be the loser, be conquered, be vanquished, be trounced, be worsted; *informal* come a cropper, go down, take a licking, be bested.
– OPPOSITES find, regain, seize, win.
■ **lose out** BE DEPRIVED OF AN OPPORTUNITY, fail to benefit, be disadvantaged, be the loser.
■ **lose out on** BE UNABLE TO TAKE ADVANTAGE OF, fail to benefit from; *informal* miss out on.
■ **lose out to** BE DEFEATED BY, be beaten by, suffer defeat at the hands of, lose to, be conquered by, be vanquished by, be trounced by, be worsted by, be beaten into second place by; *informal* go down to, be bested by.

loser ▶ noun ❶ *the loser still gets the silver medal* DEFEATED PERSON, also-ran, runner-up. ❷ (*informal*) *he's a complete loser* FAILURE, non-achiever, underachiever, ne'er-do-well, dead loss; write-off, has-been; *informal* flop, non-starter, no-hoper, washout, lemon.
– OPPOSITES winner, success.

loss ▶ noun ❶ *the loss of the documents* MISLAYING, misplacement, forgetting. ❷ *loss of earnings* DEPRIVATION, disappearance, privation, forfeiture, diminution, erosion, reduction, depletion. ❸ *the loss of her husband* DEATH, dying, demise, passing (away/on), end, quietus; bereavement; *formal* decease; *archaic* expiry. ❹ *British losses in the war* CASUALTY, fatality, victim; dead; missing; death toll, number killed/dead/wounded. ❺ *a loss of £15,000* DEFICIT, debit, debt, indebtedness, deficiency.
– OPPOSITES recovery, profit.
■ **at a loss** BAFFLED, nonplussed, mystified, puzzled, perplexed, bewildered, bemused, at sixes and sevens, confused, dumbfounded, stumped, stuck, blank; *informal* clueless, flummoxed, bamboozled, fazed, floored, beaten; *N. Amer. informal* discombobulated.

lost ▶ adjective ❶ *her lost keys* MISSING, mislaid, misplaced, vanished, disappeared, gone missing/astray, forgotten, nowhere to be found; absent, not present, strayed. ❷ *I think we're lost* OFF COURSE, off track, disorientated, having lost one's bearings, going round in circles, adrift, at sea, stray, astray. ❸ *a lost opportunity* MISSED, forfeited, neglected, wasted, squandered, gone by the board; *informal* down the drain. ❹ *lost traditional values* BYGONE, past, former, one-time, previous, old, olden, departed, vanished, forgotten, consigned to oblivion, extinct, dead, gone. ❺ *lost species and habitats* EXTINCT, died out, defunct, vanished, gone;

DESTROYED, wiped out, ruined, wrecked, exterminated, eradicated. ❻ *a lost cause* HOPELESS, beyond hope, futile, forlorn, failed, beyond remedy, beyond recovery. ❼ *lost souls* DAMNED, fallen, irredeemable, irreclaimable, irretrievable, past hope, past praying for, condemned, cursed, doomed, excommunicated; *poetic/literary* accursed. ❽ *lost in thought* ENGROSSED, absorbed, rapt, immersed, deep, intent, engaged, wrapped up.
– OPPOSITES current, saved.

lot ▶ **pronoun** *a lot of money | lots of friends* A LARGE AMOUNT, a fair amount, a good/great deal, a great quantity, quantities, an abundance, a wealth, a profusion, plenty; many, a great many, a large number, a considerable number, numerous, scores; *informal* hundreds, thousands, millions, billions, loads, masses, heaps, a pile, piles, oodles, stacks, scads, reams, wads, pots, oceans, a mountain, mountains, miles, tons, zillions, more —— than one can shake a stick at; *Brit. informal* a shedload, lashings; *N. Amer. informal* gobs, a bunch, gazillions.
– OPPOSITES a little, not much, a few, not many.
▶ **adverb** *I work in pastels a lot* A GREAT DEAL, a good deal, to a great extent, much; often, frequently, regularly.
– OPPOSITES a little, not much.
▶ **noun** ❶ (*informal*) *what do your lot think?* GROUP, set, crowd, circle, band, crew; *informal* bunch, gang, mob; *Brit. informal* shower. ❷ *the books were auctioned as a number of lots* ITEM, article; batch, set, collection, group, bundle, quantity, assortment, parcel. ❸ *his lot in life* FATE, destiny, fortune, doom; situation, circumstances, state, condition, position, plight, predicament. ❹ (*N. Amer.*) *some youngsters playing ball in a vacant lot* PATCH OF GROUND, piece of ground, plot, area, tract, parcel; *N. Amer.* plat.
■ **draw/cast lots** DECIDE RANDOMLY, spin/toss a coin, throw dice, draw straws.
■ **throw in one's lot with** JOIN FORCES WITH, join up with, form an alliance with, ally with, align oneself with, link up with, make common cause with.

lotion ▶ **noun** OINTMENT, cream, salve, balm, rub, emollient, moisturizer, lubricant, unguent, liniment, embrocation.

lottery ▶ **noun** ❶ *a national lottery* RAFFLE, (prize) draw, sweepstake, sweep, tombola, pools. ❷ *the race is something of a lottery* GAMBLE, speculation, game of chance, matter of luck.

loud ▶ **adjective** ❶ *loud music* NOISY, blaring, booming, deafening, roaring, thunderous, thundering, ear-splitting, ear-piercing, piercing; carrying, clearly audible; lusty, powerful, forceful, stentorian; *Music* forte, fortissimo. ❷ *loud complaints* VOCIFEROUS, clamorous, insistent, vehement, emphatic, urgent. ❸ *a loud T-shirt* GARISH, gaudy, flamboyant, lurid, glaring, showy, ostentatious; vulgar, tasteless; *informal* flash, flashy, naff, kitsch, tacky.
– OPPOSITES quiet, soft, gentle, sober, tasteful.

loudly ▶ **adverb** AT HIGH VOLUME, at the top of one's voice; noisily, deafeningly, thunderously, piercingly; stridently, lustily, powerfully, forcefully; *Music* forte, fortissimo; *informal* as if to wake the dead.
– OPPOSITES quietly, softly.

loudmouth ▶ **noun** (*informal*) BRAGGART, boaster, blusterer, swaggerer; *informal* blabbermouth, big mouth; *N. Amer. informal* blowhard.

loudspeaker ▶ **noun** SPEAKER, monitor, woofer, tweeter; loudhailer, megaphone; public address system, PA (system); *informal* squawk box.

lounge ▶ **verb** *he just lounges in his room* LAZE, lie, loll, lie back, lean back, recline, stretch oneself, drape oneself, relax, rest, repose, take it easy, put one's feet up, unwind, luxuriate; sprawl, slump, slouch, flop; loaf, idle, do nothing.
▶ **noun** *she sat in the lounge* LIVING ROOM, sitting room, front room, drawing room, morning room, reception room, salon, family room; *dated* parlour.

lour, lower ▶ **verb** SCOWL, frown, look sullen, glower, glare, give someone black looks, look daggers, look angry; *informal* give someone dirty looks.
– OPPOSITES smile.

louring, lowering ▶ **adjective** OVERCAST, dark, leaden, grey, cloudy, clouded, gloomy, threatening, menacing, promising rain.
– OPPOSITES sunny, bright.

lousy (*informal*) ▶ **adjective** ❶ *a lousy film. See* AWFUL sense 2. ❷ *the lousy, double-crossing snake! See* DESPICABLE. ❸ *I felt lousy. See* ILL adjective sense 1.
■ **be lousy with**. *See* CRAWL sense 3.

lout ▶ **noun** RUFFIAN, hooligan, thug, boor, oaf, hoodlum, rowdy; *informal* tough, roughneck, bruiser, yahoo, lug; *Brit. informal* yob, yobbo.
– OPPOSITES smoothie, gentleman.

loutish ▶ **adjective** UNCOUTH, rude, impolite, unmannerly, ill-mannered, ill-bred, coarse; thuggish, boorish, oafish, uncivilized, wild, rough; *informal* slobbish; *Brit. informal* yobbish.
– OPPOSITES polite, well behaved.

lovable ▶ **adjective** ADORABLE, dear, sweet, cute, charming, darling, lovely, likeable, delightful, captivating, enchanting, engaging, bewitching, pleasing, appealing, winsome, winning, fetching, endearing.
– OPPOSITES hateful, loathsome.

love ▶ **noun** ❶ *his friendship with Helen grew into love* DEEP AFFECTION, fondness, tenderness, warmth, intimacy, attachment, endearment; devotion, adoration, doting, idolization, worship; passion, ardour, desire, lust, yearning,

infatuation, besottedness. ❷ *her love of fashion* LIKING, enjoyment, appreciation, taste, delight, relish, passion, zeal, appetite, zest, enthusiasm, keenness, fondness, soft spot, weakness, bent, leaning, proclivity, inclination, disposition, partiality, predilection, penchant. ❸ *their love for their fellow human beings* COMPASSION, care, caring, regard, solicitude, concern, friendliness, friendship, kindness, charity, goodwill, sympathy, kindliness, altruism, unselfishness, philanthropy, benevolence, fellow feeling, humanity. ❹ *he was her one true love* BELOVED, loved one, love of one's life, dear, dearest, dear one, darling, sweetheart, sweet, angel, honey; lover, inamorato, inamorata, amour; *archaic* paramour. ❺ *their love will survive* RELATIONSHIP, love affair, romance, liaison, affair of the heart, amour. ❻ *my mother sends her love* BEST WISHES, regards, good wishes, greetings, kind/kindest regards.
– RELATED TERMS amatory, phil-.
– OPPOSITES hatred.

▶ **verb** ❶ *she loves him dearly* CARE VERY MUCH FOR, feel deep affection for, hold very dear, adore, think the world of, be devoted to, dote on, idolize, worship; be in love with, be infatuated with, be smitten with, be besotted with; *informal* be mad/crazy/nuts/wild/potty about, have a pash on, carry a torch for. ❷ *Laura loved painting* LIKE VERY MUCH, delight in, enjoy greatly, have a passion for, take great pleasure in, derive great pleasure from, relish, savour; have a weakness for, be partial to, have a soft spot for, have a taste for, be taken with; *informal* get a kick out of, have a thing about, be mad/crazy/nuts/wild/potty about, be hooked on, go a bundle on, get off on, get a buzz out of.
– OPPOSITES hate.

■ **fall in love with** BECOME INFATUATED WITH, give/lose one's heart to; *informal* fall for, be bowled over by, be swept off one's feet by, develop a crush on.

■ **in love with** INFATUATED WITH, besotted with, enamoured of, smitten with, consumed with desire for; captivated by, bewitched by, enthralled by, entranced by; devoted to, doting on; *informal* mad/crazy/nuts/wild/potty about.

love affair ▶ **noun** ❶ *he had a love affair with a teacher* RELATIONSHIP, affair, romance, liaison, affair of the heart, affaire de cœur, intrigue, fling, amour, involvement, romantic entanglement; flirtation, dalliance; *Brit. informal* carry-on. ❷ *a love affair with the motor car* ENTHUSIASM, mania, devotion, passion.

loveless ▶ **adjective** PASSIONLESS, unloving, unfeeling, heartless, cold, icy, frigid.
– OPPOSITES loving, passionate.

lovelorn ▶ **adjective** LOVESICK, unrequited in love, crossed in love; spurned, jilted, rejected; pining, moping.

lovely ▶ **adjective** ❶ *a lovely young woman* BEAUTIFUL, pretty, attractive, good-looking, appealing, handsome, adorable, exquisite, sweet, personable, charming; enchanting, engaging, winsome, seductive, gorgeous, alluring, ravishing, glamorous; *Scottish & N. English* bonny; *informal* tasty, knockout, stunning, drop-dead gorgeous; *Brit. informal* smashing, fit; *N. Amer. informal* cute, foxy; *formal* beauteous; *archaic* comely, fair. ❷ *a lovely view* SCENIC, picturesque, pleasing, easy on the eye; magnificent, stunning, splendid. ❸ (*informal*) *we had a lovely day* DELIGHTFUL, very pleasant, very nice, very agreeable, marvellous, wonderful, sublime, superb, fine, magical; *informal* terrific, fabulous, heavenly, divine, amazing, glorious.
– OPPOSITES ugly, horrible.

lover ▶ **noun** ❶ *she had a secret lover* BOYFRIEND, GIRLFRIEND, lady-love, beloved, love, darling, sweetheart, inamorata, inamorato; mistress; partner, significant other; *informal* bit on the side, bit of fluff, toy boy, fancy man, fancy woman; *dated* beau; *archaic* swain, concubine, paramour. ❷ *a dog lover* DEVOTEE, admirer, fan, enthusiast, aficionado; *informal* buff, freak, nut.
– RELATED TERMS -phile.

lovesick ▶ **adjective** LOVELORN, pining, languishing, longing, yearning, infatuated; frustrated.

loving ▶ **adjective** AFFECTIONATE, fond, devoted, adoring, doting, solicitous, demonstrative, caring, tender, warm, warm-hearted, close; amorous, ardent, passionate, amatory.
– OPPOSITES cold, cruel.

low¹ ▶ **adjective** ❶ *a low fence* SHORT, small, little; squat, stubby, stunted, dwarf; shallow. ❷ *she was wearing a low dress* LOW-CUT, skimpy, revealing, plunging. ❸ *low prices* CHEAP, economical, moderate, reasonable, modest, bargain, bargain-basement, rock-bottom. ❹ *supplies were low* SCARCE, scanty, scant, skimpy, meagre, sparse, few, little, paltry; reduced, depleted, diminished. ❺ *low quality* INFERIOR, substandard, poor, bad, low-grade, below par, second-rate, unsatisfactory, deficient, defective. ❻ *of low birth* HUMBLE, lowly, low-ranking, plebeian, proletarian, peasant, poor; common, ordinary. ❼ *low expectations* UNAMBITIOUS, unaspiring, modest. ❽ *a low opinion* UNFAVOURABLE, poor, bad, adverse, negative. ❾ *a rather low thing to have done* DESPICABLE, contemptible, reprehensible, lamentable, disgusting, shameful, mean, abject, unworthy, shabby, uncharitable, base, dishonourable, unprincipled, ignoble, sordid; nasty, cruel, foul, bad; *informal* rotten, low-down; *Brit. informal* beastly; *dated* dastardly; *archaic* scurvy. ❿ *low comedy* UNCOUTH, uncultured, unsophisticated, rough, rough-hewn, unrefined, tasteless, crass, common, vulgar, coarse, crude. ⓫ *a low voice* QUIET, soft, faint, gentle, muted, subdued, muffled, hushed, quietened, whispered, stifled, murmured. ⓬ *a low note* BASS, low-pitched, deep,

rumbling, booming, sonorous. ⓭ *she was feeling low* DEPRESSED, dejected, despondent, downhearted, downcast, low-spirited, down, fed up, morose, miserable, dismal, heavy-hearted, mournful, forlorn, woebegone, crestfallen, dispirited; without energy, enervated, flat, sapped, weary; *informal* down in the mouth, down in the dumps, blue.
– OPPOSITES high, expensive, plentiful, superior, noble, favourable, admirable, decent, exalted, loud, cheerful, lively.
▶ **noun** *the dollar fell to an all-time low* NADIR, low point, lowest point, lowest level, depth, rock bottom.
– OPPOSITES high.

low[2] ▶ **verb** *cattle were lowing* MOO, bellow.

lowbrow ▶ **adjective** MASS-MARKET, tabloid, popular, intellectually undemanding, lightweight, accessible, unpretentious; uncultured, unsophisticated, trashy, philistine, simplistic; *Brit.* downmarket; *informal* dumbed-down, rubbishy.
– OPPOSITES highbrow, intellectual.

low-down (*informal*) ▶ **adjective** *a low-down trick* UNFAIR, mean, despicable, reprehensible, contemptible, lamentable, disgusting, shameful, low, unworthy, shabby, base, dishonourable, unprincipled, sordid, underhand; *informal* rotten, dirty; *Brit. informal* beastly; *dated* dastardly; *archaic* scurvy.
– OPPOSITES kind, honourable.
▶ **noun** *he gave us the low-down* FACTS, information, story, data, facts and figures, intelligence, news; *informal* info, rundown, the score, the gen, the latest, the word, the dope.

lower[1] ▶ **adjective** ❶ *the lower house of parliament* SUBORDINATE, inferior, lesser, junior, minor, secondary, lower-level, subsidiary, subservient. ❷ *her lower lip* BOTTOM, bottommost, nether, under; underneath, further down, beneath. ❸ *a lower price* CHEAPER, reduced, cut, slashed.
– OPPOSITES upper, higher, increased.

lower[2] ▶ **verb** ❶ *she lowered the mask* MOVE DOWN, let down, take down, haul down, drop, let fall. ❷ *lower your voice* SOFTEN, modulate, quieten, hush, tone down, muffle, turn down, mute. ❸ *they are lowering their prices* REDUCE, decrease, lessen, bring down, mark down, cut, slash, axe, diminish, curtail, prune, pare (down). ❹ *the water level lowered* SUBSIDE, fall (off), recede, ebb, wane; abate, die down, let up, moderate, diminish, lessen. ❺ *don't lower yourself to their level* DEGRADE, debase, demean, abase, humiliate, downgrade, discredit, shame, dishonour, disgrace; belittle, cheapen, devalue; (**lower oneself**) stoop, sink, descend.
– OPPOSITES raise, increase.

lower[3] ▶ **verb** *he lowered at her. See* LOUR.

low-grade ▶ **adjective** POOR-QUALITY, inferior, substandard, second-rate; shoddy, cheap, reject, trashy, gimcrack; *Brit. informal* duff, ropy, twopenny-halfpenny, rubbishy; *N. Amer. informal* two-bit, bum, cheapjack.
– OPPOSITES top-quality, first-class.

low-key ▶ **adjective** RESTRAINED, modest, understated, muted, subtle, quiet, low-profile, inconspicuous, unostentatious, unobtrusive, discreet, toned-down.
– OPPOSITES ostentatious, obtrusive.

lowly ▶ **adjective** HUMBLE, low, low-born, low-bred, low-ranking, plebeian, proletarian; common, ordinary, plain, average, modest, simple; inferior, ignoble, subordinate, obscure.
– OPPOSITES aristocratic, exalted.

loyal ▶ **adjective** FAITHFUL, true, devoted; constant, steadfast, staunch, dependable, reliable, trusted, trustworthy, trusty, dutiful, dedicated, unchanging, unwavering, unswerving; patriotic.
– OPPOSITES treacherous.

loyalty ▶ **noun** ALLEGIANCE, faithfulness, obedience, adherence, homage, devotion; steadfastness, staunchness, true-heartedness, dependability, reliability, trustiness, trustworthiness, duty, dedication, commitment; patriotism; *historical* fealty.
– OPPOSITES treachery.

lozenge ▶ **noun** ❶ *the pattern consists of overlapping lozenges* DIAMOND, rhombus. ❷ *a throat lozenge* PASTILLE, drop; cough sweet, jujube; *dated* cachou.

lubricant ▶ **noun** GREASE, oil, lubrication, lubricator, emollient, lotion, unguent; *informal* lube.

lubricate ▶ **verb** ❶ *lubricate the washer with silicone grease* OIL, GREASE, wax, polish. ❷ *oil money lubricates an elaborate system of patronage* FACILITATE, ease, smooth the way for, oil the wheels of.
– OPPOSITES impede.

lucid ▶ **adjective** ❶ *a lucid description* INTELLIGIBLE, comprehensible, understandable, cogent, coherent, articulate; clear, transparent; plain, simple, vivid, sharp, straightforward, unambiguous, graphic; *formal* perspicuous. ❷ *he was not lucid enough to explain* RATIONAL, sane, in one's right mind, in possession of one's faculties, compos mentis, able to think clearly, balanced, clear-headed, sober, sensible; *informal* all there.
– OPPOSITES confusing, confused.

luck ▶ **noun** ❶ *with luck you'll make it* GOOD FORTUNE, good luck; fluke, stroke of luck; *informal* lucky break. ❷ *I wish you luck* SUCCESS, prosperity, good fortune, good luck. ❸ *it is a matter of luck whether it hits or misses* FORTUNE, fate, destiny, lot, stars, karma, kismet; fortuity, serendipity; chance, accident, a twist of fate; *Austral./NZ informal* mozzle.
– OPPOSITES bad luck, misfortune.

■ **in luck** FORTUNATE, lucky, blessed with good luck, born under a lucky star; successful, having a charmed life; *Brit. informal* jammy.

■ **out of luck** UNFORTUNATE, unlucky, luckless, hapless, unsuccessful, cursed, jinxed, ill-fated; *informal* down on one's luck; *poetic/literary* star-crossed.

luckily ▶ adverb FORTUNATELY, happily, providentially, opportunely, by good fortune, as luck would have it, propitiously; mercifully, thankfully.
– OPPOSITES unfortunately.

luckless ▶ adjective UNLUCKY, unfortunate, unsuccessful, hapless, out of luck, cursed, jinxed, doomed, ill-fated; *informal* down on one's luck; *poetic/literary* star-crossed.
– OPPOSITES lucky.

lucky ▶ adjective ❶ *the lucky winner* FORTUNATE, in luck, blessed, blessed with good luck, favoured, born under a lucky star, charmed; successful, prosperous; born with a silver spoon in one's mouth; *Brit. informal* jammy. ❷ *a lucky escape* PROVIDENTIAL, fortunate, advantageous, timely, opportune, serendipitous, expedient, heaven-sent, auspicious; chance, fortuitous, fluky, accidental.
– OPPOSITES unfortunate.

lucrative ▶ adjective PROFITABLE, profit-making, gainful, remunerative, moneymaking, paying, high-income, well paid, bankable; rewarding, worthwhile; thriving, flourishing, successful, booming.
– OPPOSITES unprofitable.

lucre ▶ noun MONEY, cash, funds, capital, finances, riches, wealth, spoils, ill-gotten gains, Mammon; *informal* dough, bread, loot, the ready, readies, moolah; *Brit. informal* dosh, brass, lolly, spondulicks, wonga, ackers; *archaic* pelf.

ludicrous ▶ adjective ABSURD, ridiculous, farcical, laughable, risible, preposterous, foolish, mad, insane, idiotic, stupid, inane, silly, asinine, nonsensical; *informal* crazy; *rare* derisible.
– OPPOSITES sensible.

lug ▶ verb CARRY, lift, bear, tote, heave, hoist, shoulder, manhandle; haul, drag, tug, tow, transport, move, convey, shift; *informal* hump, schlep; *Scottish informal* humph.

luggage ▶ noun BAGGAGE; bags, suitcases, cases, trunks. *See also* BAG noun sense 2.

lugubrious ▶ adjective MOURNFUL, gloomy, sad, unhappy, doleful, glum, melancholy, woeful, miserable, woebegone, forlorn, long-faced, sombre, solemn, serious, sorrowful, morose, dour, cheerless, joyless, dismal; funereal, sepulchral; *informal* down in the mouth; *poetic/literary* dolorous.
– OPPOSITES cheerful.

lukewarm ▶ adjective ❶ *lukewarm coffee* TEPID, slightly warm, warmish, blood-warm, at skin temperature, at room temperature, chambré. ❷ *a lukewarm response* INDIFFERENT, cool, half-hearted, apathetic, unenthusiastic, tepid, offhand, perfunctory, non-committal, lackadaisical; *informal* laid-back, unenthused, couldn't-care-less; *rare* Laodicean.
– OPPOSITES hot, cold, enthusiastic.

lull ▶ verb ❶ *the sound of the bells lulled us to sleep* SOOTHE, calm, hush; rock to sleep. ❷ *his suspicions were soon lulled* ASSUAGE, allay, ease, alleviate, soothe, quiet, quieten; reduce, diminish; quell, banish, dispel. ❸ *the noise had lulled* ABATE, die down, subside, let up, moderate, slacken, lessen, dwindle, decrease, diminish.
– OPPOSITES waken, agitate, arouse, intensify.
▶ noun ❶ *a lull in the fighting* PAUSE, respite, interval, break, hiatus, suspension, interlude, intermission, breathing space; *informal* let-up, breather. ❷ *the lull before the storm* CALM, stillness, quiet, tranquillity, peace, silence, hush.
– OPPOSITES agitation, activity.

lullaby ▶ noun CRADLE SONG, berceuse.

lumber[1] ▶ verb *elephants lumbered past* LURCH, stumble, trundle, shamble, shuffle, waddle; trudge, clump, stump, plod, tramp; *informal* galumph.

lumber[2] ▶ noun ❶ *a spare room packed with lumber* JUMBLE, clutter, odds and ends, bits and pieces, flotsam and jetsam, cast-offs, refuse, rubbish, litter; *N. Amer.* trash; *informal* junk, odds and sods, gubbins, clobber. ❷ *the lumber trade* TIMBER, wood.
▶ verb (*Brit. informal*) *she was lumbered with a husband and child* BURDEN, saddle, encumber, hamper; load, oppress, trouble, tax; *informal* land, dump something on someone.
– OPPOSITES free.

lumbering ▶ adjective CLUMSY, awkward, heavy-footed, slow, blundering, bumbling, inept, maladroit, uncoordinated, ungainly, ungraceful, gauche, lumpish, hulking, ponderous; *informal* clodhopping.
– OPPOSITES nimble, agile.

luminary ▶ noun LEADING LIGHT, guiding light, inspiration, role model, hero, heroine, leader, expert, master, panjandrum; lion, legend, great, giant.
– OPPOSITES nobody.

luminous ▶ adjective SHINING, bright, brilliant, radiant, dazzling, glowing, gleaming, scintillating, lustrous; luminescent, phosphorescent, fluorescent, incandescent.
– OPPOSITES dark.

lump[1] ▶ noun ❶ *a lump of coal* CHUNK, hunk, piece, mass, block, wedge, slab, cake, nugget, ball, brick, cube, pat, knob, clod, gobbet, dollop, wad; *informal* glob; *N. Amer. informal* gob. ❷ *a lump on his head* SWELLING, bump, bulge, protuberance, protrusion, growth, outgrowth, nodule, hump.

▶ verb *it is convenient to lump them together* COMBINE, put, group, bunch, aggregate, unite, pool, merge, collect, throw, consider together.

lump² ▶ verb (*informal*) *I'm afraid you'll have to lump it* PUT UP WITH, bear, endure, take, tolerate, accept.

lumpish ▶ adjective ❶ *lumpish furniture* CUMBERSOME, unwieldy, heavy, hulking, chunky, bulky, ponderous. ❷ *a lumpish young girl* STUPID, obtuse, dense, dim-witted, dull-witted, slow-witted, slow; lethargic, bovine, sluggish, listless; *informal* thick, dumb, dopey, slow on the uptake, moronic; *Brit. informal* dozy.
– OPPOSITES elegant, quick-witted, sharp.

lumpy ▶ adjective ❶ *a lumpy mattress* BUMPY, knobbly, bulging, uneven, rough, gnarled. ❷ *lumpy custard* CLOTTED, curdled, congealed, coagulated.

lunacy ▶ noun ❶ *originality demands a degree of lunacy* INSANITY, madness, mental illness, dementia, mania, psychosis; *informal* craziness. ❷ *the lunacy of gambling* FOLLY, foolishness, foolhardiness, stupidity, silliness, idiocy, madness, rashness, recklessness, imprudence, irresponsibility, injudiciousness; *informal* craziness; *Brit. informal* daftness.
– OPPOSITES sanity, sense, prudence.

lunatic ▶ noun *he drives like a lunatic* MANIAC, madman, madwoman, imbecile, psychopath, psychotic; fool, idiot; eccentric; *informal* loony, nut, nutcase, head case, psycho, moron; *Brit. informal* nutter; *N. Amer. informal* screwball.
▶ adjective ❶ *a lunatic prisoner. See* MAD sense 1. ❷ *a lunatic idea. See* MAD sense 3.

lunch ▶ noun MIDDAY MEAL, luncheon; *Brit.* dinner.

lung
– RELATED TERMS pulmonary, pneumo-.

lunge ▶ noun *Darren made a lunge at his attacker* THRUST, dive, rush, charge, grab.
▶ verb *he lunged at Finn with a knife* THRUST, dive, spring, launch oneself, rush, make a grab.

lurch ▶ verb ❶ *he lurched into the kitchen* STAGGER, stumble, wobble, sway, reel, roll, weave, pitch, totter, blunder. ❷ *the ship lurched* SWAY, reel, list, heel, rock, roll, pitch, toss, jerk, shake, judder, flounder, swerve.

lure ▶ verb *consumers are frequently lured into debt* TEMPT, entice, attract, induce, coax, persuade, inveigle, allure, seduce, win over, cajole, beguile, bewitch, ensnare.
– OPPOSITES deter, put off.
▶ noun *the lure of the stage* TEMPTATION, enticement, attraction, pull, draw, appeal; inducement, allurement, fascination, interest; magnet; *informal* come-on.

lurid ▶ adjective ❶ *lurid food colourings* BRIGHT, brilliant, vivid, glaring, shocking, fluorescent, flaming, dazzling, intense, gaudy, loud. ❷ *the lurid details* SENSATIONAL, sensationalist, exaggerated, over-dramatized, extravagant, colourful; salacious, graphic, explicit, unrestrained, prurient, shocking; gruesome, gory, grisly; *informal* tacky, shock-horror, juicy, full-frontal.
– OPPOSITES muted, restrained.

lurk ▶ verb SKULK, loiter, lie in wait, lie low, hide, conceal oneself, take cover, keep out of sight.

luscious ▶ adjective ❶ *luscious fruit* DELICIOUS, succulent, lush, juicy, mouth-watering, sweet, tasty, appetizing; *informal* scrumptious, moreish, scrummy, yummy; *N. Amer. informal* nummy; *poetic/literary* ambrosial. ❷ *a luscious Swedish beauty* SEXY, sexually attractive, nubile, ravishing, gorgeous, seductive, alluring, sultry, beautiful, stunning; *informal* fanciable, tasty, drop-dead gorgeous, curvy; *Brit. informal* fit; *N. Amer. informal* foxy, cute; *Austral./NZ informal* spunky.
– OPPOSITES unappetizing, plain, scrawny.

lush ▶ adjective ❶ *lush vegetation* LUXURIANT, rich, abundant, profuse, exuberant, riotous, prolific, vigorous; dense, thick, rank, rampant; *informal* jungly. ❷ *a lush, ripe peach* SUCCULENT, luscious, juicy, soft, tender, ripe. ❸ *a lush apartment* LUXURIOUS, de luxe, sumptuous, palatial, opulent, lavish, elaborate, extravagant, fancy; *informal* plush, ritzy, posh, swanky; *Brit. informal* swish; *N. Amer. informal* swank.
– OPPOSITES barren, sparse, shrivelled, austere.

lust ▶ noun ❶ *his lust for her* SEXUAL DESIRE, sexual appetite, sexual longing, ardour, desire, passion; libido, sex drive, sexuality, biological urge; lechery, lecherousness, lasciviousness; *informal* horniness, the hots; *Brit. informal* randiness. ❷ *a lust for power* GREED, desire, craving, covetousness, eagerness, avidity, cupidity, longing, yearning, hunger, thirst, appetite, hankering.
– OPPOSITES dread, aversion.
▶ verb ❶ *he lusted after his employer's wife* DESIRE, be consumed with desire for, find sexually attractive, crave, covet, ache for, burn for, pant for; *informal* have the hots for, lech after/over, fancy, have a thing about/for, drool over, have the horn for. ❷ *she lusted after adventure* CRAVE, desire, covet, want, wish for, long for, yearn for, dream of, hanker for, hanker after, hunger for, thirst for, ache for.
– OPPOSITES dread, avoid.

lustful ▶ adjective LECHEROUS, lascivious, libidinous, licentious, salacious, goatish; wanton, unchaste, impure, naughty, immodest, indecent, dirty, prurient; passionate, sensual, sexy, erotic; *informal* horny, randy, raunchy; *formal* concupiscent.
– OPPOSITES chaste, pure.

lustily ▶ adverb HEARTILY, vigorously, loudly, at the top of one's voice, powerfully, forcefully, strongly; *informal* like mad, like crazy.
– OPPOSITES feebly, quietly.

lustre ▶ noun ❶ *her hair lost its lustre* SHEEN, gloss, shine, glow, gleam, shimmer, burnish, polish, patina. ❷ *the lustre of the Milky Way* BRILLIANCE, brightness, radiance, sparkle, dazzle, flash, glitter, glint, gleam, luminosity, luminescence.
– OPPOSITES dullness, dark.

lustreless ▶ adjective DULL, lacklustre, matt, unpolished, tarnished, dingy, dim, dark.
– OPPOSITES lustrous, bright.

lustrous ▶ adjective SHINY, shining, satiny, glossy, gleaming, shimmering, burnished, polished; radiant, bright, brilliant, luminous; dazzling, sparkling, glistening, twinkling.
– OPPOSITES dull, dark.

lusty ▶ adjective ❶ *lusty young men* HEALTHY, strong, fit, vigorous, robust, hale and hearty, energetic; rugged, sturdy, muscular, muscly, strapping, hefty, husky, burly, powerful; *informal* beefy; *dated* stalwart. ❷ *lusty singing* LOUD, hearty, strong, powerful, forceful, vigorous.
– OPPOSITES feeble, quiet.

luxuriant ▶ adjective LUSH, rich, abundant, profuse, exuberant, riotous, prolific, vigorous; dense, thick, rank, rampant; *informal* jungly.
– OPPOSITES barren, sparse.

luxuriate ▶ verb REVEL, bask, delight, take pleasure, wallow; (**luxuriate in**) enjoy, relish, savour, appreciate; *informal* get a kick out of, get a thrill out of.
– OPPOSITES dislike.

luxurious ▶ adjective ❶ *a luxurious hotel* OPULENT, sumptuous, de luxe, grand, palatial, splendid, magnificent, well appointed, extravagant, fancy; *Brit.* upmarket; *informal* plush, posh, classy, ritzy, swanky; *Brit. informal* swish; *N. Amer. informal* swank. ❷ *a luxurious lifestyle* SELF-INDULGENT, sensual, pleasure-loving, pleasure-seeking, epicurean, hedonistic, sybaritic, lotus-eating.
– OPPOSITES plain, basic, abstemious.

luxury ▶ noun ❶ *we'll live in luxury* OPULENCE, luxuriousness, sumptuousness, grandeur, magnificence, splendour, lavishness, the lap of luxury, a bed of roses, milk and honey; *informal* the life of Riley. ❷ *a TV is his only luxury* INDULGENCE, extravagance, self-indulgence, non-essential, treat, extra, frill.
– OPPOSITES simplicity, necessity.

lying ▶ noun *she was no good at lying* UNTRUTHFULNESS, fabrication, fibbing, perjury, white lies; falseness, falsity, dishonesty, mendacity, telling stories, invention, misrepresentation, deceit, duplicity; *poetic/literary* perfidy.
– OPPOSITES honesty.
▶ adjective *he was a lying womanizer* UNTRUTHFUL, false, dishonest, mendacious, deceitful, deceiving, duplicitous, double-dealing, two-faced; *poetic/literary* perfidious.
– OPPOSITES truthful.

lynch ▶ verb EXECUTE ILLEGALLY, hang; *informal* string up.

lyric ▶ adjective ❶ *a lyric poem* EXPRESSIVE, emotional, deeply felt, personal, subjective, passionate. ❷ *a lyric soprano* LIGHT, silvery, clear, sweet.
– OPPOSITES harsh.

lyrical ▶ adjective ❶ *lyrical love poetry* EXPRESSIVE, emotional, deeply felt, personal, subjective, passionate. ❷ *she was lyrical about her success* ENTHUSIASTIC, rhapsodic, effusive, rapturous, ecstatic, euphoric, carried away.
– OPPOSITES unenthusiastic.

lyrics ▶ plural noun WORDS, libretto, book, text, lines.

Mm

macabre ▶ adjective ❶ *a macabre ritual* GRUESOME, grisly, grim, gory, morbid, ghastly, unearthly, grotesque, hideous, horrific, shocking, dreadful, loathsome, repugnant, repulsive, sickening. ❷ *a macabre joke* BLACK, weird, unhealthy; *informal* sick.

mace ▶ noun CLUB, cudgel, stick, staff, shillelagh, bludgeon, truncheon; *Brit.* life preserver; *N. Amer.* nightstick, billy, billy club, blackjack; *Brit. informal* cosh.

macerate ▶ verb PULP, mash, squash, soften, liquefy, soak.

Machiavellian ▶ adjective DEVIOUS, cunning, crafty, artful, wily, sly, scheming, treacherous, two-faced, tricky, double-dealing, unscrupulous, deceitful, dishonest; *poetic/literary* perfidious; *informal* foxy.
– OPPOSITES straightforward, ingenuous.

machinations ▶ plural noun SCHEMING, plotting, intrigues, conspiracies, ruses, tricks, wiles, stratagems, tactics, manoeuvring.

machine ▸ noun ❶ *it is quicker done by machine* APPARATUS, appliance, device, contraption, contrivance, mechanism, engine, gadget, tool. ❷ *an efficient publicity machine* ORGANIZATION, system, structure, arrangement, machinery; *informal* set-up.
– RELATED TERMS mechanical.

machinery ▸ noun ❶ *road-making machinery* EQUIPMENT, apparatus, plant, hardware, gear, tackle; mechanism; instruments, tools; gadgetry, technology. ❷ *the machinery of local government* WORKINGS, organization, system, structure, administration, institution; *informal* set-up.

machinist ▸ noun OPERATOR, operative, machine-minder.

machismo ▸ noun (AGGRESSIVE) MASCULINITY, toughness, male chauvinism, sexism, laddishness; virility, manliness.

macho ▸ adjective *a macho, non-caring image* (AGGRESSIVELY) MALE, (unpleasantly) masculine; manly, virile, red-blooded; *informal* butch, laddish.
– OPPOSITES wimpish.
▸ noun ❶ *he was a macho at heart* RED-BLOODED MALE, macho man, muscleman; *informal* he-man, tough guy. ❷ *macho is out. See* MACHISMO.
– OPPOSITES wimp.

mackintosh ▸ noun RAINCOAT, gabardine, trench coat, waterproof; *Brit.* pakamac; *N. Amer.* slicker; *Brit. informal* mac; *trademark* Burberry, Drizabone.

macrocosm ▸ noun ❶ *the law of the macrocosm* UNIVERSE, cosmos, creation, outer space. ❷ *the individual is a microcosm of the social macrocosm* SYSTEM, structure, totality, entirety, complex.
– OPPOSITES microcosm.

mad ▸ adjective ❶ *he was killed by his mad brother* INSANE, mentally ill, certifiable, deranged, demented, of unsound mind, out of one's mind, not in one's right mind, sick in the head, crazy, crazed, lunatic, non compos mentis, unhinged, disturbed, raving, psychotic, psychopathic, mad as a hatter, mad as a March hare, away with the fairies; *informal* mental, off one's head, off one's nut, nuts, nutty, off one's rocker, not right in the head, round the bend, stark staring/raving mad, bats, batty, bonkers, dotty, cuckoo, cracked, loopy, loony, doolally, bananas, loco, dippy, screwy, schizoid, touched, gaga, up the pole, not all there, not right upstairs; *Brit. informal* barmy, crackers, barking, barking mad, round the twist, off one's trolley, not the full shilling; *N. Amer. informal* nutso, out of one's tree, meshuga, wacko, gonzo; *Austral./NZ informal* bushed; *NZ informal* porangi; (**be mad**) *informal* have a screw loose, have bats in the/one's belfry; *Austral. informal* have kangaroos in the/one's top paddock; (**go mad**) lose one's reason, lose one's mind, take leave of one's senses; *informal* lose one's marbles, crack up. ❷ (*informal*) *I'm still mad at him* ANGRY, furious, infuriated, irate, raging, enraged, fuming, incensed, seeing red, beside oneself; *informal* livid, spare; *informal, dated* in a wax; *Brit. informal* aerated; *N. Amer. informal* sore; *poetic/literary* wrathful; (**go mad**) lose one's temper, get in a rage, rant and rave; *informal* explode, go off the deep end, go ape, flip, flip one's lid; *Brit. informal* do one's nut; *N. Amer. informal* flip one's wig. ❸ *some mad scheme* FOOLISH, insane, stupid, lunatic, foolhardy, idiotic, senseless, absurd, impractical, silly, inane, asinine, wild, unwise, imprudent; *informal* crazy, crackpot, crackbrained; *Brit. informal* daft. ❹ (*informal*) *he's mad about jazz* ENTHUSIASTIC, passionate; ardent, fervent, avid, fanatical; devoted to, infatuated with, in love with, hot for; *informal* crazy, dotty, nuts, wild, hooked on, gone on; *Brit. informal* potty; *N. Amer. informal* nutso. ❺ *it was a mad dash to get ready* FRENZIED, frantic, frenetic, feverish, hysterical. wild, hectic, manic.
– OPPOSITES sane, pleased, sensible, indifferent, calm.
■ **like mad** (*informal*) ❶ *I ran like mad* FAST, quickly, rapidly, speedily, hastily, hurriedly. ❷ *he had to fight like mad* ENERGETICALLY, enthusiastically, madly, furiously, with a will, for all one is worth, passionately, intensely, ardently, fervently; *informal* like crazy, hammer and tongs; *Brit. informal* like billy-o.

madcap ▸ adjective ❶ *a madcap scheme* RECKLESS, rash, foolhardy, foolish, hare-brained, wild, hasty, imprudent, ill-advised; *informal* crazy, crackpot, crackbrained. ❷ *a madcap comedy* ZANY, eccentric, unconventional.
▸ noun *she was a boisterous madcap* ECCENTRIC, crank, madman/madwoman, maniac, lunatic; oddity, character, individual; *informal* crackpot, oddball, weirdo, loony, nut; *Brit. informal* nutter; *N. Amer. informal* screwball.

madden ▸ verb ❶ *what maddens people most is his vagueness* INFURIATE, exasperate, irritate; incense, anger, enrage, provoke, upset, agitate, vex, irk, make someone's hackles rise, make someone see red; *informal* aggravate, make someone's blood boil, make livid, get up someone's nose, get someone's goat, get someone's back up; *Brit. informal* nark; *N. Amer. informal* tee off, tick off. ❷ *they were maddened with pain* DRIVE MAD, drive insane, derange, unhinge, unbalance; *informal* drive round the bend.

made-up ▸ adjective INVENTED, fabricated, trumped up, concocted, fictitious, fictional, false, untrue, specious, spurious, bogus, apocryphal, imaginary, mythical.

madhouse ▸ noun *informal* ❶ *his father is shut up in a madhouse* MENTAL HOSPITAL, mental institution, psychiatric hospital, asylum; *informal* nuthouse, funny farm, loony bin; *dated* lunatic asylum. ❷ *the place was a total madhouse* BEDLAM, mayhem, chaos, pandemonium, uproar, turmoil, disorder, madness, all hell broken loose; *N. Amer.* three-ring circus.

madly ▶ **adverb** ❶ *she was smiling madly* INSANELY, deliriously, wildly, like a lunatic; *informal* crazily, barmily. ❷ *it was fun, hurtling madly downhill* FAST, furiously, hurriedly, quickly, speedily, hastily, energetically; *informal* like mad, like crazy. ❸ (*informal*) *he loved her madly* INTENSELY, fervently, wildly, unrestrainedly, to distraction. ❹ (*informal*) *his job isn't madly glamorous* VERY, extremely, really, exceedingly, exceptionally, remarkably, extraordinarily, immensely, tremendously, wildly, all that, hugely; *informal* awfully, terribly, terrifically, fantastically.
– OPPOSITES sanely, slowly, slightly.

madman, madwoman ▶ **noun** LUNATIC, maniac, psychotic, psychopath; *informal* loony, nut, nutcase, head case, psycho; *Brit. informal* nutter; *N. Amer. informal* screwball.

madness ▶ **noun** ❶ *today madness is called mental illness* INSANITY, mental illness, dementia, derangement; lunacy, instability; mania, psychosis; *informal* craziness. ❷ *it would be madness to do otherwise* FOLLY, foolishness, idiocy, stupidity, insanity, lunacy, silliness; *informal* craziness. ❸ *it's absolute madness in here* BEDLAM, mayhem, chaos, pandemonium, uproar, turmoil, disorder, all hell broken loose; *N. Amer.* three-ring circus.
– OPPOSITES sanity, common sense, good sense, calm.

maelstrom ▶ **noun** ❶ *a maelstrom in the sea* WHIRLPOOL, vortex, eddy, swirl; *poetic/literary* Charybdis. ❷ *the maelstrom of war* TURBULENCE, tumult, turmoil, disorder, disarray, chaos, confusion, upheaval, pandemonium, bedlam, whirlwind.

maestro ▶ **noun** VIRTUOSO, master, expert, genius, wizard, prodigy; *informal* ace, whizz, pro, hotshot.
– OPPOSITES tyro, beginner.

magazine ▶ **noun** JOURNAL, periodical, supplement, colour supplement; *informal* glossy, mag, 'zine.

magenta ▶ **adjective** REDDISH-PURPLE, purplish-red, crimson, plum, carmine red, fuchsia.

maggot ▶ **noun** GRUB, larva.

magic ▶ **noun** ❶ *do you believe in magic?* SORCERY, witchcraft, wizardry, necromancy, enchantment, the supernatural, occultism, the occult, black magic, the black arts, voodoo, shamanism; charm, hex, spell, jinx; *N. Amer.* mojo. ❷ *he does magic at children's parties* CONJURING TRICKS, sleight of hand, legerdemain, illusion, prestidigitation. ❸ *the magic of the stage* ALLURE, attraction, excitement, fascination, charm, glamour. ❹ *a taste of soccer magic* SKILL, brilliance, ability, accomplishment, adeptness, adroitness, deftness, dexterity, aptitude, expertise, art, finesse, talent.
▶ **adjective** ❶ *a magic spell* SUPERNATURAL, enchanted, occult. ❷ *a magic place* FASCINATING, captivating, charming, glamorous, magical, enchanting, entrancing, spellbinding, magnetic, irresistible, hypnotic. ❸ (*informal*) *we had a magic time* MARVELLOUS, wonderful, excellent, admirable; *informal* terrific, fabulous, fab, brilliant, brill.

magical ▶ **adjective** ❶ *magical incantations* SUPERNATURAL, magic, occult, shamanistic, mystical, paranormal, preternatural, otherworldly. ❷ *the news had a magical effect* EXTRAORDINARY, remarkable, exceptional, outstanding, incredible, phenomenal, unbelievable, amazing, astonishing, astounding, stunning, staggering, marvellous, magnificent, wonderful, sensational, breathtaking, miraculous; *informal* fantastic, fabulous, stupendous, out of this world, terrific, tremendous, brilliant, mind-boggling, mind-blowing, awesome; *poetic/literary* wondrous. ❸ *this magical small land* ENCHANTING, entrancing, spellbinding, bewitching, beguiling, fascinating, captivating, alluring, enthralling, charming, attractive, lovely, delightful, beautiful; *informal* dreamy, heavenly, divine, gorgeous.
– OPPOSITES predictable, boring.

magician ▶ **noun** ❶ SORCERER, sorceress, witch, wizard, warlock, enchanter, enchantress, necromancer, shaman. ❷ CONJUROR, illusionist, prestidigitator.

magisterial ▶ **adjective** ❶ *a magisterial pronouncement* AUTHORITATIVE, masterful, assured, lordly, commanding, assertive. ❷ *his magisterial style of questioning* DOMINEERING, dictatorial, autocratic, imperious, overbearing, peremptory, high-handed, arrogant, supercilious, patronizing; *informal* bossy.
– OPPOSITES untrustworthy, humble, hesitant, tentative.

magnanimity ▶ **noun** GENEROSITY, charity, benevolence, beneficence, big-heartedness, altruism, philanthropy, humanity, chivalry, nobility; clemency, mercy, leniency, forgiveness, indulgence.
– OPPOSITES meanness, selfishness.

magnanimous ▶ **adjective** GENEROUS, charitable, benevolent, beneficent, big-hearted, handsome, princely, altruistic, philanthropic, chivalrous, noble; forgiving, merciful, lenient, indulgent, clement.
– OPPOSITES mean-spirited, selfish.

magnate ▶ **noun** TYCOON, mogul, captain of industry, baron, lord, king; industrialist, proprietor; *informal* big shot, honcho; *derogatory* fat cat.

magnet ▶ **noun** ❶ *you can tell steel by using a magnet* LODESTONE; electromagnet, solenoid. ❷ *a magnet for tourists* ATTRACTION, focus, draw, lure.

magnetic ▶ **adjective** ❶ *a magnetic personality*

ALLURING, attractive, fascinating, captivating, enchanting, enthralling, appealing, charming, prepossessing, engaging, entrancing, seductive, inviting, irresistible, charismatic.

magnetism ▶ **noun** *his sheer magnetism* ALLURE, attraction, fascination, appeal, draw, drawing power, pull, charm, enchantment, seductiveness, magic, spell, charisma.

magnification ▶ **noun** ❶ *optical magnification* ENLARGEMENT, enhancement, increase, augmentation, extension, expansion, amplification, intensification. ❷ *the magnification of marginal details* EXAGGERATION, overstatement, overemphasis, overplaying, dramatization, colouring, embroidery, embellishment, inflation, hyperbole, aggrandizement; *informal* blowing up (out of all proportion), making a big thing out of something.
– OPPOSITES reduction, understatement.

magnificence ▶ **noun** SPLENDOUR, resplendence, grandeur, impressiveness, glory, majesty, nobility, pomp, stateliness, elegance, sumptuousness, opulence, luxury, lavishness, richness, brilliance, dazzle, skill, virtuosity.
– OPPOSITES modesty, tawdriness, weakness.

magnificent ▶ **adjective** ❶ *a magnificent view of the mountains* SPLENDID, spectacular, impressive, striking, glorious, superb, majestic, awesome, awe-inspiring, breathtaking. ❷ *a magnificent apartment overlooking the lake* SUMPTUOUS, resplendent, grand, impressive, imposing, monumental, palatial, stately, opulent, luxurious, lavish, rich, dazzling, beautiful, elegant; *informal* splendiferous, ritzy, posh. ❸ *a magnificent performance* MASTERLY, skilful, virtuoso, brilliant.
– OPPOSITES uninspiring, modest, tawdry, poor, weak.

magnify ▶ **verb** ❶ *the lens magnifies the image* ENLARGE, boost, enhance, maximize, increase, augment, extend, expand, amplify, intensify; *informal* blow up. ❷ *the problem gets magnified* EXAGGERATE, overstate, overemphasize, overplay, dramatize, colour, embroider, embellish, inflate, make a mountain out of (a molehill); *informal* blow up (out of all proportion), make a big thing out of.
– OPPOSITES reduce, minimize, understate.

magnitude ▶ **noun** ❶ *the magnitude of the task* IMMENSITY, vastness, hugeness, enormity; size, extent, expanse, greatness, largeness, bigness. ❷ *events of tragic magnitude* IMPORTANCE, import, significance, weight, consequence, mark, notability, note; *formal* moment. ❸ *a change in magnitude on the Richter scale* VALUE, figure, number, measure, order, quantity, vector, index, indicator. ❹ *a star of magnitude 4.2* BRIGHTNESS, brilliance, radiance, luminosity.
– OPPOSITES smallness, triviality.
■ **of the first magnitude** OF THE UTMOST IMPORTANCE, of the greatest significance, very important, of great consequence; *formal* of great moment.

maid ▶ **noun** ❶ *the maid cleared the table* FEMALE SERVANT, maidservant, housemaid, parlourmaid, lady's maid, chambermaid, maid-of-all-work, domestic; help, cleaner, cleaning woman/lady; *Brit. informal* daily, skivvy, Mrs Mop; *Brit. dated* charwoman, charlady, char, tweeny. ❷ (*poetic/literary*) *a village maid and her swain* GIRL, young woman, young lady, lass, miss; *Scottish* (wee) lassie; *poetic/literary* maiden, damsel, nymph; *archaic* wench. ❸ (*poetic/literary*) *she was no longer a maid* VIRGIN, chaste woman, unmarried girl, celibate; *formal* virgo intacta; *poetic/literary* maiden.

maiden ▶ **noun** (*poetic/literary*). *See* MAID senses 2, 3.
▶ **adjective** ❶ *a maiden aunt* UNMARRIED, spinster, unwed, unwedded, single, husbandless, celibate. ❷ *a maiden voyage* FIRST, initial, inaugural, introductory, initiatory.

maidenly ▶ **adjective** VIRGINAL, immaculate, intact, chaste, pure, virtuous; demure, reserved, retiring, decorous, seemly.
– OPPOSITES fast, slatternly.

mail ▶ **noun** *the mail arrived* POST, letters, correspondence; postal system, postal service, post office; delivery, collection; e-mail; *informal* snail mail; *N. Amer.* the mails.
▶ **verb** *we mailed the parcels* SEND, post, dispatch, direct, forward, redirect, ship; e-mail.

maim ▶ **verb** INJURE, wound, cripple, disable, incapacitate, impair, mar, mutilate, lacerate, disfigure, deform, mangle.

main ▶ **adjective** *the main item* PRINCIPAL, chief, head, leading, foremost, most important, major, ruling, dominant, central, focal, key, prime, master, premier, primary, first, fundamental, supreme, predominant, (most) prominent, pre-eminent, paramount, overriding, cardinal, crucial, critical, pivotal, salient, elemental, essential, staple.
– OPPOSITES subsidiary, minor.
▶ **noun** (*poetic/literary*) *the Spanish Main* SEA, ocean, deep; *informal, dated* the drink; *Brit. informal, dated* the briny.
■ **in the main**. *See* MAINLY.

mainly ▶ **adverb** MOSTLY, for the most part, in the main, on the whole, largely, by and large, to a large extent, predominantly, chiefly, principally, primarily; generally, usually, typically, commonly, on average, as a rule, almost always.

mainspring ▶ **noun** MOTIVE, motivation, impetus, driving force, incentive, impulse, prime mover, reason, fountain, fount, root, generator.

mainstay ▶ **noun** CENTRAL COMPONENT, central figure, centrepiece, prop, linchpin, cornerstone, pillar, bulwark, buttress, chief support, backbone, anchor, foundation, base, staple.

mainstream ▶ **adjective** NORMAL, conventional, ordinary, orthodox, conformist, accepted, established, recognized, common, usual, prevailing, popular.
– OPPOSITES fringe.

maintain ▶ **verb** ❶ *they wanted to maintain peace* PRESERVE, conserve, keep, retain, keep going, keep alive, keep up, prolong, perpetuate, sustain, carry on, continue. ❷ *the council maintains the roads* KEEP IN GOOD CONDITION, keep in (good) repair, keep up, service, care for, take good care of, look after. ❸ *the costs of maintaining a family* SUPPORT, provide for, keep, sustain; nurture, feed, nourish. ❹ *he always maintained his innocence | he maintains that he is innocent* INSIST (ON), declare, assert, protest, affirm, avow, profess, claim, allege, contend, argue, swear (to), hold to; *formal* aver; *rare* asseverate.
– OPPOSITES break, discontinue, neglect, deny.

maintenance ▶ **noun** ❶ *the maintenance of peace* PRESERVATION, conservation, keeping, prolongation, perpetuation, carrying on, continuation, continuance. ❷ *car maintenance* UPKEEP, service, servicing, repair(s), care, aftercare. ❸ *the maintenance of his children* SUPPORT, keeping, upkeep, sustenance; nurture, feeding, nourishment. ❹ *absent fathers are forced to pay maintenance* FINANCIAL SUPPORT, child support, alimony, provision; keep, subsistence, living expenses.
– OPPOSITES breakdown, discontinuation, neglect.

majestic ▶ **adjective** STATELY, dignified, distinguished, solemn, magnificent, grand, splendid, resplendent, glorious, sumptuous, impressive, august, noble, awe-inspiring, monumental, palatial; statuesque, Olympian, imposing, marvellous, sonorous, resounding, heroic.
– OPPOSITES modest, wretched.

majesty ▶ **noun** ❶ *the majesty of the procession* STATELINESS, dignity, distinction, solemnity, magnificence, pomp, grandeur, grandness, splendour, resplendence, glory, impressiveness, augustness, nobility. ❷ *the majesty invested in the monarch* SOVEREIGNTY, authority, power, dominion, supremacy.
– OPPOSITES modesty, wretchedness.

major ▶ **adjective** ❶ *the major English poets* GREATEST, best, finest, most important, chief, main, prime, principal, capital, cardinal, leading, star, foremost, outstanding, first-rate, preeminent, arch-. ❷ *an issue of major importance* CRUCIAL, vital, great, considerable, paramount, utmost, prime. ❸ *a major factor* IMPORTANT, big, significant, weighty, crucial, key, sweeping, substantial. ❹ *major surgery* SERIOUS, radical, complicated, difficult.
– OPPOSITES minor, little, trivial.

majority ▶ **noun** ❶ *the majority of cases* LARGER PART/NUMBER, greater part/number, best/better part, most, more than half; bulk, mass, weight, (main) body, preponderance, predominance, generality, lion's share. ❷ *a majority in the election* (WINNING) MARGIN, superiority of numbers/votes; landslide. ❸ *my son has reached his majority* COMING OF AGE, legal age, adulthood, manhood/womanhood, maturity; age of consent.
– OPPOSITES minority.

make ▶ **verb** ❶ *he makes models* CONSTRUCT, build, assemble, put together, manufacture, produce, fabricate, create, form, fashion, model. ❷ *she made me drink it* FORCE, compel, coerce, press, drive, pressure, pressurize, oblige, require; have someone do something, prevail on, dragoon, bludgeon, strong-arm, impel, constrain; *informal* railroad. ❸ *don't make such a noise* CAUSE, create, give rise to, produce, bring about, generate, engender, occasion, effect, set up, establish, institute, found, develop, originate; *poetic/literary* beget. ❹ *she made a little bow* PERFORM, execute, give, do, accomplish, achieve, bring off, carry out, effect. ❺ *they made him chairman* APPOINT, designate, name, nominate, select, elect, vote in, install; induct, institute, invest, ordain. ❻ *he had made a will* FORMULATE, frame, draw up, devise, make out, prepare, compile, compose, put together; draft, write, pen. ❼ *I've made a mistake* PERPETRATE, commit, be responsible for, be guilty of, be to blame for. ❽ *he's made a lot of money* ACQUIRE, obtain, gain, get, realize, secure, win, earn; gross, net, clear; bring in, take (in). ❾ *he made tea* PREPARE, get ready, put together, concoct, cook, dish up, throw together, whip up, brew; *informal* fix; *Brit. informal* mash. ❿ *we've got to make a decision* REACH, come to, settle on, determine on, conclude. ⓫ *she made a short announcement* UTTER, give, deliver, give voice to, enunciate, recite, pronounce. ⓬ *the sofa makes a good bed* BE, act as, serve as, function as, constitute, do duty for. ⓭ *he'll make the first eleven* GAIN A PLACE IN, get into, gain access to, enter; achieve, attain. ⓮ *he just made his train* CATCH, get, arrive/be in time for, arrive at, reach; get to.
– OPPOSITES destroy, lose, miss.
▶ **noun** ❶ *what make is the car?* BRAND, marque, label. ❷ *a man of a different make from his brother* CHARACTER, nature, temperament, temper, disposition, kidney, mould, stamp.

■ **make as if/though** FEIGN, pretend, make a show/pretence of, affect, feint, make out; *informal* put it on.

■ **make away with** ❶ *she decided to make away with him* KILL, murder, dispatch, eliminate; *informal* bump off, do away with, do in, do for, knock off, top, croak, stiff, blow away; *N. Amer. informal* ice, rub out, smoke, waste; *poetic/literary* slay. ❷ *they made away with the evidence* DISPOSE OF, get rid of, destroy, throw away, jettison, ditch, dump; *informal* do away with.

■ **make believe** PRETEND, fantasize, daydream, build castles in the air, build castles in Spain, dream, imagine, play-act, play.
■ **make do** SCRAPE BY, scrape along, get by/along, manage, cope, survive, muddle through/along, improvise, make ends meet, keep the wolf from the door, keep one's head above water; *informal* make out; (**make do with**) make the best of, get by on, put up with.
■ **make for** ❶ *she made for the door* GO FOR/TOWARDS, head for/towards, aim for, make one's way towards, move towards, direct one's steps towards, steer a course towards, be bound for, make a beeline for. ❷ *constant arguing doesn't make for a happy marriage* CONTRIBUTE TO, be conducive to, produce, promote, facilitate, foster; *formal* conduce to.
■ **make it** ❶ *he never made it as a singer* SUCCEED, be a success, distinguish oneself, get ahead, make good; *informal* make the grade, arrive, crack it. ❷ *she's very ill—is she going to make it?* SURVIVE, come through, pull through, get better, recover.
■ **make love**. *See* HAVE SEX at SEX.
■ **make off** RUN AWAY/OFF, take to one's heels, beat a hasty retreat, flee, make one's getaway, make a quick exit, run for it, make a run for it, take off, take flight, bolt, make oneself scarce, decamp, do a disappearing act; *informal* clear off/out, beat it, leg it, cut and run, skedaddle, vamoose, hightail it, hotfoot it, show a clean pair of heels, fly the coop, split, scoot, scram; *Brit. informal* scarper, do a runner; *N. Amer. informal* take a powder.
■ **make off with** TAKE, steal, purloin, pilfer, abscond with, run away/off with, carry off, snatch; kidnap, abduct; *informal* walk away/off with, swipe, filch, snaffle, nab, lift, 'liberate', 'borrow', snitch; *Brit. informal* pinch, half-inch, nick, whip, knock off; *N. Amer. informal* heist, glom.
■ **make out** (*informal*) *how did you make out?* GET ON/ALONG, fare, do, proceed, go, progress, manage, survive, cope, get by.
■ **make something out** ❶ *I could just make out a figure in the distance* SEE, discern, distinguish, perceive, pick out, detect, observe, recognize; *poetic/literary* descry, espy. ❷ *he couldn't make out what she was saying* UNDERSTAND, comprehend, follow, grasp, fathom, work out, make sense of, interpret, decipher, make head or tail of, get, get the drift of, catch. ❸ *she made out that he was violent* ALLEGE, claim, assert, declare, maintain, affirm, suggest, imply, hint, insinuate, indicate, intimate, impute; *formal* aver. ❹ *he made out a receipt for $20* WRITE OUT, fill out, fill in, complete, draw up.
■ **make something over to someone** TRANSFER, sign over, turn over, hand over/on/down, give, leave, bequeath, bestow, pass on, assign, consign, entrust; *Law* devolve, convey.
■ **make up** *let's kiss and make up* BE FRIENDS AGAIN, bury the hatchet, declare a truce, make peace, forgive and forget, shake hands, become reconciled, settle one's differences, mend fences, call it quits.
■ **make something up** ❶ *exports make up 42% of earnings* COMPRISE, form, compose, constitute, account for. ❷ *Gina brought a friend to make up a foursome* COMPLETE, round off, finish. ❸ *the pharmacist made up the prescription* PREPARE, mix, concoct, put together. ❹ *he made up an excuse* INVENT, fabricate, concoct, dream up, think up, hatch, trump up; devise, manufacture, formulate, coin; *informal* cook up. ❺ *she made up her face* APPLY MAKE-UP/COSMETICS TO, powder, rouge; (**make oneself up**) *informal* put on one's face, do/paint one's face, apply one's warpaint, doll oneself up.
■ **make up for** ❶ *she tried to make up for what she'd said* ATONE FOR, make amends for, compensate for, make recompense for, make reparation for, make redress for, make restitution for, expiate. ❷ *job satisfaction can make up for low pay* OFFSET, counterbalance, counteract, compensate for; balance, neutralize, cancel out, even up, redeem.
■ **make up one's mind** DECIDE, come to a decision, make/reach a decision; settle on a plan of action, come to a conclusion, reach a conclusion; determine, resolve.
■ **make up to** (*informal*) CURRY FAVOUR WITH, cultivate, try to win over, court, ingratiate oneself with; *informal* suck up to, butter up; *N. Amer. informal* shine up to; *archaic* blandish.
■ **make way** MOVE ASIDE, clear the way, make a space, make room, stand back.

make-believe ▶ **noun** *that was sheer make-believe* FANTASY, pretence, daydreaming, imagination, invention, fancy, dream, fabrication, play-acting, charade, masquerade.
– OPPOSITES reality.
▶ **adjective** *make-believe adventures* IMAGINARY, imagined, made-up, fantasy, dreamed-up, fanciful, fictitious, fictive, feigned, fake, mock, sham, simulated; *informal* pretend, phoney.
– OPPOSITES real, actual.

maker ▶ **noun** CREATOR, manufacturer, constructor, builder, producer, fabricator.

makeshift ▶ **adjective** TEMPORARY, provisional, stopgap, standby, rough and ready, improvised, ad hoc, extempore, thrown together, cobbled together.
– OPPOSITES permanent.

make-up ▶ **noun** ❶ *she used excessive make-up* COSMETICS, maquillage; greasepaint, face paint; *informal* warpaint, slap. ❷ *the cellular make-up of plants* COMPOSITION, constitution, structure, configuration, arrangement, organization, formation. ❸ *jealousy isn't part of his make-up* CHARACTER, nature, temperament, personality, disposition, mentality, persona, psyche; *informal* what makes someone tick.

making ▶ **noun** ❶ *the making of cars* MANUFACTURE, mass-production, building, construction,

assembly, production, creation, putting together, fabrication, forming, moulding, forging. ❷ *she has the makings of a champion* QUALITIES, characteristics, ingredients; potential, promise, capacity, capability; essentials, essence, beginnings, rudiments, basics, stuff.
– OPPOSITES destruction.
■ **in the making** *a hero in the making* BUDDING, up and coming, emergent, developing, nascent, potential, promising, incipient.

maladjusted ▶ adjective DISTURBED, unstable, neurotic, unbalanced, unhinged, dysfunctional; *informal* mixed up, screwed up, hung up, messed up.
– OPPOSITES normal, stable.

maladministration ▶ noun (*formal*) MISMANAGEMENT, mishandling, misgovernment, misrule, incompetence, inefficiency, bungling; malpractice, misconduct; *Law* malfeasance; *formal* malversation.
– OPPOSITES probity, efficiency.

maladroit ▶ adjective BUNGLING, awkward, inept, clumsy, bumbling, incompetent, unskilful, heavy-handed, gauche, tactless, inconsiderate, undiplomatic, impolitic; *informal* hamfisted, cack-handed.
– OPPOSITES adroit, skilful.

malady ▶ noun ILLNESS, sickness, disease, infection, ailment, disorder, complaint, indisposition, affliction, infirmity; *informal* bug, virus; *Brit. informal* lurgy; *Austral. informal* wog.

malaise ▶ noun UNHAPPINESS, uneasiness, unease, discomfort, melancholy, depression, despondency, dejection, angst, Weltschmerz, ennui; lassitude, listlessness, languor, weariness; indisposition, ailment, infirmity, illness, sickness, disease.
– OPPOSITES comfort, well-being.

malapropism ▶ noun WRONG WORD, solecism, misuse, misapplication, infelicity, slip of the tongue.

malapropos ▶ adjective (*formal*) INAPPROPRIATE, unsuitable, inapposite, infelicitous, inapt, unseemly, inopportune, ill-timed, untimely.

malcontent ▶ noun *a group of malcontents* TROUBLEMAKER, mischief-maker, agitator, dissident, rebel; discontent, complainer, grumbler, moaner; *informal* stirrer, whinger, grouch, bellyacher; *N. Amer. informal* kvetch.
▶ adjective *a malcontent employee* DISAFFECTED, discontented, dissatisfied, disgruntled, fed up, unhappy, annoyed, irritated, displeased, resentful; rebellious, dissentient, troublemaking, grumbling, complaining; *informal* browned off, hacked off, peeved, bellyaching; *Brit. informal* cheesed off, brassed off; *N. Amer. informal* teed off, ticked off.
– OPPOSITES happy.

male ▶ adjective *male sexual jealousy* MASCULINE, virile, manly, macho, red-blooded.
– OPPOSITES female.
▶ noun *two males walked past. See* MAN noun sense 1.
– RELATED TERMS andro-.

malediction ▶ noun CURSE, damnation, oath; spell; *N. Amer.* hex; *formal* imprecation; *poetic/literary* anathema; *archaic* execration.
– OPPOSITES blessing.

malefactor ▶ noun WRONGDOER, miscreant, offender, criminal, culprit, villain, lawbreaker, felon, evil-doer, delinquent, sinner, transgressor; *informal* crook, baddy; *Austral. informal* crim; *Law* malfeasant; *archaic* trespasser.

malevolence ▶ noun MALICE, hostility, hate, hatred, ill will, enmity, ill feeling, balefulness, venom, rancour, malignity, vindictiveness, viciousness, vengefulness; *poetic/literary* maleficence.
– OPPOSITES benevolence.

malevolent ▶ adjective MALICIOUS, hostile, evil-minded, baleful, evil-intentioned, venomous, evil, malign, malignant, rancorous, vicious, vindictive, vengeful; *poetic/literary* malefic, maleficent.
– OPPOSITES benevolent.

malformation ▶ noun DEFORMITY, distortion, crookedness, misshapenness, disfigurement, abnormality, warp.

malformed ▶ adjective DEFORMED, misshapen, misproportioned, ill-proportioned, disfigured, distorted, crooked, contorted, twisted, wry, warped; abnormal, grotesque, monstrous; *Scottish* thrawn.
– OPPOSITES perfect, normal, healthy.

malfunction ▶ verb *the computer has malfunctioned* CRASH, go wrong, break down, fail, stop working; *informal* conk out, go kaput, fall over, act up; *Brit. informal* play up, pack up.
▶ noun *a computer malfunction* CRASH, breakdown, fault, failure, bug; *informal* glitch.

malice ▶ noun SPITE, malevolence, ill will, vindictiveness, vengefulness, revenge, malignity, evil intentions, animus, enmity, rancour; *informal* bitchiness, cattiness; *poetic/literary* maleficence.
– OPPOSITES benevolence.

malicious ▶ adjective SPITEFUL, malevolent, evil-intentioned, vindictive, vengeful, malign, mean, nasty, hurtful, mischievous, wounding, cruel, unkind; *informal* bitchy, catty; *poetic/literary* malefic, maleficent.
– OPPOSITES benevolent.

malign ▶ adjective *a malign influence* HARMFUL, evil, bad, baleful, hostile, inimical, destructive, malignant, injurious; *poetic/literary* malefic, maleficent.
– OPPOSITES beneficial.
▶ verb *he maligned an innocent man* DEFAME, slander, libel, blacken someone's name/character, smear, vilify, speak ill of, cast aspersions on, run down, traduce, denigrate, disparage, slur, abuse, revile; *informal* bad-mouth, knock; *Brit.*

informal rubbish, slag off; *formal* derogate, calumniate; *rare* asperse.
– OPPOSITES praise.

malignant ▸ noun ❶ *a malignant disease* VIRULENT, very infectious, invasive, uncontrollable, dangerous, deadly, fatal, life-threatening. ❷ *a malignant growth* CANCEROUS; *technical* metastatic. ❸ *a malignant thought* SPITEFUL, malicious, malevolent, evil-intentioned, vindictive, vengeful, malign, mean, nasty, hurtful, mischievous, wounding, cruel, unkind; *informal* bitchy, catty; *poetic/literary* malefic, maleficent.
– OPPOSITES benign, benevolent.

malinger ▸ verb PRETEND TO BE ILL, feign/fake illness, sham; shirk; *informal* put it on; *Brit. informal* skive, swing the lead; *N. Amer. informal* goldbrick.

malingerer ▸ noun SHIRKER, idler, layabout; *informal* slacker; *Brit. informal* skiver, lead-swinger; *N. Amer. informal* gold brick.

mall ▸ noun SHOPPING PRECINCT, shopping centre, shopping complex, arcade, galleria; *N. Amer.* plaza.

malleable ▸ adjective ❶ *a malleable substance* PLIABLE, ductile, plastic, pliant, soft, workable. ❷ *a malleable young woman* EASILY INFLUENCED, suggestible, susceptible, impressionable, pliable, amenable, compliant, tractable; biddable, complaisant, manipulable, persuadable, like putty in someone's hands.
– OPPOSITES hard, intractable.

malnutrition ▸ noun UNDERNOURISHMENT, malnourishment, poor diet, inadequate diet, unhealthy diet, lack of food.

malodorous ▸ adjective FOUL-SMELLING, evil-smelling, fetid, smelly, stinking (to high heaven), reeking, rank, high, putrid, noxious; *informal* stinky; *Brit. informal* niffy, pongy, whiffy, humming; *N. Amer. informal* funky; *poetic/literary* noisome, mephitic.
– OPPOSITES fragrant.

malpractice ▸ noun WRONGDOING, professional misconduct, breach of ethics, unprofessionalism, unethical behaviour; negligence, carelessness, incompetence.

maltreat ▸ verb ILL-TREAT, mistreat, abuse, ill-use, misuse, mishandle; knock about/around, hit, beat, strike, manhandle, harm, hurt, persecute, molest; *informal* beat up, rough up, do over.

maltreatment ▸ noun ILL-TREATMENT, mistreatment, abuse, ill use, ill usage, misuse, mishandling; violence, harm, persecution, molestation.

mammoth ▸ adjective HUGE, enormous, gigantic, giant, colossal, massive, vast, immense, mighty, stupendous, monumental, Herculean, epic, prodigious, mountainous, monstrous, titanic, towering, elephantine, king-size(d), gargantuan, Brobdingnagian; *informal* mega, monster, whopping, humongous, bumper, jumbo, astronomical; *Brit. informal* whacking, whacking great, ginormous.
– OPPOSITES tiny.

man ▸ noun ❶ *a handsome man* MALE, adult male, gentleman; youth; *informal* guy, fellow, geezer, gent; *Brit. informal* bloke, chap, lad, cove; *Scottish & Irish informal* bodach; *N. Amer. informal* dude, hombre; *Austral./NZ informal* digger. ❷ *all men are mortal* HUMAN BEING, human, person, mortal, individual, personage, soul. ❸ *the evolution of man* THE HUMAN RACE, the human species, Homo sapiens, humankind, humanity, human beings, humans, people, mankind. ❹ *the men voted to go on strike* WORKER, workman, labourer, hand, blue-collar worker. *See also* STAFF noun sense 1. ❺ *have you met her new man?* BOYFRIEND, partner, husband, spouse, lover, admirer, fiancé; common-law husband, live-in lover, significant other, cohabitee; *informal* fancy man, toy boy, sugar daddy, intended; *N. Amer. informal* squeeze; *dated* beau, steady, young man; *archaic* leman. ❻ *his man brought him a cocktail* MANSERVANT, valet, gentleman's gentleman, Jeeves, attendant, retainer; page, footman, flunkey; *Military, dated* batman; *N. Amer.* houseman.
– RELATED TERMS male, masculine, virile.
▸ verb ❶ *the office is manned from 9 a.m. to 5 p.m.* STAFF, crew, occupy, people. ❷ *firemen manned the pumps* OPERATE, work, use, utilize.
■ **man to man** FRANKLY, openly, honestly, directly, candidly, plainly, forthrightly, without beating about the bush; woman to woman.
■ **to a man** WITHOUT EXCEPTION, with no exceptions, bar none, one and all, everyone, each and every one, unanimously, as one.

manacle ▸ verb SHACKLE, fetter, chain, put/clap in irons, handcuff, restrain; secure; *informal* cuff.

manacles ▸ plural noun HANDCUFFS, shackles, chains, irons, fetters, restraints, bonds; *informal* cuffs, bracelets; *Brit. archaic* darbies.

manage ▸ verb ❶ *she manages a staff of 80 people* BE IN CHARGE OF, run, be head of, head, direct, control, preside over, lead, govern, rule, command, superintend, supervise, oversee, administer, organize, conduct, handle, guide, be at the helm of; *informal* head up. ❷ *how much work can you manage this week?* ACCOMPLISH, achieve, do, carry out, perform, undertake, bring about/off, effect, finish; succeed in, contrive, engineer. ❸ *will you be able to manage without him?* COPE, get along/on, make do, be/fare/do all right, carry on, survive, get by, muddle through/along, fend for oneself, shift for oneself, make ends meet, weather the storm; *informal* make out, hack it. ❹ *she can't manage that horse* CONTROL, handle, master; cope with, deal with.

manageable ▸ adjective ❶ *a manageable amount of work* ACHIEVABLE, doable, practicable,

possible, feasible, reasonable, attainable, viable. ❷ *a manageable child* COMPLIANT, tractable, pliant, pliable, malleable, biddable, docile, amenable, governable, controllable, accommodating, acquiescent, complaisant, yielding. ❸ *a manageable tool* USER-FRIENDLY, easy to use, handy.
– OPPOSITES difficult, impossible.

management ▶ noun ❶ *he's responsible for the management of the firm* ADMINISTRATION, running, managing, organization; charge, care, direction, leadership, control, governing, governance, ruling, command, superintendence, supervision, overseeing, conduct, handling, guidance, operation. ❷ *workers are in dispute with the management* MANAGERS, employers, directors, board of directors, board, directorate, executives, administrators, administration; owners, proprietors; *informal* bosses, top brass.

manager ▶ noun ❶ *the works manager* EXECUTIVE, head of department, line manager, supervisor, principal, administrator, head, director, managing director, employer, superintendent, foreman, forewoman, overseer; proprietor; *informal* boss, chief, head honcho, governor; *Brit. informal* gaffer, guv'nor. ❷ *the band's manager* ORGANIZER, controller, comptroller; impresario.

mandate ▶ noun ❶ *he called an election to seek a mandate for his policies* AUTHORITY, approval, acceptance, ratification, endorsement, sanction, authorization. ❷ *a mandate from the UN* INSTRUCTION, directive, decree, command, order, injunction, edict, charge, commission, bidding, ruling, fiat; *formal* ordinance.

mandatory ▶ adjective OBLIGATORY, compulsory, binding, required, requisite, necessary, essential, imperative.
– OPPOSITES optional.

manful ▶ adjective BRAVE, courageous, bold, plucky, gallant, manly, heroic, intrepid, fearless, stout-hearted, valiant, valorous, dauntless, doughty; resolute, with gritted teeth, determined; *informal* gutsy, spunky.
– OPPOSITES cowardly.

manfully ▶ adverb BRAVELY, courageously, boldly, gallantly, pluckily, heroically, intrepidly, fearlessly, valiantly, dauntlessly; resolutely, determinedly, hard, strongly, vigorously, with might and main, like a Trojan; with all one's strength, to the best of one's abilities, as best one can, desperately.

mange ▶ noun SCABIES, scab, rash, eruption, skin infection.

manger ▶ noun TROUGH, feeding trough, fodder rack, feeder, crib.

mangle ▶ verb ❶ *the bodies were mangled beyond recognition* MUTILATE, maim, disfigure, damage, injure, crush; hack, cut up, lacerate, tear apart, butcher, maul. ❷ *he's mangling the English language* SPOIL, ruin, mar, mutilate, make a mess of, wreck; *informal* murder, make a hash of, butcher.

mangy ▶ adjective ❶ *a mangy cat* SCABBY, scaly, scabious, diseased. ❷ *a mangy old armchair* SCRUFFY, moth-eaten, shabby, worn; dirty, squalid, sleazy, seedy; *informal* tatty, the worse for wear, scuzzy; *Brit. informal* grotty.

manhandle ▶ verb ❶ *he was manhandled by a gang of youths* PUSH, shove, jostle, hustle; maltreat, ill-treat, mistreat, maul, molest; *informal* paw, rough up; *N. Amer. informal* roust. ❷ *we manhandled the piano down the stairs* HEAVE, haul, push, shove; pull, tug, drag, lug, carry, lift, manoeuvre; *informal* hump.

manhood ▶ noun ❶ *the transition from boyhood to manhood* MATURITY, sexual maturity, adulthood. ❷ *an insult to his manhood* VIRILITY, manliness, machismo, masculinity, maleness; mettle, spirit, strength, fortitude, determination, bravery, courage, intrepidity, valour, heroism, boldness.

mania ▶ noun ❶ *fits of mania* MADNESS, derangement, dementia, insanity, lunacy, psychosis, mental illness; delirium, frenzy, hysteria, raving, wildness. ❷ *his mania for gadgets* OBSESSION, compulsion, fixation, fetish, fascination, preoccupation, passion, enthusiasm, desire, urge, craving; craze, fad, rage; *informal* thing, yen.

maniac ▶ noun ❶ *a homicidal maniac* LUNATIC, madman, madwoman, psychopath; *informal* loony, fruitcake, nutcase, nut, psycho, head case, headbanger, sicko; *Brit. informal* nutter; *N. Amer. informal* screwball, crazy, meshuggener. ❷ (*informal*) *a football maniac* ENTHUSIAST, fan, devotee, aficionado; *informal* freak, fiend, fanatic, nut, buff, addict.

manic ▶ adjective ❶ *a manic grin* MAD, insane, deranged, demented, maniacal, lunatic, wild, crazed, demonic, hysterical, raving, unhinged, unbalanced; *informal* crazy. ❷ *manic activity* FRENZIED, feverish, frenetic, hectic, intense; *informal* hyper, mad.
– OPPOSITES sane, calm.

manifest ▶ verb ❶ *she manifested signs of depression* DISPLAY, show, exhibit, demonstrate, betray, present, reveal; *formal* evince. ❷ *strikes manifest bad industrial relations* BE EVIDENCE OF, be a sign of, indicate, show, attest, reflect, bespeak, prove, establish, evidence, substantiate, corroborate, confirm; *poetic/literary* betoken.
– OPPOSITES hide, mask.

▶ adjective *his manifest lack of interest* OBVIOUS, clear, plain, apparent, evident, patent, palpable, distinct, definite, blatant, overt, glaring, barefaced, explicit, transparent, conspicuous, undisguised, unmistakable, noticeable, perceptible, visible, recognizable.
– OPPOSITES secret.

manifestation ▶ noun ❶ *the manifestation of anxiety* DISPLAY, demonstration, show, exhibition, presentation. ❷ *manifestations of global warming* SIGN, indication, evidence, token, symptom, testimony, proof, substantiation, mark, reflection, example, instance. ❸ *a supernatural manifestation* APPARITION, appearance, materialization, visitation.

manifesto ▶ **noun** POLICY STATEMENT, mission statement, platform, programme, declaration, proclamation, pronouncement, announcement.

manifold ▶ **adjective** MANY, numerous, multiple, multifarious, legion, diverse, various, several, varied, different, miscellaneous, assorted, sundry; *poetic/literary* myriad, divers.

manikin ▶ **noun** MIDGET, dwarf, homunculus, pygmy, Tom Thumb.

manipulate ▶ **verb** ❶ *he manipulated some knobs and levers* OPERATE, work; turn, pull. ❷ *she manipulated the muscles of his back* MASSAGE, rub, knead, feel, palpate. ❸ *the government tried to manipulate the situation* CONTROL, influence, use/turn to one's advantage, exploit, manoeuvre, engineer, steer, direct; twist someone round one's little finger. ❹ *they accused him of manipulating the data* FALSIFY, rig, distort, alter, change, doctor, massage, juggle, tamper with, tinker with, interfere with, misrepresent; *informal* cook, fiddle.

manipulative ▶ **adjective** SCHEMING, calculating, cunning, crafty, wily, shrewd, devious, designing, conniving, Machiavellian, artful, guileful, slippery, slick, sly, unscrupulous, disingenuous; *informal* foxy.

manipulator ▶ **noun** EXPLOITER, user, manoeuvrer, conniver, puppet master, wheeler-dealer; *informal* operator, thimblerigger.

mankind ▶ **noun** THE HUMAN RACE, man, humanity, human beings, humans, Homo sapiens, humankind, people, men and women.

manly ▶ **adjective** ❶ *his manly physique* VIRILE, masculine, strong, all-male, muscular, muscly, strapping, well built, sturdy, robust, rugged, tough, powerful, brawny, red-blooded, vigorous; *informal* hunky. ❷ *their manly deeds* BRAVE, courageous, bold, valiant, valorous, fearless, plucky, macho, manful, intrepid, daring, lionhearted, heroic, gallant, chivalrous, swashbuckling, adventurous, stout-hearted, dauntless, doughty, resolute, determined, stalwart; *informal* gutsy, spunky.
–OPPOSITES effeminate, cowardly.

man-made ▶ **adjective** ARTIFICIAL, synthetic, manufactured; imitation, ersatz, simulated, mock, fake, plastic.
–OPPOSITES natural, real.

mannequin ▶ **noun** ❶ *mannequins in a shop window* DUMMY, model, figure. ❷ *mannequins on the catwalk* MODEL, fashion model, supermodel; *informal* clothes horse.

manner ▶ **noun** ❶ *it was dealt with in a very efficient manner* WAY, fashion, mode, means, method, system, style, approach, technique, procedure, process, methodology, modus operandi, form. ❷ (*archaic*) *what manner of person is he?* KIND, sort, type, variety, nature, breed, brand, stamp, class, category, genre, order. ❸ *her rather unfriendly manner* DEMEANOUR, air, aspect, attitude, bearing, cast, behaviour, conduct; mien; *formal* comportment. ❹ *the life and manners of Victorian society* CUSTOMS, habits, ways, practices, conventions, usages. ❺ *it's bad manners to stare* BEHAVIOUR, conduct, way of behaving; form. ❻ *you ought to teach him some manners* CORRECT BEHAVIOUR, etiquette, social graces, good form, protocol, politeness, decorum, propriety, gentility, civility, Ps and Qs, breeding; *informal* the done thing; *archaic* convenances.

mannered ▶ **adjective** AFFECTED, pretentious, unnatural, artificial, contrived, stilted, stiff, forced, put-on, theatrical, precious, stagy, camp; *informal* pseudo.
–OPPOSITES natural.

mannerism ▶ **noun** IDIOSYNCRASY, quirk, oddity, foible, trait, peculiarity, habit, characteristic.

mannerly ▶ **adjective**. *See* POLITE sense 1.

mannish ▶ **adjective** UNFEMININE, unwomanly, masculine, unladylike, Amazonian; *informal* butch.
–OPPOSITES feminine, girlish.

manoeuvre ▶ **verb** ❶ *I manoeuvred the car into the space* STEER, guide, drive, negotiate, navigate, pilot, direct, manipulate, move, work, jockey. ❷ *he manoeuvred things to suit himself* MANIPULATE, contrive, manage, engineer, devise, plan, fix, organize, arrange, set up, orchestrate, choreograph, stage-manage; *informal* wangle. ❸ *he began manoeuvring for the party leadership* INTRIGUE, plot, scheme, plan, lay plans, conspire, pull strings.
▶ **noun** ❶ *a tricky parking manoeuvre* OPERATION, exercise, activity, move, movement, action. ❷ *diplomatic manoeuvres* STRATAGEM, tactic, gambit, ploy, trick, dodge, ruse, plan, scheme, operation, device, plot, machination, artifice, subterfuge, intrigue. ❸ *military manoeuvres* TRAINING EXERCISES, exercises, war games, operations.

manse ▶ **noun** MINISTER'S HOUSE, vicarage, parsonage, rectory, deanery.

manservant ▶ **noun** VALET, attendant, retainer, equerry, gentleman's gentleman, man, Jeeves; steward, butler, footman, flunkey, page, houseboy, lackey; *N. Amer.* houseman; *Military, dated* batman.

mansion ▶ **noun** STATELY HOME, hall, seat, manor, manor house, country house; *informal* palace, pile; *formal* residence.
–OPPOSITES hovel.

mantle ▶ **noun** ❶ *a dark green velvet mantle*

CLOAK, cape, shawl, wrap, stole; *historical* pelisse. ❷ *a thick mantle of snow* COVERING, layer, blanket, sheet, veil, curtain, canopy, cover, cloak, pall, shroud. ❸ *the mantle of leadership* ROLE, burden, onus, duty, responsibility.

▶ **verb** *heavy mists mantled the forest* COVER, envelop, veil, cloak, curtain, shroud, swathe, wrap, blanket, conceal, hide, disguise, mask, obscure, surround, clothe; *poetic/literary* enshroud.

manual ▶ **adjective** ❶ *manual work* DONE WITH ONE'S HANDS, labouring, physical, blue-collar. ❷ *a manual typewriter* HAND-OPERATED, hand, non-automatic.

▶ **noun** *a training manual* HANDBOOK, instruction book, instructions, guide, companion, ABC, guidebook; *informal* bible.

manufacture ▶ **verb** ❶ *the company manufactures laser printers* MAKE, produce, mass-produce, build, construct, assemble, put together, create, fabricate, prefabricate, turn out, process, engineer. ❷ *a story manufactured by the press* MAKE UP, invent, fabricate, concoct, hatch, dream up, think up, trump up, devise, formulate, frame, contrive; *informal* cook up.

▶ **noun** *the manufacture of aircraft engines* PRODUCTION, making, manufacturing, mass-production, construction, building, assembly, creation, fabrication, prefabrication, processing.

manufacturer ▶ **noun** MAKER, producer, builder, constructor, creator; factory owner, industrialist, captain/baron of industry.

manure ▶ **noun** DUNG, muck, excrement, droppings, ordure, guano, cowpats; fertilizer; *N. Amer. informal* cow chips, horse apples.

manuscript ▶ **noun** DOCUMENT, text, script, paper, typescript; codex, palimpsest, scroll; autograph, holograph.

many ▶ **determiner & adjective** ❶ *many animals were killed* NUMEROUS, a great/good deal of, a lot of, plenty of, countless, innumerable, scores of, crowds of, droves of, an army of, a horde of, a multitude of, a multiplicity of, multitudinous, multiple, untold; several, various, sundry, diverse, assorted, multifarious; copious, abundant, profuse, an abundance of, a profusion of; frequent; *informal* lots of, umpteen, loads of, masses of, stacks of, scads of, heaps of, piles of, bags of, tons of, oodles of, dozens of, hundreds of, thousands of, millions of, billions, of, zillions of, a slew of, more —— than one can shake a stick at; *Brit. informal* a shedload of; *N. Amer. informal* gazillions of; *Austral./NZ informal* a swag of; *poetic/literary* myriad, divers. ❷ *sacrificing the individual for the sake of the many* THE PEOPLE, the common people, the masses, the multitude, the populace, the public, the rank and file; *derogatory* the hoi polloi, the common herd, the mob, the proletariat, the riff-raff, the great unwashed, the proles.

– RELATED TERMS multi-, poly-.

– OPPOSITES few.

map ▶ **noun** PLAN, chart, cartogram; road map, A to Z, street plan, guide; atlas, globe; sketch map, relief map, contour map; Mercator projection, Peters projection; *N. Amer.* plat, plot.

– RELATED TERMS cartography.

▶ **verb** *the region was mapped from the air* CHART, plot, delineate, draw, depict, portray.

■ **map something out** OUTLINE, set out, lay out, sketch out, trace out, rough out, block out, delineate, detail, draw up, formulate, work out, frame, draft, plan, plot out, arrange, design, programme.

mar ▶ **verb** ❶ *an ugly scar marred his features* SPOIL, impair, disfigure, detract from, blemish, scar; mutilate, deface, deform. ❷ *the celebrations were marred by violence* SPOIL, ruin, impair, damage, wreck; harm, hurt, blight, taint, tarnish, sully, stain, pollute; *informal* foul up; *formal* vitiate.

– OPPOSITES enhance.

marauder ▶ **noun** RAIDER, plunderer, pillager, looter, robber, pirate, freebooter, bandit, highwayman, rustler; *poetic/literary* brigand; *archaic* buccaneer, corsair, reaver, cateran, moss-trooper.

marauding ▶ **adjective** PREDATORY, rapacious, thieving, plundering, pillaging, looting, freebooting, piratical.

march ▶ **verb** ❶ *the men marched past* STRIDE, walk, troop, step, pace, tread; footslog, slog, tramp, hike, trudge; parade, file, process; *Brit. informal* yomp. ❷ *she marched in without even knocking* STALK, stride, strut, flounce, storm, stomp, sweep. ❸ *time marches on* ADVANCE, progress, move on, roll on.

▶ **noun** ❶ *a 20-mile march* HIKE, trek, tramp, slog, footslog, walk; route march, forced march; *Brit. informal* yomp. ❷ *police sought to ban the march* PARADE, procession, march past, cortège; demonstration; *informal* demo. ❸ *the march of technology* PROGRESS, advance, progression, development, evolution; passage.

marches ▶ **plural noun** *the Welsh marches* BORDERS, boundaries, borderlands, frontiers; *historical* marcher lands.

margin ▶ **noun** ❶ *the margin of the lake* EDGE, side, verge, border, perimeter, brink, brim, rim, fringe, boundary, limits, periphery, bound, extremity; *poetic/literary* marge, bourn, skirt. ❷ *there's no margin for error* LEEWAY, latitude, scope, room, room for manoeuvre, space, allowance, extra, surplus. ❸ *they won by a narrow margin* GAP, majority, amount, difference.

marginal ▶ **adjective** ❶ *the difference is marginal* SLIGHT, small, tiny, minute, insignificant, minimal, negligible. ❷ *a very marginal case* BORDERLINE, disputable, questionable, doubtful.

marijuana ▶ **noun** CANNABIS, hashish, bhang, hemp, kif, ganja, sinsemilla, skunkweed; *informal* dope, hash, grass, pot, blow, draw, the weed, skunk; *Brit. informal* wacky baccy; *N. Amer. informal* locoweed.

marinate ▶ verb SOUSE, soak, steep, immerse, marinade.

marine ▶ adjective ❶ *marine plants* SEAWATER, sea, saltwater, oceanic; aquatic; *technical* pelagic, thalassic. ❷ *a marine insurance company* MARITIME, nautical, naval; seafaring, seagoing, ocean-going.

mariner ▶ noun SAILOR, seaman, seafarer; *informal* Jack tar, tar, sea dog, salt, bluejacket, matelot; *N. Amer. informal* shellback.

marital ▶ adjective MATRIMONIAL, married, wedded, conjugal, nuptial, marriage, wedding; *Law* spousal; *poetic/literary* connubial, epithalamic.

maritime ▶ adjective ❶ *maritime law* NAVAL, marine, nautical; seafaring, seagoing, sea, ocean-going. ❷ *maritime regions* COASTAL, seaside, littoral.

mark ▶ noun ❶ *a dirty mark* BLEMISH, streak, spot, fleck, dot, blot, stain, smear, speck, speckle, blotch, smudge, smut, fingermark, fingerprint; bruise, discoloration; birthmark; *informal* splotch, splodge; *technical* stigma; *poetic/literary* smirch. ❷ *a punctuation mark* SYMBOL, sign, character; diacritic. ❸ *books bearing the mark of a well-known bookseller* LOGO, seal, stamp, imprint, symbol, emblem, device, insignia, badge, brand, trademark, monogram, hallmark, logotype, watermark. ❹ *unemployment passed the three million mark* POINT, level, stage, degree. ❺ *a mark of respect* SIGN, token, symbol, indication, badge, emblem; symptom, evidence, proof. ❻ *the war left its mark on him* IMPRESSION, imprint, traces; effect, impact, influence. ❼ *the mark of a civilized society* CHARACTERISTIC, feature, trait, attribute, quality, hallmark, badge, stamp, property, indicator. ❽ *he got good marks for maths* GRADE, grading, rating, score, percentage. ❾ *the bullet missed its mark* TARGET, goal, aim, bullseye; objective, object, end.

▶ verb ❶ *be careful not to mark the paintwork* DISCOLOUR, stain, smear, smudge, streak, blotch, blemish; dirty, pockmark, bruise; *informal* splotch, splodge; *poetic/literary* smirch. ❷ *her possessions were clearly marked* PUT ONE'S NAME ON, name, initial, label; hallmark, watermark, brand. ❸ *I've marked the relevant passages* INDICATE, label, flag, tick; show, identify, designate, delineate, denote. ❹ *a festival to mark the town's 200th anniversary* CELEBRATE, observe, recognize, acknowledge, keep, honour, solemnize, pay tribute to, salute, commemorate, remember, memorialize. ❺ *the incidents marked a new phase in their campaign* REPRESENT, signify, be a sign of, indicate, herald. ❻ *his style is marked by simplicity and concision* CHARACTERIZE, distinguish, identify, typify, brand, signalize, stamp. ❼ *I have a pile of essays to mark* ASSESS, evaluate, appraise, correct; *N. Amer.* grade. ❽ *it'll cause trouble, you mark my words!* TAKE HEED OF, pay heed to, heed, listen to, take note of, pay attention to, attend to, note, mind, bear in mind, take into consideration.

■ **make one's mark** BE SUCCESSFUL, distinguish oneself, succeed, be a success, prosper, get ahead/on, make good; *informal* make it, make the grade, find a place in the sun.

■ **mark something down** REDUCE, decrease, lower, cut, put down, discount; *informal* slash.

■ **mark someone out** ❶ *his honesty marked him out from the rest* SET APART, separate, single out, differentiate, distinguish. ❷ *she is marked out for fame* DESTINE, ordain, predestine, preordain.

■ **mark something up** INCREASE, raise, up, put up, hike (up), escalate; *informal* jack up.

■ **of mark** (*dated*) IMPORTANT, distinguished, eminent, pre-eminent, prominent, notable, famous, great, prestigious; of importance, of consequence, of note, of high standing, of distinction.

■ **quick off the mark** ALERT, quick, quick-witted, bright, clever, perceptive, sharp, sharp-witted, observant, wide awake, on one's toes; *informal* on the ball, quick on the uptake.

■ **wide of the mark** INACCURATE, incorrect, wrong, erroneous, off target, off beam, out, mistaken, misguided, misinformed.

marked ▶ adjective NOTICEABLE, pronounced, decided, distinct, striking, clear, glaring, blatant, unmistakable, obvious, plain, manifest, patent, palpable, prominent, signal, significant, conspicuous, notable, recognizable, identifiable, distinguishable, discernible, apparent, evident; written all over one.

– OPPOSITES imperceptible.

market ▶ noun ❶ SHOPPING CENTRE, marketplace, mart, flea market, bazaar, souk, fair; *archaic* emporium. ❷ *there's no market for such goods* DEMAND, call, want, desire, need, requirement. ❸ *the market is sluggish* TRADE, trading, business, commerce, buying and selling, dealing.

▶ verb *the product was marketed worldwide* SELL, retail, vend, merchandise, trade, peddle, hawk; advertise, promote.

■ **on the market** ON SALE, (up) for sale, on offer, available, obtainable; *N. Amer.* on the block.

marksman, markswoman ▶ noun SNIPER, sharpshooter, good shot; *informal* crack shot; *N. Amer. informal* deadeye, shootist.

maroon ▶ verb STRAND, cast away, cast ashore; abandon, leave behind, leave, leave in the lurch, desert; *informal* leave high and dry.

marriage ▶ noun ❶ *a proposal of marriage* (HOLY) MATRIMONY, wedlock. ❷ *the marriage took place at St Margaret's* WEDDING, wedding ceremony, marriage ceremony, nuptials, union; *archaic* espousal. ❸ *a marriage of jazz, pop, and*

gospel UNION, alliance, fusion, mixture, mix, blend, amalgamation, combination, merger.
– RELATED TERMS conjugal, marital, matrimonial.
– OPPOSITES divorce, separation.

married ▶ adjective ❶ *a married couple* WEDDED, wed; *informal* spliced, hitched. ❷ *married bliss* MARITAL, matrimonial, conjugal, nuptial; *Law* spousal; *poetic/literary* connubial.
– OPPOSITES single.

marrow ▶ noun *the marrow of his statement* ESSENCE, core, nucleus, pith, kernel, heart, quintessence, gist, substance, sum and substance, meat, nub; *informal* nitty-gritty.

marry ▶ verb ❶ *the couple married last year* GET/BE MARRIED, wed, be wed, become man and wife, plight/pledge one's troth; *informal* tie the knot, walk down the aisle, take the plunge, get spliced, get hitched, say 'I do'. ❷ *John wanted to marry her* WED, take to wife/husband; *informal* make an honest woman of; *archaic* espouse. ❸ *the show marries poetry with art* JOIN, unite, combine, fuse, mix, blend, merge, amalgamate, link, connect, couple, knit, yoke.
– OPPOSITES divorce, separate.

marsh ▶ noun SWAMP, marshland, bog, peat bog, swampland, morass, mire, quagmire, slough, fen, fenland, wetland; *N. Amer.* bayou; *Scottish & N. English* moss; *archaic* quag.

marshal ▶ verb ❶ *the king marshalled an army* ASSEMBLE, gather together, collect, muster, call together, draw up, line up, align, array, organize, group, arrange, deploy, position, order, dispose; mobilize, rally, round up. ❷ *guests were marshalled to their seats* USHER, guide, escort, conduct, lead, shepherd, steer, take.

marshy ▶ adjective BOGGY, swampy, muddy, squelchy, soggy, waterlogged, miry, fenny; *Scottish & N. English* mossy; *Ecology* paludal.
– OPPOSITES dry, firm.

martial ▶ adjective MILITARY, soldierly, soldier-like, army, naval; warlike, fighting, combative, militaristic; *informal* gung-ho.

martinet ▶ noun DISCIPLINARIAN, slave-driver, stickler for discipline, (hard) taskmaster, authoritarian, tyrant.

martyr ▶ verb PUT TO DEATH, kill, martyrize; burn, burn at the stake, immolate, stone to death, throw to the lions, crucify.

martyrdom ▶ noun DEATH, suffering, torture, torment, agony, ordeal; killing, sacrifice, crucifixion, immolation, burning, auto-da-fé; *Christianity* Passion.

marvel ▶ verb *she marvelled at their courage* BE AMAZED, be astonished, be surprised, be awed, stand in awe, wonder; stare, gape, goggle, not believe one's eyes/ears, be dumbfounded; *informal* be flabbergasted.
▶ noun *the marvels of technology* WONDER, miracle, sensation, spectacle, phenomenon; *informal* something else, something to shout about, eye-opener.

marvellous ▶ adjective ❶ *his solo climb was marvellous* AMAZING, astounding, astonishing, awesome, breathtaking, sensational, remarkable, spectacular, stupendous, staggering, stunning; phenomenal, prodigious, miraculous, extraordinary, incredible, unbelievable; *poetic/literary* wondrous. ❷ *marvellous weather* EXCELLENT, splendid, wonderful, magnificent, superb, glorious, sublime, lovely, delightful, too good to be true; *informal* super, great, amazing, fantastic, terrific, tremendous, sensational, heavenly, divine, gorgeous, grand, fabulous, fab, awesome, to die for, magic, ace, wicked, mind-blowing, far out, out of this world; *Brit. informal* smashing, brilliant, brill; *N. Amer. informal* boss; *Austral./NZ informal* beaut, bonzer; *Brit. informal, dated* champion, wizard, corking, ripping, spiffing, top-hole; *N. Amer. informal, dated* swell.
– OPPOSITES commonplace, awful.

masculine ▶ adjective ❶ *a masculine trait* MALE, man's, men's; male-oriented. ❷ *a powerfully masculine man* VIRILE, macho, manly, all-male, muscular, muscly, strong, strapping, well built, rugged, robust, brawny, powerful, red-blooded, vigorous; *informal* hunky. ❸ *a rather masculine woman* MANNISH, unfeminine, unwomanly, unladylike, Amazonian; *informal* butch.
– OPPOSITES feminine, effeminate.

masculinity ▶ noun VIRILITY, manliness, maleness, machismo, vigour, strength, muscularity, ruggedness, robustness.

mash ▶ verb *mash the potatoes* PULP, crush, purée, cream, smash, squash, pound, beat.
▶ noun *first pound the garlic to a mash* PULP, purée, mush, paste.

mask ▶ noun ❶ *she wore a mask to conceal her face* DISGUISE, false face; *historical* domino, visor; *archaic* vizard. ❷ *he dropped his mask of good humour* PRETENCE, semblance, veil, screen, front, false front, facade, veneer, blind, false colours, disguise, guise, concealment, cover, cover-up, cloak, camouflage.
▶ verb *poplar trees masked the factory* HIDE, conceal, disguise, cover up, obscure, screen, cloak, camouflage, veil.

masquerade ▶ noun ❶ *a grand masquerade* MASKED BALL, masque, fancy-dress party. ❷ *he couldn't keep up the masquerade much longer* PRETENCE, deception, pose, act, front, facade, disguise, dissimulation, cover-up, bluff, play-acting, make-believe; *informal* put-on.
▶ verb *a woman masquerading as a man* PRETEND TO BE, pose as, pass oneself off as, impersonate, disguise oneself as; *formal* personate.

Mass ▶ noun EUCHARIST, Holy Communion, Communion, the Lord's Supper.

mass ▶ noun ❶ *a soggy mass of fallen leaves* PILE, heap; accumulation, aggregation, accretion, concretion, build-up. ❷ *a mass of cyclists* CROWD, horde, large group, throng, host, troop, army, herd, flock, drove, swarm, mob, pack, press, crush, flood, multitude. ❸ *the mass of the population* MAJORITY, greater part/number, best/better part, major part, most, bulk, main body, lion's share. ❹ THE COMMON PEOPLE, the populace, the public, the people, the rank and file, the crowd, the third estate; *derogatory* the hoi polloi, the mob, the proletariat, the common herd, the great unwashed. ❺ (*informal*) *masses of food. See* LOT pronoun.

▶ **adjective** *mass hysteria* WIDESPREAD, general, wholesale, universal, large-scale, extensive, pandemic.

▶ **verb** *they began massing troops in the region* ASSEMBLE, marshal, gather together, muster, round up, mobilize, rally.

massacre ▶ **noun** ❶ *a cold-blooded massacre of innocent civilians* SLAUGHTER, wholesale/mass slaughter, indiscriminate killing, mass murder, mass execution, annihilation, liquidation, decimation, extermination; carnage, butchery, bloodbath, bloodletting, pogrom, genocide, ethnic cleansing, holocaust, Shoah, night of the long knives; *poetic/literary* slaying. ❷ (*informal*) *the match was an 8–0 massacre. See* ROUT noun sense 2.

▶ **verb** ❶ *thousands were brutally massacred* SLAUGHTER, butcher, murder, kill, annihilate, exterminate, execute, liquidate, eliminate, decimate, wipe out, mow down, cut down, put to the sword, put to death; *poetic/literary* slay. ❷ (*informal*) *they were massacred in the final. See* TROUNCE.

massage ▶ **noun** RUB, rub-down, rubbing, kneading, palpation, manipulation, pummelling; shiatsu, reflexology, acupressure, hydromassage, Swedish massage, osteopathy; effleurage, tapotement, Rolfing.

▶ **verb** ❶ *he massaged her tired muscles* RUB, knead, palpate, manipulate, pummel, work. ❷ *the statistics have been massaged* ALTER, tamper with, manipulate, doctor, falsify, juggle, fiddle with, tinker with, distort, change, rig, interfere with, misrepresent; *informal* fix, cook, fiddle.

massive ▶ **adjective** HUGE, enormous, vast, immense, large, big, mighty, great, colossal, tremendous, prodigious, gigantic, gargantuan, mammoth, monstrous, monumental, giant, towering, elephantine, mountainous, titanic; epic, Herculean, Brobdingnagian; *informal* monster, jumbo, mega, whopping, humongous, hulking, bumper, astronomical; *Brit. informal* whacking, ginormous.
– OPPOSITES tiny.

mast ▶ **noun** ❶ *a ship's mast* spar, boom, yard, gaff, foremast, mainmast, topmast, mizzenmast, mizzen, royal mast. ❷ *the mast on top of the building* FLAGPOLE, flagstaff, pole, post, rod, upright; aerial, transmitter, pylon.

master ▶ **noun** ❶ (*historical*) *he acceded to his master's wishes* LORD, overlord, lord and master, ruler, sovereign, monarch, liege (lord), suzerain. ❷ *the dog's master* OWNER, keeper. ❸ *a chess master* EXPERT, adept, genius, past master, maestro, virtuoso, professional, doyen, authority; *informal* ace, pro, wizard, whizz, hotshot; *Brit. informal* dab hand; *N. Amer. informal* maven, crackerjack. ❹ *the master of the ship* CAPTAIN, commander; *informal* skipper. ❺ *the geography master* TEACHER, schoolteacher, schoolmaster, tutor, instructor, preceptor; *formal* pedagogue. ❻ *their spiritual master* GURU, teacher, leader, guide, mentor; swami, Maharishi; Roshi.
– OPPOSITES servant, amateur, pupil.

▶ **verb** ❶ *I managed to master my fears* OVERCOME, conquer, beat, quell, quash, suppress, control, overpower, triumph over, subdue, vanquish, subjugate, prevail over, govern, curb, check, bridle, tame, defeat, get the better of, get a grip on, get over; *informal* lick. ❷ *it took ages to master the technique* LEARN, become proficient in, know inside out, know backwards; pick up, grasp, understand; *informal* get the hang of.

▶ **adjective** ❶ *a master craftsman* EXPERT, adept, proficient, skilled, skilful, deft, dexterous, adroit, practised, experienced, masterly, accomplished, complete, demon, brilliant; *informal* crack, ace, mean, wizard; *N. Amer. informal* crackerjack. ❷ *the master bedroom* PRINCIPAL, main, chief; biggest.

masterful ▶ **adjective** ❶ *a masterful man* COMMANDING, powerful, imposing, magisterial, lordly, authoritative; dominating, domineering, overbearing, overweening, imperious. ❷ *their masterful handling of the situation* EXPERT, adept, clever, masterly, skilful, skilled, adroit, proficient, deft, dexterous, accomplished, polished, consummate; *informal* crack, ace.
– OPPOSITES weak, inept.

masterly ▶ **adjective**. *See* MASTERFUL sense 2.

mastermind ▶ **verb** *he masterminded the whole campaign* PLAN, control, direct, be in charge of, run, conduct, organize, arrange, preside over, orchestrate, stage-manage, engineer, manage, coordinate; conceive, devise, originate, initiate, think up, frame, hatch, come up with; *informal* be the brains behind.

▶ **noun** *the mastermind behind the project* GENIUS, mind, intellect, author, architect, organizer, originator, prime mover, initiator, inventor; *informal* brain, brains, bright spark.

masterpiece ▶ **noun** CHEF-D'ŒUVRE, pièce de résistance, masterwork, magnum opus, finest/best work, tour de force.

master stroke ▶ **noun** STROKE OF GENIUS, coup, triumph, coup de maître, tour de force.

mastery ▶ **noun** ❶ *her mastery of the language* PROFICIENCY, ability, capability; knowledge, understanding, comprehension, familiarity, command, grasp, grip. ❷ *they played with tact-*

ical mastery SKILL, skilfulness, expertise, dexterity, finesse, adroitness, virtuosity, prowess, deftness, proficiency; *informal* know-how. ❸ *man's mastery over nature* CONTROL, domination, command, ascendancy, supremacy, pre-eminence, superiority; triumph, victory, the upper hand, the whip hand, rule, government, power, sway, authority, jurisdiction, dominion, sovereignty.

masticate ▶ **verb** CHEW, munch, champ, chomp, crunch, eat; ruminate, chew the cud; *formal* manducate.

mat ▶ **noun** ❶ *the hall mat* RUG, runner, carpet, drugget; doormat, welcome mat, hearthrug; dhurrie, numdah; kilim, flokati; *N. Amer.* floorcloth. ❷ *he placed his glass on the mat* COASTER, beer mat, doily; table mat, place mat; *Brit.* drip mat. ❸ *a thick mat of hair* MASS, tangle, knot, mop, thatch, shock, mane.

▶ **verb** *his hair was matted with blood* TANGLE, entangle, knot, ravel, snarl up.

match ▶ **noun** ❶ *a football match | a boxing match* CONTEST, competition, game, tournament, tie, cup tie, event, fixture, trial, test, meet, bout, fight; friendly, (local) derby; play-off, replay, rematch; *archaic* tourney. ❷ *he was no match for the champion* EQUAL, rival, equivalent, peer, counterpart; *formal* compeer. ❸ *the vase was an exact match of the one she already owned* LOOKALIKE, double, twin, duplicate, mate, fellow, companion, counterpart, pair; replica, copy; *informal* spitting image, spit and image, dead spit, dead ringer. ❹ *a love match* MARRIAGE, betrothal, relationship, partnership, union.

▶ **verb** ❶ *the curtains matched the duvet cover* GO WITH, coordinate with, complement, suit; be the same as, be similar to. ❷ *did their statements match?* CORRESPOND, be in agreement, tally, agree, match up, coincide, accord, conform, square. ❸ *no one can match him at chess* EQUAL, be a match for, measure up to, compare with, parallel, be in the same league as, be on a par with, touch, keep pace with, keep up with, emulate, rival, vie with, compete with, contend with; *informal* hold a candle to.

■ **match up to** MEASURE UP TO, come up to, meet with, be equal to, be as good as, satisfy, fulfil, answer to.

matching ▶ **adjective** CORRESPONDING, equivalent, parallel, analogous; coordinating, complementary, toning; paired, twin, identical, like, like (two) peas in a pod, alike.

– OPPOSITES different, clashing.

matchless ▶ **adjective** INCOMPARABLE, unrivalled, inimitable, beyond compare/comparison, unparalleled, unequalled, without equal, peerless, second to none, unsurpassed, unsurpassable, nonpareil, unique, consummate, perfect, rare, transcendent, surpassing; *formal* unexampled.

matchmaker ▶ **noun** MARRIAGE BROKER, shadchan; marriage bureau, dating agency; go-between.

mate ▶ **noun** ❶ (*Brit. informal*) *he's gone out with his mates* FRIEND, companion, boon companion, intimate, familiar, confidant; playmate, playfellow, schoolmate, classmate, workmate; *informal* pal, chum; *Brit. informal* china, mucker; *N. English informal* marra; *N. Amer. informal* buddy, amigo, compadre, homeboy; *archaic* compeer. ❷ *she's finally found her ideal mate* PARTNER, husband, wife, spouse, lover, live-in lover, significant other, companion, helpmate, helpmeet, consort; *informal* better half, hubby, missus, missis; *Brit. informal* other half, dutch, trouble and strife. ❸ *I can't find the mate to this sock* MATCH, fellow, twin, companion, pair, other half, equivalent. ❹ *a plumber's mate* ASSISTANT, helper, apprentice.

▶ **verb** *pandas rarely mate in captivity* BREED, couple, copulate.

material ▶ **noun** ❶ *the decomposition of organic material* MATTER, substance, stuff, medium. ❷ *the materials for a new building* CONSTITUENT, raw material, element, component. ❸ *cleaning materials* THINGS, items, articles, stuff, necessaries; *Brit. informal* gubbins. ❹ *curtain material* FABRIC, cloth, textiles. ❺ *material for a magazine article* INFORMATION, data, facts, facts and figures, statistics, evidence, details, particulars, background, notes; *informal* info, gen, dope, low-down.

▶ **adjective** ❶ *the material world* PHYSICAL, corporeal, tangible, non-spiritual, mundane, worldly, earthly, secular, temporal, concrete, real, solid, substantial. ❷ *she was too fond of material pleasures* SENSUAL, physical, carnal, corporal, fleshly, bodily. ❸ *information that could be material to the inquiry* RELEVANT, pertinent, applicable, germane; apropos, to the point; vital, essential, key. ❹ *the storms caused material damage* SIGNIFICANT, major, important.

– OPPOSITES spiritual, aesthetic, irrelevant.

materialistic ▶ **adjective** CONSUMERIST, acquisitive, money-oriented, greedy; worldly, capitalistic, bourgeois.

materialize ▶ **verb** ❶ *the forecast investment boom did not materialize* HAPPEN, occur, come about, take place, come into being, transpire; *informal* come off; *formal* eventuate; *poetic/literary* come to pass. ❷ *Harry materialized at the door* APPEAR, turn up, arrive, make/put in an appearance, present oneself/itself, emerge, surface, reveal oneself/itself, show one's face, pop up; *informal* show up, fetch up, pitch up.

materially ▶ **adverb** SIGNIFICANTLY, greatly, much, very much, to a great extent, considerably, substantially, a great deal, appreciably, markedly, fundamentally, seriously, gravely.

maternal ▶ **adjective** ❶ *her maternal instincts* MOTHERLY, protective, caring, nurturing, loving, devoted, affectionate, fond, warm, tender, gentle, kind, kindly, comforting. ❷ *his maternal grandparents* ON ONE'S MOTHER'S SIDE, on the distaff side.

mathematical ▶ adjective ❶ *mathematical symbols* ARITHMETICAL, numerical; statistical, algebraic, geometric, trigonometric. ❷ *mathematical precision* RIGOROUS, meticulous, scrupulous, punctilious, scientific, strict, precise, exact, accurate, pinpoint, correct, careful, unerring.

matrimonial ▶ adjective MARITAL, conjugal, married, wedded; nuptial; *Law* spousal; *poetic/literary* connubial.

matrimony ▶ noun MARRIAGE, wedlock, union; nuptials.
– OPPOSITES divorce.

matted ▶ adjective TANGLED, tangly, knotted, knotty, tousled, dishevelled, uncombed, unkempt, ratty; *black English* natty.

matter ▶ noun ❶ *decaying vegetable matter* MATERIAL, substance, stuff. ❷ *the heart of the matter* AFFAIR, business, proceeding, situation, circumstance, event, happening, occurrence, incident, episode, experience; subject, topic, issue, question, point, point at issue, case, concern. ❸ *it is of little matter now* IMPORTANCE, consequence, significance, note, import, weight; *formal* moment. ❹ *what's the matter?* PROBLEM, trouble, difficulty, complication; upset, worry. ❺ *the matter of the sermon* CONTENT, subject matter, text, argument, substance. ❻ *an infected wound full of matter* PUS, suppuration, purulence, discharge.
▶ verb *it doesn't matter what you wear* BE IMPORTANT, make any/a difference, be of importance, be of consequence, signify, be relevant, count; *informal* cut any ice.
■ **as a matter of fact** ACTUALLY, in (actual) fact, in point of fact, as it happens, really, believe it or not, in reality, in truth, to tell the truth.
■ **no matter** IT DOESN'T MATTER, it makes no difference/odds, it's not important, never mind, don't worry about it.

matter-of-fact ▶ adjective UNEMOTIONAL, practical, down-to-earth, sensible, realistic, rational, sober, unsentimental, pragmatic, businesslike, commonsensical, level-headed, hard-headed, no-nonsense, factual, literal, straightforward, plain, unembellished, unvarnished, unadorned.

mature ▶ adjective ❶ *a mature woman* ADULT, grown-up, grown, fully grown, full-grown, of age, fully developed, in one's prime. ❷ *he's very mature for his age* SENSIBLE, responsible, adult, level-headed, reliable, dependable; wise, discriminating, shrewd, sophisticated. ❸ *mature cheese* RIPE, ripened, mellow; ready to eat/drink. ❹ *on mature reflection, he decided not to go* CAREFUL, thorough, deep, considered.
– OPPOSITES adolescent, childish.
▶ verb ❶ *kittens mature when they are about a year old* BE FULLY GROWN, be full-grown; come of age, reach adulthood, reach maturity. ❷ *he's matured since he left home* GROW UP, become more sensible/adult; blossom. ❸ *leave the cheese to mature* RIPEN, mellow; age. ❹ *their friendship didn't have time to mature* DEVELOP, grow, evolve, bloom, blossom, flourish, thrive.

maturity ▶ noun ❶ *her progress from childhood to maturity* ADULTHOOD, majority, coming-of-age, manhood/womanhood. ❷ *he displayed a maturity beyond his years* RESPONSIBILITY, sense, level-headedness; wisdom, discrimination, shrewdness, sophistication.

maudlin ▶ adjective ❶ *maudlin self-pity* SENTIMENTAL, over-sentimental, emotional, over-emotional, tearful, lachrymose; *informal* weepy. ❷ *a maudlin ballad* MAWKISH, sentimental, over-sentimental; *Brit.* twee; *informal* mushy, slushy, sloppy, schmaltzy, cheesy, corny, toe-curling; *Brit. informal* soppy; *N. Amer. informal* cornball, three-hankie.

maul ▶ verb ❶ *he had been mauled by a lion* SAVAGE, attack, tear to pieces, lacerate, claw, scratch. ❷ *she hated being mauled by men* MOLEST, feel, fondle, manhandle; *informal* grope, paw, touch up. ❸ *his book was mauled by the critics.* See CRITICIZE.

maunder ▶ verb ❶ *he maundered on about his problems* RAMBLE, prattle, blather, blether, rattle, chatter, jabber, babble; *informal* yak, yatter; *Brit. informal* rabbit, witter, waffle, natter, chunter. ❷ *she maundered across the road* WANDER, drift, meander, amble, potter; *Brit. informal* mooch.

mausoleum ▶ noun TOMB, sepulchre, crypt, vault, charnel house, burial chamber, catacomb, undercroft.

maverick ▶ noun INDIVIDUALIST, nonconformist, free spirit, unorthodox person, original, eccentric; rebel, dissenter, dissident.
– OPPOSITES conformist.

maw ▶ noun MOUTH, jaws, muzzle; throat, gullet; *informal* trap, chops, kisser; *Brit. informal* gob.

mawkish ▶ adjective SENTIMENTAL, over-sentimental, maudlin, cloying, sickly, saccharine, sugary, syrupy, nauseating; *Brit.* twee; *informal* mushy, slushy, sloppy, schmaltzy, weepy, cutesy, lovey-dovey, cheesy, corny, sick-making, toe-curling; *Brit. informal* soppy; *N. Amer. informal* cornball, hokey, three-hankie.

maxim ▶ noun SAYING, adage, aphorism, proverb, motto, saw, axiom, apophthegm, dictum, precept, epigram; truism, cliché.

maximum ▶ adjective *the maximum amount* GREATEST, highest, biggest, largest, top, topmost, most, utmost, maximal.
– OPPOSITES minimum.
▶ noun *production levels are near their maximum*

UPPER LIMIT, limit, utmost, uttermost, greatest, most, extremity, peak, height, ceiling, top.
– OPPOSITES minimum.

maybe ▶ **adverb** PERHAPS, possibly, conceivably, it could be, it is possible, for all one knows; *N. English* happen; *poetic/literary* peradventure, perchance.

mayhem ▶ **noun** CHAOS, disorder, havoc, bedlam, pandemonium, tumult, uproar, turmoil, commotion, all hell broken loose, maelstrom, trouble, disturbance, confusion, riot, anarchy, violence; *informal* madhouse.

maze ▶ **noun** LABYRINTH, complex network, warren; web, tangle, jungle, snarl.

meadow ▶ **noun** FIELD, paddock; pasture, pastureland; *poetic/literary* lea, mead.

meagre ▶ **adjective** ❶ *their meagre earnings* INADEQUATE, scanty, scant, paltry, limited, restricted, modest, insufficient, sparse, deficient, negligible, skimpy, slender, poor, miserable, pitiful, puny, miserly, niggardly, beggarly; *informal* measly, stingy, pathetic, piddling; *formal* exiguous. ❷ *a tall, meagre man* THIN, lean, skinny, spare, scrawny, scraggy, gangling, gangly, spindly, stringy, bony, rawboned, gaunt, underweight, underfed, undernourished, emaciated, skeletal, cadaverous.
– OPPOSITES abundant, fat.

meal ▶ **noun** snack; feast, banquet; *informal* bite (to eat), spread, blowout, feed; *Brit. informal* nosh-up; *formal* repast, collation; *poetic/literary* refection.
– RELATED TERMS prandial.

mean¹ ▶ **verb** ❶ *flashing lights mean the road is blocked* SIGNIFY, convey, denote, designate, indicate, connote, show, express, spell out; stand for, represent, symbolize; imply, suggest, intimate, hint at, insinuate, drive at, refer to, allude to; *poetic/literary* betoken. ❷ *she didn't mean to break it* INTEND, aim, plan, design, have in mind, contemplate, purpose, propose, set out, aspire, desire, want, wish, expect. ❸ *he was hit by a bullet meant for a soldier* INTEND, design; destine, predestine. ❹ *the closures will mean a rise in unemployment* ENTAIL, involve, necessitate, lead to, result in, give rise to, bring about, cause, engender, produce. ❺ *this means a lot to me* MATTER, be important, be significant. ❻ *a red sky in the morning usually means rain* PRESAGE, portend, foretell, augur, promise, foreshadow, herald, signal, bode; *poetic/literary* betoken, foretoken.

mean² ▶ **adjective** ❶ *he's too mean to leave a tip* MISERLY, niggardly, close-fisted, parsimonious, penny-pinching, cheese-paring, Scrooge-like; *informal* tight-fisted, stingy, tight, mingy, money-grubbing; *N. Amer. informal* cheap; *formal* penurious; *archaic* near, niggard. ❷ *a mean trick* UNKIND, nasty, unpleasant, spiteful, malicious, unfair, cruel, shabby, foul, despicable, contemptible, obnoxious, vile, odious, loathsome, base, low; *informal* horrible, horrid, hateful, rotten, low-down; *Brit. informal* beastly. ❸ *the truth was obvious to even the meanest intelligence* INFERIOR, poor, limited, restricted. ❹ *her flat was mean and cold* SQUALID, shabby, dilapidated, sordid, seedy, slummy, sleazy, insalubrious, wretched, dismal, dingy, miserable, run down, down at heel; *informal* scruffy, scuzzy, crummy, grungy; *Brit. informal* grotty. ❺ *a man of mean birth* LOWLY, humble, ordinary, low, low-born, modest, common, base, proletarian, plebeian, obscure, undistinguished, ignoble; *archaic* baseborn. ❻ (*informal*) *he's a mean cook.* See EXCELLENT.
– OPPOSITES generous, kind, luxurious, noble.

mean³ ▶ **noun** *a mean between saving and splashing out* MIDDLE COURSE, middle way, midpoint, happy medium, golden mean, compromise, balance; median, norm, average.
▶ **adjective** *the mean temperature* AVERAGE, median, middle, medial, medium, normal, standard.

meander ▶ **verb** ❶ *the river meandered gently* ZIGZAG, wind, twist, turn, curve, curl, bend, snake. ❷ *we meandered along the path* STROLL, saunter, amble, wander, ramble, drift, maunder; *Scottish* stravaig; *informal* mosey, tootle.

meandering ▶ **adjective** ❶ *a meandering stream* WINDING, windy, zigzag, twisting, turning, curving, serpentine, sinuous, twisty. ❷ *meandering reminiscences* RAMBLING, maundering, circuitous, roundabout, digressive, discursive, indirect, tortuous, convoluted.
– OPPOSITES straight, succinct.

meaning ▶ **noun** ❶ *the meaning of his remark* SIGNIFICANCE, sense, signification, import, gist, thrust, drift, implication, tenor, message, essence, substance, purport, intention. ❷ *the word has several different meanings* DEFINITION, sense, explanation, denotation, connotation, interpretation. ❸ *my life has no meaning* VALUE, validity, worth, consequence, account, use, usefulness, significance, point. ❹ *his smile was full of meaning* EXPRESSIVENESS, significance, eloquence, implications, insinuations.
– RELATED TERMS semantic.
▶ **adjective** *a meaning look. See* MEANINGFUL sense 3.

meaningful ▶ **adjective** ❶ *a meaningful remark* SIGNIFICANT, relevant, important, consequential, telling, material, valid, worthwhile. ❷ *a meaningful relationship* SINCERE, deep, serious, in earnest, significant, important. ❸ *a meaningful glance* EXPRESSIVE, eloquent, pointed, significant, meaning; pregnant, speaking, telltale, revealing, suggestive.
– OPPOSITES inconsequential.

meaningless ▶ **adjective** ❶ *a jumble of meaningless words* UNINTELLIGIBLE, incomprehensible, incoherent. ❷ *she felt her life was meaningless* FUTILE, pointless, aimless, empty, hollow,

vain, purposeless, valueless, useless, of no use, worthless, senseless, trivial, trifling, unimportant, insignificant, inconsequential.
– OPPOSITES worthwhile.

means ▶ plural noun ❶ *the best means to achieve your goal* METHOD, way, manner, mode, measure, technique, expedient, agency, medium, instrument, channel, vehicle, avenue, course, process, procedure. ❷ *she doesn't have the means to support herself* MONEY, resources, capital, income, finance, funds, cash, the wherewithal, assets; *informal* dough, bread; *Brit. informal* dosh, brass, lolly, spondulicks, ackers. ❸ *a man of means* WEALTH, riches, affluence, substance, fortune, property, money, capital.

■ **by all means** OF COURSE, certainly, definitely, surely, absolutely, with pleasure; *N. Amer. informal* sure thing.

■ **by means of** USING, utilizing, employing, through, with the help of; as a result of, by dint of, by way of, by virtue of.

■ **by no means** NOT AT ALL, in no way, not in the least, not in the slightest, not the least bit, not by a long shot, certainly not, absolutely not, definitely not, on no account, under no circumstances; *Brit.* not by a long chalk; *informal* no way.

meantime ▶ adverb. *See* MEANWHILE.

meanwhile ▶ adverb ❶ *meanwhile, I'll stay here* FOR NOW, for the moment, for the present, for the time being, meantime, in the meantime, in the interim, in the interval. ❷ *cook for a further half hour; meanwhile, make the stuffing* AT THE SAME TIME, simultaneously, concurrently, the while.

measurable ▶ adjective ❶ *a measurable amount* QUANTIFIABLE, assessable, gaugeable, computable. ❷ *a measurable improvement* APPRECIABLE, noticeable, significant, visible, perceptible, definite, obvious.

measure ▶ verb ❶ *they measured the length of the room* CALCULATE, compute, count, meter, quantify, weigh, size, evaluate, assess, gauge, plumb, determine. ❷ *I had better measure my words* CHOOSE CAREFULLY, consider, plan. ❸ *she did not need to measure herself against some ideal* COMPARE WITH, pit against, set against, test against, judge by.

▶ noun ❶ *cost-cutting measures* ACTION, act, course (of action), deed, proceeding, procedure, step, means, expedient; manoeuvre, initiative, programme, operation. ❷ *the Senate passed the measure* STATUTE, act, bill, law, legislation. ❸ *the original dimensions were in imperial measure* SYSTEM, standard, units, scale. ❹ *use a measure to check the size* RULER, tape measure, rule, gauge, meter, scale, level, yardstick. ❺ *a measure of egg white* QUANTITY, amount, portion. ❻ *the states retain a measure of independence* CERTAIN AMOUNT, degree; some. ❼ *sales are the measure of the company's success* YARDSTICK, test, standard, barometer, touchstone, litmus test, criterion, benchmark. ❽ *poetic measure* METRE, cadence, rhythm; foot.

■ **beyond measure** IMMENSELY, extremely, vastly, greatly, excessively, immeasurably, incalculably, infinitely.

■ **for good measure** AS A BONUS, as an extra, into the bargain, to boot, in addition, besides, as well.

■ **get/have the measure of** EVALUATE, assess, gauge, judge, weigh up; understand, fathom, read, be wise to, see through; *informal* have someone's number.

■ **measure something off** MARK OFF, measure out, demarcate, delimit, delineate, outline, describe, define, stake out.

■ **measure up** PASS MUSTER, match up, come up to standard, fit/fill the bill, be acceptable; *informal* come up to scratch, make the grade, cut the mustard, be up to snuff.

■ **measure someone up** EVALUATE, rate, assess, appraise, judge, weigh up; *informal* size up.

■ **measure up to** MEET, come up to, equal, match, bear comparison with, be on a level with; achieve, satisfy, fulfil.

measured ▶ adjective ❶ *his measured tread* REGULAR, steady, even, rhythmic, rhythmical, unfaltering; slow, dignified, stately, sedate, leisurely, unhurried. ❷ *his measured tones* THOUGHTFUL, careful, carefully chosen, studied, calculated, planned, considered, deliberate, restrained.

measureless ▶ adjective BOUNDLESS, limitless, unlimited, unbounded, untold, immense, vast, endless, inexhaustible, infinite, illimitable, immeasurable, incalculable.
– OPPOSITES limited.

measurement ▶ noun ❶ *measurement of the effect is difficult* QUANTIFICATION, computation, calculation, mensuration; evaluation, assessment, gauging. ❷ *all measurements are given in metric form* SIZE, dimension, proportions, magnitude, amplitude; mass, bulk, volume, capacity, extent; value, amount, quantity, area, length, height, depth, weight, width, range.

meat ▶ noun ❶ FLESH, animal flesh. ❷ (*archaic*) *meat and drink* FOOD, nourishment, sustenance, provisions, rations, fare, foodstuff(s), provender, daily bread; *informal* grub, eats, chow, nosh; *Brit. informal* scoff; *formal* comestibles; *dated* victuals; *poetic/literary* viands; *archaic* commons. ❸ *the meat of the matter* SUBSTANCE, pith, marrow, heart, kernel, core, nucleus, nub, essence, essentials, gist, fundamentals, basics; *informal* nitty-gritty.

meaty ▶ adjective ❶ *a tall, meaty young man* BEEFY, brawny, burly, muscular, muscly, powerful, sturdy, strapping, well built, solidly built, thickset; fleshy, stout. ❷ *a good, meaty story* INTERESTING, thought-provoking, three-dimensional, stimulating; substantial, satisfying, meaningful, deep, profound.

mechanical ▶ adjective ❶ *a mechanical device* MECHANIZED, machine-driven, automated, automatic, power-driven, robotic. ❷ *a mechanical response* AUTOMATIC, unthinking, robotic, involuntary, reflex, knee-jerk, habitual, routine, unemotional, unfeeling, lifeless; perfunctory, cursory, careless, casual.
– OPPOSITES manual, conscious.

mechanism ▶ noun ❶ *an electrical mechanism* MACHINE, piece of machinery, appliance, apparatus, device, instrument, contraption, gadget; *informal* gizmo. ❷ *the train's safety mechanism* MACHINERY, workings, works, movement, action, gears, components. ❸ *a formal mechanism for citizens to lodge complaints* PROCEDURE, process, system, operation, method, technique, means, medium, agency, channel.

mechanize ▶ verb AUTOMATE, industrialize, motorize, computerize.

medal ▶ noun DECORATION, ribbon, star, badge, laurel, palm, award; honour; *Military slang* fruit salad; *Brit. informal* gong.

meddle ▶ verb ❶ *don't meddle in my affairs* INTERFERE, butt in, intrude, intervene, pry; *informal* poke one's nose in, horn in on, muscle in on, snoop, put/stick one's oar in; *N. Amer. informal* kibitz. ❷ *someone had been meddling with her things* FIDDLE, interfere, tamper, tinker, finger; *Brit. informal* muck about/around.

meddlesome ▶ adjective INTERFERING, meddling, intrusive, prying, busybody; *informal* nosy, nosy-parker.

mediate ▶ verb ❶ *Austria tried to mediate between the belligerents* ARBITRATE, conciliate, moderate, act as peacemaker, make peace; intervene, step in, intercede, act as an intermediary, liaise. ❷ *a tribunal was set up to mediate disputes* RESOLVE, settle, arbitrate in, umpire, reconcile, referee; mend, clear up; *informal* patch up. ❸ *he attempted to mediate a solution to the conflict* NEGOTIATE, bring about, effect; *formal* effectuate.

mediation ▶ noun ARBITRATION, conciliation, reconciliation, intervention, intercession, good offices; negotiation, shuttle diplomacy.

mediator ▶ noun ARBITRATOR, arbiter, negotiator, conciliator, peacemaker, go-between, middleman, intermediary, moderator, intervenor, intercessor, broker, honest broker, liaison officer; umpire, referee, adjudicator, judge.

medicinal ▶ adjective CURATIVE, healing, remedial, therapeutic, restorative, corrective, health-giving; medical; *archaic* sanative.

medicine ▶ noun MEDICATION, medicament, drug, prescription, dose, treatment, remedy, cure; nostrum, panacea, cure-all; *archaic* physic.
– RELATED TERMS pharmaceutical.

medieval ▶ adjective ❶ *medieval times* OF THE MIDDLE AGES, of the Dark Ages, Dark-Age; Gothic. ❷ (*informal*) *the plumbing's a bit medieval* PRIMITIVE, antiquated, archaic, antique, antediluvian, old-fashioned, out of date, outdated, outmoded, anachronistic, passé, obsolete; *informal* out of the ark; *N. Amer. informal* horse-and-buggy, clunky.
– OPPOSITES modern.

mediocre ▶ adjective ORDINARY, average, middling, middle-of-the-road, uninspired, undistinguished, indifferent, unexceptional, unexciting, unremarkable, run-of-the-mill, pedestrian, prosaic, lacklustre, forgettable, amateur, amateurish; *informal* OK, so-so, (plain) vanilla, fair-to-middling, no great shakes, not up to much; *Brit. informal* not much cop; *N. Amer. informal* bush-league; *NZ informal* half-pie.
– OPPOSITES excellent.

meditate ▶ verb CONTEMPLATE, think, consider, ponder, muse, reflect, deliberate, ruminate, chew the cud, brood, mull over; be in a brown study, be deep/lost in thought, debate with oneself; pray; *informal* put on one's thinking cap; *formal* cogitate.

meditation ▶ noun CONTEMPLATION, thought, thinking, musing, pondering, consideration, reflection, deliberation, rumination, brooding, reverie, brown study, concentration; prayer; *formal* cogitation.

meditative ▶ adjective PENSIVE, thoughtful, contemplative, reflective, musing, ruminative, introspective, brooding, deep/lost in thought, in a brown study; prayerful; *formal* cogitative.

medium ▶ noun ❶ *using technology as a medium for job creation* MEANS, method, way, form, agency, avenue, channel, vehicle, organ, instrument, mechanism. ❷ *organisms growing in their natural medium* HABITAT, element, environment, surroundings, milieu, setting, conditions. ❸ *she consulted a medium* SPIRITUALIST, spiritist, necromancer. ❹ *a happy medium* MIDDLE WAY, middle course, middle ground, middle, mean, median, midpoint; compromise, golden mean.
▶ adjective *medium height* AVERAGE, middling, medium-sized, middle-sized, moderate, normal, standard.

medley ▶ noun ASSORTMENT, miscellany, mixture, melange, variety, mixed bag, mix, collection, selection, pot-pourri, patchwork; motley collection, ragbag, gallimaufry, mishmash, hotchpotch, jumble; *N. Amer.* hodgepodge.

meek ▶ adjective SUBMISSIVE, yielding, obedient, compliant, tame, biddable, tractable, acquiescent, deferential, timid, unprotesting, unresisting, like a lamb to the slaughter; quiet, mild, gentle, docile, lamblike, shy, diffident, unassuming, self-effacing.
– OPPOSITES assertive.

meet ▶ verb ❶ *I met an old friend on the train* ENCOUNTER, meet up with, come face to face with, run into, run across, come across/upon, chance on, happen on, light on, stumble across/on; *informal* bump into. ❷ *she first met Paul at a party* GET TO KNOW, be introduced to, make the acquaintance of. ❸ *the committee met on Saturday* ASSEMBLE, gather, come together, get together, congregate, convene; *formal* foregather. ❹ *the place where three roads meet* CONVERGE, connect, touch, link up, intersect, cross, join. ❺ *he met death bravely* FACE, encounter, undergo, experience, go through, suffer, endure, bear; cope with, handle. ❻ *the announcement was met with widespread hostility* GREET, receive, answer, treat. ❼ *he does not meet the job's requirements* FULFIL, satisfy, fill, measure up to, match (up to), conform to, come up to, comply with, answer. ❽ *shipowners would meet the cost of oil spills* PAY, settle, clear, honour, discharge, pay off, square.

▶ **noun** *an athletics meet. See* MEETING sense 5.

■ **meet someone halfway**. *See* HALFWAY.

meeting ▶ **noun** ❶ *he stood up to address the meeting* GATHERING, assembly, conference, congregation, convention, summit, forum, convocation, conclave, council of war, rally; *N. Amer.* caucus; *informal* get-together. ❷ *she demanded a meeting with the minister* CONSULTATION, audience, interview. ❸ *he intrigued her on their first meeting* ENCOUNTER, contact; appointment, assignation, rendezvous; *poetic/literary* tryst. ❹ *the meeting of land and sea* CONVERGENCE, coming together, confluence, conjunction, union, junction, abutment; intersection, T-junction, crossing. ❺ *an athletics meeting* EVENT, tournament, meet, rally, competition, match, game, contest.

megalomania ▶ **noun** DELUSIONS OF GRANDEUR, folie de grandeur, thirst for power; self-importance, egotism, conceit, conceitedness.

melancholy ▶ **adjective** *a melancholy expression* SAD, sorrowful, unhappy, desolate, mournful, lugubrious, gloomy, despondent, dejected, depressed, downhearted, downcast, disconsolate, glum, miserable, wretched, dismal, morose, woeful, woebegone, doleful, joyless, heavy-hearted; *informal* down in the dumps, down in the mouth, blue.

– OPPOSITES cheerful.

▶ **noun** *a feeling of melancholy* SADNESS, sorrow, unhappiness, woe, desolation, melancholia, dejection, depression, despondency, gloom, gloominess, misery; *informal* the dumps, the blues.

melange ▶ **noun** MIXTURE, medley, assortment, blend, variety, mixed bag, mix, miscellany, selection, pot-pourri, patchwork; motley collection, ragbag, gallimaufry, mishmash, hotchpotch, jumble; *N. Amer.* hodgepodge.

melee, mêlée ▶ **noun** FRACAS, disturbance, rumpus, tumult, commotion, disorder, fray; brawl, fight, scuffle, struggle, skirmish, free-for-all, tussle; *informal* scrap, set-to, ruction; *N. Amer. informal* rough house.

mellifluous ▶ **adjective** SWEET-SOUNDING, dulcet, honeyed, mellow, soft, liquid, silvery, soothing, rich, smooth, euphonious, harmonious, tuneful, musical.

– OPPOSITES cacophonous.

mellow ▶ **adjective** ❶ *the mellow tone of his voice* DULCET, sweet-sounding, tuneful, melodious, mellifluous; soft, smooth, warm, full, rich. ❷ *a mellow wine* FULL-BODIED, mature, well matured, full-flavoured, rich, smooth. ❸ *a mellow mood* GENIAL, affable, amiable, good-humoured, good-natured, amicable, pleasant, relaxed, easy-going; jovial, jolly, cheerful, happy, merry.

melodious ▶ **adjective** TUNEFUL, melodic, musical, mellifluous, dulcet, sweet-sounding, silvery, silvery-toned, harmonious, euphonious, lyrical; *informal* easy on the ear.

– OPPOSITES discordant.

melodramatic ▶ **adjective** EXAGGERATED, histrionic, extravagant, over-dramatic, overdone, over-sensational, sensationalized, over-emotional, sentimental; theatrical, stagy, actressy; *informal* hammy.

melody ▶ **noun** ❶ *familiar melodies* TUNE, air, strain, theme, song, refrain, piece of music. ❷ *his unique gift for melody* MELODIOUSNESS, tunefulness, lyricism, musicality, euphony.

melt ▶ **verb** ❶ *the snow was beginning to melt* LIQUEFY, thaw, defrost, soften, dissolve, deliquesce. ❷ *his smile melted her heart* SOFTEN, disarm, touch, affect, move. ❸ *his anger melted away* VANISH, disappear, fade away, dissolve, evaporate; *poetic/literary* evanesce.

member ▶ **noun** ❶ *a member of the club* SUBSCRIBER, associate, fellow, life member, founder member, card-carrying member. ❷ *a member of a mathematical set* CONSTITUENT, element, component, part, portion, piece, unit. ❸ (*archaic*) *many victims had injured members* LIMB, organ; arm, leg, appendage.

membrane ▶ **noun** LAYER, sheet, skin, film, tissue, integument, overlay; *technical* pellicle.

memento ▶ **noun** SOUVENIR, keepsake, reminder, remembrance, token, memorial; trophy, relic.

memoir ▶ **noun** ❶ *a touching memoir of her childhood* ACCOUNT, history, record, chronicle, narrative, story, portrayal, depiction, sketch, portrait, profile, biography, monograph. ❷ *he published his memoirs in 1955* AUTOBIOGRAPHY, life story, life, memories, recollections, reminiscences; journal, diary.

memorable ▶ **adjective** UNFORGETTABLE, indelible, catchy, haunting; momentous, significant, historic, notable, noteworthy, important, consequential, remarkable, special, signal, outstanding, extraordinary, striking, vivid, arresting, impressive, distinctive, distinguished, famous, celebrated, renowned, illustrious, glorious.

memorandum ▶ noun ❶ *a memorandum from the managing director* MESSAGE, communication, note, e-mail, letter, missive; *informal* memo. ❷ *hasty memoranda and jottings-down* RECORD, minute, note, aide-memoire, reminder.

memorial ▶ noun ❶ *the war memorial* MONUMENT, cenotaph, mausoleum; statue, plaque, cairn; shrine; tombstone, gravestone, headstone. ❷ *the Festschrift is a memorial to his life's work* TRIBUTE, testimonial; remembrance, memento.
▶ adjective *a memorial service* COMMEMORATIVE, remembrance, commemorating; monumental.

memorize ▶ verb COMMIT TO MEMORY, remember, learn by heart, get off by heart, learn, learn by rote, become word-perfect in, get off pat; *archaic* con.

memory ▶ noun ❶ *she is losing her memory* ABILITY TO REMEMBER, powers of recall. ❷ *happy memories of her young days* RECOLLECTION, remembrance, reminiscence; impression. ❸ *the town built a statue in memory of him* COMMEMORATION, remembrance; honour, tribute, recognition, respect. ❹ *a computer's memory* MEMORY BANK, store, cache, disk, RAM, ROM.
– RELATED TERMS mnemonic.

menace ▶ noun ❶ *an atmosphere full of menace* THREAT, ominousness, intimidation, warning, ill omen. ❷ *a menace to British society* DANGER, peril, risk, hazard, threat; jeopardy. ❸ *that child is a menace* NUISANCE, pest, annoyance, plague, torment, troublemaker, mischief-maker, thorn in someone's side/flesh.
▶ verb ❶ *the elephants are still menaced by poaching* THREATEN, be a danger to, put at risk, jeopardize, imperil. ❷ *a gang of skinheads menaced local residents* INTIMIDATE, threaten, terrorize, frighten, scare, terrify.

menacing ▶ adjective THREATENING, ominous, intimidating, frightening, terrifying, alarming, forbidding, black, thunderous, glowering, unfriendly, hostile, sinister, baleful, warning; *formal* minatory.
– OPPOSITES friendly.

mend ▶ verb ❶ *workmen were mending faulty cabling* REPAIR, fix, put back together, piece together, restore; sew (up), stitch, darn, patch, cobble; rehabilitate, renew, renovate; *informal* patch up. ❷ *'How's Walter?' 'He'll mend.'* GET BETTER, get well, recover, recuperate, improve; be well, be cured, heal. ❸ *quarrels could be mended by talking* PUT/SET RIGHT, set straight, straighten out, sort out, rectify, remedy, cure, right, resolve, square, settle, put to rights, correct, retrieve, improve, make better. ❹ *he mended the fire* STOKE (UP), make up, add fuel to.
– OPPOSITES break, worsen.

mendacious ▶ adjective LYING, untruthful, dishonest, deceitful, false, dissembling, insincere, disingenuous, hypocritical, fraudulent, double-dealing, two-faced, two-timing, duplicitous, perjured; untrue, fictitious, falsified, fabricated, fallacious, invented, made up; *euphemistic* economical with the truth; *poetic/literary* perfidious.
– OPPOSITES truthful.

mendicant ▶ noun BEGGAR, tramp, vagrant, vagabond; *N. Amer.* hobo; *informal* scrounger, sponger; *N. Amer. informal* bum, mooch, moocher, schnorrer.

menial ▶ adjective *a menial job* UNSKILLED, lowly, humble, low-grade, low-status, inferior, degrading; routine, humdrum, boring, dull.
▶ noun *they were treated like menials* SERVANT, drudge, minion, factotum, lackey; *informal* wage slave, gofer; *Brit. informal* dogsbody, skivvy; *N. Amer. informal* peon; *archaic* scullion.

menstruation ▶ noun PERIODS, menses, menorrhoea, menstrual cycle; menarche; *informal* the curse, monthlies, one's/the time of the month.

mensuration ▶ noun MEASUREMENT, measuring, calculation, computation, quantification.

mental ▶ adjective ❶ *mental faculties* INTELLECTUAL, cerebral, brain, rational, cognitive. ❷ *a mental disorder* PSYCHIATRIC, psychological, psychogenic. ❸ (*informal*) *he's completely mental. See* MAD sense 1.
– OPPOSITES physical.

mentality ▶ noun ❶ *I can't understand the mentality of these people* WAY OF THINKING, mind set, cast of mind, frame of mind, turn of mind, mind, psychology, mental attitude, outlook, disposition, make-up. ❷ *a person of limited mentality* INTELLECT, intellectual capabilities, intelligence, IQ, (powers of) reasoning, rationality.

mentally ▶ adverb IN ONE'S MIND, in one's head, inwardly, intellectually, cognitively.

mention ▶ verb ❶ *don't mention the war* ALLUDE TO, refer to, touch on/upon; bring up, raise, broach, introduce, moot. ❷ *Jim mentioned that he'd met them before* STATE, say, indicate, let someone know, disclose, divulge, reveal. ❸ *I'll gladly mention your work to my friends* RECOMMEND, commend, put in a good word for, speak well of.
▶ noun ❶ *he made no mention of your request* REFERENCE, allusion, remark, statement, announcement, indication. ❷ *a mention in dispatches* TRIBUTE, citation, acknowledgement, recognition. ❸ *my book got a mention on the show* RECOMMENDATION, commendation, a good word.
■ **don't mention it** DON'T APOLOGIZE, it doesn't matter, it makes no difference/odds, it's not important, never mind, don't worry.
■ **not to mention** IN ADDITION TO, as well as; not counting, not including, to say nothing of, aside from, besides.

mentor ▶ noun ❶ *his political mentors* ADVISER, guide, guru, counsellor, consultant; confidant(e). ❷ *regular meetings between mentor and trainee* TRAINER, teacher, tutor, instructor.

menu ▶ **noun** BILL OF FARE, carte du jour, set menu, table d'hôte.

mephitic ▶ **adjective** (*poetic/literary*). *See* MALODOROUS.

mercantile ▶ **adjective** COMMERCIAL, trade, trading, business, merchant, sales.

mercenary ▶ **adjective** ❶ *mercenary self-interest* MONEY-ORIENTED, grasping, greedy, acquisitive, avaricious, covetous, bribable, venal, materialistic; *informal* money-grubbing. ❷ *mercenary soldiers* HIRED, paid, bought, professional.
▶ **noun** *a group of mercenaries* SOLDIER OF FORTUNE, professional soldier, hired soldier; *informal* hired gun; *historical* freelance, condottiere.

merchandise ▶ **noun** *a wide range of merchandise* GOODS, wares, stock, commodities, lines, produce, products.
▶ **verb** *a new product that can be easily merchandised* PROMOTE, market, sell, retail; advertise, publicize, push; *informal* hype (up), plug.

merchant ▶ **noun** TRADER, dealer, wholesaler, broker, agent, seller, buyer, buyer and seller, vendor, distributor.

merciful ▶ **adjective** ❶ *God is merciful* FORGIVING, compassionate, clement, pitying, forbearing, lenient, humane, mild, kind, soft-hearted, tender-hearted, gracious, sympathetic, humanitarian, liberal, tolerant, indulgent, generous, magnanimous, benign, benevolent. ❷ *a merciful silence fell* WELCOME, blessed.
–OPPOSITES cruel.
■ **be merciful to** HAVE MERCY ON, have pity on, show mercy to, spare, pardon, forgive, be lenient on/to; *informal* go/be easy on, let off.

mercifully ▶ **adverb** LUCKILY, fortunately, happily, thank goodness/God/heavens.

merciless ▶ **adjective** RUTHLESS, remorseless, pitiless, unforgiving, unsparing, implacable, inexorable, relentless, inflexible, inhumane, inhuman, unsympathetic, unfeeling, intolerant, rigid, severe, cold-blooded, hard-hearted, stony-hearted, heartless, harsh, callous, cruel, brutal, barbarous, cut-throat.
–OPPOSITES compassionate.

mercurial ▶ **adjective** VOLATILE, capricious, temperamental, excitable, fickle, changeable, unpredictable, variable, protean, mutable, erratic, quicksilver, inconstant, inconsistent, unstable, unsteady, fluctuating, ever-changing, moody, flighty, wayward, whimsical, impulsive; *technical* labile.
–OPPOSITES stable.

mercy ▶ **noun** ❶ *he showed no mercy to the others* LENIENCY, clemency, compassion, grace, pity, charity, forgiveness, forbearance, quarter, humanity; soft-heartedness, tender-heartedness, kindness, sympathy, liberality, indulgence, tolerance, generosity, magnanimity, beneficence. ❷ *we must be thankful for small mercies* BLESSING, godsend, boon, favour, piece/stroke of luck.
–OPPOSITES ruthlessness, cruelty.
■ **at the mercy of** ❶ *they found themselves at the mercy of the tyrant* IN THE POWER OF, under/in the control of, in the clutches of, under the heel of, subject to. ❷ *he was at the mercy of the elements* DEFENCELESS AGAINST, vulnerable to, exposed to, susceptible to, prey to, (wide) open to.

mere ▶ **adjective** NO MORE THAN, just, only, merely; no better than.

merely ▶ **adverb** ONLY, purely, solely, simply, just, but.

meretricious ▶ **adjective** WORTHLESS, valueless, cheap, tawdry, trashy, Brummagem, tasteless, kitsch; false, artificial, fake, imitation; *informal* tacky.

merge ▶ **verb** ❶ *the company merged with a European firm* JOIN (TOGETHER), join forces, amalgamate, unite, affiliate, team up, link (up). ❷ *the two organizations were merged* AMALGAMATE, bring together, join, consolidate, conflate, unite, unify, combine, incorporate, integrate, link (up), knit, yoke. ❸ *the two colours merged* MINGLE, blend, fuse, mix, intermix, intermingle, coalesce; *poetic/literary* commingle.
–OPPOSITES separate.

merger ▶ **noun** AMALGAMATION, combination, union, fusion, coalition, affiliation, unification, incorporation, consolidation, link-up, alliance.
–OPPOSITES split.

merit ▶ **noun** ❶ *composers of outstanding merit* EXCELLENCE, quality, calibre, worth, worthiness, credit, value, distinction, eminence. ❷ *the merits of the scheme* GOOD POINT, strong point, advantage, benefit, value, asset, plus.
–OPPOSITES inferiority, fault, disadvantage.
▶ **verb** *the accusation did not merit a response* DESERVE, earn, be deserving of, warrant, rate, justify, be worthy of, be worth, be entitled to, have a right to, have a claim to/on.

meritorious ▶ **adjective** PRAISEWORTHY, laudable, commendable, admirable, estimable, creditable, worthy, deserving, excellent, exemplary, good.
–OPPOSITES discreditable.

merriment ▶ **noun** HIGH SPIRITS, high-spiritedness, exuberance, cheerfulness, gaiety, fun, effervescence, verve, buoyancy, levity, zest, liveliness, cheer, joy, joyfulness, joyousness, jolliness, jollity, happiness, gladness, jocularity, conviviality, festivity, merrymaking, revelry, mirth, glee, gleefulness, laughter, hilarity, light-heartedness, amusement, pleasure.
–OPPOSITES misery.

merry ▶ **adjective** ❶ *merry throngs of students* CHEERFUL, cheery, in high spirits, high-spirited, bright, sunny, smiling, light-hearted, buoyant, lively, carefree, without a care in the world, joyful, joyous, jolly, convivial, festive, mirthful, gleeful, happy, glad, laughing; *informal*

chirpy; *formal* jocund; *dated* gay; *poetic/literary* blithe, blithesome. ❷ (*Brit. informal*) *after three beers he began to feel quite merry* TIPSY, mellow, slightly drunk; *Brit. informal* tiddly, squiffy.
– OPPOSITES miserable.
■ **make merry** HAVE FUN, have a good time, enjoy oneself, have a party, celebrate, carouse, feast, {eat, drink, and be merry}, revel, roister; *informal* party, have a ball.

merry-go-round ▶ noun CAROUSEL; *Brit.* roundabout.

mesh ▶ noun ❶ *wire mesh* NETTING, net, network; web, webbing, lattice, latticework. ❷ *a mesh of political intrigue* ENTANGLEMENT, net, tangle, web.
▶ verb ❶ *one gear meshes with the input gear* ENGAGE, connect, lock, interlock. ❷ *don't get meshed in the weeds* ENTANGLE, enmesh, snare, trap, catch. ❸ *our ideas just do not mesh* HARMONIZE, fit together, match, dovetail.

mesmerize ▶ verb ENTHRAL, spellbind, entrance, dazzle, bewitch, charm, captivate, enchant, fascinate, transfix, grip, hypnotize.

mess ▶ noun ❶ *please clear up the mess* UNTIDINESS, disorder, disarray, clutter, shambles, jumble, muddle, chaos; *Brit. informal* tip. ❷ *cat mess* EXCREMENT, muck, faeces, excreta. ❸ *I've got to get out of this mess* PLIGHT, predicament, tight spot/corner, difficulty, trouble, quandary, dilemma, problem, muddle, mix-up, imbroglio; *informal* jam, fix, pickle, stew, hole, scrape. ❹ *he made a mess of the project* MUDDLE, bungle; *informal* botch, hash, foul-up; *Brit. informal* cock-up; *N. Amer. informal* snafu.
■ **make a mess of** MISMANAGE, mishandle, bungle, fluff, spoil, ruin, wreck; *informal* mess up, botch, make a hash of, muck up, foul up; *Brit. informal* make a pig's ear of, make a Horlicks of, cock up.
■ **mess about/around** POTTER ABOUT, pass the time, fiddle about/around, footle about/around, play about/around, fool about/around; fidget, toy, trifle, tamper, tinker, interfere, meddle, monkey (about/around); *informal* piddle about/around; *Brit. informal* muck about/around, lark (about/around).
■ **mess something up** ❶ *he messed up my kitchen* DIRTY; clutter up, disarrange, jumble, dishevel, rumple; *N. Amer. informal* muss up; *poetic/literary* befoul. ❷ (*informal*) *Eddie messed things up. See* MAKE A MESS OF.

message ▶ noun ❶ *are there any messages for me?* COMMUNICATION, piece of information, news, note, memorandum, memo, e-mail, letter, missive, report, bulletin, communiqué, dispatch. ❷ *the message of his teaching* MEANING, sense, import, idea; point, thrust, gist, essence, content, subject (matter), substance, implication, drift, lesson.
■ **get the message** (*informal*) UNDERSTAND, get the point, comprehend; *informal* catch on, latch on, get the picture.

messenger ▶ noun MESSAGE-BEARER, postman, courier, runner, dispatch rider, envoy, emissary, agent, go-between; *historical* herald; *archaic* legate.

messy ▶ adjective ❶ *messy oil spills | messy hair* DIRTY, filthy, grubby, soiled, grimy; mucky, muddy, slimy, sticky, sullied, spotted, stained, smeared, smudged; dishevelled, scruffy, unkempt, rumpled, matted, tousled, bedraggled, tangled; *informal* yucky; *Brit. informal* gungy. ❷ *a messy kitchen* DISORDERLY, disordered, in a muddle, chaotic, confused, disorganized, in disarray, disarranged; untidy, cluttered, in a jumble; *informal* like a bomb's hit it; *Brit. informal* shambolic. ❸ *a messy legal battle* COMPLEX, intricate, tangled, confused, convoluted; unpleasant, nasty, bitter, acrimonious.
– OPPOSITES clean, tidy.

metallic ▶ adjective ❶ *a metallic sound* TINNY, jangling, jingling; grating, harsh, jarring, dissonant. ❷ *metallic paint* METALLIZED, burnished; shiny, glossy, lustrous.

metamorphose ▶ verb TRANSFORM, change, mutate, transmute, transfigure, convert, alter, modify, remodel, recast, reconstruct; *humorous* transmogrify; *formal* transubstantiate.

metamorphosis ▶ noun TRANSFORMATION, mutation, transmutation, change, alteration, conversion, modification, remodelling, reconstruction; *humorous* transmogrification; *formal* transubstantiation.

metaphor ▶ noun FIGURE OF SPEECH, image, trope, analogy, comparison, symbol, word painting/picture.

metaphorical ▶ adjective FIGURATIVE, allegorical, symbolic; imaginative, extended.
– OPPOSITES literal.

metaphysical ▶ adjective ❶ *metaphysical questions* ABSTRACT, theoretical, conceptual, notional, philosophical, speculative, intellectual, academic. ❷ *Good and Evil are inextricably linked in a metaphysical battle* TRANSCENDENTAL, spiritual, supernatural, paranormal.

mete
■ **mete something out** DISPENSE, hand out, allocate, allot, apportion, issue, deal out, dole out, dish out, assign, administer.

meteor ▶ noun FALLING STAR, shooting star, meteorite, meteoroid, bolide.

meteoric ▶ adjective RAPID, lightning, swift, fast, quick, speedy, accelerated, instant, sudden, spectacular.
– OPPOSITES gradual.

meteorologist ▶ noun WEATHER FORECASTER, met officer, weatherman, weatherwoman.

method ▶ noun ❶ *they use very old-fashioned methods* PROCEDURE, technique, system, practice, routine, modus operandi, process; strategy, tactic, plan. ❷ *there's method in his madness*

ORDER, orderliness, organization, structure, form, system, logic, planning, design.
– OPPOSITES disorder.

methodical ▶ adjective ORDERLY, well ordered, well organized, (well) planned, efficient, businesslike, systematic, structured, logical, analytic, disciplined; meticulous, punctilious.

meticulous ▶ adjective CAREFUL, conscientious, diligent, scrupulous, punctilious, painstaking, accurate; thorough, studious, rigorous, detailed, perfectionist, fastidious, methodical, particular.
– OPPOSITES careless.

métier ▶ noun ❶ *he had another métier besides the priesthood* OCCUPATION, job, work, profession, business, employment, career, vocation, trade, craft, line (of work); *N. Amer.* specialty. ❷ *television is more my métier* FORTE, strong point, strength, speciality, talent, bent; *informal* thing, cup of tea.

metropolis ▶ noun CAPITAL (CITY), chief town, county town; big city, conurbation, megalopolis; *informal* big smoke; *archaic* wen.

mettle ▶ noun ❶ *a man of mettle* SPIRIT, fortitude, strength of character, moral fibre, steel, determination, resolve, resolution, backbone, grit, courage, courageousness, bravery, valour, fearlessness, daring; *informal* guts, spunk; *Brit. informal* bottle. ❷ *Frazer was of a very different mettle* CALIBRE, character, disposition, nature, temperament, personality, make-up, stamp.

mettlesome ▶ adjective SPIRITED, game, gritty, intrepid, fearless, courageous, brave, plucky, daring; tenacious, determined, resolved, resolute, indomitable.

mew ▶ verb ❶ *the cat mewed plaintively* MIAOW, mewl, cry. ❷ *above them, seagulls mewed* CRY, screech.

mewl ▶ verb WHIMPER, cry, whine; *informal* grizzle; *poetic/literary* pule.

miasma ▶ noun (*poetic/literary*) STINK, reek, stench, smell, odour, malodour; *Brit. informal* pong, niff, whiff.

miasmic, miasmal ▶ adjective (*poetic/literary*) FOUL-SMELLING, fetid, smelly, stinking (to high heaven), reeking, rank, noxious, malodorous; *Brit. informal* niffy, pongy, whiffy; *poetic/literary* noisome, mephitic.

microbe ▶ noun MICRO-ORGANISM, bacillus, bacterium, virus, germ; *informal* bug.

microscopic ▶ adjective TINY, very small, minute, infinitesimal, minuscule; little, micro, diminutive; *Scottish* wee; *informal* teeny, weeny, teensy-weensy, itsy-bitsy, eensy-weensy; *Brit. informal* titchy, tiddly.
– OPPOSITES huge.

midday ▶ noun NOON, twelve noon, high noon, noontide, noonday.
– OPPOSITES midnight.

middle ▶ noun ❶ *a shallow dish with a spike in the middle* CENTRE, midpoint, halfway point, dead centre, focus, hub; eye, heart, core, kernel. ❷ *he had a towel round his middle* MIDRIFF, waist, belly, stomach; *informal* tummy, tum.
– OPPOSITES outside.
▶ adjective ❶ *the middle point* CENTRAL, mid, mean, medium, medial, median, midway, halfway. ❷ *the middle level* INTERMEDIATE, intermediary.
– RELATED TERMS meso-.

middleman ▶ noun INTERMEDIARY, go-between; dealer, broker, agent, factor, wholesaler, distributor.

middling ▶ adjective AVERAGE, standard, normal, middle-of-the-road; moderate, ordinary, commonplace, everyday, workaday, tolerable, passable; run-of-the-mill, fair, mediocre, undistinguished, unexceptional, unremarkable; *informal* OK, so-so, bog-standard, fair-to-middling, (plain) vanilla; *NZ informal* half-pie.

midget ▶ noun *the inhabitants must have been midgets* SMALL PERSON, dwarf, homunculus, Lilliputian, manikin, gnome, pygmy; *informal* shrimp.
▶ adjective ❶ *a story about midget matadors* DIMINUTIVE, dwarfish, petite, very small, pygmy; *informal* pint-sized; *N. Amer. informal* sawn-off. ❷ *a midget camera* MINIATURE, pocket, dwarf, baby.
– OPPOSITES giant.

midnight ▶ noun TWELVE MIDNIGHT, the middle of the night, the witching hour.
– OPPOSITES midday.

midst (*poetic/literary*) ▶ noun MIDDLE, centre, heart, core, midpoint, kernel, nub; depth(s), thick; (**in the midst of**) in the course of, halfway through, at the heart/core of.
■ **in our midst** AMONG US, amid us, in our group, with us.

midway ▶ adverb HALFWAY, in the middle, at the midpoint, in the centre; part-way, at some point.

mien ▶ noun APPEARANCE, look, expression, countenance, aura, demeanour, attitude, air, manner, bearing; *formal* comportment.

miffed ▶ adjective (*informal*). *See* ANNOYED.

might ▶ noun STRENGTH, force, power, vigour, energy, brawn, powerfulness, forcefulness.
■ **with might and main** WITH ALL ONE'S STRENGTH, as hard as one can, as hard as possible, (with) full force, forcefully, powerfully, strongly, vigorously.

mightily ▶ adverb ❶ *he is mightily impressive* EXTREMELY, exceedingly, enormously, immensely, tremendously, hugely, dreadfully, very (much); *informal* awfully, majorly, mega; *N. Amer. informal* mighty, plumb; *informal, dated* devilish. ❷ *Ann and I laboured mightily* STRENUOUSLY, energetically, powerfully, hard, with all one's might, with might and main, all out, heartily, vigorously, diligently, assiduously, persistently, indefatigably; *informal* like mad, like crazy; *Brit. informal* like billy-o.

mighty ▶ adjective ❶ *a mighty blow* POWERFUL, forceful, violent, vigorous, hefty, thunderous. ❷ *a mighty warrior* FEARSOME, ferocious; big, tough, robust, muscular, strapping. ❸ *mighty industrial countries* DOMINANT, influential, strong, powerful, important, predominant. ❹ *mighty oak trees* HUGE, enormous, massive, gigantic, big, large, giant, colossal, mammoth, immense; *informal* monster, whopping (great), thumping (great), humongous, jumbo(-sized); *Brit. informal* whacking (great), ginormous.
– OPPOSITES feeble, puny, tiny.
▶ adverb (*N. Amer. informal*) *I'm mighty pleased to see you* EXTREMELY, exceedingly, enormously, immensely, tremendously, hugely, mightily, very (much); *informal* awfully, dreadfully, majorly, mega; *Brit. informal* well, jolly; *N. Amer. informal* plumb; *informal, dated* devilish, frightfully.

migrant ▶ noun *economic migrants* IMMIGRANT, EMIGRANT; nomad, itinerant, traveller, vagrant, transient, rover, wanderer, drifter.
▶ adjective *migrant workers* TRAVELLING, wandering, drifting, nomadic, roving, roaming, itinerant, vagrant, transient.

migrate ▶ verb ❶ *rural populations migrated to urban areas* RELOCATE, resettle, move (house); emigrate, go abroad, go overseas; *N. Amer.* pull up stakes; *Brit. informal* up sticks; *dated* remove. ❷ *wildebeest migrate across the Serengeti* ROAM, wander, drift, rove, travel (around).

migratory ▶ adjective MIGRANT, migrating, moving, travelling.

mild ▶ adjective ❶ *a mild tone of voice* GENTLE, tender, soft-hearted, tender-hearted, sensitive, sympathetic, warm, placid, calm, tranquil, serene, peaceable, good-natured, amiable, affable, genial, easy-going. ❷ *a mild punishment* LENIENT, light, compassionate, merciful, humane. ❸ *he was eyeing her with mild interest* SLIGHT, faint, vague, minimal, nominal, token, feeble. ❹ *mild weather* WARM, balmy, temperate, clement. ❺ *a mild curry* BLAND, insipid.
– OPPOSITES harsh, strong, severe.

mildewy ▶ adjective MOULDY, mildewed, rotten, decaying.

milieu ▶ noun ENVIRONMENT, sphere, background, backdrop, setting, context, atmosphere; location, conditions, surroundings, environs.

militant ▶ adjective *militant supporters* AGGRESSIVE, violent, belligerent, bellicose, vigorous, forceful, active, fierce, combative, pugnacious; radical, extremist, extreme, zealous, fanatical.
▶ noun *the demands of the militants* ACTIVIST, extremist, radical, young turk, zealot.

militaristic ▶ adjective WARMONGERING, warlike, martial, hawkish, pugnacious, combative, aggressive, belligerent, bellicose; *informal* gung-ho.
– OPPOSITES peaceable.

military ▶ adjective *military activity* FIGHTING, service, army, armed, defence, martial.
– OPPOSITES civilian.
▶ noun *the military took power* (ARMED) FORCES, services, militia; army, navy, air force, marines.

militate ▶ verb TEND TO PREVENT, work against, hinder, discourage, prejudice, be detrimental to.

milk ▶ verb ❶ *Pam was milking the cows* DRAW MILK FROM, express milk from. ❷ *milk a little of the liquid* DRAW OFF, siphon (off), pump off, tap, drain, extract. ❸ *milking rich clients* EXPLOIT, take advantage of, cash in on, suck dry; *informal* bleed, squeeze, fleece.
– RELATED TERMS dairy, lactic.

milksop ▶ noun NAMBY-PAMBY, coward, weakling; *informal* drip, mummy's boy, sissy, jellyfish, wimp; *Brit. informal* wet, big girl's blouse; *N. Amer. informal* pantywaist, pussy; *archaic* poltroon.

milky ▶ adjective PALE, white, milk-white, whitish, off-white, cream, creamy, chalky, pearly, nacreous, ivory, alabaster.
– OPPOSITES swarthy.

mill ▶ noun ❶ *a steel mill* FACTORY, (processing) plant, works, workshop, shop, foundry, industrial unit. ❷ *a pepper mill* GRINDER, quern, crusher.
▶ verb *the wheat is milled into flour* GRIND, pulverize, powder, granulate, pound, crush, press; *technical* comminute, triturate; *archaic* bray, levigate.
■ **mill around/about** THRONG, swarm, seethe, crowd.

millstone ▶ noun BURDEN, encumbrance, dead weight, cross to bear, albatross; duty, obligation, liability, misfortune; *archaic* cumber.

mime ▶ noun *a mime of someone fencing* DUMB SHOW, pantomime.
▶ verb *she mimed picking up a phone* ACT OUT, pantomime, gesture, simulate, represent, indicate by dumb show.

mimic ▶ verb ❶ *she mimicked his accent* IMITATE, copy, impersonate, do an impression of, ape, caricature, parody, lampoon, burlesque; *informal* send up, take off, spoof; *archaic* monkey. ❷ *most hoverflies mimic wasps* RESEMBLE, look like, have the appearance of, simulate; *N. Amer. informal* make like.
▶ noun *he was a superb mimic* IMPERSONATOR, impressionist, imitator, mimicker; parodist, caricaturist, lampooner, lampoonist; *informal* copycat; *historical* zany; *archaic* ape.
▶ adjective *they were waging mimic war* SIMULATED, mock, imitation, make-believe, sham; *informal* pretend, copycat.

mimicry ▶ noun IMITATION, imitating, impersonation, copying, aping; *archaic* apery.

minatory ▶ adjective (*rare*) MENACING, threatening, baleful, intimidating, admonitory, warning, cautionary; *rare* minacious, comminatory.

mince ▶ verb ❶ *mince the meat and onions* GRIND, chop up, cut up, dice; *N. Amer.* hash. ❷ *she minced out of the room* WALK AFFECTEDLY; *N. Amer. informal* sashay.

■ **not mince (one's) words** TALK STRAIGHT, not beat about the bush, call a spade a spade, speak straight from the shoulder, pull no punches; *informal* tell it like it is; *N. Amer. informal* talk turkey.

mincing ▶ adjective AFFECTED, dainty, effeminate, niminy-piminy; pretentious; *informal* camp, sissy; *Brit. informal* poncey.

mind ▶ noun ❶ *a good teacher must stretch pupils' minds* BRAIN, intelligence, intellect, intellectual capabilities, brains, brainpower, wits, understanding, reasoning, judgement, sense, head; *informal* grey matter, brainbox, brain cells; *Brit. informal* loaf; *N. Amer. informal* smarts. ❷ *he kept his mind on the job* ATTENTION, thoughts, concentration, attentiveness. ❸ *the tragedy affected her mind* SANITY, mental faculties, senses, wits, reason, reasoning, judgement; *informal* marbles. ❹ *his words stuck in her mind* MEMORY, recollection. ❺ *a great mind* INTELLECT, thinker, brain, scholar, academic. ❻ *I've a mind to complain* INCLINATION, desire, wish, urge, notion, fancy, intention, will. ❼ *of the same mind* OPINION, way of thinking, outlook, attitude, view, viewpoint, point of view.

– RELATED TERMS mental.

▶ verb ❶ *do you mind if I smoke?* CARE, object, be bothered, be annoyed, be upset, take offence, disapprove, dislike it, look askance; *informal* give/care a damn, give/care a toss, give/care a hoot, give/care a rap. ❷ *mind the step!* BE CAREFUL OF, watch out for, look out for, beware of, be on one's guard for, be wary of. ❸ *mind you wipe your feet* BE/MAKE SURE (THAT), see (that); remember to, don't forget to. ❹ *her husband was minding the baby* LOOK AFTER, take care of, keep an eye on, attend to, care for, tend. ❺ *mind what your mother says* PAY ATTENTION TO, heed, pay heed to, attend to, take note/notice of, note, mark, listen to, be mindful of; obey, follow, comply with; *archaic* regard.

■ **be in two minds** BE UNDECIDED, be uncertain, be unsure, hesitate, waver, vacillate, dither; *Brit.* haver, hum and haw; *informal* dilly-dally, shilly-shally.

■ **bear/keep in mind** REMEMBER, note, be mindful of, take note of; *formal* take cognizance of.

■ **cross one's mind** OCCUR TO ONE, enter one's mind/head, strike one, hit one, dawn on one.

■ **give someone a piece of one's mind.** *See* REPRIMAND verb.

■ **have something in mind** THINK OF, contemplate; intend, plan, propose, desire, want, wish.

■ **mind out** TAKE CARE, be careful, watch out, look out, beware, be on one's guard, be wary.

■ **never mind** ❶ *never mind the cost* DON'T BOTHER ABOUT, don't worry about, disregard, forget. ❷ *never mind, it's all right now* DON'T APOLOGIZE, forget it, don't worry about it, it doesn't matter.

■ **out of one's mind** ❶ *you must be out of your mind! See* MAD sense 1. ❷ *I've been out of my mind with worry* FRANTIC, beside oneself, distraught, in a frenzy.

■ **put someone in mind of** REMIND OF, recall, conjure up, suggest; RESEMBLE, look like.

■ **to my mind** IN MY OPINION, in my view, as I see it, personally, in my estimation, in my book, if you ask me.

mindful ▶ adjective AWARE, conscious, sensible, alive, alert, acquainted, heedful, wary, chary; *informal* wise, hip; *formal* cognizant, regardful.

– OPPOSITES heedless.

mindless ▶ adjective ❶ *a mindless idiot* STUPID, idiotic, brainless, imbecilic, imbecile, asinine, witless, foolish, empty-headed, slow-witted, obtuse, feather-brained, doltish; *informal* dumb, pig-ignorant, brain-dead, cretinous, moronic, thick, birdbrained, pea-brained, dopey, dim, half-witted, dippy, fat-headed, boneheaded; *N. Amer. informal* chowderheaded. ❷ *mindless acts of vandalism* UNTHINKING, thoughtless, senseless, gratuitous, wanton, indiscriminate, unreasoning. ❸ *a mindless task* MECHANICAL, automatic, routine; tedious, boring, monotonous, brainless, mind-numbing.

■ **mindless of** INDIFFERENT TO, heedless of, unaware of, unmindful of, careless of, blind to.

mine ▶ noun ❶ *a coal mine* PIT, excavation, quarry, workings, diggings; strip mine; *Brit.* opencast mine; *N. Amer.* open-pit mine. ❷ *a mine of information* RICH SOURCE, repository, store, storehouse, reservoir, gold mine, treasure house, treasury, reserve, fund, wealth, stock. ❸ *he was killed by a mine* EXPLOSIVE, landmine, limpet mine, magnetic mine, depth charge.

▶ verb ❶ *the iron ore was mined from shallow pits* QUARRY, excavate, dig (up), extract, remove; strip-mine. ❷ *medical data was mined for relevant statistics* SEARCH, delve into, scour, scan, read through, survey. ❸ *the entrance to the harbour had been mined* DEFEND WITH MINES, lay with mines.

miner ▶ noun PITMAN, digger, collier, faceworker, haulier; tinner; *dated* hewer.

mingle ▶ verb ❶ *fact and fiction are skilfully mingled in his novels* MIX, blend, intermingle, intermix, interweave, interlace, combine, merge, fuse, unite, join, amalgamate, meld, mesh; *poetic/literary* commingle; *archaic* commix. ❷ *wedding guests mingled in the marquee* SOCIALIZE, circulate, fraternize, get together, associate with others; *informal* hobnob.

– OPPOSITES separate.

miniature ▶ adjective *a miniature railway* SMALL-SCALE, mini; tiny, little, small, minute,

baby, toy, pocket, dwarf, pygmy, minuscule, diminutive; *Scottish* wee; *N. Amer.* vest-pocket; *informal* teeny, teeny-weeny, teensy, teensy-weensy, itsy-bitsy, eensy, eensy-weensy; *Brit. informal* titchy, tiddly.
– OPPOSITES giant.

minimal ▶ **adjective** VERY LITTLE, minimum, the least (possible); nominal, token, negligible.
– OPPOSITES maximum.

minimize ▶ **verb** ❶ *the aim is to minimize costs* KEEP DOWN, keep at/to a minimum, reduce, decrease, cut down, lessen, curtail, diminish, prune; *informal* slash. ❷ *we should not minimize his contribution* BELITTLE, make light of, play down, underestimate, underrate, downplay, undervalue, understate; *informal* pooh-pooh; *archaic* hold cheap; *rare* misprize.
– OPPOSITES maximize, exaggerate.

minimum ▶ **noun** *costs will be kept to the minimum* LOWEST LEVEL, lower limit, bottom level, rock bottom; least, lowest, slightest.
– OPPOSITES maximum.
▶ **adjective** *the minimum amount of effort* MINIMAL, least, smallest, least possible, slightest, lowest, minutest.

minion ▶ **noun** UNDERLING, henchman, flunkey, lackey, hanger-on, follower, servant, hireling, vassal, stooge; *informal* yes-man, bootlicker; *Brit. informal* poodle; *N. Amer. informal* suck-up.

minister ▶ **noun** ❶ *a government minister* MEMBER OF THE GOVERNMENT, cabinet minister, secretary of state, undersecretary. ❷ *a minister of religion* CLERGYMAN, clergywoman, cleric, ecclesiastic, pastor, vicar, rector, priest, parson, father, man/woman of the cloth, man/woman of God, churchman, churchwoman; curate, chaplain; *informal* reverend, padre, Holy Joe, sky pilot; *Austral. informal* josser. ❸ *the British minister in Egypt* AMBASSADOR, chargé d'affaires, plenipotentiary, envoy, emissary, diplomat, consul, representative; *archaic* legate.
▶ **verb** *doctors were ministering to the injured* TEND, care for, take care of, look after, nurse, treat, attend to, see to, administer to, help, assist.

ministrations ▶ **plural noun** ATTENTION, treatment, help, assistance, aid, care, services.

ministry ▶ **noun** ❶ *the ministry for foreign affairs* (GOVERNMENT) DEPARTMENT, bureau, agency, office. ❷ *he's training for the ministry* HOLY ORDERS, the priesthood, the cloth, the church. ❸ *the ministry of Jesus* TEACHING, preaching, evangelism. ❹ *Gladstone's first ministry* PERIOD OF OFFICE, term (of office), administration.

minor ▶ **adjective** ❶ *a minor problem* SLIGHT, small; unimportant, insignificant, inconsequential, inconsiderable, subsidiary, negligible, trivial, trifling, paltry, petty; *N. Amer.* nickel-and-dime; *informal* piffling, piddling. ❷ *a minor poet* LITTLE KNOWN, unknown, lesser, unimportant, insignificant, obscure; *N. Amer.* minor-league; *informal* small-time; *N. Amer. informal* two-bit. ❸ (*Brit.*) *Smith minor* JUNIOR, younger.
– OPPOSITES major, important.
▶ **noun** *the heir to the throne was a minor* CHILD, infant, youth, adolescent, teenager, boy, girl; *informal* kid, kiddie.
– OPPOSITES adult.

minstrel ▶ **noun** (*historical*) MUSICIAN, singer, balladeer; *historical* troubadour, jongleur; *poetic/literary* bard.

mint ▶ **noun** ❶ COINAGE FACTORY, money factory. ❷ (*informal*) *the bank made a mint out of the deal* A VAST SUM OF MONEY, a king's ransom, millions, billions; *informal* a (small) fortune, a tidy sum, a bundle, a packet, a pile; *Brit. informal* a bomb, big money; *N. Amer. informal* big bucks; *Austral. informal* big bickies, motser.
▶ **adjective** *in mint condition* BRAND NEW, pristine, perfect, immaculate, unblemished, undamaged, unmarked, unused, first-class, excellent.
▶ **verb** ❶ *the shilling was minted in 1742* COIN, stamp, strike, cast, forge, manufacture. ❷ *the slogan had been freshly minted* CREATE, invent, make up, think up, dream up.

minuscule ▶ **adjective** TINY, minute, microscopic, very small, little, micro, diminutive, miniature, baby, dwarf; *Scottish* wee; *informal* teeny, teeny-weeny, teensy, teensy-weensy, itsy-bitsy, eensy, eensy-weensy, tiddly; *Brit. informal* titchy.
– OPPOSITES huge.

minute[1] ▶ **noun** ❶ *it'll only take a minute* MOMENT, short time, little while, second, bit, instant; *informal* sec, jiffy; *Brit. informal* tick, mo, two ticks. ❷ *at that minute, Tony walked in* POINT (IN TIME), moment, instant, juncture. ❸ *their objection was noted in the minutes* RECORD(S), proceedings, log, notes; transcript, summary, résumé.
■ **at the minute** (*Brit. informal*) AT PRESENT, at the moment, now, currently.
■ **in a minute** VERY SOON, in a moment/second/instant, in a trice, shortly, any minute (now), in a short time, in (less than) no time, before long; *N. Amer.* momentarily; *informal* anon, in a jiffy, in two shakes, before you can say Jack Robinson; *Brit. informal* in a tick, in a mo, in two ticks; *N. Amer. informal* in a snap; *poetic/literary* ere long.
■ **this minute** AT ONCE, immediately, directly, this second, instantly, straight away, right away/now, forthwith; *informal* pronto, straight off, right off, toot sweet; *archaic* straight.
■ **up to the minute** LATEST, newest, up to date, modern, fashionable, smart, chic, stylish, all the rage, in vogue; *informal* trendy, with it, in.
■ **wait a minute** BE PATIENT, wait a moment/second, just a moment/minute/second, hold on; *informal* hang on, hold your horses; *Brit. informal* hang about.

minute[2] ▶ **adjective** ❶ *minute particles* TINY,

minuscule, microscopic, very small, little, micro, diminutive, miniature, baby, toy, dwarf, pygmy, Lilliputian; *Scottish* wee; *informal* teeny, teeny-weeny, teensy, teensy-weensy, itsy-bitsy, eensy, eensy-weensy; *Brit. informal* titchy, tiddly. ❷ *a minute chance of success* NEGLIGIBLE, slight, infinitesimal, minimal, insignificant, inappreciable. ❸ *minute detail* EXHAUSTIVE, painstaking, meticulous, rigorous, scrupulous, punctilious, detailed.
– OPPOSITES huge.

minutely ▶ **adverb** EXHAUSTIVELY, painstakingly, meticulously, rigorously, scrupulously, punctiliously, in detail.

minutiae ▶ **plural noun** DETAILS, niceties, finer points, particulars, trivia, trivialities.

minx ▶ **noun** TEASE, seductress, coquette, slut, Lolita; *informal* floozie, tart, vamp; *Brit. informal* scrubber, slapper; *N. Amer. informal* tramp; *dated* hussy; *archaic* strumpet, trollop.

miracle ▶ **noun** ❶ *Christ's first miracle* SUPERNATURAL PHENOMENON, mystery, prodigy. ❷ *Germany's economic miracle* WONDER, marvel, sensation, phenomenon.

miraculous ▶ **adjective** ❶ *the miraculous help of St Blaise* SUPERNATURAL, preternatural, inexplicable, unaccountable, magical. ❷ *a miraculous escape* AMAZING, astounding, remarkable, extraordinary, incredible, unbelievable, sensational; *informal* mind-boggling, mind-blowing.

mirage ▶ **noun** OPTICAL ILLUSION, hallucination, phantasmagoria, apparition, fantasy, chimera, vision, figment of the imagination; *poetic/literary* phantasm.

mire ▶ **noun** ❶ *it's a mire out there* SWAMP, bog, morass, quagmire, slough; swampland, wetland, marshland. ❷ *her horse was spattered with mire* MUD, slime, dirt, filth, muck. ❸ *struggling to pull Russia out of the mire* MESS, difficulty, plight, predicament, tight spot, trouble, quandary, muddle; *informal* jam, fix, pickle, hot water.
▶ **verb** ❶ *Frank's horse got mired in a bog* BOG DOWN, sink (down). ❷ *the children were mired* DIRTY, soil, muddy; *poetic/literary* begrime. ❸ *he has become mired in lawsuits* ENTANGLE, tangle up, embroil, catch up, mix up, involve.

mirror ▶ **noun** ❶ *a quick look in the mirror* LOOKING GLASS, reflecting surface; full-length mirror, hand mirror, wing mirror, rear-view mirror; *Brit.* glass. ❷ *the Frenchman's life was a mirror of his own* REFLECTION, twin, replica, copy, match, parallel.
– RELATED TERMS catoptric, specular.
▶ **verb** *pop music mirrored the mood of desperation* REFLECT, match, reproduce, imitate, simulate, copy, mimic, echo, parallel, correspond to.

mirth ▶ **noun** MERRIMENT, high spirits, mirthfulness, cheerfulness, cheeriness, hilarity, glee, laughter, gaiety, buoyancy, blitheness, euphoria, exhilaration, light-heartedness, joviality, joy, joyfulness, joyousness.
– OPPOSITES misery.

mirthful ▶ **adjective** MERRY, high-spirited, gleeful, cheerful, cheery, jocular, buoyant, exhilarated, euphoric, elated, light-hearted, jovial, joyous, jolly, festive.

mirthless ▶ **adjective** HUMOURLESS, unamused, grim, sour, surly, dour, sullen, sulky, gloomy, mournful, melancholy, doleful, miserable, grumpy.
– OPPOSITES cheerful.

miry ▶ **adjective** MUDDY, slushy, slimy, swampy, marshy, boggy, squelchy, waterlogged.

misadventure ▶ **noun** ACCIDENT, problem, difficulty, misfortune, mishap; setback, reversal (of fortune), stroke of bad luck, blow; failure, disaster, tragedy, calamity, woe, trial, tribulation, catastrophe.

misanthrope ▶ **noun** HATER OF MANKIND, cynic; recluse, hermit; *informal* grouch, grump; *historical* anchorite.

misanthropic ▶ **adjective** ANTISOCIAL, unsociable, unfriendly, reclusive, uncongenial, cynical, jaundiced.

misapply ▶ **verb** MISUSE, mishandle, misemploy, abuse; distort, garble, warp, misinterpret, misconstrue, misrepresent.

misapprehend ▶ **verb** MISUNDERSTAND, misinterpret, misconstrue, misconceive, mistake, misread, get the wrong idea about, take something the wrong way.

misapprehension ▶ **noun** MISUNDERSTANDING, misinterpretation, misreading, misjudgement, misconception, misbelief, the wrong idea, false impression, delusion.

misappropriate ▶ **verb** EMBEZZLE, expropriate, steal, thieve, pilfer, pocket, help oneself to, make off with; *informal* swipe, filch, rip off, snitch; *Brit. informal* pinch, nick, whip, knock off; *formal* peculate.

misappropriation ▶ **noun** EMBEZZLEMENT, expropriation, stealing, theft, thieving, pilfering; *formal* peculation.

misbegotten ▶ **adjective** ❶ *a misbegotten scheme* ILL-CONCEIVED, ill-advised, badly planned, badly thought-out, hare-brained. ❷ *you misbegotten hound!* CONTEMPTIBLE, despicable, wretched, miserable, confounded; *informal* infernal, damned, flaming; *dated* cursed, accursed. ❸ (*archaic*) *poor misbegotten children. See* ILLEGITIMATE sense 2.

misbehave ▶ **verb** BEHAVE BADLY, be misbehaved, be naughty, be disobedient, get up to mischief, get up to no good; be bad-mannered, be rude; *informal* carry on, act up.

misbehaviour ▶ **noun** BAD BEHAVIOUR, misconduct, naughtiness, disobedience, mischief, mischievousness; bad/poor manners, rudeness; *informal* acting-up.

misbelief ▶ noun FALSE BELIEF, delusion, illusion, fallacy, error, mistake, misconception, misapprehension.

miscalculate ▶ verb MISJUDGE, make a mistake (about), calculate wrongly, estimate wrongly, overestimate, underestimate, overvalue, undervalue; go wrong, err, be wide of the mark.

miscalculation ▶ noun ERROR OF JUDGEMENT, misjudgement, mistake, overestimate, underestimate.

miscarriage ▶ noun ❶ *she's had a miscarriage* (SPONTANEOUS) ABORTION, stillbirth. ❷ *the miscarriage of the project* FAILURE, foundering, ruin, ruination, collapse, breakdown, thwarting, frustration, undoing, non-fulfilment, mismanagement.

miscarry ▶ verb ❶ *the shock caused her to miscarry* LOSE ONE'S BABY, have a miscarriage, abort, have a (spontaneous) abortion. ❷ *our plan miscarried* GO WRONG, go awry, go amiss, be unsuccessful, be ruined, fail, misfire, abort, founder, come to nothing, fall through, fall flat; *informal* flop, go up in smoke.
– OPPOSITES succeed.

miscellaneous ▶ adjective VARIOUS, varied, different, assorted, mixed, sundry, diverse, disparate; diversified, motley, multifarious, heterogeneous; *poetic/literary* divers.

miscellany ▶ noun ASSORTMENT, mixture, melange, blend, variety, mixed bag, mix, medley, diversity, collection, selection, assemblage, pot-pourri, mishmash, hotchpotch, ragbag, salmagundi, gallimaufry, omnium gatherum; *N. Amer.* hodgepodge.

mischance ▶ noun ACCIDENT, misfortune, mishap, misadventure, setback, disaster, tragedy, calamity, catastrophe, reversal, upset, blow; bad luck, ill fortune.

mischief ▶ noun ❶ *the boys are always getting up to mischief* NAUGHTINESS, bad behaviour, misbehaviour, mischievousness, misconduct, disobedience; pranks, tricks, larks, capers, nonsense, devilry, funny business; *informal* monkey business, shenanigans, hanky-panky; *Brit. informal* monkey tricks, carryings-on, jiggery-pokery. ❷ *the mischief in her eyes* IMPISHNESS, roguishness, devilment. ❸ (*informal*) *you'll do yourself a mischief* HARM, hurt, injury, damage.

mischievous ▶ adjective ❶ *a mischievous child* NAUGHTY, badly behaved, misbehaving, disobedient, troublesome, full of mischief; rascally, roguish. ❷ *a mischievous smile* PLAYFUL, teasing, wicked, impish, roguish, arch. ❸ *a mischievous allegation* MALICIOUS, malevolent, spiteful, venomous, poisonous, evil-intentioned, evil, baleful, vindictive, vengeful, vitriolic, rancorous, malign, malignant, pernicious, mean, nasty, harmful, hurtful, cruel, unkind; *informal* bitchy, catty; *poetic/literary* malefic, maleficent.
– OPPOSITES well behaved.

misconceive ▶ verb MISUNDERSTAND, misinterpret, misconstrue, misapprehend, mistake, misread; miscalculate, err, be mistaken, get the wrong idea.

misconception ▶ noun MISAPPREHENSION, misunderstanding, mistake, error, misinterpretation, misconstruction, misreading, misjudgement, misbelief, miscalculation, false impression, illusion, fallacy, delusion.

misconduct ▶ noun ❶ *allegations of misconduct* WRONGDOING, unlawfulness, lawlessness, crime, felony, criminality, sin, sinfulness; unprofessionalism, unethical behaviour, malpractice, negligence, impropriety; *formal* maladministration, malversation. ❷ *misconduct in the classroom* MISBEHAVIOUR, bad behaviour, misdeeds, misdemeanours, disorderly conduct, mischief, naughtiness, rudeness.

misconstruction ▶ noun MISUNDERSTANDING, misinterpretation, misapprehension, misconception, misreading, misjudgement, misbelief, miscalculation, false impression.

misconstrue ▶ verb MISUNDERSTAND, misinterpret, misconceive, misapprehend, mistake, misread; be mistaken about, get the wrong idea about, get it/someone wrong.

miscreant ▶ noun CRIMINAL, culprit, wrongdoer, malefactor, offender, villain, lawbreaker, evil-doer, delinquent, reprobate; *Law* malfeasant.

misdeed ▶ noun WRONGDOING, wrong, evil deed, crime, felony, misdemeanour, misconduct, offence, error, transgression, sin; *archaic* trespass.

misdemeanour ▶ noun WRONGDOING, evil deed, crime, felony; misdeed, misconduct, offence, error, peccadillo, transgression, sin; *archaic* trespass.

miser ▶ noun PENNY-PINCHER, pinchpenny, niggard, cheese-parer, Scrooge; *informal* skinflint, meanie, money-grubber, cheapskate; *N. Amer. informal* tightwad.
– OPPOSITES spendthrift.

miserable ▶ adjective ❶ *I'm too miserable to eat* UNHAPPY, sad, sorrowful, dejected, depressed, downcast, downhearted, down, despondent, disconsolate, wretched, glum, gloomy, dismal, melancholy, woebegone, doleful, forlorn, heartbroken; *informal* blue, down in the mouth/dumps. ❷ *their miserable surroundings* DREARY, dismal, gloomy, drab, wretched, depressing, grim, cheerless, bleak, desolate; poor, shabby, squalid, seedy, dilapidated. ❸ *miserable weather* UNPLEASANT, disagreeable, depressing; wet, rainy, stormy; *informal* rotten. ❹ *a miserable old grouch* GRUMPY, sullen, gloomy, bad-tempered, ill-tempered, dour, surly, sour, glum, moody, unsociable, saturnine, lugubrious, irritable, churlish, cantankerous, crotchety, cross, crabby, grouchy, testy, peevish, crusty, waspish. ❺ *miserable*

wages INADEQUATE, meagre, scanty, paltry, small, poor, pitiful, niggardly; *informal* measly, stingy, pathetic; *formal* exiguous. ❻ *all that fuss about a few miserable pounds* WRETCHED, confounded; *informal* blithering, flaming, blessed, damned, blasted; *dated* accursed.
– OPPOSITES cheerful, lovely.

miserliness ▶ noun MEANNESS, niggardliness, close-fistedness, closeness, parsimony, parsimoniousness; *informal* stinginess, tight-fistedness; *N. Amer.* cheapness; *archaic* nearness.

miserly ▶ adjective ❶ *his miserly great-uncle* MEAN, niggardly, parsimonious, close, close-fisted, penny-pinching, cheese-paring, grasping, Scrooge-like; *informal* stingy, tight, tight-fisted; *N. Amer. informal* cheap; *archaic* near. ❷ *the prize is a miserly £300* MEAGRE, inadequate, paltry, negligible, miserable, pitiful, niggardly, beggarly; *informal* measly, stingy, pathetic; *formal* exiguous.
– OPPOSITES generous.

misery ▶ noun ❶ *periods of intense misery* UNHAPPINESS, distress, wretchedness, suffering, anguish, anxiety, angst, torment, pain, grief, heartache, heartbreak, despair, despondency, dejection, depression, desolation, gloom, melancholy, melancholia, woe, sadness, sorrow; *informal* the dumps, the blues; *poetic/literary* dolour. ❷ *the miseries of war* AFFLICTION, misfortune, difficulty, problem, ordeal, trouble, hardship, deprivation; pain, sorrow, trial, tribulation, woe. ❸ (*Brit. informal*) *he's a real old misery* KILLJOY, dog in the manger, spoilsport; *informal* sourpuss, grouch, grump, party-pooper.
– OPPOSITES contentment, pleasure.

misfire ▶ verb GO WRONG, go awry, be unsuccessful, fail, founder, fall through/flat; backfire; *informal* flop, go up in smoke.

misfit ▶ noun NONCONFORMIST, eccentric, maverick, individualist, square peg in a round hole; *informal* oddball, weirdo, freak; *N. Amer. informal* screwball.

misfortune ▶ noun PROBLEM, difficulty, setback, trouble, adversity, stroke of bad luck, reversal (of fortune), misadventure, mishap, blow, failure, accident, disaster; sorrow, misery, woe, trial, tribulation.

misgiving ▶ noun QUALM, doubt, reservation; suspicion, distrust, mistrust, lack of confidence, second thoughts; trepidation, scepticism, unease, uneasiness, anxiety, apprehension, disquiet.

misguided ▶ adjective ❶ *the policy is misguided* ERRONEOUS, fallacious, unsound, misplaced, misconceived, ill-advised, ill-considered, ill-judged, inappropriate, unwise, injudicious, imprudent. ❷ *you are quite misguided* MISINFORMED, misled, labouring under a misapprehension, wrong, mistaken, deluded.

mishandle ▶ verb ❶ *the officer mishandled the situation* BUNGLE, fluff, make a mess of, mismanage, spoil, ruin, wreck; *informal* botch, make a hash of, mess up, muck up; *Brit. informal* make a pig's ear of, make a Horlicks of. ❷ *he mishandled his wife* BULLY, persecute, ill-treat, mistreat, maltreat, abuse, knock about/around, hit, beat; *informal* beat up. ❸ *the equipment could be dangerous if mishandled* MISUSE, abuse, handle/treat roughly.

mishap ▶ noun ACCIDENT, trouble, problem, difficulty, setback, adversity, reversal (of fortune), misfortune, blow; failure, disaster, tragedy, catastrophe, calamity.

mishmash ▶ noun JUMBLE, confusion, hotchpotch, ragbag, patchwork, farrago, assortment, medley, miscellany, mixture, melange, blend, mix, pot-pourri, conglomeration, gallimaufry, omnium gatherum, salmagundi; *N. Amer.* hodgepodge.

misinform ▶ verb MISLEAD, misguide, give wrong information, delude, take in, deceive, lie to, hoodwink; *informal* lead up the garden path, take for a ride; *N. Amer. informal* give someone a bum steer.

misinformation ▶ noun DISINFORMATION, false/misleading information; lie, fib; *N. Amer. informal* bum steer.

misinterpret ▶ verb MISUNDERSTAND, misconceive, misconstrue, misapprehend, mistake, misread; confuse, take amiss, be mistaken, get the wrong idea.

misjudge ▶ verb GET THE WRONG IDEA ABOUT, get wrong, judge incorrectly, estimate wrongly, be wrong about, miscalculate, misread; overestimate, underestimate, overvalue, undervalue, underrate.

mislay ▶ verb LOSE, misplace, put in the wrong place, be unable to find, forget the whereabouts of.
– OPPOSITES find.

mislead ▶ verb DECEIVE, delude, take in, lie to, fool, hoodwink, throw off the scent, pull the wool over someone's eyes, misguide, misinform, give wrong information to; *informal* lead up the garden path, take for a ride; *N. Amer. informal* give someone a bum steer.

misleading ▶ adjective DECEPTIVE, confusing, deceiving, equivocal, ambiguous, fallacious, specious, spurious, false.

mismanage ▶ verb BUNGLE, fluff, make a mess of, mishandle, misconduct, spoil, ruin, wreck; *informal* botch, make a hash of, mess up, muck up; *Brit. informal* make a pig's ear of, make a Horlicks of.

mismatch ▶ noun DISCREPANCY, inconsistency, contradiction, incongruity, incongruousness, conflict, discord, irreconcilability.

mismatched ▶ adjective ILL-ASSORTED, ill-matched, incongruous, unsuited, incompatible, inconsistent, at odds; out of keeping, clashing, dissimilar, unalike, different, at

variance, disparate, unrelated, divergent, contrasting.
– OPPOSITES matching.

misogynist ▶ **noun** WOMAN-HATER, anti-feminist, (male) chauvinist, sexist; *informal* male chauvinist pig, MCP.

misplace ▶ **verb** LOSE, mislay, put in the wrong place, be unable to find, forget the whereabouts of.
– OPPOSITES find.

misplaced ▶ **adjective** ❶ *his comments were misplaced* MISGUIDED, unwise, ill-advised, ill-considered, ill-judged, inappropriate. ❷ *misplaced keys* LOST, mislaid, missing.

misprint ▶ **noun** MISTAKE, error, typographical mistake/error, typing mistake/error, corrigendum, erratum; *Brit.* literal; *informal* typo.

misquote ▶ **verb** MISREPORT, misrepresent, misstate, take/quote out of context, distort, twist, slant, bias, put a spin on, falsify.

misrepresent ▶ **verb** GIVE A FALSE ACCOUNT/IDEA OF, misstate, misreport, misquote, quote/take out of context, misinterpret, put a spin on, falsify, distort.

misrule ▶ **noun** ❶ *the misrule of Edward IV* BAD GOVERNMENT, misgovernment, mismanagement, malpractice, incompetence; *formal* maladministration. ❷ *the misrule at football games* LAWLESSNESS, anarchy, disorder, chaos, mayhem.
– OPPOSITES order.

miss[1] ▶ **verb** ❶ *the shot missed her by inches* FAIL TO HIT, be/go wide of, fall short of. ❷ *Mandy missed the catch* FAIL TO CATCH, drop, fumble, fluff, mishandle, misfield, mishit. ❸ *I've missed my bus* BE TOO LATE FOR, fail to catch/get. ❹ *I missed what you said* FAIL TO HEAR, mishear. ❺ *you can't miss the station* FAIL TO SEE/NOTICE, overlook. ❻ *she never missed a meeting* FAIL TO ATTEND, be absent from, play truant from, cut, skip; *Brit. informal* skive off. ❼ *don't miss this exciting opportunity!* LET SLIP, fail to take advantage of, let go/pass, pass up. ❽ *I left early to miss the rush-hour traffic* AVOID, beat, evade, escape, dodge, sidestep, elude, circumvent, steer clear of, find a way round, bypass. ❾ *she missed him when he was away* PINE FOR, yearn for, ache for, long for, long to see.
– OPPOSITES hit, catch.

▶ **noun** *one hit and three misses* FAILURE, omission, slip, blunder, error, mistake.

■ **miss someone/something out** LEAVE OUT, exclude, miss (off), fail to mention, pass over, skip; *Brit. informal* give something a miss.

miss[2] ▶ **noun** *a headstrong young miss* YOUNG WOMAN, young lady, girl, schoolgirl, missy; *Scottish* lass, lassie; *Irish* colleen; *informal* girlie, chick, bit, doll; *Brit. informal* bird, bint; *N. Amer. informal* broad, dame; *Austral./NZ informal* sheila; *poetic/literary* maiden, maid, damsel; *archaic* wench.

misshapen ▶ **adjective** DEFORMED, malformed, distorted, crooked, twisted, warped, out of shape, bent, asymmetrical, irregular, misproportioned, ill-proportioned, disfigured, grotesque.

missing ▶ **adjective** ❶ *his wallet is missing* LOST, mislaid, misplaced, absent, gone (astray), unaccounted for. ❷ *passion was missing from her life* ABSENT, not present, lacking, wanting.
– OPPOSITES present.

mission ▶ **noun** ❶ *a mercy mission to Romania* ASSIGNMENT, commission, expedition, journey, trip, undertaking, operation; task, job, labour, work, duty, charge, trust. ❷ *her mission in life* VOCATION, calling, goal, aim, quest, purpose, function. ❸ *a trade mission* DELEGATION, deputation, commission, legation, delegacy. ❹ *a teacher in a mission* missionary post, missionary station. ❺ *a bombing mission* SORTIE, operation, raid.

missionary ▶ **noun** EVANGELIST, apostle, proselytizer, preacher, minister, priest.

missive ▶ **noun** MESSAGE, communication, letter, word, note, memorandum, line, communiqué, dispatch, news; *informal* memo; *formal* epistle; *poetic/literary* tidings.

misspent ▶ **adjective** WASTED, dissipated, squandered, thrown away, frittered away, misused, misapplied.

misstate ▶ **verb** MISREPORT, misrepresent, take/quote out of context, distort, twist, put a spin on, falsify.

mist ▶ **noun** *the mist was clearing* HAZE, fog, smog, murk, cloud, Scotch mist; *poetic/literary* brume, fume.

■ **mist over/up** STEAM UP, become misty, fog over/up, film over, cloud over.

mistake ▶ **noun** ❶ *I assumed it had been a mistake* ERROR, fault, inaccuracy, omission, slip, blunder, miscalculation, misunderstanding, oversight, misinterpretation, gaffe, faux pas, solecism; *informal* slip-up, boo-boo, howler, boner; *Brit. informal* boob, clanger, bloomer; *N. Amer. informal* goof. ❷ *spelling mistakes* MISPRINT, typographical error/mistake, typing error/mistake, corrigendum, erratum; *Brit.* literal; *informal* typo.

▶ **verb** ❶ *men are apt to mistake their own feelings* MISUNDERSTAND, misinterpret, get wrong, misconstrue, misread. ❷ *children often mistake vitamin pills for sweets* CONFUSE WITH, mix up with, take for, misinterpret as.

■ **be mistaken** BE WRONG, be in error, be under a misapprehension, be misinformed, be misguided; *informal* be barking up the wrong tree, get the wrong end of the stick.

■ **make a mistake** GO WRONG, err, make an error, blunder, trip up, miscalculate; *informal* slip up, make a boo-boo, make a howler; *Brit. informal* boob; *N. Amer. informal* drop the ball, goof (up).

mistaken ▶ adjective WRONG, erroneous, inaccurate, incorrect, off beam, false, fallacious, unfounded, misguided, misinformed.
– OPPOSITES correct.

mistakenly ▶ adverb ❶ *we often mistakenly imagine that when a problem is diagnosed it is solved* WRONGLY, in error, erroneously, incorrectly, falsely, fallaciously, inaccurately. ❷ *Matt mistakenly opened the letter* BY ACCIDENT, accidentally, inadvertently, unintentionally, unwittingly, unconsciously, by mistake.
– OPPOSITES correctly, intentionally.

mistimed ▶ adjective ILL-TIMED, badly timed, inopportune, inappropriate, untimely, unseasonable.
– OPPOSITES opportune.

mistreat ▶ verb ILL-TREAT, maltreat, abuse, knock about/around, hit, beat, strike, molest, injure, harm, hurt; misuse, mishandle; *informal* beat up, rough up.

mistreatment ▶ noun ILL-TREATMENT, maltreatment, abuse, beating, molestation, injury, harm; mishandling, manhandling.

mistress ▶ noun LOVER, girlfriend, kept woman; courtesan, concubine; *informal* fancy woman, bit on the side; *archaic* paramour.

mistrust ▶ verb ❶ *I mistrust his motives* BE SUSPICIOUS OF, be mistrustful of, be distrustful of, be sceptical of, be wary of, be chary of, distrust, have doubts about, have misgivings about, have reservations about, suspect. ❷ *don't mistrust your impulses* QUESTION, challenge, doubt, have no confidence/faith in.
▶ noun ❶ *mistrust of Russia was widespread* SUSPICION, distrust, doubt, misgivings, wariness. ❷ *their mistrust of David's competence* QUESTIONING, lack of confidence/faith in, doubt about.

mistrustful ▶ adjective SUSPICIOUS, chary, wary, distrustful, doubtful, dubious, uneasy, sceptical, leery.

misty ▶ adjective ❶ *misty weather* HAZY, foggy, cloudy; smoggy. ❷ *a misty figure* BLURRY, fuzzy, blurred, dim, indistinct, unclear, vague. ❸ *misty memories* VAGUE, unclear, indefinite, hazy, nebulous.
– OPPOSITES clear.

misunderstand ▶ verb MISAPPREHEND, misinterpret, misconstrue, misconceive, mistake, misread; be mistaken, get the wrong idea, receive a false impression; *informal* be barking up the wrong tree, get (hold of) the wrong end of the stick.

misunderstanding ▶ noun ❶ *a fundamental misunderstanding of juvenile crime* MISINTERPRETATION, misconstruction, misreading, misapprehension, misconception, the wrong idea, false impression. ❷ *we have had some misunderstandings* DISAGREEMENT, difference (of opinion), dispute, falling-out, quarrel, argument, altercation, squabble, wrangle, row, clash; *informal* spat, scrap, tiff.

misuse ▶ verb ❶ *misusing public funds* PUT TO WRONG USE, misemploy, embezzle, use fraudulently; abuse, squander, waste. ❷ *she had been misused by her husband* ILL-TREAT, maltreat, mistreat, abuse, knock about/around, hit, beat, strike, molest, injure, harm, hurt; mishandle, manhandle; *informal* beat up, rough up.
▶ noun ❶ *a misuse of company assets* WRONG USE, embezzlement, fraud; squandering, waste. ❷ *the misuse of drugs* ILLEGAL USE, abuse.

mitigate ▶ verb ALLEVIATE, reduce, diminish, lessen, weaken, lighten, attenuate, take the edge off, allay, ease, assuage, palliate, relieve, tone down.
– OPPOSITES aggravate.

mitigating ▶ adjective EXTENUATING, exonerative, justificatory, justifying, vindicatory, vindicating, qualifying; *formal* exculpatory.

mitigation ▶ noun ❶ *the mitigation of the problems* ALLEVIATION, reduction, diminution, lessening, easing, weakening, assuagement, palliation, relief. ❷ *what did she say in mitigation?* EXTENUATION, explanation, excuse.

mix ▶ verb ❶ *mix all the ingredients together* BLEND, mix up, mingle, combine, put together, jumble; fuse, unite, unify, join, amalgamate, incorporate, meld, marry, coalesce, homogenize, intermingle, intermix; *technical* admix; *poetic/literary* commingle; *archaic* commix. ❷ *she mixes with all sorts* ASSOCIATE, socialize, fraternize, keep company, consort; mingle, circulate; *N. Amer.* rub elbows; *informal* hang out/around, knock about/around, hobnob; *Brit. informal* hang about. ❸ *we just don't mix* BE COMPATIBLE, get along/on, be in harmony, see eye to eye, agree; *informal* hit it off, click, be on the same wavelength.
– OPPOSITES separate.
▶ noun *a mix of ancient and modern* MIXTURE, blend, mingling, combination, compound, fusion, alloy, union, amalgamation; medley, melange, collection, selection, assortment, variety, mixed bag, miscellany, pot-pourri, jumble, hotchpotch, ragbag, patchwork, farrago, gallimaufry, omnium gatherum, salmagundi; *N. Amer.* hodgepodge.

■ **mix something up** ❶ *mix up the rusk with milk. See* MIX verb sense 1. ❷ *I mixed up the dates* CONFUSE, get confused, muddle (up), get muddled up, mistake.

■ **mixed up in** INVOLVED IN, embroiled in, caught up in.

mixed ▶ adjective ❶ *a mixed collection* ASSORTED, varied, variegated, miscellaneous, disparate, diverse, diversified, motley, sundry, jumbled, heterogeneous. ❷ *chickens of mixed breeds* HYBRID, half-caste, cross-bred, interbred. ❸ *mixed reactions* AMBIVALENT, equivocal, contradictory, conflicting, confused, muddled.
– OPPOSITES homogeneous.

mixed up ▶ adjective (*informal*) CONFUSED, (all) at sea, befuddled, bemused, bewildered, muddled; maladjusted, disturbed, neurotic, unbalanced; *informal* hung up, messed up.

mixer ▶ noun ❶ *a kitchen mixer* BLENDER, food processor, liquidizer, beater, churn. ❷ *she was never really a mixer* SOCIABLE PERSON, socializer, extrovert, socialite.

mixture ▶ noun ❶ *the pudding mixture* BLEND, mix, brew, combination, concoction; composition, compound, alloy, amalgam. ❷ *a strange mixture of people* ASSORTMENT, miscellany, medley, melange, blend, variety, mixed bag, mix, diversity, collection, selection, pot-pourri, mishmash, hotchpotch, ragbag, patchwork, farrago, gallimaufry, omnium gatherum, salmagundi; *N. Amer.* hodgepodge. ❸ *the animals were a mixture of genetic strands* CROSS, crossbreed, mongrel, hybrid, half-breed, half-caste.

mix-up ▶ noun CONFUSION, muddle, misunderstanding, mistake, error.

moan ▶ noun ❶ *moans of pain* GROAN, wail, whimper, sob, cry. ❷ *the moan of the wind* SOUGH, sigh, murmur. ❸ (*informal*) *there were moans about the delay* COMPLAINT, complaining, grouse, grousing, grumble, grumbling, whine, whining, carping; *informal* gripe, griping, grouch, grouching, bellyache, bitch, whinge, whingeing, beef, beefing.
▶ verb ❶ *he moaned in agony* GROAN, wail, whimper, sob, cry. ❷ *the wind moaned in the trees* SOUGH, sigh, murmur. ❸ (*informal*) *you're always moaning about the weather* COMPLAIN, grouse, grumble, whine, carp; *informal* gripe, grouch, bellyache, bitch, beef, whinge; *N. English informal* mither.

mob ▶ noun ❶ *troops dispersed the mob* CROWD, horde, multitude, rabble, mass, throng, group, gang, gathering, assemblage; *archaic* rout. ❷ *the mob were excluded from political life* THE COMMON PEOPLE, the masses, the rank and file, the commonality, the commonalty, the third estate, the plebeians, the proletariat; the hoi polloi, the lower classes, the rabble, the riff-raff, the great unwashed; *informal* the proles, the plebs. ❸ (*Brit. informal*) *he stood out from the rest of the mob* GROUP, set, crowd, lot, circle, coterie, clan, faction, pack, band, ring; *informal* gang, bunch.
▶ verb ❶ *the Chancellor was mobbed when he visited Berlin* SURROUND, swarm around, besiege, jostle. ❷ *reporters mobbed her hotel* CROWD (INTO), fill, pack, throng, press into, squeeze into.

mobile ▶ adjective ❶ *both patients are mobile* ABLE TO MOVE (AROUND), moving, walking; *Zoology* motile; *Medicine* ambulant. ❷ *her mobile face* EXPRESSIVE, eloquent, revealing, animated. ❸ *a mobile library* TRAVELLING, transportable, portable, movable; itinerant, peripatetic. ❹ *highly mobile young people* ADAPTABLE, flexible, versatile, adjustable.
– OPPOSITES motionless, static.

mobility ▶ noun ❶ *restricted mobility* ABILITY TO MOVE, movability. ❷ *the mobility of Billy's face* EXPRESSIVENESS, eloquence, animation. ❸ *mobility in the workforce* ADAPTABILITY, flexibility, versatility, adjustability.

mobilize ▶ verb ❶ *the government mobilized the troops* MARSHAL, deploy, muster, rally, call up, assemble, mass, organize, prepare. ❷ *mobilizing support for the party* GENERATE, arouse, awaken, excite, incite, provoke, foment, prompt, stimulate, stir up, galvanize, encourage, inspire, whip up; *poetic/literary* waken.

mock ▶ verb ❶ *the local children mocked the old people* RIDICULE, jeer at, sneer at, deride, scorn, make fun of, laugh at, scoff at, tease, taunt; *informal* take the mickey out of, josh; *N. Amer. informal* goof on, rag on, pull someone's chain; *Austral./NZ informal* poke mullock at, sling off at. ❷ *they mocked the way he speaks* PARODY, ape, take off, satirize, lampoon, imitate, mimic; *informal* send up.
▶ adjective *mock leather* IMITATION, artificial, man-made, simulated, synthetic, ersatz, fake, reproduction, dummy, sham, false, spurious, bogus, counterfeit, pseudo; *informal* pretend, phoney.
– OPPOSITES genuine.

mockery ▶ noun ❶ *the mockery in his voice* RIDICULE, derision, jeering, sneering, contempt, scorn, scoffing, teasing, taunting, sarcasm. ❷ *the trial was a mockery* TRAVESTY, charade, farce, parody.

mocking ▶ adjective SNEERING, derisive, contemptuous, scornful, sardonic, ironic, sarcastic.

mode ▶ noun ❶ *an informal mode of policing* MANNER, way, fashion, means, method, system, style, approach, technique, procedure, process, practice. ❷ *the camera is in manual mode* FUNCTION, position, operation. ❸ *the mode for active wear* FASHION, vogue, style, look, trend; craze, rage, fad.

model ▶ noun ❶ *a working model* REPLICA, copy, representation, mock-up, dummy, imitation, duplicate, reproduction, facsimile. ❷ *the American model of airline deregulation* PROTOTYPE, stereotype, archetype, type, version; mould, template, framework, pattern, design, blueprint. ❸ *she was a model as a teacher* IDEAL, paragon, perfect example/specimen; perfection, acme, epitome, nonpareil, crème de la crème. ❹ *a top model* FASHION MODEL, supermodel, mannequin; *informal* clothes horse. ❺ *an artist's model* SITTER, poser, subject. ❻ *the latest model of car* VERSION, type, design, variety, kind, sort. ❼ *this dress is a model* ORIGINAL (DESIGN), exclusive; *informal* one-off.
▶ adjective ❶ *model trains* REPLICA, TOY, miniature, dummy, imitation, duplicate, reproduction, facsimile. ❷ *model farms* PROTOTYPICAL, prototypal, archetypal. ❸ *a model teacher* IDEAL, perfect, exemplary, classic, flawless, faultless.

moderate ▶ adjective ❶ *moderate success* AVER-

AGE, modest, medium, middling, ordinary, common, commonplace, everyday, workaday; tolerable, passable, adequate, fair; mediocre, indifferent, unexceptional, unremarkable, run-of-the-mill; *informal* OK, so-so, bog-standard, fair-to-middling, (plain) vanilla, no great shakes, not up to much; *NZ informal* half-pie. ❷ *moderate prices* REASONABLE, acceptable; inexpensive, low, fair, modest. ❸ *moderate views* MIDDLE-OF-THE-ROAD, non-extreme, non-radical. ❹ *moderate behaviour* RESTRAINED, controlled, sober; tolerant, lenient.

– OPPOSITES great, unreasonable, extreme.

▶ **verb** ❶ *the wind has moderated* DIE DOWN, abate, let up, calm down, lessen, decrease, diminish; recede, weaken, subside. ❷ *you can help to moderate her anger* CURB, control, check, temper, restrain, subdue; repress, tame, lessen, decrease, lower, reduce, diminish, alleviate, allay, appease, assuage, ease, soothe, calm, tone down; *archaic* remit. ❸ *the Speaker moderates the assembly* CHAIR, take the chair of, preside over.

– OPPOSITES increase.

moderately ▶ **adverb** SOMEWHAT, quite, rather, fairly, reasonably, comparatively, relatively, to some extent; tolerably, passably, adequately; *informal* pretty.

moderation ▶ **noun** ❶ *he urged them to show moderation* SELF-RESTRAINT, restraint, self-control, self-discipline; moderateness, temperance, leniency, fairness. ❷ *a moderation of their confrontational style* RELAXATION, easing (off), reduction, abatement, weakening, slackening, tempering, softening, diminution, diminishing, lessening; decline, modulation, modification, mitigation, allaying; *informal* let-up.

■ **in moderation** IN MODERATE QUANTITIES/AMOUNTS, within (sensible) limits; moderately.

modern ▶ **adjective** ❶ *modern times* PRESENT-DAY, contemporary, present, current, twenty-first-century, latter-day, recent. ❷ *her clothes are very modern* FASHIONABLE, in fashion, in style, in vogue, up to date, all the rage, trendsetting, stylish, voguish, modish, chic, à la mode; the latest, new, newest, newfangled, modernistic, advanced; *informal* trendy, cool, in, with it, now, hip, happening; *N. Amer. informal* tony.

– OPPOSITES past, old-fashioned.

modernity ▶ **noun** CONTEMPORANEITY, contemporaneousness, modernness, modernism; fashionableness, vogue; *informal* trendiness.

modernize ▶ **verb** ❶ *they are modernizing their manufacturing facilities* UPDATE, bring up to date, streamline, rationalize, overhaul; renovate, remodel, refashion, revamp. ❷ *we must modernize to survive* GET UP TO DATE, move with the times, innovate; *informal* get in the swim, get with it.

modest ▶ **adjective** ❶ *she was modest about her poetry* SELF-EFFACING, self-deprecating, humble, unpretentious, unassuming, unostentatious; shy, bashful, self-conscious, diffident, reserved, reticent, coy. ❷ *modest success* MODERATE, fair, limited, tolerable, passable, adequate, satisfactory, acceptable, unexceptional. ❸ *a modest house* SMALL, ordinary, simple, plain, humble, inexpensive, unostentatious, unpretentious. ❹ *her modest dress* DECOROUS, decent, seemly, demure, proper.

– OPPOSITES conceited, great, grand.

modesty ▶ **noun** ❶ *Hannah's modesty cloaks many talents* SELF-EFFACEMENT, humility, unpretentiousness; shyness, bashfulness, self-consciousness, reserve, reticence, timidity. ❷ *the modesty of his aspirations* LIMITED SCOPE, moderation. ❸ *the modesty of his home* UNPRETENTIOUSNESS, simplicity, plainness. ❹ *her maidenly modesty* DECORUM, decorousness, decency, seemliness, demureness.

modicum ▶ **noun** SMALL AMOUNT, particle, speck, fragment, scrap, crumb, grain, morsel, shred, dash, drop, pinch, jot, iota, whit, atom, smattering, scintilla, hint, suggestion; *informal* smidgen, tad; *archaic* scantling.

modification ▶ **noun** ❶ *the design is undergoing modification* ALTERATION, adjustment, change, adaptation, refinement, revision. ❷ *some minor modifications were made* REVISION, refinement, improvement, amendment, adaptation, adjustment, change, alteration. ❸ *the modification of his views* SOFTENING, moderation, tempering, qualification.

modify ▶ **verb** ❶ *their economic policy has been modified* ALTER, change, adjust, adapt, amend, revise, reshape, refashion, restyle, revamp, rework, remodel, refine; *informal* tweak. ❷ *he modified his more extreme views* MODERATE, revise, temper, soften, tone down, qualify.

modish ▶ **adjective** FASHIONABLE, stylish, chic, modern, contemporary, all the rage, in vogue, voguish, up to the minute, à la mode; *informal* trendy, cool, with it, in, now, hip, happening; *N. Amer. informal* kicky, tony.

modulate ▶ **verb** ❶ *the cells modulate the body's response* REGULATE, adjust, set, modify, moderate. ❷ *she modulated her voice* ADJUST, change the tone of.

modus operandi ▶ **noun** METHOD (OF WORKING), way, MO, manner, technique, style, procedure, approach, methodology, strategy, plan, formula; *formal* praxis.

mogul ▶ **noun** MAGNATE, tycoon, VIP, notable, personage, baron, captain, king, lord, grandee, nabob; *informal* bigwig, big shot, big noise, top dog; *N. Amer. informal* top banana, big enchilada.

moist ▶ **adjective** ❶ *the air was moist* DAMP, dampish, steamy, humid, muggy, clammy, dank, wet, wettish, soggy, sweaty, sticky. ❷ *a moist fruitcake* SUCCULENT, juicy, soft. ❸ *her eyes grew moist* TEARFUL, watery, misty.

– OPPOSITES dry.

moisten ▶ verb DAMPEN, wet, damp, water, humidify; *poetic/literary* bedew.

moisture ▶ noun WETNESS, wet, water, liquid, condensation, steam, vapour, dampness, damp, humidity, clamminess, mugginess, dankness, wateriness.

moisturizer ▶ noun LOTION, cream, balm, emollient, salve, unguent, lubricant; *technical* humectant.

mole[1] ▶ noun *the mole on his left cheek* MARK, freckle, blotch, spot, blemish.

mole[2] ▶ noun *a well-placed mole* SPY, (secret) agent, undercover agent, operative, plant, infiltrator; *N. Amer. informal* spook; *archaic* intelligencer.

mole[3] ▶ noun *the mole protecting the harbour* BREAKWATER, groyne, dyke, pier, sea wall, causeway.

molest ▶ verb ❶ *the crowd were molesting the police* HARASS, harry, pester, beset, persecute, torment; *N. Amer. informal* roust. ❷ *he molested a ten-year-old boy* (SEXUALLY) ABUSE, (sexually) assault, interfere with, rape, violate; *informal* grope, paw; *poetic/literary* ravish.

mollify ▶ verb ❶ *they mollified the protesters* APPEASE, placate, pacify, conciliate, soothe, calm (down). ❷ *mollifying the fears of the public* ALLAY, assuage, alleviate, mitigate, ease, reduce, moderate, temper, tone down.
– OPPOSITES enrage.

mollycoddle ▶ verb *his parents mollycoddle him* PAMPER, cosset, coddle, spoil, indulge, overindulge, pet, baby, nanny, nursemaid, wait on hand and foot, wrap in cotton wool.
▶ noun (*informal*) *the boy's a mollycoddle! See* DRIP noun sense 2.

molten ▶ adjective LIQUEFIED, liquid, fluid, melted, flowing.

moment ▶ noun ❶ *he thought for a moment* LITTLE WHILE, short time, bit, minute, instant, (split) second; *informal* sec, jiffy; *Brit. informal* tick, mo, two ticks. ❷ *the moment they met* POINT (IN TIME), time, hour. ❸ (*formal*) *issues of little moment* IMPORTANCE, import, significance, consequence, note, weight, concern, interest.
■ **in a moment** VERY SOON, in a minute, in a second, in a trice, shortly, any minute (now), in the twinkling of an eye, in (less than) no time, in no time at all; *N. Amer.* momentarily; *informal* in a jiffy, in two shakes (of a lamb's tail), before you can say Jack Robinson, in the blink of an eye; *Brit. informal* in a tick, in two ticks, in a mo; *N. Amer. informal* in a snap; *poetic/literary* ere long.

momentarily ▶ adverb ❶ *he paused momentarily* BRIEFLY, fleetingly, for a moment, for a second, for an instant. ❷ (*N. Amer.*) *my husband will be here momentarily. See* IN A MOMENT at MOMENT.

momentary ▶ adjective BRIEF, short, short-lived, fleeting, passing, transient, ephemeral; *poetic/literary* evanescent.
– OPPOSITES lengthy.

momentous ▶ adjective IMPORTANT, significant, historic, portentous, critical, crucial, life-and-death, decisive, pivotal, consequential, of consequence, far-reaching, earth-shattering; *formal* of moment.
– OPPOSITES insignificant.

momentum ▶ noun IMPETUS, energy, force, power, strength, thrust, speed, velocity.

monarch ▶ noun SOVEREIGN, ruler, Crown, crowned head, potentate; king, queen, emperor, empress, prince, princess.

monarchy ▶ noun ❶ *a constitutional monarchy* KINGDOM, sovereign state, principality, empire. ❷ *hereditary monarchy* KINGSHIP, sovereignty, autocracy, monocracy, absolutism.

monastery ▶ noun RELIGIOUS COMMUNITY; friary, abbey, priory, cloister.

monastic ▶ adjective ❶ *a monastic community* CLOISTERED, cloistral, claustral. ❷ *a monastic existence* AUSTERE, ascetic, simple, solitary, monkish, celibate, quiet, cloistered, sequestered, secluded, reclusive, hermit-like, hermitic.

monetary ▶ adjective FINANCIAL, fiscal, pecuniary, money, cash, economic, budgetary.

money ▶ noun ❶ *I haven't got enough money* (HARD) CASH, ready money; the means, the wherewithal, funds, capital, finances, (filthy) lucre; banknotes, notes, coins, change, specie, silver, copper, currency; *Brit.* sterling; *N. Amer.* bills; *N. Amer. & Austral.* roll; *informal* dough, bread, loot, readies, shekels, moolah, the necessary; *Brit. informal* dosh, brass, lolly, spondulicks; *N. Amer. informal* dinero, bucks, mazuma; *US informal* greenbacks, simoleons, jack, rocks; *Austral./NZ informal* Oscar; *Brit. dated* l.s.d.; *archaic* pelf. ❷ *she married him for his money* WEALTH, riches, fortune, affluence, (liquid) assets, resources, means. ❸ *the money here is better* PAY, salary, wages, remuneration; *formal* emolument.
– RELATED TERMS pecuniary, monetary, numismatic.
■ **for my money** IN MY OPINION, to my mind, in my view, as I see it, personally, in my estimation, in my judgement, if you ask me.
■ **in the money** (*informal*) RICH, wealthy, affluent, well-to-do, well off, prosperous, moneyed, in clover, opulent; *informal* rolling in it, loaded, stinking rich, well heeled, made of money.

moneyed ▶ adjective RICH, wealthy, affluent, well-to-do, well off, prosperous, in clover, opulent, of means, of substance; *informal* in the money, rolling in it, loaded, stinking/filthy rich, well heeled, made of money.
– OPPOSITES poor.

money-grubbing ▶ adjective (*informal*) ACQUISITIVE, avaricious, grasping, money-grabbing, rapacious, mercenary, materialistic; *N. Amer. informal* grabby.

moneymaking ▶ adjective PROFITABLE, profit-making, remunerative, lucrative, successful, financially rewarding.
– OPPOSITES loss-making.

mongrel ▶ noun *a rough-haired mongrel* CROSS-BREED, cross, mixed breed, half-breed; tyke, cur, mutt; *NZ* kuri; *Austral. informal* mong, bitzer.
▶ adjective *a mongrel bitch* CROSS-BRED, of mixed breed, half-breed.
– OPPOSITES pedigree.

monitor ▶ noun ❶ *monitors covered all entrances* DETECTOR, scanner, recorder; security camera, CCTV. ❷ *UN monitors* OBSERVER, watchdog, overseer, supervisor. ❸ *a computer monitor* SCREEN, visual display unit, VDU. ❹ (*Brit.*) *a school monitor* PREFECT, praepostor; senior boy/girl, senior pupil.
▶ verb *his movements were closely monitored* OBSERVE, watch, track, keep an eye on, keep under observation, keep watch on, keep under surveillance, record, note, oversee; *informal* keep tabs on, keep a beady eye on.

monk ▶ noun brother, religious, coenobite, contemplative, mendicant; friar; abbot, prior; novice, oblate, postulant; Benedictine, Black Monk, Cluniac, Carthusian, Cistercian, White Monk.
– RELATED TERMS monastic, monastery.

monkey ▶ noun ❶ SIMIAN, primate, ape. ❷ *you little monkey!* See RASCAL.
■ **make a monkey (out) of** MAKE SOMEONE LOOK FOOLISH, make a fool of, make a laughing stock of, ridicule, make fun of, poke fun at.
■ **monkey about/around** FOOL ABOUT/AROUND, play about/around, clown about/around, footle about/around; *informal* mess about/around, horse about/around, lark (about/around); *Brit. informal* muck about/around.
■ **monkey with** TAMPER WITH, fiddle with, interfere with, meddle with, tinker with, play with; *informal* mess with; *Brit. informal* muck about/around with.

monkey business ▶ noun (*informal*) MISCHIEF, misbehaviour, mischievousness, devilry, devilment, tomfoolery; dishonesty, trickery, chicanery, skulduggery; *informal* shenanigans, funny business, hanky-panky; *Brit. informal* monkey tricks, jiggery-pokery; *N. Amer. informal* monkeyshines.

monocle ▶ noun EYEGLASS, glass.

monolith ▶ noun STANDING STONE, menhir, sarsen (stone), megalith.

monolithic ▶ adjective ❶ *a monolithic building* MASSIVE, huge, vast, colossal, gigantic, immense, giant, enormous; featureless, characterless. ❷ *the old monolithic Communist party* INFLEXIBLE, rigid, unbending, unchanging, fossilized.

monologue ▶ noun SOLILOQUY, speech, address, lecture, sermon; *formal* oration.

monomania ▶ noun OBSESSION, fixation, consuming passion, mania, compulsion.

monopolize ▶ verb ❶ *the company has monopolized the market* CORNER, control, take over, gain control/dominance over; *archaic* engross. ❷ *he monopolized the conversation* DOMINATE, take over; *informal* hog. ❸ *she monopolized the guest of honour* TAKE UP ALL THE ATTENTION OF, keep to oneself; *informal* tie up.

monotonous ▶ adjective ❶ *a monotonous job* TEDIOUS, boring, dull, uninteresting, unexciting, wearisome, tiresome, repetitive, repetitious, unvarying, unchanging, unvaried, humdrum, routine, mechanical, mind-numbing, soul-destroying; colourless, featureless, dreary; *informal* deadly; *Brit. informal* samey; *N. Amer. informal* dullsville. ❷ *a monotonous voice* TONELESS, flat, uninflected, soporific.
– OPPOSITES interesting.

monotony ▶ noun ❶ *the monotony of everyday life* TEDIUM, tediousness, lack of variety, dullness, boredom, repetitiveness, repetitiousness, uniformity, routineness, wearisomeness, tiresomeness; lack of excitement, uneventfulness, dreariness, colourlessness, featurelessness; *informal* deadliness. ❷ *the monotony of her voice* TONELESSNESS, flatness.

monster ▶ noun ❶ *legendary sea monsters* FABULOUS CREATURE, mythical creature. ❷ *her husband is a monster* BRUTE, fiend, beast, devil, demon, barbarian, savage, animal; *informal* swine, pig. ❸ *the boy's a little monster* RASCAL, imp, monkey, wretch, devil; *informal* horror, scamp, scallywag, tyke; *Brit. informal* perisher, pickle; *N. Amer. informal* varmint, hellion; *archaic* scapegrace, rapscallion. ❹ *he's a monster of a man* GIANT, mammoth, colossus, leviathan, titan; *informal* jumbo.
▶ adjective (*informal*) *a monster carp.* See HUGE.

monstrosity ▶ noun ❶ *a concrete monstrosity* EYESORE, blot on the landscape, carbuncle, excrescence. ❷ *a biological monstrosity* MUTANT, mutation, freak (of nature), monster, abortion.

monstrous ▶ adjective ❶ *a monstrous creature* GROTESQUE, hideous, ugly, ghastly, gruesome, horrible, horrific, horrifying, grisly, disgusting, repulsive, repellent, dreadful, frightening, terrifying, malformed, misshapen. ❷ *a monstrous tidal wave.* See HUGE. ❸ *monstrous acts of violence* APPALLING, heinous, egregious, evil, wicked, abominable, terrible, horrible, dreadful, vile, outrageous, shocking, disgraceful; unspeakable, despicable, vicious, savage, barbaric, barbarous, inhuman; *Brit. informal* beastly.
– OPPOSITES lovely, small.

monument ▶ noun ❶ *a stone monument* MEMORIAL, statue, pillar, column, obelisk, cross; cenotaph, tomb, mausoleum, shrine. ❷ *a monument was placed over the grave* GRAVESTONE, headstone, tombstone. ❸ *a monument to a past* *era of aviation* TESTAMENT, record, reminder, remembrance, memorial, commemoration.

monumental ▶ adjective ❶ *a monumental task* HUGE, great, enormous, gigantic, massive, colossal, mammoth, immense, tremendous, mighty, stupendous. ❷ *a monumental error of judgement* TERRIBLE, dreadful, awful, colossal, staggering, huge, enormous, unforgivable, egregious. ❸ *Beethoven's monumental works* IMPRESSIVE, striking, outstanding, remarkable, magnificent, majestic, stupendous, ambitious, large-scale, grand, awe-inspiring, important, significant, distinguished, memorable, immortal. ❹ *a monumental inscription* COMMEMORATIVE, memorial, celebratory, commemorating.

mood ▶ noun ❶ *she's in a good mood* FRAME/STATE OF MIND, humour, temper; disposition, spirit, tenor. ❷ *he's obviously in a mood* BAD MOOD, (bad) temper, sulk, pet, fit of pique; low spirits, the doldrums, the blues; *informal* the dumps, grump; *Brit. informal* paddy. ❸ *the mood of the film* ATMOSPHERE, feeling, spirit, ambience, aura, character, tenor, flavour, feel, tone.

■ **in the mood** IN THE RIGHT FRAME OF MIND, feeling like, wanting to, inclined to, disposed to, minded to, eager to, willing to.

moody ▶ adjective TEMPERAMENTAL, emotional, volatile, capricious, changeable, mercurial; sullen, sulky, morose, glum, depressed, dejected, despondent, doleful, dour, sour, saturnine; *informal* blue, down in the dumps/mouth.
– OPPOSITES cheerful.

moon ▶ noun SATELLITE.
– RELATED TERMS lunar.
▶ verb ❶ *stop mooning about* WASTE TIME, loaf, idle, mope; *Brit. informal* mooch; *N. Amer. informal* lollygag. ❷ *he's mooning over her photograph* MOPE, pine, brood, daydream, fantasize, be in a reverie.

■ **many moons ago** (*informal*) A LONG TIME AGO, ages ago, years ago; *informal* donkey's years ago; *Brit. informal* yonks ago.

■ **once in a blue moon** (*informal*) HARDLY EVER, scarcely ever, rarely, very seldom.

■ **over the moon** (*informal*). *See* ECSTATIC.

moonshine ▶ noun. *See* RUBBISH noun sense 2.

moor[1] ▶ verb *a boat was moored to the quay* TIE UP, secure, make fast, fix firmly, anchor, berth, dock.

moor[2] ▶ noun *a walk on the moor* UPLAND, moorland; grouse moor; *Brit.* heath, fell, wold.

moot ▶ adjective *a moot point* DEBATABLE, open to discussion/question, arguable, questionable, at issue, open to doubt, disputable, controversial, contentious, disputed, unresolved, unsettled, up in the air.
▶ verb *the idea was first mooted in the 1930s* RAISE, bring up, broach, mention, put forward, introduce, advance, propose, suggest.

mop ▶ noun *her tousled mop of hair* SHOCK, mane, tangle, mass.
▶ verb *a man was mopping the floor* WASH, clean, wipe.

■ **mop something up** ❶ *I mopped up the spilt coffee* WIPE UP, clean up, sponge up. ❷ *troops mopped up the last pockets of resistance* FINISH OFF, deal with, dispose of, take care of, clear up, eliminate.

mope ▶ verb ❶ *it's no use moping* BROOD, sulk, be miserable, be despondent, pine, eat one's heart out, fret, grieve; *informal* be down in the dumps/mouth; *poetic/literary* repine. ❷ *she was moping about the house* LANGUISH, moon, idle, loaf; *Brit. informal* mooch; *N. Amer. informal* lollygag.
▶ noun *she's regarded as a mope* MELANCHOLIC, depressive, pessimist, killjoy; *informal* sourpuss, party-pooper, spoilsport, grouch, grump; *Brit. informal* misery.

moral ▶ adjective ❶ *moral issues* ETHICAL, social, having to do with right and wrong. ❷ *a very moral man* VIRTUOUS, good, righteous, upright, upstanding, high-minded, principled, honourable, honest, just, noble, incorruptible, scrupulous, respectable, decent, clean-living, law-abiding. ❸ *moral support* PSYCHOLOGICAL, emotional, mental.
– OPPOSITES dishonourable.
▶ noun ❶ *the moral of the story* LESSON, message, meaning, significance, signification, import, point, teaching. ❷ *he has no morals* MORAL CODE, code of ethics, moral standards/values, principles, standards, (sense of) morality, scruples.

morale ▶ noun CONFIDENCE, self-confidence, self-esteem, spirit(s), team spirit.

moral fibre ▶ noun STRENGTH OF CHARACTER, fibre, fortitude, resolve, backbone, spine, mettle, firmness of purpose.

morality ▶ noun ❶ *the morality of nuclear weapons* ETHICS, rights and wrongs, ethicality. ❷ *a sharp decline in morality* VIRTUE, goodness, good behaviour, righteousness, rectitude, uprightness; morals, principles, honesty, integrity, propriety, honour, justice, decency. ❸ *orthodox Christian morality* MORAL STANDARDS, morals, ethics, standards/principles of behaviour, mores, standards.

moralize ▶ verb PONTIFICATE, sermonize, lecture, preach; *informal* preachify.

morass ▶ noun ❶ *the muddy morass* QUAGMIRE, swamp, bog, marsh, mire, marshland, slough; *N. Amer.* moor. ❷ *a morass of paperwork* CONFUSION, chaos, muddle, tangle, entanglement, imbroglio, jumble, clutter.

moratorium ▶ noun EMBARGO, ban, prohibition, suspension, postponement, stay, stoppage, halt, freeze, standstill, respite.

morbid ▶ adjective ❶ *a morbid fascination with contemporary warfare* GHOULISH, macabre, unhealthy, gruesome, unwholesome; *informal* sick. ❷ *I felt decidedly morbid* GLOOMY, glum, melancholy, morose, dismal, sombre, doleful, despondent, dejected, sad, depressed, down-

cast, down, disconsolate, miserable, unhappy, downhearted, dispirited, low; *informal* blue, down in the dumps/mouth.
– OPPOSITES wholesome, cheerful.

mordant ▶ **adjective** CAUSTIC, trenchant, biting, cutting, acerbic, sardonic, sarcastic, scathing, acid, sharp, keen; critical, bitter, virulent, vitriolic; *formal* mordacious.

more ▶ **determiner** *I could do with some more clothes* ADDITIONAL, further, added, extra, increased, new, other, supplementary.
– OPPOSITES less, fewer.
▶ **adverb** ❶ *he was able to concentrate more on his writing* TO A GREATER EXTENT, further, some more, better. ❷ *he was rich, and more, he was handsome* MOREOVER, furthermore, besides, what's more, in addition, also, as well, too, to boot, on top of that, into the bargain; *archaic* withal, forbye.
▶ **pronoun** *we're going to need more* EXTRA, an additional amount/number, an addition, an increase.
– OPPOSITES less, fewer.
■ **more or less** APPROXIMATELY, roughly, nearly, almost, close to, about, of the order of, in the region of.

moreover ▶ **adverb** BESIDES, furthermore, what's more, in addition, also, as well, too, to boot, additionally, on top of that, into the bargain, more; *archaic* withal, forbye.

mores ▶ **plural noun** CUSTOMS, conventions, ways, way of life, traditions, practices, habits; *formal* praxis.

morgue ▶ **noun** MORTUARY, funeral parlour; *Brit.* chapel of rest.

moribund ▶ **adjective** ❶ *the patient was moribund* DYING, expiring, on one's deathbed, near death, at death's door, not long for this world. ❷ *the moribund shipbuilding industry* DECLINING, in decline, waning, dying, stagnating, stagnant, crumbling, on its last legs.
– OPPOSITES thriving.

morning ▶ **noun** ❶ *I've got a meeting this morning* BEFORE NOON, before lunch(time), a.m.; *poetic/literary* morn; *Nautical* & *N. Amer.* forenoon. ❷ *morning is on its way* DAWN, daybreak, sunrise, first light, cockcrow; *N. Amer.* sunup; *poetic/literary* dayspring, dawning, aurora.
– RELATED TERMS matutinal.
■ **morning, noon, and night** ALL THE TIME, without a break, constantly, continually, incessantly, ceaselessly, perpetually, unceasingly; *informal* 24-7.

moron ▶ **noun**. *See* FOOL noun sense 1.

moronic ▶ **adjective**. *See* STUPID sense 1.

morose ▶ **adjective** SULLEN, sulky, gloomy, bad-tempered, ill-tempered, dour, surly, sour, glum, moody, ill-humoured, melancholy, melancholic, doleful, miserable, depressed, dejected, despondent, downcast, unhappy, in low spirits, low, down, fed up, grumpy, irritable, churlish, cantankerous, crotchety, cross, crabby, grouchy, testy, snappish, peevish, crusty; *informal* blue, down in the dumps/mouth.
– OPPOSITES cheerful.

morsel ▶ **noun** MOUTHFUL, bite, nibble, bit, soupçon, taste, spoonful, forkful, sliver, drop, dollop, spot, gobbet; titbit, bonne bouche; *informal* smidgen.

mortal ▶ **adjective** ❶ *mortal remains | all men are mortal* PERISHABLE, physical, bodily, corporeal, fleshly, earthly; human, impermanent, transient, ephemeral. ❷ *a mortal blow* DEADLY, fatal, lethal, death-dealing, murderous, terminal. ❸ *mortal enemies* IRRECONCILABLE, deadly, sworn, bitter, out-and-out, implacable. ❹ *a mortal sin* UNPARDONABLE, unforgivable. ❺ *living in mortal fear* EXTREME, (very) great, terrible, awful, dreadful, intense, severe, grave, dire, unbearable. ❻ *the punishment is out of all mortal proportion* CONCEIVABLE, imaginable, perceivable, possible, earthly.
– OPPOSITES venial.
▶ **noun** *we are mere mortals* HUMAN (BEING), person, man/woman; earthling.

mortality ▶ **noun** ❶ *a sense of his own mortality* IMPERMANENCE, transience, ephemerality, perishability; humanity; corporeality. ❷ *the causes of mortality* DEATH, loss of life, dying.

mortification ▶ **noun** ❶ *scarlet with mortification* EMBARRASSMENT, humiliation, chagrin, discomfiture, discomposure, shame. ❷ *the mortification of the flesh* SUBDUING, suppression, subjugation, control, controlling; disciplining, chastening, punishment.

mortify ▶ **verb** ❶ *I'd be mortified if my friends found out* EMBARRASS, humiliate, chagrin, discomfit, shame, abash, horrify, appal. ❷ *he was mortified at being excluded* HURT, wound, affront, offend, put out, pique, irk, annoy, vex; *informal* rile. ❸ *mortifying the flesh* SUBDUE, suppress, subjugate, control; discipline, chasten, punish. ❹ *the cut had mortified* BECOME GANGRENOUS, fester, putrefy, gangrene, rot, decay, decompose.

mortuary ▶ **noun** MORGUE, funeral parlour; *Brit.* chapel of rest.

most ▶ **pronoun** *most of the guests brought flowers* NEARLY ALL, almost all, the greatest part/number, the majority, the bulk, the preponderance.
– OPPOSITES little, few.
■ **for the most part** MOSTLY, mainly, in the main, on the whole, largely, by and large, to a large extent, predominantly, chiefly, principally, basically, generally, usually, typically, commonly, as a rule, on balance, on average.

mostly ▶ **adverb** ❶ *the other passengers were mostly businessmen* MAINLY, for the most part, on the whole, in the main, largely, chiefly, predominantly, principally, primarily. ❷ *I mostly wear jeans* USUALLY, generally, in general, as a rule, ordinarily, normally, customarily, typically, most of the time, almost always.

mote ▶ **noun** SPECK, particle, grain, spot, fleck, atom, scintilla.

moth-eaten ▶ **adjective** THREADBARE, worn (out), well worn, old, shabby, scruffy, tattered, ragged; *informal* tatty, the worse for wear; *N. Amer. informal* raggedy.

mother ▶ **noun** ❶ *I will ask my mother* FEMALE PARENT, materfamilias, matriarch; *informal* ma, mam, mammy, old lady, old woman; *Brit. informal* mum, mummy; *N. Amer. informal* mom, mommy; *Brit. informal, dated* mater. ❷ *the foal's mother* DAM. ❸ *the wish was mother of the deed* SOURCE, origin, genesis, fountainhead, inspiration, stimulus; *poetic/literary* wellspring.
– RELATED TERMS maternal, matri-.
– OPPOSITES child, father.
▶ **verb** ❶ *she mothered her husband* LOOK AFTER, care for, take care of, nurse, protect, tend, raise, rear; pamper, coddle, cosset, fuss over. ❷ *she mothered an illegitimate daughter* GIVE BIRTH TO, have, bear, produce; *N. Amer.* birth; *archaic* be brought to bed of.
– OPPOSITES neglect.

motherly ▶ **adjective** MATERNAL, maternalistic, protective, caring, loving, devoted, affectionate, fond, warm, tender, gentle, kind, kindly, understanding, compassionate.

motif ▶ **noun** ❶ *a colourful tulip motif* DESIGN, pattern, decoration, figure, shape, device, emblem, ornament. ❷ *a recurring motif in Pinter's work* THEME, idea, concept, subject, topic, leitmotif, element.

motion ▶ **noun** ❶ *the rocking motion of the boat | a planet's motion around the sun* MOVEMENT, moving, locomotion, rise and fall, shifting; progress, passage, passing, transit, course, travel, travelling. ❷ *a motion of the hand* GESTURE, movement, signal, sign, indication; wave, nod, gesticulation. ❸ *the motion failed to obtain a majority* PROPOSAL, proposition, recommendation, suggestion.
– RELATED TERMS kinetic.
▶ **verb** *he motioned her to sit down* GESTURE, signal, direct, indicate; wave, beckon, nod, gesticulate.
■ **in motion** MOVING, on the move, going, travelling, running, functioning, operational.
■ **set in motion** START, commence, begin, activate, initiate, launch, get under way, get going, get off the ground; trigger off, set off, spark off, generate, cause.

motionless ▶ **adjective** UNMOVING, still, stationary, stock-still, immobile, static, not moving a muscle, rooted to the spot, transfixed, paralysed, frozen.
– OPPOSITES moving.

motivate ▶ **verb** ❶ *she was primarily motivated by the desire for profit* PROMPT, drive, move, inspire, stimulate, influence, activate, impel, push, propel, spur (on). ❷ *it's the teacher's job to motivate the child* INSPIRE, stimulate, encourage, spur (on), excite, inspirit, incentivize, fire with enthusiasm.

motivation ▶ **noun** ❶ *his motivation was financial* MOTIVE, motivating force, incentive, stimulus, stimulation, inspiration, inducement, incitement, spur, reason. ❷ *staff motivation* ENTHUSIASM, drive, ambition, initiative, determination, enterprise; *informal* get-up-and-go.

motive ▶ **noun** ❶ *the motive for the attack* REASON, motivation, motivating force, rationale, grounds, cause, basis, object, purpose, intention; incentive, inducement, incitement, lure, inspiration, stimulus, stimulation, spur. ❷ *religious motives in art* MOTIF, theme, idea, concept, subject, topic, leitmotif.
▶ **adjective** *motive power* KINETIC, driving, impelling, propelling, propulsive, motor.

motley ▶ **adjective** MISCELLANEOUS, disparate, diverse, assorted, varied, diversified, heterogeneous.
– OPPOSITES homogeneous.

mottled ▶ **adjective** BLOTCHY, blotched, spotted, spotty, speckled, streaked, streaky, marbled, flecked, freckled, dappled, stippled, piebald, skewbald, brindled, brindle; *N. Amer.* pinto; *informal* splotchy.

motto ▶ **noun** MAXIM, saying, proverb, aphorism, adage, saw, axiom, apophthegm, formula, expression, phrase, dictum, precept; slogan, catchphrase; truism, cliché, platitude.

mould[1] ▶ **noun** ❶ *the molten metal is poured into a mould* CAST, die, form, matrix, shape, template, pattern, frame. ❷ *an actress in the traditional Hollywood mould* PATTERN, form, shape, format, model, kind, type, style; archetype, prototype. ❸ *he is a figure of heroic mould* CHARACTER, nature, temperament, disposition; calibre, kind, sort, variety, stamp, type.
▶ **verb** ❶ *a figure moulded from clay* SHAPE, form, fashion, model, work, construct, make, create, manufacture, sculpt, sculpture; forge, cast. ❷ *moulding US policy* DETERMINE, direct, control, guide, lead, influence, shape, form, fashion, make.

mould[2] ▶ **noun** *walls stained with mould* MILDEW, fungus, must, mouldiness, mustiness.

mould[3] ▶ **noun** *leaf mould* EARTH, soil, dirt, loam, humus.

moulder ▶ **verb** DECAY, decompose, rot (away), go mouldy, go off, go bad, spoil, putrefy.

mouldy ▶ **adjective** MILDEWED, mildewy, musty, mouldering, fusty; decaying, decayed, rotting, rotten, bad, spoiled, spoilt, decomposing.

mound ▶ **noun** ❶ *a mound of leaves* HEAP, pile, stack, mountain; mass, accumulation, assemblage. ❷ *high on the mound* HILLOCK, hill, knoll, rise, hummock, hump, embankment, bank, ridge, elevation, acclivity; *Scottish* brae; *Geology* drumlin. ❸ *a burial mound* BARROW, tumulus; motte.

▶ **verb** *mound up the rice on a serving plate* PILE (UP), heap (up).

mount ▶ **verb** ❶ *he mounted the stairs* GO UP, ascend, climb (up), scale. ❷ *the committee mounted the platform* CLIMB ON TO, jump on to, clamber on to, get on to. ❸ *they mounted their horses* GET ASTRIDE, bestride, get on to, hop on to. ❹ *the museum is mounting an exhibition* (PUT ON) DISPLAY, exhibit, present, install; organize, put on, stage. ❺ *the company mounted a takeover bid* ORGANIZE, stage, prepare, arrange, set up; launch, set in motion, initiate. ❻ *their losses mounted rapidly* INCREASE, grow, rise, escalate, soar, spiral, shoot up, rocket, climb, accumulate, build up, multiply. ❼ *cameras were mounted above the door* INSTALL, place, fix, set, put up, put in position.

– OPPOSITES descend.

▶ **noun** ❶ *he hung on to his mount's bridle* HORSE; *archaic* steed. ❷ *a decorated photograph mount* SETTING, backing, support, mounting, frame, stand.

mountain ▶ **noun** ❶ *a range of mountains* PEAK, height, mount, prominence, summit, pinnacle, alp; (**mountains**) range, massif, sierra; *Scottish* ben, Munro. ❷ *a mountain of work* GREAT DEAL, lot, profusion, abundance, quantity, backlog; *informal* heap, pile, stack, slew, lots, loads, heaps, piles, tons, masses; *N. Amer. informal* gobs. ❸ *a butter mountain* SURPLUS, surfeit, glut, oversupply.

■ **move mountains** ❶ *faith can move mountains* PERFORM MIRACLES, work/do wonders. ❷ *his fans move mountains to attend his performances* MAKE EVERY EFFORT, pull out all the stops, do one's utmost/best; *informal* bend/lean over backwards.

mountainous ▶ **adjective** ❶ *a mountainous region* HILLY, craggy, rocky, alpine; upland, highland. ❷ *mountainous waves* HUGE, enormous, gigantic, massive, giant, colossal, immense, tremendous, mighty; *informal* whopping, thumping, humongous; *Brit. informal* whacking, ginormous.

– OPPOSITES flat, tiny.

mountebank ▶ **noun** SWINDLER, charlatan, confidence trickster, fraud, fraudster, impostor, trickster, hoaxer, quack; *informal* con man, flimflammer, sharp; *N. Amer. informal* grifter, bunco artist; *Austral. informal* magsman, illywhacker.

mourn ▶ **verb** ❶ *Isobel mourned her husband* GRIEVE FOR, sorrow over, lament for, weep for, wail/keen over; *archaic* plain for. ❷ *he mourned the loss of the beautiful buildings* DEPLORE, bewail, bemoan, rue, regret.

mournful ▶ **adjective** SAD, sorrowful, doleful, melancholy, melancholic, woeful, grief-stricken, miserable, unhappy, heartbroken, broken-hearted, gloomy, dismal, desolate, dejected, despondent, depressed, downcast, disconsolate, woebegone, forlorn, rueful, lugubrious, joyless, cheerless; *poetic/literary* dolorous.

– OPPOSITES cheerful.

mourning ▶ **noun** ❶ *a period of mourning* GRIEF, grieving, sorrowing, lamentation, lament, keening, wailing, weeping; *poetic/literary* dole. ❷ *she was dressed in mourning* BLACK (CLOTHES), (widow's) weeds; *archaic* sables.

moustache ▶ **noun** WHISKERS, mustachios, handlebar moustache, walrus moustache, burnsides; *informal* tash; *N. Amer. informal* stash.

mousy ▶ **adjective** ❶ *mousy hair* LIGHTISH BROWN, brownish, brownish-grey, dun-coloured; dull, lacklustre. ❷ *a small, mousy woman* TIMID, quiet, fearful, timorous, shy, self-effacing, diffident, unassertive, unforthcoming, withdrawn, introverted, introvert.

mouth ▶ **noun** ❶ *open your mouth* lips, jaws; maw, muzzle; *informal* trap, chops, kisser; *Brit. informal* gob, cakehole; *N. Amer. informal* puss, bazoo. ❷ *the mouth of the cave* ENTRANCE, opening, entry, way in, access, ingress. ❸ *the mouth of the bottle* OPENING, rim, lip. ❹ *the mouth of the river* OUTFALL, outlet, debouchment; estuary, firth. ❺ (*informal*) *he's all mouth* BOASTING, bragging, idle talk, bombast, braggadocio; *informal* hot air. ❻ (*informal*) *you've got a lot of mouth* IMPUDENCE, cheek, cheekiness, insolence, impertinence, effrontery, presumption, presumptuousness, rudeness, disrespect; *informal* lip, (brass) neck; *Brit. informal* sauce, backchat; *N. Amer. informal* sass, sassiness, back talk.

▶ **verb** *he mouthed platitudes* UTTER, speak, say; pronounce, enunciate, articulate, voice, express; say insincerely, say for form's sake.

■ **down in the mouth** (*informal*). *See* UNHAPPY sense 1.

■ **keep one's mouth shut** (*informal*) SAY NOTHING, keep quiet, not breathe a word, not tell a soul; *informal* keep mum, not let the cat out of the bag.

■ **mouth off** (*informal*) RANT, spout, declaim, sound off.

mouthful ▶ **noun** ❶ *a mouthful of pizza* BITE, nibble, taste, bit, piece; spoonful, forkful. ❷ *a mouthful of beer* DRAUGHT, sip, swallow, drop, gulp, slug; *informal* swig. ❸ *'sesquipedalian' is a bit of a mouthful* TONGUE-TWISTER, long word, difficult word.

mouthpiece ▶ **noun** ❶ *the flute's mouthpiece* EMBOUCHURE. ❷ *a mouthpiece for the government* SPOKESPERSON, spokesman, spokeswoman, agent, representative, propagandist, voice.

movable ▶ **adjective** ❶ *movable objects* PORTABLE, transportable, transferable; mobile. ❷ *movable feasts* VARIABLE, changeable, alterable.

– OPPOSITES fixed.

movables ▶ **plural noun** POSSESSIONS, belongings, effects, property, goods, chattels, paraphernalia, impedimenta; *informal* gear.
– OPPOSITES fixtures, fittings.

move ▶ **verb** ❶ *she moved to the door | don't move!* GO, walk, proceed, progress, advance; budge, stir, shift, change position. ❷ *he moved the chair closer to the fire* CARRY, transport, transfer, shift. ❸ *things were moving too fast* (MAKE) PROGRESS, make headway, advance, develop. ❹ *he urged the council to move quickly* TAKE ACTION, act, take steps, do something, take measures; *informal* get moving. ❺ *she's moved to Cambridge* RELOCATE, move house, move away/out, change address/house, leave, go away, decamp; *Brit. informal* up sticks; *N. Amer. informal* pull up stakes. ❻ *I was deeply moved by the story* AFFECT, touch, impress, shake, upset, disturb, make an impression on. ❼ *she was moved to find out more about it* INSPIRE, prompt, stimulate, motivate, provoke, influence, rouse, induce, incite. ❽ *they are not prepared to move on this issue* CHANGE, budge, shift one's ground, change one's tune, change one's mind, have second thoughts; do a U-turn, do an about-face; *Brit.* do an about-turn. ❾ *she moves in the art worlds* CIRCULATE, mix, socialize, keep company, associate; *informal* hang out/around; *Brit. informal* hang about. ❿ *I move that we adjourn* PROPOSE, submit, suggest, advocate, recommend, urge.
▶ **noun** ❶ *his eyes followed her every move* MOVEMENT, motion, action; gesture, gesticulation. ❷ *his recent move to London* RELOCATION, change of house/address, transfer, posting. ❸ *the latest move in the war against drugs* INITIATIVE, step, action, act, measure, manoeuvre, tactic, stratagem. ❹ *it's your move* TURN, go; opportunity, chance.
■ **get a move on** (*informal*) HURRY UP, speed up, move faster; *informal* get cracking, get moving, step on it, shake a leg; *Brit. informal* get one's skates on, stir one's stumps; *N. Amer. informal* get a wiggle on; *dated* make haste.
■ **make a move** ❶ *waiting for the other side to make a move* DO SOMETHING, take action, act, take the initiative; *informal* get moving. ❷ (*Brit.*) *I'd better be making a move* LEAVE, take one's leave, be on one's way, get going, depart, be off; *informal* push off, shove off, split.
■ **on the move** ❶ *she's always on the move* TRAVELLING, in transit, moving, journeying, on the road; *informal* on the go. ❷ *the economy is on the move* PROGRESSING, making progress, advancing, developing.

movement ▶ **noun** ❶ *Rachel made a sudden movement | there was almost no movement* MOTION, move; gesture, gesticulation, sign, signal; action, activity. ❷ *the movement of supplies* TRANSPORTATION, shift, shifting, conveyance, moving, transfer. ❸ *the labour movement* POLITICAL GROUP, party, faction, wing, lobby, camp. ❹ *a movement to declare war on poverty* CAMPAIGN, crusade, drive, push. ❺ *there have been movements in the financial markets* DEVELOPMENT, change, fluctuation, variation. ❻ *the movement towards equality* TREND, tendency, drift, swing. ❼ *some movement will be made by the end of the month* PROGRESS, progression, advance. ❽ *a symphony in three movements* PART, section, division. ❾ *the clock's movement* MECHANISM, machinery, works, workings; *informal* innards, guts.

movie ▶ **noun** ❶ *a horror movie* FILM, (motion) picture, feature (film); *informal* flick; *dated* moving picture. ❷ *let's go to the movies* THE CINEMA, the pictures, the silver screen; *informal* the flicks, the big screen.

moving ▶ **adjective** ❶ *moving parts | a moving train* IN MOTION, operating, operational, working, going, on the move, active; movable, mobile. ❷ *a moving book* AFFECTING, touching, poignant, heart-warming, heart-rending, emotional, disturbing; inspiring, inspirational, stimulating, stirring. ❸ *the party's moving force* DRIVING, motivating, dynamic, stimulating, inspirational.
– OPPOSITES fixed, stationary.

mow ▶ **verb** *she had mown the grass* CUT (DOWN), trim; crop, clip.
■ **mow someone/something down** KILL, gun down, shoot down, cut down, cut to pieces, butcher, slaughter, massacre, annihilate, wipe out; *informal* blow away.

much ▶ **determiner** *did you get much help?* A LOT OF, a great/good deal of, a great/large amount of, plenty of, ample, copious, abundant, plentiful, considerable; *informal* lots of, loads of, heaps of, masses of, tons of.
– OPPOSITES little.
▶ **adverb** ❶ *it didn't hurt much* GREATLY, to a great extent/degree, a great deal, a lot, considerably, appreciably. ❷ *does he come here much?* OFTEN, frequently, many times, repeatedly, regularly, habitually, routinely, usually, normally, commonly; *informal* a lot.
▶ **pronoun** *he did so much for our team* A LOT, a great/good deal, plenty; *informal* lots, loads, heaps, masses.
■ **much of a muchness** (*informal*) VERY SIMILAR, much the same, very alike, practically identical.

muck ▶ **noun** ❶ *I'll just clean off the muck* DIRT, grime, filth, mud, slime, mess; *informal* crud, gunk, grunge, gloop; *Brit. informal* gunge, grot; *N. Amer. informal* guck, glop. ❷ *spreading muck on the fields* DUNG, manure, ordure, excrement, excreta, droppings, faeces, sewage; *N. Amer. informal* cow chips, horse apples.
■ **muck something up** (*informal*) MAKE A MESS OF, mess up, bungle, spoil, ruin, wreck; *informal* botch, make a hash of, muff, fluff, foul up, louse up; *Brit. informal* make a pig's ear of, make a Horlicks of; *N. Amer. informal* goof up.
■ **muck about/around** (*Brit. informal*) ❶ *he was mucking about with his mates* FOOL ABOUT/AROUND,

play about/around, clown about/around, footle about/around; *informal* mess about/around, horse about/around, lark (about/around). ❷ *someone's been mucking about with the video* INTERFERE, fiddle (about/around), play about/around, tamper, meddle, tinker; *informal* mess (about/around).

mucky ▶ **adjective** DIRTY, filthy, grimy, muddy, grubby, messy, soiled, stained, smeared, slimy, sticky, bespattered; *informal* cruddy, grungy, gloopy; *Brit. informal* gungy, grotty; *Austral./NZ informal* scungy; *poetic/literary* besmirched, begrimed, befouled.
– OPPOSITES clean.

mud ▶ **noun** MIRE, sludge, ooze, silt, clay, dirt, soil.

muddle ▶ **verb** ❶ *the papers have got muddled up* CONFUSE, mix up, jumble (up), disarrange, disorganize, disorder, disturb, mess up. ❷ *it would only muddle you* BEWILDER, confuse, bemuse, perplex, puzzle, baffle, nonplus, mystify.
▶ **noun** ❶ *the files are in a muddle* MESS, confusion, jumble, tangle, hotchpotch, mishmash, chaos, disorder, disarray, disorganization; *N. Amer.* hodgepodge. ❷ *a bureaucratic muddle* BUNGLE, mix-up, misunderstanding; *informal* foul-up; *N. Amer. informal* snafu.
■ **muddle along/through** COPE, manage, get by/along, scrape by/along, make do.

muddled ▶ **adjective** ❶ *a muddled pile of photographs* JUMBLED, in a jumble, in a muddle, in a mess, chaotic, in disorder, in disarray, topsy-turvy, disorganized, disordered, disorderly, mixed up, at sixes and sevens; *informal* higgledy-piggledy. ❷ *she felt muddled* CONFUSED, bewildered, bemused, perplexed, disorientated, disoriented, in a muddle, befuddled; *N. Amer. informal* discombobulated. ❸ *muddled thinking* INCOHERENT, confused, muddle-headed, woolly.
– OPPOSITES orderly, clear.

muddy ▶ **adjective** ❶ *muddy ground* WATERLOGGED, boggy, marshy, swampy, squelchy, squishy, mucky, slimy, spongy, wet, soft, heavy; *archaic* quaggy. ❷ *muddy boots* MUD-CAKED, muddied, dirty, filthy, mucky, grimy, soiled; *poetic/literary* begrimed. ❸ *muddy water* MURKY, cloudy, muddied, turbid; *N. Amer.* riled, roily. ❹ *a muddy pink* DINGY, dirty, drab, dull, sludgy.
– OPPOSITES clean, clear.
▶ **verb** ❶ *don't muddy your boots* MAKE MUDDY, dirty, soil, spatter, bespatter; *poetic/literary* besmirch, begrime. ❷ *these results muddy the situation* MAKE UNCLEAR, obscure, confuse, obfuscate, blur, cloud, befog.
– OPPOSITES clarify.

muff ▶ **verb** MISHANDLE, mismanage, mess up, make a mess of, bungle; *informal* botch, make a hash of, fluff, foul up, louse up; *Brit. informal* make a pig's ear of, make a Horlicks of; *N. Amer. informal* goof up.

muffle ▶ **verb** ❶ *everyone was muffled up in coats* WRAP (UP), swathe, enfold, envelop, cloak. ❷ *the sound of their footsteps was muffled* DEADEN, dull, dampen, damp down, mute, soften, quieten, tone down, mask, stifle, smother.

muffled ▶ **adjective** INDISTINCT, faint, muted, dull, soft, stifled, smothered.
– OPPOSITES loud.

mug[1] ▶ **noun** ❶ *a china mug* BEAKER, cup; tankard, glass, stein, flagon; *dated* seidel; *archaic* stoup. ❷ (*informal*) *her ugly mug. See* FACE noun sense 1. ❸ (*Brit. informal*) *he's no mug. See* FOOL noun sense 1.
▶ **verb** (*informal*) *he was mugged by three youths* ASSAULT, attack, set upon, beat up, rob; *informal* jump, rough up, lay into; *Brit. informal* duff up, do over.

mug[2]
■ **mug something up** (*informal*) *she's mugging up the Highway Code* STUDY, read up, cram; *informal* bone up (on); *Brit. informal* swot; *archaic* con.

muggy ▶ **adjective** HUMID, close, sultry, sticky, oppressive, airless, stifling, suffocating, stuffy, clammy, damp, heavy, fuggy.
– OPPOSITES fresh.

mulish ▶ **adjective** OBSTINATE, stubborn, pig-headed, recalcitrant, intransigent, unyielding, inflexible, bull-headed, stiff-necked; *Brit. informal* bloody-minded, bolshie.

mull
■ **mull something over** PONDER, consider, think over/about, reflect on, contemplate, turn over in one's mind, chew over, cogitate on, give some thought to; *archaic* pore on.

multicoloured ▶ **adjective** KALEIDOSCOPIC, psychedelic, colourful, multicolour, many-coloured, many-hued, rainbow, jazzy, varicoloured, variegated, harlequin, polychromatic.
– OPPOSITES monochrome.

multifarious ▶ **adjective** DIVERSE, many, numerous, various, varied, diversified, multiple, multitudinous, multiplex, manifold, multifaceted, different, heterogeneous, miscellaneous, assorted; *poetic/literary* myriad, divers.
– OPPOSITES homogeneous.

multiple ▶ **adjective** NUMEROUS, many, various, different, diverse, several, manifold, multifarious, multitudinous; *poetic/literary* myriad, divers.
– OPPOSITES single.

multiplicity ▶ **noun** ABUNDANCE, scores, mass, host, array, variety; range, diversity, heterogeneity, plurality, profusion; *informal* loads, stacks, heaps, masses, tons; *poetic/literary* myriad.

multiply ▶ **verb** ❶ *their difficulties seem to be multiplying* INCREASE, grow, become more numerous, accumulate, proliferate, mount up,

mushroom, snowball. ❷ *the rabbits have multiplied* BREED, reproduce, procreate.
– OPPOSITES decrease.

multitude ▶ noun ❶ *a multitude of birds* A LOT, a great/large number, a great/large quantity, host, horde, mass, swarm, abundance, profusion; scores, quantities, droves; *informal* slew, lots, loads, masses, stacks, heaps, tons, dozens, hundreds, thousands, millions; *N. Amer. informal* gazillions. ❷ *Father Peter addressed the multitude* CROWD, gathering, assembly, congregation, flock, throng, horde, mob; *formal* concourse. ❸ *political power in the hands of the multitude* THE (COMMON) PEOPLE, the populace, the masses, the rank and file, the commonality, the commonalty, the plebeians; the hoi polloi, the mob, the proletariat, the common herd, the rabble, the proles, the plebs.

multitudinous ▶ adjective NUMEROUS, many, abundant, profuse, prolific, copious, multifarious, innumerable, countless, numberless, infinite; *poetic/literary* divers, myriad.

mum[1] ▶ noun (*Brit. informal*) *my mum looks after me. See* MOTHER noun sense 1.

mum[2] (*informal*) ▶ adjective *he was keeping mum* SILENT, quiet, mute, dumb, tight-lipped, unforthcoming, reticent; *archaic* mumchance.
■ **mum's the word** (*informal*) SAY NOTHING, keep quiet, don't breathe a word, don't tell a soul, keep it secret, keep it to yourself, keep it under your hat; *informal* don't let on, keep shtum, don't let the cat out of the bag.

mumble ▶ verb MUTTER, murmur, speak indistinctly, talk under one's breath.

mumbo-jumbo ▶ noun NONSENSE, gibberish, claptrap, rubbish, balderdash, blather, hocus-pocus; *informal* gobbledegook, double Dutch, argle-bargle.

munch ▶ verb CHEW, champ, chomp, masticate, crunch, eat; *formal* manducate.

mundane ▶ adjective ❶ *her mundane life* HUMDRUM, dull, boring, tedious, monotonous, tiresome, wearisome, unexciting, uninteresting, uneventful, unvarying, unremarkable, repetitive, repetitious, routine, ordinary, everyday, day-to-day, run-of-the-mill, commonplace, workaday; *informal* (plain) vanilla. ❷ *the mundane world* EARTHLY, worldly, terrestrial, material, temporal, secular; *poetic/literary* sublunary.
– OPPOSITES extraordinary, spiritual.

municipal ▶ adjective CIVIC, civil, metropolitan, urban, city, town, borough.
– OPPOSITES rural.

municipality ▶ noun BOROUGH, town, city, district; *N. Amer.* precinct, township; *Scottish* burgh.

munificence ▶ noun GENEROSITY, bountifulness, open-handedness, magnanimity, lavishness, liberality, philanthropy, charitableness, largesse, big-heartedness, beneficence; *poetic/literary* bounty, bounteousness.

munificent ▶ adjective GENEROUS, bountiful, open-handed, magnanimous, philanthropic, princely, handsome, lavish, liberal, charitable, big-hearted, beneficent; *poetic/literary* bounteous.
– OPPOSITES mean.

murder ▶ noun ❶ *a brutal murder* KILLING, homicide, assassination, liquidation, extermination, execution, slaughter, butchery, massacre; manslaughter; *poetic/literary* slaying. ❷ (*informal*) *driving there was murder* HELL (ON EARTH), a nightmare, an ordeal, a trial, misery, torture, agony.
▶ verb ❶ *someone tried to murder him* KILL, put/do to death, assassinate, execute, liquidate, eliminate, dispatch, butcher, slaughter, massacre, wipe out; *informal* bump off, do in, do away with, knock off, blow away, blow someone's brains out, take out, dispose of; *N. Amer. informal* ice, rub out, smoke, waste; *poetic/literary* slay. ❷ (*informal*) *Anna was murdering a Mozart sonata. See* MANGLE sense 2. ❸ (*informal*) *he murdered his opponent. See* TROUNCE.

murderer, murderess ▶ noun KILLER, assassin, serial killer, butcher, slaughterer; *informal* hit man, hired gun; *dated* homicide; *poetic/literary* slayer.

murderous ▶ adjective ❶ *a murderous attack* HOMICIDAL, brutal, violent, savage, ferocious, fierce, vicious, bloodthirsty, barbarous, barbaric; fatal, lethal, deadly, mortal, death-dealing; *archaic* sanguinary. ❷ (*informal*) *a murderous schedule* ARDUOUS, gruelling, strenuous, punishing, onerous, exhausting, taxing, difficult, rigorous; *informal* killing, hellish.

murky ▶ adjective ❶ *a murky winter afternoon* DARK, gloomy, grey, leaden, dull, dim, overcast, cloudy, clouded, sunless, dismal, dreary, bleak; *poetic/literary* tenebrous. ❷ *murky water* DIRTY, muddy, cloudy, turbid; *N. Amer.* riled, roily. ❸ *her murky past* QUESTIONABLE, suspicious, suspect, dubious, dark, mysterious, secret; *informal* shady.
– OPPOSITES bright, clear.

murmur ▶ noun ❶ *his voice was a murmur* WHISPER, undertone, mutter, mumble. ❷ *there were murmurs in Tory ranks* COMPLAINT, grumble, grouse; *informal* gripe, moan. ❸ *the murmur of bees* HUM, humming, buzz, buzzing, thrum, thrumming, drone; sigh, rustle; *poetic/literary* susurration, murmuration.
▶ verb ❶ *he heard them murmuring in the hall* MUTTER, mumble, whisper, talk under one's breath, speak softly. ❷ *no one murmured at the delay* COMPLAIN, mutter, grumble, grouse; *informal* gripe, moan. ❸ *the wind was murmuring through the trees* RUSTLE, sigh; burble, purl; *poetic/literary* whisper.

muscle ▶ noun ❶ *he had muscle but no brains*

STRENGTH, power, muscularity, brawn, burliness; *informal* beef, beefiness; *poetic/literary* thew. ❷ *financial muscle* INFLUENCE, power, strength, might, force, forcefulness, weight; *informal* clout.

■ **muscle in** (*informal*) INTERFERE WITH, force one's way into, impose oneself on, encroach on; *informal* horn in on.

muscular ▶ adjective ❶ *muscular tissue* FIBROUS, sinewy. ❷ *he's very muscular* STRONG, brawny, muscly, sinewy, powerfully built, well muscled, burly, strapping, sturdy, powerful, athletic; *Physiology* mesomorphic; *informal* hunky, beefy; *poetic/literary* thewy. ❸ *a muscular economy* VIGOROUS, robust, strong, powerful, dynamic, potent, active.

muse¹ ▶ noun *the poet's muse* INSPIRATION, creative influence, stimulus; *formal* afflatus.

muse² ▶ verb *I mused on Toby's story* PONDER, consider, think over/about, mull over, reflect on, contemplate, turn over in one's mind, chew over, give some thought to, cogitate on; think, be lost in contemplation/thought, daydream; *archaic* pore on.

mush ▶ noun ❶ *some sort of greyish mush* PAP, pulp, slop, paste, purée, mash; *informal* gloop, goo, gook; *N. Amer. informal* glop. ❷ *romantic mush* SENTIMENTALITY, mawkishness; *informal* schmaltz, corn, slush; *N. Amer. informal* slop.

mushroom ▶ noun FUNGUS, field mushroom, chanterelle, button mushroom, cep, champignon, shiitake, oyster mushroom.

▶ verb *ecotourism mushroomed in the 1980s* PROLIFERATE, grow/develop rapidly, burgeon, spread, increase, expand, boom, explode, snowball, rocket, skyrocket; thrive, flourish, prosper.
– OPPOSITES contract.

mushy ▶ adjective ❶ *cook until the fruit is mushy* SOFT, semi-liquid, pulpy, pappy, sloppy, spongy, squashy, squelchy, squishy; *informal* gooey, gloopy; *Brit. informal* squidgy. ❷ (*informal*) *a mushy film* SENTIMENTAL, mawkish, emotional, saccharine; *informal* slushy, schmaltzy, weepy, corny; *Brit. informal* soppy; *N. Amer. informal* cornball, sappy, hokey, three-hankie.
– OPPOSITES firm.

musical ▶ adjective TUNEFUL, melodic, melodious, harmonious, sweet-sounding, sweet, mellifluous, euphonious, euphonic; *rare* mellifluent.
– OPPOSITES discordant.

musician ▶ noun PLAYER, performer, instrumentalist, accompanist, soloist, virtuoso, maestro; *historical* minstrel.

musing ▶ noun MEDITATION, thinking, contemplation, deliberation, pondering, reflection, rumination, introspection, daydreaming, reverie, dreaming, preoccupation, brooding; *formal* cogitation.

muss ▶ verb (*N. Amer. informal*) RUFFLE, tousle, dishevel, rumple, mess up, make a mess of, disarrange, make untidy.

must¹ ▶ verb *I must go* OUGHT TO, should, have (got) to, need to, be obliged to, be required to, be compelled to.

▶ noun (*informal*) *this video is a must* NOT TO BE MISSED, very good; necessity, essential, requirement, requisite.

must² ▶ noun *a smell of must* MOULD, mustiness, mouldiness, mildew, fustiness.

muster ▶ verb ❶ *they mustered 50,000 troops* ASSEMBLE, mobilize, rally, raise, summon, gather (together), mass, collect, convene, call up, call to arms, recruit, conscript; *US* draft; *archaic* levy. ❷ *reporters mustered outside her house* CONGREGATE, assemble, gather together, come together, collect together, convene, mass, rally; *formal* foregather. ❸ *she mustered her courage* SUMMON (UP), screw up, call up, rally.

▶ noun *the colonel called a muster* ROLL-CALL, assembly, rally, meeting, gathering, assemblage, congregation, convention; parade, review.

■ **pass muster** BE GOOD ENOUGH, come up to standard, come up to scratch, measure up, be acceptable/adequate, fill/fit the bill; *informal* make the grade, come/be up to snuff.

musty ▶ adjective ❶ *the room smelled musty* MOULDY, stale, fusty, damp, dank, mildewy, smelly, stuffy, airless, unventilated; *N. Amer. informal* funky. ❷ *the play seemed musty* UNORIGINAL, uninspired, unimaginative, hackneyed, stale, flat, tired, banal, trite, clichéd, old-fashioned, outdated; *informal* old hat.
– OPPOSITES fresh.

mutable ▶ adjective *the mutable nature of fashion* CHANGEABLE, variable, varying, fluctuating, shifting, inconsistent, unpredictable, inconstant, uneven, unstable, protean; *poetic/literary* fluctuant.
– OPPOSITES invariable.

mutant ▶ noun FREAK (OF NATURE), deviant, monstrosity, monster, mutation.

mutate ▶ verb CHANGE, metamorphose, evolve; transmute, transform, convert; *humorous* transmogrify.

mutation ▶ noun ❶ ALTERATION, change, variation, modification, transformation, metamorphosis, transmutation; *humorous* transmogrification. ❷ *a genetic mutation* MUTANT, freak (of nature), deviant, monstrosity, monster.

mute ▶ adjective ❶ *Yasmin remained mute* SILENT, speechless, dumb, unspeaking, tight-lipped, taciturn; *informal* mum; *archaic* mumchance. ❷ *a mute appeal* WORDLESS, silent, dumb, unspoken, unvoiced, unexpressed. ❸ *the church was mute* QUIET, silent, hushed. ❹ *he was deaf and mute* DUMB, unable to speak; *Medicine* aphasic.
– OPPOSITES voluble, spoken.

▶ verb ❶ *the noise was muted by the heavy curtains* DEADEN, muffle, dampen, soften, quieten;

stifle, smother, suppress. ❷ *Bruce muted his criticisms* RESTRAIN, soften, tone down, moderate, temper.
– OPPOSITES intensify.

muted ▶ adjective ❶ *the muted hum of traffic* MUFFLED, faint, indistinct, quiet, soft, low. ❷ *muted tones* SUBDUED, pastel, delicate, subtle, understated, restrained.

mutilate ▶ verb ❶ *the bodies had been mutilated* MANGLE, maim, disfigure, butcher, dismember; cripple. ❷ *the carved screen had been mutilated* VANDALIZE, damage, deface, ruin, destroy, wreck, violate, desecrate; *N. Amer. informal* trash.

mutinous ▶ adjective REBELLIOUS, insubordinate, subversive, seditious, insurgent, insurrectionary, rebel, riotous.

mutiny ▶ noun *a mutiny over pay arrears* INSURRECTION, rebellion, revolt, riot, uprising, insurgence, insubordination.
▶ verb *thousands of soldiers mutinied* RISE UP, rebel, revolt, riot, disobey/defy authority, be insubordinate.

mutt ▶ noun (*informal*) ❶ *a long-haired mutt* MONGREL, hound, dog, cur; *Austral. informal* mong, bitzer. ❷ *he pitied the poor mutt.* See FOOL noun sense 1.

mutter ▶ verb ❶ *a group of men stood muttering* TALK UNDER ONE'S BREATH, murmur, mumble, whisper, speak in an undertone. ❷ *back-benchers muttered about the reshuffle* GRUMBLE, complain, grouse, carp, whine; *informal* moan, gripe, beef, whinge; *Brit. informal* chunter; *N. Amer. informal* kvetch.

mutual ▶ adjective RECIPROCAL, reciprocated, requited, returned; common, joint, shared.

muzzle ▶ noun *the dog's velvety muzzle* SNOUT, nose, mouth, maw.
▶ verb *attempts to muzzle the media* GAG, silence, censor, stifle, restrain, check, curb, fetter.

muzzy ▶ adjective ❶ *she felt muzzy* GROGGY, light-headed, faint, dizzy, befuddled, befogged; *informal* dopey, woozy. ❷ *a slightly muzzy picture* BLURRED, blurry, fuzzy, unfocused, unclear, ill-defined, foggy, hazy.
– OPPOSITES clear.

myopic ▶ adjective ❶ *a myopic patient* SHORT-SIGHTED, near-sighted. ❷ *the government's myopic attitude* UNIMAGINATIVE, uncreative, unadventurous, narrow-minded, small-minded, short-term.
– OPPOSITES long-sighted, far-sighted.

myriad (*poetic/literary*) ▶ noun *myriads of insects* MULTITUDE, a large/great number, a large/great quantity, scores, quantities, mass, host, droves, horde; *informal* lots, loads, masses, stacks, tons, hundreds, thousands, millions; *N. Amer. informal* gazillions.
▶ adjective *the myriad lights of the city* INNUMERABLE, countless, infinite, numberless, untold, unnumbered, immeasurable, multitudinous, numerous; *poetic/literary* divers.

mysterious ▶ adjective ❶ *he vanished in mysterious circumstances* PUZZLING, strange, peculiar, curious, funny, queer, odd, weird, bizarre, mystifying, inexplicable, baffling, perplexing, incomprehensible, unexplainable, unfathomable. ❷ *he was being very mysterious* ENIGMATIC, inscrutable, secretive, reticent, evasive, furtive, surreptitious.
– OPPOSITES straightforward.

mystery ▶ noun ❶ *his death remains a mystery* PUZZLE, enigma, conundrum, riddle, secret, (unsolved) problem. ❷ *her past is shrouded in mystery* SECRECY, obscurity, uncertainty, mystique. ❸ *a murder mystery* THRILLER, detective story/novel, murder story; *informal* whodunnit.

mystic, mystical ▶ adjective ❶ *a mystic experience* SPIRITUAL, religious, transcendental, paranormal, other-worldly, supernatural, occult, metaphysical. ❷ *mystic rites* SYMBOLIC, symbolical, allegorical, representational, metaphorical. ❸ *a figure of mystical significance* CRYPTIC, concealed, hidden, abstruse, arcane, esoteric, inscrutable, inexplicable, unfathomable, mysterious, secret, enigmatic.

mystify ▶ verb BEWILDER, puzzle, perplex, baffle, confuse, confound, bemuse, nonplus, throw; *informal* flummox, stump, bamboozle, faze, fox.

mystique ▶ noun CHARISMA, glamour, romance, mystery, magic, charm, appeal, allure.

myth ▶ noun ❶ *ancient Greek myths* (FOLK) TALE, (folk) story, legend, fable, saga, mythos, mythus; lore, folklore. ❷ *the myths surrounding childbirth* MISCONCEPTION, fallacy, false notion, old wives' tale, fairy story/tale, fiction; *informal* (tall) story, cock and bull story.

mythical ▶ adjective ❶ *mythical beasts* LEGENDARY, mythological, fabled, fabulous, folkloric, fairy-tale, storybook; fantastical, imaginary, imagined, fictitious. ❷ *her mythical child* IMAGINARY, fictitious, make-believe, fantasy, invented, made-up, non-existent; *informal* pretend.

mythological ▶ adjective FABLED, fabulous, folkloric, fairy-tale, legendary, mythical, mythic, traditional; fictitious, imaginary.

mythology ▶ noun MYTH(S), legend(s), folklore, folk tales/stories, lore, tradition.

Nn

nab ▶ **verb** (*informal*) CATCH, capture, apprehend, arrest, seize; *informal* nail, cop, pull in, pick up; *Brit. informal* nick.

nabob ▶ **noun** VERY RICH PERSON, tycoon, magnate, millionaire, billionaire, multimillionaire; *informal* fat cat.

nadir ▶ **noun** THE LOWEST POINT/LEVEL, the all-time low, the bottom, rock-bottom; *informal* the pits.
–OPPOSITES zenith.

nag¹ ▶ **verb** ❶ *she's constantly nagging me* HARASS, keep on at, go on at, badger, give someone a hard time, chivvy, hound, harry, criticize, find fault with, moan at, grumble at; henpeck; *informal* hassle; *N. Amer. informal* ride; *Austral. informal* heavy. ❷ *this has been nagging me for weeks* TROUBLE, worry, bother, plague, torment, niggle, prey on one's mind; annoy, irritate; *informal* bug, aggravate.
▶ **noun** *she's such a nag* SHREW, nagger, harpy, termagant, harridan; *archaic* scold.

nag² ▶ **noun** *she rode the old nag* WORN-OUT HORSE, old horse, hack; *N. Amer. informal* plug, crowbait; *Austral./NZ informal* moke; *archaic* jade.

nagging ▶ **adjective** ❶ *his nagging wife* SHREWISH, complaining, grumbling, fault-finding, scolding, carping, criticizing. ❷ *a nagging pain* PERSISTENT, continuous, niggling, unrelenting, unremitting, unabating.

naiad ▶ **noun** (WATER) NYMPH.

nail ▶ **noun** ❶ *fastened with nails* TACK, spike, pin, rivet; hobnail. ❷ *biting her nails* FINGERNAIL, thumbnail, toenail.
–RELATED TERMS ungual.
▶ **verb** ❶ *a board was nailed to the wall* FASTEN, attach, fix, affix, secure, tack, hammer, pin. ❷ (*informal*) *nailing suspects* CATCH, capture, apprehend, arrest, seize; *informal* collar, nab, cop, pull in, pick up; *Brit. informal* nick. ❸ *the pictures had nailed the lie* EXPOSE, reveal, uncover, unmask, bring to light, detect, identify.
■ **hard as nails** CALLOUS, hard-hearted, heartless, unfeeling, unsympathetic, uncaring, insensitive, unsentimental, hardbitten, tough, lacking compassion.
■ **on the nail** IMMEDIATELY, at once, without delay, straight away, right away, promptly, directly, now, this minute; *N. Amer.* on the barrelhead.

naive ▶ **adjective** INNOCENT, unsophisticated, artless, ingenuous, inexperienced, guileless, unworldly, trusting; gullible, credulous, immature, callow, raw, green; *informal* wet behind the ears.
–OPPOSITES worldly.

naivety ▶ **noun** INNOCENCE, ingenuousness, guilelessness, unworldliness, trustfulness; gullibility, credulousness, credulity, immaturity, callowness.

naked ▶ **adjective** ❶ *a naked woman* NUDE, bare, in the nude, stark naked, having nothing on, stripped, unclothed, undressed, in a state of nature; *informal* without a stitch on, in one's birthday suit, in the raw/buff, in the altogether, in the nuddy, mother naked; *Brit. informal* starkers; *N. Amer. informal* buck naked. ❷ *a naked flame* UNPROTECTED, uncovered, exposed, unguarded. ❸ *the naked branches of the trees* BARE, barren, denuded, stripped, uncovered. ❹ *I felt naked and exposed* VULNERABLE, helpless, weak, powerless, defenceless, exposed, open to attack. ❺ *the naked truth | naked hostility* UNDISGUISED, plain, unadorned, unvarnished, unqualified, stark, bald; overt, obvious, open, patent, evident, apparent, manifest, unmistakable, blatant.
–OPPOSITES clothed, covered.

nakedness ▶ **noun** ❶ *she covered her nakedness* NUDITY, state of undress, bareness. ❷ *the nakedness of the landscape* BARENESS, barrenness, starkness.

namby-pamby ▶ **adjective** WEAK, feeble, spineless, effeminate, effete, limp-wristed, ineffectual; *informal* wet, weedy, wimpy, sissy.

name ▶ **noun** ❶ *her name's Gemma* designation, honorific, title, tag, epithet, label; *informal* moniker, handle; *formal* denomination, appellation. ❷ *the top names in the fashion industry* CELEBRITY, star, superstar, VIP, leading light, big name, luminary, expert, authority; *informal* celeb, somebody, megastar, big noise, big shot, bigwig, big gun. ❸ *the good name of the firm* REPUTATION, character, repute, standing, stature, esteem, prestige, cachet, kudos; renown, popularity, notability, distinction.
–RELATED TERMS nominal, onomastic.
▶ **verb** ❶ *they named the child Phoebe* CALL, give a name to, dub; label, style, term, title, entitle; baptize, christen; *formal* denominate. ❷ *the driver was named as Jason Penter* IDENTIFY, specify. ❸ *he has named his successor* CHOOSE, select, pick, decide on, nominate, designate.

named ▶ **adjective** ❶ *a girl named Anne* CALLED, by the name of, baptized, christened, known as; dubbed, entitled, styled, termed, labelled. ❷ *named individuals* SPECIFIED, designated, identified, cited, mentioned, singled out.

nameless ▶ **adjective** ❶ *a nameless photographer* UNNAMED, unidentified, anonymous, incognito, unspecified, unacknowledged, uncredited; unknown, unsung, uncelebrated. ❷ *nameless fears* UNSPEAKABLE, unutterable, inexpressible, indescribable; indefinable, vague, unspecified, unspecifiable.

namely ▶ **adverb** THAT IS (TO SAY), to be specific, specifically, viz, to wit.

nanny ▶ **noun** *the children's nanny* NURSEMAID, au pair, childminder, childcarer; governess; *dated* nurse.

▶ **verb** *stop nannying me* MOLLYCODDLE, cosset, coddle, wrap in cotton wool, baby, feather-bed; spoil, pamper, indulge, overindulge.

nap[1] ▶ **verb** *they were napping on the sofa* DOZE, sleep (lightly), take a nap, catnap, rest, take a siesta; *informal* snooze, snatch forty winks, get some shut-eye; *Brit. informal* have a kip, get some zizz; *N. Amer. informal* catch some Zs, catch a few Zs.

▶ **noun** *she is taking a nap* (LIGHT) SLEEP, catnap, siesta, doze, lie-down, rest; *informal* snooze, forty winks, shut-eye; *Brit. informal* kip, zizz.

■ **catch someone napping** CATCH OFF GUARD, catch unawares, (take by) surprise, catch out, find unprepared; *informal* catch someone with their trousers/pants down; *Brit. informal* catch on the hop.

nap[2] ▶ **noun** *the nap of the velvet* PILE, fibres, threads, weave, surface, grain.

nappy ▶ **noun** *N. Amer.* diaper; *Brit. dated* napkin.

narcissism ▶ **noun** VANITY, self-love, self-admiration, self-absorption, self-obsession, conceit, self-centredness, self-regard, egotism, egoism.

– OPPOSITES modesty.

narcissistic ▶ **adjective** VAIN, self-loving, self-admiring, self-absorbed, self-obsessed, conceited, self-centred, self-regarding, egotistic, egotistical, egoistic.

narcotic ▶ **noun** SOPORIFIC (DRUG), opiate, sleeping pill; painkiller, pain reliever, analgesic, anodyne, palliative, anaesthetic; tranquillizer, sedative; *informal* downer; *Medicine* stupefacient.

▶ **adjective** SOPORIFIC, sleep-inducing, opiate; painkilling, pain-relieving, analgesic, anodyne, anaesthetic, tranquillizing, sedative; *Medicine* stupefacient.

narked ▶ **adjective** (*Brit. informal*). *See* ANNOYED.

narrate ▶ **verb** TELL, relate, recount, describe, chronicle, give a report of, report; voice-over.

narration ▶ **noun** ❶ *a narration of past events* ACCOUNT, narrative, chronicle, description, report, relation, chronicling. ❷ *his narration of the story* VOICE-OVER, commentary.

narrative ▶ **noun** ACCOUNT, chronicle, history, description, record, report.

narrator ▶ **noun** ❶ *the narrator of 'the Arabian Nights'* STORYTELLER, teller of tales, relater, chronicler, romancer; raconteur, anecdotalist; *Austral. informal* magsman. ❷ *the film's narrator* VOICE-OVER, commentator.

– OPPOSITES listener, audience.

narrow ▶ **adjective** ❶ *the path became narrower* SMALL, tapered, tapering, narrowing; *archaic* strait. ❷ *her narrow waist* SLENDER, slim, slight, spare, attenuated, thin. ❸ *a narrow space* CONFINED, cramped, tight, restricted, limited, constricted. ❹ *a narrow range of products* LIMITED, restricted, circumscribed, small, inadequate, insufficient, deficient. ❺ *a narrow view of the world. See* NARROW-MINDED. ❻ *nationalism in the narrowest sense of the word* STRICT, literal, exact, precise. ❼ *a narrow escape* BY A VERY SMALL MARGIN, close, near, by a hair's breadth; *informal* by a whisker.

– OPPOSITES wide, broad.

▶ **verb** *the path narrowed | narrowing the gap between rich and poor* GET/BECOME/MAKE NARROWER, get/become/make smaller, taper, diminish, decrease, reduce, contract, shrink, constrict; *archaic* straiten.

narrowly ▶ **adverb** ❶ *one bullet narrowly missed him* (ONLY) JUST, barely, scarcely, hardly, by a hair's breadth; *informal* by a whisker. ❷ *she looked at me narrowly* CLOSELY, carefully, searchingly, attentively.

narrow-minded ▶ **adjective** INTOLERANT, illiberal, reactionary, conservative, parochial, provincial, insular, small-minded, petty, blinkered, inward-looking, narrow, hidebound, prejudiced, bigoted; *Brit.* parish-pump, blimpish; *N. Amer. informal* jerkwater.

– OPPOSITES tolerant.

narrows ▶ **plural noun** STRAIT(S), sound, channel, waterway, (sea) passage.

nascent ▶ **adjective** JUST BEGINNING, budding, developing, growing, embryonic, incipient, young, fledgling, evolving, emergent, dawning, burgeoning.

nastiness ▶ **noun** ❶ *my mother tried to shut herself off from nastiness* UNPLEASANTNESS, disagreeableness, offensiveness, vileness, foulness. ❷ *her uncharacteristic nastiness* UNKINDNESS, unpleasantness, unfriendliness, disagreeableness, rudeness, churlishness, spitefulness, maliciousness, meanness, ill temper, ill nature, viciousness, malevolence; *informal* bitchiness, cattiness. ❸ *I abhor such nastiness* OBSCENITY, indecency, offensiveness, crudity, vulgarity, pornography, smuttiness, lewdness, licentiousness.

nasty ▶ **adjective** ❶ *a nasty smell* UNPLEASANT, disagreeable, disgusting, distasteful, awful, dreadful, horrible, terrible, vile, foul, abominable, frightful, loathsome, revolting, repul-

sive, odious, sickening, nauseating, repellent, repugnant, horrendous, appalling, atrocious, offensive, objectionable, obnoxious, unsavoury, unappetizing, off-putting; noxious, foul-smelling, smelly, stinking, rank, fetid, malodorous, mephitic; *informal* ghastly, horrid, gruesome, diabolical, yucky, skanky, God-awful, gross; *Brit. informal* beastly, grotty, whiffy, pongy, niffy; *N. Amer. informal* lousy, funky; *Austral. informal* on the nose; *poetic/literary* miasmal, noisome. ❷ *the weather turned nasty* UNPLEASANT, disagreeable, foul, filthy, inclement; wet, stormy, cold, blustery. ❸ *she can be really nasty* UNKIND, unpleasant, unfriendly, disagreeable, rude, churlish, spiteful, malicious, mean, ill-tempered, ill-natured, vicious, malevolent, obnoxious, hateful, hurtful; *informal* bitchy, catty. ❹ *a nasty accident | a nasty cut* SERIOUS, dangerous, bad, awful, dreadful, terrible, severe; painful, ugly. ❺ *she had the nasty habit of appearing unannounced* ANNOYING, irritating, infuriating, disagreeable, unpleasant, maddening, exasperating. ❻ *they wrote nasty things on the wall* OBSCENE, indecent, offensive, crude, rude, dirty, filthy, vulgar, foul, gross, disgusting, pornographic, smutty, lewd; *informal* sick.
–OPPOSITES nice.

nation ▶ **noun** COUNTRY, (sovereign/nation) state, land, realm, kingdom, republic; fatherland, motherland; people, race.

national ▶ **adjective** ❶ *national politics* STATE, public, federal, governmental; civic, civil, domestic, internal. ❷ *a national strike* NATIONWIDE, countrywide, state, general, widespread.
–OPPOSITES local, international.
▶ **noun** *a French national* CITIZEN, subject, native; voter.

nationalism ▶ **noun** PATRIOTISM, patriotic sentiment, xenophobia, chauvinism, jingoism.

nationalistic ▶ **adjective** PATRIOTIC, nationalist, xenophobic, chauvinistic, jingoistic.

nationality ▶ **noun** ❶ *British nationality* CITIZENSHIP. ❷ *all the main nationalities of Ethiopia* ETHNIC GROUP, ethnic minority, tribe, clan, race, nation.

nationwide ▶ **adjective** NATIONAL, countrywide, state, general, widespread, extensive.
–OPPOSITES local.

native ▶ **noun** *a native of Sweden* INHABITANT, resident, local; citizen, national; aborigine, autochthon; *formal* dweller.
–OPPOSITES foreigner.
▶ **adjective** ❶ *the native population* INDIGENOUS, original, first, earliest, aboriginal, autochthonous. ❷ *native produce | native plants* DOMESTIC, home-grown, home-made, local; indigenous. ❸ *a native instinct for politics* INNATE, inherent, inborn, instinctive, intuitive, natural; hereditary, inherited, congenital, inbred, connate, connatural. ❹ *her native tongue* MOTHER, vernacular.
–OPPOSITES immigrant.

nativity ▶ **noun** BIRTH, childbirth, delivery; *formal* parturition.

natter (*Brit. informal*) ▶ **verb** *they nattered away. See* CHAT verb.
▶ **noun** *she rang up for a natter. See* CHAT noun.

natty ▶ **adjective** (*informal*) SMART, stylish, fashionable, dapper, debonair, dashing, spruce, well dressed, chic, elegant, trim; *N. Amer.* trig; *informal* snazzy, trendy, snappy, nifty; *N. Amer. informal* sassy, spiffy, fly, kicky.
–OPPOSITES scruffy.

natural ▶ **adjective** ❶ *a natural occurrence* NORMAL, ordinary, everyday, usual, regular, common, commonplace, typical, routine, standard, established, customary, accustomed, habitual. ❷ *natural produce* UNPROCESSED, organic, pure, wholesome, unrefined, pesticide-free, additive-free. ❸ *Alex is a natural leader* BORN, naturally gifted, untaught. ❹ *his natural instincts* INNATE, inborn, inherent, native, instinctive, intuitive; hereditary, inherited, inbred, congenital, connate, connatural. ❺ *she seemed very natural* UNAFFECTED, spontaneous, uninhibited, relaxed, unselfconscious, genuine, open, artless, guileless, ingenuous, unpretentious, without airs. ❻ *it was quite natural to think she admired him* REASONABLE, logical, understandable, (only) to be expected, predictable. ❼ (*archaic*) *his natural son* ILLEGITIMATE, born out of wedlock; *dated* born on the wrong side of the blanket; *archaic* bastard, misbegotten, baseborn.
–OPPOSITES abnormal, artificial, affected.

naturalist ▶ **noun** NATURAL HISTORIAN, life scientist, wildlife expert; biologist, botanist, zoologist, ornithologist, entomologist, ecologist, conservationist, environmentalist.

naturalistic ▶ **adjective** REALISTIC, real-life, true-to-life, lifelike, graphic, representational, photographic.
–OPPOSITES abstract.

naturalize ▶ **verb** ❶ *he was naturalized in 1950* GRANT CITIZENSHIP TO, make a citizen, give a passport to, enfranchise. ❷ *coriander has now been naturalized in southern Britain* ESTABLISH, introduce, acclimatize, domesticate; *N. Amer.* acclimate.

naturally ▶ **adverb** ❶ *he's naturally shy* BY NATURE, by character, inherently, innately, congenitally. ❷ *try to act naturally* NORMALLY, in a natural manner/way, unaffectedly, spontaneously, genuinely, unpretentiously; *informal* natural. ❸ *naturally, they wanted everything kept quiet* OF COURSE, as might be expected, needless to say; obviously, clearly, it goes without saying.
–OPPOSITES self-consciously.

naturalness ▶ **noun** UNSELFCONSCIOUSNESS, spontaneity, spontaneousness, straightforwardness, genuineness, openness, ingenuousness, lack of sophistication, unpretentiousness.

nature ▶ noun ❶ *the beauty of nature* THE NATURAL WORLD, Mother Nature, Mother Earth, the environment; the universe, the cosmos; wildlife, flora and fauna, the countryside. ❷ *such crimes are, by their very nature, difficult to hide* ESSENCE, inherent/basic/essential qualities, inherent/basic/essential features, character, complexion. ❸ *it was not in Daisy's nature to be bitchy* CHARACTER, personality, disposition, temperament, make-up, psyche, constitution. ❹ *experiments of a similar nature* KIND, sort, type, variety, category, ilk, class, species, genre, style, cast, order, kidney, mould, stamp; *N. Amer.* stripe.

naturist ▶ noun NUDIST.

naught ▶ noun (*archaic*) NOTHING (AT ALL), nil, zero; *N. English* nowt; *informal* zilch, sweet Fanny Adams, sweet FA; *Brit. informal* damn all, not a sausage; *N. Amer. informal* zip, nada, diddly-squat; *archaic* nought.

naughty ▶ adjective ❶ *a naughty boy* BADLY BEHAVED, disobedient, bad, misbehaved, misbehaving, wayward, defiant, unruly, insubordinate, wilful, delinquent, undisciplined, uncontrollable, ungovernable, unbiddable, disorderly, disruptive, fractious, recalcitrant, wild, wicked, obstreperous, difficult, troublesome, awkward, contrary, perverse, incorrigible; mischievous, playful, impish, roguish, rascally; *informal* brattish; *formal* refractory. ❷ *naughty jokes* INDECENT, risqué, rude, racy, ribald, bawdy, suggestive, improper, indelicate, indecorous; vulgar, dirty, filthy, smutty, crude, coarse, obscene, lewd, pornographic; *informal* raunchy; *Brit. informal* fruity, saucy; *N. Amer. informal* gamy; *euphemistic* adult.
– OPPOSITES well behaved, decent.

nausea ▶ noun ❶ *symptoms include nausea and a headache* SICKNESS, biliousness, queasiness; vomiting, retching, gagging; travel-sickness, seasickness, carsickness, airsickness. ❷ *it induces a feeling of nausea* DISGUST, revulsion, repugnance, repulsion, distaste, aversion, loathing, abhorrence.

nauseate ▶ verb CAUSE TO FEEL SICK, sicken, make sick, turn someone's stomach, make someone's gorge rise; *N. Amer. informal* gross out.

nauseating ▶ adjective SICKENING, stomach-churning, nauseous, emetic, sickly; disgusting, revolting, offensive, loathsome, obnoxious, foul; *N. Amer.* vomitous; *informal* sick-making, gross, gut-churning.

nauseous ▶ adjective ❶ *the food made her feel nauseous* SICK, nauseated, queasy, bilious, green about/at the gills, ill, unwell; seasick, carsick, airsick, travel-sick; *N. Amer. informal* barfy. ❷ *a nauseous stench. See* NAUSEATING.

nautical ▶ adjective MARITIME, marine, naval, seafaring; boating, sailing.

navel ▶ noun ❶ *informal* belly button, tummy button; *Anatomy* umbilicus. ❷ *the navel of Byzantine culture* CENTRE, central point, hub, focal point, focus, nucleus, heart, core; *poetic/literary* omphalos.
– RELATED TERMS umbilical, omphalo-.

navigable ▶ adjective PASSABLE, negotiable, traversable; clear, open, unobstructed, unblocked.

navigate ▶ verb ❶ *he navigated the yacht across the Atlantic* STEER, pilot, guide, direct, helm, captain; *Nautical* con; *informal* skipper. ❷ *the upper reaches are dangerous to navigate* SAIL (ACROSS/OVER), cross, traverse, negotiate. ❸ *I'll drive—you can navigate* MAP-READ, give directions.

navigation ▶ noun ❶ *the navigation of the ship* STEERING, piloting, sailing, guiding, directing, guidance. ❷ *the skills of navigation* HELMSMANSHIP, steersmanship, seamanship, map-reading, chart-reading.

navigator ▶ noun HELMSMAN, steersman, pilot, guide; *N. Amer.* wheelman.

navvy ▶ noun LABOURER, manual worker, workman, worker, hand, coolie, roustabout; *Austral./NZ* rouseabout; *archaic* mechanic.

navy ▶ noun ❶ *a 600-ship navy* FLEET, flotilla, armada. ❷ *a navy suit* NAVY BLUE, dark blue, indigo.

nay ▶ adverb OR RATHER, (and) indeed, and even, in fact, actually, in truth.

near ▶ adverb ❶ *her children all live near* CLOSE (BY), nearby, close/near at hand, in the neighbourhood, in the vicinity, at hand, within reach, on the doorstep, a stone's throw away; *informal* within spitting distance; *archaic* nigh. ❷ *near perfect conditions* ALMOST, just about, nearly, practically, virtually; *poetic/literary* well-nigh.
▶ preposition *a hotel near the seafront* CLOSE TO, close by, by, a short distance from, in the vicinity of, in the neighbourhood of, within reach of, a stone's throw away from; *informal* within spitting distance of.
▶ adjective ❶ *the nearest house* CLOSE, nearby, close/near at hand, at hand, a stone's throw away, within reach, accessible, handy, convenient; *informal* within spitting distance. ❷ *the final judgement is near* IMMINENT, in the offing, close/near at hand, at hand, (just) round the corner, impending, looming. ❸ *a near relation* CLOSELY RELATED, close, related. ❹ *a near escape* NARROW, close, by a hair's breadth; *informal* by a whisker.
– OPPOSITES far, distant.
▶ verb ❶ *by dawn we were nearing Moscow* APPROACH, draw near/nearer to, get close/closer to, advance towards, close in on. ❷ *the death toll is nearing 3,000* VERGE ON, border on, approach.

nearby ▶ adjective *one of the nearby villages* NOT FAR AWAY/OFF, close/near at hand, close (by),

near, within reach, at hand, neighbouring; accessible, handy, convenient.
–OPPOSITES faraway.
▶ **adverb** *her mother lives nearby* CLOSE (BY), close/near at hand, near, a short distance away, in the neighbourhood, in the vicinity, at hand, within reach, on the doorstep, (just) round the corner.

nearly ▶ **adverb** ALMOST, (just) about, more or less, practically, virtually, all but, as good as, not far off, to all intents and purposes; not quite; *informal* pretty much, pretty well; *poetic/literary* well-nigh.

near miss ▶ **noun** CLOSE THING, near thing, narrow escape; *informal* close shave.

nearness ▶ **noun** ❶ *the town's nearness to Rome* CLOSENESS, proximity, propinquity; accessibility, handiness; *archaic* vicinity. ❷ *the nearness of death* IMMINENCE, closeness, immediacy.

near-sighted ▶ **adjective** SHORT-SIGHTED, myopic.

neat ▶ **adjective** ❶ *the bedroom was neat and clean* TIDY, orderly, well ordered, in (good) order, shipshape (and Bristol fashion), in apple-pie order, spick and span, uncluttered, straight, trim. ❷ *he's very neat* SMART, spruce, dapper, trim, well groomed, well turned out; *N. Amer.* trig; *informal* natty. ❸ *her neat script* WELL FORMED, regular, precise, elegant, well proportioned. ❹ *this neat little gadget* COMPACT, well designed, handy; *Brit. informal* dinky. ❺ *his neat footwork* SKILFUL, deft, dexterous, adroit, adept, expert; *informal* nifty. ❻ *a neat solution* CLEVER, ingenious, inventive. ❼ *neat gin* UNDILUTED, straight, unmixed; *N. Amer. informal* straight up. ❽ (*N. Amer. informal*) *we had a really neat time. See* WONDERFUL.
–OPPOSITES untidy.

neaten ▶ **verb** TIDY (UP), make neat/neater, straighten (up), smarten (up), spruce up, put in order; *N. Amer. informal* fix up.

neatly ▶ **adverb** ❶ *neatly arranged papers* TIDILY, methodically, systematically; smartly, sprucely. ❷ *the point was neatly put* CLEVERLY, aptly, elegantly. ❸ *a neatly executed header* SKILFULLY, deftly, adroitly, adeptly, expertly.

neatness ▶ **noun** ❶ *the neatness of the cottage* TIDINESS, orderliness, trimness, spruceness; smartness. ❷ *the neatness of her movements* GRACE, gracefulness, nimbleness, deftness, dexterity, adroitness, agility.

nebulous ▶ **adjective** ❶ *the figure was nebulous* INDISTINCT, indefinite, unclear, vague, hazy, cloudy, fuzzy, misty, blurred, blurry, foggy; faint, shadowy, obscure, formless, amorphous. ❷ *nebulous ideas* VAGUE, ill-defined, unclear, hazy, uncertain, indefinite, indeterminate, imprecise, unformed, muddled, confused, ambiguous.
–OPPOSITES clear.

necessarily ▶ **adverb** AS A CONSEQUENCE, as a result, automatically, as a matter of course, certainly, surely, definitely, incontrovertibly, undoubtedly, inevitably, unavoidably, inescapably, ineluctably, of necessity; *formal* perforce.

necessary ▶ **adjective** ❶ *planning permission is necessary* OBLIGATORY, requisite, required, compulsory, mandatory, imperative, needed, de rigueur; essential, indispensable, vital. ❷ *a necessary consequence* INEVITABLE, unavoidable, inescapable, inexorable, ineluctable; predetermined, preordained.
▶ **noun** (*informal*) *could you lend me the necessary? See* MONEY sense 1.

necessitate ▶ **verb** MAKE NECESSARY, entail, involve, mean, require, demand, call for, be grounds for, warrant, constrain, force.

necessitous ▶ **adjective** NEEDY, poor, short of money, disadvantaged, underprivileged, in straitened circumstances, impoverished, poverty-stricken, penniless, impecunious, destitute, pauperized, indigent; *Brit.* on the breadline, without a penny to one's name; *informal* on one's uppers, hard up, without two pennies to rub together; *Brit. informal* in Queer Street; *formal* penurious.
–OPPOSITES wealthy.

necessity ▶ **noun** ❶ *the VCR is now regarded as a necessity* ESSENTIAL, indispensable item, requisite, prerequisite, necessary, basic, sine qua non, desideratum. ❷ *political necessity forced him to resign* FORCE OF CIRCUMSTANCE, obligation, need, call, exigency; force majeure. ❸ *the necessity of growing old* INEVITABILITY, certainty, inescapability, inexorability, ineluctability. ❹ *necessity made them steal* POVERTY, need, neediness, want, deprivation, privation, penury, destitution, indigence.
■ **of necessity** NECESSARILY, inevitably, unavoidably, inescapably, ineluctably; as a matter of course, naturally, automatically, certainly, surely, definitely, incontrovertibly, undoubtedly; *formal* perforce.

neck ▶ **noun** *technical* cervix; *archaic, informal* scrag.
–RELATED TERMS cervical, jugular.
▶ **verb** (*informal*) KISS, caress, pet; *informal* smooch, canoodle; *Brit. informal* snog; *N. Amer. informal* make out; *informal, dated* spoon.
■ **neck and neck** LEVEL, equal, tied, side by side; *Brit.* level pegging; *informal* even-steven(s).

necklace ▶ **noun** CHAIN, choker, necklet; beads, pearls; pendant, locket; *historical* torc.

necromancer ▶ **noun** SORCERER, sorceress, (black) magician, wizard, warlock, witch, enchantress, occultist, diviner; spiritualist, medium.

necromancy ▶ **noun** SORCERY, (black) magic, witchcraft, witchery, wizardry, the occult, occultism, voodoo, hoodoo; divination; spiritualism.

necropolis ▶ **noun** CEMETERY, graveyard, churchyard, burial ground; *informal* boneyard; *historical* potter's field; *archaic* God's acre.

née ▶ **adjective** *Jill Wyatt, née Peters* BORN, formerly, previously; *formal* heretofore.

need ▶ **verb** ❶ *do you need money?* REQUIRE, be in need of, have need of, want; be crying out for, be desperate for; demand, call for, necessitate, entail, involve; lack, be without, be short of. ❷ *you needn't come* HAVE TO, be obliged to, be compelled to. ❸ *she needed him so much* YEARN FOR, pine for, long for, desire, miss.
▶ **noun** ❶ *there's no need to apologize* NECESSITY, obligation, requirement, call, demand. ❷ *basic human needs* REQUIREMENT, essential, necessity, want, requisite, prerequisite, demand, desideratum. ❸ *their need was particularly pressing* NEEDINESS, want, poverty, deprivation, privation, hardship, destitution, indigence. ❹ *my hour of need* DIFFICULTY, trouble, distress; crisis, emergency, urgency, extremity.
■ **in need** NEEDY, necessitous, deprived, disadvantaged, underprivileged, poor, impoverished, poverty-stricken, destitute, impecunious, indigent; *Brit.* on the breadline; *formal* penurious.

needed ▶ **adjective** NECESSARY, required, wanted, desired, lacking; essential, requisite, compulsory, obligatory, mandatory.
– OPPOSITES optional.

needful ▶ **adjective** (*formal*) NECESSARY, needed, required, requisite; essential, imperative, vital, indispensable.

needle ▶ **noun** ❶ *a needle and thread* darner, bodkin. ❷ *the virus is transmitted via needles* hypodermic needle; *informal* hype, spike. ❸ *the needle on the meter* INDICATOR, pointer, marker, arrow, hand. ❹ *put the needle on the record* STYLUS.
▶ **verb** (*informal*) *he needled her too much. See* ANNOY.

needless ▶ **adjective** UNNECESSARY, inessential, non-essential, unneeded, undesired, unwanted, uncalled for; gratuitous, pointless; dispensable, expendable, superfluous, redundant, excessive, supererogatory.
– OPPOSITES necessary.
■ **needless to say** OF COURSE, as one would expect, not unexpectedly, it goes without saying, obviously, naturally; *informal* natch.

needlework ▶ **noun** SEWING, stitching, embroidery, needlepoint, needlecraft, tapestry, crewel work.

needy ▶ **adjective** POOR, deprived, disadvantaged, underprivileged, necessitous, in need, needful, hard up, in straitened circumstances, poverty-stricken, indigent, impoverished, pauperized, destitute, impecunious, penniless, moneyless; *Brit.* on the breadline; *informal* on one's uppers, broke, strapped (for cash), without two pennies to rub together; *Brit. informal* skint, stony broke, in Queer Street; *N. Amer. informal* stone broke; *formal* penurious.
– OPPOSITES wealthy.

ne'er-do-well ▶ **noun** GOOD-FOR-NOTHING, layabout, loafer, idler, shirker, sluggard, slugabed, drone; *informal* waster, lazybones; *Brit. informal* skiver; *N. Amer. informal* bum, gold brick; *archaic* wastrel.

nefarious ▶ **adjective** WICKED, evil, sinful, iniquitous, egregious, heinous, atrocious, vile, foul, abominable, odious, depraved, monstrous, fiendish, diabolical, unspeakable, despicable; villainous, criminal, corrupt, illegal, unlawful; *dated* dastardly.
– OPPOSITES good.

negate ▶ **verb** ❶ *they negated the court's ruling* INVALIDATE, nullify, neutralize, cancel; undo, reverse, annul, void, revoke, rescind, repeal, retract, countermand, overrule, overturn; *Law* avoid; *formal* abrogate. ❷ *he negates the political nature of education* DENY, dispute, contradict, controvert, refute, rebut, reject, repudiate; *formal* gainsay.
– OPPOSITES validate, confirm.

negation ▶ **noun** ❶ *negation of the findings* DENIAL, contradiction, repudiation, refutation, rebuttal; nullification, cancellation, revocation, repeal, retraction; *Law* disaffirmation; *formal* abrogation. ❷ *evil is not just the negation of goodness* OPPOSITE, reverse, antithesis, contrary, inverse, converse; absence, want.

negative ▶ **adjective** ❶ *a negative reply* OPPOSING, opposed, contrary, anti-, dissenting, dissentient; saying 'no', in the negative. ❷ *stop being so negative* PESSIMISTIC, defeatist, gloomy, cynical, fatalistic, dismissive, antipathetic; unenthusiastic, uninterested, unresponsive. ❸ *a negative effect on the economy* HARMFUL, bad, adverse, damaging, detrimental, unfavourable, disadvantageous.
– OPPOSITES positive, optimistic, favourable.
▶ **noun** *he murmured a negative* 'NO', refusal, rejection, veto; dissension, contradiction; denial.
▶ **verb** ❶ *the bill was negatived by the house* REJECT, turn down, refuse, veto, squash; *informal* give the thumbs down to. ❷ *his arguments were negatived* DISPROVE, belie, invalidate, refute, rebut, discredit; contradict, deny, negate; *formal* gainsay. ❸ *they tried to negative the effect of the tax* NEUTRALIZE, cancel out, counteract, nullify, negate; offset, balance, counterbalance.
– OPPOSITES ratify, prove.

negativity ▶ **noun** PESSIMISM, defeatism, gloom, cynicism, hopelessness, despair, despondency; apathy, indifference.

neglect ▶ **verb** ❶ *she neglected the children* FAIL TO LOOK AFTER, leave alone, abandon; *poetic/literary* forsake. ❷ *he's neglecting his work* PAY NO ATTENTION TO, let slide, not attend to, be remiss about, be lax about, leave undone, shirk. ❸ *don't neglect our advice* DISREGARD, ignore, pay no attention to, take no notice of, pay no

heed to, overlook; disdain, scorn, spurn. ❹ *I neglected to inform her* FAIL, omit, forget.
– OPPOSITES cherish, heed, remember.
▸ **noun** ❶ *the place had an air of neglect* DISREPAIR, dilapidation, deterioration, shabbiness, disuse, abandonment. ❷ *her doctor was guilty of neglect* NEGLIGENCE, dereliction of duty, remissness, carelessness, heedlessness, unconcern, laxity, slackness, irresponsibility; *formal* delinquency. ❸ *the relative neglect of women* DISREGARD, ignoring, overlooking; inattention to, indifference to, heedlessness to.
– OPPOSITES care, attention.

neglected ▸ **adjective** ❶ *neglected animals* UNCARED FOR, abandoned; mistreated, maltreated; *poetic/literary* forsaken. ❷ *a neglected cottage* DERELICT, dilapidated, tumbledown, ramshackle, untended. ❸ *a neglected masterpiece of prose* DISREGARDED, forgotten, overlooked, ignored, unrecognized, unnoticed, unsung, underestimated, undervalued, unappreciated.

neglectful ▸ **adjective.** *See* NEGLIGENT.

negligent ▸ **adjective** NEGLECTFUL, remiss, careless, lax, irresponsible, inattentive, heedless, thoughtless, unmindful, forgetful; slack, sloppy; *N. Amer.* derelict; *formal* delinquent.
– OPPOSITES dutiful.

negligible ▸ **adjective** TRIVIAL, trifling, insignificant, unimportant, minor, inconsequential; minimal, small, slight, inappreciable, infinitesimal, nugatory, petty; paltry, inadequate, insufficient, meagre, pitiful; *informal* minuscule, piddling, measly, poxy; *formal* exiguous.
– OPPOSITES significant.

negotiable ▸ **adjective** ❶ *the salary will be negotiable* OPEN TO DISCUSSION, discussable, flexible, open to modification; unsettled, undecided. ❷ *the path was negotiable* PASSABLE, navigable, crossable, traversable; clear, unblocked, unobstructed. ❸ *negotiable cheques* transferable; valid.

negotiate ▸ **verb** ❶ *she refused to negotiate* DISCUSS TERMS, talk, consult, parley, confer, debate; compromise; mediate, intercede, arbitrate, moderate, conciliate; bargain, haggle. ❷ *he negotiated a new contract* ARRANGE, broker, work out, thrash out, agree on; settle, clinch, conclude, pull off, bring off, transact; *informal* sort out, swing. ❸ *I negotiated the obstacles* GET ROUND, get past, get over, clear, cross; surmount, overcome, deal with, cope with.

negotiation ▸ **noun** ❶ *the negotiations resume next week* DISCUSSION(S), talks, deliberations; conference, debate, dialogue, consultation; mediation, arbitration, conciliation. ❷ *the negotiation of the deal* ARRANGEMENT, brokering; settlement, conclusion, completion, transaction.

negotiator ▸ **noun** MEDIATOR, arbitrator, arbiter, moderator, go-between, middleman, intermediary, intercessor, intervener, conciliator; representative, spokesperson, broker, bargainer.

neigh ▸ **verb** WHINNY, bray, nicker, snicker, whicker.

neighbourhood ▸ **noun** ❶ *a quiet neighbourhood* DISTRICT, area, locality, locale, quarter, community; part, region, zone; *informal* neck of the woods; *Brit. informal* manor; *N. Amer. informal* hood, nabe. ❷ *in the neighbourhood of Canterbury* VICINITY, environs, purlieus, precincts, vicinage.
■ **in the neighbourhood of** APPROXIMATELY, about, around, roughly, in the region of, of the order of, nearly, almost, close to, just about, practically, there or thereabouts, circa; *Brit.* getting on for.

neighbouring ▸ **adjective** ADJACENT, adjoining, bordering, connecting, abutting; proximate, near, close (at hand), next-door, nearby, in the vicinity, vicinal.
– OPPOSITES remote.

neighbourly ▸ **adjective** OBLIGING, helpful, friendly, kind, amiable, amicable, affable, genial, agreeable, hospitable, companionable, well disposed, civil, cordial, good-natured, nice, pleasant, generous; considerate, thoughtful, unselfish; *Brit. informal* decent.
– OPPOSITES unfriendly.

nemesis ▸ **noun** ❶ *this could be the bank's nemesis* DOWNFALL, undoing, ruin, ruination, destruction, Waterloo. ❷ *the nemesis that his crime deserved* RETRIBUTION, vengeance, punishment, just deserts; fate, destiny.

neologism ▸ **noun** NEW WORD, new expression, new term, new phrase, coinage; made-up word, nonce-word.

neophyte ▸ **noun** ❶ *a neophyte of the monastery* NOVICE, novitiate; postulant, catechumen. ❷ *cooking classes are offered to neophytes* BEGINNER, learner, novice, newcomer; initiate, tyro, fledgling; trainee, apprentice, probationer; *N. Amer.* tenderfoot; *informal* rookie, newbie, newie; *N. Amer. informal* greenhorn.

ne plus ultra ▸ **noun** THE LAST WORD, the ultimate, the perfect example, the height, the acme, the zenith, the epitome, the quintessence; *archaic* the nonsuch.

nepotism ▸ **noun** FAVOURITISM, preferential treatment, the old boy network, looking after one's own, bias, partiality, partisanship; *Brit.* jobs for the boys, the old school tie.
– OPPOSITES impartiality.

nerd ▸ **noun** (*informal*) BORE; *informal* dork, dweeb, geek; *Brit. informal* anorak, spod; *N. Amer. informal* Poindexter.

nerve ▸ **noun** ❶ *the nerves that transmit pain* nerve fibre, neuron, axon; *Physiology* dendrite. ❷ *the match will be a test of nerve* CONFIDENCE, assurance, cool-headedness, self-possession; courage, bravery, pluck, boldness, intrepidity,

fearlessness, daring; determination, will power, spirit, backbone, fortitude, mettle, grit, stout-heartedness; *informal* guts, spunk; *Brit. informal* bottle; *N. Amer. informal* moxie. ❸ *he had the nerve to chat her up* AUDACITY, cheek, effrontery, gall, temerity, presumption, boldness, brazenness, impudence, impertinence, arrogance, cockiness; *informal* face, front, brass neck, chutzpah; *Brit. informal* sauce. ❹ *pre-wedding nerves* ANXIETY, tension, nervousness, stress, worry, cold feet, apprehension; *informal* butterflies (in one's stomach), collywobbles, the jitters, the shakes; *Brit. informal* the (screaming) abdabs.
– RELATED TERMS neural, neuro-.

■ **get on someone's nerves** IRRITATE, annoy, irk, anger, bother, vex, provoke, displease, exasperate, infuriate, gall, pique, needle, ruffle someone's feathers, try someone's patience; jar on, grate on, rankle; *Brit.* rub up the wrong way; *informal* aggravate, get to, bug, miff, peeve, rile, nettle, get up someone's nose, hack off, get someone's goat; *Brit. informal* nark, get on someone's wick, wind up.

■ **nerve oneself** BRACE ONESELF, steel oneself, summon one's courage, gear oneself up, prepare oneself; fortify oneself; *informal* psych oneself up; *poetic/literary* gird one's loins.

nerveless ▶ adjective ❶ *her nerveless fingers* INERT, lifeless; weak, powerless, feeble. ❷ *a nerveless lack of restraint* CONFIDENT, self-confident, self-assured, self-possessed, cool, calm, {cool, calm, and collected}, composed, relaxed.
– OPPOSITES nervous.

nerve-racking ▶ adjective STRESSFUL, anxious, worrying, fraught, nail-biting, tense, difficult, trying, worrisome, daunting, frightening; *informal* scary, hairy.

nervous ▶ adjective ❶ *a nervous woman* HIGHLY STRUNG, anxious, edgy, tense, excitable, jumpy, skittish, brittle, neurotic; timid, mousy, shy, fearful; *Brit.* nervy. ❷ *he was so nervous he couldn't eat* ANXIOUS, worried, apprehensive, on edge, edgy, tense, stressed, agitated, uneasy, restless, worked up, keyed up, overwrought, jumpy; fearful, frightened, scared, shaky, in a cold sweat; *informal* with butterflies in one's stomach, jittery, twitchy, in a state, uptight, wired, in a flap, het up; *Brit. informal* strung up, having kittens; *N. Amer. informal* spooky, squirrelly. ❸ *a nervous disorder* NEUROLOGICAL, neural.
– OPPOSITES relaxed, calm.

nervous breakdown ▶ noun (MENTAL) COLLAPSE, breakdown, crisis, trauma; nervous exhaustion, mental illness; *informal* crack-up.

nervousness ▶ noun ANXIETY, edginess, tension, agitation, stress, worry, apprehension, uneasiness, disquiet, fear, trepidation, perturbation, alarm; *Brit.* nerviness; *informal* butterflies (in one's stomach), collywobbles, the jitters, the willies, the heebie-jeebies, the shakes; *Brit. informal* the (screaming) abdabs.

nervy ▶ adjective. *See* NERVOUS senses 1, 2.

nest ▶ noun ❶ *the birds built a nest* ROOST, eyrie. ❷ *the animals disperse rapidly from the nest* LAIR, den, burrow, set. ❸ *a cosy love nest* HIDEAWAY, hideout, retreat, shelter, refuge, snuggery, den; *informal* hidey-hole. ❹ *a nest of intrigue* HOTBED, den, breeding ground, cradle.

nest egg ▶ noun (LIFE) SAVINGS, cache, funds, reserve.

nestle ▶ verb SNUGGLE, cuddle, huddle, nuzzle, settle, burrow, snug down.

nestling ▶ noun CHICK, fledgling, baby bird.

net[1] ▶ noun ❶ *fishermen mending their nets* FISHING NET, dragnet, drift net, trawl net, landing net, gill net, cast net. ❷ *a dress of green net* NETTING, meshwork, webbing, tulle, fishnet, openwork, lace, latticework. ❸ *he managed to escape the net* TRAP, snare.
▶ verb *they netted big criminals* CATCH, capture, trap, entrap, snare, ensnare, bag, hook, land; *informal* nab, collar.

net[2] ▶ adjective ❶ *net earnings* AFTER TAX, after deductions, take-home, final; *informal* bottom line. ❷ *the net result* FINAL, end, ultimate, closing; overall, actual, effective.
– OPPOSITES gross.
▶ verb *she netted £50,000* EARN, make, get, gain, obtain, acquire, accumulate, take home, bring in, pocket, realize, be paid; *informal* rake in.

nether ▶ adjective LOWER, low, bottom, bottommost, under, basal; underground.
– OPPOSITES upper.

netherworld ▶ noun HELL, the underworld, the infernal regions, the abyss; eternal damnation, perdition; Hades, Acheron, Gehenna, Tophet, Sheol; *poetic/literary* the pit.
– OPPOSITES heaven.

nettle ▶ verb IRRITATE, annoy, irk, gall, vex, anger, exasperate, infuriate, provoke; upset, displease, offend, affront, pique, get on someone's nerves, try someone's patience, ruffle someone's feathers; *Brit.* rub up the wrong way; *N. Amer.* rankle; *informal* peeve, aggravate, miff, rile, needle, get to, bug, get up someone's nose, hack off, get someone's goat; *Brit. informal* nark, get on someone's wick, wind up; *N. Amer. informal* tick off.

network ▶ noun ❶ *a network of arteries* WEB, lattice, net, matrix, mesh, criss-cross, grid, reticulum, reticulation; *Anatomy* plexus. ❷ *a network of lanes* MAZE, labyrinth, warren, tangle. ❸ *a network of friends* SYSTEM, complex, nexus, web.

neurosis ▶ noun MENTAL ILLNESS, mental disorder, psychological disorder; psychoneurosis, psychopathy; obsession, phobia, fixation; *Medicine* neuroticism.

neurotic ▶ adjective ❶ (*Medicine*) *neurotic patients* MENTALLY ILL, mentally disturbed, un-

stable, unbalanced, maladjusted; psychopathic, phobic, obsessive-compulsive. ❷ *a neurotic, self-obsessed woman* OVER-ANXIOUS, oversensitive, nervous, tense, highly strung, paranoid; obsessive, fixated, hysterical, overwrought, irrational; *Brit.* nervy; *informal* twitchy.
– OPPOSITES stable, calm.

neuter ▶ **adjective** ASEXUAL, sexless, unsexed; androgynous, epicene.
▶ **verb** *have your pets neutered* STERILIZE, castrate, spay, geld, cut, fix, desex; *N. Amer. & Austral.* alter; *Brit. informal* doctor; *archaic* emasculate.

neutral ▶ **adjective** ❶ *she's neutral on this issue* IMPARTIAL, unbiased, unprejudiced, objective, open-minded, non-partisan, disinterested, dispassionate, detached, impersonal, unemotional, indifferent, uncommitted. ❷ *Switzerland remained neutral* UNALIGNED, non-aligned, unaffiliated, unallied, uninvolved; non-combatant. ❸ *a neutral topic of conversation* INOFFENSIVE, bland, unobjectionable, unexceptionable, anodyne, unremarkable, ordinary, commonplace; safe, harmless, innocuous. ❹ *a neutral background* PALE, light; beige, cream, taupe, oatmeal, ecru, buff, fawn, grey; colourless, uncoloured, achromatic; indeterminate, insipid, nondescript, dull, drab.
– OPPOSITES biased, partisan, provocative, colourful.

neutralize ▶ **verb** COUNTERACT, offset, counterbalance, balance, counterpoise, countervail, compensate for, make up for; cancel out, nullify, negate, negative; equalize.

never ▶ **adverb** ❶ *his room is never tidy* NOT EVER, at no time, not at any time, not once; *poetic/literary* ne'er. ❷ *she will never agree to it* NOT AT ALL, certainly not, not for a moment, under no circumstances, on no account; *informal* no way, not on your life, not in a million years; *Brit. informal* not on your nelly.
– OPPOSITES always, definitely.

never-ending ▶ **adjective** ❶ *never-ending noise* INCESSANT, continuous, unceasing, ceaseless, constant, continual, perpetual, uninterrupted, unbroken, steady, unremitting, relentless, persistent, interminable, non-stop, endless, unending, everlasting, eternal. ❷ *never-ending tasks* ENDLESS, countless, innumerable, untold, unlimited, limitless, boundless; *poetic/literary* myriad.

never-never
■ **the never-never** (*Brit. informal*). *See* HIRE PURCHASE.

nevertheless ▶ **adverb** NONETHELESS, even so, however, but, still, yet, though; in spite of that, despite that, be that as it may, for all that, that said, just the same, all the same; notwithstanding, regardless, anyway, anyhow; *informal* still and all.

new ▶ **adjective** ❶ *new technology* RECENTLY DEVELOPED, up to date, latest, current, state-of-the-art, contemporary, advanced, recent, modern. ❷ *new ideas* NOVEL, original, fresh, imaginative, creative, experimental; contemporary, modernist, up to date; newfangled, ultra-modern, avant-garde, futuristic; *informal* way out, far out. ❸ *is your boat new?* UNUSED, brand new, pristine, fresh, in mint condition. ❹ *new neighbours moved in* DIFFERENT, another, alternative; unfamiliar, unknown, strange; unaccustomed, untried. ❺ *they had a new classroom built* ADDITIONAL, extra, supplementary, further, another, fresh. ❻ *I came back a new woman* REINVIGORATED, restored, revived, improved, refreshed, regenerated, reborn.
– RELATED TERMS neo-.
– OPPOSITES old, hackneyed, second-hand, present.

newborn ▶ **adjective** *newborn babies* JUST BORN, recently born.
▶ **noun** *the bacteria are fatal to newborns* YOUNG BABY, tiny baby, infant; *Medicine* neonate.

newcomer ▶ **noun** ❶ *a newcomer to the village* (NEW) ARRIVAL, immigrant, incomer, settler; stranger, outsider, foreigner, alien; *N. English* offcomer; *informal* johnny-come-lately, new kid on the block; *Austral. informal* blow-in. ❷ *photography tips for the newcomer* BEGINNER, novice, learner; trainee, apprentice, probationer, tyro, initiate, neophyte; *N. Amer.* tenderfoot; *informal* rookie, newbie; *N. Amer. informal* greenhorn.

newfangled ▶ **adjective** NEW, the latest, modern, ultra-modern, up to the minute, state-of-the-art, advanced, contemporary; new-fashioned; *informal* trendy, flash.
– OPPOSITES dated.

newly ▶ **adverb** RECENTLY, (only) just, lately, freshly; not long ago, a short time ago, only now, of late; new-.

news ▶ **noun** REPORT, announcement, story, account; article, news flash, newscast, headlines, press release, communication, communiqué, bulletin; message, dispatch, statement, intelligence; disclosure, revelation, word, talk, gossip; *informal* scoop; *poetic/literary* tidings.

newspaper ▶ **noun** PAPER, journal, gazette, news-sheet; tabloid, broadsheet, quality (paper), national (paper), local (paper), daily (paper), weekly (paper); free sheet, scandal sheet; *informal* rag; *N. Amer. informal* tab.

newsworthy ▶ **adjective** INTERESTING, topical, notable, noteworthy, important, significant, momentous, historic, remarkable, sensational.
– OPPOSITES unremarkable.

next ▶ **adjective** ❶ *the next chapter* FOLLOWING, succeeding, upcoming, to come. ❷ *the next house in the street* NEIGHBOURING, adjacent, adjoining, next-door, bordering, connected, attached; closest, nearest.
– OPPOSITES previous.

▶ **adverb** *where shall we go next?* THEN, after, afterwards, after this/that, following that/this, later, subsequently; *formal* thereafter, thereupon.
– OPPOSITES before.
■ **next to** BESIDE, by, alongside, by the side of, next door to, adjacent to, side by side with; close to, near, neighbouring, adjoining.

nibble ▶ **verb** ❶ *they nibbled at mangoes* TAKE SMALL BITES (FROM), pick, gnaw, peck, snack on; toy with; taste, sample; *informal* graze (on). ❷ *the mouse nibbled his finger* PECK, nip, bite.
▶ **noun** ❶ *the fish enjoyed a nibble on the lettuce* BITE, gnaw, chew; taste. ❷ *nuts and nibbles* MORSEL, mouthful, bite; snack, titbit, canapé, hors d'oeuvre, bonne bouche.

nice ▶ **adjective** ❶ *have a nice time* ENJOYABLE, pleasant, agreeable, good, satisfying, gratifying, delightful, marvellous; entertaining, amusing, diverting; *informal* lovely, great; *N. Amer. informal* neat. ❷ *nice people* PLEASANT, likeable, agreeable, personable, congenial, amiable, affable, genial, friendly, charming, delightful, engaging; sympathetic, compassionate, good. ❸ *nice manners* POLITE, courteous, civil, refined, polished, genteel, elegant. ❹ *that's a rather nice distinction* SUBTLE, fine, delicate, minute, precise, strict, close; careful, meticulous, scrupulous. ❺ *it's a nice day* FINE, pleasant, agreeable; dry, sunny, warm, mild.
– OPPOSITES unpleasant, nasty, rough.

nicety ▶ **noun** ❶ *legal niceties* SUBTLETY, fine point, nuance, refinement, detail. ❷ *great nicety of control* PRECISION, accuracy, exactness, meticulousness.

niche ▶ **noun** ❶ *a niche in the wall* RECESS, alcove, nook, cranny, hollow, bay, cavity, cubbyhole, pigeonhole. ❷ *he found his niche in life* IDEAL POSITION, place, function, vocation, calling, métier, job.

nick ▶ **noun** ❶ *a slight nick in the blade* CUT, scratch, incision, snick, notch, chip, gouge, gash; dent, indentation. ❷ (*Brit. informal*) *she's in the nick. See* PRISON. ❸ (*Brit. informal*) *he's under arrest at the nick* POLICE STATION, station; *N. Amer.* precinct, station house; *informal* cop shop. ❹ (*Brit. informal*) *the car's in good nick* CONDITION, repair, shape, state, order, form, fettle, trim.
▶ **verb** ❶ *I nicked my toe* CUT, scratch, incise, snick, gouge, gash, score. ❷ (*Brit. informal*) *she nicked his wallet. See* STEAL verb sense 1. ❸ (*Brit. informal*) *Steve's been nicked. See* ARREST verb sense 1.
■ **in the nick of time** JUST IN TIME, not a moment too soon, at the critical moment; *N. Amer. informal* under the wire.

nickname ▶ **noun** SOBRIQUET, byname, tag, label, epithet, cognomen; pet name, diminutive, endearment; *informal* moniker; *formal* appellation.

nifty ▶ **adjective** (*informal*) ❶ *nifty camerawork* SKILFUL, deft, agile, capable. ❷ *a nifty little gadget* USEFUL, handy, practical. ❸ *a nifty suit* FASHIONABLE, stylish, smart.
– OPPOSITES clumsy.

niggardly ▶ **adjective** ❶ *a niggardly person* MEAN, miserly, parsimonious, close-fisted, penny-pinching, cheese-paring, grasping, ungenerous, illiberal; *informal* stingy, tight, tight-fisted; *N. Amer. informal* cheap. ❷ *niggardly rations* MEAGRE, inadequate, scanty, scant, skimpy, paltry, sparse, insufficient, deficient, short, lean, small, slender, poor, miserable, pitiful, puny; *informal* measly, stingy, pathetic, piddling.
– OPPOSITES generous.

niggle ▶ **verb** ❶ *his behaviour does niggle me* IRRITATE, annoy, bother, provoke, exasperate, upset, gall, irk, rankle with; *informal* rile, get to, bug. ❷ *he niggles on about taxes* COMPLAIN, fuss, carp, cavil, grumble, grouse; *informal* moan, nit-pick.
▶ **noun** *niggles about the lack of equipment* QUIBBLE, trivial complaint, criticism, grumble, grouse, cavil; *informal* gripe, moan, beef, grouch.

night ▶ **noun** night-time; (hours of) darkness, dark.
– RELATED TERMS nocturnal.
– OPPOSITES day.
■ **night and day** ALL THE TIME, around the clock, {morning, noon, and night}, {day in, day out}, ceaselessly, endlessly, incessantly, unceasingly, interminably, constantly, perpetually, continually, relentlessly; *informal* 24-7.

nightclub ▶ **noun** DISCO, discotheque, night spot, club, bar; *N. Amer.* cafe; *informal* niterie.

nightfall ▶ **noun** SUNSET, sundown, dusk, twilight, evening, close of day, dark; *poetic/literary* eventide.
– OPPOSITES dawn.

nightly ▶ **adjective** ❶ *nightly raids* EVERY NIGHT, each night, night after night. ❷ *his nightly wanderings* NOCTURNAL, night-time.
▶ **adverb** *a band plays there nightly* EVERY NIGHT, each night, night after night.

nightmare ▶ **noun** ❶ *she woke from a nightmare* BAD DREAM, night terrors; *archaic* incubus. ❷ *the journey was a nightmare* ORDEAL, trial, torment, horror, hell, misery, agony, torture, murder; curse, bane.

nightmarish ▶ **adjective** UNEARTHLY, spine-chilling, hair-raising, horrific, macabre, hideous, unspeakable, gruesome, grisly, ghastly, harrowing, disturbing; *informal* scary, creepy.

nihilism ▶ **noun** SCEPTICISM, disbelief, unbelief, agnosticism, atheism; negativity, cynicism, pessimism; rejection, denial.

nihilist ▶ **noun** SCEPTIC, disbeliever, unbeliever, agnostic, atheist; negativist, cynic, pessimist.

nil ▶ **noun** NOTHING, none; nought, zero, 0; *Tennis* love; *Cricket* a duck; *N. English* nowt; *informal* zilch, nix, not a dicky bird; *Brit. informal* sweet Fanny Adams, sweet FA, not a sausage; *N. Amer. informal* zip, nada, a goose egg; *dated* cipher; *archaic* naught.

nimble ▶ adjective ❶ *he was nimble on his feet* AGILE, sprightly, light, spry, lively, quick, graceful, lithe, limber; skilful, deft, dextrous, adroit; *informal* nippy, twinkle-toed; *poetic/literary* lightsome. ❷ *a nimble mind* QUICK-WITTED, quick, alert, lively, wide awake, observant, astute, perceptive, penetrating, discerning, shrewd, sharp; intelligent, bright, smart, clever, brilliant; *informal* brainy, quick on the uptake.
– OPPOSITES clumsy, dull.

nincompoop ▶ noun (*informal*). *See* IDIOT.

nine ▶ cardinal number NONET.
– RELATED TERMS nona-.

nip ▶ verb ❶ *the child nipped her* BITE, nibble, peck; pinch, tweak, squeeze, grip. ❷ (*Brit. informal*) *I'm just nipping out* RUSH, dash, dart, hurry, scurry, scamper; go; *informal* pop, whip.
▶ noun *penguins can give a serious nip* BITE, peck, nibble; pinch, tweak.
■ **nip something in the bud** CUT SHORT, curtail, check, curb, thwart, frustrate, stop, halt, arrest, stifle, obstruct, block, squash, quash, subdue, crack down on, stamp out; *informal* put the kibosh on.
■ **nip something off** CUT, snip, trim, clip, prune, lop, dock, crop; remove, take off.

nipple ▶ noun TEAT, dug; *Anatomy* mamilla.

nippy ▶ adjective (*informal*) ❶ *he's too big to be nippy* AGILE, light-footed, nimble, light on one's feet, spry, supple, limber; *informal* twinkle-toed; *poetic/literary* lightsome. ❷ *a nippy hatchback* FAST, quick, lively; *informal* zippy. ❸ *it's a bit nippy in here* COLD, chilly, icy, bitter, raw.
– OPPOSITES lumbering, slow, warm.

nirvana ▶ noun PARADISE, heaven; bliss, ecstasy, joy, peace, serenity, tranquillity; enlightenment.
– OPPOSITES hell.

nit-picking ▶ adjective (*informal*). *See* PEDANTIC.

nitty-gritty ▶ noun (*informal*) BASICS, essentials, fundamentals, substance, quintessence, heart of the matter; nub, crux, gist, meat, kernel, marrow; *informal* brass tacks, nuts and bolts.

nitwit ▶ noun (*informal*). *See* IDIOT.

no ▶ adverb absolutely not, most certainly not, of course not, under no circumstances, by no means, not at all, negative, never, not really; *informal* nope, nah, not on your life, no way; *Brit. informal* no fear, not on your nelly; *archaic* nay.
– OPPOSITES yes.

nobble ▶ verb (*Brit. informal*) ❶ *he nobbled the jury* BRIBE, suborn, buy, pay off, corrupt, get at; influence, persuade, win over, sway, control, manipulate; *informal* grease someone's palm, oil someone's palm. ❷ *a stable lad nobbled the horse* DRUG, dope; tamper with, interfere with; disable, incapacitate. ❸ *I stopped him nobbling her money* STEAL, thieve, embezzle; *informal* rob. ❹ *people tried to nobble her at parties* ACCOST, waylay, detain, catch, confront, importune; *informal* buttonhole.

nobility ▶ noun ❶ *a member of the nobility* ARISTOCRACY, aristocrats, peerage, peers (of the realm), lords, nobles, noblemen, noblewomen, patricians; *informal* aristos; *Brit. informal* nobs. ❷ *the nobility of his deed* VIRTUE, goodness, honour, decency, integrity; magnanimity, generosity, selflessness.

noble ▶ adjective ❶ *a noble family* ARISTOCRATIC, patrician, blue-blooded, high-born, titled; *archaic* gentle. ❷ *a noble cause* RIGHTEOUS, virtuous, good, honourable, upright, decent, worthy, moral, ethical, reputable; magnanimous, unselfish, generous. ❸ *a noble pine forest* MAGNIFICENT, splendid, grand, stately, imposing, dignified, proud, striking, impressive, majestic, glorious, awesome, monumental, statuesque, regal, imperial.
– OPPOSITES humble, dishonourable, base.
▶ noun *Scottish nobles* ARISTOCRAT, nobleman, noblewoman, lord, lady, peer (of the realm), peeress, patrician; *informal* aristo; *Brit. informal* nob.

nod ▶ verb ❶ *she nodded her head* INCLINE, bob, bow, dip, wag. ❷ *he nodded to me to start* SIGNAL, gesture, gesticulate, motion, sign, indicate.
▶ noun ❶ *she gave a nod to the manager* SIGNAL, indication, sign, cue; gesture. ❷ *a quick nod of his head* INCLINATION, bob, bow, dip.
■ **give someone the nod** ❶ *the winger was given the nod* SELECT, choose, pick, go for; *Brit.* cap. ❷ *the Lords will give the treaty the nod* APPROVE, agree to, sanction, ratify, endorse, rubber-stamp; *informal* OK, give something the green light, give something the thumbs up.
■ **nod off** FALL ASLEEP, go to sleep, doze off, drop off; *informal* drift off, flake out, go out like a light; *N. Amer. informal* sack out.

node ▶ noun JUNCTION, intersection, interchange, fork, confluence, convergence, crossing.

noise ▶ noun SOUND, din, hubbub, clamour, racket, uproar, tumult, commotion, pandemonium, babel; *informal* hullabaloo; *Brit. informal* row.
– OPPOSITES silence.

noisome ▶ adjective (*poetic/literary*). *See* ODIOUS.

noisy ▶ adjective ❶ *a noisy crowd* ROWDY, clamorous, boisterous, turbulent, rackety; chattering, talkative, vociferous, shouting, screaming. ❷ *noisy music* LOUD, fortissimo, blaring, booming, deafening, thunderous, tumultuous, clamorous, ear-splitting, piercing, strident, cacophonous, raucous.
– OPPOSITES quiet, soft.

nomad ▶ noun ITINERANT, traveller, migrant, wanderer, roamer, rover; gypsy, Bedouin; transient, drifter, vagabond, vagrant, tramp; *dated* bird of passage.

nominal ▶ adjective ❶ *the nominal head of the campaign* IN NAME ONLY, titular, formal, official; theoretical, supposed, ostensible, so-called. ❷ *a nominal rent* TOKEN, symbolic; tiny, minute, minimal, small, insignificant, trifling; *Brit.* peppercorn; *informal* minuscule, piddling, piffling; *N. Amer. informal* nickel-and-dime.
– OPPOSITES real, considerable.

nominate ▶ verb ❶ *you may nominate a candidate* PROPOSE, recommend, suggest, name, put forward, present, submit. ❷ *he nominated his assistant* APPOINT, select, choose, elect, commission, designate, name, delegate.

non-believer ▶ noun UNBELIEVER, disbeliever, sceptic, doubter, doubting Thomas, cynic, nihilist; atheist, agnostic, freethinker; infidel, pagan, heathen.

nonce
■ **for the nonce** FOR THE TIME BEING, temporarily, pro tem, for now, for the moment, for the interim, for a while, for the present, in the meantime; provisionally.

nonchalant ▶ adjective CALM, composed, unconcerned, cool, {cool, calm, and collected}, cool as a cucumber; indifferent, blasé, dispassionate, apathetic, casual, insouciant; *informal* laid-back.
– OPPOSITES anxious.

non-combatant ▶ adjective NON-FIGHTING, non-participating, civilian; pacifist, neutral, non-aligned.

non-committal ▶ adjective EVASIVE, equivocal, guarded, circumspect, reserved; discreet, uncommunicative, tactful, diplomatic, vague; *informal* cagey.
■ **be non-committal** PREVARICATE, give nothing away, dodge the issue, sidestep the issue, hedge, fence, pussyfoot around, beat about the bush, equivocate, temporize, shilly-shally, vacillate, waver; *Brit.* hum and haw; *informal* sit on the fence.

non compos mentis ▶ adjective. *See* INSANE sense 1.

nonconformist ▶ noun DISSENTER, dissentient, protester, rebel, renegade, schismatic; freethinker, apostate, heretic; individualist, free spirit, maverick, eccentric, original, deviant, misfit, dropout, outsider; *informal* freak, oddball, odd fish, weirdo; *N. Amer. informal* screwball, kook.

nondescript ▶ adjective UNDISTINGUISHED, unremarkable, unexceptional, featureless, characterless, unmemorable; ordinary, commonplace, average, run-of-the-mill, mundane; uninteresting, uninspiring, colourless, bland; *informal* bog-standard; *Brit. informal* common or garden.
– OPPOSITES distinctive.

none ▶ pronoun ❶ *none of the fish are unusual* NOT ONE, not a one. ❷ *none of this concerns me* NO PART, not a bit, not any. ❸ *none can know better than you* NOT ONE, no one, nobody, not a soul, not a single person, no man.
– OPPOSITES all.
■ **none the ——** *we were left none the wiser* NOT AT ALL, not a bit, not the slightest bit, in no way, by no means any.

nonentity ▶ noun NOBODY, unimportant person, cipher, non-person, nothing, small fry, lightweight, mediocrity; *informal* no-hoper, non-starter.
– OPPOSITES celebrity.

non-essential ▶ adjective UNNECESSARY, inessential, unessential, needless, unneeded, superfluous, uncalled for, redundant, dispensable, expendable, unimportant, extraneous.

nonetheless ▶ adverb NEVERTHELESS, even so, however, but, still, yet, though; in spite of that, despite that, be that as it may, for all that, that said, just the same, all the same; notwithstanding, regardless, anyway, anyhow; *informal* still and all.

non-existent ▶ adjective IMAGINARY, imagined, unreal, fictional, fictitious, made up, invented, fanciful; fantastic, mythical; illusory, hallucinatory, chimerical, notional, shadowy, insubstantial; missing, absent; *poetic/literary* illusive.
– OPPOSITES real.

non-intervention ▶ noun LAISSEZ-FAIRE, non-participation, non-interference, inaction, passivity, neutrality; live and let live.

non-observance ▶ noun INFRINGEMENT, breach, violation, contravention, transgression, non-compliance, infraction; dereliction, neglect.

nonpareil ▶ adjective *a nonpareil storyteller* INCOMPARABLE, matchless, unrivalled, unparalleled, unequalled, peerless, beyond compare, second to none, unsurpassed, unbeatable, inimitable; unique, consummate, superlative, supreme; *formal* unexampled.
– OPPOSITES mediocre.
▶ noun *Britain's nonpareil of the 1980s* BEST, finest, crème de la crème, peak of perfection, elite, jewel in the crown, ne plus ultra, paragon; *archaic* nonsuch.

nonplus ▶ verb SURPRISE, stun, dumbfound, confound, take aback, disconcert, throw (off balance); puzzle, perplex, baffle, bemuse, bewilder; *informal* faze, flummox, stump, bamboozle, fox; *N. Amer. informal* discombobulate.

nonsense ▶ noun ❶ *he was talking nonsense* RUBBISH, balderdash, gibberish, claptrap, blarney, blather, garbage; *informal* hogwash, rot, guff, baloney, tripe, drivel, gobbledegook, bilge, bosh, bunk, hot air, piffle, poppycock, phooey, twaddle; *Brit. informal* cobblers, codswal-

lop, tosh, double Dutch; *Scottish & N. English informal* havers; *N. Amer. informal* flapdoodle, bushwa, applesauce; *informal, dated* bunkum, tommyrot. ❷ *she stands no nonsense* MISCHIEF, naughtiness, bad behaviour, misbehaviour, misconduct, misdemeanour; pranks, tricks, clowning, buffoonery, funny business; *informal* tomfoolery, monkey business, shenanigans, hanky-panky; *Brit. informal* monkey tricks, jiggery-pokery. ❸ *they dismissed the concept as a nonsense* ABSURDITY, folly, stupidity, ludicrousness, inanity, foolishness, idiocy, insanity, madness.
– OPPOSITES sense, wisdom.

nonsensical ▶ **adjective** ❶ *her nonsensical way of talking* MEANINGLESS, senseless, illogical. ❷ *a nonsensical generalization* FOOLISH, insane, stupid, idiotic, illogical, irrational, senseless, absurd, silly, inane, hare-brained, ridiculous, ludicrous, preposterous; *informal* crazy, crackpot, nutty; *Brit. informal* daft.
– OPPOSITES logical, sensible.

non-stop ▶ **adjective** *non-stop entertainment* CONTINUOUS, constant, continual, perpetual, incessant, unceasing, ceaseless, uninterrupted, round-the-clock; unremitting, relentless, persistent.
– OPPOSITES occasional.
▶ **adverb** *we worked non-stop* CONTINUOUSLY, continually, incessantly, unceasingly, ceaselessly, all the time, constantly, perpetually, round the clock, steadily, relentlessly, persistently; *informal* 24-7.
– OPPOSITES occasionally.

nook ▶ **noun** RECESS, corner, alcove, niche, bay, inglenook, cavity, cubbyhole, pigeonhole; opening, gap, aperture; hideaway, hiding place, hideout, shelter; *informal* hidey-hole.

noon ▶ **noun** MIDDAY, twelve o'clock, twelve hundred hours, twelve noon, high noon, noonday; *poetic/literary* noontime, noontide.
– RELATED TERMS meridian.

no one ▶ **pronoun** NOBODY, not a soul, not anyone, not a single person, never a one, none.

norm ▶ **noun** ❶ *norms of diplomatic behaviour* CONVENTION, standard; criterion, yardstick, benchmark, touchstone, rule, formula, pattern, guide, guideline, model, exemplar. ❷ *such teams are now the norm* STANDARD, usual, the rule; normal, typical, average, unexceptional, par for the course, expected.

normal ▶ **adjective** ❶ *they issue books in the normal way* USUAL, standard, ordinary, customary, conventional, habitual, accustomed, expected, wonted; typical, stock, common, everyday, regular, routine, established, set, fixed, traditional. ❷ *a normal couple* ORDINARY, average, typical, run-of-the-mill, middle-of-the-road, common, conventional, mainstream, unremarkable, unexceptional; *N. Amer.* garden-variety; *informal* bog-standard, a dime a dozen; *Brit. informal* common or garden; *N. Amer. informal* ornery. ❸ *the man was not normal* SANE, in one's right mind, right in the head, of sound mind, compos mentis, lucid, rational, coherent; *informal* all there.
– OPPOSITES unusual, insane.

normality ▶ **noun** NORMALCY, business as usual, the daily round; routine, order, regularity.

normally ▶ **adverb** ❶ *she wanted to walk normally* NATURALLY, conventionally, ordinarily; as usual, as normal. ❷ *normally we'd keep quiet about this* USUALLY, ordinarily, as a rule, generally, in general, mostly, for the most part, by and large, mainly, most of the time, on the whole; typically, customarily, traditionally.

north ▶ **adjective** NORTHERN, northerly, boreal.

North American Indian ▶ **noun** NATIVE AMERICAN, American Indian; *dated* Red Indian.

nose ▶ **noun** ❶ *a punch on the nose* snout, muzzle, proboscis, trunk; *informal* beak, conk, snoot, schnozzle, hooter, sniffer. ❷ *he has a good nose* SENSE OF SMELL. ❸ *a nose for scandal* INSTINCT, feeling, sixth sense, intuition, insight, perception. ❹ *wine with a fruity nose* SMELL, bouquet, aroma, fragrance, perfume, scent, odour. ❺ *the plane's nose dipped* nose-cone, bow, prow, front end; *informal* droop-snoot.
– RELATED TERMS nasal, rhinal.
▶ **verb** ❶ *the dog nosed the ball* NUZZLE, nudge, push. ❷ *she's nosing into my business* PRY, inquire, poke about/around, interfere (in), meddle (in); be a busybody, stick/poke one's nose in; *informal* be nosy (about), snoop; *Austral./NZ informal* stickybeak. ❸ *he nosed the car into the traffic* EASE, inch, edge, move, manoeuvre, steer, guide.
■ **by a nose** (ONLY) JUST, barely, narrowly, by a hair's breadth, by the skin of one's teeth; *informal* by a whisker.
■ **nose around/about/round** INVESTIGATE, explore, ferret (about/around), rummage, search; delve into, peer into; prowl around; *informal* snoop about/around/round.
■ **nose something out** DETECT, find, discover, bring to light, track down, dig up, ferret out, root out, uncover, unearth, sniff out.
■ **on the nose** (*informal*) EXACTLY, precisely, sharp, on the dot, promptly, prompt, dead (on); *informal* bang (on); *Brit. informal* spot on; *N. Amer informal* on the button.

nosedive ▶ **noun** ❶ *the plane went into a nosedive* DIVE, descent, drop, plunge, plummet, fall. ❷ (*informal*) *sterling took a nosedive* FALL, drop, plunge, plummet, tumble, decline, slump; *informal* crash.
– OPPOSITES climb, rise.
▶ **verb** ❶ *the device nosedived to earth* DIVE, plunge, pitch, drop, plummet. ❷ (*informal*) *costs have nosedived* FALL, take a header, drop, sink, plunge, plummet, tumble, slump, go down, decline; *informal* crash.
– OPPOSITES soar, rise.

nosegay ▶ noun POSY, bouquet, bunch, spray, sprig, buttonhole, corsage, boutonnière, tussie-mussie.

nosh (*informal*) ▶ noun *all kinds of nosh. See* FOOD sense 1.
▶ verb *they nosh smoked salmon. See* EAT sense 1.

nostalgia ▶ noun REMINISCENCE, remembrance, recollection; wistfulness, regret, sentimentality.

nostalgic ▶ adjective WISTFUL, evocative, romantic, sentimental; regretful, dewy-eyed, maudlin.

nostrum ▶ noun ❶ *they have to prove their nostrums work* MEDICINE, quack remedy, potion, elixir, panacea, cure-all, wonder drug; *informal* magic bullet. ❷ *right-wing nostrums* MAGIC FORMULA, recipe for success, remedy, cure, prescription, answer.

nosy ▶ adjective (*informal*) PRYING, inquisitive, curious, busybody, spying, eavesdropping, intrusive; *informal* snooping, snoopy.

notability ▶ noun ❶ *the village has always enjoyed notability* NOTEWORTHINESS, prominence, importance, significance, eminence; fame, renown, notoriety. ❷ *the patronage of notabilities. See* NOTABLE noun.

notable ▶ adjective ❶ *notable examples of workmanship* NOTEWORTHY, remarkable, outstanding, important, significant, momentous, memorable; marked, striking, impressive; uncommon, unusual, special, exceptional, signal. ❷ *a notable author* PROMINENT, important, well known, famous, famed, noted, distinguished, great, eminent, illustrious, respected, esteemed, renowned, celebrated, acclaimed, influential, prestigious, of note.
– OPPOSITES unremarkable, unknown.
▶ noun *movie stars and other notables* CELEBRITY, public figure, VIP, personage, notability, dignitary, worthy, luminary; star, superstar, (big) name; *informal* celeb, somebody, bigwig, big shot, big cheese, big fish, megastar; *Brit. informal* nob; *N. Amer. informal* kahuna, high muckamuck.
– OPPOSITES nonentity.

notably ▶ adverb ❶ *other countries, notably the USA* IN PARTICULAR, particularly, especially, specially; primarily, principally. ❷ *these are notably short-lived birds* REMARKABLY, especially, specially, very, extremely, exceptionally, singularly, particularly, peculiarly, distinctly, significantly, unusually, extraordinarily, uncommonly, incredibly, really, decidedly, surprisingly, conspicuously; *informal* seriously; *Brit. informal* jolly, dead.

notation ▶ noun ❶ *algebraic notation* SYMBOLS, alphabet, syllabary, script; code, cipher, hieroglyphics. ❷ *notations in the margin* ANNOTATION, jotting, comment, footnote, entry, memo, gloss, explanation; *historical* scholium.

notch ▶ noun ❶ *a notch in the end of the arrow* NICK, cut, incision, score, scratch, slit, snick, slot, groove, cleft, indentation. ❷ *her opinion of Nick dropped a notch* DEGREE, level, rung, point, mark, measure, grade.
▶ verb *notch the plank* NICK, cut, score, incise, carve, scratch, slit, snick, gouge, groove, furrow.
■ **notch something up** SCORE, achieve, attain, gain, earn, make; rack up, chalk up; register, record.

note ▶ noun ❶ *a note in her diary* RECORD, entry, item, notation, jotting, memorandum, reminder, aide-memoire; *informal* memo. ❷ *he will take notes of the meeting* MINUTES, records, details; report, account, commentary, transcript, proceedings, transactions; synopsis, summary, outline. ❸ *notes in the margins* ANNOTATION, footnote, commentary, comment; marginalia, exegesis; *historical* scholium. ❹ *he dropped me a note* MESSAGE, communication, letter, line; *formal* epistle, missive. ❺ (*Brit.*) *a £20 note* BANKNOTE; *N. Amer.* bill; *US informal* greenback; (**notes**) paper money. ❻ *this is worthy of note* ATTENTION, consideration, notice, heed, observation, regard. ❼ *a composer of note* DISTINCTION, importance, eminence, prestige, fame, celebrity, acclaim, renown, repute, stature, standing, consequence, account. ❽ *a note of hopelessness in her voice* TONE, intonation, inflection, sound; hint, indication, sign, element, suggestion.
▶ verb ❶ *we will note your suggestion* BEAR IN MIND, be mindful of, consider, observe, heed, take notice of, pay attention to, take in. ❷ *the letter noted the ministers' concern* MENTION, refer to, touch on, indicate, point out, make known, state. ❸ *note the date in your diary* WRITE DOWN, put down, jot down, take down, inscribe, enter, mark, record, register, pencil.

notebook ▶ noun NOTEPAD, exercise book; register, logbook, log, diary, daybook, journal, record; *Brit.* jotter, pocketbook; *N. Amer.* scratch pad; *informal* memo pad.

noted ▶ adjective RENOWNED, well known, famous, famed, prominent, celebrated; notable, of note, important, eminent, distinguished, illustrious, acclaimed, esteemed; of distinction, of repute.
– OPPOSITES unknown.

noteworthy ▶ adjective NOTABLE, interesting, significant, important; remarkable, impressive, striking, outstanding, memorable, unique, special; unusual, extraordinary, singular, rare.
– OPPOSITES unexceptional.

nothing ▶ noun ❶ *there's nothing I can do* NOT A THING, not anything, nil, zero; *N. English* nowt; *informal* zilch, sweet Fanny Adams, sweet FA, nix, not a dicky bird; *Brit. informal* damn all, not a sausage; *N. Amer. informal* zip, nada; *archaic* naught. ❷ *forget it—it's nothing* A TRIFLING MATTER, a trifle; neither here nor there; *informal* no big deal. ❸ *he treats her as nothing* A NOBODY, an unimportant person, a nonentity, a cipher, a non-person; *Brit.* small beer. ❹ *the share value fell to nothing* ZERO, nought, 0; *Tennis* love; *Cricket* a duck.

– OPPOSITES something.

■ **be/have nothing to do with** ❶ *it has nothing to do with you* BE UNCONNECTED WITH, be unrelated to; be irrelevant to, be inapplicable to, be inapposite to. ❷ *I'll have nothing to do with him* AVOID, have no truck with, have no contact with, steer clear of, give a wide berth to.

■ **for nothing** ❶ *she hosted the show for nothing* FREE (OF CHARGE), gratis, without charge, at no cost; *informal* for free, on the house. ❷ *all this trouble for nothing* IN VAIN, to no avail, to no purpose, with no result, needlessly, pointlessly.

■ **nothing but** *he's nothing but a nuisance* MERELY, only, just, solely, simply, purely, no more than.

nothingness ▶ **noun** ❶ *the nothingness of death* OBLIVION, nullity, blankness; void, vacuum; *rare* nihility. ❷ *the nothingness of it all overwhelmed him* UNIMPORTANCE, insignificance, triviality, pointlessness, uselessness, worthlessness.

notice ▶ **noun** ❶ *nothing escaped his notice* ATTENTION, observation, awareness, consciousness, perception; regard, consideration, scrutiny; watchfulness, vigilance, attentiveness. ❷ *a notice on the wall* POSTER, bill, handbill, advertisement, announcement, bulletin; flyer, leaflet, pamphlet; sign, card; *informal* ad; *Brit. informal* advert. ❸ *times may change without notice* NOTIFICATION, (advance) warning, announcement; information, news, communication, word. ❹ *I handed in my notice* RESIGNATION. ❺ *the film got bad notices* REVIEW, write-up, critique, criticism; *Brit. informal* crit.

▶ **verb** *I noticed that the door was open* OBSERVE, perceive, note, see, discern, detect, spot, distinguish, mark, remark; *Brit. informal* clock; *poetic/literary* behold.

– OPPOSITES overlook.

■ **take no notice (of)** IGNORE, pay no attention (to), disregard, pay no heed (to), take no account (of), brush aside, shrug off, turn a blind eye (to), pass over, let go, overlook, look the other way.

noticeable ▶ **adjective** DISTINCT, evident, obvious, apparent, manifest, patent, plain, clear, marked, conspicuous, unmistakable, undeniable, pronounced, prominent, striking, arresting; perceptible, discernible, detectable, observable, visible, appreciable.

noticeboard ▶ **noun** PINBOARD, cork board, bulletin board; hoarding.

notification ▶ **noun** ❶ *the notification of the victim's wife* INFORMING, telling, alerting. ❷ *she received notification that he was on the way* INFORMATION, word, advice, news, intelligence; communication, message; *poetic/literary* tidings.

notify ▶ **verb** ❶ *we will notify you as soon as possible* INFORM, tell, advise, apprise, let someone know, put in the picture; alert, warn. ❷ *births should be notified to the registrar* REPORT, make known, announce, declare, communicate, disclose.

notion ▶ **noun** ❶ *he had a notion that something was wrong* IDEA, belief, conviction, opinion, view, thought, impression, perception; hypothesis, theory; (funny) feeling, (sneaking) suspicion, hunch. ❷ *Claire had no notion of what he meant* UNDERSTANDING, idea, awareness, knowledge, clue, inkling. ❸ *he got a notion to return* IMPULSE, inclination, whim, desire, wish, fancy.

notional ▶ **adjective** HYPOTHETICAL, theoretical, speculative, conjectural, suppositional, putative, conceptual; imaginary, fanciful, unreal, illusory.

– OPPOSITES actual.

notoriety ▶ **noun** INFAMY, disrepute, ill repute, bad name, dishonour, discredit; *dated* ill fame.

notorious ▶ **adjective** INFAMOUS, scandalous; well known, famous, famed, legendary.

notwithstanding ▶ **preposition** *notwithstanding his workload, he is a dedicated father* DESPITE, in spite of, regardless of, for all.

▶ **adverb** *she is bright—notwithstanding, she is now jobless* NEVERTHELESS, nonetheless, even so, all the same, in spite of this, despite this, however, still, yet, that said, just the same, anyway, in any event, at any rate.

▶ **conjunction** *notwithstanding that there was no space, they played on* ALTHOUGH, even though, though, in spite of the fact that, despite the fact that.

nought ▶ **noun** ❶ *the batsman was out for nought* NIL, zero, 0; *Tennis* love; *Cricket* a duck. ❷ (*archaic*) *my work has all been for nought. See* NAUGHT.

nourish ▶ **verb** ❶ *patients must be well nourished* FEED, provide for, sustain, maintain. ❷ *we nourish the talents of children* ENCOURAGE, promote, foster, nurture, cultivate, stimulate, boost, advance, assist, help, aid, strengthen, enrich. ❸ *the hopes Ursula nourished* CHERISH, nurture, foster, harbour, nurse, entertain, maintain, hold, have.

nourishing ▶ **adjective** NUTRITIOUS, nutritive, wholesome, good for one, healthy, health-giving, healthful, beneficial, sustaining.

– OPPOSITES unhealthy.

nourishment ▶ **noun** FOOD, sustenance, nutriment, nutrition, subsistence, provisions, provender, fare; *informal* grub, nosh, chow, eats; *Brit. informal* scoff; *N. Amer. informal* chuck; *formal* comestibles; *dated* victuals.

nouveau riche ▶ **plural noun** the new rich, parvenus, arrivistes, upstarts, social climbers, vulgarians.

novel[1] ▶ **noun** *curl up with a good novel* BOOK,

paperback, hardback; STORY, tale, narrative, romance; best-seller; *informal* blockbuster.

novel[2] ▶ **adjective** *a novel way of making money* NEW, original, unusual, unfamiliar, unconventional, unorthodox; different, fresh, imaginative, innovative, innovatory, innovational, inventive, modern, neoteric, avant-garde, pioneering, ground-breaking, revolutionary; rare, unique, singular, unprecedented; experimental, untested, untried; strange, exotic, newfangled.
– OPPOSITES traditional.

novelist ▶ **noun** WRITER, author, fictionist, man/woman of letters; *informal* penman, scribbler.

novelty ▶ **noun** ❶ *the novelty of our approach* ORIGINALITY, newness, freshness, unconventionality, unfamiliarity; difference, imaginativeness, creativity, innovation, modernity. ❷ *we sell seasonal novelties* KNICK-KNACK, trinket, bauble, toy, trifle, gewgaw, gimcrack, ornament; *N. Amer.* kickshaw.

novice ▶ **noun** ❶ *a five-day course for novices* BEGINNER, learner, neophyte, newcomer, initiate, tyro, fledgling; apprentice, trainee, probationer, student, pupil; *N. Amer.* tenderfoot; *informal* rookie, newie, newbie; *N. Amer. informal* greenhorn. ❷ *a novice who was never ordained* NEOPHYTE, novitiate; postulant, proselyte, catechumen.
– OPPOSITES expert, veteran.

novitiate ▶ **noun** ❶ *a three-year novitiate* PROBATIONARY PERIOD, probation, trial period, test period, apprenticeship, training period, traineeship, training, initiation. ❷ *two young novitiates* NOVICE, neophyte; postulant, proselyte, catechumen.

now ▶ **adverb** ❶ *I'm extremely busy now* AT THE MOMENT, at present, at the present (time/moment), at this moment in time, currently, *N. Amer.* presently; *Brit. informal* at the minute. ❷ *television is now the main source of news* NOWADAYS, today, these days, in this day and age; in the present climate. ❸ *you must leave now* AT ONCE, straight away, right away, right now, this minute, this instant, immediately, instantly, directly, without further ado, promptly, without delay, as soon as possible; *informal* pronto, straight off, a.s.a.p.
■ **as of now** FROM THIS TIME ON, from now on, henceforth, henceforward, from this day forward, in future; *formal* hereafter.
■ **for now** FOR THE TIME BEING, for the moment, for the present, for the meantime; *archaic* for the nonce.
■ **not now** LATER (ON), sometime, one day, some day, one of these days, sooner or later, in due course, by and by, eventually, ultimately.
■ **now and again** OCCASIONALLY, now and then, from time to time, sometimes, every so often, (every) now and again, at times, on occasion(s), (every) once in a while; periodically, once in a blue moon.

nowadays ▶ **adverb** THESE DAYS, today, at the present time, in these times, in this day and age, now, currently, at the moment, at present, at this moment in time; in the present climate; *N. Amer.* presently.

noxious ▶ **adjective** POISONOUS, toxic, deadly, harmful, dangerous, pernicious, damaging, destructive; unpleasant, nasty, disgusting, awful, dreadful, horrible, terrible; vile, revolting, foul, nauseating, appalling, offensive; malodorous, fetid, putrid; *informal* ghastly, horrid; *poetic/literary* noisome; *archaic* disgustful.
– OPPOSITES innocuous.

nuance ▶ **noun** FINE DISTINCTION, subtle difference; shade, shading, gradation, variation, degree; subtlety, nicety, overtone.

nub ▶ **noun** CRUX, central point, main point, core, heart (of the matter), nucleus, essence, quintessence, kernel, marrow, meat, pith; gist, substance; *informal* nitty-gritty.

nubile ▶ **adjective** SEXUALLY MATURE, marriageable; sexually attractive, desirable, sexy, luscious; *informal* beddable.

nucleus ▶ **noun** ❶ *the nucleus of the banking world* CORE, centre, central part, heart, nub, hub, middle, eye, focus, focal point, pivot, crux. ❷ *a nucleus of union men supported him* SMALL GROUP, caucus, cell, coterie, clique, faction.

nude ▶ **adjective** (STARK) NAKED, bare, unclothed, undressed, disrobed, stripped, unclad, in a state of nature, au naturel; *informal* without a stitch on, in one's birthday suit, in the raw, in the altogether, in the buff, in the nuddy; *Brit. informal* starkers; *Scottish informal* in the scud; *N. Amer. informal* buck naked.
– OPPOSITES clothed.

nudge ▶ **verb** ❶ *he nudged Ben* POKE, elbow, dig, prod, jog, jab. ❷ *the canoe nudged a bank* TOUCH, bump (against), push (against), run into. ❸ *we nudged them into action* PROMPT, encourage, stimulate, prod, galvanize. ❹ *unemployment was nudging 3,000,000* APPROACH, near, come close to, be verging on, border on.
▶ **noun** ❶ *Maggie gave him a nudge* POKE, dig (in the ribs), prod, jog, jab, push. ❷ *after a nudge, she remembered Lilian* REMINDER, prompt, prompting, prod, encouragement.

nugatory ▶ **adjective** ❶ *a nugatory observation* WORTHLESS, unimportant, inconsequential, valueless, trifling, trivial, insignificant, meaningless. ❷ *the shortages will render nugatory our hopes* FUTILE, useless, vain, unavailing, null, invalid.

nugget ▶ **noun** LUMP, nub, chunk, piece, hunk, wad, gobbet; *N. Amer. informal* gob.

nuisance ▶ **noun** ANNOYANCE, inconvenience, bore, bother, irritation, problem, trouble,

trial, burden; pest, plague, thorn in one's side/flesh; *informal* pain (in the neck), hassle, bind, drag, aggravation, headache; *Scottish informal* nyaff, skelf; *N. Amer. informal* nudnik; *Austral./NZ informal* nark.
– OPPOSITES blessing.

null ▶ adjective ❶ *their marriage was declared null* INVALID, null and void, void; annulled, nullified, cancelled, revoked. ❷ *his null life* CHARACTERLESS, colourless, empty, insipid, vapid, dull, boring.
– OPPOSITES valid, interesting.

nullify ▶ verb ❶ *they nullified the legislation* ANNUL, render null and void, void, invalidate; repeal, reverse, rescind, revoke, cancel, abolish; countermand, do away with, terminate, quash; *Law* vacate; *formal* abrogate. ❷ *the costs would nullify any tax relief* CANCEL OUT, neutralize, negate, negative.
– OPPOSITES ratify.

numb ▶ adjective *his fingers were numb* WITHOUT SENSATION, without feeling, numbed, benumbed, desensitized, insensible, senseless, unfeeling; anaesthetized; dazed, stunned, stupefied, paralysed, immobilized, frozen.
– OPPOSITES sensitive.
▶ verb *the cold numbed her senses* DEADEN, benumb, desensitize, dull; anaesthetize; daze, stupefy, paralyse, immobilize, freeze.
– OPPOSITES sensitize.

number ▶ noun ❶ *a whole number* NUMERAL, integer, figure, digit; character, symbol; decimal, unit; cardinal number, ordinal number. ❷ *a large number of complaints* AMOUNT, quantity; total, aggregate, tally; quota. ❸ *the wedding of one of their number* GROUP, company, crowd, circle, party, band, crew, set; *informal* gang. ❹ *the band performed another number* SONG, piece (of music), tune, track; routine, sketch, dance, act.
– RELATED TERMS numerical.
▶ verb ❶ *visitors numbered more than two million* ADD UP TO, amount to, total, come to. ❷ *he numbers the fleet at a thousand* CALCULATE, count, total, compute, reckon, tally; assess; *Brit.* tot up; *formal* enumerate. ❸ *each paragraph is numbered* assign a number to, mark with a number; itemize, enumerate. ❹ *he numbers her among his friends* INCLUDE, count, reckon, deem. ❺ *his days are numbered* LIMIT, restrict, fix.
■ **a number of** SEVERAL, various, quite a few, sundry.
■ **without number** COUNTLESS, innumerable, unlimited, endless, limitless, untold, numberless, uncountable, uncounted; numerous, many, multiple, manifold, legion.

numberless ▶ adjective INNUMERABLE, countless, unlimited, endless, limitless, untold, uncountable, uncounted; numerous, many, multiple, manifold, legion; *informal* more —— than one can shake a stick at; *poetic/literary* myriad.

numbing ▶ adjective ❶ *menthol has a numbing action* DESENSITIZING, deadening, benumbing, anaesthetic, anaesthetizing. ❷ *numbing cold* FREEZING, raw, bitter, biting, arctic. ❸ *numbing boredom* STUPEFYING, mind-numbing, stultifying, paralysing; soporific.

numbskull ▶ noun (*informal*). *See* IDIOT.

numeral ▶ noun NUMBER, integer, figure, digit; character, symbol, unit.

numerous ▶ adjective (VERY) MANY, a lot of, scores of, countless, numberless, innumerable; several, quite a few, various; plenty of, copious, a quantity of, an abundance of, a profusion of, a multitude of; frequent; *informal* umpteen, lots of, loads of, masses of, stacks of, heaps of, bags of, tons of, oodles of, hundreds of, thousands of, millions of, more —— than one can shake a stick at; *Brit. informal* a shedload of; *N. Amer. informal* gazillions of; *Austral./NZ informal* a swag of; *poetic/literary* myriad.
– OPPOSITES few.

numinous ▶ adjective SPIRITUAL, religious, divine, holy, sacred; mysterious, other-worldly, unearthly, transcendent.

nun ▶ noun sister, abbess, prioress, Mother Superior, Reverend Mother; novice; bride of Christ, religious, conventual, contemplative, canoness; *poetic/literary* vestal; *historical* anchoress.

nuncio ▶ noun (PAPAL) AMBASSADOR, legate, envoy, messenger.

nunnery ▶ noun CONVENT, priory, abbey, cloister, religious community.

nuptial ▶ adjective MATRIMONIAL, marital, marriage, wedding, conjugal, bridal; married, wedded; *poetic/literary* connubial; *Law* spousal.

nuptials ▶ plural noun WEDDING (CEREMONY), marriage, union; *archaic* espousal.

nurse ▶ noun ❶ *skilled nurses* CARER, caregiver; *informal* Florence Nightingale, nursey; *N. Amer. informal* candy-striper. ❷ *she had been his nurse in childhood* NANNY, nursemaid, nursery nurse, childminder, governess, au pair, childcarer, babysitter, ayah.
▶ verb ❶ *they nursed smallpox patients* CARE FOR, take care of, look after, tend, minister to. ❷ *I nursed my sore finger* TREAT, medicate, tend; dress, bandage, soothe; *informal* doctor. ❸ *Rosa was nursing her baby* BREASTFEED, suckle, feed. ❹ *they nursed old grievances* HARBOUR, foster, entertain, bear, have, hold (on to), cherish, cling to, retain. ❺ *our unity needs to be nursed* NURTURE, encourage, promote, boost, assist, help, cultivate; protect, safeguard.

nursemaid ▶ noun. *See* NURSE noun sense 2.

nurture ▶ verb ❶ *she nurtured her children into adulthood* BRING UP, care for, take care of, look after, tend, rear, raise, support, foster; parent, mother. ❷ *we nurtured these plants* CULTIVATE, grow, keep, tend. ❸ *he nurtured my love of art*

ENCOURAGE, promote, stimulate, develop, foster, cultivate, boost, contribute to, assist, help, abet, strengthen, fuel.
– OPPOSITES neglect, hinder.
▶ **noun** ❶ *we are what nature and nurture have made us* UPBRINGING, rearing, raising, childcare; training, education. ❷ *the nurture of ideas* ENCOURAGEMENT, promotion, fostering, development, cultivation.
– OPPOSITES nature.

nut ▶ **noun** ❶ *nuts in their shells* kernel. ❷ (*informal*) *he smacked her on the nut* HEAD, skull, cranium, crown; *informal* noodle, noggin, dome; *Brit. informal* bonce; *informal, dated* conk, noddle. ❸ (*informal*) *some nut arrived at the office* MANIAC, lunatic, madman, madwoman; eccentric; *informal* loony, nutcase, fruitcake, head case, crank, crackpot, weirdo; *Brit. informal* nutter; *N. Amer. informal* screwball, crazy; *N. Amer. & Austral./NZ informal* dingbat. ❹ (*informal*) *a movie nut* ENTHUSIAST, fan, devotee, aficionado; *informal* freak, fiend, fanatic, addict, buff; *N. Amer. informal* jock.
■ **do one's nut** (*informal*) BE VERY ANGRY, be furious, lose one's temper, go into a rage; *informal* go mad, go crazy, go wild, go bananas, have a fit, blow one's top, hit the roof, go off the deep end, go ape, flip, lose one's rag; *Brit. informal* go spare.
■ **off one's nut** (*informal*). *See* MAD sense 1.

nutriment ▶ **noun** NOURISHMENT, nutrients, sustenance, goodness, nutrition, food.

nutrition ▶ **noun** NOURISHMENT, nutriment, nutrients, sustenance, food; *informal* grub, chow, nosh; *Brit. informal* scoff; *poetic/literary* viands; *dated* victuals; *archaic* aliment.
– RELATED TERMS trophic.

nutritious ▶ **adjective** NOURISHING, good for one, full of nutrients, nutritive, nutrimental; wholesome, healthy, healthful, beneficial, sustaining.

nuts ▶ **adjective** (*informal*) ❶ *they thought we were nuts. See* MAD sense 1. ❷ *he's nuts about her* INFATUATED WITH, keen on, devoted to, in love with, smitten with, enamoured of, hot for; *informal* mad, crazy, nutty, wild, hooked on, gone on; *Brit. informal* potty.

nuts and bolts ▶ **plural noun** PRACTICAL DETAILS, fundamentals, basics, practicalities, essentials, mechanics; *informal* nitty-gritty, ins and outs, brass tacks.

nutty ▶ **adjective** (*informal*) ❶ *they're all nutty. See* MAD sense 1. ❷ *she's nutty about Elvis. See* NUTS sense 2.

nuzzle ▶ **verb** ❶ *the horse nuzzled at her pocket* NUDGE, nose, prod, push. ❷ *she nuzzled up to her boyfriend* SNUGGLE, cuddle, nestle, burrow, embrace, hug.

nymph ▶ **noun** ❶ *a nymph with winged sandals* SPRITE, sylph, spirit. ❷ (*poetic/literary*) *a skinny nymph with brown eyes* GIRL, belle, nymphet, sylph; young woman, young lady; *Scottish & N. English* lass; *Brit. dated* rosebud; *poetic/literary* maid, maiden, damsel.

oaf ▶ **noun** LOUT, boor, barbarian, Neanderthal, churl, bumpkin, yokel; fool, idiot, imbecile; *informal* cretin, ass, goon, oik, yahoo, ape, lump, clod, meathead, bonehead, lamebrain; *Brit. informal* clot, plonker, berk, pillock, yob, yobbo; *Scottish informal* nyaff, gowk; *N. Amer. informal* bozo, dumbhead, lummox, klutz, goofus, clunk, turkey; *Austral. informal* hoon, dingbat, galah, drongo; *archaic* lubber.

oafish ▶ **adjective** STUPID, foolish, idiotic; loutish, awkward, gawkish, clumsy, lumbering, ape-like, cloddish, Neanderthal, uncouth, uncultured, boorish, rough, coarse, brutish, ill-mannered, unrefined; *informal* clodhopping, blockheaded, boneheaded, thickheaded; *Brit. informal* yobbish; *archaic* lubberly.

oasis ▶ **noun** ❶ *an oasis near Cairo* WATERING HOLE, watering place, water hole, spring. ❷ *a cool oasis in a hot summer* REFUGE, haven, retreat, sanctuary, sanctum, harbour, asylum.

oath ▶ **noun** ❶ *an oath of allegiance* VOW, pledge, promise, avowal, affirmation, word (of honour), bond, guarantee; *formal* troth. ❷ *he uttered a stream of oaths* SWEAR WORD, profanity, expletive, four-letter word, dirty word, obscenity, vulgarity, curse, malediction; *informal* cuss (word); *formal* imprecation.

obdurate ▶ **adjective** STUBBORN, obstinate, intransigent, inflexible, unyielding, unbending, pig-headed, mulish, stiff-necked; headstrong, unshakeable, intractable, unpersuadable, immovable, inexorable, uncompromising, iron-willed, adamant, firm, determined; *Brit. informal* bloody-minded.
– OPPOSITES malleable.

obedient ▶ **adjective** COMPLIANT, biddable, acquiescent, tractable, amenable, malleable, pliable, pliant; dutiful, good, law-abiding, deferential, respectful, duteous, well trained, well disciplined, manageable, governable, docile, tame, meek, passive, submissive, unresisting, yielding.
– OPPOSITES rebellious.

obeisance ▶ **noun** ❶ *a gesture of obeisance* RESPECT, homage, worship, adoration, reverence, veneration, honour, submission, deference. ❷ *she made a deep obeisance* BOW, curtsy, bob, genuflection, salaam; *historical* kowtow.

obelisk ▶ **noun** COLUMN, pillar, needle, shaft, monolith, monument.

obese ▶ **adjective** FAT, overweight, corpulent, gross, stout, fleshy, heavy, portly, paunchy, pot-bellied, beer-bellied, well upholstered, well padded, broad in the beam, bulky, bloated, flabby; *informal* porky, roly-poly, blubbery; *Brit. informal* podgy; *archaic* pursy.
– OPPOSITES thin.

obey ▶ **verb** ❶ *I obeyed him without question* DO WHAT SOMEONE SAYS, carry out someone's orders; submit to, defer to, bow to, yield to. ❷ *he refused to obey the order* CARRY OUT, perform, act on, execute, discharge, implement, fulfil. ❸ *health and safety regulations have to be obeyed* COMPLY WITH, adhere to, observe, abide by, act in accordance with, conform to, respect, follow, keep to, stick to; play it by the book, toe the line.
– OPPOSITES defy, ignore.

obfuscate ▶ **verb** OBSCURE, confuse, blur, muddle, complicate, muddy, cloud, befog; muddy the waters.
– OPPOSITES clarify.

obituary ▶ **noun** DEATH NOTICE; *informal* obit; *formal* necrology.

object ▶ **noun** ❶ *wooden objects* THING, article, item, device, gadget; *informal* doodah, thingamajig, thingamabob, thingummy, whatsit, whatchamacallit, thingy; *Brit. informal* gubbins; *N. Amer. informal* doodad, dingus. ❷ *he became the object of criticism* TARGET, butt, focus, recipient, victim. ❸ *his object was to resolve the crisis* OBJECTIVE, aim, goal, target, purpose, end (in view), plan, object of the exercise, point; ambition, design, intent, intention, idea.
▶ **verb** *teachers objected to the scheme* PROTEST ABOUT, oppose, raise objections to, express disapproval of, take exception to, take issue with, take a stand against, argue against, quarrel with, condemn, draw the line at, demur at, mind, complain about, cavil at, quibble about; beg to differ; *informal* kick up a fuss/stink about.
– OPPOSITES approve, accept.

objection ▶ **noun** PROTEST, protestation, demur, demurral, complaint, expostulation, grievance, cavil, quibble; opposition, argument, counter-argument, disagreement, disapproval, dissent; *informal* niggle.

objectionable ▶ **adjective** UNPLEASANT, disagreeable, distasteful, displeasing, off-putting, undesirable, obnoxious, offensive, nasty, horrible, horrid, disgusting, awful, terrible, dreadful, frightful, appalling, insufferable, odious, vile, foul, unsavoury, repulsive, repellent, repugnant, revolting, abhorrent, loathsome, hateful, detestable, reprehensible, deplorable; *informal* ghastly; *Brit. informal* beastly; *formal* exceptionable, rebarbative.
– OPPOSITES pleasant.

objective ▶ **adjective** ❶ *an interviewer must try to be objective* IMPARTIAL, unbiased, unprejudiced, non-partisan, disinterested, neutral, uninvolved, even-handed, equitable, fair, fair-minded, just, open-minded, dispassionate, detached. ❷ *the world of objective knowledge* FACTUAL, actual, real, empirical, verifiable.
– OPPOSITES biased, subjective.
▶ **noun** *our objective is to build a profitable business* AIM, intention, purpose, target, goal, intent, object, object of the exercise, point, end (in view); idea, design, plan, ambition, aspiration, desire, hope.

objectively ▶ **adverb** IMPARTIALLY, without bias, without prejudice, even-handedly, dispassionately, detachedly, equitably, fairly, justly, with an open mind, without fear or favour.

objectivity ▶ **noun** IMPARTIALITY, lack of bias/prejudice, fairness, fair-mindedness, neutrality, even-handedness, justice, open-mindedness, disinterest, detachment, dispassion, dispassionateness.

oblation ▶ **noun** RELIGIOUS OFFERING, offering, sacrifice, peace offering, burnt offering, first fruits, libation.

obligate ▶ **verb** OBLIGE, compel, commit, bind, require, constrain, force, impel, make.

obligation ▶ **noun** ❶ *his professional obligations* DUTY, commitment, responsibility; function, task, job, assignment, commission, burden, charge, onus, liability, accountability, requirement, debt; *archaic* devoir. ❷ *a sense of obligation* DUTY, compulsion, indebtedness; duress, necessity, pressure, constraint.
■ **under an obligation** BEHOLDEN, obliged, in someone's debt, indebted, obligated, owing someone a debt of gratitude, duty-bound, honour-bound.

obligatory ▶ **adjective** COMPULSORY, mandatory, prescribed, required, demanded, statutory, enforced, binding, incumbent; requisite, necessary, imperative, unavoidable, inescapable, essential.
– OPPOSITES optional.

oblige ▶ **verb** ❶ *both parties are obliged to accept the decision* REQUIRE, compel, bind, constrain, obligate, leave someone no option, force.

❷ *I'll be happy to oblige you* DO SOMEONE A FAVOUR, accommodate, help, assist, serve; gratify someone's wishes, indulge, humour.

obliged ▶ **adjective** THANKFUL, grateful, appreciative, much obliged; beholden, indebted, in someone's debt.

obliging ▶ **adjective** HELPFUL, accommodating, willing, cooperative, considerate, complaisant, agreeable, amenable, generous, kind, neighbourly, hospitable, pleasant, good-natured, amiable, gracious, unselfish, civil, courteous, polite; *Brit. informal* decent.
– OPPOSITES unhelpful.

oblique ▶ **adjective** ❶ *an oblique line* SLANTING, slanted, sloping, at an angle, angled, diagonal, aslant, slant, slantwise, skew, on the skew, askew, squint; *N. Amer.* cater-cornered. ❷ *an oblique reference* INDIRECT, inexplicit, roundabout, circuitous, circumlocutory, implicit, implied, elliptical, evasive, backhanded. ❸ *an oblique glance* SIDELONG, sideways, furtive, covert, sly, surreptitious.
– OPPOSITES straight, direct.
▶ **noun** SLASH, solidus, backslash, diagonal, virgule.

obliquely ▶ **adverb** ❶ *the sun shone obliquely across the tower* DIAGONALLY, at an angle, slantwise, sideways, sidelong, aslant. ❷ *he referred obliquely to the war* INDIRECTLY, in a roundabout way, not in so many words, circuitously, evasively.

obliterate ▶ **verb** ❶ *he tried to obliterate the memory* ERASE, eradicate, expunge, efface, wipe out, blot out, rub out, remove all traces of. ❷ *a nuclear explosion that would obliterate a city* DESTROY, wipe out, annihilate, demolish, liquidate, wipe off the face of the earth, wipe off the map; *informal* zap. ❸ *clouds were darkening, obliterating the sun* HIDE, obscure, blot out, block, cover, screen.

oblivion ▶ **noun** ❶ *they drank themselves into oblivion* UNCONSCIOUSNESS, insensibility, stupor, stupefaction; coma, blackout; *poetic/literary* the waters of Lethe. ❷ *they rescued him from artistic oblivion* OBSCURITY, limbo, anonymity, neglect, disregard.
– OPPOSITES consciousness, fame.

oblivious ▶ **adjective** UNAWARE, unconscious, heedless, unmindful, insensible, unheeding, ignorant, blind, deaf, unsuspecting, unobservant; unconcerned, impervious, unaffected.
– OPPOSITES conscious.

obloquy ▶ **noun** ❶ *he endured years of contempt and obloquy* VILIFICATION, opprobrium, vituperation, condemnation, denunciation, abuse, criticism, censure, defamation, denigration, revilement, calumny, insults; *informal* flak; *formal* castigation, excoriation; *archaic* contumely. ❷ *conduct to which no moral obloquy could reasonably attach* DISGRACE, dishonour, shame, discredit, stigma, humiliation, loss of face, ignominy, odium, opprobrium, disfavour, disrepute, ill repute, infamy, stain, notoriety, scandal.
– OPPOSITES praise, honour.

obnoxious ▶ **adjective** UNPLEASANT, disagreeable, nasty, distasteful, offensive, objectionable, unsavoury, unpalatable, awful, terrible, dreadful, frightful, revolting, repulsive, repellent, repugnant, disgusting, odious, vile, foul, abhorrent, loathsome, nauseating, sickening, hateful, insufferable, intolerable; *informal* horrible, horrid, ghastly, gross, putrid, sick-making, yucky, God-awful; *Brit. informal* beastly; *archaic* disgustful, loathly.
– OPPOSITES delightful.

obscene ▶ **adjective** ❶ *obscene literature* PORNOGRAPHIC, indecent, smutty, dirty, filthy, X-rated, 'adult', explicit, lewd, rude, vulgar, coarse, crude, immoral, improper, off colour; scatological, profane; *informal* blue, porn, porno, skin. ❷ *an obscene crime* SHOCKING, scandalous, vile, foul, atrocious, outrageous, heinous, odious, abhorrent, abominable, disgusting, hideous, repugnant, repulsive, revolting, repellent, loathsome, nauseating, sickening, awful, dreadful, terrible, frightful.

obscenity ▶ **noun** ❶ *the book was banned on the grounds of obscenity* INDECENCY, immorality, impropriety, smuttiness, smut, lewdness, rudeness, vulgarity, dirt, filth, coarseness, crudity; profanity, profaneness. ❷ *the men scowled and muttered obscenities* EXPLETIVE, swear word, oath, profanity, curse, four-letter word, dirty word, blasphemy; *informal* cuss, cuss word; *formal* imprecation.

obscure ▶ **adjective** ❶ *his origins and parentage remain obscure* UNCLEAR, uncertain, unknown, in doubt, doubtful, dubious, mysterious, hazy, vague, indeterminate, concealed, hidden. ❷ *obscure references to Proust* MYSTIFYING, puzzling, perplexing, baffling, ambiguous, cryptic, enigmatic, Delphic, oracular, oblique, opaque, elliptical, unintelligible, incomprehensible, impenetrable, unfathomable; abstruse, recondite, arcane, esoteric; *informal* as clear as mud. ❸ *an obscure Peruvian painter* LITTLE KNOWN, unknown, unheard of, undistinguished, unimportant, nameless, minor; unsung, unrecognized, forgotten. ❹ *an obscure shape* INDISTINCT, faint, vague, nebulous, ill-defined, unclear, blurred, blurry, misty, hazy.
– OPPOSITES clear, plain, famous, distinct.
▶ **verb** ❶ *grey clouds obscured the sun* HIDE, conceal, cover, veil, shroud, screen, mask, cloak, cast a shadow over, shadow, block, obliterate, eclipse, darken. ❷ *recent events have obscured the issue* CONFUSE, complicate, obfuscate, cloud, blur, muddy; muddy the waters; *poetic/literary* befog.
– OPPOSITES reveal, clarify.

obscurity ▶ **noun** ❶ *the discovery rescued him from relative obscurity* INSIGNIFICANCE, inconspicu-

ousness, unimportance, anonymity; limbo, twilight, oblivion. ❷ *poems of impenetrable obscurity* INCOMPREHENSIBILITY, impenetrability, unintelligibility, opacity. ❸ *the obscurities in his poems and plays* ENIGMA, puzzle, mystery, difficulty, problem.
– OPPOSITES fame, clarity.

obsequies ▶ plural noun FUNERAL RITES, funeral service, funeral, burial, interment, entombment, inhumation, last offices; *formal* exequies; *archaic* sepulture.

obsequious ▶ adjective SERVILE, ingratiating, sycophantic, fawning, unctuous, oily, oleaginous, grovelling, cringing, subservient, submissive, slavish; *informal* slimy, bootlicking, smarmy.

observable ▶ adjective NOTICEABLE, visible, perceptible, perceivable, detectable, distinguishable, discernible, recognizable, evident, apparent, manifest, obvious, patent, clear, distinct, plain, unmistakable; *archaic* sensible.

observance ▶ noun ❶ *strict observance of the rules* COMPLIANCE, adherence, accordance, respect, observation, fulfilment, obedience; keeping, obeying. ❷ *religious observances* RITE, ritual, ceremony, ceremonial, celebration, practice, service, office, festival, tradition, custom, usage, formality, form.

observant ▶ adjective ALERT, sharp-eyed, sharp, eagle-eyed, hawk-eyed, having eyes like a hawk, keen-eyed, watchful, heedful, aware; on the lookout, on the qui vive, on guard, attentive, vigilant, having one's eyes open/peeled; *informal* beady-eyed, not missing a trick, on the ball.
– OPPOSITES inattentive.

observation ▶ noun ❶ *detailed observation of the animal's behaviour* MONITORING, watching, scrutiny, examination, inspection, survey, surveillance, attention, consideration, study. ❷ *his observations were concise and to the point* REMARK, comment, statement, utterance, pronouncement, declaration; opinion, impression, thought, reflection. ❸ *the observation of the law* OBSERVANCE, compliance, adherence, respect, obedience; keeping, obeying.

observe ▶ verb ❶ *she observed that all the chairs were occupied* NOTICE, see, note, perceive, discern, spot; *poetic/literary* espy, descry. ❷ *she was alarmed to discover he had been observing her* WATCH, look at, eye, contemplate, view, survey, regard, keep an eye on, scrutinize, keep under observation, keep watch on, keep under surveillance, monitor, keep a weather eye on; *informal* keep tabs on, keep a beady eye on; *poetic/literary* behold. ❸ *'You look tired,' she observed* REMARK, comment, say, mention, declare, announce, state, pronounce; *formal* opine. ❹ *both countries agreed to observe the ceasefire* COMPLY WITH, abide by, keep, obey, adhere to, heed, honour, fulfil, respect, follow, consent to, acquiesce in, accept. ❺ *townspeople observed the one-year anniversary of the flood* COMMEMORATE, mark, keep, memorialize, remember, celebrate.

observer ▶ noun ❶ *a casual observer might not have noticed* SPECTATOR, onlooker, watcher, looker-on, fly on the wall, viewer, witness; *informal* rubberneck; *poetic/literary* beholder. ❷ *industry observers expect the deal to be finalized today* COMMENTATOR, reporter; monitor.

obsess ▶ verb PREOCCUPY, be uppermost in someone's mind, prey on someone's mind, prey on, possess, haunt, consume, plague, torment, hound, bedevil, beset, take control of, take over, have a hold on, eat up, grip.

obsessed ▶ adjective FIXATED, possessed, consumed; infatuated, besotted; *informal* smitten, hung up; *N. Amer. informal* hipped.

obsession ▶ noun FIXATION, ruling/consuming passion, passion, mania, idée fixe, compulsion, preoccupation, infatuation, addiction, fetish, craze; hobby horse; phobia, complex, neurosis; *informal* bee in one's bonnet, hang-up, thing.

obsessive ▶ adjective ALL-CONSUMING, consuming, compulsive, controlling, obsessional, fanatical, neurotic, excessive, besetting, tormenting, inescapable; *informal* pathological.

obsolescent ▶ adjective DYING OUT, on the decline, declining, waning, on the wane, disappearing, past its prime, ageing, moribund, on its last legs, out of date, outdated, old-fashioned, outmoded; *informal* on the way out, past it.

obsolete ▶ adjective OUT OF DATE, outdated, outmoded, old-fashioned, démodé, passé; no longer in use, disused, fallen into disuse, superannuated, outworn, antiquated, antediluvian, anachronistic, discontinued, old, dated, archaic, ancient, fossilized, extinct, defunct, dead, bygone; *informal* out of the ark, prehistoric; *Brit. informal* past its sell-by date.
– OPPOSITES current, modern.

obstacle ▶ noun BARRIER, hurdle, stumbling block, obstruction, bar, block, impediment, hindrance, snag, catch, drawback, hitch, handicap, deterrent, complication, difficulty, problem, disadvantage, curb, check; *informal* fly in the ointment; *Brit. informal* spanner in the works; *poetic/literary* trammel.
– OPPOSITES advantage, aid.

obstinacy ▶ noun STUBBORNNESS, inflexibility, intransigence, intractability, obduracy, mulishness, pig-headedness, wilfulness, contrariness, perversity, recalcitrance, implacability; persistence, tenacity, tenaciousness, doggedness, single-mindedness, determination; *Brit. informal* bloody-mindedness, bolshiness; *formal* refractoriness, pertinacity.

obstinate ▶ adjective STUBBORN, unyielding, inflexible, unbending, intransigent, intract-

able, obdurate, mulish, stubborn as a mule, pig-headed, self-willed, strong-willed, headstrong, wilful, contrary, perverse, recalcitrant, uncooperative, unmanageable, stiff-necked, uncompromising, implacable, unrelenting, immovable, unshakeable; persistent, tenacious, dogged, single-minded, adamant, determined; *Brit. informal* bloody-minded, bolshie; *N. Amer. informal* balky; *formal* refractory, pertinacious.
– OPPOSITES compliant.

obstreperous ▶ adjective UNRULY, unmanageable, disorderly, undisciplined, uncontrollable, rowdy, disruptive, truculent, difficult, rebellious, mutinous, riotous, out of control, wild, turbulent, uproarious, boisterous; noisy, loud, clamorous, raucous, vociferous; *Brit. informal* stroppy, bolshie, rumbustious; *N. Amer. informal* rambunctious; *formal* refractory.
– OPPOSITES quiet, restrained.

obstruct ▶ verb ❶ *ensure that air bricks and vents are not obstructed* BLOCK (UP), clog (up), get in the way of, occlude, cut off, shut off, bung up, choke, dam up; barricade, bar; *Brit. informal* gunge up. ❷ *he was charged with obstructing the traffic* HOLD UP, bring to a standstill, stop, halt, block. ❸ *fears that the regime would obstruct the distribution of food* IMPEDE, hinder, interfere with, hamper, block, interrupt, hold up, stand in the way of, frustrate, thwart, baulk, inhibit, hamstring, sabotage; slow down, retard, delay, stonewall, stop, halt, restrict, limit, curb, put a brake on, bridle; *N. Amer. informal* bork.
– OPPOSITES clear, facilitate.

obstruction ▶ noun OBSTACLE, barrier, stumbling block, hurdle, bar, block, impediment, hindrance, snag, difficulty, catch, drawback, hitch, handicap, deterrent, curb, check, restriction; blockage, stoppage, congestion, bottleneck, hold-up; *Medicine* occlusion; *informal* fly in the ointment; *Brit. informal* spanner in the works.

obstructive ▶ adjective UNHELPFUL, uncooperative, awkward, difficult, unaccommodating, disobliging, perverse, contrary; *Brit. informal* bloody-minded, bolshie; *N. Amer. informal* balky.
– OPPOSITES helpful.

obtain ▶ verb ❶ *the newspaper obtained a copy of the letter* GET, acquire, come by, secure, procure, come into the possession of, pick up, be given; gain, earn, achieve, attain; *informal* get hold of, get/lay one's hands on, get one's mitts on, land. ❷ (*formal*) *rules obtaining in other jurisdictions* PREVAIL, be in force, apply, exist, be in use, be in effect, stand, hold, be the case.
– OPPOSITES lose.

obtainable ▶ adjective AVAILABLE, to be had, in circulation, on the market, on offer, in season, at one's disposal, at hand, attainable, procurable, accessible; *informal* up for grabs, on tap, get-at-able.

obtrusive ▶ adjective CONSPICUOUS, prominent, noticeable, obvious, unmistakable, intrusive, out of place; *informal* sticking out a mile, sticking out like a sore thumb.
– OPPOSITES inconspicuous.

obtuse ▶ adjective STUPID, foolish, slow-witted, slow, dull-witted, unintelligent, ignorant, simple-minded; insensitive, imperceptive, uncomprehending; *informal* dim, dim-witted, dense, dumb, slow on the uptake, half-witted, brain-dead, moronic, cretinous, thick, dopey, dozy, wooden-headed, boneheaded; *Brit. informal* divvy; *Scottish & N. English informal* glaikit; *N. Amer. informal* dumb-ass, chowderheaded.
– OPPOSITES clever.

obviate ▶ verb PRECLUDE, prevent, remove, get rid of, do away with, get round, rule out, eliminate, make unnecessary.

obvious ▶ adjective CLEAR, crystal clear, plain, evident, apparent, manifest, patent, conspicuous, pronounced, transparent, palpable, prominent, marked, decided, distinct, noticeable, perceptible, visible, discernible; unmistakable, indisputable, self-evident, incontrovertible, incontestable, undeniable, as plain as a pikestaff, as clear as day, staring someone in the face; overt, open, undisguised, unconcealed, frank, glaring, blatant, written all over someone; *informal* as plain as the nose on your face, sticking out like a sore thumb, sticking out a mile.
– OPPOSITES imperceptible.

obviously ▶ adverb CLEARLY, evidently, plainly, patently, visibly, discernibly, manifestly, noticeably; unmistakably, undeniably, incontrovertibly, demonstrably, unquestionably, undoubtedly, without doubt, doubtless; of course, naturally, needless to say, it goes without saying.
– OPPOSITES perhaps.

occasion ▶ noun ❶ *a previous occasion* TIME, instance, juncture, point; event, occurrence, affair, incident, episode, experience; situation, case, circumstance. ❷ *a family occasion* SOCIAL EVENT, event, affair, function, celebration, party, get-together, gathering; *informal* do, bash. ❸ *I doubt if the occasion will arise* OPPORTUNITY, right moment, chance, opening, window. ❹ *it's the first time I've had occasion to complain* REASON, cause, call, grounds, justification, need, motive.
▶ verb *her situation occasioned a good deal of sympathy* CAUSE, give rise to, bring about, result in, lead to, prompt, elicit, call forth, produce, create, arouse, generate, engender, precipitate, provoke, stir up, inspire, spark off, trigger; *poetic/literary* beget.
■ **on occasion**. *See* OCCASIONALLY.

occasional ▶ adjective INFREQUENT, intermittent, irregular, periodic, sporadic, odd, random, uncommon, few and far between, isolated, rare; *N. Amer.* sometime.

– OPPOSITES regular, frequent.

occasionally ▶ adverb SOMETIMES, from time to time, (every) now and then, (every) now and again, at times, every so often, (every) once in a while, on occasion, periodically, at intervals, irregularly, sporadically, infrequently, intermittently, on and off, off and on.
– OPPOSITES often.

occlude ▶ verb BLOCK (UP), stop (up), obstruct, clog (up), close, shut, bung up, choke.

occult ▶ noun *his interest in the occult* THE SUPERNATURAL, supernaturalism, magic, black magic, witchcraft, sorcery, necromancy, wizardry, the black arts, occultism, diabolism, devil worship, devilry, voodoo, hoodoo, white magic, mysticism; *NZ* makutu.
▶ adjective ❶ *occult powers* SUPERNATURAL, magic, magical, mystical, mystic, psychic, preternatural, transcendental; cabbalistic, hermetic. ❷ *the typically occult language of the time* ESOTERIC, arcane, recondite, abstruse, secret; obscure, incomprehensible, impenetrable, puzzling, perplexing, mystifying, mysterious, enigmatic.

occupancy ▶ noun OCCUPATION, tenancy, tenure, residence, residency, inhabitation, habitation, living, lease, holding, owner-occupancy; *formal* dwelling.

occupant ▶ noun ❶ *the occupants of the houses* RESIDENT, inhabitant, owner, householder, tenant, renter, leaseholder, lessee; addressee; *Brit.* occupier, owner-occupier; *formal* dweller. ❷ *the first occupant of the post* INCUMBENT, holder.

occupation ▶ noun ❶ *his father's occupation* JOB, profession, (line) of work, trade, employment, position, post, situation, business, career, métier, vocation, calling, craft; *Austral. informal* grip; *archaic* employ. ❷ *her leisure occupations* PASTIME, activity, hobby, pursuit, interest, entertainment, recreation, amusement, divertissement. ❸ *a property suitable for occupation by older people* RESIDENCE, residency, habitation, inhabitation, occupancy, tenancy, tenure, lease, living in; *formal* dwelling. ❹ *the Roman occupation of Britain* CONQUEST, capture, invasion, seizure, takeover, annexation, overrunning, subjugation, subjection, appropriation; colonization, rule, control, suzerainty.

occupational ▶ adjective JOB-RELATED, work, professional, vocational, employment, business, career.

occupied ▶ adjective ❶ *tasks which kept her occupied all day* BUSY, engaged, working, at work, active; *informal* tied up, hard at it, on the go. ❷ *all the tables were occupied* IN USE, full, engaged, taken. ❸ *only two of the flats are occupied* INHABITED, lived-in, tenanted, settled.
– OPPOSITES free, vacant.

occupy ▶ verb ❶ *Carol occupied the basement flat* LIVE IN, inhabit, be the tenant of, lodge in; move into, take up residence in; people, populate, settle; *Scottish* stay in; *formal* reside in, dwell in. ❷ *two windows occupied almost the whole of the end wall* TAKE UP, fill, fill up, cover, use up. ❸ *he occupies a senior post at the Treasury* HOLD, fill, have; *informal* hold down. ❹ *I need something to occupy my mind* ENGAGE, busy, employ, distract, absorb, engross, preoccupy, hold, interest, involve, entertain, amuse, divert. ❺ *the region was occupied by Soviet troops* CAPTURE, seize, take possession of, conquer, invade, overrun, take over, colonize, garrison, annex, subjugate.

occur ▶ verb ❶ *the accident occurred at about 3.30* HAPPEN, take place, come about, transpire, materialize, arise, crop up; *N. Amer. informal* go down; *poetic/literary* come to pass, befall, betide; *archaic* hap; *formal* eventuate. ❷ *the disease occurs chiefly in tropical climates* BE FOUND, be present, exist, appear, prevail, present itself, manifest itself, turn up. ❸ *an idea occurred to her* ENTER ONE'S HEAD/MIND, cross one's mind, come to mind, spring to mind, strike one, hit one, dawn on one, suggest itself.

occurrence ▶ noun ❶ *vandalism used to be a rare occurrence* EVENT, incident, happening, phenomenon, affair, matter, circumstance. ❷ *the occurrence of cancer increases with age* EXISTENCE, instance, appearance, manifestation, materialization, development; frequency, incidence, rate, prevalence; *Statistics* distribution.

ocean ▶ noun ❶ *the ocean was calm* THE SEA; *informal* the drink; *Brit. informal* the briny; *poetic/literary* the deep, the waves, the main. ❷ (*informal*) *she had oceans of energy.* See LOT pronoun.

odd ▶ adjective ❶ *an odd man* STRANGE, peculiar, weird, queer, funny, bizarre, eccentric, unusual, unconventional, outlandish, quirky, zany; *informal* wacky, kooky, screwy, oddball, offbeat, off the wall. ❷ *quite a few odd things had happened* STRANGE, unusual, peculiar, funny, curious, bizarre, weird, uncanny, queer, outré, unexpected, unfamiliar, abnormal, atypical, anomalous, different, out of the ordinary, out of the way, exceptional, rare, extraordinary, remarkable, puzzling, mystifying, mysterious, perplexing, baffling, unaccountable, uncommon, irregular, singular, deviant, aberrant, freak, freakish. ❸ *we have the odd drink together | he does odd jobs for friends* OCCASIONAL, casual, irregular, isolated, random, sporadic, periodic; miscellaneous, various, varied, sundry. ❹ *odd shoes* MISMATCHED, unmatched, unpaired; single, lone, solitary, extra, surplus, leftover, remaining.
– OPPOSITES normal, ordinary, regular.
■ **odd man out** OUTSIDER, exception, oddity, nonconformist, maverick, individualist, misfit, fish out of water, square peg in a round hole.

oddity ▶ noun ❶ *she was regarded as a bit of an oddity* ECCENTRIC, crank, misfit, maverick, nonconformist, rare bird; *informal* character, oddball, weirdo, crackpot, nut, freak; *Brit. informal* nutter; *N. Amer. informal* screwball, kook; *informal, dated* case. ❷ *his work remains an oddity in some respects* ANOMALY, aberration, curiosity, rarity. ❸ *the oddities of human nature* PECULIARITY, idiosyncrasy, eccentricity, quirk, irregularity, twist.

oddments ▶ **plural noun** ❶ *oddments of material* SCRAPS, remnants, odds and ends, bits, pieces, bits and pieces, bits and bobs, leftovers, fragments, snippets, offcuts, ends, shreds, tail ends; *Brit. informal* fag ends. ❷ *a cellar full of oddments. See* ODDS AND ENDS at ODDS.

odds ▶ **plural noun** ❶ *the odds are that he is no longer alive* LIKELIHOOD, probability, chances, chance, balance. ❷ *the odds are in our favour* ADVANTAGE, edge; superiority, supremacy, ascendancy.

■ **at odds** ❶ *he was at odds with his colleagues* IN CONFLICT, in disagreement, on bad terms, at cross purposes, at loggerheads, quarrelling, arguing, at daggers drawn, at each other's throats; *N. Amer.* on the outs. ❷ *behaviour at odds with the interests of the company* AT VARIANCE, out of keeping, out of line, in opposition, conflicting, contrary, incompatible, inconsistent, irreconcilable.

■ **odds and ends** BITS AND PIECES, bits and bobs, bits, pieces, stuff, paraphernalia, things, sundries, miscellanea, bric-a-brac, knick-knacks, oddments; *informal* junk; *Brit. informal* odds and sods, clobber, gubbins.

odious ▶ **adjective** REVOLTING, repulsive, repellent, repugnant, disgusting, offensive, objectionable, vile, foul, abhorrent, loathsome, nauseating, sickening, hateful, detestable, execrable, abominable, monstrous, appalling, reprehensible, deplorable, insufferable, intolerable, despicable, contemptible, unspeakable, atrocious, awful, terrible, dreadful, frightful, obnoxious, unsavoury, unpalatable, unpleasant, disagreeable, nasty, distasteful; *informal* ghastly, horrible, horrid, gross, God-awful; *Brit. informal* beastly; *archaic* disgustful, loathly.

– OPPOSITES delightful.

odium ▶ **noun** DISGUST, abhorrence, repugnance, revulsion, loathing, detestation, hatred, hate, obloquy, dislike, distaste, disfavour, antipathy, animosity, animus, enmity, hostility, contempt; disgrace, shame, opprobrium, discredit, dishonour.

– OPPOSITES approval.

odorous ▶ **adjective** SMELLY, malodorous, pungent, acrid, foul-smelling, evil-smelling, stinking, reeking, fetid, rank; *informal* stinky; *Brit. informal* pongy, niffy; *poetic/literary* miasmic, noisome, mephitic.

odour ▶ **noun** ❶ *an odour of sweat* SMELL, stench, stink, reek; *Brit. informal* pong, whiff, niff, hum; *N. Amer. informal* funk; *poetic/literary* miasma. ❷ *an odour of suspicion* ATMOSPHERE, air, aura, quality, flavour, savour, hint, suggestion, impression, whiff.

odyssey ▶ **noun** JOURNEY, voyage, trek, travels, quest, crusade, pilgrimage, wandering, journeying; *archaic* peregrination.

off ▶ **adjective** ❶ *Kate's off today* AWAY, absent, unavailable, not at work, off duty, on holiday, on leave; free, at leisure; *N. Amer.* on vacation. ❷ *the game's off* CANCELLED, postponed, called off. ❸ *strawberries are off* UNAVAILABLE, finished, sold out. ❹ *the fish was a bit off* ROTTEN, bad, stale, mouldy, high, sour, rancid, turned, spoiled, putrid, putrescent. ❺ (*Brit. informal*) *I felt decidedly off. See* OFF COLOUR sense 1. ❻ (*Brit. informal*) *that remark was a bit off* UNFAIR, unjust, uncalled for, below the belt, unjustified, unjustifiable, unreasonable, unwarranted, unnecessary; *informal* a bit much; *Brit. informal* out of order. ❼ (*Brit. informal*) *he was really off with me* UNFRIENDLY, aloof, cool, cold, distant, frosty; *informal* stand-offish.

■ **off and on** PERIODICALLY, at intervals, on and off, (every) once in a while, every so often, (every) now and then/again, from time to time, occasionally, sometimes, intermittently, irregularly.

offbeat ▶ **adjective** (*informal*) UNCONVENTIONAL, unorthodox, unusual, eccentric, idiosyncratic, outré, strange, bizarre, weird, peculiar, odd, freakish, outlandish, out of the ordinary, Bohemian, alternative, left-field, zany, quirky; *informal* wacky, freaky, way-out, off the wall, kooky, oddball.

– OPPOSITES conventional.

off colour ▶ **adjective** ❶ (*Brit.*) *I'm feeling a bit off colour* UNWELL, ill, poorly, out of sorts, indisposed, not oneself, sick, queasy, nauseous, peaky, liverish, green about the gills, run down, washed out, below par; *informal* under the weather, rough; *Brit. informal* ropy, off; *Scottish informal* wabbit, peely-wally; *Austral./NZ informal* crook. ❷ *off-colour jokes* SMUTTY, dirty, rude, crude, suggestive, indecent, indelicate, risqué, racy, bawdy, naughty, blue, vulgar, ribald, broad, salacious, coarse; *informal* raunchy; *Brit. informal* fruity, saucy; *euphemistic* adult.

– OPPOSITES well.

offence ▶ **noun** ❶ *he denied having committed any offence* CRIME, illegal/unlawful act, misdemeanour, breach of the law, felony, wrongdoing, wrong, misdeed, peccadillo, sin, transgression, infringement; *Law* malfeasance; *archaic* trespass. ❷ *an offence to basic justice* AFFRONT, slap in the face, insult, outrage, violation. ❸ *I do not want to cause offence* ANNOYANCE, anger, resentment, indignation, irritation, exasperation, wrath, displeasure, hard/bad/ill feelings, disgruntlement, pique, vexation, animosity.

■ **take offence** BE OFFENDED, take exception, take something personally, feel affronted, feel resentful, take something amiss, take umbrage, get upset, get annoyed, get angry, get into a huff; *Brit. informal* get the hump.

offend ▶ **verb** ❶ *I'm sorry if I offended him* HURT SOMEONE'S FEELINGS, give offence to, affront, displease, upset, distress, hurt, wound; annoy, anger, exasperate, irritate, vex, pique, gall, irk, nettle, tread on someone's toes; *Brit.* rub up the wrong way; *informal* rile, rattle, peeve, needle, put someone's nose out of joint, put someone's back up. ❷ *the smell of cigarette smoke offended him* DISPLEASE, be distasteful to, be disagreeable to, be offensive to, disgust, repel, revolt, sicken, nauseate; *informal* turn off; *N. Amer. informal* gross out. ❸ *criminals who offend again and again* BREAK THE LAW, commit a crime, do wrong, sin, transgress; *archaic* trespass.

offended ▶ **adjective** AFFRONTED, insulted, aggrieved, displeased, upset, hurt, wounded, disgruntled, put out, annoyed, angry, cross, exasperated, indignant, irritated, piqued, vexed, irked, stung, galled, nettled, resentful, in a huff, huffy, in high dudgeon; *informal* riled, miffed, peeved, aggravated; *Brit. informal* narked; *N. Amer. informal* sore.
– OPPOSITES pleased.

offender ▶ **noun** WRONGDOER, criminal, lawbreaker, miscreant, malefactor, felon, delinquent, culprit, guilty party, sinner, transgressor; *Law* malfeasant.

offensive ▶ **adjective** ❶ *offensive remarks* INSULTING, rude, impertinent, insolent, derogatory, disrespectful, personal, hurtful, wounding, abusive; annoying, exasperating, irritating, galling, provocative, outrageous; discourteous, uncivil, impolite; *formal* exceptionable. ❷ *an offensive smell* UNPLEASANT, disagreeable, nasty, distasteful, displeasing, objectionable, off-putting, awful, terrible, dreadful, frightful, obnoxious, abominable, disgusting, repulsive, repellent, repugnant, revolting, abhorrent, loathsome, odious, vile, foul, sickening, nauseating; *informal* ghastly, horrible, horrid, gross, God-awful; *Brit. informal* beastly; *archaic* disgustful. ❸ *an offensive air action* HOSTILE, attacking, aggressive, invading, combative, belligerent, on the attack.
– OPPOSITES complimentary, pleasant, defensive.
▶ **noun** *a military offensive* ATTACK, assault, onslaught, drive, invasion, push, thrust, charge, sortie, sally, foray, raid, incursion, blitz, campaign.

offer ▶ **verb** ❶ *Frank offered another suggestion* PUT FORWARD, proffer, give, present, come up with, suggest, recommend, propose, advance, submit, tender, render. ❷ *she offered to help* VOLUNTEER, volunteer one's services, be at someone's disposal, be at someone's service, step/come forward, show willing. ❸ *the product is offered at a competitive price* PUT UP FOR SALE, put on the market, sell, market, put under the hammer; *Law* vend. ❹ *he offered $200* BID, tender, put in a bid of, put in an offer of. ❺ *a job offering good career prospects* PROVIDE, afford, supply, give, furnish, present, hold out. ❻ *she offered no resistance* ATTEMPT, try, give, show, express; *formal* essay. ❼ *birds were offered to the gods* SACRIFICE, offer up, immolate.
– OPPOSITES withdraw, refuse.
▶ **noun** ❶ *offers of help* PROPOSAL, proposition, suggestion, submission, approach, overture. ❷ *the highest offer* BID, tender, bidding price.
■ **on offer** ON SALE, up for sale, on the market; available, obtainable, to be had; *N. Amer.* on the block.

offering ▶ **noun** ❶ *you may place offerings in the charity box* CONTRIBUTION, donation, gift, present, handout, widow's mite; charity; *formal* benefaction; *historical* alms. ❷ *many offerings were made to the goddess* SACRIFICE, oblation, burnt offering, immolation, libation, first fruits.

offhand ▶ **adjective** *an offhand manner* CASUAL, careless, uninterested, unconcerned, indifferent, cool, nonchalant, blasé, insouciant, cavalier, glib, perfunctory, cursory, unceremonious, ungracious, dismissive, discourteous, uncivil, impolite, terse, abrupt, curt; *informal* off, couldn't-care-less, take-it-or-leave-it.
▶ **adverb** *I can't think of a better answer offhand* ON THE SPUR OF THE MOMENT, without consideration, extempore, impromptu, ad lib; extemporaneously, spontaneously; *informal* off the cuff, off the top of one's head, just like that.

office ▶ **noun** ❶ *her office in Aldersgate Street* PLACE OF WORK, place of business, workplace, workroom. ❷ *the newspaper's Paris office* BRANCH, division, section, bureau, department; agency. ❸ *he assumed the office of President* POST, position, appointment, job, occupation, role, situation, function, capacity. ❹ *he was saved by the good offices of his uncle* ASSISTANCE, help, aid, services, intervention, intercession, mediation, agency. ❺ (*dated*) *the offices of a nurse* DUTY, job, task, chore, obligation, assignment, responsibility, charge, commission.

officer ▶ **noun** ❶ *an officer in the army* military officer, commissioned officer, non-commissioned officer, NCO, commanding officer, CO. ❷ *all officers carry warrant cards. See* POLICE OFFICER. ❸ *the officers of the society* OFFICIAL, office-holder, committee member, board member; public servant, administrator, executive, functionary, bureaucrat; *derogatory* apparatchik.

official ▶ **adjective** ❶ *an official inquiry* AUTHORIZED, approved, validated, authenticated, certified, accredited, endorsed, sanctioned, licensed, recognized, accepted, legitimate, legal, lawful, valid, bona fide, proper, excathedra; *informal* kosher. ❷ *an official function* CEREMONIAL, formal, solemn, ceremonious; bureaucratic; *informal* stuffed-shirt.

–OPPOSITES unauthorized, informal.

▶ **noun** *a union official* OFFICER, office-holder, administrator, executive, appointee, functionary; bureaucrat, mandarin; representative, agent; *Brit.* jack-in-office; *derogatory* apparatchik.

officiate ▶ **verb** ❶ *he officiated in the first two matches* BE IN CHARGE OF, take charge of, preside over; oversee, superintend, supervise, conduct, run. ❷ *Father Buckley officiated at the wedding service* CONDUCT, perform, celebrate, solemnize.

officious ▶ **adjective** SELF-IMPORTANT, bumptious, self-assertive, pushy, overbearing, overzealous, domineering, opinionated, interfering, intrusive, meddlesome, meddling; *informal* bossy.
–OPPOSITES self-effacing.

offing
■ **in the offing** ON THE WAY, coming, (close) at hand, near, imminent, in prospect, on the horizon, in the wings, just around the corner, in the air, in the wind, brewing, upcoming, forthcoming; *informal* on the cards.

off-key ▶ **adjective** ❶ *an off-key rendition of 'Amazing Grace'* OUT OF TUNE, flat, tuneless, discordant, unharmonious. ❷ *the cinematic effects are distractingly off-key* INCONGRUOUS, inappropriate, unsuitable, out of place, out of keeping, jarring, dissonant, inharmonious.
–OPPOSITES harmonious.

offload ▶ **verb** ❶ *the cargo was being offloaded* UNLOAD, remove, empty (out), tip (out); *archaic* unlade. ❷ *he offloaded 5,000 of the shares* DISPOSE OF, dump, jettison, get rid of, transfer, shift; palm off, foist, fob off.

off-putting ▶ **adjective** ❶ *an off-putting aroma* UNPLEASANT, unappealing, uninviting, unattractive, disagreeable, offensive, distasteful, unsavoury, unpalatable, unappetizing, objectionable, nasty, disgusting, repellent; *informal* horrid, horrible. ❷ *her manner was off-putting* DISCOURAGING, disheartening, demoralizing, dispiriting, daunting, disconcerting, unnerving, unsettling; *formal* rebarbative.

offset ▶ **verb** COUNTERBALANCE, balance (out), cancel (out), even out/up, counteract, countervail, neutralize, compensate for, make up for, make good, redeem.

offshoot ▶ **noun** ❶ *the plant's offshoots* SIDE SHOOT, shoot, sucker, tendril, runner, scion, slip, offset, stolon; twig, branch, bough, limb. ❷ *an offshoot of Cromwell's line* DESCENDANT, scion. ❸ *an offshoot of the growth of interest in heritage* OUTCOME, result, effect, consequence, upshot, product, by-product, spin-off, development, ramification.

offspring ▶ **noun** CHILDREN, sons and daughters, progeny, family, youngsters, babies, infants, brood; descendants, heirs, successors; *Law* issue; *informal* kids; *Brit. informal* sprogs, brats; *derogatory* spawn; *archaic* fruit of one's loins.

often ▶ **adverb** FREQUENTLY, many times, many a time, on many/numerous occasions, a lot, as often as not, repeatedly, again and again; regularly, routinely, usually, habitually, commonly, generally, in many cases/instances, ordinarily; *N. Amer.* oftentimes; *poetic/literary* oft.
–OPPOSITES seldom.

ogle ▶ **verb** LEER AT, stare at, eye, make eyes at; *informal* eye up, give someone the glad eye, lech after, undress with one's eyes, give someone the come-on; *Austral./NZ informal* perv on.

ogre ▶ **noun** ❶ *an ogre with two heads* MONSTER, giant, troll. ❷ *he is not the ogre he sometimes seems to be* BRUTE, fiend, monster, beast, barbarian, savage, animal, tyrant; *informal* bastard, swine, pig.

ogress ▶ **noun** ❶ *a one-eyed ogress* MONSTER, giantess. ❷ *the French teacher was a real ogress* HARRIDAN, tartar, termagant, gorgon, virago; *informal* battleaxe.

oily ▶ **adjective** ❶ *oily substances* GREASY, oleaginous; *technical* sebaceous; *formal* pinguid. ❷ *oily food* GREASY, fatty, buttery, swimming in oil/fat. ❸ *an oily man* UNCTUOUS, ingratiating, smooth-talking, fulsome, flattering; obsequious, sycophantic, oleaginous; *informal* smarmy, slimy.

ointment ▶ **noun** LOTION, cream, salve, liniment, embrocation, rub, gel, balm, emollient, unguent; *technical* humectant.

OK, okay (*informal*) ▶ **exclamation** *OK, I'll go with him* ALL RIGHT, right, right then, right you are, very well, very good, fine; *informal* okey-doke(y); *Brit. informal* righto, righty-ho.

▶ **adjective** ❶ *the film was OK* SATISFACTORY, all right, acceptable, competent; adequate, tolerable, passable, reasonable, fair, decent, not bad, average, middling, moderate, unremarkable, unexceptional; *informal* so-so, fair-to-middling. ❷ *Jo's feeling OK now* FINE, all right, well, in good shape, in good health, fit, healthy, as fit as a fiddle/flea. ❸ *it is OK for me to come?* PERMISSIBLE, allowable, acceptable, all right, in order, permitted, fitting, suitable, appropriate.
–OPPOSITES unsatisfactory, ill.

▶ **noun** *he's just given me the OK* AUTHORIZATION, approval, seal of approval, agreement, consent, assent, permission, endorsement, ratification, sanction, approbation, confirmation, blessing, leave; *informal* the go-ahead, the green light, the thumbs up, say-so.
–OPPOSITES refusal.

▶ **verb** *the move must be okayed by the president* AUTHORIZE, approve, agree to, consent to, sanction, pass, ratify, endorse, allow, give something the nod, rubber-stamp; *informal* give the go-ahead, give the green light, give the thumbs up; *formal* accede to.
–OPPOSITES refuse, veto.

old ▶ **adjective** ❶ *old people* ELDERLY, aged, older, senior, advanced in years, venerable; in one's

dotage, long in the tooth, grey-haired, grizzled, hoary, past one's prime, not as young as one was, ancient, decrepit, doddering, doddery, not long for this world, senescent, senile, superannuated; *informal* getting on, past it, over the hill, no spring chicken. ❷ *old farm buildings* DILAPIDATED, broken-down, run down, tumbledown, ramshackle, decaying, crumbling, disintegrating. ❸ *old clothes* WORN, worn out, shabby, threadbare, holey, torn, frayed, patched, tattered, moth-eaten, ragged; old-fashioned, out of date, outmoded; cast-off, hand-me-down; *informal* tatty. ❹ *old cars* ANTIQUE, veteran, vintage. ❺ *she's old for her years* MATURE, wise, sensible, experienced, worldly-wise, knowledgeable. ❻ *in the old days* BYGONE, past, former, olden, of old, previous, early, earlier, earliest; medieval, ancient, classical, primeval, primordial, prehistoric. ❼ *the same old phrases* HACKNEYED, hack, banal, trite, overused, overworked, tired, worn out, stale, clichéd, platitudinous, unimaginative, stock, conventional; out of date, outdated, old-fashioned, outmoded, hoary; *informal* old hat, corny, played out. ❽ *an old girlfriend* FORMER, previous, ex-, one-time, sometime, erstwhile; *formal* quondam.
– OPPOSITES young, new, modern.

■ **old age** DECLINING YEARS, advanced years, age, oldness, winter/autumn of one's life, senescence, senility, dotage.

■ **old man** ❶ SENIOR CITIZEN, pensioner, OAP, elder, grandfather; patriarch; *informal* greybeard, codger; *Brit. informal* buffer; *archaic* grandsire, ancient. ❷ (*informal*) *her old man was away.* See HUSBAND noun.

■ **old person** SENIOR CITIZEN, senior, (old-age) pensioner, OAP, elder, geriatric, dotard, Methuselah; *N. Amer.* golden ager; *informal* old stager, old-timer, oldie, wrinkly, crock, crumbly; *N. Amer. informal* oldster, woopie.

■ **old woman** ❶ SENIOR CITIZEN, pensioner, OAP, crone; *informal* old dear; *archaic* beldam, grandam. ❷ (*informal*) *his old woman threw him out.* See WIFE. ❸ (*informal*) *he's such an old woman* WORRIER; *informal* fusspot; *N. Amer. informal* fussbudget.

old-fashioned ▶ adjective OUT OF DATE, outdated, dated, out of fashion, outmoded, unfashionable, passé, démodé, frumpy; outworn, old, old-time, behind the times, archaic, obsolescent, obsolete, ancient, antiquated, superannuated, defunct; medieval, prehistoric, antediluvian, old-fogeyish, conservative, backward-looking, quaint, anachronistic, fusty, moth-eaten, olde worlde; *informal* old hat, square, not with it, out of the ark; *N. Amer. informal* horse-and-buggy, clunky, rinky-dink.
– OPPOSITES modern.

old-time ▶ adjective FORMER, past, bygone, old-fashioned; traditional, folk, old-world, quaint.
– OPPOSITES modern.

Olympian ▶ adjective ALOOF, distant, remote, unfriendly, uncommunicative, unforthcoming, cool; *informal* stand-offish.
– OPPOSITES friendly.

omen ▶ noun PORTENT, sign, signal, token, forewarning, warning, foreshadowing, prediction, forecast, prophesy, harbinger, augury, auspice, presage; writing on the wall, indication, hint; *poetic/literary* foretoken.

ominous ▶ adjective THREATENING, menacing, baleful, forbidding, sinister, inauspicious, unpropitious, portentous, unfavourable, unpromising; black, dark, gloomy; *formal* minatory; *poetic/literary* direful.
– OPPOSITES promising.

omission ▶ noun ❶ *the omission of recent publications from his biography* EXCLUSION, leaving out; deletion, cut, excision, elimination. ❷ *the damage was not caused by any omission on behalf of the carrier* NEGLIGENCE, neglect, neglectfulness, dereliction, forgetfulness, oversight, default, lapse, failure.

omit ▶ verb ❶ *they omitted his name from the list* LEAVE OUT, exclude, leave off, take out, miss out, miss, drop, cut; delete, eliminate, rub out, cross out, strike out. ❷ *I omitted to mention our guest lecturer* FORGET, neglect, fail; leave undone, overlook, skip.
– OPPOSITES add, include, remember.

omnipotence ▶ noun ALL-POWERFULNESS, supremacy, pre-eminence, supreme power, unlimited power; invincibility.

omnipotent ▶ adjective ALL-POWERFUL, almighty, supreme, pre-eminent; invincible, unconquerable.

omnipresent ▶ adjective UBIQUITOUS, all-pervasive, everywhere; rife, pervasive, prevalent.

omniscient ▶ adjective ALL-KNOWING, all-wise, all-seeing.

omnivorous ▶ adjective ❶ *most duck species are omnivorous* ABLE TO EAT ANYTHING; *rare* pantophagous, omnivorant. ❷ *an omnivorous reader* UNDISCRIMINATING, indiscriminate, unselective.

on ▶ adjective *the computer's on* FUNCTIONING, in operation, working, in use, operating.
– OPPOSITES off.

▶ adverb *she droned on* INTERMINABLY, at length, for a long time, continuously, endlessly, ceaselessly, without a pause/break.

■ **on and off**. *See* OFF AND ON at OFF.

■ **on and on** FOR A LONG TIME, for ages, for hours, at (great) length, incessantly, ceaselessly, constantly, continuously, continually, endlessly, unendingly, eternally, forever, interminably, unremittingly, relentlessly, indefatigably, without let-up, without a pause/break, without cease.

once ▶ adverb ❶ *I only met him once* ON ONE OCCASION, one time, one single time. ❷ *he did not* *once help* EVER, at any time, on any occasion, at all. ❸ *they were friends once* FORMERLY, previously, in the past, at one time, at one point, once upon a time, time was when, in days/times gone by, in times past, in the (good) old days, long ago; *archaic* sometime, erstwhile, whilom; *poetic/literary* in days/times of yore.

– OPPOSITES often, now.

▶ **conjunction** *he'll be all right once she's gone* AS SOON AS, when, after.

■ **at once** ❶ *you must leave at once* IMMEDIATELY, right away, right now, this moment/instant/second/minute, now, straight away, instantly, directly, forthwith, promptly, without delay/hesitation, without further ado; quickly, as fast as possible, as soon as possible, a.s.a.p., speedily; *informal* like a shot, in/like a flash, before you can say Jack Robinson. ❷ *all the guests arrived at once* AT THE SAME TIME, at one and the same time, (all) together, simultaneously; as a group, in unison, in concert, in chorus.

■ **once and for all** CONCLUSIVELY, decisively, finally, positively, definitely, definitively, irrevocably; for good, for always, forever, permanently.

■ **once in a while** OCCASIONALLY, from time to time, (every) now and then/again, every so often, on occasion, at times, sometimes, off and on, at intervals, periodically, sporadically, intermittently.

oncoming ▶ **adjective** APPROACHING, advancing, nearing, forthcoming, on the way, imminent, impending, looming, gathering, (close) at hand, about to happen, to come.

one ▶ **cardinal number** ❶ UNIT, item; *technical* monad. ❷ *only one person came* A SINGLE, a solitary, a sole, a lone. ❸ *her one concern was her daughter* ONLY, single, solitary, sole. ❹ *they have now become one* UNITED, a unit, unitary, amalgamated, consolidated, integrated, combined, incorporated, allied, affiliated, linked, joined, unified, in league, in partnership; wedded, married.

– RELATED TERMS mono-, uni-.

onerous ▶ **adjective** BURDENSOME, arduous, strenuous, difficult, hard, severe, heavy, back-breaking, oppressive, weighty, uphill, effortful, formidable, laborious, Herculean, exhausting, tiring, taxing, demanding, punishing, gruelling, exacting, wearing, wearisome, fatiguing; *archaic* toilsome.

– OPPOSITES easy.

oneself

■ **by oneself**. *See* BY.

one-sided ▶ **adjective** ❶ *a one-sided account* BIASED, prejudiced, partisan, partial, preferential, discriminatory, slanted, inequitable, unfair, unjust. ❷ *a one-sided game* UNEQUAL, uneven, unbalanced.

– OPPOSITES impartial.

one-time ▶ **adjective** FORMER, ex-, old, previous, sometime, erstwhile; lapsed; *formal* quondam.

ongoing ▶ **adjective** ❶ *negotiations are ongoing* IN PROGRESS, under way, going on, continuing, taking place, proceeding, progressing, advancing; unfinished. ❷ *an ongoing struggle* CONTINUOUS, continuing, uninterrupted, unbroken, non-stop, constant, ceaseless, unceasing, unending, endless, never-ending, unremitting, relentless, unfaltering.

onlooker ▶ **noun** EYEWITNESS, witness, observer, looker-on, fly on the wall, spectator, watcher, viewer, bystander; sightseer; *informal* rubberneck; *poetic/literary* beholder.

only ▶ **adverb** ❶ *there was only enough for two* AT MOST, at best, (only) just, no/not more than; barely, scarcely, hardly. ❷ *he only works on one picture at a time* EXCLUSIVELY, solely, to the exclusion of everything else. ❸ *you're only saying that* MERELY, simply, just.

▶ **adjective** *their only son* SOLE, single, one (and only), solitary, lone, unique; exclusive.

onomatopoeic ▶ **adjective** IMITATIVE, echoic.

onset ▶ **noun** START, beginning, commencement, arrival, (first) appearance, inception, day one; outbreak.

– OPPOSITES end.

onslaught ▶ **noun** ASSAULT, attack, offensive, advance, charge, onrush, rush, storming, sortie, sally, raid, descent, incursion, invasion, foray, push, thrust, drive, blitz, bombardment, barrage, salvo; *historical* broadside.

onus ▶ **noun** BURDEN, responsibility, liability, obligation, duty, weight, load, charge, encumbrance; cross to bear, millstone round one's neck, albatross.

ooze ▶ **verb** ❶ *blood oozed from the wound* SEEP, discharge, flow, exude, trickle, drip, dribble, issue, filter, percolate, escape, leak, drain, empty, bleed, sweat, well; *Medicine* extravasate. ❷ *she was positively oozing charm* EXUDE, gush, drip, pour forth, emanate, radiate.

▶ **noun** ❶ *the ooze of blood* SEEPAGE, seeping, discharge, flow, exudation, trickle, drip, dribble, percolation, escape, leak, leakage, drainage; secretion; *Medicine* extravasation. ❷ *the ooze on the ocean floor* MUD, slime, alluvium, silt, mire, sludge, muck, dirt, deposit.

opalescent ▶ **adjective** IRIDESCENT, prismatic, rainbow-like, kaleidoscopic, multicoloured, many-hued, lustrous, shimmering, glittering, sparkling, variegated, shot, moire, opaline, milky, pearly, nacreous.

opaque ▶ **adjective** ❶ *opaque glass* NON-TRANSPARENT, cloudy, filmy, blurred, smeared, smeary, misty, dirty, muddy, muddied, grimy. ❷ *the technical jargon was opaque to her* OBSCURE, unclear, mysterious, puzzling, perplexing, baffling, mystifying, confusing, unfathomable, incomprehensible, unintellig-

ible, impenetrable, hazy, foggy; *informal* as clear as mud.
– OPPOSITES transparent, clear.

open ▶ adjective ❶ *the door's open* NOT SHUT, not closed, unlocked, unbolted, unlatched, off the latch, unfastened, unsecured; ajar, gaping, yawning. ❷ *a blue silk shirt, open at the neck* UNFASTENED, not done up, undone, unbuttoned, unzipped, loose. ❸ *the main roads are open* CLEAR, passable, navigable, unblocked, unobstructed. ❹ *open countryside | open spaces* UNENCLOSED, rolling, sweeping, extensive, wide (open), unfenced, exposed, unsheltered; spacious, airy, uncrowded, uncluttered; undeveloped, unbuilt-up. ❺ *a map was open beside him* SPREAD OUT, unfolded, unfurled, unrolled, extended, stretched out. ❻ *the bank wasn't open* OPEN FOR BUSINESS, open to the public. ❼ *the position is still open* AVAILABLE, vacant, free, unfilled; *informal* up for grabs. ❽ *the system is open to abuse* VULNERABLE, subject, susceptible, liable, exposed, an easy target for, at risk of. ❾ *she was open about her feelings* FRANK, candid, honest, forthcoming, communicative, forthright, direct, unreserved, plain-spoken, outspoken, free-spoken, not afraid to call a spade a spade; *informal* upfront. ❿ *open hostility* OVERT, obvious, patent, manifest, palpable, conspicuous, plain, undisguised, unconcealed, clear, apparent, evident; blatant, flagrant, barefaced, brazen. ⓫ *the case is still open* UNRESOLVED, undecided, unsettled, up in the air; open to debate, open for discussion, arguable, debatable, moot. ⓬ *an open mind* IMPARTIAL, unbiased, unprejudiced, objective, disinterested, non-partisan, non-discriminatory, neutral, dispassionate, detached. ⓭ *I'm open to suggestions* RECEPTIVE, amenable, willing/ready to listen, responsive. ⓮ *what other options are open to us?* AVAILABLE, accessible, on hand, obtainable, on offer. ⓯ *an open meeting* PUBLIC, general, unrestricted, non-exclusive, non-restrictive.
– OPPOSITES shut.

▶ verb ❶ *she opened the front door* UNFASTEN, unlatch, unlock, unbolt, unbar; throw wide. ❷ *Katherine opened the parcel* UNWRAP, undo, untie, unseal. ❸ *shall I open another bottle?* UNCORK, broach, crack (open). ❹ *Adam opened the map* SPREAD OUT, unfold, unfurl, unroll, straighten out. ❺ *he opened his heart to her* REVEAL, uncover, expose, lay bare, bare, pour out, disclose, divulge. ❻ *we're hoping to open next month* START TRADING, open for business, set up shop, put up one's plate; *N. Amer. informal* hang out one's shingle. ❼ *Sir Bryan opened the meeting* BEGIN, start, commence, initiate, set in motion, launch, get going, get under way, set the ball rolling, get off the ground; inaugurate; *informal* kick off, get the show on the road. ❽ *the lounge opens on to a terrace* GIVE ACCESS, lead, be connected, communicate with.
– OPPOSITES close, shut, end.

open air ▶ adjective OUTDOOR, out-of-doors, outside, alfresco.
– OPPOSITES indoor.

open-handed ▶ adjective GENEROUS, magnanimous, charitable, benevolent, beneficent, munificent, bountiful, altruistic, philanthropic; *poetic/literary* bounteous.
– OPPOSITES tight-fisted.

opening ▶ noun ❶ *an opening in the centre of the roof* HOLE, gap, aperture, orifice, vent, crack, slit, chink; spyhole, peephole; *Anatomy* foramen. ❷ *the opening in the wall* DOORWAY, gateway, entrance, (means of) entry, way in/out, exit. ❸ *United created openings but were unable to score* OPPORTUNITY, chance, window (of opportunity), possibility. ❹ *an opening with a stockbroker* VACANCY, position, job. ❺ *the opening of the session* BEGINNING, start, commencement, outset; introduction, prefatory remarks, opening statement; *informal* kick-off; *formal* proem. ❻ *a gallery opening* OPENING CEREMONY, official opening, launch, inauguration; opening/first night, premiere.

openly ▶ adverb ❶ *drugs were openly on sale* PUBLICLY, blatantly, flagrantly, overtly. ❷ *he spoke openly of his problems* FRANKLY, candidly, explicitly, honestly, sincerely, forthrightly, bluntly, without constraint, without holding back, straight from the shoulder.
– OPPOSITES secretly.

open-minded ▶ adjective ❶ *open-minded attitudes* UNBIASED, unprejudiced, neutral, non-judgemental, non-discriminatory, objective, disinterested; tolerant, liberal, permissive, broad-minded. ❷ *musicians need to be open-minded* RECEPTIVE, open (to suggestions), amenable, flexible, willing to change.
– OPPOSITES prejudiced, narrow-minded.

open-mouthed ▶ adjective ASTOUNDED, amazed, in amazement, surprised, stunned, bowled over, staggered, thunderstruck, aghast, stupefied, taken aback, shocked, speechless, dumbfounded, dumbstruck; *informal* flabbergasted; *Brit. informal* gobsmacked.

operate ▶ verb ❶ *he can operate the machine* WORK, make go, run, use, utilize, handle, control, manage; drive, steer, manoeuvre. ❷ *the machine ceased to operate* FUNCTION, work, go, run, be in working/running order, be operative. ❸ *the way the law operates in practice* TAKE EFFECT, act, apply, be applied, function. ❹ *Hechstetter operated the mines until 1634* DIRECT, control, manage, run, govern, administer, superintend, head (up), supervise, oversee, be in control/charge of. ❺ *doctors decided to operate* do an operation, perform surgery.

operation ▶ noun ❶ *the slide bars ensure smooth operation* FUNCTIONING, working, running, performance, action. ❷ *the operation of the factory* MANAGEMENT, running, governing, administration, supervision. ❸ *a heart bypass* *operation* SURGERY, surgical operation. ❹ *a military operation* ACTION, activity, exercise, undertaking, enterprise, manoeuvre, campaign. ❺ *their mining operations* BUSINESS, enterprise, company, firm; *informal* outfit.

■ **in operation**. *See* OPERATIONAL.

operational ▶ **adjective** (UP AND) RUNNING, working, functioning, operative, in operation, in use, in action; in working order, workable, serviceable, functional, usable.

operative ▶ **adjective** ❶ *the act is not operative at the moment* IN FORCE, in operation, in effect, valid. ❷ *the steam railway is operative. See* OPERATIONAL. ❸ *the operative word* KEY, significant, relevant, applicable, pertinent, apposite, germane, crucial, critical, pivotal.

– OPPOSITES invalid.

▶ **noun** ❶ *the operatives clean the machines* MACHINIST, (machine) operator, mechanic, engineer, worker, workman, (factory) hand, blue-collar worker. ❷ *an operative of the CIA* (SECRET) AGENT, undercover agent, spy, mole, plant, double agent, *N. Amer. informal* spook; *archaic* intelligencer. ❸ *a private operative* (PRIVATE) DETECTIVE, (private) investigator, sleuth; *informal* private eye; *N. Amer. informal* gumshoe.

operator ▶ **noun** ❶ *a machine operator* MACHINIST, mechanic, operative, engineer, worker. ❷ *a tour operator* CONTRACTOR, entrepreneur, promoter, arranger, fixer. ❸ (*informal*) *a ruthless operator* MANIPULATOR, manoeuvrer, string-puller, mover and shaker, wheeler-dealer; *N. Amer. informal* wire-puller.

opiate ▶ **noun** DRUG, narcotic, sedative, tranquillizer, depressant, soporific, anaesthetic, painkiller, analgesic, anodyne; morphine, opium; *informal* dope; *Medicine* stupefacient.

opine ▶ **verb** (*formal*) SUGGEST, say, declare, observe, comment, remark; think, believe, consider, maintain, imagine, reckon, guess, assume, presume, take it, suppose; *N. Amer. informal* allow.

opinion ▶ **noun** *she did not share her husband's opinion* BELIEF, judgement, thought(s), (way of) thinking, mind, (point of) view, viewpoint, attitude, stance, position, standpoint.

■ **a matter of opinion** OPEN TO QUESTION, debatable, open to debate, a moot point.

■ **be of the opinion** BELIEVE, think, consider, maintain, reckon, estimate, feel, be convinced; *N. Amer. informal* allow; *formal* opine.

■ **in my opinion** AS I SEE IT, to my mind, (according) to my way of thinking, personally, in my estimation, if you ask me.

opinionated ▶ **adjective** DOGMATIC, of fixed views; inflexible, uncompromising, prejudiced, bigoted.

opponent ▶ **noun** ❶ *his Republican opponent* RIVAL, adversary, opposer, the opposition, fellow contestant, (fellow) competitor, enemy, antagonist, combatant, contender, challenger; *poetic/literary* foe. ❷ *an opponent of the reforms* OPPOSER, objector, dissenter.

– OPPOSITES ally, supporter.

opportune ▶ **adjective** AUSPICIOUS, propitious, favourable, advantageous, golden, felicitous; timely, convenient, suitable, appropriate, apt, fitting.

– OPPOSITES disadvantageous.

opportunism ▶ **noun** EXPEDIENCY, pragmatism, Machiavellianism; striking while the iron is hot, making hay while the sun shines.

opportunity ▶ **noun** (LUCKY) CHANCE, golden opportunity, favourable time/occasion/moment; time, occasion, moment, opening, option, window (of opportunity), possibility, scope, freedom; *informal* shot, break, look-in.

oppose ▶ **verb** BE AGAINST, object to, be hostile to, be in opposition to, disagree with, dislike, disapprove of; resist, take a stand against, put up a fight against, stand up to, fight, challenge; take issue with, dispute, argue with/against, quarrel with; *informal* be anti; *formal* gainsay.

– OPPOSITES support.

opposed ▶ **adjective** ❶ *the population is opposed to the nuclear power plants* AGAINST, (dead) set against; in opposition, averse, hostile, antagonistic, antipathetic, resistant; *informal* anti. ❷ *their interests were opposed* CONFLICTING, contrasting, incompatible, irreconcilable, antithetical, contradictory, clashing, at variance, at odds, divergent, poles apart.

– OPPOSITES in favour of.

■ **as opposed to** IN CONTRAST WITH, as against, as contrasted with, rather than, instead of.

opposing ▶ **adjective** ❶ *the two opposing points of view* CONFLICTING, contrasting, opposite, incompatible, irreconcilable, contradictory, antithetical, clashing, at variance, at odds, divergent, opposed, poles apart. ❷ *opposing sides in the war* RIVAL, opposite, enemy. ❸ *the opposing page* OPPOSITE, facing.

opposite ▶ **adjective** ❶ *they sat opposite each other* FACING, face to face with, across from; *informal* eyeball to eyeball with. ❷ *the opposite page* FACING, opposing. ❸ *opposite views* CONFLICTING, contrasting, incompatible, irreconcilable, antithetical, contradictory, clashing, at variance, at odds, different, differing, divergent, dissimilar, unalike, disagreeing, opposed, opposing, poles apart. ❹ *opposite sides in a war* RIVAL, opposing, enemy.

– OPPOSITES same.

▶ **noun** *in fact the opposite was true* REVERSE, converse, antithesis, contrary, inverse, obverse, antipode; the other side of the coin; *informal* flip side.

opposition ▶ **noun** ❶ *the proposal met with opposition* RESISTANCE, hostility, antagonism, antipathy, objection, dissent, disapproval; defiance, non-compliance, obstruction. ❷ *they* *beat the opposition* OPPONENTS, opposing side, other side/team, competition, opposers, rivals, adversaries. ❸ *the opposition between the public and the private domains* CONFLICT, clash, disparity, antithesis, polarity.

oppress ▶ verb ❶ *the invaders oppressed the people* PERSECUTE, abuse, maltreat, ill-treat, tyrannize, crush, repress, suppress, subjugate, subdue, keep down, grind down, rule with a rod of iron, ride roughshod over. ❷ *the gloom oppressed her* DEPRESS, make gloomy/despondent, weigh down, weigh heavily on, cast down, dampen someone's spirits, dispirit, dishearten, discourage, sadden, get down; *archaic* deject.

oppressed ▶ adjective PERSECUTED, downtrodden, abused, maltreated, ill-treated, subjugated, tyrannized, repressed, subdued, crushed; disadvantaged, underprivileged.

oppression ▶ noun PERSECUTION, abuse, maltreatment, ill-treatment, tyranny, repression, suppression, subjection, subjugation; cruelty, brutality, injustice, hardship, suffering, misery.

oppressive ▶ adjective ❶ *an oppressive dictatorship* HARSH, cruel, brutal, repressive, tyrannical, autocratic, dictatorial, despotic, undemocratic; ruthless, merciless, pitiless. ❷ *an oppressive sense of despair* OVERWHELMING, overpowering, unbearable, unendurable, intolerable. ❸ *it was grey and oppressive* MUGGY, close, heavy, hot, humid, sticky, steamy, airless, stuffy, stifling, sultry.
– OPPOSITES lenient.

oppressor ▶ noun PERSECUTOR, tyrant, despot, autocrat, dictator, subjugator, tormentor.

opprobrious ▶ adjective ABUSIVE, vituperative, derogatory, disparaging, denigratory, pejorative, deprecatory, insulting, offensive; scornful, contemptuous, derisive; *informal* bitchy; *archaic* contumelious.

opprobrium ▶ noun ❶ *the government endured months of opprobrium* VILIFICATION, abuse, vituperation, condemnation, criticism, censure, denunciation, defamation, denigration, disparagement, obloquy, derogation, slander, revilement, calumny, calumniation, execration, bad press, invective; *informal* flak, mud-slinging, bad-mouthing; *Brit. informal* stick; *formal* castigation, excoriation; *archaic* contumely. ❷ *the opprobrium of being associated with thugs* DISGRACE, shame, dishonour, stigma, humiliation, loss of face, ignominy, disrepute, infamy, notoriety, scandal.
– OPPOSITES praise, honour.

opt ▶ verb CHOOSE, select, pick (out), decide on, go for, settle on, plump for/on.

optimism ▶ noun HOPEFULNESS, hope, confidence, buoyancy, sanguineness, positiveness, positive attitude.

optimistic ▶ adjective ❶ *she felt optimistic about the future* POSITIVE, confident, hopeful, sanguine, bullish, buoyant; *informal* upbeat. ❷ *the forecast is optimistic* ENCOURAGING, promising, hopeful, reassuring, favourable, auspicious, propitious.
– OPPOSITES pessimistic.

optimum ▶ adjective BEST, most favourable, most advantageous, ideal, perfect, prime, optimal.

option ▶ noun CHOICE, alternative, possibility, course of action.

optional ▶ adjective VOLUNTARY, discretionary, non-compulsory, non-mandatory; *Law* permissive.
– OPPOSITES compulsory.

opulence ▶ noun ❶ *the opulence of the room* LUXURIOUSNESS, sumptuousness, lavishness, richness, luxury, luxuriance, splendour, magnificence, grandeur, splendidness; *informal* plushness. ❷ *a display of opulence* WEALTH, affluence, wealthiness, richness, riches, prosperity, prosperousness, money.
– OPPOSITES poverty.

opulent ▶ adjective ❶ *his opulent home* LUXURIOUS, sumptuous, palatial, lavishly appointed, rich, splendid, magnificent, grand, grandiose, fancy; *informal* plush, swanky; *Brit. informal* swish; *N. Amer. informal* swank. ❷ *an opulent family* WEALTHY, rich, affluent, well off, well-to-do, moneyed, prosperous, of substance; *informal* well heeled, rolling in money, loaded, stinking/filthy rich, made of money. ❸ *her opulent red hair* COPIOUS, abundant, profuse, prolific, plentiful, luxuriant.
– OPPOSITES spartan, poor.

opus ▶ noun COMPOSITION, work (of art), oeuvre.

oracle ▶ noun ❶ *the oracle of Apollo* PROPHET, PROPHETESS, sibyl, seer, augur, prognosticator, diviner, soothsayer, fortune teller. ❷ *our oracle on Africa* AUTHORITY, expert, specialist, pundit, mentor, adviser.

oracular ▶ adjective ❶ *his every utterance was given oracular significance* PROPHETIC, prophetical, sibylline, predictive, prescient, prognostic, divinatory, augural. ❷ *oracular responses* ENIGMATIC, cryptic, abstruse, unclear, obscure, confusing, mystifying, puzzling, mysterious, arcane; ambiguous, equivocal.

oral ▶ adjective *an oral agreement* SPOKEN, verbal, unwritten, vocal, uttered, said.
– OPPOSITES written.
▶ noun *a French oral* ORAL EXAMINATION; *Brit.* viva (voce).

orate ▶ verb DECLAIM, make a speech, hold forth, speak, discourse, pontificate, preach, sermonize, sound off, spout off; *informal* spiel; *formal* perorate.

oration ▶ noun SPEECH, address, lecture, talk, homily, sermon, discourse, declamation; *informal* spiel.

orator ▶ **noun** (PUBLIC) SPEAKER, speech-maker, lecturer, declaimer, rhetorician, rhetor; *informal* spieler.

oratorical ▶ **adjective** RHETORICAL, grandiloquent, magniloquent, high-flown, orotund, bombastic, grandiose, pompous, pretentious, overblown, turgid, flowery, florid.

oratory ▶ **noun** RHETORIC, eloquence, grandiloquence, magniloquence, public speaking, speech-making, declamation.

orb ▶ **noun** SPHERE, globe, ball, circle.

orbit ▶ **noun** ❶ *the earth's orbit around the sun* COURSE, path, circuit, track, trajectory, rotation, revolution, circle. ❷ *the problem comes outside our orbit* SPHERE (OF INFLUENCE), area of activity, range, scope, ambit, compass, jurisdiction, authority, remit, domain, realm, province, territory; *informal* bailiwick.

▶ **verb** *Mercury orbits the sun* REVOLVE ROUND, circle round, go round, travel round.

orchestra ▶ **noun** ENSEMBLE; *informal* band.

orchestrate ▶ **verb** ❶ *the piece was orchestrated by Mozart* ARRANGE, adapt, score. ❷ *orchestrating a campaign of civil disobedience* ORGANIZE, arrange, plan, set up, bring about, mobilize, mount, stage, stage-manage, mastermind, coordinate, direct, engineer.

ordain ▶ **verb** ❶ *the Church of England voted to ordain women* CONFER HOLY ORDERS ON, appoint, anoint, consecrate. ❷ *the path ordained by God* PREDETERMINE, predestine, preordain, determine, prescribe, designate. ❸ *he ordained that anyone hunting in the forest was to pay a fine* DECREE, rule, order, command, lay down, legislate, prescribe, pronounce.

ordeal ▶ **noun** UNPLEASANT EXPERIENCE, painful experience, trial, tribulation, nightmare, trauma, hell (on earth), trouble, difficulty, torture, torment, agony.

order ▶ **noun** ❶ *alphabetical order* SEQUENCE, arrangement, organization, disposition, system, series, succession; grouping, classification, categorization, codification, systematization. ❷ *some semblance of order* TIDINESS, neatness, orderliness, trimness. ❸ *the police were needed to keep order* PEACE, control, law (and order), lawfulness, discipline, calm, (peace and) quiet, peacefulness, peaceableness. ❹ *his sense of order* ORDERLINESS, organization, method, system; symmetry, uniformity, regularity; routine. ❺ *the equipment was in good order* CONDITION, state, repair, shape. ❻ *I had to obey his orders* COMMAND, instruction, directive, direction, decree, edict, injunction, mandate, dictate, commandment, rescript; law, rule, regulation, diktat; demand, bidding, requirement, stipulation; *informal* say-so; *formal* ordinance; *poetic/literary* behest. ❼ *the company has won the order* COMMISSION, purchase order, request, requisition; booking, reservation. ❽ *the lower orders of society* CLASS, level, rank, grade, degree, position, category; *dated* station. ❾ *the established social order* (CLASS) SYSTEM, hierarchy, pecking order, grading, ranking, scale. ❿ *the higher orders of insects* TAXONOMIC GROUP, class, family, species, breed; taxon. ⓫ *a religious order* COMMUNITY, brotherhood, sisterhood. ⓬ *the Orange Order* ORGANIZATION, association, society, fellowship, fraternity, confraternity, sodality, lodge, guild, league, union, club; sect. ⓭ *skills of a very high order* TYPE, kind, sort, nature, variety; quality, calibre, standard.

– OPPOSITES chaos.

▶ **verb** ❶ *he ordered me to return* INSTRUCT, command, direct, enjoin, tell, require, charge; *formal* adjure; *poetic/literary* bid. ❷ *he ordered that their assets be confiscated* DECREE, ordain, rule, legislate, dictate, prescribe. ❸ *you can order your tickets by phone* REQUEST, apply for, place an order for; book, reserve; *formal* bespeak. ❹ *the messages are ordered chronologically* ORGANIZE, put in order, arrange, sort out, marshal, dispose, lay out; group, classify, categorize, catalogue, codify, systematize, systemize.

■ **in order** ❶ *list the dates in order* IN SEQUENCE, in alphabetical order, in numerical order, in order of priority. ❷ *he found everything in order* TIDY, neat, orderly, straight, trim, shipshape (and Bristol fashion), in apple-pie order; in position, in place. ❸ *I think it's in order for me to take the credit* APPROPRIATE, fitting, suitable, acceptable, (all) right, permissible, permitted, allowable; *informal* okay.

■ **order someone about/around** TELL SOMEONE WHAT TO DO, give orders to, dictate to; lay down the law; *informal* boss about/around, push about/around.

■ **out of order** ❶ *the lift's out of order* NOT WORKING, not in working order, not functioning, broken, broken-down, out of service, out of commission, faulty, defective, inoperative; down; *informal* conked out, bust, (gone) kaput; *N. Amer. informal* on the fritz, out of whack. ❷ (*Brit. informal*) *that's really out of order* UNACCEPTABLE, unfair, unjust, unjustified, uncalled for, below the belt, unreasonable, unwarranted, beyond the pale; *informal* not on, a bit much; *Brit. informal* a bit thick, off, not cricket; *Austral./NZ informal* over the fence.

orderly ▶ **adjective** ❶ *an orderly room* NEAT, tidy, well ordered, in order, trim, in apple-pie order, spick and span; *Brit. informal, dated* shipshape (and Bristol fashion). ❷ *the orderly presentation of information* (WELL) ORGANIZED, efficient, methodical, systematic, meticulous, punctilious; coherent, structured, logical, well planned, well regulated, systematized. ❸ *the crowd was orderly* WELL BEHAVED, law-abiding, disciplined, peaceful, peaceable, non-violent.

– OPPOSITES untidy, disorganized.

ordinance ▶ **noun** (*formal*) ❶ *the president issued an ordinance* EDICT, decree, law, injunction, fiat, command, order, rule, ruling, dictum, dictate, directive, mandate. ❷ *religious ordinances* RITE, ritual, ceremony, sacrament, observance, service.

ordinarily ▶ adverb USUALLY, normally, as a (general) rule, generally, in general, for the most part, mainly, mostly, most of the time, typically, habitually, commonly, routinely.

ordinary ▶ adjective ❶ *the ordinary course of events* USUAL, normal, standard, typical, common, customary, habitual, everyday, regular, routine, day-to-day. ❷ *my life seemed very ordinary* AVERAGE, normal, run-of-the-mill, standard, typical, middle-of-the-road, conventional, unremarkable, unexceptional, workaday, undistinguished, nondescript, colourless, commonplace, humdrum, mundane, unmemorable, pedestrian, prosaic, quotidian, uninteresting, uneventful, dull, boring, bland, suburban, hackneyed; *N. Amer.* garden-variety; *informal* bog-standard, (plain) vanilla, nothing to write home about, no great shakes; *Brit. informal* common or garden; *N. Amer. informal* ornery.
– OPPOSITES unusual.
■ **out of the ordinary** UNUSUAL, exceptional, remarkable, extraordinary, unexpected, surprising, unaccustomed, unfamiliar, abnormal, atypical, different, special, exciting, memorable, noteworthy, unique, singular, outstanding; unconventional, unorthodox, strange, peculiar, odd, queer, curious, bizarre, outlandish; *informal* offbeat.

ordnance ▶ noun GUNS, cannon, artillery, weapons, arms; munitions.

ordure ▶ noun EXCREMENT, excreta, dung, manure, muck, droppings, faeces, stools, night soil, sewage; *informal* pooh; *Brit. informal* cack, big jobs; *N. Amer. informal* poop.

organ ▶ noun ❶ *the internal organs* BODY PART, biological structure. ❷ *the official organ of the Communist Party* NEWSPAPER, paper, journal, periodical, magazine, newsletter, gazette, publication, mouthpiece; *informal* rag.

organic ▶ adjective ❶ *organic matter* LIVING, live, animate, biological, biotic. ❷ *organic vegetables* PESTICIDE-FREE, additive-free, natural. ❸ *the love scenes were an organic part of the drama* ESSENTIAL, fundamental, integral, intrinsic, vital, indispensable, inherent. ❹ *a society is an organic whole* STRUCTURED, organized, coherent, integrated, coordinated, ordered, harmonious.

organism ▶ noun ❶ *fish and other organisms* LIVING THING, being, creature, animal, plant, life form. ❷ *a complex political organism* STRUCTURE, system, organization, entity.

organization ▶ noun ❶ *the organization of conferences* PLANNING, arrangement, coordination, administration, organizing, running, management. ❷ *the overall organization of the book* STRUCTURE, arrangement, plan, pattern, order, form, format, framework, composition, constitution. ❸ *his lack of organization* EFFICIENCY, order, orderliness, planning. ❹ *a large international organization* COMPANY, firm, corporation, institution, group, consortium, conglomerate, agency, association, society; *informal* outfit.

organize ▶ verb ❶ *organizing and disseminating information* (PUT IN) ORDER, arrange, sort (out), assemble, marshal, put straight, group, classify, collocate, categorize, catalogue, codify, systematize, systemize; *rare* methodize. ❷ *they organized a search party* MAKE ARRANGEMENTS FOR, arrange, coordinate, sort out, put together, fix up, set up, orchestrate, take care of, see to/about, deal with, manage, conduct, administrate, mobilize; schedule, timetable, programme; *formal* concert.

organized ▶ adjective (WELL) ORDERED, well run, well regulated, structured; orderly, efficient, neat, tidy, methodical; *informal* together.
– OPPOSITES inefficient.

orgiastic ▶ adjective DEBAUCHED, wild, riotous, wanton, dissolute, depraved.

orgy ▶ noun ❶ *a drunken orgy* WILD PARTY, debauch, carousal, carouse, revel, revelry; *informal* binge, booze-up, bender, love-in; *Brit. informal* rave-up; *N. Amer. informal* toot; *poetic/literary* bacchanal; *archaic* wassail. ❷ *an orgy of violence* BOUT, excess, spree, surfeit; *informal* binge.

orient, orientate ▶ verb ❶ *there were no street names to enable her to orient herself* GET/FIND ONE'S BEARINGS, establish one's location. ❷ *you need to orientate yourself to your new way of life* ADAPT, adjust, familiarize, acclimatize, accustom, attune; *N. Amer.* acclimate. ❸ *magazines oriented to the business community* AIM, direct, pitch, design, intend. ❹ *the fires are oriented in line with the sunset* ALIGN, place, position, dispose.

oriental ▶ adjective EASTERN, Far Eastern, Asian; *poetic/literary* orient.

orientation ▶ noun ❶ *the orientation of the radar station* POSITIONING, location, position, situation, placement, alignment. ❷ *his orientation to his new way of life* ADAPTATION, adjustment, acclimatization. ❸ *broadly Marxist in orientation* ATTITUDE, inclination. ❹ *orientation courses* INDUCTION, training, initiation, briefing.

orifice ▶ noun OPENING, hole, aperture, slot, slit, cleft.

origin ▶ noun ❶ *the origins of life* BEGINNING, start, commencement, origination, genesis, birth, dawning, dawn, emergence, creation, birthplace, cradle; source, basis, cause, root(s); *formal* radix. ❷ *the Latin origin of the word* SOURCE, derivation, root(s), provenance, etymology; *N. Amer.* provenience. ❸ *his Scottish origins* DESCENT, ancestry, parentage, pedigree, lineage, line (of descent), heritage, birth, extraction, family, stock, blood, bloodline.

original ▶ adjective ❶ *the original inhabitants* INDIGENOUS, native, aboriginal, autochthonous; first, earliest, early. ❷ *original Rembrandts* AUTHENTIC, genuine, actual, true, bona fide; *informal* pukka, kosher. ❸ *the film is highly original* INNOVATIVE, creative, imaginative, innovatory, inventive; new, novel, fresh, refreshing; unusual, unconventional, unorthodox, groundbreaking, pioneering, avant-garde, unique, distinctive.
▶ noun ❶ *a copy of the original* ARCHETYPE, prototype, source, master. ❷ *he really is an original* INDIVIDUALIST, individual, eccentric, nonconformist, free spirit, maverick; *informal* character, oddball; *Brit. informal* one-off, odd bod; *N. Amer. informal* screwball, kook.

originality ▶ noun INVENTIVENESS, ingenuity, creativeness, creativity, innovation, novelty, freshness, imagination, imaginativeness, individuality, unconventionality, uniqueness, distinctiveness.

originally ▶ adverb (AT) FIRST, in/at the beginning, to begin with, initially, in the first place, at the outset.

originate ▶ verb ❶ *the disease originates from Africa* ARISE, have its origin, begin, start, stem, spring, emerge, emanate. ❷ *Bill Levy originated the idea* INVENT, create, initiate, devise, think up, dream up, conceive, formulate, form, develop, generate, engender, produce, mastermind, pioneer; *poetic/literary* beget.

originator ▶ noun INVENTOR, creator, architect, author, father, mother, initiator, innovator, founder, pioneer, mastermind; *poetic/literary* begetter.

ornament ▶ noun ❶ *small tables covered with ornaments* KNICK-KNACK, trinket, bauble, bibelot, gewgaw, gimcrack, furbelow; *informal* whatnot, doodah; *N. Amer. informal* tchotchke; *archaic* whim-wham, kickshaw, bijou. ❷ *the dress had no ornament at all* DECORATION, adornment, embellishment, ornamentation, trimming, accessories.
▶ verb *the room was highly ornamented* DECORATE, adorn, embellish, trim, bedeck, deck (out), festoon; *poetic/literary* bedizen, furbelow.

ornamental ▶ adjective DECORATIVE, fancy, ornate, ornamented.

ornamentation ▶ noun DECORATION, adornment, embellishment, ornament, trimming, accessories.

ornate ▶ adjective ❶ *an ornate mirror* ELABORATE, decorated, embellished, adorned, ornamented, fancy, fussy, ostentatious, showy; *informal* flash, flashy. ❷ *ornate language* ELABORATE, flowery, florid; grandiose, pompous, pretentious, high-flown, orotund, magniloquent, grandiloquent, rhetorical, oratorical, bombastic, overwrought, overblown; *informal* highfalutin, purple.
– OPPOSITES plain.

orotund ▶ adjective ❶ *Halliwell's orotund voice* DEEP, sonorous, strong, powerful, full, rich, resonant, loud, booming. ❷ *the orotund rhetoric of his prose* POMPOUS, pretentious, affected, fulsome, grandiose, ornate, overblown, flowery, florid, high-flown, magniloquent, grandiloquent, rhetorical, oratorical; *informal* highfalutin, purple.

orthodox ▶ adjective ❶ *orthodox views* CONVENTIONAL, mainstream, conformist, (well) established, traditional, traditionalist, prevalent, popular, conservative, unoriginal. ❷ *an orthodox Hindu* CONSERVATIVE, traditional, observant, devout, strict.
– OPPOSITES unconventional.

orthodoxy ▶ noun ❶ *a pillar of orthodoxy* CONVENTIONALITY, conventionalism, conformism, conservatism, traditionalism, conformity. ❷ *Christian orthodoxies* DOCTRINE, belief, conviction, creed, dogma, credo, theory, tenet, teaching.

oscillate ▶ verb ❶ *the pendulum started to oscillate* SWING (TO AND FRO), swing back and forth, sway; *N. Amer. informal* wigwag. ❷ *oscillating between fear and bravery* WAVER, swing, fluctuate, alternate, see-saw, yo-yo, sway, vacillate, hover; *informal* wobble.

oscillation ▶ noun ❶ *the oscillation of the pendulum* SWINGING (TO AND FRO), swing, swaying. ❷ *his oscillation between commerce and art* WAVERING, swinging, fluctuation, see-sawing, yo-yoing, vacillation.

ossify ▶ verb ❶ *these cartilages may ossify* TURN INTO BONE, become bony, harden, solidify, rigidify, petrify. ❷ *ossified political institutions* BECOME INFLEXIBLE, become rigid, fossilize, rigidify, stagnate.

ostensible ▶ adjective APPARENT, outward, superficial, professed, supposed, alleged, purported.
– OPPOSITES genuine.

ostensibly ▶ adverb APPARENTLY, seemingly, on the face of it, to all intents and purposes, outwardly, superficially, allegedly, supposedly, purportedly.

ostentation ▶ noun SHOWINESS, show, ostentatiousness, pretentiousness, vulgarity, conspicuousness, display, flamboyance, gaudiness, brashness, extravagance, ornateness, exhibitionism; *informal* flashiness, glitz, glitziness, ritziness.

ostentatious ▶ adjective SHOWY, pretentious, conspicuous, flamboyant, gaudy, brash, vulgar, loud, extravagant, fancy, ornate, overelaborate; *informal* flash, flashy, over the top, OTT, glitzy, ritzy; *N. Amer. informal* superfly.
– OPPOSITES restrained.

ostracism ▶ noun EXCLUSION, rejection, shunning, spurning, the cold shoulder, snubbing, avoidance; blackballing, blacklisting.

ostracize ▶ verb EXCLUDE, shun, spurn, cold-shoulder, reject, shut out, avoid, ignore, snub, cut dead, keep at arm's length, leave out in the cold; blackball, blacklist; *Brit.* send to Coventry; *informal* freeze out; *Brit. informal* blank.
– OPPOSITES welcome.

other ▶ adjective ❶ *these homes use other fuels* ALTERNATIVE, different, dissimilar, disparate, distinct, separate, contrasting. ❷ *are there any other questions?* MORE, further, additional, extra, added, supplementary.

otherwise ▶ adverb ❶ *hurry up, otherwise we'll be late* OR (ELSE), if not. ❷ *she's exhausted, but otherwise she's fine* IN OTHER RESPECTS, apart from that. ❸ *he could not have acted otherwise* IN ANY OTHER WAY, differently.

other-worldly ▶ adjective ETHEREAL, dreamy, spiritual, mystic, mystical; unearthly, unworldly, supernatural.
– OPPOSITES realistic.

ounce ▶ noun PARTICLE, scrap, bit, speck, iota, whit, jot, trace, atom, shred, crumb, fragment, grain, drop, spot; *informal* smidgen.

oust ▶ verb DRIVE OUT, expel, force out, throw out, remove (from office/power), eject, get rid of, depose, topple, unseat, overthrow, bring down, overturn, dismiss, dislodge, displace; *informal* boot out, kick out; *Brit. informal* turf out; *dated* out.

out ▶ adjective & adverb ❶ *she's out at the moment* NOT HERE, not at home, not in, (gone) away, elsewhere, absent. ❷ *the secret was out* REVEALED, (out) in the open, common/public knowledge, known, disclosed, divulged. ❸ *the roses are out* IN FLOWER, flowering, in (full) bloom, blooming, in blossom, blossoming, open. ❹ *the book should be out soon* AVAILABLE, obtainable, in the shops, published, in print. ❺ *the fire was nearly out* EXTINGUISHED, no longer alight. ❻ (*informal*) *grunge is out* UNFASHIONABLE, out of fashion, dated, outdated, passé; *informal* old hat, not with it, not in. ❼ *smoking is out* FORBIDDEN, not permitted, not allowed, proscribed, unacceptable; *informal* not on. ❽ *he was slightly out in his calculations* MISTAKEN, inaccurate, incorrect, wrong, in error.
– OPPOSITES in.
▶ verb (*informal*) *it was not our intention to out him* EXPOSE, unmask.
■ **out cold** UNCONSCIOUS, knocked out, out for the count; *informal* KO'd, kayoed.

out-and-out ▶ adjective UTTER, downright, thoroughgoing, absolute, complete, thorough, total, unmitigated, outright, real, perfect, consummate; *N. Amer.* full-bore; *informal* deep-dyed; *Brit. informal* right; *Austral./NZ informal* fair.
– OPPOSITES partial.

outbreak ▶ noun ❶ *a fresh outbreak of killings* ERUPTION, flare-up, upsurge, outburst, rash, wave, spate, flood, explosion, burst, flurry; *formal* boutade. ❷ *on the outbreak of war* START, beginning, commencement, onset, outset.

outburst ▶ noun ERUPTION, explosion, burst, outbreak, flare-up, access, rush, flood, storm, outpouring, surge, upsurge, outflowing; *formal* boutade.

outcast ▶ noun PARIAH, persona non grata, reject, outsider.

outclass ▶ verb SURPASS, be superior to, be better than, outshine, overshadow, eclipse, outdo, outplay, outmanoeuvre, outstrip, get the better of, upstage; top, cap, beat, defeat, exceed; *informal* be a cut above, be head and shoulders above, run rings round; *archaic* outrival.

outcome ▶ noun (END) RESULT, consequence, net result, upshot, after-effect, aftermath, conclusion, issue, end (product).

outcry ▶ noun ❶ *an outcry of passion* SHOUT, exclamation, cry, yell, howl, roar, scream; *informal* holler. ❷ *public outcry* PROTEST(S), protestation(s), complaints, objections, furore, fuss, commotion, uproar, outbursts, opposition, dissent; *informal* hullabaloo, ballyhoo, ructions, stink.

outdated ▶ adjective OLD-FASHIONED, out of date, outmoded, out of fashion, unfashionable, dated, passé, old, behind the times, behindhand, obsolete, antiquated; *informal* out, old hat, square, not with it, out of the ark; *N. Amer. informal* horse-and-buggy, clunky.
– OPPOSITES modern.

outdistance ▶ verb ❶ *the colt outdistanced the train* OUTRUN, outstrip, outpace, leave behind, get (further) ahead of; overtake, pass. ❷ *the mill outdistanced all its rivals* SURPASS, outshine, outclass, outdo, exceed, transcend, top, cap, beat, better, leave behind; *informal* leave standing; *archaic* outrival.

outdo ▶ verb SURPASS, outshine, overshadow, eclipse, outclass, outmanoeuvre, get the better of, put in the shade, upstage; exceed, transcend, top, cap, beat, better, leave behind, get ahead of; *informal* be a cut above, be head and shoulders above, run rings round; *archaic* outrival.

outdoor ▶ adjective OPEN AIR, out-of-doors, outside, al fresco, not under cover.
– OPPOSITES indoor.

outer ▶ adjective ❶ *the outer layer* OUTSIDE, outermost, outward, exterior, external, surface. ❷ *outer areas of the city* OUTLYING, distant, remote, faraway, furthest, peripheral; suburban.
– OPPOSITES inner.

outface ▶ verb STAND UP TO, face down, cow, overawe, intimidate.

outfit ▶ noun ❶ *a new outfit* COSTUME, suit, uniform, ensemble, attire, clothes, clothing, dress, garb; *informal* get-up, gear, togs; *Brit. informal* kit, rig-out; *formal* apparel; *archaic* habit, rai-

ment. ❷ *a studio lighting outfit* KIT, equipment, tools, implements, tackle, apparatus, paraphernalia, things, stuff. ❸ *a local manufacturing outfit* ORGANIZATION, set-up, enterprise, company, firm, business; group, band, body, team.
▶ **verb** *enough swords to outfit an army* EQUIP, kit out, fit out/up, rig out, supply, arm; dress, attire, clothe, deck out; *archaic* apparel, invest, habit.

outfitter ▶ **noun** CLOTHIER, tailor, couturier, costumier, dressmaker, seamstress; *dated* modiste.

outflow ▶ **noun** DISCHARGE, outflowing, outpouring, outrush, rush, flood, deluge, issue, spurt, jet, cascade, stream, torrent, gush, outburst; flow, flux; *technical* efflux.

outgoing ▶ **adjective** ❶ *outgoing children* EXTROVERT, uninhibited, unreserved, demonstrative, affectionate, warm, friendly, genial, cordial, affable, easy-going, sociable, convivial, lively, gregarious; communicative, responsive, open, forthcoming, frank. ❷ *the outgoing president* DEPARTING, retiring, leaving.
– OPPOSITES introverted, incoming.

outgoings ▶ **plural noun** EXPENSES, expenditure, spending, outlay, payments, costs, overheads.

outgrowth ▶ **noun** PROTUBERANCE, swelling, excrescence, growth, lump, bump, bulge; tumour, cancer, boil, carbuncle, pustule.

outing ▶ **noun** ❶ *family outings* (PLEASURE) TRIP, excursion, jaunt, expedition, day out, (mystery) tour, drive, ride, run; *informal* junket, spin. ❷ (*informal*) *the outing of public figures* EXPOSURE, unmasking, revelation.

outlandish ▶ **adjective** WEIRD, queer, far out, quirky, zany, eccentric, idiosyncratic, unconventional, unorthodox, funny, bizarre, unusual, singular, extraordinary, strange, unfamiliar, peculiar, odd, curious; *informal* offbeat, off the wall, way-out, wacky, freaky, kooky, kinky, oddball; *N. Amer. informal* in left field.
– OPPOSITES ordinary.

outlast ▶ **verb** OUTLIVE, survive, live/last longer than; ride out, weather, withstand.

outlaw ▶ **noun** *bands of outlaws* FUGITIVE, (wanted) criminal, outcast, exile, pariah; bandit, robber; *dated* desperado.
▶ **verb** ❶ *they voted to outlaw fox-hunting* BAN, bar, prohibit, forbid, veto, make illegal, proscribe, interdict. ❷ *she feared she would be outlawed* BANISH, exile, expel.
– OPPOSITES permit.

outlay ▶ **noun** EXPENDITURE, expenses, spending, outgoings, cost, price, payment, investment.
– OPPOSITES profit.

outlet ▶ **noun** ❶ *a central-heating outlet* VENT (HOLE), way out, egress; outfall, opening, channel, conduit, duct. ❷ *an outlet for farm produce* MARKET, retail outlet, marketplace, shop, store. ❸ *an outlet for their energies* MEANS OF EXPRESSION, (means of) release, vent, avenue, channel.

outline ▶ **noun** ❶ *the outline of the building* SILHOUETTE, profile, shape, contours, form, line, delineation; diagram, sketch; *poetic/literary* lineaments. ❷ *an outline of expenditure for each department* ROUGH IDEA, thumbnail sketch, (quick) rundown, summary, synopsis, résumé, precis; essence, main points, gist, (bare) bones, draft, sketch.
▶ **verb** ❶ *the plane was outlined against the sky* SILHOUETTE, define, demarcate; sketch, delineate, trace. ❷ *she outlined the plan briefly* ROUGH OUT, sketch out, draft, give a rough idea of, summarize, precis.

outlive ▶ **verb** LIVE ON AFTER, live longer than, outlast, survive.

outlook ▶ **noun** ❶ *the two men were wholly different in outlook* POINT OF VIEW, viewpoint, views, opinion, (way of) thinking, perspective, attitude, standpoint, stance, frame of mind. ❷ *a lovely open outlook* VIEW, vista, prospect, panorama, scene, aspect. ❸ *the outlook for the economy* PROSPECTS, expectations, hopes, future, lookout.

outlying ▶ **adjective** DISTANT, remote, outer, out of the way, faraway, far-flung, inaccessible, off the beaten track.

outmanoeuvre ▶ **verb** ❶ *the English army were outmanoeuvred* OUTFLANK, circumvent, bypass. ❷ *he outmanoeuvred his critics* OUTWIT, outsmart, out-think, outplay, steal a march on, trick, get the better of; *informal* outfox, put one over on.

outmoded ▶ **adjective** OUT OF DATE, old-fashioned, out of fashion, outdated, dated, behind the times, antiquated, obsolete, passé; *informal* old hat, out of the ark.

out of date ▶ **adjective** ❶ *this design is out of date* OLD-FASHIONED, outmoded, out of fashion, unfashionable, frumpish, frumpy, outdated, dated, old, passé, behind the times, behindhand, obsolete, antiquated; *informal* out, old hat, square, not with it, out of the ark; *N. Amer. informal* horse-and-buggy, clunky. ❷ *many of the facts are out of date* SUPERSEDED, obsolete, expired, lapsed, invalid, (null and) void.
– OPPOSITES fashionable, current.

out of the way ▶ **adjective** ❶ *out-of-the-way places* OUTLYING, distant, remote, faraway, far-flung, isolated, lonely, godforsaken, inaccessible, off the beaten track. ❷ *I find his methods out of the way* STRANGE, unusual, peculiar, odd, funny, curious, bizarre, weird, queer, unfamiliar, out of the ordinary, extraordinary, remarkable, singular.
– OPPOSITES accessible.

out of work ▶ **adjective** UNEMPLOYED, jobless, out of a job; redundant, laid off; *Brit. informal* on the dole; *Austral. informal* on the wallaby track.

outpouring ▶ noun OUTFLOW, outflowing, outrush, rush, flood, deluge, discharge, issue, spurt, jet, cascade, stream, torrent, gush, outburst, flow, flux; *technical* efflux.

output ▶ noun PRODUCTION, amount/quantity produced, yield, gross domestic product, outturn; works, writings.

outrage ▶ noun ❶ *widespread public outrage* INDIGNATION, fury, anger, rage, disapproval, wrath, resentment. ❷ *it is an outrage* SCANDAL, offence, insult, injustice, disgrace. ❸ *the bomb outrage* ATROCITY, act of violence/wickedness, crime, wrong, barbarism, inhumane act.
▶ verb *his remarks outraged his parishioners* ENRAGE, infuriate, incense, anger, scandalize, offend, give offence to, affront, shock, horrify, disgust, appal.

outrageous ▶ adjective ❶ *outrageous acts of cruelty* SHOCKING, disgraceful, scandalous, atrocious, appalling, monstrous, heinous; evil, wicked, abominable, terrible, horrendous, dreadful, foul, nauseating, sickening, vile, nasty, odious, loathsome, unspeakable; *Brit. informal* beastly. ❷ *the politician's outrageous promises* FAR-FETCHED, (highly) unlikely, doubtful, dubious, questionable, implausible, unconvincing, unbelievable, incredible, preposterous, extravagant, excessive. ❸ *outrageous clothes* EYE-CATCHING, flamboyant, showy, gaudy, ostentatious; shameless, brazen, shocking; *informal* saucy, flashy.

outré ▶ adjective WEIRD, queer, outlandish, far out, freakish, quirky, zany, eccentric, off-centre, unconventional, unorthodox, funny, bizarre, fantastic, unusual, singular, extraordinary, strange, unfamiliar, peculiar, odd, out of the way; *informal* way-out, wacky, freaky, kooky, oddball, off the wall; *N. Amer. informal* offbeat, in left field.

outright ▶ adverb ❶ *he rejected the proposal outright* COMPLETELY, entirely, wholly, fully, totally, categorically, absolutely, utterly, flatly, unreservedly. ❷ *I told her outright* EXPLICITLY, directly, forthrightly, openly, frankly, candidly, honestly, sincerely, bluntly, plainly, in plain language, truthfully, to someone's face, straight from the shoulder; *Brit. informal* straight up. ❸ *they were killed outright* INSTANTLY, instantaneously, immediately, at once, straight away, then and there, on the spot. ❹ *paintings have to be bought outright* ALL AT ONCE, in one go.
▶ adjective ❶ *an outright lie* OUT-AND-OUT, absolute, complete, downright, utter, sheer, categorical, unqualified, unconditional. ❷ *the outright winner* DEFINITE, unequivocal, clear, unqualified, incontestable, unmistakable.

outrun ▶ verb RUN FASTER THAN, outstrip, outdistance, outpace, leave behind, lose; *informal* leave standing.

outset ▶ noun START, starting point, beginning, commencement, dawn, birth, origin, inception, opening, launch, inauguration; *informal* the word go.
–OPPOSITES end.

outshine ▶ verb SURPASS, overshadow, eclipse, outclass, put in the shade, upstage, exceed, transcend, top, cap, beat, better; *informal* be a cut above, be head and shoulders above, run rings round; *archaic* outrival.

outside ▶ noun *the outside of the building* OUTER/EXTERNAL SURFACE, exterior, outer side/layer, case, skin, shell, covering, facade.
–RELATED TERMS ecto-, exo-, extra-.
▶ adjective ❶ *outside lights* EXTERIOR, external, outer, outdoor, out-of-doors. ❷ *outside contractors* INDEPENDENT, hired, temporary, freelance, casual, external, extramural. ❸ *an outside chance* SLIGHT, slender, slim, small, tiny, faint, negligible, remote, vague.
▶ adverb *they went outside | shall we eat outside?* OUTDOORS, out of doors.
–OPPOSITES inside.

outsider ▶ noun STRANGER, visitor, non-member; foreigner, alien, immigrant, emigrant, émigré; incomer, newcomer, parvenu.

outsize ▶ adjective ❶ *her outsize handbag* HUGE, oversized, enormous, gigantic, very big/large, great, giant, colossal, massive, mammoth, vast, immense, tremendous, monumental, prodigious, mountainous, king-sized; *informal* mega, monster, whopping (great), thumping (great), humongous, jumbo, bumper; *Brit. informal* whacking (great), ginormous. ❷ *an outsize actor* VERY LARGE, big, massive, fat, corpulent, stout, heavy, plump, portly, ample, bulky; *informal* pudgy, tubby; *Brit. informal* podgy; *archaic* pursy.

outskirts ▶ plural noun OUTLYING DISTRICTS, edges, fringes, suburbs, suburbia; purlieus, borders, environs.

outsmart ▶ verb OUTWIT, outmanoeuvre, outplay, steal a march on, trick, get the better of; *informal* outfox, pull a fast one on, put one over on.

outspoken ▶ adjective FORTHRIGHT, direct, candid, frank, straightforward, honest, open, straight from the shoulder, plain-spoken; blunt, abrupt, bluff, brusque; *archaic* free-spoken.

outspread ▶ adjective FULLY EXTENDED, outstretched, spread out, fanned out, unfolded, unfurled, (wide) open, opened out.

outstanding ▶ adjective ❶ *an outstanding painter* EXCELLENT, marvellous, magnificent, superb, fine, wonderful, superlative, exceptional, first-class, first-rate; *informal* great, terrific, tremendous, super, amazing, fantastic, sensational, fabulous, ace, crack, A1, mean, awesome, out of this world; *Brit. informal* smashing, brilliant; *N. Amer. informal* neat; *Austral. informal* bonzer. ❷ *an outstanding decorative element* REMARKABLE, extraordinary, exceptional, striking, eye-catching, arresting, impressive, distinct-

ive, unforgettable, memorable, special, momentous, significant, notable, noteworthy; *informal* out of this world. ❸ *how much work is still outstanding?* TO BE DONE, undone, unattended to, unfinished, incomplete, remaining, pending, ongoing. ❹ *outstanding debts* UNPAID, unsettled, owing, owed, to be paid, payable, due, overdue, undischarged; *N. Amer.* delinquent.
– OPPOSITES unexceptional.

outstrip ▶ **verb** ❶ *he outstripped the police cars* GO FASTER THAN, outrun, outdistance, outpace, leave behind, get (further) ahead of, lose; *informal* leave standing. ❷ *demand far outstrips supply* SURPASS, exceed, be more than, top, eclipse.

outward ▶ **adjective** EXTERNAL, outer, outside, exterior; surface, superficial, seeming, apparent, ostensible.
– OPPOSITES inward.

outwardly ▶ **adverb** EXTERNALLY, on the surface, superficially, on the face of it, to all intents and purposes, apparently, ostensibly, seemingly.

outweigh ▶ **verb** BE GREATER THAN, exceed, be superior to, prevail over, have the edge on/over, override, supersede, offset, cancel out, (more than) make up for, outbalance, compensate for.

outwit ▶ **verb** OUTSMART, outmanoeuvre, outplay, steal a march on, trick, gull, get the better of; *informal* outfox, pull a fast one on, put one over on.

outworn ▶ **adjective** OUT OF DATE, outdated, old-fashioned, out of fashion, outmoded, dated, behind the times, antiquated, obsolete, defunct, passé; *informal* old hat, out of the ark.
– OPPOSITES up to date.

oval ▶ **adjective** EGG-SHAPED, ovoid, ovate, oviform, elliptical; *Botany* obovate.

ovation ▶ **noun** (ROUND OF) APPLAUSE, handclapping, clapping, cheering, cheers, bravos, acclaim, acclamation, tribute, standing ovation; *informal* (big) hand.

oven ▶ **noun** (KITCHEN) STOVE, microwave (oven), (kitchen) range; roaster.

over ▶ **preposition** ❶ *there will be cloud over most of the country* ABOVE, on top of, higher (up) than, atop; covering. ❷ *he walked over the grass* ACROSS, around, throughout. ❸ *he has three people over him* SUPERIOR TO, above, higher up than, in charge of, responsible for. ❹ *over 200,000 people live in the area* MORE THAN, above, in excess of, upwards of. ❺ *a discussion over unemployment* ON THE SUBJECT OF, about, concerning, apropos of, with reference to, regarding, relating to, in connection with.
– OPPOSITES under.
▶ **adverb** ❶ *a flock of geese flew over* OVERHEAD, on high, above, past, by. ❷ *the relationship is over* AT AN END, finished, concluded, terminated, ended, no more, a thing of the past. ❸ *he had some money over* LEFT (OVER), remaining, unused, surplus, in excess, in addition.
■ **over and above** IN ADDITION TO, on top of, plus, as well as, besides, along with.
■ **over and over** REPEATEDLY, again and again, over and over again, time and (time) again, many times over, frequently, constantly, continually, persistently, ad nauseam.

overact ▶ **verb** EXAGGERATE, overdo it, overplay it; *informal* ham it up, camp it up.

overall ▶ **adjective** *the overall cost* ALL-INCLUSIVE, general, comprehensive, universal, all-embracing, gross, net, final, inclusive; wholesale, complete, across the board, global, worldwide.
▶ **adverb** *overall, things have improved* GENERALLY (SPEAKING), in general, altogether, all in all, on balance, on average, for the most part, in the main, on the whole, by and large, to a large extent.

overawe ▶ **verb** INTIMIDATE, daunt, cow, disconcert, unnerve, subdue, dismay, frighten, alarm, scare, terrify; *informal* psych out; *N. Amer. informal* buffalo.

overbalance ▶ **verb** FALL OVER, topple over, lose one's balance, tip over, keel over; push over, upend, upset.

overbearing ▶ **adjective** DOMINEERING, dominating, autocratic, tyrannical, despotic, oppressive, high-handed, bullying; *informal* bossy.

overblown ▶ **adjective** OVERWRITTEN, florid, grandiose, pompous, over-elaborate, flowery, overwrought, pretentious, high-flown, turgid, grandiloquent, magniloquent, orotund; *informal* highfalutin.

overcast ▶ **adjective** CLOUDY, clouded (over), sunless, darkened, dark, grey, black, leaden, heavy, dull, murky, dismal, dreary.
– OPPOSITES bright.

overcharge ▶ **verb** ❶ *clients are being overcharged* SWINDLE, charge too much, cheat, defraud, fleece, short-change; *informal* rip off, sting, screw, rob, diddle, do, rook; *N. Amer. informal* gouge. ❷ *the decoration is overcharged* OVERSTATE, overdo, exaggerate, over-embroider, over-embellish; overwrite, overdraw.

overcome ▶ **verb** ❶ *we overcame the home team* DEFEAT, beat, conquer, trounce, thrash, rout, vanquish, overwhelm, overpower, get the better of, triumph over, prevail over, win over/against, outdo, outclass, worst, crush; *informal* drub, slaughter, clobber, hammer, lick, best, crucify, demolish, wipe the floor with, make mincemeat of, blow out of the water, take to the cleaners; *Brit. informal* stuff; *N. Amer. informal* shellac, skunk. ❷ *they overcame their fear of flying* GET THE BETTER OF, prevail over, control, get/bring under control, master, conquer, defeat, beat; get over, get a grip on, curb, subdue; *informal* lick, best.
▶ **adjective** *I was overcome* OVERWHELMED, emotional, moved, affected, speechless.

overconfident ▶ adjective COCKSURE, cocky, smug, conceited, self-assured, brash, blustering, overbearing, presumptuous, heading for a fall, riding for a fall; *informal* too big for one's boots.

overcritical ▶ adjective FAULT-FINDING, hypercritical, captious, carping, cavilling, quibbling, hair-splitting, over-particular; fussy, finicky, fastidious, pedantic, over-scrupulous, punctilious; *informal* nit-picking, pernickety; *archaic* overnice.

overcrowded ▶ adjective OVERFULL, overflowing, full to overflowing/bursting, crammed full, congested, overpopulated, crowded, overpeopled, swarming, teeming; *informal* bursting/bulging at the seams, full to the gunwales, jam-packed.
– OPPOSITES empty.

overdo ▶ verb ❶ *she overdoes the cockney scenes* EXAGGERATE, overstate, overemphasize, overplay, go overboard with, over-dramatize; *informal* ham up, camp up. ❷ *don't overdo the drink* HAVE/USE/EAT/DRINK TOO MUCH OF, overindulge in, have/use/eat/drink to excess. ❸ *they overdid the beef* OVERCOOK, burn.
– OPPOSITES understate.
■ **overdo it** WORK TOO HARD, overwork, do too much, burn the candle at both ends, overtax oneself, drive/push oneself too hard, work/run oneself into the ground, wear oneself to a shadow, wear oneself out, bite off more than one can chew, strain oneself; *informal* kill oneself, knock oneself out.

overdone ▶ adjective ❶ *the flattery was overdone* EXCESSIVE, too much, undue, immoderate, inordinate, disproportionate, inflated, overstated, overworked, exaggerated, overemphasized, over-enthusiastic, over-effusive; *informal* a bit much, over the top, OTT. ❷ *overdone food* OVERCOOKED, dried out, burnt.
– OPPOSITES understated, underdone.

overdue ▶ adjective ❶ *the ship is overdue* LATE, behind schedule, behind time, delayed, unpunctual. ❷ *overdue payments* UNPAID, unsettled, owing, owed, payable, due, outstanding, undischarged; *N. Amer.* delinquent.
– OPPOSITES early, punctual.

overeat ▶ verb EAT TOO MUCH, be greedy, gorge (oneself), overindulge (oneself), feast, gourmandize, gluttonize; *informal* binge, make a pig of oneself, pig out, have eyes bigger than one's stomach; *N. Amer. informal* scarf out.
– OPPOSITES starve.

overemphasize ▶ verb PLACE/LAY TOO MUCH EMPHASIS ON, overstress, place/lay too much stress on, exaggerate, make too much of, overplay, overdo, over-dramatize; *informal* make a big thing about/of, blow up out of all proportion.
– OPPOSITES understate, play down.

overflow ▶ verb *a lot of cream had overflowed the edges of the shallow dish* SPILL OVER, flow over, brim over, well over, pour forth, stream forth, flood.
▶ noun ❶ *an overflow from the tank* OVERSPILL, spill, spillage, flood. ❷ *to accommodate the overflow, five more offices were built* SURPLUS, excess, additional people/things, extra people/things, remainder, overspill.

overflowing ▶ adjective OVERFULL, full to overflowing/bursting, spilling over, running over, crammed full, overcrowded, overloaded; *informal* bursting/bulging at the seams, jam-packed.
– OPPOSITES empty.

overhang ▶ verb STICK OUT (OVER), stand out (over), extend (over), project (over), protrude (over), jut out (over), bulge out (over), hang over.

overhaul ▶ verb ❶ *I've been overhauling the gearbox* SERVICE, maintain, repair, mend, fix up, rebuild, renovate, recondition, refit, refurbish; *informal* do up, patch up. ❷ *Kenyon overhauled him in the race* OVERTAKE, pass, go past/by, go faster than, get/pull ahead of, outstrip.

overhead ▶ adverb *a burst of thunder erupted overhead* (UP) ABOVE, high up, (up) in the sky, on high, above/over one's head.
– OPPOSITES below.
▶ adjective *overhead lines* AERIAL, elevated, raised, suspended.
– OPPOSITES underground.

overheads ▶ plural noun (RUNNING) COSTS, operating costs, fixed costs, expenses; *Brit.* oncosts.
– OPPOSITES profit.

overindulge ▶ verb ❶ *we all overindulge at Christmas* DRINK/EAT TOO MUCH, overeat, overdrink, be greedy, be intemperate, overindulge oneself, overdo it, drink/eat to excess, gorge (oneself), feast, gourmandize, gluttonize; *informal* binge, stuff oneself, go overboard, make a pig of oneself, pig oneself; *N. Amer. informal* scarf out. ❷ *his mother had overindulged him* SPOIL, give in to, indulge, humour, pander to, pamper, mollycoddle, baby.
– OPPOSITES abstain.

overindulgence ▶ noun INTEMPERANCE, immoderation, excess, overeating, overdrinking, gorging; *informal* binge.
– OPPOSITES abstention.

overjoyed ▶ adjective ECSTATIC, euphoric, thrilled, elated, delighted, on cloud nine/seven, in seventh heaven, jubilant, rapturous, jumping for joy, delirious, blissful, in raptures, as pleased as Punch, cock-a-hoop, as happy as a sandboy, as happy as Larry; *informal* over the moon, on top of the world, tickled pink; *N. Amer. informal* as happy as a clam; *Austral. informal* wrapped.
– OPPOSITES unhappy.

overlay ▶ **verb** *the area was overlaid with marble* COVER, face, surface, veneer, inlay, laminate, plaster; coat, varnish, glaze.
▶ **noun** *an overlay of glass-fibre insulation* COVERING, cover, layer, face, surface, veneer, lamination; coat, varnish, glaze, wash.

overload ▶ **verb** ❶ *avoid overloading the ship* OVERBURDEN, put too much in, overcharge, weigh down. ❷ *don't overload the wiring* STRAIN, overtax, overwork, overuse, swamp, oversupply, overwhelm.
▶ **noun** *there was an overload of demands* EXCESS, overabundance, superabundance, profusion, glut, surfeit, surplus, superfluity; avalanche, deluge, flood.

overlook ▶ **verb** ❶ *he overlooked the mistake* FAIL TO NOTICE, fail to spot, miss. ❷ *his work has been overlooked* DISREGARD, neglect, ignore, pay no attention/heed to, pass over, forget. ❸ *she was willing to overlook his faults* DELIBERATELY IGNORE, not take into consideration, disregard, take no notice of, make allowances for, turn a blind eye to, excuse, pardon, forgive. ❹ *the breakfast room overlooks the garden* HAVE A VIEW OF, look over/across, look on to, look out on/over, give on to, command a view of.

overly ▶ **adverb** UNDULY, excessively, inordinately, too; wildly, absurdly, ridiculously, outrageously, unreasonably, exorbitantly, impossibly.

overpower ▶ **verb** ❶ *the prisoners might overpower the crew* GAIN CONTROL OVER, overwhelm, prevail over, get the better of, gain mastery over, overthrow, overturn, subdue, suppress, subjugate, repress, bring someone to their knees, conquer, defeat, triumph over, worst, trounce; *informal* thrash, lick, best, clobber, wipe the floor with. ❷ *he was overpowered by grief* OVERCOME, overwhelm, move, stir, affect, touch, stun, shake, devastate, take aback, leave speechless; *informal* bowl over, knock sideways; *Brit. informal* knock/hit for six.

overpowering ▶ **adjective** ❶ *overpowering grief* OVERWHELMING, oppressive, unbearable, unendurable, intolerable, shattering. ❷ *an overpowering smell* STIFLING, suffocating, strong, pungent, powerful; nauseating, offensive, acrid, fetid, mephitic. ❸ *overpowering evidence* IRREFUTABLE, undeniable, indisputable, incontestable, incontrovertible, compelling, conclusive.

overrate ▶ **verb** OVERESTIMATE, overvalue, think too much of, attach too much importance to, praise too highly.
– OPPOSITES underestimate.

overreach
■ **overreach oneself** TRY TO DO TOO MUCH, overestimate one's ability, overdo it, overstretch oneself, wear/burn oneself out, bite off more than one can chew.

overreact ▶ **verb** REACT DISPROPORTIONATELY, act irrationally, lose one's sense of proportion, blow something up out of all proportion; *Brit. informal* go over the top.

override ▶ **verb** ❶ *the court could not override her decision* DISALLOW, overrule, countermand, veto, quash, overturn, overthrow; cancel, reverse, rescind, revoke, repeal, annul, nullify, invalidate, negate, void; *Law* vacate; *formal* abrogate; *archaic* recall. ❷ *the government can override all opposition* DISREGARD, pay no heed to, take no account of, turn a deaf ear to, ignore, ride roughshod over. ❸ *a positive attitude will override any negative thoughts* OUTWEIGH, supersede, take precedence over, take priority over, offset, cancel out, (more than) make up for, outbalance, compensate for.

overriding ▶ **adjective** MOST IMPORTANT, of greatest importance, of greatest significance, uppermost, top, first (and foremost), highest, pre-eminent, predominant, principal, primary, paramount, chief, main, major, foremost, central, key, focal, pivotal; *informal* number-one.

overrule ▶ **verb** COUNTERMAND, cancel, reverse, rescind, repeal, revoke, retract, disallow, override, veto, quash, overturn, overthrow, annul, nullify, invalidate, negate, void; *Law* vacate; *formal* abrogate; *archaic* recall.

overrun ▶ **verb** ❶ *guerrillas overran the barracks* INVADE, storm, occupy, swarm into, surge into, inundate, overwhelm. ❷ *the talks overran the deadline* EXCEED, go beyond/over, run over.

oversee ▶ **verb** SUPERVISE, superintend, be in charge/control of, be responsible for, look after, keep an eye on, inspect, administer, organize, manage, direct, preside over.

overseer ▶ **noun** SUPERVISOR, foreman, forewoman, team leader, controller, (line) manager, manageress, head (of department), superintendent, captain; *informal* boss, chief, governor; *Brit. informal* gaffer, guv'nor; *N. Amer. informal* straw boss; *Austral. informal* pannikin boss; *Mining* overman.

overshadow ▶ **verb** ❶ *a massive hill overshadows the town* CAST A SHADOW OVER, shade, darken, conceal, obscure, screen; dominate, overlook. ❷ *this feeling of tragedy overshadowed his story* CAST GLOOM OVER, blight, take the edge off, mar, spoil, ruin. ❸ *he was overshadowed by his brilliant elder brother* OUTSHINE, eclipse, surpass, exceed, be superior to, outclass, outstrip, outdo, upstage; *informal* be head and shoulders above.

oversight ▶ **noun** ❶ *a stupid oversight* MISTAKE, error, omission, lapse, slip, blunder; *informal* slip-up, boo-boo; *Brit. informal* boob; *N. Amer. informal* goof. ❷ *the omission was due to oversight* CARELESSNESS, inattention, negligence, forgetfulness, laxity. ❸ *school governors have oversight of the curriculum* SUPERVISION, surveillance, superintendence, charge, care, administration, management.

overstate ▶ verb EXAGGERATE, overdo, overemphasize, overplay, dramatize, embroider, embellish; *informal* blow up out of all proportion.
– OPPOSITES understate.

overstatement ▶ noun EXAGGERATION, overemphasis, dramatization, embroidery, embellishment, enhancement, hyperbole.

overt ▶ adjective UNDISGUISED, unconcealed, plain (to see), clear, apparent, conspicuous, obvious, noticeable, manifest, patent, open, blatant.
– OPPOSITES covert.

overtake ▶ verb ❶ *a green car overtook the taxi* PASS, go past/by, get/pull ahead of, leave behind, outdistance, outstrip. ❷ *tourism overtook coffee as the main earner of foreign currency* OUTSTRIP, surpass, overshadow, eclipse, outshine, outclass; dwarf, put in the shade, exceed, top, cap; *archaic* outrival. ❸ *the calamity which overtook us* BEFALL, happen to, come upon, hit, strike, overwhelm, overcome, be visited on; *poetic/literary* betide.

overthrow ▶ verb ❶ *the President was overthrown* REMOVE (FROM OFFICE/POWER), bring down, topple, depose, oust, displace, unseat. ❷ *an attempt to overthrow Soviet rule* PUT AN END TO, defeat, conquer.
▶ noun ❶ *the overthrow of the Shah* REMOVAL (FROM OFFICE/POWER), downfall, fall, toppling, deposition, ousting, displacement, supplanting, unseating. ❷ *the overthrow of capitalism* ENDING, defeat, displacement, fall, collapse, downfall, demise.

overtone ▶ noun CONNOTATION, hidden meaning, implication, association, undercurrent, undertone, echo, vibrations, hint, suggestion, insinuation, intimation, suspicion, feeling, nuance.

overture ▶ noun ❶ *the overture to Don Giovanni* PRELUDE, introduction, opening, introductory movement. ❷ *the overture to a long debate* PRELIMINARY, prelude, introduction, lead-in, precursor, start, beginning. ❸ *peace overtures* (OPENING) MOVE, approach, advances, feeler, signal, proposal, proposition.

overturn ▶ verb ❶ *the boat overturned* CAPSIZE, turn turtle, keel over, tip over, topple over, turn over; *Nautical* pitchpole; *archaic* overset. ❷ *I overturned the stool* UPSET, tip over, topple over, turn over, knock over, upend. ❸ *the Senate may overturn this ruling* CANCEL, reverse, rescind, repeal, revoke, retract, countermand, disallow, override, overrule, veto, quash, overthrow, annul, nullify, invalidate, negate, void; *Law* vacate; *formal* abrogate; *archaic* recall.

overused ▶ adjective HACKNEYED, overworked, worn out, time-worn, tired, played out, clichéd, stale, trite, banal, stock, unoriginal.

overweening ▶ adjective OVERCONFIDENT, conceited, cocksure, cocky, smug, haughty, supercilious, lofty, patronizing, arrogant, proud, vain, self-important, imperious, overbearing; *informal* high and mighty, uppish.
– OPPOSITES unassuming.

overweight ▶ adjective FAT, obese, stout, corpulent, gross, fleshy, plump, portly, chubby, rotund, paunchy, pot-bellied, flabby, well upholstered, well padded, broad in the beam; *informal* porky, tubby, blubbery; *Brit. informal* podgy, fubsy; *archaic* pursy.
– OPPOSITES skinny.

overwhelm ▶ verb ❶ *advancing sand dunes could overwhelm the village* SWAMP, submerge, engulf, bury, deluge, flood, inundate. ❷ *Spain overwhelmed Russia in the hockey* DEFEAT (UTTERLY/HEAVILY), trounce, rout, beat (hollow), conquer, vanquish, be victorious over, triumph over, worst, overcome, overthrow, crush; *informal* thrash, lick, best, clobber, wipe the floor with. ❸ *she was overwhelmed by a sense of tragedy* OVERCOME, move, stir, affect, touch, strike, dumbfound, shake, devastate, floor, leave speechless; *informal* bowl over, knock sideways; *Brit. informal* knock/hit for six.

overwhelming ▶ adjective ❶ *an overwhelming number of players were unavailable* VERY LARGE, enormous, immense, inordinate, massive, huge. ❷ *overwhelming desire to laugh* VERY STRONG, forceful, uncontrollable, irrepressible, irresistible, overpowering, compelling.

overwork ▶ verb ❶ *we should not overwork* WORK TOO HARD, work/run oneself into the ground, wear oneself to a shadow, work one's fingers to the bone, burn the candle at both ends, overtax oneself, burn oneself out, do too much, overdo it, strain oneself, overload oneself, drive/push oneself too hard; *informal* kill oneself, knock oneself out. ❷ *my colleagues did not overwork me* DRIVE (TOO HARD), exploit, drive into the ground, tax, overtax, overburden, put upon, impose on.

overworked ▶ adjective ❶ *overworked staff* STRESSED (OUT), stress-ridden, overtaxed, overburdened, overloaded, exhausted, worn out. ❷ *an overworked phrase* HACKNEYED, overused, worn out, tired, played out, clichéd, threadbare, stale, trite, banal, stock, unoriginal.
– OPPOSITES relaxed, original.

overwrought ▶ adjective ❶ *she was too overwrought to listen* TENSE, agitated, nervous, on edge, edgy, keyed up, worked up, highly strung, neurotic, overexcited, beside oneself, distracted, distraught, frantic, hysterical; *informal* in a state, in a tizzy, uptight, wound up, het up; *Brit. informal* strung up. ❷ *the painting is overwrought* OVER-ELABORATE, over-ornate, overblown, overdone, contrived, overworked, strained.
– OPPOSITES calm, understated.

owe ▶ **verb** BE IN DEBT (TO), be indebted (to), be in arrears (to), be under an obligation (to).

owing ▶ **adjective** *the rent was owing* UNPAID, to be paid, payable, due, overdue, undischarged, owed, outstanding, in arrears; *N. Amer.* delinquent.
– OPPOSITES paid.
■ **owing to** BECAUSE OF, as a result of, on account of, due to, as a consequence of, thanks to, in view of; *formal* by reason of.

own ▶ **adjective** *he has his own reasons* PERSONAL, individual, particular, private, personalized, unique.
▶ **verb** ❶ *I own this house* BE THE OWNER OF, possess, be the possessor of, have in one's possession, have (to one's name). ❷ *she had to own that she agreed* ADMIT, concede, grant, accept, acknowledge, agree, confess.
■ **get one's own back** (*informal*) HAVE/GET/TAKE ONE'S REVENGE (ON), be revenged (on), hit back, get (back at), get even (with), settle accounts (with), repay, pay someone back, give someone their just deserts, retaliate (against/on), take reprisals (against), exact retribution (on), give someone a taste of their own medicine.
■ **hold one's own** STAND FIRM, stand one's ground, keep one's end up, keep one's head above water, compete, survive, cope, get on/along.
■ **on one's own** ❶ *I am all on my own* (ALL) ALONE, (all) by oneself, solitary, unaccompanied, companionless; *informal* by one's lonesome; *Brit. informal* on one's tod, on one's Jack Jones. ❷ *she works well on her own* UNAIDED, unassisted, without help, without assistance, (all) by oneself, independently.
■ **own up** CONFESS (TO), admit to, admit guilt, plead guilty, accept blame/responsibility, tell the truth (about), make a clean breast of it, tell all; *informal* come clean (about).

owner ▶ **noun** POSSESSOR, holder, proprietor/proprietress, homeowner, freeholder, landlord, landlady.
– RELATED TERMS proprietary.

ownership ▶ **noun** (RIGHT OF) POSSESSION, freehold, proprietorship, proprietary rights, title.

ox ▶ **noun** bull, bullock, steer; *Farming* beef.

pace ▶ **noun** ❶ *he stepped back a pace* STEP, stride. ❷ *a slow, steady pace* GAIT, stride, walk, march. ❸ *he drove home at a furious pace* SPEED, rate, velocity; *informal* clip, lick.
▶ **verb** *she paced up and down* WALK, stride, tread, march, pound, patrol.

pacific ▶ **adjective** ❶ *a pacific community* PEACE-LOVING, peaceable, pacifist, non-violent, non-aggressive, non-belligerent. ❷ *their pacific intentions* CONCILIATORY, peacemaking, placatory, propitiatory, appeasing, mollifying, mediatory, dovish; *formal* irenic. ❸ *pacific waters* CALM, still, smooth, tranquil, placid, waveless, unruffled, like a millpond.
– OPPOSITES aggressive, stormy.

pacifism ▶ **noun** PEACEMAKING, conscientious objection(s), passive resistance, peace-mongering, non-violence.

pacifist ▶ **noun** PEACE-LOVER, conscientious objector, passive resister, peacemaker, peacemonger, dove; *Brit. informal* conchie.
– OPPOSITES warmonger.

pacify ▶ **verb** PLACATE, appease, calm (down), conciliate, propitiate, assuage, mollify, soothe.
– OPPOSITES enrage.

pack ▶ **noun** ❶ *a pack of cigarettes* PACKET, container, package, box, carton, parcel. ❷ *a 45lb pack* BACKPACK, rucksack, knapsack, kitbag, bag, load. ❸ *a pack of wolves* GROUP, herd, troop. ❹ *a pack of youngsters* CROWD, mob, group, band, troupe, party, set, clique, gang, rabble, horde, throng, huddle, mass, assembly, gathering, host; *informal* crew, bunch.
▶ **verb** ❶ *she helped pack the hamper* FILL (UP), put things in, load. ❷ *they packed their belongings* STOW, put away, store, box up. ❸ *the glasses were packed in straw* WRAP (UP), package, parcel, swathe, swaddle, encase, enfold, envelop, bundle. ❹ *Christmas shoppers packed the store* THRONG, crowd (into), fill (to overflowing), cram, jam, squash into, squeeze into. ❺ *pack the cloth against the wall* COMPRESS, press, squash, squeeze, jam, tamp.
■ **pack something in** (*informal*) ❶ *she has packed in her job* RESIGN FROM, leave, give up; *informal* quit, chuck; *Brit. informal* jack in. ❷ *he should pack in smoking* GIVE UP, abstain from, drop, desist from, refrain from, discontinue; *informal* quit, leave off; *formal* forswear.
■ **pack someone off** (*informal*) SEND OFF, dispatch, bundle off.

■ **pack up** ❶ (*Brit. informal*) *something is bound to pack up over Christmas* BREAK (DOWN), stop working, fail, develop a fault, malfunction, go wrong; *informal* act up, conk out, go kaput. ❷ (*informal*) *it's time to pack up* STOP, call it a day, finish, cease; *informal* knock off, quit, pack/jack it in.

■ **pack something up** PUT AWAY, tidy up/away, clear up/away.

package ▶ **noun** ❶ *the delivery of a package* PARCEL, packet, container, box. ❷ *a complete package of services* COLLECTION, bundle, combination.

▶ **verb** *goods packaged in recyclable materials* WRAP (UP), gift-wrap; pack (up), parcel (up), box, encase.

packaging ▶ **noun** WRAPPING, wrappers, packing, covering.

packed ▶ **adjective** CROWDED, full, filled (to capacity), crammed, jammed, solid, overcrowded, overfull, teeming, seething, swarming; *informal* jam-packed, chock-full, chock-a-block, full to the gunwales, bursting/bulging at the seams.

packet ▶ **noun** ❶ *a packet of cigarettes* PACK, carton, (cardboard) box, container, case, package. ❷ (*informal*) *that must have cost a packet* A CONSIDERABLE/LARGE SUM OF MONEY, a king's ransom, millions, billions; *informal* a (small) fortune, pots/heaps of money, a mint, a bundle, a pile, a tidy sum, a pretty penny, big money; *Brit. informal* a bomb, loadsamoney; *N. Amer. informal* big bucks, gazillions; *Austral. informal* big bickies, motser.

pact ▶ **noun** AGREEMENT, treaty, entente, protocol, deal, settlement, concordat; armistice, truce; *formal* concord.

pad[1] ▶ **noun** ❶ *a pad over the eye* PIECE OF COTTON WOOL, dressing, pack, padding, wadding, wad. ❷ *a seat pad* CUSHION, squab. ❸ *making notes on a pad* NOTEBOOK, notepad, writing pad, memo pad, jotter, block, sketch pad, sketchbook; *N. Amer.* scratch pad.

▶ **verb** *a quilted jacket padded with duck feathers* STUFF, fill, pack, wad.

■ **pad something out** EXPAND UNNECESSARILY, fill out, amplify, increase, flesh out, lengthen, spin out, overdo, elaborate.

pad[2] ▶ **verb** *he padded along towards the bedroom* WALK QUIETLY, tread warily, creep, tiptoe, steal, pussyfoot.

padding ▶ **noun** ❶ *padding around the ankle* WADDING, cushioning, stuffing, packing, filling, lining. ❷ *a concise style with no padding* VERBIAGE, verbosity, wordiness, prolixity; *Brit. informal* waffle.

paddle[1] ▶ **noun** *use the paddles to row ashore* OAR, scull, blade.

▶ **verb** *we paddled around the bay* ROW GENTLY, pull, scull.

paddle[2] ▶ **verb** *children were paddling in the water* SPLASH ABOUT, wade; dabble.

paddock ▶ **noun** FIELD, meadow, pasture; pen, pound; *N. Amer.* corral.

paddy ▶ **noun** (*Brit. informal*) RAGE, (bad) temper, (bad) mood, pet, fit of pique, tantrum; *informal* grump, stress; *Brit. informal* strop; *N. Amer. informal* blowout, hissy fit.

padlock ▶ **verb** LOCK (UP), fasten, secure.

padre ▶ **noun** PRIEST, chaplain, minister (of religion), pastor, father, parson, clergyman, cleric, ecclesiastic, man of the cloth, churchman, vicar, rector, curate, preacher; *informal* reverend, Holy Joe, sky pilot; *Austral. informal* josser.

paean ▶ **noun** SONG OF PRAISE, hymn, alleluia; plaudit, glorification, eulogy, tribute, panegyric, accolade, acclamation; *formal* encomium.

pagan ▶ **noun** *pagans worshipped the sun* HEATHEN, infidel, idolater, idolatress; *archaic* paynim.

▶ **adjective** *the pagan festival* HEATHEN, ungodly, irreligious, infidel, idolatrous; *rare* nullifidian.

page[1] ▶ **noun** ❶ *a book of 672 pages* FOLIO, sheet, side, leaf. ❷ *a glorious page in his life* PERIOD, time, stage, phase, epoch, era, chapter.

page[2] ▶ **noun** ❶ *a page in a hotel* ERRAND BOY, messenger boy; *N. Amer.* bellboy, bellhop. ❷ *a page at a wedding* ATTENDANT, pageboy, trainbearer.

▶ **verb** *could you please page Mr Johnson?* CALL (FOR), summon, send for.

pageant ▶ **noun** PARADE, procession, cavalcade, tableau (vivant); spectacle, extravaganza, show.

pageantry ▶ **noun** SPECTACLE, display, ceremony, magnificence, pomp, splendour, grandeur, show; *informal* razzle-dazzle, razzmatazz.

pain ▶ **noun** ❶ *she endured great pain* SUFFERING, agony, torture, torment, discomfort. ❷ *a pain in the stomach* ACHE, aching, soreness, throb, throbbing, sting, stinging, twinge, shooting pain, stab, pang; discomfort, irritation, tenderness. ❸ *the pain of losing a loved one* SORROW, grief, heartache, heartbreak, sadness, unhappiness, distress, desolation, misery, wretchedness, despair; agony, torment, torture. ❹ (*informal*) *that child is a pain. See* NUISANCE. ❺ *he took great pains to hide his feelings* CARE, effort, bother, trouble.

▶ **verb** ❶ *her foot is still paining her* HURT, cause pain, be painful, be sore, be tender, ache, throb, sting, twinge, cause discomfort; *informal* kill. ❷ *the memory pains her* SADDEN, grieve, distress, trouble, perturb, oppress, cause anguish to.

■ **be at pains** TRY HARD, make a great effort, take (great) pains, put oneself out; strive, endeavour, try, do one's best, do one's utmost, go all out; *informal* bend/fall/lean over backwards.

pained ▶ adjective UPSET, hurt, wounded, injured, insulted, offended, aggrieved, displeased, disgruntled, annoyed, angered, angry, cross, indignant, irritated, resentful; *informal* riled, miffed, aggravated, peeved, hacked off, browned off; *Brit. informal* narked, cheesed off; *N. Amer. informal* teed off, ticked off, sore.

painful ▶ adjective ❶ *a painful arm* SORE, hurting, tender, aching, throbbing. ❷ *a painful experience* DISAGREEABLE, unpleasant, nasty, bitter, distressing, upsetting, traumatic, miserable, sad, heartbreaking, agonizing, harrowing.

painfully ▶ adverb DISTRESSINGLY, disturbingly, unendurably, unbearably, uncomfortably, unpleasantly; dreadfully; *informal* terribly, awfully; *informal, dated* frightfully.

painkiller ▶ noun ANALGESIC, pain reliever, anodyne, anaesthetic, narcotic; palliative.

painless ▶ adjective ❶ *any killing of animals should be painless* WITHOUT PAIN, pain-free. ❷ *getting rid of him proved painless* EASY, trouble-free, effortless, simple, plain sailing; *informal* as easy as pie, a piece of cake, child's play, a cinch.
– OPPOSITES painful, difficult.

painstaking ▶ adjective CAREFUL, meticulous, thorough, assiduous, sedulous, attentive, diligent, industrious, conscientious, punctilious, scrupulous, rigorous, particular; pedantic, fussy.
– OPPOSITES slapdash.

paint ▶ noun COLOURING, colourant, tint, dye, stain, pigment, colour.
▶ verb ❶ *simply paint the ceiling* COLOUR, apply paint to, decorate, whitewash, emulsion, gloss, spray-paint, airbrush. ❷ *painting slogans on a wall* DAUB, smear, spray-paint, airbrush. ❸ *Rembrandt painted his mother* PORTRAY, picture, paint a picture of, depict, represent. ❹ *you paint a very stark picture of the suffering* TELL, recount, outline, sketch, describe, depict, evoke, conjure up.
■ **paint the town red** (*informal*) CELEBRATE, carouse, enjoy oneself, have a good/wild time, have a party; *informal* go out on the town, whoop it up, make whoopee, live it up, party, have a ball, push the boat out.

painting ▶ noun PICTURE, illustration, portrayal, depiction, representation, image, artwork; oil (painting), watercolour, canvas.

pair ▶ noun ❶ *a pair of gloves* SET (OF TWO), matching set, two of a kind. ❷ *the pair were arrested* TWO, couple, duo, brace, twosome, duplet; twins; *archaic* twain. ❸ *a pair of lines* COUPLET; *Prosody* distich. ❹ *the happy pair* COUPLE, man/husband and wife.
▶ verb *a cardigan paired with a matching skirt* MATCH, put together, couple, twin.
■ **pair off/up** GET TOGETHER, team up, form a couple, make a twosome.

pal (*informal*) ▶ noun *my best pal. See* FRIEND sense 1.
■ **pal up** BECOME FRIENDLY, make friends, form a friendship; *N. Amer. informal* buddy up.

palace ▶ noun ROYAL/OFFICIAL RESIDENCE, castle, château, schloss, mansion, stately home.
– RELATED TERMS palatial.

palatable ▶ adjective ❶ *palatable meals* TASTY, appetizing, flavourful, flavoursome, delicious, mouth-watering, toothsome, succulent; *informal* scrumptious, yummy, scrummy, moreish; *formal* comestible. ❷ *the truth is not always palatable* PLEASANT, acceptable, pleasing, agreeable, to one's liking.
– OPPOSITES disagreeable.

palate ▶ noun ❶ *the tea burned her palate* ROOF OF THE MOUTH, hard/soft palate. ❷ *menus to suit the tourist palate* (SENSE OF) TASTE, appetite, stomach. ❸ *wine with a peachy palate* FLAVOUR, savour, taste.

palatial ▶ adjective LUXURIOUS, de luxe, magnificent, sumptuous, splendid, grand, opulent, lavish, stately, regal; fancy; *Brit.* upmarket; *informal* plush, swanky, posh, ritzy, swish.
– OPPOSITES modest.

palaver (*informal*) ▶ noun ❶ *what was all that palaver about?* FUSS (AND BOTHER), bother, commotion, trouble, rigmarole, folderol; *informal* song and dance, performance, to-do, carrying-on, kerfuffle, hoo-ha, hullabaloo, ballyhoo. ❷ (*dated*) *they were having a palaver. See* PARLEY noun.
▶ verb *don't stand there palavering. See* TALK verb sense 3.

pale¹ ▶ noun ❶ *the pales of a fence* STAKE, post, pole, picket, upright. ❷ *outside the pale of decency* BOUNDARY, confines, bounds, limits.
■ **beyond the pale** UNACCEPTABLE, unseemly, improper, unsuitable, unreasonable, intolerable, disgraceful, deplorable, outrageous, scandalous, shocking; *informal* not on, not the done thing, out of order, out of line; *Austral./NZ informal* over the fence; *formal* exceptionable.

pale² ▶ adjective ❶ *she looked pale and drawn* WHITE, pallid, pasty, wan, colourless, anaemic, bloodless, washed out, peaky, ashen, grey, whitish, whey-faced, drained, sickly, sallow, as white as a sheet, deathly pale; milky, creamy, cream, ivory, milk-white, alabaster; *informal* like death warmed up. ❷ *pale colours* LIGHT, light-coloured, pastel, muted, subtle, soft; faded, bleached, washed out. ❸ *the pale light of morning* DIM, faint, weak, feeble. ❹ *a pale imitation* FEEBLE, weak, insipid, bland, poor, inadequate; uninspired, unimaginative, lacklustre, spiritless, lifeless; *informal* pathetic.
– OPPOSITES dark.
▶ verb ❶ *his face paled* GO/TURN WHITE, grow/turn pale, blanch, lose colour. ❷ *everything else pales by comparison* DECREASE IN IMPORTANCE, lose significance, pale into insignificance.

palisade ▶ noun FENCE, paling, barricade, stockade.

pall¹ ▶ **noun** ❶ *a rich velvet pall* FUNERAL CLOTH, coffin covering. ❷ *a pall of black smoke* CLOUD, covering, cloak, veil, shroud, layer, blanket.

■ **cast a pall over** SPOIL, cast a shadow over, overshadow, cloud, put a damper on.

pall² ▶ **verb** *the high life was beginning to pall* BECOME/GROW TEDIOUS, become/grow boring, lose its/their interest, lose attraction, wear off; weary, sicken, nauseate; irritate, irk.

palliate ▶ **verb** ❶ *the treatment works by palliating symptoms* ALLEVIATE, ease, relieve, soothe, take the edge off, assuage, moderate, temper, diminish, decrease, blunt, deaden. ❷ *there is no way to palliate his dirty deed* DISGUISE, hide, gloss over, conceal, cover (up), camouflage, mask; excuse, justify, extenuate, mitigate.

palliative ▶ **adjective** *palliative medicine* SOOTHING, alleviating, sedative, calmative.

▶ **noun** *antibiotics and palliatives* PAINKILLER, analgesic, pain reliever, sedative, tranquillizer, anodyne, calmative, opiate, bromide.

pallid ▶ **adjective** ❶ *a pallid child* PALE, white, pasty, wan, colourless, anaemic, washed out, peaky, whey-faced, ashen, grey, whitish, drained, sickly, sallow; *informal* like death warmed up. ❷ *pallid watercolours* INSIPID, uninspired, colourless, uninteresting, unexciting, unimaginative, lifeless, spiritless, sterile, bland.

pallor ▶ **noun** PALENESS, pallidness, lack of colour, wanness, ashen hue, pastiness, peakiness, greyness, sickliness, sallowness.

pally ▶ **adjective** (*informal*) FRIENDLY, on good terms, close, intimate; *informal* matey, buddy-buddy.

palm¹

■ **grease someone's palm** (*informal*) BRIBE, buy (off), corrupt, suborn, give an inducement to; *informal* give a backhander to, give a sweetener to.

■ **have someone in the palm of one's hand** HAVE CONTROL OVER, have influence over, have someone eating out of one's hand, have someone on a string; *N. Amer.* have someone in one's hip pocket.

■ **palm something off** FOIST, fob off, get rid of, dispose of, unload.

palm² ▶ **noun** *the palm of victory* PRIZE, trophy, award, crown, laurel wreath, laurels, bays.

palmistry ▶ **noun** FORTUNE TELLING, palm-reading, clairvoyancy, chiromancy.

palmy ▶ **adjective** HAPPY, fortunate, glorious, prosperous, halcyon, golden, rosy.

palpable ▶ **adjective** ❶ *a palpable bump* TANGIBLE, touchable, noticeable, detectable. ❷ *his reluctance was palpable* PERCEPTIBLE, perceivable, visible, noticeable, discernible, detectable, observable, tangible, unmistakable, transparent, self-evident; obvious, clear, plain (to see), evident, apparent, manifest, staring one in the face, written all over someone.

–OPPOSITES imperceptible.

palpitate ▶ **verb** ❶ *her heart began to palpitate* BEAT RAPIDLY, pound, throb, pulsate, pulse, thud, thump, hammer, race. ❷ *palpitating with terror* TREMBLE, quiver, quake, shake (like a leaf).

paltry ▶ **adjective** ❶ *a paltry sum of money* SMALL, meagre, trifling, insignificant, negligible, inadequate, insufficient, derisory, pitiful, pathetic, miserable, niggardly, beggarly; *informal* measly, piddling, poxy; *formal* exiguous. ❷ *naval glory struck him as paltry* WORTHLESS, petty, trivial, unimportant, insignificant, inconsequential, of little account.

–OPPOSITES considerable.

pamper ▶ **verb** SPOIL, indulge, overindulge, cosset, mollycoddle, coddle, baby, wait on someone hand and foot.

pamphlet ▶ **noun** BROCHURE, leaflet, booklet, circular, flyer, handbill; *N. Amer.* mailer, folder, dodger.

pan¹ ▶ **noun** ❶ *a heavy pan* SAUCEPAN, frying pan, wok, skillet. ❷ *salt pans* HOLLOW, pit, depression, dip, crater, concavity.

▶ **verb** ❶ (*informal*) *the movie was panned by the critics. See* CRITICIZE. ❷ *prospectors panned for gold* SIFT FOR, search for, look for.

–OPPOSITES praise.

■ **pan out** ❶ *Harold's idea hadn't panned out* SUCCEED, be successful, work (out), turn out well. ❷ *the deal panned out badly* TURN OUT, work out, end (up), come out, fall out, evolve; *formal* eventuate.

pan² ▶ **verb** *the camera panned to the building* SWING (ROUND), sweep, move, turn, circle.

panacea ▶ **noun** UNIVERSAL CURE, cure-all, cure for all ills, universal remedy, elixir, wonder drug; *informal* magic bullet.

panache ▶ **noun** FLAMBOYANCE, confidence, self-assurance, style, flair, elan, dash, verve, zest, spirit, brio, éclat, vivacity, gusto, liveliness, vitality, energy; *informal* pizzazz, oomph, zip, zing.

pancake ▶ **noun** CRÊPE, galette; blin, tortilla, tostada, chapatti, dosa, latke, blintze; *N. Amer.* flapjack, slapjack.

pandemic ▶ **adjective** WIDESPREAD, prevalent, pervasive, rife, rampant.

pandemonium ▶ **noun** BEDLAM, chaos, mayhem, uproar, turmoil, tumult, commotion, confusion, anarchy, furore, hubbub, rumpus; *informal* hullabaloo.

–OPPOSITES peace.

pander

■ **pander to** INDULGE, gratify, satisfy, cater to, give in to, accommodate, comply with.

pane ▶ **noun** SHEET OF GLASS, windowpane.

panegyric ▶ **noun** EULOGY, speech of praise, paean, accolade, tribute.

panel ▶ noun ❶ *a control panel* CONSOLE, instrument panel, dashboard; instruments, controls, dials. ❷ *a panel of judges* GROUP, team, body, committee, board.

pang ▶ noun ❶ *hunger pangs* (SHARP) PAIN, shooting pain, twinge, stab, spasm. ❷ *a pang of remorse* QUALM, twinge, prick.

panic ▶ noun *a wave of panic* ALARM, anxiety, nervousness, fear, fright, trepidation, dread, terror, agitation, hysteria, consternation, perturbation, dismay, apprehension; *informal* flap, fluster, cold sweat, funk, tizzy; *N. Amer. informal* swivet.
– OPPOSITES calm.
▶ verb ❶ *there's no need to panic* BE ALARMED, be scared, be nervous, be afraid, take fright, be agitated, be hysterical, lose one's nerve, get overwrought, get worked up; *informal* flap, get in a flap, lose one's cool, get into a tizzy, run around like a headless chicken, freak out, get in a stew; *Brit. informal* get the wind up, go into a (flat) spin, have kittens. ❷ *talk of love panicked her* FRIGHTEN, alarm, scare, unnerve; *informal* throw into a tizzy, freak out; *Brit. informal* put the wind up.

panic-stricken ▶ adjective ALARMED, frightened, scared (stiff), terrified, terror-stricken, petrified, horrified, horror-stricken, fearful, afraid, panicky, frantic, in a frenzy, nervous, agitated, hysterical, beside oneself, worked up, overwrought; *informal* in a cold sweat, in a (blue) funk, in a flap, in a fluster, in a tizzy; *Brit. informal* in a flat spin.

panoply ▶ noun ❶ *the full panoply of America's military might* ARRAY, range, collection. ❷ *all the panoply of religious liturgy* TRAPPINGS, regalia; splendour, spectacle, ceremony, ritual.

panorama ▶ noun ❶ *he surveyed the panorama* (SCENIC) VIEW, vista, prospect, scene, scenery, landscape, seascape. ❷ *a panorama of the art scene* OVERVIEW, survey, review, presentation, appraisal.

panoramic ▶ adjective ❶ *a panoramic view* SWEEPING, wide, extensive, scenic, commanding. ❷ *a panoramic look at the 20th century* WIDE-RANGING, extensive, broad, far-reaching, comprehensive, all-embracing.

pant ▶ verb ❶ *he was panting as they reached the top* BREATHE HEAVILY, breathe hard, puff (and blow), huff and puff, gasp, wheeze. ❷ *it makes you pant for more* YEARN FOR, long for, crave, hanker after/for, ache for, hunger for, thirst for, be hungry for, be thirsty for, wish for, desire, want; *informal* itch for, be dying for; *archaic* be athirst for.
▶ noun *breathing in shallow pants* GASP, puff, wheeze, breath.

panting ▶ adjective OUT OF BREATH, breathless, short of breath, puffed out, puffing (and blowing), huffing and puffing, gasping (for breath), wheezing, wheezy.

pantry ▶ noun LARDER, store, storeroom; *Brit. historical* still room; *archaic* spence.

pants ▶ plural noun ❶ (*Brit.*) UNDERPANTS, briefs, Y-fronts, boxer shorts, boxers, long johns, (French) knickers, bikini briefs; *Brit.* cami-knickers; *N. Amer.* shorts, undershorts; *informal* panties; *Brit. informal* kecks, knicks, smalls; *dated* drawers, bloomers, unmentionables; *N. Amer. dated* step-ins. ❷ (*N. Amer.*). *See* TROUSERS.

pap ▶ noun ❶ *tasteless pap* SOFT FOOD, mush, slop, pulp, purée, mash; *informal* goo, gloop, gook; *N. Amer. informal* glop. ❷ *commercial pap* TRIVIA, pulp (fiction), rubbish, nonsense, froth; *Brit.* candyfloss; *informal* dreck, drivel, trash, twaddle.

paper ▶ noun ❶ *a sheet of paper* writing paper, notepaper, foolscap. ❷ *the local paper* NEWSPAPER, journal, gazette, periodical; tabloid, broadsheet, quality paper, daily, weekly, evening paper, Sunday paper; *informal* rag; *N. Amer. informal* tab. ❸ *the paper was peeling off the walls* WALLPAPER, wallcovering; *Brit.* woodchip; *trademark* Anaglypta. ❹ *toffee papers* WRAPPER, wrapping. ❺ *a three-hour paper* EXAM, examination, test. ❻ *he has just published a paper* ESSAY, article, monograph, thesis, work, dissertation, treatise, study, report, analysis, tract, critique, exegesis, review; *N. Amer.* theme. ❼ *personal papers* DOCUMENTS, certificates, letters, files, deeds, records, archives, paperwork, documentation; *Law* muniments. ❽ *they asked us for our papers* IDENTIFICATION PAPERS/DOCUMENTS, identity card, ID, credentials.
▶ verb *we papered the walls* WALLPAPER, hang wallpaper on.
■ **paper something over** COVER UP, hide, conceal, disguise, camouflage, gloss over.
■ **on paper** ❶ *he put his thoughts down on paper* IN WRITING, in black and white, in print. ❷ *the combatants were evenly matched on paper* IN THEORY, theoretically, supposedly.

papery ▶ adjective THIN, paper-thin, flimsy, delicate, insubstantial, light, lightweight.

par
■ **below par** ❶ *their performances have been below par* SUBSTANDARD, inferior, not up to scratch, under par, below average, second-rate, mediocre, poor, undistinguished; *informal* not up to snuff; *N. Amer. informal* bush-league. ❷ *I'm feeling below par* SLIGHTLY UNWELL, not (very) well, not oneself, out of sorts; ill, unwell, poorly, washed out, run down, peaky; *Brit.* off (colour); *informal* under the weather, not up to snuff, lousy, rough; *Brit. informal* ropy, grotty; *Austral./NZ informal* crook; *dated* queer.
■ **on a par with** AS GOOD AS, comparable with, in the same class/league as, equivalent to, equal to, on a level with, of the same standard as.
■ **par for the course** NORMAL, typical, standard, usual, what one would expect.
■ **up to par** GOOD ENOUGH, up to the mark,

satisfactory, acceptable, adequate, up to scratch; *informal* up to snuff.

parable ▶ noun ALLEGORY, moral story/tale, fable, exemplum, apologue.

parade ▶ noun ❶ *a St George's Day parade* PROCESSION, march, cavalcade, motorcade, spectacle, display, pageant; review, dress parade, tattoo; *Brit.* march past. ❷ *she made a great parade of doing the housework* EXHIBITION, show, display, performance, spectacle, fuss; *informal* hoo-ha, to-do. ❸ *she walked along the parade* PROMENADE, walkway, esplanade, mall; *N. Amer.* boardwalk; *Brit. informal* prom.

▶ verb ❶ *the teams paraded through the city* MARCH, process, file, troop. ❷ *she paraded up and down* STRUT, swagger, stride. ❸ *he was keen to parade his knowledge* DISPLAY, exhibit, make a show of, flaunt, show (off), demonstrate.

paradigm ▶ noun MODEL, pattern, example, exemplar, standard, prototype, archetype.

paradisal ▶ adjective HEAVENLY, idyllic, blissful, divine, sublime, perfect.

paradise ▶ noun ❶ *the souls in paradise* (THE KINGDOM OF) HEAVEN, the heavenly kingdom, Elysium, the Elysian Fields, Valhalla, Avalon. ❷ *Adam and Eve's expulsion from Paradise* THE GARDEN OF EDEN, Eden. ❸ *a tropical paradise* UTOPIA, Shangri-La, heaven, idyll, nirvana. ❹ *this is sheer paradise!* BLISS, heaven, ecstasy, delight, joy, happiness, nirvana, heaven on earth.
– OPPOSITES hell.

paradox ▶ noun CONTRADICTION (IN TERMS), self-contradiction, inconsistency, incongruity, conflict, anomaly; enigma, puzzle, mystery, conundrum.

paradoxical ▶ adjective CONTRADICTORY, self-contradictory, inconsistent, incongruous, anomalous; illogical, puzzling, baffling, incomprehensible, inexplicable.

paragon ▶ noun PERFECT EXAMPLE, shining example, model, epitome, archetype, ideal, exemplar, nonpareil, embodiment, personification, quintessence, apotheosis, acme; jewel, gem, angel, treasure; *informal* one in a million, the tops; *archaic* a nonsuch.

paragraph ▶ noun ❶ *the concluding paragraph* SECTION, subdivision, part, subsection, division, portion, segment, passage. ❷ *a paragraph in the newspaper* REPORT, article, item, piece, write-up, mention.

parallel ▶ adjective ❶ *parallel lines* SIDE BY SIDE, aligned, collateral, equidistant. ❷ *parallel careers* SIMILAR, analogous, comparable, corresponding, like, of a kind, akin, related, equivalent, matching. ❸ *a parallel universe* COEXISTING, coexistent, concurrent; contemporaneous, simultaneous, synchronous.
– OPPOSITES divergent.

▶ noun ❶ *an exact parallel* COUNTERPART, analogue, equivalent, likeness, match, twin, duplicate, mirror. ❷ *there is an interesting parallel between these figures* SIMILARITY, likeness, resemblance, analogy, correspondence, equivalence, correlation, relation, symmetry, parity.

▶ verb ❶ *his experiences parallel mine* RESEMBLE, be similar to, be like, bear a resemblance to; correspond to, be analogous to, be comparable/equivalent to, equate with/to, correlate with, imitate, echo, remind one of, duplicate, mirror, follow, match. ❷ *her performance has never been paralleled* EQUAL, match, rival, emulate.

paralyse ▶ verb ❶ *both of his legs were paralysed* DISABLE, cripple, immobilize, incapacitate, debilitate; *formal* torpefy. ❷ *Maisie was paralysed by the sight of him* IMMOBILIZE, transfix, become rooted to the spot, freeze, stun, render motionless. ❸ *the capital was paralysed by a general strike* BRING TO A STANDSTILL, immobilize, bring to a (grinding) halt, freeze, cripple, disable.

paralysed ▶ adjective DISABLED, crippled, handicapped, incapacitated, paralytic, powerless, immobilized, useless; *Medicine* paraplegic, quadriplegic, tetraplegic, monoplegic, hemiplegic, paretic, paraparetic.

paralysis ▶ noun ❶ *the disease can cause paralysis* IMMOBILITY, powerlessness, incapacity, debilitation; *Medicine* paraplegia, quadriplegia, tetraplegia, monoplegia, hemiplegia, diplegia, paresis, paraparesis. ❷ *complete paralysis of the ports* SHUTDOWN, immobilization, stoppage.

paralytic ▶ adjective ❶ *her hands became paralytic* PARALYSED, crippled, disabled, incapacitated, powerless, immobilized, useless. ❷ (*Brit. informal*) *everyone was paralytic.* See DRUNK adjective.

parameter ▶ noun FRAMEWORK, variable, limit, boundary, limitation, restriction, criterion, guideline.

paramount ▶ adjective MOST IMPORTANT, of greatest/prime importance; uppermost, supreme, chief, overriding, predominant, foremost, prime, primary, principal, highest, main, key, central, leading, major, top; *informal* number-one.

paramour ▶ noun (*archaic*) LOVER, significant other; mistress, girlfriend, kept woman, other woman, inamorata; boyfriend, other man, inamorato; *informal* fancy woman/man, toy boy, sugar daddy, bit on the side, bit of fluff; *archaic* concubine, courtesan.

paranoia ▶ noun PERSECUTION COMPLEX, delusions, obsession, psychosis.

paranoid ▶ adjective OVER-SUSPICIOUS, paranoiac, suspicious, mistrustful, fearful, insecure; *Brit. informal* para.

parapet ▶ noun ❶ *Marian leaned over the parapet* BALUSTRADE, barrier, wall. ❷ *the sandbags making up the parapet* BARRICADE, rampart, bulwark, bank, embankment, fortification, defence, earthwork, bastion.

paraphernalia ▶ plural noun EQUIPMENT, stuff, things, apparatus, kit, implements, tools, utensils, material(s), appliances, accoutrements, appurtenances, odds and ends, bits and pieces; *informal* gear; *Brit. informal* clobber; *archaic* equipage.

paraphrase ▶ **verb** *paraphrasing literary texts* REWORD, rephrase, put/express in other words, rewrite, gloss.
▶ **noun** *this paraphrase of St Paul's words* REWORDING, rephrasing, rewriting, rewrite, rendition, rendering, gloss.

parasite ▶ **noun** HANGER-ON, cadger, leech, passenger; *informal* bloodsucker, sponger, scrounger, freeloader; *N. Amer. informal* mooch; *Austral./NZ informal* bludger.

parcel ▶ **noun** ❶ *a parcel of clothes* PACKAGE, packet; pack, bundle, box, case, bale. ❷ *a parcel of land* PLOT, piece, patch, tract; *Brit.* allotment; *N. Amer.* lot, plat.
▶ **verb** ❶ *she parcelled up the papers* PACK (UP), package, wrap (up), gift-wrap, tie up, bundle up. ❷ *parcelling out commercial farmland* DIVIDE UP, portion out, distribute, share out, allocate, allot, apportion, hand out, dole out, dish out; *informal* divvy up.

parched ▶ **adjective** ❶ *the parched earth* (BONE) DRY, dried up/out, arid, desiccated, dehydrated, baked, burned, scorched; withered, shrivelled. ❷ (*informal*) *I'm parched. See* THIRSTY sense 1.
– OPPOSITES soaking.

pardon ▶ **noun** ❶ *pardon for your sins* FORGIVENESS, absolution, clemency, mercy, lenience, leniency. ❷ *he offered them a full pardon* REPRIEVE, free pardon, amnesty, exoneration, release, acquittal, discharge; *formal* exculpation.
▶ **verb** ❶ *I know she will pardon me* FORGIVE, absolve, have mercy on; excuse, condone, overlook. ❷ *they were subsequently pardoned* EXONERATE, acquit, amnesty; reprieve, release, free; *informal* let off; *formal* exculpate.
– OPPOSITES blame, punish.
▶ **exclamation** *Pardon?* WHAT (DID YOU SAY), eh, pardon me, I beg your pardon, sorry, excuse me; *informal* come again.

pardonable ▶ **adjective** EXCUSABLE, forgivable, condonable, understandable, minor, venial, slight.
– OPPOSITES inexcusable.

pare ▶ **verb** ❶ *pare the peel from the lemon* CUT (OFF), trim (off), peel (off), strip (off), skin; *technical* decorticate. ❷ *domestic operations have been pared down* REDUCE, diminish, decrease, cut (back/down), trim, slim down, prune, curtail.

parent ▶ **noun** ❶ *her parents have divorced* MOTHER, FATHER, birth/biological parent, progenitor; adoptive parent, foster-parent, stepparent, guardian; *poetic/literary* begetter. ❷ *the parent of rock and roll* SOURCE, origin, genesis, root, author, architect; precursor, forerunner, predecessor, antecedent; *formal* radix.
▶ **verb** *those who parent young children* BRING UP, look after, take care of, rear, raise.

parentage ▶ **noun** ORIGINS, extraction, birth, family, ancestry, lineage, heritage, pedigree, descent, blood, stock, roots.

parenthetical ▶ **adjective** INCIDENTAL, supplementary, in brackets, in parentheses, parenthetic; explanatory, qualifying.

parenthetically ▶ **adverb** INCIDENTALLY, by the way, by the by(e), in passing, in parenthesis.

parenthood ▶ **noun** CHILDCARE, child-rearing, motherhood, fatherhood, parenting.

pariah ▶ **noun** OUTCAST, persona non grata, leper, undesirable, unperson.

parings ▶ **plural noun** PEELINGS, clippings, peel, rind, cuttings, trimmings, shavings.

parish ▶ **noun** ❶ *the parish of Poplar* DISTRICT, community. ❷ *the vicar scandalized the parish* PARISHIONERS, churchgoers, congregation, fold, flock, community.
– RELATED TERMS parochial.

parity ▶ **noun** EQUALITY, equivalence, uniformity, consistency, correspondence, congruity, levelness, unity, coequality.

park ▶ **noun** ❶ *we were playing in the park* PUBLIC GARDEN, recreation ground, playground, play area. ❷ *fifty acres of park* PARKLAND, grassland, woodland, garden(s), lawns, grounds, estate. ❸ *the liveliest player on the park* (PLAYING) FIELD, football field, pitch.
▶ **verb** ❶ *he parked his car* LEAVE, position; stop, pull up. ❷ (*informal*) *park your bag by the door* PUT (DOWN), place, deposit, leave, stick, shove, dump; *informal* plonk; *Brit. informal* bung.
■ **park oneself** (*informal*) SIT DOWN, seat oneself, settle (oneself), install oneself; *informal* plonk oneself.

parlance ▶ **noun** JARGON, language, phraseology, talk, speech, argot, patois, cant; *informal* lingo, -ese, -speak.

parley ▶ **noun** *a peace parley* NEGOTIATION, talk(s), conference, summit, discussion, powwow; *informal* confab; *formal* colloquy, confabulation; *dated* palaver.
▶ **verb** *the two parties were willing to parley* DISCUSS TERMS, talk, hold talks, negotiate, deliberate; *informal* powwow.

parliament ▶ **noun** ❶ *the Queen's speech to Parliament* THE HOUSES OF PARLIAMENT, Westminster, the (House of) Commons, the (House of) Lords. ❷ *the Russian parliament* LEGISLATURE, legislative assembly, congress, senate, (upper/lower) house, (upper/lower) chamber, diet, assembly.

parliamentary ▶ **adjective** LEGISLATIVE, lawmaking, governmental, congressional, senatorial, democratic, elected, representative.

parlour ▶ **noun** ❶ (*dated*) *tea in the parlour* SITTING ROOM, living room, lounge, front room, drawing room; *Brit.* reception room. ❷ *a beauty parlour* SALON, shop, establishment, store.

parlous ▶ adjective BAD, dire, dreadful, awful, terrible, grave, serious, desperate, precarious; sorry, poor, lamentable, hopeless; unsafe, perilous, dangerous, risky; *informal* dicey, hairy, chronic, woeful.

parochial ▶ adjective NARROW-MINDED, small-minded, provincial, narrow, small-town, conservative, illiberal, intolerant; *Brit.* parish-pump; *N. Amer. informal* jerkwater.
– OPPOSITES broad-minded.

parochialism ▶ noun NARROW-MINDEDNESS, provincialism, small-mindedness.

parody ▶ noun ❶ *a parody of the gothic novel* SATIRE, burlesque, lampoon, pastiche, pasquinade, caricature, imitation, mockery; *informal* spoof, take-off, send-up. ❷ *a parody of the truth* DISTORTION, travesty, caricature, misrepresentation, perversion, corruption, debasement.
▶ verb *parodying schoolgirl fiction* SATIRIZE, burlesque, lampoon, caricature, mimic, imitate, ape, copy, make fun of, travesty, take off; *informal* send up.

paroxysm ▶ noun SPASM, attack, fit, burst, bout, convulsion, seizure, outburst, eruption, explosion, access; *formal* boutade.

parrot ▶ noun PSITTACINE.
▶ verb *they parroted slogans without appreciating their significance* REPEAT (MINDLESSLY), repeat mechanically, echo.

parrot-fashion ▶ adverb MECHANICALLY, by rote, mindlessly, automatically.

parry ▶ verb ❶ *Sharpe parried the blow* WARD OFF, fend off; deflect, hold off, block, counter, repel, repulse. ❷ *I parried her constant questions* EVADE, sidestep, avoid, dodge, answer evasively, field, fend off.

parsimonious ▶ adjective MEAN, miserly, niggardly, close-fisted, close, penny-pinching, ungenerous, Scrooge-like; *informal* tight-fisted, tight, stingy, mingy; *N. Amer. informal* cheap; *formal* penurious; *archaic* near.
– OPPOSITES generous.

parsimony ▶ noun MEANNESS, miserliness, parsimoniousness, niggardliness, close-fistedness, closeness, penny-pinching; *informal* stinginess, minginess, tightness, tight-fistedness; *N. Amer.* cheapness; *formal* penuriousness; *archaic* nearness.

parson ▶ noun VICAR, rector, clergyman, cleric, chaplain, pastor, curate, man of the cloth, ecclesiastic, minister, priest, preacher; *informal* reverend, padre; *Austral. informal* josser.

part ▶ noun ❶ *the last part of the cake | a large part of their life* BIT, slice, chunk, lump, hunk, wedge, fragment, scrap, piece; portion, proportion, percentage, fraction. ❷ *car parts* COMPONENT, bit, constituent, element, module. ❸ *body parts* PART OF THE BODY, organ, limb, member. ❹ *the third part of the book* SECTION, division, volume, chapter, act, scene, instalment. ❺ *another part of the country* DISTRICT, neighbourhood, quarter, section, area, region. ❻ *the part of Juliet* (THEATRICAL) ROLE, character, persona. ❼ *he's learning his part* LINES, words, script, speech; libretto, lyrics, score. ❽ *he was jailed for his part in the affair* INVOLVEMENT, role, function, hand, work, responsibility, capacity, position, participation, contribution; *informal* bit.
– OPPOSITES whole.
▶ verb ❶ *the curtains parted* SEPARATE, divide (in two), split (in two), move apart. ❷ *we parted on bad terms* LEAVE, take one's leave, say goodbye/farewell, say one's goodbyes/farewells, go one's (separate) ways, go away, depart.
– OPPOSITES join, meet.
▶ adjective *a part payment* INCOMPLETE, partial, half, semi-, limited, inadequate, insufficient, unfinished.
– OPPOSITES complete.
▶ adverb *it is part finished* TO A CERTAIN EXTENT/DEGREE, to some extent/degree, partly, partially, in part, half, relatively, comparatively, (up) to a point, somewhat; not totally, not entirely, (very) nearly, almost, just about, all but.
– OPPOSITES completely.
■ **for the most part**. *See* MOST.
■ **in good part**. *See* GOOD.
■ **in part** TO A CERTAIN EXTENT/DEGREE, to some extent/degree, partly, partially, slightly, in some measure, (up) to a point.
■ **on the part of** (MADE/DONE) BY, carried out by, caused by, from.
■ **part with** GIVE UP/AWAY, relinquish, forgo, surrender, hand over, deliver up, dispose of.
■ **take part** PARTICIPATE, join in, get involved, enter, play a part/role, be a participant, contribute, have a hand, help, assist, lend a hand; *informal* get in on the act.
■ **take part in** PARTICIPATE IN, engage in, join in, get involved in, share in, play a part/role in, be a participant in, contribute to, be associated with, have a hand in.
■ **take someone's part** SUPPORT, give one's support to, take the side of, side with, stand by, stick up for, be supportive of, back (up), give one's backing to, be loyal to, defend, come to the defence of, champion.

partake ▶ verb ❶ (*formal*) *visitors can partake in golf* PARTICIPATE IN, take part in, engage in, join in, get involved in. ❷ *she had partaken of lunch* CONSUME, have, eat, drink, devour; *informal* wolf down, polish off. ❸ *Bohemia partakes of both East and West* HAVE THE QUALITIES/ATTRIBUTES OF, suggest, evoke, be characterized by.

partial ▶ adjective ❶ *a partial recovery* INCOMPLETE, limited, qualified, imperfect, fragmentary, unfinished. ❷ *a very partial view of the situation* BIASED, prejudiced, partisan, one-sided, slanted, skewed, coloured, unbalanced.
– OPPOSITES complete, unbiased.
■ **be partial to** LIKE, love, enjoy, have a liking

for, be fond of, be keen on, have a soft spot for, have a taste for, have a penchant for; *informal* adore, be mad about/on, have a thing about, be crazy about, be nutty about; *Brit. informal* be potty about; *N. Amer. informal* cotton to; *Austral./NZ informal* be shook on.

partiality ▶ **noun** ❶ *his partiality towards their cause* BIAS, prejudice, favouritism, favour, partisanship. ❷ *her partiality for brandy* LIKING, love, fondness, taste, soft spot, predilection, penchant, passion.

partially ▶ **adverb** TO A LIMITED EXTENT/DEGREE, to a certain extent/degree, partly, in part, not totally, not entirely, relatively, moderately, (up) to a point, somewhat, comparatively, slightly.

participant ▶ **noun** PARTICIPATOR, contributor, party, member; entrant, competitor, player, contestant, candidate.

participate ▶ **verb** TAKE PART, engage, join, get involved, share, play a part/role, be a participant, partake, have a hand in, be associated with; cooperate, help, assist, lend a hand.

participation ▶ **noun** INVOLVEMENT, part, contribution, association.

particle ▶ **noun** ❶ *minute particles of rock* (TINY) BIT, (tiny) piece, speck, spot, fleck; fragment, sliver, splinter. ❷ *he never showed a particle of sympathy* IOTA, jot, whit, bit, scrap, shred, crumb, drop, hint, touch, trace, suggestion, whisper, suspicion, scintilla; *informal* smidgen.

particular ▶ **adjective** ❶ *a particular group of companies* SPECIFIC, certain, distinct, separate, discrete, definite, precise; single, individual. ❷ *an issue of particular importance* (EXTRA) SPECIAL, especial, exceptional, unusual, singular, uncommon, notable, noteworthy, remarkable, unique; *formal* peculiar. ❸ *he was particular about what he ate* FUSSY, fastidious, finicky, meticulous, punctilious, discriminating, selective, painstaking, exacting, demanding; *informal* pernickety, choosy, picky; *Brit. informal* faddy.
– OPPOSITES general, careless.

▶ **noun** *the same in every particular* DETAIL, item, point, specific, element, aspect, respect, regard, particularity, fact, feature.

■ **in particular** ❶ *nothing in particular* SPECIFIC, special. ❷ *the poor, in particular, were hit by rising prices* PARTICULARLY, specifically, especially, specially.

particularity ▶ **noun** ❶ *the particularity of each human being* INDIVIDUALITY, distinctiveness, uniqueness, singularity, originality. ❷ *a great degree of particularity* DETAIL, precision, accuracy, thoroughness, scrupulousness, meticulousness.

particularize ▶ **verb** SPECIFY, detail, itemize, list, enumerate, spell out, cite, stipulate, instance.

particularly ▶ **adverb** ❶ *the acoustics are particularly good* ESPECIALLY, specially, very, extremely, exceptionally, singularly, peculiarly, unusually, extraordinarily, remarkably, outstandingly, amazingly, incredibly, really; *informal* seriously, majorly, awfully, terribly; *Brit. informal* jolly, dead, well; *informal, dated* devilish, frightfully. ❷ *he particularly asked that I should help you* SPECIFICALLY, explicitly, expressly, in particular, especially, specially.

parting ▶ **noun** ❶ *an emotional parting* FAREWELL, leave-taking, goodbye, adieu, departure; valediction. ❷ *they kept their parting quiet* SEPARATION, break-up, split, divorce, rift, estrangement; *Brit. informal* bust-up. ❸ *the parting of the Red Sea* DIVISION, dividing, separation, separating, splitting, breaking up/apart, partition, partitioning.

▶ **adjective** *a parting kiss* FAREWELL, goodbye, last, final, valedictory.

partisan ▶ **noun** ❶ *Conservative partisans* SUPPORTER, follower, adherent, devotee, champion; fanatic, fan, enthusiast, stalwart, zealot; *N. Amer.* booster. ❷ *the partisans opened fire from the woods* GUERRILLA, freedom fighter, resistance fighter, underground fighter, irregular (soldier).

▶ **adjective** *partisan attitudes* BIASED, prejudiced, one-sided, discriminatory, coloured, partial, interested, sectarian, factional.
– OPPOSITES unbiased.

partisanship ▶ **noun** BIAS, prejudice, one-sidedness, discrimination, favour, favouritism, partiality, sectarianism, factionalism.

partition ▶ **noun** ❶ *the partition of Palestine* DIVIDING UP, partitioning, separation, division, dividing, subdivision, splitting (up), breaking up, break-up. ❷ *room partitions* SCREEN, (room) divider, (dividing) wall, barrier, panel, separator.

▶ **verb** ❶ *the resolution partitioned Poland* DIVIDE (UP), subdivide, separate, split (up), break up; share (out), parcel out. ❷ *the huge hall was partitioned* SUBDIVIDE, divide (up); separate (off), section off, screen off.

partly ▶ **adverb** TO A CERTAIN EXTENT/DEGREE, to some extent/degree, in part, partially, a little, somewhat, not totally, not entirely, relatively, moderately, (up) to a point, in some measure, slightly.
– OPPOSITES completely.

partner ▶ **noun** ❶ *business partners* COLLEAGUE, associate, co-worker, fellow worker, collaborator, comrade, teammate; *Brit. informal* oppo; *Austral./NZ informal* offsider; *archaic* compeer. ❷ *his partner in crime* ACCOMPLICE, confederate, accessory, collaborator, fellow conspirator, helper; *informal* sidekick. ❸ *your relationship with your partner* SPOUSE, husband, wife, consort; lover, girlfriend, boyfriend, fiancé, fiancée, significant other, live-in lover, common-law husband/wife, man, woman, mate; *informal* hubby, missus, old man, old lady/woman, better half, intended, POSSLQ; *Brit. informal* other half.

partnership ▶ noun ❶ *close partnership* CO-OPERATION, association, collaboration, coalition, alliance, union, affiliation, relationship, connection. ❷ *thriving partnerships* COMPANY, firm, business, corporation, organization, association, consortium, syndicate.

parturition ▶ noun (*formal*) CHILDBIRTH, birth, delivery, labour; *dated* confinement; *poetic/literary* travail; *archaic* childbed, accouchement.

party ▶ noun ❶ *150 people attended the party* (SOCIAL) GATHERING, (social) function, get-together, celebration, reunion, festivity, jamboree, reception, at-home, soirée, social; dance, ball, ceilidh, frolic, carousal, carouse; *N. Amer.* fête, hoedown, shower, bake, cookout, levee; *Austral./NZ* corroboree; *informal* bash, shindig, rave, disco, do, shebang, bop, hop; *Brit. informal* rave-up, knees-up, beanfeast, beano, bunfight; *N. Amer. informal* blast, wingding, kegger; *Austral./NZ informal* shivoo, rage, ding, jollo, rort. ❷ *a party of British tourists* GROUP, company, body, gang, band, crowd, pack, contingent; *informal* bunch, crew, load. ❸ *the left-wing parties* FACTION, political party, group, grouping, cabal, junta, bloc, camp, caucus. ❹ *don't mention a certain party* PERSON, individual, somebody, someone.

▶ verb (*informal*) *let's party!* CELEBRATE, have fun, enjoy oneself, have a party, have a good/wild time, go on a spree, rave it up, carouse, make merry; *informal* go out on the town, paint the town red, whoop it up, let one's hair down, make whoopee, live it up, have a ball.

■ **be a party to** GET INVOLVED IN/WITH, be associated with, be a participant in.

parvenu ▶ noun UPSTART, social climber, arriviste.

pass[1] ▶ verb ❶ *the traffic passing through the village* GO, proceed, move, progress, make one's way, travel. ❷ *a car passed him* OVERTAKE, go past/by, pull ahead of, overhaul, leave behind. ❸ *time passed* ELAPSE, go by/past, advance, wear on, roll by, tick by. ❹ *he passed the time writing letters* OCCUPY, spend, fill, use (up), employ, while away. ❺ *pass me the salt* HAND (OVER), let someone have, give, reach. ❻ *he passed the ball back* KICK, hit, throw, lob. ❼ *her estate passed to her grandson* BE TRANSFERRED, go, be left, be bequeathed, be handed down/on, be passed on; *Law* devolve. ❽ *his death passed almost unnoticed* HAPPEN, occur, take place, come about, transpire; *poetic/literary* befall. ❾ *the storm passed* COME TO AN END, fade (away), blow over, run its course, die out, finish, end, cease. ❿ *God's peace passes all human understanding* SURPASS, exceed, transcend. ⓫ *he passed the exam* BE SUCCESSFUL IN, succeed in, gain a pass in, get through; *informal* sail through, scrape through. ⓬ *the Senate passed the bill* APPROVE, vote for, accept, ratify, adopt, agree to, authorize, endorse, legalize, enact; *informal* OK. ⓭ *she could not let that comment pass* GO (UNNOTICED), stand, go unremarked, go undisputed. ⓮ *we should not pass judgement* DECLARE, pronounce, utter, express, deliver, issue. ⓯ *passing urine* DISCHARGE, excrete, evacuate, expel, emit, release.
– OPPOSITES stop, fail, reject.

▶ noun ❶ *you must show your pass* PERMIT, warrant, authorization, licence. ❷ *a cross-field pass* KICK, hit, throw, shot.

■ **come to pass** (*poetic/literary*) HAPPEN, come about, occur, transpire, arise; *poetic/literary* befall.

■ **make a pass at** MAKE (SEXUAL) ADVANCES TO, proposition; *informal* come on to, make a play for; *N. Amer. informal* hit on, make time with, put the make on.

■ **pass away/on**. *See* DIE sense 1.

■ **pass as/for** BE MISTAKEN FOR, be taken for, be accepted as.

■ **pass off** ❶ *the rally passed off peacefully* TAKE PLACE, go off, happen, occur, be completed, turn out. ❷ *when the dizziness passed off he sat up* WEAR OFF, fade (away), pass, die down.

■ **pass someone off** MISREPRESENT, falsely represent; disguise.

■ **pass out** FAINT, lose consciousness, black out.

■ **pass something over** DISREGARD, overlook, ignore, pay no attention to, let pass, gloss over, take no notice of, pay no heed to, turn a blind eye to.

■ **pass something up** TURN DOWN, reject, refuse, decline, give up, forgo, let pass, miss (out on); *informal* give something a miss.

pass[2] ▶ noun *a pass through the mountains* ROUTE, way, road, passage, cut, gap; *N. Amer.* notch.

passable ▶ adjective ❶ *the beer was passable* ADEQUATE, all right, fairly good, acceptable, satisfactory, moderately good, not (too) bad, average, tolerable, fair; mediocre, middling, ordinary, indifferent, unremarkable, unexceptional; *informal* OK, so-so, nothing to write home about, no great shakes, not up to much; *NZ informal* half-pie. ❷ *the road is still passable* NAVIGABLE, traversable, negotiable, unblocked, unobstructed, open, clear.

passably ▶ adverb QUITE, rather, somewhat, fairly, reasonably, moderately, comparatively, relatively, tolerably; *informal* pretty.

passage ▶ noun ❶ *their passage through the country* TRANSIT, progress, passing, movement, motion, travelling. ❷ *the passage of time* PASSING, advance, course, march. ❸ *a passage from the embassy* SAFE CONDUCT, warrant, visa; admission, access. ❹ *the overnight passage* VOYAGE, crossing, trip, journey. ❺ *clearing a passage to the front door* WAY (THROUGH), route, path. ❻ *a passage to the kitchen. See* PASSAGEWAY sense 1. ❼ *a passage between the buildings. See* PASSAGEWAY sense 2. ❽ *the nasal passages* DUCT, orifice, opening, channel; inlet, outlet. ❾ *the passage to democracy* TRANSITION, development, progress, move, change, shift. ❿ *the passage of the bill*

ENACTMENT, passing, ratification, approval, adoption, authorization, legalization. ⓫ *a passage from 'Macbeth'* EXTRACT, excerpt, quotation, quote, citation, reading, piece, selection.

passageway ▶ noun ❶ *secret passageways* CORRIDOR, hall, passage, hallway, walkway, aisle. ❷ *a narrow passageway off the main street* ALLEY, alleyway, passage, lane, path, pathway, footpath, track, thoroughfare; *N. Amer.* areaway.

passé ▶ adjective. *See* OLD-FASHIONED.

passenger ▶ noun ❶ *rail passengers* TRAVELLER, commuter, fare payer. ❷ *we can't afford passengers* HANGER-ON, idler, parasite; *informal* freeloader.

passing ▶ adjective ❶ *of passing interest* FLEETING, transient, transitory, ephemeral, brief, short-lived, temporary, momentary; *poetic/literary* evanescent. ❷ *a passing glance* HASTY, rapid, hurried, brief, quick; cursory, superficial, casual, perfunctory.

▶ noun ❶ *the passing of time* PASSAGE, course, progress, advance. ❷ *Jack's passing* DEATH, demise, passing away/on, end, loss, quietus; *formal* decease. ❸ *the passing of the new bill* ENACTMENT, ratification, approval, adoption, authorization, legalization, endorsement.

■ **in passing** INCIDENTALLY, by the by/way, en passant.

passion ▶ noun ❶ *the passion of activists* FERVOUR, ardour, enthusiasm, eagerness, zeal, zealousness, vigour, fire, fieriness, energy, fervency, animation, spirit, spiritedness, fanaticism. ❷ *he worked himself up into a passion* (BLIND) RAGE, fit of anger/temper, temper, towering rage, tantrum, fury, frenzy; *Brit. informal* paddy. ❸ *hot with passion* LOVE, (sexual) desire, lust, ardour, infatuation, lasciviousness, lustfulness. ❹ *his passion for football* ENTHUSIASM, love, mania, fascination, obsession, fanaticism, fixation, compulsion, appetite, addiction; *informal* thing. ❺ *English literature is a passion with me* OBSESSION, preoccupation, craze, mania, hobby horse. ❻ *the Passion of Christ* CRUCIFIXION, suffering, agony, martyrdom.
– OPPOSITES apathy.

passionate ▶ adjective ❶ *a passionate entreaty* INTENSE, impassioned, ardent, fervent, vehement, fiery, heated, emotional, heartfelt, eager, excited, animated, spirited, energetic, fervid, frenzied, wild, consuming, violent; *poetic/literary* perfervid. ❷ *McGregor is passionate about sport* VERY KEEN, very enthusiastic, addicted; *informal* mad, crazy, hooked, nuts; *N. Amer. informal* nutso; *Austral./NZ informal* shook. ❸ *a passionate kiss* AMOROUS, ardent, hot-blooded, aroused, loving, sexy, sensual, erotic, lustful; *informal* steamy, hot, turned on. ❹ *a passionate woman* EXCITABLE, emotional, fiery, volatile, mercurial, quick-tempered, highly strung, impulsive, temperamental.
– OPPOSITES apathetic.

passionless ▶ adjective UNEMOTIONAL, cold, cold-blooded, emotionless, frigid, cool, unfeeling, unloving, unresponsive, undemonstrative, impassive.

passive ▶ adjective ❶ *a passive role* INACTIVE, non-active, non-participative, uninvolved. ❷ *passive victims* SUBMISSIVE, acquiescent, unresisting, unassertive, compliant, pliant, obedient, docile, tractable, malleable, pliable. ❸ *the woman's face was passive* EMOTIONLESS, impassive, unemotional, unmoved, dispassionate, passionless, detached, unresponsive, undemonstrative, apathetic, phlegmatic.
– OPPOSITES active.

passport ▶ noun ❶ TRAVEL PERMIT, (travel) papers, visa, laissez-passer. ❷ *qualifications are the passport to success* KEY, path, way, route, avenue, door, doorway.

password ▶ noun WORD OF IDENTIFICATION; *Military, archaic* watchword, countersign.

past ▶ adjective ❶ *memories of times past* GONE (BY), over (and done with), no more, done, bygone, former, (of) old, olden, long-ago; *poetic/literary* of yore. ❷ *the past few months* LAST, recent, preceding. ❸ *a past chairman* PREVIOUS, former, foregoing, erstwhile, one-time, sometime, ex-; *formal* quondam.
– OPPOSITES present, future.

▶ noun *details about her past* HISTORY, background, life (story).

▶ preposition ❶ *she walked past the cafe* IN FRONT OF, by. ❷ *he's past retirement age* BEYOND, in excess of.

▶ adverb *they hurried past* ALONG, by, on.

■ **in the past** FORMERLY, previously, in days/years/times gone by, in former times, in the (good) old days, in days of old, in olden times, once (upon a time); *poetic/literary* in days of yore, in yesteryear.

paste ▶ noun ❶ *blend the ingredients to a paste* PURÉE, pulp, mush, blend. ❷ *wallpaper paste* ADHESIVE, glue, gum, fixative; *N. Amer.* mucilage. ❸ *fish paste* SPREAD, pâté.

▶ verb *a notice was pasted on the door* GLUE, stick, gum, fix, affix.

pastel ▶ adjective PALE, soft, light, light-coloured, muted, subtle, subdued, soft-hued.
– OPPOSITES dark, bright.

pastiche ▶ noun ❶ *a pastiche of literary models* MIXTURE, blend, medley, melange, miscellany, mixed bag, pot-pourri, mix, compound, composite, collection, assortment, conglomeration, hotchpotch, jumble, ragbag; *N. Amer.* hodgepodge. ❷ *a pastiche of 18th-century style* IMITATION, parody; *informal* take-off.

pastille ▶ noun LOZENGE, sweet, drop; tablet, pill.

pastime ▶ noun HOBBY, leisure activity/pursuit, sport, game, recreation, amusement, diversion, entertainment, interest, sideline.

past master ▶ noun EXPERT, master, wizard, genius, old hand, veteran, maestro, connoisseur, authority, grandmaster; *informal* ace, pro, star, hotshot; *Brit. informal* dab hand; *N. Amer. informal* maven, crackerjack.

pastor ▶ noun PRIEST, minister (of religion), parson, clergyman, cleric, chaplain, padre, ecclesiastic, man of the cloth, churchman, vicar, rector, curate, preacher; *informal* reverend; *Austral. informal* josser.

pastoral ▶ adjective ❶ *a pastoral scene* RURAL, country, countryside, rustic, agricultural, bucolic; *poetic/literary* sylvan, Arcadian. ❷ *his pastoral duties* PRIESTLY, clerical, ecclesiastical, ministerial.
– OPPOSITES urban.

pastry ▶ noun ❶ *pastries for tea* TART, tartlet, pie, pasty, patty. ❷ *two layers of pastry* CRUST, piecrust, croute.

pasture ▶ noun GRAZING (LAND), grassland, grass, pastureland, pasturage, ley; meadow, field; *Austral./NZ* run; *poetic/literary* lea, mead, greensward.

pasty ▶ adjective PALE, pallid, wan, colourless, anaemic, ashen, white, grey, pasty-faced, washed out, sallow.

pat[1] ▶ verb *Brian patted her on the shoulder* TAP, slap lightly, clap, touch.
▶ noun ❶ *a pat on the cheek* TAP, light blow, clap, touch. ❷ *a pat of butter* PIECE, dab, lump, portion, knob, mass, gobbet, ball, curl.
■ **pat someone on the back** CONGRATULATE, praise, take one's hat off to; commend, compliment, applaud, acclaim.

pat[2] ▶ adjective *pat answers* GLIB, simplistic, facile, unconvincing.
▶ adverb *his reply came rather pat* OPPORTUNELY, conveniently, at just/exactly the right moment, expediently, favourably, appropriately, fittingly, auspiciously, providentially, felicitously, propitiously.
■ **off pat** WORD-PERFECT, by heart, by rote, by memory, parrot-fashion.
■ **get something off pat** MEMORIZE, commit to memory, remember, learn by heart, learn (by rote).

patch ▶ noun ❶ *a patch over one eye* COVER, eyepatch, covering, pad. ❷ *a reddish patch on her wrist* BLOTCH, mark, spot, smudge, speckle, smear, stain, streak, blemish; *informal* splodge, splotch. ❸ *a patch of ground* PLOT, area, piece, strip, tract, parcel; bed; *Brit.* allotment; *N. Amer.* lot. ❹ (*Brit. informal*) *they are going through a difficult patch* PERIOD, time, spell, phase, stretch; *Brit. informal* spot.
▶ verb *her jeans were neatly patched* MEND, repair, put a patch on, sew (up), stitch (up).
■ **patch something up** (*informal*) ❶ *the houses were being patched up* REPAIR, mend, fix hastily, do a makeshift repair on. ❷ *he's trying to patch things up with his wife* RECONCILE, make up, settle, remedy, put to rights, rectify, clear up, set right, make good, resolve, square.

patchwork ▶ noun ASSORTMENT, miscellany, mixture, melange, medley, blend, mixed bag, mix, collection, selection, assemblage, combination, pot-pourri, jumble, mishmash, ragbag, hotchpotch; *N. Amer.* hodgepodge.

patchy ▶ adjective ❶ *their teaching has been patchy* UNEVEN, bitty, varying, variable, intermittent, fitful, sporadic, erratic, irregular. ❷ *patchy evidence* FRAGMENTARY, inadequate, insufficient, rudimentary, limited, sketchy.
– OPPOSITES uniform, comprehensive.

patent ▶ noun *there is a patent on the chemical* COPYRIGHT, licence, legal protection, registered trademark.
▶ adjective ❶ *patent nonsense* OBVIOUS, clear, plain, evident, manifest, self-evident, transparent, overt, conspicuous, blatant, downright, barefaced, flagrant, undisguised, unconcealed, unmistakable. ❷ *patent medicines* PROPRIETARY, patented, licensed, branded.

paternal ▶ adjective ❶ *his face showed paternal concern* FATHERLY, fatherlike, patriarchal; protective, solicitous, compassionate, sympathetic. ❷ *his paternal grandfather* ON ONE'S FATHER'S SIDE, patrilineal.
– OPPOSITES maternal.

paternity ▶ noun FATHERHOOD.

path ▶ noun ❶ *a path down to the beach* FOOTPATH, pathway, footway, pavement, track, trail, trackway, bridleway, bridle path, lane, alley, alleyway, passage, passageway; cycle path/track; *N. Amer.* sidewalk, bikeway. ❷ *journalists blocked his path* ROUTE, way, course; direction, bearing, line; orbit, trajectory. ❸ *the best path towards a settlement* COURSE OF ACTION, route, road, avenue, line, approach, tack, strategy, tactic.

pathetic ▶ adjective ❶ *a pathetic groan* PITIFUL, pitiable, piteous, moving, touching, poignant, plaintive, distressing, upsetting, heartbreaking, heart-rending, harrowing, wretched, forlorn. ❷ (*informal*) *a pathetic excuse* FEEBLE, woeful, sorry, poor, pitiful, lamentable, deplorable, contemptible, inadequate, paltry, insufficient, insubstantial, unsatisfactory.

pathfinder ▶ noun PIONEER, ground-breaker, trailblazer, trendsetter, leader, torch-bearer, pacemaker.

pathological ▶ adjective ❶ *a pathological condition* MORBID, diseased. ❷ (*informal*) *a pathological liar* COMPULSIVE, obsessive, inveterate, habitual, persistent, chronic, hardened, confirmed.

pathos ▶ noun POIGNANCY, tragedy, sadness, pitifulness, piteousness, pitiableness.

patience ▶ noun ❶ *she tried everyone's patience* FORBEARANCE, tolerance, restraint, self-restraint, stoicism; calmness, composure, equanimity, serenity, tranquillity, imperturbability, understanding, indulgence. ❷ *a task requiring patience* PERSEVERANCE, persistence, endurance, tenacity, assiduity, application, staying power, doggedness, determination, resolve, resolution, resoluteness; *formal* pertinacity.

patient ▶ **adjective** ❶ *I must ask you to be patient* FORBEARING, uncomplaining, tolerant, resigned, stoical; calm, composed, even-tempered, imperturbable, unexcitable, accommodating, understanding, indulgent; *informal* unflappable, cool. ❷ *a good deal of patient work* PERSEVERING, persistent, tenacious, indefatigable, dogged, determined, resolved, resolute, single-minded; *formal* pertinacious.

▶ **noun** *a doctor's patient* SICK PERSON, case; invalid, convalescent, outpatient, inpatient.

patio ▶ **noun** TERRACE; courtyard, quadrangle, quad; *N. Amer.* sun deck.

patois ▶ **noun** VERNACULAR, (local) dialect, regional language; jargon, argot, cant; *informal* (local) lingo.

patriarch ▶ **noun** SENIOR FIGURE, father, paterfamilias, leader, elder.

patrician ▶ **noun** *the great patricians* ARISTOCRAT, grandee, noble, nobleman, noblewoman, lord, lady, peer, peeress.

▶ **adjective** *patrician families* ARISTOCRATIC, noble, titled, blue-blooded, high-born, upper-class, landowning; *informal* upper-crust; *archaic* gentle.

patrimony ▶ **noun** HERITAGE, inheritance, birthright; legacy, bequest, endowment, bequeathal; *Law, dated* hereditament.

patriot ▶ **noun** NATIONALIST, loyalist; chauvinist, jingoist, flag-waver.

patriotic ▶ **adjective** NATIONALIST, nationalistic, loyalist, loyal; chauvinistic, jingoistic, flag-waving.

– OPPOSITES traitorous.

patriotism ▶ **noun** NATIONALISM, patriotic sentiment, allegiance/loyalty to one's country; chauvinism, jingoism, flag-waving.

patrol ▶ **noun** ❶ *anti-poaching patrols* VIGIL, guard, watch, monitoring, policing, beat-pounding, patrolling; reconnoitre, surveillance; *informal* recce. ❷ *the patrol stopped a suspect* PATROLMAN, PATROLWOMAN, sentinel, sentry; scout, scouting party, task force.

▶ **verb** *a security guard was patrolling a housing estate* KEEP GUARD (ON), guard, keep watch (on); police, pound the beat (of), make the rounds (of); stand guard (over), keep a vigil (on), defend, safeguard.

patron ▶ **noun** ❶ *a patron of the arts* SPONSOR, backer, financier, benefactor, benefactress, contributor, subscriber, donor; philanthropist, promoter, friend, supporter; *informal* angel. ❷ *club patrons* CUSTOMER, client, frequenter, consumer, user, visitor, guest; *informal* regular.

patronage ▶ **noun** ❶ *art patronage* SPONSORSHIP, backing, funding, financing, promotion, assistance, support. ❷ *political patronage* POWER OF APPOINTMENT, favouritism, nepotism, preferential treatment. ❸ *a slight note of patronage* CONDESCENSION, patronizing, patronization, disdain, disrespect, scorn, contempt. ❹ *thank you for your patronage* CUSTOM, trade, business.

patronize ▶ **verb** ❶ *don't patronize me!* TREAT CONDESCENDINGLY, condescend to, look down on, talk down to, put down, treat like a child, treat with disdain. ❷ *they patronized local tradesmen* DO BUSINESS WITH, buy from, shop at, be a customer of, be a client of, deal with, trade with, frequent, support. ❸ *he patronized a national museum* SPONSOR, back, fund, finance, be a patron of, support, champion.

patronizing ▶ **adjective** CONDESCENDING, disdainful, supercilious, superior, imperious, scornful, contemptuous; *informal* uppity, high and mighty.

patter[1] ▶ **verb** ❶ *raindrops pattered against the window* GO PITTER-PATTER, tap, drum, beat, pound, rat-a-tat, go pit-a-pat, thrum. ❷ *she pattered across the floor* SCURRY, scuttle, skip, trip.

▶ **noun** *the patter of rain* PITTER-PATTER, tapping, pattering, drumming, beat, beating, pounding, rat-a-tat, pit-a-pat, clack, thrum, thrumming.

patter[2] ▶ **noun** ❶ *this witty patter* PRATTLE, prating, blather, blither, drivel, chatter, jabber, babble; *informal* yabbering, yatter; *archaic* twaddle. ❷ *the salesmen's patter* (SALES) PITCH, sales talk; *informal* line. ❸ *the local patter* SPEECH, language, parlance, dialect; *informal* lingo.

▶ **verb** *she pattered on incessantly* PRATTLE, prate, blather, blither, drivel, chatter, jabber, babble; *informal* yabber, yatter; *Brit. informal* rabbit, witter.

pattern ▶ **noun** ❶ *the pattern on the wallpaper* DESIGN, decoration, motif, marking, ornament, ornamentation. ❷ *working patterns* SYSTEM, order, arrangement, form, method, structure, scheme, plan, format, framework. ❸ *this would set the pattern for a generation* MODEL, example, criterion, standard, basis, point of reference, gauge, norm, yardstick, touchstone, benchmark; prototype, archetype, blueprint. ❹ *textile patterns* SAMPLE, specimen, swatch.

▶ **verb** *someone else is patterning my life* SHAPE, influence, model, fashion, mould, style, determine, control.

patterned ▶ **adjective** DECORATED, ornamented, fancy, adorned, embellished.

– OPPOSITES plain.

paucity ▶ **noun** SCARCITY, sparseness, sparsity, dearth, shortage, poverty, insufficiency, deficiency, lack, want; *formal* exiguity.

– OPPOSITES abundance.

paunch ▶ **noun** POT BELLY, beer belly; *informal* beer gut, pot; *dated* corporation.

pauper ▶ **noun** POOR PERSON, indigent, down-and-out; *informal* have-not.

pause ▶ **noun** *a pause in the conversation* STOP, cessation, break, halt, interruption, check, lull, respite, breathing space, discontinuation, hiatus, gap, interlude; adjournment, suspension, rest, wait, hesitation; *informal* let-up, breather.
▶ **verb** *Hannah paused for a moment* STOP, cease, halt, discontinue, break off, take a break; adjourn, rest, wait, hesitate, falter, waver; *informal* take a breather.

pave ▶ **verb** *the yard was paved* TILE, surface, flag.
■ **pave the way for** PREPARE (THE WAY) FOR, make preparations for, get ready for, lay the foundations for, herald, precede.

pavement ▶ **noun** FOOTPATH, walkway, footway; *N. Amer.* sidewalk.

paw ▶ **noun** FOOT, forepaw, hind paw.
▶ **verb** ❶ *their offspring were pawing each other* HANDLE ROUGHLY, pull, grab, maul, manhandle. ❷ *some Casanova tried to paw her* FONDLE, feel, maul, molest; *informal* grope, feel up, touch up, goose.

pawn[1] ▶ **verb** *he pawned his watch* PLEDGE, put in pawn, give as security, use as collateral; *informal* hock, put in hock.

pawn[2] ▶ **noun** *a pawn in the battle for the throne* PUPPET, dupe, hostage, tool, cat's paw, instrument.

pay ▶ **verb** ❶ *I must pay him for his work* REWARD, reimburse, recompense, give payment to, remunerate. ❷ *you must pay a few more pounds* SPEND, expend, pay out, dish out, disburse; *informal* lay out, shell out, fork out, cough up; *N. Amer. informal* ante up, pony up. ❸ *he paid his debts* DISCHARGE, settle, pay off, clear, liquidate. ❹ *hard work will pay dividends* YIELD, return, produce. ❺ *he made the buses pay* BE PROFITABLE, make money, make a profit. ❻ *it may pay you to be early* BE ADVANTAGEOUS TO, benefit, be of advantage to, be beneficial to. ❼ *paying compliments* BESTOW, grant, give, offer. ❽ *he will pay for his mistakes* SUFFER (THE CONSEQUENCES), be punished, atone, pay the penalty/price.
▶ **noun** *equal pay for women* SALARY, wages, payment; earnings, remuneration, reimbursement, income, revenue; *formal* emolument(s).
■ **pay someone back/out** GET ONE'S REVENGE ON, be revenged on, avenge oneself on, get back at, get even with, settle accounts with, pay someone out, exact retribution on.
■ **pay something back** REPAY, pay off, give back, return, reimburse, refund.
■ **pay for** DEFRAY THE COST OF, settle up for, finance, fund; treat someone to; *informal* foot the bill for, shell out for, fork out for, cough up for; *N. Amer. informal* ante up for, pony up for.
■ **pay someone off** ❶ *Tim paid off the driver* PAY WHAT ONE OWES, discharge. ❷ *paying off the police* BRIBE, suborn, buy (off); *informal* grease someone's palm.
■ **pay something off** PAY (IN FULL), settle, discharge, clear, liquidate.
■ **pay off** (*informal*) MEET WITH SUCCESS, be successful, be effective, get results.
■ **pay something out** SPEND, expend, pay, dish out, put up, part with, hand over; *informal* shell out, fork out/up, lay out, cough up.
■ **pay up** MAKE PAYMENT, settle up, pay (in full); *informal* cough up.

payable ▶ **adjective** DUE, owed, owing, outstanding, unpaid, overdue, in arrears; *N. Amer.* delinquent.

payment ▶ **noun** ❶ *discounts for early payment* REMITTANCE, settlement, discharge, clearance, liquidation. ❷ *monthly payments* INSTALMENT, premium. ❸ *extra payment for good performance* SALARY, wages, pay, earnings, fee(s), remuneration, reimbursement, income; *formal* emolument(s).

pay-off ▶ **noun** (*informal*) ❶ *the lure of enormous pay-offs* PAYMENT, payout, reward; bribe, inducement, 'incentive'; *N. Amer.* payola; *informal* kickback, sweetener, backhander; *Austral. informal* sling. ❷ *a pay-off of £160,000* RETURN (ON INVESTMENT), yield, payback, profit, gain, dividend. ❸ *a dramatic pay-off* OUTCOME, denouement, culmination, conclusion, development, result.

peace ▶ **noun** ❶ *can't a man get any peace around here?* TRANQUILLITY, calm, restfulness, peace and quiet, peacefulness, quiet, quietness; privacy, solitude. ❷ *peace of mind* SERENITY, peacefulness, tranquillity, equanimity, calm, calmness, composure, ease, contentment, contentedness. ❸ *we pray for peace* LAW AND ORDER, lawfulness, order, peacefulness, peaceableness, harmony, non-violence; *formal* concord. ❹ *a lasting peace* TREATY, truce, ceasefire, armistice, cessation/suspension of hostilities.
– OPPOSITES noise, war.

peaceable ▶ **adjective** ❶ *a peaceable man* PEACE-LOVING, non-violent, non-aggressive, easy-going, placid, gentle, inoffensive, good-natured, even-tempered, amiable, amicable, friendly, affable, genial, pacific, dovelike, dovish; *formal* irenic. ❷ *a peaceable society* PEACEFUL, strife-free, harmonious; law-abiding, disciplined, orderly, civilized.
– OPPOSITES aggressive.

peaceful ▶ **adjective** ❶ *everything was quiet and peaceful* TRANQUIL, calm, restful, quiet, still, relaxing, soothing, undisturbed, untroubled, private, secluded. ❷ *his peaceful mood* SERENE, calm, tranquil, composed, placid, at ease, untroubled, unworried, content. ❸ *peaceful relations* HARMONIOUS, at peace, peaceable, on good terms, amicable, friendly, cordial, non-violent.
– OPPOSITES noisy, agitated, hostile.

peacemaker ▶ **noun** ARBITRATOR, arbiter, mediator, negotiator, conciliator, go-between, intermediary, pacifier, appeaser, peace-monger, pacifist, peace-lover, dove; *informal* peacenik.

peak ▶ **noun** ❶ *the peaks of the mountains* SUMMIT, top, crest, pinnacle, apex, crown, cap. ❷ *the highest peak* MOUNTAIN, hill, height, mount, alp; *Scottish* ben, Munro. ❸ *the peak of a cap* BRIM, visor. ❹ *the peak of his career* HEIGHT, high point/spot, pinnacle, summit, top, climax, culmination, apex, zenith, crowning point, acme, apogee, prime, heyday.
▶ **verb** *Labour support has peaked* REACH ITS HEIGHT, climax, reach a climax, come to a head.
▶ **adjective** *peak loads* MAXIMUM, top, greatest, highest; ultimate, best, optimum.

peaky ▶ **adjective** PALE, pasty, wan, drained, washed out, drawn, pallid, anaemic, ashen, grey, pinched, sickly, sallow; ill, unwell, poorly, indisposed, run down; *Brit.* off (colour); *informal* under the weather, rough, lousy, seedy; *Brit. informal* grotty, ropy.

peal ▶ **noun** ❶ *a peal of bells* CHIME, carillon, ring, ringing, tintinnabulation. ❷ *peals of laughter* SHRIEK, shout, scream, howl, gale, fit, roar, hoot. ❸ *a peal of thunder* RUMBLE, roar, boom, crash, clap, crack.
▶ **verb** ❶ *the bell pealed* RING (OUT), chime (out), clang, sound, ding, jingle. ❷ *the thunder pealed* RUMBLE, roar, boom, crash, resound.

peasant ▶ **noun** ❶ *peasants working the land* AGRICULTURAL WORKER, small farmer, rustic, swain, villein, serf. ❷ (*informal*) *you peasants!* *See* BOOR.

peccadillo ▶ **noun** MISDEMEANOUR, petty offence, indiscretion, lapse, misdeed.

peck ▶ **verb** ❶ *the cockerel pecked my heel* BITE, nip, strike, hit, tap, rap, jab. ❷ *he pecked her on the cheek* KISS, give someone a peck. ❸ (*informal*) *the old lady pecked at her food* NIBBLE, pick at, take very small bites from, toy with, play with.

peculiar ▶ **adjective** ❶ *something peculiar began to happen* STRANGE, unusual, odd, funny, curious, bizarre, weird, queer, unexpected, unfamiliar, abnormal, atypical, anomalous, out of the ordinary; exceptional, extraordinary, remarkable; puzzling, mystifying, mysterious, perplexing, baffling; suspicious, eerie, unnatural; *informal* fishy, creepy, spooky. ❷ *peculiar behaviour* BIZARRE, eccentric, strange, odd, weird, queer, funny, unusual, abnormal, idiosyncratic, unconventional, outlandish, quirky; *informal* wacky, freaky, oddball, offbeat, off the wall; *N. Amer. informal* wacko. ❸ (*informal*) *I feel a bit peculiar. See* UNWELL. ❹ *mannerisms peculiar to the islanders* CHARACTERISTIC OF, typical of, representative of, indicative of, suggestive of, exclusive to. ❺ *their own peculiar contribution* DISTINCTIVE, characteristic, distinct, individual, special, unique, personal.
– OPPOSITES ordinary.

peculiarity ▶ **noun** ❶ *a legal peculiarity* ODDITY, anomaly, abnormality. ❷ *a physical peculiarity* IDIOSYNCRASY, mannerism, quirk, foible. ❸ *one of the peculiarities of the city* CHARACTERISTIC, feature, (essential) quality, property, trait, attribute, hallmark, trademark. ❹ *the peculiarity of this notion* STRANGENESS, oddness, bizarreness, weirdness, queerness, unexpectedness, unfamiliarity, anomalousness, incongruity. ❺ *there is a certain peculiarity about her appearance* OUTLANDISHNESS, bizarreness, unconventionality, idiosyncrasy, weirdness, oddness, eccentricity, unusualness, abnormality, queerness, strangeness, quirkiness; *informal* wackiness, freakiness.

pecuniary ▶ **adjective** FINANCIAL, monetary, money, fiscal, economic.

pedagogic ▶ **adjective** EDUCATIONAL, educative, pedagogical, teaching, instructional, instructive, didactic; academic, scholastic.

pedagogue (*formal*) ▶ **noun** TEACHER, schoolteacher, schoolmaster, schoolmistress, master, mistress, tutor; lecturer, academic, don, professor, instructor, educator, educationalist, educationist; *Austral./NZ informal* chalkie.

pedant ▶ **noun** DOGMATIST, purist, literalist, formalist, doctrinaire, perfectionist; quibbler, hair-splitter, casuist, sophist; *informal* nit-picker.

pedantic ▶ **adjective** OVER-SCRUPULOUS, scrupulous, precise, exact, perfectionist, punctilious, meticulous, fussy, fastidious, finical, finicky; dogmatic, purist, literalist, literalistic, formalist; casuistic, casuistical, sophistic, sophistical; captious, hair-splitting, quibbling; *informal* nit-picking, pernickety; *archaic* overnice.

pedantry ▶ **noun** DOGMATISM, purism, literalism, formalism; over-scrupulousness, scrupulousness, perfectionism, fastidiousness, punctiliousness, meticulousness; captiousness, quibbling, hair-splitting, casuistry, sophistry; *informal* nit-picking.

peddle ▶ **verb** ❶ *they are peddling water filters* SELL (FROM DOOR TO DOOR), hawk, tout, vend; trade (in), deal in, traffic in. ❷ *peddling unorthodox views* ADVOCATE, champion, preach, put forward, proclaim, propound, promote.

pedestal ▶ **noun** *a bust on a pedestal* PLINTH, base, support, mounting, stand, foundation, pillar, column, pier; *Architecture* socle.
■ **put someone on a pedestal** IDEALIZE, lionize, look up to, respect, hold in high regard, think highly of, admire, esteem, revere, worship.

pedestrian ▶ **noun** *accidents involving pedestrians* WALKER, person on foot.
– OPPOSITES driver.
▶ **adjective** *pedestrian lives* DULL, boring, tedious, monotonous, uneventful, unremarkable, tiresome, wearisome, uninspired, unimaginative, unexciting, uninteresting; unvarying, unvaried, repetitive, routine, commonplace, workaday; ordinary, everyday, run-of-the-mill, mundane, humdrum; *informal* bog-standard, (plain) vanilla; *Brit. informal* common or garden.
– OPPOSITES exciting.

pedigree ▶ **noun** *a long pedigree* ANCESTRY, descent, lineage, line (of descent), genealogy, family tree, extraction, derivation, origin(s), heritage, parentage, bloodline, background, roots.

▶ **adjective** *a pedigree cat* PURE-BRED, thoroughbred, pure-blooded.

pedlar ▶ **noun** ❶ *pedlars of watches* TRAVELLING SALESMAN, door-to-door salesman, huckster; street trader, hawker; *Brit. informal* fly-pitcher; *archaic* chapman, packman. ❷ *a drug pedlar* TRAFFICKER, dealer; *informal* pusher.

peek ▶ **verb** ❶ *they peeked from behind the curtains* (HAVE A) PEEP, have a peek, spy, take a sly/stealthy look, sneak a look; *informal* take a gander, have a squint; *Brit. informal* have a dekko, have/take a butcher's, take a shufti. ❷ *the deer's antlers peeked out from the trees* APPEAR (SLOWLY/PARTLY), show, come into view/sight, become visible, emerge, peep (out).

▶ **noun** *a peek at the map* SECRET LOOK, sly look, stealthy look, sneaky look, peep, glance, glimpse, hurried/quick look; *informal* gander, squint; *Brit. informal* dekko, butcher's, shufti.

peel ▶ **verb** ❶ *peel and core the fruit* PARE, skin, take the skin/rind off; hull, shell, husk, shuck; *technical* decorticate. ❷ *use a long knife to peel the veneer* TRIM (OFF), peel off, pare, strip (off), shave (off), remove. ❸ *the wallpaper was peeling* FLAKE (OFF), peel off, come off in layers/strips.

▶ **noun** *orange peel* RIND, skin, covering, zest; hull, pod, integument, shuck.

■ **keep one's eyes peeled** KEEP A (SHARP) LOOKOUT, look out, keep one's eyes open, keep watch, be watchful, be alert, be on the alert, be on the qui vive, be on guard; *Brit.* keep one's eyes skinned.

■ **peel something off** (*Brit. informal*) TAKE OFF, strip off, remove.

peep[1] ▶ **verb** ❶ *I peeped through the keyhole* LOOK QUICKLY, cast a brief look, take a secret look, sneak a look, (have a) peek, glance; *informal* take a gander, have a squint; *Brit. informal* have a dekko, have/take a butcher's, take a shufti. ❷ *the moon peeped through the clouds* APPEAR (SLOWLY/PARTLY), show, come into view/sight, become visible, emerge, peek, peer out.

▶ **noun** *I'll just take a peep at it* QUICK LOOK, brief look, sneaky look, peek, glance; *informal* gander, squint; *Brit. informal* dekko, butcher's, shufti.

peep[2] ▶ **noun** ❶ *I heard a quiet peep* CHEEP, chirp, chirrup, tweet, twitter, chirr, warble. ❷ *there's been not a peep out of the children* SOUND, noise, cry, word. ❸ *the painting was sold without a peep* COMPLAINT, grumble, mutter, murmur, grouse, objection, protest, protestation; *informal* moan, gripe, grouch.

▶ **verb** *the fax peeped* CHEEP, chirp, chirrup, tweet, twitter, chirr.

peephole ▶ **noun** OPENING, gap, cleft, spyhole, slit, crack, chink, keyhole, squint, judas (hole).

peer[1] ▶ **verb** *he peered at the manuscript* LOOK CLOSELY, try to see, narrow one's eyes, screw up one's eyes, squint.

peer[2] ▶ **noun** ❶ *hereditary peers* ARISTOCRAT, lord, lady, peer of the realm, peeress, noble, nobleman, noblewoman, titled man/woman, patrician. ❷ *his academic peers* EQUAL, coequal, fellow, confrère; contemporary; *formal* compeer.

peerage ▶ **noun** ARISTOCRACY, nobility, peers and peeresses, lords and ladies, patriciate; the House of Lords, the Lords.

peerless ▶ **adjective** INCOMPARABLE, matchless, unrivalled, inimitable, beyond compare/comparison, unparalleled, unequalled, without equal, second to none, unsurpassed, unsurpassable, nonpareil; unique, consummate, perfect, rare, transcendent, surpassing; *formal* unexampled.

peeve ▶ **verb** (*informal*) IRRITATE, annoy, vex, anger, exasperate, irk, gall, pique, nettle, put out, get on someone's nerves, try someone's patience, ruffle someone's feathers; *Brit.* rub up the wrong way; *informal* aggravate, rile, needle, get to, bug, hack off, get someone's goat, get/put someone's back up, get up someone's nose, give someone the hump; *Brit. informal* wind up, get on someone's wick; *N. Amer. informal* tee off, tick off.

peeved ▶ **adjective** (*informal*) IRRITATED, annoyed, cross, angry, vexed, displeased, disgruntled, indignant, exasperated, galled, irked, put out, aggrieved, offended, affronted, piqued, nettled, in high dudgeon; *informal* aggravated, miffed, riled, hacked off, browned off; *Brit. informal* narked, cheesed off, brassed off; *N. Amer. informal* teed off, ticked off, sore.

peevish ▶ **adjective** IRRITABLE, fractious, fretful, cross, petulant, querulous, pettish, crabby, crotchety, cantankerous, curmudgeonly, sullen, grumpy, bad-tempered, short-tempered, touchy, testy, tetchy, snappish, irascible, waspish, prickly, crusty, dyspeptic, splenetic, choleric; *N. English* mardy; *Brit. informal* ratty, like a bear with a sore head; *N. Amer. informal* cranky, ornery.

– OPPOSITES good-humoured.

peg ▶ **noun** PIN, nail, dowel, skewer, spike, rivet, brad, screw, bolt, hook, spigot; *Mountaineering* piton; *Golf* tee.

▶ **verb** ❶ *the flysheet is pegged to the ground* FIX, pin, attach, fasten, secure, make fast. ❷ *we decided to peg our prices* HOLD DOWN, keep down, fix, set, hold, freeze.

■ **peg away** (*informal*) WORK HARD, slog away, plod away, hammer away, grind away, slave away, exert oneself; persevere, persist, keep at it; *informal* beaver away, plug away, stick at it, soldier on; *Brit. informal* graft away.

■ **take someone down a peg or two** HUMBLE, humiliate, mortify, bring down, shame, embarrass, abash, put someone in their place, chasten, subdue, squash, deflate, make someone eat humble pie; *informal* show up, settle someone's hash, cut down to size; *N. Amer. informal* make someone eat crow.

pejorative ▶ **adjective** DISPARAGING, derogatory, denigratory, deprecatory, defamatory, slanderous, libellous, abusive, insulting, slighting; *informal* bitchy.
– OPPOSITES complimentary.

pellet ▶ **noun** ❶ *a pellet of mud* LITTLE BALL, little piece. ❷ *pellet wounds* BULLET, shot, lead shot, buckshot. ❸ *rabbit pellets* EXCREMENT, excreta, droppings, faeces, dung.

pell-mell ▶ **adverb** ❶ *men streamed pell-mell from the building* HELTER-SKELTER, headlong, (at) full tilt, hotfoot, post-haste, hurriedly, hastily, recklessly, precipitately; *archaic* hurry-scurry. ❷ *the sacks' contents were thrown pell-mell to the ground* UNTIDILY, anyhow, in disarray, in a mess, in a muddle; *informal* all over the place, every which way, any old how; *Brit. informal* all over the shop; *N. Amer. informal* all over the map, all over the lot.

pellucid ▶ **adjective** ❶ *the pellucid waters* TRANSLUCENT, transparent, clear, crystal clear, crystalline, glassy, limpid, unclouded. ❷ *pellucid prose* LUCID, limpid, clear, crystal clear, articulate; coherent, comprehensible, understandable, intelligible, straightforward, simple, well constructed; *formal* perspicuous.

pelt[1] ▶ **verb** ❶ *they pelted him with snowballs* BOMBARD, shower, attack, assail, pepper. ❷ *rain was pelting down* POUR DOWN, teem down, stream down, tip down, rain cats and dogs, rain hard; *Brit. informal* bucket down, come down in stair rods. ❸ (*informal*) *they pelted into the factory* DASH, run, race, rush, sprint, bolt, dart, career, charge, shoot, hurtle, hare, fly, speed, zoom, streak; hasten, hurry; *informal* tear, belt, hotfoot it, scoot, leg it, go like a bat out of hell; *Brit. informal* bomb; *N. Amer. informal* hightail it.

pelt[2] ▶ **noun** *an animal's pelt* SKIN, hide, fleece, coat, fur; *archaic* fell.

pen[1] ▶ **noun** *you'll need a pen and paper* fountain pen, ballpoint (pen), rollerball; fibre tip (pen), felt tip (pen), highlighter, marker pen; *Brit. trademark* biro.
▶ **verb** *he penned a number of articles* WRITE, compose, draft, dash off; write down, jot down, set down, take down, scribble.

pen[2] ▶ **noun** *a sheep pen* ENCLOSURE, fold, sheepfold, pound, compound, stockade; sty, coop; *N. Amer.* corral.
▶ **verb** *the hostages had been penned up in a basement* CONFINE, coop (up), cage, shut in, box up/in, lock up/in, trap, imprison, incarcerate, immure.

penal ▶ **adjective** ❶ *a penal institution* DISCIPLINARY, punitive, corrective, correctional. ❷ *penal rates of interest* EXORBITANT, extortionate, excessive, outrageous, preposterous, unreasonable, inflated, sky-high.

penalize ▶ **verb** ❶ *if you break the rules you will be penalized* PUNISH, discipline, inflict a penalty on. ❷ *people with certain medical positions would be penalized* HANDICAP, disadvantage, put at a disadvantage, cause to suffer.
– OPPOSITES reward.

penalty ▶ **noun** ❶ *increased penalties for dumping oil at sea* PUNISHMENT, sanction, punitive action, retribution; fine, forfeit, sentence; penance; *formal* mulct. ❷ *the penalties of old age* DISADVANTAGE, difficulty, drawback, handicap, downside, minus; trial, tribulation, bane, affliction, burden, trouble.
– OPPOSITES reward.

penance ▶ **noun** ATONEMENT, expiation, self-punishment, self-mortification, self-abasement, amends; punishment, penalty.

penchant ▶ **noun** LIKING, fondness, preference, taste, relish, appetite, partiality, soft spot, love, passion, desire, fancy, whim, weakness, inclination, bent, bias, proclivity, predilection, predisposition.

pencil ▶ **noun** ❶ *a sharpened pencil* lead pencil, propelling pencil. ❷ *a pencil of light* BEAM, ray, shaft, finger, gleam.
▶ **verb** ❶ *he pencilled his name inside the cover* WRITE, write down, jot down, scribble, note, take down. ❷ *pencil a line along the top of the moulding* DRAW, trace, sketch.

pendant ▶ **noun** NECKLACE, locket, medallion.

pendent ▶ **adjective** HANGING, suspended, dangling, pendulous, pensile, pendant, drooping, droopy, trailing.

pending ▶ **adjective** ❶ *nine cases were still pending* UNRESOLVED, undecided, unsettled, awaiting decision/action, undetermined, open, hanging fire, (up) in the air, ongoing, outstanding, not done, unfinished, incomplete; *informal* on the back burner. ❷ *with a general election pending* IMMINENT, impending, about to happen, forthcoming, upcoming, on the way, coming, approaching, looming, gathering, near, nearing, close, close at hand, in the offing, to come.
▶ **preposition** *they were released on bail pending an appeal* AWAITING, until, till, until there is/are.

pendulous ▶ **adjective** DROOPING, dangling, trailing, droopy, sagging, saggy, floppy; hanging, pendent, pensile.

penetrable ▶ **adjective** ❶ *a penetrable subsoil* PERMEABLE, pervious, porous. ❷ *books which are barely penetrable to anyone under 50* UNDERSTANDABLE, fathomable, comprehensible, intelligible.

penetrate ▶ **verb** ❶ *the knife penetrated his lungs* PIERCE, puncture, make a hole in, perforate, stab, prick, gore, spike. ❷ *they penetrated the enemy territory* INFILTRATE, slip into, sneak into, insinuate oneself into. ❸ *fear penetrated her bones* PERMEATE, pervade, fill, spread throughout, suffuse, seep through. ❹ *he* *seemed to have penetrated the mysteries of nature* UNDERSTAND, comprehend, apprehend, fathom, grasp, perceive, discern, get to the bottom of, solve, resolve, make sense of, interpret, puzzle out, work out, unravel, decipher, make head or tail of; *informal* crack, get, figure out; *Brit. informal* suss out. ❺ *his words finally penetrated* REGISTER, sink in, be understood, be comprehended, become clear, fall into place; *informal* click.

penetrating ▶ adjective ❶ *a penetrating wind* PIERCING, cutting, biting, stinging, keen, sharp, harsh, raw, freezing, chill, wintry, cold. ❷ *a penetrating voice* SHRILL, strident, piercing, carrying, loud, high, high-pitched, piping, ear-splitting, screechy, intrusive. ❸ *a penetrating smell* PUNGENT, pervasive, strong, powerful, sharp, acrid; heady, aromatic. ❹ *her penetrating gaze* OBSERVANT, searching, intent, alert, shrewd, perceptive, probing, piercing, sharp, keen. ❺ *a penetrating analysis* PERCEPTIVE, insightful, keen, sharp, sharp-witted, intelligent, clever, smart, incisive, piercing, razor-edged, trenchant, astute, shrewd, clear, acute, percipient, perspicacious, discerning, sensitive, thoughtful, deep, profound.
– OPPOSITES mild, soft.

penetration ▶ noun ❶ *skin penetration by infective larvae* PERFORATION, piercing, puncturing, puncture, stabbing, pricking. ❷ *remarks of great penetration* INSIGHT, discernment, perception, perceptiveness, intelligence, sharp-wittedness, cleverness, incisiveness, keenness, sharpness, trenchancy, astuteness, shrewdness, acuteness, clarity, acuity, percipience, perspicacity, discrimination, sensitivity, thoughtfulness, profundity; *formal* perspicuity.

peninsula ▶ noun CAPE, promontory, point, head, headland, foreland, ness, horn, bill, bluff, mull.

penitence ▶ noun REPENTANCE, contrition, regret, remorse, remorsefulness, ruefulness, sorrow, sorrowfulness, pangs of conscience, self-reproach, shame, guilt, compunction; *archaic* rue.

penitent ▶ adjective REPENTANT, contrite, remorseful, sorry, apologetic, regretful, conscience-stricken, rueful, ashamed, shamefaced, abject, in sackcloth and ashes.
– OPPOSITES unrepentant.

pen name ▶ noun PSEUDONYM, nom de plume, assumed name, alias, professional name.

pennant ▶ noun FLAG, standard, ensign, colour(s), banner, banderole, guidon; *Brit.* pendant; *Nautical* burgee.

penniless ▶ adjective DESTITUTE, poverty-stricken, impoverished, poor, indigent, impecunious, in penury, moneyless, without a sou, necessitous, needy, on one's beam-ends; bankrupt, insolvent; *Brit.* on the breadline, without a penny (to one's name); *informal* (flat) broke, cleaned out, strapped for cash, on one's uppers, without a brass farthing, bust; *Brit. informal* stony broke, skint; *N. Amer. informal* stone broke; *formal* penurious.
– OPPOSITES wealthy.

penny

■ **a pretty penny** (*informal*) A LOT OF MONEY, millions, billions, a king's ransom; *informal* a (small) fortune, lots/pots/heaps of money, a mint, a killing, a bundle, a packet, a tidy sum, big money, telephone numbers, an arm and a leg; *Brit. informal* a bomb, loadsamoney; *N. Amer. informal* big bucks; *Austral. informal* big bickies, motser, motza.

■ **two/ten a penny** (*informal*) NUMEROUS, abundant, thick on the ground, plentiful; in large numbers, by the yard; very common, ubiquitous; *N. Amer. informal* a dime a dozen.

penny-pincher ▶ noun MISER, Scrooge, niggard; *informal* skinflint, meanie, money-grubber, cheapskate; *N. Amer. informal* tightwad.
– OPPOSITES spendthrift.

penny-pinching ▶ adjective MEAN, miserly, niggardly, parsimonious, close-fisted, cheese-paring, grasping, Scrooge-like; *informal* stingy, mingy, tight, tight-fisted, money-grubbing; *formal* penurious; *archaic* near.
– OPPOSITES generous.

pension ▶ noun OLD-AGE PENSION, retirement pension, regular payment, superannuation; allowance, benefit, support, welfare.

pensioner ▶ noun RETIRED PERSON, old-age pensioner, OAP, senior citizen; *N. Amer.* senior, retiree.

pensive ▶ adjective THOUGHTFUL, reflective, contemplative, musing, meditative, introspective, ruminative, absorbed, preoccupied, deep/lost in thought, in a brown study, brooding; *formal* cogitative.

pent-up ▶ adjective REPRESSED, suppressed, stifled, smothered, restrained, confined, bottled up, held in/back, kept in check, curbed, bridled.

penurious ▶ adjective (*formal*) ❶ *a penurious student* POOR, as poor as a church mouse, poverty-stricken, destitute, necessitous, impecunious, impoverished, indigent, needy, in need/want, badly off, in reduced/straitened circumstances, hard up, on one's beam-ends, unable to make ends meet, penniless, without a sou; *Brit.* on the breadline, without a penny (to one's name); *informal* (flat) broke, strapped for cash, on one's uppers; *Brit. informal* stony broke, skint, without a brass farthing, in Queer Street; *N. Amer. informal* stone broke. ❷ *a penurious old skinflint* MEAN, miserly, niggardly, parsimonious, penny-pinching, close-fisted, cheese-paring, Scrooge-like; *informal* stingy, mingy, tight, tight-fisted, money-grubbing; *archaic* near.
– OPPOSITES wealthy, generous.

penury ▶ **noun** EXTREME POVERTY, destitution, pennilessness, impecuniousness, impoverishment, indigence, pauperism, privation, beggary.

people ▶ **noun** ❶ *crowds of people* HUMAN BEINGS, persons, individuals, humans, mortals, (living) souls, personages, {men, women, and children}; *informal* folk, peeps. ❷ *the British people* CITIZENS, subjects, electors, voters, taxpayers, residents, inhabitants, (general) public, citizenry, nation, population, populace. ❸ *a man of the people* THE COMMON PEOPLE, the proletariat, the masses, the populace, the rank and file, the commonality, the commonalty, the third estate, the plebeians; *derogatory* the hoi polloi, the common herd, the great unwashed, the proles, the plebs. ❹ *her people don't live far away* FAMILY, parents, relatives, relations, folk, kinsmen, kin, kith and kin, kinsfolk, flesh and blood, nearest and dearest; *informal* folks. ❺ *the peoples of Africa* RACE, (ethnic) group, tribe, clan.
▶ **verb** *the Indians who once peopled Newfoundland* POPULATE, settle (in), colonize, inhabit, live in, occupy; *formal* reside in, be domiciled in, dwell in.

pep (*informal*) ▶ **noun** *a performance full of pep* DYNAMISM, life, energy, spirit, liveliness, animation, bounce, sparkle, effervescence, verve, spiritedness, ebullience, high spirits, enthusiasm, vitality, vivacity, fire, dash, panache, elan, zest, exuberance, vigour, gusto, brio; *informal* feistiness, get-up-and-go, oomph, pizzazz, vim.
■ **pep something up** ENLIVEN, animate, liven up, put some/new life into, invigorate, vitalize, revitalize, vivify, ginger up, energize, galvanize, put some spark into, stimulate, get something going, perk up; brighten up, cheer up; *informal* buck up.

pepper ▶ **verb** ❶ *salt and pepper the potatoes* ADD PEPPER TO, season, flavour. ❷ *stars peppered the desert skies* SPRINKLE, fleck, dot, spot, stipple; cover, fill. ❸ *another burst of bullets peppered the tank* BOMBARD, pelt, shower, rain down on, attack, assail, batter, strafe, rake, blitz, hit.

peppery ▶ **adjective** ❶ *a peppery sauce* SPICY, spiced, peppered, hot, highly seasoned, piquant, pungent, sharp. ❷ *a peppery old man* IRRITABLE, cantankerous, irascible, bad-tempered, ill-tempered, grumpy, grouchy, crotchety, short-tempered, tetchy, testy, crusty, crabby, curmudgeonly, peevish, cross, fractious, pettish, prickly, waspish; *informal* snappish, snappy, chippy; *N. Amer. informal* cranky, ornery.
– OPPOSITES mild, bland, affable.

perceive ▶ **verb** ❶ *I immediately perceived the flaws in her story* DISCERN, recognize, become aware of, see, distinguish, realize, grasp, understand, take in, make out, find, identify, hit on, comprehend, apprehend, appreciate, sense, divine; *informal* figure out; *Brit. informal* twig; *formal* become cognizant of. ❷ *he perceived a flush creeping up her neck* SEE, discern, detect, catch sight of, spot, observe, notice. ❸ *he was perceived as too negative* REGARD, look on, view, consider, think of, judge, deem, adjudge.

perceptible ▶ **adjective** NOTICEABLE, perceivable, detectable, discernible, visible, observable, recognizable, appreciable; obvious, apparent, evident, manifest, patent, clear, distinct, plain, conspicuous.

perception ▶ **noun** ❶ *our perception of our own limitations* RECOGNITION, awareness, consciousness, appreciation, realization, knowledge, grasp, understanding, comprehension, apprehension; *formal* cognizance. ❷ *popular perceptions of old age* IMPRESSION, idea, conception, notion, thought, belief, judgement, estimation. ❸ *he talks with great perception* INSIGHT, perceptiveness, percipience, perspicacity, understanding, sharpness, sharp-wittedness, intelligence, intuition, cleverness, incisiveness, trenchancy, astuteness, shrewdness, acuteness, acuity, discernment, sensitivity, penetration, thoughtfulness, profundity; *formal* perspicuity.

perceptive ▶ **adjective** INSIGHTFUL, discerning, sensitive, intuitive, observant; piercing, penetrating, percipient, perspicacious, penetrative, clear-sighted, far-sighted, intelligent, clever, canny, keen, sharp, sharp-witted, astute, shrewd, quick, smart, acute, discriminating; *informal* on the ball; *N. Amer. informal* heads-up.
– OPPOSITES obtuse.

perch ▶ **noun** *the budgerigar's perch* POLE, rod, branch, roost, rest, resting place.
▶ **verb** ❶ *three swallows perched on the telegraph wire* ROOST, sit, rest; alight, settle, land, come to rest. ❷ *she perched her glasses on her nose* PUT, place, set, rest, balance. ❸ *the church is perched on a hill* BE LOCATED, be situated, be positioned, be sited, stand.

perchance ▶ **adverb** (*poetic/literary*) MAYBE, perhaps, possibly, for all one knows, it could be, it's possible, conceivably; *N. English* happen; *poetic/literary* peradventure.

percipient ▶ **adjective.** *See* PERCEPTIVE.

percolate ▶ **verb** ❶ *water percolated through the soil* FILTER, drain, drip, ooze, seep, trickle, dribble, leak, leach. ❷ *these views began to percolate through society as a whole* SPREAD, be disseminated, filter, pass; permeate, pervade. ❸ *he put some coffee on to percolate* BREW; *informal* perk.

perdition ▶ **noun** DAMNATION, eternal punishment; hell, hellfire, doom.

peregrinations ▶ **plural noun** (*archaic*) TRAVELS, wanderings, journeys, globetrotting, voyages, expeditions, odysseys, trips, treks, excursions; *formal* perambulations.

peremptory ▶ **adjective** ❶ *a peremptory reply* BRUSQUE, imperious, high-handed, brisk, abrupt, summary, commanding, dictatorial, autocratic, overbearing, dogmatic, arrogant, overweening, lordly, magisterial, authoritarian; emphatic, firm, insistent; *informal* bossy. ❷ *a peremptory order of the court* IRREVERSIBLE, binding, absolute, final, conclusive, decisive, definitive, categorical, irrefutable, incontrovertible; *Law* unappealable.

perennial ▸ **adjective** ABIDING, enduring, lasting, everlasting, perpetual, eternal, continuing, unending, unceasing, never-ending, endless, undying, ceaseless, persisting, permanent, constant, continual, unfailing, unchanging, never-changing.

perfect ▸ **adjective** ❶ *she strove to be the perfect wife* IDEAL, model, without fault, faultless, flawless, consummate, quintessential, exemplary, best, ultimate, copybook; unrivalled, unequalled, matchless, unparalleled, beyond compare, without equal, second to none, too good to be true, Utopian, incomparable, nonpareil, peerless, inimitable, unexcelled, unsurpassed, unsurpassable. ❷ *an E-type Jaguar in perfect condition* FLAWLESS, mint, as good as new, pristine, impeccable, immaculate, superb, superlative, optimum, prime, optimal, peak, excellent, faultless, as sound as a bell, unspoiled, unblemished, undamaged, spotless, unmarred; *informal* tip-top, A1. ❸ *a perfect copy* EXACT, precise, accurate, faithful, correct, unerring, right, true, strict; *Brit. informal* spot on; *N. Amer. informal* on the money. ❹ *the perfect Christmas present for golfers everywhere* IDEAL, just right, right, appropriate, fitting, fit, suitable, apt, made to order, tailor-made; very; *Brit. informal* spot on, just the job. ❺ *she felt a perfect idiot* ABSOLUTE, complete, total, real, out-and-out, thorough, thoroughgoing, downright, utter, sheer, arrant, unmitigated, unqualified, veritable, in every respect, unalloyed; *Brit. informal* right; *Austral./NZ informal* fair.

▸ **verb** *he's busy perfecting his bowling technique* IMPROVE, better, polish (up), hone, refine, put the finishing/final touches to, brush up, fine-tune.

perfection ▸ **noun** ❶ *the perfection of his technique* IMPROVEMENT, betterment, refinement, refining, honing. ❷ *for her, he was still perfection* THE IDEAL, a paragon, the ne plus ultra, the beau idéal, a nonpareil, the crème de la crème, the last word, the ultimate; *informal* one in a million, the tops, the best/greatest thing since sliced bread, the bee's knees; *archaic* a nonsuch.

perfectionist ▸ **noun** PURIST, stickler for perfection, idealist; pedant; *archaic* precisian.

perfectly ▸ **adverb** ❶ *a perfectly cooked meal* SUPERBLY, superlatively, excellently, flawlessly, faultlessly, to perfection, without fault, ideally, inimitably, incomparably, impeccably, immaculately, exquisitely, consummately; *N. Amer.* to a fare-thee-well; *informal* like a dream, to a T. ❷ *I think we understand each other perfectly* ABSOLUTELY, utterly, completely, altogether, entirely, wholly, totally, thoroughly, fully, in every respect. ❸ *you know perfectly well that is not what I meant* VERY, quite, full; *informal* damn, damned; *Brit. informal* jolly, bloody; *N. Amer. informal* darned; *N. English* right.

perfidious ▸ **adjective** (*poetic/literary*) TREACHEROUS, duplicitous, deceitful, disloyal, faithless, unfaithful, traitorous, treasonous, false, false-hearted, double-dealing, two-faced, untrustworthy.
– OPPOSITES faithful.

perfidy ▸ **noun** (*poetic/literary*) TREACHERY, duplicity, deceit, deceitfulness, disloyalty, infidelity, faithlessness, unfaithfulness, betrayal, treason, double-dealing, untrustworthiness, breach of trust; *poetic/literary* perfidiousness.

perforate ▸ **verb** PIERCE, penetrate, enter, puncture, prick, bore through, riddle.

perforce ▸ **adverb** (*formal*) NECESSARILY, of necessity, inevitably, unavoidably, by force of circumstances, needs must; *informal* like it or not; *formal* nolens volens.

perform ▸ **verb** ❶ *I have my duties to perform* CARRY OUT, do, execute, discharge, bring about, bring off, accomplish, achieve, fulfil, complete, conduct, effect, dispatch, work, implement; *informal* pull off; *formal* effectuate; *archaic* acquit oneself of. ❷ *a car which performs well at low speeds* FUNCTION, work, operate, run, go, respond, behave, act, acquit oneself/itself. ❸ *the play has been performed in Britain* STAGE, put on, present, mount, enact, act, produce. ❹ *the band performed live in Hyde Park* APPEAR, play, be on stage.
– OPPOSITES neglect.

performance ▸ **noun** ❶ *the evening performance* SHOW, production, showing, presentation, staging; concert, recital; *Brit.* house; *informal* gig. ❷ *their performance of Mozart's concerto in E flat* RENDITION, rendering, interpretation, playing, acting, representation. ❸ *the continual performance of a single task* CARRYING OUT, execution, discharge, accomplishment, completion, fulfilment, dispatch, implementation; *formal* effectuation. ❹ *the performance of the processor* FUNCTIONING, working, operation, running, behaviour, capabilities, capability, capacity, power, potential. ❺ (*informal*) *he made a great performance of telling her about it* FUSS, production, palaver, scene; *NZ* bobsy-die; *informal* song and dance, to-do, hoo-ha, business, pantomime.

performer ▸ **noun** ACTOR, ACTRESS, thespian, artiste, artist, entertainer, trouper, player, musician, singer, dancer, comic, comedian, comedienne.

perfume ▸ **noun** ❶ *a bottle of perfume* SCENT, fragrance, eau de toilette, toilet water, eau de cologne, cologne, aftershave. ❷ *the heady perfume of lilacs* SMELL, scent, fragrance, aroma, bouquet, redolence.

perfumed ▶ adjective SWEET-SMELLING, scented, fragrant, fragranced, perfumy, aromatic.

perfunctory ▶ adjective CURSORY, desultory, quick, brief, hasty, hurried, rapid, fleeting, token, casual, superficial, careless, half-hearted, sketchy, mechanical, automatic, routine, offhand, inattentive.
– OPPOSITES careful, thorough.

perhaps ▶ adverb MAYBE, for all one knows, it could be, it may be, it's possible, possibly, conceivably; *N. English* happen; *poetic/literary* peradventure, perchance.

peril ▶ noun DANGER, jeopardy, risk, hazard, insecurity, uncertainty, menace, threat, perilousness; pitfall, problem.

perilous ▶ adjective DANGEROUS, fraught with danger, hazardous, risky, unsafe, treacherous; precarious, vulnerable, uncertain, insecure, exposed, at risk, in jeopardy, in danger, touch-and-go; *informal* dicey.
– OPPOSITES safe.

perimeter ▶ noun ❶ *the perimeter of a circle* CIRCUMFERENCE, outside, outer edge. ❷ *the perimeter of the vast estate* BOUNDARY, border, limits, bounds, confines, edge, margin, fringe(s), periphery, borderline, verge; *poetic/literary* bourn, marge.

period ▶ noun ❶ *a six-week period* TIME, spell, interval, stretch, term, span, phase, bout, run, duration, chapter, stage; while; *Brit. informal* patch. ❷ *the post-war period* ERA, age, epoch, time, days, years; *Geology* aeon. ❸ *a double Maths period* LESSON, class, session. ❹ *women who suffer from painful periods* MENSTRUATION, menstrual flow; *informal* the curse, monthlies, time of the month; *technical* menses. ❺ (*N. Amer.*) *a comma instead of a period* FULL STOP, full point, point, stop.

periodic ▶ adjective REGULAR, periodical, at fixed intervals, recurrent, recurring, repeated, cyclical, cyclic, seasonal; occasional, infrequent, intermittent, sporadic, spasmodic, odd.

periodical ▶ noun *he wrote for two periodicals* JOURNAL, publication, magazine, newspaper, paper, review, digest, gazette, newsletter, organ, quarterly; *informal* mag, book, glossy.
▶ adjective *the island has periodical earthquakes. See* PERIODIC.

peripatetic ▶ adjective NOMADIC, itinerant, travelling, wandering, roving, roaming, migrant, migratory, unsettled.

peripheral ▶ adjective ❶ *the city's peripheral housing estates* OUTLYING, outer, on the edge/outskirts, surrounding. ❷ *peripheral issues* SECONDARY, subsidiary, incidental, tangential, marginal, minor, unimportant, lesser, inessential, non-essential, immaterial, ancillary.
– OPPOSITES central.

periphery ▶ noun EDGE, outer edge, margin, fringe, boundary, border, perimeter, rim, verge, borderline; outskirts, outer limits/reaches, bounds; *poetic/literary* bourn, marge.
– OPPOSITES centre.

periphrastic ▶ adjective CIRCUMLOCUTORY, circuitous, roundabout, indirect, tautological, pleonastic, prolix, verbose, wordy, long-winded, rambling, wandering, tortuous, diffuse.

perish ▶ verb ❶ *millions of soldiers perished* DIE, lose one's life, be killed, fall, expire, meet one's death, be lost, lay down one's life, breathe one's last, pass away, go the way of all flesh, give up the ghost, go to glory, meet one's maker, go to one's last resting place, cross the great divide; *informal* kick the bucket, turn up one's toes, shuffle off this mortal coil, buy it, croak; *Brit. informal* snuff it, pop one's clogs; *N. Amer. informal* bite the big one, buy the farm; *archaic* decease, depart this life. ❷ *must these hopes perish so soon?* COME TO AN END, die (away), disappear, vanish, fade, dissolve, evaporate, melt away, wither. ❸ *the wood had perished* GO BAD, go off, spoil, rot, go mouldy, moulder, putrefy, decay, decompose.

perjure
■ **perjure oneself** LIE UNDER OATH, lie, commit perjury, give false evidence/testimony; *formal* forswear oneself, be forsworn.

perjury ▶ noun LYING UNDER OATH, giving false evidence/testimony, making false statements, wilful falsehood.

perk[1]
■ **perk up** ❶ *you seem to have perked up* CHEER UP, brighten up, liven up, take heart; *informal* buck up. ❷ *the economy has been slow to perk up* RECOVER, rally, improve, revive, take a turn for the better, look up, pick up, bounce back.
■ **perk someone/something up** *you could do with something to perk you up* CHEER UP, liven up, brighten up, raise someone's spirits, give someone a boost/lift, revitalize, invigorate, energize, enliven, ginger up, put new life/heart into, put some spark into, rejuvenate, refresh, vitalize; *informal* buck up, pep up.

perk[2] ▶ noun *a job with a lot of perks* FRINGE BENEFIT, additional benefit, benefit, advantage, bonus, extra, plus; *informal* freebie; *Brit. informal* golden hello; *formal* perquisite.

perky ▶ adjective CHEERFUL, lively, vivacious, animated, bubbly, effervescent, bouncy, spirited, high-spirited, in high spirits, cheery, merry, buoyant, ebullient, exuberant, jaunty, frisky, sprightly, spry, bright, sunny, jolly, full of the joys of spring, sparkly, pert; *informal* full of beans, bright-eyed and bushy-tailed, chirpy, chipper; *N. Amer. informal* peppy; *dated* gay.

permanence ▶ noun STABILITY, durability, permanency, fixity, fixedness, changelessness, immutability, endurance, constancy, continuity, immortality, indestructibility, perpetuity, endlessness.

permanent ▶ adjective ❶ *permanent brain damage* LASTING, enduring, indefinite, continuing, perpetual, everlasting, eternal, abiding, constant, irreparable, irreversible, lifelong, indissoluble, indelible, standing, perennial, unending, endless, never-ending, immutable, undying, imperishable, indestructible, ineradicable; *poetic/literary* sempiternal, perdurable. ❷ *a permanent job* LONG-TERM, stable, secure, durable.
– OPPOSITES temporary.

permanently ▶ adverb ❶ *the attack left her permanently disabled* FOR ALL TIME, forever, for good, for always, for ever and ever, (for) evermore, until hell freezes over, in perpetuity, indelibly, immutably, until the end of time; *N. Amer.* forevermore; *informal* for keeps, until the cows come home, until doomsday, until kingdom come; *archaic* for aye. ❷ *I was permanently hungry* CONTINUALLY, constantly, perpetually, always.

permeable ▶ adjective POROUS, pervious, penetrable, absorbent, absorptive.

permeate ▶ verb ❶ *the delicious smell permeated the entire flat* PERVADE, spread through, fill, filter through, diffuse through, imbue, penetrate, pass through, percolate through, perfuse, charge, suffuse, steep, impregnate, inform. ❷ *these resins are able to permeate the timber* SOAK THROUGH, penetrate, seep through, saturate, percolate through, leach through.

permissible ▶ adjective PERMITTED, allowable, allowed, acceptable, legal, lawful, legitimate, admissible, licit, authorized, sanctioned, tolerated; *informal* legit, OK.
– OPPOSITES forbidden.

permission ▶ noun AUTHORIZATION, consent, leave, authority, sanction, licence, dispensation, assent, acquiescence, agreement, approval, seal of approval, approbation, endorsement, blessing, imprimatur, clearance, allowance, tolerance, sufferance, empowerment; *informal* the go-ahead, the thumbs up, the OK, the green light, say-so.

permissive ▶ adjective LIBERAL, broad-minded, open-minded, free, free and easy, easy-going, live-and-let-live, latitudinarian, laissez-faire, libertarian, unprescriptive, tolerant, forbearing, indulgent, lenient; overindulgent, lax, soft.
– OPPOSITES intolerant, strict.

permit ▶ verb *I cannot permit you to leave* ALLOW, let, authorize, give someone permission, sanction, grant, give someone the right, license, empower, enable, entitle, qualify; consent to, assent to, give one's blessing to, give the nod to, acquiesce in, agree to, tolerate, countenance, admit of; legalize, legitimatize, legitimate; *informal* give the go-ahead to, give the thumbs up to, OK, give the OK to, give the green light to, say the word; *formal* accede to; *archaic* suffer.
– OPPOSITES ban, forbid.
▶ noun *I need to see your permit* AUTHORIZATION, licence, pass, ticket, warrant, document, certification; passport, visa.

permutation ▶ noun VARIATION, alteration, modification, change, shift, transformation, transmutation, mutation; *humorous* transmogrification.

pernicious ▶ adjective HARMFUL, damaging, destructive, injurious, hurtful, detrimental, deleterious, dangerous, adverse, inimical, unhealthy, unfavourable, bad, evil, baleful, wicked, malign, malevolent, malignant, noxious, poisonous, corrupting; *poetic/literary* maleficent.
– OPPOSITES beneficial.

pernickety ▶ adjective (*informal*) FUSSY, difficult to please, difficult, finicky, over-fastidious, fastidious, over-particular, particular, faddish, punctilious, hair-splitting, critical, overcritical; *informal* nit-picking, choosy, picky; *Brit. informal* faddy; *N. Amer. informal* persnickety.
– OPPOSITES easy-going.

peroration ▶ noun ❶ *the peroration of his speech* CONCLUSION, ending, close, closing remarks; summation, summing-up. ❷ *an hour-long peroration* SPEECH, lecture, talk, address, oration, sermon, disquisition, discourse, declamation, harangue, diatribe; *informal* spiel.

perpendicular ▶ adjective ❶ *the perpendicular stones* UPRIGHT, vertical, erect, plumb, straight (up and down), on end, standing, upended. ❷ *lines perpendicular to each other* AT RIGHT ANGLES, at 90 degrees. ❸ *the perpendicular hillside* STEEP, sheer, precipitous, abrupt, bluff, vertiginous.
– OPPOSITES horizontal.

perpetrate ▶ verb COMMIT, carry out, perform, execute, do, effect, bring about, accomplish; be guilty of, be to blame for, be responsible for, inflict, wreak; *informal* pull off; *formal* effectuate.

perpetual ▶ adjective ❶ *deep caves in perpetual darkness* EVERLASTING, never-ending, eternal, permanent, unending, endless, without end, lasting, long-lasting, constant, abiding, enduring, perennial, timeless, ageless, deathless, undying, immortal; unfailing, unchanging, never-changing, changeless, unfading; *poetic/literary* sempiternal, perdurable. ❷ *a perpetual state of fear* CONSTANT, permanent, uninterrupted, continuous, unremitting, unending, unceasing, persistent, unbroken. ❸ *her mother's perpetual nagging* INTERMINABLE, incessant, ceaseless, endless, without respite, relentless, unrelenting, persistent, continual, continuous, non-stop, never-ending, recurrent, repeated, unremitting, sustained, round-the-clock, unabating; *informal* eternal.
– OPPOSITES temporary, intermittent.

perpetuate ▶ **verb** KEEP ALIVE, keep going, preserve, conserve, sustain, maintain, continue, extend, carry on, keep up, prolong; immortalize, commemorate, memorialize, eternalize.

perpetuity

■ **in perpetuity** FOREVER, permanently, for always, for good, for good and all, perpetually, (for) evermore, for ever and ever, for all time, until the end of time, until hell freezes over, eternally, for eternity, everlastingly; *N. Amer.* forevermore; *informal* for keeps, until doomsday; *archaic* for aye.

perplex ▶ **verb** PUZZLE, baffle, mystify, bemuse, bewilder, confound, confuse, nonplus, disconcert, dumbfound, throw, throw/catch off balance, exercise, worry; *informal* flummox, be all Greek to, stump, bamboozle, floor, beat, faze, fox; *N. Amer. informal* discombobulate; *archaic* wilder, maze.

perplexing ▶ **adjective** PUZZLING, baffling, mystifying, mysterious, bewildering, confusing, disconcerting, worrying, unaccountable, difficult to understand, beyond one, paradoxical, peculiar, funny, strange, weird, odd.

perplexity ▶ **noun** ❶ *he scratched his head in perplexity* CONFUSION, bewilderment, puzzlement, bafflement, incomprehension, mystification, bemusement; *informal* bamboozlement; *N. Amer. informal* discombobulation. ❷ *the perplexities of international relations* COMPLEXITY, complication, intricacy, problem, difficulty, mystery, puzzle, enigma, paradox.

perquisite ▶ **noun** (*formal*). *See* PERK².

per se ▶ **adverb** IN ITSELF, of itself, by itself, as such, intrinsically; by its very nature, in essence, by definition, essentially.

persecute ▶ **verb** ❶ *they were persecuted for their religious beliefs* OPPRESS, abuse, victimize, ill-treat, mistreat, maltreat, tyrannize, torment, torture; martyr. ❷ *she was persecuted by the press* HARASS, hound, plague, badger, harry, intimidate, pick on, pester, bother, bedevil, bully, victimize, terrorize; *N. Amer.* devil; *informal* hassle, give someone a hard time, get on someone's back; *Austral. informal* heavy.

persecution ▶ **noun** ❶ *victims of religious persecution* OPPRESSION, victimization, maltreatment, ill-treatment, mistreatment, abuse, ill-usage, discrimination, tyranny; *informal* witch hunt. ❷ *the persecution I endured at school* HARASSMENT, hounding, intimidation, bullying.

perseverance ▶ **noun** PERSISTENCE, tenacity, determination, staying power, indefatigability, steadfastness, purposefulness; patience, endurance, application, diligence, dedication, commitment, doggedness, assiduity, tirelessness, stamina; intransigence, obstinacy; *informal* stickability; *N. Amer. informal* stick-to-it-iveness; *formal* pertinacity.

persevere ▶ **verb** PERSIST, continue, carry on, go on, keep on, keep going, struggle on, hammer away, be persistent, be determined, see/follow something through, keep at it, press on/ahead, not take no for an answer, be tenacious, stand one's ground, stand fast/firm, hold on, go the distance, stay the course, plod on, plough on, stop at nothing, leave no stone unturned; *informal* soldier on, hang on, plug away, peg away, stick to one's guns, stick it out, hang in there.
– OPPOSITES give up.

persist ▶ **verb** ❶ *Corbett persisted with his questioning. See* PERSEVERE. ❷ *if dry weather persists, water the lawn thoroughly* CONTINUE, hold, carry on, last, keep on, keep up, remain, linger, stay, endure.

persistence ▶ **noun**. *See* PERSEVERANCE.

persistent ▶ **adjective** ❶ *a very persistent man* TENACIOUS, persevering, determined, resolute, purposeful, dogged, single-minded, tireless, indefatigable, patient, unflagging, untiring, insistent, importunate, relentless, unrelenting; stubborn, intransigent, obstinate, obdurate; *formal* pertinacious. ❷ *persistent rain* CONSTANT, continuous, continuing, continual, non-stop, never-ending, steady, uninterrupted, unbroken, interminable, incessant, unceasing, endless, unending, perpetual, unremitting, unrelenting, relentless, unrelieved, sustained. ❸ *a persistent cough* CHRONIC, permanent, nagging, frequent; repeated, habitual.
– OPPOSITES irresolute, intermittent.

person ▶ **noun** HUMAN BEING, individual, man/woman, human, being, (living) soul, mortal, creature; personage, character, customer; *informal* type, sort, beggar, cookie; *Brit. informal* bod; *informal, dated* body, dog, cove; *archaic* wight.

■ **in person** PHYSICALLY, in the flesh, in propria persona, personally; oneself; *informal* as large as life.

persona ▶ **noun** IMAGE, face, public face, character, personality, identity, self; front, facade, guise, exterior, role, part.

personable ▶ **adjective** PLEASANT, agreeable, likeable, nice, amiable, affable, charming, congenial, genial, engaging, pleasing; attractive, presentable, good-looking, nice-looking, pretty, appealing; *Scottish* couthy; *Scottish & N. English* bonny, canny; *dated* taking.
– OPPOSITES disagreeable, unattractive.

personage ▶ **noun** IMPORTANT PERSON, VIP, luminary, celebrity, personality, name, famous name, household name, public figure, star, leading light, dignitary, notable, notability, worthy, panjandrum; person; *informal* celeb, somebody, big shot, big noise; *Brit. informal* nob; *N. Amer. informal* big wheel, big kahuna.

personal ▶ **adjective** ❶ *a highly personal style* DISTINCTIVE, characteristic, unique, individual, one's own, particular, peculiar, idiosyncratic,

individualized, personalized. ❷ *a personal appearance* IN PERSON, in the flesh, actual, live, physical. ❸ *his personal life* PRIVATE, intimate; confidential, secret. ❹ *a personal friend* INTIMATE, close, dear, great, bosom. ❺ *I have personal knowledge of the family* DIRECT, empirical, first-hand, immediate, experiential. ❻ *personal remarks* DEROGATORY, disparaging, belittling, insulting, critical, rude, slighting, disrespectful, offensive, pejorative.
– OPPOSITES public, general.

personality ▶ noun ❶ *her cheerful personality* CHARACTER, nature, disposition, temperament, make-up, persona, psyche. ❷ *she had loads of personality* CHARISMA, magnetism, strength/force of personality, character, charm, presence. ❸ *a famous personality* CELEBRITY, VIP, star, superstar, name, famous name, household name, big name, somebody, leading light, luminary, notable, personage, notability; *informal* celeb.

personalize ▶ verb ❶ *products which can be personalized to your requirements* CUSTOMIZE, individualize. ❷ *attempts to personalize God* PERSONIFY, humanize, anthropomorphize.

personally ▶ adverb ❶ *I'd like to thank him personally* IN PERSON, oneself. ❷ *personally, I think it's a good idea* FOR MY PART, for myself, to my way of thinking, to my mind, in my estimation, as far as I am concerned, in my view/opinion, from my point of view, from where I stand, as I see it, if you ask me, for my money, in my book; privately.
■ **take something personally** TAKE OFFENCE, take something amiss, be offended, be upset, be affronted, take umbrage, take exception, feel insulted, feel hurt.

personification ▶ noun EMBODIMENT, incarnation, epitome, quintessence, essence, type, symbol, soul, model, exemplification, exemplar, image, representation.

personify ▶ verb EPITOMIZE, embody, be the incarnation of, typify, exemplify, represent, symbolize, stand for, body forth.

personnel ▶ noun STAFF, employees, workforce, workers, labour force, manpower, human resources; *informal* liveware.

perspective ▶ noun ❶ *her perspective on things had changed* OUTLOOK, view, viewpoint, point of view, standpoint, position, stand, stance, angle, slant, attitude, frame of mind, frame of reference, approach, way of looking, interpretation. ❷ *a perspective of the whole valley* VIEW, vista, panorama, prospect, bird's-eye view, outlook, aspect.

perspicacious ▶ adjective DISCERNING, shrewd, perceptive, astute, penetrating, observant, percipient, sharp-witted, sharp, smart, alert, clear-sighted, far-sighted, acute, clever, canny, intelligent, insightful, wise, sage, sensitive, intuitive, understanding, aware, discriminating; *informal* on the ball; *N. Amer. informal* heads-up.
– OPPOSITES stupid.

perspicuous ▶ adjective (*formal*). *See* CLEAR adjective sense 1.

perspiration ▶ noun SWEAT, moisture; a lather; *informal* a muck sweat; *Medicine* diaphoresis, hidrosis.

perspire ▶ verb SWEAT, be dripping/pouring with sweat, glow; *informal* be in a muck sweat.

persuadable ▶ adjective MALLEABLE, tractable, pliable, compliant, amenable, adaptable, accommodating, cooperative, flexible, acquiescent, yielding, biddable, complaisant, like putty in one's hands, suggestible.

persuade ▶ verb ❶ *he tried to persuade her to come with him* PREVAIL ON, talk into, coax, convince, make, get, induce, win over, bring round, coerce, influence, sway, inveigle, entice, tempt, lure, cajole, wheedle; *Law* procure; *informal* sweet-talk, twist someone's arm. ❷ *shortage of money persuaded them to abandon the scheme* CAUSE, lead, move, dispose, incline.
– OPPOSITES dissuade, deter.

persuasion ▶ noun ❶ *Monica needed plenty of persuasion* COAXING, persuading, coercion, inducement, convincing, blandishment, encouragement, urging, inveiglement, cajolery, enticement, wheedling; *informal* sweet-talking, arm-twisting; *formal* suasion. ❷ *various political and religious persuasions* GROUP, grouping, sect, denomination, party, camp, side, faction, affiliation, school of thought, belief, creed, credo, faith, philosophy.

persuasive ▶ adjective CONVINCING, cogent, compelling, potent, forceful, powerful, eloquent, impressive, influential, sound, valid, strong, effective, winning, telling; plausible, credible.
– OPPOSITES unconvincing.

pert ▶ adjective ❶ *a pert little hat* JAUNTY, neat, trim, stylish, smart, perky, rakish; *informal* natty; *N. Amer. informal* saucy. ❷ *a young girl with a pert manner* IMPUDENT, impertinent, cheeky, irreverent, forward, insolent, disrespectful, flippant, familiar, presumptuous, bold, as bold as brass, brazen; *informal* fresh, lippy, saucy; *N. Amer. informal* sassy; *archaic* malapert.

pertain ▶ verb ❶ *developments pertaining to the economy* CONCERN, relate to, be related to, be connected with, be relevant to, apply to, be pertinent to, refer to, have a bearing on, appertain to, bear on, affect, involve, touch; *archaic* regard. ❷ *the stock and assets pertaining to the business* BELONG TO, be a part of, be included in. ❸ *the economic situation which pertained in Britain at that time* EXIST, be the order of the day, be the case, prevail; *formal* obtain.

pertinacious ▶ adjective (*formal*) DETERMINED, tenacious, persistent, persevering, purposeful, resolute, dogged, indefatigable, insistent, sin-

gle-minded, unrelenting, relentless, tireless, unshakeable; stubborn, obstinate, inflexible, unbending.
– OPPOSITES irresolute, tentative.

pertinent ▶ adjective RELEVANT, to the point, apposite, appropriate, suitable, fitting, fit, apt, applicable, material, germane, to the purpose, apropos; *formal* ad rem.
– OPPOSITES irrelevant.

perturb ▶ verb WORRY, upset, unsettle, disturb, concern, trouble, disquiet; disconcert, discomfit, unnerve, alarm, bother, distress, dismay, gnaw at, agitate, fluster, ruffle, discountenance, exercise; *informal* rattle.
– OPPOSITES reassure.

perturbed ▶ adjective UPSET, worried, unsettled, disturbed, concerned, troubled, anxious, ill at ease, uneasy, disquieted, fretful; disconcerted, discomposed, distressed, unnerved, alarmed, bothered, dismayed, agitated, flustered, ruffled, shaken, discountenanced; *informal* twitchy, rattled, fazed; *N. Amer. informal* discombobulated.
– OPPOSITES calm.

peruse ▶ verb READ, study, scrutinize, inspect, examine, wade through, look through; browse through, leaf through, scan, run one's eye over, glance through, flick through, skim through, thumb through, dip into; *archaic* con.

pervade ▶ verb PERMEATE, spread through, fill, suffuse, be diffused through, imbue, penetrate, filter through, percolate through, infuse, perfuse, flow through; charge, steep, saturate, impregnate, inform.

pervasive ▶ adjective PREVALENT, pervading, permeating, extensive, ubiquitous, omnipresent, universal, rife, widespread, general.

perverse ▶ adjective ❶ *he is being deliberately perverse* AWKWARD, contrary, difficult, unreasonable, uncooperative, unhelpful, obstructive, disobliging, recalcitrant, stubborn, obstinate, obdurate, mulish, pig-headed, bullheaded; *informal* cussed; *Brit. informal* bloody-minded, bolshie; *N. Amer. informal* balky; *formal* refractory; *archaic* froward, contumacious. ❷ *a verdict that is manifestly perverse* ILLOGICAL, irrational, unreasonable, wrong, wrong-headed. ❸ *an evil life dedicated to perverse pleasure* PERVERTED, depraved, unnatural, abnormal, deviant, degenerate, immoral, warped, twisted, corrupt; wicked, base, evil; *informal* kinky, sick, pervy.
– OPPOSITES accommodating, reasonable.

perversion ▶ noun ❶ *a twisted perversion of the truth* DISTORTION, misrepresentation, falsification, travesty, misinterpretation, misconstruction, twisting, corruption, subversion, misuse, misapplication, debasement. ❷ *sexual perversion* DEVIANCE, abnormality; depravity, degeneracy, debauchery, corruption, vice, wickedness, immorality.

perversity ▶ noun ❶ *out of sheer perversity, he refused* CONTRARINESS, awkwardness, recalcitrance, stubbornness, obstinacy, obduracy, mulishness, pig-headedness; *informal* cussedness; *Brit. informal* bloody-mindedness; *formal* refractoriness. ❷ *the perversity of the decision* UNREASONABLENESS, irrationality, illogicality, wrong-headedness.

pervert ▶ verb ❶ *people who attempt to pervert the rules* DISTORT, corrupt, subvert, twist, bend, abuse, misapply, misuse, misrepresent, misinterpret, falsify. ❷ *men can be perverted by power* CORRUPT, lead astray, debase, warp, pollute, poison, deprave, debauch.
▶ noun *a sexual pervert* DEVIANT, degenerate; *informal* perv, dirty old man, sicko.

perverted ▶ adjective UNNATURAL, deviant, warped, corrupt, twisted, abnormal, unhealthy, depraved, perverse, aberrant, immoral, debauched, debased, degenerate, evil, wicked, vile, amoral, wrong, bad; *informal* sick, sicko, kinky, pervy.

pessimism ▶ noun DEFEATISM, negativity, doom and gloom, gloominess, cynicism, fatalism; hopelessness, depression, despair, despondency, angst; *informal* looking on the black side.

pessimist ▶ noun DEFEATIST, fatalist, prophet of doom, cynic, doomsayer, doomster, Cassandra; sceptic, doubter, doubting Thomas; misery, killjoy, Job's comforter; *informal* doom (and gloom) merchant, wet blanket; *N. Amer. informal* gloomy Gus.
– OPPOSITES optimist.

pessimistic ▶ adjective GLOOMY, negative, defeatist, downbeat, cynical, bleak, fatalistic, dark, black, despairing, despondent, depressed, hopeless; suspicious, distrustful, doubting.
– OPPOSITES optimistic.

pest ▶ noun NUISANCE, annoyance, irritation, irritant, thorn in one's flesh/side, vexation, trial, the bane of one's life, menace, trouble, problem, worry, bother; *informal* pain (in the neck), aggravation, headache; *Scottish informal* skelf; *N. Amer. informal* nudnik; *Austral./NZ informal* nark.

pester ▶ verb BADGER, hound, harass, plague, annoy, bother, trouble, keep after, persecute, torment, bedevil, harry, worry, beleaguer, chivvy, nag; *informal* hassle, bug, get on someone's back; *N. English informal* mither; *N. Amer. informal* devil.

pestilence ▶ noun (*archaic*). *See* PLAGUE noun sense 1.

pestilential ▶ adjective ❶ *pestilential fever* PLAGUE-LIKE, infectious, contagious, communicable, epidemic, virulent; *informal* catching; *poetic/literary* pestiferous. ❷ (*informal*) *a pestilential man!* ANNOYING, irritating, infuriating, exasperating, maddening, tiresome, irksome, vexing, vexatious; *informal* aggravating, pesky, infernal.

pet[1] ▶ **noun** *the teacher's pet* FAVOURITE, darling, the apple of one's eye; *Brit. informal* blue-eyed boy/girl; *N. Amer. informal* fair-haired boy/girl.
▶ **adjective** ❶ *a pet lamb* TAME, domesticated, domestic; *Brit.* house-trained; *N. Amer.* housebroken. ❷ *his pet theory* FAVOURITE, favoured, cherished, dear to one's heart; particular, special, personal.
▶ **verb** ❶ *the cats came to be petted* STROKE, caress, fondle, pat. ❷ *she had always been petted by her parents* PAMPER, spoil, mollycoddle, coddle, cosset, baby, indulge, overindulge, wrap in cotton wool. ❸ *couples were petting in their cars* KISS AND CUDDLE, kiss, cuddle, embrace, caress; *informal* canoodle, neck, smooch; *Brit. informal* snog; *N. Amer. informal* make out, get it on; *informal, dated* spoon.
■ **pet name** AFFECTIONATE NAME, term of endearment, endearment, nickname, diminutive, hypocoristic.

pet[2] ▶ **noun** *Mum's in a pet* BAD MOOD, mood, bad temper, temper, sulk, fit of pique, huff; *Brit. informal* paddy, strop.

peter
■ **peter out** FIZZLE OUT, fade (away), die away/out, dwindle, diminish, taper off, tail off, trail away/off, wane, ebb, melt away, evaporate, disappear, come to an end, subside.

petite ▶ **adjective** SMALL, dainty, diminutive, slight, little, tiny, elfin, delicate, small-boned; *Scottish* wee; *informal* pint-sized.

petition ▶ **noun** ❶ *over 1,000 people signed the petition* APPEAL, round robin. ❷ *petitions to Allah* ENTREATY, supplication, plea, prayer, appeal, request, invocation, suit; *archaic* orison.
▶ **verb** *they petitioned the king to revoke the decision* APPEAL TO, request, ask, call on, entreat, beg, implore, plead with, apply to, press, urge; *formal* adjure; *poetic/literary* beseech.

petrified ▶ **adjective** ❶ *she looked petrified* TERRIFIED, terror-stricken, horrified, scared/frightened out of one's wits, scared/frightened to death. ❷ *petrified remains of prehistoric animals* OSSIFIED, fossilized, calcified.

petrify ▶ **verb** TERRIFY, horrify, frighten, scare, scare/frighten to death, scare/frighten the living daylights out of, scare/frighten the life out of, strike terror into, put the fear of God into; paralyse, transfix; *informal* scare the pants off; *Irish informal* scare the bejesus out of.

petrol ▶ **noun** FUEL, unleaded, superunleaded, diesel; *N. Amer.* gasoline, gas; *informal* juice.

petticoat ▶ **noun** SLIP, underskirt, half-slip, underslip, undergarment; *archaic* kirtle; *historical* crinoline.

petty ▶ **adjective** ❶ *petty regulations* TRIVIAL, trifling, minor, small, unimportant, insignificant, inconsequential, inconsiderable, negligible, paltry, footling, pettifogging; *informal* piffling, piddling, fiddling. ❷ *a petty form of revenge* SMALL-MINDED, mean, ungenerous, shabby, spiteful.
–OPPOSITES important, magnanimous.

petulant ▶ **adjective** PEEVISH, bad-tempered, querulous, pettish, fretful, cross, irritable, sulky, snappish, crotchety, touchy, tetchy, testy, fractious, grumpy, disgruntled, crabbed, crabby; *informal* grouchy; *Brit. informal* ratty; *N. English informal* mardy; *N. Amer. informal* cranky.
–OPPOSITES good-humoured.

phantasmagorical ▶ **adjective** DREAMLIKE, psychedelic, kaleidoscopic, surreal, unreal, hallucinatory, fantastic, fantastical, chimerical.

phantom ▶ **noun** ❶ *a phantom who haunts lonely roads* GHOST, apparition, spirit, spectre, wraith; *informal* spook; *poetic/literary* phantasm, shade. ❷ *the phantoms of an overactive imagination* DELUSION, figment of the imagination, hallucination, illusion, chimera, vision, mirage.

phase ▶ **noun** ❶ *the final phase of the campaign* STAGE, period, chapter, episode, part, step, point, time, juncture. ❷ *he's going through a difficult phase* PERIOD, stage, time, spell; *Brit. informal* patch. ❸ *the phases of the moon* ASPECT, shape, form, appearance, state, condition.
■ **phase something in** INTRODUCE GRADUALLY, begin to use, ease in.
■ **phase something out** WITHDRAW GRADUALLY, discontinue, stop using, run down, wind down.

phenomenal ▶ **adjective** REMARKABLE, exceptional, extraordinary, amazing, astonishing, astounding, sensational, stunning, incredible, unbelievable; marvellous, magnificent, wonderful, outstanding, singular, out of the ordinary, unusual, unprecedented; *informal* fantastic, terrific, tremendous, stupendous, awesome, out of this world; *poetic/literary* wondrous.
–OPPOSITES ordinary.

phenomenon ▶ **noun** ❶ *a rare phenomenon* OCCURRENCE, event, happening, fact, situation, circumstance, experience, case, incident, episode. ❷ *the band was a pop phenomenon* MARVEL, sensation, wonder, prodigy, miracle, rarity, nonpareil.

philander ▶ **verb** WOMANIZE, have affairs, flirt; *informal* play around, carry on, play the field, play away, sleep around; *N. Amer. informal* fool around.

philanderer ▶ **noun** WOMANIZER, Casanova, Don Juan, Lothario, flirt, ladies' man, playboy, rake, roué; *informal* stud, skirt-chaser, ladykiller, wolf; *informal, dated* gay dog.

philanthropic ▶ **adjective** CHARITABLE, generous, benevolent, humanitarian, public-spirited, altruistic, magnanimous, munificent, open-handed, bountiful, liberal, generous to a fault, beneficent, caring, compassionate, unselfish, kind, kind-hearted, big-hearted; *formal* eleemosynary.
–OPPOSITES selfish, mean.

philanthropist ▶ **noun** BENEFACTOR, benefactress, patron, patroness, donor, contributor, sponsor, backer, helper, good Samaritan; do-gooder, Lady Bountiful; *historical* almsgiver.

philanthropy ▶ **noun** BENEVOLENCE, generosity, humanitarianism, public-spiritedness, altruism, social conscience, charity, charitableness, brotherly love, fellow feeling, magnanimity, munificence, liberality, largesse, openhandedness, bountifulness, beneficence, unselfishness, humanity, kindness, kindheartedness, compassion; *historical* almsgiving.

philippic ▶ **noun** (*poetic/literary*) TIRADE, diatribe, harangue, lecture, attack, onslaught, denunciation, rant, polemic, broadside, fulmination, condemnation, criticism, censure; *informal* blast.

philistine ▶ **adjective** UNCULTURED, lowbrow, anti-intellectual, uncultivated, uncivilized, uneducated, unenlightened, commercial, materialist, bourgeois; ignorant, crass, boorish, barbarian.

philosopher ▶ **noun** THINKER, theorist, theorizer, theoretician, metaphysicist, metaphysician; scholar, intellectual, sage, wise man.

philosophical ▶ **adjective** ❶ *a philosophical question* THEORETICAL, metaphysical. ❷ *a philosophical mood* THOUGHTFUL, reflective, pensive, meditative, contemplative, introspective, ruminative; *formal* cogitative. ❸ *he was philosphical about losing the contract* CALM, composed, cool, collected, {cool, calm, and collected}, self-possessed, serene, tranquil, stoical, impassive, dispassionate, phlegmatic, unperturbed, imperturbable, unruffled, patient, forbearing, long-suffering, resigned, rational, realistic.

philosophize ▶ **verb** THEORIZE, speculate; pontificate, preach, sermonize, moralize.

philosophy ▶ **noun** ❶ *the philosophy of Aristotle* THINKING, thought, reasoning. ❷ *her political philosophy* BELIEFS, credo, convictions, ideology, ideas, thinking, notions, theories, doctrine, tenets, principles, views, school of thought.

phlegm ▶ **noun** ❶ MUCUS, catarrh. ❷ *British phlegm and perseverance* CALMNESS, coolness, composure, equanimity, tranquillity, placidity, placidness, impassivity, stolidity, imperturbability, impassiveness, dispassionateness; *informal* cool, unflappability.

phlegmatic ▶ **adjective** CALM, cool, composed, {cool, calm, and collected}, controlled, serene, tranquil, placid, impassive, stolid, imperturbable, unruffled, dispassionate, philosophical; *informal* unflappable.
–OPPOSITES excitable.

phobia ▶ **noun** ABNORMAL FEAR, irrational fear, obsessive fear, dread, horror, terror, hatred, loathing, detestation, aversion, antipathy, revulsion; complex, neurosis; *informal* thing, hang-up.

phone ▶ **noun** ❶ *she spent hours on the phone* TELEPHONE, mobile (phone), cellphone, car phone, cordless phone, speakerphone; extension; *Brit. informal* blower; *Brit. rhyming slang* dog and bone. ❷ *give me a phone sometime* CALL, telephone call, phone call; *Brit.* ring; *informal* buzz; *Brit. informal* tinkle, bell.

▶ **verb** *I'll phone you later* TELEPHONE, call, give someone a call; *Brit.* ring, ring up, give someone a ring; *informal* call up, give someone a buzz; *Brit. informal* give someone a bell/tinkle, get on the blower to; *N. Amer. informal* get someone on the horn.

phoney (*informal*) ▶ **adjective** *a phoney address* BOGUS, false, fake, fraudulent, spurious; counterfeit, forged, feigned; pseudo, imitation, sham, man-made, mock, ersatz, synthetic, artificial; simulated, pretended, contrived, affected, insincere; *informal* pretend, put-on; *Brit. informal* cod.
–OPPOSITES authentic.

▶ **noun** ❶ *he's nothing but a phoney* IMPOSTOR, sham, fake, fraud, charlatan; *informal* con artist. ❷ *the diamond's a phoney* FAKE, imitation, counterfeit, forgery.

photocopy ▶ **noun** COPY, facsimile, duplicate; *trademark* Xerox, photostat, Ozalid.

photograph ▶ **noun** *a photograph of her father* PICTURE, photo, snap, snapshot, shot, likeness, print, slide, transparency, still, enlargement; *Brit.* enprint; *informal* tranny.

▶ **verb** *she was photographed leaving the castle* TAKE SOMEONE'S PICTURE/PHOTO, snap, shoot, film.

photographer ▶ **noun** LENSMAN, paparazzo; cameraman; *informal* snapper; *N. Amer. informal* shutterbug.

photographic ▶ **adjective** ❶ *a photographic record* PICTORIAL, in photographs; cinematic, filmic. ❷ *a photographic memory* DETAILED, graphic, exact, precise, accurate, vivid.

phrase ▶ **noun** *familiar words and phrases* EXPRESSION, group of words, construction, locution, term, turn of phrase; idiom, idiomatic expression; saying, tag.

▶ **verb** *how could I phrase the question?* EXPRESS, put into words, put, word, style, formulate, couch, frame, articulate, verbalize.

phraseology ▶ **noun** WORDING, choice of words, phrasing, way of speaking/writing, usage, idiom, diction, parlance, words, language, vocabulary, terminology; jargon; *informal* lingo, -speak, -ese.

physical ▶ **adjective** ❶ *physical pleasure* BODILY, corporeal, corporal, somatic; carnal, fleshly, non-spiritual. ❷ *hard physical work* MANUAL, labouring, blue-collar. ❸ *the physical universe* MATERIAL, concrete, tangible, palpable, solid, substantial, real, actual, visible.
–OPPOSITES mental, spiritual.

physician ▶ **noun** DOCTOR, doctor of medicine, MD, medical practitioner, general practitioner, GP, clinician; specialist, consultant; *informal* doc, medic, medico; *Brit. informal* quack; *informal, dated* sawbones.

physiognomy ▶ noun FACE, features, countenance, expression, look, mien; *informal* mug; *Brit. informal* phizog, phiz; *Brit. rhyming slang* boat race; *N. Amer. informal* puss; *poetic/literary* visage, lineaments.

physique ▶ noun BODY, build, figure, frame, anatomy, shape, form, proportions; muscles, musculature; *informal* vital statistics, bod.

pick ▶ verb ❶ *I got a job picking apples* HARVEST, gather (in), collect, pluck; *poetic/literary* cull. ❷ *pick the time that suits you best* CHOOSE, select, pick out, single out, take, opt for, plump for, elect, decide on, settle on, fix on, sift out, sort out; name, nominate. ❸ *Beth picked at her food* NIBBLE, toy with, play with, eat like a bird. ❹ *people were singing and picking guitars* STRUM, twang, thrum, pluck. ❺ *he tried to pick a fight* PROVOKE, start, cause, incite, stir up, whip up, instigate, prompt, bring about.

▶ noun ❶ *take your pick* CHOICE, selection, option, decision; preference, favourite. ❷ *the pick of the crop* BEST, finest, top, choice, choicest, prime, cream, flower, prize, pearl, gem, jewel, jewel in the crown, crème de la crème, elite.

■ **pick on** BULLY, victimize, tyrannize, torment, persecute, criticize, harass, hound, taunt, tease; *informal* get at, have it in for, have a down on, be down on, needle.

■ **pick something out** ❶ *one painting was picked out for special mention* CHOOSE, select, pick, single out, opt for, plump for, decide on, elect, settle on, fix on, sift out, sort out; name, nominate. ❷ *she picked out Jessica in the crowd* SEE, make out, distinguish, discern, spot, perceive, detect, notice, recognize, identify, catch sight of, glimpse; *poetic/literary* espy, behold, descry.

■ **pick up** IMPROVE, recover, be on the road to recovery, rally, make a comeback, bounce back, perk up, look up, take a turn for the better, turn the/a corner, be on the mend, make headway, make progress.

■ **pick someone/something up** LIFT, take up, raise, hoist, scoop up, gather up, snatch up.

■ **pick someone up** ❶ *I'll pick you up after lunch* FETCH, collect, call for. ❷ (*informal*) *he was picked up by the police* ARREST, apprehend, detain, take into custody, seize; *informal* nab, run in, bust; *Brit. informal* nick. ❸ (*informal*) *he picked her up in a club* TAKE UP WITH; *informal* get off with, pull, cop off with.

■ **pick something up** ❶ *we picked it up at a flea market* FIND, discover, come across, stumble across, happen on, chance on; acquire, obtain, come by, get, procure; purchase, buy; *informal* get hold of, get/lay one's hands on, get one's mitts on, bag, land. ❷ *he picked up the story in the 1950s* RESUME, take up, start again, recommence, continue, carry on with, go on with. ❸ *she picked up a virus* CATCH, contract, get, go/come down with. ❹ *he told us the bits of gossip he'd picked up* HEAR, hear tell, get wind of, be told, learn; glean, garner. ❺ *we're picking up a distress signal* RECEIVE, detect, get, hear.

picket ▶ noun ❶ *forty pickets were arrested* STRIKER, demonstrator, protester, objector, picketer; flying picket. ❷ *fences made of cedar pickets* STAKE, post, paling; upright, stanchion, pier, piling.

▶ verb *over 200 people picketed the factory* DEMONSTRATE AT, form a picket at, man the picket line at; blockade, shut off.

pickle ▶ noun ❶ *a jar of pickle* RELISH, chutney, piccalilli. ❷ *steep the vegetables in pickle* MARINADE, brine, vinegar. ❸ (*informal*) *they got into an awful pickle* PLIGHT, predicament, mess, difficulty, trouble, dire/desperate straits, problem; *informal* tight corner, tight spot, jam, fix, scrape, bind, hole, hot water, fine kettle of fish; *Brit. informal* spot of bother.

▶ verb *fish pickled in brine* PRESERVE, souse, marinate, conserve; bottle, can, tin.

pick-me-up ▶ noun ❶ *a drink that's a very good pick-me-up* TONIC, restorative, energizer, stimulant, refresher, reviver; *informal* bracer; *Medicine* analeptic. ❷ *his winning goal was a perfect pick-me-up* BOOST, boost to the spirits, fillip, stimulant, stimulus; *informal* shot in the arm.

pickpocket ▶ noun THIEF, petty thief, sneak thief; *archaic* cutpurse.

pickup ▶ noun IMPROVEMENT, recovery, revival, upturn, upswing, rally, comeback, resurgence, renewal, turn for the better.

– OPPOSITES slump.

picnic ▶ noun ❶ *a picnic on the beach* OUTDOOR MEAL, alfresco meal; *N. Amer.* cookout. ❷ (*informal*) *working for him was no picnic* EASY TASK/JOB, child's play, five-finger exercise, gift, walkover; *informal* doddle, piece of cake, money for old rope, money for jam, cinch, breeze, kids' stuff, cakewalk, pushover; *N. Amer. informal* duck soup; *Austral./NZ informal* bludge.

pictorial ▶ adjective ILLUSTRATED, in pictures, in picture form, in photographs, photographic, graphic.

picture ▶ noun ❶ *pictures in an art gallery* PAINTING, DRAWING, sketch, oil painting, watercolour, print, canvas, portrait, portrayal, illustration, artwork, depiction, likeness, representation, image, icon, miniature; fresco, mural, wall painting; *informal* oil. ❷ *we were told not to take pictures* PHOTOGRAPH, photo, snap, snapshot, shot, print, slide, transparency, exposure, still, enlargement; *Brit.* enprint. ❸ *a picture of the sort of person the child should be* CONCEPT, idea, impression, view, (mental) image, vision, visualization, notion. ❹ *the picture of health* PERSONIFICATION, embodiment, epitome, essence, quintessence, perfect example, soul, model. ❺ *a picture starring Robert de Niro* FILM, movie, feature film, motion picture; *informal* flick; *dated* moving picture. ❻ *we went to the pictures* THE CINEMA, the movies, the silver screen, the big screen; *informal* the flicks.

▶ **verb** ❶ *he was pictured with his guests* PHOTOGRAPH, take a photograph/photo of, snap, shoot, film. ❷ *in the drawing they were pictured against a snowy background* PAINT, DRAW, sketch, depict, delineate, portray, show, illustrate. ❸ *Anne still pictured Richard as he had been* VISUALIZE, see in one's mind's eye, conjure up a picture/image of, imagine, see, evoke.

■ **put someone in the picture** INFORM, fill in, explain the situation/circumstances to, bring up to date, update, brief, keep posted; *informal* clue in, bring up to speed.

picturesque ▶ **adjective** ❶ *a picturesque village* ATTRACTIVE, pretty, beautiful, lovely, scenic, charming, quaint, pleasing, delightful. ❷ *a picturesque description* VIVID, graphic, colourful, impressive, striking.
– OPPOSITES ugly, dull.

piddling ▶ **adjective** (*informal*) TRIVIAL, trifling, petty, footling, slight, small, insignificant, unimportant, inconsequential, inconsiderable, negligible; meagre, inadequate, insufficient, paltry, scant, scanty, derisory, pitiful, miserable, puny, niggardly, beggarly, mere; *informal* measly, pathetic, piffling, mingy, poxy; *N. Amer. informal* nickel-and-dime.

pie ▶ **noun** PASTRY, tart, tartlet, quiche, pasty, patty, turnover, strudel.

■ **pie in the sky** (*informal*) FALSE HOPE, illusion, delusion, fantasy, pipe dream, daydream, castle in the air, castle in Spain.

piebald ▶ **adjective.** *See* PIED.

piece ▶ **noun** ❶ *a piece of cheese | a piece of wood* BIT, slice, chunk, segment, section, lump, hunk, wedge, slab, block, cake, bar, cube, stick, length; offcut, sample, fragment, sliver, splinter, wafer, chip, crumb, scrap, remnant, shred, shard, snippet; mouthful, morsel; *Brit. informal* wodge. ❷ *the pieces of a clock* COMPONENT, part, bit, section, segment, constituent, element; unit, module. ❸ *a piece of furniture* ITEM, article, specimen. ❹ *a piece of the profit* SHARE, portion, slice, quota, part, bit, percentage, amount, quantity, ration, fraction, division; *informal* cut, rake-off; *Brit. informal* whack. ❺ *pieces from his private collection* WORK (OF ART), creation, production; composition, opus. ❻ *the reporter who wrote the piece* ARTICLE, item, story, report, essay, study, review, composition, column. ❼ *the pieces on a chess board* TOKEN, counter, man, disc, chip, marker.

■ **in one piece** ❶ *the camera was still in one piece* UNBROKEN, entire, whole, intact, undamaged, unharmed. ❷ *I'll bring her back in one piece* UNHURT, uninjured, unscathed, safe, safe and sound.

■ **in pieces** BROKEN, in bits, shattered, smashed, in smithereens; *informal* bust.

■ **go/fall to pieces** HAVE A BREAKDOWN, break down, go out of one's mind, lose control, lose one's head, fall apart; *informal* crack up, lose it, come/fall apart at the seams, freak, freak out.

pièce de résistance ▶ **noun** MASTERPIECE, magnum opus, chef-d'œuvre, masterwork, tour de force, showpiece, prize, jewel in the crown.

piecemeal ▶ **adverb** A LITTLE AT A TIME, piece by piece, bit by bit, gradually, slowly, in stages, in steps, step by step, little by little, by degrees, in/by fits and starts.

pied ▶ **adjective** PARTICOLOURED, multicoloured, variegated, black and white, brown and white, piebald, skewbald, dappled, brindle, spotted, mottled, speckled, flecked; *N. Amer.* pinto.

pier ▶ **noun** ❶ *a boat was tied to the pier* JETTY, quay, wharf, dock, landing, landing stage. ❷ *the piers of the bridge* SUPPORT, cutwater, pile, piling, abutment, buttress, stanchion, prop, stay, upright, pillar, post, column.

pierce ▶ **verb** ❶ *the metal pierced his flesh* PENETRATE, puncture, perforate, prick, lance; stab, spike, stick, impale, transfix, bore through, drill through. ❷ *his anguish pierced her to the quick* HURT, wound, pain, sting, sear, grieve, distress, upset, trouble, harrow, afflict; affect, move.

piercing ▶ **adjective** ❶ *a piercing shriek* SHRILL, ear-splitting, high-pitched, penetrating, strident, loud. ❷ *the piercing wind* BITTER, biting, cutting, penetrating, sharp, keen, stinging, raw; freezing, frigid, glacial, arctic, chill. ❸ *a piercing pain* INTENSE, excruciating, agonizing, sharp, stabbing, shooting, stinging, severe, extreme, fierce, searing, racking. ❹ *his piercing gaze* SEARCHING, probing, penetrating, penetrative, shrewd, sharp, keen. ❺ *his piercing intelligence* PERCEPTIVE, percipient, perspicacious, penetrating, discerning, discriminating, intelligent, quick-witted, sharp, sharp-witted, shrewd, insightful, keen, acute, astute, clever, smart, incisive, razor-edged, trenchant.

piety ▶ **noun** DEVOUTNESS, devotion, piousness, religion, holiness, godliness, saintliness; veneration, reverence, faith, religious duty, spirituality, religious zeal, fervour; pietism, religiosity.

piffle ▶ **noun** (*informal*). *See* NONSENSE sense 1.

piffling ▶ **adjective** (*informal*) INADEQUATE, insufficient, tiny, small, minimal, trifling, paltry, pitiful, negligible; miserly, miserable; *informal* measly, stingy, lousy, pathetic, piddling, mingy, poxy.

pig ▶ **noun** ❶ *a herd of pigs* HOG, boar, sow, porker, swine, piglet; *children's word* piggy. ❷ (*informal*) *he's eaten the lot, the pig* GLUTTON, guzzler; *informal* hog, greedy guts; *Brit. informal* gannet. ❸ (*informal*) *he's been an absolute pig lately*

informal BASTARD, beast, louse, swine; *Brit. informal* toerag; *informal, dated* rotter, heel, stinker.
– RELATED TERMS porcine.

pigeonhole ▶ **noun** *journalistic pigeonholes* CATEGORY, categorization, class, classification, group, grouping, designation, slot.
▶ **verb** ❶ *they were pigeonholed as an indie guitar band* CATEGORIZE, compartmentalize, classify, characterize, label, brand, tag, designate. ❷ *the plan was pigeonholed last year* POSTPONE, put off, put back, defer, shelve, hold over, put to one side, put on ice, mothball, put in cold storage; *N. Amer.* table; *informal* put on the back burner.

pig-headed ▶ **adjective** OBSTINATE, stubborn (as a mule), mulish, bull-headed, obdurate, headstrong, self-willed, wilful, perverse, contrary, recalcitrant, stiff-necked; uncooperative, inflexible, uncompromising, intractable, intransigent, unyielding; *Brit. informal* bloody-minded, bolshie; *formal* refractory.

pigment ▶ **noun** COLOURING MATTER, colouring, colourant, colour, tint, dye, dyestuff.

pile[1] ▶ **noun** ❶ *a pile of stones* HEAP, stack, mound, pyramid, mass, quantity; collection, accumulation, assemblage, store, stockpile, hoard. ❷ (*informal*) *I've a pile of work to do* GREAT DEAL, lot, large quantity/amount, quantities, reams, mountain; abundance, cornucopia, plethora; *informal* load, heap, mass, slew, ocean, stack, ton; *Brit. informal* shedload; *Austral./NZ informal* swag. ❸ (*informal*) *he'd made his pile in the fur trade* FORTUNE, millions, billions; *informal* small fortune, bomb, packet, bundle, wad; *Brit. informal* loadsamoney. ❹ *a huge Victorian pile* MANSION, stately home, manor, manor house, country house; edifice.
▶ **verb** ❶ *he piled up the plates* HEAP (UP), stack (up), put on top of each other. ❷ *he piled his plate with fried eggs* LOAD, heap, fill (up), lade, stack, charge, stock. ❸ *his debts were piling up* INCREASE, grow, mount up, escalate, soar, spiral, leap up, shoot up, rocket, climb, accumulate, accrue, build up, multiply. ❹ *we piled into the car* CROWD, climb, pack, squeeze, push, shove.
■ **pile it on** (*informal*) EXAGGERATE, overstate the case, make a mountain out of a molehill, overdo it, overplay it, over-dramatize; *informal* lay it on thick, lay it on with a trowel.

pile[2] ▶ **noun** *a wall supported by timber piles* POST, stake, pillar, column, support, foundation, piling, abutment, pier, cutwater, buttress, stanchion, upright.

pile[3] ▶ **noun** *a carpet with a short pile* NAP, fibres, threads.

pile-up ▶ **noun** CRASH, multiple crash, collision, multiple collision, smash, accident, road accident; *Brit.* RTA (road traffic accident); *N. Amer.* wreck; *informal* smash-up; *Brit. informal* shunt.

pilfer ▶ **verb** STEAL, thieve, take, snatch, purloin, loot; *informal* swipe, rob, nab, rip off, lift, 'liberate', 'borrow', filch, snaffle; *Brit. informal* pinch, half-inch, nick, whip, knock off, nobble; *N. Amer. informal* heist.

pilgrim ▶ **noun** worshipper, devotee, believer; traveller, crusader, haji; *poetic/literary* wayfarer; *historical* palmer.

pilgrimage ▶ **noun** RELIGIOUS JOURNEY, religious expedition, hajj, crusade, mission.

pill ▶ **noun** TABLET, capsule, caplet, pellet, lozenge, pastille; *Veterinary Medicine* bolus.

pillage ▶ **verb** ❶ *the abbey was pillaged* RANSACK, rob, plunder, despoil, raid, loot; sack, devastate, lay waste, ravage, rape. ❷ *columns pillaged from an ancient town* STEAL, pilfer, thieve, take, snatch, purloin, loot; *informal* swipe, rob, nab, rip off, lift, 'liberate', 'borrow', filch, snaffle; *Brit. informal* pinch, half-inch, nick, whip, knock off, nobble; *N. Amer. informal* heist.
▶ **noun** *the rebels were intent on pillage* ROBBERY, robbing, raiding, plunder, looting, sacking, rape, marauding; *poetic/literary* rapine.

pillar ▶ **noun** ❶ *stone pillars* COLUMN, post, support, upright, baluster, pier, pile, pilaster, stanchion, prop, newel; obelisk, monolith. ❷ *a pillar of the community* STALWART, mainstay, bastion, rock; leading light, worthy, backbone, support, upholder, champion.

pillory ▶ **noun** *offenders were put in the pillory* STOCKS.
▶ **verb** ❶ *he was pilloried by the press* ATTACK, criticize, censure, condemn, denigrate, lambaste, savage, stigmatize, denounce; *informal* knock, slam, pan, bash, crucify, hammer; *Brit. informal* slate, rubbish, slag off; *N. Amer. informal* pummel; *Austral./NZ informal* bag, monster; *formal* excoriate. ❷ *they were pilloried at school* RIDICULE, jeer at, sneer at, deride, mock, scorn, make fun of, poke fun at, laugh at, scoff at, tease, taunt, rag; *informal* kid, rib, josh, take the mickey out of; *N. Amer. informal* razz, pull someone's chain.

pillow ▶ **noun** *his head rested on the pillow* CUSHION, bolster, pad; headrest.
▶ **verb** *she pillowed her head on folded arms* CUSHION, cradle, rest, lay, support.

pilot ▶ **noun** ❶ *a fighter pilot* AIRMAN/AIRWOMAN, flyer; captain, commander, co-pilot, wingman; *informal* skipper; *N. Amer. informal* jock; *dated* aviator, aeronaut. ❷ *a harbour pilot* NAVIGATOR, helmsman, steersman, coxswain. ❸ *a pilot for a TV series* TRIAL EPISODE; sample, experiment.
▶ **adjective** *a pilot project* EXPERIMENTAL, exploratory, trial, test, sample, speculative; preliminary.
▶ **verb** ❶ *he piloted the jet to safety* NAVIGATE, guide, manoeuvre, steer, control, direct, captain, shepherd; fly, aviate; drive; sail; *informal* skipper. ❷ *the questionnaire has been piloted* TEST, trial, try out; assess, investigate, examine, appraise, evaluate.

pimp ▶**noun** PROCURER, procuress; brothel-keeper, madam; *Brit. informal* ponce; *archaic* bawd.

pimple ▶**noun** SPOT, pustule, bleb, boil, swelling, eruption, blackhead, carbuncle, blister; (**pimples**) acne; *informal* whitehead, zit; *Scottish informal* plook; *technical* comedo, papule.

pin ▶**noun** ❶ *fasten the hem with a pin* TACK, safety pin, nail, staple, fastener. ❷ *a broken pin in the machine* BOLT, peg, rivet, dowel, screw. ❸ *they wore name pins* BADGE, brooch.

▶**verb** ❶ *she pinned the brooch to her dress* ATTACH, fasten, affix, fix, tack, clip; join, secure. ❷ *they pinned him to the ground* HOLD, press, hold fast, hold down; restrain, pinion, immobilize. ❸ *they pinned the crime on him* BLAME FOR, hold responsible for, attribute to, impute to, ascribe to; lay something at someone's door; *informal* stick on.

■ **pin someone/something down** ❶ *our troops can pin down the enemy* CONFINE, TRAP, hem in, corner, close in, shut in, hedge in, pen in, restrain, entangle, enmesh, immobilize. ❷ *she tried to pin him down to a plan* CONSTRAIN, make someone commit themselves, pressure, pressurize, tie down, nail down. ❸ *it evoked a memory but he couldn't pin it down* DEFINE, put one's finger on, put into words, express, name, specify, identify, pinpoint, place.

pinch ▶**verb** ❶ *he pinched my arm* NIP, tweak, squeeze, grasp. ❷ *my new shoes pinch my toes* HURT, pain; squeeze, crush, cramp; be uncomfortable. ❸ *I scraped and pinched to afford it* ECONOMIZE, scrimp (and save), be sparing, be frugal, cut back, tighten one's belt, retrench, cut one's coat according to one's cloth; *informal* be stingy, be tight. ❹ (*informal*) *he was pinched for drink-driving* ARREST, apprehend, take into custody, detain, seize, catch, take in, haul in; *informal* collar, nab, pick up, run in, nick, bust, nail, do. ❺ (*Brit. informal*) *you pinched his biscuits* STEAL, thieve, take, snatch, pilfer, purloin, loot; *informal* swipe, rob, nab, lift, 'liberate', 'borrow', filch; *Brit. informal* nick, half-inch, whip, knock off, nobble; *N. Amer. informal* heist.

▶**noun** ❶ *he gave her arm a pinch* NIP, tweak, squeeze. ❷ *a pinch of salt* BIT, touch, dash, spot, trace, soupçon, speck, taste; *informal* smidgen, tad.

■ **at a pinch** IF NECESSARY, if need be, in an emergency, just possibly, with difficulty; *N. Amer.* in a pinch; *Brit. informal* at a push.

■ **feel the pinch** SUFFER HARDSHIP, be short of money, be poor, be impoverished.

pinched ▶**adjective** *their pinched faces* STRAINED, stressed, fraught, tense, taut; tired, worn, drained, sapped; wan, peaky, pale, grey, blanched; thin, drawn, haggard, gaunt.
– OPPOSITES healthy.

pine ▶**verb** ❶ *I am pining away from love* LANGUISH, decline, weaken, waste away, wilt, wither, fade, sicken, droop; brood, mope, moon. ❷ *he was pining for his son* YEARN, long, ache, sigh, hunger, languish; miss, mourn, lament, grieve over, shed tears for, bemoan, rue, eat one's heart out over; *informal* itch.

pinion ▶**verb** HOLD DOWN, pin down, restrain, hold fast, immobilize; tie, bind, truss (up), shackle, fetter, hobble, manacle, handcuff; *informal* cuff.

pink ▶**adjective** ROSE, rosy, rosé, pale red, salmon, coral; flushed, blushing.

▶**noun** (*informal*) *she's in the pink of condition* PRIME, perfection, best, finest, height; utmost, greatest, apex, zenith, acme, bloom.

■ **in the pink** (*informal*) IN GOOD HEALTH, very healthy, in rude health, very well, hale and hearty; blooming, flourishing, thriving, vigorous, strong, lusty, robust, in fine fettle, (as) fit as a fiddle, in excellent shape.

pinnacle ▶**noun** ❶ *pinnacles of rock* PEAK, needle, aiguille, hoodoo, crag, tor; summit, crest, apex, tip; *Geology* inselberg. ❷ *the pinnacles of the clock tower* TURRET, minaret, spire, finial, shikara, mirador. ❸ *the pinnacle of the sport* HIGHEST LEVEL, peak, height, high point, top, apex, zenith, apogee, acme.
– OPPOSITES nadir.

pinpoint ▶**noun** *a pinpoint of light* POINT, spot, speck, dot, speckle.

▶**adjective** *pinpoint accuracy* PRECISE, strict, exact, meticulous, scrupulous, punctilious, accurate, careful.

▶**verb** *pinpoint the cause of the trouble* IDENTIFY, determine, distinguish, discover, find, locate, detect, track down, spot, diagnose, recognize, pin down, home in on, put one's finger on.

pioneer ▶**noun** ❶ *the pioneers of the Wild West* SETTLER, colonist, colonizer, frontiersman/woman, explorer, trailblazer. ❷ *a pioneer of motoring* DEVELOPER, innovator, trailblazer, ground-breaker, spearhead; founder, founding father, architect, creator.

▶**verb** *he pioneered the sale of insurance* INTRODUCE, develop, evolve, launch, instigate, initiate, spearhead, institute, establish, found, be the father/mother of, originate, set in motion, create; lay the groundwork, prepare the way, blaze a trail, break new ground.

pious ▶**adjective** ❶ *a pious family* RELIGIOUS, devout, God-fearing, churchgoing, spiritual, prayerful, holy, godly, saintly, dedicated, reverent, dutiful, righteous. ❷ *a pious platitude* SANCTIMONIOUS, hypocritical, insincere, self-righteous, holier-than-thou, pietistic, churchy; *informal* goody-goody; *Brit. informal* pi. ❸ *a pious hope* FORLORN, vain, doomed, hopeless, desperate; unlikely, unrealistic.
– OPPOSITES irreligious, sincere.

pip ▶**noun** SEED, stone, pit.

pipe ▶**noun** ❶ *a central-heating pipe* TUBE, conduit, hose, main, duct, line, channel, pipeline, drain; tubing, piping, siphon. ❷ *he smokes a* *pipe* briar (pipe), meerschaum, chibouk; hookah, narghile, hubble-bubble, bong; *Brit.* churchwarden; *Scottish & N. English* cutty. ❸ *she was playing a pipe* WHISTLE, penny whistle, flute, recorder, fife; chanter. ❹ *regimental pipes and drums* BAGPIPES, uillean pipes; pan pipes.

▶ **verb** ❶ *the beer is piped into barrels* SIPHON, feed, channel, run, convey. ❷ *programmes piped in from London* TRANSMIT, feed, patch. ❸ *he heard a tune being piped* PLAY ON A PIPE, tootle, whistle; *poetic/literary* flute. ❹ *a curlew piped* CHIRP, cheep, chirrup, twitter, warble, trill, peep, sing, shrill.

■ **pipe down** (*informal*) BE QUIET, be silent, hush, stop talking, hold one's tongue; *informal* shut up, shut one's mouth, button it, button one's lip, belt up, put a sock in it.

pipe dream ▶ **noun** FANTASY, false hope, illusion, delusion, daydream, chimera; castle in the air, castle in Spain; *informal* pie in the sky.

pipeline ▶ **noun** *a gas pipeline* PIPE, conduit, main, line, duct, tube.

■ **in the pipeline** ON THE WAY, coming, forthcoming, upcoming, imminent, about to happen, near, close, brewing, in the offing, in the wind.

pipsqueak ▶ **noun** (*informal*) NOBODY, nonentity, insignificant person, non-person, cipher, small fry; upstart, stripling; *informal* squirt, whippersnapper; *N. Amer. informal* picayune; *archaic, informal* dandiprat.

piquant ▶ **adjective** ❶ *a piquant sauce* SPICY, tangy, peppery, hot; tasty, flavoursome, flavourful, appetizing, savoury; pungent, sharp, tart, zesty, strong, salty. ❷ *a piquant story* INTRIGUING, stimulating, interesting, fascinating, colourful, exciting, lively; spicy, provocative, racy; *informal* juicy.

– OPPOSITES bland, dull.

pique ▶ **noun** *a fit of pique* IRRITATION, annoyance, resentment, anger, displeasure, indignation, petulance, ill humour, vexation, exasperation, disgruntlement, discontent; offence, umbrage.

▶ **verb** ❶ *his curiosity was piqued* STIMULATE, arouse, rouse, provoke, whet, awaken, excite, kindle, stir, galvanize. ❷ *she was piqued by his neglect* IRRITATE, annoy, bother, vex, displease, upset, offend, affront, anger, exasperate, infuriate, gall, irk, nettle; *informal* peeve, aggravate, miff, rile, bug, needle, get someone's back up, hack off, get someone's goat; *Brit. informal* nark, give someone the hump; *N. Amer. informal* tick off, tee off.

piracy ▶ **noun** ❶ *piracy on the high seas* ROBBERY AT SEA, freebooting; *archaic* buccaneering. ❷ *software piracy* ILLEGAL COPYING, plagiarism, copyright infringement, bootlegging.

pirate ▶ **noun** ❶ *pirates boarded the ship* FREEBOOTER, marauder, raider; *historical* privateer; *archaic* buccaneer, corsair. ❷ *software pirates* COPYRIGHT INFRINGER, plagiarist, plagiarizer.

▶ **verb** *designers may pirate good ideas* REPRODUCE ILLEGALLY, copy illegally, plagiarize, poach, steal, appropriate, bootleg; *informal* crib, lift, rip off; *Brit. informal* nick, pinch.

pirouette ▶ **noun** *she did a little pirouette* SPIN, twirl, whirl, turn.

▶ **verb** *she pirouetted before the mirror* SPIN ROUND, twirl, whirl, turn round, revolve, pivot.

pistol ▶ **noun** REVOLVER, gun, handgun, side arm; automatic, six-shooter, thirty-eight, derringer; *informal* gat; *N. Amer. informal* piece, shooting iron; *trademark* Colt, Luger.

pit[1] ▶ **noun** ❶ *a pit in the ground* HOLE, ditch, trench, trough, hollow, excavation, cavity, crater, pothole; shaft, mineshaft. ❷ *pit closures* COAL MINE, colliery, quarry. ❸ *the pits in her skin* POCKMARK, pock, hollow, indentation, depression, dent, dint, dimple.

▶ **verb** ❶ *his skin had been pitted by acne* MARK, pockmark, scar, blemish, disfigure. ❷ *raindrops pitted the bare earth* MAKE HOLES IN, make hollows in, dent, indent, dint.

■ **pit someone/something against** SET AGAINST, match against, put in opposition to, put in competition with; compete with, contend with, vie with, wrestle with.

■ **the pits** (*informal*) THE WORST, the lowest of the low; rock-bottom, extremely bad, awful, terrible, dreadful, deplorable; *informal* appalling, lousy, abysmal, dire; *Brit. informal* chronic.

pit[2] ▶ **noun** *cherry pits* STONE, pip, seed.

pitch[1] ▶ **noun** ❶ *the pitch was unfit for cricket* PLAYING FIELD, field, ground, sports field; stadium, arena; *Brit.* park. ❷ *her voice rose in pitch* TONE, timbre, key, modulation, frequency. ❸ *the pitch of the roof* GRADIENT, slope, slant, angle, steepness, tilt, incline, inclination. ❹ *her anger reached such a pitch that she screamed* LEVEL, intensity, point, degree, height, extent. ❺ *a pitch of the ball* THROW, fling, hurl, toss, lob; delivery; *informal* chuck, heave. ❻ *his sales pitch* PATTER, talk; *informal* spiel, line. ❼ *street traders reserved their pitches* SITE, place, spot, station; *Scottish* stance; *Brit. informal* patch.

▶ **verb** ❶ *he pitched the note into the fire* THROW, toss, fling, hurl, cast, lob, flip, propel, bowl; *informal* chuck, sling, heave, bung; *N. Amer. informal* peg; *Austral. informal* hoy; *NZ informal* bish; *dated* shy. ❷ *he pitched overboard* FALL, tumble, topple, plunge, plummet. ❸ *they pitched their tents* PUT UP, set up, erect, raise. ❹ *the boat pitched* LURCH, toss (about), plunge, roll, reel, sway, rock, keel, list, wallow, labour.

■ **make a pitch for** TRY TO OBTAIN, try to acquire, try to get, bid for, make a bid for.

■ **pitch in** HELP (OUT), assist, lend a hand, join in, participate, contribute, do one's bit, chip in, cooperate, collaborate; *Brit. informal* muck in.

■ **pitch into** ATTACK, turn on, lash out at, set upon, assault, fly at, tear into, weigh into, belabour; *informal* lay into, let someone have it, take a pop at; *N. Amer. informal* light into.

pitch² ▶ noun *cement coated with pitch* bitumen, asphalt, tar.

pitch-black ▶ adjective BLACK, dark, pitch-dark, inky, jet-black, coal-black, jet, ebony; starless, moonless; *poetic/literary* Stygian.

pitcher ▶ noun JUG, ewer, jar; *N. Amer.* creamer; *historical* jorum.

piteous ▶ adjective SAD, pitiful, pitiable, pathetic, heart-rending, heartbreaking, moving, touching; plaintive, poignant, forlorn; poor, wretched, miserable.

pitfall ▶ noun HAZARD, danger, risk, peril, difficulty, catch, snag, stumbling block, drawback.

pith ▶ noun ❶ *the pith of the argument* ESSENCE, main point, fundamentals, heart, substance, nub, core, quintessence, crux, gist, meat, kernel, marrow, burden; *informal* nitty-gritty. ❷ *he writes with pith and exactitude* SUCCINCTNESS, conciseness, concision, pithiness, brevity; cogency, weight, depth, force.

pithy ▶ adjective SUCCINCT, terse, concise, compact, short (and sweet), brief, condensed, to the point, epigrammatic, crisp, thumbnail; significant, meaningful, expressive, telling; *formal* compendious.
– OPPOSITES verbose.

pitiful ▶ adjective ❶ *a child in a pitiful state* DISTRESSING, sad, piteous, pitiable, pathetic, heart-rending, heartbreaking, moving, touching, tear-jerking; plaintive, poignant, forlorn; poor, sorry, wretched, abject, miserable. ❷ *a pitiful £50 a month* PALTRY, miserable, meagre, insufficient, trifling, negligible, pitiable, derisory; *informal* pathetic, measly, piddling, mingy; *Brit. informal* poxy. ❸ *his performance was pitiful* DREADFUL, awful, terrible, lamentable, hopeless, poor, bad, feeble, pitiable, woeful, inadequate, below par, deplorable, laughable; *informal* pathetic, useless, appalling, lousy, abysmal, dire.

pitiless ▶ adjective MERCILESS, unmerciful, unpitying, ruthless, cruel, heartless, remorseless, hard-hearted, cold-hearted, harsh, callous, severe, unsparing, unforgiving, unfeeling, uncaring, unsympathetic, uncharitable, brutal, inhuman, inhumane, barbaric, sadistic.
– OPPOSITES merciful.

pittance ▶ noun A TINY AMOUNT, next to nothing, very little; *informal* peanuts, chicken feed, slave wages; *N. Amer. informal* chump change.

pitted ▶ adjective ❶ *his skin was pitted* POCK-MARKED, pocked, scarred, marked, blemished. ❷ *the pitted lane* POTHOLED, rutted, rutty, holey, bumpy, rough, uneven.
– OPPOSITES smooth.

pity ▶ noun ❶ *a voice full of pity* COMPASSION, commiseration, condolence, sympathy, fellow feeling, understanding; sorrow, regret, sadness. ❷ *it's a pity he never had children* SHAME, sad thing, bad luck, misfortune; *informal* crime, bummer, sin.
– OPPOSITES indifference, cruelty.
▶ verb *they pitied me* FEEL SORRY FOR, feel for, sympathize with, empathize with, commiserate with, take pity on, be moved by, condole with, grieve for.
■ **take pity on** FEEL SORRY FOR, relent, be compassionate towards, be sympathetic towards, have mercy on, help (out), put someone out of their misery.

pivot ▶ noun ❶ *the machine turns on a pivot* FULCRUM, axis, axle, swivel; pin, shaft, hub, spindle, hinge, kingpin, gudgeon. ❷ *the pivot of government policy* CENTRE, focus, hub, heart, nucleus, crux, keystone, cornerstone, linchpin, kingpin.
▶ verb ❶ *the panel pivots inwards* ROTATE, turn, swivel, revolve, spin. ❷ *it all pivoted on his response* DEPEND, hinge, turn, centre, hang, rely, rest; revolve around.

pivotal ▶ adjective CENTRAL, crucial, vital, critical, focal, essential, key, decisive.

pixie ▶ noun ELF, fairy, sprite, imp, brownie, puck, leprechaun; *poetic/literary* faerie, fay.

placard ▶ noun NOTICE, poster, sign, bill, advertisement; banner; *informal* ad; *Brit. informal* advert.

placate ▶ verb PACIFY, calm, appease, mollify, soothe, win over, conciliate, propitiate, make peace with, humour; *Austral./NZ* square someone off.
– OPPOSITES provoke.

place ▶ noun ❶ *an ideal place for dinner* LOCATION, site, spot, setting, position, situation, area, region, locale; venue; *technical* locus. ❷ *foreign places* COUNTRY, state, area, region, town, city; locality, district; *poetic/literary* clime. ❸ *a place of her own* HOME, house, flat, apartment; accommodation, property, pied-à-terre; rooms, quarters; *informal* pad, digs; *Brit. informal* gaff; *formal* residence, abode, dwelling (place), domicile, habitation. ❹ *if I were in your place, I'd agree* SITUATION, position, circumstances; *informal* shoes. ❺ *a place was reserved for her* SEAT, chair, space. ❻ *I offered him a place in the company* JOB, position, post, appointment, situation, office; employment. ❼ *I know my place* STATUS, position, standing, rank, niche; *dated* estate, station. ❽ *it was not her place to sort it out* RESPONSIBILITY, duty, job, task, role, function, concern, affair, charge; right, privilege, prerogative.
▶ verb ❶ *books were placed on the table* PUT (DOWN), set (down), lay, deposit, position, plant, rest, stand, station, situate, leave; *informal* stick, dump, bung, park, plonk, pop; *N. Amer. informal* plunk. ❷ *the trust you placed in me* PUT, lay, set, invest. ❸ *a survey placed the company sixth* RANK, order, grade, class, classify, categorize; put, set, assign. ❹ *Joe couldn't quite place her* IDENTIFY, recognize, remember, put a name to, pin

down; locate, pinpoint. ❺ *we were placed with foster parents* ACCOMMODATE, house; allocate, assign, appoint.

■ **in place** ❶ *the veil was held in place by pearls* IN POSITION, in situ. ❷ *the plans are in place* READY, set up, all set, established, arranged, in order.

■ **in place of** INSTEAD OF, rather than, as a substitute for, as a replacement for, in exchange for, in lieu of; in someone's stead.

■ **out of place** ❶ *she never had a hair out of place* OUT OF POSITION, out of order, in disarray, disarranged, in a mess, messy, topsy-turvy, muddled. ❷ *he said something out of place* INAPPROPRIATE, unsuitable, unseemly, improper, untoward, out of keeping, unbecoming, wrong. ❸ *she seemed out of place in a launderette* INCONGRUOUS, out of one's element, like a fish out of water; uncomfortable, uneasy.

■ **put someone in their place** HUMILIATE, take down a peg or two, deflate, crush, squash, humble; *informal* cut down to size, settle someone's hash; *N. Amer. informal* make someone eat crow.

■ **take place** HAPPEN, occur, come about, transpire, crop up, materialize, arise; *N. Amer. informal* go down; *poetic/literary* come to pass, befall, betide.

■ **take the place of** REPLACE, stand in for, substitute for, act for, fill in for, cover for, relieve.

placement ▶ noun ❶ *the placement of the chairs* POSITIONING, placing, arrangement, position, deployment, location, disposition. ❷ *teaching placements* JOB, post, assignment, posting, position, appointment, engagement.

placid ▶ adjective ❶ *she's normally very placid* EVEN-TEMPERED, calm, tranquil, equable, equanimous, unexcitable, serene, mild, {cool, calm, and collected}, composed, self-possessed, poised, easy-going, level-headed, steady, unruffled, unperturbed, phlegmatic; *informal* unflappable. ❷ *a placid village* QUIET, calm, tranquil, still, peaceful, undisturbed, restful, sleepy.

–OPPOSITES excitable, bustling.

plagiarism ▶ noun COPYING, infringement of copyright, piracy, theft, stealing; *informal* cribbing.

plagiarize ▶ verb COPY, infringe the copyright of, pirate, steal, poach, appropriate; *informal* rip off, crib, 'borrow'; *Brit. informal* pinch, nick.

plague ▶ noun ❶ *they died of the plague* BUBONIC PLAGUE, pneumonic plague, the Black Death; disease, sickness, epidemic; *dated* contagion; *archaic* pestilence. ❷ *a plague of cat fleas* INFESTATION, epidemic, invasion, swarm, multitude, host. ❸ *theft is the plague of restaurants* BANE, curse, scourge, affliction, blight.

▶ verb ❶ *he was plagued by poor health* AFFLICT, bedevil, torment, trouble, beset, dog, curse. ❷ *he plagued her with questions* PESTER, harass, badger, bother, torment, persecute, bedevil, harry, hound, trouble, irritate, nag, annoy, vex, molest; *informal* hassle, bug, aggravate; *N. English informal* mither; *N. Amer. informal* devil.

plain ▶ adjective ❶ *it was plain that something was wrong* OBVIOUS, (crystal) clear, evident, apparent, manifest, patent; discernible, perceptible, noticeable, recognizable, unmistakable, transparent; pronounced, marked, striking, conspicuous, self-evident, indisputable; as plain as a pikestaff, writ large; *informal* standing/sticking out like a sore thumb, standing/sticking out a mile. ❷ *plain English* INTELLIGIBLE, comprehensible, understandable, clear, coherent, uncomplicated, lucid, unambiguous, simple, straightforward, user-friendly; *formal* perspicuous. ❸ *plain speaking* CANDID, frank, outspoken, forthright, direct, honest, truthful, blunt, bald, explicit, unequivocal; *informal* upfront. ❹ *a plain dress* SIMPLE, ordinary, unadorned, unembellished, unornamented, unostentatious, unfussy, homely, basic, modest, unsophisticated, without frills; restrained, muted; everyday, workaday. ❺ *a plain girl* UNATTRACTIVE, unprepossessing, ugly, ill-favoured, unlovely, ordinary; *N. Amer.* homely; *informal* not much to look at; *Brit. informal* no oil painting. ❻ *it was plain bad luck* SHEER, pure, downright, out-and-out, unmitigated.

–OPPOSITES obscure, fancy, attractive, pretentious.

▶ adverb *this is just plain stupid* DOWNRIGHT, utterly, absolutely, completely, totally, really, thoroughly, positively, simply, unquestionably, undeniably; *informal* plumb.

▶ noun *the plains of North America* GRASSLAND, flatland, lowland, pasture, meadowland, prairie, savannah, steppe; tableland, tundra, pampas, veld.

plain-spoken ▶ adjective CANDID, frank, outspoken, forthright, direct, honest, truthful, open, blunt, straightforward, explicit, unequivocal, unambiguous, not afraid to call a spade a spade; *informal* upfront.

–OPPOSITES evasive.

plaintive ▶ adjective MOURNFUL, sad, wistful, doleful, pathetic, pitiful, piteous, melancholy, sorrowful, unhappy, wretched, woeful, forlorn, woebegone; *poetic/literary* dolorous.

plan ▶ noun ❶ *a plan for raising money* SCHEME, idea, proposal, proposition, suggestion; project, programme, system, method, procedure, strategy, stratagem, formula, recipe; way, means, measure, tactic. ❷ *her plan was to win a medal* INTENTION, aim, idea, intent, objective, object, goal, target, ambition. ❸ *plans for the clubhouse* BLUEPRINT, drawing, diagram, sketch, layout; illustration, representation; *N. Amer.* plat.

▶ verb ❶ *plan your route in advance* ORGANIZE, arrange, work out, design, outline, map out, prepare, schedule, formulate, frame, develop, devise, concoct; plot, scheme, hatch, brew; *N. Amer.* slate. ❷ *he plans to buy a house* INTEND, aim, propose, mean, hope, want, wish, desire, envisage; *formal* purpose. ❸ *I'm planning a new garden* DESIGN, draw up, sketch out, map out; *N. Amer.* plat.

plane[1] ▶ **noun** ❶ *a horizontal plane* FLAT SURFACE, level surface; the flat, horizontal. ❷ *a higher plane of achievement* LEVEL, degree, standard, stratum; position, rung, echelon.

▶ **adjective** *a plane surface* FLAT, level, horizontal, even; smooth, regular, uniform; *technical* planar.

▶ **verb** ❶ *seagulls planed overhead* SOAR, glide, float, drift, wheel. ❷ *boats planed across the water* SKIM, glide.

plane[2] ▶ **noun** *the plane took off* AIRCRAFT, airliner, (jumbo) jet, jetliner; flying machine; *Brit.* aeroplane; *N. Amer.* airplane, ship.

planet ▶ **noun** CELESTIAL BODY, heavenly body, satellite, moon, earth, asteroid, planetoid; *poetic/literary* orb.

plangent ▶ **adjective** (*poetic/literary*) MELANCHOLY, mournful, plaintive; sonorous, resonant, loud.

plank ▶ **noun** BOARD, floorboard, timber, stave.

planning ▶ **noun** PREPARATION(S), organization, arrangement, design; forethought, groundwork.

plant ▶ **noun** ❶ *garden plants* flower, vegetable, herb, shrub, weed; (**plants**) vegetation, greenery, flora, herbage, verdure. ❷ *a CIA plant* SPY, informant, informer, (secret) agent, mole, infiltrator, operative; *N. Amer. informal* spook. ❸ *the plant commenced production* FACTORY, works, foundry, mill, workshop, yard; *archaic* manufactory.

– RELATED TERMS phyto-, -phyte.

▶ **verb** ❶ *plant the seeds this autumn* SOW, scatter, seed; bed out, transplant. ❷ *he planted his feet on the ground* PLACE, put, set, position, situate, settle; *informal* plonk. ❸ *she planted the idea in his mind* INSTIL, implant, impress, imprint, put, place, introduce, fix, establish, lodge. ❹ *letters were planted to embarrass them* HIDE, conceal, secrete.

plaque ▶ **noun** PLATE, tablet, panel, sign, plaquette, cartouche; *Brit.* brass.

plaster ▶ **noun** ❶ *the plaster covering the bricks* PLASTERWORK, stucco, pargeting; *trademark* Artex. ❷ *a statuette made of plaster* PLASTER OF PARIS, gypsum. ❸ *waterproof plasters* STICKING PLASTER, (adhesive) dressing, bandage; *trademark* Elastoplast, Band-Aid.

▶ **verb** ❶ *bread plastered with butter* COVER THICKLY, smother, spread, smear, cake, coat. ❷ *his hair was plastered down with sweat* FLATTEN (DOWN), smooth down, slick down.

plastic ▶ **adjective** ❶ *at high temperatures the rocks become plastic* MALLEABLE, mouldable, pliable, pliant, ductile, flexible, soft, workable, bendable; *informal* bendy. ❷ *the plastic minds of children* IMPRESSIONABLE, malleable, receptive, pliable, pliant, flexible; compliant, tractable, biddable, persuadable, susceptible, manipulable. ❸ *a plastic smile* ARTIFICIAL, false, fake, superficial, pseudo, bogus, unnatural, insincere; *informal* phoney, pretend.

– OPPOSITES rigid, intractable, genuine.

plate ▶ **noun** ❶ *a dinner plate* DISH, platter, salver, paten; *historical* trencher; *archaic* charger. ❷ *a plate of spaghetti* PLATEFUL, helping, portion, serving. ❸ *steel plates* PANEL, sheet, layer, pane, slab. ❹ *a brass plate on the door* PLAQUE, sign, tablet, plaquette, cartouche; *Brit.* brass. ❺ *the book has colour plates* PICTURE, print, illustration, photograph, photo.

▶ **verb** *the roof was plated with steel* COVER, coat, overlay, laminate, veneer; electroplate, galvanize, gild.

plateau ▶ **noun** ❶ *a windswept plateau* UPLAND, tableland, plain, mesa, highland. ❷ *prices reached a plateau* quiescent period; let-up, respite, lull.

platform ▶ **noun** ❶ *he made a speech from the platform* STAGE, dais, rostrum, podium, soapbox. ❷ *the Democratic Party's platform* POLICY, programme, party line, manifesto, plan, principles, objectives, aims.

platitude ▶ **noun** CLICHÉ, truism, commonplace, banality, old chestnut, bromide.

platitudinous ▶ **adjective** HACKNEYED, overworked, overused, clichéd, banal, trite, commonplace, well worn, stale, tired, unoriginal; *informal* corny, old hat.

– OPPOSITES original.

platonic ▶ **adjective** NON-SEXUAL, non-physical, chaste; intellectual, friendly.

– OPPOSITES sexual.

platoon ▶ **noun** UNIT, patrol, troop, squad, squadron, team, company, corps, outfit, detachment, contingent.

platter ▶ **noun** PLATE, dish, salver, paten, tray; *historical* trencher; *archaic* charger.

plaudits ▶ **plural noun** PRAISE, acclaim, commendation, congratulations, accolades, compliments, cheers, applause, tributes, bouquets; a pat on the back; *informal* a (big) hand.

– OPPOSITES criticism.

plausible ▶ **adjective** CREDIBLE, reasonable, believable, likely, feasible, tenable, possible, conceivable, imaginable; convincing, persuasive, cogent, sound, rational, logical, thinkable.

– OPPOSITES unlikely.

play ▶ **verb** ❶ *the children played with toys* AMUSE ONESELF, entertain oneself, enjoy oneself, have fun; relax, occupy oneself, divert oneself; frolic, frisk, romp, caper; *informal* mess about/around, lark (about/around); *dated* sport. ❷ *I used to play football* TAKE PART IN, participate in, be involved in, compete in, do. ❸ *Liverpool play Oxford on Sunday* COMPETE AGAINST, take on, challenge, vie with. ❹ *he was to play Macbeth* ACT (THE PART OF), take the role of, appear as, portray, depict, impersonate, represent, render, perform; *formal* personate. ❺ *he learned to play the flute* PERFORM ON, make music on; blow, sound. ❻ *the sunlight played on the water* DANCE, flit, ripple, touch; sparkle, glint.

▶ **noun** ❶ *a balance between work and play* AMUSEMENT, entertainment, relaxation, recreation, diversion, distraction, leisure; enjoyment, pleasure, fun, games, fun and games; horseplay, merrymaking, revelry; *informal* living it up; *dated* sport. ❷ *a Shakespeare play* DRAMA, theatrical work; teleplay, screenplay, comedy, tragedy; production, performance, show, sketch. ❸ *she knew the play of the real world* ACTION, activity, operation, working, function; interaction, interplay. ❹ *there was a little play in the rope* MOVEMENT, slack, give; room to manoeuvre, scope, latitude.

■ **play around** (*informal*) WOMANIZE, philander, have affairs, flirt; *informal* carry on, mess about/around, play the field, sleep around; *Brit. informal* play away; *N. Amer. informal* fool around.

■ **play at** PRETEND TO BE, pass oneself off as, masquerade as, profess to be, pose as, impersonate; fake, feign, simulate, affect; *N. Amer. informal* make like.

■ **play ball** (*informal*) COOPERATE, collaborate, play the game, show willing, help, lend a hand, assist, contribute; *informal* pitch in.

■ **play something down** MAKE LIGHT OF, make little of, gloss over, de-emphasize, downplay, understate; soft-pedal, tone down, diminish, trivialize, underrate, underestimate, undervalue; disparage, belittle, scoff at, sneer at, shrug off; *informal* pooh-pooh.

■ **play for time** STALL, temporize, delay, hold back, hang fire, procrastinate, drag one's feet.

■ **play it by ear** IMPROVISE, extemporize, ad lib; *informal* busk it, wing it.

■ **play on** *they play on our fears* EXPLOIT, take advantage of, use, turn to (one's) account, profit by, capitalize on, trade on, milk, abuse.

■ **play the fool** CLOWN ABOUT/AROUND, fool about/around, mess about/around, lark about/around, monkey about/around, joke; *informal* horse about/around, act the goat; *Brit. informal* muck about/around.

■ **play the game** PLAY FAIR, be fair, play by the rules, conform, be a good sport, toe the line.

■ **play up** (*Brit. informal*) ❶ *the boys really did play up* MISBEHAVE, be bad, be naughty, get up to mischief, be disobedient, cause trouble. ❷ *the boiler's playing up* MALFUNCTION, not work, be defective, be faulty; *informal* go on the blink, act up. ❸ *his leg was playing up* BE PAINFUL, hurt, ache, be sore, cause discomfort; *informal* kill someone, give someone gyp.

■ **play something up** EMPHASIZE, accentuate, call attention to, point up, underline, highlight, spotlight, foreground, feature, stress, accent.

■ **play up to** INGRATIATE ONESELF WITH, curry favour with, court, fawn over, make up to, keep someone sweet, toady to, crawl to, pander to, flatter; *informal* soft-soap, suck up to, butter up, lick someone's boots.

playboy ▶ **noun** SOCIALITE, pleasure-seeker, sybarite; ladies' man, womanizer, philanderer, rake, roué; *informal* ladykiller.

player ▶ **noun** ❶ *a tournament for young players* PARTICIPANT, contestant, competitor, contender; sportsman/woman, athlete. ❷ *the players in the orchestra* MUSICIAN, performer, instrumentalist, soloist, virtuoso. ❸ *the players of the Royal Shakespeare Company* ACTOR, actress, performer, thespian, entertainer, artist(e), trouper.

playful ▶ **adjective** ❶ *a playful mood* FRISKY, jolly, lively, full of fun, frolicsome, sportive, high-spirited, exuberant, perky; mischievous, impish, rascally, tricksy; *informal* full of beans; *dated* gay; *formal* ludic. ❷ *a playful remark* LIGHT-HEARTED, in jest, joking, jokey, teasing, humorous, jocular, good-natured, tongue-in-cheek, facetious, frivolous, flippant, arch; *informal* waggish.

–OPPOSITES serious.

playground ▶ **noun** PLAY AREA, park, playing field, recreation ground; *Brit. informal* rec.

playmate ▶ **noun** FRIEND, playfellow, companion; *informal* chum, pal; *Brit. informal* mate; *N. Amer. informal* buddy.

plaything ▶ **noun** TOY, game.

playwright ▶ **noun** DRAMATIST, dramaturge, scriptwriter, screenwriter, writer, scenarist; tragedian.

plea ▶ **noun** ❶ *a plea for aid* APPEAL, entreaty, supplication, petition, request, call, suit, solicitation. ❷ *her plea of a headache was unconvincing* CLAIM, explanation, defence, justification; excuse, pretext.

plead ▶ **verb** ❶ *he pleaded with her to stay* BEG, implore, entreat, appeal to, supplicate, petition, request, ask, call on; *poetic/literary* beseech. ❷ *she pleaded ignorance* CLAIM, use as an excuse, assert, allege, argue, state.

pleasant ▶ **adjective** ❶ *a pleasant evening* ENJOYABLE, pleasurable, nice, agreeable, pleasing, satisfying, gratifying, good; entertaining, amusing, delightful, charming; fine, balmy; *informal* lovely, great. ❷ *the staff are pleasant* FRIENDLY, agreeable, amiable, nice, genial, cordial, likeable, amicable, good-humoured, good-natured, personable; hospitable, approachable, gracious, courteous, polite, obliging, helpful, considerate; charming, lovely, delightful, sweet, sympathetic; *N. English & Scottish* canny; *Scottish* couthy.

–OPPOSITES disagreeable.

pleasantry ▶ **noun** ❶ *we exchanged pleasant-*

ries BANTER, badinage; polite remark, casual remark; *N. Amer. informal* josh. ❷ *he laughed at his own pleasantry* JOKE, witticism, quip, jest, gag, bon mot; *informal* wisecrack, crack.

please ▶ **verb** ❶ *he'd do anything to please her* MAKE HAPPY, give pleasure to, make someone feel good; delight, charm, amuse, entertain; satisfy, gratify, humour, oblige, content, suit; *informal* tickle someone pink. ❷ *do as you please* LIKE, want, wish, desire, see fit, think fit, choose, will, prefer.
– OPPOSITES annoy.
▶ **adverb** *please sit down* IF YOU PLEASE, if you wouldn't mind, if you would be so good; kindly, pray; *archaic* prithee.

pleased ▶ **adjective** HAPPY, glad, delighted, gratified, grateful, thankful, content, contented, satisfied; thrilled, elated, overjoyed, cock-a-hoop; *informal* over the moon, tickled pink, on cloud nine; *Brit. informal* chuffed; *N. English informal* made up; *Austral. informal* wrapped; *humorous* gruntled.
– OPPOSITES unhappy.

pleasing ▶ **adjective** ❶ *a pleasing day* NICE, agreeable, pleasant, pleasurable, satisfying, gratifying, good, enjoyable, entertaining, amusing, delightful; *informal* lovely, great. ❷ *her pleasing manner* FRIENDLY, amiable, pleasant, agreeable, affable, nice, genial, likeable, good-humoured, charming, engaging, delightful; *informal* lovely.

pleasurable ▶ **adjective** PLEASANT, enjoyable, delightful, nice, pleasing, agreeable, gratifying; fun, entertaining, amusing, diverting; *informal* lovely, great.

pleasure ▶ **noun** ❶ *she smiled with pleasure* HAPPINESS, delight, joy, gladness, glee, satisfaction, gratification, contentment, enjoyment, amusement. ❷ *his greatest pleasures in life* JOY, amusement, diversion, recreation, pastime; treat, thrill. ❸ *don't mix business and pleasure* ENJOYMENT, fun, entertainment; recreation, leisure, relaxation; *informal* jollies. ❹ *a life of pleasure* HEDONISM, indulgence, self-indulgence, self-gratification, lotus-eating. ❺ *what's your pleasure?* WISH, desire, preference, will, inclination, choice.
■ **take pleasure in** ENJOY, delight in, love, like, adore, appreciate, relish, savour, revel in, glory in; *informal* get a kick out of, get a thrill out of.
■ **with pleasure** GLADLY, willingly, happily, readily; by all means, of course; *archaic* fain.

pleat ▶ **noun** *a curtain pleat* FOLD, crease, gather, tuck, crimp; pucker.
▶ **verb** *the dress is pleated at the front* FOLD, crease, gather, tuck, crimp; pucker.

plebeian ▶ **noun** *plebeians and gentry lived together* PROLETARIAN, commoner, working-class person, worker; peasant; *informal* pleb, prole.
– OPPOSITES aristocrat.
▶ **adjective** ❶ *people of plebeian descent* LOWER-CLASS, working-class, proletarian, common, peasant; mean, humble, lowly. ❷ *plebeian tastes* UNCULTURED, uncultivated, unrefined, lowbrow, philistine, uneducated; coarse, uncouth, common, vulgar; *informal* plebby; *Brit. informal* non-U.
– OPPOSITES noble, refined.

plebiscite ▶ **noun** VOTE, referendum, ballot, poll.

pledge ▶ **noun** ❶ *his election pledge* PROMISE, undertaking, vow, word (of honour), commitment, assurance, oath, guarantee. ❷ *he gave it as a pledge to a creditor* SURETY, bond, security, collateral, guarantee, deposit. ❸ *a pledge of my sincerity* TOKEN, symbol, sign, earnest, mark, testimony, proof, evidence.
▶ **verb** ❶ *he pledged to root out corruption* PROMISE, vow, swear, undertake, engage, commit oneself, declare, affirm, avow. ❷ *they pledged £100 million* PROMISE (TO GIVE), donate, contribute, give, put up; *Brit.* covenant. ❸ *his home is pledged as security against the loan* MORTGAGE, put up as collateral, guarantee, pawn.

plenary ▶ **adjective** ❶ *the council has plenary powers* UNCONDITIONAL, unlimited, unrestricted, unqualified, absolute, sweeping, comprehensive; plenipotentiary. ❷ *a plenary session of the parliament* FULL, complete, entire.

plenipotentiary ▶ **noun** *a plenipotentiary in Paris* DIPLOMAT, dignitary, ambassador, minister, emissary, chargé d'affaires, envoy.
▶ **adjective** *plenipotentiary powers. See* PLENARY sense 1.

plenitude ▶ **noun** (*formal*) ABUNDANCE, lot, wealth, profusion, cornucopia, plethora, superabundance; *informal* load, slew, heap, ton; *Brit. informal* shedload.

plenteous ▶ **adjective** (*poetic/literary*). *See* PLENTIFUL.

plentiful ▶ **adjective** ABUNDANT, copious, ample, profuse, rich, lavish, generous, bountiful, large, great, bumper, superabundant, inexhaustible, prolific; *informal* a gogo, galore; *poetic/literary* plenteous.
– OPPOSITES scarce.

plenty ▶ **noun** *times of plenty* PROSPERITY, affluence, wealth, opulence, comfort, luxury; plentifulness, abundance; *poetic/literary* plenteousness.
▶ **pronoun** *there are plenty of books* A LOT OF, many, a great deal of, a plethora of, enough (and to spare), no lack of, sufficient, a wealth of; *informal* loads of, lots of, heaps of, stacks of, masses of, tons of, oodles of, scads of, a slew of.

plethora ▶ **noun** EXCESS, abundance, superabundance, surplus, glut, superfluity, surfeit, profusion, too many, too much, enough and to spare; *informal* more —— than one can shake a stick at.
– OPPOSITES dearth.

pliable ▶ adjective ❶ *leather is pliable* FLEXIBLE, pliant, bendable, elastic, supple, malleable, workable, plastic, springy, ductile; *informal* bendy. ❷ *pliable teenage minds* MALLEABLE, impressionable, flexible, adaptable, pliant, compliant, biddable, tractable, yielding, amenable, susceptible, suggestible, persuadable, manipulable, receptive.
– OPPOSITES rigid, obdurate.

pliant ▶ adjective. *See* PLIABLE senses 1, 2.

plight ▶ noun PREDICAMENT, difficult situation, dire straits, trouble, difficulty, extremity, bind; *informal* dilemma, tight corner, tight spot, hole, pickle, jam, fix.

plod ▶ verb ❶ *Mum plodded wearily upstairs* TRUDGE, walk heavily, clump, stomp, tramp, lumber, slog; *Brit. informal* trog. ❷ *I have to plod through the whole book* WADE, plough, trawl, toil, labour; *informal* slog.

plot ▶ noun ❶ *a plot to overthrow him* CONSPIRACY, intrigue, secret plan; machinations. ❷ *the plot of her novel* STORYLINE, story, scenario, action, thread; *formal* diegesis. ❸ *a three-acre plot* PIECE OF GROUND, patch, area, tract, acreage; *Brit.* allotment; *N. Amer.* lot, plat; *N. Amer. & Austral./NZ* homesite.
▶ verb ❶ *he plotted their downfall* PLAN, scheme, arrange, organize, hatch, concoct, devise, dream up; *informal* cook up. ❷ *his brother was plotting against him* CONSPIRE, scheme, intrigue, collude, connive, machinate. ❸ *the fifty-three sites were plotted* MARK, chart, map, represent, graph.

plotter ▶ noun CONSPIRATOR, schemer, intriguer, machinator; planner.

plough ▶ verb ❶ *the fields were ploughed* TILL, furrow, harrow, cultivate, work, break up. ❷ *the car ploughed into a lamp post* CRASH, smash, career, plunge, bulldoze, hurtle, cannon, run, drive; *N. Amer. informal* barrel. ❸ *they ploughed through deep snow* TRUDGE, plod, toil, wade; *informal* slog; *Brit. informal* trog.

ploy ▶ noun RUSE, tactic, move, device, stratagem, scheme, trick, gambit, plan, manoeuvre, dodge, subterfuge, wile; *Brit. informal* wheeze.

pluck ▶ verb ❶ *he plucked a thread from his lapel* REMOVE, pick (off), pull (off/out), extract, take (off). ❷ *she plucked at his T-shirt* PULL (AT), tug (at), clutch (at), snatch (at), grab, catch (at), tweak, jerk; *informal* yank. ❸ *the turkeys are plucked* DEPLUME, remove the feathers from. ❹ *she plucked the guitar strings* STRUM, pick, thrum, twang; play pizzicato.
▶ noun *the task took a lot of pluck* COURAGE, bravery, nerve, backbone, spine, daring, spirit, intrepidity, fearlessness, mettle, grit, determination, fortitude, resolve, stout-heartedness, dauntlessness, valour, heroism, audacity; *informal* guts, spunk, gumption; *Brit. informal* bottle; *N. Amer. informal* moxie.

plucky ▶ adjective BRAVE, courageous, bold, daring, fearless, intrepid, spirited, game, valiant, valorous, stout-hearted, dauntless, resolute, determined, undaunted, unflinching, audacious, unafraid, doughty, mettlesome; *informal* gutsy, spunky.
– OPPOSITES timid.

plug ▶ noun ❶ *she pulled out the plug* STOPPER, bung, cork, seal, spigot, spile; *N. Amer.* stopple. ❷ *a plug of tobacco* WAD, quid, twist, chew. ❸ (*informal*) *a plug for his new book* ADVERTISEMENT, promotion, commercial, recommendation, mention, good word; *informal* hype, push, puff, ad, boost, ballyhoo; *Brit. informal* advert.
▶ verb ❶ *plug the holes* STOP (UP), seal (up/off), close (up/off), cork, stopper, bung, block (up/off), fill (up); *N. Amer.* stopple. ❷ (*informal*) *she plugged her new film* PUBLICIZE, promote, advertise, mention, bang the drum for, draw attention to; *informal* hype (up), push, puff. ❸ (*informal*) *don't move or I'll plug you* SHOOT, gun down; *informal* blast, pump full of lead.
■ **plug away** (*informal*) TOIL, labour, slave away, soldier on, persevere, persist, keep on, plough on; *informal* slog away, beaver away, peg away.

plum ▶ adjective (*informal*) *a plum job* EXCELLENT, very good, wonderful, marvellous, choice, first-class; *informal* great, terrific, cushy.

plumb[1] ▶ verb *an attempt to plumb her psyche* EXPLORE, probe, delve into, search, examine, investigate, fathom, penetrate, understand.
▶ adverb ❶ (*informal*) *it went plumb through the screen* RIGHT, exactly, precisely, directly, dead, straight; *informal* (slap) bang. ❷ (*N. Amer. informal*) UTTERLY, absolutely, completely, downright, totally, quite, thoroughly. ❸ (*archaic*) *the bell hangs plumb* VERTICALLY, perpendicularly, straight down.
▶ adjective *a plumb drop* VERTICAL, perpendicular, straight.
■ **plumb the depths** FIND, experience the extremes, reach the lowest point; reach rock bottom.

plumb[2] ▶ verb *he plumbed in the washing machine* INSTALL, put in, fit.

plume ▶ noun *ostrich plumes* FEATHER, quill; *Ornithology* plumule, covert.
■ **plume oneself** CONGRATULATE ONESELF, preen oneself, pat oneself on the back, pride oneself, boast about.

plummet ▶ verb ❶ *the plane plummeted to the ground* PLUNGE, nosedive, dive, drop, fall, descend, hurtle. ❷ *share prices plummeted* FALL STEEPLY, plunge, tumble, drop rapidly, go down, slump; *informal* crash, nosedive.

plummy ▶ adjective (*Brit. informal*) *a plummy voice* UPPER-CLASS, refined, aristocratic, grand; *Brit.* Home Counties; *Scottish* Kelvinside, Morningside; *Brit. informal* posh, Sloaney.

plump[1] ▶ adjective *a plump child* CHUBBY, fat, stout, rotund, well padded, ample, round, chunky, portly, overweight, fleshy, paunchy, bulky, corpulent; *informal* tubby, roly-poly,

pudgy, beefy, porky, blubbery; *Brit. informal* podgy, fubsy; *N. Amer. informal* zaftig, corn-fed.
–OPPOSITES thin.

plump[2] ▶ verb ❶ *Jack plumped down on to a chair* FLOP, COLLAPSE, sink, fall, drop, slump; *informal* plonk oneself; *N. Amer. informal* plank oneself. ❷ *she plumped her bag on the table* PUT (DOWN), set (down), place, deposit, dump, stick; *informal* plonk; *Brit. informal* bung; *N. Amer. informal* plunk. ❸ *I plumped for a cream cake* CHOOSE, decide on, go for, opt for, pick, settle on, select, take, elect.

plunder ▶ verb ❶ *they plundered the countryside* PILLAGE, loot, rob, raid, ransack, despoil, strip, ravage, lay waste, devastate, sack, rape. ❷ *money plundered from pension funds* STEAL, purloin, thieve, seize, pillage; embezzle.
▶ noun ❶ *the plunder of the villages* LOOTING, pillaging, plundering, raiding, ransacking, devastation, sacking; *poetic/literary* rapine. ❷ *the army took huge quantities of plunder* BOOTY, loot, stolen goods, spoils, ill-gotten gains; *informal* swag.

plunge ▶ verb ❶ *Joy plunged into the sea* DIVE, jump, throw oneself, launch oneself. ❷ *the aircraft plunged to the ground* PLUMMET, nosedive, drop, fall, pitch, tumble, descend. ❸ *the car plunged down an alley* CHARGE, hurtle, career, plough, cannon, tear; *N. Amer. informal* barrel. ❹ *oil prices plunged* FALL SHARPLY, plummet, drop, go down, tumble, slump; *informal* crash, nosedive. ❺ *he plunged the dagger into her back* THRUST, jab, stab, sink, stick, ram, drive, push, shove, force. ❻ *plunge the pears into water* IMMERSE, submerge, dip, dunk. ❼ *the room was plunged into darkness* THROW, cast, pitch.
▶ noun ❶ *a plunge into the deep end* DIVE, jump, nosedive, fall, pitch, drop, plummet, descent. ❷ *a plunge in profits* FALL, drop, slump; *informal* nosedive, crash.
■ **take the plunge** COMMIT ONESELF, go for it, throw caution to the wind(s), risk it; *informal* jump in at the deep end, go for broke.

plurality ▶ noun *a plurality of theories* WIDE VARIETY, diversity, range, lot, multitude, multiplicity, galaxy, wealth, profusion, abundance, plethora, host; *informal* load, stack, heap, mass.

plus ▶ preposition ❶ *three plus three makes six* AND, added to. ❷ *he wrote four novels plus various poems* AS WELL AS, together with, along with, in addition to, and, not to mention, besides.
–OPPOSITES minus.
▶ noun *one of the pluses of the job* ADVANTAGE, good point, asset, pro, (fringe) benefit, bonus, extra, attraction; *informal* perk; *formal* perquisite.
–OPPOSITES disadvantage.

plush ▶ adjective (*informal*) LUXURIOUS, luxury, de luxe, sumptuous, palatial, lavish, opulent, magnificent, lush, rich, expensive, fancy, grand; *Brit.* upmarket; *informal* posh, ritzy, swanky, classy; *Brit. informal* swish; *N. Amer. informal* swank.
–OPPOSITES austere.

plutocrat ▶ noun RICH PERSON, magnate, millionaire, billionaire, multimillionaire; nouveau riche; *informal* fat cat, moneybags.

ply[1] ▶ verb ❶ *the gondolier plied his oar* USE, wield, work, manipulate, handle, operate, utilize, employ. ❷ *he plied a profitable trade* ENGAGE IN, carry on, pursue, conduct, practise; *archaic* prosecute. ❸ *ferries ply between all lake resorts* GO REGULARLY, travel, shuttle, go back and forth. ❹ *she plied me with scones* PROVIDE, supply, lavish, shower, regale. ❺ *he plied her with questions* BOMBARD, assail, beset, pester, plague, harass, importune; *informal* hassle.

ply[2] ▶ noun *a three-ply tissue* LAYER, thickness, strand, sheet, leaf.

poach ▶ verb ❶ *he's been poaching salmon* HUNT ILLEGALLY, catch illegally; steal. ❷ *workers were poached by other firms* STEAL, appropriate, purloin, take; *informal* nab, swipe; *Brit. informal* nick, pinch.

pocket ▶ noun ❶ *a bag with two pockets* POUCH, compartment. ❷ *the jewellery was beyond her pocket* MEANS, budget, resources, finances, funds, money, wherewithal; *N. Amer.* pocketbook. ❸ *pockets of disaffection* (ISOLATED) AREA, patch, region, island, cluster, centre.
▶ adjective *a pocket dictionary* SMALL, little, miniature, mini, compact, concise, abridged, potted, portable; *N. Amer.* vest-pocket.
▶ verb *he pocketed $900,000 of their money* STEAL, take, appropriate, thieve, purloin, misappropriate, embezzle; *informal* filch, swipe, snaffle; *Brit. informal* pinch, nick, whip.

pockmark ▶ noun SCAR, pit, pock, mark, blemish.

pod ▶ noun SHELL, husk, hull, case; *N. Amer.* shuck; *Botany* pericarp, capsule.

podgy ▶ adjective (*Brit. informal*) CHUBBY, plump, fat, stout, rotund, well padded, ample, round, chunky, portly, overweight, fleshy, paunchy, bulky, corpulent; *informal* tubby, roly-poly, pudgy, beefy, porky, blubbery; *N. Amer. informal* zaftig, corn-fed.
–OPPOSITES thin.

podium ▶ noun PLATFORM, stage, dais, rostrum, stand, soapbox.

poem ▶ noun VERSE, rhyme, piece of poetry, song, verselet.

poet ▶ noun WRITER OF POETRY, versifier, rhymester, rhymer, sonneteer, lyricist, lyrist; laureate; *poetic/literary* bard; *derogatory* poetaster; *historical* troubadour, balladeer; *archaic* rhymist.

poetic ▶ adjective ❶ *poetic compositions* POETICAL, verse, metrical, lyrical, lyric, elegiac. ❷ *poetic language* EXPRESSIVE, figurative, symbolic, flowery, artistic, elegant, fine, beautiful; sensitive, imaginative, creative.

poetry ▶ noun POEMS, verse, versification, metrical composition, rhymes, balladry; *archaic* poesy.

pogrom ▶ **noun** MASSACRE, slaughter, mass murder, annihilation, extermination, decimation, carnage, bloodbath, bloodletting, butchery, genocide, holocaust, ethnic cleansing.

poignancy ▶ **noun** PATHOS, pitifulness, piteousness, sadness, sorrow, mournfulness, wretchedness, misery, tragedy.

poignant ▶ **adjective** TOUCHING, moving, sad, affecting, pitiful, piteous, pathetic, sorrowful, mournful, wretched, miserable, distressing, heart-rending, tear-jerking, plaintive, tragic.

point[1] ▶ **noun** ❶ *the point of a needle* TIP, (sharp) end, extremity; prong, spike, tine, nib, barb. ❷ *points of light* PINPOINT, dot, spot, speck, fleck. ❸ *a meeting point* PLACE, position, location, site, spot, area. ❹ *this point in her life* TIME, stage, juncture, period, phase. ❺ *the tension had reached such a high point* LEVEL, degree, stage, pitch, extent. ❻ *an important point* DETAIL, item, fact, thing, argument, consideration, factor, element; subject, issue, topic, question, matter. ❼ *get to the point* HEART OF THE MATTER, most important part, essence, nub, keynote, core, pith, crux; meaning, significance, gist, substance, thrust, burden, relevance; *informal* brass tacks, nitty-gritty. ❽ *what's the point of this?* PURPOSE, aim, object, objective, goal, intention; use, sense, value, advantage. ❾ *he had his good points* ATTRIBUTE, characteristic, feature, trait, quality, property, aspect, side.

▶ **verb** ❶ *she pointed the gun at him* AIM, direct, level, train. ❷ *the evidence pointed to his guilt* INDICATE, suggest, evidence, signal, signify, denote, bespeak, reveal, manifest.

■ **beside the point** IRRELEVANT, immaterial, unimportant, neither here nor there, inconsequential, incidental, out of place, unconnected, peripheral, tangential, extraneous.

■ **in point of fact** IN FACT, as a matter of fact, actually, in actual fact, really, in reality, as it happens, in truth.

■ **make a point of** MAKE AN EFFORT TO, go out of one's way to, put emphasis on.

■ **on the point of** (JUST) ABOUT TO, on the verge of, on the brink of, going to, all set to.

■ **point of view** OPINION, view, belief, attitude, feeling, sentiment, thoughts; position, perspective, viewpoint, standpoint, outlook.

■ **point something out** IDENTIFY, show, designate, draw attention to, indicate, specify, detail, mention.

■ **point something up** EMPHASIZE, highlight, draw attention to, accentuate, underline, spotlight, foreground, put emphasis on, stress, play up, accent, bring to the fore.

■ **to the point** RELEVANT, pertinent, apposite, germane, applicable, apropos, appropriate, apt, fitting, suitable, material; *formal* ad rem.

■ **up to a point** PARTLY, to some extent, to a certain degree, in part, somewhat, partially.

point[2] ▶ **noun** *the ship rounded the point* PROMONTORY, headland, foreland, cape, peninsula, bluff, ness, horn.

point-blank ▶ **adverb** ❶ *he fired the pistol point-blank* AT CLOSE RANGE, close up, close to. ❷ *she couldn't say it point-blank* BLUNTLY, directly, straight, frankly, candidly, openly, explicitly, unequivocally, unambiguously, plainly, flatly, categorically, outright.

▶ **adjective** *a point-blank refusal* BLUNT, direct, straight, straightforward, frank, candid, forthright, explicit, unequivocal, plain, clear, flat, decisive, unqualified, categorical, outright.

pointed ▶ **adjective** ❶ *a pointed stick* SHARP, tapering, tapered, conical, jagged, spiky, spiked, barbed; *informal* pointy. ❷ *a pointed remark* CUTTING, trenchant, biting, incisive, acerbic, caustic, scathing, venomous, sarcastic; *informal* sarky; *N. Amer. informal* snarky.

pointer ▶ **noun** ❶ *the pointer moved to 100rpm* INDICATOR, needle, arrow, hand. ❷ *he used a pointer on the chart* STICK, rod, cane; cursor. ❸ *a pointer to the outcome of the election* INDICATION, indicator, clue, hint, sign, signal, evidence, intimation, inkling, suggestion. ❹ *I can give you a few pointers* TIP, hint, suggestion, guideline, recommendation.

pointless ▶ **adjective** SENSELESS, futile, hopeless, fruitless, useless, needless, in vain, unavailing, aimless, idle, worthless, valueless; absurd, insane, stupid, silly, foolish.
– OPPOSITES valuable.

poise ▶ **noun** ❶ *poise and good deportment* GRACE, gracefulness, elegance, balance, control. ❷ *in spite of the setback she retained her poise* COMPOSURE, equanimity, self-possession, aplomb, presence of mind, self-assurance, self-control, nerve, calm, sangfroid, dignity; *informal* cool, unflappability.

▶ **verb** ❶ *she was poised on one foot* BALANCE, hold (oneself) steady, be suspended, remain motionless, hang, hover. ❷ *he was poised for action* PREPARE ONESELF, ready oneself, brace oneself, gear oneself up, stand by.

poison ▶ **noun** ❶ *a deadly poison* TOXIN, toxicant, venom; *archaic* bane. ❷ *Marianne would spread her poison* MALICE, ill will, hate, malevolence, bitterness, spite, spitefulness, venom, acrimony, rancour; bad influence, cancer, corruption, pollution.
– RELATED TERMS toxic.

▶ **verb** ❶ *her mother poisoned her* GIVE POISON TO; murder. ❷ *a blackmailer poisoning baby foods* CONTAMINATE, put poison in, adulterate, spike, lace, doctor. ❸ *the Amazon is being poisoned* POLLUTE, contaminate, taint, blight, spoil; *poetic/literary* befoul. ❹ *they poisoned his mind* PREJUDICE, bias, jaundice, embitter, sour, envenom, warp, corrupt, subvert.

poisonous ▶ **adjective** ❶ *a poisonous snake* VENOMOUS, deadly. ❷ *a poisonous chemical* TOXIC, noxious, deadly, fatal, lethal, mortal, death-

dealing. ❸ *a poisonous glance* MALICIOUS, malevolent, hostile, vicious, spiteful, bitter, venomous, vindictive, vitriolic, rancorous, malign, pernicious, mean, nasty; *informal* bitchy, catty.
– OPPOSITES harmless, non-toxic, benevolent.

poke ▶ **verb** ❶ *she poked him in the ribs* PROD, jab, dig, nudge, butt, shove, jolt, stab, stick. ❷ *leave the cable poking out* STICK OUT, jut out, protrude, project, extend.
▶ **noun** ❶ *Carrie gave him a poke* PROD, jab, dig, elbow, nudge. ❷ *a poke in the arm* JAB, dig, nudge, shove, stab.
■ **poke about/around** SEARCH, hunt, rummage (around), forage, grub, root about/around, scavenge; nose around, ferret (about/around); sift through, rifle through, scour, comb, probe; *Brit. informal* rootle (around).
■ **poke fun at** MOCK, make fun of, ridicule, laugh at, jeer at, sneer at, deride, scorn, scoff at, pillory, lampoon, tease, taunt, rag, chaff, jibe at; *informal* send up, take the mickey out of, kid, rib; *Brit. informal* wind up; *N. Amer. informal* goof on, rag on; *Austral./NZ informal* poke mullock at.
■ **poke one's nose into** PRY INTO, interfere in, intrude on, butt into, meddle with; *informal* snoop into.

poky ▶ **adjective** SMALL, little, tiny, cramped, confined, restricted, boxy; *euphemistic* compact, bijou.
– OPPOSITES spacious.

polar ▶ **adjective** ❶ *polar weather* ARCTIC, cold, freezing, icy, glacial, chilly, gelid. ❷ *two polar types of interview* OPPOSITE, opposed, dichotomous, extreme, contrary, contradictory, antithetical.

polarity ▶ **noun** DIFFERENCE, dichotomy, separation, opposition, contradiction, antithesis, antagonism.

pole[1] ▶ **noun** POST, pillar, stanchion, paling, stake, stick, support, prop, batten, bar, rail, rod, beam; staff, stave, cane, baton.

pole[2] ▶ **noun** *points of view at opposite poles* EXTREMITY, extreme, limit, antipode.
■ **poles apart** COMPLETELY DIFFERENT, directly opposed, antithetical, incompatible, irreconcilable, worlds apart, at opposite extremes; *Brit.* like chalk and cheese.

polemic ▶ **noun** ❶ *a polemic against injustice* DIATRIBE, invective, rant, tirade, broadside, attack, harangue, condemnation, criticism, stricture, admonition, rebuke; abuse; *informal* blast; *formal* castigation; *poetic/literary* philippic. ❷ *he is skilled in polemics* ARGUMENTATION, argument, debate, contention, disputation, discussion, altercation; *formal* contestation.
▶ **adjective** *his famous polemic book. See* POLEMICAL.

polemical ▶ **adjective** CRITICAL, hostile, bitter, polemic, virulent, vitriolic, venomous, caustic, trenchant, cutting, acerbic, sardonic, sarcastic, scathing, sharp, incisive, devastating.

police ▶ **noun** the police force, police officers, policemen, policewomen, officers of the law, the forces of law and order; *Brit.* constabulary; *informal* the cops, the fuzz, (the long arm of) the law, the boys in blue; *Brit. informal* the (Old) Bill, coppers, bobbies, busies, the force; *N. Amer. informal* the heat; *informal, derogatory* pigs, the filth.
▶ **verb** ❶ *we must police the area* GUARD, watch over, protect, defend, patrol; control, regulate. ❷ *the regulations will be policed by the ministry* ENFORCE, regulate, oversee, supervise, monitor, observe, check.

police officer ▶ **noun** POLICEMAN, POLICEWOMAN, officer (of the law); *Brit.* constable; *N. Amer.* patrolman, trooper, roundsman; *informal* cop; *Brit. informal* copper, bobby, rozzer, busy, (PC) plod; *N. Amer. informal* uniform; *informal, derogatory* pig; *archaic* peeler.

policy ▶ **noun** ❶ *government policy* PLANS, strategy, stratagem, approach, code, system, guidelines, theory; line, position, stance, attitude. ❷ (*archaic*) *it's good policy to listen* PRACTICE, custom, procedure, conduct, convention.

polish ▶ **verb** ❶ *I polished his shoes* SHINE, wax, buff, rub up/down; gloss, burnish; varnish, oil, glaze, lacquer, japan, shellac. ❷ *polish up your essay* PERFECT, refine, improve, hone, enhance; brush up, revise, edit, correct, rewrite, go over, touch up; *informal* clean up.
▶ **noun** ❶ *furniture polish* WAX, glaze, varnish; lacquer, japan, shellac. ❷ *a good surface polish* SHINE, gloss, lustre, sheen, sparkle, patina, finish. ❸ *his polish made him stand out* SOPHISTICATION, refinement, urbanity, suaveness, elegance, style, grace, finesse, cultivation, civility, gentility, breeding, courtesy, (good) manners; *informal* class.
■ **polish something off** (*informal*) ❶ *he polished off an apple pie* EAT, finish, consume, devour, guzzle, wolf down, down, bolt; drink up, drain, quaff, gulp (down); *informal* binge on, stuff oneself with, get outside of, murder, put away, scoff, shovel down, pig out on, sink, swill, knock back; *Brit. informal* shift, gollop; *N. Amer. informal* scarf (down/up), snarf (down/up). ❷ *the enemy tried to polish him off* DESTROY, finish off, despatch, do away with, eliminate, kill, liquidate; *informal* bump off, knock off, do in, take out, dispose of; *N. Amer. informal* rub out. ❸ *I'll polish off the last few pages* COMPLETE, finish, deal with, accomplish, discharge, do; end, conclude, close, finalize, round off, wind up; *informal* wrap up, sew up.

polished ▶ **adjective** ❶ *a polished table* SHINY, glossy, gleaming, lustrous, glassy; waxed, buffed, burnished; varnished, glazed, lacquered, japanned, shellacked. ❷ *a polished performance* EXPERT, accomplished, masterly, masterful, skilful, adept, adroit, dexterous; impeccable, flawless, perfect, consummate, exquisite, outstanding, excellent, superb, superlative, first-rate, fine; *informal* ace. ❸ *polished*

manners REFINED, cultivated, civilized, well bred, polite, courteous, genteel, decorous, respectable, urbane, suave, sophisticated.
– OPPOSITES dull, inexpert, gauche.

polite ▶ adjective ❶ *a very polite girl* WELL MANNERED, civil, courteous, mannerly, respectful, deferential, well behaved, well bred, gentlemanly, ladylike, genteel, gracious, urbane; tactful, diplomatic. ❷ *polite society* CIVILIZED, refined, cultured, sophisticated, genteel, courtly.
– OPPOSITES rude, uncivilized.

politic ▶ adjective WISE, prudent, sensible, judicious, canny, sagacious, shrewd, astute; recommended, advantageous, beneficial, profitable, desirable, advisable; appropriate, suitable, fitting, apt.
– OPPOSITES unwise.

political ▶ adjective ❶ *the political affairs of the nation* GOVERNMENTAL, government, constitutional, ministerial, parliamentary, diplomatic, legislative, administrative, bureaucratic; public, civic, state. ❷ *he's a political man* POLITICALLY ACTIVE, party (political); militant, factional, partisan.

politician ▶ noun LEGISLATOR, elected official, Member of Parliament, MP, minister, statesman, stateswoman, public servant; senator, congressman/woman; *informal* politico, pol.

politics ▶ noun ❶ *a career in politics* GOVERNMENT, affairs of state, public affairs; diplomacy. ❷ *he studies politics* POLITICAL SCIENCE, civics, statecraft. ❸ *what are his politics?* POLITICAL VIEWS, political leanings, party politics. ❹ *office politics* POWER STRUGGLE, machinations, manoeuvring, opportunism, realpolitik.

poll ▶ noun ❶ *a second-round poll* VOTE, ballot, show of hands, referendum, plebiscite; election. ❷ *the poll was unduly low* VOTING FIGURES, vote, returns, count, tally. ❸ *a poll to investigate holiday choices* SURVEY, opinion poll, straw poll, canvass, market research, census.
▶ verb ❶ *most of those polled supported him* CANVASS, survey, ask, question, interview, ballot. ❷ *she polled 119 votes* GET, gain, register, record, return.

pollute ▶ verb ❶ *fish farms will pollute the lake* CONTAMINATE, adulterate, taint, poison, foul, dirty, soil, infect; *poetic/literary* befoul. ❷ *propaganda polluted this nation* CORRUPT, poison, warp, pervert, deprave, defile, blight, sully; *poetic/literary* besmirch.
– OPPOSITES purify.

pollution ▶ noun ❶ *pollution in the rivers* CONTAMINATION, adulteration, impurity; dirt, filth, infection. ❷ *the pollution of young minds* CORRUPTION, defilement, poisoning, warping, depravation, sullying, violation.

pomp ▶ noun CEREMONY, ceremonial, solemnity, ritual, display, spectacle, pageantry; show, showiness, ostentation, splendour, grandeur, magnificence, majesty, stateliness, glory, opulence, brilliance, drama, resplendence, splendidness; *informal* razzmatazz.

pompous ▶ adjective SELF-IMPORTANT, imperious, overbearing, domineering, magisterial, pontifical, sententious, grandiose, affected, pretentious, puffed up, arrogant, vain, haughty, proud, conceited, egotistic, supercilious, condescending, patronizing; *informal* snooty, uppity, uppish.
– OPPOSITES modest.

pond ▶ noun POOL, waterhole, lake, tarn, reservoir, swim; *Brit.* stew; *Scottish* lochan; *N. Amer.* pothole; *Austral./NZ* tank.

ponder ▶ verb THINK ABOUT, contemplate, consider, review, reflect on, mull over, meditate on, muse on, deliberate about, cogitate on, dwell on, brood on, ruminate on, chew over, puzzle over, turn over in one's mind.

ponderous ▶ adjective ❶ *a ponderous dance* CLUMSY, heavy, awkward, lumbering, slow, cumbersome, ungainly, graceless, uncoordinated, blundering; *informal* clodhopping, clunky. ❷ *his ponderous sentences* LABOURED, laborious, awkward, clumsy, forced, stilted, unnatural, artificial; stodgy, lifeless, plodding, pedestrian, boring, dull, tedious, monotonous; over-elaborate, convoluted, windy.
– OPPOSITES light, lively.

pontifical ▶ adjective POMPOUS, cocksure, self-important, arrogant, superior; opinionated, dogmatic, doctrinaire, authoritarian, domineering; adamant, obstinate, stubborn, single-minded, inflexible.
– OPPOSITES humble.

pontificate ▶ verb HOLD FORTH, expound, declaim, preach, lay down the law, sound off, dogmatize, sermonize, moralize, lecture; *informal* preachify, mouth off.

pooh-pooh ▶ verb (*informal*) DISMISS, reject, spurn, rebuff, wave aside, disregard, discount; play down, make light of, belittle, deride, mock, scorn, scoff at, sneer at; *Austral./NZ informal* wipe.

pool[1] ▶ noun ❶ *pools of water* PUDDLE, pond; *poetic/literary* plash. ❷ *the hotel has a pool* SWIMMING POOL, baths, lido; *Brit.* swimming bath(s); *N. Amer.* natatorium.

pool[2] ▶ noun ❶ *a pool of skilled labour* SUPPLY, reserve(s), reservoir, fund; store, stock, accumulation, cache. ❷ *a pool of money for emergencies* FUND, reserve, kitty, pot, bank, purse.
▶ verb *they pooled their skills* COMBINE, amalgamate, group, join, unite, merge; fuse, conglomerate, integrate; share.

poor ▶ adjective ❶ *a poor family* POVERTY-STRICKEN, penniless, moneyless, impoverished, necessitous, impecunious, indigent, needy, destitute, pauperized, on one's beam-ends, unable to make ends meet, without a sou; insolvent, in debt; *Brit.* on the breadline, without a penny (to one's name); *informal* (flat) broke, hard up, cleaned out, strapped, on one's uppers, without two pennies to rub together; *Brit. informal* skint, in Queer Street; *formal* penurious. ❷ *poor workmanship* SUBSTANDARD, below par, bad, deficient, defective, faulty, imperfect, inferior; appalling, abysmal, atrocious, awful, terrible, dreadful, unsatisfactory, second-rate, third-rate, shoddy, crude, lamentable, deplorable, inadequate, unacceptable; *informal* crummy, rubbishy, dire, dismal, bum, rotten, tenth-rate; *Brit. informal* ropy, duff, rubbish, dodgy. ❸ *a poor crop* MEAGRE, scanty, scant, paltry, disappointing, limited, reduced, modest, insufficient, inadequate, sparse, spare, deficient, insubstantial, skimpy, short, small, lean, slender; *informal* measly, stingy, pathetic, piddling; *formal* exiguous. ❹ *poor soil* UNPRODUCTIVE, barren, unyielding, unfruitful, uncultivatable; arid, sterile. ❺ *the waters are poor in nutrients* DEFICIENT, lacking, wanting; short of, low on. ❻ *you poor thing!* UNFORTUNATE, unlucky, luckless, unhappy, hapless, ill-fated, ill-starred, pitiable, pitiful, wretched.

– OPPOSITES rich, superior, good, fertile, lucky.

poorly ▶ **adverb** *the text is poorly written* BADLY, deficiently, defectively, imperfectly, incompetently; appallingly, abysmally, atrociously, awfully, dreadfully; crudely, shoddily, inadequately.

▶ **adjective** *she felt poorly* ILL, unwell, not (very) well, ailing, indisposed, out of sorts, under/below par, peaky; sick, queasy, nauseous; *Brit.* off colour; *informal* under the weather, funny, peculiar, lousy, rough; *Brit. informal* ropy, grotty; *Scottish informal* wabbit; *Austral./NZ informal* crook; *Brit. informal, dated* queer; *dated* seedy.

pop ▶ **verb** ❶ *champagne corks popped* GO BANG, go off; crack, snap, burst, explode. ❷ *I'm just popping home* GO; drop in, stop by, visit; *informal* tootle, whip; *Brit. informal* nip. ❸ *pop a bag over the pot* PUT, place, slip, slide, stick, set, lay, install, position, arrange.

▶ **noun** ❶ *the balloons burst with a pop* BANG, crack, snap; explosion, report. ❷ (*informal*) *a bottle of pop* FIZZY DRINK, soft drink, carbonated drink; *N. Amer.* soda; *Scottish informal* scoosh.

■ **pop up** APPEAR (SUDDENLY), occur (suddenly), arrive, materialize, come along, happen, emerge, arise, crop up, turn up, present itself, come to light; *informal* show up.

pope ▶ **noun** PONTIFF, Bishop of Rome, Holy Father, Vicar of Christ, His Holiness.

– RELATED TERMS papal, pontifical.

pop music ▶ **noun** POP, popular music, chart music.

poppycock ▶ **noun** (*informal*) NONSENSE, rubbish, claptrap, balderdash, blather, moonshine, garbage; *informal* rot, tripe, hogwash, baloney, drivel, bilge, bosh, bunk, eyewash, piffle, phooey, twaddle; *Brit. informal* cobblers, codswallop, tosh; *N. Amer. informal* applesauce, bushwa; *informal, dated* bunkum, tommyrot.

populace ▶ **noun** POPULATION, inhabitants, residents, natives; community, country, (general) public, people, nation; common people, man/woman in the street, masses, multitude, rank and file, commonality, commonalty, third estate, plebeians, proletariat; *informal* proles, plebs; *Brit. informal* Joe Public; *formal* denizens; *derogatory* the hoi polloi, common herd, rabble, riff-raff.

popular ▶ **adjective** ❶ *the restaurant is very popular* WELL LIKED, favoured, sought-after, in demand, desired, wanted; commercial, marketable, fashionable, in vogue, all the rage, hot; *informal* in, cool, big; *Brit. informal, dated* all the go. ❷ *popular science* NON-SPECIALIST, non-technical, amateur, lay person's, general, middle-of-the-road; accessible, simplified, plain, simple, easy, straightforward, understandable; mass-market, middlebrow, lowbrow, pop. ❸ *popular opinion* WIDESPREAD, general, common, current, prevalent, prevailing, standard, stock; ordinary, usual, accepted, established, acknowledged, conventional, orthodox. ❹ *a popular movement for independence* MASS, general, communal, collective, social, collaborative, group, civil, public.

– OPPOSITES highbrow.

popularize ▶ **verb** ❶ *tobacco was popularized by Sir Walter Raleigh* MAKE POPULAR, make fashionable; market, publicize; *informal* hype. ❷ *he popularized the subject* SIMPLIFY, make accessible, give mass-market appeal to. ❸ *the report popularized the unfounded notion* GIVE CURRENCY TO, spread, propagate, give credence to.

popularly ▶ **adverb** ❶ *old age is popularly associated with illness* WIDELY, generally, universally, commonly, usually, customarily, habitually, conventionally, traditionally, as a rule. ❷ *the rock was popularly known as 'Arthur's Seat'* INFORMALLY, unofficially; by lay people. ❸ *the President is popularly elected* DEMOCRATICALLY, by the people.

populate ▶ **verb** ❶ *the state is populated by 40,000 people* INHABIT, occupy, people; live in, reside in. ❷ *an attempt to populate the island* SETTLE, colonize, people, occupy, move into, make one's home in.

population ▶ **noun** INHABITANTS, residents, people, citizens, citizenry, public, community, populace, society, natives, occupants; *formal* denizens.

– RELATED TERMS demo-.

populous ▶ **adjective** DENSELY POPULATED, heavily populated, congested, crowded, packed, jammed, crammed, teeming, swarming, seething, crawling; *informal* jam-packed.

– OPPOSITES deserted.

porch ▶ **noun** VESTIBULE, foyer, entrance (hall),

entry, portico, lobby; *N. Amer.* ramada, stoop; *Architecture* lanai, tambour, narthex.

pore¹ ▶ **noun** *pores in the skin* OPENING, orifice, aperture, hole, outlet, inlet, vent; *Biology* stoma, foramen.

pore² ▶ **verb** *they pored over the map* STUDY, read intently, peruse, scrutinize, scan, examine, go over.

pornographic ▶ **adjective** OBSCENE, indecent, crude, lewd, dirty, vulgar, smutty, filthy; erotic, titillating, arousing, suggestive, sexy, risqué; off colour, adult, X-rated, hardcore, soft-core; *informal* porn, porno, blue, skin.
– OPPOSITES wholesome.

pornography ▶ **noun** EROTICA, pornographic material, dirty books; smut, filth, vice; *informal* (hard/soft) porn, porno, girlie magazines, skin flicks.

porous ▶ **adjective** PERMEABLE, penetrable, pervious, cellular, holey; absorbent, absorptive, spongy.
– OPPOSITES impermeable.

port¹ ▶ **noun** ❶ *the German port of Kiel* SEAPORT, entrepôt. ❷ *shells exploded down by the port* HARBOUR, dock(s), haven, marina; anchorage, moorage, harbourage, roads.

port² ▶ **noun** *push the supply pipes into the ports* APERTURE, opening, outlet, inlet, socket, vent.

portable ▶ **adjective** TRANSPORTABLE, movable, mobile, travel; lightweight, compact, handy, convenient.

portal ▶ **noun** DOORWAY, gateway, entrance, exit, opening; door, gate; *N. Amer.* entryway; *formal* egress.

portend ▶ **verb** PRESAGE, augur, foreshadow, foretell, prophesy; be a sign, warn, be an omen, indicate, herald, signal, bode, promise, threaten, signify, spell, denote; *poetic/literary* betoken, foretoken, forebode.

portent ▶ **noun** ❶ *a portent of things to come* OMEN, sign, signal, token, forewarning, warning, foreshadowing, prediction, forecast, prophesy, harbinger, augury, auspice, presage; writing on the wall, indication, hint; *poetic/literary* foretoken. ❷ *the word carries terrifying portent* SIGNIFICANCE, importance, import, consequence, meaning, weight; *formal* moment.

portentous ▶ **adjective** ❶ *portentous signs* OMINOUS, warning, premonitory, prognosticatory; threatening, menacing, ill-omened, foreboding, inauspicious, unfavourable. ❷ *portentous dialogue* POMPOUS, bombastic, self-important, pontifical, solemn, sonorous, grandiloquent.

porter¹ ▶ **noun** *a porter helped with the bags* CARRIER, bearer; *N. Amer.* redcap, skycap.

porter² ▶ **noun** (*Brit.*) *the college porter* DOORMAN, doorkeeper, commissionaire, gatekeeper.

portion ▶ **noun** ❶ *the upper portion of the chimney* PART, piece, bit, section, segment. ❷ *her portion of the allowance* SHARE, slice, quota, quantum, part, percentage, amount, quantity, ration, fraction, division, allocation, measure; *informal* cut, rake-off; *Brit. informal* whack. ❸ *a portion of cake* HELPING, serving, amount, quantity; plateful, bowlful; slice, piece, chunk, wedge, slab, hunk; *Brit. informal* wodge. ❹ (*archaic*) *poverty was certain to be his portion.* See DESTINY sense 1.

▶ **verb** *she portioned out the food* SHARE OUT, allocate, allot, apportion; distribute, hand out, deal out, dole out, give out, dispense, mete out; *informal* divvy up.

portly ▶ **adjective** STOUT, plump, fat, overweight, heavy, corpulent, fleshy, paunchy, pot-bellied, well padded, rotund, stocky, bulky; *informal* tubby, roly-poly, beefy, porky, pudgy; *Brit. informal* podgy; *N. Amer. informal* corn-fed.
– OPPOSITES slim.

portrait ▶ **noun** ❶ *a portrait of the King* PAINTING, picture, drawing, sketch, likeness, image, study, miniature; *informal* oil; *formal* portraiture. ❷ *a vivid portrait of Italy* DESCRIPTION, portrayal, representation, depiction, impression, account; sketch, vignette, profile.

portray ▶ **verb** ❶ *he portrays Windermere in sunny weather* PAINT, draw, sketch, picture, depict, represent, illustrate, render. ❷ *the dons portrayed by Waugh* DESCRIBE, depict, characterize, represent, delineate, evoke. ❸ *he portrays her as a doormat* REPRESENT, depict, characterize, describe, present. ❹ *the actor portrays a spy* PLAY, act the part of, take the role of, represent, appear as; *formal* personate.

portrayal ▶ **noun** ❶ *a portrayal of a parrot* PAINTING, picture, portrait, drawing, sketch, representation, depiction, study. ❷ *her portrayal of adolescence* DESCRIPTION, representation, characterization, depiction, evocation. ❸ *Brando's portrayal of Corleone* PERFORMANCE AS, representation, interpretation, rendering; *formal* personation.

pose ▶ **verb** ❶ *pollution poses a threat to health* CONSTITUTE, present, create, cause, produce, be. ❷ *the question posed earlier* RAISE, ask, put, set, submit, advance, propose, suggest, moot. ❸ *she posed for the artist* BE A MODEL, model, sit. ❹ *he posed her on the sofa* POSITION, place, put, arrange, dispose, locate, situate. ❺ *fashion victims were posing at the bar* BEHAVE AFFECTEDLY, strike a pose, posture, attitudinize, put on airs; *informal* show off.

▶ **noun** ❶ *a sexy pose* POSTURE, position, stance, attitude, bearing. ❷ *her pose of aggrieved innocence* PRETENCE, act, affectation, facade, show, front, display, masquerade, posture.

■ **pose as** PRETEND TO BE, impersonate, pass oneself off as, masquerade as, profess to be, represent oneself as; *formal* personate.

poser¹ ▶ **noun** *this situation's a bit of a poser* DIFFICULT QUESTION, vexed question, awkward problem, tough one, puzzle, mystery, conundrum, puzzler, enigma, riddle; *informal* dilemma, facer, toughie, stumper.

poser² ▶ noun *he's such a poser* EXHIBITIONIST, poseur, poseuse, posturer; *informal* show-off, pseud.

poseur ▶ noun. *See* POSER².

posh ▶ adjective ❶ (*informal*) *a posh hotel* SMART, stylish, fancy, high-class, fashionable, chic, luxurious, luxury, de luxe, exclusive, opulent, lavish, grand, showy; *Brit.* upmarket; *informal* classy, swanky, snazzy, plush, ritzy, flash, la-di-da; *Brit. informal* swish; *N. Amer. informal* swank, tony. ❷ (*Brit. informal*) *a posh accent* UPPER-CLASS, aristocratic; *Brit.* upmarket, Home Counties; *informal* upper-crust, top-drawer; *Brit. informal* plummy, Sloaney, U.

posit ▶ verb POSTULATE, put forward, advance, propound, submit, hypothesize, propose, assert.

position ▶ noun ❶ *the aircraft's position* LOCATION, place, situation, spot, site, locality, setting, area; whereabouts, bearings, orientation; *technical* locus. ❷ *a standing position* POSTURE, stance, attitude, pose. ❸ *our financial position* SITUATION, state, condition, circumstances; predicament, plight, strait(s). ❹ *the two parties jockeyed for position* ADVANTAGE, the upper hand, the edge, the whip hand, primacy; *Austral./NZ* the box seat; *N. Amer. informal* the catbird seat. ❺ *their position in society* STATUS, place, level, rank, standing; stature, prestige, influence, reputation, importance, consequence, class; *dated* station. ❻ *a secretarial position* JOB, post, situation, appointment, role, occupation, employment; office, capacity, duty, function; opening, vacancy, placement. ❼ *the government's position on the matter* VIEWPOINT, opinion, outlook, attitude, stand, standpoint, stance, perspective, approach, slant, thinking, policy, feelings.

▶ verb *he positioned a chair between them* PUT, place, locate, situate, set, site, stand, station; plant, stick, install; arrange, dispose; *informal* plonk, park.

positive ▶ adjective ❶ *a positive response* AFFIRMATIVE, favourable, good, approving, enthusiastic, supportive, encouraging. ❷ *do something positive* CONSTRUCTIVE, practical, useful, productive, helpful, worthwhile, beneficial, effective. ❸ *she seems a lot more positive* OPTIMISTIC, hopeful, confident, cheerful, sanguine, buoyant; *informal* upbeat. ❹ *positive economic signs* FAVOURABLE, good, promising, encouraging, heartening, propitious, auspicious. ❺ *positive proof* DEFINITE, conclusive, certain, categorical, unequivocal, incontrovertible, indisputable, undeniable, unmistakable, irrefutable, reliable, concrete, tangible, clear-cut, explicit, firm, decisive, real, actual. ❻ *I'm positive he's coming back* CERTAIN, sure, convinced, confident, satisfied, assured; as sure as eggs is eggs.

–OPPOSITES negative, pessimistic, doubtful, unsure.

positively ▶ adverb ❶ *I could not positively identify the voice* CONFIDENTLY, definitely, emphatically, categorically, with certainty, conclusively, unquestionably, undoubtedly, indisputably, unmistakably, assuredly. ❷ *he was positively livid* ABSOLUTELY, really, downright, thoroughly, completely, utterly, totally, extremely, fairly; *informal* plain.

possess ▶ verb ❶ *the only hat she possessed* OWN, have (to one's name), hold. ❷ *he did not possess a sense of humour* HAVE, be blessed with, be endowed with; enjoy, boast. ❸ *a supernatural force possessed him* TAKE CONTROL OF, take over, control, dominate, influence; bewitch, enchant, enthral. ❹ *she was possessed by a need to talk to him* OBSESS, haunt, preoccupy, consume; eat someone up, prey on one's mind.

■ **possess oneself of** ACQUIRE, obtain, get (hold of), procure, get one's hands on; take, seize; *informal* get one's mitts on.

possessed ▶ adjective MAD, demented, insane, crazed, berserk, out of one's mind; bewitched, enchanted, haunted, under a spell.

possession ▶ noun ❶ *the estate came into their possession* OWNERSHIP, control, hands, keeping, care, custody, charge, hold, title, guardianship. ❷ *her possession of the premises* OCCUPANCY, occupation, tenure, holding, tenancy. ❸ *she packed her possessions* BELONGINGS, things, property, (worldly) goods, (personal) effects, assets, chattels, movables, valuables; stuff, bits and pieces; luggage, baggage; *informal* gear, junk; *Brit. informal* clobber. ❹ *colonial possessions* COLONY, dependency, territory, holding, protectorate.

■ **take possession of** SEIZE, appropriate, impound, expropriate, sequestrate, sequester, confiscate; take, get, acquire, obtain, procure, possess oneself of, get hold of, get one's hands on; capture, commandeer, requisition; *Law* distrain; *Scottish Law* poind; *informal* get one's mitts on.

possessive ▶ adjective ❶ *he was very possessive* PROPRIETORIAL, overprotective, controlling, dominating, jealous, clingy. ❷ *kids are possessive of their own property* COVETOUS, selfish, unwilling to share; grasping, greedy, acquisitive; *N. Amer. informal* grabby.

possibility ▶ noun ❶ *there is a possibility that he might be alive* CHANCE, likelihood, probability, hope; risk, hazard, danger, fear. ❷ *they discussed the possibility of launching a new project* FEASIBILITY, practicability, chances, odds, achievability, probability. ❸ *buying a smaller house is one possibility* OPTION, alternative, choice, course of action, solution. ❹ *the idea has distinct possibilities* POTENTIAL, promise, prospects.

possible ▶ adjective ❶ *it's not possible to check the figures* FEASIBLE, practicable, viable, within

the bounds/realms of possibility, attainable, achievable, workable; *informal* on, doable. ❷ *a possible reason for his disappearance* CONCEIVABLE, plausible, imaginable, believable, likely, potential, probable, credible. ❸ *a possible future leader* POTENTIAL, prospective, likely, probable.
– OPPOSITES unlikely.

possibly ▶ adverb ❶ *possibly he took the boy with him* PERHAPS, maybe, it is possible, for all one knows, very likely; *poetic/literary* peradventure, perchance, mayhap. ❷ *you can't possibly refuse* CONCEIVABLY, under any circumstances, by any means. ❸ *could you possibly help me?* PLEASE, kindly, be so good as to.

post[1] ▶ noun *wooden posts* POLE, stake, upright, shaft, prop, support, picket, strut, pillar, pale, paling, stanchion, puncheon.
▶ verb ❶ *the notice posted on the wall* AFFIX, attach, fasten, display, pin (up), put up, stick (up), tack (up). ❷ *the group posted a net profit* ANNOUNCE, report, make known, publish.

post[2] ▶ noun (*Brit.*) ❶ *the winners will be notified by post* MAIL, the postal service; airmail, surface mail, registered mail; *informal* snail mail. ❷ *did we get any post?* LETTERS, correspondence, mail.
▶ verb ❶ (*Brit.*) *post the order form today* SEND (OFF), mail, put in the post/mail, get off. ❷ *post the transaction in the second column* RECORD, write in, enter, register.
■ **keep someone posted** KEEP INFORMED, keep up to date, keep in the picture, keep briefed, update, fill in; *informal* keep up to speed.

post[3] ▶ noun ❶ *there were seventy candidates for the post* JOB, position, appointment, situation, place; vacancy, opening; *Austral. informal* grip. ❷ *Back to your posts!* (ASSIGNED) POSITION, station, observation post.
▶ verb ❶ *he'd been posted to Berlin* SEND, assign to a post, dispatch. ❷ *armed guards were posted beside the exit* PUT ON DUTY, station, position, situate, locate.

poster ▶ noun NOTICE, placard, bill, sign, advertisement, affiche, playbill; *Brit.* fly-poster.

posterior ▶ adjective ❶ *the posterior part of the skull* REAR, hind, back, hinder; *technical* dorsal, caudal. ❷ (*formal*) *a date posterior to the Reform Bill* LATER THAN, subsequent to, following, after.
– OPPOSITES anterior, previous.
▶ noun (*humorous*) *her plump posterior*. See BOTTOM noun sense 6.

posterity ▶ noun ❶ *their names are recorded for posterity* FUTURE GENERATIONS, the future. ❷ (*archaic*) *the posterity of Abraham* DESCENDANTS, heirs, successors, offspring, children, progeny; *Law* issue; *archaic* seed.

post-haste ▶ adverb AS QUICKLY AS POSSIBLE, without delay, (very) quickly, speedily, without further/more ado, with all speed, promptly, immediately, at once, straight away, right away; *informal* pronto, straight off.

postman, postwoman ▶ noun POSTAL WORKER; *N. Amer.* mailman; *Brit. informal* postie.

post-mortem ▶ noun ❶ *the hospital carried out a post-mortem* AUTOPSY, post-mortem examination, PM, necropsy. ❷ *a post-mortem of her failed relationship* ANALYSIS, evaluation, assessment, appraisal, examination, review.

postpone ▶ verb PUT OFF/BACK, delay, defer, reschedule, adjourn, shelve; *N. Amer.* put over, take a rain check on; *informal* put on ice, put on the back burner; *rare* remit, respite.
– OPPOSITES bring forward.

postponement ▶ noun DEFERRAL, deferment, delay, putting off/back, rescheduling, adjournment, shelving.

postscript ▶ noun ❶ *a handwritten postscript* AFTERTHOUGHT, PS, additional remark. ❷ *he added postscripts of his own* ADDENDUM, supplement, appendix, codicil, afterword, addition.

postulate ▶ verb PUT FORWARD, suggest, advance, posit, hypothesize, propose; assume, presuppose, presume, take for granted.

posture ▶ noun ❶ *a kneeling posture* POSITION, pose, attitude, stance. ❷ *good posture* BEARING, carriage, stance, comportment; *Brit.* deportment. ❸ *trade unions adopted a militant posture* ATTITUDE, stance, standpoint, point of view, opinion, position, frame of mind.
▶ verb *Keith postured, flexing his biceps* POSE, strike an attitude, strut.

posy ▶ noun BOUQUET, bunch (of flowers), spray, nosegay, corsage; buttonhole, boutonnière.

pot ▶ noun ❶ *pots and pans* COOKING UTENSIL, pan, saucepan, casserole, stewpot, stockpot, dixie. ❷ *earthenware pots* FLOWERPOT, planter, jardinière. ❸ *Jim raked in half the pot* BANK, kitty, pool, purse, jackpot.
■ **go to pot** (*informal*) DETERIORATE, decline, degenerate, go to (rack and) ruin, go downhill, go to seed, become run down; *informal* go to the dogs, go down the tubes; *Austral./NZ informal* go to the pack.

pot-bellied ▶ adjective PAUNCHY, beer-bellied, portly, rotund; *informal* tubby, roly-poly.

pot belly ▶ noun PAUNCH, (beer) belly; *informal* beer gut, pot, tummy.

potency ▶ noun ❶ *the potency of his words* FORCEFULNESS, force, effectiveness, persuasiveness, cogency, influence, strength, authoritativeness, authority, power, powerfulness; *poetic/literary* puissance. ❷ *the potency of the drugs* STRENGTH, powerfulness, power, effectiveness; *formal* efficacy; efficaciousness.

potent ▶ adjective ❶ *a potent political force* POWERFUL, strong, mighty, formidable, influential, dominant, forceful; *poetic/literary* puissant. ❷ *a potent argument* FORCEFUL, convincing, cogent, compelling, persuasive, powerful, strong. ❸ *a potent drug* STRONG, powerful, ef-

fective; *formal* efficacious.
– OPPOSITES weak.

potentate ▶ noun RULER, monarch, sovereign, king, queen, emperor, empress.

potential ▶ adjective *a potential source of conflict* POSSIBLE, likely, prospective, future, probable; latent, inherent, undeveloped.
▶ noun *economic potential* POSSIBILITIES, potentiality, prospects; promise, capability, capacity.

potion ▶ noun CONCOCTION, mixture, brew, elixir, philtre, drink, decoction; medicine, tonic; *poetic/literary* draught.

pot-pourri ▶ noun MIXTURE, assortment, collection, selection, assemblage, medley, miscellany, mix, variety, mixed bag, patchwork; ragbag, hotchpotch, mishmash, jumble, farrago; *N. Amer.* hodge-podge.

potter ▶ verb *we pottered down to the library* AMBLE, wander, meander, stroll, saunter, maunder; *informal* mosey, tootle, toddle; *N. Amer. informal* putter.
■ **potter about/around** DO NOTHING MUCH, fiddle about/around, footle about/around; *informal* mess about/around; *Brit. informal* muck about/around; *N. Amer. informal* putter about/around, lollygag.

pottery ▶ noun CHINA, crockery, ceramics, earthenware, stoneware.

potty ▶ adjective (*Brit. informal*) ❶ *I'm going potty.* See CRAZY sense 1. ❷ *she's potty about you.* See CRAZY sense 3.

pouch ▶ noun ❶ *a leather pouch* BAG, purse, sack, sac, pocket; *Scottish* sporran. ❷ *a kangaroo's pouch Zoology* marsupium.

pounce ▶ verb *two men pounced on him* JUMP ON, spring, leap, dive, lunge, fall on, set on, attack suddenly; *informal* jump, mug.
▶ noun *a sudden pounce* LEAP, spring, jump, dive, lunge, bound.

pound[1] ▶ verb ❶ *the two men pounded him with their fists* BEAT, strike, hit, batter, thump, pummel, punch, rain blows on, belabour, hammer, thrash, set on, tear into; *informal* bash, clobber, wallop, beat the living daylights out of, whack, thwack, lay into, pitch into; *Brit. informal* slosh; *N. Amer. informal* light into, whale. ❷ *waves pounded the seafront* BEAT AGAINST, crash against, batter, dash against, lash, buffet. ❸ *gunships pounded the capital* BOMBARD, bomb, shell, fire on; *archaic* cannonade. ❹ *pound the cloves with salt* CRUSH, grind, pulverize, mill, mash, pulp; *technical* triturate; *archaic* levigate. ❺ *I heard him pounding along the gangway* WALK/RUN HEAVILY, stomp, lumber, clomp, clump, tramp, trudge. ❻ *her heart was pounding* THROB, thump, thud, hammer, pulse, race, go pit-a-pat; *poetic/literary* pant, thrill.

pound[2] ▶ noun ❶ *a pound of apples* pound weight, lb. ❷ *ten pounds* pound sterling, £; *Brit. informal* quid, smacker, nicker.

pound[3] ▶ noun *a dog pound* ENCLOSURE, compound, pen, yard.

pour ▶ verb ❶ *blood was pouring from his nose* STREAM, flow, run, gush, course, jet, spurt, surge, spill. ❷ *Amy poured wine into his glass* TIP, let flow, splash, spill, decant; *informal* slosh, slop. ❸ *it was pouring with rain* RAIN HEAVILY/HARD, teem down, pelt down, tip down, come down in torrents/sheets, rain cats and dogs; *informal* be chucking it down; *Brit. informal* bucket down, come down in stair rods; *N. Amer. informal* rain pitchforks. ❹ *people poured off the train* THRONG, crowd, swarm, stream, flood.

pout ▶ verb *Crystal pouted sullenly* LOOK PETULANT, pull a face, look sulky.
▶ noun *a childish pout* PETULANT EXPRESSION, sulky expression, moue.

poverty ▶ noun ❶ *abject poverty* PENURY, destitution, pauperism, pauperdom, indigence, pennilessness, impoverishment, neediness, need, hardship, impecuniousness. ❷ *the poverty of choice* SCARCITY, deficiency, dearth, shortage, paucity, insufficiency, absence, lack. ❸ *the poverty of her imagination* INFERIORITY, mediocrity, poorness, sterility.
– OPPOSITES wealth, abundance.

poverty-stricken ▶ adjective EXTREMELY POOR, impoverished, destitute, penniless, on one's beam-ends, as poor as a church mouse, in penury, impecunious, indigent, needy, in need/want; *Brit.* on the breadline, without a penny (to one's name); *informal* on one's uppers, without two pennies/farthings to rub together; *Brit. informal* in Queer Street; *formal* penurious.

powder ▶ noun DUST, fine particles; talcum powder, talc; *historical* pounce.
▶ verb ❶ *she powdered her face* DUST, sprinkle/cover with powder. ❷ *the grains are powdered* CRUSH, grind, pulverize, pound, mill; *technical* comminute; *archaic* levigate. ❸ *powdered milk* dry, freeze-dry; *technical* lyophilize.

powdered ▶ adjective dried, freeze-dried; *technical* lyophilized.

powdery ▶ adjective FINE, dry, fine-grained, powder-like, dusty, chalky, floury, sandy, crumbly, friable.

power ▶ noun ❶ *the power of speech* ABILITY, capacity, capability, potential, faculty, competence. ❷ *the unions wield enormous power* CONTROL, authority, influence, dominance, mastery, domination, dominion, sway, weight, leverage; *informal* clout, teeth; *N. Amer. informal* drag; *poetic/literary* puissance. ❸ *police have the power to stop and search* AUTHORITY, right, authorization, warrant, licence. ❹ *a major European power* STATE, country, nation. ❺ *he hit the ball with as much power as he could* STRENGTH, powerfulness, might, force, forcefulness, vigour, energy; brawn, muscle; *informal* punch; *Brit. informal* welly; *poetic/literary* thew. ❻ *the power of his arguments* FORCEFULNESS, powerfulness, potency, strength, force, cogency, persuasiveness. ❼ *the new engine has more power* DRIVING FORCE, horsepower, hp, acceleration; *informal* oomph, grunt. ❽ *generating power from waste* ENERGY, electrical power. ❾ (*informal*) *the holiday did him a power of good* A GREAT DEAL OF, a lot of, much; *informal* lots of, loads of.

– OPPOSITES inability, weakness.

■ **have someone in/under one's power** HAVE CONTROL OVER, have influence over, have under one's thumb, have at one's mercy, have in one's clutches, have in the palm of one's hand; *N. Amer.* have in one's hip pocket; *informal* have over a barrel.

■ **the powers that be** THE AUTHORITIES, the people in charge, the government.

powerful ▶ adjective ❶ *powerful shoulders* STRONG, muscular, muscly, sturdy, strapping, robust, brawny, burly, athletic, manly, well built, solid; *informal* beefy, hunky; *dated* stalwart; *poetic/literary* stark, thewy. ❷ *a powerful drink* INTOXICATING, hard, strong, stiff; *formal* spirituous. ❸ *a powerful blow* VIOLENT, forceful, hard, mighty. ❹ *he felt a powerful desire to kiss her* INTENSE, keen, fierce, passionate, ardent, burning, strong, irresistible, overpowering, overwhelming. ❺ *a powerful nation* INFLUENTIAL, strong, important, dominant, commanding, potent, forceful, formidable; *poetic/literary* puissant. ❻ *a powerful critique* COGENT, compelling, convincing, persuasive, forceful; dramatic, graphic, vivid, moving.

– OPPOSITES weak, gentle.

powerless ▶ adjective IMPOTENT, helpless, ineffectual, ineffective, useless, defenceless, vulnerable; *poetic/literary* impuissant.

practicable ▶ adjective REALISTIC, feasible, possible, within the bounds/realms of possibility, viable, reasonable, sensible, workable, achievable; *informal* doable.

practical ▶ adjective ❶ *practical experience* EMPIRICAL, hands-on, actual, active, applied, heuristic, experiential. ❷ *there are no practical alternatives* FEASIBLE, practicable, realistic, viable, workable, possible, reasonable, sensible; *informal* doable. ❸ *practical clothes* FUNCTIONAL, sensible, utilitarian, workaday. ❹ *try to be more practical* REALISTIC, sensible, down-to-earth, businesslike, commonsensical, hard-headed, no-nonsense; *informal* hard-nosed. ❺ *a practical certainty* VIRTUAL, effective, near.

– OPPOSITES theoretical.

practicality ▶ noun ❶ *the practicality of the proposal* FEASIBILITY, practicability, viability, workability. ❷ *practicality of design* FUNCTIONALISM, functionality, serviceability, utility. ❸ *his calm practicality* (COMMON) SENSE, realism, pragmatism. ❹ *the practicalities of army life* PRACTICAL DETAILS; *informal* nitty gritty, nuts and bolts.

practical joke ▶ noun TRICK, joke, prank, jape, hoax; *informal* leg-pull.

practically ▶ adverb ❶ *the cinema was practically empty* ALMOST, (very) nearly, virtually, just about, all but, more or less, as good as, to all intents and purposes, verging on, bordering on; *informal* pretty nearly, pretty well; *poetic/literary* well-nigh. ❷ *'You can't afford it,' he pointed out practically* REALISTICALLY, sensibly, reasonably.

practice ▶ noun ❶ *the practice of radiotherapy* APPLICATION, exercise, use, operation, implementation, execution. ❷ *common practice* CUSTOM, procedure, policy, convention, tradition; *formal* praxis. ❸ *it takes lots of practice | the team's final practice* TRAINING, rehearsal, repetition, preparation; practice session, dummy run, run-through; *informal* dry run. ❹ *the practice of medicine* PROFESSION, career, business, work. ❺ *a small legal practice* BUSINESS, firm, office, company; *informal* outfit.

■ **in practice** IN REALITY, realistically, practically.

■ **out of practice** RUSTY, unpractised.

■ **put something into practice** USE, make use of, put to use, utilize, apply.

practise ▶ verb ❶ *he practised the songs every day* REHEARSE, run through, go over/through, work on/at; polish, perfect. ❷ *the performers were practising* TRAIN, rehearse, prepare, go through one's paces. ❸ *we still practise these rituals today* CARRY OUT, perform, observe. ❹ *she practises medicine* WORK AT, pursue a career in.

practised ▶ adjective EXPERT, experienced, seasoned, skilled, skilful, accomplished, proficient, talented, able, adept, consummate, master, masterly; *informal* crack, ace, mean; *N. Amer. informal* crackerjack.

pragmatic ▶ adjective PRACTICAL, matter of fact, sensible, down-to-earth, commonsensical, businesslike, having both/one's feet on the ground, hard-headed, no-nonsense; *informal* hard-nosed.

– OPPOSITES impractical.

praise ▶ verb ❶ *the police praised Pauline for her courage* COMMEND, express admiration for, applaud, pay tribute to, speak highly of, eulogize, compliment, congratulate, sing the praises of, rave about, go into raptures about, heap praise on, wax lyrical about, make much of, pat on the back, take one's hat off to, lionize, admire, hail; *N. Amer. informal* ballyhoo; *formal* laud. ❷ *we praise God* WORSHIP, glorify, honour, exalt, adore, pay tribute to, give thanks to, venerate, reverence; *formal* laud; *archaic* magnify.

– RELATED TERMS laudatory.

– OPPOSITES criticize.

▶ noun ❶ *James was full of praise for the medical teams* APPROVAL, acclaim, admiration, approbation, acclamation, plaudits, congratulations, commendation; tribute, accolade, compliment, a pat on the back, eulogy, panegyric;

formal laudation, encomium. ❷ *give praise to God* HONOUR, thanks, glory, worship, devotion, adoration, reverence.

praiseworthy ▶ **adjective** COMMENDABLE, admirable, laudable, worthy (of admiration), meritorious, estimable, exemplary.

pram ▶ **noun** (*Brit.*) pushchair; *N. Amer.* baby carriage, stroller; *formal* perambulator.

prance ▶ **verb** CAVORT, dance, jig, trip, caper, jump, leap, spring, bound, skip, hop, frisk, romp, frolic.

prank ▶ **noun** (PRACTICAL) JOKE, trick, piece of mischief, escapade, stunt, caper, jape, game, hoax, antic; *informal* lark, leg-pull.

prattle ▶ **verb** *he prattled on for ages. See* CHAT verb.
▶ **noun** *childish prattle. See* CHATTER noun.

pray ▶ **verb** ❶ *let us pray* SAY ONE'S PRAYERS, make one's devotions, offer a prayer/prayers. ❷ *she prayed God to forgive her* INVOKE, call on, implore, appeal to, entreat, beg, petition, supplicate; *poetic/literary* beseech.

prayer ▶ **noun** ❶ *the priest's murmured prayers* INVOCATION, intercession, devotion; *archaic* orison. ❷ *a quick prayer that she wouldn't bump into him* APPEAL, plea, entreaty, petition, supplication, invocation; *rare* obsecration.
■ **not have a prayer** (*informal*) HAVE NO HOPE, have/stand no chance, not have/stand (the ghost of) a chance; *informal* not have a hope in hell, not have/stand an earthly; *Austral./NZ informal* not have Buckley's (chance).

preach ▶ **verb** ❶ *he preached to a large congregation* GIVE A SERMON, sermonize, address, speak. ❷ *preaching the good news of Jesus* PROCLAIM, teach, spread, propagate, expound. ❸ *they preach toleration* ADVOCATE, recommend, advise, urge, teach, counsel. ❹ *who are you to preach at me?* MORALIZE, sermonize, pontificate, lecture, harangue; *informal* preachify.
– RELATED TERMS homiletic.

preacher ▶ **noun** MINISTER (OF RELIGION), parson, clergyman, clergywoman, member of the clergy, priest, man/woman of the cloth, man/woman of God, cleric, churchman, churchwoman, evangelist; *informal* reverend, padre, Holy Joe, sky pilot; *N. Amer. informal* preacher man; *Austral. informal* josser.

preaching ▶ **noun** RELIGIOUS TEACHING, message, sermons.

preachy ▶ **adjective** (*informal*) MORALISTIC, moralizing, sanctimonious, self-righteous, holier-than-thou, sententious.

preamble ▶ **noun** INTRODUCTION, preface, prologue; foreword, prelude, front matter; *informal* intro, prelims; *formal* exordium, proem, prolegomenon.

pre-arranged ▶ **adjective** ARRANGED BEFOREHAND, agreed in advance, predetermined, pre-established, pre-planned.

precarious ▶ **adjective** UNCERTAIN, insecure, unpredictable, risky, parlous, hazardous, dangerous, unsafe; unsettled, unstable, unsteady, shaky; *informal* dicey, chancy, iffy; *Brit. informal* dodgy.
– OPPOSITES safe.

precaution ▶ **noun** SAFEGUARD, preventative/preventive measure, safety measure, insurance; *informal* backstop.

precautionary ▶ **adjective** PREVENTATIVE, preventive, safety.

precede ▶ **verb** ❶ *adverts preceded the film* GO/COME BEFORE, lead (up) to, pave/prepare the way for, herald, introduce, usher in; *archaic* forgo. ❷ *Catherine preceded him into the studio* GO AHEAD OF, go in front of, go before, go first, lead the way. ❸ *he preceded the book with a poem* PREFACE, introduce, begin, open.
– OPPOSITES follow.

precedence ▶ **noun** *quarrels over precedence* PRIORITY, rank, seniority, superiority, primacy, pre-eminence, eminence.
■ **take precedence over** TAKE PRIORITY OVER, outweigh, prevail over, come before.

precedent ▶ **noun** MODEL, exemplar, example, pattern, previous case, prior instance/example; paradigm, criterion, yardstick, standard.

preceding ▶ **adjective** FOREGOING, previous, prior, former, precedent, earlier, above, aforementioned, antecedent; *formal* anterior, prevenient.

precept ▶ **noun** ❶ *the precepts of Orthodox Judaism* PRINCIPLE, rule, tenet, canon, doctrine, command, order, decree, dictate, dictum, injunction, commandment; *Judaism* mitzvah; *formal* prescript. ❷ *precepts that her grandmother used to quote* MAXIM, saying, adage, axiom, aphorism, apophthegm.

precinct ▶ **noun** ❶ *a pedestrian precinct* AREA, zone, sector. ❷ *within the precincts of the City* BOUNDS, boundaries, limits, confines. ❸ *the cathedral precinct* ENCLOSURE, close, court.

precious ▶ **adjective** ❶ *precious works of art* VALUABLE, costly, expensive; invaluable, priceless, beyond price. ❷ *her most precious possession* VALUED, cherished, treasured, prized, favourite, dear, dearest, beloved, darling, adored, loved, special. ❸ *his precious manners* AFFECTED, over-refined, pretentious; *informal* la-di-da; *Brit. informal* poncey.

precipice ▶ **noun** CLIFF (FACE), steep cliff, rock face, sheer drop, crag, bluff, escarpment, scarp; *poetic/literary* steep.

precipitate ▶ **verb** ❶ *the incident precipitated a crisis* BRING ABOUT/ON, cause, lead to, give rise to, instigate, trigger, spark, touch off, provoke, hasten, accelerate, expedite. ❷ *they were precipitated down the mountain* HURL, catapult, throw, plunge, launch, fling, propel.

▶ **adjective** ❶ *their actions were precipitate* HASTY, overhasty, rash, hurried, rushed; impetuous, impulsive, spur-of-the-moment, precipitous, incautious, imprudent, injudicious, ill-advised, reckless, harum-scarum; *informal* previous; *poetic/literary* temerarious. ❷ *a precipitate decline. See* PRECIPITOUS sense 2.

precipitous ▶ **adjective** ❶ *a precipitous drop* STEEP, sheer, perpendicular, abrupt, sharp, vertical. ❷ *his fall from power was precipitous* SUDDEN, rapid, swift, abrupt, headlong, speedy, quick, fast. ❸ *he was too precipitous. See* PRECIPITATE adjective sense 1.

precis ▶ **noun** *a precis of the report* SUMMARY, synopsis, résumé, abstract, outline, summarization, summation; abridgement, digest, overview, epitome; *N. Amer.* wrap-up; *rare* conspectus.

▶ **verb** *precising a passage* SUMMARIZE, sum up, give a summary/precis of, give the main points of; abridge, condense, shorten, synopsize, abstract, outline, abbreviate; *archaic* epitomize.

precise ▶ **adjective** ❶ *precise measurements* EXACT, accurate, correct, specific, detailed, explicit, unambiguous, definite. ❷ *at that precise moment the car stopped* EXACT, particular, very, specific. ❸ *the attention to detail is very precise* METICULOUS, careful, exact, scrupulous, punctilious, conscientious, particular, methodical, strict, rigorous.

–OPPOSITES inaccurate.

precisely ▶ **adverb** ❶ *at 2 o'clock precisely* EXACTLY, sharp, on the dot; promptly, prompt, dead (on), on the stroke of ——, on the dot of ——; *informal* bang (on); *Brit. informal* spot on; *N. Amer. informal* on the button/nose. ❷ *precisely the kind of man I am looking for* EXACTLY, absolutely, just, in all respects; *informal* to a T. ❸ *fertilization can be timed precisely* ACCURATELY, exactly; clearly, distinctly, strictly. ❹ *'So it's all done?' 'Precisely.'* YES, exactly, absolutely, (that's) right, quite so, indubitably, definitely; *informal* you bet, I'll say.

precision ▶ **noun** EXACTNESS, exactitude, accuracy, correctness, preciseness; care, carefulness, meticulousness, scrupulousness, punctiliousness, methodicalness, rigour, rigorousness.

preclude ▶ **verb** PREVENT, make it impossible for, rule out, stop, prohibit, debar, bar, hinder, impede, inhibit, exclude.

precocious ▶ **adjective** ADVANCED FOR ONE'S AGE, forward, mature, gifted, talented, clever, intelligent, quick; *informal* smart.

–OPPOSITES backward.

preconceived ▶ **adjective** PREDETERMINED, prejudged; prejudiced, biased.

preconception ▶ **noun** PRECONCEIVED IDEA/NOTION, presupposition, assumption, presumption, prejudgement; prejudice.

precondition ▶ **noun** PREREQUISITE, (necessary/essential) condition, requirement, necessity, essential, imperative, sine qua non; *informal* must.

precursor ▶ **noun** ❶ *a three-stringed precursor of the guitar* FORERUNNER, predecessor, forefather, father, antecedent, ancestor, forebear. ❷ *a precursor of disasters to come* HARBINGER, herald, sign, indication, portent, omen.

precursory ▶ **adjective** PRELIMINARY, prior, previous, introductory, preparatory, prefatory; *formal* anterior, prevenient.

predatory ▶ **adjective** ❶ *predatory birds* PREDACIOUS, carnivorous, hunting, raptorial; of prey. ❷ *a predatory gleam in his eyes* EXPLOITATIVE, wolfish, rapacious, vulturine, vulturous.

predecessor ▶ **noun** ❶ *the Prime Minister's predecessor* FORERUNNER, precursor, antecedent. ❷ *our Victorian predecessors* ANCESTOR, forefather, forebear, antecedent.

–OPPOSITES successor, descendant.

predestined ▶ **adjective** PREORDAINED, ordained, predetermined, destined, fated.

predetermined ▶ **adjective** ❶ *a predetermined budget* PRE-ARRANGED, established in advance, preset, set, fixed, agreed. ❷ *our predetermined fate* PREDESTINED, preordained.

predicament ▶ **noun** DIFFICULT SITUATION, mess, difficulty, plight, quandary, muddle, mare's nest; *informal* hole, fix, jam, pickle, scrape, bind, tight spot/corner, dilemma.

predicate ▶ **verb** BASE, be dependent, found, establish, rest, ground, premise.

predict ▶ **verb** FORECAST, foretell, foresee, prophesy, anticipate, tell in advance, envision, envisage; *poetic/literary* previse; *archaic* augur, presage.

predictable ▶ **adjective** FORESEEABLE, (only) to be expected, anticipated, foreseen, unsurprising; *informal* inevitable.

prediction ▶ **noun** FORECAST, prophecy, prognosis, prognostication, augury; projection, conjecture, guess.

predilection ▶ **noun** LIKING, fondness, preference, partiality, taste, penchant, weakness, soft spot, fancy, inclination, leaning, bias, propensity, bent, proclivity, predisposition, appetite.

–OPPOSITES dislike.

predispose ▶ **verb** ❶ *lack of exercise may predispose an individual to high blood pressure* MAKE SUSCEPTIBLE, make liable, make prone, make vulnerable, put at risk of. ❷ *attitudes which predispose people to behave badly* LEAD, influence, sway, induce, prompt, dispose; bias, prejudice.

predisposed ▶ **adjective** INCLINED, prepared, ready, of a mind, disposed, minded, willing.

predisposition ▶ **noun** ❶ *a predisposition to heart disease* SUSCEPTIBILITY, proneness, tendency, liability, inclination, disposition, vulnerability. ❷ *their political predispositions* PREFERENCE, predilection, inclination, leaning.

predominance ▶ noun ❶ *the predominance of women carers* PREVALENCE, dominance, preponderance. ❷ *Soviet military predominance* SUPREMACY, mastery, control, power, ascendancy, dominance, pre-eminence, superiority.

predominant ▶ adjective ❶ *our predominant objectives* MAIN, chief, principal, most important, primary, prime, central, leading, foremost, key, paramount; *informal* number-one. ❷ *the predominant political forces* CONTROLLING, dominant, predominating, more/most powerful, pre-eminent, ascendant, superior, in the ascendancy.
– OPPOSITES subsidiary.

predominantly ▶ adverb MAINLY, mostly, for the most part, chiefly, principally, primarily, predominately, in the main, on the whole, largely, by and large, typically, generally, usually.

predominate ▶ verb ❶ *small-scale producers predominate* BE IN THE MAJORITY, preponderate, be predominant, prevail, be most prominent. ❷ *private interest predominates over the public good* PREVAIL, dominate, be dominant, carry most weight; override, outweigh.

pre-eminence ▶ noun SUPERIORITY, supremacy, greatness, excellence, distinction, prominence, predominance, eminence, importance, prestige, stature, fame, renown, celebrity.

pre-eminent ▶ adjective GREATEST, leading, foremost, best, finest, chief, outstanding, excellent, distinguished, prominent, eminent, important, top, famous, renowned, celebrated, illustrious, supreme; *N. Amer.* marquee.
– OPPOSITES undistinguished.

pre-eminently ▶ adverb PRIMARILY, principally, above all, chiefly, mostly, mainly, in particular.

pre-empt ▶ verb ❶ *his action may have pre-empted war* FORESTALL, prevent. ❷ *many tables were already pre-empted by family parties* COMMANDEER, occupy, seize, arrogate, appropriate, take over, secure, reserve.

preen ▶ verb ❶ *the robin preened its feathers* CLEAN, tidy, groom, smooth, arrange; *archaic* plume. ❷ *she preened before the mirror* ADMIRE ONESELF, primp oneself, prink oneself, groom oneself, spruce oneself up; *informal* titivate oneself, doll oneself up; *Brit. informal* tart oneself up; *N. Amer. informal* gussy oneself up.
■ **preen oneself** CONGRATULATE ONESELF, be pleased with oneself, be proud of oneself, pat oneself on the back, feel self-satisfied.

preface ▶ noun *the preface to the novel* INTRODUCTION, foreword, preamble, prologue, prelude; front matter; *informal* prelims, intro; *formal* exordium, proem, prolegomenon.
▶ verb *the chapter is prefaced by a poem* PRECEDE, introduce, begin, open, start.

prefatory ▶ adjective INTRODUCTORY, preliminary, opening, initial, preparatory, initiatory, precursory.
– OPPOSITES closing.

prefect ▶ noun (*Brit.*) MONITOR; *Brit.* praepostor.

prefer ▶ verb ❶ *I prefer white wine to red* LIKE BETTER, would rather (have), would sooner (have), favour, be more partial to; choose, select, pick, opt for, go for, plump for. ❷ (*formal*) *do you want to prefer charges?* BRING, press, file, lodge, lay. ❸ (*archaic*) *he was preferred to the post* PROMOTE, upgrade, raise, elevate.

preferable ▶ adjective BETTER, best, more desirable, more suitable, advantageous, superior, preferred, recommended.

preferably ▶ adverb IDEALLY, if possible, for preference, from choice.

preference ▶ noun ❶ *her preference for boys' games* LIKING, partiality, predilection, proclivity, fondness, taste, inclination, leaning, bias, bent, penchant, predisposition. ❷ *my preference is rock* FAVOURITE, (first) choice, selection; *informal* cup of tea, thing; *N. Amer. informal* druthers. ❸ *preference will be given to applicants speaking Japanese* PRIORITY, favour, precedence, preferential treatment.
■ **in preference to** RATHER THAN, instead of, in place of, sooner than.

preferential ▶ adjective SPECIAL, better, privileged, superior, favourable; partial, discriminatory, partisan, biased.

preferment ▶ noun PROMOTION, advancement, elevation, being upgraded, a step up (the ladder); *informal* a kick upstairs.
– OPPOSITES demotion.

prefigure ▶ verb FORESHADOW, presage, be a harbinger of, herald; *poetic/literary* foretoken.

pregnancy ▶ noun gestation.
– RELATED TERMS antenatal, maternity.

pregnant ▶ adjective ❶ *she is heavily pregnant* EXPECTING A BABY, expectant, carrying a child; *informal* expecting, in the family way, preggers, with a bun in the oven; *Brit. informal* up the duff, in the (pudding) club, up the spout; *N. Amer. informal* knocked up, having swallowed a watermelon seed; *Austral. informal* with a joey in the pouch; *informal, dated* in trouble; *archaic* with child, in a delicate condition, in an interesting condition; *technical* gravid, parturient. ❷ *a ceremony pregnant with religious significance* FILLED, charged, heavy; full of. ❸ *a pregnant pause* MEANINGFUL, significant, suggestive, expressive, charged.

prehistoric ▶ adjective ❶ *prehistoric times* PRIMITIVE, primeval, primordial, primal, ancient, early, antediluvian. ❷ *the special effects look prehistoric* OUT OF DATE, outdated, outmoded, old-fashioned, passé, antiquated,

archaic, behind the times, primitive, antediluvian; *informal* out of the ark; *N. Amer. informal* horse and buggy, clunky.
– RELATED TERMS archaeo-.
– OPPOSITES modern.

prejudice ▶ noun ❶ *male prejudices about women* PRECONCEIVED IDEA, preconception, prejudgement. ❷ *they are motivated by prejudice* BIGOTRY, bias, partisanship, partiality, intolerance, discrimination, unfairness, inequality. ❸ *without prejudice to the interests of others* DETRIMENT, harm, damage, injury, hurt, loss.
▶ verb ❶ *the article could prejudice the jury* BIAS, influence, sway, predispose, make biased, make partial, colour. ❷ *this could prejudice his chances of victory* DAMAGE, be detrimental to, be prejudicial to, injure, harm, hurt, spoil, impair, undermine, hinder, compromise.

prejudiced ▶ adjective BIASED, bigoted, discriminatory, partisan, intolerant, narrow-minded, unfair, unjust, inequitable, coloured.
– OPPOSITES impartial.

prejudicial ▶ adjective DETRIMENTAL, damaging, injurious, harmful, disadvantageous, hurtful, deleterious.
– OPPOSITES beneficial.

preliminary ▶ adjective *the discussions are still at a preliminary stage* PREPARATORY, introductory, initial, opening, prefatory, precursory; early, exploratory.
– OPPOSITES final.
▶ noun ❶ *he began without any preliminaries* INTRODUCTION, preamble, opening/prefatory remarks, formalities. ❷ *a preliminary to the resumption of war* PRELUDE, preparation, preparatory measure, preliminary action.
■ **preliminary to** IN PREPARATION FOR, before, in advance of, prior to, preparatory to.

prelims ▶ plural noun (*informal*) FRONT MATTER, preliminary material, introduction, foreword, preface, preamble; *informal* intro; *formal* exordium, proem, prolegomenon.

prelude ▶ noun ❶ *a ceasefire was a prelude to peace negotiations* PRELIMINARY, overture, opening, preparation, introduction, start, commencement, beginning, lead-in, precursor. ❷ *an orchestral prelude* OVERTURE, introductory movement, introduction, opening. ❸ *the passage forms a prelude to Part III* INTRODUCTION, preface, prologue, foreword, preamble; *informal* intro; *formal* exordium, proem, prolegomenon.

premature ▶ adjective ❶ *his premature death* UNTIMELY, (too) early, unseasonable, before time. ❷ *a premature baby* PRETERM; *informal* prem. ❸ *such a step would be premature* RASH, overhasty, hasty, precipitate, precipitous, impulsive, impetuous; *informal* previous.
– OPPOSITES overdue.

prematurely ▶ adverb ❶ *Sam was born prematurely* TOO SOON, too early, ahead of time; preterm. ❷ *don't act prematurely* RASHLY, overhastily, hastily, precipitately, precipitously.

premeditated ▶ adjective PLANNED, intentional, deliberate, pre-planned, calculated, cold-blooded, conscious, pre-arranged.
– OPPOSITES spontaneous.

premeditation ▶ noun (ADVANCE) PLANNING, forethought, pre-planning, (criminal) intent; *Law* malice aforethought.

premier ▶ adjective *a premier chef* LEADING, foremost, chief, principal, head, top-ranking, top, prime, primary, first, highest, pre-eminent, senior, outstanding, master; *N. Amer.* ranking; *informal* top-notch.
▶ noun *the Italian premier* HEAD OF GOVERNMENT, prime minister, PM, president, chancellor.

premiere ▶ noun FIRST PERFORMANCE, first night, opening night.

premise ▶ noun *the premise that human life consists of a series of choices* PROPOSITION, assumption, hypothesis, thesis, presupposition, postulation, postulate, supposition, presumption, surmise, conjecture, speculation, assertion, belief.
▶ verb *they premised that the cosmos is indestructible* POSTULATE, hypothesize, conjecture, posit, theorize, suppose, presuppose, surmise, assume.

premises ▶ plural noun BUILDING(S), property, site, office.

premium ▶ noun ❶ *monthly premiums of £30* (REGULAR) PAYMENT, instalment. ❷ *you must pay a premium for organic fruit* SURCHARGE, additional payment, extra amount. ❸ *a foreign service premium* BONUS, extra; incentive, inducement; *informal* perk; *formal* perquisite.
■ **at a premium** SCARCE, in great demand, hard to come by, in short supply, thin on the ground.
■ **put/place a premium on** ❶ *I place a high premium on our relationship* VALUE GREATLY, attach great/special importance to, set great store by, put a high value on. ❷ *the high price of oil put a premium on the coal industry* MAKE VALUABLE, make invaluable, make important.

premonition ▶ noun FOREBODING, presentiment, intuition, (funny) feeling, hunch, suspicion, feeling in one's bones; misgiving, apprehension, fear; *archaic* presage.

preoccupation ▶ noun ❶ *an air of preoccupation* PENSIVENESS, concentration, engrossment, absorption, self-absorption, musing, thinking, deep thought, brown study, brooding; abstraction, absent-mindedness, distraction, forgetfulness, inattentiveness, woolgathering, daydreaming. ❷ *their main preoccupation was feeding their family* OBSESSION, concern; passion, enthusiasm, hobby horse.

preoccupied ▶ adjective ❶ *officials preoccupied with their careers* OBSESSED, concerned, absorbed, engrossed, intent, involved, wrapped up. ❷ *she looked preoccupied* LOST/DEEP IN THOUGHT, in a brown study, pensive, absent-minded, distracted, abstracted.

preoccupy ▸ **verb** ENGROSS, concern, absorb, take up someone's attention, distract, obsess, occupy, prey on someone's mind.

preordain ▸ **verb** PREDESTINE, destine, foreordain, ordain, fate, predetermine, determine.

preparation ▸ **noun** ❶ *the preparation of contingency plans* DEVISING, putting together, drawing up, construction, composition, production, getting ready, development. ❷ *preparations for the party* ARRANGEMENTS, planning, plans, preparatory measures. ❸ *preparation for exams* INSTRUCTION, teaching, coaching, training, tutoring, drilling, priming. ❹ *a preparation to kill off mites* MIXTURE, compound, concoction, solution, tincture, medicine, potion, cream, ointment, lotion.

preparatory ▸ **adjective** *preparatory work* PRELIMINARY, initial, introductory, prefatory, opening, preparative, precursory.
■ **preparatory to** IN PREPARATION FOR, before, prior to, preliminary to.

prepare ▸ **verb** ❶ *I want you to prepare a report* MAKE/GET READY, put together, draw up, produce, arrange, assemble, construct, compose, formulate. ❷ *the meal was easy to prepare* COOK, make, get, put together, concoct; *informal* fix, rustle up; *Brit. informal* knock up. ❸ *preparing for war* GET READY, make preparations, arrange things, make provision, get everything set. ❹ *athletes preparing for the Olympics* TRAIN, get into shape, practise, get ready. ❺ *I must prepare for my exams* STUDY, revise; *Brit. informal* swot. ❻ *this course prepares students for their exams* INSTRUCT, coach, train, tutor, drill, prime. ❼ *prepare yourself for a shock* BRACE, make ready, tense, steel, steady.

prepared ▸ **adjective** ❶ *he needs to be well prepared* READY, (all) set, equipped, primed; waiting, on hand, poised, in position. ❷ *I'm not prepared to cut the price* WILLING, ready, disposed, predisposed, (favourably) inclined, of a mind, minded.

preponderance ▸ **noun** ❶ *the preponderance of women among older people* PREVALENCE, predominance, dominance. ❷ *the preponderance of the evidence* BULK, majority, greater quantity, larger part, best/better part, most; almost all. ❸ *the preponderance of the trade unions* PREDOMINANCE, dominance, ascendancy, supremacy, power.

preponderant ▸ **adjective** DOMINANT, predominant, pre-eminent, in control, more/most powerful, superior, supreme, ascendant, in the ascendancy.

preponderate ▸ **verb** BE IN THE MAJORITY, predominate, be predominant; be more/most important, prevail, dominate.

prepossessing ▸ **adjective** ATTRACTIVE, beautiful, pretty, handsome, good-looking, fetching, charming, delightful, enchanting, captivating; *archaic* fair.
– OPPOSITES ugly.

preposterous ▸ **adjective** ABSURD, ridiculous, foolish, stupid, ludicrous, farcical, laughable, comical, risible, nonsensical, senseless, insane; outrageous, monstrous; *informal* crazy.
– OPPOSITES sensible.

prerequisite ▸ **noun** *a prerequisite for the course* (NECESSARY) CONDITION, precondition, essential, requirement, requisite, necessity, sine qua non; *informal* must.
▸ **adjective** *the prerequisite qualifications* NECESSARY, required, called for, essential, requisite, obligatory, compulsory.
– OPPOSITES unnecessary.

prerogative ▸ **noun** ENTITLEMENT, right, privilege, advantage, due, birthright.

presage ▸ **verb** *the owl's hooting presages death* PORTEND, augur, foreshadow, foretell, prophesy, be an omen of, herald, be a sign of, be the harbinger of, warn of, be a presage of, signal, bode, promise, threaten; *poetic/literary* betoken, foretoken, forebode.
▸ **noun** *a sombre presage of his final illness* OMEN, sign, indication, portent, warning, forewarning, harbinger, augury, prophecy, foretoken.

prescience ▸ **noun** FAR-SIGHTEDNESS, foresight, foreknowledge; psychic powers, clairvoyance; prediction, prognostication, divination, prophesy, augury; insight, intuition, perception, percipience.

prescient ▸ **adjective** PROPHETIC, predictive, visionary; psychic, clairvoyant; far-sighted, prognostic, divinatory; insightful, intuitive, perceptive, percipient.

prescribe ▸ **verb** ❶ *the doctor prescribed antibiotics* WRITE A PRESCRIPTION FOR, authorize. ❷ *traditional values prescribe a life of domesticity* ADVISE, recommend, advocate, suggest, endorse, champion, promote. ❸ *rules prescribing your duty* STIPULATE, lay down, dictate, specify, determine, establish, fix.

prescription ▸ **noun** ❶ *the doctor wrote a prescription* INSTRUCTION, authorization; *informal* script; *archaic* recipe. ❷ *he fetched the prescription from the chemist* MEDICINE, drug, medication. ❸ *a painless prescription for improvement* METHOD, measure; recommendation, suggestion, recipe, formula.

prescriptive ▸ **adjective** DICTATORIAL, narrow, rigid, authoritarian, arbitrary, repressive, dogmatic.

presence ▸ **noun** ❶ *presence of a train was indicated electrically* EXISTENCE, being there. ❷ *I requested the presence of an adjudicator* ATTENDANCE, appearance; company, companionship. ❸ *a woman of great presence* AURA, charisma, (strength/force of) personality; poise, self-assurance, self-confidence. ❹ *she felt a presence in the castle* GHOST, spirit, spectre, phantom, apparition, supernatural being; *informal* spook; *poetic/literary* shade.

– OPPOSITES absence.

■ **presence of mind** COMPOSURE, equanimity, self-possession, level-headedness, self-assurance, calmness, sangfroid, imperturbability; alertness, quick-wittedness; *informal* cool, unflappability.

present[1] ▶ **adjective** ❶ *a doctor must be present at the ringside* IN ATTENDANCE, here, there, near, nearby, (close/near) at hand, available. ❷ *organic compounds are present in the waste* IN EXISTENCE, existing, existent. ❸ *the present economic climate* CURRENT, present-day, existing; *archaic* instant.

– OPPOSITES absent.

▶ **noun** *forget the past and think about the present* NOW, today, the present time/moment, the here and now.

– OPPOSITES past, future.

■ **at present** AT THE MOMENT, just now, right now, at the present time, currently, at this moment in time.

■ **for the present** FOR THE TIME BEING, for now, for the moment, for a while, temporarily, pro tem.

■ **the present day** MODERN TIMES, nowadays.

present[2] ▶ **verb** ❶ *Eddy presented a cheque to the winner* HAND OVER/OUT, give (out), confer, bestow, award, grant, accord. ❷ *the committee presented its report* SUBMIT, set forth, put forward, proffer, offer, tender, table. ❸ *may I present my wife?* INTRODUCE, make known, acquaint someone with. ❹ *I called to present my warmest compliments* OFFER, give, express. ❺ *they presented their new product last month* DEMONSTRATE, show, put on show/display, exhibit, display, launch, unveil. ❻ *presenting good quality opera* STAGE, put on, produce, perform. ❼ *she presents a TV show* HOST, introduce, compère, be the presenter of; *N. Amer. informal* emcee. ❽ *the authorities present him as a common criminal* REPRESENT, describe, portray, depict.

■ **present oneself** ❶ *he presented himself at ten* BE PRESENT, make an appearance, appear, turn up, arrive. ❷ *an opportunity that presented itself* OCCUR, arise, happen, come about/up, appear, crop up, turn up.

present[3] ▶ **noun** *a birthday present* GIFT, donation, offering, contribution; *informal* prezzie, freebie; *formal* benefaction.

presentable ▶ **adjective** ❶ *I'm making the place look presentable* TIDY, neat, straight, clean, spick and span, in good order, shipshape (and Bristol fashion). ❷ *make yourself presentable* SMARTLY DRESSED, tidily dressed, tidy, well groomed, trim, spruce; *informal* natty. ❸ *presentable videos* FAIRLY GOOD, passable, all right, satisfactory, moderately good, not (too) bad, average, fair; *informal* OK.

presentation ▶ **noun** ❶ *the presentation of his certificate* AWARDING, presenting, giving, handing over/out, bestowal, granting, award. ❷ *the presentation of food* APPEARANCE, arrangement, packaging, disposition, display, layout. ❸ *her presentation to the Queen* INTRODUCTION, making known. ❹ *the presentation of new proposals* SUBMISSION, proffering, offering, tendering, advancing, proposal, suggestion, mooting, tabling. ❺ *a sales presentation* DEMONSTRATION, talk, lecture, address, speech, show, exhibition, display, introduction, launch, launching, unveiling. ❻ *a presentation of his latest play* STAGING, production, performance, mounting, showing.

present-day ▶ **adjective** CURRENT, present, contemporary, latter-day, present-time, modern, twenty-first-century; up to date, up to the minute, fashionable, trendsetting, the latest, new, newest, newfangled; *informal* trendy, now.

presentiment ▶ **noun** PREMONITION, foreboding, intuition, (funny) feeling, hunch, feeling in one's bones, sixth sense; *archaic* presage.

presently ▶ **adverb** ❶ *I shall see you presently* SOON, shortly, directly, quite soon, in a short time, in a little while, at any moment/minute/second, in next to no time, before long; *N. Amer.* momentarily; *informal* pretty soon, any moment now, in a jiffy, before you can say Jack Robinson, in two shakes of a lamb's tail; *Brit. informal* in a mo; *poetic/literary* ere long. ❷ *he is presently abroad* AT PRESENT, currently, at the/this moment, at the present moment/time, now, nowadays, these days; *Brit. informal* at the minute.

preservation ▶ **noun** ❶ *wood preservation* CONSERVATION, protection, care. ❷ *the preservation of the status quo* CONTINUATION, conservation, maintenance, upholding, sustaining, perpetuation. ❸ *the preservation of food* CONSERVING, bottling, canning, freezing, drying; curing, smoking, pickling.

preserve ▶ **verb** ❶ *oil helps preserve wood* CONSERVE, protect, maintain, care for, look after. ❷ *they wish to preserve the status quo* CONTINUE (WITH), conserve, keep going, maintain, uphold, sustain, perpetuate. ❸ *preserving him from harassment* GUARD, protect, keep, defend, safeguard, shelter, shield. ❹ *spices enable us to preserve food* CONSERVE, bottle, can, freeze, dry; cure, smoke, pickle.

▶ **noun** ❶ *strawberry preserve* JAM, jelly, marmalade, conserve. ❷ *the preserve of an educated middle-class* DOMAIN, area, field, sphere, orbit, realm, province, territory; *informal* turf, bailiwick. ❸ *a game preserve* SANCTUARY, (game) reserve, reservation.

preside ▶ **verb** *the chairman presides at the meeting* CHAIR, be chairman/chairwoman/chairperson, officiate (at), conduct, lead.

■ **preside over** BE IN CHARGE OF, be responsible for, be at the head/helm of, head, be head of, manage, administer, be in control of, control, direct, lead, govern, rule, command, supervise, oversee; *informal* head up, be boss of, be in the driving/driver's seat, be in the saddle.

president ▶ **noun** ❶ *terrorists assassinated the president* HEAD OF STATE. ❷ *the president of the society* HEAD, chief, director, leader, governor, principal, master; *N. Amer. informal* prexy. ❸ *the president of the company* CHAIRMAN, chairwoman; managing director, MD, chief executive (officer), CEO.

press ▶ **verb** ❶ *press the paper down firmly* PUSH (DOWN), press down, depress, hold down, force, thrust, squeeze, compress. ❷ *his shirt was pressed* SMOOTH (OUT), iron, remove creases from. ❸ *we pressed the grapes* CRUSH, squeeze, squash, mash, pulp, pound, pulverize, macerate. ❹ *she pressed the child to her bosom* CLASP, hold close, hug, cuddle, squeeze, clutch, grasp, embrace. ❺ *Winnie pressed his hand* SQUEEZE, grip, clutch. ❻ *the crowd pressed round* CLUSTER, gather, converge, congregate, flock, swarm, throng, crowd. ❼ *the government pressed its claim* PLEAD, urge, advance insistently, present, submit, put forward. ❽ *they pressed him to agree* URGE, put pressure on, pressurize, force, push, coerce, dragoon, steamroller, browbeat; *informal* lean on, put the screws on, twist someone's arm, railroad, bulldoze. ❾ *they pressed for a ban on the ivory trade* CALL, ask, clamour, push, campaign, demand.

▶ **noun** ❶ *a private press* PUBLISHING HOUSE, printing company; printing press. ❷ *the freedom of the press* THE MEDIA, the newspapers, the papers, the news media, the fourth estate; journalists, reporters, newspapermen, newsmen, newspaper women, pressmen, presswomen; *informal* journos, news hounds; *N. Amer. informal* newsies; *Brit. dated* Fleet Street. ❸ *the company had some bad press* (PRESS) REPORTS, press coverage, press articles, press reviews.

■ **be pressed for** HAVE TOO LITTLE, be short of, have insufficient, lack, be lacking (in), be deficient in, need, be/stand in need of; *informal* be strapped for.

■ **press on** PROCEED, keep going, continue, carry on, make progress, make headway, press ahead, forge on/ahead, push on, keep on, struggle on, persevere, keep at it, stay with it, plod on, plough on; *informal* soldier on, plug away, peg away, stick at it.

pressing ▶ **adjective** ❶ *a pressing problem* URGENT, critical, crucial, acute, desperate, serious, grave, life-and-death. ❷ *a pressing engagement* IMPORTANT, high-priority, critical, crucial, compelling, inescapable.

pressure ▶ **noun** ❶ *a confined gas exerts a constant pressure* PHYSICAL FORCE, load, stress, thrust; compression, weight. ❷ *they put pressure on us to borrow money* COERCION, force, compulsion, constraint, duress; pestering, harassment, nagging, badgering, intimidation, arm-twisting, pressurization, persuasion. ❸ *she had a lot of pressure from work* STRAIN, stress, tension, trouble, difficulty; *informal* hassle.

▶ **verb** *they pressured him into resigning. See* PRESSURIZE.

pressurize ▶ **verb** *he tried to pressurize Buffy into selling* COERCE, pressure, put pressure on, press, push, persuade, force, bulldoze, hound, harass, nag, harry, badger, goad, pester, browbeat, bully, bludgeon, intimidate, dragoon, twist someone's arm; *informal* railroad, lean on; *N. Amer. informal* hustle.

prestige ▶ **noun** STATUS, standing, stature, prestigiousness, reputation, repute, regard, fame, note, renown, honour, esteem, celebrity, importance, prominence, influence, eminence; kudos, cachet; *informal* clout.

prestigious ▶ **adjective** ❶ *prestigious journals* REPUTABLE, distinguished, respected, esteemed, eminent, august, highly regarded, well thought of, acclaimed, authoritative, celebrated, illustrious, leading, renowned. ❷ *a prestigious job* IMPRESSIVE, important, prominent, high-ranking, influential, powerful, glamorous; well paid, expensive; *Brit.* upmarket.

–OPPOSITES obscure, minor.

presumably ▶ **adverb** I PRESUME, I expect, I assume, I take it, I suppose, I imagine, I dare say, I guess, in all probability, probably, in all likelihood, as likely as not, doubtless, undoubtedly, no doubt.

presume ▶ **verb** ❶ *I presumed that it had once been an attic* ASSUME, suppose, dare say, imagine, take it, expect, believe, think, surmise, guess, judge, conjecture, speculate, postulate, presuppose. ❷ *let me presume to give you some advice* VENTURE, dare, have the audacity/effrontery, be so bold as, take the liberty of.

■ **presume on** TAKE (UNFAIR) ADVANTAGE OF, exploit, take liberties with; count on, bank on, place reliance on.

presumption ▶ **noun** ❶ *this presumption may be easily rebutted* ASSUMPTION, supposition, presupposition, belief, guess, judgement, surmise, conjecture, speculation, hypothesis, postulation, inference, deduction, conclusion. ❷ *he apologized for his presumption* BRAZENNESS, audacity, boldness, audaciousness, temerity, arrogance, presumptuousness, forwardness; cockiness, insolence, impudence, bumptiousness, impertinence, effrontery, cheek, cheekiness; rudeness, impoliteness, disrespect, familiarity; *informal* nerve, brass neck, chutzpah; *N. Amer. informal* sass, sassiness; *archaic* assumption.

presumptive ▶ **adjective** ❶ *a presumptive diagnosis* CONJECTURAL, speculative, tentative; theoretical, unproven, unconfirmed. ❷ *the heir presumptive* PROBABLE, likely, prospective, assumed, supposed, expected.

presumptuous ▶ adjective BRAZEN, overconfident, arrogant, bold, audacious, forward, familiar, impertinent, insolent, impudent, cocky; cheeky, rude, impolite, uncivil, bumptious; *N. Amer. informal* sassy; *archaic* assumptive.

presuppose ▶ verb ❶ *this presupposes the existence of a policy-making group* REQUIRE, necessitate, imply, entail, mean, involve, assume. ❷ *I had presupposed that theme parks make people happy* PRESUME, assume, take it for granted, take it as read, suppose, surmise, think, accept, consider.

presupposition ▶ noun PRESUMPTION, assumption, preconception, supposition, hypothesis, surmise, thesis, theory, premise, belief, postulation.

pretence ▶ noun ❶ *cease this pretence* MAKE-BELIEVE, putting on an act, acting, dissembling, shamming, faking, feigning, simulation, dissimulation, play-acting, posturing; deception, deceit, deceitfulness, fraud, fraudulence, duplicity, subterfuge, trickery, dishonesty, hypocrisy, falsity, lying, mendacity. ❷ *he made a pretence of being unconcerned* (FALSE) SHOW, semblance, affectation, (false) appearance, outward appearance, impression, (false) front, guise, facade, display. ❸ *she had dropped any pretence to faith* CLAIM, profession. ❹ *he was absolutely without pretence* PRETENTIOUSNESS, display, ostentation, affectation, showiness, posturing, humbug.
– OPPOSITES honesty.

pretend ▶ verb ❶ *they just pretend to listen* MAKE AS IF, profess, affect; dissimulate, dissemble, put it on, put on a false front, go through the motions, sham, fake it. ❷ *I'll pretend to be the dragon* PUT ON AN ACT, make believe, play at, act, play-act, impersonate. ❸ *it was useless to pretend innocence* FEIGN, sham, fake, simulate, put on, counterfeit, affect. ❹ *he cannot pretend to sophistication* CLAIM, lay claim to, purport to have, profess to have.
▶ adjective (*informal*) *a pretend conversation* IMAGINARY, imagined, pretended, make-believe, made-up, fantasy, fantasized, dreamed-up, unreal, invented, fictitious, mythical, feigned, fake, mock, sham, simulated, artificial, ersatz, false, pseudo; *informal* phoney.

pretended ▶ adjective FAKE, faked, affected, assumed, professed, spurious, mock, imitation, simulated, make-believe, pseudo, sham, false, bogus; *informal* pretend, phoney.

pretender ▶ noun CLAIMANT, aspirant.

pretension ▶ noun ❶ *the author has no pretension to exhaustive coverage* ASPIRATION, claim, assertion, pretence, profession. ❷ *she spoke without pretension* PRETENTIOUSNESS, affectation, affectedness, ostentation, ostentatiousness, artificiality, airs, posing, posturing, show, flashiness; pomposity, pompousness, grandiosity, grandiloquence, magniloquence.

pretentious ▶ adjective AFFECTED, ostentatious, showy; overambitious, pompous, artificial, inflated, overblown, high-sounding, flowery, grandiose, elaborate, extravagant, flamboyant, ornate, grandiloquent, magniloquent; *N. Amer.* sophomoric; *informal* flashy, highfalutin, la-di-da, pseudo; *Brit. informal* poncey.

preternatural ▶ adjective EXTRAORDINARY, exceptional, unusual, uncommon, singular, unprecedented, remarkable, phenomenal, abnormal, inexplicable, unaccountable; strange, mysterious, fantastic.

pretext ▶ noun (FALSE) EXCUSE, ostensible reason, alleged reason; guise, ploy, pretence, ruse.

prettify ▶ verb BEAUTIFY, make attractive, make pretty, titivate, adorn, ornament, decorate, smarten (up); *informal* doll up, do up, give something a facelift; *Brit. informal* tart up.

pretty ▶ adjective *a pretty child* ATTRACTIVE, lovely, good-looking, nice-looking, personable, fetching, prepossessing, appealing, charming, delightful, cute, as pretty as a picture; *Scottish & N. English* bonny; *informal* easy on the eye; *poetic/literary* beauteous; *archaic* fair, comely.
– OPPOSITES plain, ugly.
▶ adverb *a pretty large sum* QUITE, rather, somewhat, fairly, reasonably, comparatively, relatively.
▶ verb *she's prettying herself* BEAUTIFY, make attractive, make pretty, prettify, titivate, adorn, ornament, smarten; *informal* do oneself up; *Brit. informal* tart oneself up.

prevail ▶ verb ❶ *common sense will prevail* WIN (OUT/THROUGH), triumph, be victorious, carry the day, come out on top, succeed, prove superior, conquer, overcome; rule, reign. ❷ *the conditions that prevailed in the 1950s* EXIST, be in existence, be present, be the case, occur, be prevalent, be current, be the order of the day, be customary, be common, be widespread, be in force/effect; *formal* obtain.
■ **prevail on/upon** PERSUADE, induce, talk someone into, coax, convince, make, get, press someone into, argue someone into, urge, pressure someone into, pressurize someone into, coerce; *informal* sweet-talk, soft-soap.

prevailing ▶ adjective CURRENT, existing, prevalent, usual, common, general, widespread.

prevalence ▶ noun COMMONNESS, currency, widespread presence, generality, popularity, pervasiveness, universality, extensiveness; rampancy, rifeness.

prevalent ▶ adjective WIDESPREAD, prevailing, frequent, usual, common, current, popular, general, universal; endemic, rampant, rife.
– OPPOSITES rare.

prevaricate ▶ verb BE EVASIVE, beat about the bush, hedge, fence, shilly-shally, dodge (the issue), sidestep (the issue), equivocate; temporize, stall (for time); *Brit.* hum and haw; *archaic* palter; *rare* tergiversate.

prevent ▶ verb STOP, put a stop to, avert, nip in the bud, fend off, stave off, ward off; hinder, impede, hamper, obstruct, baulk, foil, thwart, forestall, counteract, inhibit, curb, restrain, preclude, pre-empt, save, help; disallow, prohibit, forbid, proscribe, exclude, debar, bar; *poetic/literary* stay.
– OPPOSITES allow.

preventive ▶ adjective ❶ *preventive maintenance* PRE-EMPTIVE, deterrent, precautionary, protective. ❷ *preventive medicine* PROPHYLACTIC, disease-preventing.
▶ noun ❶ *a preventive against crime* PRECAUTIONARY MEASURE, deterrent, safeguard, security, protection, defence. ❷ *disease preventives* PROPHYLACTIC (DEVICE), prophylactic medicine, preventive drug.

previous ▶ adjective ❶ *the previous five years | her previous boyfriend* FOREGOING, preceding, antecedent; old, earlier, prior, former, ex-, past, last, sometime, one-time, erstwhile; *formal* quondam, anterior; *archaic* whilom. ❷ (*informal*) *I was a bit previous* OVERHASTY, hasty, premature, precipitate, impetuous; *informal* ahead of oneself.
– OPPOSITES next.
■ **previous to** BEFORE, prior to, until, (leading) up to, earlier than, preceding; *formal* anterior to.

previously ▶ adverb FORMERLY, earlier (on), before, hitherto, once, at one time, in the past, in days/times gone by, in bygone days, in times past, in former times; in advance, already, beforehand; *formal* heretofore.

prey ▶ noun ❶ *the lions killed their prey* QUARRY, kill. ❷ *she was easy prey* VICTIM, target, dupe, gull; *informal* sucker, soft touch, pushover; *N. Amer. informal* patsy, sap, schlemiel; *Austral./NZ informal* dill.
– OPPOSITES predator.
■ **prey on** ❶ *hoverfly larvae prey on aphids* HUNT, catch; eat, feed on, live on/off. ❷ *they prey on the elderly* EXPLOIT, victimize, pick on, take advantage of; trick, swindle, cheat, hoodwink, fleece; *informal* con. ❸ *the problem preyed on his mind* OPPRESS, weigh (heavily) on, lie heavy on, gnaw at; trouble, worry, beset, disturb, distress, haunt, nag, torment, plague, obsess.

price ▶ noun ❶ *the purchase price* COST, asking price, charge, fee, fare, levy, amount, sum; outlay, expense, expenditure; valuation, quotation, estimate; *informal, humorous* damage. ❷ *spinsterhood was the price of her career* CONSEQUENCE, result, cost, penalty, sacrifice; downside, snag, drawback, disadvantage, minus. ❸ *he had a price on his head* REWARD, bounty, premium.
▶ verb *a ticket is priced at £5.00* FIX/SET THE PRICE OF, cost, value, rate; estimate.
■ **at a price** AT A HIGH PRICE/COST, at considerable cost, for a great deal of money.
■ **at any price** WHATEVER THE PRICE, at whatever cost, no matter (what) the cost.
■ **beyond price**. *See* PRICELESS sense 1.

priceless ▶ adjective ❶ *priceless works of art* OF INCALCULABLE VALUE/WORTH, of immeasurable value/worth, invaluable, beyond price; irreplaceable, incomparable, unparalleled. ❷ (*informal*) *that's priceless! See* HILARIOUS sense 1.
– OPPOSITES worthless, cheap.

pricey ▶ adjective (*informal*). *See* EXPENSIVE.

prick ▶ verb ❶ *prick the potatoes with a fork* PIERCE, puncture, make/put a hole in, stab, perforate, nick, jab. ❷ *his eyes began to prick* STING, smart, burn, prickle. ❸ *his conscience pricked him* TROUBLE, worry, distress, perturb, disturb, cause someone anguish, afflict, torment, plague, prey on, gnaw at. ❹ *ambition pricked him on to greater effort* GOAD, prod, incite, provoke, urge, spur, stimulate, encourage, inspire, motivate, push, propel, impel. ❺ *the horse pricked up its ears* RAISE, erect.
▶ noun ❶ *a prick in the leg* JAB, sting, pinprick, stab. ❷ *the prick of tears behind her eyelids* STING, stinging, smart, smarting, burning. ❸ *the prick of conscience* PANG, twinge, stab.
■ **prick up one's ears** LISTEN CAREFULLY, pay attention, become attentive, begin to take notice, attend; *informal* be all ears; *poetic/literary* hark.

prickle ▶ noun ❶ *the cactus is covered with prickles* THORN, needle, barb, spike, point, spine; *technical* spicule. ❷ *Willie felt a cold prickle of fear* TINGLE, tingling (sensation), prickling sensation, chill, thrill; *Medicine* paraesthesia.
▶ verb *its tiny spikes prickled his skin* STING, prick.

prickly ▶ adjective ❶ *a prickly hedgehog* SPIKY, spiked, thorny, barbed, spiny; briary, brambly; rough, scratchy; *technical* spiculate, spicular, aculeate, spinose. ❷ *my skin feels prickly* TINGLY, tingling, prickling. ❸ *a prickly character. See* IRRITABLE. ❹ *the prickly question of the refugees* PROBLEMATIC, awkward, ticklish, tricky, delicate, sensitive, difficult, knotty, thorny, irksome, tough, troublesome, bothersome, vexatious.

pride ▶ noun ❶ *their triumphs were a source of pride* SELF-ESTEEM, dignity, honour, self-respect, self-worth, self-regard, pride in oneself. ❷ *take pride in a good job well done* PLEASURE, joy, delight, gratification, fulfilment, satisfaction, sense of achievement. ❸ *he refused her offer out of pride* ARROGANCE, vanity, self-importance, hubris, conceit, conceitedness, self-love, self-adulation, self-admiration, narcissism, egotism, superciliousness, haughtiness, snobbery, snobbishness; *informal* big-headedness; *poetic/literary* vainglory. ❹ *the bull is the pride of the herd* BEST, finest, top, cream, pick, choice, prize, glory, the jewel in the crown. ❺ *the vegetable garden was the pride of the gardener* SOURCE

OF SATISFACTION, pride and joy, treasured possession, joy, delight.
– OPPOSITES shame, humility.
■ **pride oneself on** BE PROUD OF, be proud of oneself for, take pride in, take satisfaction in, congratulate oneself on, pat oneself on the back for; *archaic* pique oneself on/in.

priest ▶ noun CLERGYMAN, CLERGYWOMAN, minister (of religion), cleric, ecclesiastic, pastor, vicar, rector, parson, churchman, churchwoman, man/woman of the cloth, man/woman of God, father, curate, chaplain, curé, evangelist, preacher; *Scottish* kirkman; *N. Amer.* dominie; *informal* reverend, padre, Holy Joe, sky pilot; *Austral. informal* josser; *dated* divine.

priestly ▶ adjective CLERICAL, pastoral, priestlike, ecclesiastical, sacerdotal, hieratic, rectorial; *archaic* vicarial.

prig ▶ noun PRUDE, puritan, killjoy, Mrs Grundy; *informal* goody-goody, holy Joe; *N. Amer. informal* bluenose.

priggish ▶ adjective SELF-RIGHTEOUS, holier-than-thou, sanctimonious, moralistic, prudish, puritanical, prim, strait-laced, stuffy, prissy, narrow-minded; *informal* goody-goody, starchy.
– OPPOSITES broad-minded.

prim ▶ adjective DEMURE, (prim and) proper, formal, stuffy, strait-laced, prudish; prissy, mimsy, priggish, puritanical; *Brit.* po-faced; *informal* starchy.

primacy ▶ noun GREATER IMPORTANCE, priority, precedence, pre-eminence, superiority, supremacy, ascendancy, dominance, dominion, leadership.

prima donna ▶ noun LEADING SOPRANO, leading lady, diva, (opera) star, principal singer.

primal ▶ adjective ❶ *primal masculine instincts* BASIC, fundamental, essential, elemental, vital, central, intrinsic, inherent. ❷ *the primal source of living things* ORIGINAL, initial, earliest, first, primitive, primeval.

primarily ▶ adverb ❶ *the bishop was primarily a leader of the local community* FIRST (AND FOREMOST), firstly, essentially, in essence, fundamentally, principally, predominantly, basically. ❷ *such work is undertaken primarily for large institutions* MOSTLY, for the most part, chiefly, mainly, in the main, on the whole, largely, to a large extent, especially, generally, usually, typically, commonly, as a rule.

primary ▶ adjective ❶ *our primary role* MAIN, chief, key, prime, central, principal, foremost, first, most important, predominant, paramount; *informal* number-one. ❷ *the primary cause* ORIGINAL, earliest, initial, first; essential, fundamental, basic.
– OPPOSITES secondary.

prime[1] ▶ adjective ❶ *his prime reason for leaving* MAIN, chief, key, primary, central, principal, foremost, first, most important, paramount, major; *informal* number-one. ❷ *the prime cause of flooding* FUNDAMENTAL, basic, essential, primary, central. ❸ *prime agricultural land* TOP-QUALITY, top, best, first-class, first-rate, grade A, superior, supreme, choice, select, finest; excellent, superb, fine; *informal* tip-top, A1, top-notch. ❹ *a prime example* ARCHETYPAL, prototypical, typical, classic, excellent, characteristic, quintessential.
– OPPOSITES secondary, inferior.
▶ noun *he is in his prime* HEYDAY, best days/years, prime of one's life; youth, salad days; peak, pinnacle, high point/spot, zenith.

prime[2] ▶ verb ❶ *he primed the gun* PREPARE, load, get ready. ❷ *Lucy had primed him carefully* BRIEF, fill in, prepare, put in the picture, inform, advise, instruct, coach, drill; *informal* clue in, give someone the low-down.

prime minister ▶ noun PREMIER, first minister, head of the government.

primeval ▶ adjective ❶ *primeval forest* ANCIENT, earliest, first, prehistoric, antediluvian, primordial; pristine, original, virgin. ❷ *primeval fears* INSTINCTIVE, primitive, basic, primal, primordial, intuitive, inborn, innate, inherent.

primitive ▶ adjective ❶ *primitive times* ANCIENT, earliest, first, prehistoric, antediluvian, primordial, primeval, primal. ❷ *primitive peoples* UNCIVILIZED, barbarian, barbaric, barbarous, savage, ignorant, uncultivated. ❸ *primitive tools* CRUDE, simple, rough (and ready), basic, rudimentary, unrefined, unsophisticated, rude, makeshift. ❹ *primitive art* SIMPLE, natural, unsophisticated, unaffected, undeveloped, unpretentious.
– OPPOSITES sophisticated, civilized.

primordial ▶ adjective ❶ *the primordial oceans* ANCIENT, earliest, first, prehistoric, antediluvian, primeval. ❷ *their primordial desires* INSTINCTIVE, primitive, basic, primal, primeval, intuitive, inborn, innate, inherent.

primp ▶ verb GROOM, tidy, arrange, brush, comb; smarten (up), spruce up; *informal* titivate, doll up; *Brit. informal* tart up; *N. Amer. informal* gussy up.

prince ▶ noun RULER, sovereign, monarch, king, princeling; crown prince; emir, sheikh, sultan, maharaja, raja.

princely ▶ adjective ❶ *princely buildings. See* SPLENDID sense 1. ❷ *a princely sum. See* HANDSOME sense 3.

principal ▶ adjective *the principal cause of poor air quality* MAIN, chief, primary, leading, foremost, first, most important, predominant, dominant, (most) prominent; key, crucial, vital, essential, basic, prime, central, focal; premier, paramount, major, overriding, cardinal, pre-eminent, uppermost, highest, top, topmost; *informal* number-one.
– OPPOSITES minor.

▶ **noun** ❶ *the principal of the firm* CHIEF, chief executive (officer), CEO, chairman, chairwoman, managing director, MD, president, director, manager, head; *informal* boss; *Brit. informal* gaffer, governor. ❷ *the school's principal* HEAD (TEACHER), headmaster, headmistress; dean, rector, chancellor, vice-chancellor, president, provost; *N. Amer. informal* prexy. ❸ *a principal in a soap opera* LEADING ACTOR/ACTRESS, leading player/performer, leading role, lead, star. ❹ *repayment of the principal* CAPITAL (SUM), debt, loan.

principally ▶ **adverb** MAINLY, mostly, chiefly, for the most part, in the main, on the whole, largely, to a large extent, predominantly, basically, primarily.

principle ▶ **noun** ❶ *elementary principles* TRUTH, proposition, concept, idea, theory, assumption, fundamental, essential. ❷ *the principle of laissez-faire* DOCTRINE, belief, creed, credo, (golden) rule, criterion, tenet, code, ethic, dictum, canon, law. ❸ *a woman of principle | sticking to one's principles* MORALS, morality, (code of) ethics, beliefs, ideals, standards; integrity, uprightness, righteousness, virtue, probity, (sense of) honour, decency, conscience, scruples.

■ **in principle** ❶ *there is no reason, in principle, why we couldn't work together* IN THEORY, theoretically, on paper. ❷ *he has accepted the idea in principle* IN GENERAL, in essence, on the whole, in the main.

principled ▶ **adjective** MORAL, ethical, virtuous, righteous, upright, upstanding, high-minded, honourable, honest, incorruptible.

prink ▶ **verb** GROOM, tidy, arrange, smarten (up), spruce up, preen, primp; *informal* titivate, doll up; *Brit. informal* tart up; *N. Amer. informal* gussy up.

print ▶ **verb** ❶ *four newspapers are printed in the town* SET IN PRINT, send to press, run off, reprint. ❷ *patterns were printed on the cloth* IMPRINT, impress, stamp, mark. ❸ *they printed 30,000 copies* PUBLISH, issue, release, circulate. ❹ *the incident is printed on her memory* REGISTER, record, impress, imprint, engrave, etch, stamp, mark.

▶ **noun** ❶ *small print* TYPE, printing, letters, lettering, characters, type size, typeface, font. ❷ *prints of his left hand* IMPRESSION, fingerprint, footprint. ❸ *sporting prints* PICTURE, design, engraving, etching, lithograph, linocut, woodcut. ❹ *prints and negatives* PHOTOGRAPH, photo, snap, snapshot, picture, still; *Brit.* enprint. ❺ *soft floral prints* PRINTED CLOTH/FABRIC, patterned cloth/fabric, chintz.

■ **in print** PUBLISHED, printed, available in bookshops.

■ **out of print** NO LONGER AVAILABLE, unavailable, unobtainable.

prior ▶ **adjective** *by prior arrangement* EARLIER, previous, preceding, foregoing, antecedent, advance; *formal* anterior.

– OPPOSITES subsequent.

■ **prior to** BEFORE, until, till, up to, previous to, earlier than, preceding, leading up to; *formal* anterior to.

priority ▶ **noun** ❶ *safety is our priority* PRIME CONCERN, most important consideration, primary issue. ❷ *giving priority to primary education* PRECEDENCE, greater importance, preference, pre-eminence, predominance, primacy, first place. ❸ *traffic on the roundabout has priority* RIGHT OF WAY.

priory ▶ **noun** RELIGIOUS HOUSE, abbey, cloister; monastery, friary; convent, nunnery.

prise ▶ **verb** ❶ *I prised the lid off* LEVER, jemmy; wrench, wrest, twist; *N. Amer.* pry, jimmy. ❷ *he had to prise information from them* WRING, wrest, worm out, winkle out, screw, squeeze, extract.

prison ▶ **noun** JAIL, lock-up, penal institution, detention centre; *Brit.* young offender institution; *N. Amer.* jailhouse, penitentiary, correctional facility; *informal* clink, slammer, stir, jug, brig; *Brit. informal* nick; *N. Amer. informal* can, pen, cooler, pokey, slam; *Brit. informal, dated* chokey, quod; *Brit. historical* approved school, borstal, bridewell; *Brit. Military* glasshouse; (**be in prison**) *informal* be inside, be behind bars, do time; *Brit. informal* do bird, do porridge.

– RELATED TERMS custodial.

prisoner ▶ **noun** ❶ *a prisoner serving a life sentence* CONVICT, detainee, inmate; *informal* jailbird, con; *Brit. informal* (old) lag; *N. Amer. informal* yardbird. ❷ *the army took many prisoners* PRISONER OF WAR, POW, internee, captive.

prissy ▶ **adjective** PRUDISH, priggish, prim, prim and proper, strait-laced, Victorian, old-maidish, schoolmistressy, schoolmarmish; *Brit.* po-faced; *informal* starchy.

– OPPOSITES broad-minded.

pristine ▶ **adjective** IMMACULATE, perfect, in mint condition, as new, unspoilt, spotless, flawless, clean, fresh, new, virgin, pure, unused.

– OPPOSITES dirty, spoilt.

privacy ▶ **noun** SECLUSION, solitude, isolation, freedom from disturbance, freedom from interference.

private ▶ **adjective** ❶ *his private plane* PERSONAL, own, individual, special, exclusive, privately owned. ❷ *private talks* CONFIDENTIAL, secret, classified, unofficial, off the record, closet, in camera; backstage, privileged, one-on-one, tête-à-tête. ❸ *private thoughts* INTIMATE, personal, secret; innermost, undisclosed, unspoken, unvoiced. ❹ *a very private man* RESERVED, introvert, introverted, self-contained, reticent, discreet, uncommunicative, unforthcoming, retiring, unsociable, withdrawn, solitary, reclusive, hermitic. ❺ *they found a private place in which to talk* SECLUDED, solitary, undisturbed, concealed, hidden, remote, isolated, out of the way, sequestered. ❻ *we can be private here* UNDISTURBED, uninterrupted; alone, by ourselves. ❼ *the Queen attended in a private capacity* UNOFFICIAL, personal. ❽ *private industry* INDEPENDENT, non-state; privatized, denationalized; commercial, private-enterprise.

– OPPOSITES public, open, extrovert, busy, crowded, official, state, nationalized.

▶ **noun** *a private in the army* PRIVATE SOLDIER, common soldier; trooper; *Brit.* sapper, gunner, ranker; *US* GI; *Brit. informal* Tommy, squaddie.

■ **in private** IN SECRET, secretly, privately, behind closed doors, in camera, à huis clos; in confidence, confidentially, between ourselves, entre nous, off the record; *formal* sub rosa.

private detective ▶ **noun** PRIVATE INVESTIGATOR; *Brit.* enquiry agent; *informal* private eye, PI, sleuth, snoop; *N. Amer. informal* shamus, gumshoe; *informal, dated* private dick.

privately ▶ **adverb** ❶ *we must talk privately* IN SECRET, secretly, in private, behind closed doors, in camera, à huis clos; in confidence, confidentially, between ourselves, entre nous, off the record; *formal* sub rosa. ❷ *privately, I am glad* SECRETLY, inwardly, deep down, personally, unofficially. ❸ *he lived very privately* OUT OF THE PUBLIC EYE, out of public view, in seclusion, in solitude, alone.

– OPPOSITES publicly.

privation ▶ **noun** DEPRIVATION, hardship, destitution, impoverishment, want, need, neediness, austerity.

– OPPOSITES plenty, luxury.

privilege ▶ **noun** ❶ *senior pupils have certain privileges* ADVANTAGE, benefit; prerogative, entitlement, right; concession, freedom, liberty. ❷ *it was a privilege to meet her* HONOUR, pleasure. ❸ *parliamentary privilege* IMMUNITY, exemption, dispensation.

privileged ▶ **adjective** ❶ *a privileged background* WEALTHY, rich, affluent, prosperous; LUCKY, fortunate, elite, favoured; (socially) advantaged. ❷ *privileged information* CONFIDENTIAL, private, secret, restricted, classified, not for publication, off the record, inside; *informal* hush-hush. ❸ *MPs are privileged* IMMUNE (FROM PROSECUTION), protected, exempt, excepted.

– OPPOSITES underprivileged, disadvantaged, public, liable.

privy ▶ **adjective** *he was not privy to the discussions* IN THE KNOW ABOUT, acquainted with, in on, informed of, advised of, apprised of; *informal* genned up on, clued up on, wise to; *formal* cognizant of.

▶ **noun** *he went out to the privy. See* TOILET sense 1.

prize ▶ **noun** ❶ *an art prize* AWARD, reward, premium, purse; trophy, medal; honour, accolade, crown, laurels, palm. ❷ *the prizes of war* SPOILS, booty, plunder, loot, pickings.

▶ **adjective** ❶ *a prize bull* CHAMPION, award-winning, prize-winning, winning, top, best. ❷ *a prize example* OUTSTANDING, excellent, superlative, superb, supreme, very good, prime, fine, magnificent, marvellous, wonderful; *informal* great, terrific, tremendous, fantastic. ❸ *a prize idiot* UTTER, complete, total, absolute, real, perfect, positive, veritable; *Brit. informal* right, bloody; *Austral./NZ informal* fair.

– OPPOSITES second-rate.

▶ **verb** *many collectors prize his work* VALUE, set great store by, rate highly, attach great importance to, esteem, hold in high regard, think highly of, treasure, cherish.

prized ▶ **adjective** TREASURED, precious, cherished, much loved, beloved, valued, esteemed, highly regarded.

prizewinner ▶ **noun** CHAMPION, winner, gold medallist, victor; *informal* champ, number one.

probability ▶ **noun** ❶ *the probability of winning* LIKELIHOOD, prospect, expectation, chance, chances, odds. ❷ *relegation is a distinct probability* PROBABLE EVENT, prospect, possibility, good/fair/reasonable bet.

probable ▶ **adjective** LIKELY, most likely, odds-on, expected, anticipated, predictable, foreseeable, ten to one; *informal* on the cards, a good/fair/reasonable bet.

– OPPOSITES unlikely.

probably ▶ **adverb** IN ALL LIKELIHOOD, in all probability, as like(ly) as not, (very/most) likely, ten to one, the chances are, doubtless, no doubt; *archaic* like enough.

probation ▶ **noun** TRIAL PERIOD, test period, experimental period, trial.

probe ▶ **noun** *a probe into an air crash* INVESTIGATION, enquiry, examination, inquest, exploration, study, analysis.

▶ **verb** ❶ *hands probed his body* EXAMINE, feel, feel around, explore, prod, poke, check. ❷ *police probed the tragedy* INVESTIGATE, enquire into, look into, study, examine, scrutinize, go into, carry out an inquest into.

probity ▶ **noun** INTEGRITY, honesty, uprightness, decency, morality, rectitude, goodness, virtue, right-mindedness, trustworthiness, truthfulness, honour.

– OPPOSITES untrustworthiness.

problem ▶ **noun** ❶ *they ran into a problem* DIFFICULTY, trouble, worry, complication, difficult situation; snag, hitch, drawback, stumbling block, obstacle, hurdle, hiccup, setback, catch; predicament, plight; misfortune, mishap, misadventure; *informal* dilemma, headache, prob, facer. ❷ *I don't want to be a problem* NUISANCE, bother, pest, irritant, thorn in one's side/flesh, vexation; *informal* drag, pain, pain in the neck. ❸ *arithmetical problems* PUZZLE, question, poser, enigma, riddle, conundrum; *informal* teaser, brain-teaser.

▶ **adjective** *a problem child* TROUBLESOME, difficult, unmanageable, unruly, disobedient, uncontrollable, recalcitrant, delinquent.

– OPPOSITES well behaved, manageable.

problematic ▶ adjective DIFFICULT, hard, taxing, troublesome, tricky, awkward, controversial, ticklish, complicated, complex, knotty, thorny, prickly, vexed; *informal* sticky; *Brit. informal* dodgy.
– OPPOSITES easy, simple, straightforward.

procedure ▶ noun COURSE OF ACTION, line of action, policy, series of steps, method, system, strategy, way, approach, formula, mechanism, methodology, MO (modus operandi), technique; routine, drill, practice.

proceed ▶ verb ❶ *she was uncertain how to proceed* BEGIN, make a start, get going, move, set something in motion; TAKE ACTION, act, go on, go ahead, make progress, make headway. ❷ *he proceeded down the road* GO, make one's way, advance, move, progress, carry on, press on, push on. ❸ *we should proceed with the talks* GO AHEAD, carry on, go on, continue, keep on, get on, get ahead; pursue, prosecute. ❹ *there is not enough evidence to proceed against him* TAKE SOMEONE TO COURT, start/take proceedings against, start an action against, sue. ❺ *all power proceeds from God* ORIGINATE, spring, stem, come, derive, arise, issue, flow, emanate.
– OPPOSITES stop.

proceedings ▶ plural noun ❶ *the evening's proceedings* EVENTS, activities, happenings, goings-on, doings. ❷ *the proceedings of the meeting* REPORT, transactions, minutes, account, record(s); annals, archives. ❸ *legal proceedings* LEGAL ACTION, court/judicial proceedings, litigation; lawsuit, case, prosecution.

proceeds ▶ plural noun PROFITS, earnings, receipts, returns, takings, income, revenue; *Sport* gate (money/receipts); *N. Amer.* take.

process ▶ noun ❶ *investigation is a long process* PROCEDURE, operation, action, activity, exercise, affair, business, job, task, undertaking. ❷ *a new canning process* METHOD, system, technique, means, practice, way, approach, methodology.
▶ verb *applications are processed rapidly* DEAL WITH, attend to, see to, sort out, handle, take care of, action.
■ **in the process of** IN THE MIDDLE OF, in the course of, in the midst of, in the throes of, busy with, occupied in/with, taken up with/by, involved in.

procession ▶ noun ❶ *a procession through the town* PARADE, march, march past, cavalcade, motorcade, cortège; column, file, train. ❷ *a procession of dance routines* SERIES, succession, stream, string, sequence, run.

proclaim ▶ verb ❶ *messengers proclaimed the good news* DECLARE, announce, pronounce, state, make known, give out, advertise, publish, broadcast, promulgate, trumpet, blazon. ❷ *the men proclaimed their innocence* ASSERT, declare, profess, maintain, protest. ❸ *he proclaimed himself president* DECLARE, pronounce, announce. ❹ *cheap paint soon proclaims its cheapness* DEMONSTRATE, indicate, show, reveal, manifest, betray, testify to, signify.

proclamation ▶ noun DECLARATION, announcement, pronouncement, statement, notification, publication, broadcast, promulgation, blazoning; assertion, profession, protestation; DECREE, order, edict, ruling.

proclivity ▶ noun INCLINATION, tendency, leaning, disposition, proneness, propensity, bent, bias, penchant, predisposition; predilection, partiality, liking, preference, taste, fondness, weakness.

procrastinate ▶ verb DELAY, put off doing something, postpone action, defer action, be dilatory, use delaying tactics, stall, temporize, drag one's feet/heels, take one's time, play for time, play a waiting game.

procreate ▶ verb PRODUCE OFFSPRING, reproduce, multiply, propagate, breed.

procure ▶ verb ❶ *he managed to procure a coat* OBTAIN, acquire, get, find, come by, secure, pick up; buy, purchase; *informal* get hold of, get one's hands on. ❷ *the police found that he was procuring* PIMP; *Brit. informal* ponce.

prod ▶ verb ❶ *Cassie prodded him in the chest* POKE, jab, dig, elbow, butt, stab. ❷ *they hoped to prod the government into action* SPUR, stimulate, stir, rouse, prompt, drive, galvanize; persuade, urge, chivvy; incite, goad, egg on, provoke.
▶ noun ❶ *a prod in the ribs* POKE, jab, dig, elbow, butt, thrust. ❷ *they need a prod to get them to do act* STIMULUS, push, prompt, reminder, spur; incitement, goad.

prodigal ▶ adjective ❶ *prodigal habits die hard* WASTEFUL, extravagant, spendthrift, profligate, improvident, imprudent. ❷ *a composer who is prodigal with his talents* GENEROUS, lavish, liberal, unstinting, unsparing; *poetic/literary* bounteous. ❸ *a dessert prodigal with whipped cream* ABOUNDING IN, abundant in, rich in, covered in, awash with.
– OPPOSITES thrifty, mean, deficient.

prodigious ▶ adjective ENORMOUS, huge, colossal, immense, vast, great, massive, gigantic, mammoth, tremendous, inordinate, monumental; amazing, astonishing, astounding, staggering, stunning, remarkable, phenomenal, terrific, miraculous, impressive, striking, startling, sensational, spectacular, extraordinary, exceptional, breathtaking, incredible; *informal* humongous, stupendous, fantastic, fabulous, mega, awesome; *Brit. informal* ginormous; *poetic/literary* wondrous.
– OPPOSITES small, unexceptional.

prodigy ▶ noun ❶ *a seven-year-old prodigy* GENIUS, mastermind, virtuoso, wunderkind, wonder child; *informal* whizz-kid, whizz, wizard. ❷ *Germany seemed a prodigy of industrial discipline* MODEL, classic example, paragon, paradigm, epitome, exemplar, archetype.

produce ▶ verb ❶ *the company produces furniture* MANUFACTURE, make, construct, build, fabricate, put together, assemble, turn out, create; mass-produce; *informal* churn out. ❷ *the vineyards produce excellent wines* YIELD, grow, give, supply, provide, furnish, bear, bring forth. ❸ *she produced ten puppies* GIVE BIRTH TO, bear, deliver, bring forth, bring into the world. ❹ *he produced five novels* CREATE, originate, fashion, turn out; compose, write, pen; paint. ❺ *she produced an ID card* PULL OUT, extract, fish out; present, offer, proffer, show. ❻ *no evidence was produced* PRESENT, offer, provide, furnish, advance, put forward, bring forward, come up with. ❼ *that will produce a reaction* GIVE RISE TO, bring about, cause, occasion, generate, engender, lead to, result in, effect, induce, set off; provoke, precipitate, breed, spark off, trigger; *poetic/literary* beget. ❽ *James produced the play* STAGE, put on, mount, present.
– RELATED TERMS -facient, -genic.
▶ noun *fresh produce* FOOD, foodstuff(s), products; harvest, crops, fruit, vegetables, greens; *Brit.* greengrocery.

producer ▶ noun ❶ *a car producer* MANUFACTURER, maker, builder, constructor, fabricator. ❷ *coffee producers* GROWER, farmer. ❸ *the producer of the show* IMPRESARIO, manager, administrator, promoter, regisseur.

product ▶ noun ❶ *a household product* ARTEFACT, commodity, manufactured article; creation, invention; (**products**) goods, wares, merchandise, produce. ❷ *his skill is a product of experience* RESULT, consequence, outcome, effect, upshot, fruit, by-product, spin-off.

production ▶ noun ❶ *the production of cars* MANUFACTURE, making, construction, building, fabrication, assembly, creation; mass-production. ❷ *the production of literary works* CREATION, origination, fashioning; composition, writing. ❸ *literary productions* WORK, opus, creation; publication, composition, piece; work of art, painting, picture. ❹ *agricultural production* OUTPUT, yield; productivity. ❺ *admission only on production of a ticket* PRESENTATION, proffering, showing. ❻ *a theatre production* PERFORMANCE, staging, presentation, show, piece, play.

productive ▶ adjective ❶ *a productive artist* PROLIFIC, inventive, creative; energetic. ❷ *productive talks* USEFUL, constructive, profitable, fruitful, gainful, valuable, effective, worthwhile, helpful. ❸ *productive land* FERTILE, fruitful, rich, fecund.
– OPPOSITES sterile, barren.

productivity ▶ noun ❶ *workers have boosted productivity* EFFICIENCY, work rate; output, yield, production. ❷ *the productivity of the soil* FRUITFULNESS, fertility, richness, fecundity.
– OPPOSITES sterility, barrenness.

profane ▶ adjective ❶ *subjects both sacred and profane* SECULAR, lay, non-religious, temporal; *formal* laic. ❷ *a profane man* IRREVERENT, irreligious, ungodly, godless, unbelieving, impious, disrespectful, sacrilegious. ❸ *profane language* OBSCENE, blasphemous, indecent, foul, vulgar, crude, filthy, dirty, smutty, coarse, rude, offensive, indecorous.
– OPPOSITES religious, sacred, reverent, decorous.
▶ verb *invaders profaned our temples* DESECRATE, violate, defile, treat sacrilegiously.

profanity ▶ noun ❶ *he hissed a profanity | an outburst of profanity* OATH, swear word, expletive, curse, obscenity, four-letter word, dirty word; blasphemy, swearing, foul language, bad language, cursing; *informal* cuss, cuss word; *formal* imprecation; *archaic* execration. ❷ *some traditional festivals were tainted with profanity* SACRILEGE, blasphemy, irreligion, ungodliness, impiety, irreverence, disrespect.

profess ▶ verb ❶ *he professed his love* DECLARE, announce, proclaim, assert, state, affirm, avow, maintain, protest; *formal* aver. ❷ *she professed to loathe publicity* CLAIM, pretend, purport, affect; make out; *informal* let on. ❸ *the Emperor professed Christianity* AFFIRM ONE'S FAITH IN, affirm one's allegiance to, avow, confess.

professed ▶ adjective ❶ *his professed ambition* CLAIMED, supposed, ostensible, self-styled, apparent, pretended, purported. ❷ *a professed Christian* DECLARED, self-acknowledged, self-confessed, confessed, sworn, avowed, confirmed.

profession ▶ noun ❶ *his chosen profession of teaching* CAREER, occupation, calling, vocation, métier, line (of work), walk of life, job, business, trade, craft; *informal* racket. ❷ *a profession of allegiance* DECLARATION, affirmation, statement, announcement, proclamation, assertion, avowal, vow, claim, protestation; *formal* averment.

professional ▶ adjective ❶ *people in professional occupations* WHITE-COLLAR, non-manual. ❷ *a professional cricketer* PAID, salaried. ❸ *a thoroughly professional performance* EXPERT, accomplished, skilful, masterly, masterful, fine, polished, skilled, proficient, competent, able, experienced, practised, trained, seasoned, businesslike, deft; *informal* ace, crack, top-notch. ❹ *not a professional way to behave* APPROPRIATE, fitting, proper, honourable, ethical, correct, comme il faut.
– OPPOSITES manual, amateur, amateurish, inappropriate, unethical.
▶ noun ❶ *affluent young professionals* WHITE-COLLAR WORKER, office worker. ❷ *his first season as a professional* PROFESSIONAL PLAYER, paid player, salaried player; *informal* pro. ❸ *she was a real professional on stage* EXPERT, virtuoso, old hand, master, maestro, past master; *informal* pro, ace, wizard, whizz, hotshot; *Brit. informal* dab hand; *N. Amer. informal* maven, crackerjack.
– OPPOSITES manual worker, amateur.

professor ▶ **noun** holder of a chair, head of faculty, head of department; *N. Amer.* full professor; *informal* prof.

proffer ▶ **verb** OFFER, tender, submit, extend, volunteer, suggest, propose, put forward; hold out.
– OPPOSITES refuse, withdraw.

proficiency ▶ **noun** SKILL, expertise, experience, accomplishment, competence, mastery, prowess, professionalism, deftness, adroitness, dexterity, finesse, ability, facility; *informal* know-how.
– OPPOSITES incompetence.

proficient ▶ **adjective** SKILLED, skilful, expert, experienced, accomplished, competent, masterly, adept, adroit, deft, dexterous, able, professional, consummate, complete, master; *informal* crack, ace, mean.
– OPPOSITES incompetent.

profile ▶ **noun** ❶ *his handsome profile* SIDE VIEW, outline, silhouette, contour, shape, form, figure, lines. ❷ *she wrote a profile of the organization* DESCRIPTION, account, study, portrait, portrayal, depiction, rundown, sketch, outline.
▶ **verb** *he was profiled in the Irish Times* DESCRIBE, write about, give an account of, portray, depict, sketch, outline.
■ **keep a low profile** LIE LOW, keep quiet, keep out of the public eye, avoid publicity, keep out of sight.

profit ▶ **noun** ❶ *the firm made a profit* (FINANCIAL) GAIN, return(s), yield, proceeds, earnings, winnings, surplus, excess; *informal* pay dirt, bottom line. ❷ *there was little profit in going on* ADVANTAGE, benefit, value, use, good, avail; *informal* mileage.
– OPPOSITES loss, disadvantage.
▶ **verb** ❶ *the company will not profit from the disposal* MAKE MONEY, make a profit; *informal* rake it in, clean up, make a packet, make a killing, make a bundle; *N. Amer. informal* make big bucks, make a fast/quick buck. ❷ *how will that profit us?* BENEFIT, be beneficial to, be of benefit to, be advantageous to, be of advantage to, be of use to, be of value to, do someone good, help, be of service to, serve, assist, aid.
– OPPOSITES lose, disadvantage.
■ **profit by/from** BENEFIT FROM, take advantage of, derive benefit from, capitalize on, make the most of, turn to one's advantage, put to good use, do well out of, exploit, gain from; *informal* cash in on.

profitable ▶ **adjective** ❶ *a profitable company* MONEYMAKING, profit-making, commercial, successful, money-spinning, solvent, in the black, gainful, remunerative, financially rewarding, paying, lucrative, bankable. ❷ *profitable study* BENEFICIAL, useful, advantageous, valuable, productive, worthwhile; rewarding, fruitful, illuminating, informative, well spent.
– OPPOSITES loss-making, fruitless, useless.

profiteer ▶ **verb** *a shopkeeper was charged with profiteering* OVERCHARGE, racketeer; cheat someone, fleece someone; *informal* rip someone off, rob someone.
▶ **noun** *he was a war profiteer* RACKETEER, exploiter, black marketeer; *informal* bloodsucker.

profligate ▶ **adjective** ❶ *profligate local authorities* WASTEFUL, extravagant, spendthrift, improvident, prodigal. ❷ *a profligate lifestyle* DISSOLUTE, degenerate, dissipated, debauched, corrupt, depraved; PROMISCUOUS, loose, wanton, licentious, libertine, decadent, abandoned, fast; SYBARITIC, voluptuary.
– OPPOSITES thrifty, frugal, moral, upright.
▶ **noun** *he was an out-and-out profligate* LIBERTINE, debauchee, degenerate, dissolute, roué, rake, loose-liver; sybarite, voluptuary; *dated* rip.

profound ▶ **adjective** ❶ *profound relief* HEARTFELT, intense, keen, great, extreme, acute, severe, sincere, earnest, deep, deep-seated, overpowering, overwhelming, fervent, ardent. ❷ *profound silence* COMPLETE, utter, total, absolute. ❸ *a profound change* FAR-REACHING, radical, extensive, sweeping, exhaustive, thoroughgoing. ❹ *a profound analysis* WISE, learned, clever, intelligent, scholarly, sage, erudite, discerning, penetrating, perceptive, astute, thoughtful, insightful, percipient, perspicacious; *rare* sapient. ❺ *profound truths* COMPLEX, abstract, deep, weighty, difficult, abstruse, recondite, esoteric.
– OPPOSITES superficial, mild, slight, simple.

profuse ▶ **adjective** ❶ *profuse apologies* COPIOUS, prolific, abundant, liberal, unstinting, fulsome, effusive, extravagant, lavish, gushing; *informal* over the top, gushy. ❷ *profuse blooms* LUXURIANT, plentiful, copious, abundant, lush, rich, exuberant, riotous, teeming, rank, rampant; *informal* jungly.
– OPPOSITES meagre, sparse.

profusion ▶ **noun** ABUNDANCE, mass, host, cornucopia, riot, plethora, superabundance; *informal* sea, wealth; *formal* plenitude.

progenitor ▶ **noun** ❶ *the progenitor of an illustrious family* ANCESTOR, forefather, forebear, parent, primogenitor; law stirps; *archaic* begetter. ❷ *the progenitor of modern jazz* ORIGINATOR, creator, founder, architect, inventor, pioneer.

progeny ▶ **noun** OFFSPRING, young, babies, children, sons and daughters, family, brood; DESCENDANTS, heirs, scions; *Law* issue; *archaic* seed, fruit of one's loins.

prognosis ▶ **noun** FORECAST, prediction, prognostication, prophecy, divination, augury.

prognosticate ▶ **verb** FORECAST, predict, prophesy, foretell, foresee, forewarn of.

prognostication ▶ **noun** PREDICTION, forecast, prophecy, prognosis, divination, augury.

programme ▶ **noun** ❶ *our programme for the day* SCHEDULE, agenda, calendar, timetable;

order of events, line-up. ❷ *the government's reform programme* SCHEME, plan of action, series of measures, strategy. ❸ *a television programme* BROADCAST, production, show, presentation, transmission, performance, telecast; *informal* prog. ❹ *a programme of study* COURSE, syllabus, curriculum. ❺ *a theatre programme* GUIDE, list of performers; *N. Amer.* playbill.

▶ **verb** *they programmed the day well* ARRANGE, organize, schedule, plan, map out, timetable, line up; *N. Amer.* slate.

progress ▶ **noun** ❶ *boulders made progress difficult* FORWARD MOVEMENT, advance, going, progression, headway, passage. ❷ *scientific progress* DEVELOPMENT, advance, advancement, headway, step(s) forward; improvement, betterment, growth.

– OPPOSITES relapse.

▶ **verb** ❶ *they progressed slowly down the road* GO, make one's way, move, move forward, go forward, proceed, advance, go on, continue, make headway, work one's way. ❷ *the school has progressed rapidly* DEVELOP, make progress, advance, make headway, take steps forward, move on, get on, gain ground; improve, get better, come on, come along, make strides; thrive, prosper, blossom, flourish; *informal* be getting there.

– OPPOSITES relapse.

■ **in progress** UNDER WAY, going on, ongoing, happening, occurring, taking place, proceeding, continuing; unfinished, on the stocks; *N. Amer.* in the works.

progression ▶ **noun** ❶ *progression to the next stage* PROGRESS, advancement, movement, passage, march; development, evolution, growth. ❷ *a progression of peaks on the graph* SUCCESSION, series, sequence, string, stream, chain, concatenation, train, row, cycle.

progressive ▶ **adjective** ❶ *progressive deterioration* CONTINUING, continuous, increasing, growing, developing, ongoing, accelerating, escalating; gradual, step-by-step, cumulative. ❷ *progressive views* MODERN, liberal, advanced, forward-thinking, enlightened, enterprising, innovative, pioneering, dynamic, bold, avant-garde, reforming, reformist, radical; *informal* go-ahead.

– OPPOSITES conservative, reactionary.

▶ **noun** *he is very much a progressive* INNOVATOR, reformer, reformist, liberal, libertarian.

prohibit ▶ **verb** ❶ *state law prohibits gambling* FORBID, ban, bar, interdict, proscribe, make illegal, embargo, outlaw, disallow, veto; *Law* enjoin. ❷ *a cash shortage prohibited the visit* PREVENT, stop, rule out, preclude, make impossible.

– OPPOSITES allow.

prohibited ▶ **adjective** ILLEGAL, illicit, against the law, verboten; *Islam* haram; *informal* not on, out, no go; *formal* non licet.

– OPPOSITES permitted.

prohibition ▶ **noun** ❶ *the prohibition of cannabis* BANNING, forbidding, prohibiting, barring, debarment, vetoing, proscription, interdiction, outlawing. ❷ *a prohibition was imposed* BAN, bar, interdict, veto, embargo, injunction, moratorium.

prohibitive ▶ **adjective** ❶ *prohibitive costs* EXCESSIVELY HIGH, sky-high, over-inflated; out of the question, beyond one's means; extortionate, unreasonable, exorbitant; *informal* steep, criminal. ❷ *prohibitive regulations* PROSCRIPTIVE, prohibitory, restrictive, repressive.

project ▶ **noun** ❶ *an engineering project* SCHEME, plan, programme, enterprise, undertaking, venture; proposal, idea, concept. ❷ *a history project* ASSIGNMENT, piece of work, piece of research, task.

▶ **verb** ❶ *profits are projected to rise* FORECAST, predict, expect, estimate, calculate, reckon. ❷ *his projected book* INTEND, plan, propose, devise, design, outline. ❸ *balconies projected over the lake* STICK OUT, jut (out), protrude, extend, stand out, bulge out, poke out, thrust out, cantilever. ❹ *seeds are projected from the tree* PROPEL, discharge, launch, throw, cast, fling, hurl, shoot. ❺ *the sun projected his shadow on the wall* CAST, throw, send, shed, shine. ❻ *she tried to project a calm image* CONVEY, put across, put over, communicate, present, promote.

projectile ▶ **noun** MISSILE.

projecting ▶ **adjective** STICKING OUT, protuberant, protruding, prominent, jutting, overhanging, proud, bulging; *informal* sticky-out.

– OPPOSITES sunken, flush.

projection ▶ **noun** ❶ *a sales projection* FORECAST, prediction, prognosis, expectation, estimate. ❷ *tiny projections on the cliff face* PROTUBERANCE, protrusion, sticking-out bit, prominence, eminence, outcrop, outgrowth, jut, jag, snag; overhang, ledge, shelf; *informal* sticky-out bit.

proletarian ▶ **adjective** *a proletarian background* WORKING-CLASS, plebeian, cloth-cap, common.

– OPPOSITES aristocratic.

▶ **noun** *disaffected proletarians* WORKING-CLASS PERSON, worker, plebeian, commoner, man/woman/person in the street; *derogatory* prole.

– OPPOSITES aristocrat.

proletariat ▶ **noun** THE WORKERS, working-class people, wage-earners, the labouring classes, the common people, the lower classes, the masses, the commonalty, the rank and file, the third estate, the plebeians; *derogatory* the hoi polloi, the plebs, the proles, the great unwashed, the mob, the rabble.

– OPPOSITES aristocracy.

proliferate ▶ **verb** INCREASE RAPIDLY, grow rapidly, multiply, rocket, mushroom, snowball, burgeon, run riot.

– OPPOSITES decrease, dwindle.

prolific ▶ adjective ❶ *a prolific crop of tomatoes* PLENTIFUL, abundant, bountiful, profuse, copious, luxuriant, rich, lush; fruitful, fecund; *poetic/literary* plenteous, bounteous. ❷ *a prolific composer* PRODUCTIVE, creative, inventive, fertile.

prolix ▶ adjective LONG-WINDED, verbose, wordy, pleonastic, discursive, rambling, long-drawn-out, overlong, lengthy, protracted, interminable; *informal* windy; *Brit. informal* waffly.

prologue ▶ noun INTRODUCTION, foreword, preface, preamble, prelude; *informal* intro; *formal* exordium, proem, prolegomenon.
– OPPOSITES epilogue.

prolong ▶ verb LENGTHEN, extend, draw out, drag out, protract, spin out, stretch out, string out, elongate; carry on, continue, keep up, perpetuate.
– OPPOSITES shorten.

promenade ▶ noun ❶ *the tree-lined promenade* ESPLANADE, front, seafront, parade, walk, boulevard, avenue; *N. Amer.* boardwalk; *Brit. informal* prom. ❷ *our nightly promenade* WALK, stroll, turn, amble, airing; *dated* constitutional.
▶ verb *we promenaded in the park* WALK, stroll, saunter, wander, amble, stretch one's legs, take a turn.

prominence ▶ noun ❶ *his rise to prominence* FAME, celebrity, eminence, pre-eminence, importance, distinction, greatness, note, notability, prestige, stature, standing, position, rank. ❷ *the press gave prominence to the reports* GOOD COVERAGE, importance, precedence, weight, a high profile, top billing. ❸ *a rocky prominence* HILLOCK, hill, hummock, mound; outcrop, crag, spur, rise; ridge, arête; peak, pinnacle; promontory, cliff, headland.

prominent ▶ adjective ❶ *a prominent surgeon* IMPORTANT, well known, leading, eminent, distinguished, notable, noteworthy, noted, illustrious, celebrated, famous, renowned, acclaimed, famed, influential; *N. Amer.* major-league. ❷ *prominent cheekbones* PROTUBERANT, protruding, projecting, jutting (out), standing out, sticking out, proud, bulging, bulbous. ❸ *a prominent feature of the landscape* CONSPICUOUS, noticeable, easily seen, obvious, unmistakable, eye-catching, pronounced, salient, striking, dominant; obtrusive.
– OPPOSITES unimportant, unknown, inconspicuous.

promiscuity ▶ noun LICENTIOUSNESS, wantonness, immorality; *informal* sleeping around, sluttishness, whorishness; *dated* looseness.
– OPPOSITES chastity, virtue.

promiscuous ▶ adjective ❶ *a promiscuous woman* LICENTIOUS, sexually indiscriminate, wanton, immoral, of easy virtue, fast; *informal* easy, swinging, sluttish, whorish; *N. Amer. informal* roundheeled; *Brit. informal* slaggy; *dated* loose, fallen; *archaic* light. ❷ *promiscuous reading* INDISCRIMINATE, undiscriminating, unselective, random, haphazard, irresponsible, unthinking, unconsidered.
– OPPOSITES chaste, virtuous, selective.

promise ▶ noun ❶ *you broke your promise* WORD (OF HONOUR), assurance, pledge, vow, guarantee, oath, bond, undertaking, agreement, commitment, contract, convenant. ❷ *he shows promise* POTENTIAL, ability, aptitude, capability, capacity. ❸ *a promise of fine weather* INDICATION, hint, suggestion, sign.
▶ verb ❶ *she promised to go* GIVE ONE'S WORD, swear, pledge, vow, undertake, guarantee, contract, engage, give an assurance, commit oneself, bind oneself, swear/take an oath, covenant; *archaic* plight. ❷ *the skies promised sunshine* INDICATE, lead one to expect, point to, denote, signify, be a sign of, be evidence of, give hope of, bespeak, presage, augur, herald, bode, portend; *poetic/literary* betoken, foretoken, forebode.

promising ▶ adjective ❶ *a promising start* GOOD, encouraging, favourable, hopeful, full of promise, auspicious, propitious, bright, rosy, heartening, reassuring. ❷ *a promising actor* WITH POTENTIAL, budding, up-and-coming, rising, coming, in the making.
– OPPOSITES unfavourable, hopeless.

promontory ▶ noun HEADLAND, point, cape, head, foreland, horn, bill, ness, naze, peninsula; *Scottish* mull.

promote ▶ verb ❶ *she's been promoted at work* UPGRADE, give promotion to, elevate, advance, move up; *archaic* prefer. ❷ *an organization promoting justice* ENCOURAGE, further, advance, assist, aid, help, contribute to, foster, nurture, develop, boost, stimulate, forward, work for. ❸ *she is promoting her new film* ADVERTISE, publicize, give publicity to, beat/bang the drum for, market, merchandise; *informal* push, plug, hype, puff, boost; *N. Amer. informal* ballyhoo, flack.
– OPPOSITES demote, obstruct, play down.

promoter ▶ noun ADVOCATE, champion, supporter, backer, proponent, protagonist, campaigner; *N. Amer.* booster.

promotion ▶ noun ❶ *her promotion at work* UPGRADING, preferment, elevation, advancement, step up (the ladder). ❷ *the promotion of justice* ENCOURAGEMENT, furtherance, furthering, advancement, assistance, aid, help, contribution to, fostering, boosting, stimulation; *N. Amer.* boosterism. ❸ *the promotion of her new film* ADVERTISING, publicizing, marketing; publicity, campaign, propaganda; *informal* hard sell, plug, hype, puff; *N. Amer. informal* ballyhoo.

prompt ▶ verb ❶ *curiosity prompted him to look* INDUCE, make, move, motivate, lead, dispose, persuade, incline, encourage, stimulate, prod, impel, spur on, inspire. ❷ *the statement prompted a hostile reaction* GIVE RISE TO, bring

about, cause, occasion, result in, lead to, elicit, produce, bring on, engender, induce, precipitate, trigger, spark off, provoke. ❸ *the actors needed prompting* REMIND, cue, feed, help out; jog someone's memory.
– OPPOSITES deter.
▶ **adjective** *a prompt reply* QUICK, swift, rapid, speedy, fast, direct, immediate, instant, expeditious, early, punctual, in good time, on time, timely.
– OPPOSITES slow, late.
▶ **adverb** *at 3.30 prompt* EXACTLY, precisely, sharp, on the dot, dead, punctually, on the nail; *informal* bang on; *N. Amer. informal* on the button, on the nose.
▶ **noun** *he stopped, and Julia supplied a prompt* REMINDER, cue, feed.

promptly ▶ **adverb** ❶ *William arrived promptly at 7.30* PUNCTUALLY, on time; *informal* on the dot, bang on; *Brit. informal* spot on; *N. Amer. informal* on the button, on the nose. ❷ *I expect the matter to be dealt with promptly* WITHOUT DELAY, straight away, right away, at once, immediately, now, as soon as possible; QUICKLY, swiftly, rapidly, speedily, fast, expeditiously; *N. Amer.* momentarily; *informal* pronto, a.s.a.p., p.d.q. (pretty damn quick).
– OPPOSITES late, slowly.

promulgate ▶ **verb** ❶ *they promulgated their own views* MAKE KNOWN, make public, publicize, spread, communicate, propagate, disseminate, broadcast, promote, preach; *poetic/literary* bruit abroad. ❷ *the law was promulgated in 1942* PUT INTO EFFECT, enact, implement, enforce.

prone ▶ **adjective** ❶ *softwood is prone to rotting | prone to rot* SUSCEPTIBLE, vulnerable, subject, open, liable, given, predisposed, likely, disposed, inclined, apt; at risk of. ❷ *his prone body* (LYING) FACE DOWN, face downwards, on one's stomach/front; LYING FLAT/DOWN, horizontal, prostrate.
– OPPOSITES resistant, immune, upright.

prong ▶ **noun** TINE, spike, point, tip, projection.

pronounce ▶ **verb** ❶ *his name is difficult to pronounce* SAY, enunciate, articulate, utter, voice, sound, vocalize, get one's tongue round. ❷ *the doctor pronounced that I had a virus* ANNOUNCE, proclaim, declare, affirm, assert; judge, rule, decree; *rare* asseverate.

pronounced ▶ **adjective** NOTICEABLE, marked, strong, conspicuous, striking, distinct, prominent, unmistakable, obvious, recognizable, identifiable.
– OPPOSITES slight.

pronouncement ▶ **noun** ANNOUNCEMENT, proclamation, declaration, assertion; judgement, ruling, decree; *formal* ordinance; *rare* asseveration.

pronunciation ▶ **noun** ACCENT, manner of speaking, speech, diction, delivery, elocution, intonation; articulation, enunciation, voicing, vocalization, sounding; *rare* orthoepy.

proof ▶ **noun** ❶ *proof of ownership* EVIDENCE, verification, corroboration, authentication, confirmation, certification, documentation, validation, attestation, substantiation. ❷ *the proofs of a book* PAGE PROOF, galley proof, galley, pull, slip; revise.
▶ **adjective** *no system is proof against theft* RESISTANT, immune, unaffected, invulnerable, impenetrable, impervious, repellent.

prop ▶ **noun** ❶ *the roof is held up by props* POLE, post, support, upright, brace, buttress, stay, strut, stanchion, shore, pier, pillar, pile, piling, bolster, truss, column. ❷ *a prop for the economy* MAINSTAY, pillar, anchor, backbone, support, foundation, cornerstone.
▶ **verb** ❶ *he propped his bike against the wall* LEAN, rest, stand, balance, steady. ❷ *this post is propping the wall up* HOLD UP, shore up, bolster up, buttress, support, brace, underpin. ❸ *they prop up loss-making industries* SUBSIDIZE, underwrite, fund, finance.

propaganda ▶ **noun** INFORMATION, promotion, advertising, publicity; agitprop, disinformation, counter-information, the big lie; *informal* info, hype, plugging.

propagandist ▶ **noun** PROMOTER, champion, supporter, proponent, advocate, campaigner, crusader, publicist, evangelist, apostle; *informal* plugger.

propagate ▶ **verb** ❶ *an easy plant to propagate* BREED, grow, cultivate. ❷ *these shrubs propagate easily* REPRODUCE, multiply, proliferate, increase, spread, self-seed, self-sow. ❸ *they propagated socialist ideas* SPREAD, disseminate, communicate, make known, promulgate, circulate, broadcast, publicize, proclaim, preach, promote; *poetic/literary* bruit abroad.

propel ▶ **verb** ❶ *a boat propelled by oars* MOVE, power, push, drive. ❷ *he propelled the ball into the air* THROW, thrust, toss, fling, hurl, launch, pitch, project, send, shoot. ❸ *confusion propelled her into action* SPUR, drive, prompt, precipitate, catapult, motivate, force, impel.

propeller ▶ **noun** ROTOR, screw, airscrew; *informal* prop.

propensity ▶ **noun** TENDENCY, inclination, predisposition, proneness, proclivity, readiness, liability, disposition, leaning, weakness.

proper ▶ **adjective** ❶ *he's not a proper scientist* REAL, genuine, actual, true, bona fide; *informal* kosher. ❷ *the proper channels* RIGHT, correct, accepted, orthodox, conventional, established, official, formal, regular, acceptable, appropriate; *archaic* meet. ❸ *they were terribly proper* RESPECTABLE, decorous, seemly, decent, refined, ladylike, gentlemanly, genteel; formal, conventional, correct, comme il faut, done, orthodox, polite, punctilious. ❹ (*Brit. informal*) *a proper mess* COMPLETE, absolute, real, perfect, total,

thorough, utter, out-and-out, positive, unmitigated, consummate; *Brit. informal* right; *Austral./NZ informal* fair.
– OPPOSITES fake, inappropriate, wrong, unconventional.

property ▶ **noun** ❶ *lost property* POSSESSIONS, belongings, things, effects, stuff, chattels, movables; resources, assets, valuables, fortune, capital, riches, wealth; *Law* personalty, goods and chattels; *informal* gear. ❷ *private property* BUILDING(S), premises, house(s), land, estates; *Law* real property, realty; *N. Amer.* real estate. ❸ *healing properties* QUALITY, attribute, characteristic, feature, power, trait, mark, hallmark.

prophecy ▶ **noun** ❶ *her prophecy is coming true* PREDICTION, forecast, prognostication, prognosis, divination, augury. ❷ *the gift of prophecy* FORETELLING THE FUTURE, fortune telling, crystal-gazing, prediction, second sight, prognostication, divination, augury, soothsaying.

prophesy ▶ **verb** PREDICT, foretell, forecast, foresee, forewarn of, prognosticate.

prophet, prophetess ▶ **noun** SEER, soothsayer, fortune teller, clairvoyant, diviner; oracle, augur, sibyl.
■ **prophet of doom** PESSIMIST, doom-monger, doomsayer, doomster, Cassandra, Jeremiah; *informal* doom (and gloom) merchant.

prophetic ▶ **adjective** PRESCIENT, predictive, far-seeing, prognostic, divinatory, sibylline, apocalyptic; *rare* vatic, mantic.

prophylactic ▶ **adjective** *prophylactic measures* PREVENTIVE, preventative, precautionary, protective, inhibitory.
▶ **noun** *a prophylactic against malaria* PREVENTIVE MEASURE, precaution, safeguard, safety measure; preventive medicine.

prophylaxis ▶ **noun** PREVENTIVE TREATMENT, prevention, protection, precaution.

propitiate ▶ **verb** APPEASE, placate, mollify, pacify, make peace with, conciliate, make amends to, soothe, calm.
– OPPOSITES provoke.

propitious ▶ **adjective** FAVOURABLE, auspicious, promising, providential, advantageous, optimistic, bright, rosy, heaven-sent, hopeful; opportune, timely.
– OPPOSITES inauspicious, unfortunate.

proponent ▶ **noun** ADVOCATE, champion, supporter, backer, promoter, protagonist, campaigner; *N. Amer.* booster.

proportion ▶ **noun** ❶ *a small proportion of the land* PART, portion, amount, quantity, bit, piece, percentage, fraction, section, segment, share. ❷ *the proportion of water to alcohol* RATIO, distribution, relative amount/number; relationship. ❸ *the drawing is out of proportion* BALANCE, symmetry, harmony, correspondence, correlation, agreement. ❹ *men of huge proportions* SIZE, dimensions, magnitude, measurements; mass, volume, bulk; expanse, extent, width, breadth.

proportional ▶ **adjective** CORRESPONDING, proportionate, comparable, in proportion, pro rata, commensurate, equivalent, consistent, relative, analogous.
– OPPOSITES disproportionate.

proposal ▶ **noun** ❶ *the proposal was rejected* SCHEME, plan, idea, project, programme, manifesto, motion, proposition, suggestion, submission. ❷ *the proposal of a new constitution* PUTTING FORWARD, proposing, suggesting, submitting.
– OPPOSITES withdrawal.

propose ▶ **verb** ❶ *he proposed a solution* PUT FORWARD, suggest, submit, advance, offer, present, move, come up with, lodge, table, nominate. ❷ *do you propose to go?* INTEND, mean, plan, have in mind/view, resolve, aim, purpose, think of, aspire, want. ❸ *you've proposed to her!* ASK SOMEONE TO MARRY YOU, make an offer of marriage, offer marriage; *informal* pop the question; *dated* ask for someone's hand in marriage.
– OPPOSITES withdraw.

proposition ▶ **noun** ❶ *the analysis derives from one proposition* THEORY, hypothesis, thesis, argument, premiss, theorem, concept, idea, statement. ❷ *a business proposition* PROPOSAL, scheme, plan, project, idea, programme, bid. ❸ *doing it for real is a very different proposition* TASK, job, undertaking, venture, activity, affair, problem.
▶ **verb** *he never dared proposition her* PROPOSE SEX WITH, make sexual advances to, make an indecent proposal to, make an improper suggestion to; *informal* give someone the come-on.

propound ▶ **verb** PUT FORWARD, advance, offer, proffer, present, set forth, submit, tender, suggest, introduce, postulate, propose, pose, posit; advocate, promote, peddle, spread.

proprietor, proprietress ▶ **noun** OWNER, possessor, holder, master/mistress; landowner, landlord/landlady; innkeeper, hotelkeeper, hotelier, shopkeeper; *Brit.* publican.

propriety ▶ **noun** ❶ *he behaves with the utmost propriety* DECORUM, respectability, decency, correctness, protocol, appropriateness, suitability, good manners, courtesy, politeness, rectitude, morality, civility, modesty, demureness; sobriety, refinement, discretion. ❷ *he was careful to preserve the proprieties in public* ETIQUETTE, convention(s), social grace(s), niceties, one's Ps and Qs, protocol, standards, civilities, formalities, accepted behaviour, good form, the done thing, the thing to do, punctilio.
– OPPOSITES indecorum.

propulsion ▶ **noun** THRUST, motive force, impetus, impulse, drive, driving force, actuation, push, pressure, power.

prosaic ▶ **adjective** ORDINARY, everyday, commonplace, conventional, straightforward, routine, run-of-the-mill, workaday; UNIMAGINATIVE, uninspired, uninspiring, matter-of-fact, dull, dry, dreary, tedious, boring, humdrum, mundane, pedestrian, tame, plodding; bland, insipid, banal, trite, literal, factual, unpoetic, unemotional, unsentimental.
– OPPOSITES interesting, imaginative, inspired.

proscribe ▶ **verb** ❶ *gambling was proscribed* FORBID, prohibit, ban, bar, interdict, make illegal, embargo, outlaw, disallow, veto; *Law* enjoin. ❷ *the book was proscribed by the Church* CONDEMN, denounce, attack, criticize, censure, damn, reject.
– OPPOSITES allow, authorize, accept.

proscription ▶ **noun** ❶ *the proscription of alcohol* BANNING, forbidding, prohibition, prohibiting, barring, debarment, vetoing, interdiction, outlawing. ❷ *a proscription was imposed* BAN, prohibition, bar, interdict, veto, embargo, moratorium. ❸ *the proscription of his recordings* CONDEMNATION, denunciation, attacking, criticism, censuring, damning, rejection.
– OPPOSITES allowing, authorization, acceptance.

prosecute ▶ **verb** ❶ *they prosecute offenders* TAKE TO COURT, bring/institute legal proceedings against, bring an action against, take legal action against, sue, try, bring to trial, put on trial, put in the dock, bring a suit against, indict, arraign; *N. Amer.* impeach; *informal* have the law on. ❷ *they helped him prosecute the war* PURSUE, fight, wage, carry on, conduct, direct, engage in, proceed with, continue (with), keep on with.
– OPPOSITES defend, let off, give up.

proselyte ▶ **noun** CONVERT, new believer, catechumen.

proselytize ▶ **verb** ❶ *I'm not here to proselytize* EVANGELIZE, convert, save, redeem, win over, preach (to), recruit, act as a missionary. ❷ *he wanted to proselytize his ideas* PROMOTE, advocate, champion, advance, further, spread, proclaim, peddle, preach, endorse, urge, recommend, boost.

prospect ▶ **noun** ❶ *there is little prospect of success* LIKELIHOOD, hope, expectation, anticipation, (good/poor) chance, odds, probability, possibility, promise, lookout; fear, danger. ❷ *her job prospects* POSSIBILITIES, potential, promise, expectations, outlook. ❸ *a daunting prospect* VISION, thought, idea; task, undertaking. ❹ *Jimmy is an exciting prospect* CANDIDATE, possibility; *informal* catch. ❺ *there is a pleasant prospect from the lounge* VIEW, vista, outlook, perspective, panorama, aspect, scene; picture, spectacle, sight.
▶ **verb** *they are prospecting for oil* SEARCH, look, explore, survey, scout, hunt, reconnoitre, examine, inspect.
■ **in prospect** EXPECTED, likely, coming soon, on the way, to come, at hand, near, imminent, in the offing, in store, on the horizon, just around the corner, in the air, in the wind, brewing, looming; *informal* on the cards.

prospective ▶ **adjective** POTENTIAL, possible, probable, likely, future, eventual, -to-be, soon-to-be, in the making; intending, aspiring, would-be; forthcoming, approaching, coming, imminent.

prospectus ▶ **noun** BROCHURE, pamphlet, description, particulars, announcement, advertisement; syllabus, curriculum, catalogue, programme, list, scheme, schedule.

prosper ▶ **verb** FLOURISH, thrive, do well, bloom, blossom, burgeon, progress, do all right for oneself, get ahead, get on (in the world), be successful; *informal* go places.
– OPPOSITES fail, flounder.

prosperity ▶ **noun** SUCCESS, profitability, affluence, wealth, opulence, luxury, the good life, milk and honey, (good) fortune, ease, plenty, comfort, security, well-being.
– OPPOSITES hardship, failure.

prosperous ▶ **adjective** THRIVING, flourishing, successful, strong, vigorous, profitable, lucrative, expanding, booming, burgeoning; AFFLUENT, wealthy, rich, moneyed, well off, well-to-do, opulent, substantial, in clover; *informal* on a roll, on the up and up, in the money.
– OPPOSITES ailing, poor.

prostitute ▶ **noun** WHORE, sex worker, call girl; rent boy; *informal* tart, pro, moll, working girl, member of the oldest profession; *Brit. informal* tom, woman on the game, renter; *N. Amer. informal* hooker, hustler, chippy; *black English* ho; *dated* streetwalker, woman of the streets, lady/woman of the night, scarlet woman, cocotte; *archaic* courtesan, strumpet, harlot, trollop, woman of ill repute, lady of pleasure, wench.
▶ **verb** *they prostituted their art* BETRAY, sacrifice, sell, sell out, debase, degrade, demean, devalue, cheapen, lower, shame, misuse, pervert; abandon one's principles, be untrue to oneself.

prostitution ▶ **noun** WHORING, the sex industry, streetwalking, Mrs Warren's profession, sex tourism; *informal* the oldest profession, the trade; rough trade; *Brit. informal* the game; *N. Amer. informal* hooking, hustling; *dated* whoredom; *archaic* harlotry.

prostrate ▶ **adjective** ❶ *the prostrate figure on the ground* PRONE, lying flat, lying down, stretched out, spreadeagled, sprawling, horizontal, recumbent; *rare* procumbent. ❷ *his wife was prostrate with shock* OVERWHELMED, overcome, overpowered, brought to one's knees, stunned, dazed; speechless, helpless; *informal* knocked/hit for six. ❸ *the fever left me prostrate* WORN OUT, exhausted, fatigued, tired out, sapped, dog-tired, spent, drained, debilitated, enervated, laid low; *informal* all in, done in, dead, dead beat, dead on one's feet, ready to drop, fagged out, bushed, frazzled, worn to a frazzle; *Brit. informal* whacked, knackered; *N. Amer. informal* pooped.

– OPPOSITES upright, fresh.

▶ **verb** *she was prostrated by the tragedy* OVERWHELM, overcome, overpower, bring to one's knees, devastate, debilitate, weaken, enfeeble, enervate, lay low, wear out, exhaust, tire out, drain, sap, wash out, take it out of; *informal* knacker, frazzle, do in; *N. Amer. informal* poop.

■ **prostrate oneself** THROW ONESELF FLAT/DOWN, lie down, stretch oneself out, throw oneself at someone's feet; *dated* measure one's length.

prostration ▶ **noun** COLLAPSE, weakness, debility, lassitude, exhaustion, fatigue, tiredness, enervation, emotional exhaustion.

protagonist ▶ **noun** ❶ *the protagonist in the plot* CHIEF/CENTRAL/PRINCIPAL/MAIN/LEADING CHARACTER, chief etc. participant/figure/player, principal, hero/heroine, leading man/lady, title role, lead. ❷ *a protagonist of deregulation* CHAMPION, advocate, upholder, supporter, backer, promoter, proponent, exponent, campaigner, fighter, crusader; apostle, apologist; *N. Amer.* booster.

– OPPOSITES opponent.

protean ▶ **adjective** ❶ *the protean nature of mental disorders* EVER-CHANGING, variable, changeable, mutable, kaleidoscopic, inconstant, inconsistent, unstable, shifting, unsettled, fluctuating, fluid, wavering, vacillating, mercurial, volatile; *technical* labile. ❷ *a remarkably protean composer* VERSATILE, adaptable, flexible, all-round, multifaceted, multitalented, many-sided.

– OPPOSITES constant, consistent, limited.

protect ▶ **verb** KEEP SAFE, keep from harm, save, safeguard, preserve, defend, shield, cushion, insulate, hedge, shelter, screen, secure, fortify, guard, watch over, look after, take care of, keep; inoculate.

– OPPOSITES expose, neglect, attack, harm.

protection ▶ **noun** ❶ *protection against frost* DEFENCE, security, shielding, preservation, conservation, safe keeping, safeguarding, safety, sanctuary, shelter, refuge, lee, immunity, insurance, indemnity. ❷ *under the protection of the Church* SAFE KEEPING, care, charge, keeping, protectorship, guidance, aegis, auspices, umbrella, guardianship, support, patronage, championship, providence. ❸ *good protection against noise* BARRIER, buffer, shield, screen, hedge, cushion, preventative, armour, refuge, bulwark.

protective ▶ **adjective** ❶ *protective clothing* PRESERVATIVE, protecting, safeguarding, shielding, defensive, safety, precautionary, preventive, preventative. ❷ *he felt protective towards the girl* SOLICITOUS, caring, warm, paternal/maternal, fatherly/motherly, gallant, chivalrous; overprotective, possessive, jealous.

protector ▶ **noun** ❶ *a protector of the environment* DEFENDER, preserver, guardian, guard, champion, watchdog, ombudsman, knight in shining armour, guardian angel, patron, chaperon, escort, keeper, custodian, bodyguard, minder; *informal* hired gun. ❷ *ear protectors* GUARD, shield, buffer, cushion, pad, screen.

protégé, fem. **protégée** ▶ **noun** PUPIL, student, trainee, apprentice; disciple, follower; discovery, find, ward.

protest ▶ **noun** ❶ *he resigned as a protest* OBJECTION, complaint, exception, disapproval, challenge, dissent, demurral, remonstration, fuss, outcry. ❷ *women staged a protest* DEMONSTRATION, (protest) march, rally; sit-in, occupation; work-to-rule, industrial action, stoppage, strike, walkout, mutiny, picket, boycott; *informal* demo.

– OPPOSITES support, approval.

▶ **verb** ❶ *residents protested at the plans* EXPRESS OPPOSITION, object, dissent, take issue, make/take a stand, put up a fight, kick, take exception, complain, express disapproval, disagree, demur, remonstrate, make a fuss; cry out, speak out, rail, inveigh, fulminate; *informal* kick up a fuss/stink. ❷ *people protested outside the cathedral* DEMONSTRATE, march, hold a rally, sit in, occupy somewhere; work to rule, take industrial action, stop work, down tools, strike, go on strike, walk out, mutiny, picket somewhere; boycott something. ❸ *he protested his innocence* INSIST ON, maintain, assert, affirm, announce, proclaim, declare, profess, contend, argue, claim, vow, swear (to), stress; *formal* aver, asseverate.

– OPPOSITES acquiesce, support, deny.

protestation ▶ **noun** ❶ *his protestations of innocence* DECLARATION, announcement, profession, assertion, insistence, claim, affirmation, assurance, oath, vow; *rare* aver, asseveration. ❷ *we helped him despite his protestations* OBJECTION, protest, exception, complaint, disapproval, opposition, challenge, dissent, demurral, remonstration, fuss, outcry; *informal* stink.

– OPPOSITES denial, acquiescence, support.

protester ▶ **noun** ❶ *the council lost protesters' letters* OBJECTOR, opposer, opponent, complainant, complainer, dissenter, dissident, nonconformist. ❷ *the protesters were moved on* DEMONSTRATOR, protest marcher; striker, mutineer, picket.

protocol ▶ **noun** ❶ *a stickler for protocol* ETIQUETTE, conventions, formalities, customs, rules of conduct, procedure, ritual, accepted behaviour, propriety, proprieties, one's Ps and Qs, decorum, good form, the done thing, the thing to do, punctilio. ❷ *the two countries signed a protocol* AGREEMENT, treaty, entente, concordat, convention, deal, pact, contract, compact; *formal* concord.

prototype ▸ noun ❶ *a protoype of the weapon* ORIGINAL, first example/model, master, mould, template, framework, mock-up, pattern, sample; DESIGN, guide, blueprint. ❷ *the prototype of an ideal wife* TYPICAL EXAMPLE, paradigm, archetype, exemplar.

protract ▸ verb PROLONG, lengthen, extend, draw out, drag out, spin out, stretch out, string out, elongate; carry on, continue, keep up, perpetuate.
–OPPOSITES curtail, shorten.

protracted ▸ adjective PROLONGED, long-lasting, extended, long-drawn-out, spun out, dragged out, strung out, lengthy, long.
–OPPOSITES short.

protrude ▸ verb STICK OUT, jut (out), project, extend, stand out, bulge out, poke out, thrust out, cantilever.

protruding ▸ adjective STICKING OUT, protuberant, projecting, prominent, jutting, overhanging, proud, bulging; *informal* sticky-out.
–OPPOSITES sunken, flush.

protrusion ▸ noun ❶ *the neck vertebrae have short vertical protrusions* BUMP, lump, knob; protuberance, projection, sticking-out bit, prominence, swelling, eminence, outcrop, outgrowth, jut, jag, snag; ledge, shelf, ridge; *informal* sticky-out bit. ❷ *protrusion of the lips* STICKING OUT, jutting, projection, obtrusion, prominence; swelling, bulging.

protuberance ▸ noun ❶ *a protuberance can cause drag* BUMP, lump, knob, projection, protrusion, sticking-out bit, prominence, swelling, eminence, outcrop, outgrowth, jut, jag, snag; ledge, shelf, ridge; *informal* sticky-out bit. ❷ *the protuberance of the incisors* STICKING OUT, jutting, projection, obtrusion, prominence; swelling, bulging.

protuberant ▸ adjective STICKING OUT, protruding, projecting, prominent, jutting, overhanging, proud, bulging; *informal* sticky-out.
–OPPOSITES sunken, flush.

proud ▸ adjective ❶ *the proud parents beamed* PLEASED, glad, happy, delighted, joyful, overjoyed, thrilled, satisfied, gratified, content. ❷ *a proud day* PLEASING, gratifying, satisfying, cheering, heart-warming; happy, good, glorious, memorable, notable, red-letter. ❸ *they were poor but proud* SELF-RESPECTING, dignified, noble, worthy; independent. ❹ *I'm not too proud to admit I'm wrong* ARROGANT, conceited, vain, self-important, full of oneself, puffed up, jumped-up, smug, complacent, disdainful, condescending, scornful, supercilious, snobbish, imperious, pompous, overbearing, bumptious, haughty; *informal* big-headed, swollen-headed, too big for one's boots, high and mighty, stuck-up, uppity, snooty, highfalutin; *Brit. informal* toffee-nosed; *poetic/literary* vainglorious; *rare* hubristic. ❺ *the proud ships* MAGNIFICENT, splendid, resplendent, grand, noble, stately, imposing, dignified, striking, impressive, majestic, glorious, awe-inspiring, awesome, monumental. ❻ *the switch is proud of the wall* PROJECTING, sticking out/up, jutting (out), protruding, prominent, raised, convex, elevated.
–OPPOSITES ashamed, shameful, humble, modest, unimpressive, concave, flush.

prove ▸ verb ❶ *that proves I'm right* SHOW (TO BE TRUE), demonstrate (the truth of), show beyond doubt, manifest, produce proof/evidence; witness to, give substance to, determine, substantiate, corroborate, verify, ratify, validate, authenticate, document, bear out, confirm; *formal* evince. ❷ *the rumour proved to be correct* TURN OUT, be found, happen.
–OPPOSITES disprove.
■ **prove oneself** DEMONSTRATE ONE'S ABILITIES/QUALITIES, show one's (true) mettle, show what one is made of.

provenance ▸ noun ORIGIN, source, place of origin; birthplace, fount, roots, pedigree, derivation, root, etymology; *N. Amer.* provenience; *formal* radix.

proverb ▸ noun SAYING, adage, saw, maxim, axiom, motto, bon mot, aphorism, apophthegm, epigram, gnome, dictum, precept; words of wisdom.

proverbial ▸ adjective WELL KNOWN, famous, famed, renowned, traditional, time-honoured, legendary; notorious, infamous.

provide ▸ verb ❶ *the Foundation will provide funds* SUPPLY, give, issue, furnish, come up with, dispense, bestow, impart, produce, yield, bring forth, bear, deliver, donate, contribute, pledge, advance, spare, part with, allocate, distribute, allot, put up; *informal* fork out, lay out; *N. Amer. informal* ante up, pony up. ❷ *he was provided with enough tools* EQUIP, furnish, issue, supply, outfit; fit out, rig out, kit out, arm, provision; *informal* fix up. ❸ *he had to provide for his family* FEED, nurture, nourish; SUPPORT, maintain, keep, sustain, provide sustenance for, fend for, finance, endow. ❹ *the test may provide the answer* MAKE AVAILABLE, present, offer, afford, give, add, bring, yield, impart. ❺ *we have provided for further restructuring* PREPARE, allow, make provision, be prepared, arrange, get ready, plan, cater. ❻ *the banks have to provide against bad debts* TAKE PRECAUTIONS, take steps/measures, guard, forearm oneself; make provision for. ❼ *the Act provides that factories must be kept clean* STIPULATE, lay down, make it a condition, require, order, ordain, demand, prescribe, state, specify.
–OPPOSITES refuse, withhold, deprive, neglect.

provided ▸ conjunction IF, on condition that, providing (that), provided that, presuming (that), assuming (that), on the assumption that, as long as, given (that), with the provision/proviso that, with/on the understanding that, contingent on.

providence ▶ noun ❶ *a life mapped out by providence* FATE, destiny, nemesis, kismet, God's will, divine intervention, predestination, predetermination, the stars; one's lot (in life); *archaic* one's portion. ❷ *he had a streak of providence* PRUDENCE, foresight, forethought, far-sightedness, judiciousness, shrewdness, circumspection, wisdom, sagacity, common sense; careful budgeting, thrift, economy.

provident ▶ adjective PRUDENT, far-sighted, judicious, shrewd, circumspect, forearmed, wise, sagacious, sensible; thrifty, economical.
– OPPOSITES improvident.

providential ▶ adjective OPPORTUNE, advantageous, favourable, auspicious, propitious, heaven-sent, welcome, golden, lucky, happy, fortunate, felicitous, timely, well timed, seasonable, convenient, expedient.
– OPPOSITES inopportune.

provider ▶ noun SUPPLIER, donor, giver, contributor, source.

providing ▶ conjunction. *See* PROVIDED.

province ▶ noun ❶ *a province of the Ottoman Empire* TERRITORY, region, state, department, canton, area, district, sector, zone, division. ❷ *people in the provinces* NON-METROPOLITAN AREAS/COUNTIES, the rest of the country, middle England/America, rural areas/districts, the countryside, the backwoods, the wilds; *informal* the sticks, the middle of nowhere; *N. Amer. informal* the boondocks. ❸ *that's outside my province* RESPONSIBILITY, area of activity, area of interest, knowledge, department, sphere, world, realm, field, domain, territory, orbit, preserve, line of country; business, affair, concern; speciality, forte; jurisdiction, authority; *informal* pigeon, bailiwick, turf.

provincial ▶ adjective ❶ *the provincial government* REGIONAL, state, territorial, district, local; sectoral, zonal, cantonal, county. ❷ *provincial areas* NON-METROPOLITAN, small-town, non-urban, outlying, rural, country, rustic, backwoods, backwater; *informal* one-horse; *N. Amer. informal* hick, freshwater. ❸ *they're so dull and provincial* UNSOPHISTICATED, narrow-minded, parochial, small-town, suburban, insular, parish-pump, inward-looking, conservative; small-minded, blinkered, bigoted, prejudiced; *N. Amer. informal* jerkwater, corn-fed.
– OPPOSITES national, metropolitan, cosmopolitan, sophisticated, broad-minded.
▶ noun *they were dismissed as provincials* (COUNTRY) BUMPKIN, country cousin, rustic, yokel, village idiot, peasant; *Irish informal* culchie; *N. Amer. informal* hayseed, hick, rube, hillbilly.
– OPPOSITES sophisticate.

provision ▶ noun ❶ *the provision of weapons to guerrillas* SUPPLYING, supply, providing, giving, presentation, donation; equipping, furnishing. ❷ *there has been limited provision for gifted children* FACILITIES, services, amenities, resource(s), arrangements; means, funds, benefits, assistance, allowance(s). ❸ *provisions for the trip* SUPPLIES, food and drink, stores, groceries, foodstuff(s), provender, rations; *informal* grub, eats, nosh; *N. Amer. informal* chuck; *formal* comestibles; *poetic/literary* viands; *dated* victuals. ❹ *he made no provision for the future* PREPARATIONS, plans, arrangements, pre-arrangement, precautions, contingency. ❺ *the provisions of the Act* TERM, clause; requirement, specification, stipulation; proviso, condition, qualification, restriction, limitation.

provisional ▶ adjective INTERIM, temporary, pro tem; transitional, changeover, stopgap, short-term, fill-in, acting, caretaker, TBC (to be confirmed), subject to confirmation; pencilled in, working, tentative, contingent.
– OPPOSITES permanent, definite.

provisionally ▶ adverb TEMPORARILY, short-term, pro tem, for the interim, for the present, for the time being, for now, for the nonce; subject to confirmation, in an acting capacity, conditionally, tentatively.

proviso ▶ noun CONDITION, stipulation, provision, clause, rider, qualification, restriction, caveat.

provocation ▶ noun ❶ *he remained calm despite severe provocation* GOADING, prodding, egging on, incitement, pressure; ANNOYANCE, irritation, nettling; harassment, plaguing, molestation; teasing, taunting, torment; affront, insults; *informal* hassle, aggravation. ❷ *without provocation, Jones punched Mr Cartwright* JUSTIFICATION, excuse, pretext, occasion, call, motivation, motive, cause, grounds, reason, need.

provocative ▶ adjective ❶ *provocative remarks* ANNOYING, irritating, exasperating, infuriating, maddening, vexing, galling; insulting, offensive, inflammatory, incendiary, controversial; *informal* aggravating, in-your-face. ❷ *a provocative pose* SEXY, sexually arousing, sexually exciting, alluring, seductive, suggestive, inviting, tantalizing, titillating; indecent, pornographic, indelicate, immodest, shameless; erotic, sensuous, slinky, coquettish, amorous, flirtatious; *informal* tarty, come-hither.
– OPPOSITES soothing, calming, modest, decorous.

provoke ▶ verb ❶ *the plan has provoked outrage* AROUSE, produce, evoke, cause, give rise to, occasion, call forth, elicit, induce, excite, spark off, touch off, kindle, generate, engender, instigate, result in, lead to, bring on, precipitate, prompt, trigger; *poetic/literary* beget. ❷ *he was provoked into replying* GOAD, spur, prick, sting, prod, egg on, incite, rouse, stir, move, stimulate, motivate, excite, inflame, work/fire up, impel. ❸ *he wouldn't be provoked* ANNOY, anger, incense, enrage, irritate, infuri-

ate, exasperate, madden, nettle, get/take a rise out of, ruffle, ruffle someone's feathers, make someone's hackles rise; harass, harry, plague, molest; tease, taunt, torment; *Brit.* rub up the wrong way; *informal* peeve, aggravate, hassle, miff, rile, needle, get, bug, hack off, make someone's blood boil, get under someone's skin, get in someone's hair, get/put someone's back up, get up someone's nose, get someone's goat, get across someone; *Brit. informal* wind up, nark; *N. Amer. informal* rankle, ride, gravel.
– OPPOSITES allay, deter, pacify, appease.

prow ▶ noun BOW(S), stem, front, nose, head, cutwater; *Brit. humorous* sharp end.

prowess ▶ noun ❶ *his prowess as a winemaker* SKILL, expertise, mastery, facility, ability, capability, capacity, savoir faire, talent, genius, adeptness, aptitude, dexterity, deftness, competence, accomplishment, proficiency, finesse; *informal* know-how. ❷ *the knights' prowess in battle* COURAGE, bravery, gallantry, valour, heroism, intrepidity, nerve, pluck, pluckiness, boldness, daring, audacity, fearlessness; *informal* bottle, guts, spunk; *N. Amer. informal* moxie, sand.
– OPPOSITES inability, ineptitude, cowardice.

prowl ▶ verb MOVE STEALTHILY, slink, skulk, steal, nose, pussyfoot, sneak, stalk, creep; *informal* snoop.

proximity ▶ noun CLOSENESS, nearness, propinquity; accessibility, handiness; *archaic* vicinity.

proxy ▶ noun DEPUTY, representative, substitute, delegate, agent, surrogate, stand-in, attorney, go-between.

prude ▶ noun PURITAN, prig, killjoy, moralist, pietist; *informal* goody-goody; *N. Amer. informal* bluenose.

prudence ▶ noun ❶ *you have gone beyond the bounds of prudence* WISDOM, judgement, good judgement, common sense, sense, sagacity, shrewdness, advisability. ❷ *financial prudence* CAUTION, care, providence, far-sightedness, foresight, forethought, shrewdness, circumspection; thrift, economy.
– OPPOSITES folly, recklessness, extravagance.

prudent ▶ adjective ❶ *it is prudent to obtain consent* WISE, well judged, sensible, politic, judicious, sagacious, sage, shrewd, advisable, well advised. ❷ *a prudent approach to borrowing* CAUTIOUS, careful, provident, far-sighted, judicious, shrewd, circumspect; thrifty, economical.
– OPPOSITES unwise, reckless, extravagant.

prudish ▶ adjective PURITANICAL, priggish, prim, prim and proper, moralistic, pietistic, sententious, censorious, strait-laced, Victorian, old-maidish, stuffy; *informal* goody-goody; *rare* Grundyish, starchy.
– OPPOSITES permissive.

prune ▶ verb ❶ *I pruned the roses* CUT BACK, trim, thin, pinch back, clip, shear, pollard, top, dock. ❷ *prune lateral shoots of wisteria* CUT OFF, lop (off), chop off, clip, snip (off), nip off, dock. ❸ *staff numbers have been pruned* REDUCE, cut (back/down), pare (down), slim down, make reductions in, make cutbacks in, trim, decrease, diminish, downsize, axe, shrink; *informal* slash.
– OPPOSITES increase.

prurient ▶ adjective SALACIOUS, licentious, voyeuristic, lascivious, lecherous, lustful, lewd, libidinous, lubricious; *formal* concupiscent.

pry ▶ verb ENQUIRE IMPERTINENTLY, be inquisitive, be curious, poke about/around, ferret (about/around), spy, be a busybody; eavesdrop, listen in, tap someone's phone, intrude; *informal* stick/poke one's nose in/into, be nosy, nose, snoop; *Austral./NZ informal* stickybeak.
– OPPOSITES mind one's own business.

psalm ▶ noun SACRED SONG, religious song, hymn, song of praise; chant, plainsong; (**psalms**) psalmody, psalter.

pseud ▶ noun PRETENTIOUS PERSON, poser, poseur, sham, fraud; *informal* show-off, phoney.

pseudo ▶ adjective BOGUS, sham, phoney, artificial, mock, ersatz, quasi-, fake, false, spurious, deceptive, misleading, assumed, contrived, affected, insincere; *informal* pretend, put-on; *Brit. informal* cod.
– OPPOSITES genuine.

pseudonym ▶ noun PEN NAME, nom de plume, assumed name, false name, alias, professional name, sobriquet, stage name, nom de guerre.

psych (*informal*)
■ **psych someone out** INTIMIDATE, daunt, browbeat, bully, cow, tyrannize, scare, terrorize, frighten, dishearten, unnerve, subdue; *informal* bulldoze; *N. Amer. informal* buffalo.
■ **psych oneself up** NERVE ONESELF, steel oneself, brace oneself, summon one's courage, prepare oneself, gear oneself up, urge oneself on, gird (up) one's loins.

psyche ▶ noun SOUL, spirit, (inner) self, ego, true being, inner man/woman, persona, subconscious, mind, intellect; *technical* anima, pneuma.
– OPPOSITES body.

psychiatrist ▶ noun PSYCHOTHERAPIST, psychoanalyst; *informal* shrink, head doctor; *Brit. humorous* trick cyclist.

psychic ▶ adjective ❶ *psychic powers* SUPERNATURAL, paranormal, other-worldly, supernormal, preternatural, metaphysical, extrasensory, magic, magical, mystical, mystic, occult. ❷ *I'm not psychic* CLAIRVOYANT, telepathic, having second sight, having a sixth sense. ❸ *psychic development* EMOTIONAL, spiritual, inner; cog-

nitive, psychological, intellectual, mental, psychiatric, psychogenic.
– OPPOSITES normal, physical.
▶ noun *she is a psychic* CLAIRVOYANT, fortune teller, crystal-gazer; medium, spiritualist; telepathist, telepath, mind-reader, palmist, palm-reader.

psychological ▶ adjective ❶ *his psychological state* MENTAL, emotional, intellectual, inner, cerebral, brain, rational, cognitive. ❷ *her pain was psychological* (ALL) IN THE MIND, psychosomatic, emotional, irrational, subjective, subconscious, unconscious.
– OPPOSITES physical.

psychology ▶ noun ❶ *a degree in psychology* STUDY OF THE MIND, science of the mind. ❷ *the psychology of the road user* MINDSET, mind, mental processes, thought processes, way of thinking, cast of mind, mentality, persona, psyche, (mental) attitude(s), make-up, character; *informal* what makes someone tick.

psychopath ▶ noun MADMAN, MADWOMAN, maniac, lunatic, psychotic, sociopath; *informal* loony, fruitcake, nutcase, nut, psycho, schizo, head case, headbanger, sicko; *Brit. informal* nutter; *N. Amer. informal* screwball, crazy, kook, meshuggener.

psychopathic. ▶ adjective. *See* MAD sense 1.

psychosomatic ▶ adjective (ALL) IN THE MIND, psychological, irrational, stress-related, stress-induced, subjective, subconscious, unconscious.

psychotic ▶ adjective. *See* MAD sense 1.

pub ▶ noun (*Brit.*) BAR, inn, tavern, hostelry, wine bar, taproom, roadhouse; *Brit.* public house; *Austral./NZ* hotel; *informal* watering hole; *Brit. informal* local, boozer; *dated* alehouse; *historical* pothouse, beerhouse; *N. Amer. historical* saloon.

puberty ▶ noun ADOLESCENCE, pubescence, sexual maturity, growing up; youth, young adulthood, teenage years, teens, the awkward age; *formal* juvenescence.

public ▶ adjective ❶ *public affairs* STATE, national, federal, government; constitutional, civic, civil, official, social, municipal, community, communal, local; nationalized. ❷ *by public demand* POPULAR, general, common, communal, collective, shared, joint, universal, widespread. ❸ *a public figure* PROMINENT, well known, important, leading, eminent, distinguished, notable, noteworthy, noted, celebrated, household, famous, famed, influential; *N. Amer.* major-league. ❹ *public places* OPEN (TO THE PUBLIC), communal, accessible to all, available, free, unrestricted, community. ❺ *the news became public* KNOWN, published, publicized, in circulation, exposed, overt, plain, obvious.
– OPPOSITES private, obscure, unknown, restricted, secret.
▶ noun ❶ *the British public* PEOPLE, citizens, subjects, general public, electors, electorate, voters, taxpayers, residents, inhabitants, citizenry, population, populace, community, society, country, nation, world; everyone. ❷ *his adoring public* AUDIENCE, spectators, followers, following, fans, devotees, aficionados, admirers; patrons, clientele, market, consumers, buyers, customers, readers.
■ **in public** PUBLICLY, in full view of people, openly, in the open, for all to see, undisguisedly, blatantly, flagrantly, brazenly, with no attempt at concealment, overtly; *formal* coram populo.

publication ▶ noun ❶ *the author of this publication* BOOK, volume, title, work, tome, opus; newspaper, paper, magazine, periodical, newsletter, bulletin, journal, report; organ, booklet, brochure, catalogue; daily, weekly, monthly, quarterly, annual; *informal* rag, mag, 'zine. ❷ *the publication of her new book* ISSUING, announcement, publishing, printing, notification, reporting, declaration, communication, proclamation, broadcasting, publicizing, advertising, distribution, spreading, dissemination, promulgation, issuance, appearance.

publicity ▶ noun ❶ *the blaze of publicity* PUBLIC ATTENTION, public interest, public notice, media attention/interest, exposure, glare, limelight. ❷ *publicity should boost sales* PROMOTION, advertising, propaganda; boost, push; *informal* hype, ballyhoo, puff, puffery, build-up, razzmatazz; plug.

publicize ▶ verb ❶ *I never publicize the fact* MAKE KNOWN, make public, publish, announce, report, post, communicate, broadcast, issue, put out, distribute, spread, promulgate, disseminate, circulate, air; disclose, reveal, divulge, leak. ❷ *he just wants to publicize his book* ADVERTISE, promote, build up, talk up, push, beat the drum for, boost; *informal* hype, plug, puff (up).
– OPPOSITES conceal, suppress.

public-spirited ▶ adjective COMMUNITY-MINDED, socially concerned, philanthropic, charitable; ALTRUISTIC, humanitarian, generous, unselfish.

publish ▶ verb ❶ *we publish novels* ISSUE, bring out, produce, print. ❷ *he ought to publish his views* MAKE KNOWN, make public, publicize, announce, report, post, communicate, broadcast, issue, put out, distribute, spread, promulgate, disseminate, circulate, air; disclose, reveal, divulge, leak.

pucker ▶ verb *she puckered her forehead* WRINKLE, crinkle, crease, furrow, crumple, rumple, ruck up, scrunch up, corrugate, ruffle, screw up, shrivel; cockle.
▶ noun *a pucker in the sewing* WRINKLE, crinkle, crumple, corrugation, furrow, line, fold.

puckish ▶ adjective MISCHIEVOUS, naughty, impish, roguish, playful, arch, prankish; *informal* waggish.

pudding ▶ **noun** DESSERT, sweet, second course, last course; *Brit. informal* afters, pud.

puddle ▶ **noun** POOL, spill, splash; *poetic/literary* plash.

puerile ▶ **adjective** CHILDISH, immature, infantile, juvenile, babyish; silly, inane, fatuous, jejune, asinine, foolish, petty.
– OPPOSITES mature, sensible.

puff ▶ **noun** ❶ *a puff of wind* GUST, blast, flurry, rush, draught, waft, breeze, breath. ❷ *he took a puff at his cigar* PULL; *informal* drag. ❸ (*informal*) *they expected a puff in our review column* FAVOURABLE MENTION, review, recommendation, good word, advertisement, promotion, commercial; *informal* ad; *Brit. informal* advert. ❹ (*informal*) *a salesman's puff* PUBLICITY, advertising, promotion, marketing, propaganda, build-up; patter, line, pitch, sales talk; *informal* spiel.
▶ **verb** ❶ *he walked fast, puffing a little* BREATHE HEAVILY, pant, blow; gasp, fight for breath. ❷ *she puffed at her cigarette* SMOKE, draw on, drag on, suck at/on. ❸ (*informal*) *new ways to puff our products* ADVERTISE, promote, publicize, push, recommend, endorse, beat the drum for; *informal* hype (up), plug.
■ **puff out/up** BULGE, swell (out), stick out, distend, tumefy, balloon (up/out), expand, inflate, enlarge.
■ **puff something out/up** DISTEND, expand, dilate, inflate, blow up, pump up, enlarge, bloat.

puffed ▶ **adjective** OUT OF BREATH, breathless, short of breath; panting, puffing, gasping, wheezing, wheezy, winded; *informal* out of puff.

puffed-up ▶ **adjective** SELF-IMPORTANT, conceited, arrogant, bumptious, pompous, overbearing; affected, stiff, vain, proud; *informal* snooty, uppity, uppish.

puffy ▶ **adjective** SWOLLEN, puffed up, distended, enlarged, inflated, dilated, bloated, engorged, bulging, tumid, tumescent.

pugilism ▶ **noun** (*dated*) BOXING, prizefighting, bare-knuckle boxing, sparring; fisticuffs; the ring.

pugilist ▶ **noun** (*dated*) BOXER, fighter, prizefighter; *informal* bruiser, pug.

pugnacious ▶ **adjective** COMBATIVE, aggressive, antagonistic, belligerent, bellicose, warlike, quarrelsome, argumentative, contentious, disputatious, hostile, threatening, truculent; fiery, hot-tempered.
– OPPOSITES peaceable.

puke ▶ **verb** (*informal*). *See* VOMIT verb senses 1, 2.

pukka ▶ **adjective** (*informal*) ❶ *the pukka thing to do* RESPECTABLE, decorous, proper, genteel, polite; conventional, right, correct, accepted, decent. ❷ *pukka racing cars* GENUINE, authentic, proper, actual, real, true, bona fide, veritable, legitimate; *informal* kosher, the real McCoy. ❸ *a pukka meal* EXCELLENT, very good, outstanding, exceptional, marvellous, wonderful, first-class; *informal* A1, ace, great, terrific, fantastic, fabulous, fab, awesome, wicked; *Brit. informal* brilliant, brill.
– OPPOSITES improper, imitation, bad.

pull ▶ **verb** ❶ *he pulled the box towards him* TUG, haul, drag, draw, tow, heave, lug, jerk, wrench; *informal* yank. ❷ *he pulled the bad tooth out* EXTRACT, take out, remove. ❸ *she pulled a muscle* STRAIN, sprain, wrench, turn, rick, tear; damage. ❹ *race day pulled big crowds* ATTRACT, draw, bring in, pull in, lure, seduce, entice, tempt, beckon, interest, fascinate.
– OPPOSITES push, repel.
▶ **noun** ❶ *give the chain a pull* TUG, jerk, heave; *informal* yank. ❷ *she took a pull on her beer* GULP, draught, drink, swallow, mouthful, slug; *informal* swill, swig. ❸ *a pull on a cigarette* PUFF; *informal* drag. ❹ *she felt the pull of the sea* ATTRACTION, draw, lure, allurement, enticement, magnetism, temptation, fascination, appeal. ❺ *he has a lot of pull in finance* INFLUENCE, sway, power, authority, say, prestige, standing, weight, leverage, muscle, teeth; *informal* clout.
■ **pull something apart** DISMANTLE, disassemble, take/pull to pieces, take/pull to bits, take apart, strip down; demolish, destroy, break up.
■ **pull back** WITHDRAW, retreat, fall back, back off; pull out, retire, disengage; flee, turn tail.
■ **pull something down** DEMOLISH, knock down, tear down, dismantle, raze (to the ground), level, flatten, bulldoze, destroy.
■ **pull in** STOP, halt, come to a halt, pull over, pull up, draw up, brake, park.
■ **pull someone/something in** ❶ *they pulled in big audiences. See* PULL verb sense 4. ❷ (*informal*) *the police pulled him in* ARREST, apprehend, detain, take into custody, seize, capture, catch; *informal* collar, nab, nick, pinch, run in, bust, feel someone's collar.
■ **pull someone's leg** TEASE, fool, play a trick on, rag, pull the wool over someone's eyes; *informal* kid, rib, lead up the garden path, take for a ride; *Brit. informal* wind up, have on.
■ **pull something off** ACHIEVE, fulfil, succeed in, accomplish, bring off, carry off, perform, discharge, complete, clinch, fix, effect, engineer.
■ **pull out** WITHDRAW, resign, leave, retire, step down, bow out, back out, give up; *informal* quit.
■ **pull through** GET BETTER, get well again, improve, recover, rally, come through, recuperate.
■ **pull something to pieces** ❶ *don't pull my radio to pieces. See* PULL SOMETHING APART. ❷ *they pulled the plan to pieces* CRITICIZE, attack, censure, condemn, find fault with, pillory, maul, savage; *informal* knock, slam, pan, bash, crucify, lay into, roast; *Brit. informal* slate, rubbish, slag off.
■ **pull oneself together** REGAIN ONE'S COMPOSURE, recover, get a grip on oneself, get over it; *informal* snap out of it, get one's act together, buck up.

■ **pull up**. *See* PULL IN.

■ **pull someone up** REPRIMAND, rebuke, scold, chide, chastise, upbraid, berate, reprove, reproach, censure, take to task, admonish, lecture, read someone the Riot Act, haul over the coals; *informal* tell off, bawl out, dress down, give someone hell, give someone an earful; *Brit. informal* tick off, carpet, give someone a rollicking; *N. Amer. informal* chew out; *Austral. informal* monster; *formal* castigate.

pulp ▶ **noun** ❶ *he kneaded it into a pulp* MUSH, mash, paste, purée, pomace, pap, slop, slush, mulch; *informal* gloop, goo; *N. Amer. informal* glop. ❷ *the sweet pulp on cocoa seeds* FLESH, marrow, meat.

▶ **verb** *pulp the gooseberries* MASH, purée, cream, crush, press, liquidize, liquefy, sieve, squash, pound, macerate, grind, mince.

▶ **adjective** *pulp fiction* TRASHY, cheap, sensational, lurid, tasteless; *informal* tacky, rubbishy.

pulpit ▶ **noun** STAND, lectern, platform, podium, stage, dais, rostrum.

pulsate ▶ **verb** PALPITATE, pulse, throb, pump, undulate, surge, heave, rise and fall; beat, thump, drum, thrum; flutter, quiver.

pulse¹ ▶ **noun** ❶ *the pulse in her neck* HEARTBEAT, pulsation, pulsing, throbbing, pounding. ❷ *the pulse of the train wheels* RHYTHM, beat, tempo, cadence, pounding, thudding, drumming. ❸ *pulses of ultrasound* BURST, blast, spurt, impulse, surge.

▶ **verb** *music pulsed through the building* THROB, pulsate, vibrate, beat, pound, thud, thump, drum, thrum, reverberate, echo.

pulse² ▶ **noun** *eat plenty of pulses* LEGUME, pea, bean, lentil.

pulverize ▶ **verb** ❶ *the seeds are pulverized into flour* GRIND, crush, pound, powder, mill, crunch, squash, press, pulp, mash, sieve, mince, macerate; *technical* comminute. ❷ (*informal*) *he pulverized the opposition. See* TROUNCE.

pummel ▶ **verb** BATTER, pound, belabour, drub, beat; punch, strike, hit, thump, thrash; *informal* clobber, wallop, bash, whack, beat the living daylights out of, give someone a (good) hiding, belt, biff, lay into, lam; *Brit. informal* slosh; *N. Amer. informal* bust, slug; *Austral./NZ informal* quilt; *poetic/literary* smite.

pump ▶ **verb** ❶ *I pumped air out of the tube* FORCE, drive, push; suck, draw, tap, siphon, withdraw, expel, extract, bleed, drain. ❷ *she pumped up the tyre* INFLATE, aerate, blow up, fill up; swell, enlarge, distend, expand, dilate, puff up. ❸ *blood was pumping from his leg* SPURT, spout, squirt, jet, surge, spew, gush, stream, flow, pour, spill, well, cascade, run, course. ❹ (*informal*) *I pumped them for information* INTERROGATE, cross-examine, ask, question, quiz, probe, sound out, catechize, give someone the third degree; *informal* grill.

pun ▶ **noun** PLAY ON WORDS, wordplay, double entendre, innuendo, witticism, quip, bon mot.

punch¹ ▶ **verb** *Jim punched him in the face* HIT, strike, thump, jab, smash, welt, cuff, clip; batter, buffet, pound, pummel; *informal* sock, slug, biff, bop, wallop, clobber, bash, whack, thwack, clout, lam, whomp; *Brit. informal* stick one on, dot, slosh; *N. Amer. informal* boff, bust; *Austral./NZ informal* quilt; *poetic/literary* smite.

▶ **noun** ❶ *a punch on the nose* BLOW, hit, knock, thump, box, jab, clip, welt; uppercut, hook; *informal* sock, slug, biff, bop, wallop, bash, whack, clout, belt; *N. Amer. informal* boff, bust; *dated* buffet. ❷ *the album is full of punch* VIGOUR, liveliness, vitality, drive, strength, zest, verve, enthusiasm; impact, bite, kick; *informal* oomph, zing.

punch² ▶ **verb** *he punched her ticket* MAKE A HOLE IN, perforate, puncture, pierce, prick, hole, spike, skewer; *poetic/literary* transpierce.

punch-up ▶ **noun** (*Brit. informal*). *See* FIGHT noun sense 1.

punchy ▶ **adjective** *punchy dialogue* FORCEFUL, incisive, strong, powerful, vigorous, dynamic, effective, impressive, telling, compelling; dramatic, passionate, graphic, vivid, potent, authoritative, aggressive; *informal* in-your-face.
– OPPOSITES ineffectual.

punctilio ▶ **noun** ❶ *a stickler for punctilio* CONFORMITY, conscientiousness, punctiliousness; etiquette, protocol, conventions, formalities, propriety, decorum, manners, politesse, good form, the done thing. ❷ *the punctilios of court procedure* NICETY, detail, fine point, subtlety, nuance, refinement.
– OPPOSITES informality.

punctilious ▶ **adjective** METICULOUS, conscientious, diligent, scrupulous, careful, painstaking, rigorous, perfectionist, methodical, particular, strict; fussy, fastidious, finicky, pedantic; *informal* nit-picking, pernickety; *N. Amer. informal* persnickety; *archaic* nice.
– OPPOSITES careless.

punctual ▶ **adjective** ON TIME, prompt, on schedule, in (good) time; *informal* on the dot.
– OPPOSITES late.

punctuate ▶ **verb** ❶ *how to punctuate direct speech* ADD PUNCTUATION TO, put punctuation marks in, dot, apostrophize. ❷ *slides punctuated the talk* BREAK UP, interrupt, intersperse, pepper, sprinkle, scatter.

puncture ▶ **noun** ❶ *the tyre developed a puncture* HOLE, perforation, rupture; cut, slit; leak. ❷ *my car has a puncture* FLAT TYRE; *informal* flat.

▶ **verb** ❶ *he punctured her balloon* MAKE A HOLE IN, pierce, rupture, perforate, stab, cut, slit, prick, spike, stick, lance; deflate. ❷ *she knows how to puncture his speeches* PUT AN END TO, cut short, deflate, reduce.

pundit ▶ **noun** EXPERT, authority, specialist,

doyen(ne), master, guru, sage, savant; *informal* buff, whizz.

pungent ▶ adjective ❶ *a pungent marinade* STRONG, powerful, pervasive, penetrating; sharp, acid, sour, biting, bitter, tart, vinegary, tangy; highly flavoured, aromatic, spicy, piquant, peppery, hot. ❷ *pungent remarks* CAUSTIC, biting, trenchant, cutting, acerbic, sardonic, sarcastic, scathing, acrimonious, barbed, sharp, tart, incisive, bitter, venomous, waspish.
– OPPOSITES bland, mild.

punish ▶ verb ❶ *they punished their children* DISCIPLINE, bring someone to book, teach someone a lesson; tan someone's hide; *informal* murder, wallop, come down on (like a ton of bricks), have someone's guts for garters; *Brit. informal* give someone what for; *dated* chastise. ❷ *higher charges would punish the poor* PENALIZE, unfairly disadvantage, handicap, hurt, wrong, ill-use, maltreat. ❸ *the strikers punished the defence's mistakes* EXPLOIT, take advantage of, turn to account, profit from, capitalize on, cash in on; *informal* walk all over.

punishable ▶ adjective ILLEGAL, unlawful, illegitimate, criminal, felonious, actionable, indictable, penal; blameworthy, dishonest, fraudulent, unauthorized, outlawed, banned, forbidden, prohibited, interdicted, proscribed.

punishing ▶ adjective *a punishing schedule* ARDUOUS, demanding, taxing, onerous, burdensome, strenuous, rigorous, stressful, trying; hard, difficult, tough, exhausting, tiring, gruelling, crippling, relentless; *informal* killing.
– OPPOSITES easy.

punishment ▶ noun ❶ *the punishment of the guilty* PENALIZING, punishing, disciplining; retribution; *dated* chastisement. ❷ *the teacher imposed punishments* PENALTY, penance, sanction, sentence, one's just deserts; discipline, correction, vengeance, justice, judgement; *informal* comeuppance. ❸ *both boxers took punishment* A BATTERING, a thrashing, a beating, a drubbing; *informal* a hiding. ❹ *ovens take continual punishment* MALTREATMENT, mistreatment, abuse, ill-use, manhandling; damage, harm.
– RELATED TERMS punitive, penal.

punitive ▶ adjective ❶ *punitive measures* PENAL, disciplinary, corrective, correctional, retributive. ❷ *punitive taxes* HARSH, severe, stiff, stringent, burdensome, demanding, crushing, crippling; high, sky-high, inflated, exorbitant, extortionate, excessive, inordinate, unreasonable; *Brit.* swingeing.

punter ▶ noun ❶ (*informal*) *each punter has a 1:39 chance* GAMBLER, backer, staker, speculator, bettor; *informal* plunger, high roller. ❷ (*Brit. informal*) *sales bring the punters in* CUSTOMER, client, patron; buyer, purchaser, shopper, consumer; (**punters**) clientele, audience, trade, business; *Brit. informal* bums on seats.

puny ▶ adjective ❶ *he grew up puny* UNDERSIZED, undernourished, underfed, stunted, slight, small, little; weak, feeble, sickly, delicate, frail, fragile; *informal* weedy, pint-sized. ❷ *puny efforts to save their homes* PITIFUL, pitiable, inadequate, insufficient, derisory, miserable, sorry, meagre, paltry, trifling, inconsequential; *informal* pathetic, measly, piddling; *formal* exiguous.
– OPPOSITES sturdy, substantial.

pupil ▶ noun ❶ *former pupils of the school* STUDENT, scholar; schoolchild, schoolboy, schoolgirl. ❷ *the guru's pupils* DISCIPLE, follower, student, protégé, apprentice, trainee, novice.

puppet ▶ noun ❶ *a show with puppets* MARIONETTE; glove puppet, hand puppet, finger puppet. ❷ *a puppet of the government* PAWN, tool, instrument, cat's paw, poodle, creature, dupe; mouthpiece, minion, stooge.

purchase ▶ verb *we purchased the software* BUY, pay for, acquire, obtain, pick up, snap up, take, procure; invest in; *informal* get hold of, score.
– OPPOSITES sell.
▶ noun ❶ *he's happy with his purchase* ACQUISITION, buy, investment, order, bargain; shopping, goods. ❷ *he could get no purchase on the wall* GRIP, grasp, hold, foothold, toehold, anchorage, attachment, support; resistance, friction, leverage.
– OPPOSITES sale.

purchaser ▶ noun BUYER, shopper, customer, consumer, patron; *Law* vendee.

pure ▶ adjective ❶ *pure gold* UNADULTERATED, uncontaminated, unmixed, undiluted, unalloyed, unblended; sterling, solid, refined, 100%; clarified, clear, filtered; flawless, perfect, genuine, real. ❷ *the air is so pure* CLEAN, clear, fresh, sparkling, unpolluted, uncontaminated, untainted; wholesome, natural, healthy; sanitary, uninfected, disinfected, germ-free, sterile, sterilized, aseptic. ❸ *pure in body and mind* VIRTUOUS, moral, ethical, good, righteous, saintly, honourable, reputable, wholesome, clean, honest, upright, upstanding, exemplary, irreproachable; chaste, virginal, maidenly; decent, worthy, noble, blameless, guiltless, spotless, unsullied, uncorrupted, undefiled; *informal* squeaky clean. ❹ *pure maths* THEORETICAL, abstract, conceptual, academic, hypothetical, speculative, conjectural. ❺ *three hours of pure magic* SHEER, utter, absolute, out-and-out, complete, total, perfect, unmitigated.
– OPPOSITES adulterated, polluted, immoral, practical.

pure-bred ▶ adjective PEDIGREE, thoroughbred, full-bred, blooded, pedigreed, pure.
– OPPOSITES hybrid.

purely ▶ adverb ENTIRELY, completely, absolutely, wholly, exclusively, solely, only, just, merely.

purgative ▶ adjective *purgative medicine* LAXATIVE, evacuant; *Medicine* aperient; *Medicine, archaic* lenitive.
▶ noun *orris root is a purgative* LAXATIVE, evacuant; *Medicine* aperient; *Medicine, archaic* lenitive; *dated* purge.

purgatory ▶ noun TORMENT, torture, misery, suffering, affliction, anguish, agony, woe, hell; an ordeal, a nightmare.
– OPPOSITES paradise.

purge ▶ verb ❶ *he purged them of their doubt* CLEANSE, clear, purify, wash, shrive, absolve; *rare* lustrate. ❷ *lawbreakers were purged from the army* REMOVE, get rid of, expel, eject, exclude, dismiss, sack, oust, eradicate, clear out, weed out.
▶ noun *the purge of dissidents* REMOVAL, expulsion, ejection, exclusion, eviction, dismissal, sacking, ousting, eradication.

purify ▶ verb ❶ *trees help to purify the air* CLEAN, cleanse, refine, decontaminate; filter, clarify, clear, freshen, deodorize; sanitize, disinfect, sterilize. ❷ *they purify themselves before the ceremony* PURGE, cleanse, unburden, deliver; redeem, shrive, exorcize, sanctify; *rare* lustrate.

purist ▶ noun PEDANT, perfectionist, formalist, literalist, stickler, traditionalist, doctrinaire, quibbler, dogmatist; *informal* nit-picker; *archaic* precisian.

puritan ▶ noun MORALIST, pietist, prude, prig, killjoy; ascetic; *informal* goody-goody, Holy Joe; *N. Amer. informal* bluenose.

puritanical ▶ adjective MORALISTIC, puritan, pietistic, strait-laced, stuffy, prudish, prim, priggish; narrow-minded, sententious, censorious; austere, severe, ascetic, abstemious; *informal* goody-goody, starchy.
– OPPOSITES permissive.

purity ▶ noun ❶ *the purity of our tap water* CLEANNESS, clearness, clarity, freshness; sterility. ❷ *they sought purity in a foul world* VIRTUE, morality, goodness, righteousness, saintliness, piety, honour, honesty, integrity, decency, ethicality, impeccability; innocence, chastity.

purloin ▶ verb (*formal*) STEAL, thieve, rob, take, snatch, pilfer, loot, appropriate; *informal* swipe, nab, rip off, lift, 'liberate', 'borrow', filch, snaffle; *Brit. informal* pinch, half-inch, nick, whip, knock off, nobble; *N. Amer. informal* heist.

purport ▶ verb *this work purports to be authoritative* CLAIM, profess, pretend; appear, seem; be ostensibly, pose as, impersonate, masquerade as, pass for.
▶ noun ❶ *the purport of his remarks* GIST, substance, drift, implication, intention, meaning, significance, sense, essence, thrust, message. ❷ *the purport of the attack* INTENTION, purpose, object, objective, aim, goal, target, end, design, idea.

purpose ▶ noun ❶ *the purpose of his visit* MOTIVE, motivation, grounds, cause, occasion, reason, point, basis, justification. ❷ *their purpose was to subvert the economy* INTENTION, aim, object, objective, goal, end, plan, scheme, target; ambition, aspiration. ❸ *I cannot see any purpose in it* ADVANTAGE, benefit, good, use, value, merit, worth, profit; *informal* mileage, percentage. ❹ *the original purpose of the porch* FUNCTION, role, use. ❺ *they started the game with purpose* DETERMINATION, resolution, resolve, steadfastness, backbone, drive, push, enthusiasm, ambition, motivation, commitment, conviction, dedication; *informal* get-up-and-go.
▶ verb (*formal*) *they purposed to reach the summit* INTEND, mean, aim, plan, design, have the intention; decide, resolve, determine, propose, aspire, set one's sights on.
■ **on purpose** DELIBERATELY, intentionally, purposely, by design, wilfully, knowingly, consciously, of one's own volition; expressly, specifically, especially, specially.

purposeful ▶ adjective DETERMINED, resolute, steadfast, single-minded; enthusiastic, motivated, committed, dedicated, persistent, dogged, unfaltering, unshakeable.
– OPPOSITES aimless.

purposely ▶ adverb. *See* ON PURPOSE at PURPOSE.

purse ▶ noun ❶ *the money fell out of her purse* WALLET, money bag; *N. Amer.* change purse, billfold. ❷ (*N. Amer.*) *a woman's purse. See* HANDBAG. ❸ *the public purse* FUND(S), kitty, coffers, pool, bank, treasury, exchequer, money, finances, wealth, reserves, cash, capital, assets. ❹ *the fight will net him a $75,000 purse* PRIZE, reward, award; winnings, stake(s).
▶ verb *he pursed his lips* PRESS TOGETHER, compress, tighten, pucker, pout.

pursuance ▶ noun (*formal*) ❶ *he was arrested in pursuance of this Act* EXECUTION, discharge, implementation, performance, accomplishment, fulfilment, dispatch, prosecution, enforcement. ❷ *their pursuance of power* SEARCH FOR, pursuit of, quest for, hunt for.

pursue ▶ verb ❶ *I pursued him down the garden* FOLLOW, run after, chase; hunt, stalk, track, trail, shadow, hound, course; *informal* tail. ❷ *pursue the goal of political union* STRIVE FOR, work towards, seek, search for, aim at/for, aspire to. ❸ *he had been pursuing her for weeks* WOO, pay court to, chase, run after; *informal* make up to; *dated* court, make love to, romance, set one's cap at. ❹ *she pursued a political career* ENGAGE IN, be occupied in, practise, follow, prosecute, conduct, ply, take up, undertake, carry on. ❺ *we will not pursue the matter* INVESTIGATE, research, inquire into, look into, examine, scrutinize, analyse, delve into, probe.
– OPPOSITES avoid, shun.

pursuit ▶ noun ❶ *the pursuit of profit* STRIVING TOWARDS, quest after/for, search for; aim, goal, objective, dream. ❷ *a worthwhile pursuit* ACTIVITY, hobby, pastime, diversion, recreation, relaxation, divertissement, amusement; occupation, trade, vocation, business, work, job, employment.

purvey ▶ verb SELL, supply, provide, furnish, cater, retail, deal in, trade, stock, offer; peddle, hawk, tout, traffic in; *informal* flog.

purveyor ▶ noun SELLER, vendor, retailer, supplier, stockist, trader, pedlar, hawker; *Brit.* tout.

pus ▶ noun SUPPURATION, matter; discharge, secretion.
– RELATED TERMS purulent.

push ▶ verb ❶ *she tried to push him away* SHOVE, thrust, propel; send, drive, force, prod, poke, nudge, elbow, shoulder; sweep, bundle, hustle, manhandle. ❷ *she pushed her way into the flat* FORCE, shove, thrust, squeeze, jostle, elbow, shoulder, bundle, hustle; work, inch. ❸ *he pushed the panic button* PRESS, depress, bear down on, hold down, squeeze; operate, activate. ❹ *don't push her to join in* URGE, press, pressure, pressurize, force, impel, coerce, nag; prevail on, browbeat into; *informal* lean on, twist someone's arm, bulldoze. ❺ *they push their own products* ADVERTISE, publicize, promote, bang the drum for; sell, market, merchandise; *informal* plug, hype (up), puff, flog; *N. Amer. informal* ballyhoo.
– OPPOSITES pull.
▶ noun ❶ *I felt a push in the back* SHOVE, thrust, nudge, ram, bump, jolt, butt, prod, poke. ❷ *the enemy's eastward push* ADVANCE, drive, thrust, charge, attack, assault, onslaught, onrush, offensive, sortie, sally, incursion.
■ **at a push** (*Brit. informal*) IF NECESSARY, if need be, if needs must, if all else fails, in an emergency.
■ **push someone around** BULLY, domineer, ride roughshod over, trample on, bulldoze, browbeat, tyrannize, intimidate, threaten, victimize, pick on; *informal* lean on, boss about/around.
■ **push for** DEMAND, call for, request, press for, campaign for, lobby for, speak up for; urge, promote, advocate, champion, espouse.
■ **push off** (*informal*) GO AWAY, depart, leave, get out; go, get moving, be off (with you), shoo; *informal* skedaddle, split, scram, run along, beat it, get lost, shove off, buzz off, clear off, on your bike; *Brit. informal* get stuffed, sling your hook, hop it, bog off, naff off; *N. Amer. informal* bug off, take a powder, take a hike; *Austral./NZ informal* rack off, nick off; *poetic/literary* begone.
■ **push on** PRESS ON, continue one's journey, carry on, advance, proceed, go on, progress, make headway, forge ahead.

pushover ▶ noun ❶ *the teacher was a pushover* WEAKLING, feeble opponent, man of straw; *informal* soft touch, easy touch, easy meat. ❷ *this course is no pushover* EASY TASK, walkover, five-finger exercise, gift; child's play; *informal* doddle, piece of cake, picnic, money for old rope, cinch, breeze; *Brit. informal* doss; *N. Amer. informal* duck soup, snap; *Austral./NZ informal* bludge; *dated* snip.

pushy ▶ adjective ASSERTIVE, self-assertive, overbearing, domineering, aggressive, forceful, forward, bold, bumptious, officious; thrusting, ambitious, overconfident, cocky; *informal* bossy; *dated* pushful.
– OPPOSITES submissive.

pusillanimous ▶ adjective TIMID, timorous, cowardly, fearful, faint-hearted, lily-livered, spineless, craven, shrinking; *informal* chicken, gutless, wimpy, wimpish, sissy, yellow, yellow-bellied.
– OPPOSITES brave.

pussyfoot ▶ verb ❶ *you can't pussyfoot around with this* EQUIVOCATE, tergiversate, be evasive, be non-committal, sidestep the issue, prevaricate, quibble, hedge, beat about the bush; *Brit.* hum and haw; *informal* duck the question, sit on the fence, shilly-shally. ❷ *I had to pussyfoot over the gravel* CREEP, tiptoe, pad, soft-shoe, steal, sneak, slink.

pustule ▶ noun PIMPLE, spot, bleb, boil, swelling, eruption, carbuncle, blister, abscess; *informal* whitehead, zit; *Scottish informal* plook; *technical* comedo, papule.

put ▶ verb ❶ *she put the parcel on a chair* PLACE, set (down), lay (down), deposit, position, settle; leave, plant; *informal* stick, dump, bung, park, plonk, pop; *N. Amer. informal* plunk. ❷ *he didn't want to be put in a category* ASSIGN TO, consign to, allocate to, place in. ❸ *don't put the blame on me* LAY, pin, place, fix; attribute to, impute to, assign to, allocate to, ascribe to. ❹ *the proposals put to the committee* SUBMIT, present, tender, offer, proffer, advance, suggest, propose. ❺ *she put it bluntly* EXPRESS, word, phrase, frame, formulate, render, convey, couch; state, say, utter. ❻ *he put the cost at £8,000* ESTIMATE, calculate, reckon, gauge, assess, evaluate, value, judge, measure, compute, fix, set; *informal* guesstimate.
■ **put about** *the ship put about* TURN ROUND, come about, change course.
■ **put something about** *the rumour had been put about* SPREAD, circulate, make public, disseminate, broadcast, publicize, pass on, propagate, bandy about.
■ **put something across/over** COMMUNICATE, convey, get across/over, explain, make clear, spell out, clarify; get through to someone.
■ **put something aside** ❶ *we've got a bit put aside in the bank* SAVE, put by, set aside, deposit, reserve, store, stockpile, hoard, stow, cache; *informal* salt away, squirrel away, stash away. ❷ *they put aside their differences* DISREGARD, set aside, ignore, forget, discount, bury.
■ **put someone away** (*informal*) ❶ *they put him away for life* JAIL, imprison, put in prison, put behind bars, lock up, incarcerate; *informal* cage; *Brit. informal* bang up, send down; *N. Amer. informal* jug. ❷ *you should be put away!* CERTIFY, commit, hospitalize, institutionalize, put in a psychiatric hospital.

■ **put something away** ❶ *I put away some money. See* PUT SOMETHING ASIDE sense 1. ❷ *she never puts her things away* REPLACE, put back, tidy away, tidy up, clear away. ❸ (*informal*) *she can put away a lot of food. See* EAT sense 1.

■ **put something back** ❶ *he put the books back* REPLACE, return, restore, put away, tidy away. ❷ *they put back the film's release date. See* PUT SOMETHING OFF.

■ **put someone down** ❶ (*informal*) *he often puts me down* CRITICIZE, belittle, disparage, deprecate, denigrate, slight, humiliate, shame, crush, squash, deflate; *informal* show up, cut down to size. ❷ *I put him down as shy* CONSIDER TO BE, judge to be, reckon to be, take to be; regard, have down, take for.

■ **put something down** ❶ *he put his ideas down on paper* WRITE DOWN, note down, jot down, take down, set down; list, record, register, log. ❷ *they put down the rebellion* SUPPRESS, check, crush, quash, squash, quell, overthrow, stamp out, repress, subdue. ❸ *the horse had to be put down* DESTROY, put to sleep, put out of its misery, put to death, kill. ❹ *put it down to the heat* ATTRIBUTE, ascribe, chalk up, impute; blame on.

■ **put something forward**. *See* PUT sense 4.

■ **put in for** APPLY FOR, put in an application for, try for; request, seek, ask for.

■ **put someone off** DETER, discourage, dissuade, daunt, unnerve, intimidate, scare off, repel, repulse; distract, disturb, divert, sidetrack; *informal* turn off.

■ **put something off** POSTPONE, defer, delay, put back, adjourn, hold over, reschedule, shelve, table; *informal* put on ice, put on the back burner.

■ **put it on** PRETEND, play-act, make believe, fake it, go through the motions.

■ **put something on** ❶ *she put on jeans* DRESS IN, don, pull on, throw on, slip into, change into; *informal* doll oneself up in. ❷ *I put the light on* SWITCH ON, turn on, activate. ❸ *they put on an extra train* PROVIDE, lay on, supply, make available. ❹ *the museum put on an exhibition* ORGANIZE, stage, mount, present, produce. ❺ *she put on an American accent* FEIGN, fake, simulate, affect; assume. ❻ *he put a fiver on Oxford United* BET, gamble, stake, wager; place, lay; risk, chance, hazard.

■ **put one over on** (*informal*). *See* HOODWINK.

■ **put someone out** ❶ *Maria was put out by the slur* ANNOY, anger, irritate, offend, affront, displease, irk, vex, pique, nettle, gall, upset; *informal* rile, miff, peeve; *Brit. informal* nark. ❷ *I don't want to put you out* INCONVENIENCE, trouble, bother, impose on, disoblige; *informal* put someone on the spot; *formal* discommode.

■ **put something out** ❶ *firemen put out the blaze* EXTINGUISH, quench, douse, smother; blow out, snuff out. ❷ *he put out a press release* ISSUE, publish, release, bring out, circulate, publicize, post.

■ **put someone up** ❶ *we can put him up for a few days* ACCOMMODATE, house, take in, lodge, quarter, billet; give someone a roof over their head. ❷ *they put up a candidate* NOMINATE, propose, put forward, recommend.

■ **put something up** ❶ *the building was put up 100 years ago* BUILD, construct, erect, raise. ❷ *she put up a poster* DISPLAY, pin up, stick up, hang up, post. ❸ *we put up alternative schemes* PROPOSE, put forward, present, submit, suggest, tender. ❹ *the chancellor put up taxes* INCREASE, raise; *informal* jack up, hike, bump up. ❺ *he put up most of the funding* PROVIDE, supply, furnish, give, contribute, donate, pledge, pay; *informal* fork out, cough up, shell out; *N. Amer. informal* ante up, pony up.

■ **put upon** (*informal*) TAKE ADVANTAGE OF, impose on, exploit, use, misuse; *informal* walk all over.

■ **put someone up to something** (*informal*) PERSUADE TO, encourage to, urge to, egg on to, incite to, goad into.

■ **put up with** TOLERATE, take, stand (for), accept, stomach, swallow, endure, bear, support, take something lying down; *informal* abide, lump it; *Brit. informal* stick, be doing with; *formal* brook; *archaic* suffer.

putative ▶ **adjective** SUPPOSED, assumed, presumed; accepted, recognized; commonly regarded, presumptive, alleged, reputed, reported, rumoured.

put-down ▶ **noun** (*informal*) SNUB, slight, affront, rebuff, sneer, disparagement, humiliation, barb, jibe, criticism; *informal* dig.

putrefy ▶ **verb** DECAY, rot, decompose, go bad, go off, spoil, fester, perish, deteriorate; moulder.

putrid ▶ **adjective** DECOMPOSING, decaying, rotting, rotten, bad, off, putrefied, putrescent, rancid, mouldy; foul, fetid, rank.

puzzle ▶ **verb** ❶ *her decision puzzled me* PERPLEX, confuse, bewilder, bemuse, baffle, mystify, confound, nonplus; *informal* flummox, faze, stump, beat; *N. Amer. informal* discombobulate. ❷ *she puzzled over the problem* THINK HARD ABOUT, mull over, muse over, ponder, contemplate, meditate on, consider, deliberate on, chew over, wonder about. ❸ *she tried to puzzle out what he meant* WORK OUT, understand, comprehend, sort out, reason out, solve, make sense of, make head or tail of, unravel, decipher; *informal* figure out, suss out.

▶ **noun** *the poem has always been a puzzle* ENIGMA, mystery, paradox, conundrum, poser, riddle, problem; *informal* stumper.

puzzled ▶ **adjective** PERPLEXED, confused, bewildered, bemused, baffled, mystified, confounded, nonplussed, at a loss, at sea; *informal* flummoxed, stumped, fazed, clueless; *N. Amer. informal* discombobulated.

puzzling ▶ **adjective** BAFFLING, perplexing, be-

wildering, confusing, complicated, unclear, mysterious, enigmatic, ambiguous, obscure, abstruse, unfathomable, incomprehensible, impenetrable, cryptic.
–OPPOSITES clear.

pygmy ▶ noun ❶ *a Congo pygmy* VERY SMALL PERSON, person of restricted growth, midget, dwarf, homunculus, manikin; Lilliputian; *informal* shrimp. ❷ *an intellectual pygmy* LIGHTWEIGHT, mediocrity, nonentity, nobody, cipher; small fry; *informal* pipsqueak, no-hoper; *Brit. informal* squit; *N. Amer. informal* picayune.
–OPPOSITES giant.

pyromaniac ▶ noun ARSONIST, incendiary; *Brit.* fire-raiser; *informal* firebug, pyro; *N. Amer. informal* torch.

Qq

quack ▶ noun ❶ *a quack selling fake medicines* SWINDLER, charlatan, mountebank, trickster, fraud, fraudster, impostor, hoaxer, sharper; *informal* con man, shark; *Brit. informal* twister; *N. Amer. informal* grifter; *Austral. informal* shicer. ❷ (*Brit. informal*) *get the quack to examine you*. See DOCTOR noun.

quadrangle ▶ noun COURTYARD, quad, court, cloister, precinct; square, plaza, piazza.

quaff ▶ verb DRINK, swallow, gulp (down), guzzle, slurp, down, drain, empty; imbibe, partake of, consume, sup, sip; *informal* sink, kill, glug, swig, swill, slug, knock back, toss off; *Brit. informal* get outside (of), shift, murder, neck; *N. Amer. informal* chug, snarf (down).

quagmire ▶ noun ❶ *the field became a quagmire* SWAMP, morass, bog, marsh, mire, slough; *archaic* quag. ❷ *a judicial quagmire* MUDDLE, mix-up, mess, predicament, mare's nest, quandary, tangle, imbroglio; trouble, confusion, difficulty; *informal* sticky situation, pickle, stew, dilemma, fix, bind.

quail ▶ verb COWER, cringe, flinch, shrink, recoil, shy (away), pull back; shiver, tremble, shake, quake, blench, blanch.

quaint ▶ adjective ❶ *a quaint town* PICTURESQUE, charming, sweet, attractive, old-fashioned, old-world; *Brit.* twee; *N. Amer.* cunning; *pseudo-archaic* olde (worlde). ❷ *quaint customs* UNUSUAL, different, out of the ordinary, curious, eccentric, quirky, bizarre, whimsical, unconventional; *informal* offbeat.
–OPPOSITES ugly, ordinary.

quake ▶ verb ❶ *the ground quaked* SHAKE, tremble, quiver, shudder, sway, rock, wobble, move, heave, convulse. ❷ *we quaked when we saw the soldiers* TREMBLE, shake, quiver, shiver; blench, blanch, flinch, shrink, recoil, cower, cringe.

qualification ▶ noun ❶ *a teaching qualification* CERTIFICATE, diploma, degree, licence, document, warrant; eligibility, acceptability, adequacy; proficiency, skill, ability, capability, aptitude. ❷ *I can't accept it without qualification* MODIFICATION, limitation, reservation, stipulation; alteration, amendment, revision, moderation, mitigation; condition, proviso, caveat.

qualified ▶ adjective CERTIFIED, certificated, chartered, licensed, professional; trained, fit, competent, accomplished, proficient, skilled, experienced, expert.

qualify ▶ verb ❶ *I qualify for free travel* BE ELIGIBLE, meet the requirements; be entitled to, be permitted. ❷ *they qualify as refugees* COUNT, be considered, be designated, be eligible. ❸ *she qualified as a solicitor* BE CERTIFIED, be licensed; pass, graduate, make the grade, succeed, pass muster. ❹ *the course qualified them to teach* AUTHORIZE, empower, allow, permit, license; equip, prepare, train, educate, teach. ❺ *they qualified their findings* MODIFY, limit, restrict, make conditional; moderate, temper, modulate, mitigate.

quality ▶ noun ❶ *a poor quality of signal* STANDARD, grade, class, calibre, condition, character, nature, form, rank, value, level; sort, type, kind, variety. ❷ *work of such quality* EXCELLENCE, superiority, merit, worth, value, virtue, calibre, eminence, distinction, incomparability; talent, skill, virtuosity, craftsmanship. ❸ *her good qualities* FEATURE, trait, attribute, characteristic, point, aspect, facet, side, property.

qualm ▶ noun MISGIVING, doubt, reservation, second thought, worry, concern, anxiety; (**qualms**) hesitation, hesitance, hesitancy, demur, reluctance, disinclination, apprehension, trepidation, unease; scruples, remorse, compunction.

quandary ▶ noun PREDICAMENT, plight, difficult situation, awkward situation; trouble, muddle, mess, confusion, difficulty, mare's nest; *informal* dilemma, sticky situation, pickle, hole, stew, fix, bind, jam.

quantity ▶ noun ❶ *the quantity of food collected* AMOUNT, total, aggregate, sum, quota, mass, weight, volume, bulk; quantum, proportion, portion, part. ❷ *a quantity of ammunition* AMOUNT, lot, great deal, good deal, an abundance, a wealth, a profusion, plenty; *informal* piles, oodles, tons, lots, loads, heaps, masses, stacks, bags; *Brit. informal* shedloads.

quarrel ▶ noun *they had a quarrel about money* ARGUMENT, disagreement, squabble, fight, dispute, wrangle, clash, altercation, feud, contretemps, disputation, falling-out, war of words, shouting match; *informal* tiff, slanging match, run-in; *Brit. informal* barney, row, bust-up.

▶ verb *don't quarrel over it* ARGUE, fight, disagree, fall out; differ, be at odds; bicker, squabble, cross swords, lock horns, be at each other's throats; *informal* argufy; *Brit. informal* row.

■ **quarrel with** *you can't quarrel with the verdict* FAULT, criticize, object to, oppose, take exception to; attack, take issue with, impugn, contradict, dispute, controvert; *informal* knock; *formal* gainsay.

quarrelsome ▶ adjective ARGUMENTATIVE, disputatious, confrontational, captious, pugnacious, combative, antagonistic, bellicose, belligerent, cantankerous, choleric; *Brit. informal* stroppy; *N. Amer. informal* scrappy.

– OPPOSITES peaceable.

quarry ▶ noun PREY, victim; object, goal, target; kill, game.

quarter ▶ noun ❶ *the Latin quarter* DISTRICT, area, region, part, side, neighbourhood, precinct, locality, sector, zone; ghetto, community, enclave. ❷ *help from an unexpected quarter* SOURCE, direction, place, location; person. ❸ *the servants' quarters* ACCOMMODATION, lodgings, rooms, chambers; home; *informal* pad, digs; *formal* abode, residence, domicile. ❹ *the riot squads gave no quarter* MERCY, leniency, clemency, lenity, compassion, pity, charity, sympathy, tolerance.

▶ verb ❶ *they were quartered in a villa* ACCOMMODATE, house, board, lodge, put up, take in, install, shelter; *Military* billet. ❷ *I quartered the streets* PATROL, range over, tour, reconnoitre, traverse, survey, scout; *Brit. informal* recce.

quash ▶ verb ❶ *he may quash the sentence* CANCEL, reverse, rescind, repeal, revoke, retract, countermand, withdraw, overturn, overrule, veto, annul, nullify, invalidate, negate, void; *Law* vacate; *formal* abrogate. ❷ *we want to quash these rumours* PUT AN END TO, put a stop to, stamp out, crush, put down, check, curb, nip in the bud, squash, quell, subdue, suppress, extinguish, stifle; *informal* squelch, put the kibosh on.

– OPPOSITES validate.

quasi- ▶ combining form ❶ *quasi-scientific* SUPPOSEDLY, seemingly, apparently, allegedly, ostensibly, on the face of it, on the surface, to all intents and purposes, outwardly, superficially, purportedly, nominally; pseudo-. ❷ *a quasi-autonomous organization* PARTLY, partially, part, to a certain extent, to some extent, half, relatively, comparatively, (up) to a point; almost, nearly, just about, all but.

quaver ▶ verb TREMBLE, waver, quiver, shake, vibrate, oscillate, fluctuate, falter, warble.

quay ▶ noun WHARF, pier, jetty, landing stage, berth; marina, dock, harbour.

queasy ▶ adjective NAUSEOUS, nauseated, bilious, sick; ill, unwell, poorly, green about the gills; *Brit.* off colour.

queen ▶ noun ❶ *the Queen was crowned* MONARCH, sovereign, ruler, head of state; Her Majesty; king's consort, queen consort. ❷ (*informal*) *the queen of soul music* DOYENNE, star, superstar, leading light, big name, queen bee, prima donna, idol, heroine, favourite, darling, goddess.

queer ▶ adjective ❶ *it seemed queer to see him here* ODD, strange, unusual, funny, peculiar, curious, bizarre, weird, uncanny, freakish, eerie, unnatural; unconventional, unorthodox, unexpected, unfamiliar, abnormal, anomalous, atypical, untypical, out of the ordinary, incongruous, irregular; puzzling, perplexing, baffling, unaccountable; *informal* fishy, creepy, spooky, freaky; *Brit. informal* rum. ❷ (*Brit. informal, dated*) *the pills made her feel queer. See* ILL adjective sense 1.

– OPPOSITES normal, well.

▶ verb *he queered the whole deal* SPOIL, ruin, wreck, destroy, scotch, disrupt, undo, thwart, foil, blight, cripple, jeopardize, threaten, undermine, compromise; *informal* botch, blow, put the kibosh on; *Brit. informal* scupper.

quell ▶ verb ❶ *troops quelled the unrest* PUT AN END TO, put a stop to, end, crush, put down, check, crack down on, curb, nip in the bud, squash, quash, subdue, suppress, overcome; *informal* squelch. ❷ *he quelled his misgivings* CALM, soothe, pacify, settle, quieten, quiet, silence, allay, assuage, mitigate, moderate; *poetic/literary* stay.

quench ▶ verb ❶ *they quenched their thirst* SATISFY, slake, sate, satiate, gratify, relieve, assuage, take the edge off, indulge; lessen, reduce, diminish, check, suppress, extinguish, overcome. ❷ *the flames were quenched* EXTINGUISH, put out, snuff out, smother, douse.

querulous ▶ adjective PETULANT, peevish, pettish, complaining, fractious, fretful, irritable, testy, tetchy, cross, snappish, crabby, crotchety, cantankerous, miserable, moody, grumpy, bad-tempered, sullen, sulky, sour, churlish; *informal* snappy, grouchy, whingy; *Brit. informal* ratty, cranky; *N. English informal* mardy; *N. Amer. informal* soreheaded.

query ▶ noun ❶ *we are happy to answer any queries* QUESTION, enquiry; *Brit. informal* quiz. ❷ *there was a query as to who owned the hotel* DOUBT, uncertainty, question (mark), reservation; scepticism.

▶ **verb** ❶ *'Why do that?' queried Isobel* ASK, enquire, question; *Brit. informal* quiz. ❷ *folk may query his credentials* QUESTION, call into question, challenge, dispute, cast aspersions on, doubt, have suspicions about, have reservations about.

quest ▶ **noun** ❶ *their quest for her killer* SEARCH, hunt; pursuance of. ❷ *Sir Galahad's quest* EXPEDITION, journey, voyage, trek, travels, odyssey, adventure, exploration, search; crusade, mission, pilgrimage.

■ **in quest of** IN SEARCH OF, in pursuit of, seeking, looking for, on the lookout for, after.

question ▶ **noun** ❶ *please answer my question* ENQUIRY, query; interrogation; *Brit. informal* quiz. ❷ *there is no question that he is ill* DOUBT, dispute, argument, debate, uncertainty, dubiousness, reservation; *formal* dubiety. ❸ *the political questions of the day* ISSUE, matter, business, problem, concern, topic, theme, case; debate, argument, dispute, controversy.

– RELATED TERMS interrogative.

– OPPOSITES answer, certainty.

▶ **verb** ❶ *the magistrate questions the suspect* INTERROGATE, cross-examine, cross-question, quiz, catechize; interview, debrief, examine, give the third degree to; *informal* grill, pump. ❷ *she questioned his motives* QUERY, call into question, challenge, dispute, cast aspersions on, doubt, suspect, have suspicions about, have reservations about.

■ **beyond question** ❶ *her loyalty is beyond question* UNDOUBTED, beyond doubt, certain, indubitable, indisputable, incontrovertible, unquestionable, undeniable, clear, patent, manifest. ❷ *the results demonstrated this beyond question* INDISPUTABLY, irrefutably, incontestably, incontrovertibly, unquestionably, undeniably, undoubtedly, beyond doubt, without doubt, clearly, patently, obviously.

■ **in question** AT ISSUE, under discussion, under consideration, on the agenda, to be decided.

■ **out of the question** IMPOSSIBLE, impracticable, unfeasible, unworkable, inconceivable, unimaginable, unrealizable, unsuitable; *informal* not on.

questionable ▶ **adjective** ❶ *jokes of questionable taste* CONTROVERSIAL, contentious, doubtful, dubious, uncertain, debatable, arguable; unverified, unprovable, unresolved, unconvincing, implausible, improbable; borderline, marginal, moot; *informal* iffy; *Brit. informal* dodgy. ❷ *questionable financial dealings* SUSPICIOUS, suspect, dubious, irregular, odd, strange, murky, dark, unsavoury, disreputable; *informal* funny, fishy, shady, iffy; *Brit. informal* dodgy.

– OPPOSITES indisputable, honest.

questionnaire ▶ **noun** QUESTION SHEET, survey form, opinion poll; test, exam, examination, quiz; *Medicine* questionary.

queue ▶ **noun** ❶ *a queue of people* LINE, row, column, file, chain, string; procession, train, cavalcade; waiting list; *N. Amer.* wait list; *Brit. informal* crocodile. ❷ *a traffic queue* (TRAFFIC) JAM, tailback, gridlock; *N. Amer.* back-up; *informal* snarl-up.

▶ **verb** *we queued for ice creams* LINE UP, form a queue, queue up, wait in line, form a line, fall in.

quibble ▶ **noun** *I have just one quibble* CRITICISM, objection, complaint, protest, argument, exception, grumble, grouse, cavil; *informal* niggle, moan, gripe, beef, grouch.

▶ **verb** *no one quibbled with the title* OBJECT TO, find fault with, complain about, cavil at; split hairs, chop logic; criticize, query, fault, pick holes in; *informal* nit-pick; *archaic* pettifog.

quick ▶ **adjective** ❶ *a quick worker* FAST, swift, rapid, speedy, high-speed, expeditious, brisk, smart; lightning, whirlwind, fast-track, whistle-stop, breakneck; *informal* nippy, zippy; *poetic/literary* fleet. ❷ *she took a quick look* HASTY, hurried, cursory, perfunctory, desultory, superficial, summary; brief, short, fleeting, transient, transitory, short-lived, lightning, momentary. ❸ *a quick end to the recession* SUDDEN, instantaneous, immediate, instant, abrupt, precipitate. ❹ *she isn't as quick as the others* INTELLIGENT, bright, clever, gifted, able, astute, quick-witted, sharp-witted, smart; observant, alert, sharp, perceptive; *informal* brainy, on the ball, quick on the uptake.

– OPPOSITES slow, long.

quicken ▶ **verb** ❶ *she quickened her pace* SPEED UP, accelerate, step up, hasten, hurry (up); *informal* gee up. ❷ *the film quickened his interest in nature* STIMULATE, excite, arouse, rouse, stir up, activate, galvanize, whet, inspire, kindle; invigorate, revive, revitalize.

quickly ▶ **adverb** ❶ *he walked quickly* FAST, swiftly, briskly, rapidly, speedily, at the speed of light, at full tilt, as fast as one's legs can carry one, at a gallop, at the double, post-haste, hotfoot; *informal* double quick, p.d.q. (pretty damn quick), like (greased) lightning, hell for leather, like mad, like blazes, like the wind; *Brit. informal* like the clappers, like billy-o; *N. Amer. informal* lickety-split; *poetic/literary* apace. ❷ *you'd better leave quickly* IMMEDIATELY, directly, at once, now, straight away, right away, instantly, forthwith, without delay, without further ado; soon, promptly, early; *N. Amer.* momentarily; *informal* like a shot, a.s.a.p. (as soon as possible), pronto, before you can say Jack Robinson, straight off. ❸ *he quickly inspected it* BRIEFLY, fleetingly, briskly; hastily, hurriedly, cursorily, perfunctorily, superficially, desultorily.

quick-tempered ▶ **adjective** IRRITABLE, irascible, hot-tempered, short-tempered, snappish, fiery, touchy, volatile; cross, crabby, crotchety, cantankerous, grumpy, ill-tempered, bad-tempered, testy, tetchy, prickly, choleric; *informal* snappy, chippy, grouchy,

cranky, on a short fuse; *Brit. informal* narky, ratty, eggy, like a bear with a sore head; *N. Amer. informal* soreheaded.
– OPPOSITES placid.

quick-witted ▶ **adjective** INTELLIGENT, bright, clever, gifted, able, astute, quick, smart, sharp-witted; observant, alert, sharp, perceptive; *informal* brainy, on the ball, quick on the uptake.
– OPPOSITES slow.

quid pro quo ▶ **noun** EXCHANGE, trade, trade-off, swap, switch, barter, substitute, reciprocation, return; amends, compensation, recompense, restitution, reparation.

quiescent ▶ **adjective** INACTIVE, inert, idle, dormant, at rest, inoperative, deactivated, quiet; still, motionless, immobile, passive.
– OPPOSITES active.

quiet ▶ **adjective** ❶ *the whole pub went quiet* SILENT, still, hushed, noiseless, soundless; mute, dumb, speechless. ❷ *a quiet voice* SOFT, low, muted, muffled, faint, indistinct, inaudible, hushed, whispered, suppressed. ❸ *a quiet village* PEACEFUL, sleepy, tranquil, calm, still, restful, undisturbed, untroubled; unfrequented. ❹ *can I have a quiet word?* PRIVATE, confidential, secret, discreet, unofficial, off the record, between ourselves. ❺ *quiet colours* UNOBTRUSIVE, restrained, muted, understated, subdued, subtle, low-key; soft, pale, pastel. ❻ *you can't keep it quiet for long* SECRET, confidential, classified, unrevealed, undisclosed, unknown, under wraps; *informal* hush-hush, mum; *formal* sub rosa. ❼ *business is quiet* SLOW, stagnant, slack, sluggish, inactive, idle.
– OPPOSITES loud, busy, public.
▶ **noun** *the quiet of the countryside* PEACEFULNESS, peace, restfulness, calm, tranquillity, serenity; silence, quietness, stillness, still, quietude, hush, soundlessness.

quieten ▶ **verb** ❶ *quieten the children down* SILENCE, hush, shush, quiet; *informal* shut up. ❷ *her companions quietened* FALL SILENT, stop talking, break off, shush, hold one's tongue; *informal* shut up, clam up, shut it, pipe down, shut one's mouth, put a sock in it, button it. ❸ *he tried to quieten manic patients* PACIFY, calm (down), soothe, subdue, tranquillize, relax, comfort, compose.

quietly ▶ **adverb** ❶ *she quietly entered the room* SILENTLY, in silence, noiselessly, soundlessly, inaudibly; mutely, dumbly. ❷ *he spoke quietly* SOFTLY, in a low voice, in a whisper, in a murmur, under one's breath, in an undertone, sotto voce, gently, faintly, weakly, feebly. ❸ *some bonds were sold quietly* DISCREETLY, privately, confidentially, secretly, unofficially, off the record. ❹ *she is quietly confident* CALMLY, patiently, placidly, serenely.

quilt ▶ **noun** DUVET, cover(s); *Brit.* eiderdown; *N. Amer.* comforter, puff; *Austral. trademark* Doona.

quintessence ▶ **noun** ❶ *it's the quintessence of the modern home* PERFECT EXAMPLE, exemplar, prototype, stereotype, picture, epitome, embodiment, ideal; best, pick, prime, acme, crème de la crème. ❷ *the quintessence of intelligence* ESSENCE, soul, spirit, nature, core, heart, crux, kernel, marrow, substance; *informal* nitty-gritty; *Philosophy* quiddity, esse.

quintessential ▶ **adjective** TYPICAL, prototypical, stereotypical, archetypal, classic, model, standard, stock, representative, conventional; ideal, consummate, exemplary, best, ultimate.

quip ▶ **noun** *the quip provoked a smile* JOKE, witty remark, witticism, jest, pun, sally, pleasantry, bon mot; *informal* one-liner, gag, crack, wisecrack, funny.
▶ **verb** *'Enjoy your trip?' he quipped* JOKE, jest, pun, sally; *informal* gag, wisecrack.

quirk ▶ **noun** ❶ *they all know his quirks* IDIOSYNCRASY, peculiarity, oddity, eccentricity, foible, whim, vagary, caprice, fancy, crotchet, habit, characteristic, trait, fad; *informal* hang-up. ❷ *a quirk of fate* CHANCE, fluke, freak, anomaly, twist.

quirky ▶ **adjective** ECCENTRIC, idiosyncratic, unconventional, unorthodox, unusual, strange, bizarre, peculiar, odd, outlandish, zany; *informal* wacky, freaky, kinky, way-out, far out, kooky, offbeat.
– OPPOSITES conventional.

quisling ▶ **noun** COLLABORATOR, fraternizer, colluder, sympathizer; traitor, turncoat, backstabber, double-crosser, defector, Judas, snake in the grass, fifth columnist.

quit ▶ **verb** ❶ *he quit the office at 12.30* LEAVE, vacate, exit, depart from, withdraw from; abandon, desert. ❷ (*informal*) *he's decided to quit his job* RESIGN FROM, leave, give up, hand in one's notice, stand down from, relinquish, vacate, walk out on, retire from; *informal* chuck, pack in. ❸ (*informal*) *quit living in the past* GIVE UP, stop, cease, discontinue, drop, break off, abandon, abstain from, desist from, refrain from, avoid, forgo; *informal* pack (it) in, leave off.

quite ▶ **adverb** ❶ *two quite different types* COMPLETELY, entirely, totally, wholly, absolutely, utterly, thoroughly, altogether. ❷ *red hair was quite common* FAIRLY, rather, somewhat, slightly, relatively, comparatively, moderately, reasonably, to a certain extent; *informal* pretty, kind of, sort of.

quiver ▶ **verb** ❶ *I quivered with terror* TREMBLE, shake, shiver, quaver, quake, shudder. ❷ *the bird quivers its wings* FLUTTER, flap, beat, agitate, vibrate.
▶ **noun** *a quiver in her voice* TREMOR, tremble, shake, quaver, flutter, fluctuation, waver.

quixotic ▶ **adjective** IDEALISTIC, romantic, visionary, Utopian, extravagant, starry-eyed, unrealistic, unworldly; impracticable, unworkable, impossible.

quiz ▶ **noun** ❶ *a music quiz* COMPETITION, test of knowledge. ❷ (*informal*) *jockey faces quiz over*

bribes INTERROGATION, questioning, interview, examination, the third degree; *informal* grilling.
▶ **verb** *a man was being quizzed by police* QUESTION, interrogate, cross-examine, cross-question, interview, sound out, give someone the third degree; *informal* grill, pump.

quizzical ▶ **adjective** ENQUIRING, questioning, curious; puzzled, perplexed, baffled, mystified; amused, mocking, teasing.

quota ▶ **noun** ALLOCATION, share, allowance, limit, ration, portion, dispensation, slice (of the cake); percentage, commission; proportion, fraction, bit, amount, quantity; *informal* cut, rake-off; *Brit. informal* whack.

quotation ▶ **noun** ❶ *a quotation from Dryden* CITATION, quote, excerpt, extract, passage, line, paragraph, verse, phrase; reference, allusion; *N. Amer.* cite. ❷ *a quotation for the building work* ESTIMATE, quote, price, tender, bid, costing, charge, figure.

quote ▶ **verb** ❶ *he quoted a sentence from the book* RECITE, repeat, reproduce, retell, echo, iterate; take, extract. ❷ *she quoted one case in which a girl died* CITE, mention, refer to, name, instance, specify, identify; relate, recount; allude to, point out, present, offer, advance.
▶ **noun** ❶ *a Shakespeare quote. See* QUOTATION sense 1. ❷ *ask the contractor for a quote. See* QUOTATION sense 2.

quotidian ▶ **adjective** ❶ *the quotidian routine* DAILY, everyday, day-to-day, diurnal. ❷ *her dreadfully quotidian car* ORDINARY, average, run-of-the-mill, everyday, standard, typical, middle-of-the-road, common, conventional, mainstream, unremarkable, unexceptional, workaday, commonplace, mundane, uninteresting; *informal* bog-standard, nothing to write home about, a dime a dozen; *Brit. informal* common or garden.
– OPPOSITES unusual.

Rr

rabbit ▶ **noun** buck, doe; *Brit.* coney; *informal* bunny.

rabble ▶ **noun** ❶ *a rabble of noisy youths* MOB, crowd, throng, gang, swarm, horde, pack, mass, group. ❷ *rule by the rabble* THE COMMON PEOPLE, the masses, the populace, the multitude, the rank and file, the commonality, the commonalty, the plebeians, the proletariat, the peasantry, the hoi polloi, the lower classes, the riff-raff; *informal* the proles, the plebs.
– OPPOSITES nobility.

rabble-rouser ▶ **noun** AGITATOR, troublemaker, instigator, firebrand, revolutionary, demagogue.

rabid ▶ **adjective** ❶ *a rabid dog* rabies-infected, mad. ❷ *a rabid anti-royalist* EXTREME, fanatical, overzealous, extremist, maniacal, passionate, fervent, diehard, uncompromising, illiberal; *informal* gung-ho.
– OPPOSITES moderate.

race[1] ▶ **noun** ❶ *Dave won the race* CONTEST, competition, event, fixture, heat, trial(s). ❷ *the race for naval domination* COMPETITION, rivalry, contention; quest. ❸ *the mill race* CHANNEL, waterway, conduit, sluice, spillway.
▶ **verb** ❶ *he will race in the final* COMPETE, contend; run. ❷ *Claire raced after him* HURRY, dash, rush, run, sprint, bolt, dart, gallop, career, charge, shoot, hurtle, hare, fly, speed, scurry; *informal* tear, belt, pelt, scoot, hotfoot it, leg it; *Brit. informal* bomb; *N. Amer. informal* hightail it. ❸ *her heart was racing* POUND, beat rapidly, throb, pulsate, thud, thump, hammer, palpitate, flutter, pitter-patter, quiver, pump.

race[2] ▶ **noun** ❶ *pupils of many different races* ETHNIC GROUP, racial type, (ethnic) origin. ❷ *a bloodthirsty race* PEOPLE, nation.

racial ▶ **adjective** ETHNIC, ethnological, race-related; cultural, national, tribal.

racism ▶ **noun** RACIAL DISCRIMINATION, racialism, racial prejudice, xenophobia, chauvinism, bigotry; anti-Semitism.

racist ▶ **noun** *he was exposed as a racist* RACIAL BIGOT, racialist, xenophobe, chauvinist; anti-Semite.
▶ **adjective** *a racist society* (RACIALLY) DISCRIMINATORY, racialist, prejudiced, bigoted; anti-Semitic.

rack ▶ **noun** *put the cake on a wire rack* FRAME, framework, stand, holder, trestle, support, shelf.
▶ **verb** *she was racked with guilt* TORMENT, afflict, torture, agonize, harrow; plague, bedevil, persecute, trouble, worry.
■ **on the rack** UNDER PRESSURE, under stress, under a strain, in distress; in trouble, in difficulties, having problems.
■ **rack one's brains** THINK HARD, concentrate, cudgel one's brains; *informal* scratch one's head.

racket ▶ noun ❶ *the engine makes such a racket* NOISE, din, hubbub, clamour, uproar, tumult, commotion, rumpus, pandemonium, babel; *informal* hullabaloo; *Brit. informal* row. ❷ (*informal*) *a gold-smuggling racket* ILLEGAL SCHEME, fraud, swindle; *informal* rip-off; *N. Amer. informal* shakedown.

raconteur ▶ noun STORYTELLER, narrator, anecdotalist; *Austral. informal* magsman.

racy ▶ adjective RISQUÉ, suggestive, naughty, sexy, spicy, ribald; indecorous, indecent, immodest, off colour, dirty, rude, smutty, crude, salacious; *N. Amer.* gamy; *informal* raunchy, blue; *Brit. informal* saucy; *euphemistic* adult.
– OPPOSITES prim.

raddled ▶ adjective HAGGARD, gaunt, drawn, tired, fatigued, drained, exhausted, worn out, washed out; unwell, unhealthy; *informal* the worse for wear.

radiance ▶ noun ❶ *the radiance of the sun* LIGHT, brightness, brilliance, luminosity, beams, rays, illumination, blaze, glow, gleam, lustre, glare; luminescence, incandescence. ❷ *her face flooded with radiance* JOY, elation, jubilance, ecstasy, rapture, euphoria, delirium, happiness, delight, pleasure.

radiant ▶ adjective ❶ *the radiant moon* SHINING, bright, illuminated, brilliant, gleaming, glowing, ablaze, luminous, luminescent, lustrous, incandescent, dazzling, shimmering; *archaic* splendent. ❷ *she looked radiant* JOYFUL, elated, thrilled, overjoyed, jubilant, rapturous, ecstatic, euphoric, in seventh heaven, on cloud nine, delighted, very happy; *informal* on top of the world, over the moon; *Austral. informal* wrapped.
– OPPOSITES dark, gloomy.

radiate ▶ verb ❶ *the stars radiate energy* EMIT, give off, give out, discharge, diffuse; shed, cast. ❷ *light radiated from the hall* SHINE, beam, emanate. ❸ *their faces radiate hope* DISPLAY, show, exhibit; emanate, breathe, be a picture of. ❹ *four spokes radiate from the hub* FAN OUT, spread out, branch out/off, extend, issue.

radical ▶ adjective ❶ *radical reform* THOROUGHGOING, thorough, complete, total, comprehensive, exhaustive, sweeping, far-reaching, wide-ranging, extensive, profound, major, stringent, rigorous. ❷ *radical differences between the two theories* FUNDAMENTAL, basic, essential, quintessential; structural, deep-seated, intrinsic, organic, constitutive. ❸ *a radical political movement* REVOLUTIONARY, progressive, reformist, revisionist, progressivist; extreme, extremist, fanatical, militant, diehard.
– OPPOSITES superficial, minor, conservative.
▶ noun *the arrested man was a radical* REVOLUTIONARY, progressive, reformer, revisionist; militant, zealot, extremist, fanatic, diehard; *informal* ultra.
– OPPOSITES conservative.

raffish ▶ adjective RAKISH, unconventional, bohemian; devil-may-care, casual, careless; louche, disreputable, dissolute, decadent.

raffle ▶ noun LOTTERY, (prize) draw, sweepstake, sweep, tombola; *N. Amer.* lotto.

rag[1] ▶ noun ❶ *an oily rag* CLOTH, scrap of cloth; *N. Amer. informal* schmatte. ❷ *a man dressed in rags* TATTERS, torn clothing, old clothes; cast-offs, hand-me-downs.

rag[2] ▶ noun (*Brit.*) *the student rag* FUND-RAISING EVENT, charity event, charitable event.
▶ verb (*informal*) *he was ragged mercilessly. See* TEASE.

ragamuffin ▶ noun URCHIN, waif, guttersnipe; *informal* scarecrow; *dated* gamin(e).

ragbag ▶ noun JUMBLE, hotchpotch, mishmash, mess, hash; assortment, mixture, miscellany, medley, mixed bag, melange, variety, diversity, pot-pourri; *N. Amer.* hodgepodge.

rage ▶ noun ❶ *his rage is due to frustration* FURY, anger, wrath, outrage, indignation, temper, spleen, resentment, pique, annoyance, vexation, displeasure; pet, tantrum, (bad) mood; *informal* grump, strop; *poetic/literary* ire, choler. ❷ *the current rage for DIY* CRAZE, passion, fashion, taste, trend, vogue, fad, enthusiasm, obsession, compulsion, fixation, fetish, mania, preoccupation; *informal* thing.
▶ verb ❶ *she raged silently* BE ANGRY, be furious, be enraged, be incensed, seethe, be beside oneself, rave, storm, fume, spit; *informal* be livid, be wild, foam at the mouth, have a fit, be steamed up. ❷ *he raged against the reforms* PROTEST ABOUT, complain about, oppose, denounce; fulminate, storm, rail; *informal* kick up a stink about. ❸ *a storm was raging* BE VIOLENT, be turbulent, be tempestuous; thunder, rampage.
■ **(all) the rage** POPULAR, fashionable, in fashion, in vogue, the (latest) thing, in great demand, sought-after, le dernier cri; *informal* in, the in thing, cool, big, trendy, hot, hip.

ragged ▶ adjective ❶ *ragged jeans* TATTERED, in tatters, torn, ripped, holey, in holes, moth-eaten, frayed, worn (out), falling to pieces, threadbare, scruffy, shabby; *informal* tatty. ❷ *a ragged child* SHABBY, scruffy, down at heel, unkempt, dressed in rags. ❸ *a ragged coastline* JAGGED, craggy, rugged, uneven, rough, irregular; serrated, sawtooth, indented; *technical* crenulate, crenulated.
– OPPOSITES smart.

raging ▶ adjective ❶ *a raging mob* ANGRY, furious, enraged, incensed, infuriated, irate, fuming, seething, ranting; *informal* livid, wild; *poetic/literary* wrathful. ❷ *raging seas* STORMY, violent, wild, turbulent, tempestuous. ❸ *a raging headache* EXCRUCIATING, agonizing, painful, throbbing, acute, bad. ❹ *her raging thirst* SEVERE, extreme, great, excessive.

raid ▶ noun ❶ *the raid on Dieppe* ATTACK, assault, descent, blitz, incursion, sortie; onslaught, storming, charge, offensive, invasion, blitzkrieg. ❷ *a raid on a shop* ROBBERY, burglary, hold-up, break-in, ram raid; looting, plunder; *informal* smash-and-grab, stick-up; *Brit. informal* blag; *N. Amer. informal* heist. ❸ *a police raid on the flat* SWOOP, search; *N. Amer. informal* bust, takedown.

▶ **verb** ❶ *they raided shipping in the harbour* ATTACK, assault, set upon, descend on, swoop on, blitz, assail, storm, rush. ❷ *armed men raided the store* ROB, hold up, break into; plunder, steal from, pillage, loot, ransack, sack; *informal* stick up. ❸ *homes were raided by police* SEARCH, swoop on; *N. Amer. informal* bust.

raider ▶ **noun** ROBBER, burglar, thief, housebreaker, plunderer, pillager, looter, marauder; attacker, assailant, invader.

rail ▶ **verb** *he rails against injustice* PROTEST, fulminate, inveigh, rage, speak out, make a stand; expostulate about, criticize, denounce, condemn; object to, oppose, complain about, challenge; *informal* kick up a fuss about.

railing ▶ **noun** FENCE, fencing, rail(s), paling, palisade, balustrade, banister, hurdle.

raillery ▶ **noun** TEASING, mockery, chaff, ragging; banter, badinage; *informal* leg-pulling, ribbing, kidding; *N. Amer. informal* josh.

rain ▶ **noun** ❶ *the rain had stopped* RAINFALL, precipitation, raindrops, wet weather; drizzle, mizzle, shower, rainstorm, cloudburst, torrent, downpour, deluge, storm. ❷ *a rain of hot ash* SHOWER, deluge, flood, torrent, avalanche, flurry; storm, hail.

– RELATED TERMS pluvial.

▶ **verb** ❶ *it rained heavily* POUR (DOWN), pelt down, tip down, teem down, beat down, lash down, sheet down, rain cats and dogs; fall, drizzle, spit; *informal* be chucking it down; *Brit. informal* bucket down. ❷ *bombs rained on the city* FALL, hail, drop, shower.

rainy ▶ **adjective** WET, showery, drizzly, damp, inclement.

raise ▶ **verb** ❶ *he raised a hand in greeting* LIFT (UP), hold aloft, elevate, uplift, upraise, upthrust; hoist, haul up, hitch up; *Brit. informal* hoick up. ❷ *he raised himself in the bed* SET UPRIGHT, set vertical; sit up, stand up. ❸ *they raised prices* INCREASE, put up, push up, up, mark up, escalate, inflate; *informal* hike (up), jack up, bump up. ❹ *he raised his voice* AMPLIFY, louden, magnify, intensify, boost, lift, increase, heighten, augment. ❺ *the temple was raised in 900 BC* BUILD, construct, erect, assemble, put up. ❻ *how will you raise the money?* GET, obtain, acquire; accumulate, amass, collect, fetch, net, make. ❼ *the city raised troops to fight for them* RECRUIT, enlist, sign up, conscript, call up, mobilize, rally, assemble; *US* draft. ❽ *a tax raised on imports* LEVY, impose, exact, demand, charge. ❾ *he raised several objections* BRING UP, air, ventilate; present, table, propose, submit, advance, suggest, moot, put forward. ❿ *the disaster raised doubts about safety* GIVE RISE TO, occasion, cause, produce, engender, elicit, create, result in, lead to, prompt, awaken, arouse, induce, kindle, incite, stir up, trigger, spark off, provoke, instigate, foment, whip up; *poetic/literary* beget. ⓫ *most parents raise their children well* BRING UP, rear, nurture, look after, care for, provide for, mother, parent, tend, cherish; educate, train. ⓬ *he raised cattle* BREED, rear, nurture, keep, tend; grow, farm, cultivate, produce. ⓭ *he was raised to the peerage* PROMOTE, advance, upgrade, elevate, ennoble; *informal* kick upstairs; *archaic* prefer. ⓮ (*Brit. informal*) *raise them on the radio* CONTACT, get hold of, reach, get in touch with, communicate with, call.

– OPPOSITES lower, reduce, demolish.

▶ **noun** *the workers wanted a raise* PAY RISE, pay increase, increment.

■ **raise hell** (*informal*). *See* HELL.

raised ▶ **adjective** EMBOSSED, relief, relievo, die-stamped.

rake[1] ▶ **verb** ❶ *he raked the leaves into a pile* SCRAPE UP, collect, gather. ❷ *she raked the gravel* SMOOTH (OUT), level, even out, flatten, comb. ❸ *the cat raked his arm with its claws* SCRATCH, lacerate, scrape, rasp, graze, grate; *Medicine* excoriate. ❹ *she raked a hand through her hair* DRAG, pull, scrape, tug, comb. ❺ *I raked through my pockets* RUMMAGE, search, hunt, sift, rifle. ❻ *machine-gun fire raked the streets* SWEEP, enfilade, pepper, strafe.

■ **rake something in** (*informal*) EARN, make, get, gain, obtain, acquire, accumulate, bring in, pull in, pocket, realize, fetch, return, yield, raise, net, gross.

■ **rake something up** REMIND PEOPLE OF, recollect, remember, call to mind; drag up, dredge up.

rake[2] ▶ **noun** *he was something of a rake* PLAYBOY, libertine, profligate; degenerate, roué, debauchee; lecher, seducer, womanizer, philanderer, adulterer, Don Juan, Lothario, Casanova; *informal* ladykiller, ladies' man, lech.

rake-off ▶ **noun** (*informal*). *See* CUT noun sense 3.

rakish ▶ **adjective** DASHING, debonair, stylish, jaunty, devil-may-care; raffish, disreputable, louche; *informal* sharp.

rally ▶ **verb** ❶ *the troops rallied and held their ground* REGROUP, reassemble, re-form, reunite. ❷ *he rallied an army* MUSTER, marshal, mobilize, raise, call up, recruit, enlist, conscript; assemble, gather, round up; *US* draft; *formal* convoke. ❸ *ministers rallied to denounce the rumours* GET TOGETHER, band together, assemble, join forces, unite, ally, collaborate, cooperate, pull together. ❹ *share prices rallied* RECOVER, improve, get better, pick up, revive, bounce back, perk up, look up, turn a corner.

– OPPOSITES disperse, disband, slump.

▶ **noun** ❶ *a rally in support of the strike* (MASS) MEETING, gathering, assembly; demonstration, (protest) march; *informal* demo. ❷ *a rally in oil prices*

RECOVERY, upturn, improvement, comeback, resurgence; *Stock Exchange* dead cat bounce.
– OPPOSITES slump.

ram ▶ **verb** ❶ *he rammed his sword into its sheath* FORCE, thrust, plunge, stab, push, sink, dig, stick, cram, jam, stuff, pack. ❷ *a van rammed the police car* HIT, strike, crash into, collide with, impact, run into, smash into, bump (into), butt.

ramble ▶ **verb** ❶ *we rambled around the lanes* WALK, hike, tramp, trek, backpack; wander, stroll, saunter, amble, roam, range, rove, traipse; *Scottish & Irish* stravaig; *informal* mosey, tootle; *Brit. informal* pootle; *formal* perambulate. ❷ *she does ramble on* CHATTER, babble, prattle, prate, blather, gabble, jabber, twitter, rattle, maunder; *informal* jaw, gas, gab, yak, yabber; *Brit. informal* witter, chunter, natter, waffle, rabbit.
▶ **noun** *a ramble in the hills* WALK, hike, trek; wander, stroll, saunter, amble, roam, traipse, jaunt, promenade; *informal* mosey, tootle; *Brit. informal* pootle; *formal* perambulation.

rambler ▶ **noun** WALKER, hiker, backpacker, wanderer, rover; *poetic/literary* wayfarer.

rambling ▶ **adjective** ❶ *a rambling speech* LONG-WINDED, verbose, wordy, prolix; digressive, maundering, roundabout, circuitous, circumlocutory; disconnected, disjointed, incoherent. ❷ *rambling streets* WINDING, twisting, twisty, labyrinthine; sprawling. ❸ *a rambling rose* TRAILING, creeping, climbing, vining.
– OPPOSITES concise.

ramification ▶ **noun** CONSEQUENCE, result, aftermath, outcome, effect, upshot; development, implication; product, by-product.

ramp ▶ **noun** SLOPE, bank, incline, gradient, tilt; rise, ascent, acclivity; drop, descent, declivity.

rampage ▶ **verb** *mobs rampaged through the streets* RIOT, run riot, go on the rampage, run amok, go berserk; storm, charge, tear.
■ **go on the rampage** RIOT, rampage, go berserk, get out of control, run amok; *N. Amer. informal* go postal.

rampant ▶ **adjective** ❶ *rampant inflation* UNCONTROLLED, unrestrained, unchecked, unbridled, widespread; out of control, out of hand, rife. ❷ *rampant dislike* VEHEMENT, strong, violent, forceful, intense, passionate, fanatical. ❸ *rampant vegetation* LUXURIANT, exuberant, lush, rich, riotous, rank, profuse, vigorous; *informal* jungly. ❹ *(Heraldry) a lion rampant* UPRIGHT, erect, standing (up), rearing up.
– OPPOSITES controlled, mild.

rampart ▶ **noun** DEFENSIVE WALL, embankment, earthwork, parapet, breastwork, battlement, bulwark, outwork.

ramshackle ▶ **adjective** TUMBLEDOWN, dilapidated, derelict, decrepit, neglected, run down, gone to rack and ruin, crumbling, decaying; rickety, shaky, unsound; *informal* shambly; *N. Amer. informal* shacky.
– OPPOSITES sound.

rancid ▶ **adjective** SOUR, stale, turned, rank, putrid, foul, rotten, bad, off; gamy, high, fetid, stinking, malodorous, foul-smelling; *poetic/literary* noisome.
– OPPOSITES fresh.

rancorous ▶ **adjective** BITTER, spiteful, hateful, resentful, acrimonious, malicious, malevolent, hostile, venomous, vindictive, baleful, vitriolic, vengeful, pernicious, mean, nasty; *informal* bitchy, catty.
– OPPOSITES amicable.

rancour ▶ **noun** BITTERNESS, spite, hate, hatred, resentment, malice, ill will, malevolence, animosity, antipathy, enmity, hostility, acrimony, venom, vitriol.

random ▶ **adjective** ❶ *random spot checks* UNSYSTEMATIC, unmethodical, arbitrary, unplanned, undirected, casual, indiscriminate, non-specific, haphazard, stray, erratic; chance, accidental.
– OPPOSITES systematic.
■ **at random** UNSYSTEMATICALLY, arbitrarily, randomly, unmethodically, haphazardly.

range ▶ **noun** ❶ *his range of vision* SPAN, scope, compass, sweep, extent, area, field, orbit, ambit, horizon, latitude; limits, bounds, confines, parameters. ❷ *a range of mountains* ROW, chain, sierra, ridge, massif; line, string, series. ❸ *a range of quality foods* ASSORTMENT, variety, diversity, mixture, collection, array, selection, choice. ❹ *she put the dish into the range* STOVE, cooker; *trademark* Aga. ❺ *cows grazed on open range* PASTURE, pasturage, pastureland, grass, grassland, grazing land, bocage, veld; *Scottish* shieling; *poetic/literary* greensward.
▶ **verb** ❶ *charges range from 1% to 5%* VARY, fluctuate, differ; extend, stretch, reach, cover, go, run. ❷ *on the stalls are ranged fresh foods* ARRANGE, line up, order, position, dispose, set out, array. ❸ *they ranged over the steppes* ROAM, rove, traverse, travel, journey, wander, drift, ramble, meander, stroll, traipse, walk, hike, trek.

rangy ▶ **adjective** LONG-LEGGED, long-limbed, leggy, tall; slender, slim, lean, thin, gangling, gangly, lanky, spindly, skinny, spare.
– OPPOSITES squat.

rank[1] ▶ **noun** ❶ *he was elevated to ministerial rank* POSITION, level, grade, echelon; class, status, standing; *dated* station. ❷ *a family of rank* HIGH STANDING, blue blood, high birth, nobility, aristocracy; eminence, distinction, prestige; prominence, influence, consequence, power. ❸ *a rank of riflemen* ROW, line, file, column, string, train, procession.
▶ **verb** ❶ *the plant is ranked as endangered* CLASSIFY, class, categorize, rate, grade, bracket, group, pigeonhole, designate; catalogue, file, list.

❷ *he ranked below the others* HAVE A RANK, be graded, have a status, be classed, be classified, be categorized; belong. ❸ *tulips ranked like guardsmen* LINE UP, align, order, arrange, dispose, set out, array, range.

■ **the rank and file** ❶ *the officers and the rank and file* OTHER RANKS, soldiers, NCOs, lower ranks; men, troops. ❷ *a speech appealing to the rank and file* THE (COMMON) PEOPLE, the proletariat, the masses, the populace, the commonality, the commonalty, the third estate, the plebeians; the hoi polloi, the rabble, the riff-raff, the great unwashed; *informal* the proles, the plebs.

rank[2] ▶ **adjective** ❶ *rank vegetation* ABUNDANT, lush, luxuriant, dense, profuse, vigorous, overgrown; *informal* jungly. ❷ *a rank smell* OFFENSIVE, unpleasant, nasty, revolting, sickening, obnoxious, noxious; foul, fetid, smelly, stinking, reeking, high, off, rancid, putrid, malodorous; *Brit. informal* niffy, pongy, whiffy, humming; *poetic/literary* noisome. ❸ *rank stupidity* DOWNRIGHT, utter, outright, out-and-out, absolute, complete, sheer, arrant, thoroughgoing, unqualified, unmitigated, positive, perfect, patent, pure, total.

– OPPOSITES sparse, pleasant.

rankle ▶ **verb** CAUSE RESENTMENT, annoy, upset, anger, irritate, offend, affront, displease, provoke, irk, vex, pique, nettle, gall; *informal* rile, miff, peeve, aggravate, hack off; *Brit. informal* nark; *N. Amer. informal* tick off.

ransack ▶ **verb** PLUNDER, pillage, raid, rob, loot, sack, strip, despoil; ravage, devastate, turn upside down; scour, rifle, comb, search.

ransom ▶ **noun** *they demanded a huge ransom* PAY-OFF, payment, sum, price.

▶ **verb** *the girl was ransomed for £4 million* RELEASE, free, deliver, liberate, rescue; exchange for a ransom, buy the freedom of.

rant ▶ **verb** *she ranted on about the unfairness* HOLD FORTH, go on, fulminate, vociferate, sound off, spout, pontificate, bluster, declaim; shout, yell, bellow; *informal* mouth off.

▶ **noun** *he went into a rant about them* TIRADE, diatribe, broadside; *poetic/literary* philippic.

rap[1] ▶ **verb** ❶ *she rapped his fingers with a ruler* HIT, strike; *informal* whack, thwack, bash, wallop; *poetic/literary* smite. ❷ *I rapped on the door* KNOCK, tap, bang, hammer, pound. ❸ (*informal*) *banks were rapped for high charges. See* REPRIMAND verb.

▶ **noun** ❶ *a rap on the knuckles* BLOW, hit, knock, bang, crack; *informal* whack, thwack, bash, wallop. ❷ *a rap at the door* KNOCK, tap, rat-tat, bang, hammering, pounding.

■ **take the rap** (*informal*) BE PUNISHED, take the blame, suffer (the consequences), pay (the price).

rap[2] ▶ **noun** *they didn't care a rap* WHIT, iota, jot, hoot, scrap, bit, fig; *informal* damn, monkey's.

rapacious ▶ **adjective** GRASPING, greedy, avaricious, acquisitive, covetous; mercenary, materialistic; insatiable, predatory; *informal* money-grubbing; *N. Amer. informal* grabby.

– OPPOSITES generous.

rape ▶ **noun** ❶ *he was charged with rape* SEXUAL ASSAULT, sexual abuse; *archaic* ravishment, defilement. ❷ *the rape of rainforest* DESTRUCTION, violation, ravaging, pillaging, plundering, desecration, defilement, sacking, sack.

▶ **verb** ❶ *he raped her at knifepoint* SEXUALLY ASSAULT, sexually abuse, violate, force oneself on; *poetic/literary* ravish; *archaic* defile. ❷ *they raped our country* RAVAGE, violate, desecrate, defile, plunder, pillage, despoil; lay waste, ransack, sack.

rapid ▶ **adjective** QUICK, fast, swift, speedy, expeditious, express, brisk; lightning, meteoric, whirlwind; sudden, instantaneous, instant, immediate; hurried, hasty, precipitate; *informal* p.d.q. (pretty damn quick); *poetic/literary* fleet.

– OPPOSITES slow.

rapidly ▶ **adverb** QUICKLY, fast, swiftly, speedily, at the speed of light, post-haste, hotfoot, at full tilt, briskly; hurriedly, hastily, in haste, in a rush, precipitately; *informal* like a shot, double quick, p.d.q. (pretty damn quick), in a flash, hell for leather, at the double, like a bat out of hell, like (greased) lightning, like mad, like the wind; *Brit. informal* like the clappers, at a rate of knots, like billy-o; *N. Amer. informal* lickety-split; *poetic/literary* apace.

– OPPOSITES slowly.

rapport ▶ **noun** AFFINITY, close relationship, (mutual) understanding, bond, empathy, sympathy, accord.

rapt ▶ **adjective** FASCINATED, enthralled, spellbound, captivated, riveted, gripped, mesmerized, enchanted, entranced, bewitched; transported, enraptured, thrilled, ecstatic.

– OPPOSITES inattentive.

rapture ▶ **noun** *she gazed at him in rapture* ECSTASY, bliss, exaltation, euphoria, elation, joy, enchantment, delight, happiness, pleasure.

■ **go into raptures** ENTHUSE, rhapsodize, rave, gush, wax lyrical; praise something to the skies.

rapturous ▶ **adjective** ECSTATIC, joyful, elated, euphoric, enraptured, on cloud nine, in seventh heaven, transported, enchanted, blissful, happy; enthusiastic, delighted, thrilled, overjoyed, rapt; *informal* over the moon, on top of the world, blissed out; *Austral. informal* wrapped.

rara avis ▶ **noun** RARITY, rare bird, wonder, marvel, nonpareil, nonsuch, one of a kind; curiosity, oddity, freak; *Brit. informal* one-off.

rare ▶ **adjective** ❶ *rare moments of privacy* INFREQUENT, scarce, sparse, few and far between, thin on the ground, like gold dust; occasional, limited, odd, isolated, unaccustomed, un-

wonted; *Brit.* out of the common. ❷ *rare stamps* UNUSUAL, recherché, uncommon, unfamiliar, atypical, singular. ❸ *a man of rare talent* EXCEPTIONAL, outstanding, unparalleled, peerless, matchless, unique, unrivalled, inimitable, beyond compare, without equal, second to none, unsurpassed; consummate, superior, superlative, first-class; *informal* A1, top-notch.
– OPPOSITES common, commonplace.

rarefied ▶ **adjective** ESOTERIC, exclusive, select; elevated, lofty.

rarely ▶ **adverb** SELDOM, infrequently, hardly (ever), scarcely, not often; once in a while, now and then, occasionally; *informal* once in a blue moon.
– OPPOSITES often.

raring ▶ **adjective** EAGER, keen, enthusiastic; impatient, longing, desperate; ready; *informal* dying, itching, gagging.

rarity ▶ **noun** ❶ *the rarity of earthquakes in the UK* INFREQUENCY, rareness, unusualness, uncommonness, scarcity, scarceness. ❷ *this book is a rarity* COLLECTOR'S ITEM, rare thing, rare bird, rara avis; wonder, nonpareil, one of a kind; curiosity, oddity; *Brit. informal* one-off.

rascal ▶ **noun** SCALLYWAG, imp, monkey, mischief-maker, wretch; *informal* scamp, tyke, horror, monster; *Brit. informal* perisher; *N. Amer. informal* varmint; *archaic* rapscallion.

rash[1] ▶ **noun** ❶ *he broke out in a rash* SPOTS, breakout, eruption; hives; *Medicine* erythema, exanthema, urticaria. ❷ *a rash of articles in the press* SERIES, succession, spate, wave, flood, deluge, torrent; outbreak, epidemic, flurry.

rash[2] ▶ **adjective** *a rash decision* RECKLESS, impulsive, impetuous, hasty, foolhardy, incautious, precipitate; careless, heedless, thoughtless, imprudent, foolish; ill-advised, injudicious, ill-judged, misguided, hare-brained; *poetic/literary* temerarious.
– OPPOSITES prudent.

rasp ▶ **verb** ❶ *enamel is rasped off the teeth* SCRAPE, rub, abrade, grate, grind, sand, file, scratch, scour; *Medicine* excoriate. ❷ *'Help!' he rasped* CROAK, squawk, caw, say hoarsely.

rasping ▶ **adjective** HARSH, grating, jarring; raspy, scratchy, hoarse, rough, gravelly, croaky, gruff, husky, throaty, guttural.

rat (*informal*) ▶ **noun** ❶ *her rat of a husband* SCOUNDREL, wretch, rogue; *informal* beast, pig, swine, creep, louse, lowlife, scumbag, heel, dog, weasel; *N. Amer. informal* rat fink; *dated* cad; *informal, dated* rotter. ❷ *the most famous rat in mob history* INFORMER, betrayer, stool pigeon; *informal* snitch, squealer; *Brit. informal* grass, supergrass, nark, snout; *Scottish & N. Irish informal* tout; *N. Amer. informal* fink, stoolie.
■ **rat on** ❶ *we don't rat on our friends* INFORM ON, betray, be unfaithful to, stab in the back; *informal* tell on, sell down the river, blow the whistle on, squeal on, stitch up, peach on, do the dirty on; *Brit. informal* grass on, shop; *N. Amer. informal* rat out, finger. ❷ *he ratted on his pledge* BREAK, renege on, go back on, welsh on.

rate ▶ **noun** ❶ *a fixed rate of interest* PERCENTAGE, ratio, proportion; scale, standard. ❷ *an hourly rate of £30* CHARGE, price, cost, tariff, fare, levy, toll; fee, remuneration, payment, wage, allowance. ❸ *the rate of change* SPEED, pace, tempo, velocity, momentum.
▶ **verb** ❶ *they rated their ability at driving* ASSESS, evaluate, appraise, judge, weigh up, estimate, calculate, gauge, measure, adjudge; grade, rank, classify, categorize. ❷ *the scheme was rated effective* CONSIDER, judge, reckon, think, hold, deem, find; regard as, look on as, count as. ❸ *he rated only a brief mention* MERIT, deserve, warrant, be worthy of, be deserving of. ❹ (*informal*) *Ben doesn't rate him* THINK HIGHLY OF, think much of, set much store by; admire, esteem, value.
■ **at any rate** IN ANY CASE, anyhow, anyway, in any event, nevertheless; whatever happens, come what may, regardless, notwithstanding.

rather ▶ **adverb** ❶ *I'd rather you went* SOONER, by preference, preferably, by choice. ❷ *it's rather complicated* QUITE, a bit, a little, fairly, slightly, somewhat, relatively, to some degree, comparatively; *informal* pretty, sort of, kind of. ❸ *her true feelings—or rather, lack of feelings* MORE PRECISELY, to be precise, to be exact, strictly speaking. ❹ *she seemed sad rather than angry* MORE; as opposed to, instead of. ❺ *it was not impulsive, but rather a considered decision* ON THE CONTRARY, instead.

ratify ▶ **verb** CONFIRM, approve, sanction, endorse, agree to, accept, uphold, authorize, formalize, validate, recognize; sign.
– OPPOSITES reject.

rating ▶ **noun** GRADE, grading, classification, ranking, rank, category, designation; assessment, evaluation, appraisal; mark, score.

ratio ▶ **noun** PROPORTION, comparative number, correlation, relationship, correspondence; percentage, fraction, quotient.

ration ▶ **noun** ❶ *a daily ration of chocolate* ALLOWANCE, allocation, quota, quantum, share, portion, helping; amount, quantity, measure, proportion, percentage. ❷ *the garrison ran out of rations* SUPPLIES, provisions, food, foodstuffs, eatables, edibles, provender; stores; *informal* grub, eats; *N. Amer. informal* chuck; *formal* comestibles; *dated* victuals.
▶ **verb** *fuel supplies were rationed* CONTROL, limit, restrict; conserve.

rational ▶ **adjective** ❶ *a rational approach* LOGICAL, reasoned, sensible, reasonable, cogent, intelligent, judicious, shrewd, common-sense, commonsensical, sound, prudent; down-to-earth, practical, pragmatic. ❷ *she was not rational at the time of signing* SANE, compos mentis, in one's right mind, of sound mind;

normal, balanced, lucid, coherent; *informal* all there. ❸ *man is a rational being* INTELLIGENT, thinking, reasoning; cerebral, logical, analytical; *formal* ratiocinative.
– OPPOSITES illogical, insane.

rationale ▶ noun REASON(S), reasoning, thinking, logic, grounds, sense; principle, theory, argument, case; motive, motivation, explanation, justification, excuse; the whys and wherefores.

rationalize ▶ verb ❶ *he tried to rationalize his behaviour* JUSTIFY, explain (away), account for, defend, vindicate, excuse. ❷ *an attempt to rationalize the industry* STREAMLINE, reorganize, modernize, update; trim, hone, simplify, downsize, prune.

rattle ▶ verb ❶ *hailstones rattled against the window* CLATTER, patter; clink, clunk. ❷ *he rattled some coins* JINGLE, jangle, clink, tinkle. ❸ *the bus rattled along* JOLT, bump, bounce, jounce, shake, judder. ❹ *the government were rattled by the strike* UNNERVE, disconcert, disturb, fluster, shake, perturb, discompose, discomfit, ruffle, throw; *informal* faze.
▶ noun *the rattle of the bottles* CLATTER, clank, clink, clang; jingle, jangle.
■ **rattle something off** REEL OFF, recite, list, fire off, run through, enumerate.
■ **rattle on/away** PRATTLE, babble, chatter, gabble, prate, go on, jabber, gibber, blether, ramble; *informal* gab, yak, yap; *Brit. informal* witter, rabbit, chunter, waffle.

ratty ▶ adjective (*Brit. informal*). *See* IRRITABLE.

raucous ▶ adjective ❶ *raucous laughter* HARSH, strident, screeching, piercing, shrill, grating, discordant, dissonant; noisy, loud, cacophonous. ❷ *a raucous hen night* ROWDY, noisy, boisterous, roisterous, wild.
– OPPOSITES soft, quiet.

raunchy ▶ adjective (*informal*). *See* SEXY sense 2.

ravage ▶ verb LAY WASTE, devastate, ruin, destroy, wreak havoc on, leave desolate; pillage, plunder, despoil, ransack, sack, loot; *poetic/literary* rape; *archaic* spoil.

ravages ▶ plural noun ❶ *the ravages of time* DAMAGING EFFECTS, ill effects. ❷ *the ravages of man* (ACTS OF) DESTRUCTION, damage, devastation, ruin, havoc, depredation(s).

rave ▶ verb ❶ *he was raving about the fires of hell* TALK WILDLY, babble, jabber, talk incoherently. ❷ *I raved and swore at them* RANT (AND RAVE), rage, lose one's temper, storm, fulminate, fume; shout, roar, thunder, bellow; *informal* fly off the handle, blow one's top, go up the wall, hit the roof; *Brit. informal* go spare; *N. Amer. informal* flip one's wig. ❸ *he raved about her talent* PRAISE ENTHUSIASTICALLY, go into raptures about/over, wax lyrical about, sing the praises of, rhapsodize over, enthuse about/over, acclaim, eulogize, extol; *N. Amer. informal* ballyhoo; *formal* laud; *archaic* panegyrize.
– OPPOSITES criticize.
▶ noun (*informal*) ❶ *the food won raves from the critics* ENTHUSIASTIC/LAVISH PRAISE, a rapturous reception, tribute, plaudits, acclaim. ❷ *a fancy-dress rave. See* PARTY noun sense 1.
– OPPOSITES criticism.
▶ adjective (*informal*) *rave reviews* VERY ENTHUSIASTIC, rapturous, glowing, ecstatic, excellent, highly favourable.

raven ▶ noun.
– RELATED TERMS corvine.
▶ adjective *raven hair* BLACK, jet-black, ebony; *poetic/literary* sable.

ravenous ▶ adjective ❶ *I'm absolutely ravenous* VERY HUNGRY, starving, famished; *rare* esurient. ❷ *her ravenous appetite* VORACIOUS, insatiable; greedy, gluttonous; *poetic/literary* insatiate.

rave-up ▶ noun (*Brit. informal*). *See* PARTY noun sense 1.

ravine ▶ noun GORGE, canyon, gully, defile, couloir; chasm, abyss, gulf; *S. English* chine; *N. English* clough, gill, thrutch; *N. Amer.* gulch, coulee.

raving ▶ adjective ❶ *she's raving mad. See* MAD sense 1. ❷ *a raving beauty* VERY GREAT, remarkable, extraordinary, singular, striking, outstanding, stunning.

ravings ▶ plural noun GIBBERISH, rambling, babbling, wild/incoherent talk.

ravish ▶ verb ❶ (*poetic/literary*) *he tried to ravish her* RAPE, sexually assault/abuse, violate, force oneself on, molest; *archaic* dishonour, defile. ❷ (*poetic/literary*) *you will be ravished by this wine* ENRAPTURE, enchant, delight, charm, entrance, enthral, captivate. ❸ (*archaic*) *her child was ravished from her breast* SEIZE, snatch, carry off/away, steal, abduct.

ravishing ▶ adjective VERY BEAUTIFUL, gorgeous, stunning, wonderful, lovely, striking, magnificent, dazzling, radiant, delightful, charming, enchanting; *informal* amazing, sensational, fantastic, fabulous, terrific; *Brit. informal* smashing; *N. Amer. informal* bodacious.
– OPPOSITES hideous.

raw ▶ adjective ❶ *raw carrot* UNCOOKED, fresh. ❷ *raw materials* UNPROCESSED, untreated, unrefined, crude, natural. ❸ *raw recruits* INEXPERIENCED, new, untrained, untried, untested; callow, immature, green, naive; *informal* wet behind the ears. ❹ *his skin is raw* SORE, red, painful, tender; abraded, chafed; *Medicine* excoriated. ❺ *a raw morning* BLEAK, cold, chilly, freezing, icy, icy-cold, wintry, bitter; *informal* nippy; *Brit. informal* parky. ❻ *raw emotions* STRONG, intense, passionate, fervent, powerful, violent; undisguised, unconcealed, unrestrained, uninhibited. ❼ *raw images of Latin America* REALISTIC, unembellished, unvarnished, brutal, harsh.
– OPPOSITES cooked, processed.
■ **in the raw** (*informal*). *See* NAKED sense 1.

raw-boned ▶ adjective THIN, lean, gaunt, bony, skinny, spare.
– OPPOSITES plump.

ray ▶ noun ❶ *rays of light* BEAM, shaft, streak, stream. ❷ *a ray of hope* GLIMMER, flicker, spark, hint, suggestion, sign.
▶ verb *her hair rayed out in the water* SPREAD OUT, fan out.

raze ▶ verb DESTROY, demolish, raze to the ground, tear down, pull down, knock down, level, flatten, bulldoze, wipe out, lay waste.

re ▶ preposition ABOUT, concerning, regarding, with regard to, relating to, apropos (of), on the subject of, in respect of, with reference to, in connection with.

reach ▶ verb ❶ *Travis reached out a hand* STRETCH OUT, hold out, extend, outstretch, thrust out, stick out. ❷ *reach me that book* PASS, hand, give, let someone have. ❸ *soon she reached Helen's house* ARRIVE AT, get to, come to; end up at. ❹ *the temperature reached 94 degrees* ATTAIN, get to; rise to, climb to; fall to, sink to, drop to; *informal* hit. ❺ *the leaders reached an agreement* ACHIEVE, work out, draw up, put together, negotiate, thrash out, hammer out. ❻ *I have been trying to reach you all day* GET IN TOUCH WITH, contact, get through to, get, speak to; *informal* get hold of. ❼ *our concern is to reach more people* INFLUENCE, sway, get (through) to, make an impression on, have an impact on.
▶ noun ❶ *Bobby moved out of her reach* GRASP, range. ❷ *small goals within your reach* CAPABILITIES, capacity. ❸ *beyond the reach of the law* JURISDICTION, authority, influence; scope, range, compass, ambit.

react ▶ verb ❶ *how he would react if she told him the truth?* BEHAVE, act, take it, conduct oneself; respond, reply, answer. ❷ *he reacted against the new regulations* REBEL AGAINST, oppose, rise up against.

reaction ▶ noun ❶ *his reaction had bewildered her* RESPONSE, answer, reply, rejoinder, retort, riposte; *informal* comeback. ❷ *a reaction against modernism* BACKLASH, counteraction. ❸ *the forces of reaction* CONSERVATISM, the right (wing), the extreme right.

reactionary ▶ adjective *a reactionary policy* RIGHT-WING, conservative, rightist, traditionalist, conventional, unprogressive.
– OPPOSITES progressive.
▶ noun *an extreme reactionary* RIGHT-WINGER, conservative, rightist, traditionalist, conventionalist.
– OPPOSITES radical.

read ▶ verb ❶ *he was reading the newspaper* PERUSE, study, scrutinize, look through; pore over, be absorbed in; run one's eye over, cast an eye over, leaf through, scan, flick through, skim through, thumb through. ❷ *he read a passage of the letter* READ OUT/ALOUD, recite, declaim. ❸ *I can't read my own writing* DECIPHER, make out, make sense of, interpret, understand. ❹ *his remark could be read as a criticism* INTERPRET, take (to mean), construe, see, understand. ❺ *the dial read 70mph* INDICATE, register, record, display, show. ❻ *he read modern history* STUDY, take; *N. Amer. & Austral./NZ* major in.
– RELATED TERMS legible.
▶ noun *have a read of this* PERUSAL, study, scan; look (at), browse (through), leaf (through), flick (through), skim (through).
■ **read something into something** INFER FROM, interpolate from, assume from, attribute to; read between the lines.
■ **read up on** STUDY; *informal* bone up on; *Brit. informal* mug up on, swot; *archaic* con.

readable ▶ adjective ❶ *the inscription is perfectly readable* LEGIBLE, easy to read, decipherable, clear, intelligible, comprehensible. ❷ *her novels are immensely readable* ENJOYABLE, entertaining, interesting, absorbing, gripping, enthralling, engrossing, stimulating; *informal* unputdownable.
– OPPOSITES illegible.

readily ▶ adverb ❶ *Durkin readily offered to drive him* WILLINGLY, without hesitation, unhesitatingly, ungrudgingly, gladly, happily, eagerly, promptly. ❷ *the island is readily accessible* EASILY, with ease, without difficulty.
– OPPOSITES reluctantly.

readiness ▶ noun ❶ *their readiness to accept change* WILLINGNESS, enthusiasm, eagerness, keenness; promptness, quickness, alacrity. ❷ *a state of readiness* PREPAREDNESS, preparation. ❸ *the readiness of his reply* PROMPTNESS, quickness, rapidity, swiftness, speed, speediness.
■ **in readiness** (AT THE) READY, available, on hand, accessible, handy; prepared, primed, on standby, standing by, on full alert.

reading ▶ noun ❶ *a cursory reading of the financial pages* PERUSAL, study, scan, scanning; browse (through), look (through), glance (through), leaf (through), flick (through), skim (through). ❷ *a man of wide reading* (BOOK) LEARNING, scholarship, education, erudition. ❸ *readings from the Bible* PASSAGE, lesson; section, piece; recital, recitation. ❹ *my reading of the situation* INTERPRETATION, construal, understanding, explanation, analysis. ❺ *a meter reading* RECORD, figure, indication, measurement.

ready ▶ adjective ❶ *are you ready?* PREPARED, (all) set, organized, primed; *informal* fit, psyched up, geared up. ❷ *everything is ready* COMPLETED, finished, prepared, organized, done, arranged, fixed, in readiness. ❸ *he's always ready to help* WILLING, prepared, pleased, inclined, disposed, predisposed; eager, keen, happy, glad; *informal* game. ❹ *she looked ready to collapse* ABOUT TO, on the point of, on the verge of, close to, liable to, likely to. ❺ *a ready supply of food* (EASILY) AVAILABLE, accessible; handy, close/near at hand, to/on hand, convenient, within reach, at the ready, near, at one's fingertips. ❻ *a ready an-*

swer PROMPT, quick, swift, speedy, fast, immediate, unhesitating; clever, sharp, astute, shrewd, keen, perceptive, discerning; *poetic/literary* rathe.

▶ **verb** *he needed time to ready himself* PREPARE, get/make ready, organize; gear oneself up; *informal* psych oneself up.

■ **at the ready** IN POSITION, poised, ready for use/action, waiting; *N. Amer.* on deck.

■ **make ready** PREPARE, make preparations, get everything ready, gear up for.

ready-made ▶ **adjective** ❶ *ready-made clothing* READY-TO-WEAR; *Brit.* off the peg; *N. Amer.* off the rack. ❷ *ready-made meals* PRE-COOKED, oven-ready, convenience.
– OPPOSITES tailor-made.

real ▶ **adjective** ❶ *is she a fictional character or a real person?* ACTUAL, non-fictional, factual; historical; material, physical, tangible, concrete, palpable. ❷ *real gold* GENUINE, authentic, bona fide; *informal* pukka, kosher. ❸ *my real name* TRUE, actual. ❹ *tears of real grief* SINCERE, genuine, true, unfeigned, heartfelt, unaffected. ❺ *a real man* PROPER, true; *informal* regular; *archaic* very. ❻ *you're a real idiot* COMPLETE, utter, thorough, absolute, total, prize, perfect; *Brit. informal* right, proper; *Austral./NZ informal* fair.
– OPPOSITES imaginary, imitation.

▶ **adverb** (*N. Amer. informal*) *that's real good of you. See* VERY adverb.

realism ▶ **noun** ❶ *optimism tinged with realism* PRAGMATISM, practicality, common sense, level-headedness. ❷ *a degree of realism* AUTHENTICITY, fidelity, verisimilitude, truthfulness, faithfulness.

realistic ▶ **adjective** ❶ *you've got to be realistic* PRACTICAL, pragmatic, matter-of-fact, down-to-earth, sensible, commonsensical; rational, reasonable, level-headed, clear-sighted, businesslike; *informal* having both/one's feet on the ground, hard-nosed, no-nonsense. ❷ *a realistic aim* ACHIEVABLE, attainable, feasible, practicable, viable, reasonable, sensible, workable; *informal* doable. ❸ *a realistic portrayal of war* TRUE (TO LIFE), lifelike, truthful, faithful, real-life, naturalistic, graphic.
– OPPOSITES idealistic, impracticable.

reality ▶ **noun** ❶ *distinguishing fantasy from reality* THE REAL WORLD, real life, actuality; truth; physical existence. ❷ *the harsh realities of life* FACT, actuality, truth. ❸ *the reality of the detail* VERISIMILITUDE, authenticity, realism, fidelity, faithfulness.
– OPPOSITES fantasy.

■ **in reality** IN (ACTUAL) FACT, in point of fact, as a matter of fact, actually, really, in truth; in practice; *archaic* in sooth.

realization ▶ **noun** ❶ *a growing realization of the danger* AWARENESS, understanding, comprehension, consciousness, appreciation, recognition, discernment; *formal* cognizance. ❷ *the realization of our dreams* FULFILMENT, achievement, accomplishment, attainment; *formal* effectuation.

realize ▶ **verb** ❶ *he suddenly realized what she meant* REGISTER, perceive, discern, be/become aware of (the fact that), be/become conscious of (the fact that), notice; understand, grasp, comprehend, see, recognize, work out, fathom (out), apprehend; *informal* latch on to, cotton on to, tumble to, savvy, figure out, get (the message); *Brit. informal* twig, suss; *formal* be/become cognizant of. ❷ *they realized their dream* FULFIL, achieve, accomplish, make a reality, make happen, bring to fruition, bring about/off, carry out/through; *formal* effectuate. ❸ *the company realized significant profits* MAKE, clear, gain, earn, return, produce. ❹ *the goods realized £3000* BE SOLD FOR, fetch, go for, make, net. ❺ *he realized his assets* CASH IN, liquidate, capitalize.

really ▶ **adverb** ❶ *he is really very wealthy* IN (ACTUAL) FACT, actually, in reality, in point of fact, as a matter of fact, in truth, to tell the truth; *archaic* in sooth. ❷ *he really likes her* GENUINELY, truly, honestly; undoubtedly, without a doubt, indubitably, certainly, assuredly, unquestionably; *archaic* verily. ❸ *they were really kind to me* VERY, extremely, thoroughly, decidedly, dreadfully, exceptionally, exceedingly, immensely, tremendously, uncommonly, remarkably, eminently, extraordinarily, most, downright; *Scottish* unco; *N. Amer.* quite; *informal* awfully, terribly, terrifically, fearfully, right, devilishly, ultra, too —— for words, seriously, majorly; *Brit. informal* jolly, ever so, dead, well, fair; *N. Amer. informal* real, mighty, awful, plumb, powerful, way; *informal, dated* devilish, frightfully; *archaic* exceeding.

▶ **exclamation** *'They've split up.' 'Really?'* IS THAT SO, is that a fact, well I never (did); *informal* {well, knock/blow me down with a feather}; *Brit. informal* {well, I'll be blowed}.

realm ▶ **noun** ❶ *peace in the realm* KINGDOM, country, land, dominion, nation. ❷ *the realm of academia* DOMAIN, sphere, area, field, world, province, territory.

reap ▶ **verb** ❶ *the corn has been reaped* HARVEST, garner, gather in, bring in. ❷ *reaping the benefits* RECEIVE, obtain, get, acquire, secure, realize.

rear[1] ▶ **verb** ❶ *I was reared in Newcastle* BRING UP, care for, look after, nurture, parent; educate; *N. Amer.* raise. ❷ *he reared cattle* BREED, raise, keep. ❸ *laboratory-reared plants* GROW, cultivate. ❹ *Harry reared his head* RAISE, lift (up), hold up, uplift. ❺ *Creagan Hill reared up before them* RISE (UP), tower, soar, loom.

rear[2] ▶ **noun** ❶ *the rear of the building* BACK (PART), hind part, back end; *Nautical* stern. ❷ *the rear of the queue* (TAIL) END, rear end, back end, tail; *N. Amer.* tag end. ❸ *he slapped her on the rear. See* BOTTOM noun sense 6.
– OPPOSITES front.

▶ **adjective** *the rear bumper* BACK, end, rearmost; hind, hinder, hindmost; *technical* posterior.

rearrange ▶ **verb** ❶ *the furniture has been rearranged* REPOSITION, move round, change round, arrange differently. ❷ *Tony had rearranged his schedule* REORGANIZE, alter, adjust, change (round), reschedule; *informal* jigger.

reason ▶ **noun** ❶ *the main reason for his decision* CAUSE, ground(s), basis, rationale; motive, motivation, purpose, point, aim, intention, objective, goal; explanation, justification, argument, defence, vindication, excuse, pretext. ❷ *postmodern voices railing against reason* RATIONALITY, logic, logical thought, reasoning, cognition; *formal* ratiocination. ❸ *he was losing his reason* SANITY, mind, mental faculties; senses, wits; *informal* marbles. ❹ *he continues, against reason, to love her* GOOD SENSE, good judgement, common sense, wisdom, sagacity, reasonableness.

▶ **verb** ❶ *a young child is unable to reason* THINK RATIONALLY, think logically, use one's common sense, use one's head/brain; *formal* cogitate, ratiocinate. ❷ *Scott reasoned that Annabel might be ill* CALCULATE, come to the conclusion, conclude, reckon, think, judge, deduce, infer, surmise; *informal* figure. ❸ *her husband tried to reason with her* TALK ROUND, bring round, win round, persuade, prevail on, convince, make someone see the light.

■ **by reason of** (*formal*) BECAUSE OF, on account of, as a result of, owing to, due to, by virtue of, thanks to.

■ **reason something out** WORK OUT, think through, make sense of, get to the bottom of, puzzle out; *informal* figure out.

■ **reason with someone** TALK ROUND, bring round, persuade, prevail on, convince; make someone see the light.

■ **with reason** JUSTIFIABLY, justly, legitimately, rightly, reasonably.

reasonable ▶ **adjective** ❶ *a reasonable man | a reasonable explanation* SENSIBLE, rational, logical, fair, fair-minded, just, equitable; intelligent, wise, level-headed, practical, realistic; sound, (well) reasoned, valid, commonsensical; tenable, plausible, credible, believable. ❷ *you must take all reasonable precautions* WITHIN REASON, practicable, sensible; appropriate, suitable. ❸ *cars in reasonable condition* FAIRLY GOOD, acceptable, satisfactory, average, adequate, fair, all right, tolerable, passable; *informal* OK. ❹ *reasonable prices* INEXPENSIVE, moderate, low, cheap, budget, bargain; competitive.

reasoned ▶ **adjective** LOGICAL, rational, well thought out, clear, lucid, coherent, cogent, well expressed, well presented, considered, sensible.

reasoning ▶ **noun** THINKING, reason, (train of) thought, thought process, logic, analysis, interpretation, explanation, rationalization; reasons, rationale, arguments; *formal* ratiocination.

reassure ▶ **verb** PUT/SET SOMEONE'S MIND AT REST, put someone at ease, encourage, inspirit, hearten, buoy up, cheer up; comfort, soothe.
– OPPOSITES alarm.

rebate ▶ **noun** (PARTIAL) REFUND, repayment; discount, deduction, reduction, decrease.

rebel ▶ **noun** ❶ *the rebels took control of the capital* REVOLUTIONARY, insurgent, revolutionist, mutineer, insurrectionist, insurrectionary, guerrilla, terrorist, freedom fighter. ❷ *the concept of the artist as a rebel* NONCONFORMIST, dissenter, dissident, iconoclast, maverick.

▶ **verb** ❶ *the citizens rebelled* REVOLT, mutiny, riot, rise up, take up arms, stage/mount a rebellion, be insubordinate. ❷ *his stomach rebelled at the thought of food* RECOIL, show/feel repugnance. ❸ *teenagers rebelling against their parents* DEFY, disobey, refuse to obey, kick against, challenge, oppose, resist.
– OPPOSITES obey.

▶ **adjective** ❶ *rebel troops* INSURGENT, revolutionary, mutinous, rebellious, insurrectionary, insurrectionist. ❷ *rebel MPs* REBELLIOUS, defiant, disobedient, insubordinate, subversive, resistant, recalcitrant; nonconformist, maverick, iconoclastic; *archaic* contumacious.
– OPPOSITES compliant.

rebellion ▶ **noun** ❶ *troops suppressed the rebellion* UPRISING, revolt, insurrection, mutiny, revolution, insurgence, insurgency; rioting, riot, disorder, unrest. ❷ *an act of rebellion* DEFIANCE, disobedience, rebelliousness, insubordination, subversion, subversiveness, resistance.

rebellious ▶ **adjective** ❶ *rebellious troops* REBEL, insurgent, mutinous, mutinying, rebelling, rioting, riotous, insurrectionary, insurrectionist, revolutionary. ❷ *a rebellious adolescent* DEFIANT, disobedient, insubordinate, unruly, mutinous, wayward, obstreperous, recalcitrant, intractable; *Brit. informal* bolshie; *formal* refractory; *archaic* contumacious.

rebirth ▶ **noun** REVIVAL, renaissance, resurrection, reawakening, renewal, regeneration; revitalization, rejuvenation; *formal* renascence.

rebound ▶ **verb** ❶ *the ball rebounded off the wall* BOUNCE (BACK), spring back, ricochet, boomerang; *N. Amer.* carom. ❷ *later sterling rebounded* RECOVER, rally, pick up, make a recovery. ❸ *Thomas's tactics rebounded on him* BACKFIRE, boomerang, have unwelcome repercussions; *archaic* redound on.

rebuff ▶ **verb** *his offer was rebuffed* REJECT, turn down, spurn, refuse, decline, repudiate; snub, slight, repulse, repel, dismiss, brush off, give someone the cold shoulder; *informal* give someone the brush-off; *N. Amer. informal* give someone the bum's rush.
– OPPOSITES accept.

▶ **noun** *the rebuff did little to dampen his ardour* REJECTION, snub, slight, repulse; refusal, spurning, cold-shouldering, discouragement; *informal* brush-off, kick in the teeth, slap in the face.

rebuild ▶ verb RECONSTRUCT, renovate, restore, remodel, remake, reassemble.
– OPPOSITES demolish.

rebuke ▶ verb *she never rebuked him in front of others* REPRIMAND, reproach, scold, admonish, reprove, chastise, upbraid, berate, take to task, criticize, censure; *informal* tell off, give someone a telling-off, give someone a talking-to, give someone a dressing-down, give someone an earful; *Brit. informal* tick off; *N. Amer. informal* chew out, ream out; *Austral. informal* monster; *formal* castigate.
– OPPOSITES praise.
▶ noun *Damian was silenced by the rebuke* REPRIMAND, reproach, reproof, scolding, admonishment, admonition, reproval, upbraiding; *informal* telling-off, dressing-down; *Brit. informal* ticking-off; *formal* castigation.
– OPPOSITES compliment.

rebut ▶ verb REFUTE, deny, disprove; invalidate, negate, contradict, controvert, counter, discredit, give the lie to, explode; *informal* shoot full of holes; *formal* confute.
– OPPOSITES confirm.

rebuttal ▶ noun REFUTATION, denial, countering, invalidation, negation, contradiction.

recalcitrant ▶ adjective UNCOOPERATIVE, intractable, insubordinate, defiant, rebellious, wilful, wayward, headstrong, self-willed, contrary, perverse, difficult, awkward; *Brit. informal* bloody-minded, bolshie, stroppy; *formal* refractory; *archaic* contumacious, froward.
– OPPOSITES amenable.

recall ▶ verb ❶ *he recalled his student days* REMEMBER, recollect, call to mind; think back on/to, look back on, reminisce about. ❷ *their exploits recall the days of chivalry* BRING TO MIND, call to mind, put one in mind of, call up, conjure up, evoke. ❸ *the ambassador was recalled* SUMMON BACK, order back, call back. ❹ (*archaic*) *he recalled his earlier communication* REVOKE, rescind, cancel, retract, countermand, withdraw; *formal* abrogate.
– OPPOSITES forget.
▶ noun ❶ *the recall of the ambassador* SUMMONING BACK, ordering back, calling back. ❷ *their recall of dreams* RECOLLECTION, remembrance, memory.

recant ▶ verb ❶ *he was forced to recant his political beliefs* RENOUNCE, disavow, deny, repudiate, renege on; *formal* forswear, abjure. ❷ *he refused to recant* CHANGE ONE'S MIND, be apostate; *rare* tergiversate. ❸ *he recanted his testimony* RETRACT, take back, withdraw.

recantation ▶ noun RENUNCIATION, renouncement, disavowal, denial, repudiation, retraction, withdrawal.

recapitulate ▶ verb SUMMARIZE, sum up; restate, repeat, reiterate, go over, review; *informal* recap.

recede ▶ verb ❶ *the flood waters receded* RETREAT, go back/down, move back/away, withdraw, ebb, subside, abate. ❷ *the lights receded into the distance* DISAPPEAR FROM VIEW, fade into the distance, be lost to view. ❸ *fears of violence have receded* DIMINISH, lessen, decrease, dwindle, fade, abate, subside, ebb, wane.
– OPPOSITES advance, grow.

receipt ▶ noun ❶ *the receipt of a letter* RECEIVING, getting, obtaining, gaining; arrival, delivery. ❷ *make sure you get a receipt* PROOF OF PURCHASE, sales ticket, till receipt. ❸ *receipts from house sales* PROCEEDS, takings, money/payment received, income, revenue, earnings; profits, (financial) return(s); *N. Amer.* take.

receive ▶ verb ❶ *Tony received an award | they received £650 in damages* BE GIVEN, be presented with, be awarded, collect; get, obtain, gain, acquire; win, be paid, earn, gross, net. ❷ *she received a letter* BE SENT, be in receipt of, accept (delivery of). ❸ *Alec received the news on Monday* BE TOLD, be informed of, be notified of, hear, discover, find out (about), learn; *informal* get wind of. ❹ *he received her suggestion with a complete lack of interest* HEAR, listen to; respond to, react to. ❺ *she received a serious injury* EXPERIENCE, sustain, undergo, meet with; suffer, bear. ❻ *they received their guests* GREET, welcome, say hello to. ❼ *she's not receiving visitors* ENTERTAIN, be at home to.
– OPPOSITES give, send.

receiver ▶ noun ❶ *the receiver of a gift* RECIPIENT, beneficiary, donee. ❷ *a telephone receiver* HANDSET.
– OPPOSITES donor.

recent ▶ adjective ❶ *recent research* NEW, the latest, current, fresh, modern, contemporary, up to date, up to the minute. ❷ *his recent visit* NOT LONG PAST, occurring recently, just gone.
– OPPOSITES old.

recently ▶ adverb NOT LONG AGO, a short time ago, in the past few days/weeks/months, a little while back; lately, latterly, just now.

receptacle ▶ noun CONTAINER, holder, repository; box, tin, bin, can, canister, case, pot, bag.

reception ▶ noun ❶ *the reception of the goods* RECEIPT, receiving, getting. ❷ *the reception of foreign diplomats* GREETING, welcoming, entertaining. ❸ *a chilly reception* RESPONSE, reaction, treatment. ❹ *a wedding reception* (FORMAL) PARTY, function, social occasion, soirée; *N. Amer.* levee; *informal* do, bash; *Brit. informal* rave-up, knees-up, beanfeast, bunfight, beano.

receptive ▶ adjective OPEN-MINDED, responsive, amenable, well disposed, flexible, approachable, accessible; *archaic* susceptive.
– OPPOSITES unresponsive.

recess ▶ noun ❶ *two recesses fitted with bookshelves* ALCOVE, bay, niche, nook, corner, hollow, oriel. ❷ *the deepest recesses of Broadcasting House* INNERMOST PARTS/REACHES, remote/secret places, heart, depths, bowels. ❸ *the Christmas recess* ADJOURNMENT, break, interlude, interval, rest; holiday, vacation; *informal* breather.

▶ **verb** *let's recess for lunch* ADJOURN, take a recess, stop, (take a) break; *informal* take five.

recession ▶ **noun** ECONOMIC DECLINE, downturn, depression, slump, slowdown.
– OPPOSITES boom.

recherché ▶ **adjective** OBSCURE, rare, esoteric, abstruse, arcane, recondite, exotic, strange, unusual, unfamiliar, out of the ordinary.

recipe ▶ **noun** ❶ *a tasty recipe* cooking instructions/directions; *archaic* receipt. ❷ *a recipe for success* MEANS/WAY OF ACHIEVING, prescription, formula, blueprint.

recipient ▶ **noun** RECEIVER, beneficiary, legatee, donee.
– OPPOSITES donor.

reciprocal ▶ **adjective** ❶ *reciprocal love* GIVEN/FELT IN RETURN, requited, reciprocated. ❷ *reciprocal obligations and duties* MUTUAL, common, shared, joint, corresponding, complementary.

reciprocate ▶ **verb** ❶ *I was happy to reciprocate* DO THE SAME (IN RETURN), return the favour. ❷ *love that was not reciprocated* REQUITE, return, give back.

recital ▶ **noun** ❶ *a piano recital* CONCERT, (musical) performance, solo (performance); *informal* gig. ❷ *her recital of Adam's failures* ENUMERATION, list, litany, catalogue, listing, detailing; account, report, description, recapitulation, recounting. ❸ *a recital of the Lord's Prayer. See* RECITATION sense 1.

recitation ▶ **noun** ❶ *the recitation of his poem* RECITAL, saying aloud, declamation, rendering, rendition, delivery, performance. ❷ *a recitation of her life story* ACCOUNT, description, narration, narrative, story. ❸ *songs and recitations* READING, passage; poem, verse, monologue.

recite ▶ **verb** ❶ *he began to recite verses of the Koran* REPEAT FROM MEMORY, say aloud, declaim, quote, deliver, render. ❷ *he stood up and started reciting* GIVE A RECITATION, say a poem. ❸ *Sir John recited the facts they knew* ENUMERATE, list, detail, reel off; recount, relate, describe, narrate, give an account of, recapitulate, repeat.

reckless ▶ **adjective** RASH, careless, thoughtless, heedless, unheeding, hasty, overhasty, precipitate, precipitous, impetuous, impulsive, daredevil, devil-may-care; irresponsible, foolhardy, over-adventurous, audacious; ill-advised, injudicious, madcap, imprudent, unwise, ill-considered; *poetic/literary* temerarious.
– OPPOSITES careful.

reckon ▶ **verb** ❶ *the cost was reckoned at £6,000* CALCULATE, compute, work out, put a figure on, figure; count (up), add up, total; *Brit.* tot up. ❷ *Anselm reckoned Hugh among his friends* INCLUDE, count, consider to be, regard as, look on as. ❸ (*informal*) *I reckon I can manage that* BELIEVE, think, be of the opinion/view, be convinced, dare say, imagine, guess, suppose, consider; *informal* figure. ❹ *it was reckoned a failure* REGARD AS, consider, judge, hold to be, think of as; deem, rate, gauge, count. ❺ *I reckon to get good value for money* EXPECT, anticipate, hope to, be looking to; count on, rely on, depend on, bank on; *N. Amer. informal* figure on.

■ **to be reckoned with** IMPORTANT, of considerable importance, significant; influential, powerful, strong, potent, formidable, redoubtable.

■ **reckon with** ❶ *it's her mother you'll have to reckon with* DEAL WITH, contend with, face (up to). ❷ *they hadn't reckoned with her burning ambition* TAKE INTO ACCOUNT, take into consideration, bargain for/on, anticipate, foresee, be prepared for, consider; *formal* take cognizance of.

■ **reckon without** OVERLOOK, fail to take account of, disregard.

reckoning ▶ **noun** ❶ *by my reckoning, this comes to £2 million* CALCULATION, estimation, computation, working out, summation, addition. ❷ *by her reckoning, the train was late* OPINION, view, judgement, evaluation, estimate, estimation. ❸ *the terrible reckoning that he deserved* RETRIBUTION, fate, doom, nemesis, punishment.

■ **day of reckoning** JUDGEMENT DAY, day of retribution, doomsday.

reclaim ▶ **verb** ❶ *travelling expenses can be reclaimed* GET BACK, claim back, recover, regain, retrieve, recoup. ❷ *Henrietta had reclaimed him from a life of vice* SAVE, rescue, redeem; reform.

recline ▶ **verb** LIE (DOWN/BACK), lean back; be recumbent; relax, repose, loll, lounge, sprawl, stretch out; *poetic/literary* couch.

recluse ▶ **noun** ❶ *a religious recluse* HERMIT, ascetic, eremite; *historical* anchorite, anchoress. ❷ *a natural recluse* LONER, solitary, lone wolf.

reclusive ▶ **adjective** SOLITARY, secluded, isolated, hermit-like, hermitic, eremitic, eremitical, cloistered.
– OPPOSITES gregarious.

recognition ▶ **noun** ❶ *there was no sign of recognition on his face* IDENTIFICATION, recollection, remembrance. ❷ *his recognition of his lack of experience* ACKNOWLEDGEMENT, acceptance, admission; realization, awareness, consciousness, knowledge, appreciation; *formal* cognizance. ❸ *official recognition* OFFICIAL APPROVAL, certification, accreditation, endorsement, validation. ❹ *you deserve recognition for the tremendous job you are doing* APPRECIATION, gratitude, thanks, congratulations, credit, commendation, acclaim, acknowledgement; *informal* bouquets.

recognizable ▶ **adjective** IDENTIFIABLE, noticeable, perceptible, discernible, detectable, distinguishable, observable, perceivable; distinct, unmistakable, clear; *archaic* sensible.
– OPPOSITES imperceptible.

recognize ▶ verb ❶ *Hannah recognized him at once* IDENTIFY, place, know, put a name to; remember, recall, recollect; know by sight; *Scottish & N. English* ken. ❷ *they recognized Alan's ability* ACKNOWLEDGE, accept, admit; realize, be aware of, be conscious of, perceive, discern, appreciate; *formal* be cognizant of. ❸ *psychotherapists who are recognized* OFFICIALLY APPROVE, certify, accredit, endorse, sanction, validate. ❹ *the Trust recognized their hard work* PAY TRIBUTE TO, show appreciation of, appreciate, be grateful for, acclaim, commend.

recoil ▶ verb ❶ *she instinctively recoiled* DRAW BACK, jump back, pull back; flinch, shy away, shrink (back), blench. ❷ *he recoiled from the thought* FEEL REVULSION AT, feel disgust at, be unable to stomach, shrink from, baulk at. ❸ *his rifle recoiled* KICK (BACK), jerk back, spring back. ❹ *this will eventually recoil on him* HAVE AN ADVERSE EFFECT ON, rebound on, affect badly, backfire, boomerang; *archaic* redound on.
▶ noun *the recoil of the gun* KICKBACK, kick.

recollect ▶ verb REMEMBER, recall, call to mind, think of; think back to, look back on, reminisce about.
– OPPOSITES forget.

recollection ▶ noun MEMORY, remembrance, impression, reminiscence.

recommend ▶ verb ❶ *his former employer recommended him for the post* ADVOCATE, endorse, commend, suggest, put forward, propose, nominate, put up; speak favourably of, speak well of, put in a good word for, vouch for; *informal* plug. ❷ *the committee recommended a cautious approach* ADVISE, counsel, urge, exhort, enjoin, prescribe, argue for, back, support; suggest, advocate, propose. ❸ *there was little to recommend her* HAVE IN ONE'S FAVOUR, give an advantage to; *informal* have going for one.

recommendation ▶ noun ❶ *the advisory group's recommendations* ADVICE, counsel, guidance, direction, enjoinder; suggestion, proposal. ❷ *a personal recommendation* COMMENDATION, endorsement, good word, favourable mention, testimonial; suggestion, tip; *informal* plug. ❸ *a place whose only recommendation is that it has very few women* ADVANTAGE, good point/feature, benefit, asset, boon, attraction, appeal.

recompense ▶ verb ❶ *offenders should recompense their victims* COMPENSATE, indemnify, repay, reimburse, make reparation to, make restitution to, make amends to. ❷ *she wanted to recompense him* REWARD, pay back; *archaic* guerdon. ❸ *nothing could recompense her loss* MAKE UP FOR, compensate for, make amends for, make restitution for, make reparation for, redress, make good.
▶ noun *damages were paid in recompense* COMPENSATION, reparation, restitution, indemnification, indemnity; reimbursement, repayment, redress; *archaic* guerdon.

reconcilable ▶ adjective COMPATIBLE, consistent, congruous, congruent.

reconcile ▶ verb ❶ *the news reconciled us* REUNITE, bring (back) together (again), restore friendly relations between, make peace between; pacify, appease, placate, mollify; *formal* conciliate. ❷ *her divorced parents have reconciled* SETTLE ONE'S DIFFERENCES, make (one's) peace, (kiss and) make up, bury the hatchet, declare a truce. ❸ *trying to reconcile his religious beliefs with his career* MAKE COMPATIBLE, harmonize, square, make congruent, balance. ❹ *the quarrel was reconciled* SETTLE, resolve, sort out, mend, remedy, heal, rectify; *informal* patch up. ❺ *they had to reconcile themselves to drastic losses* (COME TO) ACCEPT, resign oneself to, come to terms with, learn to live with, get used to.
– OPPOSITES estrange, quarrel.

reconciliation ▶ noun ❶ *the reconciliation of the disputants* REUNITING, reunion, bringing together (again), conciliation, reconcilement; pacification, appeasement, placating, mollification. ❷ *a reconciliation of their differences* RESOLUTION, settlement, settling, resolving, mending, remedying. ❸ *there was little hope of reconciliation* RESTORATION OF HARMONY, agreement, compromise, understanding, peace; *formal* concord. ❹ *the reconciliation of theory with practice* HARMONIZING, harmonization, squaring, balancing.

recondite ▶ adjective OBSCURE, abstruse, arcane, esoteric, recherché, profound, difficult, complex, complicated, involved; incomprehensible, unfathomable, impenetrable, cryptic, opaque.

recondition ▶ verb OVERHAUL, rebuild, renovate, restore, repair, reconstruct, remodel, refurbish; *informal* do up, revamp.

reconnaissance ▶ noun (PRELIMINARY) SURVEY, exploration, observation, investigation, examination, inspection; patrol, search; reconnoitring; *informal* recce; *N. Amer. informal* recon.

reconnoitre ▶ verb SURVEY, make a reconnaissance of, explore; investigate, examine, scrutinize, inspect, observe, take a look at; patrol; *informal* recce, make a recce of, check out; *N. Amer. informal* recon.

reconsider ▶ verb RETHINK, review, revise, re-examine, re-evaluate, reassess, reappraise; change, alter, modify; have second thoughts, change one's mind.

reconsideration ▶ noun REVIEW, rethink, re-examination, reassessment, re-evaluation, reappraisal.

reconstruct ▶ verb ❶ *the building had to be reconstructed* REBUILD, restore, renovate, recreate, remake, reassemble, remodel, refashion, revamp, recondition, refurbish. ❷ *reconstructing the events of that day* RECREATE, build up a picture/impression of, piece together, re-enact.

record ▶ noun ❶ *written records of the past* ACCOUNT(S), document(s), documentation, data, file(s), dossier(s), evidence, report(s); annal(s), archive(s), chronicle(s); minutes, transactions, proceedings, transcript(s); certificate(s), instrument(s), deed(s); register, log, logbook; *Law* muniment(s). ❷ *listening to records* album, vinyl; *dated* gramophone record, LP, EP, single, forty-five, seventy-eight. ❸ *his previous good record* PREVIOUS CONDUCT/PERFORMANCE, track record, (life) history, reputation. ❹ *he's got a record* CRIMINAL RECORD, police record; previous; *Brit. informal* form; *N. Amer. informal* rap sheet. ❺ *a new British record* BEST PERFORMANCE, highest achievement; best time, fastest time; world record. ❻ *a lasting record of what they have achieved* REMINDER, memorial, souvenir, memento, remembrance, testament.

▶ **adjective** *record profits* RECORD-BREAKING, best ever, unsurpassed, unparalleled, unequalled, second to none.

▶ **verb** ❶ *the doctor recorded her blood pressure* WRITE DOWN, put in writing, take down, note, make a note of, jot down, put down on paper; document, put on record, enter, minute, register, log; list, catalogue. ❷ *the thermometer recorded a high temperature* INDICATE, register, show, display. ❸ *the team recorded their fourth away win* ACHIEVE, accomplish, chalk up, notch up; *informal* clock up. ❹ *the recital was recorded live* MAKE A RECORD/RECORDING OF, tape, tape-record; video-record, videotape, video.

■ **off the record** ❶ *his comments were off the record* UNOFFICIAL, confidential, in (strict) confidence, not to be made public. ❷ *they admitted, off the record, that they had made a mistake* UNOFFICIALLY, privately, in (strict) confidence, confidentially, between ourselves.

recorder ▶ noun ❶ *he put a tape in the recorder* tape recorder, cassette recorder; video (recorder), VCR, videotape recorder. ❷ *a recorder of rural life* RECORD KEEPER, archivist, annalist, diarist, chronicler, historian.

recount ▶ verb TELL, relate, narrate, give an account of, describe, report, outline, delineate, relay, convey, communicate, impart.

recoup ▶ verb GET BACK, regain, recover, win back, retrieve, redeem, recuperate.

recourse ▶ noun *surgery may be the only recourse* OPTION, possibility, alternative, resort, way out, hope, remedy, choice, expedient.

■ **have recourse to** RESORT TO, make use of, avail oneself of, turn to, call on, look to, fall back on.

recover ▶ verb ❶ *he's recovering from a heart attack* RECUPERATE, get better, convalesce, regain one's strength, get stronger, get back on one's feet; be on the mend, be on the road to recovery, pick up, rally, respond to treatment, improve, heal, pull through, bounce back. ❷ *later, shares recovered* RALLY, improve, pick up, make a recovery, rebound, bounce back. ❸ *the stolen material has been recovered* RETRIEVE, regain (possession of), get back, recoup, reclaim, repossess, redeem, recuperate, find (again), track down. ❹ *gold coins recovered from a wreck* SALVAGE, save, rescue, retrieve.

– OPPOSITES deteriorate.

■ **recover oneself** PULL ONESELF TOGETHER, regain one's composure, regain one's self-control; *informal* get a grip (on oneself).

recovery ▶ noun ❶ *her recovery may be slow* RECUPERATION, convalescence. ❷ *the economy was showing signs of recovery* IMPROVEMENT, rallying, picking up, upturn, upswing. ❸ *the recovery of the stolen goods* RETRIEVAL, regaining, repossession, getting back, reclamation, recouping, redemption, recuperation.

– OPPOSITES relapse, deterioration.

recreation ▶ noun ❶ *she cycles for recreation* PLEASURE, leisure, relaxation, fun, enjoyment, entertainment, amusement; play, sport; *informal* R and R; *N. Amer. informal* rec; *archaic* disport. ❷ *his favourite recreations* PASTIME, hobby, leisure activity.

– OPPOSITES work.

recrimination ▶ noun ACCUSATION(S), counter-accusation(s), countercharge(s), counterattack(s), retaliation(s).

recruit ▶ verb ❶ *more soldiers were recruited* ENLIST, call up, conscript; *US* draft, muster in; *archaic* levy. ❷ *the king recruited an army* MUSTER, form, raise, mobilize. ❸ *the company is recruiting staff* HIRE, employ, take on; enrol, sign up, engage.

– OPPOSITES disband, dismiss.

▶ **noun** ❶ *new recruits were enlisted* CONSCRIPT, new soldier; *US* draftee; *Brit. informal* sprog; *N. Amer. informal* yardbird. ❷ *top-quality recruits* NEW MEMBER, new entrant, newcomer, initiate, beginner, novice; *N. Amer.* tenderfoot, hire; *informal* rookie, newbie; *N. Amer. informal* greenhorn.

rectify ▶ verb CORRECT, (put) right, put to rights, sort out, deal with, amend, remedy, repair, fix, make good, resolve, settle; *informal* patch up.

rectitude ▶ noun RIGHTEOUSNESS, goodness, virtue, morality, honour, honourableness, integrity, principle, probity, honesty, trustworthiness, uprightness, decency, good character.

recumbent ▶ adjective LYING, flat, horizontal, stretched out, sprawled (out), reclining, prone, prostrate, supine; lying down.

– OPPOSITES upright.

recuperate ▶ verb ❶ *he went to France to recuperate* GET BETTER, recover, convalesce, get well, regain one's strength/health, get over something. ❷ *he recuperated the money* GET BACK, regain, recover, recoup, retrieve, reclaim, repossess, redeem.

recur ▶ verb HAPPEN AGAIN, reoccur, occur

again, repeat (itself); come back (again), return, reappear, appear again; *formal* recrudesce.

recurrent ▶ **adjective** REPEATED, recurring, repetitive, periodic, cyclical, seasonal, perennial, regular, frequent; intermittent, sporadic, spasmodic.

recycle ▶ **verb** REUSE, reprocess, reclaim, recover; salvage, save.

red ▶ **adjective** ❶ *a red dress* scarlet, vermilion, ruby, cherry, cerise, cardinal, carmine, wine, blood-red; coral, cochineal, rose; brick-red, maroon, rusty, rufous; reddish; *poetic/literary* damask, vermeil, sanguine. ❷ *he was red in the face* FLUSHED, reddish, pink, pinkish, florid, rubicund; ruddy, rosy, glowing; burning, feverish; *poetic/literary* rubescent; *archaic* sanguine. ❸ *his eyes were red* BLOODSHOT, swollen, sore. ❹ *red hair* reddish, auburn, Titian, chestnut, carroty, ginger.

▶ **noun** (*informal, derogatory*) *the war against the Reds* COMMUNIST, socialist, left-winger, leftist; *informal* Commie, lefty.

■ **in the red** OVERDRAWN, in debt, in debit, in deficit, in arrears.

■ **see red** (*informal*) BECOME VERY ANGRY, become enraged, lose one's temper; *informal* go mad, go crazy, go wild, go bananas, hit the roof, go up the wall, fly off the handle, blow one's top, flip (one's lid), go ballistic; *Brit. informal* go spare, do one's nut; *N. Amer. informal* flip one's wig, blow one's lid/stack.

red-blooded ▶ **adjective** MANLY, masculine, virile, macho.

redden ▶ **verb** GO/TURN RED, blush, flush, colour (up), burn.

redeem ▶ **verb** ❶ *one feature redeems the book* SAVE, compensate for the defects of, vindicate. ❷ *he fully redeemed himself next time* VINDICATE, free from blame, absolve. ❸ *you cannot redeem their sins* ATONE FOR, make amends for, make restitution for. ❹ *redeeming sinners* SAVE, deliver from sin, convert. ❺ *Billy redeemed his drums from the pawnbrokers* RETRIEVE, regain, recover, get back, reclaim, repossess; buy back. ❻ *this voucher can be redeemed at any branch* (GIVE IN) EXCHANGE, cash in, convert, trade in. ❼ *they could not redeem their debts* PAY OFF/BACK, clear, discharge, honour. ❽ *he made no effort to redeem his promise* FULFIL, carry out, discharge, make good; keep (to), stick to, hold to, adhere to, abide by, honour.

redeeming ▶ **adjective** COMPENSATING, compensatory, extenuating, redemptive.

redemption ▶ **noun** ❶ *God's redemption of his people* SAVING, freeing from sin, absolution. ❷ *the redemption of their possessions* RETRIEVAL, recovery, reclamation, repossession, return. ❸ *the redemption of credit vouchers* EXCHANGE, cashing in, conversion. ❹ *the redemption of the mortgage* PAYING OFF/BACK, discharge, clearing, honouring. ❺ *the redemption of his obligations* FULFILMENT, carrying out, discharge, performing, honouring, meeting.

red-handed ▶ **adjective** IN THE ACT, with one's fingers/hand in the till, in flagrante delicto; *Brit. informal* with one's trousers down; *N. Amer. informal* with one's pants down.

redolent ▶ **adjective** ❶ *names redolent of history* EVOCATIVE, suggestive, reminiscent. ❷ (*poetic/literary*) *the air was redolent of incense* SMELLING OF, scented with, fragrant with, perfumed with.

redoubtable ▶ **adjective** FORMIDABLE, awe-inspiring, fearsome, daunting; impressive, commanding, indomitable, invincible, doughty, mighty.

redound ▶ **verb** ❶ (*formal*) *his effort will redound to his credit* CONTRIBUTE TO, be conducive to, result in, lead to, have an effect; *formal* conduce to. ❷ (*archaic*) *the consequences redounded upon them* REBOUND ON, have an adverse effect on, backfire.

redress ▶ **verb** ❶ *we redressed the problem* RECTIFY, correct, right, put to rights, compensate for, amend, remedy, make good, resolve, settle. ❷ *we aim to redress the balance* EVEN UP, regulate, equalize.

▶ **noun** *your best hope of redress* COMPENSATION, reparation, restitution, recompense, repayment, indemnity, indemnification, retribution, satisfaction; justice.

reduce ▶ **verb** ❶ *the aim to reduce pollution* LESSEN, make smaller, lower, bring down, decrease, diminish, minimize; shrink, narrow, contract, shorten; axe, cut (back/down), make cutbacks in, trim, slim (down), prune; *informal* chop. ❷ *he reduced her to tears* BRING TO, bring to the point of, drive to. ❸ *he was reduced to the ranks* DEMOTE, downgrade, lower (in rank). ❹ *bread has been reduced* MAKE CHEAPER, lower the price of, cut (in price), mark down, discount, put on sale; *informal* slash, knock down.
–OPPOSITES increase, put up.

■ **in reduced circumstances** IMPOVERISHED, in straitened circumstances, ruined, bankrupted; poor, indigent, impecunious, in penury, poverty-stricken, destitute; needy, badly off, hard up; *informal* flat (broke), without two pennies to rub together, strapped for cash; *Brit. informal* stony broke, skint, in Queer Street; *N. Amer. informal* stone broke; *formal* penurious.

reduction ▶ **noun** ❶ *a reduction in pollution* LESSENING, lowering, decrease, diminution. ❷ *a reduction in staff* CUT, cutback, scaling down, trimming, pruning, axing, chopping. ❸ *a reduction in inflationary pressure* EASING, lightening, moderation, alleviation. ❹ *a reduction in status* DEMOTION, downgrading, lowering. ❺ *substantial reductions* DISCOUNT, markdown, deduction, (price) cut, concession.

redundancy ▶ **noun** ❶ *redundancy in language* SUPERFLUITY, unnecessariness, excess. ❷ *redun-*

dancies are in the offing SACKING, dismissal, lay-off, discharge; unemployment.

redundant ▶ **adjective** ❶ *many churches are now redundant* UNNECESSARY, not required, unneeded, uncalled for, surplus (to requirements), superfluous. ❷ *2,000 workers were made redundant* SACKED, dismissed, laid off, discharged; unemployed, jobless, out of work.
– OPPOSITES employed.

reef ▶ **noun** SHOAL, bar, sandbar, sandbank, spit; *Scottish* skerry.

reek ▶ **verb** *the whole place reeked* STINK, smell (bad), stink to high heaven.
▶ **noun** *the reek of cattle dung* STINK, bad smell, stench, malodour; *Brit. informal* niff, pong, whiff; *poetic/literary* miasma.

reel ▶ **verb** ❶ *he reeled as the ship began to roll* STAGGER, lurch, sway, rock, stumble, totter, wobble, falter. ❷ *we were reeling from the crisis* BE SHAKEN, be stunned, be in shock, be shocked, be taken aback, be staggered, be aghast, be upset. ❸ *the room reeled* GO ROUND (AND ROUND), whirl, spin, revolve, swirl, twirl, turn, swim.
■ **reel something off** RECITE, rattle off, list rapidly, run through, enumerate, detail, itemize.

refer ▶ **verb** ❶ *he referred to errors in the article* MENTION, make reference to, allude to, touch on, speak of/about, talk of/about, write about, comment on, deal with, point out, call attention to. ❷ *the matter has been referred to my insurers* PASS, hand on/over, send on, transfer, remit, entrust, assign. ❸ *these figures refer only to 2001* APPLY TO, be relevant to, concern, relate to, be connected with, pertain to, appertain to, be pertinent to, have a bearing on, cover. ❹ *the name refers to a Saxon village* DENOTE, describe, indicate, mean, signify, designate. ❺ *the constable referred to his notes* CONSULT, turn to, look at, have recourse to.

referee ▶ **noun** ❶ *the referee blew his whistle* UMPIRE, judge; *informal* ref. ❷ *include the names of two referees* SUPPORTER, character witness, advocate.
▶ **verb** ❶ *he refereed the game* UMPIRE, judge. ❷ *they asked him to referee in the dispute* ARBITRATE, mediate.

reference ▶ **noun** ❶ *his journal contains many references to railways* MENTION OF, allusion to, comment on, remark about. ❷ *references are given in the bibliography* (INFORMATION) SOURCE, citation, authority, credit; bibliographical data. ❸ *reference to a higher court* REFERRAL, transfer, remission. ❹ *a glowing reference* TESTIMONIAL, character reference, recommendation; credentials; *dated* character.
■ **with reference to** APROPOS, with regard to, regarding, with respect to, on the subject of, re; in relation to, relating to, in connection with.

referendum ▶ **noun** (POPULAR) VOTE, plebiscite, ballot, poll.

refine ▶ **verb** ❶ *refining our cereal foods* PURIFY, process, treat. ❷ *helping students to refine their language skills* IMPROVE, perfect, polish (up), hone, fine-tune.

refined ▶ **adjective** ❶ *refined sugar* PURIFIED, processed, treated. ❷ *a refined lady* CULTIVATED, cultured, polished, stylish, elegant, sophisticated, urbane; polite, gracious, well mannered, well bred, gentlemanly, ladylike, genteel. ❸ *a person of refined taste* DISCRIMINATING, discerning, fastidious, exquisite, impeccable, fine.
– OPPOSITES crude, coarse.

refinement ▶ **noun** ❶ *the refinement of sugar* PURIFICATION, refining, processing, treatment, treating. ❷ *all writing needs endless refinement* IMPROVEMENT, polishing, honing, fine-tuning, touching up, finishing off, revision, editing. ❸ *a woman of refinement* STYLE, elegance, finesse, polish, sophistication, urbanity; politeness, grace, graciousness, good manners, good breeding, gentility; cultivation, taste, discrimination.

reflect ▶ **verb** ❶ *the snow reflects light* SEND BACK, throw back, cast back. ❷ *their expressions reflected their feelings* INDICATE, show, display, demonstrate, be evidence of, register, reveal, betray, disclose; express, communicate; *formal* evince. ❸ *he reflected on his responsibilities* THINK ABOUT, give thought to, consider, give consideration to, review, mull over, contemplate, cogitate about/on, meditate on, muse on, brood on/over, turn over in one's mind; *archaic* pore on; *rare* cerebrate.
■ **reflect badly on** DISCREDIT, disgrace, shame, put in a bad light, damage, tarnish the reputation of, give a bad name to, bring into disrepute.

reflection ▶ **noun** ❶ *the reflection of light* SENDING BACK, throwing back, casting back. ❷ *her reflection in the mirror* (MIRROR) IMAGE, likeness. ❸ *your hands are a reflection of your well-being* INDICATION, display, demonstration, manifestation; expression, evidence. ❹ *a sad reflection on society* SLUR, aspersion, imputation, reproach, shame, criticism. ❺ *after some reflection, he turned it down* THOUGHT, thinking, consideration, contemplation, deliberation, pondering, meditation, musing, rumination; *formal* cogitation; *rare* cerebration. ❻ *write down your reflections* OPINION, thought, view, belief, feeling, idea, impression, conclusion, assessment; comment, observation, remark.

reflex ▶ **adjective** INSTINCTIVE, automatic, involuntary, reflexive, impulsive, intuitive, spontaneous, unconscious, unconditioned, untaught, unlearned.
– OPPOSITES conscious.

reform ▶ **verb** ❶ *a plan to reform the system* IMPROVE, (make) better, ameliorate, refine; alter, make alterations to, change, adjust, make adjustments to, adapt, amend, revise, reshape, refashion, redesign, restyle, revamp, rebuild, reconstruct, remodel, reorganize. ❷ *after his marriage he reformed* MEND ONE'S WAYS, change for the better, turn over a new leaf, improve.

▶ **noun** *the reform of the prison system* IMPROVEMENT, amelioration, refinement; alteration, change, adaptation, amendment, revision, reshaping, refashioning, redesigning, restyling, revamp, revamping, renovation, rebuilding, reconstruction, remodelling, reorganizing, reorganization.

refractory ▶ **adjective** (*formal*) OBSTINATE, stubborn, mulish, pig-headed, obdurate, headstrong, self-willed, wayward, wilful, perverse, contrary, recalcitrant, obstreperous, disobedient; *Brit. informal* bloody-minded, bolshie, stroppy; *N. Amer. informal* balky; *archaic* contumacious, froward.
– OPPOSITES obedient.

refrain ▶ **verb** ABSTAIN, desist, hold back, stop oneself, forbear, avoid, eschew, shun, renounce; *informal* swear off; *formal* forswear, abjure.

refresh ▶ **verb** ❶ *the cool air will refresh me* REINVIGORATE, revitalize, revive, restore, fortify, enliven, perk up, stimulate, freshen, energize, exhilarate, reanimate, wake up, revivify, inspirit; blow away the cobwebs; *informal* buck up, pep up. ❷ *let me refresh your memory* JOG, stimulate, prompt, prod. ❸ (*N. Amer.*) *I refreshed his glass* REFILL, top up, replenish, recharge.
– OPPOSITES weary.

refreshing ▶ **adjective** ❶ *a refreshing drink* INVIGORATING, revitalizing, reviving, restoring, bracing, fortifying, enlivening, inspiriting, stimulating, energizing, exhilarating. ❷ *a refreshing change of direction* WELCOME, stimulating, fresh, imaginative, innovative, innovatory.

refreshment ▶ **noun** ❶ *refreshments were available in the interval* FOOD AND DRINK, sustenance, provender; snacks, titbits, eatables; *informal* nibbles, eats, grub, nosh; *formal* comestibles; *poetic/literary* viands; *dated* victuals; *archaic* aliment. ❷ *spiritual refreshment* INVIGORATION, revival, stimulation, reanimation, revivification, rejuvenation, regeneration, renewal.

refrigerate ▶ **verb** KEEP COLD, cool (down), chill.
– OPPOSITES heat.

refuge ▶ **noun** ❶ *homeless people seeking refuge in subway stations* SHELTER, protection, safety, security, asylum, sanctuary. ❷ *a refuge for mountain gorillas* SANCTUARY, shelter, place of safety, (safe) haven, sanctum; retreat, bolt-hole, hiding place, hideaway, hideout.

refugee ▶ **noun** DISPLACED PERSON, DP, fugitive, asylum seeker, exile, émigré, stateless person; *Austral. informal* reffo.

refund ▶ **verb** ❶ *we will refund your money if you're not satisfied* REPAY, give back, return, pay back. ❷ *they refunded the subscribers* REIMBURSE, compensate, recompense, remunerate, indemnify.

▶ **noun** *a full refund* REPAYMENT, reimbursement, rebate.

refurbish ▶ **verb** RENOVATE, recondition, rehabilitate, revamp, overhaul, restore, renew, redevelop, rebuild, reconstruct; redecorate, spruce up, upgrade, refit; *N. Amer.* bring up to code; *informal* do up; *N. Amer. informal* rehab.

refusal ▶ **noun** ❶ *we had one refusal to our invitation* NON-ACCEPTANCE, no, dissent, demurral, negation, turndown; regrets. ❷ *you can have first refusal* OPTION, choice, opportunity to purchase. ❸ *the refusal of planning permission* WITHHOLDING, denial, turndown.

refuse[1] ▶ **verb** ❶ *he refused their invitation* DECLINE, turn down, say no to; reject, spurn, rebuff, dismiss; send one's regrets; *informal* pass up. ❷ *the Council refused planning permission* WITHHOLD, not grant, deny.
– OPPOSITES accept, grant.

refuse[2] ▶ **noun** *piles of refuse* RUBBISH, waste, debris, litter, detritus, dross; dregs, leftovers; *N. Amer.* garbage, trash; *Austral./NZ* mullock; *informal* dreck, junk.

refute ▶ **verb** ❶ *attempts to refute Einstein's theory* DISPROVE, prove wrong/false, controvert, rebut, give the lie to, explode, debunk, discredit, invalidate; *informal* shoot full of holes; *formal* confute. ❷ *she refuted the allegation* DENY, reject, repudiate, rebut; contradict; *formal* gainsay.

regain ▶ **verb** ❶ *government troops regained the capital* RECOVER, get back, win back, recoup, retrieve, reclaim, repossess; take back, retake, recapture, reconquer. ❷ *they regained dry land* RETURN TO, get back to, reach again, rejoin.

regal ▶ **adjective** ❶ *a regal feast. See* SPLENDID sense 1. ❷ *his regal forebears* ROYAL, kingly, queenly, princely.

regale ▶ **verb** ❶ *they were lavishly regaled* ENTERTAIN, wine and dine, fête, feast, serve, feed. ❷ *he regaled her with colourful stories* ENTERTAIN, amuse, divert, delight, fascinate, captivate.

regard ▶ **verb** ❶ *we regard these results as encouraging* CONSIDER, look on, view, see, think of, judge, deem, estimate, assess, reckon, adjudge, rate, gauge. ❷ *he regarded her coldly* LOOK AT, contemplate, eye, gaze at, stare at; watch, observe, view, study, scrutinize; *poetic/literary* behold. ❸ (*archaic*) *he seldom regards her advice* HEED, pay heed to, pay attention to, listen to, take notice of.

▶ **noun** ❶ *he has no regard for human life* CONSIDERATION, care, concern, thought, notice, heed, attention. ❷ *doctors are held in high regard* ESTEEM, respect, acclaim, admiration, approval, approbation, estimation. ❸ *Jamie sends his regards* BEST WISHES, good wishes, greetings, kind/kindest regards, felicitations, salutations, respects, compliments, best, love. ❹ *his steady regard* (FIXED) LOOK, gaze, stare; observation, contemplation, study, scrutiny. ❺ *in this regard I disagree with you* RESPECT, aspect, point, item, particular, detail, specific; matter, issue, topic, question.

■ **with regard to**. *See* REGARDING.

regarding ▶ **preposition** CONCERNING, as regards, with/in regard to, with respect to, with reference to, relating to, respecting, re, about, apropos, on the subject of, in connection with, vis-à-vis.

regardless ▶ **adverb** *he decided to go, regardless* ANYWAY, anyhow, in any case, nevertheless, nonetheless, despite everything, in spite of everything, even so, all the same, in any event, come what may; *informal* irregardless.

■ **regardless of** IRRESPECTIVE OF, without regard to, without reference to, disregarding, without consideration of, discounting, ignoring, notwithstanding, no matter; *informal* irregardless of.

regenerate ▶ **verb** REVIVE, revitalize, renew, restore, breathe new life into, revivify, rejuvenate, reanimate, resuscitate; *informal* give a shot in the arm to.

regime ▶ **noun** ❶ *the former Communist regime* (SYSTEM OF) GOVERNMENT, authorities, rule, authority, control, command, administration, leadership. ❷ *a health regime* SYSTEM, arrangement, scheme; order, pattern, method, procedure, routine, course, plan, programme.

regiment ▶ **noun** *the regiment was fighting in France* UNIT, outfit, force, corps, division, brigade, battalion, squadron, company, platoon.

▶ **verb** *their life is strictly regimented* ORGANIZE, order, systematize, control, regulate, manage, discipline.

regimented ▶ **adjective** STRICTLY REGULATED, organized, disciplined, controlled, ordered, systematic, orderly.

region ▶ **noun** *the western region of the country* DISTRICT, province, territory, division, area, section, sector, zone, belt, part, quarter; *informal* parts.

■ **in the region of**. *See* APPROXIMATELY.

regional ▶ **adjective** ❶ *regional variation* GEOGRAPHICAL, territorial; by region. ❷ *a regional parliament* LOCAL, localized, provincial, district, parochial.

–OPPOSITES national.

register ▶ **noun** ❶ *the register of electors* OFFICIAL LIST, listing, roll, roster, index, directory, catalogue, inventory. ❷ *the parish register* RECORD, chronicle, log, logbook, ledger, archive; annals, files. ❸ *the lower register of the piano* RANGE, reaches; notes, octaves.

▶ **verb** ❶ *I wish to register a complaint* RECORD, put on record, enter, file, lodge, write down, put in writing, submit, report, note, minute, log. ❷ *it is not too late to register* ENROL, put one's name down, enlist, sign on/up, apply. ❸ *the dial registered a speed of 100mph* INDICATE, read, record, show, display. ❹ *her face registered anger* DISPLAY, show, express, exhibit, betray, evidence, reveal, manifest, demonstrate, bespeak; *formal* evince. ❺ *the content of her statement did not register* MAKE AN IMPRESSION, get through, sink in, penetrate, have an effect, strike home.

regress ▶ **verb** REVERT, retrogress, relapse, lapse, backslide, slip back; deteriorate, decline, worsen, degenerate, get worse; *informal* go downhill.

–OPPOSITES progress.

regret ▶ **verb** ❶ *they came to regret their decision* BE SORRY ABOUT, feel contrite about, feel remorse about/for, be remorseful about, rue, repent (of), feel repentant about, be regretful at/about. ❷ *regretting the passing of youth* MOURN, grieve for/over, feel grief at, weep over, sigh over, feel sad about, lament, sorrow for, deplore.

–OPPOSITES welcome.

▶ **noun** ❶ *both players later expressed regret* REMORSE, sorrow, contrition, contriteness, repentance, penitence, guilt, compunction, remorsefulness, ruefulness. ❷ *please give your grandmother my regrets* APOLOGY, apologies; refusal. ❸ *they left with genuine regret* SADNESS, sorrow, disappointment, unhappiness, grief.

–OPPOSITES satisfaction.

regretful ▶ **adjective** SORRY, remorseful, contrite, repentant, rueful, penitent, conscience-stricken, apologetic, guilt-ridden, ashamed, shamefaced.

–OPPOSITES unrepentant.

regrettable ▶ **adjective** UNDESIRABLE, unfortunate, unwelcome, sorry, woeful, disappointing; deplorable, lamentable, shameful, disgraceful.

regular ▶ **adjective** ❶ *plant them at regular intervals* UNIFORM, even, consistent, constant, unchanging, unvarying, fixed. ❷ *a regular beat* RHYTHMIC, steady, even, uniform, constant, unchanging, unvarying. ❸ *the subject of regular protests* FREQUENT, repeated, continual, recurrent, periodic, constant, perpetual, numerous. ❹ *regular methods of business* ESTABLISHED, conventional, orthodox, proper, official, approved, bona fide, standard, usual, traditional, tried and tested. ❺ *a regular procedure* METHODICAL, systematic, structured, well ordered, well organized, orderly, efficient. ❻ *his regular route to work* USUAL, normal, customary, habitual, routine, typical, accustomed, established. ❼ (*informal, dated*) *he's a regular charmer* UTTER, real, absolute, complete, thorough, total, out-and-out, perfect; *N. Amer.* full-bore; *Brit. informal* right, proper; *Austral./NZ informal* fair.

–OPPOSITES erratic, occasional.

regulate ▶ **verb** ❶ *the flow of the river has been regulated* CONTROL, adjust, manage. ❷ *a new act regulating businesses* SUPERVISE, police, monitor, check (up on), be responsible for; control, manage, direct, guide, govern.

regulation ▶ noun ❶ *EC regulations* RULE, ruling, order, directive, act, law, by-law, statute, edict, canon, pronouncement, dictate, dictum, decree, fiat, command, precept. ❷ *the regulation of blood sugar* ADJUSTMENT, control, management, balancing. ❸ *the regulation of financial services* SUPERVISION, policing, superintendence, monitoring, inspection; control, management, responsibility for.

▶ adjective *regulation dress* OFFICIAL, prescribed, set, fixed, mandatory, compulsory, obligatory.
– OPPOSITES unofficial.

regurgitate ▶ verb ❶ *a ruminant continually regurgitates food* DISGORGE, bring up; *archaic* regorge. ❷ *regurgitating facts* REPEAT, say again, restate, reiterate, recite, parrot; *informal* trot out.

rehabilitate ▶ verb ❶ *efforts to rehabilitate patients* RESTORE TO NORMALITY, reintegrate, readapt; *N. Amer. informal* rehab. ❷ *former dissidents were rehabilitated* REINSTATE, restore, bring back; pardon, absolve, exonerate, forgive; *formal* exculpate. ❸ *rehabilitating vacant housing* RECONDITION, restore, renovate, refurbish, revamp, overhaul, redevelop, rebuild, reconstruct; redecorate, spruce up; upgrade, refit, modernize; *informal* do up; *N. Amer. informal* rehab.

rehearsal ▶ noun PRACTICE (SESSION), trial performance, read-through, run-through; *informal* dry run.

rehearse ▶ verb ❶ *I rehearsed the role* PREPARE, practise, read through, run through/over, go over. ❷ *he rehearsed the Vienna Philharmonic* TRAIN, drill, prepare, coach, put someone through their paces. ❸ *the document rehearsed all the arguments* ENUMERATE, list, itemize, detail, spell out, catalogue, recite, rattle off; restate, repeat, reiterate, recapitulate, go over, run through; *informal* recap.

reign ▶ verb ❶ *Robert II reigned for nineteen years* BE KING/QUEEN, be monarch, be sovereign, sit on the throne, wear the crown, rule. ❷ *chaos reigned* PREVAIL, exist, be present, be the case, occur, be prevalent, be current, be rife, be rampant, be the order of the day, be in force, be in effect; *formal* obtain.

▶ noun ❶ *during Henry's reign* RULE, sovereignty, monarchy. ❷ *his reign as manager* PERIOD IN OFFICE, incumbency, managership, leadership.

reigning ▶ adjective ❶ *the reigning monarch* RULING, regnant; on the throne. ❷ *the reigning world champion* INCUMBENT, current. ❸ *the reigning legal conventions* PREVAILING, existing, current; usual, common, recognized, established, accepted, popular, widespread.

reimburse ▶ verb ❶ *they will reimburse your travel costs* REPAY, refund, return, pay back. ❷ *we'll reimburse you* COMPENSATE, recompense, repay.

rein ▶ noun *there is no rein on his behaviour* RESTRAINT, check, curb, constraint, restriction, limitation, control, brake.

▶ verb *they reined back costs* RESTRAIN, check, curb, constrain, hold back/in, keep under control, regulate, restrict, control, curtail, limit.

■ **free rein** FREEDOM, a free hand, leeway, latitude, flexibility, liberty, independence, free play, licence, room to manoeuvre, carte blanche.

■ **keep a tight rein on** EXERCISE STRICT CONTROL OVER, regulate, discipline, regiment, keep in line.

reincarnation ▶ noun REBIRTH, transmigration of the soul, metempsychosis.

reinforce ▶ verb ❶ *troops reinforced the dam* STRENGTHEN, fortify, bolster up, shore up, buttress, prop up, underpin, brace, support. ❷ *reinforcing links between colleges and companies* STRENGTHEN, fortify, support; cement, boost, promote, encourage, deepen, enrich, enhance, intensify, improve. ❸ *the need to reinforce NATO troops* AUGMENT, increase, add to, supplement, boost, top up.

reinforcement ▶ noun ❶ *the reinforcement of our defences* STRENGTHENING, fortification, bolstering, shoring up, buttressing, bracing. ❷ *reinforcement of the bomber force* AUGMENTATION, increase, supplementing, boosting, topping up. ❸ *they returned later with reinforcements* ADDITIONAL TROOPS, fresh troops, auxiliaries, reserves; support, back-up, help.

reinstate ▶ verb RESTORE, return to power, put back, bring back, reinstitute, reinstall.

reiterate ▶ verb REPEAT, say again, restate, recapitulate, go over (and over), rehearse.

reject ▶ verb ❶ *the miners rejected the offer* TURN DOWN, refuse, decline, say no to, spurn; *informal* give the thumbs down to. ❷ *Jamie rejected her* REBUFF, spurn, shun, snub, repudiate, cast off/aside, discard, abandon, desert, turn one's back on, have nothing (more) to do with, wash one's hands of; *informal* give someone the brush-off; *poetic/literary* forsake.
– OPPOSITES accept.

▶ noun ❶ *it is only a reject* SUBSTANDARD ARTICLE, discard, second. ❷ *what a reject!* FAILURE, loser, incompetent.

rejection ▶ noun ❶ *a rejection of the offer* REFUSAL, declining, turning down, dismissal, spurning. ❷ *Madeleine's rejection of him* REPUDIATION, rebuff, spurning, abandonment, desertion; *informal* brush-off; *poetic/literary* forsaking.

rejoice ▶ verb ❶ *they rejoiced when she returned* BE JOYFUL, be happy, be pleased, be glad, be delighted, be elated, be ecstatic, be euphoric, be overjoyed, be as pleased as Punch, be cock-a-hoop, be jubilant, be in raptures, be beside oneself with joy, be delirious, be thrilled, be on cloud nine, be in seventh heaven; celebrate, make merry; *informal* be over the moon,

be on top of the world; *Austral. informal* be wrapped; *poetic/literary* joy; *archaic* jubilate. ❷ *he rejoiced in their success* TAKE DELIGHT, find/take pleasure, feel satisfaction, find joy, enjoy, revel in, glory in, delight in, relish, savour.
–OPPOSITES mourn.

rejoicing ▶ **noun** HAPPINESS, pleasure, joy, gladness, delight, elation, jubilation, exuberance, exultation, celebration, revelry, merrymaking.

rejoin[1] ▶ **verb** *the path rejoins the main road further on* RETURN TO, be reunited with, join again, reach again, regain.

rejoin[2] ▶ **verb** *Eugene rejoined that you couldn't expect much* ANSWER, reply, respond, return, retort, riposte, counter.

rejoinder ▶ **noun** ANSWER, reply, response, retort, riposte, counter; *informal* comeback.

rejuvenate ▶ **verb** REVIVE, revitalize, regenerate, breathe new life into, revivify, reanimate, resuscitate, refresh, reawaken, put new life into; *informal* give a shot in the arm to, pep up, buck up.

relapse ▶ **verb** ❶ *a few patients relapse* GET ILL/WORSE AGAIN, have/suffer a relapse, deteriorate, degenerate, take a turn for the worse. ❷ *she relapsed into silence* REVERT, lapse; regress, retrogress, slip back, slide back, degenerate.
–OPPOSITES improve.
▶ **noun** ❶ *one patient suffered a relapse* DETERIORATION, turn for the worse. ❷ *a relapse into alcoholism* DECLINE, lapse, deterioration, degeneration, reversion, regression, retrogression, fall, descent, slide.

relate ▶ **verb** ❶ *he related many stories* TELL, recount, narrate, report, chronicle, outline, delineate, retail, recite, repeat, communicate, impart. ❷ *mortality is related to unemployment levels* CONNECT (WITH), associate (with), link (with), correlate (with), ally (with), couple (with). ❸ *the charges relate to offences committed in August* APPLY, be relevant, concern, pertain to, be pertinent to, have a bearing on, appertain to, involve; *archaic* regard. ❹ *she cannot relate to her step-father* HAVE A RAPPORT, get on (well), feel sympathy, feel for, identify with, empathize with, understand; *informal* hit it off with.

related ▶ **adjective** ❶ *related ideas* CONNECTED, interconnected, associated, linked, coupled, allied, affiliated, concomitant, corresponding, analogous, kindred, parallel, comparable, homologous, equivalent. ❷ *are you two related?* OF THE SAME FAMILY, kin, akin, kindred, consanguineous; *formal* cognate.
–OPPOSITES unconnected.

relation ▶ **noun** ❶ *the relation between church and state* CONNECTION, relationship, association, link, correlation, correspondence, parallel, alliance, bond, interrelation, interconnection. ❷ *this had no relation to national security* RELEVANCE, applicability, reference, pertinence, bearing. ❸ *are you a relation of his?* RELATIVE, member of the family, kinsman, kinswoman; (**relations**) family, (kith and) kin, kindred. ❹ *improving relations with India* DEALINGS, communication, relationship, connections, contact, interaction. ❺ *sexual relations. See* SEX sense 1.

relationship ▶ **noun** ❶ *the relationship between diet and diabetes* CONNECTION, relation, association, link, correlation, correspondence, parallel, alliance, bond, interrelation, interconnection. ❷ *evidence of their relationship to a common ancestor* FAMILY TIES/CONNECTIONS, blood relationship, kinship, affinity, consanguinity, common ancestry/lineage. ❸ *the end of their relationship* ROMANCE, (love) affair, love, liaison, amour.

relative ▶ **adjective** ❶ *the relative importance of each factor* COMPARATIVE, respective, comparable, correlative, parallel, corresponding. ❷ *the food required is relative to body weight* PROPORTIONATE, proportional, in proportion, commensurate, corresponding. ❸ *relative ease* MODERATE, reasonable, a fair degree of, considerable, comparative.
▶ **noun** *he's a relative of mine* RELATION, member of someone's/the family, kinsman, kinswoman; (**relatives**) family, (kith and) kin, kindred, kinsfolk.

relatively ▶ **adverb** COMPARATIVELY, by comparison; quite, fairly, reasonably, rather, somewhat, to a certain degree/degree, tolerably, passably; *informal* pretty, kind of, sort of.

relax ▶ **verb** ❶ *yoga is helpful in learning to relax* UNWIND, loosen up, ease up/off, slow down, destress, unbend, rest, put one's feet up, take it easy; *informal* unbutton; *N. Amer. informal* hang loose, chill out. ❷ *a walk will relax you* CALM (DOWN), unwind, loosen up, make less tense/uptight, soothe, pacify, compose. ❸ *he relaxed his grip* LOOSEN, loose, slacken, unclench, weaken, lessen. ❹ *her muscles relaxed* BECOME LESS TENSE, loosen, slacken, unknot. ❺ *they relaxed the restrictions* MODERATE, modify, temper, ease (up on), loosen, lighten, dilute, weaken, reduce, decrease; *informal* let up on.
–OPPOSITES tense, tighten.

relaxation ▶ **noun** ❶ *a state of relaxation* (MENTAL) REPOSE, calm, tranquillity, peacefulness, loosening up, unwinding. ❷ *I just play for relaxation* RECREATION, enjoyment, amusement, entertainment, fun, pleasure, leisure; *informal* R and R. ❸ *muscle relaxation* LOOSENING, slackening, loosing. ❹ *relaxation of censorship rules* MODERATION, easing, loosening, lightening; alleviation, mitigation, dilution, weakening, reduction; *informal* letting up.

relay ▶ **noun** *a live relay of the performance* BROADCAST, transmission, showing.
▶ **verb** *relaying messages through a third party* PASS ON, hand on, transfer, repeat, communicate, send, transmit, disseminate, spread, circulate.

release ▶ verb ❶ *all prisoners were released* (SET) FREE, let go/out, allow to leave, liberate, set at liberty. ❷ *Burke released the animal* UNTIE, undo, loose, let go, unleash, unfetter. ❸ *this released staff for other duties* MAKE AVAILABLE, free (up), put at someone's disposal, supply, furnish, provide. ❹ *she released Stephen from his promise* EXCUSE, exempt, discharge, deliver, absolve; *informal* let off. ❺ *police released the news yesterday* MAKE PUBLIC, make known, issue, break, announce, declare, report, reveal, divulge, disclose, publish, broadcast, circulate, communicate, disseminate. ❻ *the film has been released on video* LAUNCH, put on the market, put on sale, bring out, make available.
–OPPOSITES imprison, tie up.
▶ noun ❶ *the release of political prisoners* FREEING, liberation, deliverance; freedom, liberty. ❷ *the release of the news* ISSUING, announcement, declaration, reporting, revealing, divulging, disclosure, publication, communication, dissemination. ❸ *a press release* ANNOUNCEMENT, bulletin, newsflash, dispatch, proclamation. ❹ *the group's last release* CD, album, single, record; video, film; book.

relegate ▶ verb DOWNGRADE, lower (in rank/status), put down, move down; demote, degrade.
–OPPOSITES upgrade.

relent ▶ verb ❶ *the government finally relented* CHANGE ONE'S MIND, do a U-turn, back-pedal, back down, give way/in, capitulate; become merciful, become lenient, agree to something, allow something, concede something; *Brit.* do an about-turn; *formal* accede. ❷ *the rain has relented* EASE (OFF/UP), slacken, let up, abate, drop, die down, lessen, decrease, subside, weaken, tail off.

relentless ▶ adjective ❶ *their relentless pursuit of quality* PERSISTENT, continuing, constant, continual, continuous, non-stop, never-ending, unabating, interminable, incessant, unceasing, endless, unending, unremitting, unrelenting, unrelieved; unfaltering, unflagging, untiring, unwavering, dogged, single-minded, tireless, indefatigable; *formal* pertinacious. ❷ *a relentless taskmaster* HARSH, grim, cruel, severe, strict, remorseless, merciless, pitiless, ruthless, unmerciful, heartless, hard-hearted, unforgiving; inflexible, unbending, uncompromising, obdurate, unyielding.

relevant ▶ adjective PERTINENT, applicable, apposite, material, apropos, to the point, germane; connected, related, linked.

reliable ▶ adjective ❶ *reliable evidence* DEPENDABLE, good, well founded, authentic, valid, genuine, sound, true. ❷ *a reliable friend* TRUSTWORTHY, dependable, good, true, faithful, devoted, steadfast, staunch, constant, loyal, trusty, dedicated, unfailing; truthful, honest. ❸ *reliable brakes* DEPENDABLE, safe, fail-safe. ❹ *a reliable firm* REPUTABLE, dependable, trustworthy, honest, responsible, established, proven.
–OPPOSITES untrustworthy.

reliance ▶ noun ❶ *reliance on the state* DEPENDENCE, dependency. ❷ *reliance on his own judgement* TRUST, confidence, faith, belief, conviction.

relic ▶ noun ❶ *a Viking relic* ARTEFACT, historical object, ancient object, antiquity, antique. ❷ *a saint's relics* REMAINS, corpse, bones, reliquiae; *Medicine* cadaver.

relief ▶ noun ❶ *it was such a relief to share my worries* REASSURANCE, consolation, comfort, solace. ❷ *the relief of pain* ALLEVIATION, alleviating, relieving, assuagement, assuaging, palliation, allaying, soothing, easing, lessening, reduction. ❸ *relief from her burden* FREEDOM, release, liberation, deliverance. ❹ *a little light relief* RESPITE, amusement, diversion, entertainment, jollity, jollification, recreation. ❺ *bringing relief to the starving* HELP, aid, assistance, succour, sustenance; charity, gifts, donations. ❻ *his relief arrived to take over* REPLACEMENT, substitute, deputy, reserve, cover, stand-in, supply, locum (tenens), understudy.
–OPPOSITES intensification.
■ **throw something into relief** HIGHLIGHT, spotlight, give prominence to, point up, show up, emphasize, bring out, stress, accent, underline, underscore, accentuate.

relieve ▶ verb ❶ *this helps relieve pain* ALLEVIATE, mitigate, assuage, ease, dull, reduce, lessen, diminish. ❷ *relieving the boredom* COUNTERACT, reduce, alleviate, mitigate; interrupt, vary, stop, dispel, prevent. ❸ *the helpers relieved us* REPLACE, take over from, stand in for, fill in for, substitute for, deputize for, cover for. ❹ *this relieves the teacher of a heavy load* (SET) FREE, release, exempt, excuse, absolve, let off, discharge.
–OPPOSITES aggravate.

relieved ▶ adjective GLAD, thankful, grateful, pleased, happy, easy/easier in one's mind, reassured.
–OPPOSITES worried.

religion ▶ noun FAITH, belief, worship, creed; sect, cult, church, denomination.

religious ▶ adjective ❶ *a religious person* DEVOUT, pious, reverent, godly, God-fearing, churchgoing, practising, faithful, devoted, committed. ❷ *religious beliefs* SPIRITUAL, theological, scriptural, doctrinal, ecclesiastical, church, churchly, holy, divine, sacred. ❸ *religious attention to detail* SCRUPULOUS, conscientious, meticulous, sedulous, punctilious, strict, rigorous, close.
–OPPOSITES atheistic, secular.

relinquish ▶ verb ❶ *he relinquished control of the company* RENOUNCE, give up/away, hand over, let go of. ❷ *he relinquished his post* LEAVE, resign from, stand down from, bow out of,

give up; *informal* quit, chuck. ❸ *he relinquished his pipe-smoking* DISCONTINUE, stop, cease, give up, desist from; *informal* quit, leave off, kick; *formal* forswear. ❹ *she relinquished her grip* LET GO, release, loose, loosen, relax.
– OPPOSITES retain, continue.

relish ▶ noun ❶ *he dug into his food with relish* ENJOYMENT, gusto, delight, pleasure, glee, rapture, satisfaction, contentment, appreciation, enthusiasm, appetite; *humorous* delectation. ❷ *a hot relish* CONDIMENT, sauce, dressing, flavouring, seasoning, dip.
– OPPOSITES dislike.
▶ verb ❶ *he was relishing his moment of glory* ENJOY, delight in, love, adore, take pleasure in, rejoice in, appreciate, savour, revel in, luxuriate in, glory in. ❷ *I don't relish the drive* LOOK FORWARD TO, fancy, anticipate with pleasure.

reluctance ▶ noun UNWILLINGNESS, disinclination; hesitation, wavering, vacillation; doubts, second thoughts, misgivings; *archaic* disrelish.

reluctant ▶ adjective ❶ *her parents were reluctant* UNWILLING, disinclined, unenthusiastic, resistant, resisting, opposed; hesitant. ❷ *a reluctant smile* SHY, bashful, coy, diffident, reserved, timid, timorous. ❸ *he was reluctant to leave* LOATH, unwilling, disinclined, indisposed; not in favour of, against, opposed to.
– OPPOSITES willing, eager.

rely ▶ verb ❶ *we can rely on his discretion* DEPEND, count, bank, place reliance, reckon; be confident of, be sure of, believe in, have faith in, trust in; *informal* swear by; *N. Amer. informal* figure on. ❷ *we rely on government funding* BE DEPENDENT, depend, be unable to manage without.

remain ▶ verb ❶ *the problem will remain* CONTINUE TO EXIST, endure, last, abide, carry on, persist, stay (around), prevail, survive, live on. ❷ *he remained in hospital* STAY (BEHIND/PUT), wait (around), be left, hang on; *informal* hang around/round; *Brit. informal* hang about; *archaic* bide. ❸ *union leaders remain sceptical* CONTINUE TO BE, stay, keep, persist in being, carry on being. ❹ *the few minutes that remain* BE LEFT (OVER), be still available, be unused; have not yet passed.

remainder ▶ noun RESIDUE, balance, remaining part/number, rest, others, those left, remnant(s), surplus, extra, excess, overflow; *technical* residuum.

remaining ▶ adjective ❶ *the remaining workers* RESIDUAL, surviving, left (over); extra, surplus, spare, superfluous, excess. ❷ *his remaining jobs* UNSETTLED, outstanding, unfinished, incomplete, to be done, unattended to. ❸ *my only remaining memories* SURVIVING, lasting, enduring, continuing, persisting, abiding, (still) existing.

remains ▶ plural noun ❶ *the remains of her drink* REMAINDER, residue, remaining part/number, rest, remnant(s); *technical* residuum. ❷ *Roman remains* ANTIQUITIES, relics, reliquiae. ❸ *the saint's remains* CORPSE, (dead) body, carcass; bones, skeleton; *Medicine* cadaver.

remark ▶ verb ❶ *'You're quiet,' he remarked* COMMENT, say, observe, mention, reflect, state, declare, announce, pronounce, assert; *formal* opine. ❷ *many critics remarked on their rapport* COMMENT, mention, refer to, speak of, pass comment on. ❸ *he remarked the absence of policemen* NOTE, notice, observe, take note of, perceive, discern.
▶ noun ❶ *his remarks have been misinterpreted* COMMENT, statement, utterance, observation, declaration, pronouncement. ❷ *worthy of remark* ATTENTION, notice, comment, mention, observation, acknowledgement.

remarkable ▶ adjective EXTRAORDINARY, exceptional, amazing, astonishing, astounding, marvellous, wonderful, sensational, stunning, incredible, unbelievable, phenomenal, outstanding, momentous; out of the ordinary, unusual, uncommon, surprising; *informal* fantastic, terrific, tremendous, stupendous, awesome; *poetic/literary* wondrous.
– OPPOSITES ordinary.

remediable ▶ adjective CURABLE, treatable, operable; solvable, reparable, rectifiable, resolvable.
– OPPOSITES incurable.

remedy ▶ noun ❶ *herbal remedies* TREATMENT, cure, medicine, medication, medicament, drug; *archaic* physic. ❷ *a remedy for all kinds of problems* SOLUTION, answer, cure, antidote, curative, nostrum, panacea, cure-all; *informal* magic bullet.
▶ verb ❶ *remedying the situation* PUT/SET RIGHT, put/set to rights, right, rectify, solve, sort out, straighten out, resolve, correct, repair, mend, make good. ❷ *anaemia can be remedied by iron tablets* CURE, treat, heal, make better; relieve, ease, alleviate, palliate.

remember ▶ verb ❶ *remembering happy times* RECALL, call to mind, recollect, think of; reminisce about, look back on; *archaic* bethink oneself of. ❷ *can you remember all that?* MEMORIZE, commit to memory, retain; learn off by heart. ❸ *you must remember she's only five* BEAR/KEEP IN MIND, be mindful of the fact; take into account, take into consideration. ❹ *remember to feed the cat* BE SURE, be certain; mind that you, make sure that you. ❺ *remember me to Alice* SEND ONE'S BEST WISHES TO, send one's regards to, give one's love to, send one's compliments to, say hello to. ❻ *the nation remembered those who gave their lives* COMMEMORATE, pay tribute to, honour, salute, pay homage to. ❼ *she remembered them in her will* BEQUEATH SOMETHING TO, leave something to, bestow something on.
– OPPOSITES forget.

remembrance ▶ noun ❶ *an expression of remembrance* RECOLLECTION, reminiscence; remembering, recalling, recollecting, reminiscing. ❷ *she smiled at the remembrance* MEMORY, recollection, reminiscence, thought. ❸ *we sold poppies in remembrance* COMMEMORATION, memory, recognition. ❹ *a remembrance of my father* MEMENTO, reminder, keepsake, souvenir, memorial, token.

remind ▶ **verb** ❶ *I left a note to remind him* JOG SOMEONE'S MEMORY, help someone remember, prompt. ❷ *the song reminded me of my sister* MAKE ONE THINK OF, cause one to remember, put one in mind of, bring/call to mind, evoke.

reminder ▶ **noun** PROMPT, prompting, aide-memoire.

reminisce ▶ **verb** REMEMBER (WITH PLEASURE), cast one's mind back to, look back on, be nostalgic about, recall, recollect, reflect on, call to mind.

reminiscences ▶ **plural noun** MEMORIES, recollections, reflections, remembrances.

reminiscent ▶ **adjective** SIMILAR TO, comparable with, evocative of, suggestive of, redolent of.

remiss ▶ **adjective** NEGLIGENT, neglectful, irresponsible, careless, thoughtless, heedless, lax, slack, slipshod, lackadaisical; *N. Amer.* derelict; *informal* sloppy; *formal* delinquent.
– OPPOSITES careful.

remission ▶ **noun** ❶ *the remission of all fees* CANCELLATION, setting aside, suspension, revocation; *formal* abrogation. ❷ *the cancer is in remission* RESPITE, abeyance. ❸ *the wind howled without remission* RESPITE, lessening, abatement, easing, decrease, reduction, diminution, dying down, slackening, lull; *informal* let-up. ❹ *the remission of sins* FORGIVENESS, pardoning, absolution, exoneration; *formal* exculpation.

remit ▶ **verb** ❶ *the fines were remitted* CANCEL, set aside, suspend, revoke; *formal* abrogate. ❷ *remitting duties to the authorities* SEND, dispatch, forward, hand over; pay. ❸ *the case was remitted to the Court of Appeal* PASS (ON), refer, send on, transfer. ❹ (*rare*) *we remitted all further discussion* POSTPONE, defer, put off/back, shelve, delay, suspend; *N. Amer.* table; *informal* put on the back burner, put on ice. ❺ *remitting their sins* PARDON, forgive; excuse. ❻ (*archaic*) *the fever remitted* DIMINISH, lessen, decrease, ease (up), abate, moderate, subside.
▶ **noun** *that is outside his remit* AREA OF RESPONSIBILITY, sphere, orbit, scope, ambit, province; brief, instructions, orders; *informal* bailiwick.

remittance ▶ **noun** ❶ *send the form with your remittance* PAYMENT, money, fee; cheque; *formal* monies. ❷ *a monthly remittance* ALLOWANCE, sum of money.

remnant ▶ **noun** ❶ *the remnants of the picnic* REMAINS, remainder, leftovers, residue, rest; *technical* residuum. ❷ *remnants of cloth* SCRAP, piece, bit, fragment, shred, offcut, oddment.

remonstrate ▶ **verb** ❶ *'I'm not a child!' he remonstrated* PROTEST, complain, expostulate; argue with, take issue with. ❷ *we remonstrated against this proposal* OBJECT STRONGLY TO, complain vociferously about, protest against, argue against, oppose strongly, make a fuss about, challenge; deplore, condemn, denounce, criticize; *informal* kick up a fuss/stink about.

remorse ▶ **noun** CONTRITION, deep regret, repentance, penitence, guilt, compunction, remorsefulness, ruefulness, contriteness; pangs of conscience.

remorseful ▶ **adjective** SORRY, full of regret, regretful, contrite, repentant, penitent, guilt-ridden, conscience-stricken, guilty, chastened, self-reproachful.
– OPPOSITES unrepentant.

remorseless ▶ **adjective** ❶ HEARTLESS, pitiless, merciless, ruthless, callous, cruel, hard-hearted, inhumane, unmerciful, unforgiving, unfeeling. ❷ *remorseless cost-cutting* RELENTLESS, unrelenting, unremitting, unabating, inexorable, unstoppable.
– OPPOSITES compassionate.

remote ▶ **adjective** ❶ *areas remote from hospitals* FARAWAY, distant, far (off), far removed. ❷ *a remote mountain village* ISOLATED, out of the way, off the beaten track, secluded, lonely, in the back of beyond, godforsaken, inaccessible; *N. Amer.* in the backwoods, lonesome; *Austral./NZ* in the backblocks, in the booay; *informal* in the sticks, in the middle of nowhere; *N. Amer. informal* in the tall timbers; *Austral./NZ informal* beyond the black stump; *archaic* unapproachable. ❸ *events remote from modern times* IRRELEVANT TO, unrelated to, unconnected to, unconcerned with, not pertinent to, immaterial to, unassociated with; foreign to, alien to. ❹ *a remote possibility* UNLIKELY, improbable, implausible, doubtful, dubious; faint, slight, slim, small, slender. ❺ *she seems very remote* ALOOF, distant, detached, withdrawn, reserved, uncommunicative, unforthcoming, unapproachable, unresponsive, unfriendly, unsociable, introspective, introverted; *informal* stand-offish.
– OPPOSITES close, central.

removal ▶ **noun** ❶ *the removal of heavy artillery* TAKING AWAY, moving, carrying away. ❷ *his removal from office* DISMISSAL, ejection, expulsion, ousting, displacement, deposition; *N. Amer.* ouster; *informal* sacking, firing. ❸ *the removal of customs barriers* WITHDRAWAL, elimination, taking away. ❹ *the removal of errors* DELETION, elimination, erasing, effacing, obliteration. ❺ *the removal of weeds* UPROOTING, eradication. ❻ *the removal of old branches* CUTTING OFF, chopping off, hacking off. ❼ *her removal to France* MOVE, transfer, relocation. ❽ *the removal of a rival* KILLING, murder, elimination; *informal* liquidation.
– OPPOSITES installation.

remove ▶ **verb** ❶ *remove the plug* DETACH, unfasten; pull out, take out, disconnect. ❷ *she removed the lid* TAKE OFF, undo, unfasten. ❸ *he*

removed a note from his wallet TAKE OUT, produce, bring out, get out, pull out, withdraw. ❹ *police removed boxes of documents* TAKE AWAY, carry away, move, transport; confiscate; *informal* cart off. ❺ *Sheila removed the mud* CLEAN OFF, wash off, wipe off, rinse off, scrub off, sponge out. ❻ *Henry removed his coat* TAKE OFF, pull off, slip out of; *Brit. informal* peel off. ❼ *he was removed from his post* DISMISS, discharge, get rid of, dislodge, displace, expel, oust, depose; *informal* sack, fire, kick out, boot out; *Brit. informal* turf out. ❽ *tax relief was removed* WITHDRAW, abolish, eliminate, get rid of, do away with, stop, cut, axe. ❾ *Gabriel removed two words* DELETE, erase, rub out, cross out, strike out, score out. ❿ *weeds have to be removed* UPROOT, pull out, eradicate. ⓫ *removing branches* CUT OFF, chop off, lop off, hack off. ⓬ (*dated*) *he removed to Edinburgh* MOVE (HOUSE), relocate, transfer; emigrate; *Brit. informal* up sticks; *N. Amer. informal* pull up stakes. ⓭ *the mobsters removed their enemies.* See KILL verb sense 1.
–OPPOSITES attach, insert, replace.
▶ **noun** *it is impossible, at this remove, to reconstruct the accident* DISTANCE, space of time, interval.

removed ▶ **adjective** DISTANT, remote, disconnected; unrelated, unconnected, alien, foreign.

remunerate ▶ **verb** PAY, reward, reimburse, recompense.

remuneration ▶ **noun** PAYMENT, pay, salary, wages; earnings, fee(s), reward, recompense, reimbursement; *formal* emolument(s).

remunerative ▶ **adjective** LUCRATIVE, well paid, financially rewarding; profitable.

renaissance ▶ **noun** REVIVAL, renewal, resurrection, reawakening, re-emergence, rebirth, reappearance, resurgence, regeneration; *formal* renascence.

rend ▶ **verb** TEAR/RIP APART, tear/rip in two, split, rupture, sever; *poetic/literary* tear/rip asunder, sunder; *rare* dissever; *archaic* rive.

render ▶ **verb** ❶ *her fury rendered her speechless* MAKE, cause to be/become, leave. ❷ *rendering assistance* GIVE, provide, supply, furnish, contribute; offer, proffer. ❸ *the invoices rendered by the accountants* SEND IN, present, submit. ❹ *the jury rendered their verdict* DELIVER, return, hand down, give, announce. ❺ *paintings rendered in vivid colours* PAINT, draw, depict, portray, represent, execute; *poetic/literary* limn. ❻ *she rendered all three verses* PERFORM, sing. ❼ *the characters are vividly rendered* ACT, perform, play, depict, interpret. ❽ *the phrase was rendered into English* TRANSLATE, put, express, rephrase, reword. ❾ *he rendered up the stolen money* GIVE BACK, return, restore, pay back, repay, hand over, give up, surrender. ❿ *the fat can be rendered* MELT DOWN, clarify.

rendezvous ▶ **noun** *Edward was late for their rendezvous* MEETING, appointment, assignation; *informal* date; *poetic/literary* tryst.
▶ **verb** *the bar where they had agreed to rendezvous* MEET, come together, gather, assemble.

rendition ▶ **noun** ❶ *our rendition of Beethoven's Fifth* PERFORMANCE, rendering, interpretation, presentation, execution, delivery. ❷ *the artist's rendition of Adam and Eve* DEPICTION, portrayal, representation. ❸ *an interpreter's rendition of the message* TRANSLATION, interpretation, version.

renegade ▶ **noun** ❶ *he was denounced as a renegade* TRAITOR, defector, deserter, turncoat, rebel, mutineer; *rare* tergiversator. ❷ (*archaic*) *a religious renegade* APOSTATE, heretic, dissenter; *archaic* recreant.
▶ **adjective** ❶ *renegade troops* TREACHEROUS, traitorous, disloyal, treasonous, rebel, mutinous. ❷ *a renegade monk* APOSTATE, heretic, heretical, dissident; *archaic* recreant.
–OPPOSITES loyal.

renege ▶ **verb** DEFAULT ON, fail to honour, go back on, break, back out of, withdraw from, retreat from, welsh on, backtrack on; break one's word/promise.
–OPPOSITES honour.

renew ▶ **verb** ❶ *I renewed my search* RESUME, return to, take up again, come back to, begin again, start again, restart, recommence; continue (with), carry on (with). ❷ *they renewed their vows* REAFFIRM, reassert; repeat, reiterate, restate. ❸ *something to renew her interest in life* REVIVE, regenerate, revitalize, reinvigorate, restore, resuscitate, breathe new life into; *archaic* renovate. ❹ *the hotel was completely renewed* RENOVATE, restore, refurbish, modernize, overhaul, redevelop, rebuild, reconstruct, remodel; *N. Amer.* bring something up to code; *informal* do up; *N. Amer. informal* rehab. ❺ *they renewed Jackie's contract* EXTEND, prolong. ❻ *I renewed my supply of toilet paper* REPLENISH, restock, resupply, top up, replace.

renewal ▶ **noun** ❶ *the renewal of our friendship* RESUMPTION, recommencement, re-establishment; continuation. ❷ *spiritual renewal* REGENERATION, revival, reinvigoration, revitalization; *archaic* renovation. ❸ *the renewal of older urban areas* RENOVATION, restoration, modernization, reconditioning, overhauling, redevelopment, rebuilding, reconstruction.

renounce ▶ **verb** ❶ *Edward renounced his claim to the throne* GIVE UP, relinquish, abandon, abdicate, surrender, waive, forego; *Law* disclaim; *formal* abnegate. ❷ *Hungary renounced the agreement* REJECT, refuse to abide by, repudiate. ❸ *she renounced her family* REPUDIATE, deny, reject, abandon, wash one's hands of, turn one's back on, disown, spurn, shun; *poetic/literary* forsake. ❹ *he renounced alcohol* ABSTAIN FROM, give up, desist from, refrain from, keep off, eschew; *informal* quit, pack in, lay off; *formal* forswear.
–OPPOSITES assert, accept.

■ **renounce the world** BECOME A RECLUSE, turn one's back on society, cloister oneself, hide oneself away.

renovate ▶ verb MODERNIZE, restore, refurbish, revamp, recondition, rehabilitate, overhaul, redevelop; update, upgrade, refit; *N. Amer.* bring something up to code; *informal* do up; *N. Amer. informal* rehab.

renown ▶ noun FAME, distinction, eminence, pre-eminence, prominence, repute, reputation, prestige, acclaim, celebrity, notability.

renowned ▶ adjective FAMOUS, celebrated, famed, eminent, distinguished, acclaimed, illustrious, pre-eminent, prominent, great, esteemed, of note, of repute, well known, well thought of.
– OPPOSITES unknown.

rent[1] ▶ noun *I can't afford to pay the rent* HIRE CHARGE, rental.
▶ verb ❶ *she rented a car* HIRE, lease, charter. ❷ *why don't you rent it out?* LET (OUT), lease (out), hire (out); sublet, sublease.

rent[2] ▶ noun ❶ *the rent in his trousers* RIP, tear, split, hole, slash, slit. ❷ *a vast rent in the mountains* GORGE, chasm, fault, rift, fissure, crevasse.

renunciation ▶ noun ❶ *Henry's renunciation of his throne* RELINQUISHMENT, giving up, abandonment, abdication, surrender, waiving, foregoing; *Law* disclaimer; *rare* abnegation. ❷ *his renunciation of luxury* ABSTENTION, refraining, going without, giving up, eschewal; *formal* forswearing. ❸ *their renunciation of terrorism* REPUDIATION, rejection, abandonment.

reorganize ▶ verb RESTRUCTURE, change, alter, adjust, transform, shake up, rationalize, rearrange, reshape, overhaul.

repair[1] ▶ verb ❶ *the car was repaired* MEND, fix (up), put/set right, restore (to working order), overhaul, service; *informal* patch up. ❷ *they repaired the costumes* MEND, darn; *informal* patch up. ❸ *repairing relations with other countries* PUT/SET RIGHT, mend, fix, straighten out, improve; *informal* patch up. ❹ *she sought to repair the wrong she had done* RECTIFY, make good, (put) right, correct, make up for, make amends for, make reparation for.
▶ noun ❶ *in need of repair* RESTORATION, fixing (up), mending, renovation; *archaic* reparation. ❷ *an invisible repair* MEND, darn. ❸ *in good repair* CONDITION, working order, state, shape, fettle; *Brit. informal* nick.
■ **beyond repair** IRREPARABLE, irreversible, irretrievable, irremediable, irrecoverable, past hope.

repair[2] ▶ verb (*formal*) *we repaired to the sitting room* GO TO, head for, adjourn, wend one's way; *formal* remove; *poetic/literary* betake oneself.

reparable ▶ adjective RECTIFIABLE, remediable, curable, restorable, recoverable, retrievable, salvageable.

reparation ▶ noun AMENDS, restitution, redress, compensation, recompense, repayment, atonement.

repartee ▶ noun BANTER, badinage, bantering, raillery, witticism(s), ripostes, sallies, quips, joking, jesting, chaff, chaffing; *formal* persiflage.

repast ▶ noun (*formal*) MEAL, feast, banquet; *informal* spread, feed, bite (to eat); *Brit. informal* nosh-up; *formal* collation; *poetic/literary* refection.

repay ▶ verb ❶ *repaying customers who have been cheated* REIMBURSE, refund, pay back/off, recompense, compensate, indemnify. ❷ *the grants have to be repaid* PAY BACK, return, refund, reimburse. ❸ *I'd like to repay her generosity* RECIPROCATE, return, requite, recompense, reward. ❹ *interesting books that would repay further study* BE WELL WORTH, be worth one's while.

repayment ▶ noun ❶ *the repayment of tax* REFUND, reimbursement, paying back. ❷ *repayment for all they have done* RECOMPENSE, reward, compensation.

repeal ▶ verb *the Act was repealed* REVOKE, rescind, cancel, reverse, annul, nullify, declare null and void, quash, abolish; *Law* vacate; *formal* abrogate; *archaic* recall.
– OPPOSITES enact.
▶ noun *the repeal of the law* REVOCATION, rescinding, cancellation, reversal, annulment, nullification, quashing, abolition; *formal* abrogation; *archaic* recall.

repeat ▶ verb ❶ *she repeated her story* SAY AGAIN, restate, reiterate, go/run through again, recapitulate; *informal* recap. ❷ *children can repeat large chunks of text* RECITE, quote, parrot, regurgitate; *informal* trot out. ❸ *Steele was invited to repeat his work* DO AGAIN, redo, replicate, duplicate. ❹ *the episodes were repeated* REBROADCAST, rerun, reshow.
▶ noun ❶ *a repeat of the previous year's final* REPETITION, duplication, replication, duplicate. ❷ *repeats of his TV show* RERUN, rebroadcast, reshowing.
■ **repeat itself** REOCCUR, recur, occur again, happen again.

repeated ▶ adjective RECURRENT, frequent, persistent, continual, incessant, constant; regular, periodic, numerous, (very) many, a great many.
– OPPOSITES occasional.

repeatedly ▶ adverb FREQUENTLY, often, again and again, over and over (again), time and (time) again, many times, many a time; persistently, recurrently, constantly, continually, regularly; *N. Amer.* oftentimes; *informal* 24-7; *poetic/literary* oft, oft-times.

repel ▶ verb ❶ *the rebels were repelled* FIGHT OFF, repulse, drive back/away, force back, beat back, push back; hold off, ward off, keep at bay; *Brit.* see off; *archaic* rebut. ❷ *the coating will repel water* BE IMPERVIOUS TO, be impermeable to, keep out, resist. ❸ *the thought of kissing him repelled me* REVOLT, disgust, repulse, sicken, nauseate, turn someone's stomach, be repulsive, be distasteful, be repugnant; *informal* turn off; *N. Amer. informal* gross out.

repellent ▶ adjective ❶ *a repellent stench* REVOLTING, repulsive, disgusting, repugnant, sickening, nauseating, stomach-turning, nauseous, vile, nasty, foul, horrible, awful, dreadful, terrible, obnoxious, loathsome, offensive, objectionable; abhorrent, despicable, reprehensible, contemptible, odious, hateful, execrable; *N. Amer.* vomitous; *informal* ghastly, horrid, gross, yucky, icky; *poetic/literary* noisome; *archaic* disgustful. ❷ *a repellent coating* IMPERMEABLE, impervious, resistant; -proof.
– OPPOSITES delightful.

repent ▶ verb FEEL REMORSE, regret, be sorry, rue, reproach oneself, be ashamed, feel contrite; be penitent, be remorseful, be repentant.

repentance ▶ noun REMORSE, contrition, contriteness, penitence, regret, ruefulness, remorsefulness, shame, guilt; *archaic* rue.

repentant ▶ adjective PENITENT, contrite, regretful, rueful, remorseful, apologetic, chastened, ashamed, shamefaced.
– OPPOSITES impenitent.

repercussion ▶ noun ❶ *political repercussions* CONSEQUENCE, result, effect, outcome; reverberation, backlash, aftermath, fallout. ❷ (*archaic*) *a vicious repercussion* REVERBERATION, recoil, kickback.

repertoire ▶ noun COLLECTION, stock, range, repertory, reserve, store, repository, supply.

repetition ▶ noun ❶ *the statistics bear repetition* REITERATION, repeating, restatement, retelling. ❷ *the repetition the of words* REPEATING, echoing, parroting. ❸ *a repetition of the scene in the kitchen* RECURRENCE, reoccurrence, rerun, repeat. ❹ *there is some repetition* REPETITIOUSNESS, repetitiveness, redundancy, tautology.

repetitious ▶ adjective *repetitious work. See* REPETITIVE.

repetitive ▶ adjective MONOTONOUS, tedious, boring, humdrum, mundane, dreary, tiresome; unvaried, unchanging, unvarying, recurrent, recurring, repeated, repetitious, routine, mechanical, automatic.

rephrase ▶ verb REWORD, put in other words, express differently, paraphrase.

repine ▶ verb (*poetic/literary*) FRET, be/feel unhappy, mope, eat one's heart out, brood; lament, grieve, mourn, sorrow, pine.

replace ▶ verb ❶ *Adam replaced the receiver* PUT BACK, return, restore. ❷ *a new chairman came in to replace him* TAKE THE PLACE OF, succeed, take over from, supersede; stand in for, substitute for, deputize for, cover for, relieve; *informal* step into someone's shoes/boots. ❸ *she replaced the spoon with a fork* SUBSTITUTE, exchange, change, swap.
– OPPOSITES remove.

replacement ▶ noun ❶ *we have to find a replacement* SUCCESSOR; SUBSTITUTE, stand-in, locum, relief, cover. ❷ *the wiring was in need of replacement* RENEWAL, replacing.

replenish ▶ verb ❶ *she replenished their glasses* REFILL, top up, fill up, recharge; *N. Amer.* freshen. ❷ *their supplies were replenished* STOCK UP, restock, restore, replace.
– OPPOSITES empty, exhaust.

replete ▶ adjective ❶ *the guests were replete* WELL FED, sated, satiated, full (up); glutted, gorged; *informal* stuffed. ❷ *a sumptuous environment replete with antiques* FILLED, full, well stocked, well supplied, crammed, packed, jammed, teeming, overflowing, bursting; *informal* jam-packed, chock-a-block.

replica ▶ noun ❶ *is it real or a replica?* (CARBON) COPY, model, duplicate, reproduction, replication; dummy, imitation, facsimile. ❷ *a replica of her mother* PERFECT LIKENESS, double, lookalike, (living) image, twin, clone; *informal* spitting image, (dead) ringer.

replicate ▶ verb COPY, reproduce, duplicate, recreate, repeat, perform again; clone.

reply ▶ verb ❶ *Rachel didn't reply* ANSWER, respond, come back, write back. ❷ *he replied defensively* RESPOND, answer, rejoin, retort, riposte, counter, come back.
▶ noun *he waited for a reply* ANSWER, response, rejoinder, retort, riposte; *informal* comeback.

report ▶ verb ❶ *the government reported a fall in inflation* ANNOUNCE, describe, give an account of, detail, outline, communicate, divulge, disclose, reveal, make public, publish, broadcast, proclaim, publicize. ❷ *the newspapers reported on the scandal* INVESTIGATE, look into, inquire into; write about, cover, describe, give details of, commentate on. ❸ *I reported him to the police* INFORM ON, tattle on; *informal* shop, tell on, squeal on, rat on, peach on; *Brit. informal* grass on. ❹ *Juliet reported for duty* PRESENT ONESELF, arrive, turn up, clock in, sign in; *Brit.* clock on; *N. Amer.* punch in; *informal* show up.
▶ noun ❶ *a full report on the meeting* ACCOUNT, review, record, description, statement; transactions, proceedings, transcripts, minutes. ❷ *reports of drug dealing* NEWS, information, word, intelligence; *poetic/literary* tidings. ❸ *newspaper reports* STORY, account, article, piece, item, column, feature, bulletin, dispatch. ❹ (*Brit.*) *a school report* ASSESSMENT, evaluation, appraisal; *N. Amer.* report card. ❺ *reports of his imminent resignation* RUMOUR, whisper; *informal* buzz; *archaic* bruit. ❻ *the report of a gun* BANG, blast, crack, shot, gunshot, explosion, boom. ❼ (*archaic*) *of good report. See* REPUTATION.

reporter ▶ noun JOURNALIST, correspondent, newspaperman, newspaperwoman, newsman, newswoman, columnist; *Brit.* pressman;

N. Amer. legman, wireman; *Austral.* roundsman; *informal* news hound, hack, stringer, journo; *N. Amer. informal* newsy.

repose ▶ **noun** ❶ *a face in repose* REST, relaxation, inactivity; sleep, slumber. ❷ *they found true repose* PEACE (AND QUIET), peacefulness, quiet, quietness, calm, tranquillity. ❸ *he lost his repose* COMPOSURE, serenity, equanimity, poise, self-possession, aplomb.

▶ **verb** ❶ *the diamond reposed on a bed of velvet* LIE, rest, be placed, be situated. ❷ (*poetic/literary*) *the trust he had reposed in her* PUT, place, invest, entrust. ❸ *the beds where we reposed* LIE (DOWN), recline, rest, sleep; *poetic/literary* slumber.

repository ▶ **noun** STORE, storehouse, depository; reservoir, bank, cache, treasury, fund, mine.

reprehensible ▶ **adjective** DEPLORABLE, disgraceful, discreditable, despicable, blameworthy, culpable, wrong, bad, shameful, dishonourable, objectionable, opprobrious, repugnant, inexcusable, unforgivable, indefensible, unjustifiable; criminal, sinful, scandalous, iniquitous; *formal* exceptionable.
– OPPOSITES praiseworthy.

represent ▶ **verb** ❶ *a character representing a single quality* SYMBOLIZE, stand for, personify, epitomize, typify, embody, illustrate. ❷ *the initials which represent her qualification* STAND FOR, designate, denote; *poetic/literary* betoken. ❸ *Hathor is represented as a woman with cow's horns* DEPICT, portray, render, picture, delineate, show, illustrate; *poetic/literary* limn. ❹ *he represented himself as the owner of the factory* DESCRIBE AS, present as, profess to be, claim to be, pass oneself off as, pose as, pretend to be. ❺ *ageing represents a threat to one's independence* CONSTITUTE, be, amount to, be regarded as. ❻ *a panel representing a cross section of the public* BE A TYPICAL SAMPLE OF, be representative of, typify. ❼ *his solicitor represented him in court* APPEAR FOR, act for, speak on behalf of. ❽ *the Queen was represented by Lord Lewin* DEPUTIZE FOR, substitute for, stand in for. ❾ (*formal*) *I represented the case as I saw it* POINT OUT, state, present, put forward. ❿ (*formal*) *the vendors represented that the information was accurate* CLAIM, maintain, state, affirm, contend; *rare* asseverate.

representation ▶ **noun** ❶ *Rossetti's representation of women* PORTRAYAL, depiction, delineation, presentation, rendition. ❷ *representations of the human form* LIKENESS, painting, drawing, picture, illustration, sketch, image, model, figure, figurine, statue, statuette. ❸ (*formal*) *making representations to the council* STATEMENT, deposition, allegation, declaration, exposition, report, protestation.

representative ▶ **adjective** ❶ *a representative sample* TYPICAL, prototypical, characteristic, illustrative, archetypal. ❷ *a female figure representative of Britain* SYMBOLIC, emblematic. ❸ *representative government* ELECTED, elective, democratic, popular.
– OPPOSITES atypical, totalitarian.

▶ **noun** ❶ *a representative of the Royal Society* SPOKESPERSON, spokesman, spokeswoman, agent, official, mouthpiece. ❷ *a sales representative* (COMMERCIAL) TRAVELLER, (travelling) salesman, saleswoman, agent; *informal* rep; *N. Amer. informal* drummer. ❸ *the Cambodian representative at the UN* DELEGATE, commissioner, ambassador, attaché, envoy, emissary, chargé d'affaires, deputy. ❹ *our representatives in parliament* MEMBER (OF PARLIAMENT), MP; councillor; *N. Amer.* Member of Congress, senator. ❺ *he acted as his father's representative* DEPUTY, substitute, stand-in, proxy. ❻ *fossil representatives of lampreys* EXAMPLE, specimen, exemplar, exemplification.

repress ▶ **verb** ❶ *the rebellion was repressed* SUPPRESS, quell, quash, subdue, put down, crush, extinguish, stamp out, defeat, conquer, rout, overwhelm, contain. ❷ *the peasants were repressed* OPPRESS, subjugate, keep down, rule with a rod of iron, intimidate, tyrannize, crush. ❸ *these emotions may well be repressed* RESTRAIN, hold back/in, keep back, suppress, keep in check, control, keep under control, curb, stifle, bottle up; *informal* button up, keep the lid on.

repressed ▶ **adjective** ❶ *a repressed country* OPPRESSED, subjugated, subdued, tyrannized. ❷ *repressed feelings* RESTRAINED, suppressed, held back/in, kept in check, stifled, pent up, bottled up. ❸ *emotionally repressed* INHIBITED, frustrated, restrained; *informal* uptight, hung up.
– OPPOSITES democratic, uninhibited.

repression ▶ **noun** ❶ *the repression of the protests* SUPPRESSION, quashing, subduing, crushing, stamping out. ❷ *political repression* OPPRESSION, subjugation, suppression, tyranny, despotism, authoritarianism. ❸ *the repression of sexual urges* RESTRAINT, restraining, holding back, keeping back, suppression, keeping in check, control, keeping under control, stifling, bottling up.

repressive ▶ **adjective** OPPRESSIVE, authoritarian, despotic, tyrannical, dictatorial, fascist, autocratic, totalitarian, undemocratic.

reprieve ▶ **verb** ❶ *she was reprieved* GRANT A STAY OF EXECUTION TO, pardon, spare, grant an amnesty to, amnesty; *informal* let off (the hook); *archaic* respite. ❷ *the project has been reprieved* SAVE, rescue; *informal* take off the hit list.

▶ **noun** *a last-minute reprieve* STAY OF EXECUTION, remission, pardon, amnesty; *US Law* continuance; *informal* let-off.

reprimand ▶ **verb** *he was publicly reprimanded* REBUKE, admonish, chastise, chide, upbraid, reprove, reproach, scold, berate, take to task, lambaste, give someone a piece of one's mind, haul over the coals, lecture, criticize, censure;

informal tell off, give someone a telling-off, give someone a talking-to, dress down, give someone a dressing-down, give someone an earful, give someone a roasting, rap over the knuckles, slap someone's wrist, bawl out, pitch into, lay into, lace into, blast; *Brit. informal* tick off, carpet, tear off a strip, give someone what for, give someone a wigging, give someone a rocket, give someone a rollicking; *N. Amer. informal* chew out, ream out; *Austral. informal* monster; *formal* castigate; *dated* give someone a rating; *rare* reprehend, objurgate.
– OPPOSITES praise.
▶ **noun** *they received a severe reprimand* REBUKE, reproof, admonishment, admonition, reproach, reproval, scolding, upbraiding, censure; *informal* telling-off, rap over the knuckles, slap on the wrist, flea in one's ear, dressing-down, earful, roasting, tongue-lashing; *Brit. informal* ticking-off, carpeting, wigging, rocket, rollicking; *formal* castigation; *dated* rating.
– OPPOSITES commendation.

reprisal ▶ **noun** RETALIATION, counter-attack, comeback; revenge, vengeance, retribution, requital; *informal* a taste of one's own medicine.

reproach ▶ **verb** *Albert reproached him for being late. See* REPRIMAND verb.
▶ **noun** ❶ *an expression of reproach. See* REPRIMAND noun. ❷ *this party is a reproach to British politics* DISGRACE, discredit, source of shame, blemish, stain, blot; *poetic/literary* smirch.
■ **beyond/above reproach** PERFECT, blameless, above suspicion, without fault, faultless, flawless, irreproachable, exemplary, impeccable, immaculate, unblemished, spotless, untarnished, stainless, unsullied, whiter than white; *informal* squeaky clean.

reproachful ▶ **adjective** DISAPPROVING, reproving, critical, censorious, disparaging, withering, accusatory, admonitory; *formal* castigatory.
– OPPOSITES approving.

reprobate ▶ **noun** *a hardened reprobate* ROGUE, rascal, scoundrel, miscreant, good-for-nothing, villain, wretch, rake, degenerate, libertine, debauchee; *informal, dated* rotter, bounder; *dated* cad; *archaic* blackguard, knave, rapscallion, scapegrace.
▶ **adjective** *reprobate behaviour* UNPRINCIPLED, bad, roguish, wicked, rakish, shameless, immoral, degenerate, dissipated, debauched, depraved; *archaic* knavish.
▶ **verb** (*archaic*) *they reprobated his conduct* CRITICIZE, condemn, censure, denounce.

reproduce ▶ **verb** ❶ *each artwork is reproduced in colour* COPY, duplicate, replicate; photocopy, xerox, photostat, print. ❷ *this work has not been reproduced in other laboratories* REPEAT, replicate, recreate, redo; simulate, imitate, emulate, mirror, mimic. ❸ *some animals reproduce prolifically* BREED, produce offspring, procreate, propagate, multiply.

reproduction ▶ **noun** ❶ *colour reproduction* COPYING, duplication, duplicating; photocopying, xeroxing, photostatting, printing. ❷ *a reproduction of the original* PRINT, copy, reprint, duplicate, facsimile, carbon copy, photocopy; *trademark* Xerox. ❸ *the process of reproduction* BREEDING, procreation, multiplying, propagation.

reproductive ▶ **adjective** GENERATIVE, procreative, propagative; sexual, genital.

reproof ▶ **noun** REBUKE, reprimand, reproach, admonishment, admonition; disapproval, censure, criticism, condemnation; *informal* telling-off, dressing down; *Brit. informal* ticking-off; *dated* rating.

reprove ▶ **verb** REPRIMAND, rebuke, reproach, scold, admonish, chastise, chide, upbraid, berate, take to task, haul over the coals, criticize, censure; *informal* tell off, give someone a telling-off, give someone a talking-to, dress down, give someone a dressing-down, give someone an earful, give someone a roasting, rap over the knuckles, slap someone's wrist; *Brit. informal* tick off, carpet, tear off a strip, give someone a rocket, give someone a rollicking; *formal* castigate; *dated* give someone a rating; *rare* reprehend, objurgate.

reptile
– RELATED TERMS saurian.

reptilian ▶ **adjective** ❶ *reptilian species* REPTILE, reptile-like, saurian; cold-blooded. ❷ *a reptilian smirk* UNPLEASANT, distasteful, nasty, disagreeable, unattractive, off-putting, horrible, horrid; unctuous, ingratiating, oily, oleaginous; *informal* smarmy, slimy, creepy.

repudiate ▶ **verb** ❶ *she repudiated communism* REJECT, renounce, abandon, give up, turn one's back on, disown, cast off, lay aside; *formal* forswear, abjure; *poetic/literary* forsake. ❷ *Cranham repudiated the allegations* DENY, refute, contradict, controvert, rebut, dispute, dismiss, brush aside; *formal* gainsay. ❸ *Egypt repudiated the treaty* CANCEL, revoke, rescind, reverse, overrule, overturn, invalidate, nullify; disregard, flout, renege on; *Law* disaffirm; *formal* abrogate.
– OPPOSITES embrace, confirm.

repudiation ▶ **noun** ❶ *the repudiation of one's religion* REJECTION, renunciation, abandonment, forswearing, giving up; *rare* abjuration. ❷ *his repudiation of the allegations* DENIAL, refutation, rebuttal, rejection. ❸ *a repudiation of the contract* CANCELLATION, revocation, rescindment, reversal, invalidation, nullification; *Law* disaffirmation; *formal* abrogation.

repugnance ▶ **noun** REVULSION, disgust, abhorrence, repulsion, loathing, hatred, detestation, aversion, distaste, antipathy, contempt; *archaic* disrelish.

repugnant ▶ **adjective** ❶ *the idea of cannibalism is repugnant* ABHORRENT, revolting, repulsive, repellent, disgusting, offensive, objectionable,

vile, foul, nasty, loathsome, sickening, nauseating, hateful, detestable, execrable, abominable, monstrous, appalling, insufferable, intolerable, unacceptable, contemptible, unsavoury, unpalatable; *informal* ghastly, gross, horrible, horrid; *poetic/literary* noisome. ❷ (*formal*) *the restriction is repugnant to the tenancy* INCOMPATIBLE WITH, in conflict with, contrary to, at variance with, inconsistent with.
– OPPOSITES pleasant.

repulse ▶ verb ❶ *the rebels were repulsed* REPEL, drive back/away, fight back/off, put to flight, force back, beat off/back; ward off, hold off; *Brit.* see off; *archaic* rebut. ❷ *her advances repulsed* REBUFF, reject, spurn, snub, cold-shoulder; *informal* give someone the brush-off, freeze out; *Brit. informal* knock back; *N. Amer. informal* give someone the bum's rush. ❸ *his bid for the company was repulsed* REJECT, turn down, refuse, decline. ❹ *the brutality repulsed her* REVOLT, disgust, repel, sicken, nauseate, turn someone's stomach, be repugnant to; *informal* turn off; *N. Amer. informal* gross out.
▶ noun ❶ *the repulse of the attack* REPELLING, driving back; warding off, holding off. ❷ *he was mortified by this repulse* REBUFF, rejection, snub, slight; *informal* brush-off, knock-back.

repulsion ▶ noun DISGUST, revulsion, abhorrence, repugnance, nausea, horror, aversion, abomination, distaste; *archaic* disrelish.

repulsive ▶ adjective REVOLTING, disgusting, abhorrent, repellent, repugnant, offensive, objectionable, vile, foul, nasty, loathsome, sickening, nauseating, hateful, detestable, execrable, abominable, monstrous, noxious, horrendous, awful, terrible, dreadful, frightful, obnoxious, unsavoury, unpleasant, disagreeable, distasteful; ugly, hideous, grotesque; *informal* ghastly, horrible, horrid, gross; *poetic/literary* noisome; *archaic* disgustful, loathly.
– OPPOSITES attractive.

reputable ▶ adjective WELL THOUGHT OF, highly regarded, (well) respected, respectable, of (good) repute, prestigious, established; reliable, dependable, trustworthy; *archaic* of good report.
– OPPOSITES untrustworthy.

reputation ▶ noun (GOOD) NAME, character, repute, standing, stature, status, position, renown, esteem, prestige; *N. Amer. informal* rep, rap; *archaic* honour, report.

repute ▶ noun ❶ *a woman of ill repute* REPUTATION, name, character; *archaic* report. ❷ *a firm of international repute* FAME, renown, celebrity, distinction, high standing, stature, prestige.

reputed ▶ adjective ❶ *they are reputed to be very rich* THOUGHT, said, reported, rumoured, believed, held, considered, regarded, deemed, alleged. ❷ *his reputed father* SUPPOSED, putative. ❸ *a reputed naturalist* WELL THOUGHT OF, (well) respected, highly regarded, of good repute.

reputedly ▶ adverb SUPPOSEDLY, by all accounts, so I'm told, so people say, allegedly.

request ▶ noun ❶ *requests for assistance* APPEAL, entreaty, plea, petition, application, demand, call; *formal* adjuration; *poetic/literary* behest. ❷ *Charlotte spoke, at Ursula's request* BIDDING, entreaty, demand, insistence. ❸ *indicate your requests on the form* REQUIREMENT, wish, desire; choice.
▶ verb ❶ *the government requested military aid* ASK FOR, appeal for, call for, seek, solicit, plead for, apply for, demand; *formal* adjure. ❷ *I requested him to help* CALL ON, beg, entreat, implore; *poetic/literary* beseech.

require ▶ verb ❶ *the child required hospital treatment* NEED, be in need of. ❷ *a situation requiring patience* NECESSITATE, demand, call for, involve, entail. ❸ *unquestioning obedience is required* DEMAND, insist on, call for, ask for, expect. ❹ *she was required to pay costs* ORDER, instruct, command, enjoin, oblige, compel, force. ❺ *do you require anything else?* WANT, wish to have, desire; lack, be short of.

required ▶ adjective ❶ *required reading* ESSENTIAL, vital, indispensable, necessary, compulsory, obligatory, mandatory, prescribed. ❷ *cut it to the required length* DESIRED, preferred, chosen; correct, proper, right.
– OPPOSITES optional.

requirement ▶ noun NEED, wish, demand, want, necessity, essential, prerequisite, stipulation.

requisite ▶ adjective *he lacks the requisite skills* NECESSARY, required, prerequisite, essential, indispensable, vital.
– OPPOSITES optional.
▶ noun ❶ *toilet requisites* REQUIREMENT, need, necessity, essential. ❷ *a requisite for a successful career* NECESSITY, essential (requirement), prerequisite, precondition, sine qua non; *informal* must.

requisition ▶ noun ❶ *requisitions for staff* ORDER, request, call, application, claim, demand; *Brit.* indent. ❷ *the requisition of cultural treasures* APPROPRIATION, commandeering, seizure, confiscation, expropriation.
▶ verb ❶ *the house was requisitioned by the army* COMMANDEER, appropriate, take over, take possession of, occupy, seize, confiscate, expropriate. ❷ *she requisitioned statements* REQUEST, order, call for, demand.

requital ▶ noun ❶ *in requital of your kindness* REPAYMENT, return, payment, recompense. ❷ *personal requital* REVENGE, vengeance, retribution, redress.

requite ▶ verb ❶ *requiting their hospitality* RETURN, reciprocate, repay. ❷ *Drake had requited the wrongs inflicted on them* AVENGE, exact revenge for, revenge, pay someone back for; take reprisals, settle the score, get even. ❸ *she did not requite his love* RECIPROCATE, return.

rescind ▶ **verb** REVOKE, repeal, cancel, reverse, overturn, overrule, annul, nullify, void, invalidate, quash, abolish; *Law* vacate; *formal* abrogate; *archaic* recall.
– OPPOSITES enforce.

rescission ▶ **noun** (*formal*) REVOCATION, repeal, rescindment, annulment, nullification, invalidation, voiding; *formal* abrogation; *archaic* recall.

rescue ▶ **verb** ❶ *an attempt to rescue the hostages* SAVE (FROM DANGER), save the life of, come to the aid of; (set) free, release, liberate. ❷ *Boyd rescued his papers* RETRIEVE, recover, salvage, get back.
▶ **noun** *the rescue of 10 crewmen* SAVING, rescuing; release, freeing, liberation, deliverance, redemption.
■ **come to someone's rescue** HELP, assist, lend a (helping) hand to, bail out; *informal* save someone's bacon, save someone's neck, save someone's skin.

research ▶ **noun** ❶ *medical research* INVESTIGATION, experimentation, testing, analysis, fact-finding, examination, scrutiny, scrutinization. ❷ *he continued his researches* EXPERIMENTS, experimentation, tests, inquiries, studies.
▶ **verb** ❶ *the phenomenon has been widely researched* INVESTIGATE, study, inquire into, look into, probe, explore, analyse, examine, scrutinize, review. ❷ *I researched all the available material* STUDY, read (up on), sift through; *informal* check out.

resemblance ▶ **noun** SIMILARITY, likeness, similitude, correspondence, congruity, congruence, coincidence, conformity, agreement, equivalence, comparability, parallelism, uniformity, sameness.

resemble ▶ **verb** LOOK LIKE, be similar to, be like, bear a resemblance to, remind one of, take after, favour, have the look of; approximate to, smack of, have (all) the hallmarks of, correspond to, echo, mirror, parallel.

resent ▶ **verb** BEGRUDGE, feel aggrieved at/about, feel bitter about, grudge, be annoyed at/about, be resentful of, dislike, take exception to, object to, take amiss, take offence at, take umbrage at, bear/harbour a grudge about.
– OPPOSITES welcome.

resentful ▶ **adjective** AGGRIEVED, indignant, irritated, piqued, put out, in high dudgeon, dissatisfied, disgruntled, discontented, offended, bitter, jaundiced; envious, jealous; *informal* miffed, peeved; *Brit. informal* narked; *N. Amer. informal* sore.

resentment ▶ **noun** BITTERNESS, indignation, irritation, pique, dissatisfaction, disgruntlement, discontentment, discontent, resentfulness, bad feelings, hard feelings, ill will, acrimony, rancour, animosity, jaundice; envy, jealousy.

reservation ▶ **noun** ❶ *grave reservations* DOUBT, qualm, scruple; misgivings, scepticism, unease, hesitation, objection. ❷ *group reservations* (ADVANCE) BOOKING; *dated* engagement. ❸ *the reservation of the room* BOOKING, ordering, securing; *dated* engagement. ❹ *Indian reservation* RESERVE, enclave, sanctuary, territory, homeland.
■ **without reservation** WHOLEHEARTEDLY, unreservedly, without qualification, fully, completely, totally, entirely, wholly, unconditionally.

reserve ▶ **verb** ❶ *ask your newsagent to reserve you a copy* PUT TO ONE SIDE, put aside, set aside, keep (back), save, hold back, keep in reserve, earmark. ❷ *he reserved a table* BOOK, make a reservation for, order, arrange for, secure; *formal* bespeak; *dated* engage. ❸ *the management reserves the right to alter the programme* RETAIN, keep, hold. ❹ *reserve your judgement until you know him better* DEFER, postpone, put off, delay, withhold.
▶ **noun** ❶ *reserves of petrol* STOCK, store, supply, stockpile, pool, hoard, cache. ❷ *the army are calling up reserves* REINFORCEMENTS, extras, auxiliaries. ❸ *a nature reserve* NATIONAL PARK, sanctuary, preserve, conservation area. ❹ *his natural reserve* RETICENCE, detachment, distance, remoteness, coolness, aloofness, constraint, formality; shyness, diffidence, timidity, taciturnity, inhibition; *informal* stand-offishness. ❺ *she trusted him without reserve* RESERVATION, qualification, condition, limitation, hesitation, doubt.
▶ **adjective** *a reserve goalkeeper* SUBSTITUTE, stand-in, relief, replacement, fallback, spare, extra.
■ **in reserve** AVAILABLE, to/on hand, ready, in readiness, set aside, at one's disposal.

reserved ▶ **adjective** ❶ *Sewell is rather reserved* RETICENT, quiet, private, uncommunicative, unforthcoming, undemonstrative, unsociable, formal, constrained, cool, aloof, detached, distant, remote, unapproachable, unfriendly, withdrawn, secretive, silent, taciturn; shy, retiring, diffident, timid, self-effacing, inhibited, introverted; *informal* stand-offish. ❷ *that table is reserved* BOOKED, taken, spoken for, pre-arranged; *dated* engaged; *formal* bespoken.
– OPPOSITES outgoing.

reservoir ▶ **noun** ❶ *sailing on the reservoir* lake, pool, pond; water supply; *Scottish* loch. ❷ *an ink reservoir* RECEPTACLE, container, holder, repository, tank. ❸ *the reservoir of managerial talent* STOCK, store, stockpile, reserve(s), supply, bank, pool, fund.

reshuffle ▶ **verb** *the prime minister reshuffled his cabinet* REORGANIZE, restructure, rearrange, change (around), shake up, shuffle.
▶ **noun** *a management reshuffle* REORGANIZATION, restructuring, change, rearrangement; *informal* shake-up.

reside ▶ **verb** ❶ *most students reside in flats* LIVE IN, occupy, inhabit, stay in, lodge in; *formal* dwell in, be domiciled in. ❷ *the paintings reside* *in an air-conditioned vault* BE SITUATED, be found, be located, lie. ❸ *executive power resides in the president* BE VESTED IN, be bestowed on, be conferred on, be in the hands of. ❹ *the qualities that reside within each individual* BE INHERENT, be present, exist.

residence ▶ **noun** ❶ (*formal*) *her private residence* HOME, house, place of residence, address; quarters, lodgings; *informal* pad; *formal* dwelling (place), domicile, abode. ❷ *his place of residence* OCCUPANCY, habitation, residency; *formal* abode.

resident ▶ **noun** ❶ *the residents of New York City* INHABITANT, local, citizen, native; householder, homeowner, occupier, tenant; *formal* denizen. ❷ (*Brit.*) *the bar is open to residents only* GUEST, lodger.

▶ **adjective** ❶ *resident in the UK* LIVING, residing, in residence; *formal* dwelling. ❷ *a resident nanny* LIVE-IN, living in. ❸ *the resident registrar in obstetrics* PERMANENT, incumbent.

residential ▶ **adjective** SUBURBAN, commuter, dormitory.

residual ▶ **adjective** ❶ *residual heat* REMAINING, leftover, unused, unconsumed. ❷ *residual affection* LINGERING, enduring, abiding, surviving, vestigial.

residue ▶ **noun** REMAINDER, remaining part, rest, remnant(s); surplus, extra, excess; remains, leftovers; *technical* residuum.

resign ▶ **verb** ❶ *the senior manager resigned* LEAVE, hand in one's notice, give notice, stand down, step down; *informal* quit. ❷ *19 MPs resigned their seats* GIVE UP, leave, vacate, stand down from; *informal* quit, pack in; *archaic* demit. ❸ *he resigned his right to the title* RENOUNCE, relinquish, give up, abandon, surrender, forego, cede; *Law* disclaim; *poetic/literary* forsake. ❹ *we resigned ourselves to a long wait* RECONCILE ONESELF TO, become resigned to, come to terms with.

resignation ▶ **noun** ❶ *his resignation from his post* DEPARTURE, leaving, standing down, stepping down; *informal* quitting. ❷ *she handed in her resignation* NOTICE (TO QUIT), letter of resignation. ❸ *he accepted his fate with resignation* PATIENCE, forbearance, stoicism, fortitude, fatalism, acceptance, acquiescence, compliance, passivity.

resigned ▶ **adjective** PATIENT, long-suffering, uncomplaining, forbearing, stoical, philosophical, fatalistic, acquiescent, compliant, passive.

resilient ▶ **adjective** ❶ *resilient materials* FLEXIBLE, pliable, supple; durable, hard-wearing, stout, strong, sturdy, tough. ❷ *young and resilient* STRONG, tough, hardy; quick to recover, buoyant, irrepressible.

resist ▶ **verb** ❶ *built to resist cold winters* WITHSTAND, be proof against, combat, weather, endure, be resistant to, keep out. ❷ *they resisted his attempts to change things* OPPOSE, fight against, refuse to accept, object to, defy, set one's face against, kick against; obstruct, impede, hinder, block, thwart, frustrate; *informal* be anti. ❸ *I resisted the urge to retort* REFRAIN FROM, abstain from, forbear from, desist from, not give in to, restrain oneself from, stop oneself from. ❹ *she tried to resist him* STRUGGLE WITH/AGAINST, fight (against), stand up to, withstand, hold off; fend off, ward off.

– OPPOSITES welcome, submit.

■ **cannot resist** LOVE, adore, relish, have a weakness for, be very keen on, like, delight in, enjoy, take great pleasure in; *informal* be mad about, get a kick/thrill out of.

resistance ▶ **noun** ❶ *resistance to change* OPPOSITION, hostility, refusal to accept. ❷ *a spirited resistance* OPPOSITION, fight, stand, struggle. ❸ *the body's resistance to disease* ABILITY TO FIGHT OFF, immunity from, defences against. ❹ *the French resistance* RESISTANCE MOVEMENT, freedom fighters, underground, partisans.

resistant ▶ **adjective** ❶ *resistant to water* IMPERVIOUS, unsusceptible, immune, invulnerable, proof against, unaffected by. ❷ *resistant to change* OPPOSED, averse, hostile, inimical, against; *informal* anti.

resolute ▶ **adjective** DETERMINED, purposeful, resolved, adamant, single-minded, firm, unswerving, unwavering, steadfast, staunch, stalwart, unfaltering, unhesitating, persistent, indefatigable, tenacious, strong-willed, unshakeable; stubborn, dogged, obstinate, obdurate, inflexible, intransigent, implacable, unyielding, unrelenting; spirited, brave, bold, courageous, plucky, indomitable; *N. Amer.* rock-ribbed; *informal* gutsy, spunky; *formal* pertinacious.

– OPPOSITES half-hearted.

resolution ▶ **noun** ❶ *her resolution not to smoke* INTENTION, resolve, decision, intent, aim, plan; commitment, pledge, promise. ❷ *the committee passed the resolution* MOTION, proposal, proposition; *N. Amer.* resolve. ❸ *she handled the work with resolution* DETERMINATION, purpose, purposefulness, resolve, resoluteness, single-mindedness, firmness (of purpose); steadfastness, staunchness, perseverance, persistence, indefatigability, tenacity, tenaciousness, staying power, dedication, commitment; stubbornness, doggedness, obstinacy, obduracy; boldness, spiritedness, braveness, bravery, courage, pluck, grit, courageousness; *informal* guts, spunk; *formal* pertinacity. ❹ *a satisfactory resolution of the problem* SOLUTION, answer, end, ending, settlement, conclusion.

resolve ▶ **verb** ❶ *this matter cannot be resolved overnight* SETTLE, sort out, solve, find a solution to, fix, straighten out, deal with, put right, put to rights, rectify; *informal* hammer out, thrash out, figure out. ❷ *Charity resolved not to wait any longer* DETERMINE, decide, make up one's mind, take a decision. ❸ *the committee resolved that the* *project should proceed* VOTE, pass a resolution, rule, decide formally, agree. ❹ *the compounds were resolved into their active constituents* BREAK DOWN/UP, separate, reduce, divide. ❺ *the ability to resolve facts into their legal categories* ANALYSE, dissect, break down. ❻ *the grey smudge resolved into a sandy beach* TURN, change, be transformed.

▶ **noun** ❶ *their intimidation merely strengthened his resolve. See* RESOLUTION sense 3. ❷ (*N. Amer.*) *he made a resolve not to go there again* DECISION, resolution, commitment.

resolved ▶ **adjective** DETERMINED, hell bent, intent, set.

resonant ▶ **adjective** ❶ *a resonant voice* DEEP, low, sonorous, full, full-bodied, vibrant, rich, clear, ringing; loud, booming, thunderous. ❷ *valleys resonant with the sound of church bells* REVERBERATING, reverberant, resounding, echoing, filled. ❸ *resonant words* EVOCATIVE, suggestive, expressive, redolent.

resort ▶ **noun** ❶ *a seaside resort* HOLIDAY DESTINATION, (tourist) centre; *informal* honeypot. ❷ *settle the matter without resort to legal proceedings* RECOURSE TO, turning to, the use of, utilizing. ❸ *strike action is our last resort* EXPEDIENT, measure, step, recourse, alternative, option, choice, possibility, hope.

■ **in the last resort** ULTIMATELY, in the end, at the end of the day, in the long run, when all is said and done.

■ **resort to** HAVE RECOURSE TO, fall back on, turn to, make use of, use, employ, avail oneself of; stoop to, descend to, sink to.

resound ▶ **verb** ❶ *the explosion resounded round the silent street* ECHO, re-echo, reverberate, ring out, boom, thunder, rumble. ❷ *resounding with the clang of hammers* REVERBERATE, echo, re-echo, resonate, ring. ❸ *nothing will resound like their earlier achievements* BE ACCLAIMED, be celebrated, be renowned, be famed, be glorified, be trumpeted.

resounding ▶ **adjective** ❶ *a resounding voice* REVERBERANT, reverberating, resonant, resonating, echoing, ringing, sonorous, deep, rich, clear; loud, booming. ❷ *a resounding success* ENORMOUS, huge, very great, tremendous, terrific, colossal; emphatic, decisive, conclusive, outstanding, remarkable, phenomenal.

resource ▶ **noun** ❶ *use your resources efficiently* ASSETS, funds, wealth, money, capital; staff; supplies, materials, store(s), stock(s), reserve(s). ❷ *your tutor is there as a resource* FACILITY, amenity, aid, help, support. ❸ *tears were her only resource* EXPEDIENT, resort, course, scheme, stratagem; trick, ruse, device. ❹ *a person of resource* INITIATIVE, resourcefulness, enterprise, ingenuity, inventiveness; talent, ability, capability; *informal* gumption.

resourceful ▶ **adjective** INGENIOUS, enterprising, inventive, creative; clever, talented, able, capable.

respect ▶ **noun** ❶ *the respect due to a great artist* ESTEEM, regard, high opinion, admiration, reverence, deference, honour. ❷ *he spoke to her with respect* DUE REGARD, politeness, courtesy, civility, deference. ❸ *paying one's respects* (KIND) REGARDS, compliments, greetings, best/good wishes, felicitations, salutations; *archaic* remembrances. ❹ *the report was accurate in every respect* ASPECT, regard, facet, feature, way, sense, particular, point, detail.

– OPPOSITES contempt.

▶ **verb** ❶ *he is highly respected for his industry* ESTEEM, admire, think highly of, have a high opinion of, hold in high regard, hold in (high) esteem, look up to, revere, reverence, honour. ❷ *they respected our privacy* SHOW CONSIDERATION FOR, have regard for, observe, be mindful of, be heedful of; *formal* take cognizance of. ❸ *father respected her wishes* ABIDE BY, comply with, follow, adhere to, conform to, act in accordance with, defer to, obey, observe, keep (to).

– OPPOSITES despise, disobey.

■ **with respect to/in respect of** CONCERNING, regarding, in/with regard to, with reference to, respecting, re, about, apropos, on the subject of, in connection with, vis-à-vis.

respectable ▶ **adjective** ❶ *a respectable middle-class background* REPUTABLE, of good repute, upright, honest, honourable, trustworthy, decent, good, well bred, clean-living. ❷ *a respectable salary* FAIRLY GOOD, decent, fair, reasonable, moderately good; substantial, considerable, sizable.

– OPPOSITES disreputable, paltry.

respectful ▶ **adjective** DEFERENTIAL, reverent, reverential, dutiful; polite, well mannered, civil, courteous, gracious.

– OPPOSITES rude.

respective ▶ **adjective** SEPARATE, personal, own, particular, individual, specific, special, appropriate, different, various.

respite ▶ **noun** ❶ *a brief respite* REST, break, breathing space, interval, intermission, interlude, recess, lull, pause, time out; relief, relaxation, repose; *informal* breather, let-up. ❷ *respite from debts* POSTPONEMENT, deferment, delay, reprieve; *US Law* continuance.

resplendent ▶ **adjective** SPLENDID, magnificent, brilliant, dazzling, glittering, gorgeous, impressive, imposing, spectacular, striking, stunning, majestic; *informal* splendiferous.

respond ▶ **verb** ❶ *they do not respond to questions* ANSWER, reply, make a response, make a rejoinder. ❷ *'No,' she responded* SAY IN RESPONSE, answer, reply, rejoin, retort, riposte, counter. ❸ *they were slow to respond* REACT, make a response, reciprocate, retaliate.

response ▶ **noun** ❶ *his response to the question* ANSWER, reply, rejoinder, retort, riposte; *informal* comeback. ❷ *an angry response* REACTION, reply, retaliation; *informal* comeback.

– OPPOSITES question.

responsibility ▶ noun ❶ *it was his responsibility to find witnesses* DUTY, task, function, job, role, business; *Brit. informal* pigeon. ❷ *they denied responsibility for the bomb attack* BLAME, fault, guilt, culpability, liability. ❸ *a sense of responsibility* TRUSTWORTHINESS, (common) sense, maturity, reliability, dependability. ❹ *managerial responsibility* AUTHORITY, control, power, leadership.

responsible ▶ adjective ❶ *who is responsible for prisons?* IN CHARGE OF, in control of, at the helm of, accountable for, liable for. ❷ *I am responsible for the mistake* ACCOUNTABLE, answerable, to blame, guilty, culpable, blameworthy, at fault, in the wrong. ❸ *a responsible job* IMPORTANT, powerful, executive. ❹ *he is responsible to the president* ANSWERABLE, accountable. ❺ *a responsible tenant* TRUSTWORTHY, sensible, mature, reliable, dependable.

responsive ▶ adjective QUICK TO REACT, reactive, receptive, open to suggestions, amenable, flexible, forthcoming.

rest[1] ▶ verb ❶ *he needed to rest* RELAX, take a rest, ease up/off, let up, slow down, have/take a break, unbend, unwind, recharge one's batteries, be at leisure, take it easy, put one's feet up; lie down, go to bed, have/take a nap, catnap, doze, sleep; *informal* take five, have/take a breather, snatch forty winks, get some shut-eye; *Brit. informal* have a kip; *N. Amer. informal* chill out, catch some Zs. ❷ *his hands rested on the rail* LIE, be laid, repose, be placed, be positioned, be supported by. ❸ *she rested her basket on the ground* SUPPORT, prop (up), lean, lay, set, stand, position, place, put. ❹ *the film script rests on an improbable premise* BE BASED, depend, be dependent, rely, hinge, turn on, be contingent, revolve around.

▶ noun ❶ *get some rest* REPOSE, relaxation, leisure, respite, time off, breathing space; sleep, nap, doze; *informal* shut-eye, snooze, lie-down, forty winks; *Brit. informal* kip. ❷ *a short rest from work* HOLIDAY, vacation, break, breathing space, interval, interlude, intermission, time off/out; *informal* breather. ❸ *she took the poker from its rest* STAND, base, holder, support, rack, frame, shelf. ❹ *we came to rest 100 metres lower* A STANDSTILL, a halt, a stop.

rest[2] ▶ noun *the rest of the board are appointees* REMAINDER, residue, balance, remaining part/number/quantity, others, those left, remains, remnant(s), surplus, excess; *technical* residuum.

▶ verb *you may rest assured that he is there* REMAIN, continue to be, stay, keep, carry on being.

restaurant ▶ noun EATING PLACE, bistro, cafe, cafeteria, carvery, brasserie; *N. Amer.* diner; *informal* eatery.

restful ▶ adjective RELAXED, relaxing, quiet, calm, calming, tranquil, soothing, peaceful, placid, reposeful, leisurely, undisturbed, untroubled.

–OPPOSITES exciting.

restitution ▶ noun ❶ *restitution of the land seized* RETURN, restoration, handing back, surrender. ❷ *restitution for the damage caused* COMPENSATION, recompense, reparation, damages, indemnification, indemnity, reimbursement, repayment, remuneration, redress; *archaic* guerdon.

restive ▶ adjective ❶ *Edward is getting restive. See* RESTLESS sense 1. ❷ *the militants are increasingly restive* UNRULY, disorderly, uncontrollable, unmanageable, wilful, recalcitrant, insubordinate; *Brit. informal* bolshie; *formal* refractory; *archaic* contumacious.

restless ▶ adjective ❶ *Maria was restless* UNEASY, ill at ease, restive, fidgety, edgy, on edge, tense, worked up, nervous, agitated, anxious, on tenterhooks, keyed up; *Brit.* nervy; *informal* jumpy, jittery, twitchy, uptight, like a cat on a hot tin roof; *Brit. informal* like a cat on hot bricks. ❷ *a restless night* SLEEPLESS, wakeful; fitful, broken, disturbed, troubled, unsettled; *rare* insomnolent.

restlessness ▶ noun UNEASE, restiveness, edginess, tenseness, nervousness, agitation, anxiety, fretfulness, apprehension, disquiet; *informal* jitteriness.

restoration ▶ noun ❶ *the restoration of democracy* REINSTATEMENT, reinstitution, re-establishment, reimposition, return. ❷ *the restoration of derelict housing* REPAIR, repairing, fixing, mending, refurbishment, reconditioning, rehabilitation, rebuilding, reconstruction, overhaul, redevelopment, renovation; *N. Amer. informal* rehab.

restore ▶ verb ❶ *the aim to restore democracy* REINSTATE, bring back, reinstitute, reimpose, reinstall, re-establish. ❷ *he restored it to its rightful owner* RETURN, give back, hand back. ❸ *the building has been restored* REPAIR, fix, mend, refurbish, recondition, rehabilitate, rebuild, reconstruct, remodel, overhaul, redevelop, renovate; *informal* do up; *N. Amer. informal* rehab. ❹ *a good sleep can restore you* REINVIGORATE, revitalize, revive, refresh, energize, fortify, revivify, regenerate, stimulate, freshen.

–OPPOSITES abolish.

restrain ▶ verb ❶ *Charles restrained his anger* CONTROL, keep under control, check, hold/keep in check, curb, suppress, repress, contain, dampen, subdue, smother, choke back, stifle, bottle up, rein back/in; *informal* keep the lid on. ❷ *she could barely restrain herself from swearing* PREVENT, stop, keep, hold back. ❸ *the insane used to be restrained* TIE UP, bind, tether, chain (up), fetter, shackle, manacle, put in irons.

restrained ▶ adjective ❶ *Julie was quite restrained* SELF-CONTROLLED, self-restrained, not given to excesses, sober, steady, unemotional, undemonstrative. ❷ *restrained elegance* MUTED, soft, discreet, subtle, quiet, unobtrusive, unostentatious, understated, tasteful.

restraint ▶ noun ❶ *a restraint on their impulsiveness* CONSTRAINT, check, control, restriction, limitation, curtailment; rein, bridle, brake, damper, impediment, obstacle. ❷ *the customary restraint of the police* SELF-CONTROL, self-restraint, self-discipline, control, moderation, prudence, judiciousness. ❸ *the room has been decorated with restraint* SUBTLETY, understatedness, taste, tastefulness, discretion, discrimination. ❹ *a child restraint* BELT, harness, strap.

restrict ▶ verb ❶ *a busy working life restricted his leisure activities* LIMIT, keep within bounds, regulate, control, moderate, cut down. ❷ *the cuff supports the ankle without restricting movement* HINDER, interfere with, impede, hamper, obstruct, block, check, curb. ❸ *he restricted himself to a 15-minute speech* CONFINE, limit.

restricted ▶ adjective ❶ *restricted space* CRAMPED, confined, constricted, small, narrow, tight; *archaic* strait. ❷ *a restricted calorie intake* LIMITED, controlled, regulated, reduced. ❸ *a restricted zone* OUT OF BOUNDS, off limits, private, exclusive. ❹ *restricted information* (TOP) SECRET, classified; *informal* hush-hush.
– OPPOSITES unlimited.

restriction ▶ noun ❶ *there is no restriction on the number of places* LIMITATION, limit, constraint, control, check, curb; condition, proviso, qualification. ❷ *the restriction of personal freedom* REDUCTION, limitation, diminution, curtailment. ❸ *restriction of movement* HINDRANCE, impediment, slowing, reduction, limitation.

result ▶ noun ❶ *stress is the result of overwork* CONSEQUENCE, outcome, upshot, sequel, effect, reaction, repercussion, ramification, conclusion, culmination. ❷ *what is your result?* ANSWER, solution; sum, total, product. ❸ *exam results* MARK, score, grade. ❹ *the result of the trial* VERDICT, decision, outcome, conclusion, judgement, findings, ruling.
– OPPOSITES cause.
▶ verb ❶ *differences between species could result from their habitat* FOLLOW, ensue, develop, stem, spring, arise, derive, evolve, proceed; occur, happen, take place, come about; be caused by, be brought about by, be produced by, originate in, be consequent on. ❷ *the shooting resulted in five deaths* END IN, culminate in, finish in, terminate in, lead to, prompt, precipitate, trigger; cause, bring about, occasion, effect, give rise to, produce, engender, generate; *poetic/literary* beget.

resume ▶ verb ❶ *the government resumed negotiations* RESTART, recommence, begin again, start again, reopen; renew, return to, continue with, carry on with. ❷ *the priest resumed his kneeling posture* RETURN TO, come back to, take up again, reoccupy.
– OPPOSITES suspend, abandon.

résumé ▶ noun SUMMARY, precis, synopsis, abstract, outline, summarization, summation, epitome; abridgement, digest, condensation, abbreviation, overview, review.

resumption ▶ noun RESTART, restarting, recommencement, reopening; continuation, carrying on, renewal, return to.

resurgence ▶ noun RENEWAL, revival, recovery, comeback, reawakening, resurrection, reappearance, re-emergence, regeneration; resumption, recommencement, continuation; *formal* renascence.

resurrect ▶ verb ❶ *Jesus was resurrected* RAISE FROM THE DEAD, restore to life, revive. ❷ *resurrecting his career* REVIVE, restore, regenerate, revitalize, breathe new life into, reinvigorate, resuscitate, rejuvenate, stimulate, re-establish, relaunch.

resuscitate ▶ verb ❶ *medics resuscitated him* BRING ROUND, revive, bring back to consciousness; give artificial respiration to, give the kiss of life to. ❷ *measures to resuscitate the economy* REVIVE, resurrect, restore, regenerate, revitalize, breathe new life into, reinvigorate, rejuvenate, stimulate.

retain ▶ verb ❶ *the government retained a share in the industries* KEEP (POSSESSION OF), keep hold of, hold on to, hang on to. ❷ *existing footpaths are to be retained* MAINTAIN, keep, preserve, conserve. ❸ *some students retain facts easily* REMEMBER, memorize, keep in one's mind/memory. ❹ *solicitors can retain a barrister* EMPLOY, contract, keep on the payroll.
– OPPOSITES give up, abolish.

retainer ▶ noun ❶ *they're paid a retainer* (RETAINING) FEE, periodic payment, advance, standing charge. ❷ *a faithful retainer. See* SERVANT sense 1.

retaliate ▶ verb FIGHT BACK, hit back, respond, react, reply, reciprocate, counter-attack, return like for like, get back at someone, give tit for tat, give someone a taste of their own medicine; have/get/take one's revenge, be revenged, avenge oneself, take reprisals, get even, pay someone back; *informal* get one's own back; *archaic* give someone a Roland for an Oliver.

retaliation ▶ noun REVENGE, vengeance, reprisal, retribution, requital, recrimination, repayment; response, reaction, reply, counterattack; *archaic* a Roland for an Oliver.

retard ▶ verb DELAY, slow down/up, hold back/up, set back, postpone, put back, detain, decelerate; hinder, hamper, obstruct, inhibit, impede, check, restrain, restrict, trammel; *poetic/literary* stay.
– OPPOSITES accelerate.

retch ▶ verb ❶ *the sour taste made her retch* GAG, heave; *informal* keck. ❷ *he retched all over the table. See* VOMIT verb sense 1.

reticence ▶ noun RESERVE, restraint, inhibition, diffidence, shyness; unresponsiveness, quietness, taciturnity, secretiveness.

reticent ▶adjective RESERVED, withdrawn, introverted, inhibited, diffident, shy; uncommunicative, unforthcoming, unresponsive, tight-lipped, quiet, taciturn, silent, guarded, secretive.
–OPPOSITES expansive.

retinue ▶noun ENTOURAGE, escort, company, court, staff, personnel, household, train, suite, following, bodyguard; aides, attendants, servants, retainers.

retire ▶verb ❶ *he has retired* GIVE UP WORK, stop working, stop work. ❷ *we've retired him on full pension* PENSION OFF, force to retire. ❸ *Gillian retired to her office* WITHDRAW, go away, take oneself off, decamp, shut oneself away; *formal* repair; *poetic/literary* betake oneself. ❹ *their forces retired* RETREAT, withdraw, pull back, fall back, disengage, back off, give ground. ❺ *everyone retired early* GO TO BED, call it a day, go to sleep; *informal* turn in, hit the hay/sack.

retired ▶adjective *a retired schoolteacher* FORMER, ex-, past, in retirement, elderly.
▶noun *apartments for the retired* RETIRED PEOPLE, (old-age) pensioners, OAPs, senior citizens, the elderly; *N. Amer.* seniors.

retirement ▶noun ❶ *they are nearing retirement* GIVING UP WORK, stopping working, stopping work. ❷ *retirement in an English village* SECLUSION, retreat, solitude, isolation, obscurity.

retiring ▶adjective ❶ *the retiring president* DEPARTING, outgoing. ❷ *a retiring man* SHY, diffident, self-effacing, unassuming, unassertive, reserved, reticent, quiet, timid, modest; private, secret, secretive, withdrawn, reclusive, unsociable.
–OPPOSITES incoming, outgoing.

retort ▶verb *'Oh, sure,' she retorted* ANSWER, reply, respond, say in response, return, counter, rejoin, riposte, retaliate, snap back.
▶noun *a sarcastic retort* ANSWER, reply, response, return, counter, rejoinder, riposte, retaliation; *informal* comeback.

retract ▶verb ❶ *the sea otter can retract its claws* PULL IN/BACK, draw in. ❷ *he retracted his allegation* TAKE BACK, withdraw, recant, disavow, disclaim, repudiate, renounce, reverse, revoke, rescind, go back on, backtrack on; *formal* abjure.

retreat ▶verb ❶ *the army retreated* WITHDRAW, retire, draw back, pull back/out, fall back, give way, give ground, beat a retreat. ❷ *the tide was retreating* GO OUT, ebb, recede, fall, go down. ❸ *the government had to retreat* CHANGE ONE'S MIND, change one's plans; back down, climb down, do a U-turn, backtrack, back-pedal, give in, concede defeat; *Brit.* do an about-turn.
–OPPOSITES advance.
▶noun ❶ *the retreat of the army* WITHDRAWAL, pulling back. ❷ *the President's retreat* CLIMBDOWN, backdown, about-face; *Brit.* about-turn. ❸ *her rural retreat* REFUGE, haven, sanctuary; hideaway, hideout, hiding place; *informal* hidey-hole. ❹ *a period of retreat from the world* SECLUSION, withdrawal, retirement, solitude, isolation, sanctuary.

retrench ▶verb ❶ *we have to retrench* ECONOMIZE, cut back, make cutbacks, make savings, make economies, reduce expenditure, be economical, be frugal, tighten one's belt. ❷ *services have to be retrenched* REDUCE, cut (back/down), pare (down), slim down, make reductions in, make cutbacks in, trim, prune; *informal* slash.

retribution ▶noun PUNISHMENT, penalty, one's just deserts; revenge, reprisal, requital, retaliation, vengeance, an eye for an eye (and a tooth for a tooth), tit for tat; redress, reparation, restitution, recompense, repayment, indemnification, atonement, amends.

retrieve ▶verb ❶ *I retrieved our balls from their garden* GET BACK, bring back, recover, regain (possession of), recoup, reclaim, repossess, redeem, recuperate. ❷ *they were trying to retrieve the situation* PUT/SET RIGHT, rectify, remedy, restore, sort out, straighten out, resolve.

retrograde ▶adjective ❶ *a retrograde step* FOR THE WORSE, regressive, negative, downhill, unwelcome. ❷ *retrograde motion* BACKWARD(S), reverse, rearward.
–OPPOSITES positive.

retrospect
■ **in retrospect** LOOKING BACK, on reflection, in/with hindsight.

retrospective ▶adjective BACKDATED, retroactive, ex post facto.

return ▶verb ❶ *he returned to London* GO BACK, come back, arrive back, come home. ❷ *the symptoms returned* RECUR, reoccur, occur again, repeat (itself); reappear, appear again. ❸ *he returned the money* GIVE BACK, hand back; pay back, repay. ❹ *Peter returned the book to the shelf* RESTORE, put back, replace, reinstall. ❺ *he returned the volley* HIT BACK, throw back. ❻ *she returned his kiss* RECIPROCATE, requite, give in return, repay, give back. ❼ *'Later,' returned Isabel* ANSWER, reply, respond, counter, rejoin, retort. ❽ *the jury returned a unanimous verdict* DELIVER, bring in, hand down. ❾ *the club returned a profit* YIELD, earn, realize, net, gross, clear. ❿ *the Labour candidate was returned* ELECT, vote in, choose, select.
–OPPOSITES depart, disappear, keep.
▶noun ❶ *his return to Paris* HOMECOMING. ❷ *the return of hard times* RECURRENCE, reoccurrence, repeat, repetition, reappearance, revival, resurrection, re-emergence, resurgence. ❸ *I requested the return of my books* GIVING BACK, handing back, replacement, restoration, reinstatement, restitution. ❹ *two returns to London* RETURN TICKET/FARE; *N. Amer.* round trip ticket/fare. ❺ *a quick return on investments* YIELD, profit, gain, revenue, interest, dividend. ❻ *a census*

return STATEMENT, report, submission, record, dossier; document, form.
– OPPOSITES departure, disappearance, single.
■ **in return for** IN EXCHANGE FOR, as a reward for, as compensation for.

revamp ▶ verb RENOVATE, redecorate, refurbish, recondition, rehabilitate, overhaul, make over; upgrade, refit, re-equip; remodel, refashion, redesign, restyle; *informal* do up, give something a facelift, vamp up; *Brit. informal* tart up; *N. Amer. informal* rehab.

reveal ▶ verb ❶ *the police can't reveal his whereabouts* DIVULGE, disclose, tell, let slip/drop, give away/out, blurt (out), release, leak; make known, make public, broadcast, publicize, circulate, disseminate; *informal* let on; *archaic* discover. ❷ *he revealed his new car* SHOW, display, exhibit, disclose, uncover; *poetic/literary* uncloak. ❸ *the data reveal a good deal of information* BRING TO LIGHT, uncover, lay bare, unearth, unveil; *formal* evince; *poetic/literary* uncloak.
– OPPOSITES hide.

revel ▶ verb ❶ *they revelled all night* CELEBRATE, make merry, have a party, carouse, roister, go on a spree; *informal* party, live it up, whoop it up, make whoopee, rave, paint the town red. ❷ *he revelled in the applause* ENJOY, delight in, love, like, adore, be pleased by, take pleasure in, appreciate, relish, lap up, savour; *informal* get a kick out of.
▶ noun *late-night revels* CELEBRATION, festivity, jollification, merrymaking, carousal, carouse, spree; party, jamboree; *informal* rave, shindig, bash; *Brit. informal* rave-up, knees-up; *N. Amer. informal* wingding, blast; *Austral. informal* rage, ding, jollo.

revelation ▶ noun ❶ *revelations about his personal life* DISCLOSURE, surprising fact, announcement, report; admission, confession. ❷ *the revelation of a secret* DIVULGING, divulgence, disclosure, disclosing, letting slip/drop, giving away/out, leaking, leak, betrayal, unveiling, making known, making public, broadcasting, publicizing, dissemination, reporting, report, declaring, declaration.

reveller ▶ noun MERRYMAKER, partygoer, carouser, roisterer; *archaic* wassailer.

revelry ▶ noun CELEBRATION(S), parties, revels, festivity, festivities, jollification, merrymaking, carousing, carousal, roistering; *informal* partying.

revenge ▶ noun ❶ *she is seeking revenge* VENGEANCE, retribution, retaliation, reprisal, requital, recrimination, an eye for an eye (and a tooth for a tooth), redress, satisfaction. ❷ *they were filled with revenge* VENGEFULNESS, vindictiveness, vitriol, spite, spitefulness, malice, maliciousness, malevolence, ill will, animosity, hate, hatred, rancour, bitterness; *poetic/literary* maleficence.
▶ verb ❶ *he revenged his brother's murder* AVENGE, take/exact revenge for, exact retribution for, take reprisals for, get redress for, get satisfaction for. ❷ *I'll be revenged on the whole pack of you* TAKE REVENGE ON, get one's revenge on, avenge oneself on, take vengeance on, get even with, settle a/the score with, pay back, take reprisals against; *informal* get one's own back on; *archaic* give someone a Roland for an Oliver.

revenue ▶ noun INCOME, takings, receipts, proceeds, earnings; profit(s).
– OPPOSITES expenditure.

reverberate ▶ verb RESOUND, echo, re-echo, resonate, ring, boom, rumble.

reverberation ▶ noun ❶ *natural reverberation* RESONANCE, echo, echoing, re-echoing, resounding, ringing, booming, rumbling. ❷ *political reverberations* REPERCUSSIONS, ramifications, consequences, shock waves; aftermath, fallout, backlash.

revere ▶ verb RESPECT, admire, think highly of, have a high opinion of, esteem, hold in high esteem/regard, look up to.
– OPPOSITES despise.

reverence ▶ noun *reverence for the countryside* HIGH ESTEEM, high regard, great respect, acclaim, admiration, appreciation, estimation, favour.
– OPPOSITES scorn.
▶ verb *they reverence modern jazz. See* REVERE.

reverent ▶ adjective RESPECTFUL, reverential, admiring, devoted, devout, dutiful, awed, deferential.

reverie ▶ noun DAYDREAM, daydreaming, trance, musing; inattention, inattentiveness, wool-gathering, preoccupation, absorption, abstraction, lack of concentration.

reversal ▶ noun ❶ *there was no reversal on this issue* TURNAROUND, turnabout, about-face, volte-face, change of heart, U-turn, backtracking; *Brit.* about-turn; *rare* tergiversation. ❷ *a reversal of roles* SWAP, exchange, change, swapping, interchange. ❸ *the reversal of the decision* ALTERATION, changing; countermanding, undoing, overturning, overthrow, disallowing, overriding, overruling, veto, vetoing, revocation, repeal, rescinding, annulment, nullification, voiding, invalidation; *formal* rescission, abrogation. ❹ *they suffered a reversal* SETBACK, reverse, upset, failure, misfortune, mishap, disaster, blow, disappointment, adversity, hardship, affliction, vicissitude, defeat; bad luck.

reverse ▶ verb ❶ *the car reversed into a lamp post* BACK, drive back/backwards, move back/backwards. ❷ *reverse the bottle in the ice bucket* TURN UPSIDE DOWN, turn over, upend, upturn, invert; *archaic* overset. ❸ *I reversed my jacket* TURN INSIDE OUT. ❹ *reverse your roles* SWAP (ROUND), change (round), exchange, interchange, switch (round). ❺ *the umpire reversed the decision* ALTER, change; overturn, overthrow, disallow, override, overrule, veto, revoke, repeal, rescind, annul, nullify, void, invalidate; *Brit.* do an about-turn on; *formal* abrogate.

▶ **adjective** *in reverse order* BACKWARD(S), reversed, inverted, transposed.

▶ **noun** ❶ *the reverse is the case* OPPOSITE, contrary, converse, inverse, obverse, antithesis. ❷ *successes and reverses. See* REVERSAL sense 4. ❸ *the reverse of the page* OTHER SIDE, reverse side, back, underside, wrong side, verso.

revert ▶ **verb** ❶ *life will soon revert to normal* RETURN, go back, change back, default; fall back, regress, relapse. ❷ *the property reverted to the landlord* BE RETURNED; *historical* escheat.

review ▶ **noun** ❶ *the Council undertook a review* ANALYSIS, evaluation, assessment, appraisal, examination, investigation, inquiry, probe, inspection, study. ❷ *the rent is due for review* RECONSIDERATION, reassessment, re-evaluation, reappraisal; change, alteration, modification, revision. ❸ *book reviews* CRITICISM, critique, assessment, evaluation, commentary; *Brit. informal* crit. ❹ *a scientific review* JOURNAL, periodical, magazine, publication. ❺ *their review of the economy* SURVEY, report, study, account, description, statement, overview. ❻ *a military review* INSPECTION, parade, tattoo, procession; *Brit.* march past.

▶ **verb** ❶ *I reviewed the evidence* SURVEY, study, research, consider, analyse, examine, scrutinize, explore, look into, probe, investigate, inspect, assess, appraise; *informal* size up. ❷ *the referee reviewed his decision* RECONSIDER, re-examine, reassess, re-evaluate, reappraise, rethink; change, alter, modify, revise. ❸ *he reviewed the day* REMEMBER, recall, reflect on, think through, go over in one's mind, look back on. ❹ *reviewing troops* INSPECT, view. ❺ *she reviewed the play* COMMENT ON, evaluate, assess, appraise, judge, critique, criticize.

reviewer ▶ **noun** CRITIC, COMMENTATOR, judge, observer, pundit, analyst.

revile ▶ **verb** CRITICIZE, censure, condemn, attack, inveigh against, rail against, lambaste, denounce; slander, libel, malign, vilify, besmirch, abuse; *informal* knock, slam, pan, crucify, roast, bad-mouth; *Brit. informal* slate, rubbish, slag off; *N. Amer. informal* pummel; *Austral./NZ informal* bag, monster; *formal* excoriate, calumniate.

–OPPOSITES praise.

revise ▶ **verb** ❶ *she revised her opinion* RECONSIDER, review, re-examine, reassess, re-evaluate, reappraise, rethink; change, alter, modify. ❷ *the editor revised the text* AMEND, emend, correct, alter, change, edit, rewrite, redraft, rephrase, rework. ❸ (*Brit.*) *revise your lecture notes* GO OVER, reread, memorize; cram; *informal* bone up on; *Brit. informal* swot up (on), mug up (on).

revision ▶ **noun** ❶ *a revision of the Prayer Book* EMENDATION, correction, alteration, adaptation, editing, rewriting, redrafting. ❷ *a new revision* VERSION, edition, rewrite. ❸ *a major revision of the system* RECONSIDERATION, review, re-examination, reassessment, re-evaluation, reappraisal, rethink; change, alteration, modification. ❹ (*Brit.*) *he was doing some revision* REREADING, memorizing, cramming; *Brit. informal* swotting.

revitalize ▶ **verb** REINVIGORATE, re-energize, boost, regenerate, revive, revivify, rejuvenate, reanimate, resuscitate, refresh, stimulate, breathe new life into; *informal* give a shot in the arm to, pep up, buck up.

revival ▶ **noun** ❶ *a revival in the economy* IMPROVEMENT, rallying, picking up, amelioration, turn for the better, upturn, upswing, resurgence. ❷ *the revival of traditional crafts* COMEBACK, re-establishment, reintroduction, restoration, reappearance, resurrection, regeneration, rejuvenation.

–OPPOSITES downturn, disappearance.

revive ▶ **verb** ❶ *attempts to revive her failed* RESUSCITATE, bring round, bring back to consciousness. ❷ *the man soon revived* REGAIN CONSCIOUSNESS, come round, wake up. ❸ *a cup of tea revived her* REINVIGORATE, revitalize, refresh, energize, reanimate, resuscitate, revivify, rejuvenate, regenerate, enliven, stimulate. ❹ *reviving old traditions* REINTRODUCE, re-establish, restore, resurrect, bring back, regenerate, resuscitate.

revoke ▶ **verb** CANCEL, repeal, rescind, reverse, annul, nullify, void, invalidate, countermand, retract, withdraw, overrule, override; *Law* vacate; *formal* abrogate.

revolt ▶ **verb** ❶ *the people revolted* REBEL, rise (up), take to the streets, riot, mutiny. ❷ *the smell revolted him* DISGUST, sicken, nauseate, make someone sick, make someone's gorge rise, turn someone's stomach, be repugnant to, be repulsive to, put off, be offensive to; *informal* turn off; *N. Amer. informal* gross out.

▶ **noun** *an armed revolt* REBELLION, revolution, insurrection, mutiny, uprising, riot, rioting, insurgence, seizure of power, coup (d'état).

revolting ▶ **adjective** DISGUSTING, sickening, nauseating, stomach-turning, stomach-churning, repulsive, repellent, repugnant, appalling, abominable, hideous, horrible, awful, dreadful, terrible, obnoxious, vile, nasty, foul, loathsome, offensive, objectionable, off-putting, distasteful, disagreeable; *N. Amer.* vomitous; *informal* ghastly, putrid, horrid, gross, gut-churning, yucky, skanky, icky; *formal* rebarbative; *poetic/literary* noisome; *archaic* disgustful, loathly.

–OPPOSITES attractive, pleasant.

revolution ▶ **noun** ❶ *the French Revolution* REBELLION, revolt, insurrection, mutiny, uprising, riot, rioting, insurgence, seizure of power, coup (d'état). ❷ *a revolution in printing techniques* DRAMATIC CHANGE, radical alteration, sea change, metamorphosis, transformation, innovation, reorganization, restructuring; *informal* shake-up; *N. Amer. informal* shakedown. ❸ *one revolution of a wheel* (SINGLE) TURN, rotation, circle, spin; circuit, lap. ❹ *the revolution of the earth* TURNING, rotation, circling; orbit.

revolutionary ▶ adjective ❶ *revolutionary troops* REBELLIOUS, rebel, insurgent, rioting, mutinous, renegade, insurrectionary, insurrectionist, seditious, subversive, extremist. ❷ *revolutionary change* THOROUGHGOING, thorough, complete, total, absolute, utter, comprehensive, sweeping, far-reaching, extensive, profound. ❸ *a revolutionary kind of wheelchair* NEW, novel, original, unusual, unconventional, unorthodox, newfangled, innovative, innovatory, innovational, modern, state-of-the-art, futuristic, pioneering.

▶ noun *political revolutionaries* REBEL, insurgent, revolutionist, mutineer, insurrectionist, agitator, subversive.

revolutionize ▶ verb TRANSFORM, alter dramatically, shake up, turn upside down, restructure, reorganize, transmute, metamorphose; *humorous* transmogrify.

revolve ▶ verb ❶ *a fan revolved slowly* GO ROUND, turn round, rotate, spin. ❷ *the moon revolves around the earth* CIRCLE, travel, orbit. ❸ *his life revolves around cars* BE CONCERNED WITH, be preoccupied with, focus on, centre around. ❹ *her mind revolved the possibilities* THINK ABOUT/OVER, give thought to, consider, reflect on, mull over, muse on, cogitate about/on, chew over, weigh up; *archaic* pore on.

revulsion ▶ noun DISGUST, repulsion, abhorrence, repugnance, nausea, horror, aversion, abomination, distaste; *archaic* disrelish.
– OPPOSITES delight.

reward ▶ noun *a reward for its safe return* RECOMPENSE, prize, award, honour, decoration, bonus, premium, bounty, present, gift, payment; *informal* pay-off, perk; *formal* perquisite.

▶ verb *they were well rewarded* RECOMPENSE, pay, remunerate, make something worth someone's while; give an award to.
– OPPOSITES punish.

rewarding ▶ adjective SATISFYING, gratifying, pleasing, fulfilling, enriching, edifying, beneficial, illuminating, worthwhile, productive, fruitful.

reword ▶ verb REWRITE, rephrase, recast, put in other words, express differently, redraft, revise; paraphrase.

rewrite ▶ verb REVISE, recast, reword, rephrase, redraft.

rhetoric ▶ noun ❶ *a form of rhetoric* ORATORY, eloquence, command of language, way with words. ❷ *empty rhetoric* BOMBAST, turgidity, grandiloquence, magniloquence, pomposity, extravagant language, purple prose; wordiness, verbosity, prolixity; *informal* hot air; *rare* fustian.

rhetorical ▶ adjective ❶ *rhetorical devices* STYLISTIC, oratorical, linguistic, verbal. ❷ *rhetorical hyperbole* EXTRAVAGANT, grandiloquent, magniloquent, high-flown, orotund, bombastic, grandiose, pompous, pretentious, overblown, oratorical, turgid, flowery, florid; *informal* highfalutin; *rare* fustian.

rhyme ▶ noun POEM, piece of poetry, verse; (**rhymes**) poetry, doggerel.

rhythm ▶ noun ❶ *the rhythm of the music* BEAT, cadence, tempo, time, pulse, throb, swing. ❷ *poetic features such as rhythm* METRE, measure, stress, accent, cadence. ❸ *the rhythm of daily life* PATTERN, flow, tempo.

rhythmic ▶ adjective RHYTHMICAL, with a steady pulse, measured, throbbing, beating, pulsating, regular, steady, even.

rib
– RELATED TERMS costal.

ribald ▶ adjective. *See* CRUDE sense 3.

rich ▶ adjective ❶ *rich people* WEALTHY, affluent, moneyed, well off, well-to-do, prosperous, opulent; *N. Amer.* silk-stocking; *informal* rolling in money, in the money, loaded, stinking rich, filthy rich, well heeled, made of money; *informal, dated* oofy. ❷ *rich furnishings* SUMPTUOUS, opulent, luxurious, luxury, de luxe, lavish, gorgeous, splendid, magnificent, costly, expensive, fancy; *informal* posh, plush, ritzy, swanky, classy; *Brit. informal* swish; *N. Amer. informal* swank. ❸ *a garden rich in flowers* ABOUNDING, well provided, well stocked, crammed, packed, teeming, bursting; *informal* jam-packed, chock-a-block, chock-full; *Austral./NZ informal* chocker. ❹ *a rich supply of restaurants* PLENTIFUL, abundant, copious, ample, profuse, lavish, liberal, generous, bountiful; *poetic/literary* plenteous, bounteous. ❺ *rich soil* FERTILE, productive, fecund, fruitful. ❻ *a rich sauce* CREAMY, fatty, heavy, full-flavoured. ❼ *a rich wine* FULL-BODIED, heavy, fruity. ❽ *rich colours* STRONG, deep, full, intense, vivid, brilliant. ❾ *her rich voice* SONOROUS, full, resonant, deep, clear, mellow, mellifluous; *rare* mellifluent. ❿ (*informal*) *that's rich!* PREPOSTEROUS, outrageous, absurd, ridiculous, ludicrous, laughable, risible; *informal* a bit much; *Brit. informal* a bit thick.
– OPPOSITES poor, light.

riches ▶ plural noun ❶ *his new-found riches* MONEY, wealth, funds, (hard) cash, (filthy) lucre, wherewithal, means, (liquid) assets, capital, resources, reserves; opulence, affluence, prosperity; *informal* dough, bread, loot, readies, shekels, moolah, the necessary; *Brit. informal* dosh, brass, lolly, spondulicks; *N. Amer. informal* bucks, mazuma, dinero; *US informal* greenbacks, simoleons, jack, rocks; *Austral./NZ informal* Oscar; *Brit. dated* l.s.d.; *archaic* pelf. ❷ *underwater riches* RESOURCES, treasure(s), bounty, jewels, gems.

richly ▶ adverb ❶ *the richly furnished chamber* SUMPTUOUSLY, opulently, luxuriously, lavishly,

gorgeously, splendidly, magnificently; *informal* poshly, plushly, ritzily, swankily, classily; *Brit. informal* swishly. ❷ *the joy she richly deserves* FULLY, thoroughly, in full measure, well, completely, wholly, totally, entirely, absolutely, amply, utterly.
– OPPOSITES meanly.

rickety ▶ **adjective** SHAKY, unsteady, unsound, unsafe, tumbledown, broken-down, dilapidated, ramshackle; *informal* shambly; *N. Amer. informal* shacky.

rid ▶ **verb** *ridding the building of asbestos* CLEAR, free, purge, empty, strip.
■ **get rid of** ❶ *we must get rid of some stuff* DISPOSE OF, throw away/out, clear out, discard, scrap, dump, bin, jettison; *informal* chuck (away), ditch, junk, get shut of; *Brit. informal* get shot of; *N. Amer. informal* trash. ❷ *the cats got rid of the rats* DESTROY, eliminate, annihilate, obliterate, wipe out, kill.

riddle[1] ▶ **noun** *an answer to the riddle* PUZZLE, conundrum, brain-teaser, (unsolved) problem, question, poser, enigma, mystery; *informal* stumper.

riddle[2] ▶ **verb** ❶ *his car was riddled by gunfire* PERFORATE, hole, pierce, puncture, pepper. ❷ *he was riddled with cancer* PERMEATE, suffuse, fill, pervade, spread through, imbue, saturate, overrun, beset. ❸ *the soil must be riddled* SIEVE, sift, strain, screen, filter; *archaic* griddle.

ride ▶ **verb** ❶ *she can ride a horse* SIT ON, mount, bestride; manage, handle, control. ❷ *riding round the town on motor bikes* TRAVEL, move, proceed, make one's way; drive, cycle; trot, canter, gallop.
▶ **noun** *he took us for a ride* TRIP, journey, drive, run, excursion, outing, jaunt; lift; *informal* spin.

ridicule ▶ **noun** *he was subjected to ridicule* MOCKERY, derision, laughter, scorn, scoffing, contempt, jeering, sneering, sneers, jibes, jibing, teasing, taunts, taunting, ragging, chaffing, sarcasm, satire; *informal* kidding, ribbing, joshing; *N. Amer. informal* goofing, razzing; *Austral./NZ informal* chiacking; *dated* sport.
– OPPOSITES respect.
▶ **verb** *his theory was ridiculed* DERIDE, mock, laugh at, heap scorn on, jeer at, jibe at, sneer at, treat with contempt, scorn, make fun of, poke fun at, scoff at, satirize, lampoon, burlesque, caricature, parody, tease, taunt, rag, chaff; *informal* kid, rib, josh, take the mickey out of; *N. Amer. informal* goof on, rag on, razz, pull someone's chain; *Austral./NZ informal* chiack, poke mullock at, sling off at; *dated* make sport of, twit.

ridiculous ▶ **adjective** ❶ *that looks ridiculous* LAUGHABLE, absurd, comical, funny, hilarious, risible, droll, amusing, farcical, silly, ludicrous; *rare* derisible. ❷ *a ridiculous suggestion* SENSELESS, silly, foolish, foolhardy, stupid, inane, fatuous, childish, puerile, half-baked, hare-brained, ill-thought-out, crackpot, idiotic. ❸ *a ridiculous exaggeration* ABSURD, preposterous, ludicrous, laughable, risible, nonsensical, senseless, outrageous.
– OPPOSITES sensible.

rife ▶ **adjective** ❶ *violence is rife* WIDESPREAD, general, common, universal, extensive, ubiquitous, omnipresent, endemic, inescapable, insidious, prevalent. ❷ *the village was rife with gossip* OVERFLOWING, bursting, alive, teeming, abounding.
– OPPOSITES unknown.

riff-raff ▶ **noun** RABBLE, scum, the lowest of the low, good-for-nothings, undesirables; *informal* peasants.
– OPPOSITES elite.

rifle ▶ **verb** ❶ *she rifled through her wardrobe* RUMMAGE, search, hunt, forage. ❷ *a thief rifled her home* BURGLE, rob, steal from, loot, raid, plunder, ransack.

rift ▶ **noun** ❶ *a deep rift in the ice* CRACK, fault, flaw, split, break, breach, fissure, fracture, cleft, crevice, cavity, opening. ❷ *the rift between them* BREACH, division, split; quarrel, squabble, disagreement, falling-out, row, argument, dispute, conflict, feud; estrangement; *informal* spat, scrap; *Brit. informal* bust-up.

rig[1] ▶ **verb** ❶ *the boats were rigged with a single sail* EQUIP, kit out, fit out, supply, furnish, provide, arm. ❷ *I rigged myself out in black* DRESS, clothe, attire, robe, garb, array, deck out, drape, accoutre, outfit, get up, trick out/up; *informal* doll up; *archaic* apparel. ❸ *he will rig up a shelter* SET UP, erect, assemble; throw together, cobble together, put together, whip up, improvise, contrive; *Brit. informal* knock up.
▶ **noun** ❶ *a CB radio rig* APPARATUS, appliance, machine, device, instrument, contraption, system; tackle, gear, kit, outfit. ❷ *the rig of the American Army Air Corps* UNIFORM, costume, ensemble, outfit, livery, attire, clothes, clothing, garments, dress, garb, regimentals, regalia, trappings; *Brit.* strip; *informal* get-up, gear, togs; *Brit. informal* kit; *formal* apparel; *archaic* raiment, vestments.

rig[2] ▶ **verb** *they rigged the election* MANIPULATE, engineer, distort, misrepresent, pervert, tamper with, doctor; falsify, fake, trump up; *informal* fix; *Brit. informal* fiddle.

right ▶ **adjective** ❶ *it wouldn't be right to do that* JUST, fair, proper, good, upright, righteous, virtuous, moral, ethical, honourable, honest; lawful, legal. ❷ *the right answer* CORRECT, accurate, exact, precise; proper, valid, conventional, established, official, formal; *Brit. informal* spot on. ❸ *the right person for the job* SUITABLE, appropriate, fitting, correct, proper, desirable, preferable, ideal; *archaic* meet. ❹ *you've come at the right time* OPPORTUNE, advantageous, favourable, propitious, good, lucky, happy, fortunate, providential, felicitous; timely, seasonable, convenient, expedient, suitable, appropriate. ❺ *he's not right in the head* SANE, lucid, rational, balanced, compos mentis; *informal* all there. ❻ *he does not look right* HEALTHY, well, (fighting) fit, normal, up to par; *informal* up to scratch, in the pink. ❼ *my right hand* DEXTRAL. ❽ (*informal*) *it's a right mess* ABSOLUTE, complete, total, real, thorough, perfect, utter, sheer, unmitigated, veritable.

– OPPOSITES wrong, insane, unhealthy.

▶ **adverb** ❶ *she was right at the limit of her patience* COMPLETELY, fully, totally, absolutely, utterly, thoroughly, quite. ❷ *right in the middle of the village* EXACTLY, precisely, directly, immediately, just, squarely, dead; *informal* (slap) bang, smack, plumb; *N. Amer. informal* smack dab. ❸ *keep going right on* STRAIGHT, directly, as the crow flies. ❹ (*informal*) *he'll be right down* STRAIGHT, immediately, instantly, at once, straight away, now, right now, this minute, directly, forthwith, without further ado, promptly, quickly, a.s.a.p., as soon as possible; *N. Amer.* in short order; *informal* straight off, p.d.q. (pretty damn quick), pronto; *N. Amer. informal* lickety-split. ❺ *I think I heard right* CORRECTLY, accurately, properly, precisely, aright, rightly, perfectly. ❻ *make sure you're treated right* WELL, properly, justly, fairly, equitably, impartially, honourably, lawfully, legally. ❼ *things will turn out right* WELL, for the best, favourably, happily, advantageously, profitably, providentially, luckily, conveniently.

– OPPOSITES wrong, badly.

▶ **noun** ❶ *the difference between right and wrong* GOODNESS, righteousness, virtue, integrity, rectitude, propriety, morality, truth, honesty, honour, justice, fairness, equity; lawfulness, legality. ❷ *you have the right to say no* ENTITLEMENT, prerogative, privilege, advantage, due, birthright, liberty, authority, power, licence, permission, dispensation, leave, sanction; *Law, historical* droit.

– OPPOSITES wrong.

▶ **verb** ❶ *the way to right a capsized dinghy* SET UPRIGHT, turn back over. ❷ *we must right the situation* REMEDY, put right, rectify, retrieve, fix, resolve, sort out, settle, square; straighten out, correct, repair, mend, redress, make good, ameliorate, better.

■ **by rights** PROPERLY, correctly, technically, in fairness; legally, de jure.

■ **in the right** JUSTIFIED, vindicated, right.

■ **put something to rights**. *See* RIGHT verb sense 2.

■ **right away** AT ONCE, straight away, (right) now, this (very) minute, this instant, immediately, instantly, directly, forthwith, without further ado, promptly, quickly, without delay, a.s.a.p., as soon as possible; *N. Amer.* in short order; *informal* straight off, p.d.q. (pretty damn quick), pronto; *N. Amer. informal* lickety-split.

■ **within one's rights** ENTITLED, permitted, allowed, at liberty, empowered, authorized, qualified, licensed, justified.

righteous ▶ **adjective** ❶ *righteous living* GOOD, virtuous, upright, upstanding, decent; ethical, principled, moral, high-minded, law-abiding, honest, honourable, blameless, irreproachable, noble; saintly, angelic, pure. ❷ *righteous anger* JUSTIFIABLE, justified, legitimate, defensible, supportable, rightful; admissible, allowable, understandable, excusable, acceptable, reasonable.

– OPPOSITES sinful, unjustifiable.

rightful ▶ **adjective** ❶ *the car's rightful owner* LEGAL, lawful, real, true, proper, correct, recognized, genuine, authentic, acknowledged, approved, licensed, valid, bona fide, de jure; *informal* legit, kosher. ❷ *their rightful place in society* DESERVED, merited, due, just, right, fair, proper, fitting, appropriate, suitable.

right-wing ▶ **adjective** CONSERVATIVE, rightist, ultra-conservative, blimpish, diehard; reactionary, traditionalist, conventional, unprogressive.

– OPPOSITES left-wing.

rigid ▶ **adjective** ❶ *a rigid container* STIFF, hard, firm, inflexible, unbending, unyielding, inelastic. ❷ *a rigid routine* FIXED, set, firm, inflexible, unalterable, unchangeable, immutable, unvarying, invariable, hard and fast, cast-iron. ❸ *a rigid approach to funding* STRICT, severe, stern, stringent, rigorous, inflexible, uncompromising, intransigent.

– OPPOSITES flexible, lenient.

rigmarole ▶ **noun** ❶ *the rigmarole of dressing up* FUSS, bother, trouble, folderol, ado, pother; *NZ* bobsy-die; *informal* palaver, song and dance, performance, to-do, pantomime, hassle; *Brit. informal* carry-on. ❷ *that rigmarole about the house being haunted* TALE, saga, yarn, shaggy-dog story; *informal* spiel.

rigorous ▶ **adjective** ❶ *rigorous attention to detail* METICULOUS, conscientious, punctilious, careful, diligent, attentive, scrupulous, painstaking, exact, precise, accurate, thorough, particular, strict, demanding, exacting; *informal* pernickety. ❷ *the rigorous enforcement of rules* STRICT, severe, stern, stringent, tough, harsh, rigid, relentless, unsparing, inflexible, draconian, intransigent, uncompromising, exacting. ❸ *rigorous yachting conditions* HARSH, severe, bad, bleak, extreme, inclement; unpleasant, disagreeable, foul, nasty, filthy; stormy, wild, tempestuous.

– OPPOSITES slapdash, lax, mild.

rigour ▶ **noun** ❶ *a mine operated under conditions of rigour* STRICTNESS, severity, stringency, toughness, harshness, rigidity, inflexibility, intransigence. ❷ *intellectual rigour* METICULOUSNESS, thoroughness, carefulness, diligence, scrupulousness, exactness, exactitude, precision, accuracy, correctness, strictness. ❸ *the rigours of the journey* HARDSHIP, harshness, severity, adversity; ordeal, misery, trial; discomfort, inconvenience, privation.

rile ▶ **verb** (*informal*). *See* ANNOY.

rim ▶ **noun** ❶ *the rim of her cup* BRIM, edge, lip. ❷ *the rim of the crater* EDGE, border, side, margin, brink, fringe, boundary, perimeter, limits, periphery; *archaic* skirt.

rind ▶ **noun** SKIN, peel, zest, integument; *Botany* pericarp.

ring[1] ▶ **noun** ❶ *a ring round the moon* CIRCLE, band, halo, disc. ❷ *she wore a ring* WEDDING RING, band. ❸ *a circus ring* ARENA, enclosure, field, ground; amphitheatre, stadium. ❹ *a ring of onlookers* CIRCLE, group, knot, cluster, bunch, band, throng, crowd, flock, pack. ❺ *a spy ring* GANG, syndicate, cartel, mob, band, circle, organization, association, society, alliance, league, coterie, cabal.

▶ **verb** *police ringed the building* SURROUND, circle, encircle, encompass, girdle, enclose, hem in, confine, seal off.

ring[2] ▶ **verb** ❶ *church bells rang all day* TOLL, sound, peal, chime, clang, bong, ding, jingle, tinkle; *poetic/literary* knell. ❷ *the room rang with laughter* RESOUND, reverberate, resonate, echo. ❸ *I'll ring you tomorrow* TELEPHONE, phone (up), call (up); reach, dial; *informal* give someone a buzz; *Brit. informal* give someone a bell, give someone a tinkle, get on the blower to; *N. Amer. informal* get someone on the horn.

▶ **noun** ❶ *the ring of a bell* CHIME, toll, peal, clang, clink, ding, jingle, tinkle, tintinnabulation, sound; *poetic/literary* knell. ❷ *I'll give Chris a ring* CALL, telephone call, phone call; *informal* buzz; *Brit. informal* bell, tinkle.

■ **ring something in** HERALD, signal, announce, proclaim, usher in, introduce; mark, signify, indicate; *poetic/literary* betoken, knell.

rinse ▶ **verb** WASH (OUT), clean, cleanse, bathe; dip, drench, splash, swill, sluice, hose down.

riot ▶ **noun** ❶ *a riot in the capital* UPROAR, commotion, upheaval, disturbance, furore, tumult, melee, scuffle, fracas, fray, brawl, free-for-all; violence, fighting, vandalism, mayhem, turmoil, lawlessness, anarchy; *N. Amer. informal* wilding; *Law, dated* affray. ❷ *the garden was a riot of colour* MASS, sea, splash, show, exhibition.

▶ **verb** *the miners rioted* (GO ON THE) RAMPAGE, run riot, fight in the streets, run wild, run amok, go berserk; *informal* raise hell.

■ **run riot** ❶ *the children ran riot* (GO ON THE) RAMPAGE, riot, run amok, go berserk, go out of control; *informal* raise hell. ❷ *the vegetation has run riot* GROW PROFUSELY, spread uncontrolled, grow rapidly, spread like wildfire; burgeon, multiply, rocket.

riotous ▶ **adjective** ❶ *the demonstration turned riotous* UNRULY, rowdy, disorderly, uncontrollable, unmanageable, undisciplined, uproarious, tumultuous; violent, wild, ugly, lawless, anarchic. ❷ *a riotous party* BOISTEROUS, lively, loud, noisy, unrestrained, uninhibited, uproarious, unruly, rollicking; *Brit. informal* rumbustious; *N. Amer. informal* rambunctious.

–OPPOSITES peaceable.

rip ▶ **verb** ❶ *he ripped the posters down* TEAR, wrench, wrest, pull, snatch, tug, prise, heave, drag, peel, pluck; *informal* yank. ❷ *she ripped Leo's note into pieces* TEAR, claw, hack, slit, cut; *poetic/literary* rend.

▶ **noun** *a rip in my sleeve* TEAR, slit, split, rent, laceration, cut, gash, slash.

ripe ▶ **adjective** ❶ *a ripe tomato* MATURE, ripened, full grown, ready to eat; luscious, juicy, tender, sweet. ❷ *the dock is ripe for development* READY, fit, suitable, right. ❸ *the ripe old age of ninety* ADVANCED, hoary, venerable, old. ❹ *the time is ripe for his return* OPPORTUNE, advantageous, favourable, auspicious, propitious, promising, good, right, fortunate, benign, providential, felicitous, seasonable; convenient, suitable, appropriate, apt, fitting.

–OPPOSITES unsuitable, young.

ripen ▶ **verb** BECOME RIPE, mature, mellow.

rip-off ▶ **noun** (*informal*) FRAUD, swindle, confidence trick; *informal* con, scam, flimflam, gyp; *Brit. informal* swizz, daylight robbery; *N. Amer. informal* rip, shakedown, bunco; *Austral. informal* rort.

riposte ▶ **noun** *an indignant riposte* RETORT, counter, rejoinder, sally, return, answer, reply, response; *informal* comeback.

▶ **verb** *'Heaven help you,' riposted Sally* RETORT, counter, rejoin, return, retaliate, hurl back, answer, reply, respond, come back.

ripple ▶ **noun** *he blew ripples in his coffee* WAVELET, wave, undulation, ripplet, ridge, ruffle.

▶ **verb** *a breeze rippled the lake* FORM RIPPLES ON, ruffle, wrinkle.

rise ▶ **verb** ❶ *the sun rose* MOVE UP/UPWARDS, come up, make one's/its way up, arise, ascend, climb, mount, soar. ❷ *the mountains rising above us* LOOM, tower, soar, rise up, rear (up). ❸ *prices rose* GO UP, increase, soar, shoot up, surge, leap, jump, rocket, escalate, spiral. ❹ *living standards have risen* IMPROVE, get better, advance, go up, soar, shoot up. ❺ *his voice rose* GET HIGHER, grow, increase, become louder, swell, intensify. ❻ *he rose from his chair* STAND UP, get to one's feet, get up, jump up, leap up; *formal* arise. ❼ *he rises at dawn* GET UP, get out of bed, rouse oneself, stir, bestir oneself, be up and about; *informal* rise and shine, shake a leg, surface; *formal* arise. ❽ *the court rose at midday* ADJOURN, recess, be suspended, pause, take a break; *informal* knock off, take five. ❾ *he rose through the ranks* MAKE PROGRESS, climb, advance, get on, work one's way, be promoted. ❿ *he wouldn't rise to the bait* REACT, respond; take. ⓫ *Christ rose again* COME BACK TO LIFE, be resurrected, revive. ⓬ *the dough started to rise* SWELL, expand, enlarge, puff up. ⓭ *the nation rose against its oppressors* REBEL, revolt, mutiny, riot, take up arms. ⓮ *the Rhine rises in the Alps* ORIGINATE, begin, start, emerge; issue from, spring from, flow from, emanate from. ⓯ *her spirits rose* BRIGHTEN, lift, cheer up, improve, pick up; *informal* buck up. ⓰ *the ground rose gently* SLOPE UPWARDS, go uphill, incline, climb.

–OPPOSITES fall, descend, drop, sit, retire, resume, die, shelve.

▶**noun** ❶ *a price rise* INCREASE, hike, leap, upsurge, upswing, climb, escalation. ❷ *he got a rise of 11%* RAISE, pay increase, wage increase; hike, increment. ❸ *a rise in standards* IMPROVEMENT, amelioration, upturn, leap. ❹ *his rise to power* PROGRESS, climb, promotion, elevation, aggrandizement. ❺ *we walked up the rise* SLOPE, incline, acclivity, hillock, hill; *formal* eminence.

risible ▶**adjective** LAUGHABLE, ridiculous, absurd, comical, comic, amusing, funny, hilarious, humorous, droll, farcical, silly, ludicrous, hysterical; *informal* rib-tickling, priceless; *informal, dated* killing.

risk ▶**noun** ❶ *there is a certain amount of risk* CHANCE, uncertainty, unpredictability, precariousness, instability, insecurity, perilousness, riskiness. ❷ *the risk of fire* POSSIBILITY, chance, probability, likelihood, danger, peril, threat, menace, fear, prospect.

–OPPOSITES safety, impossibility.

▶**verb** ❶ *he risked his life to save them* ENDANGER, imperil, jeopardize, hazard, gamble (with), chance; put on the line, put in jeopardy. ❷ *you risk getting cold and wet* CHANCE, stand a chance of.

■ **at risk** IN DANGER, in peril, in jeopardy, under threat.

risky ▶**adjective** DANGEROUS, hazardous, perilous, fraught with danger, unsafe, insecure, precarious, parlous, touch-and-go, treacherous; uncertain, unpredictable; *informal* chancy, dicey, hairy; *N. Amer. informal* gnarly.

risqué ▶**adjective** RIBALD, rude, bawdy, racy, earthy, indecent, suggestive, improper, naughty, locker-room; vulgar, dirty, smutty, crude, coarse, obscene, lewd, X-rated; *informal* blue, raunchy; *Brit. informal* fruity, off colour, saucy; *N. Amer. informal* gamy.

rite ▶**noun** CEREMONY, ritual, ceremonial; service, sacrament, liturgy, worship, office; act, practice, custom, tradition, convention, institution, procedure.

ritual ▶**noun** *an elaborate civic ritual* CEREMONY, rite, ceremonial, observance; service, sacrament, liturgy, worship; act, practice, custom, tradition, convention, formality, procedure, protocol.

▶**adjective** *a ritual burial* CEREMONIAL, ritualistic, prescribed, set, formal; sacramental, liturgical; traditional, conventional.

ritzy ▶**adjective** (*informal*). *See* POSH sense 1.

rival ▶**noun** ❶ *his rival for the nomination* OPPONENT, challenger, competitor, contender; adversary, antagonist, enemy; *poetic/literary* foe. ❷ *the tool has no rival* EQUAL, match, peer, equivalent, counterpart, like.

–OPPOSITES ally.

▶**verb** *few countries can rival it for scenery* MATCH, compare with, compete with, vie with, equal, measure up to, be in the same league as, be on a par with, touch, challenge; *informal* hold a candle to.

▶**adjective** *rival candidates* COMPETING, opposing, contending.

rivalry ▶**noun** COMPETITIVENESS, competition, contention, vying; opposition, conflict, feuding, antagonism, friction, enmity; *informal* keeping up with the Joneses.

riven ▶**adjective** *a country riven by civil war* TORN APART, split, rent, severed; *poetic/literary* cleft, torn asunder.

river ▶**noun** ❶ WATERCOURSE, waterway, tributary, stream, rivulet, brook, inlet, rill, runnel, freshet; *Scottish & N. English* burn; *N. English* beck; *S. English* bourn; *N. Amer. & Austral./NZ* creek; *Austral.* billabong. ❷ *a river of molten lava* STREAM, torrent, flood, deluge, cascade.

–RELATED TERMS fluvial, fluvio-.

■ **sell someone down the river** (*informal*). *See* DOUBLE-CROSS.

riveted ▶**adjective** ❶ *she stood riveted to the spot* FIXED, rooted, frozen, unable to move; motionless, unmoving, immobile, stock-still. ❷ *he was riveted by the newsreels* FASCINATED, engrossed, gripped, captivated, enthralled, spellbound, mesmerized, transfixed. ❸ *their eyes were riveted on the teacher* FIXED, fastened, focused, concentrated, locked.

–OPPOSITES bored.

riveting ▶**adjective** FASCINATING, gripping, engrossing, interesting, intriguing, absorbing, captivating, enthralling, compelling, spellbinding, mesmerizing; *informal* unputdownable.

–OPPOSITES boring.

road ▶**noun** ❶ *the roads were crowded with traffic* STREET, thoroughfare, roadway, avenue, broadway, bypass, ring road, trunk road, byroad; lane, crescent, drive, parade, row; *Brit.* dual carriageway, clearway, motorway; *N. Amer.* highway, freeway, parkway, throughway, expressway; *US* turnpike, interstate. ❷ *a step on the road to recovery* WAY, path, route, course. ❸ *oil tankers waiting in the roads* ANCHORAGE, channel, haven, roadstead.

■ **on the road** ON TOUR, touring, travelling.

roam ▶**verb** WANDER, rove, ramble, drift, walk, traipse; range, travel, tramp, traverse, trek; *Scottish & Irish* stravaig; *informal* cruise, mosey; *formal* perambulate; *archaic* peregrinate.

roar ▶**noun** ❶ *the roars of the crowd* SHOUT, bellow, yell, cry, howl; clamour; *informal* holler. ❷ *the roar of the sea* BOOM, crash, rumble, roll, thundering. ❸ *roars of laughter* GUFFAW, howl, hoot, shriek, gale, peal.

▶ **verb** ❶ *'Get out!' roared Angus* BELLOW, yell, shout, bawl, howl; *informal* holler. ❷ *thunder roared* BOOM, rumble, crash, roll, thunder. ❸ *the movie left them roaring* GUFFAW, laugh, hoot; *informal* split one's sides, be rolling in the aisles, be doubled up, crack up, be in stitches, die laughing; *Brit. informal* crease up, fall about. ❹ *a motorbike roared past* SPEED, zoom, whizz, flash; *informal* belt, tear, zip; *Brit. informal* bomb.

roaring ▶ **adjective** ❶ *a roaring fire* BLAZING, burning, flaming. ❷ (*informal*) *a roaring success* ENORMOUS, huge, massive, (very) great, tremendous; complete, out-and-out, thorough; *informal* rip-roaring, whopping, fantastic.

roast ▶ **verb** ❶ *potatoes roasted in olive oil* COOK, bake, grill; *N. Amer.* broil. ❷ (*informal*) *they roasted him for wasting time. See* CRITICIZE.

roasting (*informal*) ▶ **adjective** *a roasting day* HOT, sweltering, scorching, blistering, searing, torrid; *informal* boiling (hot), baking (hot).

▶ **noun** *the boss gave him a roasting. See* LECTURE noun sense 2.

rob ▶ **verb** ❶ *the gang robbed the local bank* BURGLE, steal from, hold up, break into; raid, loot, plunder, pillage; *N. Amer.* burglarize; *informal* do, turn over, knock off, stick up. ❷ *he robbed an old woman* STEAL FROM; *informal* mug, jump; *N. Amer. informal* clip. ❸ *he was robbed of his savings* CHEAT, swindle, defraud; *informal* do out of, con out of, fleece; *N. Amer. informal* stiff. ❹ (*informal*) *it cost £70—I was robbed* OVERCHARGE; *informal* rip off, sting, do, diddle; *N. Amer. informal* gouge. ❺ *defeat robbed him of his title* DEPRIVE, strip, divest; deny.

robber ▶ **noun** BURGLAR, thief, housebreaker, mugger, shoplifter; stealer, pilferer, raider, looter, plunderer, pillager; bandit, highwayman; *informal* crook, cracksman; *Brit. informal* tea leaf; *N. Amer. informal* yegg; *poetic/literary* brigand.

robbery ▶ **noun** ❶ *they were arrested for the robbery* BURGLARY, theft, thievery, stealing, breaking and entering, housebreaking, larceny, shoplifting; embezzlement, fraud; hold-up, break-in, raid; *informal* mugging, smash-and-grab, stick-up; *Brit. informal* blag; *N. Amer. informal* heist. ❷ (*informal*) *Six quid? That's robbery.* A SWINDLE; *informal* a con, a rip-off; *Brit. informal* daylight robbery.

robe ▶ **noun** ❶ *the women wore black robes* CLOAK, kaftan, djellaba, wrap, mantle, cape; *N. Amer.* wrapper. ❷ *coronation robes* GARB, regalia, costume, finery; garments, clothes; *formal* apparel; *archaic* raiment, habiliments, vestments. ❸ *priestly robes* VESTMENT, surplice, cassock, rochet, alb, dalmatic, chasuble; canonicals. ❹ *a towelling robe* DRESSING GOWN, bathrobe, housecoat; *N. Amer.* wrapper.

▶ **verb** *he robed for Mass* DRESS, clothe oneself; *formal* enrobe.

robot ▶ **noun** AUTOMATON, android, golem; *informal* bot, droid.

robust ▶ **adjective** ❶ *a large, robust man* STRONG, vigorous, sturdy, tough, powerful, solid, muscular, sinewy, rugged, hardy, strapping, brawny, burly, husky; healthy, (fighting) fit, hale and hearty, lusty, in fine fettle; *informal* beefy, hunky. ❷ *these knives are robust* DURABLE, resilient, tough, hard-wearing, long-lasting, sturdy, strong. ❸ *her usual robust view of things* DOWN-TO-EARTH, practical, realistic, pragmatic, common-sense, commonsensical, matter-of-fact, businesslike, sensible, unromantic, unsentimental; *informal* no-nonsense. ❹ *a robust red wine* STRONG, full-bodied, flavourful, flavoursome, rich.

– OPPOSITES frail, fragile, romantic, insipid.

rock¹ ▶ **verb** ❶ *the ship rocked on the water* MOVE TO AND FRO, move back and forth, sway, seesaw; roll, pitch, plunge, toss, lurch, reel, list; wobble, oscillate. ❷ *the building began to rock* SHAKE, vibrate, quake, tremble. ❸ *Wall Street was rocked by the news* STUN, shock, stagger, astonish, startle, surprise, shake (up), take aback, throw, unnerve, disconcert.

rock² ▶ **noun** ❶ *a gully strewn with rocks* BOULDER, stone, pebble; *Austral. informal* goolie. ❷ *a castle built on a rock* CRAG, cliff, outcrop. ❸ *he was the rock on which they relied* FOUNDATION, cornerstone, support, prop, mainstay; tower of strength, bulwark, anchor. ❹ (*informal*) *she wore a massive rock* DIAMOND (RING), jewel, precious stone.

– RELATED TERMS litho-, petro-.

■ **on the rocks** (*informal*) ❶ *her marriage is on the rocks* IN DIFFICULTY, in trouble, breaking up, over; in tatters, in ruins, ruined. ❷ *a Scotch on the rocks* WITH ICE, on ice.

rocket ▶ **noun** ❶ *guerrillas fired rockets at them* MISSILE, projectile. ❷ *they lit some colourful rockets* FIREWORK, Roman candle, banger. ❸ (*Brit. informal*) *he got a rocket from the boss. See* LECTURE noun sense 2.

▶ **verb** ❶ *prices have rocketed* SHOOT UP, soar, increase, rise, escalate, spiral; *informal* go through the roof. ❷ *they rocketed into the alley* SPEED, zoom, shoot, whizz, tear, career; *Brit. informal* bomb; *N. Amer. informal* barrel, hightail it.

– OPPOSITES plummet.

rocky¹ ▶ **adjective** *a rocky path* STONY, pebbly, shingly; rough, bumpy; craggy, mountainous.

rocky² ▶ **adjective** ❶ *that table's rocky* UNSTEADY, shaky, unstable, wobbly, tottery, rickety, flimsy. ❷ *a rocky marriage* DIFFICULT, problematic, precarious, unstable, unreliable, undependable; *informal* iffy, up and down.

– OPPOSITES steady, stable.

rococo ▶ **adjective** ORNATE, fancy, elaborate, extravagant, baroque; fussy, busy, ostenta-

tious, showy; flowery, florid, flamboyant, high-flown, magniloquent, orotund, bombastic, overwrought, overblown, inflated, turgid; *informal* highfalutin.
– OPPOSITES plain.

rod ▶ **noun** ❶ *an iron rod* BAR, stick, pole, baton, staff; shaft, strut, rail, spoke. ❷ *the ceremonial rod* STAFF, mace, sceptre. ❸ *instruction was accompanied by the rod* CORPORAL PUNISHMENT, the cane, the lash, the birch; beating, flogging, caning, birching.

rogue ▶ **noun** ❶ *a rogue without ethics* SCOUNDREL, villain, miscreant, reprobate, rascal, good-for-nothing, ne'er-do-well, wretch; *informal* rat, dog, louse, crook; *informal, dated* rotter, bounder, blighter; *dated* cad; *archaic* blackguard, knave. ❷ *your boy's a little rogue* RASCAL, imp, devil, monkey; *informal* scamp, scallywag, monster, horror, terror, tyke; *Brit. informal* perisher; *N. Amer. informal* hellion.

roguish ▶ **adjective** ❶ *a roguish character* UNPRINCIPLED, dishonest, deceitful, unscrupulous, untrustworthy, shameless; wicked, villainous; *informal* shady, scoundrelly, rascally; *archaic* knavish. ❷ *a roguish grin* MISCHIEVOUS, playful, teasing, cheeky, naughty, wicked, impish, devilish, arch; *informal* waggish.

roister ▶ **verb** ENJOY ONESELF, celebrate, revel, carouse, frolic, romp, have fun, make merry, rollick; *informal* party, live it up, whoop it up, have a ball, make whoopee.

role ▶ **noun** ❶ *a small role in the film* PART; character. ❷ *his role as President of the EC* CAPACITY, position, job, post, office, duty, responsibility, mantle, place; function, part.

roll ▶ **verb** ❶ *the bottle rolled down the table* BOWL, turn over and over, spin, rotate. ❷ *waiters rolled in the trolleys* WHEEL, push, trundle. ❸ *we rolled past fields* TRAVEL, go, move, pass, cruise, sweep. ❹ *the months rolled by* PASS, go by, slip by, fly by, elapse, wear on, march on. ❺ *tears rolled down her cheeks* FLOW, run, course, stream, pour, spill, trickle. ❻ *the mist rolled in* BILLOW, undulate, tumble. ❼ *he rolled his handkerchief into a ball* WIND, coil, fold, curl; twist. ❽ *roll out the pastry* FLATTEN, level; even out. ❾ *they rolled about with laughter* STAGGER, lurch, reel, totter, teeter, wobble. ❿ *the ship began to roll* LURCH, toss, rock, pitch, plunge, sway, reel, list, keel. ⓫ *thunder rolled* RUMBLE, reverberate, echo, resound, boom, roar, grumble.
▶ **noun** ❶ *a roll of wrapping paper* CYLINDER, tube, scroll; bolt. ❷ *a roll of film* REEL, spool. ❸ *a roll of notes* WAD, bundle. ❹ *a roll of the dice* THROW, toss, turn, spin. ❺ *crusty rolls* BREAD ROLL, bun, bagel; *Brit.* bap, muffin; *N. English* barm; *N. Amer.* hoagie; *Military slang* wad. ❻ *the electoral roll* LIST, register, directory, record, file, index, catalogue, inventory; census. ❼ *a roll of thunder* RUMBLE, reverberation, echo, boom, clap, crack, roar, grumble.
■ **roll in** (*informal*) ❶ *money has been rolling in* POUR IN, flood in, flow in. ❷ *he rolled in at nine o'clock* ARRIVE, turn up, appear, show one's face; *informal* show up, roll up, blow in.
■ **rolling in it** (*informal*). *See* RICH sense 1.
■ **roll something out** UNROLL, spread out, unfurl, unfold, open (out), unwind, uncoil.
■ **roll something up** FOLD (UP), furl, wind up, coil (up), bundle up.
■ **roll up** (*informal*). *See* ROLL IN sense 2.

rollicking[1] ▶ **noun** (*Brit. informal*) *I got a rollicking for being late. See* LECTURE noun sense 2.

rollicking[2] ▶ **adjective** *a rollicking party* LIVELY, boisterous, exuberant, spirited; riotous, noisy, wild, rowdy, roisterous; *Brit. informal* rumbustious; *N. Amer. informal* rambunctious.

roly-poly ▶ **adjective** (*informal*) CHUBBY, plump, fat, stout, rotund, round, dumpy, chunky, portly, overweight, fleshy, paunchy, bulky, corpulent; *informal* tubby, pudgy, beefy, porky, blubbery; *Brit. informal* podgy; *N. Amer. informal* zaftig, corn-fed.
– OPPOSITES skinny.

romance ▶ **noun** ❶ *their romance blossomed* LOVE, passion, ardour, adoration, devotion; affection, fondness, attachment. ❷ *he's had many romances* LOVE AFFAIR, relationship, liaison, courtship, attachment; flirtation, dalliance. ❸ *an author of historical romances* LOVE STORY, novel; romantic fiction; *informal* tear-jerker. ❹ *the romance of the Far East* MYSTERY, glamour, excitement, exoticism, mystique; appeal, allure, charm.
▶ **verb** ❶ (*dated*) *he was romancing Meg* WOO, chase, pursue; go out with, pay court to; *informal* see, go steady with, date; *dated* court, make love to. ❷ *I am romancing the past* ROMANTICIZE, idealize, paint a rosy picture of.

romantic ▶ **adjective** ❶ *he's so romantic* LOVING, amorous, passionate, tender, affectionate; *informal* lovey-dovey. ❷ *romantic songs* SENTIMENTAL, hearts-and-flowers; mawkish, sickly, saccharine, syrupy; *informal* slushy, mushy, sloppy, schmaltzy, gooey, treacly, cheesy, corny; *Brit. informal* soppy; *N. Amer. informal* cornball, sappy. ❸ *a romantic setting* IDYLLIC, picturesque, fairytale; beautiful, lovely, charming, pretty. ❹ *romantic notions of rural communities* IDEALISTIC, idealized, unrealistic, fanciful, impractical; head-in-the-clouds, starry-eyed, optimistic, hopeful, visionary, utopian, fairy-tale.
– OPPOSITES unsentimental, realistic.
▶ **noun** *an incurable romantic* IDEALIST, sentimentalist, romanticist; dreamer, visionary, utopian, Don Quixote, fantasist; *N. Amer.* fantast.
– OPPOSITES realist.

Romeo ▶ **noun** LADIES' MAN, Don Juan, Casanova, Lothario, womanizer, playboy, lover, seducer, philanderer, flirt; gigolo; *informal* ladykiller, stud.

romp ▶ **verb** ❶ *two fox cubs romped playfully* PLAY,

frolic, frisk, gambol, skip, prance, caper, cavort, rollick; *dated* sport. ❷ *South Africa romped to a win* SAIL, coast, sweep; win hands down, run away with it; *informal* win by a mile, walk it.

roof

■ **hit the roof** (*informal*) BE VERY ANGRY, be furious, lose one's temper; *informal* go mad, go crazy, go wild, go bananas, have a fit, blow one's top, do one's nut, go up the wall, go off the deep end, go ape, flip, lose one's rag; *Brit. informal* go spare.

room ▶ **noun** ❶ *there isn't much room* SPACE; headroom, legroom; area, expanse, extent; *informal* elbow room. ❷ *room for improvement* SCOPE, capacity, leeway, latitude, freedom; opportunity, chance. ❸ *he wandered around the room* CHAMBER. ❹ *he had rooms in the Pepys building* LODGINGS, quarters; accommodation; a suite, an apartment; *informal* a pad, digs.

▶ **verb** *he roomed there in September* LODGE, board, live, stay; be quartered, be housed; *formal* dwell, reside, sojourn.

roomy ▶ **adjective** SPACIOUS, capacious, sizeable, generous, big, large, extensive; voluminous, ample; *formal* commodious.

– OPPOSITES cramped.

root ▶ **noun** ❶ *a plant's roots* rootstock, tuber, rootlet; *Botany* rhizome, radicle. ❷ *the root of the problem* SOURCE, origin, germ, beginnings, genesis; cause, reason, basis, foundation, bottom, seat; core, heart, nub, essence; *formal* radix. ❸ *he rejected his roots* ORIGINS, beginnings, family, ancestors, predecessors, heritage; birthplace, homeland.

– RELATED TERMS radical, rhizo-.

▶ **verb** ❶ *has the shoot rooted?* TAKE ROOT, grow roots, establish, strike, take. ❷ *root the cuttings* PLANT, bed out, sow. ❸ *he rooted around in the cupboard* RUMMAGE, hunt, search, rifle, delve, forage, dig, nose, poke; *Brit. informal* rootle.

■ **put down roots** SETTLE, establish oneself, set up home.

■ **root and branch** ❶ *the firm should be eradicated, root and branch* COMPLETELY, entirely, wholly, totally, thoroughly. ❷ *a root-and-branch reform* COMPLETE, total, thorough, radical.

■ **root for** (*informal*) CHEER (ON), applaud, support, encourage.

■ **root something out** ❶ *the hedge was rooted out* UPROOT, deracinate, pull up, grub out. ❷ *root out corruption* ERADICATE, eliminate, weed out, destroy, wipe out, stamp out, extirpate, abolish, end, put a stop to. ❸ *he rooted out a dark secret* UNEARTH, dig up, bring to light, uncover, discover, dredge up, ferret out, expose.

■ **take root** ❶ *leave the plants to take root* GERMINATE, sprout, establish, strike, take. ❷ *Christianity took root in Persia* BECOME ESTABLISHED, take hold; develop, thrive, flourish.

rooted ▶ **adjective** ❶ *views rooted in Indian culture* EMBEDDED, fixed, established, entrenched, ingrained. ❷ *Neil was rooted to the spot* FROZEN, riveted, paralysed, glued, fixed; stock-still, motionless, unmoving.

rootless ▶ **adjective** ITINERANT, unsettled, drifting, roving, footloose; homeless, of no fixed abode.

rope ▶ **noun** CORD, cable, line, hawser; string.

– RELATED TERMS funicular.

▶ **verb** *his feet were roped together* TIE, bind, lash, truss; secure, moor, fasten, attach; hitch, tether, lasso.

■ **know the ropes** (*informal*) KNOW WHAT TO DO, know the routine, know one's way around, know one's stuff, know what's what; be experienced; *informal* know the drill, know the score.

■ **rope someone in/into** PERSUADE TO/INTO, talk into, inveigle into; enlist, engage.

ropy ▶ **adjective** ❶ *ropy strands of lava* STRINGY, thready, fibrous, filamentous; viscous, sticky, mucilaginous, thick. ❷ (*Brit. informal*) *I feel a bit ropy. See* ILL adjective sense 1. ❸ (*Brit. informal*) *ropy defending from the home team. See* SUBSTANDARD.

roster ▶ **noun** SCHEDULE, list, listing, register, agenda, calendar, table; *Brit.* rota.

rostrum ▶ **noun** DAIS, platform, podium, stage; soapbox.

rosy ▶ **adjective** ❶ *a rosy complexion* PINK, pinkish, roseate, reddish; glowing, healthy, fresh, radiant, blooming; blushing, flushed; ruddy, high-coloured, florid. ❷ *his future looks rosy* PROMISING, optimistic, auspicious, hopeful, encouraging, favourable, bright, golden; *informal* upbeat.

– OPPOSITES pale, bleak.

rot ▶ **verb** ❶ *the floorboards rotted* DECAY, decompose, become rotten; disintegrate, crumble, perish. ❷ *the meat began to rot* GO BAD, go off, spoil; moulder, putrefy, fester. ❸ *poor neighbourhoods have been left to rot* DETERIORATE, degenerate, decline, decay, go to rack and ruin, go to seed, go downhill; *informal* go to pot, go to the dogs.

– RELATED TERMS sapro-.

– OPPOSITES improve.

▶ **noun** ❶ *the leaves turned black with rot* DECAY, decomposition, mould, mouldiness, mildew, blight, canker; putrefaction, putrescence. ❷ *traditionalists said the rot had set in* DETERIORATION, decline; corruption, cancer. ❸ (*informal*) *stop talking rot. See* NONSENSE sense 1.

– OPPOSITES sense.

rota ▶ **noun** (*Brit.*). *See* ROSTER.

rotary ▶ **adjective** ROTATING, rotatory, rotational, revolving, turning, spinning, gyrating, gyratory.

rotate ▶ **verb** ❶ *the wheels rotate continually* REVOLVE, go round, turn (round), spin, gyrate, whirl, twirl, swivel, circle, pivot. ❷ *many nurses* *rotate jobs* ALTERNATE, take turns, change, switch, interchange, exchange, swap; move around.

rotation ▶ **noun** ❶ *the rotation of the wheels* REVOLVING, turning, spinning, gyration, circling. ❷ *a rotation of the Earth* TURN, revolution, orbit, spin. ❸ *each member is chair for six months in rotation* SEQUENCE, succession; alternation, cycle.
– RELATED TERMS gyro-.

rote
■ **by rote** MECHANICALLY, automatically, parrot-fashion, unthinkingly, mindlessly; from memory, by heart.

rotten ▶ **adjective** ❶ *rotten meat* DECAYING, rotting, bad, off, decomposing, putrid, putrescent, perished, mouldy, mouldering, mildewy, rancid, festering, fetid; addled; maggoty, wormy, flyblown. ❷ *rotten teeth* DECAYING, decayed, carious, black; disintegrating, crumbling. ❸ *he's rotten to the core* CORRUPT, unprincipled, dishonest, dishonourable, unscrupulous, untrustworthy, immoral; villainous, bad, wicked, evil, iniquitous, venal; *informal* crooked, warped; *Brit. informal* bent. ❹ (*informal*) *a rotten thing to do* NASTY, unkind, unpleasant, obnoxious, vile, contemptible, despicable, shabby; spiteful, mean, malicious, hateful, hurtful; unfair, uncharitable, uncalled for; *informal* dirty, low-down; *Brit. informal* out of order. ❺ (*informal*) *he was a rotten singer* BAD, poor, dreadful, awful, terrible, frightful, atrocious, hopeless, inadequate, inferior, substandard; *informal* crummy, pathetic, useless, lousy, appalling, abysmal, dire; *Brit. informal* duff, rubbish, a load of pants. ❻ (*informal*) *I feel rotten about it* GUILTY, conscience-stricken, remorseful, ashamed, shamefaced, chastened, contrite, sorry, regretful, repentant, penitent. ❼ (*informal*) *I felt rotten with that cold. See* ILL adjective sense 1.
– OPPOSITES fresh, honourable, kind, good, well.

rotter ▶ **noun** (*informal, dated*). *See* SCOUNDREL.

rotund ▶ **adjective** ❶ *a small, rotund man* PLUMP, chubby, fat, stout, portly, dumpy, round, chunky, overweight, heavy, paunchy, ample; flabby, fleshy, bulky, corpulent, obese; *informal* tubby, roly-poly, pudgy, beefy, porky, blubbery; *Brit. informal* podgy; *N. Amer. informal* zaftig, corn-fed. ❷ *rotund cauldrons* ROUND, bulbous, spherical, spheric; *poetic/literary* orbicular.
– OPPOSITES thin.

roué ▶ **noun** LIBERTINE, rake, debauchee, degenerate, profligate; lecher, seducer, womanizer, philanderer, adulterer, Don Juan, Lothario; *informal* ladykiller, lech, dirty old man.

rough ▶ **adjective** ❶ *rough ground* UNEVEN, irregular, bumpy, lumpy, knobbly, stony, rocky, rugged, rutted, pitted, rutty. ❷ *the terrier's rough coat* COARSE, bristly, scratchy, prickly, shaggy, hairy, bushy. ❸ *rough skin* DRY, leathery, weather-beaten; chapped, calloused, scaly, scabrous. ❹ *his voice was rough* GRUFF, hoarse, harsh, rasping, raspy, husky, throaty, gravelly, guttural. ❺ *rough red wine* SHARP, sour, acidic, acid, vinegary, acidulous. ❻ *he gets rough when he's drunk* VIOLENT, brutal, vicious; AGGRESSIVE, belligerent, pugnacious, thuggish; boisterous, rowdy, disorderly, unruly, riotous. ❼ *a machine that can take rough handling* CARELESS, clumsy, inept, unskilful. ❽ *rough manners* BOORISH, loutish, oafish, brutish, coarse, crude, uncouth, vulgar, unrefined, unladylike, ungentlemanly, uncultured; unmannerly, impolite, discourteous, uncivil, ungracious, rude. ❾ *rough seas* TURBULENT, stormy, tempestuous, violent, heavy, heaving, choppy. ❿ (*informal*) *I've had a rough time* DIFFICULT, hard, tough, bad, unpleasant; demanding, arduous. ⓫ (*informal*) *you were a bit rough on her* HARSH, hard, tough, stern, severe, unfair, unjust; insensitive, nasty, cruel, unkind, unsympathetic, brutal, heartless, merciless. ⓬ (*informal*) *I'm feeling rough. See* ILL adjective sense 1. ⓭ *a rough draft* PRELIMINARY, hasty, quick, sketchy, cursory, basic, crude, rudimentary, raw, unpolished; incomplete, unfinished. ⓮ *a rough estimate* APPROXIMATE, inexact, imprecise, vague, estimated, hazy; *N. Amer. informal* ballpark. ⓯ *the accommodation is rather rough* PLAIN, BASIC, simple, rough and ready, rude, crude, primitive, spartan.
– OPPOSITES smooth, sleek, soft, dulcet, sweet, gentle, careful, refined, calm, easy, kind, well, exact, luxurious.
▶ **noun** ❶ *the artist's initial roughs* SKETCH, draft, outline, mock-up. ❷ (*Brit.*) *a bunch of roughs attacked him* RUFFIAN, thug, lout, hooligan, hoodlum, rowdy; *informal* tough, roughneck, bruiser, gorilla, yahoo; *Brit. informal* yob, yobbo.
▶ **verb** *rough the surface with sandpaper* ROUGHEN.
■ **rough something out** DRAFT, sketch out, outline, block out, mock up; *formal* adumbrate.
■ **rough someone up** (*informal*) BEAT UP, attack, assault, knock about/around, batter, manhandle; *informal* do over, beat the living daylights out of; *Brit. informal* duff up.

rough and ready ▶ **adjective** BASIC, simple, crude, unrefined, unsophisticated; makeshift, provisional, stopgap, improvised, extemporary, ad hoc; hurried, sketchy.

rough and tumble ▶ **noun** SCUFFLE, fight, brawl, melee, free-for-all, fracas, rumpus; horseplay; *Law, dated* affray; *informal* scrap, dust-up, punch-up, shindy; *N. Amer. informal* rough house.

roughly ▶ **adverb** ❶ *he shoved her roughly away* VIOLENTLY, forcefully, forcibly, abruptly, unceremoniously. ❷ *they treated him roughly* HARSHLY, unkindly, unsympathetically; brutally, savagely, mercilessly, cruelly, heartlessly. ❸ *roughly £2.4 million* APPROXIMATELY, (round) about, around, circa, in the region of, something like, of the order of, or so, or thereabouts, more or less, give or take; nearly, close to, approaching; *Brit.* getting on for.

roughneck ▶ noun (*informal*). *See* RUFFIAN.

round ▶ adjective ❶ *a round window* CIRCULAR, disc-shaped, ring-shaped, hoop-shaped; spherical, spheroidal, globular, globe-shaped, orb-shaped; cylindrical; bulbous, rounded, rotund; *technical* annular, discoid, discoidal; *poetic/literary* orbicular. ❷ *a short, round man* PLUMP, chubby, fat, stout, rotund, portly, dumpy, chunky, overweight, pot-bellied, paunchy; flabby, corpulent, fleshy, bulky, obese; *informal* tubby, roly-poly, pudgy, beefy, porky, blubbery; *Brit. informal* podgy; *N. Amer. informal* zaftig, corn-fed. ❸ *his deep, round voice* SONOROUS, resonant, rich, full, mellow, mellifluous, orotund. ❹ *a round dozen* COMPLETE, entire, whole, full. ❺ *she berated him in round terms* CANDID, frank, direct, honest, truthful, straightforward, plain, blunt, forthright, bald, explicit, unequivocal.
–OPPOSITES thin, reedy.
▶ noun ❶ *mould the dough into rounds* BALL, sphere, globe, orb, circle, disc, ring, hoop; *technical* annulus. ❷ *a policeman on his rounds* CIRCUIT, beat, route, tour. ❸ *the first round of the contest* STAGE, level; heat, game, bout, contest. ❹ *an endless round of parties* SUCCESSION, sequence, series, cycle. ❺ *the gun fires thirty rounds a second* BULLET, cartridge, shell, shot.
▶ preposition & adverb ❶ *the alleys round the station* AROUND, about, encircling; near, in the vicinity of; orbiting. ❷ *casinos dotted round France* THROUGHOUT, all over, here and there in.
▶ verb *the ship rounded the point* GO ROUND, travel round, skirt, circumnavigate, orbit.
■ **round about** APPROXIMATELY, about, around, circa, roughly, of the order of, something like, more or less, as near as dammit to, close to, near to, practically; or so, or thereabouts, give or take a few; not far off, nearly, almost, approaching; *Brit.* getting on for.
■ **round the bend** (*informal*). *See* MAD sense 1.
■ **round the clock** ❶ *we're working round the clock* DAY AND NIGHT, night and day, all the time, {morning, noon, and night}, continuously, non-stop, steadily, unremittingly; *informal* 24-7. ❷ *round-the-clock supervision* CONTINUOUS, constant, non-stop, continual, uninterrupted.
■ **round something off** ❶ *the square edges were rounded off* SMOOTH OFF, plane off, sand off, level off. ❷ *the party rounded off a successful year* COMPLETE, finish off, crown, cap, top; conclude, close, end.
■ **round on someone** SNAP AT, attack, turn on, weigh into, let fly at, lash out at, hit out at; *informal* bite someone's head off, jump down someone's throat, lay into, tear into; *Brit. informal* have a go at; *N. Amer. informal* light into.
■ **round someone/something up** GATHER TOGETHER, herd together, muster, marshal, rally, assemble, collect, group; *N. Amer.* corral.

roundabout ▶ adjective ❶ *a roundabout route* CIRCUITOUS, indirect, meandering, serpentine, tortuous. ❷ *I asked in a roundabout sort of way* INDIRECT, oblique, circuitous, circumlocutory, periphrastic, digressive, long-winded; evasive.
–OPPOSITES direct.
▶ noun (*Brit.*) ❶ *go straight on at the roundabout* *N. Amer.* rotary, traffic circle. ❷ *a roundabout with wooden horses* MERRY-GO-ROUND, carousel; *archaic* whirligig.

roundly ▶ adverb ❶ *he was roundly condemned* VEHEMENTLY, emphatically, fiercely, forcefully, severely; plainly, frankly, candidly. ❷ *she was roundly defeated* UTTERLY, completely, thoroughly, decisively, conclusively, heavily, soundly.

round-up ▶ noun ❶ *a cattle round-up* ASSEMBLY, muster, rally; *N. Amer.* rodeo. ❷ *the sports round-up* SUMMARY, synopsis, overview, review, outline, digest, precis; *N. Amer.* wrap-up; *informal* recap.

rouse ▶ verb ❶ *he roused Ralph at dawn* WAKE (UP), awaken, arouse; *Brit. informal* knock up; *formal* waken. ❷ *she roused and looked around* WAKE UP, awake, awaken, come to, get up, rise, bestir oneself; *formal* arise. ❸ *he roused the crowd* STIR UP, excite, galvanize, electrify, stimulate, inspire, inspirit, move, inflame, agitate, goad, provoke; incite, spur on; *N. Amer.* light a fire under. ❹ *he's got a temper when he's roused* PROVOKE, annoy, anger, infuriate, madden, incense, vex, irk; *informal* aggravate. ❺ *her disappearance roused my suspicions* AROUSE, awaken, prompt, provoke, stimulate, pique, trigger, spark off, touch off, kindle, elicit.
–OPPOSITES calm, pacify, allay.

rousing ▶ adjective STIRRING, inspiring, exciting, stimulating, moving, electrifying, invigorating, energizing, exhilarating; enthusiastic, vigorous, spirited; inflammatory.

rout ▶ noun ❶ *the army's ignominious rout* RETREAT, flight. ❷ *Newcastle scored 13 tries in the rout* CRUSHING DEFEAT, trouncing, annihilation; debacle, fiasco; *informal* licking, hammering, thrashing, pasting, drubbing, massacre.
–OPPOSITES victory.
▶ verb ❶ *his army was routed* PUT TO FLIGHT, drive off, scatter; defeat, beat, conquer, vanquish, crush, overpower. ❷ *he routed the defending champion* BEAT HOLLOW, trounce, defeat, get the better of; *informal* lick, hammer, clobber, thrash, paste, demolish, annihilate, drub, cane, wipe the floor with, walk all over, make mincemeat of, massacre, slaughter; *Brit. informal* stuff; *N. Amer. informal* cream, shellac, skunk.
–OPPOSITES lose.

route ▶ noun *a different route to the shops* WAY, course, road, path, direction; passage, journey.
▶ verb *enquiries are routed to the relevant desk* DIRECT, send, convey, dispatch, forward.

routine ▶ noun ❶ *his morning routine* PROCEDURE, practice, pattern, drill, regime, regimen; programme, schedule, plan; formula, method, system; customs, habits; wont. ❷ *a stand-up routine* ACT, performance, number, turn, piece; *informal* spiel, patter.
▶ adjective ❶ *a routine health check* STANDARD, regular, customary, normal, usual, ordinary, typical; everyday, common, commonplace, conventional, habitual, wonted. ❷ *a routine action movie* BORING, tedious, tiresome, wearisome, monotonous, humdrum, run-of-the-mill, prosaic, dreary, pedestrian; predictable, hackneyed, stock, unimaginative, unoriginal, banal, trite.
– OPPOSITES unusual.

rove ▶ verb WANDER, roam, ramble, drift, meander; range, travel; *Scottish* stravaig; *archaic* peregrinate.

rover ▶ noun WANDERER, traveller, globetrotter, drifter, bird of passage, roamer, itinerant, transient; nomad, gypsy, Romany; tramp, vagrant, vagabond; *N. Amer.* hobo.

row[1] ▶ noun ❶ *rows of children* LINE, column, file, queue; procession, chain, string, succession; *informal* crocodile. ❷ *the middle row of seats* TIER, line, rank, bank.
■ **in a row** *three days in a row* CONSECUTIVELY, in succession; running, straight; *informal* on the trot.

row[2] (*Brit. informal*) ▶ noun ❶ *have you two had a row?* ARGUMENT, quarrel, squabble, fight, contretemps, falling-out, disagreement, dispute, clash, altercation, shouting match; *informal* tiff, set-to, run-in, slanging match, spat; *Brit. informal* barney, bust-up. ❷ *the row the crowd was making* DIN, noise, racket, clamour, uproar, tumult, hubbub, commotion, brouhaha, rumpus, pandemonium, babel; *informal* hullabaloo. ❸ *Mum give me a row* REPRIMAND, rebuke, reproof, admonition, reproach, remonstration, lecture, criticism; *informal* telling-off, slap on the wrist, dressing-down, roasting, tongue-lashing; *Brit. informal* ticking-off, carpeting, rollicking, rocket.
▶ verb *they rowed about money* ARGUE, quarrel, squabble, bicker, fight, fall out, disagree, have words, dispute, wrangle, cross swords, lock horns, be at loggerheads; *informal* scrap, argufy.

rowdy ▶ adjective *rowdy youths* UNRULY, disorderly, obstreperous, riotous, undisciplined, uncontrollable, ungovernable, disruptive, out of control, rough, wild, lawless; boisterous, uproarious, noisy, loud, clamorous; *Brit. informal* rumbustious; *N. Amer. informal* rambunctious.
– OPPOSITES peaceful.
▶ noun *the pub filled up with rowdies* RUFFIAN, troublemaker, lout, hooligan, thug, hoodlum; *Brit.* tearaway; *informal* tough, bruiser, yahoo; *Brit. informal* rough, yob, yobbo.

royal ▶ adjective ❶ *the royal prerogative* REGAL, kingly, queenly, princely; sovereign, monarchical. ❷ *a royal welcome* EXCELLENT, fine, magnificent, splendid, superb, wonderful, first-rate, first-class; *informal* fantastic, great, tremendous.

rub ▶ verb ❶ *Polly rubbed her arm* MASSAGE, knead; stroke, pat. ❷ *he rubbed sun lotion on her back* APPLY, smear, spread, work in. ❸ *my shoes rub painfully* CHAFE, pinch; hurt, be painful.
▶ noun ❶ *she gave his back a rub* MASSAGE, rubdown. ❷ *I gave my shoes a rub* POLISH, wipe, clean. ❸ *it's too complicated—that's the rub* PROBLEM, difficulty, trouble, drawback, hindrance, impediment; snag, hitch, catch.
■ **rub along** (*Brit. informal*) MANAGE, cope, get by, make do, muddle along/through; *informal* make out.
■ **rub something down** CLEAN, sponge, wash; groom.
■ **rub it in** (*informal*) EMPHASIZE, stress, underline, highlight; go on, harp on; *informal* rub someone's nose in it.
■ **rub off on** BE TRANSFERRED TO, be passed on to, be transmitted to, be communicated to; affect, influence.
■ **rub something out** ERASE, delete, remove, efface, obliterate, expunge.
■ **rub shoulders with** ASSOCIATE WITH, mingle with, fraternize with, socialize with, mix with, keep company with, consort with; *N. Amer.* rub elbows with; *informal* hang around/out with, hobnob with, knock about/around with.
■ **rub something up** POLISH, buff up, burnish, shine, wax, clean, wipe.
■ **rub someone up the wrong way** (*Brit.*). *See* ANNOY.

rubbish ▶ noun ❶ *throw away that rubbish* REFUSE, waste, litter, debris, detritus, scrap, dross; flotsam and jetsam, lumber; sweepings, scraps, dregs; *N. Amer.* garbage, trash; *informal* dreck, junk. ❷ *she's talking rubbish* NONSENSE, balderdash, gibberish, claptrap, blarney, moonshine, garbage; *informal* hogwash, baloney, tripe, drivel, bilge, bunk, piffle, poppycock, phooey, twaddle, gobbledegook; *Brit. informal* codswallop, cobblers, tosh, cack; *Scottish & N. English informal* havers; *N. Amer. informal* bushwa, applesauce.
▶ verb (*Brit. informal*) *they often rubbish trade unions. See* CRITICIZE.
▶ adjective (*Brit. informal*) *a rubbish team. See* HOPELESS sense 3.

rubbishy ▶ adjective (*informal*) WORTHLESS, substandard, trashy, inferior, second-rate, third-rate, poor-quality, cheap, shoddy; bad, poor, dreadful, awful, terrible; *informal* crummy, appalling, lousy, dire, tacky; *Brit. informal* duff, chronic, rubbish.

rubble ▶ noun DEBRIS, remains, ruins, wreckage.

ruction ▶ noun (*informal*) DISTURBANCE, noise, racket, din, commotion, fuss, uproar, furore, hue and cry, rumpus, fracas; (**ructions**) trouble, hell to pay; *informal* to-do, hullabaloo, hoo-ha, ballyhoo, stink, kerfuffle; *Brit. informal* row, carry-on.

ruddy ▶ adjective ❶ *a ruddy complexion* ROSY, red, pink, roseate, rubicund; healthy, glowing, fresh; flushed, blushing; florid, high-coloured; *poetic/literary* rubescent. ❷ (*Brit. informal*) *you ruddy idiot! See* DAMNED sense 2.
– OPPOSITES pale.

rude ▶ adjective ❶ *a rude man* ILL-MANNERED, bad-mannered, impolite, discourteous, uncivil, unmannerly, mannerless; impertinent, insolent, impudent, disrespectful, cheeky; churlish, curt, brusque, brash, offhand, short, sharp; offensive, insulting, derogatory, disparaging, abusive; tactless, undiplomatic, uncomplimentary. ❷ *rude jokes* VULGAR, coarse, smutty, dirty, filthy, crude, lewd, obscene, off colour, offensive, indelicate, tasteless; risqué, naughty, ribald, bawdy, racy; *informal* blue; *Brit. informal* near the knuckle; *N. Amer. informal* gamy; *euphemistic* adult. ❸ *a rude awakening* ABRUPT, sudden, sharp, startling; unpleasant, nasty, harsh. ❹ (*dated*) *a rude cabin* PRIMITIVE, crude, rudimentary, rough, simple, basic. ❺ (*archaic*) *a rude and barbarous people* UNEDUCATED, ignorant, illiterate; uncultured, uncivilized, unrefined; rough, coarse, uncouth, boorish.
– OPPOSITES polite, clean, luxurious, civilized.

rudimentary ▶ adjective ❶ *rudimentary carpentry skills* BASIC, elementary, primary, fundamental, essential. ❷ *the equipment was rudimentary* PRIMITIVE, crude, simple, unsophisticated, rough (and ready), makeshift. ❸ *a rudimentary thumb* VESTIGIAL, undeveloped, incomplete; *Biology* abortive, primitive.
– OPPOSITES advanced, sophisticated, developed.

rudiments ▶ plural noun BASICS, fundamentals, essentials, first principles, foundation; *informal* nuts and bolts, ABC.

rue ▶ verb REGRET, be sorry about, feel remorseful about, repent of, reproach oneself for; deplore, lament, bemoan, bewail.

rueful ▶ adjective REGRETFUL, apologetic, sorry, remorseful, shamefaced, sheepish, hangdog, contrite, repentant, penitent, conscience-stricken, self-reproachful; sorrowful, sad.

ruffian ▶ noun THUG, lout, hooligan, hoodlum, vandal, delinquent, rowdy, scoundrel, villain, rogue, bully boy, brute; *informal* tough, bruiser, heavy, yahoo; *Brit. informal* rough, yob, yobbo; *N. Amer. informal* goon.

ruffle ▶ verb ❶ *he ruffled her hair* DISARRANGE, tousle, dishevel, rumple, riffle, disorder, mess up, tangle; *N. Amer. informal* muss up. ❷ *the wind ruffled the water* RIPPLE, riffle. ❸ *don't let him ruffle you* ANNOY, irritate, vex, nettle, anger, exasperate; disconcert, unnerve, fluster, agitate, harass, upset, disturb, discomfit, put off, perturb, unsettle, bother, worry, trouble; *informal* rattle, faze, throw, get to, rile, needle, aggravate, bug, peeve; *Brit. informal* wind up, nark.
– OPPOSITES smooth, soothe.
▶ noun *a shirt with ruffles* FRILL, flounce, ruff, ruche, jabot, furbelow.

rug ▶ noun ❶ *they sat on the rug* MAT, carpet, drugget, runner; hearthrug; *N. Amer.* floorcloth. ❷ *he was wrapped in a tartan rug* BLANKET, coverlet, throw, wrap; *N. Amer.* lap robe. ❸ (*informal*) *he's wearing a ridiculous rug* TOUPEE, wig, hairpiece.

rugged ▶ adjective ❶ *the rugged coast path* ROUGH, uneven, bumpy, rocky, stony, pitted, jagged, craggy. ❷ *a rugged vehicle* ROBUST, durable, sturdy, strong, tough, resilient. ❸ *rugged manly types* WELL BUILT, burly, strong, muscular, muscly, brawny, strapping, husky, hulking; tough, hardy, robust, sturdy, lusty, solid; *informal* hunky, beefy. ❹ *his rugged features* STRONG, craggy, rough-hewn; manly, masculine; irregular, weathered.
– OPPOSITES smooth, flimsy, weedy, delicate.

ruin ▶ noun ❶ *the buildings were saved from ruin* DISINTEGRATION, decay, disrepair, dilapidation, ruination; destruction, demolition, wreckage. ❷ *the ruins of a church* REMAINS, remnants, fragments, relics; rubble, debris, wreckage. ❸ *electoral ruin for Labour* DOWNFALL, collapse, defeat, undoing, failure, breakdown, ruination; Waterloo. ❹ *shopkeepers are facing ruin* BANKRUPTCY, insolvency, penury, poverty, destitution, impoverishment, indigence; failure.
– OPPOSITES preservation, triumph, wealth.
▶ verb ❶ *don't ruin my plans* WRECK, destroy, spoil, mar, blight, shatter, dash, torpedo, scotch, mess up; sabotage; *informal* screw up, foul up, put the kibosh on, do for, nix, queer; *Brit. informal* scupper. ❷ *the bank's collapse ruined them all* BANKRUPT, make insolvent, impoverish, pauperize, wipe out, break, cripple; bring someone to their knees. ❸ *a country ruined by civil war* DESTROY, devastate, lay waste, ravage; raze, demolish, wreck, wipe out, flatten.
– OPPOSITES save, rebuild.
■ **in ruins** ❶ *the abbey is in ruins* DERELICT, ruined, in disrepair, falling to pieces, dilapidated, tumbledown, ramshackle, decrepit, decaying, ruinous. ❷ *his career is in ruins* DESTROYED, ruined, in pieces, in ashes; over, finished; *informal* in tatters, on the rocks, done for.

ruined ▶ adjective DERELICT, in ruins, dilapidated, ruinous, tumbledown, ramshackle, decrepit, falling to pieces, crumbling, decaying, disintegrating; *informal* shambly.

ruinous ▶ adjective ❶ *a ruinous trade war* DISASTROUS, devastating, catastrophic, calamitous, crippling, crushing, damaging, destructive, harmful; costly. ❷ *ruinous interest rates* EXTORTIONATE, exorbitant, excessive, sky-high, outrageous, inflated; *Brit.* over the odds; *informal* criminal, steep. ❸ *a ruinous chapel. See* RUINED.

rule ▶ noun ❶ *health and safety rules* REGULATION, ruling, directive, order, act, law, statute, edict, canon, mandate, command, dictate, decree, fiat, injunction, commandment, stipulation, requirement, guideline, direction; *formal* ordinance. ❷ *church attendance on Sunday was the general rule* PROCEDURE, practice, protocol, convention, norm, routine, custom, habit, wont; *formal* praxis. ❸ *moderation is the golden rule* PRECEPT, principle, standard, axiom, truth, maxim. ❹ *Punjab came under British rule* CONTROL, jurisdiction, command, power, dominion; government, administration, sovereignty, leadership, supremacy, authority; raj.

– RELATED TERMS hegemonic, -cracy, -archy.

▶ verb ❶ *El Salvador was ruled by Spain* GOVERN, preside over, control, lead, dominate, run, head, administer, manage. ❷ *Mary ruled for six years* BE IN POWER, be in control, be in command, be in charge, govern; reign, be monarch, be sovereign. ❸ *the judge ruled that they be set free* DECREE, order, pronounce, judge, adjudge, ordain; decide, find, determine, resolve, settle. ❹ *subversion ruled* PREVAIL, predominate, be the order of the day, reign supreme; *formal* obtain.

■ **as a rule** USUALLY, generally, in general, normally, ordinarily, customarily, for the most part, on the whole, by and large, in the main, mainly, mostly, commonly, typically.

■ **rule something out** EXCLUDE, eliminate, disregard; preclude, prohibit, prevent, disallow.

ruler ▶ noun LEADER, sovereign, monarch, potentate, king, queen, emperor, empress, prince, princess; crowned head, head of state, president, premier, governor; overlord, chief, chieftain, lord; dictator, autocrat.

– OPPOSITES subject.

ruling ▶ noun *the judge's ruling* JUDGEMENT, decision, adjudication, finding, verdict; pronouncement, resolution, decree, injunction.

▶ adjective ❶ *the ruling monarch* REIGNING, sovereign, regnant. ❷ *Japan's ruling party* GOVERNING, controlling, commanding, supreme, leading, dominant, ascendant. ❸ *football was their ruling passion* MAIN, chief, principal, major, prime, dominating, foremost; predominant, central, focal; *informal* number-one.

rum ▶ adjective (*Brit. informal, dated*). *See* PECULIAR sense 1.

rumble ▶ verb BOOM, thunder, roll, roar, resound, reverberate, echo, grumble.

rumbustious ▶ adjective (*Brit. informal*). *See* BOISTEROUS sense 1.

ruminate ▶ verb ❶ *we ruminated on life* THINK ABOUT, contemplate, consider, meditate on, muse on, mull over, ponder on/over, deliberate about/on, chew over, puzzle over; *formal* cogitate about. ❷ *cows ruminating* CHEW THE CUD.

rummage ▶ verb SEARCH, hunt, root about/around, ferret about/around, fish about/around, poke around in, dig, delve, go through, explore, sift through, rifle through; *Brit. informal* rootle around.

rumour ▶ noun GOSSIP, hearsay, talk, tittle-tattle, speculation, word, on dit; (**rumours**) reports, stories, whispers, canards; *informal* the grapevine, the word on the street, the buzz; *N. Amer. informal* scuttlebutt.

rump ▶ noun ❶ *a smack on the rump* REAR (END), backside, seat; buttocks, cheeks; *Brit.* bottom; *informal* behind, BTM, sit-upon, derrière; *Brit. informal* bum, botty, jacksie; *N. Amer. informal* butt, fanny, tush, tail, buns, booty, heinie; *humorous* fundament, posterior, stern; *Anatomy* nates. ❷ *the rump of the army* REMAINDER, rest, remnant, remains.

rumple ▶ verb ❶ *the sheet was rumpled* CRUMPLE, crease, wrinkle, crinkle, ruck (up), scrunch up; *Brit.* ruckle. ❷ *Ian rumpled her hair* RUFFLE, disarrange, tousle, dishevel, riffle; mess up; *N. Amer. informal* muss up.

– OPPOSITES smooth.

rumpus ▶ noun DISTURBANCE, commotion, uproar, furore, brouhaha, hue and cry, ruckus; fracas, melee, tumult, noise, racket, din; *informal* to-do, hullabaloo, hoo-ha, kerfuffle, ballyhoo; *Brit. informal* row, carry-on; *Scottish informal* stushie.

run ▶ verb ❶ *she ran across the road* SPRINT, race, dart, rush, dash, hasten, hurry, scurry, scamper, hare, bolt, fly, gallop, career, charge, shoot, hurtle, speed, zoom, go like lightning, go hell for leather, go like the wind; jog, trot; *informal* tear, pelt, scoot, hotfoot it, leg it, belt, zip, whip; *Brit. informal* bomb; *N. Amer. informal* hightail it, barrel. ❷ *the robbers turned and ran* FLEE, run away, run off, run for it, take flight, make off, take off, take to one's heels, make a break for it, bolt, make one's getaway, escape; *informal* beat it, clear off/out, vamoose, skedaddle, split, leg it, scram; *Brit. informal* do a runner, scarper, do a bunk; *N. Amer. informal* light out, take a powder, skidoo; *Austral. informal* shoot through. ❸ *he ran in the marathon* COMPETE, take part, participate. ❹ *a shiver ran down my spine* GO, pass, slide, move, travel. ❺ *he ran his eye down the list* CAST, pass, skim, flick. ❻ *the road runs the length of the valley* EXTEND, stretch, reach, continue. ❼ *water ran from the eaves* FLOW, pour, stream, gush, flood, cascade, roll, course, spill, trickle, drip, dribble, leak. ❽ *a bus runs to Sorrento* TRAVEL, shuttle, go. ❾ *I'll run you home* DRIVE, take, bring, ferry, chauffeur, give someone a lift. ❿ *he runs a transport company* BE IN CHARGE OF, manage, direct, control, head, govern, supervise, superintend, oversee; operate, conduct, own. ⓫ *it's expensive to run a car* MAINTAIN, keep, own, possess, have; drive. ⓬ *they ran some tests* CARRY OUT, do, perform, execute. ⓭ *he left the engine running* OPERATE, function, work, go; tick over, idle. ⓮ *the lease runs for twenty years* BE VALID, last, be in effect, be operative, continue, be effective. ⓯ *the show ran for two years* BE STAGED, be performed, be on, be mounted, be screened. ⓰ *he ran for president* STAND FOR, be a candidate for, be a contender for. ⓱ *the paper ran the story* PUBLISH, print, feature, carry, put out, release, issue. ⓲ *they run drugs* SMUGGLE, traffic in, deal in. ⓳ *they were run out of town* CHASE, drive, hound.

▶ **noun** ❶ *his morning run* SPRINT, jog, dash, gallop, trot. ❷ *she did the school run* ROUTE, journey; circuit, round, beat. ❸ *a run in the car* DRIVE, ride, turn; trip, excursion, outing, jaunt, airing; *informal* spin, tootle; *Scottish informal* hurl. ❹ *an unbeaten run of victories* SERIES, succession, sequence, string, chain, streak, spell, stretch, spate. ❺ *a run on sterling* DEMAND FOR, rush on. ❻ *they had the run of her home* FREE USE OF, unrestricted access to. ❼ *the usual run of cafes* TYPE, kind, sort, variety, class. ❽ *against the run of play, he scored again* TREND, tendency, course, direction, movement, drift, tide. ❾ *a chicken run* ENCLOSURE, pen, coop. ❿ *a ski run* SLOPE, track, piste; *N. Amer.* trail. ⓫ *a run in her tights* LADDER, rip, tear, snag, hole.

■ **in the long run** EVENTUALLY, in the end, ultimately, when all is said and done, in the fullness of time; *Brit. informal* at the end of the day.

■ **on the run** ON THE LOOSE, at large, loose; running away, fleeing, fugitive; *informal* AWOL; *N. Amer. informal* on the lam.

■ **run across** MEET (BY CHANCE), come across, run into, chance on, stumble on, happen on; *informal* bump into.

■ **run after** (*informal*) PURSUE, chase; make advances to, flirt with; *informal* make up to, come on to, be all over, vamp; *dated* set one's cap at.

■ **run along** (*informal*) GO AWAY, be off with you, shoo; *informal* scram, buzz off, skedaddle, scat, beat it, get lost, shove off, clear off; *Brit. informal* hop it; *poetic/literary* begone.

■ **run around** (*informal*) BE UNFAITHFUL, have affairs, philander; *informal* play the field, sleep around; *Brit. informal* play away; *N. Amer. informal* fool around.

■ **run away** ❶ *her attacker ran away. See* RUN verb sense 2. ❷ *she ran away with the championship* WIN EASILY, win hands down; *informal* win by a mile, walk it, romp home.

■ **run down** DECLINE, degenerate, go downhill, go to seed, decay, go to rack and ruin; *informal* go to pot, go to the dogs.

■ **run someone down** ❶ *he was run down by joyriders* RUN OVER, knock down/over; hit, strike. ❷ *she ran him down in front of other people* CRITICIZE, denigrate, belittle, disparage, deprecate, find fault with; *informal* put down, knock, badmouth; *Brit. informal* rubbish, slag off; *formal* derogate.

■ **run something down** ❶ *she finally ran a copy of the book down* FIND, discover, locate, track down, trace, unearth. ❷ *employers ran down their workforces gradually* REDUCE, cut back on, downsize, decrease, trim; phase out, wind down/up.

■ **run for it**. *See* RUN verb sense 2.

■ **run high** *feelings were running high* BE STRONG, be fervent, be passionate, be intense.

■ **run in** *heart disease runs in the family* BE COMMON IN, be inherent in.

■ **run someone in** (*informal*). *See* ARREST verb sense 1.

■ **run into** ❶ *a car ran into his van* COLLIDE WITH, hit, strike, crash into, smash into, plough into, ram, impact. ❷ *I ran into Hugo the other day* MEET (BY CHANCE), run across, chance on, stumble on, happen on; *informal* bump into. ❸ *we ran into a problem* EXPERIENCE, encounter, meet with, be faced with, be confronted with. ❹ *his debts run into six figures* REACH, extend to, be as much as.

■ **run low** *supplies were running low* DWINDLE, diminish, become depleted, be used up, be in short supply, be tight.

■ **run off** ❶ *the youths ran off. See* RUN verb sense 2. ❷ (*informal*) *he ran off with her money. See* STEAL verb sense 1.

■ **run something off** ❶ *would you run off that list for me?* COPY, photocopy, xerox, duplicate, print, produce, do. ❷ *run off some of the excess water* DRAIN, bleed, draw off, pump out.

■ **run on** ❶ *the call ran on for hours* CONTINUE, go on, carry on, last, keep going, stretch. ❷ *your mother does run on* TALK INCESSANTLY, talk a lot, go on, chatter on, ramble on; *informal* yak, gab, yabber; *Brit. informal* rabbit on, witter on, chunter on, talk the hind leg off a donkey; *N. Amer. informal* run off at the mouth.

■ **run out** ❶ *supplies ran out* BE USED UP, dry up, be exhausted, be finished, peter out. ❷ *they ran out of cash* BE OUT OF; use up, consume, eat up; *informal* be fresh out of, be cleaned out of. ❸ *her contract ran out* EXPIRE, end, terminate, finish; lapse.

■ **run out on someone** (*informal*). *See* ABANDON verb sense 3.

■ **run over** ❶ *the bathwater ran over* OVERFLOW, spill over, brim over; *archaic* overbrim. ❷ *the project ran over budget* EXCEED, go over, overshoot, overreach. ❸ *he quickly ran over the story* RECAPITULATE, repeat, run through, go over, reiterate, review; look over, read through; *informal* recap on.

■ **run someone over**. *See* RUN SOMEONE DOWN sense 1.

■ **run the show** (*informal*) BE IN CHARGE, be in control, be at the helm, be in the driving seat, be at the wheel; *informal* be the boss, call the shots.

■ **run through** ❶ *they quickly ran through their money* SQUANDER, spend, fritter away, dissipate, waste, go through, consume, use up; *informal* blow. ❷ *the attitude that runs through his writing* PERVADE, permeate, suffuse, imbue, inform. ❸ *he ran through his notes. See* RUN OVER sense 3. ❹ *let's run through scene three* REHEARSE, practise, go over, repeat; *N. Amer.* run down; *informal* recap on.

■ **run someone through** STAB, pierce, transfix, impale.

■ **run to** ❶ *the bill ran to £22,000* AMOUNT TO, add up to, total, come to, equal, reach, be as much as. ❷ *we can't run to champagne* AFFORD, stretch to, manage. ❸ *he was running to fat* TEND TO, become, get, grow.

runaway ▶ noun *a teenage runaway* FUGITIVE, escaper, escapee; refugee; truant; absconder, deserter.

▶ adjective ❶ *a runaway horse* OUT OF CONTROL, escaped, loose, on the loose. ❷ *a runaway victory* EASY, effortless; *informal* as easy as pie. ❸ *runaway inflation* RAMPANT, out of control, unchecked, unbridled.

rundown ▶ noun SUMMARY, synopsis, precis, run-through, summarization, summation, review, overview, briefing, sketch, outline; *informal* low-down, recap.

run down ▶ adjective ❶ *a run-down area of London* DILAPIDATED, tumbledown, ramshackle, derelict, ruinous, in ruins, crumbling, decaying; neglected, uncared-for, depressed, seedy, shabby, slummy, squalid; *informal* shambly; *Brit. informal* grotty. ❷ *she was feeling rather run down* UNWELL, ill, poorly, unhealthy, peaky; tired, drained, exhausted, fatigued, worn out, below par, washed out; *Brit.* off colour; *informal* under the weather; *Brit. informal* off, ropy, knackered; *Scottish informal* wabbit; *Austral./NZ informal* crook; *dated* seedy.

run-in ▶ noun (*informal*) DISAGREEMENT, argument, dispute, altercation, confrontation, contretemps, quarrel; brush, encounter, tangle, fight, clash; *informal* set-to, spat, scrap; *Brit. informal* row.

runner ▶ noun ❶ *the runners were limbering up* ATHLETE, sprinter, hurdler, racer, jogger. ❷ *a strawberry runner* SHOOT, offshoot, sprout, tendril; *Botany* stolon. ❸ *the bookmaker employed runners* MESSENGER, courier, errand boy; *informal* gofer.

■ **do a runner** (*Brit. informal*). *See* ABSCOND.

running ▶ noun ❶ *his running was particularly fast* SPRINTING, sprint, racing, jogging, jog. ❷ *the running of the school* ADMINISTRATION, management, organization, coordination, orchestration, handling, direction, control, regulation, supervision. ❸ *the smooth running of her department* OPERATION, working, function, performance.

▶ adjective ❶ *running water* FLOWING, gushing, rushing, moving. ❷ *a running argument* ONGOING, sustained, continuous, incessant, ceaseless, constant, perpetual; recurrent, recurring. ❸ *she was late two days running* IN SUCCESSION, in a row, in sequence, consecutively; straight, together; *informal* on the trot.

■ **in the running** *he's in the running for a prize* LIKELY TO GET, a candidate for, in line for, on the shortlist for, up for.

runny ▶ adjective LIQUEFIED, liquid, fluid, melted, molten; watery, thin.

– OPPOSITES solid.

run-of-the-mill ▶ adjective ORDINARY, average, middle-of-the-road, commonplace, humdrum, mundane, standard, nondescript, characterless, conventional; unremarkable, unexceptional, uninteresting, dull, boring, routine, bland, lacklustre; *N. Amer.* garden-variety; *informal* bog-standard, nothing to write home about, nothing special, a dime a dozen; *Brit. informal* common or garden.

– OPPOSITES exceptional.

rupture ▶ noun ❶ *pipeline ruptures* BREAK, fracture, crack, burst, split, fissure. ❷ *a rupture due to personal differences* RIFT, estrangement, falling-out, break-up, breach, split, separation, parting, division, schism; *informal* bust-up. ❸ *an abdominal rupture* HERNIA.

▶ verb ❶ *the reactor core might rupture* BREAK, fracture, crack, breach, burst, split; *informal* bust. ❷ *the problem ruptured their relationships* SEVER, break off, breach, disrupt; *poetic/literary* sunder.

rural ▶ adjective COUNTRY, countryside, bucolic, rustic, pastoral; agricultural, agrarian; *poetic/literary* sylvan, georgic.

– OPPOSITES urban.

ruse ▶ noun PLOY, stratagem, tactic, scheme, trick, gambit, cunning plan, dodge, subterfuge, machination, wile; *Brit. informal* wheeze.

rush ▶ verb ❶ *she rushed home* HURRY, dash, run, race, sprint, bolt, dart, gallop, career, charge, shoot, hurtle, hare, fly, speed, zoom, scurry, scuttle, scamper, hasten; *informal* tear, belt, pelt, scoot, zip, whip, hotfoot it, leg it; *Brit. informal* bomb; *N. Amer. informal* hightail it. ❷ *water rushed along gutters* FLOW, pour, gush, surge, stream, cascade, run, course. ❸ *the tax was rushed through parliament* PUSH, hurry, hasten, speed, hustle, press, force. ❹ *they rushed the cordon of troops* ATTACK, charge, run at, assail, storm.

▶ noun ❶ *Tim made a rush for the exit* DASH, run, sprint, dart, bolt, charge, scramble, break. ❷ *the lunchtime rush* HUSTLE AND BUSTLE, commotion, hubbub, hurly-burly, stir. ❸ *a last minute rush for flights* DEMAND, clamour, call, request; run on. ❹ *he was in no rush to leave* HURRY, haste, urgency. ❺ *a rush of adrenalin* SURGE, flow, flood, spurt, stream; dart, thrill, flash. ❻ *a rush of cold air* GUST, draught, flurry. ❼ *I made a sudden rush at him* CHARGE, onslaught, attack, assault, onrush.

▶ adjective *a rush job* URGENT, high-priority, emergency; hurried, hasty, fast, quick, swift; *N. Amer. informal* hurry-up.

rushed ▶ adjective ❶ *a rushed divorce* HASTY, fast, speedy, quick, swift, rapid, hurried. ❷ *he was too rushed to enjoy his stay* PUSHED FOR TIME, pressed for time, busy, in a hurry, run off one's feet.

rust ▶ **verb** CORRODE, oxidize, become rusty, tarnish.
– RELATED TERMS ferruginous.

rustic ▶ **adjective** ❶ *a rustic setting* RURAL, country, countryside, countrified, pastoral, bucolic; agricultural, agrarian; *poetic/literary* sylvan, georgic. ❷ *rustic wooden tables* PLAIN, simple, homely, unsophisticated; rough, rude, crude. ❸ *rustic peasants* UNSOPHISTICATED, uncultured, unrefined, simple; artless, unassuming, guileless, naive, ingenuous; coarse, rough, uncouth, boorish; *N. Amer. informal* hillbilly, hick.
– OPPOSITES urban, ornate, sophisticated.
▶ **noun** *the rustics were carousing* PEASANT, countryman, countrywoman, bumpkin, yokel, country cousin; *N. Amer. informal* hillbilly, hayseed, hick; *Austral./NZ informal* bushy; *archaic* swain, cottier.

rustle ▶ **verb** ❶ *her dress rustled as she moved* SWISH, whoosh, whisper, sigh. ❷ *he was rustling cattle* STEAL, thieve, take; abduct, kidnap.
▶ **noun** *the rustle of the leaves* SWISH, whisper, rustling; *poetic/literary* susurration, susurrus.
■ **rustle something up** (*informal*) PREPARE HASTILY, throw together, make; *informal* fix; *Brit. informal* knock up.

rusty ▶ **adjective** ❶ *rusty wire* RUSTED, rust-covered, corroded, oxidized; tarnished, discoloured. ❷ *his hair was a rusty colour* REDDISH-BROWN, chestnut, auburn, tawny, russet, coppery, copper, Titian, red. ❸ *my French is a little rusty* OUT OF PRACTICE, below par; unpractised, deficient, impaired, weak.

rut ▶ **noun** ❶ *the car bumped across the ruts* FURROW, groove, trough, ditch, hollow, pothole, crater. ❷ *he was stuck in a rut* BORING ROUTINE, humdrum existence, groove, dead end.

ruthless ▶ **adjective** MERCILESS, pitiless, cruel, heartless, hard-hearted, cold-hearted, cold-blooded, harsh, callous, unmerciful, unforgiving, uncaring, unsympathetic, uncharitable; remorseless, unbending, inflexible, implacable; brutal, inhuman, inhumane, barbarous, barbaric, savage, sadistic, vicious.
– OPPOSITES merciful.

Ss

sable ▶ **adjective** BLACK, jet-black, pitch-black, ebony, raven, sooty, dusky, inky, coal-black.

sabotage ▶ **noun** VANDALISM, wrecking, destruction, impairment, incapacitation, damage; subversion, obstruction, disruption, spoiling, undermining; *Brit. informal* a spanner in the works.
▶ **verb** VANDALIZE, wreck, damage, destroy, cripple, impair, incapacitate; obstruct, disrupt, spoil, ruin, undermine, threaten, subvert.

sac ▶ **noun** BAG, pouch; *Medicine* blister, cyst; *Anatomy* bladder, bursa, saccule, vesicle.

saccharine ▶ **adjective** SENTIMENTAL, sickly, mawkish, cloying, sugary, sickening, nauseating; *informal* mushy, slushy, schmaltzy, weepy, gooey, drippy, cheesy, corny, toe-curling; *Brit. informal* soppy, twee; *N. Amer. informal* cornball, sappy.

sack[1] ▶ **noun** ❶ *a sack of flour* BAG, pouch, pocket, pack. ❷ (*informal*) *work hard or you'll get the sack* DISMISSAL, discharge, redundancy; *informal* the boot, the bullet, the axe, the heave-ho, one's marching orders, the elbow, the push; *Brit. informal* one's cards. ❸ (*informal*) *she stayed in the sack* BED; *informal* kip; *Brit. informal* pit.
▶ **verb** (*informal*) *she was sacked for stealing* DISMISS, discharge, lay off, make redundant, let go, throw out; *Military* cashier; *informal* fire, kick out, boot out, give someone the bullet, give someone the sack, give someone their marching orders, show someone the door, send packing; *Brit. informal* give someone their cards.
■ **hit the sack** (*informal*) GO TO BED, retire, go to sleep; *informal* turn in, hit the hay.

sack[2] ▶ **verb** *raiders sacked the town* RAVAGE, lay waste, devastate, raid, ransack, strip, plunder, despoil, pillage, loot, rob.

sackcloth ▶ **noun** HESSIAN, sacking, hopsack, burlap; *N. Amer.* gunny.
■ **wearing sackcloth and ashes** PENITENT, contrite, regretful, sorrowful, rueful, remorseful, apologetic, ashamed, guilt-ridden, chastened, shamefaced, self-reproachful, guilty.

sacred ▶ **adjective** ❶ *the priest entered the sacred place* HOLY, hallowed, blessed, consecrated, sanctified, venerated, revered; *archaic* blest. ❷ *sacred music* RELIGIOUS, spiritual, devotional, church, ecclesiastical. ❸ *the hill is sacred to the tribe* SACROSANCT, inviolable, inviolate, invulnerable, untouchable, protected, defended, secure.
– RELATED TERMS hiero-.
– OPPOSITES secular, profane.

sacrifice ▶ noun ❶ *the sacrifice of animals* RITUAL SLAUGHTER, offering, oblation, immolation. ❷ *the calf was a sacrifice* (VOTIVE) OFFERING, burnt offering, gift, oblation. ❸ *the sacrifice of sovereignty* SURRENDER, giving up, abandonment, renunciation, forfeiture, relinquishment, resignation, abdication.
▶ verb ❶ *two goats were sacrificed* OFFER UP, immolate, slaughter. ❷ *he sacrificed his principles* GIVE UP, abandon, surrender, forgo, renounce, forfeit, relinquish, resign, abdicate; betray.

sacrificial ▶ adjective VOTIVE, oblatory, oblational; expiatory, propitiatory.

sacrilege ▶ noun DESECRATION, profanity, profanation, blasphemy, impiety, irreligion, unholiness, irreverence, disrespect.
– OPPOSITES piety.

sacrilegious ▶ adjective PROFANE, blasphemous, impious, sinful, irreverent, irreligious, unholy, disrespectful.

sacrosanct ▶ adjective SACRED, hallowed, respected, inviolable, inviolate, unimpeachable, invulnerable, untouchable, inalienable; protected, defended, secure, safe.

sad ▶ adjective ❶ *we felt sad when we left* UNHAPPY, sorrowful, dejected, depressed, downcast, miserable, down, despondent, despairing, disconsolate, desolate, wretched, glum, gloomy, doleful, dismal, melancholy, mournful, woebegone, forlorn, crestfallen, heartbroken, inconsolable; *informal* blue, down in the mouth, down in the dumps. ❷ *they knew her sad story* TRAGIC, unhappy, unfortunate, awful, miserable, wretched, sorry, pitiful, pathetic, traumatic, heartbreaking, heart-rending, harrowing. ❸ *a sad state of affairs* UNFORTUNATE, regrettable, sorry, deplorable, lamentable, pitiful, shameful, disgraceful.
– OPPOSITES happy, cheerful, fortunate.

sadden ▶ verb DEPRESS, dispirit, deject, dishearten, grieve, desolate, discourage, upset, get down, bring down, break someone's heart.

saddle ▶ verb *they were saddled with the children* BURDEN, encumber, lumber, hamper; land, charge; impose something on, thrust something on, fob something off on to.

sadism ▶ noun CALLOUSNESS, schadenfreude, barbarity, brutality, cruelty, cold-bloodedness, inhumanity, ruthlessness, heartlessness; perversion.

sadistic ▶ adjective CALLOUS, barbarous, vicious, brutal, cruel, fiendish, cold-blooded, inhuman, ruthless, heartless; perverted.

sadness ▶ noun UNHAPPINESS, sorrow, dejection, depression, misery, despondency, despair, desolation, wretchedness, gloom, gloominess, dolefulness, melancholy, mournfulness, woe, heartache, grief.

safe ▶ adjective ❶ *the jewels are safe in the bank* SECURE, protected, shielded, sheltered, guarded, out of harm's way. ❷ *the lost children are all safe* UNHARMED, unhurt, uninjured, unscathed, all right, well, in one piece, out of danger; *informal* OK. ❸ *a safe place to hide* SECURE, sound, impregnable, unassailable, invulnerable. ❹ *a safe driver* CAUTIOUS, circumspect, prudent, attentive; unadventurous, conservative, unenterprising. ❺ *the drug is safe* HARMLESS, innocuous, benign, non-toxic, non-poisonous; wholesome.
– OPPOSITES insecure, dangerous, reckless, harmful.
▶ noun *I keep the ring in a safe* STRONGBOX, safety-deposit box, safe-deposit box, coffer, casket; strongroom, vault.

safeguard ▶ noun *a safeguard against crises* PROTECTION, defence, guard, screen, buffer, preventive, precaution, provision, security; surety, cover, insurance, indemnity.
▶ verb *the contract will safeguard 1000 jobs* PROTECT, preserve, conserve, save, secure, shield, guard, keep safe.
– OPPOSITES jeopardize.

safety ▶ noun ❶ *the safety of the residents* WELFARE, well-being, protection, security. ❷ *the safety of ferries* SECURITY, soundness, dependability, reliability. ❸ *we reached the safety of the shore* SHELTER, sanctuary, refuge.

sag ▶ verb ❶ *he sagged back in his chair* SINK, slump, loll, flop, crumple. ❷ *the floors all sag* DIP, droop; bulge, bag. ❸ *production has sagged* DECLINE, fall (off), drop, decrease, diminish, slump, plummet; *informal* nosedive.

saga ▶ noun ❶ *Celtic tribal sagas* EPIC, chronicle, legend, folk tale, romance, history, narrative, adventure, myth, fairy story. ❷ *the saga of how they met* LONG STORY, rigmarole; chain of events; *informal* spiel.

sagacious ▶ adjective WISE, clever, intelligent, knowledgeable, sensible, sage; discerning, judicious, canny, perceptive, astute, shrewd, prudent, thoughtful, insightful, perspicacious; *informal* streetwise; *formal* sapient.
– OPPOSITES foolish.

sage ▶ noun *the Chinese sage Confucius* WISE MAN/WOMAN, learned person, philosopher, thinker, scholar, savant; authority, expert, guru.
▶ adjective *some very sage comments. See* SAGACIOUS.

sail ▶ noun *the ship's sails* canvas.
▶ verb ❶ *we sailed across the Atlantic* VOYAGE, travel by water, steam, navigate, cruise. ❷ *you can learn to sail here* YACHT, boat, go sailing; crew, helm. ❸ *we sail tonight* SET SAIL, put to sea, leave port, hoist sail, weigh anchor, shove off. ❹ *he is sailing the ship* STEER, pilot, navigate, con, helm, captain; *informal* skipper. ❺ *clouds were sailing past* GLIDE, drift, float, flow, sweep, skim, coast, flit. ❻ *a pencil sailed past his ear* WHIZZ, speed, streak, shoot, whip, buzz, zoom, flash; fly, wing, soar; *informal* zip.
■ **sail into** ATTACK, set upon, set about, fall on,

assault, assail, lay into, pitch into, hit out at, thump, batter, pummel, beat, thrash, belabour; berate, abuse, round on; *informal* let someone have it; *Brit. informal* have a go at; *N. Amer. informal* light into.

■ **sail through** SUCCEED EASILY AT, pass easily, romp through, walk through.

sailor ▶ **noun** SEAMAN, seafarer, mariner; boatman, yachtsman, yachtswoman; hand; *informal* (old) salt, sea dog, bluejacket; *Brit. informal* matelot; *Brit. informal, dated* Jack tar.

saintly ▶ **adjective** HOLY, godly, pious, religious, devout, spiritual, prayerful; virtuous, righteous, good, moral, innocent, sinless, guiltless, irreproachable, spotless, uncorrupted, pure, angelic.
– OPPOSITES ungodly.

sake ▶ **noun** ❶ *this is simplified for the sake of clarity* PURPOSE, reason, aim, end, objective, object, goal, motive. ❷ *she had to be brave for the her daughter's sake* BENEFIT, advantage, good, well-being, welfare, interest, profit.

salacious ▶ **adjective** ❶ *salacious writing* PORNOGRAPHIC, obscene, indecent, crude, lewd, vulgar, dirty, filthy; erotic, titillating, arousing, suggestive, sexy, risqué, ribald, smutty, bawdy; X-rated; *informal* porn, porno, blue; *euphemistic* adult. ❷ *salacious women* LUSTFUL, lecherous, licentious, lascivious, libidinous, prurient, lewd; debauched, wanton, loose, fast, impure, unchaste, degenerate, sinful, depraved, promiscuous; *informal* randy, horny, raunchy, pervy.

salary ▶ **noun** PAY, wages, earnings, payment, remuneration, fee(s), stipend, income; *formal* emolument.

sale ▶ **noun** ❶ *the sale of firearms* SELLING, vending; dealing, trading. ❷ *they make a sale every minute* DEAL, transaction, bargain.
– OPPOSITES purchase.

■ **for sale** ON THE MARKET, on sale, on offer, available, purchasable, obtainable.

salesperson ▶ **noun** SALES ASSISTANT, salesman, saleswoman, shop assistant, seller, agent; shopkeeper, trader, merchant, dealer, pedlar, hawker; *N. Amer.* clerk; *informal* counter-jumper, rep.

salient ▶ **adjective** IMPORTANT, main, principal, major, chief, primary; notable, noteworthy, outstanding, conspicuous, striking, noticeable, obvious, remarkable, prominent, predominant, dominant; key, crucial, vital, essential, pivotal, prime, central, paramount.
– OPPOSITES minor.

saliva ▶ **noun** SPIT, spittle, dribble, drool, slaver, slobber, sputum.

sallow ▶ **adjective** YELLOWISH, jaundiced, pallid, wan, pale, anaemic, bloodless, pasty; unhealthy, sickly, washed out, peaky; *informal* like death warmed up.

sally ▶ **noun** ❶ *the garrison made a sally against us* SORTIE, charge, foray, thrust, drive, offensive, attack, assault, raid, incursion, invasion, onset, onslaught. ❷ *a fruitless sally into Wales* EXPEDITION, excursion, trip, outing, jaunt, visit. ❸ *he was delighted with his sally* WITTICISM, smart remark, quip, barb, pleasantry; joke, pun, jest, bon mot; retort, riposte, counter, rejoinder; *informal* gag, wisecrack, comeback.

salon ▶ **noun** ❶ *a hairdressing salon* SHOP, parlour, establishment, premises; boutique, store. ❷ *the chateau's mirrored salon* RECEPTION ROOM, drawing room, sitting room, living room, lounge; *dated* parlour.

salt ▶ **noun** ❶ *the potatoes need salt* SODIUM CHLORIDE. ❷ (*poetic/literary*) *danger is the salt of pleasure* ZEST, spice, piquancy, bite, edge; vitality, spirit, sparkle; *informal* zing, punch.
– RELATED TERMS saline.

▶ **adjective** *salt water* SALTY, salted, saline, briny, brackish.

■ **salt something away** (*informal*) SAVE, put aside, put by, set aside, reserve, keep, store, stockpile, hoard, stow away; *informal* squirrel away, stash away.

■ **with a pinch of salt** WITH RESERVATIONS, with misgivings, sceptically, cynically, doubtfully, doubtingly, suspiciously, quizzically, incredulously.

salty ▶ **adjective** ❶ *salty water* SALT, salted, saline, briny, brackish. ❷ *a salty sense of humour* EARTHY, colourful, spicy, racy, naughty, vulgar, rude; piquant, biting.

salubrious ▶ **adjective** ❶ *I found the climate salubrious* HEALTHY, health-giving, healthful, beneficial, wholesome; *archaic* salutary. ❷ *a salubrious area of London* PLEASANT, agreeable, nice, select, high-class; *Brit.* upmarket; *informal* posh, swanky, classy; *Brit. informal* swish; *N. Amer. informal* swank.
– OPPOSITES unhealthy, unpleasant.

salutary ▶ **adjective** ❶ *a salutary lesson on the fragility of nature* BENEFICIAL, advantageous, good, profitable, productive, helpful, useful, valuable, worthwhile; timely. ❷ (*archaic*) *the salutary Atlantic air* HEALTHY, health-giving, healthful, salubrious, beneficial.
– OPPOSITES unwelcome, unhealthy.

salutation ▶ **noun** GREETING, salute, address, welcome.

salute ▶ **noun** ❶ *he gave the Brigadier a salute* GREETING, salutation, gesture of respect, obeisance, acknowledgement, welcome, address. ❷ *a salute to British courage* TRIBUTE, testimonial, homage, toast, honour, eulogy; celebration of, acknowledgement of.

▶ **verb** ❶ *he saluted the ambassadors* GREET, address, hail, welcome, acknowledge, toast; make obeisance to. ❷ *we salute a great photographer* PAY TRIBUTE TO, pay homage to, honour, celebrate, acknowledge, take one's hat off to.

salvage ▶ **verb** ❶ *an attempt to salvage the vessel* RESCUE, save, recover, retrieve, raise, reclaim. ❷ *he salvaged a precious point for his club* RETAIN, preserve, conserve; regain, recoup, redeem, snatch.

▶ **noun** *the salvage is taking place off the coast* RESCUE, recovery, reclamation.

salvation ▶ **noun** ❶ *salvation by way of repentance* REDEMPTION, deliverance, reclamation. ❷ *that conviction was her salvation* LIFELINE, preservation; means of escape, help.
– OPPOSITES damnation.

salve ▶ **noun** *lip salve* OINTMENT, cream, balm, unguent, emollient; embrocation, liniment; *archaic* unction.

▶ **verb** *she did it to salve her conscience* SOOTHE, assuage, ease, allay, lighten, alleviate, comfort, mollify.

salver ▶ **noun** PLATTER, plate, dish, paten, tray; *archaic* charger.

same ▶ **adjective** ❶ *we stayed at the same hotel* IDENTICAL, selfsame, very same, one and the same. ❷ *they had the same symptoms* MATCHING, identical, alike, duplicate, carbon-copy, twin; indistinguishable, interchangeable, corresponding, equivalent, parallel, like, comparable, similar, congruent, concordant, consonant. ❸ *it happened that same month* SELFSAME; aforesaid, aforementioned. ❹ *they provide the same menu worldwide* UNCHANGING, unvarying, unvaried, invariable, consistent, uniform, regular.
– RELATED TERMS homo-.
– OPPOSITES another, different, dissimilar, varying.

▶ **noun** *Louise said the same* THE SAME THING, the aforementioned, the aforesaid, the above-mentioned.

■ **all the same** ❶ *I was frightened all the same* IN SPITE OF EVERYTHING, despite that, nevertheless, nonetheless, even so, however, but, still, yet, though, be that as it may, just the same, at the same time, in any event, notwithstanding, regardless, anyway, anyhow; *informal* still and all. ❷ *it's all the same to me* IMMATERIAL, of no importance, of no consequence, inconsequential, unimportant, of little account, irrelevant, insignificant, trivial, petty.

sample ▶ **noun** ❶ *a sample of the fabric* SPECIMEN, example, bit, snippet, swatch, exemplification, representative piece; prototype, test piece, dummy, pilot, trial, taste, taster, tester. ❷ *a sample of 10,000 people nationwide* CROSS SECTION, variety, sampling, test.

▶ **verb** *we sampled the culinary offerings* TRY (OUT), taste, test, put to the test, experiment with; appraise, evaluate; *informal* check out.

▶ **adjective** ❶ *the sample group is small* REPRESENTATIVE, illustrative, selected, specimen, test, trial, typical. ❷ *a sample copy can be obtained* SPECIMEN, test, trial, pilot, dummy.

sanatorium ▶ **noun** INFIRMARY, clinic, hospital, medical centre, hospice; sickbay, sickroom; *N. Amer.* sanitarium; *informal* san.

sanctify ▶ **verb** ❶ *he came to sanctify the site* CONSECRATE, bless, make holy, hallow, make sacred, dedicate to God. ❷ *they sanctified themselves* PURIFY, cleanse, free from sin, absolve, unburden, redeem; *rare* lustrate. ❸ *we must not sanctify this outrage* APPROVE, sanction, condone, vindicate, endorse, support, back, permit, allow, authorize, legitimize, legitimatize.

sanctimonious ▶ **adjective** SELF-RIGHTEOUS, holier-than-thou, pious, pietistic, churchy, moralizing, smug, superior, priggish, hypocritical, insincere; *informal* goody-goody, pi.

sanction ▶ **noun** ❶ *trade sanctions* PENALTY, punishment, deterrent; punitive action, discipline, penalization, restriction; embargo, ban, prohibition, boycott. ❷ *the scheme has the sanction of the court* AUTHORIZATION, consent, leave, permission, authority, warrant, licence, dispensation, assent, acquiescence, agreement, approval, approbation, endorsement, accreditation, ratification, validation, blessing, imprimatur; *informal* the go-ahead, the thumbs up, the OK, the green light.
– OPPOSITES reward, prohibition.

▶ **verb** ❶ *the rally was sanctioned by the government* AUTHORIZE, permit, allow, warrant, accredit, license, endorse, approve, accept, back, support; *informal* OK. ❷ *the penalties available to sanction crime* PUNISH, discipline someone for.
– OPPOSITES prohibit.

sanctity ▶ **noun** ❶ *the sanctity of St Francis* HOLINESS, godliness, blessedness, saintliness, spirituality, piety, piousness, devoutness, righteousness, goodness, virtue, purity; *formal* sanctitude. ❷ *the sanctity of the family meal* SACROSANCTITY, inviolability; importance, paramountcy.

sanctuary ▶ **noun** ❶ *the sanctuary at Delphi* HOLY PLACE, temple; shrine, altar; sanctum, sacrarium, holy of holies, sanctum sanctorum. ❷ *the island is our sanctuary* REFUGE, haven, harbour, port in a storm, oasis, shelter, retreat, bolt-hole, hideaway, fastness. ❸ *he was given sanctuary in the embassy* SAFETY, protection, shelter, immunity, asylum. ❹ *a bird sanctuary* RESERVE, park, reservation, preserve.

sanctum ▶ **noun** ❶ *the sanctum in the temple* HOLY PLACE, shrine, sanctuary, holy of holies, sanctum sanctorum. ❷ *a private sanctum for the bar's regulars* REFUGE, retreat, bolt-hole, hideout, hideaway, den.

sand ▶ **noun** *she ran across the sand* BEACH, sands, shore, seashore; (sand) dunes; *poetic/literary* strand.

sane ▶ **adjective** ❶ *the accused is presumed to be sane* OF SOUND MIND, in one's right mind, compos mentis, lucid, rational, balanced, stable, normal; *informal* all there. ❷ *it isn't sane to use nuclear*

weapons SENSIBLE, practical, advisable, responsible, realistic, prudent, wise, reasonable, rational, level-headed, commonsensical, judicious, politic.
– OPPOSITES mad, foolish.

sangfroid ▶ **noun** COMPOSURE, equanimity, self-possession, equilibrium, aplomb, poise, self-assurance, self-control, nerve, calm, presence of mind; *informal* cool, unflappability.

sanguine ▶ **adjective** ❶ *he is sanguine about the advance of technology* OPTIMISTIC, bullish, hopeful, buoyant, positive, confident, cheerful, cheery; *informal* upbeat. ❷ (*archaic*) *a sanguine complexion. See* FLORID sense 1.
– OPPOSITES gloomy.

sanitary ▶ **adjective** HYGIENIC, clean, antiseptic, aseptic, sterile, uninfected, disinfected, unpolluted, uncontaminated; salubrious, healthy, wholesome.

sanitize ▶ **verb** ❶ *the best way to sanitize a bottle* STERILIZE, disinfect, clean, cleanse, purify, fumigate, decontaminate. ❷ *the diaries have not been sanitized* MAKE PRESENTABLE, make acceptable, make palatable, clean up; expurgate, bowdlerize, censor.

sanity ▶ **noun** ❶ *she was losing her sanity* MENTAL HEALTH, faculties, reason, rationality, saneness, stability, lucidity; sense, wits, mind. ❷ *sanity has prevailed* (COMMON) SENSE, wisdom, prudence, judiciousness, rationality, soundness, sensibleness.

sap[1] ▶ **noun** ❶ *sap from the roots of trees* JUICE, secretion, fluid, liquid. ❷ *they're full of youthful sap* VIGOUR, energy, drive, dynamism, life, spirit, liveliness, sparkle, verve, ebullience, enthusiasm, gusto, vitality, vivacity, fire, zest, zeal, exuberance; *informal* get-up-and-go, oomph, vim.
▶ **verb** *they sapped the will of the troops* ERODE, wear away/down, deplete, reduce, lessen, attenuate, undermine, exhaust, drain, bleed.

sap[2] ▶ **noun** (*informal*) *he fell for it—what a sap! See* IDIOT.

sarcasm ▶ **noun** DERISION, mockery, ridicule, scorn, sneering, scoffing; irony.

sarcastic ▶ **adjective** SARDONIC, ironic, ironical; derisive, snide, scornful, contemptuous, mocking, sneering, jeering; caustic, scathing, trenchant, cutting, sharp, acerbic; *Brit. informal* sarky; *N. Amer. informal* snarky.

sardonic ▶ **adjective** MOCKING, satirical, sarcastic, ironical, ironic; cynical, scornful, contemptuous, derisive, derisory, sneering, jeering; scathing, caustic, trenchant, cutting, sharp, acerbic; *Brit. informal* sarky.

sash ▶ **noun** BELT, cummerbund, waistband, girdle, obi; *poetic/literary* cincture.

Satan ▶ **noun**. *See* DEVIL sense 1.

satanic ▶ **adjective** DIABOLICAL, fiendish, devilish, demonic, demoniacal, ungodly, hellish, infernal, wicked, evil, sinful, iniquitous, nefarious, vile, foul, abominable, unspeakable, loathsome, monstrous, heinous, hideous, horrible, horrifying, shocking, appalling, dreadful, awful, terrible, ghastly, abhorrent, despicable, damnable.

sate ▶ **verb**. *See* SATIATE.

satellite ▶ **noun** ❶ *the European Space Agency's ERS-1 satellite* SPACE STATION, space capsule, spacecraft; sputnik. ❷ *the two small satellites of Mars* MOON, secondary planet. ❸ *Bulgaria was then a Russian satellite* DEPENDENCY, colony, protectorate, possession, holding; *historical* fief, vassal.
▶ **adjective** *a satellite state* DEPENDENT, subordinate, subsidiary; puppet.

satiate ▶ **verb** FILL, satisfy, sate; slake, quench; gorge, stuff, surfeit, glut, cloy, sicken, nauseate.

satiety ▶ **noun** SATIATION, satisfaction, repleteness, repletion, fullness; surfeit.

satiny ▶ **adjective** SMOOTH, shiny, glossy, shining, gleaming, lustrous, sleek, silky.

satire ▶ **noun** ❶ *a satire on American politics* PARODY, burlesque, caricature, lampoon, skit, pasquinade; *informal* spoof, take-off, send-up. ❷ *he has become the subject of satire* MOCKERY, ridicule, derision, scorn, caricature; irony, sarcasm.

satirical ▶ **adjective** MOCKING, ironic, ironical, satiric, sarcastic, sardonic; caustic, trenchant, mordant, biting, cutting, stinging, acerbic; critical, irreverent, disparaging, disrespectful.

satirize ▶ **verb** MOCK, ridicule, deride, make fun of, poke fun at, parody, lampoon, burlesque, caricature, take off; criticize; *informal* send up, take the mickey out of.

satisfaction ▶ **noun** ❶ *he derived great satisfaction from his work* CONTENTMENT, content, pleasure, gratification, fulfilment, enjoyment, happiness, pride; self-satisfaction, smugness, complacency. ❷ *the satisfaction of consumer needs* FULFILMENT, gratification; appeasement, assuaging. ❸ *investors turned to the courts for satisfaction* COMPENSATION, recompense, redress, reparation, restitution, repayment, payment, settlement, reimbursement, indemnification, indemnity.

satisfactory ▶ **adjective** ADEQUATE, all right, acceptable, good enough, sufficient, reasonable, quite good, competent, fair, decent, average, passable; fine, in order, up to scratch, up to the mark, up to standard, up to par; *informal* OK, so-so.
– OPPOSITES inadequate, poor.

satisfied ▶ **adjective** ❶ *a satisfied smile* PLEASED, well pleased, content, contented, happy, proud, triumphant; smug, self-satisfied, pleased with oneself, complacent; *Brit. informal* like the cat that's got the cream. ❷ *the*

pleasure of satisfied desire FULFILLED, gratified. ❸ *I am satisfied that she is happy with the decision* CONVINCED, certain, sure, positive, persuaded, easy in one's mind.
– OPPOSITES discontented, unhappy.

satisfy ▶ verb ❶ *a last chance to satisfy his hunger for romance* FULFIL, gratify, meet, fill; indulge, cater to, pander to; appease, assuage; quench, slake, satiate, sate, take the edge off. ❷ *she satisfied herself that it had been an accident* CONVINCE, persuade, assure; reassure, put someone's mind at rest. ❸ *products which satisfy the EC's criteria* COMPLY WITH, meet, fulfil, answer, conform to; measure up to, come up to; suffice, be good enough, fit/fill the bill. ❹ *there was insufficient collateral to satisfy the loan* REPAY, pay (off), settle, make good, discharge, square, liquidate, clear.
– OPPOSITES frustrate.

satisfying ▶ adjective FULFILLING, rewarding, gratifying, pleasing, enjoyable, pleasurable, to one's liking.

saturate ▶ verb ❶ *heavy rain saturated the ground* SOAK, drench, waterlog, wet through; souse, steep, douse. ❷ *the air was saturated with the stench of joss sticks* PERMEATE, suffuse, imbue, pervade, charge, infuse, fill. ❸ *the company has saturated the market* FLOOD, glut, oversupply, overfill, overload.

saturated ▶ adjective ❶ *his trousers were saturated* SOAKED, soaking (wet), wet through, sopping (wet), sodden, dripping, wringing wet, drenched; soaked to the skin, like a drowned rat. ❷ *the saturated ground* WATERLOGGED, soggy, squelchy, heavy, muddy, boggy.
– OPPOSITES dry.

saturnine ▶ adjective ❶ *a saturnine temperament* GLOOMY, sombre, melancholy, moody, lugubrious, dour, glum, morose, unsmiling, humourless. ❷ *his saturnine good looks* SWARTHY, dark, dark-skinned, dark-complexioned; mysterious, mercurial, moody.
– OPPOSITES cheerful.

sauce ▶ noun ❶ *a piquant sauce* RELISH, condiment, ketchup; dip, dressing; jus, coulis. ❷ (*Brit. informal*) *'I'll have less of your sauce,' said Aunt Edie* IMPUDENCE, impertinence, cheek, cheekiness, effrontery, forwardness, brazenness; insolence, rudeness, disrespect; *informal* mouth, lip; *N. Amer. informal* sassiness.

saucepan ▶ noun PAN, pot, casserole, skillet, stockpot, stewpot; billy, billycan.

saucy ▶ adjective (*informal*) ❶ (*Brit.*) *saucy postcards* SUGGESTIVE, titillating, risqué, rude, bawdy, racy, ribald, spicy; *informal* raunchy, smutty, nudge-nudge; *Brit. informal* fruity; *N. Amer. informal* gamy. ❷ *you saucy little minx!* CHEEKY, impudent, impertinent, irreverent, forward, disrespectful, bold, as bold as brass, brazen; *informal* fresh, lippy, mouthy; *N. Amer. informal* sassy; *archaic* malapert. ❸ (*N. Amer.*) *the cap sat at a saucy angle on her black hair* JAUNTY, rakish, sporty, raffish.
– OPPOSITES demure, polite.

saunter ▶ verb STROLL, amble, wander, meander, drift, walk; stretch one's legs, take the air; *informal* mosey, tootle; *Brit. informal* pootle; *formal* promenade.

savage ▶ adjective ❶ *savage dogs* FEROCIOUS, fierce; wild, untamed, undomesticated, feral. ❷ *a savage assault* VICIOUS, brutal, cruel, sadistic, ferocious, fierce, violent, bloody, murderous, homicidal, bloodthirsty; *poetic/literary* fell; *archaic* sanguinary. ❸ *a savage attack on European free-trade policy* FIERCE, blistering, scathing, searing, stinging, devastating, mordant, trenchant, caustic, cutting, biting, withering, virulent, vitriolic. ❹ *a savage race* PRIMITIVE, uncivilized, unenlightened, non-literate, in a state of nature. ❺ *a savage landscape* RUGGED, rough, wild, inhospitable, uninhabitable. ❻ *a savage blow for the town* SEVERE, crushing, devastating, crippling, terrible, awful, dreadful, dire, catastrophic, calamitous, ruinous.
– OPPOSITES tame, mild, civilized.
▶ noun ❶ *she'd expected mud huts and savages* BARBARIAN, wild man, wild woman, primitive. ❷ *she described her son's assailants as savages* BRUTE, beast, monster, barbarian, sadist, animal.
▶ verb ❶ *he was savaged by a dog* MAUL, attack, tear to pieces, lacerate, claw, bite. ❷ *critics savaged the film* CRITICIZE SEVERELY, attack, lambaste, condemn, denounce, pillory, revile; *informal* pan, tear to pieces, hammer, slam, do a hatchet job on, crucify; *Brit. informal* slate, rubbish; *N. Amer. informal* trash; *Austral./NZ informal* bag, monster; *formal* excoriate.

savant ▶ noun INTELLECTUAL, scholar, sage, philosopher, thinker, wise/learned person; guru, master, pandit.
– OPPOSITES ignoramus.

save ▶ verb ❶ *the captain was saved by his crew* RESCUE, come to someone's rescue, save someone's life; set free, free, liberate, deliver, extricate; bail out; *informal* save someone's bacon/neck/skin. ❷ *the farmhouse has been saved from demolition* PRESERVE, keep safe, keep, protect, safeguard; salvage, retrieve, reclaim, rescue. ❸ *start saving old newspapers for wrapping china* PUT ASIDE, set aside, put by, put to one side, save up, keep, retain, reserve, conserve, stockpile, store, hoard, save for a rainy day; *informal* salt away, squirrel away, stash away, hang on to. ❹ *asking me first would have saved a lot of trouble* PREVENT, obviate, forestall, spare; stop; avoid, avert.
▶ preposition & conjunction (*formal*) *no one needed to know save herself* EXCEPT, apart from, but, other than, besides, aside from, bar, barring, excluding, leaving out, saving; *informal* outside of.

saving ▶ noun ❶ *a considerable saving in development costs* REDUCTION, cut, decrease, economy. ❷ *I'll have to use some of my savings* NEST EGG, money put by for a rainy day, life savings; capital, assets, funds, resources, reserves.

saving grace ▶ **noun** REDEEMING FEATURE, good point, thing in its/one's favour, advantage, asset, selling point.

saviour ▶ **noun** ❶ *the country's saviour* RESCUER, liberator, deliverer, emancipator; champion, knight in shining armour, friend in need, good Samaritan. ❷ *the Saviour is depicted with two archangels* CHRIST, Jesus (Christ), the Redeemer, the Messiah, Our Lord, the Lamb of God, the Son of God, the Son of Man, the Prince of Peace.

savoir faire ▶ **noun** SOCIAL SKILL, social grace(s), urbanity, suavity, finesse, sophistication, poise, aplomb, adroitness, polish, style, smoothness, tact, tactfulness, diplomacy, discretion, delicacy, sensitivity; *informal* savvy.
–OPPOSITES gaucheness.

savour ▶ **verb** ❶ *she wanted to savour every moment* RELISH, enjoy (to the full), appreciate, delight in, revel in, smack one's lips over, luxuriate in, bask in. ❷ *such a declaration savoured of immodesty* SUGGEST, smack of, have the hallmarks of, seem like, have the air of, show signs of.
▶ **noun** ❶ *the subtle savour of wood smoke* SMELL, aroma, fragrance, scent, perfume, bouquet; TASTE, flavour, tang, smack. ❷ *a savour of bitterness seasoned my feelings for him* TRACE, hint, suggestion, touch, smack. ❸ *her usual diversions had lost their savour* PIQUANCY, interest, attraction, flavour, spice, zest, excitement, enjoyment; *informal* zing.

savoury ▶ **adjective** ❶ *sweet or savoury dishes* SALTY, spicy, piquant, tangy. ❷ *a rich, savoury aroma* APPETIZING, mouth-watering, delicious, delectable, luscious; tasty, flavoursome, flavourful, palatable, toothsome; *informal* scrumptious, finger-licking, yummy, scrummy, moreish. ❸ *one of the less savoury aspects of the affair* ACCEPTABLE, pleasant, respectable, wholesome, honourable, proper, seemly.
–OPPOSITES sweet, unappetizing.
▶ **noun** *cocktail savouries* CANAPÉ, hors d'oeuvre, appetizer, titbit.

savvy (*informal*) ▶ **noun** *his political savvy. See* ACUMEN.
▶ **adjective** *a savvy investor. See* SHREWD.

saw ▶ **noun** SAYING, maxim, proverb, aphorism, axiom, adage, apophthegm, epigram, gnome.

say ▶ **verb** ❶ *she felt her stomach flutter as he said her name* SPEAK, utter, voice, pronounce, give voice to, vocalize. ❷ *'I must go,' she said* DECLARE, state, announce, remark, observe, mention, comment, note, add; reply, respond, answer, rejoin; *informal* come out with. ❸ *Newall says he's innocent* CLAIM, maintain, assert, hold, insist, contend; allege, profess; *formal* opine, aver; *rare* asseverate. ❹ *I can't conjure up the words to say how I feel* EXPRESS, put into words, phrase, articulate, communicate, make known, put/get across, convey, verbalize; reveal, divulge, impart, disclose; imply, suggest. ❺ *they sang hymns and said a prayer* RECITE, repeat, utter, deliver, perform, declaim, orate. ❻ *the dial of her watch said one twenty* INDICATE, show, read. ❼ *I'd say it's about five miles* ESTIMATE, judge, guess, hazard a guess, predict, speculate, surmise, conjecture, venture; *informal* reckon. ❽ *let's say you'd just won a million pounds* SUPPOSE, assume, imagine, presume, hypothesize, postulate, posit.
▶ **noun** ❶ *everyone is entitled to their say* CHANCE TO SPEAK, turn to speak, opinion, view, voice; *informal* twopence worth, twopenn'orth. ❷ *don't I have any say in the matter?* INFLUENCE, sway, weight, voice, input, share, part.
■ **that is to say** IN OTHER WORDS, to put it another way; i.e., that is, to wit, viz, namely.
■ **to say the least** TO PUT IT MILDLY, putting it mildly, without any exaggeration, at the very least.

saying ▶ **noun** PROVERB, maxim, aphorism, axiom, adage, saw, tag, motto, apophthegm, epigram, dictum, gnome; expression, phrase, formula; slogan, catchphrase; platitude, cliché, commonplace, truism.
■ **it goes without saying** OF COURSE, naturally, needless to say, it's taken for granted, it's understood/assumed, it's taken as read, it's an accepted fact; obviously, self-evidently, manifestly; *informal* natch.

say-so ▶ **noun** (*informal*) AUTHORIZATION, (seal of) approval, agreement, consent, assent, permission, endorsement, sanction, ratification, approbation, acquiescence, blessing, leave; *informal* the OK, the go-ahead, the green light, the thumbs up.
–OPPOSITES refusal, denial.

scalding ▶ **adjective** EXTREMELY HOT, burning, blistering, searing, red-hot; piping hot; *informal* boiling (hot), sizzling.

scale[1] ▶ **noun** ❶ *the reptile's scales* plate; *technical* lamella, lamina, squama, scute, scutum. ❷ *scales on the skin* FLAKE; (**scales**) scurf, dandruff. ❸ *scale in kettles* LIMESCALE, deposit, incrustation; *Brit.* fur.

scale[2] ▶ **noun** ❶ *the Celsius scale of temperature* CALIBRATED SYSTEM, graduated system, system of measurement. ❷ *opposite ends of the social scale* HIERARCHY, ladder, ranking, pecking order, order, spectrum; succession, sequence, series. ❸ *the scale of the map* RATIO, proportion, relative size. ❹ *no one foresaw the scale of the disaster* EXTENT, size, scope, magnitude, dimensions, range, breadth, compass, degree, reach.
▶ **verb** *thieves scaled an 8ft high fence* CLIMB, ascend, clamber up, shin (up), scramble up, mount; *N. Amer.* shinny (up).
■ **scale something down** REDUCE, cut down, cut back, cut, decrease, lessen, lower, trim, slim down, prune.

■ **scale something up** INCREASE, expand, augment, build up, add to; step up, boost, escalate.

scaly ▶ adjective ❶ *the dragon's scaly hide technical* squamous, squamulose, squamate, lamellate. ❷ *scaly patches of dead skin* DRY, flaky, flaking, scurfy, rough, scabrous, mangy, scabious; *technical* furfuraceous.

scam ▶ noun (*informal*) FRAUD, swindle, racket, trick, diddle; *informal* con (trick); *Brit. informal* ramp; *N. Amer. informal* hustle, grift, bunco.

scamp ▶ noun (*informal*) RASCAL, monkey, devil, imp, wretch, mischief-maker; *informal* scallywag, horror, monster, tyke; *Brit. informal* perisher; *N. English informal* scally; *N. Amer. informal* varmint; *archaic* rapscallion, scapegrace.

scamper ▶ verb SCURRY, scuttle, dart, run, rush, race, dash, hurry, hasten; *informal* scoot; *dated* make haste.

scan ▶ verb ❶ *Adam scanned the horizon* SCRUTINIZE, examine, study, inspect, survey, search, scour, sweep, rake; look at, stare at, gaze at, eye, watch; *informal* check out; *N. Amer. informal* scope. ❷ *I scanned the papers* GLANCE THROUGH, look through, have a look at, run/cast one's eye over, skim through, flick through, flip through, leaf through, thumb through.

▶ noun ❶ *a careful scan of the terrain* INSPECTION, scrutiny, examination, survey. ❷ *a quick scan through the report* GLANCE, look, flick, browse. ❸ *a brain scan* EXAMINATION, screening.

scandal ▶ noun ❶ *revelation of the sex scandal forced him to resign* WRONGDOING, impropriety, misconduct, immoral behaviour, unethical behaviour; offence, transgression, crime, sin; skeleton in the closet; *informal* -gate. ❷ *it's a scandal that the disease is not adequately treated* DISGRACE, outrage, injustice; (crying) shame. ❸ *no scandal attached to her name* MALICIOUS GOSSIP, malicious rumour(s), slander, libel, calumny, defamation, aspersions, muckraking; *informal* dirt.

scandalize ▶ verb SHOCK, appal, outrage, horrify, disgust; offend, affront, insult, cause raised eyebrows.
– OPPOSITES impress.

scandalous ▶ adjective ❶ *a scandalous waste of taxpayers' money* DISGRACEFUL, shocking, outrageous, monstrous, criminal, wicked, shameful, appalling, deplorable, reprehensible, inexcusable, intolerable, insupportable, unforgivable, unpardonable. ❷ *a series of scandalous liaisons* DISCREDITABLE, disreputable, dishonourable, improper, unseemly, sordid. ❸ *scandalous rumours* SCURRILOUS, malicious, slanderous, libellous, defamatory.

scant ▶ adjective LITTLE, little or no, minimal, limited, negligible, meagre; insufficient, inadequate, deficient; *formal* exiguous.
– OPPOSITES abundant, ample.

scanty ▶ adjective ❶ *their scanty wages* MEAGRE, scant, minimal, limited, modest, restricted, sparse; tiny, small, paltry, negligible, insufficient, inadequate, deficient; scarce, in short supply, thin on the ground, few and far between; *informal* measly, piddling, mingy, pathetic; *formal* exiguous. ❷ *her scanty nightdress* SKIMPY, revealing, short, brief; low, low-cut; indecent.
– OPPOSITES ample, plentiful.

scapegoat ▶ noun WHIPPING BOY, Aunt Sally; *informal* fall guy; *N. Amer. informal* patsy.

scar ▶ noun ❶ *the scar on his left cheek* CICATRIX, mark, blemish, disfigurement, discoloration; pockmark, pock, pit; lesion, stigma; birthmark, naevus. ❷ *deep psychological scars* TRAUMA, damage, injury.

▶ verb ❶ *he's likely to be scarred for life* DISFIGURE, mark, blemish; pockmark, pit; *Christianity* stigmatize. ❷ *a landscape which has been scarred by strip mining* DAMAGE, spoil, mar, deface, injure. ❸ *she was profoundly scarred by the incident* TRAUMATIZE, damage, injure; distress, disturb, upset.

scarce ▶ adjective ❶ *food was scarce* IN SHORT SUPPLY, scant, scanty, meagre, sparse, hard to find, hard to come by, insufficient, deficient, inadequate; at a premium, like gold dust; paltry, negligible; *informal* not to be had for love nor money; *formal* exiguous. ❷ *birds that prefer dense forest are becoming scarcer* RARE, few and far between, thin on the ground; uncommon, unusual; *Brit.* out of the common.
– OPPOSITES plentiful.

scarcely ▶ adverb ❶ *she could scarcely hear what he was saying* HARDLY, barely, only just; almost not. ❷ *I scarcely ever see him* RARELY, seldom, infrequently, not often, hardly ever, every once in a while; *informal* once in a blue moon. ❸ *this could scarcely be accidental* SURELY NOT, not, hardly, certainly not, not at all, on no account, under no circumstances, by no means; *N. Amer.* noway.
– OPPOSITES often.

scarcity ▶ noun SHORTAGE, dearth, lack, undersupply, insufficiency, paucity, scantness, meagreness, sparseness, poverty; deficiency, inadequacy; unavailability, absence; *formal* exiguity.

scare ▶ verb *stop it, you're scaring me* FRIGHTEN, startle, alarm, terrify, petrify, unnerve, intimidate, terrorize, cow; strike terror into, put the fear of God into, chill someone to the bone/marrow, make someone's blood run cold; *informal* frighten/scare the living daylights out of, scare stiff, frighten/scare someone out of their wits, scare witless, frighten/scare to death, scare the pants off, make someone's hair stand on end, throw into a blue funk, make someone jump out of their skin; *Brit. informal* put the wind up, make someone's hair curl; *N. Amer. informal* spook; *Irish informal* scare the bejesus out of; *archaic* affright.

▶ **noun** *you gave me a scare—how did you get here?* FRIGHT, shock, start, turn, jump.

scared ▶ **adjective** FRIGHTENED, afraid, fearful, nervous, panicky; terrified, petrified, horrified, panic-stricken, scared stiff, frightened/scared out of one's wits, scared witless, frightened/scared to death; *Scottish* feart; *informal* in a cold sweat, in a (blue) funk; *Brit. informal* funky, windy; *N. Amer. informal* spooked; *dialect* frit; *archaic* afeared, affrighted.

scaremonger ▶ **noun** ALARMIST, prophet of doom, Cassandra, voice of doom, doom-monger; *informal* doom (and gloom) merchant.

scarf ▶ **noun** MUFFLER, headscarf, headsquare, square; mantilla, stole, tippet; *N. Amer.* babushka.

scarper ▶ **verb** (*Brit. informal*). *See* RUN verb sense 2.

scary ▶ **adjective** (*informal*) FRIGHTENING, alarming, terrifying, hair-raising, spine-chilling, blood-curdling, horrifying, nerve-racking, unnerving; eerie, sinister; *informal* creepy, spine-tingling, spooky, hairy.

scathing ▶ **adjective** WITHERING, blistering, searing, devastating, fierce, ferocious, savage, severe, stinging, biting, cutting, mordant, trenchant, virulent, caustic, vitriolic, scornful, sharp, bitter, harsh, unsparing; *formal* mordacious.
– OPPOSITES mild.

scatter ▶ **verb** ❶ *scatter the seeds as evenly as possible* THROW, strew, toss, fling; sprinkle, spread, distribute, sow, broadcast, disseminate. ❷ *the crowd scattered | onlookers were scattered in all directions* DISPERSE, break up, disband, separate, go separate ways, dissolve; drive, send, put to flight, chase. ❸ *the sky was scattered with stars* FLECK, stud, dot, cover, sprinkle, stipple, spot, pepper; *poetic/literary* bestrew.
– OPPOSITES gather, assemble.

scatterbrained ▶ **adjective** ABSENT-MINDED, forgetful, disorganized; dreamy, wool-gathering, with one's head in the clouds, feather-brained, giddy; *informal* scatty, with a mind/memory like a sieve, dizzy, dippy.

scavenge ▶ **verb** SEARCH, hunt, look, forage, rummage, root about/around, grub about/around.

scenario ▶ **noun** ❶ *Walt wrote scenarios for a major Hollywood studio* PLOT, outline, storyline, framework; screenplay, script; *formal* diegesis. ❷ *every possible scenario must be explored* SEQUENCE OF EVENTS, course of events, chain of events, situation. ❸ *this film has a more contemporary scenario* SETTING, background, context, scene, milieu.

scene ▶ **noun** ❶ *the scene of the accident* LOCATION, site, place, position, point, spot; locale, whereabouts; *technical* locus. ❷ *the scene is London, in the late 1890s* BACKGROUND, setting, context, milieu, backdrop, mise en scène. ❸ *terrible scenes of violence* INCIDENT, event, episode, happening. ❹ *an impressive mountain scene* VIEW, vista, outlook, panorama, sight; landscape, scenery. ❺ *she made an embarrassing scene* FUSS, exhibition of oneself, performance, tantrum, commotion, disturbance, row, upset, furore, brouhaha; *informal* to-do; *Brit. informal* carry-on. ❻ *the political scene* ARENA, stage, sphere, world, milieu, realm, domain; area of interest, field, province, preserve. ❼ *a scene from a Laurel and Hardy film* CLIP, section, segment, part, sequence.
■ **behind the scenes** SECRETLY, in secret, privately, in private, behind closed doors, surreptitiously; *informal* on the quiet, on the q.t.; *formal* sub rosa.

scenery ▶ **noun** ❶ *the beautiful scenery of west Wales* LANDSCAPE, countryside, country, terrain, topography, setting, surroundings, environment; view, vista, panorama. ❷ *we all helped with the scenery and costumes* STAGE SET, set, mise en scène, flats, backdrop, drop curtain; *Brit.* backcloth.

scenic ▶ **adjective** PICTURESQUE, pretty, pleasing, attractive, lovely, beautiful, charming, pretty as a picture, easy on the eye; impressive, striking, spectacular, breathtaking; panoramic.

scent ▶ **noun** ❶ *the scent of freshly cut hay* SMELL, fragrance, aroma, perfume, redolence, savour, odour; bouquet, nose. ❷ *a bottle of scent* PERFUME, fragrance, toilet water, eau de toilette, cologne; eau de cologne. ❸ *the hounds picked up the scent of a hare* SPOOR, trail, track; *Hunting* foil, wind.
▶ **verb** ❶ *a shark can scent blood from over half a kilometre away* SMELL, detect the smell of, get a whiff of. ❷ *Rose looked at him, scenting a threat* SENSE, become aware of, detect, discern, recognize, get wind of.

scented ▶ **adjective** PERFUMED, fragranced, perfumy; sweet-smelling, fragrant, aromatic.

sceptic ▶ **noun** ❶ *sceptics said the marriage wouldn't last* CYNIC, doubter; pessimist, prophet of doom. ❷ *sceptics who have found faith* AGNOSTIC, atheist, unbeliever, non-believer, disbeliever, doubting Thomas; *rare* nullifidian.

sceptical ▶ **adjective** DUBIOUS, doubtful, taking something with a pinch of salt, doubting; cynical, distrustful, mistrustful, suspicious, disbelieving, unconvinced, incredulous, scoffing; pessimistic, defeatist.
– OPPOSITES certain, convinced.

scepticism ▶ **noun** ❶ *his ideas were met with scepticism* DOUBT, doubtfulness, a pinch of salt; disbelief, cynicism, distrust, mistrust, suspicion, incredulity; pessimism, defeatism; *formal* dubiety. ❷ *he passed from scepticism to religious belief* AGNOSTICISM, doubt; atheism, unbelief, non-belief.

schedule ▸ noun ❶ *we need to draw up a production schedule* PLAN, programme, timetable, scheme. ❷ *I have a very busy schedule* TIMETABLE, agenda, diary, calendar; itinerary.
▸ verb *another meeting was scheduled for April 20* ARRANGE, organize, plan, programme, timetable, set up, line up; *N. Amer.* slate.
■ **behind schedule** LATE, running late, overdue, behind time, behind, behindhand.

scheme ▸ noun ❶ *adventurous fund-raising schemes* PLAN, project, plan of action, programme, strategy, stratagem, tactic, game plan, course/line of action; system, procedure, design, formula, recipe; *Brit. informal* wheeze; *archaic* shift. ❷ *police uncovered a scheme to steal the paintings* PLOT, intrigue, conspiracy; ruse, ploy, stratagem, manoeuvre, subterfuge; machinations; *informal* game, racket. ❸ *the sonnet's rhyme scheme* ARRANGEMENT, system, organization, configuration, pattern, format; *technical* schema.
▸ verb *he schemed to bring about the collapse of the government* PLOT, hatch a plot, conspire, intrigue, connive, manoeuvre, plan.

scheming ▸ adjective CUNNING, crafty, calculating, devious, designing, conniving, wily, sly, tricky, artful, guileful, slippery, slick, manipulative, Machiavellian, unscrupulous, disingenuous; duplicitous, deceitful, underhand, treacherous.
– OPPOSITES ingenuous, honest.

schism ▸ noun DIVISION, split, rift, breach, rupture, break, separation, severance; chasm, gulf; discord, disagreement, dissension.

schismatic ▸ adjective SEPARATIST, heterodox, dissident, dissentient, dissenting, heretical; breakaway, splinter.
– OPPOSITES orthodox.

schmaltzy ▸ adjective (*informal*). *See* SENTIMENTAL sense 2.

scholar ▸ noun ❶ *a leading biblical scholar* ACADEMIC, intellectual, learned person, man/woman of letters, mind, intellect, savant, polymath, highbrow, bluestocking; authority, expert; *informal* egghead; *N. Amer. informal* pointyhead; *archaic* bookman. ❷ (*archaic*) *the school had 28 scholars* PUPIL, student, schoolchild, schoolboy, schoolgirl.

scholarly ▸ adjective ❶ *an earnest, scholarly man* LEARNED, erudite, academic, well read, widely read, intellectual, literary, lettered, educated, knowledgeable, highbrow; studious, bookish, donnish, bluestocking, cerebral; *N. Amer. informal* pointy-headed; *archaic* clerkly. ❷ *a scholarly career* ACADEMIC, scholastic, pedagogic.
– OPPOSITES uneducated, illiterate.

scholarship ▸ noun ❶ *a centre of medieval scholarship* LEARNING, book learning, knowledge, erudition, education, letters, culture, academic study, academic achievement. ❷ *a scholarship of £200 per term* GRANT, award, endowment, payment; *Brit.* bursary, exhibition.

scholastic ▸ adjective ACADEMIC, educational, school, scholarly.

school ▸ noun ❶ *their children went to the village school* EDUCATIONAL INSTITUTION; academy, college; seminary; alma mater. ❷ *the university's School of English* DEPARTMENT, faculty, division. ❸ *the Barbizon school* GROUP, set, circle; followers, following, disciples, apostles, admirers, devotees, votaries; proponents, adherents. ❹ *the school of linguistics associated with his ideas* WAY OF THINKING, school of thought, persuasion, creed, credo, doctrine, belief, faith, opinion, point of view; approach, method, style.
– RELATED TERMS scholastic.
▸ verb ❶ *he was born in Paris and schooled in Lyon* EDUCATE, teach, instruct. ❷ *he schooled her in horsemanship* TRAIN, teach, tutor, coach, instruct, drill, discipline, direct, guide, prepare, groom; prime, verse.

schooling ▸ noun ❶ *his parents paid for his schooling* EDUCATION, teaching, tuition, instruction, tutoring, tutelage; lessons; (book) learning. ❷ *the schooling of horses* TRAINING, coaching, instruction, drill, drilling, discipline, disciplining.

schoolteacher ▸ noun TEACHER, schoolmaster, schoolmistress, tutor, educationist; *Brit.* master, mistress; *N. Amer. informal* schoolmarm; *Austral./NZ informal* chalkie, schoolie; *formal* pedagogue.

science ▸ noun ❶ *a science teacher* physics, chemistry, biology; physical sciences, life sciences. ❷ *the science of criminology* BRANCH OF KNOWLEDGE, body of knowledge/information, area of study, discipline, field.

scientific ▸ adjective ❶ *scientific research* technological, technical; research-based, knowledge-based, empirical. ❷ *you need to approach it in a more scientific way* SYSTEMATIC, methodical, organized, well organized, ordered, orderly, meticulous, rigorous; exact, precise, accurate, mathematical; analytical, rational.

scintilla ▸ noun PARTICLE, iota, jot, whit, atom, speck, bit, trace, ounce, shred, crumb, fragment, grain, drop, spot, mite, modicum, hint, touch, suggestion, whisper, suspicion; *informal* smidgen, tad; *archaic* scantling.

scintillate ▸ verb SPARKLE, shine, gleam, glitter, flash, shimmer, twinkle, glint, glisten, wink; *poetic/literary* glister, coruscate.

scintillating ▸ adjective ❶ *a scintillating diamond necklace* SPARKLING, shining, bright, brilliant, gleaming, glittering, twinkling, shimmering. ❷ *a scintillating second-half performance* BRILLIANT, dazzling, exciting, exhilarating, stimulating; sparkling, lively, vivacious, vibrant, animated, ebullient, effervescent; witty, clever; *poetic/literary* coruscating.
– OPPOSITES dull, boring.

scion ▶ noun ❶ *a scion of the tree* CUTTING, graft, slip; shoot, offshoot, twig. ❷ *the scion of an aristocratic family* DESCENDANT; heir, successor; child, offspring; *Law* issue.

scoff[1] ▶ verb *they scoffed at her article* MOCK, deride, ridicule, sneer at, jeer at, jibe at, taunt, make fun of, poke fun at, laugh at, scorn, laugh to scorn, dismiss, make light of, belittle; *informal* pooh-pooh.

scoff[2] ▶ verb (*Brit. informal*) *the bears scoffed our packed lunch* EAT, devour, consume, guzzle, gobble, wolf down, bolt; *informal* put away, nosh, polish off, demolish, shovel down, stuff one's face with, pig oneself on, pig out on; *Brit. informal* gollop, shift; *N. Amer. informal* scarf (down/up), snarf (down/up).

scold ▶ verb *Mum took Anna away, scolding her for her bad behaviour* REBUKE, reprimand, reproach, reprove, admonish, remonstrate with, chastise, chide, upbraid, berate, take to task, read someone the Riot Act, give someone a piece of one's mind, haul over the coals; *informal* tell off, dress down, give someone an earful, give someone a roasting, rap over the knuckles, let someone have it, bawl out, give someone hell; *Brit. informal* tick off, have a go at, carpet, tear someone off a strip, give someone what for, give someone some stick, give someone a rollicking/rocket/row; *N. Amer. informal* chew out, ream out; *Austral. informal* monster; *formal* castigate.
– OPPOSITES praise.
▶ noun (*archaic*) *she is turning into a scold* NAG, shrew, fishwife, harpy, termagant, harridan; complainer, moaner, grumbler; *N. Amer. informal* kvetch.

scolding ▶ noun REBUKE, reprimand, reproach, reproof, admonishment, reproval, remonstration, lecture, upbraiding; *informal* telling-off, talking-to, rap over the knuckles, dressing-down, earful, roasting; *Brit. informal* ticking-off, carpeting, rocket, rollicking; *formal* castigation.

scoop ▶ noun ❶ *a measuring scoop* SPOON, ladle, dipper; bailer. ❷ *a scoop of vanilla ice cream* SPOONFUL, ladleful, portion, lump, ball; *informal* dollop. ❸ (*informal*) *reporters competed for scoops* EXCLUSIVE (STORY), inside story, exposé, revelation.
▶ verb ❶ *a hole was scooped out in the floor* HOLLOW OUT, gouge out, dig, excavate, cut out. ❷ *cut the tomatoes in half and scoop out the flesh* REMOVE, take out, spoon out, scrape out. ❸ *she scooped up armfuls of clothes* PICK UP, gather up, lift, take up; snatch up, grab.

scoot ▶ verb (*informal*). *See* DASH verb sense 1.

scope ▶ noun ❶ *the scope of the investigation* EXTENT, range, breadth, width, reach, sweep, purview, span, horizon; area, sphere, field, realm, compass, orbit, ambit, terms/field of reference, jurisdiction, remit; confine, limit; gamut. ❷ *the scope for change is limited by political realities* OPPORTUNITY, freedom, latitude, leeway, capacity, liberty, room (to manoeuvre), elbow room; possibility, chance.

scorch ▶ verb ❶ *the buildings were scorched by the fire* BURN, sear, singe, char, blacken, discolour. ❷ *grass scorched by the sun* DRY UP, desiccate, parch, wither, shrivel; burn, bake.

scorching ▶ adjective ❶ *the scorching July sun* EXTREMELY HOT, red-hot, blazing, flaming, fiery, burning, blistering, searing, sweltering, torrid; *N. Amer.* broiling; *informal* boiling (hot), baking (hot), sizzling. ❷ *scorching criticism* FIERCE, savage, scathing, withering, blistering, searing, devastating, stringent, severe, harsh, stinging, biting, mordant, trenchant, caustic, virulent, vitriolic.
– OPPOSITES freezing, mild.

score ▶ noun ❶ *the final score was 4–3* RESULT, outcome; total, sum total, tally, count. ❷ *an IQ score of 161* RATING, grade, mark, percentage. ❸ *I've got a score to settle with you* GRIEVANCE, bone to pick, axe to grind, grudge, complaint; dispute, bone of contention. ❹ (*informal*) *he knew the score before he got here* THE SITUATION, the position, the facts, the truth of the matter, the (true) state of affairs, the picture, how things stand, the lie of the land; *Brit.* the state of play; *N. Amer.* the lay of the land; *informal* the set-up, what's what. ❺ *scores of complaints* A GREAT MANY, a lot, a great/good deal, large quantities, plenty; *informal* lots, umpteen, a slew, loads, masses, stacks, scads, heaps, piles, bags, tons, oodles, dozens, hundreds, thousands, millions, billions; *Brit. informal* shedloads; *N. Amer. informal* a bunch, gazillions; *Austral./NZ informal* a swag.
▶ verb ❶ *he's already scored 13 goals this season* GET, gain, chalk up, achieve, make; record, rack up, notch up; *informal* bag, knock up. ❷ (*informal*) *his new movie really scored* BE SUCCESSFUL, be a success, triumph, make an impression, go down well; *informal* be a hit, be a winner, be a sell-out, go down a storm. ❸ *the piece was scored for flute, violin, and continuo* ORCHESTRATE, arrange, set, adapt; write, compose. ❹ *score the wood in criss-cross patterns* SCRATCH, cut, notch, incise, scrape, nick, snick, chip, gouge; mark; *archaic* scotch.
■ **score points off** GET THE BETTER OF, gain the advantage over, outdo, worst, have the edge over; have the last laugh on, make a fool of, humiliate; *informal* get/be one up on, get one over on, best.
■ **score something out/through** CROSS OUT, strike out, put a line through, ink out, blue-pencil, scratch out; delete, obliterate, expunge.

scorn ▶ noun *he was unable to hide the scorn in his voice* CONTEMPT, derision, contemptuousness, disdain, derisiveness, mockery, sneering; *archaic* contumely, despite.
– OPPOSITES admiration, respect.

▶ **verb** ❶ *critics scorned the painting* DERIDE, hold in contempt, treat with contempt, pour/heap scorn on, look down on, look down one's nose at, disdain, curl one's lip at, mock, scoff at, sneer at, jeer at, laugh at, laugh out of court; disparage, slight; dismiss, cock a snook at, spit in the eye/face of, thumb one's nose at; *informal* turn one's nose up at; *archaic* contemn. ❷ *'I am a woman scorned,' she thought* SPURN, rebuff, reject, ignore, shun, snub. ❸ *she would have scorned to stoop to such tactics* REFUSE TO, refrain from, not lower oneself to; be above, consider it beneath one.
– OPPOSITES admire, respect.

scornful ▶ **adjective** CONTEMPTUOUS, derisive, withering, mocking, scoffing, sneering, jeering, scathing, snide, disparaging, supercilious, disdainful, superior; *archaic* contumelious.
– OPPOSITES admiring, respectful.

scotch ▶ **verb** PUT AN END TO, put a stop to, nip in the bud, put the lid on; ruin, wreck, destroy, smash, shatter, demolish, queer; frustrate, thwart; *informal* put paid to, put the kibosh on; *Brit. informal* scupper.

scot-free ▶ **adverb** UNPUNISHED, without punishment; unscathed, unhurt, unharmed, without a scratch.

Scotland ▶ **noun** Caledonia; *Brit.* north of the border; *informal* the land of cakes.

scoundrel ▶ **noun** ROGUE, rascal, miscreant, good-for-nothing, reprobate; cheat, swindler, fraudster, trickster, charlatan; *informal* villain, bastard, beast, son of a bitch, SOB, rat, louse, swine, dog, skunk, heel, snake (in the grass), wretch, scumbag; *Irish informal* sleeveen, spalpeen; *N. Amer. informal* rat fink; *informal, dated* rotter, hound, bounder, blighter; *dated* cad; *archaic* blackguard, knave, varlet, whoreson.

scour[1] ▶ **verb** *she scoured the cooker and cleaned out the cupboards* SCRUB, rub, clean, wash, cleanse, wipe; polish, buff (up), shine, burnish; abrade.

scour[2] ▶ **verb** *Christine scoured the shops for a gift* SEARCH, comb, hunt through, rummage through, go through with a fine-tooth comb, root through, rake through, leave no stone unturned, look high and low in; ransack, turn upside-down; *Austral./NZ informal* fossick through.

scourge ▶ **noun** ❶ (*historical*) *he was beaten with a scourge* WHIP, horsewhip, lash, strap, birch, switch; *N. Amer.* bullwhip, rawhide; *historical* cat-o'-nine-tails. ❷ *inflation was the scourge of the mid-1970s* AFFLICTION, bane, curse, plague, menace, evil, misfortune, burden, cross to bear; blight, cancer, canker.
– OPPOSITES blessing, godsend.

▶ **verb** ❶ (*historical*) *he was publicly scourged* FLOG, whip, beat, horsewhip, lash, flagellate, strap, birch, cane, thrash, belt, leather; *informal* tan someone's hide, take a strap to. ❷ *a disease which scourged the English for centuries* AFFLICT, plague, torment, torture, curse, oppress, burden, bedevil, beset.

scout ▶ **noun** ❶ *scouts reported that the enemy were massing ahead* LOOKOUT, outrider, advance guard, vanguard; spy. ❷ *a lengthy scout round the area* RECONNAISSANCE, reconnoitre; exploration, search, expedition; *informal* recce; *Brit. informal* shufti; *N. Amer. informal* recon. ❸ *a record company scout* TALENT SPOTTER, talent scout; *N. Amer. informal* bird dog.

▶ **verb** ❶ *I scouted around for some logs* SEARCH, look, hunt, ferret about/around, root about/around. ❷ *a night patrol was sent to scout out the area* RECONNOITRE, explore, make a reconnaissance of, inspect, investigate, spy out, survey; examine, scan, study, observe; *informal* make a recce of, check out, case; *Brit. informal* take a shufti round; *N. Amer. informal* recon.

scowl ▶ **verb** GLOWER, frown, glare, grimace, lour, look daggers at, give someone a black look; make a face, pull a face, turn the corner's of one's mouth down, pout; *informal* give someone a dirty look.
– OPPOSITES smile, grin.

scraggy ▶ **adjective** SCRAWNY, thin, as thin as a rake, skinny, skin-and-bones, gaunt, bony, angular, gawky, raw-boned; *dated* spindle-shanked.
– OPPOSITES fat.

scram ▶ **verb** (*informal*) *scram or I'll call the police* GO AWAY, leave, get out; go, get moving, be off (with you), shoo; *informal* skedaddle, split, run along, beat it, get lost, shove off, buzz off, push off, clear off, on your bike; *Brit. informal* get stuffed, sling your hook, hop it, bog off, naff off; *N. Amer. informal* bug off, take a powder, take a hike; *Austral./NZ informal* rack off; *poetic/literary* begone.

scramble ▶ **verb** ❶ *we scrambled over the boulders* CLAMBER, climb, crawl, claw one's way, scrabble, grope one's way, struggle; *N. Amer.* shinny. ❷ *small children scrambled for the scattered coins* JOSTLE, scuffle, tussle, struggle, strive, compete, contend, vie, jockey. ❸ *the alcohol has scrambled his brains* MUDDLE, confuse, mix up, jumble (up), disarrange, disorganize, disorder, disturb, mess up.

▶ **noun** ❶ *a short scramble over the rocks* CLAMBER, climb, trek. ❷ *I lost Tommy in the scramble for a seat* TUSSLE, jostle, scrimmage, scuffle, struggle, free-for-all, competition, contention, vying, jockeying; muddle, confusion, melee.

scrap[1] ▶ **noun** ❶ *a scrap of paper* FRAGMENT, piece, bit, snippet, shred; offcut, oddment, remnant. ❷ *there wasn't a scrap of evidence* BIT, speck, iota, particle, ounce, whit, jot, atom, shred, scintilla, tittle, jot or tittle; *informal* smidgen, tad. ❸ *he slept rough and lived on scraps* LEFTOVERS, leavings, crumbs, scrapings, remains, remnants, residue, odds and ends, bits and pieces. ❹ *the whole thing was made from bits* *of scrap* WASTE, rubbish, refuse, litter, debris, detritus; flotsam and jetsam; *N. Amer.* garbage, trash; *informal* junk.

▶ **verb** ❶ *old cars which are due to be scrapped* THROW AWAY, throw out, dispose of, get rid of, toss out, throw on the scrap heap, discard, remove, dispense with, lose, bin; decommission, recycle, break up, demolish; *informal* chuck (away/out), ditch, dump, junk, get shut of; *Brit. informal* get shot of; *N. Amer. informal* trash. ❷ *campaigners called for the plans to be scrapped* ABANDON, drop, abolish, withdraw, throw out, do away with, put an end to, cancel, axe, jettison; *informal* ditch, dump, junk.

– OPPOSITES keep, preserve.

scrap[2] (*informal*) ▶ **noun** *he and Joe had several scraps* QUARREL, argument, row, fight, disagreement, difference of opinion, falling-out, dispute, squabble, contretemps, clash, altercation, brawl, tussle, conflict, shouting match; *informal* tiff, set-to, run-in, slanging match, shindy, spat, dust-up, ruction; *Brit. informal* barney, ding-dong, bust-up.

▶ **verb** *the older boys started scrapping with me* QUARREL, argue, row, fight, squabble, brawl, bicker, spar, wrangle, lock horns, be at each other's throats.

scrape ▶ **verb** ❶ *we scraped all the paint off the windows* ABRADE, grate, sand, sandpaper, scour, scratch, rub, file, rasp. ❷ *their boots scraped along the floor* GRATE, creak, rasp, grind, scratch. ❸ *she scraped her hair back behind her ears* RAKE, drag, pull, tug, draw. ❹ *he scraped a hole in the ground* SCOOP OUT, hollow out, dig (out), excavate, gouge out. ❺ *Ellen had scraped her shins on the wall* GRAZE, scratch, abrade, scuff, rasp, skin, rub raw, cut, lacerate, bark, chafe; *Medicine* excoriate.

▶ **noun** ❶ *the scrape of her key in the lock* GRATING, creaking, grinding, rasp, rasping, scratch, scratching. ❷ *there was a long scrape on his shin* GRAZE, scratch, abrasion, cut, laceration, wound. ❸ (*informal*) *he's always getting into scrapes* PREDICAMENT, plight, tight corner/spot, ticklish/tricky situation, problem, crisis, mess, muddle; *informal* jam, fix, stew, bind, hole, hot water, a pretty/fine kettle of fish; *Brit. informal* spot of bother.

■ **scrape by** MANAGE, cope, survive, muddle through/along, make ends meet, get by/along, make do, keep the wolf from the door, keep one's head above water, eke out a living; *informal* make out.

scrappy ▶ **adjective** DISORGANIZED, untidy, disjointed, unsystematic, uneven, bitty, sketchy; piecemeal; fragmentary, incomplete, unfinished.

scratch ▶ **verb** ❶ *the paintwork was scratched* SCORE, abrade, scrape, scuff. ❷ *thorns scratched her skin* GRAZE, scrape, abrade, skin, rub raw, cut, lacerate, bark, chafe; wound; *Medicine* excoriate. ❸ *many names had been scratched out* CROSS OUT, strike out, score out, delete, erase, remove, eliminate, expunge, obliterate. ❹ *she was forced to scratch from the race* WITHDRAW, pull out of, back out of, bow out of, stand down.

▶ **noun** ❶ *he had two scratches on his cheek* GRAZE, scrape, abrasion, cut, laceration, wound. ❷ *a scratch on the paintwork* SCORE, mark, line, scrape.

■ **up to scratch** GOOD ENOUGH, up to the mark, up to standard, up to par, satisfactory, acceptable, adequate, passable, sufficient, all right; *informal* OK, up to snuff.

scrawl ▶ **verb** *he scrawled his name at the bottom of the page* SCRIBBLE, write hurriedly, write untidily, dash off.

▶ **noun** *pages of handwritten scrawl* SCRIBBLE, squiggle(s), hieroglyphics; *rare* cacography.

scrawny ▶ **adjective** SKINNY, thin, as thin as a rake, skin-and-bones, gaunt, bony, angular, gawky, scraggy, raw-boned; *dated* spindle-shanked.

– OPPOSITES fat.

scream ▶ **verb** *he screamed in pain* SHRIEK, screech, yell, howl, shout, bellow, bawl, cry out, call out, yelp, squeal, wail, squawk; *informal* holler.

▶ **noun** ❶ *a scream of pain* SHRIEK, screech, yell, howl, shout, bellow, bawl, cry, yelp, squeal, wail, squawk; *informal* holler. ❷ (*informal*) *the whole thing's a scream* LAUGH, hoot; *informal* gas, giggle, riot, bundle of fun/laughs. ❸ (*informal*) *he's an absolute scream* WIT, hoot, comedian, comic, entertainer, joker, clown, character; *informal* gas, giggle, riot; *informal, dated* caution, case, card.

screech ▶ **verb**. *See* SCREAM verb.

screen ▶ **noun** ❶ *he dressed hurriedly behind the screen* PARTITION, (room) divider; windbreak. ❷ *a computer with a 15-inch screen* DISPLAY, monitor, visual display unit, VDU; cathode-ray tube, CRT. ❸ *every window has a screen because of mosquitoes* MESH, net, netting. ❹ *the hedge acts as a screen against the wind* BUFFER, protection, shield, shelter, guard. ❺ *the earth must be put through a screen* SIEVE, riddle, strainer, colander, filter.

▶ **verb** ❶ *the end of the hall had been screened of* PARTITION OFF, divide off, separate off, curtain off. ❷ *the cottage was screened by the trees* CONCEAL, hide, veil; shield, shelter, shade, protect, guard, safeguard. ❸ *the prospective candidates will have to be screened* VET, check, check up on, investigate; *informal* check out. ❹ *all donated blood is screened for the virus* CHECK, test, examine, investigate. ❺ *coal used to be screened by hand* SIEVE, riddle, sift, strain, filter, winnow. ❻ *the programme is screened on Thursday evenings* SHOW, broadcast, transmit, televise, put out, put on the air.

screw ▶ **noun** ❶ *stainless steel screws* bolt, fastener; nail, pin, tack, spike, rivet, brad. ❷ *the handle needs a couple of screws to tighten it* TURN, twist, wrench. ❸ *the ship's twin screws* PROPELLER, rotor.

▶ **verb** ❶ *he screwed the lid back on the jar* TIGHTEN, turn, twist, wind. ❷ *the bracket was screwed in place* FASTEN, secure, fix, attach. ❸ (*informal*) *she intended to screw money out of them* EXTORT, force, extract, wrest, wring, squeeze; *informal* bleed.

■ **put the screws on** (*informal*) PRESSURIZE, put pressure on, pressure, coerce, browbeat, use strong-arm tactics on; hold a gun to someone's head; *informal* put the heat on, lean on.

■ **screw something up** ❶ *Christina screwed up her face in disgust* WRINKLE (UP), pucker, crumple, crease, furrow, contort, distort, twist, purse. ❷ (*informal*) *they'll screw up the whole economy* WRECK, ruin, destroy, wreak havoc on, damage, spoil, mar; dash, shatter, scotch, make a mess of, mess up; *informal* louse up, foul up, put the kibosh on, banjax, do for, nix, queer; *Brit. informal* scupper, cock up.

scribble ▶ **verb** *he scribbled a few lines on a piece of paper* SCRAWL, write hurriedly, write untidily, scratch, dash off, jot (down); doodle.

▶ **noun** *a page of scribble* SCRAWL, squiggle(s), jottings; doodle, doodlings; *rare* cacography.

scribe ▶ **noun** ❶ (*historical*) *a medieval scribe* CLERK, secretary, copyist, transcriber, amanuensis; *historical* penman, scrivener. ❷ (*informal*) *a local cricket scribe* WRITER, author, penman; journalist, reporter; *informal* hack.

scrimmage ▶ **noun** FIGHT, tussle, brawl, struggle, fracas, free-for-all, rough and tumble; *Law, dated* affray; *informal* scrap, dust-up, punch-up, set-to, shindy; *Brit. informal* scrum; *N. Amer. informal* rough house.

scrimp ▶ **verb** ECONOMIZE, skimp, scrimp and save, save; be thrifty, be frugal, tighten one's belt, cut back, husband one's resources, draw in one's horns, watch one's pennies; *N. Amer.* pinch the pennies.

script ▶ **noun** ❶ *her neat, tidy script* HANDWRITING, writing, hand, pen, penmanship, calligraphy. ❷ *the script of the play* TEXT, screenplay; libretto, score; lines, dialogue, words.

scripture ▶ **noun** THE BIBLE, the Holy Bible, Holy Writ, the Gospel, the Good Book, the Word of God, the Book of Books; sacred text(s).

Scrooge ▶ **noun** MISER, penny-pincher, pinchpenny, niggard; *informal* skinflint, meanie, money-grubber, cheapskate; *N. Amer. informal* tightwad.
– OPPOSITES spendthrift.

scrounge ▶ **verb** BEG, borrow; *informal* cadge, sponge, bum, touch someone for; *Brit. informal* scab; *N. Amer. informal* mooch; *Austral./NZ informal* bludge.

scrounger ▶ **noun** BEGGAR, borrower, parasite, cadger; *informal* sponger, freeloader; *N. Amer. informal* mooch, moocher, schnorrer; *Austral./NZ informal* bludger.

scrub[1] ▶ **verb** ❶ *he scrubbed the kitchen floor* SCOUR, rub; clean, cleanse, wash, wipe. ❷ (*informal*) *the plans were scrubbed* ABANDON, scrap, drop, cancel, call off, axe, jettison, discard, discontinue, abort; *informal* ditch, dump, junk.

scrub[2] ▶ **noun** *there the buildings ended and the scrub began* BRUSH, brushwood, scrubland, undergrowth.

scruffy ▶ **adjective** SHABBY, worn, down at heel, ragged, tattered, mangy, dirty; untidy, unkempt, bedraggled, messy, dishevelled, ill-groomed; *informal* tatty, the worse for wear; *N. Amer. informal* raggedy.
– OPPOSITES smart, tidy.

scrumptious ▶ **adjective** (*informal*) DELICIOUS, delectable, mouth-watering, tasty, appetizing, rich, savoury, flavoursome, flavourful, toothsome; succulent, luscious; *informal* scrummy, yummy; *Brit. informal* moreish; *N. Amer. informal* finger-licking, nummy.
– OPPOSITES unpalatable.

scrunch ▶ **verb** CRUMPLE, crunch, crush, rumple, screw up, squash, squeeze, compress; *informal* squidge.

scruple ▶ **verb** *she would not scruple to ask them for money* HESITATE, be reluctant, be loath, have qualms, have scruples, have misgivings, have reservations, think twice, baulk, demur; recoil from, shrink from, shy away from, flinch from.

scruples ▶ **plural noun** *he had no scruples about eavesdropping* QUALMS, compunction, pangs/twinges of conscience, hesitation, reservations, second thoughts, doubt(s), misgivings, uneasiness, reluctance.

scrupulous ▶ **adjective** ❶ *scrupulous attention to detail* CAREFUL, meticulous, painstaking, thorough, assiduous, sedulous, attentive, conscientious, punctilious, searching, close, minute, rigorous, particular, strict. ❷ *a scrupulous man* HONEST, honourable, upright, upstanding, high-minded, right-minded, moral, ethical, good, virtuous, principled, incorruptible.
– OPPOSITES careless, dishonest.

scrutinize ▶ **verb** EXAMINE, inspect, survey, study, look at, peruse; investigate, explore, probe, inquire into, go into, check.

scrutiny ▶ **noun** EXAMINATION, inspection, survey, study, perusal; investigation, exploration, probe, inquiry; *informal* going-over.

scud ▶ **verb** SPEED, race, rush, sail, shoot, sweep, skim, whip, whizz, flash, fly, scurry, flit, scutter.

scuff ▶ **verb** SCRAPE, scratch, rub, abrade; mark.

scuffle ▶ **noun** *there was a scuffle outside the pub* FIGHT, struggle, tussle, brawl, fracas, free-for-all, rough and tumble, scrimmage; *Law, dated* affray; *informal* scrap, dust-up, punch-up, set-to, shindy; *N. Amer. informal* rough house.

▶ **verb** *demonstrators scuffled with police* FIGHT, struggle, tussle, exchange blows, come to blows, brawl, clash; *informal* scrap.

sculpt ▶ **verb** CARVE, model, chisel, sculpture, fashion, form, shape, cast, cut, hew.

sculpture ▶ **noun** *a bronze sculpture* MODEL, carving, statue, statuette, figure, figurine, effigy, bust, head, likeness.

▶ **verb** *the choir stalls were carefully sculptured. See* SCULPT.

scum ▶ **noun** ❶ *the water was covered with a thick green scum* FILM, layer, covering, froth; filth, dross, dirt. ❷ (*informal*) *drug dealers are scum* DESPICABLE PEOPLE, the lowest of the low, the dregs of society, vermin, riff-raff; *informal* the scum of the earth, dirt.

scupper (*Brit.*) ▶ **verb** ❶ *the captain decided to scupper the ship* SINK, scuttle, submerge, send to the bottom. ❷ (*informal*) *he denied trying to scupper the agreement* RUIN, wreck, destroy, sabotage, torpedo, spoil, ruin, mess up; *informal* screw up, foul up, put the kibosh on, banjax, do for; *archaic* bring to naught.

scurrilous ▶ **adjective** DEFAMATORY, slanderous, libellous, scandalous, insulting, offensive, gross; abusive, vituperative, malicious; *informal* bitchy.

scurry ▶ **verb** *pedestrians scurried for cover* HURRY, hasten, run, rush, dash; scamper, scuttle, scramble; *Brit.* scutter; *informal* scoot, beetle; *dated* make haste.

–OPPOSITES amble.

▶ **noun** *there was a scurry to get out* RUSH, race, dash, run, hurry; scramble, bustle.

scuttle ▶ **verb**. *See* SCURRY verb.

sea ▶ **noun** ❶ *the sea sparkled in the sun* (THE) OCEAN, the waves; *informal* the drink; *Brit. informal* the briny; *poetic/literary* the deep, the main, the foam. ❷ *the boat overturned in the heavy seas* WAVES, swell, breakers, rollers, combers; *informal* boomers. ❸ *a sea of roofs and turrets* EXPANSE, stretch, area, tract, sweep, blanket, sheet, carpet, mass; multitude, host, profusion, abundance, plethora.

–RELATED TERMS marine, maritime, nautical.

–OPPOSITES land.

▶ **adjective** *sea creatures* MARINE, ocean, oceanic; saltwater, seawater; ocean-going, seagoing, seafaring; maritime, naval, nautical; *technical* pelagic, thalassic.

■ **at sea** CONFUSED, perplexed, puzzled, baffled, mystified, bemused, bewildered, nonplussed, disconcerted, disoriented, dumbfounded, at a loss, at sixes and sevens; *informal* flummoxed, bamboozled, fazed; *N. Amer. informal* discombobulated; *archaic* wildered, mazed.

seafaring ▶ **adjective** MARITIME, nautical, naval, seagoing, sea.

seal ▶ **noun** ❶ *the seal round the bath* SEALANT, sealer, adhesive. ❷ *the king put his seal on the letter* EMBLEM, symbol, insignia, device, badge, crest, coat of arms, mark, monogram, stamp. ❸ *the Minister gave his seal of approval to the project* RATIFICATION, approval, blessing, consent, agreement, permission, sanction, endorsement, clearance.

▶ **verb** ❶ *she quietly sealed the door behind her* FASTEN, secure, shut, close, lock, bolt. ❷ *seal each bottle while it is hot* STOP UP, seal up, make airtight/watertight, cork, stopper, plug. ❸ *police sealed off the High Street* CLOSE OFF, shut off, cordon off, fence off, isolate. ❹ *he held out his hand to seal the bargain* CLINCH, secure, settle, conclude, complete, establish, set the seal on, confirm, guarantee; *informal* sew up.

seam ▶ **noun** ❶ *the seam was coming undone* JOIN, stitching; *Surgery* suture. ❷ *a seam of coal* LAYER, stratum, vein, lode. ❸ *the seams of his face* WRINKLE, line, crow's foot, furrow, crease, corrugation, crinkle, pucker, groove, ridge.

seaman ▶ **noun** SAILOR, seafarer, mariner, boatman, hand; *informal* (old) salt, sea dog, bluejacket; *Brit. informal* matelot; *informal, dated* tar, Jack Tar.

–OPPOSITES landlubber.

seamy ▶ **adjective** SORDID, disreputable, seedy, sleazy, squalid, insalubrious, unwholesome, unsavoury, rough, unpleasant.

–OPPOSITES salubrious.

sear ▶ **verb** ❶ *the heat of the blast seared his face* SCORCH, burn, singe, char. ❷ *sear the meat before adding the other ingredients* FLASH-FRY, seal, brown. ❸ *his betrayal had seared her terribly* HURT, wound, pain, cut to the quick, sting; distress, grieve, upset, trouble, harrow, torment, torture.

search ▶ **verb** ❶ *I searched for the key in my handbag* HUNT, look, seek, forage, fish about/around, look high and low, cast about/around, ferret about/around, root about/around, rummage about/around; *Brit. informal* rootle about/around. ❷ *he searched the house thoroughly* LOOK THROUGH, hunt through, explore, scour, rifle through, go through, sift through, comb, go through with a fine-tooth comb; turn upside down, turn inside out, leave no stone unturned in; *Austral./NZ informal* fossick through. ❸ *the guards searched him for weapons* EXAMINE, inspect, check, frisk.

▶ **noun** *we continued our search for a hotel* HUNT, look, quest; pursuit.

■ **in search of** SEARCHING FOR, hunting for, seeking, looking for, on the lookout for, in pursuit of.

■ **search me!** (*informal*) I DON'T KNOW, how should I know?, it's a mystery, I haven't a clue, I haven't the least idea, I've no idea; *informal* dunno, don't ask me, I haven't the faintest/foggiest (idea/notion), it beats me, ask me another.

searching ▶ **adjective** PENETRATING, piercing,

probing, penetrative, keen, shrewd, sharp, intent.

searing ▶ adjective ❶ *the searing heat* SCORCHING, blistering, sweltering, blazing (hot), burning, fiery, torrid; *informal* boiling (hot), baking (hot), sizzling, roasting. ❷ *searing pain* INTENSE, excruciating, agonizing, sharp, stabbing, shooting, stinging, severe, extreme, racking. ❸ *a searing attack* FIERCE, savage, blistering, scathing, stinging, devastating, mordant, trenchant, caustic, cutting, biting, withering.

seaside ▶ noun COAST, shore, seashore, waterside; beach, sand, sands; *poetic/literary* strand.
– RELATED TERMS littoral.

season ▶ noun *the rainy season | the opera season* PERIOD, time, time of year, spell, term.
▶ verb ❶ *season the casserole to taste* FLAVOUR, add flavouring to, add salt/pepper to, spice. ❷ *his albums include standard numbers seasoned with a few of his own tunes* ENLIVEN, leaven, spice (up), liven up; *informal* pep up.
■ **in season** AVAILABLE, obtainable, to be had, on offer, on the market; plentiful, abundant.

seasonable ▶ adjective USUAL, expected, predictable, normal for the time of year.

seasoned ▶ adjective EXPERIENCED, practised, well versed, knowledgeable, established, habituated, veteran, hardened, battle-scarred.
– OPPOSITES inexperienced.

seasoning ▶ noun FLAVOURING, salt and pepper, herbs, spices, condiments.

seat ▶ noun ❶ *a wooden seat* CHAIR, bench, stool, settle, stall; (**seats**) seating, room; *Brit. informal* pew. ❷ *the seat of government* HEADQUARTERS, base, centre, nerve centre, hub, heart; location, site, whereabouts, place. ❸ *the family's country seat* RESIDENCE, ancestral home, mansion, stately home; *formal* abode.
▶ verb ❶ *they seated themselves round the table* POSITION, put, place; ensconce, install, settle; *informal* plonk, park. ❷ *the hall seats 500* HAVE ROOM FOR, contain, take, sit, hold, accommodate.

seating ▶ noun SEATS, room, places, chairs, accommodation.

secede ▶ verb *the Kingdom of Belgium seceded from the Netherlands in 1830* WITHDRAW FROM, break away from, break with, separate (oneself) from, leave, split with, split off from, disaffiliate from, resign from, pull out of; *informal* quit.
– OPPOSITES join.

secluded ▶ adjective SHELTERED, private, concealed, hidden, unfrequented, sequestered, tucked away.
– OPPOSITES busy.

seclusion ▶ noun ISOLATION, solitude, retreat, privacy, retirement, withdrawal, purdah, concealment, hiding, secrecy.

second[1] ▶ adjective ❶ *the second day of the trial* NEXT, following, subsequent, succeeding. ❷ *he keeps a second pair of glasses in his office* ADDITIONAL, extra, alternative, another, spare, back-up, relief, fallback; *N. Amer.* alternate. ❸ *he dropped down to captain the second team* SECONDARY, lower, subordinate, subsidiary, lesser, inferior. ❹ *the conflict could turn into a second Vietnam* ANOTHER, new; repeat of, copy of, carbon copy of.
– OPPOSITES first.
▶ noun ❶ *Eva had been working as his second* ASSISTANT, attendant, helper, aide, supporter, auxiliary, right-hand man/woman, girl/man Friday, second in command, number two, deputy, understudy, subordinate; *informal* sidekick. ❷ (*informal*) *he enjoyed the pie and asked for seconds* A SECOND HELPING, a further helping, more.
▶ verb *George Beale seconded the motion* FORMALLY SUPPORT, give one's support to, vote for, back, approve, endorse.
■ **second to none** INCOMPARABLE, matchless, unrivalled, inimitable, beyond compare/comparison, unparalleled, without parallel, unequalled, without equal, in a class of its own, peerless, unsurpassed, unsurpassable, nonpareil, unique; perfect, consummate, transcendent, surpassing, superlative, supreme; *formal* unexampled.

second[2] ▶ noun *I'll only be gone for a second* MOMENT, bit, little while, short time, instant, split second; *informal* sec, jiffy; *Brit. informal* mo, tick, two ticks.
■ **in a second** VERY SOON, in a minute, in a moment, in a trice, shortly, any minute (now), in the twinkling of an eye, in (less than) no time, in no time at all; *N. Amer.* momentarily; *informal* in a jiffy, in two shakes (of a lamb's tail), before you can say Jack Robinson, in the blink of an eye; *Brit. informal* in a tick, in two ticks, in a mo; *N. Amer. informal* in a snap; *poetic/literary* ere long.

second[3] ▶ verb *he was seconded to their Welsh office* ASSIGN TEMPORARILY, lend; transfer, move, shift, relocate, assign, reassign, send.

secondary ▶ adjective ❶ *a secondary issue* LESS IMPORTANT, subordinate, lesser, minor, peripheral, incidental, ancillary, subsidiary, nonessential, inessential, of little account, unimportant. ❷ *secondary infections* ACCOMPANYING, attendant, concomitant, consequential, resulting, resultant.
– OPPOSITES primary, main.

second-class ▶ adjective SECOND-RATE, second-best, inferior, lesser, unimportant.

second-hand ▶ adjective ❶ *second-hand clothes* USED, old, worn, pre-owned, handed-down, hand-me-down, cast-off; *Brit. informal* reach-me-down. ❷ *second-hand information* INDIRECT, derivative; vicarious.
– OPPOSITES new, direct.
▶ adverb *I was discounting anything I heard second-hand* INDIRECTLY, at second-hand, on the bush telegraph; *informal* on the grapevine.
– OPPOSITES directly.

second in command ▶noun DEPUTY, number two, subordinate, right-hand man/woman; understudy.

secondly ▶adverb FURTHERMORE, also, moreover; second, in the second place, next; secondarily.

second-rate ▶adjective INFERIOR, substandard, low-quality, below par, bad, poor, deficient, defective, faulty, imperfect, shoddy, inadequate, insufficient, unacceptable; *Brit. informal* ropy, duff, rubbish.
– OPPOSITES first-rate, excellent.

secrecy ▶noun ❶ *the secrecy of the material* CONFIDENTIALITY, classified nature. ❷ *a government which thrived on secrecy* SECRETIVENESS, covertness, furtiveness, surreptitiousness, stealth, stealthiness.

secret ▶adjective ❶ *a secret plan* CONFIDENTIAL, top secret, classified, undisclosed, unknown, private, under wraps; *informal* hush-hush; *formal* sub rosa. ❷ *a secret drawer in the table* HIDDEN, concealed, disguised; invisible. ❸ *a secret operation to infiltrate terrorist groups* CLANDESTINE, covert, undercover, underground, surreptitious, stealthy, furtive, cloak-and-dagger, hole-and-corner, closet; *informal* hush-hush. ❹ *a secret message* | *a secret code* CRYPTIC, encoded, coded; mysterious, abstruse, recondite, arcane, esoteric, cabbalistic. ❺ *a secret place* SECLUDED, private, concealed, hidden, unfrequented, out of the way, tucked away. ❻ *a very secret person. See* SECRETIVE.
– OPPOSITES public, open.
▶noun ❶ *he just can't keep a secret* CONFIDENTIAL MATTER, confidence, private affair; skeleton in the cupboard. ❷ *the secrets of the universe* MYSTERY, enigma, paradox, puzzle, conundrum, poser, riddle. ❸ *the secret of their success* RECIPE, (magic) formula, blueprint, key, answer, solution.
■ **in secret** SECRETLY, in private, privately, behind closed doors, behind the scenes, in camera, under cover, under the counter, discreetly, behind someone's back, furtively, stealthily, on the sly, on the quiet, conspiratorially, covertly, clandestinely, on the side; *informal* on the q.t.; *formal* sub rosa.

secret agent ▶noun SPY, double agent, counterspy, undercover agent, operative, plant, mole; *N. Amer. informal* spook.

secretary ▶noun ASSISTANT, personal assistant, PA, administrator, amanuensis, girl/man Friday.

secrete[1] ▶verb *a substance secreted by the prostate gland* PRODUCE, discharge, emit, excrete, release, send out.
– OPPOSITES absorb.

secrete[2] ▶verb *we secreted ourselves in the bushes* CONCEAL, hide, cover up, veil, shroud, screen, stow away; bury, cache; *informal* stash away.
– OPPOSITES reveal.

secretive ▶adjective UNCOMMUNICATIVE, secret, unforthcoming, playing one's cards close to one's chest, reticent, reserved, silent, non-communicative, quiet, tight-lipped, close-mouthed, taciturn.
– OPPOSITES open, communicative.

secretly ▶adverb ❶ *they met secretly for a year* IN SECRET, in private, privately, behind closed doors, in camera, behind the scenes, under cover, under the counter, behind someone's back, furtively, stealthily, on the sly, on the quiet, conspiratorially, covertly, clandestinely, on the side; *informal* on the q.t.; *formal* sub rosa. ❷ *he was secretly jealous of Bartholomew* PRIVATELY, in one's heart (of hearts), deep down.

sect ▶noun (RELIGIOUS) CULT, religious group, denomination, persuasion, religious order; splinter group, faction.

sectarian ▶adjective FACTIONAL, separatist, partisan, parti pris; doctrinaire, dogmatic, extreme, fanatical, rigid, inflexible, bigoted, hidebound, narrow-minded.
– OPPOSITES tolerant, liberal.

section ▶noun ❶ *the separate sections of a train* PART, piece, bit, segment, component, division, portion, element, unit, constituent. ❷ *the last section of the questionnaire* SUBDIVISION, part, subsection, division, portion, bit, chapter, passage, clause. ❸ *the reference section of the library* DEPARTMENT, area, part, division. ❹ *a residential section of the capital. See* SECTOR sense 2.

sector ▶adjective ❶ *every sector of the industry is affected* PART, branch, arm, division, area, department, field, sphere. ❷ *the north-eastern sector of the town* DISTRICT, quarter, part, section, zone, region, area, belt.

secular ▶adjective NON-RELIGIOUS, lay, temporal, worldly, earthly, profane; *formal* laic.
– OPPOSITES holy, religious.

secure ▶adjective ❶ *check to ensure that all bolts are secure* FASTENED, fixed, secured, done up; closed, shut, locked. ❷ *an environment in which children can feel secure* SAFE, protected from harm/danger, out of from danger, sheltered, safe and sound, out of harm's way, in a safe place, in safe hands, invulnerable; at ease, unworried, relaxed, happy, confident. ❸ *a secure future* CERTAIN, assured, reliable, dependable, settled, fixed.
– OPPOSITES loose, vulnerable, uncertain.
▶verb ❶ *pins secure the handle to the main body* FIX, attach, fasten, affix, connect, couple. ❷ *the doors had not been properly secured* FASTEN, close, shut, lock, bolt, chain, seal. ❸ *he leapt out to secure the boat* TIE UP, moor, make fast; anchor. ❹ *they sought to secure the country against attack* PROTECT, make safe, fortify, strengthen. ❺ *a written constitution would secure the rights of the individual* ASSURE, ensure, guarantee, protect, confirm, establish. ❻ *the division secured a*

major contract OBTAIN, acquire, gain, get, get possession of; *informal* get hold of, land.

security ▶ **noun** ❶ *the security of the nation's citizens* SAFETY, freedom from danger, protection, invulnerability. ❷ *he could give her the security she needed* PEACE OF MIND, feeling of safety, stability, certainty, happiness, confidence. ❸ *security at the court was tight* SAFETY MEASURES, safeguards, surveillance, defence, protection. ❹ *additional security for your loan may be required* GUARANTEE, collateral, surety, pledge, bond; *archaic* gage.
– OPPOSITES vulnerability, danger.

sedate[1] ▶ **verb** *the patient had to be sedated* TRANQUILLIZE, put under sedation, drug.

sedate[2] ▶ **adjective** ❶ *a sedate pace* SLOW, steady, dignified, unhurried, relaxed, measured, leisurely, slow-moving, easy, easy-going, gentle. ❷ *he had lived a sedate and straightforward life* CALM, placid, tranquil, quiet, uneventful; boring, dull.
– OPPOSITES exciting, fast.

sedative ▶ **adjective** *sedative drugs* TRANQUILLIZING, calming, calmative, relaxing, soporific; depressant; *Medicine* neuroleptic.
▶ **noun** *the doctor gave him a sedative* TRANQUILLIZER, calmative, sleeping pill, narcotic, opiate; depressant; *informal* trank, sleeper, downer.

sedentary ▶ **adjective** SITTING, seated, desk-bound; inactive.
– OPPOSITES active.

sediment ▶ **noun** DREGS, lees, precipitate, deposit, grounds, settlings, residue, remains; silt, alluvium; *technical* residuum; *archaic* grouts.

sedition ▶ **noun** RABBLE-ROUSING, incitement to rebel, subversion, troublemaking, provocation; rebellion, insurrection, mutiny, insurgence, civil disorder.

seditious ▶ **adjective** RABBLE-ROUSING, provocative, inflammatory, subversive, troublemaking; rebellious, insurrectionist, mutinous, insurgent.

seduce ▶ **verb** ❶ *he took her to his hotel room and tried to seduce her* persuade to have sex; *euphemistic* have one's (wicked) way with, take advantage of; *dated* debauch. ❷ *a firm which had seduced customers into buying worthless products* ATTRACT, allure, lure, tempt, entice, beguile, inveigle, manoeuvre.

seducer ▶ **noun** WOMANIZER, philanderer, Romeo, Don Juan, Lothario, Casanova, playboy, ladies' man; *informal* ladykiller, wolf, skirt-chaser.

seductive ▶ **adjective** SEXY, alluring, tempting, exciting, provocative, sultry, slinky; coquettish, flirtatious; *informal* vampish, come-hither, come-to-bed.

seductress ▶ **noun** TEMPTRESS, siren, femme fatale, Mata Hari; flirt, coquette; *informal* vamp.

sedulous ▶ **adjective** DILIGENT, careful, meticulous, thorough, assiduous, attentive, industrious, conscientious, ultra-careful, punctilious, scrupulous, painstaking, minute, rigorous, particular.

see[1] ▶ **verb** ❶ *he saw her running across the road* DISCERN, spot, notice, catch sight of, glimpse, catch/get a glimpse of, make out, pick out, spy, distinguish, detect, perceive, note; *informal* clap/lay/set eyes on, clock; *poetic/literary* behold, descry, espy. ❷ *I saw a documentary about it last week* WATCH, look at, view; catch. ❸ *would you like to see over the house?* INSPECT, view, look round, tour, survey, examine, scrutinize; *informal* give something a/the once-over. ❹ *I finally saw what she meant* UNDERSTAND, grasp, comprehend, follow, take in, realize, appreciate, recognize, work out, get the drift of, perceive, fathom (out); *informal* get, latch on to, cotton on to, catch on to, tumble to, savvy, figure out, get a fix on; *Brit. informal* twig, suss (out). ❺ *I must go and see what Victor is up to* FIND OUT, discover, learn, ascertain, determine, establish. ❻ *see that no harm comes to him* ENSURE, make sure/certain, see to it, take care, mind. ❼ *I see trouble ahead* FORESEE, predict, forecast, prophesy, anticipate, envisage, picture, visualize. ❽ *about a year later, I saw him in town* ENCOUNTER, meet, run into/across, come across, stumble on/across, happen on, chance on; *informal* bump into; *archaic* run against. ❾ *they see each other from time to time* MEET, meet up with, get together with, socialize with. ❿ *you'd better see a doctor* CONSULT, confer with, talk to, speak to, have recourse to, call on, call in, turn to, ask. ⓫ *he's seeing someone else now* GO OUT WITH, date, take out, be involved with; *informal* go steady with; *Brit. informal, dated* walk out with; *N. Amer. informal, dated* step out with; *dated* court. ⓬ *he saw her to her car* ESCORT, accompany, show, walk, conduct, lead, take, usher, attend.
■ **see about** ARRANGE, see to, deal with, take care of, look after, attend to, sort out.
■ **see through** UNDERSTAND, get/have the measure of, read like a book; *informal* be wise to, have someone's number, know someone's (little) game.
■ **see someone through** SUSTAIN, encourage, buoy up, keep going, support, be a tower of strength to, comfort, help (out), stand by, stick by.
■ **see something through** PERSEVERE WITH, persist with, continue (with), carry on with, keep at, follow through, stay with; *informal* stick at, stick it out, hang in there.
■ **see to** ATTEND TO, deal with, see about, take care of, look after, sort out, fix, organize, arrange.

see[2] ▶ **noun** *a bishop's see* DIOCESE, bishopric.

seed ▶ **noun** ❶ *sow the seeds in trays or pots* pip, stone, kernel; ovule. ❷ *each war contains within it the seeds of a fresh war* GENESIS, source, origin, root, starting point, germ, beginnings, potential (for); cause, reason, motivation, motive, grounds. ❸ *(archaic) Abraham and his seed* DESCENDANTS, heirs, successors, scions; offspring, children, sons and daughters, progeny, family; *Law* issue; *derogatory* spawn; *archaic* fruit of someone's loins.

– RELATED TERMS seminal.

■ **go/run to seed** DETERIORATE, degenerate, decline, decay, fall into decay, go to rack and ruin, go downhill, moulder, rot; *informal* go to pot, go to the dogs, go down the toilet.

seedy ▶ **adjective** ❶ *the seedy world of prostitution* SORDID, disreputable, seamy, sleazy, squalid, unwholesome, unsavoury. ❷ *a seedy block of flats* DILAPIDATED, tumbledown, ramshackle, falling to pieces, decrepit, gone to rack and ruin, run down, down at heel, shabby, dingy, slummy, insalubrious, squalid; *informal* crummy; *Brit. informal* grotty.

– OPPOSITES high-class.

seek ▶ **verb** ❶ *they sought shelter from the winter snows* SEARCH FOR, try to find, look for, be on the lookout for, be after, hunt for, be in quest of. ❷ *the company is seeking a judicial review of the decision* TRY TO OBTAIN, work towards, be intent on, aim at/for. ❸ *he sought help from the police* ASK FOR, request, solicit, call for, entreat, beg for, petition for, appeal for, apply for, put in for. ❹ *we constantly seek to improve the service* TRY, attempt, endeavour, strive, work, do one's best; *formal* essay.

seem ▶ **verb** APPEAR (TO BE), have the appearance/air of being, give the impression of being, look, look as though one is, look like, show signs of, look to be; come across as, strike someone as, sound.

seeming ▶ **adjective** APPARENT, ostensible, supposed, outward, surface, superficial; pretended, feigned.

– OPPOSITES actual, genuine.

seemingly ▶ **adverb** APPARENTLY, on the face of it, to all appearances, as far as one can see/tell, on the surface, to all intents and purposes, outwardly, superficially, supposedly.

seemly ▶ **adjective** DECOROUS, proper, decent, becoming, fitting, suitable, appropriate, apt, apposite, meet, in good taste, genteel, polite, the done thing, right, correct, acceptable, comme il faut.

– OPPOSITES unseemly, unbecoming.

seep ▶ **verb** OOZE, trickle, exude, drip, dribble, flow, issue, escape, leak, drain, bleed, filter, percolate, soak.

seer ▶ **noun** SOOTHSAYER, oracle, prophet(ess), augur, prognosticator, diviner, fortune teller, crystal-gazer, clairvoyant, psychic; *Scottish* spaewife; *poetic/literary* sibyl.

see-saw ▶ **verb** FLUCTUATE, swing, go up and down, rise and fall, oscillate, alternate, yo-yo, vary.

seethe ▶ **verb** ❶ *the brew seethed* BOIL, bubble, simmer, foam, froth, fizz, effervesce. ❷ *the water seethed with fish* TEEM, swarm, boil, swirl, churn, surge. ❸ *I seethed at the injustice of it all* BE ANGRY, be furious, be enraged, be incensed, be beside oneself, boil, simmer, rage, rant, rave, storm, fume, smoulder; *informal* be livid, be wild, foam at the mouth, be steamed up, be hot under the collar; *Brit. informal* do one's nut, throw a wobbly.

see-through ▶ **adjective** TRANSPARENT, translucent, clear, limpid, pellucid; thin, lightweight, flimsy, sheer, diaphanous, filmy, gossamer, chiffony, gauzy.

– OPPOSITES opaque.

segment ▶ **noun** ❶ *orange segments* PIECE, bit, section, part, chunk, portion, division, slice; fragment, wedge, lump, tranche. ❷ *all segments of society* PART, section, sector, division, portion, constituent, element, unit, compartment; branch, wing.

▶ **verb** *they plan to segment their market share* DIVIDE (UP), subdivide, separate, split, cut up, carve up, slice up, break up; segregate, divorce, partition, section.

– OPPOSITES amalgamate.

segregate ▶ **verb** SEPARATE, set apart, keep apart, isolate, quarantine, closet; partition, divide, detach, disconnect, sever, dissociate.

– OPPOSITES amalgamate.

seize ▶ **verb** ❶ *she seized the microphone* GRAB, grasp, snatch, take hold of, get one's hands on; grip, clutch; *Brit. informal* nab. ❷ *rebels seized the air base* CAPTURE, take, overrun, occupy, conquer, take over. ❸ *the drugs were seized by customs* CONFISCATE, impound, commandeer, requisition, appropriate, expropriate, take away; *Law* distrain; *Scottish Law* poind. ❹ *terrorists seized his wife* KIDNAP, abduct, take captive, take prisoner, take hostage, hold to ransom; *informal* snatch.

– OPPOSITES relinquish, release.

■ **seize on** *they seized on the opportunity* TAKE ADVANTAGE OF, exploit, grasp with both hands, leap at, jump at, pounce on.

seizure ▶ **noun** ❶ *Napoleon's seizure of Spain* CAPTURE, takeover, annexation, invasion, occupation, colonization. ❷ *the seizure of defaulters' property* CONFISCATION, appropriation, expropriation, sequestration; *Law* distraint; *Scottish Law* poind. ❸ *the seizure of UN staff by rebels* KIDNAPPING, kidnap, abduction. ❹ *the baby suffered a seizure* CONVULSION, fit, spasm, paroxysm; *Medicine* ictus; *dated* apoplexy.

seldom ▶ **adverb** RARELY, infrequently, hardly (ever), scarcely (ever), almost never; now and then, occasionally, sporadically; *informal* once in a blue moon.

– OPPOSITES often.

select ▶ **verb** *select the correct tool for the job* CHOOSE, pick (out), single out, sort out, take;

opt for, decide on, settle on, determine, nominate, appoint, elect.

▶ adjective ❶ *a select group of SAS members* CHOICE, hand-picked, prime, first-rate, first-class, superior, finest, best, top-class, supreme, superb, excellent; *informal* A1, top-notch. ❷ *a select clientele* EXCLUSIVE, elite, favoured, privileged; wealthy; *informal* posh.
– OPPOSITES inferior.

selection ▶ noun ❶ *Jim made his selection of toys* CHOICE, pick; option, preference. ❷ *a wide selection of dishes* RANGE, array, diversity, variety, assortment, mixture. ❸ *a selection of his poems* ANTHOLOGY, assortment, collection, assemblage; miscellany, medley, pot-pourri.

selective ▶ adjective DISCERNING, discriminating, discriminatory, critical, exacting, demanding, particular; fussy, fastidious, faddish; *informal* choosy, pernickety, picky; *Brit. informal* faddy.

self ▶ noun EGO, I, oneself, persona, person, identity, character, personality, psyche, soul, spirit, mind, inner self.
– OPPOSITES other.

self-assembly ▶ noun *kits for self-assembly* DO-IT-YOURSELF, DIY.

▶ adjective *self-assembly furniture* FLAT-PACK, kit, self-build, do-it-yourself, DIY.

self-assurance ▶ noun SELF-CONFIDENCE, confidence, assertiveness, self-reliance, self-possession, composure, presence of mind, aplomb.
– OPPOSITES diffidence.

self-assured ▶ adjective SELF-CONFIDENT, confident, assertive, assured, authoritative, commanding, self-reliant, self-possessed, poised.

self-centred ▶ adjective EGOCENTRIC, egotistic, egotistical, egomaniacal, self-absorbed, self-obsessed, self-seeking, self-interested, self-serving; narcissistic, vain; inconsiderate, thoughtless; *informal* looking after number one.

self-confidence ▶ noun MORALE, confidence, self-assurance, assurance, assertiveness, self-reliance, self-possession, composure.

self-conscious ▶ adjective EMBARRASSED, uncomfortable, uneasy, nervous; unnatural, inhibited, gauche, awkward; modest, shy, diffident, bashful, retiring, shrinking.
– OPPOSITES confident.

self-contained ▶ adjective ❶ *each train was a self-contained unit* COMPLETE, independent, separate; free-standing, enclosed. ❷ *a very self-contained child* INDEPENDENT, self-sufficient, self-reliant; introverted, quiet, private, aloof, insular, reserved, reticent, secretive.

self-control ▶ noun SELF-DISCIPLINE, restraint, self-possession, will power, composure, coolness; moderation, temperance, abstemiousness; *informal* cool.

self-denial ▶ noun SELF-SACRIFICE, selflessness, unselfishness; self-discipline, asceticism, self-deprivation, abstemiousness, abstinence, abstention; moderation, temperance.
– OPPOSITES self-indulgence.

self-discipline ▶ noun SELF-CONTROL; restraint, self-restraint; will power, purposefulness, strong-mindedness, resolve, moral fibre; doggedness, persistence, determination, grit.

self-employed ▶ adjective FREELANCE, independent, casual; consultant, consulting; temporary, jobbing, visiting, outside, external, extramural, peripatetic.

self-esteem ▶ noun SELF-RESPECT, pride, dignity, self-regard, faith in oneself; morale, self-confidence, confidence, self-assurance.

self-evident ▶ adjective OBVIOUS, clear, plain, evident, apparent, manifest, patent; distinct, transparent, overt, conspicuous, palpable, unmistakable, undeniable.
– OPPOSITES unclear.

self-explanatory ▶ adjective EASILY UNDERSTOOD, comprehensible, intelligible, straightforward, unambiguous, accessible, crystal clear, user-friendly, simple, self-evident, obvious.
– OPPOSITES impenetrable.

self-governing ▶ noun INDEPENDENT, sovereign, autonomous, free; self-legislating, self-determining.
– OPPOSITES dependent.

self-important ▶ adjective CONCEITED, arrogant, bumptious, full of oneself, puffed up, swollen-headed, pompous, overbearing, opinionated, cocky, presumptuous, sententious, vain, overweening, proud, egotistical; *informal* snooty, uppity, uppish.
– OPPOSITES humble.

self-indulgent ▶ adjective HEDONISTIC, pleasure-seeking, sybaritic, indulgent, luxurious, lotus-eating, epicurean; intemperate, immoderate, overindulgent, excessive, extravagant, licentious, dissolute, decadent.
– OPPOSITES abstemious.

self-interest ▶ noun SELF-SEEKING, self-serving, self-obsession, self-absorption, self-regard, egocentrism, egotism, egomania, selfishness; *informal* looking after number one.
– OPPOSITES altruism.

self-interested ▶ adjective SELF-SEEKING, self-serving, self-obsessed, self-absorbed, wrapped up in oneself, egocentric, egotistic, egotistical, egomaniacal, selfish.

selfish ▶ adjective EGOCENTRIC, egotistic, egotistical, egomaniacal, self-centred, self-absorbed, self-obsessed, self-seeking, self-serving, wrapped up in oneself; inconsiderate, thoughtless, unthinking, uncaring, uncharitable; mean, miserly, grasping, greedy, mercenary, acquisitive, opportunistic; *informal* looking after number one.
– OPPOSITES altruistic.

selfless ▶ **adjective** UNSELFISH, altruistic, self-sacrificing, self-denying; considerate, compassionate, kind, noble, generous, magnanimous, ungrudging, charitable, benevolent, open-handed.
– OPPOSITES inconsiderate.

self-possessed ▶ **adjective** ASSURED, self-assured, calm, cool, composed, at ease, unperturbed, unruffled, confident, self-confident, poised, imperturbable; *informal* together, unfazed, unflappable.
– OPPOSITES unsure.

self-possession ▶ **noun** COMPOSURE, assurance, self-assurance, self-control, imperturbability, impassivity, equanimity, nonchalance, confidence, self-confidence, poise, aplomb, presence of mind, nerve, sangfroid; *informal* cool.

self-reliant ▶ **adjective** SELF-SUFFICIENT, self-supporting, self-sustaining, able to stand on one's own two feet; independent, autarkic.

self-respect ▶ **noun** SELF-ESTEEM, self-regard, amour propre, faith in oneself, pride, dignity, morale, self-confidence.

self-restraint ▶ **noun** SELF-CONTROL, restraint, self-discipline, self-possession, will power, moderation, temperance, abstemiousness, abstention.
– OPPOSITES self-indulgence.

self-righteous ▶ **adjective** SANCTIMONIOUS, holier-than-thou, self-satisfied, smug, priggish, complacent, pious, moralizing, superior, hypocritical; *informal* goody-goody.
– OPPOSITES humble.

self-sacrifice ▶ **noun** SELF-DENIAL, selflessness, unselfishness; self-discipline, abstinence, asceticism, abnegation, self-deprivation, moderation, austerity, temperance, abstention.

self-satisfied ▶ **adjective** COMPLACENT, self-congratulatory, smug, superior, puffed up, pleased with oneself; *informal* goody-goody, I'm-all-right-Jack; *Brit. informal* like the cat that's got the cream.

self-seeking ▶ **adjective** SELF-INTERESTED, self-serving, selfish; egocentric, egotistic, egotistical, self-obsessed, self-absorbed; inconsiderate, thoughtless, unthinking; *informal* looking after number one.
– OPPOSITES altruistic.

self-styled ▶ **adjective** WOULD-BE, so-called, self-appointed, self-titled, professed, self-confessed, soi-disant.

self-sufficient ▶ **adjective** SELF-SUPPORTING, self-reliant, self-sustaining, able to stand on one's own two feet; independent, autarkic.

self-willed ▶ **adjective** WILFUL, contrary, perverse, uncooperative, wayward, headstrong, stubborn, obstinate, obdurate, pig-headed, mulish, intransigent, recalcitrant, intractable; *Brit. informal* bloody-minded; *formal* refractory.
– OPPOSITES biddable.

sell ▶ **verb** ❶ *they are selling their house* PUT UP FOR SALE, offer for sale, put on sale, dispose of, vend, auction (off); trade, barter. ❷ *he sells cakes* TRADE IN, deal in, traffic in, stock, carry, offer for sale, peddle, hawk, retail, market. ❸ *the book should sell well* GO, be bought, be purchased; move, be in demand. ❹ *it sells for £79.95* COST, be priced at, retail at, go for, be. ❺ *he still has to sell the deal to Congress* PROMOTE; persuade someone to accept, talk someone into, bring someone round to, win someone over to, win approval for.
– OPPOSITES buy.

■ **sell someone down the river** (*informal*). *See* DOUBLE-CROSS.

■ **sell out** ❶ *we've sold out of petrol* HAVE NONE LEFT, be out of stock, have run out; *informal* be fresh out, be cleaned out. ❷ *the edition sold out quickly* BE BOUGHT UP, be depleted, be exhausted. ❸ *they say the band has sold out* ABANDON ONE'S PRINCIPLES, prostitute oneself, sell one's soul, betray one's ideals, be untrue to oneself; debase oneself, degrade oneself, demean oneself.

■ **sell someone out** BETRAY, inform on; be disloyal to, be unfaithful to, double-cross, break faith with, stab in the back; *informal* tell on, sell down the river, blow the whistle on, squeal on, stitch up, peach on, do the dirty on; *Brit. informal* grass on, shop; *N. Amer. informal* finger.

■ **sell someone short** UNDERVALUE, underrate, underestimate, disparage, deprecate, belittle; *formal* derogate.

seller ▶ **noun** VENDOR, retailer, purveyor, supplier, stockist, trader, merchant, dealer; shopkeeper, salesperson, salesman, saleswoman, sales assistant, shop assistant, travelling salesperson, pedlar, hawker; auctioneer; *N. Amer.* clerk; *informal* counter-jumper.

semblance ▶ **noun** (OUTWARD) APPEARANCE, air, show, facade, front, veneer, guise, pretence.

seminal ▶ **adjective** INFLUENTIAL, formative, ground-breaking, pioneering, original, innovative; major, important.

seminar ▶ **noun** ❶ *a seminar for education officials* CONFERENCE, symposium, meeting, convention, forum, summit, discussion, consultation. ❷ *teaching in the form of seminars* STUDY GROUP, workshop, tutorial, class, lesson.

seminary ▶ **noun** THEOLOGICAL COLLEGE, rabbinical college, Talmudical college; academy, training college, training institute, school.

send ▶ **verb** ❶ *they sent a message to HQ* DISPATCH, post, mail, address, consign, direct, forward; transmit, convey, communicate; telephone, phone, broadcast, radio, fax, e-mail; *dated* telegraph, wire, cable. ❷ *we sent for a doctor* CALL, summon, contact; ask for, request, order.

❸ *the pump sent out a jet of petrol* PROPEL, project, eject, deliver, discharge, spout, fire, shoot, release; throw, let fly; *informal* chuck. ❹ *the barrels send off nasty fumes* EMIT, give off, discharge, exude, send out, release, leak. ❺ *it's enough to send one mad* MAKE, drive, turn. ❻ (*informal*) *it's the music that sends us* EXCITE, stimulate, move, rouse, stir, thrill, electrify, intoxicate, enrapture, enthral, grip; charm, delight; *informal* blow away, give someone a kick.

– OPPOSITES receive.

■ **send someone down** ❶ (*Brit.*) *she was sent down from Cambridge* EXPEL, exclude; *Brit.* rusticate. ❷ (*informal*) *he was sent down for life* SEND TO PRISON, imprison, jail, incarcerate, lock up, confine, detain, intern; *informal* put away; *Brit. informal* bang up.

■ **send someone off** (*Sport*) ORDER OFF, dismiss; show someone the red card; *informal* red-card, send for an early bath, sin-bin.

■ **send someone/something up** (*informal*) SATIRIZE, ridicule, make fun of, parody, lampoon, mock, caricature, imitate, ape; *informal* take off, spoof, take the mickey out of.

send-off ▶ noun FAREWELL, goodbye, adieu, leave-taking, valediction; funeral; *archaic* vale.

– OPPOSITES welcome.

send-up ▶ noun (*informal*) SATIRE, burlesque, lampoon, pastiche, caricature, imitation, impression, impersonation; mockery, mimicry, travesty; *informal* spoof, take-off, mickey-take.

senile ▶ adjective DODDERING, doddery, decrepit, senescent, declining, infirm, feeble; aged, long in the tooth, in one's dotage; mentally confused, having Alzheimer's (disease), having senile dementia; *informal* past it, gaga.

senior ▶ adjective ❶ *senior school pupils* OLDER, elder. ❷ *a senior officer* SUPERIOR, higher-ranking, high-ranking, more important; top, chief; *N. Amer.* ranking. ❸ *Albert Stone Senior* THE ELDER; *Brit.* major; *N. Amer.* I.

– OPPOSITES junior, subordinate.

senior citizen ▶ noun RETIRED PERSON, (old-age) pensioner, OAP; old person, elderly person, geriatric, dotard, Methuselah; *N. Amer.* senior, retiree, golden ager; *informal* old stager, old-timer, oldie, oldster, wrinkly, crumbly; *Brit. informal* buffer, josser.

seniority ▶ noun RANK, superiority, standing, primacy, precedence, priority; age.

sensation ▶ noun ❶ *a sensation of light* FEELING, sense, awareness, consciousness, perception, impression. ❷ *I caused a sensation by donating £1m* COMMOTION, stir, uproar, furore, scandal, impact; interest, excitement; *informal* splash, to-do, hullabaloo. ❸ *the new cars were a sensation* TRIUMPH, success, sell-out; talking point; *informal* smash (hit), hit, winner, crowd-puller, wow, knockout.

sensational ▶ adjective ❶ *a sensational murder trial* SHOCKING, scandalous, appalling; amazing, startling, astonishing, staggering; stirring, exciting, thrilling, electrifying; fascinating, interesting, noteworthy, significant, remarkable, momentous, historic, newsworthy. ❷ *sensational stories* OVER-DRAMATIZED, dramatic, melodramatic, exaggerated, sensationalist, sensationalistic; graphic, explicit, lurid; *informal* shock-horror, juicy. ❸ (*informal*) *she looked sensational* GORGEOUS, stunning, wonderful, exquisite, lovely, radiant, delightful, charming, enchanting, captivating; striking, spectacular, remarkable, outstanding, arresting, eye-catching; marvellous, superb, excellent, fine, first-class; *informal* great, terrific, tremendous, super, fantastic, fabulous, fab, heavenly, divine, knockout, delectable, scrumptious, awesome, magic, wicked, out of this world; *Brit. informal* smashing, brilliant, brill.

– OPPOSITES dull, understated, unremarkable.

sense ▶ noun ❶ *the sense of touch* SENSORY FACULTY, feeling, sensation, perception; sight, hearing, touch, taste, smell. ❷ *a sense of guilt* FEELING, awareness, sensation, consciousness, recognition. ❸ *a sense of humour* APPRECIATION, awareness, understanding, comprehension, discernment. ❹ *she had the sense to press the panic button* WISDOM, common sense, sagacity, discernment, perception; wit, intelligence, cleverness, shrewdness, judgement, reason, logic, brain(s); *informal* gumption, nous, horse sense, savvy; *Brit. informal* loaf, common; *N. Amer. informal* smarts. ❺ *I can't see the sense in this* PURPOSE, point, reason, object, motive; use, value, advantage, benefit. ❻ *the different senses of 'well'* MEANING, definition, import, signification, significance, purport, implication, nuance; drift, gist, thrust, tenor, message.

– OPPOSITES stupidity.

▶ verb *she sensed their hostility* DISCERN, feel, observe, notice, recognize, pick up, be aware of, distinguish, make out, identify; comprehend, apprehend, see, appreciate, realize; suspect, have a funny feeling about, have a hunch, divine, intuit; *informal* catch on to; *Brit. informal* twig.

senseless ▶ adjective ❶ *they found him senseless on the floor* UNCONSCIOUS, stunned, insensible, insensate, comatose, knocked out, out cold, out for the count; numb; *informal* KO'd, dead to the world; *Brit. informal* spark out. ❷ *a senseless waste* POINTLESS, futile, useless, needless, unavailing, in vain, purposeless, meaningless, unprofitable; absurd, foolish, insane, stupid, idiotic, ridiculous, ludicrous, mindless, illogical.

– OPPOSITES conscious, wise.

sensibility ▶ noun ❶ *study leads to the growth of sensibility* SENSITIVITY, finer feelings, delicacy, taste, discrimination, discernment; understanding, insight, empathy, appreciation; feeling, intuition, responsiveness, receptiveness, perceptiveness, awareness. ❷ *the wording might offend their sensibilities* (FINER) FEELINGS, emotions, sensitivities, moral sense.

sensible ▶ adjective PRACTICAL, realistic, responsible, reasonable, commonsensical, rational, logical, sound, balanced, sober, no-nonsense, pragmatic, level-headed, thoughtful, down-to-earth, wise, prudent, judicious, sagacious, shrewd.
–OPPOSITES foolish.

sensitive ▶ adjective ❶ *she's sensitive to changes in temperature* RESPONSIVE TO, reactive to, sentient of, sensitized to; aware of, conscious of, alive to; susceptible to, affected by, vulnerable to; attuned to. ❷ *sensitive skin* DELICATE, fragile; tender, sore, raw. ❸ *the matter needs sensitive handling* TACTFUL, careful, thoughtful, diplomatic, delicate, subtle, kid-glove; sympathetic, compassionate, understanding, intuitive, responsive, insightful. ❹ *he's sensitive about his bald patch* TOUCHY, oversensitive, hypersensitive, easily offended, easily upset, easily hurt, thin-skinned, defensive; paranoid, neurotic; *informal* twitchy, uptight. ❺ *a sensitive issue* DIFFICULT, delicate, tricky, awkward, problematic, ticklish, precarious; controversial, emotive; *informal* sticky.
–OPPOSITES impervious, resilient, clumsy, thick-skinned, uncontroversial.

sensitivity ▶ noun ❶ *the sensitivity of the skin* RESPONSIVENESS, sensitiveness, reactivity; susceptibility, vulnerability. ❷ *the job calls for sensitivity* CONSIDERATION, care, thoughtfulness, tact, diplomacy, delicacy, subtlety, finer feelings; understanding, empathy, sensibility, feeling, intuition, responsiveness, receptiveness; perception, discernment, insight; savoir faire. ❸ *her sensitivity on the subject of boyfriends* TOUCHINESS, oversensitivity, hypersensitivity, defensiveness. ❹ *the sensitivity of the issue* DELICACY, trickiness, awkwardness, ticklishness.

sensual ▶ adjective ❶ *sensual pleasure* PHYSICAL, carnal, bodily, fleshly, animal; hedonistic, epicurean, sybaritic, voluptuary. ❷ *a beautiful, sensual woman* SEXUALLY ATTRACTIVE, sexy, voluptuous, sultry, seductive, passionate; sexually arousing, erotic, sexual.
–OPPOSITES spiritual, passionless.

sensualist ▶ noun HEDONIST, pleasure-seeker, sybarite, voluptuary; epicure, gastronome; bon vivant, bon viveur.

sensuality ▶ noun SEXINESS, sexual attractiveness, sultriness, seductiveness; sexuality, eroticism; physicality, carnality.

sensuous ▶ adjective ❶ *big sensuous canvases* AESTHETICALLY PLEASING, gratifying, rich, sumptuous, luxurious; sensory, sensorial. ❷ *sensuous lips* SEXUALLY ATTRACTIVE, sexy, seductive, voluptuous, luscious, lush.

sentence ▶ noun PRISON TERM, prison sentence; punishment; *informal* time, stretch, stint; *Brit. informal* porridge, bird.
▶ verb *they were sentenced to death* PASS JUDGEMENT ON, punish, convict; condemn, doom.

sententious ▶ adjective MORALISTIC, moralizing, sanctimonious, self-righteous, pietistic, pious, priggish, judgemental; pompous, pontifical, self-important; *informal* preachifying, preachy; *Brit. informal* pi.

sentient ▶ adjective (CAPABLE OF) FEELING, living, live; conscious, aware, responsive, reactive.

sentiment ▶ noun ❶ *the comments echo my own sentiments* VIEW, feeling, attitude, thought, opinion, belief. ❷ *there's no room for sentiment in sport* SENTIMENTALITY, sentimentalism, mawkishness, emotionalism; emotion, sensibility, soft-heartedness, tender-heartedness; *informal* schmaltz, mush, slushiness, corniness, cheese; *Brit. informal* soppiness; *N. Amer. informal* sappiness.

sentimental ▶ adjective ❶ *she kept the vase for sentimental reasons* NOSTALGIC, tender, emotional, affectionate. ❷ *the film is too sentimental* MAWKISH, over-emotional, cloying, sickly, saccharine, sugary; romantic, hearts-and-flowers, touching; *Brit.* twee; *informal* slushy, mushy, weepy, tear-jerking, schmaltzy, lovey-dovey, gooey, drippy, cheesy, corny; *Brit. informal* soppy; *N. Amer. informal* cornball, sappy, hokey. ❸ *she is sentimental about animals* SOFT-HEARTED, tender-hearted, soft; *informal* soppy.
–OPPOSITES practical, gritty.

sentry ▶ noun GUARD, sentinel, lookout, watch, watchman, patrol.

separable ▶ adjective DIVISIBLE, distinct, independent, distinguishable; detachable, removable.

separate ▶ adjective ❶ *his personal life was separate from his job* UNCONNECTED, unrelated, different, distinct, discrete; detached, divorced, disconnected, independent, autonomous. ❷ *the infirmary was separate from the school* SET APART, detached, disjoined; fenced off, cut off, segregated, isolated; free-standing, self-contained.
–OPPOSITES linked, attached.
▶ verb ❶ *they separated two rioting mobs* SPLIT (UP), break up, part, pull apart, divide; *poetic/literary* sunder. ❷ *the connectors can be separated* DISCONNECT, detach, disengage, uncouple, unyoke, disunite, disjoin; split, divide, sever; disentangle. ❸ *the wall that separated the two estates* PARTITION, divide, come between, keep apart; bisect, intersect. ❹ *the south aisle was separated off* ISOLATE, partition off, section off; close off, shut off, cordon off, fence off, screen off. ❺ *they separated at the airport* PART (COMPANY), go their separate ways, split up; say goodbye; disperse, disband, scatter. ❻ *the road separated* FORK, divide, branch, bifurcate, diverge. ❼ *her parents separated* SPLIT UP, break up, part, be estranged, divorce. ❽ *separate fact from fiction*

ISOLATE, set apart, segregate; distinguish, differentiate, dissociate; sort out, sift out, filter out, remove, weed out. ❾ *those who separate themselves from society* BREAK AWAY FROM, break with, secede from, withdraw from, leave, quit, dissociate oneself from, resign from, drop out of, repudiate, reject.
–OPPOSITES unite, join, link, meet, merge, marry.

separately ▸ adverb INDIVIDUALLY, one by one, one at a time, singly, severally; apart, independently, alone, by oneself, on one's own.

separation ▸ noun ❶ *the separation of the two companies* DISCONNECTION, detachment, severance, dissociation, disunion, disaffiliation, segregation, partition. ❷ *her parent's separation* BREAK-UP, split, parting (of the ways), estrangement, rift, rupture, breach; divorce; *Brit. informal* bust-up. ❸ *the separation between art and life* DISTINCTION, difference, differentiation, division, dividing line; gulf, gap, chasm.

septic ▸ adjective INFECTED, festering, suppurating, pus-filled, putrid, putrefying, poisoned, diseased; *Medicine* purulent.

sepulchral ▸ adjective GLOOMY, lugubrious, sombre, melancholy, melancholic, sad, sorrowful, mournful, doleful, dismal; *poetic/literary* dolorous.
–OPPOSITES cheerful.

sepulchre ▸ noun TOMB, vault, burial chamber, mausoleum, crypt, undercroft, catacomb; grave.

sequel ▸ noun ❶ *the film inspired a sequel* FOLLOW-UP, continuation. ❷ *the sequel was an armed uprising* CONSEQUENCE, result, upshot, outcome, development, issue, postscript; effect, after-effect, aftermath; *informal* pay-off.

sequence ▸ noun ❶ *the sequence of events* SUCCESSION, order, course, series, chain, train, string, progression, chronology; pattern, flow; *formal* concatenation. ❷ *a sequence from his film* EXCERPT, clip, extract, episode, section.

sequester ▸ verb ❶ *he sequestered himself from the world* ISOLATE ONESELF, hide away, shut oneself away, seclude oneself, cut oneself off, segregate oneself; closet oneself, withdraw, retire. ❷ *the government sequestered his property.* See SEQUESTRATE.

sequestrate ▸ verb CONFISCATE, seize, take, sequester, appropriate, expropriate, impound, commandeer; *Law* distrain; *Scottish Law* poind.

seraphic ▸ adjective BLISSFUL, beatific, sublime, rapturous, ecstatic, joyful, rapt; serene, ethereal; cherubic, saintly, angelic.

serendipitous ▸ adjective CHANCE, accidental, coincidental; lucky, fluky, fortuitous; unexpected, unforeseen.

serendipity ▸ noun (HAPPY) CHANCE, (happy) accident, fluke; luck, good luck, good fortune, fortuity, providence; happy coincidence.

serene ▸ adjective ❶ *on the surface she seemed serene* CALM, composed, tranquil, peaceful, untroubled, relaxed, at ease, unperturbed, unruffled, unworried; placid, equable; *N. Amer.* centered; *informal* together, unflappable. ❷ *serene valleys* PEACEFUL, tranquil, quiet, still, restful, relaxing, undisturbed.
–OPPOSITES agitated, turbulent.

series ▸ noun ❶ *a series of lectures* SUCCESSION, sequence, string, chain, run, round; spate, wave, rash; set, course, cycle; row, line; *formal* concatenation. ❷ *a new drama series* SERIAL, programme; soap opera; *informal* soap.

serious ▸ adjective ❶ *a serious expression* SOLEMN, earnest, grave, sombre, sober, unsmiling, poker-faced, stern, grim, dour, humourless, stony-faced; thoughtful, preoccupied, pensive. ❷ *serious decisions* IMPORTANT, significant, consequential, momentous, weighty, far-reaching, major, grave; urgent, pressing, crucial, critical, vital, life-and-death, high-priority. ❸ *give serious consideration to this* CAREFUL, detailed, in-depth, deep, profound, meaningful. ❹ *a serious play* INTELLECTUAL, highbrow, heavyweight, deep, profound, literary, learned, scholarly; *informal* heavy. ❺ *serious injuries* SEVERE, grave, bad, critical, acute, terrible, dire, dangerous, perilous, parlous; *formal* grievous. ❻ *we're serious about equality* IN EARNEST, earnest, sincere, wholehearted, genuine; committed, resolute, determined.
–OPPOSITES light-hearted, trivial, superficial, lowbrow, minor, half-hearted.

seriously ▸ adverb ❶ *Faye nodded seriously* SOLEMNLY, earnestly, gravely, soberly, sombrely, sternly, grimly, dourly, humourlessly; pensively, thoughtfully. ❷ *she was seriously injured* SEVERELY, gravely, badly, critically, acutely, dangerously; *formal* grievously. ❸ *do you seriously expect me to come?* REALLY, actually, honestly. ❹ *seriously, I'm very pleased* JOKING ASIDE, to be serious, honestly, truthfully, truly, I mean it; *informal* Scout's honour; *Brit. informal* straight up; *dated* honest Injun. ❺ (*infor-mal*) *'I've resigned.' 'Seriously?'* REALLY, is that so, is that a fact, you're joking, well I never, go on, you don't say; *informal* you're kidding; *Brit. informal* {well, I'll be blowed}. ❻ (*informal*) *he was seriously rich.* See EXTREMELY.

sermon ▸ noun ❶ *he preached a sermon* HOMILY, address, speech, talk, discourse, oration; lesson. ❷ *the headmaster gave them a lengthy sermon* LECTURE, tirade, harangue, diatribe; speech, disquisition, monologue; reprimand, reproach, reproof, admonishment, admonition, reproval, remonstration, criticism; *informal* telling-off, talking-to, dressing-down, earful; *Brit. informal* ticking-off, row, rocket, rollicking; *formal* castigation.

serpentine ▸ adjective ❶ *a serpentine path* WINDING, windy, zigzag, twisty, twisting and turning, meandering, sinuous, snaky, tortu-

ous. ❷ *serpentine election rules* COMPLICATED, complex, intricate, involved, tortuous, convoluted, elaborate, knotty, confusing, bewildering, baffling, impenetrable.
– OPPOSITES straight, simple.

serrated ▶ **adjective** JAGGED, sawtoothed, sawtooth, zigzag, notched, indented, toothed, denticulate, denticulated; *Botany* serrate; *technical* crenulated.
– OPPOSITES smooth.

serried ▶ **adjective** CLOSE TOGETHER, packed together, close-set, dense, tight, compact.

servant ▶ **noun** ❶ *servants were cleaning the hall* ATTENDANT, retainer; domestic (worker), (hired) help, cleaner; lackey, flunkey, minion; maid, housemaid, footman, page (boy), valet, butler, batman, manservant; housekeeper, steward; drudge, menial, slave; *Brit. informal* Mrs Mop, daily (woman), skivvy, scout; *Brit. dated* charwoman, charlady, boots; *archaic* abigail, scullion. ❷ *a servant of the Labour Party* HELPER, supporter, follower.

serve ▶ **verb** ❶ *they served their masters faithfully* WORK FOR, be in the service of, be employed by; obey. ❷ *this job serves the community* BE OF SERVICE TO, be of use to, help, assist, aid, make a contribution to, do one's bit for, do something for, benefit. ❸ *she served on the committee for years* BE A MEMBER OF, work on, be on, sit on, have a place on. ❹ *he served his apprenticeship in Scotland* CARRY OUT, perform, do, fulfil, complete, discharge; spend. ❺ *serve the soup hot* DISH UP/OUT, give out, distribute; present, provide, supply; eat. ❻ *she served another customer* ATTEND TO, deal with, see to; ASSIST, help, look after. ❼ *they served him with a writ* PRESENT, deliver, give, hand over. ❽ *a saucer serving as an ashtray* ACT AS, function as, do the work of, be a substitute for. ❾ *official forms will serve in most cases* SUFFICE, be adequate, be good enough, fit/fill the bill, do, answer, be useful, meet requirements, suit.

service ▶ **noun** ❶ *your conditions of service* WORK, employment, employ, labour. ❷ *he has done us a service* FAVOUR, kindness, good turn, helping hand; (**services**) ASSISTANCE, help, aid, offices, ministrations. ❸ *the food and service were excellent* WAITING, waitressing, serving, attendance. ❹ *products which give reliable service* USE, usage; functioning. ❺ *he took his car in for a service* OVERHAUL, maintenance check, servicing. ❻ *a marriage service* CEREMONY, ritual, rite, observance; liturgy, sacrament; *formal* ordinance. ❼ *a range of local services* AMENITY, facility, resource, utility. ❽ *soldiers leaving the services* (ARMED) FORCES, armed services, military; army, navy, air force.
▶ **verb** *the appliances are serviced regularly* OVERHAUL, check, go over, maintain; repair, mend, recondition.
■ **be of service** HELP, assist, benefit, be of assistance, be beneficial, serve, be useful, be of use, be valuable; do someone a good turn.
■ **out of service** OUT OF ORDER, broken, broken-down, out of commission, unserviceable, faulty, defective, inoperative, in disrepair; down; *informal* conked out, bust, kaput, on the blink, acting up, shot; *Brit. informal* knackered.

serviceable ▶ **adjective** ❶ *a serviceable heating system* IN WORKING ORDER, working, functioning, functional, operational, operative; usable, workable, viable. ❷ *serviceable lace-up shoes* FUNCTIONAL, utilitarian, sensible, practical; HARD-WEARING, durable, tough, robust.
– OPPOSITES unusable, impractical.

servile ▶ **adjective** OBSEQUIOUS, sycophantic, deferential, subservient, fawning, ingratiating, unctuous, grovelling, toadyish, slavish, humble, self-abasing; *informal* slimy, bootlicking, smarmy, sucky; *N. Amer. informal* apple-polishing.
– OPPOSITES assertive.

serving ▶ **noun** PORTION, helping, plateful, plate, bowlful; amount, quantity, ration.

servitude ▶ **noun** SLAVERY, enslavement, bondage, subjugation, subjection, domination; *historical* serfdom.
– OPPOSITES liberty.

session ▶ **noun** ❶ *a special session of the committee* MEETING, sitting, assembly, conclave, plenary; hearing; conference, discussion, forum, symposium; *Scottish* sederunt, diet; *N. Amer. & NZ* caucus. ❷ *training sessions* PERIOD, time, spell, stretch, bout. ❸ *the next college session begins in August* ACADEMIC YEAR, school year; term, semester; *N. Amer.* trimester.

set[1] ▶ **verb** ❶ *Beth set the bag on the table* PUT (DOWN), place, lay, deposit, position, settle, leave, stand, plant, posit; *informal* stick, dump, bung, park, plonk, pop; *N. Amer. informal* plunk. ❷ *the cottage is set on a hill* BE SITUATED, be located, lie, stand, be sited, be perched. ❸ *the fence is set in concrete* FIX, embed, insert; mount. ❹ *a ring set with precious stones* ADORN, ornament, decorate, embellish; *poetic/literary* bejewel. ❺ *I'll go and set the table* LAY, prepare, arrange. ❻ *we set them some easy tasks* ASSIGN, allocate, give, allot, prescribe. ❼ *just set your mind to it* APPLY, address, direct, aim, turn, focus, concentrate. ❽ *they set a date for the election* DECIDE ON, select, choose, arrange, schedule; fix (on), settle on, determine, designate, name, appoint, specify, stipulate. ❾ *he set his horse towards her* DIRECT, steer, orientate, point, aim, train. ❿ *his jump set a national record* ESTABLISH, create, institute. ⓫ *he set his watch* ADJUST, regulate, synchronize; calibrate; put right, correct; programme, activate, turn on. ⓬ *the adhesive will set in an hour* SOLIDIFY, harden, stiffen, thicken, gel, gelatinize; cake, congeal, coagulate, clot; freeze, crystallize. ⓭ *the sun was setting* GO DOWN, sink, dip; vanish, disappear.
– OPPOSITES melt, rise.

■ **set about** ❶ *Mike set about raising £5000* BEGIN, start, commence, go about, get to work on, get down to, embark on, tackle, address oneself to, undertake. ❷ *the youths set about him* ATTACK, assail, assault, hit, strike, beat, thrash, pummel, wallop, tear into, set upon, fall on; *informal* lay into, lace into, pitch into, let someone have it, do over, work over, rough up, knock about/around; *Brit. informal* duff up, have a go at; *N. Amer. informal* beat up on.

■ **set someone against someone else** ALIENATE FROM, estrange from; drive a wedge between, sow dissension, set at odds.

■ **set someone apart** DISTINGUISH, differentiate, mark out, single out, separate, demarcate.

■ **set something apart** ISOLATE, separate, segregate, put to one side.

■ **set something aside** ❶ *set aside some money each month* SAVE, put by, put aside, put away, lay by, keep, reserve; store, stockpile, hoard, stow away, cache, withhold; *informal* salt away, squirrel away, stash away. ❷ *he set aside his cup* PUT DOWN, cast aside, discard, abandon, dispense with. ❸ *set aside your differences* DISREGARD, put aside, ignore, forget, discount, shrug off, bury. ❹ *the Appeal Court set aside the decision* OVERRULE, overturn, reverse, revoke, countermand, nullify, annul, cancel, quash, dismiss, reject, repudiate; *Law* disaffirm; *formal* abrogate.

■ **set someone back** (*informal*). *See* COST verb sense 1.

■ **set someone/something back** DELAY, hold up, hold back, slow down/up, retard, check, decelerate; hinder, impede, obstruct, hamper, inhibit, frustrate, thwart.

■ **set something down** ❶ *he set down his thoughts* WRITE DOWN, put in writing, jot down, note down, make a note of; record, register, log. ❷ *we set down a code of practice* FORMULATE, draw up, establish, frame; lay down, determine, fix, stipulate, specify, prescribe, impose, ordain. ❸ *I set it down to the fact that he was drunk* ATTRIBUTE, put down, ascribe, assign, chalk up; blame on, impute.

■ **set something forth** PRESENT, describe, set out, detail, delineate, explain, expound; state, declare, announce; submit, offer, put forward, advance, propose, propound.

■ **set someone free** RELEASE, free, let go, turn loose, let out, liberate, deliver, emancipate.

■ **set in** *bad weather set in* BEGIN, start, arrive, come, develop.

■ **set off** SET OUT, start out, sally forth, leave, depart, embark, set sail; *informal* hit the road.

■ **set something off** ❶ *the bomb was set off* DETONATE, explode, blow up, touch off, trigger; ignite. ❷ *it set off a wave of protest* GIVE RISE TO, cause, lead to, set in motion, occasion, bring about, initiate, precipitate, prompt, trigger (off), spark (off), touch off, provoke, incite. ❸ *the blue dress set off her auburn hair* ENHANCE, bring out, emphasize, show off, throw into relief; complement.

■ **set on/upon** ATTACK, assail, assault, hit, strike, beat, thrash, pummel, wallop, set about, fall on; *informal* lay into, lace into, let someone have it, get stuck into, work over, rough up, knock about/around; *Brit. informal* duff up, have a go at; *N. Amer. informal* beat up on, light into.

■ **set one's heart on** WANT DESPERATELY, wish for, desire, long for, yearn for, hanker after, ache for, hunger for, thirst for, burn for; *informal* be itching for, be dying for.

■ **set out** ❶ *he set out early. See* SET OFF. ❷ *you've done what you set out to achieve* AIM, intend, mean, seek; hope, aspire, want.

■ **set something out** ❶ *the gifts were set out on tables* ARRANGE, lay out, put out, array, dispose, display, exhibit. ❷ *they set out some guidelines* PRESENT, set forth, detail; state, declare, announce; submit, put forward, advance, propose, propound.

■ **set someone up** ❶ *his father set him up in business* ESTABLISH, finance, fund, back, subsidize. ❷ (*informal*) *she set him up for Newley's murder* FALSELY INCRIMINATE, frame, entrap; *Brit. informal* fit up.

■ **set something up** ❶ *a monument to her memory was set up* ERECT, put up, construct, build, raise, elevate. ❷ *she set up her own business* ESTABLISH, start, begin, initiate, institute, found, create. ❸ *set up a meeting* ARRANGE, organize, fix (up), schedule, timetable, line up.

set² ▶ **noun** ❶ *a set of colour postcards* GROUP, collection, series; assortment, selection, compendium, batch, number; arrangement, array. ❷ *the literary set* CLIQUE, coterie, circle, crowd, group, crew, band, company, ring, camp, fraternity, school, faction, league; *informal* gang, bunch. ❸ *a chemistry set* KIT, apparatus, equipment, outfit. ❹ *a set of cutlery* CANTEEN, box, case. ❺ *a set of china* SERVICE. ❻ *he's in the bottom set at school* CLASS, form, group; stream, band. ❼ *the set of his shoulders* POSTURE, position, cast, attitude; bearing, carriage. ❽ *a stage set* SCENERY, setting, backdrop, flats; mise en scène.

set³ ▶ **adjective** ❶ *a set routine* FIXED, established, predetermined, hard and fast, pre-arranged, prescribed, specified, defined; unvarying, unchanging, invariable, unvaried, rigid, inflexible, cast-iron, strict, settled, predictable; routine, standard, customary, regular, usual, habitual, accustomed, wonted. ❷ *she had set ideas* INFLEXIBLE, rigid, fixed, firm, deep-rooted, deep-seated, ingrained, entrenched. ❸ *he had a set speech for such occasions* STOCK, standard, routine, rehearsed, well worn, formulaic, conventional. ❹ *I was all set for the evening* READY, prepared, organized, equipped, primed; *informal* geared up, psyched up. ❺ *he's set on marrying her* DETERMINED TO, intent on, (hell) bent on, resolute about, insistent about. ❻ *you were dead set against the idea* OPPOSED TO, averse to,

hostile to, resistant to, antipathetic to, unsympathetic to; *informal* anti.
–OPPOSITES variable, flexible, original, unprepared, uncertain.

setback ▶noun PROBLEM, difficulty, hitch, complication, upset, disappointment, misfortune, mishap, reversal; blow, stumbling block, hindrance, impediment, obstruction; delay, hold-up; *informal* glitch, hiccup.
–OPPOSITES breakthrough.

settee ▶noun SOFA, couch, divan, chaise longue, chesterfield; *Brit.* put-you-up; *N. Amer.* davenport, day bed.

setting ▶noun ❶ *a rural setting* SURROUNDINGS, position, situation, environment, background, backdrop, milieu, environs, habitat; spot, place, location, locale, site, scene; area, region, district. ❷ *a garnet in a gold setting* MOUNT, fixture, surround.

settle ▶verb ❶ *they settled the dispute* RESOLVE, sort out, solve, clear up, end, fix, work out, iron out, straighten out, set right, rectify, remedy, reconcile; *informal* patch up. ❷ *she settled their affairs* PUT IN ORDER, sort out, tidy up, arrange, organize, order, clear up. ❸ *they settled on a date for the wedding* DECIDE ON, set, fix, agree on, name, establish, arrange, appoint, designate, assign; choose, select, pick. ❹ *she went down to the lobby to settle her bill* PAY, settle up, square, clear, defray. ❺ *they settled for a 4.2% pay rise* ACCEPT, agree to, assent to; *formal* accede to. ❻ *he settled in London* MAKE ONE'S HOME, set up home, take up residence, put down roots, establish oneself; live, move to, emigrate to. ❼ *immigrants settled much of Australia* COLONIZE, occupy, inhabit, people, populate. ❽ *Catherine settled down to her work* APPLY ONESELF TO, get down to, set about, attack; concentrate on, focus on, devote oneself to. ❾ *the class wouldn't settle down* CALM DOWN, quieten down, be quiet, be still; *informal* shut up. ❿ *a brandy will settle your nerves* CALM, quieten, quiet, soothe, pacify, quell; sedate, tranquillize. ⓫ *he settled into an armchair* SIT DOWN, seat oneself, install oneself, ensconce oneself, plant oneself; *informal* park oneself, plonk oneself. ⓬ *a butterfly settled on the flower* LAND, come to rest, alight, descend, perch; *archaic* light. ⓭ *sediment settles at the bottom* SINK, subside, fall, gravitate.
–OPPOSITES agitate, rise.

settlement ▶noun ❶ *a pay settlement* AGREEMENT, deal, arrangement, resolution, bargain, understanding, pact. ❷ *the settlement of the dispute* RESOLUTION, settling, solution, reconciliation. ❸ *a frontier settlement* COMMUNITY, colony, outpost, encampment, post; village, commune; *historical* plantation. ❹ *the settlement of the area* COLONIZATION, settling, populating; *historical* plantation. ❺ *the settlement of their debts* PAYMENT, discharge, defrayal, liquidation, clearance.

settler ▶noun COLONIST, colonizer, frontiersman, frontierswoman, pioneer; immigrant, newcomer, incomer; *N. Amer. historical* homesteader.
–OPPOSITES native.

set-up ▶noun ❶ *a telecommunications set-up* SYSTEM, structure, organization, arrangement, framework, layout, configuration. ❷ *a set-up called Film International* ORGANIZATION, group, body, agency, association, operation; company, firm; *informal* outfit. ❸ (*informal*) *the whole thing was a set-up* TRICK, trap; conspiracy; *informal* put-up job, frame-up.

seven ▶cardinal number SEPTET, septuplets; *technical* heptad.
–RELATED TERMS hepta-, septi-.

sever ▶verb ❶ *the head was severed from the body* CUT OFF, chop off, detach, disconnect, dissever, separate, part; amputate, dock; *poetic/literary* sunder. ❷ *a knife had severed the artery* CUT (THROUGH), rupture, split, pierce. ❸ *they severed diplomatic relations* BREAK OFF, discontinue, suspend, end, terminate, cease, dissolve.
–OPPOSITES join, maintain.

several ▶adjective ❶ *several people* SOME, a number of, a few; various, assorted, sundry, diverse; *poetic/literary* divers. ❷ *they sorted out their several responsibilities* RESPECTIVE, individual, own, particular, specific; separate, different, disparate, distinct; various.

severe ▶adjective ❶ *severe injuries* ACUTE, very bad, serious, grave, critical, dreadful, terrible, awful; dangerous, parlous, life-threatening; *formal* grievous. ❷ *severe storms* FIERCE, violent, strong, powerful, intense; tempestuous, turbulent. ❸ *a severe winter* HARSH, bitter, cold, bleak, freezing, icy, arctic, extreme. ❹ *a severe headache* EXCRUCIATING, agonizing, intense, dreadful, awful, terrible, unbearable, intolerable; *informal* splitting, pounding. ❺ *a severe test of their stamina* DIFFICULT, demanding, tough, arduous, formidable, exacting, rigorous, punishing, onerous, gruelling. ❻ *severe criticism* HARSH, scathing, sharp, strong, fierce, savage, scorching, devastating, trenchant, caustic, biting, withering. ❼ *severe tax penalties* EXTORTIONATE, excessive, unreasonable, inordinate, outrageous, sky-high, harsh, stiff; punitive; *Brit.* swingeing. ❽ *they received severe treatment* HARSH, stern, hard, inflexible, uncompromising, unrelenting, merciless, pitiless, ruthless, draconian, oppressive, repressive, punitive; brutal, cruel, savage. ❾ *his severe expression* STERN, dour, grim, forbidding, disapproving, unsmiling, unfriendly, sombre, grave, serious, stony, steely; cold, frosty. ❿ *a severe style of architecture* PLAIN, simple, austere, unadorned, unembellished, unornamented, stark, spartan, ascetic; clinical, uncluttered.
–OPPOSITES minor, gentle, mild, easy, lenient, friendly, ornate.

severely ▶ adjective ❶ *he was severely injured* BADLY, seriously, critically; fatally; *formal* grievously. ❷ *she was severely criticized* SHARPLY, roundly, soundly, fiercely, savagely. ❸ *murderers should be treated more severely* HARSHLY, strictly, sternly, rigorously, mercilessly, pitilessly, roughly, sharply; with a rod of iron; brutally, cruelly, savagely. ❹ *she looked severely at Harriet* STERNLY, grimly, dourly, disapprovingly; coldly, frostily. ❺ *she dressed severely in black* PLAINLY, simply, austerely, starkly.

sew ▶ verb *she sewed the seams of the tunic* STITCH, tack, baste, seam, hem; embroider.

■ **sew something up** ❶ *the tear was sewn up* DARN, mend, repair, patch. ❷ (*informal*) *the company sewed up a deal with IBM* SECURE, clinch, pull off, bring off, settle, conclude, complete, finalize, tie up; *informal* swing.

sewing ▶ noun STITCHING, needlework, needlecraft, fancy-work.

sex ▶ noun ❶ *they talked about sex* SEXUAL INTERCOURSE, intercourse, lovemaking, making love, sex act, (sexual) relations; mating, copulation; *informal* nooky; *Brit. informal* bonking, rumpy pumpy, how's your father; *formal* fornication; *technical* coitus, coition; *dated* carnal knowledge. ❷ *teach your children about sex* THE FACTS OF LIFE, reproduction; *informal* the birds and the bees. ❸ *adults of both sexes* GENDER.

■ **have sex** HAVE SEXUAL INTERCOURSE, make love, sleep with, go to bed; mate, copulate; seduce, rape; *informal* do it, go all the way, know in the biblical sense; *Brit. informal* bonk; *N. Amer. informal* get it on; *euphemistic* be intimate; *poetic/literary* ravish; *formal* fornicate.

sex appeal ▶ noun SEXINESS, seductiveness, sexual attractiveness, desirability, sensuality, sexuality; *informal* it, SA.

sexism ▶ noun SEXUAL DISCRIMINATION, chauvinism, prejudice, bias.

sexless ▶ adjective ASEXUAL, non-sexual, neuter; androgynous, epicene.

sexual ▶ adjective ❶ *the sexual organs* REPRODUCTIVE, genital, sex, procreative. ❷ *sexual activity* CARNAL, erotic; *formal* venereal; *technical* coital. ❸ *she's so sexual. See* SEXY sense 1.

sexual intercourse ▶ noun. *See* SEX sense 1.

sexuality ▶ noun ❶ *she had a powerful sexuality* SENSUALITY, sexiness, seductiveness, desirability, eroticism, physicality; sexual appetite, passion, desire, lust. ❷ *I'm open about my sexuality* SEXUAL ORIENTATION, sexual preference, leaning, persuasion; heterosexuality, homosexuality, lesbianism, bisexuality. ❸ *sexuality within holy matrimony* SEXUAL ACTIVITY, sexual relations, sexual intercourse, sex, procreation.

sexy ▶ adjective ❶ *she's so sexy* SEXUALLY ATTRACTIVE, seductive, desirable, alluring, sensual, sultry, slinky, provocative, tempting, tantalizing; nubile, voluptuous, luscious, lush; *informal* fanciable, beddable; *Brit. informal* fit; *N. Amer. informal* foxy, cute; *Austral. informal* spunky. ❷ *sexy videos* EROTIC, sexually explicit, arousing, exciting, stimulating, hot, titillating, racy, naughty, risqué, adult, X-rated; rude, pornographic, crude, lewd; *informal* raunchy, steamy, porno, blue, skin. ❸ *they weren't feeling sexy* (SEXUALLY) AROUSED, sexually excited, amorous, lustful, passionate; *informal* horny, hot, turned on, sexed up; *Brit. informal* randy. ❹ (*informal*) *a sexy sales promotion* EXCITING, stimulating, interesting, appealing, intriguing.

shabby ▶ adjective ❶ *a shabby little bar* RUN DOWN, down at heel, scruffy, dilapidated, ramshackle, tumbledown; seedy, slummy, insalubrious, squalid, sordid; *informal* crummy, scuzzy, shambly; *Brit. informal* grotty; *N. Amer. informal* shacky. ❷ *a shabby grey coat* SCRUFFY, old, worn out, threadbare, ragged, frayed, tattered, battered, faded, moth-eaten, mangy; *informal* tatty, ratty, the worse for wear; *N. Amer. informal* raggedy. ❸ *her shabby treatment of Ben* CONTEMPTIBLE, despicable, dishonourable, discreditable, mean, low, dirty, hateful, shameful, sorry, ignoble, unfair, unworthy, unkind, shoddy, nasty; *informal* rotten, low-down; *Brit. informal* beastly.

– OPPOSITES smart, honourable.

shack ▶ noun HUT, shanty, cabin, lean-to, shed; hovel; *Scottish* bothy, shieling.

■ **shack up with** (*informal*) COHABIT, live with; *informal, dated* live in sin.

shackle ▶ verb ❶ *he was shackled to the wall* CHAIN, fetter, manacle; secure, tie (up), bind, tether, hobble; put in chains, clap in irons, handcuff. ❷ *journalists were shackled by a new law* RESTRAIN, restrict, limit, constrain, handicap, hamstring, hamper, hinder, impede, obstruct, inhibit, check, curb.

shackles ▶ plural noun ❶ *the men filed through their shackles* CHAINS, fetters, irons, leg-irons, manacles, handcuffs; bonds; *informal* cuffs, bracelets. ❷ *the shackles of bureaucracy* RESTRICTIONS, restraints, constraints, impediments, hindrances, obstacles, barriers, obstructions, checks, curbs; *poetic/literary* trammels.

shade ▶ noun ❶ *they sat in the shade* SHADOW(S), shadiness, shelter, cover; cool. ❷ *shades of blue* COLOUR, hue, tone, tint, tinge. ❸ *shades of meaning* NUANCE, gradation, degree, difference, variation, variety; nicety, subtlety; undertone, overtone. ❹ *her skirt was a shade too short* A LITTLE, a bit, a trace, a touch, a modicum, a tinge; slightly, rather, somewhat; *informal* a tad, a smidgen. ❺ *the window shade* BLIND, curtain, screen, cover, covering; awning, canopy. ❻ (*informal*) *he was wearing shades* SUNGLASSES, dark glasses; *Austral. informal* sunnies.

– OPPOSITES light.

▶ verb ❶ *vines shaded the garden* CAST A SHADOW OVER, shadow, shelter, cover, screen; darken.

❷ *she shaded in the picture* DARKEN, colour in, pencil in, block in, fill in; cross-hatch. ❸ *the sky shaded from turquoise to blue* CHANGE, transmute, turn, go; merge, blend.

■ **put someone/something in the shade** SURPASS, outshine, outclass, overshadow, eclipse, transcend, cap, top, outstrip, outdo, put to shame, beat, outperform, upstage; *informal* run rings around, be a cut above, leave standing.

■ **shades of** ECHOES OF, a reminder of, memories of, suggestions of, hints of.

shadow ▶ **noun** ❶ *he saw her shadow in the doorway* SILHOUETTE, outline, shape, contour, profile. ❷ *he emerged from the shadows* SHADE, darkness, twilight; gloom, murkiness; *archaic* umbrage. ❸ *the shadow of war* (BLACK) CLOUD, pall; gloom, blight; threat. ❹ *she knew without any shadow of doubt* TRACE, scrap, shred, crumb, iota, scintilla, jot, whit, grain; *informal* smidgen, smidge, tad. ❺ *a shadow of a smile* TRACE, hint, suggestion, suspicion, ghost, glimmer. ❻ *he's a shadow of his former self* INFERIOR VERSION, poor imitation, apology, travesty; remnant. ❼ *the dog became her shadow* CONSTANT COMPANION, alter ego, second self; close friend, bosom friend, fidus Achates; *informal* Siamese twin.

▶ **verb** ❶ *the market is shadowed by the church* OVERSHADOW, shade; darken, dim. ❷ *he is shadowing a poacher* FOLLOW, trail, track, stalk, pursue, hunt; *informal* tail, keep tabs on.

shadowy ▶ **adjective** ❶ *a shadowy corridor* DARK, dim, gloomy, murky, crepuscular, shady, shaded; *poetic/literary* tenebrous. ❷ *a shadowy figure* INDISTINCT, hazy, indefinite, vague, nebulous, ill-defined, faint, blurred, blurry, unclear, indistinguishable, unrecognizable; ghostly, spectral, wraithlike.

–OPPOSITES bright, clear.

shady ▶ **adjective** ❶ *a shady garden* SHADED, shadowy, dim, dark; sheltered, screened, shrouded; leafy; *poetic/literary* bosky, tenebrous. ❷ (*informal*) *shady deals* SUSPICIOUS, suspect, questionable, dubious, doubtful, disreputable, untrustworthy, dishonest, dishonourable, devious, underhand, unscrupulous, irregular, unethical; *N. Amer.* snide; *informal* fishy, murky; *Brit. informal* dodgy; *Austral./NZ informal* shonky.

–OPPOSITES bright, honest.

shaft ▶ **noun** ❶ *the shaft of a golf club* POLE, shank, stick, rod, staff; handle, hilt, stem. ❷ *the shaft of a feather* QUILL; *Ornithology* rachis. ❸ *shafts of sunlight* RAY, beam, gleam, streak, finger. ❹ *he directs his shafts against her* CUTTING REMARK, barb, gibe, taunt; *informal* dig. ❺ *a ventilation shaft* MINESHAFT, tunnel, passage, pit, adit, downcast, upcast; borehole, bore; duct, well, flue, vent.

shaggy ▶ **adjective** HAIRY, bushy, thick, woolly; tangled, tousled, unkempt, dishevelled, untidy, matted; *formal* hirsute.

–OPPOSITES sleek.

shake ▶ **verb** ❶ *the whole building shook* VIBRATE, tremble, quiver, quake, shiver, shudder, judder, jiggle, wobble, rock, sway; convulse. ❷ *she shook the bottle* JIGGLE, joggle, agitate; *informal* waggle. ❸ *he shook his stick at them* BRANDISH, wave, flourish, swing, wield; *informal* waggle. ❹ *the look in his eyes really shook her* UPSET, distress, disturb, unsettle, disconcert, discompose, disquiet, unnerve, trouble, throw off balance, agitate, fluster; shock, alarm, frighten, scare, worry; *informal* rattle. ❺ *this will shake their confidence* WEAKEN, undermine, damage, impair, harm; reduce, diminish, decrease.

–OPPOSITES soothe, strengthen.

▶ **noun** ❶ *he gave his coat a shake* JIGGLE, joggle; *informal* waggle. ❷ *a shake of his fist* FLOURISH, brandish, wave. ❸ *it gives me the shakes* TREMORS, delirium tremens; *informal* DTs, jitters, willies, heebie-jeebies, yips; *Austral. informal* Joe Blakes.

■ **in two shakes (of a lamb's tail)** (*informal*). *See* IN A MOMENT at MOMENT.

■ **no great shakes** (*informal*) NOT VERY GOOD, unexceptional, unmemorable, forgettable, uninspired, uninteresting, indifferent, unimpressive, lacklustre; *informal* nothing to write home about, nothing special, not up to much.

■ **shake a leg** (*informal*). *See* HURRY verb sense 1.

■ **shake someone off** GET AWAY FROM, escape, elude, dodge, lose, leave behind, get rid of, give someone the slip, throw off the scent; *Brit. informal* get shot of.

■ **shake something off** RECOVER FROM, get over; get rid of, free oneself from; *Brit. informal* get shot of; *N. Amer. informal* shuck off.

■ **shake someone/something up** ❶ *the accident shook him up. See* SHAKE verb sense 4. ❷ *plans to shake up the legal profession* REORGANIZE, restructure, revolutionize, alter, change, transform, reform, overhaul.

shake-up ▶ **noun** (*informal*) REORGANIZATION, restructuring, reshuffle, change, overhaul, makeover; upheaval; *N. Amer. informal* shakedown.

shaky ▶ **adjective** ❶ *shaky legs* TREMBLING, shaking, tremulous, quivering, quivery, unsteady, wobbly, weak; tottering, tottery, teetering, doddery; *informal* trembly. ❷ *I feel a bit shaky* FAINT, dizzy, light-headed, giddy; weak, wobbly, quivery, groggy, muzzy; *informal* trembly, woozy. ❸ *a shaky table* UNSTEADY, unstable, wobbly, precarious, rocky, rickety, ramshackle; *Brit. informal* wonky. ❹ *the evidence is shaky* UNRELIABLE, untrustworthy, questionable, dubious, doubtful, tenuous, suspect, flimsy, weak, unsound, unsupported, unsubstantiated, unfounded; *informal* iffy; *Brit. informal* dodgy.

–OPPOSITES steady, stable, sound.

shallow ▶ **adjective** SUPERFICIAL, facile, simplistic, oversimplified; flimsy, insubstantial, lightweight, empty, trivial, trifling; surface, skin-deep; frivolous, foolish, silly.

–OPPOSITES profound.

sham ▶ noun ❶ *his tenderness had been a sham* PRETENCE, fake, act, fiction, simulation, fraud, feint, lie, counterfeit; humbug. ❷ *the doctor was a sham* CHARLATAN, fake, fraud, impostor, pretender; quack, mountebank; *informal* phoney.
▶ adjective *sham togetherness* FAKE, pretended, feigned, simulated, false, artificial, bogus, insincere, contrived, affected, make-believe, fictitious; imitation, mock, counterfeit, fraudulent; *informal* pretend, put-on, phoney, pseudo; *Brit. informal* cod.
– OPPOSITES genuine.
▶ verb ❶ *she shams indifference* FEIGN, fake, pretend, put on, simulate, affect. ❷ *was he ill or just shamming?* PRETEND, fake, dissemble; malinger; *informal* put it on; *Brit. informal* swing the lead.

shaman ▶ noun WITCH DOCTOR, medicine man/woman, healer, kahuna.

shamble ▶ verb SHUFFLE, drag one's feet, lumber, totter, dodder; hobble, limp.

shambles ▶ plural noun ❶ *we have to sort out this shambles* CHAOS, mess, muddle, confusion, disorder, havoc, mare's nest; *Brit. informal* dog's dinner/breakfast. ❷ *the room was a shambles* MESS, pigsty; *informal* disaster area; *Brit. informal* tip.

shambolic ▶ adjective (*Brit. informal*). *See* CHAOTIC.

shame ▶ noun ❶ *her face was scarlet with shame* HUMILIATION, mortification, chagrin, ignominy, embarrassment, indignity, abashment, discomfort. ❷ *I felt shame at telling a lie* GUILT, remorse, contrition, compunction. ❸ *he brought shame on the family* DISGRACE, dishonour, discredit, degradation, ignominy, disrepute, infamy, scandal, opprobrium, contempt; *dated* disesteem. ❹ *it's a shame she never married* PITY, misfortune, sad thing; bad luck; *informal* bummer, crime, sin.
– OPPOSITES pride, honour.
▶ verb ❶ *you shamed your family's name* DISGRACE, dishonour, discredit, degrade, debase; stigmatize, taint, sully, tarnish, besmirch, blacken, drag through the mud. ❷ *he was shamed in public* HUMILIATE, mortify, chagrin, embarrass, abash, chasten, humble, take down a peg or two, cut down to size; *informal* show up; *N. Amer. informal* make someone eat crow.
– OPPOSITES honour.
■ **put someone/something to shame** OUTSHINE, outclass, eclipse, surpass, excel, outstrip, outdo, put in the shade, upstage; *informal* run rings around, leave standing; *Brit. informal* knock spots off.

shamefaced ▶ adjective ASHAMED, abashed, sheepish, guilty, conscience-stricken, guilt-ridden, contrite, sorry, remorseful, repentant, penitent, regretful, rueful, apologetic; embarrassed, mortified, red-faced, chagrined, humiliated; *informal* with one's tail between one's legs.
– OPPOSITES unrepentant.

shameful ▶ adjective ❶ *shameful behaviour* DISGRACEFUL, deplorable, despicable, contemptible, dishonourable, discreditable, reprehensible, low, unworthy, ignoble, shabby; shocking, scandalous, outrageous, abominable, atrocious, appalling, vile, odious, heinous, egregious, loathsome, bad; inexcusable, unforgivable; *informal* low-down, hateful. ❷ *a shameful secret* EMBARRASSING, mortifying, humiliating, degrading, ignominious.
– OPPOSITES admirable.

shameless ▶ adjective FLAGRANT, blatant, barefaced, overt, brazen, brash, audacious, outrageous, undisguised, unconcealed, transparent; immodest, indecorous; unabashed, unashamed, unblushing, unrepentant.
– OPPOSITES modest.

shanty ▶ noun SHACK, hut, cabin, lean-to, shed; hovel; *Scottish* bothy, shieling.

shape ▶ noun ❶ *the shape of the dining table* FORM, appearance, configuration, formation, structure; figure, build, physique, body; contours, lines, outline, silhouette, profile. ❷ *a spirit in the shape of a fox* GUISE, likeness, semblance, form, appearance, image. ❸ *you're in pretty good shape* CONDITION, health, trim, fettle, order; *Brit. informal* nick.
– RELATED TERMS morpho-.
▶ verb ❶ *the metal is shaped into tools* FORM, fashion, make, mould, model, cast; sculpt, sculpture, carve, cut, whittle. ❷ *attitudes were shaped by his report* DETERMINE, form, fashion, mould, define, develop; influence, affect.
■ **shape up** ❶ *her work is shaping up nicely* IMPROVE, get better, progress, show promise; develop, take shape, come on, come along. ❷ *a regime to help you shape up* GET FIT, get into shape, tone up; slim, lose weight.
■ **take shape** BECOME CLEAR, become definite, become tangible, crystallize, come together, fall into place.

shapeless ▶ adjective ❶ *shapeless lumps* FORMLESS, amorphous, unformed, indefinite. ❷ *a shapeless dress* BAGGY, saggy, ill-fitting, sacklike, oversized, unshapely, formless.

shapely ▶ adjective WELL PROPORTIONED, clean-limbed, curvaceous, voluptuous, full-figured, Junoesque; attractive, sexy; *informal* curvy; *archaic* comely.

shard ▶ noun FRAGMENT, sliver, splinter, shiver, chip, piece, bit, particle.

share ▶ noun *her share of the profits* PORTION, part, division, quota, quantum, allowance, ration, allocation, measure, due; percentage, commission, dividend; helping, serving; *informal* cut, slice, rake-off; *Brit. informal* whack, divvy.
▶ verb ❶ *we share the bills* SPLIT, divide, go halves on; *informal* go fifty-fifty, go Dutch. ❷ *they shared*

out the peanuts APPORTION, divide up, allocate, portion out, ration out, parcel out, measure out; carve up; *Brit. informal* divvy up. ❸ *we all share in the learning process* PARTICIPATE IN, take part in, play a part in, be involved in, contribute to, have a hand in, partake in.

sharp ▶ **adjective** ❶ *a sharp knife* KEEN, razor-edged; sharpened, honed. ❷ *a sharp pain* EXCRUCIATING, agonizing, intense, stabbing, shooting, severe, acute, keen, fierce, searing; exquisite. ❸ *a sharp taste* TANGY, piquant, strong; ACIDIC, acid, sour, tart, pungent, acrid, bitter, acidulous. ❹ *a sharp cry of pain* LOUD, piercing, shrill, high-pitched, penetrating, harsh, strident, ear-splitting, deafening. ❺ *a sharp wind* COLD, chilly, chill, brisk, keen, penetrating, biting, icy, bitter, freezing, raw; *informal* nippy; *Brit. informal* parky. ❻ *sharp words* HARSH, bitter, cutting, scathing, caustic, barbed, trenchant, acrimonious, acerbic, sarcastic, sardonic, spiteful, venomous, malicious, vitriolic, vicious, hurtful, nasty, cruel, abrasive; *informal* bitchy, catty. ❼ *a sharp sense of loss* INTENSE, acute, keen, strong, bitter, fierce, heartfelt, overwhelming. ❽ *her nose is sharp* POINTED, tapering, tapered; spiky; *informal* pointy. ❾ *the lens brings it into sharp focus* DISTINCT, clear, crisp; stark, obvious, marked, definite, pronounced. ❿ *a sharp increase* SUDDEN, abrupt, rapid; steep, precipitous. ⓫ *a sharp corner* HAIRPIN, tight. ⓬ *a sharp drop* STEEP, sheer, abrupt, precipitous, vertical. ⓭ *sharp eyes* KEEN, perceptive, observant, acute, beady, hawklike. ⓮ *she was sharp and witty* PERCEPTIVE, percipient, perspicacious, incisive, sensitive, keen, acute, quick-witted, clever, shrewd, canny, astute, intelligent, intuitive, bright, alert, smart, quick off the mark, insightful, knowing; *informal* on the ball, quick on the uptake, savvy; *Brit. informal* suss; *Scottish & N. English informal* pawky; *N. Amer. informal* heads-up. ⓯ (*informal*) *a sharp suit* SMART, stylish, fashionable, chic, modish, elegant; *informal* trendy, cool, snazzy, classy, flash, snappy, natty, nifty; *N. Amer. informal* fly, spiffy.
–OPPOSITES blunt, mild, sweet, soft, kind, rounded, indistinct, gradual, slow, weak, stupid, naive, untidy.
▶ **adverb** ❶ *nine o'clock sharp* PRECISELY, exactly, on the dot; promptly, prompt, punctually, dead on; *informal* on the nose; *N. Amer. informal* on the button. ❷ *the recession pulled people up sharp* ABRUPTLY, suddenly, sharply, unexpectedly.
–OPPOSITES roughly.

sharpen ▶ **verb** ❶ *sharpen the carving knife* HONE, whet, strop, grind, file. ❷ *the players are sharpening up their skills* IMPROVE, brush up, polish up, better, enhance; hone, fine-tune, perfect.

sharp-eyed ▶ **adjective** OBSERVANT, perceptive, eagle-eyed, hawk-eyed, keen-eyed, gimlet-eyed; watchful, vigilant, alert, on the lookout; *informal* beady-eyed.

shatter ▶ **verb** ❶ *the glasses shattered* SMASH, break, splinter, crack, fracture, fragment, disintegrate, shiver; *informal* bust. ❷ *the announcement shattered their hopes* DESTROY, wreck, ruin, dash, crush, devastate, demolish, torpedo, scotch; *informal* put the kibosh on, banjax, do for, put paid to; *Brit. informal* scupper. ❸ *we were shattered by the news* DEVASTATE, shock, stun, daze, traumatize, crush, distress; *informal* knock sideways; *Brit. informal* knock for six.

shattered ▶ **adjective** ❶ *he was shattered by the reviews* DEVASTATED, shocked, stunned, dazed, traumatized, crushed; heartbroken. ❷ (*informal*) *I feel too shattered to move. See* EXHAUSTED sense 1.
–OPPOSITES thrilled.

shave ▶ **verb** ❶ *he shaved his beard* CUT OFF, snip off; crop, trim, barber. ❷ *shave off excess wood* PLANE, pare, whittle, scrape. ❸ *shave parmesan over the top* GRATE, shred. ❹ *he shaved the MP's majority to 2,000* REDUCE, cut, lessen, decrease, pare down, shrink, slim down. ❺ *his shot shaved the post* GRAZE, brush, touch, glance off, kiss.

sheaf ▶ **noun** BUNDLE, bunch, stack, pile, heap, mass; *Brit. informal* wodge.

sheath ▶ **noun** ❶ *put the sword in its sheath* SCABBARD, case. ❷ *the wire has a plastic sheath* COVERING, cover, case, casing, envelope, sleeve, wrapper, capsule. ❸ *a contraceptive sheath. See* CONDOM.

shed¹ ▶ **noun** *the rabbit lives in the shed* HUT, lean-to, outhouse, outbuilding; shack; potting shed, woodshed; *Brit.* lock-up.

shed² ▶ **verb** ❶ *the trees shed their leaves* DROP, scatter, spill. ❷ *the caterpillar shed its skin* SLOUGH OFF, cast off, moult; *technical* exuviate. ❸ *we shed our jackets* TAKE OFF, remove, shrug off, discard, doff, climb out of, slip out of, divest oneself of; *Brit. informal* peel off. ❹ *much blood has been shed* SPILL, discharge. ❺ *the firm is to shed ten workers* MAKE REDUNDANT, dismiss, let go, discharge, get rid of, discard; *informal* sack, fire, give someone their marching orders, send packing, give someone the push, boot out. ❻ *they must shed their illusions* DISCARD, get rid of, dispose of, do away with, drop, abandon, jettison, scrap, cast aside, dump, reject, repudiate; *informal* ditch, junk, get shut of; *Brit. informal* get shot of. ❼ *the moon shed a watery light* CAST, radiate, diffuse, disperse, give out.
–OPPOSITES don, hire, keep.
■ **shed tears** WEEP, cry, sob; lament, grieve, mourn; *Scottish* greet; *informal* blub, blubber, boohoo.

sheen ▶ **noun** SHINE, lustre, gloss, patina, shininess, burnish, polish, shimmer, brilliance, radiance.

sheep ▶ **noun** ram, ewe, lamb, wether, bellwether, tup; *Austral. informal* jumbuck, woolly.
–RELATED TERMS ovine.

sheepish ▶ adjective EMBARRASSED, uncomfortable, hangdog, self-conscious; shamefaced, ashamed, abashed, mortified, chastened, remorseful, contrite, apologetic, rueful, regretful, penitent, repentant.

sheer[1] ▶ adjective ❶ *the sheer audacity of the plan* UTTER, complete, absolute, total, pure, downright, out-and-out, arrant, thorough, thoroughgoing, patent, veritable, unmitigated, plain; *Austral./NZ informal* fair. ❷ *a sheer drop* PRECIPITOUS, steep, vertical, perpendicular, abrupt, bluff, sharp. ❸ *a sheer dress* DIAPHANOUS, gauzy, filmy, floaty, gossamer, thin, translucent, transparent, see-through, insubstantial.
– OPPOSITES gradual, thick.

sheer[2] ▶ verb ❶ *the boat sheered off along the coast* SWERVE, veer, slew, skew, swing, change course. ❷ *her mind sheered away from his image* TURN AWAY, flinch, recoil, shy away; avoid.

sheet ▶ noun ❶ *she changed the sheets* BED LINEN, linen, bedclothes. ❷ *a sheet of ice* LAYER, stratum, covering, blanket, coating, coat, film, skin. ❸ *a sheet of glass* PANE, panel, piece, plate; slab. ❹ *she put a fresh sheet in the typewriter* PIECE OF PAPER, leaf, page, folio. ❺ *a sheet of water* EXPANSE, area, stretch, sweep.

shelf ▶ noun ❶ *the plant on the shelf* LEDGE, sill, bracket, rack; mantelpiece; shelving. ❷ *the waters above the shelf* SANDBANK, sandbar, bank, bar, reef, shoal.
■ **on the shelf** UNMARRIED, single, unattached; lonely, unloved, neglected.

shell ▶ noun ❶ *a crab shell* CARAPACE, exterior; armour; *Zoology* exoskeleton. ❷ *peanut shells* POD, husk, hull, casing, case, covering, integument; *N. Amer.* shuck. ❸ *shells passing overhead* PROJECTILE, bomb, explosive; grenade; bullet, cartridge. ❹ *the metal shell of the car* FRAMEWORK, frame, chassis, skeleton; hull, exterior.
– RELATED TERMS conchoidal, concho-.
▶ verb ❶ *they were shelling peas* HULL, pod, husk; *N. Amer.* shuck. ❷ *rebel artillery shelled the city* BOMBARD, fire on, shoot at, attack, bomb, blitz, strafe.
■ **shell something out** (*informal*). *See* PAY verb sense 2.

shellfish ▶ noun CRUSTACEAN, bivalve, mollusc.

shelter ▶ noun ❶ *the trees provide shelter for animals* PROTECTION, cover, screening, shade; safety, security, refuge, sanctuary, asylum. ❷ *a shelter for abandoned cats* SANCTUARY, refuge, home, haven, safe house; harbour, port in a storm.
– OPPOSITES exposure.
▶ verb ❶ *the hut sheltered him from the wind* PROTECT, shield, screen, cover, shade, save, safeguard, preserve, defend, cushion, guard, insulate. ❷ *the anchorage where the convoy sheltered* TAKE SHELTER, take refuge, seek sanctuary, take cover; *informal* hole up.
– OPPOSITES expose.

sheltered ▶ adjective ❶ *a sheltered stretch of water* PROTECTED, screened, shielded, covered; shady; cosy. ❷ *she led a sheltered life* SECLUDED, cloistered, isolated, protected, withdrawn, sequestered, reclusive; privileged, secure, safe, quiet.

shelve ▶ verb POSTPONE, put off, delay, defer, put back, reschedule, hold over/off, put to one side, suspend, stay, keep in abeyance, mothball; abandon, drop, give up, stop, cancel, jettison, axe; *N. Amer.* put over, table, take a rain check on; *informal* put on ice, put on the back burner, ditch, dump, junk.
– OPPOSITES execute.

shepherd ▶ noun *he worked as a shepherd* shepherdess, herdsman, herder, sheepman.
▶ verb *we shepherded them away* USHER, steer, herd, lead, take, escort, guide, conduct, marshal, walk; show, see, chaperone.

shield ▶ noun ❶ *he used his shield to fend off blows* *Heraldry* escutcheon; *historical* buckler, target; *archaic* targe. ❷ *a shield against dirt* PROTECTION, guard, defence, cover, screen, security, shelter, safeguard, protector.
▶ verb *he shielded his eyes* PROTECT, cover, screen, shade; save, safeguard, preserve, defend, secure, guard; cushion, insulate.
– OPPOSITES expose.

shift ▶ verb ❶ *he shifted some chairs* MOVE, carry, transfer, transport, convey, lug, haul, fetch, switch, relocate, reposition, rearrange; *informal* cart. ❷ *she shifted her position* CHANGE, alter, adjust, vary; modify, revise, reverse, retract; do a U-turn. ❸ *the cargo has shifted* MOVE, slide, slip, be displaced. ❹ *the wind shifted* VEER, alter, change, turn, swing round. ❺ (*Brit.*) *this brush really shifts the dirt* GET RID OF, remove, get off, budge, lift, expunge.
– OPPOSITES keep.
▶ noun ❶ *the southward shift of people* MOVEMENT, move, transference, transport, transposition, relocation. ❷ *a shift in public opinion* CHANGE, alteration, adjustment, amendment, variation, modification, revision, reversal, retraction, U-turn; *Brit.* about-turn. ❸ *they worked three shifts* STINT, stretch, spell of work. ❹ *the night shift went home* WORKERS, crew, gang, team, squad, patrol. ❺ (*archaic*) *dubious shifts to make money* STRATAGEM, scheme, subterfuge, expedient, dodge, trick, ruse, wile, strategy, device, plan.
■ **shift for oneself** COPE, manage, survive, make it, fend for oneself, take care of oneself, make do, get by/along, scrape by/along, muddle through; stand on one's own two feet; *informal* make out.

shiftless ▶ adjective LAZY, idle, indolent, slothful, lethargic, lackadaisical; spiritless, apathetic, feckless, good-for-nothing, worthless; unambitious, unenterprising.

shifty ▶ adjective (*informal*) DEVIOUS, evasive, slippery, duplicitous, false, deceitful, underhand,

untrustworthy, dishonest, shady, wily, crafty, tricky, sneaky, treacherous, artful, sly, scheming; *N. Amer.* snide; *Brit. informal* dodgy; *Austral./NZ informal* shonky.
– OPPOSITES honest.

shilly-shally ▶ **verb** DITHER, be indecisive, be irresolute, vacillate, waver, hesitate, blow hot and cold, falter, drag one's feet; *Brit.* haver, hum and haw; *Scottish* swither; *informal* dilly-dally.

shimmer ▶ **verb** *the lake shimmered* GLINT, glisten, twinkle, sparkle, flash, scintillate, gleam, glow, glimmer, glitter, wink; *poetic/literary* coruscate.
▶ **noun** *the shimmer of lights from the traffic* GLINT, twinkle, sparkle, flash, gleam, glow, glimmer, lustre, glitter; *poetic/literary* coruscation.

shin ▶ **verb** CLIMB, clamber, scramble, swarm, shoot, go; mount, ascend, scale; descend; *N. Amer.* shinny.

shine ▶ **verb** ❶ *the sun shone* EMIT LIGHT, beam, radiate, gleam, glow, glint, glimmer, sparkle, twinkle, glitter, glisten, shimmer, flash, flare, glare, fluoresce, luminesce; *poetic/literary* glister, coruscate. ❷ *she shone his shoes* POLISH, burnish, buff, wax, gloss, rub up. ❸ *they shone at university* EXCEL, be outstanding, be brilliant, be successful, stand out.
▶ **noun** ❶ *the shine of the moon on her face* LIGHT, brightness, gleam, glow, glint, glimmer, sparkle, twinkle, glitter, glisten, shimmer, beam, glare, radiance, illumination, luminescence, luminosity, incandescence. ❷ *linseed oil restores the shine* POLISH, burnish, gleam, gloss, lustre, sheen, patina.

shining ▶ **adjective** ❶ *a shining expanse of water* GLEAMING, bright, brilliant, illuminated, lustrous, glowing, glinting, sparkling, twinkling, glittering, glistening, shimmering, dazzling, luminous, luminescent, incandescent; *poetic/literary* glistering, coruscating. ❷ *a shining face* GLOWING, beaming, radiant, happy. ❸ *shining chromium tubes* SHINY, bright, polished, gleaming, glossy, glassy, sheeny, lustrous.
■ **a shining example** PARAGON, model, epitome, archetype, ideal, exemplar, nonpareil, paradigm, quintessence, the crème de la crème, the beau idéal, acme, jewel, flower, treasure; *informal* one in a million, the bee's knees.

shiny ▶ **adjective** GLOSSY, glassy, bright, polished, gleaming, satiny, sheeny, lustrous.
– OPPOSITES matt.

ship ▶ **noun** BOAT, vessel, craft.
– RELATED TERMS marine, maritime, naval.

shirk ▶ **verb** ❶ *she didn't shirk any task* EVADE, dodge, avoid, get out of, sidestep, shrink from, shun, slide out of, skip, miss; neglect; *informal* duck (out of), cop out of; *Brit. informal* skive off; *N. Amer. informal* cut; *Austral./NZ informal* duck-shove. ❷ *no one shirked* AVOID ONE'S DUTY, be remiss, be negligent, play truant; *Brit. informal* skive (off), swing the lead, scrimshank, slack off; *N. Amer. informal* goof off, play hookey.

shirker ▶ **noun** DODGER, truant, absentee, layabout, loafer, idler; *informal* slacker; *Brit. informal* skiver, scrimshanker; *archaic* shirk.

shiver[1] ▶ **verb** *she was shivering with fear* TREMBLE, quiver, shake, shudder, quaver, quake.
▶ **noun** *she gave a shiver as the door opened* TREMBLE, quiver, shake, shudder, quaver, quake, tremor, twitch.

shiver[2] ▶ **noun** *a shiver of glass* SPLINTER, sliver, shard, fragment, chip, shaving, smithereen, particle, bit, piece.
▶ **verb** *the window shivered into thousands of pieces* SHATTER, splinter, smash, fragment, crack, break.

shivery ▶ **adjective** TREMBLING, trembly, quivery, shaky, shuddering, shuddery, quavery, quaking; cold, chilly.

shoal ▶ **noun** SANDBANK, bank, mudbank, bar, sandbar, tombolo, shelf, cay.

shock[1] ▶ **noun** ❶ *the news came as a shock* BLOW, upset, disturbance; surprise, revelation, a bolt from the blue, thunderbolt, bombshell, rude awakening, eye-opener; *informal* whammy. ❷ *you gave me a shock* FRIGHT, scare, jolt, start; *informal* turn. ❸ *she was suffering from shock* TRAUMA, traumatism, prostration; collapse, breakdown. ❹ *the first shock of the earthquake* VIBRATION, reverberation, shake, jolt, jar, jerk; impact, blow.
▶ **verb** *the murder shocked the nation* APPAL, horrify, outrage, revolt, disgust, nauseate, sicken; traumatize, distress, upset, disturb, disquiet, unsettle; stun, rock, stagger, astound, astonish, amaze, startle, surprise, dumbfound, shake, take aback, throw, unnerve.

shock[2] ▶ **noun** *a shock of red hair* MASS, mane, mop, thatch, head, crop, bush, frizz, tangle, cascade, halo.

shocking ▶ **adjective** APPALLING, horrifying, horrific, dreadful, awful, frightful, terrible; scandalous, outrageous, disgraceful, vile, abominable, abhorrent, atrocious; odious, repugnant, disgusting, nauseating, sickening, loathsome; distressing, upsetting, disturbing, disquieting, unsettling; staggering, amazing, astonishing, startling, surprising.

shoddy ▶ **adjective** ❶ *shoddy goods* POOR-QUALITY, inferior, second-rate, third-rate, cheap, cheapjack, trashy, jerry-built; *informal* tacky, rubbishy, junky; *Brit. informal* duff, rubbish. ❷ *shoddy workmanship* CARELESS, slapdash, sloppy, slipshod, scrappy, crude; negligent, cursory.
– OPPOSITES quality, careful.

shoemaker ▶ **noun** COBBLER, bootmaker, clogger; *Scottish & N. English* souter.

shoot ▶ **verb** ❶ *they shot him in the street* GUN

DOWN, mow down, hit, wound, injure; put a bullet in, pick off, bag, fell, kill; *informal* pot, blast, pump full of lead, plug. ❷ *they shot at the enemy* FIRE, open fire, aim, snipe, let fly; bombard, shell. ❸ *faster than a gun can shoot bullets* DISCHARGE, fire, launch, loose off, let fly, emit. ❹ *a car shot past* RACE, speed, flash, dash, dart, rush, hurtle, streak, whizz, go like lightning, go hell for leather, zoom, charge; career, sweep, fly, wing; *informal* belt, scoot, scorch, tear, zip, whip, step on it, burn rubber; *Brit. informal* bomb, bucket, shift; *N. Amer. informal* clip, hightail it, barrel. ❺ *the plant failed to shoot* SPROUT, bud, burgeon, germinate. ❻ *the film was shot in Tunisia* FILM, photograph, take, snap, capture, record; televise, video.

▶ **noun** *nip off the new shoots* SPROUT, bud, offshoot, scion, sucker, spear, runner, tendril, sprig.

shop ▶ **noun** ❶ *a shop selling clothes* STORE, (retail) outlet, boutique, cash and carry, emporium, department store, supermarket, hypermarket, superstore, chain store, concession, market, mart, trading post; *N. Amer.* minimart. ❷ *he works in the machine shop* WORKSHOP, workroom, plant, factory, works, industrial unit, mill, foundry, yard.

▶ **verb** ❶ *he was shopping for spices* GO SHOPPING, go to the shops; buy, purchase, get, acquire, obtain, pick up, snap up, procure, stock up on; *humorous* indulge in retail therapy. ❷ (*Brit. informal*) *he shopped his fellow robbers.* See BETRAY sense 1.

shopkeeper ▶ **noun** SHOP-OWNER, shop manager, vendor, retailer, dealer, seller, trader, wholesaler, salesperson, tradesman, distributor; *N. Amer.* storekeeper.

shopper ▶ **noun** BUYER, purchaser, customer, consumer, client, patron; *Law* vendee.

shopping centre ▶ **noun** SHOPPING PRECINCT, (shopping) mall, (shopping) arcade, galleria, parade; marketplace, mart; *N. Amer.* plaza.

shore[1] ▶ **noun** *he swam out from the shore* SEASHORE, beach, foreshore, sand(s), shoreline, waterside, front, coast, seaboard; *poetic/literary* strand.

– RELATED TERMS littoral.

shore[2] ▶ **verb** *we had to shore up the building* PROP UP, hold up, bolster, support, brace, buttress, strengthen, fortify, reinforce, underpin.

short ▶ **adjective** ❶ *a short piece of string* SMALL, little, tiny; *informal* teeny. ❷ *short people* SMALL, little, petite, tiny, diminutive, stubby, elfin, dwarfish, midget, pygmy, Lilliputian, minuscule, miniature; *Scottish* wee; *informal* pint-sized, teeny, knee-high to a grasshopper. ❸ *a short report* CONCISE, brief, succinct, compact, summary, economical, crisp, pithy, epigrammatic, laconic, thumbnail, abridged, abbreviated, condensed, synoptic, summarized, contracted, truncated; *formal* compendious. ❹ *a short time* BRIEF, momentary, temporary, short-lived, impermanent, cursory, fleeting, passing, fugitive, lightning, transitory, transient, ephemeral, quick. ❺ *money is a bit short* SCARCE, in short supply, scant, meagre, sparse, insufficient, deficient, inadequate, lacking, wanting. ❻ *he was rather short with her* CURT, sharp, abrupt, blunt, brusque, terse, offhand, gruff, surly, testy, rude, uncivil; *informal* snappy.

– OPPOSITES long, tall, plentiful, courteous.

▶ **adverb** *she stopped short* ABRUPTLY, suddenly, sharply, all of a sudden, all at once, unexpectedly, without warning, out of the blue.

■ **in short** BRIEFLY, in a word, in a nutshell, in precis, in essence, to come to the point; in conclusion, in summary, to sum up.

■ **short of** ❶ *we are short of nurses* DEFICIENT IN, lacking, wanting, in need of, low on, short on, missing; *informal* strapped for, pushed for, minus. ❷ *short of searching everyone, there is nothing we can do* APART FROM, other than, aside from, besides, except (for), excepting, without, excluding, not counting, save (for).

shortage ▶ **noun** SCARCITY, sparseness, sparsity, dearth, paucity, poverty, insufficiency, deficiency, inadequacy, famine, lack, want, deficit, shortfall, rarity.

– OPPOSITES abundance.

shortcoming ▶ **noun** DEFECT, fault, flaw, imperfection, deficiency, limitation, failing, drawback, weakness, weak point, foible, frailty, vice.

– OPPOSITES strength.

shorten ▶ **verb** MAKE SHORTER, abbreviate, abridge, condense, precis, synopsize, contract, compress, reduce, shrink, diminish, cut (down); dock, trim, crop, pare down, prune; curtail, truncate.

– OPPOSITES extend.

short-lived ▶ **adjective** BRIEF, short, momentary, temporary, impermanent, cursory, fleeting, passing, fugitive, lightning, transitory, transient, ephemeral, quick.

shortly ▶ **adverb** ❶ *she will be with you shortly* SOON, presently, in a little while, at any moment, in a minute, in next to no time, before long, by and by; *N. Amer.* momentarily; *informal* anon, any time now, pretty soon, before one can say Jack Robinson, in a jiffy; *Brit. informal* in a mo, sharpish; *dated* directly. ❷ *'I know,' he replied shortly* CURTLY, sharply, abruptly, bluntly, brusquely, tersely, gruffly, snappily, testily, rudely.

short-sighted ▶ **adjective** ❶ *I'm a little short-sighted* MYOPIC, near-sighted; *informal* as blind as a bat. ❷ *short-sighted critics* NARROW-MINDED, unimaginative, improvident, small-minded, insular, parochial, provincial.

– OPPOSITES long-sighted, imaginative.

short-staffed ▶ **adjective** UNDERSTAFFED, short-handed, undermanned, below strength.

short-tempered ▶ **adjective** IRRITABLE, irascible, hot-tempered, quick-tempered, snappish, fiery, touchy, volatile; cross, crabby, crotchety, cantankerous, grumpy, ill-tempered, bad-tempered, testy, tetchy, prickly, choleric; *informal* snappy, chippy, grouchy, cranky, on a short fuse; *Brit. informal* narky, ratty, eggy, like a bear with a sore head; *N. Amer. informal* soreheaded.
–OPPOSITES placid.

shot[1] ▶ **noun** ❶ *a shot rang out* report of a gun, crack, bang, blast; (**shots**) gunfire. ❷ *the cannon have run out of shot* BULLETS, cannonballs, pellets, ammunition. ❸ *a winning shot* STROKE, hit, strike; kick, throw, pitch, lob. ❹ *Mike was an excellent shot* MARKSMAN, markswoman, shooter. ❺ *a shot of us on holiday* PHOTOGRAPH, photo, snap, snapshot, picture, print, slide, still; *Brit.* enprint. ❻ (*informal*) *it's nice to get a shot at driving* ATTEMPT, try; turn, chance, opportunity; *informal* go, stab, crack, bash; *formal* essay. ❼ *tetanus shots* INJECTION, inoculation, immunization, vaccination, booster; *informal* jab.
■ **a shot in the arm** (*informal*) BOOST, fillip, tonic, stimulus, spur, impetus, encouragement.
■ **a shot in the dark** (WILD) GUESS, surmise, supposition, conjecture, speculation.
■ **like a shot** (*informal*) WITHOUT HESITATION, unhesitatingly, eagerly, enthusiastically; immediately, at once, right away/now, straight away, instantly, instantaneously, without delay; *informal* in/like a flash, before one can say Jack Robinson.
■ **not by a long shot** BY NO (MANNER OF) MEANS, not at all, in no way, certainly not, absolutely not, definitely not; *Brit.* not by a long chalk.

shot[2] ▶ **adjective** *shot silk* VARIEGATED, mottled; multicoloured, varicoloured; iridescent, opalescent.

shoulder ▶ **verb** ❶ *Britain shouldered the primary responsibility* TAKE ON (ONESELF), undertake, accept, assume; bear, carry. ❷ *another lad shouldered him aside* PUSH, shove, thrust, jostle, force, bulldoze, bundle.
■ **give someone the cold shoulder** SNUB, shun, cold-shoulder, ignore, cut (dead), rebuff, spurn, ostracize; *informal* give someone the brush-off, freeze out; *Brit. informal* send to Coventry; *N. Amer. informal* give someone the brush.
■ **put one's shoulder to the wheel** GET (DOWN) TO WORK, apply oneself, set to work, buckle down, roll up one's sleeves; work hard, be diligent, be industrious, exert oneself.
■ **shoulder to shoulder** ❶ *the regiment lined up shoulder to shoulder* SIDE BY SIDE, abreast, alongside (each other). ❷ *he fought shoulder to shoulder with the others* UNITED, (working) together, jointly, in partnership, in collaboration, in cooperation, side by side, in alliance.

shout ▶ **verb** *'Help,' he shouted* YELL, cry (out), call (out), roar, howl, bellow, bawl, call at the top of one's voice, clamour, shriek, scream; raise one's voice, vociferate; *informal* holler.
–OPPOSITES whisper.
▶ **noun** *a shout of pain* YELL, cry, call, roar, howl, bellow, bawl, clamour, vociferation, shriek, scream; *informal* holler.

shove ▶ **verb** ❶ *she shoved him back into the chair* PUSH, thrust, propel, drive, force, ram, knock, elbow, shoulder; jostle, bundle, hustle, manhandle. ❷ *she shoved past him* PUSH (ONE'S WAY), force one's way, barge (one's way), elbow (one's way), shoulder one's way.
▶ **noun** *a hefty shove* PUSH, thrust, bump, jolt.
■ **shove off** (*informal*) *shove off!* GO AWAY, get out (of my sight); get going, take oneself off, be off (with you), shoo; *informal* scram, make yourself scarce, be on your way, beat it, get lost, push off, buzz off, clear off, go (and) jump in the lake; *Brit. informal* hop it, bog off, naff off; *N. Amer. informal* bug off, haul off, take a hike; *Austral. informal* nick off; *Austral./NZ informal* rack off; *poetic/literary* begone.

shovel ▶ **noun** *a pick and shovel* SPADE; *Austral./NZ* banjo.
▶ **verb** *shovelling snow* SCOOP (UP), dig, excavate.

show ▶ **verb** ❶ *the stitches do not show* BE VISIBLE, be seen, be in view, be obvious. ❷ *he wouldn't show the picture* DISPLAY, exhibit, put on show/display, put on view, parade, uncover, reveal. ❸ *Frank showed his frustration* MANIFEST, exhibit, reveal, convey, communicate, make known; express, proclaim, make plain, make obvious, disclose, betray; *formal* evince. ❹ *I'll show you how to make a daisy chain* DEMONSTRATE, explain, describe, illustrate; teach, instruct, give instructions. ❺ *recent events show this to be true* PROVE, demonstrate, confirm, show beyond doubt; substantiate, corroborate, verify, establish, attest, certify, testify, bear out; *formal* evince. ❻ *a young woman showed them to their seats* ESCORT, accompany, take, conduct, lead, usher, guide, direct, steer, shepherd. ❼ (*informal*) *they never showed* APPEAR, arrive, come, get here/there, put in an appearance, materialize, turn up; *informal* show up.
–OPPOSITES conceal.
▶ **noun** ❶ *a spectacular show of bluebells* DISPLAY, array, exhibition, presentation, exposition, spectacle. ❷ *the motor show* EXHIBITION, exposition, fair, extravaganza, spectacle; *N. Amer.* exhibit. ❸ *they took in a show* (THEATRICAL) PERFORMANCE, musical, play. ❹ *she's only doing it for show* APPEARANCE, display, impression, ostentation, image. ❺ *Drew made a show of looking busy* PRETENCE, outward appearance, (false) front, guise, semblance, pose, parade. ❻ (*informal*) *I don't run the show* UNDERTAKING, affair, operation, proceedings, enterprise, business, venture.
■ **show off** (*informal*) BEHAVE AFFECTEDLY, put on airs, put on an act, swagger around, swank, strut, strike an attitude, posture; draw atten-

tion to oneself; *N. Amer. informal* cop an attitude.

■ **show something off** DISPLAY, show to advantage, exhibit, demonstrate, parade, draw attention to, flaunt.

■ **show up** ❶ *cancers show up on X-rays* BE VISIBLE, be obvious, be seen, be revealed. ❷ (*informal*) *only two waitresses showed up. See* SHOW verb sense 7.

■ **show someone/something up** ❶ *the sun showed up the shabbiness of the room* EXPOSE, reveal, make visible, make obvious, highlight. ❷ (*informal*) *they showed him up in front of his friends. See* HUMILIATE.

showdown ▶ noun CONFRONTATION, clash, face-off.

shower ▶ noun ❶ *a shower of rain* (LIGHT) FALL, drizzle, sprinkling, mizzle. ❷ *a shower of arrows* VOLLEY, hail, salvo, bombardment, barrage, fusillade, cannonade. ❸ *a shower of awards* AVALANCHE, deluge, flood, spate, flurry; profusion, abundance, plethora.

▶ verb ❶ *confetti showered down on us* RAIN, fall, hail. ❷ *she showered them with gifts* DELUGE, flood, inundate, swamp, engulf; overwhelm, overload, snow under. ❸ *showering honours on his cronies* LAVISH, heap, bestow freely.

showing ▶ noun ❶ *another showing of the series* PRESENTATION, broadcast, airing, televising. ❷ *the party's present showing* PERFORMANCE, (track) record, results, success, achievement.

showman ▶ noun ❶ *a travelling showman* IMPRESARIO, stage manager; ringmaster, host, compère, master of ceremonies, MC; presenter; *N. Amer. informal* emcee. ❷ *he is a great showman* ENTERTAINER, performer, virtuoso.

show-off ▶ noun (*informal*) EXHIBITIONIST, extrovert, poser, poseur, peacock, swaggerer, self-publicist; *informal* pseud.

showy ▶ adjective OSTENTATIOUS, conspicuous, pretentious, flamboyant, gaudy, garish, brash, vulgar, loud, extravagant, fancy, ornate, overelaborate, kitsch; *informal* flash, flashy, glitzy, ritzy, swanky; *N. Amer. informal* superfly.

– OPPOSITES restrained.

shred ▶ noun ❶ *her dress was torn to shreds* TATTER, scrap, strip, ribbon, rag, fragment, sliver, (tiny) bit/piece. ❷ *not a shred of evidence* SCRAP, bit, speck, iota, particle, ounce, whit, jot, crumb, morsel, fragment, grain, drop, trace, scintilla, spot; *informal* smidgen.

▶ verb *shredding vegetables* CHOP FINELY, cut up, tear up, grate, mince, macerate, grind.

shrew ▶ noun VIRAGO, dragon, termagant, fishwife, witch, tartar, hag; *informal* battleaxe, old bag, old bat; *archaic* scold.

shrewd ▶ adjective ASTUTE, sharp-witted, sharp, smart, acute, intelligent, clever, canny, perceptive, perspicacious, sagacious, wise; *informal* on the ball, savvy; *N. Amer. informal* heads-up; *formal* sapient.

– OPPOSITES stupid.

shrewdness ▶ noun ASTUTENESS, sharp-wittedness, acuteness, acumen, acuity, intelligence, cleverness, smartness, wit, canniness, common sense, discernment, insight, understanding, perception, perceptiveness, perspicacity, perspicaciousness, discrimination, sagacity, sageness; *informal* nous, horse sense, savvy; *formal* sapience.

shrewish ▶ adjective BAD-TEMPERED, quarrelsome, spiteful, sharp-tongued, scolding, nagging; venomous, rancorous, bitchy.

shriek ▶ verb *she shrieked with laughter* SCREAM, screech, squeal, squawk, roar, howl, shout, yelp; *informal* holler.

▶ noun *a shriek of laughter* SCREAM, screech, squeal, squawk, roar, howl, shout, yelp; *informal* holler.

shrill ▶ adjective HIGH-PITCHED, piercing, high, sharp, ear-piercing, ear-splitting, penetrating, screeching, shrieking, screechy.

shrine ▶ noun ❶ *the shrine of St James* HOLY PLACE, temple, church, chapel, tabernacle, sanctuary, sanctum. ❷ *a shrine to the Beatles* MEMORIAL, monument.

shrink ▶ verb ❶ *the number of competitors shrank* GET SMALLER, become/grow smaller, contract, diminish, lessen, reduce, decrease, dwindle, decline, fall off, drop off. ❷ *he shrank back against the wall* DRAW BACK, recoil, back away, retreat, withdraw, cringe, cower, quail. ❸ *he doesn't shrink from naming names* RECOIL, shy away, demur, flinch, have scruples, have misgivings, have qualms, be loath, be reluctant, be unwilling, be averse, fight shy of, be hesitant, be afraid, hesitate, baulk at; *archaic* disrelish something.

– OPPOSITES expand, increase.

shrivel ▶ verb WITHER, shrink; wilt; dry up, desiccate, dehydrate, parch, frazzle.

shroud ▶ noun ❶ *the Turin Shroud* WINDING SHEET; *historical* cerements. ❷ *a shroud of mist | a shroud of secrecy* COVERING, cover, cloak, mantle, blanket, layer, cloud, veil.

▶ verb *a mist shrouded the jetties* COVER, envelop, veil, cloak, blanket, screen, conceal, hide, mask, obscure; *poetic/literary* enshroud.

shrub ▶ noun BUSH, woody plant.

shrug

■ **shrug something off** DISREGARD, dismiss, take no notice of, ignore, pay no heed to, play down, make light of.

shudder ▶ verb *she shuddered at the thought* SHAKE, shiver, tremble, quiver, vibrate, palpitate.

▶ noun *a shudder racked his body* SHAKE, shiver, tremor, tremble, trembling, quiver, quivering, vibration, palpitation.

shuffle ▶ verb ❶ *they shuffled along the passage* SHAMBLE, drag one's feet, totter, dodder. ❷ *she shuffled her feet* SCRAPE, drag, scuffle, scuff. ❸ *he* *shuffled the cards* MIX (UP), mingle, rearrange, jumble.

shun ▶ **noun** AVOID, evade, eschew, steer clear of, shy away from, fight shy of, keep one's distance from, give a wide berth to, have nothing to do with; snub, give someone the cold shoulder, cold-shoulder, ignore, cut (dead), look right through; reject, rebuff, spurn, ostracize; *informal* give someone the brush-off, freeze out, stiff-arm; *Brit. informal* send to Coventry; *N. Amer. informal* give someone the bum's rush, give someone the brush.
– OPPOSITES welcome.

shut ▶ **verb** *please shut the door* CLOSE, pull/push to, slam, fasten; put the lid on, bar, lock, secure.
– OPPOSITES open, unlock.
■ **shut down** CEASE ACTIVITY, close (down), cease operating, cease trading, be shut (down); *informal* fold.
■ **shut someone/something in** CONFINE, enclose, impound, shut up, pen (in/up), fence in, immure, lock up/in, cage, imprison, intern, incarcerate; *N. Amer.* corral.
■ **shut someone/something out** ❶ *he shut me out of the house* LOCK OUT, keep out, refuse entrance to. ❷ *she shut out the memories* BLOCK, suppress. ❸ *the bamboo shut out the light* KEEP OUT, block out, screen, veil.
■ **shut up** (*informal*) BE QUIET, keep quiet, hold one's tongue, keep one's lips sealed; stop talking, quieten (down); *informal* keep mum, button it, cut the cackle, shut it, shut your face/mouth/trap, belt up, put a sock in it, give it a rest; *Brit. informal* shut your gob; *N. Amer. informal* save it.
■ **shut someone/something up** ❶ *I haven't shut the hens up yet. See* SHUT SOMEONE/SOMETHING IN. ❷ (*informal*) *that should shut them up* QUIETEN (DOWN), silence, hush, shush, quiet, gag, muzzle.

shuttle ▶ **verb** PLY, run, commute, go/travel back and forth, go/travel to and fro; ferry.

shy[1] ▶ **adjective** *I was painfully shy* BASHFUL, diffident, timid, sheepish, reserved, reticent, introverted, retiring, self-effacing, withdrawn, timorous, mousy, nervous, insecure, unconfident, inhibited, repressed, self-conscious, embarrassed.
– OPPOSITES confident.
■ **shy away from** FLINCH, demur, recoil, hang back, have scruples, have misgivings, have qualms, be chary, be diffident, be bashful, fight shy, be coy; be loath, be reluctant, be unwilling, be disinclined, be hesitant, hesitate, baulk at; *informal* boggle at; *archaic* disrelish.

shy[2] ▶ **verb** (*dated*) *they began shying stones* THROW, toss, fling, hurl, cast, lob, launch, pitch; *informal* chuck, heave, sling, bung.

shyness ▶ **noun** BASHFULNESS, diffidence, sheepishness, reserve, reservedness, introversion, reticence, timidity, timidness, timorousness, mousiness, lack of confidence, inhibitedness, self-consciousness, embarrassment, coyness, demureness.

sibling ▶ **noun** brother, sister; *Zoology* sib.

sick ▶ **adjective** ❶ *the children are sick* ILL, unwell, poorly, ailing, indisposed, not oneself; *Brit.* off colour; *informal* laid up, under the weather; *Austral./NZ informal* crook. ❷ *he was feeling sick* NAUSEOUS, nauseated, queasy, bilious, green about the gills; seasick, carsick, airsick, travel-sick; *informal* about to throw up. ❸ (*informal*) *we're sick about the plans* DISAPPOINTED, depressed, dejected, despondent, downcast, unhappy; angry, cross, annoyed, displeased, disgruntled, fed up; *Brit. informal* cheesed off. ❹ *I'm sick of this music* FED UP, bored, tired, weary. ❺ (*informal*) *a sick joke* MACABRE, black, ghoulish, morbid, perverted, gruesome, sadistic, cruel.
– OPPOSITES well.
■ **be sick** (*Brit.*) VOMIT, throw up, retch, heave, gag; *informal* chunder, chuck up, hurl, spew, keck; *Brit. informal* honk; *N. Amer. informal* spit up, barf, upchuck, toss one's cookies.

sicken ▶ **verb** ❶ *the stench sickened him* CAUSE TO FEEL SICK/NAUSEOUS, make sick, turn someone's stomach, revolt, disgust; *informal* make someone want to throw up; *N. Amer. informal* gross out. ❷ *she sickened and died* BECOME ILL, fall ill, be taken ill/sick, catch something. ❸ *I'm sickening for something* BECOME ILL WITH, fall ill with, be taken ill with, show symptoms of, develop, come down with; *Brit.* go down with; *N. Amer. informal* take sick with.
– OPPOSITES recover.

sickening ▶ **adjective** NAUSEATING, stomach-turning, stomach-churning, repulsive, revolting, disgusting, repellent, repugnant, appalling, obnoxious, nauseous, vile, nasty, foul, loathsome, offensive, objectionable, off-putting, distasteful, obscene, gruesome, grisly; *N. Amer.* vomitous; *informal* gross; *formal* rebarbative; *archaic* disgustful.

sickly ▶ **adjective** ❶ *a sickly child* UNHEALTHY, in poor health, delicate, frail, weak. ❷ *sickly faces* PALE, wan, pasty, sallow, pallid, ashen, anaemic. ❸ *a sickly green* INSIPID, pale, light, light-coloured, washed out, faded. ❹ *sickly love songs* SENTIMENTAL, mawkish, cloying, sugary, syrupy, saccharine; *informal* mushy, slushy, schmaltzy, weepy, lovey-dovey, corny; *Brit. informal* soppy; *N. Amer. informal* cornball, sappy, hokey, three-hankie.
– OPPOSITES healthy.

sickness ▶ **noun** ❶ *she was absent through sickness* ILLNESS, disease, ailment, complaint, infection, malady, infirmity, indisposition; *informal* bug, virus; *Brit. informal* lurgy; *Austral. informal* wog. ❷ *a wave of sickness* NAUSEA, biliousness, queasiness. ❸ *he suffered sickness and diarrhoea* VOMITING, retching, gagging; travel-sickness, seasickness, carsickness, airsickness, motion sickness; *informal* throwing up, puking.

side ▶ **noun** ❶ *the side of the road* EDGE, border, verge, boundary, margin, fringe(s), flank, bank, perimeter, extremity, periphery, (outer) limit, limits, bounds; *poetic/literary* marge, bourn. ❷ *the wrong side of the road* HALF, part; carriageway, lane. ❸ *the east side of the city* DISTRICT, quarter, area, region, part, neighbourhood, sector, section, zone, ward. ❹ *one side of the paper* SURFACE, face, plane. ❺ *his side of the argument* POINT OF VIEW, viewpoint, perspective, opinion, way of thinking, standpoint, position, outlook, slant, angle. ❻ *the losing side in the war* FACTION, camp, bloc, party, wing. ❼ *the players in their side* TEAM, squad, line-up. ❽ (*Brit. informal*) *there's absolutely no side about her. See* AFFECTATION sense 1.
– RELATED TERMS lateral.
– OPPOSITES centre, end.

▶ **adjective** ❶ *elaborate side pieces* LATERAL, wing, flanking. ❷ *a side issue* SUBORDINATE, lesser, lower-level, secondary, minor, peripheral, incidental, ancillary, subsidiary, of little account, extraneous.
– OPPOSITES front, central.

▶ **verb** *siding with the underdog. See* TAKE SOMEONE'S SIDE.

■ **side by side** ❶ *they cycled along side by side* ALONGSIDE (EACH OTHER), beside each other, abreast, shoulder to shoulder, close together. ❷ *most transactions proceed side by side* AT (ONE AND) THE SAME TIME, simultaneously, contemporaneously.

■ **take someone's side** SUPPORT, take someone's part, side with, be on someone's side, stand by, back, give someone one's backing, be loyal to, defend, champion, ally (oneself) with, sympathize with, favour.

sideline ▶ **noun** *he founded the company as a sideline* SECONDARY OCCUPATION, second job; hobby, leisure activity/pursuit, recreation.

■ **on the sidelines** WITHOUT TAKING PART, without getting involved.

sidelong ▶ **adjective** *a sidelong glance* INDIRECT, oblique, sideways, sideward; surreptitious, furtive, covert, sly.
– OPPOSITES overt.

▶ **adverb** *he looked sidelong at her* INDIRECTLY, obliquely, sideways, out of the corner of one's eye; surreptitiously, furtively, covertly, slyly.

side-splitting ▶ **adjective** (*informal*). *See* FUNNY sense 1.

sidestep ▶ **verb** AVOID, evade, dodge, circumvent, skirt round, bypass; *informal* duck.

sidetrack ▶ **verb** DISTRACT, divert, deflect, draw away.

sideways ▶ **adverb** ❶ *I slid off sideways* TO THE SIDE, laterally. ❷ *the expansion slots are mounted sideways* EDGEWISE, sidewards, side first, edgeways, end on. ❸ *he looked sideways at her. See* SIDELONG adverb.

▶ **adjective** ❶ *sideways force* LATERAL, sideward, on the side, side to side. ❷ *a sideways look. See* SIDELONG adjective.

sidle ▶ **verb** CREEP, sneak, slink, slip, slide, steal, edge, inch, move furtively.

siege ▶ **noun** BLOCKADE, encirclement; *archaic* investment.
– OPPOSITES relief.

siesta ▶ **noun** AFTERNOON SLEEP, nap, catnap, doze, rest; *informal* snooze, lie-down, forty winks, a bit of shut-eye; *Brit. informal* kip, zizz.

sieve ▶ **noun** *use a sieve to strain the mixture* STRAINER, sifter, filter, riddle, screen.

▶ **verb** ❶ *sieve the mixture into a bowl* STRAIN, sift, screen, filter, riddle; *archaic* bolt. ❷ *the coins were sieved from the ash* SEPARATE OUT, filter out, sift, sort out, divide, segregate, extract.

sift ▶ **verb** ❶ *sift the flour into a large bowl* SIEVE, strain, screen, filter, riddle; *archaic* bolt. ❷ *we sift out unsuitable applications* SEPARATE OUT, filter out, sort out, put to one side, weed out, get rid of, remove. ❸ *investigators are sifting through the wreckage* SEARCH THROUGH, look through, examine, inspect, scrutinize, pore over, investigate, analyse, dissect, review.

sigh ▶ **verb** ❶ *she sighed with relief* BREATHE OUT, exhale; groan, moan. ❷ *the wind sighed in the trees* RUSTLE, whisper, murmur, sough. ❸ *he sighed for days gone by* YEARN, long, pine, ache, grieve, cry for/over, weep for/over, rue, miss, mourn, lament, hanker for/after.

sight ▶ **noun** ❶ *she has excellent sight* EYESIGHT, vision, eyes, faculty of sight, visual perception. ❷ *her first sight of it* VIEW, glimpse, glance, look. ❸ *within sight of the enemy* RANGE OF VISION, field of vision, view. ❹ (*dated*) *we are all equal in the sight of God* PERCEPTION, judgement, belief, opinion, point of view, view, viewpoint, mind, perspective, standpoint. ❺ *historic sights* LANDMARK, place of interest, monument, spectacle, view, marvel, wonder. ❻ (*informal*) *I must look a sight* EYESORE, spectacle, mess; *informal* fright.
– RELATED TERMS optical, visual.

▶ **verb** *one of the helicopters sighted wreckage* GLIMPSE, catch/get a glimpse of, catch sight of, see, spot, spy, notice, observe; *poetic/literary* espy, descry.

■ **catch sight of** GLIMPSE, catch/get a glimpse of, see, spot, spy, make out, pick out, sight, have sight of; *poetic/literary* espy, descry.

■ **set one's sights on** ASPIRE TO, aim at/for, try for, strive for/towards, work towards.

sightseer ▶ **noun** ❶ *sightseers to the city* TOURIST, visitor, tripper, holidaymaker; *Brit. informal* grockle. ❷ *gawping sightseers* BUSYBODY, gawker; *informal* rubberneck; *Brit. informal* gawper.

sign ▶ **noun** ❶ *a sign of affection* INDICATION, signal, symptom, pointer, suggestion, intimation, mark, manifestation, demonstration, token, evidence; *poetic/literary* sigil. ❷ *a sign of things to come* PORTENT, omen, warning, forewarning, augury, presage; promise, threat. ❸ *at his sign the soldiers followed* GESTURE, signal, wave, gesticulation, cue, nod. ❹ *signs saying 'keep out'* NOTICE, signpost, signboard, warning sign, road sign, traffic sign. ❺ *the dancers were daubed with signs* SYMBOL, mark, cipher, letter, character, figure, hieroglyph, ideogram, rune, emblem, device, logo.

▶ **verb** ❶ *he signed the letter* WRITE ONE'S NAME ON, autograph, endorse, initial, countersign; *formal* subscribe. ❷ *the government signed the agreement* ENDORSE, validate, certify, authenticate, sanction, authorize; agree to, approve, ratify, adopt, give one's approval to; *informal* give something the go-ahead, give something the green light, give something the thumbs up. ❸ *he signed his name* WRITE, inscribe, pen. ❹ *we have signed a new player* RECRUIT, hire, engage, employ, take on, appoint, sign on/up, enlist. ❺ *she signed to Susan to leave* GESTURE, signal, give a sign to, motion; wave, beckon, nod.

■ **sign on/up** ENLIST, take a job, join (up), enrol, register, volunteer.

■ **sign someone on/up** *See* SIGN verb sense 4.

■ **sign something over** TRANSFER, make over, hand over, bequeath, pass on, transmit, cede; *Law* devolve, convey.

signal[1] ▶ **noun** ❶ *a signal to stop* GESTURE, sign, wave, gesticulation, cue, indication, warning, motion. ❷ *a clear signal that the company is in trouble* INDICATION, sign, symptom, hint, pointer, intimation, clue, demonstration, evidence, proof. ❸ *the encroaching dark is a signal for people to emerge* CUE, prompt, impetus, stimulus; *informal* go-ahead.

▶ **verb** ❶ *the driver signalled to her to cross* GESTURE, sign, give a sign to, direct, motion; wave, beckon, nod. ❷ *they signalled displeasure by refusing to cooperate* INDICATE, show, express, communicate, proclaim, declare. ❸ *his death signals the end of an era* MARK, signify, mean, be a sign of, be evidence of, herald; *poetic/literary* betoken, foretoken.

signal[2] ▶ **adjective** *a signal failure* NOTABLE, noteworthy, remarkable, striking, glaring, significant, momentous, memorable, unforgettable, obvious, special, extraordinary, exceptional, conspicuous.

significance ▶ **noun** ❶ *a matter of considerable significance* IMPORTANCE, import, consequence, seriousness, gravity, weight, magnitude, momentousness; *formal* moment. ❷ *the significance of his remarks* MEANING, sense, signification, import, thrust, drift, gist, implication, message, essence, substance, point.

significant ▶ **adjective** ❶ *a significant increase* NOTABLE, noteworthy, worthy of attention, remarkable, important, of importance, of consequence; serious, crucial, weighty, momentous, uncommon, unusual, rare, extraordinary, exceptional, special; *formal* of moment. ❷ *a significant look* MEANINGFUL, expressive, eloquent, suggestive, knowing, telling.

significantly ▶ **adverb** ❶ *significantly better* NOTABLY, remarkably, outstandingly, importantly, crucially, materially, appreciably; markedly, considerably, obviously, conspicuously, strikingly, signally. ❷ *he paused significantly* MEANINGFULLY, expressively, eloquently, revealingly, suggestively, knowingly.

signify ▶ **verb** ❶ *this signified a fundamental change* BE EVIDENCE OF, be a sign of, mark, signal, mean, spell, be symptomatic of, herald, indicate; *poetic/literary* betoken. ❷ *the egg signifies life* MEAN, denote, designate, represent, symbolize, stand for; *poetic/literary* betoken. ❸ *signify your agreement by signing below* EXPRESS, indicate, show, proclaim, declare. ❹ *the locked door doesn't signify* MEAN ANYTHING, be of importance, be important, be significant, be of significance, be of account, count, matter, be relevant.

silence ▶ **noun** ❶ *the silence of the night* QUIETNESS, quiet, quietude, still, stillness, hush, tranquillity, noiselessness, soundlessness, peacefulness, peace (and quiet). ❷ *she was reduced to silence* SPEECHLESSNESS, wordlessness, dumbness, muteness, taciturnity. ❸ *the politicians kept their silence* SECRETIVENESS, secrecy, reticence, taciturnity, uncommunicativeness.

–OPPOSITES sound.

▶ **verb** ❶ *he silenced her with a kiss* QUIETEN, quiet, hush, shush; gag, muzzle, censor. ❷ *silencing outside noises* MUFFLE, deaden, soften, mute, smother, dampen, damp down, mask, suppress, reduce. ❸ *this would silence their complaints* STOP, put an end to, put a stop to.

silent ▶ **adjective** ❶ *the night was silent* COMPLETELY QUIET, still, hushed, inaudible, noiseless, soundless. ❷ *the right to remain silent* SPEECHLESS, quiet, unspeaking, dumb, mute, taciturn, uncommunicative, tight-lipped; *informal* mum. ❸ *silent thanks* UNSPOKEN, wordless, unsaid, unexpressed, unvoiced, tacit, implicit, understood.

–OPPOSITES audible, noisy.

silently ▶ **adverb** ❶ *Nancy crept silently up the stairs* QUIETLY, inaudibly, noiselessly, soundlessly, in silence. ❷ *they drove on silently* WITHOUT A WORD, saying nothing, in silence. ❸ *I silently said goodbye* WITHOUT WORDS, wordlessly, in one's head, tacitly, implicitly.

–OPPOSITES audibly, out loud.

silhouette ▶ **noun** *the silhouette of the dome* OUTLINE, contour(s), profile, form, shape, figure, shadow.

▶ **verb** *the castle was silhouetted against the sky* OUTLINE, delineate, define; stand out.

silky ▶ **adjective** SMOOTH, soft, sleek, fine, glossy, satiny, silken.

silly ▶ **adjective** ❶ *don't be so silly* FOOLISH, stupid, unintelligent, idiotic, brainless, mindless, witless, imbecilic, doltish; imprudent, thoughtless, rash, reckless, foolhardy, irresponsible;

mad, scatterbrained, feather-brained; frivolous, giddy, inane, immature, childish, puerile, empty-headed; *informal* crazy, dotty, scatty, loopy, screwy, thick, thickheaded, bird-brained, pea-brained, dopey, dim, dim-witted, half-witted, dippy, blockheaded, boneheaded, lamebrained; *Brit. informal* daft, divvy; *N. Amer. informal* chowderheaded; *dated* tomfool. ❷ *that was a silly thing to do* UNWISE, imprudent, thoughtless, foolish, stupid, idiotic, senseless, mindless; rash, reckless, foolhardy, irresponsible, injudicious, misguided, irrational; *informal* crazy; *Brit. informal* daft. ❸ *he would brood about silly things* TRIVIAL, trifling, frivolous, footling, petty, small, insignificant, unimportant; *informal* piffling, piddling; *N. Amer. informal* small-bore. ❹ *he drank himself silly* SENSELESS, insensible, unconscious, stupid, into a stupor, into senselessness, stupefied.
– OPPOSITES sensible.
▶ noun (*informal*) *you are a silly!* *See* FOOL noun sense 1.

silt ▶ noun *the flooding brought more silt* SEDIMENT, deposit, alluvium, mud.
▶ verb *the harbour had silted up* BECOME BLOCKED, become clogged, fill up (with silt).

silver ▶ noun ❶ *freshly polished silver* SILVERWARE, (silver) plate; cutlery, {knives, forks, and spoons}. ❷ *a handful of silver* COINS, coinage, specie; (small) change, loose change. ❸ *she won three silvers* SILVER MEDAL, second prize.
▶ adjective ❶ *silver hair* GREY, greyish, white. ❷ *the silver water* SILVERY, shining, lustrous, gleaming; *poetic/literary* argent.

similar ▶ adjective ❶ *you two are very similar* ALIKE, (much) the same, indistinguishable, almost identical, homogeneous; *informal* much of a muchness. ❷ *northern India and similar areas* COMPARABLE, like, corresponding, homogeneous, equivalent, analogous. ❸ *other parts were similar to Wales* LIKE, much the same as, comparable to.
– OPPOSITES different, unlike.
■ **be similar to** RESEMBLE, look like, have the appearance of.

similarity ▶ noun RESEMBLANCE, likeness, sameness, similitude, comparability, correspondence, parallel, equivalence, homogeneity, indistinguishability, uniformity; *archaic* semblance.

similarly ▶ adverb LIKEWISE, in similar fashion, in like manner, comparably, correspondingly, uniformly, indistinguishably, analogously, homogeneously, equivalently, in the same way, the same, identically.

similitude ▶ noun. *See* SIMILARITY.

simmer ▶ verb ❶ *the soup was simmering on the stove* BOIL GENTLY, cook gently, bubble. ❷ *she was simmering with resentment* BE FURIOUS, be enraged, be angry, be incensed, be infuriated, seethe, fume, smoulder; *informal* be steamed up, be hot under the collar.
■ **simmer down** BECOME LESS ANGRY, cool off/down, be placated, control oneself, become calmer, calm down, become quieter, quieten down.

simper ▶ verb SMILE AFFECTEDLY, smile coquettishly, look coy.

simple ▶ adjective ❶ *it's really pretty simple* STRAIGHTFORWARD, easy, uncomplicated, uninvolved, effortless, painless, undemanding, elementary, child's play; *informal* as easy as falling off a log, as easy as pie, as easy as ABC, a piece of cake, a cinch, no sweat, a doddle, a pushover, money for old rope, kids' stuff, a breeze; *Brit. informal* easy-peasy, a doss; *N. Amer. informal* duck soup, a snap; *Austral./NZ informal* a bludge, a snack. ❷ *simple language* CLEAR, plain, straightforward, intelligible, comprehensible, uncomplicated, in words of one syllable, accessible; *informal* user-friendly. ❸ *a simple white blouse* PLAIN, unadorned, undecorated, unembellished, unornamented, unelaborate, basic, unsophisticated, no-frills; classic, understated, uncluttered, restrained. ❹ *the simple truth* CANDID, frank, honest, sincere, plain, absolute, unqualified, bald, stark, unadorned, unvarnished, unembellished. ❺ *simple country people* UNPRETENTIOUS, unsophisticated, ordinary, unaffected, unassuming, natural, honest-to-goodness; *N. Amer.* cracker-barrel. ❻ *he's a bit simple* HAVING LEARNING DIFFICULTIES, having special (educational) needs; of low intelligence, simple-minded, unintelligent, backward, (mentally) retarded; *dated* (mentally) subnormal, educationally subnormal, ESN. ❼ *simple chemical substances* NON-COMPOUND, non-complex, uncombined, unblended, unalloyed, pure, single.
– OPPOSITES difficult, complex, fancy, compound.

simpleton ▶ noun. *See* FOOL noun sense 1.

simplicity ▶ noun ❶ *the simplicity of the recipes* STRAIGHTFORWARDNESS, ease, easiness, simpleness, effortlessness. ❷ *the simplicity of the language* CLARITY, clearness, plainness, simpleness, intelligibility, comprehensibility, understandability, straightforwardness, accessibility. ❸ *the building's simplicity* PLAINNESS, lack/absence of adornment, lack/absence of decoration, austerity, spareness, clean lines. ❹ *the simplicity of their lifestyle* UNPRETENTIOUSNESS, ordinariness, lack of sophistication, lack of affectation, naturalness.

simplify ▶ verb MAKE SIMPLE/SIMPLER, make easy/easier to understand, make plainer, clarify, make more comprehensible/intelligible; paraphrase, put in words of one syllable.
– OPPOSITES complicate.

simplistic ▶ adjective FACILE, superficial, oversimple, oversimplified; shallow, jejune, naive; *N. Amer. informal* dime-store.

simply ▶ adverb ❶ *he spoke simply and forcefully* STRAIGHTFORWARDLY, directly, clearly, plainly, intelligibly, lucidly, unambiguously. ❷ *she was dressed simply* PLAINLY, without adornment, without decoration, without ornament/ornamentation, soberly, unfussily, unelaborately, classically. ❸ *they lived simply* UNPRETENTIOUSLY, modestly, quietly. ❹ *they are welcomed simply because they have plenty of money* MERELY, just, purely, solely, only. ❺ *Mrs Marks was simply livid* UTTERLY, absolutely, completely, positively, really; *informal* plain. ❻ *it's simply the best thing ever written* WITHOUT DOUBT, unquestionably, undeniably, incontrovertibly, certainly, categorically.

simulate ▶ **verb** ❶ *they simulated pleasure* FEIGN, pretend, fake, sham, affect, put on, give the appearance of. ❷ *simulating conditions in space* IMITATE, reproduce, replicate, duplicate, mimic.

simulated ▶ **adjective** ❶ *simulated fear* FEIGNED, fake, mock, affected, sham, insincere, false, bogus; *informal* pretend, put-on, phoney. ❷ *simulated leather* ARTIFICIAL, imitation, fake, mock, synthetic, man-made, ersatz.
– OPPOSITES real.

simultaneous ▶ **adjective** CONCURRENT, happening at the same time, contemporaneous, concomitant, coinciding, coincident, synchronous, synchronized.

simultaneously ▶ **adverb** AT (ONE AND) THE SAME TIME, at the same instant/moment, at once, concurrently, concomitantly; (all) together, in unison, in concert, in chorus.

sin ▶ **noun** ❶ *a sin in the eyes of God* IMMORAL ACT, wrong, wrongdoing, act of evil/wickedness, transgression, crime, offence, misdeed, misdemeanour; *archaic* trespass. ❷ *the human capacity for sin* WICKEDNESS, wrongdoing, wrong, evil, evil-doing, sinfulness, immorality, iniquity, vice, crime. ❸ (*informal*) *wasting money—it's a sin* SCANDAL, crime, disgrace, outrage.
– OPPOSITES virtue.
▶ **verb** *I have sinned* COMMIT A SIN, commit an offence, transgress, do wrong, commit a crime, break the law, misbehave, go astray; *archaic* trespass.

sincere ▶ **adjective** ❶ *our sincere gratitude* HEARTFELT, wholehearted, profound, deep; genuine, real, unfeigned, unaffected, true, honest, bona fide. ❷ *a sincere person* HONEST, genuine, truthful, unhypocritical, straightforward, direct, frank, candid; *informal* straight, upfront, on the level; *N. Amer. informal* on the up and up.

sincerely ▶ **adverb** GENUINELY, honestly, really, truly, truthfully, wholeheartedly, earnestly, fervently.

sincerity ▶ **noun** HONESTY, genuineness, truthfulness, integrity, probity, trustworthiness; straightforwardness, openness, candour, candidness.

sinecure ▶ **noun** EASY JOB, soft option; *informal* cushy number, money for old rope, picnic, doddle, cinch; *Austral. informal* bludge.

sinewy ▶ **adjective** MUSCULAR, muscly, brawny, powerfully built, burly, strapping, sturdy, rugged, strong, powerful, athletic, muscle-bound; *informal* hunky, beefy; *dated* stalwart; *poetic/literary* thewy.
– OPPOSITES puny.

sinful ▶ **adjective** ❶ *sinful conduct* IMMORAL, wicked, (morally) wrong, wrongful, evil, bad, iniquitous, corrupt, criminal, nefarious, depraved, degenerate; *rare* peccable. ❷ *a sinful waste of money* REPREHENSIBLE, scandalous, disgraceful, deplorable, shameful, criminal.
– OPPOSITES virtuous.

sinfulness ▶ **noun** IMMORALITY, wickedness, sin, wrongdoing, evil, evil-doing, iniquitousness, corruption, depravity, degeneracy, vice; *formal* turpitude; *rare* peccability.
– OPPOSITES virtue.

sing ▶ **verb** ❶ *Miguelito began to sing* croon, carol, trill, troll, chant, intone, chorus. ❷ *the birds were singing* WARBLE, trill, chirp, chirrup, cheep, peep. ❸ *he sang out a greeting* CALL (OUT), cry (out), shout, yell; *informal* holler. ❹ (*informal*) *he's going to sing to the police* INFORM (ON SOMEONE); *informal* squeal, rat on someone, blow the whistle on someone, peach (on someone), snitch (on someone); *Brit. informal* grass (on someone), shop someone; *N. Amer. informal* finger someone, fink on someone, drop a/the dime on someone; *Austral. informal* pimp on someone.

singe ▶ **verb** SCORCH, burn, sear, char.

singer ▶ **noun** VOCALIST, soloist, songster, songstress, cantor.

single ▶ **adjective** ❶ *a single red rose* ONE (ONLY), sole, lone, solitary, by itself/oneself, unaccompanied, alone. ❷ *she wrote down every single word* INDIVIDUAL, separate, distinct, particular. ❸ *is she single?* UNMARRIED, unwed, unwedded, unattached, free, a bachelor, a spinster; *archaic* sole.
– OPPOSITES double, married.
■ **single someone/something out** SELECT, pick out, choose, decide on; target, earmark, mark out, separate out, set apart/aside.

single-handed ▶ **adverb** BY ONESELF, alone, on one's own, solo, unaided, unassisted, without help.

single-minded ▶ **adjective** DETERMINED, committed, unswerving, unwavering, resolute, purposeful, devoted, dedicated, uncompromising, tireless, tenacious, persistent, indefatigable, dogged; *formal* pertinacious.
– OPPOSITES half-hearted.

singly ▶ **adverb** ONE BY ONE, one at a time, one after the other, individually, separately, by oneself, on one's own.
– OPPOSITES together.

singular ▶ **adjective** ❶ *the gallery's singular capacity to attract sponsors* REMARKABLE, extraordinary, exceptional, outstanding, signal, notable, noteworthy; rare, unique, unparalleled, unprecedented, amazing, astonishing, phenomenal, astounding; *informal* fantastic, terrific. ❷ *why was Betty was behaving in so singular a fashion?* STRANGE, unusual, odd, peculiar, funny, curious, extraordinary, bizarre, eccentric, weird, queer, unexpected, unfamiliar, abnormal, atypical, unconventional, out of the ordinary, untypical, puzzling, mysterious, perplexing, baffling, unaccountable.

singularity ▶ **noun** ❶ *the singularity of their concerns* UNIQUENESS, distinctiveness. ❷ *his singularities* IDIOSYNCRASY, quirk, foible, peculiarity, oddity, eccentricity.

singularly ▶ **adverb**. *See* EXTREMELY.

sinister ▶ **adjective** ❶ *there was a sinister undertone in his words* MENACING, threatening, ominous, forbidding, baleful, frightening, alarming, disturbing, disquieting, dark, black; *formal* minatory; *poetic/literary* direful. ❷ *a sinister motive* EVIL, wicked, criminal, corrupt, nefarious, villainous, base, vile, malevolent, malicious; *informal* shady.
– OPPOSITES innocent.

sink ▶ **verb** ❶ *the coffin sank below the waves* BECOME SUBMERGED, be engulfed, go down, drop, fall, descend. ❷ *the cruise liner sank yesterday* FOUNDER, go under, submerge. ❸ *they sank their ships* SCUTTLE, send to the bottom; *Brit.* scupper. ❹ *the announcement sank hopes of a recovery* DESTROY, ruin, wreck, put an end to, demolish, smash, shatter, dash; *informal* put the kibosh on, put paid to; *Brit. informal* scupper; *archaic* bring to naught. ❺ *they agreed to sink their differences* IGNORE, overlook, disregard, forget, put aside, set aside, bury. ❻ *I sank myself in student life* IMMERSE, plunge, lose, bury. ❼ *the plane sank towards the airstrip* DESCEND, drop, go down/downwards. ❽ *the sun was sinking* SET, go down/downwards. ❾ *Loretta sank into an armchair* LOWER ONESELF, flop, collapse, drop down, slump; *informal* plonk oneself. ❿ *her voice sank to a whisper* FALL, drop, become/get quieter, become/get softer. ⓫ *she would never sink to your level* STOOP, lower oneself, descend. ⓬ *he was sinking fast* DETERIORATE, decline, fade, grow weak, flag, waste away; be at death's door, be on one's deathbed, be slipping away; *informal* go downhill, be on one's last legs, be giving up the ghost. ⓭ *sink the pots into the ground* EMBED, insert, drive, plant. ⓮ *sinking a gold mine* DIG, excavate, bore, drill. ⓯ (*informal*) *he sank five pints of lager* DRINK, quaff; *informal* down, knock back, polish off; *N. Amer. informal* chug, scarf down. ⓰ *they sank their life savings in the company* INVEST, venture, risk.
– OPPOSITES float, rise.

▶ **noun** *he washed himself at the sink* BASIN, washbasin, handbasin; *dated* lavabo.

■ **sink in** REGISTER, be understood, be comprehended, be grasped, get through.

sinless ▶ **adjective** INNOCENT, pure, virtuous, as pure as the driven snow, uncorrupted, faultless, blameless, guiltless, immaculate.
– OPPOSITES wicked.

sinner ▶ **noun** WRONGDOER, evil-doer, transgressor, miscreant, offender, criminal; *archaic* trespasser.

sinuous ▶ **adjective** ❶ *a sinuous river* WINDING, windy, serpentine, curving, twisting, meandering, snaking, zigzag, curling, coiling. ❷ *sinuous grace* LITHE, supple, agile, graceful, loose-limbed, limber, lissom.

sip ▶ **verb** *Amanda sipped her coffee* DRINK (SLOWLY); *dated* sup.

▶ **noun** *a sip of whisky* MOUTHFUL, swallow, drink, drop, dram, nip; *informal* swig; *dated* sup.

siren ▶ **noun** ❶ *an air-raid siren* ALARM (BELL), warning bell, danger signal; *archaic* tocsin. ❷ *the siren's allure* SEDUCTRESS, temptress, femme fatale; flirt, coquette; *informal* mantrap, vamp.

sissy (*informal*) ▶ **noun** *he's a real sissy. See* DRIP noun sense 2.

▶ **adjective** *don't be so sissy* COWARDLY, weak, feeble, spineless, effeminate, effete, unmanly; *informal* wet, weedy, wimpish, wimpy.

sister ▶ **noun** ❶ *I have two sisters* SIBLING. ❷ *our European sisters* COMRADE, partner, colleague. ❸ *the sisters in the convent* NUN, novice, abbess, prioress.
– RELATED TERMS sororal.

sit ▶ **verb** ❶ *you'd better sit down* TAKE A SEAT, seat oneself, be seated, perch, ensconce oneself, plump oneself, flop; *informal* take the load/weight off one's feet, plonk oneself; *Brit. informal* take a pew. ❷ *she sat the package on the table* PUT (DOWN), place, set (down), lay, deposit, rest, stand; *informal* stick, bung, dump, park, plonk. ❸ *the chapel sat about 3,000 people* HOLD, seat, have seats for, have space/room for, accommodate. ❹ *she sat for Picasso* POSE, model. ❺ *a hotel sitting on the bank of the River Dee* BE SITUATED, be located, be sited, stand. ❻ *the committee sits on Saturday* BE IN SESSION, meet, be convened. ❼ *women jurists sit on the tribunal* SERVE ON, have a seat on, be a member of. ❽ *his shyness doesn't sit easily with Hollywood tradition* BE HARMONIOUS, go, fit in, harmonize. ❾ *Mrs Hillman will sit for us* BABYSIT, childmind.
– OPPOSITES stand.

■ **sit back** RELAX, unwind, lie back; *informal* let it all hang out, veg out; *N. Amer. informal* hang loose, chill out.

■ **sit in for** STAND IN FOR, fill in for, cover for, substitute for, deputize for; *informal* sub for.

■ **sit in on** ATTEND, be present at, be an observer at, observe; *N. Amer.* audit.

■ **sit tight** (*informal*) ❶ *just sit tight* STAY PUT, wait there, remain in one's place. ❷ *we're advising our clients to sit tight* TAKE NO ACTION, wait, hold back, bide one's time; *informal* hold one's horses.

site ▶ **noun** *the site of the battle* LOCATION, place, position, situation, locality, whereabouts; *technical* locus.
▶ **verb** *bins sited at police stations* PLACE, put, position, situate, locate.

sitting ▶ **noun** *all-night sittings* SESSION, meeting, assembly; hearing.
▶ **adjective** *a sitting position* SEDENTARY, seated.
– OPPOSITES standing.

sitting room ▶ **noun** LIVING ROOM, lounge, front room, drawing room, reception room, family room; *dated* parlour.

situate ▶ **verb** LOCATE, site, position, place, station, build.

situation ▶ **noun** ❶ *their financial situation* CIRCUMSTANCES, (state of) affairs, state, condition. ❷ *I'll fill you in on the situation* THE FACTS, how things stand, the lie of the land, what's going on; *Brit.* the state of play; *N. Amer.* the lay of the land; *informal* the score. ❸ *the hotel's pleasant situation* LOCATION, position, spot, site, setting, environment; *technical* locus. ❹ *he was offered a situation in America* JOB, post, position, appointment; employment; *archaic* employ.

six ▶ **cardinal number** SEXTET, sextuplets; *technical* hexad.
– RELATED TERMS hexa-, sexi-.

size ▶ **noun** *the room was of medium size* DIMENSIONS, measurements, proportions, magnitude, largeness, bigness, area, expanse; breadth, width, length, height, depth; immensity, hugeness, vastness.
▶ **verb** *the drills are sized in millimetres* SORT, categorize, classify.
■ **size someone/something up** (*informal*) ASSESS, appraise, form an estimate of, take the measure of, judge, take stock of, evaluate; *Brit. informal* suss out.

sizeable ▶ **adjective** FAIRLY LARGE, substantial, considerable, respectable, significant, largish, biggish, goodly.
– OPPOSITES small.

sizzle ▶ **verb** CRACKLE, frizzle, sputter, spit.

sizzling ▶ **adjective** (*informal*) ❶ *sizzling temperatures* EXTREMELY HOT, unbearably hot, blazing, burning, scorching, sweltering; *N. Amer.* broiling; *informal* boiling (hot), baking (hot). ❷ *a sizzling affair* PASSIONATE, torrid, ardent, lustful, erotic; *informal* steamy, hot.
– OPPOSITES freezing.

skedaddle ▶ **verb** (*informal*). *See* RUN verb sense 2.

skeletal ▶ **adjective** ❶ *a skeletal man* EMACIATED, very thin, as thin as a rake, cadaverous, skin-and-bones, skinny, bony, gaunt; *informal* anorexic. ❷ *a skeletal account* LACKING IN DETAIL, incomplete, outline, fragmentary, sketchy; thumbnail.
– OPPOSITES fat, detailed.

skeleton ▶ **noun** ❶ *the human skeleton* BONES. ❷ *she was no more than a skeleton* SKIN AND BONE; *informal* bag of bones. ❸ *a concrete skeleton* FRAMEWORK, frame, shell. ❹ *the skeleton of a report* OUTLINE, (rough) draft, abstract, (bare) bones.
▶ **adjective** *a skeleton staff* MINIMUM, minimal, basic; essential.

sketch ▶ **noun** ❶ *a sketch of the proposed design* (PRELIMINARY) DRAWING, outline; diagram, design, plan; *informal* rough. ❷ *she gave a rough sketch of what had happened* OUTLINE, brief description, rundown, main points, thumbnail sketch, (bare) bones; summary, synopsis, summarization, precis, résumé; *N. Amer.* wrap-up. ❸ *a biographical sketch* DESCRIPTION, portrait, profile, portrayal, depiction. ❹ *a hilarious sketch* SKIT, scene, piece, act, item, routine.
▶ **verb** ❶ *he sketched the garden* DRAW, make a drawing of, draw a picture of, pencil, rough out, outline. ❷ *the company sketched out its plans* DESCRIBE, outline, give a brief idea of, rough out; summarize, precis.

sketchily ▶ **adverb** PERFUNCTORILY, cursorily, incompletely, patchily, vaguely, imprecisely; hastily, hurriedly.

sketchy ▶ **adjective** INCOMPLETE, patchy, fragmentary, cursory, perfunctory, scanty, vague, imprecise; hurried, hasty.
– OPPOSITES detailed.

skew-whiff ▶ **adjective** (*Brit. informal*). *See* CROOKED sense 3.

skilful ▶ **adjective** EXPERT, accomplished, skilled, masterly, master, virtuoso, consummate, proficient, talented, gifted, adept, adroit, deft, dexterous, able, good, competent, capable, brilliant, handy; *informal* mean, wicked, crack, ace, wizard; *N. Amer. informal* crackerjack.

skill ▶ **noun** ❶ *his skill as a politician* EXPERTISE, skilfulness, expertness, adeptness, adroitness, deftness, dexterity, ability, prowess, mastery, competence, capability, aptitude, artistry, virtuosity, talent. ❷ *bringing up a family gives you many skills* ACCOMPLISHMENT, strength, gift.
– OPPOSITES incompetence.

skilled ▶ **adjective** EXPERIENCED, trained, qualified, proficient, practised, accomplished, expert, skilful, talented, gifted, adept, adroit, deft, dexterous, able, good, competent; *informal* crack; *N. Amer. informal* crackerjack.
– OPPOSITES inexperienced.

skim ▶ **verb** ❶ *skim off the scum* REMOVE, cream off, scoop off. ❷ *the boat skimmed over the water* GLIDE, move lightly, slide, sail, skate, float. ❸ *he skimmed the pebble across the water* THROW, toss, cast, pitch; bounce. ❹ *she skimmed through the newspaper* GLANCE, flick, flip, leaf, thumb, read quickly, scan, run one's eye over. ❺ *Hannah skimmed over this part of the story* MENTION

BRIEFLY, pass over quickly, skate over, gloss over.
– OPPOSITES elaborate on.

skimp ▶ **verb** ❶ *don't skimp on the quantity* STINT ON, scrimp on, economize on, cut back on, be sparing, be frugal, be mean, be parsimonious, cut corners; *informal* be stingy, be mingy, be tight. ❷ *the process cannot be skimped* DO HASTILY, do carelessly.

skimpy ▶ **adjective** ❶ *a skimpy black dress* REVEALING, short, low, low-cut; flimsy, thin, see-through, indecent. ❷ *my information is rather skimpy* MEAGRE, scanty, sketchy, limited, paltry, deficient, sparse.

skin ▶ **noun** ❶ *these chemicals could damage the skin* EPIDERMIS, dermis, derma. ❷ *Mary's fair skin* COMPLEXION, colouring, skin colour/tone, pigmentation. ❸ *leopard skins* HIDE, pelt, fleece; *archaic* fell. ❹ *a banana skin* PEEL, rind, integument. ❺ *milk with a skin on it* FILM, layer, membrane. ❻ *the plane's skin was damaged* CASING, exterior.
– RELATED TERMS cutaneous.
▶ **verb** ❶ *skin the tomatoes* PEEL, pare, hull; *technical* decorticate. ❷ *he skinned his knee* GRAZE, scrape, abrade, bark, rub something raw, chafe; *Medicine* excoriate. ❸ (*informal*) *Dad would skin me alive if I forgot it* PUNISH SEVERELY; *informal* murder, come down on someone (like a ton of bricks); *Brit. informal* give someone what for.
■ **by the skin of one's teeth** (ONLY) JUST, narrowly, by a hair's breadth, by a very small margin; *informal* by a whisker.
■ **get under someone's skin** (*informal*) ❶ *the children really got under my skin. See* IRRITATE sense 1. ❷ *she got under my skin* OBSESS, intrigue, captivate, charm; enthral, enchant, entrance.
■ **it's no skin off my nose** (*informal*) I DON'T CARE, I don't mind, I'm not bothered, it doesn't bother me, it doesn't matter to me; *informal* I don't give a damn, I don't give a monkey's.

skin-deep ▶ **adjective** SUPERFICIAL, (on the) surface, external, outward, shallow.

skinflint ▶ **noun** (*informal*). *See* MISER.

skinny ▶ **adjective**. *See* THIN adjective sense 3.

skip ▶ **verb** ❶ *skipping down the path* CAPER, prance, trip, dance, bound, bounce, gambol, frisk, romp, cavort. ❷ *we skipped the boring stuff* OMIT, leave out, miss out, dispense with, pass over, skim over, disregard; *informal* give something a miss. ❸ *I skipped school* PLAY TRUANT FROM, miss; *N. Amer.* cut; *Brit. informal* skive off; *N. Amer. informal* play hookey from; *Austral./NZ informal* play the wag from. ❹ *I skipped through the magazine* HAVE A QUICK LOOK AT, flick through, flip through, leaf through. ❺ (*informal*) *they skipped off again* RUN OFF/AWAY, take off; *informal* beat it, clear off, cut and run; *Brit. informal* do a runner, do a bunk, scarper; *N. Amer. informal* light out, cut out; *Austral. informal* shoot through.

skirmish ▶ **noun** ❶ *the unit was caught up in a skirmish* FIGHT, battle, clash, conflict, encounter, engagement, fray, combat. ❷ *there was a skirmish over the budget* ARGUMENT, quarrel, squabble, contretemps, disagreement, difference of opinion, falling-out, dispute, clash, altercation; *informal* tiff, spat; *Brit. informal* row, barney, ding-dong.
▶ **verb** *they skirmished with enemy soldiers* FIGHT, (do) battle with, engage with, close with, combat, clash with.

skirt ▶ **verb** ❶ *he skirted the city* GO ROUND, walk round, circle. ❷ *the fields that skirt the highway* BORDER, edge, flank, line, lie alongside. ❸ *he carefully skirted round the subject* AVOID, evade, sidestep, dodge, pass over, gloss over; *informal* duck; *Austral./NZ informal* duck-shove.

skit ▶ **noun** COMEDY SKETCH, comedy act, parody, pastiche, burlesque, satire, pasquinade; *informal* spoof, take-off, send-up.

skittish ▶ **adjective** ❶ *she grew increasingly skittish* PLAYFUL, lively, high-spirited, sportive, frisky; *poetic/literary* frolicsome, wanton. ❷ *his horse was skittish* RESTIVE, excitable, nervous, skittery, jumpy, highly strung.

skive ▶ **verb** (*Brit. informal*) MALINGER, play truant, truant, shirk, idle; *N. Amer.* cut; *Brit. informal* bunk off, swing the lead, scrimshank; *N. Amer. informal* gold-brick, play hookey, goof off; *Austral./NZ informal* play the wag.

skulduggery ▶ **noun** TRICKERY, fraudulence, sharp practice, underhandedness, chicanery; *informal* shenanigans, funny business, monkey business; *Brit. informal* monkey tricks, jiggery-pokery; *N. Amer. informal* monkeyshines.

skulk ▶ **verb** LURK, loiter, hide; creep, sneak, slink, prowl, pussyfoot.

skull
– RELATED TERMS cranial.

sky ▶ **noun** *the sun was shining in the sky* the upper atmosphere; *poetic/literary* the heavens, the firmament, the blue, the (wide) blue yonder, the welkin, the azure, the empyrean.
– RELATED TERMS celestial.
■ **to the skies** EFFUSIVELY, profusely, very highly, very enthusiastically, unreservedly, fervently, fulsomely, extravagantly.

slab ▶ **noun** PIECE, block, hunk, chunk, lump; cake, tablet, brick.

slack ▶ **adjective** ❶ *the rope went slack* LOOSE, limp, hanging, flexible. ❷ *slack skin* FLACCID, flabby, loose, sagging, saggy. ❸ *business is slack* SLUGGISH, slow, quiet, slow-moving, flat, depressed, stagnant. ❹ *slack accounting procedures* LAX, negligent, remiss, careless, slapdash, slipshod, lackadaisical, inefficient, casual; *informal* sloppy, slap-happy.
– OPPOSITES tight, taut.
▶ **noun** ❶ *the rope had some slack in it* LOOSENESS, play, give. ❷ *foreign demand will help pick up the*

slack SURPLUS, excess, residue, spare capacity. ❸ *a little slack in the daily routine* LULL, pause, respite, break, hiatus, breathing space; *informal* let-up, breather.

▶ **verb** ❶ *the horse slacked his pace* REDUCE, lessen, slacken, slow. ❷ (*Brit. informal*) *no slacking!* IDLE, shirk, be lazy, be indolent, waste time, lounge about; *Brit. informal* skive; *N. Amer. informal* goof off.

■ **slack off** ❶ *the rain has slacked off* DECREASE, subside, let up, ease off, abate, diminish, die down, fall off. ❷ *slack off a bit!* RELAX, take things easy, let up, ease up/off, loosen up, slow down; *N. Amer. informal* hang loose, chill out.

■ **slack up** *the horse slacked up* SLOW (DOWN), decelerate, reduce speed.

slacken ▶ **verb** ❶ *he slackened his grip* LOOSEN, release, relax, loose, lessen, weaken. ❷ *he slackened his pace* SLOW (DOWN), become/get/make slower, decelerate, slack (up). ❸ *the rain is slackening* DECREASE, lessen, subside, ease up/off, let up, abate, slack off, diminish, die down, fall off.

– OPPOSITES tighten.

slacker ▶ **noun** (*informal*). *See* LAYABOUT.

slag

■ **slag someone/something off** (*Brit. informal*). *See* CRITICIZE.

slake ▶ **verb** QUENCH, satisfy, sate, satiate, relieve, assuage.

slam ▶ **verb** ❶ *he slammed the door behind him* BANG, shut/close with a bang, shut/close noisily, shut/close with force. ❷ *the car slammed into a lamp post* CRASH INTO, smash into, collide with, hit, strike, ram, plough into, run into, bump into; *N. Amer.* impact. ❸ (*informal*) *he was slammed by the critics. See* CRITICIZE.

slander ▶ **noun** *he could sue us for slander* DEFAMATION (OF CHARACTER), character assassination, calumny, libel; scandalmongering, malicious gossip, disparagement, denigration, aspersions, vilification, traducement, obloquy; lie, slur, smear, false accusation; *informal* mudslinging, bad-mouthing; *archaic* contumely.

▶ **verb** *they were accused of slandering the minister* DEFAME (SOMEONE'S CHARACTER), blacken someone's name, tell lies about, speak ill/evil of, sully someone's reputation, libel, smear, cast aspersions on, spread scandal about, besmirch, tarnish, taint; malign, traduce, vilify, disparage, denigrate, run down; *N. Amer.* slur; *formal* derogate, calumniate.

slanderous ▶ **adjective** DEFAMATORY, denigratory, disparaging, libellous, pejorative, false, misrepresentative, scurrilous, scandalous, malicious, abusive, insulting; *informal* mudslinging.

– OPPOSITES complimentary.

slang ▶ **noun** INFORMAL LANGUAGE, colloquialisms, patois, argot, cant.

slanging match ▶ **noun** (*informal*). *See* QUARREL noun.

slant ▶ **verb** ❶ *the floor was slanting* SLOPE, tilt, incline, be at an angle, tip, cant, lean, dip, pitch, shelve, list, bank. ❷ *their findings were slanted in our favour* BIAS, distort, twist, skew, weight, give a bias to.

▶ **noun** ❶ *the slant of the roof* SLOPE, incline, tilt, gradient, pitch, angle, cant, camber, inclination. ❷ *a feminist slant* POINT OF VIEW, viewpoint, standpoint, stance, angle, perspective, approach, view, attitude, position; bias, leaning.

slanting ▶ **adjective** OBLIQUE, sloping, at an angle, on an incline, inclined, tilting, tilted, slanted, aslant, diagonal, canted, cambered.

slap ▶ **verb** ❶ *he slapped her hard* HIT, strike, smack, clout, cuff, thump, punch, spank; *informal* whack, thwack, wallop, biff, bash; *Brit. informal* slosh; *N. Amer. informal* boff, slug, bust; *Austral./NZ informal* dong, quilt; *archaic* smite. ❷ *he slapped down a £10 note* FLING, throw, toss, slam, bang; *informal* plonk. ❸ *slap on a coat of paint* DAUB, plaster, spread. ❹ (*informal*) *they slapped a huge tax on imports* IMPOSE, levy, put on.

▶ **noun** *a slap across the cheek* SMACK, blow, thump, cuff, clout, punch, spank; *informal* whack, thwack, wallop, clip, biff, bash.

▶ **adverb** (*informal*) *the bypass goes slap through the green belt* STRAIGHT, right, directly, plumb; *informal* smack, (slap) bang; *N. Amer. informal* spang, smack dab.

■ **a slap in the face** REBUFF, rejection, snub, insult, put-down, humiliation.

■ **a slap on the back** CONGRATULATIONS, commendation, approbation, approval, accolades, compliments, tributes, a pat on the back, praise, acclaim, acclamation; *formal* laudation.

■ **a slap on the wrist** REPRIMAND, rebuke, reproof, scolding, admonishment; *informal* telling-off, rap over the knuckles, dressing-down; *Brit. informal* ticking-off, wigging; *Austral./NZ informal* serve.

■ **slap someone down** (*informal*). *See* BERATE.

slapdash ▶ **adjective** CARELESS, slipshod, hurried, haphazard, unsystematic, untidy, messy, hit-or-miss, negligent, neglectful, lax; *informal* sloppy, slap-happy; *Brit. informal* shambolic.

– OPPOSITES meticulous.

slap-happy ▶ **adverb** (*informal*) ❶ *his slap-happy friend* HAPPY-GO-LUCKY, devil-may-care, carefree, easy-going, nonchalant, insouciant, blithe, airy, casual. ❷ *slap-happy work. See* SLAPDASH. ❸ *she's a bit slap-happy after such a narrow escape* DAZED, stupefied, punch-drunk.

slap-up ▶ **adjective** (*Brit. informal*) LAVISH, sumptuous, elaborate, expensive, fit for a king, princely, splendid.

– OPPOSITES meagre.

slash ▶ **verb** ❶ *her tyres had been slashed* CUT (OPEN), gash, slit, split open, lacerate, knife, make an incision in. ❷ (*informal*) *the company slashed prices* REDUCE, cut, lower, bring down, mark down. ❸ (*informal*) *they have slashed 10,000 jobs* GET RID OF, axe, cut, shed.

▶ **noun** ❶ *a slash across his temple* CUT, gash, laceration, slit, incision; wound. ❷ *sentence breaks are indicated by slashes* SOLIDUS, oblique, backslash.

slate ▶ **verb** (*Brit. informal*). *See* CRITICIZE.

slatternly ▶ **adjective** SLOVENLY, untidy, messy, scruffy, unkempt, ill-groomed, dishevelled, frowzy; *N. Amer. informal* raggedy.

slaughter ▶ **verb** ❶ *the animals were slaughtered* KILL, butcher. ❷ *innocent civilians are being slaughtered* MASSACRE, murder, butcher, kill (off), annihilate, exterminate, liquidate, eliminate, destroy, decimate, wipe out, put to death; *poetic/literary* slay. ❸ (*informal*) *their team were slaughtered. See* DEFEAT verb sense 1.

▶ **noun** ❶ *the slaughter of 20 demonstrators* MASSACRE, murdering, (mass) murder, mass killing, mass execution, annihilation, extermination, liquidation, decimation, carnage, butchery, genocide; *poetic/literary* slaying. ❷ *a scene of slaughter* CARNAGE, bloodshed, bloodletting, bloodbath. ❸ (*informal*) *their electoral slaughter. See* DEFEAT noun sense 1.

slaughterhouse ▶ **noun** ABATTOIR; *Brit.* butchery; *archaic* shambles.

slave ▶ **noun** ❶ *the work was done by slaves historical* serf, vassal, thrall; *archaic* bondsman, bondswoman. ❷ *Anna was his willing slave* DRUDGE, servant, man/maid of all work, lackey; *informal* gofer; *Brit. informal* skivvy, dogsbody, poodle.
– RELATED TERMS servile.
– OPPOSITES freeman, master.

▶ **verb** *slaving away for a pittance* TOIL, labour, grind, sweat, work one's fingers to the bone, work like a Trojan/dog; *informal* work one's socks off, kill oneself, sweat blood, slog away; *Brit. informal* graft; *Austral./NZ informal* bullock; *poetic/literary* travail; *archaic* drudge, moil.

slaver ▶ **verb** DROOL, slobber, dribble, salivate; *archaic* drivel.

slavery ▶ **noun** ❶ *thousands were sold into slavery* BONDAGE, enslavement, servitude, thraldom, thrall, serfdom, vassalage. ❷ *this work is sheer slavery* DRUDGERY, toil, (hard) slog, hard labour, grind; *poetic/literary* travail; *archaic* moil.
– OPPOSITES freedom.

slavish ▶ **adjective** ❶ *slavish lackeys of the government* SERVILE, subservient, fawning, obsequious, sycophantic, toadying, unctuous; *informal* bootlicking, forelock-tugging; *N. Amer. informal* apple-polishing. ❷ *slavish copying* UNORIGINAL, uninspired, unimaginative, uninventive, imitative.

slay ▶ **verb** ❶ (*poetic/literary*) *8,000 men were slain* KILL, murder, put to death, butcher, cut down, cut to pieces, slaughter, massacre, shoot down, gun down, mow down, eliminate, annihilate, exterminate, liquidate; *informal* wipe out, bump off, do in/for. ❷ (*informal*) *you slay me, you really do* AMUSE GREATLY, entertain greatly, make someone laugh; *informal* have people rolling in the aisles, kill, knock dead, be a hit with.

slaying ▶ **noun** (*poetic/literary*) MURDER, killing, butchery, slaughter, massacre, extermination, liquidation.

sleazy ▶ **adjective** ❶ *sleazy arms dealers* CORRUPT, immoral, unsavoury, disreputable; *informal* shady, sleazoid. ❷ *a sleazy bar* SQUALID, seedy, seamy, sordid, insalubrious, mean, cheap, low-class, run down; *informal* scruffy, scuzzy, crummy, skanky; *Brit. informal* grotty.
– OPPOSITES reputable, upmarket.

sledge ▶ **noun** TOBOGGAN, bobsleigh, sleigh; *N. Amer.* sled.

sleek ▶ **adjective** ❶ *his sleek dark hair* SMOOTH, glossy, shiny, shining, lustrous, silken, silky. ❷ *the car's sleek lines* STREAMLINED, trim, elegant, graceful. ❸ *sleek young men in city suits* WELL GROOMED, stylish, wealthy-looking.

sleep ▶ **noun** *go and have a sleep* NAP, doze, siesta, catnap, beauty sleep; *informal* snooze, forty winks, a bit of shut-eye; *Brit. informal* kip, zizz; *children's language* bye-byes; *poetic/literary* slumber.

▶ **verb** *she slept for about an hour* BE ASLEEP, doze, take a siesta, take a nap, catnap, sleep like a log/top; *informal* snooze, snatch forty winks, get some shut-eye; *Brit. informal* (have a) kip, get one's head down, (get some) zizz; *N. Amer. informal* catch some Zs; *humorous* be in the land of Nod; *poetic/literary* slumber.
– OPPOSITES wake up.

■ **go to sleep** FALL ASLEEP, get to sleep; *informal* drop off, nod off, drift off, crash out, flake out; *N. Amer. informal* sack out, zone out.

■ **put something to sleep** PUT DOWN, destroy.

sleepiness ▶ **noun** DROWSINESS, tiredness, somnolence, languor, languidness, doziness; lethargy, sluggishness, lassitude, enervation.

sleepless ▶ **adjective** WAKEFUL, restless, without sleep, insomniac; (wide) awake, unsleeping, tossing and turning; *archaic* watchful.

sleeplessness ▶ **noun** INSOMNIA, wakefulness.

sleepwalker ▶ **noun** SOMNAMBULIST; *rare* noctambulist.

sleepy ▶ **adjective** ❶ *she felt very sleepy* DROWSY, tired, somnolent, languid, languorous, heavy-eyed, asleep on one's feet; lethargic, sluggish, enervated, torpid; *informal* dopey; *poetic/literary* slumberous. ❷ *the sleepy heat of the afternoon* SOPORIFIC, sleep-inducing, somnolent. ❸ *a sleepy little village* QUIET, peaceful, tranquil, placid, slow-moving; dull, boring.
– OPPOSITES awake, alert.

sleight of hand ▶ **noun** ❶ *impressive sleight of hand* DEXTERITY, adroitness, deftness, skill. ❷ *financial sleight of hand* DECEPTION, deceit, dissimulation, chicanery, trickery, sharp practice.

slender ▶ **adjective** ❶ *her tall slender figure* SLIM, lean, willowy, sylphlike, svelte, lissom, graceful; slight, slightly built, thin, skinny. ❷ *slender evidence* MEAGRE, limited, slight, scanty, scant, sparse, paltry, insubstantial, insufficient, deficient, negligible; *formal* exiguous. ❸ *the chances seemed slender* FAINT, remote, flimsy, tenuous, fragile, slim; unlikely, improbable.
– OPPOSITES plump.

sleuth ▶ **noun** (*informal*) (PRIVATE) DETECTIVE, (private) investigator; *informal* private eye, snoop, sleuth-hound; *N. Amer. informal* shamus, gumshoe.

slice ▶ **noun** ❶ *a slice of fruitcake* PIECE, portion, slab, rasher, sliver, wafer, shaving. ❷ *a huge slice of public spending* SHARE, part, portion, tranche, piece, proportion, allocation, percentage.
▶ **verb** ❶ *slice the cheese thinly* CUT (UP), carve. ❷ *one man had his ear sliced off* CUT OFF, sever, chop off, shear off.

slick ▶ **adjective** ❶ *a slick advertising campaign* EFFICIENT, smooth, smooth-running, polished, well organized, well run, streamlined. ❷ *his slick use of words* GLIB, smooth, fluent, plausible. ❸ *a slick salesman* SUAVE, urbane, polished, assured, self-assured, smooth-talking, glib; *informal* smarmy. ❹ *her slick brown hair* SHINY, glossy, shining, sleek, smooth, oiled. ❺ *the pavements were slick with rain* SLIPPERY, slithery, wet, greasy; *informal* slippy.
▶ **verb** *his hair was slicked down* SMOOTH, sleek, grease, oil, gel; *informal* smarm.

slide ▶ **verb** ❶ *the glass slid across the table* GLIDE, move smoothly, slip, slither, skim, skate; skid, slew. ❷ *tears slid down her cheeks* TRICKLE, run, flow, pour, stream. ❸ *four men slid out of the shadows* CREEP, steal, slink, slip, tiptoe, sidle. ❹ *the country is sliding into recession* SINK, fall, drop, descend; decline, degenerate.
▶ **noun** ❶ *the current slide in house prices* FALL, decline, drop, slump, downturn, downswing. ❷ *a slide show* TRANSPARENCY, diapositive.
– OPPOSITES rise.
■ **let something slide** NEGLECT, pay little/no attention to, not attend to, be remiss about, let something go downhill.

slight ▶ **adjective** ❶ *the chance of success is slight* SMALL, modest, tiny, minute, inappreciable, negligible, insignificant, minimal, remote, slim, faint; *informal* minuscule; *formal* exiguous. ❷ *the book is a slight work* MINOR, inconsequential, trivial, unimportant, lightweight, superficial, shallow. ❸ *Elizabeth's slight figure* SLIM, slender, petite, diminutive, small, delicate, dainty.
– OPPOSITES considerable.
▶ **verb** *he had been slighted* INSULT, snub, rebuff, repulse, spurn, treat disrespectfully, give someone the cold shoulder, cut (dead), scorn; *informal* give someone the brush-off, freeze out, stiff-arm.
– OPPOSITES respect.
▶ **noun** *an unintended slight* INSULT, affront, snub, rebuff; *informal* put-down, dig.
– OPPOSITES compliment.

slighting ▶ **adjective** INSULTING, disparaging, derogatory, disrespectful, denigratory, pejorative, abusive, offensive, defamatory, slanderous, scurrilous; disdainful, scornful, contemptuous; *archaic* contumelious.

slightly ▶ **adverb** A LITTLE, a bit, somewhat, rather, moderately, to a certain extent, faintly, vaguely, a shade.
– OPPOSITES very.

slim ▶ **adjective** ❶ *she was tall and slim* SLENDER, lean, thin, willowy, sylphlike, svelte, lissom, trim, slight, slightly built. ❷ *a slim silver bracelet* NARROW, slender, slimline. ❸ *a slim chance of escape* SLIGHT, small, slender, faint, poor, remote, unlikely, improbable.
– OPPOSITES plump.
▶ **verb** ❶ *I'm trying to slim* LOSE WEIGHT, get thinner, lose some pounds/inches, get into shape; *N. Amer.* slenderize. ❷ *the number of staff had been slimmed down* REDUCE, cut (down/back), scale down, decrease, diminish, pare down.

slime ▶ **noun** OOZE, sludge, muck, mud, mire; *informal* goo, gunk, gook, gloop; *Brit. informal* gunge; *N. Amer. informal* guck, glop.

slimy ▶ **adjective** ❶ *the floor was slimy* SLIPPERY, slithery, greasy, muddy, mucky, sludgy, wet, sticky; *informal* slippy, gunky, gooey, gloopy. ❷ (*informal*) *her slimy press agent. See* OBSEQUIOUS.

sling ▶ **noun** ❶ *she had her arm in a sling* (SUPPORT) BANDAGE, support, strap. ❷ *armed only with a sling* CATAPULT, slingshot; *Austral./NZ* shanghai.
▶ **verb** ❶ *a hammock was slung between two trees* HANG, suspend, string, swing. ❷ (*informal*) *she slung her jacket on the sofa. See* THROW verb sense 1.

slink ▶ **verb** CREEP, sneak, steal, slip, slide, sidle, tiptoe, pussyfoot.

slinky ▶ **adjective** (*informal*) ❶ *a slinky black dress* TIGHT-FITTING, close-fitting, figure-hugging, sexy. ❷ *her slinky elegance* SINUOUS, willowy, graceful, sleek.

slip[1] ▶ **verb** ❶ *she slipped on the ice* SLIDE, skid, slither, glide; fall (over), lose one's balance, tumble. ❷ *the envelope slipped through Luke's fingers* FALL, drop, slide. ❸ *we slipped out by a back door* CREEP, steal, sneak, slide, sidle, slope, slink, tiptoe. ❹ *standards have slipped* DECLINE, deteriorate, degenerate, worsen, get worse, fall (off), drop; *informal* go downhill, go to the dogs, go to pot. ❺ *the bank's shares slipped 1.5p* DROP, go down, sink, slump, decrease, depreciate. ❻ *the hours slipped by* PASS, elapse, go by/past, roll by/past, fly by/past, tick by/past. ❼ *she slipped the map into her pocket* PUT, tuck, shove; *informal* pop, stick, stuff. ❽ *Sarah slipped into a black skirt* PUT ON, pull on, don, dress/clothe oneself in; change into. ❾ *she slipped out of her clothes* TAKE OFF, remove, pull off, doff; *Brit. informal* peel off. ❿ *he slipped the knot of his tie* UNTIE, unfasten, undo.

▶ **noun** ❶ *a single slip could send them plummeting downwards* FALSE STEP, misstep, slide, skid, fall, tumble. ❷ *a careless slip* MISTAKE, error, blunder, gaffe, slip of the tongue/pen; oversight, omission, lapse, inaccuracy; *informal* slip-up, boo-boo, howler; *Brit. informal* boob, clanger, bloomer; *N. Amer. informal* goof, blooper, bloop. ❸ *a silk slip* UNDERSKIRT, petticoat, underslip.

■ **give someone the slip** (*informal*) ESCAPE FROM, get away from, evade, dodge, elude, lose, shake off, throw off (the scent), get clear of.

■ **let something slip** REVEAL, disclose, divulge, let out, give away, blurt out; give the game away; *informal* let on, blab, let the cat out of the bag, spill the beans; *Brit. informal* blow the gaff.

■ **slip away** ❶ *they managed to slip away* ESCAPE, get away, break free; *informal* fly the coop; *Brit. informal* do a bunk, do a runner; *N. Amer. informal* take a powder. ❷ *she slipped away in her sleep. See* DIE sense 1.

■ **slip up** (*informal*) MAKE A MISTAKE, (make a) blunder, get something wrong, make an error, err; *informal* make a bloomer, make a boo-boo; *Brit. informal* boob, drop a clanger; *N. Amer. informal* goof up.

slip[2] ▶ **noun** ❶ *a slip of paper* PIECE OF PAPER, scrap of paper, sheet, note; chit; *informal* stickie. ❷ *they took slips from rare plants* CUTTING, graft; scion, shoot, offshoot.

■ **a slip of a ——** SMALL, slender, slim, slight, slightly built, petite, little, tiny, diminutive; *informal* pint-sized.

slipper ▶ **noun** ❶ *he pulled on his slippers* carpet slipper, bedroom slipper, house shoe; *N. Amer.* slipperette. ❷ *satin slippers* pump, mule.

slippery ▶ **adjective** ❶ *the roads are slippery* SLITHERY, greasy, oily, icy, glassy, smooth, slimy, wet; *informal* slippy. ❷ *a slippery customer* EVASIVE, unreliable, unpredictable; devious, crafty, cunning, wily, tricky, artful, slick, sly, sneaky, scheming, untrustworthy, deceitful, duplicitous, dishonest, treacherous, two-faced; *N. Amer.* snide; *informal* shady, shifty; *Brit. informal* dodgy; *Austral./NZ informal* shonky.

slipshod ▶ **adjective** CARELESS, lackadaisical, slapdash, disorganized, haphazard, hit-or-miss, untidy, messy, unsystematic, unmethodical, casual, negligent, neglectful, remiss, lax, slack; *informal* sloppy, slap-happy.
– OPPOSITES meticulous.

slip-up ▶ **noun** (*informal*) MISTAKE, slip, error, blunder, oversight, omission, gaffe, slip of the tongue/pen, inaccuracy; *informal* boo-boo, howler; *Brit. informal* boob, clanger, bloomer; *N. Amer. informal* goof, blooper, bloop.

slit ▶ **noun** ❶ *three diagonal slits* CUT, incision, split, slash, gash, laceration. ❷ *a slit in the curtains* OPENING, gap, chink, crack, aperture, slot.

▶ **verb** *he threatened to slit her throat* CUT, slash, split open, slice open, gash, lacerate, make an incision in.

slither ▶ **verb** SLIDE, slip, glide, wriggle, crawl; skid.

sliver ▶ **noun** SPLINTER, shard, shiver, chip, flake, shred, scrap, slither, shaving, paring, piece, fragment.

slob ▶ **noun** (*informal*) LAYABOUT, good-for-nothing, sluggard, laggard; *informal* slacker, couch potato; *archaic* sloven.

slobber ▶ **verb** DROOL, slaver, dribble, salivate; *archaic* drivel.

slog ▶ **verb** ❶ *they were all slogging away* WORK HARD, toil, labour, work one's fingers to the bone, work like a Trojan/dog, exert oneself, grind, slave, grub, plough, plod, peg; *informal* beaver, plug, work one's guts out, work one's socks off, sweat blood; *Brit. informal* graft; *Austral./NZ informal* bullock; *poetic/literary* travail; *archaic* drudge, moil. ❷ *they slogged around the streets* TRUDGE, tramp, traipse, toil, plod, trek, footslog, drag oneself.
– OPPOSITES relax.

▶ **noun** ❶ *10 months' hard slog* HARD WORK, toil, toiling, labour, effort, exertion, grind, drudgery; *informal* sweat; *Brit. informal* graft; *Austral./NZ informal* (hard) yakka; *poetic/literary* travail; *archaic* moil. ❷ *a steady uphill slog* TRUDGE, tramp, traipse, plod, trek, footslog.
– OPPOSITES leisure.

slogan ▶ **noun** CATCHPHRASE, catchline, jingle; *N. Amer. informal* tag line.

slop ▶ **verb** *water slopped over the edge* SPILL, flow, overflow, run, slosh, splash.

■ **slop around/about** (*Brit. informal*) LAZE (AROUND/ABOUT), lounge (around/about), loll (around/about), loaf (around/about), slouch (about/around); *informal* hang around; *Brit. informal* hang about, mooch about/around; *N. Amer. informal* bum around, lollygag.

slope ▶ **noun** ❶ *the slope of the roof* GRADIENT, incline, angle, slant, inclination, pitch, decline, ascent, declivity, acclivity, rise, fall, tilt, tip, downslope, upslope; *N. Amer.* grade, downgrade, upgrade. ❷ *a grassy slope* HILL, hillside, hillock, bank, escarpment, scarp; *poetic/literary* steep. ❸ *the ski slopes* PISTE, run, nursery slope, dry slope; *N. Amer.* trail.

▶ **verb** *the garden sloped down to a stream* SLANT, incline, tilt; drop away, fall away, decline, descend, shelve, lean; rise, ascend, climb.

■ **slope off** (*informal*) LEAVE, go away, slip away, steal away, slink off, creep off, sneak off; *informal* push off, clear off.

sloping ▶ **adjective** AT A SLANT, on the slant, at an angle, slanting, slanted, leaning, inclining, inclined, angled, cambered, canted, tilting, tilted, dipping, declivitous, acclivitous.
–OPPOSITES level.

sloppy ▶ **adjective** ❶ *sloppy chicken curry* RUNNY, watery, thin, liquid, semi-liquid, mushy; *informal* gloopy. ❷ *their defending was sloppy* CARELESS, slapdash, slipshod, lackadaisical, haphazard, lax, slack, slovenly; *informal* slaphappy; *Brit. informal* shambolic. ❸ *sloppy T-shirts* BAGGY, loose-fitting, loose, generously cut; shapeless, sack-like, oversized. ❹ *sloppy letters* SENTIMENTAL, mawkish, cloying, saccharine, sugary, syrupy; romantic, hearts-and-flowers; *informal* slushy, schmaltzy, lovey-dovey; *Brit. informal* soppy; *N. Amer. informal* cornball, sappy, hokey, three-hankie.

slosh ▶ **verb** ❶ *beer sloshed over the side of the glass* SPILL, slop, splash, flow, overflow. ❷ *workers sloshed round in boots* SPLASH, swash, squelch, wade; *informal* splosh. ❸ *she sloshed more wine into her glass* POUR, slop, splash. ❹ (*Brit. informal*) *Gary sloshed him. See* HIT verb sense 1.

slot ▶ **noun** ❶ *he slid a coin into the slot* APERTURE, slit, crack, hole, opening. ❷ *a mid-morning slot* SPOT, time, period, niche, space; *informal* window.
▶ **verb** *he slotted a cassette into the machine* INSERT, put, place, slide, slip.

sloth ▶ **noun** LAZINESS, idleness, indolence, slothfulness, inactivity, inertia, sluggishness, shiftlessness, apathy, accidie, listlessness, lassitude, lethargy, languor, torpidity; *poetic/literary* hebetude.
–OPPOSITES industriousness.

slothful ▶ **adjective** LAZY, idle, indolent, workshy, inactive, sluggish, apathetic, lethargic, listless, languid, torpid; *informal* bone idle; *archaic* otiose.

slouch ▶ **verb** SLUMP, hunch; loll, droop.

slovenly ▶ **adjective** ❶ *his slovenly appearance* SCRUFFY, untidy, messy, unkempt, ill-groomed, slatternly, dishevelled, bedraggled, tousled, rumpled, frowzy; *informal* slobbish, slobby; *N. Amer. informal* raggedy, raunchy. ❷ *his work is slovenly* CARELESS, slapdash, slipshod, haphazard, hit-or-miss, untidy, messy, negligent, lax, lackadaisical, slack; *informal* sloppy, slaphappy.
–OPPOSITES tidy, careful.

slow ▶ **adjective** ❶ *their slow walk home* UNHURRIED, leisurely, steady, sedate, slow-moving, plodding, dawdling, sluggish, sluggardly. ❷ *a slow process* LONG-DRAWN-OUT, time-consuming, lengthy, protracted, prolonged, gradual. ❸ *he can be so slow* OBTUSE, stupid, unperceptive, insensitive, bovine, stolid, slow-witted, dull-witted, unintelligent, doltish, witless; *informal* dense, dim, dim-witted, thick, slow on the uptake, dumb, dopey, boneheaded; *Brit. informal* dozy; *N. Amer. informal* chowderheaded. ❹ *they were slow to voice their opinions* RELUCTANT, unwilling, disinclined, loath, hesitant, afraid, chary, shy. ❺ *the slow season* SLUGGISH, slack, quiet, inactive, flat, depressed, stagnant, dead. ❻ *a slow narrative* DULL, boring, uninteresting, unexciting, uneventful, tedious, tiresome, wearisome, monotonous, dreary, lacklustre.
–OPPOSITES fast.
▶ **verb** ❶ *the traffic forced him to slow down* REDUCE SPEED, go slower, decelerate, brake. ❷ *you need to slow down* TAKE IT EASY, relax, ease up/off, take a break, slack off, let up; *N. Amer. informal* chill out, hang loose. ❸ *this would slow down economic growth* HOLD BACK/UP, delay, retard, set back; restrict, check, curb, inhibit, impede, obstruct, hinder, hamper; *archaic* stay.
–OPPOSITES accelerate.

slowly ▶ **adverb** ❶ *Rose walked off slowly* AT A SLOW PACE, without hurrying, unhurriedly, steadily, at a leisurely pace, at a snail's pace; *Music* adagio, lento, largo. ❷ *her health is improving slowly* GRADUALLY, bit by bit, little by little, slowly but surely, step by step.
–OPPOSITES quickly.

sludge ▶ **noun** MUD, muck, mire, ooze, silt, alluvium; *informal* gunk, crud, gloop, gook, goo; *Brit. informal* gunge, grot; *N. Amer. informal* guck, glop.

sluggish ▶ **adjective** ❶ *Alex felt tired and sluggish* LETHARGIC, listless, lacking in energy, lifeless, inert, inactive, slow, torpid, languid, apathetic, weary, tired, fatigued, sleepy, drowsy, enervated; lazy, idle, indolent, slothful, sluggardly; *Medicine* asthenic; *N. Amer.* logy; *informal* dozy, dopey. ❷ *the economy is sluggish* INACTIVE, quiet, slow, slack, flat, depressed, stagnant.
–OPPOSITES vigorous.

sluice ▶ **verb** ❶ *crews sluiced down the decks* WASH (DOWN), rinse, clean, cleanse. ❷ *the water sluiced out* POUR, flow, run, gush, stream, course, flood, surge, spill.

slum ▶ **noun** HOVEL; (**slums**) ghetto, shanty town.

slumber (*poetic/literary*) ▶ **verb** *the child slumbered fitfully. See* SLEEP verb.
▶ **noun** *an uneasy slumber. See* SLEEP noun.

slummy ▶ **adjective** SEEDY, insalubrious, squalid, sleazy, run down, down at heel, shabby, dilapidated; *informal* scruffy, skanky; *Brit. informal* grotty; *N. Amer. informal* shacky.
–OPPOSITES upmarket.

slump ▶ **verb** ❶ *he slumped into a chair* SIT HEAVILY, flop, flump, collapse, sink, fall; *informal* plonk oneself. ❷ *houses prices slumped* FALL STEEPLY, plummet, tumble, drop, go down; *informal* crash, nosedive. ❸ *reading standards have slumped* DECLINE, deteriorate, degenerate, worsen, slip; *informal* go downhill.
▶ **noun** ❶ *a slump in profits* STEEP FALL, drop, tum-

ble, downturn, downswing, slide, decline, decrease; *informal* nosedive. ❷ *an economic slump* RECESSION, economic decline, depression, slowdown, stagnation.
– OPPOSITES rise, boom.

slur ▶ **verb** *she was slurring her words* MUMBLE, speak unclearly, garble.
▶ **noun** *a gross slur* INSULT, slight, slander, slanderous statement, aspersion, smear, allegation.

slush ▶ **noun** ❶ *he wiped the slush off his shoes* MELTING SNOW, wet snow, mush, sludge. ❷ (*informal*) *the slush of romantic films* SENTIMENTALITY, mawkishness, sentimentalism; *informal* schmaltz, mush, slushiness, corniness; *Brit. informal* soppiness; *N. Amer. informal* sappiness, hokeyness.

slut ▶ **noun** PROMISCUOUS WOMAN, prostitute, whore; *informal* tart, floozie, pro; *Brit. informal* scrubber, slag, slapper; *N. Amer. informal* tramp, hooker, hustler, roundheel; *dated* scarlet woman, loose woman, hussy, trollop; *archaic* harlot, strumpet, wanton.

sly ▶ **adjective** ❶ *she's rather sly* CUNNING, crafty, clever, wily, artful, guileful, tricky, scheming, devious, deceitful, duplicitous, dishonest, underhand, sneaky; *archaic* subtle. ❷ *a sly grin* ROGUISH, mischievous, impish, playful, wicked, arch, knowing. ❸ *she took a sly sip of water* SURREPTITIOUS, furtive, stealthy, covert.
■ **on the sly** IN SECRET, secretly, furtively, surreptitiously, covertly, clandestinely, on the quiet, behind someone's back.

smack[1] ▶ **noun** ❶ *she gave him a smack* SLAP, clout, cuff, blow, spank, rap, swat, crack, thump, punch; *informal* whack, thwack, clip, biff, wallop, swipe, bop, belt, bash, sock. ❷ *the parcel landed with a smack* BANG, crash, crack, thud, thump. ❸ (*informal*) *a smack on the lips* KISS, peck; *informal* smacker.
▶ **verb** ❶ *he tried to smack her* SLAP, hit, strike, spank, cuff, clout, thump, punch, swat; box someone's ears; *informal* whack, clip, wallop, biff, swipe, bop, belt, bash, sock; *Scottish & N. English informal* skelp; *N. Amer. informal* boff, slug, bust. ❷ *the waiter smacked a plate down* BANG, slam, crash, thump; sling, fling; *informal* plonk; *N. Amer. informal* plunk.
▶ **adverb** (*informal*) *smack in the middle* EXACTLY, precisely, straight, right, directly, squarely, dead, plumb, point-blank; *informal* slap, bang; *N. Amer. informal* smack dab.

smack[2] ▶ **noun** ❶ *the beer has a smack of hops* TASTE, flavour, savour. ❷ *a smack of bitterness in his words* TRACE, tinge, touch, suggestion, hint, overtone, suspicion, whisper.
■ **smack of** ❶ *the tea smacked of tannin* TASTE OF, have the flavour of. ❷ *the plan smacked of self-promotion* SUGGEST, hint at, have overtones of, give the impression of, have the stamp of, seem like; smell of, reek of.

small ▶ **adjective** ❶ *a small flat* LITTLE, compact, bijou, tiny, miniature, mini; minute, microscopic, minuscule; toy, baby; poky, cramped, boxy; *Scottish* wee; *informal* tiddly, teeny, teensy, itsy-bitsy, itty-bitty, pocket-sized, half-pint, dinky, ickle; *Brit. informal* titchy; *N. Amer. informal* little-bitty. ❷ *a very small man* SHORT, little, petite, diminutive, elfin, tiny; puny, undersized, stunted, dwarfish, midget, pygmy, Lilliputian; *Scottish* wee; *informal* teeny, pint-sized. ❸ *a few small changes* SLIGHT, minor, unimportant, trifling, trivial, insignificant, inconsequential, negligible, nugatory, infinitesimal; *informal* minuscule, piffling, piddling. ❹ *small helpings* INADEQUATE, meagre, insufficient, ungenerous; *informal* measly, stingy, mingy, pathetic. ❺ *they made him feel small* FOOLISH, stupid, insignificant, unimportant; embarrassed, humiliated, uncomfortable, mortified, ashamed; crushed. ❻ *a small farmer* SMALL-SCALE, small-time; modest, unpretentious, humble.
– RELATED TERMS micro-, mini-, nano-.
– OPPOSITES big, tall, major, ample, substantial.

small change ▶ **noun** COINS, change, coppers, silver, cash, specie.

small-minded ▶ **adjective** NARROW-MINDED, petty, mean-spirited, uncharitable; close-minded, short-sighted, myopic, blinkered, inward-looking, unimaginative, parochial, provincial, insular, small-town; intolerant, illiberal, conservative, hidebound, dyed-in-the-wool, set in one's ways, inflexible; prejudiced, bigoted; *Brit.* parish-pump, blimpish.
– OPPOSITES tolerant.

small-time ▶ **adjective** MINOR, small-scale; petty, unimportant, insignificant, inconsequential; *N. Amer.* minor-league; *informal* penny-ante, piddling; *N. Amer. informal* two-bit, bush-league, picayune.
– OPPOSITES major.

smarmy ▶ **adjective** (*informal*) UNCTUOUS, ingratiating, slick, oily, greasy, obsequious, sycophantic, fawning; *informal* slimy, sucky.

smart ▶ **adjective** ❶ *you look very smart* WELL DRESSED, stylish, chic, fashionable, modish, elegant, neat, spruce, trim, dapper; *N. Amer.* trig; *informal* snazzy, natty, snappy, sharp, cool; *N. Amer. informal* sassy, spiffy, fly, kicky. ❷ *a smart restaurant* FASHIONABLE, stylish, high-class, exclusive, chic, fancy; *Brit.* upmarket; *N. Amer.* high-toned; *informal* trendy, posh, ritzy, plush, classy, swanky, glitzy; *Brit. informal* swish; *N. Amer. informal* swank. ❸ (*informal*) *he's the smart one* CLEVER, bright, intelligent, sharp-witted, quick-witted, shrewd, astute, able; perceptive, percipient; *informal* brainy, savvy, quick on the uptake. ❹ *a smart pace* BRISK, quick, fast, rapid, swift, lively, spanking, energetic, vigorous; *informal* snappy, cracking. ❺ *a smart blow on the snout* SHARP, severe, forceful, violent.
– OPPOSITES untidy, downmarket, stupid, slow, gentle.

▶ **verb** ❶ *her eyes were smarting* STING, burn, tingle, prickle; hurt, ache. ❷ *she smarted at the accusations* FEEL ANNOYED, feel upset, take offence, feel aggrieved, feel indignant, be put out, feel hurt.

■ **look smart** (*Brit.*) BE QUICK, hurry up, speed up; *informal* make it snappy, get cracking, get moving, step on it; *Brit. informal* get one's skates on, stir one's stumps; *N. Amer. informal* get a wiggle on.

smarten ▶ **verb** SPRUCE UP, clean up, tidy up, neaten, tidy; groom, freshen, preen, primp, beautify; redecorate, refurbish, modernize; *informal* do up, titivate, doll up; *Brit. informal* tart up, posh up; *N. Amer. informal* gussy up.

smash ▶ **verb** ❶ *he smashed a window* BREAK, shatter, splinter, crack, shiver; *informal* bust. ❷ *she's smashed the car* CRASH, wreck; *Brit.* write off; *Brit. informal* prang; *N. Amer. informal* total. ❸ *they smashed into a wall* CRASH INTO, collide with, hit, strike, ram, smack into, slam into, plough into, run into, bump into; *N. Amer.* impact. ❹ *Don smashed him over the head* HIT, strike, thump, punch, smack; *informal* whack, bash, biff, bop, clout, wallop, crown; *Brit. informal* slosh, dot; *N. Amer. informal* slug. ❺ *he smashed their hopes of glory* DESTROY, wreck, ruin, shatter, dash, crush, devastate, demolish, overturn, scotch; *informal* put the kibosh on, do for, put paid to, queer; *Brit. informal* scupper.

▶ **noun** ❶ *the smash of glass* BREAKING, shattering, crash. ❷ *a motorway smash* CRASH, collision, accident, bump; *Brit.* RTA; *N. Amer.* wreck; *informal* pile-up, smash-up; *Brit. informal* prang, shunt. ❸ (*informal*) *a box-office smash* SUCCESS, sensation, sell-out, triumph; *informal* (smash) hit, winner, crowd-puller, knockout, wow, biggie.

smashing ▶ **adjective** (*Brit. informal*). *See* MARVELLOUS sense 2.

smattering ▶ **noun** BIT, little, modicum, touch, soupçon; nodding acquaintance; rudiments, basics; *informal* smidgen, smidge, tad.

smear ▶ **verb** ❶ *the table was smeared with grease* STREAK, smudge, mark, soil, dirty; *informal* splotch, splodge; *poetic/literary* besmear. ❷ *smear the meat with olive oil* COVER, coat, grease; *poetic/literary* bedaub. ❸ *she smeared sunblock on her skin* SPREAD, rub, daub, slap, slather, smother, plaster, cream, slick; apply; *poetic/literary* besmear. ❹ *they are trying to smear our reputation* SULLY, tarnish, blacken, drag through the mud, taint, damage, defame, discredit, malign, slander, libel; *N. Amer.* slur; *informal* do a hatchet job on; *formal* calumniate; *poetic/literary* besmirch.

▶ **noun** ❶ *smears of blood* STREAK, smudge, daub, dab, spot, patch, blotch, mark; *informal* splotch, splodge. ❷ *press smears about his closest aides* FALSE ACCUSATION, lie, untruth, slur, slander, libel, defamation, calumny.

smell ▶ **noun** *the smell of the kitchen* ODOUR, aroma, fragrance, scent, perfume, redolence; bouquet, nose; stench, stink, reek; *Brit. informal* pong, niff, whiff, hum; *Scottish informal* guff; *N. Amer. informal* funk; *poetic/literary* miasma.

– RELATED TERMS osmic, olfactory.

▶ **verb** ❶ *he smelled her perfume* SCENT, get a sniff of, detect. ❷ *the dogs smelled each other* SNIFF, nose. ❸ *the cellar smells* STINK, reek, have a bad smell; *Brit. informal* pong, hum, niff, whiff. ❹ *it smells like a hoax to me* SMACK OF, have the hallmarks of, seem like, have the air of, suggest.

smelly ▶ **adjective** FOUL-SMELLING, stinking, reeking, fetid, malodorous, pungent, rank, noxious; off, gamy, high; musty, fusty; *informal* stinky; *Brit. informal* pongy, whiffy, humming; *N. Amer. informal* funky; *poetic/literary* miasmic, noisome.

smile ▶ **verb** *he smiled at her* BEAM, grin (from ear to ear), dimple, twinkle; smirk, simper; leer.

– OPPOSITES frown.

▶ **noun** *the smile on her face* BEAM, grin, twinkle; smirk, simper; leer.

smirk ▶ **verb** SMILE SMUGLY, simper, snigger; leer.

smitten ▶ **adjective** ❶ *he was smitten with cholera* STRUCK DOWN, laid low, suffering, affected, afflicted, plagued, stricken. ❷ *Jane's smitten with you* INFATUATED, besotted, in love, obsessed, head over heels; enamoured of, attracted to, taken with; captivated, enchanted, under someone's spell; *informal* bowled over, swept off one's feet, crazy about, mad about, keen on, gone on, sweet on; *Brit. informal* potty about.

smog ▶ **noun** FOG, haze; fumes, smoke, pollution; *Brit. informal* pea-souper.

smoke ▶ **verb** ❶ *the fire was smoking* SMOULDER, emit smoke; *archaic* reek. ❷ *he smoked his cigarette* PUFF ON, draw on, pull on; inhale; light; *informal* drag on. ❸ *they smoke their salmon* CURE, preserve, dry.

▶ **noun** *the smoke from the bonfire* FUMES, exhaust, gas, vapour; smog.

smoky ▶ **adjective** ❶ *the smoky atmosphere* SMOKE-FILLED, sooty, smoggy, hazy, foggy, murky, thick; *Brit. informal* fuggy. ❷ *her smoky eyes* GREY, sooty, dark, black.

smooth ▶ **adjective** ❶ *the smooth flat rocks* EVEN, level, flat, plane; unwrinkled, featureless; glassy, glossy, silky, polished. ❷ *his face was smooth* CLEAN-SHAVEN, hairless. ❸ *a smooth sauce* CREAMY, velvety, blended. ❹ *a smooth sea* CALM, still, tranquil, undisturbed, unruffled, even, flat, waveless, like a millpond. ❺ *the smooth running of the equipment* STEADY, regular, uninterrupted, unbroken, fluid, fluent; straightforward, easy, effortless, trouble-free. ❻ *a smooth wine* MELLOW, mild, agreeable, pleasant. ❼ *the smooth tone of the clarinet* DULCET, soft, soothing, mellow, sweet, silvery, honeyed, mellifluous, melodious, lilting, lyrical, harmonious. ❽ *a smooth, confident man* SUAVE, urbane, sophisticated, polished, debonair; courteous, gracious, glib, slick, ingratiating, unctuous; *informal* smarmy.

– OPPOSITES uneven, rough, hairy, lumpy, irregular, raucous, gauche.

▶ **verb** ❶ *she smoothed the soil* FLATTEN, level (out/off), even out/off; press, roll, steamroll, iron, plane. ❷ *a plan to smooth the way for the agreement* EASE, facilitate, clear the way for, pave the way for, expedite, assist, aid, help, oil the wheels of, lubricate.

smoothly ▶ **adverb** ❶ *her hair was combed smoothly back* EVENLY, level, flat, flush. ❷ *the door closed smoothly* FLUIDLY, fluently, steadily, frictionlessly, easily; quietly. ❸ *the plan had gone smoothly* WITHOUT A HITCH, like clockwork, without difficulty, easily, effortlessly, according to plan, swimmingly, satisfactorily, very well; *informal* like a dream.

smooth-talking ▶ **adjective** (*informal*) PERSUASIVE, glib, plausible, silver-tongued, slick, eloquent, fast-talking; ingratiating, flattering, unctuous, obsequious, sycophantic; *informal* smarmy.

– OPPOSITES blunt.

smother ▶ **verb** ❶ *she tried to smother her baby* SUFFOCATE, asphyxiate, stifle, choke. ❷ *we smothered the flames* EXTINGUISH, put out, snuff out, dampen, douse, stamp out, choke. ❸ *we smothered ourselves with suncream* SMEAR, daub, spread, cover; *poetic/literary* besmear, bedaub. ❹ *their granny always smothers them* OVERWHELM, inundate, envelop, cocoon; *Brit.* wrap someone in cotton wool. ❺ *she smothered a sigh* STIFLE, muffle, strangle, repress, suppress, hold back, fight back, bite back, swallow, contain, bottle up, conceal, hide; bite one's lip; *informal* keep a/the lid on.

smoulder ▶ **verb** ❶ *the bonfire still smouldered* SMOKE, glow, burn; *archaic* reek. ❷ *she was smouldering with resentment* SEETHE, boil, fume, burn, simmer, be boiling over, be beside oneself; *informal* be livid.

smudge ▶ **noun** *a smudge of blood* STREAK, smear, mark, stain, blotch, stripe, blob, dab; *informal* splotch, splodge.

▶ **verb** ❶ *her face was smudged with dust* STREAK, mark, dirty, soil, blotch, blacken, smear, blot, daub, stain; *informal* splotch, splodge; *poetic/literary* bedaub, besmirch. ❷ *she smudged her make-up* SMEAR, streak, mess up.

smug ▶ **adjective** SELF-SATISFIED, self-congratulatory, complacent, superior, pleased with oneself, self-approving; *Brit. informal* like the cat that got the cream, I'm-all-right-Jack.

smuggle ▶ **verb** IMPORT/EXPORT ILLEGALLY, traffic in, run.

smuggler ▶ **noun** CONTRABANDIST, runner, courier; *informal* mule, moonshiner.

smutty ▶ **adjective** VULGAR, rude, crude, dirty, filthy, salacious, coarse, obscene, lewd, pornographic, X-rated; risqué, racy, earthy, bawdy, suggestive, naughty, ribald, off colour; *informal* blue, raunchy; *Brit. informal* near the knuckle, saucy; *N. Amer. informal* gamy; *euphemistic* adult.

snack ▶ **noun** *she made herself a snack* LIGHT MEAL, sandwich, treat, refreshments, nibbles, titbit(s); *informal* bite (to eat); *Brit. informal* elevenses.

▶ **verb** *don't snack on sugary foods* EAT BETWEEN MEALS, nibble, munch; *informal* graze.

snaffle ▶ **verb** (*informal*). *See* STEAL verb sense 1.

snag ▶ **noun** ❶ *the snag is that this might affect inflation* COMPLICATION, difficulty, catch, hitch, obstacle, stumbling block, pitfall, problem, impediment, hindrance, inconvenience, setback, hurdle, disadvantage, downside, drawback. ❷ *smooth rails with no snags* SHARP PROJECTION, jag; thorn, spur. ❸ *a snag in her tights* TEAR, rip, hole, gash, slash; ladder, run.

▶ **verb** ❶ *she snagged her tights* TEAR, rip, ladder. ❷ *the zip snagged on the fabric* CATCH, get caught, hook.

snake ▶ **noun** *the snake shed its skin poetic/literary* serpent; *Zoology* ophidian; *Austral./NZ rhyming slang* Joe Blake.

– RELATED TERMS colubrine, serpentine.

▶ **verb** *the road snakes inland* TWIST, wind, meander, zigzag, curve.

■ **snake in the grass** TRAITOR, turncoat, betrayer, informer, back-stabber, double-crosser, quisling, Judas; fraudster, trickster, charlatan; *informal* two-timer, rat.

snap ▶ **verb** ❶ *the ruler snapped* BREAK, fracture, splinter, come apart, split, crack; *informal* bust. ❷ *she snapped after years of violence* FLARE UP, lose one's self-control, freak out, go to pieces, get worked up; *informal* crack up, lose one's cool, blow one's top, fly off the handle; *Brit. informal* throw a wobbly. ❸ *a dog was snapping at his heels* BITE; gnash its teeth. ❹ *'Shut up!' Anna snapped* SAY ROUGHLY, say brusquely, say abruptly, say angrily, bark, snarl, growl; retort, rejoin, retaliate; round on someone; *informal* jump down someone's throat. ❺ *photographers snapped the royals* PHOTOGRAPH, picture, take, shoot, film, capture.

▶ **noun** ❶ *she closed her purse with a snap* CLICK, crack, pop. ❷ *a cold snap* PERIOD, spell, time, interval, stretch; *Brit. informal* patch. ❸ (*informal*) *holiday snaps* PHOTOGRAPH, picture, photo, shot, snapshot, print, slide, frame, still; *Brit.* enprint.

■ **snap out of it** (*informal*) RECOVER, get a grip, pull oneself together, get over it, get better, cheer up, perk up; *informal* buck up.

■ **snap something up** BUY EAGERLY, accept eagerly, jump at, take advantage of, grab, seize (on), grasp with both hands, pounce on.

snappy ▶ **adjective** (*informal*) ❶ *a snappy mood* IRRITABLE, irascible, short-tempered, hot-tempered, quick-tempered, snappish, fiery, touchy, volatile; cross, crabby, crotchety, cantankerous, grumpy, bad-tempered, testy, tetchy; *informal* chippy, grouchy, cranky, on a short fuse; *Brit. informal* narky, ratty, eggy, like a bear with a sore head; *N. Amer. informal* sore-headed. ❷ *a snappy catchphrase* CONCISE, succinct, memorable, catchy, neat, clever, crisp, pithy, witty, incisive, brief, short. ❸ *a snappy dresser* SMART, fashionable, stylish, chic, modish, elegant, neat, spruce, trim, dapper; *informal* snazzy, natty, sharp, nifty, cool; *N. Amer. informal* sassy, spiffy, fly.

–OPPOSITES peaceable, long-winded, slovenly.

■ **make it snappy** HURRY (UP), be quick (about it), get a move on, look lively, speed up; *informal* get cracking, step on it, move it, buck up, shake a leg; *Brit. informal* get your skates on; *N. Amer. informal* get a wiggle on; *dated* make haste.

snare ▶ **noun** ❶ *the hare was caught in a snare* TRAP, gin, net, noose. ❷ *avoid the snares of the new law* PITFALL, trap, catch, danger, hazard, peril; web, mesh; *poetic/literary* toils.

▶ **verb** ❶ *game birds were snared* TRAP, catch, net, bag, ensnare, entrap. ❷ *he managed to snare an heiress* ENSNARE, catch, get hold of, bag, hook, land.

snarl[1] ▶ **verb** ❶ *the wolves are snarling* GROWL, gnash one's teeth. ❷ *'Shut it!' he snarled* SAY ROUGHLY, say brusquely, say nastily, bark, snap, growl; *informal* jump down someone's throat.

snarl[2] ▶ **verb** ❶ *the rope got snarled up in a bush* TANGLE, entangle, entwine, enmesh, ravel, knot, foul. ❷ *this case has snarled up the court process* COMPLICATE, confuse, muddle, jumble; *informal* mess up.

snarl-up ▶ **noun** (*informal*) ❶ *a snarl-up in Edinburgh* TRAFFIC JAM, tailback, gridlock. ❷ *a snarl-up in terminology* MUDDLE, mess, tangle, jumble; misunderstanding, misinterpretation, misconception, confusion; mistake, mix-up, bungle; *informal* hash, foul-up, screw-up; *N. Amer. informal* snafu.

snatch ▶ **verb** ❶ *she snatched the sandwich* GRAB, seize, take hold of, get one's hands on, take, pluck; grasp at, clutch at. ❷ (*informal*) *someone snatched my bag. See* STEAL verb sense 1. ❸ (*informal*) *she snatched the newborn from the hospital. See* ABDUCT. ❹ *he snatched victory* SEIZE, pluck, wrest, achieve, secure, obtain; scrape.

▶ **noun** ❶ *brief snatches of sleep* PERIOD, spell, time, fit, bout, interval, stretch. ❷ *a snatch of conversation* FRAGMENT, snippet, bit, scrap, part, extract, excerpt, portion.

snazzy ▶ **adjective** (*informal*). *See* STYLISH.

sneak ▶ **verb** ❶ *I sneaked out* CREEP, slink, steal, slip, slide, sidle, edge, move furtively, tiptoe, pussyfoot, pad, prowl. ❷ *she sneaked a camera in* BRING/TAKE SURREPTITIOUSLY, bring/take secretly, bring/take illicitly, smuggle, spirit, slip. ❸ *he sneaked a doughnut* TAKE FURTIVELY, take surreptitiously; steal; *informal* snatch. ❹ (*Brit. informal*) *the little squirt sneaked on me* INFORM, tell tales; report, give someone away, be disloyal, sell out, stab in the back; *informal* squeal, rat, blow the whistle, peach, snitch, stitch up; *Brit. informal* grass, split, shop; *Scottish informal* clype; *N. Amer. informal* finger; *Austral./NZ informal* dob.

▶ **noun** (*Brit. informal*) *Ethel was the class sneak* INFORMER, traitor; *informal* snitch, squealer, rat, whistle-blower; *Brit. informal* grass; *Scottish informal* clype; *N. Amer. informal* fink; *Austral./NZ informal* dobber.

▶ **adjective** *a sneak preview* FURTIVE, secret, stealthy, sly, surreptitious, clandestine, covert; private, quick.

sneaking ▶ **adjective** ❶ *she had a sneaking admiration for him* SECRET, private, hidden, concealed, unvoiced, undisclosed, undeclared, unavowed. ❷ *a sneaking feeling* NIGGLING, nagging, lurking, insidious, lingering, gnawing, persistent.

sneaky ▶ **adjective** SLY, crafty, cunning, wily, artful, scheming, devious, guileful, deceitful, duplicitous, underhand, unscrupulous; furtive, secretive, secret, stealthy, surreptitious, clandestine, covert; *informal* foxy, shifty, dirty.

–OPPOSITES honest.

sneer ▶ **noun** ❶ *she had a sneer on her face* SMIRK, curl of the lip, disparaging smile, contemptuous smile, cruel smile. ❷ *the sneers of others* JIBE, barb, jeer, taunt, insult, slight, affront, slur; *informal* dig.

▶ **verb** ❶ *he looked at me and sneered* SMIRK, curl one's lip, smile disparagingly, smile contemptuously, smile cruelly. ❷ *it is easy to sneer at them* SCOFF AT, scorn, disdain, mock, jeer at, hold in contempt, ridicule, deride, insult, slight; *N. Amer.* slur.

snicker ▶ **verb** *they all snickered at her* SNIGGER, titter, giggle, chortle, simper.

▶ **noun** *he could not suppress a snicker* SNIGGER, titter, giggle, chortle, simper.

snide ▶ **adjective** DISPARAGING, derogatory, deprecating, denigratory, insulting, contemptuous; mocking, taunting, sneering, scornful, derisive, sarcastic, spiteful, nasty, mean; *Brit. informal* sarky.

sniff ▶ **verb** ❶ *she sniffed and blew her nose* INHALE, breathe in; snuffle. ❷ *Tom sniffed the fruit* SMELL, scent, get a whiff of.

▶ **noun** ❶ *she gave a loud sniff* SNUFFLE, inhalation. ❷ *a sniff of fresh air* SMELL, scent, whiff; lungful. ❸ (*informal*) *the first sniff of trouble* INDICATION, hint, whiff, inkling, suggestion, whisper, trace, sign, suspicion.

■ **sniff at** SCORN, disdain, hold in contempt, look down one's nose at, treat as inferior, look down on, sneer at, scoff at; *informal* turn one's nose up at.

■ **sniff something out** (*informal*) DETECT, find, discover, bring to light, track down, dig up, hunt out, ferret out, root out, uncover, unearth, run to earth/ground.

snigger ▶ **verb** *they snigger at him behind his back* SNICKER, titter, giggle, chortle, laugh; sneer, smirk.

▶ **noun** *the joke got hardly a snigger* SNICKER, titter, giggle, chortle, laugh; sneer, smirk.

snip ▶ **verb** ❶ *an usher snipped our tickets* CUT, clip, snick, slit, nick, notch. ❷ *snip off the faded flowers* CUT OFF, trim (off), clip, prune, chop off, lop (off), dock, crop, sever, detach, remove, take off.

▶ **noun** ❶ *make snips along the edge* CUT, slit, snick, nick, notch, incision. ❷ *snips of wallpaper* SCRAP, snippet, cutting, shred, remnant, fragment, sliver, bit, piece. ❸ (*Brit. informal*) *the book was a snip. See* BARGAIN noun sense 2. ❹ (*informal*) *the job was a snip. See* CINCH sense 1.

snippet ▶ **noun** PIECE, bit, scrap, fragment, particle, shred; excerpt, extract.

snivel ▶ **verb** ❶ *he slumped in a chair, snivelling* SNIFFLE, snuffle, whimper, whine, weep, cry; *Scottish* greet; *informal* blub, blubber, boohoo; *Brit. informal* grizzle. ❷ *don't snivel about what you get* COMPLAIN, mutter, grumble, grouse, groan, carp, bleat, whine, *informal* gripe, moan, grouch, beef, bellyache, whinge, sound off; *Brit. informal* create; *N. Amer. informal* kvetch.

snobbery ▶ **noun** AFFECTATION, pretension, pretentiousness, arrogance, haughtiness, airs and graces, elitism; disdain, condescension, superciliousness; *informal* snootiness, uppitiness; *Brit. informal* side.

snobbish ▶ **adjective** ELITIST, snobby, superior, supercilious; arrogant, haughty, disdainful, condescending; pretentious, affected; *informal* snooty, uppity, high and mighty, la-di-da, stuck-up, hoity-toity, snotty; *Brit. informal* toffee-nosed.

snoop (*informal*) ▶ **verb** ❶ *don't snoop into our affairs* PRY, inquire, be inquisitive, be curious, poke about/around, be a busybody, poke one's nose into; interfere (in/with), meddle (in/with), intrude (on); *informal* be nosy; *Austral./NZ informal* stickybeak. ❷ *they snooped around the building* INVESTIGATE, explore, search, nose, have a good look; prowl around.

▶ **noun** ❶ *he went for a snoop around* SEARCH, nose, look, prowl, ferret, poke, investigation. ❷ *radio snoops. See* SNOOPER.

snooper ▶ **noun** MEDDLER, busybody, eavesdropper; investigator, detective; *informal* nosy parker, Paul Pry, snoop, private eye, PI, sleuth; *N. Amer. informal* gumshoe; *Austral./NZ informal* stickybeak.

snooty ▶ **adjective** (*informal*) ARROGANT, proud, haughty, conceited, aloof, superior, self-important, disdainful, supercilious, snobbish, snobby, patronizing, condescending; *informal* uppity, high and mighty, la-di-da, stuck-up, hoity-toity; *Brit. informal* toffee-nosed.

– OPPOSITES modest.

snooze (*informal*) ▶ **noun** *a good place for a snooze* NAP, doze, sleep, rest, siesta, catnap; *informal* forty winks; *Brit. informal* kip; *poetic/literary* slumber.

▶ **verb** *she gently snoozed* NAP, doze, sleep, rest, take a siesta, catnap; *informal* snatch forty winks, get some shut-eye; *Brit. informal* kip, get one's head down; *N. Amer. informal* catch some Zs; *poetic/literary* slumber.

snout ▶ **noun** MUZZLE, nose, proboscis, trunk; *Scottish & N. English* neb.

snow ▶ **noun** SNOWFLAKES, flakes, snowfall, snowstorm, blizzard, sleet; snowdrift, avalanche.

– RELATED TERMS niveous, nival.

snub ▶ **verb** *they snubbed their hosts* REBUFF, spurn, repulse, cold-shoulder, brush off, give the cold shoulder to, keep at arm's length; cut (dead), ignore; insult, slight, affront, humiliate; *informal* freeze out, knock back; *N. Amer. informal* stiff.

▶ **noun** *a very public snub* REBUFF, repulse, slap in the face; humiliation, insult, slight, affront; *informal* brush-off, put-down.

snuff ▶ **verb** EXTINGUISH, put out, douse, smother, choke, blow out, quench, stub out.

snug ▶ **adjective** ❶ *our tents were snug* COSY, comfortable, warm, homely, welcoming, restful, reassuring, intimate, sheltered, secure; *informal* comfy. ❷ *a snug dress* TIGHT, skintight, close-fitting, figure-hugging, slinky.

– OPPOSITES bleak, loose.

snuggle ▶ **verb** NESTLE, curl up, huddle (up), cuddle up, nuzzle, settle; *N. Amer.* snug down.

soak ▶ **verb** ❶ *soak the beans in water* IMMERSE, steep, submerge, submerse, dip, dunk, bathe, douse, marinate, souse. ❷ *we got soaked outside* DRENCH, wet through, saturate, waterlog, deluge, inundate, submerge, drown, swamp. ❸ *the sweat soaked through his clothes* PERMEATE, penetrate, percolate, seep into, spread through, infuse, impregnate. ❹ *use towels to soak up the water* ABSORB, suck up, blot (up), mop (up), sponge up, sop up.

soaking ▶ **adjective** DRENCHED, wet (through), soaked (through), sodden, soggy, waterlogged, saturated, sopping wet, dripping wet, wringing wet.

– OPPOSITES parched.

soar ▶ **verb** ❶ *the bird soared into the air* FLY, wing, ascend, climb, rise; take off, take flight. ❷ *the gulls soared on the winds* GLIDE, plane, float, drift, wheel, hover. ❸ *the cost of living soared* INCREASE, escalate, shoot up, rise, spiral; *informal* go through the roof, skyrocket.

– OPPOSITES plummet.

sob ▶ **verb** WEEP, cry, shed tears, snivel, whimper; howl, bawl; *Scottish* greet; *informal* blub, blubber, boohoo; *Brit. informal* grizzle.

sober ▶ **adjective** ❶ *the driver was clearly sober* NOT DRUNK, clear-headed; teetotal, abstinent,

abstemious, dry; *informal* on the wagon. ❷ *a sober view of life* SERIOUS, solemn, sensible, thoughtful, grave, sombre, staid, level-headed, businesslike, down-to-earth, commonsensical, pragmatic, conservative; unemotional, dispassionate, objective, matter-of-fact, no-nonsense, rational, logical, straightforward; *Scottish* douce. ❸ *a sober suit* SOMBRE, subdued, severe; conventional, traditional, quiet, drab, plain.
– OPPOSITES drunk, frivolous, sensational, flamboyant.
▶ **verb** ❶ *I ought to sober up* BECOME SOBER; *informal* dry out. ❷ *his expression sobered her* MAKE SERIOUS, subdue, calm down, quieten, steady; bring down to earth, make someone stop and think, give someone pause for thought.

sobriety ▶ **noun** ❶ *she noted his sobriety* SOBERNESS, clear-headedness; abstinence, teetotalism, non-indulgence, abstemiousness, temperance. ❷ *the mayor is a model of sobriety* SERIOUSNESS, solemnity, gravity, dignity, level-headedness, common sense, pragmatism, practicality, self-control, self-restraint, conservatism.

so-called ▶ **adjective** INAPPROPRIATELY NAMED, supposed, alleged, presumed, ostensible, reputed; nominal, titular, self-styled, professed, would-be, self-appointed, soi-disant.

sociable ▶ **adjective** FRIENDLY, affable, companionable, gregarious, convivial, clubbable, amicable, cordial, warm, genial; communicative, responsive, forthcoming, open, outgoing, extrovert, hail-fellow-well-met, approachable; *informal* chummy, clubby; *Brit. informal* matey.
– OPPOSITES unfriendly.

social ▶ **adjective** ❶ *a major social problem* COMMUNAL, community, collective, group, general, popular, civil, public, societal. ❷ *a social club* RECREATIONAL, leisure, entertainment, amusement. ❸ *a uniquely social animal* GREGARIOUS, interactional; organized.
– OPPOSITES individual.
▶ **noun** *the club has a social once a month* PARTY, gathering, function, get-together; celebration, reunion, jamboree; *informal* bash, shindig, do; *Brit. informal* rave-up, knees-up, beano, bunfight, jolly.

socialism ▶ **noun** LEFTISM, Fabianism, labourism, welfarism; radicalism, progressivism, social democracy; communism, Marxism, Leninism, Maoism; *historical* Bolshevism.

socialist ▶ **adjective** *the socialist movement* LEFT-WING, leftist, Labour, Labourite, labourist, Fabian, progressive, reform; radical, revolutionary, militant, red; communist, Marxist, Leninist, Maoist; *informal, derogatory* lefty, Bolshie, Commie.
– OPPOSITES conservative.
▶ **noun** *a well-known socialist* LEFT-WINGER, leftist, Fabian, Labourite, labourist, progressive, progressivist, reformer; radical, revolutionary, militant, red; communist, Marxist, Leninist, Maoist; *informal, derogatory* lefty, Bolshie, Commie.
– OPPOSITES conservative.

socialize ▶ **verb** INTERACT, converse, be sociable, mix, mingle, get together, meet, fraternize, consort; entertain, go out; *informal* hobnob.

society ▶ **noun** ❶ *a danger to society* THE COMMUNITY, the (general) public, the people, the population; civilization, humankind, mankind, humanity. ❷ *an industrial society* CULTURE, community, civilization, nation, population. ❸ *Lady Angela will help you enter society* HIGH SOCIETY, polite society, the upper classes, the elite, the county set, the smart set, the beautiful people, the beau monde, the haut monde; *informal* the upper crust, the top drawer. ❹ *a local history society* ASSOCIATION, club, group, circle, fellowship, guild, lodge, fraternity, brotherhood, sisterhood, sorority, league, union, alliance. ❺ *the society of others* COMPANY, companionship, fellowship, friendship, comradeship, camaraderie.

sodden ▶ **adjective** ❶ *his clothes were sodden* SOAKING, soaked (through), wet (through), saturated, drenched, sopping wet, wringing wet. ❷ *sodden fields* WATERLOGGED, soggy, saturated, boggy, swampy, miry, marshy; heavy, squelchy, soft.
– OPPOSITES arid.

sofa ▶ **noun** SETTEE, couch, divan, chaise longue, chesterfield; *Brit.* put-you-up; *N. Amer.* davenport, day bed.

soft ▶ **adjective** ❶ *soft fruit* MUSHY, squashy, pulpy, pappy, slushy, squelchy, squishy, doughy; *informal* gooey; *Brit. informal* squidgy. ❷ *soft ground* SWAMPY, marshy, boggy, miry, oozy; heavy, squelchy. ❸ *a soft cushion* SQUASHY, spongy, compressible, supple, springy, pliable, pliant, resilient, malleable. ❹ *soft fabric* VELVETY, smooth, fleecy, downy, furry, silky, silken, satiny. ❺ *a soft wind* GENTLE, light, mild, moderate. ❻ *soft light* DIM, low, faint, subdued, muted, mellow. ❼ *soft colours* PALE, pastel, muted, understated, restrained, subdued, subtle. ❽ *soft voices* QUIET, low, faint, muted, subdued, muffled, hushed, whispered, stifled, murmured, gentle, dulcet; indistinct, inaudible. ❾ *soft outlines* BLURRED, vague, hazy, misty, foggy, nebulous, fuzzy, blurry, indistinct, unclear. ❿ *he seduced her with soft words* KIND, gentle, sympathetic, soothing, tender, sensitive, affectionate, loving, warm, sweet, sentimental; *informal* mushy, slushy, schmaltzy. ⓫ *she's too soft with her pupils* LENIENT, easygoing, tolerant, forgiving, forbearing, indulgent, clement, permissive, liberal, lax. ⓬ (*informal*) *he's soft in the head* FOOLISH, stupid, simple, brainless, mindless; mad, scatterbrained, feather-brained; slow, weak, feeble; *informal*

dopey, dippy, dotty, scatty, loopy; *Brit. informal* daft; *Scottish & N. English informal* glaikit.
– OPPOSITES hard, firm, rough, strong, harsh, lurid, strident, sharp, strict, sensible.

soften ▶ **verb** ❶ *he tried to soften the blow of new taxes* ALLEVIATE, ease, relieve, soothe, take the edge off, assuage, cushion, moderate, mitigate, palliate, diminish, blunt, deaden. ❷ *the winds softened* DIE DOWN, abate, subside, moderate, let up, calm, diminish, slacken, weaken.
■ **soften someone up** CHARM, win over, persuade, influence, weaken, disarm, sweeten, butter up, soft-soap.

soft-hearted ▶ **adjective** KIND, kindly, tender-hearted, tender, gentle, sympathetic, compassionate, humane; generous, indulgent, lenient, merciful, benevolent.

softly-softly ▶ **adjective** CAUTIOUS, circumspect, discreet, gentle, patient, tactful, diplomatic.

soggy ▶ **adjective** MUSHY, squashy, pulpy, slushy, squelchy, squishy; swampy, marshy, boggy, miry; soaking, soaked through, wet, saturated, drenched; *Brit. informal* squidgy.

soil[1] ▶ **noun** ❶ *acid soil* EARTH, loam, dirt, clay, sod, turf; ground. ❷ *British soil* TERRITORY, land, domain, dominion, region, country.

soil[2] ▶ **verb** ❶ *he soiled his tie* DIRTY, stain, splash, spot, spatter, splatter, smear, smudge, sully, spoil, foul; *informal* muck up; *poetic/literary* begrime. ❷ *our reputation is being soiled* DISHONOUR, damage, sully, stain, blacken, tarnish, taint, blemish, defile, blot, smear, drag through the mud; *poetic/literary* besmirch.

sojourn (*formal*) ▶ **noun** *a sojourn in France* STAY, visit, stop, stopover; holiday, vacation.
▶ **verb** *they sojourned in the monastery* STAY, live, put up, stop (over), lodge, room, board; holiday, vacation.

solace ▶ **noun** *they found solace in each other* COMFORT, consolation, cheer, support, relief.
▶ **verb** *she was solaced with tea and sympathy* COMFORT, console, cheer, support, soothe, calm.

soldier ▶ **noun** FIGHTER, trooper, serviceman, servicewoman; warrior; *US* GI; *Brit. informal* squaddie; *archaic* man-at-arms.
■ **soldier on** (*informal*). *See* PERSEVERE.

sole ▶ **adjective** ONLY, one (and only), single, solitary, lone, unique, exclusive.

solecism ▶ **noun** ❶ *a poem marred by solecisms* (GRAMMATICAL) MISTAKE, error, blunder; *informal* howler, blooper; *Brit. informal* boob. ❷ *it would have been a solecism to answer* FAUX PAS, gaffe, impropriety, social indiscretion, infelicity, slip, error, blunder, lapse; *informal* slip-up, boo-boo; *Brit. informal* boob, clanger, bloomer; *N. Amer. informal* goof, blooper.

solely ▶ **adverb** ONLY, simply, just, merely, uniquely, exclusively, entirely, wholly; alone.

solemn ▶ **adjective** ❶ *a solemn occasion* DIGNIFIED, ceremonious, ceremonial, stately, formal, courtly, majestic; imposing, awe-inspiring, splendid, magnificent, grand. ❷ *he looked very solemn* SERIOUS, grave, sober, sombre, unsmiling, stern, grim, dour, humourless; pensive, meditative. ❸ *a solemn promise* SINCERE, earnest, honest, genuine, firm, heartfelt, wholehearted, sworn.
– OPPOSITES frivolous, light-hearted, insincere.

solemnize ▶ **verb** PERFORM, celebrate; formalize, officiate at.

solicit ▶ **verb** ❶ *Phil tried to solicit his help* ASK FOR, request, seek, apply for, put in for, call for, press for, beg, plead for; *dated* crave. ❷ *they are solicited for their opinions* ASK, beg, implore, plead with, entreat, appeal to, lobby, petition, importune, supplicate, call on, press; *poetic/literary* beseech. ❸ *the girls gathered to solicit* WORK AS A PROSTITUTE, make sexual advances, tout (for business); *N. Amer. informal* hustle.

solicitor ▶ **noun** (*Brit.*) LAWYER, legal representative, legal practitioner, notary (public), advocate, attorney; *Brit.* articled clerk; *Scottish* law agent; *informal* brief.

solicitous ▶ **adjective** CONCERNED, caring, considerate, attentive, mindful, thoughtful, interested; anxious, worried.

solid ▶ **adjective** ❶ *the ice cream was solid* HARD, rock-hard, rigid, firm, solidified, set, frozen, concrete. ❷ *solid gold* PURE, 24-carat, unalloyed, unadulterated, genuine. ❸ *a solid line* CONTINUOUS, uninterrupted, unbroken, non-stop, undivided. ❹ *solid houses* WELL BUILT, sound, substantial, strong, sturdy, durable. ❺ *a solid argument* WELL FOUNDED, valid, sound, reasonable, logical, authoritative, convincing, cogent, plausible, credible, reliable. ❻ *a solid friendship* DEPENDABLE, reliable, firm, unshakeable, trustworthy, stable, steadfast, staunch, constant. ❼ *solid citizens* SENSIBLE, dependable, trustworthy, decent, law-abiding, upright, upstanding, worthy. ❽ *the company is very solid* FINANCIALLY SOUND, secure, creditworthy, profit-making, solvent, in credit, in the black; *Finance* ungeared, unlevered. ❾ *solid support from their colleagues* UNANIMOUS, united, consistent, undivided.
– OPPOSITES liquid, alloyed, broken, flimsy, untenable, unreliable.

solidarity ▶ **noun** UNANIMITY, unity, like-mindedness, agreement, accord, harmony, consensus, concurrence, cooperation, cohesion; *formal* concord.

solidify ▶ **verb** HARDEN, set, freeze, thicken, stiffen, congeal, cake, dry, bake; ossify, fossilize, petrify.
– OPPOSITES liquefy.

soliloquy ▶ **noun** MONOLOGUE, speech, address, lecture, oration, sermon, homily, aside.

solitary ▶ **adjective** ❶ *a solitary life* LONELY,

companionless, unaccompanied, by oneself, on one's own, alone, friendless; antisocial, unsociable, withdrawn, reclusive, cloistered, hermitic; *N. Amer.* lonesome. ❷ *solitary farmsteads* ISOLATED, remote, lonely, out of the way, in the back of beyond, outlying, off the beaten track, godforsaken, obscure, inaccessible, cut-off; secluded, private, sequestered, desolate; *N. Amer.* in the backwoods; *Austral./NZ* in the backblocks; *informal* in the sticks, in the middle of nowhere; *N. Amer. informal* in the boondocks; *Austral./NZ informal* beyond the black stump; *poetic/literary* lone. ❸ *a solitary piece of evidence* SINGLE, lone, sole, unique; only, one, individual; odd.
– OPPOSITES sociable, accessible.
▶ **noun** *he became a solitary* RECLUSE, loner, hermit, eremite; *historical* anchorite.

solitude ▶ **noun** ❶ *she savoured her solitude* LONELINESS, solitariness, isolation, seclusion, sequestration, withdrawal, privacy, peace. ❷ *solitudes like the area around the loch* WILDERNESS, rural area, wilds, backwoods; desert, emptiness, wasteland; *Austral.* the bush, the outback; *N. Amer. & Austral./NZ* backcountry; *informal* the sticks; *N. Amer. informal* the boondocks.

solo ▶ **adjective** *a solo flight* UNACCOMPANIED, single-handed, companionless, unescorted, unattended, unchaperoned, independent, solitary; alone, on one's own, by oneself.
– OPPOSITES accompanied.
▶ **adverb** *she sailed solo* UNACCOMPANIED, alone, on one's own, single-handed(ly), by oneself, unescorted, unattended, unchaperoned, unaided, independently.
– OPPOSITES accompanied.

solution ▶ **noun** ❶ *an easy solution to the problem* ANSWER, result, resolution, way out, panacea; key, formula, explanation, interpretation. ❷ *a solution of ammonia in water* MIXTURE, mix, blend, compound, suspension, tincture, infusion, emulsion.

solve ▶ **verb** RESOLVE, answer, work out, find a solution to, find the key to, puzzle out, fathom, decipher, decode, clear up, straighten out, get to the bottom of, unravel, piece together, explain; *informal* figure out, crack; *Brit. informal* suss out.

solvent ▶ **adjective** FINANCIALLY SOUND, debt-free, in the black, in credit, creditworthy, solid, secure, profit-making; *Finance* ungeared, unlevered.

sombre ▶ **adjective** ❶ *sombre clothes* DARK, drab, dull, dingy; restrained, subdued, sober, funereal. ❷ *a sombre expression* SOLEMN, earnest, serious, grave, sober, unsmiling, stern, grim, dour, humourless; gloomy, depressed, sad, melancholy, dismal, doleful, mournful, lugubrious.
– OPPOSITES bright, cheerful.

somebody ▶ **noun** *she wanted to be a somebody* IMPORTANT PERSON, VIP, public figure, notable, dignitary, worthy; someone, (big/household) name, celebrity, star, superstar; grandee, luminary; *informal* celeb, bigwig, big shot, big cheese, hotshot, megastar.
– OPPOSITES nonentity.

some day ▶ **adverb** SOMETIME, one day, one of these (fine) days, at a future date, sooner or later, by and by, in due course, in the fullness of time, in the long run.
– OPPOSITES never.

somehow ▶ **adverb** BY SOME MEANS, by any means, in some way, one way or another, no matter how, by fair means or foul, by hook or by crook, come what may.

sometime ▶ **adverb** ❶ *I'll visit sometime* SOME DAY, one day, one of these (fine) days, at a future date, sooner or later, by and by, in due course, in the fullness of time, in the long run. ❷ *it happened sometime on Sunday* AT SOME TIME, at some point; during, in the course of.
– OPPOSITES never.
▶ **adjective** *the sometime editor of the paper* FORMER, past, previous, prior, foregoing, late, erstwhile, one-time, ex-; *formal* quondam.

sometimes ▶ **adverb** OCCASIONALLY, from time to time, now and then, every so often, once in a while, on occasion, at times, off and on, at intervals, periodically, sporadically, spasmodically, intermittently.

somewhat ▶ **adverb** ❶ *matters have improved somewhat* A LITTLE, a bit, to some extent, (up) to a point, in some measure, rather, quite; *N. Amer. informal* some; *informal* kind of, sort of. ❷ *a somewhat thicker book* SLIGHTLY, relatively, comparatively, moderately, fairly, rather, quite, marginally.
– OPPOSITES greatly.

somnolent ▶ **adjective** ❶ *he felt somnolent after lunch* SLEEPY, drowsy, tired, languid, dozy, groggy, lethargic, sluggish, enervated, torpid; *informal* snoozy, dopey, yawny; *poetic/literary* slumberous. ❷ *a somnolent village* QUIET, restful, tranquil, calm, peaceful, relaxing, soothing, undisturbed, untroubled.

son ▶ **noun** MALE CHILD, boy, heir; descendant, offspring; *informal* lad.
– RELATED TERMS filial.

song ▶ **noun** ❶ *a beautiful song* AIR, strain, ditty, melody, tune, number, track. ❷ *the song of the birds* CALL(S), chirping, cheeping, peeping, chirruping, warble(s), warbling, trilling, twitter; birdsong.
■ **song and dance** (*informal*). *See* FUSS noun sense 1.

songster, songstress ▶ **noun** SINGER, vocalist, soloist, crooner, chorister, choirboy, choirgirl; alto, bass, baritone, contralto, tenor, soprano; balladeer; *informal* warbler, popster, soulster, folkie; *historical* minstrel, troubadour; *archaic* melodist.

sonorous ▶ adjective ❶ *a sonorous voice* RESONANT, rich, full, round, booming, deep, clear, mellow, orotund, fruity, strong, resounding, reverberant. ❷ *sonorous words of condemnation* IMPRESSIVE, imposing, grandiloquent, magniloquent, high-flown, lofty, orotund, bombastic, grandiose, pompous, pretentious, overblown, turgid; oratorical, rhetorical; *informal* highfalutin.

soon ▶ adverb ❶ *we'll be there soon* SHORTLY, presently, in the near future, before long, in a little while, in a minute, in a moment, in an instant, in the twinkling of an eye, in no time, before you know it, any minute (now), any day (now), by and by; *informal* pronto, in a jiffy, before you can say Jack Robinson, anon; *Brit. informal* sharpish, in a tick, in two ticks; *dated* directly. ❷ *how soon can you get here?* EARLY, quickly, promptly, speedily, punctually.

sooner ▶ adverb ❶ *he should have done it sooner* EARLIER, before, beforehand, in advance, ahead of time; already. ❷ *I would sooner stay* RATHER, preferably, by preference, by choice, more willingly, more readily.

soothe ▶ verb ❶ *Rachel tried to soothe him* CALM (DOWN), pacify, comfort, hush, quiet, subdue, settle (down), lull, tranquillize; appease, conciliate, mollify; *Brit.* quieten (down). ❷ *an anaesthetic to soothe the pain* ALLEVIATE, ease, relieve, take the edge off, assuage, allay, lessen, palliate, diminish, decrease, dull, blunt, deaden.
– OPPOSITES agitate, aggravate.

soothing ▶ adjective ❶ *soothing music* RELAXING, restful, calm, calming, tranquil, peaceful, reposeful, tranquillizing, soporific. ❷ *soothing ointment* PALLIATIVE, mild, calmative.

soothsayer ▶ noun SEER, oracle, augur, prophet(ess), sage, prognosticator, diviner, fortune teller, crystal-gazer, clairvoyant, psychic; *Scottish* spaewife; *poetic/literary* sibyl.

sophisticated ▶ adjective ❶ *sophisticated techniques* ADVANCED, modern, state of the art, the latest, new, up to the minute; innovatory, trailblazing, revolutionary, futuristic, avant-garde; complex, complicated, intricate. ❷ *a sophisticated woman* WORLDLY, worldly-wise, experienced, enlightened, cosmopolitan, knowledgeable; urbane, cultured, cultivated, civilized, polished, refined; elegant, stylish; *informal* cool.
– OPPOSITES crude, naive.

sophistication ▶ noun WORLDLINESS, experience; urbanity, culture, civilization, polish, refinement; elegance, style, poise, finesse, savoir faire; *informal* cool.

sophistry ▶ noun ❶ *to claim this is pure sophistry* SPECIOUS REASONING, fallacy, sophism, casuistry. ❷ *he went along with her sophistry* FALLACIOUS ARGUMENT, sophism, fallacy; *Logic* paralogism.

soporific ▶ adjective *soporific drugs* SLEEP-INDUCING, sedative, somnolent, calmative, tranquillizing, narcotic, opiate; drowsy, sleepy, somniferous; *Medicine* hypnotic.
– OPPOSITES invigorating.
▶ noun *she was given a soporific* SLEEPING PILL, sedative, calmative, tranquillizer, narcotic, opiate; *Medicine* hypnotic.
– OPPOSITES stimulant.

soppy ▶ adjective (*Brit. informal*) ❶ *the songs are really soppy. See* SENTIMENTAL sense 2. ❷ *they were too soppy for our games. See* FEEBLE sense 3.

sorcerer, sorceress ▶ noun WIZARD, witch, magician, warlock, enchanter, enchantress, magus; shaman, witch doctor; *archaic* mage.

sorcery ▶ noun (BLACK) MAGIC, the black arts, witchcraft, wizardry, enchantment, spells, incantation, witching, witchery, thaumaturgy; shamanism; *Irish* pishogue.

sordid ▶ adjective ❶ *a sordid love affair* SLEAZY, seedy, seamy, unsavoury, tawdry, cheap, debased, degenerate, dishonourable, disreputable, discreditable, contemptible, ignominious, shameful, wretched, abhorrent. ❷ *a sordid little street* SQUALID, slummy, dirty, filthy, mucky, grimy, shabby, messy, soiled, scummy, unclean; *informal* cruddy, grungy, crummy, scuzzy; *Brit. informal* grotty.
– OPPOSITES respectable, immaculate.

sore ▶ adjective ❶ *a sore leg* PAINFUL, hurting, hurt, aching, throbbing, smarting, stinging, agonizing, excruciating; inflamed, sensitive, tender, raw, bruised, wounded, injured. ❷ *we are in sore need of you* DIRE, urgent, pressing, desperate, parlous, critical, crucial, acute, grave, serious, drastic, extreme, life-and-death, great, terrible; *formal* exigent. ❸ (*N. Amer. informal*) *they were sore at us* UPSET, angry, annoyed, cross, furious, vexed, displeased, disgruntled, dissatisfied, exasperated, irritated, galled, irked, put out, aggrieved, offended, affronted, piqued, nettled; *informal* aggravated, miffed, peeved, hacked off, riled; *Brit. informal* narked, cheesed off, brassed off; *N. Amer. informal* teed off, ticked off.
▶ noun *a sore on his leg* INFLAMMATION, swelling, lesion; wound, scrape, abrasion, cut, laceration, graze, contusion, bruise; ulcer, boil, abscess, carbuncle.

sorrow ▶ noun ❶ *he felt sorrow at her death* SADNESS, unhappiness, misery, despondency, regret, depression, despair, desolation, dejection, wretchedness, gloom, dolefulness, melancholy, woe, heartache, grief; *poetic/literary* dolour. ❷ *the sorrows of life* TROUBLE, difficulty, problem, adversity, misery, woe, affliction, trial, tribulation, misfortune, setback, reverse, blow, failure, tragedy.
– OPPOSITES joy.
▶ verb *they sorrowed over her grave* MOURN, lament, grieve, be sad, be miserable, be despondent,

despair, suffer, ache, agonize, anguish, pine, weep, wail.
– OPPOSITES rejoice.

sorrowful ▶ adjective ❶ *sorrowful eyes* SAD, unhappy, dejected, regretful, downcast, miserable, downhearted, despondent, despairing, disconsolate, desolate, glum, gloomy, doleful, dismal, melancholy, mournful, woeful, woebegone, forlorn, crestfallen, heartbroken; *informal* blue, down in the mouth, down in the dumps. ❷ *sorrowful news* TRAGIC, sad, unhappy, awful, miserable, sorry, pitiful; traumatic, upsetting, depressing, distressing, dispiriting, heartbreaking, harrowing; *formal* grievous.

sorry ▶ adjective ❶ *I was sorry to hear about his accident* SAD, unhappy, sorrowful, distressed, upset, downcast, downhearted, disheartened, despondent; heartbroken, inconsolable, grief-stricken. ❷ *he felt sorry for her* FULL OF PITY, sympathetic, compassionate, moved, consoling, empathetic, concerned. ❸ *I'm sorry if I was brusque* REGRETFUL, remorseful, contrite, repentant, rueful, penitent, apologetic, abject, guilty, self-reproachful, ashamed, sheepish, shamefaced. ❹ *he looks a sorry sight* PITIFUL, pitiable, heart-rending, distressing; unfortunate, unhappy, wretched, unlucky, shameful, regrettable, awful.
– OPPOSITES glad, unsympathetic, unrepentant.

sort ▶ noun ❶ *what sort of book is it?* TYPE, kind, nature, manner, variety, class, category, style; calibre, quality, form, group, set, bracket, genre, species, family, order, generation, vintage, make, model, brand, stamp, ilk, kidney, cast, grain, mould; *N. Amer.* stripe. ❷ (*informal*) *he's a good sort* PERSON, individual, soul, creature, human being; character, customer; *informal* fellow, type, beggar, cookie; *Brit. informal* bod; *informal, dated* body, dog, cove.
▶ verb ❶ *they sorted things of similar size* CLASSIFY, class, categorize, catalogue, grade, group; organize, arrange, order, marshal, assemble, systematize, systemize, pigeonhole. ❷ *the problem was soon sorted* RESOLVE, settle, solve, fix, work out, straighten out, deal with, put right, set right, rectify, iron out; answer, explain, fathom, unravel, clear up; *informal* sew up, hammer out, thrash out, patch up, figure out.
■ **out of sorts** ❶ *I'm feeling out of sorts* UNWELL, ill, poorly, sick, queasy, nauseous, peaky, run down, below par; *Brit.* off colour; *informal* under the weather, funny, rough, lousy, rotten, awful; *Brit. informal* off, ropy; *Scottish informal* wabbit, peely-wally; *Austral./NZ informal* crook; *dated* seedy. ❷ *I've been out of sorts and I'd like a chat* UNHAPPY, sad, miserable, down, depressed, melancholy, gloomy, glum, dispirited, despondent, forlorn, woebegone, fed up, low, in the doldrums; *informal* blue, down in the dumps, down in the mouth.
■ **sort of** (*informal*) ❶ *you look sort of familiar* SLIGHTLY, faintly, remotely, vaguely; somewhat, moderately, quite, rather, fairly, reasonably, relatively; *informal* pretty, kind of. ❷ *he sort of pirouetted* AS IT WERE, kind of, somehow.
■ **sort something out** ❶ *she sorted out the clothes. See* SORT verb sense 1. ❷ *they must sort out their problems. See* SORT verb sense 2.

sortie ▶ noun ❶ *a sortie against their besiegers* FORAY, sally, charge, offensive, attack, assault, onset, onslaught, thrust, drive. ❷ *a bomber sortie* RAID, flight, mission, operation.

so-so ▶ adjective (*informal*) MEDIOCRE, indifferent, average, middle-of-the-road, middling, moderate, ordinary, adequate, fair; uninspired, undistinguished, unexceptional, unremarkable, run-of-the-mill, lacklustre; *informal* bog-standard, no great shakes, not up to much; *NZ informal* half-pie.

soul ▶ noun ❶ *seeing the soul through the eyes* SPIRIT, psyche, (inner) self, inner being, life force, vital force; individuality, make-up, subconscious, anima; *Philosophy* pneuma; *Hinduism* atman. ❷ *he is the soul of discretion* EMBODIMENT, personification, incarnation, epitome, quintessence, essence; model, exemplification, exemplar, image, manifestation. ❸ *not a soul in sight* PERSON, human being, individual, man, woman, mortal, creature. ❹ *their music lacked soul* INSPIRATION, feeling, emotion, passion, animation, intensity, fervour, ardour, enthusiasm, warmth, energy, vitality, spirit.

soulful ▶ adjective EMOTIONAL, deep, profound, fervent, heartfelt, sincere, passionate; meaningful, significant, eloquent, expressive; moving, stirring; sad, mournful, doleful.

soulless ▶ adjective ❶ *a soulless room* CHARACTERLESS, featureless, bland, dull, colourless, lacklustre, dreary, drab, uninspiring, undistinguished, anaemic, insipid. ❷ *it was soulless work* BORING, dull, tedious, dreary, humdrum, tiresome, wearisome, uninteresting, uninspiring, unexciting, soul-destroying, mind-numbing, dry; monotonous, repetitive.
– OPPOSITES exciting.

sound[1] ▶ noun ❶ *the sound of the car* NOISE, note; din, racket, row, hubbub; resonance, reverberation. ❷ *she did not make a sound* UTTERANCE, cry, word, noise, peep; *informal* cheep. ❸ *the sound of the flute* MUSIC, tone, notes. ❹ *I don't like the sound of that* IDEA, thought, concept, prospect, description. ❺ *we're within sound of the sea* EARSHOT, hearing (distance), range.
– RELATED TERMS acoustic, sonic, aural, audio-, sono-.
– OPPOSITES silence.
▶ verb ❶ *the buzzer sounded* MAKE A NOISE, resonate, resound, reverberate, go off, blare; ring, chime, peal. ❷ *drivers must sound their horns* BLOW, blast, toot, blare; operate, set off; ring. ❸ *do you sound the 'h'?* PRONOUNCE, verbalize, voice, enunciate, articulate, vocalize, say.

❹ *she sounded a warning* UTTER, voice, deliver, express, speak, announce, pronounce. ❺ *it sounds a crazy idea* APPEAR, look (like), seem, strike someone as being, give every indication of being.

sound[2] ▶ **adjective** ❶ *your heart is sound* HEALTHY, in good condition, in good shape, fit, hale and hearty, in fine fettle; undamaged, unimpaired. ❷ *a sound building* WELL BUILT, solid, substantial, strong, sturdy, durable, stable, intact, unimpaired. ❸ *sound advice* WELL FOUNDED, valid, reasonable, logical, weighty, authoritative, reliable. ❹ *a sound judge of character* RELIABLE, dependable, trustworthy, fair; good, sensible, wise, judicious, sagacious, shrewd, perceptive. ❺ *financially sound* SOLVENT, debt-free, in the black, in credit, creditworthy, secure. ❻ *a sound sleep* DEEP, undisturbed, uninterrupted, untroubled, peaceful. ❼ *a sound thrashing* THOROUGH, proper, real, complete, unqualified, out-and-out, thoroughgoing, severe; *informal* right (royal).
– OPPOSITES unhealthy, unsafe, unreliable, insolvent, light.

sound[3] ▶ **verb** *sound the depth of the river* MEASURE, gauge, determine, test, investigate, survey, plumb, fathom, probe.
■ **sound someone/something out** INVESTIGATE, test, check, examine, probe, research, look into; canvass, survey, poll, question, interview, sample; *informal* pump.

sound[4] ▶ **noun** *an oil spill in Prince William Sound* CHANNEL, (sea) passage, strait(s), narrows, waterway; inlet, arm (of the sea), fjord, creek, bay; estuary, firth.

soup ▶ **noun** BROTH, potage, consommé, bouillon, chowder, bisque.

sour ▶ **adjective** ❶ *sour wine* ACID, acidic, acidy, acidulated, tart, bitter, sharp, vinegary, pungent; *N. Amer.* acerb; *technical* acerbic. ❷ *sour milk* BAD, off, turned, curdled, rancid, high, rank, foul, fetid. ❸ *a sour old man* EMBITTERED, resentful, rancorous, jaundiced, bitter; nasty, spiteful, irritable, peevish, fractious, cross, crabby, crotchety, cantankerous, disagreeable, petulant, querulous, grumpy, bad-tempered, ill-humoured, sullen, surly, sulky, churlish; *informal* snappy, grouchy; *Brit. informal* ratty, stroppy, shirty; *N. Amer. informal* cranky, soreheaded.
– OPPOSITES sweet, fresh, amiable.
▶ **verb** ❶ *the war had soured him* EMBITTER, disillusion, disenchant, poison, alienate; dissatisfy, frustrate. ❷ *the dispute soured relations* SPOIL, mar, damage, harm, impair, wreck, upset, poison, blight, tarnish.
– OPPOSITES improve.

source ▶ **noun** ❶ *the source of the river* SPRING, origin, (well) head, headspring, headwater(s); *poetic/literary* wellspring. ❷ *the source of the rumour* ORIGIN, birthplace, spring, fountainhead, fount, starting point; history, provenance, derivation, root, beginning, genesis, start, rise; author, originator, initiator, inventor; *N. Amer.* provenience. ❸ *a historian uses primary and secondary sources* REFERENCE, authority, informant; document.

souse ▶ **verb** DRENCH, douse, soak, steep, saturate, plunge, immerse, submerge, dip, sink, dunk.

soused ▶ **adjective** ❶ *a soused herring* PICKLED, marinated, soaked, steeped. ❷ (*informal*) *he was well and truly soused. See* DRUNK adjective.

south ▶ **adjective** SOUTHERN, southerly, meridional, austral.

souvenir ▶ **noun** MEMENTO, keepsake, reminder, remembrance, token, memorial; trophy, relic.

sovereign ▶ **noun** RULER, monarch, crowned head, head of state, potentate, suzerain, overlord, dynast, leader; king, queen, emperor, empress, prince, princess, tsar, royal duke, regent, mogul, emir, sheikh, sultan, maharaja, raja.
– RELATED TERMS regal.
▶ **adjective** ❶ *sovereign control* SUPREME, absolute, unlimited, unrestricted, boundless, ultimate, total, unconditional, full; principal, chief, dominant, predominant, ruling; royal, regal, monarchical. ❷ *a sovereign state* INDEPENDENT, autonomous, self-governing, self-determining; non-aligned, free. ❸ (*dated*) *a sovereign remedy for all ills* EFFECTIVE, effectual, efficient, powerful, potent; useful, helpful, valuable, worthwhile; excellent, reliable, unfailing; *informal* sure-fire; *formal* efficacious.

sovereignty ▶ **noun** ❶ *their sovereignty over the islands* JURISDICTION, rule, supremacy, dominion, power, ascendancy, suzerainty, hegemony, domination, authority, control, influence. ❷ *full sovereignty was achieved in 1955* AUTONOMY, independence, self-government, self-rule, home rule, self-determination, freedom.

sow ▶ **verb** ❶ *sow the seeds in rows* PLANT, scatter, spread, broadcast, disperse, strew, disseminate, distribute; drill, dibble, seed. ❷ *the new policy has sown confusion* CAUSE, bring about, occasion, create, lead to, produce, engender, generate, prompt, initiate, precipitate, trigger, provoke; culminate in, entail, necessitate; foster, foment; *poetic/literary* beget.

space ▶ **noun** ❶ *there was not enough space* ROOM, capacity, area, volume, expanse, extent, scope, latitude, margin, leeway, play, clearance. ❷ *green spaces in London* AREA, expanse, stretch, sweep, tract. ❸ *the space between the timbers* GAP, interval, opening, aperture, cavity, cranny, fissure, crack, interstice, lacuna. ❹ *write your name in the appropriate space* BLANK, gap, box. ❺ *a space of seven years* PERIOD, span, time, duration, stretch, course, interval. ❻ *the first woman in space* OUTER SPACE, deep space; the universe, the galaxy, the solar system; infinity.

▶ **verb** *the chairs were spaced widely* POSITION, arrange, range, array, dispose, lay out, locate, situate, set, stand.

spaceman, spacewoman ▶ **noun** ASTRONAUT, cosmonaut, space traveller, space cadet; *N. Amer. informal* jock.

spacious ▶ **adjective** ROOMY, capacious, palatial, airy, sizable, generous, large, big, vast, immense; extensive, expansive, sweeping, rolling, rambling, open; *formal* commodious.
– OPPOSITES cramped.

spadework ▶ **noun** GROUNDWORK, preliminary work, preliminaries, preparatory measures, preparations, planning, foundations; hard work, donkey work, labour, drudgery, toil; *informal* grind; *Brit. informal* graft.

span ▶ **noun** ❶ *a six-foot wing span* EXTENT, length, width, reach, stretch, spread, distance, range. ❷ *the span of one working day* PERIOD, space, time, duration, course, interval.

▶ **verb** ❶ *an arch spanned the stream* BRIDGE, cross, traverse, pass over. ❷ *his career spanned twenty years* LAST, cover, extend, spread over, comprise.

spank ▶ **verb** SMACK, slap, hit, cuff; *informal* wallop, belt, whack, give someone a hiding; *Scottish & N. English* skelp.

spar ▶ **verb** QUARREL, argue, fight, disagree, differ, be at odds, be at variance, fall out, dispute, squabble, wrangle, bandy words, cross swords, lock horns, be at loggerheads; *informal* scrap, argufy, spat; *Brit. informal* row.

spare ▶ **adjective** ❶ *a spare set of keys* EXTRA, supplementary, additional, second, other, alternative; emergency, reserve, back-up, relief, fallback, substitute; fresh; *N. Amer.* alternate. ❷ *they sold off the spare land* SURPLUS, superfluous, excessive; redundant, unnecessary, inessential, unessential, unneeded, uncalled for, dispensable, disposable, expendable, unwanted; *informal* going begging. ❸ *your spare time* FREE, leisure, own. ❹ *a spare woman* SLENDER, lean, willowy, svelte, lissom, rangy, clean limbed, trim, slight; thin, skinny, gaunt, lanky, spindly; *informal* skin and bone.

▶ **verb** ❶ *he could not spare any money* AFFORD, do without, manage without, dispense with, part with, give, provide. ❷ *they were spared by their captors* PARDON, let off, forgive, reprieve, release, free; leave uninjured, leave unhurt; be merciful to, show mercy to, have mercy on, be lenient to, have pity on.

■ **go spare** (*Brit. informal*). *See* GET ANGRY at ANGRY.

■ **to spare** LEFT (OVER), remaining, unused, unneeded, not required, still available, surplus (to requirements), superfluous, extra; *informal* going begging.

sparing ▶ **adjective** THRIFTY, economical, frugal, canny, careful, prudent, cautious; mean, miserly, niggardly, parsimonious, close-fisted, penny-pinching, cheese-paring, ungenerous, close, grasping; *informal* stingy, tight-fisted, tight, mingy, money-grubbing; *N. Amer. informal* cheap.
– OPPOSITES lavish.

spark ▶ **noun** ❶ *a spark of light* FLASH, glint, twinkle, flicker, flare, pinprick. ❷ *not a spark of truth in the story* PARTICLE, iota, jot, whit, glimmer, atom, bit, trace, vestige, ounce, shred, crumb, grain, mite, hint, touch, suggestion, whisper, scintilla; *informal* smidgen, tad.

▶ **verb** *the trial sparked a furious row* CAUSE, give rise to, lead to, occasion, bring about, start, initiate, precipitate, prompt, trigger (off), provoke, stimulate, stir up.

sparkle ▶ **verb** ❶ *her earrings sparkled* GLITTER, glint, glisten, twinkle, flash, blink, wink, shimmer, shine, gleam; *poetic/literary* coruscate, glister. ❷ *she sparkled as the hostess* BE LIVELY, be vivacious, be animated, be ebullient, be exuberant, be bubbly, be effervescent, be witty, be full of life.

▶ **noun** *the sparkle of the pool* GLITTER, glint, twinkle, flicker, shimmer, flash, shine, gleam; *poetic/literary* coruscation.

sparkling ▶ **adjective** ❶ *sparkling wine* EFFERVESCENT, fizzy, carbonated, aerated, gassy, bubbly, frothy; mousseux, spumante. ❷ *a sparkling performance* BRILLIANT, dazzling, scintillating, exciting, exhilarating, stimulating, invigorating; vivacious, lively, vibrant, animated.
– OPPOSITES still, dull.

sparse ▶ **adjective** SCANT, scanty, scattered, scarce, infrequent, few and far between; meagre, paltry, skimpy, limited, in short supply.
– OPPOSITES abundant.

spartan ▶ **adjective** AUSTERE, harsh, hard, frugal, stringent, rigorous, strict, stern, severe; ascetic, abstemious; bleak, joyless, grim, bare, stark, plain.
– OPPOSITES luxurious.

spasm ▶ **noun** ❶ *a muscle spasm* CONTRACTION, convulsion, cramp; twitch, jerk, tic, shudder, shiver, tremor. ❷ *a spasm of coughing* FIT, paroxysm, attack, burst, bout, seizure, outburst, outbreak, access; *informal* splurt; *formal* boutade.

spasmodic ▶ **adjective** INTERMITTENT, fitful, irregular, sporadic, erratic, occasional, infrequent, scattered, patchy, isolated, periodic, periodical, on and off.

spate ▶ **noun** SERIES, succession, run, cluster, string, rash, epidemic, outbreak, wave, flurry, rush, flood, deluge, torrent.

spatter ▶ **verb** SPLASH, bespatter, splatter, spray, sprinkle, shower, speck, speckle, fleck, mottle, blotch, mark, cover; *informal* splotch; *Brit. informal* splodge.

spawn ▶ **verb** GIVE RISE TO, bring about, occasion, generate, engender, originate; lead to, result in, effect, induce, initiate, start, set off, precipitate, trigger; breed, bear; *poetic/literary* beget.

speak ▶ **verb** ❶ *she refused to speak about it* TALK, say anything/something; utter, state, declare, tell, voice, express, pronounce, articulate, enunciate, vocalize, verbalize. ❷ *we spoke the other day* CONVERSE, have a conversation, talk, communicate, chat, pass the time of day, have a word, gossip; *informal* have a confab, chew the fat; *Brit. informal* natter; *N. Amer. informal* shoot the breeze; *formal* confabulate. ❸ *the Minister spoke for two hours* GIVE A SPEECH, talk, lecture, hold forth, discourse, expound, expatiate, orate, sermonize, pontificate; *informal* spout, spiel, speechify, jaw, sound off. ❹ *he was spoken of as a promising student* MENTION, talk about, discuss, refer to, remark on, allude to. ❺ *his expression spoke disbelief* INDICATE, show, display, register, reveal, betray, exhibit, manifest, express, convey, impart, bespeak, communicate, evidence; suggest, denote, reflect; *formal* evince. ❻ *you must speak to him about his rudeness* REPRIMAND, rebuke, admonish, chastise, chide, upbraid, reprove, reproach, scold, remonstrate with, take to task, pull up; *informal* tell off, dress down, rap over the knuckles, come down on; *Brit. informal* tick off, have a go at, tear someone off a strip, give someone what for; *formal* castigate.

■ **speak for** ❶ *she speaks for the Liberal Democrats* REPRESENT, act for, appear for, express the views of, be spokesperson for. ❷ *I spoke for the motion* ADVOCATE, champion, uphold, defend, support, promote, recommend, back, endorse, sponsor, espouse.

■ **speak out** SPEAK PUBLICLY, speak openly, speak frankly, speak one's mind, sound off, stand up and be counted.

■ **speak up** SPEAK LOUDLY, speak clearly, raise one's voice; shout, yell, bellow; *informal* holler.

speaker ▶ **noun** SPEECH-MAKER, lecturer, talker, speechifier, orator, declaimer, rhetorician; spokesperson, spokesman/woman, mouthpiece; reader, lector, commentator, broadcaster, narrator; *informal* tub-thumper, spieler; *historical* demagogue, rhetor.

spear ▶ **noun** JAVELIN, lance, assegai, harpoon, bayonet; gaff, leister; *historical* pike.

spearhead ▶ **noun** ❶ *a Bronze Age spearhead* SPEAR TIP, spear point. ❷ *the spearhead of the struggle against Fascism* LEADER(S), driving force; forefront, front runner(s), front line, vanguard, van, cutting edge.

▶ **verb** *she spearheaded the campaign* LEAD, head, front; lead the way, be in the van, be in the vanguard.

special ▶ **adjective** ❶ *a very special person* EXCEPTIONAL, unusual, singular, uncommon, notable, noteworthy, remarkable, outstanding, unique. ❷ *our town's special character* DISTINCTIVE, distinct, individual, particular, specific, peculiar. ❸ *a special occasion* MOMENTOUS, significant, memorable, signal, important, historic, festive, gala, red-letter. ❹ *a special tool for cutting tiles* SPECIFIC, particular, purpose-built, tailor-made, custom-built.

– OPPOSITES ordinary, general.

specialist ▶ **noun** EXPERT, authority, pundit, professional; connoisseur; master, maestro, adept, virtuoso; *informal* pro, buff, ace, whizz, hotshot; *Brit. informal* dab hand; *N. Amer. informal* maven.

– OPPOSITES amateur.

speciality ▶ **noun** ❶ *his speciality was watercolours* FORTE, strong point, strength, métier, strong suit, talent, skill, bent, gift; *informal* bag, thing, cup of tea. ❷ *a speciality of the region* DELICACY, specialty, fine food/product, traditional food/product.

species ▶ **noun** TYPE, kind, sort; genus, family, order, breed, strain, variety, class, classification, category, set, bracket; style, manner, form, genre; generation, vintage.

specific ▶ **adjective** ❶ *a specific purpose* PARTICULAR, specified, fixed, set, determined, distinct, definite; single, individual, peculiar, discrete, express, precise. ❷ *I gave specific instructions* DETAILED, explicit, express, clear-cut, unequivocal, precise, exact, meticulous, strict, definite.

– OPPOSITES general, vague.

specification ▶ **noun** ❶ *clear specification of objectives* STATEMENT, identification, definition, description, setting out, framing, designation, detailing, enumeration; stipulation, prescription. ❷ *a shelter built to their specifications* INSTRUCTIONS, guidelines, parameters, stipulations, requirements, conditions, provisions, restrictions, order; description, details.

specify ▶ **verb** STATE, name, identify, define, describe, set out, frame, itemize, detail, list, spell out, enumerate, particularize, cite, instance; stipulate, prescribe.

specimen ▶ **noun** SAMPLE, example, instance, illustration, demonstration, exemplification; bit, snippet; model, prototype, pattern, dummy, pilot, trial, taster, tester.

specious ▶ **adjective** MISLEADING, deceptive, false, fallacious, unsound, casuistic, sophistic; plausible.

speck ▶ **noun** ❶ *a mere speck in the distance* DOT, pinprick, spot, fleck, speckle. ❷ *a speck of dust* PARTICLE, grain, atom, molecule; bit, trace.

speckled ▶ **adjective** FLECKED, speckly, specked, freckled, freckly, spotted, spotty, dotted, mottled, dappled.

spectacle ▶ **noun** ❶ *a spectacle fit for a monarch* DISPLAY, show, pageant, parade, performance, exhibition, extravaganza, spectacular. ❷ *they were rather an odd spectacle* SIGHT, vision, scene, prospect, vista, picture. ❸ *don't make a* *spectacle of yourself* EXHIBITION, laughing stock, fool, curiosity.

spectacles ▶ **plural noun** GLASSES, eyewear; *N. Amer.* eyeglasses; *informal* specs.

spectacular ▶ **adjective** ❶ *a spectacular victory* IMPRESSIVE, magnificent, splendid, dazzling, sensational, dramatic, remarkable, outstanding, memorable, unforgettable. ❷ *a spectacular view* STRIKING, picturesque, eye-catching, breathtaking, arresting, glorious; *informal* out of this world.

– OPPOSITES unimpressive, dull.

▶ **noun** *a spectacular put on for the tourists. See* SPECTACLE sense 1.

spectator ▶ **noun** WATCHER, viewer, observer, onlooker, bystander, witness; commentator, reporter, monitor; *poetic/literary* beholder.

– OPPOSITES participant.

spectral ▶ **adjective** GHOSTLY, phantom, wraithlike, shadowy, incorporeal, insubstantial, disembodied, unearthly, other-worldly; *informal* spooky.

spectre ▶ **noun** ❶ *the spectres in the crypt* GHOST, phantom, apparition, spirit, wraith, shadow, presence; *informal* spook; *poetic/literary* phantasm, shade. ❷ *the looming spectre of war* THREAT, menace, shadow, cloud; prospect; danger, peril, fear, dread.

spectrum ▶ **noun** RANGE, gamut, sweep, scope, span; compass, orbit, ambit.

speculate ▶ **verb** ❶ *they speculated about my private life* CONJECTURE, theorize, hypothesize, guess, surmise; think, wonder, muse. ❷ *investors speculate on the stock market* GAMBLE, take a risk, venture, wager; invest, play the market; *Brit. informal* have a flutter, punt.

speculative ▶ **adjective** ❶ *any discussion is largely speculative* CONJECTURAL, suppositional, theoretical, hypothetical, putative, academic, notional, abstract; tentative, unproven, unfounded, groundless, unsubstantiated. ❷ *a speculative investment* RISKY, hazardous, unsafe, uncertain, unpredictable; *informal* chancy, dicey, iffy; *Brit. informal* dodgy.

speech ▶ **noun** ❶ *he doesn't have the power of speech* SPEAKING, talking, verbal expression, verbal communication. ❷ *her speech was slurred* DICTION, elocution, articulation, enunciation, pronunciation; utterance, words. ❸ *an after-dinner speech* TALK, address, lecture, discourse, oration, disquisition, peroration, deliverance, presentation; sermon, homily; monologue, soliloquy; *informal* spiel. ❹ *Spanish popular speech* LANGUAGE, tongue, parlance, idiom, dialect, vernacular, patois; *informal* lingo, patter, -speak, -ese.

– RELATED TERMS lingual, oral, phono-, -phone, -phasia.

speechless ▶ **adjective** LOST FOR WORDS, dumbstruck, bereft of speech, tongue-tied, inarticulate, mute, dumb, voiceless, silent; *informal* mum; *archaic* mumchance.

– OPPOSITES verbose.

speed ▶ **noun** ❶ *the speed of their progress* RATE, pace, tempo, momentum. ❷ *the speed with which they responded* RAPIDITY, swiftness, speediness, quickness, dispatch, promptness, immediacy, briskness, sharpness; haste, hurry, precipitateness; acceleration, velocity; *informal* lick, clip; *poetic/literary* celerity.

– RELATED TERMS tacho-, tachy-.

▶ **verb** ❶ *I sped home* HURRY, rush, dash, run, race, sprint, bolt, dart, gallop, career, charge, shoot, hurtle, hare, fly, zoom, scurry, scuttle, scamper, hasten; *informal* tear, belt, pelt, scoot, zip, whip, hotfoot it, leg it; *Brit. informal* bomb; *N. Amer. informal* hightail it. ❷ *he was caught speeding* DRIVE TOO FAST, exceed the speed limit. ❸ *a holiday will speed his recovery* HASTEN, expedite, speed up, accelerate, advance, further, promote, boost, stimulate, aid, assist, facilitate.

– OPPOSITES slow, hinder.

■ **speed up** HURRY UP, accelerate, go faster, get a move on, put a spurt on, pick up speed, gather speed; *informal* get cracking, get moving, step on it, shake a leg; *Brit. informal* get one's skates on; *N. Amer. informal* get a wiggle on.

speedily ▶ **adverb** RAPIDLY, swiftly, quickly, fast, post-haste, at the speed of light, at full tilt; promptly, immediately, briskly; hastily, hurriedly, precipitately; *informal* p.d.q. (pretty damn quick), double quick, hell for leather, at the double, like the wind, like (greased) lightning; *Brit. informal* like the clappers, like billy-o; *N. Amer. informal* lickety-split; *poetic/literary* apace.

speedy ▶ **adjective** ❶ *a speedy reply* RAPID, swift, quick, fast; prompt, immediate, expeditious, express, brisk, sharp; whirlwind, lightning, meteoric; hasty, hurried, precipitate, breakneck, rushed; *informal* p.d.q. (pretty damn quick), snappy, quickie. ❷ *a speedy hatchback* FAST, high-speed; *informal* nippy, zippy; *poetic/literary* fleet.

– OPPOSITES slow.

spell[1] ▶ **verb** *the drought spelled disaster for them* SIGNAL, signify, mean, amount to, add up to, constitute; portend, augur, herald, bode, promise; involve; *poetic/literary* betoken, foretoken, forebode.

■ **spell something out** EXPLAIN, make clear, make plain, elucidate, clarify; specify, itemize, detail, enumerate, list, expound, particularize, catalogue.

spell[2] ▶ **noun** ❶ *the witch recited a spell* INCANTATION, charm, conjuration, formula; (**spells**) magic, sorcery, witchcraft; *N. Amer.* hex. ❷ *she surrendered to his spell* INFLUENCE, (animal) magnetism, charisma, allure, lure, charm, attraction, enticement; magic, romance, mystique.

■ **cast a spell on** BEWITCH, enchant, entrance; curse, jinx, witch; *N. Amer.* hex.

spell[3] ▶ **noun** ❶ *a spell of dry weather* PERIOD, time, interval, season, stretch, run, course, streak; *Brit. informal* patch. ❷ *a spell of dizziness* BOUT, fit, attack.

spellbinding ▶ **adjective** FASCINATING, enthralling, entrancing, bewitching, captivating, riveting, engrossing, gripping, absorbing, compelling, compulsive, mesmerizing, hypnotic; *informal* unputdownable.
– OPPOSITES boring.

spellbound ▶ **adjective** ENTHRALLED, fascinated, rapt, riveted, transfixed, gripped, captivated, bewitched, enchanted, mesmerized, hypnotized; *informal* hooked.

spend ▶ **verb** ❶ *she spent £185 on shoes* PAY OUT, dish out, expend, disburse; squander, waste, fritter away; lavish; *informal* fork out, lay out, shell out, cough up, blow, splash out, splurge; *Brit. informal* stump up, blue; *N. Amer. informal* pony up. ❷ *the morning was spent gardening* PASS, occupy, fill, take up, while away. ❸ *I've spent hours on this essay* PUT IN, devote; waste. ❹ *the storm had spent its force* USE UP, consume, exhaust, deplete, drain.

spendthrift ▶ **noun** *he is such spendthrift* PROFLIGATE, prodigal, squanderer, waster; *informal* big spender.
– OPPOSITES miser.
▶ **adjective** *his spendthrift father* PROFLIGATE, improvident, thriftless, wasteful, extravagant, prodigal.
– OPPOSITES frugal.

spent ▶ **adjective** ❶ *a spent force* USED UP, consumed, exhausted, finished, depleted, drained; *informal* burnt out. ❷ *that's enough—I'm spent* EXHAUSTED, tired (out), weary, worn out, dog-tired, on one's last legs, drained, fatigued, ready to drop; *informal* done in, all in, dead on one's feet, dead beat, bushed, wiped out, frazzled; *Brit. informal* knackered, whacked; *N. Amer. informal* pooped, tuckered out.

spew ▶ **verb** ❶ *factories spewed out yellow smoke* EMIT, discharge, eject, expel, belch out, pour out, spout, gush, spurt, disgorge. ❷ (*informal*) *he wanted to spew. See* VOMIT verb sense 1.

sphere ▶ **noun** ❶ *a glass sphere* GLOBE, ball, orb, spheroid, globule, round; bubble. ❷ *our sphere of influence* AREA, field, compass, orbit; range, scope, extent. ❸ *the sphere of foreign affairs* DOMAIN, realm, province, field, area, territory, arena, department.

spherical ▶ **adjective** ROUND, globular, globose, globoid, globe-shaped, spheroidal, spheric; *poetic/literary* orbicular.

spice ▶ **noun** ❶ *the spices in curry powder* SEASONING, flavouring, condiment. ❷ *the risk added spice to their affair* EXCITEMENT, interest, colour, piquancy, zest; an edge; *informal* a kick; *poetic/literary* salt.
■ **spice something up** ENLIVEN, make more exciting, vitalize, perk up, put some life into, ginger up, galvanize, electrify, boost; *informal* pep up, jazz up, buck up.

spick and span ▶ **adjective** NEAT, tidy, orderly, well kept, shipshape (and Bristol fashion), in apple-pie order; immaculate, uncluttered, trim, spruce; spotless.
– OPPOSITES untidy.

spicy ▶ **adjective** ❶ *a spicy casserole* PIQUANT, tangy, peppery, hot, picante; spiced, seasoned; tasty, flavoursome, zesty, strong, pungent. ❷ *spicy stories* ENTERTAINING, colourful, lively, spirited, exciting, piquant, zesty; risqué, racy, scandalous, ribald, titillating, bawdy, naughty, salacious, dirty, smutty; *informal* raunchy, juicy; *Brit. informal* saucy, fruity; *N. Amer. informal* gamy.
– OPPOSITES bland, boring.

spiel ▶ **noun** (*informal*) SPEECH, patter, (sales) pitch, talk; monologue; rigmarole, story, saga.

spike ▶ **noun** ❶ *a metal spike* PRONG, barb, point; skewer, stake, spit; tine, pin; spur; *Mountaineering* piton. ❷ *the spikes of a cactus* THORN, spine, prickle, bristle; *Zoology* spicule.
▶ **verb** ❶ *she spiked an oyster* IMPALE, spear, skewer; pierce, penetrate, perforate, stab, stick, transfix; *poetic/literary* transpierce. ❷ (*informal*) *his drink was spiked with drugs* ADULTERATE, contaminate, drug, lace; *informal* dope, doctor, cut.

spill ▶ **verb** ❶ *Kevin spilled his drink* KNOCK OVER, tip over, upset, overturn. ❷ *the bath water spilled on to the floor* OVERFLOW, flow, pour, run, slop, slosh, splash; leak, escape; *archaic* overbrim. ❸ *students spilled out of the building* STREAM, pour, surge, swarm, flood, throng, crowd. ❹ *the horse spilled his rider* UNSEAT, throw, dislodge, unhorse. ❺ (*informal*) *he's spilling out his troubles to her* REVEAL, disclose, divulge, blurt out, babble, betray, tell; *informal* blab.
▶ **noun** ❶ *an oil spill* SPILLAGE, leak, leakage, overflow, flood. ❷ *he took a spill in the opening race* FALL, tumble; *informal* header, cropper, nosedive.
■ **spill the beans** (*informal*) REVEAL ALL, tell all, give the game away, talk; *informal* let the cat out of the bag, blab, come clean.

spin ▶ **verb** ❶ *the bike wheels are spinning* REVOLVE, rotate, turn, go round, whirl, gyrate, circle. ❷ *she spun round to face him* WHIRL, wheel, twirl, turn, swing, twist, swivel, pirouette, pivot. ❸ *her head was spinning* REEL, whirl, go round, swim. ❹ *she spun me a yarn* TELL, recount, relate, narrate; weave, concoct, invent, fabricate, make up.
– RELATED TERMS rotary.
▶ **noun** ❶ *a spin of the wheel* ROTATION, revolution, turn, whirl, twirl, gyration. ❷ *a positive spin on the campaign* SLANT, angle, twist, bias. ❸ *a spin in the car* TRIP, jaunt, outing, excursion, journey; drive, ride, run, turn, airing; *informal* tootle; *Scottish informal* hurl.
■ **in a flat spin** (*Brit. informal*). *See* AGITATED.

■ **spin something out** PROLONG, protract, draw out, drag out, string out, extend, carry on, continue; fill out, pad out; *archaic* wire-draw.

spindle ▶ **noun** pivot, pin, rod, axle, capstan; axis.

spindly ▶ **adjective** ❶ *he was pale and spindly* LANKY, thin, skinny, lean, spare, gangling, gangly, scrawny, bony, rangy, angular; *dated* spindle-shanked. ❷ *spindly chairs* RICKETY, flimsy, wobbly, shaky.
– OPPOSITES stocky.

spine ▶ **noun** ❶ *he injured his spine* BACKBONE, spinal column, vertebral column; back; *technical* rachis. ❷ *the spine of his philosophy* CORE, centre, cornerstone, foundation, basis. ❸ *the spines of a hedgehog* NEEDLE, quill, bristle, barb, spike, prickle; thorn; *technical* spicule.
– RELATED TERMS vertebral.

spine-chilling ▶ **adjective** TERRIFYING, blood-curdling, petrifying, hair-raising, frightening, scaring, chilling, horrifying, fearsome; eerie, sinister, ghostly; *Scottish* eldritch; *informal* scary, creepy, spooky.
– OPPOSITES comforting, reassuring.

spineless ▶ **adjective** WEAK, weak-willed, weak-kneed, feeble, soft, ineffectual, irresolute, indecisive; COWARDLY, timid, timorous, fearful, faint-hearted, pusillanimous, craven, unmanly, namby-pamby, lily-livered, chicken-hearted; *informal* wimpish, wimpy, sissy, chicken, yellow, yellow-bellied, gutless; *Brit. informal* wet.
– OPPOSITES bold, brave, strong-willed.

spiny ▶ **adjective** PRICKLY, spiky, thorny, bristly, bristled, spiked, barbed, scratchy, sharp; *technical* spinose, spinous.

spiral ▶ **adjective** *a spiral column of smoke* COILED, helical, corkscrew, curling, winding, twisting, whorled; *technical* voluted, helicoid, helicoidal.
▶ **noun** *a spiral of smoke* COIL, helix, corkscrew, curl, twist, gyre, whorl, scroll; *technical* volute, volution.
▶ **verb** ❶ *smoke spiralled up* COIL, wind, swirl, twist, wreathe, snake, gyrate; *poetic/literary* gyre. ❷ *prices spiralled* SOAR, shoot up, rocket, increase rapidly, rise rapidly, escalate, climb; *informal* skyrocket, go through the roof. ❸ *the economy is spiralling downward* DETERIORATE, decline, degenerate, worsen, get worse; *informal* go downhill, take a nosedive, go to pot, go to the dogs, hit the skids, go down the tubes.
– OPPOSITES fall, improve.

spire ▶ **noun** STEEPLE, flèche.

spirit ▶ **noun** ❶ *harmony between body and spirit* SOUL, psyche, (inner) self, inner being, inner man/woman, mind, ego, id; *Philosophy* pneuma. ❷ *a spirit haunts the island* GHOST, phantom, spectre, apparition, wraith, presence; *informal* spook; *poetic/literary* shade. ❸ *that's the spirit* ATTITUDE, frame of mind, way of thinking, point of view, outlook, thoughts, ideas. ❹ *she was in good spirits when I left* MOOD, frame of mind, state of mind, emotional state, humour, temper. ❺ *team spirit* MORALE, esprit de corps. ❻ *the spirit of the age* ETHOS, prevailing tendency, motivating force, essence, quintessence; atmosphere, mood, feeling, climate; attitudes, beliefs, principles, standards, ethics. ❼ *his spirit never failed him* COURAGE, bravery, pluck, valour, strength of character, fortitude, backbone, mettle, stout-heartedness, determination, resolution, resolve, fight, grit; *informal* guts, spunk; *Brit. informal* bottle; *N. Amer. informal* sand, moxie. ❽ *they played with great spirit* ENTHUSIASM, eagerness, keenness, liveliness, vivacity, vivaciousness, animation, energy, verve, vigour, dynamism, zest, dash, elan, panache, sparkle, exuberance, gusto, brio, pep, fervour, zeal, fire, passion; *informal* get-up-and-go. ❾ *the spirit of the law* REAL/TRUE MEANING, true intention, essence, substance. ❿ *he drinks spirits* STRONG LIQUOR/DRINK; *informal* hard stuff, firewater, hooch; *Brit. informal* short.
– OPPOSITES body, flesh.

■ **spirit someone/something away** WHISK AWAY/OFF, vanish with, make off with, make someone/something disappear, run away with, abscond with, carry off, steal someone/something away, abduct, kidnap, snatch, seize.

spirited ▶ **adjective** LIVELY, vivacious, vibrant, full of life, vital, animated, high-spirited, sparkling, sprightly, energetic, active, vigorous, dynamic, dashing, enthusiastic, passionate; determined, resolute, purposeful; *informal* feisty, spunky, have-a-go, gutsy; *N. Amer. informal* peppy.
– OPPOSITES timid, apathetic, lifeless.

spiritless ▶ **adjective** APATHETIC, passive, unenthusiastic, lifeless, listless, weak, feeble, spineless, languid, bloodless, insipid, characterless, submissive, meek, irresolute, indecisive; lacklustre, flat, colourless, passionless, uninspired, wooden, dry, anaemic, vapid, dull, boring, wishy-washy.
– OPPOSITES spirited, lively.

spiritual ▶ **adjective** ❶ *your spiritual self* NON-MATERIAL, incorporeal, intangible; inner, mental, psychological; transcendent, ethereal, other-worldly, mystic, mystical, metaphysical; *rare* extramundane. ❷ *spiritual writings* RELIGIOUS, sacred, divine, holy, non-secular, church, ecclesiastical, devotional.
– OPPOSITES physical, secular.

spit[1] ▶ **verb** ❶ *Cranston coughed and spat* EXPECTORATE, hawk; *Brit. informal* gob. ❷ *'Go to hell,' she spat* SNAP, say angrily, hiss. ❸ *the fat began to spit* SIZZLE, hiss; crackle, sputter. ❹ (*Brit.*) *it began to spit* RAIN LIGHTLY, drizzle, spot; *N. English* mizzle; *N. Amer.* sprinkle.
▶ **noun** ❶ *spit dribbled from his mouth* SPITTLE, saliva, sputum, slobber, dribble; *Brit. informal* gob.

❷ (*informal*) *he is the spit of his father* EXACT LIKENESS, image, very/living image, double, twin, lookalike, duplicate, copy, Doppelgänger; *informal* spitting image, ringer, dead ringer.

spit² ▶ **noun** *chicken cooked on a spit* SKEWER, brochette, rotisserie.

spite ▶ **noun** *he said it out of spite* MALICE, malevolence, ill will, vindictiveness, vengefulness, revenge, malignity, evil intentions, animus, enmity; *informal* bitchiness, cattiness; *poetic/literary* maleficence.
– OPPOSITES benevolence.
▶ **verb** *he did it to spite me* UPSET, hurt, make miserable, grieve, distress, wound, pain, torment, injure.
– OPPOSITES please.
■ **in spite of** DESPITE, notwithstanding, regardless of, for all; undeterred by, in defiance of, in the face of; even though, although.

spiteful ▶ **adjective** MALICIOUS, malevolent, evil-intentioned, vindictive, vengeful, malign, mean, nasty, hurtful, mischievous, wounding, cruel, unkind; *informal* bitchy, catty; *poetic/literary* malefic, maleficent.
– OPPOSITES benevolent.

splash ▶ **verb** ❶ *splash your face with cool water* SPRINKLE, spray, shower, splatter, slosh, slop, squirt; daub; wet. ❷ *his boots were splashed with mud* SPATTER, bespatter, splatter, speck, speckle, blotch, smear, stain, mark; *Scottish & Irish* slabber; *informal* splotch, splodge; *poetic/literary* bedabble. ❸ *waves splashed on the beach* SWASH, wash, break, lap; dash, beat, lash, batter, crash, buffet; *poetic/literary* plash. ❹ *children splashed in the water* PADDLE, wade, slosh; wallow; *informal* splosh. ❺ *the story was splashed across the front pages* BLAZON, display, spread, plaster, trumpet, publicize; *informal* splatter.
▶ **noun** ❶ *a splash of fat on his shirt* SPOT, blob, dab, daub, smudge, smear, speck, fleck; mark, stain; *informal* splotch, splodge. ❷ *a splash of lemonade* DROP, dash, bit, spot, soupçon, dribble, driblet; *Scottish informal* scoosh. ❸ *a splash of colour* PATCH, burst, streak.
■ **make a splash** (*informal*) CAUSE A SENSATION, cause a stir, attract attention, draw attention to oneself/itself, get noticed, make an impression, make an impact.
■ **splash out** (*Brit. informal*) BE EXTRAVAGANT, go on a spending spree, spare no expense, spend lavishly; *informal* lash out, splurge; *Brit. informal* push the boat out.

spleen ▶ **noun** BAD TEMPER, bad mood, ill temper, ill humour, anger, wrath, vexation, annoyance, irritation, displeasure, dissatisfaction, resentment, rancour; spite, ill feeling, malice, maliciousness, bitterness, animosity, antipathy, hostility, malevolence, venom, gall, malignance, malignity, acrimony, bile, hatred, hate; *poetic/literary* ire, choler.
– OPPOSITES good humour.

splendid ▶ **adjective** ❶ *splendid costumes* MAGNIFICENT, sumptuous, grand, impressive, imposing, superb, spectacular, resplendent, opulent, luxurious, de luxe, rich, fine, costly, expensive, lavish, ornate, gorgeous, glorious, dazzling, elegant, handsome, beautiful; stately, majestic, princely, noble, proud, palatial; *informal* plush, posh, swanky, ritzy, splendiferous; *Brit. informal* swish; *N. Amer. informal* swank; *poetic/literary* brave. ❷ (*informal*) *we had a splendid holiday* EXCELLENT, wonderful, marvellous, superb, glorious, sublime, lovely, delightful, first-class, first-rate; *informal* super, great, amazing, fantastic, terrific, tremendous, phenomenal, sensational, heavenly, gorgeous, dreamy, grand, fabulous, fab, awesome, magic, ace, cool, mean, bad, wicked, mega, crucial, far out, A1, sound, out of this world; *Brit. informal* smashing, brilliant, brill; *N. Amer. informal* dandy, neat; *Austral./NZ informal* beaut, bonzer; *black English* def; *informal, dated* divine, capital; *Brit. informal, dated* champion, wizard, ripping, cracking, spiffing, top-hole; *N. Amer. informal, dated* swell; *archaic* goodly.
– OPPOSITES modest, awful.

splendour ▶ **noun** MAGNIFICENCE, sumptuousness, grandeur, impressiveness, resplendence, opulence, luxury, richness, fineness, lavishness, ornateness, glory, beauty, elegance; majesty, stateliness; *informal* ritziness, splendiferousness.
– OPPOSITES ordinariness, simplicity, modesty.

splenetic ▶ **adjective** BAD-TEMPERED, ill-tempered, angry, cross, peevish, petulant, pettish, irritable, irascible, choleric, dyspeptic, testy, tetchy, snappish, waspish, crotchety, crabby, querulous, resentful, rancorous, bilious; SPITEFUL, malicious, ill-natured, hostile, acrimonious, sour, bitter, malevolent, malignant, malign; *informal* bitchy.
– OPPOSITES good-humoured.

splice ▶ **verb** *the ropes are spliced together* INTERWEAVE, braid, plait, entwine, intertwine, interlace, knit, mesh; *Nautical* marry.
■ **get spliced** (*informal*). *See* MARRY sense 1.

splinter ▶ **noun** *a splinter of wood* SLIVER, shiver, chip, shard; fragment, piece, bit, shred; *Scottish* skelf; (**splinters**) matchwood, flinders.
▶ **verb** *the windscreen splintered* SHATTER, break into tiny pieces, smash, smash into smithereens, fracture, split, crack, disintegrate, crumble.

split ▶ **verb** ❶ *the axe split the wood* BREAK, chop, cut, hew, lop, cleave; snap, crack. ❷ *the ice cracked and split* BREAK APART, fracture, rupture, fissure, snap, come apart, splinter. ❸ *her dress was split* TEAR, rip, slash, slit; *poetic/literary* rend. ❹ *the issue could split the Party* DIVIDE, disunite, separate, sever; bisect, partition; *poetic/literary* tear asunder. ❺ *they split the money between them* SHARE (OUT), divide (up), apportion, allocate, allot, distribute, dole out, parcel out,

measure out; carve up, slice up; *informal* divvy up. ❻ *the path split* FORK, divide, bifurcate, diverge, branch. ❼ *they split up last year* BREAK UP, separate, part, part company, become estranged; divorce, get divorced; *Brit. informal* bust up. ❽ (*informal*) *let's split. See* LEAVE[1] sense 1.
– RELATED TERMS fissile, schizo-.
– OPPOSITES mend, join, unite, pool, converge, get together, marry.
▶ **noun** ❶ *a split in the rock face* CRACK, fissure, cleft, crevice, break, fracture, breach. ❷ *a split in the curtain* RIP, tear, cut, rent, slash, slit. ❸ *a split in the Party* DIVISION, rift, breach, schism, rupture, partition, separation, severance, scission, break-up. ❹ *the acrimonious split with his wife* BREAK-UP, split-up, separation, parting, estrangement, rift; divorce; *Brit. informal* bust-up.
– OPPOSITES marriage.
■ **split hairs** QUIBBLE, cavil, carp, niggle, chop logic; *informal* nit-pick; *archaic* pettifog.
■ **split on someone** (*Brit. informal*). *See* BETRAY sense 1.

split-up ▶ **noun** BREAK-UP, separation, split, parting, estrangement, rift; divorce; *Brit. informal* bust-up.

spoil ▶ **verb** ❶ *too much sun spoils the complexion* MAR, damage, impair, blemish, disfigure, blight, flaw, deface, scar, injure, harm; ruin, destroy, wreck; be a blot on the landscape; *rare* disfeature. ❷ *rain spoiled my plans* RUIN, wreck, destroy, upset, undo, mess up, make a mess of, dash, sabotage, scotch, torpedo; *informal* foul up, louse up, muck up, screw up, put the kibosh on, banjax, do for; *Brit. informal* cock up, scupper, throw a spanner in the works of; *archaic* bring to naught. ❸ *his sisters spoil him* OVERINDULGE, pamper, indulge, mollycoddle, cosset, coddle, baby, wait on hand and foot, kill with kindness; nanny; *archaic* cocker. ❹ *stockpiled food may spoil* GO BAD, go off, go rancid, turn, go sour, go mouldy, go rotten, rot, perish.
– OPPOSITES improve, enhance, further, help, neglect, be strict with, keep.
■ **spoiling for** EAGER FOR, itching for, looking for, keen to have, after, bent on, longing for.

spoils ▶ **plural noun** ❶ *the spoils of war* BOOTY, loot, stolen goods, plunder, ill-gotten gains, haul, pickings; *informal* swag, boodle. ❷ *the spoils of office* BENEFITS, advantages, perks, prize; *formal* perquisites.

spoilsport ▶ **noun** KILLJOY, dog in the manger, misery, damper; *informal* wet blanket, party-pooper.

spoken ▶ **adjective** *spoken communication* VERBAL, oral, vocal, viva voce, uttered, said, stated; unwritten; by word of mouth.
– OPPOSITES non-verbal, written.
■ **spoken for** ❶ *the money is spoken for* RESERVED, set aside, claimed, owned, booked. ❷ *Claudine is spoken for* ATTACHED, going out with someone, in a relationship; *informal* going steady; *dated* courting.

spokesman, spokeswoman ▶ **noun** SPOKESPERSON, representative, agent, mouthpiece, voice, official; *informal* spin doctor.

sponge ▶ **verb** ❶ *I'll sponge your face* WASH, clean, wipe, swab; mop, rinse, sluice, swill. ❷ (*informal*) *he lived by sponging off others* SCROUNGE, be a parasite, beg; live off; *informal* freeload, cadge, bum; *N. Amer. informal* mooch; *Austral./NZ* bludge.

sponger ▶ **noun** (*informal*) PARASITE, hanger-on, leech, scrounger, beggar; *informal* freeloader, cadger, bum, bloodsucker; *N. Amer. informal* mooch, moocher, schnorrer; *Austral./NZ informal* bludger.

spongy ▶ **adjective** SOFT, squashy, cushioned, cushiony, compressible, yielding; springy, resilient, elastic; porous, absorbent, permeable; *technical* spongiform; *Brit. informal* squidgy.
– OPPOSITES hard, solid.

sponsor ▶ **noun** *the money came from sponsors* BACKER, patron, promoter, benefactor, benefactress, supporter, contributor, subscriber, friend, guarantor, underwriter; *informal* angel.
▶ **verb** *a bank sponsored the event* FINANCE, put up the money for, fund, subsidize, back, promote, support, contribute to, be a patron of, guarantee, underwrite; *informal* foot the bill for, pick up the tab for; *N. Amer. informal* bankroll.

sponsorship ▶ **noun** BACKING, support, promotion, patronage, subsidy, funding, financing, aid, financial assistance.

spontaneous ▶ **adjective** ❶ *a spontaneous display of affection* UNPLANNED, unpremeditated, unrehearsed, impulsive, impetuous, unstudied, impromptu, spur-of-the-moment, extempore, extemporaneous; unforced, voluntary, unconstrained, unprompted, unbidden, unsolicited; *informal* off-the-cuff. ❷ *a spontaneous reaction to danger* REFLEX, automatic, mechanical, natural, knee-jerk, involuntary, unthinking, unconscious, instinctive, instinctual; *informal* gut. ❸ *a spontaneous kind of person* NATURAL, uninhibited, relaxed, unselfconscious, unaffected, open, genuine, easy, free and easy; impulsive, impetuous.
– OPPOSITES planned, calculated, conscious, voluntary, inhibited.

spontaneously ▶ **adverb** ❶ *they applauded spontaneously* WITHOUT BEING ASKED, of one's own accord, voluntarily, on impulse, impulsively, on the spur of the moment, extempore, extemporaneously; *informal* off the cuff. ❷ *he reacted spontaneously* WITHOUT THINKING, automatically, mechanically, unthinkingly, involuntarily, instinctively, naturally, by oneself/itself.

spooky ▶ **adjective** (*informal*) EERIE, sinister, ghostly, uncanny, weird, unearthly, mysterious; FRIGHTENING, spine-chilling, hair-raising; *informal* creepy, scary, spine-tingling.

sporadic ▶ **adjective** OCCASIONAL, infrequent, irregular, periodic, scattered, patchy, isolated, odd; intermittent, spasmodic, fitful, desultory, erratic, unpredictable.
– OPPOSITES frequent, steady, continuous.

sport ▶ **noun** ❶ *we did a lot of sport* (COMPETITIVE) GAME(S), physical recreation, physical activity, physical exercise; pastime. ❷ (*dated*) *they were rogues out for a bit of sport* FUN, pleasure, enjoyment, entertainment, amusement, diversion.
▶ **verb** *he sported a beard* WEAR, have on, dress in; DISPLAY, exhibit, show off, flourish, parade, flaunt.

sporting ▶ **adjective** SPORTSMANLIKE, generous, gentlemanly, considerate; fair, just, honourable; *Brit. informal* decent.
– OPPOSITES dirty, unfair.

sporty ▶ **adjective** (*informal*) ❶ *he's quite a sporty type* ATHLETIC, fit, active, energetic. ❷ *a sporty outfit* STYLISH, smart, jaunty; CASUAL, informal; *informal* trendy, cool, snazzy; *N. Amer. informal* sassy. ❸ *a sporty car* FAST, speedy; *informal* nippy, zippy.
– OPPOSITES unfit, lazy, formal, sloppy, slow.

spot ▶ **noun** ❶ *a grease spot on the wall* MARK, patch, dot, fleck, smudge, smear, stain, blotch, blot, splash; *informal* splotch, splodge. ❷ *a spot on his nose* PIMPLE, pustule, blackhead, boil, swelling, eruption, wen, sty; (**spots**) acne; *technical* comedo, papule; *informal* zit, whitehead; *Scottish informal* plook. ❸ *a secluded spot* PLACE, location, site, position, point, situation, scene, setting, locale, locality, area, neighbourhood, region; venue; *technical* locus. ❹ *social policy has a regular spot on the agenda* POSITION, place, slot, space. ❺ *a spot to eat or drink* BIT, little, some, small amount, morsel, bite, mouthful; drop, splash; *informal* smidgen, tad. ❻ (*informal*) *in a tight spot* PREDICAMENT, mess, difficulty, trouble, plight, corner, quandary, dilemma; *informal* fix, jam, hole, sticky situation, pickle, scrape, hot water.
▶ **verb** ❶ *she spotted him in his car* NOTICE, see, observe, note, discern, detect, perceive, make out, recognize, identify, locate; catch sight of, glimpse; *Brit. informal* clock; *poetic/literary* behold, espy. ❷ *her clothes were spotted with grease* STAIN, mark, fleck, speckle, smudge, streak, splash, spatter; *informal* splotch, splodge. ❸ *it was spotting with rain* RAIN LIGHTLY, drizzle; *Brit.* spit; *N. English* mizzle; *N. Amer.* sprinkle.
■ **on the spot** IMMEDIATELY, at once, straight away, right away, without delay, without hesitation, that instant, directly, there and then, then and there, forthwith, instantly, summarily; *N. Amer.* in short order; *archaic* straightway, instanter.
■ **spot on** (*Brit. informal*) ACCURATE, correct, right, perfect, exact, unerring; *Brit. informal* bang on; *N. Amer. informal* on the money, on the nose.

spotless ▶ **adjective** ❶ *the kitchen was spotless* PERFECTLY CLEAN, ultra-clean, pristine, immaculate, shining, shiny, gleaming, spick and span. ❷ *a spotless reputation* UNBLEMISHED, unsullied, untarnished, untainted, unstained, pure, whiter than white, innocent, impeccable, blameless, irreproachable, above reproach; *informal* squeaky clean.
– OPPOSITES dirty, tarnished, impure.

spotlight ▶ **noun** *she was constantly in the spotlight* PUBLIC EYE, glare of publicity, limelight; focus of public/media attention.
▶ **verb** *this article spotlights the problem* FOCUS ATTENTION ON, highlight, point up, draw/call attention to, give prominence to, throw into relief, turn the spotlight on, bring to the fore.

spotted ▶ **adjective** ❶ *the spotted leaves* MOTTLED, dappled, speckled, flecked, freckled, freckly, dotted, stippled, brindle(d); *informal* splotchy. ❷ *a black-and-white spotted dress* POLKA-DOT, spotty, dotted.
– OPPOSITES plain.

spotty ▶ **adjective** ❶ *a spotty dog* SPOTTED, mottled, speckled, speckly, flecked, specked, stippled; *informal* splodgy, splotchy. ❷ *a spotty dress* POLKA-DOT, spotted, dotted. ❸ (*Brit.*) *his spotty face* PIMPLY, pimpled, acned; *Scottish informal* plooky.

spouse ▶ **noun** PARTNER, mate, consort; *informal* better half; *Brit. informal* other half. *See also* HUSBAND noun, WIFE.

spout ▶ **verb** ❶ *lava was spouting from the crater* SPURT, gush, spew, erupt, shoot, squirt, spray; disgorge, discharge, emit, belch forth. ❷ *he spouts on foreign affairs* HOLD FORTH, sound off, go on, talk at length, expatiate; *informal* mouth off, speechify, spiel.
▶ **noun** *a can with a spout* NOZZLE, lip, rose.
■ **up the spout** (*Brit. informal*) ❶ *my computer's up the spout. See* BROKEN sense 3. ❷ *his daughter's up the spout. See* PREGNANT sense 1.

sprawl ▶ **verb** ❶ *he sprawled on a sofa* STRETCH OUT, lounge, loll, lie, recline, drape oneself, slump, flop, slouch. ❷ *the town sprawled ahead of them* SPREAD, stretch, extend, be strung out, be scattered, straggle, spill.

spray[1] ▶ **noun** ❶ *a spray of water* SHOWER, sprinkling, sprinkle, jet, mist, drizzle; spume, spindrift; foam, froth. ❷ *a perfume spray* ATOMIZER, vaporizer, aerosol, sprinkler; nebulizer.
▶ **verb** ❶ *water was sprayed around* SPRINKLE, shower, spatter; scatter, disperse, diffuse; mist; douche; *poetic/literary* besprinkle. ❷ *water sprayed into the air* SPOUT, jet, gush, spurt, shoot, squirt.

spray[2] ▶ **noun** ❶ *a spray of holly* SPRIG, twig. ❷ *a spray of flowers* BOUQUET, bunch, posy, nosegay; corsage, buttonhole, boutonnière.

spread ▶ verb ❶ *he spread the map out* LAY OUT, open out, unfurl, unroll, roll out; straighten out, fan out; stretch out, extend; *poetic/literary* outspread. ❷ *the landscape spread out below* EXTEND, stretch, open out, be displayed, be exhibited, be on show; sprawl. ❸ *papers were spread all over his desk* SCATTER, strew, disperse, distribute. ❹ *he's been spreading rumours* DISSEMINATE, circulate, pass on, put about, communicate, diffuse, make public, make known, purvey, broadcast, publicize, propagate, promulgate; repeat; *poetic/literary* bruit about/abroad. ❺ *she spread cold cream on her face* SMEAR, daub, plaster, slather, lather, apply, put; smooth, rub. ❻ *he spread the toast with butter* COVER, coat, layer, daub, smother; butter.
– OPPOSITES fold up, suppress.
▶ noun ❶ *the spread of learning* EXPANSION, proliferation, extension, growth; dissemination, diffusion, transmission, propagation. ❷ *a spread of six feet* SPAN, width, extent, stretch, reach. ❸ *the immense spread of the heavens* EXPANSE, area, sweep, stretch. ❹ *a wide spread of subjects* RANGE, span, spectrum, sweep; variety. ❺ (*informal*) *his mother laid on a huge spread* LARGE/ELABORATE MEAL, feast, banquet; *informal* blowout, nosh; *Brit. informal* nosh-up, slap-up meal.

spree ▶ noun ❶ *a shopping spree* UNRESTRAINED BOUT, orgy; *informal* binge, splurge; *humorous* retail therapy. ❷ *a drinking spree* DRINKING BOUT, debauch; *informal* binge, bender, session, booze-up, blind; *Scottish informal* skite; *N. Amer. informal* jag, toot; *poetic/literary* bacchanal, bacchanalia; *archaic* wassail.

sprig ▶ noun SMALL STEM, spray, twig.

sprightly ▶ adjective SPRY, lively, agile, nimble, energetic, active, full of energy, vigorous, spirited, animated, vivacious, frisky; *informal* full of vim and vigour; *N. English informal* wick.
– OPPOSITES doddery, lethargic.

spring ▶ verb ❶ *the cat sprang off her lap* LEAP, jump, bound, vault, hop. ❷ *the branch sprang back* FLY, whip, flick, whisk, kick, bounce. ❸ *all art springs from feelings* ORIGINATE, derive, arise, stem, emanate, proceed, issue, evolve, come. ❹ *fifty men sprang from nowhere* APPEAR SUDDENLY, appear unexpectedly, materialize, pop up, shoot up, sprout, develop quickly; proliferate, mushroom. ❺ *he sprang the truth on me* ANNOUNCE SUDDENLY/UNEXPECTEDLY, reveal suddenly/unexpectedly, surprise someone with.
▶ noun ❶ *with a sudden spring he leapt on to the table* LEAP, jump, bound, vault, hop; pounce. ❷ *the mattress has lost its spring* SPRINGINESS, bounciness, bounce, resilience, elasticity, flexibility, stretch, stretchiness, give. ❸ *there was a spring in his step* BUOYANCY, bounce, energy, liveliness, jauntiness, sprightliness, confidence. ❹ *a mineral spring* WELL HEAD, source; spa, geyser; *poetic/literary* wellspring, fount. ❺ *the springs of his own emotions* ORIGIN, source, fountainhead, root, roots, basis.
– RELATED TERMS vernal.

springy ▶ adjective ELASTIC, stretchy, stretchable, tensile; flexible, pliant, pliable, whippy; bouncy, resilient, spongy.
– OPPOSITES rigid, squashy.

sprinkle ▶ verb ❶ *he sprinkled water over the towel* SPLASH, trickle, spray, shower; spatter. ❷ *sprinkle sesame seeds over the top* SCATTER, strew; drizzle. ❸ *sprinkle the cake with icing sugar* DREDGE, dust. ❹ *the sky was sprinkled with stars* DOT, stipple, stud, fleck, speckle, spot, pepper; scatter, cover; *poetic/literary* besprinkle.

sprinkling ▶ noun ❶ *a sprinkling of nutmeg* SCATTERING, sprinkle, scatter, dusting; pinch, dash. ❷ *mainly women, but a sprinkling of men* FEW, one or two, couple, handful, small number, trickle, scattering.

sprint ▶ verb RUN, race, dart, rush, dash, hasten, hurry, scurry, scamper, hare, bolt, fly, gallop, career, charge, shoot, hurtle, speed, zoom, go like lightning, go hell for leather, go like the wind; jog, trot; *informal* tear, pelt, scoot, hotfoot it, leg it, belt, zip, whip; *Brit. informal* bomb; *N. Amer. informal* hightail it, barrel.
– OPPOSITES walk.

sprite ▶ noun FAIRY, elf, pixie, imp, brownie, puck, peri, kelpie, leprechaun; nymph, nixie, sylph, naiad.

sprout ▶ verb ❶ *the weeds begin to sprout* GERMINATE, put/send out shoots, bud, burgeon. ❷ *he had sprouted a beard* GROW, develop, put/send out. ❸ *parsley sprouted from the pot* SPRING UP, shoot up, come up, grow, burgeon, develop, appear.

spruce ▶ adjective *the Captain looked very spruce* NEAT, well groomed, well turned out, well dressed, smart, trim, dapper, elegant, chic; *informal* natty, snazzy; *N. Amer. informal* spiffy, trig.
– OPPOSITES untidy.
▶ verb ❶ *the cottage had been spruced up* SMARTEN, tidy, neaten, put in order, clean; *informal* do up; *Brit. informal* tart up, posh up; *N. Amer. informal* gussy up. ❷ *Sarah had spruced herself up* GROOM, tidy, smarten, preen, primp, prink; *N. Amer.* trig; *informal* titivate, doll up; *Brit. informal* tart up.

spry ▶ adjective SPRIGHTLY, lively, agile, nimble, energetic, active, full of energy, vigorous, spirited, animated, vivacious, frisky; *informal* full of vim and vigour; *N. English informal* wick.
– OPPOSITES doddery, lethargic.

spume ▶ noun FOAM, froth, surf, spindrift, bubbles.

spunk ▶ noun (*informal*) COURAGE, bravery, valour, nerve, confidence, daring, audacity, pluck, spirit, grit, mettle, spine, backbone; *informal* guts, gumption; *Brit. informal* bottle; *N. Amer. informal* moxie.

spur ▶ noun ❶ *competition can be a spur* STIMULUS, incentive, encouragement, inducement, fillip, impetus, prod, motivation, inspiration; *informal*

kick up the backside, shot in the arm. ❷ *a spur of bone* PROJECTION, spike, point; *technical* process.
– OPPOSITES disincentive, discouragement.
▶ **verb** *the thought spurred him into action* STIMULATE, encourage, prompt, propel, prod, induce, impel, motivate, move, galvanize, inspire, incentivize, urge, drive, egg on, stir; incite, goad, provoke, prick, sting; *N. Amer.* light a fire under.
– OPPOSITES discourage.
■ **on the spur of the moment** IMPULSIVELY, on impulse, impetuously, without thinking, without premeditation, unpremeditatedly, impromptu, extempore, spontaneously; *informal* off the cuff.

spurious ▶ **adjective** BOGUS, fake, false, counterfeit, forged, fraudulent, sham, artificial, imitation, simulated, feigned, deceptive, misleading; *informal* phoney, pretend; *Brit. informal* cod.
– OPPOSITES genuine.

spurn ▶ **verb** REJECT, rebuff, scorn, turn down, treat with contempt, disdain, look down one's nose at, despise; snub, slight, jilt, dismiss, brush off, turn one's back on; give someone the cold shoulder, cold-shoulder; *informal* turn one's nose up at, give someone the brush-off, kick in the teeth; *Brit. informal* knock back; *N. Amer. informal* give someone the bum's rush.
– OPPOSITES welcome, accept.

spurt ▶ **verb** *water spurted from the tap* SQUIRT, shoot, jet, erupt, gush, pour, stream, pump, surge, spew, course, well, spring, burst; disgorge, discharge, emit, belch forth, expel, eject; *Brit. informal* sloosh.
▶ **noun** ❶ *a spurt of water* SQUIRT, jet, spout, gush, stream, rush, surge, flood, cascade, torrent. ❷ *a spurt of courage* BURST, fit, bout, rush, spate, surge, attack, outburst, blaze. ❸ *Daisy put on a spurt* BURST OF SPEED, turn of speed, sprint, rush, burst of energy.

spy ▶ **noun** *a foreign spy* SECRET AGENT, intelligence agent, double agent, counterspy, mole, plant, scout; *informal* snooper; *N. Amer. informal* spook; *archaic* intelligencer.
▶ **verb** ❶ *he spied for the West* BE A SPY, gather intelligence, work for the secret service; *informal* snoop. ❷ *investigators spied on them* OBSERVE FURTIVELY, keep under surveillance/observation, watch, keep a watch on, keep an eye on. ❸ *she spied a coffee shop* NOTICE, observe, see, spot, sight, catch sight of, glimpse, make out, discern, detect; *informal* clap/lay/set eyes on; *poetic/literary* espy, behold, descry.

spying ▶ **noun** ESPIONAGE, intelligence gathering, surveillance, infiltration, undercover work, cloak-and-dagger activities.

squabble ▶ **noun** *there was a squabble over which way they should go* QUARREL, disagreement, row, argument, contretemps, falling-out, dispute, clash, altercation, shouting match, exchange, war of words; *informal* tiff, set-to, run-in, slanging match, shindig, shindy, stand-up, spat, scrap, dust-up; *Brit. informal* barney, ding-dong; *N. Amer. informal* rhubarb.
▶ **verb** *the boys were squabbling over a ball* QUARREL, row, argue, bicker, fall out, disagree, have words, dispute, spar, cross swords, lock horns, be at loggerheads; *informal* scrap, argufy.

squad ▶ **noun** ❶ *an assassination squad* TEAM, crew, gang, band, cell, body, mob, outfit, force. ❷ *a firing squad* DETACHMENT, detail, unit, platoon, battery, troop, patrol, squadron, cadre, commando.

squalid ▶ **adjective** ❶ *a squalid prison* DIRTY, filthy, grubby, grimy, mucky, slummy, foul, vile, poor, sorry, wretched, miserable, mean, seedy, shabby, sordid, insalubrious; NEGLECTED, uncared-for, broken-down, run down, down at heel, depressed, dilapidated, ramshackle, tumbledown, gone to rack and ruin, crumbling, decaying; *informal* scruffy, crummy, shambly, ratty; *Brit. informal* grotty; *N. Amer. informal* shacky. ❷ *a squalid deal with the opposition* IMPROPER, sordid, unseemly, unsavoury, sleazy, seedy, seamy, shoddy, cheap, base, low, corrupt, dishonest, dishonourable, disreputable, despicable, discreditable, disgraceful, contemptible, shameful; *informal* sleazoid.
– OPPOSITES clean, pleasant, smart, upmarket, proper, decent.

squall ▶ **noun** GUST, storm, blast, flurry, shower, gale, blow, rush.

squally ▶ **adjective** STORMY, gusty, gusting, blustery, blustering, windy, blowy; wild, tempestuous, rough.

squalor ▶ **noun** DIRT, filth, grubbiness, grime, muck, foulness, vileness, poverty, wretchedness, meanness, seediness, shabbiness, sordidness, sleaziness, insalubrity; NEGLECT, decay, dilapidation; *informal* scruffiness, crumminess, grunge, rattiness; *Brit. informal* grottiness.
– OPPOSITES cleanliness, pleasantness, smartness.

squander ▶ **verb** WASTE, misspend, misuse, throw away, fritter away, spend recklessly, spend unwisely, spend like water; *informal* blow, go through, splurge, pour down the drain; *Brit. informal* blue.
– OPPOSITES manage, make good use of, save.

square ▶ **noun** ❶ *a shop in the square* market square, marketplace, plaza, piazza. ❷ (*informal*) *you're such a square!* (OLD) FOGEY, conservative, traditionalist, conventionalist, conformist, bourgeois, fossil; *Brit.* museum piece; *informal* stick-in-the-mud, fuddy-duddy, back number, stuffed shirt.
– OPPOSITES trendy.
▶ **adjective** ❶ *a square table* QUADRILATERAL, rectangular, oblong, right-angled, at right angles, perpendicular; straight, level, parallel, horizontal, upright, vertical, true, plane. ❷ *the*

sides were square at half-time LEVEL, even, drawn, equal, tied; neck and neck, level pegging, nip and tuck, side by side, evenly matched; *informal* even-steven(s). ❸ *I'm going to be square with you* FAIR, honest, just, equitable, straight, true, upright, above board, ethical, decent, proper; *informal* on the level. ❹ (*informal*) *don't be square!* OLD-FASHIONED, behind the times, out of date, conservative, traditionalist, conventional, conformist, bourgeois, strait-laced, fogeyish, stuffy; *informal* stick-in-the-mud, fuddy-duddy.
– OPPOSITES crooked, uneven, underhand, trendy.

▶ **verb** ❶ *the theory does not square with the data* AGREE, tally, be in agreement, be consistent, match up, correspond, fit, coincide, accord, conform, be compatible. ❷ *his goal squared the match 1–1* LEVEL, even, make equal. ❸ *would you square up the bill?* PAY, settle, discharge, clear, meet. ❹ (*informal*) *they tried to square the press* BRIBE, buy off, buy, corrupt, suborn; *informal* grease someone's palm, give a backhander to. ❺ *Tom squared things with his boss* RESOLVE, sort out, settle, clear up, work out, iron out, smooth over, straighten out, deal with, put right, set right, put to rights, rectify, remedy; *informal* patch up.

squash ▶ **verb** ❶ *the fruit got squashed* CRUSH, squeeze, flatten, compress, press, smash, distort, pound, trample, stamp on; pulp, mash, cream, liquidize, beat, pulverize. ❷ *she squashed her clothes inside the bag* FORCE, ram, thrust, push, cram, jam, stuff, pack, compress, squeeze, wedge, press. ❸ *the proposal was immediately squashed* REJECT, block, cancel, scotch, frustrate, thwart, suppress, put a stop to, nip in the bud, put the lid on; *informal* put paid to, put the kibosh on, stymie; *Brit. informal* dish, scupper.

squashy ▶ **adjective** ❶ *a squashy pillow* SPRINGY, resilient, spongy, soft, pliant, pliable, yielding, elastic, cushiony, compressible. ❷ *squashy pears* MUSHY, pulpy, pappy, slushy, squelchy, squishy, oozy, doughy, soft; *Brit. informal* squidgy.
– OPPOSITES firm, hard.

squat ▶ **verb** *I was squatting on the floor* CROUCH (DOWN), hunker (down), sit on one's haunches, sit on one's heels.

▶ **adjective** *he was muscular and squat* STOCKY, thickset, dumpy, stubby, stumpy, short, small; *Brit. informal* fubsy.

squawk ▶ **verb & noun** *a pheasant squawked | the gull gave a squawk* SCREECH, squeal, shriek, scream, croak, crow, caw, cluck, cackle, hoot, cry, call.

squeak ▶ **noun & verb** ❶ *the vole's dying squeak | the rat squeaked* PEEP, cheep, pipe, piping, squeal, tweet, yelp, whimper. ❷ *the squeak of the hinge | the hinges of the gate squeaked* SCREECH, creak, scrape, grate, rasp, jar, groan.

squeal ▶ **noun** *the harsh squeal of a fox* SCREECH, scream, shriek, squawk.

▶ **verb** ❶ *a dog squealed* SCREECH, scream, shriek, squawk. ❷ *the bookies only squealed because we beat them* COMPLAIN, protest, object, grouse, grumble, whine, wail, carp, squawk; *informal* kick up a fuss, kick up a stink, gripe, grouch, bellyache, moan, bitch, beef, whinge; *N. English informal* mither. ❸ (*informal*) *he squealed on the rest of the gang to the police* INFORM, tell tales, sneak; report, give away, be disloyal, sell out, stab in the back; *informal* rat, peach, snitch, put the finger on, sell down the river, stitch up; *Brit. informal* grass, split, shop; *N. Amer. informal* rat out, finger, drop a/the dime on; *Austral. informal* dob, pimp on, pool.

squeamish ▶ **adjective** ❶ *I'm too squeamish to gut fish* EASILY NAUSEATED, nervous; (**be squeamish about**) BE PUT OFF BY, cannot stand the sight of, —— makes one feel sick. ❷ *less squeamish nations will sell them arms* SCRUPULOUS, principled, fastidious, particular, punctilious, honourable, upright, upstanding, high-minded, righteous, right-minded, moral, ethical.

squeeze ▶ **verb** ❶ *I squeezed the bottle* COMPRESS, press, crush, squash, pinch, nip, grasp, grip, clutch, flatten. ❷ *squeeze the juice from both oranges* EXTRACT, press, force, express. ❸ *Sally squeezed her feet into the sandals* FORCE, thrust, cram, ram, jam, stuff, pack, wedge, press, squash. ❹ *we all squeezed into Steve's van* CROWD, crush, cram, pack, jam, squash, wedge oneself, shove, push, force one's way. ❺ *he would squeeze more money out of Bill* EXTORT, force, extract, wrest, wring, milk; *informal* bleed someone of something.

▶ **noun** ❶ *he gave her hand a squeeze* PRESS, pinch, nip; grasp, grip, clutch, hug, clasp; compression. ❷ *it was a tight squeeze in the tiny hall* CRUSH, jam, squash, press, huddle; congestion. ❸ *a squeeze of lemon juice* FEW DROPS, dash, splash, dribble, trickle, spot, hint, touch.

squint ▶ **verb** ❶ *the sun made them squint* SCREW UP ONE'S EYES, narrow one's eyes, peer, blink. ❷ *he has squinted from birth* BE CROSS-EYED, have a squint, suffer from strabismus; *Scottish* be skelly; *Brit. informal* be boss-eyed.

▶ **noun** ❶ (*informal*) *we must have another squint at his record card* LOOK, glance, peep, peek, glimpse; view, examination, study, inspection, scan, sight; *informal* eyeful, dekko, butcher's, gander, look-see, once-over, shufti. ❷ *does he have a squint?* CROSS-EYES, strabismus; *Brit. informal* boss-eye.

squire ▶ **noun** ❶ *the squire of the village* LANDOWNER, landholder, landlord, lord of the manor, country gentleman. ❷ (*historical*) *his squire carried a banner* ATTENDANT, courtier, equerry, aide, steward, page boy.

squirm ▶ **verb** ❶ *I tried to squirm away* WRIGGLE, wiggle, writhe, twist, slide, slither, turn, shift, fidget, jiggle, twitch, thresh, flounder, flail, toss and turn. ❷ *he squirmed as everyone laughed* WINCE, shudder, feel embarrassed, feel ashamed.

squirrel
– RELATED TERMS sciurine.
■ **squirrel something away** SAVE, put aside, put by, lay by, set aside, lay aside, keep in reserve, stockpile, accumulate, stock up with/on, hoard; *informal* salt away, stash away.

squirt ▶ **verb** ❶ *a jet of ink squirted out of the tube* SPURT, shoot, spray, fountain, jet, erupt; gush, rush, pump, surge, stream, spew, well, spring, burst, issue, emanate; emit, belch forth, expel, eject; *Brit. informal* sloosh. ❷ *she squirted me with scent* SPLASH, wet, spray, shower, spatter, splatter, sprinkle; *Scottish & Irish* slabber; *poetic/literary* besprinkle.
▶ **noun** ❶ *a squirt of water* SPURT, jet, spray, fountain, gush, stream, surge. ❷ (*informal*) *he was just a little squirt* IMPUDENT PERSON, insignificant person, gnat, insect; *informal* pipsqueak, whippersnapper; *Brit. informal* squit; *Scottish informal* nyaff; *N. Amer. informal* bozo, picayune, pisher.

stab ▶ **verb** ❶ *he stabbed him in the stomach* KNIFE, run through, skewer, spear, bayonet, gore, spike, stick, impale, transfix, pierce, prick, puncture; *poetic/literary* transpierce. ❷ *she stabbed at the earth with a fork* LUNGE, thrust, jab, poke, prod, dig.
▶ **noun** ❶ *a stab in the leg* KNIFE WOUND, puncture, incision, prick, cut, perforation. ❷ *they made stabs into the air* LUNGE, thrust, jab, poke, prod, dig, punch. ❸ *a stab of pain* TWINGE, pang, throb, spasm, cramp, dart, blaze, prick, flash, thrill. ❹ (*informal*) *he had a stab at writing* ATTEMPT, try, effort, endeavour; guess; *informal* go, shot, crack, bash, whack; *formal* essay.
■ **stab someone in the back** BETRAY, be disloyal to, be unfaithful to, desert, break one's promise to, double-cross, break faith with, sell out, play false, inform on/against; *informal* tell on, sell down the river, squeal on, stitch up, peach on, do the dirty on; *Brit. informal* grass on, shop; *N. Amer. informal* rat out, finger, drop a/the dime on; *Austral. informal* pimp on, pool, put someone's pot on.

stability ▶ **noun** ❶ *the stability of play equipment* FIRMNESS, solidity, steadiness, strength, security, safety. ❷ *his mental stability* BALANCE OF MIND, mental health, sanity, normality, soundness, rationality, reason, sense. ❸ *the stability of their relationship* STEADINESS, firmness, solidity, strength, durability, lasting nature, enduring nature, permanence, changelessness, invariability, immutability, indestructibility, reliability, dependability.

stable ▶ **adjective** ❶ *a stable tent* FIRM, solid, steady, secure, fixed, fast, safe, moored, anchored, stuck down, immovable. ❷ *a stable person* WELL BALANCED, of sound mind, compos mentis, sane, normal, right in the head, rational, steady, reasonable, sensible, sober, down-to-earth, matter-of-fact, having both one's feet on the ground; *informal* all there. ❸ *a stable relationship* SECURE, solid, strong, steady, firm, sure, steadfast, unwavering, unvarying, unfaltering, unfluctuating; established, abiding, durable, enduring, lasting, permanent, reliable, dependable.
– OPPOSITES loose, wobbly, unbalanced, rocky, lasting, changeable.

stack ▶ **noun** ❶ *a stack of boxes* HEAP, pile, mound, mountain, pyramid, tower. ❷ *a stack of hay* HAYSTACK, rick, hayrick, stook, mow, shock; *dated* cock. ❸ (*informal*) *a stack of money*. See LOT pronoun. ❹ CHIMNEY, smokestack, funnel, exhaust pipe.
– OPPOSITES few, little.
▶ **verb** ❶ *Leo was stacking plates* HEAP (UP), pile (up), make a heap/pile/stack of; assemble, put together, collect, hoard, store, stockpile. ❷ *they stacked the shelves* LOAD, fill (up), lade, pack, charge, stuff, cram; stock.
– OPPOSITES empty.

stadium ▶ **noun** ARENA, field, ground, pitch; bowl, amphitheatre, coliseum, ring, dome, manège; track, course, racetrack, racecourse, speedway, velodrome; (*in ancient Rome*) circus.

staff ▶ **noun** ❶ *there is a reluctance to take on new staff* EMPLOYEES, workers, workforce, personnel, human resources, manpower, labour; *informal* liveware. ❷ *he carried a wooden staff* STICK, stave, pole, crook. ❸ *a staff of office* ROD, tipstaff, cane, mace, wand, sceptre, crozier, verge; *Greek Mythology* caduceus.
▶ **verb** *the centre is staffed by teachers* MAN, people, crew, work, operate, occupy.

stage ▶ **noun** ❶ *this stage of the development* PHASE, period, juncture, step, point, time, moment, instant, level. ❷ *the last stage of the race* PART, section, portion, stretch, leg, lap, circuit. ❸ *a theatre stage* PLATFORM, dais, stand, grandstand, staging, apron, rostrum, podium. ❹ *she has written for the stage* THEATRE, drama, dramatics, dramatic art, thespianism; *informal* the boards. ❺ *the political stage* SCENE, setting; context, frame, sphere, field, realm, arena, backdrop; affairs.
▶ **verb** ❶ *they staged two plays* PUT ON, put before the public, present, produce, mount, direct; perform, act, give. ❷ *workers staged a protest* ORGANIZE, arrange, coordinate, lay on, put together, get together, set up; orchestrate, choreograph, mastermind, engineer; take part in, participate in, join in.

stagger ▶ **verb** ❶ *he staggered to the door* LURCH, walk unsteadily, reel, sway, teeter, totter, stumble, wobble. ❷ *I was absolutely staggered* AMAZE, astound, astonish, surprise, startle, stun, confound, dumbfound, stupefy, daze, nonplus, take aback, leave open-mouthed, leave aghast; *informal* flabbergast, bowl over; *Brit. informal* knock for six. ❸ *meetings are stag-*

gered throughout the day SPREAD (OUT), space (out), time at intervals, overlap. ❹ *stagger the screws at each joint* ALTERNATE, step, arrange in a zigzag.

stagnant ▶ **adjective** ❶ *stagnant water* STILL, motionless, static, stationary, standing, dead, slack; FOUL, stale, putrid, smelly. ❷ *a stagnant economy* INACTIVE, sluggish, slow-moving, lethargic, static, flat, depressed, declining, moribund, dying, dead, dormant.
– OPPOSITES flowing, fresh, active, vibrant.

stagnate ▶ **verb** ❶ *obstructions allow water to stagnate* STOP FLOWING, become stagnant, become trapped; stand; become foul, become stale; fester, putrefy. ❷ *exports stagnated* LANGUISH, decline, deteriorate, fall, become stagnant, do nothing, stand still, be sluggish.
– OPPOSITES flow, rise, boom.

staid ▶ **adjective** SEDATE, respectable, quiet, serious, serious-minded, steady, conventional, traditional, unadventurous, unenterprising, set in one's ways, sober, proper, decorous, formal, stuffy, stiff; *informal* starchy, stick-in-the-mud.
– OPPOSITES frivolous, daring, informal.

stain ▶ **verb** ❶ *her clothing was stained with blood* DISCOLOUR, blemish, soil, mark, muddy, spot, spatter, splatter, smear, splash, smudge, blotch, blacken. ❷ *the report stained his reputation* DAMAGE, injure, harm, sully, blacken, tarnish, taint, smear, bring discredit to, dishonour, drag through the mud; *poetic/literary* besmirch. ❸ *the wood was stained* COLOUR, tint, dye, tinge, pigment, colour-wash.
▶ **noun** ❶ *a mud stain* MARK, spot, spatter, splatter, blotch, smudge, smear. ❷ *a stain on his character* BLEMISH, injury, taint, blot, smear, discredit, dishonour; damage. ❸ *dark wood stain* TINT, colour, dye, tinge, pigment, colourant, colour wash.

stake[1] ▶ **noun** *a stake in the ground* POST, pole, stick, spike, upright, support, prop, strut, pale, paling, picket, pile, piling, cane.
▶ **verb** ❶ *the plants have to be staked* PROP UP, tie up, tether, support, hold up, brace, truss. ❷ *he staked his claim* ASSERT, declare, proclaim, state, make, lay, put in.
■ **stake something out** ❶ *builders staked out the plot* MARK OFF/OUT, demarcate, measure out, delimit, fence off, section off, close off, shut off, cordon off. ❷ (*informal*) *the police staked out his flat* OBSERVE, watch, keep an eye on, keep under observation, keep watch on, monitor, keep under surveillance, surveil; *informal* keep tabs on, keep a tab on, case.

stake[2] ▶ **noun** ❶ *playing dice for high stakes* BET, wager, ante. ❷ *they are racing for record stakes* PRIZE MONEY, purse, pot, winnings. ❸ *low down in the popularity stakes* COMPETITION, contest, battle, challenge, rivalry, race, running, struggle, scramble. ❹ *a 40% stake in the business* SHARE, interest, ownership, involvement.
▶ **verb** *he staked all his week's pay* BET, wager, lay, put on, gamble, chance, venture, risk, hazard.

stale ▶ **adjective** ❶ *stale food* OLD, past its best, past its sell-by date; off, dry, hard, musty, rancid. ❷ *stale air* STUFFY, close, musty, fusty, stagnant, frowzy; *Brit.* frowsty, fuggy. ❸ *stale beer* FLAT, turned, spoiled, off, insipid, tasteless. ❹ *stale jokes* HACKNEYED, tired, worn out, overworked, threadbare, warmed-up, banal, trite, clichéd, platitudinous, unoriginal, unimaginative, uninspired, flat; out of date, outdated, outmoded, passé, archaic, obsolete; *N. Amer.* warmed-over; *informal* old hat, corny, out of the ark, played out.
– OPPOSITES fresh, original.

stalemate ▶ **noun** DEADLOCK, impasse, standoff; draw, tie, dead heat.

stalk[1] ▶ **noun** *the stalk of a plant* STEM, shoot, trunk, stock, cane, bine, bent, haulm, straw, reed.
– RELATED TERMS cauline.

stalk[2] ▶ **verb** ❶ *a stoat was stalking a rabbit* CREEP UP ON, trail, follow, shadow, track down, go after, be after, course, hunt; *informal* tail. ❷ *she stalked out* STRUT, stride, march, flounce, storm, stomp, sweep.

stall ▶ **noun** ❶ *a market stall* STAND, table, counter, booth, kiosk. ❷ *stalls for larger animals* PEN, coop, sty, corral, enclosure, compartment. ❸ (*Brit.*) *theatre stalls N. Amer.* orchestra, parterre.
▶ **verb** ❶ *the Government has stalled the project* OBSTRUCT, impede, interfere with, hinder, hamper, block, interrupt, hold up, hold back, thwart, baulk, sabotage, delay, stonewall, check, stop, halt, derail, put a brake on; *informal* stymie; *N. Amer. informal* bork. ❷ *quit stalling* USE DELAYING TACTICS, play for time, temporize, gain time, procrastinate, hedge, beat about the bush, drag one's feet, delay, filibuster, stonewall. ❸ *stall him for a bit* DELAY, divert, distract; HOLD OFF, stave off, fend off, keep off, ward off, keep at bay.

stalwart ▶ **adjective** STAUNCH, loyal, faithful, committed, devoted, dedicated, dependable, reliable, steady, constant, trusty, hard-working, steadfast, redoubtable, unwavering.
– OPPOSITES disloyal, unfaithful, unreliable.

stamina ▶ **noun** ENDURANCE, staying power, tirelessness, fortitude, strength, energy, toughness, determination, tenacity, perseverance, grit.

stammer ▶ **verb** *he began to stammer* STUTTER, stumble over one's words, hesitate, falter, pause, halt, splutter.
▶ **noun** *he had a stammer* STUTTER, speech impediment, speech defect.

stamp ▶ **verb** ❶ *he stamped on my toe* TRAMPLE, step, tread, tramp; CRUSH, squash, flatten. ❷ *John stamped off, muttering* STOMP, stump, clomp, clump. ❸ *the name is stamped on the cover* IMPRINT, print, impress, punch, inscribe, emboss, brand, frank. ❹ *his face was stamped on Martha's memory* FIX, inscribe, etch, carve, imprint, impress. ❺ *his style stamps him as a player to watch* IDENTIFY, characterize, brand, distinguish, classify, mark out, set apart, single out.

▶ **noun** ❶ *the stamp of authority* MARK, hallmark, indication, sign, seal, sure sign, telltale sign, quality, smack, smell, savour, air. ❷ *he was of a very different stamp* TYPE, kind, sort, variety, class, category, classification, style, description, condition, calibre, status, quality, nature, ilk, kidney, cast, grain, mould; *N. Amer.* stripe.

■ **stamp something out** PUT AN END/STOP TO, end, stop, crush, put down, crack down on, curb, nip in the bud, scotch, squash, quash, quell, subdue, suppress, extinguish, stifle, abolish, get rid of, eliminate, eradicate, beat, overcome, defeat, destroy, wipe out; *informal* put the kibosh on.

stamp collecting ▶ **noun** PHILATELY.

stampede ▶ **noun** *the noise caused a stampede* CHARGE, panic, rush, flight, rout.

▶ **verb** *the sheep stampeded* BOLT, charge, flee, take flight; race, rush, career, sweep, run.

stance ▶ **noun** ❶ *a natural golfer's stance* POSTURE, body position, pose, attitude. ❷ *a liberal stance* ATTITUDE, stand, point of view, viewpoint, opinion, way of thinking, outlook, standpoint, position, angle, perspective, approach, line, policy.

stand ▶ **verb** ❶ *Lionel stood in the doorway* BE ON ONE'S FEET, be upright, be erect, be vertical. ❷ *the men stood up* RISE, get/rise to one's feet, get up, straighten up, pick oneself up, find one's feet, be upstanding; *formal* arise. ❸ *today a house stands on the site* BE, be situated, be located, be positioned, be sited, have been built. ❹ *he stood the book on the shelf* PUT, set, set up, erect, up-end, place, position, locate, prop, lean, stick, install, arrange; *informal* park. ❺ *my decision stands* REMAIN IN FORCE, remain valid/effective/operative, remain in operation, hold, hold good, apply, be the case, exist; *formal* obtain. ❻ *his heart could not stand the strain* WITHSTAND, endure, bear, put up with, take, cope with, handle, sustain, resist, stand up to. ❼ (*informal*) *I won't stand cheek* ENDURE, tolerate, bear, put up with, take, abide, support, countenance; *Scottish* thole; *informal* swallow, stomach; *Brit. informal* stick, wear; *formal* brook.

– OPPOSITES sit, lie, sit down, lie down.

▶ **noun** ❶ *the party's stand on immigration* ATTITUDE, stance, point of view, viewpoint, opinion, way of thinking, outlook, standpoint, position, approach, thinking, policy, line. ❷ *a stand against tyranny* OPPOSITION, resistance, objection, hostility, animosity. ❸ *a large mirror on a stand* BASE, support, mounting, platform, rest, plinth, bottom; tripod, rack, trivet. ❹ *a beer stand* STALL, counter, booth, kiosk, tent. ❺ *a taxi stand* RANK, station, park, bay. ❻ *the train drew to a stand* STOP, halt, standstill, dead stop. ❼ *a stand of trees* COPSE, spinney, thicket, grove.

■ **stand by** WAIT, be prepared, be in (a state of) readiness, be ready for action, be on full alert, wait in the wings.

■ **stand by someone/something** ❶ *she stood by her husband* REMAIN/BE LOYAL TO, stick with/by, remain/be true to, stand up for, support, back up, defend, stick up for. ❷ *the government must stand by its pledges* ABIDE BY, keep (to), adhere to, hold to, stick to, observe, comply with.

■ **stand down** RELAX, stand easy, come off full alert.

■ **stand for** ❶ *V stands for volts* MEAN, be an abbreviation of, represent, signify, denote, indicate, symbolize. ❷ (*informal*) *I won't stand for any nonsense* PUT UP WITH, endure, tolerate, accept, take, abide, stand, support, countenance; *informal* swallow, stomach; *Brit. informal* stick, wear; *formal* brook. ❸ *we stand for animal welfare* ADVOCATE, champion, uphold, defend, stand up for, support, back, endorse, be in favour of, promote, recommend, urge.

■ **stand in** DEPUTIZE, act, act as deputy, substitute, fill in, sit in, do duty, take over, act as locum, be a proxy, cover, hold the fort, step into the breach; replace, relieve, take over from; *informal* sub, fill someone's shoes, step into someone's shoes; *N. Amer.* pinch-hit.

■ **stand out** ❶ *his veins stood out* PROJECT, stick out, bulge (out), be proud, jut (out). ❷ *she stood out in the crowd* BE NOTICEABLE, be visible, be obvious, be conspicuous, stick out, be striking, be distinctive, be prominent, attract attention, catch the eye, leap out, show up; *informal* stick/stand out a mile, stick/stand out like a sore thumb.

■ **stand up** REMAIN/BE VALID, be sound, be plausible, hold water, hold up, stand questioning, survive investigation, bear examination, be verifiable.

■ **stand someone up** FAIL TO KEEP A DATE WITH, fail to meet, fail to keep an appointment with, jilt.

■ **stand up for someone/something** SUPPORT, defend, back, back up, stick up for, champion, promote, uphold, take someone's part, take the side of, side with.

■ **stand up to someone/something** ❶ *she stood up to her parents* DEFY, confront, challenge, resist, take on, put up a fight against, argue with, take a stand against. ❷ *the old house has stood up to the war* WITHSTAND, survive, come through (unscathed), outlast, outlive, weather, ride out, ward off.

standard ▶ **noun** ❶ *the standard of her work* QUALITY, level, grade, calibre, merit, excellence. ❷ *a safety standard* GUIDELINE, norm, yardstick, benchmark, measure, criterion, guide, touchstone, model, pattern, example, exemplar. ❸ *a standard to live by* PRINCIPLE, ideal; (**standards**) code of behaviour, code of honour, morals, scruples, ethics. ❹ *the regiment's stand-*

ard FLAG, banner, pennant, ensign, colour(s), banderole, guidon; *Brit.* pendant; *Nautical* burgee.

▶ **adjective** ❶ *the standard way of doing it* NORMAL, usual, typical, stock, common, ordinary, customary, conventional, wonted, established, settled, set, fixed, traditional, prevailing. ❷ *the standard work on the subject* DEFINITIVE, established, classic, recognized, accepted, authoritative, most reliable, exhaustive.
– OPPOSITES unusual, special.

standardize ▶ **verb** SYSTEMATIZE, make consistent, make uniform, make comparable, regulate, normalize, bring into line, equalize, homogenize, regiment.

stand-in ▶ **noun** *a stand-in for the minister* SUBSTITUTE, replacement, deputy, surrogate, proxy, understudy, locum, supply, fill-in, cover, relief, stopgap; *informal* temp; *N. Amer. informal* pinch-hitter.

▶ **adjective** *a stand-in goalkeeper* SUBSTITUTE, replacement, deputy, fill-in, stopgap, supply, surrogate, relief, acting, temporary, provisional, caretaker; *N. Amer. informal* pinch-hitting.

standing ▶ **noun** ❶ *his standing in the community* STATUS, rank, ranking, position; reputation, estimation, stature; *dated* station. ❷ *a person of some standing* SENIORITY, rank, eminence, prominence, prestige, repute, stature, esteem, importance, account, consequence, influence, distinction; *informal* clout; *dated* mark. ❸ *a squabble of long standing* DURATION, existence, continuance, endurance, life.

▶ **adjective** ❶ *standing stones* UPRIGHT, erect, vertical, plumb, upended, on end, perpendicular; on one's feet; not yet reaped; *Heraldry* rampant. ❷ *standing water* STAGNANT, still, motionless, static, stationary, dead, slack. ❸ *a standing invitation* PERMANENT, perpetual, everlasting, continuing, abiding, indefinite, open-ended; regular, repeated.
– OPPOSITES flat, lying down, seated, flowing, temporary, occasional.

stand-off ▶ **noun** DEADLOCK, stalemate, impasse; draw, tie, dead heat; suspension of hostilities, lull.

stand-offish ▶ **adjective** (*informal*) ALOOF, distant, remote, detached, withdrawn, reserved, uncommunicative, unforthcoming, unapproachable, unresponsive, unfriendly, unsociable, introspective, introverted.
– OPPOSITES friendly, approachable, sociable.

standpoint ▶ **noun** POINT OF VIEW, viewpoint, vantage point, attitude, stance, view, opinion, position, way of thinking, outlook, perspective.

standstill ▶ **noun** HALT, stop, dead stop, stand.

staple ▶ **adjective** MAIN, principal, chief, major, primary, leading, foremost, first, most important, predominant, dominant, (most) prominent, basic, standard, prime, premier; *informal* number-one.

star ▶ **noun** ❶ *the sky was full of stars* CELESTIAL BODY, heavenly body, sun; asteroid, planet. ❷ *the stars of the film* PRINCIPAL, leading lady/man, lead, female/male lead, hero, heroine. ❸ *a star of the world of chess* CELEBRITY, superstar, big name, famous name, household name, someone, somebody, lion, leading light, VIP, personality, personage, luminary; *informal* celeb, big shot, big noise, megastar.
– RELATED TERMS astral, astro-, sidereal, sidero-, stellar.
– OPPOSITES nobody.

▶ **adjective** ❶ *a star pupil* BRILLIANT, talented, gifted, able, exceptional, outstanding, bright, clever, masterly, consummate, precocious, prodigious. ❷ *the star attraction* TOP, leading, best, greatest, foremost, major, pre-eminent, champion.
– OPPOSITES poor, minor.

starchy ▶ **adjective** (*informal*). *See* STAID.

stare ▶ **verb** GAZE, gape, goggle, glare, ogle, peer; *informal* gawk, rubberneck; *Brit. informal* gawp.

stark ▶ **adjective** ❶ *a stark silhouette* SHARP, sharply defined, well focused, crisp, distinct, obvious, evident, clear, clear-cut, graphic, striking. ❷ *a stark landscape* DESOLATE, bare, barren, arid, vacant, empty, forsaken, godforsaken, bleak, sombre, depressing, cheerless, joyless; *poetic/literary* drear. ❸ *a stark room* AUSTERE, severe, bleak, plain, simple, bare, unadorned, unembellished, undecorated. ❹ *stark terror* SHEER, utter, complete, absolute, total, pure, downright, out-and-out, outright; rank, thorough, consummate, unqualified, unmitigated, unalloyed. ❺ *the stark facts* BLUNT, bald, bare, simple, basic, plain, unvarnished, harsh, grim.
– OPPOSITES fuzzy, indistinct, pleasant, ornate, disguised.

▶ **adverb** *stark naked* COMPLETELY, totally, utterly, absolutely, downright, dead, entirely, wholly, fully, quite, altogether, thoroughly, truly.

start ▶ **verb** ❶ *the meeting starts at 7.45* BEGIN, commence, get under way, go ahead, get going; *informal* kick off. ❷ *this was how her illness had started* COME INTO BEING, begin, commence, be born, come into existence, appear, arrive, come forth, emerge, erupt, burst out, arise, originate, develop. ❸ *she started her own charity* ESTABLISH, set up, found, create, bring into being, institute, initiate, inaugurate, introduce, open, launch, float, kick-start, get something off the ground, pioneer, organize, mastermind; *informal* kick something off. ❹ *we had better start on the work* MAKE A START, begin, commence, take the first step, make the first move, get going, go ahead, set things moving, start/get/set the ball rolling, buckle to/down, turn to; *informal* get moving, get cracking, get

stuck in, get down to it, get to it, get down to business, get one's finger out, get the show on the road, take the plunge, kick off, get off one's backside, fire away; *Brit. informal* get weaving. ❺ *he started across the field* SET OFF, set out, start out, set forth, begin one's journey, get on the road, depart, leave, get under way, make a start, sally forth, embark, sail; *informal* hit the road. ❻ *you can start the machine* ACTIVATE, set in motion, switch on, start up, turn on, fire up; energize, actuate, set off, start off, set something going/moving. ❼ *the machine started* BEGIN WORKING, start up, get going, spring into life. ❽ *'Oh my!' she said, starting* FLINCH, jerk, jump, twitch, recoil, shy, shrink, blench, wince.
– OPPOSITES finish, stop, clear up, wind up, hang about, give up, arrive, stay, close down.
▶ **noun** ❶ *the start of the event* BEGINNING, commencement, inception. ❷ *the start of her illness* ONSET, commencement, emergence, (first) appearance, arrival, eruption, dawn, birth. ❸ *a quarter of an hour's start* LEAD, head start, advantage. ❹ *a start in life* ADVANTAGEOUS BEGINNING, flying start, helping hand, lift, assistance, support, encouragement, boost, kick-start; *informal* break, leg up. ❺ *she awoke with a start* JERK, twitch, flinch, wince, spasm, convulsion, jump.
– OPPOSITES end, finish, handicap.

startle ▶ **verb** SURPRISE, frighten, scare, alarm, give someone a shock/fright/jolt, make someone jump; PERTURB, unsettle, agitate, disturb, disconcert, disquiet; *informal* give someone a turn, make someone jump out of their skin.
– OPPOSITES put at ease.

startling ▶ **adjective** SURPRISING, astonishing, amazing, unexpected, unforeseen, staggering, shocking, stunning; extraordinary, remarkable, dramatic; disturbing, unsettling, perturbing, disconcerting, disquieting; frightening, alarming, scary.
– OPPOSITES predictable, ordinary.

starvation ▶ **noun** EXTREME HUNGER, lack of food, famine, undernourishment, malnourishment, fasting; deprivation of food; death from lack of food.

starving ▶ **adjective** DYING OF HUNGER, deprived of food, undernourished, malnourished, starved, half-starved; very hungry, ravenous, famished, empty, hollow; fasting.
– OPPOSITES full.

stash (*informal*) ▶ **verb** *he stashed his things away* STORE, stow, pack, load, cache, hide, conceal, secrete; hoard, save, stockpile; *informal* salt away, squirrel away.
▶ **noun** *a stash of money* CACHE, hoard, stock, stockpile, store, supply, accumulation, collection, reserve.

state[1] ▶ **noun** ❶ *the state of the economy* CONDITION, shape, situation, circumstances, position; predicament, plight. ❷ (*informal*) *don't get into a state* FLUSTER, frenzy, fever, fret, panic, state of agitation/anxiety; *informal* flap, tizzy, tiz-woz, dither, stew, sweat; *N. Amer. informal* twit. ❸ (*informal*) *your room is in a state* MESS, chaos, disorder, disarray, confusion, muddle, heap, shambles; clutter, untidiness, disorganization. ❹ *an autonomous state* COUNTRY, nation, land, sovereign state, nation state, kingdom, realm, power, republic, confederation, federation. ❺ *the country is divided into thirty-two states* PROVINCE, federal state, region, territory, canton, department, county, district; *Brit.* shire. ❻ *the power of the state* GOVERNMENT, parliament, administration, regime, authorities.
▶ **adjective** *a state visit to China* CEREMONIAL, official, formal, governmental, national, public.
– OPPOSITES unofficial, private, informal.

state[2] ▶ **verb** *I stated my views* EXPRESS, voice, utter, put into words, declare, affirm, assert, announce, make known, put across/over, communicate, air, reveal, disclose, divulge, proclaim, present, expound; set out, set down; *informal* come out with.

stated ▶ **adjective** SPECIFIED, fixed, settled, set, agreed, declared, designated, laid down.
– OPPOSITES undefined, irregular, tacit.

stately ▶ **adjective** DIGNIFIED, majestic, ceremonious, courtly, imposing, impressive, solemn, awe-inspiring, regal, elegant, grand, glorious, splendid, magnificent, resplendent; slow-moving, measured, deliberate.

statement ▶ **noun** DECLARATION, expression of views/facts, affirmation, assertion, announcement, utterance, communication, proclamation, presentation, expounding; account, testimony, evidence, report, bulletin, communiqué.

state-of-the-art ▶ **adjective** MODERN, ultra-modern, the latest, new, the newest, up to the minute; advanced, highly developed, innovatory, trailblazing, revolutionary; sophisticated.

statesman, stateswoman ▶ **noun** SENIOR POLITICIAN, respected political figure, elder statesman, political leader, national leader.

static ▶ **adjective** ❶ *static prices* UNCHANGED, fixed, stable, steady, unchanging, changeless, unvarying, invariable, constant, consistent. ❷ *a static display* STATIONARY, motionless, immobile, unmoving, still, stock-still, at a standstill, at rest, not moving a muscle, like a statue, rooted to the spot, frozen, inactive, inert, lifeless, inanimate.
– OPPOSITES variable, mobile, active, dynamic.

station ▶ **noun** ❶ *a railway station* STOPPING PLACE, stop, halt, stage; terminus, terminal, depot. ❷ *a research station* ESTABLISHMENT, base, camp; post, depot; mission; site, facility, installation, yard. ❸ *a police station* OFFICE, depot, base, headquarters; *N. Amer.* precinct, station house; *informal* cop shop; *Brit. informal* nick. ❹ *a radio station* CHANNEL, broadcasting organization; wavelength. ❺ (*Austral./NZ*) *a sheep station* RANCH, range; farm. ❻ *the lookout resumed his station* POST, position, place. ❼ (*dated*) *Karen was getting ideas above her station* RANK, place, status, position in society, social class, stratum, level, grade; caste; *archaic* condition, degree.

▶ **verb** *the regiment was stationed at Woolwich* PUT ON DUTY, post, position, place; establish, install; deploy, base, garrison.

stationary ▶ **adjective** ❶ *a stationary car* STATIC, parked, stopped, motionless, immobile, unmoving, still, stock-still, at a standstill, at rest; not moving a muscle, like a statue, rooted to the spot, frozen, inactive, inert, lifeless, inanimate. ❷ *a stationary population* UNCHANGING, unvarying, invariable, constant, consistent, unchanged, changeless, fixed, stable, steady.
– OPPOSITES moving, shifting.

statue ▶ **noun** SCULPTURE, figure, effigy, statuette, figurine, idol; carving, bronze, graven image, model; bust, head.

statuesque ▶ **adjective** TALL AND DIGNIFIED, imposing, striking, stately, majestic, noble, magnificent, splendid, impressive, regal.

stature ▶ **noun** ❶ *she was small in stature* HEIGHT, tallness; size, build. ❷ *an architect of international stature* REPUTATION, repute, standing, status, position, prestige, distinction, eminence, pre-eminence, prominence, importance, influence, note, fame, celebrity, renown, acclaim.

status ▶ **noun** ❶ *the status of women* STANDING, rank, ranking, position, social position, level, place, estimation; *dated* station. ❷ *wealth and status* PRESTIGE, kudos, cachet, standing, stature, regard, fame, note, renown, honour, esteem, image, importance, prominence, consequence, distinction, influence, authority, eminence.

statute ▶ **noun** LAW, regulation, enactment, act, bill, decree, edict, rule, ruling, resolution, dictum, command, order, directive, pronouncement, proclamation, dictate, diktat, fiat, by-law; *N. Amer. formal* ordinance.

staunch[1] ▶ **adjective** *a staunch supporter* STALWART, loyal, faithful, committed, devoted, dedicated, dependable, reliable, steady, constant, trusty, hard-working, steadfast, redoubtable, unwavering.
– OPPOSITES disloyal, unfaithful, unreliable.

staunch[2] ▶ **verb** *she tried to staunch the flow of blood* STEM, stop, halt, check, hold back, restrain, restrict, control, contain, curb; block, dam; slow, lessen, reduce, diminish, retard; *N. Amer.* stanch; *archaic* stay.

stave

■ **stave something in** BREAK IN, smash in, put a hole in, push in, kick in, cave in.

■ **stave something off** AVERT, prevent, avoid, counter, preclude, forestall, nip in the bud; ward off, fend off, head off, keep off, keep at bay.

stay[1] ▶ **verb** ❶ *he stayed where he was* REMAIN (BEHIND), stay behind, stay put; wait, linger, stick, be left, hold on, hang on, lodge; *informal* hang around/round; *Brit. informal* hang about; *archaic* bide, tarry. ❷ *they won't stay hidden* CONTINUE (TO BE), remain, keep, persist in being, carry on being, go on being. ❸ *our aunt is staying with us* VISIT, spend time, put up, stop (off/over); holiday; lodge, room, board, have rooms, be housed, be accommodated, be quartered, be billeted; *N. Amer.* vacation; *formal* sojourn; *archaic* bide. ❹ *legal proceedings were stayed* POSTPONE, put off, delay, defer, put back, hold over/off; adjourn, suspend, prorogue; *N. Amer.* put over, table, lay on the table, take a rain check on; *US Law* continue; *informal* put on ice, put on the back burner. ❺ (*poetic/literary*) *we must stay the enemy's advance* DELAY, slow down/up, hold back/up, set back, keep back, put back, put a brake on, retard; hinder, hamper, obstruct, inhibit, impede, curb, check, restrain, restrict, arrest; *Brit. informal* throw a spanner in the works of; *N. Amer. informal* throw a monkey wrench in the works of.
– OPPOSITES leave, advance, promote.

▶ **noun** ❶ *a stay at a hotel* VISIT, stop, stop-off, stopover, break, holiday; *N. Amer.* vacation; *formal* sojourn. ❷ *a stay of judgement* POSTPONEMENT, putting off, delay, deferment, deferral, putting back; adjournment, suspension, prorogation; *N. Amer.* tabling; *US Law* continuance.

stay[2] ▶ **noun** *the stays holding up the mast* STRUT, WIRE, brace, tether, guy, prop, rod, support, truss; *Nautical* shroud.

▶ **verb** *her masts were well stayed* BRACE, tether, strut, wire, guy, prop, support, truss.

steadfast ▶ **adjective** ❶ *a steadfast friend* LOYAL, faithful, committed, devoted, dedicated, dependable, reliable, steady, true, constant, staunch, trusty. ❷ *a steadfast policy* FIRM, determined, resolute, relentless, implacable, single-minded; unchanging, unwavering, unhesitating, unfaltering, unswerving, unyielding, unflinching, uncompromising.
– OPPOSITES disloyal, irresolute.

steady ▶ **adjective** ❶ *the ladder must be steady* STABLE, firm, fixed, secure, fast, safe, immovable, unshakeable, dependable; anchored, moored, jammed, rooted, braced. ❷ *keep the camera steady* MOTIONLESS, still, unshaking, static, stationary, unmoving. ❸ *a steady gaze* FIXED, intent, unwavering, unfaltering. ❹ *a steady young man* SENSIBLE, level-headed, rational, settled, mature, down-to-earth, full of common sense, reliable, dependable, sound, sober, serious-minded, responsible, serious. ❺ *a steady income* CONSTANT, unchanging, regu-

lar, consistent, invariable; continuous, continual, unceasing, ceaseless, perpetual, unremitting, unwavering, unfaltering, unending, endless, round-the-clock, all-year-round. ❻ *a steady boyfriend* REGULAR, usual, established, settled, firm, devoted, faithful.
– OPPOSITES unstable, loose, shaky, darting, flighty, immature, fluctuating, sporadic, occasional.
▶ **verb** ❶ *he steadied the rifle* STABILIZE, hold steady; brace, support; balance, poise; secure, fix, make fast. ❷ *she needed to steady her nerves* CALM, soothe, quieten, compose, settle; subdue, quell, control, get a grip on.

steal ▶ **verb** ❶ *the raiders stole a fax machine* PURLOIN, thieve, take, take for oneself, help oneself to, loot, pilfer, run off with, carry off, shoplift; embezzle, misappropriate; have one's fingers/hand in the till; *informal* walk off with, rob, swipe, nab, rip off, lift, 'liberate', 'borrow', filch, snaffle, snitch; *Brit. informal* nick, pinch, half-inch, whip, knock off, nobble; *N. Amer. informal* heist; *formal* peculate. ❷ *his work was stolen by his tutor* PLAGIARIZE, copy, pass off as one's own, pirate, poach, borrow; *informal* rip off, lift, pinch, nick, crib. ❸ *he stole a kiss* SNATCH, sneak, get stealthily/surreptitiously. ❹ *he stole out of the room* CREEP, sneak, slink, slip, slide, glide, tiptoe, sidle, slope, edge.
▶ **noun** (*informal*) *at £30 it's a steal. See* BARGAIN noun sense 2.

stealing ▶ **noun** THEFT, thieving, thievery, robbery, larceny, burglary, shoplifting, pilfering, pilferage, looting, misappropriation; embezzlement; *formal* peculation.

stealth ▶ **noun** FURTIVENESS, secretiveness, secrecy, surreptitiousness, sneakiness, slyness.
– OPPOSITES openness.

stealthy ▶ **adjective** FURTIVE, secretive, secret, surreptitious, sneaking, sly, clandestine, covert, conspiratorial.
– OPPOSITES open.

steam ▶ **noun** ❶ *steam from the kettle* WATER VAPOUR, condensation, mist, haze, fog, moisture. ❷ *he ran out of steam* ENERGY, vigour, vitality, stamina, enthusiasm; MOMENTUM, impetus, force, strength, thrust, impulse, push, drive; speed, pace.
▶ **verb** (*informal*) *he steamed into the shop. See* RUN verb sense 1.
■ **steamed up** (*informal*) ❶ *he got steamed up about forgetting his papers. See* AGITATED. ❷ *they get steamed up about the media. See* ANGRY sense 1.
■ **let off steam** (*informal*) GIVE VENT TO ONE'S FEELINGS, speak one's mind, speak out, sound off, lose one's inhibitions, let oneself go; use up surplus energy.
■ **steam up** MIST (UP/OVER), fog (up), become misty/misted.

steamy ▶ **adjective** ❶ *the steamy jungle* HUMID, muggy, sticky, dripping, moist, damp, clammy, sultry, sweaty, steaming. ❷ (*informal*) *a steamy love scene. See* EROTIC. ❸ (*informal*) *they had a steamy affair* PASSIONATE, torrid, amorous, ardent, lustful; *informal* sizzling, hot, red-hot.

steel
■ **steel oneself** BRACE ONESELF, nerve oneself, summon (up) one's courage, screw up one's courage, gear oneself up, prepare oneself, get in the right frame of mind; fortify oneself, harden oneself; *informal* psych oneself up; *poetic/literary* gird (up) one's loins.

steely ▶ **adjective** ❶ *steely light* BLUE-GREY, grey, steel-coloured, steel-grey, iron-grey. ❷ *steely muscles* HARD, firm, toned, rigid, stiff, tense, tensed, taut. ❸ *steely eyes* CRUEL, unfeeling, merciless, ruthless, pitiless, heartless, hard-hearted, hard, stony, cold-blooded, cold-hearted, harsh, callous, severe, unrelenting, unpitying, unforgiving, uncaring, unsympathetic; *poetic/literary* adamantine. ❹ *steely determination* RESOLUTE, firm, steadfast, dogged, single-minded; bitter, burning, ferocious, fanatical; ruthless, iron, grim, gritty; unquenchable, unflinching, unswerving, unfaltering, untiring, unwavering.
– OPPOSITES flabby, kind, half-hearted.

steep[1] ▶ **adjective** ❶ *steep cliffs* PRECIPITOUS, sheer, abrupt, sharp, perpendicular, vertical, bluff, vertiginous. ❷ *a steep increase* SHARP, sudden, precipitate, precipitous, rapid. ❸ (*informal*) *steep prices* EXPENSIVE, dear, costly, high, stiff; unreasonable, excessive, exorbitant, extortionate, outrageous, prohibitive; *Brit.* over the odds.
– OPPOSITES gentle, gradual, reasonable.

steep[2] ▶ **verb** ❶ *the ham is then steeped in brine* MARINADE, marinate, soak, souse, macerate; pickle. ❷ *winding sheets were steeped in mercury sulphate* SOAK, saturate, immerse, wet through, drench; *technical* ret. ❸ *a city steeped in history* IMBUE WITH, fill with, permeate with, pervade with, suffuse with, infuse with, soak in.

steeple ▶ **noun** SPIRE, tower; bell tower, belfry, campanile; minaret.

steer ▶ **verb** ❶ *he steered the boat* GUIDE, direct, manoeuvre, drive, pilot, navigate; *Nautical* con, helm. ❷ *Luke steered her down the path* GUIDE, conduct, direct, lead, take, usher, shepherd, marshal, herd.
■ **steer clear of** KEEP AWAY FROM, keep one's distance from, keep at arm's length, give a wide berth to, avoid, avoid dealing with, have nothing to do with, shun, eschew.

stem[1] ▶ **noun** *a plant stem* STALK, shoot, trunk, stock, cane, bine.
– RELATED TERMS cauline.
■ **stem from** HAVE ITS ORIGINS IN, arise from, originate from, spring from, derive from, come from, emanate from, flow from, proceed from; BE CAUSED BY, be brought on/about by, be produced by.

stem[2] ▶ **verb** *he stemmed the flow of blood*

STAUNCH, stop, halt, check, hold back, restrict, control, contain, curb; block, dam; slow, lessen, reduce, diminish; *N. Amer.* stanch; *archaic* stay.

stench ▶**noun** STINK, reek; *Brit. informal* niff, pong, whiff, hum; *Scottish informal* guff; *N. Amer. informal* funk; *poetic/literary* miasma.

stentorian ▶**adjective** LOUD, thundering, thunderous, ear-splitting, deafening; powerful, strong, carrying; booming, resonant; strident.
– OPPOSITES quiet, soft.

step ▶**noun** ❶ *Frank took a step forward* PACE, stride. ❷ *she heard a step on the stairs* FOOTSTEP, footfall, tread. ❸ *she left the room with a springy step* GAIT, walk, tread. ❹ *it is only a step to the river* SHORT DISTANCE, stone's throw, spitting distance; *informal* {a hop, skip, and jump}. ❺ *the top step* STAIR, tread; (**steps**) STAIRS, staircase, stairway. ❻ *each step of the ladder* RUNG, tread. ❼ *resigning is a very serious step* COURSE OF ACTION, measure, move, act, action, initiative, manoeuvre, operation. ❽ *a significant step towards a ceasefire* ADVANCE, development, move, movement; breakthrough. ❾ *the first step on the managerial ladder* STAGE, level, grade, rank, degree; notch.
▶**verb** ❶ *she stepped forward* WALK, move, tread, pace, stride. ❷ *the bull had stepped on his hat* TREAD, stamp, trample; squash, crush, flatten.
■ **in step** *he is in step with mainstream thinking* IN ACCORD, in harmony, in agreement, in tune, in line, in keeping, in conformity.
■ **mind/watch one's step** BE CAREFUL, take care, step/tread carefully, exercise care/caution, mind how one goes, look out, watch out, be wary, be on one's guard, be on the qui vive.
■ **out of step** *the paper was often out of step with public opinion* AT ODDS, at variance, in disagreement, out of tune, out of line, not in keeping, out of harmony.
■ **step by step** ONE STEP AT A TIME, bit by bit, gradually, in stages, by degrees, slowly, steadily.
■ **step down** RESIGN, stand down, give up one's post/job, bow out, abdicate; *informal* quit.
■ **step in** ❶ *nobody stepped in to save the bank* INTERVENE, intercede, involve oneself, become/get involved, take a hand. ❷ *I stepped in for a sick colleague* STAND IN, sit in, fill in, cover, substitute, take over; replace, take someone's place; *informal* sub.
■ **step on it** (*informal*) HURRY UP, get a move on, speed up, go faster, be quick; *informal* get cracking, get moving, step on the gas; *Brit. informal* get one's skates on; *N. Amer. informal* get a wiggle on; *dated* make haste.
■ **step something up** ❶ *the army stepped up its offensive* INCREASE, intensify, strengthen, augment, escalate; *informal* up, crank up. ❷ *I stepped up my pace* SPEED UP, increase, accelerate, quicken, hasten.

stereotype ▶**noun** *the stereotype of the rancher* STANDARD/CONVENTIONAL IMAGE, received idea, cliché, hackneyed idea, formula.
▶**verb** *women are often stereotyped as scheming* TYPECAST, pigeonhole, conventionalize, categorize, label, tag.

stereotyped ▶**adjective** STOCK, conventional, stereotypical, standard, formulaic, predictable; hackneyed, clichéd, cliché-ridden, banal, trite, unoriginal; typecast; *informal* corny, old hat.
– OPPOSITES unconventional, original.

sterile ▶**adjective** ❶ *mules are sterile* INFERTILE, unable to reproduce/conceive, unable to have children/young; *technical* infecund; *archaic* barren. ❷ *sterile desert* UNPRODUCTIVE, infertile, unfruitful, uncultivatable, barren. ❸ *a sterile debate* POINTLESS, unproductive, unfruitful, unrewarding, useless, unprofitable, profitless, futile, vain, idle; *archaic* bootless. ❹ *sterile academicism* UNIMAGINATIVE, uninspired, uninspiring, unoriginal, stale, lifeless, musty. ❺ *sterile conditions* ASEPTIC, sterilized, germ-free, antiseptic, disinfected; uncontaminated, unpolluted, pure, clean; sanitary, hygienic.
– OPPOSITES fertile, productive, creative, original, septic.

sterilize ▶**verb** ❶ *the scalpel was first sterilized* DISINFECT, fumigate, decontaminate, sanitize; pasteurize; clean, cleanse, purify; *technical* autoclave. ❷ *over 6.5 million people were sterilized* MAKE UNABLE TO HAVE CHILDREN, make infertile, hysterectomize, vasectomize. ❸ *stray pets are usually sterilized* NEUTER, castrate, spay, geld, cut, fix, desex; *N. Amer. & Austral.* alter; *Brit. informal* doctor.
– OPPOSITES contaminate.

sterling ▶**adjective** (*Brit.*) EXCELLENT, first-rate, first-class, exceptional, outstanding, splendid, superlative, praiseworthy, laudable, commendable, admirable, valuable, worthy, deserving.
– OPPOSITES poor, unexceptional.

stern[1] ▶**adjective** ❶ *a stern expression* SERIOUS, unsmiling, frowning, severe, forbidding, grim, unfriendly, austere, dour, stony, flinty, steely, unrelenting, unforgiving, unbending, unsympathetic, disapproving. ❷ *stern measures* STRICT, severe, stringent, harsh, drastic, hard, tough, extreme, rigid, ruthless, rigorous, exacting, demanding, uncompromising, unsparing, inflexible, authoritarian, draconian.
– OPPOSITES genial, friendly, lenient, lax.

stern[2] ▶**noun** *the stern of the ship* REAR (END), back, after end, poop, transom, tail.
– OPPOSITES bow.

stew ▶**noun** ❶ *a beef stew* CASSEROLE, hotpot, ragout, goulash, carbonnade, daube, grillade; *N. Amer.* burgoo. ❷ (*informal*) *she's in a right old stew* PANIC, fluster, fret, fuss, fever; *informal* flap, sweat, lather, tizzy, dither, twitter, state; *N.*

Amer. informal twit; *poetic/literary* pother.

▶ **verb** ❶ *stew the meat for an hour* BRAISE, casserole, simmer, boil; jug; *archaic* seethe. ❷ (*informal*) *there's no point stewing over it.* See WORRY verb sense 1. ❸ (*informal*) *the girls sat stewing in the heat* SWELTER, be very hot, perspire, sweat; *informal* roast, bake, be boiling.

steward ▶ **noun** ❶ *an air steward* FLIGHT ATTENDANT, cabin attendant; stewardess, air hostess; *N. Amer. informal* stew. ❷ *the race stewards* OFFICIAL, marshal, organizer. ❸ *the steward of the estate* (ESTATE) MANAGER, agent, overseer, custodian, caretaker; *Brit.* land agent, bailiff; *Scottish* factor; *historical* reeve.

stick[1] ▶ **noun** ❶ *a fire made of sticks* PIECE OF WOOD, twig, small branch. ❷ *he walks with a stick* WALKING STICK, cane, staff, alpenstock, crook, crutch; *trademark* Zimmer frame. ❸ *the plants need supporting on sticks* CANE, pole, post, stake, upright. ❹ *he beat me with a stick* CLUB, cudgel, bludgeon, shillelagh; truncheon, baton; cane, birch, switch, rod; *Brit. informal* cosh. ❺ (*Brit. informal*) *he'll get stick for this.* See CRITICISM sense 1.

– OPPOSITES praise, commendation.

■ **the sticks** (*informal*) THE COUNTRY, the countryside, rural areas, the provinces; the backwoods, the back of beyond, the wilds, the hinterland, a backwater; *N. Amer.* the backcountry, the backland; *Austral./NZ* the backblocks, the booay; *S. African* the backveld, the platteland; *informal* the middle of nowhere; *N. Amer. informal* the boondocks, the boonies; *Austral./NZ informal* Woop Woop, beyond the black stump.

stick[2] ▶ **verb** ❶ *he stuck his fork into the sausage* THRUST, push, insert, jab, poke, dig, plunge. ❷ *the bristles stuck into his skin* PIERCE, penetrate, puncture, prick, stab. ❸ *the cup stuck to its saucer* ADHERE, cling, be fixed, be glued. ❹ *stick the stamp there* AFFIX, attach, fasten, fix; paste, glue, gum, tape, sellotape, pin, tack. ❺ *the wheels stuck fast* BECOME TRAPPED, become jammed, jam, catch, become wedged, become lodged, become fixed, become embedded. ❻ *that sticks in his mind* REMAIN, stay, linger, dwell, persist, continue, last, endure. ❼ *the charges won't stick* BE UPHELD, hold, be believed; *informal* hold water. ❽ (*informal*) *just stick that sandwich on my desk* PUT (DOWN), place, set (down), lay (down), deposit, position; leave, stow; *informal* dump, bung, park, plonk, pop; *N. Amer. informal* plunk. ❾ (*Brit. informal*) *I can't stick it any longer* TOLERATE, put up with, take, stand, stomach, endure, bear; *Scottish* thole; *informal* abide.

■ **stick at** PERSEVERE WITH, persist with, keep at, work at, continue with, carry on with, not give up with, hammer away at, stay with; go the distance, stay the course; *informal* soldier on with, hang in there.

■ **stick by** BE LOYAL TO, be faithful to, be true to, stand by, keep faith with, keep one's promise to.

■ **stick it out** PUT UP WITH IT, grin and bear it, keep at it, keep going, stay with it, see it through; persevere, persist, carry on, struggle on; *informal* hang in there, soldier on, tough it out.

■ **stick out** ❶ *his front teeth stuck out* PROTRUDE, jut (out), project, stand out, extend, poke out; bulge, overhang. ❷ *they stuck out in their strange clothes* BE NOTICEABLE, be visible, be obvious, be conspicuous, stand out, be obtrusive, be prominent, attract attention, catch the eye, leap out, show up; *informal* stick/stand out a mile, stick/stand out like a sore thumb.

■ **stick to** *he stuck to his promise* ABIDE BY, keep, adhere to, hold to, comply with, fulfil, make good, stand by.

■ **stick up for** SUPPORT, take someone's side, side with, be on the side of, stand by, stand up for, take someone's part, defend, come to the defence of, champion, speak up for, fight for.

stick-in-the-mud ▶ **noun** (*informal*) (OLD) FOGEY, conservative, fossil, troglodyte; *Brit.* museum piece; *informal* fuddy-duddy, square, stuffed shirt.

sticky ▶ **adjective** ❶ *sticky tape* (SELF-)ADHESIVE, gummed; *technical* adherent. ❷ *sticky clay* GLUTINOUS, viscous, viscid, ropy; gluey, tacky, gummy, treacly, syrupy; mucilaginous; *Brit.* claggy; *informal* gooey, gloopy, icky; *Brit. informal* gungy; *N. Amer. informal* gloppy. ❸ *sticky weather* HUMID, muggy, close, sultry, steamy, sweaty. ❹ *a sticky situation* AWKWARD, difficult, tricky, ticklish, problematic, delicate, touch-and-go, embarrassing, sensitive, uncomfortable; *informal* hairy.

– OPPOSITES dry, fresh, cool, easy.

stiff ▶ **adjective** ❶ *stiff cardboard* RIGID, hard, firm, inelastic, inflexible. ❷ *a stiff paste* SEMI-SOLID, viscous, viscid, thick, stiffened, firm. ❸ *I'm stiff all over* ACHING, achy, painful; arthritic, rheumatic; *informal* creaky, rheumaticky, rusty. ❹ *a rather stiff manner* FORMAL, reserved, unfriendly, chilly, cold, frigid, icy, austere, wooden, forced, strained, stilted; *informal* starchy, uptight, stand-offish. ❺ *a stiff fine* HARSH, severe, heavy, crippling, punishing, stringent, drastic, draconian; *Brit.* swingeing. ❻ *stiff resistance* VIGOROUS, determined, full of determination, strong, spirited, resolute, tenacious, steely, four-square, unflagging, unyielding, dogged, stubborn, obdurate; *N. Amer.* rock-ribbed. ❼ *a stiff climb* DIFFICULT, hard, arduous, tough, strenuous, laborious, uphill, exacting, tiring, demanding, formidable, challenging, punishing, gruelling; *informal* killing, hellish; *Brit. informal* knackering. ❽ *a stiff breeze* STRONG, fresh, brisk. ❾ *a stiff drink* STRONG, potent, alcoholic.

– OPPOSITES flexible, plastic, limp, runny, supple, limber, relaxed, informal, lenient, mild, half-hearted, easy, gentle, weak.

stiffen ▶ **verb** ❶ *stir until the mixture stiffens* BE-

COME STIFF, thicken; set, become solid, solidify, harden, gel, congeal, coagulate, clot. ❷ *she stiffened her muscles | without exercise, joints will stiffen* MAKE/BECOME STIFF, tense (up), tighten, tauten. ❸ *intimidation stiffened their resolve* STRENGTHEN, harden, toughen, fortify, reinforce, give a boost to.
– OPPOSITES soften, liquefy, relax, weaken.

stifle ▶ verb ❶ *she stifled him with a bolster* SUFFOCATE, choke, asphyxiate, smother. ❷ *Eleanor stifled a giggle* SUPPRESS, smother, restrain, fight back, choke back, gulp back, check, swallow, curb, silence. ❸ *cartels stifle competition* CONSTRAIN, hinder, hamper, impede, hold back, curb, check, restrain, prevent, inhibit, suppress.
– OPPOSITES let out, encourage.

stifling ▶ adjective AIRLESS, suffocating, oppressive; very hot, sweltering; humid, close, muggy; *informal* boiling.
– OPPOSITES fresh, airy, cold.

stigma ▶ noun SHAME, disgrace, dishonour, ignominy, opprobrium, humiliation.
– OPPOSITES honour, credit.

stigmatize ▶ verb CONDEMN, denounce; brand, label, mark out; disparage, vilify, pillory, pour scorn on, defame.

still ▶ adjective ❶ *Polly lay still* MOTIONLESS, unmoving, not moving a muscle, stock-still, immobile, like a statue, as if turned to stone, rooted to the spot, transfixed, static, stationary. ❷ *a still night* QUIET, silent, hushed, soundless, noiseless, undisturbed; CALM, peaceful, serene, windless; *poetic/literary* stilly. ❸ *the lake was still* CALM, flat, even, smooth, placid, tranquil, pacific, waveless, glassy, like a millpond, unruffled.
– OPPOSITES moving, active, noisy, rough.
▶ noun *the still of the night* QUIETNESS, quiet, quietude, silence, stillness, hush, soundlessness; calm, tranquillity, peace, serenity.
– OPPOSITES noise, disturbance, hubbub.
▶ adverb ❶ *he's still here* UP TO THIS TIME, up to the present time, until now, even now, yet. ❷ *He's crazy. Still, he's harmless* NEVERTHELESS, nonetheless, all the same, just the same, anyway, anyhow, even so, yet, but, however, notwithstanding, despite that, in spite of that, for all that, be that as it may, in any event, at any rate; *informal* still and all.
▶ verb ❶ *he stilled the crowd* QUIETEN, quiet, silence, hush; calm, settle, pacify, soothe, lull, allay, subdue. ❷ *the wind stilled* ABATE, die down, lessen, subside, ease up/off, let up, moderate, slacken, weaken.
– OPPOSITES stir up, get stronger, get up.

stilted ▶ adjective STRAINED, forced, contrived, constrained, laboured, stiff, self-conscious, awkward, unnatural, wooden.
– OPPOSITES natural, effortless, spontaneous.

stimulant ▶ noun ❶ *caffeine is a stimulant* TONIC, restorative; antidepressant; *informal* pep pill, upper, pick-me-up, bracer; *Medicine* analeptic. ❷ *a stimulant to discussion* STIMULUS, incentive, encouragement, impetus, inducement, fillip, boost, spur, prompt; *informal* shot in the arm.
– OPPOSITES sedative, downer, deterrent.

stimulate ▶ verb ENCOURAGE, act as a stimulus/incentive/impetus/fillip/spur to, prompt, prod, move, motivate, trigger, spark, spur on, galvanize, activate, kindle, fire, fire with enthusiasm, fuel, whet, nourish; inspire, incentivize, inspirit, rouse, excite, animate, electrify; *N. Amer.* light a fire under, spirit someone up.
– OPPOSITES discourage.

stimulating ▶ adjective ❶ *a stimulating effect on the circulation* RESTORATIVE, tonic, invigorating, bracing, energizing, reviving, refreshing, revitalizing, revivifying; *Medicine* analeptic. ❷ *a stimulating lecture* THOUGHT-PROVOKING, interesting, fascinating, inspiring, inspirational, lively, sparkling, exciting, stirring, rousing, intriguing, giving one food for thought, refreshing; provocative, challenging.
– OPPOSITES sedative, uninspiring, uninteresting, boring.

stimulus ▶ noun SPUR, stimulant, encouragement, impetus, boost, prompt, prod, incentive, inducement, inspiration, fillip; motivation, impulse; *informal* shot in the arm.
– OPPOSITES deterrent, discouragement.

sting ▶ noun ❶ *a bee sting* PRICK, wound, injury, puncture. ❷ *this cream will take the sting away* SMART, pricking; pain, soreness, hurt, irritation. ❸ *the sting of his betrayal* HEARTACHE, heartbreak, agony, torture, torment, hurt, pain, anguish. ❹ *there was a sting in her words* SHARPNESS, severity, bite, edge, pointedness, asperity; sarcasm, acrimony, malice, spite, venom. ❺ (*informal*) *the victim of a sting* SWINDLE, fraud, deception; trickery, sharp practice; *informal* rip-off, con, con trick, fiddle; *N. Amer. informal* bunco.
▶ verb ❶ *she was stung by a scorpion* PRICK, wound; poison. ❷ *the smoke made her eyes sting* SMART, burn, hurt, be irritated, be sore. ❸ *the criticism stung her* UPSET, wound, cut to the quick, sear, grieve, hurt, pain, torment, mortify. ❹ *he was stung into action* PROVOKE, goad, incite, spur, prick, prod, rouse, drive, galvanize. ❺ (*informal*) swindle defraud, cheat, fleece, gull; *informal* rip off, screw, shaft, bilk, do, rook, diddle, take for a ride, skin; *N. Amer. informal* chisel, gouge; *Brit. informal, dated* rush.
– OPPOSITES deter.

stingy ▶ adjective (*informal*) MEAN, miserly, niggardly, close-fisted, parsimonious, penny-pinching, cheese-paring, Scrooge-like; *informal* tight-fisted, tight, mingy, money-grubbing; *N. Amer. informal* cheap; *formal* penurious; *archaic* near, niggard.
– OPPOSITES generous, liberal.

stink ▶ verb ❶ *his clothes stank of sweat* REEK, smell (foul/bad/disgusting), stink/smell to high heaven. ❷ (*informal*) *the whole idea stinks* BE VERY UNPLEASANT, be abhorrent, be despicable, be contemptible, be disgusting, be vile, be foul; *N. Amer. informal* suck. ❸ (*informal*) *the whole affair stinks of a set-up* SMACK, reek, give the impression, have all the hallmarks; strongly suggest.
▶ noun ❶ *the stink of sweat* STENCH, reek, foul/bad smell, malodour; *Brit. informal* pong, niff, hum; *Scottish informal* guff; *N. Amer. informal* funk; *poetic/literary* miasma. ❷ (*informal*) *she kicked up a stink* FUSS, commotion, rumpus, ruckus, trouble, outcry, uproar, brouhaha, furore; *informal* song and dance, to-do, kerfuffle, hoo-ha; *Brit. informal* row, carry-on.

stinking ▶ adjective ❶ *stinking rubbish* FOUL-SMELLING, smelly, reeking, fetid, malodorous, rank, putrid, noxious; *informal* stinky, reeky; *Brit. informal* niffing, niffy, pongy, whiffy, humming; *N. Amer. informal* funky; *poetic/literary* miasmic, noisome. ❷ (*informal*) *a stinking cold* DREADFUL, awful, terrible, frightful, ghastly, nasty, foul, vile; *Brit. informal* rotten, shocking.
– OPPOSITES sweet-smelling, aromatic, mild, slight.

stint ▶ verb *we saved by stinting on food* SKIMP, scrimp, be economical, economize, be sparing, hold back, be frugal; be mean, be parsimonious; limit, restrict; *informal* be stingy, be mingy, be tight.
▶ noun *a two-week stint in the office* SPELL, stretch, turn, session, term, shift, tour of duty.

stipulate ▶ verb SPECIFY, set down, set out, lay down; demand, require, insist on, make a condition of, prescribe, impose; *Law* provide.

stipulation ▶ noun CONDITION, precondition, proviso, provision, prerequisite, specification; demand, requirement; rider, caveat, qualification.

stir ▶ verb ❶ *stir the mixture well* MIX, blend, agitate; beat, whip, whisk, fold in; *N. Amer.* muddle. ❷ *Travis stirred in his sleep* MOVE SLIGHTLY, change one's position, shift. ❸ *a breeze stirred the leaves* DISTURB, rustle, shake, move, flutter, agitate. ❹ *he finally stirred at ten o'clock* GET UP, get out of bed, rouse oneself, rise; WAKE (UP), awaken; *informal* rise and shine, surface, show signs of life; *formal* arise; *poetic/literary* waken. ❺ *I never stirred from here* MOVE, budge, make a move, shift, go away; leave. ❻ *symbolism can stir the imagination* AROUSE, rouse, fire, kindle, inspire, stimulate, excite, awaken, quicken; *poetic/literary* waken. ❼ *the war stirred him to action* SPUR, drive, rouse, prompt, propel, prod, motivate, encourage; urge, impel; provoke, goad, prick, sting, incite; *N. Amer.* light a fire under.
– OPPOSITES go to bed, retire, go to sleep, stultify, stay, stay put.
▶ noun *the news caused a stir* COMMOTION, disturbance, fuss, excitement, turmoil, sensation; *informal* to-do, hoo-ha, hullabaloo, flap, splash.
■ **stir something up** WHIP UP, work up, foment, fan the flames of, trigger, spark off, precipitate, excite, provoke, incite.

stirring ▶ adjective EXCITING, thrilling, rousing, stimulating, moving, inspiring, inspirational, passionate, impassioned, emotional, heady.
– OPPOSITES boring, pedestrian.

stitch ▶ noun *he was panting and had a stitch* SHARP PAIN, stabbing pain, shooting pain, stab of pain, pang, twinge, spasm.
▶ verb *the seams are stitched by hand* SEW, baste, tack; seam, hem; darn.
■ **stitch someone up** (*Brit. informal*) FALSELY INCRIMINATE, get someone into trouble; *informal* frame, set up; *Brit. informal* fit someone up, drop someone in it.

stock ▶ noun ❶ *the shop carries little stock* MERCHANDISE, goods, wares, items/articles for sale, inventory. ❷ *a stock of fuel* STORE, supply, stockpile, reserve, hoard, cache, bank, accumulation, quantity, collection. ❸ *farm stock* ANIMALS, livestock, beasts; flocks, herds. ❹ *blue-chip stocks* SHARES, securities, equities, bonds. ❺ *his stock is low with most voters* POPULARITY, favour, regard, estimation, standing, status, reputation, name, prestige. ❻ *his mother was of French stock* DESCENT, ancestry, origin(s), parentage, pedigree, lineage, line (of descent), heritage, birth, extraction, family, blood, bloodline. ❼ *chicken stock* BOUILLON, broth. ❽ *the stock of a weapon* HANDLE, butt, haft, grip, shaft, shank.
▶ adjective ❶ *a stock size* STANDARD, regular, normal, established, set; common, readily/widely available; staple. ❷ *the stock response* USUAL, routine, predictable, set, standard, staple, customary, familiar, conventional, traditional, stereotyped, clichéd, hackneyed, unoriginal, formulaic.
– OPPOSITES non-standard, original, unusual.
▶ verb ❶ *we do not stock GM food* SELL, carry, keep (in stock), offer, have (for sale), retail, supply. ❷ *the fridge was well stocked with milk* SUPPLY, provide, furnish, provision, equip, fill, load.
■ **in stock** FOR/ON SALE, (immediately) available, on the shelf.
■ **stock up on/with** AMASS SUPPLIES OF, stockpile, hoard, cache, lay in, buy up/in, put away/by, put/set aside, collect, accumulate, save; *informal* squirrel away, salt away, stash away.
■ **take stock of** REVIEW, assess, weigh up, appraise, evaluate; *informal* size up.

stockings ▶ plural noun NYLONS, stay-ups; tights; hosiery, hose; *N. Amer.* pantyhose.

stockpile ▶ noun *a stockpile of weapons* STOCK, store, supply, accumulation, collection, reserve, hoard, cache; *informal* stash.
▶ verb *food had been stockpiled* STORE UP, amass, accumulate, store (up), stock up on, hoard, cache, collect, lay in, put away, put/set aside,

put by, put away for a rainy day, stow away, save; *informal* salt away, stash away.

stock-still ▶ **adjective** MOTIONLESS, completely still, unmoving, not moving a muscle, immobile, like a statue, as if turned to stone, rooted to the spot, transfixed, static, stationary.
– OPPOSITES moving, active.

stocky ▶ **adjective** THICKSET, sturdy, heavily built, chunky, burly, strapping, brawny, solid, heavy, hefty, beefy.
– OPPOSITES slender, skinny.

stodgy ▶ **adjective** ❶ *a stodgy pudding* SOLID, substantial, filling, hearty, heavy, starchy, indigestible. ❷ *stodgy writing* BORING, dull, uninteresting, dreary, turgid, tedious, dry, heavy going, unimaginative, uninspired, unexciting, unoriginal, monotonous, humdrum, prosaic, staid; *informal* deadly, square.
– OPPOSITES light, interesting, lively.

stoical ▶ **adjective** LONG-SUFFERING, uncomplaining, patient, forbearing, accepting, tolerant, resigned, phlegmatic, philosophical.
– OPPOSITES complaining, intolerant.

stoicism ▶ **noun** PATIENCE, forbearance, resignation, fortitude, endurance, acceptance, tolerance, philosophicalness, phlegm.
– OPPOSITES intolerance.

stoke ▶ **verb** ADD FUEL TO, mend, keep burning, tend.

stolid ▶ **adjective** IMPASSIVE, phlegmatic, unemotional, cool, calm, placid, unexcitable; dependable; unimaginative, dull.
– OPPOSITES emotional, lively, imaginative.

stomach ▶ **noun** ❶ *a stomach pain* ABDOMEN, belly, gut, middle; *informal* tummy, tum, breadbasket, insides. ❷ *his fat stomach* PAUNCH, pot belly, beer belly, girth; *informal* beer gut, pot, tummy, spare tyre, middle-aged spread; *N. Amer. informal* bay window; *dated, humorous* corporation. ❸ *he had no stomach for it* APPETITE, taste, hunger, thirst; inclination, desire, relish, fancy.
– RELATED TERMS gastric.
▶ **verb** ❶ *I can't stomach butter* DIGEST, keep down, manage to eat/consume, tolerate, take. ❷ *they couldn't stomach the sight* TOLERATE, put up with, take, stand, endure, bear; *Scottish* thole; *informal* hack, abide; *Brit. informal* stick.

stomach ache ▶ **noun** INDIGESTION, dyspepsia; colic, gripe; *informal* bellyache, tummy ache, gut ache, collywobbles.

stone ▶ **noun** ❶ *someone threw a stone at me* ROCK, pebble, boulder. ❷ *a commemorative stone* TABLET, monument, monolith, obelisk; gravestone, headstone, tombstone. ❸ *paving stones* SLAB, flagstone, flag, sett. ❹ *a precious stone* GEM, gemstone, jewel, semi-precious stone, brilliant; *informal* rock, sparkler. ❺ *a peach stone* KERNEL, seed, pip, pit.
– RELATED TERMS lithic, lapidary.

stony ▶ **adjective** ❶ *a stony path* ROCKY, pebbly, gravelly, shingly; rough, hard. ❷ *a stony stare* UNFRIENDLY, hostile, cold, chilly, frosty, icy; hard, flinty, steely, stern, severe; fixed, expressionless, blank, poker-faced, deadpan; unfeeling, uncaring, unsympathetic, indifferent, cold-hearted, callous, heartless, hard-hearted, stony-hearted, merciless, pitiless.
– OPPOSITES smooth, friendly, sympathetic.

stooge ▶ **noun** ❶ *a government stooge* UNDERLING, minion, lackey, subordinate; henchman; PUPPET, pawn, cat's paw; *informal* sidekick; *Brit. informal* dogsbody, poodle. ❷ *a comedian's stooge* BUTT, foil, straight man.

stoop ▶ **verb** ❶ *she stooped to pick up the pen* BEND (OVER/DOWN), lean over/down, crouch (down). ❷ *he stooped his head* LOWER, bend, incline, bow, duck. ❸ *he stoops when he walks* HUNCH ONE'S SHOULDERS, walk with a stoop, be round-shouldered. ❹ *Davis would stoop to crime* LOWER ONESELF, sink, descend, resort; go as far as, sink as low as.
▶ **noun** *a man with a stoop* HUNCH, round shoulders; curvature of the spine; *Medicine* kyphosis.

stop ▶ **verb** ❶ *we can't stop the decline* PUT AN END/STOP/HALT TO, bring to an end/stop/halt/close/standstill, end, halt; finish, terminate, wind up, discontinue, cut short, interrupt, nip in the bud; deactivate, shut down. ❷ *he stopped running* CEASE, discontinue, desist from, break off; give up, abandon, abstain from, cut out; *informal* quit, leave off, knock off, pack in, lay off, give over; *Brit. informal* jack in. ❸ *the car stopped* PULL UP, draw up, come to a stop/halt, come to rest, pull in, pull over; park. ❹ *the music stopped* COME TO AN END/STOP/STANDSTILL, cease, end, finish, draw to a close, be over, conclude, terminate; pause, break off; peter out, fade away. ❺ *divers stopped the flow of oil* STEM, staunch, hold back, check, curb, block, dam; *N. Amer.* stanch; *archaic* stay. ❻ *the police stopped her leaving* PREVENT, hinder, obstruct, impede, block, bar, preclude; dissuade from. ❼ *the council stopped the Kilmarnock scheme* THWART, baulk, foil, frustrate, stand in the way of; scotch, derail; *informal* put paid to, put the kibosh on, do for, stymie; *Brit. informal* scupper. ❽ *the firm stops your tax* WITHHOLD, keep back, hold back, deduct, take away, refuse to pay. ❾ *just stop the bottle with your thumb* BLOCK (UP), plug, close (up), fill (up); seal, caulk, bung up; *technical* occlude.
– OPPOSITES start, begin, continue, allow, encourage, expedite, pay, open.
▶ **noun** ❶ *all business came to a stop* HALT, end, finish, close, standstill; cessation, conclusion, stoppage, discontinuation. ❷ *a brief stop in the town* BREAK, stopover, stop-off, stay, visit; *formal* sojourn. ❸ *the next stop is Oxford Street* STOPPING PLACE, halt, station, stage. ❹ *a full stop* (FULL) POINT; *N. Amer.* period.
– OPPOSITES start, beginning, continuation.

■ **put a stop to**. *See* STOP verb senses 1, 7.

■ **stop off/over** BREAK ONE'S JOURNEY, take a break, pause; stay, remain, put up, lodge, rest; *formal* sojourn.

stopgap ▸ **noun** *that old plane was merely a stopgap* TEMPORARY SOLUTION, expedient, makeshift; substitute, stand-in.

▸ **adjective** *a stopgap measure* TEMPORARY, provisional, interim, pro tem, short-term, working, makeshift, emergency; caretaker, acting, stand-in, fill-in.

– OPPOSITES permanent.

stopover ▸ **noun** BREAK, stop, stop-off, visit, stay; *formal* sojourn.

stoppage ▸ **noun** ❶ *the stoppage of production* DISCONTINUATION, stopping, halting, cessation, termination, end, finish; interruption, suspension, breaking off. ❷ *a stoppage of the blood supply* OBSTRUCTION, blocking, blockage, block; *Medicine* occlusion, stasis. ❸ *a stoppage over pay* STRIKE, walkout; industrial action. ❹ (*Brit.*) *she was paid £3.40 an hour before stoppages* DEDUCTION, subtraction.

– OPPOSITES start, continuation.

stopper ▸ **noun** BUNG, plug, cork, spigot, spile, seal; *N. Amer.* stopple.

store ▸ **noun** ❶ *a store of food* STOCK, supply, stockpile, hoard, cache, reserve, bank, pool. ❷ *a grain store* STOREROOM, storehouse, repository, depository, stockroom, depot, warehouse, magazine; *informal* lock-up. ❸ *ship's stores* SUPPLIES, provisions, stocks, necessities; food, rations, provender; materials, equipment, hardware; *Military* materiel, accoutrements; *Nautical* chandlery. ❹ *a DIY store* SHOP, (retail) outlet, boutique, department store, chain store, emporium; supermarket, hypermarket, superstore, megastore.

▸ **verb** *rabbits don't store food* KEEP, keep in reserve, stockpile, lay in, put/set aside, put away/by, put away for a rainy day, save, collect, accumulate, hoard, cache; *informal* squirrel away, salt away, stash away.

– OPPOSITES use, discard.

■ **set (great) store by** VALUE, attach great importance to, put a high value on, put a premium on; THINK HIGHLY OF, hold in (high) regard, have a high opinion of; *informal* rate.

storehouse ▸ **noun** WAREHOUSE, depository, repository, store, storeroom, depot.

storey ▸ **noun** FLOOR, level, deck.

storm ▸ **noun** ❶ *battered by a storm* TEMPEST, squall; gale, hurricane, tornado, cyclone, typhoon; thunderstorm, rainstorm, monsoon, hailstorm, snowstorm, blizzard; *N. Amer.* williwaw, windstorm. ❷ *a storm of bullets* VOLLEY, salvo, fusillade, barrage, cannonade; shower, spray, hail, rain. ❸ *there was a storm over his remarks* UPROAR, outcry, fuss, furore, brouhaha, rumpus, trouble, hue and cry, controversy; *informal* to-do, hoo-ha, hullabaloo, ballyhoo, ructions, stink; *Brit. informal* row. ❹ *a storm of protest* OUTBURST, outbreak, explosion, eruption, outpouring, surge, blaze, flare-up, wave.

▸ **verb** ❶ *she stormed out* STRIDE ANGRILY, stomp, march, stalk, flounce, stamp, fling. ❷ *his mother stormed at him* RANT, rave, shout, bellow, roar, thunder, rage. ❸ *police stormed the building* ATTACK, charge, rush, assail, descend on, swoop on.

stormy ▸ **adjective** ❶ *stormy weather* BLUSTERY, squally, windy, gusty, blowy; rainy, thundery; wild, tempestuous, turbulent, violent, rough, foul. ❷ *a stormy debate* ANGRY, heated, fiery, fierce, furious, passionate, 'lively'.

– OPPOSITES calm, fine, peaceful.

story ▸ **noun** ❶ *an adventure story* TALE, narrative, account, anecdote; *informal* yarn, spiel. ❷ *the novel has a good story* PLOT, storyline, scenario; *formal* diegesis. ❸ *the story appeared in the papers* NEWS ITEM, news report, article, feature, piece. ❹ *there have been a lot of stories going round* RUMOUR, piece of gossip, whisper; speculation; *Austral./NZ informal* furphy. ❺ *Harper changed his story* TESTIMONY, statement, report, account, version. ❻ *Ellie never told stories. See* FALSEHOOD sense 1.

storyteller ▸ **noun** NARRATOR, teller of tales, raconteur, raconteuse, fabulist, anecdotalist; *Austral. informal* magsman.

stout ▸ **adjective** ❶ *a short stout man* FAT, plump, portly, rotund, dumpy, chunky, corpulent; stocky, burly, bulky, hefty, solidly built, thickset; *informal* tubby, pudgy; *Brit. informal* podgy, fubsy; *N. Amer. informal* zaftig, corn-fed; *archaic* pursy. ❷ *stout leather shoes* STRONG, sturdy, solid, substantial, robust, tough, durable, hard-wearing. ❸ *stout resistance* DETERMINED, vigorous, forceful, spirited; staunch, steadfast, stalwart, firm, resolute, unyielding, dogged; brave, bold, courageous, valiant, valorous, gallant, fearless, doughty, intrepid; *informal* gutsy, spunky.

– OPPOSITES thin, flimsy, feeble.

stout-hearted ▸ **adjective** BRAVE, determined, courageous, bold, plucky, spirited, valiant, valorous, gallant, fearless, doughty, intrepid, stalwart; *informal* gutsy, spunky.

stove ▸ **noun** OVEN, range, cooker.

stow ▸ **verb** *Barney stowed her luggage in the boot* PACK, load, store, place, put (away), deposit, stash.

– OPPOSITES unload.

■ **stow away** HIDE, conceal oneself, travel secretly.

straddle ▸ **verb** ❶ *she straddled the motorbike* SIT/STAND ASTRIDE, bestride, mount, get on. ❷ *a mountain range straddling the border* LIE ON BOTH SIDES OF, extend across, span. ❸ (*N. Amer.*) *he straddled the issue of taxes* BE EQUIVOCAL ABOUT, be undecided about, equivocate about, vacillate about, waver about; *informal* sit on the fence.

strafe ▶ **verb** BOMB, shell, bombard, fire on, machine-gun, rake with gunfire, enfilade; *archaic* fusillade.

straggle ▶ **verb** TRAIL, lag, dawdle, walk slowly; fall behind, bring up the rear.

straggly ▶ **adjective** UNTIDY, messy, unkempt, straggling, dishevelled.

straight ▶ **adjective** ❶ *a long, straight road* UNSWERVING, undeviating, linear, as straight as an arrow, uncurving, unbending. ❷ *that picture isn't straight* LEVEL, even, in line, aligned, square; vertical, upright, perpendicular; horizontal. ❸ *we must get the place straight* IN ORDER, (neat and) tidy, neat, shipshape (and Bristol fashion), orderly, spick and span, organized, arranged, sorted out, straightened out. ❹ *a straight answer* HONEST, direct, frank, candid, truthful, sincere, forthright, straightforward, plain-spoken, blunt, straight from the shoulder, unequivocal, unambiguous; *informal* upfront. ❺ *straight thinking* LOGICAL, rational, clear, lucid, sound, coherent. ❻ *three straight wins* SUCCESSIVE, in succession, consecutive, in a row, running; *informal* on the trot. ❼ *straight brandy* UNDILUTED, neat, pure; *N. Amer. informal* straight up. ❽ (*informal*) *she's very straight* RESPECTABLE, conventional, conservative, traditional, old-fashioned, strait-laced; *informal* stuffy, square, fuddy-duddy.

–OPPOSITES winding, crooked, untidy, evasive.

▶ **adverb** ❶ *he looked me straight in the eyes* RIGHT, directly, squarely, full; *informal* smack, (slap) bang; *N. Amer. informal* spang, smack dab. ❷ *she drove straight home* DIRECTLY, right, by a direct route. ❸ *I'll call you straight back* RIGHT AWAY, straight away, immediately, directly, at once; *archaic* straightway. ❹ *I told her straight* FRANKLY, directly, candidly, honestly, forthrightly, plainly, point-blank, bluntly, flatly, straight from the shoulder, without beating about the bush, without mincing words, unequivocally, unambiguously, in plain English, to someone's face; *Brit. informal* straight up. ❺ *he can't think straight* LOGICALLY, rationally, clearly, lucidly, coherently, cogently.

■ **go straight** REFORM, mend one's ways, turn over a new leaf, get back on the straight and narrow.

■ **straight away** AT ONCE, right away, (right) now, this/that (very) minute, this/that instant, immediately, instantly, directly, forthwith, without further/more ado, promptly, quickly, without delay, then and there, here and now, a.s.a.p., as soon as possible, as quickly as possible; *N. Amer.* in short order; *informal* straight off, in double quick time, p.d.q., pretty damn quick, pronto, before you can say Jack Robinson; *N. Amer. informal* lickety-split; *archaic* straight, straightway.

■ **straight from the shoulder**. *See* STRAIGHT adverb sense 4.

straighten ▶ **verb** ❶ *Rory straightened his tie* MAKE STRAIGHT, adjust, arrange, rearrange, (make) tidy, spruce up. ❷ *we must straighten things out with Viola* PUT/SET RIGHT, sort out, clear up, settle, resolve, put in order, regularize, rectify, remedy; *informal* patch up. ❸ *he straightened up* STAND UP (STRAIGHT), stand upright.

straightforward ▶ **adjective** ❶ *the process was remarkably straightforward* UNCOMPLICATED, simple, easy, effortless, painless, undemanding, plain sailing, child's play; *informal* as easy as falling off a log, as easy as pie, a piece of cake, a cinch, a snip, a doddle, a breeze, a cakewalk; *Brit. informal* easy-peasy, a doss; *N. Amer. informal* duck soup, a snap; *Austral./NZ informal* a bludge, a snack. ❷ *a straightforward man* HONEST, frank, candid, open, truthful, sincere, on the level; forthright, plain-speaking, direct, unambiguous; *informal* upfront; *N. Amer. informal* on the up and up.

–OPPOSITES complicated.

strain[1] ▶ **verb** ❶ *take care that you don't strain yourself* OVERTAX, overwork, overextend, overreach, drive too far, overdo it; exhaust, wear out; *informal* knacker, knock oneself out. ❷ *you have strained a muscle* INJURE, damage, pull, wrench, twist, sprain. ❸ *we strained to haul the guns up the slope* STRUGGLE, labour, toil, make every effort, try very hard, break one's back, push/drive oneself to the limit; *informal* pull out all the stops, go all out, bust a gut; *Austral. informal* go for the doctor. ❹ *the flood of refugees is straining the relief services* MAKE EXCESSIVE DEMANDS ON, overtax, be too much for, test, tax, put a strain on. ❺ *the bear strained at the chain* PULL, tug, heave, haul, jerk; *informal* yank. ❻ (*archaic*) *she strained the infant to her bosom* CLASP, press, clutch, hold tight; embrace, hug, enfold, envelop. ❼ *strain the mixture* SIEVE, sift, filter, screen, riddle; *rare* filtrate.

▶ **noun** ❶ *the rope snapped under the strain* TENSION, tightness, tautness. ❷ *muscle strain* INJURY, sprain, wrench, twist. ❸ *the strain of her job* PRESSURE, demands, burdens; stress; *informal* hassle. ❹ *Melissa was showing signs of strain* STRESS, (nervous) tension; exhaustion, fatigue, pressure of work, overwork. ❺ *the strains of Brahms's lullaby* SOUND, music; melody, tune.

strain[2] ▶ **noun** ❶ *a different strain of flu* VARIETY, kind, type, sort; breed, genus. ❷ *Hawthorne was of Puritan strain* DESCENT, ancestry, origin(s), parentage, lineage, extraction, family, roots. ❸ *there was a strain of insanity in the family* TENDENCY, susceptibility, propensity, proneness; trait, disposition. ❹ *a strain of solemnity* ELEMENT, strand, vein, note, trace, touch, suggestion, hint.

strained ▶ **adjective** ❶ *relations between them were strained* AWKWARD, tense, uneasy, uncom-

fortable, edgy, difficult, troubled. ❷ *Jean's strained face* DRAWN, careworn, worn, pinched, tired, exhausted, drained, haggard. ❸ *a strained smile* FORCED, constrained, unnatural; artificial, insincere, false, affected, put-on.
– OPPOSITES friendly.

strainer ▶ noun SIEVE, colander, filter, sifter, riddle, screen; *archaic* griddle.

strait ▶ noun ❶ *a strait about six miles wide* CHANNEL, sound, inlet, stretch of water. ❷ *the company is in desperate straits* A BAD/DIFFICULT SITUATION, difficulty, trouble, crisis, a mess, a predicament, a plight; *informal* hot/deep water, a jam, a hole, a bind, a fix, a scrape.

straitened ▶ adjective IMPOVERISHED, poverty-stricken, poor, destitute, penniless, on one's beam-ends, as poor as a church mouse, in penury, impecunious, unable to make ends meet, in reduced circumstances; *Brit.* on the breadline; *informal* (flat) broke, strapped for cash, on one's uppers; *Brit. informal* stony broke, skint, in Queer Street; *N. Amer. informal* stone broke; *formal* penurious.

strait-laced ▶ adjective PRIM (AND PROPER), prudish, puritanical, prissy, mimsy, niminy-piminy; conservative, old-fashioned, stuffy, staid, narrow-minded; *informal* starchy, square, fuddy-duddy.
– OPPOSITES broad-minded.

strand[1] ▶ noun ❶ *strands of wool* THREAD, filament, fibre; length, ply. ❷ *the various strands of the ecological movement* ELEMENT, component, factor, ingredient, aspect, feature, strain.

strand[2] ▶ noun (*poetic/literary*) *a walk along the strand* SEASHORE, shore, beach, sands, foreshore, shoreline, seaside, waterfront, front, waterside.

stranded ▶ adjective ❶ *a stranded ship* BEACHED, grounded, run aground, high and dry; shipwrecked, wrecked, marooned. ❷ *she was stranded in a strange city* HELPLESS, without resources, in difficulties; in the lurch, abandoned, deserted.

strange ▶ adjective ❶ *strange things have been happening* UNUSUAL, odd, curious, peculiar, funny, bizarre, weird, uncanny, queer, unexpected, unfamiliar, atypical, anomalous, out of the ordinary, extraordinary, puzzling, mystifying, mysterious, perplexing, baffling, unaccountable, inexplicable, singular, freakish; suspicious, questionable; eerie, unnatural; *informal* fishy, creepy, spooky. ❷ *strange clothes* WEIRD, eccentric, odd, peculiar, funny, bizarre, unusual; unconventional, outlandish, freakish, quirky, zany; *informal* wacky, way out, freaky, kooky, offbeat, off the wall; *N. Amer. informal* screwy, wacko. ❸ *visiting a strange house* UNFAMILIAR, unknown, new. ❹ *Jean was feeling strange* ILL, unwell, poorly, peaky; *Brit.* off colour; *informal* under the weather, funny, peculiar, lousy; *Brit. informal* off, ropy, grotty; *Austral./NZ informal* crook; *dated* queer. ❺ *she felt strange with him* ILL AT EASE, uneasy, uncomfortable, awkward, self-conscious. ❻ (*archaic*) *I am strange to the work. See* A STRANGER TO at STRANGER.
– OPPOSITES ordinary, familiar.

strangeness ▶ noun ODDITY, eccentricity, peculiarity, curiousness, bizarreness, weirdness, queerness, unusualness, abnormality, unaccountability, inexplicability, incongruousness, outlandishness, singularity.

stranger ▶ noun NEWCOMER, new arrival, visitor, outsider; *Austral. informal* blow-in.
■ **a stranger to** UNACCUSTOMED TO, unfamiliar with, unused to, new to, fresh to, inexperienced in; *archaic* strange to.

strangle ▶ verb ❶ *the victim was strangled with a scarf* THROTTLE, choke, garrotte; *informal* strangulate. ❷ *she strangled a sob* SUPPRESS, smother, stifle, repress, restrain, fight back, choke back. ❸ *bureaucracy is strangling commercial activity* HAMPER, hinder, impede, restrict, inhibit, curb, check, constrain, squash, crush, suppress, repress.

strap ▶ noun *thick leather straps* THONG, tie, band, belt.
▶ verb ❶ *a bag was strapped to the bicycle* FASTEN, secure, tie, bind, make fast, lash, truss. ❷ *his knee was strapped up* BANDAGE, bind. ❸ *his father strapped him. See* LASH verb sense 1.

strapping ▶ adjective BIG, strong, well built, brawny, burly, broad-shouldered, muscular, rugged; *informal* hunky, beefy; *dated* stalwart.
– OPPOSITES weedy.

stratagem ▶ noun PLAN, scheme, tactic, manoeuvre, ploy, device, trick, ruse, plot, machination, dodge; subterfuge, artifice; *Brit. informal* wheeze; *Austral. informal* lurk; *archaic* shift.

strategic ▶ adjective PLANNED, calculated, tactical, politic, judicious, prudent, shrewd.

strategy ▶ noun ❶ *the government's economic strategy* MASTER PLAN, grand design, game plan, plan (of action), policy, programme; tactics. ❷ *military strategy* THE ART OF WAR, (military) tactics.

stratum ▶ noun ❶ *a stratum of flint* LAYER, vein, seam, lode, bed. ❷ *this stratum of society* LEVEL, class, echelon, rank, grade, group, set; caste; *dated* station, estate.

stray ▶ verb ❶ *the gazelle had strayed from the herd* WANDER OFF, go astray, get separated, get lost. ❷ *we strayed from our original topic* DIGRESS, deviate, wander, get sidetracked, go off at a tangent; get off the subject. ❸ *the young men were likely to stray* BE UNFAITHFUL, have affairs, philander; *informal* play around, play the field. ❹ *he strayed from the path of righteousness* SIN, transgress, err, go astray; *archaic* trespass. ❺ (*poetic/literary*) *straying about in a strange place* ROAM, rove, wander, drift.

▶ **adjective** ❶ *a stray dog* HOMELESS, lost, strayed, gone astray, abandoned. ❷ *a stray bullet* RANDOM, chance, freak, unexpected, isolated, lone, single.

▶ **noun** *wardens who deal with strays* HOMELESS ANIMAL, stray dog/cat, waif.

streak ▶ **noun** ❶ *a streak of orange light* BAND, line, strip, stripe, vein, slash, ray. ❷ *green streaks on her legs* MARK, smear, smudge, stain, blotch; *informal* splotch. ❸ *a streak of self-destructiveness* ELEMENT, vein, touch, strain; trait, characteristic. ❹ *a winning streak* PERIOD, spell, stretch, run; *Brit. informal* patch.

▶ **verb** ❶ *the sky was streaked with red* STRIPE, band, fleck; *archaic* freak. ❷ *overalls streaked with paint* MARK, daub, smear; *informal* splotch. ❸ *Miranda streaked across the road. See* RUN verb sense 1.

streaky ▶ **adjective** STRIPED, stripy, streaked, banded, veined, brindled.

stream ▶ **noun** ❶ *a mountain stream* BROOK, rivulet, rill, runnel, streamlet, freshet; tributary; *Scottish & N. English* burn; *N. English* beck; *S. English* bourn; *N. Amer. & Austral./NZ* creek; *Austral.* billabong. ❷ *a stream of boiling water* JET, flow, rush, gush, surge, torrent, flood, cascade, outpouring, outflow; *technical* efflux. ❸ *a steady stream of visitors* SUCCESSION, series, string.

▶ **verb** ❶ *tears were streaming down her face* FLOW, pour, course, run, gush, surge, flood, cascade, spill. ❷ *children streamed out of the classrooms* POUR, surge, flood, swarm, pile, crowd. ❸ *a flag streamed from the mast* FLUTTER, float, flap, fly, blow, waft, wave.

streamer ▶ **noun** PENNANT, pennon, flag, banderole, banner.

streamlined ▶ **adjective** ❶ *streamlined cars* AERODYNAMIC, smooth, sleek, elegant. ❷ *a streamlined organization* EFFICIENT, smooth-running, well run, slick; time-saving, labour-saving.

street ▶ **noun** *Amsterdam's narrow cobbled streets* ROAD, thoroughfare, avenue, drive, boulevard, parade; side street/road, lane; *N. Amer.* highway.

■ **the man/woman in the street** AN ORDINARY PERSON, Mr/ Mrs Average; *Brit. informal* Joe Bloggs, Joe Public, the man on the Clapham omnibus; *N. Amer. informal* John Doe, Joe Sixpack.

■ **on the streets** HOMELESS, sleeping rough, down and out.

strength ▶ **noun** ❶ *enormous physical strength* POWER, brawn, muscle, muscularity, burliness, sturdiness, robustness, toughness, hardiness; vigour, force, might; *informal* beef; *poetic/literary* thew. ❷ *Oliver began to regain his strength* HEALTH, fitness, vigour, stamina. ❸ *her great inner strength* FORTITUDE, resilience, spirit, backbone, strength of character; courage, bravery, pluck, pluckiness, courageousness, grit; *informal* guts, spunk. ❹ *the strength of the retaining wall* ROBUSTNESS, sturdiness, firmness, toughness, soundness, solidity, durability. ❺ *Europe's military strength* POWER, influence, dominance, ascendancy, supremacy; *informal* clout; *poetic/literary* puissance. ❻ *the strength of feeling against the president* INTENSITY, vehemence, force, forcefulness, depth, ardour, fervour. ❼ *the strength of their argument* COGENCY, forcefulness, force, weight, power, potency, persuasiveness, soundness, validity. ❽ *what are your strengths?* STRONG POINT, advantage, asset, forte, aptitude, talent, skill; speciality. ❾ (*poetic/literary*) *my strength and shield* SUPPORT, mainstay, anchor. ❿ *the strength of the army* SIZE, extent, magnitude.

– OPPOSITES weakness.

■ **on the strength of** BECAUSE OF, by virtue of, on the basis of.

strengthen ▶ **verb** ❶ *calcium strengthens growing bones* MAKE STRONG/STRONGER, build up, give strength to. ❷ *engineers strengthened the walls* REINFORCE, make stronger, buttress, shore up, underpin. ❸ *strengthened glass* TOUGHEN, temper, anneal. ❹ *the wind had strengthened* BECOME STRONG/STRONGER, gain strength, intensify, pick up. ❺ *his insistence strengthened her determination* FORTIFY, bolster, make stronger, boost, reinforce, harden, stiffen, toughen, fuel. ❻ *they strengthened their efforts* STEP UP, increase, escalate; *informal* up, crank up, beef up. ❼ *the argument is strengthened by this evidence* REINFORCE, lend more weight to; support, back up, confirm, bear out, corroborate.

– OPPOSITES weaken.

strenuous ▶ **adjective** ❶ *a strenuous climb* ARDUOUS, difficult, hard, tough, taxing, demanding, exacting, exhausting, tiring, gruelling, back-breaking; *informal* killing; *Brit. informal* knackering; *archaic* toilsome. ❷ *strenuous efforts* VIGOROUS, energetic, zealous, forceful, strong, spirited, intense, determined, resolute, tenacious, tireless, indefatigable, dogged; *formal* pertinacious.

– OPPOSITES easy, half-hearted.

stress ▶ **noun** ❶ *he's under a lot of stress* STRAIN, pressure, (nervous) tension, worry, anxiety, trouble, difficulty; *informal* hassle. ❷ *laying greater stress on education* EMPHASIS, importance, weight. ❸ *the stress falls on the first syllable* EMPHASIS, accent, accentuation; beat; *Prosody* ictus. ❹ *the stress is uniform across the bar* PRESSURE, tension, strain.

▶ **verb** ❶ *they stressed the need for reform* EMPHASIZE, draw attention to, underline, underscore, point up, place emphasis on, lay stress on, highlight, accentuate, press home. ❷ *the last syllable is stressed* PLACE THE EMPHASIS ON, emphasize, place the accent on. ❸ *all the staff were stressed* OVERSTRETCH, overtax, push to the limit, pressurize, pressure, make tense, worry, harass; *informal* hassle.

– OPPOSITES play down.

stressful ▶ **adjective** DEMANDING, trying, taxing, difficult, hard, tough; fraught, traumatic,

pressured, tense, frustrating.
– OPPOSITES relaxing.

stretch ▶ verb ❶ *this material stretches* BE ELASTIC, be stretchy, be tensile. ❷ *he stretched the elastic* PULL (OUT), draw out, extend, lengthen, elongate, expand. ❸ *stretch your weekend into a vacation* PROLONG, lengthen, make longer, extend, spin out. ❹ *my budget won't stretch to a new car* BE SUFFICIENT FOR, be enough for, cover; afford, have the money for. ❺ *the court case stretched their finances* PUT A STRAIN ON, overtax, overextend, drain, sap. ❻ *stretching the truth* BEND, strain, distort, exaggerate, embellish. ❼ *she stretched out her hand to him* REACH OUT, hold out, extend, outstretch, proffer; *poetic/literary* outreach. ❽ *he stretched his arms* EXTEND, straighten (out). ❾ *she stretched out on the sofa* LIE DOWN, recline, lean back, be recumbent, sprawl, lounge, loll. ❿ *the desert stretches for miles* EXTEND, spread, continue.
– OPPOSITES shorten.
▶ noun ❶ *magnificent stretches of forest* EXPANSE, area, tract, belt, sweep, extent. ❷ *a four-hour stretch* PERIOD, time, spell, run, stint, session, shift. ❸ (*informal*) *a ten-year stretch* (PRISON) SENTENCE; *N. Amer. informal* rap.
▶ adjective *stretch fabrics* STRETCHY, stretchable, elastic.

strew ▶ verb SCATTER, spread, disperse, litter, toss; *poetic/literary* bestrew.

stricken ▶ adjective TROUBLED, (deeply) affected, afflicted, struck, hit.

strict ▶ adjective ❶ *a strict interpretation of the law* PRECISE, exact, literal, faithful, accurate, careful, meticulous, rigorous. ❷ *strict controls on spending* STRINGENT, rigorous, severe, harsh, hard, rigid, tough. ❸ *strict parents* STERN, severe, harsh, uncompromising, authoritarian, firm, austere. ❹ *this will be treated in strict confidence* ABSOLUTE, utter, complete, total. ❺ *a strict Roman Catholic* ORTHODOX, devout, conscientious.
– OPPOSITES loose, liberal.

strictness ▶ noun ❶ *the strictness of the laws* SEVERITY, harshness, rigidity, rigidness, stringency, rigorousness, sternness. ❷ *the provision has been interpreted with strictness* PRECISION, preciseness, accuracy, exactness, faithfulness; meticulousness, scrupulousness.
– OPPOSITES imprecision.

stricture ▶ noun ❶ *the constant strictures of the nuns* CRITICISM, censure, condemnation, reproof, reproach, admonishment. ❷ *the strictures on Victorian women* CONSTRAINT, restriction, limitation, restraint, curb, impediment, barrier, obstacle. ❸ *an intestinal stricture* NARROWING, constriction.
– OPPOSITES praise, freedom.

stride ▶ verb *she came striding down the path* MARCH, pace, step.
▶ noun *long swinging strides* (LONG/LARGE) STEP, pace.
■ **take something in one's stride** DEAL WITH EASILY, cope with easily, not bat an eyelid.

strident ▶ adjective HARSH, raucous, rough, grating, rasping, jarring, loud, shrill, screeching, piercing, ear-piercing.
– OPPOSITES soft.

strife ▶ noun CONFLICT, friction, discord, disagreement, dissension, dispute, argument, quarrelling, wrangling, bickering, controversy; ill/bad feeling, falling-out, bad blood, hostility, animosity.
– OPPOSITES peace.

strike ▶ verb ❶ *the teacher struck Mary* HIT, slap, smack, beat, thrash, spank, thump, punch, cuff; cane, lash, whip, club; *Austral./NZ informal* quilt; *informal* clout, wallop, belt, whack, thwack, bash, clobber, bop, biff; *poetic/literary* smite. ❷ *he struck the gong* BANG, beat, hit; *informal* bash, wallop. ❸ *the car struck a tree* CRASH INTO, collide with, hit, run into, bump into, smash into; *N. Amer.* impact. ❹ *Jennifer struck the ball* HIT, drive, propel; *informal* clout, wallop, swipe. ❺ *he struck a match* IGNITE, light. ❻ *she was asleep when the killer struck* ATTACK, set upon someone, fall on someone, assault someone. ❼ *the disease is striking 3,000 people a year* AFFECT, afflict, attack, hit. ❽ *striking a balance* ACHIEVE, reach, arrive at, find, attain, establish. ❾ *we have struck a bargain* AGREE (ON), come to an agreement on, settle on; *informal* clinch. ❿ *he struck a heroic pose* ASSUME, adopt, take on/up, affect; *N. Amer. informal* cop. ⓫ *they have struck oil* DISCOVER, find, come upon. ⓬ *a thought struck her* OCCUR TO, come to (mind), dawn on one, hit, spring to mind, enter one's head. ⓭ *you strike me as intelligent* SEEM TO, appear to, give the impression to. ⓮ *train drivers are striking* TAKE INDUSTRIAL ACTION, go on strike, down tools, walk out. ⓯ *they struck the big tent* TAKE DOWN, pull down. ⓰ *Lord Bridport struck his flag* LOWER, take down, bring down. ⓱ *we should strike south* GO, make one's way, head.
▶ noun ❶ *a 48-hour strike* INDUSTRIAL ACTION, walkout. ❷ *a military strike* (AIR) ATTACK, assault, bombing. ❸ *a gold strike* FIND, discovery.
■ **strike something out** DELETE, cross out, erase, rub out.
■ **strike something up** ❶ *the band struck up another tune* BEGIN TO PLAY, start playing. ❷ *we struck up a friendship* BEGIN, start, commence, embark on, establish.

striking ▶ adjective ❶ *Lizzie bears a striking resemblance to her sister* NOTICEABLE, obvious, conspicuous, evident, marked, notable, unmistakable, strong; remarkable, extraordinary, incredible, amazing, astounding, astonishing, staggering. ❷ *Kenya's striking landscape* IMPRESSIVE, imposing, grand, splendid, magnificent, spectacular, breathtaking, superb, marvellous, wonderful, stunning, staggering, sensational, dramatic. ❸ *striking good looks* STUNNING, attractive, good-looking, beautiful, glamorous,

gorgeous, prepossessing, ravishing, handsome, pretty; *informal* knockout; *archaic* fair, comely.
–OPPOSITES unremarkable.

string ▶ **noun** ❶ *a ball of string* TWINE, cord, yarn, thread, strand. ❷ *a string of brewers* CHAIN, group, firm, company. ❸ *a string of convictions* SERIES, succession, chain, sequence, run, streak. ❹ *a string of wagons* QUEUE, procession, line, file, column, convoy, train, cavalcade. ❺ *a string of pearls* STRAND, rope, necklace. ❻ *a guaranteed loan with no strings* CONDITIONS, qualifications, provisions, provisos, caveats, stipulations, riders, prerequisites, limitations, limits, constraints, restrictions; *informal* catches.
▶ **verb** ❶ *lights were strung across the promenade* HANG, suspend, sling, stretch, run; thread, loop, festoon. ❷ *beads strung on a silver chain* THREAD, loop, link.
■ **string along** GO ALONG, come too, accompany, join (up with).
■ **string someone along** (*informal*) MISLEAD, deceive, take advantage of, dupe, hoax, fool, make a fool of, play with, toy with, dally with, trifle with; *informal* lead up the garden path, take for a ride.
■ **string something out** ❶ *stringing out a story* SPIN OUT, drag out, lengthen. ❷ *airfields strung out along the Gulf* SPREAD OUT, space out, distribute, scatter.
■ **string someone up** (*informal*) HANG, lynch, gibbet.

stringent ▶ **adjective** STRICT, firm, rigid, rigorous, severe, harsh, tough, tight, exacting, demanding, inflexible, hard and fast.

stringy ▶ **adjective** ❶ *stringy hair* STRAGGLY, lank, thin. ❷ *a stringy brunette* LANKY, gangling, gangly, rangy, wiry, bony, skinny, scrawny, thin, spare, gaunt. ❸ *stringy meat* FIBROUS, gristly, sinewy, chewy, tough, leathery.

strip[1] ▶ **verb** ❶ *he stripped and got into bed* UNDRESS, strip off, take one's clothes off, unclothe, disrobe, strip naked. ❷ *stripping off paint* PEEL, remove, take off, scrape, rub, clean. ❸ *they stripped him of his doctorate* TAKE AWAY FROM, dispossess, deprive, confiscate, divest, relieve. ❹ *they stripped down my engine* DISMANTLE, disassemble, take to bits/pieces, take apart. ❺ *the house had been stripped* EMPTY, clear, clean out, plunder, rob, burgle, loot, pillage, ransack, despoil, sack; *archaic* spoil.
–OPPOSITES dress.
▶ **noun** *the team's new strip* OUTFIT, clothes, clothing, garments, dress, garb; *Brit.* kit; *informal* gear, get-up; *Brit. informal* rig-out.

strip[2] ▶ **noun** *a strip of paper* (NARROW) PIECE, bit, band, belt, ribbon, slip, shred.

stripe ▶ **noun** LINE, band, strip, belt, bar, streak, vein, flash, blaze; *technical* stria, striation.

striped ▶ **adjective**. *See* STRIPY.

stripling ▶ **noun** YOUTH, adolescent, youngster, boy, schoolboy, lad, teenager, juvenile, minor, young man; *Scottish* laddie; *informal* kid, young 'un, nipper, whippersnapper, shaver.

stripy ▶ **adjective** STRIPED, barred, lined, banded; streaky, variegated; *technical* striated.

strive ▶ **verb** ❶ *I shall strive to be virtuous* TRY (HARD), attempt, endeavour, aim, venture, make an effort, exert oneself, do one's best, do all one can, do one's utmost, labour, work; *informal* go all out, give it one's best shot, pull out all the stops; *formal* essay. ❷ *scholars must strive against bias* STRUGGLE, fight, battle, combat; campaign, crusade.

stroke ▶ **noun** ❶ *five strokes of the axe* BLOW, hit, thump, punch, slap, smack, cuff, knock; *informal* wallop, clout, whack, thwack, bash, biff, swipe; *archaic* smite. ❷ *cricket strokes* SHOT, hit, strike. ❸ *light upward strokes* MOVEMENT, action, motion. ❹ *a stroke of genius* FEAT, accomplishment, achievement, master stroke. ❺ *broad brush strokes* MARK, line. ❻ *the budget was full of bold strokes* DETAIL, touch, point. ❼ *he suffered a stroke* THROMBOSIS, seizure; *Medicine* ictus.
▶ **verb** *she stroked the cat* CARESS, fondle, pat, pet, touch, rub, massage, soothe.

stroll ▶ **verb** *they strolled along the river* SAUNTER, amble, wander, meander, ramble, promenade, walk, go for a walk, stretch one's legs, get some air; *informal* mosey; *formal* perambulate.
▶ **noun** *a stroll in the park* SAUNTER, amble, wander, walk, turn, promenade; *informal* mosey; *dated* constitutional; *formal* perambulation.

strong ▶ **adjective** ❶ *a strong lad* POWERFUL, muscular, brawny, powerfully built, strapping, sturdy, burly, meaty, robust, athletic, tough, rugged, lusty, strong as an ox/horse; *informal* beefy, hunky, husky; *dated* stalwart. ❷ *she isn't very strong* WELL, healthy, in good health, (fighting) fit, robust, vigorous, blooming, thriving, hale and hearty, in fine fettle; *informal* in the pink. ❸ *a strong character* FORCEFUL, determined, spirited, self-assertive, tough, tenacious, formidable, redoubtable, strong-minded; *informal* gutsy, feisty. ❹ *a strong fortress* SECURE, well built, indestructible, well fortified, well protected, impregnable, solid. ❺ *strong cotton bags* DURABLE, hard-wearing, heavy-duty, tough, sturdy, well made, long-lasting. ❻ *the current is very strong* FORCEFUL, powerful, vigorous, fierce, intense. ❼ *a strong interest in literature* KEEN, eager, passionate, fervent. ❽ *strong feelings* INTENSE, forceful, passionate, ardent, fervent, fervid, deep-seated; *poetic/literary* perfervid. ❾ *a strong supporter* KEEN, eager, enthusiastic, dedicated, staunch, loyal, steadfast. ❿ *strong arguments* COMPELLING, cogent, forceful, powerful, potent, weighty, convincing, sound, valid, well founded, persuasive, influential. ⓫ *a need for*

strong action FIRM, forceful, drastic, extreme. ⓬ *she bore a very strong resemblance to Vera* MARKED, noticeable, pronounced, distinct, definite, unmistakable, notable. ⓭ *a strong voice* LOUD, powerful, forceful, resonant, sonorous, rich, deep, booming. ⓮ *strong language* BAD, foul, obscene, profane. ⓯ *a strong blue colour* INTENSE, deep, rich, bright, brilliant, vivid. ⓰ *strong lights* BRIGHT, brilliant, dazzling, glaring. ⓱ *strong black coffee* CONCENTRATED, undiluted. ⓲ *strong cheese* HIGHLY FLAVOURED, flavourful, flavoursome; piquant, tangy, spicy. ⓳ *strong drink* ALCOHOLIC, intoxicating, hard, stiff; *formal* spirituous.
– OPPOSITES weak, gentle, mild.

strong-arm ▶ **adjective** AGGRESSIVE, forceful, bullying, coercive, threatening, intimidatory; *informal* bully-boy.

strongbox ▶ **noun** SAFE, safe-deposit box, cash/money box.

stronghold ▶ **noun** ❶ *the enemy stronghold* FORTRESS, fort, castle, citadel, garrison. ❷ *a Tory stronghold* BASTION, centre, hotbed.

strong-minded ▶ **adjective** DETERMINED, firm, resolute, purposeful, strong-willed, uncompromising, unbending, forceful, persistent, tenacious, dogged; *informal* gutsy, spunky.

strong point ▶ **noun** STRENGTH, strong suit, forte, speciality.
– OPPOSITES weakness.

strong-willed ▶ **adjective** DETERMINED, resolute, stubborn, obstinate, wilful, headstrong, strong-minded, self-willed, unbending, unyielding, intransigent, intractable, obdurate, recalcitrant; *formal* refractory.

stroppy ▶ **adjective** (*Brit. informal*). *See* BAD-TEMPERED.

structure ▶ **noun** ❶ *a vast Gothic structure* BUILDING, edifice, construction, erection, pile. ❷ *the structure of local government* CONSTRUCTION, form, formation, shape, composition, anatomy, make-up, constitution; organization, system, arrangement, design, framework, configuration, pattern.
▶ **verb** *the programme is structured around periods of residential study* ARRANGE, organize, design, shape, construct, build, put together.

struggle ▶ **verb** ❶ *they struggled to do better* STRIVE, try hard, endeavour, make every effort, do one's best/utmost, bend over backwards, put oneself out; *informal* go all out, give it one's best shot; *formal* essay. ❷ *James struggled with the raiders* FIGHT, grapple, wrestle, scuffle, brawl, spar; *informal* scrap. ❸ *the teams struggled to be first* COMPETE, contend, vie, fight, battle, jockey. ❹ *she struggled over the dunes* SCRAMBLE, flounder, stumble, fight/battle one's way, labour.
▶ **noun** ❶ *the struggle for justice* ENDEAVOUR, striving, effort, exertion, labour; campaign, battle, crusade, drive, push. ❷ *they were arrested without a struggle* FIGHT, scuffle, brawl, tussle, wrestling bout, skirmish, fracas, melee; breach of the peace; *informal* scrap, dust-up, punch-up; *Brit. informal* bust-up, ding-dong; *Law, dated* affray. ❸ *many perished in the struggle* CONFLICT, fight, battle, confrontation, clash, skirmish; hostilities, fighting, war, warfare, campaign. ❹ *a struggle within the leadership* CONTEST, competition, fight, clash; rivalry, friction, feuding, conflict. ❺ *life has been a struggle for me* EFFORT, trial, trouble, stress, strain, battle; *informal* grind, hassle.

strumpet ▶ **noun** (*archaic*). *See* PROSTITUTE noun.

strut ▶ **verb** SWAGGER, swank, parade, stride, sweep; *N. Amer. informal* sashay.

stub ▶ **noun** ❶ *a cigarette stub* BUTT, (tail) end; *informal* dog-end. ❷ *a ticket stub* COUNTERFOIL, ticket slip, tab. ❸ *a stub of pencil* STUMP, remnant, (tail) end.

stubble ▶ **noun** ❶ *a field of stubble* STALKS, straw. ❷ *grey stubble* BRISTLES, whiskers, facial hair; *informal* five o'clock shadow.

stubbly ▶ **adjective** BRISTLY, unshaven, whiskered; prickly, rough, coarse, scratchy.

stubborn ▶ **adjective** ❶ *you're too stubborn to admit it* OBSTINATE, stubborn as a mule, headstrong, wilful, strong-willed, pig-headed, obdurate, difficult, contrary, perverse, recalcitrant, inflexible, iron-willed, uncompromising, unbending; *informal* stiff-necked; *Brit. informal* bolshie, bloody-minded; *N. Amer. informal* balky; *formal* pertinacious, refractory; *archaic* contumacious, froward. ❷ *stubborn stains* INDELIBLE, permanent, persistent, tenacious, resistant.
– OPPOSITES compliant.

stubby ▶ **adjective** DUMPY, stocky, chunky, chubby, squat; short, stumpy, dwarfish.
– OPPOSITES slender, tall.

stuck ▶ **adjective** ❶ *a message was stuck to his screen* FIXED, fastened, attached, glued, pinned. ❷ *the gate was stuck* IMMOVABLE, stuck fast, jammed. ❸ *if you get stuck, leave a blank* BAFFLED, beaten, at a loss, at one's wits' end; *informal* stumped, bogged down, flummoxed, fazed, bamboozled.

■ **get stuck into** (*informal*) GET DOWN TO, make a start on, commence, embark on, get to work at, tackle, throw oneself into.

■ **stuck on** (*informal*) INFATUATED WITH, besotted with, smitten with, (head over heels) in love with, obsessed with; *informal* struck on, crazy about, mad about, wild about, carrying a torch for.

■ **stuck with** LUMBERED WITH, left with, made responsible for.

stuck-up ▶ **adjective** (*informal*). *See* CONCEITED.

studded ▶ **adjective** DOTTED, scattered, sprinkled, covered, spangled; *poetic/literary* bespangled, bejewelled.

student ▶ noun ❶ *a university student* UNDERGRADUATE, postgraduate, scholar; freshman, freshwoman, finalist; *N. Amer.* sophomore; *Brit. informal* fresher. ❷ *a former student* PUPIL, schoolchild, schoolboy, schoolgirl, scholar. ❸ *a nursing student* TRAINEE, apprentice, probationer, recruit, novice; *informal* rookie.

studied ▶ adjective DELIBERATE, careful, considered, conscious, calculated, intentional; affected, forced, strained, artificial.

studio ▶ noun WORKSHOP, workroom, atelier.

studious ▶ adjective ❶ *a studious nature* SCHOLARLY, academic, bookish, intellectual, erudite, learned, donnish. ❷ *studious attention* DILIGENT, careful, attentive, assiduous, painstaking, thorough, meticulous. ❸ *his studious absence from public view* DELIBERATE, wilful, conscious, intentional.

study ▶ noun ❶ *two years of study* LEARNING, education, schooling, academic work, scholarship, tuition, research; *informal* swotting, cramming. ❷ *a study of global warming* INVESTIGATION, enquiry, research, examination, analysis, review, survey. ❸ *Father was in his study* OFFICE, workroom, studio. ❹ *a critical study* ESSAY, article, work, review, paper, dissertation, disquisition.

▶ verb ❶ *Anne studied hard* WORK, revise; *informal* swot, cram, mug up; *archaic* con. ❷ *he studied electronics* LEARN, read, be taught. ❸ *Thomas was studying child development* INVESTIGATE, inquire into, research, look into, examine, analyse, explore, review, appraise, conduct a survey of. ❹ *she studied her friend thoughtfully* SCRUTINIZE, examine, inspect, consider, regard, look at, eye, observe, watch, survey; *informal* check out; *N. Amer. informal* eyeball.

■ **in a brown study** LOST IN THOUGHT, in a reverie, musing, ruminating, cogitating, dreaming, daydreaming; *informal* miles away.

stuff ▶ noun ❶ *suede is tough stuff* MATERIAL, fabric, cloth, textile; matter, substance. ❷ *first-aid stuff* ITEMS, articles, objects, goods; *informal* things, bits and pieces, odds and ends. ❸ *all my stuff is in the suitcase* BELONGINGS, (personal) possessions, effects, goods (and chattels), paraphernalia; *informal* gear, things, kit; *Brit. informal* clobber, gubbins. ❹ *he knows his stuff* FACTS, information, data, subject; *informal* onions.

▶ verb ❶ *stuffing pillows* FILL, pack, pad, upholster. ❷ *Robyn stuffed her clothes into a bag* SHOVE, thrust, push, ram, cram, squeeze, force, jam, pack, pile, stick. ❸ (*informal*) *they stuffed themselves with chocolate* FILL, gorge, overindulge; gobble, devour, wolf; *informal* pig (out), make a pig of oneself. ❹ *my nose was stuffed up* BLOCK, bung, congest, obstruct. ❺ (*Brit. informal*) *Scotland stuffed Chile. See* TROUNCE.

■ **stuff and nonsense** (*Brit. informal*). *See* NONSENSE sense 1.

stuffing ▶ noun ❶ *the stuffing is coming out of the armchair* PADDING, wadding, filling, upholstery, packing, filler. ❷ *sage and onion stuffing* FILLING, forcemeat, salpicon; *N. Amer.* dressing.

■ **knock the stuffing out of** (*informal*) DEVASTATE, shatter, crush, shock; *informal* knock sideways; *Brit. informal* knock for six.

stuffy ▶ adjective ❶ *a stuffy atmosphere* AIRLESS, close, musty, stale; *Brit.* frowsty; *Brit. informal* fuggy. ❷ *a stuffy young man* STAID, sedate, sober, prim, priggish, strait-laced, conformist, conservative, old-fashioned; *informal* square, straight, starchy, fuddy-duddy. ❸ *a stuffy nose* BLOCKED, stuffed up, bunged up.

–OPPOSITES airy, clear.

stultify ▶ verb ❶ *the free market was stultified by the welfare state* HAMPER, impede, thwart, frustrate, foil, suppress, smother. ❷ *he stultifies her with too much gentleness* BORE, make bored, dull, numb, benumb, stupefy.

stumble ▶ verb ❶ *he stumbled and fell heavily* TRIP (OVER/UP), lose one's balance, lose/miss one's footing, slip. ❷ *he stumbled back home* STAGGER, totter, teeter, dodder, blunder, hobble, move clumsily. ❸ *he stumbled through his speech* STAMMER, stutter, hesitate, falter, speak haltingly; *informal* fluff one's lines.

■ **stumble across/on** COME ACROSS/UPON, chance on, happen on, light on; discover, find, unearth, uncover; *informal* dig up.

stumbling block ▶ noun OBSTACLE, hurdle, barrier, bar, hindrance, impediment, handicap, disadvantage; snag, hitch, catch, drawback, difficulty, problem, weakness, defect, pitfall; *informal* fly in the ointment, hiccup.

stump ▶ verb ❶ (*informal*) *they were stumped by the question* BAFFLE, perplex, puzzle, confuse, confound, nonplus, defeat, put at a loss; *informal* flummox, fox, throw, floor; *N. Amer. informal* discombobulate. ❷ *she stumped along the landing* STOMP, stamp, clomp, clump, lumber, thump, thud.

■ **stump something up** (*Brit. informal*) PAY (UP), dish out, contribute; *informal* fork out, shell out, lay out, cough up, chip in; *N. Amer. informal* ante up, pony up.

stumpy ▶ adjective SHORT, stubby, squat, stocky, chunky.

–OPPOSITES long, thin.

stun ▶ verb ❶ *a glancing blow stunned Gary* DAZE, stupefy, knock unconscious, knock out, lay out. ❷ *she was stunned by the news* ASTOUND, amaze, astonish, dumbfound, stupefy, stagger, shock, take aback; *informal* flabbergast, knock sideways, bowl over; *Brit. informal* knock for six.

stunner ▶ noun (*informal*). *See* BEAUTY sense 2.

stunning ▶ adjective ❶ *a stunning win* REMARKABLE, extraordinary, staggering, incredible, outstanding, amazing, astonishing, marvellous, phenomenal, splendid; *informal* fabulous, fantastic, tremendous. ❷ *she was looking stunning. See* BEAUTIFUL.

–OPPOSITES ordinary.

stunt[1] ▶ **verb** *a disease that stunts growth* INHIBIT, impede, hamper, hinder, restrict, retard, slow, curb, check.
– OPPOSITES encourage.

stunt[2] ▶ **noun** *acrobatic stunts* FEAT, exploit, trick.

stunted ▶ **adjective** SMALL, undersize(d), diminutive.

stupefaction ▶ **noun** ❶ *alcoholic stupefaction* OBLIVION, obliviousness, unconsciousness, insensibility, stupor, daze. ❷ *Don shook his head in stupefaction* BEWILDERMENT, confusion, perplexity, wonder, amazement, astonishment.

stupefy ▶ **verb** ❶ *the blow had stupefied her* STUN, daze, knock unconscious, knock out, lay out. ❷ *they were stupefied* DRUG, sedate, tranquillize, intoxicate, inebriate; *informal* dope. ❸ *the amount stupefied us* SHOCK, stun, astound, dumbfound, overwhelm, stagger, amaze, astonish, take aback, take someone's breath away; *informal* flabbergast, knock sideways, bowl over, floor; *Brit. informal* knock for six.

stupendous ▶ **adjective** ❶ *stupendous achievements* AMAZING, astounding, astonishing, extraordinary, remarkable, phenomenal, staggering, breathtaking; *informal* fantastic, mind-boggling, awesome; *poetic/literary* wondrous. ❷ *a building of stupendous size* COLOSSAL, immense, vast, gigantic, massive, mammoth, huge, enormous.
– OPPOSITES ordinary.

stupid ▶ **adjective** ❶ *they're rather stupid* UNINTELLIGENT, ignorant, dense, foolish, dull-witted, slow, simple-minded, vacuous, vapid, idiotic, imbecilic, imbecile, obtuse, doltish; *informal* thick (as two short planks), dim, dumb, dopey, dozy, moronic, cretinous, pea-brained, half-witted, soft in the head, boneheaded, thickheaded, wooden-headed, muttonheaded; *Brit. informal* barmy, daft, not the full shilling. ❷ *a stupid mistake* FOOLISH, silly, unintelligent, idiotic, scatterbrained, nonsensical, senseless, unthinking, ill-advised, ill-considered, unwise, injudicious; inane, absurd, ludicrous, ridiculous, laughable, risible, fatuous, asinine, mad, insane, lunatic; *informal* crazy, dopey, cracked, half-baked, cock-eyed, hare-brained, nutty, dotty, batty, gormless, cuckoo, loony, loopy, off one's head, off one's trolley; *Brit. informal* potty. ❸ *he drank himself stupid* INTO A STUPOR, into a daze, into oblivion; stupefied, dazed, unconscious.
– OPPOSITES intelligent, sensible.

stupidity ▶ **noun** ❶ *he cursed their stupidity* LACK OF INTELLIGENCE, foolishness, denseness, brainlessness, ignorance, dull-wittedness, slow-wittedness, doltishness, slowness; *informal* thickness, dimness, dopiness, doziness. ❷ *she blushed at her stupidity* FOOLISHNESS, folly, silliness, idiocy, brainlessness, senselessness, injudiciousness, ineptitude, inaneness, inanity, absurdity, ludicrousness, ridiculousness, fatuousness, madness, insanity, lunacy; *informal* craziness; *Brit. informal* daftness.

stupor ▶ **noun** DAZE, state of unconsciousness, torpor, insensibility, oblivion.

sturdy ▶ **adjective** ❶ *a sturdy lad* STRAPPING, well built, muscular, athletic, strong, hefty, brawny, powerful, solid, burly, rugged, robust, tough, hardy, lusty; *informal* husky, beefy, meaty; *dated* stalwart; *poetic/literary* thewy, stark. ❷ *sturdy boots* ROBUST, strong, strongly made, well built, solid, stout, tough, resilient, durable, long-lasting, hard-wearing. ❸ *sturdy resistance* VIGOROUS, strong, stalwart, firm, determined, resolute, staunch, steadfast.
– OPPOSITES weak.

stutter ▶ **verb** *he stuttered over a word* STAMMER, stumble, falter.
▶ **noun** *a bad stutter* STAMMER, speech impediment, speech defect.

Stygian ▶ **adjective** (*poetic/literary*). *See* DARK adjective sense 1.

style ▶ **noun** ❶ *differing styles of management* MANNER, way, technique, method, methodology, approach, system, mode, form, modus operandi; *informal* MO. ❷ *a non-directive style of counselling* TYPE, kind, variety, sort, genre, school, brand, pattern, model. ❸ *wearing clothes with style* FLAIR, stylishness, elegance, grace, gracefulness, poise, polish, suaveness, sophistication, urbanity, chic, dash, panache, elan; *informal* class, pizzazz. ❹ *Laura travelled in style* COMFORT, luxury, elegance, opulence, lavishness. ❺ *modern styles* FASHION, trend, vogue, mode.
▶ **verb** ❶ *sportswear styled by Karl* DESIGN, fashion, tailor. ❷ *men who were styled 'knight'* CALL, name, title, entitle, dub, designate, term, label, tag, nickname; *formal* denominate.

stylish ▶ **adjective** FASHIONABLE, modish, voguish, modern, up to date; smart, sophisticated, elegant, chic, dapper, dashing; *informal* trendy, natty, classy, nifty, ritzy, snazzy; *N. Amer. informal* fly, kicky, tony, spiffy.
– OPPOSITES unfashionable.

stymie ▶ **verb** (*informal*). *See* HAMPER[2].

suave ▶ **adjective** CHARMING, sophisticated, debonair, urbane, polished, refined, poised, self-possessed, dignified, civilized, gentlemanly, gallant; smooth, polite, well mannered, civil, courteous, affable, tactful, diplomatic.
– OPPOSITES unsophisticated.

suavity ▶ **noun** CHARM, sophistication, polish, urbanity, suaveness, refinement, poise; politeness, courtesy, courteousness, civility, tact.

subconscious ▶ **adjective** *subconscious desires* UNCONSCIOUS, latent, suppressed, repressed, subliminal, dormant, underlying, innermost; *informal* bottled up.
▶ **noun** *the creative powers of the subconscious* (UNCON-

SCIOUS) MIND, imagination, inner(most) self, psyche.

subdue ▶ verb ❶ *he subdued all his enemies* CONQUER, defeat, vanquish, overcome, overwhelm, crush, quash, beat, trounce, subjugate, suppress, bring someone to their knees; *informal* lick, thrash, hammer. ❷ *she could not subdue her longing* CURB, restrain, hold back, constrain, contain, repress, suppress, stifle, smother, keep in check, rein in, control, master, quell; *informal* keep a/the lid on.

subdued ▶ adjective ❶ *Lewis's subdued air* SOMBRE, low-spirited, downcast, sad, dejected, depressed, gloomy, despondent, dispirited, disheartened, forlorn, woebegone; withdrawn, preoccupied; *informal* down in the mouth, down in the dumps, in the doldrums. ❷ *subdued voices* HUSHED, muted, quiet, low, soft, faint, muffled, indistinct. ❸ *subdued light* DIM, muted, softened, soft, lowered, subtle.
– OPPOSITES cheerful, bright.

subject ▶ noun ❶ *the subject of this chapter* THEME, subject matter, topic, issue, question, concern, point; substance, essence, gist. ❷ *popular university subjects* BRANCH OF STUDY, discipline, field. ❸ *six subjects did the trials* PARTICIPANT, volunteer; *informal* guinea pig. ❹ *British subjects* CITIZEN, national; taxpayer, voter. ❺ *a loyal subject* LIEGE, liegeman, vassal, henchman, follower.
▶ verb *they were subjected to violence* PUT THROUGH, treat with, expose to.
■ **subject to** ❶ *it is subject to budgetary approval* CONDITIONAL ON, contingent on, dependent on. ❷ *horses are subject to coughs* SUSCEPTIBLE TO, liable to, prone to, vulnerable to, predisposed to, at risk of; *archaic* susceptive of. ❸ *we are all subject to the law* BOUND BY, constrained by, accountable to.

subjection ▶ noun SUBJUGATION, domination, oppression, mastery, repression, suppression.

subjective ▶ adjective PERSONAL, individual, emotional, instinctive, intuitive.
– OPPOSITES objective.

subjugate ▶ verb CONQUER, vanquish, defeat, crush, quash, bring someone to their knees, enslave, subdue, suppress.
– OPPOSITES liberate.

sublimate ▶ verb CHANNEL, control, divert, transfer, redirect, convert.

sublime ▶ adjective ❶ *sublime music* EXALTED, elevated, noble, lofty, awe-inspiring, majestic, magnificent, glorious, superb, wonderful, marvellous, splendid; *informal* fantastic, fabulous, terrific, heavenly, divine, out of this world. ❷ *the sublime confidence of youth* SUPREME, total, complete, utter, consummate.

subliminal ▶ adjective SUBCONSCIOUS; hidden, concealed.
– OPPOSITES explicit.

submerge ▶ verb ❶ *the U-boat submerged* GO UNDER WATER, dive, sink. ❷ *submerge the bowl in water* IMMERSE, plunge, sink. ❸ *the farmland was submerged* FLOOD, inundate, deluge, swamp. ❹ *she was submerged in work* OVERWHELM, inundate, deluge, swamp, bury, engulf, snow under.
– OPPOSITES surface.

submission ▶ noun ❶ *submission to authority* YIELDING, capitulation, acceptance, consent, compliance. ❷ *Tim raised his hands in submission* SURRENDER, capitulation, resignation, defeat. ❸ *he wanted her total submission* COMPLIANCE, submissiveness, acquiescence, passivity, obedience, docility, deference, subservience, servility, subjection. ❹ *a report for submission to the Board* PRESENTATION, presenting, proffering, tendering, proposal, proposing. ❺ *his original submission* PROPOSAL, suggestion, proposition, recommendation. ❻ *the judge rejected his submission* ARGUMENT, assertion, contention, statement, claim, allegation.
– OPPOSITES defiance, resistance.

submissive ▶ adjective COMPLIANT, yielding, acquiescent, unassertive, passive, obedient, biddable, dutiful, docile, pliant; *informal* under someone's thumb.

submit ▶ verb ❶ *she submitted under duress* GIVE IN/WAY, yield, back down, cave in, capitulate; surrender, knuckle under. ❷ *he refused to submit to their authority* BE GOVERNED BY, abide by, be regulated by, comply with, accept, adhere to, be subject to, agree to, consent to, conform to. ❸ *we submitted an unopposed bid* PUT FORWARD, present, offer, proffer, tender, propose, suggest; put in, send in, register. ❹ *they submitted that the judgement was inappropriate* CONTEND, assert, argue, state, claim, posit, postulate.
– OPPOSITES resist, withdraw.

subnormal ▶ adjective ❶ *subnormal trade activity* BELOW AVERAGE, below normal, low, poor. ❷ (*dated*) *subnormal children* HAVING LEARNING DIFFICULTIES, having special (educational) needs, of low intelligence, backward; *dated* ESN.

subordinate ▶ adjective ❶ *subordinate staff* LOWER-RANKING, junior, lower, supporting. ❷ *a subordinate rule* SECONDARY, lesser, minor, subsidiary, subservient, ancillary, auxiliary, peripheral, marginal; supplementary, accessory.
– OPPOSITES senior.
▶ noun *the manager and his subordinates* JUNIOR, assistant, second (in command), number two, right-hand man/woman, deputy, aide, underling, minion; *informal* sidekick.
– OPPOSITES superior.

subordination ▶ noun INFERIORITY, subjection, subservience, submission, servitude.

sub rosa ▶ adverb (*formal*) IN SECRET, secretly, in private, privately, behind closed doors, in camera.
– OPPOSITES openly.

subscribe ▶ **verb** ❶ *we subscribe to 'Punch'* PAY A SUBSCRIPTION, take, buy regularly. ❷ *millions subscribe to the NSPCC* DONATE, make a donation, make a subscription, give (money), contribute towards. ❸ *I can't subscribe to that theory* AGREE WITH, accept, believe in, endorse, back, support, champion; *formal* accede to. ❹ (*formal*) *he subscribed the document* SIGN, countersign, initial, autograph, witness.

subscriber ▶ **noun** (REGULAR) READER, member, patron, supporter, backer, contributor.

subscription ▶ **noun** ❶ *the club's subscription* MEMBERSHIP FEE, dues, annual payment, charge. ❷ *we put your subscription to good use* DONATION, contribution, gift, grant; *formal* benefaction. ❸ *their subscription to capitalism* AGREEMENT, belief, endorsement, backing, support. ❹ (*formal*) *the subscription was witnessed* SIGNATURE, initials; addition, appendage.

subsequent ▶ **adjective** *the subsequent months* FOLLOWING, ensuing, succeeding, later, future, coming, to come, next.
– OPPOSITES previous.
■ **subsequent to** FOLLOWING, after, at the close/end of.

subsequently ▶ **adverb** LATER (ON), at a later date, afterwards, in due course, following this/that, eventually; *informal* after a bit; *formal* thereafter.

subservient ▶ **adjective** ❶ *subservient women* SUBMISSIVE, deferential, compliant, obedient, dutiful, biddable, docile, passive, unassertive, subdued, downtrodden; *informal* under someone's thumb. ❷ *individual rights are subservient to the interests of the state* SUBORDINATE, secondary, subsidiary, peripheral, ancillary, auxiliary, less important.
– OPPOSITES independent.

subside ▶ **verb** ❶ *wait until the storm subsides* ABATE, let up, quieten down, calm, slacken (off), ease (up), relent, die down, recede, lessen, soften, diminish, decline, dwindle, weaken, fade, wane, ebb; *archaic* remit. ❷ *the flood has subsided* RECEDE, ebb, fall, go down, get lower, abate. ❸ *the volcano is gradually subsiding* SINK, settle, cave in, collapse, crumple, give way. ❹ *Sarah subsided into a chair* SLUMP, flop, sink, collapse; *informal* flump, plonk oneself.
– OPPOSITES intensify, rise.

subsidiary ▶ **adjective** *a subsidiary company* SUBORDINATE, secondary, ancillary, auxiliary, subservient, supplementary, peripheral.
– OPPOSITES principal.
▶ **noun** *two major subsidiaries* SUBORDINATE COMPANY, branch, division, subdivision, derivative, offshoot.

subsidize ▶ **verb** GIVE MONEY TO, pay a subsidy to, contribute to, invest in, sponsor, support, fund, finance, underwrite; *informal* shell out for, fork out for, cough up for; *N. Amer. informal* bankroll.

subsidy ▶ **noun** GRANT, allowance, endowment, contribution, donation, bursary, handout; backing, support, sponsorship, finance, funding; *formal* benefaction.

subsist ▶ **verb** ❶ *he subsists on his pension* SURVIVE, live, stay alive, exist, eke out an existence; support oneself, manage, get along/by, make (both) ends meet. ❷ *the tenant's rights of occupation subsist* CONTINUE, last, persist, endure, prevail, carry on, remain.

subsistence ▶ **noun** ❶ *they depend on fish for subsistence* SURVIVAL, existence, living, life, sustenance, nourishment. ❷ *the money needed for his subsistence* MAINTENANCE, keep, upkeep, livelihood, board (and lodging), nourishment, food.

substance ▶ **noun** ❶ *an organic substance* MATERIAL, matter, stuff. ❷ *ghostly figures with no substance* SOLIDITY, body, corporeality; density, mass, weight, shape, structure. ❸ *none of the objections has any substance* MEANINGFULNESS, significance, importance, import, validity, foundation; *formal* moment. ❹ *the substance of the tale is very thin* CONTENT, subject matter, theme, message, essence. ❺ *Rangers are a team of substance* CHARACTER, backbone, mettle. ❻ *independent men of substance* WEALTH, fortune, riches, affluence, prosperity, money, means.

substandard ▶ **adjective** INFERIOR, second-rate, low-quality, poor, below par, imperfect, faulty, defective, shoddy, shabby, unsound, unsatisfactory; *informal* tenth-rate, crummy, lousy; *Brit. informal* duff, ropy, rubbish, chronic.

substantial ▶ **adjective** ❶ *substantial beings* REAL, true, actual; physical, solid, material, concrete, corporeal. ❷ *substantial progress had been made* CONSIDERABLE, real, significant, important, notable, major, valuable, useful. ❸ *substantial damages* SIZEABLE, considerable, significant, large, ample, appreciable, goodly. ❹ *substantial Victorian villas* STURDY, solid, stout, strong, well built, durable, long-lasting, hardwearing. ❺ *substantial country gentlemen* HEFTY, stout, sturdy, large, solid, bulky, burly, well built, portly. ❻ *substantial City companies* SUCCESSFUL, profitable, prosperous, wealthy, affluent, moneyed, well-to-do, rich; *informal* loaded, stinking rich. ❼ *substantial agreement* FUNDAMENTAL, essential, basic.

substantially ▶ **adverb** ❶ *the cost has fallen substantially* CONSIDERABLY, significantly, to a great/large extent, greatly, markedly, appreciably. ❷ *the draft was substantially accepted* LARGELY, for the most part, by and large, on the whole, in the main, mainly, in essence, basically, fundamentally, to all intents and purposes.
– OPPOSITES slightly.

substantiate ▶ **verb** PROVE, show to be true, give substance to, support, uphold, bear out, justify, vindicate, validate, corroborate, verify,

authenticate, confirm, endorse, give credence to.
– OPPOSITES disprove.

substitute ▶ noun *substitutes for permanent employees* REPLACEMENT, deputy, relief, proxy, reserve, surrogate, cover, stand-in, locum (tenens), understudy; *informal* sub.
▶ adjective *a substitute teacher* ACTING, replacement, deputy, relief, reserve, surrogate, stand-in, temporary, caretaker, interim, provisional.
– OPPOSITES permanent.
▶ verb ❶ *curd cheese can be substituted for yogurt* EXCHANGE, replace with, use instead of, use as an alternative to, use in place of, swap. ❷ *the Senate was empowered to substitute for the President* DEPUTIZE, act as deputy, act as a substitute, stand in, cover; replace, relieve, take over from; *informal* sub, fill someone's boots/shoes.

substitution ▶ noun EXCHANGE, change; replacement, replacing, swapping, switching.

subterfuge ▶ noun ❶ *the use of subterfuge by journalists* TRICKERY, intrigue, deviousness, deceit, deception, dishonesty, cheating, duplicity, guile, cunning, craftiness, chicanery, pretence, fraud, fraudulence. ❷ *a disreputable subterfuge* TRICK, hoax, ruse, wile, ploy, stratagem, artifice, dodge, bluff, pretence, deception, fraud, blind, smokescreen; *informal* con, scam.

subtle ▶ adjective ❶ *subtle colours* UNDERSTATED, muted, subdued; delicate, faint, pale, soft, indistinct. ❷ *subtle distinctions* FINE, fine-drawn, nice, overnice, hair-splitting. ❸ *a subtle mind* ASTUTE, keen, quick, fine, acute, sharp, shrewd, perceptive, discerning, discriminating, penetrating, sagacious, wise, clever, intelligent. ❹ *a subtle plan* INGENIOUS, clever, cunning, crafty, wily, artful, devious.

subtlety ▶ noun ❶ *the subtlety of the flavour* DELICACY, delicateness, subtleness; understatedness, mutedness, softness. ❷ *classification is fraught with subtlety* FINENESS, subtleness, niceness, nicety, nuance. ❸ *the subtlety of the human mind* ASTUTENESS, keenness, acuteness, sharpness, canniness, shrewdness, perceptiveness, discernment, discrimination, percipience, perspicacity, wisdom, cleverness, intelligence. ❹ *the subtlety of their tactics* INGENUITY, cleverness, skilfulness, adroitness, cunning, guile, craftiness, wiliness, artfulness, deviousness.

subtract ▶ verb TAKE AWAY/OFF, deduct, debit, dock; *informal* knock off, minus.
– OPPOSITES add.

suburb ▶ noun RESIDENTIAL AREA, dormitory area, commuter belt; suburbia.

suburban ▶ adjective ❶ *a suburban area* RESIDENTIAL, commuter, dormitory. ❷ *her drab suburban existence* DULL, boring, uninteresting, conventional, ordinary, commonplace, unremarkable, unexceptional; provincial, unsophisticated, parochial, bourgeois, middle-class.

subversive ▶ adjective *subversive activities* DISRUPTIVE, troublemaking, inflammatory, insurrectionary; seditious, revolutionary, rebellious, rebel, renegade, dissident.
▶ noun *a dangerous subversive* TROUBLEMAKER, dissident, agitator, revolutionary, renegade, rebel.

subvert ▶ verb ❶ *a plot to subvert the state* DESTABILIZE, unsettle, overthrow, overturn; bring down, topple, depose, oust; disrupt, wreak havoc on, sabotage, ruin, undermine, weaken, damage. ❷ *attempts to subvert Soviet youth* CORRUPT, pervert, deprave, contaminate, poison, embitter.

subway ▶ noun ❶ *he walked through the subway* UNDERPASS, (pedestrian) tunnel. ❷ *Tokyo's subway* UNDERGROUND (RAILWAY), metro; *Brit. informal* tube.

succeed ▶ verb ❶ *Darwin succeeded where others had failed* TRIUMPH, achieve success, be successful, do well, flourish, thrive; *informal* make it, make the grade, make a name for oneself. ❷ *the plan succeeded* BE SUCCESSFUL, turn out well, work (out), be effective; *informal* come off, pay off. ❸ *Rosebery succeeded Gladstone as Prime Minister* REPLACE, take the place of, take over from, follow, supersede; *informal* step into someone's shoes. ❹ *he succeeded to the throne* INHERIT, assume, acquire, attain; *formal* accede to. ❺ *embarrassment was succeeded by fear* FOLLOW, come after, follow after.
– OPPOSITES fail, precede.

succeeding ▶ adjective SUBSEQUENT, successive, following, ensuing, later, future, coming.

success ▶ noun ❶ *the success of the scheme* FAVOURABLE OUTCOME, successfulness, successful result, triumph. ❷ *the trappings of success* PROSPERITY, prosperousness, affluence, wealth, riches, opulence. ❸ *a West End success* TRIUMPH, best-seller, box-office success, sell-out; *informal* (smash) hit, winner. ❹ *an overnight success* STAR, superstar, celebrity, big name, household name; *informal* celeb, megastar.
– OPPOSITES failure.

successful ▶ adjective ❶ *a successful campaign* VICTORIOUS, triumphant; fortunate, lucky. ❷ *a successful designer* PROSPEROUS, affluent, wealthy, rich; doing well, famous, eminent, top; *informal* on the up and up. ❸ *successful companies* FLOURISHING, thriving, booming, buoyant, doing well, profitable, moneymaking, lucrative; *informal* on the up and up.

succession ▶ noun ❶ *a succession of exciting events* SEQUENCE, series, progression, chain, cycle, round, string, train, line, run, flow, stream. ❷ *his succession to the throne* ACCESSION, elevation, assumption.
■ **in succession** ONE AFTER THE OTHER, in a row, consecutively, successively, in sequence; running; *informal* on the trot.

successive ▶ adjective CONSECUTIVE, in a row, straight, sequential, in succession, running; *informal* on the trot.

successor ▶ **noun** HEIR (APPARENT), inheritor, next-in-line.
– OPPOSITES predecessor.

succinct ▶ **adjective** CONCISE, short (and sweet), brief, compact, condensed, crisp, laconic, terse, to the point, pithy, epigrammatic, synoptic, gnomic; *formal* compendious.
– OPPOSITES verbose.

succour ▶ **noun** *providing succour in times of need* AID, help, a helping hand, assistance; comfort, ease, relief, support.
▶ **verb** *the prisoners were succoured* HELP, aid, bring aid to, give/render assistance to, assist, lend a (helping) hand to; minister to, care for, comfort, bring relief to, support, take care of, look after, attend to.

succulent ▶ **adjective** JUICY, moist, luscious, soft, tender; choice, mouth-watering, appetizing, flavoursome, tasty, delicious; *informal* scrumptious, scrummy.
– OPPOSITES dry.

succumb ▶ **verb** ❶ *she succumbed to temptation* YIELD, give in/way, submit, surrender, capitulate, cave in. ❷ *he succumbed to the disease* DIE FROM/OF; catch, develop, contract, fall ill with; *informal* come/go down with.
– OPPOSITES resist.

suck ▶ **verb** ❶ *they sucked orange juice through straws* SIP, sup, siphon, slurp, draw, drink. ❷ *Fran sucked in a deep breath* DRAW, pull, breathe, gasp; inhale, inspire. ❸ *they got sucked into petty crime* IMPLICATE IN, involve in, draw into; *informal* mix up in. ❹ (*N. Amer. informal*) *the weather sucks* BE VERY BAD, be awful, be terrible, be dreadful, be horrible; *informal* stink.
■ **suck up** (*informal*) *they suck up to him, hanging on to his every word* GROVEL, creep, toady, be obsequious, be sycophantic, kowtow, bow and scrape, truckle; fawn on; *informal* lick someone's boots, be all over.

suckle ▶ **verb** BREASTFEED, feed, nurse.

sudden ▶ **adjective** UNEXPECTED, unforeseen, unanticipated, unlooked-for; immediate, instantaneous, instant, precipitous, precipitate, abrupt, rapid, swift, quick.

suddenly ▶ **adverb** IMMEDIATELY, instantaneously, instantly, straight away, all of a sudden, all at once, promptly, abruptly, swiftly; unexpectedly, without warning, without notice, out of the blue; *informal* straight off, in a flash, like a shot.
– OPPOSITES gradually.

suds ▶ **plural noun** LATHER, foam, froth, bubbles, soap.

sue ▶ **verb** ❶ *he sued for negligence* TAKE LEGAL ACTION, take to court, bring an action/suit, proceed against; *informal* have the law on. ❷ *suing for peace* APPEAL, petition, ask, solicit, request, seek.

suffer ▶ **verb** ❶ *I hate to see him suffer* HURT, ache, be in pain, feel pain; be in distress, be upset, be miserable. ❷ *he suffers from asthma* BE AFFLICTED BY, be affected by, be troubled with, have. ❸ *England suffered a humiliating defeat* UNDERGO, experience, be subjected to, receive, endure, face. ❹ *the school's reputation has suffered* BE IMPAIRED, be damaged, deteriorate, decline. ❺ (*archaic*) *he was obliged to suffer her intimate proximity* TOLERATE, put up with, bear, stand, abide, endure; *formal* brook. ❻ (*archaic*) *my conscience would not suffer me to accept* ALLOW, permit, let, give leave to, sanction.

suffering ▶ **noun** HARDSHIP, distress, misery, wretchedness, adversity, tribulation; pain, agony, anguish, trauma, torment, torture, hurt, affliction, sadness, unhappiness, sorrow, grief, woe, angst, heartache, heartbreak, stress; *poetic/literary* dolour.

suffice ▶ **verb** BE ENOUGH, be sufficient, be adequate, do, serve, meet requirements, satisfy demands, answer/meet one's needs, answer/serve the purpose; *informal* fit/fill the bill, hit the spot.

sufficient ▶ **adjective & determiner** ENOUGH, adequate, plenty of, ample.
– OPPOSITES inadequate.

suffocate ▶ **verb** ❶ *she suffocated her victim* SMOTHER, asphyxiate, stifle; choke, strangle. ❷ *she was suffocating in the heat* BE BREATHLESS, be short of air, struggle for air; be too hot, swelter; *informal* roast, bake, boil.

suffrage ▶ **noun** FRANCHISE, right to vote, the vote, enfranchisement, ballot.

suffuse ▶ **verb** PERMEATE, spread over, spread throughout, cover, bathe, pervade, wash, saturate, imbue.

sugar
– RELATED TERMS saccharine, glyco-.

sugary ▶ **adjective** ❶ *sugary snacks* SWEET, sugared, sickly. ❷ *sugary romance* SENTIMENTAL, mawkish, cloying, sickly (sweet), saccharine, syrupy; *informal* soppy, schmaltzy, slushy, mushy, sloppy, cutesy, corny.
– OPPOSITES sour.

suggest ▶ **verb** ❶ *Ruth suggested a holiday* PROPOSE, put forward, recommend, advocate; advise, urge, encourage, counsel. ❷ *evidence suggests that teenagers are responsive to price increases* INDICATE, lead to the belief, argue, demonstrate, show; *formal* evince. ❸ *sources suggest that the Prime Minister will change his cabinet* HINT, insinuate, imply, intimate, indicate. ❹ *the seduction scenes suggest his guilt and her loneliness* CONVEY, express, impart, imply, intimate, smack of, evoke, conjure up; *formal* evince.

suggestion ▶ **noun** ❶ *some suggestions for tackling this problem* PROPOSAL, proposition, motion, submission, recommendation; advice, counsel, hint, tip, clue, idea. ❷ *the suggestion of a smirk* HINT, trace, touch, suspicion, dash, soupçon; ghost, semblance, shadow, glimmer, impression, whisper. ❸ *there is no suggestion that he was party to a conspiracy* INSINUATION, hint, implication, intimation, innuendo, imputation.

suggestive ▶ adjective ❶ *suggestive remarks* INDECENT, indelicate, improper, unseemly, sexual, sexy, smutty, dirty, ribald, bawdy, racy, risqué, lewd, vulgar, coarse, salacious. ❷ *an odour suggestive of a brewery* REDOLENT, evocative, reminiscent; characteristic, indicative, typical.

suicide ▶ noun SELF-DESTRUCTION, taking one's own life, self-murder; *informal* topping oneself.

suit ▶ noun ❶ *a pinstriped suit* OUTFIT, set of clothes, ensemble. ❷ (*informal*) *suits in faraway boardrooms* BUSINESSMAN, BUSINESSWOMAN, executive, bureaucrat, administrator, manager. ❸ *a medical malpractice suit* LEGAL ACTION, lawsuit, (court) case, action, (legal/judicial) proceedings, litigation. ❹ *they spurned his suit* ENTREATY, request, plea, appeal, petition, supplication, application. ❺ *his suit came to nothing* COURTSHIP, wooing, attentions.

▶ verb ❶ *blue really suits you* LOOK ATTRACTIVE ON, enhance the appearance of, look good on, become, flatter. ❷ *savings schemes to suit all pockets* BE CONVENIENT FOR, be acceptable to, be suitable for, meet the requirements of; *informal* fit the bill. ❸ *recipes ideally suited to students* MAKE APPROPRIATE TO/FOR, tailor, fashion, adjust, adapt, modify, fit, gear, design.

suitable ▶ adjective ❶ *suitable employment opportunities* ACCEPTABLE, satisfactory, fitting; *informal* right up someone's street. ❷ *a drama suitable for all ages* APPROPRIATE, fitting, fit, acceptable, right. ❸ *music suitable for a lively dinner party* APPROPRIATE, suited, befitting, in keeping with; *informal* cut out for. ❹ *they treated him with suitable respect* PROPER, seemly, decent, appropriate, fitting, befitting, correct, due. ❺ *suitable candidates* WELL QUALIFIED, well suited, appropriate, fitting.
– OPPOSITES inappropriate.

suitcase ▶ noun TRAVELLING BAG, travel bag, case, valise, overnight case, portmanteau, vanity case; (**suitcases**) luggage, baggage.

suite ▶ noun ❶ *a penthouse suite* APARTMENT, flat, (set of) rooms. ❷ *the Queen and her suite* RETINUE, entourage, train, escort, royal household, court; attendants, retainers, servants.

suitor ▶ noun ADMIRER, wooer, boyfriend, sweetheart, lover; *poetic/literary* swain; *dated* beau.

sulk ▶ verb *Dad was sulking* MOPE, brood, be sullen, have a long face, be in a bad mood, be in a huff, be grumpy, be moody; *informal* be down in the dumps.

▶ noun *he sank into a deep sulk* (BAD) MOOD, fit of ill humour, fit of pique, pet, huff, (bad) temper, the sulks, the blues; *informal* grump.

sulky ▶ adjective *sulky faces* SULLEN, surly, moping, pouting, moody, sour, piqued, petulant, disgruntled, ill-humoured, in a bad mood, having a fit of the sulks, out of humour, fed up, put out; bad-tempered, grumpy, huffy, glum, gloomy, morose; *informal* grouchy.
– OPPOSITES cheerful.

sullen ▶ adjective SURLY, sulky, pouting, sour, morose, resentful, glum, moody, gloomy, grumpy, bad-tempered, ill-tempered; unresponsive, uncommunicative, uncivil, unfriendly.
– OPPOSITES cheerful.

sully ▶ verb TAINT, defile, soil, tarnish, stain, blemish, pollute, spoil, mar; *poetic/literary* besmirch, befoul.

sultry ▶ adjective ❶ *a sultry day* HUMID, close, airless, stifling, oppressive, muggy, sticky, sweltering, tropical, heavy; hot; *informal* boiling, roasting. ❷ *a sultry film star* PASSIONATE, attractive, sensual, sexy, voluptuous, erotic, seductive.
– OPPOSITES refreshing.

sum ▶ noun ❶ *a large sum of money* AMOUNT, quantity, volume. ❷ *just a small sum* AMOUNT OF MONEY, price, charge, fee, cost. ❸ *the sum of two numbers* (SUM) TOTAL, grand total, tally, aggregate, summation. ❹ *the sum of his wisdom* ENTIRETY, totality, total, whole, aggregate, summation, beginning and end. ❺ *we did sums at school* (ARITHMETICAL) PROBLEM, calculation; (**sums**) arithmetic, mathematics, computation; *Brit. informal* maths; *N. Amer. informal* math.
– OPPOSITES difference.

■ **sum up** SUMMARIZE THE EVIDENCE, review the evidence, give a summing-up.

■ **sum someone/something up** ❶ *one reviewer summed it up as 'compelling'* EVALUATE, assess, appraise, rate, weigh up, gauge, judge, deem, adjudge, estimate, form an opinion of. ❷ *he summed up his reasons* SUMMARIZE, make/give a summary of, precis, outline, give an outline of, recapitulate, review; *informal* recap.

summarily ▶ adverb IMMEDIATELY, instantly, right away, straight away, at once, on the spot, promptly; speedily, swiftly, rapidly, without delay; arbitrarily, without formality, peremptorily, without due process.

summarize ▶ verb SUM UP, abridge, condense, encapsulate, outline, give an outline of, put in a nutshell, recapitulate, give/make a summary of, give a synopsis of, precis, give a résumé of, give the gist of; *informal* recap; *archaic* epitomize.

summary ▶ noun *a summary of the findings* SYNOPSIS, precis, résumé, abstract, digest, encapsulation, abbreviated version; outline, sketch, rundown, review, summing-up, overview, recapitulation, epitome, conspectus; *informal* recap.

▶ adjective ❶ *a summary financial statement* ABRIDGED, abbreviated, shortened, condensed, concise, succinct, short, brief, pithy; *formal* compendious. ❷ *summary execution* IMMEDIATE, instant, instantaneous, on-the-spot; speedy, swift, rapid, without delay, sudden; arbitrary, without formality, peremptory.

summer
– RELATED TERMS aestival.

summer house ▶ **noun** GAZEBO, pavilion, belvedere; *poetic/literary* bower.

summit ▶ **noun** ❶ *the summit of Mont Blanc* (MOUNTAIN) TOP, peak, crest, crown, apex, tip, cap, hilltop. ❷ *the summits of world literature* ACME, peak, height, pinnacle, zenith, climax, high point/spot, highlight, crowning glory, best, finest, nonpareil. ❸ *the next superpower summit* MEETING, negotiation, conference, talk(s), discussion.
– OPPOSITES base, nadir.

summon ▶ **verb** ❶ *he was summoned to the Embassy* SEND FOR, call for, request the presence of; ask, invite. ❷ *they were summoned as witnesses* SERVE WITH A SUMMONS, summons, subpoena, cite, serve with a citation. ❸ *the chair summoned a meeting* CONVENE, assemble, order, call, announce; *formal* convoke. ❹ *he summoned the courage to move closer* MUSTER, gather, collect, rally, screw up. ❺ *summoning up their memories of home* CALL TO MIND, call up/forth, conjure up, evoke, recall, revive, arouse, kindle, awaken, spark (off). ❻ *they summoned spirits of the dead* CONJURE UP, call up, invoke.

summons ▶ **noun** ❶ *the court issued a summons* WRIT, subpoena, warrant, court order; *Law* citation. ❷ *a summons to go to the boss's office* ORDER, directive, command, instruction, demand, decree, injunction, edict, call, request.
▶ **verb** *he was summonsed to appear in court* SERVE WITH A SUMMONS, summon, subpoena, cite, serve with a citation.

sumptuous ▶ **adjective** LAVISH, luxurious, opulent, magnificent, resplendent, gorgeous, splendid, grand, lavishly appointed, palatial, rich; *informal* plush, ritzy; *Brit. informal* swish.
– OPPOSITES plain.

sun ▶ **noun** SUNSHINE, sunlight, daylight, light, warmth; beams, rays.
– RELATED TERMS solar, helio-.
■ **sun oneself**. *See* SUNBATHE.

sunbathe ▶ **verb** SUN ONESELF, bask, get a tan, tan oneself; *informal* catch some rays.

sunburnt ▶ **adjective** ❶ *his sunburnt shoulders* BURNT, sunburned, red, scarlet. ❷ *a handsome sunburnt face* TANNED, suntanned, brown, bronzed, bronze.
– OPPOSITES pale.

Sunday ▶ **noun** THE LORD'S DAY, the Sabbath.
– RELATED TERMS dominical.

sunder ▶ **verb** (*poetic/literary*) DIVIDE, split, cleave, separate, rend, sever, rive.

sundry ▶ **adjective** VARIOUS, varied, miscellaneous, assorted, mixed, diverse, diversified; several, numerous, many, manifold, multifarious, multitudinous; *poetic/literary* divers.

sunken ▶ **adjective** ❶ *sunken eyes* HOLLOWED, hollow, depressed, deep-set, concave, indented. ❷ *a sunken garden* BELOW GROUND LEVEL, at a lower level, lowered.

sunless ▶ **adjective** ❶ *a cold sunless day* DARK, overcast, cloudy, grey, gloomy, dismal, murky, dull. ❷ *the sunless side of the house* SHADY, shadowy, dark, gloomy.

sunlight ▶ **noun** DAYLIGHT, sun, sunshine, sun's rays, (natural) light.

sunny ▶ **adjective** ❶ *a sunny day* BRIGHT, sunshiny, sunlit, clear, fine, cloudless, without a cloud in the sky. ❷ *a sunny disposition* CHEERFUL, cheery, happy, light-hearted, bright, merry, joyful, bubbly, blithe, jolly, jovial, animated, buoyant, ebullient, upbeat, vivacious. ❸ *look on the sunny side* OPTIMISTIC, rosy, bright, hopeful, auspicious, favourable.
– OPPOSITES dull, miserable.

sunrise ▶ **noun** (CRACK OF) DAWN, daybreak, break of day, first light, (early) morning, cockcrow; *N. Amer.* sunup; *poetic/literary* aurora, dayspring.

sunset ▶ **noun** NIGHTFALL, close of day, twilight, dusk, evening; *N. Amer.* sundown; *poetic/literary* eventide, gloaming.

sunshine ▶ **noun** ❶ *relaxing in the sunshine* SUNLIGHT, sun, sun's rays, daylight, (natural) light. ❷ *his smile was all sunshine* HAPPINESS, cheerfulness, cheer, gladness, laughter, gaiety, merriment, joy, joyfulness, blitheness, joviality, jollity. ❸ (*Brit. informal*) *hello, sunshine* MY FRIEND; *informal* pal, chum; *Brit. informal* mate, matey, squire, mush; *N. Amer. informal* bud, buddy, buster.

super ▶ **adjective** (*informal*) EXCELLENT, superb, superlative, first-class, outstanding, marvellous, magnificent, wonderful, splendid, glorious; *informal* great, fantastic, fabulous, terrific, ace, divine, A1, wicked, cool; *Brit. informal* smashing, brilliant, brill.
– OPPOSITES rotten.

superannuated ▶ **adjective** ❶ *a superannuated civil servant* PENSIONED (OFF), retired; elderly, old. ❷ *superannuated computing equipment* OLD, old-fashioned, antiquated, out of date, outmoded, broken-down, obsolete, disused, defunct; *informal* clapped out.

superb ▶ **adjective** ❶ *he scored a superb goal* EXCELLENT, superlative, first-rate, first-class, outstanding, remarkable, marvellous, magnificent, wonderful, splendid, admirable, noteworthy, impressive, fine, exquisite, exceptional, glorious; *informal* great, fantastic, fabulous, terrific, super, awesome, ace, cool, A1; *Brit. informal* brilliant, brill, smashing. ❷ *a superb diamond necklace* MAGNIFICENT, majestic, splendid, grand, impressive, imposing, awe-inspiring, breathtaking; gorgeous.
– OPPOSITES poor, inferior.

supercilious ▶ adjective ARROGANT, haughty, conceited, disdainful, overbearing, pompous, condescending, superior, patronizing, imperious, proud, snobbish, snobby, smug, scornful, sneering; *informal* hoity-toity, high and mighty, uppity, snooty, stuck-up, snotty, jumped up, too big for one's boots.

superficial ▶ adjective ❶ *superficial burns* SURFACE, exterior, external, outer, outside, slight. ❷ *a superficial friendship* SHALLOW, surface, skin-deep, artificial; empty, hollow, meaningless. ❸ *a superficial investigation* CURSORY, perfunctory, casual, sketchy, desultory, token, slapdash, offhand, rushed, hasty, hurried. ❹ *a superficial resemblance* APPARENT, seeming, outward, ostensible, cosmetic, slight. ❺ *a superficial biography* TRIVIAL, lightweight. ❻ *a superficial person* FACILE, shallow, flippant, empty-headed, trivial, frivolous, silly, inane.
– OPPOSITES deep, thorough.

superficially ▶ adverb APPARENTLY, seemingly, ostensibly, outwardly, on the surface, on the face of it, to all intents and purposes, at first glance, to the casual eye.

superfluity ▶ noun SURPLUS, excess, overabundance, glut, surfeit, profusion, plethora.
– OPPOSITES shortage.

superfluous ▶ adjective ❶ *superfluous material* SURPLUS (TO REQUIREMENTS), redundant, unneeded, excess, extra, (to) spare, remaining, unused, left over, in excess, waste. ❷ *words seemed superfluous* UNNECESSARY, unneeded, redundant, uncalled for, unwarranted.
– OPPOSITES necessary.

superhuman ▶ adjective ❶ *a superhuman effort* EXTRAORDINARY, phenomenal, prodigious, stupendous, exceptional, immense, heroic. ❷ *superhuman power* DIVINE, holy, heavenly. ❸ *superhuman beings* SUPERNATURAL, preternatural, paranormal, other-worldly, unearthly; *rare* extramundane.
– OPPOSITES mundane.

superintend ▶ verb SUPERVISE, oversee, be in charge of, be in control of, preside over, direct, administer, manage, run, be responsible for.

superintendent ▶ noun ❶ *the superintendent of the museum* MANAGER, director, administrator, supervisor, overseer, controller, chief, head, governor; *informal* boss. ❷ (*N. Amer.*) *the building's superintendent* CARETAKER, janitor, warden, porter.

superior ▶ adjective ❶ *a superior officer* HIGHER-RANKING, higher-level, senior, higher, higher-up. ❷ *the superior candidate* BETTER, more expert, more skilful; worthier, fitter, preferred. ❸ *superior workmanship* FINER, better, higher-grade, of higher quality, greater; accomplished, expert. ❹ *superior chocolate* GOOD-QUALITY, high-quality, first-class, first-rate, top-quality; choice, select, exclusive, prime, prize, fine, excellent, best, choicest, finest. ❺ *a superior hotel* HIGH-CLASS, upper-class, select, exclusive; *Brit.* upmarket; *informal* classy, posh. ❻ *Jake regarded her with superior amusement* CONDESCENDING, supercilious, patronizing, haughty, disdainful, pompous, snobbish; *informal* high and mighty, hoity-toity, snooty, stuck-up.
– OPPOSITES junior, inferior.
▶ noun *my immediate superior* MANAGER, chief, supervisor, senior, controller, foreman; *informal* boss.
– OPPOSITES subordinate.

superiority ▶ noun SUPREMACY, advantage, lead, dominance, primacy, ascendancy, eminence.

superlative ▶ adjective EXCELLENT, magnificent, wonderful, marvellous, supreme, consummate, outstanding, remarkable, fine, choice, first-rate, first-class, premier, prime, unsurpassed, unequalled, unparalleled, unrivalled, pre-eminent; *informal* crack, ace, wicked; *Brit. informal* brilliant.
– OPPOSITES mediocre.

supernatural ▶ adjective ❶ *supernatural powers* PARANORMAL, psychic, magic, magical, occult, mystic, mystical, superhuman, supernormal; *rare* extramundane. ❷ *a supernatural being* GHOSTLY, phantom, spectral, otherworldly, unearthly, unnatural.

supersede ▶ verb REPLACE, take the place of, take over from, succeed; supplant, displace, oust, overthrow, remove, unseat; *informal* fill someone's shoes/boots.

superstition ▶ noun ❶ *the old superstitions held by sailors* MYTH, belief, old wives' tale; legend, story. ❷ *medicine was riddled with superstition* UNFOUNDED BELIEF, credulity, fallacy, delusion, illusion; magic, sorcery.

superstitious ▶ adjective ❶ *superstitious beliefs* MYTHICAL, irrational, illusory, groundless, unfounded; traditional. ❷ *he's incredibly superstitious* CREDULOUS, naive, gullible.
– OPPOSITES factual, sceptical.

supervise ▶ verb ❶ *he had to supervise the loading* SUPERINTEND, oversee, be in charge of, preside over, direct, manage, run, look after, be responsible for, govern, organize, handle. ❷ *you may need to supervise the patient* WATCH, oversee, keep an eye on, observe, monitor, mind.

supervision ▶ noun ❶ *the supervision of the banking system* ADMINISTRATION, management, control, charge; superintendence, regulation, government, governance. ❷ *keep your children under supervision* OBSERVATION, guidance, custody, charge, safe keeping, care, guardianship; control.

supervisor ▶ noun MANAGER, director, overseer, controller, superintendent, governor, chief, head; steward, foreman; *Brit.* ganger; *informal* boss; *Brit. informal* gaffer.

supine ▶ adjective ❶ *she lay supine on the sand*

FLAT ON ONE'S BACK, face upwards, flat, horizontal, recumbent, stretched out. ❷ *a supine media* WEAK, spineless, yielding, effete; docile, acquiescent, pliant, submissive, passive, inert, spiritless.
– OPPOSITES prostrate, strong.

supper ▶ **noun** DINNER, evening meal, main meal; snack, bite to eat; *Brit.* tea; *formal* repast; *poetic/literary* refection.

supplant ▶ **verb** ❶ *motorways supplanted the network of A-roads* REPLACE, supersede, displace, take over from, substitute for, override. ❷ *the man he supplanted as Prime Minister* OUST, usurp, overthrow, remove, topple, unseat, depose, dethrone; succeed, come after; *informal* fill someone's shoes/boots.

supple ▶ **adjective** ❶ *her supple body* LITHE, limber, lissom(e), willowy, flexible, loose-limbed, agile, acrobatic, nimble, double-jointed. ❷ *supple leather* PLIANT, pliable, flexible, soft, bendable, workable, malleable, stretchy, elastic, springy, yielding, rubbery.
– OPPOSITES stiff, rigid.

supplement ▶ **noun** ❶ *a mouse is a keyboard supplement* ADDITION, supplementation, supplementary, extra, add-on, accessory, adjunct, appendage; *Computing* peripheral. ❷ *a single room supplement* SURCHARGE, addition, increase. ❸ *a supplement to the essay* APPENDIX, addendum, end matter, tailpiece, codicil, postscript, addition, coda. ❹ *a special supplement with today's paper* PULL-OUT, insert, extra section.

▶ **verb** *they supplemented their incomes by spinning* AUGMENT, increase, add to, boost, swell, amplify, enlarge, top up.

supplementary ▶ **adjective** ❶ *supplementary income* ADDITIONAL, supplemental, extra, more, further; add-on, subsidiary, auxiliary, ancillary. ❷ *a supplementary index* APPENDED, attached, added, extra, accompanying.

suppliant ▶ **noun** *they were not mere suppliants* PETITIONER, supplicant, pleader, beggar, applicant.

▶ **adjective** *those around her were suppliant* PLEADING, begging, imploring, entreating, supplicating; on bended knee.

supplicate ▶ **verb** ENTREAT, beg, plead with, implore, petition, appeal to, call on, urge, enjoin, importune, sue, ask, request; *poetic/literary* beseech.

supply ▶ **verb** ❶ *they supplied money to rebels* GIVE, contribute, provide, furnish, donate, bestow, grant, endow, impart; dispense, disburse, allocate, assign; *informal* fork out, shell out. ❷ *the lake supplies the city with water* PROVIDE, furnish, endow, serve, confer; equip, arm. ❸ *windmills supply their power needs* SATISFY, meet, fulfil, cater for.

▶ **noun** ❶ *a limited supply of food* STOCK, store, reserve, reservoir, stockpile, hoard, cache; storehouse, repository; fund, mine, bank. ❷ *the supply of alcoholic liquor* PROVISION, dissemination, distribution, serving. ❸ *go to a supermarket for supplies* PROVISIONS, stores, stocks, rations, food, foodstuffs, eatables, produce, necessities; *informal* eats; *formal* comestibles.

▶ **adjective** *a supply teacher* SUBSTITUTE, stand-in, fill-in, locum, temporary, stopgap.

support ▶ **verb** ❶ *a roof supported by pillars* HOLD UP, bear, carry, prop up, keep up, brace, shore up, underpin, buttress, reinforce. ❷ *he struggled to support his family* PROVIDE FOR, maintain, sustain, keep, take care of, look after. ❸ *she supported him to the end* COMFORT, encourage, sustain, buoy up, hearten, fortify, console, solace, reassure; *informal* buck up. ❹ *evidence to support the argument* SUBSTANTIATE, back up, bear out, corroborate, confirm, attest to, verify, prove, validate, authenticate, endorse, ratify. ❺ *the money supports charitable projects* HELP, aid, assist; contribute to, back, subsidize, fund, finance; *N. Amer. informal* bankroll. ❻ *an independent candidate supported by locals* BACK, champion, help, assist, aid, abet, favour, encourage; vote for, stand behind, defend; sponsor, second, promote, endorse, sanction; *informal* throw one's weight behind. ❼ *they support human rights* ADVOCATE, promote, champion, back, espouse, be in favour of, recommend, defend, subscribe to. ❽ *I could not support the grief* ENDURE, bear, tolerate, stand, put up with, abide, stomach, sustain; *formal* brook; *archaic* suffer.
– OPPOSITES neglect, contradict, oppose.

▶ **noun** ❶ *bridge supports* PILLAR, post, prop, upright, crutch, plinth, brace, buttress; base, substructure, foundation, underpinning. ❷ *he pays support for his wife* MAINTENANCE, keep, sustenance, subsistence. ❸ *I was lucky to have their support* ENCOURAGEMENT, friendship, strength, consolation, solace, succour, relief. ❹ *he was a great support* COMFORT, help, assistance, tower of strength, prop, mainstay. ❺ *support for community services* CONTRIBUTIONS, backing, donations, money, subsidy, funding, funds, finance, capital. ❻ *they voiced their support for him* BACKING, help, assistance, aid, endorsement, approval; votes, patronage. ❼ *a surge in support for decentralization* ADVOCACY, backing, promotion, championship, espousal, defence, recommendation.

supporter ▶ **noun** ❶ *supporters of gun control* ADVOCATE, backer, adherent, promoter, champion, defender, upholder, crusader, proponent, campaigner, apologist. ❷ *Labour supporters* BACKER, helper, adherent, follower, ally, voter, disciple; member. ❸ *the charity relies on its supporters* CONTRIBUTOR, donor, benefactor, sponsor, backer, patron, subscriber, well-wisher. ❹ *the team's supporters* FAN, follower, enthusiast, devotee, admirer; *informal* buff, addict.

supportive ▶ **adjective** ❶ *a supportive teacher* ENCOURAGING, caring, sympathetic, reassuring, understanding, concerned, helpful, kind, kindly. ❷ *we are supportive of the proposal* IN FAVOUR OF, favourable to, pro, on the side of, sympathetic to, well disposed to, receptive to.

suppose ▶ verb ❶ *I suppose he's used to this* ASSUME, presume, expect, dare say, take it (as read); believe, think, fancy, suspect, sense, trust; guess, surmise, reckon, conjecture, deduce, infer, gather; *formal* opine. ❷ *suppose you had a spacecraft* ASSUME, imagine, (let's) say; hypothesize, theorize, speculate. ❸ *the theory supposes rational players* REQUIRE, presuppose, imply, assume; call for, need.

supposed ▶ adjective ❶ *the supposed phenomena* APPARENT, ostensible, seeming, alleged, putative, reputed, rumoured, claimed, purported; professed, declared, assumed, presumed. ❷ *I'm supposed to meet him at 8.30* MEANT, intended, expected; required, obliged.

supposition ▶ noun BELIEF, surmise, idea, notion, suspicion, conjecture, speculation, inference, theory, hypothesis, postulation, guess, feeling, hunch, assumption, presumption.

suppress ▶ verb ❶ *they could suppress the rebellion* SUBDUE, repress, crush, quell, quash, squash, stamp out; defeat, conquer, overpower, put down, crack down on; end, stop, terminate, halt. ❷ *she suppressed her irritation* CONCEAL, restrain, stifle, smother, bottle up, hold back, control, check, curb, contain, bridle, inhibit, keep a rein on, put a lid on. ❸ *the report was suppressed* CENSOR, keep secret, conceal, hide, hush up, gag, withhold, cover up, stifle; ban, proscribe, outlaw; sweep under the carpet.
–OPPOSITES incite, reveal.

suppurate ▶ verb FESTER, form pus, discharge, run, weep, become septic; *Medicine* maturate.

supremacy ▶ noun ASCENDANCY, predominance, primacy, dominion, hegemony, authority, mastery, control, power, rule, sovereignty, influence; dominance, superiority, advantage, the upper hand, the whip hand, the edge; distinction, greatness.

supreme ▶ adjective ❶ *the supreme commander* HIGHEST RANKING, chief, head, top, foremost, principal, superior, premier, first, prime; greatest, dominant, predominant, pre-eminent. ❷ *a supreme achievement* EXTRAORDINARY, remarkable, incredible, phenomenal, rare, exceptional, outstanding, great, incomparable, unparalleled, peerless. ❸ *the supreme sacrifice* ULTIMATE, final, last; utmost, extreme, greatest, highest.
–OPPOSITES subordinate, insignificant.

sure ▶ adjective ❶ *I am sure that they didn't* CERTAIN, positive, convinced, confident, definite, assured, satisfied, persuaded; unhesitating, unwavering, unshakeable. ❷ *someone was sure to be blamed* BOUND, likely, destined, fated. ❸ *a sure winner with the children* GUARANTEED, unfailing, infallible, unerring, assured, certain, inevitable, as sure as eggs is eggs; *informal* surefire. ❹ *he entered in the sure knowledge that he would win* UNQUESTIONABLE, indisputable, irrefutable, incontrovertible, undeniable, indubitable, undoubted, absolute, categorical, true, certain; obvious, evident, plain, clear, conclusive, definite. ❺ *a sure sign that he's worried* RELIABLE, dependable, trustworthy, unfailing, infallible, certain, unambiguous, true, foolproof, established, effective; *informal* sure-fire; *formal* efficacious. ❻ *the sure hand of the soloist* FIRM, steady, stable, secure, confident, steadfast, unfaltering, unwavering.
–OPPOSITES uncertain, unlikely.
▶ exclamation *'Can I come too?' 'Sure.'* YES, all right, of course, indeed, certainly, absolutely, agreed; *informal* OK, yeah, yep, uh-huh, you bet, I'll say, sure thing.
■ **be sure to** REMEMBER TO, don't forget to, see that you, mind that you, take care to, be certain to.
■ **for sure** (*informal*) DEFINITELY, surely, certainly, without doubt, without question, undoubtedly, indubitably, absolutely, undeniably, unmistakably.
■ **make sure** CHECK, confirm, make certain, ensure, assure; verify, corroborate, substantiate.

surely ▶ adverb ❶ *surely you remembered?* IT MUST BE THE CASE THAT, assuredly, without question. ❷ *I will surely die* CERTAINLY, for sure, definitely, undoubtedly, without doubt, doubtless, indubitably, unquestionably, without fail, inevitably. ❸ *slowly but surely manipulating the public* FIRMLY, steadily, confidently, assuredly, unhesitatingly, unfalteringly, unswervingly, determinedly, doggedly.

surety ▶ noun ❶ *she's a surety for her his obligations* GUARANTOR, sponsor. ❷ *bail of £10,000 with a further £10,000 surety* PLEDGE, collateral, guaranty, guarantee, bond, assurance, insurance, deposit; security, indemnity, indemnification; earnest.

surface ▶ noun ❶ *the surface of the door* OUTSIDE, exterior; top, side; finish, veneer. ❷ *the surface of police culture* OUTWARD APPEARANCE, façade. ❸ *a floured surface* WORKTOP, top, work surface, counter, table.
–OPPOSITES inside, interior.
▶ adjective *surface appearances* SUPERFICIAL, external, exterior, outward, ostensible, apparent, cosmetic, skin deep.
–OPPOSITES underlying.
▶ verb ❶ *a submarine surfaced* COME TO THE SURFACE, come up, rise. ❷ *the idea first surfaced in the sixties* EMERGE, arise, appear, come to light, crop up, materialize, spring up. ❸ (*informal*) *she eventually surfaces for breakfast* GET UP, get out of bed, rise, wake, awaken, appear.
–OPPOSITES dive.

■ **on the surface** AT FIRST GLANCE, to the casual eye, outwardly, to all appearances, apparently, ostensibly, superficially, externally.

surfeit ▶ **noun** *a surfeit of apples* EXCESS, surplus, abundance, oversupply, superabundance, superfluity, glut, avalanche, deluge; overdose; too much; *informal* bellyful.
– OPPOSITES lack.
▶ **verb** *we'll all be surfeited with food* SATIATE, gorge, overfeed, overfill, glut, cram, stuff, overindulge, fill.

surge ▶ **noun** ❶ *a surge of water* GUSH, rush, outpouring, stream, flow. ❷ *a surge in oil production* INCREASE, rise, growth, upswing, upsurge, escalation, leap. ❸ *a sudden surge of anger* RUSH, storm, torrent, blaze, outburst, eruption. ❹ *the surge of sea* SWELL, heaving, rolling, roll, swirling; tide.
▶ **verb** ❶ *the water surged into people's homes* GUSH, rush, stream, flow, burst, pour, cascade, spill, overflow, sweep, roll. ❷ *the Dow Jones index surged 47.63 points* INCREASE, rise, grow, escalate, leap. ❸ *the sea surged* SWELL, heave, rise, roll.

surly ▶ **adjective** SULLEN, sulky, moody, sour, unfriendly, unpleasant, scowling, unsmiling; bad-tempered, grumpy, crotchety, prickly, cantankerous, irascible, testy, short-tempered; abrupt, brusque, curt, gruff, churlish, ill-humoured, crabby, uncivil; *informal* grouchy.
– OPPOSITES pleasant.

surmise ▶ **verb** GUESS, conjecture, suspect, deduce, infer, conclude, theorize, speculate, divine; assume, presume, suppose, understand, gather, feel, sense, think, believe, imagine, fancy, reckon; *formal* opine.

surmount ▶ **verb** ❶ *his reputation surmounts language barriers* OVERCOME, conquer, prevail over, triumph over, beat, vanquish; clear, cross, pass over; resist, endure. ❷ *they surmounted the ridge* CLIMB OVER, top, ascend, scale, mount. ❸ *the dome is surmounted by a statue* CAP, top, crown, finish.
– OPPOSITES descend.

surname ▶ **noun** FAMILY NAME, last name; patronymic.

surpass ▶ **verb** EXCEL, exceed, transcend; outdo, outshine, outstrip, outclass, overshadow, eclipse; improve on, top, trump, cap, beat, better, outperform.

surplus ▶ **noun** *a surplus of grain* EXCESS, surfeit, superabundance, superfluity, oversupply, glut, profusion, plethora; remainder, residue, remains, leftovers.
– OPPOSITES dearth.
▶ **adjective** *surplus adhesive* EXCESS, leftover, unused, remaining, extra, additional, spare; superfluous, redundant, unwanted, unneeded, dispensable, expendable.
– OPPOSITES insufficient.

surprise ▶ **noun** ❶ *Kate looked at me in surprise* ASTONISHMENT, amazement, wonder, incredulity, bewilderment, stupefaction, disbelief. ❷ *the test came as a big surprise* SHOCK, bolt from the blue, bombshell, revelation, rude awakening, eye-opener; *informal* turn up for the books, shocker.
▶ **verb** ❶ *I was so surprised that I dropped it* ASTONISH, amaze, startle, astound, stun, stagger, shock; leave open-mouthed, take someone's breath away, dumbfound, daze, take aback, shake up; *informal* bowl over, floor, flabbergast; *Brit. informal* knock for six. ❷ *she surprised a burglar* TAKE BY SURPRISE, catch unawares, catch off guard, catch red-handed, catch in the act, catch out; *Brit. informal* catch on the hop.

surprised ▶ **adjective** ASTONISHED, amazed, astounded, startled, stunned, staggered, nonplussed, shocked, taken aback, stupefied, dumbfounded, dumbstruck, speechless, thunderstruck, confounded, shaken up; *informal* bowled over, flabbergasted, floored, flummoxed.

surprising ▶ **adjective** UNEXPECTED, unforeseen, unpredictable; astonishing, amazing, startling, astounding, staggering, incredible, extraordinary, breathtaking, remarkable; *informal* mind-blowing.

surrender ▶ **verb** ❶ *the army surrendered* CAPITULATE, give in, give (oneself) up, give way, yield, concede (defeat), submit, climb down, back down, cave in, relent, crumble; lay down one's arms, raise the white flag, throw in the towel/sponge. ❷ *they surrendered power to the government* GIVE UP, relinquish, renounce, forgo, forswear; cede, abdicate, waive, forfeit, sacrifice; hand over, turn over, yield, resign, transfer, grant. ❸ *surrender all hope of changing things* ABANDON, give up, cast aside.
– OPPOSITES resist, seize.
▶ **noun** ❶ *the surrender of the hijackers* CAPITULATION, submission, yielding, succumbing, acquiescence; fall, defeat. ❷ *a surrender of power to the shop floor* RELINQUISHMENT, renunciation, cession, abdication, resignation, transfer.

surreptitious ▶ **adjective** SECRET, secretive, stealthy, clandestine, sneaky, sly, furtive; concealed, hidden, undercover, covert, veiled, cloak-and-dagger.
– OPPOSITES blatant.

surrogate ▶ **noun** SUBSTITUTE, proxy, replacement; deputy, representative, stand-in, standby, stopgap, relief, understudy.

surround ▶ **verb** *we were surrounded by cops* ENCIRCLE, enclose, encompass, ring; fence in, hem in, confine, bound, circumscribe, cut off; besiege, trap.
▶ **noun** *a fireplace with a wood surround* BORDER, edging, edge, perimeter, boundary, margin, skirting, fringe.

surrounding ▶ **adjective** NEIGHBOURING, nearby, near, neighbourhood, local; adjoining, adjacent, bordering, abutting; encircling, encompassing.

surroundings ▶ **plural noun** ENVIRONMENT, setting, milieu, background, backdrop; conditions, circumstances, situation, context; vicinity, locality, habitat.

surveillance ▶ **noun** OBSERVATION, scrutiny, watch, view, inspection, supervision; spying, espionage, infiltration, reconnaissance; *informal* bugging, wiretapping, recon.

survey ▶ **verb** ❶ *he surveyed his work* LOOK AT, look over, observe, view, contemplate, regard, gaze at, stare at, eye; scrutinize, examine, inspect, scan, study, consider, review, take stock of; *informal* size up; *poetic/literary* behold. ❷ *they surveyed 4000 drug users* INTERVIEW, question, canvass, poll, cross-examine, investigate, research, study, probe, sample. ❸ *he was asked to survey the house* APPRAISE, assess, prospect; make a survey of, value.

▶ **noun** ❶ *a survey of the current literature* STUDY, review, consideration, overview; scrutiny, examination, inspection, appraisal. ❷ *a survey of sexual behaviour* POLL, review, investigation, inquiry, study, probe, questionnaire, census, research. ❸ *a thorough survey of the property* APPRAISAL, assessment, valuation, estimate, estimation.

survive ▶ **verb** ❶ *he survived by escaping through a hole* REMAIN ALIVE, live, sustain oneself, pull through, get through, hold on/out, make it, keep body and soul together. ❷ *the theatre must survive* CONTINUE, remain, persist, endure, live on, persevere, abide, go on, carry on, be extant, exist. ❸ *he was survived by his sons* OUTLIVE, outlast; live longer than.

susceptible ▶ **adjective** ❶ *susceptible children* IMPRESSIONABLE, credulous, gullible, innocent, ingenuous, naive, easily led; defenceless, vulnerable; persuadable, tractable; sensitive, responsive, thin-skinned. ❷ *people susceptible to blackmail* OPEN TO, receptive to, vulnerable to; an easy target for. ❸ *he is susceptible to ulcers* LIABLE TO, prone to, subject to, inclined to, predisposed to, disposed to, given to, at risk of; *archaic* susceptive of. ❹ *the database will be susceptible of exploitation* OPEN TO, capable of, admitting of, receptive of, responsive to.
– OPPOSITES sceptical, immune, resistant.

suspect ▶ **verb** ❶ *I suspected she'd made a mistake* HAVE A SUSPICION, have a feeling, feel, (be inclined to) think, fancy, reckon, guess, surmise, conjecture, conclude, have a hunch; suppose, presume, deduce, infer, sense, imagine; fear. ❷ *he had no reason to suspect my honesty* DOUBT, distrust, mistrust, have misgivings about, be sceptical about, have qualms about, be suspicious of, be wary of, harbour reservations about; *informal* smell a rat.

▶ **noun** *a murder suspect* SUSPECTED PERSON, accused, defendant.

▶ **adjective** *a suspect package* SUSPICIOUS, dubious, doubtful, untrustworthy; odd, queer; *informal* fishy, funny, shady; *Brit. informal* dodgy.

suspend ▶ **verb** ❶ *the court case was suspended* ADJOURN, interrupt, break off, postpone, delay, defer, shelve, put off, intermit, prorogue, hold over, hold in abeyance; cut short, discontinue, dissolve, disband, terminate; *N. Amer.* table; *informal* put on ice, put on the back burner, mothball; *N. Amer. informal* take a rain check on. ❷ *he was suspended from his duties* EXCLUDE, debar, remove, eliminate, expel, eject. ❸ *lights were suspended from the ceiling* HANG, sling, string; swing, dangle.

suspense ▶ **noun** *I can't bear the suspense* TENSION, uncertainty, doubt, anticipation, expectation, expectancy, excitement, anxiety, apprehension, strain.

■ **in suspense** EAGERLY, agog, with bated breath, on tenterhooks; on edge, anxious, edgy, jumpy, keyed up, uneasy; *informal* uptight, jittery.

suspension ▶ **noun** ❶ *the suspension of army operations* ADJOURNMENT, interruption, postponement, delay, deferral, deferment, stay, prorogation; armistice; cessation, end, halt, stoppage, dissolution, disbandment, termination. ❷ *his suspension from school* EXCLUSION, debarment, removal, elimination, expulsion, ejection; *Brit.* rustication.

suspicion ▶ **noun** ❶ *she had a suspicion that he didn't like her* INTUITION, feeling, impression, inkling, hunch, fancy, notion, supposition, belief, idea, theory; presentiment, premonition; *informal* gut feeling, sixth sense. ❷ *I confronted him with my suspicions* MISGIVING, doubt, qualm, reservation, hesitation, question; scepticism, uncertainty, distrust, mistrust. ❸ *wine with a suspicion of soda* TRACE, touch, suggestion, hint, soupçon, tinge, shade, whiff, bit, drop, dash, taste, jot, mite.

suspicious ▶ **adjective** ❶ *she gave him a suspicious look* DOUBTFUL, unsure, dubious, wary, chary, sceptical, distrustful, mistrustful, disbelieving, cynical. ❷ *a highly suspicious character* DISREPUTABLE, unsavoury, dubious, suspect, dishonest-looking, funny-looking, slippery; *informal* shifty, shady; *Brit. informal* dodgy. ❸ *she disappeared in suspicious circumstances* QUESTIONABLE, odd, strange, dubious, irregular, queer, funny, doubtful, mysterious, murky; *informal* fishy; *Brit. informal* dodgy.
– OPPOSITES trusting, honest, innocent.

sustain ▶ **verb** ❶ *the balcony might not sustain the weight* BEAR, support, carry, stand, keep up, prop up, shore up, underpin. ❷ *her memories sustained her* COMFORT, help, assist, encourage, succour, support, give strength to, buoy up, carry, cheer up, hearten; *informal* buck up. ❸ *they were unable to sustain a coalition* CONTINUE, carry on, keep up, keep alive, maintain, preserve, conserve, perpetuate, retain. ❹ *she had* *bread and cheese to sustain her* NOURISH, feed, nurture; maintain, preserve, keep alive, keep going, provide for. ❺ *she sustained slight injuries* UNDERGO, experience, suffer, endure. ❻ *the allegation was not sustained* UPHOLD, validate, ratify, vindicate, confirm, endorse; verify, corroborate, substantiate, bear out, prove, authenticate, back up, evidence, justify.

sustained ▶ **adjective** CONTINUOUS, ongoing; steady, continual, constant, prolonged, persistent, non-stop, perpetual, unabating, relentless, unrelieved, unbroken, never-ending, incessant, unceasing, ceaseless, round the clock.
– OPPOSITES sporadic.

sustenance ▶ **noun** ❶ *the creature needs sustenance* NOURISHMENT, food, nutriment, nutrition, provisions, provender, rations; *informal* grub, chow; *Brit. informal* scoff; *formal* comestibles; *poetic/literary* viands; *dated* victuals. ❷ *the sustenance of his family* SUPPORT, maintenance, keep, living, livelihood, subsistence, income.

swagger ▶ **verb** ❶ *we swaggered into the arena* STRUT, parade, stride; walk confidently; *informal* sashay. ❷ *he likes to swagger about his kindness* BOAST, brag, bluster, crow, gloat; strut, posture, blow one's own trumpet, lord it; *informal* show off, swank.
▶ **noun** ❶ *a slight swagger in his stride* STRUT; confidence, arrogance, ostentation. ❷ *he was full of swagger* BLUSTER, braggadocio, bumptiousness, vainglory; *informal* swank.

swallow ▶ **verb** ❶ *she couldn't swallow anything* EAT, gulp down, consume, devour, put away; ingest, assimilate; drink, guzzle, quaff, imbibe, sup, slug; *informal* polish off, swig, swill, down; *Brit. informal* scoff. ❷ *I can't swallow any more of your insults* TOLERATE, endure, stand, put up with, bear, abide, countenance, stomach, take, accept; *informal* hack; *Brit. informal* stick; *formal* brook. ❸ *he swallowed my story* BELIEVE, credit, accept, trust; *informal* fall for, buy, go for, {swallow hook, line, and sinker}. ❹ *she swallowed her pride* RESTRAIN, repress, suppress, hold back, fight back; overcome, check, control, curb, rein in; silence, muffle, stifle, smother, hide, bottle up; *informal* keep a/the lid on.
■ **swallow someone/something up** ❶ *the darkness swallowed them up* ENGULF, swamp, devour, overwhelm, overcome. ❷ *the colleges were swallowed up by universities* TAKE OVER, engulf, absorb, assimilate, incorporate.

swamp ▶ **noun** *his horse got stuck in a swamp* MARSH, bog, quagmire, mire, morass, fen; quicksand; *N. Amer.* bayou; *archaic* quag.
▶ **verb** ❶ *the rain was swamping the dry roads* FLOOD, inundate, deluge, immerse; soak, drench, saturate. ❷ *he was swamped by media attention* OVERWHELM, inundate, flood, deluge, engulf, snow under, overload, overpower, weigh down, besiege, beset.

swampy ▶ **adjective** MARSHY, boggy, fenny, miry; soft, soggy, muddy, spongy, heavy, squelchy, waterlogged, sodden, wet; *archaic* quaggy.

swap ▶ **verb** ❶ *I swapped some toys for a set of dice* EXCHANGE, trade, barter, interchange, bargain; switch, change, replace. ❷ *we swapped jokes* BANDY, exchange, trade, reciprocate.
▶ **noun** *a job swap* EXCHANGE, interchange, trade, switch, trade-off, substitution.

swarm ▶ **noun** ❶ *a swarm of bees* HIVE, flock, collection. ❷ *a swarm of gendarmes* CROWD, multitude, horde, host, mob, gang, throng, mass, army, troop, herd, pack; *poetic/literary* myriad.
▶ **verb** *reporters were swarming all over the place* FLOCK, crowd, throng, surge, stream.
■ **be swarming with** BE CROWDED WITH, be thronged with, be overrun with, be full of, abound in, be teeming with, bristle with, be alive with, be crawling with, be infested with, overflow with, be prolific in, be abundant in; *informal* be thick with.

swarthy ▶ **adjective** DARK-SKINNED, olive-skinned, dusky, tanned, saturnine, black; *archaic* swart.
– OPPOSITES pale.

swashbuckling ▶ **adjective** DARING, heroic, daredevil, dashing, adventurous, bold, valiant, valorous, fearless, lionhearted, dauntless, devil-may-care; gallant, chivalrous, romantic.
– OPPOSITES timid.

swathe ▶ **verb** WRAP, envelop, bind, swaddle, bandage, cover, shroud, drape, wind, enfold, sheathe.

sway ▶ **verb** ❶ *the curtains swayed in the breeze* SWING, shake, oscillate, undulate, move to and fro, move back and forth. ❷ *she swayed on her feet* STAGGER, wobble, rock, lurch, reel, roll, list, stumble, pitch. ❸ *we are swayed by the media* INFLUENCE, affect, bias, persuade, talk round, win over; manipulate, bend, mould. ❹ *you must not be swayed by emotion* RULE, govern, dominate, control, guide.
▶ **noun** ❶ *the sway of her hips* SWING, roll, shake, oscillation, undulation. ❷ *a province under the sway of the Franks* JURISDICTION, rule, government, sovereignty, dominion, control, command, power, authority, ascendancy, domination, mastery.
■ **hold sway** HOLD POWER, wield power, exercise power, rule, be in control, predominate; have the upper hand, have the edge, have the whip hand; *informal* run the show, be in the driving seat, be in the saddle.

swear ▶ **verb** ❶ *they swore to marry each other* PROMISE, vow, pledge, give one's word, take an oath, undertake, guarantee; *Law* depose; *formal* aver. ❷ *she swore she would never go back* INSIST, avow, pronounce, declare, proclaim, assert, profess, maintain, contend, emphasize, stress; *formal* aver. ❸ *Kate spilled wine and swore* CURSE, blaspheme, utter profanities, utter oaths, use bad language, take the Lord's name in vain; *informal* cuss, eff and blind; *archaic* execrate.

■ **swear by** (*informal*) EXPRESS CONFIDENCE IN, have faith in, trust, believe in; set store by, value; *informal* rate.

■ **swear off** (*informal*) RENOUNCE, forswear, forgo, abstain from, go without, shun, avoid, eschew, steer clear of; give up, dispense with, stop, discontinue, drop; *informal* kick, quit; *Brit. informal* jack in.

swearing ▶ **noun** BAD LANGUAGE, strong language, cursing, blaspheming, blasphemy; profanities, obscenities, curses, oaths, expletives, swear words; *informal* cussing, effing and blinding, four-letter words; *formal* imprecation.

sweat ▶ **noun** ❶ *he was drenched with sweat* PERSPIRATION, moisture, dampness, wetness; *Medicine* diaphoresis, hidrosis. ❷ (*informal*) *he got into such a sweat about that girl* FLUSTER, panic, frenzy, fever, pother; *informal* state, flap, tizzy, dither, stew, lather; *N. Amer. informal* twit. ❸ (*informal*) *the sweat of the working classes* LABOUR, hard work, toil(s), effort(s), exertion(s), industry, drudgery, slog; *informal* graft, grind, elbow grease.

– RELATED TERMS sudatory.

▶ **verb** ❶ *she was sweating heavily* PERSPIRE, swelter, glow; be damp, be wet; secrete. ❷ *I've sweated over this for six months* WORK (HARD), work like a Trojan, labour, toil, slog, slave, work one's fingers to the bone; *informal* graft, plug away; *archaic* drudge. ❸ (*N. Amer. informal*) *I sweated over my mistakes* WORRY, agonize, fuss, panic, fret, dither, lose sleep; *informal* be on pins and needles, be in a state, be in a flap, be in a stew, torture oneself, torment oneself.

sweaty ▶ **adjective** PERSPIRING, sweating, clammy, sticky, glowing; moist, damp.

sweep ▶ **verb** ❶ *she swept the floor* BRUSH, clean, scrub, wipe, mop, dust, scour; *informal* do. ❷ *I swept the crumbs off* REMOVE, brush, clean, clear, whisk. ❸ *he was swept out to sea* CARRY, pull, drag, tow. ❹ *riots swept the country* ENGULF, overwhelm, flood. ❺ *he swept down the stairs* GLIDE, sail, breeze, drift, flit, flounce; stride, stroll, swagger. ❻ *a limousine swept past* GLIDE, sail, rush, race, streak, speed, fly, zoom, whizz, hurtle; *informal* tear, whip. ❼ *police swept the conference room* SEARCH, probe, check, explore, go through, scour, comb.

▶ **noun** ❶ *a great sweep of his hand* GESTURE, stroke, wave, movement. ❷ *a security sweep* SEARCH, hunt, exploration, probe. ❸ *a long sweep of golden sand* EXPANSE, tract, stretch, extent, plain. ❹ *the broad sweep of our interests* RANGE, span, scope, compass, reach, spread, ambit, remit, gamut, spectrum, extent.

■ **sweep something aside** DISREGARD, ignore, take no notice of, dismiss, shrug off, forget about, brush aside.

■ **sweep something under the carpet** HIDE, conceal, suppress, hush up, keep quiet about, censor, gag, withhold, cover up, stifle.

sweeping ▶ **adjective** ❶ *sweeping changes* EXTENSIVE, wide-ranging, global, broad, comprehensive, all-inclusive, all-embracing, far-reaching, across the board; thorough, radical; *informal* wall-to-wall. ❷ *a sweeping victory* OVERWHELMING, decisive, thorough, complete, total, absolute, out-and-out, unqualified. ❸ *sweeping statements* WHOLESALE, blanket, generalized, all-inclusive, unqualified, indiscriminate, universal, oversimplified, imprecise. ❹ *sweeping banks of heather* BROAD, extensive, expansive, vast, spacious, boundless, panoramic.

– OPPOSITES limited, narrow, focused, small.

sweet ▶ **adjective** ❶ *sweet biscuits* SUGARY, sweetened, saccharine; sugared, honeyed, candied, glacé; sickly, cloying. ❷ *the sweet scent of roses* FRAGRANT, aromatic, perfumed; *poetic/literary* ambrosial. ❸ *her sweet voice* DULCET, melodious, lyrical, mellifluous, musical, tuneful, soft, harmonious, silvery, honeyed, mellow, rich, golden. ❹ *life was still sweet* PLEASANT, pleasing, agreeable, delightful, nice, satisfying, gratifying, good, acceptable, fine; *informal* lovely, great. ❺ *the sweet March air* PURE, wholesome, fresh, clean, clear. ❻ *she has a sweet nature* LIKEABLE, appealing, engaging, amiable, pleasant, agreeable, genial, friendly, nice, kind, thoughtful, considerate; charming, enchanting, captivating, delightful, lovely. ❼ *she looks quite sweet* CUTE, lovable, adorable, endearing, charming, attractive, dear. ❽ *my sweet Lydia* DEAR, dearest, darling, beloved, loved, cherished, precious, treasured.

– OPPOSITES sour, savoury, harsh, disagreeable.

▶ **noun** ❶ *sweets for the children* CONFECTIONERY, chocolate, bonbon, fondant, toffee; *N. Amer.* candy; *informal* sweetie; *archaic* sweetmeat. ❷ *a delicious sweet for the guests* DESSERT, pudding, second course, last course; *Brit. informal* afters, pud. ❸ *happy birthday my sweet!* DEAR, darling, dearest, love, sweetheart, beloved, honey, pet, treasure, angel.

■ **sweet on** (*informal*) FOND OF, taken with, attracted to, in love with, enamoured of, captivated by, infatuated with, keen on, devoted to, smitten with; *informal* gone on, mad about, bowled over by; *Brit. informal* daft about.

sweeten ▶ **verb** ❶ *sweeten the milk with honey* MAKE SWEET, add sugar to, sugar, sugar-coat. ❷ *he chewed gum to sweeten his breath* FRESHEN, refresh, purify, deodorize, perfume. ❸ *try to sweeten the bad news* SOFTEN, ease, alleviate, mitigate, temper, cushion; embellish, embroider. ❹ (*informal*) *a bigger dividend to sweeten shareholders* MOLLIFY, placate, soothe, soften up, pacify, appease, win over.

sweetheart ▶ **noun** ❶ *you look lovely, sweetheart* DARLING, dear, dearest, love, beloved, sweet; *informal* honey, sweetie, sugar, baby, babe, poppet. ❷ *my high-school sweetheart* LOVER, love, girlfriend, boyfriend, beloved, significant other, lady love, loved one, suitor, admirer; *informal* steady, flame; *poetic/literary* swain; *dated* beau; *archaic* paramour.

swell ▶ **verb** ❶ *her lip swelled up* EXPAND, bulge, distend, inflate, dilate, bloat, puff up, balloon, fatten, fill out, tumefy; *rare* intumesce. ❷ *the population swelled* GROW, enlarge, increase, expand, rise, escalate, multiply, proliferate, snowball, mushroom. ❸ *she swelled with pride* BE FILLED, be bursting, brim, overflow. ❹ *the graduate scheme swelled entry numbers* INCREASE, enlarge, augment, boost, top up, step up, multiply. ❺ *the music swelled to fill the house* GROW LOUD, grow louder, amplify, intensify, heighten.
– OPPOSITES shrink, decrease, quieten.
▶ **noun** ❶ *a brief swell in the volume* INCREASE, rise, escalation, surge, boost. ❷ *a heavy swell on the sea* SURGE, wave, undulation, roll. ❸ (*informal, dated*) *he was an elegant swell* DANDY, fop, beau, poseur; *informal* trendsetter; *Brit. informal* toff; *dated* popinjay; *archaic* coxcomb.
– OPPOSITES decrease, dip.
▶ **adjective** (*N. Amer. informal, dated*) *a swell idea* EXCELLENT, marvellous, wonderful, splendid, magnificent, superb; *informal* super, great, fantastic.
– OPPOSITES bad.

swelling ▶ **noun** BUMP, lump, bulge, protuberance, enlargement, distension, prominence, protrusion, node, nodule, tumescence; boil, blister, bunion, carbuncle.

sweltering ▶ **adjective** HOT, stifling, humid, sultry, sticky, muggy, close, stuffy; tropical, torrid, searing, blistering; *informal* boiling (hot), baking, roasting, sizzling.
– OPPOSITES freezing.

swerve ▶ **verb** *a car swerved into her path* VEER, deviate, skew, diverge, sheer, weave, zigzag, change direction; *Sailing* tack.
▶ **noun** *the bowler regulated his swerve* CURVE, curl, deviation, twist; *N. Amer.* English.

swift ▶ **adjective** ❶ *a swift decision* PROMPT, rapid, sudden, immediate, instant, instantaneous; abrupt, hasty, hurried, precipitate, headlong. ❷ *swift runners* FAST, rapid, quick, speedy, high-speed, brisk, lively; express, breakneck; fleet-footed; *informal* nippy, supersonic.
– OPPOSITES slow, leisurely.

swill ▶ **verb** ❶ (*informal*) *she was swilling pints* DRINK, quaff, swallow, down, gulp, drain, imbibe, sup, slurp, consume, slug; *informal* swig, knock back, toss off, put away; *Brit. informal* bevvy; *N. Amer. informal* chug. ❷ *he swilled out a glass* WASH, rinse, sluice, clean, flush.
▶ **noun** ❶ (*informal*) *he took a swill of coffee* GULP, swallow, drink, draught, mouthful, slug; *informal* swig. ❷ *swill for the pigs* PIGSWILL, mash, slops, scraps, refuse, scourings, leftovers; *archaic* hogwash.

swim ▶ **verb** ❶ *they swam in the pool* BATHE, take a dip, splash around; float, tread water. ❷ *his food was swimming in gravy* BE SATURATED IN, be drenched in, be soaked in, be steeped in, be immersed in, be covered in, be full of.

swimmingly ▶ **adverb** WELL, smoothly, easily, effortlessly, like clockwork, without a hitch, as planned, to plan; *informal* like a dream, like magic.

swimming pool ▶ **noun** POOL, baths, lido, piscina; *Brit.* swimming bath(s); *N. Amer.* natatorium.

swimsuit ▶ **noun** BATHING SUIT, bathing dress, (swimming) trunks, bikini; swimwear; *Brit.* bathing costume, swimming costume; *informal* cossie; *Austral./NZ informal* bathers.

swindle ▶ **verb** *I was swindled out of money* DEFRAUD, cheat, trick, dupe, deceive, fool, hoax, hoodwink, bamboozle; *informal* fleece, do, con, sting, diddle, swizzle, rip off, take for a ride, pull a fast one on, put one over on, take to the cleaners, gull; *N. Amer. informal* stiff, euchre; *poetic/literary* cozen; *archaic* sharp.
▶ **noun** *an insurance swindle* FRAUD, trick, deception, deceit, cheat, sham, artifice, ruse, dodge, racket, wile; sharp practice; *informal* con, fiddle, diddle, rip-off, flimflam, swizzle, swizz; *N. Amer. informal* bunco.

swindler ▶ **noun** FRAUDSTER, fraud, (confidence) trickster, cheat, rogue, mountebank, charlatan, impostor, hoaxer; *informal* con man, con artist, shark, sharp, hustler, phoney, crook.

swing ▶ **verb** ❶ *the sign swung in the wind* SWAY, oscillate, move back and forth, move to and fro, wave, wag, rock, flutter, flap. ❷ *Helen swung the bottle* BRANDISH, wave, flourish, wield, shake, wag, twirl. ❸ *this road swings off to the north* CURVE, bend, veer, turn, bear, wind, twist, deviate, slew, skew, drift, head. ❹ *the balance swung from one party to the other* CHANGE, fluctuate, shift, alter, oscillate, waver, alternate, see-saw, yo-yo, vary. ❺ (*informal*) *their persistence finally swung it for him* ACCOMPLISH, achieve, obtain, acquire, get, secure, net, win, attain, bag, hook; *informal* wangle, land, fix (up).
▶ **noun** ❶ *a swing of the pendulum* OSCILLATION, sway, wave. ❷ *the swing to the Conservatives* CHANGE, move; turnaround, turnabout, reversal, about turn, about face, volte face, change of heart, U-turn, sea change. ❸ *a swing towards plain food* TREND, tendency, drift, movement. ❹ *a mood swing* FLUCTUATION, change, shift, variation, oscillation.

swingeing ▶ **adjective** (*Brit.*) SEVERE, extreme, serious, substantial, drastic, harsh, punishing, excessive, heavy.
– OPPOSITES minor.

swipe (*informal*) ▶ **verb** ❶ *he swiped at her head* SWING, lash out; strike, hit, slap, cuff; *informal* belt, wallop, sock, biff, clout. ❷ *they're always* *swiping sweets* STEAL, thieve, take, pilfer, purloin, snatch, shoplift; *informal* filch, lift, snaffle, rob, nab; *Brit. informal* nick, pinch, whip; *N. Amer. informal* glom.

▶ **noun** *she took a swipe at his face* SWING, stroke, strike, hit, slap, cuff, clip; *informal* belt, wallop.

swirl ▶ **verb** WHIRL, eddy, billow, spiral, circulate, revolve, spin, twist; flow, stream, surge, seethe.

switch ▶ **noun** ❶ *the switch on top of the telephone* BUTTON, lever, control, dial. ❷ *a switch from direct to indirect taxation* CHANGE, move, shift, transition, transformation; reversal, turnaround, U-turn, changeover, transfer, conversion; substitution, exchange. ❸ *a switch of willow* BRANCH, twig, stick, rod.

▶ **verb** ❶ *he switched sides* CHANGE, shift; reverse; *informal* chop and change. ❷ *he managed to switch envelopes* EXCHANGE, swap, interchange, trade, substitute, replace, rotate.

■ **switch something on** TURN ON, put on, activate, start, set going, set in motion, operate, initiate, actuate, initialize, energize.

■ **switch something off** TURN OFF, shut off, stop, cut, halt, deactivate.

swivel ▶ **verb** TURN, rotate, revolve, pivot, swing; spin, twirl, whirl, wheel, gyrate, pirouette.

swollen ▶ **adjective** DISTENDED, expanded, enlarged, bulging, inflated, dilated, bloated, puffed up, puffy, tumescent; inflamed.

swoop ▶ **verb** ❶ *pigeons swooped down after the grain* DIVE, descend, sweep, pounce, plunge, pitch, nosedive; rush, dart, speed, zoom. ❷ *police swooped on the flat* RAID, search; pounce on, attack, assault, assail, charge; *N. Amer. informal* bust.

▶ **noun** *an early morning swoop by police* RAID; attack, assault; *N. Amer. informal* bust, takedown.

sword ▶ **noun** *a ceremonial sword* BLADE, foil, épée, cutlass, rapier, sabre, scimitar; *poetic/literary* brand.

■ **cross swords** QUARREL, disagree, dispute, wrangle, bicker, be at odds, be at loggerheads, lock horns; fight, contend; *informal* scrap.

■ **put to the sword** KILL, execute, put to death, murder, butcher, slaughter, massacre, cut down; *poetic/literary* slay.

sybarite ▶ **noun** HEDONIST, sensualist, voluptuary, libertine, pleasure-seeker, epicure, bon vivant, bon viveur.

– OPPOSITES puritan.

sybaritic ▶ **adjective** LUXURIOUS, extravagant, lavish, self-indulgent, pleasure-seeking, sensual, voluptuous, hedonistic, epicurean, lotus-eating, libertine, debauched, decadent.

– OPPOSITES ascetic.

sycophant ▶ **noun** TOADY, creep, crawler, fawner, flatterer, truckler, groveller, doormat, lickspittle, kowtower, Uriah Heep; *informal* bootlicker, yes-man.

sycophantic ▶ **adjective** OBSEQUIOUS, servile, subservient, deferential, grovelling, toadying, fawning, flattering, ingratiating, cringing, unctuous, slavish; *informal* smarmy, bootlicking.

syllabus ▶ **noun** CURRICULUM, course (of study), programme of study, course outline; timetable, schedule.

symbol ▶ **noun** ❶ *the lotus is the symbol of purity* EMBLEM, token, sign, representation, figure, image; metaphor, allegory. ❷ *the chemical symbol for helium* SIGN, character, mark, letter, ideogram. ❸ *the Red Cross symbol* LOGO, emblem, badge, stamp, trademark, crest, insignia, coat of arms, seal, device, monogram, hallmark, flag, motif.

symbolic ▶ **adjective** ❶ *the Colosseum is symbolic of the Roman Empire* EMBLEMATIC, representative, typical, characteristic, symptomatic. ❷ *symbolic language* FIGURATIVE, representative, illustrative, emblematic, metaphorical, allegorical, parabolic, allusive, suggestive; meaningful, significant.

– OPPOSITES literal.

symbolize ▶ **verb** REPRESENT, stand for, be a sign of, exemplify; denote, signify, mean, indicate, convey, express, imply, suggest, allude to; embody, epitomize, encapsulate, personify, typify; *poetic/literary* betoken.

symmetrical ▶ **adjective** REGULAR, uniform, consistent; evenly shaped, aligned, equal; mirror-image; balanced, proportional, regular, even.

symmetry ▶ **noun** REGULARITY, evenness, uniformity, consistency, conformity, correspondence, equality; balance, proportions; *formal* concord.

sympathetic ▶ **adjective** ❶ *a sympathetic listener* COMPASSIONATE, caring, concerned, solicitous, empathetic, understanding, sensitive; commiserative, pitying, consoling, comforting, supportive, encouraging; considerate, kind, tender-hearted. ❷ *the most sympathetic character in the book* LIKEABLE, pleasant, agreeable, congenial, friendly, genial. ❸ *I was sympathetic to his cause* IN FAVOUR OF, in sympathy with, pro, on the side of, supportive of, encouraging of; well disposed to, favourably disposed to, receptive to.

– OPPOSITES unfeeling, opposed.

sympathize ▶ **verb** ❶ *he sympathized with his wife* PITY, feel sorry for, show compassion for, commiserate, offer condolences to, feel for, show concern, show interest; console, comfort, solace, soothe, support, encourage; empathize with, identify with, understand, relate to. ❷ *they sympathize with the critique* AGREE WITH, support, be in favour of, go along with, favour, approve of, back, side with.

sympathizer ▶ **noun** SUPPORTER, backer,

well-wisher, advocate, ally, partisan; collaborator, fraternizer, conspirator, quisling.

sympathy ▶ noun ❶ *he shows sympathy for the poor* COMPASSION, caring, concern, solicitude, empathy; commiseration, pity, condolence, comfort, solace, support, encouragement; consideration, kindness. ❷ *sympathy with a fellow journalist* RAPPORT, fellow feeling, affinity, empathy, harmony, accord, compatibility; fellowship, camaraderie. ❸ *their sympathy with the Republicans* AGREEMENT, favour, approval, approbation, support, encouragement, partiality; association, alignment, affiliation.
– OPPOSITES indifference, hostility.

symptom ▶ noun ❶ *the symptoms of the disease* MANIFESTATION, indication, indicator, sign, mark, feature, trait; *Medicine* prodrome. ❷ *a symptom of the country's present turmoil* EXPRESSION, sign, indication, mark, token, manifestation; portent, warning, clue, hint; testimony, evidence, proof.

symptomatic ▶ adjective INDICATIVE, characteristic, suggestive, typical, representative, symbolic.

synopsis ▶ noun SUMMARY, summarization, precis, abstract, outline, digest, rundown, round-up, abridgement.

synthesis ▶ noun COMBINATION, union, amalgam, blend, mixture, compound, fusion, composite, alloy; unification, amalgamation, marrying.

synthetic ▶ adjective ARTIFICIAL, fake, imitation, mock, simulated, ersatz, substitute; pseudo, so-called; man-made, manufactured, fabricated; *informal* phoney, pretend.
– OPPOSITES natural.

syrupy ▶ adjective ❶ *syrupy medicine* OVERSWEET, sweet, sugary, treacly, honeyed, saccharine; thick, sticky, gluey, viscid, glutinous; *informal* gooey. ❷ *syrupy romantic drivel* SENTIMENTAL, mawkish, cloying, sickly, saccharine, trite; *informal* soppy, schmaltzy, mushy, slushy, sloppy, lovey-dovey, cheesy, corny.

system ▶ noun ❶ *a system of canals* STRUCTURE, organization, arrangement, complex, network; *informal* set-up. ❷ *a system for regulating sales* METHOD, methodology, technique, process, procedure, approach, practice; means, way, mode, framework, modus operandi; scheme, plan, policy, programme, regimen, formula, routine. ❸ *there was no system in his work* ORDER, method, orderliness, systematization, planning, logic, routine. ❹ *youngsters have no faith in the system* THE ESTABLISHMENT, the administration, the authorities, the powers that be; bureaucracy, officialdom; the status quo.

systematic ▶ adjective STRUCTURED, methodical, organized, orderly, planned, systematized, regular, routine, standardized, standard; logical, coherent, consistent; efficient, businesslike, practical.
– OPPOSITES disorganized.

Tt

tab ▶ noun ❶ *his name is on the tab of his jacket* TAG, label, flap. ❷ (*informal*) *the company will pick up the tab* BILL, invoice, account, charge, expense, cost; *N. Amer.* check.

table ▶ noun ❶ *put the plates on the table* bench, buffet, stand, counter, work surface, worktop; desk, bar. ❷ *he provides an excellent table* MEAL, food, fare, menu, nourishment; eatables, provisions; *informal* spread, grub, chow, eats, nosh; *poetic/literary* viands; *dated* victuals. ❸ *the report has numerous tables* CHART, diagram, figure, graph, plan; list, tabulation, index.
▶ verb *she tabled a question in parliament* SUBMIT, put forward, propose, suggest, move, lodge, file, introduce, air, moot.

tableau ▶ noun ❶ *mythic tableaux* PICTURE, painting, representation, illustration, image. ❷ *the first act consists of a series of tableaux* PAGEANT, tableau vivant, parade, diorama, scene. ❸ *a domestic tableau around the fireplace* SCENE, arrangement, grouping, group; picture, spectacle, image, vignette.

tablet ▶ noun ❶ *a carved tablet* SLAB, stone, panel, plaque, plate, sign. ❷ *a headache tablet* PILL, capsule, lozenge, caplet, pastille, drop, pilule; *informal* tab. ❸ *a tablet of soap* BAR, cake, slab, brick, block, chunk, piece.

taboo ▶ noun *the taboo against healing on the sabbath* PROHIBITION, proscription, veto, interdiction, interdict, ban, restriction.
▶ adjective *taboo language* FORBIDDEN, prohibited, banned, proscribed, interdicted, non licet, outlawed, illegal, illicit, unlawful, restricted, off limits; unmentionable, unspeakable, unutterable, ineffable; rude, impolite; *Islam* haram; *NZ* tapu; *informal* no go.
– OPPOSITES acceptable.

tabulate ▶ **verb** CHART, arrange, order, organize, systematize, systemize, catalogue, list, index, classify, class, codify; compile, group, log, grade, rate.

tacit ▶ **adjective** IMPLICIT, understood, implied, inferred, hinted, suggested; unspoken, unstated, unsaid, unexpressed, unvoiced; taken for granted, taken as read.
– OPPOSITES explicit.

taciturn ▶ **adjective** UNTALKATIVE, uncommunicative, reticent, unforthcoming, quiet, secretive, tight-lipped, close-mouthed; silent, mute, dumb, inarticulate; reserved, withdrawn.
– OPPOSITES talkative.

tack ▶ **noun** ❶ *tacks held the carpet down* PIN, drawing pin, nail, staple, rivet, stud. ❷ *the brig bowled past on the opposite tack* HEADING, bearing, course, track, path, line. ❸ *the defender changed his tack* APPROACH, way, method; policy, procedure, technique, tactic, plan, strategy, stratagem; path, line, angle, direction, course.
▶ **verb** ❶ *a photo tacked to the wall* PIN, nail, staple, fix, fasten, attach, secure, affix. ❷ *the dress was roughly tacked together* STITCH, baste, sew, bind. ❸ *the yachts tacked back and forth* CHANGE COURSE, change direction, swerve, zigzag, veer; *Nautical* go/come about, beat. ❹ *poems tacked on at the end of the book* ADD, append, join, tag.

tackle ▶ **noun** ❶ *fishing tackle* GEAR, equipment, apparatus, kit, hardware; implements, instruments, accoutrements, paraphernalia, trappings, appurtenances; *informal* things, stuff, clobber, bits and pieces; *archaic* equipage. ❷ *lifting tackle* PULLEYS, gear, hoist, crane, winch, davit, windlass, sheave. ❸ *a tackle by the scrum half* INTERCEPTION, challenge, block, attack.
▶ **verb** ❶ *we must tackle environmental problems* GET TO GRIPS WITH, address, get to work on, set one's hand to, approach, take on, attend to, see to, try to sort out; deal with, take care of, handle, manage; *informal* get stuck into, have a crack at, have a go at. ❷ *I tackled Nina about it* CONFRONT, speak to, interview, question, cross-examine; accost, waylay; remonstrate with. ❸ *he tackled a masked intruder* CONFRONT, face up to, take on, contend with, challenge; seize, grab, grapple with, intercept, block, stop; bring down, floor, fell; *informal* have a go at. ❹ *the winger got tackled* INTERCEPT, challenge, block, stop, attack.

tacky[1] ▶ **adjective** *the paint was still tacky* STICKY, wet, gluey, gummy, adhesive, viscous, viscid, treacly; *informal* gooey.

tacky[2] ▶ **adjective** *a tacky game show* TAWDRY, tasteless, kitsch, vulgar, crude, garish, gaudy, showy, trashy, cheap, common, second-rate; *Brit. informal* naff.
– OPPOSITES tasteful.

tact ▶ **noun** DIPLOMACY, tactfulness, sensitivity, understanding, thoughtfulness, consideration, delicacy, discretion, prudence, judiciousness, subtlety, savoir faire; *informal* savvy.

tactful ▶ **adjective** DIPLOMATIC, discreet, considerate, sensitive, understanding, thoughtful, delicate, judicious, politic, perceptive, subtle; courteous, polite, decorous, respectful; *informal* savvy.

tactic ▶ **noun** ❶ *a tax-saving tactic* STRATEGY, scheme, stratagem, plan, manoeuvre; method, expedient, gambit, move, approach, tack; device, trick, ploy, dodge, ruse, machination, contrivance; *informal* wangle; *archaic* shift. ❷ *our fleet's superior tactics* STRATEGY, policy, campaign, battle plans, game plans, manoeuvres, logistics; generalship, organization, planning, direction, orchestration.

tactical ▶ **adjective** CALCULATED, planned, strategic; prudent, politic, diplomatic, judicious, shrewd, cunning, artful.

tactless ▶ **adjective** INSENSITIVE, inconsiderate, thoughtless, indelicate, undiplomatic, impolitic, indiscreet, unsubtle, clumsy, heavy-handed, graceless, awkward, inept, gauche; blunt, frank, outspoken, abrupt, gruff, rough, crude, coarse; imprudent, injudicious, unwise; rude, impolite, uncouth, discourteous, crass, tasteless, disrespectful, boorish.

tag ▶ **noun** ❶ *a price tag* LABEL, ticket, badge, mark, marker, tab, sticker, docket, stub, counterfoil, flag. ❷ *his jacket was hung up by its tag* TAB, loop, label. ❸ *he gained a 'bad boy' tag* DESIGNATION, label, description, characterization, identity; nickname, name, epithet, title, sobriquet; *informal* handle, moniker; *formal* denomination, appellation. ❹ *tags from Shakespeare* QUOTATION, quote, phrase, platitude, cliché, excerpt; saying, proverb, maxim, adage, aphorism, motto, epigram; slogan, catchphrase.
▶ **verb** ❶ *bottles tagged with coloured stickers* LABEL, mark, ticket, identify, flag, indicate. ❷ *he is tagged as a 'thinking' actor* LABEL, class, categorize, characterize, designate, describe, identify, classify; mark, stamp, brand, pigeonhole, stereotype, typecast, compartmentalize, typify; name, call, title, entitle, dub, term, style. ❸ *a poem tagged on as an afterthought* ADD, tack, join; attach, append. ❹ *he was tagging along behind her* FOLLOW, trail; come after, go after, shadow, dog; accompany, attend, escort; *informal* tail.

tail ▶ **noun** ❶ *the dog's tail* brush, scut, dock; tailpiece, tail feathers; hindquarters. ❷ *the tail of the queue* REAR, end, back, extremity; bottom; *Brit. informal* fag end. ❸ *the tail of the hunting season* CLOSE, end, conclusion, tail end. ❹ (*informal*) *put a tail on that man* DETECTIVE, investigator, shadow; *informal* sleuth, private eye, tec; *N. Amer. informal* gumshoe.
– RELATED TERMS caudal, cercal.
– OPPOSITES head, front, start.

▶ **verb** (*informal*) *the paparazzi tailed them* FOLLOW, shadow, stalk, trail, track, hunt, hound, dog, pursue, chase.

■ **on someone's tail** CLOSE BEHIND, following closely, (hard) on someone's heels.

■ **tail off/away** FADE, wane, ebb, dwindle, decrease, lessen, diminish, decline, subside, abate, drop off, peter out, taper off; let up, ease off, die away, die down, come to an end.

■ **turn tail** RUN AWAY, flee, bolt, make off, take to one's heels, cut and run, beat a (hasty) retreat; *informal* scram, scarper, skedaddle, vamoose.

tailback ▶ **noun** TRAFFIC JAM, queue, line; congestion.

tailor ▶ **noun** OUTFITTER, dressmaker, couturier, (fashion) designer; clothier, costumier, seamstress; *dated* modiste.

– RELATED TERMS sartorial.

▶ **verb** *services can be tailored to customer requirements* CUSTOMIZE, adapt, adjust, modify, change, convert, alter, attune, mould, gear, fit, cut, shape, tune.

taint ▶ **noun** *the taint of corruption* TRACE, touch, suggestion, hint, tinge; stain, blot, blemish, stigma, black mark, blot on one's escutcheon; discredit, dishonour, disgrace, shame.

▶ **verb** ❶ *the wilderness is tainted by pollution* CONTAMINATE, pollute, adulterate, infect, blight, spoil, soil, ruin, destroy; *poetic/literary* befoul. ❷ *fraudulent firms taint our firm's reputation* TARNISH, sully, blacken, stain, blot, blemish, stigmatize, mar, corrupt, defile, soil, muddy, damage, harm, hurt; drag through the mud; *poetic/literary* besmirch.

– OPPOSITES clean, improve.

take ▶ **verb** ❶ *she took his hand* LAY HOLD OF, get hold of; grasp, grip, clasp, clutch, grab. ❷ *he took an envelope from his pocket* REMOVE, pull, draw, withdraw, extract, fish. ❸ *a passage taken from my book* EXTRACT, quote, cite, excerpt, derive, abstract, copy, cull. ❹ *she took a little wine* DRINK, imbibe; consume, swallow, eat, ingest. ❺ *many prisoners were taken* CAPTURE, seize, catch, arrest, apprehend, take into custody; carry off, abduct. ❻ *someone's taken my car* STEAL, remove, appropriate, make off with, pilfer, purloin; *informal* filch, swipe, snaffle; *Brit. informal* pinch, nick. ❼ *take four from the total* SUBTRACT, deduct, remove; discount; *informal* knock off, minus. ❽ *all the seats had been taken* OCCUPY, use, utilize, fill, hold; reserve, engage; *informal* bag. ❾ *I have taken a room nearby* RENT, lease, hire, charter; reserve, book, engage. ❿ *I took the job* ACCEPT, undertake. ⓫ *I'd take this over the other option* PICK, choose, select; prefer, favour, opt for, plump for, vote for. ⓬ *take, for instance, the English* CONSIDER, contemplate, ponder, think about, weigh up, mull over, examine, study, meditate over, ruminate about. ⓭ *he takes 'The Observer'* SUBSCRIBE TO, buy, read. ⓮ *she took his temperature* ASCERTAIN, determine, establish, measure, find out, discover; calculate, compute, evaluate, rate, assess, appraise, gauge. ⓯ *he took notes* WRITE, note (down), jot (down), scribble, scrawl, record, register, document, minute. ⓰ *I took it back to London* BRING, carry, bear, transport, convey, move, transfer, shift, ferry; *informal* cart, tote. ⓱ *the priest took her home* ESCORT, accompany, help, assist, show, lead, guide, see, usher, convey. ⓲ *he took the train* TRAVEL ON/BY, journey on, go via; use. ⓳ *the town takes its name from the lake* DERIVE, get, obtain, come by, acquire, pick up. ⓴ *she took the prize for best speaker* RECEIVE, obtain, gain, get, acquire, collect, accept, be awarded; secure, come by, win, earn, pick up, carry off; *informal* land, bag, net, scoop. ㉑ *I took the chance to postpone it* ACT ON, take advantage of, capitalize on, use, exploit, make the most of, leap at, jump at, pounce on, seize, grasp, grab, accept. ㉒ *he took great pleasure in painting* DERIVE, draw, acquire, obtain, get, gain, extract, procure; experience, undergo, feel. ㉓ *Liz took the news badly* RECEIVE, respond to, react to, meet, greet; deal with, cope with. ㉔ *do you take me for a fool?* REGARD AS, consider to be, view as, see as, believe to be, reckon to be, imagine to be, deem to be. ㉕ *I take it that you are hungry* ASSUME, presume, suppose, imagine, expect, reckon, gather, dare say, trust, surmise, deduce, guess, conjecture, fancy, suspect. ㉖ *I take your point* UNDERSTAND, grasp, get, comprehend, apprehend, see, follow; accept, appreciate, acknowledge, sympathize with, agree with. ㉗ *Shirley was rather taken with him* CAPTIVATE, enchant, charm, delight, attract, beguile, enthral, entrance, infatuate, dazzle; amuse, divert, entertain; *informal* tickle someone's fancy. ㉘ *I can't take much more* ENDURE, bear, tolerate, stand, put up with, abide, stomach, accept, allow, countenance, support, shoulder; *formal* brook; *archaic* suffer. ㉙ *applicants must take a test* CARRY OUT, do, complete, conduct, perform, execute, discharge, accomplish, fulfil. ㉚ *I took English and French* STUDY, learn, have lessons in; take up, pursue; *Brit.* read; *informal* do. ㉛ *the journey took six hours* LAST, continue for, go on for, carry on for; require, call for, need, necessitate, entail, involve. ㉜ *it would take an expert to know that* REQUIRE, need, necessitate, demand, call for, entail, involve. ㉝ *I take size three shoes* WEAR, use; require, need. ㉞ *the dye did not take* BE EFFECTIVE, take effect, hold, root, be productive, be effectual, be useful; work, operate, succeed, function; *formal* be efficacious.

– OPPOSITES give, free, add, refuse, miss.

▶ **noun** ❶ *the whalers' commercial take* CATCH, haul, bag, yield, net. ❷ *the state's tax take* REVENUE, income, gain, profit; takings, proceeds, returns, receipts, winnings, pickings, earnings, spoils; purse. ❸ *a clapperboard for the start of each take* SCENE, sequence, (film) clip. ❹ *a wry* *take on gender issues* VIEW OF, reading of, version of, interpretation of, understanding of, account of, analysis of, approach to.

■ **take after** RESEMBLE, look like; remind one of, make one think of, recall, conjure up, suggest, evoke; *informal* favour, be a chip off the old block, be the spitting image of.

■ **take against** TAKE A DISLIKE TO, feel hostile towards, view with disfavour, look askance at.

■ **take something apart** ❶ *we took the machine apart* DISMANTLE, pull to pieces, pull apart, disassemble, break up; tear down, demolish, destroy, wreck. ❷ (*informal*) *the scene was taken apart by the director. See* CRITICIZE.

■ **take someone back** ❶ *the dream took me back to Vienna* EVOKE, remind one of, conjure up, summon up; echo, suggest. ❷ *I will never take that girl back* BE RECONCILED TO, forgive, pardon, excuse, exonerate, absolve; let bygones be bygones, bury the hatchet.

■ **take something back** ❶ *I take back every word* RETRACT, withdraw, renounce, disclaim, unsay, disavow, recant, repudiate; *formal* abjure. ❷ *I must take the keys back* RETURN, bring back, give back, restore.

■ **take something down** WRITE DOWN, note down, jot down, set down, record, commit to paper, register, draft, document, minute, pen.

■ **take someone in** ❶ *she took in paying guests* ACCOMMODATE, board, house, feed, put up, admit, receive; harbour. ❷ *you were taken in by a hoax* DECEIVE, delude, hoodwink, mislead, trick, dupe, fool, cheat, defraud, swindle, outwit, gull, hoax, bamboozle; *informal* con, put one over on.

■ **take something in** ❶ *she could hardly take in the news* COMPREHEND, understand, grasp, follow, absorb; *informal* get. ❷ *this route takes in some great scenery* INCLUDE, encompass, embrace, contain, comprise, cover, incorporate, comprehend, hold.

■ **take someone in hand** CONTROL, be in charge of, dominate, master; reform, improve, correct, change, rehabilitate.

■ **take something in hand** DEAL WITH, apply oneself to, get to grips with, set one's hand to, grapple with, take on, attend to, see to, sort out, take care of, handle, manage; *informal* get stuck into.

■ **take it out of someone** EXHAUST, drain, enervate, tire, fatigue, wear out, weary, debilitate; *informal* knacker, poop.

■ **take off** ❶ *the horse took off at great speed* RUN AWAY/OFF, flee, abscond, take flight, decamp, leave, go, depart, make off, bolt, take to one's heels, escape; *informal* split, clear off, skedaddle, vamoose. ❷ *the plane took off* BECOME AIRBORNE, take to the air, take wing; lift off, blast off. ❸ *the idea really took off* SUCCEED, do well, become popular, catch on, prosper, flourish, thrive, boom.

■ **take someone off** MIMIC, impersonate, imitate, ape, parody, mock, caricature, satirize, burlesque, lampoon, ridicule; *informal* spoof, send up.

■ **take oneself off** WITHDRAW, retire, leave, exit, depart, go away, quit; *informal* clear off.

■ **take on** (*Brit. informal*) *don't take on so!* GET UPSET, make a fuss, get excited, overreact; *informal* lose one's cool.

■ **take someone on** ❶ *there was no challenger to take him on* COMPETE AGAINST, oppose, challenge, confront, face, fight, vie with, contend with, stand up to. ❷ *we took on extra staff* ENGAGE, hire, employ, enrol, enlist, sign up; *informal* take on board.

■ **take something on** ❶ *he took on more responsibility* UNDERTAKE, accept, assume, shoulder, acquire, carry, bear. ❷ *the study took on political meaning* ACQUIRE, assume, come to have.

■ **take one's time** GO SLOWLY, dally, dawdle, delay, linger, drag one's feet, waste time, kill time; *informal* dilly-dally; *archaic* tarry.

■ **take someone out** ❶ *he asked if he could take her out* GO OUT WITH, escort, partner, accompany, go with; romance, woo; *informal* date, see, go steady with; *dated* court. ❷ (*informal*) *the sniper took them all out* KILL, murder, assassinate, dispatch, execute, finish off, eliminate, exterminate, terminate; *informal* do in, do away with, bump off, rub out, mow down, top; *poetic/literary* slay.

■ **take something over** ASSUME CONTROL OF, take charge of, take command of.

■ **take to** ❶ *he took to carrying his money in his sock* MAKE A HABIT OF, resort to, turn to, have recourse to; start, commence. ❷ *Ruth took to him instantly* LIKE, get on with, be friendly towards; *informal* take a shine to. ❸ *the dog has really taken to racing* BECOME GOOD AT, develop an ability for; like, enjoy.

■ **take something up** ❶ *he took up abstract painting* ENGAGE IN, practise; begin, start, commence. ❷ *the meetings took up all her time* CONSUME, fill, absorb, use, occupy; waste, squander. ❸ *her cousin took up the story* RESUME, recommence, restart, carry on, continue, pick up, return to. ❹ *he took up their offer of a job* ACCEPT, say yes to, agree to, adopt; *formal* accede to. ❺ *take the skirt up an inch* SHORTEN, turn up; raise, lift.

■ **take up with** BECOME FRIENDS WITH, go around with, fall in with, string along with, get involved with, start seeing; *informal* knock around with, hang out with.

take-off ▶ **noun** ❶ *the plane crashed on take-off* DEPARTURE, lift-off, launch, blast-off; ascent, flight. ❷ (*informal*) *a take-off of a talent show* PARODY, pastiche, mockery, caricature, travesty, satire, lampoon, mimicry, imitation, impersonation, impression; *informal* send-up, spoof.
– OPPOSITES touchdown.

takeover ▶ **noun** BUYOUT, merger, amalgamation; purchase, acquisition.

taking ▶ **adjective** (*dated*). *See* WINNING sense 2.

takings ▶ plural noun PROCEEDS, returns, receipts, earnings, winnings, pickings, spoils; profit, gain, income, revenue; gate, purse.

tale ▶ noun ❶ *a tale of witches* STORY, narrative, anecdote, report, account, history; legend, fable, myth, parable, allegory, saga; *informal* yarn. ❷ *she told tales to her mother* LIE, fib, falsehood, story, untruth, fabrication, fiction; *informal* tall story, fairy story/tale, cock-and-bull story.

talent ▶ noun FLAIR, aptitude, facility, gift, knack, technique, touch, bent, ability, expertise, capacity, faculty; strength, forte, genius, brilliance; dexterity, skill, artistry.

talented ▶ adjective GIFTED, skilful, skilled, accomplished, brilliant, expert, consummate, masterly, adroit, dexterous, able, competent, capable, apt, deft, adept, proficient; *informal* crack, ace.
– OPPOSITES inept.

talisman ▶ noun (LUCKY) CHARM, fetish, amulet, mascot, totem, juju.

talk ▶ verb ❶ *I was talking to a friend* SPEAK, chat, chatter, gossip, prattle, babble, rattle on, blather; *informal* yak, gab, jaw, chew the fat; *Brit. informal* natter, rabbit, witter, chunter; *N. Amer. informal* rap; *Austral./NZ informal* mag. ❷ *you're talking rubbish* UTTER, speak, say, voice, express, articulate, pronounce, verbalize, vocalize. ❸ *they were able to talk in peace* CONVERSE, communicate, speak, confer, consult; negotiate, parley; *informal* have a confab, chew the fat/rag, rap; *formal* confabulate. ❹ *he talked of suicide* MENTION, refer to, speak about, discuss. ❺ *I was able to talk English* SPEAK (IN), talk in, communicate in, converse in, express oneself in; use. ❻ *nothing would make her talk* CONFESS, speak out/up, reveal all, tell tales, give the game away, open one's mouth; *informal* come clean, blab, squeal, let the cat out of the bag, spill the beans, grass, sing, rat. ❼ *the others will talk* GOSSIP, pass comment, make remarks; criticize.
▶ noun ❶ *he was bored with all this talk* CHATTER, gossip, prattle, jabbering, babbling, gabbling; *informal* yakking, gabbing; *Brit. informal* nattering, rabbit. ❷ *she needed a talk with Vi* CONVERSATION, chat, discussion, tête-à-tête, heart-to-heart, dialogue, parley, powwow, consultation, conference, meeting; *informal* confab, jaw, chitchat, gossip; *formal* colloquy, confabulation. ❸ *peace talks* NEGOTIATIONS, discussions; conference, summit, meeting, consultation, dialogue, symposium, seminar, conclave, parley; mediation, arbitration; *informal* powwow. ❹ *she gave a talk on her travels* LECTURE, speech, address, discourse, oration, presentation, report, sermon; *informal* spiel. ❺ *there was talk of a takeover* GOSSIP, rumour, hearsay, tittle-tattle; news, report. ❻ *baby talk* SPEECH, language, slang, idiom, idiolect; words; *informal* lingo.
■ **talk back** ANSWER BACK, be impertinent, be cheeky, be rude; contradict, argue with, disagree with.
■ **talk big** (*informal*). *See* BOAST verb sense 1.
■ **talk something down** DENIGRATE, deprecate, disparage, belittle, diminish, criticize; *informal* knock, put down.
■ **talk down to** CONDESCEND TO, patronize, look down one's nose at, put down.
■ **talk someone into something** PERSUADE INTO, argue into, cajole into, coax into, bring round to, inveigle into, wheedle into, sweet-talk into, prevail on someone to; *informal* hustle, fast-talk.

talkative ▶ adjective CHATTY, loquacious, garrulous, voluble, conversational, communicative; gossipy, babbling, blathering; long-winded, wordy, verbose; *informal* gabby, mouthy.
– OPPOSITES taciturn.

talker ▶ noun CONVERSATIONALIST, speaker, communicator; chatterbox, gossip.

talking-to ▶ noun (*informal*). *See* REPRIMAND noun.

tall ▶ adjective ❶ *a tall man* BIG, large, huge, towering, colossal, gigantic, giant, monstrous; leggy; *informal* long. ❷ *tall buildings* HIGH, big, lofty, towering, elevated, sky-high; multistorey. ❸ *she's five feet tall* IN HEIGHT, high, from head to toe; from top to bottom. ❹ *a tall tale* UNLIKELY, improbable, exaggerated, far-fetched, implausible, dubious, unbelievable, incredible, absurd, untrue; *informal* cock-and-bull. ❺ *a tall order* DEMANDING, exacting, difficult; unreasonable, impossible.
– OPPOSITES short, low, wide, credible, easy.

tally ▶ noun ❶ *he keeps a tally of the score* RUNNING TOTAL, count, record, reckoning, register, account, roll; census, poll. ❷ *his tally of 1,816 wickets* TOTAL, score, count, sum.
▶ verb ❶ *these statistics tally with government figures* CORRESPOND, agree, accord, concur, coincide, match, fit, be consistent, conform, equate, harmonize, be in tune, dovetail, correlate, parallel; *informal* square; *N. Amer. informal* jibe. ❷ *votes were tallied with abacuses* COUNT, calculate, add up, total, compute; figure out, work out, reckon, measure, quantify; *Brit.* tot up; *formal* enumerate.
– OPPOSITES disagree.

tame ▶ adjective ❶ *a tame elephant* DOMESTICATED, domestic, docile, tamed, broken, trained; gentle, mild; pet; *Brit.* house-trained; *N. Amer.* housebroken. ❷ (*informal*) *he has a tame lawyer* AMENABLE, biddable, cooperative, willing, obedient, tractable, acquiescent, docile, submissive, compliant, meek. ❸ *it was a pretty tame affair* UNEXCITING, uninteresting, uninspiring, dull, bland, flat, insipid, spiritless, pedestrian, colourless, run-of-the-mill, mediocre, ordinary, humdrum, boring; harmless, safe, inoffensive.
– OPPOSITES wild, uncooperative, exciting.

▶ **verb** ❶ *wild rabbits can be tamed* DOMESTICATE, break, train, master, subdue. ❷ *she learned to tame her emotions* SUBDUE, curb, control, calm, master, moderate, overcome, discipline, suppress, repress, mellow, temper, soften, bridle, get a grip on; *informal* lick.

tamper ▶ **verb** ❶ *she saw them tampering with her car* INTERFERE, monkey around, meddle, tinker, fiddle, fool around, play around; doctor, alter, change, adjust, damage, deface, vandalize; *informal* mess about/around; *Brit. informal* muck about/around. ❷ *the defendant tampered with the jury* INFLUENCE, get at, rig, manipulate, bribe, corrupt, bias; *informal* fix; *Brit. informal* nobble.

tan ▶ **adjective** *a tan waistcoat* YELLOWISH-BROWN, light brown, pale brown, tawny.

▶ **verb** ❶ *use a sunscreen to help you tan* BECOME SUNTANNED, get a suntan, (go) brown, bronze. ❷ (*informal*) *I'll tan his hide. See* THRASH sense 1.

tang ▶ **noun** FLAVOUR, taste, savour; sharpness, zest, bite, edge, smack, piquancy, spice; smell, odour, aroma, fragrance, perfume, redolence; *informal* kick, pep.

tangible ▶ **adjective** TOUCHABLE, palpable, material, physical, real, substantial, corporeal, solid, concrete; visible, noticeable; actual, definite, clear, clear-cut, distinct, manifest, evident, unmistakable, perceptible, discernible.
– OPPOSITES abstract.

tangle ▶ **verb** ❶ *the wool got tangled up* ENTANGLE, snarl, catch, entwine, twist, ravel, knot, enmesh, coil, mat, jumble, muddle. ❷ *he tangled with his old rival* COME INTO CONFLICT, dispute, argue, quarrel, fight, wrangle, squabble, contend, cross swords, lock horns.

▶ **noun** ❶ *a tangle of branches* SNARL, mass, knot, mesh, mishmash. ❷ *the defence got into an awful tangle* MUDDLE, jumble, mix-up, confusion, shambles.

tangled ▶ **adjective** ❶ *tangled hair* KNOTTED, knotty, ravelled, entangled, snarled (up), twisted, matted, tangly, messy; tousled, unkempt, ratty; *informal* mussed up. ❷ *a tangled bureaucratic mess* CONFUSED, jumbled, mixed up, messy, chaotic, complicated, involved, complex, intricate, knotty, tortuous.
– OPPOSITES simple.

tangy ▶ **adjective** ZESTY, sharp, acid, acidic, tart, sour, bitter, piquant, spicy, tasty, flavoursome, pungent.
– OPPOSITES bland.

tank ▶ **noun** ❶ *a hot water tank* CONTAINER, receptacle, vat, cistern, repository, reservoir, basin. ❷ *a tank full of fish* AQUARIUM, bowl. ❸ *the army's use of tanks* ARMOURED VEHICLE, armoured car, combat vehicle; Panzer.

tantalize ▶ **verb** TEASE, torment, torture, bait; tempt, entice, lure, allure, beguile; excite, fascinate, titillate, intrigue.

tantamount ▶ **adjective** *this is tantamount to mutiny* EQUIVALENT TO, equal to, as good as, more or less, much the same as, comparable to, on a par with, commensurate with.

tantrum ▶ **noun** FIT OF TEMPER, fit of rage, fit, outburst, pet, paroxysm, frenzy, (bad) mood, huff, scene; *informal* paddy, wax, wobbly; *Brit. informal, dated* bate; *N. Amer. informal* hissy fit.

tap[1] ▶ **noun** ❶ *she turned the tap on* VALVE, stopcock, cock, spout; *N. Amer.* faucet, spigot, spile. ❷ *a phone tap in the embassy* LISTENING DEVICE, wiretap, wire, bug, bugging device, microphone, receiver.

▶ **verb** ❶ *several barrels were tapped* DRAIN, bleed, milk; broach, open. ❷ *butlers were tapping ale* POUR (OUT), draw off, siphon off, pump out, decant. ❸ *their telephones were tapped* BUG, wiretap, monitor, overhear, eavesdrop on, spy on. ❹ *the resources were to be tapped for our benefit* DRAW ON, exploit, milk, mine, use, utilize, turn to account.

■ **on tap** ❶ *beers on tap* ON DRAUGHT, cask-conditioned, real-ale, from barrels. ❷ (*informal*) *trained staff are on tap* ON HAND, at hand, available, ready, handy, accessible, standing by.

tap[2] ▶ **verb** ❶ *she tapped on the door* KNOCK, rap, strike, beat, drum. ❷ *Dad tapped me on the knee* PAT, hit, strike, slap, jab, poke, dig.

▶ **noun** ❶ *a sharp tap at the door* KNOCK, rap, drumming. ❷ *a tap on the shoulder* PAT, blow, slap, jab, poke, dig.

tape ▶ **noun** ❶ *a package tied with tape* BINDING, ribbon, string, braid. ❷ *secure the bandage with tape* ADHESIVE TAPE, sticky tape, masking tape; *trademark* Sellotape. ❸ *they listened to tapes* (AUDIO) CASSETTE, (tape) recording, audio tape, reel, spool; video.

▶ **verb** ❶ *a card was taped to the box* BIND, stick, fix, fasten, secure, attach; tie, strap. ❷ *they taped off the area* CORDON, seal, close, shut, mark, fence; isolate, segregate. ❸ *police taped his confession* RECORD, tape-record; video.

taper ▶ **verb** ❶ *the leaves taper at the tip* NARROW, thin (out), come to a point, attenuate. ❷ *the meetings soon tapered off* DECREASE, lessen, dwindle, diminish, reduce, decline, die down, peter out, wane, ebb, slacken (off), fall off, let up, thin out.
– OPPOSITES thicken, increase.

▶ **noun** *a lighted taper* CANDLE, spill, sconce; *historical* rushlight.

tardy ▶ **adjective** LATE, unpunctual, behind schedule, running late; behind, overdue, belated, delayed; slow, dilatory.
– OPPOSITES punctual.

target ▶ **noun** ❶ *targets at a range of 200 yards* MARK, bullseye, goal. ❷ *eagles can spot their targets from half a mile* PREY, quarry, game, kill. ❸ *their profit target* OBJECTIVE, goal, aim, end; plan, intention, intent, design, aspiration, ambition, ideal, desire, wish. ❹ *she was the target* *for a wave of abuse* VICTIM, butt, recipient, focus, object, subject.

▶ **verb** ❶ *he was targeted by a gunman* PICK OUT, single out, earmark, fix on; attack, aim at, fire at. ❷ *the product is targeted at a specific market* AIM, direct, level, intend, focus.

■ **on target** ❶ *the striker was bang on target* ACCURATE, precise, unerring, sure, on the mark; *Brit. informal* spot on. ❷ *the project was on target* ON SCHEDULE, on track, on course, on time.

tariff ▶ **noun** TAX, duty, toll, excise, levy, charge, rate, fee; price list.

tarnish ▶ **verb** ❶ *gold does not tarnish easily* DISCOLOUR, rust, oxidize, corrode, stain, dull, blacken. ❷ *it tarnished his reputation* SULLY, blacken, stain, blemish, blot, taint, soil, ruin, disgrace, mar, damage, harm, hurt, undermine, dishonour, stigmatize; *poetic/literary* besmirch.

– OPPOSITES polish, enhance.

▶ **noun** ❶ *the tarnish on the candlesticks* DISCOLORATION, oxidation, rust; film. ❷ *the tarnish on his reputation* SMEAR, stain, blemish, blot, taint, stigma.

tarry ▶ **verb** (*archaic*) LINGER, loiter, procrastinate, delay, wait, dawdle; *informal* hang around/round.

– OPPOSITES hurry.

tart[1] ▶ **noun** *a jam tart* PASTRY, flan, tartlet, quiche, pie.

tart[2] (*informal*) ▶ **noun** *a tart on a street corner. See* PROSTITUTE noun.

▶ **verb** ❶ *she tarted herself up* DRESS UP, make up, smarten up, preen oneself, beautify oneself, groom oneself; *informal* doll oneself up, titivate oneself. ❷ *we must tart this place up a bit* DECORATE, renovate, refurbish, redecorate; smarten up; *informal* do up, fix up.

tart[3] ▶ **adjective** ❶ *a tart apple* SOUR, sharp, acid, acidic, zesty, tangy, piquant; lemony, acetic. ❷ *a tart reply* ACERBIC, sharp, biting, cutting, astringent, caustic, trenchant, incisive, barbed, scathing, sarcastic, acrimonious, nasty, rude, vicious, spiteful, venomous.

– OPPOSITES sweet, kind.

task ▶ **noun** *a daunting task* JOB, duty, chore, charge, assignment, detail, mission, engagement, occupation, undertaking, exercise, business, responsibility, burden, endeavour, enterprise, venture.

■ **take someone to task** REBUKE, reprimand, reprove, reproach, remonstrate with, upbraid, scold, berate, lecture, censure, criticize, admonish, chide, chasten, arraign; *informal* tell off, bawl out, give someone a dressing-down; *Brit. informal* tick off, carpet; *formal* castigate.

taste ▶ **noun** ❶ *a distinctive sharp taste* FLAVOUR, savour, relish, tang, smack. ❷ *a taste of brandy* MOUTHFUL, drop, bit, sip, nip, swallow, touch, soupçon, dash, modicum. ❸ *it's too sweet for my taste* PALATE, taste buds, appetite, stomach. ❹ *a taste for adventure* LIKING, love, fondness, fancy, desire, preference, penchant, predilection, inclination, partiality; hankering, appetite, hunger, thirst, relish. ❺ *my first taste of prison* EXPERIENCE, impression; exposure to, contact with, involvement with. ❻ *the house was furnished with taste* JUDGEMENT, discrimination, discernment, tastefulness, refinement, finesse, elegance, grace, style. ❼ *the photo was rejected on grounds of taste* DECORUM, propriety, etiquette, politeness, delicacy, nicety, sensitivity, discretion, tastefulness.

– RELATED TERMS gustative, gustatory.

– OPPOSITES dislike.

▶ **verb** ❶ *Adam tasted the wine* SAMPLE, test, try, savour; sip, sup. ❷ *he could taste blood* PERCEIVE, discern, make out, distinguish. ❸ *a beer that tasted of cashews* HAVE A FLAVOUR, savour, smack, be reminiscent; suggest. ❹ *it'll be good to taste real coffee again* CONSUME, drink, partake of; eat, devour. ❺ *he tasted defeat* EXPERIENCE, encounter, come face to face with, come up against, undergo; know.

tasteful ▶ **adjective** ❶ *the decor is simple and tasteful* AESTHETICALLY PLEASING, in good taste, refined, cultured, elegant, stylish, smart, chic, attractive, exquisite. ❷ *this video is erotic but tasteful* DECOROUS, proper, seemly, respectable, appropriate, modest.

– OPPOSITES tasteless, improper.

tasteless ▶ **adjective** ❶ *the vegetables are tasteless* FLAVOURLESS, bland, insipid, unappetizing, savourless, watery, weak. ❷ *tasteless leather panelling* VULGAR, crude, tawdry, garish, gaudy, loud, trashy, showy, ostentatious, cheap, inelegant; *informal* flash, flashy, tacky, kitsch; *Brit. informal* naff. ❸ *a tasteless remark* CRUDE, vulgar, indelicate, uncouth, crass, tactless, undiplomatic, indiscreet, inappropriate, offensive.

– OPPOSITES tasty, tasteful, seemly.

tasty ▶ **adjective** DELICIOUS, palatable, luscious, mouth-watering, delectable, ambrosial, toothsome, dainty, flavoursome, flavourful; appetizing, tempting; *informal* yummy, scrummy, scrumptious, finger-licking, moreish; *dated* flavorous.

– OPPOSITES bland.

tatters ▶ **plural noun** *the satin had frayed to tatters* RAGS, scraps, shreds, bits, pieces, ribbons.

■ **in tatters** ❶ *his clothes were in tatters* RAGGED, tattered, torn, ripped, frayed, in pieces, worn out, moth-eaten, falling to pieces, threadbare. ❷ *her marriage is in tatters* IN RUINS, on the rocks, destroyed, finished, devastated.

tattle ▶ **verb** ❶ *we were tattling about him* GOSSIP, tittle-tattle, chatter, chat, prattle, babble, jabber, gabble, rattle on; *informal* chinwag, jaw, yak, gab; *Brit. informal* natter, chit-chat. ❷ *I would tattle on her if I had evidence* INFORM; report, talk, tell all, spill the beans; *informal* squeal, sing, let the cat out of the bag.

▶ **noun** *tabloid tattle* GOSSIP, rumour, tittle-tattle, hearsay, scandal.

taunt ▶ **noun** *the taunts of his classmates* JEER, gibe, sneer, insult, barb, catcall; (**taunts**) teasing, provocation, goading, derision, mockery; *informal* dig, put-down.

▶ **verb** *she taunted him about his job* JEER AT, sneer at, scoff at, poke fun at, make fun of, get at, insult, tease, chaff, torment, goad, ridicule, deride, mock, heckle; *N. Amer.* ride; *informal* rib, needle, rag, guy.

taut ▶ **adjective** ❶ *the rope was pulled taut* TIGHT, stretched, rigid. ❷ *his muscles remained taut* FLEXED, tense, hard, solid, firm, rigid, stiff. ❸ *a taut expression* FRAUGHT, strained, stressed, tense; *informal* uptight. ❹ *a taut tale of gang life* CONCISE, controlled, crisp, pithy, sharp, succinct, compact, terse. ❺ *he ran a taut ship* ORDERLY, tight, trim, neat, disciplined, tidy, spruce, smart, shipshape (and Bristol fashion).
– OPPOSITES slack, relaxed.

tavern ▶ **noun** BAR, inn, hostelry, taphouse; *Brit.* pub, public house; *informal* watering hole; *Brit. informal* local, boozer; *dated* alehouse; *N. Amer. historical* saloon.

tawdry ▶ **adjective** GAUDY, flashy, showy, garish, loud; tasteless, vulgar, trashy, junky, cheap (and nasty), cheapjack, shoddy, shabby, gimcrack; *informal* rubbishy, tacky, kitsch.
– OPPOSITES tasteful.

tax ▶ **noun** ❶ *they have to pay tax on the interest* DUTY, excise, customs, dues; levy, tariff, toll, impost, tithe, charge, fee. ❷ *a heavy tax on one's attention* BURDEN, load, weight, demand, strain, pressure, stress, drain, imposition.
– RELATED TERMS fiscal.
– OPPOSITES rebate.

▶ **verb** ❶ *they tax foreign companies more harshly* CHARGE (DUTY ON), tithe; *formal* mulct. ❷ *his whining taxed her patience* STRAIN, stretch, overburden, overload, encumber, push too far; overwhelm, try, wear out, exhaust, sap, drain, weary, weaken.

taxing ▶ **adjective** DEMANDING, exacting, challenging, burdensome, arduous, onerous, difficult, hard, tough, laborious, back-breaking, strenuous, rigorous, punishing; tiring, exhausting, enervating, wearing, stressful; *informal* murderous.
– OPPOSITES easy.

teach ▶ **verb** ❶ *she teaches small children* EDUCATE, instruct, school, tutor, coach, train; enlighten, illuminate, verse, edify, indoctrinate; drill, discipline. ❷ *I taught English* GIVE LESSONS IN, lecture in, be a teacher of. ❸ *teach your teenager how to negotiate* TRAIN, show, guide, instruct, demonstrate; instil, inculcate.
– RELATED TERMS didactic, pedagogic.

teacher ▶ **noun** EDUCATOR, tutor, instructor, master, mistress, schoolmarm, governess, educationist, preceptor; coach, trainer; lecturer, professor, don; guide, mentor, guru, counsellor; *informal* teach; *Brit. informal* beak; *Austral./NZ informal* chalkie, schoolie; *formal* pedagogue; *historical* schoolman.

team ▶ **noun** ❶ *the sales team* GROUP, squad, company, party, crew, troupe, band, side, line-up; *informal* bunch, gang, posse. ❷ *a team of horses* PAIR, span, yoke, duo, set, tandem.

▶ **verb** ❶ *the horses are teamed in pairs* HARNESS, yoke, hitch, couple. ❷ *team a T-shirt with matching shorts* MATCH, coordinate, complement, pair up. ❸ *team up with another artist for an exhibition* JOIN (FORCES), collaborate, get together, work together; unite, combine, cooperate, link, ally, associate, club together.

tear[1] ▶ **verb** ❶ *I tore up the letter* RIP UP, rip in two, pull to pieces, shred. ❷ *his flesh was torn* LACERATE, cut (open), gash, slash, scratch, hack, pierce, stab; injure, wound. ❸ *the traumas tore her family apart* DIVIDE, split, sever, break up, disunite, rupture; *poetic/literary* rend, sunder, cleave. ❹ *Gina tore the book from his hands* SNATCH, grab, seize, rip, wrench, wrest, pull, pluck; *informal* yank. ❺ (*informal*) *Jack tore down the street* SPRINT, race, run, dart, rush, dash, hasten, hurry, hare, bolt, fly, career, charge, shoot, hurtle, speed, whizz, zoom, go like lightning, go like the wind; *informal* pelt, scoot, hotfoot it, leg it, belt, zip, whip; *Brit. informal* go like the clappers, bomb, bucket; *N. Amer. informal* hightail it.
– OPPOSITES unite.

▶ **noun** *a tear in her dress* RIP, hole, split, slash, slit; ladder, snag.

■ **tear something down** DEMOLISH, knock down, raze (to the ground), flatten, level, bulldoze; dismantle, disassemble.

tear[2] ▶ **noun** *tears in her eyes* TEARDROP.
– RELATED TERMS lachrymal, lachrymose.

■ **in tears** CRYING, weeping, sobbing, wailing, howling, bawling, whimpering; tearful, upset; *informal* weepy, teary, blubbing, blubbering.

tearaway ▶ **noun** HOOLIGAN, hoodlum, ruffian, lout, rowdy, roughneck; *Austral.* larrikin; *informal* yahoo; *Brit. informal* yob, yobbo; *Scottish informal* ned; *Austral./NZ informal* roughie.

tearful ▶ **adjective** ❶ *Georgina was tearful* CLOSE TO TEARS, emotional, upset, distressed, sad, unhappy; in tears, crying, weeping, sobbing, snivelling; *informal* weepy, teary; *formal* lachrymose. ❷ *a tearful farewell* EMOTIONAL, upsetting, distressing, sad, heartbreaking, sorrowful; poignant, moving, touching, tear-jerking; *poetic/literary* dolorous.
– OPPOSITES cheerful.

tease ▶ **verb** MAKE FUN OF, poke fun at, chaff, laugh at, guy, make a monkey (out) of; taunt, bait, goad, pick on; deride, mock, ridicule; *informal* take the mickey out of, rag, send up, rib, josh, have on, pull someone's leg; *Brit. informal* wind up; *N. Amer. informal* pull someone's chain, razz; *Austral./NZ informal* poke mullock at; *dated* twit.

technical ▶ **adjective** ❶ *an important technical achievement* practical, scientific, technological, high-tech. ❷ *this might seem very technical* SPECIALIST, specialized, scientific; complex, complicated, esoteric. ❸ *a technical fault* MECHANICAL.

technique ▶ **noun** ❶ *different techniques for solving the problem* METHOD, approach, procedure, system, modus operandi, MO, way; means, strategy, tack, tactic, line; routine, practice. ❷ *I was impressed with his technique* SKILL, ability, proficiency, expertise, mastery, talent, genius, artistry, craftsmanship; aptitude, adroitness, deftness, dexterity, facility, competence; performance, delivery; *informal* know-how.

tedious ▶ **adjective** BORING, dull, monotonous, repetitive, unrelieved, unvaried, uneventful; characterless, colourless, lifeless, insipid, uninteresting, unexciting, uninspiring, flat, bland, dry, stale, tired, lacklustre, stodgy, dreary, humdrum, mundane; mind-numbing, soul-destroying, wearisome, tiring, tiresome, irksome, trying, frustrating; *informal* deadly, not up to much; *Brit. informal* samey; *N. Amer. informal* dullsville.
– OPPOSITES exciting.

tedium ▶ **noun** MONOTONY, boredom, ennui, uniformity, routine, dreariness, dryness, banality, vapidity, insipidity.
– OPPOSITES variety.

teem[1] ▶ **verb** *the pond was teeming with fish* BE FULL OF, be filled with, be alive with, be brimming with, abound in, be swarming with; be packed with, be crawling with, be overrun by, bristle with, seethe with, be thick with; *informal* be jam-packed with, be chock-a-block with, be chock-full with.

teem[2] ▶ **verb** *the rain was teeming down* POUR, pelt, tip, beat, lash, sheet; come down in torrents, rain cats and dogs; *informal* be chucking it down; *Brit. informal* bucket down.

teenage ▶ **adjective** ADOLESCENT, teenaged, youthful, young, juvenile; *informal* teen.

teenager ▶ **noun** ADOLESCENT, youth, young person, minor, juvenile; *informal* teen, teenybopper.

teeny ▶ **adjective** (*informal*). *See* TINY.

teeter ▶ **verb** ❶ *Daisy teetered towards them* TOTTER, wobble, toddle, sway, stagger, stumble, reel, lurch, pitch. ❷ *the situation teetered between tragedy and farce* SEE-SAW, veer, fluctuate, oscillate, swing, alternate, waver.

teetotal ▶ **adjective** ABSTINENT, abstemious; sober, dry; *informal* on the wagon.
– OPPOSITES alcoholic.

telegram ▶ **noun** TELEMESSAGE, telex; *informal* wire; *dated* radiogram; *historical* cable, cablegram.

telepathic ▶ **adjective** PSYCHIC, clairvoyant.

telepathy ▶ **noun** MIND-READING, thought transference; extrasensory perception, ESP; clairvoyance, sixth sense; psychometry.

telephone ▶ **noun** *Sophie picked up the telephone* PHONE, handset, receiver; *informal* blower; *N. Amer. informal* horn.
▶ **verb** *he telephoned me last night* PHONE, call, dial; get, reach; *Brit.* ring (up); *informal* call up, give someone a buzz, get on the blower to; *Brit. informal* give someone a bell, give someone a tinkle; *N. Amer. informal* get someone on the horn.

telescope ▶ **noun** SPYGLASS; *informal* scope.
▶ **verb** ❶ *the front of the car was telescoped* CONCERTINA, compact, compress, crush, squash. ❷ *his experience can be telescoped into a paragraph* CONDENSE, shorten, reduce, abbreviate, abridge, summarize, precis, abstract, shrink, consolidate; truncate, curtail.

televise ▶ **verb** BROADCAST, screen, air, telecast; transmit, relay.

television ▶ **noun** TV; *informal* the small screen; *Brit. informal* telly, the box; *N. Amer. informal* the tube.

tell ▶ **verb** ❶ *why didn't you tell me before?* INFORM, notify, apprise, let know, make aware, acquaint with, advise, put in the picture, brief, fill in; alert, warn; *informal* clue in/up. ❷ *she told the story slowly* RELATE, recount, narrate, unfold, report, recite, describe, sketch, weave, spin; utter, voice, state, declare, communicate, impart, divulge. ❸ *she told him to leave* INSTRUCT, order, command, direct, charge, enjoin, call on, require; *poetic/literary* bid. ❹ *I tell you, I did nothing wrong* ASSURE, promise, give one's word, swear, guarantee. ❺ *the figures tell a different story* REVEAL, show, indicate, be evidence of, disclose, convey, signify. ❻ *promise you won't tell?* GIVE THE GAME AWAY, talk, tell tales, tattle; *informal* spill the beans, let the cat out of the bag, blab; *Brit. informal* blow the gaff. ❼ *she was bound to tell on him* INFORM ON, tell tales on, give away, denounce, sell out; *informal* split on, blow the whistle on, rat on, peach on, squeal on; *Brit. informal* grass on, sneak on, shop; *N. Amer. informal* finger; *Austral./NZ informal* dob on. ❽ *it was hard to tell what he said* ASCERTAIN, determine, work out, make out, deduce, discern, perceive, see, identify, recognize, understand, comprehend; *informal* figure out; *Brit. informal* suss out. ❾ *he couldn't tell one from the other* DISTINGUISH, differentiate, discriminate. ❿ *the strain began to tell on him* TAKE ITS TOLL, leave its mark; affect.
■ **tell someone off** (*informal*). *See* REPRIMAND verb.

teller ▶ **noun** ❶ *a bank teller* CASHIER, clerk. ❷ *a teller of tales* NARRATOR, raconteur; storyteller, anecdotalist.

telling ▶ **adjective** REVEALING, significant,

weighty, important, meaningful, influential, striking, potent, powerful, compelling.
– OPPOSITES insignificant.

telling-off ▶ noun (*informal*). *See* REPRIMAND noun.

telltale ▶ adjective *the telltale blush on her face* REVEALING, revelatory, suggestive, meaningful, significant, meaning; *informal* giveaway.
▶ noun *'Sue did it,' said a telltale* INFORMER, whistleblower; *N. Amer.* tattletale; *informal* snitch, squealer; *Brit. informal* sneak; *Scottish informal* clype; *dated* talebearer.

temerity ▶ noun AUDACITY, nerve, effrontery, impudence, impertinence, cheek, gall, presumption; daring; *informal* face, front, (brass) neck, chutzpah.

temper ▶ noun ❶ *he walked out in a temper* (FIT OF) RAGE, fury, fit of pique, tantrum, (bad) mood, pet, sulk, huff; *informal* grump, snit; *Brit. informal* strop, paddy; *Brit. informal, dated* bate, wax; *N. Amer. informal* hissy fit. ❷ *a display of temper* ANGER, fury, rage, annoyance, vexation, irritation, irritability, ill humour, spleen, pique, petulance, testiness, tetchiness, crabbiness; *Brit. informal* stroppiness; *poetic/literary* ire, choler. ❸ *she struggled to keep her temper* COMPOSURE, equanimity, self-control, self-possession, sangfroid, calm, good humour; *informal* cool.
▶ verb ❶ *the steel is tempered by heat* HARDEN, strengthen, toughen, fortify, anneal. ❷ *their idealism is tempered with realism* MODERATE, modify, modulate, mitigate, alleviate, reduce, weaken, lighten, soften.
■ **lose one's temper** GET ANGRY, fly into a rage, erupt, lose control, go berserk, breathe fire, flare up, boil over; *informal* go mad, go crazy, go bananas, have a fit, see red, fly off the handle, blow one's top, do one's nut, hit the roof, go off the deep end, go ape, flip, lose one's rag, freak out; *Brit. informal* go spare, go crackers, throw a wobbly.

temperament ▶ noun DISPOSITION, nature, character, personality, make-up, constitution, mind, spirit; stamp, mettle, mould; mood, frame of mind, attitude, outlook, humour.

temperamental ▶ adjective ❶ *a temperamental chef* VOLATILE, excitable, emotional, mercurial, capricious, erratic, unpredictable, changeable, inconsistent; hot-headed, fiery, quick-tempered, irritable, irascible, impatient; touchy, moody, sensitive, oversensitive, highly strung, neurotic, melodramatic. ❷ *a temperamental dislike of conflict* INHERENT, innate, natural, inborn, constitutional, deep-rooted, ingrained, congenital.
– OPPOSITES placid.

temperance ▶ noun TEETOTALISM, abstinence, abstention, sobriety, self-restraint; prohibition.
– OPPOSITES alcoholism.

temperate ▶ adjective ❶ *temperate climates* MILD, clement, benign, gentle, balmy. ❷ *he was temperate in his consumption* SELF-RESTRAINED, restrained, moderate, self-controlled, disciplined; abstemious, self-denying, austere, ascetic; teetotal, abstinent.
– OPPOSITES extreme.

tempest ▶ noun STORM, gale, hurricane; tornado, whirlwind, cyclone, typhoon.

tempestuous ▶ adjective ❶ *the day was tempestuous* STORMY, blustery, squally, wild, turbulent, windy, gusty, blowy, rainy; foul, nasty, inclement. ❷ *the tempestuous political environment* TURBULENT, stormy, tumultuous, wild, lively, heated, explosive, feverish, frenetic, frenzied. ❸ *a tempestuous woman* EMOTIONAL, passionate, impassioned, fiery, intense; temperamental. volatile, excitable, mercurial, capricious, unpredictable, quick-tempered.
– OPPOSITES calm, peaceful, placid.

temple ▶ noun HOUSE OF GOD, shrine, sanctuary; church, cathedral, mosque, synagogue, shul; *archaic* fane.

tempo ▶ noun ❶ *the tempo of the music* CADENCE, speed, rhythm, beat, time, pulse; measure, metre. ❷ *the tempo of life in Western society* PACE, rate, speed, velocity.

temporal ▶ adjective SECULAR, non-spiritual, worldly, profane, material, mundane, earthly, terrestrial; non-religious, lay.
– OPPOSITES spiritual.

temporarily ▶ adverb ❶ *the girl was temporarily placed with a foster-family* FOR THE TIME BEING, for the moment, for now, for the present, in the interim, for the nonce, in/for the meantime, in the meanwhile; provisionally, pro tem; *informal* for the minute. ❷ *he was temporarily blinded by the light* BRIEFLY, for a short time, momentarily, fleetingly.
– OPPOSITES permanently.

temporary ▶ adjective ❶ *temporary accommodation | the temporary captain* NON-PERMANENT, short-term, interim; provisional, pro tem, makeshift, stopgap; acting, fill-in, stand-in, caretaker. ❷ *a temporary loss of self-control* BRIEF, short-lived, momentary, fleeting, passing.
– OPPOSITES permanent, lasting.

temporize ▶ verb EQUIVOCATE, procrastinate, play for time, play a waiting game, stall, use delaying tactics, delay, hang back, prevaricate; *Brit.* hum and haw; *rare* tergiversate.

tempt ▶ verb ❶ *the manager tried to tempt him to stay* ENTICE, persuade, convince, inveigle, induce, cajole, coax, woo; *informal* sweet-talk. ❷ *more customers are being tempted by credit* ALLURE, attract, appeal to, whet the appetite of; lure, seduce, beguile, tantalize, draw.
– OPPOSITES discourage, deter.

temptation ▶ noun ❶ *Mary resisted the temptation to answer back* DESIRE, urge, itch, impulse, inclination. ❷ *the temptations of London* LURE, allurement, enticement, seduction, attraction, draw, pull; siren song. ❸ *the temptation of travel to exotic locations* ALLURE, appeal, attraction, fascination.

tempting ▶ adjective ❶ *the tempting shops of the Via Nazionale* ENTICING, alluring, attractive, appealing, inviting, captivating, seductive, beguiling, fascinating, tantalizing; irresistible. ❷ *a plate of tempting cakes* APPETIZING, mouthwatering, delicious, toothsome; *informal* scrummy, scrumptious, yummy.
– OPPOSITES off-putting, uninviting.

temptress ▶ noun SEDUCTRESS, siren, femme fatale, Mata Hari; *informal* vamp.

ten ▶ cardinal number DECADE.
– RELATED TERMS decimal, deca-, deci-.

tenable ▶ adjective DEFENSIBLE, justifiable, supportable, sustainable, arguable, able to hold water, reasonable, rational, sound, viable, plausible, credible, believable, conceivable.
– OPPOSITES indefensible.

tenacious ▶ adjective ❶ *his tenacious grip* FIRM, tight, fast, clinging; strong, forceful, powerful, unshakeable, immovable, iron. ❷ *a tenacious man* PERSEVERING, persistent, determined, dogged, strong-willed, tireless, indefatigable, resolute, patient, purposeful, unflagging, staunch, steadfast, untiring, unwavering, unswerving, unshakeable, unyielding, insistent; stubborn, intransigent, obstinate, obdurate, stiff-necked; *N. Amer.* rock-ribbed; *formal* pertinacious.
– OPPOSITES weak, irresolute.

tenacity ▶ noun PERSISTENCE, determination, perseverance, doggedness, strength of purpose, bulldog spirit, tirelessness, indefatigability, resolution, resoluteness, resolve, firmness, patience, purposefulness, staunchness, steadfastness, staying power, application; stubbornness, intransigence, obstinacy, obduracy; *formal* pertinacity.

tenancy ▶ noun OCCUPANCY, occupation, period of occupancy/occupation, residence, habitation, holding, possession; tenure, lease, rental, leasehold.

tenant ▶ noun OCCUPANT, resident, inhabitant; leaseholder, lessee, renter; *Brit.* occupier, sitting tenant.
– OPPOSITES owner, freeholder.

tend[1] ▶ verb ❶ *I tend to get very involved in my work* BE INCLINED, be apt, be disposed, be prone, be liable, have a tendency, have a propensity. ❷ *younger voters tended towards the tabloid press* INCLINE, lean, gravitate, move; prefer, favour; *N. Amer.* trend.

tend[2] ▶ verb *she tended her cattle* LOOK AFTER, take care of, care for, minister to, attend to, see to, wait on; watch over, keep an eye on, mind, protect, watch, guard; nurse, nurture, cherish.
– OPPOSITES neglect.

tendency ▶ noun ❶ *his tendency to take the law into his own hands* PROPENSITY, proclivity, proneness, aptness, likelihood, inclination, disposition, predisposition, bent, leaning, penchant, predilection, susceptibility, liability; readiness; habit. ❷ *this tendency towards cohabitation* TREND, movement, drift, swing, gravitation, direction, course; orientation, bias.

tender[1] ▶ adjective ❶ *a gentle, tender man* CARING, kind, kindly, kind-hearted, soft-hearted, tender-hearted, compassionate, sympathetic, warm, warm-hearted, fatherly, motherly, maternal, gentle, mild, benevolent, generous, giving, humane. ❷ *a tender kiss* AFFECTIONATE, fond, loving, emotional, warm, gentle, soft; amorous, adoring; *informal* lovey-dovey. ❸ *tender love songs* ROMANTIC, sentimental, emotional, emotive, touching, moving, poignant; *Brit. informal* soppy. ❹ *simmer until the meat is tender* EASILY CHEWED, chewable, soft; succulent, juicy; tenderized. ❺ *tender plants* DELICATE, easily damaged, fragile. ❻ *her ankle was swollen and tender* SORE, painful, sensitive, inflamed, raw, red, chafed, bruised; hurting, aching, throbbing, smarting. ❼ *the tender age of fifteen* YOUNG, youthful; impressionable, inexperienced, immature, unsophisticated, unseasoned, juvenile, callow, green, raw; *informal* wet behind the ears. ❽ *the issue of conscription was a particularly tender one* DIFFICULT, delicate, tricky, awkward, problematic, troublesome, ticklish; controversial, emotive; *informal* sticky.
– OPPOSITES hard-hearted, callous, tough.

tender[2] ▶ verb ❶ *she tendered her resignation* OFFER, proffer, present, put forward, propose, suggest, advance, submit, extend, give, render; hand in. ❷ *firms of interior decorators tendered for the work* PUT IN A BID, bid, quote, give an estimate.
▶ noun *six contractors were invited to submit tenders* BID, offer, quotation, quote, estimate, price; proposal, submission.

tender-hearted ▶ adjective. See TENDER[1] sense 1.

tenderness ▶ noun ❶ *I felt an enormous tenderness for her* AFFECTION, fondness, love, devotion, loving kindness, emotion, sentiment. ❷ *with unexpected tenderness, he told her what had happened* KINDNESS, kindliness, kind-heartedness, tender-heartedness, compassion, care, concern, sympathy, warmth, fatherliness, motherliness, gentleness, benevolence, generosity. ❸ *abdominal tenderness* SORENESS, pain, inflammation, bruising; ache, aching, smarting, throbbing.

tenet ▶ noun PRINCIPLE, belief, doctrine, precept, creed, credo, article of faith, dogma, canon; theory, thesis, conviction, idea, view, opinion, position, hypothesis, postulation; (**tenets**) ideology, code of belief, teaching(s).

tenor ▶ noun ❶ *the general tenor of his speech* SENSE, meaning, theme, drift, thread, import, purport, intent, intention, burden, thrust, significance, message; gist, essence, substance, spirit. ❷ *the even tenor of life in the village* COURSE, direction, movement, drift, current, trend.

tense ▶ **adjective** ❶ *the tense muscles of his neck* TAUT, tight, rigid, stretched, strained, stiff. ❷ *Loretta was feeling tense and irritable* ANXIOUS, nervous, on edge, edgy, strained, stressed, under pressure, agitated, ill at ease, uneasy, restless, worked up, keyed up, overwrought, jumpy, on tenterhooks, with one's stomach in knots, worried, apprehensive, panicky; *Brit.* nervy; *informal* a bundle of nerves, jittery, twitchy, uptight, stressed out; *N. Amer. informal* spooky, squirrelly. ❸ *a tense moment* NERVE-RACKING, stressful, anxious, worrying, fraught, charged, strained, nail-biting, difficult, uneasy, uncomfortable; exciting, cliffhanging, knife-edge.
– OPPOSITES slack, calm.
▶ **verb** *Hebden tensed his muscles* TIGHTEN, tauten, tense up, flex, contract, brace, stiffen; screw up, knot, strain, stretch; *N. Amer.* squinch up.
– OPPOSITES relax.

tension ▶ **noun** ❶ *the tension of the rope* TIGHTNESS, tautness, rigidity; pull, traction. ❷ *the tension was unbearable* STRAIN, stress, anxiety, pressure; worry, apprehensiveness, apprehension, agitation, nerves, nervousness, jumpiness, edginess, restlessness; suspense, uncertainty, anticipation, excitement; *informal* butterflies (in one's stomach), collywobbles. ❸ *months of tension between the military and the government* STRAINED RELATIONS, strain; ill feeling, friction, antagonism, antipathy, hostility, enmity.

tentative ▶ **adjective** ❶ *tentative arrangements | a tentative conclusion* PROVISIONAL, unconfirmed, pencilled in, preliminary, to be confirmed, TBC, subject to confirmation; speculative, conjectural, untried, unproven, exploratory, experimental, trial, test, pilot. ❷ *he took a few tentative steps* HESITANT, uncertain, cautious, timid, hesitating, faltering, shaky, unsteady, halting; wavering, unsure.
– OPPOSITES definite, confident.

tenterhooks
■ **on tenterhooks** IN SUSPENSE, waiting with bated breath; anxious, nervous, nervy, apprehensive, worried, worried sick, on edge, edgy, tense, strained, stressed, agitated, restless, worked up, keyed up, jumpy, with one's stomach in knots, with one's heart in one's mouth, like a cat on a hot tin roof; *informal* with butterflies in one's stomach, jittery, twitchy, in a state, uptight; *N. Amer. informal* spooky, squirrelly.

tenuous ▶ **adjective** ❶ *a tenuous connection* SLIGHT, insubstantial, flimsy, weak, doubtful, dubious, questionable, suspect; vague, nebulous, hazy. ❷ *a tenuous thread* FINE, thin, slender, delicate, gossamer, fragile.
– OPPOSITES convincing, strong.

tenure ▶ **noun** ❶ *residents should have security of tenure* TENANCY, occupancy, holding, occupation, residence; possession, title, ownership. ❷ *his tenure as Secretary of State for Industry* INCUMBENCY, term (of office), period (of/in office), time (in office).

tepid ▶ **adjective** ❶ *tepid water* LUKEWARM, warmish, slightly warm; at room temperature. ❷ *a tepid response* UNENTHUSIASTIC, apathetic, half-hearted, indifferent, cool, lukewarm, uninterested; *informal* unenthused.
– OPPOSITES hot, cold, enthusiastic.

term ▶ **noun** ❶ *scientific and technical terms* WORD, expression, phrase, turn of phrase, idiom, locution; name, title, designation, label; *formal* appellation, denomination. ❷ *a protest in the strongest terms* LANGUAGE, mode of expression, manner of speaking, phraseology, terminology; words, phrases, expressions. ❸ *the terms of the contract* CONDITIONS, stipulations, specifications, provisions, provisos; restrictions, qualifications; particulars, details, points. ❹ *a policy offering more favourable terms* RATES, prices, charges, costs, fees; tariff. ❺ *the President is elected for a four-year term* PERIOD, period of time, time, length of time, spell, stint, duration; stretch, run; period of office, incumbency. ❻ (*archaic*) *the whole term of your natural life* DURATION, length, span. ❼ *the summer term* SESSION; *N. Amer.* semester, trimester, quarter.
▶ **verb** *he has been termed the father of modern theology* CALL, name, entitle, title, style, designate, describe as, dub, label, tag; nickname; *formal* denominate.
■ **come to terms** ❶ *the two sides came to terms* REACH AN AGREEMENT/UNDERSTANDING, make a deal, reach a compromise, meet each other halfway. ❷ *she eventually came to terms with her situation* ACCEPT, come to accept, reconcile oneself to, learn to live with, become resigned to, make the best of; face up to.

terminal ▶ **adjective** ❶ *a terminal illness* INCURABLE, untreatable, inoperable; fatal, mortal, deadly. ❷ *terminal patients* DYING, near death; incurable. ❸ *a terminal bonus may be payable when a policy matures* FINAL, last, concluding, closing, end. ❹ (*informal*) *you're making a terminal ass of yourself* COMPLETE, utter, absolute, total, real, thorough, out-and-out, downright, perfect; *Brit. informal* right, proper; *Austral./NZ informal* fair.
▶ **noun** ❶ *a railway terminal* STATION, last stop, end of the line; depot; *Brit.* terminus. ❷ *a computer terminal* WORKSTATION, VDU, visual display unit.

terminate ▶ **verb** ❶ *treatment was terminated* BRING TO AN END, end, bring to a close/conclusion, close, conclude, finish, stop, put an end to, wind up, discontinue, cease, cut short, abort, axe; *informal* pull the plug on. ❷ *the train will terminate in Stratford* END ITS JOURNEY, finish up, stop. ❸ *the pregnancy was terminated* ABORT, end.

– OPPOSITES begin, start, continue.

termination ▶ noun ❶ *the termination of a contract* ENDING, end, closing, close, conclusion, finish, stopping, winding up, discontinuance, discontinuation; cancellation, dissolution; *informal* wind-up. ❷ *she had a termination* ABORTION; *rare* feticide.

– OPPOSITES start, beginning.

terminology ▶ noun PHRASEOLOGY, terms, expressions, words, language, parlance, vocabulary, nomenclature; usage, idiom; jargon, cant, argot; *informal* lingo, -speak, -ese.

terminus ▶ noun (*Brit.*) *the bus terminus* STATION, last stop, end of the line, terminal; depot, garage.

terrain ▶ noun LAND, ground, territory; topography, landscape, countryside, country.

terrestrial ▶ adjective EARTHLY, worldly, mundane, earthbound; *poetic/literary* sublunary.

terrible ▶ adjective ❶ *a terrible crime | terrible injuries* DREADFUL, awful, appalling, horrific, horrifying, horrible, horrendous, atrocious, abominable, abhorrent, frightful, shocking, hideous, ghastly, grim, dire, unspeakable, gruesome, monstrous, sickening, heinous, vile; serious, grave, acute; *formal* grievous. ❷ *a terrible smell* NASTY, disgusting, awful, dreadful, ghastly, horrid, horrible, vile, foul, abominable, frightful, loathsome, revolting, repulsive, odious, nauseating, repellent, horrendous, hideous, appalling, offensive, objectionable, obnoxious; *informal* gruesome, putrid, diabolical, yucky, sick-making, God-awful, gross; *Brit. informal* beastly; *archaic* disgustful. ❸ *he was in terrible pain* SEVERE, extreme, intense, excruciating, agonizing, unbearable, intolerable, unendurable. ❹ *that's a terrible thing to say* UNKIND, nasty, unpleasant, foul, obnoxious, vile, contemptible, despicable, wretched, shabby; spiteful, mean, malicious, poisonous, mean-spirited, cruel, hateful, hurtful; unfair, uncharitable, uncalled for, below the belt, unwarranted; *Brit. informal* beastly. ❺ *the film was terrible* VERY BAD, dreadful, awful, frightful, atrocious, hopeless, poor; *informal* pathetic, pitiful, useless, lousy, appalling, abysmal, dire; *Brit. informal* duff, chronic, poxy, rubbish, a load of pants. ❻ (*informal*) *you're a terrible flirt* INCORRIGIBLE, outrageous; real, awful, dreadful, frightful, shocking; *informal* impossible, fearful; *Brit. informal* right, proper. ❼ *I feel terrible—I've been in bed all day* ILL, poorly, sick, queasy, nauseous, nauseated, green about the gills; faint, dizzy; *informal* rough, lousy, awful, dreadful; *Brit. informal* grotty, ropy. ❽ *he still feels terrible about what he did to John* GUILTY, conscience-stricken, remorseful, guilt-ridden, ashamed, chastened, contrite, sorry.

– OPPOSITES minor, slight, pleasant, wonderful.

terribly ▶ adverb ❶ (*informal*) *she's terribly upset* VERY, extremely, really, terrifically, tremendously, immensely, thoroughly, dreadfully, exceptionally, remarkably, extraordinarily, exceedingly; *N. English* right; *informal* awfully, devilishly, seriously, majorly; *Brit. informal* jolly, ever so, dead, well; *N. Amer. informal* real, mighty, awful; *informal, dated* frightfully; *archaic* exceeding. ❷ *he played terribly* VERY BADLY, atrociously, awfully, dreadfully, appallingly, execrably; *informal* abysmally, pitifully, diabolically. ❸ (*informal*) *I shall miss you terribly* VERY MUCH, greatly, a great deal, a lot; *informal* loads.

terrific ▶ adjective ❶ *a terrific bang* TREMENDOUS, huge, massive, gigantic, colossal, mighty, great, prodigious, formidable, sizeable, considerable; intense, extreme, extraordinary; *informal* mega, whopping great, humongous; *Brit. informal* whacking great, ginormous. ❷ (*informal*) *a terrific game of top-quality football* MARVELLOUS, wonderful, sensational, outstanding, superb, excellent, first-rate, first-class, dazzling, out of this world, breathtaking; *informal* great, fantastic, fabulous, fab, mega, super, ace, magic, cracking, cool, wicked, awesome; *Brit. informal* brilliant, brill, smashing; *Austral./NZ informal* bonzer; *Brit. informal, dated* spiffing. ❸ (*archaic*) *terrific scenes of slaughter and destruction* DREADFUL, terrible, appalling, awful, horrific, horrible, horrendous, horrifying, hideous, grim, ghastly, gruesome, frightful, fearful.

terrified ▶ adjective PETRIFIED, frightened, scared, scared/frightened to death, scared stiff, scared/frightened out of one's wits, scared witless, horrified, with one's heart in one's mouth, shaking in one's shoes.

terrify ▶ verb PETRIFY, horrify, frighten, scare, scare/frighten to death, scare/frighten the living daylights out of, scare/frighten the life out of, scare/frighten someone out of their wits, scare witless, strike terror into, put the fear of God into; paralyse, transfix; *informal* scare the pants off; *Irish informal* scare the bejesus out of.

territory ▶ noun ❶ *British overseas territories* AREA OF LAND, area, region, enclave; country, state, land, dependency, colony, dominion, protectorate, fief, possession, holding. ❷ *mountainous territory* TERRAIN, land, ground, countryside. ❸ *the territory of biblical scholarship* DOMAIN, area of concern/interest/knowledge, province, department, field, preserve, sphere, arena, realm, world. ❹ *Sheffield was his territory* SPHERE OF OPERATIONS, area, section; *informal* turf; *Brit. informal* patch, manor.

terror ▶ noun ❶ *she screamed in terror* EXTREME FEAR, dread, horror, fear and trembling, fright, alarm, panic, shock. ❷ *the terrors of her own mind* DEMON, fiend, devil, monster; horror, nightmare. ❸ (*informal*) *he turned out to be a right little terror* RASCAL, devil, imp, monkey, scallywag, mischief-maker; *informal* scamp, horror; *Brit. informal* perisher; *N. English informal* scally; *N. Amer. informal* varmint.

terrorist ▶ **noun** bomber, arsonist, incendiary; gunman, assassin; hijacker; revolutionary, radical, guerrilla, urban guerrilla, anarchist, freedom fighter.

terrorize ▶ **verb** PERSECUTE, victimize, torment, tyrannize, intimidate, menace, threaten, bully, browbeat; scare, frighten, terrify, petrify; *Brit. informal* put the frighteners on.

terse ▶ **adjective** BRIEF, short, to the point, concise, succinct, crisp, pithy, incisive, short and sweet, laconic, elliptical; BRUSQUE, abrupt, curt, clipped, blunt, ungracious.
– OPPOSITES long-winded, polite.

test ▶ **noun** ❶ *a series of scientific tests* TRIAL, experiment, pilot study, try-out; check, examination, assessment, evaluation, appraisal, investigation, inspection, analysis, scrutiny, study, probe, exploration; screening; *technical* assay. ❷ *candidates may be required to take a test* EXAM, examination; *N. Amer.* quiz. ❸ *the test of a good sparkling wine* CRITERION, proof, indication, yardstick, touchstone, standard, measure, litmus test, acid test.
▶ **verb** ❶ *a small-scale prototype was tested* TRY OUT, trial, put to the test, put through its paces, experiment with, pilot; check, examine, assess, evaluate, appraise, investigate, analyse, scrutinize, study, probe, explore; sample; screen; *technical* assay. ❷ *such behaviour would test any marriage* PUT A STRAIN ON, strain, tax, try; make demands on, stretch, challenge.

testament ▶ **noun** *an achievement which is a testament to his professionalism and dedication* TESTIMONY, witness, evidence, proof, attestation; demonstration, indication, exemplification; monument, tribute.

testify ▶ **verb** ❶ *you may be required to testify in court* GIVE EVIDENCE, bear witness, be a witness, give one's testimony, attest; *Law* make a deposition. ❷ *he testified that he had been threatened by a fellow officer* ATTEST, swear, state on oath, state, declare, assert, affirm; allege, submit, claim; *Law* depose. ❸ *the exhibits testify to the talents of the local sculptors* BE EVIDENCE/PROOF OF, attest to, confirm, prove, corroborate, substantiate, bear out; show, demonstrate, bear witness to, indicate, reveal, bespeak.

testimonial ▶ **noun** REFERENCE, character reference, letter of recommendation, commendation.

testimony ▶ **noun** ❶ *Smith was in court to hear her testimony* EVIDENCE, sworn statement, attestation, affidavit; statement, declaration, assertion, affirmation; allegation, submission, claim; *Law* deposition. ❷ *the work is a testimony to his professional commitment* TESTAMENT, proof, evidence, attestation, witness; confirmation, corroboration; demonstration, indication.

testing ▶ **adjective** DIFFICULT, challenging, tough, hard, demanding, taxing, stressful.
– OPPOSITES easy.

testy ▶ **adjective**. *See* TETCHY.

tetchy ▶ **adjective** IRRITABLE, cantankerous, irascible, bad-tempered, grumpy, grouchy, crotchety, crabby, testy, crusty, curmudgeonly, ill-tempered, ill-humoured, peevish, cross, fractious, pettish, crabbed, prickly, waspish; *informal* snappish, snappy, chippy; *Brit. informal* shirty, stroppy, narky, ratty; *N. Amer. informal* cranky, ornery.
– OPPOSITES good-humoured.

tête-à-tête ▶ **noun** CONVERSATION, chat, talk, heart-to-heart, one-on-one, one-to-one; *informal* confab, chinwag; *Brit. informal* natter; *formal* confabulation.

tether ▶ **verb** *the horse had been tethered to a post* TIE (UP), hitch, rope, chain; fasten, secure.
– OPPOSITES unleash.
▶ **noun** *a dog on a tether* ROPE, chain, cord, lead, leash; restraint; halter.
■ **at the end of one's tether** AT ONE'S WITS' END, desperate, not knowing which way to turn, unable to cope; *N. Amer.* at the end of one's rope.

text ▶ **noun** ❶ *a text which explores pain and grief* BOOK, work, written/printed work. ❷ *the pictures are clear and relate well to the text* WORDS, wording; content, body, main body. ❸ *academic texts* TEXTBOOK, book; set book. ❹ *a text from the First Book of Samuel* PASSAGE, extract, quotation, verse, line; reading. ❺ *he took as his text the fact that Australia is a paradise* THEME, subject, topic, motif; thesis, argument.

textiles ▶ **plural noun** FABRICS, cloths, materials.

texture ▶ **noun** FEEL, touch; appearance, finish, surface, grain; quality, consistency; weave, nap.

thank ▶ **verb** EXPRESS (ONE'S) GRATITUDE TO, express one's thanks to, offer/extend thanks to, say thank you to, show one's appreciation to.

thankful ▶ **adjective** GRATEFUL, filled with gratitude, relieved, pleased, glad.

thankless ▶ **adjective** ❶ *a thankless task* UNENVIABLE, difficult, unpleasant, unrewarding; unappreciated, unrecognized, unacknowledged. ❷ *her thankless children* UNGRATEFUL, unappreciative, unthankful.
– OPPOSITES rewarding, grateful.

thanks ▶ **plural noun** *they expressed their thanks and wished her well* GRATITUDE, appreciation; acknowledgement, recognition, credit.
▶ **exclamation** *thanks for being so helpful* THANK YOU, many thanks, thanks very much, thanks a lot, thank you kindly, much obliged, much appreciated, bless you; *informal* cheers, thanks a million; *Brit. informal* ta.
■ **thanks to** AS A RESULT OF, owing to, due to, because of, through, as a consequence of, on

account of, by virtue of, by dint of; *formal* by reason of.

thaw ▶ **verb** MELT, unfreeze, soften, liquefy, dissolve; defrost; *N. Amer.* unthaw.
– OPPOSITES freeze.

theatre ▶ **noun** ❶ *the local theatre* PLAYHOUSE, auditorium, amphitheatre. ❷ *what made you want to go into the theatre?* ACTING, performing, the stage; drama, the dramatic arts, dramaturgy, the thespian art; show business; *informal* the boards, show biz. ❸ *the lecture theatre* HALL, room, auditorium. ❹ *the theatre of war* SCENE, arena, field/sphere/place of action.

theatrical ▶ **adjective** ❶ *a theatrical career* STAGE, dramatic, thespian, dramaturgical; show-business; *informal* showbiz; *formal* histrionic. ❷ *Henry looked over his shoulder with theatrical caution* EXAGGERATED, ostentatious, actressy, stagy, showy, melodramatic, overacted, overdone, histrionic, affected, mannered; *informal* hammy, ham, camp.

theft ▶ **noun** ROBBERY, stealing, thieving, larceny, thievery, shoplifting, burglary, misappropriation, embezzlement; raid, hold-up; *informal* smash and grab; *N. Amer. informal* heist, stick-up; *formal* peculation.
– RELATED TERMS kleptomania.

theme ▶ **noun** ❶ *the theme of her speech* SUBJECT, topic, subject matter, matter, thesis, argument, text, burden, thrust; thread, motif, keynote. ❷ *the first violin takes up the theme* MELODY, tune, air; motif, leitmotif.

then ▶ **adverb** ❶ *I was living in Cairo then* AT THAT TIME, in those days; at that point (in time), at that moment, on that occasion. ❷ *she won the first and then the second game* NEXT, after that, afterwards, subsequently. ❸ *and then there's another problem* IN ADDITION, also, besides, as well, additionally, on top of that, over and above that, moreover, furthermore, what's more, to boot; too. ❹ *well, if that's what he wants, then he should leave* IN THAT CASE, that being so, it follows that.

theological ▶ **adjective** RELIGIOUS, scriptural, ecclesiastical, doctrinal; divine, holy.

theoretical ▶ **adjective** HYPOTHETICAL, conjectural, academic, suppositional, speculative, notional, postulatory, assumed, presumed, untested, unproven, unsubstantiated.
– OPPOSITES actual, real.

theorize ▶ **verb** SPECULATE, conjecture, hypothesize, postulate, propose, posit, suppose.

theory ▶ **noun** ❶ *I reckon that confirms my theory* HYPOTHESIS, thesis, conjecture, supposition, speculation, postulation, postulate, proposition, premise, surmise, assumption, presupposition; opinion, view, belief, contention. ❷ *modern economic theory* PRINCIPLES, ideas, concepts; philosophy, ideology, system of ideas, science.

■ **in theory** IN PRINCIPLE, on paper, in the abstract, all things being equal, in an ideal world; hypothetically.

therapeutic ▶ **adjective** HEALING, curative, remedial, medicinal, restorative, health-giving, tonic, reparative, corrective, beneficial, good, salutary; *archaic* sanative.
– OPPOSITES harmful.

therapist ▶ **noun** PSYCHOLOGIST, psychotherapist, analyst, psychoanalyst, psychiatrist; *informal* shrink; *Brit. humorous* trick cyclist.

therapy ▶ **noun** ❶ *a wide range of complementary therapies* TREATMENT, remedy, cure. ❷ *he's currently in therapy* PSYCHOTHERAPY, psychoanalysis, analysis.

thereabouts ▶ **adverb** ❶ *the land thereabouts* NEAR THERE, around there. ❷ *they sold it for five million or thereabouts* APPROXIMATELY, or so, give or take a bit, plus or minus a bit, in round numbers, not far off; *Brit.* getting on for; *N. Amer. informal* in the ballpark of.

thereafter ▶ **adverb** AFTER THAT, following that, afterwards, subsequently, then, next.

therefore ▶ **adverb** CONSEQUENTLY, so, as a result, hence, thus, accordingly, for that reason, ergo, that being the case, on that account; *formal* whence; *archaic* wherefore.

thesis ▶ **noun** ❶ *the central thesis of his lecture* THEORY, contention, argument, line of argument, proposal, proposition, premise, assumption, hypothesis, postulation, surmise, supposition. ❷ *a doctoral thesis* DISSERTATION, essay, paper, treatise, disquisition, composition, monograph, study; *N. Amer.* theme.

thick ▶ **adjective** ❶ *the walls are five feet thick* IN EXTENT/DIAMETER, across, wide, broad, deep. ❷ *his short, thick legs* STOCKY, sturdy, chunky, hefty, thickset, beefy, meaty, big, solid; fat, stout, plump. ❸ *a thick Aran sweater* CHUNKY, bulky, heavy, cable-knit; woollen, woolly. ❹ *the station was thick with people* CROWDED, full, filled, packed, teeming, seething, swarming, crawling, crammed, thronged, bursting at the seams, solid, overflowing, choked, jammed, congested; *informal* jam-packed, chock-a-block, stuffed; *Austral./NZ informal* chocker. ❺ *the thick summer vegetation* PLENTIFUL, abundant, profuse, luxuriant, bushy, rich, riotous, exuberant; rank, rampant; dense, close-packed, impenetrable, impassable; serried; *informal* jungly. ❻ *a thick paste* SEMI-SOLID, firm, stiff, stiffened, heavy; clotted, coagulated, viscid, viscous, gelatinous; concentrated. ❼ *thick fog* DENSE, heavy, opaque, impenetrable, soupy, murky. ❽ (*informal*) *he's a bit thick. See* STUPID sense 1. ❾ *Guy's voice was thick with desire* HUSKY, hoarse, throaty, guttural, gravelly, rough. ❿ *a thick Scottish accent* OBVIOUS, pronounced, marked, broad, strong, rich, decided, distinct. ⓫ *she's very thick with him* FRIENDLY, intimate, familiar, on the best of

terms, hand in glove; close to, devoted to, inseparable from; *informal* pally, chummy, matey, buddy-buddy, as thick as thieves, well in.
– OPPOSITES thin, slender, sparse.
▶ **noun** *in the thick of the crisis* MIDST, centre, hub, middle, core, heart.
■ **a bit thick** (*Brit. informal*) UNREASONABLE, unfair, unjust, unjustified, uncalled for, unwarranted, unnecessary, excessive; *informal* below the belt, a bit much; *Brit. informal* out of order.

thicken ▶ **verb** BECOME THICK/THICKER, stiffen, condense; solidify, set, gel, congeal, clot, coagulate, cake, inspissate.

thicket ▶ **noun** COPSE, coppice, grove, brake, covert, clump; wood; *Brit.* spinney; *archaic* hurst.

thickhead ▶ **noun** (*informal*). *See* FOOL noun sense 1.

thickness ▶ **noun** ❶ *the gateway is several feet in thickness* WIDTH, breadth, depth, diameter. ❷ *several thicknesses of limestone* LAYER, stratum, stratification, seam, vein; sheet, lamina.

thickset ▶ **adjective** STOCKY, sturdy, heavily built, well built, chunky, burly, strapping, brawny, solid, heavy, hefty, beefy, meaty; *Physiology* pyknic.
– OPPOSITES slight.

thick-skinned ▶ **adjective** INSENSITIVE, unfeeling, tough, impervious, hardened, case-hardened; *informal* hard-boiled.
– OPPOSITES sensitive.

thief ▶ **noun** ROBBER, burglar, housebreaker, cat burglar, shoplifter, pickpocket, sneak thief, mugger; embezzler, swindler; criminal, villain; kleptomaniac; bandit, pirate, highwayman; *informal* crook, cracksman; *Brit. rhyming slang* tea leaf; *poetic/literary* brigand.

thieve ▶ **verb** STEAL, take, purloin, help oneself to, snatch, pilfer; embezzle, misappropriate; have one's fingers/hand in the till; *informal* rob, swipe, nab, rip off, lift, 'liberate', 'borrow', filch, snaffle; *Brit. informal* nick, pinch, half-inch, whip, knock off, nobble; *N. Amer. informal* heist; *formal* peculate.

thievery ▶ **noun**. *See* THIEVING.

thieving ▶ **noun** THEFT, stealing, thievery, robbery, larceny, pilfering; burglary, shoplifting, embezzlement; *formal* peculation.

thin ▶ **adjective** ❶ *a thin white line* NARROW, fine, attenuated. ❷ *a thin cotton nightdress* LIGHTWEIGHT, light, fine, delicate, floaty, flimsy, diaphanous, gossamer, insubstantial; sheer, gauzy, filmy, chiffony, transparent, see-through. ❸ *a tall, thin woman* SLIM, lean, slender, rangy, willowy, svelte, sylphlike, spare, slight; SKINNY, underweight, scrawny, scraggy, bony, angular, raw-boned, hollow-cheeked, gaunt, as thin as a rake/reed, stick-like, skin-and-bones, emaciated, skeletal, wasted, pinched, undernourished, underfed; lanky, spindly, gangly, gangling, weedy; *informal* anorexic, like a bag of bones; *dated* spindle-shanked; *archaic* starveling. ❹ *his thin grey hair* SPARSE, scanty, wispy, thinning. ❺ *a bowl of thin soup* WATERY, weak, dilute, diluted; runny, sloppy. ❻ *her thin voice* WEAK, faint, feeble, small, soft; reedy, high-pitched. ❼ *the plot is very thin* INSUBSTANTIAL, flimsy, slight, feeble, lame, poor, weak, tenuous, inadequate, insufficient, unconvincing, unbelievable, implausible.
– OPPOSITES thick, broad, fat, abundant.
▶ **verb** ❶ *some paint must be thinned down before use* DILUTE, water down, weaken. ❷ *the crowds were beginning to thin out* DISPERSE, dissipate, scatter; become less dense/numerous, decrease, diminish, dwindle.

thing ▶ **noun** ❶ *the room was full of strange things* OBJECT, article, item, artefact, commodity; device, gadget, instrument, utensil, tool, implement; entity, body; *informal* doodah, whatsit, whatchamacallit, thingummy, thingy, thingamabob, thingamajig; *Brit. informal* gubbins; *N. Amer. informal* doodad, dingus. ❷ *I'll come back tomorrow to collect my things* BELONGINGS, possessions, stuff, property, worldly goods, (personal) effects, paraphernalia, bits and pieces, bits and bobs; luggage, baggage, bags; *Law* goods and chattels; *informal* gear, junk; *Brit. informal* clobber. ❸ *his gardening things* EQUIPMENT, apparatus, gear, kit, tackle, stuff; implements, tools, utensils; accoutrements. ❹ *I've got several things to do today* ACTIVITY, act, action, deed, undertaking, exploit, feat; task, job, chore. ❺ *I've got other things on my mind just now* THOUGHT, notion, idea; concern, matter, worry, preoccupation. ❻ *I keep remembering things he said* REMARK, statement, comment, utterance, observation, declaration, pronouncement. ❼ *quite a few odd things happened* INCIDENT, episode, event, happening, occurrence, phenomenon. ❽ *how are things with you?* MATTERS, affairs, circumstances, conditions, relations; state of affairs, situation, life. ❾ *one of the things I like about you is your optimism* CHARACTERISTIC, quality, attribute, property, trait, feature, point, aspect, facet. ❿ *there's another thing you should know* FACT, piece of information, point, detail, particular, factor. ⓫ *the thing is, I'm not sure if it's what I want* FACT OF THE MATTER, fact, point, issue, problem. ⓬ *you lucky thing!* PERSON, soul, creature, wretch; *informal* devil, beggar, bastard. ⓭ *Dora developed a thing about noise* PHOBIA, fear, dislike, aversion; obsession, fixation; complex, neurosis; *informal* hang-up, bee in one's bonnet. ⓮ *she had a thing about men who wore glasses* PENCHANT, preference, taste, inclination, partiality, predilection, soft spot, weakness, fancy, fondness, liking, love; fetish, obsession, fixation. ⓯ *books aren't really my thing* WHAT ONE LIKES, what interests one; *informal* one's cup of tea, one's bag, what turns one on. ⓰ *it's the latest thing* FASHIONABLE, in fashion, popular, all the rage; *informal* trendy, cool, big, hip, happening.

think ▶ verb ❶ *I think he's gone home* BELIEVE, be of the opinion, be of the view, be under the impression; expect, imagine, anticipate; surmise, suppose, conjecture, guess, fancy; conclude, determine, reason; *informal* reckon, figure; *formal* opine; *archaic* ween. ❷ *his family was thought to be enormously rich* DEEM, judge, hold, reckon, consider, presume, estimate; regard as, view as. ❸ *Jack thought for a moment* PONDER, reflect, deliberate, consider, meditate, contemplate, muse, ruminate, be lost in thought, be in a brown study, brood; concentrate, rack one's brains; *informal* put on one's thinking cap, sleep on it; *formal* cogitate. ❹ *she thought of all the visits she had made to her father* RECALL, remember, recollect, call to mind, think back to. ❺ *she forced herself to think of how he must be feeling* IMAGINE, picture, visualize, envisage; dream about, fantasize about.

■ **think better of** HAVE SECOND THOUGHTS ABOUT, think twice about, think again about, change one's mind about; reconsider, decide against; *informal* get cold feet about.

■ **think something over** CONSIDER, contemplate, deliberate about, weigh up, consider the pros and cons of, mull over, ponder, reflect on, muse on, ruminate on.

■ **think something up** DEVISE, dream up, come up with, invent, create, concoct, make up; hit on.

thinker ▶ noun THEORIST, ideologist, philosopher, scholar, savant, sage, intellectual, intellect, mind; *informal* brain.

thinking ▶ adjective *he seemed a thinking man* INTELLIGENT, sensible, reasonable, rational; logical, analytical; thoughtful, reflective, meditative, contemplative, pensive, philosophical.
– OPPOSITES stupid, irrational.

▶ noun *the thinking behind the campaign* REASONING, idea(s), theory, thoughts, line of thought, philosophy, beliefs; opinion(s), view(s), position, judgement, assessment, evaluation.

thin-skinned ▶ adjective SENSITIVE, oversensitive, hypersensitive, easily offended/hurt, touchy, defensive.
– OPPOSITES insensitive.

third-rate ▶ adjective SUBSTANDARD, bad, inferior, poor, poor-quality, low-grade, inadequate, unsatisfactory, unacceptable; appalling, abysmal, atrocious, awful, terrible, dreadful, execrable, frightful, miserable, wretched, pitiful; jerry-built, shoddy, tinny, trashy; *N. Amer.* cheapjack; *informal* lousy, diabolical, rotten, dire, bum, crummy, rubbishy; *Brit. informal* ropy, duff.
– OPPOSITES excellent.

thirst ▶ noun ❶ *I need a drink—I'm dying of thirst* THIRSTINESS, dryness; dehydration; *Medicine* polydipsia; *archaic* drought. ❷ *his thirst for knowledge* CRAVING, desire, longing, yearning, hunger, hankering, keenness, eagerness, lust, appetite; *informal* yen, itch; *archaic* appetency.

▶ verb *she thirsted for power* CRAVE, want, covet, desire, hunger for, lust after, hanker after, have one's heart set on; wish, long.

thirsty ▶ adjective ❶ *the boys were hot and thirsty* LONGING FOR A DRINK, dry, dehydrated; *informal* parched, gasping; *Brit. informal* spitting feathers; *Austral./NZ informal* spitting chips. ❷ *the thirsty soil* DRY, arid, dried up/out, as dry as a bone, parched, baked, desiccated. ❸ *she was thirsty for power* EAGER, hungry, greedy, thirsting, craving, longing, yearning, lusting, burning, desirous, hankering; *informal* itching, dying.

thorn ▶ noun PRICKLE, spike, barb, spine.

thorny ▶ adjective ❶ *dense thorny undergrowth* PRICKLY, spiky, barbed, spiny, sharp; *technical* spinose, spinous. ❷ *the thorny subject of confidentiality* PROBLEMATIC, tricky, ticklish, delicate, controversial, awkward, difficult, knotty, tough, taxing, trying, troublesome; complicated, complex, involved, intricate; vexed; *informal* sticky.

thorough ▶ adjective ❶ *a thorough investigation* RIGOROUS, in-depth, exhaustive, thoroughgoing, minute, detailed, close, meticulous, methodical, careful, complete, comprehensive, full, extensive, widespread, sweeping, all-embracing, all-inclusive. ❷ *he is slow but thorough* METICULOUS, scrupulous, assiduous, conscientious, painstaking, punctilious, methodical, careful, diligent, industrious, hardworking. ❸ *the child is being a thorough nuisance* UTTER, downright, thoroughgoing, absolute, complete, total, out-and-out, arrant, real, perfect, proper, sheer, unqualified, unmitigated; *Brit. informal* right; *Austral./NZ informal* fair.
– OPPOSITES superficial, cursory, careless.

thoroughbred ▶ adjective PURE-BRED, pedigree, pure, pure-blooded.

thoroughfare ▶ noun ❶ *the park is being used as a thoroughfare* THROUGH ROUTE, access route; *Brit. informal* rat run. ❷ *the teeming thoroughfares of central London* STREET, road, roadway, avenue, boulevard, main road, high road, A road, B road; *N. Amer.* highway, freeway, throughway.

thoroughly ▶ adverb ❶ *we will investigate all complaints thoroughly* RIGOROUSLY, in depth, exhaustively, from top to bottom, minutely, closely, in detail, meticulously, scrupulously, assiduously, conscientiously, painstakingly, methodically, carefully, comprehensively, fully. ❷ *she is thoroughly spoilt* UTTERLY, downright, absolutely, completely, totally, entirely, really, perfectly, positively, in every respect, through and through; *informal* plain, clean.

though ▶ conjunction *though she smiled bravely, she looked pale and tired* ALTHOUGH, even though/if, in spite of the fact that, despite the fact that, notwithstanding (the fact) that, for all that.

▶ adverb *You can't always do that. You can try, though.* NEVERTHELESS, nonetheless, even so, however, be that as it may, for all that, despite that, having said that; *informal* still and all.

thought ▶ **noun** ❶ *what are your thoughts on the matter?* IDEA, notion, opinion, view, impression, feeling, theory; judgement, assessment, conclusion. ❷ *he gave up any thought of taking a degree* HOPE, aspiration, ambition, dream; intention, idea, plan, design, aim. ❸ *it only took a moment's thought* THINKING, contemplation, musing, pondering, consideration, reflection, introspection, deliberation, rumination, meditation, brooding, reverie, brown study, concentration; *formal* cogitation. ❹ *have you no thought for others?* COMPASSION, sympathy, care, concern, regard, solicitude, empathy; consideration, understanding, sensitivity, thoughtfulness, charity.

thoughtful ▶ **adjective** ❶ *a thoughtful expression* PENSIVE, reflective, contemplative, musing, meditative, introspective, philosophical, ruminative, absorbed, engrossed, rapt, preoccupied, deep/lost in thought, in a brown study, brooding; *formal* cogitative. ❷ *how very thoughtful of you!* CONSIDERATE, caring, attentive, understanding, sympathetic, solicitous, concerned, helpful, friendly, obliging, accommodating, neighbourly, unselfish, kind, compassionate, charitable.
– OPPOSITES vacant, inconsiderate.

thoughtless ▶ **adjective** ❶ *I'm so sorry—how thoughtless of me* INCONSIDERATE, uncaring, insensitive, uncharitable, unkind, tactless, undiplomatic, indiscreet, careless. ❷ *a few minutes of thoughtless pleasure* UNTHINKING, heedless, careless, unmindful, absent-minded, injudicious, ill-advised, ill-considered, imprudent, unwise, foolish, silly, stupid, reckless, rash, precipitate, negligent, neglectful, remiss.
– OPPOSITES considerate, careful.

thousand ▶ **cardinal number** *informal* K, thou.
– RELATED TERMS millenary, kilo-, milli-.

thrall ▶ **noun** POWER, clutches, hands, control, grip, yoke, enslavement, subjection, subjugation, tyranny.

thrash ▶ **verb** ❶ *she thrashed him across the head and shoulders* HIT, beat, strike, batter, thump, hammer, pound, rain blows on; assault, attack; cudgel, club, birch; *informal* wallop, belt, bash, whack, thwack, clout, clobber, slug, tan, biff, bop, sock, beat the living daylights out of, give someone a good hiding. ❷ (*informal*) *Newcastle were thrashed 8–1. See* TROUNCE. ❸ *he was thrashing around in pain* FLAIL, writhe, thresh, jerk, toss, twist, twitch.
■ **thrash something out** ❶ *it's better if we can thrash out our difficulties first* RESOLVE, settle, sort out, straighten out, iron out, clear up; talk through, discuss, debate, air, ventilate. ❷ *they tried to thrash out an agreement* WORK OUT, negotiate, agree on, bring about, hammer out, produce, effect.

thread ▶ **noun** ❶ *a needle and thread* COTTON, yarn, filament, fibre. ❷ (*poetic/literary*) *the Thames was a thread of silver below them* STREAK, strand, stripe, line, strip, seam, vein. ❸ *she lost the thread of the conversation* TRAIN OF THOUGHT, drift, direction, theme, motif, tenor; storyline, plot.
▶ **verb** ❶ *he threaded the rope through a pulley* PASS, string, work, ease, push, poke. ❷ *she threaded her way through the tables* WEAVE ONE'S WAY, inch one's way, wind one's way, squeeze one's way, make one's way.

threadbare ▶ **adjective** WORN, well worn, old, thin, worn out, holey, moth-eaten, mangy, ragged, frayed, tattered, battered; decrepit, shabby, scruffy, unkempt; having seen better days, falling apart at the seams, falling to pieces; *informal* tatty, ratty, the worse for wear; *N. Amer. informal* raggedy.

threat ▶ **noun** ❶ *Maggie ignored his threats* THREATENING REMARK, warning, ultimatum. ❷ *a possible threat to aircraft* DANGER, peril, hazard, menace, risk. ❸ *the company faces the threat of liquidation proceedings* POSSIBILITY, chance, probability, likelihood, risk.

threaten ▶ **verb** ❶ *how dare you threaten me?* MENACE, intimidate, browbeat, bully, terrorize; make/issue threats to. ❷ *these events could threaten the stability of Europe* ENDANGER, be a danger/threat to, jeopardize, imperil, put at risk, put in jeopardy. ❸ *the grey skies threatened snow* HERALD, bode, warn of, presage, augur, portend, foreshadow, be a harbinger of, indicate, point to, be a sign of, signal, spell; *poetic/literary* foretoken. ❹ *as rain threatened, the party moved indoors* SEEM LIKELY, seem imminent, be on the horizon, be brewing, be gathering, be looming, be on the way, be impending; hang over someone.

threatening ▶ **adjective** ❶ *a threatening letter* MENACING, intimidating, bullying, frightening, hostile; *formal* minatory. ❷ *banks of threatening clouds* OMINOUS, sinister, menacing, dark, black, thunderous.

three ▶ **cardinal number** TRIO, threesome, triple, triad, trinity, troika, triumvirate, trilogy, triptych, trefoil, three-piece, triplets.
– RELATED TERMS triple, treble, ter-, tri-.

threesome ▶ **noun** TRIO, triumvirate, triad, trinity, troika; triplets.

threnody ▶ **noun** LAMENT, dirge, requiem, elegy, monody; *Irish* keen; *Irish & Scottish* coronach.

threshold ▶ **noun** ❶ *the threshold of the church* DOORSTEP, doorway, entrance, entry, door, gate, gateway, portal. ❷ *the threshold of a new era* START, beginning, commencement, brink, verge, dawn, inception, day one, opening, debut; *informal* kick-off. ❸ *the human threshold of pain* LOWER LIMIT, minimum; *Psychology* limen.
– RELATED TERMS liminal.

thrift ▸ **noun** FRUGALITY, economy, economizing, thriftiness, providence, prudence, good management/husbandry, saving, scrimping and saving, abstemiousness, parsimony, penny-pinching.
– OPPOSITES extravagance.

thriftless ▸ **adjective** EXTRAVAGANT, profligate, spendthrift, wasteful, improvident, imprudent, free-spending, prodigal, lavish; immoderate, excessive, reckless, irresponsible.

thrifty ▸ **adjective** FRUGAL, economical, sparing, careful with money, provident, prudent, abstemious, parsimonious, penny-pinching; *N. Amer.* forehanded.
– OPPOSITES extravagant.

thrill ▸ **noun** ❶ *the thrill of jumping out of an aeroplane* (FEELING OF) EXCITEMENT, stimulation, pleasure, tingle; fun, enjoyment, amusement, delight, joy; *informal* buzz, kick; *N. Amer. informal* charge. ❷ *a thrill of excitement ran through her* WAVE, rush, surge, flash, blaze, stab, dart, throb, tremor, quiver, flutter, shudder.
▸ **verb** ❶ *his words thrilled her* EXCITE, stimulate, arouse, rouse, inspire, delight, exhilarate, intoxicate, stir, electrify, galvanize, move, fire (with enthusiasm), fire someone's imagination; *informal* give someone a buzz, give someone a kick; *N. Amer. informal* give someone a charge. ❷ *he thrilled at the sound of her voice* BE/FEEL EXCITED, tingle; *informal* get a buzz out of, get a kick out of; *N. Amer. informal* get a charge out of. ❸ *shivers of anticipation thrilled through her* RUSH, race, surge, course, flood, flow, wash, sweep, flash, blaze.
– OPPOSITES bore.

thrilling ▸ **adjective** EXCITING, stirring, action-packed, rip-roaring, gripping, riveting, fascinating, dramatic, hair-raising; rousing, stimulating, moving, inspiring, inspirational, electrifying, heady, soul-stirring.
– OPPOSITES boring.

thrive ▸ **verb** FLOURISH, prosper, burgeon, bloom, blossom, do well, advance, make strides, succeed, boom.
– OPPOSITES decline, wither.

thriving ▸ **adjective** FLOURISHING, prosperous, prospering, growing, developing, burgeoning, blooming, healthy, successful, booming, profitable, expanding; *informal* going strong.
– OPPOSITES moribund.

throat ▸ **noun** GULLET, oesophagus; windpipe, trachea; maw; *informal, dated* the red lane; *archaic* throttle, gorge.
– RELATED TERMS guttural, jugular.

throaty ▸ **adjective** GRAVELLY, husky, rough, guttural, deep, thick, gruff, growly, growling, hoarse, croaky, croaking; rasping, raspy.
– OPPOSITES high-pitched.

throb ▸ **verb** *her arms and legs throbbed with tiredness* PULSATE, beat, pulse, palpitate, pound, thud, thump, drum, thrum, vibrate, pitter-patter, go pit-a-pat, quiver.
▸ **noun** *the throb of the ship's engines* PULSATION, beat, beating, pulse, palpitation, pounding, thudding, thumping, drumming, thrumming, pit-a-pat, pitter-patter.

throes ▸ **plural noun** *the throes of childbirth* AGONY, pain, pangs, suffering, torture; *poetic/literary* travail.
■ **in the throes of** IN THE MIDDLE OF, in the process of, in the midst of, busy with, occupied with, taken up with/by, involved in; struggling with, wrestling with, grappling with.

thrombosis ▸ **noun** BLOOD CLOT, embolism, embolus, thrombus, infarction.

throne ▸ **noun** ❶ *a golden throne* seat of state, royal seat. ❷ *the tsar risked losing his throne* SOVEREIGN POWER, sovereignty, rule, dominion.

throng ▸ **noun** *throngs of people blocked her way* CROWD, horde, mass, multitude, host, army, herd, flock, drove, swarm, sea, troupe, pack, press, crush; collection, company, gathering, assembly, assemblage, congregation; *informal* gaggle, bunch, gang; *archaic* rout.
▸ **verb** ❶ *the pavements were thronged with tourists* FILL, crowd. pack, cram, jam. ❷ *people thronged to see the play* FLOCK, stream, swarm, troop. ❸ *visitors thronged round him* CROWD, cluster, mill, swarm, congregate, gather.

throttle ▸ **verb** ❶ *he tried to throttle her* CHOKE, strangle, strangulate, garrotte. ❷ *attempts to throttle the criminal supply of drugs* SUPPRESS, inhibit, stifle, control, restrain, check, contain, put a/the lid on; stop, put an end to, end, stamp out.

through ▸ **preposition** ❶ *we drove through the tunnel* INTO AND OUT OF, to the other/far side of, from one side to the other of. ❷ *he got the job through an advertisement* BY MEANS OF, by way of, by dint of, via, using, thanks to, by virtue of, as a result of, as a consequence of, on account of, owing to, because of. ❸ *he worked through the night* THROUGHOUT, all through, for the duration of, until/to the end of.
▸ **adverb** ❶ *as soon as we opened the gate they came streaming through* FROM ONE SIDE TO THE OTHER, from one end to another, in and out the other side. ❷ *I woke up, but Anthony slept through* THE WHOLE TIME, all the time, from start to finish, without a break, without an interruption, non-stop, continuously, throughout.
▸ **adjective** *a through train* DIRECT, non-stop.
■ **through and through** IN EVERY RESPECT, to the core; thoroughly, utterly, absolutely, completely, totally, wholly, fully, entirely, unconditionally, unreservedly, altogether, out-and-out.

throughout ▸ **preposition** ❶ *it had repercussions throughout Europe* ALL OVER, in every part of, everywhere in, all through, right through, all round. ❷ *Rose had generally been very fit* *throughout her life* ALL THROUGH, all, for the duration of, for the whole of, until the end of.

throw ▶ verb ❶ *she threw the ball back* HURL, toss, fling, pitch, cast, lob, launch, catapult, project, propel; bowl; *informal* chuck, heave, sling, bung; *N. Amer. informal* peg; *Austral. informal* hoy; *NZ informal* bish; *dated* shy. ❷ *he threw the door open* PUSH, thrust, fling, bang, force. ❸ *a chandelier threw its light over the walls* CAST, send, give off, emit, radiate, project. ❹ *he threw another punch* DELIVER, give, land. ❺ *she threw a withering glance at him* DIRECT, cast, send, dart, shoot. ❻ *the horse threw his rider* UNSEAT, dislodge. ❼ *his question threw me* DISCONCERT, unnerve, fluster, ruffle, agitate, discomfit, put off, throw off balance, discountenance, unsettle, confuse; *informal* rattle, faze; *N. Amer. informal* discombobulate. ❽ *the pots were thrown on a wheel* SHAPE, form, mould, fashion. ❾ *he threw a farewell party for them* GIVE, host, hold, have, provide, put on, lay on, arrange, organize.

▶ noun ❶ *we were allowed two throws each* LOB, pitch; go; bowl, ball. ❷ (*informal*) *drinks are only £1 a throw* EACH, apiece, per item.

■ **throw something away** ❶ *she hated throwing old clothes away* DISCARD, throw out, dispose of, get rid of, do away with, toss out, scrap, throw on the scrap heap, clear out, dump, jettison; *informal* chuck (away/out), ditch, bin, junk, get shut of; *Brit. informal* get shot of. ❷ *Cambridge threw away a 15–0 lead* SQUANDER, waste, fritter away, fail to exploit, lose, let slip; *informal* blow, throw something down the drain.

■ **throw someone off** SHAKE OFF, get away from, escape, elude, give someone the slip, throw off the scent, dodge, lose.

■ **throw someone out** EXPEL, eject, evict, drive out, force out, oust, remove; get rid of, depose, topple, unseat, overthrow, bring down, overturn, dislodge, displace, supplant, show someone the door; banish, deport, exile; *informal* boot out, kick out, give someone the boot; *Brit. informal* turf out.

■ **throw something out** ❶ *throw out food that's past its sell-by date*. See THROW SOMETHING AWAY sense 1. ❷ *his case was thrown out by the magistrate* REJECT, dismiss, turn down, refuse, disallow, veto; *informal* give the thumbs down to. ❸ *a thermal light bulb throws out a lot of heat* RADIATE, emit, give off, send out, diffuse.

■ **throw someone over** ABANDON, leave, desert, discard, turn one's back on, cast aside/off; jilt, break up with, finish with, leave in the lurch, leave high and dry; *informal* dump, ditch, chuck, drop, walk out on, run out on, leave flat, give someone the push/elbow, give someone the big E; *poetic/literary* forsake.

■ **throw up** (*informal*). See VOMIT verb sense 1.

■ **throw something up** GIVE UP, abandon, relinquish, resign (from), leave; *informal* quit, chuck, pack in; *Brit. informal* jack in.

throwaway ▶ adjective ❶ *throwaway packaging* DISPOSABLE, non-returnable; biodegradable, photodegradable. ❷ *throwaway remarks* CASUAL, passing, careless, unthinking, unstudied, unconsidered, offhand.

thrust ▶ verb ❶ *she thrust her hands into her pockets* SHOVE, push, force, plunge, stick, drive, propel, ram, poke. ❷ *fame had been thrust on him* FORCE, foist, impose, inflict. ❸ *he thrust his way past her* PUSH, shove, force, elbow, shoulder, barge.

▶ noun ❶ *a hard thrust* SHOVE, push, lunge, poke. ❷ *a thrust by the Third Army* ADVANCE, push, drive, attack, assault, onslaught, offensive, charge, sortie, foray, raid, sally, invasion, incursion. ❸ *only one engine is producing thrust* FORCE, propulsive force, propulsion, power, impetus, momentum. ❹ *the thrust of the speech* GIST, substance, drift, burden, meaning, significance, signification, sense, theme, message, import, tenor.

thrusting ▶ adjective AMBITIOUS, pushy, forceful, aggressive, assertive, self-assertive, full of oneself, determined, power-hungry.
– OPPOSITES meek.

thud ▶ noun & verb THUMP, clunk, clonk, crash, smack, bang; stomp, stamp, clump, clomp; *informal* wham.

thug ▶ noun RUFFIAN, lout, hooligan, bully boy, vandal, hoodlum, gangster, villain, criminal; *informal* tough, bruiser, heavy, hired gun; *Brit. informal* rough, bovver boy; *N. Amer. informal* hood, goon.

thumb ▶ noun *technical* pollex, opposable digit.

▶ verb ❶ *he thumbed through his notebook* LEAF, flick, flip, riffle, skim, browse, look. ❷ *his dictionaries were thumbed and ink-stained* SOIL, mark, make dog-eared. ❸ *he was thumbing his way across France* HITCH-HIKE; *informal* hitch, hitch/thumb a lift.

■ **all thumbs** (*Brit. informal*) CLUMSY, awkward, maladroit, inept, unskilful, heavy-handed, inexpert; *informal* butterfingered, cack-handed, ham-fisted, having two left feet; *Brit. informal* all fingers and thumbs; *N. Amer. informal* klutzy.

■ **thumbs down** (*informal*) REJECTION, refusal, veto, no, negation, rebuff; *informal* red light, knock-back.

■ **thumbs up** (*informal*) APPROVAL, seal of approval, endorsement; permission, authorization, consent, yes, leave, authority, sanction, ratification, licence, dispensation, nod, assent, blessing, rubber stamp, clearance; *informal* go-ahead, OK, green light, say-so.

thumbnail ▶ adjective CONCISE, short, brief, succinct, to the point, compact, crisp, short and sweet, quick, rapid; potted.

thump ▶ verb ❶ *the two men kicked and thumped him* HIT, strike, smack, cuff, punch; beat, thrash, batter, belabour, pound, pummel, box someone's ears; *informal* whack, wallop, bash, biff, bop, lam, clout, clobber, sock, swipe, crown, beat the living daylights out of, give someone a (good) hiding, belt, tan, lay into, let someone have it; *Brit. informal* stick one on, slosh; *N. Amer. informal* slug, boff; *poetic/literary* smite. ❷ *her heart thumped with fright* THROB, pound, thud, hammer, pulsate, pulse, pump, palpitate, race, beat heavily.

▶ **noun** ❶ *a well-aimed thump on the jaw* BLOW, punch, box, cuff, smack; thrashing, hiding; *informal* whack, thwack, wallop, bash, belt, biff, clout, swipe; *Brit. informal* slosh; *N. Amer. informal* boff, slug. ❷ *she put the box down with a thump* THUD, clunk, clonk, crash, smack, bang.

thumping ▶ **adjective** ❶ *the thumping beat of her heart* THUDDING, pounding, throbbing, pulsating, banging, hammering, drumming. ❷ (*informal*) *a thumping 64 per cent majority | a thumping victory* ENORMOUS, huge, massive, vast, tremendous, substantial, prodigious, gigantic, giant, terrific, fantastic, colossal, immense, mammoth, monumental, stupendous; emphatic, decisive, conclusive, striking, impressive, outstanding, notable, memorable, remarkable, extraordinary, resounding, phenomenal; *informal* whopping, thundering; *Brit. informal* whacking.

▶ **adverb** (*informal*) *a thumping good read. See* VERY adverb.

thunder ▶ **noun** ❶ *thunder and lightning* THUNDERCLAP, roll/rumble of thunder, crack/crash of thunder; *poetic/literary* thunderbolt. ❷ *the ceaseless thunder of the traffic* RUMBLE, rumbling, boom, booming, roar, roaring, pounding, thud, thudding, crash, crashing, reverberation.

▶ **verb** ❶ *below me the surf thrashed and thundered* RUMBLE, boom, roar, pound, thud, thump, bang; resound, reverberate, beat. ❷ *he thundered against the evils of the age* RAIL, fulminate, inveigh, rage; condemn, denounce. ❸ *'Answer me!' he thundered* ROAR, bellow, bark, yell, shout, bawl; *informal* holler.

thundering ▶ **adjective** *a thundering noise. See* THUNDEROUS.

▶ **adverb** *a thundering good read. See* VERY adverb.

thunderous ▶ **adjective** VERY LOUD, tumultuous, booming, roaring, resounding, reverberating, reverberant, ringing, deafening, earsplitting, noisy.

thunderstruck ▶ **adjective** ASTONISHED, amazed, astounded, staggered, surprised, startled, stunned, shocked, aghast, taken aback, dumbfounded, dumbstruck, stupefied, dazed, speechless; *informal* flabbergasted; *Brit. informal* gobsmacked, knocked for six.

thus ▶ **adverb** ❶ *the studio handled production, thus cutting its costs* CONSEQUENTLY, as a consequence, in consequence, so, that being so, therefore, ergo, accordingly, hence, as a result, for that reason, because of that, on that account. ❷ *legislation forbids such data being held thus* LIKE THAT, in that way, so, like so.

■ **thus far** SO FAR, (up) until now, up to now, up to this point, hitherto.

thwack ▶ **verb** (*informal*) HIT, strike, slap, smack, cuff, punch, thump; beat, thrash, batter, belabour, pound, pummel, box someone's ears; whip, flog, cane; *informal* whack, wallop, bash, biff, bop, lam, clout, clobber, sock, swipe, crown, beat the living daylights out of, give someone a (good) hiding, belt, tan, lay into, let someone have it, deck, floor; *Brit. informal* stick one on, slosh; *N. Amer. informal* slug, boff; *poetic/literary* smite.

thwart ▶ **verb** FOIL, frustrate, baulk, stand in the way of, forestall, derail, dash; stop, check, block, prevent, defeat, impede, obstruct, snooker, hinder, hamper; spike someone's guns; *informal* put paid to, put the kibosh on, do for, stymie; *Brit. informal* scupper, queer someone's pitch.

– OPPOSITES facilitate.

tic ▶ **noun** TWITCH, spasm, jerk, tremor.

tick ▶ **noun** ❶ *put a tick against the item of your choice* mark, stroke; *N. Amer.* check, check mark. ❷ *the tick of his watch* TICKING, tick-tock, click, clicking, tap, tapping. ❸ (*Brit. informal*) *I won't be a tick* MOMENT, second, minute, bit, little while, instant; *informal* sec, jiffy; *Brit. informal* mo, two ticks.

▶ **verb** ❶ *tick the appropriate box* PUT A TICK IN/AGAINST, mark, check off, indicate; *N. Amer.* check. ❷ *I could hear the clock ticking* TICK-TOCK, click; tap.

■ **in a tick** (*Brit. informal*) (VERY) SOON, in a second, in a minute, in a moment, in a trice, in a flash, shortly, any second, any minute, in no time (at all); *N. Amer.* momentarily; *informal* in a sec, in a jiffy, in two shakes (of a lamb's tail), before you can say Jack Robinson; *Brit. informal* in two ticks, in a mo; *N. Amer. informal* in a snap; *dated* directly.

■ **tick someone off** (*Brit. informal*). *See* REPRIMAND verb.

ticket ▶ **noun** ❶ *can I see your ticket?* PASS, authorization, permit; token, coupon, voucher. ❷ *a price ticket* LABEL, tag, sticker, tab, marker, docket.

tickle ▶ **verb** ❶ *he tried to tickle her under the chin* STROKE, pet, chuck. ❷ *he found something that tickled his imagination* STIMULATE, interest, appeal to, arouse, excite. ❸ *the idea tickled Lewis* AMUSE, entertain, divert, please, delight; *informal* tickle someone pink.

ticklish ▶ **adjective** DIFFICULT, problematic, tricky, delicate, sensitive, awkward, prickly, thorny, tough; vexed; *informal* sticky.

tide ▶ **noun** ❶ *ships come up the river with the tide* TIDAL FLOW, ebb and flow, tidewater, ebb, current. ❷ *the tide of history* COURSE, movement, direction, trend, current, drift, run, turn, tendency, tenor.

■ **tide someone over** SUSTAIN, keep someone going, keep someone's head above water, see someone through; keep the wolf from the door; help out, assist, aid.

tidings ▶ **plural noun** (*poetic/literary*) NEWS, information, intelligence, word, reports, notification, communication, the latest; *informal* info, the low down.

tidy ▶ **adjective** ❶ *a tidy room* NEAT, neat and tidy, as neat as a new pin, orderly, well ordered, in (good) order, well kept, shipshape (and Bristol fashion), in apple-pie order, immaculate, spick and span, uncluttered, straight, trim, spruce. ❷ *he's a very tidy person* NEAT, trim, spruce, dapper, well groomed, well turned out; organized, well organized, methodical, meticulous; fastidious; *informal* natty. ❸ (*informal*) *a tidy sum* LARGE, sizeable, considerable, substantial, generous, significant, appreciable, handsome, respectable, decent, goodly; *informal* not to be sneezed at.
– OPPOSITES messy.
▶ **verb** ❶ *I'd better tidy up the living room* PUT IN ORDER, clear up, sort out, straighten (up), clean up, spruce up. ❷ *she tidied herself up in the bathroom* GROOM ONESELF, spruce oneself up, freshen oneself up, smarten oneself up; *informal* titivate oneself.

tie ▶ **verb** ❶ *they tied Max to a chair* BIND, tie up, tether, hitch, strap, truss, fetter, rope, chain, make fast, moor, lash, attach, fasten, fix, secure, join, connect, link, couple. ❷ *he bent to tie his shoelaces* DO UP, lace, knot. ❸ *women can feel tied by childcare responsibilities* RESTRICT, restrain, limit, tie down, constrain, trammel, confine, cramp, hamper, handicap, hamstring, encumber, shackle, inhibit; cramp someone's style. ❹ *a pay deal tied to a productivity agreement* LINK, connect, couple, relate, join, marry; make conditional on, bind up with. ❺ *they tied for second place* DRAW, be equal, be even, be neck and neck.
▶ **noun** ❶ *he tightened the ties of his robe* LACE, string, cord, fastening, fastener. ❷ *a collar and tie* NECKTIE, bow tie, string tie; *Brit.* bootlace tie. ❸ *family ties* BOND, connection, link, relationship, attachment, affiliation, allegiance, friendship; kinship, interdependence. ❹ *pets can be a tremendous tie* RESTRICTION, constraint, curb, limitation, restraint, hindrance, encumbrance, handicap; obligation, commitment. ❺ *there was a tie for first place* DRAW, dead heat, deadlock. ❻ (*Brit.*) *Turkey's World Cup tie against Holland* MATCH, game, contest, fixture, event.
■ **tie someone down** *she was afraid of being tied down. See* TIE verb sense 3.
■ **tie in** BE CONSISTENT, tally, agree, be in agreement, accord, concur, fit in, harmonize, be in tune, dovetail, correspond, match; *informal* square; *N. Amer. informal* jibe.
■ **tie someone/something up** ❶ *robbers tied her up and ransacked her home* BIND, bind hand and foot, fasten together, truss (up), fetter, chain up. ❷ *he is tied up in meetings all morning* OCCUPY, engage, keep busy. ❸ *they were anxious to tie up the contract* FINALIZE, conclude, complete, finish off, seal, set the seal on, settle, secure, clinch; *informal* wrap up.

tie-in ▶ **noun** CONNECTION, link, association, correlation, tie-up, interrelation, relationship, relation, interconnection; parallel, similarity.

tier ▶ **noun** ❶ *tiers of empty seats* ROW, rank, bank, line; layer, level. ❷ *the most senior tier of management* GRADE, gradation, echelon, rung on the ladder.

tiff ▶ **noun** (*informal*) QUARREL, squabble, argument, disagreement, fight, falling-out, difference of opinion, dispute, wrangle, altercation, contretemps, disputation, shouting match; *informal* slanging match, run-in, spat, set-to; *Brit. informal* barney, row, bust-up.

tight ▶ **adjective** ❶ *a tight grip* FIRM, fast, secure, fixed, clenched. ❷ *the rope was pulled tight* TAUT, rigid, stiff, tense, stretched, strained. ❸ *tight jeans* TIGHT-FITTING, close-fitting, narrow, figure-hugging, skintight; *informal* sprayed on. ❹ *a tight mass of fibres* COMPACT, compacted, compressed, dense, solid. ❺ *a tight space* SMALL, tiny, narrow, limited, restricted, confined, cramped, constricted, uncomfortable. ❻ *the joint will be perfectly tight against petrol leaks* IMPERVIOUS, impenetrable, sealed, sound, hermetic; watertight, airtight. ❼ *tight limits on the use of pesticides* STRICT, rigorous, stringent, tough, rigid, firm, uncompromising. ❽ *he's in a tight spot* DIFFICULT, tricky, delicate, awkward, problematic, worrying, precarious; *informal* sticky; *Brit. informal* dodgy. ❾ *a tight piece of writing* SUCCINCT, concise, pithy, incisive, crisp, condensed, well structured, to the point. ❿ *a tight race* CLOSE, even, evenly matched, well matched; hard-fought, neck and neck. ⓫ *money is a bit tight just now* LIMITED, restricted, in short supply, scarce, depleted, diminished, low, inadequate, insufficient. ⓬ (*informal*) *he's tight with his money* MEAN, miserly, parsimonious, niggardly, close-fisted, penny-pinching, cheese-paring, Scrooge-like, close; *informal* stingy, tight-fisted; *N. Amer. informal* cheap; *formal* penurious; *archaic* near. ⓭ (*informal*) *he came home tight from the pub. See* DRUNK adjective.
– OPPOSITES slack, loose, generous.

tighten ▶ **verb** ❶ *I tightened up the screws* MAKE TIGHTER, make fast, screw up. ❷ *he tightened his grip* STRENGTHEN, make stronger, harden. ❸ *she tightened the rope* TAUTEN, make/draw taut, make/draw tight, stretch, strain, stiffen, tense. ❹ *he tightened his lips* NARROW, constrict, contract, compress, screw up, pucker, purse; *N. Amer.* squinch. ❺ *security in the area has been tightened up* INCREASE, make stricter, toughen up, heighten, scale up.
– OPPOSITES loosen, slacken, relax.

tight-fisted ▶ **adjective** MEAN, miserly, parsimonious, niggardly, close-fisted, penny-pinching, cheese-paring, Scrooge-like, close; *informal* stingy, tight; *N. Amer. informal* cheap; *formal* penurious; *archaic* near.
– OPPOSITES generous.

tight-lipped ▶ **adjective** RETICENT, uncommunicative, unforthcoming, playing one's cards close to one's chest, close-mouthed, silent, taciturn; *informal* mum.
– OPPOSITES forthcoming.

till[1] ▶ **preposition & conjunction** *he stayed till 7 | I'll stay here till you get back.* See UNTIL senses 1, 2.

till[2] ▶ **noun** *she counted the money in the till* CASH REGISTER, cash box, cash drawer, strongbox; checkout, cash desk.

till[3] ▶ **verb** *he went back to tilling the land* CULTIVATE, work, farm, plough, dig, turn over, prepare.

tilt ▶ **verb** ❶ *the ground seemed to tilt* SLOPE, tip, lean, list, bank, slant, incline, pitch, cant, careen, angle. ❷ (*historical*) *he tilts at his prey* CHARGE, rush, run; lunge, thrust, jab. ❸ (*historical*) *knights tilting at a tournament* JOUST, tourney, enter the lists; contend, spar, fight.
▶ **noun** ❶ *a tilt of some 45°* SLOPE, list, camber, gradient, bank, slant, incline, pitch, cant, bevel, angle. ❷ (*historical*) *knights would take part in a tilt* JOUST, tournament, tourney, lists, combat, contest, fight, duel. ❸ *another tilt at the European Cup* ATTEMPT, bid; *informal* go, crack, shot.
■ **(at) full tilt** ❶ *they charged full tilt down the side of the hill* (AT) FULL SPEED, (at) full pelt, as fast as one's legs can carry one, at a gallop, helter-skelter, headlong, pell-mell, at breakneck speed; *informal* hell for leather, at the double, a mile a minute, like the wind, like a bat out of hell, like a scalded cat, like (greased) lightning; *Brit. informal* like the clappers, at a rate of knots, like billy-o; *N. Amer. informal* lickety-split; *poetic/literary* apace. ❷ *the marketing blitz has raged at full tilt for some time now* WITH GREAT FORCE, with full force, full blast, with all the stops out, all out, with a vengeance; *informal* like crazy, like mad.

timber ▶ **noun** ❶ *houses built of timber* WOOD; *N. Amer.* lumber. ❷ *the timbers of wrecked ships* BEAM, spar, plank, batten, lath, board, joist, rafter.

timbre ▶ **noun** TONE, sound, sound quality, voice, voice quality, colour, tone colour, tonality, resonance.

time ▶ **noun** ❶ *what time is it?* HOUR; *dated* o'clock. ❷ *late at night was the best time to leave* MOMENT, point (in time), occasion, hour, minute, second, instant, juncture, stage. ❸ *he worked there for a time* WHILE, spell, stretch, stint, span, season, interval, period (of time), length of time, duration, run, space, phase, stage, term; *Brit. informal* patch. ❹ *the time of the dinosaurs* ERA, age, epoch, period, years, days; generation, date. ❺ *I've known a lot of women in my time* LIFETIME, life, life span, days, time on earth, existence, threescore years and ten. ❻ *he had been a professional actor in his time* HEYDAY, day, best days/years, prime. ❼ *times are hard at the moment* CONDITIONS, circumstances, life, state of affairs, experiences. ❽ *tunes in waltz time* RHYTHM, tempo, beat; metre, measure, cadence, pattern.
– RELATED TERMS chronological, temporal.
▶ **verb** *the meeting was timed for three o'clock* SCHEDULE, set, set up, arrange, organize, fix, fix up, book, line up, slot in, pre-arrange, timetable, plan; *N. Amer.* slate.
■ **ahead of time** EARLY, in good time, with time to spare, in advance.
■ **ahead of one's/its time** REVOLUTIONARY, avant-garde, futuristic, innovatory, innovative, trailblazing, pioneering, ground-breaking, advanced.
■ **all the time** CONSTANTLY, the entire time, around the clock, day and night, night and day, {morning, noon, and night}, {day in, day out}, at all times, always, without a break, ceaselessly, endlessly, incessantly, perpetually, permanently, interminably, continuously, continually, eternally, unremittingly, remorselessly, relentlessly; *N. Amer.* without surcease; *informal* 24-7.
■ **at one time** FORMERLY, previously, once, in the past, at one point, once upon a time, time was when, in days/times gone by, in times past, in the (good) old days, long ago; *poetic/literary* in days/times of yore; *archaic* erstwhile, whilom.
■ **at the same time** ❶ *they arrived at the same time* SIMULTANEOUSLY, at the same instant/moment, together, all together, as a group, at once, at one and the same time; in unison, in concert, in chorus, as one. ❷ *I can't really explain it, but at the same time I'm not convinced* NONETHELESS, even so, however, but, still, yet, though; in spite of that, despite that, be that as it may, for all that, that said; notwithstanding, regardless, anyway, anyhow; *informal* still and all.
■ **at times** OCCASIONALLY, sometimes, from time to time, now and then, every so often, once in a while, on occasion, off and on, at intervals, periodically, sporadically.
■ **behind time** LATE, behind, behind schedule, behindhand, running late, overdue.
■ **behind the times** OLD-FASHIONED, out of date, outmoded, outdated, dated, old, passé; *informal* square, not with it, out of the ark; *N. Amer. informal* horse-and-buggy, clunky.
■ **for the time being** FOR NOW, for the moment, for the present, in the interim, for the nonce, in/for the meantime, in the meanwhile, for a short time, briefly; temporarily, provisionally, pro tem; *informal* for the minute.
■ **from time to time** OCCASIONALLY, some-

times, now and then, every so often, once in a while, on occasion, off and on, at intervals, periodically, sporadically.

■ **in no time** (VERY) SOON, in a second, in a minute, in a moment, in a trice, in a flash, shortly, any second, any minute (now); *N. Amer.* momentarily; *informal* in a sec, in a jiffy, in two shakes (of a lamb's tail), before you can say Jack Robinson; *Brit. informal* in a tick, in two ticks, in a mo; *N. Amer. informal* in a snap; *dated* directly.

■ **in good time** PUNCTUALLY, on time, early, with time to spare, ahead of time/schedule.

■ **in time** ❶ *I came back in time for the party* EARLY ENOUGH, in good time, punctually, on time, not too late, with time to spare, on schedule. ❷ *in time, she forgot about it* EVENTUALLY, in the end, in due course, by and by, finally; one day, some day, sometime, sooner or later.

■ **many a time** FREQUENTLY, regularly, often, very often, all the time, habitually, customarily, routinely; again and again, time and again, over and over again, repeatedly, recurrently, continually; *N. Amer.* oftentimes; *poetic/literary* oft, oft-times.

■ **on time** PUNCTUALLY, in good time, to/on schedule, when expected; *informal* on the dot, bang on time.

■ **time after time** REPEATEDLY, frequently, often, again and again, over and over (again), time and (time) again, many times, many a time; persistently, recurrently, constantly, continually; *N. Amer.* oftentimes; *poetic/literary* oft, oft-times.

time-honoured ▸ **adjective** TRADITIONAL, established, long-established, long-standing, long-lived, age-old, enduring, lasting, tried and tested.

timeless ▸ **adjective** LASTING, enduring, classic, ageless, permanent, perennial, abiding, unfailing, unchanging, unvarying, never-changing, changeless, unfading, unending, undying, deathless, immortal, eternal, everlasting, immutable.
–OPPOSITES ephemeral.

timely ▸ **adjective** OPPORTUNE, well timed, at the right time, convenient, appropriate, expedient, seasonable, felicitous.
–OPPOSITES ill-timed.

timetable ▸ **noun** *a bus timetable | I have a very full timetable* SCHEDULE, programme, agenda, calendar; list, itinerary.
▸ **verb** *German lessons were timetabled on Wednesday* SCHEDULE, set, arrange, organize, fix, time, line up; *N. Amer.* slate.

time-worn ▸ **adjective** ❶ *the carpet was old and time-worn* WORN OUT, worn, well worn, old, tattered, battered, dog-eared, shabby, having seen better days; *informal* tatty. ❷ *time-worn faces* OLD, aged, weathered, lined, wrinkled, hoary. ❸ *a time-worn aphorism* HACKNEYED, trite, banal, platitudinous, clichéd, stock, conventional, unoriginal, overused, overworked, tired, stale; *informal* old hat.
–OPPOSITES new, fresh.

timid ▸ **adjective** EASILY FRIGHTENED, fearful, afraid, faint-hearted, timorous, nervous, scared, frightened, cowardly, pusillanimous, lily-livered, spineless; shy, diffident, self-effacing; *informal* wimpish, wimpy, chicken, gutless.
–OPPOSITES bold.

timorous ▸ **adjective.** *See* TIMID.

tincture ▸ **noun** ❶ *tincture of iodine* SOLUTION, suspension, infusion, elixir. ❷ *a tincture of bitterness* TRACE, note, tinge, touch, suggestion, hint, bit, element, suspicion, soupçon.

tinge ▸ **verb** ❶ *a mass of white blossom tinged with pink* TINT, colour, stain, shade, wash. ❷ *his optimism is tinged with realism* INFLUENCE, affect, touch, flavour, colour, modify.
▸ **noun** ❶ *the light had a blue tinge to it* TINT, colour, shade, tone, hue. ❷ *a tinge of cynicism* TRACE, note, touch, suggestion, hint, bit, scintilla, savour, flavour, element, streak, vein, suspicion, soupçon, tincture.

tingle ▸ **verb** *her flesh still tingled from the shock* PRICKLE, sting; tremble, quiver, shiver.
▸ **noun** *she felt a tingle of anticipation* PRICKLING, tingling, pricking, sting, stinging; tremor, thrill, quiver, shiver; goose pimples; *N. Amer.* goosebumps.

tinker ▸ **verb** *a workman was tinkering with the engine* FIDDLE WITH, adjust, try to mend, play about with; tamper with, interfere with, mess about with, meddle with; *informal* rearrange the deckchairs on the Titanic; *Brit. informal* muck about with.

tinkle ▸ **verb** ❶ *the bell tinkled* RING, jingle, jangle, chime, peal, ding, ping. ❷ *cool water tinkled in the stone fountain* SPLASH, purl, babble, burble; *poetic/literary* plash.
▸ **noun** ❶ *the tinkle of the doorbell* RING, chime, peal, ding, ping, jingle, jangle, tintinnabulation. ❷ *the faint tinkle of water* SPLASH, purl, babble, burble; *poetic/literary* plash. ❸ (*Brit. informal*) *I'll give them a tinkle* TELEPHONE CALL, phone call, call; *informal* buzz; *Brit. informal* ring, bell.

tinny ▸ **adjective** ❶ *tinny music* JANGLY, jangling, jingling, jingly. ❷ *a tinny little car* CHEAP, cheapjack, poor-quality, inferior, low-grade, gimcrack, shoddy, jerry-built; *informal* tacky, tatty, rubbishy.

tinsel ▸ **noun** *the tinsel of Hollywood* OSTENTATION, showiness, show, glitter, flamboyance, gaudiness; attractiveness, glamour; *informal* flashiness, glitz, glitziness, razzle-dazzle, razzmatazz.
▸ **adjective** *tinsel stardom* OSTENTATIOUS, showy, glittering, flamboyant, gaudy; *informal* flash, flashy, over the top, OTT, glitzy, ritzy; *N. Amer. informal* superfly.

tint ▶ noun ❶ *the sky was taking on an apricot tint* SHADE, colour, tone, hue, tinge, cast, tincture, flush, blush. ❷ *a hair tint* DYE, colourant, colouring, wash; highlights, lowlights.

tiny ▶ adjective MINUTE, minuscule, microscopic, very small, little, mini, diminutive, miniature, scaled down, baby, toy, dwarf, pygmy, Lilliputian; *Scottish* wee; *informal* teeny, teeny-weeny, teensy, teensy-weensy, itsy-bitsy, eensy, eensy-weensy, tiddly, pint-sized; *Brit. informal* titchy; *N. Amer. informal* little-bitty.
– OPPOSITES huge.

tip[1] ▶ noun ❶ *the tip of the spear* POINT, end, extremity, head, sharp end, spike, prong, tine, nib. ❷ *the tips of the mountains* PEAK, point, top, summit, apex, crown, crest, pinnacle. ❸ *the sticks have tips fitted to protect them* CAP, cover, ferrule.
▶ verb *mountains tipped with snow* CAP, top, crown.

tip[2] ▶ verb ❶ *the boat tipped over* OVERTURN, turn over, topple (over), fall (over); keel over, capsize, turn turtle; *Nautical* pitchpole. ❷ *a whale could tip over a small boat* UPSET, overturn, topple over, turn over, knock over, push over, upend, capsize; *informal* roll; *archaic* overset. ❸ *the car tipped to one side* LEAN, tilt, list, slope, bank, slant, incline, pitch, cant, heel, careen. ❹ *she tipped the water into the trough* POUR, empty, drain, unload, dump, discharge; decant.
▶ noun (*Brit.*) *rubbish must be taken to the tip* DUMP, rubbish dump; *Canadian* nuisance grounds.

tip[3] ▶ noun ❶ *a generous tip* GRATUITY, baksheesh; present, gift, reward; *Brit. informal* dropsy. ❷ *useful tips* PIECE OF ADVICE, suggestion, word of advice, pointer, recommendation; clue, hint; *informal* wrinkle, tip-off.

tip-off ▶ noun (*informal*) PIECE OF INFORMATION, warning, lead, forewarning; hint, clue; advice, information, notification.

tipple ▶ verb *boys discovered tippling were punished* DRINK ALCOHOL, drink; *informal* booze, wet one's whistle, hit the bottle, take to the bottle; *Brit. informal* bevvy; *N. Amer. informal* bend one's elbow; *archaic* tope.
▶ noun (*informal*) *their favourite tipple was claret* ALCOHOLIC DRINK, drink, liquor; *informal* booze, poison.

tippler ▶ noun DRINKER, imbiber; alcoholic, drunk, drunkard, dipsomaniac, inebriate, sot; *informal* boozer, alky, lush, barfly, sponge, dipso, wino, soak; *Austral./NZ informal* hophead; *archaic* toper.
– OPPOSITES teetotaller.

tipsy ▶ adjective MERRY, mellow, slightly drunk; *Brit. informal* tiddly, squiffy.
– OPPOSITES sober.

tirade ▶ noun DIATRIBE, harangue, rant, onslaught, attack, polemic, denunciation, broadside, fulmination, condemnation, censure, criticism, tongue-lashing; *informal* blast; *poetic/literary* philippic.

tire ▶ verb ❶ *the ascent grew steeper and he began to tire* GET TIRED, weaken, grow weak, flag, droop. ❷ *the journey had tired him* FATIGUE, tire out, exhaust, wear out, drain, weary, wash out, overtire, enervate; *informal* knock out, take it out of, do in, fag out, wear to a frazzle; *Brit. informal* knacker. ❸ *they tired of his difficult behaviour* WEARY, get tired, get fed up, get sick, get bored; *informal* have had something up to here.

tired ▶ adjective ❶ *you're just tired from travelling* EXHAUSTED, worn out, weary, fatigued, dog-tired, bone-tired, ready to drop, drained, enervated, jaded; *informal* done in, all in, dead beat, shattered, bushed, knocked out, wiped out, bushwhacked; *Brit. informal* knackered, whacked (out), jiggered; *N. Amer. informal* pooped, tuckered out; *Austral./NZ informal* stonkered. ❷ *are you tired of having him here?* FED UP WITH, weary of, bored with/by, sick (and tired) of; *informal* up to here with. ❸ *tired jokes* HACKNEYED, overused, overworked, worn out, stale, clichéd, hoary, stock, stereotyped, predictable, unimaginative, unoriginal, uninspired, dull, boring, routine; *informal* old hat, corny, played out.
– OPPOSITES energetic, lively, fresh.

tiredness ▶ noun FATIGUE, weariness, exhaustion, enervation, inertia; sleepiness, drowsiness, somnolence.
– OPPOSITES energy.

tireless ▶ adjective VIGOROUS, energetic, industrious, determined, enthusiastic, keen, zealous, spirited, dynamic, dogged, tenacious, persevering, stout, untiring, unwearying, indefatigable, unflagging.
– OPPOSITES lazy.

tiresome ▶ adjective BORING, dull, tedious, wearisome, wearing, uninteresting, uneventful, humdrum; annoying, irritating, trying, irksome, vexatious, troublesome; *informal* aggravating, pesky.
– OPPOSITES interesting, pleasant.

tiring ▶ adjective EXHAUSTING, wearying, taxing, fatiguing, wearing, enervating, draining; hard, heavy, arduous, strenuous, onerous, uphill, demanding, gruelling; *informal* killing, murderous; *Brit. informal* knackering.

tissue ▶ noun ❶ *living tissue* MATTER, material, substance; flesh. ❷ *a box of tissues* PAPER HANDKERCHIEF, paper towel; *trademark* Kleenex. ❸ *a tissue of lies* WEB, network, nexus, complex, mass, set, series, chain.

titanic ▶ adjective HUGE, great, enormous, gigantic, massive, colossal, monumental, mammoth, immense, tremendous, terrific, mighty, stupendous, prodigious, gargantuan, Herculean; *informal* humongous, whopping, thumping, mega; *Brit. informal* whacking, ginormous.

titbit ▶ noun ❶ *tasty titbits* DELICACY, tasty morsel, dainty, bonne bouche, treat; snack, nibble, savoury, appetizer; *informal* goody; *N. Amer.* tidbit. ❷ *a fascinating titbit* PIECE OF GOSSIP, bit of scandal, piece of information.

tit for tat ▶ **noun** RETALIATION, reprisal, counter-attack, counterstroke, comeback; revenge, vengeance, retribution, an eye for an eye, a tooth for a tooth, as good as one gets, payback; *informal* a taste of someone's own medicine.

titillate ▶ **verb** AROUSE, excite, tantalize, stimulate, stir, thrill, interest, attract, fascinate; *informal* turn on.
– OPPOSITES bore.

titillating ▶ **adjective** AROUSING, exciting, stimulating, sexy, thrilling, provocative, tantalizing, interesting, fascinating; suggestive, salacious, lurid; *Brit. informal* saucy.
– OPPOSITES boring.

titivate ▶ **verb** (*informal*) *she titivated herself in front of the hall mirror* GROOM, smarten (up), spruce up, freshen up, preen, primp, prink; tidy, arrange; *informal* doll up, tart up; *N. Amer. informal* gussy up.

title ▶ **noun** ❶ *the title of the book* NAME. ❷ *the cartoon title* CAPTION, legend, inscription, label, heading, sub-heading; credit. ❸ *the company publishes 400 titles a year* PUBLICATION, work, book, newspaper, paper, magazine, periodical. ❹ *the title of Duke of Marlborough* DESIGNATION, name, form of address; epithet, style; rank, office, position; *informal* moniker, handle; *formal* appellation, denomination. ❺ *an Olympic title* CHAMPIONSHIP, crown, first place; laurels, bays, palm. ❻ *the vendor is obliged to prove his title to the land* OWNERSHIP, proprietorship, possession, holding, freehold, entitlement, right, claim.
▶ **verb** *a policy paper titled 'Law and Order'* CALL, entitle, name, dub, designate, style, term; *formal* denominate.

titter ▶ **verb & noun** GIGGLE, snigger, snicker, tee-hee, chuckle, laugh; *informal* chortle.

tittle ▶ **noun**. *See* IOTA.

tittle-tattle ▶ **noun** *she would never listen to tittle-tattle* GOSSIP, rumour(s), idle talk, hearsay, whispers, titbits; scandal; *informal* dirt, buzz; *Brit. informal* goss; *N. Amer. informal* scuttlebutt.
▶ **verb** *he was tittle-tattling all over the village* GOSSIP, spread rumours, spread gossip, tattle, talk, whisper, tell tales.

titular ▶ **adjective** ❶ *the titular head of a university* NOMINAL, in title/name only, ceremonial; token, puppet. ❷ *the work's titular song* EPONYMOUS, identifying.

toady ▶ **noun** *a conniving little toady* SYCOPHANT, fawner, flatterer, creep, crawler, lickspittle; *informal* bootlicker, yes-man; *archaic* toad-eater.
▶ **verb** *she imagined him toadying to his rich clients* GROVEL TO, ingratiate oneself with, be obsequious to, kowtow to, pander to, crawl to, truckle to, bow and scrape to, dance attendance on, curry favour with, make up to, fawn on/over; *informal* suck up to, lick someone's boots, butter up.

toast ▶ **noun** ❶ *he raised his glass in a toast* TRIBUTE, salute, salutation; *archaic* pledge. ❷ *he was the toast of the West End* DARLING, favourite, pet, heroine, hero; talk; *Brit. informal* blue-eyed boy/girl; *N. Amer. informal* fair-haired boy/girl.
▶ **verb** ❶ *she toasted her hands in front of the fire* WARM (UP), heat, heat (up). ❷ *we toasted the couple with champagne* DRINK (TO) THE HEALTH OF, drink to, salute, honour, pay tribute to; *archaic* pledge.

today ▶ **adverb** ❶ *the work must be finished today* THIS (VERY) DAY, this morning, this afternoon, this evening. ❷ *the complex tasks demanded of computers today* NOWADAYS, these days, at the present time, in these times, in this day and age, now, currently, at the moment, at present, at this moment in time; in the present climate; *N. Amer.* presently.

toddle ▶ **verb** ❶ *the child toddled towards him* TOTTER, teeter, wobble, falter, waddle, stumble. ❷ (*informal*) *I toddled down to the quay* AMBLE, potter, wander, meander, stroll, saunter; *informal* mosey, tootle; *N. Amer. informal* putter.

to-do ▶ **noun** (*informal*) COMMOTION, fuss, ado, excitement, agitation, bother, stir, palaver, confusion, disturbance, brouhaha, uproar, furore, storm in a teacup, much ado about nothing; *informal* hoo-ha, ballyhoo, kerfuffle, song and dance, performance, pantomime; *Brit. informal* carry-on; *N. Amer. informal* fuss and feathers.

together ▶ **adverb** ❶ *friends who work together* WITH EACH OTHER, in conjunction, jointly, in cooperation, in collaboration, in partnership, in combination, in league, side by side, hand in hand, shoulder to shoulder, cheek by jowl; in collusion, hand in glove; *informal* in cahoots. ❷ *they both spoke together* SIMULTANEOUSLY, at the same time, at one and the same time, at once, all together, as a group, in unison, in concert, in chorus, as one, with one accord. ❸ *I was not able to get up for days together* IN SUCCESSION, in a row, at a time, successively, consecutively, running, straight, on end, one after the other, continuously, without a break, without interruption; *informal* on the trot.
– OPPOSITES separately.
▶ **adjective** (*informal*) *a very together young woman. See* LEVEL-HEADED.

toil ▶ **verb** ❶ *she toiled all night* WORK HARD, labour, exert oneself, slave (away), grind away, strive, work one's fingers to the bone, work like a Trojan/slave, keep one's nose to the grindstone; *informal* slog away, plug away, peg away, beaver away, work one's guts out, work one's socks off, sweat blood; *Brit. informal* graft; *poetic/literary* travail; *archaic* moil. ❷ *she began to toil up the cliff path* STRUGGLE, trudge, tramp, traipse, slog, plod, trek, footslog, drag oneself; *Brit. informal* yomp; *N. Amer. informal* schlep.
– OPPOSITES rest, relax.

▶ **noun** *a life of toil* HARD WORK, labour, exertion, slaving, drudgery, effort, industry, {blood, sweat, and tears}; *informal* slog, elbow grease; *Brit. informal* graft; *poetic/literary* travail; *archaic* moil.

toilet ▶ **noun** ❶ *he had to go to the toilet* LAVATORY, WC, water closet, (public) convenience, cloakroom, powder room, urinal, privy, latrine, jakes; *N. Amer.* washroom, bathroom, rest room, men's/ladies' room, commode, comfort station; *Nautical* head; *informal* little girls'/boys' room, smallest room; *Brit. informal* loo, bog, the Ladies, the Gents, khazi, lav; *N. Amer. informal* can, john; *Austral./NZ informal* dunny; *archaic* closet, garderobe. ❷ *she had always taken a long time over her toilet* WASHING, bathing, showering; grooming, dressing, make-up; *formal or humorous* ablutions; *dated* toilette.

toils ▶ **plural noun** (*poetic/literary*) TRAP, net, snare.

token ▶ **noun** ❶ *a token of our appreciation* SYMBOL, sign, emblem, badge, representation, indication, mark, manifestation, expression, pledge, demonstration, recognition; evidence, proof. ❷ *he kept the menu as a token of their golden wedding* MEMENTO, souvenir, keepsake, reminder, remembrance, memorial. ❸ *a book token* VOUCHER, coupon. ❹ *a telephone token* COUNTER, disc, jetton, chip, piece, man.

▶ **adjective** ❶ *a one-day token strike* SYMBOLIC, emblematic, indicative; peppercorn. ❷ *the practice now meets only token resistance* PERFUNCTORY, slight, nominal, minimal, minor, mild, superficial, inconsequential.

tolerable ▶ **adjective** ❶ *a tolerable noise level* BEARABLE, endurable, supportable, acceptable. ❷ *he had a tolerable voice* FAIRLY GOOD, passable, adequate, all right, acceptable, satisfactory, not (too) bad, average, fair; mediocre, middling, ordinary, indifferent, unremarkable, unexceptional; *informal* OK, so-so, nothing to write home about, no great shakes.
– OPPOSITES unacceptable.

tolerance ▶ **noun** ❶ *an attitude of tolerance towards other people* ACCEPTANCE, toleration; open-mindedness, broad-mindedness, forbearance, liberality, liberalism; patience, charity, indulgence, understanding. ❷ *the plant's tolerance of pollution* ENDURANCE, resilience, resistance, immunity. ❸ *a 1% maximum tolerance in measurement* DEVIATION, variation, play; inaccuracy, imprecision.

tolerant ▶ **adjective** OPEN-MINDED, forbearing, broad-minded, liberal, unprejudiced, unbiased; patient, long-suffering, understanding, charitable, lenient, indulgent, permissive, free and easy, easy-going, lax.
– OPPOSITES intolerant.

tolerate ▶ **verb** ❶ *a regime unwilling to tolerate serious dissent* ALLOW, permit, condone, accept, swallow, countenance; *formal* brook; *archaic* suffer. ❷ *he couldn't tolerate her moods any longer* ENDURE, put up with, bear, take, stand, support, stomach; *informal* hack, abide; *Brit. informal* stick, wear, be doing with.

toleration ▶ **noun** ACCEPTANCE, tolerance, endurance; forbearance, liberality, open-mindedness, broad-mindedness, liberalism; patience, charity, indulgence, understanding.

toll[1] ▶ **noun** ❶ *a motorway toll* CHARGE, fee, payment, levy, tariff, tax. ❷ *the toll of dead and injured* NUMBER, count, tally, total, sum total, grand total, sum; record, list, listing. ❸ *the toll on the environment has been high* ADVERSE EFFECT(S), detriment, harm, damage, injury, hurt; cost, price, loss, disadvantage, suffering, penalty.

toll[2] ▶ **verb** *I heard the bell toll* RING (OUT), chime, strike, peal; sound, clang, resound, reverberate; *poetic/literary* knell.

tomb ▶ **noun** BURIAL CHAMBER, sepulchre, mausoleum, vault, crypt, undercroft, catacomb; last/final resting place, grave, barrow, burial mound; *historical* charnel house.
– RELATED TERMS sepulchral.

tombstone ▶ **noun** GRAVESTONE, headstone, stone; memorial, monument.

tome ▶ **noun** VOLUME, book, work, opus, publication, title.

tomfoolery ▶ **noun** SILLINESS, fooling around, clowning, capers, antics, pranks, tricks, buffoonery, skylarking, nonsense, horseplay, mischief, foolishness, foolery; *informal* larks, shenanigans.

tone ▶ **noun** ❶ *the tone of the tuba* TIMBRE, sound, sound quality, voice, voice quality, colour, tone colour, tonality. ❷ *his friendly tone* INTONATION, tone of voice, modulation, accentuation. ❸ *the somewhat impatient tone of his letter* MOOD, air, feel, flavour, note, attitude, character, temper; tenor, vein, drift, gist. ❹ *a dialling tone* NOTE, signal, beep, bleep. ❺ *tones of primrose, lavender, and rose* SHADE, colour, hue, tint, tinge.

▶ **verb** *the caramel shirt toned well with her cream skirt* HARMONIZE, go, blend, coordinate, team; match, suit, complement.

■ **tone something down** ❶ *the colour needs to be toned down a bit* SOFTEN, lighten, mute, subdue. ❷ *the papers refused to tone down their criticism* MODERATE, modify, modulate, mitigate, temper, dampen, soften, subdue.

tongue ▶ **noun** ❶ *a foreign tongue* LANGUAGE, dialect, patois, vernacular, mother tongue, native tongue; *informal* lingo. ❷ *her sharp tongue* WAY/MANNER OF SPEAKING, speech, parlance.

tongue-tied ▶ **adjective** LOST FOR WORDS, speechless, unable to get a word out, struck dumb, dumbstruck; mute, dumb, silent; *informal* mum.
– OPPOSITES loquacious.

tonic ▶ **noun** ❶ *ginseng can be used as a natural*

tonic STIMULANT, restorative, refresher; *informal* pick-me-up, bracer; *Medicine* analeptic. ❷ *we found the change of scene a tonic* STIMULANT, boost, fillip; *informal* shot in the arm, pick-me-up.

too ▶ **adverb** ❶ *invasion would be too risky* EXCESSIVELY, overly, over, unduly, immoderately, inordinately, unreasonably, extremely, very; *informal* too-too. ❷ *he was unhappy, too, you know* ALSO, as well, in addition, additionally, into the bargain, besides, furthermore, moreover, on top of that, to boot.

tool ▶ **noun** ❶ *garden tools* IMPLEMENT, utensil, instrument, device, apparatus, gadget, appliance, machine, contrivance, contraption; *informal* gizmo. ❷ *the beautiful Estella is Miss Havisham's tool* PUPPET, pawn, creature, cat's paw; minion, lackey; *informal* stooge.
▶ **verb** *red leather, tooled in gold* ORNAMENT, embellish, decorate, work, cut, chase.

tooth ▶ **noun** FANG, tusk; *Zoology* denticle; *informal* gnasher; *Brit. informal* pearly white.
– RELATED TERMS dental.

toothsome ▶ **adjective** TASTY, delicious, luscious, mouth-watering, delectable, succulent; tempting, appetizing, inviting; *informal* scrumptious, yummy, scrummy, finger-licking; *Brit. informal* moreish.

top ▶ **noun** ❶ *the top of the cliff* SUMMIT, peak, pinnacle, crest, crown, brow, head, tip, apex, vertex. ❷ *the top of the table* UPPER PART, upper surface, upper layer. ❸ *the carrots' green tops* LEAVES, shoots, stem, stalk. ❹ *the top of the coffee jar* LID, cap, cover, stopper, cork. ❺ *a short-sleeved top* SWEATER, jumper, jersey, sweat shirt; T-shirt, shirt; blouse. ❻ *by 1981 he was at the top of his profession* HIGH POINT, height, peak, pinnacle, zenith, acme, culmination, climax, crowning point; prime.
– OPPOSITES bottom, base.
▶ **adjective** ❶ *the top floor* HIGHEST, topmost, uppermost, upmost. ❷ *the world's top scientists* FOREMOST, leading, principal, pre-eminent, greatest, best, finest, elite; *informal* top-notch. ❸ *the organization's top management* CHIEF, principal, main, leading, highest, highest-ranking, ruling, commanding, most powerful, most important. ❹ *a top Paris hotel* PRIME, excellent, superb, superior, choice, select, top-quality, top-grade, first-rate, first-class, grade A, best, finest, premier, superlative, second to none; *informal* A1, top-notch. ❺ *they are travelling at top speed* MAXIMUM, maximal, greatest, utmost.
– OPPOSITES bottom, lowest, minimum.
▶ **verb** ❶ *sales are expected to top £1.3 billion* EXCEED, surpass, go beyond, better, best, beat, outstrip, outdo, outshine, eclipse, go one better than. ❷ *their debut CD is currently topping the charts* LEAD, head, be at the top of. ❸ *they topped the rise of a mist-shrouded valley* REACH THE TOP OF, crest, climb, scale, ascend, mount. ❹ *chocolate mousse topped with cream* COVER, cap, coat, smother; finish, garnish.
■ **over the top** (*informal*) EXCESSIVE, immoderate, inordinate, extreme, exaggerated, extravagant, overblown, too much, unreasonable, disproportionate, undue, unwarranted, uncalled for, unnecessary, going too far; *informal* a bit much, OTT.
■ **top something up** FILL, refill, refresh, freshen, replenish, recharge, resupply; supplement, add to, augment.

topcoat ▶ **noun** OVERCOAT, coat, greatcoat.

topic ▶ **noun** SUBJECT, subject matter, theme, issue, matter, point, talking point, question, concern, argument, thesis, text, keynote.

topical ▶ **adjective** CURRENT, up to date, up to the minute, contemporary, recent, relevant; newsworthy, in the news.
– OPPOSITES out of date.

topmost ▶ **adjective** ❶ *the tree's topmost branches* HIGHEST, top, uppermost, upmost. ❷ *the topmost authority on the subject* FOREMOST, leading, principal, premier, prime, top, greatest, best, supreme, pre-eminent, outstanding, most important, main, chief; *N. Amer.* ranking; *informal* number-one.

top-notch ▶ **adjective** (*informal*) FIRST-CLASS, first-rate, top-quality, five-star; superior, prime, premier, premium, grade A, superlative, best, finest, select, exclusive, excellent, superb, outstanding, splendid; *informal* tip-top, A1.

topple ▶ **verb** ❶ *she toppled over* FALL, tumble, overbalance, overturn, tip, keel; lose one's balance. ❷ *protesters toppled a huge statue* KNOCK OVER, upset, push over, tip over, upend. ❸ *a plot to topple the government* OVERTHROW, oust, unseat, overturn, bring down, defeat, get rid of, dislodge, eject.

topsy-turvy ▶ **adjective** ❶ *a topsy-turvy flag* UPSIDE DOWN, the wrong way/side up, inverted. ❷ *everything in the flat was topsy-turvy* IN DISARRAY, in a mess, in a muddle, in disorder, disordered, in chaos, chaotic, disorganized, awry, upside down, at sixes and sevens; *informal* every which way, higgledy-piggledy.
– OPPOSITES neat.

torch ▶ **noun** ❶ *an electric torch* LAMP, light, flashlight. ❷ (*historical*) *a flaming torch* FIREBRAND, brand; *historical* cresset, flambeau.
▶ **verb** (*informal*) *one of the shops had been torched* BURN, set fire to, set on fire, set light to, set alight, incinerate, put/set a match to.

torment ▶ **noun** ❶ *months of mental and emotional torment* AGONY, suffering, torture, pain, anguish, misery, distress, affliction, trauma, wretchedness; hell, purgatory. ❷ *it was a torment to see him like that* ORDEAL, affliction, scourge, curse, plague, bane, thorn in someone's side/flesh, cross to bear; sorrow, tribulation, trouble.
▶ **verb** ❶ *she was tormented by shame* TORTURE, afflict, rack, harrow, plague, haunt, distress,

agonize. ❷ *she began to torment the two younger boys* TEASE, taunt, bait, harass, provoke, goad, plague, bother, trouble, persecute; *informal* needle.

torn ▶ **adjective** ❶ *a torn shirt* RIPPED, rent, cut, slit; ragged, tattered, in tatters, in ribbons. ❷ *she was torn between the two options* WAVERING, vacillating, irresolute, dithering, uncertain, unsure, undecided, in two minds.

tornado ▶ **noun** WHIRLWIND, windstorm, cyclone, typhoon, storm, hurricane; *N. Amer. informal* twister.

torpid ▶ **adjective** LETHARGIC, sluggish, inert, inactive, slow, lifeless; languid, listless, lazy, idle, indolent, slothful, supine, passive, apathetic, somnolent, sleepy, weary, tired.
– OPPOSITES energetic.

torpor ▶ **noun** LETHARGY, sluggishness, inertia, inactivity, lifelessness, listlessness, languor, lassitude, laziness, idleness, indolence, sloth, accidie, passivity, somnolence, weariness, sleepiness.

torrent ▶ **noun** ❶ *a torrent of water* FLOOD, deluge, inundation, spate, cascade, rush, stream, current, flow, overflow, tide. ❷ *a torrent of abuse* OUTBURST, outpouring, stream, flood, volley, barrage, tide, spate.
– OPPOSITES trickle.

torrential ▶ **adjective** COPIOUS, heavy, teeming, severe, relentless, violent.

torrid ▶ **adjective** ❶ *a torrid summer* HOT, dry, scorching, searing, blazing, blistering, sweltering, burning; *informal* boiling (hot), baking (hot), sizzling. ❷ *a torrid affair* PASSIONATE, ardent, lustful, amorous; *informal* steamy, sizzling, hot.
– OPPOSITES cold.

tortuous ▶ **adjective** ❶ *a tortuous route* TWISTING, twisty, twisting and turning, winding, windy, zigzag, sinuous, snaky, meandering, serpentine. ❷ *a tortuous argument* CONVOLUTED, complicated, complex, labyrinthine, involved, confusing, difficult to follow, lengthy, overlong.
– OPPOSITES straight, straightforward.

torture ▶ **noun** ❶ *the torture of political prisoners* INFLICTION OF PAIN, abuse; ill-treatment, maltreatment, persecution. ❷ *the torture of losing a loved one* TORMENT, agony, suffering, pain, anguish, misery, distress, heartbreak, affliction, trauma, wretchedness; hell, purgatory.
▶ **verb** ❶ *the security forces routinely tortured suspects* INFLICT PAIN ON, ill-treat, abuse, mistreat, maltreat, persecute; *informal* work over, give someone the works. ❷ *he was tortured by grief* TORMENT, rack, afflict, harrow, plague, agonize, crucify.

toss ▶ **verb** ❶ *he tossed his tools into the boot* THROW, hurl, fling, sling, cast, pitch, lob, propel, project, launch; *informal* heave, chuck, bung; *dated* shy. ❷ *he tossed a coin and it landed heads up* FLIP, flick, spin. ❸ *the ship tossed about on the waves* PITCH, lurch, rock, roll, plunge, reel, list, keel, sway, wallow, make heavy weather. ❹ *toss the salad ingredients together* SHAKE, stir, turn, mix, combine.

tot[1] ▶ **noun** ❶ *the tot looks just like her mum* INFANT, baby, toddler, tiny tot, child, little one, mite; *Scottish* bairn, wean. ❷ *a tot of rum* DRAM, drink, nip, drop, slug; *informal* shot, finger, snifter.

tot[2] ▶ **verb** ❶ *he totted up some figures* ADD, total, count, calculate, compute, reckon, tally. ❷ *we've totted up 89 victories* ACCUMULATE, build up, amass, accrue.

total ▶ **adjective** ❶ *the total cost* ENTIRE, complete, whole, full, comprehensive, combined, aggregate, gross, overall. ❷ *a total disaster* COMPLETE, utter, absolute, thorough, perfect, downright, out-and-out, outright, thoroughgoing, all-out, sheer, arrant, positive, prize, rank, unmitigated, unqualified; *Brit. informal* right, proper.
– OPPOSITES partial.
▶ **noun** *a total of £160,000* SUM, sum total, grand total, aggregate; whole, entirety, totality.
▶ **verb** ❶ *the prize money totalled £33,050* ADD UP TO, amount to, come to, run to, make, work out as. ❷ *he totalled up his score* ADD (UP), count, reckon, tot up, compute, work out.

totalitarian ▶ **adjective** AUTOCRATIC, undemocratic, one-party, dictatorial, tyrannical, despotic, fascist, oppressive, repressive, illiberal; authoritarian, autarchic, absolute, absolutist; dystopian.
– OPPOSITES democratic.

totality ▶ **noun** ENTIRETY, whole, total, aggregate, sum, sum total; all, everything.

totally ▶ **adverb** COMPLETELY, entirely, wholly, thoroughly, fully, utterly, absolutely, perfectly, unreservedly, unconditionally, quite, altogether, downright; in every way, in every respect, one hundred per cent, every inch, to the hilt; *informal* dead, deadly.
– OPPOSITES partly.

totter ▶ **verb** ❶ *he tottered off down the road* TEETER, walk unsteadily, stagger, wobble, stumble, shuffle, shamble, toddle; reel, sway, roll, lurch. ❷ *the foundations began to heave and totter* SHAKE, sway, tremble, quiver, teeter, shudder, judder, rock, quake.

touch ▶ **verb** ❶ *his shoes were touching the end of the bed* BE IN CONTACT WITH, come into contact with, meet, join, connect with, converge with, be contiguous with, be against. ❷ *he touched her cheek* PRESS LIGHTLY, tap, pat; feel, stroke, fondle, caress, pet; brush, graze. ❸ *sales touched twenty grand last year* REACH, attain, come to, make; rise to, soar to; sink to, plummet to; *informal* hit. ❹ *nobody can touch him when he's on form* COMPARE WITH, be on a par with, equal, match, be a match for, be in the same class/league as, parallel, rival, come/get close to, measure up to; better, beat; *informal* hold a candle to. ❺ *you're not supposed to touch the computer* HANDLE, hold, pick up, move; meddle with, play about with, fiddle with, interfere with, tamper with, disturb, lay a finger on; use, employ, make use of. ❻ *state companies which have been touched by privatization* AFFECT, have an effect/impact on, make a difference to. ❼ *Lisa felt touched by her kindness* AFFECT, move, tug at someone's heartstrings; leave an impression on, have an effect on.

▶ **noun** ❶ *her touch on his shoulder* TAP, pat; stroke, caress; brush, graze. ❷ *his political touch* SKILL, skilfulness, expertise, dexterity, deftness, adroitness, adeptness, ability, talent, flair, facility, proficiency, knack, technique, approach, style. ❸ *there was a touch of bitterness in her voice | add a touch of vinegar* TRACE, bit, suggestion, suspicion, hint, scintilla, tinge, overtone, undertone; dash, taste, spot, drop, dab, pinch, speck, soupçon. ❹ *the gas lights are a nice touch* DETAIL, feature, point; addition, accessory. ❺ *have you been in touch with him?* CONTACT, communication, correspondence; connection, association.

– RELATED TERMS tactile.

■ **touch down** LAND, alight, come down, put down, arrive.

■ **touch something off** ❶ *he touched off two of the bombs* DETONATE, set off, trigger, explode. ❷ *the plan touched off a major political storm* CAUSE, spark off, trigger (off), start, set in motion, ignite, stir up, provoke, give rise to, lead to, generate.

■ **touch on/upon** ❶ *many television programmes have touched on the subject* REFER TO, mention, comment on, remark on, bring up, raise, broach, allude to; cover, deal with. ❷ *a self-confident manner touching on the arrogant* COME CLOSE TO, verge on, border on, approach.

■ **touch someone up** (*Brit. informal*) FONDLE, molest, feel up; *informal* grope, paw, maul, goose; *N. Amer. informal* cop a feel.

■ **touch something up** ❶ *these paints are handy for touching up small areas* REPAINT, retouch, patch up, fix up; renovate, refurbish, revamp; *informal* do up. ❷ *touch up your CV and improve your interview skills* IMPROVE, enhance, make better, refine; *informal* tweak.

touch-and-go ▶ **adjective** UNCERTAIN, precarious, risky, hazardous, dangerous, critical, suspenseful, cliffhanging, hanging by a thread.

– OPPOSITES certain.

touched ▶ **adjective** ❶ *he was visibly touched by their plight* AFFECTED, moved. ❷ (*informal*) *her mother was a bit touched. See* MAD sense 1.

touching ▶ **adjective** MOVING, affecting, heartwarming, emotional, emotive, tender, sentimental; poignant, sad, tear-jerking.

touchstone ▶ **noun** CRITERION, standard, yardstick, benchmark, barometer, litmus test; measure, point of reference, norm, gauge, test, guide, exemplar, model, pattern.

touchy ▶ **adjective** ❶ *she can be so touchy* SENSITIVE, oversensitive, hypersensitive, easily offended, thin-skinned, highly strung, tense; irritable, tetchy, testy, crotchety, peevish, querulous, bad-tempered, petulant, pettish; *informal* snappy, ratty; *N. Amer. informal* cranky. ❷ *a touchy subject* DELICATE, sensitive, tricky, ticklish, embarrassing, awkward, difficult; contentious, controversial.

– OPPOSITES affable.

tough ▶ **adjective** ❶ *tough leather gloves* DURABLE, strong, resilient, sturdy, rugged, solid, stout, hard-wearing, long-lasting, heavy-duty, well built, made to last. ❷ *the steak was tough* CHEWY, leathery, gristly, stringy, fibrous. ❸ *he'll survive—he's pretty tough* ROBUST, resilient, strong, hardy, rugged, fit; *informal* hard, (as) tough as old boots; *dated* stalwart. ❹ *tough sentencing for persistent offenders* STRICT, stern, severe, stringent, rigorous, hard, firm, hard-hitting, uncompromising; unsentimental, unsympathetic. ❺ *the training was pretty tough* ARDUOUS, onerous, strenuous, gruelling, exacting, difficult, demanding, hard, heavy, taxing, tiring, exhausting, punishing, laborious, stressful, Herculean; *archaic* toilsome. ❻ *these are tough questions for American policy-makers* DIFFICULT, hard, knotty, thorny, tricky.

– OPPOSITES soft, weak, easy.

▶ **noun** *a gang of toughs* RUFFIAN, thug, hoodlum, hooligan, bully boy; *Brit.* rough; *informal* roughneck, heavy, bruiser, gorilla, yahoo; *Brit. informal* yob, yobbo.

toughen ▶ **verb** ❶ *the process toughens the wood fibres* STRENGTHEN, fortify, reinforce, harden, temper, anneal. ❷ *measures to toughen up prison discipline* MAKE STRICTER, make more severe, stiffen, tighten up; *informal* beef up.

tour ▶ **noun** ❶ *a three-day walking tour* TRIP, excursion, journey, expedition, jaunt, outing; trek, safari; *archaic* peregrination. ❷ *a tour of the factory* VISIT, inspection, guided tour, walkabout. ❸ *his tour of duty in Ulster* STINT, stretch, spell, turn, assignment, period of service.

▶ **verb** ❶ *this hotel is well placed for touring Somerset* TRAVEL ROUND, explore, holiday in; *informal* do. ❷ *the prince toured a local factory* VISIT, go round, walk round, inspect.

tourist ▶ **noun** HOLIDAYMAKER, traveller, sightseer, visitor, backpacker, globetrotter, day tripper, tripper; *N. Amer.* vacationer, vacationist, out-of-towner; *Brit. informal* grockle.

– OPPOSITES local.

tournament ▶ **noun** ❶ *a golf tournament* COMPETITION, contest, championship, meeting, meet, event, match, fixture. ❷ (*historical*) *a knight preparing for a tournament* JOUST, tourney, tilt; the lists.

tousled ▶ **adjective** UNTIDY, dishevelled, windblown, messy, disordered, disarranged, messed up, rumpled, uncombed, ungroomed,

tangled, wild, unkempt; *informal* mussed up.
– OPPOSITES neat, tidy.

tout ▶ **verb** ❶ *street merchants were touting their wares* PEDDLE, sell, hawk, offer for sale; *informal* flog. ❷ *minicab drivers were touting for business* SOLICIT, seek, drum up; ask, petition, appeal, canvas. ❸ *he's being touted as the next Scotland manager* RECOMMEND, speak of, talk of; predict; *Brit.* tip.

tow ▶ **verb** *the car was towed back to the garage* PULL, haul, drag, draw, tug, lug.
■ **in tow** *he arrived with his new girlfriend in tow* IN ATTENDANCE, by one's side, in one's charge; accompanying, following.

towards ▶ **preposition** ❶ *they were driving towards her flat* IN THE DIRECTION OF, to; on the way to, on the road to, en route for. ❷ *towards evening dark clouds gathered* JUST BEFORE, shortly before, near, nearing, around, approaching, close to, coming to, getting on for. ❸ *her attitude towards politics* WITH REGARD TO, as regards, regarding, in/with regard to, respecting, in relation to, concerning, about, apropos. ❹ *a grant towards the cost of new buses* AS A CONTRIBUTION TO, for, to help with.

tower ▶ **noun** *a church tower* STEEPLE, spire; minaret; turret; bell tower, belfry, campanile.
▶ **verb** ❶ *snow-capped peaks towered over the valley* SOAR, rise, rear; overshadow, overhang, hang over, dominate. ❷ *he towered over most other theologians of his generation* DOMINATE, overshadow, outshine, outclass, eclipse, be head and shoulders above, put someone/something in the shade.

towering ▶ **adjective** ❶ *a towering skyscraper* HIGH, tall, lofty, soaring, sky-high, sky-scraping, multi-storey; giant, gigantic, enormous, huge, massive; *informal* ginormous. ❷ *a towering intellect* OUTSTANDING, pre-eminent, leading, foremost, finest, top, surpassing, supreme, great, incomparable, unrivalled, unsurpassed, peerless. ❸ *a towering rage* EXTREME, fierce, terrible, intense, overpowering, mighty, violent, vehement, passionate.

town ▶ **noun** URBAN AREA, conurbation, municipality; city, metropolis, megalopolis; *Brit.* borough; *Scottish* burgh.
– RELATED TERMS municipal, urban.
– OPPOSITES country.

toxic ▶ **adjective** POISONOUS, virulent, noxious, dangerous, harmful, injurious, pernicious.
– OPPOSITES harmless.

toy ▶ **noun** ❶ *a cuddly toy* PLAYTHING, game. ❷ *an executive toy* GADGET, device; trinket, knick-knack; *informal* gizmo.
▶ **adjective** ❶ *a toy gun* MODEL, imitation, replica; miniature. ❷ *a toy poodle* MINIATURE, small, tiny, diminutive, dwarf, midget, pygmy.
■ **toy with** ❶ *I was toying with the idea of writing a book* THINK ABOUT, consider, flirt with, entertain the possibility of; *informal* kick around. ❷ *Adam toyed with his glasses* FIDDLE WITH, play with, fidget with, twiddle; finger. ❸ *she toyed with her food* NIBBLE, pick at, peck at, eat listlessly, eat like a bird.

trace ▶ **verb** ❶ *police hope to trace the owner of the jewellery* TRACK DOWN, find, discover, detect, unearth, turn up, hunt down, ferret out, run to ground. ❷ *she traced a pattern in the sand with her toe* DRAW, outline, mark. ❸ *the analysis traces out the consequences of such beliefs* OUTLINE, map out, sketch out, delineate, depict, show, indicate.
▶ **noun** ❶ *no trace had been found of the missing plane* VESTIGE, sign, mark, indication, evidence, clue; remains, remnant, relic, survival. ❷ *a trace of bitterness crept into her voice* BIT, touch, hint, suggestion, suspicion, shadow, whiff; drop, dash, tinge, speck, shred, jot, iota; *informal* smidgen, tad. ❸ *the ground was hard and they left no traces* TRAIL, tracks, marks, prints, footprints; spoor.

track ▶ **noun** ❶ *a gravel track* PATH, pathway, footpath, lane, trail, route, way, course. ❷ *the final lap of the track* COURSE, racecourse, racetrack; velodrome; *Brit.* circuit. ❸ *he found the tracks of a grey fox* TRACES, marks, prints, footprints, trail, spoor. ❹ *Orkney lies on the track of the Atlantic winds* COURSE, path, line, route, way, trajectory. ❺ *commuters had to walk along the tracks* RAIL, line, railway line. ❻ *the album's title track* SONG, recording, number, piece.
▶ **verb** *he tracked a bear for 40 km* FOLLOW, trail, trace, pursue, shadow, stalk, keep an eye on, keep in sight; *informal* tail.
■ **keep track of** MONITOR, follow, keep up with, keep an eye on; keep in touch with, keep up to date with; *informal* keep tabs on.
■ **track someone/something down** DISCOVER, find, detect, hunt down/out, unearth, uncover, turn up, dig up, ferret out, bring to light, run to earth, run to ground.

tract[1] ▶ **noun** *large tracts of land* AREA, region, expanse, sweep, stretch, extent, belt, swathe, zone.

tract[2] ▶ **noun** *a political tract* TREATISE, essay, article, paper, work, monograph, disquisition, dissertation, thesis, homily; pamphlet, booklet, leaflet.

tractable ▶ **adjective** MALLEABLE, manageable, amenable, pliable, governable, yielding, complaisant, compliant, persuadable, accommodating, docile, biddable, obedient, submissive, meek.
– OPPOSITES recalcitrant.

traction ▶ **noun** GRIP, purchase, friction, adhesion.

trade ▶ **noun** ❶ *the illicit trade in stolen cattle* COMMERCE, buying and selling, dealing, traffic, trafficking, business, marketing, merchandising; dealings, transactions. ❷ *the glazier's trade* CRAFT, occupation, job, career, profession,

business, line (of work), métier, vocation, calling, walk of life, field; work, employment.
– RELATED TERMS mercantile.

▶ **verb** ❶ *he made his fortune trading in beaver pelts* DEAL, buy and sell, traffic, market, merchandise, peddle; *informal* hawk, flog. ❷ *the business is trading at a loss* OPERATE, run, do business. ❸ *I traded the old machine for a newer model* SWAP, exchange, switch; barter.

■ **trade on** EXPLOIT, take advantage of, capitalize on, profit from, use, make use of; milk; *informal* cash in on.

trademark ▶ **noun** ❶ *the company's trademark* LOGO, emblem, sign, mark, stamp, symbol, device, badge, crest, monogram, colophon; trade name, brand name, proprietary name. ❷ *it had all the trademarks of a Mafia hit* CHARACTERISTIC, hallmark, telltale sign, sign, trait, quality, attribute, feature, peculiarity, idiosyncrasy.

trader ▶ **noun** DEALER, merchant, buyer, seller, buyer and seller, marketeer, merchandiser, broker, agent; distributor, vendor, purveyor, supplier, trafficker; shopkeeper, retailer, wholesaler.

tradesman, tradeswoman ▶ **noun** ❶ *tradesmen standing nonchalantly outside their stores* SHOPKEEPER, retailer, vendor, wholesaler; *N. Amer.* storekeeper. ❷ *a qualified tradesman* CRAFTSMAN, workman, artisan.

tradition ▶ **noun** ❶ *during a maiden speech, by tradition, everyone keeps absolutely silent* HISTORICAL CONVENTION, unwritten law; oral history, lore, folklore. ❷ *an age-old tradition* CUSTOM, practice, convention, ritual, observance, way, usage, habit, institution; *formal* praxis.

traditional ▶ **adjective** ❶ *traditional Christmas fare* LONG-ESTABLISHED, customary, time-honoured, established, classic, wonted, accustomed, standard, regular, normal, conventional, usual, orthodox, habitual, set, fixed, routine, ritual; old, age-old. ❷ *traditional beliefs* HANDED-DOWN, folk, unwritten, oral.

traduce ▶ **verb** DEFAME, slander, speak ill of, misrepresent, malign, vilify, denigrate, disparage, slur, impugn, smear, besmirch, run down, blacken the name of, cast aspersions on; *informal* bad-mouth; *formal* calumniate.

traffic ▶ **noun** ❶ *the bridge is not open to traffic* VEHICLES, cars, lorries, trucks. ❷ *they might be stuck in traffic* TRAFFIC JAMS, congestion, gridlock, tailbacks, hold-ups, queues; *informal* snarl-ups. ❸ *the increased use of railways for goods traffic* TRANSPORT, transportation, freight, conveyancing, shipping. ❹ *the illegal traffic in stolen art* TRADE, trading, trafficking, dealing, commerce, business, buying and selling; smuggling, bootlegging, black market; dealings, transactions. ❺ (*archaic*) *he has little traffic with his neighbours* CONTACT, communication, intercourse, dealings, relations.

▶ **verb** *he confessed to trafficking in gold and ivory* TRADE, deal, do business, buy and sell; smuggle, bootleg; *informal* run.

tragedy ▶ **noun** DISASTER, calamity, catastrophe, cataclysm, misfortune, reverse, vicissitude, trial, tribulation, affliction, adversity.

tragic ▶ **adjective** ❶ *a tragic accident* DISASTROUS, calamitous, catastrophic, cataclysmic, devastating, terrible, dreadful, awful, appalling, horrendous; fatal, deadly, mortal, lethal. ❷ *a tragic tale* SAD, unhappy, pathetic, moving, distressing, painful, harrowing, heart-rending, piteous, wretched, sorry; melancholy, doleful, mournful. ❸ *a tragic waste of talent* DREADFUL, terrible, awful, deplorable, lamentable, regrettable; *formal* grievous.
– OPPOSITES fortunate, happy.

trail ▶ **noun** ❶ *he left a trail of clues | a trail of devastation* SERIES, string, chain, succession, sequence; aftermath. ❷ *wolves on the trail of their prey* TRACK, spoor, path, scent; traces, marks, signs, prints, footprints. ❸ *the plane's vapour trail* WAKE, tail, stream. ❹ *a trail of ants* LINE, column, train, file, procession, string, chain, convoy; queue. ❺ *country parks with nature trails* PATH, pathway, way, footpath, track, course, route.

▶ **verb** ❶ *her robe trailed along the ground* DRAG, sweep, be drawn; dangle, hang (down), droop. ❷ *the roses grew wild, their stems trailing over the banks* HANG, droop, fall, spill, cascade. ❸ *Sharpe suspected that they were trailing him* FOLLOW, pursue, track, shadow, stalk, hunt (down); run to earth, run to ground; *informal* tail. ❹ *the defending champions were trailing 10–5 at half time* LOSE, be down, be behind, lag behind. ❺ *I hate trailing round the shops* TRUDGE, plod, drag oneself, traipse, trek; *N. Amer. informal* schlep. ❻ *her voice trailed off* FADE, tail off/away, grow faint, die away, dwindle, subside, peter out, fizzle out.

train ▶ **verb** ❶ *an engineer trained in remote-sensing techniques* INSTRUCT, teach, coach, tutor, school, educate, prime, drill, ground; inculcate, indoctrinate. ❷ *she's training to be a hairdresser* STUDY, learn, prepare, take instruction. ❸ *with the Olympics in mind, athletes are training hard* EXERCISE, do exercises, work out, get into shape, practise. ❹ *she trained the gun on his chest* AIM, point, direct, level, focus; take aim, zero in on.

▶ **noun** ❶ *the train for London* locomotive, railway train; *baby talk* choo choo. ❷ *a minister and his train of attendants* RETINUE, entourage, cortège, following, staff, household, court, suite, attendants, retainers, followers, bodyguards. ❸ *a train of elephants* PROCESSION, line, file, column, convoy, cavalcade, caravan, queue, string, succession. ❹ *a bizarre train of events* CHAIN, string, series, sequence, succession, set, course, cycle, concatenation.

trainer ▶ **noun** COACH, instructor, teacher, tutor; handler.

training ▶ **noun** ❶ *in-house training for staff* INSTRUCTION, teaching, coaching, tuition, tutoring, schooling, education; indoctrination, inculcation. ❷ *four months' hard training before the match* EXERCISE, exercises, working out; practice, preparation.

traipse ▶ **verb** TRUDGE, trek, tramp, trail, plod, drag oneself, slog; *Brit. informal* trog; *N. Amer. informal* schlep.

trait ▶ **noun** CHARACTERISTIC, attribute, feature, (essential) quality, property; habit, custom, mannerism, idiosyncrasy, peculiarity, quirk, oddity, foible.

traitor ▶ **noun** BETRAYER, back-stabber, double-crosser, double-dealer, renegade, Judas, quisling, fifth columnist; turncoat, defector, deserter; collaborator, informer, double agent; *informal* snake in the grass, two-timer.

traitorous ▶ **adjective** TREACHEROUS, disloyal, treasonous, back-stabbing; double-crossing, double-dealing, faithless, unfaithful, two-faced, false-hearted, duplicitous, deceitful, false; *informal* two-timing; *poetic/literary* perfidious.
– OPPOSITES loyal.

trajectory ▶ **noun** COURSE, path, route, track, line, orbit.

trammel (*poetic/literary*) ▶ **noun** *the trammels of tradition* RESTRAINT, constraint, curb, check, impediment, obstacle, barrier, handicap, bar, hindrance, encumbrance, disadvantage, drawback, snag, stumbling block; shackles, fetters, bonds.
▶ **verb** *those less trammelled by convention than himself* RESTRICT, restrain, constrain, hamper, confine, hinder, handicap, obstruct, impede, hold back, hamstring, shackle, fetter.

tramp ▶ **verb** ❶ *men were tramping through the shrubbery* TRUDGE, plod, stamp, trample, lumber, clump, clomp, stump, stomp; *informal* traipse, galumph. ❷ *he spent ten days tramping through the jungle* TREK, slog, footslog, trudge, drag oneself, walk, hike, march; *informal* traipse; *Brit. informal* yomp; *N. Amer. informal* schlep.
▶ **noun** ❶ *a dirty old tramp* VAGRANT, vagabond, homeless person, down-and-out; traveller, drifter, beachcomber; beggar, mendicant; *N. Amer.* hobo; *Austral./NZ* bagman; *informal* bag lady; *N. Amer. informal* bum. ❷ *the regular tramp of the sentry's boots* FOOTSTEP, step, footfall, tread, stamp, stomp. ❸ *a tramp round Norwich* TREK, slog, trudge, hike, march, walk; *Brit. informal* yomp; *N. Amer. informal* schlep.

trample ▶ **verb** ❶ *someone had trampled on the tulips* TREAD, tramp, stamp, stomp, walk over; squash, crush, flatten. ❷ *we do nothing but trample over their feelings* TREAT WITH CONTEMPT, ride roughshod over, disregard, set at naught, show no consideration for, abuse; encroach on, infringe.

trance ▶ **noun** DAZE, stupor, hypnotic state, half-conscious state, dream; *Scottish* dwam.

tranquil ▶ **adjective** ❶ *a wonderfully tranquil village* PEACEFUL, calm, restful, quiet, still, relaxing, undisturbed. ❷ *Martha smiled, perfectly tranquil* CALM, serene, relaxed, unruffled, unperturbed, unflustered, untroubled, composed, {cool, calm, and collected}; equable, even-tempered, placid, phlegmatic; *informal* unflappable.
– OPPOSITES busy, excitable.

tranquillity ▶ **noun** ❶ *the tranquillity of the Norfolk countryside* PEACE, peacefulness, restfulness, repose, calm, calmness, quiet, quietness, stillness. ❷ *the incident jolted her out of her tranquillity* COMPOSURE, calmness, serenity; equanimity, equability, placidity; *informal* cool, unflappability.

tranquillize ▶ **verb** SEDATE, put under sedation, narcotize, drug.

tranquillizer ▶ **noun** SEDATIVE, barbiturate, calmative, sleeping pill, narcotic, opiate; *informal* trank, downer.
– OPPOSITES [illegible]

transact ▶ **verb** CONDUCT, carry out, negotiate, do, perform, execute, take care of; settle, conclude, finish, clinch, accomplish.

transaction ▶ **noun** ❶ *property transactions* DEAL, business deal, undertaking, arrangement, bargain, negotiation, agreement, settlement; proceedings. ❷ *the transactions of the Historical Society* PROCEEDINGS, report, record(s), minutes, account; archives. ❸ *the transaction of government business* CONDUCT, carrying out, negotiation, performance, execution.

transcend ▶ **verb** ❶ *an issue that transcended party politics* GO BEYOND, rise above, cut across. ❷ *his military exploits far transcended those of his predecessors* SURPASS, exceed, beat, top, cap, outdo, outclass, outstrip, leave behind, outshine, eclipse, overshadow, throw into the shade, upstage.

transcendence ▶ **noun** EXCELLENCE, supremacy, incomparability, matchlessness, peerlessness, magnificence.

transcendent ▶ **adjective** ❶ *the search for a transcendent level of knowledge* MYSTICAL, mystic, transcendental, spiritual; metaphysical. ❷ *a transcendent genius* INCOMPARABLE, matchless, peerless, unrivalled, inimitable, beyond compare/comparison, unparalleled, unequalled, without equal, second to none, unsurpassed, unsurpassable, nonpareil; exceptional, consummate, unique, perfect, rare, surpassing, magnificent; *formal* unexampled.

transcendental ▶ **adjective**. *See* TRANSCENDENT sense 1.

transcribe ▶ **verb** ❶ *each interview was taped and transcribed* WRITE OUT, copy out, put in writing, put on paper. ❷ *a person who can take and* *transcribe shorthand* TRANSLITERATE, interpret, translate.

transcript ▶ **noun** WRITTEN VERSION, printed version, text, transliteration, record, reproduction.

transfer ▶ **verb** ❶ *the hostages were transferred to a safe house* MOVE, convey, take, bring, shift, remove, carry, transport; transplant, relocate, resettle. ❷ *the property was transferred to his wife* HAND OVER, pass on, make over, turn over, sign over, consign, devolve, assign, delegate.
▶ **noun** *he died shortly after his transfer to hospital* MOVE, conveyance, transferral, transference, relocation, removal, transplantation.

transfigure ▶ **verb** TRANSFORM, transmute, change, alter, metamorphose; *humorous* transmogrify.

transfix ▶ **verb** ❶ *he was transfixed by the images on the screen* MESMERIZE, hypnotize, spellbind, bewitch, captivate, entrance, enthral, fascinate, enrapture, grip, rivet; root to the spot, paralyse. ❷ *a field mouse is transfixed by the owl's curved talons* IMPALE, stab, spear, pierce, spike, skewer, gore, stick, run through; *poetic/literary* transpierce.

transform ▶ **verb** CHANGE, alter, convert, metamorphose, transfigure, transmute; revolutionize, overhaul; remodel, reshape, remould, redo, reconstruct, rebuild, reorganize, rearrange, rework, renew, revamp, remake; *humorous* transmogrify.

transformation ▶ **noun** CHANGE, alteration, conversion, metamorphosis, transfiguration, transmutation, sea change; revolution, overhaul; remodelling, reshaping, remoulding, redoing, reconstruction, rebuilding, reorganization, rearrangement, reworking, renewal, revamp, remaking; *humorous* transmogrification.

transgress ▶ **verb** ❶ *if they transgress the punishment is harsh* MISBEHAVE, behave badly, break the law, err, fall from grace, stray from the straight and narrow, sin, do wrong, go astray; *archaic* trespass. ❷ *she had transgressed an unwritten social law* INFRINGE, breach, contravene, disobey, defy, violate, break, flout.

transgression ▶ **noun** ❶ *a punishment for past transgressions* OFFENCE, crime, sin, wrong, wrongdoing, misdemeanour, misdeed, lawbreaking; error, lapse, fault; *archaic* trespass. ❷ *Adam's transgression of God's law* INFRINGEMENT, breach, contravention, violation, defiance, disobedience, non-observance.

transgressor ▶ **noun** WRONGDOER, offender, miscreant, lawbreaker, criminal, villain, felon, malefactor, guilty party, culprit; sinner, evil-doer; *archaic* trespasser.

transient ▶ **adjective** TRANSITORY, temporary, short-lived, short-term, ephemeral, impermanent, brief, short, momentary, fleeting, passing, fugitive, here today and gone tomorrow; *poetic/literary* evanescent.
–OPPOSITES permanent.

transit ▶ **noun** *the transit of goods between states* TRANSPORT, transportation, movement, conveyance, shipment, haulage, freightage, carriage, transfer.
■ **in transit** EN ROUTE, on the journey, on the way, along/on the road, during transport.

transition ▶ **noun** CHANGE, passage, move, transformation, conversion, metamorphosis, alteration, changeover, shift, switch, jump, leap, progression, progress, development, evolution.

transitional ▶ **adjective** ❶ *a transitional period* INTERMEDIATE, interim, changeover; changing, fluid, unsettled. ❷ *the transitional government* INTERIM, temporary, provisional, pro tem, acting, caretaker.

transitory ▶ **adjective** TRANSIENT, temporary, brief, short, short-lived, short-term, impermanent, ephemeral, momentary, fleeting, passing, fugitive, here today and gone tomorrow; *poetic/literary* evanescent.
–OPPOSITES permanent.

translate ▶ **verb** ❶ *the German original had been translated into English* RENDER, put, express, convert, change; transcribe, transliterate. ❷ *be prepared to translate the jargon into normal English* RENDER, paraphrase, reword, rephrase, convert, decipher, decode, gloss, explain. ❸ *interesting ideas cannot always be translated into effective movies* CHANGE, convert, transform, alter, adapt, turn, transmute; *humorous* transmogrify. ❹ *in 1228 the bishop was translated from Salisbury to Durham* RELOCATE, transfer, move, remove, shift, transplant.

translation ▶ **noun** ❶ *the translation of the Bible into English* RENDITION, rendering, conversion; transcription, transliteration. ❷ *the translation of these policies into practice* CONVERSION, change, transformation, alteration, adaptation, transmutation; *humorous* transmogrification.

translucent ▶ **adjective** SEMI-TRANSPARENT, pellucid, limpid, clear; diaphanous, gossamer, sheer.
–OPPOSITES opaque.

transmission ▶ **noun** ❶ *the transmission of knowledge and culture* TRANSFERENCE, transferral, communication, conveyance; dissemination, spreading, circulation. ❷ *the transmission of the film* BROADCASTING, relaying, airing, televising. ❸ *a live transmission* BROADCAST, programme, show.

transmit ▶ **verb** ❶ *the use of computers to transmit information* TRANSFER, pass on, hand on, communicate, convey, impart, channel, carry, relay, dispatch; disseminate, spread, circulate. ❷ *the programme will be transmitted on Sunday* BROADCAST, relay, send out, air, televise.

transmute ▶ **verb** CHANGE, alter, adapt, transform, convert, metamorphose, translate; *humorous* transmogrify.

transparency ▶ noun ❶ *the transparency of the glass* TRANSLUCENCY, limpidity, glassiness, clearness, clarity. ❷ *colour transparencies* SLIDE, diapositive.

transparent ▶ adjective ❶ *transparent blue water* CLEAR, crystal clear, see-through, translucent, pellucid, limpid, glassy. ❷ *fine transparent fabrics* SEE-THROUGH, sheer, filmy, gauzy, diaphanous. ❸ *the symbolism of this myth is transparent* OBVIOUS, unambiguous, unequivocal, clear, crystal clear, plain, (as) plain as the nose on your face, apparent, unmistakable, manifest, conspicuous, patent, palpable, indisputable, evident, self-evident, undisguised, unconcealed.

– OPPOSITES opaque, obscure.

transpire ▶ verb ❶ *it transpired that her family had moved away* BECOME KNOWN, emerge, come to light, be revealed, turn out, come out, be discovered, prove to be the case. ❷ *I'm going to find out exactly what transpired* HAPPEN, occur, take place, arise, come about, turn up, chance, befall; *poetic/literary* come to pass.

transplant ▶ verb ❶ *it was proposed to transplant the club to the vacant site* TRANSFER, move, remove, shift, relocate, take. ❷ *the seedlings should be transplanted in larger pots* REPLANT, repot, relocate. ❸ *kidneys must be transplanted within 48 hours of removal* TRANSFER, implant.

transport ▶ verb ❶ *the concrete blocks were transported by lorry* CONVEY, carry, take, transfer, move, shift, send, deliver, bear, ship, ferry; *informal* cart. ❷ *he was convicted of theft and transported* BANISH, exile, deport, expatriate, extradite. ❸ *she was completely transported by the excitement* THRILL, delight, carry away, enrapture, entrance, enchant, enthral, electrify, captivate, bewitch, fascinate, spellbind, charm; *informal* send; *poetic/literary* ravish.

▶ noun ❶ *alternative forms of transport* CONVEYANCE, transportation; vehicle, car, lorry, truck. train. ❷ *the transport of crude oil* TRANSPORTATION, conveyance, carriage, freight, freightage, shipment, shipping, haulage; transit. ❸ *transports of delight* RAPTURE, ecstasy, elation, exaltation, exhilaration, euphoria, bliss, seventh heaven, heaven, paradise, high; passion, strong feeling/emotion; *informal* cloud nine.

transpose ▶ verb ❶ *the blue and black plates were transposed* INTERCHANGE, exchange, switch, swap (round), reverse, invert. ❷ *the themes are transposed from the sphere of love to that of work* TRANSFER, shift, relocate, transplant, move, displace.

transverse ▶ adjective CROSSWISE, crossways, cross, horizontal, diagonal, oblique.

trap ▶ noun ❶ *an animal caught in a trap* SNARE, net, mesh, gin, springe; *N. Amer.* deadfall. ❷ *the question was set as a trap* TRICK, ploy, ruse, deception, subterfuge; booby trap; *informal* set-up. ❸ (*informal*) *shut your trap! See* MOUTH *noun sense* 1.

▶ verb ❶ *police trapped the two men, who admitted blackmail* SNARE, entrap, ensnare, lay a trap for; capture, catch, corner, ambush; *archaic* ambuscade. ❷ *a rat trapped in a barn* CONFINE, cut off, corner, shut in, pen in, hem in; imprison, hold captive. ❸ *I hoped to trap him into an admission* TRICK, dupe, deceive, lure, inveigle, beguile, fool, hoodwink; catch out, trip up.

trappings ▶ plural noun ACCESSORIES, accoutrements, appurtenances, trimmings, frills, accompaniments, extras, ornamentation, adornment, decoration; regalia, panoply, paraphernalia, apparatus, finery, equipment, gear, effects, things.

trash ▶ noun ❶ (*N. Amer.*) *the subway entrance was blocked with trash* RUBBISH, refuse, waste, litter, junk, detritus; *N. Amer.* garbage. ❷ (*informal*) *if they read at all, they read trash* RUBBISH, nonsense, trivia, pulp (fiction), pap; *N. Amer.* garbage; *informal* drivel, dreck. ❸ (*informal*) *they're just trash* SCUM, vermin, the dregs of society, the scum of the earth, the lowest of the low; *informal* dirt.

▶ verb (*N. Amer. informal*) ❶ *the apartment had been totally trashed* WRECK, ruin, destroy, wreak havoc on, devastate; vandalize; *informal* total. ❷ *his play was trashed by the critics. See* LAMBASTE.

trauma ▶ noun ❶ *the trauma of divorce* SHOCK, upheaval, distress, stress, strain, pain, anguish, suffering, upset, agony, misery, sorrow, grief, heartache, heartbreak, torture; ordeal, trial, tribulation, trouble, worry, anxiety; nightmare. ❷ *the trauma to the liver* INJURY, damage, wound; cut, laceration, lesion, abrasion, contusion.

traumatic ▶ adjective DISTURBING, shocking, distressing, upsetting, heartbreaking, painful, agonizing, hurtful, stressful, damaging, injurious, harmful, awful, terrible, devastating, harrowing.

travail (*poetic/literary*) ▶ noun ❶ *years of bitter travail* ORDEALS, trials, tribulations, trials and tribulations, trouble, hardship, privation, stress; drudgery, toil, slog, effort, exertion, labour, work, endeavour, sweat, struggle. ❷ *a woman in travail* LABOUR, childbirth; contractions, labour pains; *archaic* childbed.

travel ▶ verb ❶ *he spent much of his time travelling abroad* JOURNEY, tour, take a trip, voyage, go sightseeing, globetrot, backpack; *informal* gallivant; *archaic* peregrinate. ❷ *we travelled the length and breadth of the island* JOURNEY THROUGH, cross, traverse, cover; roam, rove, range, trek. ❸ *light travels faster than sound* MOVE, be transmitted.

▶ noun *he amassed great wealth during his travels* JOURNEYS, expeditions, trips, tours, excursions, voyages, treks, safaris, explorations, wanderings, odysseys, pilgrimages, jaunts; travelling, touring, sightseeing, backpacking, globetrotting; *informal* gallivanting; *archaic* peregrinations.

traveller ▶ **noun** ❶ *thousands of travellers were left stranded* TOURIST, tripper, holidaymaker, sightseer, visitor, globetrotter, backpacker; pilgrim; passenger, commuter, fare; *N. Amer.* vacationer, vacationist. ❷ *a travellers' site* GYPSY, Romany, tzigane; nomad, migrant, wanderer, itinerant, drifter; tramp, vagrant; *dialect* didicoi; *Brit. derogatory* tinker.

travelling ▶ **adjective** ❶ *the travelling population* NOMADIC, itinerant, peripatetic, wandering, roaming, roving, wayfaring, migrant, vagrant, of no fixed address/abode; gypsy, Romany. ❷ *a little travelling clock* PORTABLE, easily carried, easy to carry, lightweight, compact.

traverse ▶ **verb** ❶ *he traversed the deserts of Persia* TRAVEL OVER/ACROSS, cross, journey over/across, pass over; cover; ply; wander, roam, range. ❷ *a ditch traversed by a wooden bridge* CROSS, bridge, span; extend across, lie across, stretch across.

travesty ▶ **noun** *a travesty of justice* MISREPRESENTATION, distortion, perversion, corruption, poor imitation, poor substitute, mockery, parody, caricature; farce, charade, pantomime, sham; *informal* apology for, excuse for.

treacherous ▶ **adjective** ❶ *her treacherous brother betrayed her* TRAITOROUS, disloyal, faithless, unfaithful, duplicitous, false-hearted, deceitful, false, back-stabbing, double-crossing, double-dealing, two-faced, untrustworthy, unreliable; apostate, renegade; *informal* two-timing; *poetic/literary* perfidious. ❷ *treacherous driving conditions* DANGEROUS, hazardous, perilous, unsafe, precarious, risky, deceptive, unreliable; *informal* dicey, hairy.
– OPPOSITES loyal, faithful, reliable.

treachery ▶ **noun** BETRAYAL, disloyalty, faithlessness, unfaithfulness, infidelity, breach of trust, duplicity, deceit, deception, stab in the back, back-stabbing, double-dealing, untrustworthiness; treason; *informal* two-timing; *poetic/literary* perfidy.

tread ▶ **verb** ❶ *he trod purposefully down the hall* WALK, step, stride, pace, go; march, tramp, plod, stomp, trudge. ❷ *the snow had been trodden down by the horses* CRUSH, flatten, press down, squash; trample on, tramp on, stamp on, stomp on.
▶ **noun** *we heard his heavy tread on the stairs* STEP, footstep, footfall, tramp.

treason ▶ **noun** TREACHERY, lese-majesty; disloyalty, betrayal, faithlessness; sedition, subversion, mutiny, rebellion; high treason; *poetic/literary* perfidy.
– OPPOSITES allegiance, loyalty.

treasonable ▶ **adjective** TRAITOROUS, treacherous, disloyal; seditious, subversive, mutinous, rebellious; *poetic/literary* perfidious.
– OPPOSITES loyal.

treasure ▶ **noun** ❶ *a casket of treasure* RICHES, valuables, jewels, gems, gold, silver, precious metals, money, cash; wealth, fortune; *Brit.* treasure trove. ❷ *art treasures* VALUABLE OBJECT, valuable, work of art, objet of virtu, masterpiece. ❸ (*informal*) *she's a real treasure* PARAGON, gem, angel, nonpareil; find, prize; *informal* star, one of a kind, one in a million, the tops.
▶ **verb** *I treasure the photographs I took of Jack* CHERISH, hold dear, prize, set great store by, value greatly; adore, dote on, love dearly, be devoted to, worship.

treasury ▶ **noun** ❶ *the national treasury* EXCHEQUER, purse; bank, coffers; revenues, finances, funds, moneys. ❷ *the area is a treasury of early fossils* RICH SOURCE, repository, storehouse, treasure house; fund, mine, bank. ❸ *a treasury of stories* ANTHOLOGY, collection, miscellany, compilation, compendium.

treat ▶ **verb** ❶ *Charlotte treated him very badly* BEHAVE TOWARDS, act towards, use; deal with, handle. ❷ *police are treating the fires as arson* REGARD, consider, view, look on; put down as. ❸ *the book treats its subject with insight and responsibility* DEAL WITH, tackle, handle, discuss, explore, investigate; consider, study, analyse. ❹ *she was treated at Addenbrooke's Hospital* GIVE MEDICAL CARE TO, nurse, tend, attend to; medicate. ❺ *the plants may prove useful in treating cancer* CURE, heal, remedy. ❻ *he treated her to a slap-up lunch* BUY, take out for, stand, give; pay for; entertain, wine and dine; *informal* foot the bill for. ❼ *delegates were treated to authentic Indonesian dance performances* REGALE WITH, entertain with/by, fête with, amuse with, divert with. ❽ (*formal*) *propagandists claimed that he was treating with the enemy* NEGOTIATE, discuss terms, have talks, consult, parley, talk, confer.
▶ **noun** ❶ *a birthday treat* CELEBRATION, entertainment, amusement; surprise; party, excursion, outing. ❷ *I bought you some chocolate as a treat* PRESENT, gift; titbit, delicacy, luxury, indulgence, extravagance; *informal* goodie. ❸ *it was a real treat to see them* PLEASURE, delight, thrill, joy.

treatise ▶ **noun** DISQUISITION, essay, paper, work, exposition, discourse, dissertation, thesis, monograph, study, critique; tract, pamphlet.

treatment ▶ **noun** ❶ *the company's treatment of its workers* BEHAVIOUR TOWARDS, conduct towards; handling of, dealings with. ❷ *she's responding well to treatment* MEDICAL CARE, therapy, nursing; medication, drugs, medicaments; cure, remedy. ❸ *her treatment of the topic* DISCUSSION, handling, investigation, exploration, consideration, study, analysis, critique.

treaty ▶ **noun** AGREEMENT, settlement, pact, deal, entente, concordat, accord, protocol, compact, convention, contract, covenant, bargain, pledge; *formal* concord.

tree ▶ noun sapling, conifer, evergreen.
– RELATED TERMS arboreal.

trek ▶ noun *a three-day trek across the desert* JOURNEY, trip, expedition, safari, odyssey; hike, march, slog, footslog, tramp, walk; long haul; *Brit. informal* yomp, trog.
▶ verb *we trekked through the jungle* HIKE, tramp, march, slog, footslog, trudge, traipse, walk; travel, journey; *Brit. informal* yomp, trog.

trellis ▶ noun LATTICE, framework, espalier; network, mesh, tracery; grille, grid, grating; latticework, trelliswork; *technical* reticulation.

tremble ▶ verb ❶ *Joe's hands were trembling* SHAKE, shake like a leaf, quiver, twitch; quaver, waver. ❷ *the entire building trembled* SHAKE, shudder, judder, wobble, rock, vibrate, move, sway, totter, teeter. ❸ *she trembled at the thought of what he had in store for her* BE AFRAID, be frightened, be apprehensive, worry, shake in one's shoes; quail, shrink, blench; *informal* be in a blue funk, be all of a tremble.
▶ noun *the slight tremble in her hands* TREMOR, shake, shakiness, trembling, quiver, twitch.
– OPPOSITES steadiness.

tremendous ▶ adjective ❶ *tremendous sums of money* HUGE, enormous, immense, colossal, massive, prodigious, stupendous, monumental, mammoth, vast, gigantic, giant, mighty, epic, titanic, towering, king-size(d), gargantuan, Herculean; substantial, considerable; *informal* whopping, thumping, astronomical, humongous; *Brit. informal* whacking, ginormous. ❷ *a tremendous explosion* VERY LOUD, deafening, ear-splitting, booming, thundering, thunderous, resounding. ❸ (*informal*) *I've seen him play and he's tremendous* EXCELLENT, splendid, wonderful, marvellous, magnificent, superb, glorious, sublime, lovely, delightful, too good to be true; *informal* super, great, amazing, fantastic, terrific, sensational, heavenly, divine, gorgeous, grand, fabulous, fab, awesome, to die for, magic, ace, wicked, mind-blowing, far out, out of this world; *Brit. informal* smashing, brilliant, brill; *N. Amer. informal* boss; *Austral./NZ informal* beaut, bonzer; *Brit. informal, dated* champion, wizard, corking, ripping, spiffing, top-hole; *N. Amer. informal, dated* swell.
– OPPOSITES tiny, small, poor.

tremor ▶ noun ❶ *the sudden tremor of her hands* TREMBLING, shaking, shakiness, tremble, shake, quivering, quiver, twitching, twitch, tic; quavering, quaver. ❷ *a tremor of fear ran through her* FRISSON, shiver, spasm, thrill, tingle, stab, dart, shaft; wave, surge, rush, ripple. ❸ *the epicentre of the tremor* EARTHQUAKE, earth tremor, shock; *informal* quake; *N. Amer. informal* tremblor.

tremulous ▶ adjective ❶ *a tremulous voice* SHAKY, trembling, shaking, unsteady, quavering, wavering, quivering, quivery, quaking, weak; *informal* trembly, all of a tremble. ❷ *a tremulous smile* TIMID, diffident, shy, hesitant, uncertain, nervous, timorous, fearful, frightened, scared, anxious, apprehensive.
– OPPOSITES steady, confident.

trench ▶ noun DITCH, channel, trough, excavation, furrow, rut, conduit, cut, drain, waterway, watercourse; earthwork, entrenchment, moat; *Archaeology* fosse.

trenchant ▶ adjective INCISIVE, penetrating, sharp, keen, acute, shrewd, razor-sharp, rapier-like, piercing; vigorous, forceful, strong, telling, emphatic, forthright; mordant, cutting, biting, pungent.
– OPPOSITES vague.

trend ▶ noun ❶ *an upward trend in unemployment* TENDENCY, movement, drift, swing, shift, course, current, direction, inclination, leaning; bias, bent. ❷ *the latest trend in dance music* FASHION, vogue, style, mode, craze, mania, rage; *informal* fad, thing.
▶ verb *interest rates are trending up* MOVE, go, head, drift, gravitate, swing, shift, turn, incline, tend, lean, veer.

trendy ▶ adjective (*informal*) FASHIONABLE, in fashion, in vogue, popular, (bang) up to date, up to the minute, modern, all the rage, modish, à la mode, trendsetting; stylish, chic, designer; *informal* cool, funky, in, the in thing, hot, big, hip, happening, sharp, groovy, snazzy, with it; *N. Amer. informal* tony, kicky.
– OPPOSITES unfashionable.

trepidation ▶ noun FEAR, apprehension, dread, fearfulness, agitation, anxiety, worry, nervousness, tension, misgivings, unease, uneasiness, foreboding, disquiet, dismay, consternation, alarm, panic; *informal* butterflies, jitteriness, the jitters, a cold sweat, a blue funk, the heebie-jeebies, the willies, the shakes, the jim-jams, collywobbles, cold feet; *Brit. informal* the (screaming) abdabs/habdabs.
– OPPOSITES equanimity, composure.

trespass ▶ verb ❶ *there is no excuse for trespassing on railway property* INTRUDE ON, encroach on, enter without permission, invade. ❷ *I must not trespass on your good nature* TAKE ADVANTAGE OF, impose on, play on, exploit, abuse; encroach on, infringe. ❸ (*archaic*) *he would be the last among us to trespass* SIN, transgress, offend, do wrong, err, go astray, fall from grace, stray from the straight and narrow.
▶ noun ❶ *his alleged trespass on council land* UNLAWFUL ENTRY, intrusion, encroachment, invasion. ❷ (*archaic*) *he asked forgiveness for his trespasses* SIN, wrong, wrongdoing, transgression, crime, offence, misdeed, misdemeanour, error, lapse, fall from grace.

trespasser ▶ noun ❶ *a high stone wall discouraged would-be trespassers* INTRUDER, interloper, unwelcome visitor, encroacher. ❷ (*archaic*) *trespassers asking for forgiveness* SINNER, transgressor, wrongdoer, evil-doer, malefactor, offender, criminal.

tresses ▸ plural noun HAIR, head of hair, mane, mop of hair, shock of hair; locks, curls, ringlets.

trial ▸ noun ❶ *the trial is expected to last several weeks* COURT CASE, case, lawsuit, suit, hearing, inquiry, tribunal, litigation, (legal/judicial) proceedings, legal action; court martial; appeal, retrial. ❷ *the drug is undergoing clinical trials* TEST, try-out, experiment, pilot study; examination, check, assessment, evaluation, appraisal; trial/test period, trial/test run, dummy run; *informal* dry run. ❸ *she could be a bit of a trial at times* NUISANCE, pest, bother, irritant, problem, inconvenience, plague, thorn in one's flesh, the bane of one's life, one's cross to bear; bore; *informal* pain, pain in the neck/backside, headache, drag, nightmare; *Scottish informal* skelf; *N. Amer. informal* pain in the butt, nudnik, burr under/in someone's saddle. ❹ *a long account of her trials and tribulations* TROUBLE, anxiety, worry, burden, affliction, ordeal, tribulation, adversity, hardship, tragedy, trauma, reverse, setback, difficulty, problem, misfortune, bad luck, mishap, misadventure; *informal* hassle; *poetic/literary* travails.
▸ adjective *a three-month trial period* TEST, experimental, pilot, exploratory, probationary, provisional.
▸ verb *the electronic cash card has been trialled by several banks* TEST, try out, put to the test, put through its paces; pilot.

tribe ▸ noun ❶ *the nomadic tribes of the Sahara* ETHNIC GROUP, people; family, dynasty, house; clan, sept. ❷ *a tribe of children trailed after her* GROUP, crowd, gang, company, body, band, host, bevy, party, pack, army, herd, flock, drove, horde; *informal* bunch, crew, gaggle, posse.

tribulation ▸ noun ❶ *the tribulations of her personal life* TROUBLE, difficulty, problem, worry, anxiety, burden, cross to bear, ordeal, trial, adversity, hardship, tragedy, trauma, affliction; reverse, setback, blow; *informal* hassle. ❷ *his time of tribulation was just beginning* SUFFERING, distress, trouble, misery, wretchedness, unhappiness, sadness, heartache, woe, grief, pain, anguish, agony; *poetic/literary* travail.

tribunal ▸ noun ❶ *a rent tribunal* ARBITRATION BOARD/PANEL, board, panel, committee. ❷ *an international war-crimes tribunal* COURT, court of justice, court of law, law court; court of inquiry; *N. Amer.* forum.

tributary ▸ noun HEADWATER, branch, feeder, side stream, influent; *N. Amer. & Austral./NZ* creek.

tribute ▸ noun ❶ *tributes flooded in from friends and colleagues* ACCOLADE, praise, commendation, salute, testimonial, homage, eulogy, paean, panegyric; congratulations, compliments, plaudits; gift, present, offering; *informal* bouquet; *formal* laudation, encomium. ❷ *it is a tribute to his determination that he ever played again* TESTIMONY, indication, manifestation, evidence, proof, attestation. ❸ *the Vikings demanded tributes in silver* PAYMENT, contribution, dues, levy, tax, duty, impost.
– OPPOSITES criticism, condemnation.
■ **pay tribute to** PRAISE, sing the praises of, speak highly of, commend, acclaim, take one's hat off to, applaud, salute, honour, show appreciation of, recognize, acknowledge, pay homage to, extol; *formal* laud.

trice
■ **in a trice** VERY SOON, in a moment/second/instant, shortly, any minute (now), in a short time, in (less than) no time, in the twinkling of an eye, in a flash, before you know it, before long; *N. Amer.* momentarily; *informal* anon, in a jiffy, in two shakes (of a lamb's tail), before you can say Jack Robinson; *Brit. informal* in a tick, in a mo, in two ticks; *N. Amer. informal* in a snap; *dated* directly.

trick ▸ noun ❶ *he's capable of any mean trick* STRATAGEM, ploy, ruse, scheme, device, manoeuvre, contrivance, machination, artifice, wile, dodge; deceit, deception, trickery, subterfuge, chicanery, sharp practice; swindle, hoax, fraud, confidence trick; *informal* con (trick), set-up, game, scam, sting, flimflam; *Brit. informal* wheeze; *N. Amer. informal* bunco; *archaic* shift. ❷ *I think he's playing a trick on us* PRACTICAL JOKE, joke, prank, jape; *informal* leg-pull, spoof, put-on; *Brit. informal* cod. ❸ *conjuring tricks* FEAT, stunt; (**tricks**) SLEIGHT OF HAND, legerdemain, prestidigitation; magic. ❹ *it was probably a trick of the light* ILLUSION, optical illusion, figment of the imagination; mirage. ❺ *the tricks of the trade* KNACK, art, skill, technique; secret. ❻ *he sat biting his fingernails, a trick of his when he was excited* MANNERISM, habit, quirk, idiosyncrasy, peculiarity, foible, way; characteristic, trait.
▸ verb *many people have been tricked by villains with false identity cards* DECEIVE, delude, hoodwink, mislead, take in, dupe, fool, double-cross, cheat, defraud, swindle, catch out, gull, hoax, bamboozle; *informal* con, diddle, rook, put one over on, pull a fast one on, pull the wool over someone's eyes, take for a ride, lead up the garden path, shaft, do, flimflam; *N. Amer. informal* sucker, snooker, gold-brick; *Austral. informal* pull a swifty on; *poetic/literary* cozen.
■ **do the trick** (*informal*) BE EFFECTIVE, work, solve the problem, fill/fit the bill; *N. Amer.* turn the trick; *informal* do the necessary.
■ **trick someone/something out** DRESS (UP), attire, array, rig out, garb, get up; adorn, decorate, deck (out), bedeck, embellish, ornament, festoon; *poetic/literary* bedizen, caparison; *archaic* apparel.

trickery ▸ noun DECEPTION, deceit, dishonesty, cheating, duplicity, double-dealing, legerdemain, sleight of hand, guile, craftiness, devi-

ousness, subterfuge, skulduggery, chicanery, fraud, fraudulence, swindling, sharp practice; *informal* monkey business, funny business, jiggery-pokery.
– OPPOSITES honesty.

trickle ▶ verb *blood was trickling from two cuts in his lip* DRIP, dribble, ooze, leak, seep, spill.
– OPPOSITES pour, gush.
▶ noun *trickles of water* DRIBBLE, drip, thin stream, rivulet.

trickster ▶ noun SWINDLER, cheat, fraud, fraudster; charlatan, mountebank, quack, impostor, sham, hoaxer; rogue, villain, scoundrel; *informal* con man, sharp, flimflammer; *Brit. informal* twister; *N. Amer. informal* grifter, bunco artist; *Austral. informal* illywhacker, magsman; *dated* confidence man.

tricky ▶ adjective ❶ *a tricky situation* DIFFICULT, awkward, problematic, delicate, ticklish, sensitive, embarrassing, touchy; risky, uncertain, precarious, touch-and-go; thorny, knotty; *informal* sticky, dicey; *N. Amer. informal* gnarly. ❷ *a tricky and unscrupulous politician* CUNNING, crafty, wily, guileful, artful, devious, sly, scheming, calculating, designing, sharp, shrewd, astute, canny; duplicitous, dishonest, deceitful; *informal* foxy.
– OPPOSITES straightforward, honest.

tried and trusted ▶ adjective RELIABLE, dependable, trustworthy, trusted, certain, sure; proven, proved, tested, tried and tested, put to the test, established, fail-safe; reputable.

trifle ▶ noun ❶ *we needn't bother the headmaster over such trifles* UNIMPORTANT THING, trivial thing, triviality, thing of no importance/consequence, bagatelle, inessential, nothing; technicality; (**trifles**) trivia, minutiae. ❷ *he bought it for a trifle* NEXT TO NOTHING, very small amount; pittance; *informal* peanuts; *N. Amer. informal* chump change. ❸ *he went to buy a few trifles for Christmas* BAUBLE, trinket, knick-knack, gimcrack, gewgaw, toy.
■ **a trifle** A LITTLE, a bit, somewhat, a touch, a spot, a mite, a whit; *informal* a tad.
■ **trifle with** PLAY WITH, amuse oneself with, toy with, dally with, flirt with, play fast and loose with; *informal* mess about with; *dated* sport with.

trifling ▶ adjective TRIVIAL, unimportant, insignificant, inconsequential, petty, minor, of little/no account, of little/no consequence, footling, pettifogging, incidental; silly, idle, superficial, small, tiny, inconsiderable, nominal, negligible, nugatory; *informal* piffling, piddling, fiddling; *formal* exiguous.
– OPPOSITES important.

trigger ▶ verb ❶ *the incident triggered an acrimonious debate* PRECIPITATE, prompt, trigger off, set off, spark (off), touch off, provoke, stir up; cause, give rise to, lead to, set in motion, occasion, bring about, generate, engender, begin, start, initiate; *poetic/literary* enkindle. ❷ *burglars triggered the alarm* ACTIVATE, set off, set going, trip.

trill ▶ verb WARBLE, sing, chirp, chirrup, tweet, twitter, cheep, peep.

trim ▶ verb ❶ *his hair had been washed and trimmed* CUT, barber, crop, bob, shorten, clip, snip, shear; neaten, shape, tidy up. ❷ *trim off the lower leaves using a sharp knife* CUT OFF, remove, take off, chop off, lop off; prune, pollard. ❸ *production costs need to be trimmed* REDUCE, decrease, cut down, cut back on, scale down, prune, slim down, pare down, dock. ❹ *the story was severely trimmed for the film version* SHORTEN, abridge, condense, abbreviate, telescope, truncate. ❺ *a pair of black leather gloves trimmed with fake fur* DECORATE, adorn, ornament, embellish; edge, pipe, border, hem, fringe.
▶ noun ❶ *white curtains with a blue trim* DECORATION, trimming, ornamentation, adornment, embellishment; border, edging, piping, rickrack, hem, fringe, frill; *archaic* purfle. ❷ *an unruly mop in desperate need of a trim* HAIRCUT, cut, barbering, clip, snip; pruning; tidy-up.
▶ adjective ❶ *a cropped, fitted jacket looks trim with a long-line skirt* SMART, stylish, chic, spruce, dapper, elegant, crisp; *N. Amer.* trig; *informal* natty, sharp; *N. Amer. informal* spiffy. ❷ *a trim little villa* NEAT, tidy, neat and tidy, as neat as a new pin, orderly, in (good) order, uncluttered, well kept, well maintained, shipshape (and Bristol fashion), in apple-pie order, immaculate, spick and span. ❸ *her trim figure* SLIM, slender, lean, clean-limbed, sleek, willowy, lissom, sylph-like, svelte; streamlined.
– OPPOSITES untidy, messy.
■ **in trim** FIT, fighting fit, as fit as a fiddle, in good health, in fine fettle; slim, in shape.

trimming ▶ noun ❶ *a black party dress with lace trimming* DECORATION, trim, ornamentation, adornment, passementerie, embroidery; border, edging, piping, rickrack, fringes, fringing, frills; *archaic* purfles. ❷ *roast turkey with all the trimmings* ACCOMPANIMENTS, extras, frills, accessories, accoutrements, trappings, paraphernalia; garnishing, garnish. ❸ *hedge trimmings* CUTTINGS, clippings, parings, shavings.

trinket ▶ noun KNICK-KNACK, bauble, ornament, bibelot, curio, trifle, toy, novelty, gimcrack, gewgaw; *N. Amer.* kickshaw; *N. Amer. informal* tchotchke; *archaic* whim-wham, bijou, gaud.

trio ▶ noun THREESOME, three, triumvirate, triad, troika, trinity; trilogy, triptych; triplets.

trip ▶ verb ❶ *he tripped on the loose stones* STUMBLE, lose one's footing, catch one's foot, slip, lose one's balance, fall (down), tumble, topple, take a spill. ❷ *taxpayers often trip up by not declaring taxable income* MAKE A MISTAKE, miscalculate, make a blunder, blunder, go wrong, make an error, err; *informal* slip up, screw up, make a boo-boo; *Brit. informal* boob; *N. Amer. informal* goof up. ❸ *the question was intended to trip him up* CATCH OUT, trick, outwit, outsmart; throw off balance, disconcert, unsettle, discountenance, discomfit; *informal* throw, wrong-foot; *Brit. informal* catch on the hop. ❹ *they tripped up the terrace steps* SKIP, run, dance, prance, bound, spring, scamper. ❺ *Hoffman tripped the alarm* SET OFF, activate, trigger; turn on, switch on, throw.

▶ **noun** ❶ *a trip to Paris* EXCURSION, outing, jaunt; HOLIDAY, visit, tour, journey, expedition, voyage; drive, run, day out, day trip; *informal* junket, spin. ❷ *trips and falls cause nearly half such accidents* STUMBLE, slip, misstep, false step; fall, tumble, spill.

tripe ▶ **noun** (*informal*). *See* NONSENSE sense 1.

triple ▶ **adjective** ❶ *a triple alliance* THREE-WAY, tripartite; threefold. ❷ *they paid him triple the going rate* THREE TIMES, treble.

tripper ▶ **noun** (*Brit. informal*) TOURIST, holiday-maker, sightseer, day tripper, visitor, traveller; *N. Amer.* vacationer, vacationist, out-of-towner; *Brit. informal* grockle.

trite ▶ **adjective** BANAL, hackneyed, clichéd, platitudinous, vapid, commonplace, stock, conventional, stereotyped, overused, overdone, overworked, stale, worn out, time-worn, tired, hoary, hack, unimaginative, unoriginal, uninteresting, dull; *informal* old hat, corny, played out; *N. Amer. informal* cornball.
– OPPOSITES original, imaginative.

triumph ▶ **noun** ❶ *Napoleon's many triumphs* VICTORY, win, conquest, success; achievement. ❷ *his eyes shone with triumph* JUBILATION, exultation, elation, delight, joy, happiness, glee, pride, satisfaction. ❸ *a triumph of Victorian engineering* TOUR DE FORCE, masterpiece, crowning example, coup, wonder, sensation, master stroke.
– OPPOSITES defeat, disappointment.

▶ **verb** ❶ *he triumphed in the British Grand Prix* WIN, succeed, come first, be victorious, carry the day, carry all before one, prevail, take the honours, come out on top. ❷ *they had no chance of triumphing over the Nationalists* DEFEAT, beat, conquer, trounce, vanquish, worst, overcome, overpower, overwhelm, get the better of; bring someone to their knees, prevail against, subdue, subjugate; *informal* lick, best. ❸ *'You can't touch me,' she triumphed* CROW, gloat; rejoice, exult.
– OPPOSITES lose.

triumphant ▶ **adjective** ❶ *the triumphant British team* VICTORIOUS, successful, winning, conquering; undefeated, unbeaten. ❷ *a triumphant expression* JUBILANT, exultant, elated, rejoicing, joyful, joyous, delighted, gleeful, proud, cock-a-hoop; gloating.
– OPPOSITES unsuccessful, despondent.

trivia ▶ **plural noun** (PETTY) DETAILS, minutiae, niceties, technicalities, trivialities, trifles, non-essentials.

trivial ▶ **adjective** ❶ *trivial problems* UNIMPORTANT, insignificant, inconsequential, minor, of no account, of no consequence, of no importance; incidental, inessential, non-essential, petty, trifling, pettifogging, footling, small, slight, little, inconsiderable, negligible, paltry, nugatory; *informal* piddling, piffling, fiddling, penny-ante. ❷ *I used to be quite a trivial person* FRIVOLOUS, superficial, shallow, unthinking, empty-headed, feather-brained, lightweight, foolish, silly.
– OPPOSITES important, significant, serious.

triviality ▶ **noun** ❶ *the triviality of the subject matter* UNIMPORTANCE, insignificance, inconsequence, inconsequentiality, pettiness. ❷ *he need not concern himself with such trivialities* MINOR DETAIL, petty detail, thing of no importance/consequence, trifle, non-essential, nothing; technicality; (**trivialities**) trivia, minutiae.

trivialize ▶ **verb** TREAT AS UNIMPORTANT, minimize, play down, underestimate, underplay, make light of, treat lightly, dismiss; *informal* pooh-pooh.

troop ▶ **noun** ❶ *a troop of tourists* GROUP, party, band, gang, bevy, body, company, troupe, crowd, throng, horde, pack, drove, flock, swarm, multitude, host, army; *informal* bunch, gaggle, crew, posse. ❷ *British troops were stationed here* SOLDIERS, armed forces, service men/women; the services, the army, the military, soldiery.

▶ **verb** ❶ *we trooped out of the hall* WALK, march, file; flock, crowd, throng, stream, swarm, surge, spill. ❷ *Caroline trooped wearily home* TRUDGE, plod, traipse, trail, drag oneself, tramp; *N. Amer. informal* schlep.

trophy ▶ **noun** ❶ *a swimming trophy* CUP, medal; prize, award. ❷ *a cabinet full of trophies from his travels* SOUVENIR, memento, keepsake; spoils, booty.

tropical ▶ **adjective** *tropical weather* VERY HOT, sweltering, humid, sultry, steamy, sticky, oppressive, stifling, suffocating, heavy; *informal* boiling.
– OPPOSITES cold, arctic.

trot ▶ **verb** *Doyle trotted across the patio* RUN, jog, jogtrot, dogtrot; scuttle, scurry, bustle, scamper.

■ **on the trot** (*Brit. informal*) IN SUCCESSION, one after the other, in a row, consecutively, successively; running, straight.

■ **trot something out** (*informal*) RECITE, repeat, regurgitate, churn out; come out with, produce.

troubadour ▶ **noun** (*historical*) MINSTREL, singer, balladeer, poet; *historical* jongleur, trouvère.

trouble ▶ **noun** ❶ *you've caused enough trouble*

already PROBLEMS, difficulty, bother, inconvenience, worry, anxiety, distress, stress, agitation, harassment, unpleasantness; *informal* hassle. ❷ *she poured out all her troubles* PROBLEM, misfortune, difficulty, trial, tribulation, trauma, burden, pain, woe, grief, heartache, misery, affliction, suffering. ❸ *he's gone to a lot of trouble to help you* BOTHER, inconvenience, fuss, effort, exertion, work, labour; pains, care, attention, thought. ❹ *I wouldn't want to be a trouble to her* NUISANCE, bother, inconvenience, irritation, irritant, problem, trial, pest, thorn in someone's flesh/side; *informal* headache, pain, pain in the neck/backside, drag; *N. Amer. informal* pain in the butt, burr in/under someone's saddle, nudnik. ❺ *you're too gullible, that's your trouble* SHORTCOMING, weakness, weak point, failing, fault, imperfection, defect, blemish; problem, difficulty. ❻ *he had a history of heart trouble* DISEASE, illness, sickness, ailments, complaints, problems; disorder, disability. ❼ *the crash was due to engine trouble* MALFUNCTION, dysfunction, failure, breakdown. ❽ *a match marred by serious crowd trouble* DISTURBANCE, disorder, unrest, fighting, ructions, fracas, breach of the peace; *Law, dated* affray.

▶ **verb** ❶ *this matter had been troubling her for some time* WORRY, bother, concern, disturb, upset, agitate, distress, perturb, annoy, irritate, vex, irk, nag, niggle, prey on someone's mind, weigh down, burden; *informal* bug. ❷ *he was troubled by bouts of ill health* AFFLICT, burden; suffer from, be cursed with; *informal* be a martyr to. ❸ *there is nothing you need trouble about* WORRY, upset oneself, fret, be anxious, be concerned, concern oneself. ❹ *don't trouble to see me out* BOTHER, take the trouble, go to the trouble, exert oneself, go out of one's way. ❺ *I'm sorry to trouble you* INCONVENIENCE, bother, impose on, disturb, put out, disoblige; *informal* hassle; *formal* discommode.

■ **in trouble** IN DIFFICULTY, in difficulties, in a mess, in a bad way, in a predicament; *informal* in a tight corner/spot, in a fix, in a hole, in hot water, in a pickle, in the soup, up against it; *Brit. informal* up a gum tree.

troubled ▶ **adjective** ❶ *Joanna looked troubled* ANXIOUS, worried, concerned, perturbed, disturbed, bothered, ill at ease, uneasy, unsettled, agitated; distressed, upset, dismayed. ❷ *we live in troubled times* DIFFICULT, problematic, full of problems, unsettled, hard, tough, stressful, dark.

troublemaker ▶ **noun** MISCHIEF-MAKER, rabble-rouser, firebrand, agitator, agent provocateur, ringleader, incendiary; demagogue; scandalmonger, gossipmonger, meddler; *informal* stirrer.

troublesome ▶ **adjective** ❶ *a troublesome problem* ANNOYING, irritating, exasperating, maddening, infuriating, irksome, vexatious, vexing, bothersome, tiresome, worrying, worrisome, disturbing, upsetting, niggling, nagging; difficult, awkward, problematic, taxing; *informal* aggravating; *N. Amer. informal* pesky. ❷ *a troublesome child* DIFFICULT, awkward, trying, demanding, uncooperative, rebellious, unmanageable, unruly, obstreperous, disruptive, badly behaved, disobedient, naughty, recalcitrant; *formal* refractory.

– OPPOSITES simple, cooperative.

trough ▶ **noun** ❶ *a large feeding trough* MANGER, feedbox, feeder, fodder rack, crib. ❷ *a thirty-yard trough* CHANNEL, conduit, trench, ditch, gully, drain, culvert, cut, flume, gutter.

trounce ▶ **verb** DEFEAT UTTERLY, beat hollow, rout, crush, overwhelm; *informal* hammer, clobber, thrash, drub, pulverize, massacre, crucify, demolish, destroy, annihilate, wipe the floor with, make mincemeat of, murder; *Brit. informal* stuff; *N. Amer. informal* shellac, cream, skunk.

troupe ▶ **noun** GROUP, company, band, ensemble, set; cast.

trousers ▶ **plural noun** SLACKS, chinos, jeans; *N. Amer.* pants; *Brit. informal* trews, strides, kecks, breeches; *Austral. informal* daks.

truant ▶ **noun** ABSENTEE; *Brit. informal* skiver; *Austral./NZ informal* wag.

▶ **verb** *pupils who truant.* See PLAY TRUANT.

■ **play truant** stay away from school, truant; *Brit. informal* skive (off), bunk off; *Irish informal* mitch (off); *N. Amer. informal* play hookey, goof off; *Austral./NZ informal* play the wag.

truce ▶ **noun** CEASEFIRE, armistice, suspension of hostilities, peace; respite, lull; *informal* let-up.

truck[1] ▶ **noun** *a heavily laden truck* LORRY, heavy goods vehicle, juggernaut; van, pickup (truck); *Brit.* HGV; *dated* pantechnicon.

truck[2] ▶ **noun** *we are to have no truck with him* DEALINGS, association, contact, communication, connection, relations; business, trade.

truckle ▶ **verb** *an ambitious woman who truckled to no man* KOWTOW, submit, defer, yield, bow and scrape, be obsequious, pander, toady, prostrate oneself, grovel; fawn on, dance attendance on, curry favour with, ingratiate oneself with; *informal* suck up, crawl, lick someone's boots; *Austral./NZ informal* smoodge.

truculent ▶ **adjective** DEFIANT, aggressive, antagonistic, belligerent, pugnacious, confrontational, ready for a fight, obstreperous, argumentative, quarrelsome, uncooperative; bad-tempered, short-tempered, cross, snappish; *informal* feisty, spoiling for a fight; *Brit. informal* stroppy, bolshie.

– OPPOSITES cooperative, amiable.

trudge ▶ **verb** PLOD, tramp, drag oneself, walk heavily/slowly, plough, slog, footslog, toil, trek; *informal* traipse, galumph; *Brit. informal* trog.

true ▶ **adjective** ❶ *you'll see that what I say is true* CORRECT, accurate, right, verifiable, in accordance with the facts, what actually/really

happened, the case, so; faithful, literal, factual, unelaborated, unvarnished. ❷ *people are still willing to pay for true craftsmanship* GENUINE, authentic, real, actual, bona fide, proper; *informal* honest-to-goodness, kosher, pukka, legit, the real McCoy; *Austral./NZ informal* dinkum. ❸ *the true owner of the goods* RIGHTFUL, legitimate, legal, lawful, authorized, bona fide, de jure. ❹ *the necessity for true repentance* SINCERE, genuine, real, unfeigned, heartfelt, from the heart. ❺ *a true friend* LOYAL, faithful, constant, devoted, staunch, steadfast, unswerving, unwavering; trustworthy, trusty, reliable, dependable. ❻ *a true reflection of life in the 50s* ACCURATE, true to life, faithful, telling it like it is, fact-based, realistic, close, lifelike.
– OPPOSITES untrue, false, disloyal, inaccurate.

true-blue ▶ adjective STAUNCH, loyal, faithful, stalwart, committed, card-carrying, confirmed, dyed-in-the-wool, devoted, dedicated, firm, steadfast, unswerving, unwavering, unfaltering; *informal* deep-dyed.

truism ▶ noun PLATITUDE, commonplace, cliché, stock phrase, banality, old chestnut, old saw, bromide.

truly ▶ adverb ❶ *tell me truly what you want* TRUTHFULLY, honestly, frankly, candidly, openly, to someone's face, laying one's cards on the table; *informal* pulling no punches. ❷ *I'm truly grateful to them* SINCERELY, genuinely, really, indeed, from the bottom of one's heart, heartily, profoundly; very, extremely, dreadfully, immensely, tremendously, incredibly, most; *informal* awfully, terribly, terrifically, fearfully; *Brit. informal* jolly, ever so; *informal, dated* frightfully. ❸ *a truly dreadful song* REALLY, absolutely, simply, utterly, totally, perfectly, thoroughly, positively, completely. ❹ *this is truly a miracle* WITHOUT (A) DOUBT, unquestionably, undoubtedly, certainly, surely, definitely, beyond doubt/question, indubitably, undeniably, beyond the shadow of a doubt; in truth, really, in reality, actually, in fact; *archaic* forsooth, in sooth, verily. ❺ *the streaming system does not truly reflect children's ability* ACCURATELY, correctly, exactly, precisely, faithfully.

trump ▶ verb *by wearing the simplest of dresses, she had trumped them all* OUTSHINE, outclass, upstage, put in the shade, eclipse, surpass, outdo, outperform; beat, better, top, cap; *informal* be a cut above, be head and shoulders above, leave standing; *Brit. informal* knock spots off; *archaic* outrival.
■ **trump something up** INVENT, make up, fabricate, concoct, contrive, manufacture, devise, hatch; fake, falsify; *informal* cook up.

trumped-up ▶ adjective BOGUS, spurious, specious, false, fabricated, invented, manufactured, contrived, made-up, fake, factitious; *informal* phoney.
– OPPOSITES genuine.

trumpery ▶ noun (*archaic*) TRINKETS, baubles, knick-knacks, ornaments, bibelots, gewgaws, gimcracks.

trumpet ▶ verb ❶ *'Come on!' he trumpeted* SHOUT, bellow, roar, yell, cry out, call out; *informal* holler. ❷ *companies trumpeted their enthusiasm for the multimedia revolution* PROCLAIM, announce, declare, noise abroad, shout from the rooftops.
■ **blow one's own trumpet** BOAST, brag, sing one's own praises, show off, swank, congratulate oneself; *N. Amer. informal* blow/toot one's own horn; *Austral./NZ informal* skite.

truncate ▶ verb SHORTEN, cut, cut short, curtail, bring to an untimely end; abbreviate, condense, reduce.
– OPPOSITES lengthen, extend.

truncheon ▶ noun (*Brit.*) CLUB, baton, cudgel, bludgeon; stick, staff; *Brit.* life preserver; *N. Amer.* billy, blackjack, nightstick; *Brit. informal* cosh.

trunk ▶ noun ❶ *the trunk of a tree* MAIN STEM, bole, stock. ❷ *his powerful trunk* TORSO, body. ❸ *an elephant's trunk* PROBOSCIS, nose, snout. ❹ *an enormous tin trunk* CHEST, box, crate, coffer; case, portmanteau. ❺ (*N. Amer.*) *the trunk of his car* LUGGAGE COMPARTMENT; *Brit.* boot.

truss ▶ noun ❶ *the bridge is supported by three steel trusses* SUPPORT, buttress, joist, brace, prop, strut, stay, stanchion, pier. ❷ *a hernia truss* SURGICAL APPLIANCE, support, pad.
▶ verb *they trussed us up with ropes and chains* TIE UP, bind, chain up; pinion, fetter, tether, secure.

trust ▶ noun ❶ *good relationships are built on trust* CONFIDENCE, belief, faith, certainty, assurance, conviction, credence; reliance. ❷ *a position of trust* RESPONSIBILITY, duty, obligation. ❸ *the money is to be held in trust for his son* SAFE KEEPING, keeping, protection, charge, care, custody; trusteeship, guardianship.
– OPPOSITES distrust, mistrust, doubt.
▶ verb ❶ *I should never have trusted her* PUT ONE'S TRUST IN, have faith in, have (every) confidence in, believe in, pin one's hopes/faith on. ❷ *he can be trusted to carry out an impartial investigation* RELY ON, depend on, bank on, count on, be sure of. ❸ *I trust we shall meet again* HOPE, expect, take it, assume, presume. ❹ *they don't like to trust their money to anyone outside the family* ENTRUST, consign, commit, give, hand over, turn over, assign; *formal* commend.
– OPPOSITES distrust, mistrust, doubt.

trustee ▶ noun ADMINISTRATOR, agent; custodian, keeper, steward, depositary; executor, executrix; *Law* fiduciary, feoffee.

trustful ▶ adjective. *See* TRUSTING.

trusting ▶ adjective TRUSTFUL, unsuspecting, unquestioning, unguarded, unwary; naive, innocent, childlike, ingenuous, wide-eyed, credulous, gullible, easily taken in.
– OPPOSITES distrustful, suspicious.

trustworthy ▶ adjective RELIABLE, dependable, honest, honourable, upright, principled, true, truthful, as good as one's word, ethical, virtuous, incorruptible, unimpeachable, above suspicion; responsible, sensible, level-headed; loyal, faithful, staunch, steadfast, trusty; safe, sound, reputable; *informal* on the level; *N. Amer. informal* straight-up.
– OPPOSITES unreliable.

trusty ▶ adjective RELIABLE, dependable, trustworthy, never-failing, unfailing, trusted; loyal, faithful, true, staunch, steadfast, constant, unswerving, unwavering.
– OPPOSITES unreliable.

truth ▶ noun ❶ *he doubted the truth of her statement* VERACITY, truthfulness, verity, sincerity, candour, honesty; accuracy, correctness, validity, factuality, authenticity. ❷ *it's the truth, I swear it* WHAT ACTUALLY HAPPENED, the case, so; gospel (truth), the honest truth. ❸ *truth is stranger than fiction* FACT(S), reality, real life, actuality. ❹ *scientific truths* FACT, verity, certainty, certitude; law, principle.
– OPPOSITES lies, fiction, falsehood.
■ **in truth** IN (ACTUAL) FACT, in point of fact, in reality, really, actually, to tell the truth, if truth be told.

truthful ▶ adjective ❶ *a truthful answer* HONEST, sincere, trustworthy, genuine; candid, frank, open, forthright, straight; *informal* upfront, on the level; *N. Amer. informal* on the up and up. ❷ *a truthful account* TRUE, accurate, correct, factual, faithful, reliable; unvarnished, unembellished; *formal* veracious, veridical.
– OPPOSITES deceitful, untrue.

try ▶ verb ❶ *try to help him* ATTEMPT, endeavour, make an effort, exert oneself, strive, do one's best, do one's utmost, move heaven and earth; undertake, aim, take it on oneself; *informal* have a go, give it one's best shot, bend over backwards, bust a gut, do one's damnedest, pull out all the stops, go all out, knock oneself out; *formal* essay; *archaic* assay. ❷ *try it and see what you think* TEST, put to the test, sample, taste, inspect, investigate, examine, appraise, evaluate, assess; *informal* check out, give something a whirl. ❸ *Mary tried everyone's patience* TAX, strain, test, stretch, sap, drain, exhaust, wear out. ❹ *the case is to be tried by a jury* ADJUDICATE, consider, hear, adjudge, examine.
▶ noun *I'll have one last try* ATTEMPT, effort, endeavour; *informal* go, shot, crack, stab, bash, whack; *formal* essay.
■ **try something out** TEST, trial, experiment with, pilot; put through its paces; assess, evaluate.

trying ▶ adjective ❶ *a trying day* STRESSFUL, taxing, demanding, difficult, tough, hard, pressured, frustrating, fraught; arduous, gruelling, tiring, exhausting; *informal* hellish. ❷ *Steve was very trying* ANNOYING, irritating, exasperating, maddening, infuriating; tiresome, irksome, troublesome, bothersome; *informal* aggravating.
– OPPOSITES easy, accommodating.

tub ▶ noun ❶ *a wooden tub* CONTAINER, butt, barrel, cask, drum, keg. ❷ *a tub of yogurt* POT, carton. ❸ *a soak in the tub* BATH, bathtub; hot tub.

tubby ▶ adjective (*informal*) CHUBBY, plump, stout, dumpy, chunky, portly, rotund, round, fat, overweight, fleshy, paunchy, pot-bellied, corpulent; *informal* pudgy, beefy, porky, roly-poly, blubbery; *Brit. informal* podgy; *N. Amer. informal* corn-fed.
– OPPOSITES skinny.

tuck ▶ verb ❶ *he tucked his shirt into his trousers* PUSH, insert, slip; thrust, stuff, stick, cram; *informal* pop. ❷ *the dress was tucked all over* PLEAT, gather, fold, ruffle. ❸ *he tucked the knife behind his seat* HIDE, conceal, secrete; store, stow; *informal* stash.
▶ noun ❶ *a dress with tucks* PLEAT, gather, fold, ruffle. ❷ (*Brit. informal*) *they pinched his tuck* FOOD; *informal* eats, grub, nosh, chow; *Brit. informal* scoff; *N. Amer. informal* chuck; *poetic/literary* viands; *dated* victuals.
■ **tuck someone in/up** MAKE COMFORTABLE, settle down, cover up; put to bed.
■ **tuck in/into** (*informal*) EAT HEARTILY, devour, consume, gobble up, wolf down; *informal* get stuck into, dispose of, polish off, get outside of, put away, scoff (down); *Brit. informal* shift; *N. Amer. informal* scarf (down/up), snarf (down/up).

tuft ▶ noun CLUMP, bunch, knot, cluster, tussock, tuffet; lock, wisp; crest, topknot; tassel.

tug ▶ verb ❶ *Ben tugged at her sleeve* PULL, pluck, tweak, twitch, jerk, wrench; catch hold of; *informal* yank. ❷ *she tugged him towards the door* DRAG, pull, lug, draw, haul, heave, tow, trail.
▶ noun *one good tug would loosen it* PULL, jerk, wrench, heave; *informal* yank.

tuition ▶ noun INSTRUCTION, teaching, coaching, tutoring, tutelage, lessons, education, schooling; training, drill, preparation, guidance.

tumble ▶ verb ❶ *he tumbled over* FALL (OVER/DOWN), topple over, lose one's balance, keel over, take a spill, go headlong, go head over heels, trip (up), stumble; *informal* come a cropper. ❷ *they all tumbled from the room* HURRY, rush, scramble, scurry, bound, pile, bundle. ❸ *a brook tumbled over the rocks* CASCADE, fall, flow, pour, spill, stream. ❹ *oil prices tumbled* PLUMMET, plunge, fall, dive, nosedive, drop, slump, slide, decrease, decline; *informal* crash. ❺ (*informal*) *I tumbled to what was happening. See* REALIZE sense 1.
– OPPOSITES rise.
▶ noun ❶ *I took a tumble in the nettles* FALL, trip, spill; *informal* nosedive, header, cropper. ❷ *a tumble in share prices* DROP, fall, plunge, dive, nosedive, slump, decline, collapse; *informal* crash.
– OPPOSITES rise.

tumbledown ▶ adjective DILAPIDATED, ramshackle, decrepit, neglected, run down, gone to rack and ruin, falling to pieces, decaying, derelict, crumbling; rickety, shaky; *N. Amer. informal* shacky.

tumbler ▶ noun (DRINKING) GLASS, beaker, highball glass.

tumid ▶ adjective ❶ *her tumid belly* SWOLLEN, distended, tumescent, engorged, enlarged, bloated, bulging, protuberant, bulbous. ❷ *tumid oratory* BOMBASTIC, pompous, turgid, overblown, inflated, high-flown, pretentious, grandiose, florid, flowery, magniloquent, grandiloquent, orotund; *informal* highfalutin, purple, windy.
– OPPOSITES shrunken, simple.

tummy ▶ noun (*informal*) STOMACH, abdomen, belly, gut, middle; *informal* tum, insides; *Austral. informal* bingy.

tumour ▶ noun CANCEROUS GROWTH, malignant growth, cancer, malignancy; lump, growth, swelling; *Medicine* carcinoma, sarcoma.
– RELATED TERMS onco-, -oma.

tumult ▶ noun ❶ *she added her voice to the tumult* CLAMOUR, din, noise, racket, uproar, commotion, ruckus, rumpus, hubbub, pandemonium, babel, bedlam, brouhaha, furore, fracas, melee, frenzy; *Scottish & N. English* stramash; *informal* hullabaloo; *Brit. informal* row. ❷ *years of political tumult* TURMOIL, confusion, disorder, disarray, unrest, chaos, turbulence, mayhem, havoc, upheaval, ferment, agitation, trouble.
– OPPOSITES tranquillity.

tumultuous ▶ adjective ❶ *tumultuous applause* LOUD, deafening, thunderous, uproarious, noisy, clamorous, vociferous. ❷ *a tumultuous crowd* DISORDERLY, unruly, rowdy, turbulent, boisterous, excited, agitated, restless, wild, riotous, frenzied; *Brit. informal* rumbustious.
– OPPOSITES soft, orderly.

tune ▶ noun *she hummed a cheerful tune* MELODY, air, strain, theme; song, jingle, ditty.
▶ verb ❶ *they tuned their guitars* ADJUST, fine-tune. ❷ *a body clock tuned to the tides* ATTUNE, adapt, adjust, fine-tune; regulate, modulate.
■ **change one's tune** CHANGE ONE'S MIND, do a U-turn, have a change of heart; *Brit.* do an about-turn.
■ **in tune** IN ACCORD, in keeping, in accordance, in agreement, in harmony, in step, in line, in sympathy.

tuneful ▶ adjective MELODIOUS, melodic, musical, mellifluous, dulcet, euphonious, harmonious, lyrical, lilting, sweet.
– OPPOSITES discordant.

tuneless ▶ adjective DISCORDANT, unmelodious, dissonant, harsh, cacophonous.
– OPPOSITES melodious.

tunnel ▶ noun *a tunnel under the hills* UNDERGROUND PASSAGE, underpass, subway; shaft; burrow, hole; *historical* mine, sap.
▶ verb *he tunnelled under the fence* DIG, burrow, mine, bore, drill.

turbid ▶ adjective MURKY, opaque, cloudy, muddy, thick; *N. Amer.* roily.
– OPPOSITES clear.

turbulent ▶ adjective ❶ *the country's turbulent past* TEMPESTUOUS, stormy, unstable, unsettled, tumultuous, chaotic; violent, anarchic, lawless. ❷ *turbulent seas* ROUGH, stormy, tempestuous, storm-tossed, heavy, violent, wild, seething, choppy, agitated, boisterous.
– OPPOSITES peaceful, calm.

turf ▶ noun ❶ *they walked across the turf* GRASS, lawn, sod; *poetic/literary* sward, greensward. ❷ *devotees of the turf* HORSE RACING; racecourses, racetracks. ❸ (*informal*) *he was keen to protect his turf* TERRITORY, domain, province, preserve, sphere of influence; stamping ground; *informal* bailiwick; *Brit. informal* patch, manor.
▶ verb *the lawns have been turfed* GRASS (OVER).
■ **turf someone/something out** (*informal*). *See* EJECT sense 3.

turgid ▶ adjective ❶ *his turgid prose* BOMBASTIC, pompous, overblown, inflated, tumid, high-flown, affected, pretentious, grandiose, florid, ornate, magniloquent, grandiloquent, orotund; *informal* highfalutin, purple, windy. ❷ *the tissues become turgid* SWOLLEN, distended, tumescent, engorged, bloated.
– OPPOSITES simple.

turmoil ▶ noun *political turmoil* CONFUSION, upheaval, turbulence, tumult, disorder, disturbance, agitation, ferment, unrest, trouble, disruption, chaos, mayhem; uncertainty; *N. Amer. informal* tohubohu.
– OPPOSITES peace.
■ **in turmoil** CONFUSED, in a whirl, at sixes and sevens; reeling, disorientated; *informal* all over the place.

turn ▶ verb ❶ *the wheels were still turning* GO ROUND, revolve, rotate, spin, roll, circle, wheel, whirl, gyrate, swivel, pivot. ❷ *I turned and headed back* CHANGE DIRECTION, change course, make a U-turn, turn about/round, wheel round. ❸ *the car turned the corner* GO ROUND, round, negotiate, take. ❹ *the path turned to right and left* BEND, curve, wind, twist, meander, snake, zigzag. ❺ *he turned his pistol on Liam* AIM AT, point at, level at, direct at, train on. ❻ *he turned his ankle* SPRAIN, twist, wrench; hurt. ❼ *their honeymoon turned into a nightmare* BECOME, develop into, turn out to be; be transformed into, metamorphose into. ❽ *Emma turned red* BECOME, go, grow, get. ❾ *he turned the house into flats* CONVERT, change, transform, make; adapt, modify, rebuild, reconstruct. ❿ *I've just turned forty* REACH, get to, become; *informal* hit. ⓫ *the milk had turned* (GO) SOUR, go off, curdle, become rancid, go bad, spoil. ⓬ *he turned to politics* TAKE UP, become involved in, go in for, enter, undertake. ⓭ *we can now turn to another topic* MOVE ON TO, go on to, consider, attend to, address; take up. ⓮ *she turned a somersault* PERFORM, execute, do, carry out. ⓯ *an object turned on a lathe* FASHION, make, shape, form.

▶ **noun** ❶ *a turn of the wheel* ROTATION, revolution, spin, whirl, gyration, swivel. ❷ *a turn to the left* CHANGE OF DIRECTION, veer, divergence. ❸ *we're approaching the turn* BEND, corner, dog-leg; turning, junction, crossroads; *N. Amer.* turnout; *Brit.* hairpin bend. ❹ *you'll get your turn in a minute* OPPORTUNITY, chance, say; stint, time; try; *informal* go, shot, stab, crack. ❺ *a comic turn* ACT, routine, performance, number, piece. ❻ *a turn around the garden* STROLL, walk, saunter, amble, wander, airing, promenade; outing, excursion, jaunt; *informal* mosey, tootle, spin; *Brit. informal* pootle. ❼ *you gave me quite a turn!* SHOCK, start, surprise, jolt; fright, scare. ❽ *she did me some good turns* SERVICE, deed, act; favour, kindness; disservice, wrong.

■ **at every turn** REPEATEDLY, recurrently, all the time, always, constantly, again and again.

■ **in turn** ONE AFTER THE OTHER, one by one, one at a time, in succession, successively, sequentially.

■ **take a turn for the better** IMPROVE, pick up, look up, perk up, rally, turn the corner; recover, revive.

■ **take a turn for the worse** DETERIORATE, worsen, decline; *informal* go downhill.

■ **to a turn** PERFECTLY, just right, to perfection; *informal* to a T.

■ **turn of events** DEVELOPMENT, incident, occurrence, happening, circumstance.

■ **turn against someone** BECOME HOSTILE TO, take a dislike to.

■ **turn someone away** SEND AWAY, reject, rebuff, repel, cold-shoulder; *informal* send packing.

■ **turn back** RETRACE ONE'S STEPS, go back, return; retreat.

■ **turn someone/something down** ❶ *his novel was turned down* REJECT, spurn, rebuff, refuse, decline; *Brit. informal* knock back. ❷ *Pete turned the sound down* REDUCE, lower, decrease, lessen; muffle, mute.

■ **turn in** (*informal*) GO TO BED, retire, call it a day; *informal* hit the hay, hit the sack.

■ **turn someone in** BETRAY, inform on, denounce, sell out, stab someone in the back; *informal* split on, blow the whistle on, rat on, peach on, squeal on; *Brit. informal* grass on, shop; *N. Amer. informal* finger; *Austral./NZ informal* dob on.

■ **turn something in** ❶ *your documents must be turned in* HAND IN/OVER, give in, submit, surrender, give up; deliver, return. ❷ *he turned in a score of 199* ACHIEVE, attain, reach, make; notch up, chalk up, rack up, record.

■ **turn of mind** DISPOSITION, inclination, tendency, propensity, bias, bent.

■ **turn off** *they turned off the road* LEAVE, branch off; *informal* take a left/right; *N. Amer. informal* hang a left/right.

■ **turn someone off** (*informal*) PUT OFF, leave cold, repel, disgust, revolt, offend; disenchant, alienate; bore; *N. Amer. informal* gross out.

■ **turn something off** SWITCH OFF, shut off, put off, extinguish, deactivate; *informal* kill, cut.

■ **turn on** *the decision turned on the law* DEPEND ON, rest on, hinge on, be contingent on, be decided by.

■ **turn someone on** (*informal*). *See* AROUSE sense 3.

■ **turn something on** SWITCH ON, put on, start up, activate, trip.

■ **turn on someone** ATTACK, set on, fall on, let fly at, lash out at, hit out at, round on; *informal* lay into, tear into, let someone have it, bite someone's head off, jump down someone's throat; *Brit. informal* have a go at; *N. Amer. informal* light into.

■ **turn out** ❶ *a huge crowd turned out* COME, be present, attend, appear, turn up, arrive; assemble, gather; *informal* show up. ❷ *it turned out that she had been abroad* TRANSPIRE, emerge, come to light, become apparent. ❸ *things didn't turn out as I'd intended* HAPPEN, occur, come about, develop, work out, come out, end up; *informal* pan out; *formal* eventuate.

■ **turn someone out** THROW OUT, eject, evict, expel, oust, drum out, banish; *informal* kick out, send packing, boot out, show someone the door, turf out.

■ **turn something out** ❶ *turn out the light. See* TURN SOMETHING OFF. ❷ *they turn out a million engines a year* PRODUCE, make, manufacture, fabricate, put out, churn out. ❸ *she turned out the cupboards* CLEAR OUT, clean out, empty (out).

■ **turn over** OVERTURN, upturn, capsize, keel over, turn turtle, be upended.

■ **turn something over** ❶ *I turned over a few pages* FLIP OVER, flick through, leaf through. ❷ *she turned the proposal over in her mind* THINK ABOUT/OVER, consider, weigh up, ponder, contemplate, reflect on, chew over, mull over, muse on, ruminate on. ❸ *he turned over the business to his brother* TRANSFER, hand over, pass on, consign, commit.

■ **turn of phrase** EXPRESSION, idiom, phrase, term, word.

■ **turn someone's stomach** NAUSEATE, sicken, make someone's gorge rise.

■ **turn to someone/something** SEEK HELP FROM, have recourse to, approach, apply to, appeal to; take to, resort to.

■ **turn up** ❶ *the missing documents turned up* BE FOUND, be discovered, be located, reappear. ❷ *the police turned up* ARRIVE, appear, present oneself; *informal* show (up), show one's face. ❸ *something better will turn up* PRESENT ITSELF, occur, happen, crop up.

■ **turn something up** ❶ *she turned up the volume* INCREASE, raise, amplify, intensify. ❷ *they turned up lots of information* DISCOVER, uncover, unearth, find, dig up, ferret out, root out, expose. ❸ *I turned up the hem* TAKE UP, raise; shorten.

turncoat ▶ **noun** TRAITOR, renegade, defector, deserter, betrayer, Judas; fifth columnist, quisling; *informal* rat.

turning ▶ **noun** TURN-OFF, turn, side road, exit; *N. Amer.* turnout.

turning point ▶ **noun** WATERSHED, critical moment, decisive moment, moment of truth, crossroads, crisis.

turnout ▶ **noun** ❶ *the lecture attracted a good turnout* ATTENDANCE, audience, house; crowd, gathering, throng, assembly, assemblage, congregation. ❷ *his turnout was very elegant* OUTFIT, clothes, clothing, dress, garb, attire, ensemble; *informal* get-up, gear, togs; *Brit. informal* clobber, kit; *formal* apparel.

turnover ▶ **noun** ❶ *an annual turnover of £2.25 million* (GROSS) REVENUE, income, yield; sales. ❷ *a high turnover of staff* rate of replacement, change, movement.

turpitude ▶ **noun** (*formal*). *See* DEPRAVITY.

tussle ▶ **noun** *his glasses were smashed in the tussle* SCUFFLE, fight, struggle, skirmish, brawl, scrum, rough and tumble, free-for-all, fracas, fray, rumpus, melee; *Irish, N. Amer., & Austral.* donnybrook; *informal* scrap, dust-up, punch-up, spat, ruck; *Brit. informal* ding-dong, bust-up; *Scottish informal* rammy; *Law, dated* affray.

▶ **verb** *demonstrators tussled with police* SCUFFLE, fight, struggle, brawl, grapple, wrestle, clash; *informal* scrap; *N. Amer. informal* rough-house.

tutor ▶ **noun** *a history tutor* TEACHER, instructor, educator, educationalist, lecturer, trainer, mentor; *informal* teach; *formal* pedagogue.

▶ **verb** *he was tutored at home* TEACH, instruct, educate, school, coach, train, drill.

tutorial ▶ **noun** LESSON, class, seminar.

twaddle ▶ **noun** (*informal*). *See* NONSENSE sense 1.

tweak ▶ **verb** ❶ *he tweaked the boy's ear* PULL, jerk, tug, twist, twitch, pinch, squeeze. ❷ (*informal*) *the programme can be tweaked to suit your needs* ADJUST, modify, alter, change, adapt; refine.

▶ **noun** ❶ *he gave her hair a tweak* PULL, jerk, tug, twist, pinch, twitch, squeeze. ❷ (*informal*) *a few minor tweaks were required* ADJUSTMENT, modification, alteration, change; refinement.

twee ▶ **adjective** (*Brit.*) ❶ *twee little shops* QUAINT, sweet, dainty, pretty; *informal* cute, cutesy. ❷ *the lyrics are too twee in places* SENTIMENTAL, over-sentimental, mawkish, sickly; *Brit. informal* soppy.

twelve ▶ **cardinal number** DOZEN, zodiac.
– RELATED TERMS duodecimal, dodeca-.

twenty ▶ **cardinal number** SCORE.
– RELATED TERMS icos-.

twiddle ▶ **verb** *she twiddled the dials* TURN, twist, swivel, twirl; adjust, move, jiggle; fiddle with, play with.

■ **twiddle one's thumbs** BE IDLE, kick one's heels, kill time, waste time; *informal* hang around/round; *Brit. informal* hang about.

twig[1] ▶ **noun** *leafy twigs* STICK, sprig, withy, shoot, stem, branchlet.

twig[2] ▶ **verb** (*Brit. informal*) *she finally twigged what I was on about* REALIZE, understand, grasp, comprehend, take in, fathom, see, recognize; *informal* latch on to, cotton on to, tumble to, get, get wise to, figure out; *Brit. informal* suss.

twilight ▶ **noun** ❶ *we arrived at twilight* DUSK, sunset, sundown, nightfall, evening, close of day; *poetic/literary* eventide. ❷ *it was scarcely visible in the twilight* HALF-LIGHT, semi-darkness, gloom. ❸ *the twilight of his career* DECLINE, waning, ebb; autumn, final years.
– RELATED TERMS crepuscular.
– OPPOSITES dawn.

▶ **adjective** *a twilight world* SHADOWY, dark, shady, dim, gloomy, obscure.

twin ▶ **noun** *a sitting room that was the twin of her own* DUPLICATE, double, carbon-copy, exact likeness, mirror image, replica, lookalike, clone; counterpart, match, pair; *informal* spitting image, dead ringer.

▶ **adjective** ❶ *the twin towers of the stadium* MATCHING, identical, matched, paired. ❷ *the twin aims of conservation and recreation* TWOFOLD, double, dual; related, linked, connected; corresponding, parallel, complementary, equivalent.

▶ **verb** *the company twinned its brewing with distilling* COMBINE, join, link, couple, pair.

twine ▶ **noun** *a ball of twine* STRING, cord, thread, yarn.

▶ **verb** ❶ *she twined her arms around him* WIND, entwine, wrap, wreathe. ❷ *convolvulus twined around the tree* ENTWINE ITSELF, coil, loop, twist, spiral, curl. ❸ *a bloom was twined in her hair* WEAVE, interlace, intertwine, braid, twist.

twinge ▶ **noun** ❶ *twinges in her stomach* PAIN, spasm, ache, throb; cramp, stitch. ❷ *a twinge of guilt* PANG, prick, dart; qualm, scruple, misgiving.

twinkle ▶ **verb** ❶ *the lights of the city twinkled* GLITTER, sparkle, shine, glimmer, shimmer, glint, gleam, glisten, flicker, flash, wink; *poetic/literary* coruscate, glister. ❷ *his feet twinkled over the ground* DART, dance, skip, flit, glide.

▶ **noun** *the twinkle of the lights* GLITTER, sparkle, glimmer, shimmer, glint, gleam, flicker, flash, wink; *poetic/literary* coruscation.

twinkling ▶ **adjective** SPARKLING, glistening, glittering, glimmering, glinting, gleaming, flickering, winking, shining, scintillating; *poetic/literary* coruscating.

twirl ▶ **verb** ❶ *she twirled her parasol* SPIN, whirl, turn, gyrate, pivot, swivel, twist, revolve, rotate. ❷ *she twirled her hair round her fingers* WIND, twist, coil, curl, wrap.

▶ **noun** *she did a quick twirl* PIROUETTE, spin, whirl, turn, twist, rotation, revolution, gyration.

twist ▶ **verb** ❶ *the impact twisted the chassis* CRUMPLE, crush, buckle, mangle, warp, deform, distort. ❷ *her face twisted with rage* CONTORT, screw up. ❸ *Ma anxiously twisted a handkerchief* WRING, squeeze. ❹ *he twisted round in his seat* TURN (ROUND), swivel (round), spin (round), pivot, rotate, revolve. ❺ *she twisted out of his grasp* WRIGGLE, squirm, worm, wiggle. ❻ *I twisted my ankle* SPRAIN, wrench, turn, rick, crick. ❼ *you are twisting my words* DISTORT, misrepresent, change, alter, pervert, falsify, warp, skew, misinterpret, misconstrue, misstate, misquote; garble. ❽ *he twisted the radio knob* TWIDDLE, adjust, turn, rotate, swivel. ❾ *she twisted her hair round her finger* WIND, twirl, coil, curl, wrap. ❿ *the wires were twisted together* INTERTWINE, twine, interlace, weave, plait, braid, coil, wind. ⓫ *the road twisted and turned* WIND, bend, curve, turn, meander, weave, zigzag, swerve, snake.

▶ **noun** ❶ *the twist of a dial* TURN, twirl, spin. ❷ *a personality twist* QUIRK, idiosyncrasy, foible, eccentricity, peculiarity, oddity, kink; aberration, fault, flaw, imperfection, defect, failing, weakness. ❸ (*Brit.*) *a twist of tobacco* WAD, quid, plug, chew; *Brit.* screw. ❹ *long twists of black hair* RINGLET, curl, corkscrew, coil; lock, hank. ❺ *the twists of the road* BEND, curve, turn, zigzag, kink, dog-leg; *Brit.* hairpin bend. ❻ *the twists of the plot* CONVOLUTION, complication, complexity, intricacy; surprise, revelation. ❼ *a new twist on an old theme* INTERPRETATION, slant, outlook, angle, approach, treatment; variation.

■ **twist someone's arm** (*informal*) PRESSURIZE, coerce, force; persuade; *informal* lean on, bulldoze, railroad, put the screws on.

twisted ▶ **adjective** ❶ *twisted metal* CRUMPLED, bent, crushed, buckled, warped, misshapen, distorted, deformed. ❷ *a twisted smile* CROOKED, lopsided; contorted, wry. ❸ *his twisted mind* PERVERTED, warped, deviant, depraved, corrupt, abnormal, unhealthy, aberrant, distorted, corrupted, debauched, debased; *informal* sick, kinky, pervy.

twisty ▶ **adjective** WINDING, windy, twisting, bendy, zigzag, meandering, curving, sinuous, snaky.

– OPPOSITES straight.

twit ▶ **noun** (*Brit. informal*). *See* FOOL noun sense 1.

twitch ▶ **verb** ❶ *he twitched and then lay still* JERK, convulse, have a spasm, quiver, tremble, shiver, shudder. ❷ *he twitched the note out of my hand* SNATCH, tweak, pluck, pull, tug; *informal* yank.

▶ **noun** ❶ *a twitch of her lips* SPASM, convulsion, quiver, tremor, shiver, shudder; tic. ❷ *he gave a twitch at his moustache* PULL, tug, tweak; *informal* yank. ❸ *he felt a twitch of annoyance* PANG, twinge, dart, stab, prick.

twitter ▶ **verb** ❶ *sparrows twittered under the eaves* CHIRP, chirrup, cheep, tweet, peep, chatter, trill, warble, sing. ❷ *stop twittering about Francis* PRATTLE, babble, chatter, gabble, jabber, go on, yap, blether, blither, ramble; *informal* yak, yabber; *Brit. informal* witter, rabbit, chunter, waffle.

▶ **noun** ❶ *a bird's twitter* CHIRP, chirrup, cheep, tweet, peep, trill, warble, song. ❷ *her non-stop twitter* PRATTLE, chatter, babble, talk, gabble, blether; *informal* yackety-yak; *Brit. informal* wittering, nattering, chuntering. ❸ *she got into a real twitter* (*informal*). *See* STEW noun sense 2.

two ▶ **cardinal number** PAIR, duo, duet, double, dyad, duplet, tandem; *archaic* twain.

– RELATED TERMS binary, dual, bi-, di-, duo-.

two-faced ▶ **adjective** DECEITFUL, insincere, double-dealing, hypocritical, back-stabbing, false, untrustworthy, duplicitous, deceiving, dissembling, dishonest; disloyal, treacherous, faithless; *poetic/literary* perfidious.

– OPPOSITES sincere.

twosome ▶ **noun** COUPLE, pair, duo.

tycoon ▶ **noun** MAGNATE, mogul, businessman, captain of industry, industrialist, financier, entrepreneur; millionaire, multimillionaire; *informal* big shot, bigwig, honcho; *Brit. informal* supremo; *N. Amer. informal* big wheel, kahuna; *derogatory* fat cat.

type ▶ **noun** ❶ *a curate of the old-fashioned type* KIND, sort, variety, class, category, set, genre, species, order, breed, race; style, nature, manner, rank; generation, vintage; stamp, ilk, kidney, cast, grain, mould; *N. Amer.* stripe. ❷ (*informal*) *sporty types* PERSON, individual, character, sort; *Brit. informal* bod. ❸ *his sayings are the type of modern wisdom* EPITOME, quintessence, essence, archetype, paradigm, model, embodiment. ❹ *italic type* PRINT, typeface, face, characters, lettering, letters; font; *Brit.* fount.

typhoon ▶ **noun** CYCLONE, tropical storm, storm, tornado, hurricane, whirlwind; *N. Amer. informal* twister.

typical ▶ **adjective** ❶ *a typical example of art deco* REPRESENTATIVE, classic, quintessential, archetypal, model, prototypical, stereotypical. ❷ *a fairly typical day* NORMAL, average, ordinary, standard, regular, routine, run-of-the-mill, conventional, unremarkable, unexceptional; *informal* bog-standard. ❸ *it's typical of him to forget* CHARACTERISTIC, in keeping, usual, normal, par for the course, predictable, true to form; customary, habitual.

– OPPOSITES unusual, exceptional, uncharacteristic.

typify ▶ **verb** ❶ *he typified the civil servant* EPITOMIZE, exemplify, characterize, be representative of; personify, embody. ❷ *the sun typified the Greeks* SYMBOLIZE, represent, stand for, be emblematic of.

tyrannical ▶ **adjective** DICTATORIAL, despotic,

autocratic, oppressive, repressive, totalitarian, undemocratic, illiberal; authoritarian, high-handed, imperious, harsh, strict, iron-handed, severe, cruel, brutal, ruthless.
– OPPOSITES liberal.

tyrannize ▶ **verb** DOMINATE, dictate to, browbeat, intimidate, bully, lord it over; persecute, victimize, torment; oppress, rule with a rod of iron, repress, crush, subjugate; *informal* push around.

tyranny ▶ **noun** DESPOTISM, absolute power, autocracy, dictatorship, totalitarianism, Fascism; oppression, repression, subjugation, enslavement; authoritarianism, bullying, severity, cruelty, brutality, ruthlessness.

tyrant ▶ **noun** DICTATOR, despot, autocrat, authoritarian, oppressor; slave-driver, martinet, bully.

tyro ▶ **noun** NOVICE, beginner, learner, neophyte, newcomer, initiate, fledgling; apprentice, trainee, probationer; *N. Amer.* tenderfoot; *informal* rookie, newie, newbie; *N. Amer. informal* greenhorn.
– OPPOSITES veteran.

Uu

ubiquitous ▶ **adjective** OMNIPRESENT, ever-present, everywhere, all over the place, all-pervasive; universal, worldwide, global; rife, prevalent, far-reaching, inescapable.
– OPPOSITES rare.

ugly ▶ **adjective** ❶ *an ugly face* UNATTRACTIVE, ill-favoured, hideous, plain, unlovely, unprepossessing, unsightly, horrible, frightful, awful, ghastly, unpleasant, vile, revolting, repellent, repugnant; grotesque, monstrous, reptilian, misshapen, deformed, disfigured; *N. Amer.* homely; *informal* not much to look at; *Brit. informal* no oil painting. ❷ *things got pretty ugly* UNPLEASANT, nasty, disagreeable, alarming, tense, charged, serious, grave; dangerous, perilous, threatening, menacing, hostile, ominous, sinister. ❸ *an ugly rumour* HORRIBLE, despicable, reprehensible, nasty, appalling, objectionable, offensive, obnoxious, vile, dishonourable, rotten, vicious, spiteful.
– OPPOSITES beautiful, pleasant.

ulcer ▶ **noun** SORE, ulceration, abscess, boil, carbuncle, blister, gumboil, wen; *Medicine* aphtha, chancre, furuncle.

ulterior ▶ **adjective** UNDERLYING, undisclosed, undivulged, concealed, hidden, covert, secret, personal, private, selfish.
– OPPOSITES overt.

ultimate ▶ **adjective** ❶ *the ultimate collapse of the Empire* EVENTUAL, final, concluding, terminal, end; resulting, ensuing, consequent, subsequent. ❷ *ultimate truths about civilization* FUNDAMENTAL, basic, primary, elementary, elemental, absolute, central, key, crucial, essential, pivotal. ❸ *the ultimate gift for cat lovers* BEST, ideal, greatest, supreme, paramount, superlative, highest, utmost, optimum, quintessential.
▶ **noun** *the ultimate in luxury living* UTMOST, optimum, last word, height, epitome, peak, pinnacle, acme, zenith, nonpareil, dernier cri, ne plus ultra; *informal* the bee's knees, the cat's pyjamas/whiskers.

ultimately ▶ **adverb** ❶ *the cost will ultimately fall on us* EVENTUALLY, in the end, in the long run, at length, finally, sooner or later, in time, in the fullness of time, when all is said and done, one day, some day, sometime; *informal* when push comes to shove; *Brit. informal* at the end of the day. ❷ *two ultimately contradictory reasons* FUNDAMENTALLY, basically, primarily, essentially, at heart, deep down.

ultra- ▶ **combining form** *an ultra-conservative view* EXTREMELY, exceedingly, excessively, immensely, especially, exceptionally; *N. English* right; *informal* mega, mucho, majorly, oh-so; *Brit. informal* dead, ever so, well; *N. Amer. informal* real; *informal, dated* devilish; *archaic* exceeding.
▶ **noun** *ultras in the animal rights movement* EXTREMIST, radical, fanatic, zealot, diehard, militant.

umbrage
■ **take umbrage** TAKE OFFENCE, take exception, be aggrieved, be affronted, be annoyed, be angry, be indignant, be put out, be insulted, be hurt, be piqued, be resentful, be disgruntled, go into a huff; *informal* be miffed, have one's nose put out of joint; *Brit. informal* get the hump.

umbrella ▶ **noun** ❶ *they huddled under the umbrella* parasol, sunshade; *Brit. informal* brolly; *Brit. informal, dated* gamp. ❷ *the groups worked under the umbrella of the Liberal Party* AEGIS, auspices, patronage, protection, guardianship, support, backing, agency, guidance, care, charge, responsibility, cover.

umpire ▶ noun *the umpire reversed his decision* REFEREE, linesman, adjudicator, arbitrator, judge, moderator; *informal* ref; *N. Amer. informal* ump.
▶ verb *he umpired a boat race* REFEREE, adjudicate, arbitrate, judge, moderate, oversee; *Cricket* stand; *informal* ref.

umpteen ▶ adjective (*informal*). *See* COUNTLESS.

unabashed ▶ adjective UNASHAMED, shameless, unembarrassed, brazen, audacious, barefaced, blatant, flagrant, bold, cocky, unrepentant, undaunted, unconcerned, fearless.
– OPPOSITES sheepish.

unable ▶ adjective POWERLESS, impotent, at a loss, inadequate, incompetent, unfit, unqualified, incapable.

unabridged ▶ adjective COMPLETE, entire, whole, intact, uncut, unshortened, unexpurgated.

unacceptable ▶ adjective INTOLERABLE, insufferable, unsatisfactory, inadmissible, inappropriate, unsuitable, undesirable, unreasonable, insupportable; offensive, obnoxious, disagreeable, disgraceful, deplorable, beyond the pale, bad; *informal* not on, a bit much, too much, out of order; *Brit. informal* a bit thick, a bit off, not cricket; *formal* exceptionable.
– OPPOSITES satisfactory.

unaccompanied ▶ adjective ALONE, on one's own, by oneself, solo, lone, solitary, single-handed; unescorted, unattended, unchaperoned; *informal* by one's lonesome; *Brit. informal* on one's tod, on one's Jack Jones; *Austral./NZ informal* on one's Pat Malone.

unaccomplished ▶ adjective ❶ *unaccomplished works* UNCOMPLETED, incomplete, unfinished, undone, half-done, unfulfilled, neglected. ❷ *an unaccomplished poet* INEXPERT, unskilful, unskilled, amateur, amateurish, unqualified, untrained; incompetent, maladroit.
– OPPOSITES complete, skilful.

unaccountable ▶ adjective ❶ *for some unaccountable reason* INEXPLICABLE, insoluble, incomprehensible, unfathomable, impenetrable, puzzling, perplexing, baffling, bewildering, mystifying, mysterious, inscrutable, peculiar, strange, queer, odd, obscure; *informal* weird, freaky; *Brit. informal* rum. ❷ *the Council is unaccountable to anyone* UNANSWERABLE, not liable; free, exempt, immune; unsupervised.

unaccustomed ▶ adjective ❶ *she was unaccustomed to being bossed about* UNUSED, new, fresh; unfamiliar with, inexperienced in, unconversant with, unacquainted with. ❷ *he showed unaccustomed emotion* UNUSUAL, unfamiliar, uncommon, unwonted, exceptional, extraordinary, rare, surprising, abnormal, atypical.
– OPPOSITES habitual.

unacquainted ▶ adjective UNFAMILIAR, unaccustomed, unused; inexperienced, ignorant, uninformed, unenlightened, unconversant; *informal* in the dark; *poetic/literary* nescient.
– OPPOSITES familiar.

unadorned ▶ adjective UNEMBELLISHED, unornamented, undecorated, unfussy, no-nonsense, no-frills; plain, basic, restrained; bare, bald, austere, stark, spartan, clinical.
– OPPOSITES ornate.

unadventurous ▶ adjective CAUTIOUS, careful, circumspect, wary, hesitant, timid; conservative, conventional, unenterprising, unexciting, unimaginative; boring, strait-laced, stuffy, narrow-minded; *informal* square, straight, stick-in-the-mud.
– OPPOSITES enterprising.

unaffected ▶ adjective ❶ *they are unaffected by the cabinet reshuffle* UNCHANGED, unaltered, uninfluenced; untouched, unmoved, unresponsive to; proof against, impervious to, immune to. ❷ *his manner was unaffected* UNASSUMING, unpretentious, down-to-earth, natural, easy, uninhibited, open, artless, guileless, ingenuous, unsophisticated. ❸ *she was welcomed with unaffected warmth* GENUINE, real, sincere, honest, earnest, wholehearted, heartfelt, true, bona fide, frank, open; *informal* upfront.
– OPPOSITES influenced, pretentious, false, feigned.

unafraid ▶ adjective UNDAUNTED, unabashed, fearless, brave, courageous, plucky, intrepid, stout-hearted, bold, daring, confident, audacious, mettlesome, unshrinking; *informal* gutsy, spunky.
– OPPOSITES timid.

unanimous ▶ adjective ❶ *doctors were unanimous about the effects* UNITED, in agreement, in accord, of one mind, in harmony, concordant, undivided. ❷ *a unanimous vote* UNIFORM, consistent, united, concerted, congruent.
– OPPOSITES divided.

unanswerable ▶ adjective ❶ *an unanswerable case* IRREFUTABLE, indisputable, undeniable, incontestable, incontrovertible; conclusive, absolute, positive. ❷ *unanswerable questions* INSOLUBLE, unsolvable, insolvable, inexplicable, unexplainable.
– OPPOSITES weak, obvious.

unanswered ▶ adjective UNRESOLVED, undecided, unsettled, undetermined; pending, open to question, up in the air, doubtful, disputed.

unappetizing ▶ adjective UNPALATABLE, uninviting, unappealing, unpleasant, off-putting, disagreeable, distasteful, unsavoury, insipid, tasteless, flavourless, dull; inedible, uneatable, revolting; *informal* yucky, gross.
– OPPOSITES tempting.

unapproachable ▶ adjective ❶ *unapproachable islands* INACCESSIBLE, unreachable, remote,

out of the way, isolated, far-flung; *informal* off the beaten track, in the middle of nowhere, in the sticks, unget-at-able. ❷ *her boss appeared unapproachable* ALOOF, distant, remote, detached, reserved, withdrawn, uncommunicative, guarded, undemonstrative, unresponsive, unforthcoming, unfriendly, unsympathetic, unsociable; cool, cold, frosty, stiff, formal; *informal* stand-offish.
– OPPOSITES accessible, friendly.

unarmed ▶ adjective DEFENCELESS, weaponless; unprotected, undefended, unguarded, unshielded, vulnerable, exposed, assailable, pregnable.

unassailable ▶ adjective ❶ *an unassailable fortress* IMPREGNABLE, invulnerable, impenetrable, inviolable, invincible, unconquerable; secure, safe, strong, indestructible. ❷ *his logic was unassailable* INDISPUTABLE, undeniable, unquestionable, incontestable, incontrovertible, irrefutable, indubitable, watertight, sound, good, sure, manifest, patent, obvious.
– OPPOSITES defenceless.

unassertive ▶ adjective PASSIVE, retiring, unforthcoming, submissive, unassuming, self-effacing, modest, humble, meek, unconfident, diffident, shy, timid, insecure; *informal* mousy.
– OPPOSITES bold.

unassuming ▶ adjective MODEST, self-effacing, humble, meek, reserved, diffident; unobtrusive, unostentatious, unpretentious, unaffected, natural, artless, ingenuous.

unattached ▶ adjective ❶ *they were both unattached* SINGLE, unmarried, unwed, partnerless, uncommitted, available, footloose and fancy free, on one's own; on the shelf, unloved. ❷ *we are unattached to any organization* UNAFFILIATED, unallied; autonomous, independent, non-aligned, self-governing, neutral, separate, unconnected, detached.
– OPPOSITES married.

unattended ▶ adjective ❶ *his cries went unattended* IGNORED, disregarded, neglected, passed over. ❷ *an unattended vehicle* UNGUARDED, unwatched, alone, solitary; abandoned. ❸ *she had to walk there unattended* UNACCOMPANIED, unescorted, partnerless, unchaperoned, alone, on one's own, by oneself, solo; *informal* by one's lonesome; *Brit. informal* on one's tod, on one's Jack Jones; *Austral./NZ informal* on one's Pat Malone.

unattractive ▶ adjective PLAIN, ugly, ill-favoured, unappealing, unsightly, unlovely, unprepossessing, displeasing; hideous, monstrous, grotesque; *N. Amer.* homely; *informal* not much to look at, as ugly as sin; *Brit. informal* no oil painting.
– OPPOSITES beautiful.

unauthorized ▶ adjective UNOFFICIAL, unsanctioned, unaccredited, unlicensed, unwarranted, unapproved; disallowed, prohibited, banned, barred, forbidden, outlawed, illegal, illegitimate, illicit, proscribed.
– OPPOSITES official.

unavailing ▶ adjective INEFFECTIVE, ineffectual, inefficacious, vain, futile, useless, unsuccessful, fruitless, profitless, unprofitable, to no avail, abortive; *archaic* bootless.
– OPPOSITES effective.

unavoidable ▶ adjective INESCAPABLE, inevitable, inexorable, assured, certain, predestined, predetermined, ineluctable; necessary, compulsory, required, obligatory, mandatory.

unaware ▶ adjective IGNORANT, unknowing, unconscious, heedless, unmindful, oblivious, unsuspecting, uninformed, unenlightened, unwitting, innocent; inattentive, unobservant, unperceptive, blind, deaf; *informal* in the dark; *poetic/literary* nescient.
– OPPOSITES conscious.

unawares ▶ adverb ❶ *brigands caught them unawares* BY SURPRISE, unexpectedly, without warning, suddenly, abruptly, unprepared, off-guard; *informal* with one's trousers down, napping; *Brit. informal* on the hop. ❷ *the roach approached the pike unawares* UNKNOWINGLY, unwittingly, unconsciously; unintentionally, inadvertently, accidentally, by mistake.
– OPPOSITES prepared, knowingly.

unbalanced ▶ adjective ❶ *he is unbalanced and dangerous* UNSTABLE, mentally ill, deranged, demented, disturbed, unhinged, insane, mad, out of one's mind, non compos mentis; *informal* crazy, loopy, loony, nuts, nutty, cracked, screwy, batty, dotty, cuckoo, bonkers, mental, off one's head, round the bend/twist; *Brit. informal* barmy, potty, crackers, barking, off one's rocker; *N. Amer. informal* nutso, squirrelly; *dated* touched. ❷ *a most unbalanced article* BIASED, prejudiced, one-sided, partisan, inequitable, unjust, unfair, parti pris.
– OPPOSITES sane, unbiased.

unbearable ▶ adjective INTOLERABLE, insufferable, insupportable, unendurable, unacceptable, unmanageable, more than flesh and blood can stand, overpowering; *informal* too much.
– OPPOSITES tolerable.

unbeatable ▶ adjective INVINCIBLE, unstoppable, unassailable, indomitable, unconquerable, unsurpassable, matchless, peerless; supreme.

unbeaten ▶ adjective UNDEFEATED, unconquered, unsurpassed, unequalled, unrivalled; triumphant, victorious, supreme, matchless, second to none.

unbecoming ▶ adjective ❶ *an unbecoming sundress* UNFLATTERING, unattractive, unsightly, plain, ugly, hideous; unsuitable. ❷ *conduct unbecoming to the Senate* INAPPROPRIATE, unfitting, unbefitting, unsuitable, unsuited, inapt, out of keeping, untoward, incorrect, unacceptable;

unworthy, improper, unseemly, undignified.
– OPPOSITES flattering, appropriate.

unbelief ▶ **noun** ATHEISM, non-belief, agnosticism, apostasy, irreligion, godlessness, nihilism; scepticism, cynicism, disbelief, doubt.
– OPPOSITES faith.

unbelievable ▶ **adjective** INCREDIBLE, beyond belief, inconceivable, unthinkable, unimaginable; unconvincing, far-fetched, implausible, improbable; *informal* hard to swallow.
– OPPOSITES credible.

unbend ▶ **verb** ❶ *I couldn't unbend my knees* STRAIGHTEN (OUT), extend, flex, uncurl. ❷ *if you'd only unbend a little* RELAX, unwind, de-stress, loosen up, let oneself go; *informal* let one's hair down, let it all hang out, hang loose.

unbending ▶ **adjective** ❶ *an unbending man* ALOOF, formal, stiff, reserved, remote, forbidding, cool, unfeeling, unemotional, unfriendly, austere; *informal* uptight, stand-offish. ❷ *unbending attitudes* UNCOMPROMISING, inflexible, unyielding, hard-line, tough, strict, firm, resolute, determined, unrelenting, relentless, inexorable, intransigent, immovable.

unbiased ▶ **adjective** IMPARTIAL, unprejudiced, neutral, non-partisan, disinterested, detached, dispassionate, objective, open-minded, equitable, even-handed, fair.
– OPPOSITES prejudiced.

unbidden ▶ **adjective** ❶ *an unbidden guest* UNINVITED, unasked, unsolicited; unwanted, unwelcome. ❷ *unbidden excitement* SPONTANEOUS, unprompted, voluntary, unforced, unplanned, unpremeditated; *informal* off-the-cuff.

unbind ▶ **verb** UNTIE, unchain, unfetter, unshackle, unfasten, untether, undo, loosen; release, free, liberate.

unblemished ▶ **adjective** IMPECCABLE, flawless, faultless, perfect, pure, whiter than white, clean, spotless, unsullied, unspoilt, undefiled, untouched, untarnished, unpolluted; incorrupt, guiltless, sinless, innocent, blameless; *informal* squeaky clean.
– OPPOSITES flawed.

unborn ▶ **adjective** ❶ *your unborn child* EMBRYONIC, fetal, in utero; expected. ❷ *the unborn generations* FUTURE, coming, forthcoming, subsequent.

unbounded ▶ **adjective** UNLIMITED, boundless, limitless, illimitable; unrestrained, unrestricted, unconstrained, uncontrolled, unchecked, unbridled; untold, immeasurable, endless, unending, interminable, everlasting, infinite, inexhaustible.
– OPPOSITES limited.

unbreakable ▶ **adjective** SHATTERPROOF, indestructible, imperishable, durable, long-lasting; toughened, sturdy, stout, resistant, hard-wearing, heavy-duty.
– OPPOSITES fragile.

unbridled ▶ **adjective** UNRESTRAINED, unconstrained, uncontrolled, uninhibited, unrestricted, unchecked, uncurbed, rampant, runaway, irrepressible, unstoppable, intemperate, immoderate.
– OPPOSITES restrained.

unbroken ▶ **adjective** ❶ *the last unbroken window* UNDAMAGED, unimpaired, unharmed, unscathed, untouched, sound, intact, whole, perfect. ❷ *an unbroken horse* UNTAMED, undomesticated, wild, feral. ❸ *an unbroken chain of victories* UNINTERRUPTED, continuous, endless, constant, unremitting, ongoing. ❹ *his record is still unbroken* UNBEATEN, undefeated, unsurpassed, unrivalled, unmatched, supreme.

unburden ▶ **verb** *she had a sudden wish to unburden herself* OPEN ONE'S HEART, confess, tell all; *informal* come clean; *archaic* unbosom oneself.

uncalled
■ **uncalled for** GRATUITOUS, unnecessary, needless, inessential; undeserved, unmerited, unwarranted, unjustified, unreasonable, unfair, inappropriate, pointless; unasked, unsolicited, unrequested, unprompted, unprovoked, unwelcome.

uncanny ▶ **adjective** ❶ *the silence was uncanny* EERIE, unnatural, unearthly, other-worldly, ghostly, strange, abnormal, weird, bizarre, freakish; *Scottish* eldritch; *informal* creepy, spooky, freaky. ❷ *an uncanny resemblance* STRIKING, remarkable, extraordinary, exceptional, incredible, noteworthy, notable, arresting.

unceasing ▶ **adjective** INCESSANT, ceaseless, constant, continual, unabating, interminable, endless, unending, never-ending, everlasting, eternal, perpetual, continuous, non-stop, uninterrupted, unbroken, unremitting, persistent, relentless, unrelenting, unrelieved, sustained.

unceremonious ▶ **adjective** ❶ *an unceremonious dismissal* ABRUPT, sudden, hasty, hurried, summary, perfunctory, undignified; rude, impolite, discourteous, offhand. ❷ *an unceremonious man* INFORMAL, casual, relaxed, easy-going, familiar, natural, open; *informal* laid-back.
– OPPOSITES formal.

uncertain ▶ **adjective** ❶ *the effects are uncertain* UNKNOWN, debatable, open to question, in doubt, undetermined, unsure, in the balance, up in the air; unpredictable, unforeseeable, incalculable; risky, chancy; *informal* iffy. ❷ *uncertain weather* CHANGEABLE, variable, changeful, irregular, unpredictable, unreliable, unsettled, erratic, fluctuating. ❸ *Ed was uncertain about the decision* UNSURE, doubtful, dubious, undecided, irresolute, hesitant, blowing hot and cold, vacillating, vague, unclear, ambivalent, in two minds. ❹ *an uncertain smile* HESITANT, tentative, faltering, unsure, unconfident.
– OPPOSITES predictable, sure, confident.

unchangeable ▶ **adjective** UNALTERABLE, immutable, invariable, changeless, fixed, hard and fast, cast-iron, set in stone, established, permanent, enduring, abiding, lasting, indestructible, ineradicable, irreversible.
– OPPOSITES variable.

unchanging ▶ **adjective** CONSISTENT, constant, regular, unvarying, predictable, stable, steady, fixed, permanent, perpetual, eternal; sustained, lasting, persistent.

uncharitable ▶ **adjective** MEAN, mean-spirited, unkind, selfish, self-centred, inconsiderate, thoughtless, insensitive, unfriendly, unsympathetic, uncaring, ungenerous, ungracious, unfair.

uncharted ▶ **adjective** UNEXPLORED, undiscovered, unmapped, untravelled, unfamiliar, unplumbed, unknown.

uncivil ▶ **adjective** IMPOLITE, rude, discourteous, disrespectful, unmannerly, bad-mannered, impertinent, impudent, ungracious; brusque, sharp, curt, offhand, gruff, churlish; *informal* off, fresh.
– OPPOSITES polite.

uncivilized ▶ **adjective** UNCOUTH, coarse, rough, boorish, vulgar, philistine, uneducated, uncultured, uncultivated, benighted, unsophisticated, unpolished; ill-bred, ill-mannered, thuggish, loutish; barbarian, primitive, savage, brutish; *archaic* rude.

unclean ▶ **adjective** ❶ *unclean premises* DIRTY, filthy, grubby, grimy, mucky, foul, impure, tainted, soiled, unwashed; polluted, contaminated, infected, insanitary, unhygienic, unhealthy, germy, disease-ridden; *informal* yucky, cruddy; *Brit. informal* grotty, gungy. ❷ *sex was considered unclean* SINFUL, immoral, bad, wicked, evil, corrupt, impure, unwholesome, sordid, disgusting, debased, degenerate, depraved. ❸ *an unclean meat* IMPURE; forbidden, taboo.
– OPPOSITES pure, halal, kosher.

unclear ▶ **adjective** UNCERTAIN, unsure, unsettled, up in the air, debatable, open to question, in doubt, doubtful; ambiguous, equivocal, indefinite, vague, mysterious, obscure, hazy, foggy, nebulous; *informal* iffy.
– OPPOSITES evident.

unclothed ▶ **adjective** NAKED, bare, nude, stripped, undressed, in a state of nature; *informal* in one's birthday suit, in the buff, in the raw, in the altogether, in the nuddy; *Brit. informal* starkers; *Scottish informal* in the scud; *N. Amer. informal* buck naked.
– OPPOSITES dressed.

uncomfortable ▶ **adjective** ❶ *an uncomfortable chair* PAINFUL, disagreeable, intolerable, unbearable, confining, cramped. ❷ *I felt uncomfortable in her presence* UNEASY, awkward, nervous, tense, strained, edgy, restless, embarrassed, troubled, worried, anxious, unquiet, fraught; *informal* rattled, twitchy; *N. Amer. informal* discombobulated, antsy.
– OPPOSITES relaxed.

uncommitted ▶ **adjective** ❶ *uncommitted voters* FLOATING, undecided, non-partisan, unaffiliated, neutral, impartial, independent, undeclared, uncertain; *informal* sitting on the fence. ❷ *the uncommitted male* UNMARRIED, unattached, unwed, partnerless; footloose and fancy free, available, single, lone.
– OPPOSITES aligned, attached.

uncommon ▶ **adjective** ❶ *an uncommon plant* UNUSUAL, abnormal, rare, atypical, unconventional, unfamiliar, strange, odd, curious, extraordinary, outlandish, novel, singular, peculiar, queer, bizarre; alien; *informal* weird, oddball, offbeat. ❷ *abductions are uncommon* RARE, scarce, few and far between, exceptional, abnormal, isolated, infrequent, irregular; *Brit.* out of the common. ❸ *an uncommon capacity for hard work* REMARKABLE, extraordinary, exceptional, singular, particular, marked, outstanding, noteworthy, significant, especial, special, signal, superior, unique, unparalleled, prodigious; *informal* mind-boggling.

uncommonly ▶ **adverb** UNUSUALLY, remarkably, extraordinarily, exceptionally, singularly, particularly, especially, decidedly, notably, eminently, extremely, very; *N. English* right; *informal* awfully, terribly, seriously; *Brit. informal* jolly, dead.

uncommunicative ▶ **adjective** TACITURN, quiet, unforthcoming, reserved, reticent, laconic, tongue-tied, mute, silent, tight-lipped; guarded, secretive, close, private; distant, remote, aloof, withdrawn, unsociable; *informal* mum, stand-offish.
– OPPOSITES talkative.

uncomplicated ▶ **adjective** SIMPLE, straightforward, clear, accessible, undemanding, unchallenging, unsophisticated, trouble-free, painless, effortless, easy, elementary, idiot-proof, plain sailing; *informal* a piece of cake, child's play, a cinch, a doddle, a breeze; *Brit. informal* easy-peasy.
– OPPOSITES complex.

uncompromising ▶ **adjective** INFLEXIBLE, unbending, unyielding, unshakeable, resolute, rigid, hard-line, immovable, intractable, firm, determined, iron-willed, obstinate, stubborn, adamant, obdurate, intransigent, headstrong, pig-headed; *Brit. informal* bloody-minded.
– OPPOSITES flexible.

unconcerned ▶ **adjective** ❶ *he is unconcerned about their responses* INDIFFERENT, unmoved, apathetic, uninterested, incurious, dispassionate, heedless, unmindful; cool, lukewarm, unenthusiastic. ❷ *she tried to look unconcerned* UNTROUBLED, unworried, unruffled, insouciant, nonchalant, blasé, carefree, casual, relaxed, at ease, {cool, calm, and collected}; *informal* laid-back.
– OPPOSITES interested, anxious.

unconditional ▶ adjective UNQUESTIONING, unqualified, unreserved, unlimited, unrestricted, wholehearted; complete, total, entire, full, absolute, out-and-out, unequivocal.

unconnected ▶ adjective ❶ *the earth wire was unconnected* DETACHED, disconnected, loose. ❷ *unconnected tasks* UNRELATED, dissociated, separate, independent, distinct, different, disparate, discrete. ❸ *unconnected chains of thought* DISJOINTED, incoherent, disconnected, rambling, wandering, diffuse, disorderly, haphazard, disorganized, garbled, mixed, muddled, aimless.
– OPPOSITES attached, related, coherent.

unconscionable ▶ adjective ❶ *the unconscionable use of test animals* UNETHICAL, amoral, immoral, unprincipled, indefensible, wrong; unscrupulous, unfair, underhand, dishonourable. ❷ *we had to wait an unconscionable time* EXCESSIVE, unreasonable, unwarranted, uncalled for, unfair, inordinate, immoderate, undue, inexcusable, unnecessary, needless; *informal* over the top, OTT.
– OPPOSITES ethical, acceptable.

unconscious ▶ adjective ❶ *she made sure he was unconscious* INSENSIBLE, senseless, insentient, insensate, comatose, inert, knocked out, stunned; motionless, immobile, prostrate; *informal* out cold, out for the count, dead to the world; *Brit. informal* spark out. ❷ *she was unconscious of the pain* HEEDLESS, unmindful, disregarding, oblivious to, insensible to, impervious to, unaffected by, unconcerned by, indifferent to; unaware, unknowing. ❸ *an unconscious desire* SUBCONSCIOUS, latent, suppressed, subliminal, sleeping, inherent, instinctive, involuntary, uncontrolled, spontaneous; unintentional, unthinking, unwitting, inadvertent; *informal* gut.
– OPPOSITES aware, voluntary.
▶ noun *fantasies raging in the unconscious* SUBCONSCIOUS, psyche, ego, id, inner self.

uncontrollable ▶ adjective ❶ *the crowds were uncontrollable* UNMANAGEABLE, out of control, ungovernable, wild, unruly, disorderly, recalcitrant, turbulent, disobedient, delinquent, defiant, undisciplined; *formal* refractory. ❷ *an uncontrollable rage* UNGOVERNABLE, irrepressible, unstoppable, unquenchable; wild, violent, frenzied, furious, mad, hysterical, passionate.
– OPPOSITES compliant.

unconventional ▶ adjective UNUSUAL, irregular, unorthodox, unfamiliar, uncommon, unwonted, out of the ordinary, atypical, singular, alternative, different; new, novel, innovative, ground-breaking, pioneering, original, unprecedented; eccentric, idiosyncratic, quirky, odd, strange, bizarre, weird, outlandish, curious; abnormal, anomalous, aberrant, extraordinary; nonconformist, bohemian, avant-garde; *informal* way out, far out, offbeat, wacky, madcap, zany, hippy; *Brit. informal* rum; *N. Amer. informal* kooky, wacko.
– OPPOSITES orthodox.

unconvincing ▶ adjective IMPROBABLE, unlikely, implausible, incredible, unbelievable, questionable, dubious, doubtful; strained, laboured, far-fetched, unrealistic, fanciful, fantastic; feeble, weak, transparent, poor, lame, ineffectual, half-baked; *informal* hard to swallow.
– OPPOSITES persuasive.

uncooperative ▶ adjective UNHELPFUL, awkward, disobliging, recalcitrant, perverse, contrary, stubborn, wilful, stiff-necked, unyielding, unbending, inflexible, immovable, obstructive, difficult, obstreperous, disobedient; *Brit. informal* bloody-minded.
– OPPOSITES obliging.

uncoordinated ▶ adjective CLUMSY, awkward, blundering, bumbling, lumbering, flat-footed, heavy-handed, graceless, gawky, ungainly, ungraceful; inept, unhandy, unskilful, inexpert, maladroit, bungling; *informal* butter-fingered, cack-handed, ham-fisted; *Brit. informal* all (fingers and) thumbs; *N. Amer. informal* klutzy.
– OPPOSITES dexterous.

uncouth ▶ adjective UNCIVILIZED, uncultured, uncultivated, unrefined, unpolished, unsophisticated, common, low, rough, coarse, crude, loutish, boorish, oafish; churlish, uncivil, rude, impolite, discourteous, disrespectful, unmannerly, bad-mannered, ill-bred, indecorous, vulgar, crass, indelicate; *Brit. informal* yobbish.
– OPPOSITES refined.

uncover ▶ verb ❶ *she uncovered the sandwiches* EXPOSE, reveal, lay bare; unwrap, unveil; strip, denude. ❷ *they uncovered a money-laundering plot* DETECT, discover, come across, stumble on, chance on, find, turn up, unearth, dig up; expose, bring to light, unmask, unveil, reveal, lay bare, make known, make public, betray, give away; *informal* blow the whistle on, pull the plug on.

unctuous ▶ adjective SYCOPHANTIC, ingratiating, obsequious, fawning, servile, grovelling, subservient, cringing, humble, hypocritical, insincere, gushing, effusive; glib, smooth, slick, slippery, oily, greasy; *informal* smarmy, slimy, sucky, soapy.

undaunted ▶ adjective UNAFRAID, undismayed, unflinching, unshrinking, unabashed, fearless, dauntless, intrepid, bold, valiant, brave, courageous, plucky, mettlesome, gritty, indomitable, confident, audacious, daring; *informal* gutsy, spunky.
– OPPOSITES fearful.

undecided ▶ adjective UNRESOLVED, uncertain, unsure, unclear, unsettled, indefinite, undetermined, unknown, in the balance, up in the air, debatable, arguable, moot, open to

question, doubtful, dubious, borderline, ambiguous, vague; indecisive, irresolute, hesitant, tentative, wavering, vacillating, uncommitted, ambivalent, in two minds; *informal* iffy.
– OPPOSITES certain.

undefined ▶ adjective ❶ *some matters are still undefined* UNSPECIFIED, unexplained, unspecific, indeterminate, unsettled; unclear, woolly, imprecise, inexact, indefinite, vague. ❷ *undefined shapes* INDISTINCT, indefinite, formless, indistinguishable, vague, hazy, misty, shadowy, nebulous, blurred, blurry.
– OPPOSITES definite, distinct.

undemonstrative ▶ adjective UNEMOTIONAL, unaffectionate, impassive, dispassionate, restrained, reserved, unresponsive, uncommunicative, unforthcoming, stiff, guarded, aloof, distant, detached, remote, withdrawn; cool, cold, frosty, frigid; *informal* stand-offish.

undeniable ▶ adjective INDISPUTABLE, indubitable, unquestionable, beyond doubt, beyond question, undebatable, incontrovertible, incontestable, irrefutable, unassailable; certain, sure, definite, positive, conclusive, plain, obvious, unmistakable, self-evident, patent, emphatic, categorical, unequivocal.
– OPPOSITES questionable.

under ▶ preposition ❶ *they hid under a bush* BENEATH, below, underneath. ❷ *the rent is under £250* LESS THAN, lower than, below. ❸ *branch managers are under the retail director* SUBORDINATE TO, junior to, inferior to, subservient to, answerable to, responsible to, subject to, controlled by. ❹ *forty homes are under construction* UNDERGOING, in the process of. ❺ *the town was under water* FLOODED BY, immersed in, submerged by, sunk in, engulfed by, inundated by. ❻ *our finances are under pressure* SUBJECT TO, liable to, at the mercy of.
– OPPOSITES above, over.
▶ adverb *coughing and spluttering she went under* DOWN, lower, below, underneath, beneath; underwater.

underclothes ▶ plural noun UNDERWEAR, undergarments, underclothing, underthings, lingerie; *informal* undies, frillies; *Brit. informal* smalls; *archaic* underlinen.

undercover ▶ adjective COVERT, secret, clandestine, underground, surreptitious, furtive, cloak-and-dagger, hole-and-corner, hugger-mugger, stealthy, hidden, concealed; *informal* hush-hush, sneaky.
– OPPOSITES overt.

undercurrent ▶ noun ❶ *dangerous undercurrents in the cove* UNDERTOW, underflow, underswell, underset. ❷ *the undercurrent of despair in his words* UNDERTONE, overtone, suggestion, connotation, intimation, hint, nuance, trace, suspicion, whisper, tinge; feeling, atmosphere, aura, echo; *informal* vibes.

undercut ▶ verb ❶ *the firm undercut their rivals* CHARGE LESS THAN, undersell, underbid. ❷ *his authority was being undercut* UNDERMINE, weaken, impair, sap, threaten, subvert, sabotage, ruin, destabilize, wreck.

underdog ▶ noun WEAKER PARTY, victim, loser, scapegoat; *informal* little guy, fall guy, stooge.

underestimate ▶ verb UNDERRATE, undervalue, do an injustice to, be wrong about, sell short, play down, understate; minimize, de-emphasize, underemphasize, diminish, downgrade, gloss over, trivialize; miscalculate, misjudge, misconstrue, misread.
– OPPOSITES exaggerate.

undergo ▶ verb GO THROUGH, experience, undertake, face, submit to, be subjected to, come in for, receive, sustain, endure, brave, bear, tolerate, stand, withstand, weather; *Brit. informal* wear.

underground ▶ adjective ❶ *an underground car park* SUBTERRANEAN, buried, sunken, basement. ❷ *underground organizations* CLANDESTINE, secret, surreptitious, covert, undercover, closet, hole-and-corner, cloak-and-dagger, hugger-mugger, back-alley, hidden, sneaky, furtive; resistance, subversive; *informal* hush-hush. ❸ *the underground art scene* ALTERNATIVE, radical, revolutionary, unconventional, unorthodox, avant-garde, experimental, innovative.
▶ adverb ❶ *the insects live underground* BELOW GROUND, in the earth. ❷ *the rebels went underground* INTO HIDING, into seclusion, undercover.
▶ noun ❶ *he took the underground* UNDERGROUND RAILWAY, metro; *N. Amer.* subway; *Brit. informal* tube. ❷ *information from the French underground* RESISTANCE (MOVEMENT); partisans, guerrillas, freedom fighters; (*historical*) Maquis.

undergrowth ▶ noun SHRUBBERY, vegetation, greenery, ground cover, underwood, brushwood, brush, scrub, covert, thicket, copse; bushes, plants, brambles, herbage; *N. Amer.* underbrush.

underhand ▶ adjective DECEITFUL, dishonest, dishonourable, disreputable, unethical, unprincipled, immoral, unscrupulous, fraudulent, dubious, unfair; treacherous, duplicitous, double-dealing; devious, artful, crafty, conniving, scheming, sly, wily; clandestine, sneaky, furtive, covert, cloak-and-dagger; *N. Amer.* snide; *informal* crooked, shady, bent, low-down; *Brit. informal* dodgy; *Austral./NZ informal* shonky.
– OPPOSITES honest.

underline ▶ verb ❶ *she underlined a phrase* UNDERSCORE, mark, pick out, emphasize, highlight. ❷ *the programme underlines the benefits of exercise* EMPHASIZE, stress, highlight, accentuate, accent, focus on, spotlight, point up, play up; *informal* rub in.

underling ▶ noun SUBORDINATE, inferior, junior, minion, lackey, flunkey, menial, retainer, vassal, subject, hireling, servant, hench-

man, factotum; *informal* dogsbody, gofer; *Brit. informal* skivvy.
– OPPOSITES boss.

underlying ▶ adjective ❶ *the underlying aims of the research* FUNDAMENTAL, basic, primary, prime, central, principal, chief, key, elementary, intrinsic, essential. ❷ *an underlying feeling of irritation* LATENT, repressed, suppressed, unrevealed, undisclosed, unexpressed, concealed, hidden, masked.

undermine ▶ verb ❶ *their integrity is being undermined* SUBVERT, sabotage, threaten, weaken, compromise, diminish, reduce, impair, mar, spoil, ruin, damage, hurt, injure, cripple, sap, shake; *informal* drag through the mud. ❷ *we undermined the building* TUNNEL UNDER, dig under, burrow under, sap. ❸ *the damp had so undermined the wall that it collapsed* ERODE, wear away, eat away at.
– OPPOSITES strengthen, support.

underprivileged ▶ adjective NEEDY, deprived, disadvantaged, poor, destitute, in straitened circumstances, impoverished, poverty-stricken, indigent; *Brit.* on the breadline; *informal* on one's uppers, on one's beam-ends; *formal* penurious.
– OPPOSITES wealthy.

underrate ▶ verb UNDERVALUE, underestimate, do an injustice to, sell short, play down, understate, minimize, diminish, downgrade, trivialize.
– OPPOSITES exaggerate.

undersized ▶ adjective UNDERDEVELOPED, stunted, small, short, little, tiny, petite, slight, compact, miniature, mini, diminutive, dwarfish, pygmy; *Scottish* wee; *informal* pint-sized, pocket-sized, knee-high to a grasshopper, baby, teeny-weeny, itsy-bitsy.
– OPPOSITES overgrown.

understand ▶ verb ❶ *he couldn't understand anything we said* COMPREHEND, grasp, take in, see, apprehend, follow, make sense of, fathom; unravel, decipher, interpret; *informal* work out, figure out, make head or tail of, get one's head around, take on board, get the drift of, catch on to, get; *Brit. informal* twig, suss (out). ❷ *she understood how hard he'd worked* APPRECIATE, recognize, realize, acknowledge, know, be aware of, be conscious of; *informal* be wise to; *formal* be cognizant of. ❸ *I understand that you wish to go* BELIEVE, gather, take it, hear (tell), notice, see, learn; conclude, infer, assume, surmise, fancy.

understandable ▶ adjective ❶ *make it understandable to the layman* COMPREHENSIBLE, intelligible, coherent, clear, explicit, unambiguous, transparent, plain, straightforward, digestible, user-friendly. ❷ *an understandable desire to be happy* UNSURPRISING, expected, predictable, inevitable; reasonable, acceptable, logical, rational, normal, natural; justifiable, justified, defensible, excusable, pardonable, forgivable.

understanding ▶ noun ❶ *test your understanding of the language* COMPREHENSION, apprehension, grasp, mastery, appreciation, assimilation, absorption; knowledge, awareness, insight, skill, expertise, proficiency; *informal* know-how; *formal* cognizance. ❷ *a young man of brilliant understanding* INTELLECT, intelligence, brainpower, brains, judgement, reasoning, mentality; insight, intuition, shrewdness, acumen, sagacity, wisdom, wit; *informal* nous, savvy, know-how. ❸ *it was my understanding that this was free* BELIEF, perception, view, conviction, feeling, opinion, intuition, impression, assumption, supposition. ❹ *he treated me with understanding* COMPASSION, sympathy, pity, feeling, concern, consideration, kindness, sensitivity, decency, humanity, charity, goodwill, mercy, tolerance. ❺ *we had a tacit understanding* AGREEMENT, arrangement, deal, bargain, settlement, pledge, pact, compact, contract, covenant, bond.
– OPPOSITES ignorance, indifference.
▶ adjective *an understanding friend* COMPASSIONATE, sympathetic, sensitive, considerate, tender, kind, thoughtful, tolerant, patient, forbearing, lenient, merciful, forgiving, humane; approachable, supportive, perceptive.

understate ▶ verb PLAY DOWN, downplay, underrate, underplay, de-emphasize, trivialize, minimize, diminish, downgrade, brush aside, gloss over; *informal* soft-pedal, sell short.
– OPPOSITES exaggerate.

understudy ▶ noun STAND-IN, substitute, replacement, reserve, fill-in, locum, proxy, back-up, relief, standby, stopgap, second, ancillary; *informal* sub; *N. Amer. informal* pinch-hitter.

undertake ▶ verb TACKLE, take on, assume, shoulder, handle, manage, deal with, be responsible for; engage in, take part in, go about, set about, get down to, get to grips with, embark on; attempt, try, endeavour; *informal* have a go at; *formal* essay.

undertaker ▶ noun FUNERAL DIRECTOR; *N. Amer.* mortician.

undertaking ▶ noun ❶ *a risky undertaking* ENTERPRISE, venture, project, campaign, scheme, plan, operation, endeavour, effort, task, activity, pursuit, exploit, business, affair, procedure; mission, quest. ❷ *sign this undertaking to comply with the rules* PLEDGE, agreement, promise, oath, covenant, vow, commitment, guarantee, assurance, contract.

undertone ▶ noun ❶ *he said something in an undertone* LOW VOICE, murmur, whisper, mutter. ❷ *the story's dark undertones* UNDERCURRENT, overtone, suggestion, nuance, vein, atmosphere, aura, tenor, flavour; vibrations.

undervalue ▶ verb UNDERRATE, underestimate, play down, understate, underemphasize, diminish, minimize, downgrade, reduce, brush aside, gloss over, trivialize, hold cheap; *informal* sell short.

underwater ▶ adjective SUBMERGED, immersed, sunken, subaqueous; undersea, submarine.

underwear ▶ noun UNDERCLOTHES, underclothing, undergarments, underthings, lingerie; *informal* undies, frillies; *Brit. informal* smalls; *archaic* underlinen.

underworld ▶ noun ❶ *Osiris, god of the underworld* THE NETHERWORLD, the nether regions, hell, the abyss; eternal damnation; Gehenna, Tophet, Sheol, Hades; *Brit.* the other place; *poetic/literary* the pit. ❷ *the violent underworld of Southwark* CRIMINAL WORLD, gangland; criminals, gangsters; *informal* mobsters.
– OPPOSITES heaven.

underwrite ▶ verb SPONSOR, support, back, insure, indemnify, subsidize, pay for, finance, fund; *informal* foot the bill for; *N. Amer. informal* bankroll.

undesirable ▶ adjective ❶ *undesirable side effects* UNPLEASANT, disagreeable, nasty, unwelcome, unwanted, unfortunate, infelicitous. ❷ *some very undesirable people* UNPLEASANT, disagreeable, obnoxious, nasty, awful, terrible, dreadful, frightful, repulsive, repellent, abhorrent, loathsome, hateful, detestable, deplorable, appalling, insufferable, intolerable, despicable, contemptible, odious, vile, unsavoury; *informal* ghastly, horrible, horrid; *Brit. informal* beastly.
– OPPOSITES pleasant, agreeable.

undignified ▶ adjective UNSEEMLY, demeaning, unbecoming, unworthy, unbefitting, degrading, shameful, dishonourable, ignominious, discreditable, ignoble, untoward, unsuitable; scandalous, disgraceful, indecent, low, base; *informal* infra dig.

undisciplined ▶ adjective UNRULY, disorderly, disobedient, badly behaved, recalcitrant, wilful, wayward, delinquent, naughty, rebellious, insubordinate, disruptive, errant, out of control, uncontrollable, wild; disorganized, unsystematic, unmethodical, lax, slapdash, slipshod, sloppy; *Brit. informal* stroppy, bolshie; *formal* refractory.

undisguised ▶ adjective OBVIOUS, evident, patent, manifest, transparent, overt, unconcealed, unhidden, unmistakable, undeniable, plain, clear, clear-cut, explicit, naked, visible; blatant, flagrant, glaring, bold; *informal* standing/sticking out a mile.

undisputed ▶ adjective UNDOUBTED, indubitable, uncontested, incontestable, unchallenged, incontrovertible, unequivocal, undeniable, irrefutable, unmistakable, sure, certain, definite, accepted, acknowledged, recognized.
– OPPOSITES doubtful.

undistinguished ▶ adjective UNEXCEPTIONAL, indifferent, run-of-the-mill, middle-of-the-road, ordinary, average, commonplace, mediocre, humdrum, lacklustre, forgettable, uninspired, uneventful, unremarkable, inconsequential, featureless, nondescript, middling, moderate; *N. Amer.* garden-variety; *informal* nothing special, no great shakes, nothing to write home about, OK, so-so, bog standard; *Brit. informal* common or garden; *N. Amer. informal* bush-league.
– OPPOSITES extraordinary.

undivided ▶ adjective COMPLETE, full, total, whole, entire, absolute, unqualified, unreserved, unmitigated, unbroken, consistent, thorough, exclusive, dedicated; focused, engrossed, absorbed, attentive, committed.

undo ▶ verb ❶ *he undid another button* UNFASTEN, unbutton, unhook, untie, unlace; unlock, unbolt; loosen, disentangle, extricate, release, detach, free, open; disconnect, disengage, separate. ❷ *they will undo a decision by the law lords* REVOKE, overrule, overturn, repeal, rescind, reverse, countermand, cancel, annul, nullify, invalidate, void, negate; *Law* vacate; *formal* abrogate. ❸ *she undid much of the good work done* RUIN, undermine, subvert, overturn, scotch, sabotage, spoil, impair, mar, destroy, wreck, eradicate, obliterate; cancel out, neutralize, thwart, foil, frustrate, hamper, hinder, obstruct; *informal* blow, put the kibosh on, foul up, muck up; *Brit. informal* scupper, throw a spanner in the works of; *N. Amer. informal* rain on someone's parade.
– OPPOSITES fasten, ratify, enhance.

undoing ▶ noun ❶ *she plotted the king's undoing* DOWNFALL, defeat, conquest, deposition, overthrow, ruin, ruination, elimination, end, collapse, failure, debasement; Waterloo. ❷ *their complacency was their undoing* FATAL FLAW, Achilles' heel, weakness, weak point, failing, misfortune, affliction, curse.

undone ▶ adjective ❶ *some work was left undone* UNFINISHED, incomplete, half-done, unaccomplished, unfulfilled, unconcluded; omitted, neglected, disregarded, ignored; remaining, outstanding, deferred, pending, on ice; *informal* on the back burner. ❷ (*formal*) *she had lost and was utterly undone* DONE FOR, finished, ruined, destroyed, doomed, lost, defeated, beaten; *informal* washed up.
– OPPOSITES finished, successful.

undoubted ▶ adjective UNDISPUTED, unchallenged, unquestioned, indubitable, incontrovertible, irrefutable, incontestable, sure, certain, unmistakable; definite, accepted, acknowledged, recognized.

undoubtedly ▶ adverb DOUBTLESS, indubitably, doubtlessly, no doubt, without (a) doubt; unquestionably, indisputably, undeniably, incontrovertibly, clearly, obviously, patently, certainly, definitely, surely, of course, indeed.

undress ▶ verb *he undressed and got into bed* STRIP (OFF), disrobe, take off one's clothes; *Brit. informal* peel off.
■ **in a state of undress** NAKED, (in the) nude, bare, stripped, unclothed, undressed, in a state of nature; *informal* in one's birthday suit, in the raw, in the buff, in the nuddy; *Brit. informal* starkers.

undue ▶ adjective EXCESSIVE, immoderate, intemperate, inordinate, disproportionate; uncalled for, unneeded, unnecessary, non-essential, needless, unwarranted, unjustified, unreasonable; inappropriate, unmerited, unsuitable, improper.
– OPPOSITES appropriate.

undulate ▶ verb RISE AND FALL, surge, swell, heave, ripple, flow; wind, wobble, oscillate.

undying ▶ adjective ABIDING, lasting, enduring, permanent, constant, infinite; unceasing, perpetual, ceaseless, incessant, unending, never-ending; immortal, eternal, deathless.

unearth ▶ verb ❶ *workmen unearthed an artillery shell* DIG UP, excavate, exhume, disinter, root out, unbury. ❷ *I unearthed an interesting fact* DISCOVER, uncover, find, come across, hit on, bring to light, expose, turn up, hunt out, nose out.

unearthly ▶ adjective ❶ *an unearthly chill in the air* OTHER-WORLDLY, supernatural, preternatural, alien; ghostly, spectral, phantom, mysterious, spine-chilling, hair-raising; uncanny, eerie, strange, weird, unnatural, bizarre; *Scottish* eldritch; *informal* spooky, creepy, scary. ❷ (*informal*) *they rose at some unearthly hour* UNREASONABLE, preposterous, abnormal, extraordinary, absurd, ridiculous, unheard of; *informal* ungodly, unholy.
– OPPOSITES normal, reasonable.

uneasy ▶ adjective ❶ *the doctor made him feel uneasy* WORRIED, anxious, troubled, disturbed, agitated, nervous, tense, overwrought, edgy, apprehensive, restless, discomfited, perturbed, fearful, uncomfortable, unsettled; *informal* jittery, nervy. ❷ *he had an uneasy feeling* WORRYING, disturbing, troubling, alarming, dismaying, disquieting, unsettling, disconcerting, upsetting. ❸ *the victory ensured an uneasy peace* TENSE, awkward, strained, fraught; precarious, unstable, insecure.
– OPPOSITES calm, stable.

uneconomic, uneconomical ▶ adjective UNPROFITABLE, uncommercial, non-viable, loss-making, worthless; wasteful, inefficient, improvident.

uneducated ▶ adjective UNTAUGHT, unschooled, untutored, untrained, unread, unscholarly, illiterate, unlettered, ignorant, ill-informed, uninformed; uncouth, unsophisticated, uncultured, unaccomplished, unenlightened, philistine, benighted, backward.
– OPPOSITES learned.

unemotional ▶ adjective RESERVED, undemonstrative, sober, restrained, passionless, emotionless, unsentimental, unexcitable, impassive, phlegmatic, stoical, equable; cold, cool, unfeeling.

unemployed ▶ adjective JOBLESS, out of work, between jobs, unwaged, unoccupied, redundant, laid off; on benefit; *Brit.* signing on; *N. Amer.* on welfare; *Brit. informal* on the dole, 'resting'.

unending ▶ adjective ENDLESS, never-ending, interminable, perpetual, eternal, ceaseless, incessant, unceasing, non-stop, uninterrupted, continuous, continual, constant, persistent, unbroken, unabating, unremitting, relentless.

unendurable ▶ adjective INTOLERABLE, unbearable, insufferable, insupportable, more than flesh and blood can stand.

unenthusiastic ▶ adjective INDIFFERENT, apathetic, half-hearted, lukewarm, casual, cool, lacklustre, offhand, unmoved; cursory, perfunctory.
– OPPOSITES keen.

unenviable ▶ adjective DISAGREEABLE, nasty, unpleasant, undesirable, horrible, thankless; unwanted, unwished-for.

unequal ▶ adjective ❶ *they are unequal in length* DIFFERENT, dissimilar, unlike, unalike, disparate, unmatched, uneven, irregular, varying, variable. ❷ *the unequal distribution of wealth* UNFAIR, unjust, disproportionate, inequitable, biased. ❸ *an unequal contest* ONE-SIDED, uneven, unfair, ill-matched, unbalanced, lopsided. ❹ *she felt unequal to the task* INADEQUATE FOR, incapable of, unqualified for, unsuited to, incompetent at, not up to; *informal* not cut out for.
– OPPOSITES identical, fair.

unequalled ▶ adjective UNBEATEN, matchless, unmatched, unrivalled, unsurpassed, unparalleled, peerless, incomparable, inimitable, second to none, unique.

unequivocal ▶ adjective UNAMBIGUOUS, unmistakable, indisputable, incontrovertible, indubitable, undeniable; clear, clear-cut, plain, explicit, specific, categorical, straightforward, blunt, candid, emphatic, manifest.
– OPPOSITES ambiguous.

unerring ▶ adjective UNFAILING, infallible, perfect, flawless, faultless, impeccable, unimpeachable; sure, true, assured, deadly; *informal* sure-fire.

unethical ▶ adjective IMMORAL, amoral, unprincipled, unscrupulous, dishonourable, dishonest, wrong, deceitful, unconscionable, fraudulent, underhand, wicked, evil, corrupt; unprofessional, improper.

uneven ▶ adjective ❶ *uneven ground* BUMPY, rough, lumpy, stony, rocky, potholed, rutted, pitted, jagged. ❷ *uneven teeth* IRREGULAR, unequal, unbalanced, lopsided, askew, crooked,

asymmetrical, unsymmetrical. ❸ *uneven quality* INCONSISTENT, variable, varying, fluctuating, irregular, erratic, patchy. ❹ *an uneven contest* ONE-SIDED, unequal, unfair, unjust, inequitable, ill-matched, unbalanced.
– OPPOSITES flat, regular, equal.

uneventful ▸ adjective UNEXCITING, uninteresting, monotonous, boring, dull, tedious, humdrum, routine, unvaried, ordinary, run-of-the-mill, pedestrian, mundane, predictable.
– OPPOSITES exciting.

unexceptional ▸ adjective ORDINARY, average, typical, everyday, mediocre, run-of-the-mill, middle-of-the-road, indifferent; *informal* OK, so-so, nothing special, no great shakes, fair-to-middling.

unexpected ▸ adjective UNFORESEEN, unanticipated, unpredicted, unlooked for, without warning; sudden, abrupt, surprising, out of the blue.

unfailing ▸ adjective *his unfailing good humour* CONSTANT, reliable, dependable, steadfast, steady; endless, undying, unfading, inexhaustible, boundless, ceaseless.

unfair ▸ adjective ❶ *the trial was unfair* UNJUST, inequitable, prejudiced, biased, discriminatory; one-sided, unequal, uneven, unbalanced, partisan. ❷ *his comments were unfair* UNDESERVED, unmerited, uncalled for, unreasonable, unjustified; *Brit. informal* out of order. ❸ *unfair play* UNSPORTING, unsportsmanlike, dirty, below the belt, underhand, dishonourable. ❹ *you're being very unfair* INCONSIDERATE, thoughtless, insensitive, selfish, mean, unkind, unreasonable.
– OPPOSITES just, justified.

unfaithful ▸ adjective ❶ *her husband had been unfaithful* ADULTEROUS, faithless, fickle, untrue, inconstant; *informal* cheating, two-timing. ❷ *an unfaithful friend* DISLOYAL, treacherous, traitorous, untrustworthy, unreliable, undependable, false, two-faced, double-crossing, deceitful; *poetic/literary* perfidious.
– OPPOSITES loyal.

unfaltering ▸ adjective STEADY, resolute, resolved, firm, steadfast, fixed, decided, unswerving, unwavering, tireless, indefatigable, persistent, unyielding, relentless, unremitting, unrelenting.
– OPPOSITES unsteady.

unfamiliar ▸ adjective ❶ *an unfamiliar part of the city* UNKNOWN, new, strange, foreign, alien. ❷ *the unfamiliar sounds* UNUSUAL, uncommon, unconventional, novel, different, exotic, unorthodox, odd, peculiar, curious, uncharacteristic, anomalous, out of the ordinary. ❸ *investors unfamiliar with the stock market* UNACQUAINTED, unused, unaccustomed, unconversant, inexperienced, uninformed, unenlightened, ignorant, new to, a stranger to.

unfashionable ▸ adjective OUT OF FASHION, outdated, old-fashioned, outmoded, out of style, dated, unstylish, passé, démodé; *informal* out, square, out of the ark.

unfasten ▸ verb UNDO, open, disconnect, remove, untie, unbutton, unzip, loose, loosen, free, unlock, unbolt.

unfathomable ▸ adjective ❶ *dark unfathomable eyes* INSCRUTABLE, incomprehensible, enigmatic, indecipherable, obscure, esoteric, mysterious, mystifying, deep, profound. ❷ *unfathomable water* DEEP, immeasurable, unfathomed, unplumbed, bottomless.
– OPPOSITES penetrable.

unfavourable ▸ adjective ❶ *unfavourable comment* ADVERSE, critical, hostile, inimical, unfriendly, unsympathetic, negative; discouraging, disapproving, uncomplimentary, unflattering. ❷ *the unfavourable economic climate* DISADVANTAGEOUS, adverse, inauspicious, unpropitious, gloomy; unsuitable, inappropriate, inopportune.
– OPPOSITES positive.

unfeeling ▸ adjective UNCARING, unsympathetic, unemotional, uncharitable; heartless, hard-hearted, hard, harsh, austere, cold, cold-hearted.
– OPPOSITES compassionate.

unfeigned ▸ adjective SINCERE, genuine, real, true, honest, unaffected, unforced, heartfelt, wholehearted.
– OPPOSITES insincere.

unfettered ▸ adjective UNRESTRAINED, unrestricted, unconstrained, free, unbridled, unchecked, uncontrolled.
– OPPOSITES restricted.

unfinished ▸ adjective ❶ *an unfinished essay* INCOMPLETE, uncompleted; partial, undone, half-done; imperfect, unpolished, unrefined, sketchy, fragmentary, rough. ❷ *the door can be supplied unfinished* UNPAINTED, unvarnished, untreated.
– OPPOSITES complete.

unfit ▸ adjective ❶ *the film is unfit for children | unfit for duty* UNSUITABLE, unsuited, inappropriate, unequipped, inadequate, not designed; incapable of, unable to do something, not up to, not equal to; *informal* not cut out for, not up to scratch. ❷ *I am unfit* UNHEALTHY, out of condition/shape, in poor condition/shape.
– OPPOSITES suitable.

unflagging ▸ adjective TIRELESS, persistent, dogged, tenacious, determined, resolute, staunch, single-minded, unrelenting, unfaltering, unfailing.
– OPPOSITES inconstant.

unflappable ▸ adjective (*informal*) IMPERTURBABLE, unexcitable, cool, calm, {cool, calm, and collected}, self-controlled, cool-headed, level-headed; *informal* laid-back.
– OPPOSITES excitable.

unflattering ▶ adjective ❶ *an unflattering review* UNFAVOURABLE, uncomplimentary, harsh, unsympathetic, critical, hostile, scathing. ❷ *an unflattering dress* UNATTRACTIVE, unbecoming, unsightly, ugly, plain, ill-fitting.
– OPPOSITES complimentary, becoming.

unflinching ▶ adjective RESOLUTE, determined, single-minded, dogged, resolved, firm, committed, steady, unwavering, unflagging, unswerving, unfaltering, untiring, undaunted, fearless.

unfold ▶ verb ❶ *May unfolded the map* OPEN OUT, spread out, flatten, straighten out, unroll. ❷ *she unfolded her tale to Joanna* NARRATE, relate, recount, tell, reveal, disclose, divulge, communicate, report, recite, give an account of. ❸ *I watched the events unfold* DEVELOP, evolve, happen, take place, occur, transpire, progress.

unforeseen ▶ adjective UNPREDICTED, unexpected, unanticipated, unplanned, unlooked for, not bargained for.
– OPPOSITES expected.

unforgettable ▶ adjective MEMORABLE, not/never to be forgotten, haunting, catchy; striking, impressive, outstanding, extraordinary, exceptional.
– OPPOSITES unexceptional.

unforgivable ▶ adjective INEXCUSABLE, unpardonable, unjustifiable, indefensible, inexpiable, irremissible.
– OPPOSITES venial.

unfortunate ▶ adjective ❶ *unfortunate people* UNLUCKY, hapless, out of luck, luckless, wretched, miserable, forlorn, poor, pitiful; *informal* down on one's luck. ❷ *an unfortunate start to our holiday* ADVERSE, disadvantageous, unfavourable, unlucky, unwelcome, unpromising, inauspicious, unpropitious; *formal* grievous. ❸ *an unfortunate remark* REGRETTABLE, inappropriate, unsuitable, infelicitous, tactless, injudicious.
– OPPOSITES lucky, auspicious.

unfortunately ▶ adverb UNLUCKILY, sadly, regrettably, unhappily, alas, sad to say; *informal* worse luck.

unfounded ▶ adjective GROUNDLESS, baseless, unsubstantiated, unproven, unsupported, uncorroborated, unconfirmed, unverified, unattested, without basis, without foundation, speculative, conjectural.
– OPPOSITES proven.

unfriendly ▶ adjective ❶ *an unfriendly look* HOSTILE, disagreeable, antagonistic, aggressive; ill-natured, unpleasant, surly, sour, unamicable, uncongenial; inhospitable, unneighbourly, unwelcoming, unkind, unsympathetic; unsociable, antisocial; aloof, cold, cool, frosty, distant, unapproachable; *informal* stand-offish, starchy. ❷ *unfriendly terrain* UNFAVOURABLE, disadvantageous, unpropitious, inauspicious, hostile.
– OPPOSITES amiable, favourable.

ungainly ▶ adjective AWKWARD, clumsy, ungraceful, graceless, inelegant, gawky, maladroit, gauche, uncoordinated; *archaic* lubberly.
– OPPOSITES graceful.

ungodly ▶ adjective ❶ *ungodly behaviour* UNHOLY, godless, irreligious, impious, blasphemous, sacrilegious; immoral, corrupt, depraved, sinful, wicked, evil, iniquitous. ❷ (*informal*) *he called at an ungodly hour* UNREASONABLE, unsocial, antisocial; *informal* unearthly.

ungovernable ▶ adjective UNCONTROLLABLE, unmanageable, anarchic, intractable; unruly, disorderly, rebellious, riotous, wild, mutinous, undisciplined.

ungracious ▶ adjective RUDE, impolite, uncivil, discourteous, ill-mannered, bad-mannered, uncouth, disrespectful, insolent, impertinent, offhand.
– OPPOSITES polite.

ungrateful ▶ adjective UNAPPRECIATIVE, unthankful, ungracious.
– OPPOSITES thankful.

unguarded ▶ adjective ❶ *an unguarded frontier* UNDEFENDED, unprotected, unfortified; vulnerable, insecure, open to attack. ❷ *an unguarded remark* CARELESS, ill-considered, incautious, thoughtless, rash, foolhardy, foolish, indiscreet, imprudent, injudicious, ill-judged, insensitive; *poetic/literary* temerarious. ❸ *an unguarded moment* UNWARY, inattentive, off guard, distracted, absent-minded.

unhappiness ▶ noun SADNESS, sorrow, dejection, depression, misery, cheerlessness, downheartedness, despondency, despair, desolation, wretchedness, glumness, gloom, gloominess, dolefulness; melancholy, low spirits, mournfulness, woe, heartache, distress, chagrin, grief, pain; *informal* the blues.

unhappy ▶ adjective ❶ *an unhappy childhood* SAD, miserable, sorrowful, dejected, despondent, disconsolate, morose, broken-hearted, heartbroken, down, downcast, dispirited, downhearted, depressed, melancholy, mournful, gloomy, glum, despairing, doleful, forlorn, woebegone, woeful, long-faced, joyless, cheerless; *informal* down in the mouth/dumps, fed up, blue. ❷ *in the unhappy event of litigation* UNFORTUNATE, unlucky, luckless; ill-starred, ill-fated, doomed; *informal* jinxed; *poetic/literary* star-crossed. ❸ *I was unhappy with the service I received* DISSATISFIED, displeased, discontented, disappointed, disgruntled. ❹ *'disorganized capitalism' seems an unhappy term* INAPPROPRIATE, unsuitable, inapt, unfortunate; regrettable, ill-chosen.
– OPPOSITES cheerful.

unharmed ▶ adjective ❶ *they released the hostage unharmed* UNINJURED, unhurt, unscathed, safe (and sound), alive and well, in one piece,

without a scratch. ❷ *the tomb was unharmed* UNDAMAGED, unbroken, unmarred, unspoiled, unsullied, unmarked; sound, intact, perfect, unblemished, pristine.
– OPPOSITES injured, damaged.

unhealthy ▶ adjective ❶ *an unhealthy lifestyle* HARMFUL, detrimental, destructive, injurious, damaging, deleterious; malign, noxious, poisonous, insalubrious, baleful. ❷ *an unhealthy pallor* ILL-LOOKING, ill, unwell, in poor health, ailing, sick, sickly, poorly, indisposed, weak, frail, delicate, infirm, washed out, run down, peaky. ❸ *an unhealthy obsession with drugs* UNWHOLESOME, morbid, macabre, twisted, abnormal, warped, depraved, unnatural; *informal* sick.

unheard of ▶ adjective ❶ *such behaviour was unheard of* UNPRECEDENTED, exceptional, extraordinary, out of the ordinary, unthought of, undreamed of, unbelievable, inconceivable, unimaginable, unthinkable; *formal* unexampled. ❷ *a game unheard of in the UK* UNKNOWN, unfamiliar, new.
– OPPOSITES common, well known.

unheeded ▶ adjective DISREGARDED, ignored, neglected, overlooked, unnoted, unrecognized.

unhinged ▶ adjective DERANGED, demented, unbalanced, out of one's mind, crazed, mad, insane, disturbed; *informal* crazy, mental, bonkers, batty, loopy, bananas, touched.
– OPPOSITES sane.

unholy ▶ adjective ❶ *a grin of unholy amusement* UNGODLY, godless, irreligious, impious, blasphemous, sacrilegious, profane, irreverent; wicked, evil, immoral, corrupt, depraved, sinful. ❷ (*informal*) *an unholy row* SHOCKING, dreadful, outrageous, appalling, terrible, horrendous, frightful. ❸ *an unholy alliance* UNNATURAL, unusual, improbable, made in Hell.

unhoped for ▶ adjective UNEXPECTED, unanticipated, unforeseen, unlooked-for, undreamed of, out of the blue.
– OPPOSITES expected.

unhurried ▶ adjective LEISURELY, easy, easygoing, relaxed, slow, deliberate, measured, calm.
– OPPOSITES hasty.

unhygienic ▶ adjective INSANITARY, unsanitary, dirty, filthy, contaminated, unhealthy, unwholesome, insalubrious, polluted, foul.
– OPPOSITES sanitary.

unidentified ▶ adjective UNKNOWN, unnamed, anonymous, incognito, nameless, unfamiliar, strange.
– OPPOSITES known.

unification ▶ noun UNION, merger, fusion, fusing, amalgamation, coalition, combination, confederation, federation, synthesis, joining.

uniform ▶ adjective ❶ *a uniform temperature* CONSTANT, consistent, steady, invariable, unvarying, unfluctuating, unchanging, stable, static, regular, fixed, even, equal. ❷ *pieces of uniform size* IDENTICAL, matching, similar, equal; same, like, homogeneous, consistent.
– OPPOSITES variable.
▶ noun *a soldier in uniform* COSTUME, livery, regalia, suit, ensemble, outfit; regimentals, colours; *informal* get-up, rig, gear; *archaic* habit.

uniformity ▶ noun ❶ *uniformity in tax law* CONSTANCY, consistency, conformity, invariability, stability, regularity, evenness, homogeneity, homogeneousness, equality. ❷ *a dull uniformity* MONOTONY, tedium, tediousness, dullness, dreariness, flatness, sameness.
– OPPOSITES variation, variety.

unify ▶ verb UNITE, bring together, join (together), merge, fuse, amalgamate, coalesce, combine, blend, mix, bind, consolidate.
– OPPOSITES separate.

unimaginable ▶ adjective UNTHINKABLE, inconceivable, incredible, unbelievable, unheard of, unthought of, untold, undreamed of, beyond one's wildest dreams.

unimaginative ▶ adjective UNINSPIRED, uninventive, unoriginal, uncreative, commonplace, pedestrian, mundane, ordinary, routine, humdrum, workaday, run-of-the-mill, hackneyed, trite.

unimpeachable ▶ adjective TRUSTWORTHY, reliable, dependable, above suspicion, irreproachable.
– OPPOSITES unreliable.

unimpeded ▶ adjective UNRESTRICTED, unhindered, unblocked, unhampered, free, clear.

unimportant ▶ adjective INSIGNIFICANT, inconsequential, trivial, minor, trifling, of little/no importance, of little/no consequence, of no account, irrelevant, peripheral, extraneous, petty, paltry; *informal* piddling; *formal* of no moment.

uninhabited ▶ adjective ❶ *much of this land was uninhabited* UNPOPULATED, unpeopled, unsettled. ❷ *an uninhabited hut* VACANT, empty, unoccupied, untenanted, to let.

uninhibited ▶ adjective ❶ *uninhibited dancing* UNRESTRAINED, unrepressed, abandoned, wild, reckless; unrestricted, uncontrolled, unchecked, intemperate, wanton. ❷ *I'm pretty uninhibited* UNRESERVED, unrepressed, liberated, unselfconscious, free and easy, relaxed, informal, open, outgoing, extrovert, outspoken, frank, forthright; *informal* upfront.
– OPPOSITES repressed.

uninspired ▶ adjective UNIMAGINATIVE, uninventive, pedestrian, mundane, unoriginal, commonplace, ordinary, routine, humdrum, run-of-the-mill, hackneyed, trite; spiritless, passionless.

uninspiring ▶ adjective BORING, dull, dreary, unexciting, unstimulating; dry, colourless, bland, lacklustre, tedious, humdrum, run-of-the-mill.

unintelligent ▶ adjective STUPID, ignorant, dense, brainless, mindless, foolish, dull-witted, slow, simple-minded, vacuous, vapid, idiotic, obtuse; *informal* thick, dim, dumb, dopey, half-witted, dozy.

unintelligible ▶ adjective ❶ *unintelligible sounds* INCOMPREHENSIBLE, indiscernible, mumbled, indistinct, unclear, slurred, inarticulate, incoherent, garbled. ❷ *unintelligible graffiti* ILLEGIBLE, indecipherable, unreadable.

unintentional ▶ adjective UNINTENDED, accidental, inadvertent, involuntary, unwitting, unthinking, unpremeditated, unconscious.
– OPPOSITES deliberate.

uninterested ▶ adjective INDIFFERENT, unconcerned, uninvolved, apathetic, lukewarm, unenthusiastic.

uninteresting ▶ adjective UNEXCITING, boring, dull, tiresome, wearisome, tedious, dreary, lifeless, humdrum, colourless, bland, insipid, banal, dry, pedestrian; *informal* samey.
– OPPOSITES exciting.

uninterrupted ▶ adjective UNBROKEN, continuous, continual, undisturbed, untroubled.
– OPPOSITES intermittent.

uninvited ▶ adjective ❶ *an uninvited guest* UNASKED, unexpected; unwelcome, unwanted. ❷ *uninvited suggestions* UNSOLICITED, unrequested, unsought.

uninviting ▶ adjective UNAPPEALING, unattractive, unappetizing, off-putting; bleak, cheerless, dreary, dismal, depressing, grim, inhospitable.
– OPPOSITES tempting.

union ▶ noun ❶ *the union of art and nature* UNIFICATION, uniting, joining, merging, merger, fusion, fusing, amalgamating, amalgamation, coalition, combination, synthesis, blend, blending, mingling. ❷ *the crowd moved in union* UNITY, accord, unison, harmony, agreement, concurrence; *formal* concord. ❸ *his daughter's union* MARRIAGE, wedding, alliance; coupling, intercourse, copulation. ❹ *representation by a union* ASSOCIATION, trade union, league, guild, confederation, federation.
– OPPOSITES separation, parting.

unique ▶ adjective ❶ *each site is unique* DISTINCTIVE, individual, special, idiosyncratic; single, sole, lone, unrepeated, unrepeatable, solitary, exclusive, rare, uncommon, unusual; *informal* one-off. ❷ *a unique insight into history* REMARKABLE, special, singular, noteworthy, notable, extraordinary; unequalled, unparalleled, unmatched, unsurpassed, incomparable; *formal* unexampled. ❸ *species unique to the island* PECULIAR, specific.

unison
■ **in unison** ❶ *they lifted their arms in unison* SIMULTANEOUSLY, at (one and) the same time, (all) at once, (all) together. ❷ *we are in complete unison* IN AGREEMENT, in accord, in harmony, as one; *formal* in concord.

unit ▶ noun ❶ *the family is the fundamental unit of society* COMPONENT, element, constituent, subdivision. ❷ *a unit of currency* QUANTITY, measure, denomination. ❸ *a guerrilla unit* DETACHMENT, contingent, division, company, squadron, corps, regiment, brigade, platoon, battalion; cell, faction.

unite ▶ verb ❶ *uniting the nation* UNIFY, join, link, connect, combine, amalgamate, fuse, weld, bond, bring together, knit together. ❷ *environmentalists and activists united* JOIN TOGETHER, join forces, combine, band together, ally, cooperate, collaborate, work together, pull together, team up. ❸ *he sought to unite comfort with elegance* MERGE, mix, blend, mingle, combine; *poetic/literary* commingle.
– OPPOSITES divide.

united ▶ adjective ❶ *a united Germany* UNIFIED, integrated, amalgamated, joined, merged; federal, confederate. ❷ *a united response* COMMON, shared, joint, combined, communal, cooperative, collective, collaborative, concerted. ❸ *they were united in their views* IN AGREEMENT, agreed, in unison, of the same opinion, like-minded, as one, in accord, in harmony, in unity.

United States of America ▶ noun AMERICA; *informal* the States, the US of A, Uncle Sam; *poetic/literary* Columbia.

unity ▶ noun ❶ *European unity* UNION, unification, integration, amalgamation; coalition, federation, confederation. ❷ *unity between opposing factions* HARMONY, accord, cooperation, collaboration, agreement, consensus, solidarity; *formal* concord. ❸ *the organic unity of the universe* ONENESS, singleness, wholeness, uniformity, homogeneity.
– OPPOSITES division, discord.

universal ▶ adjective GENERAL, ubiquitous, comprehensive, common, omnipresent, all-inclusive; global, worldwide, international, widespread.

universally ▶ adverb INVARIABLY, always, without exception, in all cases; everywhere, worldwide, globally, internationally; widely, commonly, generally.

universe ▶ noun ❶ *the physical universe* COSMOS, macrocosm, totality; infinity, all existence. ❷ *the universe of computer hardware* PROVINCE, world, sphere, preserve, domain.
– RELATED TERMS cosmic.

university ▶ noun COLLEGE, academy, institute; *N. Amer.* school; *historical* polytechnic.

unjust ▶ adjective ❶ *the attack was unjust* BIASED, prejudiced, unfair, inequitable, discrimin-

atory, partisan, partial, one-sided. ❷ *an unjust law* WRONGFUL, unfair, undeserved, unmerited, unwarranted, uncalled for, unreasonable, unjustifiable, indefensible.
– OPPOSITES fair.

unjustifiable ▶ adjective ❶ *an unjustifiable extravagance* INDEFENSIBLE, inexcusable, unforgivable, unpardonable, uncalled for, without justification, unwarrantable; excessive, immoderate. ❷ *an unjustifiable slur on his character* GROUNDLESS, unfounded, baseless, unsubstantiated, unconfirmed, uncorroborated.
– OPPOSITES reasonable.

unkempt ▶ adjective UNTIDY, messy, scruffy, disordered, dishevelled, disarranged, rumpled, wind-blown, ungroomed, bedraggled, in a mess, messed up; tousled, uncombed; *N. Amer. informal* mussed up.
– OPPOSITES tidy.

unkind ▶ adjective ❶ *everyone was being unkind to him* UNCHARITABLE, unpleasant, disagreeable, nasty, mean, mean-spirited, cruel, vicious, spiteful, malicious, callous, unsympathetic, unfeeling, uncaring, hurtful, ill-natured, hard-hearted, cold-hearted; unfriendly, uncivil, inconsiderate, insensitive, hostile; *informal* bitchy, catty; *Brit. informal* beastly. ❷ *unkind weather* INCLEMENT, intemperate, rough, severe, filthy.

unkindness ▶ noun NASTINESS, unpleasantness, disagreeableness, cruelty, malice, meanness, mean-spiritedness, viciousness, callousness, hard-heartedness, cold-heartedness; unfriendliness, inconsiderateness, hostility; *informal* bitchiness, cattiness.

unknown ▶ adjective ❶ *the outcome was unknown* UNDISCLOSED, unrevealed, secret; undetermined, undecided, unresolved, unsettled, unsure, unascertained. ❷ *unknown country* UNEXPLORED, uncharted, unmapped, untravelled, undiscovered. ❸ *persons unknown* UNIDENTIFIED, unnamed, nameless, anonymous. ❹ *firearms were unknown to the Indians* UNFAMILIAR, unheard of, new, novel, strange. ❺ *unknown artists* OBSCURE, unheard of, unsung, minor, insignificant, unimportant, undistinguished.
– OPPOSITES familiar.

unlawful ▶ adjective ILLEGAL, illicit, illegitimate, against the law; criminal, felonious; prohibited, banned, outlawed, proscribed, forbidden.
– OPPOSITES legal.

unleash ▶ verb LET LOOSE, release, (set) free, unloose, untie, untether, unchain.

unlettered ▶ adjective ILLITERATE, uneducated, poorly educated, unschooled, unlearned, ignorant.
– OPPOSITES educated.

unlike ▶ preposition ❶ *England is totally unlike Jamaica* DIFFERENT FROM, unalike, dissimilar to. ❷ *unlike Linda, Chrissy was a bit of a radical* IN CONTRAST TO, as opposed to.
– OPPOSITES similar too.
▶ adjective *a meeting of unlike minds* DISSIMILAR, unalike, disparate, contrasting, antithetical, different, diverse, heterogeneous, divergent, at variance, varying, at odds; *informal* like chalk and cheese.

unlikely ▶ adjective ❶ *it is unlikely they will ever recover* IMPROBABLE, doubtful, dubious. ❷ *an unlikely story* IMPLAUSIBLE, improbable, questionable, unconvincing, far-fetched, unrealistic, incredible, unbelievable, inconceivable, unimaginable; *informal* tall, cock and bull.
– OPPOSITES probable, believable.

unlimited ▶ adjective ❶ *unlimited supplies of water* INEXHAUSTIBLE, limitless, illimitable, boundless, immeasurable, incalculable, untold, infinite, endless, never-ending. ❷ *unlimited travel* UNRESTRICTED, unconstrained, unrestrained, unchecked, unbridled, uncurbed. ❸ *unlimited power* TOTAL, unqualified, unconditional, unrestricted, absolute, supreme.
– OPPOSITES finite, restricted.

unload ▶ verb ❶ *we unloaded the van* UNPACK, empty; *archaic* unlade. ❷ *they unloaded the cases from the lorry* REMOVE, offload, discharge. ❸ *the state unloaded its 25 per cent stake* SELL, discard, jettison, offload, get rid of, dispose of; palm something off on someone, foist something on someone, fob something off on someone; *informal* dump, junk, get shot/shut of.

unlock ▶ verb UNBOLT, unlatch, unbar, unfasten, open.

unlooked-for ▶ adjective UNEXPECTED, unforeseen, unanticipated, unsought, unpredicted, undreamed of, fortuitous, chance, serendipitous.

unloved ▶ adjective UNCARED-FOR, unwanted, friendless, unvalued; rejected, unwelcome, shunned, spurned, neglected, abandoned.

unlucky ▶ adjective ❶ *he was unlucky not to score* UNFORTUNATE, luckless, out of luck, hapless, ill-fated, ill-starred, unhappy; *informal* down on one's luck; *poetic/literary* star-crossed. ❷ *an unlucky number* UNFAVOURABLE, inauspicious, unpropitious, ominous, cursed, ill-fated, ill-omened, disadvantageous, unfortunate.
– OPPOSITES fortunate, favourable.

unmanageable ▶ adjective ❶ *the huge house was unmanageable* TROUBLESOME, awkward, inconvenient; cumbersome, bulky, unwieldy. ❷ *his behaviour was becoming unmanageable* UNCONTROLLABLE, ungovernable, unruly, disorderly, out of hand, difficult, disruptive, undisciplined, wayward; *informal* stroppy; *archaic* contumacious.

unmanly ▶ adjective EFFEMINATE, effete, unmasculine; weak, soft, timid, timorous, limp-wristed; *informal* sissy, wimpish, wimpy.
– OPPOSITES virile.

unmannerly ▶ adjective RUDE, impolite, uncivil, discourteous, bad-mannered, ill-man-

nered, disrespectful, impertinent, impudent, insolent; uncouth, boorish, oafish, loutish, ill-bred, coarse.
– OPPOSITES polite.

unmarried ▶ adjective UNWED(DED), single; spinster, bachelor; unattached, available, eligible, free.

unmatched ▶ adjective ❶ *a talent for publicity unmatched by any other politician* UNEQUALLED, unrivalled, unparalleled, unsurpassed. ❷ *unmatched clarity and balance* PEERLESS, matchless, without equal, without parallel, incomparable, inimitable, superlative, second to none, in a class of its own.

unmentionable ▶ adjective TABOO, censored, forbidden, banned, proscribed, prohibited, not to be spoken of, ineffable, unspeakable, unutterable, unprintable, off limits; *informal* no go.

unmerciful ▶ adjective RUTHLESS, cruel, harsh, merciless, pitiless, cold-blooded, hard-hearted, callous, brutal, severe, unforgiving, inhumane, inhuman, heartless, unsympathetic, unfeeling.

unmistakable ▶ adjective DISTINCTIVE, distinct, telltale, indisputable, indubitable, undoubted; plain, clear, definite, obvious, evident, self-evident, manifest, patent, unambiguous, unequivocal, pronounced, as plain as the nose on your face.

unmitigated ▶ adjective ABSOLUTE, unqualified, categorical, complete, total, downright, outright, utter, out-and-out, undiluted, unequivocal, veritable, perfect, consummate, pure, sheer.

unmoved ▶ adjective ❶ *he was totally unmoved by her outburst* UNAFFECTED, untouched, unimpressed, undismayed, unworried; aloof, cool, cold, dry-eyed; unconcerned, uncaring, indifferent, impassive, unemotional, stoical, phlegmatic, equable; impervious (to), oblivious (to), heedless (of), deaf to. ❷ *he remained unmoved on the crucial issues* STEADFAST, firm, unwavering, unswerving, resolute, decided, resolved, inflexible, unbending, implacable, adamant.

unnatural ▶ adjective ❶ *the life of a battery hen is completely unnatural* ABNORMAL, unusual, uncommon, extraordinary, strange, freak, odd, peculiar, unorthodox, exceptional, irregular, untypical. ❷ *a flash of unnatural colour* ARTIFICIAL, man-made, synthetic, manufactured. ❸ *unnatural vice* PERVERTED, warped, twisted, deviant, depraved, degenerate; *informal* kinky, pervy, sick. ❹ *her voice sounded unnatural* AFFECTED, artificial, stilted, forced, laboured, strained, false, fake, insincere; *informal* put on, phoney. ❺ *they condemned her as an unnatural woman* UNCARING, unfeeling, heartless, cold-blooded, hard-hearted, callous, cruel, inhumane.
– OPPOSITES normal, genuine.

unnecessary ▶ adjective UNNEEDED, inessential, not required, uncalled for, useless, unwarranted, unwanted, undesired, dispensable, unimportant, optional, extraneous, expendable, disposable, redundant, pointless, purposeless.
– OPPOSITES essential.

unnerve ▶ verb DEMORALIZE, discourage, dishearten, dispirit, daunt, alarm, frighten, dismay, disconcert, discompose, perturb, upset, discomfit, take aback, unsettle, disquiet, fluster, agitate, shake, ruffle, throw off balance; *informal* rattle, faze, shake up; *Brit. informal* put the wind up; *N. Amer. informal* discombobulate.
– OPPOSITES hearten.

unobtrusive ▶ adjective ❶ *she was unobtrusive and shy* SELF-EFFACING, retiring, unassuming, quiet; shy, bashful, timid, timorous, reserved, withdrawn, introvert(ed), unforthcoming, unassertive. ❷ *unobtrusive service* INCONSPICUOUS, unnoticeable, low-key, discreet, circumspect, understated, unostentatious.
– OPPOSITES extrovert, conspicuous.

unoccupied ▶ adjective ❶ *an unoccupied house* VACANT, empty, uninhabited; free, available, to let. ❷ *an unoccupied territory* UNINHABITED, unpopulated, unpeopled, unsettled. ❸ *many young people were unoccupied* AT LEISURE, idle, free, with time on one's hands, at a loose end.
– OPPOSITES inhabited, populated, busy.

unofficial ▶ adjective ❶ *unofficial figures* UNAUTHENTICATED, unconfirmed, uncorroborated, unsubstantiated, off the record. ❷ *an unofficial committee* INFORMAL, casual; unauthorized, unsanctioned, unaccredited.
– OPPOSITES confirmed, formal.

unorthodox ▶ adjective ❶ *unorthodox views on management* UNCONVENTIONAL, unusual, radical, nonconformist, avant-garde, eccentric; *informal* off the wall, way out, offbeat. ❷ *unorthodox religious views* HETERODOX, heretical, nonconformist, dissenting.
– OPPOSITES conventional.

unpaid ▶ adjective ❶ *unpaid bills* UNSETTLED, outstanding, due, overdue, owing, owed, payable, undischarged; *N. Amer.* delinquent, past due. ❷ *unpaid charity work* VOLUNTARY, volunteer, honorary, unremunerative, unsalaried, pro bono (publico).

unpalatable ▶ adjective ❶ *unpalatable food* UNAPPETIZING, unappealing, unsavoury, inedible, uneatable; disgusting, revolting, nauseating, tasteless, flavourless. ❷ *the unpalatable truth* DISAGREEABLE, unpleasant, regrettable, unwelcome, lamentable, dreadful, hateful.
– OPPOSITES tasty.

unparalleled ▶ adjective EXCEPTIONAL, unique, singular, rare, unequalled, unprecedented, without parallel, without equal; matchless, peerless, unrivalled, unsurpassed, unexcelled, incomparable, second to none; *formal* unexampled.

unperturbed ▶ adjective UNTROUBLED, undisturbed, unworried, unconcerned, unmoved, unflustered, unruffled, undismayed; calm, composed, cool, collected, unemotional, self-possessed, self-assured, level-headed, unfazed, laid-back.

unpleasant ▶ adjective ❶ *a very unpleasant situation* DISAGREEABLE, irksome, troublesome, annoying, irritating, vexatious, displeasing, distressing, nasty, horrible, terrible, awful, dreadful, hateful, miserable, invidious, objectionable, offensive, obnoxious, repugnant, repulsive, repellent, revolting, disgusting, distasteful, nauseating, unsavoury. ❷ *an unpleasant man* UNLIKABLE, unlovable, disagreeable; unfriendly, rude, impolite, obnoxious, nasty, spiteful, mean, mean-spirited; insufferable, unbearable, annoying, irritating. ❸ *an unpleasant taste* UNAPPETIZING, unpalatable, unsavoury, unappealing, bitter, sour, rancid; disgusting, revolting, nauseating, sickening.
–OPPOSITES agreeable, likable.

unpolished ▶ adjective ❶ *unpolished wood* UNVARNISHED, unfinished, untreated, natural. ❷ *his unpolished ways* UNSOPHISTICATED, unrefined, uncultured, uncultivated, coarse, vulgar, crude, rough (and ready), awkward, clumsy, gauche. ❸ *an unpolished performance* SLIPSHOD, rough, crude, uneven.
–OPPOSITES varnished, sophisticated.

unpopular ▶ adjective DISLIKED, friendless, unliked, unloved; unwelcome, avoided, ignored, rejected, shunned, spurned, cold-shouldered.

unprecedented ▶ adjective UNPARALLELED, unequalled, unmatched, unrivalled, without parallel, without equal, out of the ordinary, unusual, exceptional, singular, remarkable, unique; unheard of, unknown, new, groundbreaking, revolutionary, pioneering; *formal* unexampled.

unpredictable ▶ adjective ❶ *unpredictable results* UNFORESEEABLE, uncertain, unsure, doubtful, dubious, in the balance, up in the air, arbitrary. ❷ *unpredictable behaviour* ERRATIC, moody, volatile, unstable, capricious, temperamental, mercurial, changeable, variable.

unprejudiced ▶ adjective ❶ *unprejudiced observation* OBJECTIVE, impartial, unbiased, neutral, non-partisan, detached, disinterested. ❷ *unprejudiced attitudes* UNBIASED, tolerant, non-discriminatory, liberal, broad-minded, unbigoted.
–OPPOSITES partisan, intolerant.

unpremeditated ▶ adjective UNPLANNED, spontaneous, unprepared, impromptu, spur-of-the-moment, unrehearsed; *informal* off-the-cuff.
–OPPOSITES planned.

unprepared ▶ adjective ❶ *we were unprepared for the new VAT regime* UNREADY, off (one's) guard, surprised, taken aback; *informal* caught napping, caught on the hop. ❷ *they are unprepared to support the reforms* UNWILLING, disinclined, loath, reluctant, resistant, opposed.
–OPPOSITES ready, willing.

unpretentious ▶ adjective ❶ *he was thoroughly unpretentious* UNAFFECTED, modest, unassuming, without airs, natural, straightforward, open, honest, sincere, frank. ❷ *an unpretentious hotel* SIMPLE, plain, modest, humble, unostentatious, homely, unsophisticated.

unprincipled ▶ adjective IMMORAL, unethical, unscrupulous, dishonourable, dishonest, deceitful, devious, corrupt, crooked, wicked, evil, villainous, shameless, base, low.
–OPPOSITES ethical.

unproductive ▶ adjective ❶ *unproductive soil* STERILE, barren, infertile, unfruitful, poor. ❷ *unproductive meetings* FRUITLESS, futile, vain, idle, useless, worthless, valueless, pointless, ineffective, ineffectual, unprofitable, unrewarding.
–OPPOSITES fruitful.

unprofessional ▶ adjective ❶ *unprofessional conduct* IMPROPER, unethical, unprincipled, unscrupulous, dishonourable, disreputable, unseemly, unbecoming, indecorous; *informal* shady, crooked. ❷ *he accused the detectives of being unprofessional* AMATEURISH, amateur, unskilled, unskilful, inexpert, unqualified, inexperienced, incompetent, second-rate, inefficient.

unpromising ▶ adjective INAUSPICIOUS, unfavourable, unpropitious, discouraging, disheartening, gloomy, bleak, black, portentous, ominous, ill-omened.
–OPPOSITES auspicious.

unqualified ▶ adjective ❶ *an unqualified accountant* UNCERTIFICATED, unlicensed, untrained, inexperienced. ❷ *those unqualified to look after children* UNSUITABLE, unfit, ineligible, incompetent, unable, incapable. ❸ *unqualified support* UNCONDITIONAL, unreserved, unlimited, without reservations, categorical, unequivocal, unambiguous, wholehearted; complete, absolute, downright, undivided, total, utter.

unquestionable ▶ adjective INDUBITABLE, undoubted, beyond question, beyond doubt, indisputable, undeniable, irrefutable, incontestable, incontrovertible, unequivocal; certain, sure, definite, self-evident, evident, manifest, obvious, apparent, patent.

unravel ▶ verb ❶ *he unravelled the strands* UNTANGLE, disentangle, separate out, unwind, untwist. ❷ *detectives are trying to unravel the mystery* SOLVE, resolve, clear up, puzzle out, get to the bottom of, explain, clarify, make head or tail of; *informal* figure out, suss (out). ❸ *society is starting to unravel* FALL APART, fail, collapse, go wrong.
–OPPOSITES entangle.

unreadable ▶ adjective ❶ *unreadable writing*

ILLEGIBLE, hard to read, indecipherable, unintelligible, scrawled, crabbed. ❷ *heavy, unreadable novels* DULL, tedious, boring, uninteresting, dry, wearisome, difficult, heavy. ❸ *Nathan's expression was unreadable* INSCRUTABLE, enigmatic, impenetrable, cryptic, mysterious, deadpan; *informal* poker-faced.
– OPPOSITES legible, accessible.

unreal ▶ **adjective** IMAGINARY, fictitious, pretend, make-believe, made-up, dreamed-up, mock, false, illusory, mythical, fanciful; hypothetical, theoretical; *informal* phoney.

unrealistic ▶ **adjective** ❶ *it is unrealistic to expect changes overnight* IMPRACTICAL, impracticable, unfeasible, non-viable; unreasonable, irrational, illogical, senseless, silly, foolish, fanciful, idealistic, romantic, starry-eyed. ❷ *unrealistic images* UNLIFELIKE, non-realistic, unnatural, non-representational, abstract.
– OPPOSITES pragmatic, lifelike.

unreasonable ▶ **adjective** ❶ *an unreasonable woman* UNCOOPERATIVE, unhelpful, disobliging, unaccommodating, awkward, contrary, difficult; obstinate, obdurate, wilful, headstrong, pig-headed, intractable, intransigent, inflexible; irrational, illogical, prejudiced, intolerant. ❷ *unreasonable demands* UNACCEPTABLE, preposterous, outrageous; excessive, immoderate, disproportionate, undue, inordinate, intolerable, unjustified, unwarranted, uncalled for.

unrecognizable ▶ **adjective** UNIDENTIFIABLE, unknowable; disguised.

unrefined ▶ **adjective** ❶ *unrefined clay* UNPROCESSED, untreated, crude, raw, natural, unprepared, unfinished. ❷ *unrefined men* UNCULTURED, uncultivated, uncivilized, uneducated, unsophisticated; boorish, oafish, loutish, coarse, vulgar, rude, uncouth.
– OPPOSITES processed.

unrelated ▶ **adjective** ❶ *unrelated incidents* SEPARATE, unconnected, independent, unassociated, distinct, discrete, disparate. ❷ *a reason unrelated to my work* IRRELEVANT, immaterial, inapplicable, unconcerned, off the subject, beside the point, not pertinent, not germane.

unrelenting ▶ **adjective** ❶ *the unrelenting heat* CONTINUAL, constant, continuous, relentless, unremitting, unabating, unrelieved, incessant, unceasing, endless, unending, persistent. ❷ *an unrelenting opponent* IMPLACABLE, inflexible, uncompromising, unyielding, unbending, relentless, determined, dogged, tireless, unflagging, unshakeable, unswerving, unwavering.
– OPPOSITES intermittent.

unreliable ▶ **adjective** ❶ *unreliable volunteers* UNDEPENDABLE, untrustworthy, irresponsible, fickle, capricious, erratic, unpredictable, inconstant, faithless. ❷ *an unreliable indicator* QUESTIONABLE, open to doubt, doubtful, dubious, suspect, unsound, tenuous, fallible; risky, chancy, inaccurate; *informal* iffy, dicey.

unremitting ▶ **adjective** RELENTLESS, unrelenting, continual, constant, continuous, unabating, unrelieved, sustained, unceasing, ceaseless, endless, unending, persistent, perpetual, interminable.

unrepentant ▶ **adjective** IMPENITENT, unrepenting, remorseless, unashamed, unapologetic, unabashed.

unreserved ▶ **adjective** ❶ *unreserved support* UNCONDITIONAL, unqualified, without reservations, unlimited, categorical, unequivocal, unambiguous; absolute, complete, thorough, wholehearted, total, utter, undivided. ❷ *an unreserved young man* UNINHIBITED, extrovert, outgoing, unrestrained, open, unconstrained, unselfconscious, outspoken, frank, candid. ❸ *unreserved seats* UNBOOKED, unallocated, unoccupied, free, empty, vacant.
– OPPOSITES qualified, reticent, booked.

unresolved ▶ **adjective** UNDECIDED, unsettled, undetermined, uncertain, open, pending, open to debate/question, doubtful, in doubt, up in the air.
– OPPOSITES decided.

unrest ▶ **noun** DISRUPTION, disturbance, trouble, turmoil, disorder, chaos, anarchy; discord, dissension, dissent, strife, protest, rebellion, uprising, rioting.
– OPPOSITES peace.

unrestrained ▶ **adjective** UNCONTROLLED, unconstrained, unrestricted, unchecked, unbridled, unlimited, unfettered, uninhibited, unbounded, undisciplined.

unrestricted ▶ **adjective** UNLIMITED, open, free, clear, unhindered, unimpeded, unhampered, unchecked, unrestrained, unconstrained, unblocked, unbounded, unconfined, unqualified.
– OPPOSITES limited.

unripe ▶ **adjective** IMMATURE, unready, green, sour.

unrivalled ▶ **adjective** UNEQUALLED, without equal, unparalleled, without parallel, unmatched, unsurpassed, unexcelled, incomparable, beyond compare, inimitable, second to none.

unruffled ▶ **adjective** ❶ *an unruffled voice* CALM, composed, self-controlled, self-possessed, untroubled, unperturbed, at ease, relaxed, serene, cool, {cool, calm, and collected}, cool-headed, unemotional, equanimous, equable, stoical; *informal* unfazed. ❷ *an unruffled sea* TRANQUIL, calm, smooth, still, flat, motionless, placid, waveless, pacific, like a millpond.

unruly ▶ **adjective** DISORDERLY, rowdy, wild, unmanageable, uncontrollable, disobedient, disruptive, undisciplined, wayward, wilful, headstrong, irrepressible, obstreperous, difficult,

intractable, out of hand, recalcitrant; boisterous, lively; *formal* refractory; *archaic* contumacious.
– OPPOSITES disciplined.

unsafe ▶ adjective ❶ *the building was unsafe* DANGEROUS, risky, perilous, hazardous, life-threatening, high-risk, treacherous, insecure, unsound; harmful, injurious, toxic. ❷ *the verdict was unsafe* UNRELIABLE, insecure, unsound, questionable, open to question/doubt, doubtful, dubious, suspect, fallible; *informal* iffy.
– OPPOSITES harmless, secure.

unsaid ▶ adjective UNSPOKEN, unuttered, unstated, unexpressed, unvoiced, untalked-of, suppressed; tacit, implicit, understood, not spelt out, taken as read, inferred, implied.

unsanitary ▶ adjective UNHYGIENIC, insanitary, dirty, filthy, unclean, contaminated, unhealthy, germ-ridden, disease-ridden, infested, insalubrious, polluted.
– OPPOSITES hygienic.

unsatisfactory ▶ adjective DISAPPOINTING, dissatisfying, undesirable, disagreeable, displeasing; inadequate, unacceptable, poor, bad, substandard, weak, mediocre, not good enough, not up to par, defective, deficient, imperfect, inferior; *informal* leaving a lot to be desired, no great shakes, not much cop.

unsavoury ▶ adjective ❶ *unsavoury portions of food* UNPALATABLE, unappetizing, distasteful, disagreeable, unappealing, unattractive; inedible, uneatable, disgusting, revolting, nauseating, sickening, foul, nasty, vile; tasteless, bland, flavourless; *informal* yucky. ❷ *an unsavoury character* DISREPUTABLE, unpleasant, disagreeable, nasty, mean, rough; immoral, degenerate, dishonourable, dishonest, unprincipled, unscrupulous, low, villainous; *informal* shady, crooked.
– OPPOSITES tasty, appetizing.

unscathed ▶ adjective UNHARMED, unhurt, uninjured, undamaged, in one piece, intact, safe (and sound), unmarked, untouched, unscratched.
– OPPOSITES harmed, injured.

unscrupulous ▶ adjective UNPRINCIPLED, unethical, immoral, conscienceless, shameless, reprobate, exploitative, corrupt, dishonest, dishonourable, deceitful, devious, underhand, unsavoury, disreputable, evil, wicked, villainous; *informal* crooked, shady; *dated* dastardly.

unseat ▶ verb ❶ *the horse unseated his rider* DISLODGE, throw, dismount, upset, unhorse. ❷ *an attempt to unseat the party leader* DEPOSE, oust, remove from office, topple, overthrow, bring down, dislodge, supplant, usurp, overturn, eject.

unseemly ▶ adjective INDECOROUS, improper, unbecoming, unfitting, unbefitting, unworthy, undignified, indiscreet, indelicate, ungentlemanly, unladylike.
– OPPOSITES decorous.

unseen ▶ adjective HIDDEN, concealed, obscured, camouflaged, out of sight, imperceptible, undetectable, unnoticeable, unnoticed, unobserved.

unselfish ▶ adjective ALTRUISTIC, disinterested, selfless, self-denying, self-sacrificing; generous, philanthropic, public-spirited, charitable, benevolent, caring, kind, considerate, noble.

unsettle ▶ verb DISCOMPOSE, unnerve, upset, disturb, disquiet, perturb, discomfit, disconcert, alarm, dismay, trouble, bother, agitate, fluster, ruffle, shake (up), throw, unbalance, destabilize; *informal* rattle, faze.

unsettled ▶ adjective ❶ *an unsettled life* AIMLESS, directionless, purposeless, without purpose; rootless, nomadic. ❷ *an unsettled child* RESTLESS, restive, fidgety, anxious, worried, troubled, fretful; agitated, ruffled, uneasy, disconcerted, discomposed, unnerved, ill at ease, edgy, on edge, tense, nervous, apprehensive, disturbed, perturbed; *informal* rattled, fazed. ❸ *unsettled weather* CHANGEABLE, changing, variable, varying, inconstant, inconsistent, ever-changing, erratic, unstable, undependable, unreliable, uncertain, unpredictable, protean. ❹ *the question remains unsettled* UNDECIDED, to be decided, unresolved, undetermined, uncertain, open to debate, doubtful, in doubt, up in the air, in a state of uncertainty. ❺ *the debt remains unsettled* UNPAID, payable, outstanding, owing, owed, to be paid, due, undischarged; *N. Amer.* delinquent, past due. ❻ *unsettled areas* UNINHABITED, unpopulated, unpeopled, desolate, lonely.

unshakeable ▶ adjective STEADFAST, resolute, staunch, firm, decided, determined, unswerving, unwavering; unyielding, inflexible, dogged, obstinate, persistent, indefatigable, tireless, unflagging, unremitting, unrelenting, relentless.

unsightly ▶ adjective UGLY, unattractive, unprepossessing, unlovely, disagreeable, displeasing, hideous, horrible, repulsive, revolting, offensive, grotesque, monstrous, ghastly.
– OPPOSITES attractive.

unskilful ▶ adjective INEXPERT, incompetent, inept, unskilled, amateurish, unprofessional, inexperienced, untrained, unpractised; *informal* ham-fisted, ham-handed, cack-handed.

unskilled ▶ adjective UNTRAINED, unqualified; manual, blue-collar, labouring, menial; inexpert, inexperienced, unpractised, amateurish, unprofessional.

unsociable ▶ adjective UNFRIENDLY, uncongenial, unneighbourly, unapproachable, introverted, reticent, reserved, withdrawn, aloof, distant, remote, detached, unsocial, antisocial, taciturn, silent, quiet; *informal* stand-offish.
– OPPOSITES friendly.

unsolicited ▶ adjective UNINVITED, unsought, unasked for, unrequested.

unsophisticated ▶ adjective ❶ *she seemed terribly unsophisticated* UNWORLDLY, naive, simple, innocent, ignorant, green, immature, callow, inexperienced, childlike, artless, guileless, ingenuous, natural, unaffected, unassuming, unpretentious. ❷ *unsophisticated software* SIMPLE, crude, basic, rudimentary, primitive, rough and ready; straightforward, uncomplicated, uninvolved.

unsound ▶ adjective ❶ *structurally unsound* RICKETY, flimsy, wobbly, unstable, crumbling, damaged, rotten, ramshackle, insubstantial, unsafe, dangerous. ❷ *this submission appears unsound* UNTENABLE, flawed, defective, faulty, ill-founded, flimsy, unreliable, questionable, dubious, tenuous, suspect, fallacious, fallible; *informal* iffy. ❸ *of unsound mind* DISORDERED, deranged, disturbed, demented, unstable, unbalanced, unhinged, insane; *informal* touched.
– OPPOSITES strong.

unsparing ▶ adjective ❶ *he is unsparing in his criticism* MERCILESS, pitiless, ruthless, relentless, remorseless, unmerciful, unforgiving, implacable, uncompromising; stern, strict, severe, harsh, tough, rigorous. ❷ *unsparing approval* UNGRUDGING, unstinting, willingly given, free, free-handed, ready; lavish, liberal, generous, magnanimous, open-handed.

unspeakable ▶ adjective ❶ *unspeakable delights* INDESCRIBABLE, beyond description, inexpressible, unutterable, indefinable, unimaginable, inconceivable, marvellous, wonderful. ❷ *an unspeakable crime* DREADFUL, awful, appalling, horrific, horrifying, horrendous, abominable, frightful, fearful, shocking, ghastly, gruesome, monstrous, heinous, egregious, deplorable, despicable, execrable, vile.

unspecified ▶ adjective UNNAMED, unstated, unidentified, undesignated, undefined, unfixed, undecided, undetermined, uncertain; nameless, unknown, indefinite, indeterminate, vague.

unspectacular ▶ adjective UNREMARKABLE, unexceptional, undistinguished, unmemorable; ordinary, average, commonplace, mediocre, run-of-the-mill, indifferent.
– OPPOSITES remarkable.

unspoilt ▶ adjective UNIMPAIRED, as good as new/before, perfect, pristine, immaculate, unblemished, unharmed, unflawed, undamaged, untouched, unmarked, untainted.

unspoken ▶ adjective UNSTATED, unexpressed, unuttered, unsaid, unvoiced, unarticulated, undeclared, not spelt out; tacit, implicit, implied, understood, taken as read.
– OPPOSITES explicit.

unstable ▶ adjective ❶ *icebergs are notoriously unstable* UNSTEADY, rocky, wobbly, rickety, shaky, unsafe, insecure, precarious. ❷ *unstable coffee prices* CHANGEABLE, volatile, variable, fluctuating, irregular, unpredictable, erratic. ❸ *he was mentally unstable* UNBALANCED, of unsound mind, mentally ill, deranged, demented, disturbed, unhinged.
– OPPOSITES steady, firm.

unsteady ▶ adjective ❶ *she was unsteady on her feet* UNSTABLE, rocky, wobbly, rickety, shaky, tottery, doddery, insecure. ❷ *an unsteady flow* IRREGULAR, uneven, varying, variable, erratic, spasmodic, changeable, changing, fluctuating, inconstant, intermittent, fitful.
– OPPOSITES stable, regular.

unstinted, unstinting ▶ adjective *unstinted praise* LAVISH, liberal, generous, open-handed, ungrudging, unsparing, willingly given, ready, profuse, abundant, ample.

unstudied ▶ adjective NATURAL, easy, unaffected, unforced, uncontrived, unstilted, unpretentious, without airs, artless.

unsubstantiated ▶ adjective UNCONFIRMED, unsupported, uncorroborated, unverified, unattested, unproven; unfounded, groundless, baseless, without foundation.

unsuccessful ▶ adjective ❶ *an unsuccessful attempt* FAILED, without success, abortive, ineffective, fruitless, profitless, unproductive; vain, futile, useless, pointless, worthless. ❷ *an unsuccessful business* UNPROFITABLE, loss-making. ❸ *an unsuccessful candidate* FAILED, losing, beaten; unlucky, out of luck.

unsuitable ▶ adjective ❶ *an unsuitable product* INAPPROPRIATE, unsuited, ill-suited, inapt, inapposite, unacceptable, unfitting, unbefitting, incompatible, out of place/keeping. ❷ *an unsuitable moment* INOPPORTUNE, infelicitous; *formal* malapropos.
– OPPOSITES appropriate, opportune.

unsullied ▶ adjective SPOTLESS, untarnished, unblemished, untainted, unspoilt, impeccable, undamaged, unimpaired, stainless, immaculate, unflawed.
– OPPOSITES tarnished.

unsung ▶ adjective UNACKNOWLEDGED, uncelebrated, unacclaimed, unapplauded, unhailed; neglected, unrecognized, overlooked, forgotten.
– OPPOSITES celebrated.

unsure ▶ adjective ❶ *she felt very unsure* UNCONFIDENT, unassertive, insecure, hesitant, diffident, anxious, apprehensive. ❷ *Sally was unsure what to do* UNDECIDED, irresolute, dithering, equivocating, in two minds, in a quandary. ❸ *some teachers are unsure about the proposed strike* DUBIOUS, doubtful, sceptical, uncertain, unconvinced. ❹ *the date is unsure* NOT FIXED, undecided, uncertain.
– OPPOSITES confident.

unsurpassed ▶ adjective UNMATCHED, unrivalled, unparalleled, unequalled, matchless, peerless, without equal, inimitable, incomparable, unsurpassable; *formal* unexampled.

unsurprising ▶ **adjective** PREDICTABLE, foreseeable, (only) to be expected, foreseen, anticipated, par for the course; *informal* inevitable, on the cards.

unsuspecting ▶ **adjective** UNSUSPICIOUS, unwary, unaware, unconscious, ignorant, unwitting; trusting, gullible, credulous, ingenuous, naive.
– OPPOSITES wary.

unswerving ▶ **adjective** UNWAVERING, unfaltering, steadfast, unshakeable, staunch, firm, resolute, stalwart, dedicated, committed, constant, single-minded, dogged, indefatigable, unyielding, unbending, indomitable.

unsympathetic ▶ **adjective** ❶ *unsympathetic staff* UNCARING, unconcerned, unfeeling, insensitive, unkind, pitiless, heartless, hard-hearted. ❷ *the government was unsympathetic to these views* OPPOSED, against, (dead) set against, antagonistic, ill-disposed; *informal* anti. ❸ *an unsympathetic character* UNLIKEABLE, disagreeable, unpleasant, objectionable, unsavoury; uncongenial, unfriendly, unneighbourly, unapproachable.
– OPPOSITES caring.

unsystematic ▶ **adjective** UNMETHODICAL, uncoordinated, disorganized, unplanned, indiscriminate; random, inconsistent, irregular, erratic, casual, haphazard, chaotic.

untamed ▶ **adjective** WILD, feral, undomesticated, unbroken.

untangle ▶ **verb** ❶ *I untangled the fishing tackle* DISENTANGLE, unravel, unsnarl, straighten out, untwist, untwine, unknot. ❷ *untangling a mystery* SOLVE, find the/an answer to, resolve, puzzle out, fathom, clear up, clarify, get to the bottom of; *informal* figure out; *Brit. informal* suss out.

untarnished ▶ **adjective** UNSULLIED, unblemished, untainted, impeccable, undamaged, unspoilt, unimpaired, spotless, stainless.

untenable ▶ **adjective** INDEFENSIBLE, undefendable, insupportable, unsustainable, unjustified, unjustifiable, flimsy, weak, shaky.

unthinkable ▶ **adjective** UNIMAGINABLE, inconceivable, unbelievable, incredible, beyond belief, implausible.

unthinking ▶ **adjective** ❶ *an unthinking woman* THOUGHTLESS, inconsiderate, insensitive; tactless, undiplomatic, indiscreet. ❷ *an unthinking remark* ABSENT-MINDED, heedless, thoughtless, careless, injudicious, imprudent, unwise, foolish, reckless, rash, precipitate; involuntary, inadvertent, unintentional, spontaneous, impulsive, unpremeditated.
– OPPOSITES thoughtful, intentional.

untidy ▶ **adjective** ❶ *untidy hair* SCRUFFY, tousled, dishevelled, unkempt, messy, disordered, disarranged, messed up, rumpled, bedraggled, uncombed, ungroomed, straggly, ruffled, tangled, matted, wind-blown; *informal* mussed up; *N. Amer. informal* raggedy. ❷ *the room was untidy* DISORDERED, messy, in a mess, disorderly, disorganized, in disorder, cluttered, in a muddle, muddled, in chaos, chaotic, haywire, topsy-turvy, in disarray, at sixes and sevens; *informal* higgledy-piggledy.
– OPPOSITES neat, orderly.

untie ▶ **verb** UNDO, unknot, unbind, unfasten, unlace, untether, unhitch, unmoor; loose, (set) free, release, let go.

until ▶ **preposition & conjunction** ❶ *I was working until midnight* (UP) TILL, up to, up until, as late as; *N. Amer.* through. ❷ *this did not happen until 1998* BEFORE, prior to, previous to, up to, up until, (up) till, earlier than.

untimely ▶ **adjective** ❶ *an untimely interruption* ILL-TIMED, badly timed, mistimed; inopportune, inappropriate; inconvenient, unwelcome, infelicitous; *formal* malapropos. ❷ *his untimely death* PREMATURE, (too) early, too soon, before time.
– OPPOSITES opportune.

untiring ▶ **adjective** VIGOROUS, energetic, determined, resolute, enthusiastic, keen, zealous, spirited, dogged, tenacious, persistent, persevering, staunch; tireless, unflagging, unfailing, unfaltering, unwavering, indefatigable, unrelenting, unswerving; *formal* pertinacious.

untold ▶ **adjective** ❶ *untold damage* BOUNDLESS, measureless, limitless, unlimited, infinite, immeasurable, incalculable. ❷ *untold billions* COUNTLESS, innumerable, endless, limitless, numberless, an infinite number of, without number, uncountable; numerous, many, multiple; *poetic/literary* multitudinous, myriad. ❸ *the untold story* UNREPORTED, unrecounted, unrevealed, undisclosed, undivulged, unpublished.
– OPPOSITES limited.

untouched ▶ **adjective** ❶ *the food was untouched* UNEATEN, unconsumed, undrunk. ❷ *one of the few untouched areas* UNSPOILT, unmarked, unblemished, unsullied, undefiled, undamaged, unharmed; pristine, natural, immaculate, in perfect condition, unaffected, unchanged, unaltered.

untoward ▶ **adjective** UNEXPECTED, unanticipated, unforeseen, unpredictable, unpredicted, surprising, unusual; unwelcome, unfavourable, adverse, unfortunate, infelicitous; *formal* malapropos.

untrained ▶ **adjective** UNSKILLED, untaught, unschooled, untutored, unpractised, inexperienced; unqualified, unlicensed, amateur, non-professional.

untried ▶ **adjective** UNTESTED, unestablished, new, experimental, unattempted, trial, test, pilot, unproven.
– OPPOSITES established.

untroubled ▶ adjective UNWORRIED, unperturbed, unconcerned, unruffled, undismayed, unbothered, unagitated, unflustered; insouciant, nonchalant, blasé, carefree, serene, relaxed, at ease, happy-go-lucky; *informal* laid-back.

untrue ▶ adjective ❶ *these suggestions are totally untrue* FALSE, untruthful, fabricated, made up, invented, concocted, trumped up; erroneous, wrong, incorrect, inaccurate; fallacious, unsound, unfounded, misguided. ❷ *he was untrue to his friends* UNFAITHFUL, disloyal, faithless, false, treacherous, traitorous, deceitful, deceiving, duplicitous, double-dealing, insincere, unreliable, undependable, inconstant; *informal* two-timing; *poetic/literary* perfidious.
– OPPOSITES correct, faithful.

untrustworthy ▶ adjective DISHONEST, deceitful, double-dealing, treacherous, traitorous, two-faced, duplicitous, dishonourable, unprincipled, unscrupulous, corrupt; unreliable, undependable.
– OPPOSITES reliable.

untruth ▶ noun ❶ *a patent untruth* LIE, falsehood, fib, fabrication, invention, falsification, cock-and-bull story, half-truth, exaggeration; story, myth, piece of fiction; *informal* tall story, fairy tale, whopper; *Brit. informal* porky (pie). ❷ *the total untruth of the story* FALSITY, falsehood, falseness, untruthfulness, fallaciousness, fictitiousness; fabrication, dishonesty, deceit, deceitfulness.

untruthful ▶ adjective ❶ *the answers may be untruthful* FALSE, untrue, fabricated, made up, invented, trumped up; erroneous, wrong, incorrect, inaccurate, fallacious, fictitious. ❷ *an untruthful person* LYING, mendacious, dishonest, deceitful, duplicitous, false, double-dealing, two-faced; *informal* crooked, bent; *poetic/literary* perfidious.
– OPPOSITES honest.

untutored ▶ adjective UNEDUCATED, untaught, unschooled, ignorant, unsophisticated, uncultured, unenlightened.
– OPPOSITES educated.

untwine ▶ verb. *See* UNTWIST.

untwist ▶ verb UNTWINE, disentangle, unravel, unsnarl, unwind, unroll, uncoil, unfurl, open (out), straighten (out).

unused ▶ adjective ❶ *the notebook is unused | unused food* UNUTILIZED, unemployed, unexploited, not in service; left over, remaining, uneaten, unconsumed, unneeded, not required, to spare, surplus. ❷ *he was unused to such directness* UNACCUSTOMED, new, a stranger, unfamiliar, unconversant, unacquainted; *archaic* strange.
– OPPOSITES accustomed.

unusual ▶ adjective ❶ *an unusual sight* UNCOMMON, abnormal, atypical, unexpected, surprising, unfamiliar, different; strange, odd, curious, out of the ordinary, extraordinary, unorthodox, unconventional, outlandish, singular, peculiar, bizarre; rare, scarce, few and far between, thin on the ground, exceptional, isolated, occasional, infrequent; *informal* weird, offbeat, way out, freaky. ❷ *a man of unusual talent* REMARKABLE, extraordinary, exceptional, singular, particular, outstanding, notable, noteworthy, distinctive, striking, significant, special, unique, unparalleled, prodigious.
– OPPOSITES common.

unutterable ▶ adjective ❶ *an existence of unutterable boredom* INDESCRIBABLE, beyond description, inexpressible, unspeakable, undefinable, inconceivable; extreme, great, overwhelming; dreadful, awful, appalling, terrible. ❷ *unutterable joy* MARVELLOUS, wonderful, superb, splendid, unimaginable, profound, deep.

unvarnished ▶ adjective ❶ *unvarnished wood* BARE, unpainted, unpolished, unfinished, untreated. ❷ *the unvarnished truth* STRAIGHTFORWARD, plain, simple, stark; truthful, realistic, candid, honest, frank, forthright, direct, blunt, straight from the shoulder.

unveil ▶ verb REVEAL, present, disclose, divulge, make known, make public, communicate, publish, broadcast; display, show, exhibit, put on display; release, bring out.

unwanted ▶ adjective ❶ *an unwanted development* UNWELCOME, undesirable, undesired, unpopular, unfortunate, unlucky, unfavourable, untoward; unpleasant, disagreeable, displeasing, distasteful, objectionable; regrettable, deplorable, lamentable; unacceptable, intolerable, awful, terrible, wretched, appalling. ❷ *tins of unwanted pet food* UNUSED, left over, surplus, superfluous; uneaten, unconsumed, untouched. ❸ *an unwanted guest* UNINVITED, unbidden, unasked, unrequested, unsolicited. ❹ *many ageing people feel unwanted* FRIENDLESS, unloved, uncared-for, forsaken, rejected, shunned; superfluous, useless, unnecessary.
– OPPOSITES welcome.

unwarranted ▶ adjective ❶ *the criticism is unwarranted* UNJUSTIFIED, unjustifiable, indefensible, inexcusable, unforgivable, unpardonable, uncalled for, unnecessary, unreasonable, unjust, groundless, excessive, immoderate, disproportionate. ❷ *an unwarranted invasion of privacy* UNAUTHORIZED, unsanctioned, unapproved, uncertified, unlicensed; illegal, unlawful, illicit, illegitimate, criminal, actionable.
– OPPOSITES justified.

unwary ▶ adjective INCAUTIOUS, careless, thoughtless, heedless, inattentive, unwatchful, off one's guard.

unwavering ▶ adjective STEADY, fixed, resolute, resolved, firm, steadfast, unswerving, unfaltering, untiring, tireless, indefatigable, un-

yielding, relentless, unremitting, unrelenting, sustained.
– OPPOSITES unsteady.

unwelcome ▶ adjective ❶ *I was made to feel unwelcome* UNWANTED, uninvited. ❷ *even a small increase is unwelcome* UNDESIRABLE, undesired, unpopular, unfortunate, unlucky; disappointing, upsetting, distressing, disagreeable, displeasing; regrettable, deplorable, lamentable.

unwell ▶ adjective ILL, sick, poorly, indisposed, ailing, not (very) well, not oneself, under/below par, peaky, queasy, nauseous; *Brit.* off colour; *informal* under the weather, not up to snuff, funny, peculiar, lousy, rough; *Brit. informal* grotty; *Austral./NZ informal* crook; *dated* queer.

unwholesome ▶ adjective ❶ *unwholesome air* UNHEALTHY, noxious, poisonous; insalubrious, unhygienic, insanitary; harmful, injurious, detrimental, destructive, damaging, deleterious, baleful. ❷ *unwholesome Web pages* IMPROPER, immoral, indecent, corrupting, depraving, salacious.
– OPPOSITES healthy, seemly.

unwieldy ▶ adjective CUMBERSOME, unmanageable, unmanoeuvrable; awkward, clumsy, massive, heavy, hefty, bulky, weighty.
– OPPOSITES manageable.

unwilling ▶ adjective ❶ *unwilling conscripts* RELUCTANT, unenthusiastic, hesitant, resistant, grudging, involuntary, forced. ❷ *he was unwilling to take on that responsibility* DISINCLINED, reluctant, averse, loath; (**be unwilling to do something**) not have the heart to, baulk at, demur at, shy away from, flinch from, shrink from, have qualms about, have misgivings about, have reservations about.
– OPPOSITES keen.

unwillingness ▶ adjective DISINCLINATION, reluctance, hesitation, diffidence, wavering, vacillation, resistance, objection, opposition, doubts, second thoughts, scruples, qualms, misgivings; *archaic* disrelish.

unwind ▶ verb ❶ *Ella unwound the scarf from her neck* UNROLL, uncoil, unravel, untwine, untwist, disentangle, open (out), straighten (out). ❷ *unwinding after work* RELAX, loosen up, ease up/off, slow down, de-stress, unbend, rest, put one's feet up, take it easy; *informal* wind down, let it all hang out, unbutton; *N. Amer. informal* hang loose, chill out.

unwise ▶ adjective INJUDICIOUS, ill-advised, imprudent, foolish, silly, inadvisable, impolitic, misguided, foolhardy, irresponsible, rash, hasty, overhasty, reckless.
– OPPOSITES sensible.

unwitting ▶ adjective ❶ *an unwitting accomplice* UNKNOWING, unconscious, unsuspecting, oblivious, unaware, innocent. ❷ *an unwitting mistake* UNINTENTIONAL, unintended, inadvertent, involuntary, unconscious, accidental.
– OPPOSITES conscious.

unwonted ▶ adjective UNUSUAL, uncommon, unaccustomed, unfamiliar, unprecedented, exceptional, extraordinary, remarkable, singular, surprising.
– OPPOSITES usual.

unworldly ▶ adjective ❶ *a gauche, unworldly girl* NAIVE, simple, inexperienced, innocent, green, raw, callow, immature, unsophisticated, gullible, ingenuous, artless, guileless, childlike, trusting, credulous. ❷ *unworldly beauty* UNEARTHLY, other-worldly, ethereal, ghostly, preternatural, supernatural, paranormal, mystical; *rare* extramundane. ❸ *an unworldly religious order* NON-MATERIALISTIC, spiritualistic, religious.

unworthy ▶ adjective ❶ *he was unworthy of trust* UNDESERVING, ineligible, unqualified, unfit. ❷ *unworthy behaviour* UNBECOMING, unsuitable, inappropriate, unbefitting, unfitting, unseemly, improper; discreditable, shameful, dishonourable, despicable, ignoble, contemptible, reprehensible.
– OPPOSITES deserving, becoming.

unwritten ▶ adjective TACIT, implicit, unvoiced, taken for granted, accepted, recognized, understood; traditional, customary, conventional; oral, verbal, spoken, vocal, word-of-mouth.

unyielding ▶ adjective ❶ *unyielding spikes of cane* STIFF, inflexible, unbending, inelastic, firm, hard, solid, tough, tight, compact, compressed, dense. ❷ *an unyielding policy* RESOLUTE, inflexible, uncompromising, unbending, unshakeable, unwavering, immovable, intractable, intransigent, rigid, stiff, firm, determined, dogged, obstinate, stubborn, adamant, obdurate, tenacious, relentless, implacable, single-minded; *formal* pertinacious.

up-and-coming ▶ adjective PROMISING, budding, rising, on the up and up, with potential; talented, gifted, able.

upbeat ▶ adjective (*informal*) OPTIMISTIC, cheerful, cheery, positive, confident, hopeful, sanguine, bullish, buoyant.
– OPPOSITES pessimistic, negative.

upbraid ▶ verb REPRIMAND, rebuke, admonish, chastise, chide, reprove, reproach, scold, berate, take to task, lambaste, give someone a piece of one's mind, haul over the coals, lecture; *informal* tell off, give someone a talking-to, dress down, give someone an earful, rap over the knuckles, bawl out, lay into; *Brit. informal* tick off, carpet, tear off a strip, give someone what for, give someone a rocket/rollicking; *N. Amer. informal* chew out, ream out; *Austral. informal* monster; *formal* castigate; *rare* reprehend.

upbringing ▶ noun CHILDHOOD, early life, formative years, teaching, instruction, care, bringing-up, rearing.

update ▶ verb ❶ *security measures are continually updated* MODERNIZE, upgrade, bring up to date, improve, overhaul; *N. Amer.* bring up to code. ❷ *I'll update him on today's developments* BRIEF, bring up to date, inform, fill in, tell, notify, apprise, keep posted; *informal* clue in, put in the picture, bring/keep up to speed.

upgrade ▸ **verb** ❶ *there are plans to upgrade the rail system* IMPROVE, modernize, update, bring up to date, make better, ameliorate, reform; rehabilitate, recondition, refurbish, renovate; *N. Amer.* bring up to code. ❷ *he was upgraded to a seat in the cabinet* PROMOTE, give promotion to, elevate, move up, raise; *archaic* prefer.
– OPPOSITES downgrade, demote.

upheaval ▸ **noun** DISRUPTION, disturbance, trouble, turbulence, disorder, confusion, turmoil, pandemonium, chaos, mayhem, cataclysm; revolution, change.

uphill ▸ **adjective** ❶ *an uphill path* UPWARD, rising, ascending, climbing. ❷ *an uphill job* ARDUOUS, difficult, hard, tough, taxing, demanding, exacting, stiff, formidable, exhausting, tiring, wearisome, laborious, gruelling, back-breaking, punishing, burdensome, onerous, Herculean; *informal* no picnic, killing; *archaic* toilsome.
– OPPOSITES downhill.

uphold ▸ **verb** ❶ *the court upheld his claim for damages* CONFIRM, endorse, sustain, approve, support, back (up), stand by, champion, defend. ❷ *they've a tradition to uphold* MAINTAIN, sustain, continue, preserve, protect, keep, hold to, keep alive, keep going.
– OPPOSITES overturn, oppose.

upkeep ▸ **noun** ❶ *the upkeep of the road* MAINTENANCE, repair(s), service, servicing, care, preservation, conservation; running. ❷ *the child's upkeep* (FINANCIAL) SUPPORT, maintenance, keep, subsistence, care.

uplift ▸ **verb** *she needs something to uplift her spirits* BOOST, raise, buoy up, lift, cheer up, perk up, enliven, brighten up, lighten, stimulate, inspire, ginger up, revive, restore; *informal* buck up.

uplifted ▸ **adjective** RAISED, upraised, elevated, upthrust; held high, erect, proud.

uplifting ▸ **adjective** INSPIRING, stirring, inspirational, rousing, moving, touching, affecting, cheering, heartening, encouraging.

upper ▸ **adjective** ❶ *the upper floor* HIGHER, superior; top. ❷ *the upper echelons of the party* SENIOR, superior, higher-level, higher-ranking, top.
– OPPOSITES lower.
■ **the upper hand** AN ADVANTAGE, the edge, the whip hand, a lead, a head start, ascendancy, superiority, supremacy, sway, control, power, mastery, dominance, command.

upper-class ▸ **adjective** ARISTOCRATIC, noble, of noble birth, patrician, titled, blue-blooded, high-born, well born, elite, landowning, landed, born with a silver spoon in one's mouth; *Brit.* county, upmarket; *informal* upper-crust, top-drawer, {huntin', shootin', and fishin'}, classy; *Brit. informal* posh; *archaic* gentle, of gentle birth.

uppermost ▸ **adjective** ❶ *the uppermost branches* HIGHEST, top, topmost. ❷ *their own problems remained uppermost in their minds* PREDOMINANT, of greatest importance, to the fore, foremost, dominant, principal, chief, main, paramount, major.

uppish ▸ **adjective** (*informal*) ARROGANT, bumptious, full of oneself, puffed up, conceited, swollen-headed, pompous, self-assertive, overbearing, throwing one's weight about, cocky, cocksure, haughty, self-important, superior, presumptuous, overweening; *informal* snooty, uppity, high and mighty, too big for one's boots.

upright ▸ **adjective** ❶ *an upright position* VERTICAL, perpendicular, plumb, straight (up), straight up and down, bolt upright, erect, on end; on one's feet; *Heraldry* rampant. ❷ *an upright member of the community* HONEST, honourable, upstanding, respectable, high-minded, law-abiding, right-minded, worthy, moral, ethical, righteous, decent, good, virtuous, principled, high-principled, of principle, noble, incorruptible.
– OPPOSITES horizontal, dishonourable.

uprising ▸ **noun** REBELLION, revolt, insurrection, mutiny, revolution, insurgence, rioting, riot; civil disobedience, unrest, anarchy, fighting in the streets; coup, coup d'état, putsch.

uproar ▸ **noun** ❶ *the uproar in the kitchen continued for some time* TURMOIL, disorder, confusion, chaos, commotion, disturbance, rumpus, tumult, turbulence, mayhem, pandemonium, bedlam, noise, din, clamour, hubbub, racket; shouting, yelling, babel; *informal* hullabaloo; *Brit. informal* row. ❷ *there was an uproar when he was dismissed* OUTCRY, furore, howl of protest; fuss, commotion, hue and cry, rumpus, ruckus, brouhaha; *informal* hullabaloo, stink, ructions; *Brit. informal* row.
– OPPOSITES calm.

uproarious ▸ **adjective** ❶ *an uproarious party* RIOTOUS, rowdy, noisy, loud, wild, unrestrained, unruly, rip-roaring, rollicking, boisterous; *Brit. informal* rumbustious; *N. Amer. informal* rambunctious. ❷ *an uproarious joke* HILARIOUS, hysterically funny, too funny for words, rib-tickling; *informal* priceless, side-splitting, a scream, a hoot; *informal, dated* killing.
– OPPOSITES quiet.

uproot ▸ **verb** ❶ *don't pick or uproot wild flowers* PULL UP, root out, deracinate, grub out/up. ❷ *a revolution is necessary to uproot the social order* ERADICATE, get rid of, eliminate, root out, destroy, put an end to, do away with, wipe out, stamp out.
– OPPOSITES plant.

upset ▶ verb ❶ *the accusation upset her* DISTRESS, trouble, perturb, dismay, disturb, discompose, unsettle, disconcert, disquiet, worry, bother, agitate, fluster, throw, ruffle, unnerve, shake; hurt, sadden, grieve. ❷ *he upset a tureen of soup* KNOCK OVER, overturn, upend, tip over, topple (over); spill; *archaic* overset. ❸ *the dam will upset the ecological balance* DISRUPT, interfere with, disturb, throw out, turn topsy-turvy, throw into confusion, mess up.

▶ noun ❶ *a legal dispute will cause worry and upset* DISTRESS, trouble, perturbation, dismay, disquiet, worry, bother, agitation; hurt, grief. ❷ *a stomach upset* DISORDER, complaint, ailment, illness, sickness, malady; *informal* bug; *Brit. informal* lurgy.

▶ adjective ❶ *I was upset by the news* DISTRESSED, troubled, perturbed, dismayed, disturbed, unsettled, disconcerted, worried, bothered, anxious, agitated, flustered, ruffled, unnerved, shaken; hurt, saddened, grieved; *informal* cut up, choked; *Brit. informal* gutted. ❷ *an upset stomach* DISTURBED, unsettled, queasy, bad, poorly; *informal* gippy.

– OPPOSITES unperturbed, calm.

upshot ▶ noun RESULT, end result, consequence, outcome, conclusion; effect, repercussion, reverberations, ramification; *dated* issue.

– OPPOSITES cause.

upside down ▶ adjective ❶ *an upside-down canoe* UPTURNED, upended, wrong side up, overturned, inverted; capsized. ❷ *they left the flat upside down* IN DISARRAY, in disorder, jumbled up, in a muddle, untidy, disorganized, chaotic, all over the place, in chaos, in confusion, topsy-turvy, at sixes and sevens; *informal* higgledy-piggledy.

upstanding ▶ adjective ❶ *an upstanding member of the community* HONEST, honourable, upright, respectable, high-minded, law-abiding, right-minded, worthy, moral, ethical, righteous, decent, good, virtuous, principled, high-principled, of principle, noble, incorruptible. ❷ *the upstanding feathered plumes* UPRIGHT, erect, vertical; standing, in a standing position, on one's feet; *Heraldry* rampant.

– OPPOSITES dishonourable.

upstart ▶ noun PARVENU(E), arriviste, nouveau riche, vulgarian; status seeker, social climber.

up to date ▶ adjective ❶ *up-to-date equipment* MODERN, contemporary, the latest, state-of-the-art, new, present-day, up to the minute; advanced; *informal* bang up to date, mod. ❷ *the newsletter will keep you up to date* INFORMED, up to speed, in the picture, in touch, au fait, au courant, conversant, familiar, knowledgeable, acquainted, aware.

– OPPOSITES out of date, old-fashioned.

upturn ▶ noun IMPROVEMENT, upswing, turn for the better; recovery, revival, rally, resurgence, increase, rise, jump, leap, upsurge, boost, escalation.

– OPPOSITES fall, slump.

upward ▶ adjective *an upward trend* RISING, on the rise, ascending, climbing, mounting; uphill.

– OPPOSITES downward.

▶ adverb *the smoke drifts upward. See* UPWARDS.

upwards ▶ adverb *he inched his way upwards* UP, upward, uphill; to the top.

– OPPOSITES downward.

■ **upward(s) of** MORE THAN, above, over, in excess of, exceeding, beyond.

urban ▶ adjective TOWN, city, municipal, metropolitan, built-up, inner-city, suburban.

– OPPOSITES rural.

urbane ▶ adjective SUAVE, sophisticated, debonair, worldly, cultivated, cultured, civilized; smooth, polished, refined, self-possessed; courteous, polite, civil, well mannered, mannerly, charming, gentlemanly, gallant.

– OPPOSITES uncouth, unsophisticated.

urchin ▶ noun RAGAMUFFIN, waif, stray; imp, rascal; *derogatory* guttersnipe; *dated* gamin; *archaic* mudlark, scapegrace, street Arab.

urge ▶ verb ❶ *she urged him to try again* ENCOURAGE, exhort, enjoin, press, entreat, implore, call on, appeal to, beg, plead with; egg on, spur, push, pressure, pressurize; *formal* adjure; *poetic/literary* beseech. ❷ *she urged her horse down the lane* SPUR (ON), force, drive, impel. ❸ *I urge caution in interpreting these results* ADVISE, counsel, advocate, recommend.

▶ noun *his urge to travel* DESIRE, wish, need, compulsion, longing, yearning, hankering, craving, appetite, hunger, thirst; fancy, impulse; *informal* yen, itch.

urgent ▶ adjective ❶ *the urgent need for more funding* ACUTE, pressing, dire, desperate, critical, serious, grave, intense, crying, burning, compelling, extreme, high-priority, top-priority; life-and-death. ❷ *an urgent whisper* INSISTENT, persistent, importunate, earnest, pleading, begging.

urinate ▶ verb PASS WATER, relieve oneself; *informal* spend a penny, have/take a leak, pee, piddle, widdle, have a tinkle; *Brit. informal* wee, have a Jimmy (Riddle), have a slash; *N. Amer. informal* take a whizz; *formal* micturate.

usable ▶ adjective READY/FIT FOR USE, able to be used, at someone's disposal, disposable; working, in working order, functioning, functional, serviceable, operational, up and running.

usage ▶ noun ❶ *energy usage* USE, consumption, utilization. ❷ *the usage of equipment* USE, utilization, operation, manipulation, running, handling. ❸ *the intricacies of English usage* PHRASEOLOGY, parlance, idiom, way of speaking/writing, mode of expression; idiolect. ❹ *the usages of polite society* CUSTOM, practice, habit, tradition, convention, rule, observance; way, procedure, form, wont; *formal* praxis; (**usages**) mores.

use ▶ verb ❶ *she used her key to open the front door* UTILIZE, make use of, avail oneself of, employ, work, operate, wield, ply, apply, manoeuvre, manipulate, put to use, put into service. ❷ *the court will use its discretion in making an order* EXERCISE, employ, bring into play, practise, apply. ❸ *use your troops well and they will not let you down* MANAGE, handle, treat, deal with, behave/act towards, conduct oneself towards. ❹ *I couldn't help feeling that she was using me* TAKE ADVANTAGE OF, exploit, manipulate, take liberties with, impose on, abuse; capitalize on, profit from, trade on, milk; *informal* cash in on, walk all over. ❺ *we have used all the available funds* CONSUME, get/go through, exhaust, deplete, expend, spend; waste, fritter away, squander, dissipate.

▶ noun ❶ *the use of such weapons* UTILIZATION, usage, application, employment, operation, manipulation. ❷ *his use of other people for his own ends* EXPLOITATION, manipulation; abuse. ❸ *what is the use of that?* ADVANTAGE, benefit, service, utility, usefulness, help, good, gain, avail, profit, value, worth, point, object, purpose, sense, reason. ❹ *composers have not found much use for the device* NEED, necessity, call, demand, requirement.

used ▶ adjective *a used car* SECOND-HAND, pre-owned, nearly new, old; worn, hand-me-down, handed-down, cast-off; *Brit. informal* reach-me-down.

– OPPOSITES new.

■ **used to** ACCUSTOMED TO, no stranger to, familiar with, at home with, in the habit of, experienced in, versed in, conversant with, acquainted with.

useful ▶ adjective ❶ *a useful multi-purpose tool* FUNCTIONAL, practical, handy, convenient, utilitarian, serviceable, of use, of service; *informal* nifty. ❷ *a useful experience* BENEFICIAL, advantageous, helpful, worthwhile, profitable, rewarding, productive, constructive, valuable, fruitful. ❸ (*informal*) *they had some very useful players* COMPETENT, capable, able, skilful, skilled, talented, proficient, accomplished, good, handy.

– OPPOSITES useless, disadvantageous, incompetent.

useless ▶ adjective ❶ *it was useless to try | a piece of useless knowledge* FUTILE, to no avail, in vain, vain, pointless, to no purpose, unavailing, hopeless, ineffectual, ineffective, to no effect, fruitless, unprofitable, profitless, unproductive; broken, kaput; *archaic* bootless. ❷ (*informal*) *he was useless at his job* INCOMPETENT, inept, ineffective, incapable, inadequate, hopeless, bad; *informal* pathetic, a dead loss.

– OPPOSITES useful, beneficial, competent.

usher ▶ verb *she ushered him to a window seat* ESCORT, accompany, take, show, see, lead, conduct, guide, steer, shepherd.

▶ noun *ushers showed them to their seats* GUIDE, attendant, escort.

■ **usher something in** HERALD, mark the start of, signal, ring in, show in, set the scene for, pave the way for; start, begin, introduce, open the door to, get going, set in motion, get under way, kick off, launch.

usual ▶ adjective HABITUAL, customary, accustomed, wonted, normal, routine, regular, standard, typical, established, set, settled, stock, conventional, traditional, expected, predictable, familiar; average, general, ordinary, everyday.

– OPPOSITES exceptional.

usually ▶ adverb NORMALLY, generally, habitually, customarily, routinely, typically, ordinarily, commonly, conventionally, traditionally; as a rule, in general, more often than not, in the main, mainly, mostly, for the most part.

usurp ▶ verb ❶ *Richard usurped the throne* SEIZE, take over, take possession of, take, commandeer, assume. ❷ *the Hanoverian dynasty had usurped the Stuarts* OUST, overthrow, remove, topple, unseat, depose, dethrone; supplant, replace.

utensil ▶ noun IMPLEMENT, tool, instrument, device, apparatus, gadget, appliance, contrivance, contraption, aid; *informal* gizmo.

utilitarian ▶ adjective PRACTICAL, functional, serviceable, useful, sensible, efficient, utility, workaday; plain, unadorned, undecorative.

– OPPOSITES decorative.

utility ▶ noun USEFULNESS, use, benefit, value, advantage, advantageousness, help, helpfulness, profitability, practicality, effectiveness, avail, service; *formal* efficacy.

utilize ▶ verb USE, make use of, put to use, employ, avail oneself of, bring/press into service, bring into play, deploy, draw on, exploit.

utmost ▶ adjective ❶ *a matter of the utmost importance* GREATEST, highest, maximum, most, uttermost; extreme, supreme, paramount. ❷ *the utmost tip of Shetland* FURTHEST, farthest, furthermost, farthermost, extreme, very, uttermost, outermost, endmost.

▶ noun *a plot that stretches credulity to the utmost* UTTERMOST, maximum, limit.

Utopia ▶ noun PARADISE, heaven, heaven on earth, Eden, Garden of Eden, Shangri-La, Elysium; idyll, nirvana, ideal place; *poetic/literary* Arcadia.

Utopian ▶ adjective IDEALISTIC, visionary, romantic, starry-eyed, fanciful, unrealistic; ideal, perfect, paradisal, heavenly, idyllic, blissful, Elysian; *poetic/literary* Arcadian.

utter[1] ▶ adjective *that's utter nonsense* COMPLETE, total, absolute, thorough, perfect, downright, out-and-out, outright, thoroughgoing, all-out, sheer, arrant, positive, prize, rank, pure, real, veritable, consummate, categorical, unmitigated, unqualified, unadulterated, unalloyed.

utter² ▶ verb ❶ *he uttered an exasperated snort* EMIT, let out, give, produce. ❷ *he hardly uttered a word* SAY, speak, voice, express, articulate, pronounce, enunciate, verbalize, vocalize.

utterance ▶ noun REMARK, comment, word, statement, observation, declaration, pronouncement.

utterly ▶ adverb COMPLETELY, totally, absolutely, entirely, wholly, fully, thoroughly, quite, altogether, one hundred per cent, downright, outright, in all respects, unconditionally, perfectly, really, to the hilt, to the core; *informal* dead.

uttermost ▶ adjective & noun. *See* UTMOST.

U-turn ▶ noun *a complete U-turn in economic policy* VOLTE-FACE, turnaround, about-face, reversal, shift, change of heart, change of mind, backtracking, change of plan; *Brit.* about-turn.

Vv

vacancy ▶ noun ❶ *there are vacancies for computer technicians* OPENING, position, situation vacant, post, job, opportunity, place. ❷ *Cathy stared into vacancy, seeing nothing* EMPTY SPACE, emptiness, nothingness, void. ❸ *a vacancy of mind* EMPTY-HEADEDNESS, lack of intelligence, brainlessness, vacuousness, vacuity, stupidity.

vacant ▶ adjective ❶ *a vacant house* EMPTY, unoccupied, available, not in use, free, unfilled; uninhabited, untenanted. ❷ *a vacant look* BLANK, expressionless, unresponsive, emotionless, impassive, uninterested, vacuous, empty, glazed, glassy; unintelligent, dull-witted, dense, brainless, empty-headed.
– OPPOSITES full, occupied, expressive.

vacate ▶ verb ❶ *he was forced to vacate the premises* LEAVE, move out of, evacuate, quit, depart from; abandon, desert. ❷ *he will be vacating his post next year* RESIGN FROM, leave, stand down from, give up, bow out of, relinquish, retire from; *informal* quit.
– OPPOSITES occupy, take up.

vacation ▶ noun ❶ *his summer vacations in France* HOLIDAY, trip, tour, break, mini-break; leave, time off, recess, furlough; *informal* hol, vac; *formal* sojourn. ❷ *the squatters' vacation of the occupied land* DEPARTURE, evacuation, abandonment, desertion.

vacillate ▶ verb DITHER, be indecisive, be undecided, waver, hesitate, be in two minds, blow hot and cold, keep changing one's mind; *Brit.* haver, hum and haw; *informal* dilly-dally, shilly-shally.

vacillating ▶ adjective IRRESOLUTE, indecisive, dithering, undecided, hesitant, wavering, ambivalent, divided, uncertain, in two minds, blowing hot and cold; *informal* dilly-dallying, shilly-shallying.
– OPPOSITES resolute.

vacuous ▶ adjective SILLY, inane, unintelligent, foolish, stupid, fatuous, idiotic, brainless, witless, vapid, vacant, empty-headed; *informal* dumb, gormless, moronic, brain-dead.
– OPPOSITES intelligent.

vacuum ▶ noun ❶ *people longing to fill the spiritual vacuum in their lives* EMPTINESS, void, nothingness, vacancy. ❷ *the political vacuum left by the Emperor's death* GAP, space, lacuna, void. ❸ (*informal*) *I use the vacuum for cleaning the rug* VACUUM CLEANER; *Brit. informal* vac; *trademark* Hoover.

vagabond ▶ noun. *See* VAGRANT noun.

vagary ▶ noun CHANGE, fluctuation, variation, quirk, peculiarity, oddity, eccentricity, unpredictability, caprice, foible, whim, whimsy, fancy.

vagrant ▶ noun *a temporary home for vagrants* TRAMP, drifter, down-and-out, derelict, beggar, itinerant, wanderer, nomad, traveller, vagabond, transient, homeless person, beachcomber; *informal* knight of the road; *N. Amer.* hobo; *Austral.* bagman; *informal* bag lady; *N. Amer. informal* bum; *poetic/literary* wayfarer.
▶ adjective *vagrant beggars* HOMELESS, drifting, transient, roving, roaming, itinerant, wandering, nomadic, travelling, vagabond, rootless, of no fixed address/abode.

vague ▶ adjective ❶ *a vague shape* INDISTINCT, indefinite, indeterminate, unclear, ill-defined; hazy, fuzzy, misty, blurred, blurry, out of focus, faint, shadowy, dim, obscure, nebulous, amorphous. ❷ *a vague description* IMPRECISE, rough, approximate, inexact, non-specific, generalized, ambiguous, equivocal, hazy, woolly. ❸ *they had only vague plans* HAZY, uncertain, undecided, unsure, unclear, unsettled, indefinite, indeterminate, unconfirmed, up in the air, speculative. ❹ *she was so vague in everyday life* ABSENT-MINDED, forgetful, dreamy, abstracted, with one's head in the clouds; *informal* scatty, not with it.
– OPPOSITES clear, precise, certain.

vaguely ▸ adverb ❶ *she looks vaguely familiar* SLIGHTLY, a little, a bit, somewhat, rather, in a way; faintly, obscurely; *informal* sort of, kind of. ❷ *he fired his rifle vaguely in our direction* ROUGHLY, more or less, approximately. ❸ *he smiled vaguely* ABSENT-MINDEDLY, abstractedly, vacantly.
– OPPOSITES very, exactly.

vain ▸ adjective ❶ *he was vain about his looks* CONCEITED, narcissistic, self-loving, in love with oneself, self-admiring, self-regarding, egotistic, egotistical; proud, arrogant, boastful, cocky, immodest, swaggering; *informal* bigheaded; *poetic/literary* vainglorious. ❷ *a vain attempt* FUTILE, useless, pointless, to no purpose, in vain; ineffective, ineffectual, inefficacious, impotent, unavailing, to no avail, fruitless, profitless, unproductive, unsuccessful, failed, abortive, for nothing; thwarted, frustrated, foiled; *archaic* bootless.
– OPPOSITES modest, successful.
▪ **in vain** ❶ *they tried in vain to save him* UNSUCCESSFULLY, without success, to no avail, to no purpose, fruitlessly. ❷ *his efforts were in vain. See* VAIN sense 2.

valediction ▸ noun FAREWELL, goodbye, adieu, leave-taking.

valedictory ▸ adjective FAREWELL, goodbye, leaving, parting; last, final.

valet ▸ noun MANSERVANT, man, personal attendant, gentleman's gentleman, Jeeves; *Military, dated* batman.

valetudinarian ▸ noun *an elderly valetudinarian* HYPOCHONDRIAC; invalid.
▸ adjective *he was earnest, fussy, and valetudinarian* HYPOCHONDRIAC, obsessed with one's health, neurotic; sickly, ailing, poorly, in poor health, weak, infirm, valetudinary.

valiant ▸ adjective BRAVE, courageous, plucky, valorous, intrepid, heroic, gallant, lionhearted, bold, fearless, daring, audacious; unflinching, unshrinking, unafraid, dauntless, undaunted, doughty, indomitable, mettlesome, stout-hearted, spirited; *informal* game, gutsy, spunky.
– OPPOSITES cowardly.

valid ▸ adjective ❶ *a valid criticism* WELL FOUNDED, sound, reasonable, rational, logical, justifiable, defensible, viable, bona fide; cogent, effective, powerful, convincing, credible, forceful, strong, weighty. ❷ *a valid contract* LEGALLY BINDING, lawful, legal, official, signed and sealed, contractual; in force, in effect, effective.

validate ▸ verb ❶ *clinical trials now exist to validate this claim* PROVE, substantiate, corroborate, verify, support, back up, bear out, confirm, justify, vindicate, authenticate. ❷ *250 course proposals were validated* RATIFY, endorse, approve, agree to, accept, authorize, legalize, legitimize, warrant, license, certify, recognize.
– OPPOSITES disprove.

valley ▸ noun DALE, vale; hollow, gully, gorge, ravine, canyon, rift; *Brit.* combe, dene; *N. English* clough; *Scottish* glen, strath; *poetic/literary* dell, dingle.

valour ▸ noun BRAVERY, courage, pluck, intrepidity, nerve, daring, fearlessness, audacity, boldness, dauntlessness, stout-heartedness, heroism, backbone, spirit; *informal* guts, spunk; *Brit. informal* bottle; *N. Amer. informal* moxie.
– OPPOSITES cowardice.

valuable ▸ adjective ❶ *a valuable watch* PRECIOUS, costly, high-priced, high-cost, expensive, dear; worth its weight in gold, worth a king's ransom, priceless. ❷ *a valuable contribution* USEFUL, helpful, beneficial, invaluable, productive, constructive, effective, advantageous, worthwhile, worthy, important.
– OPPOSITES cheap, worthless, useless.

valuables ▸ plural noun PRECIOUS ITEMS, costly items, prized possessions, personal effects, treasures.

value ▸ noun ❶ *houses exceeding £250,000 in value* PRICE, cost, worth; market price, monetary value, face value. ❷ *the value of adequate preparation cannot be understated* WORTH, usefulness, advantage, benefit, gain, profit, good, help, helpfulness, avail; importance, significance. ❸ *society's values are passed on to us as children* PRINCIPLES, ethics, moral code, morals, standards, code of behaviour.
▸ verb ❶ *his estate was valued at £45,000* EVALUATE, assess, estimate, appraise, price, put/set a price on. ❷ *she valued his opinion* THINK HIGHLY OF, have a high opinion of, hold in high regard, rate highly, esteem, set (great) store by, appreciate, respect; prize, cherish, treasure.

valued ▸ adjective CHERISHED, treasured, dear, prized; esteemed, respected, highly regarded.

valueless ▸ adjective WORTHLESS, of no value, useless, to no purpose, (of) no use, profitless, futile, pointless, vain, in vain, to no avail, to no effect, fruitless, unproductive, idle, ineffective, unavailing; *archaic* bootless.

vamp[1] ▸ verb (*informal*) *the design had been vamped up* IMPROVE, revamp, redesign, remodel, restyle, rework, make over; renovate, refurbish, redecorate, recondition, rehabilitate, overhaul, repair; *informal* do up, give something a facelift; *N. Amer. informal* rehab.

vamp[2] ▸ noun (*informal*) *a raven-haired vamp* SEDUCTRESS, temptress, siren, femme fatale, Mata Hari; flirt, coquette, tease.

van ▸ noun *he was in the van of the movement. See* VANGUARD.

vanguard ▸ noun FOREFRONT, van, advance guard, spearhead, front, front line, fore, lead, cutting edge; leaders, founders, founding fathers, pioneers, trailblazers, trendsetters, innovators, ground-breakers.
– OPPOSITES rear.

vanish ▶ verb ❶ *he vanished into the darkness* DISAPPEAR, be lost to sight/view, become invisible, vanish into thin air, recede from view. ❷ *all hope of freedom vanished* FADE (AWAY), evaporate, melt away, come to an end, end, cease to exist, pass away, die out, be no more.
– OPPOSITES appear, materialize.

vanity ▶ noun ❶ *she had none of the vanity often associated with beautiful women* CONCEIT, narcissism, self-love, self-admiration, self-regard, egotism; pride, arrogance, boastfulness, cockiness, swagger; *informal* big-headedness; *poetic/literary* vainglory. ❷ *the vanity of all desires of the will* FUTILITY, uselessness, pointlessness, worthlessness, fruitlessness.
– OPPOSITES modesty.

vanquish ▶ verb CONQUER, defeat, beat, trounce, rout, triumph over, be victorious over, get the better of, worst; overcome, overwhelm, overpower, overthrow, subdue, subjugate, quell, quash, crush, bring someone to their knees; *informal* lick, hammer, clobber, thrash, demolish, wipe the floor with, make mincemeat of, massacre, slaughter, annihilate; *Brit. informal* stuff; *N. Amer. informal* cream, shellac.

vapid ▶ adjective INSIPID, uninspired, colourless, uninteresting, feeble, flat, dull, boring, tedious, tired, unexciting, uninspiring, unimaginative, lifeless, tame, vacuous, bland, trite.
– OPPOSITES lively, colourful.

vapour ▶ noun HAZE, mist, steam, condensation; fumes, exhalation, fog, smog, smoke.

variable ▶ adjective CHANGEABLE, changing, varying, shifting, fluctuating, changeful, irregular, inconstant, inconsistent, fluid, unsteady, unstable, unsettled, fitful, mutable, protean, wavering, vacillating, capricious, fickle, volatile, unpredictable, unreliable; *informal* up and down.
– OPPOSITES constant.

variance ▶ noun DIFFERENCE, variation, discrepancy, dissimilarity, disagreement, conflict, divergence, deviation, contrast, contradiction, imbalance, incongruity.
■ **at variance** ❶ *his recollections were at variance with documentary evidence* INCONSISTENT, at odds, not in keeping, out of keeping, out of line, out of step, in conflict, in disagreement, different, differing, divergent, discrepant, dissimilar, contrary, incompatible, contradictory, irreconcilable, incongruous. ❷ *they were at variance with their previous allies* IN DISAGREEMENT, at odds, at cross purposes, at loggerheads, in conflict, in dispute, at outs, quarrelling.

variant ▶ noun *there are a number of variants of the same idea* VARIATION, form, alternative, adaptation, alteration, modification, permutation.
▶ adjective *a variant spelling* ALTERNATIVE, other, different, divergent, derived, modified.

variation ▶ noun ❶ *regional variations in farming practice* DIFFERENCE, dissimilarity; disparity, contrast, discrepancy, imbalance; *technical* differential; *formal* dissimilitude. ❷ *opening times are subject to variation* CHANGE, alteration, modification; diversification. ❸ *there was very little variation from an understood pattern* DEVIATION, variance, divergence, departure, fluctuation. ❹ *hurling is an Irish variation of hockey* VARIANT, form, alternative form; development, adaptation, alteration, diversification, modification.

varied ▶ adjective DIVERSE, assorted, miscellaneous, mixed, sundry, heterogeneous, wide-ranging, multifarious; disparate, motley.

variegated ▶ adjective MULTICOLOURED, particoloured, multicolour, many-coloured, many-hued, polychromatic, colourful, prismatic, rainbow-like, kaleidoscopic; mottled, striated, marbled, streaked, speckled, flecked, dappled; *informal* splotchy, splodgy.
– OPPOSITES plain, monochrome.

variety ▶ noun ❶ *the lack of variety in the curriculum* DIVERSITY, variation, diversification, multifariousness, heterogeneity, many-sidedness; change, difference. ❷ *a wide variety of flowers and shrubs* ASSORTMENT, miscellany, range, array, collection, selection, mixture, medley, multiplicity; mixed bag, motley collection, pot-pourri. ❸ *fifty varieties of pasta* SORT, kind, type, class, category, style, form; make, model, brand; strain, breed, genus.
– OPPOSITES uniformity.

various ▶ adjective DIVERSE, different, differing, varied, varying, a variety of, assorted, mixed, sundry, miscellaneous, heterogeneous, disparate, motley; *poetic/literary* divers.

varnish ▶ noun & verb LACQUER, shellac, japan, enamel, glaze; polish.

vary ▶ verb ❶ *estimates of the development cost vary* DIFFER, be different, be dissimilar. ❷ *rates of interest vary over time* FLUCTUATE, rise and fall, go up and down, change, alter, shift, swing. ❸ *the diaphragm is used for varying the aperture of the lens* MODIFY, change, alter, adjust, regulate, control, set; diversify. ❹ *the routine never varied* CHANGE, alter, deviate, differ, fluctuate.

vassal ▶ noun (*historical*) VILLEIN, liegeman, man, vavasour, serf, helot.

vast ▶ adjective HUGE, extensive, expansive, broad, wide, boundless, immeasurable, limitless, infinite; enormous, immense, great, massive, colossal, tremendous, mighty, prodigious, gigantic, gargantuan, mammoth, monumental; giant, towering, mountainous, titanic, Brobdingnagian; *informal* jumbo, mega, monster, whopping, humongous, astronomical; *Brit. informal* ginormous.
– OPPOSITES tiny.

vat ▶ noun TUB, tank, cistern, barrel, butt, cask, tun, drum, basin; vessel, receptacle, container, holder, reservoir.

vault[1] ▸ **noun** ❶ *the highest Gothic vault in Europe* ARCHED ROOF, dome, arch. ❷ *the vault under the church* CELLAR, basement, underground chamber; crypt, undercroft, catacomb, burial chamber. ❸ *valuables stored in the vault* STRONGROOM, safe deposit, safety deposit.

vault[2] ▸ **verb** *he vaulted over the gate* JUMP OVER, leap over, spring over, bound over; hurdle, clear.

vaunt ▸ **verb** BOAST ABOUT, brag about, make much of, crow about, parade, flaunt; acclaim, praise, extol, celebrate; *informal* show off about; *formal* laud.

veer ▸ **verb** TURN, swerve, swing, sheer, career, weave, wheel; change direction/course, go off course, deviate.

vegetate ▸ **verb** DO NOTHING, idle, languish, laze, lounge, loll; moulder, stagnate; *informal* veg out, slob out; *Brit. informal* slummock; *N. Amer. informal* bum around, lollygag.

vegetation ▸ **noun** PLANTS, flora; greenery, foliage, herbage, verdure.

vehemence ▸ **noun** PASSION, force, forcefulness, ardour, fervour, violence, urgency, strength, vigour, intensity, keenness, enthusiasm, zeal.

vehement ▸ **adjective** PASSIONATE, forceful, ardent, impassioned, heated, spirited, urgent, fervent, violent, fierce, strong, forcible, powerful, emphatic, vigorous, intense, earnest, keen, enthusiastic, zealous.
–OPPOSITES mild, apathetic.

vehicle ▸ **noun** ❶ *a stolen vehicle* MEANS OF TRANSPORT, conveyance; car, automobile, motorcycle, motorbike, van, bus, coach, lorry, truck; *N. Amer. informal* auto. ❷ *a vehicle for the communication of original ideas* CHANNEL, medium, means (of expression), agency, agent, instrument, mechanism, organ, apparatus.

veil ▸ **noun** *a thin veil of high cloud made the sun hazy* COVERING, cover, screen, curtain, mantle, cloak, mask, blanket, shroud, canopy, cloud, pall.
▸ **verb** *the peak was veiled in mist* ENVELOP, surround, swathe, enfold, cover, conceal, hide, screen, shield, cloak, blanket, shroud; obscure; *poetic/literary* enshroud, mantle.

veiled ▸ **adjective** *veiled threats* DISGUISED, camouflaged, masked, covert, hidden, concealed, suppressed, underlying, implicit, implied, indirect.
–OPPOSITES overt.

vein ▸ **noun** ❶ *a vein in his neck pulsed* BLOOD VESSEL. ❷ *the mineral veins in the rock* LAYER, lode, seam, stratum, stratification, deposit. ❸ *white marble with grey veins* STREAK, marking, mark, line, stripe, strip, band, thread, strand; *technical* stria, striation. ❹ *he closes the article in a humorous vein* MOOD, humour, frame of mind, temper, disposition, attitude, tenor, tone, key, spirit, character, feel, flavour, quality, atmosphere; manner, way, style.
–RELATED TERMS vascular.

velocity ▸ **noun** SPEED, pace, rate, tempo, momentum, impetus; swiftness, rapidity; *poetic/literary* fleetness, celerity.

venal ▸ **adjective** CORRUPT, corruptible, bribable, open to bribery; dishonest, dishonourable, untrustworthy, unscrupulous, unprincipled; mercenary, greedy; *informal* bent.
–OPPOSITES honourable, honest.

vendetta ▸ **noun** FEUD, blood feud, quarrel, argument, falling-out, dispute, fight, war; bad blood, enmity, rivalry, conflict, strife.

vendor ▸ **noun** SELLER, retailer, purveyor, dealer, trader, tradesman, shopkeeper, merchant, supplier, stockist; huckster, pedlar, hawker; *N. Amer.* storekeeper.

veneer ▸ **noun** ❶ *American cherry wood with a maple veneer* SURFACE, lamination, layer, overlay, facing, covering, finish, exterior. ❷ *a veneer of sophistication* FACADE, front, false front, show, outward display, appearance, impression, semblance, guise, disguise, mask, masquerade, pretence, camouflage, cover.

venerable ▸ **adjective** RESPECTED, venerated, revered, reverenced, honoured, esteemed, hallowed, august, distinguished, eminent, great.

venerate ▸ **verb** REVERE, reverence, worship, hallow, hold sacred, exalt, adore, honour, respect, esteem; *archaic* magnify.

veneration ▸ **noun** REVERENCE, worship, adoration, exaltation, devotion, honour, respect, esteem, high regard.

vengeance ▸ **noun** REVENGE, retribution, retaliation, requital, reprisal, satisfaction, an eye for an eye (and a tooth for a tooth).
■ **with a vengeance** VIGOROUSLY, strenuously, energetically, with a will, with might and main, with all the stops out, for all one is worth, all out, flat out, at full tilt; *informal* hammer and tongs, like crazy, like mad; *Brit. informal* like billy-o.

vengeful ▸ **adjective** VINDICTIVE, revengeful, out for revenge, unforgiving, grudge-bearing.
–OPPOSITES forgiving.

venial ▸ **adjective** FORGIVABLE, pardonable, excusable, allowable, permissible; slight, minor, unimportant, insignificant, trivial, trifling.
–OPPOSITES unforgivable, mortal.

venom ▸ **noun** ❶ *snake venom* POISON, toxin; *archaic* bane. ❷ *his voice was full of venom* RANCOUR, malevolence, vitriol, spite, vindictiveness, malice, maliciousness, ill will, animosity, animus, bitterness, antagonism, hostility, bile, hate, hatred; *informal* bitchiness, cattiness.

venomous ▸ **adjective** ❶ *a venomous snake | the spider's venomous bite* POISONOUS, toxic; dangerous, deadly, lethal, fatal, mortal. ❷ *venomous remarks* VICIOUS, spiteful, rancorous, malevo-

lent, vitriolic, vindictive, malicious, poisonous, virulent, bitter, acrimonious, antagonistic, hostile, cruel; *informal* bitchy, catty; *poetic/literary* malefic, maleficent.
–OPPOSITES harmless, benevolent.

vent ▶noun *an air vent* OUTLET, INLET, opening, aperture, hole, gap, orifice, space; duct, flue, shaft, well, passage, airway.
▶verb *the crowd vented their fury on the pitch* LET OUT, give vent to, give free rein to, release, pour out, express, give expression to, air, voice, give voice to, ventilate.

ventilate ▶verb ❶ *the greenhouse must be properly ventilated* AIR, aerate, oxygenate, air-condition; freshen, cool. ❷ *the workers ventilated their discontent* EXPRESS, give expression to, air, bring into the open, communicate, voice, give voice to, verbalize, discuss, debate, talk over.

venture ▶noun *a business venture* ENTERPRISE, undertaking, project, scheme, operation, endeavour, speculation, plunge, gamble, experiment.
▶verb ❶ *we ventured across the moor* SET OUT, go, travel, journey. ❷ *may I venture an opinion?* PUT FORWARD, advance, proffer, offer, air, suggest, submit, propose, moot, ventilate. ❸ *I ventured to ask her to come and dine with me* DARE, make so bold as, presume; take the liberty of; *informal* stick one's neck out, go out on a limb.

veracious ▶adjective (*formal*). *See* TRUTHFUL senses 1, 2.

verbal ▶adjective ORAL, spoken, stated, said, verbalized; unwritten.

verbatim ▶adverb WORD FOR WORD, letter for letter, line for line, to the letter, literally, exactly, precisely, closely, faithfully; *formal* literatim.

verbiage ▶noun VERBOSITY, padding, wordiness, prolixity, long-windedness; *Brit. informal* waffle.

verbose ▶adjective WORDY, loquacious, garrulous, talkative, voluble; long-winded, lengthy, prolix, tautological, pleonastic, periphrastic, circumlocutory, circuitous, discursive, digressive, rambling; *informal* mouthy, gabby; *Brit. informal* waffly.
–OPPOSITES succinct, laconic.

verbosity ▶noun WORDINESS, loquacity, garrulity, talkativeness, volubility; long-windedness, lengthiness, verbiage, prolixity, tautology, circumlocution, discursiveness; *Brit. informal* waffle.

verdant ▶adjective GREEN, leafy, grassy; lush, rich; *poetic/literary* verdured, verdurous.

verdict ▶noun JUDGEMENT, adjudication, decision, finding, ruling, resolution, pronouncement, conclusion, opinion; *Law* determination.

verge ▶noun ❶ *the verge of the lake* EDGE, border, margin, side, brink, rim, lip; fringe, boundary, perimeter; *poetic/literary* bourn, marge, skirt. ❷ *Spain was on the verge of an economic crisis* BRINK, threshold, edge, point.
▶verb *a degree of caution that verged on the obsessive* APPROACH, border on, be close/near to, be tantamount to; tend towards, approximate to, resemble.

verification ▶noun CONFIRMATION, substantiation, proof, corroboration, support, attestation, validation, authentication, endorsement.

verify ▶verb SUBSTANTIATE, confirm, prove, corroborate, back up, bear out, justify, support, uphold, attest to, testify to, validate, authenticate, endorse, certify.
–OPPOSITES refute.

vernacular ▶noun ❶ *he wrote in the vernacular to reach a wider audience* EVERYDAY LANGUAGE, colloquial language, conversational language, common parlance; dialect, regional language, regionalisms, patois; *informal* lingo, local lingo. ❷ (*informal*) *the vernacular of today's youth* LANGUAGE, parlance; idiom, slang, jargon; *informal* lingo, -speak, -ese.

versatile ▶adjective ADAPTABLE, flexible, all-round, multifaceted, multitalented, resourceful; adjustable, multi-purpose, all-purpose, handy.

verse ▶noun ❶ *Elizabethan verse* POETRY, versification; poems, balladry, lyrics; blank verse, heroic verse, free verse; *poetic/literary* poesy. ❷ *a verse he'd composed to mark my anniversary* POEM, lyric, ballad, sonnet, ode, limerick, rhyme, ditty, lay. ❸ *a poem with sixty verses* STANZA, canto, couplet; strophe.
–OPPOSITES prose.

version ▶noun ❶ *his version of events* ACCOUNT, report, statement, description, record, story, rendering, interpretation, explanation, understanding, reading, impression, side. ❷ *the English version will be published next year* EDITION, translation, impression. ❸ *they have replaced coal-burning fires with gas versions* FORM, sort, kind, type, variety, variant.

vertex ▶noun APEX, peak, tip, top.

vertical ▶adjective UPRIGHT, erect, perpendicular, plumb, straight up and down, on end, standing, upstanding, bolt upright, upended.
–OPPOSITES horizontal.

vertigo ▶noun DIZZINESS, giddiness, light-headedness, loss of balance; *Veterinary Medicine* sturdy.

verve ▶noun ENTHUSIASM, vigour, energy, pep, dynamism, go, elan, vitality, vivacity, buoyancy, liveliness, animation, zest, sparkle, spirit, ebullience, life, brio, gusto, eagerness, keenness, passion, zeal, relish, feeling, ardour, fire; *informal* zing, zip, vim, pizzazz, oomph.

very ▶adverb *that's very kind of you* EXTREMELY, exceedingly, exceptionally, extraordinarily, tremendously, immensely, hugely, intensely,

acutely, abundantly, singularly, uncommonly, unusually, decidedly, particularly, supremely, highly, remarkably, really, truly, mightily; *informal* terrifically, awfully, fearfully, terribly, devilishly, majorly, seriously, mega, ultra, damn, damned; *Brit. informal* ever so, well, hellish, dead, jolly; *N. Amer. informal* real, mighty, awful, darned; *informal, dated* devilish, frightfully; *archaic* exceeding.
– OPPOSITES slightly.
▶ **adjective** ❶ *those were his very words* EXACT, actual, precise. ❷ *the very thought of food made her feel ill* MERE, simple, pure; sheer.

vessel ▶ **noun** ❶ *a fishing vessel* BOAT, ship, craft, watercraft; *poetic/literary* barque. ❷ *pour the mixture into a heatproof vessel* CONTAINER, receptacle; basin, bowl, pan, pot; urn, cask, barrel, drum, butt, vat.

vest ▶ **verb** *executive power is vested in the President* CONFER ON, entrust to, invest in, bestow on, grant to, give to; endow, lodge, lay, place.

vestibule ▶ **noun** ENTRANCE HALL, hall, hallway, entrance, porch, portico, foyer, lobby, ante-room, antechamber, waiting room.

vestige ▶ **noun** ❶ *the last vestiges of colonialism* REMNANT, fragment, relic, echo, indication, sign, trace, mark, legacy, reminder; remains. ❷ *she showed no vestige of emotion* BIT, touch, hint, suggestion, suspicion, shadow, scrap, tinge, speck, shred, jot, iota, whit, scintilla, glimmer; *informal* smidgen, tad.

vestigial ▶ **adjective** ❶ *vestigial limbs* RUDIMENTARY, undeveloped; non-functional; *Biology* primitive. ❷ *he felt a vestigial flicker of anger from last night* REMAINING, surviving, residual, leftover, lingering.

vet ▶ **verb** *press releases are vetted by an executive council* CHECK, examine, scrutinize, investigate, inspect, look over, screen, assess, evaluate, appraise; *informal* check out.
▶ **noun** *I took the cat to the vet* VETERINARY SURGEON, animal doctor, horse doctor; *N. Amer.* veterinarian; *dated* veterinary.

veteran ▶ **noun** *a veteran of 16 political campaigns* OLD HAND, past master, doyen; *informal* old-timer, old stager, old warhorse.
– OPPOSITES novice.
▶ **adjective** *a veteran diplomat* LONG-SERVING, seasoned, old, hardened; adept, expert, well trained, practised, experienced; *informal* battle-scarred.

veto ▶ **noun** *parliament's right of veto* REJECTION, dismissal; prohibition, proscription, embargo, ban, interdict; *informal* thumbs down, red light.
– OPPOSITES approval.
▶ **verb** *the president vetoed the bill* REJECT, turn down, throw out, dismiss; prohibit, forbid, interdict, proscribe, disallow, embargo, ban; *informal* kill, put the kibosh on, give the thumbs down to, give the red light to.
– OPPOSITES approve.

vex ▶ **verb** ANNOY, irritate, anger, infuriate, exasperate, irk, gall, pique, put out, antagonize, get on someone's nerves, ruffle someone's feathers, make someone's hackles rise; *Brit.* rub up the wrong way; *informal* aggravate, peeve, miff, rile, nettle, needle, get (to), bug, hack off, get up someone's nose, get someone's goat, get someone's back up, give someone the hump, get someone's dander up; *Brit. informal* wind up, nark, get on someone's wick; *N. Amer. informal* tee off, tick off, burn up, rankle; *informal, dated* give someone the pip.

vexation ▶ **noun** ANNOYANCE, irritation, exasperation, indignation, anger, crossness, displeasure, pique, disgruntlement; *informal* aggravation.

vexatious ▶ **adjective** ANNOYING, irritating, infuriating, exasperating, maddening, trying, tiresome, troublesome, bothersome, irksome, vexing, galling; *informal* aggravating, pesky.

vexed ▶ **adjective** ❶ *a vexed expression* ANNOYED, irritated, cross, angry, infuriated, exasperated, irked, piqued, displeased, put out, disgruntled; *informal* aggravated, peeved, nettled, miffed, miffy, riled, hacked off, hot under the collar; *Brit. informal* narked, shirty; *N. Amer. informal* teed off, ticked off, sore, bent out of shape; *archaic* wroth. ❷ *the vexed issue of immigration* DISPUTED, in dispute, contested, in contention, contentious, debated, at issue, controversial, moot; problematic, difficult, knotty, thorny.

viable ▶ **adjective** FEASIBLE, workable, practicable, practical, usable, possible, realistic, achievable, attainable, realizable; *informal* doable.
– OPPOSITES impracticable.

vibrant ▶ **adjective** ❶ *a vibrant and passionate woman* SPIRITED, lively, full of life, energetic, vigorous, vital, full of vim and vigour, animated, sparkling, effervescent, vivacious, dynamic, stimulating, exciting, passionate, fiery; *informal* peppy, feisty. ❷ *she was vibrant with excitement* QUIVERING, trembling, shaking, shivering, shuddering, quavering, quaking. ❸ *vibrant colours* VIVID, bright, striking, brilliant, strong, rich. ❹ *his vibrant voice* RESONANT, sonorous, reverberant, resounding, ringing, echoing; strong, rich, full.
– OPPOSITES lifeless, pale.

vibrate ▶ **verb** ❶ *the floor beneath them vibrated* QUIVER, shake, tremble, shiver, shudder, judder, throb, pulsate; rock, oscillate, swing, sway, move to and fro. ❷ *a low rumbling sound began to vibrate through the car* REVERBERATE, resonate, resound, ring, echo.

vibration ▶ **noun** TREMOR, shaking, quivering, quaking, judder, juddering, shuddering, throb, throbbing, pulsation.

vicar ▶ **noun** MINISTER, rector, priest, parson, clergyman, clergywoman, cleric, churchman, churchwoman, ecclesiastic, pastor, father, man/woman of the cloth, man/woman of god, curate, chaplain, preacher; *Scottish* kirkman; *N. Amer.* dominie; *informal* reverend, padre, Holy Joe, sky pilot; *Austral. informal* josser; *dated* divine.

vicarious ▶ **adjective** INDIRECT, second-hand, secondary, derivative, derived, surrogate, substitute; empathetic, empathic.

vice ▶ **noun** ❶ *youngsters may be driven to vice* IMMORALITY, wrongdoing, wickedness, badness, evil, iniquity, villainy, corruption, misconduct; sin, sinfulness, ungodliness; depravity, degeneracy, dissolution, dissipation, debauchery, decadence, lechery; crime, transgression; *formal* turpitude; *archaic* trespass. ❷ *smoking is my only vice* SHORTCOMING, failing, flaw, fault, defect, weakness, deficiency, limitation, imperfection, blemish, foible, frailty.
– OPPOSITES virtue.

vice versa ▶ **adverb** CONVERSELY, inversely, contrariwise; reciprocally.

vicinity ▶ **noun** ❶ *she lives in the vicinity* NEIGHBOURHOOD, surrounding area, locality, locale, (local) area, district, region, quarter, zone; environs, surroundings, precincts; *N. Amer.* vicinage; *informal* neck of the woods. ❷ (*archaic*) *the forest's vicinity to the dockyards. See* PROXIMITY.
■ **in the vicinity of** AROUND, about, nearly, circa, approaching, roughly, something like, more or less; in the region of, in the neighbourhood of, near to, close to; *Brit.* getting on for.

vicious ▶ **adjective** ❶ *a vicious killer* BRUTAL, ferocious, savage, violent, dangerous, ruthless, remorseless, merciless, heartless, callous, cruel, harsh, cold-blooded, inhuman, fierce, barbarous, barbaric, brutish, bloodthirsty, fiendish, sadistic, monstrous, murderous, homicidal. ❷ *a vicious hate campaign* MALICIOUS, malevolent, malignant, malign, spiteful, vindictive, venomous, poisonous, rancorous, mean, cruel, bitter, acrimonious, hostile, nasty; defamatory, slanderous; *informal* catty.
– OPPOSITES gentle, kindly.

vicissitude ▶ **noun** CHANGE, alteration, transition, shift, reversal, downturn; inconstancy, instability, uncertainty, unpredictability, chanciness, fickleness, variability, changeability, fluctuation, vacillation; ups and downs.

victim ▶ **noun** ❶ *a victim of crime* SUFFERER, injured party, casualty; fatality, loss; loser. ❷ *the victim of a confidence trick* DUPE, stooge, gull, fool; target, prey, quarry, object, subject, focus, recipient; *informal* sucker, fall guy, chump, muggins, charlie; *N. Amer. informal* patsy, pigeon, sap. ❸ *a sacrificial victim* SACRIFICE, (burnt) offering, scapegoat.
■ **fall victim to** FALL ILL WITH, be stricken with, catch, develop, contract, pick up; succumb to; *informal* go down with.

victimize ▶ **verb** PERSECUTE, pick on, push around, bully, abuse, discriminate against, ill-treat, mistreat, maltreat, terrorize; exploit, prey on, take advantage of, dupe, cheat, double-cross; *informal* get at, have it in for, give someone a hard time, hassle, lean on.

victor ▶ **verb** WINNER, champion, conqueror, vanquisher, hero; prizewinner, medallist; *informal* champ, top dog.
– OPPOSITES loser.

victorious ▶ **adjective** TRIUMPHANT, conquering, vanquishing, winning, champion, successful, top, first.

victory ▶ **noun** SUCCESS, triumph, conquest, win, favourable result, landslide, coup, vanquishment; mastery, superiority, supremacy; *informal* walkover, thrashing, trouncing.
– OPPOSITES defeat.

victuals ▶ **plural noun** (*dated*). *See* FOOD sense 1.

vie ▶ **verb** COMPETE, contend, contest, struggle, fight, battle, cross swords, lock horns, jockey; war, feud.

view ▶ **noun** ❶ *the view from her flat* OUTLOOK, prospect, panorama, vista, scene, aspect, perspective, spectacle, sight; scenery, landscape. ❷ *we agree with this view* OPINION, point of view, viewpoint, belief, judgement, thinking, notion, idea, conviction, persuasion, attitude, feeling, sentiment, concept, hypothesis, theory; stance, standpoint, approach. ❸ *the church came into view* SIGHT, perspective, vision, visibility.
▶ **verb** ❶ *they viewed the landscape* LOOK AT, eye, observe, gaze at, stare at, ogle, contemplate, regard, scan, survey, inspect, scrutinize; *informal* check out, get a load of, gawp at; *Brit. informal* clock; *N. Amer. informal* eyeball; *poetic/literary* espy, behold. ❷ *the law was viewed as a last resort* CONSIDER, regard, look on, see, perceive, judge, deem, reckon.
■ **in view of** CONSIDERING, bearing in mind, taking into account, on account of, in the light of, owing to, because of, as a result of.
■ **on view** ON DISPLAY, on exhibition, on show.

viewer ▶ **noun** WATCHER, spectator, onlooker, observer; (**viewers**) audience, crowd; *poetic/literary* beholder.

viewpoint ▶ **noun**. *See* VIEW noun sense 2.

vigilant ▶ **adjective** WATCHFUL, observant, attentive, alert, eagle-eyed, hawk-eyed, on the lookout, on one's toes, on the qui vive; wide awake, on one's guard, cautious, wary, circumspect, heedful, mindful; *informal* beady-eyed.
– OPPOSITES inattentive.

vigorous ▶ **adjective** ❶ *the child was vigorous* ROBUST, healthy, hale and hearty, strong, sturdy, fit; hardy, tough, athletic; bouncing, thriving, flourishing, blooming; energetic, lively, active, perky, spirited, vibrant, vital, zestful; *informal* peppy, bouncy, in the pink. ❷ *a vigorous defence of policy* STRENUOUS, powerful, forceful, spirited, mettlesome, deter-

mined, aggressive, eager, zealous, ardent, fervent, vehement, passionate; tough, blunt, hard-hitting; *informal* punchy.
– OPPOSITES weak, feeble.

vigorously ▶ **adverb** STRENUOUSLY, strongly, powerfully, forcefully, energetically, heartily, with might and main, for dear life, for all one is worth, all out, fiercely, hard; *informal* like mad, like crazy; *Brit. informal* like billy-o.

vigour ▶ **noun** ROBUSTNESS, health, hardiness, strength, sturdiness, toughness; bloom, radiance, energy, life, vitality, verve, spirit; zeal, passion, determination, dynamism, zest, pep, drive; *informal* oomph, get-up-and-go; *Brit. informal* welly.
– OPPOSITES lethargy.

vile ▶ **adjective** FOUL, nasty, unpleasant, bad, disagreeable, horrid, horrible, dreadful, abominable, atrocious, offensive, obnoxious, odious, unsavoury, repulsive, disgusting, distasteful, loathsome, hateful, nauseating, sickening; disgraceful, appalling, shocking, sorry, shabby, shameful, dishonourable, execrable, heinous, abhorrent, deplorable, monstrous, wicked, evil, iniquitous, depraved, debased; contemptible, despicable, reprehensible; *informal* gross, God-awful, low-down, lousy; *Brit. informal* beastly; *archaic* scurvy.
– OPPOSITES pleasant.

vilify ▶ **verb** DISPARAGE, denigrate, defame, run down, revile, abuse, speak ill of, criticize, condemn; malign, slander, libel; *N. Amer.* slur; *informal* pull apart, lay into, slam, bad-mouth; *Brit. informal* rubbish, slate; *Austral./NZ informal* bag, monster; *formal* derogate, calumniate.
– OPPOSITES commend.

villain ▶ **noun** CRIMINAL, lawbreaker, offender, felon, convict, malefactor, miscreant, wrongdoer; gangster, gunman, thief, robber; rogue, scoundrel, reprobate, ruffian, hoodlum; *Law* malfeasant; *informal* crook, con, crim, baddy; *dated* cad, knave; *archaic* blackguard.

villainous ▶ **adjective** WICKED, evil, iniquitous, sinful, nefarious, vile, foul, monstrous, outrageous, atrocious, abominable, reprehensible, hateful, odious, contemptible, horrible, heinous, egregious, diabolical, fiendish, vicious, murderous; criminal, illicit, unlawful, illegal, lawless; immoral, corrupt, degenerate, sordid, depraved, dishonourable, dishonest, unscrupulous, unprincipled; *informal* crooked, bent, low-down, dirty, shady; *dated* dastardly.
– OPPOSITES virtuous.

villainy ▶ **noun** WICKEDNESS, badness, evil, iniquity, wrongdoing, dishonesty, unscrupulousness, roguery, delinquency; crime, vice, criminality, lawlessness, lawbreaking, corruption; *Law* malfeasance; *informal* crookedness; *formal* turpitude; *archaic* knavery.

vindicate ▶ **verb** ❶ *he was vindicated by the jury* ACQUIT, clear, absolve, exonerate; discharge, liberate, free, redeem; *informal* let off (the hook); *formal* exculpate. ❷ *I had fully vindicated my request* JUSTIFY, warrant, substantiate, ratify, authenticate, verify, confirm, corroborate, prove, defend, support, back, evidence, endorse.

vindictive ▶ **adjective** VENGEFUL, revengeful, unforgiving, resentful, acrimonious, bitter, spiteful, mean, rancorous, venomous, malicious, malevolent, nasty, cruel, unkind; *informal* catty.
– OPPOSITES forgiving.

vintage ▶ **noun** ❶ *1986 was a classic vintage* YEAR. ❷ *he lost a vintage through frost* (GRAPE) HARVEST, crop, yield. ❸ *furniture of Louis XV vintage* PERIOD, era, epoch, time, origin; genre, style, kind, sort, type.
▶ **adjective** ❶ *vintage French wine* HIGH-QUALITY, quality, choice, select, superior, best. ❷ *vintage motor vehicles* CLASSIC, ageless, timeless; old, antique, heritage, historic. ❸ *his reaction was vintage Francis* CHARACTERISTIC, typical, pure.

violate ▶ **verb** ❶ *this violates fundamental human rights* CONTRAVENE, breach, infringe, break, transgress, overstep, disobey, defy, flout; disregard, ignore. ❷ *the tomb was violated* DESECRATE, profane, defile, degrade, debase; damage, vandalize, deface, destroy. ❸ *he drugged and then violated her* RAPE, assault, force oneself on, abuse, molest, interfere with; *dated* deflower, defile, dishonour, ruin; *poetic/literary* ravish.
– OPPOSITES respect.

violation ▶ **noun** ❶ *a violation of human rights* CONTRAVENTION, breach, infringement, infraction, transgression, defiance; neglect. ❷ *a violation of their private lives* INVASION, breach, infraction; trespass, intrusion, encroachment. ❸ *she was threatened with violation* RAPE, (sexual) assault, (sexual) abuse, molestation, interference; *dated* defloration, defilement, dishonour; *archaic* ravishment.

violence ▶ **noun** ❶ *police violence* BRUTALITY, brute force, ferocity, savagery, cruelty, sadism, barbarity, brutishness. ❷ *the violence of the blow* FORCEFULNESS, force, power, strength, might, savagery, ferocity, brutality. ❸ *the violence of his passion* INTENSITY, severity, strength, force, vehemence, power, potency, fervency, ardency, ferocity, fury.

violent ▶ **adjective** ❶ *a violent alcoholic* BRUTAL, vicious, savage, rough, aggressive, threatening, fierce, wild, ferocious; barbarous, barbaric, thuggish, cut-throat, homicidal, murderous, cruel. ❷ *a violent blow* POWERFUL, forceful, hard, sharp, smart, strong, vigorous, mighty, hefty; savage, ferocious, brutal, vicious. ❸ *violent jealousy* INTENSE, extreme, strong, powerful, vehement, intemperate, unbridled, uncontrollable, ungovernable, inordinate, consuming, passionate.
– OPPOSITES gentle, weak, mild.

VIP ▶ noun CELEBRITY, famous person, very important person, personality, big name, star, superstar; dignitary, luminary, worthy, grandee, lion, notable, notability, personage; *informal* heavyweight, celeb, bigwig, big shot, big cheese, nob, honcho, top dog, megastar; *N. Amer. informal* big wheel, (big) kahuna, high muckamuck.

virago ▶ noun HARRIDAN, shrew, dragon, termagant, vixen; fishwife, witch, hellcat, she-devil, tartar, martinet, spitfire, ogress; *informal* battleaxe; *archaic* scold.

virgin ▶ noun *she remained a virgin* chaste woman, celibate; *formal* virgo intacta; *poetic/literary* maiden, maid, vestal.

▶ adjective ❶ *virgin forest* UNTOUCHED, unspoilt, untainted, immaculate, pristine, flawless; spotless, unsullied, unpolluted, undefiled, perfect; unchanged, intact; unexplored, uncharted, unmapped. ❷ *virgin girls* CHASTE, virginal, celibate, abstinent; unmarried, unwed, maiden, maidenly; pure, uncorrupted, incorrupt, undefiled, unsullied, innocent; *poetic/literary* vestal.

virginal ▶ adjective. *See* VIRGIN adjective sense 2.

virginity ▶ noun CHASTITY, maidenhood, honour, purity, innocence; celibacy, abstinence; *informal* cherry; *archaic* virtue.

virile ▶ adjective MANLY, masculine, male; strong, tough, vigorous, robust, muscular, muscly, brawny, rugged, sturdy, husky; red-blooded, fertile; *informal* macho, laddish, butch, beefy, hunky.
–OPPOSITES effeminate.

virtual ▶ adjective EFFECTIVE, in effect, near (enough), essential, practical, to all intents and purposes; indirect, implied, implicit, unacknowledged, tacit.

virtually ▶ adverb EFFECTIVELY, in effect, all but, more or less, practically, almost, nearly, close to, verging on, just about, as good as, essentially, to all intents and purposes, as near as dammit; roughly, approximately; *informal* pretty much, pretty well; *poetic/literary* well nigh, nigh on.

virtue ▶ noun ❶ *the simple virtue of peasant life* GOODNESS, virtuousness, righteousness, morality, integrity, dignity, rectitude, honour, decency, respectability, nobility, worthiness, purity; principles, ethics. ❷ *promptness was not one of his virtues* GOOD POINT, good quality, strong point, asset, forte, attribute, strength, talent. ❸ (*archaic*) *she lost her virtue in the city. See* VIRGINITY. ❹ *I can see no virtue in this* MERIT, advantage, benefit, usefulness, strength, efficacy.
–OPPOSITES vice, failing, disadvantage.

■ **by virtue of** BECAUSE OF, on account of, by dint of, by means of, by way of, via, through, as a result of, as a consequence of, on the strength of, owing to, thanks to, due to, by reason of.

virtuosity ▶ noun SKILL, skilfulness, mastery, expertise, prowess, proficiency, ability, aptitude; excellence, brilliance, talent, genius, artistry, flair, panache, finesse, wizardry; *informal* know-how.

virtuoso ▶ noun *the pianist is clearly a virtuoso* GENIUS, expert, (past) master, maestro, artist, prodigy, marvel, adept, professional, doyen, veteran; star, champion; *informal* hotshot, wizard, pro, ace; *Brit. informal* dab hand.
–OPPOSITES duffer.

▶ adjective *a virtuoso violinist* SKILFUL, expert, accomplished, masterly, master, consummate, proficient, talented, gifted, adept, able, good, competent, capable; impressive, outstanding, exceptional, magnificent, supreme, first-rate, brilliant, excellent; *informal* superb, mean, ace.
–OPPOSITES incompetent.

virtuous ▶ adjective RIGHTEOUS, good, moral, ethical, upright, upstanding, high-minded, principled, exemplary; law-abiding, irreproachable, blameless, guiltless, unimpeachable, honest, honourable, reputable, decent, respectable, noble, worthy, meritorious; pure, whiter than white, saintly, angelic; *informal* squeaky clean.

virulent ▶ adjective ❶ *virulent herbicides* POISONOUS, toxic, venomous, noxious, deadly, lethal, fatal, mortal, dangerous, harmful, injurious, pernicious, damaging, destructive; *poetic/literary* deathly, nocuous. ❷ *a virulent epidemic* INFECTIOUS, infective, contagious, communicable, transmittable, transmissible, spreading, pestilential; *informal* catching. ❸ *a virulent attack on morals* VITRIOLIC, malicious, malevolent, hostile, spiteful, venomous, vicious, vindictive, bitter, rancorous, acrimonious, scathing, caustic, withering, nasty, savage, harsh.
–OPPOSITES harmless, amicable.

viscous ▶ adjective STICKY, gummy, gluey, adhesive, tacky, adherent, treacly, syrupy; glutinous, gelatinous, thick, viscid, mucous, mucoid, mucilaginous; *informal* gooey, gloopy; *N. Amer. informal* gloppy.

visible ▶ adjective PERCEPTIBLE, perceivable, seeable, observable, noticeable, detectable, discernible; in sight, in/on view, on display; evident, apparent, manifest, transparent, plain, clear, conspicuous, obvious, patent, unmistakable, unconcealed, undisguised, prominent, salient, striking, glaring.

vision ▶ noun ❶ *her vision was blurred by tears* EYESIGHT, sight, observation, (visual) perception; eyes; view, perspective. ❷ *visions of the ancestral pilgrims* APPARITION, spectre, phantom, ghost, wraith, manifestation; hallucination, illusion, mirage; *informal* spook; *poetic/literary* phantasm, shade. ❸ *visions of a better future* DREAM, daydream, reverie; plan, hope; fantasy, pipe dream, delusion. ❹ *his speech lacked vision*

IMAGINATION, creativity, inventiveness, innovation, inspiration, intuition, perception, insight, foresight, prescience. ❺ *Melissa was a vision in lilac* BEAUTIFUL SIGHT, feast for the eyes, pleasure to behold, delight, dream, beauty, picture, joy, marvel, sensation; *informal* sight for sore eyes, stunner, knockout, looker, peach; *Brit. informal* smasher.

visionary ▶ **adjective** ❶ *a visionary leader* INSPIRED, imaginative, creative, inventive, ingenious, enterprising, innovative; insightful, perceptive, intuitive, prescient, discerning, shrewd, wise, clever, resourceful; idealistic, romantic, quixotic, dreamy; *informal* starry-eyed. ❷ (*archaic*) *a visionary image. See* IMAGINARY.
▶ **noun** ❶ *a visionary pictured him in hell* SEER, mystic, oracle, prophet(ess), soothsayer, augur, diviner, clairvoyant, crystal-gazer; *Scottish* spaewife; *poetic/literary* sibyl. ❷ *a visionary can't run a business effectively* DREAMER, daydreamer, idealist, romantic, fantasist, utopian.

visit ▶ **verb** ❶ *I visited my dear uncle* CALL ON, pay a visit to, go to see, look in on; stay with, holiday with; stop by, drop by; *N. Amer.* visit with, go see; *informal* pop in on, drop in on, look up. ❷ *Alex was visiting America* STAY IN, stop over in, spend time in, holiday in, vacation in; tour, explore, see; *informal* do. ❸ *they were visited with many epidemics* AFFLICT, attack, trouble, torment; *archaic* smite.
▶ **noun** ❶ *she paid a visit to her mum* (SOCIAL) CALL. ❷ *a visit to the museum* TRIP TO, tour of, look round; stopover, stay; holiday, break, vacation; *formal* sojourn.

visitation ▶ **noun** ❶ *the bishop's pastoral visitations* (OFFICIAL) VISIT, tour of inspection, survey, examination. ❷ *a visitation from God* APPARITION, vision, appearance, manifestation, materialization. ❸ *Jehovah punished them by visitations* AFFLICTION, scourge, bane, curse, plague, blight, disaster, tragedy, catastrophe; punishment, retribution, vengeance.

visitor ▶ **noun** ❶ *I am expecting a visitor* GUEST, caller; company; *archaic* visitant. ❷ *the monument attracts foreign visitors* TOURIST, traveller, holidaymaker, day tripper, tripper, vacationer, vacationist, sightseer; pilgrim; foreigner, outsider, stranger, alien; *Brit. informal* emmet, grockle.

vista ▶ **noun** VIEW, prospect, panorama, aspect, perspective, spectacle, sight; scenery, landscape.

visual ▶ **adjective** ❶ *visual defects* OPTICAL, optic, ocular, eye; vision, sight. ❷ *a visual indication that the alarm works* VISIBLE, perceptible, perceivable, discernible.

visualize ▶ **verb** ENVISAGE, envision, conjure up, picture, call to mind, see, imagine, evoke, dream up, fantasize about, conceptualize, contemplate.

vital ▶ **adjective** ❶ *it is vital that action is taken* ESSENTIAL, of the essence, critical, crucial, indispensable, all-important, imperative, mandatory, urgent, pressing, burning, compelling, high-priority; *informal* earth-shattering, world-shaking. ❷ *the vital organs* MAJOR, main, chief; essential, necessary. ❸ *he is young and vital* LIVELY, energetic, active, sprightly, spry, spirited, vivacious, exuberant, bouncy, enthusiastic, vibrant, zestful, sparkling, dynamic, vigorous, lusty, hale and hearty; *informal* peppy, spunky, full of beans, bright-eyed and bushy-tailed.
–OPPOSITES unimportant, minor, listless.

vitality ▶ **noun** LIVELINESS, life, energy, spirit, vivacity, exuberance, buoyancy, bounce, verve, vim, pep, brio, zest, sparkle, dynamism, passion, fire, vigour, drive; *informal* get-up-and-go.

vitriolic ▶ **adjective** ACRIMONIOUS, rancorous, bitter, caustic, mordant, acerbic, trenchant, virulent, spiteful, savage, venomous, poisonous, malicious, splenetic; nasty, mean, cruel, unkind, harsh, vindictive, scathing, barbed, wounding, sharp, cutting, withering, sarcastic; *informal* bitchy, catty.

vituperate ▶ **verb** (*archaic*). *See* REVILE.

vituperation ▶ **noun** INVECTIVE, revilement, condemnation, opprobrium, scolding, criticism, disapprobation, fault-finding; blame, abuse, insults, vilification, denunciation, obloquy, denigration, disparagement, slander, libel, defamation, slurs, aspersions; vitriol, venom; *informal* flak; *Brit. informal* stick; *formal* castigation.
–OPPOSITES praise.

vivacious ▶ **adjective** LIVELY, spirited, bubbly, ebullient, buoyant, sparkling, light-hearted, jaunty, merry, happy, jolly, full of fun, cheery, cheerful, perky, sunny, breezy, enthusiastic, irrepressible, vibrant, vital, zestful, energetic, dynamic; *informal* peppy, bouncy, upbeat, chirpy; *dated* gay.
–OPPOSITES dull.

vivid ▶ **adjective** ❶ *a vivid blue sea* BRIGHT, colourful, brilliant, radiant, vibrant, strong, bold, deep, intense, rich, warm. ❷ *a vivid account of urban poverty* GRAPHIC, evocative, realistic, lifelike, faithful, authentic, clear, detailed, lucid, striking, arresting, impressive, colourful, rich, dramatic, lively, stimulating, interesting, fascinating, scintillating; memorable, powerful, stirring, moving, haunting.
–OPPOSITES dull, vague.

viz. ▶ **adverb** NAMELY, that is to say, in other words, to wit, specifically; such as, as, like, for instance, for example; *formal* videlicet.

vocabulary ▶ **noun** ❶ *she has an extensive vocabulary* LEXICON, lexis. ❷ *we listed the terms in a vocabulary* WORDBOOK, dictionary, wordfinder, glossary, lexicon, thesaurus.

vocal ▶ **adjective** ❶ *vocal sounds* VOCALIZED,

voiced, uttered, articulated, oral; spoken, said. ❷ *a vocal critic of the government* VOCIFEROUS, outspoken, forthright, plain-spoken, blunt, frank, candid, open; vehement, vigorous, emphatic, insistent, forceful, zealous, clamorous.

vocation ▶ noun CALLING, life's work, mission, purpose, function; profession, occupation, career, job, employment, trade, craft, business, line (of work), métier.

vociferous ▶ adjective. *See* VOCAL sense 2.

vogue ▶ noun *the skirt is enjoying a new vogue* FASHION, trend, fad, fancy, craze, rage, enthusiasm, passion, obsession, mania; fashionableness, popularity, currency, favour; *informal* trendiness.

■ **in vogue** FASHIONABLE, voguish, stylish, modish, up to date, up to the minute, modern, current; prevalent, popular, in favour, in demand, sought-after, all the rage; chic, smart, le dernier cri; *informal* trendy, hip, cool, big, happening, now, in, with it; *N. Amer. informal* tony, kicky.

voice ▶ noun ❶ *she lost her voice* POWER OF SPEECH. ❷ *he gave voice to his anger* EXPRESSION, utterance, verbalization, vocalization. ❸ *the voice of the people* OPINION, view, feeling, wish, desire, vote, input. ❹ *a powerful voice for conservation* MOUTHPIECE, representative, spokesperson, intermediary; forum, vehicle, instrument, channel, organ, agent.

▶ verb *they voiced their opposition* EXPRESS, vocalize, communicate, declare, state, assert, reveal, proclaim, announce, table, air, ventilate, vent; utter, say, speak, articulate; *informal* come out with.

void ▶ noun *the void of space* VACUUM, emptiness, nothingness, blankness, vacuity; (empty) space, gap, cavity, chasm, abyss, gulf, pit.

▶ verb ❶ *the contract was voided* INVALIDATE, annul, nullify; negate, quash, cancel, countermand, repeal, revoke, rescind, retract, withdraw, reverse, undo, abolish; *Law* vacate; *formal* abrogate. ❷ *they voided their bladders* EVACUATE, empty, drain, clear, purge. ❸ *bacteria are voided in the urine* EJECT, expel, emit, discharge, pass, excrete, exude, eliminate.

– OPPOSITES validate, fill.

▶ adjective ❶ *vast void spaces* EMPTY, vacant, blank, bare, clear, free, unfilled, unoccupied, uninhabited. ❷ *a country void of man or beast* DEVOID OF, empty of, vacant of, bereft of, free from; lacking, wanting, without. ❸ *the election was void* INVALID, null, ineffective, non-viable, useless, worthless, nugatory.

– OPPOSITES full, occupied, valid.

volatile ▶ adjective ❶ *a volatile personality* UNPREDICTABLE, changeable, variable, inconstant, inconsistent, erratic, irregular, unstable, turbulent, blowing hot and cold, varying, shifting, fluctuating, fluid, mutable; mercurial, capricious, whimsical, fickle, flighty, impulsive, temperamental, highly strung, excitable, emotional, fiery, moody, tempestuous. ❷ *the atmosphere is too volatile for an election* TENSE, strained, fraught, uneasy, uncomfortable, charged, explosive, inflammatory, turbulent; *informal* nail-biting; *Brit. informal* dodgy. ❸ *a volatile organic compound* EVAPORATIVE, vaporous; explosive, inflammable; unstable, labile.

– OPPOSITES stable, calm.

volition

■ **of one's own volition** OF ONE'S OWN FREE WILL, of one's own accord, by choice, by preference; voluntarily, willingly, readily, freely, intentionally, consciously, deliberately, on purpose, purposely; gladly, with pleasure.

volley ▶ noun BARRAGE, cannonade, battery, bombardment, salvo, fusillade; storm, hail, shower, deluge, torrent; *historical* broadside.

voluble ▶ adjective TALKATIVE, loquacious, garrulous, verbose, wordy, chatty, gossipy, effusive, gushing, forthcoming, conversational, communicative, expansive; articulate, fluent; *informal* mouthy, gabby, gassy, windy.

– OPPOSITES taciturn.

volume ▶ noun ❶ *a volume from the library* BOOK, publication, tome, hardback, paperback, title; manual, almanac, compendium. ❷ *a glass syringe of known volume* CAPACITY, cubic measure, size, magnitude, mass, bulk, extent; dimensions, proportions, measurements. ❸ *a huge volume of water* QUANTITY, amount, proportion, measure, mass, bulk. ❹ *she turned the volume down* LOUDNESS, sound, amplification.

voluminous ▶ adjective CAPACIOUS, roomy, spacious, ample, full, big, large, generous; billowing, baggy, loose-fitting; *formal* commodious.

voluntarily ▶ adverb OF ONE'S OWN FREE WILL, of one's own accord, of one's own volition, by choice, by preference; willingly, readily, freely, intentionally, deliberately, on purpose, purposely, spontaneously; gladly, with pleasure.

voluntary ▶ adjective ❶ *attendance is voluntary* OPTIONAL, discretionary, elective, non-compulsory, volitional; *Law* permissive. ❷ *voluntary work* UNPAID, unsalaried, for free, without charge, for nothing; honorary, volunteer; *Law* pro bono (publico).

– OPPOSITES compulsory, paid.

volunteer ▶ verb ❶ *I volunteered my services* OFFER, tender, proffer, put forward, put up, venture. ❷ *he volunteered as a driver* OFFER ONE'S SERVICES, present oneself, make oneself available.

▶ noun *each volunteer was tested three times* SUBJECT, participant, case, client, patient; *informal* guinea pig.

voluptuous ▶ adjective ❶ *a voluptuous model* CURVACEOUS, shapely, ample, buxom, full-fig-

ured, Junoesque, Rubenesque; seductive, alluring, sultry, sensuous, sexy; *informal* curvy, busty, slinky. ❷ *she was voluptuous by nature* HEDONISTIC, sybaritic, epicurean, pleasure-loving, self-indulgent; decadent, intemperate, immoderate, dissolute, sensual, licentious.
– OPPOSITES scrawny, ascetic.

vomit ▶ **verb** ❶ *he needed to vomit* BE SICK, spew, fetch up; heave, retch, reach, gag; *N. Amer.* get sick; *informal* throw up, puke, chunder, chuck up, hurl; *Brit. informal* honk; *Scottish informal* boke; *N. Amer. informal* barf, upchuck. ❷ *I vomited my breakfast* REGURGITATE, bring up, spew up, cough up; *informal* chuck up, throw up, puke; *Brit. informal* sick up; *N. Amer. informal* spit up. ❸ *the printer is vomiting paper* EJECT, issue, emit, expel, discharge, disgorge, throw out, spew out, belch.
▶ **noun** *a coat stained with vomit* SICK; *informal* chunder, puke, spew; *N. Amer. informal* barf; *Medicine* vomitus.

voracious ▶ **adjective** INSATIABLE, unquenchable, unappeasable, prodigious, uncontrollable, compulsive, gluttonous, greedy, rapacious; enthusiastic, eager, keen, avid, desirous, hungry, ravenous; *informal* piggish.

vortex ▶ **noun** WHIRLWIND, whirlpool, gyre, maelstrom, eddy, swirl.

vote ▶ **noun** ❶ *a rigged vote* BALLOT, poll, election, referendum, plebiscite; show of hands. ❷ *in 1918 women got the vote* SUFFRAGE, voting rights, franchise, enfranchisement; voice, say.
▶ **verb** ❶ *only half of them voted* GO TO THE POLLS, cast one's vote. ❷ *I vote we have one more game* SUGGEST, propose, recommend, advocate, move, table, submit.
■ **vote someone in** ELECT, return, select, choose, pick, adopt, appoint, designate, opt for, plump for, decide on.

vouch
■ **vouch for** ATTEST TO, confirm, affirm, verify, swear to, testify to, bear out, back up, support, stick up for, corroborate, substantiate, prove, uphold, give credence to, endorse, certify, warrant, validate.

voucher ▶ **noun** COUPON, token, ticket, licence, permit, carnet, pass; chit, slip, stub, docket; *Brit. informal* chitty; *N. Amer. informal* ducat, comp.

vouchsafe ▶ **verb** ❶ *the grace which God had vouchsafed him* GRANT, give, accord; confer on, bestow on, favour with. ❷ *you never vouchsafed that information before* DISCLOSE, reveal, divulge, impart, give away, make known, broadcast, air; *informal* blab, spill; *Brit. informal* cough. ❸ *if he would only vouchsafe to talk with them* DEIGN, condescend, stoop, lower oneself, humble oneself, demean oneself.
– OPPOSITES withhold, conceal.

vow ▶ **noun** *a vow of silence* OATH, pledge, promise, bond, covenant, commitment, avowal, profession, affirmation, attestation, assurance, guarantee; word (of honour); *formal* troth.
– RELATED TERMS votive.
▶ **verb** *I vowed to do better* SWEAR, pledge, promise, avow, undertake, engage, make a commitment, give one's word, guarantee; *archaic* plight.

voyage ▶ **noun** *the voyage lasted 120 days* JOURNEY, trip, expedition, excursion, tour; hike, trek; pilgrimage, quest, crusade, odyssey; cruise, passage, flight, drive.
▶ **verb** *he voyaged through Peru* TRAVEL, journey, tour, globetrot; sail, steam, cruise, fly, drive; *informal* gallivant; *archaic* peregrinate.

vulgar ▶ **adjective** ❶ *a vulgar joke* RUDE, indecent, indelicate, offensive, distasteful, coarse, crude, ribald, risqué, naughty, suggestive, racy, earthy, off colour, bawdy, obscene, lewd, salacious, smutty, dirty, filthy, pornographic, X-rated; *informal* sleazy, raunchy, blue, locker-room; *Brit. informal* saucy, close to the bone; *N. Amer. informal* gamy; *euphemistic* adult. ❷ *the decor was lavish but vulgar* TASTELESS, crass, tawdry, ostentatious, flamboyant, overdone, showy, gaudy, garish, brassy, kitsch, tinselly, loud; *informal* flash, flashy, tacky, over the top. ❸ *it was vulgar for a woman to whistle* IMPOLITE, ill-mannered, unmannerly, indecorous, unseemly, ill-bred, boorish, uncouth, crude, rough; unsophisticated, unrefined, common.
– OPPOSITES tasteful, decorous.

vulnerable ▶ **adjective** ❶ *a vulnerable city* IN DANGER, in peril, in jeopardy, at risk, endangered, unsafe, unprotected, unguarded; open to attack, assailable, exposed, wide open; undefended, unfortified, unarmed, defenceless, helpless, pregnable. ❷ *he is vulnerable to criticism* EXPOSED TO, open to, liable to, prone to, prey to, susceptible to, subject to, an easy target for; *archaic* susceptive of.
– OPPOSITES resilient.

Ww

wacky ▶ **adjective** (*informal*). *See* ECCENTRIC adjective.

wad ▶ **noun** ❶ *a wad of cotton wool* LUMP, clump, mass, plug, pad, hunk, wedge, ball, cake, nugget; bit, piece; *Brit. informal* wodge. ❷ *a wad of dollar bills* BUNDLE, roll, pile, stack, sheaf; *N. Amer.* bankroll. ❸ *a wad of tobacco* QUID, twist, plug, chew.

▶ **verb** *the teddy bear was wadded with cotton* STUFF, pad, fill, pack; wrap, cover, cushion.

wadding ▶ **noun** STUFFING, filling, filler, packing, padding, cushioning, quilting.

waddle ▶ **verb** TODDLE, dodder, totter, wobble, shuffle; duckwalk.

wade ▶ **verb** ❶ *they waded in the icy water* PADDLE, wallow, dabble, squelch; *informal* splosh. ❷ *I had to wade through some hefty documents* PLOUGH, plod, trawl, labour, toil; study, browse; *informal* slog.

■ **wade in** (*informal*) SET TO WORK, buckle down, go to it, put one's shoulder to the wheel; *informal* plunge in, dive in, get stuck in, get cracking.

waffle (*Brit. informal*) ▶ **verb** *they waffled on about the baby* PRATTLE, chatter, babble, ramble, jabber, gibber, gabble, prate, drivel; *informal* blather; *Brit. informal* rabbit, witter, natter.

▶ **noun** *my panic reduced the interview to waffle* PRATTLE, drivel, nonsense, twaddle, gibberish, mumbo-jumbo; *informal* hot air, poppycock, bunk, hogwash, gobbledegook.

waft ▶ **verb** ❶ *smoke wafted through the air* DRIFT, float, glide, whirl, travel. ❷ *a breeze wafted the smell towards us* CONVEY, carry, transport, bear; blow, puff.

wag[1] ▶ **verb** ❶ *the dog's tail wagged frantically* SWING, swish, switch, sway, shake, quiver, twitch, whip; *informal* waggle. ❷ *he wagged his stick at them* SHAKE, wave, wiggle, flourish, brandish.

▶ **noun** ❶ *a feeble wag of her tail* SWING, shake, swish, switch, quiver, twitch, whip; *informal* waggle. ❷ *a wag of the finger* SHAKE, flourish, wiggle, wobble, wave; *informal* waggle.

wag[2] ▶ **noun** (*informal*) *he's a bit of a wag. See* JOKER.

wage ▶ **noun** ❶ *the farm workers' wages* PAY, payment, remuneration, salary, stipend, fee, honorarium; income, revenue; profit, gain, reward; earnings; *formal* emolument. ❷ *the wages of sin is death* REWARD, recompense, retribution; returns, deserts.

▶ **verb** *they waged war on the guerrillas* ENGAGE IN, carry on, conduct, execute, pursue, prosecute, proceed with.

wager ▶ **noun** *a wager of £100* BET, gamble, speculation; stake, pledge, ante; *Brit. informal* flutter.

▶ **verb** *I'll wager a pound on the home team* BET, gamble, lay odds, put money on; stake, pledge, risk, venture, hazard, chance; *informal* punt.

waggle ▶ **verb** (*informal*). *See* WAG[1] verb senses 1, 2.

waif ▶ **noun** RAGAMUFFIN, urchin; foundling, orphan, stray; *derogatory* guttersnipe; *dated* gamin.

wail ▶ **noun** *a wail of anguish* HOWL, bawl, yowl, cry, moan, groan; shriek, scream, yelp.

▶ **verb** *the children began to wail* HOWL, weep, cry, sob, moan, groan, keen, lament, yowl, snivel, whimper, whine, bawl, shriek, scream, yelp, caterwaul; *Scottish* greet; *informal* blubber, blub.

wait ▶ **verb** ❶ *we'll wait in the airport* STAY (PUT), remain, rest, stop, halt, pause; linger, loiter, dally; *informal* stick around; *archaic* tarry. ❷ *she had to wait until her bags arrived* STAND BY, hold back, bide one's time, hang fire, mark time, kill time, waste time, kick one's heels, twiddle one's thumbs; *informal* hold on, hang around, sit tight, hold one's horses. ❸ *they were waiting for the kettle to boil* AWAIT; anticipate, expect, be ready. ❹ *that job will have to wait* BE POSTPONED, be delayed, be put off, be deferred; *informal* be put on the back burner, be put on ice.

▶ **noun** *a long wait* DELAY, hold-up, interval, interlude, intermission, pause, break, stay, cessation, suspension, stoppage, halt, interruption, lull, respite, recess, moratorium, hiatus, gap, rest.

■ **wait on someone** SERVE, attend to, tend, cater for/to; minister to, take care of, look after, see to.

■ **wait up** STAY AWAKE, stay up.

waiter, waitress ▶ **noun** SERVER, stewardess, steward, attendant, garçon; hostess, host; butler, servant, page; *N. Amer.* waitperson.

waive ▶ **verb** ❶ *he waived his right to a hearing* RELINQUISH, renounce, give up, abandon, surrender, yield, reject, dispense with, abdicate, sacrifice, refuse, turn down, spurn. ❷ *the manager waived the rules* DISREGARD, ignore, overlook, set aside, forgo, drop.

wake[1] ▶ **verb** ❶ *at 4.30 am Mark woke up* AWAKE, waken (up), awaken, rouse oneself, stir, come to, come round, bestir oneself; get up, get out of bed; *formal* arise. ❷ *she woke her husband* ROUSE, arouse, waken; *Brit. informal* knock up. ❸ *a shock woke him up a bit* ACTIVATE, stimulate, galvanize, enliven, stir up, spur on, ginger up, buoy up, invigorate, revitalize; *informal* perk up, pep up. ❹ *they woke up to what we were saying* REALIZE, become aware of, become conscious of, become mindful of. ❺ *the name woke an old memory* EVOKE, conjure up, rouse, stir, revive, awaken, rekindle, rejuvenate, stimulate.

– OPPOSITES sleep.

▶ **noun** *a mourner at a wake* VIGIL, watch; funeral.

wake[2] ▶ **noun** *the cruiser's wake* BACKWASH, wash, slipstream, turbulence; trail, path.

■ **in the wake of** IN THE AFTERMATH OF, after, subsequent to, following, as a result of, as a consequence of, on account of, because of, owing to.

wakeful ▶ **adjective** ❶ *he had been wakeful all night* AWAKE, restless, restive, tossing and turning; *archaic* watchful. ❷ *I was suddenly wakeful* ALERT, watchful, vigilant, on the lookout, on one's guard, attentive, heedful, wary.

– OPPOSITES asleep, inattentive.

waken ▶ **verb**. *See* WAKE[1] verb senses 1, 2.

Wales ▶ **noun** Cambria; *Brit.* the Principality.

walk ▶ **verb** ❶ *they walked along the road* STROLL, saunter, amble, trudge, plod, hike, tramp, trek, march, stride, troop, patrol, step out, wander, ramble, tread, prowl, footslog, promenade, roam, traipse; stretch one's legs; *informal* mosey, pootle, hoof it; *Brit. informal* yomp; *formal* perambulate. ❷ *he walked her home* ACCOMPANY, escort, guide, show, see, usher, take, chaperone, steer, shepherd.

▶ **noun** ❶ *country walks* STROLL, saunter, amble, promenade; ramble, hike, tramp, march; turn, airing; *dated* constitutional. ❷ *her elegant walk* GAIT, step, stride, tread. ❸ *the riverside walk* PATHWAY, path, footpath, track, walkway, promenade, footway, pavement, trail, towpath.

■ **walk all over someone** (*informal*) ❶ *be firm or they'll walk all over you* TAKE ADVANTAGE OF, impose on, exploit, use, abuse, misuse, manipulate, take liberties with; *informal* take for a ride, run rings around. ❷ *we walked all over the home team. See* TROUNCE.

■ **walk off/away with** ❶ (*informal*) *she walked off with my car keys. See* STEAL verb sense 1. ❷ *he walked off with four awards* WIN EASILY, win hands down, attain, earn, gain, receive, acquire, secure, collect, pick up, net; *informal* bag.

■ **walk of life** CLASS, status, rank, caste, sphere, arena; profession, career, vocation, job, occupation, employment, business, trade, craft; province, field; *dated* station.

■ **walk out** ❶ *he walked out in a temper* LEAVE, depart, get up and go, storm off/out, flounce out, absent oneself; *informal* take off. ❷ *teachers walked out in protest* (GO ON) STRIKE, stop work; protest, mutiny, revolt; *Brit. informal* down tools.

■ **walk out on someone** DESERT, abandon, leave, betray, throw over, jilt, run out on, rat on; *informal* chuck, dump, ditch.

walker ▶ **noun** HIKER, rambler, traveller, roamer, rover, stroller; pedestrian; *poetic/literary* wayfarer.

walkout ▶ **noun** STRIKE, stoppage, industrial action; revolt, rebellion.

walkover ▶ **noun** EASY VICTORY, rout, landslide; *informal* piece of cake, doddle, pushover, cinch, breeze, picnic, whitewash; *N. Amer. informal* duck soup; *dated* snip.

wall ▶ **noun** ❶ *brick walls* BARRIER, partition, enclosure, screen, panel, separator. ❷ *an ancient city wall* FORTIFICATION, rampart, barricade, bulwark, stockade. ❸ *break down the walls that stop world trade* OBSTACLE, barrier, fence; impediment, hindrance, block, check.

– RELATED TERMS mural.

▶ **verb** ❶ *tenements walled in the courtyard* ENCLOSE, bound, encircle, confine, hem, close in, shut in, fence in. ❷ *the doorway had been walled up* BLOCK, seal, close, brick up.

■ **go to the wall** (*informal*). *See* FAIL sense 1.

■ **off the wall** (*informal*). *See* UNCONVENTIONAL.

wallet ▶ **noun** PURSE; *N. Amer.* billfold, pocketbook; *Brit. dated* notecase.

wallop ▶ **verb** (*informal*). *See* THUMP verb sense 1.

wallow ▶ **verb** ❶ *buffalo wallowed in the lake* LOLL ABOUT/AROUND, lie about/around, splash about/around; slosh, wade, paddle; *informal* splosh. ❷ *a ship wallowing in stormy seas* ROLL, lurch, toss, plunge, reel, rock, flounder, keel, list; labour. ❸ *she seems to wallow in self-pity* LUXURIATE, bask, take pleasure, take satisfaction, indulge (oneself), delight, revel, glory; enjoy, like, love, relish, savour; *informal* get a kick out of, get a buzz from.

wan ▶ **adjective** ❶ *she looked so wan and frail* PALE, pallid, ashen, white, grey; anaemic, colourless, bloodless, waxen, chalky, pasty, peaky, sickly, washed out, drained, drawn, ghostly. ❷ *the wan light of the moon* DIM, faint, weak, feeble, pale, watery.

– OPPOSITES flushed, bright.

wand ▶ **noun** BATON, stick, staff, bar, dowel, rod; twig, cane, birch, switch; *historical* caduceus.

wander ▶ **verb** ❶ *I wandered around the estate* STROLL, amble, saunter, walk, dawdle, potter, ramble, meander; roam, rove, range, drift, prowl; *Scottish & Irish* stravaig; *informal* traipse, mosey, tootle; *Brit. informal* mooch. ❷ *we are wandering from the point* STRAY, depart, diverge, veer, swerve, deviate, digress, drift, get sidetracked. ❸ *the child wandered off* GET LOST, lose one's way, go astray. ❹ *the road wanders along the shore* MEANDER, wind, twist, curve, zigzag, bend, snake.

▶ **noun** *let's go for a wander* STROLL, amble, saunter, walk, potter, ramble, prowl, promenade; turn, breather, airing; *informal* traipse, mosey, tootle; *Brit. informal* mooch; *dated* constitutional.

wanderer ▶ **noun** TRAVELLER, rambler, hiker, migrant, globetrotter, roamer, rover; itinerant, rolling stone, bird of passage, nomad; tramp, drifter, vagabond, vagrant; *Brit. informal* dosser; *N. Amer. informal* hobo, bum; *poetic/literary* wayfarer.

wane ▶ **verb** ❶ *the moon is waning* DECREASE, diminish, dwindle. ❷ *their support was waning* DECLINE, diminish, decrease, dwindle, shrink, tail off, ebb, fade (away), lessen, peter out, fall off, recede, slump, flag, weaken, give way, wither, evaporate, die out; *poetic/literary* evanesce.
– OPPOSITES wax, grow.
■ **on the wane** DECLINING, decreasing, diminishing, dwindling, shrinking, contracting, tapering off, subsiding, ebbing, fading away, dissolving, petering out, winding down, falling off, on the way out, receding, flagging, melting away, crumbling, withering, disintegrating, evaporating, dying out.

wangle ▶ **verb** (*informal*). *See* CONTRIVE.

want ▶ **verb** ❶ *do you want more coffee?* DESIRE, wish for, hope for, fancy, care for, like; long for, yearn for, crave, hanker after, hunger for, thirst for, cry out for, covet; need; *informal* have a yen for, be dying for. ❷ (*informal*) *his toaster wants repairing* NEED, require, demand, cry out for. ❸ (*informal*) *you want to be more careful* SHOULD, ought, need, must. ❹ (*archaic*) *his poem wants a name* LACK, be without, have need of, be devoid of, be bereft of.
▶ **noun** ❶ *his want of vigilance* LACK, absence, non-existence, unavailability; dearth, deficiency, inadequacy, insufficiency, paucity, shortage, scarcity, deficit. ❷ *a time of want* NEED, neediness, austerity, privation, deprivation, poverty, impoverishment, penury, destitution; famine, drought. ❸ *all her wants would be taken care of* WISH, desire, demand, longing, yearning, fancy, craving, hankering; need, requirement; *informal* yen.

wanting ▶ **adjective** ❶ *the defences were found wanting* DEFICIENT, inadequate, lacking, insufficient, imperfect, unacceptable, flawed, faulty, defective, unsound, substandard, inferior, second-rate, poor, shoddy; *Brit. informal* not much cop. ❷ *the kneecap is wanting in amphibians* ABSENT, missing, lacking, non-existent. ❸ *millions were left wanting for food* WITHOUT, lacking, deprived of, devoid of, bereft of, in need of; deficient in, short on; *informal* minus.
– OPPOSITES sufficient, present.

wanton ▶ **adjective** ❶ *wanton destruction* DELIBERATE, wilful, malicious, spiteful, wicked, cruel; gratuitous, unprovoked, motiveless, arbitrary, groundless, unjustifiable, needless, unnecessary, uncalled for, senseless, pointless, purposeless, meaningless, empty. ❷ *a wanton seductress* PROMISCUOUS, immoral, immodest, indecent, shameless, unchaste, fast, impure, abandoned, lustful, lecherous, lascivious, libidinous, licentious, dissolute, debauched, degenerate, corrupt, whorish, disreputable; *dated* loose.
– OPPOSITES justifiable, chaste.

war ▶ **noun** ❶ *the Napoleonic wars* CONFLICT, warfare, combat, fighting, (military) action, bloodshed, struggle; battle, skirmish, fight, clash, engagement, encounter; offensive, attack, campaign; hostilities; jihad, crusade. ❷ *the war against drugs* CAMPAIGN, crusade, battle, fight, struggle, movement, drive.
– RELATED TERMS belligerent, martial.
– OPPOSITES peace.
▶ **verb** *rival Emperors warred against each other* FIGHT, battle, combat, wage war, take up arms; feud, quarrel, struggle, contend, wrangle, cross swords; attack, engage, take on, skirmish with.

warble ▶ **verb** *larks warbled in the sky* TRILL, sing, chirp, chirrup, cheep, twitter, tweet, chatter, peep.
▶ **noun** *a warble pierced the air* TRILL, song, chirp, chirrup, chirr, cheep, twitter, tweet, chatter, peep, call.

ward ▶ **noun** ❶ *the surgical ward* ROOM, department, unit, area. ❷ *the most marginal ward in Westminster* DISTRICT, constituency, division, quarter, zone, parish. ❸ *the boy is my ward* DEPENDANT, charge, protégé.
■ **ward someone off** FEND OFF, repel, repulse, beat back, chase away; *informal* send packing.
■ **ward something off** ❶ *she warded off the blow* PARRY, avert, deflect, block; evade, avoid, dodge. ❷ *garlic is worn to ward off evil spirits* REBUFF, avert, keep at bay, fend off, stave off, resist, prevent, obstruct, foil, frustrate, thwart, check, stop.

warden ▶ **noun** ❶ *the flats have a resident warden* SUPERINTENDENT, caretaker, janitor, porter, custodian, watchman, concierge, doorman. ❷ *a game warden* RANGER, custodian, keeper, guardian, protector. ❸ *he was handcuffed to a warden* PRISON OFFICER, guard, jailer, warder, wardress, keeper, sentry; *informal* screw. ❹ (*Brit.*) *the college warden* PRINCIPAL, head, governor, master, mistress, rector, provost, president, director, chancellor; *N. Amer. informal* prexy.

warder, wardress ▶ **noun**. *See* WARDEN sense 3.

wardrobe ▶ **noun** ❶ *she opened the wardrobe* CUPBOARD, cabinet, locker; *N. Amer.* closet. ❷ *her wardrobe has an outfit for every mood* COLLECTION OF CLOTHES; garments, attire, outfits; trousseau.

warehouse ▶ **noun** STOREROOM, storehouse, store, depot, depository, stockroom; magazine; granary; *informal* lock-up.

wares ▶ **plural noun** MERCHANDISE, goods, products, produce, stock, commodities; lines, range.

warfare ▶ **noun** FIGHTING, war, combat, conflict, (military) action, hostilities; bloodshed, battles, skirmishes.

warlike ▶ **adjective** AGGRESSIVE, belligerent, warring, bellicose, pugnacious, combative, bloodthirsty, jingoistic, sabre-rattling; hostile, threatening, quarrelsome; militaristic, militant; *informal* gung-ho.

warlock ▶ **noun** SORCERER, wizard, magus, (black) magician, enchanter; *archaic* mage.

warm ▶ **adjective** ❶ *a warm kitchen* HOT, cosy, snug; *informal* toasty. ❷ *a warm day in spring* BALMY, summery, sultry, hot, mild, temperate; sunny, fine. ❸ *warm water* HEATED, tepid, lukewarm. ❹ *a warm sweater* THICK, chunky, thermal, winter, woolly. ❺ *a warm welcome* FRIENDLY, cordial, amiable, genial, kind, pleasant, fond; welcoming, hospitable, benevolent, benign, charitable; sincere, genuine, wholehearted, heartfelt, enthusiastic, eager, hearty. ❻ (*informal*) *they haven't found it, but they're warm* CLOSE, near; *informal* hot.
– OPPOSITES cold, chilly, light, hostile.
▶ **verb** *warm the soup in that pan* HEAT (UP), reheat, cook; thaw (out), melt; *N. Amer.* warm over; *informal* zap; *Brit. informal* hot up.
– OPPOSITES chill.
■ **warm to/towards** ❶ *everyone warmed to him* LIKE, take to, get on (well) with, hit it off with, be on good terms with. ❷ *he couldn't warm to the notion* BE ENTHUSIASTIC ABOUT, be supportive of, be excited about.
■ **warm up** LIMBER UP, loosen up, stretch, work out, exercise; prepare, rehearse.
■ **warm someone up** *the compère warmed up the crowd* ENLIVEN, liven, stimulate, animate, rouse, stir, excite; *informal* get going.

warm-blooded ▶ **adjective** ❶ *mammals are warm-blooded Zoology* HOMEOTHERMIC, homeothermal. ❷ *a warm-blooded woman* PASSIONATE, ardent, red-blooded, emotional, intense, impetuous, lively, spirited, fiery, tempestuous.
– OPPOSITES poikilothermic, reserved.

warmed-up ▶ **adjective** ❶ *a warmed-up pasty* REHEATED; *N. Amer.* warmed-over. ❷ *warmed-up ideas* UNORIGINAL, derivative, imitative, uninspired; copied, plagiarized, rehashed; hackneyed, stale, tired, banal; *informal* old hat.
– OPPOSITES original.

warm-hearted ▶ **adjective** KIND, warm, bighearted, tender-hearted, tender, loving, caring, feeling, unselfish, selfless, benevolent, humane, good-natured; friendly, sympathetic, understanding, compassionate, charitable, generous.

warmonger ▶ **noun** MILITARIST, hawk, jingoist, sabre-rattler, aggressor, belligerent.

warmth ▶ **noun** ❶ *the warmth of the fire* HEAT, warmness, hotness; cosiness. ❷ *the warmth of their welcome* FRIENDLINESS, amiability, geniality, cordiality, kindness, tenderness, fondness; benevolence, charity; enthusiasm, eagerness, ardour, fervour, effusiveness.

warn ▶ **verb** ❶ *David warned her that it was too late* NOTIFY, alert, apprise, inform, tell, make someone aware, forewarn, remind; *informal* tip off, put wise. ❷ *police are warning galleries to be alert* ADVISE, exhort, urge, counsel, caution.

warning ▶ **noun** ❶ *the earthquake came without warning* (ADVANCE) NOTICE, forewarning, alert; hint, signal, sign, alarm bells; *informal* a tip-off. ❷ *a health warning* CAUTION, notification, information; exhortation, injunction; advice. ❸ *a warning of things to come* OMEN, premonition, foreboding, prophecy, prediction, forecast, token, portent, signal, sign; *poetic/literary* foretoken. ❹ *his sentence is a warning to other drunk drivers* EXAMPLE, deterrent, lesson, caution, exemplar, message, moral. ❺ *a written warning* ADMONITION, caution, remonstrance, reprimand, censure; *informal* dressing-down, talking-to, telling-off.

warp ▶ **verb** ❶ *timber which is too dry will warp* BUCKLE, twist, bend, distort, deform, misshape, malform, curve, bow, contort. ❷ *he warped the mind of her child* CORRUPT, twist, pervert, deprave.
– OPPOSITES straighten.

warrant ▶ **noun** ❶ *a warrant for his arrest* AUTHORIZATION, order, licence, permit, document; writ, summons, subpoena; mandate, decree, fiat, edict. ❷ *a travel warrant* VOUCHER, chit, slip, ticket, coupon, pass. ❸ *there's no warrant for this assumption* JUSTIFICATION, grounds, cause, rationale, basis, authority, licence, sanction, vindication.
▶ **verb** ❶ *the charges warranted a severe sentence* JUSTIFY, vindicate, call for, sanction, validate; permit, authorize; deserve, excuse, account for, legitimize; support, license, approve of; merit, qualify for, rate, be worthy of, be deserving of. ❷ *we warrant that the texts do not infringe copyright* GUARANTEE, affirm, swear, promise, vow, pledge, undertake, state, assert, declare, profess, attest; vouch, testify, bear witness; *formal* aver.

warranty ▶ **noun** GUARANTEE, assurance, promise, commitment, undertaking, agreement.

warring ▶ **adjective** OPPOSING, conflicting, at war, fighting, battling, quarrelling; competing, hostile, rival.

warrior ▶ **noun** FIGHTER, soldier, serviceman, combatant.

wary ▶ **adjective** ❶ *he was trained to be wary* CAUTIOUS, careful, circumspect, on one's guard, chary, alert, on the lookout, on one's toes, on the qui vive; attentive, heedful, watchful, vigilant, observant; *informal* wide awake. ❷ *we are*

wary of strangers SUSPICIOUS, chary, leery, careful, distrustful, mistrustful, sceptical, doubtful, dubious.
– OPPOSITES inattentive, trustful.

wash ▶ **verb** ❶ *he washed in the bath* CLEAN ONESELF, have a wash; bathe, bath, shower, soak, freshen up; *formal* perform one's ablutions; *dated* make one's toilet. ❷ *she washed her hands* CLEAN, cleanse, sponge, scrub, wipe, scour; shampoo, lather; sluice, swill, douse, swab, disinfect. ❸ *she washed off the blood* REMOVE, expunge, eradicate; sponge off, scrub off, wipe off, rinse off. ❹ *the women were washing clothes* LAUNDER, clean, rinse; *poetic/literary* lave. ❺ *waves washed against the hull* SPLASH, lap, splosh, dash, break, beat, surge, ripple, roll. ❻ *the wreckage was washed up downriver* SWEEP, carry, convey, transport; deposit. ❼ *guilt washed over her* AFFECT, rush through, surge through, course through, flood over, flow over. ❽ *the stonework was washed with pastel paint* PAINT, colour, tint, shade, dye, stain; coat, cover. ❾ (*informal*) *this story just won't wash* BE ACCEPTED, be acceptable, be plausible, be convincing, hold up, hold water, stand up, bear scrutiny.
– OPPOSITES dirty, soil.
▶ **noun** ❶ *she needs a wash* CLEAN, shower, dip, bath, soak; *formal* ablutions. ❷ *that shirt should go in the wash* LAUNDRY, washing. ❸ *antiseptic skin wash* LOTION, salve, preparation, rinse, liquid; liniment, embrocation. ❹ *the wash of a motor boat* BACKWASH, wake, trail, path. ❺ *the wash of the waves on the beach* SURGE, flow, swell, sweep, rise and fall, roll, splash. ❻ *water thinned out the crayon into a wash* PAINT, stain, film.
■ **wash something away** ERODE, abrade, wear away, eat away, undermine.
■ **wash one's hands of** DISOWN, renounce, reject, forswear, disavow, give up on, turn one's back on, cast aside, abandon; *formal* abjure.
■ **wash up** WASH THE DISHES, do the dishes, do the washing-up.

washed out ▶ **adjective** ❶ *a washed-out denim jacket* FADED, bleached, decolorized, stonewashed; pale, light, drab, muted. ❷ *he looked washed out after his exams* EXHAUSTED, tired, worn out, weary, fatigued, spent, drained, enervated, run down; *informal* all in, done in, dog-tired, bushed, beat, zonked; *Brit. informal* knackered; *N. Amer. informal* pooped, tuckered out.
– OPPOSITES bold, energetic.

washout ▶ **noun** (*informal*). *See* FAILURE senses 2, 3.

waspish ▶ **adjective** IRRITABLE, touchy, testy, cross, snappish, cantankerous, splenetic, short-tempered, bad-tempered, moody, crotchety, crabby, ratty; *informal* grouchy.

waste ▶ **verb** ❶ *he doesn't like to waste money* SQUANDER, misspend, misuse, fritter away, throw away, lavish, dissipate, throw around; *informal* blow, splurge. ❷ *kids are wasting away in the streets* GROW WEAK, grow thin, shrink, decline, wilt, fade, flag, deteriorate, degenerate, languish. ❸ *the disease wasted his legs* EMACIATE, atrophy, wither, debilitate, shrivel, shrink, weaken, enfeeble. ❹ (*poetic/literary*) *our country was wasted by the enemy. See* DEVASTATE sense 1. ❺ (*N. Amer. informal*) *I saw them waste the guy. See* MURDER verb sense 1.
– OPPOSITES conserve, thrive.
▶ **adjective** ❶ *waste material* UNWANTED, excess, superfluous, left over, scrap, useless, worthless; unusable, unprofitable. ❷ *waste ground* UNCULTIVATED, barren, desert, arid, bare; desolate, void, uninhabited, unpopulated; wild.
▶ **noun** ❶ *a waste of money* MISUSE, misapplication, misemployment, abuse; extravagance, wastefulness, lavishness. ❷ *household waste* RUBBISH, refuse, litter, debris, dross, junk, detritus, scrap; dregs, scraps; sewage, effluent; *N. Amer.* garbage, trash. ❸ *the frozen wastes of the South Pole* DESERT, wasteland, wilderness, emptiness, wilds.
■ **lay waste**. *See* LAY[1].

wasted ▶ **adjective** ❶ *a wasted effort* SQUANDERED, misspent, misdirected, misused, dissipated; pointless, useless, needless, unnecessary. ❷ *a wasted opportunity* MISSED, lost, forfeited, neglected, squandered, bungled; *informal* down the drain. ❸ *I'm wasted in this job* UNDEREMPLOYED, underused, too good for; neglected, forgotten, disregarded. ❹ *his wasted legs* EMACIATED, atrophied, withered, shrivelled, weak, frail, shrunken, skeletal, rickety, scrawny, wizened. ❺ (*informal*) *everybody at the party was wasted. See* DRUNK adjective.

wasteful ▶ **adjective** PRODIGAL, profligate, uneconomical, extravagant, lavish, excessive, imprudent, improvident; thriftless, spendthrift; needless, useless.
– OPPOSITES frugal.

wasteland ▶ **noun** WILDERNESS, desert; wilds, wastes, badlands.

waster ▶ **noun** (*informal*) IDLER, loafer, good-for-nothing, ne'er-do-well, slob, lounger, shirker, sluggard, laggard; *informal* loser, skiver, slacker, lazybones; *N. Amer. informal* bum; *poetic/literary* wastrel.

wastrel ▶ **noun** (*poetic/literary*). *See* WASTER.

watch ▶ **verb** ❶ *she watched him as he spoke* OBSERVE, view, look at, eye, gaze at, stare at, gape at, peer at; contemplate, survey, keep an eye on; inspect, scrutinize, scan, examine, study, ogle, regard, mark; *informal* check out, get a load of, recce, eyeball; *Brit. informal* have a butcher's at; *poetic/literary* behold. ❷ *he was being watched by the police* SPY ON, keep in sight, track, monitor, survey, follow, keep under surveillance; *informal* keep tabs on, stake out. ❸ *will you watch the kids?* LOOK AFTER, mind, keep an eye on, take care of, supervise, tend, attend to; guard, safeguard, protect. ❹ *we stayed to watch the boat* GUARD, protect, shield, defend, safe-

guard; cover, patrol, police. ❺ *watch what you say* BE CAREFUL, mind, be aware of, pay attention to, consider, pay heed to.
– OPPOSITES ignore, neglect.
▶ **noun** ❶ *Bill looked at his watch* TIMEPIECE, chronometer; wristwatch, pocket watch, stopwatch. ❷ *we kept watch on the yacht* GUARD, vigil, lookout, an eye; observation, surveillance, vigilance.
■ **watch out/it/yourself** BE CAREFUL, be watchful, be on your guard, beware, be wary, be cautious, mind out, look out, pay attention, take heed, take care, keep an eye open/out, keep one's eyes peeled, be vigilant.

watchdog ▶ **noun** ❶ *they use watchdogs to ward off trespassers* GUARD DOG. ❷ *a consumer watchdog* OMBUDSMAN, monitor, scrutineer, inspector, supervisor; custodian, guardian, protector.

watcher ▶ **noun** ONLOOKER, spectator, observer, viewer, fly on the wall; witness, bystander; spy; *informal* rubberneck; *poetic/literary* beholder.

watchful ▶ **adjective** OBSERVANT, alert, vigilant, attentive, awake, aware, heedful, sharp-eyed, eagle-eyed; on the lookout, on the qui vive, wary, cautious, careful, chary.

watchman ▶ **noun** SECURITY GUARD, custodian, warden; sentry, guard, patrolman, lookout, sentinel, scout, watch.

watchword ▶ **noun** GUIDING PRINCIPLE, motto, slogan, maxim, mantra, catchword, catchphrase, byword; *informal* buzzword.

water ▶ **noun** ❶ *a glass of water technical* H_20; *dated* Adam's ale. ❷ *a house down by the water* SEA, ocean; lake, river.
– RELATED TERMS aqueous, aqua-.
▶ **verb** ❶ *water the plants* SPRINKLE, moisten, dampen, wet, spray, splash; soak, douse, souse, drench, saturate; hose (down). ❷ *my mouth watered* MOISTEN, become wet, leak; salivate. ❸ *he watered the claret. See* WATER SOMETHING DOWN sense 1.
■ **hold water** BE TENABLE, ring true, bear scrutiny, make sense, stand up, hold up, be convincing, be plausible, be sound.
■ **water something down** ❶ *staff had watered down the drinks* DILUTE, water, thin (out), weaken; adulterate, doctor, mix; *informal* cut. ❷ *the proposals were watered down* MODERATE, temper, mitigate, tone down, soften, tame; understate, play down, soft-pedal.

waterfall ▶ **noun** CASCADE, cataract, falls, rapids; *N. English* force.

waterproof ▶ **adjective** *a waterproof jacket* WATERTIGHT, water-repellent, water-resistant, damp-proof; impermeable, impervious; rubberized, waxed.
▶ **noun** (*Brit.*) *she put on a waterproof* RAINCOAT, anorak, oilskin, cagoule; *Brit.* mackintosh; *Brit. informal* mac.

watertight ▶ **adjective** ❶ *a watertight container* IMPERMEABLE, impervious, (hermetically) sealed; waterproof, water-repellent, water-resistant, damp-proof. ❷ *a watertight alibi* INDISPUTABLE, unquestionable, incontrovertible, irrefutable, unassailable, impregnable; foolproof, sound, flawless, airtight, conclusive.
– OPPOSITES leaky, flawed.

watery ▶ **adjective** ❶ *a watery discharge* LIQUID, fluid, aqueous; *technical* hydrous. ❷ *a watery meadow* WET, damp, moist, sodden, soggy, squelchy, soft; saturated, waterlogged; boggy, marshy, swampy, miry, muddy. ❸ *watery porridge* THIN, runny, weak, sloppy, dilute, diluted; tasteless, flavourless, insipid, bland. ❹ *the light was watery and grey* PALE, wan, faint, weak, feeble; *informal* wishy-washy. ❺ *watery eyes* TEARFUL, teary, weepy, moist, rheumy; *formal* lachrymose.
– OPPOSITES dry, thick, bright.

wave ▶ **verb** ❶ *he waved his flag furiously* MOVE UP AND DOWN, move to and fro, wag, shake, swish, sweep, swing, brandish, flourish, wield; flick, flutter; *informal* waggle. ❷ *the grass waved in the breeze* RIPPLE, flutter, undulate, stir, flap, sway, shake, quiver, move. ❸ *the waiter waved them closer* GESTURE, gesticulate, signal, beckon, motion.
▶ **noun** ❶ *she gave him a friendly wave* GESTURE, gesticulation; signal, sign, motion. ❷ *he surfs the big waves* BREAKER, roller, comber, boomer, ripple, white horse; (**waves**) swell, surf, froth; *Austral.* bombora; *archaic* billow. ❸ *a wave of emigration* FLOW, rush, surge, flood, stream, tide, deluge, spate. ❹ *a wave of self-pity* SURGE, rush, stab, dart, upsurge; thrill, frisson; feeling. ❺ *his hair grew in thick waves* CURL, kink, corkscrew, twist, ringlet, coil. ❻ *electromagnetic waves* ripple, vibration, oscillation.
■ **make waves** (*informal*) CAUSE TROUBLE, be disruptive, be troublesome; make an impression, get noticed.
■ **wave something aside** DISMISS, reject, brush aside, shrug off, disregard, ignore, discount, play down; *informal* pooh-pooh.
■ **wave someone/something down** FLAG DOWN, hail, stop, summon, call, accost.

waver ▶ **verb** ❶ *the candlelight wavered in the draught* FLICKER, quiver, twinkle, glimmer, wink, blink. ❷ *his voice wavered* FALTER, wobble, tremble, quaver. ❸ *he wavered between the choices* BE UNDECIDED, be irresolute, hesitate, dither, equivocate, vacillate, fluctuate; think twice, change one's mind, blow hot and cold; *Brit.* haver, hum and haw; *informal* shilly-shally, sit on the fence.

wavy ▶ **adjective** CURLY, curvy, curved, undulating, squiggly, rippled, crinkly, kinked, zigzag.

wax ▶ **verb** ❶ *the moon is waxing* GET BIGGER, increase, enlarge. ❷ (*poetic/literary*) *price sensitivity is waxing* INCREASE, grow, develop, rise, expand, escalate, intensify, spread, mushroom, snowball.

–OPPOSITES wane.

■ **wax lyrical** BE ENTHUSIASTIC, enthuse, rave, gush, get carried away.

waxen ▶ adjective PALLID, pale, pasty, wan, ashen, colourless, anaemic, bloodless, washed out, white, grey, whitish, waxy, drained, sickly.

–OPPOSITES ruddy.

waxy ▶ adjective. *See* WAXEN.

way ▶ noun ❶ *a way of reducing the damage* METHOD, process, procedure, technique, system; plan, strategy, scheme; means, mechanism, approach. ❷ *she kissed him in her brisk way* MANNER, style, fashion, mode; modus operandi, MO. ❸ *I've changed my ways* PRACTICE, wont, habit, custom, policy, procedure, convention, routine, modus vivendi; trait, attribute, peculiarity, idiosyncrasy; conduct, behaviour, manner, style, nature, personality, temperament, disposition, character. ❹ *which way leads home?* ROUTE, course, direction; road, street, track, path. ❺ *I'll go out the back way* DOOR, gate, exit, entrance, entry; route. ❻ *a short way downstream* DISTANCE, length, stretch, journey; space, interval, span. ❼ *April is a long way away* TIME, stretch, term, span, duration. ❽ *a car coming the other way* DIRECTION, bearing, course, orientation, line, tack. ❾ (*informal*) *what do they call it down your way?* AREA, region, district, neighbourhood, locality, locale; *informal* neck of the woods, parts; *Brit. informal* manor; *N. Amer. informal* hood, nabe. ❿ *in some ways, he may be better off* RESPECT, regard, aspect, facet, sense; detail, point, particular. ⓫ *the country is in a bad way* STATE, condition, situation, circumstances, position; predicament, plight; *informal* shape.

■ **by the way** INCIDENTALLY, by the by, in passing, en passant.

■ **give way** ❶ *the government gave way and passed the bill* YIELD, back down, surrender, concede defeat, give in, submit, succumb; acquiesce, agree, assent; *informal* throw in the towel/sponge, cave in. ❷ *the door gave way* COLLAPSE, give, cave in, fall in, come apart, crumple. ❸ *grief gave way to guilt* BE REPLACED BY, be succeeded by, be followed by, be supplanted by.

■ **on the way** COMING, imminent, forthcoming, approaching, impending, close, near, on us; proceeding, en route, in transit.

wayfarer ▶ noun (*poetic/literary*). *See* WANDERER.

waylay ▶ verb ❶ *we were waylaid and robbed* AMBUSH, hold up, attack, assail, rob; *informal* mug, stick up. ❷ *several people waylaid her to chat* ACCOST, detain, intercept, take aside, pounce on, importune; *informal* buttonhole.

way-out ▶ adjective (*informal*) UNCONVENTIONAL, avant-garde, outlandish, eccentric, quirky, unusual, bizarre, strange, peculiar, odd, uncommon; *informal* far out, offbeat, oddball, off the wall; *Brit. informal* rum.

–OPPOSITES ordinary.

wayward ▶ adjective WILFUL, headstrong, stubborn, obstinate, obdurate, perverse, contrary, disobedient, insubordinate, undisciplined; rebellious, defiant, uncooperative, recalcitrant, unruly, wild, unmanageable, erratic; difficult, impossible; *formal* refractory.

–OPPOSITES docile.

weak ▶ adjective ❶ *they are too weak to move* FRAIL, feeble, delicate, fragile; infirm, sick, sickly, debilitated, incapacitated, ailing, indisposed, decrepit; tired, fatigued, exhausted; *informal* weedy. ❷ *bats have weak eyes* INADEQUATE, poor, feeble; defective, faulty, deficient, imperfect, substandard. ❸ *a weak excuse* UNCONVINCING, untenable, tenuous, implausible, unsatisfactory, poor, inadequate, feeble, flimsy, lame, hollow; *informal* pathetic. ❹ *I was too weak to be a rebel* SPINELESS, craven, cowardly, pusillanimous, timid; irresolute, indecisive, ineffectual, inept, effete, meek, tame, ineffective, impotent, soft, faint-hearted; *informal* yellow, weak-kneed, gutless, chicken. ❺ *a weak light* DIM, pale, wan, faint, feeble, muted. ❻ *a weak voice* INDISTINCT, muffled, muted, hushed, faint, low. ❼ *weak coffee* WATERY, diluted, dilute, watered down, thin, tasteless, flavourless, bland, insipid, wishy-washy. ❽ *a weak smile* UNENTHUSIASTIC, feeble, half-hearted, lame.

–OPPOSITES strong, powerful, convincing, resolute, bright, loud.

weaken ▶ verb ❶ *the virus weakened him terribly* ENFEEBLE, debilitate, incapacitate, sap, enervate, tire, exhaust, wear out; wither, cripple, disable. ❷ *she tried to weaken the shock for him* REDUCE, decrease, diminish, lessen, moderate, temper, dilute, blunt, mitigate, soften. ❸ *our morale weakened* DECREASE, dwindle, diminish, wane, ebb, subside, peter out, fizzle out, tail off, decline, falter. ❹ *the move weakened her authority* IMPAIR, undermine, compromise; invalidate, negate, discredit.

weakling ▶ noun MILKSOP, namby-pamby, coward, pushover; *informal* wimp, weed, sissy, drip, softie, doormat, chicken, yellow-belly, scaredy-cat; *N. Amer. informal* wuss, pussy.

weakness ▶ noun ❶ *with old age came weakness* FRAILTY, feebleness, enfeeblement, fragility, delicacy; infirmity, sickness, sickliness, debility, incapacity, indisposition, decrepitude; *informal* weediness. ❷ *he has worked on his weaknesses* FAULT, flaw, defect, deficiency, weak point, failing, shortcoming, imperfection, Achilles' heel. ❸ *a weakness for champagne* FONDNESS, liking, partiality, preference, love, penchant, soft spot, predilection, inclination, taste, eye; enthusiasm, appetite. ❹ *the President was accused of weakness* TIMIDITY, cravenness, cowardliness, pusillanimity; indecision, irresolution, ineffectuality, ineptitude, meekness, powerlessness, ineffectiveness, impotence. ❺ *the weakness of this argument* UNTENABILITY, implausibility, poverty, inadequacy, transparency; flimsiness, hollowness. ❻ *the weakness of the sound* INDISTINCTNESS, mutedness, faintness, feebleness, lowness; dimness, paleness.

weak-willed ▶ adjective SPINELESS, weak, irresolute, indecisive; impressionable, persuadable, persuasible, submissive, unassertive, compliant, pusillanimous; *informal* wimpish, chicken.

weal ▶ noun WELT, wound, lesion, swelling; scar, cicatrix, mark, blemish.

wealth ▶ noun ❶ *a gentleman of wealth* AFFLUENCE, prosperity, riches, means, substance, fortune; money, cash, lucre, capital, treasure, finance; assets, possessions, resources, funds; property, stock, reserves, securities, holdings; *informal* wherewithal, dough, bread. ❷ *a wealth of information* ABUNDANCE, profusion, plethora, mine, store, treasury, bounty, cornucopia; *informal* lot, load, heap, mass, mountain, stack, ton; *Brit. informal* shedload; *formal* plenitude.
– OPPOSITES poverty, dearth.

wealthy ▶ adjective RICH, affluent, moneyed, well off, well-to-do, prosperous, comfortable, propertied; of substance; *informal* well heeled, rolling in it, in the money, made of money, filthy rich, stinking rich, loaded, flush, quids in; *Austral./NZ informal* financial; *informal, dated* oofy.
– OPPOSITES poor.

wear ▶ verb ❶ *he wore a suit* DRESS IN, be clothed in, have on, sport; put on, don. ❷ *Barbara wore a smile* BEAR, have (on one's face), show, display, exhibit; give, put on, assume. ❸ *the bricks have been worn down* ERODE, abrade, rub away, grind away, wash away, crumble (away), wear down; corrode, eat away (at), dissolve. ❹ *the tyres are wearing well* LAST, endure, hold up, bear up, prove durable. ❺ (*Brit. informal*) *I've asked him twice, but he won't wear it* ALLOW, permit, authorize, sanction, condone, indulge, agree to, approve of; put up with, take, stand, support; accept, swallow, tolerate, countenance; *informal* hack, abide, stomach; *Brit. informal* stick; *formal* brook; *archaic* suffer.
▶ noun ❶ *you won't get much wear out of that* USE, wearing, service, utility, value; *informal* mileage. ❷ *evening wear* CLOTHES, clothing, garments, dress, attire, garb, wardrobe; *informal* get-up, gear, togs; *Brit. informal* kit, clobber; *formal* apparel; *poetic/literary* array. ❸ *the varnish which will withstand wear* DAMAGE, friction, erosion, attrition, abrasion.
■ **wear something down** *he wore down her resistance* GRADUALLY OVERCOME, slowly reduce, erode, wear away, exhaust, undermine.
■ **wear off** *the novelty soon wore off* FADE, diminish, lessen, dwindle, decrease, wane, ebb, peter out, fizzle out, pall, disappear, vanish, run out.
■ **wear on** *the afternoon wore on* PASS, elapse, proceed, advance, progress, go by, roll by, march on, slip by/away, fly by/past.
■ **wear out** DETERIORATE, become worn, wear thin, fray, become threadbare, go into holes, wear through.
■ **wear something out** USE UP, consume, go through.
■ **wear someone out** FATIGUE, tire out, weary, exhaust, drain, sap, overtax, enervate, debilitate, jade, prostrate; *informal* whack, poop, shatter, frazzle, do in; *Brit. informal* knacker.

wearing ▶ adjective TIRING, exhausting, wearying, fatiguing, enervating, draining, sapping; demanding, exacting, taxing, arduous, gruelling, punishing, difficult, hard, tough, laborious, strenuous, rigorous.

wearisome ▶ adjective. *See* WEARING.

weary ▶ adjective ❶ *he was weary after cycling* TIRED, worn out, exhausted, fatigued, sapped, dog-tired, spent, drained, prostrate, enervated; *informal* all in, done in, dead beat, ready to drop, bushed, worn to a frazzle, shattered; *Brit. informal* knackered, whacked; *N. Amer. informal* pooped, tuckered out. ❷ *she was weary of the arguments* TIRED OF, fed up with, bored by, sick of; *informal* have had it up to here with. ❸ *a weary journey* TIRING, exhausting, wearying, fatiguing, enervating, draining, sapping, wearing, trying, demanding, taxing, arduous, gruelling, difficult, hard, tough.
– OPPOSITES fresh, keen, refreshing.
▶ verb ❶ *she was wearied by her illness* TIRE, fatigue, wear out, overtire, exhaust, drain, sap, enervate, debilitate, enfeeble, prostrate; *informal* whack, bush, shatter, frazzle, poop, do in; *Brit. informal* knacker. ❷ *don't risk wearying the reader* BORE, tire; irk, irritate, exasperate. ❸ *he wearied of the struggle* TIRE OF, become fed up with, become bored by, sicken of; have had enough of.
– OPPOSITES refresh, interest.

wearying ▶ adjective. *See* WEARING.

weather ▶ noun *what's the weather like?* FORECAST, outlook; meteorological conditions, climate, atmospheric pressure, temperature; elements.
▶ verb *we weathered the recession* SURVIVE, come through, ride out, pull through; withstand, endure, rise above, surmount, overcome, resist; *informal* stick out.
■ **under the weather** (*informal*). *See* ILL adjective sense 1.

weathered ▶ adjective WEATHER-BEATEN, worn; tanned, bronzed; lined, creased, wrinkled, gnarled.

weave[1] ▶ verb ❶ *flowers were woven into their hair* ENTWINE, lace, twist, knit, intertwine, braid, plait. ❷ *he weaves colourful plots* INVENT, make up, fabricate, construct, create, contrive, spin; tell, recount, relate.

weave² ▶ **verb** *he had to weave his way through the crowds* THREAD, wind, wend; dodge, zigzag.

web ▶ **noun** ❶ *a spider's web* MESH, net, lattice, latticework, lacework, webbing; gauze, gossamer. ❷ *a web of friendships* NETWORK, nexus, complex, set, chain.

wed ▶ **verb** ❶ *they are old enough to wed* MARRY, get married, become husband and wife; *informal* tie the knot, walk down the aisle, get spliced, get hitched. ❷ *he will wed his girlfriend* MARRY, take as one's wife/husband, lead to the altar; *informal* make an honest woman of; *archaic* espouse. ❸ *she wedded the two forms of spirituality* UNITE, unify, join, combine, amalgamate, fuse, integrate, bond, merge.
– OPPOSITES divorce, separate.

wedded ▶ **adjective** ❶ *wedded bliss* MARRIED, matrimonial, marital, conjugal, nuptial; *Law* spousal; *poetic/literary* connubial. ❷ *he is wedded to his work* DEDICATED TO, devoted to, attached to, fixated on, single-minded about.

wedding ▶ **noun** MARRIAGE (SERVICE/RITES), nuptials, union; *archaic* espousal.
– RELATED TERMS nuptial.

wedge ▶ **noun** ❶ *the door was secured by a wedge* TAPERED BLOCK, chock, stop. ❷ *a wedge of cheese* TRIANGLE, segment, slice, section; chunk, lump, slab, hunk, block, piece.
▶ **verb** *she wedged her case between two bags* SQUEEZE, cram, jam, ram, force, push, shove; *informal* stuff, bung.

wedlock ▶ **noun** MARRIAGE, (holy) matrimony, married state, union.

wee ▶ **adjective** (*Scottish*) LITTLE, small, tiny, minute, miniature, mini, compact, undersized, diminutive, dwarf, midget, infinitesimal, microscopic, minuscule; *informal* teeny, teeny-weeny, itsy-bitsy, half-pint, dinky; *Brit. informal* titchy, diddy; *N. Amer. informal* little-bitty.
– OPPOSITES big.

weed
■ **weed something/someone out** ISOLATE, separate out, sort out, sift out, winnow out, filter out, set apart, segregate; eliminate, get rid of, remove; *informal* lose.

weedy ▶ **adjective** (*informal*) PUNY, feeble, weak, frail, undersized, slight, skinny; *informal* pint-sized.

weekly ▶ **adjective** *weekly instalments* ONCE A WEEK; lasting a week; *formal* hebdomadal.
▶ **adverb** *the directors meet weekly* ONCE A WEEK, every week, each week, on a weekly basis; by the week, per week, a week.

weep ▶ **verb** *even the toughest soldiers wept* CRY, shed tears, sob, snivel, whimper, whine, wail, bawl, keen; *Scottish* greet; *informal* boohoo, blub, blubber; *Brit. informal* grizzle.
▶ **noun** *you sit and have a weep* CRY, sob, snivel, whimper, bawl; *informal* blub, blubber; *Brit. informal* grizzle.

weepy ▶ **adjective** TEARFUL, close to tears, upset, distressed, sad, unhappy; in tears, crying, weeping, snivelling; *informal* teary; *formal* lachrymose.

weigh ▶ **verb** ❶ *she weighs the vegetables* MEASURE THE WEIGHT OF, put on the scales. ❷ *he weighed 118 kg* HAVE A WEIGHT OF, tip the scales at. ❸ *the situation weighed heavily on him. See* WEIGH SOMEONE DOWN sense 2. ❹ *he has to weigh up the possibilities* CONSIDER, contemplate, think about, mull over, chew over, reflect on, ruminate about, muse on; assess, appraise, analyse, investigate, inquire into, look into, examine, review, explore, take stock of. ❺ *they need to weigh benefit against risk* BALANCE, evaluate, compare, juxtapose, contrast.
■ **weigh someone down** ❶ *my fishing gear weighed me down* BURDEN, saddle, overload, overburden, encumber, hamper, handicap. ❷ *the silence weighed me down* OPPRESS, depress, lie heavy on, burden, cast down, hang over, gnaw at, prey on (one's mind); trouble, worry, bother, disturb, upset, haunt, nag, torment, afflict, plague.

weight ▶ **noun** ❶ *the weight of the book* HEAVINESS, mass, load, burden, pressure, force; poundage, tonnage. ❷ *his recommendation will carry great weight* INFLUENCE, force, leverage, sway, pull, importance, significance, consequence, value, substance, power, authority; *informal* clout. ❸ *a weight off her mind* BURDEN, load, millstone, albatross, encumbrance; trouble, worry, strain. ❹ *the weight of the evidence is against him* PREPONDERANCE, majority, bulk, body, lion's share, predominance; most, almost all.

weighty ▶ **adjective** ❶ *a weighty tome* HEAVY, thick, bulky, hefty, cumbersome, ponderous. ❷ *a weighty subject* IMPORTANT, significant, momentous, consequential, far-reaching, key, major, vital, critical, crucial; serious, grave, solemn. ❸ *a weighty responsibility* BURDENSOME, onerous, heavy, oppressive, taxing, troublesome. ❹ *weighty arguments* COMPELLING, cogent, strong, forceful, powerful, potent, effective, sound, valid, telling; impressive, persuasive, convincing, influential, authoritative.
– OPPOSITES light, trivial, weak.

weird ▶ **adjective** ❶ *weird apparitions* UNCANNY, eerie, unnatural, supernatural, unearthly, other-worldly, ghostly, mysterious, strange, abnormal, unusual; *Scottish* eldritch; *informal* creepy, spooky, freaky. ❷ (*informal*) *a weird sense of humour* BIZARRE, quirky, outlandish, eccentric, unconventional, unorthodox, idiosyncratic, surreal, crazy, peculiar, odd, strange, queer, freakish, zany, madcap, outré; *informal* wacky, freaky, way-out, offbeat, off the wall; *Brit. informal* rum; *N. Amer. informal* wacko.
– OPPOSITES normal, conventional.

weirdo ▶ **noun** (*informal*). *See* ECCENTRIC noun.

welcome ▶ noun *a welcome from the vicar* GREETING, salutation; reception, hospitality; the red carpet.

▶ verb ❶ *welcome your guests in their own language* GREET, salute, receive, meet, usher in. ❷ *we welcomed their decision* BE PLEASED BY, be glad about, approve of, appreciate, embrace; *informal* give the thumbs up to.

▶ adjective *welcome news* PLEASING, agreeable, encouraging, gratifying, heartening, promising, favourable, pleasant; gladly received, wanted, appreciated, popular, desirable.

weld ▶ verb FUSE, bond, stick, join, attach, seal, splice, melt, solder.

welfare ▶ noun ❶ *the welfare of children* WELL-BEING, health, comfort, security, safety, protection, prosperity, success, fortune; interest, good. ❷ *we cannot claim welfare* SOCIAL SECURITY, (state) benefit, public assistance; pension, credit, support; sick pay, unemployment benefit; *Brit. informal* the dole.

well[1] ▶ adverb ❶ *please behave well* SATISFACTORILY, nicely, correctly, properly, fittingly, suitably, appropriately. ❷ *they get on well together* HARMONIOUSLY, agreeably, pleasantly, nicely, happily, amicably, amiably, peaceably; *informal* famously. ❸ *he plays the piano well* SKILFULLY, ably, competently, proficiently, adeptly, deftly, expertly, admirably, excellently. ❹ *treat your employees well* DECENTLY, fairly, kindly, generously, honestly. ❺ *mix the ingredients well* THOROUGHLY, completely; effectively, rigorously, carefully. ❻ *I know her quite well* INTIMATELY, thoroughly, deeply, profoundly, personally. ❼ *they studied the car market well* CAREFULLY, closely, attentively, rigorously, in depth, exhaustively, in detail, meticulously, scrupulously, conscientiously, methodically, completely, comprehensively, fully, extensively. ❽ *they speak well of him* ADMIRINGLY, highly, approvingly, favourably, appreciatively, warmly, enthusiastically, glowingly. ❾ *she makes enough money to live well* COMFORTABLY, in (the lap of) luxury, prosperously. ❿ *you may well be right* QUITE POSSIBLY, conceivably, probably; undoubtedly, certainly, unquestionably. ⓫ *he is well over forty* CONSIDERABLY, very much, a great deal, substantially, easily, comfortably, significantly. ⓬ *she could well afford it* EASILY, comfortably, readily, effortlessly.

– OPPOSITES badly, negligently, disparagingly, barely.

▶ adjective ❶ *she was completely well again* HEALTHY, fine, fit, robust, strong, vigorous, blooming, thriving, hale and hearty, in good shape, in good condition, in good trim, in fine fettle; *informal* in the pink. ❷ *all is not well* SATISFACTORY, all right, fine, in order, as it should be, acceptable; *informal* OK, hunky-dory; *N. Amer. & Austral./NZ informal* jake; *Brit. informal, dated* tickety-boo. ❸ *it would be well to tell us in advance* ADVISABLE, sensible, prudent, politic, commonsensical, wise, judicious, expedient, recommended, advantageous, beneficial, profitable, desirable; a good idea.

– OPPOSITES poorly, unsatisfactory, inadvisable.

■ **as well** TOO, also, in addition, additionally, into the bargain, besides, furthermore, moreover, to boot.

■ **as well as** TOGETHER WITH, along with, besides, plus, and, with, on top of, not to mention, to say nothing of, let alone.

well[2] ▶ noun ❶ *she drew water from the well* BOREHOLE, bore, spring, waterhole. ❷ *he's a bottomless well of forgiveness* SOURCE, supply, fount, reservoir, mine, fund, treasury.

▶ verb *tears welled from her eyes* FLOW, spill, stream, run, rush, gush, roll, cascade, flood, spout; seep, trickle; burst, issue.

well advised ▶ adjective WISE, prudent, sensible.

well balanced ▶ adjective. *See* BALANCED senses 1, 2, 3.

well behaved ▶ adjective ORDERLY, obedient, disciplined, peaceable, docile, controlled, restrained, cooperative, compliant; mannerly, polite, civil, courteous, respectful, proper, decorous, refined, polished.

– OPPOSITES naughty.

well-being ▶ noun. *See* WELFARE sense 1.

well bred ▶ adjective WELL BROUGHT UP, polite, civil, mannerly, courteous, respectful; ladylike, gentlemanly, genteel, cultivated, urbane, proper, refined, polished, well behaved.

well built ▶ adjective STURDY, strapping, brawny, burly, hefty, muscular, muscly, strong, rugged, lusty, Herculean; *informal* hunky, beefy, husky, hulking.

– OPPOSITES puny.

well dressed ▶ adjective SMART, fashionable, stylish, chic, modish, elegant, neat, spruce, trim, dapper; *N. Amer.* trig; *informal* snazzy, natty, snappy, sharp; *N. Amer. informal* spiffy, fly.

– OPPOSITES scruffy.

well founded ▶ adjective JUSTIFIABLE, justified, warranted, legitimate, defensible, valid, admissible, allowable, understandable, excusable, acceptable, reasonable, sensible, sound.

– OPPOSITES groundless.

well heeled ▶ adjective (*informal*). *See* WEALTHY.

well known ▶ adjective ❶ *well-known principles* FAMILIAR, widely known, popular, common, everyday, established. ❷ *a well-known family of architects* FAMOUS, famed, prominent, notable, renowned, distinguished, eminent, illustrious, celebrated, acclaimed, important.

– OPPOSITES obscure.

well mannered ▶ adjective POLITE, courteous, civil, mannerly, genteel, decorous, respectful, refined, polished, civilized, urbane, well bred.

well-nigh ▶ adverb ALMOST, nearly, just about, more or less, practically, virtually, all but, as good as, nearing, approaching; roughly, approximately; *informal* pretty much, nigh on.

well off ▶ adjective ❶ *her family's very well off.* See WELL-TO-DO. ❷ *the prisoners were relatively well off* FORTUNATE, lucky, comfortable; *informal* sitting pretty. ❸ *the island is not well off for harbours* WELL SUPPLIED WITH, well stocked with, well furnished with, well equipped with.

well read ▶ adjective KNOWLEDGEABLE, well informed, well versed, erudite, scholarly, literate, educated, cultured, bookish, studious; *dated* lettered.
– OPPOSITES ignorant.

well spoken ▶ adjective ARTICULATE, nicely spoken; refined, polite; *Brit. informal* posh.

well-to-do ▶ adjective WEALTHY, rich, affluent, moneyed, well off, prosperous, comfortable, propertied; *informal* rolling in it, in the money, loaded, well heeled, flush, made of money, quids in, worth a packet, on easy street.

welter ▶ noun CONFUSION, jumble, tangle, mess, hotchpotch, mishmash, mass.

wend ▶ verb MEANDER, wind one's way, wander, amble, stroll, saunter, drift, roam, swan, traipse, walk; journey, travel; *informal* mosey, tootle.

west ▶ adjective WESTERN, westerly, occidental.

wet ▶ adjective ❶ *wet clothes* DAMP, moist, soaked, drenched, saturated, sopping, dripping, soggy; waterlogged, squelchy. ❷ *it was cold and wet* RAINY, raining, pouring, teeming, showery, drizzly, drizzling; damp. ❸ *the paint is still wet* STICKY, tacky; fresh. ❹ *a wet mortar mix* AQUEOUS, watery, sloppy. ❺ (*Brit. informal*) *the cadets were a bit wet* FEEBLE, silly, weak, foolish, inept, ineffectual, effete, soft, namby-pamby, timid, spiritless, cowardly, spineless; *informal* sissy, pathetic, drippy, wimpish, weedy, chicken; *Brit. informal* soppy.
– OPPOSITES dry, fine, brave.
▶ verb *wet the clothes before ironing them* DAMPEN, damp, moisten; sprinkle, spray, splash; soak, saturate, flood, douse, souse, drench.
– OPPOSITES dry.
▶ noun ❶ *the wet of his tears* WETNESS, damp, moisture, moistness, sogginess; wateriness. ❷ *the race was held in the wet* RAIN, drizzle, precipitation; spray, dew, damp. ❸ (*Brit. informal*) *come on, don't be such a wet* NAMBY-PAMBY, weakling, milksop, Milquetoast, baby, coward; *informal* wimp, weed, drip, sissy, softie, chicken, scaredy-cat; *Brit. informal* big girl's blouse; *N. Amer. informal* pantywaist, pussy.

whack (*informal*) ▶ verb *she whacked him on the head.* See STRIKE verb sense 1.
▶ noun ❶ *he got a whack with a stick.* See BLOW[2] sense 1. ❷ (*Brit. informal*) *everyone will get their whack.* See SHARE noun.

wharf ▶ noun QUAY, pier, dock, berth, landing, jetty; harbour, dockyard, marina.

whatsit ▶ noun (*informal*) THING, so-and-so, whatever it's called; *informal* whatnot, doodah, what-d'you-call-it, what's-its-name, thingy, thingummy, thingamabob, thingamajig, oojamaflip; *Brit. informal* doings; *N. Amer. informal* doodad, doohickey.

wheedle ▶ verb COAX, cajole, inveigle, induce, entice, charm, tempt, beguile, flatter, persuade, influence, win someone over, bring someone round, convince, prevail on, get round; *informal* sweet-talk, soft-soap.

wheel ▶ noun *a wagon wheel* disc, hoop, ring, circle.
▶ verb ❶ *she wheeled the trolley away* PUSH, trundle, roll. ❷ *the flock of doves wheeled round* TURN, go round, circle, orbit.
■ **at/behind the wheel** DRIVING, steering, in the driving seat.

wheeze ▶ verb *the illness left her wheezing* BREATHE NOISILY, gasp, whistle, hiss, rasp, croak, pant, cough.
▶ noun ❶ *she still had a slight wheeze* RASP, croak, whistle, hiss, pant, cough. ❷ (*Brit. informal*) *I've thought of a brilliant wheeze.* See RUSE.

whereabouts ▶ noun LOCATION, position, site, place, situation, spot, point, vicinity; home, address, locale, neighbourhood; bearings, orientation.

wherewithal ▶ noun MONEY, cash, capital, finance(s), funds; resources, means, ability, capability; *informal* dough, bread, loot, readies, the necessary, boodle, dibs, ducats; *Brit. informal* dosh, brass, lolly; *N. Amer. informal* bucks; *US informal* greenbacks.

whet ▶ verb ❶ *he whetted his knife on a stone* SHARPEN, hone, strop, grind, file. ❷ *something to whet your appetite* STIMULATE, excite, arouse, rouse, kindle, trigger, spark, quicken, stir, inspire, animate, fuel, fire, activate, tempt, galvanize.
– OPPOSITES blunt.

whiff ▶ noun ❶ *I caught a whiff of perfume* FAINT SMELL, trace, sniff, scent, odour, aroma. ❷ (*Brit. informal*) *there's a terrible whiff in here* STENCH, stink, smell, reek; *Brit. informal* pong, niff, hum; *Scottish informal* guff; *N. Amer. informal* funk. ❸ *the faintest whiff of irony* TRACE, hint, suggestion, impression, suspicion, soupçon, nuance, intimation, tinge, vein, shred, whisper, air, element, overtone. ❹ *whiffs of smoke from the boiler* PUFF, gust, flurry, breath, draught, waft.

while ▶ noun *we chatted for a while* TIME, spell, stretch, stint, span, interval, period; duration, phase; *Brit. informal* patch.
▶ verb *tennis helped to while away the time* PASS, spend, occupy, use up, kill.

whim ▶ noun ❶ *she bought it on a whim* IMPULSE, urge, notion, fancy, foible, caprice, conceit, vagary, crotchet, inclination. ❷ *human whim* CAPRICIOUSNESS, whimsy, caprice, volatility, fickleness, idiosyncrasy.

whimper ▶ verb *he was whimpering in pain* WHINE, cry, sob, moan, snivel, wail, groan; *Brit. informal* grizzle.

▶ noun *she gave a whimper of protest* WHINE, cry, sob, moan, bleat, wail, groan.

whimsical ▶ adjective ❶ *a whimsical sense of humour* FANCIFUL, playful, mischievous, waggish, quaint, curious, droll; eccentric, quirky, idiosyncratic, unconventional, outlandish, queer; *informal* offbeat, freaky. ❷ *the whimsical arbitrariness of autocracy* VOLATILE, capricious, fickle, changeable, unpredictable, variable, erratic, mercurial, mutable, inconstant, inconsistent, unstable, protean.

whine ▶ noun ❶ *the dog gave a whine* WHIMPER, cry, mewl, howl, yowl. ❷ *the whine of the motor* HUM, drone. ❸ *a whine about the quality of service* COMPLAINT, grouse, grumble, murmur; *informal* gripe, moan, grouch, whinge, bellyache, beef.

▶ verb ❶ *a child was whining* WAIL, whimper, cry, mewl, moan, howl, yowl. ❷ *the lift began to whine* HUM, drone. ❸ *he's always whining about something* COMPLAIN, grouse, grouch, grumble, moan, carp, mutter, murmur; *informal* gripe, bellyache, whinge.

whinge (*informal*) ▶ verb *I whinged about the weather. See* WHINE verb sense 3.

▶ noun *his tale is one long whinge. See* WHINE noun sense 3.

whip ▶ noun *he would use a whip on his dogs* LASH, scourge, strap, belt; *historical* cat-o'-nine-tails.

▶ verb ❶ *he whipped the boy* FLOG, scourge, flagellate, lash, strap, belt, thrash, beat, tan someone's hide. ❷ *whip the cream* WHISK, beat. ❸ *he whipped his listeners into a frenzy* ROUSE, stir up, excite, galvanize, electrify, stimulate, inspire, fire up, get someone going, inflame, agitate, goad, provoke. ❹ (*informal*) *he whipped round the corner. See* DASH verb sense 1. ❺ (*informal*) *then he whipped out a revolver* PULL, whisk, snatch, pluck, jerk; *informal* yank; *Scottish informal* wheech. ❻ (*Brit. informal*) *he whipped the necklace. See* STEAL verb sense 1.

whippersnapper ▶ noun (*informal*) UPSTART, stripling; *informal* pipsqueak, squirt; *Brit. informal* squit; *N. Amer. informal* snip.

whirl ▶ verb ❶ *leaves whirled in eddies of wind* ROTATE, circle, wheel, turn, revolve, orbit, spin, twirl; *Scottish* birl. ❷ *they whirled past* HURRY, race, dash, rush, run, sprint, bolt, dart, gallop, career, charge, shoot, hurtle, hare, fly, speed, scurry; *informal* tear, belt, pelt, scoot; *Brit. informal* bomb; *N. Amer. informal* hightail it. ❸ *his mind was whirling* SPIN, reel, swim.

▶ noun ❶ *a whirl of dust* SWIRL, flurry, eddy. ❷ *the mad social whirl* HURLY-BURLY, activity, bustle, rush, flurry, fuss, turmoil, merry-go-round; *informal* to-do. ❸ *Laura's mind was in a whirl* SPIN, daze, stupor, muddle, jumble; confusion; *informal* dither. ❹ (*informal*) *go on, give it a whirl* TRY, test; *informal* go, shot, bash, stab.

whirlpool ▶ noun ❶ *a river full of whirlpools* EDDY, vortex, maelstrom; *N. Amer. informal* suckhole. ❷ *the health club has a whirlpool* JACUZZI, spa bath, hot tub.

whirlwind ▶ noun ❶ *the building was hit by a whirlwind* TORNADO, hurricane, typhoon, cyclone, vortex; *Austral.* willy-willy; *N. Amer. informal* twister. ❷ *a whirlwind of activity* MAELSTROM, welter, bedlam, mayhem, babel, swirl, tumult, hurly-burly, commotion, confusion; *informal* madhouse; *N. Amer.* three-ring circus.

▶ adjective *a whirlwind romance* RAPID, lightning, headlong, impulsive, breakneck, meteoric, sudden, swift, fast, quick, speedy; *informal* quickie.

whisk ▶ verb ❶ *the cable car will whisk you to the top* SPEED, hurry, rush, sweep, hurtle, shoot; *Scottish informal* wheech. ❷ *she whisked the cloth away* PULL, snatch, pluck, tug, jerk; *informal* whip, yank; *Scottish informal* wheech. ❸ *he whisked out of sight* DASH, rush, race, bolt, dart, gallop, career, charge, shoot, hurtle, hare, fly, speed, zoom, scurry, scuttle, scamper; *informal* tear, belt, pelt, scoot, zip, whip. ❹ *horses whisk their tails* FLICK, twitch, wave. ❺ *whisk the egg yolks* WHIP, beat, mix.

▶ noun ❶ *the horse gave a whisk of its tail* FLICK, twitch, wave, sweep. ❷ *blend the eggs with a whisk* BEATER, mixer, blender.

whisper ▶ verb ❶ *Alison whispered in his ear* MURMUR, mutter, mumble, speak softly, breathe. ❷ (*poetic/literary*) *the wind whispered in the grass* RUSTLE, murmur, sigh, moan, whoosh, whirr, swish, blow, breathe.

–OPPOSITES roar.

▶ noun ❶ *she spoke in a whisper* MURMUR, mutter, mumble, low voice, undertone. ❷ (*poetic/literary*) *the wind died to a whisper* RUSTLE, murmur, sigh, whoosh, swish. ❸ *I heard a whisper that he's left town* RUMOUR, story, report, speculation, insinuation, suggestion, hint; *informal* buzz. ❹ *not a whisper of interest. See* WHIT.

whit ▶ noun SCRAP, bit, speck, iota, jot, atom, crumb, shred, grain, mite, touch, trace, shadow, suggestion, whisper, suspicion, scintilla; *informal* smidgen, smidge.

white ▶ adjective ❶ *a clean white bandage* COLOURLESS, unpigmented, bleached, natural; snowy, milky, chalky, ivory. ❷ *her face was white with fear* PALE, pallid, wan, ashen, bloodless, waxen, chalky, pasty, peaky, washed out, drained, drawn, ghostly, deathly. ❸ *white hair* SNOWY, grey, silver, silvery, hoary, grizzled. ❹ *the early white settlers* CAUCASIAN, European. ❺ *a whiter than white government* VIRTUOUS, moral, ethical, good, righteous, honourable, reputable, wholesome, honest, upright, upstanding, irreproachable; decent, worthy,

noble; blameless, spotless, impeccable, unsullied, unblemished, uncorrupted, untainted; *informal* squeaky clean.
– OPPOSITES black, florid, immoral.

white-collar ▶ **adjective** CLERICAL, professional, executive, salaried, office.

whiten ▶ **verb** MAKE WHITE, make pale, bleach, blanch, lighten, fade; *Brit. Military* blanco; *archaic* white.

whitewash ▶ **noun** ❶ *the report was a whitewash* COVER-UP, camouflage, deception, facade, veneer, pretext. ❷ *a four-match whitewash* WALKOVER, rout, landslide; *informal* pushover, cinch, breeze.
– OPPOSITES exposé.
▶ **verb** *don't whitewash what happened* COVER UP, sweep under the carpet, hush up, suppress, draw a veil over, conceal, veil, obscure, keep secret; gloss over, downplay, soft-pedal.
– OPPOSITES expose.

whittle ▶ **verb** ❶ *he sat whittling a piece of wood* PARE, shave, trim, carve, shape, model. ❷ *his powers were whittled away* ERODE, wear away, eat away, reduce, diminish, undermine, weaken, subvert, compromise, impair, impede, hinder, cripple, disable, enfeeble, sap. ❸ *the ten teams have been whittled down to six* REDUCE, cut down, cut back, prune, trim, slim down, pare down, shrink, decrease, diminish.

whole ▶ **adjective** ❶ *the whole report* ENTIRE, complete, full, unabridged, uncut. ❷ *a whole marble mantelpiece* INTACT, in one piece, unbroken; undamaged, flawless, faultless, unmarked, perfect.
– OPPOSITES incomplete.
▶ **noun** ❶ *a single whole* ENTITY, unit, body, discrete item, ensemble. ❷ *the whole of the year* ALL, every part, the lot, the sum (total).
■ **on the whole** OVERALL, all in all, all things considered, for the most part, in the main, in general, generally (speaking), as a (general) rule, by and large; normally, usually, more often than not, almost always, most of the time, typically, ordinarily.

wholehearted ▶ **adjective** COMMITTED, positive, emphatic, devoted, dedicated, enthusiastic, unshakeable, unswerving; unqualified, unreserved, without reservations, unconditional, unequivocal, unmitigated; complete, full, total, absolute.
– OPPOSITES half-hearted.

wholesale ▶ **adverb** *the images were removed wholesale* EXTENSIVELY, on a large scale, comprehensively; indiscriminately, without exception.
– OPPOSITES selectively.
▶ **adjective** *wholesale destruction* EXTENSIVE, widespread, large-scale, wide-ranging, comprehensive, total, mass; indiscriminate.
– OPPOSITES partial.

wholesome ▶ **adjective** ❶ *wholesome food* HEALTHY, health-giving, healthful, good (for one), nutritious, nourishing; natural, uncontaminated, organic. ❷ *wholesome fun* MORAL, ethical, good, clean, virtuous, pure, innocent, chaste; uplifting, edifying, proper, correct, decent; *informal* squeaky clean.

wholly ▶ **adverb** ❶ *the measures were wholly inadequate* COMPLETELY, totally, absolutely, entirely, fully, thoroughly, utterly, quite, perfectly, downright, in every respect, in all respects; *informal* one hundred per cent. ❷ *they rely wholly on you* EXCLUSIVELY, only, solely, purely, alone.

whoop ▶ **noun** *whoops of delight* SHOUT, cry, call, yell, roar, scream, shriek, screech, cheer; *informal* holler.
▶ **verb** *he whooped for joy* SHOUT, cry, call, yell, roar, scream, shriek, screech, cheer; *informal* holler.

whopper ▶ **noun** (*informal*) ❶ *what a whopper!* MONSTER, brute, giant, colossus, mammoth, monstrosity; *informal* jumbo. ❷ *Joseph's story is a whopper. See* LIE[1] noun.

whopping ▶ **adjective** (*informal*). *See* HUGE.

whore ▶ **noun** *the whores on the street. See* PROSTITUTE noun.
▶ **verb** ❶ *she spent her life whoring* WORK AS A PROSTITUTE, sell one's body, sell oneself, be on the streets; *informal* be on the game. ❷ *the men whored and drank* USE PROSTITUTES; *archaic* wench.

whorehouse ▶ **noun**. *See* BROTHEL.

whorl ▶ **noun** LOOP, coil, hoop, ring, curl, twirl, twist, spiral, helix.

wicked ▶ **adjective** ❶ *wicked deeds* EVIL, sinful, immoral, wrong, morally wrong, wrongful, bad, iniquitous, corrupt, black-hearted, base, mean, vile; villainous, nefarious, erring, foul, monstrous, shocking, outrageous, atrocious, abominable, reprehensible, hateful, detestable, despicable, odious, contemptible, horrible, heinous, egregious, execrable, fiendish, vicious, murderous, barbarous; criminal, illicit, unlawful, illegal, lawless, felonious, dishonest, unscrupulous; *Law* malfeasant; *informal* crooked; *Brit. informal* beastly; *dated* dastardly; *rare* peccable. ❷ *the wind was wicked* DISAGREEABLE, unpleasant, foul, bad, nasty, irksome, troublesome, annoying, irritating, displeasing, uncomfortable, hateful, detestable. ❸ *a wicked sense of humour* MISCHIEVOUS, playful, naughty, impish, roguish, arch, puckish, cheeky. ❹ (*informal*) *Sophie makes wicked cakes. See* EXCELLENT.
– OPPOSITES virtuous.

wickedness ▶ **noun** EVIL-DOING, evil, sin, sinfulness, iniquity, vileness, baseness, badness, wrongdoing, dishonesty, unscrupulousness, roguery, villainy, viciousness, degeneracy, depravity, immorality, vice, corruption, corruptness, devilry, fiendishness; *Law* malfeasance; *informal* crookedness; *formal* turpitude.

wide ▶ adjective ❶ *a wide river* BROAD, extensive, spacious, vast, spread out. ❷ *their mouths were wide with shock* FULLY OPEN, agape, wide open. ❸ *a wide range of opinion* COMPREHENSIVE, ample, broad, extensive, large, large-scale, wide-ranging, exhaustive, general, all-inclusive. ❹ *his shot was wide* OFF TARGET, off the mark, wide of the mark/target, inaccurate.
– OPPOSITES narrow.
▶ adverb ❶ *he opened his eyes wide* FULLY, to the fullest/furthest extent, as far/much as possible. ❷ *he shot wide* OFF TARGET, wide of the mark/target, inaccurately.

wide awake ▶ adjective FULLY AWAKE, conscious, sleepless, insomniac; *archaic* watchful.
– OPPOSITES asleep.

wide-eyed ▶ adjective ❶ *the whole class was wide-eyed* STARING IN AMAZEMENT, goggle-eyed, open-mouthed, dumbstruck, amazed, surprised, astonished, astounded, stunned, staggered; *informal* flabbergasted; *Brit. informal* gobsmacked. ❷ *wide-eyed visitors* INNOCENT, naive, impressionable, ingenuous, childlike, credulous, trusting, unquestioning, unsophisticated, gullible.

widen ▶ verb ❶ *a proposal to widen the motorway* BROADEN, make/become wider, open up/out, expand, extend, enlarge. ❷ *the Party must widen its support* INCREASE, augment, boost, swell, enlarge.

wide open ▶ adjective ❶ *his eyes were wide open* FULLY OPEN, open wide, agape. ❷ *the championship is wide open* UNPREDICTABLE, uncertain, unsure, in the balance, up in the air; *informal* anyone's guess. ❸ *they were wide open to attacks* VULNERABLE, exposed, unprotected, defenceless, undefended, at risk, in danger.

widespread ▶ adjective GENERAL, extensive, universal, common, global, worldwide, international, omnipresent, ubiquitous, across the board, predominant, prevalent, rife, broad, rampant, pervasive.
– OPPOSITES limited.

width ▶ noun ❶ *the width of the river* WIDENESS, breadth, broadness, thickness, span, diameter, girth. ❷ *the width of experience required* RANGE, breadth, compass, scope, span, scale, extent, extensiveness, comprehensiveness.
– OPPOSITES length, narrowness.

wield ▶ verb ❶ *he was wielding a sword* BRANDISH, flourish, wave, swing; use, employ, handle. ❷ *he has wielded power since 1972* EXERCISE, exert, hold, maintain, command, control.

wife ▶ noun SPOUSE, partner, mate, consort, woman, helpmate, helpmeet, bride; *informal* old lady, wifey, better half, missus; *Brit. informal* other half, her indoors, trouble and strife.
– RELATED TERMS uxorial.

wiggle ▶ verb JIGGLE, wriggle, twitch, shimmy, joggle, wag, wobble, shake, twist, squirm, writhe; *informal* waggle.

wild ▶ adjective ❶ *wild animals* UNTAMED, undomesticated, feral; fierce, ferocious, savage. ❷ *wild flowers* UNCULTIVATED, native, indigenous. ❸ *wild tribes* PRIMITIVE, uncivilized, uncultured; savage, barbarous, barbaric. ❹ *wild hill country* UNINHABITED, unpopulated, uncultivated; rugged, rough, inhospitable, desolate, barren. ❺ *a wild night* STORMY, squally, tempestuous, turbulent, boisterous. ❻ *her wild black hair* DISHEVELLED, tousled, tangled, windswept, untidy, unkempt; *N. Amer.* mussed up. ❼ *wild behaviour* UNCONTROLLED, unrestrained, out of control, undisciplined, unruly, rowdy, disorderly, riotous. ❽ *wild with excitement* VERY EXCITED, delirious, in a frenzy; tumultuous, passionate, vehement, unrestrained. ❾ (*informal*) *I was wild with jealousy* DISTRAUGHT, frantic, beside oneself, in a frenzy, hysterical, deranged, berserk; *informal* mad, crazy. ❿ (*informal*) *Hank went wild when he found out. See* FURIOUS sense 1. ⓫ (*informal*) *his family weren't wild about me* VERY KEEN, very enthusiastic, enamoured, infatuated, smitten; *informal* crazy, mad, nutty/nuts. ⓬ *Bill's wild schemes* MADCAP, ridiculous, ludicrous, foolish, stupid, foolhardy, idiotic, absurd, silly, ill-considered, senseless, nonsensical; impractical, impracticable, unworkable; *informal* crazy, crackpot, cock-eyed. ⓭ *a wild guess* RANDOM, arbitrary, haphazard, uninformed.
– OPPOSITES tame, cultivated, calm, disciplined.
■ **run wild** ❶ *the garden had run wild* GROW UNCHECKED, grow profusely, run riot. ❷ *the children are running wild* RUN AMOK, run riot, get out of control, be undisciplined.

wilderness ▶ noun ❶ *the Siberian wilderness* WILDS, wastes, inhospitable region; desert. ❷ *a litter-strewn wilderness* WASTELAND.

wildlife ▶ noun (WILD) ANIMALS, fauna.

wilds ▶ plural noun REMOTE AREAS, wilderness; backwoods; *N. Amer.* backcountry, backland; *Austral./NZ* outback, bush, backblocks, booay; *N. Amer. informal* boondocks, tall timbers.

wiles ▶ plural noun TRICKS, ruses, ploys, schemes, dodges, manoeuvres, subterfuges, artifices; guile, artfulness, cunning, craftiness.

wilful ▶ adjective ❶ *wilful destruction* DELIBERATE, intentional, done on purpose, premeditated, planned, conscious. ❷ *a wilful child* HEADSTRONG, strong-willed, obstinate, stubborn, pig-headed, recalcitrant, uncooperative, obstreperous, ungovernable, unmanageable; *Brit. informal* bloody-minded, bolshie; *N. Amer. informal* balky; *formal* refractory; *archaic* froward, contumacious.
– OPPOSITES accidental, amenable.

will[1] ▶ verb *accidents will happen* HAVE A TENDENCY TO, are bound to, do.

will[2] ▶ noun ❶ *the will to succeed* DETERMINATION, will power, strength of character, resolution, resolve, resoluteness, single-mindedness, purposefulness, drive, commitment, dedication, doggedness, tenacity, tenaciousness, staying power. ❷ *they stayed against their will* DESIRE, wish, preference, inclination, intention, intent. ❸ *God's will* WISH, desire, decision, choice; decree, command. ❹ *his father's will* (LAST WILL AND) TESTAMENT.

▶ **verb** ❶ *do what you will* WANT, wish, please, see/think fit, think best, like, choose, prefer. ❷ *God willed it* DECREE, order, ordain, command. ❸ *she willed the money to her husband* BEQUEATH, leave, hand down, pass on, settle on; *Law* devise.

■ **at will** AS ONE PLEASES, as one thinks fit, to suit oneself, at whim.

willing ▶ **adjective** ❶ *I'm willing to give it a try* READY, prepared, disposed, inclined, of a mind, minded; happy, glad, pleased, agreeable, amenable; *informal* game. ❷ *willing help* READILY GIVEN, willingly given, ungrudging.

– OPPOSITES reluctant.

willingly ▶ **adverb** VOLUNTARILY, of one's own free will, of one's own accord; readily, without reluctance, ungrudgingly, cheerfully, happily, gladly, with pleasure.

willingness ▶ **noun** READINESS, inclination, will, wish, desire.

willowy ▶ **adjective** TALL, SLIM, slender, svelte, lissom, sylphlike, long-limbed, graceful, lithe; *informal* slinky.

will power ▶ **noun**. *See* WILL² noun sense 1.

willy-nilly ▶ **adverb** ❶ *cars were parked willy-nilly* HAPHAZARDLY, at random, randomly. ❷ *we are, willy-nilly, in a new situation* WHETHER ONE LIKES IT OR NOT, of necessity; *informal* like it or lump it; *formal* perforce, nolens volens.

wilt ▶ **verb** ❶ *the roses had begun to wilt* DROOP, sag, become limp, flop; wither, shrivel (up). ❷ *wilting in the heat* LANGUISH, flag, droop, become listless. ❸ *Shelley's happy mood wilted* FADE, ebb, wane, evaporate, melt away.

– OPPOSITES flourish.

wily ▶ **adjective** SHREWD, clever, sharp, sharp-witted, astute, canny, smart; crafty, cunning, artful, sly, scheming, calculating, devious; *informal* tricky, foxy; *archaic* subtle.

– OPPOSITES naive.

wimp ▶ **noun** (*informal*) COWARD, namby-pamby, milksop, weakling; *informal* drip, sissy, weed, wuss, pansy, scaredy-cat, chicken; *Brit. informal* wet, mummy's boy, big girl's blouse; *N. Amer. informal* cupcake, pantywaist, pussy; *Austral./NZ informal* sook; *archaic* poltroon.

win ▶ **verb** ❶ *Steve won the race* BE THE VICTOR IN, be the winner of, come first in, take first prize in, triumph in, be successful in. ❷ *she was determined to win* COME FIRST, be the winner, be victorious, carry/win the day, come out on top, succeed, triumph, prevail. ❸ *he won a cash prize* SECURE, gain, collect, pick up, walk away/off with, carry off; *informal* land, net, bag, scoop. ❹ *Ilona won his heart* CAPTIVATE, steal.

– OPPOSITES lose.

▶ **noun** *a 3–0 win* VICTORY, triumph, conquest.

– OPPOSITES defeat.

■ **win someone round/over** PERSUADE, talk round, convince, sway, prevail on.

wince ▶ **verb** *he winced at the pain* GRIMACE, pull a face, flinch, blench, start.

▶ **noun** *a wince of pain* GRIMACE, flinch, start.

wind¹ ▶ **noun** ❶ *the trees were swaying in the wind* BREEZE, current of air; gale, hurricane; *informal* blow; *poetic/literary* zephyr. ❷ *Jez got his wind back* BREATH; *informal* puff. ❸ *you do talk a lot of wind. See* HOT AIR. ❹ FLATULENCE, gas; *formal* flatus.

– RELATED TERMS aeolian.

■ **get wind of** (*informal*) HEAR ABOUT/OF, learn of, find out about, be told about, be informed of; *informal* hear something on the grapevine.

■ **in the wind** ON THE WAY, coming, about to happen, in the offing, in the air, on the horizon, approaching, looming, brewing, afoot; *informal* on the cards.

■ **put the wind up someone** (*Brit. informal*) SCARE, frighten, make afraid, make nervous, throw into a panic, alarm.

wind² ▶ **verb** ❶ *the road winds up the mountain* TWIST (AND TURN), bend, curve, loop, zigzag, weave, snake. ❷ *he wound a towel around his waist* WRAP, furl, entwine, lace. ❸ *Anne wound the wool into a ball* COIL, roll, twist, twine.

■ **wind down** ❶ (*informal*) *he needed to wind down* RELAX, unwind, calm down, cool down/off, ease up/off, take it easy, rest, put one's feet up; *N. Amer. informal* hang loose, chill (out). ❷ *the campaign was winding down* DRAW TO A CLOSE, come to an end, tail off, slack(en) off, slow down.

■ **wind something down** BRING TO A CLOSE/END, wind up, close down.

■ **wind up** (*informal*) END UP, finish up, find oneself, land up; *informal* fetch up.

■ **wind someone up** ❶ (*Brit. informal*) *Katie was just winding me up* TEASE, make fun of, chaff; *informal* take the mickey out of, send up, rib, josh, kid, have on, pull someone's leg; *N. Amer. informal* pull someone's chain; *Austral./NZ informal* poke mullock at. ❷ *David was winding him up on purpose* ANNOY, anger, irritate, exasperate, get on someone's nerves, provoke, goad; *Brit.* rub up the wrong way; *informal* aggravate, rile, niggle, bug, put someone's back up, get up someone's nose, hack off; *Brit. informal* nark; *N. Amer. informal* ride.

■ **wind something up** ❶ *Richard wound up the meeting* CONCLUDE, bring to an end/close, end, terminate; *informal* wrap up. ❷ *the company has been wound up* CLOSE (DOWN), dissolve, put into liquidation.

winded ▶ **adjective** OUT OF BREATH, breathless, gasping for breath, panting, puffing, puffed out; *informal* out of puff.

windfall ▶**noun** BONANZA, jackpot, pennies from heaven.

winding ▶**noun** *the windings of the stream* TWIST, turn, turning, bend, loop, curve, zigzag, meander.

▶**adjective** *the winding country roads* TWISTING AND TURNING, meandering, windy, twisty, bending, curving, zigzag, zigzagging, serpentine, sinuous, snaking.

– OPPOSITES straight.

windpipe ▶**noun** TRACHEA, pharynx; throat.

windswept ▶**adjective** ❶ *the windswept moors* EXPOSED, bleak, bare, desolate. ❷ *his windswept hair* DISHEVELLED, tousled, unkempt, windblown, untidy; *N. Amer.* mussed up.

windy ▶**adjective** ❶ *a windy day* BREEZY, blowy, fresh, blustery, gusty; wild, stormy, squally, tempestuous, boisterous. ❷ *a windy hillside* WINDSWEPT, exposed, open to the elements, bare, bleak. ❸ (*informal*) *windy speeches. See* LONG-WINDED. ❹ (*Brit. informal*) *she felt a bit windy. See* ANXIOUS sense 1.

– OPPOSITES still, sheltered.

wine ▶**noun** *informal* plonk, vino, the grape; *poetic/literary* vintage.

– RELATED TERMS vinous, oeno-.

wing ▶**noun** ❶ *a bird's wings poetic/literary* pinion. ❷ *the east wing of the house* PART, section, side; annexe, extension; *N. Amer.* ell. ❸ *the radical wing of the party* FACTION, camp, caucus, arm, branch, group, section, set, coterie, cabal.

▶**verb** ❶ *a seagull winged its way over the sea* FLY, glide, soar. ❷ *the bomb winged past* HURTLE, speed, shoot, whizz, zoom, streak, fly. ❸ *she was shot at and winged* WOUND, graze, hit.

■ **wing it** (*informal*) IMPROVISE, play it by ear, extemporize, ad lib; *informal* busk it.

wink ▶**verb** ❶ *he winked an eye at her* BLINK, flutter, bat. ❷ *the diamond winked in the moonlight* SPARKLE, twinkle, flash, glitter, gleam, shine, scintillate.

▶**noun** *a wink of light* GLIMMER, gleam, glint, flash, flicker, twinkle, sparkle.

■ **in the wink of an eye** (*informal*) VERY QUICKLY, very soon, in a second, in a moment, in a trice, in a flash, in an instant, in no time at all; *N. Amer.* momentarily; *informal* in a jiffy, in two shakes (of a lamb's tail), in a sec, in the blink of an eye; *Brit. informal* in a tick, in a mo; *N. Amer. informal* in a snap.

■ **wink at** TURN A BLIND EYE TO, close one's eyes to, ignore, overlook, disregard; connive at, condone, tolerate.

winkle

■ **winkle something out** WORM OUT, prise out, dig out, extract, draw out, obtain, get.

winner ▶**noun** VICTOR, champion, conqueror, vanquisher, hero; medallist; *Brit.* victor ludorum; *informal* champ, top dog.

– OPPOSITES loser.

winning ▶**adjective** ❶ *the winning team* VICTORIOUS, successful, triumphant, vanquishing, conquering; first, top. ❷ *a winning smile* ENGAGING, charming, appealing, endearing, sweet, cute, winsome, attractive, pretty, prepossessing, fetching, lovely, adorable, delightful, disarming, captivating; *dated* taking.

winnings ▶**plural noun** PRIZE MONEY, gains, prize, booty, spoils; proceeds, profits, takings, purse.

winnow ▶**verb** SEPARATE (OUT), divide, sort out, sift out, filter out; isolate, find, identify; remove, get rid of.

winsome ▶**adjective**. *See* WINNING sense 2.

wintry ▶**adjective** ❶ *wintry weather* BLEAK, cold, chilly, chill, frosty, freezing, icy, snowy, arctic, glacial, bitter, raw; *informal* nippy; *Brit. informal* parky. ❷ *a wintry smile* UNFRIENDLY, unwelcoming, cool, cold, frosty, frigid.

– OPPOSITES summery, warm.

wipe ▶**verb** ❶ *Beth wiped the table* RUB, mop, sponge, swab; clean, dry, polish. ❷ *he wiped the marks off the window* RUB OFF, clean off, clear up, remove, get rid of, take off, erase, efface. ❸ *she wiped the memory from her mind* OBLITERATE, expunge, erase, blot out, blank out.

▶**noun** *he gave the table a wipe* RUB, mop, sponge, swab; clean, polish.

■ **wipe someone/something out** DESTROY, annihilate, eradicate, eliminate; slaughter, massacre, kill, exterminate; demolish, raze to the ground; *informal* take out, zap; *N. Amer. informal* waste; *poetic/literary* slay.

wire ▶**noun** CABLE, lead, flex.

wiry ▶**adjective** ❶ *a wiry man* SINEWY, tough, athletic, strong; lean, spare, thin, stringy, skinny. ❷ *wiry hair* COARSE, rough, strong; curly, wavy.

– OPPOSITES flabby, smooth.

wisdom ▶**noun** ❶ *we questioned the wisdom of the decision* SAGACITY, intelligence, sense, common sense, shrewdness, astuteness, smartness, judiciousness, judgement, prudence, circumspection; logic, rationale, rationality, soundness, advisability. ❷ *the wisdom of the East* KNOWLEDGE, learning, erudition, scholarship, philosophy; lore.

– OPPOSITES folly.

wise ▶**adjective** *a wise old man* SAGE, sagacious, intelligent, clever, learned, knowledgeable, enlightened; astute, smart, shrewd, sharp-witted, canny, knowing; sensible, prudent, discerning, judicious, perceptive, insightful, perspicacious; rational, logical, sound, sane; *Brit. informal* fly; *formal* sapient.

– OPPOSITES foolish.

■ **put someone wise** (*informal*) TELL, inform, notify, apprise, make aware, put in the picture, fill in; warn, alert; *informal* clue in/up, tip off.

■ **wise to** (*informal*) AWARE OF, familiar with, acquainted with; *formal* cognizant of.

wisecrack ▶ **noun** (*informal*) JOKE, witticism, quip, jest, sally; pun, bon mot; *informal* crack, gag, funny, one-liner.

wish ▶ **verb** ❶ *I wished for power* DESIRE, want, hope for, covet, dream of, long for, yearn for, crave, hunger for, lust after; aspire to, set one's heart on, seek, fancy, hanker after; *informal* have a yen for, itch for; *archaic* be desirous of. ❷ *they can do as they wish* WANT, desire, feel inclined, feel like, care; choose, please, think fit. ❸ *I wish you to send them a message* WANT, desire, require. ❹ *I wished him farewell* BID.

▶ **noun** ❶ *his wish to own a Mercedes* DESIRE, longing, yearning, inclination, urge, whim, craving, hunger; hope, aspiration, aim, ambition, dream; *informal* hankering, yen, itch. ❷ *her parents' wishes* REQUEST, requirement, bidding, instruction, direction, demand, order, command; want, desire; will; *poetic/literary* behest.

wishy-washy ▶ **adjective** ❶ *he's so wishy-washy* FEEBLE, ineffectual, weak, vapid, effete, spineless, limp, namby-pamby, spiritless, indecisive; *informal* wet, pathetic. ❷ *wishy-washy soup* WATERY, weak, thin; tasteless, flavourless, insipid. ❸ *a wishy-washy colour* PALE, insipid, pallid, muted.
– OPPOSITES strong, tasty, vibrant.

wisp ▶ **noun** STRAND, tendril, lock; scrap, shred, thread.

wispy ▶ **adjective** THIN, fine, feathery, flyaway.

wistful ▶ **adjective** NOSTALGIC, yearning, longing; plaintive, regretful, rueful, melancholy, mournful; pensive, reflective, contemplative.

wit ▶ **noun** ❶ *he needed all his wits to escape* INTELLIGENCE, shrewdness, astuteness, cleverness, canniness, (common) sense, wisdom, sagacity, judgement, acumen, insight; brains, mind; *informal* nous, gumption, savvy, horse sense; *Brit. informal* common; *N. Amer. informal* smarts. ❷ *my sparkling wit* WITTINESS, humour, funniness, drollery; repartee, badinage, banter, wordplay; jokes, witticisms, quips, puns. ❸ *she's such a wit* COMEDIAN, humorist, comic, joker, jokester; *informal* wag; *informal, dated* card, caution.

witch ▶ **noun** ❶ *the witch cast a spell* SORCERESS, enchantress, hex; Wiccan; *archaic* pythoness. ❷ (*informal*) *she's a right old witch* HAG, crone, harpy, harridan, she-devil; *informal* battleaxe.

witchcraft ▶ **noun** SORCERY, (black) magic, witching, witchery, wizardry, thaumaturgy, spells, incantations; Wicca; *Irish* pishogue.

witch doctor ▶ **noun** MEDICINE MAN, shaman, healer.

with ▶ **preposition** ACCOMPANIED BY, escorted by; alongside, in addition to, as well as.

withdraw ▶ **verb** ❶ *she withdrew her hand from his* REMOVE, extract, pull out, take out; take back, take away. ❷ *the ban on advertising was withdrawn* ABOLISH, cancel, lift, set aside, end, stop, remove, reverse, revoke, rescind, repeal, annul, void. ❸ *she withdrew the allegation* RETRACT, take back, go back on, recant, disavow, disclaim, repudiate, renounce; back down, climb down, backtrack, back-pedal, do a U-turn, eat one's words. ❹ *the troops withdrew from the city* LEAVE, pull out of, evacuate, quit, retreat from. ❺ *his partner withdrew from the project* PULL OUT OF, back out of, bow out of; get cold feet. ❻ *they withdrew to their rooms* RETIRE, retreat, adjourn, decamp; leave, depart, absent oneself; *formal* repair; *dated* remove; *poetic/literary* betake oneself.
– OPPOSITES insert, introduce, deposit, enter.

withdrawal ▶ **noun** ❶ *the withdrawal of subsidies* REMOVAL, abolition, cancellation, discontinuation, termination, elimination. ❷ *the withdrawal of the troops* DEPARTURE, pull-out, exit, exodus, evacuation, retreat.

withdrawn ▶ **adjective** INTROVERTED, unsociable, inhibited, uncommunicative, unforthcoming, quiet, reticent, reserved, retiring, private, reclusive; shy, timid; aloof; *informal* standoffish.
– OPPOSITES outgoing.

wither ▶ **verb** ❶ *the flowers withered in the sun* SHRIVEL (UP), dry up; wilt, droop, go limp, fade, perish. ❷ *the muscles in his leg withered* WASTE (AWAY), shrivel (up), shrink, atrophy. ❸ *her confidence withered* DIMINISH, dwindle, shrink, lessen, fade, ebb, wane; evaporate, disappear.
– OPPOSITES thrive, grow.

withering ▶ **adjective** SCORNFUL, contemptuous, scathing, stinging, devastating; humiliating, mortifying.
– OPPOSITES admiring.

withhold ▶ **verb** ❶ *he withheld the information* HOLD BACK, keep back, refuse to give; retain, hold on to; hide, conceal, keep secret; *informal* sit on. ❷ *she could not withhold her tears* SUPPRESS, repress, hold back, fight back, choke back, control, check, restrain, contain.

within ▶ **preposition** ❶ *within the prison walls* INSIDE, in, enclosed by, surrounded by; within the bounds of, within the confines of. ❷ *within a few hours* IN LESS THAN, in under, in no more than, after only.
– OPPOSITES outside.

without ▶ **preposition** ❶ *thousands were without food* LACKING, short of, deprived of, in need of, wanting, needing, requiring. ❷ *I don't want to go without you* UNACCOMPANIED BY, unescorted by; in the absence of.

withstand ▶ **verb** RESIST, weather, survive, endure, cope with, stand, tolerate, bear, defy, brave, hold out against, bear up against; stand up to, face, confront.

witless ▶ **adjective** FOOLISH, stupid, unintelligent, idiotic, brainless, mindless; fatuous, inane, half-baked, empty-headed, slow-witted; *informal* thick, birdbrained, pea-brained, dopey, dim, dim-witted, half-witted, dippy, lame-brained, wooden-headed; *Brit. informal* daft; *Scottish & N. English informal* glaikit; *N. Amer. informal* dumb-ass.

witness ▶ noun ❶ *witnesses claimed that he started the fight* OBSERVER, onlooker, eyewitness, spectator, viewer, watcher; bystander, passer-by. ❷ *a whisky bottle was the only witness of his mood* EVIDENCE, indication, proof, testimony.
▶ verb ❶ *who witnessed the incident?* SEE, observe, watch, view, notice, spot; be present at, attend; *poetic/literary* behold. ❷ *the will is correctly witnessed* COUNTERSIGN, sign, endorse, validate; *N. Amer.* notarize. ❸ *his writings witness an inner toughness* ATTEST TO, testify to, bear witness to, confirm, evidence, prove, verify, corroborate, substantiate; show, demonstrate, indicate, reveal, bespeak.

witter ▶ verb (*Brit. informal*). *See* GABBLE verb.

witticism ▶ noun JOKE, quip, jest, pun, play on words, bon mot; *informal* one-liner, gag, funny, crack, wisecrack.

witty ▶ adjective HUMOROUS, amusing, droll, funny, comic, comical; jocular, facetious, waggish; sparkling, scintillating, entertaining; clever, quick-witted.

wizard ▶ noun ❶ *the wizard cast a spell over them* SORCERER, warlock, magus, (black) magician, enchanter; *archaic* mage. ❷ *a financial wizard* GENIUS, expert, master, virtuoso, maestro, marvel, Wunderkind; *informal* hotshot, demon, whizz-kid, buff, pro, ace; *Brit. informal* dab hand; *N. Amer. informal* maven.

wizardry ▶ noun SORCERY, witchcraft, witchery, witching, (black) magic, enchantment; spells, charms; *Irish* pishogue.

wizened ▶ adjective WRINKLED, lined, creased, shrivelled (up), withered, weather-beaten, shrunken, gnarled.

wobble ▶ verb ❶ *the table wobbled* ROCK, teeter, jiggle, sway, see-saw, shake. ❷ *he wobbled across to the door* TEETER, totter, stagger, lurch. ❸ *her voice wobbled* TREMBLE, shake, quiver, quaver, waver. ❹ *for a few days the minister wobbled* HESITATE, vacillate, waver, dither, shilly-shally, blow hot and cold; *Scottish* swither.
▶ noun ❶ *she stood up with a wobble* TOTTER, teeter, sway. ❷ *the operatic wobble in her voice* TREMOR, quiver, quaver, trembling, vibrato.

wobbly ▶ adjective ❶ *a wobbly table* UNSTEADY, unstable, shaky, rocky, rickety; unsafe, precarious; uneven, unbalanced; *informal* wonky. ❷ *her legs were a bit wobbly* SHAKY, quivery, weak, unsteady; *informal* trembly, like jelly. ❸ *I feel so wobbly* FAINT, dizzy, light-headed, giddy, weak (at the knees), groggy, muzzy; *informal* woozy.
–OPPOSITES stable.

woe ▶ noun ❶ *a tale of woe* MISERY, sorrow, distress, wretchedness, sadness, unhappiness, heartache, heartbreak, despondency, despair, depression, gloom, melancholy; adversity, misfortune, disaster, suffering, hardship; *poetic/literary* dolour. ❷ *financial woes* TROUBLE, difficulty, problem, trial, tribulation, misfortune, setback, reverse.
–OPPOSITES joy.

woebegone ▶ adjective SAD, unhappy, miserable, dejected, disconsolate, forlorn, crestfallen, downcast, glum, gloomy, doleful, downhearted, despondent, melancholy, sorrowful, mournful, woeful, depressed, wretched, desolate; *informal* down in the mouth, down in the dumps, blue.
–OPPOSITES cheerful.

woeful ▶ adjective ❶ *her face was woeful. See* WOEBEGONE. ❷ *a woeful tale* TRAGIC, sad, miserable, cheerless, gloomy, sorry, pitiful, pathetic, traumatic, depressing, heartbreaking, heart-rending, tear-jerking. ❸ *the team's woeful performance* DREADFUL, awful, terrible, atrocious, disgraceful, deplorable, shameful, hopeless, lamentable; substandard, poor, inadequate, inferior, unsatisfactory; *informal* rotten, appalling, crummy, pathetic, pitiful, lousy, abysmal, dire; *Brit. informal* duff, chronic, rubbish.
–OPPOSITES cheerful, excellent.

wolf ▶ verb DEVOUR, gobble (up), guzzle, gulp down, bolt; *informal* put away, demolish, shovel down, scoff (down), get outside of; *Brit. informal* gollop; *N. Amer. informal* scarf (down/up), snarf (down/up).

wolfish ▶ adjective (*informal*) LASCIVIOUS, lecherous, lustful; predatory, rapacious.

woman ▶ noun ❶ *a woman got out of the car* LADY, girl, female; matron; *Scottish & N. English* lass, lassie; *Irish* colleen; *informal* chick, girlie, filly, biddy; *Brit. informal* bird; *Scottish & N. English informal* wifie; *N. Amer. informal* sister, dame, broad, gal, jane; *Austral./NZ informal* sheila; *poetic/literary* maid, maiden, damsel; *archaic* wench, gentlewoman. ❷ *he found himself a new woman* GIRLFRIEND, sweetheart, partner, significant other, inamorata, lover, mistress; fiancée; wife, spouse; *informal* bird, fancy woman, missus, better half; *Brit. informal* other half, Dutch, trouble and strife; *Irish informal* mot; *N. Amer. informal* squeeze; *dated* lady friend, lady love; *archaic* leman.
–RELATED TERMS female, gynaeco-.

womanhood ▶ noun ❶ *she was on the brink of womanhood* ADULTHOOD, maturity; *poetic/literary* muliebrity. ❷ *she's an ideal of womanhood* WOMANLINESS, femininity. ❸ *the stereotype of Soviet womanhood* WOMEN, womenfolk; womankind, womenkind, woman; the female sex.

womanish ▶ adjective EFFEMINATE, girlish, girly, unmanly, unmasculine.
–OPPOSITES manly.

womanizer ▶ noun PHILANDERER, Casanova, Don Juan, Romeo, Lothario, ladies' man, playboy, seducer, rake, roué, libertine, lecher; *informal* skirt-chaser, ladykiller, lech.

womankind ▶ noun WOMEN, woman, the female sex, womenkind, womanhood, womenfolk.

womanly ▶ adjective ❶ *womanly virtues* FEMININE, female; *archaic* feminal. ❷ *her womanly figure* VOLUPTUOUS, curvaceous, shapely, ample, Junoesque, Rubenesque, buxom, full-figured; *informal* curvy, busty.
– OPPOSITES masculine, boyish.

wonder ▶ noun ❶ *she was speechless with wonder* AWE, admiration, wonderment, fascination; surprise, astonishment, amazement. ❷ *the wonders of nature* MARVEL, miracle, phenomenon, sensation, spectacle, beauty; curiosity.
▶ verb ❶ *I wondered what was on her mind* PONDER, think about, meditate on, reflect on, muse on, speculate about, conjecture; be curious about. ❷ *I wonder you were so patient* BE SURPRISED, find it surprising. ❸ *people wondered at such bravery* MARVEL, be amazed, be astonished, stand in awe, be dumbfounded, gape, goggle; *informal* be flabbergasted.

wonderful ▶ adjective MARVELLOUS, magnificent, superb, glorious, sublime, lovely, delightful; *informal* super, great, fantastic, terrific, tremendous, sensational, incredible, fabulous, fab, awesome, magic, ace, wicked, far out; *Brit. informal* smashing, brilliant, brill; *N. Amer. informal* peachy, dandy, neat; *Austral./NZ informal* beaut, bonzer; *Brit. informal, dated* champion, wizard, spiffing, topping; *N. Amer. informal, dated* swell.
– OPPOSITES awful.

wonky ▶ adjective (*Brit. informal*) ❶ *a wonky picture. See* CROOKED sense 3. ❷ *wonky stools. See* WOBBLY sense 1.

wont ▶ adjective *he was wont to arise at 5.30* ACCUSTOMED, used, given, inclined.
▶ noun *Paul drove fast, as was his wont* CUSTOM, habit, way, practice, convention, rule.

wonted ▶ adjective CUSTOMARY, habitual, usual, accustomed, familiar, normal, conventional, routine, common.

woo ▶ verb ❶ *Richard wooed Joan* PAY COURT TO, pursue, chase (after); *dated* court, romance, seek the hand of, set one's cap at, make love to. ❷ *the party wooed voters with promises* SEEK, pursue, curry favour with, try to win, try to attract, try to cultivate. ❸ *an attempt to woo him out of retirement* ENTICE, tempt, coax, persuade, wheedle; *informal* sweet-talk.

wood ▶ noun ❶ *polished wood* TIMBER, planks, planking; logs; *N. Amer.* lumber. ❷ *a walk through the woods* FOREST, woodland, trees; copse, coppice, grove; *Brit.* spinney; *archaic* greenwood.
– RELATED TERMS ligneous.

wooded ▶ adjective FORESTED, afforested, tree-covered, woody; *poetic/literary* sylvan, bosky.

wooden ▶ adjective ❶ *a wooden door* WOOD, timber, woody; ligneous. ❷ *wooden acting* STILTED, stiff, unnatural, awkward, leaden; dry, flat, stodgy, lifeless, passionless, spiritless, soulless. ❸ *her face was wooden* EXPRESSIONLESS, impassive, poker-faced, emotionless, blank, vacant, unresponsive.

woodland ▶ noun WOODS, wood, forest, trees; *archaic* greenwood.

woodwork ▶ noun CARPENTRY, joinery.

wool ▶ noun ❶ *sheep's wool* FLEECE, hair, coat; floccus. ❷ *a sweater made of cream wool* YARN.
■ **pull the wool over someone's eyes** (*informal*) DECEIVE, fool, trick, hoodwink, dupe, delude; *informal* lead up the garden path, put one over on, bamboozle, con.

wool-gathering ▶ noun DAYDREAMING, reverie, dreaming, musing, abstraction, preoccupation; absent-mindedness, forgetfulness.

woolly ▶ adjective ❶ *a woolly hat* WOOLLEN, wool, fleecy. ❷ *a sheep's woolly coat* FLEECY, shaggy, hairy, fluffy, flocculent. ❸ *woolly generalizations* VAGUE, ill-defined, hazy, unclear, fuzzy, blurry, foggy, nebulous, imprecise, inexact, indefinite; confused, muddled.
▶ noun (*informal*) SWEATER, pullover, jersey, cardigan; *Brit.* jumper; *Brit. informal* cardy.

woozy ▶ adjective (*informal*). *See* GROGGY.

word ▶ noun ❶ *the Italian word for 'ham'* TERM, name, expression, designation, locution, vocable; *formal* appellation. ❷ *his words were meant kindly* REMARK, comment, observation, statement, utterance, pronouncement. ❸ *I've got three weeks to learn the words* SCRIPT, lyrics, libretto. ❹ *I give you my word* PROMISE, word of honour, assurance, guarantee, undertaking; pledge, vow, oath, bond; *formal* troth. ❺ *I want a word with you* TALK, conversation, chat, tête-à-tête, heart-to-heart, one-to-one; discussion, consultation; *informal* confab, powwow; *formal* confabulation. ❻ *there's no word from the hospital* NEWS, information, communication, intelligence; message, report, communiqué, dispatch, bulletin; *informal* info, gen, dope; *poetic/literary* tidings. ❼ *word has it he's turned over a new leaf* RUMOUR, hearsay, talk, gossip; *informal* the grapevine, the word on the street. ❽ *I'm waiting for the word from HQ* INSTRUCTION, order, command; signal, prompt, cue, tip-off; *informal* go-ahead, thumbs up, green light. ❾ *his word was law* COMMAND, order, decree, edict; bidding, will. ❿ *our word now must be success* MOTTO, watchword, slogan, catchword, buzz word.
– RELATED TERMS verbal, lexical.
▶ verb *the question was carefully worded* PHRASE, express, put, couch, frame, formulate, style; say, utter.
■ **have words** QUARREL, argue, disagree,

squabble, bicker, fight, wrangle, dispute, fall out, clash; *Brit. informal* row.

■ **in a word** BRIEFLY, to be brief, in short, in a nutshell, to come to the point, to cut a long story short, not to put too fine a point on it; to sum up, to summarize, in summary.

■ **word for word** ❶ *they took down the speeches word for word* VERBATIM, letter for letter, to the letter; exactly, faithfully. ❷ *a word-for-word translation* VERBATIM, literal, exact, direct, accurate, faithful; unadulterated, unabridged.

wording ▶ noun PHRASING, words, phraseology, language, expression, terminology.

wordplay ▶ noun PUNNING, puns, play on words; wit, witticisms, repartee.

wordy ▶ adjective LONG-WINDED, verbose, prolix, lengthy, protracted, long-drawn-out, rambling, circumlocutory, periphrastic, pleonastic; loquacious, garrulous, voluble; *informal* windy; *Brit. informal* waffly.

– OPPOSITES succinct.

work ▶ noun ❶ *a day's work in the fields* LABOUR, toil, slog, drudgery, exertion, effort, industry, service; *informal* grind, sweat, elbow grease; *Brit. informal* graft, fag; *Austral./NZ informal* yakka; *poetic/literary* travail. ❷ *I'm looking for work* EMPLOYMENT, a job, a post, a position, a situation; occupation, profession, career, vocation, calling. ❸ *haven't you got any work?* TASKS, jobs, duties, assignments, projects; chores. ❹ *works of literature* COMPOSITION, piece, creation; opus, oeuvre. ❺ *this is the work of a radical faction* HANDIWORK, doing, act, deed. ❻ *a lifetime spent doing good works* DEEDS, acts, actions. ❼ *the complete works of Shakespeare* WRITINGS, oeuvre, canon, output. ❽ *a car works* FACTORY, plant, mill, foundry, yard, workshop, shop. ❾ *the works of a clock* MECHANISM, machinery, workings, parts, movement, action; *informal* insides. ❿ (*informal*) *for only $60 you can get the works* EVERYTHING, the full treatment; *informal* the lot, the whole shebang, the full nine yards; *Brit. informal* the full monty.

– OPPOSITES leisure.

▶ verb ❶ *staff worked late into the night* TOIL, labour, exert oneself, slave (away); keep at it, keep one's nose to the grindstone; *informal* slog (away), beaver away, plug away, put one's back into it, knock oneself out, sweat blood; *Brit. informal* graft, fag; *poetic/literary* travail. ❷ *he worked in education for years* BE EMPLOYED, have a job, earn one's living, do business. ❸ *farmers worked the land* CULTIVATE, farm, till, plough. ❹ *his car was working perfectly* FUNCTION, go, run, operate; *informal* behave. ❺ *how do I work this machine?* OPERATE, use, handle, control, manipulate, run. ❻ *their ploy worked* SUCCEED, work out, turn out well, go as planned, get results, be effective; *informal* come off, pay off, do the trick; *N. Amer. informal* turn the trick. ❼ *blusher can work miracles* BRING ABOUT, accomplish, achieve, produce, perform, create, engender, contrive, effect. ❽ (*informal*) *the chairman was prepared to work it for Phil* ARRANGE, manipulate, contrive; pull strings; *N. Amer.* pull wires; *informal* fix, swing, wangle. ❾ *he worked the crowd into a frenzy* STIR (UP), excite, drive, move, rouse, fire, galvanize; whip up, agitate. ❿ *work the mixture into a paste* KNEAD, squeeze, form; mix, stir, blend. ⓫ *he worked the blade into the padlock* MANOEUVRE, manipulate, guide, edge. ⓬ *her mouth worked furiously* TWITCH, quiver, convulse. ⓭ *he worked his way through the crowd* MANOEUVRE, make, thread, wind, weave, wend.

– OPPOSITES rest, fail.

■ **work on someone** PERSUADE, manipulate, influence; coax, cajole, wheedle, soften up; *informal* twist someone's arm, lean on.

■ **work out** ❶ *the bill works out at £50* AMOUNT TO, add up to, come to, total; *Brit.* tot up to. ❷ *my idea worked out. See* WORK verb sense 6. ❸ *things didn't work out the way she planned* END UP, turn out, go, come out, develop; happen, occur; *informal* pan out. ❹ *he works out at the local gym* EXERCISE, train.

■ **work something out** ❶ *work out what you can afford* CALCULATE, compute, reckon up, determine. ❷ *I'm trying to work out what she meant* UNDERSTAND, comprehend, puzzle out, sort out, make sense of, get to the bottom of, make head or tail of, unravel, decipher, decode; *informal* figure out; *Brit. informal* suss out. ❸ *they worked out a plan* DEVISE, formulate, draw up, put together, develop, construct, arrange, organize, contrive, concoct; hammer out, negotiate.

■ **work something up** STIMULATE, rouse, raise, arouse, awaken, excite.

workable ▶ adjective PRACTICABLE, feasible, viable, possible, achievable; realistic, reasonable, sensible, practical; *informal* doable.

– OPPOSITES impracticable.

workaday ▶ adjective ORDINARY, average, run-of-the-mill, middle-of-the-road, conventional, unremarkable, unexceptional, humdrum, undistinguished, commonplace, mundane, pedestrian; routine, everyday, day-to-day; *N. Amer.* garden-variety; *informal* bog-standard, nothing to write home about, ten a penny, a dime a dozen; *Brit. informal* common or garden.

– OPPOSITES exceptional.

worker ▶ noun ❶ *a strike by 500 workers* EMPLOYEE, member of staff; workman, labourer, hand, operative, operator; proletarian; artisan, craftsman, craftswoman; wage-earner, breadwinner. ❷ (*informal*) *I got a reputation for being a worker* HARD WORKER, toiler, workhorse; *informal* busy bee, eager beaver, workaholic; *N. Amer. informal* wheel horse.

workforce ▶ noun EMPLOYEES, staff, personnel, workers, labour force, manpower; human resources; *informal* liveware.

working ▶ adjective ❶ *working mothers* EMPLOYED, in (gainful) employment, in work,

waged. ❷ *a working waterwheel* FUNCTIONING, operating, running, active, operational, functional, serviceable; *informal* up and running. ❸ *a working knowledge of contract law* SUFFICIENT, adequate, viable; useful, effective.
– OPPOSITES unemployed, faulty.
▶ **noun** ❶ *the working of a carburettor* FUNCTIONING, operation, running, action, performance. ❷ *the workings of a watch* MECHANISM, machinery, parts, movement, action, works; *informal* insides.

workman ▶ **noun** (MANUAL) WORKER, labourer, hand, operative, operator; employee; journeyman, artisan.

workmanlike ▶ **adjective** EFFICIENT, competent, professional, proficient, skilful, adept, masterly.

workmanship ▶ **noun** CRAFTSMANSHIP, artistry, craft, art, artisanship, handiwork; skill, expertise, technique.

workout ▶ **noun** EXERCISE SESSION, keep-fit session, training session, drill; warm-up; exercises, aerobics; *informal, dated* daily dozen.

workshop ▶ **noun** ❶ *a car repair workshop* FACTORY, works, plant; garage. ❷ *the craftsmen had a chilly workshop* WORKROOM, studio, atelier. ❸ *a workshop on combating stress* STUDY GROUP, discussion group, seminar, class.

world ▶ **noun** ❶ *he travelled the world* EARTH, globe, planet, sphere. ❷ *life on other worlds* PLANET, satellite, moon, star, heavenly body, orb. ❸ *the academic world* SPHERE, society, circle, arena, milieu, province, domain, orbit, preserve, realm, field, discipline, area. ❹ *she would show the world that she was strong* EVERYONE, everybody, people, mankind, humankind, humanity, the (general) public, the population, the populace, all and sundry, every mother's son, {every Tom, Dick, and Harry}, every man jack. ❺ *a world of difference* HUGE AMOUNT, good deal, great deal, abundance, wealth, profusion, mountain; plenty; *informal* heap, lot, load, ton, masses; *Brit. informal* shedload. ❻ *she renounced the world* SOCIETY, secular interests, temporal concerns, earthly concerns.
■ **on top of the world** (*informal*). *See* OVERJOYED.
■ **out of this world** (*informal*). *See* WONDERFUL.

worldly ▶ **adjective** ❶ *his youth was wasted on worldly pursuits* EARTHLY, terrestrial, temporal, mundane; mortal, human, material, materialistic, physical, carnal, fleshly, bodily, corporeal, sensual. ❷ *a worldly man* SOPHISTICATED, experienced, worldly-wise, knowledgeable, knowing, enlightened, shrewd, mature, seasoned, cosmopolitan, urbane, cultivated, cultured.
– OPPOSITES spiritual, naive.

worldly-wise ▶ **adjective**. *See* WORLDLY sense 2.

worldwide ▶ **adjective** GLOBAL, international, intercontinental, universal; ubiquitous, extensive, widespread, far-reaching, wide-ranging, all-embracing.
– OPPOSITES local.

worn ▶ **adjective** ❶ *his hat was worn* SHABBY, worn out, threadbare, tattered, in tatters, holey, falling to pieces, ragged, frayed, motheaten, scruffy, having seen better days; *informal* tatty, ratty, the worse for wear; *N. Amer. informal* raggedy. ❷ *her face looked worn. See* WORN OUT sense 2.
– OPPOSITES smart, fresh.

worn out ▶ **adjective** ❶ *a worn-out shirt. See* WORN sense 1. ❷ *by evening they looked worn out* EXHAUSTED, fatigued, tired (out), weary, drained, worn, drawn, wan, sapped, spent; careworn, haggard, hollow-eyed, pinched, pale, peaky; *informal* all in, done in, dog-tired, dead beat, fit to drop, shattered; *Brit. informal* knackered; *N. Amer. informal* pooped, tuckered out. ❸ *worn-out ideas* OBSOLETE, antiquated, old, stale, hackneyed, trite, overused, overworked, clichéd, unoriginal, commonplace, pedestrian, prosaic, stock, conventional; *informal* played out, old hat.
– OPPOSITES smart, fresh.

worried ▶ **adjective** ANXIOUS, perturbed, troubled, bothered, concerned, upset, distressed, distraught, disquieted, uneasy, fretful, agitated, nervous, edgy, on edge, tense, overwrought, worked up, keyed up, jumpy, stressed; apprehensive, fearful, afraid, frightened, scared; *informal* uptight, a bundle of nerves, on tenterhooks, jittery, twitchy, in a stew, all of a dither, in a flap, in a sweat, het up, rattled; *Brit. informal* windy, having kittens; *N. Amer. informal* antsy, squirrelly.
– OPPOSITES carefree.

worrisome ▶ **adjective**. *See* WORRYING.

worry ▶ **verb** ❶ *she worries about his health* FRET, be concerned, be anxious, agonize, brood, panic, lose sleep, get worked up; *informal* get stressed, get in a flap, get in a state, stew, torment oneself. ❷ *is something worrying you?* TROUBLE, bother, make anxious, disturb, distress, upset, concern, disquiet, fret, agitate, unsettle, perturb, scare, fluster, stress, tax, torment, plague, bedevil; prey on one's mind, weigh down, gnaw at; *informal* rattle, bug, get to. ❸ *a dog worried his sheep* ATTACK, savage, maul, mutilate, mangle, go for; molest, torment, persecute.
▶ **noun** ❶ *I'm beside myself with worry* ANXIETY, perturbation, distress, concern, uneasiness, unease, disquiet, fretfulness, restlessness, nervousness, nerves, agitation, edginess, tension, stress; apprehension, fear, dread, trepidation, misgiving, angst; *informal* butterflies (in the stomach), the willies, the heebie-jeebies. ❷ *the rats are a worry* PROBLEM, cause for concern; nuisance, pest, plague, trial, trouble, vexation, bane, bugbear; *informal* pain (in the neck), headache, hassle, stress.

worrying ▶ adjective ALARMING, worrisome, daunting, perturbing, niggling, bothersome, troublesome, unsettling, nerve-racking; distressing, disquieting, upsetting, traumatic, problematic; *informal* scary, hairy.

worsen ▶ verb ❶ *insomnia can worsen a patient's distress* AGGRAVATE, exacerbate, compound, add to, intensify, increase, magnify, heighten, inflame, augment; *informal* add fuel to the fire. ❷ *the recession worsened* DETERIORATE, degenerate, decline; *informal* go downhill, go to pot, go to the dogs, hit the skids, nosedive.
– OPPOSITES improve.

worship ▶ noun ❶ *the worship of saints* REVERENCE, veneration, adoration, glorification, glory, exaltation; devotion, praise, thanksgiving, homage, honour; dulia, latria; *formal* laudation; *archaic* magnification. ❷ *morning worship* SERVICE, religious rite, prayer, praise, devotion, religious observance; matins, vespers, evensong. ❸ *he contemplated her with worship* ADMIRATION, adulation, idolization, lionization, hero-worship.
▶ verb *they worship pagan gods* REVERE, reverence, venerate, pay homage to, honour, adore, praise, pray to, glorify, exalt, extol; hold dear, cherish, treasure, esteem, adulate, idolize, deify, hero-worship, lionize; *informal* put on a pedestal; *formal* laud; *archaic* magnify.

worst ▶ verb DEFEAT, beat, prevail over, triumph over, trounce, rout, vanquish, conquer, master, overcome, overwhelm, overpower, crush; outdo, outclass, outstrip, surpass; *informal* thrash, lick, best, clobber, drub, slaughter, murder, wipe out, crucify, demolish, wipe the floor with, take to the cleaners, walk all over, make mincemeat of; *Brit. informal* stuff; *N. Amer. informal* shellac, cream.

worth ▶ noun ❶ *evidence of the rug's worth* VALUE, price, cost; valuation, quotation, estimate. ❷ *the intrinsic worth of education* BENEFIT, advantage, use, value, virtue, utility, service, profit, help, aid; desirability, appeal; significance, sense; *informal* mileage, percentage; *archaic* behoof. ❸ *a sense of personal worth* WORTHINESS, merit, value, excellence, calibre, quality, stature, eminence, consequence, importance, significance, distinction.

worthless ▶ adjective ❶ *the item was worthless* VALUELESS; poor quality, inferior, second-rate, low-grade, cheap, shoddy, tawdry; *informal* crummy, rubbishy, ten a penny; *Brit. informal* twopenny-halfpenny; *N. Amer. informal* nickel-and-dime. ❷ *your conclusions are worthless* USELESS, no use, ineffective, ineffectual, fruitless, unproductive, unavailing, pointless, nugatory, valueless, inadequate, deficient, meaningless, senseless, insubstantial, empty, hollow, trifling, petty, inconsequential, lame, paltry, pathetic; *informal* a dead loss. ❸ *his worthless son* GOOD-FOR-NOTHING, ne'er-do-well, useless, despicable, contemptible, low, ignominious, corrupt, villainous, degenerate, shiftless, feckless; *informal* no-good, lousy.
– OPPOSITES valuable, useful.

worthwhile ▶ adjective VALUABLE, useful, of use, of service, beneficial, rewarding, advantageous, positive, helpful, profitable, gainful, fruitful, productive, constructive, effective, effectual, meaningful, worthy.

worthy ▶ adjective *a worthy citizen* VIRTUOUS, righteous, good, moral, ethical, upright, upstanding, high-minded, principled, exemplary; law-abiding, irreproachable, blameless, guiltless, unimpeachable, honest, honourable, reputable, decent, respectable, noble, meritorious; pure, whiter than white, saintly, angelic; *informal* squeaky clean.
– OPPOSITES disreputable.
▶ noun *local worthies* DIGNITARY, personage, grandee, VIP, notable, notability, pillar of society, luminary, leading light, big name; *informal* heavyweight, bigwig, top dog, big shot, big cheese; *N. Amer. informal* big wheel, big kahuna.
– OPPOSITES nobody.
■ **be worthy of** DESERVE, merit, warrant, rate, justify, earn, be entitled to, qualify for.

would-be ▶ adjective ASPIRING, budding, promising, prospective, potential, hopeful, keen, eager, ambitious; *informal* wannabe.

wound ▶ noun ❶ *a chest wound* INJURY, lesion, cut, gash, laceration, tear, slash; graze, scratch, abrasion; bruise, contusion; *Medicine* trauma. ❷ *the wounds inflicted by the media* INSULT, blow, slight, offence, affront; hurt, damage, injury, pain, distress, grief, anguish, torment.
▶ verb ❶ *he was critically wounded* INJURE, hurt, harm; maim, mutilate, disable, incapacitate, cripple; lacerate, cut, graze, gash, stab, slash. ❷ *her words had wounded him* HURT, scar, damage, injure; insult, slight, offend, affront, distress, disturb, upset, trouble; grieve, sadden, pain, sting, shock, traumatize, torment.

wraith ▶ noun GHOST, spectre, spirit, phantom, apparition, manifestation; *informal* spook; *poetic/literary* shade, phantasm.

wrangle ▶ noun *a wrangle over money* ARGUMENT, dispute, disagreement, quarrel, falling-out, fight, squabble, altercation, war of words, shouting match, tiff; *informal* set-to, run-in, slanging match; *Brit. informal* barney, row, bust-up.
▶ verb *we wrangled over the details* ARGUE, quarrel, bicker, squabble, fall out, have words, disagree, be at odds, fight, battle, feud, clash; *informal* scrap; *Brit. informal* row.

wrap ▶ verb ❶ *she wrapped herself in a towel* SWATHE, bundle, swaddle, muffle, cloak, enfold, envelop, encase, cover, fold, wind. ❷ *I wrapped the vase carefully* PARCEL (UP), package, pack (up), bundle (up); gift-wrap.
▶ noun *he put a wrap round her* SHAWL, stole, cloak, cape, mantle, scarf, poncho, serape; *historical* pelisse.

■ **wrap up** ❶ *wrap up well—it's cold* DRESS WARMLY, muffle up. ❷ (*Brit. informal*) *tell that child to wrap up. See* SHUT UP at SHUT.

■ **wrap something up** (*informal*) CONCLUDE, finish, end, wind up, round off, terminate, stop, cease, finalize, complete, tie up; *informal* sew up.

wrapper ▶ noun ❶ *a sweet wrapper* WRAPPING, packaging, paper, cover, covering; jacket, sheath. ❷ (*N. Amer.*) *she wore a cotton wrapper* HOUSECOAT, bathrobe, dressing gown, robe, kimono, peignoir.

wrath ▶ noun ANGER, rage, fury, outrage, spleen, vexation, (high) dudgeon, crossness, displeasure, annoyance, irritation; *poetic/literary* ire, choler.

– OPPOSITES happiness.

wreak ▶ verb INFLICT, bestow, mete out, administer, deliver, impose, exact, create, cause, result in, effect, engender, bring about, perpetrate, unleash, vent; *formal* effectuate.

wreath ▶ noun GARLAND, circlet, chaplet, crown, festoon, lei; ring, loop, circle.

wreathe ▶ verb ❶ *a pulpit wreathed in holly* FESTOON, garland, drape, cover, bedeck, deck, decorate, ornament, adorn. ❷ *blue smoke wreathed upwards* SPIRAL, coil, loop, wind, curl, twist, snake, curve.

wreck ▶ noun ❶ *salvage teams landed on the wreck* SHIPWRECK, sunken ship, derelict; shell, hull. ❷ *the wreck of a stolen car* WRECKAGE, debris, remainder, ruins, remains.

▶ verb ❶ *he had wrecked her car* DEMOLISH, crash, smash up, damage, destroy; vandalize, deface, desecrate, write off; *N. Amer. informal* trash, total. ❷ *his ship was wrecked* SHIPWRECK, sink, capsize, run aground. ❸ *the crisis wrecked his plans* RUIN, spoil, disrupt, undo, put a stop to, frustrate, blight, crush, quash, dash, destroy, scotch, shatter, devastate, sabotage; *informal* mess up, screw up, foul up, put paid to, stymie, put the kibosh on, nix; *Brit. informal* scupper, dish.

wreckage ▶ noun. *See* WRECK noun senses 1, 2.

wrench ▶ noun ❶ *she felt a wrench on her shoulders* TUG, pull, jerk, jolt, heave; *informal* yank. ❷ *hold the piston with a wrench* SPANNER, monkey wrench. ❸ *a wrench in his arm* SPRAIN, twist, strain, rick, crick. ❹ *leaving was an immense wrench* PAINFUL PARTING, traumatic event; pang, trauma.

▶ verb ❶ *he wrenched the gun from her hand* TUG, pull, jerk, wrest, heave, twist, pluck, grab, seize, snatch, force, prise; *N. Amer.* pry; *informal* yank. ❷ *she wrenched her ankle* SPRAIN, twist, turn, strain, rick, crick, pull; injure, hurt.

wrest ▶ verb WRENCH, snatch, seize, grab, prise, pluck, tug, pull, jerk, dislodge; *N. Amer.* pry; *informal* yank.

wrestle ▶ verb GRAPPLE, fight, struggle, contend, vie, battle, wrangle; scuffle, tussle, brawl; *informal* scrap.

wretch ▶ noun ❶ *the wretches killed themselves* POOR CREATURE, poor soul, poor thing, poor unfortunate; *informal* poor devil, poor beggar. ❷ *I wouldn't trust the old wretch* SCOUNDREL, villain, ruffian, rogue, rascal, reprobate, criminal, miscreant, good-for-nothing; *informal* heel, creep, louse, rat, swine, dog, lowlife, scumbag; *informal, dated* rotter, bounder, blighter; *archaic* blackguard.

wretched ▶ adjective ❶ *I felt so wretched without you* MISERABLE, unhappy, sad, heartbroken, grief-stricken, sorrowful, distressed, desolate, devastated, despairing, disconsolate, downcast, dejected, crestfallen, cheerless, depressed, melancholy, morose, gloomy, mournful, doleful, dismal, forlorn, woebegone; *informal* blue; *poetic/literary* dolorous. ❷ *I feel wretched* ILL, unwell, poorly, sick, below par; *Brit.* off colour; *informal* under the weather, out of sorts. ❸ *their living conditions are wretched* HARSH, hard, grim, stark, difficult; poor, impoverished; pitiful, pathetic, miserable, cheerless, sordid, shabby, seedy, dilapidated; *informal* scummy; *Brit. informal* grotty. ❹ *the wretched dweller in the shanty town* UNFORTUNATE, unlucky, luckless, ill-starred, blighted, hapless, poor, pitiable, downtrodden, oppressed; *poetic/literary* star-crossed. ❺ *he's a wretched coward* DESPICABLE, contemptible, reprehensible, base, vile, loathsome, hateful, detestable, odious, ignoble, shameful, shabby, worthless; *informal* dirty, rotten, low-down, lousy. ❻ *wretched weather* TERRIBLE, awful, dire, atrocious, dreadful, bad, poor, lamentable, deplorable; *informal* God-awful; *Brit. informal* beastly. ❼ *I don't want the wretched money informal* damn, damned, blasted, blessed, flaming, confounded, rotten; *Brit. informal* flipping, blinking, blooming, bloody.

– OPPOSITES cheerful, well, comfortable, fortunate, excellent.

wriggle ▶ verb ❶ *she tried to hug him but he wriggled* SQUIRM, writhe, wiggle, jiggle, jerk, thresh, flounder, flail, twitch, twist and turn; snake, worm, slither. ❷ *he wriggled out of his responsibilities* AVOID, shirk, dodge, evade, elude, sidestep; escape from; *informal* duck.

▶ noun *the baby gave a wriggle* SQUIRM, jiggle, wiggle, twitch, twist.

wring ▶ verb ❶ *wring out the clothes* TWIST, squeeze, screw, scrunch, knead, press, mangle. ❷ *concessions were wrung from the government* EXTRACT, elicit, force, exact, wrest, wrench, squeeze, milk; *informal* bleed. ❸ *his expression wrung her heart* REND, tear at, harrow, pierce, stab, wound, rack; distress, pain, hurt.

wrinkle ▶ noun ❶ *fine wrinkles around her mouth* CREASE, fold, pucker, line, crinkle, furrow, ridge, groove; *informal* crow's feet. ❷ (*informal*) *learn the wrinkles from someone more experienced* GUIDELINE, hint, tip, pointer, clue, suggestion; (**wrinkles**) guidance, advice.

▶ verb *his coat tails wrinkled up* CREASE, pucker,

gather, line, crinkle, crimp, crumple, rumple, ruck up, scrunch up.

writ ▶ **noun** SUMMONS, subpoena, warrant, arraignment, indictment, citation, court order.

write ▶ **verb** ❶ *he wrote her name in the book* PUT IN WRITING, write down, put down, jot down, note (down), take down, record, register, log, list; inscribe, sign, scribble, scrawl, pencil. ❷ *I wrote a poem* COMPOSE, draft, think up, formulate, compile, pen, dash off, produce. ❸ *he had her address and promised to write* CORRESPOND, write a letter, communicate, get in touch, keep in contact; *informal* drop someone a line.

■ **write someone/something off** ❶ *they have had to write off loans* FORGET ABOUT, disregard, give up on, cancel, annul, wipe out. ❷ *he wrote off his new car* WRECK, smash up, crash, destroy, demolish, ruin; *N. Amer. informal* total. ❸ *who would write off a player of his stature?* DISREGARD, dismiss, ignore.

writer ▶ **noun** AUTHOR, wordsmith, man/woman of letters, penman; novelist, essayist, biographer; journalist, columnist, correspondent; scriptwriter, playwright, dramatist, dramaturge, tragedian; poet; *informal* scribbler, scribe, pen-pusher, hack.

writhe ▶ **verb** SQUIRM, wriggle, thrash, flail, toss, toss and turn, twist, twist and turn, struggle.

writing ▶ **noun** ❶ *I can't read his writing* HANDWRITING, hand, script, print; penmanship, calligraphy, chirography; *informal* scribble, scrawl. ❷ *the writings of Gertrude Stein* WORKS, compositions, books, publications, oeuvre; papers, articles, essays.

wrong ▶ **adjective** ❶ *the wrong answer* INCORRECT, mistaken, in error, erroneous, inaccurate, inexact, imprecise, fallacious, wide of the mark, off target, unsound, faulty; *informal* off beam, out. ❷ *he knew he had said the wrong thing* INAPPROPRIATE, unsuitable, inapt, inapposite, undesirable; ill-advised, ill-considered, ill-judged, impolitic, injudicious, infelicitous, unfitting, out of keeping, improper; *informal* out of order. ❸ *I've done nothing wrong* ILLEGAL, unlawful, illicit, criminal, dishonest, dishonourable, corrupt; unethical, immoral, bad, wicked, sinful, iniquitous, nefarious, blameworthy, reprehensible; *informal* crooked. ❹ *there's something wrong with the engine* AMISS, awry, out of order, not right, faulty, defective.

– OPPOSITES right, correct, appropriate, legal.

▶ **adverb** *she guessed wrong* INCORRECTLY, wrongly, inaccurately, erroneously, mistakenly.

▶ **noun** ❶ *the difference between right and wrong* IMMORALITY, sin, sinfulness, wickedness, evil; unlawfulness, crime, corruption, villainy, dishonesty, injustice, wrongdoing, misconduct, transgression. ❷ *an attempt to make up for past wrongs* MISDEED, offence, injury, crime, transgression, peccadillo, sin; injustice, outrage, atrocity; *Law* tort; *archaic* trespass.

– OPPOSITES right.

▶ **verb** ❶ *she was determined to forget the man who had wronged her* ILL-USE, mistreat, do an injustice to, do wrong to, ill-treat, abuse, harm, hurt, injure; *informal* do the dirty on. ❷ *perhaps I am wronging him* MALIGN, misrepresent, do a disservice to, impugn, defame, slander, libel.

■ **get someone/something wrong** MISUNDERSTAND, misinterpret, misconstrue, mistake, misread, take amiss; get the wrong idea/impression; *informal* get the wrong end of the stick, be barking up the wrong tree.

■ **go wrong** ❶ *I've gone wrong somewhere* MAKE A MISTAKE, make an error, make a blunder, blunder, miscalculate, trip up; *informal* slip up, screw up, make a boo-boo; *Brit. informal* boob. ❷ *their plans went wrong* GO AWRY, go amiss, go off course, fail, be unsuccessful, fall through, come to nothing; backfire, misfire, rebound; *informal* come to grief, come a cropper, go up in smoke; *Brit. informal* go adrift. ❸ *the radio's gone wrong* BREAK DOWN, malfunction, fail, stop working, crash, give out; *informal* be on the blink, conk out, go kaput; *Brit. informal* play up, pack up.

■ **in the wrong** TO BLAME, blameworthy, at fault, reprehensible, responsible, culpable, answerable, guilty; *archaic* peccant.

wrongdoer ▶ **noun** OFFENDER, lawbreaker, criminal, felon, delinquent, villain, culprit, evil-doer, sinner, transgressor, malefactor, miscreant, rogue, scoundrel; *informal* crook, wrong 'un; *Law* malfeasant; *archaic* trespasser.

wrongdoing ▶ **noun** CRIME, lawbreaking, lawlessness, criminality, misconduct, misbehaviour, malpractice, corruption, immorality, sin, sinfulness, wickedness, evil, vice, iniquity, villainy; offence, felony, wrong, misdeed, misdemeanour, fault, peccadillo, transgression; *Law* malfeasance, tort; *formal* malversation; *archaic* trespass.

wrongful ▶ **adjective** UNJUSTIFIED, unwarranted, unjust, unfair, undue, undeserved, unreasonable, groundless, indefensible, inappropriate, improper, unlawful, illegal, illegitimate.

– OPPOSITES rightful.

wrought up ▶ **adjective** AGITATED, tense, stressed, overwrought, nervous, on edge, edgy, keyed up, worked up, jumpy, anxious, nervy, flustered, fretful, upset; *informal* in a state, in a stew, het up, wound up, uptight, in a tizz/tizzy; *Brit. informal* strung up; *N. Amer. informal* spooky, squirrelly.

– OPPOSITES calm.

wry ▶ **adjective** ❶ *his wry humour* IRONIC, sardonic, satirical, mocking, sarcastic; dry, droll, witty, humorous. ❷ *a wry expression* UNIMPRESSED, displeased, annoyed, irritated, irked, vexed, piqued, disgruntled, dissatisfied; *informal* peeved. ❸ *a wry neck* TWISTED, crooked, contorted, distorted, deformed, misshapen; *Scottish* thrawn.

xenophobic ▶ adjective JINGOISTIC, chauvinistic, flag-waving, excessively nationalistic, isolationist; prejudiced, bigoted, intolerant.

Xerox ▶ noun (*trademark*) PHOTOCOPY, copy, duplicate, reproduction; *trademark* photostat.

Xmas ▶ noun (*informal*). *See* CHRISTMAS.

X-ray ▶ noun RADIOGRAPH, X-ray image/picture/photograph, roentgenogram, radiogram.

yahoo ▶ noun BOOR, lout, oaf, thug, barbarian, Neanderthal, brute, bully boy; *informal* clod, roughneck, bruiser; *Brit. informal* yobbo, yob, oik.

yank ▶ verb (*informal*) JERK, pull, tug, wrench; snatch, seize.

yap ▶ verb ❶ *the dogs yapped about his heels* BARK, woof, yelp. ❷ (*informal*) *what are they yapping on about? See* BABBLE verb sense 1.

yardstick ▶ noun STANDARD, measure, gauge, scale, guide, guideline, indicator, test, touchstone, barometer, criterion, benchmark, point of reference, model, pattern.

yarn ▶ noun ❶ *you need to use a fine yarn* THREAD, cotton, wool, fibre, filament; ply. ❷ (*informal*) *a far-fetched yarn* STORY, tale, anecdote, saga, narrative; *informal* tall tale/story, cock and bull story, shaggy-dog story, spiel.

yawning ▶ adjective GAPING, wide open, wide, cavernous, deep; huge, great, big.

year ▶ noun TWELVE-MONTH PERIOD, calendar year; *poetic/literary* sun, summer, winter; *archaic* twelvemonth.

– RELATED TERMS annual.

■ **year in, year out** REPEATEDLY, again and again, time and (time) again, time after time, over and over (again), {week in, week out}, {day in, day out}, recurrently, continuously, continually, constantly, habitually, regularly, without a break, unfailingly, always.

yearly ▶ adjective *a yearly payment* ANNUAL, once a year, every year, each year.

▶ adverb *the guide is published yearly* ANNUALLY, once a year, per annum, by the year, every year, each year.

yearn ▶ verb LONG, pine, crave, desire, want, wish, hanker, covet, lust, pant, hunger, thirst, ache, eat one's heart out, have one's heart set on; *informal* have a yen, itch.

yearning ▶ noun LONGING, craving, desire, want, wish, hankering, urge, hunger, thirst, appetite, lust, ache; *informal* yen, itch.

yell ▶ verb *he yelled in agony* CRY OUT, call out, call at the top of one's voice, shout, howl, yowl, wail, scream, shriek, screech, yelp, squeal; roar, bawl; *informal* holler.

▶ noun *a yell of rage* CRY, shout, howl, yowl, scream, shriek, screech, yelp, squeal; roar; *informal* holler.

yellow ▶ adjective ❶ *yellow hair | a yellow shirt* FLAXEN, golden, gold, blonde, fair; lemon, daffodil-yellow, mustard. ❷ (*informal*) *he'll have to prove he's not yellow. See* COWARDLY.

yelp ▶ noun & verb SQUEAL, shriek, howl, yowl, yell, cry, shout, yawp; *informal* holler.

yen ▶ noun (*informal*) HANKERING, yearning, longing, craving, urge, desire, want, wish, hunger, thirst, lust, appetite, ache; fancy, inclination; *informal* itch.

yes ▶ adverb ALL RIGHT, very well, of course, by all means, sure, certainly, absolutely, indeed, affirmative, in the affirmative, agreed, roger; *Scottish, N. English, & archaic* aye; *Nautical* aye aye; *informal* yeah, yep, yup, uh-huh, okay, OK, okey-dokey, okey-doke; *Brit. informal* righto, righty-ho; *N. Amer. informal* surely; *archaic or formal* yea.

– OPPOSITES no.

yes-man ▶ noun (*informal*) SYCOPHANT, toady, creep, fawner, flatterer, lickspittle, doormat; *informal* bootlicker; *Brit. informal* poodle; *N. Amer. informal* suck-up.

yet ▶ **adverb** ❶ *he hasn't made up his mind yet* SO FAR, thus far, as yet, up till/to now, until now. ❷ *don't celebrate just yet* NOW, right now, at this time; already, so soon. ❸ *he was doing nothing, yet he appeared purposeful* NEVERTHELESS, nonetheless, even so, but, however, still, notwithstanding, despite that, in spite of that, for all that, all the same, just the same, at the same time, be that as it may; *archaic* natheless. ❹ *he supplied yet more unsolicited advice* EVEN, still, further, in addition, additionally, besides, into the bargain, to boot.

yield ▶ **verb** ❶ *too many projects yield poor returns* PRODUCE, bear, give, supply, provide, afford, return, bring in, earn, realize, generate, deliver, pay out. ❷ *the nobility had yielded power to the new capitalist class* RELINQUISH, surrender, cede, remit, part with, hand over; make over, bequeath, leave. ❸ *the Duke was forced to yield* SURRENDER, capitulate, submit, relent, admit defeat, back down, climb down, give in, give up the struggle, lay down one's arms, raise/show the white flag, throw in the towel/sponge. ❹ *he yielded to her demands* GIVE IN TO, give way to, submit to, bow down to, comply with, agree to, consent to, go along with; grant, permit, allow; *informal* cave in to; *formal* accede to. ❺ *the floorboards yielded underfoot* BEND, give, give way.
– OPPOSITES withhold, resist, defy.
▶ **noun** *risky investments usually have higher yields* PROFIT, gain, return, dividend, earnings.

yob, yobbo ▶ **noun** (*Brit. informal*). *See* HOOLIGAN.

yoke ▶ **noun** ❶ *the horses were loosened from the yoke* HARNESS, collar, coupling. ❷ *countries struggling under the yoke of imperialism* TYRANNY, oppression, domination, hegemony, enslavement, servitude, subjugation, subjection, bondage, thrall; bonds, chains, fetters, shackles. ❸ *the yoke of marriage* BOND, tie, connection, link.
▶ **verb** ❶ *a pair of oxen were yoked together* HARNESS, hitch, couple, tether, fasten, attach, join. ❷ *their aim of yoking biology and mechanics* UNITE, join, link, connect; tie, bind, bond.

yokel ▶ **noun** BUMPKIN, peasant, provincial, rustic, country cousin, countryman/woman; *Irish informal* culchie; *N. Amer. informal* hayseed, hillbilly, hick; *Austral. informal* bushy.

young ▶ **adjective** ❶ *young people* YOUTHFUL, juvenile; junior, adolescent, teenage; in the springtime of life, in one's salad days. ❷ *she's very young for her age* IMMATURE, childish, inexperienced, unsophisticated, naive, unworldly; *informal* wet behind the ears. ❸ *the young microbrewery industry* FLEDGLING, developing, budding, in its infancy, emerging.
– OPPOSITES old, elderly, mature.
▶ **noun** ❶ *a robin feeding its young* OFFSPRING, progeny, family, babies. ❷ *the young don't care nowadays* YOUNG PEOPLE, children, boys and girls, youngsters, youth, the younger generation, juveniles, minors; *informal* kids, young 'uns.

youngster ▶ **noun** CHILD, teenager, adolescent, youth, juvenile, minor, junior; boy, girl; *Scottish & N. English* lass, lassie; *informal* lad, kid, whippersnapper, young 'un, teen.

youth ▶ **noun** ❶ *he had been a keen sportsman in his youth* EARLY YEARS, young days, teens, teenage years, adolescence, boyhood, girlhood, childhood; minority; *formal* juvenescence. ❷ *she had kept her youth and beauty* YOUTHFULNESS, freshness, bloom, vigour, energy. ❸ *local youths* YOUNG MAN, boy, juvenile, teenager, adolescent, junior, minor; *informal* lad, kid. ❹ *the youth of the nation* YOUNG PEOPLE, young, younger generation, next generation; *informal* kids.
– OPPOSITES adulthood, old age.

youthful ▶ **adjective** YOUNG-LOOKING, spry, sprightly, vigorous, active; young, boyish, girlish; fresh-faced, in the springtime of life, in one's salad days.
– OPPOSITES old, elderly.

Zz

zany ▶ **adjective** ECCENTRIC, peculiar, odd, unconventional, strange, bizarre, weird; mad, crazy, comic, madcap, funny, quirky, idiosyncratic; *informal* wacky, screwy, nutty, oddball, off the wall; *Brit. informal* daft; *N. Amer. informal* kooky, wacko.
– OPPOSITES conventional, sensible.

zap ▶ **verb** (*informal*) ❶ *they were zapped by anti-radar missiles. See* DESTROY sense 5. ❷ *racing cars zapped past. See* SPEED verb sense 1.

zeal ▶ **noun** PASSION, ardour, love, fervour, fire, avidity, devotion, enthusiasm, eagerness, keenness, appetite, relish, gusto, vigour, energy, intensity; fanaticism.
– OPPOSITES apathy.

zealot ▶ **noun** FANATIC, enthusiast, extremist,

radical, young Turk, diehard, activist, militant; bigot, dogmatist, sectarian, partisan; *informal* fiend, maniac, ultra, nut.

zealous ▶ **adjective** FERVENT, ardent, fervid, fanatical, passionate, impassioned, devout, devoted, committed, dedicated, enthusiastic, eager, keen, avid, vigorous, energetic, intense, fierce; *poetic/literary* perfervid.
– OPPOSITES apathetic.

zenith ▶ **noun** HIGHEST POINT, high point, crowning point, height, top, acme, peak, pinnacle, apex, apogee, crown, crest, summit, climax, culmination, prime, meridian.
– OPPOSITES nadir.

zero ▶ **noun** ❶ *the sum's wrong—you've left off a zero* NOUGHT, nothing, nil, 0; *Computing* null character; *dated* cipher; *archaic* naught. ❷ *I rated my chances as zero* NOTHING (AT ALL), nil, none; *N. English* nowt; *informal* zilch, nix, sweet Fanny Adams, sweet FA, not a dicky bird; *Brit. informal* damn all, not a sausage; *N. Amer. informal* zip, nada, diddly-squat; *archaic* naught, nought.
■ **zero in on** FOCUS ON, focus attention on, centre on, concentrate on, home in on, fix on, pinpoint, highlight, spotlight; *informal* zoom in on.

zero hour ▶ **noun** THE APPOINTED TIME, the critical moment, the moment of truth, the point/moment of decision, the Rubicon, the crux; *informal* the crunch.

zest ▶ **noun** ❶ *she had a great zest for life* ENTHUSIASM, gusto, relish, appetite, eagerness, keenness, avidity, zeal, fervour, ardour, passion; verve, vigour, liveliness, sparkle, fire, animation, vitality, dynamism, energy, brio, pep, spirit, exuberance, high spirits; *informal* zing, zip, oomph, vim, pizzazz, get-up-and-go. ❷ *he wanted to add some zest to his life* PIQUANCY, tang, flavour, savour, taste, spice, spiciness, relish, bite; excitement, interest, an edge; *informal* kick, punch, zing, oomph. ❸ *the zest of an orange* RIND, peel, skin.
– OPPOSITES apathy, indifference, blandness.

zigzag ▶ **adjective** TWISTING, twisty, full of twists and turns, serpentine, meandering, snaking, snaky, winding, crooked.
– OPPOSITES straight.

zing ▶ **noun** (*informal*). *See* ZEST sense 1.

zip (*informal*) ▶ **noun** *he's full of zip. See* ENERGY.
▶ **verb** *I zipped back along the M20. See* SPEED verb sense 1.

zone ▶ **noun** AREA, sector, section, belt, stretch, region, territory, district, quarter, precinct, locality, neighbourhood, province.

zoom ▶ **verb** (*informal*). *See* SPEED verb sense 1.